ISBN 978-0-260-11247-7
PIBN 10928696

This book is a reproduction of an important historical work. Forgotten Books uses
state-of-the-art technology to digitally reconstruct the work, preserving the original format
whilst repairing imperfections present in the aged copy. In rare cases, an imperfection in
the original, such as a blemish or missing page, may be replicated in our edition. We do,
however, repair the vast majority of imperfections successfully; any imperfections that
remain are intentionally left to preserve the state of such historical works.

ANNALS

OF

THE CONGRESS OF THE UNITED STATES.

THIRTEENTH CONGRESS.—THIRD SESSION.

PROCEEDINGS AND DEBATES

OF

THE SENATE OF THE UNITED STATES,

AT THE THIRD SESSION OF THE THIRTEENTH CONGRESS, BEGUN AT THE CITY OF WASHINGTON, MONDAY, SEPTEMBER 19, 1814.

A PROCLAMATION

By the President of the United States of America.

Whereas great and weighty matters, claiming the consideration of the Congress of the United States, form an extraordinary occasion for convening them, I do, by these presents, appoint Monday, the nineteenth day of September next, for their meeting at the City of Washington; hereby requiring the respective Senators and Representatives then and there to assemble in Congress, in order to receive such communications as may then be made to them, and to consult and determine on such measures as in their wisdom may be deemed meet for the welfare of the United States.

In testimony whereof, I have caused the seal of the United States to be hereunto affixed, and [L. S.] signed the same with my hand.

Done at the City of Washington, the eighth day of August, in the year of our Lord one thousand eight hundred and fourteen, and of the independence of the United States the thirty-ninth.

JAMES MADISON.

By the President:

JAMES MONROE,
Secretary of State.

MONDAY, September 19, 1814.

Conformably to the above Proclamation of the President of the United States of the 8th of August last, the third session of the Thirteenth Congress commenced this day at the City of Washington, and the Senate assembled.

PRESENT:

JOSEPH B. VARNUM, from Massachusetts.
JEREMIAH B. HOWELL, from Rhode Island.
JONATHAN ROBINSON, from Vermont.
ABNER LACOCK and JONATHAN ROBERTS, from Pennsylvania.
OUTERBRIDGE HORSEY, from Delaware.
RICHARD BRENT and WILLIAM B. GILES, from Virginia.
JAMES TURNER, from North Carolina.
JOHN GAILLARD, from South Carolina.
CHARLES TAIT, from Georgia.
JESSE BLEDSOE, from Kentucky.
JOSEPH ANDERSON and JESSE WHARTON, from Tennessee.

JEREMIAH MORROW and THOMAS WORTHINGTON, from Ohio.
JAMES BROWN and ELIJIUS FROMENTIN, from Louisiana.

JOHN GAILLARD, President *pro tempore*, resumed the Chair.

THOMAS W. THOMPSON, appointed a Senator by the Legislature of the State of New Hampshire, in place of Nicholas Gilman, deceased, produced his credentials, was qualified, and took his seat in the Senate.

On motion, by Mr. BLEDSOE,

Resolved, As the former Secretary of the Senate has departed this life, that the Chief Clerk do act as Secretary thereof until one shall be appointed.

Whereupon, the oath prescribed by law was administered to SAMUEL TURNER, jr.

On motion, by Mr. ANDERSON, the Secretary was directed to acquaint the House of Representatives that a quorum of the Senate is assembled, and ready to proceed to business.

On motion, by Mr. ROBINSON, Messrs. ROBINSON and VARNUM were appointed a committee on the part of the Senate, together with such committee as may be appointed by the House of Representatives on their part, to wait on the President of the United States, and notify him that a quorum of the two Houses is assembled, and ready to receive any communications that he may be pleased to make to them.

The PRESIDENT communicated the following letter from the President of the United States; which was read:

WASHINGTON, *September* 17, 1814.

SIR: The destruction of the Capitol, by the enemy, having made it necessary that other accommodations should be provided for the meeting of Congress, Chambers for the Senate and for the House of Representatives, with other requisite apartments, have been fitted up, under the direction of the Superintendent of the City, in the public building heretofore allotted for the Post and other public offices.

JAMES MADISON.

The PRESIDENT
Of the Senate of the United States.

PROCEEDINGS AND DEBATES

OF

THE SENATE OF THE UNITED STATES,

AT THE THIRD SESSION OF THE THIRTEENTH CONGRESS, BEGUN AT THE CITY OF WASHINGTON, MONDAY, SEPTEMBER 19, 1814.

A PROCLAMATION

By the President of the United States of America.

Whereas great and weighty matters, claiming the consideration of the Congress of the United States, form an extraordinary occasion for convening them, I do, by these presents, appoint Monday, the nineteenth day of September next, for their meeting at the City of Washington; hereby requiring the respective Senators and Representatives then and there to assemble in Congress, in order to receive such communications as may then be made to them, and to consult and determine on such measures as in their wisdom may be deemed meet for the welfare of the United States.

In testimony whereof, I have caused the seal of the United States to be hereunto affixed, and [L. S.] signed the same with my hand.

Done at the City of Washington, the eighth day of August, in the year of our Lord one thousand eight hundred and fourteen, and of the independence of the United States the thirty-ninth.

JAMES MADISON.

By the President:

JAMES MONROE,
Secretary of State.

MONDAY, September 19, 1814.

Conformably to the above Proclamation of the President of the United States of the 8th of August last, the third session of the Thirteenth Congress commenced this day at the City of Washington, and the Senate assembled.

PRESENT:

JOSEPH B. VARNUM, from Massachusetts.
JEREMIAH B. HOWELL, from Rhode Island.
JONATHAN ROBINSON, from Vermont.
ABNER LACOCK and JONATHAN ROBERTS, from Pennsylvania.
OUTERBRIDGE HORSEY, from Delaware.
RICHARD BRENT and WILLIAM B. GILES, from Virginia.
JAMES TURNER, from North Carolina.
JOHN GAILLARD, from South Carolina.
CHARLES TAIT, from Georgia.
JESSE BLEDSOE, from Kentucky.
JOSEPH ANDERSON and JESSE WHARTON, from Tennessee.

JEREMIAH MORROW and THOMAS WORTHINGTON, from Ohio.
JAMES BROWN and ELIJIUS FROMENTIN, from Louisiana.

JOHN GAILLARD, President *pro tempore*, resumed the Chair.

THOMAS W. THOMPSON, appointed a Senator by the Legislature of the State of New Hampshire, in place of Nicholas Gilman, deceased, produced his credentials, was qualified, and took his seat in the Senate.

On motion, by Mr. BLEDSOE,

Resolved, As the former Secretary of the Senate has departed this life, that the Chief Clerk do act as Secretary thereof until one shall be appointed.

Whereupon, the oath prescribed by law was administered to SAMUEL TURNER, jr.

On motion, by Mr. ANDERSON, the Secretary was directed to acquaint the House of Representatives that a quorum of the Senate is assembled, and ready to proceed to business.

On motion, by Mr. ROBINSON, Messrs. ROBINSON and VARNUM were appointed a committee on the part of the Senate, together with such committee as may be appointed by the House of Representatives on their part, to wait on the President of the United States, and notify him that a quorum of the two Houses is assembled, and ready to receive any communications that he may be pleased to make to them.

The PRESIDENT communicated the following letter from the President of the United States; which was read:

WASHINGTON, *September 17, 1814.*

SIR: The destruction of the Capitol, by the enemy, having made it necessary that other accommodations should be provided for the meeting of Congress, Chambers for the Senate and for the House of Representatives, with other requisite apartments, have been fitted up, under the direction of the Superintendent of the City, in the public building heretofore allotted for the Post and other public offices.

JAMES MADISON.

The PRESIDENT
Of the Senate of the United States.

On motion, by Mr. VARNUM, it was agreed that when the Senate adjourn it be to 5 o'clock this evening.

The usual resolution was adopted for supplying Senators with newspapers, and then the Senate adjourned.

Five o'clock in the Evening.

The number of Senators present not being sufficient to constitute a quorum, the Senate adjourned.

TUESDAY, September 20.

WILLIAM W. BIBB, from the State of Georgia, took his seat in the Senate.

On motion, by Mr. FROMENTIN, two hundred copies of the Constitution of the United States, and two hundred copies of the rules for conducting business in the Senate, were ordered to be printed and bound for the use of the Senate, in the form they have heretofore been.

A message from the House of Representatives informed the Senate that a quorum of the House of Representatives is assembled and ready to proceed to business. They have appointed a committee on their part to join the committee appointed on the part of the Senate, to wait on the President of the United States, and inform him that a quorum of the two Houses is assembled, and ready to receive any communications he may be pleased to make to them.

On motion, by Mr. LACOCK, a committee was appointed agreeably to the 42d rule for conducting business in the Senate, and Messrs. LACOCK, HOWELL, and MORROW, were appointed the committee.

Mr. WORTHINGTON submitted the following motion:

Resolved, That two Chaplains, of different denominations, be appointed to Congress during the present session, one by each House, who shall interchange weekly.

Mr. ROBINSON reported, from the joint committee, that they had waited on the President of the United States, and that the President informed the committee that he would make a communication to the two Houses this day, at 12 o'clock.

Mr. HOWELL submitted the following motion for consideration, which was read:

Resolved, That Mountjoy Bayly, Doorkeeper and Sergeant-at-Arms to the Senate, be and he hereby is authorized to employ one assistant and two horses, for the purpose of performing such services as are usually required by the Doorkeeper of the Senate; which expense shall be paid out of the contingent fund.

Ordered, That it pass to the second reading.

On motion, by Mr. FROMENTIN, a committee was appointed agreeably to the 22d rule for conducting business in the Senate; and Messrs. FROMENTIN, THOMPSON, and BLEDSOE, were appointed the committee.

PRESIDENT'S MESSAGE.

The following Message was received from the PRESIDENT OF THE UNITED STATES:

*Fellow-citizens of the Senate
and House of Representatives:*

Notwithstanding the early day which had been fixed for your session of the present year, I was induced to call you together still sooner, as well that any inadequacy in the existing provisions for the wants of the Treasury might be supplied, as that no delay might happen in providing for the result of the negotiations on foot with Great Britain, whether it should require arrangements adapted to a return of peace, or further and more effective provisions for prosecuting the war.

That result is not yet known. If, on one hand, the repeal of the Orders in Council, and the general pacification in Europe, which withdrew the occasion on which impressments from American vessels were practised, suggest expectations that peace and amity may be re-established, we were compelled, on the other hand, by the refusal of the British Government to accept the offered mediation of the Emperor of Russia; by the delays in giving effect to its own proposal of a direct negotiation; and, above all, by the principles and manner in which the war is now avowedly carried on, to infer that a spirit of hostility is indulged more violent than ever against the rights and prosperity of this country.

This increased violence is best explained by the two important circumstances, that the great contest in Europe for an equilibrium guaranteeing all its States against the ambition of any, has been closed without any check on the overbearing power of Great Britain on the ocean; and it has left in her hands disposable armaments with which, forgetting the difficulties of a remote war with a free people, and yielding to the intoxication of success, with the example of a great victim to it before her eyes, she cherishes hopes of still further aggrandizing a Power already formidable in its abuses to the tranquillity of the civilized and commercial world.

But, whatever may have inspired the enemy with these more violent purposes, the public councils of a nation, more able to maintain than it was to acquire its independence, and with a devotion to it rendered more ardent by the experience of its blessings, can never deliberate but on the means most effectual for defeating the extravagant views or unwarrantable passions with which alone the war can now be pursued against us.

In the events of the present campaign, the enemy, with all his augmented means, and wanton use of them, has little ground for exultation, unless he can feel it in the success of his recent enterprises against this metropolis and the neighboring town of Alexandria, from both of which his retreats were as precipitate as his attempts were bold and fortunate. In his other incursions on our Atlantic frontier, his progress, often checked and chastised by the martial spirit of the neighboring citizens, has had more effect in distressing individuals, and in dishonoring his arms, than in promoting any object of legitimate warfare. And, in the two instances mentioned, however deeply to be regretted on our part, he will find in his transient success, which interrupted for a moment only the ordinary public business at the Seat of Government, no compensation for the loss of character with the world, by his violations of private property, and by his destruction of public edifices, protected, as monuments of the arts, by the laws of civilized warfare.

On our side, we can appeal to a series of achievements which have given new lustre to the American arms. Besides the brilliant incidents in the minor operations of the campaign, the splendid victories gained on the Canadian side of the Niagara, by the American forces under Major General Brown, and Brigadiers Scott and Gaines, have gained for these heroes, and their emulating companions, the most unfading laurels; and, having triumphantly tested the progressive discipline of the American soldiery, have taught the enemy that the longer he protracts his hostile efforts, the more certain and decisive will be his final discomfiture.

On our southern border, victory has continued also to follow the American standard. The bold and skilful operations of Major General Jackson, conducting troops drawn from the militia of the States least distant, particularly of Tennessee, have subdued the principal tribes of hostile savages, and, by establishing a peace with them, preceded by recent and exemplary chastisement, has best guarded against the mischief of their co-operation with the British enterprises which may be planned against that quarter of our country. Important tribes of Indians on our Northwestern frontier have also acceded to stipulations which bind them to the interests of the United States, and to consider our enemy as theirs also.

In the recent attempt of the enemy on the city of Baltimore, defended by militia and volunteers, aided by a small body of regulars and seamen, he was received with a spirit which produced a rapid retreat to his ships; whilst a concurrent attack by a large fleet was successfully resisted by the steady and well directed fire of the fort and batteries opposed to it.

In another recent attack by a powerful force on our troops at Plattsburg, of which regulars made a part only, the enemy, after a perseverance for many hours, was finally compelled to seek safety in a hasty retreat, with our gallant bands pressing upon him.

On the Lakes, so much contested throughout the war, the great exertions for the command made on our part have been well repaid. On Lake Ontario, our squadron is now, and has been for some time, in a condition to confine that of the enemy to his own port, and to favor the operations of our land forces on that frontier.

A part of the squadron on Lake Erie has been extended into Lake Huron, and has produced the advantage of displaying our command on that lake also. One object of the expedition was the reduction of Mackinaw, which failed, with the loss of a few brave men, among whom was an officer justly distinguished for his gallant exploits. The expedition, ably conducted by both the land and the naval commanders, was otherwise highly valuable in its effects.

On Lake Champlain, where our superiority had for some time been undisputed, the British squadron lately came into action with the American, commanded by Captain Macdonough. It issued in the capture of the whole of the enemy's ships. The best praise for this officer, and his intrepid comrades, is in the likeness of his triumph to the illustrious victory which immortalized another officer, and established, at a critical moment, our command of another lake.

On the ocean, the pride of our naval arms has been amply supported. A second frigate has indeed fallen into the hands of the enemy, but the loss is hidden in the blaze of heroism with which she was defended. Captain Porter, who commanded her, and whose previous career had been distinguished by daring enterprise and by fertility of genius, maintained a sanguinary contest against two ships, one of them superior to his own, and under other severe disadvantages, till

humanity tore down the colors which valor had nailed to the mast. This officer and his brave comrades have added much to the rising glory of the American flag, and have merited all the effusions of gratitude which their country is ever ready to bestow on the champions of its rights and of its safety.

Two smaller vessels of war have also become prizes to the enemy; but, by a superiority of force which sufficiently vindicates the reputation of their commanders; whilst two others, one commanded by Captain Warrington, the other by Captain Blakely, have captured British ships of the same class, with a gallantry and good conduct which entitle them and their companions to a just share in the praise of their country.

In spite of the naval force of the enemy accumulated on our coasts, our private cruisers also have not ceased to annoy his commerce, and to bring their rich prizes into our ports; contributing thus, with other proofs, to demonstrate the incompetency and illegality of a blockade, the proclamation of which is made the pretext for vexing and discouraging the commerce of neutral Powers with the United States.

To meet the extended and diversified warfare adopted by the enemy, great bodies of militia have been taken into service for the public defence, and great expenses incurred. That the defence everywhere may be both more convenient and more economical, Congress will see the necessity of immediate measures for filling the ranks of the regular Army, and of enlarging the provision for special corps, mounted and unmounted, to be engaged for longer periods of service than are due from the militia. I earnestly renew, at the same time, a recommendation of such changes in the system of the militia, as, by classing and disciplining for the most prompt and active service the portions most capable of it, will give to that great resource for the public safety all the requisite energy and efficiency.

The moneys received into the Treasury during the nine months ending on the 30th day of June last, amounted to thirty-two millions of dollars, of which near eleven millions were the proceeds of the public revenue, and the remainder derived from loans. The disbursements for public expenditures during the same period exceeded thirty-four millions of dollars, and left in the Treasury, on the first day of July, near five millions of dollars. The demands during the remainder of the present year, already authorised by Congress, and the expenses incident to an extension of the operations of the war, will render it necessary that large sums should be provided to meet them.

From this view of the national affairs, Congress will be urged to take up, without delay, as well the subject of pecuniary supplies as that of military force, and on a scale commensurate with the extent and the character which the war has assumed. It is not to be disguised that the situation of our country calls for its greatest efforts. Our enemy is powerful in men and in money, on the land and on the water. Availing himself of fortuitous advantages, he is aiming, with his undivided force, a deadly blow at our growing prosperity, perhaps at our national existence. He has avowed his purpose of trampling on the usages of civilized warfare, and given earnests of it in the plunder and wanton destruction of private property. In his pride of maritime dominion, and in his thirst of commercial monopoly, he strikes with peculiar animosity at the progress of our navigation and of our manufactures. His barbarous policy has not even spared those monuments of the arts and models of taste with which our country had enriched and embellished its infant metropolis. From such an adversary, hostility, in its greatest force and in its worst forms, may be looked for. The American people will face it with the undaunted spirit which in their Revolutionary struggle defeated his unrighteous projects. His threats and his barbarities, instead of dismay, will kindle in every bosom an indignation not to be extinguished but in the disaster and expulsion of such cruel invaders. In providing the means necessary, the National Legislature will not distrust the heroic and enlightened patriotism of its constituents. They will cheerfully and proudly bear every burden of every kind which the safety and honor of the nation demand. We have seen them everywhere paying their taxes, direct and indirect, with the greatest promptness and alacrity. We see them rushing with enthusiasm to the scenes where danger and duty call. In offering their blood, they give the surest pledge that no other tribute will be withheld.

Having forborne to declare war until to other aggressions had been added the capture of nearly a thousand American vessels, and the impressment of thousands of American seafaring citizens, and until a final declaration had been made by the Government of Great Britain, that her hostile orders against our commerce would not be revoked, but on conditions as impossible as unjust; whilst it was known that those orders would not otherwise cease, but with a war which had lasted nearly twenty years, and which, according to appearances at that time, might last as many more; having manifested, on every occasion, and in every proper mode, a sincere desire to arrest the effusion of blood, and meet our enemy on the ground of justice and reconciliation, our beloved country, in still opposing to his persevering hostility all its energies, with an undiminished disposition towards peace and friendship on honorable terms, must carry with it the good wishes of the impartial world, and the best hopes of support from an omnipotent and kind Providence.

JAMES MADISON.

WASHINGTON, *Sept.* 20, 1814.

The Message was read, and five hundred copies thereof ordered to be printed for the use of the Senate.

WEDNESDAY, September 21.

DUDLEY CHACE, from the State of Vermont; OBADIAH GERMAN, from the State of New York; ROBERT H. GOLDSBOROUGH, from the State of Maryland; and DAVID STONE, from the State of North Carolina, severally took their seats in the Senate.

The PRESIDENT communicated the memorial of the Legislature of the Indiana Territory, praying that the time for the payment by purchasers of public lands in that Territory may be extended to two years on each instalment, and that all arrearages of interest may be released to the purchasers; also, suggesting the propriety of reducing the price of, and subdividing certain quarter sections, for reasons stated at large in the memorial; which was read, and referred to a select committee, to consist of five members, to consider and report thereon by bill or otherwise; and Messrs. MORROW, BLEDSOE, THOMPSON, CHACE, and TAIT, were appointed the committee.

The resolution for the appointment of Chaplains was read the second time, and considered as in Committee of the Whole; and, no amendment having been proposed, the President reported it to the House accordingly; and on the question, Shall this resolution be engrossed and read a third time? it was determined in the affirmative.

The resolution authorizing Mountjoy Bayly to employ one assistant and two horses was read the second time, and considered as in Committee of the Whole; and no amendment having been proposed, the President reported it to the House accordingly; and the resolution was ordered to be engrossed and read a third time. And by unanimous consent, the resolution was read the third time, and passed.

Mr. WORTHINGTON submitted the following motion for consideration:

Resolved, That so much of the Message of the President of the United States as relates to the militia of the United States, be referred to a select committee, with leave to report by bill or otherwise.

Mr. GILES submitted the following motion for consideration:

Resolved, That so much of the Message of the President of the United States as relates to military affairs, be referred to a select committee, with leave to report by bill, or otherwise.

The resolution for the appointment of Chaplains was, by unanimous consent, read the third time and passed, as follows:

Resolved, That two Chaplains, of different denominations, be appointed to Congress, during the present session, one by each House, who shall interchange weekly.

On motion, by Mr. BLEDSOE, a committee was appointed to revise the standing rules of the Senate, with leave to report such amendments and additions thereto as they may deem expedient; and Messrs. BLEDSOE, GILES, VARNUM, BIBB, and BROWN, were appointed the committee.

THURSDAY, September 22.

JOHN CONDIT, from the State of New Jersey, took his seat in the Senate.

Mr. BLEDSOE, from the committee appointed yesterday to revise the standing rules of the Senate, made report; which was read, and ordered to lie for consideration.

On motion, by Mr. THOMPSON,

Resolved, unanimously, That the members of the Senate, from a sincere desire of showing every mark of respect due to the memory of the honorable NICHOLAS GILMAN, deceased, late a member thereof, will go into mourning for him one month, by the usual mode of wearing a crape round the left arm.

The Senate resumed the motion made yesterday for the appointment of a committee on so much of the Message of the President of the United States as relates to the militia, and agreed thereto; and Messrs. WORTHINGTON, VARNUM, LACOCK, CHACE, and ANDERSON, were appointed the committee.

The Senate resumed the motion made yesterday for the appointment of a committee on so much of the Message of the President of the United States as relates to military affairs, and agreed thereto; and Messrs. GILES, BROWN, TURNER, BIBB, and GERMAN, were appointed the committee.

On motion. by Mr. BLEDSOE,

Resolved, That each member of the Senate be furnished with a copy of the last printed register of the officers of the Army of the United States; and also with a copy of the last printed register of the officers of the Navy.

Mr. GILES submitted the following motion for consideration:

Resolved, That a committee be appointed to inquire into the state of preparations for the defence of the City of Washington, and whether any further provisions by law be necessary for that object, with leave to report by bill or otherwise.

FRIDAY, September 23.

DAVID DAGGETT, from the State of Connecticut, took his seat in the Senate.

Mr. BRENT presented the memorial of the President and Directors of the Washington Bridge Company, praying compensation for the injury done the bridge on the 24th August last, by a military force of the United States, for reasons stated at large in the memorial; which was read, and referred to a select committee, to consider and report thereon by bill or otherwise; and Messrs. BRENT, GILES, and TAIT, were appointed the committee.

Mr. BRENT presented the memorial of the President and Directors of the Eastern Branch Bridge Company, praying reimbursement to the company for the loss of the bridge, which was destroyed, on the 24th August last, by a military force of the United States, for reasons therein stated; and the memorial was read, and referred to the committee last mentioned, to consider and report thereon by bill or otherwise.

Mr. FROMENTIN submitted the following motion:

Resolved, That, in furtherance of the resolution agreed to by the Senate on the 19th of April last, there be printed in future as many copies of the documents ordered to be printed by the Senate as there are printed copies of the Journal of the Senate.

On motion, by Mr. GILES, it was referred to a select committee, to consider and report thereon; and Messrs. FROMENTIN, WORTHINGTON, and GILES, were appointed the committee.

The Senate resumed the report of the select committee appointed to revise the standing rules of the Senate; and on motion, by Mr. BLEDSOE, the report was amended; and on motion, by Mr. ANDERSON, the further consideration thereof was postponed to Monday next.

The Senate resumed the motion made yesterday for the appointment of a committee to inquire into the state of the preparations for the defence of the City of Washington; and on motion, by Mr. WORTHINGTON, the motion was amended and agreed to, as follows:

Resolved, That the Committee on Military Affairs be instructed to inquire into the state of preparations for the defence of the City of Washington, and whether any further provisions by law be necessary for that object, with leave to report by bill or otherwise.

On motion, by Mr. TAIT, so much of the Message of the President of the United States as relates to naval affairs, was referred to a select committee, with leave to report by bill or otherwise; and Messrs. TAIT, HOWELL, DAGGETT, FROMENTIN, and MORROW, were appointed the committee.

Mr. GILES submitted the following motion:

Resolved, That the President of the United States be requested to cause to be laid before the Senate such information, in his possession, respecting the existing state of the relations between the United States and the Continental Powers of Europe, as he may deem not improper to be communicated.

The Senate adjourned to Monday next.

MONDAY, September 26.

JOHN TAYLOR, from the State of South Carolina, took his seat in the Senate.

Mr. ROBERTS presented the resolutions of the burgesses and inhabitants of the borough of Lancaster, in the State of Pennsylvania, pledging themselves that suitable accommodations shall be provided for the President and both Houses of Congress and for the other public offices, in case a removal to that borough should be deemed expedient; and the resolutions were read.

The Senate resumed the consideration of the report of the committee appointed to revise the standing rules of the Senate; and on motion, by Mr. WORTHINGTON, the consideration thereof was further postponed to Wednesday next.

The Senate proceeded to consider the motion, submitted the 23d instant, requesting information respecting the state of the relations between the United States and the continental Powers of Europe; and agreed thereto.

Mr. GOLDSBOROUGH submitted the following motion for consideration; which was read.

Resolved, That a committee of three members be appointed, who, with three members of the House of Representatives, to be appointed by that House, shall have the direction of the money appropriated to the purchase of books and maps, for the use of the two Houses of Congress.

Ordered, That it pass to a second reading.

On motion, by Mr. GOLDSBOROUGH, it was read a second time by unanimous consent, and considered as in Committee of the Whole, and, no amendment having been proposed, the President reported it to the House accordingly. The resolution was then ordered to be engrossed and read the third time; and it was read the third time by unanimous consent, and passed. Messrs. GOLDSBOROUGH, FROMENTIN, and TAIT, were appointed the committee on the part of the Senate.

The PRESIDENT communicated a letter from the President of the Washington Library, with a resolution of the directors, offering the use of the library to the members of Congress; which was read.

Mr. FROMENTIN, from the committee to whom was referred the motion, submitted the 23d instant, directing an additional number of copies to be printed of the public documents, reported it without amendment.

A message from the House of Representatives informed the Senate that the House of Representatives concur in the resolution of the Senate, of the 21st instant, for the appointment of Chaplains; and have appointed the Reverend OBADIAH B. BROWN Chaplain on their part.

The PRESIDENT communicated a report of the Secretary for the Department of Treasury, prepared in obedience to the "Act supplementary to the act, entitled 'An act to establish the Treasury Department;" and the report was read.

The following Message was received from the PRESIDENT OF THE UNITED STATES:

To the Senate and House of
Representatives of the United States:

I transmit to Congress, for their information, copies of a letter from Admiral Cochrane, commanding His Britannic Majesty's naval force on the American station, to the Secretary of State, with his answer, and of a reply from Admiral Cochrane.

JAMES MADISON.

SEPTEMBER 26, 1814.

The Message and documents were read.

TUESDAY, September 27.

The Senate resumed the motion, submitted the 23d instant, directing an additional number of the public documents to be printed, and agreed thereto.

The Senate proceeded to the appointment of a Chaplain on their part; and, on the ballots having been counted, it appeared that the Reverend JESSE LEE had a majority, and was elected.

On motion, by Mr. GILES, the galleries were cleared, and the doors of the Senate Chamber closed.

WEDNESDAY, September 28.

The Senate resumed the consideration of the report of the select committee appointed to revise the standing rules of the Senate; and the consideration thereof was further postponed to Tuesday next.

THURSDAY, September 29.

The PRESIDENT communicated a letter from Thomas Leiper, President of the Common Council of the city of Philadelphia, and Liberty Browne, President of the Select Council, enclosing resolutions of those bodies, "That in case Congress should deem a removal from the City of Washington necessary, under existing circumstances, they will provide suitable places for their accommodation, as well as that of the other Departments of the Government, and the offices attached to them."

The letter and resolutions were read, and laid on the table.

Ordered, That the President and Directors of the Union Bank of Alexandria have leave to withdraw their memorial presented at the last session.

On request, Mr. BRENT, was excused from the committee to whom were referred the memorials of the President and Directors of the Washington and Eastern Branch Bridge companies; and Mr. BLEDSOE was appointed in place of Mr. BRENT.

FRIDAY, September 30.

The PRESIDENT communicated a letter from Richards and Mallory, booksellers of Georgetown, offering the use of their books to the members of the Senate during the present session which was read.

Mr. BLEDSOE called up the memorial and resolutions of the Legislature of the State of Kentucky, relative to the division line between that State and the State of Tennessee, presented on the 15th February last; and, on his motion, they were referred to a select committee, to consist of five members, to consider and report thereon by bill or otherwise. Messrs. BLEDSOE, ANDERSON, DAGGETT, GILES, and BROWN, were appointed the committee.

Mr. GERMAN presented the petition of David M. Clarkson and others, citizens of New York, praying the establishment of a National Bank, for reasons therein stated; and the petition was read.

Mr. BLEDSOE submitted the following motion for consideration:

Resolved, That the Senate will, on —— next, proceed to the election of a Secretary of the Senate.

SATURDAY, October 1.

The Senate resumed the motion submitted yesterday, respecting the election of a Secretary of the Senate; and the further consideration thereof was postponed to Thursday next.

MONDAY, October 3.

WILLIAM HILL WELLS, from the State of Delaware, took his seat in the Senate.

Mr. TAYLOR presented the petition of the citizens of the districts of Chesterfield, Kershaw, and Lancaster, of the State of South Carolina, and of the county of Anson, in the State of North Carolina, praying for the establishment of certain post routes and post offices, for reasons therein stated; and the petition was read.

Mr. LACOCK submitted the following motion:

Resolved, That a committee be appointed to inquire and report to the Senate the extent of the injury done the Capitol and other public buildings of the United States, by the enemy; the best means of preserving from further damage, by the weather, the remains of those edifices, and the expediency of an appropriation for repairing the same.

FOREIGN RELATIONS.

The following Message was received from the PRESIDENT OF THE UNITED STATES:

To the Senate of the United States:

I transmit to the Senate a report from the Department of State complying with their resolution of the 26th ultimo.

JAMES MADISON.

OCTOBER 3, 1814.

21   HISTORY OF CONGRESS.   22

OCTOBER, 1814.   *Victory on Lake Champlain.*   SENATE.

DEPARTMENT OF STATE, *Oct.* 1, 1814.

The undersigned, acting as Secretary of State, to whom was referred the resolution of the Senate, requesting the President to cause to be laid before the Senate such information in his possession, respecting the existing state of the relations between the United States and the Continental Powers of Europe, as he may deem not improper to be communicated, has the honor to report:

That the relations of the United States with the Continental Powers of Europe continue to be those of peace and amity; nor is there, so far as is known to this Department, reason to believe that an unfavorable change is likely to take place.

Measures have been taken to continue our diplomatic relations with France under the existing Government, and to renew those with Spain, which have been for a time interrupted by the peculiar circumstances of that country. Diplomatic relations are also renewed with the United Provinces of the Low Countries. The new Government has sent an Envoy Extraordinary and Minister Plenipotentiary to the United States, who has been received.

With the other Powers of the Continent of Europe, our relations have undergone no change since the last session of Congress.

All which is respectfully submitted.

     JAMES MONROE.

The PRESIDENT *of the U. S.*

TUESDAY, October 4.

JEREMIAH MASON, from the State of New Hampshire, took his seat in the Senate.

The Senate resumed the consideration of the report of the select committee appointed to revise the standing rules of the Senate; and, on the question to agree thereto, it was determined in the negative.

The Senate proceeded to consider the motion, submitted yesterday, for the appointment of a committee to inquire into the extent of injury done the Capitol, and other public edifices, by the enemy, and the best means of preserving them from further damage, by the weather; and agreed thereto, and Messrs. LACOCK, TAYLOR, VARNUM, ANDERSON, and BIBB, were appointed the committee.

WEDNESDAY, October 5.

The Senate spent the day in the consideration of Executive business.

THURSDAY, October 6.

CHRISTOPHER GORE, from the State of Massachusetts; WILLIAM HUNTER, from the State of Rhode Island and Providence Plantations; and RUFUS KING, from the State of New York, severally attended.

The Senate resumed the consideration of the motion submitted by Mr. BLEDSOE, the 30th September; and, the blank having been filled, the motion was agreed to, as follows:

Resolved, That the Senate will, on Thursday next, proceed to the election of a Secretary of the Senate.

VICTORY ON LAKE CHAMPLAIN.

Mr TAIT, from the Committee on Naval Affairs, reported, in part, the following resolutions, which were read, and passed to the second reading:

Resolutions expressive of of the sense of Congress of the gallant conduct of Captain Thomas Macdonough, the officers, seamen, marines, and infantry serving as marines, on board the United States' squadron on Lake Champlain.

Resolved, by the Senate and House of Representatives of the United States of America in Congress assembled, That the thanks of Congress be and the same are hereby presented to Captain Thomas Macdonough, and, through him, to the officers, petty officers, seamen, marines, and infantry serving as marines, attached to the squadron under his command, for the decisive and splendid victory gained on Lake Champlain, on the 11th of September, in the year one thousand eight hundred and fourteen, over a British squadron of superior force.

Resolved, That the President of the United States be requested to cause gold medals to be struck, emblematical of the action between the two squadrons, and to present them to Captain Macdonough and Captain Robert Henly, and also to Lieutenant Stephen Cassin, in such manner as may be most honorable to them; and that the President be further requested to present a silver medal, with suitable emblems and devices, to each of the commissioned officers of the Navy and Army serving on board; and a sword to each of the Midshipmen and Sailingmasters, who so nobly distinguished themselves in that memorable conflict.

Resolved, That the President of the United States be requested to present a silver medal, with like emblems and devices, to the nearest male relative of Lieutenant Peter Gamble, and of Lieutenant John Stansbury, and to communicate to them the deep regret which Congress feel for the loss of those gallant men, whose names ought to live in the recollection and affection of a grateful country.

Resolved, That —— months' pay be allowed, exclusively of the common allowance, to all the petty officers, seamen, marines, and infantry serving as marines, who so gloriously supported the honor of the American flag on that memorable day.

Mr. TAIT also communicated a letter from the Secretary of the Navy, together with copies of documents in relation to the victory obtained by the United States' squadron, under the command of Captain Thomas Macdonough, over that of the enemy, on Lake Champlain; which was read, and ordered to be printed for the use of the Senate.

FRIDAY, October 7.

The resolutions expressive of the sense of Congress of the gallant conduct of Captain Thomas Macdonough, the officers, seamen, and marines, and infantry serving as marines, on board the United States' squadron on Lake Champlain, were read the second time, and considered as in Committee of the Whole; and no amendment having been proposed, the President reported them to the House accordingly; and the resolutions were ordered to be engrossed and read the third time.

The resolutions were then read the third time, by unanimous consent, and passed unanimously.

Mr. WORTHINGTON submitted the following motion:

Resolved, That the committee to whom was referred the memorial of the Legislature of the Indiana Territory, be instructed to inquire into the expediency of extending the time for locating Virginia military land warrants; and that they have leave to report by bill or otherwise.

On motion, by Mr. GORE,

Resolved, unanimously, That the Senate, from a sincere desire of testifying their respect for the long and faithful services of their late Secretary, SAMUEL A. OTIS, Esq., who performed the duties of that office with punctuality and exactness, from the commencement of this Government until the close of the last session of Congress, will go into mourning for one month, in the usual method of wearing crape round the left arm.

MR. JEFFERSON'S LIBRARY.

Mr. GOLDSBOROUGH, from the joint committee on the Library of Congress, reported a joint resolution empowering the committee to contract for the purchase of the library of Mr. Jefferson, late President of the United States, for the use of Congress; and the resolution was read, and passed to the second reading.

On motion, by Mr. GOLDSBOROUGH, the resolution was read the second time by unanimous consent and considered as in Committee of the Whole; and on motion, by Mr. KING, the further consideration thereof was postponed.

The report is as follows:

"That they have received, through Mr. Samuel H. Smith, an offer from Mr. Jefferson, late President of the United States, of the whole of his library for Congress, on such terms as they consider highly advantageous to the nation, and worthy the distinguished gentleman who tenders it. But the means placed at the disposal of the committee being very limited, and totally inadequate to the purchase of such a library as that now offered, the committee must have recourse to Congress either to extend their powers, or adopt such other as they may think most proper.

"Should it be the sense of Congress to confide this matter to the committee, they respectfully submit the following resolution:

"*Resolved, by the Senate and House of Representatives of the United States of America, in Congress assembled,* That the joint library committee of the two Houses of Congress be, and they are hereby, authorized and empowered to contract, on their part, for the purchase of the library of Mr. Jefferson, late President of the United States, for the use of both Houses of Congress."

MONDAY, October 10.

GEORGE WALKER, appointed a Senator by the Executive of the State of Kentucky, in place of George M. Bibb, resigned, produced his credentials, was qualified, and he took his seat in the Senate.

The Senate proceeded to consider the motion submitted the 7th instant, directing the committee on the memorial of the Legislature of the Indiana

Territory to inquire into the expediency of extending the time for locating Virginia military land warrants; and agreed thereto.

Mr. TAIT, from the Committee on Naval Affairs, reported, in part, a resolution expressive of the sense of Congress relative to the victory of the Peacock over the Epervier; and the resolution was read, and passed to the second reading.

Mr. TAIT communicated a letter from the Secretary for the Department of the Navy, with copies of the official account and other papers, relative to the capture of the enemy's sloop of war Epervier, by the United States' sloop of war Peacock, commanded by Captain Warrington; and the letter and documents therein referred to were read; and ordered to be printed for the use of the Senate.

A message from the House of Representatives informed the Senate that the House have passed a bill, entitled "An act further to extend the right of suffrage, and to increase the number of members of the Legislative Council in the Mississippi Territory," in which they request the concurrence of the Senate.

The bill last brought up for concurrence was read, and passed to the second reading.

The following Message was received from the PRESIDENT OF THE UNITED STATES:

To the Senate and House of Representatives of the United States:

I lay before Congress communications just received from the Plenipotentiaries of the United States, charged with negotiating peace with Great Britain, showing the conditions on which alone that Government is willing to put an end to the war.

The instructions to those Plenipotentiaries, disclosing the grounds on which they were authorized to negotiate and conclude a treaty of peace, will be the subject of another communication.

WASHINGTON, *October* 10, 1814.

The Message and documents were read, and one thousand copies thereof ordered to be printed for the use of the Senate.

MR. JEFFERSON'S LIBRARY.

Mr. GOLDSBOROUGH, chairman of the joint Library Committee of Congress, communicated a letter from Samuel H. Smith, Esq., enclosing one from Mr. Jefferson, tendering the disposition of his library to Congress; which were read.

Mr. Jefferson's letter is as follows:

MONTICELLO, *September* 21, 1814.

DEAR SIR: I learn from the newspapers that the Vandalism of our enemy has triumphed at Washington, over science as well as the arts, by the destruction of the public library, with the noble edifice in which it was deposited. Of this transaction, as of that of Copenhagen, the world will entertain but one sentiment. They will see a nation suddenly withdraw from a great war, full armed and full handed, taking advantage of another whom they had recently forced into it, unarmed and unprepared, to indulge themselves in acts of barbarism which does not belong to a civilized age. When Van Tromp destroyed their shipping at Chatham, and De Ruyter rode triumphantly up the Thames, he might, in like manner, by the acknowledgment of their own historians, have forced all their ships up to London bridge, and there have burnt them, the Tower, and city, had these examples been then set. London, when thus menaced, was near a thousand years old; Washington but in its teens.

I presume it will be among the early objects of Congress to recommence their collection. This will be difficult while the war continues, and intercourse with Europe is attended with so much risk. You know my collection, its condition and extent. I have been fifty years making it, and have spared no pains, opportunity or expense, to make it what it now is. While residing in Paris I devoted every afternoon I was disengaged, for a Summer or two, in examining all the principal bookstores, turning over every book with my own hands, and putting by everything which related to America, and, indeed, whatever was rare and valuable in every science; besides this, I had standing orders, during the whole time I was in Europe, in its principal book marts, particularly Amsterdam, Frankfort, Madrid, and London, for such works relating to America as could not be found in Paris. So that in that department, particularly, such a collection was made as probably can never again be effected; because it is hardly probable that the same opportunities, the same time, industry, perseverance, and expense, with some knowledge of the bibliography of the subject, would again happen to be in concurrence. During the same period, and after my return to America, I was led to procure also whatever related to the duties of those in the highest concerns of the nation; so that the collection, which I suppose is of between nine and ten thousand volumes, while it includes what is chiefly valuable in science and literature generally, extends more particularly to whatever belongs to the American statesman; in the diplomatic and parliamentary branches, it is particularly full. It is long since I have been sensible it ought not to continue private property, and had provided that, at my death, Congress should have the refusal of it, at their own price; but the loss they have now incurred makes the present the proper moment for their accommodation, without regard to the small remnant of time and the barren use of my enjoying it. I ask of your friendship, therefore, to make for me the tender of it to the Library Committee of Congress, not knowing myself of whom the committee consists. I enclose you a catalogue, which will enable them to judge of its contents. Nearly the whole are well bound—abundance of them elegantly, and of the choicest editions. They may be valued by the persons named by themselves, and the payment made convenient to the public; it may be, for instance, in such annual instalments as the law of Congress has left at their disposal, or in stock of any of their late loans or any loan they may institute at this session, so as to spare the present calls of our country, and await its days of peace and prosperity. They may enter, nevertheless, into immediate use of it, as eighteen or twenty wagons would place it in Washington in a single trip of a fortnight. I should be willing, indeed, to retain a few of the books to amuse the time I have yet to pass, which might be valued with the rest, but not included in the sum of valuation until they should be restored at my death, which I would cheerfully provide for, so that the whole library, as it stands in the catalogue at this moment, should be theirs, without any garbling. Those I should like to retain would be chiefly classical and mathematical, some few in other branches, and particularly one of the five Encyclopedias in the catalogue; but this, if not acceptable, would

not be urged. I must add, that I have not revised the library since I came home to live, so that it is probable some of the books may be missing, except in the chapters of law and divinity, which have been revised, and stand exactly as in the catalogue, which will of course be needed, whether the tender be accepted or not. I do not know that it contains any branch of science which Congress would wish to exclude from their collection. There is in fact no subject to which a member of Congress may not have occasion to refer. But such a wish would not correspond with my views of preventing its dismemberment. My design is either to place it in their hands entire, or preserve it so here. I am engaged in making an alphabetical index of the authors' names, to be annexed to the catalogue, in order to facilitate the finding their works in the catalogue, which I will forward to you as soon as completed. Any agreement you shall be so good as to take the trouble of entering into with the committee, I hereby confirm.

Accept the assurance of my great esteem and respect,

THOMAS JEFFERSON.

The Senate then resumed, as in Committee of the Whole, the "resolution empowering the joint library committee to contract for the purchase of Mr. Jefferson's library;" and, no amendment having been proposed, the President reported it to the House accordingly; and on the question, Shall this resolution be engrossed and read a third time? it was determined in the affirmative.

On motion by Mr. FROMENTIN, it was read a third time by unanimous consent, and passed.

TUESDAY, October 11.

The bill, entitled "An act further to extend the right of suffrage, and to increase the number of members of the Legislative Council of the Mississippi Territory," was read the second time; and referred to a select committee, to consider and report thereon; and Messrs. MORROW, BLEDSOE, and CHACE, were appointed the committee.

The resolution "expressive of the sense of Congress relative to the victory of the Peacock over the Epervier," was read the second time, and considered as in Committee of the Whole; and, no amendment having been proposed, the President reported it to the House accordingly; and the resolution was ordered to be engrossed and read a third time.

Agreeably to the resolution of the 6th instant, the Senate proceeded to the election of a Secretary, and the whole number of ballots collected was thirty-one, of which CHARLES CUTTS, had sixteen, and was accordingly elected in the place of Samuel Allyne Otis, deceased.

WEDNESDAY, October 12.

The oaths prescribed were, by the President, administered to CHARLES CUTTS, Esq., Secretary of the Senate.

Mr. FROMENTIN, from the committee, reported the resolution expressive of the sense of Congress relative to the victory of the Peacock over the Epervier, correctly engrossed; and it was read a third time.

Resolved, unanimously, That the said resolution do pass.

Mr. MORROW, from the committee to whom was referred the bill, entitled "An act further to extend the right of suffrage. and to increase the number of members of the Legislative Council in the Mississippi Territory," reported it without amendment.

THURSDAY, October 13.

The Senate resumed, as in Committee of the Whole, the consideration of the bill, entitled "An act further to extend the right of suffrage, and to increase the number of members of the Legislative Council of the Mississippi Territory; and, on motion, by Mr. GILES, the further consideration thereof was postponed to Monday next.

FRIDAY, October 14.

Mr. GOLDSBOROUGH presented the memorial of Washington Bowie, and others, owners of the ship Allegany, praying to be reimbursed the value of said vessel, which was seized and condemned at Gibraltar by the enemy, whilst employed in the service of the United States, for reasons stated at large in the memorial; which was read, and referred to a select committee, to consider and report thereon, by bill or otherwise; and Messrs. GOLDSBOROUGH, GORE, and CHACE, were appointed the committee.

The following Message was received from the PRESIDENT OF THE UNITED STATES:

To the Senate and House of
Representatives of the United States:

I now transmit to Congress copies of the instructions to the Plenipotentiaries of the United States, charged with negotiating a peace with Great Britain, as referred to in my Message of the 10th instant.
JAMES MADISON.
WASHINGTON *October* 13, 1814.

The Message and documents therein referred to, not confidentially communicated, were read, and ordered to be printed for the use of the Senate.

On motion by Mr. BIBB,

Resolved, That the Message and documents, together with several communications of the President of the United States to the Senate, since the commencement of the present session, relating to our foreign affairs, be referred to a select committee.

Ordered, That Messrs. BIBB, TAYLOR, KING, BROWN, and CHACE, be the committee.

On motion, by Mr. ANDERSON, the galleries were cleared and the doors of the Senate Chamber closed.

SATURDAY, October 15.

A message from the House of Representatives informed the Senate that the House have passed resolutions expressive of the sense of Congress of the gallantry and good conduct with which the reputation of the arms of the United States has been sustained by Major General Brown, Major General Scott, and Brigadiers Ripley, Miller,

Porter, Gaines, and Macomb," in which they request the concurrence of the Senate.

The resolutions last mentioned were read, and passed to the second reading.

On motion, by Mr. MASON, the Secretary of the Senate was required to purchase, for the use of the Senate, four copies of the laws of the United States, and two copies of Graydon's Digest of said laws.

MONDAY, October 17.

The resolutions expressive of the sense of Congress of the gallantry and good conduct with which the reputation of the arms of the United States has been sustained by Major General Brown, Major General Scott, and Brigadiers Ripley, Miller, Porter. Gaines, and Macomb," were read the second time. and referred to the Committee on Military Affairs, to consider and report thereon.

The Senate resumed, as in Committee of the Whole, the consideration of the bill, entitled "An act further to extend the right of suffrage, and to increase the number of members of the Legislative Council, in the Mississippi Territory;" and, on motion of Mr. BLEDSOE, the consideration thereof was further postponed to Wednesday next.

Mr. MORROW presented the petition of Edward Bland and others, inhabitants of the City of Washington, lately employed at the navy yard, praying indemnification for the loss of a quantity of tools, which, with the public buildings, were consumed by order of the Secretary of the Navy, as is stated in the petition; which was read, and referred to the Secretary for the Department of Navy, to consider and report thereon to the Senate.

Mr. TAYLOR presented the petition of Jeremiah Searcy, formerly a citizen of South Carolina, now a citizen of Madison county, in the State of Kentucky, an old Revolutionary soldier, praying relief, for reasons stated at large in the petition; which was read.

Mr. TAIT, from the Naval Committee, reported, in part, a resolution expressive of the sense of Congress relative to the capture of the British sloop Reindeer by the American sloop Wasp;" and the resolution was read, and passed to the second reading.

Mr. TAIT communicated a letter from the Secretary for the Department of Navy, with copies of the documents relative to the capture and destruction of the enemy's sloop of war Reindeer, by the American sloop of war Wasp, commanded by Captain Johnston Blakely; and the letter and documents therein referred to were read, and ordered to be printed for the use of the Senate.

TUESDAY, October 18.

Mr. MORROW, from the committee to whom the subject was referred, reported a bill further extending the time for locating Virginia military land warrants, and for returning the surveys thereon to the General Land Office; and the bill was read, and passed to the second reading.

The PRESIDENT communicated a letter from Peter Landais, together with a representation of his claim against the United States; which were read, and referred to a select committee, to consider and report thereon by bill or otherwise; and Messrs. FROMENTIN, WALKER, and BROWN, were appointed the committee.

The resolution expressive of the sense of Congress relative to the capture of the British sloop Reindeer by the American sloop Wasp, was read the second time, and considered as in Committee of the Whole; and no amendment having been proposed, the President reported it to the House accordingly; and the resolution was ordered to be engrossed and read a third time.

WEDNESDAY, October 19.

The bill further extending the time for locating Virginia military land warrants, and for returning the surveys thereon to the General Land Office, was read the second time.

Mr. FROMENTIN, from the committee, reported the resolution expressive of the sense of Congress relative to the capture of the British sloop Reindeer by the American sloop Wasp, correctly engrossed; which was read the third time, and passed unanimously.

Mr. GILES from the Committee on Military Affairs, to whom were referred the resolutions expressive of the sense of Congress of the gallantry and good conduct with which the reputation of the arms of the United States has been sustained by Major General Brown, Major General Scott, and Brigadiers Ripley, Miller, Porter, Gaines, and Macomb, reported them with amendments; which were read and considered as in Committee of the Whole, and agreed to; and on motion, by Mr. ROBINSON, the resolutions were further amended, and the President reported them to the House accordingly.

On the question, Shall these resolutions be read a third time as amended? it was determined in the affirmative.

The resolutions were then read a third time as amended, by unanimous consent, and passed unanimously with amendments.

On motion, by Mr. FROMENTIN, it was agreed that the title thereof be amended.

A message from the House of Representatives informed the Senate that the House have passed the resolution which originated in the Senate empowering the joint Library Committee of Congress to contract for the purchase of Mr. Jefferson's library, with an amendment, in which they request the concurrence of the Senate.

The Senate resumed, as in Committee of the Whole, the consideration of the bill, entitled "An act further to extend the right of suffrage, and to increase the number of members of the Legislative Council in the Mississippi Territory; and the President having reported it to the House without amendment, on the question, Shall this bill be read a third time? it was determined in the affirmative—yeas 16, nays 12, as follows:

YEAS—Messrs. Anderson, Bledsoe, Chace, Condit, Gaillard, German, Goldsborough, Lacock, Morrow, Roberts, Robinson, Turner, Varnum, Walker, Wharton, and Worthington.

NAYS—Messrs. Bibb, Daggett, Fromentin, Giles, Horsey, Hunter, King, Mason, Tait, Taylor, Thompson, and Wells.

THURSDAY, October 20.

SAMUEL SMITH, from the State of Maryland, took his seat in the Senate.

The Senate proceeded to consider the amendment of the House of Representatives to the resolution empowering the joint Library Committee of Congress to contract for the purchase of Mr. Jefferson's library.

On motion, by Mr. MASON, that the further consideration thereof be postponed to the first Monday in April next, it was determined in the negative—yeas 7, nays 21, as follows:

YEAS—Messrs. Daggett, German, Gore, Horsey, King, Mason, and Thompson.

NAYS—Messrs. Anderson, Bibb, Bledsoe, Brown, Chace, Condit, Fromentin, Gaillard, Giles, Goldsborough, Lacock, Morrow, Roberts, Robinson, Tait, Taylor, Turner, Varnum, Walker, Wharton, and Worthington.

Whereupon, *Resolved*, That they concur therein.

The bill, entitled "An act further to extend the right of suffrage, and to increase the number of members of the Legislative Council in the Mississippi Territory," was read the third time, and passed.

The Senate resumed, as in Committee of the Whole, the consideration of the bill further extending the time for locating Virginia military land warrants, and for returning the surveys thereon to the General Land Office; and, no amendment having been proposed, the President reported it to the House accordingly; and it was ordered to be engrossed and read a third time.

FRIDAY, October 21.

The bill further extending the time for locating Virginia military land warrants, and for returning the surveys thereon to the General Land Office, was read a third time; and on motion, by Mr. FROMENTIN, the bill was amended by unanimous consent; and on motion by Mr. MORROW, the blanks were filled, first, with "three," second, with "five."

Resolved, That this bill pass.

Mr. GERMAN submitted the following motion:

Resolved, That the committee to whom was referred that part of the President's Message which relates to the classification of the militia, be instructed to inquire into the expediency of adopting the following plan, viz: That the whole militia of the United States be divided into classes of ten men; that it be obligatory on each class to furnish, on the requisition of the President of the United States, on the first Monday of April, annually, one able-bodied man, who shall serve for the term of one year, in a corps of local militia, to be organized in each State for the defence thereof.

Mr. FROMENTIN submitted the following motion:

Resolved, That there be printed, for the use of the

Senate, a list of all the bills which have been laid before the Senate at any former session, and which have been rejected by the Senate, or by the House of Representatives; and that a similar list be thus printed at the beginning of every session of Congress.

The Senate adjourned to Monday.

MONDAY, October 24.

JOHN LAMBERT, from the State of New Jersey, took his seat in the Senate.

A message from the House of Representatives informed the Senate that the House disagree to the amendments of the Senate to the resolutions expressive of the sense of Congress of the gallantry and good conduct with which the reputation of the arms of the United States has been sustained by Major General Brown, Major General Scott, and Brigadiers Ripley, Miller, Porter, Gaines, and Macomb.

The Senate proceeded to consider the amendments disagreed to by the House of Representatives to the resolutions last mentioned.

On motion, by Mr. GILES,

Resolved, That they insist on their amendments, and ask a conference on the disagreeing votes of the two Houses; and,

Ordered, That Messrs. GILES, SMITH, and VARNUM, be the managers at the said conference on the part of the Senate.

The Senate resumed the motion made the 21st instant, by Mr. GERMAN, respecting the classification of the militia; and the further consideration thereof was postponed until to-morrow.

On motion, by Mr. GOLDSBOROUGH,

Resolved, That the President of the United States be requested to lay before the Senate (provided he shall not consider the same improper to be communicated,) the proof of any traffic carried on in the West Indies, by the sale of negroes taken from the United States by the British forces since the present war, which was alluded to in the letter of the Secretary of State to the American Plenipotentiaries at Gottenburg, of date 28th day of January, 1814, and contained in his late Message to Congress.

The Senate resumed the motion made the 21st instant, to print a list of rejected bills; and, on motion, by Mr. FROMENTIN, it was amended; and the further consideration thereof postponed.

TUESDAY, October 25.

The Senate resumed the motion made the 21st instant, respecting the classification of the militia, and the further consideration thereof was postponed until to-morrow.

The Senate resumed the motion made the 21st instant, to print a list of rejected bills; and on motion, by Mr. LACOCK, it was referred to a select committee, to consider and report thereon, and Messrs. FROMENTIN, LACOCK, and VARNUM, were appointed the committee.

WEDNESDAY, October 26.

Mr. TAIT, from the Committee on Naval Affairs,

reported, in part, a bill authorizing the President of the United States to cause to be built or purchased the vessels therein described; and the bill was read, and passed to the second reading.

A message from the House of Representatives informed the Senate that the House insist on their disagreement to the amendments of the Senate, to the resolutions "expressive of the sense of Congress of the gallantry and good conduct with which the reputation of the arms of the United States has been sustained by Major General Brown, Major General Scott, and Brigadiers Ripley, Miller, Porter, Gaines, and Macomb." They agree to the conference proposed on the subject, and have appointed managers on their part.

The Senate resumed the motion made on the 21st instant, by Mr. GERMAN, respecting the classification of the militia; and agreed thereto.

MEMORIAL OF STEPHEN GIRARD.

Mr. ROBERTS presented the memorial of Stephen Girard, of the city of Philadelphia, stating that he has established a bank upon his own fortune and credit, and for his own exclusive emolument, and that, by the construction given to the act of Congress laying duties on notes of banks, bankers, &c., he is excluded from the privileges enjoyed by other banking companies, and praying relief, for reasons stated at large in the memorial; which was read, and referred to a select committee, to consider and report thereon by bill or otherwise; and Messrs. ROBERTS, SMITH, and DAGGETT, were appointed the committee.

The memorial is as follows:

To the Senate and House of Representatives in Congress assembled, the memorial of Stephen Girard, of the city of Philadelphia, in the State of Pennsylvania, merchant and banker, respectfully showeth:

That your memorialist has established a bank in the city of Philadelphia, upon the foundation of his own individual fortune and credit, and for his own exclusive emolument, and that he is willing most cheerfully to contribute, in common with his fellow-citizens throughout the United States, a full proportion of the taxes which have been imposed for the support of the National Government according to the profits of his occupation and the value of his estate; but a construction has been given to the acts of Congress laying duties on notes of banks, &c., from which great difficulties have occurred and great inequalities daily produced to the disadvantage of his bank, that were not, it is confidently believed, within the contemplation of the Legislature.

That the first section of the act of Congress of the 2d August, 1813, having imposed a stamp duty on notes issued by any banker or bankers, as well as by any banks or companies, either incorporated or not incorporated, it is provided by the second section of the act, "that in respect to any stamp on any of the notes of the banks or companies aforesaid, now established, or which may hereafter be established within the United States, it shall be lawful for the Secretary of the Treasury to agree to an annual composition, in lieu of such stamp duty, with any of the said banks or companies, of 1½ per centum on the amount of the annual dividend made by such banks to their stockholders respectively; that your memorialist, in due season, offered to enter into the said composition, at the rate of 1½ per centum on the amount of the annual profit of this bank, deeming the annual profit of an individual banker equivalent, in language and in law, to the annual dividend of a bank established by a corporation or company. That it has been officially declared, however, that the second section of the act of Congress does not authorize a composition with an individual banker, because it speaks only of banks and companies, (not of banker and bankers,) and because it speaks only of dividends (not of profits) made to the stockholders; and that hence an individual banker, acting upon a capital of one million of dollars, and issuing bank notes to the amount of one million of dollars, is subjected to the prompt payment of a duty amounting to $10,000, while an incorporated bank, or even a private company of two or three bankers, acting upon the same amount of capital and issuing the same amount of bank notes, will only be liable, periodically, to the payment of a duty amounting to $1,500, upon the customary annual dividend of ten per cent.

That the first section of the act of Congress of the 2d August, 1813, imposes a stamp duty upon any promissory note, or notes, payable either to bearer or order, issued by any banks or companies, or by any banker or bankers; that the eighth section, of the act provided that no banks or companies, which shall not have compounded for the stamp duty, shall issue any bank bill or promissory note, unless upon paper duly stamped and whereon the respective duties shall have been paid; and the twelfth section of the act declares, that all the paper wanted for the purpose of the stamp duty, excepting paper for bank notes, shall be furnished, at the expense of the United States, by the Secretary of the Treasury. That, after the rejection of this offer to enter into a composition for the stamp duty, your memorialist has complied with the directions of the law, and has transmitted to the Commissioner of the Revenue sheets of bank notes in order to be stamped.

That, independent of the great hazard and delay to which your memorialist is exposed by these operations, it is obvious, from the texture and quality of bank paper, that the stamp, as at present impressed on bank notes, must disappear in the course of an extensive circulation, producing some uncertainty in the revenue, and probably great injustice to individuals.

And your memorialist, having submitted these considerations to the wisdom of Congress, respectfully prays, that the act of Congress may be so amended, as to permit the Secretary of the Treasury to enter into a composition for the stamp duty, in the case of private bankers as well as in the case of corporations and companies, or so as to render the duty equal in its operations upon every denomination of bankers.

　　　　　　　　　　　STEPHEN GIRARD.
PHILADELPHIA, *October* 24, 1814.

THURSDAY, October 27.

The bill authorizing the President of the United States to cause to be built or purchased the vessels therein described, was read the second time; and, on motion, by Mr. TAIT, was considered as in Committee of the Whole; and, after progress, the further consideration thereof was postponed until to-morrow.

Mr. GILES, from the managers on the part of the Senate, at the conference on the amendments of the Senate disagreed to by the House of Representatives, to the resolutions "expressive of the

13th CON. 3d SESS.—2

sense of Congress of the gallantry and good conduct with which the reputation of the arms of the United States has been sustained by Major General Brown, Major General Scott, and Brigadiers Ripley, Miller, Porter, Gaines, and Macomb," reported that the conferees had agreed to certain modifications of the amendments; and the report was read.

Resolved, That the Senate concur therein, and that the resolutions be amended accordingly.

FRIDAY, October 28.

The Senate resumed, as in Committee of the Whole, the consideration of the bill authorizing the President of the United States to cause to be built or purchased the vessels therein described.

On motion, by Mr. FROMENTIN, to insert, sec. 1, line 4, after the word "purchased," "manned, equipped, and officered," and to strike out the residue of the section, after the word "each," in the seventh line, as follows: "and to be manned, equipped, and officered, in the manner which he shall judge most expedient:"

The Senate being equally divided, the President determined the question in the affirmative; and the bill having been amended, the President reported it to the House accordingly.

On the question to agree to the said amendment, it was determined in the affirmative—yeas 20, nays 7, as follows:

YEAS—Messrs. Anderson, Brown, Chace, Daggett, Fromentin, Gaillard, German, Giles, Goldsborough, Gore, Horsey, Hunter, Lambert, Mason, Robinson, Smith, Tait, Thompson, Varnum, and Worthington.

NAYS—Messrs. Bibb, Bledsoe, Condit, Lacock, Roberts, Turner, and Wharton.

On the question, Shall this bill be engrossed and read a third time? it was determined in the affirmative. The bill as amended is as follows:

Be it enacted, &c., That, in addition to the present Naval Establishment, the President of the United States be, and he is hereby authorized to cause to be built or purchased, manned, equipped, and officered, any number of vessels, not exceeding ——, which, in his opinion, the public service may require, to carry not less than —— nor more than —— guns each, and to be manned, equipped, and officered, in the manner which he shall judge most expedient.

SEC. 2. *And be it further enacted,* That, for the building and purchase and equipping of these vessels, the sum of —— dollars be and the same is hereby appropriated, to be paid out of any money in the Treasury not otherwise appropriated.

MONDAY, October 31.

On motion, by Mr. SMITH, the petition of David M. Clarkson, and others, citizens of New York, praying the establishment of a National Bank, presented the 30th ultimo, was referred to the select committee, to consist of five members, to consider and report thereon by bill or otherwise; and Messrs. KING, SMITH, TAYLOR, BIBB, and MASON, were appointed the committee.

A message from the House of Representatives informed the Senate that the House have passed a bill, entitled "An act to authorize a loan for a sum not exceeding three millions of dollars," in which bill they request the concurrence of the Senate.

The bill last mentioned was read, and passed to the second reading.

The bill authorizing the President of the United States to cause to be built or purchased the vessels herein described having been reported by the committee correctly engrossed, was read a third time; and the blanks were filled; first with "twenty," second, with "eight," third, with "fourteen," fourth, with "six hundred thousand."

Resolved, That this bill pass, and that the title thereof be "An act authorizing the President of the United States,to cause to be built or purchased the vessels therein described."

TUESDAY, November 1.

The bill, entitled "An act to authorize a loan for a sum not exceeding three millions of dollars," was read the second time, and referred to a select committee to consider and report thereon; and Messrs. GORE, BIBB, and SMITH, were appointed the committee.

A message from the House of Representatives informed the Senate that the House have passed a resolution requesting the President of the United States to recommend a day of public humiliation, fasting, and prayer, in which they request the concurrence of the Senate.

The resolution last mentioned was read, and passed to the second reading.

Mr. LACOCK submitted the following motion:

Resolved, That the Committee of Accounts be authorised to audit and control the accounts for the funeral expenses of Samuel A. Otis, Esquire, late Secretary of the Senate, and for a monument erected to his memory; and that the expenses be paid out of the contingent fund of the Senate. And the resolution was read.

Ordered, That it pass to the second reading.

WEDNESDAY, November 2.

SAMUEL W. DANA, from the State of Connecticut, took his seat in the Senate.

Mr. ROBERTS presented the memorial of Oliver Evans, praying a general extension of the patent term, or a renewal of his patent for his improvements in steam engines; for reasons stated at large in the memorial; which was read, and referred to a select committee, to consist of five members, to consider and report thereon by bill or otherwise; and Messrs. ROBERTS, SMITH, DANA, ANDERSON, and VARNUM, were appointed the committee.

The resolution authorizing the Committee of Accounts to audit and control the accounts for the funeral expenses of Samuel A. Otis, Esquire, late Secretary of the Senate, was read the second time.

The resolution requesting the President of the United States to recommend a day of public humiliation, fasting, and prayer, was read the second time.

A message from the House of Representatives informed the Senate that the House have passed a bill, entitled "An act for the relief of the petty officers and seamen under the command of Captain Joshua Barney," in which bill they request the concurrence of the Senate.

The bill last mentioned was read, and passed to the second reading.

THURSDAY, November 3.

Mr. ROBERTS, from the committee, to whom was referred the petition of Stephen Girard, reported a bill supplementary to an act laying duties on notes of banks, bankers, and certain companies; on notes, bonds, and obligations,discounted by banks, bankers, and certain companies; and on bills of exchange of certain descriptions; and the bill was read, and passed to the second reading.

Mr. BLEDSOE submitted the following motion:

Resolved, That the Committee on Military Affairs be instructed to inquire into the expediency of establishing, by law, an additional number of military academies.

The bill, entitled "An act for the relief of the petty officers and seamen under the command of Captain Joshua Barney," was read the second time, and referred to the Committee on Naval Affairs, to consider and report thereon.

The Senate resumed, as in Committee of the Whole, the consideration of the resolution authorizing the Committee of Accounts to audit and control the accounts for the funeral expenses of Samuel A. Otis, Esquire, late Secretary of the Senate; and, no amendment having been proposed, the President reported it to the House accordingly; and the resolution was ordered to be engrossed, and read a third time.

The Senate resumed, as in Committee of the Whole, the consideration of the resolution requesting the President of the United States to recommend a day of public humiliation, fasting, and prayer; and, no amendment having been proposed, it was ordered to a third reading.

The resolution was then read a third time by unanimous consent, and passed.

Mr. GORE, from the committee, to whom was referred the bill, entitled "An act to authorize a loan for a sum not exceeding three millions of dollars," reported it without amendment; and the bill was considered as in Committee of the Whole.

On motion, by Mr. GORE, to strike out, of section 5, after the word "thereof," in the 20th line, to the end of the section, and insert, between sections 5 and 6, the following:

"SEC. 6. *And be it further enacted,* That, in addition to the annual sum of eight millions of dollars, heretofore appropriated to the Sinking Fund, a further annual sum, to be provided by permanent funds, and which shall be equal to the interest payable upon the stock created by virtue of this act, together with a sum that shall be equal to one per centum upon the whole principal of said stock, shall, during the present session of Congress, be appropriated to the said Sinking Fund, and vested in the commissioners thereof, in trust, to be by them applied to pay the interest and to reimburse the principal of the said stock created by this act;"

And, after debate, the further consideration thereof was postponed until to-morrow.

Friday, November 4.

Mr. Goldsborough, from the committee to whom was referred the memorial of Bowie and Kurtz, and others, made a report; which was read.

He also reported a bill for the relief of Bowie and Kurtz, and others, and the bill was read, and passed to the second reading.

Mr. Tait, from the Committee on Naval Affairs, to whom was referred the bill, entitled "An act for the relief of the petty officers and seamen under the command of Captain Joshua Barney," reported it without amendment.

The Senate resumed the motion made yesterday, instructing the Committee on Military Affairs to inquire into the expediency of establishing by law an additional number of military academies, and agreed thereto.

The bill supplementary to an act laying duties on notes of banks, bankers, and certain companies; on notes, bonds, and obligations, discounted by banks, bankers, and certain companies; and on bills of exchange of certain descriptions, was read the second time.

The resolution authorizing the Committee of Accounts to audit and control the accounts for the funeral expenses of Samuel A. Otis, Esquire, late Secretary of the Senate, was read a third time.

Resolved, unanimously, That this resolution pass, as follows:

"That the Committee of Accounts be authorized to audit and control the accounts for the funeral expenses of Samuel A. Otis, Esquire, late Secretary of the Senate, and for a monument erected to his memory; and that the expenses be paid out of the contingent fund of the Senate."

The Senate resumed, as in Committee of the Whole, the consideration of the bill, entitled "An act to authorize a loan for a sum not exceeding three millions of dollars," together with the amendments proposed thereto by Mr. Gore; and having agreed to the amendments, the President reported the bill to the House accordingly.

On the question, Shall the amendments be engrossed and the bill read a third time as amended? it was determined in the affirmative.

Saturday, November 5.

Mr. Anderson presented the petition of Edward Barry, sailingmaster, and George Hodge, boatswain, in the navy yard of the United States, at Washington, praying indemnification for the loss of household furniture, books, and instruments of navigation, destroyed by the fire, as is stated in the petition; which was read, and referred to a select committee, to consider and report thereon by bill or otherwise; and Messrs. Ander-

son, Dana, and Tait, were appointed the committee.

Mr. Dana submitted the following motions:

Resolved, That the committee to whom was referred so much of the President's Message as relates to naval affairs, be instructed to inquire what provision should be made for the appointment of officers above the grade of captain, in the Navy of the United States.

Resolved, That the same committee be instructed to inquire what provision should be made for conferring naval rank, by brevet, in consideration of meritorious service.

Mr. Giles, from the Committee on Military Affairs, reported, in part, a bill making further provision for filling the ranks of the Army of the United States; and the bill was read, and passed to the second reading.

[The 1st section of this bill provides that recruiting officers shall be authorized to enlist into the Army of the United States any free, effective, able-bodied men between the ages of eighteen and fifty years.

The 2d section repeals so much of former acts as requires the consent in writing of the parent, master or guardian, to authorize the enlistment of persons under 21 years of age, provided masters of apprentices who enlist shall receive a certain portion of the bounty money, &c.

The 3d section allows to future recruits three hundred and twenty acres of land, in lieu of the land bounty now allowed by law.

The 4th section provides "that any person subject to militia duty, who shall, according to law, furnish a recruit for the Army, at his own expense, to serve during the war, shall thereafter be exempt from militia duty during the war," &c.]

Mr. Giles also reported, in part, a bill to authorize the President of the United States to call upon the several States and Territories thereof for their respective quotas of —— thousand militia, for the defence of the frontiers of the United States; which was read, and passed to the second reading.

The bill for the relief of Bowie and Kurtz, and others, was read the second time.

The bill, entitled "An act to authorize a loan for a sum not exceeding three millions of dollars," was read a third time as amended, and passed, with amendments.

The Senate resumed, as in Committee of the Whole, the consideration of the bill, entitled "An act for the relief of the petty officers and seamen under the command of Captain Joshua Barney;" and the bill having been amended, the President reported it to the House accordingly; and,

On the question, to agree to the amendment, made in Committee of the Whole, to strike out of lines 6 and 7, "and losses;" it was determined in the negative.

On motion, by Mr. Brown, the further consideration thereof was postponed until Monday next.

The Senate resumed, as in Committee of the Whole, the consideration of the bill supplementary to an act laying duties on notes of banks, bankers, and certain companies; on notes, bonds, and obligations, discounted by banks, bankers, and certain companies; and on bills of exchange of certain descriptions; and, after debate, the further consideration thereof was postponed until Monday next.

MONDAY, November 7.

On motion, by Mr. GILES,

Resolved, That the Secretary of the Senate cause to be procured and delivered to each member of the Senate a copy of the military laws and rules and regulations for the Army of the United States.

The bill making further provision for filling the ranks of the Army of the United States, was read the second time, and the further consideration thereof postponed to, and made the special order of the day for to-morrow.

The bill to authorize the President of the United States to call upon the several States and Territories thereof, for their respective quotas of ———— thousand militia, for the defence of the frontiers of the United States, was read the second time.

The Senate resumed the consideration of the motions made the 5th instant, by Mr. DANA, for instructing the Committee on Naval Affairs relative to the appointment of naval officers above the grade of captain, and for conferring naval rank by brevet, in consideration of meritorious service; and agreed thereto.

Mr. FROMENTIN submitted the following motion for consideration:

Resolved, That the Committee on Naval Affairs be directed to inquire into the causes which may have prevented, till now, a compliance with the following resolutions, passed by the Senate on the 18th March, 1814:

" *Resolved,* That it be the duty of the Secretary of the Navy to devise and digest a system for the better organization of the Department of the Navy of the United States, and to report the same to the Senate at the commencement of their next session."

" *Resolved,* That it be the duty of the Secretary of the Navy to digest, or cause to be digested, all the laws now in force relative to the naval establishment and marine corps, and to report the same to the Senate at the commencement of their next session."

Mr. MASON submitted the following motion:

Resolved, That the President of the United States be, and he is hereby, requested to cause to be laid before the Senate a statement of the number of privates and non-commissioned officers enlisted within each State or Territory for the Army of the United States, since the commencement of the present war; specifying the year of their enlistments, and the term of time for which they were enlisted; and, also, the number of commissioned officers of each rank in the Army of the United States, specifying the number, with their respective ranks, belonging to each State or Territory.

Mr. SMITH presented the petition of George P. Stevenson and others, merchants and shipowners of the city of Baltimore, praying that the owners of private armed vessels may receive an adequate compensation for every ton of shipping belonging to the enemy, which they shall burn, sink, or destroy, on the high seas; for reasons stated at large in the petition; which was read, and referred to the Committee on Naval Affairs, to consider and report thereon by bill or otherwise.

TUESDAY, November 8.

The Senate resumed the consideration of the motion made yesterday, by Mr. FROMENTIN, in relation to the non-compliance with the resolutions passed by the Senate on the 18th of March, 1814; and on motion by Mr. TAIT, the further consideration thereof was postponed until Monday next.

The Senate resumed the motion made yesterday, by Mr. MASON, requesting a statement of enlistments within each State or Territory for the Army of the United States since the commencement of the present war; and, on motion, the further consideration thereof was postponed.

A message from the House of Representatives informed the Senate that the House have appointed a committee on their part, jointly with the committee to be appointed on the part of the Senate, to wait on the President of the United States and request him to recommend a day of public humiliation, fasting, and prayer, in pursuance of the joint resolution passed for that purpose.

UNIFORM MILITIA.

Mr. WORTHINGTON, from the Committee on the Militia of the United States, reported, in part, a bill further in addition to an act, entitled "An act more effectually to provide for the national defence by establishing a uniform militia throughout the United States;" and the bill was read, and passed to the second reading.

The bill is as follows:

A bill further in addition to the act, entitled an act more effectually to provide for the national defence by establishing a uniform militia throughout the United States.

Be it enacted by the Senate and House of Representatives of the United States of America in Congress assembled, That, in addition to the citizens directed to be enrolled by the first section of an act, entitled "An act more effectually to provide for the national defence by establishing a uniform militia throughout the United States," each and every free able-bodied white male citizen of the United States and Territories thereof, who is or shall be between the ages of sixteen and eighteen years, shall severally and respectively be immediately enrolled in the militia, by the Captain or commanding officer of the company within whose bounds such citizen shall reside, and, when enrolled and notified according to law, shall be holden to arm and equip himself, and to do and perform all the duties, and be subject to all the penalties in cases of neglect, as now are, or shall hereafter be, provided for by law for the government of the militia of the United States, except that such citizen shall not be subject to be draughted into the actual service of the United States while he remains under the age of eighteen years.

SEC. 2. *And be it further enacted,* That each and every free able-bodied white male citizen of the United States and Territories thereof, of the age of eighteen years, and under the age of forty-five years, who, by the laws of the United States, or any other State or Territory thereof, have been exempted from common trainings for the purpose of discipline, or from militia duty generally, with every free able-bodied white male citizen of the age of forty-five years, and under the age of fifty years, except ministers of the gospel, shall be immediately enrolled in the militia, by the Captain or commanding officer of the company within whose bounds such citizen shall reside, and, when so enrolled and notified according to law, such citizen shall be holden to arm and equip himself, and to do and perform all the duties, and be subject to all the penalties, in case of neglect, as now are, or shall hereafter be, provided for by law for the government of the militia of the United States, except that such citizen shall not be subject to attend the trainings of militia for discipline.

ARMY OF THE UNITED STATES.

The Senate resumed, as in Committee of the Whole, the consideration of the bill making further provision for filling the ranks of the Army of the United States.

On motion, by Mr. MASON, to strike out the third section of the bill amended, as follows:

"SEC. 3. *And be it further enacted,* That, in lieu of the bounty of one hundred and sixty acres of land, now allowed by law, there shall be allowed to each non-commissioned officer and soldier hereafter enlisted, when discharged from service, who shall have obtained from the commanding officer of his company, battalion, or regiment, a certificate that he had faithfully performed his duty whilst in service, three hundred and twenty acres of land, to be surveyed, laid off, and granted, under the same regulations, and in every respect in the manner, now prescribed by law; and the widow and children, and, if there be no widow nor child, the parents, of every non-commissioned officer and soldier enlisted according to law, who may be killed or die in the service of the United States, shall be entitled to receive the three hundred and twenty acres of land as aforesaid; but the same shall not pass to collateral relations; any law heretofore passed to the contrary notwithstanding."

It was determined in the negative—yeas 6, nays 22, as follows:

YEAS—Messrs. Daggett, Goldsborough, Horsey, Mason, Smith, and Thompson.

NAYS—Messrs. Anderson, Bibb, Bledsoe, Brent, Brown, Chace, Condit, Dana, Fromentin, Gaillard, German, Giles, Lacock, Lambert, Morrow, Roberts, Robinson, Tait, Taylor, Turner, Varnum, and Wheaton.

On motion, by Mr. GERMAN, to strike out, section one, line seven, after the word "years," the residue of the section, as follows: "which enlistment shall be absolute and binding upon all persons under the age of twenty-one years, as well as upon all persons of full age, such recruiting officer having complied with all the requisitions of the laws regulating the recruiting service:" it was determined in the negative—yeas 9, nays 19, as follows:

YEAS—Messrs. Daggett, Dana, German, Goldsborough, Hunter, King, Lambert, Mason, and Thompson.

NAYS—Messrs. Anderson, Bibb, Bledsoe, Brown, Chace, Condit, Fromentin, Gaillard, Giles, Lacock, Morrow, Roberts, Smith, Tait, Taylor, Turner, Varnum, Wharton, and Worthington.

WEDNESDAY, November 9.

Resolved, That a committee be appointed on the part of the Senate, jointly with the committee appointed by the House of Representatives, to wait on the President of the United States and request him to recommend a day of humiliation, fasting, and prayer, in pursuance of the joint resolution passed for that purpose.

Ordered, That Mr. ROBINSON be the committee on the part of the Senate.

Mr. ROBERTS, from the committee to whom was referred the memorial of Oliver Evans, reported a bill to extend the time of Oliver Evans's patent for his improvement on steam engines; and the bill was read, and passed to the second reading.

The Senate resumed the consideration of the motion made the 7th instant, by Mr. MASON, which was amended and agreed to, as follows:

"*Resolved,* That the President of the United States be, and he is hereby, requested to cause to be laid before the Senate a statement, as far as practicable, of the number of privates and non-commissioned officers enlisted within each State or Territory for the Army of the United States, since the commencement of the present war; specifying the year of their enlistments, and the term of time for which they were enlisted; and also the number of commissioned officers of each rank, in the Army of the United States, specifying the number, with their respective ranks, belonging to each State or Territory."

The bill further in addition to an act, entitled "An act more effectually to provide for the national defence by establishing a uniform militia throughout the United States," was read the second time.

The Senate resumed, as in Committee of the Whole, the consideration of the bill making further provision for filling the ranks of the Army of the United States.

On motion, by Mr. DANA, to strike out, section two, line one, after the word "that," so much of the fifth section of the act passed the 25th day of January, 1813, entitled "An act supplementary to the act, entitled 'An act for the more perfect organization of the Army of the United States, as requires the consent in writing of the parent, guardian, or master, to authorize the enlistment of persons under the age of twenty-one years shall be and the same is hereby repealed."

On motion, it was agreed to take the question by yeas and nays.

After debate, on motion by Mr. HORSEY, the further consideration thereof was postponed until to-morrow.

A message from the House of Representatives informed the Senate that the House have passed the bill which originated in the Senate, entitled "An act authorizing the President of the United States to cause to be built or purchased the vessels therein described," with an amendment, in which they request the concurrence of the Senate. They have also passed a bill, entitled "An act for the relief of John Castille, of the city of New Orleans;" in which they request the concurrence of the Senate. They also inform the Senate of the accidental loss of the amendments of the Senate to the bill, entitled "An act to authorize a loan for a sum not exceeding three millions of dollars;" and request a substitution of the same.

On motion, the Senate proceeded to consider the message from the House of Representatives, requesting the substitution of the amendments of the Senate to the bill, entitled "An act to authorize a loan for a sum not exceeding three millions of dollars."

On motion, by Mr. KING, it was referred to a select committee, to consider and report thereon; and Messrs. KING, BIBB, and BLEDSOE, were appointed the committee.

The bill last brought up for concurrence was read, and passed to the second reading.

The Senate proceeded to consider the amendment of the House of Representatives to the bill, entitled "An act authorizing the President of the United States to cause to be built or purchased the vessels therein described;" and, on motion by Mr. SMITH, resolved not to concur therein.

THURSDAY, November 10.

A message from the House of Representatives informed the Senate that the House insist on their amendment disagreed to by the Senate, to the bill, entitled "An act authorizing the President of the United States to cause to be built or purchased the vessels therein described;" they ask a conference on the disagreeing votes of the two Houses, and have appointed managers on their part. They have passed a bill, entitled "An act authorizing the Secretary of State, during the continuance of the present war, to make an additional allowance to the owners and masters of vessels for bringing back to the United States destitute and distressed American seamen;" in which bill they request the concurrence of the Senate.

The bill last mentioned was read, and passed to the second reading.

Mr. KING, from the committee to whom was referred the message of the House of Representatives of the 9th instant, reported the following order:

Ordered, That a copy, duly engrossed, of the amendments made by the Senate to the bill, entitled "An act authorizing a loan for a sum not exceeng a sum of three millions of dollars," be carried by the Secretary of the Senate to the House of Representatives, pursuant to the request contained in their message of the 9th instant.

On the question, Will the Senate concur in the report of the committee? it was determined in the affirmative.

Mr. FROMENTIN, from the committee, reported the amendments to the bill last mentioned duly engrossed.

On motion, by Mr. TAIT,

Resolved, That the Senate insist on their disagreement to the amendment of the House of Representatives to the bill, entitled "An act author

izing the President of the United States to cause to be built or purchased the vessels therein described," and agree to the conference proposed thereon.

Ordered, That Messrs. SMITH, FROMENTIN, and TAIT, be the managers on the part of the Senate.

The bill to extend the time of Oliver Evans's patent for his improvement on steam engines was read the second time.

The bill, entitled "An act for the relief of John Castille, of the city of New Orleans," was read the second time.

The Senate resumed, as in committee of the Whole, the consideration of the bill making further provision for filling the ranks of the Army of the United States, together with the amendment proposed thereto, yesterday, by Mr. DANA; and, after debate, on motion by Mr. ROBERTS, the further consideration thereof was postponed until tomorrow.

A message from the House of Representatives informed the Senate that the House disagree to the amendments of the Senate to the bill, entitled "An act to authorize a loan for a sum not exceeding three millions of dollars."

On motion, by Mr. BIBB, that the Senate recede from their amendments to the bill last mentioned, it was determined in the negative—yeas 6, nays 26, as follows:

YEAS—Messrs. Bibb, Brent, Dana, Morrow, Roberts, and Turner.

NAYS—Messrs. Anderson, Bledsoe, Brown, Chace, Condit, Daggett, Fromentin, Gaillard, German, Giles, Goldsborough, Gore, Horsey, Hunter, King, Lacock, Lambert, Mason, Smith, Tait, Taylor, Thompson, Varnum, Walker, Wharton, and Worthington.

On motion, by Mr. GORE,

Resolved, That they insist on their amendments, and ask a conference on the disagreeing votes of the two Houses.

Ordered, That Messrs. GORE, GILES, and KING, be the managers at the said conference on the part of the Senate.

Mr. GILES, from the Committee on Military Affairs, reported, in part, sundry documents received from the Secretary of the Department of War, showing the number of men who have been recruited in the Army of the United States during the present year; which was read, and ordered to be printed for the use of the Senate.

FRIDAY, November 11.

The bill, entitled "An act authorizing the Secretary of State, during the continuance of the present war, to make an additional allowance to the owners and masters of vessels for bringing back to the United States destitute and distressed American seamen," was read the second time.

The Senate resumed, as in Committee of the Whole, the consideration of the bill "making further provision for filling the ranks of the Army of the United States," together with the amendment proposed thereto by Mr. DANA, the ninth instant.

On the question, Will the Senate agree to the amendment proposed? it was determined in the negative—yeas 11, nays 21, as follows:

YEAS—Messrs. Daggett, Dana, German, Goldsborough, Gore, Horsey, Hunter, King, Lambert, Mason, and Thompson.

NAYS—Messrs. Anderson, Bibb, Bledsoe, Brent, Brown, Chace, Condit, Fromentin, Gaillard, Giles, Lacock, Morrow, Roberts, Robinson, Smith, Tait, Wharton, Taylor, Varnum, Walker, and Worthington.

And the PRESIDENT reported the bill to the House amended. On the question, Shall this bill be engrossed and read a third time as amended? it was determined in the affirmative.

Mr. SMITH, from the committee of conference on the amendment of the House of Representatives to the bill, entitled "An act authorizing the President of the United States to cause to be built or purchased the vessels therein described," reported, that the conferees had agreed to a modification of the amendment; and the report was read.

On the question, Will the Senate concur in the report of the committee of conference? it was determined in the affirmative. Whereupon,

Resolved, That the Senate concur in the amendment of the House of Representatives to the bill last mentioned, so as to adopt the report of the managers at the conference.

A message from the House of Representatives informed the Senate that they insist on their disagreement to the amendments of the Senate to the bill, entitled "An act to authorize a loan for a sum not exceeding three millions of dollars." They agree to the conference proposed on the subject, and have appointed managers on their part. They have passed a bill, entitled "An act to authorize the Commissioner of the Revenue to cause a clerk in his office to aid him in signing licenses;" in which bill they request the concurrence of the Senate.

The bill last mentioned was read, and passed to the second reading.

SATURDAY, November 12.

The bill making further provision for filling the ranks of the Army of the United States, having been reported by the committee correctly engrossed was read a third time, and passed.

The bill, entitled "An act to authorize the Commissioner of the Revenue to cause a clerk in his office to aid him in signing licenses," was read the second time.

A message from the House of Representatives informed the Senate that the House have passed a bill, entitled "An act to authorize the publication of the laws of the United States within the Territories of the United States;" also, a bill entitled "An act for the relief of John Chalmers, junior," in which bills they request the concurrence of the Senate.

The two bills last mentioned were read, and passed to the second reading.

The Senate resumed, as in Committee of the Whole, the consideration of the bill to authorize the President of the United States to call upon the several States and Territories thereof for their respective quotas of —— thousand men, for the defence of the frontiers of the United States.

On motion, by Mr. ANDERSON, to strike out, section 2, line 7, after the word "of," "two years;" after debate, on motion, by Mr. DAGGETT, the further consideration thereof was postponed until Monday next.

The PRESIDENT communicated a letter from the Secretary for the Department of Navy, transmitting a digest of the laws of the United States, in relation to the Naval Establishment and marine corps, made in obedience to a resolution of the Senate of the 18th March, 1814; which was read.

Mr. GORE, from the managers on the part of the Senate at the conference on the amendments of the Senate, disagreed to by the House of Representatives, to the bill, entitled "An act to authorize a loan for a sum not exceeding three millions of dollars," reported "that the Senate do recede from their amendments to the said bill, except so much thereof as strikes out the last clause of the fifth section, and do agree, as a substitute therefor, to the two following sections, viz:

"SEC. 6. *And be it further enacted,* That, in addition to the annual sum of eight millions of dollars, heretofore appropriated to the Sinking Fund, adequate and permanent funds shall, during the present session of Congress, be provided and appropriated for the payment of the interest and the reimbursement of the principal of said stock created by this act.

"SEC. 7. *And be it further enacted,* That an adequate and permanent Sinking Fund, gradually to reduce and eventually to extinguish the public debt, contracted and to be contracted during the present war, shall also be established during the present session of Congress.

"And that the 6th *section of the* said bill shall be denominated the 8th *section.*"

On the question, Will the Senate concur in the report of the committee of conference? it was determined in the affirmative.

Whereupon, *Resolved,* That the Senate so far recede from their amendments to the bill last mentioned, as to agree to the report of the committee of conference.

MONDAY, November 14.

Mr. WORTHINGTON presented the petition of Benjamin W. Ladd, Joseph Ladd, and Thomas Norvell, stating that, being proprietors of certain warrants for land granted by the State of Virginia to the officers and soldiers of the Virginia line on Continental Establishment, they have caused them to be located on the tract reserved by that State for satisfying similar claims; that, in consequence of the line of the reserve aforesaid being unsettled, the location has been made on lands previously granted by the United States, but it is believed within the limits of the reservation. They therefore pray an indemnification for surrendering the lands thus located, to the occupants claiming by purchase from the United States; and the petition was read, and referred to the committee to whose consideration, on the 21st September, the memorial of the Legislature of the Indiana Territory was referred, to consider and report thereon by bill or otherwise.

The Senate resumed, as in Committee of the Whole, the consideration of the bill, entitled "An act to authorize the Commissioner of the Revenue to cause a clerk in his office to aid him in signing licenses."

Ordered, That the further consideration thereof be postponed until to-morrow.

The bill, entitled "An act for the relief of John Chalmers, junior," was read the second time, and referred to a select committee, to consider and report thereon. Messrs. SMITH, WORTHINGTON, and DANA were appointed the committee.

The bill, entitled "An act to authorize the publication of the laws of the United States within the Territories of the United States," was read the second time.

The Senate resumed, as in Committee of the Whole, the consideration of the bill to authorize the President of the United States to call upon the several States and Territories thereof for their respective quotas of ——— thousand militia, for the frontiers of the United States, together with the amendment proposed by Mr. ANDERSON, to strike out "two years," the term of service.

On the question, Will the Senate agree to the proposed amendment? it was determined in the negative—yeas 15, nays 16, as follows:

YEAS—Messrs. Anderson, Daggett, Dana, Gaillard, German, Gore, Horsey, Hunter, King, Lambert, Mason, Robinson, Thompson, Varnum, and Wharton.

NAYS—Messrs. Bibb, Bledsoe, Brent, Brown, Chace, Condit, Fromentin, Giles, Lacock, Morrow, Smith, Tate, Taylor, Turner, Walker, and Worthington.

On motion, by Mr. GERMAN, to strike out, section 3, after the word "that," in the first line, to the word "act," inclusive, in the sixth line—on motion, the further consideration thereof was postponed until to-morrow.

TUESDAY, November 15.

Mr. SMITH, from the committee to whom was referred the bill, entitled "An act for the relief of John Chalmers, jun., reported it without amendment; and the bill was considered as in Committee of the Whole, and ordered to the third reading.

The Senate resumed, as in Committee of the Whole, the consideration of the bill, entitled "An act to authorize the publication of the laws of the United States within the Territories of the United States; and, no amendment having been proposed, it was ordered to the third reading.

The Senate resumed, as in Committee of the Whole, the consideration of the bill, entitled "An act to authorize the Commissioner of the Revenue to cause a clerk in his office to aid him in signing licenses; and no amendment having been proposed, it was ordered to the third reading.

On request, Mr. FROMENTIN had leave to withdraw the motions submitted by him the 7th instant, in relation to the non-compliance with the resolutions passed by the Senate on the 18th March, 1814.

The Senate resumed, as in Committee of the Whole, the consideration of the bill to authorize the President of the United States to call upon the several States and Territories thereof, for their respective quotas of ——— thousand militia, for the defence of the frontiers of the United States, together with the amendment proposed thereto by Mr. GERMAN; and, after debate, the Senate adjourned.

WEDNESDAY, November 16.

The bill, entitled "An act to authorize the publication of the laws of the United States within the Territories of the United States," was read a third time, and passed.

The bill, entitled "An act for the relief of John Chalmers, junior," was read a third time, and passed.

The Senate resumed, as in Committee of the Whole, the bill, entitled "An act for the relief of John Castille, of the city of New Orleans."

On motion of Mr. FROMENTIN, the bill was referred to a select committee, to consider and report thereon; and Messrs. FROMENTIN, DAGGETT, and ANDERSON, were appointed the committee.

The bill, entitled "An act to authorize the Commissioner of the Revenue to cause a clerk in his office to aid him in signing licenses," was read a third time.

On motion, by Mr. KING, it was referred to a select committee, to consider and report thereon; and Messrs. KING, GILES, and BLEDSOE, were appointed the committee.

A message from the House of Representatives informed the Senate that the House have passed a resolution for furnishing the American Antiquarian Society with a copy of the Journals of Congress, and of the documents published under their order; in which they request the concurrence of the Senate.

ORGANIZATION OF NAVY DEPARTMENT.

The PRESIDENT communicated a report of the Secretary of the Navy, containing a system for the better organization of the Department of the Navy of the United States, made in obedience to a resolution of the Senate of the 18th March, 1814. The reading thereof was dispensed with; and it was ordered to be printed for the use of the Senate, and that it be referred to the Committee on Naval Affairs to consider and report thereon.

The report is as follows:

NAVY DEPARTMENT, *Nov.* 15, 1814.

SIR: In obedience to the resolution of the Senate, passed on the 18th of March last, directing the Secretary of the Navy to devise and digest a system for the better organization of the Department of the Navy of the United States, I have now the honor to report the following system, with such prefatory observations as appear to me pertinent to the occasion.

It has been affirmed and cannot be denied, that im-

49　　　　　HISTORY OF CONGRESS.　　　　　50

NOVEMBER, 1814.　　　Organization of the Navy Department.　　　SENATE.

perfections exist in the civil administration of the Naval Establishment; hence it has been inferred that a radical change of system can alone remedy the evils. Legislative wisdom will readily discriminate between the constituent principles upon which the present establishment is predicated, and has thus far prospered, and the defects which result from the absence of an intelligent, practical, auxiliary agency, qualified to digest, arrange, and enforce a proper system of detailed regulations, calculated to insure the judicious and faithful application of public moneys; a strict accountability in the expenditures of supplies: and a rigid execution of the duties enjoined on all the officers and agents connected with the establishment.

Profusion, waste, and abuse, are the inherent offspring of all extensive public institutions; and, if we occasionally perceive these evils, in some degree, in the Naval Establishment of the United States, we are not thence to infer their absence from similar establishments in other countries, where naval science and experience may be presumed to have provided greater safeguards, and more numerous, skilful, and vigilant agencies.

But regulations, however correct and adequate to the end, become nugatory, or worse, unless the authority and the means are co-extensive, and competent to enforce the execution, or punish the violation thereof. This may account for the non-existence of many wholesome regulations in the civil administration of the Navy of the United States; and for the imperfect execution of those which exist. Breaches of the latter too frequently escape with impunity, from the impossibility of the head of the Department taking cognizance of all the multifarious concerns of the establishment. It is problematical, however, whether the excess may not be more injurious than the deficiency of regulation; in the former case, responsibility may be lost in the maze and mass of detail and multiplied agency, while in the latter, general instruction, and sound discretion, not unfrequently insure greater success and responsibility.

That the duties enjoined, or which may necessarily devolve upon the Secretary of the Navy, particularly during a period of active and diversified hostility, are beyond the powers of any individual to discharge to the best advantage, cannot be doubted; although, by great labor and assiduity, with adequate professional qualifications, he may, possibly, execute the general and most essential branches of duty with tolerable success.

In the progress of reform, while we pay due respect to that system, the establishment of which has attained the greatest celebrity, more, it is believed, from its magnitude and power, than from the excellence of its civil administration, we ought not to lose sight of its palpable and acknowledged defects, nor of those features in our own system, to which, in no trivial degree, the exalted reputation of our infant Navy may be attributed.

That our Navy is not excelled in anything which constitutes efficiency, perfect equipment, and general good qualities, it is believed, will be admitted. That our seamen are better paid, fed, and accommodated, is no less true. That all the imported, and many of the domestic articles of equipment, and of consumption in the service, are exceedingly enhanced; that the wages of mechanical labor is more than double that which is paid by Great Britain; that our expenditure is greatly increased by the interruption to navigable transportation, and the great extent of the local service, is equally obvious. Yet, under all these circumstances, it is demonstrable, that upon a comparison of an equal quantity of tonnage and number of guns and men, or in proportion to the number of men alone, our naval expenditure is considerably less than that for the Navy of Great Britain, in which "one hundred and forty-five thousand men are employed, at an expense of more than twenty millions of pounds sterling, annually."

The local service is, from its scattered, irregular, and irresponsible nature, much more expensive and wasteful than that of the regular Navy; the more perfect organization of which, and responsibility of command, insure a more faithful superintendence and accountability. Hence the current expenditure of the service would be an extravagant criterion by which to estimate that of a regular establishment under a judicious system. The force employed in local service is extended throughout a line of stations from Louisiana to Maine, and from Champlain to Huron, consequently it is so weak as readily to be penetrated, at almost any point on our maritime frontier, by the concentration of a small hostile force; and it is expensive in proportion to its diffusion. Independently of the deleterious nature of this service upon the health and habits of those employed in it, we are, from the present necessity of this system, deprived of the services of a body of officers and seamen, sufficient to man thirteen ships of-the-line, such as the Independence, Washington, and Franklin seventy-fours.

When we contemplate the effect which such a force would have when acting in conjunction upon our own coast and waters, or in squadron, pursuing the commercial fleets of the enemy on the ocean, or in the harbors of his colonies, it is impossible to avoid the conclusion, that our waters would be freed from invasion; our coast from blockade; his military and naval resources intercepted to such a degree as to paralyze his efforts on this continent; supersede the necessity of a vast Military Establishment, coextensive with our maritime, Canadian, and Indian frontiers; and our citizens from those harassing, irregular, and inconvenient calls of militia, which the predatory enterprise of the enemy so frequently produce. In short, according to my conceptions, this cheap and efficient national defence should be adopted as soon as circumstances will admit, and cherished by a well digested, energetic, and liberal system, steadily progressing with the population, commerce, and resources of the nation.

The nature, construction, and equipment of the ships which constitute a navy, form the basis of its efficiency, durability, and economy, and the most important branch in the civil administration of its affairs. With a view to the reform and extension of the Naval Establishment of the United States, these objects ought to command the first place in our attention, combined with such an organization of the civil department as shall promise the best results.

The defects in this part of the British system have been the theme of criticism and reprehension for many years past. The most minute, laborious, and able investigation, has, from time to time, taken place, under the direction and scrutiny of the Parliament; yet nothing approximating to radical amendment has been adopted; and the advocates of reform, either from the subtle ramifications of the evil, or the agency of some sinister influence, appear to despair of success.

According to the most intelligent writers, supported by well established facts, the deterioration of the British navy, owing to the injudicious selection and combination of incongruous materials in the construction, and the abortive method of preserving, is very alarming; and the diversity in the form, dimensions, and proportions, not only of the several rates, but of the numerous distinct classes of the same rate, as well in their hulls as in their masts, sails, and equipments, and in a still greater degree in their qualities for combined action, demonstrates the prevalence of caprice and prejudice, instead of science and system. "When Lord Nelson was off Cadiz, with seventeen or eighteen sail-of-the-line, he had no less than *seven* different classes of seventy-four gun ships, each requiring different masts, sails, yards, &c., so that if one ship was disabled, the others could not supply her with appropriate stores."

The consequences resulting from this defective organization and want of system are strongly illustrated in the fact, related by a recent professional writer of rank and talents, that "out of five hundred and thirty-eight ships, &c., in the British navy, now at sea, there are only sixty-nine which are in reality superior in the discharge of metal or force of blows, but inferior in sailing, to some of the American frigates; and that there are but eighteen which, unless in smooth water, are equal to contend with the United States, leaving four hundred and fifty-one, out of five hundred and thirty-eight, which are admitted to be incompetent to engage, single-handed, with an American frigate."

These facts are encouraging, and serve to show, that although the numerical force of the enemy in ships and men appears to be overwhelming; yet, if the aggregate number of officers, seamen, and marines, which the United States may, even now, engage for the public service, was concentrated in eighteen or twenty ships-of-the-line, such as have been recently built, it would place all the ships alluded to in the quotation just recited, except the eighteen, *hors de combat*, nor could our enemy protect his commerce and colonies, and combine such a force as would counteract the power and offensive enterprise of an American squadron so truly formidable. With such a force it will be perceived, that his host of frigates and smaller vessels would be struck out of the account, or added to the list of our Navy, if they came in contact. These views, it is true, are prospective, but with a stable, judicious, and liberal system, the result would be realized at no remote period.

Having noticed these exceptions to the civil administration of the British navy, it is but just to observe, that the organization of the military part of their system is much more perfect.

The regulations and instructions for the service at sea, adopted by order in Council, and published in one quarto volume, in 1806, are those which now prevail. They are excellent, and afford much matter worthy of incorporation into our system, with such modification as the peculiar circumstances of the service may require.

Of the French naval system, the Department of Construction is universally admitted to be the most perfect in existence, and is well worthy of imitation. The military part of the system, however, is less perfect in practice, and not so well adapted to the habits and usages of American seamen as that of the British.

The character of the navy of any nation will be determined by its commercial and navigating enterprise. That of America had surpassed every other, until the unexampled prosperity and rapid extension of its commerce, excited the envy, jealousy, and hostility, of those who could not meet it in fair, equal, and friendly competition. The same energy, skill, vigilance, and intrepidity, which distinguished the commercial navigators of the United States, characterize the officers and seamen of the Navy. The same superiority of construction which gave to its commercial marine the celerity and security for which it is distinguished, may be seen in the American Navy, which is truly indigenous and distinct from every other. The independent character of the nation is manifestly visible in the genius of its Navy. The classes of our ships, their form, construction, armament, and equipment, have been tested by experience, and found to have been happily adapted to our circumstances, compelling the enemy either to employ ships-of-the-line against frigates, or to construct a new class of ships. Their efficiency and perfection have extorted the praise of the enemy. The author, before quoted, says: "The carronades I saw on board the United States' brig Argus were better mounted, and the vessel more complete than those in the British navy; and she was uncommonly well manœuvred."

Our ships are excellent, and all in good condition. The classes are few, and so uniform that, without inconvenience, the masts, spars, and equipments, of any one of a class will serve, indifferently, for any other of the same class. All the new ships, of each rate, are of the same class, and are absolutely similar in all their equipments, and in the dimensions and proportions of their hulls, masts, spars, &c. This strict similarity should be carefully preserved, upon every principle of convenience, economy, and efficiency.

Timber, which forms an object of much solicitude in Great Britain, deserves the particular attention of the Department, the reorganization of which will doubtlessly be made to combine the necessary talents and means to provide for every branch of the service, by a seasonable, diligent, and judicious collection, in secure and convenient depots, of all the materials which enter into the construction and equipment of ships of war.

When it is considered that one seventy-four-gun ship requires two thousand large oak trees, equal to the estimated produce of fifty-seven acres, the importance of securing, for public use, all that valuable species of oak, which is found only on the Southern seaboard, is sufficiently obvious.

Dock yards, foundries, smitheries, and armories, in safe and eligible situations, are indispensable appendages of so important and growing an establishment. These always collect the best workmen, and as private interest cannot interfere with the execution, the materials and workmanship are better, and the work is performed with more certainty and regularity, than by contract with private individuals, whose works, in some cases, may be so remote from the seat of demand, that the transportation may cost more than the article.

There is another branch of the service which appears to me to merit the serious deliberation of the Legislature, with regard to the establishment of some regular system, by which the voluntary enlistments for the Navy may derive occasional reinforcement from the services of those seamen, who, pursuing their own private occupations, are exempt, by their itinerant habits, from public service of any kind. In my view there would be nothing incompatible with the free spirit of our institutions, or with the rights of individuals, if registers, with a particular descriptive record, were kept in the several districts, of all the seamen belonging to the United States, and provision made by law for classing and calling into the public service, in succession, for reasonable stated periods, such portions or classes, as the public service might require, and if any individual, so called, should be absent at the time, the next in succession should perform the tour of duty of the absentee, who should, on his return, be liable to serve his original tour, and his substitute be exempt from his succeeding regular tour of duty.

In the military service, should the ranks not be filled by recruits, the deficiency of regular force may be made up by draughts of militia, to assemble at a given time and place; not so in the naval service, it depends, exclusively, upon voluntary enlistments, upon which there is no reliance for any given object, at any time or place. Hence, the most important expeditions may utterly fail, though every possible exertion shall have been made to carry them into effect.

If we examine, with due attention, the nature, extent, and importance of the objects involved in the administration of naval affairs, and contemplate, in the history of ages past, the unsuccessful, though indefatigable labors of legislation, science, and genius, to perfect the system, we may learn to appreciate with more accuracy, and cherish with liberality, the life of study, observation and experience, required to arrive even at moderate attainments in a science, which, though familiar in the estimation of all, is the most complicated, critical, and interesting, that has ever engaged the attention or influenced the destinies of nations. My sole object is to invite the attention and liberality of the National Councils to the requisite talents and qualifications for the cherishing and rearing to maturity the vigorous plant, around which are entwined the affections and confidence of the country.

All these objects appear to me to be intimately connected with the revision of the civil administration of our naval affairs, the Executive branch of which should be conducted by persons of enlarged views, collectively combining all the practical knowledge and professional intelligence which these important, diversified, and comprehensive subjects, obviously require.

We have a good foundation upon which to raise a durable superstructure; and concluding that that system cannot be radically wrong, which has produced such favorable results, I should be unwilling to hazard, by an entire innovation, the benefits we have derived, and may still derive, by retaining the present organization of the Navy Department, and providing, by law, for an intelligent, practical, and efficient auxiliary agency, such as experience has suggested.

With this view, I have the honor to submit, with great deference, the following system for the organization of the Department of the Navy of the United States, distinguishing, for the sake of perspicuity, in the form of a bill, those objects which appear to require Legislative provision, from those for which Executive regulation may prescribe with more convenience and advantage; the outline of which only is given, as the ground-work may be filled up to greater benefit, when the collected experience and talents which it contemplates shall have deliberated upon the subject.

An Act for the better organization of the Navy Department.

Be it enacted, &c., That the office, duties, and powers of the Secretary of the Navy, and of the Accountant, Agents, and other officers of the Department of the Navy, be and remain as now, by law, established;

except as hereinafter modified, altered, or transferred to any other office or offices, created by this act.

SEC. 2. That the President of the United States be and he is hereby authorized to designate three officers of the Navy, and, with the advice and consent of the Senate, to appoint two other judicious persons, skilled in naval affairs, to be Inspectors of the Navy, who together shall constitute a Board of Inspectors of the Navy, three members whereof shall be necessary to form a quorum; and the business of the said board shall be transacted in such central and convenient place, for the superintendence of the affairs of the Navy, as the President of the United States shall direct; who shall also have power to designate the presiding member, and to appoint the secretary of the said board, whose duty it shall be to keep regular and correct records of all the transactions of the board, and to transmit attested copies of all such proceedings to the Secretary of the Navy, for the inspection and revision of the President of the United States, as soon as may be after the adjournment of the meeting at which any such proceedings shall have taken place; and the said board shall have power to establish such rules and regulations, for its own proceedings, and to employ such number of clerks and assistants, as well for the transacting of the business of the board, as for that of the several inspectors, and to procure such books, maps, charts, plans, drawings, models, and stationery as the public interest may require, and the President of the United States approve.

SEC. 3. That it shall be the duty of the Secretary of the Navy to arrange and class, under distinct and appropriate heads, as equally as may be, all such duties and details as may be found impracticable for the officers of the Department of the Navy, as now organized, to execute with advantage to the public, and, with the approbation of the President of the United States, to assign to each inspector of the Navy the special charge and execution of one of the classes, so arranged; for the faithful performance of which trust, the said inspectors shall severally be held responsible, under the instruction and subject to the revision of the board of inspectors, to which a statement of all the transactions of each inspector shall be submitted for revision, at each stated meeting, and an abstract thereof transmitted monthly to the Secretary of the Navy, with such remarks thereon as the nature of the case may require; and it shall also be the duty of the Secretary of the Navy to prepare a system of general regulations, defining and prescribing the respective powers and duties of the board of inspectors of the Navy, and of the several inspectors, which rules, when approved by the President of the United States, shall be respected and obeyed, until altered or revoked by the same authority; and the same general regulations, thus prepared and approved, shall be laid before Congress at their next session.

SEC. 4. That the President of the United States be and he is hereby authorized alone to appoint a person, skilled in the science and practice of naval architecture, to the office of Naval Constructer; and also to appoint two naval constructors. And it shall be the duty of the Secretary of the Navy to prepare such rules and regulations for connecting the business of the Constructor's department, as shall appear necessary and proper; which, when approved by the President of the United States, shall be respected and obeyed, until revoked by the same authority. And the naval constructor shall be allowed one clerk, to assist in transacting the business of his department.

SEC. 5. That the President of the United States be and he is hereby authorized, with the consent and advice of the Senate, to appoint a Paymaster of the Navy, who shall perform the duties of his office agreeably to the directions of the President of the United States for the time being: and, before he enters upon the duties of the same, shall give bonds, with good and sufficient sureties, in such sums as the President of the United States shall direct, for the faithful discharge of his said office, and shall take an oath to execute the duties thereof with fidelity.

SEC. 6. That all letters and packets to and from the inspectors and paymaster of the navy, which relate to their official duties, shall be free from postage.

SEC. 7. That each inspector of the navy shall be entitled to the pay and rations of a captain commanding a squadron on separate service, and also to the sum of one thousand two hundred dollars per annum, in lieu of house-rent, fuel, forage, &c.; and the salary of the naval constructor shall be three thousand dollars per annum; each of the assistant constructors, one thousand five hundred dollars per annum; the paymaster of the navy, two thousand dollars per annum; the secretary of the board of inspectors, two thousand dollars per annum; and the clerks and assistants, authorised by this act, shall receive such reasonable compensation for their services as the President of the United States shall direct.

I would also respectfully suggest the expediency of providing by law for the establishment of a Naval Academy, with suitable professors, for the instruction of the officers of the Navy, in those branches of the mathematics and experimental philosophy, and in the science and practice of gunnery, theory of naval architecture, and art of mechanical drawing, which are necessary to the accomplishment of the naval officer.

In order to illustrate the principles and operation of the proposed organization of the Navy Department, the following outline of the powers and duties which it is contemplated to assign to the board of inspectors, and to the several inspectors, is respectfully suggested:

Powers and duties of the Board.

The board shall have the general superintendence and direction of the affairs of the Navy, under the instructions from, and powers delegated by, the President of the United States, and authority over all the officers, agents, and persons, employed under the Navy Department; report to the Secretary of the Navy, from time to time, all such matters and things as may, in the opinion of the board, tend to promote the efficacy and economy of the establishment; and, upon the requisition of the Secretary of the Navy, furnish all the estimates of expenditure which the several branches of the service may require, and such other information and statements as he may deem necessary.

The board shall have the power of making contracts and purchases, either directly or through the navy agents, whose power, in this respect, should be limited to small sums, and to objects, the procuring of which may not admit of delay. In all other cases, the previous sanction, either of the Secretary of the Navy, of the board of inspectors, or of some officers authorized by the board, should be indispensable.

The naval stations within the United States should be designated by convenient boundaries; and an officer of rank, trust, and confidence, should reside in each, who should, under the instructions of the board, superintend and control the affairs of the Navy within his district, and report to the board from time to time.

All requisitions of commanding officers, pursers, and other persons, upon the agents, should be checked, and receive the sanction of the board, or of the resident officer authorized by the board, before they are complied with.

Payments and advances should be made, as heretofore, through the navy agents, (except those for the pay or the Navy;) and the sanction of the Secretary of the Navy, of the board, or of the officers authorized by the board, should precede all payments and advances, except for limited and urgent demands.

The board should establish general regulations for the conduct of its members, in the discharge of the special and important trusts severally assigned to them by the Secretary of the Navy; and should digest and report to the Department distinct regulations for the following objects:

1. Uniform regulations establishing the several classes of ships and vessels in the Navy of the United States; with tables of the dimensions, proportions, number, quantity, quality, nature, and description, of masts, spars, rigging, anchors, cables, armament, and equipments, of all kinds; and of the quantity, quality, and description, of provisions and stores, of every species, for a given period, for each class.

2. Regulations for receiving, preserving, issuing, and strictly accounting for, the expenditure of materials and stores of all kinds, and in every department of the service, within the United States.

3. Regulations for surveying and authenticating the actual state and condition of all the ships and vessels of the Navy, and of all materials and stores, of every species, reported to be decayed, damaged, or defective; and for directing the repair, conversion, sale, or other disposition of the same, as the nature of the case may require.

4. A more perfect system of general regulations for the naval service, at sea and on the Lakes.

5. General regulations for the flotilla or force employed in harbor defence, adapted to the peculiar nature of that service.

6. Uniform regulations for the navy yards, arsenals, and depots of stores and materials.

7. Regulations for the cruising ships and vessels of the Navy, while in port; for the recruiting service; and for the officers of the Navy, while on shore, on duty, or on furlough; in order to ascertain the actual state and local situation of all the officers.

8. A system of detailed regulations for the naval hospitals, and medical department of the Navy within the United States.

9. An entire and new system of regulations for the pursers in the Navy, accurately defining their duties, securing a more strict accountability; limiting their emoluments by a fixed and reasonable standard; and protecting the seamen of the Navy from the undue advantages which may be practised, with impunity, under the present system.

10. Regulations for ascertaining, by examination, the moral character and professional qualifications of all the officers of the Navy, below the grade of a master commandant, classing them in the scale of their several merits; and of the pretensions of those who may be selected for promotion, as well as of the candidates for warrant appointments in the Navy.

All which regulations, when approved by the President of the United States, should be established and obeyed, until revoked by the same authority.

The duties and details of the service, proposed to be

assigned to the several inspectors of the Navy, may be classed as follows:

1st Class. Comprehending the general correspondence of the board, and preparation of all the reports, estimates, and statements, required by the Department; and the communication of such propositions and information to the Secretary of the Navy, as the board may deem interesting; and, also, the general charge and direction of the flotilla service on the New Orleans station.

2d Class. Comprehending the general military correspondence with all the officers of the Navy; the roll of the officers of the Navy, and record of their services, merits, and qualifications, to be kept on the files of the board: orders for courts of inquiry and courts martial, and the preparation of all the documents and statements connected with these objects; also, the general charge and direction of the flotilla service on the Southern station, viz: Georgia, South Carolina, North Carolina, and Norfolk.

3d Class. Comprehending the direction of ordnance and transportation; the general superintendence of the foundries, laboratories, armories, and other works connected with the naval ordnance department; and the inspection and proof of arms, ammunition, &c. The direction of the transportation of all persons, stores, and provisions of the Navy, by land and water; and the general charge and direction of the flotilla service in the Patapsco and Delaware, and at New York.

4th Class. Comprehending the victualling and sustenance, including purser's, medical, and hospital stores; also, the general charge and direction of the flotilla service, on all the naval stations, from New York eastward, and on Lake Champlain.

5th Class. Comprehending the supply of hemp, yarns, cordage, sail duck, iron and other metals, anchors, and all other equipments and materials required for the service, except those which are included in the foregoing classes, and in the constructor's department; and, also, the general charge and direction of the service on Lake Ontario, and the upper lakes.

The superintendence and direction of these five classes of objects would be distributed among the five inspectors.

The department of construction, under the direction of the Secretary of the Navy, and of the board of inspectors, would prepare all the draughts, plans, and instructions, for the building of all the vessels of the Navy; construct the models, and, when approved, direct and superintend, under the control of the board of inspectors, the building and repairing of the ships, vessels, boats, the formation of masts, spars, &c., and the contracting for and procuring all the materials of wood, and of copper, in pigs, bolts, and sheets, necessary for the supply of the Navy; construct from the lines, in the mould loft, all the moulds requisite for moulding and bevelling the timber in the forest, under the direction of skilful persons to be employed by the constructor for that purpose; and superintend the construction of the wharves, ships, workshops, and engines, required in building and repairing ships of war.

It is a copious subject, in which it is difficult to combine brevity with perspicuity.

My aim has been to provide a practical, efficient, and economical system, with as much individual and collective responsibility as may be attainable; and I feel a persuasion that the result would not greatly disappoint the estimate I have formed; the wisdom of the Senate will better appreciate its merits.

I have the honor to be, with the highest respect, sir, your obedient servant,

W. JONES.

Hon. PRESIDENT OF SENATE.

MILITIA OF THE UNITED STATES.

The Senate resumed, as in Committee of the Whole, the consideration of the bill to authorize the President of the United States to call upon the several States and Territories thereof for their respective quotas of ——— thousand militia for the defence of the frontiers of the United States.

Mr. VARNUM addressed the President as follows: Sir, I am deeply impressed with the importance of the present crisis of our national concerns, and the importance of the adoption of strong and energetic measures, well calculated to meet and repulse the force which the enemy contemplate placing in the field against us. And, sir, no man in this Senate will go further than I shall feel disposed to go to effectuate the object which must be dear to every friend of the nation and the rights of the people, to repulse our enemy in the field, procure a just and equitable adjustment of the differences between the two nations, and produce an honorable peace, provided the measures pursued shall appear to me to be founded in justice and equity.

I am fully aware of the great responsibility which rests on the Government of the United States at the present crisis. The Constitution having confided the defence of the country to the General Government, and clothed it with authority to call upon the physical force of the nation to aid in making such defence, and to draw on the fiscal resources of the country for a revenue sufficient to meet the expenses necessarily incurred in making defence, Congress are at this period most imperiously bound, upon their responsibility, and in discharge of their important duty, to adopt measures commensurate with the exigencies of the nation; and I am fully sensible of the necessity of providing a large and ample military force before the opening of the next campaign. But, sir, the raising such forces should be predicated on ground which cannot fail of bringing it into the field early in the Spring; it ought to be placed on principles the best calculated to do equal justice to all classes of your citizens. In that way alone you will insure the confidence of the people, enlist their feelings, and secure their aid in carrying your system into effect. Surely, sir, these desirable qualities are not to be found in the bill before you.

To endeavor to substantiate the position I have taken on this occasion, I must be permitted to recur to the provisions of the bill. In doing this, it is not my intention to implicate the motives or abilities of the committee who reported the bill, nor of those gentlemen who have supported it on this floor; but the bill being public property, the errors which it contains are fair subjects of animadversion—nor shall I attempt a reply to the fine theoretical arguments which have been made use of in support of the bill; but will endeavor to point out some of its defects, and my ideas of the most practicable remedy for those defects.

The first section of the bill requires the President of the United States to call upon the Executives of the several States and Territories, for their respective quotas of eighty thousand militia, to serve for two years. It would seem, sir, by this section, that the committee were of opinion, that eighty thousand men in addition to the present Military Establishment, which consists of sixty-two thousand, making in the whole, 142,000, would be necessary for the defence of the United States, at all points, the next campaign. In this opinion of the committee, I do most cordially acquiesce; for, sir, under the existing circumstances of our situation, and the situation of Europe, it is very probable that an imposing force will assail us the next campaign; and I consider it an imperative duty, obligatory on the National Legislature, to do all in their power, to repulse the invasion of the enemy at every point—and to insure this object, I am of opinion, that a reliance upon a less number of men in the field, than that contemplated by the first section of the bill, would be highly impolitic, improper, and calculated to jeopardize the safety of the nation; yet, in some of the subsequent sections of it, we find that instead of realizing the pleasing prospect of seeing an ample force in the field, that the force is to be reduced to an indefinite amount; which contradiction in terms, inconsistency in principle, and uncertainty in effect, cannot fail to produce mortification and chagrin in every breast, entertaining the same impressions on the subject which I do.

The same section of the bill provides for calling out this force for two years, and, in subsequent sections of the bill, it is provided that the men shall be raised by draught, in the last resort. Sir, this mode of draughting men from the militia for two years, I must confess is a novel idea to me, and I do believe it will be so to the nation. I have lived to see draughts from the militia, under a colonial system, when the United States were colonies to Great Britain. I have seen and participated in the raising of men for public service, by draught and otherwise, from the commencement of the Revolutionary war up to the present time, and in no instance, which has come within my knowledge, has there been a draught from the militia, for a longer term than nine months; and generally the terms of service have been much shorter than nine months.

No such unreasonable exercise of power, as I conceive to be contained in this bill, ever was attempted under our former Colonial Governments; notwithstanding such attempts might have been fostered by the Monarchical Government under which we then acted. No such attempt was made during the Revolutionary war, notwithstanding our very existence as a nation much depended upon our placing a competent number of men in the field. No such attempt has been made since the close of the Revolutionary war, until it made its appearance in the bill before you. Sir, let us examine the law passed in 1795, authorizing the President of the United States to call out the militia for the purposes designated by the Constitution. By that law we find, that such was the del-

iency of General WASHINGTON, the then President of the United States, whose capacity for judging correctly on a subject of this kind all must acknowledge, and such was the delicacy of Congress upon this subject, at that time, that a positive provision was made in the law, that the militia called out under it should not be held to serve more than three months in any one year; and the provisions of that law, with a view to equal distribution of justice among the individuals comprising the militia, go further, and declare not only that the militia called out shall not be held to serve more than three months in any one year, but that they shall not be held to serve more than in due rotation with every other able-bodied man of the same rank in the battalion to which they belong. Such, sir, was the view taken by General WASHINGTON, and by the Congress of 1795, in regard to the impropriety of calling out the militia for long terms of service.

The principle then adopted has been sacredly adhered to ever since that period, until about the commencement of the present war; at which time provisions were made for detaining the militia to be detached for six months. Thus, sir, we shall find, that from time immemorial, the people of this nation have been in the habit of believing that draughts from the militia were not to be made for a term anything like that named in the bill before you, and that belief has been justly founded on the uniform practice of all the various Governments which have been in operation here, since the first settlement of the country by civilized man. In fact, sir, that draughts from the militia should not exceed the term of nine months, is fully established as a principle of common law, which no one has ever attempted to violate before the introduction of the bill under consideration. And I very much fear, sir, that the violation of the principle which the bill proposes to introduce, will not sit very well on the minds of the people. Surely, sir, this is not a time to introduce new principles which are in any degree calculated to alienate the people, or any part of them, from a vigorous defence of our national rights. I consider this system of draughting militiamen for two years' service, to be unnecessary, unequal, and unjust. If the nation wish for an additional force to the amount, and for the term mentioned in the bill, why not proffer terms adequate to procure it, and make it a part of the regular army? Although I admit, that the General Government have power, by the Constitution under which we act, to call on a part, or all the physical force of the nation for the defence of its rights, when necessary; yet, sir, I contend, that this power ought to be exercised under a sound discretion, calculated, as near as may be, to do equal justice. But this bill presents to my mind a very different aspect. It disregards the system of equality for military services among our citizens, and violates the principle of rotation in regard to those services, which has been held sacred by those who have gone before us, and which I consider imperiously binding upon us.

The second section of the bill provides for classing the whole of the militia, so that each class shall furnish one man by draught or contract for two years.

This mode of classification, I contend, is unequal and unjust, as it includes those only who are enrolled in the militia, and excludes all those who are not enrolled in the militia. The very act of classing the militia, and calling upon each class to furnish one man for two years, clearly demonstrates that the Government is aware that the pay given by the public is not sufficient to bring the men into the field for such length of time. This fact is corroborated by the provision in the first section of the bill which apportions the men to be raised amongst the States and Territories upon the principle of representation and direct taxation. In this principle, distributive justice is properly regarded as it relates to the States and Territories. But, sir, it is entirely abandoned as it relates to the people at large, by your mode of classification.

If the situation of the nation has become such as to make it necessary to class the people for the purpose of procuring an adequate number of soldiers, I conceive that the just and equitable mode of doing it would be to include in your classes all the taxable polls, and all the taxable property by whomsoever possessed—the classes to be so formed as that each class should contain, as near as may be, a just and due proportion of all the taxable polls and property ; each individual in a class should be holden to contribute towards procuring a soldier, by contract, in proportion to the taxables he may possess. And in order to insure the raising your men by classing the people, you must provide that each class which does not procure a soldier by contract in a given time, shall be taxed, each individual in proportion to the taxables he may possess, in a sum sufficient, at all events, to raise a man for such class; the assessment on such delinquent class should be collected by a summary process, and the money paid into the hands of a faithful officer, who would not fail to procure the man.

This is a mode of classification similar to the one adopted in the Revolutionary war, which was generally satisfactory. Contrast this system with the one contained in the bill before you, and let every man judge which of them ought to be preferred.

In the one case, all the persons and property in the nation would be called upon to disburse a due proportion of the national expense ; and, in the other case, the persons enrolled in the militia only are to bear the expense of raising and getting into the field eighty thousand troops, to serve for two years.

The persons enrolled in the militia are generally composed of farmers, mechanics, and laborers, not very affluent in their circumstances, but as respectable and useful members of society as any class of citizens which can be named. I imagine that they do not hold one-third of the property which is to be defended ; and yet, sir, this class of your citizens are to be called upon to bear the whole expense of this extensive detachment, while those who hold two-thirds of the property of the nation, if my ideas upon that subject be correct, are not to be called upon to pay a cent. I can see no reason for this discrimination ; I conceive it to be founded in error of so deep a die as to materially impede our operations of defence, if not to defeat them altogether. Pray, sir, what reason can be given why the rich merchant, the wealthy farmer, the opulent professional gentleman, those citizens holding property who are over the age of forty-five years, and all those citizens between the ages of eighteen and forty-five, who have been exempted from militia duty by the laws of the United States, and of individual States, should be exempted from a participation in the extra expense of this draught ? I confess I can see none, nor have I heard of but one attempted to be given; that was, that the militia were called on by this bill to render personal service, and not for pecuniary aid. But, sir, that assertion is proved to be fallacious by the bill itself. In the fourth section of the bill it is provided, that, "for the purpose of equalizing as 'much as possible the contributions of the re-'spective classes, in all cases where any class 'may furnish a militiaman by contract, it shall 'be the duty of such militia officer or officers, in 'laying off the respective districts comprehend-'ing each class, to apportion the same, as nearly 'as possible, according to the value of property 'and the number of militiamen subject to draught 'within each company." Here, sir, we find a direct appeal to pecuniary aid, anything which has been said to the contrary notwithstanding. But it is said the alternatives in this second section of the bill ameliorate the severities in the preceding parts of it. What are those alternatives ? The first provides, "that if any State or 'Territory shall, within three months after the 'passing of this act, furnish its quota of militia, 'or any part thereof required by this act, or any 'other troops in lieu thereof, for an equal or 'longer term of service, the same shall be re-'ceived into the service of the United States in 'substitution of the same number of militia called 'for by this act; and in that case the draught 'shall so far cease to take effect." I must confess, sir, that this alternative does not, in my view, present such beneficial features, as some gentlemen have imagined were contained in it. It is to be sure a modest appeal to the patriotism of the States and Territories to furnish their quotas of the men to be raised, pretty much of the nature of a recommendation under the old articles of Confederation, when Congress had power to recommend, but none to execute. It gives the States and Territories three months to consider of the question, and consequently suspends the whole operation of raising the men, otherwise than by State or Territorial authority, during that period. Well, sir, let us suppose, which certainly is at least a very possible case, that at the end of three months you find that the States and Territories have not thought proper to furnish the men, what then is to be done ? Why, sir, at the time when your men ought to be ready to take the field, you will have to commence raising them by the dilatory and very uncertain modes pointed out by the bill. Your militia must be then classed, and each class is to furnish a man by contract or draught; here again the bill appeals to the patriotism of the classes, and tells them if they will each furnish a man by contract, they will be exempt from the draught. Well, sir, what if the patriotism of the classes should not be sufficiently strong to induce them to procure their man by contract? The only remedy which the bill provides in that case is, for them to resort to the draught. Sir, who is authorized to make this draught? I find, by the second and fourth sections of the bill, that the classes are each imperatively called on to furnish a man for two years, either by draught or contract. I find no militia officer authorized to make the draught, nor any other person except the class itself. Hence, however novel and subversive of all military and militia principles of procedure this provision may appear, I must conclude, that the classes alone are authorized to make the draught.

Will the classes make the draught under the novel and extraordinary provisions of this bill? I imagine they will not, sir. First, because no bounty is offered them for procuring their men by contract; and, secondly, because no penalty whatever is required of them for omitting to raise their men by contract, nor for refusing to make the draught. Sir, I will quit this part of the subject for the present, in order to make some further observations on the details of the bill; but I purpose to touch upon it again before I sit down.

By the third section of the bill, every commanding officer of a company of infantry is called upon to enter upon his muster roll every person subject to militia duty within the beat or district comprehending his company, whether of artillery, cavalry, grenadiers, light infantry, volunteers, or by whatever other denomination distinguished, which muster roll is to be made on oath and returned to the commander of the battalion or regiment to which he belongs, and by such commander to the brigade inspector, and by him to the adjutant general of the State or Territory; whereupon, all the militia of every description entered upon such muster roll shall in like manner be subject to classification, for the purposes of draught or contribution required by the act.

In the first place, sir, I would inquire for what purpose the commanders of companies of infantry are called upon to enrol those of other corps? I know that it has been said, that the other corps being scattered over a more extensive territory, would not so expeditiously be called out by their own officers, as they would be by the provisions of this bill, against which statement I must most peremptorily protest. I have been a long time in the militia, and have had the superintendence of many draughts from it for public service, and I am compelled to assure you, that the officers of these select corps. to their honor be it spoken, have always on such occasions been active, persevering, and prompt, in procuring their men, and quite as early in making their returns as the

officers of the infantry, whose commands were much more compact. Besides, sir, I do conceive that you are imposing upon the commanders of infantry companies a duty which does not devolve upon them in virtue of their commissions, the oath they have taken, or the tenure of the office they hold. And, sir, if they should attempt to carry into effect the mandates of this bill, in regard to the members of select corps, I know of no constitutional, legal, or military principle which would enable them to do it. The officers and men composing these select corps, so far as I know, are honorable men, at all times willing to do their duty, and you must conceive, sir, that the degradation imposed upon them by this bill must be very mortifying to them.

That part of the third section which directs the commanders of battalions and regiments to make their returns of enrolments to the brigade inspector, is unmilitary and highly improper. It compels them to make their returns to an officer below them in rank, and that officer is directed to forward the returns to the adjutant general, passing by the brigadier generals and the major generals; officers eminently responsible for the correct performance of duty by all the officers and soldiers under their command, and who always have in their possession documents by which any attempt to commit a fraud can be checked and detected. By the provisions of the bill, you have no check upon fraud except the oaths of the captains of infantry. You require the adjutant general, by the fourth section of the bill, to determine how many men shall compose each class, and to apportion the classes and number of men to be detached from the several brigades, regiments, or battalions. This is a new duty assigned to the adjutant generals, and one which I should imagine they would not be very fond of discharging.

When the adjutant generals have completed the duty assigned them, they are to transmit copies of their doings to the brigadiers, who are charged with a transmittance of such copies to the commanding officers of regiments and battalions, leaving no responsibility for the correct distribution of the men to be draughted on the brigadiers, nor upon the commanders of regiments or battalions; but the commanders of companies are charged with dividing the men into classes, conformably to the number assigned to each class by the adjutant general. Here the militia part of the operation for raising your men ends. The captains are not charged with the duty of even informing the men how they are classed; they are not directed to keep a record of the classification, nor to make return of their doings to any superior officer. The classes are then left to perform all the remaining obligations of raising the men, and that too without being legally informed of whom they consist. Sir, the third and fourth sections of the bill appear to me to be not only destitute of every systematic military principle, but in open hostility to every military procedure heretofore in practice, or which ever can be practised with that degree of precision and certainty which the nature of this case seems to require.

A new path is taken upon ground which I believe was never occupied before, neither in this or any other country. upon a similar occasion. The responsibility of your principal militia officers is dispensed with, and the whole ground appears to me to be enveloped in doubt and uncertainty; whereas it must be acknowledged, that the crisis demands the adoption of the most prompt, expeditious, and certain mode practicable for raising the men and preparing them for the field, and this can only be done by pursuing the correct military system heretofore uniformly practised upon in raising men by draught. Permit me to state it, sir. The President of the United States calls on the Executive of a State (say Massachusetts, if you please) for a due proportion of the men to be raised. The Executive of the State always has before him, deposited in the adjutant general's office, the number of men contained in each division and brigade in the State; the Governor calls on the adjutant general, as one of his staff, to apportion the whole number of men called for among the several divisions, according to their number; for the correctness of the apportionment the Governor holds himself responsible; and, as commander-in-chief of the militia, he issues his general order, containing the apportionment among all the divisions, directing the major generals, or commanders of divisions, to cause the men assigned to their respective divisions to be raised agreeably to the principles of the law under which they are to be raised. The major general apportions the men assigned to his division among the brigades composing the division, according to their numbers, and adds his division orders, directing the brigadiers to cause the men assigned to their respective brigades to be raised in like manner. Each brigadier apportions the men to be raised in his brigade among the regiments and battalions composing the brigade, according to their numbers, and adds his brigade orders, directing the commanding officers of regiments and battalions to cause the men assigned to their respective regiments or battalions to be raised in like manner. Each commanding officer of a regiment or battalion apportions the men assigned to his regiment or battalion among the companies composing such regiment or battalion, according to their numbers, and adds his regimental or battalion orders, directing the captains or commanding officers of companies composing his regiment or battalion to raise the men assigned to them, respectively, in like manner, and to make return to him of their doing therein within a given time, together with the names of the men so raised. All the orders and apportionments, from the Governor down, are transmitted to the commanders of companies, and by them read to their respective companies, and recorded in the orderly book of the company, which is always open to the inspection of any person who may think himself aggrieved by the doings of any superior officer, and for correcting any other error which may be supposed to have been committed in the course of any official transaction of any officer of the line. The officers to command

13th CON. 3d SESS.—3

in the detachment are detailed from the division, brigade, and regimental and battalion rosters, according to their rank and standing on the roster for duty, and are all included in the general return.

All these pass through the hands of the several grades of officers which I have named, up to the Governor. The major generals, brigadiers, and commanders of regiments and battalions have their respective staff officers attached to them, whose duty it is to assist in apportioning the men, in copying and distributing the orders, in digesting, arranging, and transmitting returns, and of keeping a fair record of all orders, returns, and of all other official proceedings of the commanders of the said corps in their said capacities; but the commanding officers of corps are responsible for the accuracy of the apportionment, the correctness of the returns, and all other official transactions done and performed by them. I should not have troubled the Senate with these details, had I not been deeply impressed with the idea that the arrangement for raising the men pointed out by the bill is wholly impracticable, and that a better course might and ought to be pursued. The mode of procedure which I have named, I conceive to be founded in strict military principles. It engages the assistance and retains the responsibility which by law is justly imposed upon every officer of the militia, from the Governor to the commander of a company. It secures to you ample means for correcting any error, and for detecting any fraud which may take place in the apportionment, raising the men, or in the returns. It affords means by which the Government can at all times ascertain the exact number of men which they have engaged for the public service, easy and generally well understood.

Sir, in regard to the fifth section of the bill, I will only say, that the organization of the men detached into divisions, brigades, regiments, and companies, would, in my opinion, be more properly vested in the Governors of the States and Territories, than in the President of the United States. The Governors must know better than the President can know, the local situation of the officers detailed and men detached, and consequently are better qualified to organize them to their satisfaction, and in a manner the most useful to the public service.

The sixth section very properly provides for inflicting a penalty on the officers and soldiers who shall fail to obey the orders of a proper officer for carrying into effect any provision of the bill; but this provision must be considered as applying to those officers and soldiers only, who have been detailed or detached, if it be true, that the Government of the United States have no power to inflict punishment on the militia until they are called into the service of the United States, and therefore cannot attach to any of the officers or soldiers of the militia who may not have been detached or detailed.

The seventh section of the bill provides, that the militia to be raised under this bill shall not be compelled to serve beyond the limits of the

State or Territory who furnish them, and the limits of an adjoining State or Territory, with the exception of Tennessee, Kentucky, Pennsylvania, and Virginia. Sir, I have always imagined that the United States composed one great family for the purposes of national defence; that if an enemy should invade the State of Maryland, and the forces of the militia of Massachusetts were necessary to repel such invasion, that we were bound to afford our aid, and so *vice versa;* but, sir, if the Senate are tenacious of retaining the principles of this section, I must submit to their decision.

The eighth section of the bill I consider to be necessary and proper.

In the ninth section of the bill it is provided, that any three classes which will furnish two men for the war, shall be exempt from the militia duty required by the bill. Here I must be permitted, sir, to ask gentlemen if this provision does not come in direct contact with your recruiting service for the war? Your men which you may calculate on recruiting for the war are shrewd, calculating men, and the moment this bill shall be published they will have an eye to the bounty which they may acquire from the classes, in addition to that given by the public; and, sir, will not this retard, if not entirely suspend the recruiting service for the war, until it shall be ascertained what bounty can be obtained from the classes? I apprehend that it will, sir; and if that should prove to be the case, the suspension will be attended with very inconvenient, if not fatal consequences. The bill allows the States or Territories three months to furnish the men in their own way; if not so furnished within that period, it contemplates that, if the classification takes place, the classes are allowed twenty days to procure the man by contract before the draught can take place; then, sir, allowing that the men are to be classed immediately upon the transmission of the bill to the States and Territories, (which I can by no means conceive will be the case,) the recruiting service for the war and the operations of this bill are postponed for at least one hundred and ten days before you commence the operation of law for filling the ranks of the regular army, or for the detachment from the militia provided for by the bill, which will carry you far into April, when in fact the situation of the country requires that the regular army should be filled, and the militia contemplated by this act organized and ready to take the field, before the commencement of the operation of the one or the other system. But, sir, if all the effects contemplated by the friends to this bill, in regard to filling the ranks of the regular army, should be realized, what would be the consequence? Why, sir, instead of the force of 142,000 men. contemplated by the committee as the necessary force with which you ought to open the next campaign, you have 109,-000 only; for, sir, taking it for granted, that we have now only 40,000 regular troops in the field, 22,000 is wanting to fill up that establishment; consequently, if 22,000 men should be procured by the classes pointed out in this bill, 33,000 classes

would be exempt from the services required by this bill, which would reduce the whole number of men to be brought into the field, as I have stated, to 109,000. The tenth section provides for the supposition contained in it, that more than men enough to fill the regular army may be raised for the war under the provisions of this bill. That I imagine, sir, is a supposition which it is scarcely necessary to provide for; but it is to be remembered, that should the idea be realized, it is calculated to reduce the number of men contemplated for the field the next campaign, to the amount of one-third of the whole number contained in the surplus so raised, and consequently, instead of your having 109,000 men—which I must agree, according to the principles of the first section of the bill, is an adequate number—no man can divine how far below that number your force is to be reduced, by the very uncertain operation of this bill. Sir, while I am upon this part of the subject, permit me again to revert to the third section of the bill, which is, in a considerable degree, connected with it. That section, in violation of the principles of the law of 1795, which I have quoted and which is now in force, and been uniformly practised upon from the passage of the law to this time, subjects all the militiamen who have rendered service in the present war, be it ever so eminent, to the same chance of the draught, as it does those who have never rendered any service, totally subverting the precious principle of that law which provides for a general rotation of service: and, sir, this vital error in the bill seems to be acknowledged by the same section, inasmuch as it goes on to provide that all former services shall be deducted from the term of service for which they may be draughted under this bill. Well, sir, what becomes of the permanency of the troops to be raised under the bill? Why, sir, it vanishes like a vapor, and leaves no real substance behind. The militiamen which are made subject to this draught, and which have rendered services, are many; probably some of them may have served for two years, and some for eighteen months. And I know, sir, that many of them have served for one year, some for nine, six, and three months. Then you go on to make your organization upon the principles of the bill, your officers are all detailed to command the detachment, according to the principles of the organization. It may appear that some of the men detached have already served for two years; they must immediately be discharged, some must no doubt be discharged in six months, and I know that many must be discharged at the end of one year, at the end of eighteen months, and at the end of twenty-one months. Thus, sir, the permanency of your establishment will be gradually reduced as it relates to the men; but no provision is made for reducing the officers in the same proportion. No, sir, they are to remain in the service, and consequently in the pay of the nation, until the end of the term for which they were detailed, unless the President of the United States should undertake to discharge them, without imputing to them any fault within their power to control, which I should not imagine would be likely to take place. This is the pretended system of permanency in your Military Establishment, reduced by the bill itself to insignificance and uncertainty. Besides, sir, it is provided that the officer making the draught shall make report to the Department of War of all persons draughted by him, who have performed a tour of duty specified in the act. But who is the officer who is to make this return to the Secretary of War? I find no officer designated to make the draught; consequently none can be authorized to make return to the Secretary of War. It must therefore be left with the classes to do it, in which case a correspondence of eighty thousand may be opened, and in all probability of not less than twenty thousand will be opened between the classes and the Secretary of War upon this particular subject, when according to the mode of raising the men which I have had the honor to name, should it be adopted, each captain would be under obligation to make this statement in his return, through the proper channel, to the Governors. The Governors might direct the adjutant generals to make out an abstract of these returns from the captains, and transmit it to the Secretary of War, which would open with him a little over twenty correspondents, instead of at least twenty thousand. And for my own part, sir, I cannot see why the Governors of the States and Territories should not be vested with the authority of deciding this question, without troubling the Secretary of War with it, upon their being responsible for the return being made of their doings to the Secretary of War, for the information of the General Government.

Sir, I have thought it my duty to point out to the Senate my own ideas of what I conceive to be errors, both in principle and detail, contained in the bill. If it should pass the Senate in its present form, I shall very much regret it.

I should be extremely sorry to give my vote against any measure calculated to promote the object of general defence; but, sir, I do not conceive that this bill is calculated to further that object in the most desirable and practicable manner.

I do consider, sir, that the bill commences with unusual and arbitrary principles, never before attempted to be imposed on the militia of this country since its first settlement by civilized man.

It appears to me, sir, as I have endeavored to show, that it contains principles of the most deadly hostility to the correct military principles, now in practice in the militia, for raising men for public service. It dispenses with the responsibility of the principal militia officers in raising men, and thereby leaves the Government at all times in a state of entire uncertainty relative to the number engaged for the service. It is an extremely impolitic measure, inasmuch as it takes new and unexplored ground for its basis, which may, and I presume will, be disgusting to the people, at a time, too, when their most cordial co-operation with the Government is eminently necessary, to enable you to effect the great object which you have in view. In its most prominent features, I conceive that every discerning eye, not a member of this Senate, will, at first view, perceive the most manifest injustice exhibited to individuals of the militia—they are indiscriminately to be subjected to the draught for two years, whatever may be their situation or circumstances in life. Those who have heretofore rendered services have the miserable consolation only, of being told, that their former term of service shall be deducted from the two years, while the honorable principle of rotation, now existing by law, is totally disregarded. And inasmuch as the militia, not possessing more than one-third of the property of the nation, are called on to furnish all the pecuniary means of procuring the men, if procured by contract; and all others, possessing two-thirds of the property of the nation, and not subject to be called on to render personal service, are entirely exonerated from the burdens of this draught.

And, sir, notwithstanding the high, unusual ground which it assumes to take, I must confess that in my opinion it has sown in it the seeds of its own destruction, which are so deep rooted, that I imagine they cannot fail to effect that object. It dispenses with all the responsibility of your principal militia officers, as has been before observed; it inflicts no penalty on the classes for omitting to raise men for the war, for omitting to raise men by contract, nor for omitting to raise them by draught; and as no officer or other person is authorized to make the draught, besides the classes, I consider the whole system as resolving into a recommendation, upon the patriotism of the States and Territories, and upon the patriotism of the classes, which I am apprehensive must fail of furnishing you eighty thousand men. The system, therefore, appears to me to be inefficient, and totally incompetent to effect the object which I am sure the Senate have in view. Mr. President, from the view which I have taken of this subject, I think the Senate must perceive that it is impracticable for me to vote in favor of it in its present shape. Unless it shall undergo a radical change in its principles and details, I must vote against the bill.

Mr. DAGGETT, of Connecticut, addressed the Chair as follows:

Mr. President: By this bill, the President is authorized to call upon the several States and Territories for their respective quotas of 80,430 militia, to serve for two years, unless sooner discharged. They are to constitute part of the regular Army of the United States, and to be treated in every respect as such, with the exception that they cannot be compelled to serve beyond the limits of the State or Territory furnishing them, and the limits of an adjoining State or Territory, and that the officers are to be appointed by the State or Territorial authorities. The object of this force is declared to be "the defence of the frontiers of the United States." [The words at the end of the title, "against invasion," were inserted after the bill had passed.]

The principle is assumed, that Congress may by law, order the militia of the several State into the service of the United States, to defend their frontiers and garrison their fortresses for two years, or for any other definite period, or during the war, provided the country is invaded, or in imminent danger of invasion. This country, while engaged in war with any nation which can send either fleets or armies against it, will always be in such condition, and consequently the militia are subject to the control of Congress. There is no limit, say the advocates of this law, to the power of Congress over the militia, in time of war, except that they must be officered by the States. A conscription is thus justified. It is openly avowed by the same gentlemen as proper, just, and legal. I think these conclusions are fairly deduced from the premises. If the power of this Government over the militia is in time of war unlimited, it does indeed follow, that the freemen of this country, who are subject to the duties of militiamen, may be converted into soldiers of the Army of the United States during the war, or for any definite period. The exception that they shall not be obliged to go from the State, or an adjoining State, is a matter of form, and not of right. They may be ordered to Canada, or to any more remote region. But, sir, this whole doctrine is unconstitutional; it is an outrage, upon its face and its principles and provisions, upon the undoubted rights of freemen, and upon the charter of our liberties.

That the powers of this Government are limited—that those not granted are reserved—are positions sanctioned by an amendment to the Constitution, and universally admitted. The entire control over the militia, previous to the adoption of the Constitution, was in the States. All that control, except what has been delegated to the United States, remains. There is no article in the Constitution delegating a general power. Every word employed on the subject shows that it is limited. "Congress shall have power to provide for calling forth the militia to execute the laws of the Union, suppress insurrections, and repel invasions." Why give power to call forth the militia in those exigencies, if the entire authority over them was elsewhere given? The absurdity is too apparent to admit of argument or illustration. Again: "Congress shall have power to provide for organizing, arming, and disciplining the militia, and for *governing* such part of them as may be employed in the service of the United States, reserving to the States, respectively, the appointment of the officers, and the authority of training the militia, according to the discipline prescribed by Congress." In other language, it may provide for arranging them into companies, battalions, regiments, brigades, and divisions. It may provide that they shall be armed, and the manner in which it shall be done—prescribe the discipline to be pursued; and make laws for governing them while in that service of the United States, to which they might be called forth, in the cases before specified. All this Congress may do, to establish that uniformity and order which are so essential to a well-regulated militia. This is the obvious and

just meaning of the clause. Again: "The President shall be Commander-in-Chief of the Army and Navy of the United States, and of the militia of the several States, when called into the actual service of the United States." In these articles of the Constitution, Congress and the President are everywhere limited, and everywhere the power of the States is apparent. The militia cannot be called forth as a regular army at all—they may be called as a militia. They cannot be trained or officered, in any case, except under the authority of the States, nor commanded even by the President, except when called forth in the exigencies specified.. Who can discover in these provisions a pretence for asserting that the militia are constitutionally subjected to the general control of Congress?

But, sir, to prove the constitutionality of this bill, its friends rely on those clauses which give to Congress the right "to raise and support armies" and "to provide for calling forth the militia in the cases mentioned." These are distinct and independent powers and are always so considered. If the first gave to Congress any authority over the militia as such, it gave a general authority, and if so, the subsequent provisions regarding them, are worse than useless—they tend only to perplex and bewilder. The truth is, this clause has no reference to the militia any more than to physicians, lawyers, or merchants. It authorizes Congress to raise and support armies, in a manner and by means consistent with the great principles of civil liberty, known to the people of this country, and adopted and deemed sacred in all free Governments. But it is utterly inconsistent with those principles to compel any man to become a soldier for life, during a war, or for any fixed time. In Great Britain, a war-like nation, a nation often the theme of reproach here for the tyranny of the Government, no such practice is, or can be, resorted to; the people would revolt at it; they would shake a throne which should attempt it. It is alike odious here, and I hope it will remain so.

It is said, however, that the nation is invaded; a case of invasion—a specified case exists, and, by the second mentioned power, the militia may be called forth. It is true the militia may be called forth to "repel invasions." It cannot escape observation, that the words employed by the Constitution, "to repel invasions," seem quite unlike the words in this bill, "for the defence of the frontiers," still less are they descriptive of the object for which the gentlemen are obliged to contend the militia may be called forth. They declare that so long as there is invasion or imminent danger of invasion, and this will be our condition during the existence of the war, the militia may be converted into an army for the defence of the country, and support the war. Why did not the great, wise, and good men, as they are justly characterized by the gentleman from Virginia, (Mr. GILES,) use language expressive of such an idea? Why did they not say, that in time of war, Congress shall have power to provide for calling forth the militia to support it?

Again, sir, the militia may be called forth to repel invasions, to execute the laws of the Union, and to suppress insurrections. These occasions are, with good reasons, joined. In their nature, upon the soundest and fairest definitions, they are emergencies, sudden and unexpected, and therefore incapable of being met by a regular army. The wisdom of the Convention dictated provision in case of such occurrences. To make such provision by a standing army, always to be dreaded, and the subject of unceasing reprobation by the people of the United States, would have been unwise and impracticable. These were the views of the venerable men who formed and adopted the Constitution. It never entered their minds, that in providing to repel invasions and suppress insurrections, and to execute the laws, they were furnishing the nation with the means of sustaining a war, especially an offensive war. In this light was the subject considered in the State conventions, and had the doctrines here advanced been deemed the legitimate interpretations of that Constitution, it would have been rejected by every State in the Union.

Again, sir, did the Convention intend to give to Congress the power of converting the militia into an army, and yet reserve to the States the power of appointing the officers? It is unquestionable that neither the President nor Congress can grant a commission. You have then an army without the power of giving to it officers, an army which may be kept together, or disbanded for the defect of officers, at the pleasure of eighteen sovereign States. With such an army, you might repel an invasion, or suppress insurrections, or cause the laws to be executed, but you cannot carry on a war.

This bill is not only unconstitutional, but it is unequal, unjust, and oppressive. By the second section, the militia are to be divided into classes, and each class is compelled to furnish a man, one of their number, or a substitute, to serve as a soldier for two years. It affects no citizen who is over forty-five years of age—no exempt from military duty, no commissioned officer, except such as the State shall select to command, and those it obliges to serve, in all events; it includes apprentices, poor men, and those of every occupation, between eighteen and forty-five years of age. To illustrate these ideas, I will ask the attention of the Senate to its operation upon the State of Connecticut. The quota of that State is about three thousand and ten. Its militia consists of about twenty thousand non-commissioned officers and privates; there are not less than forty-eight thousand males above eighteen, and under forty-five; add to these the males over forty-five, and it will be seen what proportion of the male population over eighteen is subjected to this draught. Of the property, I believe, five-sixths, or more, is possessed by the exempts. In these twenty thousand militia are to be found apprentices, day laborers, mechanics, and farmers. Of these, one in seven is, by this bill, forced into the army for two years, or the seven are compelled to procure a substitute. The soldier is allowed

no bounty, either in land or money. He is to receive his clothing, subsistence, and eight dollars per month; not more than half the sum to be obtained by laboring peacefully in the ordinary occupations at home. It will be readily seen, that while the United State give a bounty of three hundred and twenty acres of land, as is established in the bill which has just passed the Senate, and one hundred and twenty-four dollars in money, no substitute can be obtained for less than two hundred and fifty or three hundred dollars. Seven of the militia, in this view of the subject, are compelled to pay from thirty to forty dollars each, or one of their number is to become a soldier for two years, while the wealthy exempt is no otherwise affected than he is obliged, with them, to bear his proportion of public taxes; and thus on twenty thousand, of the least affluent part of the community, a burden is imposed of about $75,000. The officer, also, who is appointed by the authority of the State, and detailed to this service, is not at liberty to procure a substitute; he must become an inmate of a camp for two years. Thus the apprentice may be forced away from his work-shop, for a period which will affect his whole future life, the poor man must leave his family helpless, the young farmer or mechanic relinquish his business, to be neglected or ruined, or pay an enormous tax, and the officer, be his condition what it may, is to spend two years in an army, subject to the rules and articles of war. Is this equality? Is this justice? Is it not oppression and tyranny of no ordinary character? If any position be so true as to admit of no doubt, it is, that, in support of burdens created by war, the people should be taxed according to their property. This bill is a palpable departure from that rule of political justice.

It is said, however, that our country is in great peril; men must be had, the Army must be filled. What then? Are these reasons for resorting to unconstitutional and oppressive measures? The plea of necessity is too old, too well characterized, too well understood to be admitted. This people have seen times of imminent danger. In the war of the Revolution where destruction assailed us on all sides, when did we, for a moment, admit these doctrines! The people were, in some States, classed and draughted, but for only short periods, and upon principles totally dissimilar to those contained in this bill. Every man was included and obliged to contribute. In Great Britain, whence we derive many of our maxims, usages, and laws, and whence too we have derived the law for calling forth the militia in the cases specified, every poor man with one child or more, all apprentices, and many others, are exempted from liability to be called out to repel invasions. Are we less attentive to the rights and interests of the people, than the nation towards which so much invective is constantly uttered?

The bill is incapable of being executed, as well as unconstitutional and unjust. It proceeds entirely upon the idea that the State governments will lend their aid to carry it into effect. If they refuse, it becomes inoperative. Now, sir, will the Executives who believe it a violation of the Constitution, assist in its execution? I tell you they will not. No one denies that the State governments have some power over their militia; all admit that they have, at least, a power concurrent with that of the United States. It is so admitted in this debate; the limits, however, it is said, are not, and cannot be denied. Of one thing you may be certain, that the captain general and commander-in-chief of the military force of a State, will not readily yield the whole or any portion of that force to the United States, to become a part of a regular army, and thus consent to annihilate the power of the State over its militia. For such a claim you must show him a warrant in the Constitution. If you differ with him as to the interpretation of that instrument, he is at liberty to construe it for himself; yours is a limited authority over the subject, the general authority is in the State. He is bound to maintain its lawful rights and privileges. He would be unworthy of his station if he surrendered them. It would be a flagrant violation of duty to execute an order which he deemed repugnant to the Constitution.

We are told, however, by the honorable gentleman from Virginia (Mr. GILES) that this bill will be popular. Let me assure that gentleman he is mistaken; in New England it will be viewed with extreme horror. An opinion there prevails, is engraven on every heart, it will live, you cannot destroy it, that no freeman is to be made a soldier in your army by compulsion. It is abhorrent to all the enlightened and independent people, of all parties and sects. They too well know and too highly appreciate the privileges of freemen to approve a conscription, however disguised.

Once more: Massachusetts and Connecticut have peculiar reasons for withholding their assent to laws, for calling out their militia. Those already draughted into your service, have neither been subsisted nor paid by the United States. I will speak particularly of Connecticut. On the first of July last, the President requested of the Executive of that State to furnish three hundred thousand men, with a major general and other officers, as its proportion of ninety-three thousand militia required from the several States and Territories. The quota was detached and organized. On the first of August following, Brigadier General Cushing, of the Army of the United States, commanding at New London, requested of the Executive the major part of the detachment thus organized, and that they might be under a brigadier general, and subjected to his (General Cushing's) command. As there was then in the service of the United States, of the militia, more than a brigadier's command, and as a majority of the major general's command was now called for, the major general was, with manifest propriety, directed to accompany his men, and of course it became his duty to command. General Cushing, commanding in that district, (how, and by what authority established as a military district is not now the subject of inquiry,) refused to acknowl-

edge the militia as in the service of the United States, or to pay or subsist them, assigning as a reason, that a major general could not be recognised when any number less than four thousand is required; though. on the first of July, as before stated, three thousand with a major general had been called for and detached, and though the brigadier assigning this reason had not then men sufficient to constitute a colonel's command. This course was in obedience to the orders of the Secretary of War. The militia however, did not abandon the defence of the State and nation, but remained in obedience to the orders of the enlightened and patriotic Chief Magistrate of that State, and have been subsisted and paid out of its treasury. I will not consent to any bill like that on your table, till justice shall have been done to a State which has ever been among the first to perform all her Constitutional engagements.

I shall vote against this bill on another ground. It is declared to be its object, to relieve the regular Army from the defence of the frontiers, that it may be employed in the conquest of the Canadas. I doubt if this object can be effected without first securing the command of the St. Lawrence. Our success as yet is not very flattering. Without detracting from the hard-earned fame of our Army, or the brilliant achievements of our Navy on the Lakes, that country remains entirely in full possession of the enemy. After an immense loss of money and life, the great work is yet undone.

The project, in my judgment, is inexpedient if practicable. The result would not be worth the sacrifice—it would not contribute towards a peace, an object near the heart of every good man. Great Britain is pronounced by gentlemen to be a wise, powerful, and haughty nation. True, sir, and when has she been driven into terms of peace by the invasion of one of her provinces? Should we succeed in this attempt, would her pride be so far subdued as to lessen her demands? Is it not far more probable that such an event might induce her to lay in wide and dreadful destruction an invaluable seacoast? At such a price the Canadas would be purchased at too great a sacrifice. She retaliates by no strict rules. It is not with her, "an eye for an eye, and a tooth for a tooth;" but a head for an eye, a body for a tooth. The Parliament House at Little York was destroyed, and she burnt your Capitol.

We are solemnly warned of our danger by the friends of this measure, and asked, if we shall stand still and suffer our country to be desolated? We answer, no; raise armies if you please, to any extent, by equal and Constitutional methods—arm every stick of timber that can float. Let the Navy, once despised, give new proofs, if possible, of her skill and valor; strike home at the commerce of the enemy. This is our true course. This will be felt by the merchant and manufacturer, and their voices will be heard and regarded in the British cabinet. This is the only effectual warfare which we can maintain offensively against that nation. I fear not the conquest of our territory. The attempt would be idle. Invasion will be met and resisted at the water's edge, with success, by hundreds of thousands of Americans who will not be forced into your Army.

Mr. MASON, of New Hampshire, addressed the Chair as follows :

Mr. President: I am glad, sir, that the few observations, which I made on a former day, when this bill was under consideration, have induced the honorable chairman of the Committee on Military Affairs, (Mr. GILES,) to make such an ample exposition of the views and objects of that committee, and of the Administration. I deem it fortunate that, at the commencement of the discussion of the bills on military affairs, we are possessed of the ulterior intentions and designs.

The Secretary of War, in his late report, has recommended for adoption by the Legislature, a plan of a forcible draught, or conscription, of the whole free male population of the United States, between the ages of eighteen and forty-five years, for the purpose of recruiting the regular Army. He proposes that all persons, within those ages, be formed into classes of one hundred each ; and that if any class neglect to furnish four soldiers for the Army, to be delivered over to the recruiting officer within thirty days, that number be taken out of the class by force ; that vacancies by casualty, be supplied in like manner from the class, and that the legal bounty of one hundred and twenty-four dollars to each recruit be assessed on all the taxable property within the precinct of each class. This plan must be presumed to have the approbation of the Administration ; for it cannot be supposed the Secretary of War would adventure on a measure so important, without such support and countenance.

Although the present bill certainly does not adopt the plan of the Secretary in its full extent, and although the honorable chairman has said he can support the provisions of the bill without its aid, yet he has attempted, in a formal argument, to maintain, that this Government has the Constitutional power, to be exercised at discretion as occasion may require, of placing our citizens, by force, and for an unlimited time, in the ranks of the regular Army. Till lately, such an opinion was entertained by few, if any. I believe it was expressed by none. Great and sudden changes in opinion on important political subjects are the usual forerunners of revolutions in States. This is emphatically the case, where the force of Government rests on common sentiment. Sincerely believing the doctrine contended for, to be unwarranted by the Constitution, and pregnant with consequences dangerous to the rights and liberties of the country, I cannot permit it to pass without attempting its refutation. The most monstrous opinions, when announced by high authority, and supported with plausibility, will, if permitted without contradiction to become familiar to the mind, in time lose much of their original deformity.

The honorable gentleman has been pleased, in a style somewhat monitory, to caution those opposed to his doctrine to consider the responsibility they must encounter in obstructing the measures of Government in the present state of affairs. I admit the distress of the nation exists to the full extent stated. We see and feel it, and have too much reason to believe it will soon become universal. The crisis demands all the wisdom and virtue of the country. I hold a stake in the fate of the nation in common with my fellow citizens, and do not feel inclined to shrink from doing what I think my duty requires. In times like these, no political situation is free from responsibility.

In return, I take the liberty of admonishing the friends of the Administration (and the honorable gentleman, if he includes himself in that number) to be cautious how they attempt to overleap the limits of the Constitution. Of all our dangers, I see none more alarming than the apparent disposition to exercise arbitrary power. Revolutionary measures can never, with safety, be resorted to by a regular Government. They place the magistrate and private citizen on the same level, and none can foresee into whose hands, during the boisterous commotion of the political elements, the tyrant's power will fall. A Government which should require such expedients would not be worth preserving. If sufficient powers are not granted by the people, apply to the people for their enlargement. In periods of alarm and terror, when present danger hushes all fears of that which is more remote and less obvious, inroads on the rights of the people are chiefly to be apprehended. In a case so deeply affecting the personal liberty of the whole body of the nation as the present, no extremity of danger would justify the exercise of illegal authority.

The inquiry is, whether the Constitution gives to this Government the power contended for?

The clause in the Constitution which declares that Congress shall provide for the common defence, has been cited, though very little reliance appears to be placed on it. The purpose of that clause seems to have been to impose a duty, or define an object to the attainment of which the powers granted are to be applied. The words, with others immediately connected, are, " to pay the debts and provide for the common defence and general welfare of the United States." The means or powers are afterwards prescribed, by which these great objects are to be attained. It has not been, and I trust will not be contended, that Congress is at liberty to resort to other means at their discretion. Should this be considered a grant of power, still the subsequent specification of the manner of exercising it, would limit and restrict it. Money raised to pay the debts of the United States, for instance, must be raised in the manner specially pointed out; and if it could not be obtained by taxes levied according to the Constitution, or by other methods therein directed, surely Congress could not levy taxes in any other way, or resort to other means not thereby authorized.

The authority given to Congress " to raise and support armies," comprises their whole power on this subject. This, and the authority of calling forth the militia under certain circumstances, are the means by which the common defence is to be provided for. Can the Legislature, by virtue of this grant of power, adopt the proposed plan of conscription, and place, by force, such part of the population of the United States, and for such periods as shall be deemed expedient, in the ranks of the regular Army? A power so transcendant and dangerous, must, to justify the exercise of it, be derived from plain principles, and depend on no doubtful construction or subtle reasoning.

The power to raise and support armies must be construed according to the intentions and understanding of the people of the United States, who made the Constitution, consistently with all the well known and established rights of the States and of the people—and consistently with the general principles of civil liberty.

The military power or force given by the Constitution to this Government, is of two sorts—a regular Army, and the militia of the States—the latter in certain emergencies, and with certain restrictions and limitations—the former without any restriction. It is unnecessary, for the present purpose, to point out with exact precision all the restrictions and limitations of the power over the militia. In three specified cases only, and for a service within the limits of the United States, and under the command of their own State officers, and as I think, for short periods of service, can this Government call on the States for their militia. From these restrictions, it is apparent, the power of the United States is of a very limited nature, and that the States still retain by far the greatest portion of authority over their own militia. Over the regular Army, the Government of the United States have an unlimited power. They may use it in all cases where military force is needed, in any part of the world, under such officers and for such periods as they please. There always have been in this country important distinctions between the militia and regular Army. These distinctions were always kept up, and in various instances exemplified in the war of the Revolution, and were well understood by the people of the United States at the time of forming the Constitution. There was known to be an essential difference between serving in the regular Army and performing a tour of duty in the militia. Regular armies were raised by enlistment of such as voluntarily consented to enter them. Such, for ages, had been the practice of the British Government, from which we originally derived most of our ideas on subjects of Government; and such was the practice of the Government of the United States, and of the several States during the Revolutionary war. There always has been, and I hope always will be, a jealousy of standing armies. At the time of the Revolution it was carried to an unreasonable height, and too strongly felt. When the Constitution was adopted, no power granted to the General Government was more severely criticised, than that over the military force of the country. Those opposed to the Constitution contended, that the power of the purse and of the sword were im-

properly united, and that not only the rights of the State Governments, but the freedom of the people would be endangered. If any such power as that contended for, could have been conceived to be granted by the Constitution, it would have been detected and pointed out by those so much alarmed. Yet it is believed, that such construction was not even suggested in any of the conventions, although the subject was there most ably discussed. Nor is it believed, that with this construction, the Constitution would have been adopted by a single State of the Union. If, then, voluntary enlistment was the only method by which a regular Army could be raised, according to the general opinion of the people, it follows that the power to raise armies is, by the very terms used in the Constitution, restricted to that method; for the words must be construed, as they were understood by the people who adopted the Constitution. And so the position of the honorable gentleman, that the grant of power to raise armies being general, and without any restriction of the method by which it shall be exercised, leaves the Government at liberty to adopt any method they please, is ill founded. That might be a just construction of the terms when used by a people accustomed to a despotic government, for they might so understand them.

The power claimed is, doubtless, vastly greater and more dangerous, than any other possessed by the Government. It subjects the personal freedom of every citizen, in comparison with which the rights of property are insignificant, to arbitrary discretion. Had there been an intention of granting such power, would there not have been some attempt to guard against the unjust and oppressive exercise of it, as was done in the granting of powers of less importance? Yet, this power of raising armies, unless confined to voluntary enlistment, is without any guard or restriction whatever. The exercise of it must depend wholly on arbitrary discretion.

All the recruits wanted for the Army might, if the Government should so please, be taken from one section of the Union. The power of raising money is not thus submitted to the discretion of the Government. All taxes, if indirect, must be uniform throughout the United States; if direct, they must be apportioned according to representation. No tax can be laid on exports. Why these guards where property was to be taken, and none where the owners of the property were to be taken? From the mere neglect of attempting in some way to limit the power, it may be strongly inferred that it was not intended to be granted.

Were the Government at liberty to raise armies, by forcibly taking men at its discretion, it might, by a similar construction of the Constitution, support them, by taking property in like manner. The armies, when raised, might live at free quarters, on the people. In a similar way, a navy might be provided, by seizing the ships of individuals. The right in both cases is the same; the injury and distress in taking property the least.

Has the Government a similar power to impress men for the Navy? The terms in the Constitution " to provide and maintain a Navy" are, at least, as proper for this construction, as those applied to the Army. The convenience and necessity in this instance, stronger than in the other. The British Government, before the Revolution, did attempt to exercise in this country the supposed right of impressment for the Navy, which it never did for the Army. Stronger reasons might be adduced for this method of manning the Navy, than for filling the Army. Yet the Government, in their instructions to our Envoys for treating of peace with Great Britain, say "impressment is not an American practice, but is utterly repugnant to our Constitution and laws." The honorable Secretary, when he draughted those instructions, knew not how soon he should be directed to contend for the contrary doctrine.

The power in question is inconsistent with certain well-known rights of the States recognised by the Constitution. Such a construction of a power granted to the General Government as destroys rights reserved to the States by the Constitution cannot be admitted. Because it can never be presumed that rights were intended to be surrendered, which are expressly reserved or recognised as existing in the States. The same principle applies to all rights acknowledged to belong to the States, whether recognised by the Constitution or not. The Constitution declares " the powers not delegated to the United States ' by the Constitution, nor prohibited by it to the ' States, are reserved to the States respectively or ' to the people."

The States still retaining the principal power over the militia, as has been shown, the power given this Government to raise armies must not be so construed as will destroy that power of the States. The power claimed is to take by force, for the regular Army, all persons capable of bearing arms, including the whole militia of the States. This surely annihilates all State power over their militia. The whole or any part may, at the pleasure of this Government, be converted into a regular army, and the provision of the Constitution in this particular, together with the rights of the States, be destroyed.

The right of the States, in time of war, to maintain regular troops, is recognised by the Constitution. Abandoned by the United States, it is well known that several of the States at the present time, keep considerable bodies of troops for their necessary defence. All these come within the description of persons claimed by this Government, and may be thus immediately transferred to the Army of the United States. Wretched would be the condition of such States, if this Government possessed the power contended for. Unprotected by the General Government, and deprived not only of their militia, but of the troops raised at their own expense, their sole remaining resource would be an application to the mercy of the enemy. It is impossible that these rights, thus secured to the States by the Constitution itself, should be destroyed by a power granted by the same instrument to the United States. The power of the United States to raise armies, if restricted

to voluntary enlistment, is consistent with the rights and safety of the States. Any other construction presents conflicting rights which cannot be reconciled.

It has been contended that every well constituted Government has a right to the personal services of its citizens or subjects, which it may enforce by compelling as many as its occasions require to become soldiers; and that the Government of the United States, in common with others, may have this power without any special grant in the Constitution. It is unnecessary to examine the general position, though it is believed it would by no means be found so universal as stated. This Government has no powers except what are delegated. To this particular, the article of the Constitution which has been recited is express. All powers not delegated, are reserved to the States or people. If, therefore, this power exists in our country, it rests in the State Governments, and not in that of the United States. Without resorting to this principle of inherent power, most of the State Governments possess very ample authority to call for the military services of their citizens, in the provisions of their respective constitutions. Hence might be drawn an additional argument, were it necessary, against the present claim of power in the General Government.

The Secretary of War admits, that the men cannot be taken from the militia as militiamen, by reason of the Constitutional restriction, but he says the same individuals may well be taken, in their capacity as citizens. This argument the honorable gentleman from Virginia has not seen fit to adopt. With all proper deference to the respectable authority whence it originates, I must confess my inability to comprehend its force. It would seem, that an individual, to be secure in his personal liberty, must produce a Constitutional protection for himself in each of his various capacities or relations in society. Will it afford much consolation to the miserable recruit, when driven in chains to the Army, to be told that he is taken, in his capacity as a citizen, and not as a militiaman ? A prudent Government, at least, would be cautious not to insult the understanding of the nation, when attempting to outrage its rights.

To that part of the Secretary's plan, which recommends a tax to be levied on all property within the precinct of the class, in order to raise the bounty for the recruits, objections occur which, in ordinary times, would seem insurmountable. The provision of the Constitution that direct taxes (of which sort that on land is) shall be apportioned among the States, according to representation, is wholly disregarded. This tax is to be apportioned according to the free male population, between the ages of eighteen and forty-five years. This relieves the slaveholding States from the increased tax which they are bound by the Constitution to pay, for their increased representation on account of their slaves. The difference between the sums to be paid by Virginia and Massachusetts, according to the proposed plan, and the

Constitutional apportionment, exceeds four hundred thousand dollars. This is a violation of the Constitution too plain and obvious to require any reasoning to demonstrate. It is, however, in my opinion of less importance than the other which affects the rights of personal liberty, as this does the rights of property. Reduce the people to slavery, and you may take their property when and as you please.

The honorable Secretary says, in relation to this part of his plan, " should it appear that this ' mode of raising recruits was justly objectiona- ' ble, on account of the tax on property, from the ' difficulties which may be apprehended in the ' execution, or from other causes, it may be ad- ' visable to decline the tax." But why is a project, directly and plainly violating the Constitution, brought forward at all ? Is it to try the temper of the Legislature and of the people, and to lessen the horror at first excited by such attempts by rendering them familiar ? In my opinion this system of military conscription, thus recommended by the Secretary of War, is not only inconsistent with the provisions and spirit of the Constitution, but also with all the principles of civil liberty. In atrocity it exceeds that adopted by the late Emperor of France, for the subjugation of Europe, which, after drenching a great portion of that Continent with blood, was destroyed by the most powerful confederacy of nations the world ever knew. He allowed exemptions to fathers of families, and those in certain professions and official stations. But the proposed system exempts none, except the President of the United States, and the Governors of States. All within the prescribed ages, whatever may be their pursuits or condition of life, must submit to the iron yoke; priests must be taken from the altar, and judges from the bench. The highest officers, both civil and military, must be ignominiously forced into the ranks of the Army. The seminaries of learning are to be robbed of their professors and scholars. Neither literature nor science, except what is subservient to the military art, will be held in estimation. The country will become military, and be involved in perpetual wars, often waged to gratify the ambition of rulers. History evinces that wars of ambition are not less the pests of republics than of monarchies.

Such a measure cannot, it ought not to be submitted to. If it could in no other way be averted, I not only believe but I hope, it would be resisted. The most odious and cruel slavery would be the inevitable consequence of submission.

On a former day, when this measure recommended by the Secretary of War, was mentioned by an honorable member, in his place expressed his approbation (except so far as relates to the bounty tax) in terms not doubtful, I did not hesitate to give it my most decided disapprobation. I then called it weak, violent, and wicked. On more reflection, I see no reason to alter my opinion of its character. It is weak, for it is ill calculated to effect its object ; violent, for it attempts to use force, without right ; and wicked, for, if successful, it will destroy the Constitution and liberties of the country.

The honorable gentleman (Mr. GILES) has been pleased to understand those epithets as being applied to the Administration themselves; and to express his regret that they had been used. He seems to admit, however, the truth and justice of the two first, and denies only the last. He believes the Administration, though weak and violent, are honest and patriotic. I shall spare myself the labor of discussing that point. It is difficult to ascertain with certainty the motives of statesmen, and it matters little to the country, whether its rights and liberties are lost through the weakness, or wickedness, of its rulers. Public men are to be judged by their measures. The mere attempt to carry a measure, involving such principles, is just cause of alarm. The people can never feel safe while they know the Government claims such a power, which may gradually, as opportunity shall favor, be brought into exercise. The present bill adopts it, in a small degree ; another reported by the same committee, authorizing forcible draughts from the militia, to serve for the term of two years, goes much further, with the same principle. In the mean time, among men of desperate fortunes and unprincipled ambition, the doctrine will gain friends. Honest intention and well-meaning weakness give no security, but increase the danger. They prevent alarm, and when men of such a character shall have prepared the system for operation, others of more talents and different character will drive them from their seats, and grasp the despotic power so unsuitable for weak hands. If this proposal of the Executive, though at present, it should not be adopted by the Legislature in all its most odious features, should still be treated with good natured civility, it will hereafter, at some unpropitious moment, be again urged, and perhaps with fatal success. The attempt merits from the nation, deep and full toned expressions of indignation.

After laboring to establish the right of the Government to exercise the dangerous power mentioned, the honorable gentleman (Mr. GILES) has attempted to show that the present bill does not necessarily involve that power. It is certain the bill does not follow the plan of the Secretary of War in its details, but I much doubt whether the provision authorizing the enlistment of minors without the consent of their parents, guardians, or masters, can be justified, without asserting the right to take the citizens for the Army by force. If the Government has not the right of taking persons for the Army by force, they must obtain them by voluntary enlistment. That is, they must contract with individuals to become soldiers of the regular Army, and to subject themselves to the duties of that condition. All persons competent to contract for themselves, may thus enlist into the Army. None who, for any reason whatever, are incompetent to contract for themselves, can enlist without the consent of those who have a legal right to control them and contract for them. As the very essence of a contract is the voluntary assent of the minds of the parties, it is sufficiently obvious that all are incompetent to make contracts, who are incapable for want of understanding to give such assent. Thus idiots and insane persons, and children in early childhood, being unable to understand the subject-matter and give their assent, are clearly incompetent to make contracts. No legislative power can remove the disability. You may, by a legislative act, dispose of their persons and property, but it cannot be said to be done by their consent.

In every civilized country a certain age has been fixed on, as to the period when the disability of youth shall cease. For plain reasons this period must be uniform, and applied to all. It would be impossible to inquire into the degree of capacity of each individual. The feudal system, which once prevailed in most of the States of Europe, fixed this period at the age of twenty-one years. What would seem to render this regulation peculiarly apposite to the present purpose, that system, established by warriors, chiefly with a view to military strength, fixed on this age as a time when a man was supposed to be fit to bear arms, and render the military services by which his lands were held. This rule of the feudal was adopted by the common law, and universally prevails where that law is followed. In each of the United States there is, and it is believed always has been, an entire uniformity on this subject. The disability of minority continues till the age of twenty-one years. No one rule of the common law is more universally known. It is one of the first a child learns. Till the age of twenty-one the parent has a power over the child, for government and education, and has a right to his services. Founded on this acknowledged rule of the common law, in most of the States, statutes from early times have been enacted, regulating the subject of binding to apprenticeship, and also of guardianship, in case of the parent's death. All these, either directly or by necessary inference, recognise the disability of the minor to contract for himself, and the right of the parent or guardian. Under the existence of these laws, thus universally known, the people of the United States, by the Constitution, gave to this Government the right to raise armies by voluntary enlistment. With whom may the Government, by virtue of the authority thus granted, make this contract? Surely, with such only as have a capacity to contract. The power cannot extend to enlisting minors under the age of twenty-one years, except with the consent of their parents or guardians; because in that way only can valid contracts affecting such persons be made. If the power of enlisting be not limited to that age, nothing would prevent Government from taking from their parents children of more tender years, if idly consenting, and placing them in military schools till prepared for the Army. Would it be contended that Government has power to do this? If not, to what age are they restricted? Of necessity, there must be a general rule as to the age of disability of minors, it being impossible to investigate and determine the capacity of each individual.

The enlisting of minors bound to apprenticeship wholly destroys the rights of masters to the services of their apprentices. The power of this Government to destroy a right so secured by a legal contract has been questioned. The Continental Congress, in the year 1776, though sorely pressed by the war they were then engaged in, and in great want of recruits for their Army, were so deeply impressed with the illegality and injustice of such a practice, that they ordered all apprentices enlisted without the consent of their masters to be immediately discharged. The Congress was too wise to attempt to maintain their cause by violence and injustice. By a statute of the United States of the 16th of March, 1802, the enlisting of minors without the consent of their parents, guardians, or masters, is expressly prohibited, under a heavy penalty. Before that time, though not expressly prohibited by any statute, the instructions to recruiting officers directed them not to enlist minors, without such consent; and whenever it was improperly done, they could obtain discharges by applying to the courts of law. When an attempt was made at the commencement of the present war to authorize such enlistments, it was rejected by the Legislature.

Certain sections of a British statute of March, 1812, have been read by the honorable gentleman, (Mr. GILES) for the purpose of showing that the British Government enlists minors into its army without the consent of their parents or guardians. By that statute, it appears that apprentices, bound by legal indentures, when enlisted without the consent of their masters, are on their request to be discharged. Hence it is inferred that minors, other than apprentices, though enlisted without the consent of their parents or guardians, would not be discharged. If so, it can avail nothing, unless it be shown that our Government possesses a power over its citizens equal to that of the British Government. As well may we justify the exercise of any other arbitrary power, by showing that the British Government exercises the same. It is apparent that that Government respects the contracts of apprenticeship, which by this bill are to be violated. The British statute provides that if any person shall, within four days after enlisting, declare before a magistrate that he enlisted hastily and incautiously, he shall, on refunding the money received as bounty, be discharged. It is to be regretted, that the honorable gentleman who produced this statute of a foreign Government as an example for imitation, had not introduced into this bill that humane provision, so well calculated to guard the unwary against the improper arts and enticements too often practised by recruiting officers. The better opinion seems to be, that this Government has not a right to enlist minors without the consent of their parents or guardians, and it is probable, if such enlistments are directed, the courts of law will, on application, be obliged to discharge the persons so enlisted.

But, sir, were it certain this Government had the right of enlisting into the Army improvident youth, without the consent of those to whom the policy of the law has intrusted the care and control of them, it would be highly inexpedient to resort to such a measure. It is forbidden by all the considerations which have subjected the improvidence of youth to the guide and direction of age and experience. If minors are wanted for the Army, why not address yourself to their parents and guardians? They surely can best judge whether it is suitable and proper for their children and wards to enlist. If there should be no reasonable objections, it must be presumed, they would consent. You will, then, without consent, obtain those only whom you ought not to obtain. It is to be hoped the number will not be great. This measure will tend to weaken the sacred relation between parents and children, and to lessen the power for the discipline and education of youth, the best and safest foundation of all Governments. It is a direct invitation for rebellion against parental authority.

Our infant manufactures, still requiring the fostering aid of Government, and which, in the Northern and Eastern States, are in a considerable degree carried on by the labor of apprentices, will be greatly injured. Without instructing children in manufactures, a sufficient supply of laborers can never be expected. The labor of a skilful mechanic in the line of his profession is more important to the community than his services can be in the Army.

All these objects will be injured in proportion as this attempt is attended with success. And after all the exertions which can be made, it is not probable any great number of recruits can, in this way, be provided. Can a wise Government hazard such valuable interests for the sake of a miserable project of enlisting unwary youth into the Army?

The circumstances of the country being such as to render a standing army of considerable magnitude necessary, I do not wish to excite any unreasonable jealousy against such an establishment. The plan of the Secretary of War contemplates an army of more than one hundred and forty thousand men, at the disposal of Government. It may be worthy of consideration whether such an army, in certain events, which may occur, instead of defending, may not endanger the liberties of the country. On one occasion, at least, it required all the influence and address of their great and good commander to restrain, within the bounds of their duty, the army of the Revolution; than which there is no reason to hope the present will be more patriotic. Surely, it is not to be desired that an unusual proportion of young men, of such early years as not to have become acquainted with the relations and duties of civil life, should be drawn into the Army. Persons educated from childhood in a camp become soldiers of fortune, indifferent in what cause they employ their arms. From a numerous and veteran army danger is mostly to be apprehended, when the civil power rests in feeble hands.

The honorable gentleman (Mr. GILES) has related, that Oliver Cromwell, in the war between the King and Parliament of England, defeated the royalists at the battle of Naseby, by means of a regiment of London apprentices. Has the honorable gentleman forgotten the artful address, used by that hypocritical tyrant, to entice into his army the youth of the country; and then to insinuate himself, by all methods in his power, into their confidence and affections? The same troops who put down the royal power accompanied their ambitious leader to the House of Parliament, and drove from their seats the very men who had raised him to power. They enabled Cromwell to establish a tyranny so odious and oppressive, that the English nation to avoid it, in a short time, surrendered themselves at discretion to the most unprincipled and profligate monarch that ever sat on their throne, and under him patiently bore injuries more grievous than those for which they had brought his father to the block. The people of this country are not more strongly attached to liberty than the English were at the time of Cromwell. The army now recommended will be in number three-fold what he ever possessed. We also may hereafter find a Cromwell in some military demagogue who is now flattering the people with professions of affection and devotion to their cause.

After painting, in strong colors, the distress and danger of the nation, the honorable gentleman has said that strong and energetic measures are necessary to preserve it from ruin; and that light objections ought not to be made. It seems to be supposed that those who shall oppose measures, declared to be brought forward for that purpose, will have the appearance of opposing the necessary defence of the country. But, however unpopular that course may be, it is surely our duty to examine the character and tendency of a measure before we assent to it. In my opinion, what have been called the strong and energetic measures of the Government, have caused our present distress, and nothing but a change can give relief. The various acts composing the system of commercial restrictions, and also the declaration of war, were, in their respective periods, denominated strong and energetic measures. All objections against them were deemed light and trivial. Is there an honest man in the nation who does not now lament that those objections were not heard with proper attention? All the disastrous consequences which have ensued were then foretold. What was then prophecy is now history. To the ill-judged measures of Government may be traced all our misfortunes. They arose from a war unnecessarily waged, and badly conducted; and have been increased by a profuse waste of the treasure, and by a destruction of the credit of the nation. Whether the war was declared through an erroneous estimation of injuries, suffered from a foreign nation, or for the purpose of gratifying a lust for power and patronage, makes little difference to the country. The Administration and their friends are united in opinion that the terms of peace which they have offered to the enemy, provide sufficiently for both the honor and safety of the country. By these terms the pretended causes of the war are abandoned. If, then, without obtaining satisfaction for the past, or security for the future, we can honorably and safely return to a state of peace, we surely might, with equal honor and safety, have remained in that condition. Whatever, therefore, were the injuries suffered from Great Britain, (and I have never deemed them inconsiderable,) it was unnecessary and unwise to declare war. Should a nation, extensively connected in intercourse with others, make every injury sustained a cause of war, it would never be at peace. The inquiry ought to have been, whether the injuries were of such a nature as could not, without loss of honor, be borne, and whether we had the means of obtaining redress by war. The Government has shown no more wisdom or prudence in conducting the war, than in declaring it. In modern times, the strength of a nation for carrying on war essentially consists in its revenue. An empty treasury, the consequence of waste and mismanagement, and the total loss of public credit are the immediate causes of the present distress. When the Government passed into the hands of the party now in power, the nation enjoyed peace and prosperity, an extensive commerce, and ample revenues. After having procured the repeal of the former internal taxes, so abundant was the income from commerce alone, that in his last annual Message to Congress Mr. Jefferson gravely recommended to their consideration the obtaining, by amendments of the Constitution, more enlarged powers and other objects, to enable the Government to expend the surplus of the revenue. All the causes, as far as they depended on foreign nations, which have led to our present condition then existed. At the commencement of the war the Administration proposed their plans of increased revenue to meet the increased expenditures. Their system was adopted by the Legislature in its full extent. Thus far, everything demanded has been granted. What, then, but gross mismanagement and waste can have produced the present deplorable condition of the finances? In the war of the Revolution, without the power of levying taxes, or in any way commanding the resources of the nation, the Government was able to obtain loans in foreign countries. Now, though possessing all the resources necessary for sustaining credit, Government can obtain loans neither at home nor abroad. Economy and good management then gained and established that confidence which waste and profusion have now destroyed. The debt already contracted in this war will be found to be double in amount to the whole debt of the United States at the end of the Revolutionary war. Instances of the grossest profusion are constantly occurring in every department. The cannon designed for the two seventy-four gun ships, and which have been for a long time wanted, are yet to be transported by land from Washington, more than five hundred miles. The mere expense of transportation far exceeds the sum for which they might be made in the vicinity and delivered at the places where wanted. In the war of the Revolution, and also in that of 1798 with France, cannon in abundance were cast in New England; but now, though proposed on the most favorable terms, the Government will not permit a gun to be made for their use in that section of the Union. Peculation and profusion almost universally prevail, to such an extent as could not be borne by any nation. If a remedy be not soon applied, the resources of the country will be entirely exhausted. Without means of subsistence, armies are worse than useless; they become dangerous.

The military force of the country has been no better employed than its pecuniary means.

The gallantry and good conduct of the Navy, and, in several instances, also of the Army, have merited and received the warmest approbation of the nation. Of this, however, the Executive Government is entitled to no share. In awarding the meed of praise for the important victories in the naval battles on the Lakes, Erie and Champlain, truth compelled you to declare, that they were, in both instances, gained over a superior hostile force. The Government merits censure, instead of praise, for exposing to such imminent hazard the great interest staked on the issue of those battles. On Lake Ontario, also, the enemy has been permitted to gain a decided superiority of force. The fleet, built and equipped there at great expense, has become useless. Instead of protecting our own shores from the attacks of the enemy, a large land force is now employed in defending the fleet from threatened destruction. The ships of war on the waters of the Atlantic are mostly laid up in the various harbors, and defended by bodies of militia at enormous expense. Ample appropriations were last year made, not only for all the vessels then in commission, but also for putting into service two new seventy-four gun ships and three frigates. These appropriations have been disregarded. The naval service on the Atlantic, and also the defence of the seaboard seem to be abandoned. The enemy has occupied more than a hundred miles of the eastern seacoast of the State of Massachusetts, including one of the best harbors and naval stations in the United States, all which was defended by less than one hundred troops. Of so little importance has this appeared to the Government, that the President, whose duty it is to lay before the Legislature information of the state of the Union, omitted even to mention it in his Message at the opening of the session. Not a movement has been made to regain that valuable territory; but the enemy is left to fortify and secure it at his leisure.

The military force, instead of defending the country, has been employed in the idle and fruitless attempt to conquer the provinces of Canada. With their whole power bent to that object, during three campaigns, the Government have lost their two principal fortresses, Niagara and Michilimackinac, and gained nothing. Still, this wild project is to be pursued. The Secretary of War, in his report, announces the intention of the Administration, with a hundred thousand regular troops, "to touch the feelings and excite the apprehensions of the British Government by pushing the war into Canada." These are bold counsels for men who lately, without drawing a sword, fled in dismay and disgrace from their own capitol, before a handful of the enemy. They now, in pompous language, promise forthwith to overrun two provinces, and then ascend the plains of Abraham, and storm the strongest fortress on our continent. Rashness in counsel, and imbecility in execution do not constitute strong claims to confidence. Can the nation longer repose confidence in such counsels? Is it wise and safe to expend our utmost resources in weak and extravagant projects, in which past experience destroys even the hope of future success? The conquest of Canada should in my opinion never have been undertaken; and the idle attempt ought immediately to be abandoned. Already, too much blood and treasure have been wasted in the pursuit of an object, which, were it desirable, cannot be attained. Without a naval force, to command the mouth of the St. Lawrence and prevent the arrival of troops and supplies, as they may be wanted, Canada cannot be conquered. By means of such force, the British succeeded in wresting those provinces from France; and for want of it, we failed in our attempt, in the war of the Revolution, when the regular troops there were few, and the inhabitants almost universally inclined to favor us. For the prosecution of this fruitless object, I will give no aid.

For the necessary and proper defence of the country, neither men nor pecuniary means are, in my opinion, to be withheld. Even to the present Administration, so long as they continue to be clothed with Constitutional authority, and shall not have given the most unequivocal and decisive evidence of having abandoned that defence, I will, for that purpose, and restricted to that object, grant all that could be necessary under a wise and prudent Administration. Such grants, however, must be within the limits, and in all respects according to the provisions of the Constitution. Beyond those limits, under no pressure of circumstances, will I consent to go. Should the national defence be abandoned by the General Government, I trust the people, if still retaining a good portion of their resources, may rally under their State Governments against foreign invasion, and rely with confidence on their own courage and virtue.

THURSDAY, November 17.

The resolution brought up yesterday for concurrence was read, and passed to the second reading.

The Senate resumed, as in Committee of the Whole, the consideration of the bill to authorize the President of the United States to call upon the several States and Territories thereof for their respective quotas of —— thousand militia, for the defence of the frontiers of the United States; and sundry amendments having been agreed to, on motion, by Mr. GILES, the bill, as amended, was ordered to be printed for the use of the Senate.

FRIDAY, November 18.

Mr. KING, from the committee to whom was referred the bill, entitled "An act to authorize the Commissioner of the Revenue to cause a clerk in his office to aid him in signing licenses;" reported it with amendments, which were considered as in Committee of the Whole, and agreed to; and the PRESIDENT reported the bill to the House amended accordingly.

On the question, Shall the amendments be engrossed and the bill read a third time, as amended? it was determined in the affirmative.

The resolution for furnishing the American Antiquarian Society with a copy of the Journals of Congress, and of the documents published under their order, was read the second time.

The Senate resumed, as in Committee of the Whole, the consideration of the bill to authorize the President of the United States to call upon the several States and Territories thereof for their respective quotas of —— thousand militia for the defence of the frontiers of the United States, as amended; and the bill having been further amended, on motion, the Senate adjourned.

SATURDAY, November 19.

The Senate resumed, as in Committee of the Whole, the consideration of the resolution for furnishing the American Antiquarian Society with a copy of the Journals of Congress, and of the documents published under their order; and, no amendment having been proposed, it passed to the third reading.

The amendments to the bill, entitled "An act to authorize the Commissioner of the Revenue to cause a clerk in his office to aid him in signing licenses," having been reported correct, the bill was read a third time as amended, and passed with amendments; and, on motion, the title was amended to read as follows: "An act authorizing the Secretary of the Treasury to appoint a clerk in the office of the Commissioner of the Revenue, with power to sign licenses."

Mr. HORSEY submitted the following motions for consideration:

Resolved, That the President of the United States be requested to cause to be laid before the Senate a statement of the amount of expenditures on account of the national armories, and the number of arms made and repaired at each of the said armories since the 2d day of April, 1794.

Resolved, That the President of the United States be requested to cause to be laid before the Senate a statement of the number of arms and equipments purchased or manufactured by or on account of the United States; as, also, of the number transmitted to each State and Territory, in virtue of the act of 23d April, 1808, for arming the whole body of the militia; together with a statement of the expenditures on account of the said arms and equipments.

Resolved, That the President of the United States be requested to cause to be laid before the Senate a statement, exhibiting the whole number of arms belonging to the United States, distinguishing what are fit from what are unfit for immediate use; as, also, showing the number distributed for the use of the armies or militia in the service of the United States, and the number loaned or sold to the States and Territories respectively.

MILITIA OF THE UNITED STATES.

The Senate resumed, as in Committee of the Whole, the consideration of the bill to authorize the President of the United States to call upon the several States and Territories thereof for their respective quotas of —— thousand militia, for the defence of the frontiers of the United States.

On motion, by Mr. ANDERSON, to strike out the seventh section of the bill, as follows:

SEC. 7. *And be it further enacted*, That the militia, while employed in the service of the United States in virtue of this act, shall not be compelled to serve beyond the limits of the United States, nor beyond the limits of the State or Territory furnishing the same, and the limits of an adjoining State or Territory; except that the militia from Kentucky and Tennessee may be required to serve in the defence and for the protection of Louisiana."

It was determined in the negative—yeas 6, nays 25, as follows:

YEAS—Messrs. Anderson, Bledsoe, Dana, Hunter, Varnum, and Walker.

NAYS—Messrs. Bibb, Brent, Brown, Chace, Condit, Daggett, Fromentin, Gaillard, German, Giles, Goldsborough, Gore, Horsey, King, Lacock, Lambert, Morrow, Roberts, Robinson, Smith, Taylor, Thompson, Turner, Wharton, and Worthington.

On motion, by Mr. GOLDSBOROUGH, to strike out the ninth section of the bill, as follows:

"SEC. 9. *And be it further enacted*, That, after the classification of the militia as aforesaid, any three classes within any State or Territory which shall furnish, according to law, two effective able-bodied recruits, to serve in the Army of the United States, during the war, shall thereafter be exempt from the militia service required by this act; and, to aid them in this respect, such recruits shall be entitled, respectively, to receive the bounty in money and land, according to the provisions of the act, entitled 'An act ——, which is allowed to other recruits respectively, for the Army of the United States; and in all cases where recruits shall be furnished as aforesaid, the same shall be delivered to some recruiting officer in the service of the United States, who shall immediately give his receipt therefor on account of the classes furnishing them, and shall forthwith report the same to the Department of War, specifying in such report the names and description of such recruits respectively, and the description of the classes of the militia furnishing the same; whereupon, it shall be the duty of the Secretary for the Department of War to grant, without delay, to such classes, a certificate of exemption from the militia service required by this act; which certificate shall, to all intents and purposes, be good and available to them for their absolute exemption therefrom."

It was determined in the negative—yeas 11, nays 19, as follows:

YEAS—Messrs. Daggett, Dana, Goldsborough, Gore, Horsey, Hunter, King, Lambert, Mason, Thompson, and Varnum.

NAYS—Messrs. Bibb, Bledsoe, Brent, Brown, Chace, Condit, Fromentin, German, Giles, Lacock, Morrow, Roberts, Smith, Tait, Taylor, Turner, Walker, Wharton, and Worthington.

And the President reported the bill to the Senate amended.

On motion, by Mr. GOLDSBOROUGH, to add a new section to the bill. as follows:

"SEC. 11. *And be it further enacted*, That the recruits raised by the classes as aforesaid, shall be substituted for, and employed in the service intended to be performed by, the militiamen contemplated by this act to be furnished by the several classes."

It was determined in the negative—yeas 11, nays 21, as follows:

YEAS—Messrs. Daggett, Dana, German, Goldsborough, Gore, Horsey, Hunter, King, Lambert, Mason, and Thompson.

NAYS—Messrs. Anderson, Bibb, Bledsoe, Brent, Brown, Chace, Fromentin, Gaillard, Giles, Lacock, Morrow, Roberts, Robinson, Smith, Tait, Taylor, Turner, Varnum, Walker, Wharton, and Worthington.

On the question, Shall this bill be engrossed and read a third time as amended? it was determined in the affirmative.

MONDAY, November 21.

The Senate resumed the consideration of the motions made the 19th instant, by Mr. HORSEY, which were amended and agreed to, as follows:

Resolved, That the President of the United States be requested to cause to be laid before the Senate a statement of the amount of expenditures on account of the national armories, and the number of arms made and repaired at each of the said armories since the 2d day of April 1794.

Resolved, That the President of the United States be requested to cause to be laid before the Senate a statement of the number of arms and equipments purchased or manufactured by, or on account of, the United States, in virtue of the act of April 23, 1808: as, also, of the number transmitted to each State and Territory, for arming the whole body of the militia; together with a statement of the expenditures on account of the said arms and equipments.

Resolved, That the President of the United States be requested to cause to be laid before the Senate a statement exhibiting the whole number of arms belonging to the United States, distinguishing what are fit from what are unfit for immediate use; as, also, showing the number distributed for the use of the armies or militia in the service of the United States, other than those distributed under the act of 23d April, 1808, and the number loaned or sold to the States and Territories respectively.

The bill to authorize the President of the United States to call upon the several States and Territories thereof for their respective quotas of —— thousand militia for the defence of the frontiers of the United States, having been reported by the committee correctly engrossed, was read a third time, and further amended by unanimous consent; and the blanks having been filled, on the question, Shall this bill pass? on motion, by Mr. BRENT, it was agreed to take the question by yeas and nays.

On motion, the Senate adjourned.

95 HISTORY OF CONGRESS. 96

SENATE. *Militia of the United States.* NOVEMBER, 1814.

TUESDAY, November 22.

A message from the House of Representatives informed the Senate that the House have passed a resolution appointing a committee on their part to join such committee as may be appointed on the part of the Senate, to inquire and report whether Congress may not be more conveniently accommodated, either by an alteration of the present chambers, or by procuring other rooms within a convenient distance of the public offices; in which resolution they request the concurrence of the Senate.

MILITIA OF THE UNITED STATES.

The Senate resumed the third reading of the bill to authorize the President of the United States to call upon the several States and Territories thereof for their respective quotas of —— thousand militia for the defence of the frontiers of the United States.

Mr. GORE addressed the Chair as follows: There is no truth more evident than that the general, sovereign, and uncontrolled power of the several States, over the militia, remains with them respectively, except in certain specified cases, in which the Congress has authority to provide for calling out this force, which, while so called into the service of the United States is subject to your Government, preserving always their officers and militia organization, and excluding from the command all other officers, except only the President of the United States.

The cases are, when insurrections exist, when the laws of the Union cannot be executed by the civil powers when an invasion is made.

" The Congress may provide for calling forth the militia to execute the laws, to suppress insurrections, to repel invasion."

For no other purposes can the United States call them forth, in no other service can they require their aid.

" The Congress may provide for organizing, arming, and disciplining the militia, and for governing such part of them as may be in the service of the United States, reserving to the States respectively the appointment of the officers, and the authority of training the militia, according to the discipline prescribed by Congress."

The power of organizing and disciplining the militia seems to have been granted for the purpose of enabling this force to operate efficiently. That, when called to act, the militia of the several States might manœuvre alike, and having the same military language and ideas, might understand and comprehend each other, as well as the orders of their superiors, and be usefully combined to effect the object proposed.

That Congress should provide for arming the militia was necessary to place them in a condition to act as soldiers; for if be not a contradiction to call militia without arms, soldiers, it is assuming very much the character of a petty German potentate, ambitious of military fame, who procured a large number of wax figures in warlike attitude and habiliment, which he called

his army, and then fancied himself equal to his more wealthy neighbors, who, at great expense, supported a large body of soldiers of flesh and blood, well armed and accoutred. We are told by well informed Senators on this floor, that the United States are unable, that the States respectively are unable, that the individuals themselves are unable. to arm the militia.

I truly hope, sir, that this picture of the deplorable condition of our country is founded in error. If it be not, it is a very important addition to that mass of evidence which is daily crowding on our minds, of the fatal improvidence of engaging in this destructive war.

If it be not in the power of the nation, nor of the several States, nor of the individuals, to provide arms for eighty thousand militia, why call them forth to eat the bread of idleness, and provide the certain means of victory to our foe, and defeat to ourselves? Why continue to propagate delusion? Why this empty boast of taking Canada, of expelling the British from every foot of the Continent, and dictating the conditions of peace to the Court of London?

Believe me, sir, rather believe the accounts, which are pouring into this desolated capital by every mail, from every quarter and corner of the country, that blind confidence, which, trusting to proclamations and the extravagant vaunts of ignorance and indolence, has delivered this generous people a prey to the weakest of men, and the worst of passions, is fast dissipating, and will soon cease to hide from them the dreadful abyss into which they have been plunged, and the enormity of those delinquencies which have impoverished, dishonored, and degraded them.

Whether it be true or not, that the people are capable of arming themselves, or the States of providing the arms, there is no good reason for receiving men who come without arms and equipments, and thus filling your muster rolls with such beings, as, in no sense of the word, can be considered soldiers, but mere cormorants, to devour the remnant of sustenance, which can yet be wrung from this industrious nation, whom presumptuous folly has rendered bankrupt.

We too well know the fact, that great, rich, and powerful States issue forth unarmed legions, and boast of having complied with requisitions for soldiers to fight the battles of their country.

We are told that the Executive provides such men with arms and equipments. Where the authority is to be found for thus favoring any State I am yet to learn. If allowed to some, and not to all, it is unequal, and therefore unjust.

Further, sir, some years since a law was enacted, appropriating an annual sum of money for the purchase of arms to be distributed among the States. To certain favored States arms were supplied, to others none. The neglected States have lately received a small part of their proportion. Whence was derived the authority thus to discriminate, to favor some States, and neglect others, is unknown to me. Sure I am it is consistent neither with policy nor justice.

It is, however, of the same character with that

justice, or rather injustice, which furnishes arms and equipments, rations and wages, to the unarmed soldiers of some of the States, while it refuses provisions and payment to soldiers, well armed and equipped, who are called forth to defend others, and afford that protection which the United States had expressly guarantied to them, but have totally neglected. An attempt is made to justify this refusal, on pretensions the most unfounded and illegitimate, on pretensions set up in violation of that principle in the Constitution which insures to the respective States the appointment of the officers of the militia.

I have said that the authority of the United States to govern the militia exists only when the militia is in their service.

The United States cannot govern the militia, cannot train them, until in their service, and even then the States, respectively, have the exclusive power of appointing their officers. The Constitution makes but one exception to this exclusive power, that is in favor of the President of the United States, who is declared to be Commander-in-Chief of the militia, when in the actual service of the United States. There is not a tittle of authority for any other officer of the United States to assume the command of the militia. Thus sacredly is the right of the several States to their militia guarded and secured. There is no power of the individual States, so positively and emphatically reserved. The other powers of the several States depend on the principle, that what is not granted is retained, confirmed by an express stipulation, that the powers not delegated to the United States, nor prohibited by it to the States, are reserved to the States respectively, or to the people; but this authority of the respective States over their militia, recognised in the Constitution as "necessary to the security of a free State," over and above the force attached to it by this sound principle, is guarantied and hedged about by all the securities and guards that language could prescribe; and if it can be invaded, and by the honorable members of this Senate, the Constitutional guardians of the rights and sovereignties of the States, there is an end of all security from Constitutions on paper, and we may resign ourselves to the contempt and ridicule of the weakest as well as the wisest of men.

All the other offspring of their sovereignty they had resigned, and have already attended them to that grave which has swallowed up much of the honor, most of the property, and all the public credit of the nation. This the States would not surrender, but in great emergency, and for very limited periods, always keeping them within their own sight, under their immediate and vigilant inspection, and under the peculiar care of officers in whom they had a special confidence, and who could look to them alone for patronage and support, that the affections of the men might not be alienated from their parent State. On this force do the States depend for protection and support, in every peril that can be imagined from domestic violence or foreign invasion, and in that dreaded event, which God grant may never happen, of

the powers which they had surrendered being turned to the destruction of their own liberties.

Every one, sir, who will attentively examine and consider the language of the Constitution; who will bring to his mind, either by recollection or reading, what passed in the several States when this instrument was presented to them for acceptance, will be satisfied that I have not misconceived nor misconstrued the views of those who framed, or of those who ratified, this grant of power to the United States.

As there is no pretence that insurrections exist, or that the laws cannot be executed, and there is reason for expecting invasion, it is presumed that the bill is bottomed on that clause of the Constitution which authorizes Congress to provide for calling forth the militia to repel invasion. On this ground it is to be inferred, for the bill nowhere mentions this to be the object of the requisition which it authorizes the President to make for eighty thousand militia, to serve for two years. The service to which they are called, according to the title, is to protect the frontiers against invasion. Now, sir, I contend Congress has no authority to provide for calling forth the militia, to serve for two years, in protection of the frontiers.

Congress shall have power to provide for calling forth the militia to repel invasion. What is the intent of the terms of the Constitution which grant this power, compared with the other provisions of the instrument, and the duties of the United States? To repel invasion, means to resist and drive back a sudden and hostile incursion. On an expected irruption, the militia might naturally be presumable to be the only force at command; and, from the interests they had at stake, might be expected to act with promptitude and vigor. Experience had shown that to such service, short in duration, sudden and urgent in emergency, they were well adapted; while for long campaigns, and extended times of service, they were altogether unfit. Unprepared by discipline, by regular and constant subordination, to support the fatigues and privations of a camp, such a force would be most incompetent to discharge the duties of protracted warfare. The militia consists of men of all professions and of all conditions. The enterprise of the merchant, the useful and indispensable labor of the agriculturist, the steady diligence of the mechanic, are all sacrificed by calling them to act the part of soldiers, for which most of them are singularly disqualified, and all their various branches of productive industry are ruined, to do that badly which a small portion of their earnings could procure to be well done. The Constitution never intended that the militia should prosecute the general purposes of war; it did not intend that this should be the force relied on for permanent defence and protection against invasion; for the instrument expressly guaranties to every State, that the United States would protect each of them against invasion. Such protection could be afforded only by ships of war, and fortresses, well armed and manned. This could not be done by the militia of the several States, over which the United States have no control, except a very limited one, and in certain specified cases, which do not include that of protecting against invasion, but only that of repelling invasion which actually exists.

The section that insures to each State protection against invasion, confirms the meaning I have given to the terms *repel invasion.*

The United States are bound, not only to protect each of the States from invasion, but also to provide for the common defence. This cannot be done by the militia, but must be by regular armies, which they have power to raise for any length of time, on whatever conditions they may please to prescribe, and under whatever officers they may choose to appoint. The militia does not belong to the United States; they cannot even train them, nor appoint their officers. The militia belong to the several States. It is called the militia of the several States in the very clause of the Constitution which constitutes the President Commander-in-Chief of this force when in the actual service of the United States.

Nothing could be more strange than to suppose that the Constitution imposed a duty of this importance on one power, and looked to the forces of another for its performance, over which forces the power on whom this obligation rested had not so much control as to appoint their officers, or even train them.

It would be equally strange, and more unjust, to presume, after the several States had granted to the United States unlimited powers to raise armies, and resources competent to meet the expenses, in return for which the United States obliged themselves to provide for the common defence, and to protect each State against invasion, that the United States could rightfully call on the several States to make this common defence, and protect themselves respectively against invasion, with the very force which, in terms the most unequivocal, they had reserved for their own purposes.

The language of the Constitution never can be tortured into such absurd contradictions, nor to effect such manifest injustice; yet this bill can be supported on no other construction. It authorizes a requisition on the several States for their militia to defend the frontiers, that is, for the common defence, and for the protection of each State against invasion. Duties the United States have solemnly contracted to perform for those States, on whom the call is now made to do it for themselves.

Further, the bill authorizes the President to make this requisition of militia to serve for two years. There is not a particle of authority in the Constitution to justify a call for their service for two years. When the object contemplated in the Constitution is attained, the power of the United States ceases. Its authority over the militia is spent. If you can require them for two, you may for ten years, during the war, or for life.

Neither in terms nor in fact, is this requisition made, to provide for any of the cases in which

the Constitution authorizes a call by the United States for the militia of the several States.

Although the men may possibly be suffered to repel an invasion, this is nowhere mentioned as any part of their duty, or any portion of the service they are expected to perform. They are called out generally for the defence of the frontiers, that is, to protect against invasion, a duty specially imposed on the United States, by an express provision of the Constitution, and one very different from that, viz: to repel invasion, which the militia is bound to perform at the requisition of the United States.

I therefore cannot refrain from pronouncing this bill unconstitutional, and in derogation of rights positively reserved to the several States.

The second section provides for classing the men, and procuring the number wanted, by contract or compulsion.

The United States have no authority to govern the militia, or even to train them, until they are in their service. This right is reserved to the States respectively. By this bill the United States undertake to govern the militia previously to their being brought into their service, and to direct the mode by which they shall be called forth, that is, to distribute the whole militia of each State into classes, and oblige each class, voluntarily raised by their order, to hire a man, or submit to a draught.

This is the first step on the odious ground of conscription; a plan, sir, which never will and never ought to be submitted to by this country, while it retains one idea of civil freedom—a plan, sir, which, if attempted, will be resisted by many States, and at every hazard. In my judgment, sir, it should be resisted by all who have any regard to public liberty or the rights of the several States.

This provision to class the militia into divisions, and take from each an individual by compulsion, will appear to be introduced merely for the purpose of familiarizing this arbitrary and tyrannical process to the minds of men, by making the first motion, in a manner presumed to be the least disgusting, under the direction of State officers, and only on the militia, for purposes pretendedly legitimate, as respects that body, and for an object the most interesting to them, the defence of their own firesides. The people readily discern that the next step will be for a conscription, for any purpose, and by any individual designated by the General Government.

The honey on the edges of the cup will not disguise the bitterness of the venomous drug at its bottom. The veil, sir, is too thin to conceal the hideous monster, which to be hated, to be avoided, to be destroyed, needs but to be seen.

I know of no purpose, I can conceive of none for making this bill, but to introduce provisions as the ground-work for other schemes, which have been introduced a little prematurely, and before this deluded people can be brought to receive the last chain, which shall bind them to the unrelenting will of despotism. Laws are now in full force, which provide for bringing forth the militia, in all the cases authorized by the Constitution. These have been sanctioned by time and experience, and the provisions have been found competent to their object.

There never has been, as I can learn, the smallest objection in a single State to rendering prompt obedience to any call for the militia, deemed legitimate by those on whom it was made, and whenever the requisition has been assented to, there has been no delay, no tardiness, no inability in the uncontrolled and unassisted power of the States to bring forth the militia demanded. They need neither your direction nor advice how to comply with Constitutional requisition. And they will not suffer your interference in a business which they consider, and rightly consider, their own.

There is a section, sir, which after all the pretence to provide a local force, for the defence of the homes of the militia, shows the whole to be a delusion. A large porch is made, and fine scaffolding erected, merely to introduce the General Government to the private purses of individuals to aid them in filling the ranks of the regular Army; leaving the several States, as they always have been, to take care of themselves, while the force on which they depended is marched off to perish in the wilds of Canada.

Finally, the several States, previously to the Confederation, held their respective militias in undiminished sovereignty; under the Confederation, the several States were bound to keep up a regulated and disciplined militia, sufficiently armed and accoutred; but the supreme control over this force remained with them, respectively, and unaltered. In this condition they were, when the existing Constitution was adopted.

"Every right, power, or authority, not delegated by the Constitution to the General Government, nor prohibited by it to the States, is reserved to the States respectively." No general power over the militia was delegated to the United States. The only power delegated in this respect was a limited authority, in three cases. The United States can exercise no other. If they attempt to extend an authority beyond the grant, the several States have a right, and are bound by duty to their own citizens, to resist the usurpation. The measure and manner of resistance are altogether within their own discretion. The surrender of such rights of sovereignty, and of other inferior rights, by the several States, as the Constitution contains, was with a view of attaining compensation in the reciprocal engagements of the United States.

The several States granted to the United States power to raise armies, to provide and maintain a navy, and resources sufficient to support them. In consideration for parting with rights so essential to their preservation, they received a solemn promise from the United States that they would provide for the common defence, and protect each State against invasion. Have the United States done either? Does not this bill attempt to take from the several States that force which they had respectively reserved to themselves for their own purposes, and apply it to uses which the United States are bound to provide for by other means?

All the articles of a league, or confederacy, have the force and nature of reciprocal promises and of conditions, which, by a default, are rendered null.

With a deep sense of the importance of this Union to the happiness and prosperity of all its members, I am bound to resist any infraction of the ties which unite them together, in order to render perpetual that, which seems to be dissolving under us.

In such motives, and in support of the dearest interests of the nation, the House will find the grounds of my opposition to this bill. The only thing wanted from Congress in relation to the militia, under the existing laws, is a provision for receiving into the employment and pay of the United States, at the discretion of the President, such bodies of State troops, for such terms and under such conditions as any of them may consent to raise.

An honorable friend of mine, from the State of New York, now detained from this House by indisposition, anxious to afford his aid in providing for the defence of the country by all Constitutional means, on Saturday last offered a motion, with this view. The honorable chairman of the committee which introduced the bill, declined to receive it at that time, and preferred to consider it on the third reading of the bill. He being unable, for the reason assigned, now to submit the motion, I take the liberty to offer the same, which is in the following words:

"That the committee be instructed so to modify the bill that it shall provide for calling into the service of the United States, from time to time, in execution of the provisions of the Constitution, and according to the mode heretofore practised, —— thousand militia, to serve for terms not exceeding nine months; with an option to the several States, in lieu of such detachments of militia, to raise and furnish, for the service of the United States, for the term of two years, unless sooner discharged, bodies of State troops equal in number to their respective quotas of militia; such State troops to be organized, armed, and equipped, according to law; their officers to be appointed by the respective States; their services to be limited within the States in which they shall be raised, or within an adjoining State; to be subject to the rules and articles of war, and to receive the same pay, clothing, rations, and forage, and to be entitled to the same privileges and immunities as the troops of the United States."

On the call of Mr. DANA, the question was divided, and taken on recommitting the bill; and it was determined in the negative—yeas 13, nays 19, as follows:

YEAS—Messrs. Anderson, Daggett, Dana, Gaillard, German, Goldsborough, Gore, Horsey, Hunter, Lambert, Mason, Thompson, and Varnum.

NAYS—Messrs. Bibb, Bledsoe, Brent, Brown, Chace, Condit, Fromentin, Giles, Lacock, Morrow, Roberts, Robinson, Smith, Tait, Taylor, Turner, Walker, Wharton, and Worthington.

Mr. GOLDSBOROUGH then rose and addressed the Chair as follows:

Mr. President: When the subject was first brought before the Committee, I was so unfortunate as to be absent, and have therefore only had an opportunity of passing upon some of its provisions. As the bill has now arrived at that stage of its progress when it is permitted to review it throughout, I must offer my former absence as an apology for detaining the Senate a few moments, and will limit myself, in the course of my remarks, to two points only, viz: the length of the time the militia are intended to be kept out, and the mode of classing them to force them out.

I had hoped, sir, though vainly, that, among the innumerable amendments which this bill was destined to suffer, it would have been so radically reformed in principle and so ameliorated in its provisions, that I could have voted for it. The professed object of this bill, the defence of the States, is particularly dear to me, and, if pursued in a Constitutional mode, would command my hearty concurrence; but I have to lament that the measure, which now seems likely to be adopted for that purpose, is such, that I cannot participate in it. Notwithstanding the unrelaxing exertions which have been made to bring the provisions of this bill within the fair limits of Constitutional jurisdiction, and to temper its severity to the feelings of the people, its greatest deformity still exists, the most hideous feature in its whole composition remains unsoftened, and I am therefore bound by a solemn sense of duty to the country, and acting under the awful responsibility of an oath, to oppose its passage.

There has been a marked and studied distinction preserved between the army and the militia of the country. The one is a permanent, the other a temporary force, intended for temporary purposes. In time of peace, no force is more competent, none more adapted " to repress insurrections, or to execute the laws," than the militia; but, surely, sir, it can never be intended to be exclusively relied on for defence, during a period of war. There can be little doubt, when the Constitution speaks of the militia " to repel invasion," it rather regarded the occasional irruptions of the Indians upon our back frontiers, than the disembarking of large bodies of finely trained European troops upon our shores. Those who are practically skilled in the art of war will tell you, that nothing but the system and discipline of regulars, can meet regulars with effect; and although occasions may be presented when militia have merited every honor which can be due to victory and good conduct, yet an exclusive reliance on them, in times like these, threatened, as we are, with formidable fleets and armies, would be to discard the best lessons of experience, and to jeopardize the fate of the country. That the militia, as such, would be a good auxiliary force, I am prepared to admit. Dispersed through every part of the country and formed into convenient corps, they might be made to fall upon and harass the enemy at his landing, and from their superior knowledge of the country, under brave and enterprising officers, they would gall him, impede and obstruct his progress, until the disci-

plined regulars, which, in a war like this, ought to be stationed at eligible points, and in considerable bodies, from one end of the continent to the other, could be brought to their relief. If, to remedy the defects of want of discipline in the militia, it is contemplated to confine them to a camp for two years, it is this unusual period of service, it is the mode that is intended to be used to force them out, and the conversion of the militia into regular troops that I complain of, and which, in my judgment, constitutes a palpable and flagrant violation of the Constitution.

In the general enumeration of the powers of Congress, sir, we shall find that part of the Constitution which bears upon this subject. Congress shall have power " to provide for calling forth the militia to execute the laws of the Union, suppress insurrections, and repel invasions." These are the three objects for which Congress can alone provide for calling out the militia, and when these, or either of these objects, cease to exist, the militia are no longer subject to duty. It is impossible for Congress to decide how long the militia shall be held to service, because they cannot determine how long the emergency will exist for which they are called. It is, therefore, that we are to understand the language of the Constitution as confining the power of Congress entirely to providing how and by whom the call upon the militia is to be made, leaving the responsibility both of the call and of the decision on the continuance of the service upon that power to which Congress shall think proper to assign it; and leaving it also exclusively to the States, to whom alone it rightfully belongs, to furnish the troops in their own way. So far from Congress having any Constitutional power to retain the militia in service for a fixed and determinate period of time, the Constitution has itself given another standard by which their term of service shall be measured, and that is, the continuance of the exigence they are called to meet. After Congress have provided for calling out the militia, by vesting the power, as it usually has done, in the President of the United States, it has discharged all its duties, and the President will then decide upon his responsibility to the nation, when it is necessary to exercise the power, and when the exigence for which the call was authorized ceases to exist. As Congress cannot calculate the length of time during which either insurrection, or opposition to the laws, or invasion, may continue, and as the power thus vested in the President to make the call and judge of the period of service, might, in certain events, impose a long, and painful, and ruinous duty, upon one body of the militia, the general power given to Congress to provide for calling them forth, clearly enables them to provide a succession of militia at easy intervals, to take the place of those who are on duty; so as to prevent the whole burden from falling too severely upon any one portion of the people. It was in this view of the Constitution, and with this intention, that the law of February, 1795, was passed, to provide for calling forth the militia. The fourth section of the law is, " that the militia

'employed in the service of the United States,
'shall be subject to the same rules and articles of
'war as the troops of the United States; and
'that no officer, non-commissioned officer, or pri-
'vate, of the militia, shall be compelled to serve
'more than three months after his arrival at the
'place of rendezvous, in any one year, nor more
'than in due rotation with every other able-bod-
'ied man of the same rank in the battalion to
'which he belongs.''

This early exposition of this part of the Constitution is unquestionably the surest and the safest
guide of construction: and as the powers here
granted were both to be vested in and exercised
by the illustrious President of the Convention
which formed that Constitution, and the act itself
received his sanction, I am at a loss to conjecture
how the true intent and meaning of any part of
that instrument could be more clearly and more
satisfactorily ascertained. By this law, the President of the United States is authorized to call
out the militia, but they cannot be kept in service
longer than three months after their arrival at
the place of rendezvous, nor can they be made to
serve longer than a due rotation with every other
member of the same rank in the battalion from
which they are taken. Here, then, I derive the
distinction between Congress undertaking to
provide, by law, that the militia shall be kept in
camp for two years, unless sooner discharged, and
their providing by law that the militia shall not
be kept out more than three months. In the first
case, Congress are made to prescribe the time for
which they shall be kept in camp, which they
have no power to do. In the last, so far from
designating the time they shall serve, they only
mean to prescribe the period of rotation, beyond
which the same body of militia shall not serve.
If the emergency continues beyond three months,
new calls of militiamen are to be made to relieve
those who perform the first tour of duty; and it
is not and never was intended, by the language
of the Constitution, that Congress should say how
long the militia shall serve, but merely judging
of the condition of the country, and the necessities and conveniences of the people, they govern
themselves by such considerations in exercising
their powers "to provide for calling forth the
militia" in such numbers, and in such rotation,
as the public emergency may require. The distinction, to my view, is neither subtle nor nice,
but founded in a just discretion, and exerted for a
correct and benevolent purpose, to rescue the
great body of the people from a painful and unjust oppression.

So far, sir, from vesting the Congress of the
United States with power to call the militia into
camp for two years, you well know, Mr. President, that the great contest of the Convention
was, whether this power, "to provide for calling
forth the militia," should be given to Congress at
all. And it was a question of long, dubious, and
animated debate, whether it should be left exclusively to the States, or whether it should be given
in certain specified cases, to be exercised by the
Federal Government. If, at that time, it could

have been anticipated that the power thus reluctantly and jealously yielded up and guarded by
strict limitation, would ever have been used, by
this or any other Congress, to drag the people of
this country from their homes, their families, and
their occupations, to consign them to the toils
and deprivations of a camp for two years, those
celebrated champions in that great cause, who
have been justly styled the fathers of our Constitution, would never have prevailed to have procured this power to the General Government.

But, sir, the unconstitutionality of this measure, though defect enough to justify my opposition to it, is not the only defect. There is a rigor
and severity in the provisions of this bill never
before practised, which will stir up a feeling of
uneasiness and restless displeasure, and which the
condition of the people of this country will not
endure. On whom, let me ask, sir, will this grievous oppression principally fall? It will fall upon
the middling ranks in society, upon your tenan-
try, your mechanics, your manufacturers—men
who constitute the very bone and muscle of your
population. Men of wealth will procure substitutes—the poorest and humblest in rank will be
compelled by their necessities, during a period of
war, to enlist with recruiting sergeants, or to be
absorbed by the provisions in the ninth section of
this bill; whilst the chief burden of this odious
conscription will fall upon those whose circumstances in life are too humble to afford extravagant bounties for substitutes, but whose feelings
are too proud, and habits too reputable, to suffer
them to become the corrupted hirelings of others.
This class of men, thus marked out for destruction by this bill, is infinitely the most numerous,
as well as the most useful in society. Their services, in their respective avocations, are essential
to the interest as well as to the convenience of
the community in which they live, and their personal labor and daily attention to their own affairs
are indispensably necessary to the support of
themselves and their families. To tear these men
away from home to serve in the militia for only
three months at a time, is to impose a serious evil
on them, but if you drag them off, as you here
contemplate by this bill, and keep them in camp
for two years, you complete their ruin, you entail
distress and misery upon their families, perhaps
starvation and death. During their absence, and
an absence, too, under a system of coercion before unheard of in our country, their former habitations will become the abodes of wretchedness.
Sir, I want language to depict the sufferings that
will flow from this tyrannical system. Those
whom the industry of a father or a husband may
have once clad in simple neatness, and fed with
comfortable fare, will be left disconsolate in penury, to wrap their chilled limbs in the tattered
remnants of his former bounty. Deprived, by
this your act, of their only source of comfort, their
protector and support, many who have been bred
in all the decencies of life, will be thrown, like
common mendicants, upon the world, to subsist
upon its precarious charity. Should it be ordained that the wretched father is to be restored to

his former home, after the expiration of this lingering and ruinous-period of service, he will return, not to the cheerful cottage which he left, where joy and plenty smiled, but to a comfortless dwelling, from which want and misery have chased every endearment, save only those whom Providence may have spared, to meet their benefactors' return, with haggard eye and squalid aspect, the miserable evidences of his long and cruel exile. These, sir, are to be some of the certain results of this dreadful conscription; and how few of the many who are doomed to suffer, now dream of the distress which you are at this hour preparing for them! Sir, believe me, there is no fiction in all this; it is but a faint sketch of the calamities that are destined to afflict us, the reality of which will far outstrip the anticipation of the liveliest imagination. Let me then ask you, sir, if you really intend to adopt this system as the law of the land, hostile as it is to the Constitution, and pregnant with all these ills? Have the people of this country not yet suffered enough? Will this honorable Senate, wise, discreet, and reflecting, on whom the nation rests its hopes, to whom they have been taught to look in the moment of anxiety and trial, and upon whose floor, we have been once told, the last expiring struggles of the liberties of this country would be exhibited, if they are doomed to expire—will they sanction, by their approbation, such a measure as this?

Sir, it is not wise in those who are ambitious of fame to indulge too much in prophetic views of things, but I fancy that I put little to hazard, when I say, carry this system into execution when you will, and you will find that the people of the country will not bear it; not that a party will not bear it, but the great body of the people will frown indignant upon this attempt to despoil them of the blessings of their Constitutional rights and personal liberties.

Sir, you dare not, at least I hope you dare not, attempt a conscription to fill the ranks of your regular army. When the plan of the Secretary of War made its appearance, it was gratifying to find that it met with the abhorrence of almost every man in the nation, and the merit of the bill before you, if such a measure can be supposed to have merit at all, is, that it is little else, as regards the militia, than a servile imitation of the Secretary's plan. And will you treat your militia with more rigor than you are willing to practise upon your regular soldiers? Will you adopt a system of tyranny towards them, that you are reluctant to attempt towards the Army? Availing yourselves of the popular appellation of militia, you undertake to enforce a system of conscription whose very severity must rouse those who may have been lulled into acquiescence, by a total want of suspicion. Thus, sir, it is, that the war-spirit of the nation has sunk so low that, like the fallen public credit of the country, neither banks or bounties can revive it. And the advocates of this bill, becoming rash by disaster, since neither monstrous bounties in money or in land will avail them, now call upon us to pursue the freemen of the country, even to their very hearths and firesides, to drag them forth in handcuffs to the field of battle, there to fight against the wrongs of impressment, and to conquer the freedom of the seas.

Mr. President, there is a foreboding that arises from all this which fills me with the deepest concern. The growth of tyranny, when it once begins, is strong and rapid. A few years past, and the name of conscription was never uttered but it was coupled with execration; last year, it found its way into a letter from the then Secretary of War to the chairman of the Military Committee, and it was then so odious that it was but little exposed to view. This year, we have conscription openly recommended to us by the Secretary of War in an official paper; and, worst of all, it finds champions and advocates on this floor. What have we to expect next, but that, in the ensuing year, we shall see it stalking abroad through the land, accompanied by its loathsome train of fetters and chains, and executioners. And why is all this to be done? The necessity of the crisis is offered as the plea; yes, sir, necessity, that blood-stained plea of tyrants, which has served every scheme of usurpation, to sacrifice the lives and liberties of men, to aid its projects of self-aggrandizement and ambition, is now given to justify this measure; nothing is therefore left to us, but, before it be too late, to improve the experience which the misfortunes of others have taught us, to our own and the national preservation. The necessities of the times, of which we hear so much and feel so sensibly, ought properly enough to urge us to active and animated exertions in behalf of the nation; there is a vigor and a zeal which should characterize all our conduct at this doubtful moment; but the ardor which impels to action should be watched, lest it betray us into error and excess. Times of imminent peril and alarm, are periods when public liberty is most in danger, and it is difficult to decide whether he is the worthiest patriot who goes to battle in defence of a nation's rights, or he who stands the faithful sentinel over the Constitution in times of general effervescence, to guard it from violation and abuse.

Unwilling, sir, to consume the time of the Senate, whose patience, as well as my own, has been much exhausted by the lingering progress of this bill, I shall content myself with the remarks I have made upon the point which seemed most particularly to demand an open and avowed opposition. Having before taken an occasion to express my opinion upon the other exceptionable parts of the bill, I will not trouble you with a recapitulation.

I must once more express to you, Mr. President, the deep regret I feel, at not being able to give my vote in favor of a measure, which is said to be designed to be for the defence of the States. There is not a man in this Senate, or in this nation, who is more willing, or who will go further in applying the true means of the country to its defence at this time, than myself. But, upon all questions, sir, there are certain bounds beyond which I can never consent to go; and I must be understood at all times, whatever pledges I may make, as imposing *this* restriction, this obligation upon myself, *viz:* neither to overleap the limits of the *Constitution,* or to be accessary to an invasion of the *essential* principles of civil liberty.

On the question, Shall this bill pass? it was then taken and determined in the affirmative—yeas 19, nays 12, as follows:

YEAS—Messrs. Bibb, Bledsoe, Brent, Brown, Chace, Condit, Fromentin, Gaillard, Giles, Lacock, Morrow, Roberts, Smith, Tait, Taylor, Turner, Walker, Wharton, and Worthington.

NAYS—Messrs. Anderson, Daggett, Dana, German, Goldsborough, Gore, Horsey, Hunter, Lambert, Mason, Thompson, and Varnum.

So it was *Resolved,* That this bill pass, and that the title thereof be "An act to authorize the President of the United States to call upon the several States and Territories thereof for their respective quotas of eighty thousand four hundred and thirty militia, for the defence of the frontiers of the United States against invasion."

WEDNESDAY, November 23.
DEATH OF THE VICE PRESIDENT.

About the hour of meeting, a report having reached the Senate Chamber of the death of the VICE PRESIDENT of the United States, the members from Massachusetts, Messrs. VARNUM and GORE, proceeded to his lodgings to ascertain the fact; and, on their return, having announced the fact to the Senate, the following proceeding took place, on motion of Mr. BLEDSOE,

The Senate, being informed of the death of their distinguished fellow-citizen, ELBRIDGE GERRY, Vice President of the United States,

Do Resolve, That a committee be appointed, jointly with such committee as may be appointed on the part of the House of Representatives, to consider and report measures most proper to manifest the public respect for the memory of the deceased, and expressive of the deep regret of the Congress of the United States for the loss of a citizen so highly respected and revered.

Ordered, That Messrs. GORE, VARNUM, SMITH, ANDERSON, and GAILLARD. be the committee.

On motion of Mr. BLEDSOE,

Ordered, That the Secretary inform the House of Representatives of the decease of the Vice President of the United States, and communicate the foregoing resolution.

A message from the House of Representatives informed the Senate that the House concur in the resolution of the Senate for the appointment of a joint committee, to consider and report measures proper to manifest the public respect for the memory of the VICE PRESIDENT of the United States, deceased; and have appointed a committee on their part.

The Senate then adjourned.

THURSDAY, November 24.

On motion, by Mr. GORE,

Resolved, unanimously, That from an unfeigned respect to the late ELBRIDGE GERRY, Vice President of the United States and President of the Senate, the Chair of the President of the Senate be shrouded with black during the present session; and as a further testimony of respect for the memory of the deceased, the members of the Senate will go into mourning, and wear black crape round the left arm for thirty days.

FRIDAY, November 25.

The resolution brought up from the House of Representatives the 22d instant, for appointing a joint committee, was read, and passed to the second reading.

The resolution for furnishing the American Antiquarian Society with a copy of the Journals of Congress, and of the documents published under their order, was read a third time, and passed.

The Senate resumed, as in Committee of the Whole, the consideration of the bill, entitled "An act for the relief of the petty officers and seamen under the command of Captain Joshua Barney;" and Mr. SMITH was requested to take the Chair.

On motion, by Mr. GAILLARD, the bill having been amended, so as to include the non-commissioned officers and privates of the marine corps, on motion, by Mr. BROWN, the further consideration thereof was postponed until the first Monday in April next.

The Senate resumed, as in Committee of the Whole, the consideration of the bill for the relief of Bowie and Kurtz, and others; and, on motion, the further consideration thereof was postponed until Monday next.

The Senate resumed, as in Committee of the Whole, the consideration of the bill supplementary to an act laying duties on notes of banks, bankers, and certain companies; on notes, bonds, and obligations, discounted by banks, bankers, and certain companies; and on bills of exchange of certain descriptions; and, no amendment having been proposed, the bill was ordered to be engrossed and read the third time.

ELECTION OF PRESIDING OFFICER

On motion, by Mr. BRENT, that the Senate now proceed to the election of President *pro tempore.*

Mr. GERMAN submitted the following motion :

" *Resolved,* That the Senate will on Monday next, at 12 o'clock, proceed to the choice of a President *pro tempore.*"

This question was negatived by the following vote :

For the motion—Messrs. Daggett, Dana, German, Goldsborough, Gore, Horsey, Hunter, Lambert, Mason, and Thompson—10.

Against it—Messrs. Anderson, Bibb, Bledsoe, Brent, Brown, Chace, Condit, Fromentin, Gaillard, Lacock, Morrow, Roberts, Robinson, Smith, Tait, Taylor, Turner, Varnum, Walker, and Wharton—20.

Mr. BRENT's motion was then agreed to, and the Senate proceeded to a choice accordingly.

On the first ballot, the whole number of votes being thirty, there were: For Mr. GAILLARD, 14 ;

Mr. KING, 10; Mr. CHACE, 8; Mr. ANDERSON, 1; Mr. SMITH, 1; and Mr. TAIT, 1.

On the second ballot, there were: For Mr. GAILLARD, 16; Mr. KING, 10; Mr. CHACE, 5; and Mr. ANDERSON, 1.

Mr. GAILLARD was therefore declared duly elected; and, on taking the Chair, addressed the Senate nearly as follows:

"*Honorable Gentlemen:* While I lament the sudden and melancholy event which has led to the distinguished honor conferred on me, I am so truly sensible of my own incompetency to discharge the duties of the station to which I am called, in a manner suitable to their importance, and correspondent to the dignity of this honorable body, that I approach the exercise of them with unfeigned diffidence and apprehension. All that I dare hope is, that my efforts will be considered as the result of well-meant intentions: all that I dare promise is, that my best exertions shall be directed to a faithful and impartial execution of the trust confided to me. Relying, then, on the candor and liberality which have ever characterized this respectable Assembly, I will proceed to the performance of the duties assigned me."

On motion, by Mr. BIBB,

Ordered, That the Secretary wait on the President of the United States, and acquaint him that the Senate have, in consequence of the decease of the VICE PRESIDENT of the United States, elected the Honorable JOHN GAILLARD President of the Senate *pro tempore.*

Ordered. That the Secretary make a similar communication to the House of Representatives.

SATURDAY, November 26.

On motion, by Mr. VARNUM, to amend the Journal of yesterday, by striking out the following words:

"On motion of Mr. Anderson,

"Having been required by a majority," and inserting, in lieu thereof, "being desired by one-fifth," so to read, "the yeas and nays being desired by one-fifth of the Senators present."

It was determined in the affirmative—yeas 18 nays 7.

On motion, by Mr. GERMAN, the yeas and nays having been desired by one-fifth of the Senators present, those who voted in the affirmative are—

Messrs. Bibb, Daggett, Dana, Gaillard, German, Goldsborough, Horsey, Hunter, Lambert, Mason, Morrow, Smith, Tait, Taylor, Thompson, Turner, Varnum, and Walker.

Those who voted in the negative are—

Messrs. Anderson, Chace, Condit, Fromentin, Lacock, Roberts, and Robinson.

The Senate resumed, as in Committee of the Whole, the consideration of the bill, entitled "An act authorizing the Secretary of State, during the continuance of the present war, to make an additional allowance to the owners and masters of vessels for bringing back to the United States destitute and distressed American seamen;" and the bill was ordered to the third reading.

The bill was then read a third time, by unanimous consent, and passed.

Mr. HUNTER called up the petition of Henry Nimmo, of Warren, in the State of Rhode Island, presented on the 3d of March, 1814, praying the remission of certain duties on one hundred bales of cotton, the growth and produce of the State of Georgia, as therein stated; and, on his motion, it was referred to a select committee, to consider and report thereon, by bill or otherwise; and Messrs. HUNTER, ROBERTS, and BIBB, were appointed the committee.

Mr. FROMENTIN, from the committee to whom was referred the bill, entitled "An act for the relief of John Castille, of the city of New Orleans," reported it without amendment; and, on his motion, the bill was considered as in Committee of the Whole, and it was ordered to a third reading.

The bill supplementary to an act laying duties on notes of banks, bankers, and certain companies; on notes, bonds, and obligations, discounted by banks, bankers, and certain companies; and on bills of exchange of certain descriptions, was reported by the committee correctly engrossed.

The Senate resumed, as in Committee of the Whole, the consideration of the bill to extend the time of Oliver Evans's patent for his improvement on steam engines; and, after debate, the Senate adjourned.

MONDAY, November 28.

The Senate resumed, as in Committee of the Whole, the consideration of the bill for the relief of Bowie and Kurtz, and others; and, no amendment having been proposed, on the question, Shall this bill be engrossed and read a third time? on motion, by Mr. SMITH, the further consideration thereof was postponed until to-morrow.

The resolution from the House of Representatives, appointing a committee on their part to join such committee as may be appointed on the part of the Senate, to inquire and report whether Congress may not be more conveniently accommodated, either by an alteration of the present Chambers, or by procuring other rooms within a convenient distance of the public offices, was read the second time, considered as in Committee of the Whole, and ordered to a third reading.

The engrossed bill supplementary to an act laying duties on notes of banks, bankers, and certain companies; on notes, bonds, and obligations, discounted by banks, bankers, and certain companies; and on bills of exchange of certain descriptions, having been reported correct, was read a third time.

On the question, Shall this bill pass? it was determined in the affirmative—yeas 20, nays 7, as follows:

YEAS—Messrs. Anderson, Bibb, Bledsoe, Brown, Chace, Condit, Dana, Fromentin, Gaillard, Lacock, Morrow, Roberts, Robinson, Smith, Tait, Taylor, Turner, Varnum, Walker, and Wharton.

NAYS—Messrs. Daggett, Goldsborough, Horsey, Hunter, Lambert, Mason, and Thompson.

So it was *Resolved,* That this bill pass, and that the title thereof be "An act supplementary to an act laying duties on notes of banks, bankers, and certain companies; on notes, bonds, and obligations, discounted by banks, bankers, and certain companies, and on bills of exchange of certain descriptions.

The bill, entitled "An act for the relief of John Castille, of the city of New Orleans," was read a third time, and passed.

The Senate resumed, as in Committee of the Whole, the consideration of the bill to extend the time of Oliver Evans's patent for his improvement on steam engines; and sundry amendments having been agreed to, the President reported it to the House accordingly.

On the question, Shall this bill be engrossed and read a third time as amended? it was determined in the affirmative—yeas 21, nays 8, as follows:

YEAS—Messrs. Anderson, Bledsoe, Brown, Chase, Condit, Dana, Fromentin, Gaillard, German, Horsey, Hunter, Lambert, Morrow, Roberts, Robinson, Smith, Tait, Turner, Varnum, Walker, and Wharton.

NAYS—Messrs. Bibb, Brent, Daggett, Goldsborough, Lacock, Mason, Taylor, and Thompson.

Mr. GOLDSBOROUGH, from the joint Library Committee of Congress, to whom the subject was referred, reported a bill to authorize the purchase of the library of Thomas Jefferson, late President of the United States; and the bill was read, and passed to the second reading.

NAVAL ESTABLISHMENT.

Mr. TAIT, from the Committee on Naval Affairs, to whom were referred two resolutions of the 7th instant, "instructing them to inquire what provision should be made for the appointment of officers above the grade of Captain in the Navy of the United States," and also, "to inquire what provision should be made for conferring naval rank by brevet, in consideration of meritorious service," made a report as follows:

That your committee assume it as a policy now settled, that the United States are to have a permanent Naval Establishment, which is to be gradually increased, according to circumstances, and as the ability of the Government may permit. Your committee deem it unnecessary to go into a course of reasoning to support the soundness of this policy, and to establish (what is now generally conceded) that a navy is the most appropriate, the most efficient, and the least expensive defence of this country.

The commercial and maritime habits of a large portion of the people of the United States press them to the ocean; hence have arisen competition and rivalship with other nations, pursuing the same course of industry. The history of all nations teaches us that the persons and the property of our citizens on the high seas, unprotected, must be (as indeed they have been) the subjects of frequent violence and injustice. The true remedy against these maritime wrongs is maritime force. A navy, growing up with the growth of the nation, cannot fail, before the lapse of many years, to procure respect from abroad, and safety at home.

Congress, apparently influenced by these considerations, at an early period after the establishment of the General Government, created a Naval Department, and have authorized, from time to time, the building of

ships of war, until the Navy has become respectable, both from the number and rates of its vessels, and, still more so, from the gallantry and splendor of its achievements. By the laws now in force, the Navy will consist of four seventy-fours, three thirty-sixes, eight sloops of war, besides a great number of brigs and schooners, carrying, on the whole, not less than thirteen hundred guns. Of these, there remain to be put on the stocks one of the seventy-fours and four of the forty-fours. This force is exclusive of the gunboats, the flotillas, and lake squadrons; the latter of which consist of between thirty and forty ships, some of which are large. The national vessels on the Lakes do not carry less than five hundred guns.

Your committee are not aware, nor do they believe, that any nation possessing a naval force, such as the above, is without a grade of officers above that of captain. The nation with whom the United States are now at war, is said to have about a thousand public ships; to command which, she has not less than two hundred admirals of ten different grades, ascending from rear admiral of the blue to the admiral of the fleet. At present, the Navy of the United States is commanded by commissioned officers of three grades only, lieutenants, master commandants, and post captains.

The committee would feel that they had not done justice to the subject committed to them, if they failed to contrast the situation of the Army with that of the Navy, as it respects the scope of promotion in each. The Army presents, for the encouragement of an honorable ambition, the high station of major general through ten different grades. It has also advantages in the variety of its corps unknown to the Navy. The youth of our country, ambitious of military fame, may, according to their taste, enter the Army as officers of cavalry, of artillery, of infantry, or of the rifle corps. Not so with the naval officer. All that he can expect, is, to be transferred from a subordinate station to the command of a ship of war. The rapid promotions of late in the Army cannot but strongly impress the naval officer with a deep sense of his own confined situation, and of the cheerless prospect before him. Does not justice, then, dictate that the range for promotion should be enlarged in our Naval Establishment?

Your committee are of opinion that a discreet policy and a prudent foresight, not less than a just regard to the strong claims of the Navy, call for an enlargement of the sphere of promotion. It cannot be long before the Navy will be called on to sail in squadron. The highest attainments in naval tactics should be encouraged. If you expect men to labor for the highest qualifications in their professions, it is necessary to open to them the way to the station requiring them. The surest mean by which you will probably induce the officers to qualify themselves for an admiral's command, is, to create that grade in the Navy; thereby requiring, in the same act, great professional attainments, and offering a reward for them.

Your committee are therefore of opinion, that, whether they view this subject in reference to the practice of older and more experienced nations, or in regard to the just claims and the long and meritorious services of the naval officers, or with a view to a just, prudent, and liberal policy, on the part of the Government, a grade or grades superior to that of captain should now be created in the Naval Establishment.

As to the second resolution, relative to conferring naval rank by brevet, it does occur to your committee as necessary; it having been the practice of the Government to confer actual rank without regard to seniority, in reward of brilliant achievements or meritorious service.

The committee respectfully submit the following resolutions:

Resolved, That it is expedient to authorize by law the appointment of officers above the grade of captain in the Navy of the United States.

Resolved, That it is inexpedient, at this time, to make any provision for conferring naval rank by brevet.

NAVY DEPARTMENT, *Nov.* 15, 1814.

SIR: In answer to the inquiry contained in your letter of the 8th instant, founded upon two resolutions of the Senate, passed on the 7th instant, instructing the Committee on Naval Affairs to inquire "what provision should be made for the appointment of officers above the grade of captain in the Navy of the United States," and "what provision should be made for conferring naval rank by brevet, in consideration of meritorious service," I have the honor to represent, that the high character which the American Navy has justly acquired; the general sentiment which indicates its rapid increase and permanency; and the long, faithful, and honorable service which its senior officers have rendered their country; appear to me to justify and call for the appointment of officers of a higher grade than that of captain.

Love of country, and the laudable desire of honorable fame, are strong excitements to noble action; but the prospect of progressive promotion to the highest distinction which talents, zeal, and valor, may justly aspire to, is not perhaps less active and stimulating.

Captains of long and honorable standing in the Navy cannot but contrast the cheerless prospect of promotion in the naval service, with the rapid and high distinction to which their military brethren, with equal, but not higher pretensions, have attained.

The naval force, in officers, seamen, and marines, is probably two-fifth parts of the whole military force of the United States, actually employed, in which there are, I think, eight major generals and sixteen brigadiers, exclusive of those of the staff, who enjoy the rank, pay, and emoluments, of brigadiers.

The effect of a limited grade, without hope of promotion, is to contract the range of study and professional attainment within the sphere of the command thus limited. Hold out but the prospect of elevated rank and command, and every officer of talents and worth will aspire to the highest qualifications.

Foreign example is to be received with caution; yet, the practice of nations of great maritime experience may throw some light upon the subject. A comparison of the force of the British navy, with the number of admirals in that service, will exhibit the following result, viz: of ships of seventy-four guns and upwards, there are—

Building, about	24
In ordinary, about	54
Guards, hospital, prison, store ships, &c.	33
In commission, about	99
Total	210

The list of admirals contains two hundred and nine, exclusive of twenty-seven superannuated rear admirals, upon half-pay; thus exhibiting more than two admirals for every ship of seventy-four guns and upwards, in commission.

We often see on our own coast admirals with commands inferior to those which the American Navy may even now afford.

The new grade to be established, and number of promotions, should be consistent with the scale and character of the Naval Establishment, which may not, for some years, require the distinction of flags as in the British navy, viz: red, white, and blue, at the main, fore, or mizen of each; making nine grades of admirals, rising in the order of the flags, from blue to red.

I am therefore of opinion, that it is now expedient to establish the grade of rear admiral, without any distinction of flags, leaving the promotions to vice admiral and admiral for future services, and an enlarged establishment.

I am also of opinion, that the same principle which induced the establishment of brevet rank in the Army, for gallant actions, meritorious conduct, or long service, is equally applicable to the Navy, and cannot fail to excite to those actions which it is intended to reward; but no officer so brevetted should be entitled to any additional pay or emoluments, except when commanding on separate service.

I have the honor to be, very respectfully, sir, your obedient servant,   W. JONES.

Hon. C. TAIT, *Ch'n Naval Committee, Senate.*

The report, together with the resolutions, were read, and the report ordered to be printed for the use of the Senate.

TUESDAY, November 29.

The Senate resumed, as in Committee of the Whole, the bill for the relief of Bowie and Kurtz, and others; and the following amendment was proposed, by Mr. BLEDSOE:

Strike out, from the word "of," in the seventh line, to the end of the bill, and insert, "as a full compensation for the freight of the ship Allegany from Algiers to Gibraltar."

On motion, by Mr. SMITH, the further consideration thereof was postponed to, and made the order of the day for, Friday next.

A message from the House of Representatives informed the Senate that the House have passed a bill, entitled "An act to provide additional revenues for defraying the expenses of Government, and maintaining the public credit, by laying duties on spirits distilled within the United States, and by amending the act laying duties on licenses to distillers of spirituous liquors;" in which bill they request the concurrence of the Senate.

The bill last mentioned was read, and passed to the second reading.

The resolution from the House of Representatives appointing a committee on their part, to join such committee as may be appointed on the part of the Senate, to inquire and report whether Congress may not be more conveniently accommodated, either by an alteration of the present Chambers, or by procuring other rooms within a convenient distance of the public offices, was read a third time.

On the question, Shall this resolution pass? it was determined in the negative—yeas 11, nays 19, as follows:

YEAS—Messrs. Brown, Dana, Fromentin, Gaillard,

German, Goldsborough, Gore, Horsey, Hunter, Lambert, and Mason.

NAYS—Messrs. Anderson, Bibb, Bledsoe, Brent, Chace, Condit, Daggett, Lacock, Morrow, Roberts, Robinson, Smith, Tait, Taylor, Thompson, Turner, Varnum, Walker, and Wharton.

WEDNESDAY, November 30.

Mr. FROMENTIN, from the committee, reported the bill to extend the time of Oliver Evans's patent for his improvement on steam engines correctly engrossed; and on motion, by Mr. BROWN, the further consideration thereof was postponed until to-morrow.

The bill, entitled "An act to provide additional revenues for defraying the expenses of Government, and maintaining the public credit, by laying duties on spirits distilled within the United States, and by amending the act laying duties on licenses to distillers of spirituous liquors," was read the second time.

A motion was made, by Mr. DAGGETT, to refer the said bill to a select committee; and on motion, by Mr. BLEDSOE, the consideration thereof was postponed until to-morrow.

Mr. ANDERSON submitted the following motion for consideration:

Resolved, That the committee to whom was referred so much of the Message of the President of the United States as relates to naval affairs, be instructed to inquire into the expediency of making provision by law that the officers and crews of the vessels authorized to be built or purchased, by an act passed the fifteenth day of November, one thousand eight hundred and fourteen, may be entitled to receive the whole of the prize money which may arise from the sale of such vessel or vessels and their cargoes as they may capture, and which may be condemned as good prize according to law; and that the committee have leave to report by bill or otherwise.

The Senate proceeded to consider the resolutions reported, on the 28th instant, by the Committee on Naval Affairs; and, having agreed to the first resolution, on motion, by Mr. DANA, the further consideration of the second resolution was postponed to the first Monday in January next.

On motion, by Mr. DANA, the first resolution was referred to the Committee on Naval Affairs, with instructions to report a bill agreeably to the provisions thereof.

The Senate resumed, as in Committee of the Whole, the consideration of the bill further in addition to an act, entitled "An act more effectually to provide for the national defence by establishing an uniform militia throughout the United States;" and on motion, by Mr. ANDERSON, the further consideration thereof was postponed until to-morrow.

The bill to authorize the purchase of the library of Thomas Jefferson, late President of the United States, was read the second time, and considered as in Committee of the Whole; and on motion, by Mr. HUNTER, the bill was postponed until to-morrow.

THURSDAY, December 1.

The Senate resumed the consideration of the motion made yesterday, by Mr. DAGGETT, to refer to a select committee, to consist of five members, the bill. entitled "An act to provide additional revenues for defraying the expenses of Government, and maintaining the public credit, by laying duties on spirits distilled within the United States, and by amending the act laying duties on licenses to distillers of spirituous liquors," to consider and report thereon, and agreed thereto; and Messrs. TAYLOR, BLEDSOE, BROWN, CHACE, and DAGGETT, were appointed the committee.

The Senate resumed, as in Committee of the Whole, the consideration of the bill in addition to an act, entitled "An act more effectually to provide for the national defence by establishing an uniform militia throughout the United States;" and on motion, by Mr. TURNER, the further consideration thereof was postponed until to-morrow.

The following Message was received from the PRESIDENT OF THE UNITED STATES:

To the Senate and House of
　　Representatives of the United States:

I transmit, for the information of Congress, the communications last received from the Ministers Extraordinary and Plenipotentiary of the United States at Ghent, explaining the course and actual state of their negotiations with the Plenipotentiaries of Great Britain.

　　　　　　　　　JAMES MADISON.

DECEMBER 1, 1814.

The Message and communications therein referred to were read, and five hundred copies thereof ordered to be printed for the use of the Senate.

FRIDAY, December 2.

The PRESIDENT communicated a report of the Secretary for the Department of the Navy, on the petition of Edward Bland and others, referred to him the 17th of October; and the report was read; and on motion, by Mr. MORROW, the report, together with the accompanying documents, was referred to the Committee on Naval Affairs, to consider and report thereon by bill or otherwise.

The Senate resumed the consideration of the motion made the 30th ultimo, by Mr. ANDERSON, for instructing the Committee on Naval Affairs to inquire into the expediency of making provision by law, in relation to officers and crews of certain vessels; and agreed thereto.

The Senate resumed, as in Committee of the Whole, the consideration of the bill to authorize the purchase of the library of Thomas Jefferson, late President of the United States; and, no amendment having been proposed, the bill was ordered to be engrossed and read a third time.

A message from the House of Representatives informed the Senate that the House have passed a bill, entitled "An act to provide additional revenues for defraying the expenses of Government and maintaining the public credit by duties on carriages, and the harness used therefor;" also, a bill, entitled "An act to provide additional revenues for defraying the expenses of Government and maintaining the public credit by duties on sales at auction, on the postage of letters, and on licenses to retail wines, spirituous liquors, and foreign merchandise;" in which bills they request the concurrence of the Senate.

The two bills last mentioned were read, and passed to the second reading.

The engrossed bill to extend the time of Oliver Evans's patent for his improvement on steam engines was read a third time, and passed.

The Senate resumed, as in Committee of the Whole, the consideration of the bill further in addition to an act, entitled "An act more effectually to provide for the national defence by establishing an uniform militia throughout the United States."

On motion, by Mr. HORSEY, that the further consideration thereof be postponed to the first Monday in December next, it was determined in the affirmative—yeas 16, nays 12, as follows:

YEAS—Messrs. Daggett, Dana, Fromentin, Goldsborough, Gore, Horsey, Hunter, King, Lambert, Mason, Smith, Tait, Taylor, Thompson, Turner, and Walker.

NAYS—Messrs. Anderson, Bibb, Bledsoe, Chace, Condit, Gaillard, German, Lacock, Morrow, Roberts, Varnum, and Wharton.

Mr. KING, from the committee to whom was referred, on the 31st of October, the petition of David M. Clarkson and others, citizens of New York, praying the establishment of a National Bank, reported a bill to incorporate the subscribers to the Bank of the United States of America; and the bill was read, and passed to the second reading.

The Senate resumed, as in Committee of the Whole, the consideration of the bill for the relief of Bowie and Kurtz, and others; and on motion, by Mr. SMITH, the consideration thereof was further postponed to, and made the order of the day for, Tuesday next.

SATURDAY, December 3.

The bill, entitled "An act to provide additional revenues for defraying the expenses of Government and maintaining the public credit by duties on sales at auction, on the postage of letters, and on licenses to retail wines, spirituous liquors, and foreign merchandise," was read the second time; and referred to the committee to whom was referred, the 1st instant, the bill, entitled "An act to provide additional revenues for defraying the expenses of Government and maintaining the public credit by laying duties on spirits distilled within the United States, and by amending the act laying duties on licenses to distillers of spirituous liquors," to consider and report thereon.

The bill, entitled "An act to provide additional revenues for defraying the expenses of Government and maintaining the public credit by duties on carriages, and the harness used therefor," was read the second time, and referred to the committee last mentioned, to consider and report thereon.

On motion, by Mr. BIBB, a committee was appointed to inquire into the expediency of appropriating the lands reserved for the use of schools in the Mississippi Territory, with leave to report by bill or otherwise; and Messrs. BIBB, MORROW, and WHARTON, were appointed the committee.

The bill to authorize the purchase of the library of Thomas Jefferson, late President of the United States, was read a third time, and passed.

MONDAY, December 5.

Mr. DAGGETT presented the petition of John C. Hurlburt, late of Chatham, in the district of Connecticut, now a prisoner confined in jail at Hartford, in said district, for an alleged violation of the embargo law, as stated in the petition, and praying relief, for reasons therein stated; and the petition was read, and referred to a select committee, to consider and report thereon by bill or otherwise; and Messrs. DAGGETT, THOMPSON, and CHACE, were appointed the committee.

Mr. TAYLOR, from the committee to whom was referred the bill, entitled "An act to provide additional revenues for defraying the expenses of Government and maintaining the public credit by laying duties on spirits distilled within the United States, and by amending the act laying duties on licenses to distillers of spirituous liquors," reported it with amendments.

Mr. TAYLOR, from the same committee, also reported the bill, entitled "An act to provide additional revenues for defraying the expenses of Government and maintaining the public credit by duties on carriages, and the harness used therefor," without amendment.

Mr. KING presented a memorial of a committee appointed by five of the banks in the city of New York, to take into consideration all matters relating to the state of credit in that city; remonstrating against the proposed incorporation of the subscribers to the Bank of the United States of America; and the memorial was read.

The bill to incorporate the subscribers to the Bank of the United States of America was read the second time and considered as in Committee of the Whole.

On motion, by Mr. MASON, to strike out, section 1, line 4, "fifty," and insert "twenty," in lieu thereof," reducing the proposed amount of the capital stock from fifty to twenty millions of dollars—after debate, on motion, by Mr. DANA, the further consideration thereof was postponed until to-morrow.

On motion, by Mr. TAYLOR, the Senate resumed, as in Committee of the Whole, the consideration of the bill, entitled "An act to provide additional revenues for defraying the expenses of Government and maintaining the public credit by laying duties on spirits distilled within the United States, and by amending the act laying duties on licenses to distillers of spirituous liquors," together with the amendments reported thereto by the select committee; and the amendment, in part, with further amendments, were agreed to; and on motion, by Mr. GERMAN, to strike out the 25th section of the bill, the Senate adjourned.

TUESDAY, December 6.

Mr. DAGGETT, from the committee to whom the subject was referred, reported a bill for the relief of John C. Hurlburt, of Chatham, in the State of Connecticut; and the bill was read, and passed to the second reading.

Mr. TAIT, from the Committee on Naval Affairs, reported a bill authorizing the appointment of certain naval officers therein named; and the bill was read, and passed to the second reading.

Mr. HORSEY submitted the following motion for consideration:

Resolved, That the President of the United States be requested to cause to be laid before the Senate a statement containing the specification of the various post offices in the States, respectively; the annual emoluments of the postmasters, and the amount of expenditures incident to their respective offices; as, also, the annual amount of the gross and net revenue derived therefrom between the 30th day of September, A. D. 1810, and the 1st day of October, A. D. 1814.

The Senate resumed, as in Committee of the Whole, the consideration of the bill, entitled "An act to provide additional revenues for defraying the expenses of Government and maintaining the public credit by laying duties on spirits distilled within the United States, and by amending the act laying duties on licenses to distillers of spirituous liquors;" and on the question to agree to Mr. GERMAN's motion, to strike out section 25, as follows:

"*And be it further enacted,* That in future it shall be lawful for the distiller or distillers of domestic spirits, and all persons from whose materials such spirits shall be distilled, to sell without license any quantity thereof, not less than one gallon :"

It was determined in the affirmative—yeas 15, nays 13, as follows:

YEAS—Messrs. Brown, Daggett, Dana, Fromentin, German, Goldsborough, Gore, Horsey, Hunter, King, Lambert, Mason, Smith, Thompson, and Varnum.

NAYS—Messrs. Bibb, Bledsoe, Chace, Condit, Gaillard, Lacock, Morrow, Roberts, Tait, Taylor, Turner, Walker, and Wharton.

And the PRESIDENT reported the bill to the House amended.

On motion, by Mr. BLEDSOE, to strike out, from the 1st section, the word "twenty," where it occurs, and insert, in lieu thereof, "fifteen," reducing the rate of duties; it was determined in the negative—yeas 10, nays 19, as follows:

YEAS—Messrs. Anderson, Bibb, Bledsoe, Chace, Lacock, Morrow, Roberts, Turner, Walker, and Wharton.

NAYS—Messrs. Brown, Condit, Daggett, Dana, Fromentin, Gaillard, German, Goldsborough, Gore, Horsey, Hunter, King, Lambert, Mason, Smith, Tait, Taylor, Thompson, and Varnum.

On the question, Shall the amendments be engrossed and the bill be read a third time as amended? it was determined in the affirmative—yeas 27, nays 1, as follows:

YEAS—Messrs. Anderson, Bibb, Brown, Chace, Condit, Daggett, Fromentin, Gaillard, German, Goldsborough, Gore, Horsey, Hunter, King, Lacock, Lambert, Mason, Morrow, Roberts, Smith, Tait, Taylor, Thompson, Turner, Varnum, Walker, and Wharton.

NAY—Mr. Bledsoe.

A message from the House of Representatives informed the Senate that the House have passed the bill which originated in the Senate, entitled "An act making further provision for filling the ranks of the Army of the United States," with amendments, in which they request the concurrence of the Senate.

The Senate resumed, as in Committee of the Whole, the consideration of the bill to incorporate the subscribers to the Bank of the United States of America.

On the question, to agree to the motion made yesterday by Mr. MASON, to strike out of section one, line four, the word "fifty," and insert in lieu thereof, "twenty," reducing the proposed amount of the capital stock from fifty to twenty millions of dollars—on motion, by Mr. HORSEY, it was agreed to take the question by yeas and nays; and, after debate, the further consideration thereof was postponed until to-morrow.

The Senate proceeded to consider the amendments of the House of Representatives to the bill, entitled "An act making further provision for filling the ranks of the Army of the United States;" and, on motion, the Senate adjourned.

WEDNESDAY, December 7.

The bill for the relief of John C. Hurlburt, of Chatham, in the State of Connecticut, was read the second time, and considered as in Committee of the Whole; and, no amendment having been proposed, the bill was ordered to be engrossed and read a third time.

The bill authorizing the appointment of certain naval officers therein mentioned was read the second time.

The Senate resumed the consideration of the motion made yesterday by Mr. HORSEY, requesting a specification of the various post offices, &c., and agreed thereto.

The Senate resumed, as in Committee of the Whole, the consideration of the bill for the relief of Bowie and Kurtz, and others; and the further consideration thereof was postponed until to-morrow.

The Senate resumed the consideration of the amendments of the House of Representatives to the bill, entitled "An act making further provision for filling the ranks of the Army of the United States;" and concurred therein.

A message from the House of Representatives informed the Senate that the House have passed a bill, entitled "An act directing the staff officers of the Army to comply with the requisitions of naval and marine officers, in certain cases;" a bill entitled "An act to provide for the widows and orphans of militia and volunteer soldiers who shall die or be killed in the service of the United States;" also, a bill, entitled "An act to authorize the President of the United States to accept the services of volunteers who may associate and organize themselves and offer their services to the Government of the United States," in which bills they request the concurrence of the Senate.

The Senate resumed, as in Committee of the Whole, the consideration of the bill to incorporate the subscribers to the Bank of the United States of America.

On the question to agree to the motion made on the 5th instant, by Mr. MASON, to strike out of section one, line four, the word "fifty," and insert in lieu thereof, "twenty," reducing the proposed amount of the capital stock from fifty to twenty millions of dollars; it was determined in the negative—yeas 13, nays 18, as follows:

YEAS—Messrs. Brown, Daggett, Dana, Fromentin, German, Goldsborough, Gore, Horsey, Hunter, King, Lambert, Mason, and Thompson.

NAYS—Messrs. Anderson, Bibb, Bledsoe, Brent, Chace, Condit, Gaillard, Lacock, Morrow, Roberts, Robinson, Smith, Tait, Taylor, Turner, Varnum, Walker, and Wharton.

On motion, by Mr. MASON, to strike out of section one, line six, the word "forty," and insert in lieu thereof, "thirty"—Mr. DANA called for a division of the question, and it was taken on striking out, and determined in the negative—yeas 13, nays 18, as follows:

YEAS—Messrs. Brown, Daggett, Dana, Fromentin, German, Goldsborough, Gore, Horsey, Hunter, King, Lambert, Mason, and Thompson.

NAYS—Messrs. Anderson, Bibb, Bledsoe, Brent, Chace, Condit, Gaillard, Lacock, Morrow, Roberts, Robinson, Smith, Tait, Taylor, Turner, Varnum, Walker, and Wharton.

After further progress, the Senate adjourned.

THURSDAY, December 8.

The three bills brought up yesterday for concurrence were read, and passed.

Mr. LACOCK submitted the following motion:

Resolved, That the Senate will, on the —— day of ——, proceed to the choice of an Assistant Doorkeeper.

Mr. TAIT, from the Committee on Naval Affairs, to whom was referred the resolution of the Senate of the second instant, made report, together with the following resolution:

"*Resolved*, That it is inexpedient at this time to alter the laws respecting the Navy pension fund.".

And the report and resolution were read.

A message from the House of Representatives informed the Senate that the House have passed a bill, entitled "An act making additional appropriations for the service of the year one thousand eight hundred and fourteen;" also, a bill, entitled "An act supplemental to the acts authorizing a loan for the several sums of twenty-five millions of dollars, and three millions of dollars;" in which bills they request the concurrence of the Senate.

The two bills last mentioned were read, and passed to the second reading.

The bill, entitled "An act making additional appropriations for the service of the year one thousand eight hundred and fourteen," was read the second time by unanimous consent, and re-

ferred to the committee to whom was referred, the first instant, the bill, entitled "An act to provide additional revenues for defraying the expenses of Government and maintaining the public credit by laying duties on spirits distilled within the United States, and by amending the act laying duties on licenses to distillers of spirituous liquors," to consider and report thereon.

The bill, entitled "An act supplemental to the acts authorizing a loan for the several sums of twenty-five millions of dollars, and three millions of dollars," was read the second time by unanimous consent, and referred to the committee last mentioned, to consider and report thereon.

The bill, entitled "An act directing the staff officers of the Army to comply with the requisitions of naval and marine officers in certain cases," was read the second time by unanimous consent, and referred to the Committee on Military Affairs, to consider and report thereon.

The bill, entitled "An act to authorize the President of the United States to accept the services of volunteers who may associate and organize themselves, and offer their services to the Government of the United States," was read the second time by unanimous consent, and referred to the Committee on Military Affairs, to consider and report thereon.

The bill, entitled "An act to provide for widows and orphans of militia and volunteer soldiers who shall die or be killed in the service of the United States," was read the second time by unanimous consent, and referred to the Committee on the Militia of the United States, to consider and report thereon.

The amendments to the bill, entitled "An act to provide additional revenues for defraying the expenses of Government and maintaining the public credit by laying duties on spirits distilled within the United States, and by amending the act laying duties on licenses to distillers of spirituous liquors," was read a third time as amended.

On motion, by Mr. TAYLOR, the title was amended, by inserting after "States" the words, "and Territories thereof."

Resolved, That this bill pass with amendments.

The bill for the relief of John C. Hurlburt, of Chatham, in the State of Connecticut, was read a third time, and passed.

The Senate resumed, as in Committee of the Whole, the consideration of the bill for the relief of Bowie and Kurtz, and others; and the further consideration thereof was postponed until to-morrow.

BANK OF THE UNITED STATES.

The Senate resumed, as in Committee of the Whole, the consideration of the bill to incorporate the subscribers to the Bank of the United States of America.

On motion, by Mr. KING, to strike out of section two, line eleven, after the word "States," the following words: "or in the public debt of the United States, contracted by virtue of the act of Congress, entitled "An act authorizing a loan for a sum not exceeding eleven millions of dollars," passed the fourteenth day of March, one thousand eight hundred and twelve, or contracted, or to be contracted, by virtue of any subsequent act and acts of Congress heretofore passed authorizing a loan or loans," and insert in lieu thereof, "or in any public debt of the United States, bearing at the time of payment an interest of six per cent. annually ;" it was determined in the negative— yeas 11, nays 19, as follows :

YEAS—Messrs. Daggett, Fromentin, German, Goldsborough, Gore, Horsey, Hunter, King, Lambert, Mason, and Thompson.

NAYS—Messrs. Anderson, Bibb, Bledsoe, Brent, Brown, Chace, Condit, Gaillard, Lacock, Morrow, Roberts, Robinson, Smith, Tait, Taylor, Turner, Varnum, Walker, and Wharton.

On motion, by Mr. FROMENTIN, to strike out of section two, line twenty-seven, after the word "paid," the word "twenty," and insert in lieu thereof, "sixty ;" it was determined in the negative—yeas 10, nays 19, as follows:

YEAS—Messrs. Brown, Daggett, Fromentin, Goldsborough, Gore, Horsey, Hunter, King, Lambert, and Mason.

NAYS—Messrs. Anderson, Bibb, Bledsoe, Brent, Chace, Condit, Gaillard, German, Lacock, Morrow, Roberts, Robinson, Smith, Tait, Taylor, Turner, Varnum, Walker, and Wharton.

On motion, by Mr. KING, to add a new section to the bill, as follows:

"SEC. 16. *And be it further enacted,* That if the said corporation shall do, or cause, or permit to be done or transacted, on its behalf or for its use, any matter or thing injurious to the public welfare, and not authorized by this act, or shall neglect to do any matter or thing which it shall be the duty of said corporation to do, it shall, in each and every such case, be competent and lawful for Congress to repeal so much of this act as allows the notes of the said corporation to be received in payment to the United States :"

It was determined in the negative—yeas 13; nays 18, as follows :

YEAS—Messrs. Brown, Daggett, Dana, Fromentin, German, Goldsborough, Gore, Horsey, Hunter, King, Lambert, Mason, and Thompson.

NAYS—Messrs. Anderson, Bibb, Bledsoe, Brent, Chace, Condit, Gaillard, Lacock, Morrow, Roberts, Robinson, Smith, Tait, Taylor, Turner, Varnum, Walker, and Wharton.

On motion, by Mr. GERMAN, to add a new section, as follows:

"*And be it further enacted,* That Congress may repeal so much of this act as relates to the payment of the public revenue in the bills of the said bank :"

It was determined in the negative—yeas 10, nays 21, as follows:

YEAS—Messrs. Dana, Fromentin, German, Goldsborough, Gore, Horsey, King, Lambert, Mason, and Thompson.

NAYS—Messrs. Anderson, Bibb, Bledsoe, Brent, Brown, Chace, Condit, Daggett, Gaillard, Hunter, Lacock, Morrow, Roberts, Robinson, Smith, Tait, Taylor, Turner, Varnum, Walker, and Wharton.

And the PRESIDENT reported the bill to the House amended.

On the question, Shall this bill be engrossed and read a third time as amended ? it was determined in the affirmative—yeas 18, nays 13, as follows:

YEAS—Messrs. Anderson, Bibb, Bledsoe, Brent, Chace, Condit, Gaillard, Lacock, Morrow, Roberts, Robinson, Smith, Tait, Taylor, Turner, Varnum, Walker, and Wharton.

NAYS—Messrs. Brown, Daggett, Dana, Fromentin, German, Goldsborough, Gore, Horsey, Hunter, King, Lambert, Mason, and Thompson.

FRIDAY, December 9.

The Senate resumed the consideration of the report of the Committee on Naval Affairs of the 8th instant. Whereupon,

Resolved, That it is inexpedient at this time to alter the laws respecting the Navy pension fund.

The Senate resumed the consideration of the motion made yesterday for the choice of an assistant doorkeeper ; and the further consideration thereof was further postponed until Monday next.

The Senate resumed the consideration of the bill for the relief of Bowie and Kurtz, and others ; and the consideration thereof was further postponed until Monday next.

The Senate resumed, as in Committee of the Whole, the consideration of the bill, entitled "An act to provide additional revenue for defraying the expenses of Government, and maintaining the public credit, by duties on carriages, and the harness used therefor ;" and the bill having been amended, the President reported it to the House accordingly.

On the question, Shall the amendments be engrossed, and the bill read a third time as amended ? it was determined in the affirmative.

The Senate resumed the bill authorizing the appointment of certain naval officers therein named ; and the further consideration thereof was postponed to, and made the order of the day for, Monday next.

Mr. TAYLOR, from the committee to whom was referred the bill, entitled "An act making additional appropriations for the service of the year one thousand eight hundred and fourteen," reported it without amendment ; and the bill was considered as in Committee of the Whole ; and passed to the third reading.

Mr. BROWN, from the committee to whom was referred the bill, entitled "An act directing the staff officers of the Army to comply with the requisitions of naval and marine officers in certain cases," reported it without amendment ; and the bill was considered as in Committee of the Whole ; and passed to the third reading.

The bill to incorporate the subscribers to the Bank of the United States of America, was read a third time ; and the blanks having been filled, on the question, Shall this bill pass ? it was determined in the affirmative—yeas 17, nays 14, as follows:

YEAS—Messrs. Anderson, Bibb, Bledsoe, Brent, Chace, Condit, Lacock, Morrow, Roberts, Robinson, Smith, Tait, Taylor, Turner, Varnum, Walker, and Wharton.

NAYS—Messrs. Brown, Daggett, Dana, Fromentin, Gaillard, German, Goldsborough, Gore, Horsey, Hunter, King, Lambert, Mason, and Thompson.

So it was *Resolved,* That this bill pass, and that the title thereof be "An act to incorporate the subscribers to the Bank of the United States of America."

SATURDAY, December 10.

The amendments to the bill, entitled "An act to provide additional revenues for defraying the expenses of Government, and maintaining the public credit, by duties on carriages, and the harness used therefor," was read a third time as amended, and passed with amendments.

The bill, entitled "An act directing the staff officers of the Army to comply with the requisitions of naval and marine officers in certain cases, was read a third time, and passed.

The bill, entitled "An act making additional appropriations for the service of the year 1814," was read a third time and passed.

MONDAY, December 12.

The Senate resumed, as in Committee of the Whole, the consideration of the bill authorizing the appointment of certain naval officers therein named; and the bill having been amended, the President reported it to the House accordingly.

On the question, Shall this bill be engrossed and read a third time as amended? it was determined in the affirmative.

TUESDAY, December 13.

The Senate resumed the consideration of the motion made the 8th instant for the choice of an Assistant Doorkeeper; and the further consideration thereof was postponed to the first Monday in January next.

Mr. TAYLOR, from the committee to whom was referred the bill, entitled "An act to provide additional revenue for defraying the expenses of Government, and maintaining the public credit, by duties on sales at auction, on the postage of letters, and on licenses to retail wines, spirituous liquors, and foreign merchandise;" reported it with amendments.

The Senate resumed the consideration of the bill for the relief of Bowie and Kurtz, and others; and on motion, by Mr. SMITH, the further consideration thereof was postponed until the second Monday in January next.

A bill authorizing the appointment of certain naval officers therein named, was read a third time and passed.

[The bill authorizes the President of the United States, by and with the advice and consent of the Senate, to appoint one Vice Admiral, and two Rear Admirals; and fixes their compensation.]

WEDNESDAY, December 14.

A message from the House of Representatives informed the Senate that the House concur in the amendments of the Senate to the bill, entitled "An act to provide additional revenues for defraying the expenses of Government, and maintaining the public credit, by laying duties on spirits distilled within the United States, and by amending the act laying duties on licenses to distillers of spirituous liquors, except the amendment to the tenth section, and the amendment striking out the twenty-fifth section of the bill, and that they disagree to the said amendment to the tenth section, and to the striking out the said twenty-fifth section.

The Senate resumed, as in committee of the Whole, the consideration of the bill, entitled "An act to provide additional revenues for defraying the expenses of Government, and maintaining the public credit, by duties on sales at auction, on the postage of letters, and on licenses to retail wines, spirituous liquors, and foreign merchandise," together with the amendments reported thereto by the select committee; and the amendments were agreed to.

On motion, by Mr. HORSEY, to strike out the second section of the bill, as follows:

"SEC. 2. *And be it further enacted,* That, from and after the first day of February next, there shall be added to the rates of postage, as at present established by law, a sum equal to fifty per centum upon the amount of such rates respectively, for the use of the United States. And the said additional sum of fifty per centum shall be charged, collected, paid, and accounted for, in like manner, by the same officer, subject in all respects to the same regulations and provisions, and with the like fines, penalties, forfeitures, and remedies, for breaches of the law, as are provided for charging, collecting, and paying the original rates of postage to which the said sum of fifty per centum is hereby added and attached."

It was determined in the negative—yeas 11, nays 14, as follows:

YEAS—Messrs. Daggett, Dana, German, Gore, Horsey, Hunter, King, Lambert, Mason, Smith, and Thompson.

NAYS—Messrs. Bibb, Bledsoe, Chace, Condit, Fromentin, Gaillard, Morrow, Roberts, Tait, Taylor, Turner, Varnum, Walker, and Wharton.

And the bill having been further amended, the President reported it to the House accordingly.

On motion, by Mr. TAYLOR, to insert, in section 5, line 9, after the word "act," the following words, "except the rates of postage:" it was determined in the affirmative—yeas 14, nays 12, as follows:

YEAS—Messrs. Bibb, Bledsoe, Dana, Gaillard, German, Horsey, Lambert, Roberts, Tait, Taylor, Thompson, Turner, Varnum, and Wharton.

NAYS—Messrs. Brown, Chace, Condit, Daggett, Fromentin, Gore, Hunter, King, Mason, Morrow, Smith, and Walker.

On the question, Shall the amendments be engrossed and the bill read a third time as amended? it was determined in the affirmative.

Mr. GORE gave notice, that to-morrow, he should ask leave to bring in a bill authorizing payment to ⬤ widow of Elbridge Gerry, deceased, late Vice President of the United States, of such salary as would have been payable to him during the residue of the term for which he was elected, had he so long lived.

The Senate proceeded to consider the amendments disagreed to by the House of Representatives to the bill, entitled "An act to provide additional revenues for defraying the expenses of Government and maintaining the public credit by laying duties on spirits distilled within the United States, and by amending the act laying duties on licenses to distillers of spirituous liquors."

On motion, by Mr. TAYLOR,·

Resolved, That they insist on their amendment to the tenth section.

On motion, by Mr. GERMAN, that they insist on their amendments, striking out the twenty-fifth section of the bill, it was determined in the affirmative—yeas 14, nays 9, as follows:

YEAS—Messrs. Condit, Daggett, Dana, Gaillard, German, Gore, Horsey, Hunter, King, Lambert, Mason, Smith, Thompson, and Varnum.

NAYS—Messrs. Bibb, Bledsoe, Chace, Morrow, Roberts, Tait, Taylor, Turner, and Wharton.

So it was *Resolved,* That the Senate insist on their amendments disagreed to by the House of Representatives, and ask a conference on the disagreeing votes of the two Houses.

Ordered, That Messrs. TAYLOR, KING, and BLEDSOE, be the managers at the said conference on the part of the Senate.

THURSDAY, December 15.

A message from the House of Representatives informed the Senate that the House have passed the bill which originated in the Senate, entitled "An act to authorize the President of the United States to call upon the several States and Territories thereof for their respective quotas of eighty thousand four hundred and thirty militia, for the defence of the frontiers of the United States against invasion," with amendments, in which they request the concurrence of the Senate. They insist on their disagreement to the amendment of the Senate to the tenth section, and to the amendment striking out the twenty-fifth section of the bill, entitled "An act to provide additional revenues for defraying the expenses of Government and maintaining the public credit, by laying duties on spirits distilled within the United States, and by amending the act laying duties on licenses to distillers of spirituous liquors." They agree to the conference proposed on the subject, and have appointed managers on their part.

Mr. VARNUM presented the petition of Daniel Renner and Nathaniel Heath, stating that, at the time of the incursion of the enemy, they were proprietors of an extensive manufactory of cordage, in the City of Washington, and had on hand a large quantity of materials, which were totally consumed and destroyed by them; and praying indemnification therefor, for reasons stated in the petition; which was read, and the petition, together with the accompanying documents, was referred to the committee to whom was referred, on the 23d of September, the memorial of the President and Directors of the Eastern Branch

13th CON. 3d SESS.—5

Bridge Company, to consider and report thereon by bill or otherwise.

The amendments to the bill, entitled "An act to provide additional revenues for defraying the expenses of Government, and maintaining the public credit, by duties on sales at auction, on the postage of letters, and on licenses to retail wines, spirituous liquors, and foreign merchandise," was read a third time as amended.

On the question, Shall this bill pass as amended? it was determined in the affirmative—yeas 19, nays 7, as follows:

YEAS—Messrs. Anderson, Bibb, Bledsoe, Brown, Chace, Condit, Fromentin, Gaillard, Lacock, Mason, Morrow, Roberts, Robinson, Smith, Taylor, Turner, Varnum, Walker, and Wharton.

NAYS—Messrs. Daggett, Gore, Horsey, Hunter, King, Lambert, and Thompson.

So it was *Resolved,* That this bill pass with amendments; and on motion, by Mr. FROMENTIN, the title was amended, to strike out "on the postage of letters," and insert, at the end thereof, "and for increasing the rates of postage."

Mr. GORE asked and obtained leave to bring in a bill authorizing payment to the widow of Elbridge Gerry, deceased, late Vice President of the United States, of such salary as would have been payable to him, during the residue of the term for which he was elected, had he so long lived; and the bill was read, and passed to the second reading.

The Senate proceeded to consider the amendments of the House of Representatives to the bill, entitled "An act to authorize the President of the United States to call upon the several States and Territories thereof for their respective quotas of eighty thousand four hundred and thirty militia, for the defence of the frontiers of the United States against invasion."

On motion, by Mr. SMITH, they were referred to the Committee on Military Affairs, to consider and report thereon.

Ordered, That the bill last mentioned, as amended, by the House of Representatives, be printed for the use of the Senate.

On motion, by Mr. HORSEY,

Resolved, That the resolution which passed the Senate on the 7th instant, calling for a specification of the various post offices in the States respectively, &c., be and the same is hereby rescinded.

On motion, by Mr. HORSEY,

Resolved, That the President of the United States be requested to cause to be laid before the Senate a statement containing a specification of the various post offices in the States respectively, of the emoluments of the postmasters, and the amount of expenditures incident to their respective offices, from the first day of January, 1814, to the first day of July, in the same year; and, also, the amount of the gross and net revenue derived therefrom during the same period.

FRIDAY, December 16.

The Senate spent most of this day in the consideration of Executive business.

SATURDAY, December 17.

The bill authorizing payment to the widow of Elbridge Gerry, deceased, late Vice President of the United States, of such salary as would have been payable to him during the residue of the term for which he was elected, had he so long lived, was read the second time, and considered as in Committee of the Whole; and no amendment having been agreed to, on the question, Shall this bill be engrossed and read a third time? it was determined in the affirmative—yeas 14, nays 12, as follows:

YEAS—Messrs. Brown, Chace, Daggett, Fromentin, Gaillard, Gore, Hunter, King, Mason, Robinson, Smith, Tait, Taylor, and Thompson.

NAYS—Messrs. Anderson, Bledsoe, Condit, German, Lacock, Lambert, Morrow, Roberts, Turner, Varnum, Walker, and Wharton.

Mr. TAYLOR, from the managers on the part of the Senate, at the conference on the disagreeing votes of the two Houses on the bill, entitled "An act to provide additional revenues for defraying the expenses of Government, and maintaining the public credit, by laying duties on spirits distilled within the United States and Territories thereof, and by amending the act laying duties on licenses to distillers of spirituous liquors," reported :

"That the said managers have met and conferred with the managers on the part of the House of Representatives, and have agreed with them to recommend to the Senate to amend the amendment to the tenth section, to strike out the whole of the tenth section.

"That the Senate do recede from their amendment, to strike out the 25th section of said bill.

"And, to conform the 18th section to the amendments in other parts of the bill, by which 'February' was inserted in lieu of 'January,' in line 18, of said section, to strike out 'January,' and insert 'February.'"

On motion, by Mr. TAYLOR,

The Senate proceeded to consider the report of the managers on their part, at the conference on the disagreeing votes of the two Houses, on the bill last mentioned. Whereupon,

Resolved, That they so far recede from their amendments, disagreed to by the House of Representatives, as to adopt the report of the committee of conference.

Mr. BROWN, from the committee on so much of the Message of the President of the United States as relates to military affairs, to whom were referred the amendments of the House of Representatives to the bill, entitled "An act to authorize the President of the United States to call upon the several States and Territories thereof for their respective quotas of eighty thousand four hundred and thirty militia, for the defence of the frontiers of the United States against invasion," together with the bill, reported that the Senate concur therein, in part, with certain modifications.

MONDAY, December 19.

A message from the House of Representatives informed the Senate that the House concur in all the amendments of the Senate to the bill, entitled "An act to provide additional revenues for defraying the expenses of Government, and maintaining the public credit, by duties on sales at auction, on the postage of letters, and on licenses to retail wines, spirituous liquors, and foreign merchandise," except the amendment to the fifth section, to which amendment they disagree. They have passed a bill, entitled "An act giving further time to locate certain claims to lands, confirmed by an act of Congress, entitled "An act confirming certain claims to lands in the district of Vincennes;" a bill, entitled "An act to provide additional revenues for defraying the expenses of Government, and maintaining the public credit, by laying duties on various goods, wares, and merchandise, manufactured within the United States;" also, a bill, entitled "An act to provide additional revenues for defraying the expenses of Government, and maintaining the public credit, by laying duties on household furniture, on horses kept exclusively for the saddle or carriage, and on gold and silver watches;" in which bills they request the concurrence of the Senate.

The three bills last mentioned were read, and passed to the second reading.

The Senate resumed the consideration of the amendments of the House of Representatives to the bill, entitled "An act to authorize the President of the United States to call upon the several States and Territories thereof for their respective quotas of eighty thousand four hundred and thirty militia, for the defence of the frontiers of the United States against invasion," together with the report of the select committee thereon. Whereupon,

Resolved, That they agree to some, and disagree to other amendments of the House of Representatives to this bill.

The Senate proceeded to consider their amendment, disagreed to by the House of Representatives, to the bill, entitled "An act to provide additional revenues for defraying the expenses of Government, and maintaining the public credit, by duties on sales at auction, on the postage of letters, and on licenses to retail wines, spirituous liquors, and foreign merchandise." Whereupon,

Resolved, That they recede therefrom.

The engrossed bill authorizing payment to the widow of Elbridge Gerry, deceased, late Vice President of the United States, of such salary as would have been payable to him during the residue of the term for which he was elected, had he so long lived, was read a third time, and passed.

TUESDAY, December 20.

The credentials of JONATHAN ROBERTS, appointed a Senator by the Legislature of the State of Pennsylvania, for the term of six years, commencing on the fourth of March next, were read, and laid on file.

Mr. GORE submitted the following motion for consideration; which was read, and passed to the second reading.

Resolved, That the Secretary of the Senate be authorized to pay, out of the contingent fund, the expenses incurred for the funeral of the late Vice President of the United States, whenever the same shall have been allowed and certified by the committee of arrangement.

The bill, entitled "An act giving further time to locate certain claims to lands, confirmed by an act of Congress, entitled 'An act confirming certain claims to lands in the district of Vincennes," was read the second time, and referred to the committee to whom was referred, on the 2d September, the memorial of the Legislature of the Indiana Territory, to consider and report thereon.

The bill, entitled "An act to provide additional revenues for defraying the expenses of Government, and maintaining the public credit, by laying duties on various goods, wares, and merchandise, manufactured within the United States," was read the second time, and referred to the committee to whom was referred, the 1st instant, the bill, entitled "An act to provide additional revenues for defraying the expenses of Government, and maintaining the public credit, by laying duties on spirits distilled within the United States and the Territories thereof, and by amending the act laying duties on licenses to distillers of spirituous liquors," to consider and report thereon.

The bill, entitled "An act to provide additional revenues for defraying the expenses of Government, and maintaining the public credit, by laying duties on household furniture, on horses kept exclusively for the saddle or carriage, and on gold and silver watches," was read the second time, and referred to the committee last mentioned, to consider and report thereon.

WEDNESDAY, December 21.

The resolution authorizing the Secretary of the Senate to pay, out of the contingent fund, the expenses incurred for the funeral of the late Vice President, was read the second time, and considered as in Committee of the Whole; and, no amendment having been proposed, the resolution was ordered to be engrossed, and read a third time.

Mr. TAYLOR, from the committee to whom was referred the bill, entitled "An act supplemental to the acts authorizing a loan for the several sums of twenty-five millions of dollars, and three millions of dollars," reported it with amendments. which were considered as in Committee of the Whole and agreed to; and the President reported the bill to the House amended accordingly.

On the question, Shall the amendments be engrossed, and the bill read a third time as amended? it was determined in the affirmative.

The PRESIDENT communicated a letter from the Honorable THOMAS WORTHINGTON, notifying the resignation of his seat in the Senate; which was read.

Mr. HUNTER submitted the following motion for consideration:

Resolved, That the President of the United States be requested to cause to be laid before the Senate the force and condition of the vessels of war of the United States on Lake Ontario, and such information as he

may possess of the force and condition of the vessels of war of the enemy on the same Lake; and such information as he may deem it proper to communicate of the means and preparation requisite for the purpose of acquiring and maintaining the naval ascendency on said Lake, if an intention to that effect be contemplated on the part of the United States.

THURSDAY, December 22.

The resolution authorizing the Secretary of the Senate to pay, out of the contingent fund, the expenses incurred for the funeral of the late Vice President, was read a third time, and passed, as follows:

Resolved, That the Secretary of the Senate be authorized to pay, out of the contingent fund, the expenses incurred for the funeral of the late Vice President of the United States, whenever the same shall have been allowed and certified by the committee of arrangement.

The amendments to the bill, entitled "An act supplemental to the acts authorizing a loan for the several sums of twenty-five millions of dollars, and three millions of dollars," was read a third time as amended, and passed with amendments.

The Senate resumed the consideration of the motion made yesterday, by Mr. HUNTER, relative to vessels of war on Lake Ontario.

On motion, by Mr. BIBB, it was agreed to take the question by yeas and nays; and, on motion by Mr. BIBB, the further consideration thereof, was postponed until to-morrow.

Mr. MORROW, from the committee to whom was referred the bill, entitled "An act giving further time to locate certain claims to lands confirmed by an act of Congress, entitled 'An act confirming certain claims to lands in the district of Vincennes," reported it without amendment; and the bill was considered as in Committee of the Whole, and amended; and the President reported it to the House accordingly.

On the question. shall the amendment be engrossed and the bill read a third time as amended? it was determined in the affirmative.

Mr. LACOCK, presented the memorial of William Gamble, stating that he had been appointed, on the 15th of February, 1806, inspector of the customs in the district of Niagara, and had performed the duties confided to him, for which he had not received adequate compensation, as is stated in the memorial; and praying relief; and the memorial was read.

FRIDAY, December 23.

A message from the House of Representatives informed the Senate that the House insist on their amendments, disagreed to by the Senate, to the bill, entitled "An act to authorize the President of the United States to call upon the several States and Territories thereof for their respective quotas of eighty thousand four hundred and thirty militia, for the defence of the frontiers of the United States against invasion." They ask a conference on the disagreeing votes of the two

Houses, and have appointed managers on their part. They have passed a bill, entitled "An act to provide additional revenues for defraying the expenses of Government, and maintaining the public credit, by laying a direct tax upon the United States, and to provide for assessing and collecting the same;" in which bill they request the concurrence of the Senate.

The bill last mentioned was read, and passed to the second reading.

On motion, by Mr. BROWN,

Resolved, That the Senate insist on their disagreement to the amendments of the House of Representatives to the bill, entitled "An act to authorize the President of the United States to call upon the several States and Territories thereof for their respective quotas of eighty thousand four hundred and thirty militia, for the defence of the frontiers of the United States against invasion;" and agree to the conference proposed thereon.

Ordered, That Messrs. BIBB, BROWN, and GERMAN, be the managers on the part of the Senate.

The amendment to the bill entitled "An act giving further time to locate certain claims to lands confirmed by an act of Congress, entitled 'An act confirming certain claims to lands in the district of Vincennes,'" was read a third time as amended, and further amended by unanimous consent.

Resolved, That this bill pass with amendments.

The Senate resumed the consideration of the motion made the 21st instant, by Mr. HUNTER, relative to vessels of war on Lake Ontario.

On motion by Mr. ROBERTS. that the further consideration thereof be postponed to the second Monday in March, it was determined in the affirmative—yeas 15, nays 12, as follows:

YEAS—Messrs. Bibb, Bledsoe, Chace, Condit, Gaillard, German, Lacock, Morrow, Roberts, Robinson, Taylor, Turner, Varnum, Walker, and Wharton.

NAYS—Messrs. Brown Daggett, Dana, Fromentin, Gore, Hunter, King, Lambert, Mason, Smith, Tait, and Thompson.

Mr. TAYLOR, from the committee to whom was referred the bill, entitled "An act to provide additional revenues for defraying the expenses of Government, and maintaining the public credit, by laying duties on various goods, wares, and merchandise, manufactured within the United States," reported it with amendments.

On motion, by Mr. LACOCK, the memorial of William Gamble, presented the 22d instant, was referred to a select committee, to consider and report thereon by bill or otherwise; and Messrs. LACOCK, CHACE, and GERMAN, were appointed the committee.

Mr. BIBB, from the committee, appointed the 3d instant, to consider the subject, reported a bill to provide for leasing certain lands reserved for the use of schools in the Mississippi Territory; and the bill was read, and passed to the second reading.

SATURDAY. December 24.

The bill, entitled "An act to provide additional revenues for defraying the expenses of Government, and maintaining the public credit, by laying a direct tax upon the United States, and to provide for assessing and collecting the same," was read the second time, and referred to the committee to whom was referred, the 1st instant, the bill, entitled "An act to provide additional revenues for defraying the expenses of Government, and maintaining the public credit, by laying duties on spirits distilled within the United States and Territories thereof, and by amending the act laying duties on licenses to distillers of spirituous liquors," to consider and report thereon.

The bill to provide for leasing certain lands reserved for the support of schools in the Mississippi Territory was read the second time, and considered as in Committee of the Whole; and on motion, by Mr. SMITH, the further consideration thereof was postponed to Monday next.

Mr. BIBB, from the managers apointed on the part of the Senate, to confer with those appointed by the House of Representatives, on the disagreeing votes of the two Houses on the bill " to authorize the President of the United States to call upon the several States and Territories thereof for their respective quotas of eighty thousand four hundred and thirty militia, for the defence of the frontiers of the United States against invasion," reported :

" That a conference has been had, and the managers have agreed to recommend to their respective Houses—

" 1. That, in lieu of the amendment proposed by the House of Representatives, to strike out the words ' two years,' and to insert ' one year,' in the 4th line of the first section, the words ' eighteen months' be inserted ; and that the same modification be made where the words ' two years' occur in other parts of the bill.

" 2. That the House of Representatives recede from their amendment proposed to be inserted at the end of the 4th line of the first section, after the word ' discharged."

" 3. That the Senate recede from their disagreement to the amendment which proposes to strike out the 7th section.

" 4. That the House of Representatives agree to the modifications proposed by the Senate to their amendments in the ninth section."

MONDAY, December 26.

Mr. DAGGETT presented several petitions, signed by a great number of the inhabitants of the State of Connecticut, remonstrating against the transportation and opening of the mail on the Sabbath; and the petitions were read, and referred to a select committee, to consider and report thereon by bill or otherwise; and Messrs. DAGGETT, SMITH, and MORROW, were appointed the committee.

Mr. THOMPSON presented several petitions, signed by a great number of the inhabitants of the State of New Hampshire, on the same subject; which were read; and referred to the committee last mentioned, to consider and report thereon by bill or otherwise.

Mr. KING presented the memorial of William Bryar and others, manufacturers of tobacco in the city of New York, praying that a specific duty may be laid, instead of an ad valorem, on manufactured tobacco, as proposed by the bill, entitled "An act to provide additional revenues for defraying the expenses of Government, and maintaining the public credit, by laying duties on various goods, wares, and merchandise, manufactured within the United States," for reasons stated at large in the memorial; which was read.

The Senate resumed, as in Committee of the Whole, the consideration of the bill to provide for leasing certain lands reserved for the use of schools in the Mississippi Territory; and the bill having been amended, the President reported it to the House accordingly; and on motion, by Mr. BIBB, the further consideration thereof was postponed until to-morrow.

The Senate resumed, as in Committee of the Whole, the consideration of the bill, entitled "An act to provide additional revenues, for defraying the expenses of Government, and maintaining the public credit, by laying duties on various goods, wares, and merchandise, manufactured within the United States," together with the amendments reported thereto by the select committee; and the amendments having been agreed to, the President reported the bill to the House accordingly, and it was further amended; and, on motion, by Mr. GERMAN, to strike out, of section 1, lines 12 and 13, the words, "made wholly or in part by machinery:" on motion, by Mr SMITH, the further consideration thereof was postponed until to-morrow.

The PRESIDENT communicated a representation of the commissioners appointed by the act " providing for the indemnification of certain claimants of public lands in the Mississippi Territory," stating their inability, without neglecting their official duties, to perform the duties therein enjoined; and the representation was read, and referred to a select committee, to consider and report thereon by bill or otherwise; and Messrs. TAYLOR, HUNTER, and GORE, were appointed the committee.

TUESDAY, December 27.

The Senate resumed the consideration of the bill to provide for leasing certain lands reserved for the support of schools in the Mississippi Territory; and the bill was further amended. On the question, Shall this bill be engrossed and read a third time as amended? it was determined in the affirmative.

The Senate resumed the consideration of the bill, entitled "An act to provide additional revenues for defraying the expenses of Government, and maintaining the public credit, by laying duties on various goods, wares, and merchandise, manufactured within the United States," together with the amendment proposed thereto by Mr. GERMAN; and the amendment was agreed to, and the bill further amended; and, on motion, by Mr. SMITH, to add a new section to the bill, as follows:

"*And be it further enacted,* That the duties hereby laid shall and may be drawn back upon all articles on which duty is laid by the first section of this act after the ninety days, which shall be exported from the United States: *Provided,* That no drawback shall be allowed on any exportation as aforesaid, in any instance where the same shall amount to less than twelve dollars:"

It was determined in the negative—yeas 13, nays 15, as follows:

YEAS—Messrs. Dana, Fromentin, German, Gore, Horsey, Hunter, King, Lambert, Mason, Smith, Thompson, Walker, and Wells.

NAYS—Messrs. Bibb, Bledsoe, Chase Condit, Daggett, Gaillard, Lacock. Morrow, Roberts, Robinson, Tait, Taylor, Turner, Varnum, and Wharton.

On the question, Shall the amendments be engrossed and the bill read a third time as amended? it was determined in the affirmative.

Mr. TAYLOR, from the committee to whom was referred the bill, entitled "An act to provide additional revenues for defraying the expenses of Government, and maintaining the public credit, by laying duties on household furniture, on horses kept exclusively for the saddle or carriage, and on gold and silver watches," reported it with amendments.

Mr. KING submitted the following motion for consideration:

Resolved, That the President of the United States be and is hereby requested, pursuant to the act, entitled "An act further to amend the several acts for the establishment and regulation of the Treasury, War, and Navy Departments," to cause to be laid before the Senate a statement of the contingent expenses of the Navy Department; and also, a statement of all purchases and contracts for supplies or services, made by or under the authority of the Navy Department, in the respective years 1812, 1813, and 1814, specifying the names of persons from whom purchases or with whom contracts have been made, the places of delivery, the prices, the amount of money advanced or paid, and the quantity of articles supplied.

Mr. DAGGETT submitted the following motion, which was read and passed to the second reading:

Resolved, That a committee of three members be appointed, who, jointly with such committee as may be appointed by the House of Representatives, shall be a committee to inquire into the expenses of stationery, printing, and binding, under the authority of both Houses of Congress, and into the expediency of establishing permanent rules for regulating and conducting the printing and binding, and for the supply of stationery, of the Senate and House of Representatives, and to report thereupon.

WEDNESDAY, December 28.

Mr. TAYLOR, from the committee to whom was referred the bill, entitled "An act to provide additional revenues for defraying the expenses of Government, and maintaining the public credit, by laying a direct tax upon the United States, and to provide for assessing and collecting the same," reported it without amendment.

Mr. HUNTER, from the Committee on Naval Affairs, reported a bill authorizing the President of the United States to cause to be built, equipped, and employed, one or more floating batteries, for the defence of the waters of the United States;

and the bill was read, and passed to the second reading.

The Senate resumed the motion made the 27th instant, by Mr. KING, for statements of the contingent expenses, purchases, and contracts, for the Navy Department.

On motion, by Mr. KING, it was agreed to take the question by yeas and nays; and on motion, by Mr. ROBERTS, the further consideration thereof was postponed until to-morrow.

The resolution for the appointment of a joint committee to inquire into the expenses of the printing, &c., of Congress, and into the expediency of establishing permanent rules for regulating the same, was read a second time, and considered as in Committee of the Whole; and the resolution ordered to be engrossed and read a third time.

REVENUE BILL.

The Senate resumed, as in Committee of the Whole, the consideration of the bill entitled "An act to provide additional revenues for defraying the expenses of Government and maintaining the public credit, by laying duties on household furniture, on horses kept exclusively for the saddle or carriage, and on gold and silver watches," together with the amendments reported thereto by the select committee.

On motion, by Mr. TAYLOR, to agree to the first amendment reported by the select committee, as follows:

After the word "scale," section 1, line 8, strike out to the word "dollars," in the 26th line, and in lieu thereof, insert the following:

"If above one hundred dollars and not exceeding five hundred dollars, thirty cents on every hundred dollars of the whole value.

"If above one hundred and not exceeding one thousand dollars, thirty-five cents on every hundred dollars of the whole value.

"If above one thousand and not exceeding fifteen hundred dollars, forty cents upon every hundred dollars of the whole value.

"If above fifteen hundred and not exceeding two thousand dollars, forty-five cents upon every hundred dollars of the whole value.

"If above two thousand and not exceeding three thousand dollars, fifty cents on every hundred dollars of the whole value.

"If above three thousand and not exceeding four thousand dollars, sixty cents on every hundred dollars of the whole value.

"If above four thousand and not exceeding five thousand dollars, seventy cents on every hundred dollars of the whole value.

"If above five thousand and not exceeding six thousand dollars, eighty cents on every hundred dollars of the whole value.

"If above six thousand and not exceeding seven thousand dollars, ninety-cents on every hundred dollars of the whole value.

"If above seven thousand and not exceeding eight thousand dollars, one hundred cents on every hundred dollars of the whole value.

"If above eight thousand and not exceeding nine thousand dollars, one hundred and ten cents on every hundred dollars of the whole value.

"If above nine thousand and not exceeding ten thousand dollars, one hundred and twenty cents on every hundred dollars of the whole value.

"If above ten thousand dollars, one hundred and thirty cents on every hundred dollars of the whole value."

A division of the question was called for by Mr. VARNUM, and it was taken on striking out, and determined in the affirmative—yeas 22, nays 3, as follows:

YEAS—Messrs. Bibb, Bledsoe, Chace, Daggett, Fromentin, Gaillard, Gore, Horsey, Hunter, King, Lambert, Mason, Morrow, Roberts, Robinson, Smith, Tait, Taylor, Thompson, Turner, Walker, and Wells.

NAYS—Messrs. Condit, Varnum, and Wharton.

The question recurring on inserting the proposed amendment, it was determined in the affirmative—yeas 20, nays 4, as follows:

YEAS—Messrs. Bibb, Bledsoe, Chace, Daggett, Fromentin, Gaillard, Horsey, Hunter, King, Lambert, Mason, Morrow, Roberts, Robinson, Smith, Tait, Taylor, Thompson, Turner, and Walker.

NAYS—Messrs. Condit, Varnum, Wells, and Wharton.

The second amendment reported by the committee was agreed to.

On motion, by Mr. SMITH, to strike out, section 1, lines 28 to 37, inclusive, the following:

"That there shall be, and hereby is, likewise imposed an annual duty of one dollar on every horse chiefly used for the saddle; and of one dollar and fifty cents on every horse chiefly used for any carriage liable to duty under the act, entitled 'An act to provide additional revenues for defraying the expenses of the Government, and maintaining the public credit, by duties on carriages and the harness used therefor;' and one dollar and fifty cents for every horse so kept both for the saddle and carriage; which duty shall be paid by the owner of such horse."

It was determined in the negative—yeas 11, nays 17, as follows:

YEAS—Messrs. Daggett, Dana, Fromentin, Horsey, Hunter, King, Lambert, Mason, Smith, Turner, and Wells.

NAYS—Messrs. Bibb, Bledsoe, Brown, Chace, Condit, Gaillard, German, Lacock, Morrow, Roberts, Robinson, Tait, Taylor, Thompson, Varnum, Walker, and Wharton.

And the bill having been further amended, the President reported it to the House accordingly.

On the question to agree to the amendment made in Committee of the Whole, to strike out, of section 1, line 7, the word "two," and to insert, in lieu thereof, "one;" it was determined in the negative—yeas 10, nays 19, as follows:

YEAS—Messrs. Brown, Chace, Daggett, Fromentin, Hunter, King, Mason, Morrow, Smith, and Taylor.

NAYS—Messrs. Bibb, Bledsoe, Condit, Dana, Gaillard, German, Gore, Horsey, Lacock, Lambert, Roberts, Robinson, Tait, Thompson, Turner, Varnum, Walker, Wells, and Wharton.

On motion, by Mr. TAYLOR, further to amend the bill, by striking out the word "one," in the third line of the first amendment reported by the select committee, and in lieu thereof, insert "two?" it was determined in the affirmative; and, on motion, by Mr. LACOCK, the further consideration thereof was postponed until to-morrow.

A message from the House of Representatives informed the Senate that the House disagree to the first and second recommendations of the committee of conference, on the disagreeing votes of the two Houses, on the bill, entitled "An act to authorize the President of the United States to call upon the several States and Territories thereof for their respective quotas of eighty thousand four hundred and thirty militia, for the defence of the frontiers of the United States against invasion," and they agree to the fourth recommendation of the said committee. They insist on their said disagreement, and ask further conference upon the subject-matter of the amendments depending to the bill aforesaid, and have appointed managers on their part.

On motion, by Mr. BIBB, the Senate proceeded to consider the report of the committee of conference on their part, made the 24th instant, on the disagreeing votes of the two Houses on the bill last mentioned.

On motion, by Mr. KING, that the said bill, together with the report of the conferees, be postponed to the second Monday in March next, it was determined in the affirmative—yeas 14, nays 13, as follows:

YEAS—Messrs. Chace, Daggett, Dana, Fromentin, Gore, Horsey, Hunter, King, Lambert, Mason, Robinson, Thompson, Varnum, and Wells.

NAYS—Messrs. Bibb, Bledsoe, Condit, Gaillard, Lacock, Morrow, Roberts, Smith, Tait, Taylor, Turner, Walker, and Wharton.

THURSDAY, December 29.

Mr. VARNUM submitted the following motion for consideration:

Resolved, That the committee to whom was referred so much of the Message of the President of the United States, of the 20th day of September last, as relates to the Military Establishment, be instructed to report a bill authorizing and requesting the President of the United States to call upon the proper authority of each State and Territory to furnish, according to the provisions of, and for purposes prescribed by, the Constitution of the United States, their respective proportions of —— thousand militia, officers included, armed and equipped, according to law, to serve for nine months, after they shall arrive at their respective places of rendezvous, unless sooner discharged; to be organized into companies, regiments, brigades, and divisions, by proper authority in each State and Territory, agreeable to the principles of law, which provide for the organization of the militia of the United States, and holden in readiness to take the field by the first day of April next; the apportionment among the States and Territories to be made in the bill, in conformity with the provision of the Constitution for apportioning direct taxes.

The engrossed bill, to provide for leasing certain lands reserved for the support of schools in the Mississippi Territory, was read a third time, and passed.

The amendments to the bill, entitled "An act to provide additional revenues for defraying the expenses of Government, and maintaining the public credit, by laying duties on various goods, wares, and merchandise, manufactured within the United States," was read a third time as amended.

On the question, Shall this bill pass as amended? it was determined in the affirmative—yeas 22, nays 7, as follows:

YEAS—Messrs. Anderson, Bibb, Bledsoe, Brown, Chace, Condit, Daggett, Fromentin, Gaillard, Hunter, King, Lacock, Morrow, Roberts, Robinson, Smith, Tait, Taylor, Turner, Varnum, Walker, and Wharton.

NAYS—Messrs. Dana, German, Horsey, Lambert, Mason, Thompson, and Wells.

So it was *Resolved,* That this bill pass with amendments.

The bill authorizing the President of the United States to cause to be built, equipped, and employed, one or more floating batteries, for the defence of the waters of the United States, was read the second time.

The resolution for the appointment of a joint committee, to inquire into the expenses of printing, &c., of Congress, and into the expediency of establishing permanent rules for regulating the same, was read a third time and passed.

Ordered, That Messrs. DAGGETT, FROMENTIN, and MORROW, be the committee on the part of the Senate.

Mr. TAYLOR, from the committee to whom the subject was referred on the 26th instant, reported a bill supplementary to the act, entitled "An act providing for the indemnification of certain claimants of public lands in the Mississippi Territory;" and the bill was read and passed to the second reading.

REVENUE BILL.

The Senate resumed the consideration of the bill, entitled "An act to provide additional revenues for defraying the expenses of Government, and maintaining the public credit, by laying duties on household furniture, on horses kept exclusively for the saddle or carriage, and on gold and silver watches."

On motion, by Mr. DAGGETT, to strike out, section 1, line 2, after the word "assembled," the following:

"That there shall be, and hereby is, imposed an annual duty on all household furniture kept for use, the value of which in any one family, with the exception of beds, bedding, kitchen furniture, family pictures, and articles made in the family from domestic materials, shall exceed two hundred dollars in money, according to the following scale:

"If above two hundred dollars and not exceeding five hundred dollars, thirty cents on every hundred dollars of the whole value.

"If above five hundred and not exceeding one thousand dollars, thirty-five cents on every hundred dollars of the whole value.

"If above one thousand and not exceeding fifteen hundred dollars, forty cents on every hundred dollars of the whole value.

"If above fifteen hundred and not exceeding two

thousand dollars, forty-five cents on every hundred dollars of the whole value.

"If above two thousand and not exceeding three thousand dollars, fifty cents on every hundred dollars of the whole value.

"If above three thousand and not exceeding four thousand dollars, sixty cents on every hundred dollars of the whole value.

"If above four thousand and not exceeding five thousand dollars, seventy cents on every hundred dollars of the whole value.

"If above five thousand and not exceeding six thousand dollars, eighty cents on every hundred dollars of the whole value.

"If above six thousand and not exceeding seven thousand dollars, ninety cents on every hundred dollars of the whole value.

"If above seven thousand dollars, one hundred cents on every hundred dollars of the whole value; which duty shall be paid by the owner of the said household furniture."

It was determined in the negative—yeas 11, nays 18, as follows:

YEAS—Messrs. Daggett, Dana, German, Gore, Horsey, Hunter, King, Lambert, Mason, Smith, and Thompson.

NAYS—Messrs. Anderson, Bibb Bledsoe, Brown, Chace, Condit, Fromentin, Gaillard, Lacock, Morrow, Roberts, Robinson, Tait, Taylor, Turner, Varnum, Walker, and Wharton.

And the bill having been further amended, on the question, Shall the amendments be engrossed and read a third time as amended? it was determined in the affirmative.

FRIDAY, December 30.

JOSEPH KERR, appointed a Senator by the Legislature of Ohio, in place of Thomas Worthington, resigned, produced his credentials, was qualified and took his seat in the Senate.

Mr. ROBERTS presented the memorial of the representatives of the religious society of Friends in Pennsylvania, New Jersey, and Delaware, representing that they are conscientiously prohibited from partaking in the sanguinary struggles of war, and praying a solemn act of legislative consent to the rights of conscience; and the memorial was read, and referred to the committee on the militia of the United States, to consider and report thereon by bill or otherwise.

Mr. MORROW presented several petitions, signed by a great number of the inhabitants of the State of Ohio, remonstrating against the transportation and opening of the mail on the Sabbath; and the petitions were read, and referred to the committee to whom were referred, on the 26th instant, several petitions on the same subject, to consider and report thereon by bill or otherwise.

Mr. SMITH announced the death of the Honorable RICHARD BRENT, a Senator from the State of Virginia, who deceased this morning.

Whereupon, on motion, by Mr. SMITH,

Resolved, That a committee be appointed to take order for superintending the funeral of the Honorable RICHARD BRENT; and that the Senate will attend the same; and that notice of the event be given to the House of Representatives.

Ordered, That Messrs. SMITH, VARNUM, TURNER, GORE, and DAGGETT, be the committee.

On motion, by Mr. SMITH,

Resolved, unanimously, That the members of the Senate, from a sincere desire of showing every mark of respect due to the memory of the Honorable RICHARD BRENT, deceased, late a member thereof, will go into mourning for him one month, by the usual mode of wearing a crape round the left arm.

On motion, by Mr. SMITH,

Resolved, That the President of the Senate be requested to notify the Executive of the State of Virginia of the death of the Honorable RICHARD BRENT, late a Senator of the United States from that State.

On motion, by Mr. SMITH,

Resolved, That, as an additional mark of respect for the memory of the Honorable RICHARD BRENT the Senate now adjourn.

SATURDAY, December 31.

The number of Senators present not being sufficient to constitute a quorum, on motion, the Senate adjourned.

MONDAY, January 2, 1815.

Mr. LACOCK, from the committee to whom the subject was referred, reported a bill for the relief of William Gamble; and the bill was read, and passed to the second reading.

The bill supplementary to the act, entitled "An act providing for the indemnification of certain claimants of public lands in the Mississippi Territory," was read the second time.

The bill, entitled "An act to provide additional revenues for defraying the expenses of Government, and maintaining the public credit, by duties on household furniture, on horses kept exclusively for the saddle or carriage, and on gold and silver watches," was read a third time as amended.

On the question, Shall this bill pass as amended? it was determined in the affirmative—yeas 16, nays 9, as follows:

YEAS—Messrs. Anderson, Bibb, Brown, Chace, Condit, Gaillard, Kerr, Lacock, Morrow, Roberts, Robinson, Taylor, Turner, Varnum, Walker, and Wharton.

NAYS—Messrs. Daggett, Horsey, Hunter, King, Lambert, Mason, Smith, Thompson, and Wells.

So it was *Resolved,* That this bill pass with amendments.

On motion, by Mr. TAYLOR, the title was amended by striking out the words "on horses kept exclusively for the saddle or carriage."

The Senate resumed the consideration of the motion submitted the 28th ultimo, by Mr. VARNUM, which was amended and agreed to as follows:

Resolved, That the committee to whom was referred so much of the Message of the President of the United States, of the twentieth day of September last, as relates to the Military Establishment, be instructed to inquire into the expediency of authorizing and requesting the President of the United States to call upon the proper authority in each State and Territory to furnish, according to the provisions of, and for the purposes prescribed by, the Constitution of the United States, their respective proportions of eighty thousand militia, officers included, armed and equipped according to law, to serve for nine months, after they shall arrive at their respective places of rendezvous, unless sooner discharged; to be organized into companies, regiments, brigades, and divisions, by the proper authority in each State and Territory, agreeable to the principles of law which provide for the organization of the militia of the United States; and holden in readiness to take the field by the first day of April next: the apportionment among the States and Territories to be made in the bill, in conformity with the provisions of the Constitution, for apportioning direct taxes.

The Senate resumed the consideration of the motion for the choice of an Assistant Doorkeeper to the Senate; and, on motion, by Mr. Turner, the further consideration thereof was postponed to the first Monday in February.

Mr. Horsey submitted the following motion for consideration:

Resolved, That the Fiscal Committee be instructed to prepare and report a bill allowing drawbacks of the duties imposed on goods, wares, and merchandise, manufactured within the United States, and which shall be exported from the United States to any foreign port or place.

The Senate resumed, as in Committee of the Whole, the consideration of the bill, entitled "An act to provide additional revenues for defraying the expenses of Government, and maintaining the public credit, by laying a direct tax upon the United States, and to provide for assessing and collecting the same."

On motion, by Mr. Turner, to strike out, section 1, line 3, "six millions," and to insert, in lieu thereof, "four millions five hundred thousand:" it was determined in the negative—yeas 7, nays 20, as follows:

Yeas—Messrs. Anderson, Bibb, Condit, Lambert, Smith, Turner, and Wharton.

Nays—Messrs. Bledsoe, Brown, Chace, Daggett, Fromentin, Gaillard, German, Horsey, Hunter, Kerr, King, Lacock, Mason, Morrow, Roberts, Tait, Taylor, Thompson, Varnum, and Walker.

On motion, by Mr. Brown, the further consideration thereof was postponed until to-morrow.

The following Message was received from the President of the United States:

To the Senate and House of
Representatives of the United States:

I lay before Congress a report of the Secretary of the Treasury, containing a statement of proceedings under the "Act to regulate the laying out and making a road from Cumberland, in the State of Maryland, to the State of Ohio."

JAMES MADISON.

January 2, 1815.

The Message and report therein referred to were read, and ordered to be printed for the use of the Senate.

Mr. Brown, from the committee to whom was referred the bill, entitled "An act to authorize the President of the United States to accept the services of volunteers, who may associate and organize themselves, and offer their services to the Government of the United States," reported it with amendments.

The Senate resumed, as in Committee of the Whole, the consideration of the bill authorizing the President of the United States to cause to be built, equipped, and employed, one or more floating batteries, for the defence of the waters of the United States; and the bill having been amended, the President reported it to the House accordingly.

On motion, by Mr. Daggett, the further consideration thereof was postponed until to-morrow.

Tuesday, January 3.

The bill for the relief of William Gamble was read the second time.

The Senate resumed the motion made the 2d instant, by Mr. Horsey, which was amended and agreed to, as follows:

Resolved, That a committee be appointed to prepare and report a bill allowing drawbacks of the duties imposed on goods, wares, and merchandise, manufactured within the United States, and which shall be exported from the United States to any foreign port or place.

Ordered, That Messrs. Horsey, Smith, and Dana, be the committee.

The Senate resumed the consideration of the resolution reported, on the 28th November, by the Committee on Naval Affairs, relative to the inexpediency of conferring naval rank by brevet.

On motion, by Mr. Tait, the further consideration thereof was postponed to the second Monday in March next.

The Senate resumed the consideration of the bill, entitled "An act to provide additional revenues for defraying the expenses of Government, and maintaining the public credit, by laying a direct tax upon the United States, and to provide for assessing and collecting the same."

On motion, by Mr. Mason, to amend the twenty-seventh section, by striking out the following:

"But in all cases where the property liable to a direct tax under this act, or the said act of Congress, entitled "An act to lay and collect a direct tax within the United States," shall not be divisible, so as to enable the collector, by a sale of a part thereof, to raise the whole amount of the tax, with all costs, charges, and commissions, the whole of such property shall be sold, the collector having first obtained the approbation, in writing, of the principal assessor for the district therefor; and the surplus of the proceeds of the sale, after satisfying the tax, costs, charges, and commissions, shall be paid to the owner of the property or his legal representatives, or if he or they cannot be found, or refuse to receive the same, then such surplus shall be deposited in the Treasury of the United States, to be there held for the use of the owner, or his legal representatives, until he or they shall make application therefor to the Secretary of the Treasury, who, upon such application, shall, by warrant on the Treasurer, cause the same to be paid to the applicant."

It was determined in the affirmative—yeas 13, nays 10, as follows:

YEAS—Messrs. Bledsoe, Dana, Gore, Horsey, Hunter, King, Lambert, Mason, Smith, Thompson, Varnum, Walker, and Wells.

NAYS—Messrs. Bibb, Daggett, Gaillard, German, Kerr, Lacock, Morrow, Roberts, Tait, and Taylor.

Further amendment having been proposed by Mr. BLEDSOE, on motion, the further consideration of the bill was postponed until to-morrow.

The Senate resumed, as in Committee of the Whole, the consideration of the bill supplementary to the act, entitled "An act providing for the indemnification of certain claimants of public lands in the Mississippi Territory; and on motion, by Mr. HUNTER, it was referred to a select committee, to consider and report thereon; and Messrs. GORE, HUNTER, and TAYLOR, were appointed the committee.

WEDNESDAY, January 4.

The Senate resumed the consideration of the bill authorizing the President of the United States to cause to be built, equipped, and employed, one or more floating batteries, for the defence of the waters of the United States; and, on motion, by Mr. SMITH, the further consideration thereof was postponed to Saturday next.

Mr. GORE, from the committee to whom was referred the bill supplementary to the act, entitled "An act providing for the indemnification of certain claimants of public lands in the Mississippi Territory," reported it with amendments.

A message from the House of Representatives informed the Senate that the House agree to some and disagree to other amendments of the Senate to the bill, entitled "An act to provide additional revenues for defraying the expenses of Government, and maintaining the public credit, by laying duties on various goods, wares, and merchandise, manufactured within the United States."

They disagree to all the amendments of the Senate to the bill, entitled "An act to provide additional revenues for defraying the expenses of Government, and maintaining the public credit, by laying duties on household furniture, on horses kept exclusively for the saddle or carriage, and on gold and silver watches."

The Senate resumed, as in Committee of the Whole, the consideration of the bill, entitled "An act to provide additional revenues for defraying the expenses of Government, and maintaining the public credit, by laying a direct tax upon the United States, and to provide for assessing and collecting the same," and Mr. BLEDSOE withdrew his motion to amend the bill; and the PRESIDENT reported it to the House amended.

On the question, to agree to the amendments made in Committee of the Whole, it was determined in the negative.

On motion, by Mr. ROBERTS, that the further consideration of the bill be postponed to Monday next, it was determined in the negative—yeas 8, nays 21, as follows:

YEAS—Messrs. Anderson, Chace, Condit, Hunter, Lambert, Roberts, Varnum, and Wells.

NAYS—Messrs. Bibb, Bledsoe, Brown, Daggett, Dana, Fromentin, Gaillard, German, Gore, Kerr, King, Lacock, Mason, Morrow, Smith, Tait, Taylor, Thompson, Turner, Walker, and Wharton.

On motion, by Mr. ANDERSON, to add a new section to the bill, as follows:

SEC. 4. *And be it further enacted,* That the same kind of money, bank notes, or other paper, which the United States shall have paid, or may at any time hereafter pay, to the militia of the respective States, for military services rendered to the United States, shall be receivable in the payment of the direct and other taxes, which have been, or shall hereafter be, authorized by Congress."

It was determined in the negative.

On the question, Shall this bill be read a third time? it was determined in the affirmative.

The Senate proceeded to consider the amendments disagreed to by the House of Representatives to the bill, entitled "An act to provide additional revenues for defraying the expenses of Government, and maintaining the public credit, by laying duties on various goods, wares, and merchandise, manufactured within the United States." Whereupon,

Resolved, That they recede from their amendments disagreed to by the House of Representatives, except so much of the fifth amendment, as follows: "umbrellas and parasols, if above the value of two dollars, eight per centum ad valorem;" and that they do insist on said amendment.

The Senate proceeded to consider the amendments disagreed to by the House of Representatives to the bill, entitled "An act to provide additional revenues for defraying the expenses of Government, and maintaining the public credit, by laying duties on household furniture, on horses kept exclusively for the saddle or carriage, and on gold and silver watches."

Whereupon, on motion by Mr. TAYLOR,

Resolved, That the Senate insist on their amendment disagreed to by the House of Representatives.

The Senate resumed, as in Committee of the Whole, the consideration of the bill, entitled "An act to authorize the President of the United States to accept the services of volunteers who may associate and organize themselves, and offer their services to the Government of the United States, together with the amendments reported thereto by the select committee; and Mr. BROWN submitted a new section to be added as an amendment to the bill.

On motion, it was agreed that the further consideration thereof be postponed.

The Senate resumed as in Committee of the Whole, the consideration of the bill for the relief of William Gamble; and no amendment having been proposed, on the question, Shall this bill be engrossed and read a third time? it was determined in the affirmative.

THURSDAY January 5.

On motion, by Mr. MORROW,

Resolved, That the committee appointed on the memorial of the Legislature of the Indiana Territory, be instructed to inquire into the expediency of allowing further time for completing the surveys, and obtaining the patents on locations heretofore made under land warrants issued by virtue of resolutions of the Legislature of Virginia, passed prior to the cession of the Northwestern Territory to the United States, as a bounty for military services in the Continental line; and that the committee report by bill or otherwise.

A message from the House of Representatives informed the Senate that the House insist on their disagreement to the amendment of the Senate to the bill, entitled "An act to provide additional revenues for defraying the expenses of Government, and maintaining the public credit, by laying duties on various goods, wares, and merchandise, manufactured within the United States." They also insist on their disagreement to the amendments of the Senate to the bill, entitled "An act to provide additional revenues for defraying the expenses of Government, and maintaining the public credit, by laying duties on household furniture, on horses kept exclusively for the saddle or carriage, and on gold and silver watches." They ask a conference on the disagreeing votes of the two Houses on the bill last mentioned, and have appointed managers on their part.

On motion, by Mr. TAYLOR, the Senate agreed to the conference proposed by the House of Representatives on the bill last mentioned, and Messrs. TAYLOR, BLEDSOE, and DAGGETT, were appointed the managers at the same, on their part.

On motion by Mr. BIBB,

Resolved, That the Senate ask a conference on the disagreeing votes of the two Houses on the amendment to the bill, entitled "An act to provide additional revenues for defraying the expenses of Government, and maintaining the public credit, by laying duties on various goods, wares, and merchandise, manufactured within the United States."

Ordered, That Messrs. TAYLOR, BLEDSOE, and DAGGETT, be the managers at the same, on their part.

The bill for the relief of William Gamble was read a third time, and passed.

The Senate resumed, as in Committee of the Whole, the consideration of the bill supplementary to the act, entitled "An act providing for the indemnification of certain claimants of public lands in the Mississippi Territory," together with the amendments reported thereto by the select committee; and the amendments having been agreed to, the President reported the bill to the House accordingly, and it was further amended, and the bill ordered to be engrossed and read a third time as amended.

Mr. VARNUM, from the committee to whom was referred the bill, entitled "An act to provide for the widows and orphans of militia and volunteer soldiers who shall die or be killed in the service of the United States," reported it without amendment.

The Senate resumed, as in Committee of the Whole, the bill, entitled "An act to authorize the President of the United States to accept the services of volunteers who may associate and organize themselves, and offer their services to the Government of the United States;" and Mr. MASON submitted an amendment to the bill. On motion, it was agreed that the further consideration thereof be postponed.

Mr. BLEDSOE submitted the following motion for consideration:

Resolved, That the committee on so much of the Message of the President of the United States as relates to our naval affairs, be instructed to inquire into the expediency of establishing a naval school.

DIRECT TAXES.

The bill entitled "An act to provide additional revenue for defraying the expenses of Government, and maintaining the public credit, by laying a direct tax upon the United States, and to provide for assessing and collecting the same," was read a third time.

Mr. GORE, of Massachusetts, addressed the Chair as follows—

Mr. President: This bill imposes burdens extremely heavy on all the citizens of our common country, and on those with which I am most acquainted, a load, that, under existing circumstances, will be intolerable.

With the principle of the bill, in selecting as objects of taxation the lands and buildings of the United States, I have no fault to find.

I consider them as fit and proper subjects of revenue, and such assessments calculated to equalize the burdens of the country, as imposing them on all parts, and with more impartiality than can be attained by any other mode.

And, sir, I should feel it my duty to vote for a bill, imposing such a tax, to any reasonable amount, had it not pleased the Government of the nation to place the State, which I have the honor to represent, out of the protection of the United States, and to determine, that while it shall bear a full proportion of the taxes, none of their fruits shall redound to her relief.

The motives of Congress, in granting supplies, are doubtless to provide for the defence of the country and the security of its rights, by a safe and honorable peace.

These motives are wise and irresistible; all concur in the necessity of defending our territory against the enemy; and in the assertion and maintenance of our essential rights, at every peril, and if necessary, by the sacrifice of all that conduces to private ease and personal enjoyment.

No one feels this truth more sensibly than myself—no one considers the duty more imperative. With its obligations I have no compromise to make, and in its performance I ask for no limitations, on account of the folly and improvidence with which the war was waged, nor of the de-

representatives, until he or they shall make application therefor to the Secretary of the Treasury, who, upon such application, shall, by warrant on the Treasurer, cause the same to be paid to the applicant."

It was determined in the affirmative—yeas 13, nays 10, as follows:

YEAS—Messrs. Bledsoe, Dana, Gore, Horsey, Hunter, King, Lambert, Mason, Smith, Thompson, Varnum, Walker, and Wells.

NAYS—Messrs. Bibb, Daggett, Gaillard, German, Kerr, Lacock, Morrow, Roberts, Tait, and Taylor.

Further amendment having been proposed by Mr. BLEDSOE, on motion, the further consideration of the bill was postponed until to-morrow.

The Senate resumed, as in Committee of the Whole, the consideration of the bill supplementary to the act, entitled "An act providing for the indemnification of certain claimants of public lands in the Mississippi Territory; and on motion, by Mr. HUNTER, it was referred to a select committee, to consider and report thereon; and Messrs. GORE, HUNTER, and TAYLOR, were appointed the committee.

WEDNESDAY, January 4.

The Senate resumed the consideration of the bill authorizing the President of the United States to cause to be built, equipped, and employed, one or more floating batteries, for the defence of the waters of the United States; and, on motion, by Mr. SMITH, the further consideration thereof was postponed to Saturday next.

Mr. GORE, from the committee to whom was referred the bill supplementary to the act, entitled "An act providing for the indemnification of certain claimants of public lands in the Mississippi Territory," reported it with amendments.

A message from the House of Representatives informed the Senate that the House agree to some and disagree to other amendments of the Senate to the bill, entitled "An act to provide additional revenues for defraying the expenses of Government, and maintaining the public credit, by laying duties on various goods, wares, and merchandise, manufactured within the United States."

They disagree to all the amendments of the Senate to the bill, entitled "An act to provide additional revenues for defraying the expenses of Government, and maintaining the public credit, by laying duties on household furniture, on horses kept exclusively for the saddle or carriage, and on gold and silver watches."

The Senate resumed, as in Committee of the Whole, the consideration of the bill, entitled "An act to provide additional revenues for defraying the expenses of Government, and maintaining the public credit, by laying a direct tax upon the United States, and to provide for assessing and collecting the same," and Mr. BLEDSOE withdrew his motion to amend the bill; and the PRESIDENT reported it to the House amended.

On the question, to agree to the amendments made in Committee of the Whole, it was determined in the negative.

On motion, by Mr. ROBERTS, that the further consideration of the bill be postponed to Monday next, it was determined in the negative—yeas 8, nays 21, as follows:

YEAS—Messrs. Anderson, Chace, Condit, Hunter, Lambert, Roberts, Varnum, and Wells.

NAYS — Messrs. Bibb, Bledsoe, Brown, Daggett, Dana, Fromentin, Gaillard, German, Gore, Kerr, King, Lacock, Mason, Morrow, Smith, Tait, Taylor, Thompson, Turner, Walker, and Wharton.

On motion, by Mr. ANDERSON, to add a new section to the bill, as follows:

SEC. 4. *And be it further enacted,* That the same kind of money, bank notes, or other paper, which the United States shall have paid, or may at any time hereafter pay, to the militia of the respective States, for military services rendered to the United States, shall be receivable in the payment of the direct and other taxes, which have been, or shall hereafter be, authorized by Congress."

It was determined in the negative.

On the question, Shall this bill be read a third time? it was determined in the affirmative.

The Senate proceeded to consider the amendments disagreed to by the House of Representatives to the bill, entitled "An act to provide additional revenues for defraying the expenses of Government, and maintaining the public credit, by laying duties on various goods, wares, and merchandise, manufactured within the United States." Whereupon,

Resolved, That they recede from their amendments disagreed to by the House of Representatives, except so much of the fifth amendment, as follows: " umbrellas and parasols, if above the value of two dollars, eight per centum ad valorem;" and that they do insist on said amendment.

The Senate proceeded to consider the amendments disagreed to by the House of Representatives to the bill, entitled "An act to provide additional revenues for defraying the expenses of Government, and maintaining the public credit, by laying duties on household furniture, on horses kept exclusively for the saddle or carriage, and on gold and silver watches."

Whereupon, on motion by Mr. TAYLOR, *Resolved,* That the Senate insist on their amendment disagreed to by the House of Representatives.

The Senate resumed, as in Committee of the Whole, the consideration of the bill, entitled "An act to authorize the President of the United States to accept the services of volunteers who may associate and organize themselves, and offer their services to the Government of the United States, together with the amendments reported thereto by the select committee; and Mr. BROWN submitted a new section to be added as an amendment to the bill.

On motion, it was agreed that the further consideration thereof be postponed.

The Senate resumed as in Committee of the Whole, the consideration of the bill for the relief of William Gamble; and no amendment having been proposed, on the question, Shall this bill be engrossed and read a third time? it was determined in the affirmative.

Thursday January 5.

On motion, by Mr. Morrow,

Resolved, That the committee appointed on the memorial of the Legislature of the Indiana Territory, be instructed to inquire into the expediency of allowing further time for completing the surveys, and obtaining the patents on locations heretofore made under land warrants issued by virtue of resolutions of the Legislature of Virginia, passed prior to the cession of the Northwestern Territory to the United States, as a bounty for military services in the Continental line; and that the committee report by bill or otherwise.

A message from the House of Representatives informed the Senate that the House insist on their disagreement to the amendment of the Senate to the bill, entitled "An act to provide additional revenues for defraying the expenses of Government, and maintaining the public credit, by laying duties on various goods, wares, and merchandise, manufactured within the United States." They also insist on their disagreement to the amendments of the Senate to the bill, entitled "An act to provide additional revenues for defraying the expenses of Government, and maintaining the public credit, by laying duties on household furniture, on horses kept exclusively for the saddle or carriage, and on gold and silver watches." They ask a conference on the disagreeing votes of the two Houses on the bill last mentioned, and have appointed managers on their part.

On motion, by Mr. Taylor, the Senate agreed to the conference proposed by the House of Representatives on the bill last mentioned, and Messrs. Taylor, Bledsoe, and Daggett, were appointed the managers at the same, on their part.

On motion by Mr. Bibb,

Resolved, That the Senate ask a conference on the disagreeing votes of the two Houses, on the amendment to the bill, entitled "An act to provide additional revenues for defraying the expenses of Government, and maintaining the public credit, by laying duties on various goods, wares, and merchandise, manufactured within the United States."

Ordered, That Messrs. Taylor, Bledsoe, and Daggett, be the managers at the same, on their part.

The bill for the relief of William Gamble was read a third time, and passed.

The Senate resumed, as in Committee of the Whole, the consideration of the bill supplementary to the act, entitled "An act providing for the indemnification of certain claimants of public lands in the Mississippi Territory," together with the amendments reported thereto by the select committee; and the amendments having been agreed to, the President reported the bill to the House accordingly, and it was further amended, and the bill ordered to be engrossed and read a third time as amended.

Mr. Varnum, from the committee to whom was referred the bill, entitled "An act to provide for the widows and orphans of militia and volunteer soldiers who shall die or be killed in the service of the United States," reported it without amendment.

The Senate resumed, as in Committee of the Whole, the bill, entitled "An act to authorize the President of the United States to accept the services of volunteers who may associate and organize themselves, and offer their services to the Government of the United States;" and Mr. Mason submitted an amendment to the bill. On motion, it was agreed that the further consideration thereof be postponed.

Mr. Bledsoe submitted the following motion for consideration:

Resolved, That the committee on so much of the Message of the President of the United States as relates to our naval affairs, be instructed to inquire into the expediency of establishing a naval school.

DIRECT TAXES.

The bill entitled "An act to provide additional revenue for defraying the expenses of Government, and maintaining the public credit, by laying a direct tax upon the United States, and to provide for assessing and collecting the same," was read a third time.

Mr. Gore, of Massachusetts, addressed the Chair as follows—

Mr. President: This bill imposes burdens extremely heavy on all the citizens of our common country, and on those with which I am most acquainted, a load, that, under existing circumstances, will be intolerable.

With the principle of the bill, in selecting as objects of taxation the lands and buildings of the United States, I have no fault to find.

I consider them as fit and proper subjects of revenue, and such assessments calculated to equalize the burdens of the country, as imposing them on all parts, and with more impartiality than can be attained by any other mode.

And, sir, I should feel it my duty to vote for a bill, imposing such a tax, to any reasonable amount, had it not pleased the Government of the nation to place the State, which I have the honor to represent, out of the protection of the United States, and to determine, that while it shall bear a full proportion of the taxes, none of their fruits shall redound to her relief.

The motives of Congress, in granting supplies, are doubtless to provide for the defence of the country and the security of its rights, by a safe and honorable peace.

These motives are wise and irresistible; all concur in the necessity of defending our territory against the enemy; and in the assertion and maintenance of our essential rights, at every peril, and if necessary, by the sacrifice of all that conduces to private ease and personal enjoyment.

No one feels this truth more sensibly than myself—no one considers the duty more imperative. With its obligations I have no compromises to make, and in its performance I ask for no limitations, on account of the folly and improvidence with which the war was waged, nor of the degrading imbecility and prodigal waste of treasure, of blood, and character, by which it has been prosecuted.

The enemy publicly proclaims his purpose. to spread desolation, far and wide, on our unprotected seacoast. He proceeds to execute his threats with a barbarity and baseness, in many instances, unprecedented.

The mansions of the rich, the palaces of the nation, and the cottages of the poorest citizens, feel alike his disgraceful vengeance. The opulence of the wealthy is destroyed; the means of subsistence to the impoverished inhabitants of the sands are redeemed from his rapacity by grinding impositions, which the charity of such as being out of the reach of his power are alone able to supply. Even the ashes of the dead are not suffered to repose in quiet. And, as the last act of atrocity, your slaves are seized and seduced, embodied in military array, and led to the destruction of their masters and the plunder of their possessions.

Whether those acts seek an apology in the conduct of our own Government, we cannot inquire for the purpose of weighing our duty to repel his attack. Whoever comes to our shores, in the character of an enemy, must be resisted. We must do all in our power to defend ourselves and our soil from an invading foe.

A question arises, have we any grounds for believing that the grants of men and money will be wisely applied to the purposes of defence and protection ?

Honorable gentlemen will please to go back to November, 1811, when the Executive, in winding its devious course to the fatal act of June 1842, addressed the hopes, the fears, the vanity, and pride of the people, and, avowing its duty to establish the general security, assured the nation " that ' the works of defence on our maritime frontier ' had been prosecuted with an activity, leaving ' little to be added for the completion of the most ' important ones. The land forces so disposed as ' to insure appropriate and important services, ' and embodied and marched toward the North-' western frontiers," to seek satisfaction for acts, which it was declared, had alike .'' the character and effect of war."

The subsequent course of things must be full in the mind of every one, and the result known and felt by all.

We learn that the same measures are to be pursued. The Atlantic coast is to be defended as heretofore, by attempts on Canada. This is frankly and formally told to the Congress, that no pretence can be urged, in future, of disappointment or deception.

I forbear to speak on this subject. In the actual state of things, all reasoning must be futile. The powers of language cease before the eloquent monitors constantly in our view.

We are doomed to remain in this scene, that we may not, for a moment, lose sight of our degradation and disgrace.

The Government had complete information of the designs of the enemy, months before his attack on Washington. In this city, were all the means of defence, fortresses, ships, cannon, men, and money; here, too, was concentrated all the wisdom of the Administration, to deliberate, examine, decide, and prepare for the support of the Capitol, at least sixty days prior to its destruction, by a few thousand worn down and exhausted soldiers. You have now in full view, the effect of their combined councils—of their individual and united talents, prudence, and energies.

These monuments show, in characters not to be mistaken, the future in the past, and the desolation around. They declare the fate of every place, under the influence and protection of our Government, if approached by the enemy.

Congress continues to grant, with no sparing hand, supplies of every kind to the same men, in the hope, it is imagined, that Heaven may, by some miracle, interpose for their application to the safety and relief of the country.

Permit me, sir, to crave your indulgence, and that of the honorable Senate, while I relate the condition of the country which I represent, as the grounds of the vote I am constrained to give on this occasion. The State of Massachusetts has a seacoast of about six hundred miles in extent. Its Eastern boundary joins that of the enemy. It is, of course, peculiarly liable to invasion. The President of the United States was avowedly of the opinion that it would be invaded immediately on the commencement of the war. There were several islands, and one of great importance, on the Eastern frontier, the title to which was not definitively acknowledged by Great Britain. The claim of Massachusetts had been allowed, by this Power, in a treaty made according to the instructions of the President, which treaty the United States had chosen to reject. The Government, therefore, superadded to the general obligation enjoined upon it, to protect and defend the territory of all the States, had incurred a peculiar responsibility to guard this particular frontier from falling into the hands of the enemy.

This State has been left entirely unprotected and defenceless, and has at no time had within it, and destined to its defence, sufficient force of the United States, to protect any one point against a common and ordinary hostile attack.

Shortly after the adoption of the Constitution she ceded to the United States all the fortresses in her possession. These, with all the prominent points of land and sites, appropriate for fortifications to defend the State against invasion, were, and for a long time previous to the war had been, in the exclusive possession of the United States. The State, therefore, had no authority or jurisdiction over, nor even to enter them, for any purpose; much less to assume the defence of their territory, through these means.

One great and principal object of the Constitution was to provide by this Government for the common defence, and, by the power and resources of all the States, to protect each against invasion. The preamble declares: " We, the people of ' the United States, in order to form a more per-' fect union, establish justice, insure domestic

153   HISTORY OF CONGRESS.   154

JANUARY, 1815.   *Direct Taxes.*   SENATE.

' tranquillity, provide for the common defence,
' promote the general welfare, and secure the bles-
' sings of liberty to ourselves and our posterity, do
' ordain and establish this Constitution." For
this end, the States surrendered the principal
sources of revenue, over which they, previously,
had uncontrolled dominion.

"The Congress shall have power—to lay and
' collect taxes, duties, imposts, and excises, to pay
' the debts, and provide for the common defence,"
" to borrow money on the credit of the United
' States."

Here are ample resources, and means commensurate to the duties the United States were enjoined and undertook to perform.

This cannot be denied by the men now in power; for they abolished many taxes, in full and
productive operation, at the time they received
the Government.

Power was also granted to raise and support
every kind of force necessary to insure the common defence, and to protect the States against
invasion, viz: " To raise and support armies."
"To provide and maintain a Navy." To exer-
' cise exclusive legislation over all places pur-
' chased by the consent of the Legislatures of the
' States in which the same shall be, for the erec-
' tion of forts, magazines, arsenals, dock yards, and
' other needful buildings."

The several States, having surrendered their
own resources, and afforded such ample provision
for the common defence, left no doubt of the paramount duty in the United States to perform it
punctually and faithfully.

In the present war, they are without excuse, if
this be not fully and perfectly done; for the war
was of their own choice; they made it, and at
their own time.

The several States received from the United
States a solemn obligation, that they would protect each against invasion. "The United States
' guarantee to every State a Republican form of
' Government, and shall protect each of them
' against invasion."

If anything were wanting to show the sacred-
ness of this duty in the United States, and the
absolute reliance which the States entertained of
its complete performance, it is to be found in
the restrictions and privations which the several
States imposed on themselves.

"No State shall grant letters of marque and
' reprisal. No State shall, without the consent of
' Congress, lay any imposts, or duties on imports
' or exports," except, &c. " No State shall, with-
' out the consent of Congress, lay any duty of
' tonnage, keep troops or ships of war, in time of
' peace, enter into any agreement or compact with
' another State, or with a foreign Power, or
' engage in a war, unless actually invaded, or
' in such imminent danger as will not admit of
' delay."

Having thus surrendered all the pecuniary resources, necessary to provide the means of defence,
and also the right to raise a force requisite to this
end, the several States did rely, and were justified
in relying, with perfect confidence, for complete

protection and defence, on the Government of
the United States.

No one will pretend that such defence has been
afforded to all the States in the Union. Massachusetts has been entirely abandoned. The men
raised there for the regular Army have been
marched out of the State.

Within a month after the declaration of war,
the Governor of that State was informed, by direction of the President, that the regular troops
were all ordered from the seacoast; and his threat,
if intended as such, was instantly executed. Thus,
the moment the United States had placed the
country in a situation to require defence, and
which it was their duty to provide, they wantonly
took away the only force which could afford it.

It may be said, that the President called forth
the militia, in June and July, 1812, for the purpose of making the defence, and protecting the
State against invasion, and the Governor refused
to obey the requisition. On the 12th June, 1812,
the President, by his Secretary of War, requested
Governor Strong to order into the service of the
United States, on the requisition of General
Dearborn, such parts of the militia as the General
might deem necessary for the defense of the seacoast; and, on the 22d June, the same General
informed the Governor that war was declared
against Great Britain, and requested forty-one
companies for the defence of the ports and harbors in Massachusetts, and the harbor of Newport, in Rhode Island.

The Governor of a State is obliged to comply
with every requisition of the United States for
militia, made in pursuance of the provisions of
the Constitution. He is equally bound, by his
duty to the States, to refrain from calling them
forth for purposes not within these provisions.

The only cases which authorize a call for the
militia of the several States, to act against an enemy, is to repel invasion.

The President, neither by himself nor any of
his officers, ever pretended that this case existed,
at the time the requisition was issued. The requisition was made expressly for the defence of
the ports and harbors of that State and of Rhode
Island.

The militia is a force which belongs to the several States respectively and exclusively, and is so
recognised by the Constitution of the United
States. The Government of the United States
is a Government of limited authorities, and has no
other powers than what are granted by the Constitution. A power to call forth the militia to
provide for the common defence, or to protect
against invasion, is nowhere granted to the United States in express terms. All the authority
over the militia delegated to the United States, is
to call them forth to repel invasion, to execute
the laws, and to suppress insurrection. The United States are bound to provide for the common
defence.

To repel invasion is included in the duty of
providing for the common defence; and as invasion may be sudden, even in time of profound
peace, and before the United States can bring

their forces to meet an unexpected attack, the militia of the several States is granted to the United States, from the necessity of the case, as the means by which they may provide for the common defence in such particular instance.

If the United States have authority to call forth the militia, for the ordinary purposes of war, for the common defence, or for protection against invasion, under any of the general powers granted, such as that to provide for the common defence, there would have been no necessity for the special clause authorizing Congress to provide for calling them forth, to repel invasion; for repelling invasion is undoubtedly one part of the duty of providing for the common defence.

If it were the intent of the Constitution to grant to the United States, expressly, a power over the militia for protection against invasion, it would have declared that for such purposes the United States might call forth the militia, or it would have said, to protect against, or repel invasion. And especially in the clause which enjoins on the United States the duty of protecting each State against invasion, the Constitution would have declared, and that, for this purpose, the United States shall call forth the militia. No such words, no such grants, are made in this instrument. If, therefore, the authority of the United States to call forth the militia, to protect the ports and harbors of a State, be granted, it must be by the terms to repel invasion. Common defence includes all the means by which a nation may be guarded, protected, defended, and secured against danger, both in war and in peace.

To repel invasion, is only one particular and specific act providing for the common defence. It is contrary to common sense, as well as to all the rules of logic, to say that a specific power or duty includes the general power, or duty, of which it is a part; it is to say, that a part contains the whole.

To repel invasion, is to drive back and resist that which has already happened. To protect against invasion is to prevent its happening, to secure against its existence. The one act is against an event that has occurred—the other is to insure and guard against the occurrence of such an event.

To protect against invasion, is to erect fortresses, to have them well manned, and supplied with all requisite stores, to provide and equip ships of war, to have an army and navy well organized and disciplined, in peace and in war. To repel invasion is one specific act of war, against another act of the like character.

To repel invasion is one part of the duty of providing for the common defence, and for this part a particular force is granted. To say that a grant of this force, for this special service, includes a grant of the same force for the purposes of protection and defence, is to say, that a grant for one purpose is a grant for another, and for every purpose, and that the grant of a limited, is the grant of a general authority. This would be both illogical and irrational. And if under the limitations, which were intended to control the powers granted to the Government of the United

States, and especially under the express limitation. viz : "that powers not delegated to the United States, by the Constitution, nor prohibited by it to the States, are reserved to the States, or to the people," such construction may be adopted. there remains no security for any right reserved to the States, or to the people.

However conclusive this reasoning may be, it is not to be presumed that, after the strides of power in which the spirit of party has indulged, it will have any effect on those who direct the affairs of this country. I will, sir, however, refer to opinions and authorities in confirmation of what has been advanced, that to many gentlemen did 'not formally admit either of exception or appeal.

These are to be found in the resolutions and arguments of the Legislature of Virginia, and of Mr. Madison, one of that Legislature, in the years 1799 and 1800—I refer the Senate to the third resolution passed by that body, and framed by the pen of the President, in the words following:

" 3, *Resolved,* That this Assembly doth explicitly and peremptorily declare, that it views the powers of the Federal Government, as resulting from the compact to which the States are parties, submitted by the plain sense and intention of the instrument constituting that compact, as no further valid than they are authorized by the grants enumerated in that contract; and that in case of a deliberate, palpable, and dangerous exercise of other powers, not granted by the said compact, the States who are parties thereto have a right and are in duty bound to interpose, for arresting the progress of the evil, and for maintaining within their respective limits the authorities, rights, and liberties appertaining to them."

" It is said, that Congress are, by the Constitution, to protect each State against invasion, and that the means of preventing, are included in the power of protection against it."

" The power of war in general having been before granted by the Constitution, this clause must either be a mere specification, for greater caution and certainty, of which there are other examples in the Constitution, or be the injunction of a duty, superadded to a grant of power. Under either explanation, it cannot enlarge the powers of Congress on the subject. The power and duty to protect each State against an invading enemy would be the same, under the general powers, if this regard to greater caution had been omitted."

" Invasion is an operation of war. To protect against invasion is an exercise of the power of war. A power, therefore, not incident to war, cannot be incident to a particular modification of war. And as the removal of alien friends has appeared to be no incident to a general state of war, it cannot be incident to a partial state, or to a particular modification of war."

" Nor, can it ever be granted, that a power to act on a case, when it actually occurs, includes a power over all the means that may tend to prevent the occurrence of the case. Such a latitude of construction would render unavailing every practicable definition of limited powers."—[See proceedings in the House of Delegates, of Virginia, on the 7th January, 1800, on the resolutions of the General Assembly of December 21, 1798.]

If the observations which I have made are

founded in truth, and justified by the Constitution, the following positions are established, viz:

That the United States have no right to call on the several States for the militia, to perform any act of war, but to repel invasion.

That to defend the ports and harbors of Massachusetts and Rhode Island, the purpose for which the militia was required in 1812, is not within the power delegated by the Constitution, to provide for calling forth the militia to repel invasion.

In the case alluded to in 1812, it was not declared by the President, nor even pretended by his officers, that any invasion was made. In fact, no invasion was attempted until two years after this time. If the United States had no authority to make the requisition, the Governor would have betrayed his duty to the State, in complying with the demand.

That the United States had no such authority, I think evident from the examination that has been made of the powers delegated by the Constitution. And the State of Massachusetts, instead of being a just object of censure, by the United States, has a well founded complaint against their Government, for an attempt to usurp her rights and invade her prerogatives.

A question has sometimes been suggested, whether the Governor of a State has a right to judge if the requisition be within the provisions of the Constitution. A little reflection on the nature of the Government of the United States, and of a State, and of the relation in which the Supreme Executive of the latter stands to the United States, and to the citizens of his particular State, will show that he is obliged to examine, if the case for which the requisition is made be within the provisions of the Constitution, and if the purposes for which it is declared are manifestly not within the powers delegated by that instrument, to withhold a compliance.

The Government of the United States can exercise no powers not granted by the Constitution, and so far as this Government can support such as it claims on this charter, it is sovereign, and has no other control than its own discretion.

The government of the several States is equally sovereign, with respect to every power of an independent State, which it has not delegated by the same instrument to the United States, or which is not thereby prohibited to the several States. It is, also, a sacred duty of the Government of the several States, to preserve unimpaired every right and authority retained by the State, either in its corporate capacity or for its individual citizens. Whether the militia, the peculiar force of the several States, and that which is to protect and defend every right and power they possess, is called forth by the United States according to the provisions which they made, in delegating to this Government its powers, must of necessity be a question between two sovereign independent Governments, and on which there is no tribunal authorized to judge between them. And if the Governors, who are commanders-in-chief of the militia of the several States, should surrender this force to the United States, in a case not authorized by the Constitution, they would betray the trust confided to them by the citizens of their States. They must, therefore, examine the case when called upon, and decide according to their duty, as prescribed by the Constitution of the United States, and that of their particular State, shall demand.

General Cushing, while superintendent of the military district in which Massachusetts is situated, informed Governor Strong, that he expected an order from the President of the United States, to request a detachment of militia for the defence of the seacoast, and particularly of Boston. That he had not more troops than sufficient to man one of the forts, and proposed that one should be occupied by the militia, and that, while out, they should be subject to the command of no officer of the United States, except the superintendent of the district. The Governor acceded to the proposal.

General Dearborn shortly after superseded General Cushing, and on the 8th July, by order of the President, and in confirmation of the expectation of Brigadier General Cushing, requested a detachment of eleven hundred militia to occupy the forts and harbor of Boston.

Governor Strong, although under no Constitutional obligation to call forth the militia for the purposes required, yet, seeing the forlorn condition of the country, the vast property of the United States in the navy yard, a ship-of-the-line nearly completed, and a frigate, all abandoned by the Government to the mercy of the enemy, at the same time that these offered to him great temptations to attack and destroy the capital of the State and its environs, and feeling authorized by the resolution of the Legislature of Massachusetts, detached the militia, in confidence that the agreement made with General Cushing would be fulfilled.

At the end of their term of service these men were offered an uncurrent and depreciated paper, as their only compensation.

In the beginning of September, General Dearborn notified the Governor that the enemy had taken possession of a considerable part of the State of Massachusetts, and requested a detachment of the militia for the purpose of protecting and defending such parts of that State, and New Hampshire, as were not in the occupation of the enemy.

Such complaints and objections had arisen in executing the order of July, that the Governor, although he issued an order for troops, found himself obliged to place the detachment under the command of a major general of the militia.

The Governor immediately addressed a letter to the Secretary of State, requesting to know from the President if the expenses, thus necessarily incurred for the protection of the State, would be ultimately reimbursed to that State by the United States.

The answer was, that if the force thus put into service by the Governor had been required by General Dearborn, or received by him, and put under his command, the expenses attending it would be defrayed by the United States. If otherwise, in either of these particulars, the United States were not chargeable with the expense.

Here is a distinct and plain case, in which the United States had neglected that protection which they were expressly bound to afford the State, and thereby occasioned the loss of a fifth part of its territory;* and then called upon the State itself to protect the remaining territory. The State obeyed the call, and reserved only that right which the Constitution, in express terms, reserved, viz : the appointment of officers to command the militia required; and the United States say this expense must be borne by the State, and that they will not reimburse the amount, because the militia is not placed under the command of an officer of the United States.†

For this act of injustice, for this neglect of duty in the United States towards the State of Massachusetts, for this abandonment of its territory to the violence of the enemy, I have never heard the smallest apology.

I forbear to mention the rights of the State, the necessity to which this wanton abandonment by those who ought to protect them may reduce the inhabitants. The laws of self-preservation, and of nature, confirmed by that of nations, afford the rule for any member of a confederacy thus deserted and forsaken,

I most earnestly hope, that although cruelly deserted by the Government, which contrary to their entreaties brought them into this perilous condition, that citizens of the country may be able to defend themselves. They will do all that men can do under their circumstances. But I am confident, that if this tax be collected there, and paid into the Treasury of the United States, for the exclusive support and defence of others, they will be destitute of the means of making any adequate resistance. I cannot, therefore, vote for this bill.

The present year the Commonwealth has expended more than $700,000 in her own defence. She is now called on by this bill for $632,041, to defend other parts of the territory of the United States; and her citizens, more exposed than any other, are left to provide for their own defence.

They who calculated on the ability of Massachusetts to pay, from the exactness and punctual-

---

* There were, at the attack and capture of Castine, twenty-eight men and a Lieutenant in the fort. This was all the protection for one of the most important harbors and rivers of the United States, and affording the best situation for a naval depot for Great Britain.

† In the military district, No. 1, which includes New Hampshire and Massachusetts, there were less than one thousand three hundred men. These were scattered over an extensive tract of country. In the forts, in Boston harbor, there were not two hundred and sixty men, and in the other forts in the State a very small corps, inadequate to any defence. There was, however, a Major General, a Brigadier General, and several Colonels. In no one place were there men enough to constitute a colonel's command.

ity which she has heretofore observed in the discharge of taxes, will recollect, that her faculty to meet the demands of the Treasury, even in times the most prosperous, arose principally from the daring enterprise, unrivalled industry, and rigid economy of the inhabitants; that her resources are now annihilated, and she is borne down by obloquy, insult, and oppression.

They who have observed the patience wherewith she has submitted to see the public treasure squandered, to purchase slanders against her citizens, and notwithstanding a complete failure by the full confession of the hireling, that these citizens were so far beyond all temptation as not even to be approached for dishonorable purposes, has been subjected to the most degrading insinuations, from the first authority; who have witnessed all the resources of her wealth, all the means of her industry, the object of unabating persecution from the Government, and her possessions coldly and expressly abandoned, by the same authority, to the depredations and seizure of the enemy, may conceive that taxes like these will still be paid for the exclusive protection of others; but if gentlemen will only condescend to view the people of this country as their brethren, as freemen, as men, they must come to the conclusion, that, had they the means, they could not possibly have the will.

When Mr. GORE had concluded—

The question was taken, Shall this bill pass? and determined in the affirmative—yeas 23, nays 7, as follows:

YEAS—Messrs. Anderson, Bibb, Bledsoe, Brown, Chace, Condit, Daggett, Fromentin, Gaillard, German, Giles, Hunter, Kerr, Lacock, Morrow, Roberts, Smith, Tait, Taylor, Turner, Walker, and Wharton.

NAYS—Messrs. Dana, Gore, Horsey, Lambert, Mason, Varnum, and Wells.

So it was *Resolved*, That this bill pass.

FRIDAY, January 6.

Mr. ROBERTS presented the petition of William Elliot, of the City of Washington, praying the examination of a floating battery which he has invented for the protection of the coasts and waters of the United States, as is stated in the petition; which was read, and referred to the Secretary for the Department of Navy, to consider and report thereon to the Senate.

The bill supplementary to the act, entitled "An act providing for the indemnification of certain claimants of the public lands in the Mississippi Territory," was read a third time, and passed.

Mr. LACOCK, from the committee appointed October, 4, 1814, to consider the subject, asked and obtained leave to report a bill making appropriations for repairing or rebuilding the public buildings within the City of Washington; and the bill was read, and passed to a second reading.

On motion, by Mr. SMITH,

Resolved, That the Message of the President of the United States, of 2d instant, together with the report of the Secretary of the Treasury, therewith communicated, containing a statement of the proceedings under the "Act to regulate the laying out and making a road from Cumberland, in the State of Maryland, to the State of Ohio," be referred to a select committee to consider and report thereon by bill or otherwise.

Ordered, That Messrs. SMITH, MORROW, and KING, be the committee.

The PRESIDENT communicated a report of the acting Secretary for the Department of Navy, on the expenditure and application of moneys drawn from the Treasury, from the first of October, 1813, to the 30th September, 1814, inclusive; and of the unexpended balances of former appropriations remaining in the Treasury on the 1st of October, 1813; also a report, comprehending contracts made by the Navy Department, during the years 1813 and 1814, prepared in obedience to the act of the 3d of March, 1809, entitled "An act further to amend the several acts for the establishment and regulation of the Treasury, War and Navy Departments;" and the reports were read. .

The Senate resumed, as in Committee of the Whole, the consideration of the bill, entitled "An act to authorize the President of the United States to accept the services of volunteers who may associate and organize themselves, and offer their services to the Government of the United States," together with the amendments proposed thereto; and the bill having been amended, the President reported it to the House accordingly.

On the question, Shall the amendments be engrossed and the bill read a third time as amended? it was unanimously determined in the affirmative—yeas 27, as follows:

YEAS—Messrs. Anderson, Bibb, Bledsoe, Brown, Chace, Condit, Daggett, Dana, Fromentin, Gaillard, German, Gore, Horsey, Kerr, King, Lambert, Mason, Morrow, Roberts, Robinson, Smith, Tait, Taylor, Thompson, Varnum, Walker, and Wharton.

The Senate resumed the consideration of the motion made the 5th instant, for instructing the Naval Committee to inquire into the expediency of establishing a naval school; and agreed thereto.

The Senate resumed, as in Committee of the Whole, the consideration of the bill, entitled "An act to provide for the widows and orphans of militia and volunteer soldiers who shall die or be killed in the service of the United States;" and on motion, by Mr. VARNUM, the further consideration thereof was postponed to the second Monday in March next.

SATURDAY, January 7.

Mr. GILES presented the petition of Littleburg E. Stainback and others, of the town of Petersburg, joint owners of the privateer called the Roger, praying a special circuit court may be ordered for the district of North Carolina, for reasons stated at large in the petition; which was read, and referred to a select committee to consider and report thereon by bill or otherwise; and Messrs. GILES, TURNER, and MASON, were appointed the committee.

The amendments to the bill, entitled "An act to authorize the President of the United States to

accept the services of volunteers who may associate and organize themselves, and offer their services to the Government of the United States," was read a third time as amended, and the blanks were filled.

Resolved, That this bill pass with amendments.

On motion, by Mr. BIBB, the title was amended, to insert, after "services," the words "State troops and;" and to strike out, from the word "volunteers," to the end thereof.

A Message from the House of Representatives informed the Senate that the House agree to the conference proposed by the Senate and the disagreeing votes of the two Houses on the amendment to the bill, entitled "An act to provide additional revenues for defraying the expenses of Government, and maintaining the public credit, by laying duties on various goods, wares, and merchandise, manufactured within the United States," and have appointed managers on their part. They recede from their disagreement to the amendments of the Senate to the bill, entitled "An act to provide additional revenues for defraying the expenses of Government, and maintaining the public credit, by laying duties on household furniture, on horses kept exclusively for the saddle or carriage, and on gold and silver wares," so far as to adopt the report of the committee of conference.

Mr. TAYLOR, from the managers on the part of the Senate, at the conference on the amendments of the Senate, disagreed to by the House of Representatives to the bill last mentioned, reported:

"That the Senate do recede from their amendments concerning the rates of duties on household furniture; and,

"That the House of Representatives do recede from their disagreement to all the other amendments made in the Senate to the bill."

On motion, by Mr. GILES, that the said bill, together with the report of the conferees, be postponed to the second Monday in March next; it was determined in the negative—yeas 8, nays 21, as follows:

YEAS—Messrs. Daggett, Dana, Giles, Gore, Hunter, Mason, Smith, and Wells.

NAYS—Messrs. Anderson, Bibb, Bledsoe, Brown, Chace, Condit, Fromentin, Gaillard, German, Lacock, Lambert, Morrow, Roberts, Robinson, Tait, Taylor, Thompson, Turner, Varnum, Walker, and Wharton.

On the question, Will the Senate concur in the report of the committee of conference? it was determined in the affirmative. Whereupon,

Resolved, That the Senate so far recede from their amendments to the bill last mentioned, as to adopt the report of the committee of conference.

The Senate resumed the consideration of the bill authorizing the President of the United States to cause to be built, equipped, and employed, one or more floating batteries, for the defence of the waters of the United States; and the bill was ordered to be engrossed and read a third time as amended.

The bill making appropriations for repairing

or rebuilding the public buildings within the City of Washington, was read the second time; and on motion, by Mr. LACOCK, the further consideration thereof was postponed to Monday next.

MONDAY, January 9.

Mr. ROBERTS presented the petition of Robert Kid, of the city of Philadelphia, praying certain bonds given by him on merchandise imported into the United States, which had been consigned by Samuel Guppy, a subject of Great Britain, to a house in Philadelphia, and by him innocently purchased, may be cancelled, for reasons therein stated; and the petition was read, and referred to a select committee, to consider and report thereon by bill or otherwise; and Messrs. ROBERTS, CHACE, and KERR, were appointed the committee.

Mr. ROBERTS presented the petition of the Chamber of Commerce of Philadelphia, in favor of general and uniform regulations of the estates of insolvents; and praying a law may pass on that subject, for reasons stated in the petition, which was read.

The PRESIDENT communicated the memorial of the Legislative Council and House of Representatives in the Mississippi Territory, praying the appointment of an additional judge for that part of the Territory lying east of Pearl river, for reasons therein stated; and the memorial was read, and referred to a select committee, to consider and report thereon by bill or otherwise; and Messrs. BROWN, BIBB, and CHACE, were appointed the committee.

The bill authorizing the President of the United States to cause to be built, equipped, and employed, one or more floating batteries, for the defence of the waters of the United States, was read a third time.

On motion, by Mr. KING, the bill was amended by unanimous consent, by adding thereto a new section.

Resolved, That this bill pass, and that the title thereof be "An act authorizing the President of the United States to cause to be built, equipped, and employed, one or more floating batteries, for the defence of the waters of the United States."

On motion, by Mr. DANA,

Resolved, That the committee to whom was referred so much of the Message of the President of the United States as relates to the militia, be instructed to inquire into the expediency of making provision, by law, that there shall be one Colonel, one Lieutenant Colonel, and one Major, to each regiment consisting of two battalions of militia.

On motion, by Mr. VARNUM, a member was added to the committee on so much of the Message of the President of the United States as relates to the militia, in place of Mr. WORTHINGTON; and Mr. DANA was elected.

The Senate resumed the consideration of the bill for the relief of Bowie and Kurtz and others; and, on motion, by Mr. BIBB, the further consideration thereof was postponed to Monday next.

The Senate resumed, as in Committee of the Whole, the consideration of the bill making appropriations for repairing or rebuilding the public buildings within the city of Washington; and, on motion, by Mr. BIBB, the further consideration thereof was postponed to Wednesday next.

A message from the House of Representatives informed the Senate that the House have passed a bill, entitled "An act to prohibit intercourse with the enemy, and for other purposes;" in which bill they request the concurrence of the Senate. They have also passed the bill which originated in the Senate, entitled "An act to incorporate the subscribers to the Bank of the United States of America," with amendments; in which they request the concurrence of the Senate.

The Senate proceeded to consider the amendments of the House of Representatives to the bill last mentioned; and, on motion, by Mr. SMITH, they were referred to a select committee, to consist of five members, to consider and report thereon; and Messrs. SMITH, BIBB, ANDERSON, GILES, and VARNUM, were appointed the committee.

On motion, by Mr. FROMENTIN, the bill last mentioned, as amended by the House of Representatives, was ordered to be printed for the use of the Senate.

The bill last brought up for concurrence was read, and passed to the second reading.

TUESDAY, January 10.

The bill, entitled "An act to prohibit intercourse with the enemy, and for other purposes," was read the second time, and referred to the committee to whom were referred, on the 14th October. the several communications from the President of the United States, relating to our foreign affairs, to consider and report thereon.

The two following Messages were also received from the PRESIDENT OF THE UNITED STATES:

To the Senate and House of
    Representatives of the United States:

I communicate, for the information of Congress, the report of the Director of the Mint, of the operation of that establishment during the last year.

        JAMES MADISON.
JANUARY 10, 1815.

To the Senate and House of
    Representatives of the United States:

I transmit to Congress an account of the contingent expenses of Government for the year one thousand eight hundred and fourteen.

        JAMES MADISON.
JANUARY 10, 1815.

The Messages and documents therein referred to were severally read.

Mr. MORROW, from the committee to whom the subject was referred, reported a bill giving further time to complete the surveys and obtain the patents for lands located under Virginia resolution warrants; and the bill was read, and passed to the second reading.

Mr. MASON submitted the following motion for consideration:

Resolved, That the President of the United States be, and he is hereby, requested to cause to be stated to the Senate the reasons which have prevented the communication of the information requested by their resolution of the 9th of November last.

WEDNESDAY, January 11.

JAMES BARBOUR, appointed a Senator by the Legislature of the Commonwealth of Virginia, to supply the vacancy occasioned by the decease of Richard Brent, produced his credentials, was qualified, and took his seat in the Senate.

The Senate resumed, as in Committee of the Whole, the consideration of the bill making appropriations for repairing or rebuilding the public buildings within the city of Washington; and on motion, by Mr. LACOCK, the further consideration thereof was postponed to Friday next.

A message from the House informed the Senate that the House recede from their disagreement to that part of the fifth amendment of the Senate to the bill, entitled "An act to provide additional revenues for defraying the expenses of Government, and maintaining the public credit, by laying duties on various goods, wares, and merchandise, manufactured within the United States," to insert "umbrellas and parasols, if above the value of two dollars, eight per centum ad valorem;" and that they agree to the said amendment. They have passed a bill, entitled, "An act for the relief of William H. Washington;" a bill, entitled "An act for the relief of William Robinson, and others;" a bill, entitled "An act for the relief of James Doyle;" also, a bill, entitled "An act for the relief of Jacob Shinnick and Shoultz and Vogeler, of Christian Chapman, and the legal representative of John Calef, deceased;" in which bills they request the concurrence of the Senate.

The four bills last mentioned were read, and passed to the second reading.

Mr. TAYLOR, from the managers appointed on the part of the Senate to confer with the managers on the part of the House of Representatives on the disagreeing votes of the two Houses on the bill, entitled "An act to provide additional revenues for defraying the expenses of Government, and maintaining the public credit, by laying duties on various goods, wares, and merchandise, manufactured within the United States;" reported:

"That they had conferred on the above subject, and that the managers on behalf of the House of Representatives have agreed to recommend to their House, that they do recede from their disagreement to the insertion of the following amendment, made by the Senate to the above-mentioned bill, viz: umbrellas and parasols, if above the value of two dollars, eight per centum ad valorem; and the report was read.

The Senate adjourned to Friday morning.

FRIDAY, January 13.

Mr. SMITH, from the committee to whom were referred the amendments of the House to the bill to incorporate the subscribers to the Bank of the United States of America, reported the same with a number of amendments.

[The amendments to the amendments of the House propose to increase the fixed capital of the Bank from thirty to thirty-five millions of dollars; to make the capital consist of shares of four hundred instead of one hundred dollars each; that the five millions proposed to be added to the capital, shall be added also to the amount subscribable in public debt; to disagree to the proposition of the House for striking out the section which authorizes suspension of payments in specie; to agree to the section which compels the bank to commence its operations before the first day of January, and to disagree to that which proposes to authorize a committee of Congress at any time to examine the books, &c., and prescribes the course of proceeding in the courts against the bank, in case of violation of its charter.]

The consideration of this report was postponed to and made the order of the day for to-morrow.

The bill, entitled "An act for the relief of James Doyle," was read the second time, and referred to a select committee, to consider and report thereon; and Messrs. ROBERTS, BARBOUR, and THOMPSON, were appointed the committee.

The bill giving further time to complete the surveys and obtain the patents for lands located under Virginia resolution warrants, was read the second time, considered as in Committee of the Whole, and postponed until to-morrow.

The bill, entitled "An act for the relief of William H. Washington," was read the second time; and referred to the committee to whom was referred, on the 26th of September last, the memorial of the President and Directors of the Eastern Branch Bridge Company, to consider and report thereon.

The bill, entitled "An act for the relief of Jacob Shinnick, Shoultz, and Vogeler, of Christian Chapman, and the legal representative of John Calef, deceased," was read the second time; and referred to the committee appointed on the bill, entitled "An act for the relief of James Doyle," to consider and report thereon.

The bill, entitled "An act for the relief of William Robinson and others," was read the second time; and referred to a select committee, to consider and report thereon; and Messrs. WALKER, MORROW, and CHACE, were appointed the committee.

A message from the House of Representatives informed the Senate that the House concur in the amendments of the Senate to the bill, entitled "An act to authorize the President of the United States to accept the services of volunteers who may associate and organize themselves, and offer their services to the Government of the United States," with amendments, in which they request the concurrence of the Senate.

The Senate proceeded to consider the amendments of the House of Representatives to their amendments to the bill, entitled "An act to authorize the President of the United States to accept the services of volunteers who may associate and organize themselves, and offer their services to the Government of the United States;" and, on motion, they were ordered to be printed for the use of the Senate.

The Senate proceeded to consider the motion submitted the 10th instant by Mr. MASON; and on motion, by Mr. ROBINSON, it was agreed to take the question thereon by yeas and nays; and on motion, by Mr. TAYLOR, the further consideration thereof was postponed to Friday next.

The Senate proceeded to consider the amendments reported by the committee to the amendments of the House of Representatives, to the bill, entitled "An act to incorporate the subscribers to the Bank of the United States of America;" and on motion, by Mr. MASON, the further consideration thereof was postponed to, and made the order of the day for, to-morrow.

The Senate proceeded to consider the motion submitted the 27th December last; and on motion, by Mr. KING, the further consideration thereof was postponed to Friday next.

The Senate resumed, as in Committee of the Whole, the consideration of the bill making appropriations for repairing or rebuilding the public buildings within the city of Washington; and on motion, by Mr. FROMENTIN, the consideration thereof was further postponed to, and made the order of the day for, Wednesday next.

SATURDAY, January 14.

The Senate resumed, as in Committee of the Whole, the consideration of the bill giving further time to complete the surveys and obtain the patents for lands located under Virginia resolution warrants; and, no amendment having been proposed, on the question, Shall this bill be engrossed and read a third time? it was determined in the affirmative.

The Senate resumed the consideration of the amendments of the House of Representatives to their amendments to the bill, entitled "An act to authorize the President of the United States to accept the services of volunteers who may associate and organize themselves, and offer their services to the Government of the United States." Whereupon,

Resolved, That they agree to the second and fourth amendments of the House of Representatives to their amendments to the said bill, and disagree to all their other amendments.

The Senate resumed the consideration of the amendments reported by the committee to the amendments of the House of Representatives to the bill, entitled "An act to incorporate the subscribers to the Bank of the United States of America."

On the question to agree to the first proposition of the committee, to wit: Add after the word "thirty," as often as it occurs, the word "five:" it was determined in the affirmative—yeas 17, nays 14, as follows:

YEAS—Messrs. Anderson, Barbour, Bibb, Chace, Condit, Giles, Kerr, Lacock, Morrow, Roberts, Smith, Tait, Taylor, Turner, Varnum, Walker, and Wharton.

NAYS.—Messrs. Brown, Daggett, Dana, Fromentin, Gaillard, German, Gore, Horsey, Hunter, King, Lambert, Mason, Thompson, and Wells.

On the question to agree to the first member of the second proposition of the committee, to amend the amendments of the House of Representatives, to wit: strike out "ten," and insert "fifteen:" it was determined in the affirmative—yeas 17, nays 14, as follows:

YEAS—Messrs. Anderson, Barbour, Bibb, Chace, Condit, Giles, Kerr, Lacock, Morrow, Roberts, Smith, Tait, Taylor, Turner, Varnum, Walker, and Wharton.

NAYS—Messrs. Brown, Daggett, Dana, Fromentin, Gaillard, German, Gore, Horsey, Hunter, King, Lambert, Mason, Thompson, and Wells.

After further progress, the Senate adjourned.

MONDAY, January 16.

Mr. GORE presented a petition, signed by a number of the inhabitants of the town of Union, in the District of Maine, remonstrating against the transportation and opening of the mail on the Sabbath; and the petition was read, and referred to the committee to whom was referred, on the 26th ultimo, several petitions on the same subject, to consider and report thereon by bill or otherwise.

Mr. FROMENTIN presented the memorial of Edward F. Howell, and others, midshipmen in the Navy of the United States, remonstrating against the practice, which they state has of late obtained, of promoting and commissioning sailing masters to the rank of lieutenants in the Navy; for reasons stated at large in the memorial; which was read, and referred to the Committee on Naval Affairs, to consider and report thereon by bill or otherwise.

Mr. GILES, from the Committee on Military Affairs, to whom was referred the resolution of the Senate of the 2d January instant, reported the following resolution; which was read:

Resolved, That it is inexpedient to pass a bill for calling out the militia upon the principles of the said resolution.

On motion, of Mr. GILES, a member was added to the committee to whom was referred, the 23d September, the memorial of the President and Directors of the Washington Bridge Company, in place of Mr. BLEDSOE; and Mr. MASON was elected.

The bill giving further time to complete the surveys and obtain the patents for lands located under Virginia resolution warrants, was read a third time, and passed.

BANK OF THE UNITED STATES.

The Senate resumed the consideration of the amendments reported by the committee to the amendments of the House of Representatives to the bill, entitled "An act to incorporate the subscribers to the Bank of the United States of America."

On the question, to agree to the proposition of the committee, in the 60th and 61st lines, to wit: "That the amendments to the 17th and 18th rules be disagreed to:" it was determined in the negative—yeas 15, nays 18, as follows:

YEAS—Messrs. Anderson, Bibb, Chace, Condit, Howell, Lacock, Morrow, Roberts, Robinson, Smith, Taylor, Turner, Varnum, Walker, and Wharton.

NAYS—Messrs. Barbour, Brown, Daggett, Dana, Fromentin, Gaillard, German, Giles, Gore, Horsey, Hunter, Kerr, King, Lambert, Mason, Tait, Thompson, and Wells.

On the question, to agree to the proposition of the committee, lines 64, and 65, to wit: "That the amendment which proposes to strike out the 13th section be disagreed to:" it was determined in the affirmative—yeas 17, nays 16, as follows:

YEAS—Messrs. Anderson, Barbour, Bibb, Chace, Condit, Howell, Lacock, Morrow, Roberts, Robinson, Smith, Tait, Taylor, Turner, Varnum, Walker, and Wharton.

NAYS—Messrs. Brown, Daggett, Dana, Fromentin, Gaillard, German, Giles, Gore, Horsey, Hunter, Kerr, King, Lambert, Mason, Thompson, and Wells.

On motion, by Mr. BIBB, to strike out of the 14th section, proposed as an amendment by the House of Representatives, after the word "that," in the first line, and insert, in lieu thereof, the following:

"If at any time the said corporation shall exercise powers not authorized by this act, or refuse or neglect to perform any of the stipulations of this act, for which refusal or neglect penalties are not already provided, it shall be the duty of the Secretary of the Treasury, by and with the consent of the President of the United States, to represent the same to Congress; and Congress may, thereupon, make such provision, by law, to restrain such exercise of unauthorized powers, and to enforce the stipulations, aforesaid, as the nature of the case may justify and require; anything in this act to the contrary notwithstanding: *Provided nevertheless,* That Congress shall not revoke or impair the corporate capacity of the said Bank, for and during the term of —— years, by this act provided, nor in any manner affect or impair the right and property of the stockholders respectively, in the capital stock of said Bank."

A division of the question was called for by Mr. DAGGETT, and it was taken on striking out; and determined in the affirmative—yeas 18, nays 15, as follows:

YEAS—Messrs. Anderson, Barbour, Bibb, Chace, Condit, Giles, Howell, Lacock, Morrow, Roberts, Robinson, Smith, Tait, Taylor, Turner, Varnum, Walker, and Wharton.

NAYS—Messrs. Brown, Daggett, Dana, Fromentin, Gaillard, German, Gore, Horsey, Hunter, Kerr, King, Lambert, Mason, Thompson, and Wells.

On the question, to insert the substitute proposed, it was determined in the negative—yeas 14, nays 19, as follows:

YEAS—Messrs. Anderson, Bibb, Chace, Condit, Howell, Kerr, Lacock, Morrow, Roberts, Robinson, Smith, Taylor, Varnum, and Walker.

NAYS—Messrs. Barbour, Brown, Daggett, Dana, Fromentin, Gaillard, German, Giles, Gore, Horsey, Hunter, King, Lambert, Mason, Tait, Thompson, Turner, Wells, and Wharton.

Whereupon, *Resolved,* That the Senate agree to some, and disagree to other amendments of the House of Representatives to the bill last mentioned.

TUESDAY, January 17.

The Senate resumed the bill for the relief of Bowie and Kurtz, and others; and on motion, by Mr. SMITH, the consideration thereof was further postponed to Monday next.

Mr. BROWN presented several memorials from a number of the inhabitants of the Mississippi Territory, praying to be confirmed in the possession of certain lands which they claim under patents granted by the British Government; for reasons stated in the memorials; which were read, and referred to a select committee to consider and report thereon by bill or otherwise; and Messrs. BROWN, MORROW, and TAYLOR, were appointed the committee.

Mr. WALKER, from the committee to whom was referred the bill, entitled "An act for the relief of William Robinson and others," reported it without amendment.

A message from the House of Representatives informed the Senate that the House have passed a bill, entitled "An act to amend the act, entitled 'An act to provide additional revenues for defraying the expenses of Government, and maintaining the public credit, by laying a direct tax upon the United States, and to provide for assessing and collecting the same;'" and the act, entitled "An act to provide additional revenues for defraying the expenses of Government, and maintaining the public credit, by laying duties on household furniture, and on gold and silver watches;" a bill, entitled "An act supplementary to the act, entitled 'An act laying duties on licenses to retailers of wines, spirituous liquors, and foreign merchandise, and for other purposes;'" a bill, entitled "An act to authorize the President to raise certain companies of rangers for the defence of the frontiers of the United States, and to repeal certain acts now in force for this purpose;" a bill, entitled "An act giving further time to the purchasers of public lands to complete their payments;" a bill, entitled "An act regulating the sale of reserved sections of land in the State of Ohio;" a bill, entitled "An act for the relief of the inhabitants of the late county of New Madrid, in the Missouri Territory, who suffered by earthquakes;" a bill entitled "An act attaching to the Canton district, in the State of Ohio, the tract of land lying between the foot of the rapids of the Miami of Lake Erie, and the Connecticut Western Reserve;" also, a bill, entitled "An act for the relief of the heirs of James Hynum;" in which bills they request the concurrence of the Senate. They insist on their amendments to the amendments of the Senate to the bill, entitled "An act to authorize the President of the United States to accept the services of volunteers who may associate and organize themselves, and offer their services to the Government of the United States."

On motion, by Mr. BIBB,

Resolved, That the Senate insist on their disagreement to the amendments insisted on by the House of Representatives to the bill last mentioned, and ask a conference thereon.

Ordered, That Messrs. BROWN, BIBB, and MASON, be the managers at the same, on the part of the Senate.

The eight bills last brought up for concurrence were read, and passed to the second reading.

WEDNESDAY, January 18.

The bill, entitled "An act to amend the act, entitled 'An act to provide additional revenues for defraying the expenses of Government, and maintaining the public credit, by laying a direct tax upon the United States, and to provide for assessing and collecting the same," and the act entitled "An act to provide additional revenues for defraying the expenses of Government, and maintaining the public credit, by laying duties on household furniture, and on gold and silver watches," was read the second time, and referred to a select committee, to consist of five members, to consider and report thereon; and Messrs. TAYLOR, DAGGETT, BROWN, CHACE, and SMITH, were appointed the committee.

The bill, entitled "An act supplementary to the act, entitled 'An act laying duties on licenses to retailers of wines, spirituous liquors and foreign merchandise, and for other purposes," was read the second time, and referred to the committee last mentioned, to consider and report thereon.

The bill entitled "An act attaching to the Canton district, in the State of Ohio, the tract of land lying between the foot of the rapids of the Miami of Lake Erie, and the Connecticut Western Reserve," was read the second time, and referred to the committee to whom was referred, the 21st September, the memorial of the Legislature of the Indiana Territory to consider and report thereon.

The bill, entitled "An act regulating the sale of certain reserved sections of land in the State of Ohio," was read the second time, and referred to the committee last mentioned, to consider and report thereon.

The bill, entitled "An act giving further time to the purchasers of public lands to complete their payments," was read the second time, and referred to the committee last mentioned, to consider and report thereon.

The bill, entitled "An act for the relief of the inhabitants of the late county of New Madrid, in the Missouri Territory, who suffered by earthquakes," was read the second time, and referred to a select committee, to consider and report thereon; and Messrs. FROMENTIN, MORROW, and DAGGETT, were appointed the committee.

The bill, entitled "An act for the relief of the heirs of James Hynum," was read the second time, and referred to the committee last mentioned, to consider and report thereon.

The bill, entitled "An act to authorize the President to raise certain companies of rangers for the defence of the frontiers of the United States, and to repeal certain acts now in force for this purpose," was read the second time, and referred to the Committee on Military Affairs, to consider and report thereon.

Mr. ANDERSON, from the committee to whom the subject was referred, reported a bill for the relief of Edward Barry and George Hodges; and the bill was read, and passed to the second reading.

The Senate resumed the consideration of the resolution reported the 16th instant, by the Committee on Military Affairs, and on motion, by Mr. TAYLOR, it was recommitted to the Committee on Military Affairs, together with the resolution of the Senate of the 2d instant, further to consider and report thereon.

On motion, by Mr. GILES, the Committee on Military Affairs were discharged from the further consideration of the resolution last mentioned, and that it be referred to the committee appointed on the 21st September, on so much of the Message of the President of the United States as relates to the militia, to consider and report thereon.

Mr. BIBB, from the Committee on Foreign Relations, to whom was referred the bill, entitled "An act to prohibit intercourse with the enemy and for other purposes," reported it with amendments; which were read, and on motion, by Mr. BIBB, the further consideration thereof was postponed to, and made the order of the day for, Friday next.

The Senate resumed the bill making appropriations for repairing or rebuilding the public buildings within the City of Washington, and on motion, by Mr. LACOCK, the consideration thereof was further postponed to, and made the order of the day for, Monday next.

The Senate resumed, as in Committee of the Whole, the consideration of the bill, entitled "An act for the relief of William Robinson and others;" and, no amendment having been proposed, it was ordered to the third reading.

THURSDAY, January 19.

The bill entitled "An act for the relief of William Robinson and others," was read a third time, and passed.

The bill for the relief of Edward Barry and George Hodges was read the second time.

On motion, by Mr. ROBERTS, the committee to whom was referred the memorial of the President and Directors of the Washington Bridge Company, were instructed to inquire into the expediency of providing by a general law for making compensation to individuals whose property may have been destroyed during the war, by the constituted authorities of the United States, or whose property may have been occupied for, or appropriated to, public purposes.

On motion, by Mr. ROBERTS, the committee to whom was referred the bill, entitled "An act for the relief of Jacob Shinnick, and Shoultz and Vogeler, of Christian Chapman, and the legal representative of John Calef, deceased," were discharged from the further consideration thereof.

On motion, by Mr. FROMENTIN, the Committee on Naval Affairs, to whom were referred the report of the Secretary for the Department of Navy, on the petition of Edward Bland and others, together with the accompanying documents, were discharged from the further consideration thereof, and they were referred to the said committee, to consider and report thereon by bill or otherwise.

Mr. THOMPSON presented several petitions, signed by a number of the inhabitants of the State of New Hampshire, remonstrating against the transportation and opening of the mail on the Sabbath; and the petitions were read, and referred to the committee to whom were referred, the 26th ultimo, several petitions on the same subject, to consider and report thereon by bill or otherwise.

A message from the House of Representatives informed the Senate that the House agree to the conference proposed on the amendments to the bill, entitled "An act to authorize the President of the United States to accept the services of volunteers who may associate and organize themselves, and offer their services to the Government of the United States," and have appointed managers on their part. They have passed the bill entitled "An act supplementary to the act, entitled 'An act providing for the indemnification of certain claimants of public lands in the Mississippi Territory," with amendments, in which they request the concurrence of the Senate.

They agree to some, and disagree to other amendments of the Senate to their amendments to the bill, entitled "An act to incorporate the subscribers to the Bank of the United States of America."

BANK OF THE UNITED STATES.

The Senate proceeded to the consideration of the message from the House announcing its disagreement to the amendments of the Senate to the bill, entitled "An act to incorporate the subscribers to the Bank of the United States of America."

[The state of this question is so intricately interwoven with matters of form and technicalities, that we shall, in describing the questions which came up to-day, disregard the mere form of them, and endeavor to present the substance.]

The first question was the proposition sent from the Senate, to which the House has disagreed, to increase the capital of the bank five millions, to be subscribable in public stock, created since the war.

On this proposition, Mr. BIBB proposed to insist. This motion was supported by Mr. BIBB, Mr. SMITH, Mr. ROBERTS, and Mr. TAYLOR, and opposed by Mr. BARBOUR, Mr. KING, and Mr. GILES. The able debate turned principally on the merits of the specie payment suspending section, (to which also the other House had disagreed,) which was considered as intimately connected with the question immediately before the Senate.

The first named gentlemen insisted on the advantages to the Government from the increase of the capital, and also from the proposed power to suspend payment in specie, without which, it was said, the operations of the bank must, for some time at least, be greatly restricted, &c., and wholly useless to the Government. Mr. BIBB, Mr. ROBERTS, and Mr. TAYLOR, intimated, if the Senate should yield these points to the House,

that they should vote for the indefinite postponement of the bill, under the impression that it would be rather an injury than a benefit to the community to pass it in its present shape.

Messrs. BARBOUR, KING, and GILES, urged the recession of the Senate from these amendments, principally on the ground of necessary concession (although the two latter gentlemen objected to them on principle also)—concessions which it was said the times now more than ever demand. Mr. BARBOUR, particularly, in an eloquent manner enforced the necessity of acting decisively on a subject which had so long been pending between the two Houses, and so greatly interested the feelings of the community, which turned its eyes with ceaseless anxiety on the dilatory proceedings of Congress. Mr. SMITH, in allusion to these remarks, took occasion to absolve the Executive and Senate from the blame of delay and apathy, and by inference to cast it on the shoulders of the House of Representatives.

The question being about to be taken, Mr. ROBERTS moved to postpone the subject till to-morrow, with the view of submitting a resolution that Mr. BLEDSOE (the Kentucky Senator) was entitled to a seat in the Senate, inasmuch as the election of his successor, Mr. TALBOT, had not yet been notified to the Senate. This motion was negatived, 25 to 9, by yeas and nays.

The question to insist on the first amendment, as stated above, was then decided as follows:

For insisting—Messrs. Anderson, Bibb, Chace, Condit, Howell, Lacock, Morrow, Roberts, Smith, Taylor, Turner, Varnum, and Walker—13.

Against insisting—Messrs. Barbour, Brown, Daggett, Dana, Fromentin, Gaillard, German, Giles, Goldsborough, Gore, Horsey, Hunter, Kerr, King, Lambert, Mason, Robinson, Tait, Thompson, Wells, and Wharton—21.

So the Senate refused to insist on this amendment.

Mr. GILES moved to recede from the said amendment.

Mr. ROBERTS then moved to postpone the further consideration of the whole subject to the second Monday in March (equivalent to a motion to reject.) In support of his motion, Mr. ROBERTS spoke at some length.

Mr. BIBB intimated that he should vote against the postponement now, because the amendment respecting which he was most anxious had not been decided (meaning the section respecting specie payments.)

Mr. TAYLOR said he should vote for the postponement, because he perceived the amendment referred to by Mr. BIBB would not be insisted on.

The question on the postponement (or rejection) was then decided as follows:

For the postponement—Messrs. Gaillard, German, Kerr, Lacock, Lambert, Roberts, Taylor, Turner, and Varnum—9.

Against the postponement—Messrs. Anderson, Barbour, Bibb, Brown, Chace, Condit, Daggett, Dana, Fromentin, Giles, Goldsborough, Gore, Horsey, Howell,

Hunter, King, Mason, Morrow, Robinson, Smith, Tait, Thompson, Walker, Wells, and Wharton—25.

The question on Mr. GILES's motion, to recede from the said first amendment, was then decided in the affirmative—ayes 18.

Mr. KING then moved to recede from all the other amendments to which the House had disagreed.

The Senate then receded from such of the said remaining amendments, as preceded the following:

The question on receding from the insertion of the section, authorizing the bank under certain circumstances, to suspend payment of their notes in specie, was decided as follows:

For receding—Messrs. Barbour, Brown, Daggett, Dana, Fromentin, Gaillard, German, Giles, Goldsborough, Gore, Horsey, Hunter, Kerr, King, Lambert, Mason, Thompson, and Wells—18.

Against receding—Messrs. Anderson, Bibb, Chace, Condit, Howell, Lacock, Morrow, Roberts, Robinson, Smith, Tait, Taylor, Turner, Varnum, Walker, and Wharton—16.

So the Senate virtually disagreed to the insertion of such a section. Whereupon,

Mr. BIBB moved to postpone to the second Monday in March (to reject) the further consideration of this bill.

Mr. SMITH then, expressing a desire to have a night's reflection on this question, moved to adjourn.

There were 19 ayes in favor of the motion; and the Senate adjourned at a late hour.

FRIDAY, January 20.

The PRESIDENT communicated a report of the Secretary of the Treasury, exhibiting the sums respectively paid to each clerk in the several offices of that Department, for services rendered during the year 1814, made in obedience to the provisions of the act of April 21, 1806, to regulate and fix the compensation of clerks; and the report was read.

Mr. VARNUM, from the Militia Committee, to whom the subject was referred the 9th instant, reported a bill concerning field officers and militia; and the bill was read, and passed to the second reading.

The PRESIDENT laid before the Senate a letter from the Honorable Mr. BLEDSOE, as follows:

WASHINGTON, *January* 20, 1815.

SIR: Doubts having arisen whether I have a right still to fill my seat in the Senate of the United States, with a view to have the question settled, and a precedent established, and to save my own feelings on a point of duty, I beg leave, through you, to submit the following case for the decision of that honorable body:

Previous to the 24th December last, I forwarded, by mail, my resignation to the Governor of the State of Kentucky, to take place on that day, to be by him communicated to the Legislature of that State, then, and, so far as I am informed, still in session. I was, by a letter from the Governor of that State, advised that he had received my resignation, and would hold it up in the hope of hearing from me, and of a change in my determination on that subject, until about the last

of that month, when he would communicate it to the Legislature. Newspaper information states that he did so, and that my successor has been appointed; which latter fact is also stated in a letter to a gentleman of the House of Representatives, as I have been informed. This is all the information I have received. Whether, under these circumstances, I am to be considered as still a member, will be for the honorable Senate to decide. Wishing it to be understood I have no other solicitude as to the result than to be informed of my duty, which is concerned, in continuing in my place, if I have a right to do so,

I am, with high respect, your most obedient servant,

         J. BLEDSOE.

The Honorable JOHN GAILLARD,
    President of the Senate.

And the letter was read. Whereupon, Mr. ROBERTS submitted the following motion:

Resolved, That the facts stated in the letter of the Honorable Jesse Bledsoe, addressed to the President of the Senate, do not vacate his seat in the Senate.

A motion was made, by Mr. KING, to amend the resolution, by striking out therefrom, the word "not;" and it was determined in the affirmative—yeas 25, nays 8, as follows:

YEAS—Messrs. Anderson, Barbour, Brown, Chace, Daggett, Fromentin, Gaillard, German, Giles, Goldsborough, Gore, Horsey, Howell, Hunter, Kerr, King, Lambert, Mason, Morrow, Robinson, Tait, Taylor, Thompson, Wells, and Wharton.

NAYS.—Messrs. Bibb, Condit, Dana, Lacock, Roberts, Smith, Turner, and Varnum.

On the question, Shall the resolution pass as amended? it was determined in the affirmative—yeas 27, nays 6, as follows:

YEAS—Messrs. Anderson, Barbour, Brown, Chace, Daggett, Fromentin, Gaillard, German, Giles, Goldsborough, Gore, Horsey, Howell, Hunter, Kerr, King, Lacock, Lambert, Mason, Morrow, Robinson, Tait, Taylor, Thompson, Turner, Wells, and Wharton.

NAYS—Messrs. Bibb, Condit, Dana, Roberts, Smith, and Varnum.

So it was, *Resolved,* That the facts stated in the letter of the Honorable JESSE BLEDSOE, addressed to the President of the Senate, do vacate his seat in the Senate.

A message from the House of Representatives informed the Senate that the House have passed a bill, entitled "An act for the relief of Benjamin Wells and others;" a bill, entitled "An act for the relief of James Brahany;" also, a bill, entitled "An act for the better regulation of the ordnance department;" in which bills they request the concurrence of the Senate.

The Senate resumed the consideration of their amendments, disagreed to by the House of Representatives, to the amendments to the bill, entitled "An act to incorporate the subscribers to the Bank of the United States of America."

On the question, that the said bill, together with the amendments, be postponed to the second Monday in March next, it was determined in the negative—yeas 14, nays 20, as follows:

YEAS—Messrs. Anderson, Bibb, Condit, Gaillard, Howell, Kerr, Lacock, Morrow, Roberts, Smith, Taylor, Turner, Varnum, and Walker.

NAYS—Messrs. Barbour, Brown, Chace, Daggett, Dana, Fromentin, German, Giles, Goldsborough, Gore, Horsey, Hunter, King, Lambert, Mason, Robinson, Tait, Thompson, Wells, and Wharton,

Whereupon, on motion, by Mr. GILES,

Resolved, That the Senate recede from their amendments to the amendments of the House of Representatives to the said bill, to which the said House have disagreed; and that they recede from their disagreement to, and concur in, all the other amendments of the House of Representatives thereto.

Mr. BROWN, from the managers appointed on the part of the Senate, on the disagreeing votes of the two Houses, on the bill, entitled "An act to authorize the President of the United States to accept the services of volunteers who may associate and organize themselves, and offer their services to the Government of the United States," reported:

"That they have agreed to recommend to their respective Houses a modification of the first amendment of the Senate, in lieu of the amendment proposed by the House of Representatives, by adding the following proviso, at the end of the first section:

"*And be it further provided,* That, in case the President of the United States shall hereafter call on the Executives of the several States to hold in readiness their respective quotas of militia for service, he shall consider the corps of State troops raised in any State, as part of the quota of such State.

"And in lieu of the amendment proposed by the House of Representatives to the 5th section, to modify the 5th section as proposed by the Senate, by striking out the word "forty," in the 12th line, and inserting the word "seventy."

SATURDAY, January 21.

The PRESIDENT laid before the Senate a memorial of the Legislature of the Mississippi Territory, praying that the inhabitants of said Territory may be authorized to form a convention for the adoption of a constitution, and that the said Territory may be admitted into the Union as a State; for reasons stated at large in the memorial; which was read.

The PRESIDENT also laid before the Senate another memorial of the Legislature of the said Territory, praying that the amount of losses sustained by citizens of said Territory, in the war against the Creek Indians, may be ascertained, in order that the sufferers may be indemnified in lands, acquired from said Indians, as is stated in the memorial; which was read.

The PRESIDENT laid before the Senate another memorial of the Legislature of the said Territory, praying that the power to lease out the lands set apart for the public schools in said Territory may be vested in said Legislature; for reasons therein stated; and the memorial was read.

The PRESIDENT also laid before the Senate another memorial of the Legislature of the said Territory, praying that the interest which has accrued on lands in said Territory, purchased of the United States, may be remitted, and that further

time may be given to complete the payments for the said lands; for reasons therein stated; and the memorial was read.

On motion, by Mr. MORROW,

Ordered, That it be referred to the committee to whom was referred, on the 21st of September, the memorial of the Legislature of the Indiana Territory, to consider and report thereon by bill or otherwise.

The PRESIDENT also communicated a resolution of the Legislature of the Mississippi Territory, tendering to the General Government their undivided support in repelling the aggressions and unjust demands of the enemy, and preferring a sacrifice of their lives and fortunes, to the surrender of our rights or national dignity; and the resolution was read, and ordered to be printed for the use of the Senate.

The three bills brought up yesterday for concurrence were read, and passed to the second reading.

On motion, by Mr. SMITH, the bill, entitled "An act for the better regulation of the Ordnance department," was read the second time by unanimous consent; and referred to the Committee on Military Affairs, to consider and report thereon.

The Senate proceeded to consider the amendments of the House of Representatives to the bill, entitled "An act supplementary to the act, entitled 'An act providing for the indemnification of certain claimants of the public lands in the Mississippi Territory."

Whereupon, on motion, by Mr. HUNTER,

Resolved, That they concur therein with an amendment.

The Senate proceeded to consider the report of the committee of conference on their part, on the disagreeing votes of the two Houses, on the bill, entitled "An act to authorize the President of the United States to accept the services of volunteers who may associate and organize themselves, and offer their services to the Government of the United States.

Whereupon, on motion, by Mr. BROWN,

Resolved, That they concur therein with an amendment.

The Senate resumed the bill, entitled "An act to prohibit intercourse with the enemy, and for other purposes;" and on motion, by Mr. BIBB, the consideration thereof was postponed to, and made the order of the day for, Monday next.

On motion, by Mr. ANDERSON, the bill for the relief of Edward Barry and George Hodges, together with the accompanying documents, was referred to the committee appointed on the 23d September, on the memorial of the President and Directors of the Washington Bridge Company, to consider and report thereon.

The bill concerning field officers of the militia was read the second time.

MONDAY, January 23.

The PRESIDENT laid before the Senate the credentials of OUTERBRIDGE HORSEY, appointed a Senator by the Legislature of the State of Delaware, for the term of six years, commencing on the fourth day of March next; and they were read, and laid on file.

The Senate resumed the consideration of the motion submitted on the 10th instant, by Mr. Mason, relative to information requested by their resolution of the 9th November last; and on the question, to agree thereto, it was determined in the negative—yeas 12, nays 18, as follows:

YEAS—Messrs. Dana, German, Goldsborough, Gore, Horsey, Hunter, King, Lambert, Mason, Smith, Taylor, and Thompson.

NAYS—Messrs. Anderson, Barbour, Bibb, Chace, Condit, Daggett, Gaillard, Giles, Kerr, Lacock, Morrow, Roberts, Robinson, Turner, Varnum, Walker, Wells, and Wharton.

The Senate resumed the consideration of the motion submitted on the 27th December last; and on motion, by Mr. King, the consideration thereof was further postponed to the first Monday in February next.

The bill, entitled "An act for the relief of John Brahany," was read the second time.

The bill, entitled "An act for the relief of Benjamin Wells and others," was read the second time, and referred to a select committee, to consider and report thereon; and Messrs. Roberts, Mason, and Barbour, were appointed the committee.

A message from the House of Representatives informed the Senate that the House agree to the amendments of the Senate to the bill, entitled "An act providing for the indemnification of certain claimants of public lands in the Mississippi Territory." They agree to the report of the conferees on the disagreeing votes of the two Houses on the amendments to the bill, entitled "An act to authorize the President of the United States to accept the services of volunteers who may associate and organize themselves, and offer their services to the Government of the United States," with the amendment made thereto by the Senate; and that the bill be passed accordingly. They have passed a bill, entitled "An act to alter and amend the several acts for establishing a Navy Department, by adding thereto a Board of Commissioners; a bill, entitled "An act directing the manner of contracts and purchases in the Navy Department, and for promoting economy therein," a bill, entitled "An act for the relief of Joseph Perkins;" a bill, entitled "An act concerning Matthew Guy, John Woodward, Samuel Tennison, and Wilfred Drury;" a bill, entitled "An act concerning Weston Jenkins and others;" a bill, entitled "An act for the relief of William Arnold;" also, a bill, entitled "An act for the relief of Farrington Barkelow, administrator of Mary Rappleyea;" in which bills they request the concurrence of the Senate.

Mr. Hunter, from the committee to whom the subject was referred reported a bill for the relief of Henry Nimmo; and the bill was read, and passed to the second reading.

The Senate resumed, as in Committee of the Whole, the consideration of the bill, entitled "An act to prohibit intercourse with the enemy, and for other purposes," together with the amendments reported thereto by the select committee; and the amendments were agreed to with an amendment; and the bill having been further amended, on motion, by Mr. Roberts, the further consideration thereof was postponed until to-morrow.

TUESDAY, January 24.

The seven bills brought up yesterday for concurrence were read, and passed to the second reading.

A message from the House of Representatives informed the Senate that the House have passed a bill, entitled "An act to amend the act laying duties on licenses to retailers of wines, spirituous liquors, and foreign merchandise;" in which bill they request the concurrence of the Senate.

The bill last mentioned was read, and passed to the second reading.

The bill for the relief of Henry Nimmo was read the second time.

The Senate resumed, as in Committee of the Whole, the consideration of the bill, entitled "An act to prohibit intercourse with the enemy, and for other purposes."

Mr. Daggett moved to strike out the 8th section of the bill. And after debate, on motion, by Mr. Barbour, the further consideration thereof was postponed until to-morrow.

Mr. Smith, from the committee to whom was referred the report of the Secretary of the Treasury containing a statement of proceedings under the act to regulate the laying out and making a road from Cumberland, in the State of Maryland, to the State of Ohio, made a report; which was read.

Mr. Smith, from the same committee, reported a bill in addition to the act to regulate the laying out and making a road from Cumberland, in the State of Maryland, to the State of Ohio; and the bill was read, and passed to the second reading.

Mr. Taylor, from the committee to whom was referred the bill, entitled "An act supplementary to the act, entitled 'An act laying duties on licenses to retailers of wines, spirituous liquors, and foreign merchandise, and for other purposes,'" reported it wth amendments.

On motion, by Mr. Goldsborough, the bill for the relief of Bowie and Kurtz, and others, was recommitted to Messrs. Goldsborough, Gore, and Chace, further to consider and report thereon.

On motion, by Mr. Morrow, a member was added to the committee to whom was referred, the 21st September last, the memorial of the Legislature of the Indiana Territory, in place of Mr. Bledsoe; and Mr. Barbour was elected.

The bill for the relief of Henry Nimmo was read the second time, and considered as in Committee of the Whole; and, no amendment having been proposed, the bill was ordered to be engrossed and read a third time.

WEDNESDAY, January 25.

The bill, entitled "An act to amend the act laying duties on licenses to retailers of wines, spirituous liquors, and foreign merchandise," was read the second time, and referred to the committee to whom was referred, the 18th instant, the bill, entitled "An act to amend the act, entitled 'An act to provide additional revenues for defraying the expenses of Government, and maintaining the public credit, by laying a direct tax upon the United States, and to provide for assessing and collecting the same;" and the act, entitled "An act to provide additional revenues for defraying the expenses of Government, and maintaining the public credit, by laying duties on household furniture, and on gold and silver watches," to consider and report thereon.

The bill for the relief of Henry Nimmo was read a third time, and passed.

Mr. MASON presented a petition, signed by a number of the inhabitants of the town of Hollis, in the State of New Hampshire, remonstrating against the transportation and opening of the mail on the Sabbath; and the petition was read, and referred to the committee to whom were referred, on the 26th ultimo, several petitions on the same subject, to consider and report thereon by bill or otherwise.

The bill, entitled "An act for the relief of William Arnold," was read the second time.

The bill, entitled "An act for the relief of Joseph Perkins," was read the second time, and referred to a select committee, to consider and report thereon; and Messrs. GORE, HUNTER, and MASON, were appointed the committee.

The bill, entitled "An act for the relief of Farrington Barkelow, administrator of Mary Rappleyea," was read the second time.

The bill, entitled "An act concerning Weston Jenkins and others," was read the second time.

The bill, entitled "An act concerning Matthew Guy, John Woodward, Samuel Tennison, and Wilfred Drury," was read the second time.

The bill, entitled "An act to alter and amend the several acts for establishing a Navy Department, by adding thereto a Board of Commissioners," was read the second time, and referred to the Committee on Naval Affairs, to consider and report thereon.

The bill, entitled "An act directing the manner of contracts and purchases in the Navy Department, and for promoting economy therein," was read the second time, and referred to the same committee, to consider and report thereon.

INTERCOURSE WITH THE ENEMY.

The Senate resumed, as in Committee of the Whole, the consideration of the bill, entitled "An act to prohibit intercourse with the enemy, and for other purposes;" and Mr. VARNUM was requested to take the Chair.

On the question to strike out the eighth section, as proposed by Mr. DAGGETT—on motion, by Mr. BIBB, it was agreed to take the question by yeas and nays.

On motion, by Mr. DAGGETT, that the bill be referred to a select committee, further to consider and report thereon, it was determined in the negative—yeas 13, nays 15, as follows:

YEAS—Messrs. Daggett, Dana, Fromentin, German, Goldsborough, Gore, Horsey, Hunter, King, Lambert, Mason, Thompson, and Wells.

NAYS—Messrs. Anderson, Barbour, Bibb, Chace, Condit, Kerr, Lacock, Morrow, Robinson, Smith, Tait, Taylor, Varnum, Walker, and Wharton.

On motion, by Mr. BARBOUR, to amend the eighth section of the bill, by inserting, in the fifth line, after the word "act," the words, "or under color thereof;" it was determined in the negative—(the Senate being equally divided) yeas 14, nays 14, as follows:

YEAS—Messrs. Anderson, Barbour, Bibb, Chace, Condit, Lacock, Morrow, Robinson, Tait, Taylor, Turner, Varnum, Walker, and Wharton.

NAYS—Messrs. Daggett, Dana, Fromentin, German, Goldsborough, Gore, Horsey, Hunter, King, Lambert, Mason, Smith, Thompson, and Wells.

And the question recurring on striking out the 8th section, amended as follows:

"SEC. 8. And be it further enacted, That if any suit or prosecution be commenced in any State court, against any collector, naval officer, surveyor, inspector, or any other officer, civil or military, or any other person aiding or assisting, agreeable to the provisions of this act, for anything done, or omitted to be done, as an officer of the customs, or for anything done by virtue of this act, and the defendant shall, at the time of entering his appearance in such court, file a petition for the removal of the cause for trial at the next circuit court to be holden in the district where the suit is pending, and offer good and sufficient surety for his entering in such court, on the first day of its session, copies of said process against him, and also for his there appearing at the court and entering special bail in the cause, if special bail was originally required therein, it shall then be the duty of the State court to accept the surety, and proceed no further in the cause, and the bail that shall have been originally taken, shall be discharged, and such copies being entered as aforesaid in such court of the United States, the cause shall there proceed in the same manner as if it had been brought there by original process, whatever may be the amount of the sum in dispute or damages claimed, or whatever the citizenship of the parties, any former law to the contrary notwithstanding. And any attachment of the goods or estate of the defendant, by the original process, shall hold the goods or estate so attached to answer the final judgment, in the same manner as by the laws of such State they would have been holden to answer final judgment, had it been rendered by the court in which the suit was commenced. And it shall be lawful, in any action or prosecution which may be now pending, or hereafter commenced, before any State court whatever, for anything done, or omitted to be done, by the defendant, as an inspector or other officer of the customs, after final judgment, for either party to remove and transfer, by appeal, such decision, during the session or term of said court, at which the same shall have taken place, from such court to the next circuit court of the United States, to be held in the district in which such appeal shall be taken in manner aforesaid; and it shall be the duty of the person taking such appeal and transfer, to produce and enter in the said circuit court, attested copies of the process, proceedings, and judgment, in such cause; and it shall also be competent for either party, within six months of the rendition of a judgment in any such cause, by writ of error or other process, to remove the same to the circuit court of the United States of that district in which such judgment shall have been rendered; and the said circuit court shall, thereupon, proceed to try and determine the facts and the law in such action, in the same manner as if the same had been there originally commenced; the judgment in such case notwithstanding. And any bail which may have been taken, or property attached, shall be holden on the final judgment of the said circuit court in such action, in the same manner as if no such removal and transfer had been made as aforesaid; and the State court from which any such action may be removed and transferred as aforesaid, upon the parties giving good and sufficient security for the prosecution thereof, shall allow the same to be removed and transferred, and proceed no further in the case: *Provided, however,* That if the party aforesaid shall fail duly to enter the removal and transfer as aforesaid in the circuit court, agreeable to this act, the State court, by which judgment shall have been rendered, and from which the transfer and removal shall have been made as aforesaid, shall be authorized, on motion for that purpose, to issue execution, and to carry into effect any such judgment, the same as if no such removal and transfer had been made: *Provided, nevertheless,* That this act shall not be construed to apply to any prosecution for an offence involving corporal punishment: *And, provided also,* That no such appeal shall be allowed in any criminal action or prosecution, where final judgment shall have been rendered in favor of the defendant, or respondent, by the State court; and in any action or prosecution against any person as aforesaid, it shall be lawful for such person to plead the general issue, and give this act and any special matter in evidence. And if, in any such suit, the plaintiff is nonsuit, or judgment pass against him, the defendant shall recover double costs:"

It was determined in the negative—yeas 12, nays 15, as follows:

YEAS—Messrs. Daggett, Dana, German, Goldsborough, Gore, Horsey, Hunter, King, Lambert, Mason, Thompson, and Wells.

NAYS—Messrs. Anderson, Barbour, Bibb, Chace, Condit, Gaillard, Kerr, Lacock, Morrow, Robinson, Taylor, Turner, Varnum, Walker, and Wharton.

And the bill having been amended, the PRESIDENT resumed the Chair, and Mr. VARNUM reported it to the House accordingly.

THURSDAY, January 26.

The bill in addition to the act to regulate the laying out and making a road from Cumberland, in the State of Maryland, to the State of Ohio, was read the second time.

A message from the House of Representatives informed the Senate that the House have passed the bill, entitled "An act to extend the time of Oliver Evans's patent for his improvement on steam engines," with amendments, in which they request the concurrence of the Senate. They have passed a bill, entitled "An act for the relief of Isaac Smith and Bratton Caldwell;" also, a bill, entitled "An act to authorize the purchase of a tract of land for the use of the United States;" in which bills they request the concurrence of the Senate.

INTERCOURSE WITH THE ENEMY.

The Senate resumed the consideration of the bill to prohibit intercourse with the enemy, and for other purposes; and the amendments made in Committee of the Whole were concurred in; and on motion, by Mr. BARBOUR, it was agreed to amend the 8th section of the bill, by inserting, in the 5th line, after the word "act," the words, "or under color thereof;" and, on motion by Mr. BARBOUR, to insert the same words in the 7th line of the same section, after the word "act;" it was determined in the affirmative—yeas 16, nays 15, as follows:

YEAS—Messrs. Anderson, Barbour, Bibb, Chace, Condit, Gaillard, Kerr, Lacock, Morrow, Robinson, Tait, Taylor, Turner, Varnum, Walker, and Wharton.

NAYS—Messrs. Brown, Daggett, Dana, Fromentin, German, Goldsborough, Gore, Horsey, Hunter, King, Lambert, Mason, Smith, Thompson, and Wells.

On motion, by Mr. DAGGETT, to strike out the 8th section of the bill as amended, it was determined in the negative—yeas 13, nays 18, as follows:

YEAS—Messrs. Daggett, Dana, Fromentin, German, Goldsborough, Gore, Horsey, Hunter, King, Lambert, Mason, Thompson, and Wells.

NAYS—Messrs. Anderson, Barber, Bibb, Brown, Chace, Condit, Gaillard, Kerr, Lacock, Morrow, Robinson, Smith, Taylor, Turner, Varnum, Walker, and Wharton.

On motion, by Mr. MASON, to add the following proviso at the end of the 5th section:

"*Provided,* That each inspector so appointed shall, before he enter upon the duties of his office, give bond to the United States with sufficient sureties, to the acceptance of the district judge, of the district where such inspector shall be appointed, in a sum not less than —— thousand dollars, for the faithful performance of the duties of his office, and to respond damages to any person injured by such officer under color of his office; which bond may, on application to such judge, by any person so injured by such officer, be put in suit for the benefit of such person:"

It was determined in the affirmative—yeas 16, nays 15, as follows:

YEAS—Messrs. Brown, Daggett, Dana, Fromentin, German, Goldsborough, Gore, Horsey, Hunter, Kerr, King, Lambert, Mason, Smith, Thompson, and Wells.

NAYS—Messrs. Anderson, Barbour, Bibb, Chace, Condit, Gaillard, Lacock, Morrow, Robinson, Tait, Taylor, Turner, Varnum, Walker, and Wharton.

And the bill having been further amended the amendments were engrossed and the bill read a third time as amended.

FRIDAY, January 27.

The bill from the House of Representatives, entitled "An act to authorize the purchase of a tract of land for the use of the United States," was read, and passed to a second reading.

The bill, entitled "An act for the relief of Isaac Smith and Bratton Caldwell," was read, and passed to the second reading.

The Senate proceeded to consider the amendments of the House of Representatives to the bill, entitled "An act to extend the time of Oliver Evans's patent for his improvement on steam engines," and on motion, by Mr. GILES, the further consideration thereof was postponed to Tuesday next.

Mr. MORROW, from the committee to whom was referred the bill, entitled "An act for giving further time to the purchasers of public lands to complete their payments," reported it without amendment.

Mr. MORROW, from the same committee, to whom was referred the bill, entitled "An act attaching to the Canton district, in the State of Ohio, the tract of land lying between the foot of the rapids of the Miami of Lake Erie, and the Connecticut Western Reserve," also reported it without amendment.

The Senate resumed the bill making appropriations for repairing or rebuilding the public buildings within the City of Washington; and on motion, by Mr. LACOCK, the consideration thereof was further postponed until to-morrow.

Mr. TAYLOR presented the petition of sundry inhabitants of Darlington district, in the State of South Carolina, praying an alteration in the conveyance of the mail through their district, for reasons stated in the petition; which was read.

The Senate resumed, as in Committee of the Whole, the consideration of the bill concerning field officers of the militia; and, no amendment having been proposed, the bill was ordered to be engrossed and read a third time.

The amendments to the bill, entitled "An act to prohibit intercourse with the enemy, and for other purposes," was read a third time as amended.

On motion, by Mr. KING, it was referred to a select committee, to consist of five members, further to consider and report thereon; and Messrs. GILES, MASON, BARBOUR, CHACE, and BIBB, were appointed the committee.

Mr. DAGGETT, from the committee to whom were referred the petitions of numerous citizens of the States of New Hampshire, Massachusetts, Connecticut, North Carolina, and Ohio, praying Congress to prohibit the transportation and opening of the mail on the Sabbath, made report; which was read, together with the following resolution:

Resolved, That at this time it is inexpedient to interfere and pass any laws on the subject-matter of the several petitions, praying the prohibition of the transportation and opening of the mail on the Sabbath.

The Senate resumed, as in Committee of the Whole, the consideration of the bill, entitled "An act concerning Matthew Guy, John Woodward, Samuel Tennison, and Wilfred Drury," and on motion, by Mr. TAIT, it was referred to the Committee on Naval Affairs, to consider and report thereon.

The Senate resumed, as in Committee of the Whole, the consideration of the bill, entitled "An act concerning Weston Jenkins and others," and on motion, by Mr. ANDERSON, it was referred to the same committee, to consider and report thereon.

The Senate resumed, as in Committee of the Whole, the consideration of the bill, entitled "An act for the relief of John Brahany;" and, no amendment having been proposed, it passed to a third reading.

The bill, entitled "An act for the relief of Farrington Barkelow, administrator of Mary Rappleyea," was resumed, as in Committee of the Whole; and, no amendment having been proposed, it passed to the third reading.

The Senate resumed, as in Committee of the Whole, the consideration of the bill, entitled "An act for the relief of William Arnold;" and, no amendment having been proposed, it passed to a third reading.

The Senate resumed, as in Committee of the Whole, the consideration of the bill, entitled "An act supplementary to the act, entitled 'An act laying duties on licenses to retailers of wines, spirituous liquors, and foreign merchandise, and for other purposes," together with the amendments reported thereto by the select committee; and, the amendments having been agreed to, the PRESIDENT reported the bill to the House accordingly.

On the question, Shall the amendments be engrossed and the bill read a third time as amended? it was determined in the affirmative.

SATURDAY, January 28.

On motion, by Mr. VARNUM,

Resolved, That the Secretary of the Navy Department be directed to lay before the Senate an account of the disbursements of public moneys which have been made at each navy yard in the United States, between the first day of January, 1800, and the last day of December, 1814, designating the disbursements made at each, in each year.

On motion, by Mr. VARNUM,

Resolved, That the Secretary for the Department of War be directed to lay before the Senate the amount of the expenditures in each State in the Union, for fortifications and for the ordnance department, from the commencement of the year 1800, to the end of the year 1814, designating the sums expended in each State, in each year; and, also, designating the sums expended for fortifications, from the sums expended for the ordnance department.

Mr. TAIT, from the Committee on Naval Affairs, to whom was referred the bill, entitled "An act to alter and amend the several acts for establishing a Navy Department, by adding thereto a Board of Commissioners," reported it with amendments.

The bill, entitled "An act to authorize the purchase of a tract of land for the use of the United States," was read the second time, and referred to the Committee on Military Affairs, to consider and report thereon.

The bill, entitled "An act for the relief of Isaac Smith and Bratton Caldwell," was read the second time, and referred to a select committee, to consider and report thereon; and Messrs. LACOCK,

ANDERSON, and THOMPSON, were appointed the committee.

The bill, entitled "An act for the relief of Barrington Barkelow, administrator of Mary Rappleyea," was read a third time, and passed.

The bill, entitled "An act for the relief of John Brahany," was read a third time, and passed.

The bill, entitled "An act for the relief of William Arnold," was read a third time, and passed.

The bill concerning field officers of the militia was read a third time, and passed.

The amendments to the bill, entitled "An act supplementary to the act, entitled 'An act laying duties on licenses to retailers of wines, spirituous liquors, and foreign merchandise, and for other purposes," was read a third time as amended.

Resolved, That this bill pass with amendments.

On motion, by Mr. TAYLOR, it was agreed to amend the title, by inserting, in the first line, after the word "act," and before "laying," "to amend the act."

The Senate resumed the consideration of the report of the committee to whom were referred the petitions of numerous citizens of the States of New Hampshire, Massachusetts, Connecticut, North Carolina, and Ohio, praying Congress to prohibit the transportation and opening of the mail on the Sabbath. Whereupon,

Resolved, That at this time it is inexpedient to interfere and pass any laws on the subject-matter of the several petitions praying the prohibition of transportation and opening of the mail on the Sabbath.

The Senate resumed the bill making appropriations for repairing or rebuilding the public buildings within the City of Washington; and on motion, by Mr. SMITH, the consideration thereof was further postponed to Monday next.

The Senate resumed, as in Committee of the Whole, the consideration of the bill in addition to the act to regulate the laying out and making a road from Cumberland, in the State of of Maryland, to the State of Ohio; and, no amendment having been proposed, the bill was ordered to be engrossed and read a third time.

INTERCOURSE WITH THE ENEMY.

Mr. GILES, from the committee to whom was referred the bill, entitled "An act to prohibit intercourse with the enemy, and for other purposes," reported it with amendments; which were read, and considered as in Committee of the Whole.

On the question to agree to the amendment proposed by the select committee, "to strike out of the amendments the proviso to the end of the 5th section of the bill," it was determined in the affirmative—yeas 17, nays 12, as follows:

YEAS—Messrs. Anderson, Barbour, Bibb, Chace, Condit, Gaillard, Giles, Kerr, Lacock, Morrow, Robinson, Tait, Taylor, Turner, Varnum, Walker, and Wharton.

NAYS—Messrs. Daggett, Fromentin, German, Goldsborough, Gore, Horsey, Hunter, King, Lambert, Mason, Smith, and Thompson.

On motion, by Mr. MASON, to amend the 5th section of the bill, by inserting, after the word "customs," in the 4th line, the following words: "and for whose acts and doings in their office the collector so appointing them shall be answerable to any person thereby injured :" it was determined in the negative—yeas 11, nays 18, as follows:

YEAS—Messrs. Daggett, Fromentin, German, Goldsborough, Gore, Horsey, Hunter, King, Lambert, Mason, and Thompson.

NAYS—Messrs. Anderson, Barbour, Bibb, Chace, Condit, Gaillard, Giles, Kerr, Lacock, Morrow, Robinson, Smith, Tait, Taylor, Turner, Varnum, Walker, and Wharton.

And the amendments reported by the select committee having been agreed to, the President reported the bill to the House accordingly.

On the question, Shall the amendments be engrossed, and the bill read a third time as amended? it was determined in the affirmative.

MONDAY, January 30.

The Senate resumed, as in Committee of the Whole, the consideration of the bill, entitled "An act giving further time to purchasers of public lands to complete their payments ;" and, no amendment having been proposed, it passed to a third reading.

The Senate resumed, as in Committee of the Whole, the consideration of the bill, entitled "An act attaching to the Canton district, in the State of Ohio, the tract of land lying between the foot of the rapids of the Miami of Lake Erie, and the Connecticut Western Reserve ;" and, no amendment having been proposed, it passed to a third reading.

Mr. HORSEY, from the committee to whom the subject was referred, reported a bill to allow a drawback of duties on spirits distilled, and certain goods, wares, and merchandise, manufactured within the United States; and the bill was read, and passed to the second reading.

The Senate resumed, as in Committee of the Whole, the consideration of the bill, entitled "An act to alter and amend the several acts for establishing a Navy Department, by adding thereto a Board of Commissioners, together with the amendments reported thereto by the select committee; and, on motion by Mr. SMITH, the further consideration thereof was postponed until to-morrow.

On motion, by Mr. LACOCK, the consideration of the bill making appropriations for repairing or rebuilding the public buildings within the City of Washington was postponed to, and made the order of the day for, Wednesday next.

The amendments to the bill, entitled "An act to prohibit intercourse with the enemy, and for other purposes," was read a third time, as amended.

Resolved, That this bill pass with amendments.

The bill in addition to the act to regulate the laying out and making a road from Cumberland, in the State of Maryland, to the State of Ohio, was read a third time; and on motion, by Mr. SMITH, to fill the blank with "one hundred thousand," it was determined in the affirmative, as follows:

YEAS—Messrs. Bibb, Brown, Chace, Condit, Fromentin, Gaillard, Goldsborough, Horsey, Kerr, Morrow, Smith, Tait, Taylor, Turner, Varnum, Walker, and Wharton.

NAYS—Messrs. Barbour, King, Lambert, Mason, Robinson, Thompson, and Wells.

Resolved, That this bill pass, and that the title thereof be "An act in addition to the act to regulate the laying out and making a road from Cumberland, in the State of Maryland, to the State of Ohio."

Mr. GILES, from the Committee on Military Affairs, to whom was referred the bill, entitled "An act for the better regulation of the Ordnance department," reported it with amendments.

Mr. GILES, from the same committee, to whom was referred the bill, entitled "An act to authorize the purchase of a tract of land for the use of the United States," reported it with an amendment.

BANK OF THE UNITED STATES.

The following Message was received from the PRESIDENT OF THE UNITED STATES:

To the Senate of the United States:

Having bestowed on the bill, entitled "An act to incorporate the subscribers to the Bank of the United States of America," that full consideration which is due to the great importance of the subject, and dictated by the respect which I feel for the two Houses of Congress, I am constrained, by a deep and solemn conviction that the bill ought not to become a law, to return it to the Senate, in which it originated, with my objections to the same.

Waiving the question of the Constitutional authority of the Legislature to establish an incorporated bank, as being precluded, in my judgment, by repeated recognitions, under varied circumstances, of the validity of such an institution, in acts of the Legislative, Executive, and Judicial branches of the Government, accompanied by indications, in different modes, of a concurrence of the general will of the nation; the proposed bank does not appear to be calculated to answer the purposes of reviving the public credit, of providing a national medium of circulation, and of aiding the Treasury by facilitating the indispensable anticipations of the revenue, and by affording to the public more durable loans.

1. The capital of the bank is to be compounded of specie, of public stock, and of Treasury notes convertible into stock, with a certain proportion of each of which every subscriber is to furnish himself.

The amount of the stock to be subscribed will not, it is believed, be sufficient to produce, in favor of the public credit, any considerable or lasting elevation of the market price, whilst this may be occasionally depressed by the bank itself, if it should carry into the market the allowed proportion of its capital consisting of public stock, in order to procure specie, which it may find its account in procuring, with some sacrifice on that part of its capital.

Nor will any adequate advantage arise to the public credit from the subscription of Treasury notes. The actual issue of these notes nearly equals at present, and will soon exceed, the amount to be subscribed to the bank. The direct effect of this operation is simply to convert fifteen millions of Treasury notes into fifteen millions of six per cent. stock, with the collateral effect of promoting an additional demand for Treasury notes, beyond what might otherwise be negotiable.

Public credit might indeed be expected to derive advantage from the establishment of a National Bank, without regard to the formation of its capital, if the full aid and co-operation of the institution were secured to the Government during the war, and during the period of its fiscal embarrassments. But, the bank proposed will be free from all legal obligation to co-operate with the public measures: and whatever might be the patriotic disposition of its directors to contribute to the removal of those embarrassments, and to invigorate the prosecution of the war, 'fidelity to the pecuniary and general interest of the institution, according to their estimate of it, might oblige them to decline a connexion of their operations with those of the National Treasury, during the continuance of the war and the difficulties incident to it. Temporary sacrifices of interest, though overbalanced by the future and permanent profits of the charter, not being requirable of right in behalf of the public, might not be gratuitously made, and the bank would reap the full benefit of the grant, whilst the public would lose the equivalent expected from it. For it must be kept in view, that the sole inducement to such a grant, on the part of the public, would be the prospect of substantial aids to its pecuniary means at the present crisis, and during the sequel of the war. It is evident that the stock of the bank will, on the return of peace, if not sooner, rise in the market to a value which, if the bank were established in a period of peace, would authorize and obtain for the public a bonus to a very large amount. In lieu of such a bonus the Government is fairly entitled to, and ought not to relinquish or risk, the needful services of the bank, under the pressing circumstances of war.

2. The bank, as proposed to be constituted, cannot be relied on during the war, to provide a circulating medium, nor to furnish loans, or anticipations of the public revenue.

Without a medium, the taxes cannot be collected; and, in the absence of specie, the medium understood to be the best substitute is that of notes issued by a National Bank. The proposed bank will commence and conduct its operations under an obligation to pay its notes in specie, or be subject to the loss of its charter. Without such an obligation, the notes of the bank, though not exchangeable for specie, yet resting on good pledges, and performing the uses of specie, in the payment of taxes, and in other public transactions, would, as experience has ascertained, qualify the bank to supply at once a circulating medium, and pecuniary aids to the Government. Under the fetters imposed by the bill, it is manifest that, during the actual state of things, and probably during the war, the period particularly requiring such a medium and such a resource for loans and advances to the Government, notes for which the bank would be compellable to give specie in exchange could not be kept in circulation. The most the bank could effect, and the most it could be expected to aim at, would be to keep the institution alive by limited and local transactions, which, with the interest on the public stock in the bank, might yield a dividend sufficient for the purpose, until a change from war to peace should enable it, by a flow of specie into its vaults, and a removal of the external demand for it, to derive its contemplated emoluments from a safe and full extension of its operations.

On the whole, when it is considered that the proposed establishment will enjoy a monopoly of the profits of a National bank for a period of twenty years; that the monopolized profits will be continually growing, with the progress of the national population and wealth; that the nation will, during the same period, be dependent on the notes of the bank for that species of circulating medium, whenever the precious metals may be wanted, and at all times for so much thereof as may be an eligible substitute for a specie medium; and that the extensive employment of the notes in the collection of the augmented taxes will, moreover, enable the bank greatly to extend its profitable issues of them, without the expense of specie capital to support their circulation; it is as reasonable as it is requisite, that the Government, in return for these extraordinary concessions to the bank, should have a greater security for attaining the public objects of the institution than is presented in the bill, and particularly for every practicable accommodation, both in the temporary advances necessary to anticipate the taxes, and in those more durable loans which are equally necessary to diminish the resort to taxes.

In discharging this painful duty of stating objections to a measure which has undergone the deliberations and received the sanction of the two Houses of the National Legislature, I console myself with the reflection that, if they have not the weight which I attach to them, they can be constitutionally overruled; and with a confidence that, in a contrary event, the wisdom of Congress will hasten to substitute a more commensurate and certain provision for the public exigencies.

                                  JAMES MADISON.
WASHINGTON, *January* 30, 1815.

The Message was read, and on motion, by Mr. BIBB,

Ordered, That it be printed for the use of the Senate, and that to-morrow, at twelve o'clock, the Senate will proceed to consider the bill, entitled "An act to incorporate the subscribers to the Bank of the United States of America," which has been returned by the President of the United States, with objections.

TUESDAY, January 31.

Mr. TAIT, from the Committee on Naval Affairs, to whom was referred the bill, entitled "An act concerning Weston Jenkins and others," reported it without amendment.

On motion, by Mr. ANDERSON, the consideration of the amendments of the House of Representatives to the bill, entitled "An act to extend the time of Oliver Evans's patent for his improvement on steam engines," was further postponed until to-morrow.

The bill, entitled "An act giving further time to the purchasers of public lands to complete their payments," was read a third time, and passed.

The bill, entitled "An act attaching to the Canton district, in the State of Ohio, the tract of land lying between the foot of the rapids of the Miami of Lake Erie, and the Connecticut Western Reserve," was read a third time, and passed.

BANK OF THE UNITED STATES.

Agreeably to order, the Senate proceeded to reconsider the bill passed by the two Houses, entitled "An act to incorporate the subscribers to the Bank of the United States of America," which was presented for approbation on Monday, the 23d instant, and returned by the President on the 30th instant, with objections.

The said bill was read, and is as follows:

An Act to incorporate the subscribers to the Bank of the United States of America.

Be it enacted by the Senate and House of Representatives of the United States of America in Congress assembled, That a Bank of the United States of America shall be established, the capital stock of which shall be thirty millions of dollars, divided into three hundred thousand shares, of one hundred dollars each share; and that subscriptions for thirty millions of dollars, towards constituting the said capital stock, shall be opened, on the last Monday of February next, at the following places, viz: at Portland, in Maine, Portsmouth, in New Hampshire, Windsor, in Vermont, Boston, Providence, New Haven, New York, New Brunswick, in New Jersey, Philadelphia, Baltimore, the City of Washington, Richmond, Raleigh, Charleston, Savannah, Lexington, in Kentucky, Nashville, in Tennessee, Chillicothe, in Ohio, and New Orleans, under the superintendence of the following persons, as commissioners to receive the same: at Portland, Matthew Cob, Isaac Isley, Joshua Wingate, junior; at Portsmouth, John Goddard, Nathan'l A. Haven, Henry S. Langdon; at Windsor, Elias Lyman, William Leveret, Eleazer May; at Boston, Israel Thorndike, Thos. H. Perkins, William Gray, Aaron Hill, Samuel Brown; at Providence, Seth Wheaton, Ebenezer K. Dexter, Henry Smith; at New Haven, Abraham Bishop, William W. Woolsey, Henry Jones; at New York, Robert Troup, William Paulding, junior, Robert Lenox, John Jacob Astor, Samuel Tooker, Isaac Bronson, Henry A. Coster; at New Brunswick, James Vanderpool, John Bray, Peter Gordon; at Philadelphia, Jared Ingersoll, Thomas M. Willing, Stephen Girard, Chandler Price, Anthony Taylor, John Sergeant, Cadwallader Evans; at Baltimore, James A. Buchanan, Henry Payson, William Wilson; at the City of Washington, John Mason, Robert Brent, John P. Van Ness; at Richmond, Benjamin Hatcher, John Brockenborough, John Preston; at Raleigh, Sherwood Haywood, Beverly Daniel, William Peace; at Charleston, John C. Faber, Thomas Jones, Stephen Elliot, Charles B. Cochran, Thomas Blackwood; at Savannah, John Bolton, Charles Harris, James Johnson; at Lexington, in Kentucky, Charles Wilkins, Lewis Sanders, John H. Morton; at Nashville, Robert Weakly, Felix Grundy, John R. Bedford; at Chillicothe, Samuel Finley, Thomas James, William McFarland; at New Orleans, Dominick H. Hall, Benjamin Morgan, Paul Lanuse, Thomas L. Harman, and William Flood; which subscriptions shall continue open every day, from the time of opening the same, from ten o'clock in the forenoon, until four o'clock in the afternoon, until the Saturday following, at four o'clock in the afternoon, when the same shall be closed; and immediately thereafter, the commissioners, or any two of them, at the respective places aforesaid, shall cause two transcripts or fair copies of such subscriptions to be made; one of which they shall send to the Secretary of the Treasury, one they shall retain, and the original shall, within three days from the closing of the same, be by the said commissioners transmitted to the said commissioners at Philadelphia, or to one of them: and, on the receipt thereof, the said commissioners at Philadelphia, or any three of them, shall immediately thereafter convene and proceed to take an account of the said subscriptions; and if more than the amount of thirty millions of dollars shall have been subscribed, then the said last mentioned commissioners shall apportion the same among the several subscribers, according to their several and respective subscriptions; *Provided, however,* That such commissioners shall, by such apportionment, allow and apportion to each subscriber at least one share; and, in case the aggregate amount of the said subscriptions shall exceed thirty millions of dollars, the said commissioners, after having apportioned the same as aforesaid, shall cause lists of the said apportioned subscriptions to be made out, including in each list the apportioned subscription for the place where the original subscription was made, one of which lists shall be transmitted to the commissioners, or to one of the commissioners, under whose superintendence such subscriptions were originally made, that the subscribers may ascertain from them the number of shares apportioned to such subscribers respectively; and, if the amount of thirty millions of dollars shall not be subscribed during the period aforesaid, at all the places aforesaid, the subscription to complete the said sum shall afterwards be and remain open at Philadelphia, under the superintendence of the said commissioners appointed at that place, and the subscription may be then made by any corporation, copartnership, or person, for any number of shares not exceeding the amount required to complete the said sum of thirty millions of dollars. And, in case of the death, or refusal to serve, of any of the commissioners aforesaid, it shall be lawful for the President of the United States to supply the vacancy or vacancies thus created, by appointing some suitable person or persons.

SEC. 2. *And be it further enacted,* That it shall be lawful for any person, copartnership, or body politic, to subscribe for so many shares of the said capital stock of the said bank, as he or they shall think fit, not exceeding three thousand shares, except as is hereinafter provided for the subscription on behalf of the United States, and the sums respectively subscribed, except on behalf of the United States, as is hereinafter provided, shall be payable in the manner following, that is to say: five millions of dollars thereof in gold or silver coin of the United States, or of foreign coin at the value heretofore established by the act of Congress, entitled "An act regulating the currency of foreign coins," passed the 10th day of April, one thousand eight hundred and six; ten millions of dollars thereof in gold or silver coin, as aforesaid, or in the public debt of the United States, contracted by virtue of the act of Congress, entitled "An act authorizing a loan for a sum not exceeding eleven millions of dollars," passed the fourteenth day of March one thousand eight hundred and twelve, or contracted, or to be contracted, by virtue of any subsequent act and acts of Congress heretofore passed, authorizing a loan or loans; and fifteen millions of dollars thereof in gold and silver coin, or in Treasury notes, issued under the act of Congress, entitled "An act to authorize the issuing notes," passed the thirtieth day of June, one thousand eight hundred and twelve, or issued under the authority of any subsequent act or acts of Congress, authorising, or which shall authorize, Treasury notes to be issued, previously to the final closing of the subscriptions to the said bank. And the said payment shall be made and completed in the sums and at the times hereinafter declared, that is to say: at the time of subscribing there shall be paid six dollars and sixty-six cents and two-thirds of a cent on each share, in gold or silver coin; twenty dollars in the Treasury notes

13th CON. 3d SESS.—7

aforesaid; and thirteen dollars thirty-three cents and one-third of a cent in the public debt of the United States, contracted or to be contracted, as aforesaid: at the expiration of four calendar months after the time of subscribing there shall be paid the further sum of three dollars thirty-three cents and one third of a cent on each share, in gold or silver coin; ten dollars in the Treasury notes aforesaid; and six dollars sixty-six cents and two-thirds of a cent in the public debt of the United States, contracted or to be contracted as aforesaid: at the expiration of six calendar months from the time of subscribing there shall be paid the further sum of three dollars thirty-three cents and one third of a cent on each share, in gold or silver coin; ten dollars in the Treasury notes aforesaid; and six dollars sixty-six cents and two-thirds of a cent in the public debt of the United States, contracted, or to be contracted, as aforesaid: at the expiration of eight calendar months from the time of subscribing there shall be paid the further sum of three dollars thirty-three cents and one-third of a cent, in gold or silver coin; ten dollars in the Treasury notes aforesaid; and six dollars sixty-six cents and two-thirds of a cent in the public debt of the United States, contracted, or to be contracted, as aforesaid. And the subscriptions in public stock and Treasury notes, as aforesaid, shall be taken and credited for the principal and so much of the interest thereof, respectively, as shall have accrued on the day of subscribing the same. And, at the time of subscribing to the capital stock of the said bank, as aforesaid, each and every subscriber shall deliver to the commissioners, at the place of subscribing, as well the specie amount of their subscriptions, respectively, as the certificates of stock for the stock proportion of their subscriptions, respectively, together with a power of attorney authorizing the said commissioners, or a majority of them, to transfer the said stock, in due form of law, to "The President, Directors, and Company, of the said Bank of the United States of America," as soon as the said bank shall be organized; and, also, Treasury notes for the proportion of the subscriptions, respectively, payable in Treasury notes as aforesaid: *Provided, always,* That if, in consequence of the apportionment of shares in the said bank among the subscribers, in the case and in the manner hereinbefore prescribed, any subscriber shall have delivered to the commissioners, at the time of subscribing, a greater amount of specie, stock, and Treasury notes, than shall be necessary to complete the payments for the share or shares to such subscriber, apportioned as aforesaid, the commissioners shall only retain so much of the said money, stock, and Treasury notes, as shall be necessary to complete such payments, and shall forthwith return, on application for the same, the surplus thereof to the subscriber lawfully entitled thereto. And the commissioners respectively shall deposite the gold and silver, certificates of stock, and Treasury notes, by them respectively received, as aforesaid, from the subscribers to the said bank, in some place of secure and safe keeping, so that the same may and shall be specifically delivered and transferred, as the same were by them respectively received, to the said President, Directors, and Company, of the said Bank of the United States of America, or to their order, as soon as shall be required after the organization of the said bank.

SEC. 3. *And be it further enacted,* That the United States may, at any time before the expiration of this act, in pursuance of any law which may be passed by Congress for that purpose, cause to be subscribed, for the use of the United States, to said bank, fifty thousand additional shares, to be paid in public stock, bearing an interest of four per cent. per annum, redeemable in any sums, and at any periods, which the Government may deem fit.

SEC. 4. *And be it further enacted,* That whenever and as often as any of the Treasury notes, subscribed as aforesaid, to the said capital stock of the said bank, shall be due and payable, it shall be lawful for the Secretary of the Treasury (and he is hereby authorized and required) to pay and redeem the same, principal and interest, by causing certificates of public stock for an equal amount, bearing an interest of six per cent. per annum, and redeemable in any sums, and at any periods, which the Government may deem fit, to be prepared and made in the usual form, and the same to be delivered to the president and directors of the said bank, in satisfaction and discharge of such Treasury notes.

SEC. 5. *And be it further enacted,* That the subscribers to the said Bank of the United States of America, their successors and assigns, shall be, and are hereby created, a corporation and body politic, by the name and style of "The President, Directors, and Company," of the Bank of the United States of America," and shall so continue until the third day of March, in the year one thousand eight hundred and thirty-five; and by that name shall be, and are hereby made, able and capable in law, to have, purchase, receive, possess, enjoy, and retain, to them and their successors, lands, rents, tenements, hereditaments, goods, chattels, and effects, of whatsoever kind, nature, and quality, to an amount not exceeding in the whole thirty-five millions of dollars, including the amount of the capital stock aforesaid; and the same to sell, grant, demise, alien, or dispose of, to sue and be sued, plead and be impleaded, answer and be answered, defend and be defended, in all courts and places whatsoever; and also to make, have, and use, a common seal, and the same to break, alter, and renew, at their pleasure; and, also, to ordain, establish, and put in execution, such by-laws and ordinances, and regulations, as they shall deem necessary and convenient, for the government of the said corporation, not being contrary to the Constitution and laws of the United States; and generally to do and execute all and singular the acts, matters, and things, which to them it shall or may appertain to do; subject, nevertheless, to the rules, regulations, restrictions, limitations, and provisions, hereinafter prescribed and declared.

SEC. 6. *And be it further enacted,* That, for the management of the affairs of the said corporation, there shall be twenty-five directors, who shall be elected at the banking house in Philadelphia, on the first Monday of January, in each year, by the stockholders or proprietors of the capital stock of the said corporation, and by a plurality of votes then and there actually given, according to the scale of voting hereinafter prescribed. And the directors, so duly chosen, shall be capable of serving by virtue of such choice, until the end or expiration of the first Monday in January next ensuing the time of such election, and no longer: *Provided, always,* That the first election and appointment of directors shall be at the time, and for the period, hereinafter declared.

SEC. 7. *And be it further enacted,* That, as soon as the sum of twelve millions of dollars in gold and silver coin, and in the public debt and Treasury notes, shall have been actually received on account of the subscriptions to the said capital stock, (exclusively of the sub-

scription aforesaid on the part of the United States,) notice thereof shall be given by the persons under whose superintendence the subscriptions shall have been made at Philadelphia, in at least two public newspapers, printed in each of the places where subscriptions shall have been made; and the said persons shall, at the same time, and in like manner, notify a time and place within the said city of Philadelphia, at the distance of at least twenty days from the time of such notification, for proceeding to the election of directors as aforesaid; and it shall be lawful for such election to be then and there made. And the persons who shall be then and there chosen as aforesaid, shall be the first directors, and shall proceed to elect one of their number president of the said corporation, and they shall be capable of serving by virtue of such choice until the end and expiration of the first Monday of January next ensuing the time of making the same, and shall forthwith, thereafter, commence the operations of the said bank, at the said city of Philadelphia: *Provided, always,* That in case it should at any time happen that an election of directors and president of the said corporation should not be made upon any day when, in pursuance of this act, they ought to be made, the said corporation shall not for that cause be deemed to be dissolved; but it shall be lawful on any other day to hold and make an election of directors and president of the said corporation, (as the case may be,) in such manner as shall have been regulated by the by-laws and ordinances of the said corporation; and until such election be so made, the directors and president, for the time being, shall continue in office; *And provided also,* That, in case of the death, resignation, or removal, of the president of the said corporation, the directors shall proceed to elect another president: *And provided, also,* That in case of the death, resignation, or absence from the United States, or removal of a director from office, the vacancy shall be supplied by the stockholders.

SEC. 8. *And be it further enacted,* That the directors, for the time being, shall have power to appoint such officers, clerks, and servants, under them, as shall be necessary for executing the business of the said corporation, and to allow them such compensation for their services respectively, as shall be reasonable; and shall be capable of exercising such other powers and authorities for the well governing and ordering of the affairs of the said corporation, as shall be prescribed, fixed, and determined, by the laws, regulations, and ordinances of the same.

SEC. 9. *And be it further enacted,* That the following, restrictions, limitations, and provisions, shall form and be fundamental articles of the constitution of the said corporation, to wit:

1. The number of votes to which the stockholders shall be entitled, in voting for directors, shall be according to the number of shares he, she, or they respectively, shall hold, in the proportions following, that is to say: for one share and not more than two shares, one vote; for every two shares above two and not exceeding ten, one vote; for every four shares above ten and not exceeding thirty, one vote; for every six shares above thirty and not exceeding sixty, one vote; for every eight shares above sixty and not exceeding one hundred, one vote; and for every ten shares above one hundred, one vote. But no person, copartnership, or body politic, shall be entitled to a greater number than thirty votes; and after the first election, no share or shares shall confer a right of voting, which shall have been holden three calendar months previous to the day

of election. And stockholders actually resident within the United States, and none other, may vote in elections by proxy.

2. Not more than three-fourths of the directors in office, at the time of an annual election, shall be elected for the next succeeding year, and no person shall be a director more than three out of four years ; but the director who shall be the president at the time of an election, may always be re-elected.

3. None but a resident citizen of the United States, and holding at the time of his election not less than ten shares, bona fide in his own right, shall be a director ; and if any director shall cease to be a stockholder to that amount, he shall cease to be a director.

4. No director shall be entitled to any emolument. The stockholders may make such compensation to the president, for his extraordinary attendance at the bank, as shall appear to them reasonable.

5. Not less than seven directors shall constitute a board for the transaction of business, of whom the president shall always be one, except in case of sickness or necessary absence, in which case his place may be supplied by any other director whom he, by writing, under his hand, shall depute for the purpose. And the director so deputed, may do and transact all the necessary business belonging to the office of the president of the said corporation, during the continuance of the sickness or necessary absence of the president.

6. A number of stockholders not less than sixty, who, together, shall be proprietors of one thousand shares or upwards, shall have power at any time to call a general meeting of the stockholders, for purposes relative to the institution, giving at least ten weeks' notice in two public newspapers of the place where the bank is seated, and specifying in such notice the object or objects of such meeting.

7. Every cashier or treasurer, before he enters upon the duties of his office, shall be required to give bond, with two or more sureties, to the satisfaction of the directors, in a sum not less than fifty thousand dollars, with a condition for his good behaviour, and the faithful performance of his duties to the corporation.

8. The lands, tenements, and hereditaments, which it shall be lawful for the said corporation to hold, shall be only requisite for its immediate accommodation in relation to the convenient transacting of its business, and such as shall have been bona fide mortgaged to it by way of security, or conveyed to it in satisfaction of debts previously contracted in the course of its dealings, or purchased at sales, upon judgments which shall have been obtained for such debts.

9. The total amount of debts which the said corporation shall at any time owe, whether by bond, bill, note, or other contract, over and above the debt or debts due for money deposited in the bank, shall not exceed the sum of thirty millions of dollars, unless the contracting of any greater debt shall have been previously authorized by a law of the United States. In case of excess, the directors under whose administration it shall happen, shall be liable for the same, in their natural and private capacities, and an action of debt may, in such case, be brought against them, or any of them, their or any of their heirs, executors, or administrators, in any court of record of the United States, or either of them, by any creditor or creditors of the said corporation, and may be prosecuted to judgment and execution, any condition, covenant, or agreement, to the contrary notwithstanding. But this provision shall not be construed to exempt the said corporation, or the lands, tenements, goods, or chattels, of the same, from being also liable for, and chargeable with, the said excess. Such of the said directors who may have been absent when the said excess was contracted or created, or who may have dissented from the resolution or act whereby the same was so contracted or created, may respectively exonerate themselves from being so liable, by forthwith giving notice of the fact, and of their absence or dissent, to the President of the United States, and to the stockholders, at a general meeting, which they shall have power to call for that purpose.

10. The said corporation shall not, directly or indirectly, deal or trade in anything except bills of exchange, gold or silver bullion, or in the sale of goods really and truly pledged for money lent, and not redeemed in due time, or goods which shall be the proceeds of its lands. It shall not be at liberty to purchase any public debt whatsoever ; nor shall it take more than at the rate of six per cent. per annum for or upon its loans or discounts.

11. The said corporation shall not, in any one year, sell any portion of the public debt constituting a part of its capital stock aforesaid, to an amount exceeding five millions of dollars, without the consent of Congress.

12. No loan shall be made by the said corporation, for the use, or on account, of the Government of the United States, to an amount exceeding five hundred thousand dollars ; or any particular State, to an amount exceeding fifty thousand dollars ; or to any foreign Prince or State, unless previously authorized by a law of the United States.

13. The stock of the said corporation shall be assignable and transferable according to such rules as shall be instituted in that behalf, by the laws and ordinances of the same.

14. The bills obligatory and of credit, under the seal of the said corporation, which shall be made to any person or persons, shall be assignable by endorsement thereupon, under the hand or hands of such person or persons, and his, her, or their executors or administrators, and of his, her, or their assignee or assignees, and the executors or administrators of such assignee or assignees, and so as absolutely to transfer and vest the property thereof in each and every assignee or assignees, successively, and to enable such assignee or assignees, and his, her, or their executors or administrators, to maintain an action thereupon in his, her, or their own name or names. And the bills or notes which may be issued by order of the said corporation, signed by the president and countersigned by the principal cashier or treasurer thereof, promising the payment of money to any person or persons, his, her, or their order, or to bearer, although not under the seal of the said corporation, shall be binding and obligatory upon the same, in the like manner, and with the like force and effect, as upon any private person or persons, if issued by him, her, or them, in his, her, or their private or natural capacity or capacities, and shall be assignable and negotiable in like manner as if they were so issued by such private person or persons ; that is to say : those which shall be payable to any person or persons, his, her, or their order, shall be assignable by endorsement, in like manner, and with the like effect, as foreign bills of exchange now are ; and those which are payable to bearer shall be assignable and negotiable by delivery only.

15. Half yearly dividends shall be made of so much of the profits of the bank as shall appear to the directors advisable ; and once in every three years, the directors shall lay before the stockholders, at a general meeting, for their information, an exact and particular

statement of the debts which have remained unpaid after the expiration of the original credit, for a period of treble the term of that credit, and of the surplus of profits, if any, after deducting losses and dividends. If there shall be a failure in the payment of any part of any sum subscribed by any person, copartnership, or body politic, the party failing shall lose the benefit of any dividend which may have accrued prior to the time for making such payment, and during the delay of the same.

16. The directors of said corporation shall be bound to establish a competent office of discount and deposite in the District of Columbia, whenever any law of the United States shall require such establishment; and it shall be lawful for the said directors to establish offices wheresoever they shall think fit, within the United States or the Territories thereof, for the purposes of discount, deposite, and distribution; or for the purposes of deposite and distribution only; and upon the same terms, and in the same manner, as shall be practised at the bank; and to commit the management of the said offices, and the business thereof respectively, to such persons, and under such regulations, as they shall deem proper, not being contrary to law or to the constitution of the bank. Or, instead of establishing such offices, it shall be lawful for the directors of the said corporation, from time to time, to employ any other bank or banks, at any place or places that they may deem safe and proper, to manage and transact the business proposed as aforesaid to be managed and transacted by such offices, under such agreements, and subject to such regulations, as they shall deem just and proper. But the managers and directors of every office of discount, deposite, and distribution, established as aforesaid, shall be annually appointed by the directors of the bank, to serve one year; each of them shall be a citizen of the United States, and shall hold, at the time of his appointment, not less than five shares in the said bank, bona fide in his own right; and if he shall cease to be a stockholder to that amount, he shall cease to be a manager or director of such office of discount, deposite, and distribution; and not more than three-fourths of the said managers or directors in office at the time of an annual appointment, shall be re-appointed for the next succeeding year; nor shall any person be a manager or director for more than three out of four years; but the president may be always re-appointed.

17. The said corporation, all offices of discount, deposite, and distribution, and of deposite and distribution only, which shall be established by the said directors as aforesaid, and all banks by the said directors employed in lieu of such offices as aforesaid, shall be bound to receive, upon deposite, the Treasury notes of the United States which have been or may be hereafter issued by virtue of any law or laws of the United States; but it shall be optional with the said corporation to pay and discharge the checks or drafts of the persons making such deposite, in Treasury notes, for the amount thereof, either in gold or silver coin, or in the notes of the bank, or in Treasury notes. And all banks by the said directors employed as aforesaid, shall be further bound to receive on deposite, and to circulate, the notes of the said corporation, on the same terms, and in the same manner, as the notes of the said banks respectively are received and circulated; and, from time to time, issue and exchange for the said notes of the said corporation, other notes of the said corporation, or the notes of the said banks respectively, or Treasury notes, at the option of the per-

sons applying for such issue or exchange. The said corporation shall, at all times, distribute among the offices of discount, deposite, and distribution, and of deposite and distribution only, and at all the banks employed in lieu of such offices as aforesaid, a sufficient sum, in the various denominations of the notes of the said corporation, and in the Treasury notes which it may receive upon deposite from the Government, to answer the demand therefor, and to establish a sufficient circulating medium throughout the United States and the Territories thereof.

18. The officer at the head of the Treasury Department of the United States shall be furnished, from time to time, as often as he may require, not exceeding once a week, with statements of the amount of capital stock of the said corporation, and of the debts due to the same; of the moneys deposited therein; of the notes in circulation; and of the cash in hand; and shall have a right to inspect such general accounts in the books of the bank as shall relate to the said statement: *Provided,* That this shall not be construed to imply a right of inspecting the account of any private individual or individuals with the bank.

SEC. 10. *And be it further enacted,* That if the said corporation, or any person or persons for or to the use of the same, shall deal or trade in buying or selling any goods, wares, merchandise, or commodities whatsoever, contrary to the provisions of this act, all and every person or persons by whom any order or direction for so dealing or trading shall have been given, and all and every person and persons who shall have been concerned as parties or agents therein, shall forfeit and lose treble the value of the goods, wares, merchandise, and commodities, in which such dealing and trade shall have been; one half thereof to the use of the informer, and the other half thereof to the use of the United States, to be recovered in any action at law, with costs of suit.

SEC. 11. *And be it further enacted,* That if the said corporation shall advance or lend any sum of money, for the use or on account of the Government of the United States, to an amount exceeding three hundred thousand dollars; or of any particular State, to an amount exceeding fifty thousand dollars; or of any foreign Prince or State, (unless previously authorised thereto by a law of the United States,) all and every person and persons, by and with whose order, approbation, and connivance, such unlawful advance or loan shall have been made, upon conviction thereof, shall forfeit and pay, for every such offence, treble the value or amount of the sum or sums which shall have been so unlawfully advanced or lent; one-fifth thereof to the use of the informer, and the residue thereof to the use of the United States.

SEC. 12. *And be it further enacted,* That the bills or notes of the said corporation, originally made payable, or which shall have become payable on demand, shall be receivable in all payments to the United States, until otherwise directed by act of Congress.

SEC. 13. *And be it further enacted,* That if the subscriptions and payments to the said bank shall not be made and completed, so as to enable the same to commence its operations, or if the said bank shall not commence its operations on or before the first day of March, one thousand eight hundred and sixteen, then, and in that case, this act shall be null and void.

SEC. 14. *And be it further enacted,* That it shall at all times be lawful for a committee of either House of Congress, appointed for that purpose, to inspect the books, and to examine into the proceedings, of the corporation hereby created, and to report whether the provisions of this charter have been by the same violated or not: and whenever any committee, as aforesaid, shall find and report, or the President of the United States shall have reason to believe, that the charter has been violated, it may be lawful for Congress to direct, or the President to order a scire facias to be sued out of the circuit court of the district of Pennsylvania, in the name of the United States, (which shall be executed upon the president of the corporation, for the time being, at least fifteen days before the commencement of the term of said court,) calling on the said corporation to show cause wherefore the charter hereby granted shall not be declared forfeited: and it shall be lawful for the said court, upon the return of the said scire facias, to examine into the truth of the alleged violation; and if such violation be made appear, then to pronounce and adjudge that the said charter is forfeited and annulled: *Provided, however,* Every issue of fact which may be joined between the United States and the corporation aforesaid shall be tried by jury. And it shall be lawful for the court aforesaid to require the production of such of the books of the corporation as it may deem necessary for the ascertainment of the controverted facts; and the final judgment of the court aforesaid shall be examinable in the Supreme Court of the United States, by writ of error, and may be there reversed or affirmed, according to the usages of law.

SEC. 15. *And be it further enacted,* That, during the continuance of this act, and whenever required by the Secretary of the Treasury, the said corporation shall do and perform the several and respective duties of the Commissioners of Loans for the several States, or any one or more of them, at the times, in the manner, and upon the terms, to be prescribed by the Secretary of the Treasury.

SEC. 16. *And be it further enacted,* That no other bank shall be established by any future law of the United States, during the continuance of the corporation hereby created; for which the faith of the United States is hereby pledged: *Provided,* Congress may renew existing charters for banks in the District of Columbia, not increasing the capital thereof; and may grant charters, if they deem it expedient, to any banking associations now in operation in the said District, and renew the same, not increasing the capital thereof. And notwithstanding the expiration of the term for which the said corporation is created, it shall be lawful to use the corporate name, style, and capacity, for the purpose of suits, for the final settlement and liquidation of the affairs and accounts of the corporation, and for the sale and disposition of their estate, real, personal, and mixed, but not for any other purpose, or in any other manner whatsoever: nor for a period exceeding two years, after the expiration of the said term of incorporation.

LANGDON CHEVES,
Speaker House of Representatives.
JOHN GAILLARD,
President of the Senate, pro tem.

The PRESIDENT's objections were also again read; and on motion, by Mr. BARBOUR, the further consideration thereof was postponed to, and made the order of the day for, Thursday next.

WEDNESDAY, February 1.

The bill to allow a drawback of duties on spirits distilled, and certain goods, wares, and merchandise, manufactured, within the United States, was read a second time.

On motion, by Mr. GILES, two members were added to the Committee on Military Affairs; and Messrs. SMITH and VARNUM were appointed.

A message from the House of Representatives informed the Senate that the House have passed a bill, entitled "An act giving the right of pre-emption in the purchase of lands to certain settlers in the Indiana Territory;" also, a bill, entitled "An act to authorize the payment for property lost, captured, or destroyed by the enemy, while in the military service of the United States;" in which bills they request the concurrence of the Senate.

The two bills last mentioned were read, and passed to the second reading.

Mr. VARNUM, from the Militia Committee, reported a bill to authorize a detachment from the militia of the United States; and the bill was read.

Mr. TAIT, from the Committee on Naval Affairs, to whom was referred the bill, entitled "An act concerning Matthew Guy, John Woodward, Samuel Tennison, and Wilfred Drury," reported it with amendments.

Mr. TAYLOR, from the committee to whom was referred the bill, entitled "An act to amend the act, entitled 'An act to provide additional revenues for defraying the expenses of Government, and maintaining the public credit, by laying a direct tax upon the United States, and to provide for assessing and collecting the same;'" and the act, entitled "An act to provide additional revenues for defraying the expenses of Government, and maintaining the public credit, by laying duties on household furniture, and on gold and silver watches," reported it with amendments.

The Senate resumed, as in Committee of the Whole, the consideration of the bill, entitled "An act for the better regulation of the Ordnance department," together with the amendments reported thereto by the select committee; and the amendments having been agreed to, the President reported the bill to the House accordingly.

On motion, by Mr. GILES, the bill as amended was recommitted to the Committee on Military Affairs, further to consider and report thereon.

The Senate resumed, as in Committee of the Whole, the consideration of the bill making appropriations for repairing or rebuilding the public buildings within the City of Washington.

On motion, by Mr. MASON, that the further consideration thereof be postponed to the second Monday in March next, it was determined in the negative—yeas 7, nays 22, as follows:

YEAS—Messrs. Dana, German, Hunter, King, Lambert, Mason, and Wells.

NAYS—Messrs. Barbour, Bibb, Brown, Chace, Condjt, Daggett, Fromentin, Gaillard, Giles, Goldsborough, Horsey, Kerr, Lacock, Morrow, Roberts, Smith, Tait, Taylor, Turner, Varnum, Walker, and Wharton.

Mr. FROMENTIN moved to recommit the bill to a select committee, further to consider and report thereon. The motion was postponed until to-morrow.

[There took place on the subject an interesting debate. Messrs. LACOCK, BARBOUR, DAGGETT, and KERR, were the principal advocates of the bill, and Messrs. MASON, DANA, and GERMAN, its principal opponents.]

DEFENCE OF THE CITY OF BALTIMORE.

Mr. SMITH presented the memorial of the Committee of Vigilance and Safety of the city and precincts of Baltimore, praying effectual protection against the enemy, as is stated in the memorial; which was read, and on motion, by Mr. SMITH, ordered to be printed for the use of the Senate, and that it be referred to the Committee on Military Affairs, to consider and report thereon by bill or otherwise.

The memorial is as follows:

To the President of the United States, and the Senate and House of Representatives of the United States of America, in Congress assembled, the memorial of the Committee of Vigilance and Safety of the city and precincts of Baltimore.

Your memorialists beg leave to draw your attention to the necessity of providing a force adequate to the defence of the city of Baltimore, during the next campaign, and, in doing so, they would take the liberty to submit the following statement and reflections for your consideration:

Nothing has so strikingly illustrated the easy accessibility of the city of Baltimore to an invading enemy, as the demonstration made upon it during the last Summer. It then appeared that large frigates, and any number of bomb vessels, could, without molestation from the shore, approach and lie within shell range of Fort McHenry, the chief strong hold of the city; and that, unless the channels should be seasonably and effectually obstructed, they might approach within reach of the city itself along a prong of the Patapsco, called Ferry Branch. It also appeared that any number of troops may with ease be landed on that long narrow slip of land, called Patapsco Neck, the most remote point of which is about twelve miles from Baltimore, and that, when landed, unless checked or repelled by an equal or superior force, they may, in a very short time, be marched to the assault of any part of the city. Thus much has been clearly evinced by the late attack of the enemy. The other directions from which assaults were seriously apprehended, it might be highly imprudent to point out and explain in a paper, with the contents of which the enemy may hereafter become acquainted; and the more especially since that enemy, everywhere barbarous and malignant, may well be supposed to cherish a peculiarly rancorous spirit of hostility against a city from which he has been driven back with disappointment and disgrace, and to be anxiously attentive to all the means by which he may best explore every avenue to assault, and be enabled to select the weakest and most vulnerable.

The people of Baltimore, apprized of the power and temper of the enemy with whom they had to contend, have, during the last Summer, exerted every means in their power to render their city as strong and as defensible as possible. They hold in readiness obstructions prepared to be thrown into the channels of the river leading to the city, at the shortest notice; have, chiefly by their own personal labor or contributions, caused forts, redoubts, or breastworks, to be thrown up, and nearly completed, under the direction

of the military authority, round about the whole extent of the city; and they have aided, as far as in their power, in procuring and mounting the ordnance necessary and suitable to the works so erected. When those lines and forts shall be well and fully manned, Baltimore will feel perfectly secure; its citizens may then with confidence set the enemy at defiance; but not till then.

Your memorialists deem it unnecessary to state the strength of the regular force now stationed here, because the most correct sources of information upon this subject are at the seat of Government. It is, however, confessedly very inferior, and inadequate to the defence of the city. Your memorialists have not been able to ascertain with precision the number of men requisite for the defence of Baltimore; but from a consideration of the ease with which the city may be approached, both by land and water, as manifested in the late attack; of the various points to be defended; of the reported threats and disposable force of the enemy; and also of information obtained from some of the most experienced and intelligent military characters, they are strongly impressed with a belief that a considerable permanent force of regulars is indispensable to the safety of the city. Whether such a force can be detached from the military establishment now on foot, is more than your memorialists can undertake to say; but every expectation that it would be done, has thus far been withheld from them, and they have uniformly been given to understand that their reliance must be placed, during the next campaign, as heretofore, on the militia to be called together as occasion may require. Against such an arrangement your memorialists, on behalf of their fellow-citizens, the people of Baltimore and its precincts, must beg leave warmly to remonstrate and most decidedly to protest. The inefficiency of militia alone for any regular or important operation of war, has been so often and so fully tested that it cannot now be necessary to adduce either proofs, or arguments, to show what has been so long and universally admitted. The experience of this, as well as that of the Revolutionary war, shows that, to repel the hasty predatory incursions of an enemy, militia may often be brought to act with much effect, and that they are a useful, and often powerful auxiliary force in partisan warfare; it also shows that it would be extremely unsafe to rely upon them solely for the defence of the extensive lines of a large city against any very considerable invading regular force. An army of militia, to be equal in strength to that of a regular one, must always be vastly superior in numbers; yet, however, the history of military affairs in all times has shown, that a mere mass of armed men, or undisciplined militia, beyond a certain number, brings with it little or no additional strength. Taking this principle as correct, your memorialists do humbly conceive that scarcely any militia force that could be hastily collected about their city, could secure it against a large invading army of well disciplined regulars. Your memorialists have no reason to doubt the courage of their fellow-citizens composing the militia; far otherwise; they insist only that, without the combined movement, concert, and discipline of a regular army, courage can do nothing, and numbers produce only confusion and disorder. A militia force, hastily assembled, is not only the most unsafe, it is also the most expensive. They are not, it is true, usually retained in service during a whole campaign; but being necessarily far more numerous than regulars, and infinitely more wasteful of all the munitions of war, they are in the end much more costly and burdensome. But the exclusive use of a militia force brings with it other evils, of a nature so striking and fatal, as, even if it were not liable to the charge of prodigality and insecurity, might induce us to avoid it. It interrupts the pursuits of husbandry, and embarrasses every branch of industry, to the impoverishment of individuals and the ruin of the State. It draws into the field men who are not prepared, either in mind or body, for its hazards or fatigues; possessing little capacity to annoy the enemy, and yet less to endure the privations and hardships of a camp. It is known to destroy by disease and to break down the constitutions of more than double the numbers of those who perish or are permanently injured by sickness in a regular army; and to augment the sum of human misery, far more than enlistments could, by diffusing more widely anxiety among families in proportion to the superior numbers of the militia force, and the superior importance of the greater part of it to those who are connected with or depend upon them.

Your memorialists are aware that it may be difficult, perhaps impossible, to provide a body of regulars, enlisted upon the terms of the existing laws, in season for the defence of their city during the next campaign, but they flatter themselves that a law might be framed and passed, by virtue of which the necessary number of able-bodied men might be called into the field for local, stationary, or limited service, during one campaign, at the least, if not longer.

Your memorialists would here beg leave to observe that, as among the most important powers of the General Government is that of the right to declare war, so the providing supplies, and all the means for its active prosecution, and the superintending its faithful and vigorous management, are among its most sacred trusts and binding obligations. The rapid and decisive movements of war imperatively require, to insure even safety, much more success, a corresponding promptitude and decision of the Government by which it is waged; a war of enterprise and vigor not only drives danger from the door of every citizen, calls forth a bold, manly spirit of patriotism, and adorns the nation with rays of imperishable glory, but is also the least costly, the least wasteful of human life, the least tedious, and almost always terminates in the most sure and lasting peace. While, on the other hand, the shrinking policy of bare defence paralyzes the powers of the nation, imperceptibly wastes its resources, and invites the aggressions of an enemy. Under such impressions, it would be the earnest wish of your memorialists that the energies of their country should be so actively and forcibly exerted as to drive their present enemy, with his barbarous system of warfare, far from their homes; but, since that seems to be at present impracticable, owing to his greatly superior powers, they do, therefore, humbly beg and entreat that the means for their defence may be provided by a timely and adequate exercise of the legitimate and wholesome powers of the nation. Unless the General Government does, by a seasonable and vigorous effort, provide for the common defence along the Atlantic border, your memorialists are very seriously apprehensive that they will be amongst the first, and, perhaps, the most signal, of the victims of the ruinous policy of relying altogether upon an inefficient militia force, or of leaving every State to defend itself according to its ability; for a crisis has now arrived, when not only the city of Baltimore, but the State of Maryland itself, can only hope for protection and safety through the powers and means of the National Government. Exposed and vulnerable as Maryland is, to its centre, harassed and plundered as it has been, it feels, with the most lively sensibility, that it is now, indeed, wholly dependent upon the Union for salvation; for, alone, it is utterly unequal to the contest. The present war has, however, clearly shown that the most potent of the States is not altogether equal to its own defence, and that one of the smallest has compelled the enemy to fly from its territory, when aided by the powers of the Union. When your memorialists consider how very obvious it must be to the mind of any one, who will reflect only for a moment upon the subject, that a single campaign, undertaken by Maryland alone, in defence of its own shores, would not only prostrate its finances, but, perhaps, mortgage its resources for ages to come, without, in the end, effecting any valuable purpose; they feel inspired with the highest degree of confidence that their National Government, so eminently characterized for its impartial and liberal justice, will with alacrity and promptitude afford them the succor so necessary to their safety; nor do they feel less confident that there is not a single citizen of Maryland, so lost to a just regard for his own best interests, as to hesitate one moment in co-operating with the General Government in the lawful and vigorous exercise of those powers of conducting war, by which alone they can be protected, defended, or even saved, from absolute ruin.

Your memorialists, in speaking of the merits of Baltimore, and her pretensions to the special consideration and regard of the Government, feel very sensibly the delicacy and embarrassment of the undertaking. The relative commercial importance of this city is best known at the seat of Government; it will, therefore, be sufficient barely to refer to official documents there, by which it will appear that, in this respect, it ranks as the third city of the Union. But the commercial loss and ruin, consequent upon the fall of Baltimore, certainly is not the only, nor is it, perhaps, the greatest evil to be apprehended. It is the loss of a post, the relative position of which would be so highly advantageous to the enemy, that will produce in the mind of every impartial and thinking man the greatest alarm. The prodigious extent of country commanded by Baltimore, and the facility with which the enemy might, from thence, push his predatory incursions in every direction, are obvious, and may more properly be left to the reflections of Government, than, under existing circumstances, be strongly urged or fully explained. Lest the people of Baltimore should be numbered among those who forget the duty of a citizen, when every man should struggle to be foremost in discharging it, your memorialists will take leave to say a few words of their patriotism. What they have to say shall be comprised in a small compass, and shall be no more than what they believe will be the award of an impartial world. The people of Baltimore have dearly earned the privilege of speaking in the most frank and unreserved terms to the representatives of the nation. Yet they feel too tenderly for the honor and welfare of their country, even if they could be so indulged, publicly to rebuke and reproach the rulers of their choice for any errors that are past; they had rather aid than weaken, applaud than condemn. Let the following unequivocal acts and sufferings speak their ardent love for their Government and country. The metropolis of the nation was threatened; a portion of the militia of Baltimore was called on; at a very few moments' warning, they marched, with alacrity, to the aid of their country, and, on the unfortunate 24th

August, they were posted in front; the loss sustained by the enemy was produced, in a great degree, by its militia, and some amongst the best of its citizens bled or fell. The enemy next threatened Baltimore itself, upon which its people, old and young, of all classes, exerted themselves to the utmost, and with the most uncommon energy, in erecting works of defence, and making preparations to meet him, and, by the most unremitting and indefatigable labors, their city was put into a tolerable state of defence by the time he appeared before it. And the city feels great pride in the recollection that, on the day so memorable to it, the 12th of September, the constancy, fortitude, and courage of its citizen soldiers will bear a comparison with those of any other people on earth. Its citizens, some of whom had borne arms in their country's defence in the war of the Revolution, and her youth, met the enemy in advance, and were everywhere the first among the foremost in every perilous encounter. The banking institutions and the citizens of Baltimore, it is believed, have been as prompt and as liberal in their loans to the Government as those of any other portion of the Union.

Such are the people for whom your memorialists beg and entreat aid, protection, and defence. The Government may yet provide means in time, if prompt and vigorous measures are adopted; but there is no time to be lost. And your memorialists cannot, for a moment, entertain the painful thought that the constituted authorities of their country will turn with apathy from the earnest entreaties of a people so highly deserving their regard, and leave them to the mercy of a brutal enemy, whose hostility against them, in particular, has been so lately manifested, and so strongly excited.

EDWARD JOHNSON,
Chairman Committee of
Vigilance and Safety.

BALTIMORE, *January* 26, 1815.

THURSDAY, February 2.

WILLIAM T. BARRY, appointed a Senator by the Legislature of the State of Kentucky, in the place of George M. Bibb, resigned, and ISHAM TALBOT, appointed a Senator by the Legislature of the same State, in the place of Jesse Bledsoe, resigned, respectively, produced their credentials, were qualified, and they took their seats in the Senate.

The bill to authorize a detachment from the militia of the United States was read the second time.

The bill, entitled "An act giving the right of pre-emption in the purchase of lands to certain settlers in the Indiana Territory," was read the second time, and referred to the committee appointed the 21st September, on the memorial of the Legislature of the Indiana Territory, to consider and report thereon.

The bill, entitled "An act to authorize the payment for property lost, captured, or destroyed, by the enemy, while in the military service of the United States," was read the second time.

The PRESIDENT laid before the Senate a report of the Secretary for the Department of the Navy on the petition of William Elliot, referred to him on the 6th ultimo; and the report was read.

Mr. TAYLOR, from the committee to whom was referred the bill, entitled "An act to amend the act laying duties on licenses to retailers of wines, spirituous liquors, and foreign merchandise," reported it without amendment.

The Senate resumed the consideration of the amendments of the House of Representatives to the bill, entitled "An act to extend the time of Oliver Evans's patent, for his improvement on steam engines," and concurred therein.

BANK OF THE UNITED STATES.

The Senate resumed the consideration of the bill, passed by the two Houses, entitled " An act to incorporate the subscribers to the Bank of the United States of America," which was presented to the President of the United States for approbation, on the 23d of January, and returned by him on the 30th of the same month, with objections.

Mr. KING rose and submitted the following observations:

The proposed bank would have a capital of thirty-five millions of dollars, composed of five millions specie, ten millions six per cent. stock, funded since the commencement of the war, fifteen millions Treasury notes, and five millions to be held by the United States, and paid for in four per cent stock, to be created for this purpose.

The President of the United States objects to the bill—

1st. Because the amount of stock to be subscribed to the bank is insufficient to raise and sustain the public credit.

2d. Because no adequate public advantage will arise from the subscription of Treasury notes.

3d. Because the full aid and co-operation of the bank, in the furnishing of permanent and temporary loans, is not secured to Government during the war.

4th. Because the bank cannot be relied upon during the war to provide a circulating medium.

How the public credit could be revived, and sustained by the transfer of any sum of war stock from one citizen to another, or from the present holders to the proposed bank, is not obvious. If the war stock be taken at fifty millions, a demand for one-fifth, or ten millions of it, to be united to the bank capital, would have a temporary influence upon the stock market; and if any except stockholders become subscribers to the bank, this increase of price would be advantageous to the sellers. But the advantage would be a private one, no part of which would accrue to Government. As soon as the requisite sum is transferred to the bank, the stock will be precisely as valuable, and no more so, than it was before such transfer. Government will be obliged to make the same annual provision to pay the interest after the transfer as before. The public credit, which, after employing all the cabalistical words and manœuvres of stock jobbers, always did, and always will, depend upon the ways and means, or the ability of Government, to fulfil its engagements, or to pay its debts in equivalent values, will be little, if at all affected by a transfer of stock from individuals to a corporation within the country, especially as these transfers are to be made at different times, and at periods of considerable distance from each other. The same debt would continue to exist, yielding the same dividends and representing the same sum of American capital as it now represents. No addition to domestic capital would be made by this operation. If it releases the capital of A who sells the stock, it will employ the capital of B, who purchases it; and the only difference will be, that A becomes the owner of a disposable capital, which before belonged to B.

The raising of the price of stocks may prove beneficial to a Government in two ways, if it wants to borrow; the permanent, not the casual raising of the prices of the stock market, will enable it to sell new stock dearer. If foreigners come into the market, the raising of its price increases the money which must be brought into the country to purchase stocks. It was to meet the latter case, that an operation was undertaken by Colonel Hamilton, which proved to a limited degree advantageous. But although Government desires to obtain loans, it is not probable that any permanent application of the public credit would have been produced by the transfer of a given sum of the war stock to the bank, especially when the deep wound given to the public credit, by the extraordinary terms upon which the late loans were negotiated, is considered. More favorable times; a revival of industry and of commerce; an improved state of the finances, with a public income commensurate to the public expenditures, are necessary to the revival and re-establishment of the public credit.

The discrimination which is proposed to be carried still further than the bill carries it, in favor of the war stock, is impolitic. Were Government at liberty, for its own advantage (a case not now existing) to make such discrimination, the holders of war stock ought not now to desire it in their favor, as the example might be hereafter cited as a precedent against them, and in favor of the now postponed, though equally meritorious stock of the Revolution.

There should be no discrimination; the public faith knows no favorites; the holders of the war stock ought not to contend for preferences. They ought to be satisfied that the public faith, whether formerly or recently pledged, is equally precious to an honest Government, and will be alike redeemed.

If there still remains a doubt concerning the correctness of the first objection contained in the President's Message, can there be any respecting that of the second? Will no adequate public advantage arise from the subscription of Treasury notes?

Public credit, as has already been observed, depends upon the ability and inclination of Government to fulfil its contracts. Treasury notes are contracts, promising to their holders the sums, and at the times, mentioned in them. The bill provides that fifteen millions of dollars, in these notes, shall be receivable as a part of the bank capital, and when received shall be converted into fifteen millions of six per cent. stock. If not received by the bank and converted into six per cent. stock, this sum of fifteen millions of Treasury notes will fall due, and must be paid off, in the beginning of the next year. To this end money must be borrowed; and assuming the rate of the last loans, to borrow fifteen millions of dollars Government must give eighteen millions and three-quarters of a million of dollars of six per cent. stock. So that the difference between paying them off, or allowing them to be subscribed to the bank, and then converted into six per cent. stock, would be a clear saving to the public of three millions seven hundred and fifty thousand dollars six per cent. stock.

Moreover, by this conversion of Treasury notes into an equal sum of six per cent. stock, room would be made for a further issue of Treasury notes—the finances would also be relieved by releasing Government from the obligation to pay off their notes at a fixed day, and the ways and means, whether from loans or taxes, to the amount of fifteen millions, which would have been required for this purpose, would be left at the disposition of Government.

Is then the objection correct, which alleges that no adequate public advantage will arise from the subscription of Treasury notes to the bank?

The third objection alleges that the bank is under no legal compulsion to afford that full aid and co-operation to Government, which the Message declares to be both indispensable and necessary in the administration of the finances, the bank being neither obliged to make temporary nor permanent loans to Government.

Temporary loans to Government, in advance or anticipation of the taxes, are without doubt among the chief advantages that Government derives from a National Bank; as portions of the annual expenditure are required to be made before the taxes are collected, the bank, with mutual advantage to itself and the Government, is commonly able to make the advances wanted for this purpose, waiting for their repayment until the taxes come in.

In ordinary times every bank of circulation finds its interest in affording to the Government this accommodation; which is made pursuant to the correct maxims of commercial credit, being a loan made upon "good pledges" or undoubted security, which at a fixed, and no distant period, will repay it.

But it must be evident that such advances in anticipation of the taxes, and which are to be repaid by them, can be made only upon the faith that the currency in which the taxes are paid will be of equal value with that in which the bank makes its advances.

If, as in the instance of this bank, its notes are convertible into specie, and the taxes are payable either in them or a Government paper, which is at a discount, no one will suppose that the bank can, in such case, make advances to Government, and receive in payment thereof the depreciated paper in which the taxes are paid.

If the bill pass, the bank must redeem its notes with cash ; the taxes will be receivable in bank notes or Treasury notes ; the latter being at a discount, the taxes will be paid in them. Ought any one to expect that the bank will advance to Government a million of dollars in its notes, as an anticipation of the land tax, and receive in payment a million of dollars in Treasury notes, which may be at a discount of ten or fifteen per cent ? Is it not plain that, instead of receiving a compensation for the loan, the bank would in such case suffer a positive loss, equal to the depreciation of the Treasury notes ?

It results, that neither this bank, nor any other, whose notes are of greater value, as a currency, than Treasury notes, can make advances in anticipation of taxes, payable in Treasury notes.

The objection, therefore, against the bank amounts to this, that it cannot do what can only be done by a bank which is released from those indispensable restraints. without which no bank can with safety be established.

This objection goes further, and urges the rejection of the bill because the bank is not obliged to make permanent loans to Government. No bank doing business, upon securities of short dates, can make permanent loans, and all banks of circulation are obliged to require such securities. If any exception to this rule exist, it can only be for moderate sums. Banks, acting upon the principle, that cash advance must be upon a security or pledge, which, at a short date, enables the bank to recall its advance, are called commercial banks. Those which make loans of long duration, or of a permanent character, do so with a reliance solely upon the public credit ; and without the specific pledges, demanded by banks of circulation, and which enable them to recover their money, in all cases of failure. These are called financial or governmental banks. So long as banks confine their business, whether with Governments or with individuals, to the maxims of commercial credit, receiving for their advances notes and bills of undoubted credit, and payable at early periods, or pledges of specific funds or effects—so long are they of advantage to Governments, as well as to individuals employed in any kind of business requiring the aid of credit.

But all experience has proved, and the examples are numerous throughout Europe, and as is believed without a single exception, that whenever banks become what is called financial banks, making permanent loans upon the mere pledge of the public faith, when they become the mints employed by Governments to fabricate paper to such amount, as often, and for such periods, as their wants frequently recurring, and always urgent, demand ; they never fail to accomplish an extensive revolution in personal property, sometimes produce the abolition of debts, and after preying upon the credulous and unprotected, end in their own, and the nation's bankruptcy.

It has been supposed that the Bank of England is a financial bank, and an exception from this conclusion ; it would require much time and detail to give a correct idea of the operations of this bank ; all that will now be said in reply to this suggestion is, that whoever takes the requisite pains to understand the origin, progress, maxims, and manner of conducting the business of the Bank of England, whether with Government or individuals, will become satisfied that it transacts its business strictly upon the principles and rules of commercial credit ; and that because it does so, and for that reason only, it has been enabled to afford the aid which it has done to the public, private, and commercial credit of the nation.

It would therefore seem that it is no sufficient objection to this bill that it does not oblige the bank to make large loans to Government ; since to compel a bank to make such loans, upon the pledge of the public faith, or upon depreciated public securities, especially when the bank is released from the obligation to make specie payments, would be to require it to repeat the experiment so often made in different forms, both at home and abroad, which has everywhere and always failed, and which enlightened economists will all unite to condemn.

Lastly, it is objected, that the bank cannot be relied upon during the war, to provide a circulating medium.

No bank which is obliged to redeem its notes with specie, can in the present state of commerce, credit, and alarm, issue the same beyond a very limited sum.

If to the distrust which the war, and a real, or supposed scarcity of specie, create, be united an unusual demand for specie to be hoarded, or sent abroad for security, or to compensate unfavorable balances of trade, in lieu of the produce usually exported for this purpose ; and if at the same time a considerable depreciation of the public credit takes place, a case will exist in which banks of circulation are reduced to the necessity of either a total suspension of business, or such an abridgement of it, as to render them incapable of circulating their notes in quantities commensurate to the public demands.

The objection, therefore, is not against the structure of the bank, but against the condition of the country, and the state of the public credit, which may compel the bank to curtail its circulation.

In effect, the objection amounts to the confession that no bank which confines its business to the only safe and practical test of a paper circulation will, or can afford, important aid in the furnishing of a circulating medium, in times and circumstances like the present ; that no bank, except one which is released from the obligation to pay its notes in specie, can now afford a circulating medium ; in a word, that none but a bank which would circulate a depreciated currency, and which it would be dangerous to create, ought now to be established.

It might suffice to have shown that the President's objections ought not to prevent this bill's becoming a law ; but a few words may be added concerning the bill. The amount of the capital of the bank has already been mentioned. Its duties and general provisions are conformable to those of the late Bank of the United States; they have had a fair trial, and have been approved; whatever that bank would have done, this would be able to do; and advantages such as it afforded to Government in the management of the finances, this bank would in due time be equally or more capable of affording.

It has not been contended, that at this time, owing to the condition of the finances and credit of the United States, as well as to the general stagnation of trade, and the distrust of every kind of credit, any safe bank that might now be established, could afford to Government or to individuals much, or important assistance by loans, even of a temporary kind.

But the agency of this bank would now be of service to Government; whatever it should be able to do would be well done. Its operations would all be solid, and of standard character; its business must be limited, but it would be safe and exemplary; and with regard to every other moneyed institution, conducting its affairs honestly, it would cherish and sustain it.

Moreover, by the establishment of this bank upon sound and approved maxims, although it may not now do what no safe bank can do—much good—it will do no injury. It will not contribute still further to depreciate public and private credit; and during the term of its charter, it will prevent, a circumstance worth much, the establishment of a bank upon false and dangerous principles. On the return of peace, the agency and influence of this bank will become invaluable in the recovery and re-establishment of the credit and finances of the nation.

For these reasons, therefore, which had their influence in the passage of the bill by the Congress, and the force of which remains not only undiminished, but the latter of them is increased by the objections made by the President, it is earnestly to be wished, although scarcely to be hoped, that the bill may become a law.

The concluding paragraph of the Message of the President is incomparably the most important. It is this which opens and interprets the object desired to be attained by the rejection of this bill. Congress are here admonished by the President to make haste "to substitute" (in lieu of the bill) "a more commensurate and certain provision for the public exigencies."

The President of the United States, after alluding to the exigent and perilous condition of the country, after insinuating to Congress in language not to be misunderstood, that the resources of the Treasury were exhausted, that extraordinary succor from loans were no longer attainable, that a bank created upon safe and approved principles could afford no public assistance, plainly intimates that paper money, and only paper money, will, or can assist the nation in the further prosecution of the war. If this be so, if by the neglect and mismanagement of the finances and profusion in the public expenditures, the country is already reduced to this situation, and the President announces the same to Congress, will they prove themselves the faithful friends of the people, unless they seasonably apprize them of the fact, however humiliating?

If paper money be necessary, avow it, prepare it, issue it; but under every caution and guard which can be devised to mitigate its evils.

All experience, public and personal, demonstrates that every object is attained with more certainty and greater advantage by a direct than by an indirect course.

Why, then, will Congress by the creation and employment of a bank attempt to conceal their actual condition and real object? Why establish a bank which, dealing only in paper, will fabricate and lend as many millions as Congress may desire to borrow? Why pay to this bank an interest of six per cent. for the loan of their notes, which in no single ingredient will, or ought to be thought, to be of greater value than Treasury notes. The people of this country have much natural sagacity, and will not long be deceived by this or any similar contrivance. Rather devise an improved scheme for the immediate issue of Treasury notes, let them be convertible at pleasure into a public stock, bearing a high interest; fund this stock by pledging specific taxes to pay the interest; the credit of this currency will be better than that of the notes of such a bank as it is desired should be created.

If a paper circulation alone will enable us to defend the country, prepare and make use of it; but spare us the expense of paying interest for it to a company, whose faculties, without our contributions, will enable them to make dividends equal to their utmost desires.

When Mr. KING had concluded, the question was taken, Shall this bill pass? and was determined in the negative—yeas 15, nays 19, as follows:

Those who voted in the affirmative, are,

Messrs. Brown, Daggett, Dana, Fromentin, German, Giles, Goldsborough, Gore, Horsey, Hunter, King, Lambert, Mason, Tait, and Thompson.

Those who voted in the negative, are,

Messrs. Anderson, Barbour, Barry, Bibb, Chace, Condit, Gaillard, Kerr, Lacock, Morrow, Roberts, Robinson, Smith, Talbot, Taylor, Turner, Varnum, Wells, and Wharton.

So it was,

Resolved, That this bill do not pass, two-thirds of the Senate not agreeing thereto.

FRIDAY, February 3.

On motion, by Mr. LACOCK, the bill, entitled "An act to authorize the payment for property lost, captured, or destroyed by the enemy, while in the military service of the United States," was referred to the Committee on Military Affairs, to consider and report thereon.

Mr. GILES, from the Committee on Military Affairs, to whom was recommitted the bill, enti-

215   HISTORY OF CONGRESS.   216

SENATE.   *Public Buildings in the City of Washington.*   FEBRUARY, 1815.

tled "An act for the better regulation of the Ordnance department," reported it with amendments; which were read, and considered as in Committee of the Whole; and, having been agreed to, the President reported the bill to the House accordingly; and the amendments were ordered to be engrossed and the bill read the third time as amended.

A message from the House of Representatives informed the Senate that the House have passed a bill, entitled "An act for the relief of Saltus, Son, and Company, merchants of the city of New York;" a bill, entitled "An act to authorize the President of the United States to receive into the service of the United States certain corps which may be raised and organized by any State, to serve in lieu of the militia thereof;" a bill, entitled "An act for the regulation of the courts of justice of Indiana;" a bill, entitled "An act to amend and extend the provisions of the act of the sixteenth of April, 1814, entitled 'An act confirming certain claims to land in the Illinois Territory, and providing for their location;'" also, a bill, entitled "An act making appropriations for the support of the Government for the year 1815," in which bills they request the concurrence of the Senate.

The five bills last mentioned were read, and passed to the second reading.

The Senate resumed, as in Committee of the Whole, the consideration of the bill, entitled "An act to alter and amend the several acts for establishing a Navy Department, by adding thereto a Board of Commissoners," together with the amendments reported thereto by the select committee; and, the amendments having been agreed to with further amendment, the President reported the bill to the House accordingly.

On the question, Shall the amendments be engrossed, and the bill read a third time as amended? it was determined in the affirmative.

The Senate resumed, as in Committee of the Whole, the consideration of the bill, entitled "An act to authorize the purchase of a tract of land for the use of the United States," together with the amendment reported thereto by the select committee; and on motion, by Mr. BROWN, the further consideration thereof was postponed until to-morrow.

The Senate resumed, as in Committee of the Whole, the consideration of the bill, entitled "An act concerning Weston Jenkins and others;" and, no other amendment having been proposed, it passed to the third reading.

The Senate resumed, as in Committee of the Whole, the consideration of the bill, entitled "An act concerning Matthew Guy, John Woodward, Samuel Tennison, and Wilfred Drury," together with the amendments reported thereto by the select committee; and, the amendments having been agreed to, the President reported it to the House accordingly.

On the question, Shall the amendments be engrossed and the bill read a third time as amended? it was determined in the affirmative.

The Senate resumed, as in Committee of the Whole, the consideration of the bill, entitled "An act to amend the act, entitled 'An act to provide additional revenues for defraying the expenses of Government, and maintaining the public credit, by laying a direct tax upon the United States, and to provide for assessing and collecting the same;' and the act, entitled 'An act to provide additional revenues for defraying the expenses of Government, and maintaining the public credit, by laying duties on household furniture, and on gold and silver watches," together with the amendments reported thereto by the select committee. And the amendments having been agreed to, in part, the President reported the bill to the House accordingly. And Mr. KERR moved to amend the bill, by adding thereto a new section, as follows:

"*And be it further enacted*, That, if either the States of Ohio or Louisiana shall pay its quota of the direct tax, according to the provisions of the aforesaid act, the Legislatures thereof shall be and they are hereby authorized and empowered to collect of all the purchasers of public lands, under any law of the United States, a just and equal proportion of the quota of said States, respectively, the compact between the United States and the said States to the contrary notwithstanding."

The further consideration of the bill was postponed till to-morrow.

PUBLIC BUILDINGS.

The Senate resumed, as in Committee of the Whole, the consideration of the bill making appropriations for repairing or rebuilding the public buildings within the City of Washington.

Mr. FROMENTIN had moved yesterday to recommit the bill to a select committee. On this motion Mr. F. addressed the Chair as follows:

Mr. President: I am called upon to give the reasons which prompted me to make the motion now under consideration. I will endeavor to give to the Senate such an account of my motives as will enable them to judge of the propriety of the reference.

It may, perhaps, not be useless on this occasion to take a retrospective view of the length of time which has elapsed, after the erection of those buildings was determined on, before they could be used for the purposes for which they were intended, and of the sums of money which have been spent upon their construction. We shall be the better able to anticipate the probable time when these buildings may again be occupied by Congress, and to form a correct estimate of the sums of money which we may have to appropriate for those purposes.

Sir, it is more than twenty-three years, if I am correctly informed, since the public edifices, proposed now to be rebuilt, were begun to be erected. None of them, at the time of their destruction by the enemy, were completely finished; and I believe, the south wing of the Capitol was not ready for the reception of the House of Representatives more than four or five years before it was destroyed. If it be found necessary to rebuild, instead of repairing, the other hopeless alternative offered by the bill on your table, you may reasonably expect, taking into consideration the pre-

217 HISTORY OF CONGRESS. 218

FEBRUARY, 1815. *Public Buildings in the City of Washington.* SENATE.

sent situation of the country, especially if the war should continue, and thereby the difficulty of procuring materials, and of getting workmen, should be increased, that the two wings of the Capitol may be finished, and ready for the reception of both Houses of Congress, in about ten or twelve years.

The public buildings, including the President's House, did not cost less than fifteen hundred thousand dollars. We are told that five hundred thousand dollars will replace those edifices in *statu quo*. Sir, notwithstanding my respect for the artists who have given an opinion on this subject, I have still some doubts of the practicability of making use of the walls as they are now standing. The architects themselves are not positive on that point. They gave their opinion before the very severe frost, which we had this Winter, had its effect upon those susceptible and unprotected walls. Their opinion, if a new examination was now had, might be materially different; and the committee themselves, by reporting a bill for repairing or rebuilding the public buildings, instead of confining themselves to reporting a bill for repairing, have manifested a doubt, which it cannot be improper for me to entertain. If, then, you should ultimately be compelled to rebuild (and I firmly believe you will) the expense for rebuilding cannot be much less than the original cost of construction. The materials which you may save will about pay the expense of taking down the walls before you can rebuild.

Great, indeed, I should almost say incalculable, must be the advantages presented by this favorite situation, which, under the pressure of our present emergencies, could induce this Congress to sacrifice such immense sums of money. Three principal reasons have been adduced in support of this bill by its friends. The pride of the nation has been appealed to, and pressed into the service of this bill. Sir, when gentlemen entrench themselves behind the inexpugnable bulwark of pride, it would be in vain to use any arguments directed to their sober judgment. As well might you attempt, sword in hand, to pierce the heart of your enemy, protected from your attack by a fortress, flanked with a hundred cannon. The fortress is to be taken first; and I know of no argument strong enough to batter down the fortress erected by pride. There is but one way to come at it, sir; and it is by erecting alongside of it another pride fortress, and then fairly to begin the assault on both sides.

I, too, have my pride—not a pride to be fed upon the unpaid blood of the soldier who wins our battles; not a pride to be gratified by the vain and useless display of a borrowed, ragged magnificence. No, sir; my pride is less voracious, it is less ostentatious. Provide for filling the ranks of your Army; provide for clothing, feeding, and paying, your soldiers and sailors. Instead of borrowing money for building costly edifices, borrow money for protecting against an invading foe the edifices yet standing. Drive the enemy from the country; then, indeed, my pride will be satisfied; then I will, with pleasure, vote

money, as much money as you please, for rebuilding our public edifices; and then the more magnificent the plan, the more elegant its execution, the more my pride will be gratified.

It is further said, in support of this bill, that the plan recommended by the bill was the plan of Gen. Washington, and under the sanction of that imposing name an attempt is made to mislead our understanding. True, sir, this was the plan of Washington—but, under what circumstances? Washington was then President of the United States. The country then was rich; the country was prosperous. An extensive, unrestricted, and almost unlimited commerce brought then to the remotest corner of this vast continent all the treasures of a tributary world. The anxious eye of Washington measured the distances, and his capacious mind was not discouraged by them. The rapid, the almost prodigious progress of every improvement under his auspicious Administration, justified, in the opinion of that great and modest man, the anticipated expectations of corresponding improvements under the Administration of his successors. But, sir, what has been the result? Instead of realizing the high expectations of General Washington, from causes which it is foreign to my subject here to investigate, this country once rich, is now poor; this country once prosperous, is now fallen. I hope, sir, it will rise again; but till then, speak not to me of what Washington did. Speak what Washington would now advise; I say advise. The recollection of General Washington's unshakeable firmness in the year 1795, forbids the idea of the possibility of his ever having had to act under such an accumulation of distressing circumstances.

When I cast my eyes on this wilderness, dignified with the name of a city; a city to be sure, very unlike the old-fashioned European city, alluded to by the Irishman, who, when placed in the middle of it, complained that he could not see the city, there were so many houses! Sir, we run no risk of hearing of any such complaints about this city. Every Irishman who arrives here may have a full view of the whole ground at once. None of those encumbrances called houses to limit the boundless prospects. Or, if there be a few, he may, among those few, open a complaisant gap through which his inquisitive eye may pierce to a distance, limited only by the foot of the surrounding hills. But, sir, the subject is too serious to admit of its being thus long treated with levity. Let me then return to it, and seriously inquire about the present state and future prospects of this city. What do we see here? Twelve or fifteen clusters of houses at a considerable distance from each other, bringing to our recollection the appearance of a camp of nomad Arabs, which, however, if connected together, would make a very respectable town, not much inferior, perhaps, to the capital of Virginia; and here and there an insulated house; the whole of it, when seen from the ruins of our public edifices, looking more like the place where proud Washington once stood, than where humble Washington now lies. If,

219   HISTORY OF CONGRESS.   220

SENATE.   *Public Buildings in the City of Washington.*   FEBRUARY, 1815.

sir, such is the situation of this city, after fifteen years since the Government removed here, during the six first years of which period there prevailed not only in this country, but all over Europe, a degree of enthusiasm bordering upon madness respecting the future destinies of this metropolis, and during which period of six years, too, this country enjoyed still the benefits of the Administration of Washington, whose good deeds for several years after his death were still in force—Washington, in his tomb, still securing the prosperity of this his beloved country—if, sir, such be now the situation of this city, what, in the present state of things, are our prospects for the future? Awful, indeed. How many ages must elapse before this chaos is likely to assume anything like a describable shape? How many, before these disjointed, distracted, warring elements may be brought together, so as to form a whole, which may entitle it to be what it now purports to be, but what it is not. Is it not time, then, that we should give up the unsuccessful experiment? Is it not time, that we should adopt less lofty ideas, that we should assume sentiments, that we should express opinions more conformable to our present situation. *Troja fuit, fuit Ilium.* It becomes us to be modest. Our laws to be wholesome, need not be enacted in a palace. A large, convenient, unadorned house, which will receive its lustre from Congress, instead of Congress borrowing it from the house, in the neighborhood of the public offices. in a part of the city which is best calculated by its actual improvements to afford accommodation to the members, and to facilitate their communications with each other, will answer our purpose much better than the plan recommended by the bill on your table; and if the place to erect those edifices be judiciously selected, it is to me quite immaterial in what quarter of this city. For want of the necessary information as to the quantity of ground still owned by the Government in the different parts of this city, I could not now form any opinion as to the spot where it would be proper to concentrate all our public edifices, whether temporarily or permanently. But I may be allowed to express a wish that it may be found convenient to place them as near as possible to Georgetown, not very distant from the improvements known under the appellation of the Six and Seven Buildings; and I have little doubt, but that, when in compliance with the uniform laws of nature, you shall have blown up a soul into this city by creating a heart from which the blood may uninterruptedly circulate to the remotest extremities, the improvements will, by degrees, extend in every direction, until the now most distant parts from that spot, no longer shrivelled, sickly, lingering, rootless slips, destined to vegetate a few mornings, in an uncongenial soil. being in their turn reconnected with a sturdy, robust trunk, from which they will derive an invigorating sap, will soon spread a wide hospitable foliage, and become a flourishing portion of a city, the future prosperity of which cannot now, if it come at all, be secured in any other way.

I am not unaware, sir, that such a plan will call into action against it all the private interests which will conceive themselves to be aggrieved by it. But, let private interest beware. In my opinion, unless some such plan is resorted to, without some such compromise is made, the Government will not, cannot remain here many years. The inconveniences are too serious, and they are not to be surmounted. I speak not of them with reference to the individual inconvenience of the members. I speak of them in reference to their public duties. It is unnecessary.to repeat what I before stated, when I had the honor to address you on the subject of this bill. Only reflect on the only mode in which we can transact business in this place. Selected from various places of this immense empire, we meet here, not altogether free from the prejudices which prevail more or less in every part of the country we come from. This social intercourse which ought to prevail, which I am sure should prevail, did we know each other otherwise than through the incorrect medium of party representation, is entirely prohibited by the insuperable obstacles which the present situation of this city puts in our way. To these local prejudices are to be added party spirit, prejudices which pursue us unremittingly, and will not let go their hold of us in this very sanctuary. This party spirit, instead of being softened into something like conciliation, by a constant intercourse, is hardened into unutterable asperity by ' the mode of life, we are compelled from imperious circumstances, to pursue in this place. The very houses where we board have become a test by which to ascertain the political opinions which we are supposed to profess. We never meet, but in battle array. Is it wonderful, that under these discouraging circumstances, so many months should be wasted in transacting business which, under less unfavorable auspices, might have been gone through in as many weeks. Sir, it is my firm conviction, that if we proceed on to passing this bill in its present shape, the question of removal of the seat of the Government from this place, which was advocated at the beginning of this session in the other branch of the Legislature, will soon want no advocate at all; it will soon become a matter of necessity, of sheer necessity. There may be still many unsuccessful attempts, but, sir, the best interests of the nation cannot forever be sacrificed. After some struggling, an attempt will succeed at last; and it will then be too late for the opposers of the plan which I have suggested to give themselves up to unavailing repentance.

Mr. President, I want to prevent such a state of things. I am unwilling to bring forward again, at any time, the question of a permanent seat of Government. I want this sacred spot—sacred still in my eyes, although temporarily polluted by the foot of the enemy, as long as it bears the name of Washington; I want this spot to remain forever the permanent seat of the Government of the United States. But, sir, I know of but two ways to accomplish that object; either by a temporary removal by the very act providing for which we should provide likewise for our return; not provide simply; I do not mean by a clause in the bill to that effect, but by previous appropriations, by contracts, which it should not be in the power of any succeeding Congress to repeal, or by an immediate concentration of the public buildings on a modest, economical and commodious plan. Of these two modes, I prefer the last, as likely to meet with fewer obstacles, as being much less expensive, but principally as being much more consonant to the principles of the justice which we owe to the people of this District. Sir, when this bill was reported, I inquired from the honorable chairman of the committee who reported it, for the papers relating to the original fixation of the several places for the building of the public edifices. I inquired for the contracts with the original proprietors of the soil, or with the purchasers. I was answered, that there was no such instrument. I shall take no advantage from this concession; in my view of the subject, there was a contract—a solemn contract; and if by any possible way it could be avoided, I would not now agree to altering, in its most inconsiderable dispositions, any part of the original plan. I am sensible, that by so doing, we seem to punish the people of this District for having placed too much confidence in our words. In our words, did I say? In our acts, sir! Look at the new ruins of the monuments on yonder hill. Were these massy walls, which have set at defiance the whole power of an enemy bent on destruction, intended to last only the short space of a dozen years? In these surviving walls I read, in characters not to be effaced, the contract of the nation with the people of the District. I find in these walls an agreement signed, sealed, and delivered. Certainly, sir, you must be convinced, from what I have just now said, that I do not dissemble to myself, and that I am not willing to conceal from others, the equity of the claims of the people of this District. But what is to be done? Imperious necessity commands a sacrifice of some sort. A compromise must take place. You have but a choice of evils. The very bill on your table promises a tardy relief to the people on Capitol Hill, at the end of ten or twelve years. Under these impressions, and under the belief too, that the people of the District at large are ultimately to be benefitted by a concentration, for the reasons previously advanced, however a few may appear likely to be sufferers by any ultimate determination as to the spot where the concentration is to take place; and under an unshakeable persuasion, that by a strict adherence to the old plan, in our present circumstances, as recommended by the bill on your table, the people of this District, by grasping at too much, will ultimately lose all—from motives of economy; from motives of duty to the people of the United States; from motives of indispensable convenience to ourselves to enable us faithfully to discharge our public duties; from motives of justice to the people of this District—I have been induced to make the motion to refer that bill to a committee, for the purpose of reporting another bill to concentrate the public

buildings. Sir, I am disposed to sacrifice everything, but my duty to the people of the United States at large, to keep the seat of Government here; and if you agree to concentrate the public buildings, in the hope of speedy improvements, by which many of the inconveniences which now affect the public interest will be removed, I am perfectly reconciled to remaining in this city. But, sir, if we are to remain here as we now are, with no other cheering prospects than those presented in the bill on your table, I do not hesitate to declare, that any place in the United States appears to me preferable to Washington, and the sooner we go, no matter where, no matter how heavy the amount of compensation justly due to the inhabitants of this District, the better.

When Mr. F. had concluded—

The question to recommit the bill to a select committee, was determined in the negative—yeas 13, nays 20, as follows:

YEAS—Messrs. Bibb, Barry, Brown, Dana, Fromentin, German, Gore, Hunter, King, Lambert, Mason, Thompson, and Wells.

NAYS—Messrs. Anderson, Barbour, Chace, Condit, Daggett, Gaillard, Giles, Goldsborough, Horsey, Kerr, Lacock, Morrow, Roberts, Smith, Tait, Talbot, Taylor, Turner, Varnum, and Wharton.

On motion, by Mr. LACOCK, to strike out, of section 1, line 4, after the words "Capitol," the words "and public offices;" and to insert, after "Washington," line 5, "and that two suitable buildings for public offices be erected on such part of the Capitol square as shall be designated by the President of the United States;" and to insert, in the 4th line, the word "and," before "Capitol:" a division of the question was called for by Mr. DANA. and was taken on striking out, and determined in the negative—yeas 13, nay 18, as follows:

YEAS—Messrs. Brown, Dana, Fromentin, Gaillard, German, Gore, Hunter, King, Lacock, Lambert, Mason, Tait, and Thompson.

NAYS—Messrs. Anderson, Barbour, Bibb, Barry, Chace, Condit, Daggett, Giles, Goldsborough, Kerr, Morrow, Roberts, Smith, Taylor, Turner, Varnum, and Wharton.

And the bill having been amended, by striking out the second section thereof, the President reported it to the House accordingly; and the bill was ordered to be engrossed and read the third time as amended.

SATURDAY, February 4.

The bill, entitled "An act for the relief of Saltus, Son, & Co., merchants of the city of New York," was read the second time, and referred to a select committee, to consider and report thereon; and Messrs. KING, ROBERTS, and GERMAN, were appointed the committee.

The bill, entitled "An act for the regulation of the courts of justice of Indiana, was read the second time, and referred to a select committee to consider and report thereon; and Messrs. MORROW, TALBOT, and CHACE, were appointed the committee.

The bill, entitled "An act to authorize the President of the United States to receive into the service of the United States certain corps which may be raised and organized by any State, to serve in lieu of the militia thereof," was read the second time, and referred to the Committee on Military Affairs, to consider and report thereon.

The bill, entitled "An act making appropriations for the support of the Government for the year 1815," was read the second time, and referred to a select committee, to consider and report thereon; and Messrs. TAYLOR, CHACE, and ROBERTS, were appointed the committee.

The bill, entitled "An act to amend and extend the provisions of the act of the 16th April, 1814, entitled 'An act confirming certain claims to land in the Illinois Territory, and providing for their location," was read the second time, and referred to the committee appointed on the 21st September, on the memorial of the Legislature of the Indiana Territory, to consider and report thereon.

Mr. BARBOUR gave notice that, to-morrow, he should ask leave to bring in a bill to incorporate the subscribers to the Bank of the United States of America.

The bill making appropriations for repairing or rebuilding the public buildings within the City of Washington was read a third time, and the blank filled with "five hundred thousand dollars."

Resolved, That this bill pass, and that the title thereof be "An act making appropriations for repairing or rebuilding the public buildings within the City of Washington."

The amendments to the bill, entitled "An act to alter and amend the several acts for establishing a Navy Department, by adding thereto a Board of Commissioners," was read a third time as amended.

On the question, Shall this bill pass as amended? it was determined in the affirmative—yeas 16, nays 8, as follows:

YEAS—Messrs. Barbour, Chace, Daggett, Fromentin, Gaillard, German, Giles, Gore, Horsey, Kerr, Mason, Morrow, Tait, Taylor, Thompson and Wharton.

NAYS—Messrs. Bibb, Condict, Lacock, Lambert, Roberts, Smith, Turner, and Varnum.

So it was *Resolved,* That this bill pass with amendments.

The amendments to the bill, entitled "An act for the better regulation of the Ordnance department," having been reported by the committee correctly engrossed, the bill was read a third time as amended, and passed with amendments.

The bill, entitled "An act concerning Weston Jenkins, and others," was read a third time, and passed.

The amendments to the bill, entitled "An act concerning Matthew Guy, John Woodward, Samuel Tennison, and Wilfred Drury," having been reported by the committee correctly engrossed, the bill was read a third time as amended.

On motion, by Mr. GORE, the bill was recommitted to the Committee on Naval Affairs, further to consider and report thereon.

The Senate resumed, as in Committee of the Whole, the consideration of the bill, entitled "An act to authorize the purchase of a tract of land for the use of the United States," together with the amendment reported thereto by the select committee; and, on motion by Mr. SMITH, the consideration thereof was further postponed to Monday next.

The Senate resumed the consideration of the bill, entitled "An act to amend the act, entitled 'An act to provide additional revenues for defraying the expenses of Government, and maintaining the public credit, by laying a direct tax upon the United States, and to provide for assessing and collecting the same;" and the act, entitled "An act to provide additional revenues for defraying the expenses of Government, and maintaining the public credit, by laying duties on household furniture, and on gold and silver watches."

Mr. KERR's motion to add a new section was withdrawn; and the bill having been further amended, by adding thereto a new section, proposed by Mr. KING, on the question, Shall the amendments be engrossed and the bill read a third time as amended? it was determined in the affirmative.

The Senate resumed, as in Committee of the Whole, the consideration of the bill, entitled "An act to amend the act laying duties on licenses to retailers of wines, spirituous liquors, and foreign merchandise; and, no amendment having been proposed, it passed to a third reading.

A message from the House of Representatives informed the Senate that the House have passed a bill, entitled "An act to provide additional revenues for defraying the expenses of Government, and maintaining the public credit, by laying a duty on gold, silver, and plated ware, and jewelry and paste work, manufactured within the United States;" a bill, entitled "An act concerning the College of Georgetown, in the District of Columbia;" also, a bill, entitled "An act to provide additional revenues for defraying the expenses of Government, and maintaining the public credit, by laying a duty on lotteries;" in which bills they request the concurrence of the Senate.

The three bills last mentioned were read, and passed to the second reading.

The PRESIDENT laid before the Senate a letter from the Secretary for the Department of Treasury, transmitting sundry documents, exhibiting a view of the revenues of the United States, as stated in the report made to Congress, from that department, on the 23d day of September last, not having been at that time prepared, owing to the early meeting of Congress; and the letter and documents therein referred to were read.

On motion, by Mr. SMITH, the consideration of the bill to allow a drawback of duties on spirits distilled, and certain goods, wares, and merchandise, manufactured, within the United States, was postponed to, and made the order of the day for, Monday next.

MONDAY, February 6.

The bill, entitled "An act to provide additional revenues for defraying the expenses of Government, and maintaining the public credit, by laying a duty on gold, silver, and plated ware, and jewelry and paste work, manufactured within the United States," was read the second time, and referred to the committee to whom was referred the bill, entitled "An act making appropriations for the support of Government for the year 1815," to consider and report thereon.

The bill, entitled "An act to provide additional revenues for defraying the expenses of Government, and maintaining the public credit, by laying a duty on lotteries," was read the second time, and referred to the same committee, to consider and report thereon.

On motion, by Mr. TAYLOR, two members were added to the committee last mentioned; and Mr. DAGGETT and Mr. BROWN were appointed.

The bill, entitled "An act concerning the College of Georgetown, in the District of Columbia," was read the second time.

The bill, entitled "An act to amend the act laying duties on licenses to retailers of wines, spirituous liquors, and foreign merchandise," was read the third time, and passed.

Mr. ROBERTS, from the committee to whom was referred the bill, entitled "An act for the relief of Benjamin Wells and others," reported it with amendments.

The Senate resumed the motion for the appointment of an assistant Doorkeeper; and on motion, by Mr. TURNER, the further consideration thereof was postponed to the fourth day of March next.

On motion, by Mr. VARNUM,

Resolved, That the committee to whom was referred that part of the Message of the President of the United States, of the 20th September last, which relates to the Military Establishment, be instructed to inquire into the expediency of making provision by law for the payment of the militia which have been called out by the authority of any State for the defence of any part of the United States against invasion, since the commencement of the present war, and not taken into the pay of the United States; and for reimbursing any State for any moneys advanced for pay, rations, camp equipage, and other expenses necessarily incurred in calling out such militia, according to the rules and regulations prescribed by law for defraying the expenses of calling out the militia by authority of the United States.

The PRESIDENT laid before the Senate the report of the Secretary for the Department of Treasury, prepared in conformity with the act of March 3d, 1809, further to amend the several acts for the establishment of the Treasury, War, and Navy Departments, with statements of the purchases or payments for supplies, made by the collectors of the customs, during the year 1813, in relation to the revenue, and to the temporary relief of sick and disabled seamen; and the report, together with the accompanying documents, were read.

The Senate resumed, as in Committee of the Whole, the consideration of the bill to allow a drawback of duties on spirits distilled, and certain goods, wares, and merchandise, manufactured

within the United States; and the bill having been amended, the President reported it to the House accordingly; and, on the question, Shall this bill be engrossed and read a third time as amended? it was determined in the affirmative.

The amendments to the bill, entitled "An act to amend the act, entitled 'An act to provide additional revenues for defraying the expenses of Government, and maintaining the public credit, by laying a direct tax upon the United States, and to provide for assessing and collecting the same;" and the act, entitled "An act to provide additional revenues for defraying the expenses of Government, and maintaining the public credit, by laying duties on household furniture, and on gold and silver watches," having been reported by the committee correctly engrossed, the bill was read a third time as amended; and on motion, by Mr. FROMENTIN, the bill was further amended by unanimous consent; and on motion, by Mr. MORROW, it was recommitted to a select committee, further to consider and report thereon; and Messrs. GILES, KING, and TAYLOR, were appointed the committee.

Mr. BARBOUR, agreeably to notice given, asked leave to introduce a bill to incorporate the subscribers to the Bank of the United States of America.

This was objected to, by Mr. MASON, as out of order, as a bill of a similar nature, passed by both Houses of Congress, and returned by the President of the United States with his objections to the same, had, on reconsideration, been negatived by the Senate.

The PRESIDENT decided it to be in order, considering it to be sanctioned by the practice of Congress in relation to bills thus returned by the President of the United States.

Whereupon, the bill was read, and passed to the second reading.

[The principal features of this bill are as follows: the capital to consist of fifty millions of dollars, payable, twenty millions in Treasury notes, fundable at the pleasure of the Government in stock to bear an interest of six per cent.; fifteen millions in any public stock bearing six per cent. interest; five millions in specie; and ten millions to be subscribed by the Government in stock bearing an interest of four per cent. per annum; the Government to have the capacity to borrow thirty millions of the bank at six per cent. interest; the directors not to be obliged to pay specie until the last payment on the stock shall be completed; and, upon the petition of the directors, the Government may introduce any regulation which shall be thought proper in regard to the specie payments of the bank; the subscriptions to be opened on the first Monday in April, at which time the first payment of one-fifth of the whole amount of subscription shall be payable, and the remaining four-fifths in four quarter yearly instalments; the bank to go into operation as soon as twenty millions are thus paid in. The directors for the first year are named in the bill.]

The PRESIDENT communicated a report of the Commissioners of the Sinking Fund, stating that the measures which have been authorized by the board, subsequent to their last report, of the 5th of February, 1814, so far as the same have been completed, are fully detailed in the report of the Secretary of the Treasury to this board, dated the 6th day of the present month, and in the statements therein referred to, which are herewith transmitted, and prayed to be received as part of this report; which was read.

The Senate resumed, as in Committee of the Whole, the consideration of the bill, entitled "An act to authorize the purchase of a tract of land for the use of the United States," together with the amendment reported thereto by the select committee; and the amendment having been disagreed to, the President reported the bill to the House without amendment, and it passed to a third reading.

The Senate resumed, as in Committee of the Whole, the consideration of the bill to authorize a detachment from the militia of the United States; and on motion, by Mr. GILES, the further consideration thereof was postponed to, and made the order of the day for, Thursday next.

A message from the House of Representatives informed the Senate that they have passed a bill, entitled "An act for the relief of the Anacosta Bridge Company;" also, a bill, entitled "An act for the relief of the legal representatives of David Darden;" in which bills they request the concurrence of the Senate.

The two bills last mentioned were read, and passed to the second reading.

TUESDAY, February 7.

The bill, entitled "An act for the relief of the legal representatives of David Darden," was read the second time, and referred to a select committee, to consider and report thereon; Messrs. BARBOUR, TALBOT, and VARNUM, were appointed the committee.

The bill, entitled "An act for the relief of the Anacosta Bridge Company," was read the second time, and referred to the committee to whom was referred the memorial of the President and Directors of the Washington Bridge Company, to consider and report thereon.

The Senate resumed the bill, entitled "An act concerning the College of Georgetown, in the District of Columbia."

On motion, by Mr. GOLDSBOROUGH, it was referred to a select committee, to consider and report thereon; and Messrs. GOLDSBOROUGH, FROMENTIN, and HORSEY, were appointed the committee.

Mr. BROWN, from the committee to whom was referred several memorials from a number of the inhabitants of the Mississippi Territory, reported a bill for quieting and adjusting claims to land in the Mississippi Territory; and the bill was read, and passed to the second reading.

Mr. TAIT, from the Committee on Naval Affairs, to whom was referred the bill, entitled "An act directing the manner of contracts and purchases in the Navy Department, and for promoting economy therein," reported it without amendment.

Mr. TAYLOR, from the committee to whom

was referred the bill, entitled "An act making appropriations for the support of Government for the year 1815," reported it without amendment.

Mr. GILES, from the Committee on Military Affairs, to whom was referred the bill, entitled "An act to authorize the President of the United States to receive into the service of the United States certain corps which may be raised and organized by any State, to serve in lieu of the militia thereof," reported it without amendment.

Mr. FROMENTIN, from the committee to whom was referred the bill, entitled "An act for the relief of the inhabitants of the late county of New Madrid, in the Missouri Territory, who suffered by earthquakes," reported it with an amendment.

On motion, by Mr. ROBERTS, the committee appointed on so much of the President's Message as relates to military affairs, were instructed to inquire into the expediency of providing for the appointment of a suitable number of veterinary surgeons, to be attached to the Army of the United States.

The bill, entitled "An act to authorize the purchase of a tract of land for the use of the United States," was read a third time, and passed.

The Senate resumed, as in Committee of the Whole, the consideration of the bill, entitled "An act for the relief of Benjamin Wells and others," together with the amendments reported by the select committee; and, the amendments having been agreed to, the PRESIDENT reported the bill to the House accordingly. On the question, Shall the amendments be engrossed and the bill read a third time as amended? it was determined in the affirmative.

Mr. KERR presented the petition of Nicholas Boilevin, praying reimbursement for certain property destroyed by the Indians, as stated in the petition; which was read, and referred to a select committee, to consider and report thereon by bill or otherwise; and Messrs. KERR, GILES, and ANDERSON, were appointed the committee.

Mr. GORE, from the committee to whom was referred the bill, entitled "An act for the relief of Joseph Perkins," reported it without amendment.

WEDNESDAY, February 8.

On motion, by Mr. FROMENTIN, it was agreed that a member be added to the committee appointed agreeably to the 22d rule for conducting business in the Senate, in place of Mr. BLEDSOE; and Mr. BARRY was appointed.

Mr. GOLDSBOROUGH, from the committee to whom was recommitted the bill for the relief of Bowie and Kurtz, and others, reported it without amendment.

A message from the House of Representatives informed the Senate that the House have passed a bill, entitled "An act making provision for subsisting the Army of the United States, by authorizing the appointment of commissaries of subsistence;" in which bill they request the concurrence of the Senate.

The bill to incorporate the subscribers to the

Bank of the United States (introduced by Mr. BARBOUR) was read a second time.

A motion was made by Mr. GILES to refer the bill to a select committee.

On this motion a wide debate took place. The argument for reference was, the usage in such cases, where a bill was introduced by an individual member; the argument against it was, that though the bill was recently introduced by an individual member, the subject was one which had been widely discussed and was well understood by every member.

The motion to commit the bill was negatived, 18 to 16.

The Senate proceeded, as in Committee of the Whole, to the consideration of the bill.

Mr. GILES moved an amendment, the object of which was to confine the stock (payable on account of subscriptions to the capital of the bank) to such stock as should be hereafter created.

After an animated and interesting debate, this motion was negatived—for the motion 15, against it 18, as follows:

YEAS—Messrs. Brown, Fromentin, Gaillard, German, Giles, Goldsborough, Gore, Horsey, Hunter, King, Kerr, Lambert, Mason, Thompson, and Wells.

NAYS—Messrs. Anderson, Barbour, Barry, Bibb, Chace, Condit, Dana, Howell, Lacock, Morrow, Roberts, Smith, Tait, Talbot, Taylor, Turner, Varnum, and Wharton.

THURSDAY, February 9.

The bill brought up yesterday from the House of Representatives for concurrence was read, and passed to the second reading.

The PRESIDENT communicated the report of the Secretary for the Department of War, comprehending contracts made by him in the year 1814, and those made by the Commissary General in the same year, in compliance with "An act concerning public contracts," passed the 21st April, 1813; and the report was read.

The amendments to the bill, entitled "An act for the relief of Benjamin Wells and others," having been reported by the committee correctly engrossed, the bill was read a third time as amended.

Resolved, That this bill pass with amendments.

The bill to allow a drawback of duties on spirits distilled, and certain goods, wares, and merchandise, manufactured within the United States, was read a third time; and the blanks were filled; and the bill was amended by unanimous consent.

Resolved, That this bill pass, and that the title thereof be "An act to allow a drawback of duties on spirits distilled, and certain goods, wares, and merchandise, manufactured within the United States, on the exportation thereof to any foreign port or place."

Mr. KING presented the petition of Gould Hoyt, of the city of New York, owner of the ship called the American Eagle, praying indemnification for the loss sustained by him, in consequence of the illegal seizure of said ship by the collector of the port of New York; as is stated in the petition; which was read, and referred to the Secretary for the Department of Treasury, to consider and report thereon to the Senate.

Mr. TAIT, from the Committee on Naval Affairs, to whom was recommitted the bill, entitled "An act concerning Matthew Guy, John Woodward, Samuel Tennison, and Wilfred Drury," reported it with amendment.

The bill for quieting and adjusting claims to land in the Mississippi Territory was read the second time.

Mr. GILES, from the Committee on Military Affairs, to whom was referred the resolution of the Senate, of the 7th instant, relative to the veterinary surgeons, reported the following resolution:

Resolved, That it is inexpedient to provide for the appointment of veterinary surgeons, to be attached to the Army of the United States.

Mr. GILES, from the committee to whom was referred, on the 19th January, the resolution relative to compensation to individuals whose property may have been destroyed during the war, by the constituted authorities of the United States, reported the following resolution:

Resolved, That it is inexpedient, at this time, to provide by a general law for making compensation to individuals whose property may have been destroyed during the war, by the constituted authorities of the United States, or whose property may have been occupied for, or appropriated to, public purposes.

The Senate resumed the consideration of the National Bank bill; on which there took place, as on yesterday, much animated debate. Several questions of amendment were proposed, which were variously decided.

The Senate did not get through the bill before the adjournment, which took place at a late hour.

FRIDAY, February 10.

The bill, entitled "An act making provision for subsisting the Army of the United States, by authorizing the appointment of commissaries of subsistence," was read the second time, and referred to the Committee on Military Affairs, to consider and report thereon.

Mr. GILES, from the Committee on Military Affairs, to whom was referred the resolution of the Senate, of the 6th instant, reported a bill to authorize the settlement and payment of certain claims for the services of the militia; and the bill was read, and passed to the second reading.

A message from the House of Representatives informed the Senate that they have passed a bill, entitled "An act in addition to the act regulating the Post Office Establishment," in which bill they request the concurrence of the Senate.

BANK OF THE UNITED STATES.

The Senate resumed, as in Committee of the Whole, the consideration of the bill to incorporate the subscribers to the Bank of the United States of America.

On motion, by Mr. GILES, to strike out of the twelfth rule, the following:

" But the said corporation shall be bound to lend to the Government of the United States, reimbursable at their pleasure, thirty millions of dollars, at an interest not exceeding six per centum, per annum, in such sums, and at such periods, as may be made convenient to the Government of the United States, whenever any law or laws of the United States shall authorize and require such loan or loans."

And to strike out, from the eighteenth rule, the following:

" Until the first Monday of April, eighteen hundred and sixteen, it shall not be obligatory on the said corporation to pay its notes in specie, but all the notes of the said corporation, whether payable at the seat of the bank, in Philadelphia, or elsewhere, shall be payable in other notes of the said corporation, or in Treasury notes, at the option of the applicant. And if, any time during the continuance of the present war between the United States and Great Britain, and the period of one year after the termination of the said war, demands shall be made upon the said corporation for gold or silver coin, to an amount and under circumstances which induce a reasonable and probable belief that the specie capital may be greatly diminished or endangered, it shall be lawful for Congress, on the petition of the directors, to authorize the suspension of specie payments, for such time or times as they may deem proper:"

It was determined in the negative—yeas 15, nays 18, as follows:

YEAS—Messrs. Brown, Daggett, Dana, Fromentin, Gaillard, German, Giles, Goldsborough, Gore, Hunter, King, Lambert, Mason, and Wells.

NAYS—Messrs. Anderson, Barbour, Barry, Bibb, Chace, Condit, Howell, Kerr, Lacock, Morrow, Roberts, Robinson, Smith, Talbot, Tait, Turner, Varnum, and Wharton.

And the bill having been amended, the President resumed the Chair, and Mr. ANDERSON reported the bill to the House accordingly; and the amendments made in Committee of the Whole were concurred in.

On motion, by Mr. GORE, to insert, after " applicant," in line 216, the following words: " and this authority of the bank to pay its notes otherwise than by specie, shall be expressed on such notes," it was determined in the negative—yeas 15, nays 18, as follows:

YEAS—Messrs. Brown, Daggett, Dana, Fromentin, Gaillard, German, Giles, Goldsborough, Gore, Hunter, Kerr, King, Lambert, Mason, and Thompson.

NAYS—Messrs. Anderson, Barbour, Barry, Bibb, Chace, Condit, Howell, Lacock, Morrow, Roberts, Robinson, Smith, Talbot, Tait, Turner, Varnum, Wells, and Wharton.

On the question, Shall this bill be engrossed and read a third time as amended ? it was determined in the affirmative—yeas 18, nays 15, as follows :

YEAS—Messrs. Anderson, Barbour, Barry, Bibb, Chace, Condit, Howell, Kerr, Lacock, Morrow, Roberts, Robinson, Smith, Talbot, Tait, Turner, Varnum, and Wharton.

NAYS—Messrs. Brown, Daggett, Dana, Fromentin, Gaillard, German, Giles, Goldsborough, Gore, Hunter, King, Lambert, Mason, Thompson, and Wells.

SATURDAY, February 11.

The bill brought up yesterday for concurrence was read, and passed to the second reading.

The bill to authorize the settlement and payment of certain claims for the services of the militia was read the second time.

The Senate resumed, as in Committee of the Whole, the consideration of the bill, entitled " An act making appropriations for the support of Government for the year 1815 ;" and the bill having been amended, the President reported it to the House accordingly. On the question, Shall the amendments be engrossed and the bill read a third time as amended ? it was determined in the affirmative.

The PRESIDENT communicated a report of the Postmaster General, of unproductive post roads, and also a list of contracts made in the year 1814; which were read.

Mr. GILES, from the Committee on Military Affairs, to whom was referred the bill, entitled " An act making provision for subsisting the Army of the United States, by authorizing the appointment of commissaries of subsistence," reported it with amendments.

The bill to incorporate the subscribers to the Bank of the United States of America was read a third time ; and on the question, Shall this bill pass ? it was determined in the affirmative—yeas 18, nays 16, as follows :

YEAS—Messrs. Anderson, Barbour, Barry, Bibb, Chace, Condit, Howell, Lacock, Morrow, Roberts, Robinson, Smith, Talbot, Tait, Taylor, Turner, Varnum, and Wharton.

NAYS—Messrs. Brown, Daggett, Dana, Fromentin, Gaillard, German, Giles, Goldsborough, Gore, Horsey, Hunter, Kerr, King, Lambert, Mason, and Thompson.

So it was *Resolved,* That this bill pass, and that the title thereof be " An act to incorporate the subscribers to the Bank of the United States of America."

MONDAY, February 13.

The amendments to the bill, entitled " An act making appropriations for the support of Government for the year 1815," having been reported by the committee correctly engrossed, the bill was read a third time as amended.

Resolved, That this bill pass with amendments.

The bill, entitled " An act in addition to an act regulating the Post Office Establishment," was read the second time.

A message from the House of Representatives informed the Senate that the House have passed a bill, entitled " An act to authorize the issuing of Treasury notes, for the service of the year 1815 ;" in which bill they request the concurrence of the Senate.

The bill last mentioned was read, and passed to the second reading.

The Senate resumed, as in Committee of the Whole, the consideration of the bill, entitled "An act to authorize the President of the United States to receive into the service of the United States certain corps which may be raised and organized by any State, to serve in lieu of the militia thereof."

On motion, by Mr. SMITH, it was recommitted to the Committee on Military Affairs, further to consider and report thereon.

The Senate resumed, as in Committee of the Whole, the consideration of the bill, entitled "An act directing the manner of contracts and purchases in the Navy Department, and for promoting economy therein;" and on motion, by Mr. TAIT, the further consideration thereof was postponed to the second Monday in March next.

The Senate resumed, as in Committee of the Whole, the consideration of the bill, entitled "An act for the relief of the inhabitants of the late county of New Madrid, in the Missouri Territory, who suffered by earthquakes," together with the amendment reported thereto by the select committee, which was disagreed to; and an amendment having been agreed to, the President reported the bill to the House accordingly,

On the question, Shall the amendment be engrossed and the bill be read a third time as amended? it was determined in the affirmative.

The Senate resumed, as in Committee of the Whole, the bill, entitled "An act for the relief of Joseph Perkins;" and, no amendment having been proposed, it passed to a third reading.

Mr. HUNTER presented the petition of Edward Martin, of Newport, in the State of Rhode Island, confined in prison at the suit of the United States, praying to be released therefrom, for reasons stated at large in the petition; which was read, and was referred to a select committee, to consider and report thereon by bill or otherwise; and Messrs. HUNTER, FROMENTIN, and BROWN, were appointed the committee.

The Senate resumed, as in Committee of the Whole, the bill for the relief of Bowie and Kurtz, and others; and, no amendment having been agreed to, on the question, Shall this bill be engrossed and read a third time? it was determined in the affirmative—yeas 13, nays 9, as follows:

YEAS—Messrs. Anderson, Brown, Daggett, Fromentin, Gaillard, Giles, Goldsborough, Gore, Hunter, King, Smith, Thompson, and Wells.

NAYS—Messrs. Bibb, Condit, German, Lacock, Morrow, Taylor, Turner, Varnum, and Wharton.

DEFENCE OF NEW ORLEANS.

Mr. GILES, from the Committee on Military Affairs, reported the following resolutions, which were read and passed to the second reading:

Resolved, by the Senate and House of Representatives of the United States of America in Congress assembled, That the thanks of Congress be, and they are hereby, given to Major General Jackson, and through him to the officers and soldiers of the regular army, of the militia, and the volunteers, under his immediate command, for their uniform gallantry and good conduct, conspicuously displayed against the enemy from the time of his landing before New Orleans, until his final expulsion therefrom; and particularly for their distinguished gallantry, skill, and good conduct, on the 8th of January last, in repulsing, with great slaughter, a numerous British army of chosen veteran

troops, when attempting, by a bold and daring attack, to storm and carry the works hastily thrown up for the defence of New Orleans, and by obtaining a most signal and complete victory over the enemy, with a disparity of loss, on his part, unexampled in military annals.

Resolved, That the President of the United States be requested to cause to be struck a gold medal, with devices emblematical of this splendid achievement, and presented to Major General Jackson, as a testimony of the high sense entertained by Congress of the judicious and distinguished part he acted on this glorious and memorable occasion.

Resolved, That the President of the United States be requested to cause the foregoing resolution to be communicated to Major General Jackson, in such terms as he may deem best calculated to give effect to the objects thereof.

Mr. GILES, from the same committee, also reported the following resolutions, which were read and passed to the second reading:

Resolved, by the Senate and House of Representatives of the United States of America in Congress assembled, That Congress entertain a high sense of the patriotism, fidelity, zeal, and courage, with which the people of Louisiana promptly and unanimously stepped forth, under circumstances of imminent danger from a powerful invading army, in defence of all the individual, social, and political rights held dear by man. Congress declare and proclaim, that the brave Louisianians deserve well of the whole people of the United States.

Resolved, That Congress entertain a high sense of the generosity, benevolence, and humanity displayed by the people of New Orleans, in voluntarily affording the best accommodations in their power, and giving the kindest attentions to the wounded, not only of our own army, but also to the wounded prisoners of a fallen though vindictive foe.

Resolved, That the President of the United States be requested to cause the foregoing resolutions to be communicated to his Excellency the Governor of Louisiana, accompanied with the request that he cause the greatest possible publicity to be given to them for the information of the whole people of Louisiana.

The Senate resumed, as in Committee of the Whole, the consideration of the bill for quieting and adjusting claims to land in the Mississippi Territory; and on motion, by Mr. BROWN, the further consideration thereof was postponed to, add made the order of the day for, Thursday next.

The Senate resumed, as in Committee of the Whole, the consideration of the bill, entitled "An act making provision for subsisting the Army of the United States, by authorizing the appointment of commissaries of subsistence," together with the amendments reported thereto by the select committee; and, the amendments having been agreed to, the President reported the bill to the House accordingly.

On the question, Shall the amendments be engrossed and the bill read a third time as amended? it was determined in the affirmative.

Mr. TAIT, from the Committee on Naval Affairs, reported the following resolutions, which were read and passed to the second reading:

Resolved, That Congress entertain a high sense of the valor and good conduct of Commodore D. T. Patterson, of the officers, petty officers, and seamen, attached to his command, for their prompt and efficient co-operation with General Jackson in the late gallant and successful defence of the city of New Orleans, when assailed by a powerful British force.

Resolved, That Congress entertain a high sense of the valor and good conduct of Major Daniel Carmick, of the officers, non-commissioned officers, and marines, under his command, in the defence of the said city, on the late memorable occasion.

Mr. HORSEY, submitted the following motion:

Resolved, That a committee be appointed on the part of the Senate, to join such committee as may be appointed on the part of the House of Representatives, to inquire into the expediency of causing the chambers at present occupied by the two Houses of Congress, or others in the same building, to be altered and fitted up for the better accommodation of the two Houses.

The Senate resumed, as in Committee of the Whole, the consideration of the bill, entitled "An act concerning Matthew Guy, John Woodward, Samuel Tennison, and Wilfred Drury," together with the amendments reported thereto by the select committee.

On motion, by Mr. TAYLOR, that the further consideration thereof be postponed to the second Monday in March next, it was determined in the affirmative—yeas 14, nays 11, as follows:

YEAS—Messrs. Anderson, Barry, Condit, Daggett, Fromentin, Gaillard, Goldsborough, Gore, King, Tait, Taylor, Thompson, Turner, and Varnum.

NAYS—Messrs. Bibb, German, Giles, Hunter, Kerr, Lacock, Morrow, Roberts, Smith, Wells, and Wharton.

The Senate resumed, as in Committee of the Whole, the bill to authorize the settlement and payment of certain claims for the services of the militia; and on motion, by Mr. GILES, the further consideration thereof was postponed to, and made the order of the day for, Thursday next.

The Senate resumed the consideration of the resolution reported by the Committee on Military Affairs, the 9th instant, relative to veterinary surgeons; and agreed thereto.

The Senate resumed the consideration of the resolution reported, the 9th instant, by the committee to whom was referred, on the 19th January, the resolution relative to compensation to individuals whose property may have been destroyed during the war, by the constituted authorities of the United States; and agreed thereto.

TUESDAY, February 14.

The bill, entitled "An act to authorize the issuing of Treasury notes for the service of the year 1815," was read the second time, and referred to a select committee to consider and report thereon; and Messrs. SMITH, KING, and TAYLOR, were appointed the committee.

The resolutions expressive of the thanks of Congress to Major General Jackson, and the troops under his command, for their gallantry and good conduct in the defence of New Orleans, were read the second time and considered as in Committee of the Whole, and amended; and the President reported them to the House accordingly.

On the question, Shall these resolutions be engrossed and read a third time as amended? it was determined in the affirmative.

The resolutions expressive of the high sense entertained by Congress of the patriotism and good conduct of the people of Louisiana and New Orleans, during the late military operations before that city, were read the second time and considered as in Committee of the Whole; and, having been amended, the President reported them to the House accordingly.

On the question, Shall these resolutions be engrossed and read a third time as amended? it was determined in the affirmative.

The resolutions expressive of the high sense entertained by Congress of the gallantry and good conduct of Commodore D. T. Patterson, Major D. Carmick, and of the officers, seamen, and marines, under their command, in the defence of New Orleans, were read the second time, and considered as in Committee of the Whole; and, no amendment having been proposed, on the question, Shall these resolutions be engrossed and read a third time? it was determined in the affirmative.

The amendment to the bill, entitled "An act for the relief of the inhabitants of the late county of New Madrid, in the Missouri Territory, who suffered by earthquakes, having been reported by the committee correctly engrossed, the bill was read a third time as amended.

Resolved, That this bill pass with an amendment.

The amendments to the bill, entitled "An act making provision for subsisting the army of the United States by authorizing the appointment of commissaries of subsistence," were reported by the committee correctly engrossed.

The bill, entitled "An act for the relief of Joseph Perkins," was read a third time, and passed.

The bill for the relief of Bowie and Kurtz, and others, having been reported by the committee correctly engrossed, was read a third time. On the question, Shall this bill pass? it was determined in the affirmative—yeas 15, nays 14, as follows:

YEAS—Messrs. Anderson, Daggett, Dana, Fromentin, Gaillard, Giles, Goldsborough, Gore, Horsey, Kerr, King, Lambert, Smith, Thompson, and Wells.

NAYS—Messrs. Bibb, Chace, Condit, German, Lacock, Morrow, Roberts, Robinson, Talbot, Tait, Taylor, Turner, Varnum, and Wharton.

So it was *Resolved,* That this bill pass, and that the title thereof be "An act for the relief of Bowie and Kurtz, and others."

A message from the House of Representatives informed the Senate that the House concur in the amendments of the Senate to the bill entitled "An act making appropriations for the support of Government for the year 1815," with an amendment; in which they request the concurrence of the Senate. They have passed a bill, entitled "An act making provision for clothing the militia called into the service of the United

States;" also, a bill, entitled "An act requiring the Secretary of the Senate and Clerk of the House of Representatives, in the Congress of the United States, to give security for the faithful application and disbursement of the contingent funds of the Senate and House of Representatives;" in which bills they request the concurrence of the Senate.

WEDNESDAY, February 15.

On motion, by Mr. TAIT, the further consideration of the bill, entitled "An act making provision for subsisting the Army of the United States, by authorizing the appointment of commissaries of subsistence," was postponed to Monday next.

The two bills brought up yesterday for concurrence were read, and passed to the second reading.

The resolution for the appointment of a joint committee to inquire into the expediency of causing the chambers at present occupied by the two Houses of Congress, or others in the same building, to be altered and fitted up, for their better accommodation, was read the second time, and considered as in Committee of the Whole ; and no amendment having been proposed thereto, on the question, Shall this resolution be engrossed and read a third time? it was determined in the affirmative.

The Senate proceeded to consider the amendment of the House of Representatives to their amendments to the bill, entitled "An act making appropriations for the support of Government for the year 1815," and concurred therein.

On motion, by Mr. SMITH, the further consideration of the bill to authorize a detachment from the militia of the United States was postponed to Monday next.

The Senate resumed, as in Committee of the Whole, the consideration of the bill, entitled "An act in addition to an act regulating the Post Office Establishment."

On motion, by Mr. TAYLOR, it was referred to the committee to whom was referred the bill, entitled "An act making appropriations for the support of Government for the year 1815," to consider and report thereon.

Mr. MORROW presented the petition of Michael Jones and W. Bond, the Register and Receiver of Public Moneys for the district of Kaskaskia, praying additional compensation for their services; for reasons stated at large in the petition; which was read, and referred to the committee to whom was referred, the 21st September last, the memorial of the Legislature of the Indiana Territory, to consider and report thereon, by bill or otherwise.

DEFENCE OF NEW ORLEANS.

The resolutions expressive of the high sense entertained by Congress of the patriotism and good conduct of the people of Louisiana and of New Orleans, during the late military operations before that city, having been reported by the committee correctly engrossed, were read a third time as amended, and having been further amended by unanimous consent, passed unanimously, as follows :

Resolved, by the Senate and House of Representatives of the United States of America in Congress assembled, That Congress entertain a high sense of the patriotism, fidelity, zeal, and courage, with which the people of the State of Louisiana promptly and unanimously stepped forth, under circumstances of imminent danger from a powerful invading army, in defence of all the individual, social, and political rights, held dear by man. Congress declare and proclaim, that the brave Louisianians deserve well of the whole people of the United States.

Resolved, That Congress entertain a high sense of the generosity, benevolence, and humanity, displayed by the people of New Orleans, in voluntarily affording the best accommodations in their power, and giving the kindest attentions to the wounded, not only of our own army, but also to the wounded prisoners of a vanquished foe.

Resolved, That the President of the United States be requested to cause the foregoing resolutions to be communicated to his Excellency the Governor of Louisiana, accompanied with a request that he cause the greatest possible publicity to be given to them for the information of the whole people of Louisiana.

The resolutions expressive of the high sense entertained by Congress of the gallantry and good conduct of Commodore D. T. Patterson and Major D. Carmick, and of the officers, seamen, and marines under their command, in the defence of New Orleans, having been reported by the committee correctly engrossed, were read a third time, and passed unanimously, as follows:

Resolved by the Senate and House of Representatives of the United States of America in Congress assembled, That Congress entertain a high sense of the valor and good conduct of Commodore D. T. Patterson, of the officers, petty officers, and seamen, attached to his command, for their prompt and efficient co-operation with General Jackson, in the late gallant and successful defence of the city of New Orleans, when assailed by a powerful British force.

Resolved, That Congress entertain a high sense of the valor and good conduct of Major Daniel Carmick, of the officers, non-commissioned officers, and marines, under his command, in the defence of the said city, on the late memorable occasion.

The resolutions expressive of. the thanks of Congress to Major General Jackson, and the troops under his command, for their gallantry and good conduct in the defence of New Orleans, having been reported by the committee correctly engrossed, were read a third time as amended, and passed unanimously, as follows:

Resolved, by the Senate and House of Representatives of the United States of America in Congress assembled, That the thanks of Congress be, and they are hereby, given to Major General Jackson, and, through him, to the officers and soldiers of the regular army, of the militia, and of the volunteers under his immediate command, and to the officers and soldiers charged with the defence of Fort St. Philip, for their uniform gallantry and good conduct, conspicuously displayed against the enemy, from the time of his landing before New Orleans until his final expulsion from the State of Louisiana, and particularly for their valor, skill, and good conduct, on the 8th of January last, in repulsing, with great slaughter, a numerous British army of chosen veteran troops, when attempting, by a bold and daring attack, to storm and carry the works hastily thrown up for the defence of New Orleans, and thereby obtaining a most signal and complete victory over the enemy, with a disparity of loss, on his part, unexampled in military annals.

Resolved, That the President of the United States be requested to cause to be struck a gold medal, with devices emblematical of this splendid achievement, and presented to Major General Jackson, as a testimony of the high sense entertained by Congress, of his judicious and distinguished conduct on that memorable occasion.

Resolved, That the President of the United States be requested to cause the foregoing resolutions to be communicated to Major General Jackson, in such terms as he may deem best calculated to give effect to the objects thereof.

When the above resolutions were under consideration, Mr. BROWN, of Louisiana, addressed the Chair, as follows:

Mr. President: Having the honor to represent the State which has been the theatre of the events which it is the object of these resolutions to commemorate, it might be considered an evidence of great insensibility on my part, did I not rise for the purpose of expressing my most hearty approbation of them.

The reflecting mind, in reviewing the eventful measures by which the people of Louisiana have been conducted from a position of extreme peril to a state of perfect security, is irresistibly led to acknowledge the protecting hand of an all-wise and beneficent Providence, whose dispensations it is our duty, in grateful humility, to revere.

The richest reward which a nation can bestow on its distinguished benefactors, is to be found in the unanimous expression of a nation's gratitude. On no occasion has the united voice of national feeling been more distinctly heard, than on that which is the subject of our present deliberations. The measures adopted by General Jackson for the protection of Louisiana, and their happy results, have been succinctly detailed in his own simple, perspicuous, and modest narrative. It is not now necessary to recapitulate the facts. It is enough that we fix our admiring eyes on their fortunate results. If to disconcert the gigantic plans of the enemy—to disappoint his extravagant expectations—to humble his pride—to destroy a great part of his hitherto invincible army—to expel them from our soil, and save a State to the Union, and to accomplish all with a comparative loss unexampled in military annals, can entitle a brave general and a gallant army to the thanks of a generous people, then are General Jackson and his followers entitled to the wreath prepared for them by these resolutions. I shall not follow the deliverer of Louisiana through the blaze of battle and the shouts of victory; I am not so weak as to believe that my feeble voice can add lustre to deeds like his—"to deeds without a name." The tears of admiration and gratitude which moisten every eye whilst surveying scenes like

these, admonish me, that it is best to indulge in the silent sentiment of unutterable joy.

The army of General Jackson was principally composed of militia corps, a species of force hitherto not considered as the most efficient, which had been hastily collected from the States of Kentucky, Tennessee, Louisiana, and the Mississippi Territory. It is equally honorable to these soldiers, and to their commander, that no jealousies or dissensions disturbed the harmony of their camp, and that all united in facing the foe with a courage, an energy, and enthusiasm, rarely witnessed in an army of veteran troops. All were animated by the same soul, and the only contest which existed among them was, who should be foremost in the hour of danger.

The citizens of Kentucky, since the commencement of our present struggle, have obtained a character so elevated for patriotism and devotion to the best interests of their country, that it can receive no additional lustre from any expressions I can employ. The State of Tennessee has exalted claims to the approbation of the nation. To that State we are indebted for the safety of our country when threatened by our savage neighbors, and the part which her citizens have acted on the late ever memorable occasion, will afford to their latest posterity a rich repast in the page of impartial history. One-third of the militia of this State, having no exposed frontier to protect, and threatened by no immediate danger, cheerfully left their friends and their families and flew to the assistance of Louisiana. Generous people! on behalf of those you have succored in the hour of peril, I thank you—from my heart I thank you!

Reflect, Mr. President, on the rapid march of General Coffee and his volunteers to Mobile, to Pensacola, to New Orleans, a distance of more than one thousand miles. Consider the difficulties of the route, and you will admire the perseverance of the commander, and the patience and discipline of his troops, as much as you will applaud the undaunted bravery they displayed on the memorable eighth of January. See the brave and indefatigable Carroll descending the Mississippi with an army of three thousand men, and accomplishing his voyage in a space of time considered too short to enable the greedy speculator, in search of a market, to conduct a single ark to the same point of destination. It is to such men, and to such exertions as these, that Louisiana is indebted for her safety, and so long as gratitude shall be considered a virtue, shall these brave men be held in grateful remembrance.

On so much of these resolutions, and other resolutions now under consideration, as relate to the militia and people of Louisiana, it would not, perhaps, become me to enlarge. Attached, as I feel myself, to the generous people of that State, by the recollection of a thousand proofs they have given me of their kindness and confidence, I could not profess to be their impartial eulogist. That their conduct on the late trying emergency has been such, as not only to fulfil the predictions of their friends, and efface the unfavorable prejudices of those who until now were strangers to their true character, but also to receive the approbation of the nation, is to me a source of inexpressible pleasure.

Mr. President, I fondly hope that the dawn of peace is about to break upon our beloved country. Cheered by its benignant rays we look into futurity, and calculate the influence which the recent events at New Orleans may have upon the destinies of this nation. To foreign Powers, the lesson taught by them will be full of instruction. From the fate of a powerful army invading a portion of our country, hitherto considered the most assailable, they will learn that freemen, impressed with a sense of the value of their rights, and armed in defence of their own soil, are invincible. At home, the effects of these brilliant achievements will be salutary and beneficent. Should the inhabitants of any portion of this Union, from incorrect sources of information, have received impressions unfriendly to the character of the people of Louisiana, let them reflect on the events of the 8th of January, and those impressions will be completely obliterated. The ties of interest and of affection, which have long attached the Western States to Louisiana, have now become indissoluble. The purple stream of their b est blood has united and mingled in the same channel, and has at once cemented their union and that of their country.

Mr. FROMENTIN, of Louisiana, addressed the Chair, as follows—

Mr. President: The resolutions now under consideration seem to call for a few remarks from those who have the honor to represent on this floor the country upon whose inhabitants the mark of signal favor contemplated by the resolutions is now proposed to be conferred. It would ill become me on this occasion to affect a vain modesty, equally injurious to the virtues which have deserved, and to the generous discernment which is going to bestow approbation.

Mr. President, we have often been called upon, since the beginning of this war, to give thanks to the intrepidity of our military leaders, and the undaunted bravery of their troops. We have just now, by a unanimous vote, awarded the same tribute to Jackson and to his followers. To Jackson—this name henceforth wants none of the meretricious epithets of courtesy—to Jackson, whose laurels on the ever memorable 8th of January will adorn the fairest page of American military history:—to Jackson, whose unheard of achievements, having no precedents in the past, seem to bid defiance to the future. Through this belovéd General we gave the same unanimous thanks to his followers. I will not, sir, give them the surname of invincibles ; be it enough for their glory, that they have proved to the world that if, until they landed in Louisiana, the soldiers of Lord Wellington had been unconquered, they were not unconquerable.

Sir, with heartfelt gratitude I joined in the vote just given in honor of those valiant men. Let us now pass from the review of the brilliant and exterminating virtues exhibited on the field of battle,

to the contemplation of the modest and saving virtues exhibited in the city of New Orleans.

So far had the campaign in Florida been prolonged beyond the time contemplated at its beginning, that Winter was threatening, before the Tennessee militia, under General Coffee, hastily collected for a Summer expedition, were disbanded, to be recalled again under the banners of their country before they had reached their homes, in order to defend a distant State against the invasion of an enemy more numerous and more formidable than the enemy they had subdued. So ardent and so anxious was the zeal of our Tennessee and Kentucky brethren, headed by Carroll, Thomas, and Adair, that, regardless of the inclemencies of the approaching season, they listened to no voice but the voice of their invaded country ; they were sensible of no want, but the want of meeting the enemy.

Already had the Mississippi received the brave, who were destined to add such a celebrity to its fame ; already had its rapid current brought them within a short distance of the spot polluted with the foot of an invading foe ; a more terrible enemy than the one they were ready to encounter had nearly overcome them.

Frost, threatened in his long enjoyed empire over the Northern Lakes of America, made an effort in December last to establish his empire over the mouth as it has usurped it over the head of the Mississippi.* Not far from the tropics the ruthless invader shook his icy bristles ; for a few days the mouths of our creeks were sealed up by the tyrant ; but assistance was at hand from above. This Winter, Mr. President, was fertile with prodigies. A genial sun had arisen in the West, whose powerful and revivifying rays soon expelled the monster, and compelled him to fly back to his uncontrolled patrimonial haunts in the caverns of the Lakes, and in the recesses of the wildernesses of Canada—a forerunner, Mr. President, of the fate which in a few days was to befall his co-invader and British ally. Have I, Mr. President, in attempting to give you an idea of a natural phenomenon in Louisiana, given you a true picture of the real scenes which, in the meantime, were acting on that interesting theatre ?

Yet, during the temporary reign of the tyrant, our soldiers, for the reasons above stated, unprepared to withstand his attacks, were suffering severely. Are those brave men who have sacrificed everything to run to the relief of their distant friends, to be doomed to fall a victim to their own generosity ? Forbid it humanity, forbid it patriotism, forbid it gratitude !

I wish, Mr. President, I had it in my power to delineate with proper colors the interesting spectacle which New Orleans exhibited in those distressing days. Not a man unengaged in repelling the enemy, not a woman not affording the most

---

* It is a fact, not less true than extraordinary, that, on the 23d December last, when the St. Lawrence and the Northern Lakes were quite free from ice, the Bayou St. John, behind the city of New Orleans, was frozen over.

zealous assistance and co-operation in preparing clothing and every other necessary comfort for their protectors! Accompany me, Mr. President, within those walls, a few days ago the asylum of hundreds of young females, taught by the precepts and by the examples of their pious and respectable mistresses all the virtues and all the accomplishments, which are soon to be the ornaments of society. How changed is the scene! Those grates, never before opened but to Religion, are now thrown open for the reception of suffering, of bleeding humanity! Under the pious direction of their respectable religious chief, the nunnery of New Orleans is converted into an hospital for our sick and wounded! The holy flame spreads with rapidity! Every soldier in a distant land has found a brother! Every sick individual has found a family!

Mr. President, I rejoice, that the resolution reported by the honorable Chairman of the Military Committee embraces the cases I have briefly alluded to. Sir: Valor is the natural growth of every clime of this extensive empire. Even in the very few actions during this war in which victory did not perch on our banners, as evinced by a late celebrated case connected with the capture of this city, scrutinizing justice has pronounced that examples of conspicuous individual bravery have not been wanting. I shall always be proud of the opportunity afforded to pay to courage the just tribute due to it by a grateful people. But, when it is right thus to encourage valor, can it be wrong to encourage humanity? Valor, Humanity—Inseparable sisters! The first has delivered our country from an invading foe—the second has healed the wounds of a bleeding friend, and of a bleeding enemy—since no longer with arms in their hands, to be treated as a friend. Both united will continue to secure to our arms the favor of an avenging and merciful God, and will wrest from a vanquished enemy, and obtain from an admiring world, the applause due to a conqueror terrible in battle—in victory merciful.

THURSDAY, February 16.

Mr. LACOCK from the committee to whom was referred the bill, entitled "An act for the relief of Isaac Smith and Bratton Caldwell," reported it without amendment.

Mr. MORROW, from the committee to whom was referred the bill, entitled "An act regulating the sale of certain reserved sections of land in the State of Ohio," reported it without amendment.

Mr. KING, from the committee to whom was referred the bill, entitled "An act for the relief of Saltus, Son, and Company, merchants of the city of New York," reported it without amendment; and the bill was considered as in Committee of the Whole, and passed to a third reading.

Mr. BIBB presented the petition of Thomas Law and others, inhabitants of the City of Washington, praying the division and sale of certain open squares in said city, as stated in the petition; which was read, and referred to a select com-

mittee, to consist of five members, to consider and report thereon by bill or otherwise; and Messrs. BIBB, BARBOUR, SMITH, DAGGETT, and CHACE, were appointed the committee.

A message from the House of Representatives informed the Senate that the House have passed a bill, entitled "An act for the relief of Uriah Coolidge and James Burnham," in which bill they request the concurrence of the Senate.

The bill last mentioned was read, and passed to a second reading.

Mr. BARBOUR, from the committee to whom was referred the bill, entitled "An act for the relief of the legal representatives of David Darden," reported it without amendment.

On motion, by Mr. LACOCK, a committee was appointed to inquire into the expediency of increasing the salary of the Sergeant-at-Arms of the Senate, with leave to report by bill or otherwise; and Messrs. LACOCK, ANDERSON, and BARBOUR, were appointed the committee.

Mr. VARNUM presented the petition of William Malcom and others, owners of the privateer Washington, praying the United States to release their claim to certain prizes captured by them, as stated in the petition; which was read, and referred to the Committee on Naval Affairs, to consider and report thereon by bill or otherwise.

The resolution for the appointment of a joint committee to inquire into the expediency of causing the chambers at present occupied by the two Houses of Congress, or others in the same building, to be altered and fitted up, for the better accommodation of the two Houses, was read a third time, and passed.

Ordered, That Messrs. HORSEY, FROMENTIN, and GOLDSBOROUGH, be the committee on the part of the Senate.

FRIDAY, February 17.

Mr. GILES, from the committee to whom was referred the bill, entitled "An act for the relief of Jacob Shinnick, and Shoultz and Vogeler, of Christian Chapman, and the legal representative of John Calef, deceased," reported it without amendment.

Mr. SMITH submitted the following motion:

Resolved, That the Committee on Military Affairs be instructed to consider the propriety of reducing the Military Establishment of the United States, with authority to report by bill or otherwise.

On motion, by Mr. DANA,

Resolved, That the committee to whom was referred so much of the President's Message as relates to naval affairs, be instructed to inquire what provision should be made by law for protecting the commerce and seamen of the United States against any of the Barbary Powers.

Mr. LACOCK, from the committee to whom the subject was referred, reported a bill increasing the compensation allowed the Sergeant-at-Arms of the Senate; and the bill was read, and passed to the second reading.

Mr. SMITH, from the committee to whom was referred the bill, entitled "An act to authorize the issuing of Treasury notes for the service of the year 1815," reported it with amendments, which were considered as in Committee of the Whole ; and, on motion, by Mr. GILES, the further consideration thereof was postponed until to-morrow.

The bill, entitled "An act for the relief of Saltus, Son, and Company, merchants, of the city of New York," was read a third time, and passed.

The bill, entitled "An act for the relief of Uriah Coolidge and James Burnham, was read the second time, and referred to the Committee on Naval Affairs, to consider and report thereon.

The bill, entitled "An act requiring the Secretary of the Senate and Clerk of the House of Representatives, in the Congress of the United States, to give security for the faithful application and disbursement of the contingent funds of the Senate and House of Representatives," was read the second time.

The bill, entitled "An act making provision for clothing the militia called into the service of the United States," was read the second time, and referred to the Committee on the Militia, to consider and report thereon.

The Senate resumed, as in Committee of the Whole, the consideration of the bill, entitled "An act for the relief of the legal representatives of David Darden."

On the question, Shall this bill be read a third time ? it was determined in the negative. So the bill was lost.

The Senate resumed, as in Committee of the Whole, the consideration of the bill to authorize the settlement and payment of certain claims for the services of the militia ; and, no amendment having been proposed thereto, on the question, Shall this bill be engrossed and read a third time? it was determined in the affirmative.

Mr. MORROW, from the committee to whom was referred the bill, entitled "An act giving the right of pre-emption in the purchase of lands to certain settlers in the Indiana Territory," reported it with amendments.

Mr. KING, from the committee to whom was referred the bill, entitled "An act to amend the act, entitled 'An act to provide additional revenues for defraying the expenses of Government, and maintaining the public credit, by laying a direct tax upon the United States, and to provide for assessing and collecting the same, and the act entitled "An act to provide additional revenues for defraying the expenses of Government, and maintaining the public credit, by laying duties on household furniture, and on gold and silver watches," reported it with an additional amendment.

The Senate resumed, as in Committee of the Whole, the consideration of the bill, entitled "An act for the relief of Isaac Smith and Bratton Caldwell;" and, no amendment having been proposed, it passed to a third reading.

Mr. DANA submitted the following motion :

Resolved, That the committee to whom were referred certain Messages of the President of the United States concerning foreign relations, be instructed to inquire into the expediency of making provision by law to release all or any claims of the United States to penalties or forfeitures, under acts which have imposed prohibitions or temporary restrictions on commercial intercourse, and to discontinue all prosecutions therefor, upon payment of costs legally incurred.

On motion, by Mr. MORROW,

Resolved, That a committee be appointed to inquire, whether the act for establishing trading-houses with the Indian tribes, which will expire at the end of the present session of Congress, ought not to be continued in force for a further term.

Ordered, That Messrs. MORROW, ANDERSON, and BARRY, be the committee.

ILLEGAL SEIZURE OF A VESSEL.

The PRESIDENT communicated the report of the Secretary for the Department of Treasury, on the petition of Gould Hoyt, referred to him by resolution of the Senate of the 9th instant; and the report was read. It is as follows:

The Secretary of the Treasury, to whom the petition of Gould Hoyt was referred by a resolution of the Senate, passed the 9th of February, 1815, having considered the same, in obedience to that resolution, has the honor to report:

That the petition contains various allegations which are not supported by any evidence that is either produced by the petitioner, or possessed by the Treasury Department : and that it contains various complaints, which are either founded upon such imperfections of the judicial institutions of the United States as cannot constitute the peculiar grievance of the petitioner, or upon such conduct in the public officers of the district of New York as would, it is believed, receive from them a satisfactory explanation, were an opportunity afforded for that purpose.

That, under these circumstances, the Secretary of the Treasury presumes that he shall best discharge his duty to the Senate by stating the facts of the case referred to him, according to the evidence which is in his own possession, without dwelling upon the allegations of the petition.

That, in the year 1809, the United States and France were at peace. The island of St. Domingo, a colony of France, had declared itself independent; and, after successive changes in its form of Government, two rival chiefs, Christophe and Petion, claimed the sovereignty. But France, in constant and decisive terms, asserted her parent right to the colony; and the American Government, so far from recognising the independence of St. Domingo, had passed two laws prohibiting all intercourse with such parts of the island as were in possession of the revolted subjects of France. The violation of those laws, on several occasions, had been the cause of great inconvenience to the United States.

That it was the policy of the American Government to avoid all participation in the conflict between France and her colony, as well as in the conflict between the native competitors for the sovereignty of St. Domingo ; and, therefore, whatever might be the indulgence shown to a mere commercial intercourse with that island, after the expiration of the acts of Congress, which expressly prohibited it, the Government never ceased to watch with particular attention any equipments in the ports of the United States, which were apparently destined to increase the military means of either of the parties to the insular war, or which might be directed by the Government of the island against the Government of France. The United States being at peace with all the world in the year 1809, there could hardly be a pretext for such equipments, with a view to the protection of American commerce; and the armament of the American merchant vessels had not been authorized by law.

That the ship American Eagle, which furnishes the subject of the petition under consideration, appears to have been a large frigate-built ship, formerly called the Marquis of Lansdowne, captured by the French from the British, and sold by the captors to American citizens. On the 18th of November, 1809, information was officially given to the Treasury Department, that "this ship had been for some time repairing at New York, and was then nearly completed in the very best manner, and pierced for thirty-six guns; that conjectures were various; that the object in view could not be discovered; but that some illicit, some forced trade was no doubt in view." On the —— day of December, 1809, further information was officially given to the Treasury Department, that "a vessel had lately arrived at Norfolk with a cargo of coffee, under Swedish colors, which was said to belong to ——, of New York; that the vessel was the schooner Gustavus, Captain ——, or ——, master, (for there were said to be two captains on board;) that she went in under a plea of distress, but was supposed to have only sought an opportunity of waiting for orders from the owners or consignees; that the cargo was said to be the property of the Government of Port-au-Prince, and designed to form the funds, in part, for the payment of the American Eagle, a large ship understood to be fitting out at New York for that Government, and nearly ready for sea."

That, on receiving these communications, (which were corroborated by publications in the newspapers,) a letter was addressed from this Department to the collector of New York, dated the 12th of December, 1809, stating the information "that the ship American Eagle was fitting out for Petion, who had purchased her," and observing "that if that be the fact, the President directed her departure to be stopped, as embraced by the act of the 5th of June, 1794," prohibiting armaments within the United States, in violation of their neutrality. But it does not appear that any act was done, in pursuance of this authority, conditionally given to the collector of New York.

That, on the 11th of April, 1810, further information was officially given to the Treasury Department, that "since the letter of the 12th of December, 1809, the ship American Eagle had very little done until then, when twenty or thirty men were employed, and there was every appearance of soon getting the ship ready for sea." And the answer to this information was given on the 27th of April, 1810, "that if any satisfactory evidence could be obtained of the ship's being intended to commit hostilities against a friendly Power, or for any other illegal purpose, she ought to be detained; but, if no such proof can be had, the vessel must then be watched, and not suffered to arm, or carry any military stores in her hold."

That to these official communications, and the public notices of the gazettes, it appears the Minister of France, in June, 1810, added "his remonstrances respecting the armament of the American Eagle, which he stated to be destined for one of the black chiefs of St. Domingo; and that the agent who superintended the armament was an ancient secretary of a General of Brigade, named La Plume, formerly commanding officer at Aux Cayes." On the 26th of June, this information was communicated to the collector of New York; and that officer replied, that "he would omit no legal step, in conformity to the instructions of the Treasury Department." But, in a letter from this Department, dated the 29th of June, 1810, a more particular direction was given, and the collector was required critically to investigate every circumstance relative to the ship, to consult with the district attorney, and, if it could be legally done, to prevent her departure; for her equipment, and the information given by both the collector of Baltimore and the French Minister, created a strong presumption that she was intended for one of the St. Domingo black chiefs; a destination not only contrary to the interests of the United States, but directly contravening the laws of nations, and forbidden by the third and fifth sections of the act of the 5th of June, 1794." It was added, that "the safest way, if the district attorney concurred, would be to libel the ship under the third section of the act; and that the President of the United States expressly recommended that every exertion be used to detect and prevent such gross violation of their laws and neutrality."

That, on the 30th of June, 1810, the surveyor of the port of New York, having, with the inspectors of the customs, examined the ship American Eagle, in pursuance of orders from the collector, reported, "that there was on board a person who said his name was John Howard, at present master of the vessel, and had been in that capacity at least six months last past; that, upon interrogating Captain Howard, he stated that the ship was owned by James Gillespie, merchant of New York, by whom he was employed as master, to superintend repairing the ship, which he had done till January last, at which time she was nearly finished, when Gillespie sold her to Hoyt & Tom, under whose orders he now acted, and has acted since they became owners. He did not know how or where the ship was to be employed; the only persons belonging to the ship were himself, Mr. Mooney, mate, and two or three seamen; that the surveyor proceeded to search the ship throughout, when (as near as could be ascertained) she had on board about one hundred and thirty barrels of salted provisions, twenty hogsheads of shipbread, and one hundred hogsheads of water, with a complete set of stone ballast; neither guns, small arms, ammunition, nor other implements of war, were found on board; she had a thorough repair from her keel up, with new copper, new masts, rigging, and sails; the latter all upon the yards; that the ship was calculated to carry twenty-four guns on her main deck, and fourteen on her upper deck; that her repairs and outfits, all together, were in a man-of-war style; and that nothing was wanting to send the ship to sea (if she went without guns) but a complement of seamen."

That, under all these circumstances, the collector of New York was informed, by a letter from this Department, dated the 6th of July, 1810, that "in the opinion of the President, the ship American Eagle ought to be immediately seized and libelled, as being fitted out for illegal purposes, unless the owner should give satisfactory proof of the contrary." But neither at the time of the survey, nor at any antecedent or subsequent time, nor in the petition under immediate consideration, has it appeared (so far as the evidence is possessed by this Department) for what voyage the ship American Eagle was actually equipped and provided in the manner which the survey describes, if the intention were not to prosecute the voyage to St. Domingo, for the purpose of delivering her to Petion, the asserted owner.

That, in pursuance of the instructions which have been stated, the ship American Eagle was seized on the 10th day of July, 1810, and was libelled in the district court. The indisposition of the district judge appears to have suspended all the business of that court for a considerable period; and owing entirely, it is believed, to that cause, the case of the American Eagle was not tried and decided until the 24th of August, 1812. The court acquitted the vessel, ordered her to be restored to Gould Hoyt, the claimant, and also refused to certify that there was reasonable cause for the seizure. The vessel remained in the custody of the marshal from the time of the seizure until the decision. Mr. Hoyt has since brought an action against the seizing officers, in the supreme court of the State of New York, for the damages sustained by the seizure and detention, which action is still depending. It is thought to be irregular and improper, under these circumstances, to state the opinion of the district attorney as to the probable issue of the action.

That repeated overtures have been made to this Department by Mr. Hoyt for a settlement or compromise of his claim for damages against the officers who seized the ship American Eagle, upon the presumption that they are eventually to be indemnified by the Government. But there was no power in the Department to adopt either the mode proposed for ascertaining the amount of the damages, or the mode proposed for liquidating that amount when ascertained.

That, upon the same presumption of an eventual responsibility on the part of the Government, Mr. Hoyt has presented the petition under consideration to Congress; in which he states, that "he would be well satisfied to obtain for the vessel the money that she has actually cost him, (computed at one hundred thousand dollars,) with charges and interest, in full satisfaction for any claims he may have on account of the seizure." He concludes, however, with praying "that the proper officers of the Government may be authorized to purchase the said ship upon such terms as to Congress may seem proper; or that he may have such relief in the premises as in the wisdom of Congress shall seem meet."

Upon this general view of the case, the following considerations arise:

1. Whether any, and what, damages will probably be recovered in the suit against the seizing officers?

2. Whether the seizing officers are to be eventually indemnified by the Government?

3. Whether the damages, if the payment shall be now assumed by Congress, ought to be assessed by a jury, by arbitrators, or by the accounting officers of the Treasury?

All which is respectfully submitted.

A. J. DALLAS.

SATURDAY, February 18.

Mr. VARNUM, from the Committee on the Militia, to whom was referred the bill, entitled "An act making provision for clothing the militia called into the service of the United States," reported it with an amendment.

Mr. GORE presented the petition of John Frothingham and Arthur Tappan, merchants, of Boston, stating that they are native citizens of the United States, and were residing in Montreal, for the purpose of trade, at the time war was declared between the United States and Great Britain, at which time they returned to the United States, and removed a part of their merchandise; and praying to be relieved from penalties incurred by the violation of the non-importation laws, in consequence of their withdrawing their effects from Canada; and the petitions were read, and referred to a select committee to consider and report thereon by bill or otherwise; and Messrs. GORE, ANDERSON, and SMITH, were appointed the committee.

Mr. MORROW, from the committee appointed to consider the subject, reported a bill to continue in force, for a limited time, the act, entitled "An act for establishing trading-houses with the Indian tribes;" and the bill was read, and passed to the second reading.

The bill, entitled "An act for the relief of Isaac Smith and Bratton Caldwell," was read a third time, and passed.

Mr. TAIT, from the Committee on Naval Affairs, to whom was referred the bill, entitled "An act for the relief of Uriah Coolidge and James Burnham," reported it without amendment.

Mr. TAYLOR, from the committee to whom was referred the bill, entitled "An act in addition to an act regulating the Post Office Establishment," reported it without amendment.

The Senate resumed the motion made the 17th instant, by Mr. DANA, instructing the Committee on Foreign Relations to inquire into the expediency of making provision by law to release certain claims of the United States; and agreed thereto.

The Senate resumed the bill for quieting and adjusting claims to land in the Mississippi Territory; and on motion, by Mr. GILES, the further consideration thereof was postponed to Monday next.

A message from the House of Representatives informed the Senate that the House have unanimously passed the resolutions expressive of the thanks of Congress to Major General Jackson, and the troops under his command, for their gallantry and good conduct in the defence of New Orleans, with amendments; in which they request the concurrence of the Senate. They have passed a bill, entitled "An act for the relief of Edward Hallowell;" a bill, entitled "An act for granting and securing to Anthony Shane the right of the United States to a tract of land in the State of Ohio;" also, a bill, entitled "An act to provide additional revenues for defraying the expenses of Government, and maintaining the public credit, by laying a direct tax upon the District of Columbia;" in which bills they request the concurrence of the Senate.

The three bills last mentioned were read, and passed to the second reading.

The bill to authorize the settlement and payment of certain claims for the services of the militia, was read a third time, and passed.

On motion, by Mr. TAIT, the Committee on

Naval Affairs were instructed to inquire into the expediency of repealing any act or acts respecting the flotilla establishment; with leave to report by bill or otherwise.

Mr. BARBOUR submitted the following motion:

Resolved, That the President of the United States be requested to cause an experienced engineer and naval officer to explore the Chesapeake bay, for the purpose of ascertaining the most convenient harbor in the said bay, for the reception of ships of war of the largest class; and that they particularly ascertain, whether it be practicable to establish a convenient harbor at the Chesapeake, on the middle ground, and the probable amount which may be necessary to place such harbor in the most respectable posture of defence.

Mr. HUNTER, from the committee to whom the subject was referred, reported a bill authorizing the discharge of Edward Martin from imprisonment; and the bill was read, and passed to the second reading.

The Senate proceeded to consider the amendment of the House of Representatives to the resolutions expressive of the thanks of Congress to Major General Jackson, and the troops under his command, for their gallantry and good conduct in the defence of New Orleans; and on motion, by Mr. SMITH, it was referred to the Committee on Military Affairs, to consider and report thereon.

The Senate resumed, as in Committee of the Whole, the consideration of the bill, entitled "An act regulating the sale of certain reserved sections of land in the State of Ohio;" and on the question, Shall this bill be engrossed and read a third time? It was determined in the negative. So the bill was lost.

On motion, by Mr. SMITH, a committee was appointed to consider the expediency of repealing all acts, or parts of acts, laying additional duties on goods, wares, and merchandise, imported in the ships or vessels of such foreign nations as shall agree to admit, into their ports, goods, wares, and merchandise, imported into such ports, on board of the ships or vessels of the United States. Messrs. SMITH, TAYLOR, BIBB, HUNTER, and KING, were appointed the committee.

The Senate resumed, as in Committee of the Whole, the consideration of the bill, entitled "An act for the relief of Jacob Shinnick, and Shoultz and Vogeler, of Christian Chapman, and the legal representative of John Calef, deceased;" and on motion, by Mr. MASON, the further consideration thereof was postponed to Tuesday next.

On motion, by Mr. BIBB, the committee to whom was referred the petition of Thomas Law and others, citizens of the City of Washington, praying the division and sales of certain open squares in the said city, were discharged from the further consideration thereof.

Mr. TAYLOR gave notice, that, on Monday next, he should ask leave to bring in a bill further supplementary to the act for the indemnification of certain claimants of public lands in the Mississippi Territory.

On motion, by Mr. KING, Gould Hoyt had leave to withdraw his petition, together with the report

of the Secretary for the Department of the Treasury thereon, made the 17th instant.

On motion, by Mr. TAIT, the Committee on Naval Affairs, to whom was referred the petition of William Malcom and others, were discharged from the further consideration thereof.

The Senate resumed, the consideration of the motion made the 17th instant, by Mr. SMITH, instructing the Committee on Military Affairs to consider the propriety of reducing the Military Establishment of the United States; and agreed thereto.

The Senate resumed, as in Committee of the Whole, the consideration of the bill, entitled "An act to amend the act, entitled 'An act to provide additional revenues for defraying the expenses of Government, and maintaining the public credit, by laying a direct tax upon the United States, and to provide for assessing and collecting the same;" and the act, entitled "An act to provide additional revenues for defraying the expenses of Government, and maintaining the public credit, by laying duties on household furniture, and on gold and silver watches," together with the additional amendment reported thereto by the select committee; and, having agreed to the amendment, the President reported the bill to the House accordingly.

On the question, Shall the amendment be engrossed and the bill read a third time as amended? it was determined in the affirmative.

The bill, entitled "An act requiring the Secretary of the Senate, and Clerk of the House of Representatives in the Congress of the United States, to give security for the faithful application and disbursement of the contingent funds of the Senate and House of Representatives, was resumed, as in Committee of the Whole; and passed to a third reading.

The bill increasing the compensation allowed the Sergeant-at-Arms of the Senate was read the second time, and considered as in Committee of the Whole; and on the question, Shall this bill be engrossed and read a third time? it was determined in the affirmative.

On motion, by Mr. VARNUM, the militia committee, to whom was referred the memorial of the representatives of the religious Society of Friends, in Pennsylvania, New Jersey, and Delaware, respecting the rights of conscience, were discharged from the further consideration thereof.

MONDAY, February 20.

Mr. GOLDSBOROUGH, from the Library Committee, made a report; which was read.

Mr. GOLDSBOROUGH, from the same committee, reported a bill to provide a library room, and for transporting the library lately purchased from Thomas Jefferson, Esq., to the City of Washington; and the bill was read, and passed to the second reading.

Mr. GILES, from the Committee on Military Affairs, to whom was referred the amendment of the House of Representatives to the resolutions expressive of the thanks of Congress to Major

General Jackson, and the troops under his command, for their gallantry and good conduct in the defence of New Orleans, reported an agreement therein, in part. Whereupon,

Resolved, That the Senate do concur in so much of the amendment of the House of Representatives to the said resolutions, as proposes to strike out the word "immediate," in the third line of the first resolution; and that they disagree to the residue of the said amendment.

Mr. GILES, from the Committee on Military Affairs, to whom the subject was referred, reported a bill to repeal certain acts therein mentioned; and the bill was read, and passed to the second reading.

Mr. HORSEY, from the joint committee to whom the subject was referred, reported a bill for the better temporary accommodation of the two Houses of Congress; and the bill was read, and passed to the second reading.

Mr. TAIT, from the Committee on Military Affairs, reported a bill to repeal certain acts concerning the flotilla service; and the bill was read, and passed to the second reading.

Mr. SMITH, from the committee to whom the subject was referred, reported a bill to repeal so much of the several acts imposing duties on the tonnage of ships, and vessels, and on goods, wares, and merchandise, imported into the United States, as imposes a discriminating duty on tonnage between foreign vessels and vessels of the United States, and between goods imported into the United States in foreign vessels and vessels of the United States; and the bill was read, and passed to the second reading.

Mr. TAYLOR asked and obtained leave to bring in a bill further supplementary to an act, entitled "An act providing for the indemnification of certain claimants of lands in the Mississippi Territory;" and the bill was read, and passed to the second reading.

Mr. TAYLOR presented the petition of James Lamb, of the city of Charleston, in the State of South Carolina, owner of the American brig Langdon Cheves, stating that the said vessel, with her cargo, were libelled and condemned, by a decree of the district court of the United States, for the district of Rhode Island; and praying restitution thereof, for reasons stated at large in the petition; which was read, and referred to a select committee, to consider and report thereon by bill or otherwise; and Messrs. TAYLOR, DANA, and BIBB, were appointed the committee.

The Senate resumed the consideration of the motion made the 13th, by Mr. BARBOUR, relative to establishing a naval harbor in the Chesapeake Bay, and it was referred to a select committee, to consider and report thereon by bill or otherwise; and Messrs. BARBOUR, SMITH, and KING, were appointed the committee.

The bill increasing the compensation allowed the Sergeant-at-Arms of the Senate, having been reported by the committee correctly engrossed, was read a third time, and passed.

On motion, by Mr. DANA,

Resolved, That a committee be appointed to consider what privileges should be secured by law to citizens of the United States, as preferable to foreign subjects, in navigation; and that the committee have leave to report by bill or otherwise.

Ordered, That Messrs. DANA, SMITH, GORE, HUNTER, and KING, be the committee.

The amendments to the bill, entitled "An act to amend the act, entitled 'An act to provide additional revenues for defraying the expenses of Government, and maintaining the public credit, by laying a direct tax upon the United States, and to provide for assessing and collecting the same;" and the act, entitled "An act to provide additional revenues for defraying the expenses of Government, and maintaining the public credit, by laying duties on household furniture, and on gold and silver watches," having been reported by the committee correctly engrossed, the bill was read a third time as amended.

Resolved, That this bill pass with amendments.

The bill, entitled "An act requiring the Secretary of the Senate, and Clerk of the House of Representatives, in the Congress of the United States, to give security for the faithful application and disbursement of the contingent funds of the Senate and House of Representatives," was read a third time, and passed.

The bill to continue in force for a limited time the act, entitled "An act for establishing trading-houses with the Indian tribes," was read the second time.

The bill, entitled "An act for the relief of Edward Hallowell, was read the second time, and referred to a select committee, to consider and report thereon; and Messrs. ROBERTS, HORSEY, and LACOCK, were appointed the committee.

The bill, entitled "An act granting and securing to Anthony Shane the right of the United States to a tract of land in the State of Ohio," was read the second time, and referred to the committee to whom was referred, on the 21st of September, the memorial of the Legislature of the Indiana Territory, to consider and report thereon.

The bill authorizing the discharge of Edward Martin from imprisonment was read the second time.

The bill, entitled "An act to provide additional revenues for defraying the expenses of Government, and maintaining the public credit, by laying a direct tax upon the District of Columbia," was read the second time, and referred to the committee to whom was referred the bill, entitled "An act making appropriations for the support of Government, for the year 1815," to consider and report thereon.

The Senate resumed, as in Committee of the Whole, the consideration of the bill to authorize a detachment from the militia of the United States; and on motion, by Mr. TURNER, the further consideration thereof was postponed to the fourth day of March next.

The Senate resumed, as in Committee of the Whole, the consideration of the bill for quieting and adjusting claims to land in the Mississippi

Territory; and, after debate, on motion by Mr. DAGGETT, the further consideration thereof was postponed until to-morrow.

The Senate resumed, as in Committee of the Whole, the consideration of the bill, entitled "An act to authorize the issuing of Treasury notes, for the service of the year 1815," together with the amendments reported thereto by the select committee; and, having agreed to the amendments, the PRESIDENT reported the bill to the House accordingly.

On the question. Shall the amendments be engrossed and the bill be read a third time as amended? it was determined in the affirmative.

Mr. MORROW, from the committee to whom was referred the bill, entitled "An act for the regulation of the courts of justice of Indiana," reported it with amendments.

On motion, by Mr. LACOCK, Isaac Smith and Bratton Caldwell had leave to withdraw their papers.

TREATY OF PEACE.

The following Message was received from the PRESIDENT OF THE UNITED STATES:

To the Senate and House of
Representatives of the United States:

I lay before Congress copies of the Treaty of Peace and Amity between the United States and His Britannic Majesty, which was signed by the Commissioners of both parties at Ghent, on the 24th of December, 1814, and the ratifications of which have been duly exchanged.

While performing this act, I congratulate you, and our constituents, upon an event which is highly honorable to the nation, and terminates, with peculiar felicity, a campaign signalized by the most brilliant successes.

The late war, although reluctantly declared by Congress, had become a necessary resort to assert the rights and independence of the nation. It has been waged with a success which is the natural result of the wisdom of the Legislative councils, of the patriotism of the people, of the public spirit of the militia, and of the valor of the military and naval forces of the country. Peace, at all times a blessing, is peculiarly welcome, therefore, at a period when the causes for the war have ceased to operate; when the Government has demonstrated the efficiency of its powers of defence; and when the nation can review its conduct without regret and without reproach.

I recommend to your care and beneficence the gallant men whose achievements, in every department of the military service, on the land and on the water, have so essentially contributed to the honor of the American name, and to the restoration of peace. The feelings of conscious patriotism and worth will animate such men under every change of fortune and pursuit; but their country performs a duty to itself, when it bestows those testimonials of approbation and applause which are at once the reward and the incentive to great actions.

The reduction of the public expenditures to the demands of a peace establishment will doubtless engage the immediate attention of Congress. There are, however, important considerations which forbid a sudden and general revocation of the measures that have been produced by the war. Experience has taught us that

neither the pacific dispositions of the American people, nor the pacific character of their political institutions, can altogether exempt them from that strife which appears, beyond the ordinary lot of nations, to be incident to the actual period of the world; and the same faithful monitor demonstrates that a certain degree of preparation for war is not only indispensable to avert disasters in the onset, but affords also the best security for the continuance of peace. The wisdom of Congress will, therefore, I am confident, provide for the maintenance of an adequate regular force; for the gradual advancement of the Naval Establishment; for improving all the means of harbor defence; for adding discipline to the distinguished bravery of the militia; and for cultivating the military art, in its essential branches, under the liberal patronage of Government.

The resources of our country were, at all times, competent to the attainment of every national object; but they will now be enriched and invigorated by the activity which peace will introduce into all the scenes of domestic enterprise and labor. The provision that has been made for the public creditors, during the present session of Congress, must have a decisive effect in the establishment of the public credit, both at home and abroad. The reviving interests of commerce will claim the legislative attention at the earliest opportunity; and such regulations will, I trust, be seasonably devised as shall secure to the United States their just proportion of the navigation of the world. The most liberal policy towards other nations, if met by corresponding dispositions, will, in this respect, be found the most beneficial policy towards ourselves. But there is no subject that can enter with greater force and merit into the deliberations of Congress, than a consideration of the means to preserve and promote the manufactures which have sprung into existence, and attained an unparalleled maturity throughout the United States during the period of the European wars. This source of national independence and wealth, I anxiously recommend, therefore, to the prompt and constant guardianship of Congress.

The termination of the legislative sessions will soon separate you fellow-citizens, from each other, and restore you to your constituents. I pray you to bear with you the expressions of my sanguine hope, that the peace which has been just declared will not only be the foundation of the most friendly intercourse between the United States and Great Britain, but that it will also be productive of happiness and harmony in every section of our beloved country. The influence of your precepts and example must be everywhere powerful: and while we accord in grateful acknowledgments for the protection which Providence has bestowed upon us, let us never cease to inculcate obedience to the laws, and fidelity to the Union, as constituting the palladium of the national independence and prosperity.

JAMES MADISON.

WASHINGTON, *February* 18, 1815.

The Message was read, and five hundred copies thereof, together with five hundred copies of the treaty therein referred to, were ordered to be printed for the use of the Senate.

On motion, by Mr. BIBB,

Resolved, That so much of the Message of the President of the United States, of this date, as relates to the Military Establishment, be referred to the Committee on Military Affairs, to consider and report thereon by bill or otherwise; and that so much of the Message as relates to the Naval Establishment be referred to the Committee on Naval Affairs, to consider and report thereon by bill or otherwise.

On motion, by Mr. DANA,

Resolved, That so much of the Message of the President of the United States, of this date, as relates to the militia of the United States, be referred to the Militia Committee, to consider and report thereon by bill or otherwise.

TUESDAY, February 21.

The PRESIDENT communicated the report of the Secretary for the Department of War, made conformably to the 5th section of the act of the 3d March, 1809, entitled "An act to amend the several acts for the establishment and regulation of the Treasury, War, and Navy Departments;" and the report was read.

Mr. MORROW, from the committee to whom was referred the bill, entitled "An act for granting and securing to Anthony Shane the right of the United States to a tract of land in the State of Ohio," reported it without amendment.

The bill to provide a library room, and for transporting the library lately purchased from Thomas Jefferson, Esq., to the City of Washington, was read the second time.

The bill to repeal certain acts therein mentioned was read the second time.

The bill to repeal certain acts concerning the flotilla service was read the second time.

The bill for the better temporary accommodation of the two Houses of Congress was read the second time.

The bill to repeal so much of the several acts imposing duties on the tonnage of ships and vessels, and on goods, wares, and merchandise, imported into the United States, as imposes a discriminating duty on tonnage between foreign vessels and vessels of the United States, and between goods imported into the United States in foreign vessels and vessels of the United States," was read the second time.

The bill further supplementary to an act, entitled "An act providing for the indemnification of certain claimants of public lands in the Mississippi Territory," was read the second time.

The Senate resumed the consideration of the bill for quieting and adjusting claims to land in the Mississippi Territory, as in Committee of the Whole; and on motion, by Mr. BIBB, the further consideration thereof was postponed to the second Monday in March next.

A message from the House of Representatives informed the Senate that the House insist on their amendment to the resolutions expressive of the thanks of Congress to Major General Jackson, and the troops under his command, for their gallantry and good conduct in the defence of New Orleans, disagreed to by the Senate. They have passed a bill, entitled "An act for the relief of Joshua Sands;" a bill, entitled "An act supplementary to an act, entitled "An act for the better

organization of the courts of the United States within the State of New York;" also, a bill, entitled "An act to alter and establish certain post roads;" in which bills they request the concurrence of the Senate.

The three bills last mentioned were read, and passed to the second reading.

On motion, by Mr. ROBERTS,

Resolved, That so much of the Message of the President of the United States, of the 20th instant, as relates to the preservation and promotion of manufactures, be referred to a select committee, and that the said committee have leave to report by bill or otherwise.

Ordered, That Messrs. ROBERTS, BARBOUR, TAYLOR, VARNUM, and CHACE, be the committee.

Mr. GORE, from the committee to whom the subject was referred, reported a bill for the relief of Arthur Tappan and John Frothingham; and the bill was read, and ordered to the second reading.

The amendments to the bill, entitled "An act to authorize the issuing of Treasury notes for the service of the year 1815," having been reported by the committee correctly engrossed, the bill was read a third time, as amended.

Resolved, That this bill pass with amendments.

Mr. GILES, from the Committee on Military Affairs, to whom was referred the bill, entitled "An act to authorize the President of the United States to raise certain companies of rangers for the defence of the frontiers of the United States," reported it with amendments.

Mr. GILES, from the Committee on Military Affairs, reported a bill making further provision for completing the public buildings at West Point, for the accommodation of the Military Academy; and the bill was read, and passed to the second reading.

Mr. GILES, from the Committee on Military Affairs, to whom was referred the bill, entitled "An act to authorize the President of the United States to receive into the service of the United States certain corps which may be raised and organized by any State, to serve in lieu of the militia thereof," reported it without amendment; and on motion, by Mr. GILES, the further consideration thereof was postponed to the second Monday in March next.

Mr. KERR, from the committee to whom was referred the petition of Nicholas Boilevin, made report: Whereupon, the further consideration thereof was postponed to the second Monday in March next.

On motion, by Mr. BIBB, the further consideration of the bill, entitled "An act making provision for subsisting the Army of the United States, by authorizing the appointment of commissaries of subsistence," was postponed until Monday next.

On motion, by Mr. GILES,

Resolved, That the Senate adhere to their disagreement to the amendment of the House of Representatives to the resolution expressive of the thanks of Congress to Major General Jackson, and the troops under his command, for their gallantry and good conduct in the defence of New Orleans.

The Senate resumed, as in Committee of the Whole, the consideration of the bill, entitled "An act for the relief of Jacob Shinnick, and Shoultz and Vogeler, of Christian Chapman, and the legal representative of John Calef, deceased," and on motion, by Mr. KING, the further consideration thereof was postponed to Friday next.

The Senate resumed, as in Committee of the Whole, the consideration of the bill, entitled "An act giving the right of pre-emption, in the purchase of lands to certain settlers in the Indiana Territory," together with the amendment reported thereto by the select committee; and, having agreed to the amendment, the President reported the bill to the House accordingly.

On the question, Shall the amendment be engrossed and the bill read a third time, as amended? it was determined in the affirmative.

The Senate resumed, as in Committee of the Whole, the consideration of the bill, entitled "An act making provision for clothing the militia called into the service of the United States," together with the amendment reported thereto by the select committee; and on motion, by Mr. VARNUM, the further consideration thereof was postponed to the second Monday in March next.

The Senate resumed, as in Committee of the Whole, the consideration of the bill, entitled "An act for the relief of Uriah Coolidge and James Burnham," and no amendment having been proposed, it passed to a third reading.

The Senate resumed, as in Committee of the Whole, the consideration of the bill, entitled "An act in addition to an act regulating the Post Office Establishment;" and, no amendment having been proposed, it passed to a third reading.

The Senate resumed, as in Committee of the Whole, the consideration of the bill, entitled "An act for the regulation of the courts of justice of Indiana," together with the amendments reported thereto by the select committee; and, having agreed to the amendments, the President reported the bill to the House accordingly.

On the question, Shall the amendments be engrossed and the bill read a third time as amended? it was determined in the affirmative.

The Senate resumed, as in Committee of the Whole, the consideration of the bill to continue in force for a limited time the act, entitled "An act for establishing trading houses with the Indian tribes," and on the question, Shall this bill be engrossed and read a third time? it was determined in the affirmative.

The Senate resumed, as in Committee of the Whole, the consideration of the bill authorizing the discharge of Edward Martin from imprisonment; and on the question, Shall this bill be engrossed and read a third time? it was determined in the affirmative.

The Senate resumed, as in Committee of the Whole, the consideration of the bill for the better temporary accommodation of the two Houses of Congress; and on the question, Shall this bill be engrossed and read a third time? it was determined in the affirmative—yeas 19, nays 7, as follows:

YEAS—Messrs. Barbour, Bibb, Chace, Condit, Fromentin, Gaillard, Giles, Goldsborough, Gore, Horsey, Hunter, Kerr, Morrow, Roberts, Smith, Tait, Thompson, Varnum, and Wharton.

NAYS—Messrs. German, King, Lacock, Talbot, Taylor, Turner, and Wells.

On motion, by Mr. BIBB,

Resolved, That the Committee on Foreign Relations be instructed to inquire whether any of the laws respecting foreign intercourse ought to be repealed or modified; and that they have leave to report by bill or otherwise.

The Senate resumed, as in Committee of the Whole, the consideration of the bill to repeal certain acts therein mentioned; and, no amendment having been proposed thereto, on the question, Shall this bill be engrossed and read a third time? it was determined in the affirmative.

WEDNESDAY, February 22.

The bill, entitled "An act for the relief of Joshua Sands," was read the second time, and referred to a select committee, to consider and report thereon; and Messrs. KING, GERMAN, and ROBERTS, were appointed the committee.

The bill, entitled "An act supplementary to an act, entitled 'An act for the better organization of the courts of the United States within the State of New York," was read the second time, and referred to a select committee, to consider and report thereon; and Messrs. GERMAN, DAGGETT, and KING, were appointed the committee.

The bill, entitled "An act to alter and establish certain post roads," was read the second time and referred to a select committee, to consider and report thereon; and Messrs. BARBOUR, THOMPSON, and TALBOT, were appointed the committee.

Mr. MORROW presented several petitions, signed by a number of citizens of Butler county, in the State of Ohio, praying the establishment of a post road, between Lebanon and Hamilton, in said State, for reasons therein stated; and the petitions were read, and referred to the committee last mentioned to consider and report thereon.

On motion of Mr. TAYLOR, the petition of the citizens of the districts of Chesterfield, Kershaw and Lancaster, of the State of South Carolina, and of the county of Anson, in the State of North Carolina, presented the 3d of October last, were referred to the same committee, to consider and report.

Mr. TAYLOR, from the committee to whom was referred the bill, entitled "An act to provide additional revenues for defraying the expenses of Government, and maintaining the public credit, by laying a direct tax upon the District of Columbia," reported it without amendment.

Mr. TAYLOR, from the committee to whom was referred the bill, entitled "An act to provide additional revenues for defraying the expenses of Government, and maintaining the public credit, by laying a duty on lotteries," reported it without amendment.

Mr. TAYLOR, from the committee to whom was referred the bill, entitled "An act to provide additional revenues for defraying the expenses of Government, and maintaining the public credit, by laying a duty on gold, silver, and plated ware, and jewelry, and pastework, manufactured within the United States," reported it with an amendment.

The bill for the relief of Arthur Tappan and John Frothingham, was read the second time.

The bill, entitled "An act in addition to an act regulating the Post Office Establishment," was read a third time, and passed.

The bill to repeal certain acts therein mentioned was read a third time, and passed.

The bill for the better temporary accommodation of the two Houses of Congress was read a third time, and passed.

The bill to continue in force for a limited time the act, entitled "An act for establishing trading houses with the Indian tribes," was read a third time, and on motion, by Mr. KING, it was recommitted to a select committee, further to consider and report thereon; and Messrs. KING, MORROW, and TAIT, were appointed the committee.

The bill authorizing the discharge of Edward Martin from imprisonment was read a third time, and passed.

The bill making further provision for completing the public buildings at West Point, for the accommodation of the Military Academy, was read the second time.

The bill, entitled "An act for the relief of Uriah Coolidge and James Burnham," was read a third time, and passed.

Mr. BARBOUR, from the committee to whom the subject was referred, reported a bill to provide for exploring the Chesapeake Bay and its waters, for the purposes therein mentioned; and the bill was read and passed to the second reading.

The amendments to the bill, entitled "An act giving the right of pre-emption in the purchase of lands to certain settlers in the Indiana Territory," having been reported by the committee correctly engrossed, the bill was read a third time as amended.

Resolved, That this bill pass with amendments.

The amendments to the bill, entitled "An act for the regulation of the courts of justice of Indiana," having been reported by the committee correctly engrossed, the bill was read a third time as amended.

Resolved, That this bill with amendments.

The bill, entitled "An act for granting and securing to Anthony Shane the right of the United States to a tract of land in the State of Ohio," was resumed, as in Committee of the Whole, and, no amendment having been proposed, it was passed to a third reading.

The Senate resumed, as in Committee of the Whole, the consideration of the bill, entitled "An act to authorize the President to raise certain companies of rangers for the defence of the frontiers of the United States, and to repeal certain acts now in force for this purpose," together with the amendments reported thereto by the select committee; and the amendments having been agreed to, the President reported the bill to the House accordingly. On the question, Shall the amendments be engrossed and the bill read a third time as amended? it was determined in the affirmative.

The Senate resumed, as in Committee of the Whole, the consideration of the bill to provide a library room, and for transporting the library lately purchased from Thomas Jefferson, Esquire, to the City of Washington.

On motion, by Mr. ROBERTS, the bill having been amended, the President reported it to the House accordingly. On the question, Shall this bill be engrossed and read a third time as amended? it was determined in the affirmative.

The Senate resumed, as in Committee of the Whole, the consideration of the bill further supplementary to an act, entitled "An act providing for the indemnification of certain claimants of public lands in the Mississippi Territory;" and, no amendment having been proposed thereto, on the question, Shall this bill be engrossed and read a third time? it was determined in the affirmative.

On motion, by Mr. ANDERSON,

Resolved, That a committee be appointed to consider and report upon the expediency of making provision by law for running the boundary lines designated in the treaty lately made between the United States and the chiefs, deputies, and warriors, of the Creek nation; and that the committee have leave to report by bill or otherwise.

Ordered, That Messrs. ANDERSON, BIBB, and MORROW, be the committee.

A message from the House of Representatives informed the Senate that the House ask a conference on the disagreeing votes of the two Houses on the amendment to the resolutions expressive of the thanks of Congress to Major General Jackson, and the troops under his command, for their gallantry and good conduct in defence of New Orleans, and have appointed managers on their part. They concur in the first amendment of the Senate to the bill to amend the act, entitled "An act to provide additional revenues for defraying the expenses of Government, and maintaining the public credit, by laying a direct tax upon the United States, and to provide for assessing and collecting the same," and the act, entitled "An act to provide additional revenues for defraying the expenses of Government, and maintaining the public credit, by laying duties on household furniture, and on gold and silver watches," with an amendment, in which they request the concurrence of the Senate. They concur in the second, third, and fourth, and disagree to the fifth amendments to said bill.

On motion by Mr. TAYLOR,

Resolved, That the Senate agree to the amendment of the House of Representatives to their first amendment to the bill last mentioned, and that they insist on their fifth amendment to said bill, disagreed to by the House of Representatives.

On motion, by Mr. GILES,

Resolved, That the Senate agree to the conference proposed on the disagreeing votes of the two Houses, on the amendment to the resolutions expressive of the thanks of Congress to Major General Jackson, and the troops under his command, for their gallantry and good conduct in the defence of New Orleans.

Ordered, That Messrs. GILES, BROWN, and SMITH, be the managers on the part of the Senate.

Mr. KING, from the committee to whom was referred the bill, entitled "An act for the relief of Joshua Sands," reported it without amendment.

Mr. MORROW, from the committee to whom was referred the bill, entitled "An act to amend and extend the provisions of the act of the sixteenth of April, 1814, entitled "An act confirming certain claims to land in the Illinois Territory, and providing for their location," reported it with amendments.

Mr. ROBERTS, from the committee to whom was referred the bill, entitled "An act for the relief of Edward Hallowell," reported it without amendment.

The PRESIDENT communicated the general account of the Treasurer of the United States, from October 1, 1813, to October 1, 1814; as, also, the accounts of the War and Navy Departments for the same period, together with the reports of the accounting officers of the Treasury thereon; which were read.

DISCRIMINATING DUTIES.

The Senate resumed as in Committee of the Whole, the consideration of the bill to repeal so much of the several acts imposing duties on the tonnage of ships and vessels, and on goods, wares, and merchandise, imported into the United States, as imposes a discriminating duty on tonnage between foreign vessels and vessels of the United States, and between goods imported into the United States in foreign vessels and vessels of the United States.

Mr. S. SMITH.—Mr. President: It may not be improper for me, as chairman of the committee who presented the bill now under consideration, to give a short history of the subject, and to present a few details taken from official authority. Soon after the adoption of the present Constitution, Congress passed acts laying duties on tonnage and on goods imported into the United States. The law provided that six cents per ton should be paid on ships or vessels of the United States entering any of the ports of the United States, and fifty cents per ton on all foreign ships, and that an additional duty of ten per cent. on the duties payable on all goods imported in vessels of the United States, should be paid on such goods when imported into foreign vessels. These, Mr. President, are what are called "the discriminating duties."

The advantage derived therefrom to the navigation of the United States was such, that in a very few years there was American tonnage sufficient for the carrying of all the productions of our own country, and of other nations to a great extent—in fact, our navigation was second to none but Great Britain, when the late war was commenced.

The effect of those discriminating duties was felt by those foreign nations with whom we had the greatest intercourse. Great Britain, in the Treaty of 1794, reserved the right of countervailing those duties, and the United States bound themselves not to impose any new discriminating duties if Great Britain did countervail—but the wars in which she has constantly been engaged since has prevented its effects from being felt to any considerable extent. The short peace she had after the Treaty of Amiens taught the merchants of South Carolina, however, to know, that the extra duty on cotton imported in an American vessel into Great Britain was so high that it was much better to employ British vessels than to have their cotton carried in their own. In the year 1802, a letter was received from Mr. King, then Minister of the United States at London, in which he advises the repeal of the discriminating duties. The President's Message (I believe at the opening of the next session) called the attention of Congress to the subject; and so much of the Message as related to the discriminating duties was referred to the Committee of Commerce and Manufactures, who made an ample report thereon, which report, I pray may be read—[Here the Secretary read the report, dated January 10, 1803.]

Mr. President, the resolution which accompanies and which is similar to the bill before you, was taken up and would perhaps have passed, but for the memorials which came from Boston, New York, Philadelphia, and other trading cities and towns. I now find that gentlemen, who then opposed and petitioned, have changed their opinions. I remark, with pleasure, the change in an honorable gentleman, formerly a member of the Senate, in a published letter to Mr. Randolph. He, as well as many others, who at that time opposed by memorial the repeal of our discriminating duties, are convinced that their conditional repeal will tend to the security of our navigation.

Mr. President, the report just read shows, that the British had, by their countervailing duties, secured for their ships the carrying of many of our most important objects of exportation, to wit: of fish-oil, tobacco, cotton, rice, pot and pearl ashes; and having secured the carriage of those articles, the minor articles not being (except flour and naval stores) sufficient to form entire cargoes, would also be carried by British ships. But, Mr. President, the British Parliament have since increased the old and laid new duties, which include other articles of our produce and effectually secure to her ships the carriage of all our bulky articles, to wit: on flour, 6s. 9d. sterling per cwt., or 12s. per barrel, by which the American vessel will pay 1s. 2¼d. on each barrel more than if imported in a British ship. The whole freight of a barrel of flour in time of peace is 5s. sterling. No person will agree to pay 6s. 2¼d. to an American for the freight and extra duty on a barrel of flour, when he can procure British ships who will carry for five shillings.

Hemp now pays three pounds sterling per ton more if imported into Great Britain in American, than if it be imported in a British ship; which I believe is equal to the whole freight. And hemp will soon become an object of export from New Orleans.

Cotton—the duty thereon has been increased in England. It now pays 8s. and 7d. sterling per cwt., if imported into Great Britain in British ships, and 17s. and 2d. in American; that is, cotton in an American will pay 8s. 7d. per cwt. more duty than when imported in a British ship; being more than the whole freight; so that it is better to pay freight to a British ship, than to have cotton carried free of freight in an American.

Rice pays 3s. 9d. sterling per tierce more duty in an American ship than in a British. The whole freight of a tierce of rice is 12s. sterling.

Pot and pearl ashes now pay 6d. sterling per cwt. more duty in an American, than in a British ship. A cask of ashes of three hundred weight will pay an extra duty of 1s. 6d. sterling; the freight of such a cask is presumed to be 5s. 6d. sterling; thus a cask of ashes will pay for freight and extra duty, 7s. in an American, when it will only pay 5s. 6d. in a British ship.

Tobacco pays 1s. 6d. per 100 lbs., or 18s. sterling per hhd. of 1200 net wt. more when imported into Great Britain in an American than in a British ship. The freight of a hhd. of tobacco in time of peace is 35s.

The statements I have given of the countervailing duties of Great Britain, are derived from a digest of the duties and customs brought up to the 5th August, 1811; they will show to every mind, however, prejudiced, that Great Britain has effectually secured by her system the carrying (for her own wants and her foreign commerce) of our fish-oil, tobacco, flour, cotton, pot and pearl ashes, rice, hemp, &c. I have only presented for consideration the important articles; the minor articles bear also their discriminating duties, to the disadvantage of our navigation.

Mr. President, it will be seen by the report just read, that France did, in the third year of the French Republic, lay an extra duty of near twenty-three dollars per hhd. of 1200 wt. on tobacco imported in American bottoms. It is also shown that Sweden, Denmark, Holland, and Spain have their discriminating duties.

We are now at peace with the European nations. It is our interest that there should be no cause of future misunderstanding with them. If we continue our discriminating duties, and they continue their countervailing duties, the result must be, that our ships will be rendered useless. We cannot carry on equal terms, and of course will not be employed. To prevent the destruction of our navigation, Congress would be compelled to add to the discriminating duties, which would be met by foreign nations with new countervailing duties, and thus a commercial warfare would commence. Is it not, therefore, better, Mr. President, for us to agree to meet the nations of Europe on equal terms—the ships of each to be

admitted into the ports of the other on the same terms with their own ships? Are we afraid of our want of enterprise, industry, or capital? I hope not. For one, I am ready to agree to the bill on the table, and feel confident that the American merchant is equal in a fair competition to the merchant of any other nation.

When Mr. SMITH had concluded, the bill was ordered to be engrossed and read a third time.

THURSDAY, February 23.

Mr. GOLDSBOROUGH, from the committee to whom was referred the bill, entitled "An act concerning the College of Georgetown, in the District of Columbia," reported it without amendment.

The PRESIDENT communicated a letter from the Secretary for the Department of the Treasury, together with a statement of the emoluments of the officers employed in the collection of the customs for the year 1814; which were read.

The bill, entitled "An act for granting and securing to Anthony Shane the right of the United States to a tract of land in the State of Ohio," was read a third time, and passed.

Mr. ROBINSON presented the petition of Justin and Elias Lyman, merchants of the city of New York, praying the remission of the forfeitures and penalties incurred by the violation of the non-importation laws, as stated in the petition; which was read, and referred to the Committee on Foreign Relations, to consider and report thereon by bill or otherwise.

The Senate resumed, as in Committee of the Whole, the consideration of the bill, entitled "An act to amend and extend the provisions of the act of the 16th of April, 1814, entitled "An act confirming certain claims to land in the Illinois Territory, and providing for their location," together with the amendments reported thereto by the select committee; and the amendments having been agreed to, the President reported the bill to the House accordingly.

On the question, Shall the amendments be engrossed and the bill read a third time? it was determined in the affirmative.

Mr. DANA, from the committee appointed to consider the subject, reported a bill to establish a system of navigation for the United States; and the bill was read, and passed to the second reading.

Mr. KING, from the committee to whom was recommitted the bill to continue in force for a limited time the act, entitled "An act for establishing trading houses with the Indian tribes," reported it without amendment.

The Senate resumed, as in Committee of the Whole, the consideration of the bill, entitled "An act for the relief of Joshua Sands;" and, no amendment having been proposed thereto, it passed to the third reading.

The Senate resumed, as in Committee of the Whole, the consideration of the bill for the relief of Arthur Tappan and John Frothingham; and on motion, by Mr. BIBB, the further consideration thereof was postponed to Monday next.

The bill to repeal so much of the several acts imposing duties on the tonnage of ships and vessels, and on goods, wares, and merchandise, imported into the United States, as imposes a discriminating duty on tonnage between foreign vessels and vessels of the United States, and between goods imported into the United States in foreign vessels and vessels of the United States, was read a third time, and passed—yeas 24, as follows:

YEAS—Messrs. Anderson, Barbour, Barry, Bibb, Brown, Chace, Condit, Fromentin, Gaillard, German, Gore, Horsey, Kerr, King, Lacock, Lambert, Morrow, Roberts, Smith, Talbot, Tait, Varnum, Wells, and Wharton.

So it was *Resolved, unanimously,* That this bill pass, and, that the title thereof be "An act to repeal so much of the several acts imposing duties on the tonnage of ships and vessels, and on goods, wares, and merchandise, imported into the United States, as imposes a discriminating duty on tonnage between foreign vessels and vessels of the United States, and between goods imported into the United States in foreign vessels and vessels of the United States."

The amendments to the bill, entitled "An act to authorize the President of the United States to raise certain companies of rangers for the defence of the frontiers of the United States," having been reported by the committee correctly engrossed, the bill was read a third time as amended.

Resolved, That this bill pass with amendments.

On motion, the title was amended to read, "An act to repeal certain acts now in force authorizing the President of the United States to raise certain companies of rangers."

The bill to repeal certain acts concerning the flotilla service, was read a third time.

On motion, by Mr. TAIT, the bill was further amended, by unanimous consent, by adding thereto a new section.

Resolved, That this bill pass, and that the title thereof be "An act to repeal certain acts concerning the flotilla service, and for other purposes."

The bill further supplementary to an act, entitled "An act providing for the indemnification of certain claimants of public lands in the Mississippi Territory," was read a third time, and passed.

The bill to provide a library room, and for transporting the library lately purchased from Thomas Jefferson, Esq., to the City of Washington, having been reported by the committee correctly engrossed, was read a third time, and passed.

The Senate resumed, as in Committee of the Whole, the consideration of the bill, entitled "An act for the relief of Edward Hallowell;" and, no amendment having been proposed thereto, it passed to a third reading.

The bill to provide for exploring the Chesapeake bay and its waters, for the purposes therein mentioned, was read the second time.

The Senate resumed, as in Committee of the Whole, the consideration of the bill entitled "An act to provide additional revenues for defraying the expenses of Government, and maintaining the public credit, by laying a duty on gold, silver, and plated ware, and jewelry and pastework, manufactured within the United States," together with the amendment reported thereto by the select committee; and the amendment having been disagreed to, on motion, by Mr. SMITH, that the further consideration of the bill be postponed to the second Monday in March next, it was determined in the negative—yeas 4, nays 22, as follows:

YEAS—Messrs. Fromentin, Smith, Tait, and Wells.

NAYS—Messrs. Anderson, Barbour, Barry, Chace, Condit, Dana, Gaillard, German, Horsey, Hunter, Kerr, King, Lacock, Lambert, Morrow, Roberts, Talbot, Taylor, Thompson, Turner, Varnum, and Wharton.

And no amendment having been agreed to, the bill passed to a third reading.

Mr. FROMENTIN, from the committee to whom was referred the bill, entitled "An act for the relief of the heirs of James Hynum," reported it without amendment.

The following Message was received from the PRESIDENT OF THE UNITED STATES:

To the Senate and House of
    Representatives of the United States:

I lay before Congress copies of two ratified treaties which were entered into on the part of the United States, one on the 22d day of July, 1814, with the several tribes of Indians called the Wyandots, Delawares, Shawanoes, Senacas, and Miamies; the other on the 9th day of August, 1814, with the Creek nation of Indians.

It is referred to the consideration of Congress how far Legislative provisions may be necessary for carrying any part of these stipulations into effect.

                JAMES MADISON.
WASHINGTON, *February* 22, 1815.

The Message and treaties therein referred to were read.

On motion, by Mr. ANDERSON,

Ordered, That the Message, together with the treaties, be referred to the committee appointed on the subject of providing for running the boundary lines, the 22d instant, to consider and report thereon by bill or otherwise.

The Senate resumed, as in Committee of the Whole, the consideration of the bill, entitled "An act to provide additional revenues for defraying the expenses of Government, and maintaining the public credit, by laying a duty on lotteries."

On motion, by Mr. GERMAN, that the further consideration thereof be postponed to the second Monday in March next, it was determined in the affirmative—yeas 16, nays 11, as follows:

YEAS—Messrs. Daggett, Dana, Fromentin, Gaillard, German, Goldsborough, Gore, Horsey, Hunter, Kerr, King, Lambert, Smith, Thompson, Varnum, and Wells.

NAYS—Messrs. Barbour, Barry, Bibb, Brown, Condit, Morrow, Roberts, Talbot, Taylor, Turner, and Wharton.

A message from the House of Representatives informed the Senate that the House have passed a bill, entitled "An act for the relief of Solomon Frazer, and the representatives of Charles Eccleston;" a bill, entitled "An act for the relief of Thomas Sprigg;" a bill, entitled "An act authorizing the sale of the public lands which may hereafter be forfeited within the Jeffersonville land district, at the land office of said district ;" a bill entitled "An act for the relief of William P. Bennett, of the State of New York ;" a bill, entitled "An act authorizing the discharge of Anthony B. Ross from imprisonment:" also, a bill, entitled "An act for the relief of James Savage and others ;" in which bills they request the concurrence of the Senate.

The six bills last mentioned were read, and passed to the second reading.

In Executive session—

The following Message was received from the PRESIDENT OF THE UNITED STATES:

To the Senate and House of
  Representatives of the United States:

Congress will have seen by the communication from the Consul General of the United States, at Algiers, laid before them on the 7th November, 1812, the hostile proceedings of the Dey against that functionary. These have been followed by acts of more overt and direct warfare against the citizens of the United States trading in the Mediterranean, some of whom are still detained in captivity, notwithstanding the attempts which have been made to ransom them, and are treated with the rigor usual on the coast of Barbary.

The considerations which rendered it unnecessary and unimportant to commence hostile operations on the part of the United States, being now terminated by the peace with Great Britain, which opens the prospect of an active and valuable trade of their citizens within the range of the Algerine cruisers, I recommend to Congress the expediency of an act declaring the existence of a state of war between the United States and the Dey and Regency of Algiers ; and of such provisions as may be requisite for a vigorous prosecution of it to a successful issue.

JAMES MADISON.

WASHINGTON, *February* 23, 1815.

The Message was read, and referrrd to the Committee on Foreign Relations, to consider and report thereon by bill or otherwise.

FRIDAY, February 24.

The bill, entitled 'An act for the relief of Solomon Frazer, and the representatives of Charles Eccleston," was read the second time, and referred to a select committee, to consider and report thereon, and Messrs. SMITH, VARNUM, and ANDERSON, were appointed the committee.

Mr. BARBOUR, from the committee to whom was referred the bill, entitled "An act to alter and establish certain post roads," reported it with amendments.

The PRESIDENT communicated a report from the Secretary of War, showing the expenditures on account of the National Armories, and of the number and kind of arms manufactured and repaired at the same, in the year 1814 ; which was read.

The bill, entitled "An act for the relief of James Savage and others," was read the second time, and referred to the committee to whom was referred, on the 23d September, the memorial of the President and Directors of the Eastern Branch Bridge Company, to consider and report thereon.

The bill, entitled "An act for the relief of Thomas Sprigg," was read the second time, and referred to the committee last mentioned, to consider and report thereon.

The bill, entitled "An act authorizing the discharge of Anthony B. Ross from imprisonment," was read the second time, and referred to a select committee to consider and report thereon ; and Messrs. DAGGETT, DANA, and THOMPSON, were appointed the committee.

The bill, entitled "An act for the relief of William P. Bennet, of the State of New York, was read the second time, and referred to the committee last mentioned, to consider and report thereon.

The bill, entitled "An act authorizing the sale of the public lands which may hereafter be forfeited within the Jeffersonville land district, at the land office of said district," was read the second time, and referred to the committee to whom was referred, on the 21st September, the memorial of the Legislature of the Indiana Territory, to consider and report thereon.

Mr. ANDERSON, from the committee appointed to consider the subject, reported a bill to provide for the ascertaining and surveying the boundary lines fixed by the treaty with the Creek Indians, and for other purposes ; and the bill was read, and passed to the second reading.

Mr. BIBB, from the Committee on Foreign Relations, reported a bill to repeal certain acts therein mentioned, (viz: the acts prohibiting trade and intercourse with our late enemy, and prohibiting the admission into our waters of the enemy's vessels ;) and the bill was read, and passed to the second reading.

A message from the House of Representatives informed the Senate that the House have passed a bill, entitled "An act supplemental to the act, entitled 'An act for the final adjustment of land titles in the State of Louisiana, and Territory of Missouri,' approved April 12, 1814 ;" in which bill they request the concurrence of the Senate.

The bill last mentioned was read, and passed to the second reading.

On motion, by Mr. BIBB, the Committee on Foreign Relations, to whom was referred the petition of Justin and Elias Lyman, were discharged from the further consideration thereof.

The bill, entitled "An act to provide additional revenues for defraying the expenses of Government, and maintaining the public credit, by laying a duty on gold, silver, and plated ware, and jewelry and pastework, manufactured within the United States," was read a third time ; and, on motion by Mr. FROMENTIN, that the further consideration thereof be postponed to the second Monday in March next, it was determined in the negative—yeas 8, nays 18, as follows:

YEAS—Messrs. Fromentin, Goldsborough, Gore, King, Lambert, Smith, Tait, and Wells.

NAYS—Messrs. Anderson, Barbour, Barry, Bibb, Brown, Chace, Condit, Gaillard, German, Giles, Lacock, Morrow, Roberts, Taylor, Thompson, Turner, Varnum, and Wharton.

Whereupon, *Resolved,* That this bill pass.

The amendments to the bill, entitled "An act

to amend and extend the provisions of the act of the 16th April, 1814, entitled 'An act confirming certain claims to land in the Illinois Territory, and providing for their location," having been reported by the committee correctly engrossed, the bill was read a third time as amended, and further amended by unanimous consent.

Resolved, That this bill pass with amendments.

The bill, entitled "An act for the relief of Joshua Sands," was read a third time, and passed.

The bill, entitled "An act for the relief of Edward Hallowell," was read a third time, and passed.

The Senate resumed, as in Committee of the Whole, the consideration of the bill, entitled "An act to provide additional revenues for defraying the expenses of Government, and maintaining the public credit, by laying a direct tax upon the District of Columbia;" and, on motion by Mr. TAYLOR, that the further consideration thereof be postponed to the second Monday in March next, it was determined in the negative—yeas 6, nays 20, as follows:

YEAS—Messrs. Chace, Gaillard, Morrow, Roberts, Tait, and Taylor.

NAYS—Messrs. Anderson, Barbour, Barry, Bibb, Fromentin, German, Giles, Goldsborough, Gore, Hunter, Kerr, King, Lacock, Lambert, Smith, Thompson, Turner, Varnum, Wells, and Wharton.

And no amendment having been proposed thereto, the bill was passed to a third reading.

The Senate resumed, as in Committee of the Whole, the consideration of the bill, entitled "An act for the relief of Jacob Shinnick, and Shoultz and Vogeler, of Christian Chapman, and the legal representative of John Calef, deceased; and Mr. VARNUM was requested to take the Chair.

On motion, by Mr. WELLS, that the further consideration thereof be postponed to the second Monday in March next, it was determined in the negative—yeas 8, nays 17, as follows:

YEAS—Messrs. Bibb, Gaillard, Gore, King, Morrow, Thompson, Varnum, and Wells.

NAYS—Messrs. Anderson, Barbour, Barry, Brown, Chace, Fromentin, German, Giles, Goldsborough, Kerr, Lacock, Roberts, Smith, Tait, Taylor, Turner and Wharton.

And, no amendment having been proposed thereto, the President resumed the Chair, and it was ordered that it pass to the third reading.

The Senate resumed, as in Committee of the Whole, the consideration of the bill making further provision for completing the public buildings at West Point, for the accommodation of the Military Academy; and no amendment having been proposed thereto, on the question, Shall this bill be engrossed and read a third time? it was determined in the affirmative.

On motion, by Mr. CHACE,

Resolved, That the Committee on Foreign Relations be instructed to inquire into the expediency of making further provision for the collection of the revenue.

SATURDAY, February 25.

Mr. SMITH, from the committee to whom was referred the bill, entitled "An act for the relief of Solomon Frazer, and the representatives of Charles Eccleston," reported it without amendment; and the bill was considered as in Committee of the Whole, and passed to a third reading.

Mr. ROBERTS presented the memorial of the manufacturers of the city and county of Philadelphia, praying suitable measures may be adopted for their protection; and the memorial was read, and referred to the committee to whom was referred, the 21st instant, so much of the Message of the President of the United States of the 20th instant, as relates to the preservation and promotion of the manufactures, to consider and report thereon by bill or otherwise.

The bill to provide for the ascertaining and surveying of the boundary lines fixed by the treaty with the Creek Indians, and for other purposes, was read the second time, and considered as in Committee of the Whole; and, having been amended, the President reported it to the House accordingly.

On the question, Shall this bill be engrossed and read a third time as amended? it was determined in the affirmative.

The bill to repeal certain acts therein mentioned was read the second time.

The bill, entitled "An act supplemental to the act, entitled 'An act for the final adjustment of land titles in the State of Louisiana and Territory of Missouri,' approved April 12, 1814," was read the second time, and referred to the committee to whom was referred, the 21st September, the memorial of the Legislature of the Indiana Territory, to consider and report thereon.

The engrossed bill to continue in force, for a limited time, the act, entitled "An act for establishing trading houses with the Indian tribes," was read a third time, and passed.

The bill, entitled "An act for the relief of Jacob Shinnick, and Shoultz and Vogeler, of Christian Chapman, and the legal representative of John Calef, deceased," was read a third time and passed.

Mr. GILES, from the committee to whom was referred the bill, entitled "An act for the relief of William H. Washington," reported it without amendment; and the bill was considered as in Committee of the Whole. and passed to a third reading.

The bill, entitled "An act to provide additional revenues for defraying the expenses of Government, and maintaining the public credit, by laying a direct tax upon the District of Columbia," was read the third time and passed.

The bill making further provision for completing the public buildings at West Point, for the accommodation of the Military Academy, was read a third time and passed.

A message from the House of Representatives informed the Senate that the House disagree to the report of the committee of conference on the disagreeing votes of the two Houses respecting the resolution expressive of the thanks of Congress to Major General Jackson, and the troops under his command, for their gallantry and good conduct in the defence of New Orleans; and that the resolution be modified accordingly. They have passed the bill, entitled "An act concerning the flotilla service, and for other purposes," with an amendment, in which they request the concurrence of the Senate. They have passed a resolution for the appointment of a joint committee to wait upon the President, and request that he recommend a day of thanksgiving to Almighty God, for restoring to these United States the blessings of peace. They have also passed a bill, entitled "An act to fix the compensations and increase the responsibility of the collectors of the direct tax and internal duties, and for other purposes, connected with the collection thereof;" in which resolution and bill they request the concurrence of the Senate. They insist on their disagreement to the fifth amendment insisted on by the Senate to the bill, entitled "An act to amend the act, entitled 'An act to provide additional revenues for defraying the expenses of Government, and maintaining the public credit, by laying a direct tax upon the United States, and to provide for assessing and collecting the same;" and the act, entitled "An act to provide additional revenues for defraying the expenses of Government, and maintaining the public credit, by laying duties on household furniture, and on gold and silver watches." They ask a conference thereon, and have appointed managers on their part.

On motion, by Mr. GILES,

Resolved, That the Senate agree to the conference proposed on the disagreeing votes of the two Houses on the amendment to the bill last mentioned.

Ordered, That Messrs. TAYLOR, KING, and GILES, be the managers on the part of the Senate.

The bill last brought up for concurrence was twice read by unanimous consent, and referred to a select committee to consist of five members, to consider and report thereon; and Messrs. TAYLOR, DAGGETT, BROWN, CHACE, and ROBERTS, were appointed the committee.

The resolution last brought up for concurrence was three times read by unanimous consent, concurred in, and Messrs. SMITH and TAIT appointed the committee on their part.

The Senate proceeded to consider the amendment of the House of Representatives to the bill, entitled "An act concerning the flotilla service, and for other purposes," and concurred therein.

Mr. GILES, from the committee of conference on the disagreeing votes of the two Houses respecting the resolution expressive of the thanks of Congress to Major General Jackson, and the troops under his command, for their gallantry and good conduct in the defence of New Orleans, reported,

That they have agreed to recommend to the adoption of the two Houses of Congress a modification of the original resolution and proposed amendment, to read as follows:

Resolved, by the Senate and House of Representa- tives *of the United States of America in Congress as-* sembled, That the thanks of Congress be, and they are hereby, given to Major General Jackson, and through him to the officers and soldiers of the regular army, of the militia, and of the volunteers, under his command, the greater proportion of which troops consisted of militia and volunteers suddenly collected together, for their uniform gallantry and good conduct conspicuously displayed against the enemy, from the time of his landing before New Orleans until his final expulsion therefrom; and particularly for their valor, skill, and good conduct, on the 8th of January last, in repulsing with great slaughter, a numerous British army of chosen veteran troops, when attempting, by a bold and daring attack, to carry by storm the works hastily thrown up for the protection of New Orleans; and thereby obtaining a most signal victory over the enemy, with a disparity of loss, on his part, unexampled in military annals.

The Senate proceeded to consider the said report of the committee of conference; whereupon,

Resolved, unanimously, That they concur therein, and that the resolution be modified accordingly.

The Senate resumed, as in Committee of the Whole, the consideration of the bill, entitled "An act to alter and establish certain post roads," together with the amendments reported thereto by the select committee; and the amendments having been agreed to, the President reported the bill to the House accordingly.

On the question, Shall the amendments be engrossed, and the bill read a third time as amended? it was determined in the affirmative.

The amendments to the bill last mentioned having been reported by the committee correctly engrossed, the bill was read a third time as amended, by unanimous consent.

Resolved, That this bill pass, with amendments.

The Senate resumed, as in Committee of the Whole, the consideration of the bill to provide for exploring the Chesapeake bay, and its waters, for the purposes therein mentioned; and the bill having been amended, the President reported it to the House accordingly.

On the question, Shall this bill be engrossed, and read a third time as amended? it was determined in the affirmative.

Mr. DAGGETT, from the committee to whom was referred the bill, entitled "An act authorizing the discharge of Anthony B. Ross from imprisonment," reported it without amendment; and the bill was considered as in Committee of the Whole, and passed to a third reading.

The bill, entitled "An act for the relief of the heirs of James Hynum," was resumed as in Committee of the Whole; and, no amendment having been proposed thereto, it passed to a third reading.

The Senate resumed, as in Committee of the Whole, the consideration of the bill, entitled "An act concerning the College of Georgetown, in the District of Columbia;" and, no amendment having been proposed thereto, it passed to a third reading.

The following Message was received from the PRESIDENT OF THE UNITED STATES:

To the Senate and House of
    Representatives of the United States:

Peace having happily taken place between the United States and Great Britain, it is desirable to guard against incidents, which, during periods of war in Europe, might tend to interrupt it; and, it is believed, in particular, that the navigation of American vessels exclusively by American seamen, either natives or such as are already naturalized, would not only conduce to the attainment of that object, but also to increase the number of our seamen, and, consequently, to render our commerce and navigation independent of the service of foreigners, who might be recalled by their Governments, under circumstances the most inconvenient to the United States. I recommend the subject, therefore, to the consideration of Congress, and, in deciding upon it, I am persuaded that they will sufficiently estimate the policy of manifesting to the world a desire, on all occasions, to cultivate harmony with other nations, by any reasonable accommodations which do not impair the enjoyment of any essential rights of a free and independent people. The example on the part of the American Government will merit, and may be expected to receive, a reciprocal attention from all the friendly Powers of Europe.

                      JAMES MADISON.

WASHINGTON, *Feb.* 25, 1815.

The Message was read, and referred to the Committee on Foreign Relations, to consider and report thereon by bill or otherwise.

Mr. DAGGETT, from the committee to whom was referred the bill, entitled "An act for the relief of William P. Bennett, of the State of New York," reported it without amendment, and the bill was considered as in Committee of the Whole; and the further consideration thereof postponed to Monday next.

Mr. KING presented the memorial of the Mayor, Aldermen, and Common Council, of the city of New York, praying the reimbursement of certain sums advanced and expended in the defence of the third military district, as stated in the memorial; which was read, and referred to a select committee, to consider and report thereon, by bill or otherwise; and Messrs. KING, TAIT, and VARNUM, were appointed the committee.

Mr. DAGGETT, from the joint committee appointed to consider the subject, reported the following resolution; which was read, and passed to the second reading:

Resolved, by the Senate and House of Representatives of the United States of America in Congress assembled, That the Secretary of the Senate and the Clerk of the House of Representatives be directed, immediately after the adjournment of the present and each succeeding Congress, to advertise three weeks successively, in two newspapers printed in the District of Columbia, for proposals for supplying the Senate and House of Representatives, during the succeeding Congress, with the necessary stationery and printing; which advertisement shall describe the kind of stationery and printing required; and that the proposals to be made be accompanied with sufficient security for their performance. And it shall be the duty of the Secretary and Clerk aforesaid, in the month of April thereafter, to notify the lowest bidder or bidders, (whose securities are deemed sufficient,) of the acceptance of his or their proposals: *Provided,* That this resolution shall not be so construed as to prevent the Secretary and Clerk aforesaid from contracting for separate parts of the supplies of stationery and printing required to be furnished.

On motion, by Mr. DAGGETT, the committee was discharged from the further consideration of the subject-matter thereof, referred to them.

             MONDAY, February 27.

Mr. TAIT, from the Committee on Naval Affairs, reported a bill concerning the Naval Establishment; and the bill was read and ordered to the second reading.

Mr. BIBB, from the Committee on Foreign Relations, who were instructed to inquire into the expediency of making provision by law to release all or any claims of the United States to penalties or forfeitures, under acts which have imposed prohibitions or temporary restrictions on commercial intercourse, and to discontinue prosecutions therefor, upon payment of costs legally incurred, reported the following resolution, which was read:

Resolved, That it is inexpedient to make such provision.

Mr. SMITH presented the petition of Robert and John Oliver and others, owners of property in the neighborhood of Baltimore, which, in the late attack of the enemy on that city, was destroyed or injured, for the purpose of erecting fortifications; and praying payment therefor, as stated in the petition; which was read, and referred to the committee to whom was referred the memorial of the President and Directors of the Washington Bridge Company, to consider and report thereon by bill or otherwise.

Mr. ROBERTS, from the committee to whom was referred the bill, entitled "An act for the relief of James Doyle," made a report thereupon; which was read.

Mr. ROBERTS also reported the bill without amendment.

The bill to establish a system of navigation for the United States was read the second time; and Mr. DANA proposed a new section to be added thereto; which was read.

Mr. FROMENTIN, from the committee to whom the subject was referred, reported a bill for the relief of Peter Landais; and the bill was read, and passed to the second reading.

The bill to provide for the ascertaining and surveying of the boundary lines fixed by the treaty with the Creek Indians, and for other purposes, was read a third time, and passed.

The bill to provide for exploring the Chesapeake Bay, and its waters, for the purposes therein mentioned, was read a third time, and passed.

The resolution directing the manner of providing stationery, and procuring the printing for the Senate and House of Representatives, was read the second time, and considered as in Committee of the Whole; and, no amendment having been proposed thereto, on the question, Shall this resolution be engrossed and read a third time? it was determined in the affirmative.

The PRESIDENT communicated a report of the Postmaster General, relative to the salaries of the clerks of that department; which was read.

Mr. GERMAN, from the committee to whom was referred the bill, entitled "An act supplementary to an act, entitled 'An act for the better organization of the courts of the United States within the State of New York," reported it with amendments, which were read, and considered as in Committee of the Whole; and the amendments having been agreed to, the PRESIDENT reported the bill to the House accordingly.

On the question, Shall the amendments be engrossed, and the bill read a third time as amended? it was determined in the affirmative.

Mr. GILES, from the committee to whom was referred the bill, entitled "An act for the relief of James Savage and others," reported it without amendment; and the bill was considered as in Committee of the Whole, and passed to a third reading.

The bill, entitled "An act for the relief of Solomon Frazer, and the representatives of Charles Eccleston," was read a third time, and passed.

The bill, entitled "An act for the relief of William H. Washington," was read a third time, and passed.

The bill entitled "An act for the relief of the heirs of James Hynum," was read a third time, and passed.

The bill, entitled "An act concerning the College of Georgetown, in the District of Columbia," was read a third time, and passed.

The bill, entitled "An act authorizing the discharge of Anthony B. Ross from imprisonment," was read a third time, and, on the question, Shall this bill pass? it was determined in the negative. So the bill was rejected.

Mr. GORE presented the petition of Walter and Miller, and others, owners of certain vessels sailing under foreign flags, and praying relief, as stated in the petition; which was read, and referred to the Committee on Foreign Relations, to consider and report thereon by bill or otherwise.

Mr. GILES, from the committee to whom was referred the bill, entitled "An act for the relief of the Anacosta Bridge Company," reported it without amendment; and the bill was considered as in Committe of the Whole, and passed to a third reading.

The Senate resumed, as in Committee of the Whole, the consideration of the bill to repeal certain acts therein mentioned; and no amendment having been proposed thereto, on the question, Shall this bill be engrossed and read a third time? it was determined in the affirmative.

The bill last mentioned was read a third time by unanimous consent, and passed.

The Senate resumed, as in Committee of the Whole, the consideration of the bill, entitled "An act for the relief of William P. Bennet, of the State of New York;" and, no amendment having been proposed thereto, it passed to a third reading.

Mr. BROWN submitted the following resolution; which was read, and passed to a second reading:

Resolved, by the Senate and House of Representatives of the United States of America in Congress assembled, That the Secretary of State cause to be distributed among the members of the present Congress, copies of the laws of the United States ordered by law to be printed, as soon as the same shall be printed.

TUESDAY, February 28.

Mr. GILES, from the Committee on Military Affairs, made a report on the subject of the differences of opinion existing between the Executive authority of the United States, and the authorities of some of the individual States, respecting the relative powers of the General and State Governments over the militia; and the report was read, and ordered to be printed for the use of the Senate.

Mr. BIBB, from the Committee on Foreign Relations, to whom was referred the Message of the President recommending certain regulations respecting American seamen, made a report, which was read and agreed to, as follows:

"That they fully accord in the policy recommended, of avoiding, by prudent regulations, the occurrence of circumstances which may disturb a liberal intercourse with foreign nations. They are, moreover, persuaded that the navigation of American vessels, exclusively by American seamen, either natives, or such as are already naturalized, would not only have the tendency to render our commerce and navigation independent of the service of foreigners, but that it would be calculated to remove the pretext under which the American navigation has heretofore been interrupted.

"But, while the committee consider the subject of the President's Message highly important, they regret that the session of Congress is so near its close, that questions affecting the foreign as well as the domestic policy of the nation cannot now receive the deliberate and full examination to which they are entitled.

"The committee, therefore, submit the following resolution:

"*Resolved,* That the further consideration of the Message be postponed until the next session of Congress."

Mr. BIBB, from the Committee on Foreign Relations, reported a bill further to provide for the collection of duties on imports and tonnage; and the bill was read, and passed to the second reading.

Mr. GILES, from the committee to whom the subject was referred, reported a bill for the relief of sundry persons in the service of the United States, in consequence of the destruction of their tools by fire at the navy yard; and the bill was read, and passed to the second reading.

Mr. MORROW, from the committee to whom was referred the bill, entitled "An act supplemental to the act, entitled 'An act for the final adjustment of land titles in the State of Louisiana and Territory of Missouri,' approved April 12, 1814," reported it without amendment; and, on motion by Mr. MORROW, the further consideration thereof was postponed to the second Monday in March next.

The following Message was received from the PRESIDENT OF THE UNITED STATES:

279
HISTORY OF CONGRESS.
280

Senate.
Amendments of the Constitution.
February, 1815.

To the Senate of the United States:

I transmit to the Senate a report from the Postmaster General, complying with their resolution of the 15th of December last.

JAMES MADISON.

Washington, February 23, 1815.

The Message and report therein referred to were read, and ordered to be printed.

Mr. Morrow, from the committee to whom was referred the bill, entitled "An act authorizing the sale of public lands, which may hereafter be forfeited within the Jeffersonville land district, at the land office of said district," reported it without amendment; and, on motion by Mr. Morrow, the further consideration thereof was postponed to the second Monday in March next.

The amendments to the bill, entitled "An act for the better organization of the courts of the United States within the State of New York," having been reported by the committee correctly engrossed, the bill was read a third time as amended.

Resolved, That this bill pass with amendments.

The resolution directing the manner of providing stationery, and procuring the printing for the Senate and House of Representatives, was read a third time, and passed.

On motion, by Mr. Taylor, the committee to whom was referred the petition of James Lamb, of Charleston, were discharged from the further consideration thereof.

Mr. Tait, from the Committee on Naval Affairs, reported the following resolutions, which were read and agreed to:

Resolved, That the Secretary of the Navy be requested to report to the Senate, in the first week of the next session, a system for the gradual and permanent increase of the Navy of the United States.

Resolved, That the said Secretary report, as aforesaid, the expenditures and contracts which have been made under the third section of the act of the 30th of March, 1812.

Resolved, That the Secretary of the Navy report, as aforesaid, what measures have been taken to carry into execution the laws respecting navy hospitals.

Resolved, That the said Secretary report, as aforesaid, what measures have been taken for the execution of the 4th section of the act of the 3d of March, 1813, entitled "An act supplementary to the act for increasing the Navy."

Resolved, That the Secretary lay before the Senate, at the commencement of the next session, a corrected register of the Navy and Marine Corps.

Mr. Lacock submitted the following resolution, which was read, and passed to the second reading:

Resolved, That Robert Tweedy, Benjamin G. Bowen, and Tobias Simpson, assistants to the Sergeant-at-Arms and Doorkeeper of the Senate, be paid, out of the contingent fund, two dollars a day for each day they may have attended the Senate during the present session of Congress, and that Charles Tims be allowed seventy-five dollars for his attendance during the present session.

The resolution last mentioned was read the second time, by unanimous consent, and considered as in Committee of the Whole; and, no amendment having been proposed thereto, on the question, Shall this resolution be engrossed and read a third time? it was determined in the affirmative.

The bill concerning the Naval Establishment was read the second time, and considered as in Committee of the Whole; and, no amendment having been proposed thereto, on the question, Shall this bill be engrossed and read a third time? it was determined in the affirmative.

The bill for the relief of Peter Landais was read the second time; and, on motion by Mr. Bibb, the further consideration thereof was postponed to the second Monday in March next.

The resolution directing the distribution among the members of the present Congress of copies of the Laws of the United States, was read the second time, and considered as in Committee of the Whole; and, having been amended, the President reported it to the House accordingly.

On the question, Shall this resolution be engrossed, and read a third time as amended? it was determined in the affirmative.

The Senate resumed the consideration of the resolution reported the 27th instant, by the Committee on Foreign Relations, and agreed thereto.

The bill, entitled "An act for the relief of James Savage and others," was read a third time, and passed.

The bill, entitled "An act for the relief of the Anacosta Bridge Company," was read a third time, and passed.

The bill, entitled "An act for the relief of William P. Bennet, of the State of New York," was read a third time, and passed.

The Senate resumed, as in Committee of the Whole, the consideration of the bill to establish a system of navigation for the United States; and the further consideration thereof was postponed to the second Monday in March next.

The Senate resumed, as in Committee of the Whole, the consideration of the bill, entitled "An act for the relief of James Doyle," together with the report of the select committee thereon; and, on the question, Shall this bill be read a third time? it was determined in the negative. So the bill was lost.

AMENDMENTS OF THE CONSTITUTION.

Mr. Dana submitted for consideration a resolution of the Legislature of the State of Connecticut, requesting the Senators of the State, and the Representatives of the people thereof, in Congress of the United States, to use their endeavors that Congress propose to the Legislatures of the several States, for their adoption, the following amendments of the Constitution of the United States, viz:

First. Representatives and direct taxes shall be apportioned among the several States which may be included within this Union, according to their respective numbers of free persons, including those bound to serve for a term of years, and excluding Indians not taxed, and all other persons.

Second. No new State shall be admitted into the

Union by Congress, in virtue of the power granted by the Constitution, without the concurrence of two-thirds of both Houses.

Third. Congress shall not have power to lay any embargo on the ships or vessels of the citizens of the United States, in the ports or harbors thereof, for more than sixty days.

Fourth. Congress shall not have power, without the concurrence of two-thirds of both Houses, to interdict the commercial intercourse between the United States and any foreign nation, or the dependencies thereof.

Fifth. Congress shall not make or declare war, or authorize acts of hostility against any foreign nation, without the concurrence of two-thirds of both Houses, except such acts of hostilities be in defence of the territories of the United States when actually invaded.

Sixth. No person who shall hereafter be naturalized, shall be eligible as a member of the Senate or House of Representatives of the United States, nor capable of holding any civil office under the authority of the United States.

Seventh. The same person shall not be elected President of the United States a second time; nor shall the President be elected from the same State two terms in succession.

And the resolution and proposed amendments were read.

WEDNESDAY, March 1.

On motion, by Mr. BIBB, the Committee on Foreign Relations, to whom was referred the petition of Walter and Miller, and others, were discharged from the further consideration thereof.

Mr. GILES, from the committee to whom was referred the bill, entitled "An act for the relief of Thomas Sprigg," reported it without amendment; and the bill was considered as in Committee of the Whole; and passed to a third reading.

The bill last mentioned was read a third time, by unanimous consent, and passed.

Mr. GILES, from the committee to whom was referred the bill, entitled "An act to authorize the payment for property lost, captured, or destroyed by the enemy, while in the military service of the United States," reported it with amendments; and Mr. TALBOT proposed for consideration sundry amendments to the bill; which were read; and on motion, by Mr. GILES, the further consideration of the bill and amendments were postponed until to-morrow.

Mr. TAYLOR, from the managers appointed by the Senate to confer with the managers appointed by the House of Representatives on the disagreeing votes of the two Houses on the fifth amendment made by the Senate to the bill, entitled "An act to amend the act, entitled 'An act to provide additional revenues for defraying the expenses of Government, and maintaining the public credit, by laying a direct tax upon the United States, and to provide for assessing and collecting the same," and the act, entitled "An act to provide additional revenues for defraying the expenses of Government, and maintaining the public credit, by laying duties on household furniture, and on gold and silver watches," reported:

"That they have met the said managers, and, after conferring with them, have agreed to recommend to the Senate, that as the said amendment would have no effect for the present year, the Senate do recede from said amendment."

The Senate proceeded to consider the said report of the committee of conference. Whereupon,

Resolved, That they concur therein, and that they recede from their said fifth amendment to said bill accordingly.

Mr. TAYLOR, from the committee to whom was referred the bill, entitled "An act to fix the compensations, and increase the responsibility, of the collectors of the direct tax and internal duties, and for other purposes connected with the collection thereof," reported it without amendment; and the bill was considered as in Committee of the Whole, and having been amended, the President reported it to the House accordingly.

On the question, Shall the amendment be engrossed and the bill read a third time as amended? it was determined in the affirmative.

Mr. ROBERTS, from the committee to whom was referred the petition of Robert Kid, of the city of Philadelphia, made report, together with the following resolution, which was read, and agreed to.

Resolved, That the petitioner have leave to withdraw his petition.

On motion, by Mr. MORROW, the committee to whom was referred the petition of Benjamin W. Ladd, Joseph Ladd, and Thomas Norvell, were discharged from the further consideration thereof.

Mr. LACOCK submitted the following resolution, which was read, and passed to the second reading:

Resolved, That the Secretary of the Senate pay, out of the contingent fund of the Senate, to Tobias Simpson, two hundred dollars, in consideration of his uniform good conduct, and particularly for his exertions to save the public property in the Capitol, both before and after the destruction thereof by the enemy.

The resolution last mentioned was read the second time, by unanimous consent, and considered as in Committee of the Whole; and no amendment having been proposed thereto, on the question, Shall this resolution be engrossed and read a third time? it was determined in the affirmative; and the resolution was then read a third time, by unanimous consent, and passed.

The bill further to provide for the collection of duties on imports and tonnage was read the second time, and considered as in Committee of the Whole; and, no amendment having been made thereto, on the question, Shall this bill be engrossed and read a third time? it was determined in the affirmative.

The bill for the relief of sundry persons in the service of the United States, in consequence of the destruction of their tools by fire at the navy yard, was read the second time, and considered as in Committee of the Whole; and, no amendment having been made thereto, on the question, Shall this bill be engrossed and read a third time? it was determined in the affirmative.

A message from the House of Representatives informed the Senate that the House have passed a bill, entitled "An act to vest more effectually in the State courts, and in the district courts of the United States, jurisdiction in the cases therein mentioned;" a bill, entitled "An act regulating and defining the duties of the United States' judges for the Territory of Illinois;" also, a bill, entitled "An act fixing the Military Peace Establishment of the United States;" in which bills they request the concurrence of the Senate.

The three bills last mentioned were read, and passed to the second reading.

The bill, entitled "An act fixing the Military Peace Establishment of the United States," was read the second time by unanimous consent, and on motion, by Mr. BIBB, referred to the Committee on Military Affairs, to consider and report thereon.

The bill, entitled "An act regulating and defining the duties of the United States' judges for the Territory of Illinois," was read the second time by unanimous consent, and considered as in Committee of the Whole; and, no amendment having been proposed thereto, it passed to the third reading.

The resolution relative to the distribution of the laws of the United States, as amended, was read a third time, and passed, as follows:

Resolved, by the Senate and House of Representatives of the United States of America in Congress assembled, That the Secretary of State cause to be distributed among the members of the present Congress, copies of the laws of the United States, ordered by law to be printed, as soon as the same shall be completed.

Resolved, That so many of the remaining copies of the laws as are not already distributed, be deposited in the Congressional Library.

The bill concerning the Naval Establishment was read the third time, and passed.

The resolution fixing the compensation of the messengers of the Senate was read the third time, and passed.

The credentials of the Honorable WILLIAM HUNTER, appointed a Senator by the Legislature of the State of Rhode Island and Providence Plantations, for the term of six years, commencing on the fourth day of this month, were read, and laid on file.

Mr. KING submitted the following motion:

Resolved, That the President of the United States be, and is hereby, requested to give instructions to the Secretary of War—

To prepare and lay before the Senate, at the commencement of their next session, a report concerning the annuities and presents granted to, and trade carried on with, the several Indian tribes within the limits of the United States, during four years antecedent to the 4th of March, 1815, whether such trade has been under the control or management of the Superintendent of Indian Trade, of the Governors of the several Territories, or of any other person acting in behalf of the

United States: and, in order that such report may exhibit a full view of the whole Indian trade during the term aforesaid, that the President be further requested to direct the Superintendent of Indian Trade, and every other public agent concerned therein, to furnish to the Secretary of War such accounts and statements as he may call for, to enable him to prepare and make the report aforesaid.

That the said report do contain an annual account of the Indian trade at each of the agencies or trading houses, or wheresoever else the same shall have been carried on, including therein the expenses of buildings, transportation, and all other incidental charges; and, also, a statement of losses, whether of goods or effects, intended for the Indians, or received from them.

Also, a like annual account of the whole of the Indian trade,

Also, a general account of the Indian trade, exhibiting the profit and loss thereof, during the term aforesaid.

Also, an account of the annuities and presents due, paid, and delivered, to the respective Indian tribes, during the aforesaid term; specifying the dates when the same were due, and when they were paid and delivered.

That the Secretary do, furthermore, report to the Senate his opinion, whether any alteration of the powers and duties of the several officers and agents employed in the superintendence and management of Indian affairs would be advantageous; whether the consolidation of the whole care and management thereof, and the placing of the same in a single department, would be expedient; and whether a plan may not be devised that will be equally advantageous to the Indian tribes, and more economical to the public, whereby the Indian trade may, under safeguards, be hereafter carried on by individuals, or by private companies, instead of the manner in which the same is now conducted.

In secret session—

A confidential message was received from the House of Representatives, by Mr. GASTON and Mr. FORSYTH, two members of that body; Mr. GASTON, Chairman:

Mr. President: The House of Representatives have confidentially passed a bill, entitled "An act for the protection of the commerce of the United States against the Algerine cruisers," in which they request the concurrence of the Senate.

The said bill was twice read by unanimous consent, and passed to the third reading.

THURSDAY, March 2.

Mr. VARNUM submitted for consideration a resolution of the Legislature of the Commonwealth of Massachusetts, containing the same request, and embracing the same objects, of the resolution of the Legislature of the State of Connecticut, submitted on the 28th ultimo; and the resolution and proposed amendments were read.

Mr. GILES, from the Committee on Military Affairs, to whom was referred the bill, entitled "An act fixing the Military Peace Establishment of the United States," reported it with amendments.

On motion, by Mr. GILES, the committee to

whom was referred the petition of Robert and John Oliver, and others, was discharged from the further consideration thereof.

A message from the House of Representatives informed the Senate that the House have passed a bill, entitled "An act making appropriations for the support of the Military Establishment for the year one thousand eight hundred and fifteen;" a bill, entitled "An act concerning invalid pensioners;" and a bill, entitled "An act making appropriations for the support of the Navy of the United States for the year 1815;" in which bills they request the concurrence of the Senate.

The three bills last mentioned were read, and passed to the second reading.

The bill, entitled "An act concerning invalid pensioners," was read the second time by unanimous consent, and referred to the Committee on Military Affairs, to consider and report thereon.

The bill, entitled "An act making appropriations for the support of the Military Establishment for the year 1815," was read the second time by unanimous consent, and referred to the Committee on Military Affairs, to consider and report thereon.

The bill, entitled "An act making appropriations for the support of the Navy of the United States for the year 1815," was read the second time by unanimous consent, and referred to the Committee on Naval Affairs, to consider and report thereon.

Mr. TAIT, from the Committee on Naval Affairs, to whom was referred the last mentioned bill, reported it without amendment, and the bill was considered as in Committee of the Whole, and passed to a third reading; and the bill was read a third time by unanimous consent, and passed.

The bill, entitled "An act to vest more effectually in the State courts, and in the district courts of the United States, jurisdiction in the cases therein mentioned," was read the second time, and referred to a select committee, to consider and report thereon; and Messrs. BIBB, BARBOUR, and CHACE, were appointed the committee.

The bill for the relief of sundry persons in the service of the United States, in consequence of the destruction of their tools by fire, at the Navy Yard, was read a third time, and passed.

The bill further to provide for the collection of duties on imports and tonnage, was read a third time, and amended by unanimous consent, and passed.

The amendment to the bill, entitled "An act to fix the compensations, and increase the responsibility, of the collectors of the direct tax and internal duties, and for other purposes connected with the collection thereof," having been reported by the committee correctly engrossed, the bill was read a third time as amended.

Resolved, That this bill pass with an amendment.

On motion, by Mr. BARBOUR, the committee to whom was referred so much of the President's Message, of the 20th ultimo, as relates to the pres-

ervation and promotion of manufactures, were discharged from the further consideration thereof.

On motion, by Mr. BARBOUR, the committee to whom was referred the memorial of the manufacturers of the city and county of Philadelphia, were discharged from the further consideration thereof.

A message from the House of Representatives informed the Senate that the House have passed the bill, entitled "An act increasing the compensation allowed the Sergeant-at-Arms of the Senate," with amendments, in which they request the concurrence of the Senate. They have also passed the bill, entitled "An act further supplementary to an act, entitled 'An act providing for the indemnification of certain claimants of public lands in the Mississippi Territory," with amendments, in which they request the concurrence of the Senate.

The Senate proceeded to consider the amendments of the House of Representatives to the bill last mentioned, and concurred therein.

The Senate proceeded to consider the amendments of the House of Representatives to the bill, entitled "An act increasing the compensation allowed the Sergeant-at-Arms of the Senate." Whereupon, on motion, by Mr. TURNER,

Resolved, That they concur therein with amendments.

It was agreed to amend the title, to read "An act increasing the compensation allowed the Sergeants-at-Arms of the Senate and House of Representatives, and of the Doorkeeper and Assistant Doorkeeper of the Senate and House of Representatives."

The bill, entitled "An act regulating and defining the duties of the United States' judges for the Territory of Illinois," was read a third time, and passed.

The Senate resumed, as in Committee of the Whole, the consideration of the bill, entitled "An act fixing the Military Peace Establishment of the United States," together with the amendments reported thereto by the select committee.

On the question, to agree to the first amendment proposed, to wit: Section 1, line 4, strike out "six," and insert "fifteen," a division of the question was called for by Mr. LACOCK, and it was taken on striking out, and determined in the affirmative—yeas 21, nays 6, as follows:

YEAS—Messrs. Barbour, Barry, Bibb, Brown, Chace, Fromentin, Gaillard, Giles, Gore, Horsey, Howell, Hunter, Kerr, King, Lacock, Morrow, Smith, Tait, Taylor, Varnum, and Wells.

NAYS—Messrs. Dana, Goldsborough, Talbot, Thompson, Turner, and Wharton.

On the question, to insert "fifteen," in lieu of "six," stricken out, it was determined in the affirmative—yeas 18, nays 10, as follows:

YEAS—Messrs. Barry, Bibb, Brown, Chace, Fromentin, Gaillard, Giles, Gore, Howell, Kerr, King, Lacock, Morrow, Smith, Tait, Taylor, Varnum, and Wells.

NAYS—Messrs. Barbour, Daggett, Dana, Goldsborough, Horsey, Hunter, Talbot, Thompson, Turner, and Wharton.

On the question to agree to the third amendment proposed, to wit: Section 3, line 1, strike out "one Major General," and insert "two Major Generals," it was determined in the affirmative—yeas 20, nays 5, as follows:

YEAS—Messrs. Bibb, Brown, Chace, Fromentin, Gaillard, Giles, Gore, Horsey, Howell, Hunter, King, Lacock, Morrow, Smith, Talbot, Tait, Taylor, Thompson, Varnum, and Wells.

NAYS—Messrs. Daggett, Dana, Goldsborough, Turner, and Wharton.

And the other amendments having been agreed to, the President reported the bill to the House accordingly; and, on motion, by Mr. BIBB, the bill was further amended.

On the question, Shall the amendments be engrossed, and the bill read a third time as amended? it was determined in the affirmative.

The amendments to the last mentioned bill having been reported by the Committee correctly engrossed, the bill was read a third time as amended, by unanimous consent.

Resolved, That this bill pass with amendments.

On motion, by Mr. BIBB, it was agreed to amend the title, to read "An act reducing the military establishment of the United States."

Mr. BIBB, from the committee to whom was referred the bill, entitled "An act to vest more effectually in the State courts, and in the district courts of the United States, jurisdiction in the cases therein mentioned," reported it without amendment.

The Senate resumed the bill for the relief of Arthur Tappan and John Frothingham; and, on motion, by Mr. BIBB, the further consideration thereof was postponed to the second Monday in March instant.

The Senate resumed the consideration of the motion made the 1st instant, by Mr. KING; and, on his motion having been amended, was agreed to, as follows:

Resolved, That the President of the United States be, and he is hereby, requested to give instructions to the Secretary of War—

To prepare and lay before the Senate, at the commencement of their next session, a report concerning the annuities and presents granted to, and the trade carried on with, the several Indian tribes within the limits of the United States, during four years antecedent to the 4th of March, 1815; and, in order that such report may exhibit a full view of the whole Indian trade during the term aforesaid, that the President be further requested to direct the Superintendent of Indian Trade, and every other public agent concerned therein, to furnish to the Secretary of War such accounts and statements as he may call for, to enable him to prepare and make the report aforesaid.

That the said report do contain an annual account of the Indian trade, at each of the agencies or trading houses, or wheresoever else the same shall have been carried on, including therein the expenses of buildings, transportation, and all other incidental charges; as also a statement of losses, whether of goods or effects, intended for the Indians or received from them.

Also, a like annual account of the whole of the Indian trade.

Also, a general account of the Indian trade, exhibiting the profit and loss thereof during the term aforesaid.

Also, an account of the annuities and presents due, paid, and delivered, to the respective Indian tribes during the aforesaid terms; specifying the dates when the same were due, and when they were paid and delivered.

That the Secretary do furthermore report to the Senate his opinion, whether any alteration of the powers and duties of the several officers and agents employed in the superintendence and management of Indian affairs would be advantageous; whether the consolidation of the whole care and management thereof, and the placing of the same in a single department, would be expedient; and whether a plan may not be devised that will be equally advantageous to the Indian tribes, and more economical to the public, whereby the Indian trade may, under safeguards, be hereafter carried on by individuals or by private companies, instead of the manner in which the same is now conducted.

SALE OF CAPTURED NEGROES.

The following Message was received from the PRESIDENT OF THE UNITED STATES:

To the Senate of the United States:

I transmit to the Senate a report from the acting Secretary of State, complying with their resolution of the 24th of October last.

JAMES MADISON.

WASHINGTON, *February* 28, 1815.

The Message and report therein referred to were read, and ordered to be printed.

The report is as follows:

DEPARTMENT OF STATE, *Feb.* 28, 1815.

The undersigned, acting as Secretary of State, to whom was referred the resolution of the Senate of the 24th of October last, requesting the President of the United States to lay before the Senate, (provided he shall not consider the same improper to be communicated,) the proof of any traffic carried on in the West Indies, by the sale of negroes taken from the United States, by the British forces since the present war, has the honor to state, that such proof was transmitted to the Executive by the Hon. St. George Tucker, in the form of an affidavit of Captain Williams, from which it appeared that he had been a prisoner in the Bahama islands, and that, while there, he had been present at the sale of negroes taken from the vicinity of Norfolk and Hampton. This affidavit, voluntarily given, and strengthened and corroborated by a variety of circumstances, was considered at the time as full proof of the fact, and was transmitted to our Ministers at Ghent. When the resolution of the Senate was transmitted to this Department, application was made to Judge Tucker, and subsequently to Major Griffin, for the original affidavit, or for an authenticated copy; as neither have yet been received, and as it is deemed improper longer to delay this report, the undersigned begs leave to refer to the accompanying papers, marked 1, 2, 3, and 4, from which the material facts stated in the affidavit may be collected, and the circumstances which have prevented its transmission to this Department explained. This subject will be further investigated with a view to place it, in all its circumstances, in the most satisfactory light.

All which is respectfully submitted,

JAS. MONROE.

No. 1.

RICHMOND, *November* 24, 1814.

SIR: I do myself the honor to enclose you a letter from my friend, Mr. Cabell, and one from Mr. John Tabb Smith, the magistrate before whom the affidavit was made, a copy of which I transmitted to the President. Mr. Campbell has written to Major Griffin to endeavor to procure the original, and if he should fortunately obtain it, I will lose no time in forwarding it to you.

I have the honor to be, very respectfully, sir, your most obedient servant,

ST. G. TUCKER.

JOHN GRAHAM, Esq.,
Department of State, Washington.

No. 2.

Copy of a letter from Joseph C. Cabell, Esq., to the Hon. St. George Tucker, dated

RICHMOND, *November* 22, 1814.

MY DEAR SIR: I have received your favor of the 14th instant, embracing an extract from the letter recently written to you by Mr. Graham, of the Department of State, on the subject of the resolution of the Senate of the United States, of the 24th ultimo.

I distinctly recollect all the material circumstances in regard to the affidavit, which you forwarded to the President. About the period that Major Thomas Griffin, of York, went on board the British squadron in Lynnhaven bay, for the purpose of endeavoring to recover his negroes, who had gone off to the enemy, I happened to be in Williamsburg. The destination of the slaves that had been taken or received by the British, was then a subject of curiosity and concern throughout the lower country. I understood that a seafaring man, of the name of Williams, who had been a prisoner with the enemy, and had recently arrived at Hampton, had gone in company with Major Thomas Griffin, of York, before John Tabb Smith, a respectable magistrate of the county of Elizabeth City, and had made oath that, while a prisoner in one of the Bahama islands, he had been present at the sale of the negroes that had been carried off from the vicinity of Hampton and Norfolk; that the negroes were sold at a high price, and that a negro carpenter from Norfolk was purchased for a thousand dollars. Several gentlemen of the first respectability, who had conversed with Major Griffin, informed me that he spoke of Williams as a man whose appearance entitled him to credit, and that he had, accordingly, published the affidavit in the town of York. Through the medium of Mr. Coke, of Williamsburg, I procured a copy of this paper, which I handed to you, and was forwarded by you to the President. This affidavit was a subject of general conversation about that time. The circumstances under which Williams arrived at Hampton; the manner in which he described the negroes sold in the Bahamas, and particularly the carpenter from Norfolk, and the appearance of entire sincerity in his narrative, left no doubt, I was assured, on the mind of either Mr. Smith or Major Griffin, that the alleged sale had actually taken place. I did not see Major Griffin, nor did I inquire what he intended to do with the original affidavit of Williams; my conjecture was, that he would send it on to the committee of Congress, charged with the business of collecting proofs of the barbarous conduct of the war by the enemy. As it seems he has not done so, I presume

it remains in his possession. I will write immediately to him, with the view of ascertaining whether this be the fact; and, if it be, to request the favor of him to enclose me the affidavit. The result of my inquiries of that gentleman shall be made known to you without delay.

In the interim, I remain most respectfully and sincerely, yours, &c.

JOSEPH C. CABELL.

No. 3.

Copy of a letter from John Tabb Smith Esq., to Judge Tucker, dated

HAMPTON, *Nov.* 21, 1814.

SIR: Your favor I have now before me. Some time in the year 1813, there came before me a Captain Williams (I think his name was) in company with Major Thomas Griffin, of York, with the affidavit you speak of in your letter, which he swore to before me, and I gave my certificate thereto; I then gave the affidavit to Major Griffin, and expected to see it published in one of the Richmond papers, but never heard of it since; but from your letter, I expect the original can be got from Major Griffin. But, if it is mislaid, I well recollect the substance of the affidavit, and will render you any service in my power.

I am, with respect,

JOHN TABB SMITH.

If it can be got from Major Griffin, it had better be in the Captain's own words, with my certificate.

ST. GEORGE TUCKER, Esq., &c.   J. T. S.

No. 4.

YORK, (VA.) *February* 16, 1815.

SIR: Your favor of the 6th instant has been received. I have examined my papers and cannot find the original affidavit of Captain Williams, therein alluded to. The copy I gave Mr. Cabell was literally correct; the original has been mislaid, or I fear lost in the bustle of moving papers from hence so frequently as has been done, to place them without the reach of the enemy during the war. I will again examine and endeavor to recover the affidavit, and will forward the same to the Department of State as soon as it shall be recovered.

Very respectfully, I am, sir, your obedient servant,

THOMAS GRIFFIN.

JOHN GRAHAM, Esq.,
Department of State, Washington.

Sketch of Plunder, by Admiral Cockburn and his officers, on St. Simon's Island, during his late visit there.

[From the Savannah Republican.]

Major Butler—Two hundred negroes; ten bales of cotton; a quantity of seed cotton; his iron, new and old; leather, tanned and half tanned; stock of wine, liquors, soap, candles, and poultry; plate, and stockbuckle, stolen by an officer named Horton.

John Couper—Eighty negroes, forty-eight of them prime fellows, some of them tradesmen; ten bales of cotton.

Dr. Grant—One negro woman; four bales cotton; all his furniture destroyed; gins spoiled in trying to gin cotton.

A. C. Wylly—Forty-six of the primest of his negroes; no cotton.

J. H. Geehot—Eleven negroes; a pair of razors, and part of a barrel of flour, stolen by Lieutenant DeThierry.

W. McIntosh—Five negroes; twelve bales ginned and some unginned cotton.

James Hamilton—One hundred and eighty-two negroes; only one old man left on his place, and he mad; twenty-five bales cotton—about eighteen ginned by themselves; all his plantation stores, medicines, tools, paint pots, old iron, and gin boxes; some handsaw files, pocketed by the Commander-in-Chief, Ramsay; carpet, library, and a pair of pistols, stolen by Cole, who commanded the land forces; a beautiful fowling piece stolen by Horton, the same officer who stole Major Butler's spoons and stock-buckle.

E. Matthews—Twenty-six negroes; seven bales cotton.

Mrs. Brailsford—House broken open, and robbed by a boat's crew under command of a Lieutenant Grant—some of Mrs. Brailsford's and Mrs. Troup's clothes were bought for ten dollars from the thieves by Lieutenant Locke, commanding His Britannic Majesty's brig Manly.

Mr. Abbott—Although they made headquarters of his house and lived on him only now and then, bringing in some plundered mutton, poultry, flour and liquor, lost the contents of his store and had the quicksilver scraped from the back of all the broken looking glasses in the house.

In secret session—

The bill from the House of Representatives, entitled "An act for the protection of the commerce of the United States against the Algerine cruisers," was read the third time.

On the question, Shall this bill pass? it was determined in the affirmative—yeas 27, nays 2, as follows:

YEAS—Messrs. Barbour, Barry, Bibb, Brown, Chace, Daggett, Dana, Fromentin, Gaillard, Giles, Gore, Horsey, Hunter, Kerr, King, Lacock, Morrow, Robinson, Smith, Talbot, Tait, Taylor, Thompson, Turner, Varnum, Wells, and Wharton.

NAYS—Messrs. Goldsborough and Lambert.

Resolved, That a committee be appointed to notify the House of Representatives, confidentially, that the Senate have passed the said bill.

Ordered, That Messrs. FROMENTIN and GOLDSBOROUGH be the committee.

FRIDAY, March 3.

A message from the House of Representatives informed the Senate that the House disagree to the amendments of the Senate to the bill entitled "An act fixing the Military Peace Establishment of the United States." They have passed a bill, entitled "An act to authorize a loan for a sum not exceeding eighteen millions four hundred and fifty-two thousand eight hundred dollars;" in which bill they request the concurrence of the Senate.

The bill last mentioned was read three times by unanimous consent, and passed.

The Senate proceeded to consider their amendments disagreed to by the House of Representatives to the bill, entitled "An act fixing the Military Peace Establishment of the United States." Whereupon, on motion, by Mr. GILES,

Resolved, That they insist thereon.

Mr. GILES, from the Committee on Military Affairs, to whom was referred the bill, entitled "An act concerning invalid pensioners," reported it with amendments, which were considered as in Committee of the Whole; and having been agreed to, the President reported the bill to the House accordingly.

On the question, Shall the amendments be engrossed and the bill read a third time as amended? it was determined in the affirmative.

The amendments to the last mentioned bill having been reported by the committee correctly engrossed, the bill was read a third time as amended, by unanimous consent; and was further amended by consent.

Resolved, That this bill pass with amendments.

A message from the House of Representatives informed the Senate that the House insist on their disagreement to, and ask a conference on, the disagreeing votes of the two Houses on the amendments to the bill, entitled "An act fixing the Military Peace Establishment of the United States; and have appointed managers on their part. They have passed a bill, entitled "An act authorizing the purchase of vessels captured on Lake Champlain;" in which bill they request the concurrence of the Senate.

The last mentioned bill was read three times by unanimous consent and passed.

On motion by Mr. GILES,

Resolved, That the Senate agree to the conference proposed on the disagreeing votes of the two Houses on the amendments to the bill, entitled "An act fixing the Military Peace Establishment of the United States."

Ordered, That Messrs. GILES, SMITH, and KING, be the managers on the part of the Senate.

The Senate resumed, as in Committee of the Whole, the consideration of the bill, entitled "An act to authorize the payment for property lost, captured, or destroyed by the enemy, while in the military service of the United States," together with the amendments proposed thereto.

Mr. VARNUM was requested to take the Chair, and the bill having been amended, the President resumed the Chair, and it was reported to the House accordingly.

On the question, Shall the amendments be engrossed and the bill be read a third time as amended? it was determined in the affirmative.

The amendments to the last mentioned bill having been reported by the committee correctly engrossed, the bill was read a third time as amended, by unanimous consent.

Resolved, That this bill pass with amendments.

A message from the House of Representatives informed the Senate that the House have passed a bill, entitled "An act making an additional appropriation for the service of the year 1815;" in which bill they request the concurrence of the Senate.

The bill last brought up for concurrence was read three times by unanimous consent, and passed.

The Senate resumed, as in Committee of the

293

HISTORY OF CONGRESS.

294

MARCH, 1815.

Retaliating System.

SENATE.

Whole, the consideration of the bill, entitled "An act to vest more effectually in the State courts, and in the district courts of the United States, jurisdiction in the cases therein mentioned;" and Mr. VARNUM was requested to take the Chair; and the bill having been amended, the President resumed the chair, and Mr. VARNUM reported the bill to the House accordingly.

On the question, Shall the amendment be engrossed and the bill be read a third time as amended? it was determined in the affirmative.

The amendment to the last mentioned bill having been reported by the committee correctly engrossed, the bill was read a third time as amended, by unanimous consent, and passed with an amendment.

On motion, by Mr. TAIT, the Committee on Naval Affairs, who were instructed, by the resolution of the 6th of January, to inquire into the expediency of establishing a Naval school, were discharged from the further consideration thereof.

On motion, by Mr. TAIT, the Committee on Naval Affairs, to whom was referred the memorial of George P. Stephenson, and others, merchants and ship-owners of the city of Baltimore, were discharged from the further consideration thereof.

On motion, by Mr. TAIT, the Committee on Naval Affairs, to whom was referred the memorial of a number of midshipmen in the United States' Navy, against the appointment of sailing-masters to be lieutenants, were discharged from the further consideration thereof.

The credentials of the Hon. CHRISTOPHER GORE, appointed a Senator by the Legislature of the Commonwealth of Massachusetts, for the term of six years, commencing on the fourth day of March next, were read, and laid on file.

A message from the House of Representatives informed the Senate that the House have passed a bill, entitled "An act for the relief of Charles Todd;" a bill, entitled "An act for the relief of the Eastern Branch Bridge Company;" also, the bill, entitled "An act authorizing the Board of Navy Commissioners to appoint clerks;" in which bills they request the concurrence of the Senate.

The three bills last mentioned were read, and passed to the second reading.

The bill, entitled "An act for the relief of the Eastern Branch Bridge Company," was read the second time by unanimous consent, and considered as in Committee of the Whole, and passed to a third reading; and the bill was read a third time, by unanimous consent, and passed.

The bill, entitled "An act authorizing the Board of Navy Commissioners to appoint clerks," was read the second time, and considered as in Committee of the Whole, and passed to a third reading; and the bill was read a third time, by unanimous consent, and passed.

The bill, entitled "An act for the relief of Charles Todd," was read the second time by unanimous consent, and, on motion by Mr. LACOCK, the further consideration thereof was postponed to the fourth day of March next.

RETALIATING SYSTEM.

Mr. BIBB, from the Committee on Foreign Relations, to whom was referred the Message of the President of the United States, of the 26th of September last, respecting the unauthorized mode of warfare adopted by the enemy, on the plea of retaliation, made a report; which was read, and ordered to be printed.

The report of the committee is as follows:

That, although the war has happily terminated, they deem it important to rescue the American Government from unworthy imputations, with which it has been assailed during its progress. They have, therefore, endeavored to ascertain, whether the destruction of York, in Upper Canada, and the other cases assumed by our late enemy, as authorizing a departure from the settled rules of civilized warfare, were of a character to justify or extenuate their conduct.

The result of the inquiries of the committee, manifesting to the world that the plea which has been advanced for the destruction of the American Capitol, and the plunder of private property, is without foundation, will be found in the communications of the Secretaries of the Departments of War and Navy, and of General Dearborn, commander of the American forces, in the attack on York, herewith submitted.

DEPARTMENT OF STATE, *Feb.* 28, 1815.

SIR: I have had the honor to receive your letter, requesting, on behalf of the Committee of Foreign Relations, any information which this Department possesses, relative to the misconduct that has been imputed to the American troops in Upper Canada during the late war, and in reply, I have the honor to state, that the charges appear to be confined to three: 1st, the alleged burning of York; 2d, the burning of Newark; and 3d, the burning of the Indian villages, usually called the Moravian towns.

1st. The burning of York, or of any of its public edifices, or of any its private houses, has never been presented to the view of the American Government by its own officers, as matter of information; and it never was exhibited by the British Government, or any of its officers, as matter of complaint, until it was asserted in the address of the Governor in Chief to the Provincial Parliament of Canada, on the 24th of January, 1815, "that, as a just retribution, the proud Capitol at Washington has experienced a similar fate to that inflicted by an American force on the Seat of Government in Upper Canada." This assertion having led to an inquiry, I am enabled, from official documents and general information, to state the following facts of the case, for the information of the committee.

The town of York in Upper Canada was taken by the American Army, under the command of General Dearborn, on the 27th of April 1813, and it was evacuated on the succeeding 1st of May; although it was again visited for a day, by an American squadron, under the command of Commodore Chauncey, on the 4th of August. At the time of the capture, the British troops on their retreat set fire to their magazine, and great injury was done by the explosion to property, as well as to persons, within the range of its effects. At the time of the capture, as well as at the time of Commodore Chauncey's visit, the public stores were seized, and the public storehouses were destroyed; but the destruction of public edifices for civil uses, or of private property, was not only unauthorized, but positively forbidden, by the American commanders; and it is understood that no private house was destroyed by the American troops. It has recently, however, appeared, that a public building of little value, called the Parliament House, (not the Government House,) in which it is said that an American scalp was found as a part of the decoration of the Speaker's Chair, had been burnt; whether it was so, and if it was, whether it was an accidental consequence of the confusion, in which the explosion of the magazine involved the town, or the unauthorized act of some exasperated individual, has not been ascertained. The silence of the military and civil officers of the Provincial Government of Canada seems to indicate, that the transaction was not deemed, when it occurred, a cause either for retaliation or reproach.

2d. The burning of Newark, adjacent to Fort George, occurred on the 10th of December, 1813. The act was vindicated by the American General, as necessary to his military operations; but as soon as the American Government heard of it, instructions, dated the 6th of January, 1814, were given by the Department of War, to Major General Wilkinson, "to disavow the conduct of the officer who committed it, and to transmit to Governor Prevost a copy of the order under color of which that officer had acted." This disavowal was accordingly communicated, and on the 10th of February, 1814, Governor Prevost answered, "that it had been with great satisfaction he had received the assurance, that the perpetration of the burning of the town of Newark was both unauthorized by the American Government and abhorrent to every American feeling; that if any outrages had ensued the wanton and unjustifiable destruction of Newark, passing the bounds of just retaliation, they were to be attributed to the influence of irritated passions, on the part of the unfortunate sufferers by that event, which, in a state of active warfare, it had not been possible altogether to restrain, and that it was as little congenial to the disposition of His Majesty's Government, as it was to that of the Government of the United States, deliberately to adopt any plan of policy which had for its object the devastation of private property."

But the disavowal of the American Government was not the only expiation of the unauthorized offence committed by its officer; for, the British Government undertook itself to redress the wrong. A few days after the burning of Newark, the British and Indian troops crossed the Niagara for this purpose; they surprised and seized Fort Niagara; they burnt the villages of Lewistown, Manchester, Tuscarora, Buffalo, and Black Rock, desolating the whole of the Niagara frontier, and dispersing the inhabitants, in the extremity of the Winter. Sir George Prevost himself appears to have been satisfied with the vengeance that had been inflicted; and, in his proclamation of the 12th of January, 1814, he expressly declared, that for the burning of Newark, "the opportunity of punishment had occurred; that a full measure of retaliation had taken place, and that it was not his intention to pursue further a system of warfare so revolting to his own feelings, and so little congenial to the British character, unless the future measures of the enemy should compel him again to resort to it." With his answer to Major General Wilkinson, which has been already noticed, he transmitted a copy of the proclamation, "as expressive of the determination as to his future line of conduct," and added, "that he was happy to learn that there was no probability that any measures, on the part of the American Government, would oblige him to depart from it."

3d. The places usually called the Moravian towns, were mere collections of Indian huts and cabins, on the river Retrench or Thames, not probably worth, in the whole, one thousand dollars. The Indians who inhabited them, among whom were some notoriously hostile to the United States, had made incursions the most cruel into their territory. When, therefore, the American Army under General Harrison invaded Canada on the —— of —— 1813, the huts and cabins of the hostile Indians were destroyed. But this species of warfare has been invariably pursued, by every nation engaged in war with the Indians of the American continent. However it may be regretted on the score of humanity, it appears to be the necessary means of averting the still greater calamities of savage hostilities; and it is believed that the occurrence would never have been made the subject of a charge against the American troops, if the fact had not been misrepresented or misunderstood. Many people at home, and most people abroad, have been led to suppose that the Moravian towns were the peaceable settlements of a religious sect of Christians, and not the abode of a hostile tribe of savages. I have the honor to be, &c.

           JAMES MONROE.

Hon. WILLIAM W. BIBB,
    Chairman Com. of Foreign Relations.

        NAVY DEPARTMENT, *Feb.* 18, 1815.

SIR: In compliance with the request of the committee of the Senate, communicated to me by your note of the 14th current, I have the honor to transmit to you, herewith, extracts from the letters of Commodore Chauncey to the Secretary of the Navy, on the subject of destroying the public store-houses and stores at York, in Upper Canada, and which is all the information in this Department on that subject.

I have the honor to be, very respectfully, sir, your obedient servant,

        B. W. CROWNINSHIELD.

Hon. WM. W. BIBB,
    Chairman Committee, &c.

Extract of a letter from Commodore Isaac Chauncey to the Secretary of the Navy, dated off York, U. C., April 20, 1813.

"The enemy set fire to some of his principal stores, containing large quantities of naval and military stores, as well as a large ship upon the stocks, nearly finished."

From the same to the same, dated off Niagara, August 4, 1813.

"In the evening of the 30th ultimo, we weighed and stood for York, arrived and anchored in that harbor, at about 3 P. M.; on the 31st ran the schooners into the upper harbor, landed the marines and soldiers under the command of Colonel Scott, without opposition; found several hundred barrels of flour and provisions in the public store-houses, five pieces of cannon, eleven boats, and a quantity of shot, shells, and other stores; all which was either destroyed or brought away. On the first instant, after having received on board all that the vessels could take, I directed the barracks and the public store-houses to be burned. We then re-embarked the men, and proceeded to this place, where I arrived yesterday."

Letter from Gen. Henry Dearborn to the Honorable Joseph B. Varnum, a member of the Senate.

BOSTON, *October* 17, 1814.

DEAR SIR: In reply to your letter of the 11th instant, I assure you, in the most explicit manner, that no public or private buildings were burned or destroyed by the troops under my command, at York, in Upper Canada, excepting two block-houses, and one or two sheds belonging to the Navy Yard. I placed a strong guard in the town, with positive orders to prevent any plunder or depredation on the inhabitants; and, when leaving the place, a letter was received from Judge Scott, chief justice of the superior court, in which he expressed his thanks for the humane treatment the inhabitants had experienced from our troops, and for my particular attention to the safety of their persons and property: A frigate on the stocks, and a large store-house containing their naval stores, were set on fire by the enemy subsequent to their offer of surrendering the troops and public property. Several of the most valuable public buildings, connected with their principal military positions, were destroyed by the explosion of their magazine, which proved so fatal to our troops; and although there were strong provocations for burning or destroying the town, nothing of the kind took place more than I have already mentioned, either by the army or navy.

Yours, with respectful esteem,

H. DEARBORN.

Hon. JOSEPH B. VARNUM.

The Senate adjourned to six o'clock in the evening.

Six o'clock in the evening.

A message from the House of Representatives informed the Senate that they have concurred in the report of the committee of conference in the disagreeing votes of the two Houses on the amendments to the bill, entitled "An act fixing the Military Peace Establishment of the United States," and that the bill be amended accordingly.

Mr. GILES, from the managers at the conference on the disagreeing votes of the two Houses on the amendments to the bill, entitled "An act fixing the Military Peace Establishment of the United States," made the following report:

That, after due consideration of the various questions involved therein, they have agreed to recommend to the adoption of the Senate and House of Representatives the following modification:

That the Senate recede from the first amendment proposed to the bill.

That, in lieu of the second amendment proposed, the two Houses agree to substitute the word *ten*, for the word *fifteen.*

That the House of Representatives recede from their disagreement to all the other amendments proposed by the Senate.

That the Senate recede from their amendment to the title.

The Senate proceeded to consider the said report; and, having agreed to the first member thereof, on the question to agree to the second member, to substitute the word *ten* for *fifteen*, it was determined in the affirmative—yeas 15, nays 8, as follows:

YEAS—Messrs. Barbour, Barry, Bibb, Chace, Dag-

gett, Giles, Gore, King, Lambert, Morrow, Talbot, Tait, Thompson, Turner, and Wharton.

NAYS—Messrs. Brown, Dana, Fromentin, Gaillard, Lacock, Smith, Varnum, and Wells.

And the other members of the report having been agreed to, it was *Resolved*, That the Senate concur in the report, and that the bill be amended accordingly.

Mr. DAGGETT presented the memorial of Robert Sewall, praying compensation for the loss and destruction of property in the City of Washington, by the enemy, which was occasioned by having his house converted into a military fortress, as is stated in the memorial; which was read.

On motion, by Mr. BIBB, the Committee on Foreign Relations, to whom was referred the message of the President of the United States, recommending a declaration of war, by the United States, against the Dey and Regency of Algiers, were discharged from the further consideration thereof

On motion, by Mr. DANA,

Resolved, That the injunction of secrecy be removed respecting the proceedings on the Message of the President of the United States recommending a declaration of war by the United States against the Dey and Regency of Algiers, and on the bill, entitled "An act for the protection of the commerce of the United States against the Algerine cruisers."

[For these proceedings, see February 23, and March 1 and 2, *ante*.]

Mr. SMITH, from the Committee on Military Affairs, to whom was referred the bill, entitled "An act making appropriations for the support of the Military Establishment for the year 1815," reported it with amendments, which were read, and considered as in Committee of the Whole; and, having been agreed to, the President reported the bill to the House accordingly.

On the question, Shall the amendments be engrossed and the bill be read a third time as amended? it was determined in the affirmative.

The amendments to the last mentioned bill having been reported by the committee correctly engrossed, the bill was read a third time as amended, by unanimous consent.

Resolved, That this bill pass with amendments.

On motion, by Mr. VARNUM, the Committee on the Militia of the United States, to whom was referred so much of the Message of the President of the United States, of the 20th February, as relates to the militia, were discharged from the further consideration thereof.

Mr. WHARTON presented a petition signed by a great number of the inhabitants of the State of Tennessee, remonstrating against the transportation and opening of the mail on the Sabbath; and the petition was read.

A message from the House of Representatives informed the Senate that the House agree to some, and disagree to other amendments of the Senate to the bill, entitled "An act to authorize the payment for property lost, captured, or destroyed by the enemy, while in the military service of the United States."

299   HISTORY OF CONGRESS.   300

SENATE.   *Proceedings.*   MARCH, 1815.

The Senate proceeded to consider their amendments to the last mentioned bill, which have been disagreed to by the House of Representatives.

On motion, by Mr. KING, that the further consideration thereof be postponed to the second Monday in March instant, it was determined in the affirmative—yeas 12, nays 9, as follows:

YEAS—Messrs. Bibb, Daggett, Dana, Gaillard, Goldsborough, Gore, King, Lambert, Tait, Thompson, Turner, and Varnum.

NAYS—Messrs. Barbour, Barry, Brown, Chace, Lacock, Morrow, Smith, Talbot, and Wharton.

A message from the House of Representatives informed the Senate that the House have passed a resolution for the appointment of a joint committee to wait on the President of the United States, and notify him of the intended recess, and have appointed a committee on their part, in which they request the concurrence of the Senate.

The Senate proceeded to consider the resolution last mentioned, and concurred therein.

Ordered, That Messrs. CHACE and BARBOUR be the committee on the part of the Senate.

Mr. CHACE reported, from the joint committee, that they had waited on the President of the United States, who informed them that he had no further communication to make to the two Houses of Congress.

Mr. KING submitted the following resolution, which was read, and passed to the second reading

Resolved, That the sum of three hundred dollars be advanced out of the contingent fund to Samuel Turner, John G. McDonald, and Lewis H. Machen, clerks in the office of the Secretary of the Senate, to each of them, respectively, for their services during the current year.

On the question, Shall this resolution be now read the second time? it was objected to by Mr. VARNUM as against the rule.

A message from the House of Representatives informed the Senate that the House, having finished the business before them, are about to adjourn.

Ordered, That the Secretary inform the House of Representatives that the Senate, having finished the Legislative business before them, are about to adjourn.

Whereupon, the President adjourned the Senate without day.

PROCEEDINGS AND DEBATES

OF THE

HOUSE OF REPRESENTATIVES OF THE UNITED STATES,

AT THE THIRD SESSION OF THE THIRTEENTH CONGRESS, BEGUN AT THE CITY OF WASHINGTON, MONDAY, SEPTEMBER 19, 1814.

MONDAY, September 19, 1814.

This being the day appointed by proclamation of the President of the United States, dated on the 8th day of August, 1814, for the meeting of Congress, LANGDON CHEVES, the Speaker, PATRICK MAGRUDER, the Clerk, and the following members of the House of Representatives, appeared, and took their seats, to wit:

From New Hampshire—Roger Vose.

From Massachusetts—Elijah Brigham, William Ely, Levi Hubbard, Cyrus King, Nathaniel Ruggles, and Artemas Ward.

From Connecticut—Epaphroditus Champion, John Davenport, jr., Jonathan O. Moseley, and Lewis B. Sturges.

From Vermont—William C. Bradley, James Fisk, Richard Skinner, William Strong, and Charles Rich.

From New York—Daniel Avery, Alexander Boyd, Oliver C. Comstock, Peter Denoyelles, Jonathan Fisk, James Geddes, Thomas, P. Grosvenor, Moss Kent, John Lovett, Jacob Markell, Hosea Moffit, Thomas J. Oakley, Jotham Post, jr., and Ebenezer Sage.

From Pennsylvania—William Anderson, David Bard, Robert Brown, John Conard, Roger Davis, Charles J. Ingersoll, Samuel D. Ingham, Jared Irwin, Aaron Lyle, William Piper, John Rea, Adam Seybert, Adamson Tannehill, Daniel Udree, and Thomas Wilson.

From Delaware—Thomas Cooper.

From Maryland—Stevenson Archer, Alexander C. Hanson, Joseph Kent, and Philip Stuart.

From Virginia—Thomas M. Bayly, William A. Burwell, Hugh Caperton, John W. Eppes, Thomas Gholson, Peterson Goodwyn, Aylet Hawes, John Kerr, Joseph Lewis, jr., William McCoy, Thomas Newton, James Pleasants, jr., John Roane, John Smith, and Francis White.

From North Carolina—Willis Alston, John Culpeper, Peter Forney, William Gaston, Nathaniel Macon, William H. Murfree, Joseph Pearson, Richard Stanford, and Bartlett Yancey.

From South Carolina—Langdon Cheves, (Speaker,) David R. Evans, Samuel Farrow, Theodore Gourdin, and Thomas Kershaw.

From Georgia—Alfred Cuthbert and John Forsyth.

From Kentucky—James Clarke, Joseph H. Hawkins, Joseph Desha, Richard M. Johnson, Thomas Montgomery, Stephen Ormsby, and Solomon P. Sharp,

From Tennessee—John H. Bowen, Thomas K. Harris, Perry W. Humphreys, John Rhea, and John Sevier.

From Ohio—John Alexander, James Caldwell, William Creighton, jr., and John McLean.

A quorum, consisting of a majority of the whole House, being present, a committee was appointed, on the part of this House, to join such committee as may be appointed on the part of the Senate, to wait on the President of the United States, and inform him that a quorum of the two Houses is assembled, and ready to receive any communications that he may be pleased to make to them; and Mr. MACON and Mr. OAKLEY were appointed the committee.

A new member, to wit: PHILIP P. BARBOUR, elected to supply the vacancy occasioned by the death of John Dawson, one of the members from the State of Virginia, also appeared, produced his credentials, was qualified, and took his seat.

WILLIAM LATTIMORE, the delegate from the Mississippi Territory, appeared, and took his seat.

A message from the Senate informed the House that a quorum of the Senate is assembled, and that they are ready to proceed to business. They have appointed a committee, on their part, to join such committee as may be appointed on the part of this House, to wait on the President of the United States, and notify him that a quorum of the two Houses is assembled, and ready to receive any communications he may be pleased to make to them.

On motion of Mr. FISK, of New York, the Clerk was directed to procure newspapers from any number of offices that the members may elect, provided, that the expense thereof do not exceed the price of three daily papers.

TUESDAY, September 20.

Several other members, to wit: From Massachusetts, LABAN WHEATON, JOHN REED, and WILLIAM BAYLIES; from Pennsylvania, WILLIAM CRAWFORD, and ISAAC GRIFFIN; from Virginia, JOHN G. JACKSON; from North Carolina, MESHACK FRANKLIN; from Georgia, BOLLING HALL, GEORGE M. TROUP, and WILLIAM BARNETT; and

303   **HISTORY OF CONGRESS.**   304

H. of R.   *Standing Committees—The President's Message.*   September, 1814.

from Kentucky, SAMUEL McKEE; appeared, and took their seats.

JONATHAN JENNINGS, the delegate from the Territory of Indiana, also appeared and took his seat.

Mr. MACON, from the joint committee appointed to wait on the President of the United States, and inform him that a quorum of the two Houses was assembled and ready to receive any communications he might be pleased to make to them, reported that they had performed that duty, and the President answered he would make a communication to the two Houses of Congress to-day at twelve o'clock.

A Message was then received from the PRESIDENT OF THE UNITED STATES, which was read, and committed to the Committee of the Whole on the state of the Union. [For this Message, see Senate proceedings of this date, *ante* page 12.]

WEDNESDAY, September 21.

Several other members, to wit: from Massachusetts, GEORGE BRADBURY; from Rhode Island, RICHARD JACKSON, junior; from Pennsylvania, WILLIAM FINDLEY and EDWARD CROUCH; from Maryland, CHARLES GOLDSBOROUGH; from North Carolina, WILLIAM R. KING; from South Carolina, DAVID R. EVANS and JOHN J. CHAPPELL; and from Georgia, THOMAS TELFAIR; appeared, and took their seats.

STANDING COMMITTEES.

On motion of Mr. FISK, of Vermont, the House proceeded to the appointment of the Standing Committees, pursuant to the rules and orders of the House; and the following were appointed:

Committee of Ways and Means.—Mr. Eppes, Mr. Fisk, of New York, Mr. Archer, Mr. Oakley, Mr. Gaston, Mr. Creighton, and Mr. Ingham.

Committee of Elections.—Mr. Fisk of Vermont, Mr. Goldsborough, Mr. Vose, Mr. Comstock, Mr. Anderson, Mr. Alston, and Mr. Harris.

Committee of Commerce and Manufactures.— Mr. Newton, Mr. Seybert, Mr. Murfree, Mr. Jackson of Rhode Island, Mr. Baylies, Mr. Gourdin, and Mr. Ruggles.

Committee of Claims.—Mr. Yancey, Mr. Sharp, Mr. Goodwyn, Mr. Davenport, Mr. Alexander, Mr. Bard, and Mr. Boyd.

Committee for the District of Columbia.—Mr. Kent of Maryland, Mr. Lewis, Mr. Crawford, Mr. Pearson, Mr. Bradley, Mr. White, and Mr. Denoyelles.

Committee on the Public Lands.—Mr. McKee, Mr. Humphreys, Mr. Montgomery, Mr. Moseley, Mr. Geddes, Mr. Irwin, and Mr. McCoy.

Committee on the Post Office and Post Roads.— Mr. Rhea of Tennessee, Mr. Lyle, Mr. Brigham, Mr. Bayly, Mr. Franklin, Mr. Hall, and Mr. Rich.

Committee on Pensions and Revolutionary Claims.—Mr. Chappell, Mr. Bowen, Mr. Wilson of Pennsylvania, Mr. Sage, Mr. Ely, Mr. Wilcox, and Mr. Conard.

Committee on Public Expenditures.—Mr. Macon, Mr. Findley, Mr. Champion, Mr. King of

North Carolina, Mr. Kent of New York, Mr. Hawkins, and Mr. Caldwell.

Committee of Revisal and Unfinished Business. Mr. Stanford, Mr. Wheaton, and Mr. Bradbury.

Committee of Accounts.—Mr. Kershaw. Mr. Barnett, and Mr. John Reed.

Committee on the Judiciary.—Mr. Ingersoll, Mr. Pleasants, Mr. Telfair, Mr. Sturges, Mr. Cooper, Mr. Fisk of Vermont, and Mr. Evans.

THE PRESIDENT'S MESSAGE.

The House resolved itself into a Committee of the Whole on the state of the Union; and, after some time spent therein, the Committee rose and reported the following resolutions, which were concurred in by the House:

1. *Resolved,* That so much of the Message of the President of the United States as relates to the subject of foreign affairs be referred to a select committee.

2. *Resolved,* That so much of the Message of the President of the United States as relates to our Military Establishment be referred to a select committee.

3. *Resolved,* That so much of the Message of the President of the United States as relates to our Naval Establishment be referred to a select committee.

4. *Resolved,* That so much of the Message of the President of the United States as relates to our revenue be referred to the Committee of Ways and Means.

5. *Resolved,* That so much of the Message of the President of the United States as relates to the classing and disciplining of the militia be referred to a select committee.

Mr. Forsyth, Mr. Clark, Mr. Ingersoll, Mr. Gholson, Mr. Grosvenor, Mr. Pearson, and Mr. McLean, were appointed a committee pursuant to the first resolution.

Mr. Troup, Mr. Johnson of Kentucky, Mr. Sevier, Mr. Stewart, Mr. Lovett, Mr. Tannehill, and Mr. Barbour, were appointed a committee pursuant to the second resolution.

Mr. Pleasants, Mr. Burwell, Mr. Seybert, Mr. King of Massachusetts, Mr. Ormsby, Mr. Post, and Mr. Ward, were appointed a committee pursuant to the third resolution.

Mr. Jackson of Virginia, Mr. Cuthbert, Mr. Desha, Mr. Hanson, Mr. Moseley, Mr. Piper, and Mr. Hubbard, were appointed a committee pursuant to the fifth resolution.

The following resolution was submitted by Mr. BRADLEY, for consideration:

Resolved, That, instead of the Committee of Commerce and Manufactures, there shall be appointed two standing committees, the one to be styled " a Committee of Commerce," and the other " a Committee of Manufactures," to consist of seven members each.

The resolution was read, and ordered to lie on the table.

THURSDAY, September 22.

Several other members, to wit: from New Hampshire, JEDUTHUN WILCOX; from New Jersey, RICHARD STOCKTON; from South Carolina, ELIAS EARLE; and from Kentucky, WILLIAM P. DUVALL, appeared and took their seats.

A new member, to wit: SAMUEL DANA, elected to supply the vacancy occasioned in the representation of the State of Massachusetts, by the resignation of William M. Richardson, appeared, was qualified, and took his seat.

Mr. JENNINGS presented a memorial of the Legislature of the Indiana Territory, praying that further time may be given to purchasers of public lands in said Territory, to complete their payments; that the price of the public lands may be reduced, and that the quarter sections may be subdivided.

The SPEAKER presented a memorial of the said Legislature, to the same effect with the memorial last stated.—Referred to the Committee on the Public Lands.

On motion of Mr. FISK, of Vermont,

Resolved, That the Committee on the Judiciary be instructed to inquire into the expediency of making further provisions, by law, for aiding and protecting the officers of the customs in the execution of their official duties, and for preventing intercourse with the enemy.

On motion of Mr. BRADLEY, the House proceeded to consider the resolution submitted by him yesterday, to amend the standing rules and orders, and the same being read, was again ordered to lie on the table.

On motion of Mr. DAVENPORT,

Resolved, That this House will, to-morrow, at twelve o'clock. proceed to the election of a Chaplain on their part.

The following resolution was submitted by Mr. JOHNSON, of Kentucky, for consideration:

Resolved, That a committee be appointed to inquire into the causes of the capture of this city by the enemy; also, into the manner in which the public buildings and property were destroyed, and the amount in value of the property, public and private, so destroyed; and that they have power to send for persons and papers.

Mr. GOLDSBOROUGH, of Maryland, recommended that the resolution might be laid on the table. It appeared to him that the blowing up of Fort Warburton, and the occupation of Alexandria by the enemy, should be included in the inquiry.

Mr. JOHNSON assenting to the proposition, the resolution was laid on the table.

BURNING OF THE CAPITOL.

The SPEAKER laid before the House a letter from Patrick Magruder, Clerk to this House, detailing the circumstances attending the destruction of his office by the enemy; which was read, and referred to Messrs. PEARSON, TELFAIR, DUVALL, WINTER, WARD of New Jersey, KERSHAW, and KERR.

The letter is as follows:

CLERK'S OFFICE, HOUSE OF REPRESENTATIVES, *September 20, 1814.*

SIR: Being compelled to leave home the latter part of July, for the Springs, on account of indisposition; after leaving the clerks in charge of the office, with instructions as to their official duties, and a person in charge of the library of Congress, for the purpose of opening and airing the books, pursuant to the regulations thereof; during my absence, the invasion of this city was effected by the enemy, and the destruction of public property by them, in those departments immediately under my superintendence, ensued; and, for a more particular detail of the circumstances attending that disastrous event, I must, through you, refer to a statement of facts (submitted in a letter to me from the clerks, who were left in the office after the militia marched from the District) to the House, with a request that a committee may be raised for the purpose of investigating the subject-matter thereof, and report to the House accordingly; and, also, that the Committee of Accounts may be instructed to ascertain, as near as can be, the amount of money paid on account of the contingent expenses of the House, since the first day of January last, by the Clerk, that he may have credit for the same at the Treasury, as the public vouchers for the expenditure of the public money since that period have all been destroyed in the conflagration of the Capitol. Without the aid of such an ascertainment, by a committee of the House, justice cannot be done to the undersigned or the public.

I am, sir, with respect, yours, &c.
PATRICK MAGRUDER.

The SPEAKER *of the House of Reps.*

CITY OF WASHINGTON, *Sept. 15, 1814.*

SIR: In order to correct any erroneous statements or representations which may go, or have gone, out to the public, in relation to the destruction of your office, we deem it our duty to make the following statement of facts:

At the time you left the city, (which was in the latter part of the month of July,) for the Springs in Virginia and Pennsylvania, for the recovery of your health, all was quiet, and we believe no fears were entertained for the safety of the seat of Government. Indeed, nothing was heard of the enemy, except his marauding parties in the Chesapeake, and what was seen in the newspapers, of troops being ordered from Europe to America. About the middle of August it was stated that the enemy was in the bay, in great force, and, on the 19th of that month, the whole body of the militia of the District of Columbia was called out, under which call every clerk of the office was taken into the field, except Mr. Frost, and marched to meet the enemy.

On the 21st, the first of the undersigned clerks was furloughed, by Brigadier General Smith, at the request of Colonel George Magruder, for the purpose of returning to the city, to take care of, and save such part of the books and papers of the Clerk's office, as he might be able to effect, in case the enemy should get possession of the place; he arrived here in the night of that day.

His orders from Colonel George Magruder were, not to begin packing up until it was ascertained that the clerks at the War Office were engaged in that business; and it was not until 12 o'clock, on Monday, the 22d, that we were informed that they had begun to move the effects of that office, although we were subsequently told that it had commenced the day before.

We immediately went to packing up, and Mr. Burch went out in search of wagons or other carriages, for the transportation of the books and papers; every wagon, and almost every cart, belonging to the city, had been previously impressed into the service of the

United States, for the transportation of the baggage of the army; the few he was able to find were loaded with the private effects of individuals, who were moving without the city; those he attempted to hire, but, not succeeding, he claimed a right to impress them; but, having no legal authority, or military force to aid him, he, of course, did not succeed. He then sent off three messengers into the country, one of whom obtained from Mr. John Wilson, whose residence is six miles from the city, the use of a cart and four oxen; it did not arrive at the office, until after dark on Monday night, when it was immediately laden with the most valuable records and papers, which were taken, on the same night, nine miles, to a safe and secret place in the country. We continued to remove as many of the most valuable books and papers, having removed the manuscript records, as we were able to do with our one cart, until the morning of the day of the battle of Bladensburg, after which we were unable to take away anything further.

Everything belonging to the office, together with the library of Congress, we venture to say, might have been removed in time, if carriages could have been procured; but it was altogether impossible to procure them, either for hire, or by force.

The most material papers which have been lost are, the last volumes of the manuscript records of the Committees of Ways and Means, Claims and Pensions, and Revolutionary Claims; the clerks were engaged in bringing up these records previous to the alarm, and as it was not certain that the enemy would get to the city, and being desirous to have them completed, they were not packed away with the rest, but were kept out, that they might be finished by the meeting of Congress; but with the intention of taking them to a private residence, if such removal should be found necessary. After the defeat of our troops at Bladensburg, Mr. Frost removed them to the house commonly called General Washington's, which house being unexpectedly consumed by fire, these records were thus unfortunately lost.

The secret journal of Congress was also consumed; it was kept in a private drawer in the office, and in the hurry of removal was forgotten. Its contents, however, have been, in most cases, published by order of the House.

The manuscript papers, which have not been saved, were mostly of a private nature, consisting chiefly of petitions, and unimportant papers, presented previous to the year 1799.

We regret very much the loss of your private accounts and vouchers, among which, we are sorry to add, were the receipts and accounts of the expenditure of the contingent moneys of the House of Representatives; they were in the private drawer of Mr. George Magruder, which being locked, and the key not in our possession, we delayed to break it open until the last extremity, after which it escaped our recollection.

It is well known to one of us, (Mr. Burch,) that the receipts were from the first of January last, and embraced nearly the whole amount of the appropriation for the contingent expenses of the House.

A number of the printed books were also consumed, but they were all duplicates of those which have been preserved.

We have thus given you a full account of our proceedings during the troublesome scene, and we flatter ourselves you will not see in them anything to disapprove, as we were guided solely by a zealous endeavor to discharge our duty to you, and to the public.

S. BURCH,
J. T. FROST.

To PATRICK MAGRUDER, Esq.

FRIDAY, September 23.

Several other members, to wit: from New York, MORRIS S. MILLER and ELISHA J. WINTER; from New Jersey, LEWIS CONDICT, THOMAS WARD, and WILLIAM COX; from Maryland, ALEXANDER McKIM and ROBERT WRIGHT; from North Carolina, ISRAEL PICKENS; and from South Carolina, WILLIAM LOWNDES; appeared and took their seats.

Mr. FISK, of New York, presented a petition of sundry inhabitants of the city of New York, praying that an act may be passed to incorporate a National Bank.—Referred to the Committee of Ways and Means.

On motion of Mr. LATTIMORE, the petition of the Legislature of the Mississippi Territory, relative to the right of suffrage, presented on the 12th of February, 1814, was referred to Messrs. LATTIMORE, DANA, and VOSE.

A message from the Senate informed the House that the Senate have passed a resolution for the appointment of two Chaplains, one by each House, who shall interchange weekly, in which resolution they ask the concurrence of this House.

The resolution was read, and concurred in by the House.

The House then proceeded by ballot to the election of a Chaplain to Congress on their part; and upon an examination of the ballots it appeared that the Reverend OBADIAH B. BROWN was duly elected.

CAPTURE OF THE CITY.

The House, on motion of Mr. JOHNSON, resumed the consideration of the resolution offered by him on yesterday, which was again read as follows:

"*Resolved,* That a committee be appointed to inquire into the causes of the capture of this city by the enemy, the manner in which the public buildings and property was destroyed, and also into the amount in value of the property, public and private, so destroyed; and that they have power to send for persons and papers."

Mr. LEWIS, of Virginia, expressed his regret at the absence from the House of the gentleman from Maryland (Mr. GOLDSBOROUGH) at whose suggestion this resolution had yesterday been laid on the table. Mr. L. said it was his wish that the House should also inquire into the manner and reasons of the capitulation of Alexandria, and of the destruction of Fort Warburton. As respected the town of Alexandria, he knew that its conduct had been much misunderstood, and by some, misrepresented. He desired to know the facts on this subject.

Mr. JOHNSON made a few general observations on the nature of this inquiry. His object he declared to be, an inquiry into the preparations made, and the measures authorized and adopted by the Administration for the defence of the District previous to its invasion, and into the collection and disposition of this force by the commanding officers of the various descriptions of it. He adverted to the various opinions entertained not only at a distance but even in this District, in respect to the merits of all to whom might attach praise or censure in regard to the recent transactions. If there was blame, as even those who defended all parties appeared to admit, he wished to know with whom it rested. He had no inclination, having this single object in view, to encumber the inquiry with matters unconnected with his object, and was therefore averse to retaining the clause proposing an inquiry into the amount of private property destroyed.

Mr. LEWIS said he was as desirous as the gentleman from Kentucky could possibly be for a full and early inquiry, but he did think that everything relating to the occurrence within the District would come fairly within the inquiry. The town of Alexandria was an important part of the District. The whole District is equally under the exclusive jurisdiction of Congress, and Mr. L. said it was due to all that the inquiry should be general. But, as the gentleman was unwilling to accede to such an amendment as he wished to propose, he would waive it for the present, and offer it in the shape of a distinct resolution.

Mr. GROSVENOR, of New York, said he was sorry he could not accord in the propriety of withdrawing the proposed amendment. The subject of the capitulation of Alexandria, and the previous destruction of Fort Warburton, was closely connected with that of the capture of the city. This District, under the exclusive control of Congress, had been approached by the enemy in different directions, up the Patuxent and the Potomac, by two divisions of the same force. It was premature now to give any opinion where the blame, if any, of what had happened should rest. He hoped it would rest nowhere; that the recent disaster would be found to be the result of the particular situation of the country, which precluded any adequate defence. But, if there was an inquiry, he hoped it would be a thorough one; one which would satisfy the nation where the blame ought to rest. In this view, he thought it would be idle to inquire why the Capitol fell, distinguishing it from any other part of the District. Fort Warburton was one of its defences; the destruction of it carries on its face great cause of suspicion—and ought therefore to be a particular subject of inquiry; and, certainly, if any part of the subject was worthy of inquiry, this was. The gentleman from Maryland being absent, he would therefore propose an amendment in the following words: "and into the causes which induced the destruction of Fort Warburton and capitulation of Alexandria."

Mr. JOHNSON had no objection to including Fort Warburton in the inquiry, but objected to also including Alexandria.

Mr. GASTON, of North Carolina, said he did not doubt that the object of all those who interested themselves in this matter, was to have a full investigation of the subject in a national view. Instead, then, of inquiring into the particular details, he would wish to have the inquiry general, and couched in the very terms in which the President had brought it before Congress, in his Message, and he should move to amend this motion accordingly. Mr. G. then stated his proposed amendment.

Mr. GROSVENOR withdrawing his proposed amendment, Mr. JOHNSON accepted Mr. GASTON's amendment to his motion; making it, with a further modification suggested by Mr. GROSVENOR, read as follows:

Resolved, That a committee be appointed to inquire into the causes of the success of the enemy in his late enterprises against the Metropolis, and the neighboring town of Alexandria, and into the manner in which the public buildings and property were destroyed, and the amount thereof; and that they have power to send for persons and papers.

Mr. WRIGHT, of Maryland, took occasion to state his opinion that it would have been more Parliamentary to have inquired into the causes of the failure of the United States to defend the District, than of the enemy's success in his enterprise against it. But Mr. W. did not move any amendment.

The motion as it now stands was agreed to, without a dissenting voice; and Mr. JOHNSON, of Kentucky, Mr. LOWNDES, Mr. STOCKTON, Mr. MILLER, Mr. GOLDSBOROUGH, Mr. BARBOUR, and Mr. PICKENS, were appointed a committee pursuant to the said resolution.

MONDAY, September 26.

Several other members, to wit: from New York, SAMUEL SHERWOOD, WILLIAM IRVING, and JOHN LEFFERTS, appeared and took their seats.

A new member, to wit: from Massachusetts, JOHN W. HULBERT, elected to supply the vacancy occasioned by the resignation of Daniel Dewey, appeared, was qualified, and took his seat.

Mr. KENT, of Maryland, presented a petition from the President and Directors of the Washington Bridge Company; also, a petition from the President Directors of the Eastern Branch Bridge Company; respectively praying compensation for said bridges, they having been destroyed by the armed forces of the United States.—Referred to the Secretary of War.

On motion of Mr. LATTIMORE, the committee to whom was referred the petition of the House of Representatives of the Mississippi Territory, praying an extension of the right of suffrage, were instructed to inquire into the expediency of increasing the number of the members of the Legislative Council of said Territory; with leave to report by bill or otherwise.

A message from the Senate informed the House that the Senate have passed a resolution for the appointment of a joint committee to have the application of the money appropriated for the use of the Library, in which they ask the concurrence of this House.

311   HISTORY OF CONGRESS.   312

H. of R.   *Removal of the Seat of Government.*   SEPTEMBER, 1814.

The resolution was read, and concurred in by the House; and Mr. SEYBERT, Mr. LOWNDES, and Mr. GASTON, were appointed the committee on the part of this House.

The SPEAKER laid before the House a letter from the Secretary of the Treasury, transmitting his annual report on the state of the finances of the United States; which were read, and referred to the Committee of Ways and Means.

A Message was received from the President of the United States transmitting copies of a letter from Admiral Cochrane, commanding His Britannic Majesty's naval forces on the American station, to the Secretary of State, with his answer, and of a reply from Admiral Cochrane.—Referred to the Committee on Foreign Affairs.

REMOVAL OF THE SEAT OF GOVERNMENT.

Mr. FISK, of New York, rose and addressed the House, as follows:

Mr. Speaker: Upon a subject which has for several weeks past attracted the attention of this body, and indeed of every person in this nation, I feel it my duty to submit a resolution to bring the question promptly and fully before this House for examination and discussion. After the people of this country had recovered from the surprise and astonishment they felt at hearing of the capture of this city, and the destruction of the public buildings, their first inquiry was, where shall Congress sit with safety and convenience? Some designated one place, some another; but few, if any, imagined that the Councils of the nation would continue here. It is not merely necessary that the members of the General Government should be secure in their own opinion, they must be so in the opinion of the nation. The confidence and credit of the nation is identified with the security of the public Councils, and the safety of the public records. Menace this safety, and public confidence is impaired, public credit is shaken.

It was supposed, as well in as out of this House, that Congress would at an early day take this subject into consideration.

There are, I am well aware, upon this measure, a variety of opinions. The question is one of some delicacy, much interest and importance, worthy of attentive examination and deliberate decision. If it should be agitated, as I apprehend it is, in some degree to excite inquiry, to raise expectations, or create an interest by informal discussion, it is best to bring it directly and formally before this House, that it may be here examined, decided, and put at rest. With this view, and under these impressions, I have risen to ask the attention of the House to the resolution I am about to offer. If we are to have a temporary removal of the Seat of Government until the public edifices can be rebuilt, our public library and documents replaced, the sooner this shall be decided the better; and if we are to remain here, it is, under existing circumstances, desirable that this should be determined by a vote of Congress, and preparations made accordingly. I therefore submit the following resolution:

Resolved, That a committee be appointed to inquire into the expediency of removing the Seat of Government, during the present session of Congress, to a place of greater security and less inconvenience than the City of Washington; with leave to report by bill or otherwise.

The question on taking this resolution into consideration was decided as follows, by yeas and and nays: For consideration 79, against it 37, as follows:

YEAS—Messrs. Alexander, Alston, Anderson, Archer, Avery, Barnett, Baylies of Massachusetts, Boyd, Bradbury, Bradley, Brigham, Brown, Caldwell, Champion, Chappell, Clark, Comstock, Condict, Conard, Cooper, Cox, Crawford, Creighton, Crouch, Culpeper, Dana, Davenport, Davis of Pennsylvania, Denoyelles, Desha, Duvall, Ely, Farrow, Findley, Fisk of New York, Gaston, Geddes, Gourdin, Grosvenor, Harris, Humphreys, Hulbert, Ingham, Irwin, Jackson of Rhode Island, Kent of New York, King of Massachusetts, Lovett, Lowndes, Lyle, Macon, Markell, McLean, Moffit, Moseley, Murfrey, Oakley, Piper, Post, John Reed, Rea of Pennsylvania, Rich, Ruggles, Sage, Seybert, Sharp, Sherwood, Skinner, Stanford, Sturges, Tannehill, Thompson, Udree, Vose, Ward of Massachusetts, Ward of New York, Wheaton, Wilcox, and Winter.

NAYS—Messrs. Bayly of Virginia, Bowen, Burwell, Cuthbert, Eppes, Forney, Forsyth, Franklin, Gholson, Goodwyn, Hall, Hawes, Hawkins, Hubbard, Jackson of Virginia, Kent of Maryland, Kerr, Kershaw, King of North Carolina, Lewis, McCoy, McKee, McKim, Montgomery, Newton, Pearson, Pickens, Pleasants, Roane, Sevier, Smith of Virginia, Strong, Stuart, Telfair, Troup, Wright, and Yancey.

So the House agreed to consider the resolution.

Mr. LEWIS, of Virginia, was opposed to the removal of the Seat of Government under any circumstances whatever. He was particularly opposed to it for the reasons stated in the resolution—he did not believe the City of Washington more vulnerable than any other situation east of the Alleghany Mountain, nor as much so as Baltimore, Philadelphia, or even Lancaster; to one of which, he understood, it was the wish of gentlemen to carry it. Mr. L. said, the natural situation of Washington was as well calculated to resist an enemy as any to which gentlemen could desire to remove; and the circumstance of its having been invaded, was no reason why it should be abandoned.

If proper preparations for resistance had been made by those whose duty it was to have made them, Washington had been safe against double the number of its invaders. Instead, then, of removing the Seat of Government, let us do our duty by compelling others to do theirs. Let fortifications be immediately constructed and defended by a sufficient number of men inured to the duties of the camp, and we have nothing to fear hereafter. It would, in his opinion, be degrading, under present circumstances, to remove from this place. Our enemies had exultingly declared that Congress had been driven from their seat, and should no longer continue there. Let us not, then, fulfil their predictions and gratify their wishes. On the score of accommodations, Mr.

313   HISTORY OF CONGRESS.   314

SEPTEMBER, 1814.   *Removal of the Seat of Government.*   H. OF R.

L. observed, that although the present Hall was not as spacious and magnificent as the one we had been accustomed to occupy, yet it was as convenient as any we might calculate on getting elsewhere; at all events, it would do very well until another could be built in the City of Washington. He stated, that although from the words of the resolution a temporary removal was only contemplated, yet he verily believed that, when once started, it would never again return, and he feared the consequences that would follow. The States of Virginia and Maryland had made large donations in money to aid in the improvement of the City of Washington as the permanent Seat of the General Government, and they would not willingly submit to the sacrifice. Hundreds and thousands of individuals had been induced, from a perfect confidence in the permanency of the Seat of the National Government, to expend their all in its improvement, who will be reduced to beggary and want if this resolution is adopted. The original proprietors of the ground upon which the city stands, had given to the Government two-thirds of their property for public uses; the greater part of which had been sold by the Government, and the proceeds appropriated to public purposes. Would it be just to sacrifice these people? Mr. L. exhorted the House to reflect on the consequences of adopting the resolution. He hoped, by rejecting it, that an end would be put to similar attempts hereafter, and that the good people of the District would be permitted to repose in safety upon the faith of the Constitution and the law, and would be suffered to continue their improvements here without the dread of being sacrificed. For the last ten or twelve years, Mr. L. observed, similar attempts had been made, the effect of which was to create alarm and paralyze exertion and improvement, to the great injury of the public. He hoped the vote which would now be given would silence forever attempts which could do no good, but much harm.

Mr. NEWTON, of Virginia, also opposed the resolution, in an energetic manner, on the grounds of expediency and Constitutionality. He also alluded to the danger of intrigue, in the operations of the Government; which, he said, was the species of friction most dangerous to the regularity and stability of Republican Government.

Mr. MACON, of North Carolina, in an impressive manner warned the House against listening to this proposition; and, among other observations, in his usual forcible manner, said, that if the Seat of Government was once set on wheels, there was no saying where it would stop.

Mr. FISK, of New York, expatiated on the inconveniences under which Congress legislated in this place. Their documents, he said, were stricken from their hands. This was a time, he said, requiring the united endeavors and the most intelligent exertion of the Public Councils, to save the nation. The people would not be disappointed, he said, to find Congress, with the view of promoting this paramount object, removing to a place of safety, where the means of information were more at hand than here; to a place more connected with the moneyed interest of the nation; where they could have a better opportunity to call into action the resources of the nation. As to violation of the public faith, as to any act which would have the effect to injure individuals, or to affect injuriously the States of Maryland or Virginia, he would be among the last to propose either. He did not view a temporary removal of the Seat of Government to a place of greater safety in that light. Gentlemen would admit there might be cases in which removal might be necessary, as in case of sickness, famine, threatened or actual invasion. The argument against the motion appeared to rest on this basis—that if the Government were temporarily removed, it would never return to this place. Were gentlemen aware of the bearing of this argument? It was nothing more than saying, that on a removal to any other place, the inconveniences of this would appear by contrast so strongly, that the Government could never be induced to return. He hoped arguments of this character would not induce the House to refuse an inquiry into this subject.

Mr. RHEA, of Tennessee, said he would vote against the resolution, and observed, that the reasons offered for it appear to be derived from inconvenience to Congress. That inconvenience is said to arise from loss of public documents, and inconvenience of living. In respect to living, he would make no observations. In respect to public documents, he observed, the loss thereof was great; but the probability is, that that loss can be met as well in this city as elsewhere. Congress, at the commencement of this Government, had no precedents to direct them, except what the proceedings of the Old Congress afforded. That several copies of the journals of the Old Congress, and also some copies of the journals of Congress under the present Government, may be had in this city is presumed.

He said he would pass over the Constitutional objection to a removal, and observe, that for Congress to remove from the District of Columbia because the public buildings were destroyed, may be assimilated to the removal of a man from his farm because a banditti had burned his house. For a man so to remove would be deemed an act of puerility, and display absence of wisdom and fortitude.

The eyes of Europe will be drawn to the result of the proposed resolution. A removal by them will be ascribed to a want of firmness; and at this particular time that Congress do manifest firmness and determination is safe and honorable; and so it will appear to all, on the present question. This House has an opportunity to manifest that firmness to the nation and to the world.

Mr. PEARSON, of North Carolina, said he had supposed that a gentleman who could have summoned up so much fortitude as to introduce the resolution now under consideration, would have given to the subject that reflection which would have enabled him to offer some better ground for it, some plausible reason why this most extraor-

815   **HISTORY OF CONGRESS.**   816

H. of R.   *Removal of the Seat of Government.*   September, 1814.

dinary and unheard of proposition should be adopted. If there was a man in this House, or in the nation, who could vote for the motion from motives of mere personal convenience, that man in his judgment deserved the execration of his country. If there were any great national object which required that this motion should be adopted; that the public faith should be violated; that the persons who compose the population of this city should be stripped of their property, acquired under the faith of the Government, should be turned out beggars on the community, the House would very properly enter into a consideration of such a motion. But what reasons are now offered for it? The gentleman who introduced does not say that he himself is afraid to remain here. But the gentleman says the people are agitated and uneasy, and desire the Government to remove to a place of safety. Were the people to think for the gentleman on matters coming before him here, or was he to think for himself? Were the members to consult their distant constituents whether they were safe in remaining, or was this House to determine for itself? The gentleman had said the proposed removal is only temporary; but his arguments look to a permanent removal. Where, if not here, is the gentleman to get those records, those steering oars to guide him in this difficult road? The public library is destroyed, but there are as good in this District as in any place to which it is now proposed to remove. The gentleman may, if he thinks proper, within the compass of ten miles, obtain all the books he ever read. The gentleman had intimated that Congress might, in a commercial city, obtain facilities in our financial transactions, and with more readiness procure money to carry on this war. All these arguments go to favor a permanent removal. If he was certain of any one thing, Mr. P. said, it was, that the Constitution precluded Congress from such removal. The law establishing a permanent seat of Government was bottomed on the Constitution; and, in consequence of its passage, the whole soil of the District had been transferred in fee simple to the President of the United States, upon the express condition that that act of Congress was carrying the Constitution into effect. What would gentlemen do with those thousands of people who had expended their substance in building and improving the place, and, relying on the public faith pledged by solemn acts, had given their property into the hands of the Government? The man who, in cold blood, could place the citizens of this place in the condition in which they would be in the event of removal, for considerations of a private nature, deserved eternal punishment. In another point of view, Mr. P. said, it seemed to him that gentlemen who were regardful of the honor of the country, would not be ready to heap disgrace upon disgrace, and add to the disaster of the enemy's success against this place; that they would be prevented by their national, or even party pride, from permitting the enemy to obtain a greater triumph than they have already obtained. The President had in-

formed Congress, in his Message, that the public buildings had been destroyed, but that only a momentary inconvenience had thereby resulted to the Government. If, after this, Congress should, under the impulse of terror, or any other motive, remove from here, they will only give cause of triumph to the enemy. So far from entering into the feelings of the nation, for such conduct the people would scout us from our seats. What, sir! Shall the Representatives of a country like this, with thousands and tens of thousands of citizens ready to offer up their blood in its defence—shall we go off in a panic from a place not even menaced by the enemy? To do so would be ten times more degrading than the result of the late incursion of the enemy. Mr. P. made a number of other pertinent remarks, and concluded by saying, that, in the language of his colleague, to set the Government on wheels, would give play to the worst passions of the worst men, and everything would become fair game for ambition and intrigue.

Mr. FARROW, of South Carolina, said he had voted to consider this motion, because he was desirous to treat with due respect every proposition made by a member of this House. But he asked, now, what great advantage would be derived from committing this subject, respecting which there could be no hesitation in deciding. The subject doubtless had been well considered before it was introduced into the House. For what, said he, are we now called upon to remove from this place? He was not about to say whether this place was the best that could have been selected for the Seat of Government. On that question he said he should not know what course to give to his own vote. But the question of removal at this moment was a very different one. Are we now called on, said he, to strike the standard of the nation? To say to the enemy, you have been here once, and may come again? No, sir; let us rally around it. The enemy, indeed, had once been here, and for his part he wished they might attempt to come again. It was time enough for Congress to move when they were in sight. He should doubt whether the honorable members of this House would then flee before them. Having assisted in calling the nation to war, he was ready to take part in it himself. He would rather sit under canvass in the city than remove one mile out of it to a palace. There had been no strength measured with the enemy in defending this place, and he would not, by deserting it, give him more credit than he had derived. The men of this District, led by proper officers, would, he believed, always do their duty and defend their city. Do we see any danger? Do you wish to examine the Faculty to know whether you are safe here? Or the Clergy to know if they will consent to pay the proper attention to those who could not get away in case the enemy should a second time visit the place? He hoped no committee would be raised on the subject. When the enemy were at the gate, it would be time enough to abandon their posts.

Mr. GROSVENOR, of New York, said he hoped,

817   HISTORY OF CONGRESS.   818

September, 1814.   *Removal of the Seat of Government.*   H. of R.

before the question was taken, he should be allowed to take a calm and dispassionate view of it. He agreed entirely with the gentleman from North Carolina, that whoever voted from personal motives on this question, whether for or against it, deserved condemnation. Although, said Mr. G., I might have personal or local feelings on the occasion, they shall not operate if I can throw them from me. I will look entirely to the good of the nation in the vote I am about to give. Mr. G. said he viewed the proposed temporary removal as no violation of the public faith. If it was, the public faith was so violated in 1794, when the President alone was authorized to change the place of meeting. Gentlemen had said, if the Government once began to roll, it would never return. Is this the true and proper place for the Seat of Government? If it be, how can gentlemen say it will not return immediately after the causes for its present removal shall cease? It will. The Seat of Government will in such case gravitate as certainly to this position as the needle to the pole. All the arguments, therefore, against the removal, on the ground that it would be permanent, ought to be thrown out of consideration, as they had nothing to do with the question. Let the resolution take its course and go to a committee. Suppose at the time Congress met, that the enemy could have held the place, or was in force on the water to occupy the place the next day. Would Congress, in such a case, attempt to sit here? The question was not, however, whether any exigency would justify the removal from this place, because that principle has been long ago decided by the passage of the act to which he had before alluded; the question was, whether this was such an exigency as to require the removal? He saw no reason, therefore, why the adoption of the question should excite such a feeling as appeared to prevail, unless gentlemen were desirous to place their argument on the ground they had unguardedly disclosed, that this was the very worst place in the nation for Congress to sit in. The idea of the gentleman from South Carolina was singular, who conceived that a removal would be striking our colors. Wait, says the gentleman, till the enemy comes and chases you off! That, said Mr. G., is the dishonor which I dread from remaining, the very disgrace I wish to avoid. You now sit coolly and deliberately; you may remove without disgrace or dishonor. But if this be a point which you cannot defend against an enemy, why talk like children about remaining here and having your heads cut off rather than remove? The gentleman from Tennessee, comparing the city to a farm, says, if his house was burned, he would not therefore move off his farm. But suppose a neighbor would politely offer him a clean bed, excellent food, and proper utensils for cooking and providing for his wants, would he refuse the use of them and rather sleep in his barn? The occupation of this city was one of the events of war, and was anticipated last Summer, when it was the subject of secret debate. To remove from the city temporarily

was one of those occurrences in life to which we must submit, and is no more disgrace than the ordering the necessary retreat of an army. If it shall appear folly to remain here, this is the moment to remove. If we are to stay here till the enemy comes, to sit and be dragged from our seats, the President stolen—and there is nothing now to guard against it; if we are to run all risks for false honor, let us have no argument; let us say at once we will be self-devoted. This war, gentlemen well knew, might continue for years. If a peace did not take place now, he feared it would be long before it did. What, then, was the condition of the Government in this District? Let gentlemen ask themselves fairly. Were they willing to appropriate the money of the people of the United States to build a Capitol, to plant it in this District, where it might be destroyed in twenty days? No, gentlemen said, they would defend it, at an expense of ten or twelve millions; for that much it would cost, so indefensible is this point. Did not the interest of the country, Mr. G. asked, require them to remove to a place of security, where it would not be necessary to expend ten or fifteen millions, or any other sum, in the simple defence of Congress? Would gentlemen say that Congress were safe without an army to protect them? No. For it was well known that, without such a protection, the frigates may be thrown up the river and drive Congress off. Were gentlemen ready to divert the public money from the great object of prosecuting the war, to raise an army solely for defending this place? Mr. G. slightly noticed the inconvenience of this place to the members; the want of information, &c. Where were they to go for libraries? Would gentlemen appropriate thousands and thousands to obtain another library to replace that which was burnt by the enemy? These inconveniences, added to insecurity, urged the immediate removal of Congress. He said he had steered clear of all idea of permanent removal, for he was not one of those who yielded to the opinion that, after removal to any other place, the impropriety of returning to this place will be so palpable that they could never obtain a vote for it. Indeed, if gentlemen desired it, he was, for one, willing to give a pledge, in case of the removal, in the act itself, to return here at the close of the war.

Mr. TROUP, of Georgia, the chairman of the Military Committee, made a very succinct and clear statement of the defences provided and about to be provided for the city. [This statement, however proper and necessary to be presented to the House, is not deemed by the reporter to be proper for publication, and is therefore omitted.]

Mr. T. concluded by observing that it was the opinion of those qualified to judge, and indeed it was his opinion, that the city was entirely protected from assault by land, and soon would be by water.

Mr. HAWKINS, of Kentucky, rose to offer a few ideas to the House, which he said had occurred to him since the subject had been presented this

319   HISTORY OF CONGRESS.   320

H. of R.   *Removal of the Seat of Government.*   September, 1814.

morning. Granting to gentlemen premises they had taken, and ceding the justice of a part of their reasoning, when tested and made applicable to the real question, neither one nor the other appeared to him to lead to the conclusions they had drawn. Cede the Constitutional question that the Seat of Government might be removed by Congress; cede too that there is some cause for this removal; we have yet to inquire, said he, whether or not this is an exigency requiring removal, and then, whether we can remove advantageously. First, as to the causes of removal. What are they? Famine? An invading army? Neither. An invading army has indeed penetrated to the city, and what have they done? With traits of barbarity better suited to Vandals than to Britons, they sacked a few buildings, and retired so precipitately, abandoned it so disgracefully as to leave many of their most valuable officers and soldiers even slightly wounded in our hands. Where now is that enemy? Is he at Baltimore. Philadelphia, or New York—or where is he? Perhaps, if Congress were to decide on removing, the first step would bring them to face that incursive foe whose approach gentlemen appeared to dread. When the emergency did exist, Mr. H. said he would go with gentlemen in seeking out a place of greater security. But at this moment, he could but view this as a question of panic. Remove now, said he, and what spectacle will you exhibit to the community? The enemy has retreated in such a manner as to induce no belief of his desire to return. The enterprise which made him master of this city was desperate in its character, and marked by a degree of bravery amounting to rashness; and every one will admit that had the energies of the Government been properly brought into action, he would have retreated with much greater loss. Nay, Mr. H. said, he would venture to assert, that three thousand brave men, led and kept in action, would have prevented the enemy from entering the capital; and that one thousand men in the Capitol alone with musketry would have defended the Capitol against the invaders. Grant that Congress has the power to remove the Seat of Government. Had the emergency occurred? Had the enemy presented that formidable attitude to require their flight from the Capitol? Was the enemy even at hand? Had he footing even in the borders of our country? No, even there he was flying before a small undisciplined force: the patriotic volunteers of New York and Vermont, one fourth the number of the enemy, had driven him before them. Just at this moment, too, when we are gaining most splendid victories over them in their own territory, he could not see the reason for removal from our capital. It must be a feeling of panic only which recommends it, and he would not consent to exhibit it to his or any other country. What trophy could the enemy exhibit from his visit to this place? It would be asked in Europe, what blood had been spilt in its defence—who had fallen? It would be seen the Government was again pursuing its course, unawed and uninterrupted. He would not give the world reason to say otherwise

by the removal of the Government from this place. If this was false pride, if this was false honor, Mr. H. said, let him thus ever maintain what he believed to be the real honor of the nation, of which some gentlemen had so lightly spoken. When the emergency does exist, the people will sanction the removal, but not till then. If the danger does exist, and there is an incompetent force for repelling it, said Mr. H., as gentlemen on the other side aver, let them take care that this nation, that other nations, and posterity, do not make some strong inquiries of them. Have they gone hand in hand with the Executive in making provision of the means for our defence? If this error did exist, Mr. H. said he was unwilling to add others to it. He was unwilling to add one disgrace to another, by flying now from that enemy who has so precipitately fled from us. The feelings of gentlemen were warm from seeing the situation of their Capitol, and he feared they were too much influenced by them. When danger is proved, Mr. H. said he should deem himself unwise if he did not go with gentlemen in voting for removal. But as to the inconvenience spoken of, it was certainly more nominal than real. If local considerations were to prevail in favor of removal to any other place, he thought it would not be difficult to show, go where they will, Congress will produce a pressure on a majority of that community. It was true that prominent men may take advantage of it, but it will operate as a prejudice to the people generally among whom Congress locate themselves. Remove from here momentarily or otherwise, and every prospect of the people of this city is blasted and withered. In voting for a removal, under present circumstances, he believed Congress would violate the national faith, sacrifice thousands and thousands of people who ought to be protected, and exhibit a panic to an enemy from whom we have nothing to fear, and who has of his own accord precipitately abandoned our territory.

Mr. OAKLEY, of New York, next spoke. He said, that if indeed the enemy had abandoned our country at every point, it could not be justly supposed that Congress would be influenced by a panic in removing from this place. If the enemy be entirely out of view, this question may be discussed without that sort of feeling which some appear to entertain of it. Mr. O. said he would endeavor never to debate with feeling or passion, which was not at all conducive to inquiry into truth. If they could not approach this question without appeals to the passions and fears of the members, it certainly was no proof of its indisputable inexpediency. He was well aware, he said, of the interest which this District felt in the decision of this question; but it was proper that that interest should be manifested in a becoming manner. It was proper that considerations of this kind should have their proper influence; but when he heard gentlemen tell the House that by a temporary removal they would ruin thousands and thousands of individuals, he must believe it mere fanciful declamation. It was true, that a removal might injure individuals; but he presumed no gentle-

821   HISTORY OF CONGRESS.   322

SEPTEMBER, 1814.   *Removal of the Seat of Government.*   H. OF R.

man in the House would hesitate to make a fair and liberal compensation by way of indemnity to such sufferers. It was a cardinal point in his politics, Mr. O. said, that the national faith should be preserved inviolate, even when improperly pledged, unless where considerations of a paramount nature forbade it. Gentlemen had talked about the national faith—but were they not aware that national contracts frequently cannot be fulfilled in the spirit in which they are made; and would they say that there might not be cases in which necessity would impose on them a course different from that pursued in ordinary cases? As to the expediency of removal, this was a mere proposition for inquiry, and if on inquiry it should appear that Congress cannot be more easily protected from the enemy, and better accommodated elsewhere, the arguments of gentlemen would apply, &c. &c. No temporary removal, Mr. O. said, would be a violation of the national faith. When we speak of a permanent seat of Government in the most literal sense, we speak of it subject to casualties. As to the panic alleged, were the enemy at our doors, the remark might be correct, but not otherwise. While, however, Mr. O. said he would not remove at present under the impulse of fear, he would not remain from false courage. There was courage of one kind, and courage of another kind—the one animating the soldier in the fight, the other fortifying the citizen in the discharge of his duties. To be sure, members of Congress might put themselves on a par with the miserable wretches who fill the ranks of the enemy, and march forth to battle. But when we are sent here, said he, it is to legislate, to provide the ways and means to pay those who are to fight. Whilst we transact the business of legislators, and put means into others hands to carry on the war, we are in the line of our duty. On some occasions it is glorious to gentlemen to take up arms and maintain the principles they have asserted by their votes; and there were some in this House who could boast of having done so; but, in general, legislation required tranquillity and separation from other duties. The incursion of the enemy, he said, instead of affording reasons against a removal of the Seat of Government, afforded conclusive arguments in favor of it. It had certainly shown one thing: that this was not a proper situation for the Seat of Government, because it is owing to the forbearance of the enemy that Congress had now a single roof to cover their heads whilst deliberating on the concerns of the nation. He called upon gentlemen to say whether it would be proper to remain at a place where the public documents were so much exposed to destruction, unless protected at an expense which was most disproportionate to the object. The gentleman from Georgia said the place was defensible. They had been told so always. They had been told so by the constituted authorities, as far as they could speak, at the moment when the enemy invaded the Capital. As to the defence by the militia, the force which is destined for the defence of this District as had been stated to this House, it was at once the most

13th CON. 3d SESS.—11

expensive and least efficient force. Notwithstanding the great services they had sometimes rendered, Mr. O. said he could have no dependence on the militia. It ought not to be tolerated, when every means ingenuity could devise was stretched to the utmost extent to prosecute the war, that Congress should sit here at such a cost. The enemy had retreated precipitately from this place, Mr. O. admitted, but they had immediately attacked another city; and our Government had been officially given to understand, that the enemy intended to pursue this course. He would not rely, therefore, on the forbearance or inability of an enemy who were both able and willing to annoy us. It was not disgraceful to feel alarm at the exposed situation of the place. The exposure was brought upon us by the war. Every point could not be defended; and Congress would deserve the meed of wisdom and prudence for removing hence, if by a removal they could be better accommodated, relieve the finances from the enormous burden of defending the city by a militia force, and at the same time relieve the city by taking from it the only object which could endanger its invasion by the enemy. Gentlemen discussed this question as if the Seat of Government was proposed to be finally removed, and said that such would be the practical effect of the temporary removal. Gentlemen had no right to say so. No such design was expressed or implied by the mover of the resolution; and it could only result, if at all, from the inherent circumstances of the case. If circumstances should make a permanent removal necessary, it must take place; and if the Constitution was in the way, it ought to be amended. Whatever respect he might feel for the inhabitants of the District, he would say that their interest could not for a moment enter into competition with the interests of this nation. It should never be permitted that a few thousand inhabitants should rise and say they would be ruined, if the nation could be benefited, provided the nation indemnified them for their loss. The people of the District are liable to suffer with all others the evils resulting from war. The temporary removal of the Government, is such an evil. The people of the city ought to have confidence enough in the honor of the nation to believe that, if the Government removed, they would be fully indemnified for any loss they might sustain.

Mr. HANSON, of Maryland, moved to postpone indefinitely the further consideration of the motion, and supported his motion by a speech, the substance of which was, that though he entertained very great contempt for the citizens of Washington, which he expressed in the most pointed language, he was opposed to a removal at this moment, as being derogatory to the national dignity and honor.

The motion for postponement was negatived— yeas 48, nays 79, as follows:

YEAS—Messrs. Barnett, Bayly of Virginia, Bowen, Burwell, Culpeper, Cuthbert, Earle, Eppes, Farrow, Fisk of Vermont, Forney, Forsyth, Franklin, Gaston, Gholson, Goodwyn, Hall, Hanson, Hawes, Hawkins, Humphreys, Jackson of Virginia, Kent of Maryland,

323   **HISTORY OF CONGRESS.**   324

H. of R.   *Amendments to the Constitution.*   September, 1814.

Kerr, Kershaw, King of North Carolina, Lewis, Lowndes, Macon, McCoy, McKim, Montgomery, Newton, Pearson, Pickens, Pleasants, Rhea of Tennessee, Roane, Sage, Sevier, Smith of Virginia, Strong, Stuart, Telfair, Troup, White, Wright, and Yancey.

Nays—Messrs. Alexander, Alston, Anderson, Archer, Avery, Barbour, Baylies of Massachusetts, Boyd, Bradbury, Bradley, Brigham, Brown, Caperton, Caldwell, Champion, Chappell, Clark, Comstock, Condit, Conard, Cox, Crawford, Creighton, Crouch, Dana, Davenport, Davis of Pennsylvania, Denoyelles, Desha, Duvall, Ely, Findley, Fisk of New York, Geddes, Gourdin, Griffin, Grosvenor, Harris, Hulbert, Ingersoll, Ingham, Johnson of Kentucky, Kent of New York, King of Massachusetts, Lefferts, Lovett, Lyle, Markell, McLean, Miller, Moffit, Moseley, Murfree, Oakley, Piper, Post, John Reed, Rea of Pennsylvania, Rich, Ruggles, Seybert, Sharp, Sherwood, Skinner, Stanford, Stockton, Sturges, Tannehill, Thompson, Udree, Vose, Ward of Massachusetts, Ward of New Jersey, Wheaton, Wilcox, Wilson of Pennsylvania, and Winter.

Mr. Fisk of Vermont, made an able and decided, but short speech against the resolution

The question was then taken on the resolution, and decided in the affirmative by yeas and nays, 72 to 51, as follows:

Yeas—Messrs. Alexander, Alston, Anderson, Archer, Avery, Baylies of Massachusetts, Boyd, Bradbury, Bradley, Brigham, Brown, Caldwell, Champion, Clark, Comstock, Condict, Conard, Cox, Crawford, Creighton, Crouch, Dana, Davenport, Davis of Pennsylvania, Denoyelles, Desha, Duvall, Ely, Findley, Fisk of New York, Geddes, Gourdin, Grosvenor, Harris, Hulbert, Ingersoll, Ingham, Irving, Johnson of Kentucky, Kent of New York, King of Massachusetts, Lefferts, Lovett, Lyle, Markell, McLean, Miller, Moffit, Moseley, Murfree, Oakley, Piper, Post, John Reed, Rea of Pennsylvania, Rich, Ruggles, Seybert, Sharp, Sherwood, Skinner, Stanford, Stockton, Sturges, Tannehill, Udree, Vose, Ward of Massachusetts, Ward of New Jersey, Wheaton, Wilcox, and Winter.

Nays—Messrs. Barbour, Bayly of Virginia, Bowen, Burwell, Chappell, Culpeper, Cuthbert, Earle, Eppes, Farrow, Fisk of Vermont, Forney, Forsyth, Franklin, Gaston, Gholson, Goodwyn, Griffin, Hall, Hanson, Hawes, Hawkins, Humphreys, Jackson of Virginia, Kent of Maryland, Kerr, Kershaw, King of North Carolina, Lewis, Lowndes, Macon, McCoy, McKim, Montgomery, Newton, Pearson, Pickens, Pleasants, Rhea of Tennessee, Roane, Sage, Sevier, Smith of Virginia, Strong, Stuart, Telfair, Troup, White, Wilson of Pennsylvania, Wright, and Yancey.

Mr. Fisk, of New York, Mr. McKim, Mr. Burwell, Mr. Grosvenor, Mr. Ingham, Mr. Hawkins, and Mr. Dana, were appointed the committee pursuant to the said resolution.

Tuesday, September 27.

Two other members, to wit: from Connecticut, Lyman Law, and from Virginia, John P. Hungerford, appeared, and took their seats.

Mr. Jackson, of Virginia, presented a petition of sundry inhabitants of the town of West Liberty in Virginia, and its vicinity, stating their opinion that the transportation and opening of the mail on Sunday is injurious to the morals of the community, and praying that it may be abolished in future.—Referred to the Committee on Post Roads and Post Offices.

Mr. King, of Massachusetts, adverting to the law passed in 1813, allowing a bounty for prisoners taken by private armed vessels, remarked that, by recent decisions of the proper authority, it appeared that the provisions of this act did not extend to the cases of recapture by private armed vessels, certainly a meritorious class of cases, and equally entitled, with others, to remuneration for their enterprises. To collect the sense of the House on the propriety of extending this provision to embrace such cases, he moved the following resolution:

Resolved, That the Committee on Naval Affairs be instructed to inquire into the expediency of extending the provisions of the act entitled, "An act allowing a bounty to the owners, officers, and crews, of the private armed vessels of the United States," passed on the 2d of August, 1813, to such officers and crews of merchant vessels of the United States as have recaptured, or may recapture, the same from the enemy.

The resolution was agreed to.

AMENDMENTS TO THE CONSTITUTION.

Mr. Jackson, of Virginia, said it would be recollected that at the last session he had the honor to propose a resolution to amend the Constitution of the United States. He now renewed it, that it might be decided on during the present session of Congress. He then offered a motion to amend the Constitution, embracing the following propositions:

Resolved, by the Senate and House of Representatives of the United States of America in Congress assembled, two-thirds of both Houses concurring, That the following articles be proposed to the Legislatures of the several States as amendments to the Constitution of the United States; each of which, when ratified by three-fourths of the said Legislatures, shall be valid, to all intents and purposes, as part of the said Constitution:

1. Congress shall have power to lay a tax or duty, not exceeding ten per centum ad valorem, on articles exported from any State.

2. Congress shall have power to make roads in any State.

3. Congress shall have power to make canals in any State, with the consent of the State within which the same shall be made.

4. Congress shall have power to establish a National Bank, with branches thereof, in any State.

Mr. Jackson moved to refer these propositions to a Committee of the Whole on the state of the Union; and gave notice that he should call for the consideration of the last of them on Friday next.

Mr. Fisk, of New York, called for a division of the question on the reference of these propositions to a Committee of the Whole. He said he should vote for the reference of the first three, but against the reference of the last, and assigned his reasons for discriminating between them. The first three, he said, were of an important nature, and would require mature deliberation and discussion before acted on, and he should probably vote for them. As to the fourth, he saw himself no occasion for it; and, if it were not indelicate in itself, after the precedents and numerous adjudications of twenty years, to propose giving to Congress a power to do that they have already done, it was at least in his view unnecessary. He objected to it, moreover, because the agitation of the question might interfere with the decision of the Committee of Ways and Means on the petition referred to them for the establishment of a National Bank. In the present situation of our affairs, the advantages which such an institution offered to the community were, he believed, more seriously felt and generally admitted than they had ever been before; and he hoped this proposition would not be thrown in the way of a decision on the subject. He was indeed much surprised to see this proposition revived at the present session, of the intention to do which he had no knowledge or information until he heard it read.

Mr. JACKSON said he had not indeed informed the gentleman of his intention to renew this proposition, because he had too much respect for this body to offer to its consideration any motion which, without consultation with others, he was not determined to persevere in. He might retort on the gentleman by saying that he (Mr. F.) did not inform him of his intention to remove the Seat of Government from this place; and the gentleman could not be more surprised at the proposition now offered than Mr. J. had been at the motion for that object yesterday moved by Mr. FISK. He regretted that the gentleman had on this occasion departed from the regular rule of reference of all motions similar to this; and the more so, as a refusal to refer the proposition could not preclude its discussion. Mr. J. denied the indelicacy imputed to his motion on account of former precedents recognising the power he proposed to vest in Congress; if there were indelicacy anywhere, he should suppose it to exist at least as much in the presentation of a petition to Congress for the establishment of a National Bank, after they had, in their refusal to renew the charter of the Bank of the United States, decided against the constitutionality of it. It is a fortunate thing for this country that Congress is not enchained by precedent in its legislation; that, if the Constitution be violated to-day, it is no reason why it should be violated to-morrow. The question of renewal of the charter of the Bank of the United States was argued on the Constitutional ground; many of the States have by a solemn vote declared that Congress does not possess the power to pass such an act, and it would be respectful at least to consult their opinions on the subject. Mr. J. did not at the last session, he did not now, say whether such a power was or was not already possessed by Congress; but he wished to place that power beyond question or doubt, because he believed it was a power they ought to possess.

Mr. FISK said that the gentleman had mistaken him if he supposed that it was his desire that he (Mr. J.) should communicate to Mr. F. every proposition he desired to submit. He knew that from the situation of members in this city, living in houses scattered over a surface of several miles, it was utterly impossible that they should consult together on the subjects of legislation before they were introduced into the House, &c.

Mr. WRIGHT, of Maryland, said he hoped this proposition would be suffered to go to a committee. The subject had been fully discussed and decided two or three years ago, on the proposition to renew the charter of the United States' Bank, which had failed, though under the auspices of the then Secretary of the Treasury, who possessed so greatly the confidence of the people, and justly too, because of the ability with which he managed the affairs of the nation. However necessary a National Bank may now be, having conscientiously voted it to be unconstitutional, he could not now vote for it without an amendment. Nor had the unconstitutionality of the old bank law been pronounced on light authority; the opinions of the late and present President of the United States were recorded against it. He hoped, therefore, the proposition would be permitted to take the usual course of going to a committee.

The question on the reference of Mr. JACKSON's motion to a Committee of the whole House, was then decided in the affirmative: For reference 61, against it 53.

WEDNESDAY, September 28.

Several other members, to wit: from Massachusetts, ABIJAH BIGELOW, and TIMOTHY PICKERING; from Vermont, EZRA BUTLER; and from Pennsylvania, HUGH GLASGOW, appeared, and took their seats.

Mr. SHERWOOD presented a petition of sundry inhabitants of Cairo, in the State of New York, praying that the mails may not be opened or carried on the Sabbath day.—Referred to the Committee on the Post Office and Post Roads.

On motion of Mr. HALL, the Committee of Claims were directed to inquire into the expediency of making provision by law for the payment of private property lost, killed, or destroyed, while employed in the service of the United States.

BOUNTY TO DESERTERS.

Mr. FISK, of Vermont, said he believed it was the practice of the British commanders, on land and water, to use every means in their power to induce our men to desert their guns. A direct retaliation of such practices would doubtless be justifiable. But, Mr. F. said, the resolution he was about to submit had a different motive. It was well known that desertions from the enemy were very frequent, and that those deserters were strangers in our country, without means of employment, or of purchasing lands on which to labor for an honest livelihood. It was as well known that we have an extensive frontier, much exposed, and a great quantity of wild lands, the settlement of which would be very desirable. In order to authorize an inquiry into the expediency of disposing of this species of persons, so that they might be useful rather than burdensome to the community, he proposed the following resolve:

Resolved, That the Committee on the Public Lands be instructed to inquire into the expediency of giving to each deserter from the British army, during the present war, one hundred acres of the public lands, such deserter actually settling the same; and that the committee have leave to report by bill or otherwise.

The question to take this motion into consideration, the yeas and nays having been required by Mr. OAKLEY, was decided—For consideration 82, against it 45, as follows:

YEAS—Messrs. Alexander, Alston, Anderson, Avery, Barbour, Bard, Barnett, Bradley, Brown, Burwell, Caldwell, Chappell, Clark, Condict, Conard, Crawford, Creighton, Crouch, Culpeper, Cuthbert, Dana, Davis of Pennsylvania, Denoyelles, Desha, Eppes, Evans, Findley, Fisk of Vermont, Fisk of New York, Forney, Forsyth, Franklin, Gholson, Glasgow, Goodwyn, Gourdin, Griffin, Hall, Harris, Hawes, Hawkins, Hubbard, Humphreys, Ingersoll, Ingham, Irving, Irwin, Jackson of Virginia, Johnson of Kentucky, Kent of Maryland, Kershaw, Lefferts, Lowndes, Lyle, Macon, McCoy, McKee, McKim, McLean, Montgomery, Murfree, Newton, Piper, Pleasants, Rea of Pennsylvania, Rhea of Tennessee, Rich, Roane, Sage, Sevier, Seybert, Sharp, Skinner, Stanford, Strong, Tannehill, Telfair, Troup, Udree, Ward of New Jersey, Wilson of Pennsylvania, and Yancey.

NAYS—Messrs. Baylies of Massachusetts, Bigelow, Boyd, Bradbury, Brigham, Caperton, Cooper, Cox, Davenport, Duvall, Earle, Ely, Farrow, Gaston, Geddes, Grosvenor, Hanson, Hulbert, Jackson of Rhode Island, Kent of New York, King of Massachusetts, Law, Lewis, Lovett, Markell, Miller, Moffit, Moseley, Oakley, Pearson, Pickering, Post, John Reed, Ruggles, Sherwood, Smith of Virginia, Stockton, Sturges, Thompson, Vose, Ward of Massachusetts, Wheaton, White, Wilcox, and Winter.

On the suggestion of Mr. McKEE, of Kentucky, the resolution was amended, so as to refer the subject to the Committee on Military Affairs, within the scope of whose duties it appeared to him more properly to come.

The yeas and nays having been ordered on the passage of the resolution—

Mr. OAKLEY, of New York, said he had asked for the yeas and nays on the question of considering this resolution, to mark his opposition to it in every stage. With deep regret, he might truly say, had he seen this resolution before the House. He had hoped, to whatever extent of sacrifice Congress might determine to go in the prosecution of this war, although we might all agree to lay down our lives and fortunes in its support, we shall still retain something like national honor. He was sorry to see a proposition before this House which he considered to be levelled at the root of it. He did not speak from extensive knowledge, but he believed he was justified in saying it was the only proposition of the kind ever submitted to any legislature. He did not know, at least, that it had ever entered into the scope of policy of this Government to encourage the commission of crime by those most likely to perpetrate it. The ranks of the enemy were known to

be filled by ragamuffins of all descriptions; and, by the adoption of such a measure as that proposed by this resolution, we should make a direct appeal to the worst passions of the worst men. Are we reduced to this? Have we not resources to maintain an open and manly contest without appealing to this most unheard of and disgraceful course? If such policy were pursued by the Government, he should forever despair of a successful issue to the contest in which we are engaged. He hoped gentlemen would reflect deeply on this subject, before they gave their consent to this inquiry. If considerations sufficiently powerful to arrest the measure do not press upon the feelings of men, it would be in vain for him to urge them. There were, he said, some propositions which outraged at once so greatly all the feelings of honor and propriety, that it seemed unnecessary to oppose them by argument. Since the resolution had been introduced, there must be some reasons to urge or justify its adoption. But could the invitation to and encouragement of treason come fairly within the scope of our views? Shall the United States, after having year after year held out their conduct as an example of public faith and honor; after arraigning the enemy at the bar of nations for his disregard of justice, and for his violations of the rules of warfare; shall the United States, after all this, go as far beyond the enemy in his violations of the usages of war, as he has gone beyond all other nations? Shall we, by so doing, draw a veil over the atrocity of his acts, and place us on an eminence of guilt which no nation ever before reached? He called upon gentlemen, by their regard for their own honor and the character of the nation, to stop this proposition in its outset. The House, by their vote to consider the resolution, had already gone too far in sanctioning a proposition which strikes at the root of those principles which bind together the civilized world. It would be to offer a bounty to treason. He did not know to what it might lead. There was enough of bitterness and animosity already infused into this war. Our enemy now affect (for affectation he must suppose it) to accuse us of a violation of the usages of civilized warfare, and presume to place their severest measures on the ground of retaliation. Adopt this measure, and they are justified for every measure of atrocity to which they may think fit to resort. It will not be in your mouths hereafter to complain of the burning and ravaging of your towns, or of the unreasonable rupture of negotiations. He called upon gentlemen, then, to reflect whether the adoption of this measure would not infuse into the present contest a temper which will defeat all hopes of an early peace.

Mr. FISK, of Vermont, denied that this proposition was of the character ascribed to it; and said that he was not conscious of possessing a disposition to sanction any such measure. What does the motion propose? That the deserters coming among us, instead of becoming nuisances to society, may be provided with the means of becoming good citizens. But, says the gentleman from New York, this is a violation of all principle. I have never understood that nations at peace with each other were precluded from receiving each other's deserters; and is it understood, that, when you are at war, we may not provide the means of support for those who desert from our enemy? Did gentlemen desire, in order to maintain this ideal national dignity, this high standing among nations, that we should return to the enemy those deserters who came within our lines? Would the gentleman from New York advocate such a measure? And which is more criminal, if criminality can attach to such conduct, to foster them when coming among you in time of peace, or provide the means necessary to prevent their being a burden to the community in time of war? If we take the first step of receiving deserters, why not take the other which is now proposed? But the gentleman had said, this would be inviting deserters from the enemy. Mr. F. said they were already invited by the nature of our institutions, by the freedom and protection they afforded to strangers. And would the gentleman change our form of Government, lest in its present shape it should tempt the soldiers of the enemy to desert? The resolution proposes to introduce no new principle. We do now receive deserters; and there is no gentleman who will rise in his place and move that all deserters be sent back. The gentleman supposes the measure to be without precedent. Let the gentleman read Lord Wellington's proclamation while in Spain, offering a bounty to every deserter from the French army of twelve crowns. This precedent had been set by the very nation with whom we are at war. Admiral Cockburn, too, had not long ago published a proclamation to all who wished to leave the country to appoint a place of rendezvous, and he would furnish the means to carry them off. Look also at General Brisbane's proclamation to the people of Vermont and New York, inviting them all to stay at home, in other words, to desert the standard of their country, and to furnish his army with provisions, &c. Gentlemen might even look back to times of peace, and see similar conduct on the part of the enemy. During the existence of our embargo law, which was very oppressive in its operation on our present enemy, though, to be sure, his friends in this country spoke very lightly of its effect, they invited our citizens to violate it, offering them protection and safe conduct in so doing, not only to any British port, but to any port whatever. Whatever new distinctions may be drawn on this head, yet, if we look at the effect of measures, a more direct invitation to rebellion, even in time of peace with us, could not be imagined. From some cause or other, a great deal of sensibility was always exhibited in this House when certain subjects were touched. The House was told again and again to beware of provoking the enemy's wrath. This kind of false sensibility was, Mr. F. said, fast vanishing. Ask the citizens of Plattsburg, Buffalo, Havre-de Grace, Hampton, Georgetown, and this place, whether they had rather the war should be carried into the enemy's territories or he should be permitted to carry it into ours. They would one and all decide in favor of the former. The people begin to find we are at war with a nation whom no considerations of peculiar modesty or generosity prevent from carrying into effect any measures to which her power is adequate. Still, however, could dishonor attach in any way to the measure which he proposed, he would not support it. But even humanity demanded such a provision. The deserters from the enemy now infesting our cities were at once a burden to themselves and a nuisance to society; but, planted on our frontiers, they would not only form a barrier against savage incursions, but would become useful citizens. Mr. F. compared the advantages of thus diminishing the enemy's effective force with the expense of doing it in any other way, and drew a conclusion favorable to his motion. He was determined to support this war by every proper and honorable measure; and he considered this one of that description. Desertions from the enemy, he said, were daily and numerous. Something like five or six hundred men had already deserted from the enemy at Plattsburg—many of them useful, enterprising men, who wish to become citizens. My wish, said Mr. F., is to make them useful, by giving them the means of support by honest industry.

Mr. GROSVENOR, of New York, said, that as he was bound to believe that any gentleman who made a motion in this House considered it honorable and proper, when he pronounced the measure, now proposed, to be dishonest, dishonorable and inexpedient, he did not mean to reflect personally on those who moved or advocated it. He did think so, and he did conceive also that the suggestions offered against them by the gentleman from New York had been in no degree met by the mover. Had they been met? The gentleman talked about the crimes of Britain; and seemed to infer because she had violated principle in one way, we might in another. This resolution would indeed at once reduce us to the same depth of guilt in which the gentlemen say our enemy is wallowing. The measure embraced in the motion before the House, being in the nature of retaliation, was different from all other such measures. It was wicked in itself, because it encouraged crime. It could not therefore be justified on that ground, nor indeed on any other. For his part, Mr. G. said, he had voted against the consideration of the motion, because in principle it was wrong, and therefore he would not even inquire into it. Without regard, he said, to the insinuation of particular sensibilities, the usual cant in this House, on such occasions, he should candidly discuss this question. If he knew himself, he observed, there was not a gentleman on the floor who would go further than he would at this moment, to rescue the country from the dangers which environ it, to repel the foe that tramples on the soil. But, let the danger be what it would, unless the existence of the nation was absolutely in jeopardy, he could not, under any pretence, consent to prostrate its honor and dignity by plunging into crime. The question, then, arose whether the proposed measure was or was not of a criminal nature; and this question he wished fairly to consider. What was this proposition which was to be adopted as a national principle, as a portion of our national morality, to stamp our character, now and forever? He asked gentlemen to say if they would, by adopting this proposition, offer a bounty for the commission of crime? Let gentlemen look into the books on national law, they will find desertion to be an offence of so black a dye that not even enemies are to encourage it. It is an offence in regard to which it is a common expression, that men love the treason but hate the traitor. A nation must receive the traitor, but hates him at the same time; because the crime of deserting the allegiance which a man owes to his country, is one of the deepest dye, one which you are daily punishing with death on your frontier. It is now proposed to offer a bounty on an offence, to which your own laws have decreed the punishment of death. Why stop here? Why not offer a bounty to every man who commits treason of any kind? Why stop here? Why not at once adopt the principles of the Old Man of the Mountain, as he is called, and offer a bounty for the assassination of the King, Governors and Generals of your enemy? Why stop short by giving a bounty on desertion? Why not at once give a bounty for the assassination of every man in your enemy's camp, and pay the perpetrators of the crime when their daggers reek with their blood? There is little or no distinction, in principle, between these offences. Mr. G. repeated that he was ready, and gentlemen would find it in his conduct, to travel every honorable length in defending his country. But nothing short of preserving the independence of the country, and not till that independence was prostrate on the ground, could induce him to adopt a measure, embracing a principle like this. And what would gentlemen gain by it? It was already universally understood that the soldiers of the enemy deserted whenever they could. But say, that by this measure we gained ten thousand men—would it be a feather in the scale; would this indemnify us for the black disgrace which it would stamp on the very forehead of the country? But look at the further consequences, said he. Believe you that the enemy will not retaliate? That after you have committed this crime against human nature, she would not enter the Southern department of your country, and kindle a fire which you could not quench? This she had not yet attempted, though she had the power. Believe you she would not capture your unoffending citizens on the ocean, and keep them as hostages till you delivered up those whom you had enticed away? Yes, sir, she would not stay her arm. Look at a further consequence of such a measure. We are to settle these ragamuffins on our frontiers. Was there a man who believed that these men, who were picked from the jails of Europe, these sixpenny men, would settle down as farmers? No; they were men of dissolute lives, men not acquainted with the useful arts. Mr. G. said he would not offer inducements to such poor wretches to commit a crime, for which, if detect-

ed, they would suffer death. The gentleman had talked of humanity; was there any humanity in this? In its consequences, as well as its principles, it is utterly objectionable. Whenever the nation is pushed to the last extremity, such a measure might present a question for consideration; but we are not driven to this extremity. This country is abundantly capable of defence. Let its means be brough forth; the people are ready and willing to raise their arms in its defence. There was no occasion for such degrading measures as this.

Mr. Sharp, of Kentucky, commenced some remarks by saying, that on all subjects requiring the deliberation of Congress, he was pleased to see a sentiment of jealous regard for the national honor and character pervading the House, and felt disposed to allow the sincerity and candor of every gentleman who made professions of it. After hearing very attentively, however, all that had been said on this subject, and giving due credit to the ingenuity of gentlemen, whose arguments are certainly very specious, his mind had not been convinced but that the measure now proposed to the House perfectly comported with the national honor. It was true, indeed, that when we consult the conduct of nations, and those usages which have the force of laws, we shall find many traits that do not quadrate entirely with the principles deemed honorable in social life. But, in considering subjects of this kind, we must disentangle our minds from the consideration of municipal laws which have no bearing on this subject. Treason is a crime of the highest grade against the nation to which the traitor belongs. To withdraw allegiance from one nation and transfer it to that nation's enemy, during war, is treason against the sovereign authority to which allegiance was due. But how ought we to consider this crime? Though a crime against a man's own country, it is no crime against that to which he deserts. The desertion of a soldier from our enemy is surely no crime against the United States, and therefore, as to us, no crime at all. Mr. S. examined at some length the nature of allegiance and of the obligations it imposed. To screen a criminal of any kind was participating in his crime, and becoming accessory after the fact; but it had been the practice of all nations to receive deserters from their enemies, and to permit them to settle among them if they behaved as good citizens ought to do. The nice principles of honor the gentlemen had laid down, extended far enough, would impose on a nation the necessity of restoring to an enemy his deserters, and enabling him to punish their offence with death. If, however, as public law exists, we may give them aid and comfort, and afford them an asylum, we may as well add to other inducements as those which, the gentleman says, already operate so powerfully on the soldiers of our enemy. In so doing, the principle, which is not controverted, is extended but little further than at present, and in its moral consequences is certainly not so enlarged as to affect the national honor. The force of the enemy's examples had been passed over in silence by the gentleman, and their correctness tacitly admitted—their authority being denied only by the general intimation that such conduct was contrary to national law. The proposed measure therefore derived strength from the preceding conduct of the enemy. But, examine all history, ancient and modern, what had been the usual course of all nations at war? To weaken the hands of their opponents and strengthen the hands of themselves. Perhaps precedents derived from the Revolutionary war might not be considered by gentlemen as bearing on this point, since Britain then claimed us as her colonies. Recollect, however, her proclamations inviting our citizens to withdraw from their allegiance. Our history, it is true, is not ample, owing to the recency of its date. But it will be recollected that in the war with Tripoli, our gallant officer conducting the war on the land united himself on that occasion with a pretender to the Tripolitan throne, and took advantage of his rebellion to divide the forces of the enemy. Who censured that act? Who blamed Eaton for his conduct? Yet it was thus only the Dey was compelled to come to terms which he had before refused. This measure was clearly distinguishable from a bounty for assassination, to which it had been likened. Employing persons secretly to kill an enemy was a warfare worthy only of savages; it was an unmanly way of getting rid of those whom an army dare not meet in a field of battle. But to withdraw soldiers from an enemy's standard was not of this character, and was besides more correct under present circumstances, inasmuch as the enemy's army is not composed of soldiers of his own country, but of soldiers from Germany and other countries—men who owe no national allegiance to Britain, but are mere mercenaries in her ranks—who fight for those who pay them best. They are calculated to be the most dangerous enemies, but are willing to desert their leaders and join our standard on sufficient inducements. If they employ men owing them no allegiance, have we not a right to withdraw them if we can, and employ them to strengthen our own frontier? As to the objection that they would not settle, that objection is refuted by the terms of the resolution, which require actual settlement on the land. Let gentlemen acquainted with the Revolutionary war recollect how many of the good citizens of Pennsylvania and other States were deserters from the British ranks, Hessians, Germans, &c., and have become among our best and wealthiest and most useful citizens. Mr. S. concluded by observing that this was a clear question of expediency, perfectly within the scope of our policy, not contrary to national honor, merited the attention of the House, and ought to be referred as proposed to one of its committees.

After rejecting a motion made by Mr. BRADLEY, of Vermont, to lay the motion on the table, the question on its adoption was determined: For the motion 80, against it 55, as follows:

YEAS—Messrs. Alexander, Alston, Anderson, Archer, Avery, Barbour, Bard, Barnett, Bowen, Brown, Burwell, Caldwell, Chappell, Clark, Comstock, Condict, Conard, Crawford, Creighton, Crouch, Dana, Davis of Pennsylvania, Denoyelles, Desha, Eppes, Evans, Findley, Fisk of Vermont, Fisk of New York, Forney, Forsyth, Franklin, Gholson, Glasgow, Goodwyn, Gourdin, Griffin, Hall, Harris, Hawes, Hawkins, Hubbard, Humphreys, Ingersoll, Ingham, Irving, Irwin, Jackson of Virginia, Johnson of Kentucky, Kent of Maryland, Kerr, Kershaw, Lefferts, Lowndes, Lyle, McCoy, McKee, McKim, McLean, Montgomery, Murfree, Newton, Pickens, Piper, Pleasants, Rea of Pennsylvania, Rhea of Tennessee, Rich, Roane, Sage, Sevier, Seybert, Sharp, Tannehill, Telfair, Troup, Udree, Ward of New Jersey, Wilson of Pennsylvania, and Yancey.

NAYS—Messrs. Baylies of Massachusetts, Bayly of Virginia, Bigelow, Boyd, Bradbury, Bradley, Brigham, Butler, Caperton, Champion, Cooper, Cox, Culpeper, Davenport, Duvall, Earle, Ely, Farrow, Gaston, Geddes, Goldsborough, Grosvenor, Hanson, Hulbert, Jackson of Rhode Island, Kent of New York, King of Massachusetts, King of North Carolina, Law, Lewis, Lovett, Macon, Markell, Miller, Moffit, Moseley, Oakley, Pearson, Pickering, Post, John Reed, Ruggles, Sherwood, Skinner, Smith of Virginia, Stanford, Stockton, Sturges, Thompson, Vose, Ward of Massachusetts, Wheaton, White, Wilcox, and Winter.

So it was adopted by the House.

HONOR TO THE BRAVE.

Mr. HAWKINS, of Kentucky, in introducing the following motion, adverted to the unpropitious events attending the commencement of the war, the more mortifying because unexpected, which had caused to be overlooked by the National Councils some displays of valor and military skill which deserved the notice of Congress. This omission had been the more marked because of the almost unlimited plaudits during the same time bestowed on the officers of the Navy, &c. Had the nation noticed by civil honors the merits of a Pike, a Taylor, a Croghan, a Miller, and some others, perhaps they would have done but sheer justice. But his object in rising now was to present a motion limited in its character, and confined to objects which must meet the approbation of the House. The resolution he proposed, and which he had hoped some other member would before now have offered, was in the following words:

Resolved, That the thanks of the United States, in Congress assembled, be presented to Generals Brown, Scott, and Gaines, and their companions in fame.

Resolved, That General Brown be requested to communicate to the other officers and soldiers under his command the thanks of the United States in Congress, and the high sense of gratitude entertained for victories so splendid, achieved in contests so unequal.

Considerable desultory debate took place on this motion, not in opposition to the principle, but from difference of opinion as to the mode.

Mr. OAKLEY moved to commit the same to the Committee of Military Affairs, with instructions to inquire into the expediency of returning the thanks of Congress to such other officers and soldiers of the United States as may have distinguished themselves during the present war.

A motion was made by Mr. SHARP, to amend

the motion of Mr. Oakley, by inserting, after the word "Congress," the following: "with such other testimonials of the national approbation, as said committee shall deem advisable."

A motion was then made by Mr. Lowndes, to postpone, until Monday next, the further consideration of the resolutions; which was agreed to.

Thursday, September 29.

Another member, to wit: from Virginia, John Clopton, appeared, and took his seat.

The Speaker laid before the House the copy of a resolution, transmitted under cover to him from Philadelphia, passed by the Select and Common Council of that city, offering to Congress and Government the use of buildings in that city, for their accommodation, provided it shall be deemed expedient, in consequence of inconvenience experienced from the destruction of the Capitol, &c.—Referred to the committee already raised on that subject.

Mr. Lattimore, of Massachusetts, from the select committee appointed on that subject, reported a bill further to extend the right of suffrage in the Mississippi Territory, and to increase the number of members of the Legislative Council for the same.—Twice read and committed.

No other business being offered for consideration, and none of the committees being ready to report, the House adjourned.

Friday, September 30.

Several other members, to wit: from New Hampshire, Bradbury Cilley; from New Jersey, James Schureman; from Maryland, Nicholas R. Moore; appeared, and took their seats.

The Speaker presented a petition of the Legislature of the Indiana Territory, praying that certain companies of militia, called out for the defence of that Territory, may be paid by the United States.—Referred to the Secretary of War.

AMENDMENT TO THE CONSTITUTION.

The House, pursuant to the order of the day, resolved itself into a Committee of the Whole, on the proposition of Mr. Jackson, of Virginia, to amend the Constitution. That part of the motion was taken up which goes to provide

"That Congress shall have power to establish a National Bank, with branches thereof in any State."

Mr. Jackson said he did not intend to repeat the remarks which he had made when this subject was last year before the Congress, or to say anything in anticipation of the remarks which might be made for or against this proposition. The utility of a National Bank had been demonstrated by every day's experience. We know at this day, said he, that some State banks which have stopped payment have not only refused to receive the notes of those which continue to cash their notes, but have forced their holders to sell them at ten per cent. discount in the brokers' shops. Independent of this fact, it was held by all gentlemen of all parties that it is necessary to the convenience of our fiscal operations that there should be a National Bank. The only difficulty opposed to the adoption of the proposition now under consideration would be on the part of those who believed that the power proposed to be vested, already resided in Congress, and who might contend that the passage of such a motion as this would by implication deny the present existence of the power. Mr. J. said that he did not himself believe that any gentleman would be compromitted in this way by voting for this proposition; that it was best in all cases the least doubtful of Constitutional construction to make assurance doubly sure. Many of the State Legislatures had declared their opinion that a law establishing a National Bank would be an unauthorized act. It would be better, to avoid all difficulties, to consult their opinions, or, if you please, their prejudices, and receive at their hand, by liberal grant, a power so essential to the well being of the country.

Mr. McKee, of Kentucky, said as he could not vote for the proposition, it was perhaps due to himself, as well as the Committee, to state his reasons for voting against it, and why he thought it ought not to be adopted. If it were to be adopted and sent out to the States for concurrence, would not the question of constitutionality, he asked, be completely yielded on the part of those who voted for it? Whether, as such a vote would be a disclaiming of the power by Congress, reason and probability did not altogether forbid the expectation that the States would relinquish this power to the General Government? A large majority of the States already had a deep interest in the banking establishments within their respective jurisdictions; and, so far as the paper and business of a National Bank extended, it must so far deteriorate the State bank stocks, and curtail the revenues therefrom on which some of the States entirely rely for the support of their governments. Besides this, the interest of the local banks extended through all the ramifications of society. Almost every individual in every Legislature was in some degree interested in the success and prosperity of the State banks, and would be interested to refuse to grant the power if it was once yielded by the House. The question presented in this form appears to propose a relinquishment of power, and will afford an opportunity on which the States will gladly seize to withhold from Congress the right of exercising this power. He did not believe that the question of renewal of the charter of the old United States Bank at all decided the question of the Constitutional power of Congress. The history of that bank, as found on the Journals of Congress, was this: that Congress, in 1791, by a very large majority of both branches, passed a law establishing a bank, which was sanctioned by President Washington, and went into operation; that it afterwards received the sanction of Congress under the Administration of Mr. Jefferson, by the passage of laws establishing branches of it, and for the punishment of those who counterfeited its paper. It was a fact, that every member would concur with him in declaring, that many who voted against rechartering the bank, did so, not because they did not believe that Congress possessed the power, but because they believed the measure inexpedient. He hazarded nothing in saying that more than the number of the majority on that question entertained no Constitutional scruples on the subject. In the Senate the question was decided against renewing the charter by the casting vote of the President of that body, in which there were many who did not vote against it from Constitutional considerations. So far as any decision of Congress had authority, their decisions proved that Congress had the power. This subject had been so repeatedly discussed, that he supposed it would be useless to refer to the Constitution in relation to it. The question had become a point of political faith, and acquired the stability of some theological opinions, on which argument and reason were thrown away. He did not aspire to the ability to shake opinions of such long standing as he knew were entertained by some members of the House. But even the argument of the gentleman from Virginia this morning would prove the Constitutional power of Congress to establish a National Bank. The gentleman had informed the House that such a bank was necessary and indispensable for the convenient, faithful, and economical administration of the finances. Availing himself of this admission, and applying it to the general clause in the Constitution vesting powers in Congress, he contended no doubt could remain of the power being in Congress. By the Constitutional phrase "necessary and proper" was not meant an absolutely indispensable necessity, but any agency fitted, suited, applicable to, and connected with, the faithful administration of the finances. Every man not prejudiced must, by experience and the gentleman's admission, be convinced that Congress already have the power now proposed to be given to them. He then took a retrospective view of the operation of the refusal to recharter the old bank or establish a new one, and proved conclusively that the Government had been very greatly a loser, perhaps to the amount of four or five millions, by that omission—besides the reduced interests at which the facilities it afforded would have enabled the Government to obtain the loans they have since had occasion for. It was demonstrated that a bank of this description furnished facilities which no existing institution did; and it was therefore proved that its establishment was necessary and proper to the fiscal operations of the Government, and of course within the scope of their Constitutional power.

Mr. Jackson said, it must have been observed, that he had on all occasions purposely avoided expressing his opinion on the constitutionality of any act to establish a National Bank. He did not consider the votes, however, during the time he had held a seat in the House, as recognising the power; for instance, he did not imagine that any person could be considered as sanctioning the institution referred to by voting to punish the counterfeiting the notes of the bank. Policy and every consideration dictated that an offence of this kind should be punished, and the law for that purpose was proposed without adverting at all to the Constitutional question. In regard to the question of establishing new branches to the bank, it was one of more difficulty. The Constitutional question, however, was not on that occasion stirred before Congress, and he believed the yeas and nays were not called on it. The charter of the Bank of the United States was limited in its duration; and whilst it was in existence, it was the duty, to say the least of it, of the constituted authorities to give to it efficacy, to punish offenders against it. The charter of that bank was like the contracts which the Government has made with the national creditors—of which he hoped, none in this House or nation, whatever he had heard to the contrary, would go so far as to say the national faith was not pledged to redeem the last shilling. So in regard to the charter of the Bank of the United States. Those who opposed it offered no obstacle to fulfilling it after it was granted. The gentleman had said the State Legislatures and individuals composing them would oppose the grant of any such power as this to the National Government. Once establish the almost indispensable utility and importance of a National Bank, and there would be such a direct appeal to the honor and patriotism of the State Legislatures as to forbid for a moment the idea that they would not sanction its creation. Their private interest would vanish before the national good. But even if this base and grovelling passion had influence, it would not prevent them from granting the power he proposed to ask from them. Mr. J. made some observations going to show that the advantage to the individual States from the establishment of banks within their limits would operate as a counterpoise to the effect of the collision of interest between a National Bank and the State Banks—because the branches so to be established would be a great advantage to the community in which they were located. The gentleman appeared to think the adoption of the proposition would be a virtual acknowledgment that we do not now possess the power proposed to be given. The Constitution, Mr. J. said, would never be destroyed by the omission to exercise in their fullest plenitude the powers expressly granted in it, &c. He adverted to the eloquent argument of Vice President Clinton, on giving his casting vote against the renewal of the charter of the old Bank of the United States, before the Senate, in which body it had been argued solely on the ground of constitutionality. The Constitution, Mr. J. further said, admitted of different constructions, about which the most learned and the most virtuous men differ; but if one violation were to be made a precedent for a subsequent and analogous violation, the Constitution would become a matter of convenience, instead of an instrument of obligation. He adverted to the report of the Committee of Ways and Means at the last session, on the subject of the National Bank, who had decided that Congress had no power to establish one. When the law passed establishing the old Bank of the United States there had existed much doubt as to its constitutionality; and General Washington withheld his signature for some days in consequence of it. The same doubts still existed; and yet, where they were most strongly entertained, he had heard of no objection to amending the Constitution so as to grant the power. Let us not, said he, refuse to avail ourselves of the advantage of such an institution, and of removing our own honest scruples, by refusing to apply to the States for a grant of the power. Mr. J. concluded by expressing his hope, though that hope was much weakened by the prospect, that his proposition would be agreed to.

After a few words of explanation by Mr. McKEE, the proposition was negatived in Committee, who reported their disagreement to the House.

The question on concurring with the Committee in their disagreement to the proposition, was then decided as follows:

YEAS—Messrs. Alexander, Alston, Avery, Barnett, Baylies of Massachusetts, Bayly of Virginia, Bigelow, Boyd, Bradbury, Bradley, Brigham, Butler, Caperton, Caldwell, Champion, Chappell, Cilley, Clark, Clopton, Comstock, Cooper, Cox, Culpeper, Cuthbert, Dana, Davenport, Denoyelles, Desha, Duvall, Farrow, Findley, Fisk of Vermont, Fisk of New York, Forney, Forsyth, Gaston, Geddes, Goldsborough, Grosvenor, Hanson, Hawkins, Hubbard, Hulbert, Irving, Jackson of Rhode Island, Kent of New York, Kerr, King of Massachusetts, Law, Lefferts, Lewis, Lovett, Lowndes, Markell, McKee, Miller, Moffit, Moseley, Murfree, Oakley, Pearson, Pickering, Post, John Reed, Rhea of Pennsylvania, Rich, Ruggles, Sage, Schureman, Sevier, Sharp, Sherwood, Skinner, Stanford, Stockton, Strong, Sturges, Thompson, Vose, Ward of Massachusetts, Ward of New Jersey, Wheaton, White, Wilcox, Winter, and Yancey—86

NAYS—Messrs. Anderson, Barbour, Bard, Bowen, Brown, Burwell, Condict, Conard, Crawford, Creighton, Davis of Pennsylvania, Earle, Eppes, Evans, Franklin, Gholson, Glasgow, Goodwyn, Gourdin, Griffin, Hall, Harris, Hawes, Humphreys, Ingersoll, Jackson of Virginia, Kershaw, King of North Carolina, Lyle, Macon, McCoy, McKim, McLean, Moore, Newton, Pickens, Piper, Pleasants, Rhea of Tennessee, Roane, Smith of Virginia, Tannehill, Udree, and Wilson of Pennsylvania—44

On motion of Mr. JACKSON, of Virginia, the first, second, and third articles contained in the proposition aforesaid, were recommended to a Committee of the whole House on the state of the Union.

MONDAY, October 3.

Two other members, to wit: from New York, JOHN W. TAYLOR; and from Virginia, HUGH NELSON; appeared, and took their seats.

A resolution was offered by Mr. DESHA to instruct the Military Committee to inquire into the expediency of making compensation for horses lost in the service by mounted volunteers and militia; which was overruled by the House, by a small majority, under the impression, it appeared, that the subject was already specially referred to a different committee.

Mr. MONTGOMERY, of Kentucky, in offering the following, assigned as a reason his desire to put officers and privates on the same footing in this respect. The bill which was passed in 1813 on this subject, contained, when sent from this House, a provision applying to soldiers as well as officers, but that clause embracing privates had been stricken out by the Senate. His motion was in the following terms:

Resolved, That the Committee of Claims be instructed to inquire into the expediency of making provision for the widows and orphans of militia privates slain in the service of the United States.

The motion having been amended, on suggestion of Mr. DESHA, of Kentucky, so as to include also those who may die or have died whilst in the service, and also so as to refer the subject to the Military Committee, instead of the Committee of Claims, was agreed to.

HONORARY REWARDS.

Mr. TROUP, from the Committee on Military Affairs, reported resolutions expressive of the thanks of Congress for the gallantry and good conduct with which the arms of the United States have been sustained by Major General Brown, and Brigadiers Scott, Gaines, and Macomb, during the present campaign.

Mr. FISK, of Vermont, moved to refer the resolves to the Committee of the whole House. There were two names omitted in one resolve, he meant those of General Porter and General Ripley, which had been associated in all the actions named in it; and he did not see why, if such should also be the opinion of the House, they should not be incorporated in the resolution, as their merits in his opinion entitled them to be.

Mr. TROUP, of Georgia, said it was desirable that these resolutions should be acted on with unanimity; if not, they would be deprived of half their value and consequence—he should not, therefore, object to any course the House might think proper to pursue in relation to them. The report of this morning was intended only as a report in part. In acting on a question so environed with delicacy and difficulty as this, it had been necessary for the committee to prescribe some limitations to itself, and it appeared to them that the House would acknowledge the same necessity. The first limit they had agreed on was to the present campaign—the second, to General Officers in the Army of the United States. In considering this subject, the claims of others than those expressly noticed could not have been passed over by the committee. The names mentioned by the gentleman from Vermont had particularly claimed their attention. The name of Porter was intimately associated in military fame with those already mentioned. Not only had he been distinguished by his gallantry and good conduct in the field, but by his zeal and activity in collecting together a band of patriotic militia in aid of the regular army, at a time when that army most needed the services of such reinforce-

341   HISTORY OF CONGRESS.   342

October, 1814.   Removal of the Seat of Government.   H. of R.

ments. Under these circumstances, it was impossible for the committee to pass by, nay, not to notice with special attention the claim of General Porter; but it was inconsistent with the limitation the committee had prescribed to itself, inasmuch as he was not attached to the regular service, but an officer of the militia. As to General Ripley, it had been thought proper, as he had not been first in command on these occasions, to pass by his case for the present, referring it to a future occasion, on which it was the intention of the committee to embrace other cases of meritorious conduct displayed not only during the present but preceding campaigns.

Mr. FISK, of Vermont, said it was far from his intention to object to the testimony proposed to be given by the House to the merits of the officers named in the resolve, but to incorporate in it other characters, entitled, as he thought, to the like tribute. For that purpose, he wished it referred to a Committee of Whole.

The resolution was referred to a Committee of the Whole, and ordered to be printed.

REMOVAL OF THE SEAT OF GOVERNMENT.

Mr. FISK, of New York, from the committee to whom was referred the resolution directing an inquiry into the expediency of a temporary removal of the Seat of Government from the City of Washington, &c. reported:

"That the committee had had the same under consideration, and directed the Chairman to submit to the House the following resolution:

"Resolved, That it inexpedient to remove the Seat of Government at this time from the City of Washington.

The House having agreed to consider the report—

Mr. FISK, of New York, said he had reported that resolution in conformity to the directions of a majority of the committee; but he now thought it his duty to move to strike out the word "inexpedient," and insert the word "expedient."

A short desultory conversation took place between several members in relation to the state of defence of the place, &c.

When the question on Mr. FISK's motion to amend (the effect of which was to declare it expedient to remove) was taken and decided as follows:

YEAS—Messrs. Alexander, Alston, Baylies of Massachusetts, Bigelow, Boyd, Bradbury, Bradley, Brigham, Brown, Butler, Caldwell, Champion, Cilley, Clark, Condict, Conard, Cooper, Cox, Creighton, Davenport, Davis of Pennsylvania, Denoyelles, Desha, Duvall, Ely, Fisk of New York, Geddes, Grosvenor, Hulbert, Ingersoll, Ingham, Irwin, Jackson of Rhode Island, Kent of New York, King of Massachusetts, Law, Lovett, Lyle, Markell, Miller, Moffit, Moseley, Murfree, Oakley, Pickering, Piper, Post, John Reed, Rea of Pennsylvania, Rich, Ruggles, Schureman, Seybert, Sharp, Sherwood, Skinner, Stanford, Stockton, Sturges, Tannehill, Taylor, Thompson, Udree, Vose, Ward of Massachusetts, Ward of New Jersey, Wilcox; and Winter—68.

NAYS—Messrs. Archer, Avery, Barbour, Bard, Barnett, Bayly of Virginia, Bowen, Burwell, Caperton, Chappell, Clopton, Comstock, Crawford, Culpeper, Cuthbert, Dana, Earle, Eppes, Evans, Farrow, Findley, Fisk of Vermont, Forney, Forsyth, Franklin, Gaston, Gholson, Glasgow, Goodwyn, Griffin, Hall, Hanson, Harris, Hawes, Hawkins, Hubbard, Humphreys, Jackson of Virginia, Johnson of Kentucky, Kerr, Kershaw, King of North Carolina, Lefferts, Lewis, Lowndes, Macon, McCoy, McKee, McKim, McLean, Montgomery, Moore, Newton, Pearson, Pickens, Pleasants, Rhea of Tennessee, Roane, Sage, Sevier, Smith of Virginia, Streng, Stuart, Telfair, Troup, White, Wilson of Pennsylvania, and Yancey—68.

The House being equally divided—

The SPEAKER said, he was now called on to give a vote as unexpected as painful. He would, on this occasion, as on any other, regardless of the feelings that might be thereby excited, and the impressions probably received, give that vote which he believed the interests, safety, and honor, of the nation under all the circumstances to require. He was deeply impressed with the belief that these considerations required him to vote in the affirmative. The reason for this vote was, that this District could not be defended except at an immense expense, and an expense perhaps half of that which would be necessary to carry on the war.

So the amendment was carried.

Mr. LEWIS, of Virginia, moved to refer the report as amended to the Committee of the whole House, that it might be more fully and freely discussed.

Mr. BURWELL, of Virginia, appeared to favor the reference of this motion to a select committee to report a bill. Although against his own opinion, he admired the firmness and decision with which the Speaker on this, as on every occasion, had acted. He was desirous that this question should be decided as speedily as possible—and, although no person was more sanguine than he was that, before it was finally acted on, the opinion of the House would change on this subject, he was desirous now to see this resolve referred to a select committee with instructions to report a bill in pursuance thereof.

Mr. FISK having acceded to the proposed reference to a Committee of the Whole, the business was so disposed of, and made the order of the day for to-morrow.

TUESDAY, October 4.

On motion of Mr. GHOLSON,

Resolved, That the Committee of Ways and Means be instructed to inquire into the expediency of amending the "act laying duties on licenses to retailers of wines, spirituous liquors, and foreign merchandise," so as to allow the proprietors of spirituous liquors distilled from domestic materials, of which they are themselves the growers, to sell, without license, any quantity thereof not less than one gallon.

Mr. YANCEY, from the Committee of Claims, reported unfavorably to the petition of Edwin Lewis; which report was concurred in. The report is as follows:

343　　　　　　　　HISTORY OF CONGRESS.　　　　　　344

H. of R.　　　　　*Bounty on Prisoners—Removal of the Seat of Government.*　　　　　OCTOBER, 1814.

That the petitioner states, that in the years 1804, 1805, and 1806, a Captain Thomas Swain, of the United States' Army, cut and used for the public service a large quantity of timber belonging to the petitioner; that the petitioner sued him for it, and recovered judgment, and that the said Captain Swain has since died insolvent, without making compensation for the timber. The petition is not supported by any evidence of the facts; the committee are of opinion, however, that, taking the facts as true, the petitioner is not entitled to relief. They, therefore, recommend to the House the following resolution:

Resolved, That the prayer of the petitioner ought not to be granted.

Mr. YANCEY also made an unfavorable report on the memorial of Thomas Cutts; which was read, and referred to a Committee of the Whole. The report is as follows:

That Tristram Hooper, Moses Lowell, and Benjamin Chandler, were indebted to the United States by a judgment recovered against them on a revenue bond; an execution issued against their property, and was levied by the marshal of the district on three eighth parts of the schooner Catharine. At the sale of the schooner, the petitioner, Thomas Cutts, became the purchaser at the price of four hundred and twenty-five dollars. A claim to the three-quarters of the three-eighths of this vessel was afterwards set up by Asa Stevens; and, in action against the petitioner, it appears he recovered for damages, interest, and costs, the sum of $904 35; which sum the petitioner prays to be remunerated, together with the sum of $456, which he alleges had been paid to counsel and witnesses in the suit, and expended by himself in attendance, and for which it is stated his vouchers are lost.

The committee are of opinion the petitioner is not entitled to relief; they view this as a common case of sale, under an execution in which the plaintiff cannot be considered the warranter of the property. The purchaser buys at his own risk; and it is for him to judge whether the title of the defendant in the execution is good or bad. They, therefore, recommend to the House the following resolution:

Resolved, That the prayer of the petitioner ought not to be granted.

BOUNTY ON PRISONERS.

Mr. PLEASANTS, of Virginia, from the Committee on Naval Affairs, who were instructed to inquire into the expediency of extending to merchant recaptors the provisions of the bill allowing a bounty on prisoners to the owners and crews of private armed vessels, reported, that it was inexpedient to extend the provisions of the said act to the case just stated.

Mr. KING, of Massachusetts, opposed the adoption of this report on various grounds. The risk and importance of the recapture of merchantmen was not, he said, inferior to the risk and importance of captures by private armed vessels. The cause of humanity would be also served by it, as the lives of the enemy's seamen might in some instances be preserved, in consequence of such an inducement, &c. He hoped it would never be said that this House, by a large majority, determined to offer a bounty on deserters from the army of the enemy, and yet refused a small premium on seamen of the enemy thus meritoriously

made prisoners. Mr. K. concluded his observations by moving to amend the report by striking out "inexpedient," and inserting "expedient."

Mr. PLEASANTS, of Virginia, stated the reasons which had given birth to this report. The principal reason was, that whilst the proposed extension of bounty to such cases would add very little inducement to recapture, it would add very greatly to the hardship and suffering of those of our citizens who might be captured, who would undoubtedly be more rigidly secured, perhaps in irons, in consequence of the passage of the law.

Mr. KING replied. He did not apprehend that such oppression would be exercised as the gentleman supposed, and believed the objection not valid against the proposition to afford this small reward to our brave seamen for their adventurous valor. He considered this vote as the test whether the friendship expressed on all hands for our brave tars was substantial or mere profession.

Mr. LOWNDES, of South Carolina, explained his ideas of the policy of the act now proposed to be amended, which he did not look upon in the light of a bounty to privateers, but as an inducement to them to bring in prisoners when captured instead of releasing them. The proposed amendment he did not consider as at all essential to, or connected with the policy of that act—and the inducements to recapture he considered to be quite sufficient already without it.

The motion of Mr. KING was negatived, and the report accepted by a large majority.

REMOVAL OF THE SEAT OF GOVERNMENT.

The House, on motion of Mr. LEWIS, of Virginia, having taken up this subject, and being about to resolve itself into a Committee of the Whole thereon—

Mr. NEWTON, of Virginia, observed that he believed much debate was not necessary, as gentlemen had not only deliberated but already made up their minds. He wished to come at the question, and with many others had rather render his vote on this subject than hear any discussion whatever; and, therefore, moved an indefinite postponement of the question.

This motion was opposed by Mr. PICKERING, of Massachusetts, and Mr. GOLDSBOROUGH, of Maryland, both of whom placed their opposition on the ground of a desire for further information—the one, however, declaring his present opinion in favor of, and the other against, removal.

The question was then taken on indefinite postponement, and decided in the negative, many of those opposed to removal, having, with Mr. GOLDSBOROUGH, voted against indefinite postponement of the motion. For the postponement 61, against it 77, as follows:

YEAS—Messrs. Archer, Avery, Barbour, Bard, Barnett, Bayly of Virginia, Burwell, Chappell, Clopton, Culpeper, Dana, Earle, Evans, Farrow, Fisk of Vermont, Forney, Forsyth, Franklin, Gaston, Gholson, Goodwyn, Griffin, Hall, Hanson, Harris, Hawes, Hawkins, Hubbard, Humphreys, Hungerford, Irving, Kent of Maryland, Kerr, Kershaw, King of North Carolina, Lefferts, Lewis, Lowndes, Macon, McCoy,

345   HISTORY OF CONGRESS.   346

OCTOBER, 1814.   *Removal of the Seat of Government.*   H. OF R.

McKee, McKim, McLean, Montgomery, Moore, Nelson, Newton, Pearson, Pleasants, Rhea of Tennessee, Roane, Sage, Sevier, Smith of Virginia, Strong, Stuart, Telfair, Troup, White, Wilson of Pennsylvania, and Yancey.

NAYS—Messrs. Alexander, Alston, Baylies of Massachusetts, Bigelow, Boyd, Bradbury, Bradley, Brigham, Brown, Butler, Caldwell, Champion, Cilley, Clark, Comstock, Condict, Conard, Cooper, Cox, Crawford, Creighton, Davenport, Davis of Pennsylvania, Denoyelles, Desha, Duvall, Ely, Findley, Fisk of New York, Geddes, Glasgow, Goldsborough, Gourdin, Grosvenor, Hulbert, Ingersoll, Irwin, Jackson of Rhode Island, Jackson of Virginia, Johnson of Kentucky, Kent of New York, King of Massachusetts, Law, Lovett, Lyle, Markell, Miller, Moffit, Moseley, Oakley, Ormsby, Pickering, Pickens, Piper, Post, John Reed, Rea of Pennsylvania, Rich, Ruggles, Schureman, Seybert, Sharp, Sherwood, Skinner, Stanford, Stockton, Sturges, Tannehill, Taylor, Thompson, Udree, Vose, Ward of Massachusetts, Ward of New Jersey, Wheaton, Wilcox, and Winter.

The House then resolved itself into a Committee of the Whole on the report abovementioned.

Mr. PEARSON, of North Carolina, rose to speak against the resolution, and continued to speak with great ability and force of reasoning, as well on the question of expediency as on that of Constitutionality, until about three o'clock; when the Committee rose, reported progress, and the House adjourned.

WEDNESDAY, October 5.

Another member, to wit: from Rhode Island ELISHA R. POTTER, appeared, and took his seat.

REMOVAL OF THE SEAT OF GOVERNMENT.

The House again resolved itself into a Committee of the Whole on the report of the select committee on the expediency of a temporary removal of the Seat of Government. The resolution under consideration stands as follows:

Resolved, That it is expedient at this time to remove the Seat of Government from the City of Washington.

Mr. STOCKTON, of New Jersey, said, he had at one time determined to take no part in the discussion now before the Committee, but to remain satisfied with a silent vote. The subject had always appeared to him of such a nature, as to preclude any just expectation of good resulting from much debate. We should make no proselytes on one side or the other—the subject lies level with every man's understanding. Gentlemen need only to open the Constitution of their country—cast their eyes around—survey the District, and observe what was before them, to enable them to judge correctly. He had, however, been induced to alter this resolution by the course of argument which an honorable member from North Carolina (Mr. PEARSON, who he was sorry not to see in his seat) had thought proper to pursue. That gentleman had made many remarks which were susceptible of a satisfactory answer; many which Mr. S. thought ought not to go forth without an answer;—they might, if unanswered, be thought correct, and would, he feared, delude and mislead those whom that gentlemen had with so much zeal and ability attempted to serve. No gentleman, Mr. S. said, could feel less personal interest in the question than he did; coming from a State having very humble pretensions to consequence or patronage—never himself expecting to be here again after this session—he could view the subject with coolness and impartiality. The honorable member he alluded to had indulged himself in very extensive and wide excursions. Mr. S. would not attempt to follow him in his whole course, but content himself with selecting some of his leading points, leaving it to other gentlemen to remark on the residue if they saw fit. To get at the gentleman's argument at once, he would consider it under two general heads—

1st. The legal, Constitutional right of Congress to remove the Seat of Government.

2d. The propriety or expediency of exercising that right if they had it.

The gentleman from North Carolina had denied both; he would contend for the affirmative of each proposition.

1st. Does the Government of the United States possess the legal Constitutional power of removing itself from this District? Mr. S. said, it was obvious that this point must be subdivided into two: 1st. Has the Government the power of temporary removal? 2d. Has it the power of permanent removal? Mr. S. said, that he considered the first as the only question now properly before the Committee. It was true, that the proposition contained in the resolution was general in its terms, yet it seemed to be agreed on all sides, that only a temporary removal was contemplated at present. We were not ready now to act on so extensive a subject—one involving so many considerations of public interest, of private feeling and justice, as that of a permanent removal. This great point, then, was really not before the committee. But the gentleman from North Carolina supposing, probably, that upon the question of permanent removal he was impregnable, had pressed it into his service; its discussion was, therefore, proper, and might be useful. As to the legal Constitutional right of the Government to remove itself for a season on good and sufficient reasons, who, Mr. S. asked, could seriously doubt it? What section of the Constitution, what principle of reason, common sense, or common justice, could be relied on to take from the national councils so common and necessary an attribute of sovereignty? None could be produced; the gentleman could find none; no gentleman had hazarded the assertion. The honorable gentleman himself from North Carolina, with all his zeal, industry, and talent, had not brought his mind up to such an assertion in direct terms; yet it was necessary to a successful opposition to this resolution, not only to make, but to make good this extravagant position. Why, he asked, should the people have thus fettered, thus imprisoned, their Government? Why should an act, ascertaining the place where the Government should

347   HISTORY OF CONGRESS.   348

H. of R.   *Removal of the Seat of Government.*   OCTOBER, 1814.

sit, be considered so sacred as not to be approached by the Government which enacted it? Why,
like the laws of the Medes and Persians, should
it be irrepealable? If pestilence came—if famine
or war came—were we to be enchained to the
spot, by the magic force of an act not to be altered? The proposition was monstrous; he had
no hesitation in pronouncing that such an idea
was totally destitute of foundation, either in Constitutional law, common sense, or common justice. Congress, Mr. S. said, had settled this question by passing a law, not only asserting the right
of temporary removal for sufficient reasons, but
delegating that right to the President of the United States. He alluded to the act of 1794, by
which the President is authorized, by proclamation, to convene Congress at some other place
than that fixed by law, if, in his opinion, by reason
of a contagious disease, or any other cause, Congress could not meet at the Seat of Government
without danger to the lives and healths of the
members. If this matter had been exposed to any
doubt, this law would have settled it; it is a legislative authority upon the very point; and so far
are the people of the United States from entertaining the scruples the honorable gentleman had
imputed to them, that there was a very common
expectation in that part of the Union Mr. S. was
conversant with, that after the late inroad of the
enemy, and the destruction of the public buildings here, the President would by proclamation
have convened Congress at some other place.
He might have so done with strict propriety; the
fact which was before him, the catastrophe which
had happened, would have justified the conclusion
that we could not sit here with safety to the lives
and healths of the members; the general terms
of the act alluded to seemed designed to meet
such a case as had happened, and although the
President did not think proper to execute the authority, yet the investing him with it was decisive
of the right to remove for sufficient reasons. But,
Mr. S. said, he would go further, submit with
confidence to the Committee that the two Houses
of Congress, without the assent of the President,
might by a joint resolution remove themselves
for this session, and this would of course produce
a removal of the Government, and all its departments. Mr. S. relied on the fifth section of the
Constitution to prove his position. It is there
provided, "that neither House shall, without the
consent of the other, adjourn for more than three
days, nor to any other place than that in which
the two Houses shall be sitting." This provision
not only prohibits unseasonable adjournments
and separations, but expressly admits and regulates the general power of removal; and, (if a
grant of power was in such a case necessary,
though he thought it was not,) by necessary implication, it invests in the two Houses a right by
joint vote to adjourn to any other place; and yet
this is the very power of temporary removal
which seems now to be called in question. Mr.
S. said that he felt that he had troubled the Committee already too long upon this part of the subject; he should, therefore, leave the question of

the right of temporary removal, under the persuasion that no member of the Committee entertained a doubt about it.

The honorable gentleman from North Carolina
had expressly denied the Constitutional right of
Congress to pass an act for the permanent removal
of the Government—and he had warned the committee, and particularly his political friends, not
to break the Constitution of their country nor to
disregard the sanctity of contracts by adopting a
measure which however disguised under the mask
of a temporary removal had for its real object a
final change of the Seat of Government. Mr. S.
said that it would be a sufficient answer to this
course of reasoning to say that the question of
final removal was not now before us. All that we
were now prepared to act on—all that we should
determine by negativing the proposed amendment
would be, that it was expedient to remove for this
session or during the war to a place of more safety
and convenience than this District afforded in its
present circumstances. We might hereafter take
up and determine the other great point—or we
might leave it to our successors, who, coming
from the people after this discussion, would be
the better able to express the public sentiment.
But, Mr. S. said, he thought it best to follow the
gentleman over this ground. It was due to ourselves to examine the pretensions set up that we
might be freed from the imputations thrown out—
it was due to the citizens of the District to dissipate
the delusion under which they appeared to be,
and which the gentleman's very able argument
would tend to confirm if it remained unanswered.
That argument might be thus concentrated. A
permanent Seat of Government, says the gentleman, is required by the Constitution of the United States. By that instrument a power is given
to Congress to fix upon a permanent seat. Congress have appointed the place where this permanent seat shall be. The power is executed—the
seat is finally located, and cannot be altered by
law. This is the marrow of the gentleman's reasoning—but unfortunately it is entirely destitute
of foundation from first to last. The gentleman
sat out wrong and ended wrong—his premises
have no existence, and consequently the conclusion he drew must be unsound. A permanent
Seat of Government is not required by the Constitution; the Constitution vests no express power
in Congress to appoint a permanent Seat of Government; and Congress, by passing an act fixing
the Seat of Government at this place, have executed no such special authority as the gentleman
contemplates. The Constitution of the United
States, Mr. S. said, was penned with great precision; the great men whose work it was, did not
leave express grants of power to be deduced from
obscure sentences by a course of subtle reasoning:
if it had been their intention to guard a Seat of
Government by the ramparts of the Constitution,
to place it beyond the reach of the legislative arm;
if they had meant to impart to it the great principle of irremovability, it would have been done
by the use of clear, unambiguous expressions; it
would not have been left to be extracted from the

section on which the gentleman relied; some such provision as this would have been introduced—Congress shall have power by law to appoint a place for the permanent Seat of the Government of the United States, which shall not be changed, nor shall the law fixing the same be liable to be repealed by a future Congress. This or some article of similar import would have been ingrafted in the Constitution, if the Convention had intended to do what the gentleman says they have done; but there is no such provision; the only article having any relation to the Seat of Government, the only Constitutional provision which the gentleman could press into his service, is that part of the 8th section which ordains that "Congress shall have power to exercise exclusive 'legislation in all cases whatsoever over such dis-'trict, not exceeding ten miles square, as may by 'cession of particular States and the acceptance 'of Congress become the Seat of the Government 'of the United States, and to exercise like author-'ity over all places purchased by the consent of 'the Legislature of the State in which the same 'shall be, for the erection of forts, magazines, 'dock yards, and other needful buildings." This is the section upon which the gentleman relies—and Mr. S. said he would leave it to his candor whether it was not perfectly manifest, on the bare reading of it, that it was not intended to impart any principle of irremoveability to the Seat of Government, but simply and singly to secure to Congress the right of governing each and every place where the Seat of Government might be, and where the public money might be expended in works of defence—to his mind it was perfectly clear that this was the sound interpretation of the section. Mr. S. said, that the power of exclusive legislation over the Seat of Government was important and necessary to the dignity and even to the safety of the National Legislature. It could be derived from no other source than that of express grant from the people; it is granted in clear and precise terms. In addition to the evident sense and meaning of the language made use of—the other places besides the Seat of Government, over which the same section extends the legislative power of Congress must convince every one open to conviction, that the object was not to secure the permanency of the Seat of Government at one place, but merely the right of governing the people at any place; for the same provision in the same terms is applied to forts, magazines, arsenals, and dock yards; hence it would follow, if the honorable gentleman was right, that a fort, a magazine, an arsenal, or a dock yard once established could never be removed to a better site, or be abandoned without a breach of the Constitution and of the public faith. The article then upon which the gentleman relies, has no bearing on the question; it was designed to perform another office; to effect another purpose, which it has fully and effectually done. But, Mr. S. admitted that Congress have unquestionably the right to fix the Seat of Government—it might then be demanded of him how it possessed that power if not by Constitutional grant. The answer, he

said, was plain, the right was not derived from express grant, but was necessarily annexed to the Government immediately on its creation, by force of general principles inherent and essential to the legislative power. From these principles it inevitably resulted that every legislative power possessed a right to locate itself, to prescribe and regulate its times and places of sitting at its will and pleasure, unless restrained by the Constitutional instrument—hence it was not necessary to confer such powers by express grant. Therefore it is that there is no express grant, and it will appear upon examination that these powers are never referred to in the Constitution, but for the purpose of limiting the general power. The right then is inherent; it must be possessed by every legislative body; not by a grant of express power to determine times and places of sitting, but by the general grant of legislative power; such a power must be subservient to and be regulated by the legislative will, to be expressed in the ordinary way, by vote or statute. This vote or statute being nothing but the exercise of a common legislative sanction, was subject to be modified, altered, or repealed, at the pleasure of the Legislature. The case, then, said Mr. S. stands thus: the Constitution does not fix the Seat of Government. It does not even direct Congress to fix it—it merely secures the jurisdiction of Congress over it. It leaves the Legislature, in virtue of inherent powers, to determine the place. It has done so by common legislative act or statute. This act may be repealed or altered, because it is not the act of the people sitting in convention, but of the Legislature—a statute has appointed the place—a statute may change it. The Seat of Government has no Constitutional guard to keep it stationary; it must rely on the wisdom and justice of the legislative will. And, Mr. S. added, that this was the only true and safe ground upon which it could have been left. The Convention had acted wisely in leaving it where it was. The people never would have consented to any other arrangement, and those concerned had sufficient security that their rights would be properly respected. Mr. S. said he would submit it to the liberality of gentlemen to say whether a country circumstanced as this was when the Constitution was formed, paying a just regard to its rights and prosperity, could have delegated to Congress such a power as is contended for by the honorable member from North Carolina. A power to fix the Seat of Government—for centuries—forever. Who can believe that the people of the United States would have vested such a power in the Congress of 1789? Our country was then just emerging from the dangers and difficulties attending the war of the Revolution—our resources were not ascertained—our strength had scarcely begun to develope itself. The imbecility of the old Confederation had reduced us to a state of almost convulsive despair. A great crisis had arrived—it produced the Constitution. What candid man can believe that such a power, at such a time, would have been vested in any Congress? A power to fix a permanent Seat of Gov-

351 HISTORY OF CONGRESS. 352

H. of R. *Removal of the Seat of Government.* October, 1814.

ernment, without regard to the alterations, improvements, revolutions, and changes which would naturally be produced by a good Government, an increasing population, and the settlement of the vast regions of the Western country. To establish a Seat of Government independent of the National Legislature, where by force of law it must remain, in spite of the most weighty reasons of public interest and convenience. No, sir, said Mr. S, the enlightened people of the United States would have conferred no such powers on a single Congress—if such a provision had been presented to them they would have rejected it. They left this important concern where it might safely be deposited, not in the Congress—but in every Congress. The citizens interested in a particular spot had all reasonable security that their rights would be properly respected. It could never be presumed that the Legislature would remove without solid reasons. The loss of dignity—the trouble and expense incurred by a Government often "on wheels"—the money expended in public buildings and improvements—the influence of those residing at the Seat of Government, were all so many securities against hasty or injurious removals. Nor could he believe that a bill would ever pass all the branches of the Legislature to sanction a change unless it was bottomed on strong and palpable reasons. Mr. S. said that the train of argument which he had pursued furnished a conclusive answer to all the cases put by the gentleman from North Carolina, particularly to the case of the repeal of the statute establishing the Circuit Courts of the United States. The rights of the judges were Constitutional, they were founded on the express grants of that instrument, which ordained that they should hold their offices during good behaviour, and that their salaries should not be diminished; the objection to the repealing act was, that it was a mean of depriving them at once of both office and salary, which could not be legally done either openly or covertly. In the case before us he had shown that there was no such Constitutional grant, and therefore there could exist no Constitutional obstacle.

Mr. S. said that the honorable gentleman from North Carolina had relied much upon the word *permanent*, which he had found in the acts of Congress and of cession, and had from it contended, that it was the manifest sense of Congress and of the States of Maryland and Virginia, that the District being ceded and accepted, must always remain the Seat of Government. He observed that not much reliance was to be placed upon an argument derived from a syllable or a word in a statute, unless its meaning harmonized with the context and the manifest intent of the makers; that the word permanent was not to be found in the Constitution. That instrument only spoke of the Seat of Government, and therefore if it had been introduced into the laws with design to alter, enlarge, or restrain the Constitutional provision, it would be inoperative and useless. A statute could not run counter to the Constitution—it could neither restrain nor enlarge its provisions; if the expression was introduced with

any such intent it was vain and nugatory. But Mr. S. was satisfied that this was not the case; and that the word *permanent* was introduced for another and very different purpose. It would be recollected by every member that the same act which fixed the Seat of Government here after the lapse of ten years, established it at Philadelphia during that period; hence Philadelphia was the temporary, this the permanent Seat of the Government. The word *permanent* was evidently made use of to distinguish the proposed residence here from the temporary abode in Philadelphia. Indeed, the word itself when applied to statutory provisions meant nothing more than that there was no limitation of time annexed. As to the acts of cession, in his opinion they had no bearing on the question. The cession is required by the Constitution, and could only be made or received for the purposes contemplated by the Constitution. These were to enable Congress to exercise jurisdiction over the District as long as it remained the Seat of Government; and if they went further (which was not the case) they were so far void and nugatory. They could impart no principle of irremoveability not found in the Constitution itself. Nor did the makers of these statutes intend that they should. The operation of the acts of cession was merely to surrender the jurisdiction to Congress while the Seat of Government remained. The removal of Congress would not injure the political rights or liberties of the inhabitants. While the law remained unrepealed, they would be governed by Congress; a final removal would put an end to the whole fabric, and they would revert to their ancient allegiance, which the two States would not fail to claim. For these reasons Mr. S. thought that there existed no Constitutional impediment to a removal, much less was there any breach of contract or public faith in leaving the place, if the public interest required it. Congress possessed no power to contract, and never had contracted, that the Seat of Government should remain here. It is true, said he, that they fixed it here with a *bona fide* intent that it should remain here, believing then, that under existing circumstances, it was the most fit and convenient place; but Congress did never attempt to, nor could they, deprive their successors of the inherent right of removal when the public good should require it. Mr. S. said that he hoped he had established the right of Congress to remove the Seat of Government, either for a season or finally. For one he would never give up his right, nor hear it denied without entering his protest against it; but although he claimed the right of Congress to legislate on the subject, yet he acknowledged that it was a subject of great importance as it regarded the public and the citizens concerned. It behooved Congress, for its own dignity, not to be capricious as to the place of its location, and to take care not wantonly to sport with the feelings and interests of the inhabitants. He would never consent to exercise the right on light or trivial grounds. When he did exercise it, he would endeavor to do it with a sacred regard to the principles of justice, so that no man should be the loser by it. He would make compensation where compensation was due. As to the subject of compensation, Mr. S. said that he thought it not now before the Committee; yet he would say that he thought it ought to be made to many of the citizens in case of a final removal, but not to all. He would go on the principle of preventing actual loss, not that of securing gain. The great landholder who had converted barren land into city lots, and made a fortune out of his sales, was not to be compensated because he was prevented from making more. The speculator, too, must abide by his loss. The Government minion was not to be paid for being torn from his hold; it was a more humble and more meritorious class of citizens to whom he would extend compensation; to the men of moderate means; to the poor of the District, (if he might call them so without offence,) worthy men, who had laid out their all in procuring establishments which would be worth little if a removal took place. These men he would compensate, and he would do it on a large and liberal scale. Mr. S. said he would trouble the Committee no longer on this point. He trusted that he had made good his promise; that he had established the power of the Government to remove, to the entire conviction of the Committee. He should not revert to it again, but leave what he had said to take care of itself. But the propriety of exercising the right of removal still remained to be considered. Is it now expedient to remove the Seat of Government for a season to some other place? In this question, Mr. S. said every citizen of the United States had an interest. It was a great public question, and ought to be decided on principles exclusively public, on a cool and dispassionate consideration of the public good. If the public good, if the interests of this great and growing nation require a removal under existing circumstances, we ought to go, although the people of this District might be injured. If the public good forbids it, we ought to remain here, without any regard to personal inconvenience. He had made up his mind with reluctance; but, upon a view of the whole subject, he thought a temporary removal at least was essential to the honor and interest of the nation. He had come to this conclusion on the grounds that we could not be accommodated here in such a manner as was essential to the public service, and that the Government would not be in safety here during the war, without incurring an enormous expense, which the Treasury was unable to pay, and to which it ought not to be exposed. As to accommodations, Mr. S. said he did not mourn over our losses on account of "soft seats," or "splendid furniture"—no chair was too hard, no furniture too plain for him—but are the accommodations reasonable? Such as would secure the health of the members, and enable them to do the public business with propriety and to advantage? He thought that they were not. In regard to ourselves, said Mr. S., here we are in the Patent Office; in a room not large enough

13th Con. 3d Sess.—12

to furnish a seat for each member, when all are present, although every spot, up to the fire-places and windows, is occupied. When Winter comes and fires must be lighted, or if we should have a Summer session, (which appears inevitable, if the war continues,) he did not believe that the health of the members could be preserved in that room. Some better place of sitting must be provided. Here, then, was no other resource but in repairing the public buildings—were gentlemen prepared for this? Would they follow up a vote to remain here with large appropriations for this purpose, exposed as we should be during this wretched war to other attacks? He believed not; no gentleman was prepared to do this now; every cent which we could raise would be necessary for more important concerns; concerns of vital importance, of indispensable necessity, to prop the drooping credit of the nation; to pay the soldier and sailor who are fighting our battles. Are we then to remain here in our present condition until that peace which we have wantonly thrown away shall return? Are we thus to expose ourselves because the good people of this District do not choose to part with us? He hoped not. If we removed to Philadelphia, we were offered accommodations without incurring any expense, and might remain there until this place, or any other, which the wisdom of Congress might select, was prepared for our reception.

Mr. S. said that he would dwell no longer upon this point; he was willing to acknowledge that it was the other consideration he had alluded to which most influenced him; it was the enormous expense which would be incurred in defending the Government at this place. He was very doubtful whether we could be defended at all by the description of force we could command—a militia force, to be collected principally from the neighboring States of Maryland and Virginia. He had little reliance on the efficacy of such a defence; it had once been tried, and failed, so completely and radically as to involve the nation in disgrace. The force, upon this occasion, was of as good a character as any that could be procured now, and, being under the same direction, he could see no security against the repetition of the same disgraceful scene. This District, he said, was most assailable; it might be approached by water at different points within a few hours' march. A small addition of force, a small variation of plan, would enable an enterprising and disciplined foe to repeat his triumph. The presence of Congress here would be the only inducement for the enemy again to attack the place, and he thought it a very strong inducement. It was evident that the war on the coast was, on the part of the enemy, merely predatory, intended not so much to attain objects important in a military point of view as to harass the Government, and expose it to much trouble, and expense, and mortification. The dispersion or capture of the members of Congress, now assembled, would gratify the pride and resentment of the English nation more than any other operation their army on the coast could perform. He

355   HISTORY OF CONGRESS.   356

H. OF R.   *Removal of the Seat of Government.*   OCTOBER, 1814.

thought that there was a great [probability that the enemy would make the attempt; they were yet in the neighborhood, evidently waiting the arrival of reinforcements. To his mind, there could be presented no more unfit or disgraceful a situation to which the enemy could expose us, than to oblige the National Legislature, whose deliberations should be removed from the din of arms, to be witnesses of a battle fought in their neighborhood, upon which their safety depended. If unsuccessful, (and we had no great reason to expect success,) the members might be made prisoners, or owe their safety to flight; their papers lost, themselves held up as objects of scorn to the foe, and of contempt to their own people. But if he should admit that the Government could be defended here, yet the expense would be enormous. Some days ago, the honorable chairman of the Military Committee had informed us that it was the intention of the War Department to keep up a disposable force of twenty-one thousand militia for the defence of the District; and, since, it had been intimated from the same quarter that it was to be increased to thirty thousand. Including pay of officers, waste, the wear and tear of such an expensive description of troops, the expense of each man would not be less than one dollar and fifty cents per day. Twenty thousand men would cost thirty thousand dollars a day, or ten millions nine hundred and fifty thousand dollars a year. Thirty thousand men would require forty-five thousand dollars a day, or sixteen millions four hundred and twenty-five thousand dollars a year. He considered this calculation as moderate, and he asked if such an expense could be endured; he thought it ought not to be endured; no, not for a month, a week, or a day. The country could not sustain it; the people would never submit to it; they could not, and would not, defend this District at such a cost. It had been asserted that the same force would be required, and the same expense incurred, if the Government removed; for that this place and Baltimore must be defended. Mr. S. observed, that the destruction of the public buildings, of the navy yard, and the public property here, had taken away every inducement to attack the place, except dispersing the Government. It seemed therefore to follow, that, if the Government removed, little or no force need be kept on foot here. And, with respect to Baltimore, no one could believe that the United States meant to provide twenty or thirty thousand men and keep them in service to defend that city. The Baltimore troops were numerous and respectable, and would require little aid, except when particularly threatened, and the necessary aid would soon be received from the adjoining country and States; that is to say, as many militia as would answer any valuable purpose. He had no opinion of keeping large bodies of militia in camp, they become homesick, and on a retreat would never stop until they got home. It was true that the people of the District were entitled to protection; but they must be contented with the same kind of defence as was afforded to their fellow-citizens elsewhere. But he would ask, what other spot of the same dimensions and population had such a defence as was calculated upon here? He was satisfied, for himself, that this great force, this heavy expense, would not be required if the Government should remove. It would, in a great measure, be saved to the Treasury and the people. The times, he said, called for rigid economy in every department. The people would soon be taxed for almost everything which they wore or ate; almost for the air they breathe. It could not be expected that they would, under present circumstances, be willing to see their money thus squandered only to gratify the false pride of making laws *among ruins.* For his part, he thought it unjust, and would never assent to it. Mr. S. said that, before he sat down, he would declare that he had no covert intention; that he meant to go no further than he had expressed. He had formed and would deliver no opinion as to the permanent removal; that was a great national question; it might be safely confided to the wisdom and justice of a future Congress. The people of this District, he thought, had great claims and great advantages; the inducements to return here would be strong; nothing but a conviction that, upon great principles, the good of the nation required a removal, could prevent the return of the Government. There exists a statute, having no limitation, fixing the Seat of Government here: this must be repealed, or the Government must return. There is in th e District a real estate belonging to the United States of considerable value. The inhabitants have many claims upon the justice of the Government which will not be overlooked. They have also the zealous support of a great interest from the Southern States. The probability is, that a majority will never agree upon any other place. He therefore thought that they had magnified the danger they were in. If the removal was temporary the evil would be temporary, and must be set down to the account *of this war.* If it was final, compensation would be made in all cases in which it was due. On the whole, he should vote against the amendment proposed by the honorable member from North Carolina.

Mr. GROSVENOR and Mr. FISK, of New York, spoke in favor of removal, and Mr. MACON, of North Carolina, and Mr. FISK, of Vermont, and Mr. RHEA, of Tennessee, against it.

Mr. PEARSON, of North Carolina, had yesterday made a motion to amend the above resolve by striking out the word "expedient" and inserting in lieu thereof, the word "inexpedient."

The question on this motion was decided in the negative by the following vote: For the amendment 67, and against it 70.

The Committee then rose, and reported progress.

THURSDAY, October 6.

Another member, to wit: from New York, ZEBULON R. SHIPHERD, appeared, and took his seat.

357 HISTORY OF CONGRESS. 358

OCTOBER, 1814. *Removal of the Seat of Government.* H. OF R.

REMOVAL OF THE SEAT OF GOVERNMENT.

The House resumed the consideration of the resolution declaring it expedient at this time to remove from the City of Washington.

Mr. PEARSON addressed the House as follows—

Mr. Speaker: I very much fear the House will be ill requited for their indulgence in acceding to an adjournment yesterday at my instance. This apprehension is heightened by the circumstance, that it has fallen to my lot to enter the lists with an adversary so powerful, so justly distinguished, as the honorable gentleman from New Jersey (Mr. STOCKTON.) The odds are, indeed, awful. My reliance is in the justice of my cause, and the candid and liberal judgments of those who hear me. I must, however, be permitted to say, that the argument of the honorable gentleman from New Jersey, (whom I have so often heard with conviction and delight when engaged in a better cause,) has tended to confirm rather than disturb the opinions I entertain on the question submitted for our decision.

The insulated proposition before us is, whether it be expedient or inexpedient for Congress to remove the Seat of the General Government from its present abode to some other place for a limited time. The specious garb which envelopes this proposition hides from the superficial eye much of its real deformity. It is our right and our duty to strip it and analyze it with that accuracy due to its importance—with that care which is demanded by a sacred regard for the national faith, the national interest, and above all the preservation of the union of these States.

Perhaps few articles in our Constitution have marked more fully the wisdom and foresight of those illustrious men who framed that charter of liberty, than the provision in the 8th section of the 1st article, which says, "Congress shall exer-' cise exclusive legislation, in all cases whatso-' ever, over such district (not exceeding ten miles ' square) as may, by cession of particular States ' and the acceptance of Congress, become the Seat ' of the Government of the United States," &c.

The policy of this power in Congress is as manifest as the freedom and independence of its sessions, its members and deliberations are essential. That this sentiment may not rest on my authority alone, I beg leave to enforce it by an authority which will not be disregarded by gentlemen on this side of the House, with whom in general I have the satisfaction to think and to act, but many of whom I regret to find on this occasion embodied against me. The authority alluded to, is that excellent exposition of the Constitution entitled *The Federalist.* This authority will not be objected to by the other side of the House, when they are informed that the extract I am about to read is the production of the present Chief Magistrate.

In considering the section of the Constitution to which I have referred, this author says: "The ' indispensable necessity of complete authority at ' the Seat of Government, carries its own evidence ' with it. It is a power exercised by every Legis-' lature in the Union, I might say of the world,

' by virtue of its general supremacy. Without it, ' not only the public authority might be insulted, ' and its proceedings be interrupted with impu-' nity, but a dependence of the members of the ' General Government on the State comprehend-' ing the Seat of the Government for protection ' in the exercise of its duty, might bring on the ' National Councils an imputation of awe or in-' fluence, equally dishonorable to the Government ' and dissatisfactory to the other members of the ' Confederacy."

For those reasons, and many other considerations which will suggest themselves to every reflecting man, Congress were vested with the power, and it became their duty, to establish the Seat of the General Government in the manner prescribed by the Constitution. This power has been exercised, this duty has been performed. The subject demanded and received the attention due to its importance by the first Congress which assembled after the adoption of the Constitution. Many of the members of the first Congress had also been members of the Convention, and may well be presumed to have best understood the powers given and duties enjoined by that sacred instrument which they had contributed to form. It would be little less than impious to accuse them of violating their own act; it would be the extreme of presumption to charge them with ignorance as to the limitation of powers which they themselves had prescribed.

By reference to the Congressional Register of 1789, it will be found that the first Congress had scarcely assembled before their attention was peculiarly directed to the important subject of locating the permanent Seat of the General Government in the mode pointed out by the Constitution. Those friends of union well knew the necessity of this power, and its inevitable tendency to bind faster and faster the members of this political association, some of whom were but feebly knit together, and the cement of the whole yet soft and infirm. Every effort was therefore essential to give a heart to this body, from which its several members would derive support, strength, and confidence. This great object was to be effected by embracing the earliest opportunity to establish the permanent Seat of the General Government on principles of justice and equality; having a due regard to the extent, population, and convenience of all the States; regarding, at the same time, the progressive increase of our Western settlements, the Atlantic navigation, and a convenient intercourse with the Western country. Upon these principles, it was resolved by the first Congress to fix the permanent residence of the Government.

It will be recollected by the House that, in the course of my remarks the other day, I referred to the speeches of almost every distinguished member of the first Congress in relation to this subject, from which it appeared that not one individual member questioned the Constitutional right of Congress to establish permanently the Seat of the Government. On the contrary, every member knew and admitted they were then legislating on

359   HISTORY OF CONGRESS.   360

H. of R.   *Removal of the Seat of Government.*   October, 1814.

a question not so important to themselves at that moment, but which was deemed vitally important to the perpetuity of the Union, as it would be binding for ages yet to come. With this understanding, and for this object, we find the word *permanent* emphatically used in every resolution, in every act, in every speech, syllable, or letter on this subject. It is true, in the discussion on this subject, local jealousies, local feelings and influence were not totally discarded. They were manifested as to the place which should become the centre of the Union, but entered not into the question of the perpetuity of the act about to be performed. The essence of the act was its perpetuity, its binding force on future legislatures, to put forever at rest a question, the agitation of which might in after times awaken and give new vigor to passions and jealousies, which the adoption of the Constitution had hushed, and which it was the first duty of wise legislators to keep in profound sleep; because, if again aroused, they might shake the Union to its centre.

The principles on which the permanent Seat of the General Government should be established being recognised and admitted by all, the contest solely rested between the rival pretensions of the banks of the Susquehanna and those of the Potomac. The superior claims of the Potomac ultimately prevailed, and Congress did, on the 15th of July, 1790, and by an amendatory act of March 3d, 1791, designate and accept the present District of Columbia for "the permanent Seat of the Government of the United States." By the same and subsequent acts, the President was authorized to enter into engagements for the acceptance of such quantity of land on the east side of the Potomac, within the said District, as he might deem proper for the use of the United States. He was authorized to erect public buildings, and, through the agency of commissioners, to lay off and designate the plan of this city, which bears its name. For this purpose, he was vested with power to enter into contracts and stipulations with the proprietors of lands within the limits of the city for an absolute transfer of their lands in fee simple, for the objects contemplated, and in consideration of the act of Congress establishing the permanent Seat of the Government of the United States. By virtue of the powers vested in the President, and in consideration of the objects specified in the several acts of Congress alluded to, the proprietors did cede to the United States at least three-fourths of all the lands within the limits of this city, and for which no compensation was received, except for a few acres on which public buildings were erected, and some squares exclusively designed for public purposes. In furtherance of these objects, a great variety of other powers were granted to the President, the execution of which necessarily involved the interests of numerous individuals, and for the successful completion of which public faith could and did alone constitute the guarantee. Under these powers, and for the objects contemplated, large donations were received, lots were sold, loans were obtained, and pledges given, for their re-payment, of the very property which had been surrendered by individuals to the United States.

The donations from the States of Maryland and Virginia, together with the sale of lots, which cost the Government nothing, amount to more than eight hundred thousand dollars. The public ground remaining unsold, is estimated at nearly one million of dollars. It may be worthy of remark, that soon after the establishment of this District as the *permanent* seat of the Government, foreigners were authorized to purchase and hold lands within its limits. The then President of the United States, General Washington, availed himself of this circumstance, not only to raise funds, but also to interest respectable foreigners and skilful artisans of all countries in aid of this new but extensive establishment. With this view agents were sent to Europe with official certified copies of all the laws and proceedings in relation to this subject, on the authority of which artists were induced to come from various parts of Europe and settle here. Large sales of city lots were made in different countries of Europe, particularly Holland and England, which property to the amount of three hundred thousand dollars is still held by those purchasers or those claiming under them.

Two other material parties to the compact for fixing the permanent Seat of the Government yet remain to be heard. These are the States of Virginia and Maryland. We need barely refer to the laws of those States to learn the motives and considerations which induced them to surrender their jurisdiction not only of soil but persons, to the extent of ten miles square in the most important section of their States. I will call the attention of the House for a moment to a few of the provisions of an act of Maryland, passed 19th December, 1791, entitled "An act concerning the Territory of Columbia and City of Washington." The preamble commences in these emphatic terms: "Whereas the President 'of the United States, by virtue of several acts 'of Congress, and acts of the Assemblies of Vir- 'ginia and Maryland, by his proclamation, dated 'at Georgetown, on the 30th day of March, 1791, 'did declare and make known, that the whole of 'the territory of ten miles square, for the per- 'manent Seat of Government of the United 'States, shall be located," &c. "And, whereas 'Notley Young, Daniel Carroll of Duddington, 'and many others, proprietors of the greater part 'of the land hereinafter mentioned, have been 'laid out in a city, came into an agreement, and 'have conveyed their lands in trust to Thomas 'Beall, son of George, and John Mackall Gantt, 'whereby they have subjected their lands to be 'laid out as a city, given up part to the United 'States, and subjected other parts to be sold to 'raise money as a donation to be employed ac- 'cording to the act of Congress for establishing 'the temporary and permanent Seat of the Gov- 'ernment of the United States, under and upon 'the terms and conditions contained in each of 'said deeds," &c.

By the second section of said law, it is enacted,

361   HISTORY OF CONGRESS.   362

October, 1814.   *Removal of the Seat of Government.*   H. of R.

"That all that part of the said Territory called 'Columbia, which lies within the limits of this 'State, shall be, and the same is hereby acknowl- 'edged to be, forever ceded and relinquished to 'the Congress and Government of the United 'States, in full and absolute right and exclusive 'jurisdiction, as well of soil as of persons resi- 'ding or to reside thereon, pursuant to the tenor 'and effect of the eighth section of the first arti- 'cle of the Constitution of the United States," &c. This law then proceeds to subject other lands within the limits of the city to the same terms and conditions as those which had been transferred as before recited, and concludes by making a donation of $72,000, to be applied to the erection of public buildings or other improve- ments in the City of Washington for the use of the United States. As this subject was until very lately little understood by myself, and pos- sibly less so by many members of the House, I have deemed it necessary to a correct decision, and a proper application of facts to principles, to give a general history of the establishment of the Seat of Government at this place, that we and the nation should know and reflect on the nu- merous obligations by which the Seat of Gov- ernment is bound to its present spot—obligations resting not on fluctuating notions of policy, but flowing from the Constitution, sanctioned by re- peated laws, rivetted by compacts with States and individuals, and rendered sacred by the plighted faith of the nation.

I will now endeavor, Mr. Speaker, to pursue more directly the arguments of the gentleman from New Jersey through all their divisions and subdivisions, and also notice some remarks which have fallen from the gentlemen from New York, (Messrs. Grosvenor and Fisk.) The gentle- man from New Jersey contends: 1st. That Con- gress have the right to remove the Seat of Gov- ernment for a limited time, on good and sufficient reasons. This is a position so broad and indefi- nite as not to admit of a distinct reply. That circumstances and exigencies may happen which would render the exercise of such a power not only proper but necessary, never was and never can be questioned. The very terms of the gen- tleman's position, "on good and sufficient rea- sons," do impliedly, if not expressly, admit, that this right does not exist and cannot be exercised as an ordinary discretionary legislative power. The cases put by the honorable gentleman of pestilence, famine, and invasion, are cases of *ne- cessity,* where nothing is left to legislative will, where no human laws can control; the argu- ment, then, like all arguments drawn from neces- sity, proves too much, and therefore proves no- thing at all.

The act of 1794, which the gentleman has brought to his aid, and on which he placed great reliance, is precisely of the character of the other instances adduced, and must fall into the same result. By that act the President was authorized to convene Congress at a different place from that to which it was adjourned, in the event of the prevalence of contagious sickness or other

circumstances which, in his opinion, would be hazardous to the lives or health of the members. This act was proper because it was necessary to the existence of Congress itself; it grew out of the circumstance of the yellow fever, which pre- vailed in Philadelphia about that time, and can- not be considered as an ordinary exercise of pow- er in Congress to change the seat of Government *ad libitum.* To argue from the case which the gentleman has put, that the Seat of Government may be changed whenever Congress may think proper, is, in my judgment, as absurd as it would be for me to contend that the Seat of Govern- ment must continue here, although the whole District were swallowed up by an earthquake. As to a temporary removal, my argument is sim- ply this, that Congress has not the right to re- move the Seat of Government for a limited time, unless for imperious causes, which, if they con- tinue to exist, would justify and render inevitable a permanent removal. Such cases do not exist; they are not pretended to exist. The gentleman, as if indeed hard pressed for argument, has re- sorted to the fifth section of the Constitution to prove what never was disputed—what may be termed an every day practice—That the two Houses of Congress may by joint resolution ad- journ for more than three days—may adjourn their sessions without the concurrence of the Executive, and that neither House shall without the consent of the other change the place of its sitting. The only power given to Congress by this section is, that of regulating its own ad- journment independent of the Executive branch of the Government; the other part of the sec- tion is a necessary restriction on each House separately, to produce harmony in their proceed- ings, despatch of business, and to prevent unrea- sonable adjournments and inconvenient separa- tions, or in other words, to prevent the two Houses from being too far apart for the neces- sary concurrence of legislation and despatch of public business. I appeal with confidence to the candor of the gentleman himself. I appeal to the common sense of every member of the House, whether it can for a moment be believed, that this section of the Constitution gives to Con- gress the power, (without even the form of a law,) to remove the Seat of the Government of the United States? Will it be contended (ad- mitting for a moment that we have the right ourselves to remove) that we can, without a law, compel the President and all the Departments to march off to Philadelphia or to the Alleghany mountains at the word of command, or that they would, without the authority of law, exercise at their new locations one single function of their departments? But, says the gentlemen, if we go, the President and Departments will follow, and thus we remove the Government. Thus by a sort of legislative legerdemain we put the Gov- ernment on wheels and push off at full gallop. I must confess, Mr. Speaker, I am shocked at such an argument from such a source. I had believed that the fair and lofty mind of the honorable gentleman from New Jersey could not have de-

363   HISTORY OF CONGRESS.   364

H. of R.   *Removal of the Seat of Government.*   October, 1814.

scended so low. I had been taught to believe that the pure principles of Federalism disdained to do an act indirectly which could not be done directly without a violation of the Constitution. "If you cannot take the man from the office, so neither can you take the office from the man." This I have always understood to be the creed of Federalism. If the gentleman has abjured the faith in this instance, I am disposed to consider it as one of those great errors to which *great* men are said to be liable; and that his most sanguine friends and believers on this question will admit the possibility of his being equally incorrect in the general tenor of his argument.

The next position of the honorable gentleman is, the right of Congress to remove permanently the present Seat of Government. On this question I have already, to a considerable extent, anticipated my argument in the exposition I have given of the Constitution, the laws, and contracts in relation to this subject. The remarks of the gentleman, however, demand a reply. I can justly retort the charge of having assumed premises totally incorrect, and therefore protest against the conclusions drawn from them.

The gentleman, I know, is incapable of intentional misrepresentation; but he has most strangely and most erroneously attributed to me an argument or rather an assertion which I never did or could have used. I did not say that the Constitution fixed the Seat of Government, or in express terms required Congress to establish the permanent seat.

It is, however, on this supposition that the gentleman has triumphantly turned over the pages of the Constitution, and sought in vain for any such terms or express injunctions on Congress. On this basis his argument is built, and he does, indeed, most conclusively prove what was never disputed.

Sir, my argument is that the Constitution contemplated and authorized the establishment of the Seat of the Government of the United States, at a place to be ceded by particular States and accepted by Congress, and over which Congress were to exercise exclusive jurisdiction. The time and manner of executing these powers and performing these duties, were left exclusively to Congress, without any other limitation than as to the extent of territory thus to be acquired, and the objects for which it was so to be acquired. This being an express grant of power for a definite object, necessarily requiring the consent of other parties, and deeply involving the rights and interests of States and individuals, whenever it was exercised, the objects obtained, and the acts consummated by Congress, the Government were bound to fulfil the engagements of Congress, who were *quo ad hoc* the legitimate agents of the Constitution. The first Congress after the adoption of the Constitution did thus bind the Government by establishing its permanent Seat; and in so doing did not transcend their powers. The gentleman says it is monstrous, it is absurd, to suppose that the people would have consented to vest Congress with such power. Sir, the people

did not hesitate to vest Congress with this power, and for the best reasons—to harmonize, to cement and perpetuate the union of these States. Who were to be trusted with this power? The First Congress, men chosen by the people for their firm virtue and distinguished worth, most of them members of the Convention, men to whom the people had trusted, but a little time before, their political existence. Besides, sir, if this was a dangerous power—if it has been abused—the remedy is with the people, as in all other cases of constitutional error or legislative abuse; experience has proved that neither the one or the other exists on the present subject.

The objection as to power would equally apply to all acts of Congress which are binding and irrevocable. It would apply to all cases of compact, of bargain and sale, of grants, and of vested rights of every description. As well might it be contended that Congress has not the right of disposing of all the unappropriated lands of the United States, because by possibility they may give it away or make bad or corrupt bargains. As well might it be said that this Congress may take away the premium given for the late loans; reduce the interest on the public stock, or *spunge* the debt itself. This legislative *omnipotence*, which is established by the doctrine that one Legislature can in no case bind a subsequent one, is abhorrent to the first and best principles of the Constitution, destructive of the national faith, and pregnant with evils not to be described.

This doctrine, I had thought, was long ago exposed and exploded by those whom I have considered the firmest champions of the Constitution; but, alas, all those ramparts so strongly erected by those of our political predecessors, whom we have most delighted to honor, and around which we have so often and proudly rallied, seem to me now to be prostrate; the sentinels have fled their posts; the Constitution is the plaything of every idle wind; the sport of every angry passion.

In my remarks the other day, I attempted to point out the analogy between the removal of the Seat of Government and the repeal of the Judiciary, and consequently the analogy between the erection of the two establishments and the principles upon which their permanency depends. The gentleman from New Jersey must excuse me for saying, that his reply to this part of my argument was peculiarly inconclusive. He says that the Seat of Government is not fixed by the Constitution. This is true; but it is equally true, that neither the Supreme or inferior courts are established by the Constitution. The Seat of Government was established by law, resulting from an express grant of power, if not an express requisition of the Constitution. The courts were established precisely in the same way. The immutability of the Supreme Court is admitted by all; the power to destroy the inferior courts is denied by the gentleman from New Jersey, and I presume all his political friends, on the ground of the necessary independence of the judges, and the contract, either express or implied, that they

365 **HISTORY OF CONGRESS.** 366

OCTOBER, 1814. *Removal of the Seat of Government.* H. OF R.

should not be deprived of their offices, either directly or indirectly, during good behaviour. The Constitution does not say, " that Congress shall ' have power to establish permanent courts, which ' shall not be changed, nor the law fixing the same ' shall not be altered or liable to be repealed by ' any future Congress;" which words the gentleman from New Jersey alleges would have been used had the Constitution intended to give the power to Congress to establish the permanent Seat of the Government. No, sir, the construction in both cases results from the nature of the powers granted, and the objects to be effected. The Constitution authorized but one Supreme Court to be established by Congress—when it was so established the power was executed, the injunction of the Constitution fulfilled—the law could not be repealed. The Constitution authorized but one district of territory, and that not to exceed ten miles square, to be accepted for the Seat of the Government, and that Congress should, like the judges in their respective spheres, be independent; they were to exercise exclusive jurisdiction over the territory where the Government was located. The idea, therefore, that Congress may abandon this place at pleasure, is, in my judgment, as incorrect as the destruction of the circuit courts of the United States; and to say that we may surrender the jurisdiction of this District, and acquire another territory where we shall possess the same jurisdiction, or that by the Constitution we possess exclusive jurisdiction over two or more districts of territory, not exceeding each ten miles square—is as absurd as to say that we may destroy the Supreme Court and create another, or to say that we may establish two or more Supreme Courts, with a double set of judges to each.

That I may be the more distinctly understood, and the principles involved in this question more clearly and authoritatively elucidated, I beg leave to read an extract from a celebrated speech of one of the ablest champions of the Constitution on the question of the repeal of the Judiciary, (GOUVERNEUR MORRIS.) I have selected this speech, not because it contains opinions peculiar to its author, but because it imbodies the sentiments of the whole party to which he was attached, and may be considered as the base, the pillar, and cap of the argument on that all-important question.

" But (says Mr. Morris in reply) another criticism, but for its effects I would call pleasant, has been made, the amount of which is, you shall not take the man from the office, but you may take the office from the man—you shall not drown him, but you may sink his boat under him; you shall not put him to death, but you may take away his life. The Constitution preserves to a judge his office—says he shall hold it—that is, it shall not be taken from him during good behaviour; the Legislature shall not diminish, though their bounty may increase, his salary. The Constitution provides perfectly for the inviolability of his tenure, but yet we may destroy the office which we cannot take away, as if the destruction of the office would not as effectually deprive him of it as the grant to another person. It is admitted, that no power derived from the Constitution can deprive him of the office, and yet it is contended that, by repeal of the law, that office may be destroyed. Is not this absurd? It had been said, that whatever one Legislature can do, another can undo, because no Legislature can bind its successor; and, therefore, whatever we make we can destroy. This I deny on the ground of reason, and on that of the Constitution. What! can a man destroy his own children? Can you annul your own compacts? Can you annihilate the national debt? When you have by law created a political existence, can you, by repealing the law, dissolve the corporation you had made? When by your laws you give to an individual any right whatever, can you by a subsequent law, rightfully take it away? No; when you make a compact you are bound by it; when you make a promise you must perform it. Establish the contrary doctrine, and what follows? The whim of the moment becomes the law of the land; your country will be looked upon as a den of robbers; every honest man will fly your shores. Who will trust you, when you are the first to violate your own contracts? The position, therefore, that the Legislature may rightfully repeal every law made by a preceding Legislature, when tested by reason is untrue; and it is equally untrue, when compared with the precepts of the Constitution—for what does the Constitution say? You shall make no *ex post facto* law! Is not this an *ex post facto* law?"

I now beg gentlemen, particularly those on this side of the House, to pause, to reflect, and compare the sentiments contained in this eloquent and correct extract, with the facts, principles, and obligations connected with the question now before us. I demand of gentlemen to be informed, what will be the political condition of the thirty thousand people who inhabit this District, should the Seat of Government be removed and the jurisdiction of Congress, thus as it unquestionably would be, withdrawn from them? I ask gentlemen if contracts are not in their nature reciprocal, and whether the States of Maryland and Virginia, who surrendered this territory to the United States upon certain terms and conditions, and for certain specific objects, might not with equal propriety and right demand a recession of it from the United States, if their convenience, or interest, or caprice so required as that Congress should, without their consent, throw back the territory on their hands whenever they thought proper? Are a free people, entitled to just rights and equal laws, and who are peculiarly under your guardianship and protection, thus to be sported with, thus to be bought and sold like the slaves of Jamaica? Forbid it justice, forbid it Heaven.

You, by the Constitution and the law, have given to the people of this District a " political existence." Can you rightfully destroy it? You have established here district courts, upon the same principles with the other circuit courts of the United States; the judges and other officers hold their appointments by the same tenure; can you abolish those courts, and drive the judges from their seats? Surely you cannot, consistently with those principles I have always considered as held sacred by those whom I have proudly called my political friends.

In the course of the ingenious argument of the gentleman from New Jersey, I was pleased to discover occasional successful efforts of true and correct principles forcing themselves from the toils in which they were involved. One instance of this was his admission, an admission made, too, by most gentlemen who have spoken, that, in the event of the Government being removed, indemnity was due to those classes of citizens who had settled here and expended their money, relying on the faith of the Government for its continuance at this place. This admission, in my judgment, to a great extent, if not entirely, yields the argument, for why should we indemnify the inhabitants, if we are under no obligations? Why pay them, if we have not deceived and injured them? Shall we, then, violate our obligations; shall we injure and deceive an innocent community and plead a miserable pittance, a promise of tender of amends at our discretion? I cannot think so badly of the Legislature of my country. If the honorable gentleman were acquainted with the real situation of most of the people of this District; if he knew the sacrifices which many of them have made for the promotion and establishment of this city, and the utter ruin in which they would be involved by the fatal measure now threatened, his sense of justice would not be appealed to in vain, for indemnity to an extent infinitely beyond what he now contemplates. It is possible some of the original proprietors may have profited by the establishment of the Seat of Government here, but it is equally true that other proprietors, from whose property the public have derived hundreds of thousands of dollars, have themselves realized little or nothing; their once flourishing and highly cultivated fields cut up by the Government into city lots, remain unsold and unoccupied; this property was, indeed, considered an increasing treasure, which would in time enrich its possessors, and compensate for the sacrifices made to the public. Do the unjust deed now meditated, and you cut up the hopes of those people—you make them poor indeed.

Mr. Speaker, before I close my remarks on the constitutionality of this question, I cannot avoid stating one or two observations more of the gentleman from New Jersey, which my respect for that honorable gentleman, alone, induces me to notice. In attempting to get rid of the common and plain import of the word permanent, so often used in the acts of Congress and of cession, the gentleman first tells us that the word permanent is totally to be disregarded; he then says that it was introduced to distinguish the temporary residence of ten years at Philadelphia, from the permanent residence at this place. In this I perfectly agree with him, for no other definition or meaning can be affixed to the term, than the very opposite of temporary, transitory, limited, or any other word which admits the idea of change or limitation. In the next breath we are told the word permanent meant nothing more than that there was no express limitation in the law as to the time the Seat of Government should continue here; consequently it was in the power of Congress to limit its duration and remove it at pleasure. Thus, agreeable to this course of reasoning, the seat of Government was to continue temporarily at Philadelphia for ten years, and then permanently at the City of Washington for six months, or any other period which Congress might think proper. I confess, Mr. Speaker, this reasoning is too refined for my comprehension. It is the first, and I presume will be the last time we shall ever hear that by the force of the terms alone, temporary may be made to embrace a longer time, and give a more lasting tenure, than the word permanent, when applied to the same subject matter. But, sir, admitting for a moment, the possibility of this reasoning being correct; I ask the gentleman if the word permanent was used in reference to the word temporary, in the act as before stated, how did it happen that the same word is used in the original resolution of 1789, which preceded the enactment of the law, and which had no reference or allusion whatever to the temporary residence of the Government at Philadelphia or elsewhere? How did it happen that during the discussion of the resolution, and the bill itself, by the members of the first Congress, so many of those distinguished men should have used the word permanent in its plain, old-fashioned, common sense meaning, without once dreaming of the references, limitations, and qualifications, which the gentleman from New Jersey has so heavily taxed his ingenuity to affix? Sir, the reason is this—they intended the Seat of the Government of the United States should, when established, be as perpetual as the union of these States, as durable as the Constitution itself.

The gentleman to whom I have referred, as also the gentleman from New York, (Mr. GROSVENOR,) have derived an argument in favor of the right of removal, from the second member of that section of the Constitution which authorizes the establishment of the Seat of Government. It is contended that because the authority of Congress is extended over "all places purchased, by the consent of the Legislature of the State in which the same may be, for the erection of forts, magazines, dock yards, and other needful buildings," the same obligation exists to continue those forts and other public works, at the sites first fixed upon and purchased, as there is to continue the Seat of the Government at the place ceded by particular States, accepted and established by Congress as the Seat of Government has been.

The gentleman from New York (Mr. GROSVENOR) has even gone further—he says Congress had no more right to establish the permanent Seat of Government than they had to establish a permanent post road, and that we have the same right to repeal such a law in one case as the other. Had those observations proceeded from gentlemen less entitled to respect and influence, I certainly should have deemed them unworthy of reply. Sir there is little or no analogy in the cases put by the gentlemen. In the purchase of sites

869   HISTORY OF CONGRESS.   870

OCTOBER, 1814.   *Removal of the Seat of Government.*   H. OF R.

for forts or other public buildings, nothing is stipulated for, nothing contemplated, by the Constitution or the law, other than a common bargain and sale for the purchase of so many acres of land, either from a State or from individuals, for public use. Congress are not restricted as to the limits, or number of places thus to be purchased. They require no jurisdiction over citizens residing within the limits of such purchases. On the contrary, no political existence is created, no residence permitted except of military force, no law prevails but martial law. Congress have therefore a right to remove or abandon those public works, and others at pleasure, without any violation of the public faith, or of individual interest, either pecuniary or political. Why the gentleman from New York put the case of a post road, I cannot well imagine. He might as well have told us that we had a right to repeal a tax law, which was not limited to a particular time, or the proceeds pledged to any special or general objects. I leave to gentlemen the full benefit and exclusive right of such arguments as these. But, sir, upon the ordinary principles of contracts, suppose an acre of land was purchased from an individual for the erection of a public fort, on the authority of an act of Congress, declaring the fort thus to be erected on the land purchased should be permanently continued and kept in repair—in consequence of which law, and in consideration of incidental advantages to be derived by the owner of the land, by the erection and continuance of said fort, the owner was induced to part with his property for one fourth of its value, and subject himself to other losses and sacrifices. I ask gentlemen, whether, under such circumstances, Congress could at their next session rightfully repeal the law, and violate their contract with the individual without making him a full and ample indemnity? And suppose, also, that a post road was established which would run through the farm of an individual, greatly to his injury, and, as an inducement for obtaining the privilege, Congress were to enact that the said road should be permanently continued, and authorize commissioners to enter into contracts and stipulations with the owner, by which he would be induced to change his fences, remove his buildings, or erect others, on the faith of the law and engagements entered into with the agents of the Government. Under such circumstances, I appeal to the understanding and common justice of the gentlemen themselves, to determine what would be the duty—what the obligation of Congress? Sir, I have done with this part of the subject, and trust I have sufficiently answered the arguments of the honorable gentleman from New Jersey, and established the positions I advanced in relation to the Constitution, the law, and the obligations resulting from them.

So much, Mr. Speaker, has already been said as to the expediency and inexpediency of the measure under consideration, (and in which I have borne my part,) that little now remains of use or novelty. When the subject was first ushered into notice, it was advocated solely on the ground of convenience and personal safety of the members. Those reasons appear to have vanished in succession, and a distinct one, not originally thought of, accidentally seized upon, and is made the watchword or rallying point for the advocates of this destructive project. This is, the expense of defending this District, if the Government is continued here. Every day's experience tends to reconcile gentlemen more and more with their new and more humble accommodations in this Hall. Every man who enters this room or approaches the gallery, must be convinced that the business of the session can be transacted here with equal despatch and intelligence as it could have been in the splendid apartments which we lately occupied. This reason is therefore abandoned; indeed, it never appeared to me, to bear a serious aspect; it was impossible it should; for, from the first moment, we found almost every member north of Maryland, and a few of the hardy sons of the West, apparently dissatisfied with their accommodations, while those from the other sections of the Union, with two or three exceptions, perfectly satisfied. It is perfectly evident, therefore, to me, that as this was in general not so much an individual as a sectional difference of opinion, the objection did not in reality exist. It is impossible, for instance, that the gentleman from New Jersey (Mr. STOCKTON) and myself could so essentially differ as to the size of this room, the state of its atmosphere, or the quality of our seats, whether hard or soft. The same remarks equally apply as to the danger or security of remaining here. It is not possible that gentlemen from the North and East should be filled with apprehensions for their personal safety, while those from the Southern and middle States, whose nerves may, from climate, be supposed more delicate, should remain unappalled. Sir, I know the nerve of some of those gentlemen too well to believe they would be the first to fly even on the approach of danger, much less before it approaches. I cannot believe, sir, that the bold and daring spirit of the honorable gentleman from New York (Mr. GROSVENOR) could yield to imaginary fears, while other gentlemen in this House remain unmoved. I cannot believe the young, the strong, and vigorous limbs of himself and his colleague, (Mr. FISK,) could tremble, while my venerable colleagues, (Messrs. MACON and FORNEY,) and other gentlemen whom either age or accident has disqualified for the toils and dangers of the camp, and who would certainly not be foremost in pedestrian feats, remained firm and unshaken.

Gentlemen, however, have entrenched themselves, as they conceive, on the ground of expense. They have most strangely and most erroneously misrepresented the expense which will be incurred for the defense of this District. The exaggerated statements on this subject are the more unfair and unaccountable, because they are not only contrary to fact and contrary to the express representations of the chairman of the Military Committee, but in total disregard of the estimates and plans of defence derived from the War Department. I, sir, am as regardful of public expenditure as any

371 HISTORY OF CONGRESS. 372

H. of R. *Removal of the Seat of Government.* October, 1814.

member of this House; and I have no doubt, those gentlemen who think with me on the present subject are not less economical; are not less opposed to useless or improper dispositions of the public force and public treasure than those who are in favor of incurring the expense, the loss of time, and other fatal consequences of removing the Seat of Government, are to be considered the exclusive guardians of the public safety, the public honor and the public purse. The fact is this: The military force which has been spoken of, is intended for the defence, not of the District of Columbia alone, but for the whole of the tenth military district, including the whole State of Maryland, part of Pennsylvania and Virginia. This force is to be so disposed, as conveniently to be brought into action for the protection of Baltimore, Annapolis, the District of Columbia, or any point between the Potomac and Baltimore. So that in truth, whether Congress remain here or go away, the force will be the same; the expense neither increased nor diminished one cent. But, sir, if considerable additional expense were to be incurred, I appeal to the patriots of my country to know, to what more laudable object it could be applied than to the defence of the heart of the country; to the security of the Government itself, and the protection of those institutions founded and cherished by a Washington? By his precepts and his institutions I will cling, as the anchor of our hope—the rock of our political salvation.

The gentleman from New York (Mr. Fisk) objects to the disposition of the force contemplated by the Secretary of War. He says, if they are stationed on the middle ground between this District and Baltimore, they can only be brought to action in rear of the enemy. I know not in what school that gentleman acquired his military science—whether he practises on the lessons of the great Frederick, the Prince of Conde, and other heroes of former days, or whether he relies on modern improvements in the art of war introduced by the Emperor of Elba, or even our late Secretary of War, John Armstrong. I know not, but I have always understood, that if the enemy could be outflanked or attacked in the rear, victory was half complete. I profess very little knowledge in military matters, but I will inform the gentleman that the situation where the troops are intended to be stationed will enable them to attack the enemy either in front or rear, as circumstances may justify. It is also objected that this is a militia force. I pray you, sir, what other force have we in any of the States? What other force do you expect at Philadelphia, or any other place to which we may remove? None. Permit me here to remark, that if the dispersion of Congress is an object with the enemy, as gentlemen suppose, that object can be as well obtained at Philadelphia as this place; and I have the authority (if any were necessary) of military men for saying, that Philadelphia is less defensible than this District. Consequently, if we go there, we not only increase the danger, but the expense also.

The gentleman (Mr. Grosvenor) admits that he is not afraid, and he believes few or none are afraid of remaining here; but he says he wishes to avoid the disgrace of having the Government again routed and driven away; and how is this to be done? By marching off when there is no danger? In other words, it is disgraceful to retreat when pressed by a superior force, but honorable to run before the approach of danger. This is indeed a new chapter in chivalry, and one which I am sure the gentleman will not adopt as a guide for his own conduct. This sentiment is also rather at points with what fell from the honorable gentleman only a moment before; the country, he said, was disgraced. The Administration had drank the very dregs of humiliation by permitting the enemy to pollute the soil of this District and riot in the Capitol of the country. This is but too true a picture; and I admonish gentlemen not to heighten this disgrace—not to consummate our degradation, by adopting the measure now proposed. Already has the pen fallen in pity—in shame and confusion, from the hand of the historian. Destroy your Seat of Government! Break asunder this strongest link in the Federal chain! The pen of history will be snatched up with rage and indignation, and this monstrous deed portrayed in all its blackest colors.

Mr. Speaker, the unusual combination in favor of this measure, by gentlemen of the most opposite political opinions, cannot fail to strike the attention of the House, and may well justify the apprehension that, with some at least, other and very different views may be entertained from those which have been expressed in debate. I therefore admonish gentlemen, while they are travelling the same road with their new companions, that they inquire and well understand what and where is the destined object. If political considerations are in view, it would be well for these extremes of political parties, which have met together on this single occasion, to perfectly understand each other before it is too late to return. The gentleman from New York (Mr. Grosvenor) did me no more than justice in supposing that I meant no personal reflection, when I represented the other day this novel coalition, by a figure perhaps rather ludicrous: "The horn of Federalism hooked to the tail of Democracy, or *vice versa.*" The alternative presented to gentlemen of being at the head or tail of this political association precludes the idea of any invidious distinction. The gentleman says he is fond of union. So am I, in a just and laudable object; but rather than unite in error, let me remain in everlasting exile. As I impeach not the motives of gentlemen, I will not withhold from them my congratulations on this their first political wedding. I wish them all the delights of the honeymoon. I fear it will be of short duration. Perhaps before to-morrow's noon matters of State may demand, and their divorce be pronounced.

Mr. Speaker, I have claimed your attention and that of the House longer I fear than was agreeable; but not longer, I trust, than the importance of the subject demanded. I forbear a detail of all the evil consequences to be apprehended to the nation from the adoption of the measure now before us. I will not harrow your feelings by even a feeble effort to portray the complicated sufferings, the deep distress in which this people would be involved. I yield to the admonition of the gentleman from New York, (Mr. Grosvenor,) and banish as much as possible the influence of feelings; even that gentleman, with all his sternness and zeal on this occasion, has expressed some sympathy for the fate which awaits this people. Sir, the human being who could not do more than feel for such calamity, must possess a heart colder than apathy itself. "There are occasions when the worst men only can be cool." Those alone can jest at scars who never felt a wound.

NOTES.

The following extracts are from the speeches of distinguished members of the First Congress.

On the 27th of August, 1789, *Mr. Scott,* of Pennsylvania, introduced the following resolution:

Resolved, That a permanent residence ought to be fixed for the General Government of the United States, at some convenient place, as near the centre of wealth, population, and extent of territory, as may be consistent with convenience to the navigation of the Atlantic ocean, and having due regard to the particular situation of the Western country.

Mr. Hartley, of Pennsylvania, was in favor of the motion. He thought some attention ought to be paid to the petitions of the people respecting a permanent Seat of Government.

Mr. Fitzsimons, of Pennsylvania, acknowledged there was business of great importance before Congress; but was there any more important than the subject proposed? It was a question in which the people of every part of the Union were deeply interested. It had been said that jealousies existed among the States; they were not likely to be removed by inattention to so great a concern.

Mr. Scott thought the principles of the Union were the principles of equal justice and reciprocity. He conceived the question now before the House as grand a link as any in the Federal chain. The future tranquility and well being of the United States, he said, depended as much on this as on any other question that ever had or could come before Congress. It was a justice due to the extremities of the continent to adopt such a measure.

Mr. Jackson, of Georgia, said that upon this subject depended the existence of the Union. The place of the Seat of Government was important in every point of view. It might be compared to the heart of the human body; it was a centre from which the principles of life were carried to the extremities, and from these might return again with precision.

Mr. Ames, of Massachusetts, said he ever found it a difficult task, on the most trivial occasions, to obtain unanimity. What then must be the division on a question which some gentlemen have said the existence of the Union depended upon? I believe it will involve as many passions as the human heart can display. Every principle of local interest, pride, and honor, and even patriotism itself, are engaged. He asked if the public mind ought not to be better prepared for the occasion?

September 3, 1789.

Mr. Goodhue, of Massachusetts, said the Eastern members, with the members from New York, have

agreed to fix a place on national principles, without regard to their own convenience, and have turned their minds to the banks of the Susquehanna. Motives of convenience would have led us to fix upon the banks of the Delaware, but it was supposed it would give more lasting content to go farther South. They were therefore entirely of opinion that the banks of the Susquehanna should be the place of the permanent residence of the General Government. Mr. G. then moved a resolution, "that the permanent Seat of the General Government ought to be on the east bank of the Susquehanna."

Mr. Lee, of Virginia, hoped they would be guided in this discussion and decision by the great principles on which the Government itself is founded. With this view he introduced a preamble (recognising the principles of the Constitution, and declaring that those great objects will be best effected by establishing the permanent Seat of Government as nearly central as a convenient water communication with the Atlantic and an easy access to the Western territory will permit) to the following resolution: "That a place as nearly central as a convenient communication with the Atlantic ocean and an easy access to the Western territory will permit, ought to be selected and established as the permanent Seat of the Government of the United States." Mr. L. wished the principles of the Government to be recognised, that the people of the United States may be able to judge whether, in the measures about to be adopted, they are carried into execution by this House.

Mr. Sedgwick, of Massachusetts, had thought that this was not the time consistently with the good of the country to determine the permanent residence of Congress. He was however ready to decide on the important subject.

Mr. Vining, of Delaware, agreed this was a matter of the highest importance. He wished that all exterior circumstances might combine in aid of Government, and every principle attended to which could preserve and add strength to it. While we had a Washington, and his virtues, to cement and guard this Union, it might be safe; but when he should leave us, who would inherit his virtues and possess his influence; who would remain to embrace and draw to a centre those hearts which the authority of his virtues alone kept in union?

Mr. Lee, of Virginia, said a question was to be decided which involves present and future interests, and extends to remote generations. The question is to be settled, which must determine whether this Government is to exist for ages, or be dispersed among contending winds. Will gentlemen say these principles ought not to be recognised? Will they say the centre of Government should not be the centre of the Union? Should it not be a situation which will admit an easy communication to the ocean? Will they say our Western brethren are to be disregarded? These are momentous considerations which should lead the House to a conclusion. If they are disregarded, it will be an alarming circumstance to the people of the Southern States. They have felt their alarms already.

Mr. Stone said, in fixing the permanent residence, we ought not only to have in view the immediate importance of the States, but what is likely to be their weight at a future day. After stating the probable future importance of the Western country, Mr. S. observed that the river Potomac, which had been mentioned by the Southern gentlemen, for the permanent Seat of

375   HISTORY OF CONGRESS.   376

H. of R.   *Removal of the Seat of Government.*   October, 1814.

the Government, is, as far as I am acquainted, extremely well calculated to furnish Government with the key of the country; and a river I believe richer in its exports than any I have contemplated on the face of the earth.

Mr. Madison, of Virginia, said he hoped that all would concur in the great principle on which they ought to conduct, and decide this business; an equal attention to the rights of the community. If these great rights be the basis of republics, and if there be a double necessity of attending to them in a Federal Republic, it is further to be considered, that there is no one right, of which the people can judge with more ease and certainty, and of which they will judge with more jealousy, than of the establishment of the permanent Seat of Government; and I am persuaded that however often this subject may be discussed in the representative body, or however the attention of the committee may be drawn to it, the observations I have made will be more and more verified. If we consider, sir, the effects of Legislative power on the aggregate community, we must feel equal inducements to look for the centre, in order to find the present Seat of Government. Those who are most adjacent to the seat of legislation, will always possess advantages over others. An earlier knowledge of the laws; a greater influence in enacting them; better opportunities for anticipating them, and a thousand other circumstances, will give a superiority to those who are thus situated. If it were possible to promulgate our laws, by some instantaneous operation, it would be of less consequence in that point of view where the Government might be placed; but if, on the contrary, time is necessary for this purpose, we ought, as far as possible, to put every part of the community on a level. If we consider the influence of the Government in its Executive Department, there is no less reason to conclude that it ought to be placed in the centre of the Union. It ought to be in a situation to command information relative to every part of the Union, to watch every conjuncture, to seize every circumstance that can be improved. The Executive eye ought to be placed where it can best see the dangers which may threaten, and the Executive arm, whence it may be extended most effectually to the protection of every part. In the Judiciary department, if it is not equally necessary, it is highly important that the Government should be equally accessible to all. With respect to the Western Territory, we are not to expect it, for it would be an affront to the understanding of our fellow-citizens on the Western waters, that they will be united with their Atlantic brethren, on any other principle than that of equality and justice. He was sure, that if justice required us to take any one position in preference to another, we had every inducement, both of interest and of prudence, to fix on the Potomac, as most satisfactory to our Western brethren. On a candid view of the two rivers, (Susquehanna and Potomac,) he flattered himself that the seat which would most correspond with the public interest would be found on the banks of the Potomac. It was proper that we should have some regard to the centre of territory; if that was to have weight, he begged leave to say that there was no comparison between the two rivers. He defied any gentleman to cast his eye, in the most cursory manner, over a map, and say, that the Potomac is not much nearer this centre than any part of the Susquehanna. If we measure from the banks of the Potomac to the most Eastern part of the United States, it is less distant than to the most Southern. If

we measure this great area diagonally, the Potomac will still have the advantage. If you draw a line perpendicularly, to the direction of the Atlantic coast, we shall find that it will run more equally through the Potomac than through any other part of the Union; or, if there be any difference between one side and the other, there will be a greater space on the Southwest than on the Northern. All the maps of the United States show the truth of this. He granted that the present centre of population is nearer the Susquehanna than the Potomac. But are we choosing a Seat of Government for the present moment only? He presumed not.

The adoption of the resolve was further opposed by Messrs. Johnson of Kentucky, Forsyth of Georgia, Hawkins of Kentucky, Bowen and Rhea of Tennessee; and advocated by Messrs. Sharp of Kentucky, and Ingersoll of Pennsylvania.

The question on the passage of the resolution was decided as follows:

Yeas—Messrs. Alston, Baylies of Massachusetts, Bigelow, Boyd, Bradbury, Bradley, Brigham, Brown, Butler, Caldwell, Champion, Cilley, Clark, Condict, Conard, Cooper, Cox, Creighton, Davenport, Davis of Pennsylvania, Denoyelles, Desha, Duvall, Ely, Findley, Fisk of New York, Geddes, Gourdin, Grosvenor, Hulbert, Ingersoll, Ingham, Irwin, Jackson of Rhode Island, Kent of New York, King of Massachusetts, Law, Lovett, Lyle, Markell, Miller, Moffit, Moseley, Oakley, Ormsby, Pickering, Piper, Post, John Reed, Rea of Pennsylvania, Rich, Ruggles, Schureman, Seybert, Sharp, Sherwood, Shipherd, Skinner, Stanford, Stockton, Sturges, Tannehill, Taylor, Thompson, Udree, Vose, Ward of Massachusetts, Ward of New Jersey, Wheaton, Wilcox, and Winter—73.

Nays—Messrs. Archer, Avery, Barbour, Bard, Barnett, Bayly of Virginia, Bowen, Burwell, Chappell, Clopton, Comstock, Crawford, Culpeper, Cuthbert, Dana, Earle, Eppes, Evans, Farrow, Fisk of Vermont, Forney, Forsyth, Franklin, Gaston, Gholson, Glasgow, Goldsborough, Goodwyn, Griffin, Hall, Hanson, Harris, Hawes, Hawkins, Humphreys, Hungerford, Irving, Jackson of Virginia, Johnson of Kentucky, Kent of Maryland, Kerr, King of North Carolina, Lefferts, Lowndes, Macon, McCoy, McKee, McKim, McLean, Montgomery, Moore, Nelson, Newton, Pearson, Pickens, Pleasants, Rhea of Tennessee, Roane, Sage, Sevier, Smith of Virginia, Stuart, Telfair, Troup, White, Wilson of Pennsylvania, Wright, and Yancey—71.

So the resolution was agreed to, and a committee appointed to bring in a bill in pursuance thereof.

Mr. Fisk, of New York, Mr. Grosvenor, Mr. Sharp, Mr. Ingersoll, Mr. Forsyth, Mr. Pearson, and Mr. Lewis, were appointed the said committee.

MONDAY, October 7.

Two other members, to wit: from New York, William S. Smith; and from Kentucky, Samuel Hopkins; appeared, and took their seats.

The bill for extending the right of suffrage, &c., in the Mississippi Territory, passed through a Committee of the Whole, and was ordered to be engrossed for a third reading.

According to the order of the day, the House resolved itself into a Committee of the Whole on the report of the Committee of Claims, unfavorable to the petition of Thomas Cutts, of the District of Maine, who prays reimbursement of moneys paid for property purchased at a marshal's sale, together with costs and damages on the recovery of said property from him by a third person, by due process of law.

Mr. KING, of Massachusetts, opposed the adoption of the report, which was supported by Mr. YANCEY, of North Carolina, the chairman of the committee who made it, &c.

The report of the Committee of Claims was finally reversed by the Committee of the Whole, and so reported to the House. It was then ordered to lie on the table for further consideration.

A communication was received from the Commissioner of the General Land Office, on the subject of Indian cessions; which was ordered to lie on the table. Adjourned to Monday.

MONDAY, October 10.

Several other members, to wit: from Massachusetts, SAMUEL TAGGART; from Maryland, SAMUEL RINGGOLD; from North Carolina, WILLIAM KENNEDY; and from Louisiana, THOMAS BOLLING ROBERTSON; appeared, and took their seats.

A message from the Senate informed the House that the Senate have passed joint resolutions "expressive of the sense of Congress of the gallant conduct of Captain Thomas Macdonough, the officers, seamen, marines, and infantry, acting as marines, on board the United States' squadron on Lake Champlain," in which they ask the concurrence of this House.

The resolutions were read twice, and referred to the Committee on Naval Affairs.

An engrossed bill further to extend the right of suffrage, and to increase the number of members of the Legislative Council of the Mississippi Territory, was read the third time and passed.

On motion of Mr. OAKLEY,

Resolved, That the Secretary of the Treasury be requested to lay before this House a statement of the return of the direct tax and the internal duties, established by the several acts passed at the first session of the present Congress, as far as the same have been received, showing—

First, The assessment made of houses, lands, and slaves, in the several collection districts in the several States, and the aggregate of assessments in each State.

Secondly, The amount received on account of the direct tax from each State, and from each collection district in the several States.

Thirdly, The amount received on account of each of the said internal duties, distinguishing the amount received on account of each from the States, respectively, and from each collection district in the several States.

The House resolved itself into a Committee of the whole House on the resolutions reported by the Committee on Military Affairs, expressive of the sense of Congress of the gallant conduct of Major General Brown, and Brigadiers Scott, Gaines, and Macomb; and, after some time spent therein the Committee rose, reported progress, and had leave to sit again.

A message from the Senate informed the House that the Senate have passed a joint resolution "empowering the Joint Library Committee of Congress to contract for the purchase of Mr. Jefferson's library;" in which they ask the concurrence of this House.

The said resolution was read twice, and referred to a Committee of the Whole to-morrow.

WAYS AND MEANS.

Mr. EPPES, from the Committee of Ways and Means, made a report on so much of the President's Message as relates to the finances of the United States; which was read, and referred to a Committee of the Whole on Thursday next.

The report is as follows:

That taxes, loans, and Treasury notes, appear to be the resources on which we must rely for carrying on the war. The product of the first cannot be commanded in time to meet the immediate demands on the Treasury. A reliance on loans, in the present situation of this country, would be uncertain; and the terms on which they would be obtained, not such as to induce a resort to them at the present moment. Treasury notes, combined with a system of taxation, more extended than the one heretofore adopted, will it is believed, in the present state of bank credit, be found to be a much better resource. The want of some medium, which, resting on a firm and solid basis, may unite public confidence, and have a general, instead of a local circulation, is now universally acknowledged. The stoppage of specie payments by the principal banks of the Middle States has embarrassed greatly the operations of the Treasury, and, by confining the circulation of notes to the limits of the States within which they are issued, has deprived the Government of all the facilities, in the remittance of money, which was afforded while public confidence gave to bank notes a general circulation. The notes of New York and Philadelphia will not be received in Boston; the notes of Baltimore, or of the District of Columbia, will not answer for payments in Philadelphia. If, by any new modification, Treasury notes could be made to answer the purposes of a circulating medium between the different States, they would greatly facilitate the operations of Government, and free from embarrassment the transactions of individuals. To secure their circulation, it would be necessary—1. To issue the notes in sums sufficiently small for the ordinary purposes of society; 2. To allow the individual who holds them to fund them at pleasure at any of the loan offices, and to receive their amount in stock of the United States, bearing an interest of 8 per cent.; 3. To make them payable to bearer, and transferrable by delivery: 4. To make them receivable in all payments for public lands and taxes; 5. To pledge, for the payment of the interest on the amount issued, so much of the internal duties as shall be necessary. To prevent an accumulation of circulating medium, the United States to retain the power, on giving six months' notice, of redeeming them with specie, or exchanging for them stock, bearing an interest of 8 per cent. If these provisions are adopted, and taxes imposed, which shall manifest clearly the ability of the Government to meet its engagements, our present difficulties will vanish, confidence be restored, and the capital, hoarded by avarice, or locked up from timidity, will be again restored to the accustomed channels of circulation. In presenting additional objects of taxation, care has been taken to select such as will bear equally on every portion of the community. In Europe, the price of agricultural products is not materially affected by a state of war; the produce of the earth is there consumed within the country, in peace and in war. The situation of the United States is totally different. With an extensive and fertile country, and a small population, compared to the extent of our territory, we have annually a large surplus to export to foreign markets, over and above what is necessary for consumption. On the export of this surplus, which is cut off by war, depends in a great degree the ability of the farmer to meet taxes. While, however, war depresses the agricultural interest, it gives vigor to various manufactures. By destroying all foreign competition, the war has brought many of these manufactures to a state of perfection, which will secure their successful prosecution, even after peace shall be restored. In times of difficulty and danger, we must appeal to the patriotism of every class of our citizens. These establishments, under the fostering hand of the Government, have grown to maturity, and will not hesitate to bear, with the agricultural interests, their portion of the taxes necessary to maintain, unimpaired, that character for punctuality and good faith for which the American Government has heretofore been distinguished. Several of these manufactures have been selected as proper subjects of taxation; and it is proposed to unite with the taxes a pledge of the public faith for the continuance of the double duties until the tax shall be repealed.

The committee deem it unnecessary, at present, to present any view of the expenditures for the next year, reserving a report on that subject until the estimates from the Treasury shall be forwarded. Confining, therefore, this report to the additional taxes necessary for the support of the public credit, they submit the following resolutions:

1. *Resolved,* That it is expedient to continue the direct tax, and to increase the same 50 per cent.

2. *Resolved,* That it is expedient to increase the duty on spirits distilled, by an additional duty of 12½ cents on the gallon.

3. *Resolved,* That it is expedient to add 100 per cent on the present duty on sales at auction.

4. *Resolved,* That it is expedient to add 50 per cent. to the present duty on the conveyance of papers and letters.

5. *Resolved,* That it is expedient to impose a duty on the following articles, viz: manufactured tobacco and snuff, in the hands of the manufacturer; candles, of tallow and spermaceti; hats; cotton yarn, spun by the aid of machinery, worked by steam or water; leather; pig iron; castings; bar, rolled, and slit iron, and on nails made by the aid of machinery; on furniture above a certain value, except beds, bedding, and articles of domestic manufacture, in the hands of the owner; beer, ale, and porter, in the hands of the manufacturer; boots and shoes, above a certain price, in the hands of the manufacturer; on plated harness, in the hands of the owner; on vats for the manufacture of paper; on saddles and bridles, above a certain price, in the hands of the owner; on gold and silver watches, in the hands of the owner; on pleasure horses, kept exclusively for the saddle or carriage; on playing cards; and on lotteries.

Estimate of the amount of the proposed increase, and of the new duties.

Fifty per cent on the direct tax	$1,500,000
Additional duty on distilled spirits	3,000,000
One hundred per cent on the present auction duties	150,000
Fifty per cent. on postage	250,000
Manufactured tobacco and snuff, 10,000,000 of pounds, averaged at 4 cents	400,000
Candles of tallow, 6,000,000 of pounds, at 2 cents	120,000
Spermaceti and white wax, 400,000 pounds, at 10 cents	40,000
Hats: on beaver $1, castors 75 cents, and roraims 25 cents, payable by manufacturers	600,000
Cotton yarn, spun by aid of machinery, worked by steam or water; 400,000 spindles, at 25 cents	100,000
Leather: sole, neats, harness, calf, horse, and hog, kip and seal skin; 18,000,000 of pounds, averaged at 3 cents	540,000
Goat and sheep skins tanned with sumack or otherwise, to resemble Spanish leather, at 50 cents per dozen; and all other skins tanned with alum, averaged at 3 cents per pound	60,000
Iron, 300,000 tons pig, at $1	300,000
One hundred thousand tons of castings, at $1 50	150,000
One hundred thousand tons of bar, rolled, and slit iron, at $1	100,000
On beer, ale, and porter; 6,000,000 gallons, at 1 cent	60,000
Furniture tax, excluding beds, bedding, kitchen furniture, carpets and curtains of domestic manufacture, and family pictures; and excluding also from the operation of the tax every person whose furniture, exclusive of the above articles, does not amount to $200. The estimate is made on a supposition that the United States contains 800,000 families. Families exempt, as possessing less than $200 worth of furniture, 259,000. Families owning to the amount of between—	
$200 and $400, 300,000, at $1	300,000
400 and 600, 100,000, at 1 50	150,000
600 and 1,000, 75,000, at 3	225,000
1,000 and 1,500, 25,000, at 6	150,000
1,500 and 2,000, 15,000, at 10	150,000
2,000 and 3,000, 10,000, at 17	170,000
3,000 and 4,000, 10,000, at 28	280,000
4,000 and 6,000, 10,000, at 45	457,000
6,000 and 9,000, 5,000, at 75	375,000
Above 9,000, 1,900, at 100	10,000
Boots: white-top, and full-dress military boots; 100,000 pairs, at 75 cents	75,000
Other boots or bootees, of the value of $8; 250,000 pairs, at 50 cents	125,000
Boots or bootees, not less than $5 in value, and not exceeding $8; 500,000 pairs, at 25 cents	125,000
Fine shoes, above the value of $1 75; 1,000,000 pairs, at 10 cents	100,000
Plated harness, in the hands of the owner; 50,000 pairs, at $2	100,000

381   HISTORY OF CONGRESS.   382

Octobur, 1814.   *Negotiations for Peace.*   H. of R.

On the manufacture of paper: on vats exclusively employed in making white paper, $50; on vats employed in making part white and part brown, $30; on vats exclusively employed in making brown paper, $15;—2,000 vats averaged	30,000
On nails made by the aid of machinery, 20,000,000 of pounds, at 1 cent - -	200,000
On saddles under $10 value, 50 cents; over $10 and under $15, 75 cents; and above the value of $15, $1 - - -	100,000
On bridles of less value than $2, 10 cents; $3 and under $5, 20 cents; $5 and under $10, 40 cents; above $10, $1 -	100,000
On pleasure horses, kept exclusively for the saddle, $1; horses kept exclusively for the carriage, $1 50 - -	150,000
On gold watches, 250,000, at $2 -	500,000
On silver watches, 250,000, at $1 -	'250,000
On playing cards, 400,000 packs, at 25 cts.	100,000
On lotteries, a per centum on the amount -	50,000
Total - - - - -	$11,635,000
Add the revenue for 1815, as estimated by the Secretary of the Treasury -	10,800,000
Making for 1815 a revenue of -	$22,435,000

NEGOTIATIONS FOR PEACE.

The following Message was received from the PRESIDENT OF THE UNITED STATES:

To the Senate and House of
* Representatives of the United States :*

I lay before Congress communications just received from the Plenipotentiaries of the United States, charged with negotiating peace with Great Britain; showing the conditions on which alone that Government is willing to put an end to the war.

The instructions to those Plenipotentiaries, disclosing the grounds on which they were authorized to negotiate and conclude a Treaty of Peace, will be the subject of another communication.

       JAMES MADISON.

WASHINGTON, *October* 10, 1814.

The Message and communications were referred to the Committee on Foreign Relations.

Mr. FORSYTH moved that five thousand copies be printed for the use of the members.

Mr. HANSON, of Maryland, moved to amend the resolution by inserting "ten thousand copies" in the place of "five thousand." He said he was persuaded the information communicated in the Message had awakened but one feeling throughout the House, and stamped the same impression on every member. It had always been his opinion that it became not this Government to stand on idle, frivolous etiquette, but to speak to the enemy, if indeed we desired to convert him to a friend, to speak to him frankly, plainly, and directly, to the end that all ground for his doubting our sincerity might be removed. He trusted that it would appear that our Commissioners had been instructed so to speak, and that they had so spoken. If, then, on fair and honorable terms proposed, England should have denied us peace; if other and new claims had been set up; if she has attempted to annex degrading and humiliating conditions; if she has presumed to trench upon our ascertained rights as hitherto acknowledged and enjoyed, from that moment Mr. H.'s determination had long since been formed to unite in supporting the most vigorous system of honorable war, with the hope of bringing the enemy to a sense of justice. Mr. H. was satisfied that nothing more was necessary to make the war national than to convince the people that an honest and fair effort had been made to obtain peace, and it had been denied upon terms mutually honorable. From that moment it ceased to be a party war, and of necessity became national. Mr. H. said he too well knew the party with which it had been his pride and happiness to act, to doubt of their determining to bear a just share of the sacrifices to be incurred in defending the honor of the nation in a war that becomes just. Forgetting, as far as possible, their objections to the Administration; stifling their complaints as far as might be against the party that supports it; sacrificing all minor considerations; endeavoring to bury in oblivion the numerous wrongs inflicted upon their party; omitting, to every proper extent, a retrospect of the past, and looking to the present and the future, for the purpose of staunching the bleeding wounds of their country, they would stand forth in this her hour of peril, in asserting and maintaining her established rights and honor. But, sir, said Mr. H., while we have ever been ready to sacrifice our political feelings upon the altar of our country, the sacred duty we owe to it will require of us never to cease insisting on a reform in the measures of the Government, and the choice of honorable and enlightened men, competent to conduct its affairs in a crisis so awful. Unfortunately for the country, the character of the men who now directed its destinies was not of this description; nor did they possess the confidence of the nation.

Mr. OAKLEY, of New York, said that it was not necessary for him on this occasion to reiterate the sentiments of his honorable friend (Mr. HANSON.) His friend, he was confident, had expressed the feelings and opinions of those gentlemen with whom he was accustomed to act, on the nature and character of the demands and pretensions of the British Government, as developed in the despatches just read to the House. He did not hesitate, in the fullest manner, to declare, that those demands and pretensions were utterly inadmissible under any circumstances. But, Mr. O. said, while he made this declaration, and while he felt, in common with all gentlemen, the conviction that there could be but one sentiment in the nation, as to the necessity of resisting, by all the means in our power, the unjust and arrogant claims of the enemy, he felt bound to remark, that he could never forget by whom and upon what grounds the nation had been involved in this war, upon the issue of which were now staked the essential rights and honor of the country. The character given by the enemy to the war, had put at hazard these rights and that honor, and they must now be vindicated at an incalculable expense of treasure and blood. Mr. O. said

383   HISTORY OF CONGRESS.   384

H. of R.   *Honors to the Brave—Library for Congress.*   October, 1814.

it was notorious, that, at the commencement of the war, a great portion of the people of this country thought it rash and unnecessary. If the Administration had been willing to make peace on terms which could be expected to unite the approbation of the nation, they must have been prepared to abandon some of the grounds on which it had been declared. Their conduct in the late negotiation could not be properly estimated until the instructions to our Commissioners are laid before the House. This, Mr. O. said, he perceived was to be done. It would then appear how far they had thought it important to maintain the grounds on which they had deemed it expedient to commence a war; the conclusion of which was not now within their control, and appeared to be removed to a hopeless distance.

Mr. O. said, it was indispensable to the safety of the nation, that its affairs, at this awful crisis, should be committed to the management of men who could reasonably be expected to unite the confidence of the nation; and who, when they had compelled the enemy to abandon his unjust and insulting pretensions, would not throw new obstacles in the way of peace, by setting up any unwarrantable claims on our part. He would tell gentlemen in sober earnestness, that a war which, to be successful, must be waged by the united means and vigor of the nation, could never be conducted to an honorable issue by a *party* Administration.

Besides the above remarks of Mr. Hanson and Mr. Oakley, which are reported with critical correctness, a few remarks were made by Mr. Forsyth, of Georgia, and Mr. Wright, of Maryland, the first acquiescing in Mr. Hanson's motion, and the second approving the spirit of the remarks of Mr. H., his colleague.

The motion to print ten thousand copies was agreed to.

Tuesday, October 11.

Another member, to wit: from New York, Abraham Hasbrouck, appeared, and took his seat.

The Speaker presented a petition from Peter Landais, praying to be paid his share of prize money for British vessels captured during the Revolutionary War by the American frigate the Alliance, under his command.—Laid on the table.

HONORS TO THE BRAVE.

The House again resolved itself into a Committee of the Whole, on the resolutions expressive of the sense entertained by Congress of the gallantry and good conduct with which the reputation of the arms of the United States has been sustained by Major Generals Brown, Scott, and Gaines, and Brigadier General Macomb. These resolutions were yesterday amended in committee by the insertion of the names of Generals P. B. Porter, Ripley, and Miller. These amendments were, after considerable debate, confirmed by the House. The resolution approbatory of the conduct of Brigadier General Macomb was

also amended, on the motion of Mr. Shipherd, of New York, by adding thereto the names of Major General Mooers of the New York militia, and Major General Strong of the militia of Vermont.

The resolutions thus amended, were ordered to be engrossed for a third reading—Ayes 93.

LIBRARY FOR CONGRESS.

The House resolved itself into a Committee of the Whole on the resolution authorizing the Library Committee of Congress to contract for the purchase of the library of Mr. Jefferson.

The letter of Mr. Jefferson to Samuel H. Smith, Esq., offering the library to Congress on their own terms and their own time of payment, to replace in some degree the loss sustained in this respect by the recent invasion, was read. The letter states that the collection has been the work of fifty years and of great care and attention (and said to consist of ten thousand volumes)—a collection which he had designed, at his death, to have offered the refusal of to Congress—but this intention, the letter states, is hastened by the recent events; as the few years yet left to him would afford him but a barren use of this extensive and valuable library.—[For which letter see Senate Proceedings, *ante* page 24.]

After much desultory conversation, as to the value of this library, the nature of the selection, &c., the Committee rose (in order, apparently, to give further time to the members to examine the catalogue) and obtained leave to sit again.

Wednesday, October 12.

Mr. Pleasants, of Virginia, from the Committee of Naval Affairs, reported without amendment the resolution from the Senate in honor of Captain Macdonough, his officers and crew; and they were made the order of the day for to-morrow.

The resolutions expressive of the high sense entertained by the Congress of the United States of the gallantry and good conduct with which the reputation of the arms of the United States has been sustained by Generals Brown, Scott, Gaines, Ripley, and Miller, of the Army, and General P. B. Porter of the New York militia, and General Macomb of the Army, were read a third time, as amended.

Mr. Oakley, of New York, moved to recommit the same for amendment; alleging, as a reason therefor, that the amendments which had been incorporated in the resolutions afforded a strong objection to their passage.

After a debate of about two hours, the motion of Mr. Oakley was agreed to, and the resolutions were committed to the Committee on Military Affairs.

A message was received from the Senate informing the House that they had passed a joint resolution relative to the capture of the British sloop of war L'Epervier by the Peacock; which resolve was twice read, and referred to the Committee on Naval Affairs.

385 HISTORY OF CONGRESS. 386

OCTOBER, 1814. *Honor to the Brave—Battle on Lake Champlain.* H. OF R.

The order of the day on Mr. JACKSON's motion to amend the Constitution having been called up, on motion of Mr. JACKSON, of Virginia, the further consideration of the same was postponed to, and made the order of the day for, the first Monday in December next.

THURSDAY, October 13.

Mr. EPPES, of Virginia, gave notice that he should to-morrow call up the report of the Committee of Ways and Means on the additional taxes.

Mr. HAWKINS, of Kentucky, called up the report for this day, but the House overruled his motion.

On motion of Mr. COOPER, of New York, a resolution was adopted, instructing the Secretary of War to make a report to the House, of the claims of the several States and Territories for moneys advanced in paying the expenses of the militia of any State or Territory, heretofore called out under the authority of such State or Territory, for the purpose of repelling invasion or defending it from the incursion of the enemy—specifying what calls, if any, have not been sanctioned by the President of the United States, and distinguishing the items which, under existing laws, may be adjusted and settled, and such also as cannot be settled without legislative provision.

HONOR TO THE BRAVE.

Mr. TROUP, of Georgia, from the Military Committee, reported the resolutions, yesterday referred to them, in the following amended form:

Resolved, by the Senate and House of Representatives of the United States of America in Congress assembled, That the thanks of Congress be and they are hereby presented to Major General Brown, and through him to the officers and men under his command, for their gallantry and good conduct in the successive battles of Chippewa, Niagara, and Erie, in Upper Canada, in which British veteran troops were beaten and repulsed by equal or inferior numbers, and that the President of the United States be requested to cause a gold medal to be struck, emblematical of these triumphs, and presented to Major General Brown.

Resolved, That the President of the United States be requested to cause a gold medal to be struck, with suitable emblems and devices, and presented to Major General Scott, in testimony of the high sense entertained by Congress of his distinguished services in the successive conflicts of Chippewa and Niagara, and of his uniform gallantry and good conduct in sustaining the reputation of the arms of the United States.

Resolved, That the President of the United States be requested to cause silver medals to be struck, with suitable emblems and devices, and presented to Brigadier General Ripley, Brigadier General Miller, and Brigadier General Porter, in testimony of the high sense entertained by Congress of their gallantry and good conduct in the several conflicts of Chippewa, Niagara, and Erie.

Resolved, That the thanks of Congress be and they are hereby presented to Brigadier General Gaines, and through him to the officers and men under his command, for their gallantry and good conduct in defeating the enemy at Erie, on the 15th of August, repelling with great slaughter the attack of a British veteran

army superior in numbers, and that the President of the United States be requested to cause a gold medal to be struck, emblematical of this triumph, and presented to Brigadier General Gaines.

Resolved, That the thanks of Congress be and they are hereby presented to Brigadier General Macomb, and through him to the officers and men under his command, for their gallantry and good conduct in defeating the enemy at Plattsburg, on the 11th of September, repelling with 1,500 men, aided by a body of militia and volunteers from New York and Vermont, a British veteran army greatly superior in number, and that the President of the United States be requested to cause a gold medal to be struck, emblematical of this triumph, and presented to Brigadier General Macomb.

No debate took place on this report, except a few words on the subject of an amendment proposed by Mr. GHOLSON, which he afterwards withdrew.

The report was accepted without opposition, and ordered to be read a third and last time to-day. [But, before it could be engrossed for that purpose, the House had adjourned.]

THE BATTLE ON LAKE CHAMPLAIN.

The House, on motion of Mr. PLEASANTS, of Virginia, resolved itself into a Committee of the Whole on the resolutions from the Senate, expressive of the sense of Congress of the importance and brilliancy of the decisive victory obtained by Commodore Thomas Macdonough and his brave officers and men.

The resolutions having been read—

Mr. PLEASANTS, of Virginia, said, before the question was taken upon the resolutions, he would take the liberty of submitting to the consideration of the Committee a few remarks. Whatever, said he, may be the difference of opinion among us, as to the manner or the measure of approbation which we will bestow upon our land officers and soldiers, I believe there is but one sentiment as to our seamen. Fortunately for our country, the occasions of just and honorable eulogium upon them have been so frequent, that the practice is fully settled, the precedents completely established. The subject of the resolutions before you, is the victory obtained by Commodore Macdonough and his gallant comrades on Lake Champlain, over a superior British squadron, on the memorable 11th of September last—a victory in itself equal to any one which has been achieved by our navy; in its consequences certainly surpassed by none. A view of the relative strength of the two squadrons will convince us that this victory was in itself equal to any one which has preceded it. It is sufficient to observe, that in almost every particular, perhaps in every one, the advantage was on the side of the enemy. The action was commenced by him in the fullest confidence of success. He chose his own time; he took his own distance; he was animated by the presence of a great army, spectators of the contest. He was stimulated by that spirit of emulation which never ceases to exist between the Army and Navy. He had every reason to believe that, upon the successful issue of the naval contest, depended the successful issue of the cam-

13th CON. 3d SESS.—13

387 HISTORY OF CONGRESS. 388

H. of R. *Removal of the Seat of Government.* October, 1814.

paign. Thus situated, and thus wrought upon by motives so powerful, he would probably have been successful had he not been opposed by men actuated by feelings of a character somewhat different, but perhaps of still more powerful influence. The Americans were, in every sense of the word, fighting for their country. That country was likely to fall under one of the severest scourges to which any country can be exposed. The City of Washington had just before fallen a prey to the invaders—there was good reason to believe that Baltimore was on the eve of destruction—perhaps destroyed. The determination to lay waste and destroy all the assailable parts of our country had been announced in form. A ferocious determination, sir! Adopted, we are assured, at the special instance of the Governor of Canada. A combination of more powerful incentives to exertion has seldom addressed itself to the human mind. Under its influence our 'brave countrymen fought; and under its influence they conquered. The consequences of their victory are known to all united America. To recite them would be superfluous; I shall not undertake it, sir. All I ask is, and I ask it with pleasure, because I am sure I shall receive it, the undivided sentiment of this House in favor of the resolutions.

No opposition or amendment being made, the resolutions were reported to the House, and ordered to a third reading; and were accordingly read a third time, and passed by an unanimous vote.

REMOVAL OF THE SEAT OF GOVERNMENT.

Mr. Fisk, of New York, from the select committee to whom the subject was referred, reported the following bill:

A bill for the temporary removal of the Seat of Government from the City of Washington.

Be it enacted by the Senate and House of Representatives of the United States of America in Congress assembled, That, within twenty days from and after the passing of this act, all the offices attached to the Seat of the Government of the United States shall be removed, under the direction of the respective holders thereof, from the City of Washington to ——, in the State of ——, and there opened for the transaction of public business.

Sec. 2. *And be it further enacted,* That, within the said twenty days, from and after the passing of this act, Congress shall adjourn for —— days, to meet at the expiration of the said —— days, at ——, in the State of ——, then and there to finish the session of the present Congress.

Sec. 3. *And be it further enacted,* That, within the said twenty days after the passing of this act, the Seat of the Government of the United States shall, by virtue of this act, be transferred to the said ——, in the State of ——, and shall continue and remain there, for and during the continuance of the present war between the United States and Great Britain, and until the commencement of the next session of Congress after the termination of the war aforesaid.

Sec. 4. *And be it further enacted,* That, for defraying the expenses of such removal, the sum of —— thousand dollars is hereby appropriated, to be paid out of any money in the Treasury not otherwise appropriated.

Sec. 5. *And be it further enacted,* That the first session of Congress to be held after the termination of the present war between the United States and Great Britain, shall be held at the City of Washington, in the District of Columbia, to which place the public offices attached to the Seat of the Government of the United States shall, at the commencement of the said session, together with the Seat of the Government of the United States, be transferred; and, from and after that time, shall cease to be held or exercised elsewhere.

Mr. Forsyth, of Georgia, having objected to the second reading of the bill—

Mr. Rhea, of Tennessee, moved to reject the bill, and thereon demanded the yeas and nays. The reason he assigned for it was, that instead of being engaged on a subject of this kind, the House ought to be engaged in matters of high importance, in which the destinies of the nation are involved. He would call the attention of gentlemen to the despatches from Europe, which, he thought, would clearly indicate that other objects than this ought to occupy the attention of the House.

Mr. Grosvenor, of New York, said he most sincerely regretted that this course had been taken with the bill. If gentlemen were friends to this District, if they wished the question decided in such a way as would quiet the minds of the people of the District, they ought to refrain from pushing this question now, when many were absent who did not expect it to come on. If, when all the members were present, there should appear to be a majority against the bill, the question would be fairly settled; but a surprise of this sort could not decide it. The question was one, he said, of trying importance, not only to the District, but to other parts of the nation. It ought to be decided by a full vote. Until it was so settled, if against removal, there is not one citizen who ought to have confidence in the permanence of the Seat of Government. Gentlemen ought to deal liberally, and let the business take the usual course. If this course was taken, the real question would not be decided, but would be subject to continual agitation.

Mr. Forsyth, of Georgia, said, so far as he was personally concerned, he denied the imputation of intending to obtain a vote by surprise; he was not operated upon by any such consideration. He was not, he said, peculiarly a friend to the people of this District; it was not on their account he was opposed to the bill. It was the intrinsic importance of this question to the nation at large, that demanded his attention. It was necessary this question should be settled, and promptly settled. He had no idea that any member could be taken by surprise, and he was indeed surprised at the remark. This question had been amply discussed, and there was nothing to be said on the subject, &c. By referring to the bill, it would be seen that the bill could not possibly pass, and the Seat of Government be removed within thirty days; before which time the season would afford ample security against the approach of an enemy.

389 HISTORY OF CONGRESS. 390

OCTOBER, 1814. *Removal of the Seat of Government.* H. OF R.

By that time all the arguments which had been urged in favor of a removal would be done away by the rigor of the season. As to personal inconvenience from sitting here, he did not believe any gentleman could or would be influenced by motives of that character. There was now no reason for removal. If reasons should hereafter occur, it would be then time enough for Congress to remove.

Mr. FISK, of New York, said he very much regretted that this motion had been submitted to the consideration of the House. The principles of this bill had been more than once before the House, who had decided in favor of the removal; and it could not be expected they were now prepared to reject the bill. The exposure of this place and the expense of sitting here were as great now as they had been before. As to the argument that time will render this place secure, Mr. F. said he would answer the gentleman, for the enemy, as a French marshal had once replied to some such remark, that he would not consult the enemy as to the time or place of meeting him. Mr. F. said we were now situated four hundred miles from the most important seat of war, with which daily and expeditious communication was all-important, as well to the facility of supplies as to the combination of movement and action, &c. The increase of expense thus incurred, he said, amounted to a greater sum than would the cost of removal of the public offices to Philadelphia or New York. To brave all these inconveniences merely in consideration of the interests of the people of this District, would be to pervert the Constitutional provision which gives Congress exclusive legislation over the District, and instead of that, would be giving to the District the control over Congress. Mr. F. said he viewed the interests of the citizens of this District with the same consideration as he did those of all other citizens; but they had, he presumed, too much good sense and patriotism to ask Congress, merely out of regard to their personal views, to compromit the national interests. They were not to be ruined, either, by a permanent removal; for the bill itself provided for the return of Congress to this place after the war. Congress would be equally exposed, and require the same expenditure for their protection, at every session during the war as they were now. Gentlemen had said the enemy would not come here now, because they could find no object. It had been supposed that the enemy could have no object in coming here before, but he had come. Was it not necessary, not only that the members should feel themselves secure from personal danger, but also from fear of interruption? Should not the creditors of the Government be satisfied of the safety of Congress? And when we speak of them, said Mr. F., let us not pass them over with a bare mention. On whom must we rely for the support of our finances—for the sinews to carry on the war? Where are the moneyed men? Are they here? He meant by this no invidious distinctions. The gentleman from North Carolina (Mr. MACON) had the other day called the attention of the House to the character of the votes for removal, which were all from the North and East—from the moneyed men who wielded the capital of the nation. Let gentlemen reflect that these men would not advance their money with the same confidence to the Government at this place as if it were removed. This was the explanation which he would give of those votes. Was it not true that confidence in the public securities had been for a moment withdrawn on the occupation of the city by the enemy? If we have not now the means of meeting the public creditors, if we cannot look them in the face, if, by a temporary removal from this place, we can fulfil our engagements and redeem the public faith, which would be violated by remaining here, Mr. F. asked if they ought not to remove? As to the urgency of more important business to prevent the consideration of this, Mr. F. said this complaint was without reason. Let it be recollected that Congress had met and adjourned at twelve o'clock, or a little after, every day during the present session; but if the present question had been deferred till other business of moment was prepared for discussion, the argument would have been entitled to some weight. At present no business was more important than this; and, if it were not so, the House would not have sanctioned its discussion. Mr. F. said he was not pleased at the unusual course proposed to be pursued in relation to this bill. He had often heard motions for the rejection of bills, but never knew one of them successful. Considering the history and character of this bill, it was entitled to the ordinary course of passing to a second and third reading. If, on a fair vote, there should be a majority against it, let there be an end of the question, not for this moment only, but during the war.

Mr. NEWTON, of Virginia, said he did not rise to discuss this question, because he was satisfied the House was prepared to decide on it. He rose only to ask the gentleman to be kind enough to answer him one question. The faith of the nation is to be pledged for the money which must be obtained for the support of Government. Will not the pledge to be given in Washington be as valuable as any which could be given in Philadelphia? Will a removal increase the ability of a nation to meet the demands against it? It is not so. The Government is as competent to all such purposes here as it could be in any other city. Mr. N. appealed to the side of the House on which he sat. We, said he, are the majority; it is necessary for us to carry on the war with vigor. Your army now wants supplies: the moment when you ought to vote them, a bill is introduced calculated to set everything in motion, and we know not where and when Congress will meet again if it passes. If the public interest thus suffers, the responsibility is on us, and the people will look to us for accountability for all the evils which will result from such conduct.

Mr. STOCKTON, after desiring a call of the House, (which was not in order,) moved an adjournment, and called the yeas and nays thereon, in order to ascertain what members were absent.

391 HISTORY OF CONGRESS. 392

H. OF R. *Removal of the Seat of Government.* OCTOBER, 1814.

The yeas and nays having been so taken, there were for adjournment 40, against it 103, as follows:

YEAS—Messrs. Alexander, Baylies of Massachusetts, Bigelow, Bradbury, Bradley, Brigham, Caldwell, Cilley, Condict, Cooper, Cox, Dana, Davenport, Ely, Geddes, Grosvenor, Hulbert, Irwin, Jackson of Rhode Island, Kent of New York, Law, Lovett, Markell, Moffit, Moseley, Ormsby, John Reed, Sherwood, Skinner, Smith of New York, Stanford, Stockton, Sturges, Taggart, Vose, Ward of Massachusetts, Ward of New Jersey, Wheaton, Wilcox, and Winter.

NAYS—Messrs. Alston, Archer, Avery, Barbour, Bard, Barnett, Bayly of Virginia, Bowen, Boyd, Brown, Burwell, Butler, Chappell, Clopton, Comstock, Conard, Crawford, Creighton, Crouch, Culpeper, Cuthbert, Davis of Pennsylvania, Denoyelles, Desha, Duvall, Eppes, Evans, Farrow, Findley, Fisk of Vermont, Fisk of New York, Forney, Forsyth, Franklin, Gaston, Gholson, Glasgow, Goldsborough, Goodwin, Griffin, Hall, Hanson, Harris, Hasbrouck, Hawes, Hawkins, Hopkins of Kentucky, Hubbard, Humphreys, Hungerford, Ingersoll, Irving, Jackson of Virginia, Johnson of Kentucky, Kennedy, Kent of Maryland, Kerr, King of Massachusetts, King of North Carolina, Lefferts, Lewis, Lowndes, Lyle, Macon, McCoy, McKee, Miller, Montgomery, Moore, Nelson, Newton, Oakley, Pearson, Pickens, Piper, Pleasants, Post, Potter, Rea of Pennsylvania, Rhea of Tennessee, Rich, Ringgold, Roane, Ruggles, Sage, Schureman, Sevier, Seybert, Sharp, Shipherd, Smith of Virginia, Strong, Stuart, Tannehill, Taylor, Telfair, Thompson, Troup, Udree, White, Wilson of Pennsylvania, Wright, and Yancey.

Mr. STOCKTON then said, as eight or nine members appeared to be absent, he should move to postpone the further consideration of the bill till to-morrow.

On this motion Mr. RHEA required the previous question, which was not sanctioned by a sufficient number to take it.

Mr. McKEE, of Kentucky, and Mr. GASTON, of North Carolina, though both opposed to the bill, favored the postponement, from motives of liberality, and also from a dislike to what might by the absentees and others be deemed an unfair mode of legislation.

Mr. RHEA, of Tennessee, and Mr. FORSYTH, of Georgia, opposed postponement, on the ground that the bill had been already sufficiently debated and ought by this time to be well understood, and also on the ground that there was now more than an usual number of members present, and probably more than there would be to-morrow.

Mr. GROSVENOR disclaimed any intention to impute improper motives to gentlemen by the expression that this was a surprise. He merely meant to say that such would be the effect of now taking the question.

Mr. WRIGHT, of Maryland, for the same reasons assigned by other gentlemen, was in favor of postponement. He had no doubt the final decision would be in favor of remaining here. He hoped the final question would be taken to-morrow. He was not willing any longer to suspend the people of the city by the eyelids. Even the savages destroy their victim the same day they begin to inflict the deathly tortures on him. He

hoped the decision would then put eternally to rest the question of removal, and that this city, established by WASHINGTON, will never be broken up on the pretence that moneyed men would not lend their money here. Mr. W. said, if there were men who would act in this local manner, he did not desire their aid. The violation of public faith in even a temporary removal, under present circumstances, would injure the public credit infinitely more than a removal to any Northern city would strengthen it. Every man must see the situation of the country; every part of the Atlantic borders alike exposed to attack. But we should never have had a country to defend, if our ancestors had been appalled by danger—and danger so much greater than now, that living here was considered next to death, and was inflicted by the British Government as a punishment in commutation of that of death. He saw no inconvenience to Congress from sitting here. He liked the room in which the House sat better than the old hall, for every member might now be heard without extending his voice to that of a Stentor. Having been indisposed when this subject originally came before the House, he had thought it his duty to make these remarks. Gentlemen had said, if the Government went from this place there would be no inducement to the enemy to come here. The enemy had already gone from the Chesapeake, burnt their barrack on Tangiers island, indicating no intention to return at present. Although the enemy had been successful at this place, he had met the rubbers above, and he hoped he would again wherever he attempted to land; and would be universally beaten, if all Americans would now, as they ought, unite against the evil doers, and if every man in the country whose aid was worth having would, as he believed they would, aid in the prosecution of the war. He hoped the House would to-morrow relieve the citizens from the groundless fears of removal. He knew, he said, that this place was as secure as Philadelphia, and more so, and less assailable by the enemy. The enemy might occupy any point to which they would bend their whole force, and Philadelphia as easily as any other. They had much less inducement to come here than to go there. And why, said Mr. W., act the part contemplated by the bill? We have reprobated France and Great Britain for retaliating on us the injuries they received from each other—and shall we now imitate them, and retaliate on the people interested in the permanence of the Government here, for the injuries we and they have sustained from the enemy? It is a poor reason, because the enemy has destroyed the public property, that we should destroy the private. If the Government once removed hence, he was confident the same influence would prevent its return.

Mr. RHEA said he was anxious to see this question at rest, and would, therefore, make a motion to supersede that now before the House, and give gentlemen as much procrastination as the most anxious for that course could desire. He, therefore, moved to postpone indefinitely (tantamount

393   HISTORY OF CONGRESS.   394

OCTOBER, 1814.   *Retaliating System—Seat of Government.*   H. OF R.

to a motion to reject) the bill. He had no other object in view than to get rid of the subject.

Mr. STANFORD, of North Carolina, then made a motion (superseding all the others) that the bill and all the motions should lie on the table; which motion was agreed to, yeas 94.

FRIDAY, October 14.

Two other members, to wit: from Massachusetts, JAMES PARKER; and from Virginia, JAMES JOHNSON, appeared, and took their seats.

Mr. LEWIS, of Virginia, presented, for the third time, the memorial of Joseph Forrest, praying compensation for the detention, &c., by the Spanish Government, of a vessel chartered by him to the Government to convey flour to the people of Caraccas.—Referred.

Before any further business was done, a Message was received from the President of the United States, transmitting a number of documents; on opening which, the SPEAKER ordered strangers to be excluded the House. The doors remained closed until half past two o'clock. When they were again opened, it appeared that the Message embraced the instructions to our Ministers now in Europe, which the President announced his intention to communicate to Congress. They were, with the exception of a few passages deemed improper for publication, ordered to be printed.

The resolutions expressive of the sense of Congress in relation to the achievements of our military heroes in the Northern campaign of the present year, were read a third time, and passed unanimously.

Mr. EPPES, of Virginia, said he had given notice that he would call up the tax report to day. The Committee, however, now expected a report from the Treasury, intimately connected with the subject, and had therefore instructed him to move to postpone the further consideration of the subject to Monday next; and it was ordered accordingly.

Mr. LEWIS, of Virginia, having called up the bill for a temporary removal of the Seat of Government—

Mr. GROSVENOR, of New York, assigned the lateness of the hour as a reason for moving an adjournment; which motion was adopted by a vote of 76 to 69; and, by adjournment, the subject was postponed until to-morrow.

SATURDAY, October 15.

Two other members, to wit: from New Hampshire, DANIEL WEBSTER; and from Connecticut, TIMOTHY PITKIN, appeared, and took their seats.

A new member, to wit: from Tennessee, NEWTON CANNON, elected to supply the vacancy occasioned by the resignation of Felix Grundy, appeared, was qualified, and took his seat.

The SPEAKER laid before the House a letter from the acting Secretary of the Treasury, transmitting, in pursuance of a resolution of the 10th instant, statements of the returns of the direct

tax and internal duties established by the several acts passed at the first session of the present Congress; which were referred to the Committee of Ways and Means.

Mr. PLEASANTS, of Virginia, from the Naval Committee, reported, without amendment, the resolution from the Senate, expressive of the sense of Congress relative to the victory of the Peacock over the Epervier; and it was referred to a Committee of the whole House.

Mr. JOHNSON, of Kentucky, from the committee appointed to inquire into the causes of the capture of this city by the enemy, after detailing their proceedings and their determination to bring it to as speedy a result as possible, moved for leave to sit on Tuesday next during the sitting of the House.—Granted.

Mr. BURWELL, of Virginia, laid upon the table a resolution instructing the Secretary of War to lay before the House a list of the officers of the Army, the places where they are stationed, distinguishing those engaged in recruiting, the number of men enlisted by these officers since the increase of bounty, and also what sums have been paid for that purpose. This resolution he did not call up for consideration to-day.

RETALIATING SYSTEM.

Mr. GROSVENOR, of New York, said it would be recollected the President, in his Message to Congress, at the last session, informed the House that the commanding General of the Canadas had selected a number of American prisoners of war, and sent them over to England in close confinement; and that, on that act, a system of retaliation had been commenced. It would be recollected also that, towards the close of the session, in consequence of a resolution passed by the Senate, a statement was given of the situation of the prisoners sent to England, and of those who, as hostages, had been confined on either side. Many publications since made in the public prints tended to show that the difficulty on this head had been settled—how, was not known. He deemed it all important that the public should know on what principles it had been settled. With that view, he offered the following resolution:

Resolved, That the President of the United States be requested to lay before this House, if, in his opinion, it will not be inconsistent with the public welfare, all communications to or from the Government of England, or her officers or agents, not heretofore communicated, relative to the commencement and progress of any acts or system of retaliation founded upon, or produced by, the conduct of the British commander in Canada, "in selecting and sending to Great Britain, for trial as criminals, a number of individuals" taken prisoners of war from the American Army; also, any evidence he may have in his possession relative to the present conditions of such individuals.

The resolution was agreed to without debate or opposition, and a committee appointed to present the same to the President of the United States.

REMOVAL OF THE SEAT OF GOVERNMENT.

Mr. LEWIS, of Virginia, called up for consideration the bill for the temporary removal of the

895   HISTORY OF CONGRESS.   896

H. of R.   *Removal of the Seat of Government.*   October, 1814.

Seat of Government from the City of Washington.

The question for rejection of the bill came first in order, and was stated from the Chair.

Mr. FARROW, of South Carolina, rose, and stated the reasons why, though he should eventually vote against the bill, he should now vote against the rejection of it.

Mr. RHEA, of Tennessee, replied to some of those reasons.

The question on the rejection of the bill was then put and negatived, by the following vote: For the rejection 76, against it, 79, as follows:

YEAS—Messrs. Archer, Avery, Barbour, Bard, Barnett, Bayly of Virginia, Bowen, Burwell, Cannon, Chappell, Clopton, Comstock, Crawford, Culpeper, Cuthbert, Dana, Earle, Eppes, Evans, Fisk of Vermont, Forney, Forsyth, Franklin, Gaston, Gholson, Glasgow, Goldsborough, Goodwyn, Griffin, Hall, Hanson, Harris, Hawes, Hawkins, Hopkins of Kentucky, Hubbard, Humphreys, Hungerford, Irving, Jackson of Virginia, Johnson of Virginia, Johnson of Kentucky, Kennedy, Kent of Maryland, Kerr, Kershaw, King of North Carolina, Lefferts, Lewis, Lowndes, Macon, McCoy, McKee, McKim, Montgomery, Moore, Nelson, Newton, Pearson, Pickens, Pleasants, Rhea of Tennessee, Ringgold, Roane, Robertson, Sage, Sevier, Smith of Virginia, Strong, Stuart, Telfair, Troup, White, Wilson of Pennsylvania, Wright, and Yancey.

NAYS—Messrs. Alexander, Alston, Baylies of Massachusetts, Bigelow, Boyd, Bradbury, Bradley, Brigham, Brown, Butler, Caldwell, Cilley, Clark, Condict, Conard, Cooper, Cox, Creighton, Crouch, Davenport, Davis of Pennsylvania, Denoyelles, Desha, Duvall, Ely, Farrow, Findley, Fisk of New York, Geddes, Gourdin, Grosvenor, Hasbrouck, Hulbert, Ingersoll, Irwin, Jackson of Rhode Island, Kent of New York, King of Massachusetts, Law, Lovett, Lyle, Markell, Miller, Moffit, Moseley, Oakley, Ormsby, Parker, Pickering, Piper, Pitkin, Post, Potter, John Reed, Rea of Pennsylvania, Rich, Ruggles, Schureman, Seybert, Sharp, Sherwood, Shipherd, Skinner, Smith of New York, Stanford, Stockton, Sturges, Taggart, Tannehill, Taylor, Thompson, Udree, Vose, Ward of Massachusetts, Ward of New Jersey, Webster, Wheaton, Wilcox, and Winter.

The bill was then read a second time, and referred to a Committee of the Whole; and the House immediately resolved itself into a Committee of the Whole on the said bill, it having been made the order of the day for to-day, in preference to Monday, by a majority of 86 to 65 votes.

Mr. FISK, of New York, moved to fill the blank for the place of removal with Philadelphia.

Mr. LEWIS, of Virginia, moved to fill it with Georgetown.

Mr. LEWIS, and Mr. HOPKINS, of Kentucky, spoke against the insertion of Philadelphia, and Mr. PICKERING in favor of it.

The motion to insert Philadelphia was agreed to by a large majority; and the other blanks in the bill were filled up.

Mr. LEWIS, of Virginia, then moved to insert the following section as an amendment to the bill:

"*And be it further enacted*, That the annual sum of one hundred thousand dollars be, and is hereby, appropriated, for the term of five years, to be applied, under the direction of the President of the United States, for the erection of suitable buildings within the city of Washington, for the accommodation of the President of the United States, the two Houses of Congress, and the several Departments of the Government, and that the same shall be paid annually to the order or orders of the President of the United States."

After much interesting debate this motion was agreed to, ayes 95.

The Committee rose, and reported the bill with the amendments, which were also concurred in by the House.

And the question was then put, "Shall the bill be engrossed and read the third time?" and decided as follows:

YEAS—Messrs. Alexander, Alston, Baylies of Massachusetts, Bigelow, Boyd, Bradbury, Bradley, Brigham, Brown, Butler, Caldwell, Champion, Cilley, Clark, Condict, Conard, Cooper, Cox, Creighton, Crouch, Davenport, Davis of Pennsylvania, Denoyelles, Desha, Duvall, Ely, Fisk of New York, Geddes, Gourdin, Grosvenor, Hasbrouck, Hulbert, Ingersoll, Irwin, Jackson of Rhode Island, Kent of New York, King of Massachusetts, Law, Lovett, Markell, Miller, Moffit, Moseley, Oakley, Ormsby, Pickering, Piper, Pitkin, Post, Potter, John Reed, Rea of Pennsylvania, Rich, Ruggles, Schureman, Seybert, Sharp, Sherwood, Shipherd, Skinner, Smith of New York, Stockton, Sturges, Taggart, Taylor, Thompson, Udree, Vose, Ward of Massachusetts, Ward of New Jersey, Webster, Wheaton, Wilcox, and Winter—74.

NAYS—Messrs. Archer, Avery, Barbour, Bard, Barnett, Bayly of Virginia, Bowen, Burwell, Cannon, Chappell, Clopton, Comstock, Crawford, Culpeper, Cuthbert, Dana, Earle, Eppes, Evans, Farrow, Findley, Fisk of Vermont, Forney, Forsyth, Franklin, Gaston, Gholson, Glasgow, Goldsborough, Goodwyn, Griffin, Hall, Hanson, Harris, Hawes, Hawkins, Hopkins of Kentucky, Hubbard, Humphreys, Hungerford, Irving, Jackson of Virginia, Johnson of Virginia, Johnson of Kentucky, Kennedy, Kent of Maryland, Kerr, Kershaw, King of North Carolina, Lefferts, Lewis, Lowndes, Lyle, Macon, McCoy, McKee, McKim, McLean, Montgomery, Moore, Nelson, Newton, Parker, Pearson, Pickens, Pleasants, Rhea of Tennessee, Ringgold, Roane, Robertson, Sage, Sevier, Smith of Virginia, Stanford, Strong, Stuart, Tannehill, Telfair, Troup, White, Wilson of Pennsylvania, Wright, and Yancey—88.

[*Absent on this vote.*—Mr. Anderson, from indisposition; Messrs. Caperton, Ingham, Murfree, on leave; Messrs. Breckenridge, Calhoun, Davis of Massachusetts, Hale, Hopkins of New York, Howell, Kilbourn, Reed, Ridgely, Sheffey, Smith of Pennsylvania, Tallmadge, Williams, Wilson of Massachusetts, and Wood, who have not attended at the present session.]

So the House determined that the bill should not be engrossed for a third reading; in other words, that it should be rejected.

MONDAY, October 17.

Two other members, to wit: from Massachusetts, JOHN WILSON, and from Pennsylvania, ISAAC SMITH, appeared and took their seats.

Mr. WRIGHT, of Maryland, presented the petition of Thomas Bruff, inventor of the method of manufacturing bullets and shot by compression, stating the destruction of certain of his machinery proposed to have been connected with the steam-engine belonging to the late navy yard in this city, and praying that Congress will take his case into consideration.—Referred to a select committee.

Mr. YANCEY, from the Committee of Claims, made a report on the petition of Captain Alexander Sevier, praying remuneration for certain losses sustained in the public service, admitting the equity of his claim, but recommending a rejection of it on general legal principles.—Laid on the table.

The report is as follows:

That the petitioner is a Lieutenant of Marines in the service of the United States. On the 16th October, 1812, he was ordered to go from Washington City to the encampment near St. Augustine, in East Florida; and on his way to that place, near Occoquan, his trunk was cut off the carriage in which he was, and robbed, as he states, of $200 in bank notes, and a check drawn in favor of the petitioner on the Bank of Petersburg for $200, and all his military clothes. It is stated in the petition that nearly one-half of the money belonged to the United States, having been advanced to him for public service. The petitioner asks to be remunerated for the money lost, and compensated for the apparel.

The petition was before the Committee of Claims at the last session of Congress; the committee were then of opinion that the petitioner was not entitled to relief; the present Committee of Claims accord with that opinion. In this case there is no satisfactory evidence of the loss of the property; in all cases the kind of evidence of that fact should be clear, positive, and uninterested. The committee, however, are of opinion that, taking the claim in its greatest latitude as related in the petition, sound policy requires that it should be rejected. When a public agent or officer receives money of the Government, he should keep it safe. There are but few cases in which he should be exonerated of his accountability; it is not believed this is a case of that description. They therefore recommend to the House the following resolution:

Resolved, That the prayer of the petitioner ought not to be granted.

Mr. JACKSON, of Virginia, made a motion to print two thousand additional copies of the instructions to our Ministers to treat of peace in Europe.

Mr. GROSVENOR, of New York, moved to amend the said motion so as to print these instructions entire, as received from the President, (that is, including the few passages not deemed proper for publication.)

The SPEAKER feeling a difficulty in receiving this motion under present circumstances—

Mr. GROSVENOR required the galleries to be cleared, and strangers were excluded accordingly.

The doors remained closed for two hours; when they were again opened, it appeared that the motion of Mr. GROSVENOR was rejected, and that of Mr. JACKSON was agreed to.

MR. JEFFERSON'S LIBRARY.

The House resolved itself into a Committee of the Whole, Mr. LEWIS in the Chair, on the resolution from the Senate authorizing the Library Committee to contract for the purchase of Mr. Jefferson's library.

Mr. OAKLEY, of New York, moved so to amend the resolution as to leave it open to the Library Committee to contract for the purchase of *a* library for the use of Congress.

On this motion considerable desultory debate took place; the purchase of Mr. Jefferson's library being opposed by Messrs. OAKLEY, JOHN REED, and GROSVENOR, and advocated by Messrs. WRIGHT, SEYBERT, ROBERTSON, HAWKINS, and FORSYTH.

The objections to the purchase were generally its extent, the cost of the purchase, the nature of the selection, embracing too many works in foreign languages, some of too philosophical a character, and some otherwise objectionable. Of the first description, exception was taken to Voltaire's works, &c., and of the other to Callender's Prospect Before Us.

On the other hand, those who advocated the purchase proposed to be made, contended that so valuable a library, one so admirably calculated for the substratum of a great national library, was not to be obtained in the United States; and that, although there might be some works to which gentlemen might take exception, there were others of very opposite character; that this, besides, was no reason against the purchase, because in every library of value might be found some books to which exceptions would be taken, according to the feelings or prejudices of those who examined them.

Mr. OAKLEY's motion was negatived by the following vote—For the amendment 53, against it 87.

The Committee then rose and reported the resolution to the House, who took it up.

Mr. KING, of Massachusetts, moved to amend the resolution by limiting the power of the committee to the purchase of such parts of the library as they should deem suitable to the purpose.

[Mr. Jefferson, in his letter on the subject to Mr. SMITH, declines disposing of a part without the whole of his library.]

After some discussion, the question on this proposed amendment was decided by yeas and nays, by the following vote—For the amendment 47, against it 91, as follows:

YEAS—Messrs. Baylies of Massachusetts, Bigelow, Boyd, Bradbury, Brigham, Champion, Cilley, Cooper, Cox, Culpeper, Davenport, Ely, Farrow, Geddes, Goldsborough, Grosvenor, Hanson, Jackson of Rhode Island, King of Massachusetts, Law, Lewis, Lovett, Markell, Miller, Moffit, Moseley, Oakley, Pearson, Pickering, Pitkin, Post, Potter, John Reed, Ruggles, Schureman, Sherwood, Shipherd, Smith of New York, Stockton, Sturges, Vose, Ward of Massachusetts, Webster, Wheaton, Wilcox, Wilson of Massachusetts, and Winter.

NAYS—Messrs. Alexander, Alston, Archer, Avery, Barbour, Bard, Bowen, Bradley, Brown, Butler, Cannon, Chappell, Clark, Clopton, Condict, Conard, Crawford, Creighton, Crouch, Cuthbert, Dana, Denoyelles, Desha, Duvall, Earle, Findley, Fisk of Vermont, Fisk of New York, Forney, Forsyth, Franklin, Gaston, Gholson, Glasgow, Goodwyn, Gourdin, Griffin, Hall,

Harris, Hasbrouck, Hawes, Hawkins, Hopkins of Kentucky, Hubbard, Humphreys, Hungerford, Hulbert, Irving, Irwin, Jackson of Virginia, Johnson of Virginia, Johnson of Kentucky, Kennedy, Kent of New York, Kent of Maryland, Kerr, Kershaw, King of North Carolina, Lefferts, Lowndes, Lyle, McCoy, McKim, McLean, Moore, Nelson, Newton, Ormsby, Parker, Pickens, Piper, Pleasants, Rhea of Tennessee, Rich, Ringgold, Roane, Robertson, Sage, Seybert, Sharp, Smith of Pennsylvania, Smith of Virginia, Stanford, Strong, Tannehill, Taylor, Telfair, Ward of New Jersey, Wilson of Pennsylvania, Wright, and Yancey.

Mr. JOHN REED, of Massachusetts, then moved to amend the bill by limiting the price to be given for the whole of the library to twenty-five thousand dollars.

Mr. STANFORD, of North Carolina, moved to postpone the further consideration of the subject to the first Monday in December next.

Mr. OAKLEY, of New York, moved to lay the resolution, and the last motion together with it, on the table.—Negatived.

Mr. STANFORD's motion was then also negatived.

The yeas and nays having been demanded on Mr. READ's motion, before mentioned, after further discussion, the House adjourned without deciding the same.

. TUESDAY, October 18.

Another member, to wit: from Massachusetts, WILLIAM REED, appeared, and took his seat.

Mr. McKIM presented a petition of Daniel Renner and Nathaniel H. Heath, rope makers in the City of Washington, praying compensation for their wrought and unwrought materials, which were consumed by fire, by order of the enemy, on the 25th of August last, and which they were prevented from previously removing to a place of safety by the impressment of their vehicles of transportation into the public service.—Referred to the Committee of Claims.

Mr. LEWIS, of Virginia, presented the memorial of a number of inhabitants of Alexandria, stating their indignant surprise at the slanders in circulation respecting that city, and praying a full and fair examination by Congress of their conduct during the late visit of the enemy to that town. The memorial was read.

Mr. LEWIS moved to refer the memorial to the committee of investigation appointed on the subject; which motion, after some desultory conversation, was agreed to.

Mr. STANFORD, from the Committee of Revisal and Unfinished Business, made a report, in part: which was read, and ordered to lie on the table.

Mr. PLEASANTS, from the Committee on Naval Affairs, reported a bill directing the staff officers of the Army to comply with the requisitions of naval and marine officers, in certain cases; which was read twice and committed to a Committee of the Whole on Thursday next.

Mr. PLEASANTS also reported a bill for the relief of the officers, petty officers, and seamen, under the command of Joshua Barney; which

was read twice and committed to a Committee of the Whole on Thursday next.

JUDICIARY OF INDIANA TERRITORY.

Mr. JENNINGS presented a petition of the Legislature of the Indiana Territory, praying that a law may be passed requiring the presence of two judges to hold courts; and that the duties of the courts of the United States for said Territory may be more clearly defined.

The memorial is as follows:

To the Senate and House of Representatives of the United States in Congress assembled, the memorial of the Legislature of the Indiana Territory humbly showeth:

That, by a law of Congress, one of the judges, appointed by virtue of the ordinance for the government of this Territory, is authorized to hold a court. Thus, one of the judges being competent to hold a court, may decide a principle, or a point of law, at one term, and, at the next term, if the other two judges are present, they may decide the same principle or point of law different. Thus the decisions of the superior court, organized, we presume, by the General Government, finally to settle in uniformity the principles of law and fact, which may be brought before them by the suitor, may be, and frequently are, in a state of fluctuation; hence the rights of persons and property become insecure. There is another evil, growing out of the system, of one judge being competent to hold the superior court, or that court which forms the last resort of the suitor in any Government, and particularly in the Territory; for appeals are taken from all the courts of inferior jurisdiction in the Territory, to the court organized by the ordinance, which inferior courts are never constituted of less than two judges. Thus the suitor in the Territory is frequently driven to the necessity of appealing from the judgment of two men to that of one; but this dilemma only constitutes part of the solecism for the next superior court, as the other two judges may overturn the principles of the decision of their brother judge at the preceding term. Hence the want of uniformity in the decisions of the court of the last resort. Anger and warmth in the suitors, and a confusion in our system of jurisprudence, is the result.

Your memorialists beg leave further to suggest the propriety and necessity of defining, with more precision, the duties of the judges appointed by virtue of the ordinance for the government of the Territory. The ordinance says there shall be a court to consist of three judges, who shall have a common law jurisdiction. The same instrument points out the way a Legislature may be organized; but in no part does the ordinance expressly delegate to the Legislature the power of regulating when and where the superior courts are to be held, or the manner how they are to do business. This power, by a kind of common consent of the judges, the Legislature have assumed from the necessity of the case, as the ordinance creating the courts leaves it afloat, without identifying either the time when, the place where, or the manner how, this court is to exercise their jurisdiction. Again, it would be desirable that Congress would define the jurisdiction of the superior court. We presume that it is a sound rule for the construction of a constitution or a law, that it must be construed from the face of it, and not travel to the history of other times and other Governments in search of the meaning of our ordinance, or any act of Congress. We beg leave to suggest the propriety of pointing out, by law, what common law the ordinance refers to, whether the common law of England, or France, or of the Territory over which the ordinance is the constitution. If it should be determined that, by the expression of the ordinance, a common law jurisdiction should be located on the common law of England, it is essential to define to what extent of that common law the judges shall take cognizance; whether the whole extent of feudal and gothic customs of England; whether the customs, or unwritten law shall be taken with the statute law, and that to form the common law to govern the judges; or whether the unwritten and statute law is to be taken in contradistinction to the laws, customs, and rules of chancery; or whether it includes that law which is common to all. By Congress defining the powers of the court, and not leaving them at sea without compass or chart to exercise their power of judicial legislation, as circumstances may arise, or passion or interest dictate, by defining the powers of the Legislature and jurisdiction of the court, that collision and jarring which might arise between those two bodies would be harmonized.

Your memorialists, therefore, pray that you would repeal the law first herein alluded to, and make two of the judges hold the court, and define more specifically the duties of that court.

WILLIAM HENDRICKS,
Speaker of the House of Representatives.
JESSE L. HOLMAN,
President of the Council.

The memorial was referred to the Committee on the Judiciary.

TREASURY REPORT.

Mr. EPPES, from the Committee of Ways and Means, laid before the House the copy of a letter from the chairman of that committee to the Secretary of the Treasury, upon the subject of maintaining unimpaired the public credit, together with the answer of the Secretary of the Treasury thereto; which were read, and referred to the Committee of the whole House, to whom was referred the report of the Committee of Ways and Means on that part of the President's Message which relates to our finances.

The Letter and Report are as follows:

SIR: The Committee of Ways and Means have had under their consideration the support of public credit by a system of taxation more extended than the one heretofore adopted. They have determined to suspend proceeding on their report at present before the House of Representatives, with a view to afford you an opportunity of suggesting another, or such additional provisions as may be necessary to revive and maintain unimpaired the public credit.

I have the honor to be, &c.

JOHN W. EPPES.
Hon. Mr. DALLAS,
Secretary of the Treasury.

———

TREASURY DEPARTMENT, *Oct.* 17, 1814.

SIR: I have the honor to acknowledge the receipt of your letter, dated the 14th instant, and, aware of the necessity for an early interposition of Congress on the subject to which it relates, I proceed, at the moment of entering upon the duties of office, to offer to the consideration of the Committee of Ways and Means, an answer on the several points of inquiry.

Contemplating the present state of the finances, it is obvious that a deficiency in the revenue, and a depreciation in the public credit, exist from causes which cannot in any degree be ascribed, either to the want of resources, or to the want of integrity in the nation. Different minds will conceive different opinions in relation to some of those causes; but it will be agreed on all sides, that the most operative have been the inadequacy of our system of taxation to form a foundation for public credit; and the absence even from that system of the means which are best adapted to anticipate, collect, and distribute the public revenue.

The wealth of the nation, in the value and products of its soil, in all the acquisitions of personal property, in all the varieties of industry, remains almost untouched by the hand of Government; for the national faith, and not the national wealth, has hitherto been the principal instrument of finance. It was reasonable, however, to expect, that a period must occur in the course of a protracted war, when confidence in the accumulating public engagements could only be secured by an active demonstration, both of the capacity and the disposition to perform them. In the present state of the Treasury, therefore, it is a just consolation to reflect that a prompt and resolute application of the resources of the country will effectually relieve from every pecuniary embarrassment and vindicate the fiscal honor of the Government. But it would be vain to attempt to disguise, and it would be pernicious to palliate the difficulties which are now to be overcome. The exigencies of the Government require a supply of treasure for the prosecution of the war, beyond any amount which it would be politic, even if it were practicable, to raise by an immediate and constant imposition of taxes. There must, therefore, be a resort to credit, for a considerable portion of the supply. But the public credit is at this juncture so depressed, that no hope of adequate succor, on moderate terms, can safely rest upon it. Hence, it becomes the object first and last in every practical scheme of finance, to re-animate the confidence of the citizens; and to impress on the mind of every man, who, for the public account, renders services, furnishes supplies, or advances money, a conviction of the punctuality as well as of the security of the Government. It is not to be regarded, indeed, as the case of preserving a credit which has never been impaired, but rather as the case of rescuing from reproach a credit over which doubt and apprehension (not the less injurious perhaps because they are visionary) have cast an inauspicious shade. In the former case, the ordinary means of raising and appropriating the revenue, will always be sufficient; but in the latter case, no exertion can be competent to attain the object, which does not quiet, in every mind, every fear of future loss or disappointment in consequence of trusting to the pledges of the public faith.

The condition of the circulating medium of the country presents another copious source of mischief and embarrassment. The recent exportations of specie have considerably diminished the fund of gold and silver coin; and another considerable portion of that fund has been drawn by the timid and the wary, from the use of the community, into the private coffers of individuals. On the other hand, the multiplication of banks in the several States has so increased the quantity of paper currency, that it would be difficult to calculate its amount; and still more difficult to ascertain its value, with reference to the capital on which it has been issued. But the benefit of even this paper currency is in a great measure lost, as the suspension of payments in specie at most of the banks has suddenly broken the chain of accommodation, that previously extended the credit and the circulation of the notes which were emitted in one State into every State in the Union. It may in general be affirmed, therefore, that there exists at this time no adequate circulating medium common to the citizens of the United States. The moneyed transactions of private life are at a stand; and the fiscal operations of Government labor with extreme inconvenience. It is impossible that such a state of things should be long endured; but, let it be fairly added, that with legislative aid it is not necessary that the endurance should be long. Under favorable circumstance, and to a limited extent, an emission of Treasury notes would, probably, afford relief; but Treasury notes are an expensive and precarious substitute, either for coin or for bank notes, charged as they are with a growing interest, productive of no countervailing profit or emolument, and exposed to every breath of popular prejudice or alarm. The establishment of a national institution, operating upon credit combined with capital, and regulated by prudence and good faith, is, after all, the only efficient remedy for the disordered condition of our circulating medium. While accomplishing that object, too, there will be found, under the auspices of such an institution, a safe depository for the public treasure and a constant auxiliary to the public credit. But, whether the issues of a paper currency proceed from the National Treasury or from a National Bank, the acceptance of the paper in a course of payments and receipts must be forever optional with the citizens. The extremity of that day cannot be anticipated, when any honest and enlightened statesman will again venture upon the desperate expedient of a tender law.

From this painful, but necessary developement of existing evils, we pass, with hope and confidence, to a more specific consideration of the measures from which relief may be certainly and speedily derived. Remembering always, that the objects of the Government are to place the public credit upon a solid and durable foundation; to provide a revenue commensurate with the demands of a war expenditure, and to remove from the Treasury an immediate pressure, the following propositions are submitted to the committee, with every sentiment of deference and respect.

PROPOSITIONS.

I. It is proposed, that, during the war, and until the claims contemplated by the proposition are completely satisfied, or extinct, there shall be annually raised by taxes, duties, imposts, and excises, a fund for these purposes:

1. For the support of Government	$1,500,000
2. For the principal and interest of the public debt, existing before the declaration of war, and payable according to the contract	3,500,000
3. For the interest of the public debt, contracted, and to be contracted, by loans, or otherwise, from the commencement to the termination of the war, calculated upon an annual principal of seventy-two millions of dollars	4,320,000
4. For the payment of Treasury notes, with the accruing interest	7,400,000
5. For the payment of debentures to be issued (as is hereinafter proposed) for liquidated balances, due to individuals, on account of services or supplies, authorized	

by law, but either not embraced by a specific appropriation, or exceeding the sum appropriated	$280,000
6. For a current addition to the sum raised by loan, or issues of Treasury notes, towards defraying the general expenses of the war	2,000,000
7. For the gradual establishment of a sinking fund, to extinguish the debt incurred during the war	500,000
8. For the contingent fund, to meet sudden and occasional demands upon the Treasury	1,500,000
	21,000,000

II. It is proposed, that, during the war, and until the claims contemplated by the preceding proposition are completely satisfied, or other adequate funds shall be provided and substituted by law, there shall be annually raised, by the means here specified, the following sums:

1. By the customs (which cannot be safely estimated, during the war, at a higher product)	$4,000,000
2. By the existing internal duties	2,700,000
3. By the existing direct tax	2,500,000
4. By the sales of public lands (which cannot be safely estimated, during the war, at a higher product)	800,000
5. By an addition to the existing direct tax of one hundred per cent.	2,850,000
6. By an addition of one hundred per cent. on the present auction duties	150,000
7. By an addition of one hundred per cent. on the existing duties upon carriages	200,000
8. By an addition of fifty per cent. on the existing duties on licenses to retail wines, spirituous liquors, and foreign merchandise	300,000
9. By an addition of one hundred per cent. on the existing rate of postage	500,000
10. By the proceeds of the new duties specified in the annexed schedule, marked A, making the aggregate	7,000,000
	21,000,000

III. It is proposed, that a National Bank shall be incorporated for a term of twenty years, to be established at Philadelphia, with a power to erect offices of discount and deposite elsewhere, upon the following principles:

1. That the capital of the bank shall be fifty millions of dollars, to be divided into one hundred thousand shares of five hundred dollars each. Three-fifths of the capital, being sixty thousand shares, amounting to thirty millions of dollars, to be subscribed by corporations, companies, or individuals; and two-fifths of the capital, being forty thousand shares, amounting to twenty millions of dollars, to be subscribed by the United States.

2. That the subscriptions of corporations, companies and individuals, shall be paid for in the following manner:

One-fifth part, or six millions, in gold or silver coin.

Four-fifth parts, or twenty-four millions, in gold or silver coin, or in six per cent. stock issued since the declaration of war, and Treasury notes, in the proportion of one-fifth Treasury notes and three-fifths in six per cent. stock.

3. That the subscriptions of corporations, companies, and individuals, shall be paid at the following periods :

20 dollars on each share, to be paid at the time of subscribing, in gold or silver coin - - - - -	$1,200,000
40 dollars on each share, to be paid in gold or silver coin, one month after the subscription - - - -	2,400,000
40 dollars on each share, in two months after the subscription, in gold or silver coin - - - -	2,400,000
100 dollars, specie	6,000,000
100 dollars on each share, in gold or silver coin, or in six per cent. stock, or in Treasury notes, according to the preceding apportionment, to be paid at the time of subscribing - -	6,000,000
150 dollars on each share, to be paid in like manner, in two months after subscribing - - - -	9,000,000
150 dollars on each share, to be paid in like manner, in three months after subscribing - - - -	9,000,000
500	30,000,000

4. That the subscription of the United States shall be paid in six per cent. stock, at the same periods and in the same proportions as the payments of private subscriptions, in stock and Treasury notes.

5. That the United States may substitute six per cent. stock, for the amount of the Treasury notes subscribed by corporations, companies, and individuals, as the notes respectively become due and payable.

6. That the bank shall loan to the United States thirty millions, at an interest of six per cent., at such periods, and in such sums, as shall be found mutually convenient.

7. That no part of the public stock, constituting a portion of the capital of the bank, shall be sold during the war; nor at any subsequent time, for less than par ; nor at any time to an amount exceeding one moiety, without the consent of Congress.

8. That provision shall be made for protecting the bank notes from forgery; for limiting the issue of bank notes; and for receiving them in all payments to the United States.

9. That the capital of the bank, its notes, deposites, dividends, or profits, (its real estate only excepted,) shall not be subject to taxation by the United States or by any individual State.

10. That no other bank shall be established by Congress, during the term for which the National Bank is incorporated.

11. That the National Bank shall be governed by fifteen directors, being resident citizens of the United States and stockholders. The President of the United States shall annually name five directors, and designate one of the five to be president of the bank. The other directors shall be annually chosen by the qualified stockholders, in person or by proxy, if resident within the United States, voting upon a scale graduated according to the number of shares which they respectively hold. The cashier and other officers of the bank to be appointed as is usual in similar institutions.

12. That the directors of the National Bank shall appoint seven persons, one of whom to preside, as the managers of each office of discount and deposite, and one person to be the cashier.

13. That the general powers, privileges, and regulations of the bank, shall be the same as are usual in similar institutions; but with this special provision, that the general accounts shall be subject to the inspection of the Secretary of the Treasury.

IV. It is proposed, that, after having thus provided for the punctual payment of the interest upon every denomination of public debt, for raising annually a portion of the annual expense, by taxes; for establishing a sinking fund, in relation to the new debt, as well as in relation to the old debt; and for securing to the public the efficient agency of a National Bank; the only remaining object of supply shall be accomplished by annual loans, and issues of Treasury notes, if, unexpectedly, such issues should continue to be necessary or expedient.

1. The amount of annual expenditure during the war, exceeding the sums provided for, does not admit of a prospective estimate beyond the year 1815; but for that year it may be estimated with sufficient accuracy for the general purposes of the present communication, at $28,000,000.

2. Then for the year 1815, an additional provision must be made, authorizing a loan and the issue of Treasury notes, to an equal amount, $28,000,000.

V. It is proposed that the accounts for authorized expenses being duly stated and settled, a certificate or debenture shall issue to the accountant specifying the balance; and that in all cases, where there has been no specific appropriation, or the claim exceeds the amount of the sum appropriated, the balance shall bear an interest of three per cent. until provision is made by law for paying the amount.

VI. And, finally, it is proposed to relieve the Treasury from an immediate pressure, upon the principles of the following statement :

1. The amount of demands upon the Treasury, exclusive of balances of appropriations for former years, unsatisfied, was stated in the report of the late Secretary of the Treasury of the 23d September, 1814, to be, on the 30th June   -   - $27,576,391 19

2. The accounts of the third quarter of 1814 are not yet made up, and the precise sums paid during that quarter cannot now be ascertained, but they amount to nearly   -   -   -   8,400,000 00

Leaving to be paid in the fourth quarter of 1814   -   - $19,176,391 19

3. This balance, payable during the fourth quarter of 1814, consists of the following items :

Civil, diplomatic, and miscellaneous expenses, about - - -	$353,392 99
Military, about - -	8,792,568 00
Naval, about - -	2,382,010 97
Public debt, about - -	7,648,419 23
	$19,176,391 19

4. The existing provisions by law for the payment of this balance of $19,176,391 19, may be stated as follows :

The act of the 24th March, 1814, authorized a loan of   -   -   - $25,000,000 00

The act of the 4th March, 1814, authorized an issue of Treasury notes for - 5,000,000 00

$30,000,000 00

Under these authorities, there have been borrowed, on loan, about $10,895,000 00
There have been sent to Europe, in 6 per cent. stock - - - 6,000,000 00
There has been issued, in Treasury notes - 3,504,000 00

20,399,000 00

$9,601,000 00

There remains, therefore, an unexecuted authority to borrow - 8,105,000 00
To issue Treasury notes 1,496,000 00

9,601,000 00

The demands of the fourth quarter being, then - - - $19,176,391 19
There may be applied to meet them the revenue accruing during the quarter, from all sources, about - - 2,900,000 00
Also, paym'ts to be made on account of loans already contracted for, according to the authority above stated, about 2,500,000 00

5,400,000 00

Leaving a balance to be provided for, of - - - $13,776,391 19

By the authority remaining to borrow - $8,105,000 00
By the authority remaining to issue Treasury notes - - - 1,496,000 00
By an additional authority to be granted by law to borrow, and to issue Treasury notes - - 4,175,391 19

$13,776,391 19

These estimates, however, it will be observed, are made with a view, simply, to the appropriations by law for the expenses of the year 1814, and do not embrace a provision to satisfy balances of appropriations made for the expenses of preceding years, which have not been called for at the Treasury. But, it will probably be deemed expedient to make such provision by extending the new authority to borrow from the above balance, to six millions. If the 6 per cent. stock which has been sent to Europe should be there disposed of, it will form an item in the estimates of the ensuing year.

As a portion of the amount to be provided during the present quarter consists of Treasury notes which will soon be due, it will be advisable to make them receivable in subscriptions to the loan.

It is proper to accompany these propositions with a few explanatory remarks:

1. The first proposition contemplates a permanent system; but the estimate of the particular items of claims and demands upon the public must be regarded as immediately applying to the year. 1815. In every subsequent year there will necessarily be some variation; as, for instance, the item of interest on the old debt will annually sink, while the item of interest on the new debt will annually rise, during the continuance of the war.

The items for annually raising a portion of the public expenses by taxes, and for applying to the new debt a sinking fund—gradually increasing until it becomes commensurate to its object—are essential features in the plan suggested, with a view to the revival and maintenance of public credit. The extinguishment of the old debt is already in rapid operation by the wise precaution of a similar institution.

2. The second proposition will doubtless generate many and very various objections. The endeavor has been, however, to spread the general amount of the taxes over a wide surface with a hand as light and equal as is consistent with convenience in the process, and certainty in the result.

All the opportunities of observation, and all the means of information that have been possessed, leave no doubt upon the disposition of the people to contribute generously for relieving the necessities of their country; and it has been thought unworthy of that patriotic disposition to dwell upon scanty means of supply, or short lived expedients. Whenever the war shall be happily terminated in an honorable peace, and the Treasury shall be again replenished by the tributary streams of commerce, it will be at once a duty and a pleasure to recommend an alleviation, if not an entire exoneration of the burdens which necessarily fall at present upon the agriculture and manufacture of the nation.

3. In making a proposition for the establishment of a National Bank, I cannot be insensible to the high authority of the names which have appeared in opposition to that measure upon Constitutional grounds. It would be presumptuous to conjecture that the sentiments which actuated the opposition have passed away; and yet it would be denying to experience a great practical advantage, were we to suppose that a difference of times and circumstances would not produce a corresponding difference in the opinions of the wisest as well as of the purest men. But, in the present case, a change of private opinion is not material to the success of the proposition for establishing a National Bank. In the administration of human affairs, there must be a period when discussion shall cease and decision shall become absolute. A diversity of opinion may honorably survive the contest; but, upon the genuine principles of a representative Government, the opinion of the majority can alone be carried into action. The judge, who dissents from the majority of the bench, changes not his opinion, but performs his duty, when he enforces the judgment of the court, although it is contrary to his own convictions. An oath to support the Constitution and the laws, is not, therefore, an oath to support them under all circumstances, according to the opinion of the individual who takes it, but it is, emphatically, an oath to support them according to the interpretation of the legitimate authorities. For the erroneous decisions of a court of law, there is the redress of a censorial as well as of an appellate jurisdiction. Over an act founded upon an exposition of the Constitution, made by the Legislative department of the Government, but alleged to be incorrect, we have seen the Judicial department exercise remedial power. And even if all the departments, Legislative, Execu-

tive, and Judicial, should concur in the exercise of a power, which is either thought to transcend the Constitutional -trust, or to operate injuriously upon the community, the case is still within the reach of a competent control, through the medium of an amendment to the Constitution, upon the proposition, not only of Congress but of the several States. When, therefore, we have marked the existence of a National Bank for a period of twenty years, with all the sanctions of the Legislative, Executive, and Judicial authorities; when we have seen the dissolution of one institution, and heard a loud and continued call for the establishment of another; when, under these circumstances, neither Congress nor the several States have resorted to the power of amendment; can it be deemed a violation of the right of private opinion, to consider the constitutionality of a National Bank, as a question forever settled and at rest?

But, after all, I should not merit the confidence, which it will be my ambition to acquire, if I were to suppress the declaration of an opinion, that, in these times, the establishment of a National Bank will not only be useful in promoting the general welfare, but that it is necessary and proper for carrying into execution some of the most important powers Constitutionally vested in the Government.

Upon the principles and regulations of the National Bank, it may be sufficient to remark, that they will be best unfolded in the form of a bill, which shall be immediately prepared. A compound capital is suggested, with a design equally to accommodate the subscribers, and to aid the general measures, for the revival of public credit; but the proportions of specie and stock may be varied, if the scarcity of coin should render it expedient; yet not in so great a degree, as to prevent an early commencement of the money operations of the institution.

4. The estimates of receipts from established sources of revenue and from the proposed new duties, and the estimates of expenditures, on all the objects contemplated in the present communication, have been made upon a call so sudden, and upon materials so scattered, that it is not intended to claim a perfect reliance on their accuracy. They are, however, believed to be sufficiently accurate to illustrate and support the general plan, for the revival of the public credit, the establishment of a permanent system of revenue, and the removal of the immediate pressure on the Treasury.

Upon the whole, sir, I have freely and openly assumed the responsibility of the station in which I have the honor to be placed. But, conscious of the imperfections of the judgment that dictates the answer to the important inquiries of the Committee of Ways and Means, I derive the highest satisfaction from reflecting, that the honor and safety of the nation, for war, or for peace, depend on the wisdom, patriotism, and fortitude of Congress, during times which imperiously demand a display of those qualities in the exercise of the Legislative authority. I have the honor to be, &c.,

A. J. DALLAS.

J. W. EPPES, Esq., *Chairman, &c.*

A.

Schedule of new taxes referred to in the letter of the Secretary of the Treasury to the Chairman of the Committee of Ways and Means, in which the taxes proposed in the report of the committee to the House of Representatives on the 10th instant, are principally adopted.

1. On spirits distilled from domestic or foreign ma-

terials 25 cents per gallon, computed on 24,000,000 gallons; provided the present tax on the capacity of the still should be continued. If it is thought best to lay the tax entirely on the liquor, then the tax on the capacity of the stills to be taken off, and 30 cents per gallon to be laid on the liquor. For the present estimate, it is taken at 25 cents per gallon - $6,000,000

2. On porter, ale, and strong beer, 2 cents per gallon, computed on 6,000,000 gallons - - - - -	120,000
3. On manufactured tobacco and snuff, averaged at 5 cents per pound, and computed on ten million pounds - - -	500,000
4. On leather of various kinds, averaged at three cents per pound, and computed on twenty million pounds - - - -	600,000
5. On pig-iron at $1,50 per ton, computed on 300,000 tons - - - -	450,000
6. On paper, at various rates, averaging 7 per cent. on the value of the article, computed on the annual manufacture of the value of 2,500,000 dollars - - -	175,000
7. On playing cards, at 25 cents per pack, computed on 400,000 packs - - -	100,000
8. On counsellors and attorneys at law, process in suits at law and equity, proceedings in admiralty, arbitrations and references, and other legal proceedings in the courts of the United States - -	300,000
9. On conveyances, mortgages, and other contracts relating to real estate - -	250,000
	$8,495,000
The sum to be raised by new taxes according to the estimates of the Secretary's letter, is - - - - -	7,000,000
Leaving a surplus, for the expenses of collection and errors in the estimates, of -	1,495,000

Mr. McKEE, of Kentucky, rose to move that a greater than the usual number of this document be printed. From the reading of the report, he considered it an able one, and of a nature and interest abundantly more important to the American people than many documents in respect to which this course had been pursued. He wished, for his part, to be enabled to send to his constituents some copies; and therefore moved that five thousand copies thereof be printed.

This motion was agreed to—70 to 57.

CONGRESSIONAL LIBRARY

The resolution authorizing the Library Committee of Congress to contract for the purchase of the library of Mr. Jefferson, was again resumed.

The amendment proposed yesterday, going to limit the sum to be given for the library to twenty-five thousand dollars, being yet under consideration.

The discussion which commenced yesterday was to-day continued with considerable vivacity.

The amendment was opposed by Mr. FORSYTH, and supported by Messrs. OAKLEY of New York, PICKERING and JOHN REED of Massachusetts.

Mr. HULBERT from Massachusetts, it ought to be mentioned particularly, being his first essay in this House, in a very ingenious and handsome speech opposed, the amendment and advocated the purchase of the library.

The debate before its conclusion became rather too animated, and being checked by the Speaker, the question was permitted to be taken. There appeared to be on the yeas and nays, for the amendment 37, and against it 103, as follows:

Yeas—Messrs. Baylies of Massachusetts, Bigelow, Boyd, Bradbury, Brigham, Cannon, Champion, Cilley, Culpeper, Davenport, Ely, Geddes, Grosvenor, Jackson of Rhode Island, Lewis, Macon, Markell, Moffit, Montgomery, Pearson, Pitkin, Post, Potter, John Reed, William Reed, Sherwood, Shipherd, Smith of New York, Stockton, Taggart, Thompson, Vose, Ward of Massachusetts, Ward of New York, Wheaton, Wilcox, and Wilson of Massachusetts.

Nays—Messrs. Alexander, Alston, Archer, Avery, Bard, Barnett, Bayly of Virginia, Bowen, Bradley, Brown, Burwell, Butler, Chappell, Clark, Clopton, Condict, Conard, Cooper, Cox, Crawford, Creighton, Crouch, Cuthbert, Dana, Davis of Pennsylvania, Denoyelles, Desha, Duvall, Earle, Evans, Farrow, Findley, Fisk of New York, Forney, Forsyth, Franklin, Gaston, Gholson, Goodwyn, Gourdin, Hall, Hanson, Harris, Hasbrouck, Hawes, Hawkins, Hopkins of Kentucky, Hubbard, Humphreys, Hungerford, Hulbert, Ingersoll, Irving, Jackson of Virginia, Johnson of Virginia, Kennedy, Kent of New York, Kent of Maryland, Kerr, Kershaw, King of Massachusetts, King of North Carolina, Law, Lefferts, Lovett, Lyle, McCoy, McKim, McLean, Moore, Moseley, Nelson, Newton, Oakley, Ormsby, Parker, Pickering, Piper, Pleasants, Rhea of Tennessee, Rich, Ringgold, Roane, Ruggles, Sage, Schureman, Seybert, Sharp, Skinner, Smith of Pennsylvania, Stanford, Strong, Sturges, Tannehill, Taylor, Telfair, Troup, Udree, Webster, Wilson of Pennsylvania, Winter, Wright, and Yancey.

Mr. Pickering moved an amendment, in substance the same as that moved yesterday by Mr. Oakley and negatived; the object of which was a selection of part of the library.

The amendment was negatived by yeas and nays—52 to 96.

An amendment was then adopted, on motion of Mr. Oakley, requiring the sanction of Congress to the agreement for the purchase of the library, before it should become binding. And, thus amended, the resolution was ordered to a third reading.

Wednesday, October 19.

Another member to wit: from South Carolina, John C. Calhoun, appeared and took his seat.

Mr. Humphreys presented several petitions from the inhabitants of the State of Tennessee, praying that measures may be taken by Congress to open a public road, crossing the Tennessee river, some where near the mouth of Duck river, and intersecting the road from Nashville to Natchez, below the Chickasaw Old Towns.— Referred to the Secretary of War.

Ordered, That the Committee on the Judiciary be discharged from the consideration of the resolution of the 23d ultimo, directing an inquiry into the expediency of making further provisions for protecting the officers of the customs in the dis-

charge of their duties, &c., and that it be referred to the Committee of Ways and Means.

Ordered, That Mr. Webster and Mr. Cox be appointed of the committee appointed to inquire into the causes of the late capture of the city of Washington, by the enemy, in the places of Mr. Stockton and Mr. Miller.

Mr. Ingersoll, of Pennsylvania, presented the petition of Oliver Evans (the same as presented last session) for the extension of his patent for the improvements in the steam engine.—Referred to the Committee of Commerce and Manufactures, in opposition to the wishes of Mr. Ingersoll, who desired it to be referred to a select committee.

Mr. Ingersoll, from the Committee on the Judiciary, reported a bill further to extend the judicial system of the United States; which was twice read and referred to a Committee of the Whole.

Mr. Kent, of Maryland, from the District Committee, reported a bill incorporating the Columbian Manufacturing Company of Alexandria, in the District of Columbia, which was twice read and committed.

The joint resolution from the Senate, authorizing the joint Library Committee of Congress to contract for the purchase of the library of Mr. Jefferson, was read a third time as amended, and passed.

The report of the Committee of Claims unfavorable to the petition of Alexander Sevier was taken up and agreed to.

Mr. Baylies, of Massachusetts, offered a motion similar to one adopted at his instance at the last session, out of which an act had grown, which had passed the House, but had not been definitively acted on in the Senate. The subject of the motion was, a further provision for compensating masters of vessels who bring home to the United States distressed and destitute American seamen; into the expediency of making which his motion instructed the Committee of Ways and Means to inquire. The motion was agreed to.

PEACOCK AND EPERVIER.

The House resolved itself into a Committee of the Whole, on the resolution from the Senate expressive of the sense of Congress relative to the victory of the Peacock over the Epervier. The resolution having been read—

Mr. Pleasants, of Virginia, (the chairman of the Naval Committee,) said it was not his intention to detain the Committee by any extended remarks on this subject. The action to which this resolution referred, more particularly, perhaps, than any which preceded it, demonstrated the superiority of American gunnery. To show this, Mr. P. quoted Captain Warrington's letter to the Secretary of the Navy announcing the victory; and inferred from it that no action had ever taken place, between vessels of anything like equal force, in which there had been so great a disparity of execution. He hoped the resolve would be unanimously adopted.

No objection being made or amendment proposed, the Committee rose and reported their

413   HISTORY OF CONGRESS.   414

OCTOBER, 1814.   *Military Marine—Relief of Commodore Barney.*   H. OF R.

agreement to the resolve, which was ordered to a third reading; and was accordingly read and unanimously passed.

THURSDAY, October 20.

Mr. WILSON, of Massachusetts, presented a petition of John Crosby and others, on behalf of the inhabitants of Hamden, in the District of Maine, praying that the property recovered from the wreck of the United States' late ship Adams may be given to the said inhabitants, as a compensation for the losses sustained in consequence of the late capture of that place by the British forces.—Referred to the Secretary of the Navy.

The Senate having returned the resolutions from the House, in honor of Generals Brown, Scott, Gaines, Macomb, Ripley, Miller, and Porter. with sundry amendments, (not affecting the object of the resolves,) the same were referred to the Committee on Military Affairs.

A resolution was also received from the Senate, expressive of the sense of Congress relative to the capture of the British sloop Reindeer by the American sloop Wasp.—Referred to the Committee on Naval Affairs.

Mr. BURWELL, of Virginia, stated the reasons why he had not called up the motion he laid on the table the other day, calling for an account of the officers of the Army, state of the recruiting service, &c. The Committee of Military Affairs, he was informed, had the subject before them, and had received a document embracing all the information he desired, and which, when they were prepared to make a report, they would lay before the House.

The Military Committee asked and obtained leave to sit for a week during the sittings of the House.

Ordered, That Mr. PITKIN be appointed of the committee appointed to inquire into the causes of the late capture of the City of Washington by the enemy.

PUBLIC BUILDINGS.

Mr. LEWIS, of Virginia, said, the House having decided that Congress should not remove from this place, he thought it proper some steps should be immediately taken towards making a provision for the better accommodation of the different Departments of the Government. With this opinion he moved the following resolution:

Resolved, That the Committee of the District of Columbia be instructed to inquire into the expediency of rebuilding or repairing the President's House, the Capitol, and Public Offices, and into the expenses necessary for that purpose; and whether the public interest or convenience would be promoted by any change or alteration of the sites of said buildings.

Mr. GHOLSON, of Virginia, said, he saw no reason for stirring the question of changing the sites of these buildings at present, and hoped the gentleman would expunge that part of his motion.

Mr. LEWIS said he was of the same opinion as his colleague in respect to the inexpediency of changing the sites of the public buildings; but,

as some gentlemen in the House were, he knew, of a different opinion, he had thought it best to place the question in its broadest shape before the Committee.

Mr. GROSVENOR, of New York, moved to refer the subject to a select committee, instead of the standing committee as proposed. It was a subject interesting to the whole United States, and the importance of which was not limited to the District only. He thought, therefore, it should be referred to a general committee. He took occasion to say, that the decision having been made on the question of removal, it ought to be final; and during this Congress, at least, he was not disposed to move it again. It was the duty of this Congress, he conceived. to proceed in preparing for the better accommodation of the Government here.

After some further conversation, Mr. G.'s amendment was agreed to—ayes 87; and Mr. LEWIS. Mr. KENT, of Maryland, Mr. HANSON, Mr. BOWEN, Mr. GROSVENOR, Mr. SHARP, and Mr. CONDICT, were appointed the said committee.

MILITARY MARINE.

The House resolved itself into a Committee of the Whole, on the bill requiring staff officers of the Army to comply with the requisitions of marine and naval officers in certain cases.

Mr. PLEASANTS, of Virginia, explained the object of the bill, as indicated by the title, and quoted a letter from the Secretary of the Navy, recommending its adoption.

Mr. WRIGHT, of Maryland, expressed his wish, whilst this subject was under consideration, that the subject should be thoroughly arranged; and, with that view, that a provision should be incorporated, settling the relative rank of naval to land officers, when employed, as they frequently are, in the land service.

Mr. PLEASANTS assented to the propriety of such an amendment; and, with that object, moved that the Committee now rise, and obtain leave to sit again, to allow time to digest such an amendment as would be proper.

The Committee rose accordingly.

Mr. TROUP, of Georgia, suggested the expediency of a proper understanding on this head, between the Heads of the War and Navy Departments, and some reciprocal provision for mutual accommodation of land and naval officers, when out of their peculiar element, &c. Some amendment of this kind might well be incorporated when the bill should again come under consideration.

Leave was given to the Committee of the Whole to sit again on said bill.

RELIEF OF COMMODORE BARNEY.

The House resolved itself into a Committee of the Whole, on the bill for the relief of the officers, petty officers, and seamen, under the command of Commodore Joshua Barney.

Mr. PLEASANTS stated the object of this bill to be, to compensate the officers and men of the flotilla, for the loss of their clothes sustained by the sudden destruction of the flotilla to prevent its falling into the hands of the enemy. Mr. P. adverted also to their good conduct in the defence of this place, and on every other occasion, and to the peculiar hardships of their service, &c.

Mr. WRIGHT, of Maryland, after paying a just tribute to the uniform good conduct of these men, moved to insert three instead of two months pay.

This motion was, after discussion, negatived.

Mr. POST, of New York, moved to amend the bill, by striking out so much of the bill as assigns the loss of clothes and bedding by the blowing up of the flotilla, as a reason for the grant proposed, and inserting, in lieu thereof, "for their bravery in the battle of Bladensburg, on the 24th of August last." This motion was negatived by a large majority.

The Committee rose and reported the bill. On the question, whether the bill should be ordered to a third reading—

Mr. GOLDSBOROUGH, of Maryland, said, he had no wish to defeat the passage of the bill, but he thought it would be proper to suspend its passage for the present, because it was not sufficiently guarded in its provisions. He wished it to lie over also till the Committee of Investigation should report on this and other subjects. He was inclined to believe, from all he had heard, that the destruction of that flotilla was a very unnecessary act, and that it might all have been saved, except the gunboats, by carrying it a proper distance up the river. He moved to postpone the further consideration of the bill to the first Monday in December next.

This motion was also negatived—ayes 38.

Mr. WILLIAM REED, of Massachusetts, renewed the motion to insert, instead of the reason now assigned for this grant, the words, "in reward for the extraordinary bravery displayed by them in the battle of Bladensburg, on the 24th August."

This motion Mr. R. afterwards modified, on the suggestion of Mr. LOWNDES, of South Carolina, so as to read, "in consideration of their gallantry and good conduct, and of the unusual hardship of their service."

On these several motions considerable debate took place, in which Messrs. WRIGHT, PLEASANTS, POST, STUART, GOLDSBOROUGH, KING, and REED, of Massachusetts, LOWNDES, of South Carolina, JACKSON, of Virginia, PICKERING, and TAYLOR, of New York, took part.

The objection to the bill as it now stood was, that it would afford an injurious precedent for all such cases of loss of clothing by seamen, which frequently occurred, whilst all appeared to agree that these men, by their general good conduct, particularly in the battle of Bladensburg, merited the notice of Government. It was said by General Stuart that the men had sufficient notice to have saved their clothing; and the enemy's force was not nearer than a day's march, when orders were given to blow up the flotilla. The same gentleman also took occasion to observe, that he believed if the flotilla had never been brought up the Patuxent, this place would never have been attacked, and the public buildings would still

have been standing. It was this flotilla which had caused the recent invasion of Maryland.

It was said, on the other hand, that giving pecuniary rewards for bravery, as was proposed to be done in this case by those who opposed the bill as it stood, would afford a precedent, if pursued, which would soon empty the Treasury. The case of these men, it was said, was far different from ordinary cases of loss of clothing. They had, since the 22d of August, the day the flotilla was destroyed, been engaged in the most arduous service which could be found, and had to sleep on the bare ground, without blankets, and scarcely clothes to their backs, having lost all they had, &c. As to the flotilla causing the invasion of Maryland, Mr. PLEASANTS said, they had had no flotilla in the waters of Virginia, and yet they had suffered there quite as much from the depredations of the enemy as they had in Maryland, &c.

Before the question on amendment was taken, a motion was made by Mr. TAYLOR, of New York, to lay the bill on the table. There were for the motion 66, against it 59.

So the bill was laid on the table.

FRIDAY, October 21.

On motion of Mr. YANCEY, the Committee on the Judiciary were instructed to inquire into the expediency of amending the laws of the United States, as to the effect which a judgment of record of one State shall have when offered in evidence in a suit in another State; and that they have permission to report by bill or otherwise.

A message from the Senate informed the House that the Senate have passed a bill, "further to extend the time for locating Virginia military land warrants, and for returning the process thereon to the General Land Office;" in which they ask the concurrence of this House.

Mr. LEWIS, of Virginia, presented the petition of the Union Bank of Georgetown, and of the Farmers and Mechanics' Bank of Georgetown, praying for charters; and of the Farmers and Mechanics' Bank of Alexandria, praying for an extension of its charter.—Referred to the Committee on the District of Columbia.

PETITION OF JOSEPH FORREST.

Mr. YANCEY, from the Committee of Claims, made a report on the petition of Joseph Forrest, which was read, and referred to a Committee of the Whole on Wednesday next. The report is as follows:

That in the month of May, 1812, the petitioner, by his agent, chartered to the United States his schooner, called the William Yeaton, to take a cargo of provisions from New York to the port of Laguira, in South America. The contract, according to the covenants of the charter-party, was, that the petitioner should keep the vessel sound, tight, and strong; to be well fitted and provided with the necessary and convenient things for such a schooner; to find the necessary men for the voyage; to employ and pay the officers and men for the same; and to defray all other expenses attending the voyage; to load the said schooner by the 26th of

May, 1812, and then to proceed to Laguira with all convenient and practicable expedition, where he was to discharge the cargo with convenient despatch. In consideration of such service, the United States covenanted with the petitioner to pay him for the cargo at the rate of one dollar and fifty cents for every barrel of flour, seventy-five cents for every half barrel of flour, and forty cents for every bushel of corn, as the full freight and compensation for the voyage. The schooner arrived at the port of Laguira on the first day of July, 1812; gave notice to the agent of the United States of her arrival; and, between the 14th of that month and the 1st of August following, about two-thirds of the cargo was received. On that day a Spanish force entered Laguira, and seized the vessel with about one-third of the cargo on board; that part, however, was then received and deposited by the agent of the United States; but the schooner was forcibly taken from the officer and crew, carried by her captors into Pórto Cabello, and condemned by the Spanish authorities, upon the ground that the cargo was intended by the Government of the United States to furnish the inhabitants of Venezuela with provisions, at a time when they were in a state of insurrection. It appears also to the committee, by a letter from the petitioner, addressed to a former chairman of the Committee of Claims, that the vessel remained in possession of the captors until about the 1st of October, when, by the interposition and friendship of Don Onis, she was restored to her captain and crew; she was then sold by the captain at auction, to defray the expenses of seizure, delay, and condemnation. The petitioner asks of Congress compensation for the loss of the vessel and such damages as he has sustained.

This case presents some features of hardship to the owner, but it is believed no legal obligation on the United States. If the owner has sustained damages by a breach of the contract on the part of the United States or its agent at Laguira, then it is conceded he is entitled to a compensation equivalent to the injury; but if the damages which have accrued to him were the consequence of an abuse of power in the Spanish authorities, or an illegal and hostile act of that Government, it is believed the United States are not responsible to the owner.

The committee know of no rule by which more justice can be done to the parties than that afforded by the terms of the contract. They are of opinion that, from the foregoing facts, these terms create no legal obligation on the United States to pay for the vessel. They, therefore, recommend to the House the following resolution:

Resolved, That the prayer of the petitioner ought not to be granted.

WASHINGTON, *June* 16, 1812.

SIR: In conformity to the request which, as chairman of the Committee of Commerce and Manufactures, you did me the honor to express to me this morning, relative to the vessels sent out with the donation voted by act of Congress in May, 1812, for the relief of the inhabitants of Venezuela, I take the liberty to state that the said vessels, in number six, say two from the respective ports of New York, Philadelphia, and Baltimore, arrived in the port of Laguira in the month of June, 1812. Of these vessels, addressed to me as Consul for the United States, one only, the Independence of Baltimore, brought with her a regular charter-party; their freights being paid in advance before their de-

parture from America, and no time, except in this one instance, being stipulated as to the discharge of the vessels. The Independence arrived on the 9th June, was immediately unloaded and reloaded for account of various merchants of Baltimore. She was cleared by the custom-house for Baltimore on the 17th July, 1812, but detained by a general embargo, laid by order of Miranda, then at the head of the revolutionary Government. The arrival of the other vessels was delayed until the 27th and 29th of June. Every exertion was used for their prompt unloading, but, owing to the scarcity of lighters, the deranged state of the town from the misfortune of the 26th March, and finally the impress of nearly all the laborers for the war service, the discharging of all the vessels could not be completed before the country came again under the Spanish yoke, in the beginning of August, insomuch that the Active Trader and Cumberland of Philadelphia, and Mary of New York, had part of their outward cargoes on board at this period. The ship Mary and Eliza of Baltimore, and William Yeaton from New York, were nearly loaded with return cargoes on freight for this country.

I beg leave, therefore, to repel the charge made against me, as agent for the United States, of want of due diligence on my part; it being impossible for any human activity, under similar circumstances, to do more for the prompt unloading of the vessels in question than was done by me.

For the subsequent events relative to the vessels, their libelling and condemnation by the Spanish authority at Puerto Cabello, and their final restitution on appeal to Caraccas, I beg leave to refer you to the protests made in due form before me in Laguira, and which, no doubt, will accompany the documents on which the claimants found their demand for compensation from the Congress of the United States.

I have the honor to be, very respectfully, your most obedient servant,

ROBERT K. LOWRY.

T. NEWTON, Esq., *Chairman, &c.*

PHILADELPHIA, *February* 14, 1814.

I consider it a general principle of maritime law, that, as the owner of a vessel who receives goods on freight is bound to use due diligence to convey them to the port of destination, and deliver them to order, so the consignee is bound to use due diligence in receiving those goods, and facilitating the vessel's discharge.

Each party is answerable to the other for any injury that may arise from neglect or delay, unless satisfactory reasons for delay can be assigned. When a vessel is to deliver an outward, and take in a return cargo, it is customary to have a charter-party executed, in which the number of lay-days, &c., are stipulated; but when the contract is simply to deliver an outward cargo, such charter-parties are not necessary, and I believe not usual.

The general rules of law are then to be resorted to. I took the liberty of stating in my letter to Mr. Eppes, that if the agreement for carrying provisions to Laguira had been made between Mr. Clement and an individual, and the same circumstances of delay in regard to receiving the goods which are imputed to Mr. Lowry had taken place on the part of the agent of the freighter, Mr. Clement could have obtained judicial relief.

The foregoing remarks explain the principles on which this opinion is founded.

One of Mr. Clement's vessels arrived at Laguira on the 27th, and the other on the 30th of June. Three or four days would have been sufficient for the discharge of the whole of the cargoes—allow a week; on the 7th of July they ought to have been discharged; but neither of them was discharged till the 8th or 9th of August.

Whatever damage happened after the expiration of a reasonable time, and which, in its nature, was fairly imputable to delay, would be recoverable at law of the freighter, who would be left to his remedy against his agent.

Mr. Lowry, it is understood, denies the charge against him. It is a fact to be inquired into, but it is difficult to conceive why the captains, whose duties and whose habits are to lose no time in discharging their outward cargoes and returning, should have trifled with their owners' interests in the extraordinary manner they must have done, by consuming four or five weeks in doing what might, as they themselves acknowledge, have been accomplished in one.

But Mr. Clement's right to compensation does not, I think, rest on this ground only.

His vessels were in the service of the nation; he sailed in a single degree under the protection of the United States; he, therefore, was bound to presume that the papers he received from them were competent to protect him.

It was not for him to cast about for other passports or documents of any kind than what they furnished him with; and, under these circumstances, the United States must be considered as guarantying his admission and his safety in the Spanish ports.

It must also be considered as an engagement, on the part of the United States, that his mission should not, from its nature, expose him to any extraordinary damage. If this had been apprehended, he would of course have claimed, and been considered entitled to, a larger compensation for the risk than the usual amount of freight.

Now the seizure and condemnation which, after the first detentions, produced the additional delay and eventual loss are founded on the nature of his errand and the alleged defect of the proper papers.

Mr. Clement's conduct throughout appears, and is admitted by the agents for the United States, both here and at Laguira, to have been unblameable.

His vessels took in their respective cargoes here with unexceeded promptness, and delivered them at Laguira in perfect order. Nothing was done by him or his captains that could in any manner produce any injury or disadvantage to the voyage.

I cannot but think his claim on the justice of his country a very strong one.

W. RAWLE.

WAYS AND MEANS.

The House, on motion of Mr. EPPES, of Virginia, resolved itself into a Committee of the Whole, on the report of the Committee of Ways and Means, and the subsequent letter from Mr. Secretary Dallas.

Mr. E. stated that, since the receipt of the Secretary's letter, the committee had revised their report, and had determined to recommend its modification, so as to correspond, in so far as they believed consistent with the public good, with the last report from the Treasury Department. The report of the committee having been read over, the first resolution having been read, which proposes to continue the direct tax, and to increase the same fifty per cent.

Mr. E., after some introductory remarks, moved to amend the report in conformity to the Secretary of the Treasury's report, so as to make the addition one hundred instead of fifty per cent.

Mr. OAKLEY, of New York, said that he rose for the purpose of moving to amend the amendment which had been offered to the resolution under consideration by the chairman of the Committee of Ways and Means. The resolution, as originally reported by that committee, proposed to continue the existing direct tax and to add fifty per cent. to the amount. The Secretary of the Treasury had recommended an increase of one hundred per cent., and, in pursuance of that recommendation, the committee had directed their chairman to make the motion he had just submitted; the effect of which, if successful, would be to raise by the direct tax six millions of dollars. His object, Mr. O. said, was to go still further, and to raise from that source of revenue seven millions and a half. As he was a member of the Committee of Ways and Means, it might be proper for him here to state, lest he should be considered as opposing the report of the committee, to which he might be presumed to have agreed—that they were much divided in opinion as to the point now in question, as well as to several others embraced in the report.

The honorable chairman, Mr. O. said, had correctly stated that the plan of finance adopted at the commencement of the war, was, to raise by customs, and direct and indirect taxes, a sum sufficient to defray the expenses of the Peace Establishment, and to pay the interest of the old debt, together with the interest on such new debt as might be incurred from year to year by the war, and to rely upon loans to meet all the expenditures of the war. This, Mr. O. presumed, was to be considered as the war plan of finance, which the Administration had deemed competent to carry the country safely through the contest. It was to the errors and insufficiency of this plan that the present financial embarrassments of the Government were fairly to be attributed. The principal feature and great defect of the plan was, that reliance was placed, to use the language of the Secretary of the Treasury, on "the national faith and not the national wealth." It was, simply, the plan of always borrowing and never paying; a plan which would necessarily lead to bankruptcy either in an individual or a nation. Its authors seemed to have forgotten or disregarded the first rudiments in any correct system of finance, which would have taught them never to contract a debt without creating a revenue sufficient to pay the interest and gradually discharge the principal.

Gentlemen had been warned of the inadequacy of this plan of finance in the outset; they had been told that there was nothing miraculous in this thing called "public faith;" that it was no better and frequently not as good as the faith of an individual; and that the public creditor would look not only to the honesty of the Government, but to the means provided by it to meet its engagements; indeed, a pledge of the public faith by law for the redemption of a debt, appeared to him entirely superfluous; inasmuch as it was always pledged by the very act of incurring the debt. Gentlemen had been frequently urged to resort to specific pledges of parts of the existing revenue to secure the payments of the loans, with a view to obtain them on more favorable terms. They had, however, considered such pledges unimportant, and had gone on relying upon public credit alone, without taking any steps to support it, until the nation was literally bankrupt. They had, indeed, succeeded in making some loans at first on very unfavorable terms; but their system had at length entirely exploded. It was admitted that their last attempt had failed, notwithstanding the Government had been prepared to accept terms of the most extravagant and ruinous character. The letter of the Secretary of the Treasury showed that there was a deficit in the ways and means provided for the present year of near fourteen millions of dollars. This sum it was necessary to raise immediately to meet the expenditures of the present quarter of the year. In this deficit was not included the vast amount of unascertained debt which had arisen from expenditures not comprised in the general estimate, and for which no specific appropriations had been made by law; but which, however, had as fair a claim on the Government for immediate payment as any other. He alluded particularly to the expenses which had attended the employment of the vast bodies of militia which had been called into the public service, and which the Government did not now possess funds to meet.

The correctness of the summary view he had taken of the defects in the plan of finance, he believed could not be questioned. The consequences of these defects would be strongly exemplified by a reference to the manner in which the last loans had been negotiated. He had made a statement, which he would submit to the Committee, and which he believed substantially correct, intended to show in a succinct point of light the extent of the sacrifice which the Government had been compelled to make in order to procure the partial supplies which these loans had afforded. By the act of the 24th of March, 1814, a loan of $25,000,000 was authorized. Proposals for a part of that loan, being $10,000,000, were invited by the Treasury on the second day of May. Various proposals were made, and the Government finally contracted for the sum of $9,795,056, at the rate of $100 in stock, bearing an interest of six per cent. for eighty-eight dollars in money. But what particularly deserved notice in this contract was the condition insisted on by the contractors and acceded to by the Government, that if any part of the $25,000,000 loan should be made by the Treasury, on terms more favorable to the lender, the same should be extended to that contract—a condition the most injurious to

the Government that could have been devised—inasmuch as it made it the interest of the contractors to depress rather than to sustain the price of the public stocks.

On the 22d of August proposals were again invited for $6,000,000, as a part of the loan authorized by the act of the 24th of March; and Government, on those proposals, contracted for the sum of $2,930,300, being all it could obtain at the rate of one hundred dollars in stock, at an interest of six per cent. for eighty dollars in money. The consequence was a sacrifice by the Government of twenty per cent., not only on the amount thus contracted for, but on the whole of the contract for the $9,795,056; the holders of which, by virtue of the condition annexed to their contract, had a right to demand of the Government a premium of eight per cent. in addition to the twelve per cent. they had already received. The following statement would give a view of the extent of the loss which the Government had suffered in the negotiation of these loans.

Amount of the first contract	$9,795,056
Amount of the second contract	2,930,300
Total contracted for	12,725,356
Loss to the Government, twelve per cent. on the original contract for $9,795,056	$1,175,356
Twenty per cent. on the contract for $2,930,300	586,060
Eight per cent. on $9,795,056, in consequence of the condition annexed to the first contract	783,604
One-fourth of one per cent. on $9,795,056 allowed as a commission	24,487
One-fourth of one per cent. on $2,930,300	7,326
Total loss	2,576,883
Amount of stock to be created by Government to raise the sum contracted for	$15,302,239

It would be seen, Mr. O. said, from this statement, that the Treasury, in order to raise the sum of $12,725,356, had been obliged to create stock to the amount of $15,302,237, and had thus paid a premium to the lenders of $2,576,883, or upwards of one-fifth of the whole amount.

Another view of the second contract might be presented which would be still more striking. As the eight per cent. on the sum of $9,595,056 were lost solely in consequence of that contract, the whole ought to be placed to its account. The statement of the second contract would then stand thus:

Amount contracted for	$2,930,300
Loss, 20 per cent. on that sum $586,060	
Eight per cent. on the sum of $9,795,056	783,604
One-fourth of one per cent. commission	7,326
Total loss on second contract	1,376,990
Amount of stock to be created by the second contract	$4,307,290

It would thus appear that the premium in fact paid by the Government for the sum of $2,930,300, was $1,376,990, or very nearly fifty per cent. When, Mr. O. said, the Treasury was reduced to the necessity of negotiating loans on terms like these, it required no argument to prove that the finances and credit of the nation were in a state of utter ruin.

Mr. O. had stated the one-fourth of one per cent. on the amount of the contracts as one item of the loss. That was allowed by the law authorizing the loan as a commission to any person who should collect subscriptions from others, and was not intended to be given on any sum which the contractor might offer for his own benefit. It would be seen, by a reference to the report of the late Secretary of the Treasury, that more than one-half of the first contract for $9,795,056 was taken by an individual, for anything that appeared, on his own account; yet the commission had been allowed to him, and indeed, had been expressly stipulated for in his written proposals, which could not have been necessary, had he been entitled to it by the terms of the law. He could not, therefore, help thinking, Mr. O. said, that in this instance, it had been paid contrary to the spirit, and indeed, to the plain letter of the law.

Mr. O. said, he had entered into these details for the purpose of showing to the Committee that a total and immediate change in the system of finance hitherto pursued by the Administration was absolutely necessary. It was the first step towards that reform in the management of the finances which could alone restore and maintain the public credit. Gentlemen must resort now to what it was their duty long ago to have adopted—a system of direct and internal taxes, sufficiently extended, to form the basis of loans. To make that basis firm, the proceeds of the taxes must be adequate, not only to pay the interest, but to constitute a certain fund for the reimbursement of the principal—and must be specially pledged to the public creditor by law. Had this system been pursued from the beginning, a much smaller amount of taxes would have been necessary to support public credit, than are now demanded to restore it. In proportion, as the state of the finances was desperate, the more vigorous must be the remedy applied for their relief.

In any such system of revenue, Mr. O. said, the direct tax was undoubtedly a principal feature. He had always thought that, in all countries, land was the legitimate and proper object of taxation, whenever the public exigencies required it. But in this country there were some reasons which, in his judgment, rendered it peculiarly so. By the Constitution, direct taxes were apportioned among the several States, according to their representation in that House. The representation of the States holding slaves, it was well known, was greatly increased by that species of population. It was therefore provided by the Constitution, that they should pay a greater proportion of every direct tax, as an equivalent for the undue weight which they thus acquired

in the Government. The chairman of the Committee of Ways and Means had said, that the direct tax was unequal, and therefore objectionable; being apportioned among the States according to population, and not according to wealth. In any other state of things than that presented by the Constitution, the remark would be correct. The framers of that instrument intended that it should be unequal, and that it should enter as a principal part into every system of extraordinary, if not ordinary taxation, to which the country might be compelled to resort.

He was, therefore, Mr. O. said, in favor of continuing the direct tax, and of increasing it beyond the amount proposed by the Committee of Ways and Means. Indeed, so just in a political point of view was it, and so much in conformity with the spirit of the Constitution, that he thought that much the greater part of the revenue now required ought to be raised by that tax alone. That it could be extended greatly beyond the amount proposed, did not admit of a doubt. If gentlemen would advert to the document from the Treasury laid on their tables that morning they would find, if they would make the necessary calculations, that in those States where the valuation of houses, lands, and slaves, had been made in pursuance of the existing law, the aggregate proportion of the tax to the amount of the valuation was extremely small. In New Hampshire it was about 26 cents in the 100 dollars—in Massachusetts about 33—in Vermont about 39—in Rhode Island about 16—in Connecticut 13—in New York 23—Delaware 22—Maryland 14—North Carolina 20—and Tennessee about 28. Thus in no case was the present direct tax as high as one-third of one per cent. on the amount of valuation, and in some it was no more than about one-eighth of one per cent. And the average rate of the tax in all the States he had named, was not more than one-fifth of one per cent. When it was considered that the valuation was in fact, in all cases, much below the real intrinsic worth of the property, it must be apparent that the present tax could be greatly increased without becoming burdensome.

He was in favor of an increase of the direct tax, Mr. O. said, for another reason. It operated, in consequence of the provisions of the Constitution, unequally on the slaveholding States, or in other words, generally speaking, on the Southern and Western States. This inequality was necessary to countervail the unequal operation of the internal duties on the Northern and Eastern States. The document before alluded to, if examined, in reference to that subject, would present some striking results. He would call the attention of gentlemen to the last page of the document, which contained the "aggregate amounts of internal duties ascertained on the 10th of October, 1814, to have been received in each State or Territory." Although that aggregate did not, for very evident reasons, show accurately the amount of internal duties actually accrued in each State, yet, when it was considered that the collectors were obliged by law to make their returns at very short periods, the amount known at the Treasury to have been received at any given time, was tolerable evidence of the amount accrued up to that time. At all events, it was sufficiently exact for the general purposes of his argument.

He had made some calculations, Mr. O. said, while in his seat that morning, from the data offered by that document, which he would submit to the Committee. Some allowance ought to be made in these calculations on account of the difference before alluded to, between the duties received and the duties accrued; but he believed, the general result would not, in any case, be materially varied. The whole amount of internal duties ascertained to have been received on the 10th of October, 1814, was $1,491,385. Of this amount, the States east of the river Delaware had paid $765,200; and States south and west of that, including all the Territories, and the District of Columbia, had paid $726,185, while the former had seventy-four Representatives in that House, and the latter one hundred and eight. Including Pennsylvania in the Eastern division, it would appear that that division, with ninety-four Representatives, had paid $1,045,183, while the South and West with eighty-five Representatives paid only $446,202. The State of Rhode Island, with two Representatives, had paid more than Tennessee with six, and as much nearly as Kentucky with ten, or Ohio with six. Connecticut, with seven Representatives, had paid $56,877, while Kentucky and Ohio, with sixteen Representatives, had paid only about $65,000. New Jersey with six Representatives had paid $54,202, and Kentucky with ten, $33,935. The State of New York alone had paid $303,694, while all the States of Ohio, Kentucky, Tennessee, Georgia, North and South Carolina, Delaware, and Louisiana, had paid only about $260,000; while the latter had fifty-three Representatives in that House, and sixty-nine votes in the choice of a President of the United States, while the former had twenty-seven Representatives, and twenty-nine votes for President. Under the Stamp Act alone, there had accrued in Massachusetts during the two first quarters of the year, $14,281, and in the States of Delaware, North Carolina, Ohio, Kentucky, Tennessee, and Georgia, there had accrued during the same period but $19,435. In Rhode Island, with two Representatives, there had accrued under the same act, and for the same time, more revenue, than in North Carolina, with thirteen Representatives—and gentlemen would find the same inequality running throughout the whole system. It was most evident, therefore, that the political power and influence of the Northern and Eastern States, when compared with the other parts of the Union, held no proportion to the share which they bore of the public burdens.

As gentlemen from the South and West had always contended that the duty on domestic distilled spirits pressed very unequally on that part of the Union, his attention, Mr. O. said, had been drawn particularly to that subject. He found on examination, that in the States east of the Delaware, there had accrued during the first two quarters of the year from the duty on licenses to distillers $317,795, and in the States south and west of that river $439,602; and if Pennsylvania were added to the eastern division, the States south and west would pay on that article only $167,822, while the East would pay $589,575. Connecticut, as far as the product could be estimated by the amount of the tax, made more domestic spirits than Maryland, Ohio, South Carolina, or Georgia, and about as much as either Tennessee or Kentucky; and the State of New York as much as Delaware, Maryland, North and South Carolina, Ohio, and Georgia together. It would appear, then, that the idea that the tax on domestic spirits bore unequally on the Western and Southern country was entirely erroneous—the reverse was the truth.

Such a system of internal duties, Mr. O. said, he considered both unjust and impolitic; unjust, because it imposed the public burdens on one section of the Union, while the political power resided in another; and impolitic, as it must necessarily tend to weaken the attachments of the people to the Government. The States ought not to contribute to the support of Government in proportion to wealth, while power was enjoyed according to numbers. He was, for these reasons, Mr. O. said, clearly of opinion, that the direct tax ought to be increased above, and the system of internal duties reduced below the amount recommended by the Secretary of the Treasury. From the effect of this general principle, however, he was willing to except the article of domestic spirits; although the duty on that article, like all other internal duties, operated unequally on the East and North, he thought it a proper subject of taxation. The use of it in most cases was a vice—in some a luxury, and in very few a necessary. He wished to increase the duty to the amount recommended by the Secretary of the Treasury; and when the proper period arrived, he would move, if no other gentlemen did it, to amend the report of the Committee of Ways and Means to that effect. The Chairman of the committee had thought that a duty of thirty cents on the gallon would operate as a prohibition of the manufacture of the article. When, however, it was recollected that imported spirits bore an average duty of fifty-eight cents on the gallon, and that the importation was almost entirely cut off, he could not doubt but that domestic spirits would easily bear the proposed tax without materially lessening the consumption.

There were still other reasons, Mr. O. said, which induced him to be in favor of an increase of the direct tax, and to give it a preference over any system of internal duties. It was a certain tax in its product. The Government could not be deceived in the amount they calculated to derive from it. When pledged to the public creditor, he would be under no apprehension that the revenue would fail him. The confidence inspired by any system of revenue was always in proportion to the certainty of its proceeds. The amount of the proceeds of this tax could not be materially varied by any change in the habits, customs, or business of the people, by which the internal duties were always more or less affected. It was not only a certain tax, but it was easily collected. It employed no excise officers to harass the people. The assessments it required to be made were in practice under the State laws in almost every State. In addition to this, the mode of collecting it was an effectual security against fraud on the part of the collector. He could not embezzle any part of the tax without detection. This was a consideration of no small importance, when it was considered that the Government must necessarily often make improper appointments to the office of collector, and when it was sometimes the case, that considerations entered into the appointment, other than those of the integrity and capacity of the candidate.

He was further anxious, Mr. O. said, for an increase of the direct tax, as gentlemen would perceive, if they agreed to raise an additional million and a half from this source, they would be able to dispense with the taxes on leather, candles, iron, saddles, bridles, and some other articles of real necessity, which had been placed on the list of new taxes. The tax on leather was particularly objectionable. It was proposed to tax it, not only in the first stage of the manufacture, but in harness, boots, saddles, and bridles; in almost every shape it could assume. The tax on iron was in truth a tax on the farmer and mechanic, into whose business it necessarily entered to a great degree. The farmer surely would prefer paying his tax in a gross sum, assessed upon his farm, when he could know the amount demanded of him, than to have it drawn from him indirectly, and to an extent that he could not well estimate, in duties on all the leather, and iron, and saddles, and bridles, and hats, and tobacco, and nails, which he might find it necessary to purchase.

, Mr. O. said he was utterly opposed to this system of drawing the supplies from so many sources, and running into all this detail of indirect taxation. It was better to lay hold of a few prominent objects and raise the money from them. Many of the proposed internal duties could not be collected at all by means of an excise, which was always odious and oppressive to the spirit of every free people. These smaller items, therefore, had better be omitted. They were not very productive, but still were very vexatious and harassing. It was better not to resort to them at all until other resources were exhausted. They might be reserved, at all events, until next year; when, if the war continued, there would be ample opportunity to include them in the list.

Gentlemen would perceive, also, that many of these new internal duties were to be levied on the manufactures of the country. The Government, Mr. O. said, had professed a great regard for the "infant manufactures." Iron and leather were articles of common use and necessity; and it was as essential to national independence to protect and encourage the manufacture of these articles, as the manufacture of cotton. The Committee of Ways and Means had determined to give up the tax on cotton yarn. He approved of that determination; but he could see no reason for exempting that manufacture, which did not apply with equal or greater force to the others.

He had still another reason, Mr. O. said, for increasing the direct tax beyond the amount recommended by the Committee of Ways and Means. It would be observed that the Secretary of the Treasury had recommended a National Bank, as an essential part of his plan of finance. Indeed so essential did he consider it, that it appeared to be the pivot on which his whole system turned, and without it he could not be held at all responsible for the success of his plans. Although, Mr. O. said, he was friendly to a National Bank, organized on correct and independent principles, and believed it necessary to a safe and easy management of the revenue, he could never approve of such a bank as the Secretary had proposed. It contained principles which appeared to him subversive of the very objects the Secretary had in view in its establishment. A bank with a capital of $6,000,000 in specie, and $44,000,000 in stock, for all the legitimate purposes of banking. was in truth nothing more than a bank of $6,000,000. It was impossible, in the present state of banking credit, that such a bank should loan extensively to the Government without being soon reduced to the situation of most of the other banks in the country. The effect of it, then, would be still more to sink the public credit, and embarrass the financial operations of the Government. A bank to succeed must be left perfectly free to pursue its own interests, without the interference of the Government. It must proceed in the outset with great caution, and on a limited scale, until by degrees it could draw to itself the public confidence, and restore it also to the other banking institutions in the country, and thus gradually get the whole machine again in motion. Whether it could succeed at all was extremely problematical; but it certainly could not if the wants of the Government, and not its own interests, were to be the guide of its conduct. There were other objections to the Secretary's plan, particularly the agency which the Government was to have in the appointment of directors, but he would not dwell on them. It was enough to observe that unless the proposed plan of the bank was materially modified, there was every reason to believe that it would meet with no support from the minority in the House; and perhaps it would receive but little in any shape. As there were many gentlemen in the House opposed to a bank under any circumstances, and many who would dislike its details, it became very questionable whether it would be adopted at all. Under this view of the subject, it became important to render the system of revenue, independent of the bank, more effectual and adequate.

In every point of light, therefore, in which he had been able to consider the subject, Mr. O. said he was satisfied that an increase of the direct tax beyond the amount recommended by the Committee of Ways and Means was essential. Without it, he thought the system incomplete, and he believed it would be found ineffectual.

Having thus, Mr. O. said, submitted to the Committee the remarks that had occurred to him, to show that the disastrous state of the finances could be retrieved only by an immediate and total change in the ruinous system hitherto pursued, and a resort to a vigorous and extensive plan of internal revenue, he ought perhaps no longer to occupy the attention of the Committee. But, feeling as he did, that the great addition to the existing burdens of the people, which was about to be heaped on them, had been rendered necessary by the war, he must beg the indulgence of the Committee, while he laid before them, in a summary manner, his views of the present state and character of the war, and the line of conduct in relation to it, which he felt called upon to pursue. His sentiments, Mr. O. said, as to the origin of the war, and the objects for which it was avowedly declared, had always been uniform. At its commencement he thought, and he still thought, that it was unnecessary and inexpedient, and that it was waged for objects unattainable in themselves, and if attainable, unimportant, when considered in connexion with the immense public and private sacrifice with which a successful pursuit of them must necessarily be attended. Adverting to the circumstances under which the war was declared, to the total want of preparation for it, and the carelessness manifested by its authors about its ultimate and probable consequences, it appeared to him that the history of human folly and rashness could not present an act so enormous. When he considered the extent of individual and national injury growing out of the war; the essential interests and rights of the country staked upon its issue; the treasure which has been squandered, and the blood which has been shed in its progress; with the absence of all rational hope that it could be brought to a successful termination with the means which had been thought adequate by the Government at its commencement—all of which had been distinctly pointed out, and ought to have been foreseen by its authors—he could scarcely resist the belief that they had acted under the influence of a blind infatuation, which had alike set at defiance the plainest dictates of prudence, and the lessons which the experience of every age had taught.

He had said that the avowed objects of the war, in its commencement, were unattainable in themselves, and, if attainable, too unimportant to justify the war either in its origin or continuance. That they were now impliedly admitted to be so by the Administration itself, appeared abundantly from the documents before the public. To say nothing of the question relative to the blockades, about which there was no substantial difference between the enemy and our-

selves, he would confine himself to the "principal cause of war," which had arisen out of the practice by the enemy of impressing from our merchant vessels his own seamen. It could not but be recollected that the war had been commenced, as far as it related to this branch of the quarrel, with the express design of compelling the enemy, not only to discontinue that practice in point of fact, but to *stipulate by treaty* that it should not be renewed. This was the ground decidedly taken by the Administration, many of its friends had gone further, and insisted that the enemy should be compelled to stipulate, not only to abandon the practice, but also to surrender the claim of right.

That such were the views of the Administration, on the subject of impressment, at the commencement of the war, and such the concessions from the enemy, which he expected to obtain, was apparent from its declarations at the time; the same views had been continued and the same intentions avowed in subsequent stages of the war. If gentlemen would advert to the correspondence between Admiral Warren and our Government, soon after its commencement, they would find the same spirit manifested. He did not know that he recollected accurately the purport of that correspondence. He had not been able, in consequence of the general destruction of the papers and documents of the House, conveniently to recur to it. He would therefore thank any gentleman on either side of the House to correct any impression relative to it which he might appear erroneously to entertain. He would then allege that the Government refused to accept the peace proffered on that occasion by the enemy, on the ground that no peace between the two countries could be secure or of long continuance unless the subject of impressment was so adjusted in the negotiation that the practice of it on the part of the enemy should entirely cease. [Here Mr. JACKSON, of Virginia, rose and observed, that as the gentleman from New York had desired to be corrected in any erroneous impression he might entertain in relation to the correspondence alluded to, he would take the liberty of stating that the Government had demanded as a condition of its acceptance of the armistice offered by Admiral Warren, that the enemy should agree to discontinue the practice of impressment during the negotiation which might follow.] Mr. O. said he did not question that the statement of the honorable gentleman was substantially correct. Admitting it to be so, he said the spirit of the condition insisted on by the Government fully bore him out in the remark he had made on its views, as manifested in that correspondence. If the Government refused even to assent to a negotiation until the enemy had yielded the point in dispute, by agreeing to discontinue the practice of impressment during its pendency, it could hardly be supposed that in the negotiation itself it was not determined to insist that a complete abandonment of the practice should be expressly stipulated. He felt justified, therefore, in saying, that the Government, in the correspondence with Admiral

Warren, was actuated by its uniform conviction that no treaty of peace ought to be made with England, in which the question of impressment was not satisfactorily adjusted.

On the subject of the refusal to accede to the armistice offered by Admiral Warren, Mr. O. said, he could not forbear remarking, that the conduct of the Administration appeared to him to have been, on that occasion, not less rash and unwise than in the declaration of war. An opportunity was then afforded of extricating the country from the war with honor. The effect of the proposition of the enemy, if acceded to, would have been to have re-established the relations of peace, by restoring the two countries to the state in which they were at the commencement of the war—terms which the Government appeared willing now to accept, but which he feared could not be obtained until after a protracted and bloody contest.

The determination of the Government to adhere to the ground which it assumed in the outset, on the subject of impressment, was fully manifested in the earliest instructions to our Commissioners for negotiating peace. As far as its views could be collected from those parts of the first instructions which had been made public, and which on that point were full and explicit, it was abundantly evident that the grand object of the negotiation was, as that of the war had been, to obtain from the enemy a clear and precise stipulation by treaty, that the practice of impressment should be abandoned. If gentlemen would look at these instructions they would everywhere see, in the first stages of them, the same spirit. In the letter of the 15th of April, 1813, the Secretary of State, after observing that the war would cease, when the enemy should respect the right of our seamen (by which it was presumed the Secretary meant British seamen on board of American vessels) to be exempted from impressment, had declared that the proposition made by Mr. Russell to the British Government immediately after the war, and the answer given by the Department of State to Admiral Warren, showed the ground on which the United States were willing to adjust that controversy. In the same letter it was again declared, that to secure the United States against impressment, "a clear and distinct provision must be made against the practice"—the form was not material—all that was required was, that the British Government should "stipulate in some adequate manner to terminate or forbear the practice of impressment from American vessels." Again, in the same letter, the Commissioners were told that the great object they had to secure was, "that our flag should protect the crew," and if that was not done, the United States "had appealed to arms in vain," and that if their efforts to accomplish it failed, "all further negotiation would cease."

In the letter of the 28th of January, 1814, gentlemen would find it declared that "the sentiments of the President had undergone no change" on the important subject of impressment; that the degrading practice must cease, our flag must protect the crew, or the United States could not consider themselves an independent nation;" and we were further told, that in agreeing to treat with Great Britain directly, "no concession was contemplated on any point in controversy." And in the letter of the 14th of February, 1814, it would be seen that the same ground was maintained even in the event of a peace in Europe.

It would thus be manifest, Mr. O. said, from a view of the official documents connected with the origin and progress of the negotiation to a late period, that the Government had all along considered a stipulation by treaty on the subject of impressment as essential to any secure and honorable peace; that it had assumed that ground as the main object of the war; that it had deemed such a stipulation not only attainable, but sufficiently important to justify the war; in that it had been made a "*sine qua non*" to any treaty of peace.

It was true, Mr. O. said, that the Government had occasionally varied its ground as to the limitation in point of time, of the stipulation contended for, and had gone very far in tendering to Great Britain an equivalent for such a stipulation. It had even gone the length of proposing, that the crews of our vessels should be mustered previous to the voyage, and be subjected to the examination and scrutiny of British Consuls or commercial agents. A regulation, Mr. O. said, almost, if not altogether, as degrading as the practice of impressment itself, and much more injurious to the commercial interests of the country. But, notwithstanding these concessions on subordinate points, the stipulation, in its principal feature, had been constantly adhered to in every instruction to our Ministers, down to the 25th of June, 1814.

A little previous to that time, Mr. O. said, gentlemen would recollect, that authentic intelligence was received in this country of the dethronement of the late Emperor of France. That event made it certain that peace would not only be restored in Europe, but would be restored under circumstances rendering futile any expectation which might have been entertained by our Government of reaping any advantage, in the contest with England, from the power or influence of France. The effect of this on the Administration had certainly been to lower its tone on the subject of impressment. In the letter to our Ministers of the 25th of June, 1814, the first appearance was manifested of a design to recede from the main ground. In that letter our Commissioners were instructed, that, in case no stipulation could be obtained from the British Government, either relinquishing the claim of impressment, or discontinuing the practice, they were at liberty to agree to an article, referring the subject to a future negotiation. The Government, however, still looked forward to an eventual arrangement of the difference on this point, similar to that for which it had uniformly been contending. An ultimate stipulation by treaty, discontinuing the practice of impressment, was still its object and intention. Two days afterwards, however, Mr. O. said, the views of the Government underwent a further change, and "on mature consideration" it was determined to abandon the whole ground. In the letter of the 27th of June, the Commissioners were told that they might "omit any stipulation on the subject of impressment if found indispensably necessary to terminate the war."

It was thus apparent, Mr. O. said, that a war, commenced for the purpose of vindicating the rights of the nation, which its authors considered essentially violated by the impressment of British seamen from our vessels, was to have been concluded by an absolute abandonment on the part of the Government, of all the grounds on which it had been declared, and the country, after two years of suffering and sacrifice, the extent of which was even now little understood, but which would be felt for generations to come, was to have been placed in the same situation, as it respected the question of impressment, in which it stood at the commencement of the war. This abandonment of the original objects of the war was not only total, but, in its effect, perpetual.

The Government, after having published to the enemy its intentions to have conceded the point, could scarcely hope to revive its claims with success in any future negotiation.

Mr. O. said he would submit to gentlemen, whether he was not borne out by the facts appearing on the face of the documents, when he repeated that the avowed objects of the war were unattainable by it; or, if attainable, too unimportant to justify either its commencement or continuance; and that they were now impliedly admitted to be so by the Administration itself. Would it be said, asked Mr. O., that the unexpected peace in Europe had defeated the hopes which the Government had entertained of bringing the contest to a successful issue? He had believed that, to the rashness of plunging the country into the war, the authors had added the folly of relying for its success, more on a favorable course of events in Europe, than on the strength and resources of their own country. He did not wish by this to be understood as entertaining a belief that the war had originated in any concert with France, or with a view to promote her interests. He knew of no satisfactory evidence to support such a belief, though it had certainly been entertained by many in this country; and so striking had been the circumstances under which the war had been declared, so well-timed in point of fact had been the blow aimed at England, and which, through her, reached her allies, that he had authority for saying that, in Europe, the impression was general, however unjust, that the war had originated in a coincidence of views and objects between our Government and the French Emperor; that we had now no friend on that Continent, and that the ear of every European Court was closed against us. He meant merely to state his own conviction, he said, that the authors of the war had rested chiefly on the success of France for a favorable issue of the contest; that they had done so in some degree did not now seem to be denied. It was evident

to him, from the consideration that they had begun the war without preparation, had conducted it without vigor, and had determined to give it up entirely as soon as they knew that the fate of France was decided. He did not mention this as an impeachment of the motives of the Administration. Deeming the war just and expedient, they might have thought that prudence and sound policy required them to take the opportunity afforded by the state of things in Europe, to attack the enemy to advantage, in the hope of thus compelling him to make concessions which they could not expect to obtain by an exertion of their own means. How far the friends of the Administration might discern in this consideration an excuse for the evident rashness of the attempt, he could not conjecture. He could say, however, that he never expected to see any honest statesman, who was at the same time a wise one, compelled to lay before his country such an apology for the failure of the war.

Mr. O. said, he was aware that it had been attempted to avoid the conclusion that our Government had abandoned the grounds on which the war was commenced, by resorting to a train of reasoning, in his judgment, entirely deceptive. It had been said that, as exemption from the practice of impressment was the object of the war, and as it had been continued until the practice had in fact ceased by the peace in Europe, that object had been "essentially obtained for the present." If, indeed, the practice of impressment had ceased in consequence of the peace in Europe, it had done so because Great Britain had chosen to discontinue it for considerations growing out of her own convenience, and depending entirely on her own will. The war had in no degree contributed to produce that effect. To say that the object of the war had been essentially obtained, because the practice of impressment had ceased, when it had not ceased in consequence of the war, appeared to him a course of argument entirely unsupported. In no sense, then, could the war be considered as having succeeded. If peace were made to-morrow, it would have produced no state of things advantageous to the United States which would not exist without it, and the country would be placed in no respect in a more eligible situation than it would be, had it never been declared.

It must be evident, he thought, from the observations he had offered to the Committee, that the Administration stood committed to the country in the most serious manner. They had involved it in war for objects which they had failed to obtain, and which they had now lost all hope of obtaining; and they were unable to make peace, though they were prepared to accept it on terms which had once been offered to them. Viewing their conduct in this light, considering the feeble manner in which they had conducted the war in all its stages, how they had misapplied the means, and exhausted the resources of the country in fruitless attempts at conquest, which, if successful, would be useless; and looking, as he did, with serious alarm to the future consequences of their errors, he felt bound to express an opinion thus publicly, that they were not competent to direct the affairs of this nation in the present crisis, and that no rational hope could be entertained that any peace, which the real friends of the country could approve, would ever be obtained under their auspices.

With such impressions, and, feeling as he did, little confidence that any means which might be placed in the hands of the Administration for the support of the war and the defence of the country, would be employed with any better effect than heretofore, he had thought much of the course which he ought to adopt when the question of supplies should come before the House. The result had been, that he felt it to be his duty to vote for supplies, and to assist, as far as he was able, in the organization of a system of revenue calculated to make these supplies certain and adequate. He should therefore give his support to such parts of the plan of the Committee of Ways and Means as appeared to him to operate with tolerable equality on the different sections of the Union ; and if he proposed any alterations they would not be calculated to diminish the amount of revenue, but to vary the sources from which it was to be drawn.

He was aware, he said, that he might be told that he had pursued a different course when the question of supplies was under consideration at a former session of Congress. He certainly had done so, and hence he felt it incumbent on him to state the reasons which actuated him on both occasions. He trusted his friends, with some of whom he might differ on this point, would see, from the view he had taken in the course of his remarks, that any change of conduct which might be attributed to him in this respect, had not arisen from any change in his opinions of the political character of the Administration.

Mr. O. said, as long as the war was waged on the principles on which it had been commenced, as long as it was an offensive war, a war to protect British seamen on board of American merchant vessels—and when the Administration had refused to accept an offer of peace from the enemy on terms which he thought comported with the interests, and did not infringe the honor of the nation—it had met his decided disapprobation. He had thought it not only unnecessary and inexpedient, but unjust. To a war commenced on such principles, and waged for such objects, he could never lend any countenance or support. When, therefore, on a former occasion, he had been called upon to grant supplies for carrying on the war, he had felt it, in common with his friends, to be his duty to vote against them ; and if the majority of the House had, at that time, adopted a similar course, the Administration would have been compelled to have made a peace, upon terms which could then have been obtained, and which they had since in vain attempted to obtain.

But, Mr. O. said, he now considered the war, in point of fact, as essentially changed. It was now strictly a war of defence—we were attacked

on every side. Instead of conquering the enemy's territory, a part of our own was in his hands. We were called on to repel invasion on every quarter. The enemy, losing sight of his own interests, and actuated by ambition or a desire of revenge, and feeling no doubt a contempt for the power and resources of the country, which the feeble conduct of the Administration was too well calculated to inspire, had made demands which rendered peace impossible, unless on terms which violated the essential interests and honor of the country. The war, therefore, was in fact a new war, to be waged on new principles, and for new objects. As long as it continued to be waged for such objects and upon such principles, and as long as the enemy persisted in his present demands, the war must be carried on, the country must be defended ; and it was to be hoped, with a prospect of success, when the power and resources of the nation should be placed in abler hands.

If any plan could be devised for furnishing and applying the supplies for the war, without placing them at the disposal of the present Administration, Mr. O. said he should seize it with avidity. He knew of none, without resorting to principles and acts of a revolutionary character, which would put at hazard the existence of the National Government. The men in power were the Constitutional organs, through which the Government must be administered, while they continued to hold it. He should therefore vote for the supplies. He should act on this occasion as he would if the granting of them depended on his vote alone. If they were withheld, and the Administration should refuse to resign, the Government would be dissolved and the country ruined. If they were granted, it was barely possible, that, under their management, it could be saved.

While such were declared to be his views, Mr. O. said, as to the war under its present aspect and to the supplies necessary for carrying it on, he must be permitted, again and again, to say, that he had little hope that it would be conducted with success or brought to safe and honorable issue by the men now in power. He should constantly repeat that the whole responsibility of the disastrous state of our affairs rested solely on them. They were responsible for having declared the war without necessity and for objects unattainable and unimportant—for having conducted it without vigor or foresight—for having ruined the finances of the country—and for having compelled a resort to this extensive and burdensome system of taxes as the only means of preventing absolute national ruin. They were responsible, too, for the new character which the war had assumed. But for the war, the British Government could never have made the demands which had now been set up ;—the points now in dispute between the two countries could never have been brought into question. They had, therefore, now staked the essential rights and honor of the nation on the issue of a contest, which in the nature of things must be always doubtful. Whatever sacrifice, therefore, the country might be ultimately obliged to make for the sake of peace, would be justly chargeable to the rashness and folly which had involved it in the war.

The only radical cure, Mr. O. said, for the evils under which the country suffered, would be found in a change of Administration. That, he feared, could not be hoped for except through the process pointed out by the Constitution. From the organization of the extensive branch of our Government, the operation of public opinion, especially on our foreign relations, was slow. In England, the fiftieth part of the disasters and disgrace, which attended the progress of the war, would have driven the most powerful Ministry from their places. In this country the effect was not so speedy, but he trusted it would be as certain. The people had the remedy in their own hands, and he did not doubt they would apply it. He should not cease, as far as depended on him, to keep before the public eye the real authors of the ruin with which we are threatened. If the people wished to put an end to this destructive war, if they wished to see public and private happiness restored, they must place other men in power. If the country was not to be irretrievably ruined—if its flag was not to be struck, as the flag of the Administration had been, it must wave over other heads than those which had hitherto directed this war.

Mr. EPPES replied to a part of Mr. OAKLEY's speech, and opposed his motion.

Mr. OAKLEY explained.

Mr. WRIGHT, of Maryland, opposed the motion, and replied to Mr. OAKLEY.

Mr. OAKLEY's motion to amend Mr. EPPES's amendment, was negatived by a considerable majority.

Mr. EPPES's motion was then agreed to by as large a majority.

The second resolution next came under consideration, which proposes to add to the duty on the capacity of the still a duty of twelve and a half cents per gallon on the quantity of spirits distilled.

Mr. EPPES moved to amend it, so as to make the new duty fifteen cents, instead of twelve and a half, per gallon.

Mr. FISK, of New York, moved to make the additional duty twenty-five cents.

This motion was advocated by Mr. WRIGHT, of Maryland, and opposed at considerable length by Mr. McKEE.

Mr. LOWNDES, of South Carolina, with a view to affording further time for reflection on the amended report of the Committee of Ways and Means, moved that the Committee should rise.

Previous to rising—

Mr EPPES laid upon the table resolutions embracing the further amendments which the Committee of Ways and Means proposed to make to their report, viz: a combination of a tax on paper, and an increase on the carriage tax, to produce double the present amount of the carriage tax; a classification of the licenses to retailers, and an increased duty thereon; and the establishment of a National Bank.

And then the Committee rose.—Adjourned.

SATURDAY, October 22.

Another member, to wit: from Ohio, JAMES KILBOURN, appeared, and took his seat.

Mr. EPPES, from the Committee of Ways and Means, reported a bill authorizing a loan for a sum not exceeding —— dollars; which was read twice, and committed to a Committee of the Whole on Tuesday next.

Mr. TROUP, of Georgia, from the Military Committee, to whom was referred the amendments of the Senate to the resolutions in honor of Generals Brown, Scott, Gaines, Macomb, Ripley, Miller, and Porter, recommended a disagreement to the same; which report was concurred in.

The bill from the Senate, further extending the time for locating Virginia Military Land Warrants, and for returning the surveys to the General Land Office, was twice read, and committed.

WAYS AND MEANS.

The House again resolved itself into a Committee of the Whole on the report of the Committee of Ways and Means.

The resolution for increasing the tax on spirits distilled being still under consideration, and Mr. FISK's motion to insert twenty five cents per gallon (in addition to the present tax on the capacity of the still) being the question immediately before the Committee—

Mr. BAYLY said, there was a difficulty in voting for the proposition before the Committee, until they had decided the principle by which the tax should be raised—whether entirely upon the capacity of the still, as the law now is, or upon the product of the still, or upon both, as the Committee of Ways and Means had. recommended. I consider, said Mr. B., as I always have, this article as a necessary and proper subject of taxation; but, as to the best manner of laying and collecting the tax, to make it productive to the Treasury and agreeable to the people, I differ from the honorable Chairman of the Committee of Ways and Means. It is not probable that any system of taxation could be formed that would please all parts of the United States; and in discussing a tax which will be paid by some States, or parts of States, more than other States, we ought to remember that there are other articles in this report proposed to be taxed, which will balance and equalize the burden, so that, taking the whole system, there will be no cause of complaint by any other State, of paying more into the Treasury than their proportion. It is admitted by all that the tax will be paid almost entirely by the consumer, and that, whenever a high duty was laid upon any article, the price would therefore be raised in the market. It would seem, that, as the Army and Navy of the United States consume much of domestic spirits, they would in fact raise the price in the market, and thereby enable the distiller to advance the tax, which would eventually be paid by the United States. But, this tax may be so heavy as to put down some of the distilleries, (especially the small ones,) and the revenue from this article thereby fail; and Congress ought to be cautious that they do not tax the article so as to destroy the contemplated revenue which they expect to derive from it. But, I cannot agree to this double mode of taxing the capacity of the still and the product. I am opposed to the present tax upon the capacity of the still; it is unequal and inconvenient. The Secretary of the Treasury states the tax, now established by law, equal to a duty of five cents a gallon on the spirits distilled. With some distilleries, this may be the case; and distilleries on a large scale, and in great perfection, perhaps, it will not amount to more than two and a half cents on the gallon distilled. In small distilleries, such as are used by farmers, it will amount to not less than ten cents, and often fifteen. It was inconvenient, because the farmer was compelled to tax at much trouble in obtaining the license, which he could not obtain for a shorter time than two weeks, although he might not have a use for his still half that time. The only reason the honorable Chairman of the Committee of Ways and Means gave for continuing the present tax, was, that it would be a guide by which the collector might detect fraud, when committed by the distiller. But, the collector must know the industry and skill of the distillers, (which would be difficult,) or his knowledge of the size of the still would be useless. The collector might often raise groundless suspicions of fraud in the revenue, which would inflame and irritate the public mind against the tax. without obtaining one cent into the Treasury, which it is the duty of Congress to avoid. Mr. B. believed that fraud would very seldom be practised, and would not materially affect the revenue. The duties on all imported spirits are and have been very light; yet, the American merchant held as exalted a character for honesty as the merchant of any country; and surely the farmer might with equal safety be trusted. Mr. B. wished the direct and excise taxes would be left as the last subject of taxation reported by the Committee of Ways and Means; that, after ascertaining what might be raised from other objects, we might return to them, and make up the deficiency from them. The taxes upon cotton manufactures, furniture, leather, hats, shoes, watches, &c., are very objectionable. They will disturb the public mind, now more than sufficiently excited, and thereby weaken the Government more than the taxes which they will produce will strengthen the Treasury. The excise and direct taxes, upon equal and fair principles, were always favorite taxes with him, and the best internal taxes under a popular Government; they were certain, easy of collection; and the people, knowing that they had to pay for the support of their Government, would examine into all extravagant expenditures. But, when the money is drawn from the people by indirect means, they give themselves little or no trouble to inquire how it is expended. If the Treasury had been supported partly by a direct tax, it is not probable that the people had suffered their commerce to be destroyed by your non-intercourse restrictions and embargoes, and thereby lose the revenue from our foreign trade, which must have

been supplied in part by taxes on land, their Treasury never would have been emptied by schemes and experiments, nor would this war have existed. Mr. B. observed, that no man was more averse to this war than he was, and it was well known that he was opposed to the Administration; but, opposed as he was to the war and Administration, such was the danger in which the country was placed, and the character of conquest which this war had assumed on the part of the enemy, that he would not withhold the resources of the country from the Administration, but would give every aid in his power to bring it to a glorious conclusion. And he was willing that the Administration should possess all the honors gained by such a peace. He did not agree with most of his friends with whom he acted, that the campaign now drawing to a close was inglorious to our arms. It is true, that, at the commencement of the war, the Navy far outshone the Army; and the reason is obvious; our small and gallant Navy was manned by sailors who had been long accustomed to danger, and, as soon as they were on board the ship, they were ready for action. Not so with the Army. Time was required to form the recruit into a useful soldier. Our armies are now formed, and are equal in discipline and courage to our enemy, as this campaign has proved. He would, therefore, impose taxes upon such articles as would be paid by the community without complaint, and draw a safe and productive revenue into the Treasury; and he was persuaded they would be cheerfully paid, when the people were satisfied that they were necessary to their safety. But, the honorable gentleman from Kentucky, (Mr. McKee,) and his honorable colleague, (Mr. Epps,) are opposed to a great increase of the excise and direct tax, because they bear harder upon Kentucky and Virginia than some other States now advocating these taxes. Before this war, the Eastern States paid more than a proportion of taxes to the General Government, by the aid of their extensive commerce, which is now gone. Their ships and fisheries are destroyed, and it may be recollected that this war is the cause, which Kentucky and Virginia had a great agency in producing. If, then, by raising the money to carry on this war, it should be found that these States paid a fraction more than other States, they ought to pay it with cheerfulness.

Mr. B. observed, he could not agree with many of his friends in desiring the President to take into his Administration Federal men. He believed it would be difficult to prevail upon Federal gentlemen of high and commanding talents to take any of the departments of the Government, and he should think it a misfortune to the Federal cause if such an arrangement should take place. For, the affairs of the country could not prosper with a divided Administration; and it is impossible, in a Government constituted as that of the United States, that any Administration could conduct prosperously the affairs of the country, at the present dangerous and perplexing crisis, without the confidence and support of the people. I must therefore give to the Administration now

441   HISTORY OF CONGRESS.   442

OCTOBER, 1814.   The Ways and Means.   H. OF R.

in power all the resources of the country; and I will not, in my Legislative capacity, withhold all support from them, and thereby endanger the existence of the Constitution. But, sir, at elections I shall, as I always have, use every fair and honorable exertion to displace them; and, when a complete change is made in the public sentiment, then, and not till then, do I wish to see a Federal Administration.

Mr. YANCEY, of North Carolina, moved to amend the resolution by striking out the whole of it and inserting, in place of it, "that it is expedient to lay a duty of —— cents, on every gallon of spirits distilled from domestic material in lieu of the duty now imposed." The object of this motion was to lay the tax altogether on the quantity distilled.

Mr. McKEE, of Kentucky, spoke at some length to prove that so high a tax as was proposed on distillation would be perfectly illusory, as it would amount to a prohibition of the manufacture of the article in many parts of the country; and, if it were not illusory, the tax would be so unequal in its operation as to be extremely unjust, particularly to the State which he represented.

Mr. BAYLY spoke in explanation and reply to Mr. McKEE. In the course of his observations, he said that he conceived an equalized direct tax, and a tax on spirituous liquors, as the best taxes, if not the only ones that ought to be imposed under popular government.

Mr. HAWKINS, of Kentucky, was in favor of an amendment fixing the tax wholly either on the product or on the capacity of the still, instead of retaining the tax on both as proposed by the Committee of Ways and Means. Although he knew the whiskey tax was considered as bearing with particular severity on Kentucky, he knew too, from the feelings of the people of that State, that they would pay any tax Congress should lay on the article—though he hoped it would not; therefore, he taxed higher than it would bear.

Mr. WRIGHT, of Maryland, was of opinion that Maryland paid as high a tax as any State in proportion to its capital; but he was desirous to carry into effect the project of the Secretary of the Treasury in every particular, and, therefore, although the tax would bear hard on his State, he should vote to tax the distillation of liquor thirty cents per gallon on the product of the still.

Mr. INGHAM, of Pennsylvania, entered into an argument to show that it would be highly impolitic to abandon the tax on the capacity of the still, and was, therefore, opposed to the present amendment.

Mr. CYRUS KING, of Massachusetts, spoke as follows:

Mr. Chairman, I feel that I owe to the Committee an apology for rising thus early in the debate, before gentlemen of greater experience and of longer standing on this floor have had an opportunity of expressing their sentiments. This course, however, I am compelled to pursue in consequence of what fell from the honorable gentleman from New York yesterday in debate upon this subject.

Had I been satisfied with the practical conclusion to which that honorable gentleman brought himself, I should have remained silent, and with him have united with the majority in voting for additional taxes. But this, after the most mature consideration, I cannot do. No one laments more sincerely than I do, the distressing state to which our country is reduced by corrupt men and ruinous measures. No one will go further in a correct and honorable course to relieve her from our present embarrassments. No one can more ardently desire the return of the blessings of peace on fair and honorable conditions—so necessary for the Government, so indispensable for the people. But I do not think that the road pointed out by that gentleman, will lead directly to that desirable end.

If the war, as he admits, and as every reflecting man must admit, was inexpedient in its origin, and is ruinous in its prosecution, I have seen nothing to change its character. As well might the Ethiopian change his skin, or the leopard his spots. If the Administration who declared this war were weak, corrupt, and wicked, as the gentleman will concede, have they, too, changed their natures? and if not, can honest men possibly unite with them? If, as the honorable gentleman correctly observes, the extreme depth of the folly of these men in declaring and conducting this war was such that even his intelligence could not fathom it—if, as he says, they have abused the confidence reposed in them, and lavished the blood and treasure of the nation in foolish and wicked contests, can we, in honor, unite with such monsters? Can we justify ourselves to our constituents, our consciences, or our God, in assisting to put into the power of such men the lives and the remains of the fortunes of our fellow-citizens? I believe in God we cannot.

But the honorable gentleman attempts to justify his course by saying that the nature of the war has wholly changed from offensive to defensive. Is this indeed the case? Where is the only efficient army which the Administration has? Is it not invading Canada? Is it not carrying fire and sword into the heart of that country? And shall we be seriously told that this, on the part of the Administration, is a defensive war? It is true, sir, as far as respects the people of this country and the State Governments, that it is a defensive war. It is true, sir, that the yeomanry of the country, the owners of the soil, are obliged to defend that, and their wives, and their children, and their firesides, against the attacks of the enemy, along the whole of your seacoast; while your Administration, who are bound by the Constitution to defend us, are dreaming of the conquest of Canada, and are sending their soldiers in that direction, to places where we have little property and few inhabitants to protect, but leaving exposed to the incursions of the enemy the whole Atlantic frontier. Like the dog in the fable, they catch at the shadow, and lose the substance.

The honorable gentleman has hinted, for he did not hazard the assertion, that some people in this country, and many in Europe, believe this war of French origin. I have no hints to give on this, or any other subject, but assert, as I believe, and I believe it as I do my existence, that this is a French war, and I have no doubt that a majority of this nation, and all Europe, think the same, and act upon that belief. I very well know, sir, that this Government has lately plead "not guilty" to this charge, on the ground, no doubt, that direct evidence of their guilt cannot be produced. So, sir, in our courts of justice, we every day hear the most notorious offenders plead the general issue of "not guilty," and even be acquitted by their country because there was not sufficient evidence of their guilt, though every honest man in the nation believes them guilty. But let us hear what those gentlemen, the Administration, say in their defence. "No reliance was placed on the good offices of France, in bringing the war with Great Britain to a satisfactory conclusion." But they dare not say they did not rely on the "good offices" or power of the French tyrant when they declared that war. But, they proceed: "He (the President) nevertheless knew 'that France held a place in the political system 'of Europe and of the world, which, as a check 'on England, would not fail to be useful to us." No doubt he knew it while France "held" under her tyrant, not *holds*, under her legitimate Sovereign, a place among nations; and all Europe knew it, felt it, and trembled, while our Administration were courting his "good offices." Like the contemptible jackal to the lion, while the imperial beast of France was greedily pursuing his prey, our dastardly Administration expected to extort their dirty portion from its fears. I was induced to advert to this French origin of the war, for the purpose of distinctly stating to the American people that the allies in Europe, the great and good Alexander the Deliverer among the rest, all so consider it. Nay, more sir, they believe your Administration only a branch of the power of the late imperial, now fallen tyrant, which power they are determined to destroy, root and branch. Let not the people, then, of this country, delude themselves with the hope of peace while the present men wield the destinies of this nation. Foreign nations, sir, have no confidence in the amicable professions of your Administration; they have forfeited all respect, and no honorable peace will ever be made with them. Not, sir, that any foreign nation would pretend to dictate to us, or in the smallest degree interfere with our internal regulations. To this I would not submit from any nation. But the people ought to know that England will not make peace with a set of men whom she thinks corrupt and wicked. Can we then, sir, ought we to unite with such men in the prosecution of this French war? Besides, sir, do we not condemn the friends of this Administration for supporting such weak and corrupt rulers, and shall we not condemn ourselves if we unite with them in that support? Honest men will decide.

For these, among other reasons, I cannot unite in support of the present Administration. I shall

now proceed to state some of the reasons which compel me to vote against the whole system, or rather scheme of finance reported by the Committee of Ways and Means, whereby they calculate to raise from the people of this country, directly or indirectly, by new or increased taxes, $11,635,000, in addition to the sum of $10,800,000, raised in the same manner, or to be raised the present year; making a grand total for the people to pay in taxes, for 1815, $22,435,000 to the national Government, which does not, and cannot protect them. Before I proceed to the reasons above alluded to, permit me to hold up to the view of the American people two pictures, one of the expenses of a year in peace, the other of a year of war. The expense of our Peace Establishment before the war, was (as the late Secretary of the Treasury, Mr. Campbell, informs us, in his able and faithful annual report made to the House of Representatives on the 26th of September, 1814,) - - - - - - $7,000,000
Interest on the debt existing prior to
the war - - - - - - 1,900,000

Making a total of - - - $8,900,000

He further informs us, that the sums authorized by Congress to be expended during the year 1814, and for which appropriations have been made, are as follows:
Amounting, in the whole, to $47,270,172. This sum the Government expected to provide thus:

From the customs - - - -	$6,500,000
Sales of public lands - -	600,000
Direct tax and internal duties -	3,800,00
Postage and incidental receipts -	50,000
Loans and Treasury notes -	33,592,665
Balance said to be in the Treasury -	2,727,507

Making a total of - - - $47,270,172

Of the sum the Government expected to raise by loans, after begging, hiring, and submitting to the grossest usury, they are still deficient more than thirteen millions and a half of dollars, according to the first and dashing report from the new Secretary Dallas, to the Committee of Ways and Means. This statement shows a balance in favor of peace of $38,370,172, of course the amount which one year of war costs the people.

I will now, sir, by your indulgence and that of the Committee, state some of the reasons which compel me to vote against the war taxes. Of these reasons, sir, some will be local and others general. While our attention is directed to the interest of the whole, we ought not to neglect that of any part.

First.—I shall vote against this report as a citizen of New England, because that section of the country was not represented in the committee which made it, although its inhabitants, if the taxes are imposed, will be called upon to pay a large proportion of them. How this happened, whether by design or accident, I know not; but such is the fact, that no member from New England was put upon that important committee.

But the Middle, Southern, and Western States, engrossed the whole. I would not be understood to implicate the honorable Speaker of this House, who appoints our committees, and who discharges the duties of his office with distinguished ability. It may have been accident, or he may only have followed the example of some bad predecessor. Nor, sir, would I suggest that the committee is not composed of gentlemen of ability and integrity. But, sir, they cannot understand the interest of that part of our country so well as a member therefrom. They cannot have the feelings, the interest, or the views of citizens of New England. New England appears to be proscribed; put under the ban of empire. These things create suspicions of designs against her rights and liberties. I cannot sanction this procedure by my vote.

Second.—This Administration have, by their weak and wicked measures, so impoverished our citizens, that they have not the ability to pay these oppressive taxes. Shall we lay upon them additional burdens, when they are now almost pressed to the dust by those which you have already heaped upon them? Let us hear what Mr. Secretary Dallas says upon this subject:

"The wealth of the nation, in the value and products of its soil, in all the acquisitions of personal property, and in all the varieties of industry, remains almost untouched by the hand of Government."

Is this indeed true? Let me ask the farmer in the middle States the value of his wheat and his flour now spoiling on his hands; the merchant in the East with his lumber and his fish without purchasers; his acquisition of property, deprived by the acts of the Government of the accustomed means of enterprise; the ship owner, the rich return of his vessels, now only food for worms; the sailor and mechanic, the value of their industry in all its varieties. These will all exclaim, that they have been sorely touched by the hand of this Government. That "the little finger of this oppressive Administration is thicker than the loins" of the Father of his Country. That this Administration has afflicted them as the great enemy of mankind was permitted to afflict the perfect and upright man, by touching all they possess, and they are almost ready to "curse them to their faces." But what does the chairman of the Committee of Ways and Means say on this subject?

"In Europe, the price of agricultural products is not materially affected by a state of war: the produce of the earth is there consumed within the country in peace and in war. The situation of the United States is entirely different; with an extensive and fertile country, and a small population compared to the extent of our territory, we have annually a large surplus to export to foreign markets, over and above what is necessary for consumption. On the export of this surplus, which is cut off by the war, depends in a great degree the ability of the farmer to meet taxes."

By this it appears that the wealth of the nation, composed by the wealth of every individual in that nation, subject to taxation, does but remain almost untouched by the hand of Government. And, sir, I consider this war, for every purpose of misery and distress, as having existed for nearly eight years—since the embargo, by Mr. Jefferson, in 1807. A constant hostility has, since that period, been maintained by the Government against the industry, property, and enterprise of our citizens, by their restrictive and oppressive acts, whereby thousands of our citizens are reduced to beggary; to a situation that scarce any change can be for the worse.

In New England, too, sir, we are obliged to pay our State tax, county tax, town tax, and parish tax—(the latter, some gentlemen on this floor may not understand.) Consider, too, sir, that our citizens are deprived of the usual means of obtaining supplies for these objects, and for the maintenance of their families. Lumber, the fisheries, and commerce, were our chief dependence. Our lumber, which before the war found a ready market at ten and fifteen dollars the thousand, is now merely nominal, at four or five. The bank fisheries are destroyed; and it now seems, from the terms of the enemy, that we are in a fair way to lose the best portion of our coast fishery. Our vessels are now confined to our ports. It must be known likewise that the inhabitants of the seaport towns in Maine were accustomed to receive two-thirds of the provisions required for their support, in articles of the first necessity, coastwise. And in proportion as their means of purchasing provisions have decreased, the price of provisions has increased. Flour, which was formerly bought for six or eight dollars, has, for some time past, been fifteen and sixteen dollars the barrel. Indian corn, which sold for seventy-five cents the bushel before the war, was, the last Summer, one dollar and a half and two dollars the bushel, and so of many other articles of prime necessity. The consequence of this has been such as was probably expected and wished by the Government. Many of our respectable citizens, sailors, and mechanics, have, for subsistence, been forced into the ranks of your Army, and marched into Canada. Yes, sir, I have to regret, nay, to lament, the fate of many valuable citizens, some personal friends, who have thus fallen victims to the diseases of that climate, or the sword of the enemy—far distant from their homes, with no friendly hand to relieve their sufferings or soothe their distress; in death they cast a fond recollection back upon their country and the dear objects of their affection, then closed their eyes in despair. With the hope of giving some relief, I have since entered the dwellings of their families, once the abodes of prosperity and happiness, now of wretchedness and woe. I have beheld their disconsolate widows and helpless parents in misery and want, and their children crying for bread. Do then, Oh God, now their only supporter, according to the petition in thy prayer, give them each day their daily bread.

But when the poor have thus cried, Madison has not wept; "ambition is made of sterner stuff" than this.

Third reason.—As a citizen of New England I am opposed to laying this additional burden upon my fellow-citizens, because no part of the money, thus to be raised, will be applied to the payment of the expense incurred by those States in calling out and subsisting their militia, for the defence of their soil and families. This information we have from the Secretary of War himself, in his answer to the letter of His Excellency, Governor Strong, upon that subject. That no part of the expense thus incurred would be reimbursed, unless our troops were placed under the orders of the commanders of their military districts. This is a species of command we know nothing of. Military districts!—by what right, what authority, what usurpation established?—they are unknown to our laws, unknown to our Constitution, and abhorrent to our feelings. For what purpose is our country gerrymandered into military districts? Can you inform me, sir? I did indeed once hear on this floor the purpose avowed for which they were established, and the use to which they were destined. I did hear an honorable gentleman in debate, and I heard him with horror and detestation, alluding to some rumors of dissatisfaction in the East, thank his God, that there was within each military district of this country a physical force sufficient to put down the first movements of popular discontent. What, sir, are we under a military despotism? Must we be butchered if we dare complain of our wrongs. Is this the Republican form of Government guarantied to us by the Constitution? Is this the freedom for which our ancestors fought and bled? If so, then Warren and the succeeding martyrs of the Revolution died in vain. No, sir, New England will not submit to it. No military despot shall ever reign there. I, too, thank my God that there is within each State in New England the brave yeomanry of the country, hearts of oak, ready and determined to beat down tyranny and oppression under their feet.

But who are the officers under whose command your President wishes to place our hardy soldiers? In Massachusetts he is an officer whom your President himself has recalled from a command in Canada with every mark of disgrace. In New Hampshire is an officer, who, when in command in Canada, suffered himself to be taken by a handful of the enemy; and of so little consequence was he, in the view of your Government, that they let him rust in Canada, unexchanged, until he almost became a subject of his Britannic Majesty. His pay and rations, however, went on, which was some consolation. Sir, our militia officers would think themselves disgraced, and throw up their commissions, if they were ordered under such commanders. But, sir, the principle on which this military gerrymander is formed is what I most deprecate. If your President can thus divide the States into military sections, and place over each a general officer, what prevents his appointment of all the subordinate officers in the same districts, ready to take from our militia officers their commands as soon as they take the field—thus violating, in the very letter, that part of the Constitution which reserves "to the States respectively the appointment of the officers of the militia"? There is nothing that will prevent his doing this, seeing he has the disposition, but the determined resistance of the people, who are accustomed "to anticipate the evil, and judge of the pressure of the grievance by the badness of the principle. "They augur misgovernment at a distance, and snuff up the approach of tyranny in every tainted breeze." If then, sir, you will not defend New England, New England will defend herself, and will keep her resources for her own occasions. "Millions for our defence, but not a cent for tribute."

Fourth reason.—I cannot unite in supporting this Administration, with Mr. Madison at their head, because he has always shown a settled and determined spirit of hostility against the enterprise, the commerce, the rights, and above all, the patriots of New England. In confirmation of this, with mingled sensations of pride and disdain, I descend to notice the mean, dastardly connexion between this Government and one John Henry; where your President gave to that scoundrel and traitor, fifty thousand dollars of the people's money, to purchase up, as he fondly hoped, calumny and detraction against the first patriots in New England; that he was disappointed in his malicious and revengeful hopes and designs was not his fault. The traitor received his fifty thousand dollars from the hand of your President, who sent him, in one of our public ships, out of the reach of justice, even to the imperial Bonaparte. Sir, this impotent attempt by your President, to sully the character of New England, will never be forgotten. It will be forgiven, for our holy religion commands us to forgive our greatest enemies, persecutors, and slanderers. Thank God, New England is covered with the heavenly panoply of integrity and patriotism; the arrows of malevolence fall harmless at her feet.

But this Government has, since 1806, constantly manifested a deadly hostility against the commerce and rights of New England; by their embargoes, non-intercourse, and non-importations; some of the provisions of which were infinitely more unjust and oppressive than the writs of assistance, so justly complained of, at the commencement of the Revolution. These writs gave to the custom-house officers and their deputies power to enter any private houses, &c. "that they would say they suspected." Now, sir, some of the provisions of your laws authorized them to do this, without saying anything—without writ, or right. I have before asserted on this floor, and now, after the most deliberate consideration, I repeat, that this Administration have brought upon this nation many of the evils which produced the Revolution; that they are in fact, acting over the tyranny of Britain, against New England, with increased aggravation. What, let me ask, was a Boston port bill compared with a general embargo? what a duty on a few unimportant articles, compared with the taxes and oppressions which this Administration have brought upon this people? As much as I detest and abhor the tyranny and oppression of a Grafton, a North, or a Bute, and their hireling associates in different

449   HISTORY OF CONGRESS.   450

October, 1814.   *The Ways and Means.*   H. of R.

Ministries in England, against this country, I would not do them the injustice to compare them with a set of men and measures which would disgrace them. If a simple King of England, by his corrupt servants, chastised New England with whips, this Administration have chastised her with scorpions. A repetition of the same grievances will remind us of the remedy. I very well know the apology that is offered by gentlemen on this occasion—that our situation is changed—that New England is represented on this floor, but was not in Parliament. Is she indeed represented here? What influence has New England in this Congress, more than she had in the Parliament of England? She has members here to state her grievances, and demand redress. She had friends there, able and distinguished, to do the same. Has the interest of New England been at all consulted for these eight years past? Have her grievances been redressed? Let her impoverished, ruined citizens, answer the question. We complain of grievances, and we are told that we are represented here. We complain of the oppression of Administration, and are told that they are the choice of the people. The people do not choose rulers to oppress and tyrannize. The moment they thus act, they forfeit their character of rulers, and ought to be deposed. What, sir, shall we be told that a hereditary Sovereign in Europe, may, for his crimes, be deposed and brought to the block—while a petty tyrant of four years standing, "strong enough to suppress, but unable to protect," shall, in this free country, live out his political life. No, sir, the same crime which would bring one man to the block, ought to bring the other to the halter.

What influence, I repeat, has New England in the Administration, or in Congress, when the whole of the Administration, and a majority of both Houses of Congress, live south and west of the Delaware? Will you appeal to their measures as an evidence? In them we see nothing but ruin and oppression. Will honorable gentlemen come nearer home, and examine the Journals of this House; here we see a rank majority ranged against New England. Look at your committees, even the least important; do you find a majority of New England interest, or of Federal Republicans (to speak plain) in either. No, sir, New England influence is carefully excluded from the walls of this House, and was excluded from the palace (before Mr. Madison permitted the enemy to burn it) lest the pure slave spirit should be contaminated. Yes, sir, I consider this Administration as alien to us. So much so, that New England would be justified in declaring them, like all foreign nations, "enemies in war, in peace friends." The States of New England, sir, can never be satellites in any system. But, like primary planets, they will revolve round the sun of Federalism, until the Almighty hand which created, shall dash them from their orbits forever.

To show the wonderful consistency of the men now in power, they have not only acted over the tyranny of England against this country, but they are now actually acting over what in times past

they affected to call the tyranny and oppression of Washington and Adams, in excise laws and internal taxes. If honorable gentlemen acted on principle in their opposition then they were, and have continued, unprincipled. If it be retorted that we ought to support these laws, we answer that we do not deem them necessary, that our support is not necessary to their passage. Sir, allegiance and protection are reciprocal—the people of the United States ordained the Constitution, among other important provisions, "to pro-'vide for the common defence, promote the 'general welfare, and secure the blessings of lib-'erty to ourselves and our posterity." This defence, this welfare, and these blessings, it was the duty of this Administration to provide for the people. How they have done it, our defenceless country will show. Nay, sir, we have ocular demonstration, within sight of this Hall; nay, more, this Hall itself is demonstration, driven as we have been by the enemy and the neglect of the Government from our splendid Capitol to the places of mere patent machines. And that we have the honor of occupying the places of patent machines, we owe to the charity of the enemy, begged by Dr. Thornton of the Patent Office, that he might have where to bestow these models of the arts and of taste. Yes, sir, every part of your city exhibits vestiges of the enemy, and of the criminal neglect of your Government. Yes, sir, the proud banner of that enemy has waved over the Capitol, and all your public edifices are in ruins. Add to this—your Government with the President at their head, pale with fear, flying before a few thousand British troops. The patriot turns from this scene with horror and disgust. Is this the man whom the people have chosen to go in and out before them and lead their armies to battle and to conquest? Is this the kind of protection which he affords to this bleeding country? From such protection and such protectors O Lord deliver my country!

It may be demanded of me, if I am willing to abandon our Navy and Army, without pay, without reward; far, very far from it. My sentiments on this subject cannot be unknown or mistaken. The steady bravery and perfect discipline of our gallant seamen, evinced by their repeated and splendid victories; the heroism lately displayed by some of our Generals, their officers and troops, in many sanguinary and successful battles, flash like lightning upon the surrounding darkness, rendering it more palpable.

New England will not give up the ship, nor the seamen either! She is prepared to swim or sink, conquer or die, with them. But, sir, this Administration have not the ability to reward them; they have lost the confidence of the people, and cannot command the resources of the nation. It will devolve on the first, fast friends of the Navy to reward our brave tars, when the "troubled night" of this Administration departs, "and the star of peace returns."

In relation to the subject more immediately before the Committee, as to the increase of taxes, for the reasons which I have given, and as to the scheme of a National Bank, reported by Mr. Dallas, for reasons which I may assign when that subject may be taken up—I shall vote against the whole. In relation to the detail of this business, as it respects a proper selection of articles or of equalizing them through the States, I shall endeavour correctly to do my duty.

Before I conclude, sir, there is one subject upon which I wish correctly to be understood, and upon which some of the gentlemen on this side of the House have been misrepresented. I allude to the motives and views of gentlemen in and out of this House, opposed to the Administration of Mr. Madison. Could I for a moment believe that a base and corrupt desire of office, or emolument, or power, influenced them; that moment would I abandon them, and esteem them as base as those they oppose. Could I believe, that any other desire actuated them, than to relieve the people from distress, and our country from ruin—I should consider them unworthy the name of patriots—unworthy the name of Americans—unworthy the air and light of Heaven. Let honorable gentlemen consult their own breasts upon this subject, they will find the charge of corrupt motives impossible. Do they find the taste of power so sweet, the couch of ambition so soft, that they are to be courted for enjoyment, and not for the elevated object of rendering happy a whole people? If they have discharged their duty to their country and to their God, they will have no difficulty in answering the question.

But union it seems is now the watch word. Does the Administration desire it? Do the majority in this House desire it? Had either made the least advance or concession for it? Though urged by the nation, has Mr. Madison called round him the wise and the good without distinction of party? Let his Cabinet answer. One important office vacant, and a continual fluctuation and succession of officers, at a time when he ought to have the constant and best advice of the wisest men of the nation. Another office sold in fee to a foreigner by birth, or held by him for another naturalized citizen, now abroad on an important mission, and who qualified himself in the school of insurrection, for his distinction. Is our Treasury always to be a prey to foreigners and traitors, Henry and others? The American people will correct this precedure, or not complain of an empty Treasury. But what advances have the majority in this House made towards a coalition? Do they not, upon every important subject of debate, unsheath the sword of contention, and cast away its scabbard? And how were even the advances of the honorable gentleman from New York, received yesterday? With coldness—no, sir, they were rejected with contempt. Conscious of their strength, they do not want our assistance; they fear that some on this side of the House may stand between them and office. They do not want our assistance to pass their laws, and God forbid they should have it, for on some of these laws are impressed the image and superscription of oppression—I will not, by my vote, give currency to such base coin.

If, sir, this Administration will abandon the evil course and evil advice which they have pursued so long, will return to a sense of duty to themselves, and justice to their country—if Mr. Madison will cease to hearken to evil counsellors, and will give up his inefficient and corrupt agents; will form a Cabinet of the most experienced and wisest statesmen of our country, and will surrender the conduct of affairs wholly to them—I will be among the first with heart and hand to support them. Until Mr. Madison does this, I can only advise him, in the words of an experienced statesman, " to retract his odious exertions of authority; and to remember that the first step towards making New England contribute to his wants, is to reconcile her to his Government.

[Mr. King was called to order soon after commencing his speech, as wandering from the order of debate, by debating questions of a general nature on a proposition to change the tax from the capacity to the product of the still. The Chairman decided that, according to the general practice, the gentleman was in order. From this decision Mr. Fisk, of New York, appealed. After some conversation on the point of order—

The decision of the Chairman was reversed by the Committee.

Mr. King, of Massachusetts then moved indefinitely to postpone the consideration of this question; which motion was declared not in order in Committee of the Whole.

Mr. King then declared himself in favor of continuing the tax on the capacity of the still, and imposing the additional duty on the product of the still—though he should vote against any increase of the present taxes.]

Mr. Oakley, of New York, was also of opinion that a combination of the tax on the capacity and on the product was most expedient, and was for adhering in all respects to the report of the Secretary of the Treasury.

Mr. Eppes assigned the reasons why the Committee of Ways and Means had been in favor of retaining the present tax on the capacity—they were, to secure the collection of the product, and to abridge as much as possible the domiciliary visits of the excise officers for proving the liquor, &c., which would then be unnecessary.

Mr. Ingham said he was fully justified in stating the opinion of the Secretary of the Treasury to be, that the communication of the capacity-tax was indispensable to the due collection of the product-tax.

Mr. Yancey advocated the adoption of the amendment he had proposed. He considered the arguments against it, though specious, to be fallacious. The present system, he contended, operated unequally, and would continue to do so under the increased duty, unless the system was changed. He saw no occasion for the employment of excise officers at all in the collection of the tax, which might be as well collected by compelling distillers to make monthly returns on oath.

The question was then taken on Mr. Yancey's motion (going to throw the tax altogether on the product of the still) and negatived. For the motion 45, against it 76.

The question on Mr. FISK's motion to insert twenty-five cents per gallon was then decided in the negative. For the motion 57, against it 64.

The question being taken a second time, by request, there were for the motion 62, against it 71.

Mr. FISK, of New York, then moved to strike out twelve and a half, and insert twenty. For the motion there were 69, against it 70.

Another count being demanded, there appeared to be for the motion 67, against it 69.

So the motion was negatived.

The question was then taken on the motion of Mr. EPPES to insert fifteen, and decided as follows: For the motion 68, against it 62.

So the House resolved that an additional duty on distillation of fifteen cents per gallon on the product of the still, ought to be laid.

The Committee then rose and reported the two resolutions agreed to in committee, and asked and obtained leave to sit again on the remainder of the report.

MONDAY, October 24.

Another member, to wit: from New Hampshire, WILLIAM HALE, appeared and took his seat.

Mr. BIGELOW presented a petition of sundry members of an association of Ministers, known by the name of the Westminister Association, in the country of Worcester, and State of Massachusetts, praying that the mails may not be transported or opened on the Sabbath day.—Referred to the Committee on the Post Office and Post Roads.

Mr. ROBERTSON presented a petition of sundry inhabitants of the State of Louisiana, praying a confirmation of their respective titles to lands held by virtue of a requette or petition to the Governors of that country, whilst under the jurisdiction of the French and Spanish Governments.—Referred to the Committee on the Public Lands.

On motion of Mr. SEYBERT,

Resolved, That the Secretaries of State, Treasury, War, and Navy Departments, and the Postmaster General, be directed to communicate to this House such information as may be in their power, in relation to the destruction of official books and papers, in their respective Departments, in consequence of the incursion of the enemy in the month of August, 1814; designating particularly what description of books and papers has been lost thereby, and what the probable effect of such loss will be in the adjustment of the unsettled accounts of the United States.

A message from the Senate informed the House that the Senate insist on their amendments to the resolutions " expressive of the sense of Congress of the gallantry and good conduct with which the reputation of the arms of the United States has been sustained by Major General Brown, Major General Scott, and Brigadiers Ripley, Miller, Porter, Gaines, and Macomb," and ask a conference upon the subject of the said amendments; to which conference they have appointed managers on their part.

WAYS AND MEANS.

The House then resolved itself into a Committee of the Whole, on the remainder of the report of the Committee of Ways and Means.

The third resolution came first next under consideration, in the following words:

Resolved, That it is expedient to add one hundred per cent. on the present duty on sales at auction.

Some conversation took place between Mr. WRIGHT, of Maryland, and Mr. EPPES, of Virginia, as to the equality of the general system of taxation proposed.

Mr. FISK, of New York, moved to amend the motion by striking out one hundred and inserting fifty per cent.; under the impression that the proposed increase would have the effect, by throwing sales into the hands of commission merchants, to diminish the present product of the tax.

Mr. EPPES made some observations in reply. He saw no reason why, when other taxes were to be so generally increased, this item should be excepted.

Mr. JOHNSON, of Kentucky, made some observations to show the extreme inequality and oppressiveness of the additional tax on distillation, compared with any other tax proposed, which he said, by the way, would, he feared, operate nearly as a prohibition of that manufacture. He was surprised, after gentlemen had so strenuously insisted on the enormous increase of that tax, that they should oppose the paltry increase of the tax now proposed.

Mr. POST made a statement to show that the increase of the tax would not increase the revenue at all. The only taxes, he appeared to conceive, on which solid reliance could be placed, to insure the requisite amount of revenue, were the land tax and the whiskey tax. The consumption of whiskey, he argued, would not be diminished essentially if it were taxed an hundred, instead of fifteen cents per gallon; and, whatever was the amount of that tax, it eventually came out of the pocket of the consumer, though immediately paid by the manufacturer.

Mr. ROBERTSON, of Louisiana, expressed his regret at the sectional discussion of the taxes. He entreated gentlemen to abandon their local objections to the various taxes, as he should himself do. The State which he represented paid much more than a due proportion, according to its representation, of the internal taxes. But no system of taxation could ever be carried into effect in this country without a reciprocal spirit of compromise, which he therefore hoped to see superseding the local feelings which were displayed on this occasion.

Mr. WRIGHT said, so far from entertaining any sectional feeling on this occasion, he was prepared to agree to the whole system proposed by the Secretary of the Treasury; but protested against dividing it, and taking it by piecemeal.

The question on Mr. FISK's motion was decided in the negative by a considerable majority; and the original resolution was adopted.

The fourth resolution, " that it is expedient to

add fifty per cent. to the present duties on the conveyance of papers and letters," was next considered, and having been amended, on motion of Mr. Eppes, by striking out fifty and inserting an hundred per cent., it was agreed to, without debate.

The next resolution, "that the carriage tax ought to be increased, and a duty on plated harness so imposed as to produce double the amount of the present duty on carriages," was agreed to.

The next resolution that came under consideration was, that "it is expedient to class the retailers of wines, spirituous liquors, and foreign merchandise, and impose an additional duty thereon of fifty per cent."

Mr. Post vehemently objected to this tax as applying exclusively to one class of the community.

Mr. Wright and Mr. Eppes replied; and

The resolution was agreed to without a division.

The next resolution which came under consideration was the following:

"*Resolved*, That it is expedient to impose a duty on the following articles, viz: manufactured tobacco and snuff, in the hands of the manufacturer; candles, of tallow and spermaceti; hats; yarn, spun by the aid of machinery worked by steam or water; leather; pig iron; castings; bar, rolled, and slit iron; and on nails made by the aid of machinery; on furniture above a certain value, except beds, bedding, and articles of domestic manufacture, in the hands of the owner; beer, ale, and porter, in the hands of the manufacturer; boots and shoes, above a certain price, in the hands of the manufacturer; on plated harness, in the hands of the owner; on vats for the manufacture of paper; on saddles and bridles, above a certain price, in the hands of the owner; on gold and silver watches, in the hands of the owner; on pleasure horses, kept exclusively for the saddle or carriage; on playing cards, and on lotteries."

Mr. Eppes, in pursuance of the further instructions of the Committee of Ways and Means, moved to strike out several articles of the above enumeration.

The first he moved to be stricken out was cotton yarn.

Mr. Eppes assigned as a reason for this motion the fear of destroying manufactures yet in their infancy, and information received that this manufacture was not as profitable as at first believed.

Mr. Goldsborough, of Maryland, objected to this motion, believing that no manufacture would better bear or be more able to pay a pretty considerable tax.

The motion was decided thus: For the motion 74, against it 46.

So cotton yarn was exempted from taxation.

The next article proposed to be stricken out was shoes.

As a reason for this motion, Mr. Eppes assigned the great difficulty of discrimination between the large manufactories, and those of an individual or domestic character.

The motion was agreed to without a division.

The next motion was to change the tax on paper vats to a tax of five per cent. on all paper manufactured. Agreed to, without opposition.

The next question was to strike out lotteries; which motion was negatived without debate.

Mr. Goldsborough moved to strike out the furniture tax; assigning as reasons therefor its odious character, because rendering necessary valuations of property, domiciliary visits, &c.

Mr. Eppes defended the tax, and stated that no inquisitions were intended to be made into property, the amount of which was proposed to be ascertained by voluntary declaration of the possessors. He considered it a very proper tax on luxury and superfluity.

Mr. Barbour, of Virginia, also opposed the proposed amendment in an argumentative manner, on the grounds of policy and justice, convinced as he was of the necessity of raising a substantial revenue to supply the wants and support the credit of the Government; he was opposed to the subduction of so great a proportion of the proposed amount of taxation as the erasure of this tax would occasion. Mr. B. spoke at some length and with much ability on the subject of taxation generally.

Mr. Wright supported his colleague's motion. He was opposed to the tax, as an inquisition into private property; as vexatious, if the property was valued by inspection; and encouraging immorality, if valued by assessment on the oath of the proprietors. He was opposed to it, too, because it would in fact operate as a tax on matrimony, from which those who lived their whole lives in violation of the first law of nature would generally be exempt. He considered it, too, in the nature of a direct tax, and which therefore ought to be apportioned according to representation.

Mr. Potter, of Rhode Island, also advocated the motion. The property proposed to be reached by this tax belonged generally to those who have seen better times, but, by the operation of the war, are thrown out of their regular income, and are many of them obliged to sell this very furniture to supply them with bread.

Mr. Gaston, of North Carolina, also supported the motion of Mr. Goldsborough, principally on account of the novelty of the tax, it being a tax never before laid, if ever proposed in any Government. There were other strong reasons against it, particularly the mode in which the tax must be assessed, &c. In opposing this tax, Mr. G. said he at least was not influenced by sectional motives, as it would fall as lightly on the section of country which he represented, as perhaps any other. He was opposed to any tax of a questionable expediency, because all the taxes were to be pledged to the public creditor, and would therefore be irrepealable until his demands were satisfied.

Mr. Hopkins, of Kentucky, in reply to the argument of novelty against the tax, said, that this had been frequently called the age of experiments. Our Government itself was a novelty, which had established its utility; and there were many novelties as well of invention as policy, in our country, which reflected on it the highest honor; and he hoped this would be attended with the same result.

Mr. BRADLEY, of Vermont, opposed the tax on furniture, principally on account of its difficulty, if not impracticability, of collection, as opening the door to fraud, perjury. and favoritism.

Mr. OAKLEY, of New York, on the same side of the question, said he was opposed in principle to the tax, which he believed would not produce anything like the estimated amount. He wished to dispense with this tax, and add the amount of it to the direct tax, or lay it on other articles.

Mr. EPPES rose to defend this tax. He had no idea, when the United States had for years collected a revenue from imports of twenty millions of dollars, on the oaths of the merchants, that they could not collect a tax of a million of dollars from property to be valued on the oaths of the possessors. As to the tax discouraging matrimony, and consequently population, he denied this operation to it; because beds, blankets, sheets, and every article essential to these objects, were exempted from taxation. He denied the inequality and oppressiveness of the tax. Its novelty was an objection, which would equally apply to various others, all internal taxes being new to the Government. It was a tax the rich would pay, and the poor be exempt from; and, therefore, he was in favor of it.

Mr. POST stated that, in collecting the duties on imports, there was a collateral examination of goods entered to verify the statement made on oath; so that the gentleman was mistaken in likening the mode of collection proposed to that existing in relation to import duties. Mr. P. again insisted on the propriety of laying the whole amount of tax on the direct and distillation tax.

Mr. GASTON, of North Carolina, spoke a few words in explanation, and Mr. EPPES replied.

The House then decided on Mr. GOLDSBOROUGH's motion, as follows: For the motion 51, against it 69.

So the Committee determined to retain the tax proposed to be laid on furniture.

Mr. OAKLEY moved to strike out the duty on tallow candles in the hands of the manufacturer. He conceived the tax would be rendered nugatory by the increase of domestic manufacture, and the very poorest people only, those who are unable to purchase materials for making candles, will pay the tax.

The motion was negatived—40 only rising in favor of it, 66 against it.

Mr. BIGELOW, of Massachusetts, moved to strike out the article of leather. His objection was that leather was an article of first necessity, of which the poor consumed nearly as much as the rich, and which, therefore, ought not to be taxed.

The motion was negatived—30 only rising in favor of it.

The question on the resolution, as amended, was then decided in the affirmative.

The next and last resolution was in the following words:

"*Resolved*, That it is expedient to establish a National Bank, with branches in the several States."

The House decided on this question without debate: For the resolution 66, against it 40.

The Committee then reported the several resolutions as agreed to, with the amendments made thereto.

The resolution for increasing the direct tax came up for concurrence. The resolution, as reported by the Committee of the Whole, proposes to add 100 per cent. to the present amount of the direct tax.

Mr. OAKLEY moved to amend the resolve, by inserting one hundred and fifty in lieu of one hundred, so as to make the present amount of that tax 150 per cent.; in other words, to lay a direct tax for the ensuing year of seven and a half millions.

This motion was negatived: For the motion 20, against it 116, as follows:

YEAS—Messrs. Chappell, Cilley, Dana, Fisk of New York, Grosvenor, Hanson, Hawkins, Hopkins of Kentucky, Ingersoll, Irving, Jackson of Rhode Island, Oakley, Post, Potter, Rich, Seybert, Sherwood, Skinner, Taylor, and Thompson.

NAYS—Messrs. Alexander, Alston, Anderson, Avery, Barbour, Bard, Baylies of Massachusetts, Bayly of Virginia, Bigelow, Bowen, Bradbury, Bradley, Brigham, Brown, Burwell, Butler, Caperton, Caldwell, Calhoun, Cannon, Champion, Clark, Condict, Conard, Crawford, Creighton, Crouch, Culpeper, Cuthbert, Davenport, Davis of Pennsylvania, Denoyelles, Desha, Earle, Eppes, Farrow, Forney, Forsyth, Franklin, Gaston, Geddes, Gholson, Goldsborough, Goodwyn, Griffin, Hale, Hall, Harris, Hasbrouck, Hawes, Hubbard, Humphreys, Hungerford, Hulbert, Ingham, Jackson of Virginia, Johnson of Virginia, Johnson of Kentucky, Kennedy, Kent of New York, Kent of Maryland, Kerr, Kershaw, Kilbourn, King of Massachusetts, King of North Carolina, Law, Lefferts, Lovett, Lowndes, Lyle, Macon, Markell, McCoy, McKee, McLean, Moffit, Montgomery, Moore, Moseley, Newton, Ormsby, Pearson, Pickering, Pickens, Piper, Pitkin, Pleasants, John Reed, William Reed, Rhea of Tennessee, Ringgold, Robertson, Ruggles, Sage, Schureman, Sharp, Shipherd, Smith of New York, Smith of Virginia, Strong, Sturges, Tannehill, Telfair, Udree, Vose, Ward of Massachusetts, Webster, Wheaton, White, Wilcox, Wilson of Massachusetts, Wilson of Pennsylvania, Winter, Wright, and Yancey.

So Mr. OAKLEY's motion was lost.

On the question to concur with the Committee in amending the resolution, so as to increase the direct tax 100 per cent. on its present amount, making the total direct tax to be raised six millions of dollars—

Mr. GOLDSBOROUGH, of Maryland, opposed the tax, on the ground that the country was not adequate to pay it without oppression, if not absolute destruction.

The question on inserting 100 per cent. in lieu of 50, was decided as follows: For the amendment 100, against it 38, as follows:

YEAS—Messrs. Alexander, Alston, Anderson, Avery, Barbour, Bard, Barnett, Bayly of Virginia, Bowen, Bradley, Brown, Burwell, Butler, Caldwell, Calhoun, Cannon, Chappell, Cilley, Clark, Comstock, Condict, Conard, Cooper, Crawford, Creighton, Cuthbert, Dana, Davis of Pennsylvania, Denoyelles, Desha, Earle, Farrow, Fisk of Vermont, Fisk of New York, Forsyth, Gholson, Goodwyn, Griffin, Grosvenor, Hall, Hanson, Harris, Hasbrouck, Hawes, Hawkins, Hopkins of Kentucky, Hubbard, Humphreys, Hungerford, Ingersoll, Ingham, Irving, Jackson of Rhode Island, Jackson of Virginia, Johnson of Virginia, Johnson of Kentucky, Kennedy, Kent of New York, Kerr, Kershaw, Kilbourn, King of North Carolina, Lefferts, Lowndes, Lyle, McCoy, McKee, McLean, Montgomery, Moore, Newton, Oakley, Ormsby, Pickens, Piper, Pitkin, Pleasants, Potter, William Reed, Rhea of Tennessee, Rich, Ringgold, Robertson, Sage, Schureman, Seybert, Sharp, Sherwood, Skinner, Smith of Virginia, Strong, Tannehill, Taylor, Telfair, Thompson, Udree, Wilson of Pennsylvania, Winter, Wright, and Yancey.

NAYS—Messrs. Baylies of Massachusetts, Bigelow, Bradbury, Brigham, Caperton, Champion, Culpeper, Davenport, Ely, Eppes, Forney, Franklin, Gaston, Goldsborough, Hale, Hulbert, King of Massachusetts, Law, Lovett, Macon, Markell, Moffit, Moseley, Pearson, Pickering, Post, John Reed, Ruggles, Shipherd, Smith of New York, Sturges, Vose, Ward of Massachusetts, Webster, Wheaton, White, Wilcox, and Wilson of Massachusetts.

The question then being on agreeing to the resolution as amended, going to increase the present direct tax, as before stated, and the yeas and nays having been demanded thereon—

Mr. WEBSTER, of New Hampshire, said, the proposition was to grant a new land tax, of twice the amount of the last. Before he gave his vote, he wished to be permitted to state the reasons which would govern and decide it. It had often happened that public bodies, or the majorities in public bodies, having the general power of adopting laws and resolutions binding on and controlling the whole, had supposed themselves capable of reducing dissenting members to a situation, in which any course of conduct pursued by them might be liable to unfavorable construction. But cases of this sort, attended with real difficulty, he thought to be rare. At any rate, the present occasion presented no such difficulty.

He did not feel himself under the necessity, either of obstructing the passage of the taxes through the House, or of taking upon himself any portion of the responsibility of laying them. A case might arise, in which it would rest with those who have been in the minority of the House, on leading measures of Government, to say whether the supplies should be granted or withheld. Whenever such a condition of things shall happen, it will bring its own rule of action along with it. At present, no such case exists. It is not put to us who opposed the war in its origin, and have steadily reprobated the manner in which it has been prosecuted, to say now, whether a burdensome system of taxes shall be imposed on the people to replenish the exhausted Treasury. That is for those to determine, who have made the taxes necessary. Our votes are not asked for now, any more than they were upon the declaration of hostilities. It was not then left for us to say, whether there should be war. It is not left with us now to say, whether there shall be taxes. Those who took upon themselves the responsibility of the first, must bear also the responsibility

of the last. And it must be presumed, that gentlemen are ready and willing to sustain the consequences of their own measures. Whoever has power to grant revenue, has also the power of directing its expenditure; and if the question of supplies or no supplies, should ever come to rest on the decision of those who have heretofore differed in opinion from the course pursued by the Administration, they then will be able to accompany the supplies with such other measures as shall insure the appropriation of the revenue to proper objects, and place its expenditure in competent hands. But if we were now to say, we will vote for the taxes, if the Administration will apply the means which we shall grant it, to proper and sensible objects, and will call to its aid, in this exigency of affairs, the most prominent men in the nation, without regard to political party or connexion, we should be told—"Gentlemen, 'you are very obliging, but we happen to be able 'to carry through our taxes upon our own strength. 'We do not choose to submit to such terms and 'limitations as you propose, and must beg leave, 'therefore, to dispense both with your conditions 'and your votes."

If, he said, the taxes depended on his vote; if the Administration could show it had made fair and reasonable offers for peace, which the enemy had refused; if it would now consent to apply its means to the first great object of all Governments, the protection of the people, to carry on the war in a manner agreeable to the common sense of the community, and would endeavour to call forth the talents of the nation to aid the cause of the nation, most assuredly he should vote for whatever supplies the occasion called for. He should only be anxious in such a case to grant enough; because he did not represent those who would weigh, very scrupulously, essential national rights and national security against the price necessary for their preservation. But as no such change of system is intimated, and as the system of taxation now proposed does not depend at all for adoption or rejection on his vote, he should hardly give what might be deemed a sanction to the measures of Government, by a general and voluntary support of its present plans of finance. At the same time he did not see that other gentlemen, equally opposed to the war with himself, and expecting as little as he did any successful issue to it, without a change, might not, nevertheless, deem the present exigency to be one, in which they were at liberty, if they so should choose, to vote for revenue, without making themselves in any degree answerable for its probable misapplication. The whole responsibility, he thought, belonged to the other side of the House. They had undertaken both to put the country into a state of war, and to get it well out again. In the former, they had succeeded; how well they will be able to perform the latter, time would show.

If it was said, continued Mr. W., that, public credit depends on adopting this system of taxes, and that it cannot be refused without refusing the means of restoring public credit, he certainly hoped that gentlemen would adopt that system of finance which suited them best, as well for the restoration of the public credit, as for other purposes of Government. He did not wish to limit their choice. He only disclaimed any share in the responsibility of measures, in the production of which those whose political opinions he respected had no concern. A high public credit was one of the treasures which the country had committed to the hands of the present Administration. How they are to restore it, buried as it now is under a mass of depreciated stocks, unfilled loans, discredited Treasury notes, debts unpaid and debts unliquidated, they must determine for themselves, looking to that account to which the country may call them.

It was worth our while to inquire, how it has happened that public credit has received such a tremendous shock. Whose is the fault? When those measures were begun, which have at length brought us where we now are, the public credit of the United States was as high as that of any nation on earth. To whom are imputable the shame and disgrace of its prostration and fall? To what is it owing? Not to any deficiency in the national resources to sustain the credit of the Government. Both the Secretary of the Treasury and the Committee of Ways and Means tell us, and they tell us truly, that the real means of the nation have been abundant. If then, the Administration received the public credit in a high and honorable condition; if the nation has at all times possessed the means of keeping it so, and the Administration has possessed, as it has, a sufficient control of these means; and if after all, the public credit has gone to fearful wreck and ruin, who alone is answerable for such a state of things? or who can refer our present condition to any other cause than an incompetent management of the powers of Government? The basis of public credit is confidence in the national resources, in the duration and stability of Government, and in the competency and character of those who administer it. It is owing to no distrust of the resources of the nation, nor of the general organization and structure of the Government, that the public credit had sunk so low. The true cause of this was to be sought elsewhere. No system of taxation, merely as such, will prove an adequate remedy, especially at this late hour. Unless the Administration can court back a general confidence, not only in the wealth of the nation, but also in its own ability and the wisdom and fitness of its own measures, public credit has gone far beyond its grasp.

As to a more able or successful prosecution of the war, he professed not to be sanguine in that hope. That the people will defend themselves, with spirit, whenever attacked, admits no doubt; but as far as the prosecution of the war rests with the Government, he despaired of any change in the manner, or any difference in the result. The Administration appeared to him not to have changed its habits. It continued to go on in its old party path—to revolve round its party centre, and to draw all its heat and its light, its animation and its being, from party sources. The measure

of ability with which the war had been conducted, was about equal to the measure of prudence with which it was declared; and the success of the issue, without a change of auspices, would probably be proportionate to both.

He had been struck with a paragraph in Mr. Jefferson's late letter. Speaking of the invasion of this place by the enemy, he says, he took advantage of this nation unarmed and unprepared. For the partial judgment of a friend, this is sufficiently severe. The Government took its own time to go to war. It invited the enemy to the conflict. It is attacked, two years afterward, in the centre of the nation, on the very threshold of the Capitol, and even there is found unarmed and unprepared.

The Government was indeed unprepared when it went to war. It has been unprepared ever since; and if the contest should not last more than twice as long as the war of the Greeks and the Trojans, it will come to an end, before the country, upon the present system of things, will be prepared for its beginning.

A state of mere unpreparedness, however, was not exactly the whole of our case, when war was declared. There was something in it worse than that, even aside from the character of the war itself, and the opinion which one half the nation had of it.

The country had had commerce, the abundant source of its revenue. A barbarous and unrelenting series of acts of self-murder, called restrictions, had put an end to that commerce. It had had a sinking fund, containing the sustaining, redeeming principles of public credit. This was abandoned. It had an useful National Banking Institution, with solid capital and on sound principles; and which had proved itself, by twenty years experience, to be capable of offering the most important facilities to the operations of finance. This also was destroyed. Having made these provisions for revenue, for public credit, and financial operations, the Government felt itself in a condition to invite a war.

From such a beginning, what else could be expected than we have seen to happen? While it remained on our part a war of invasion, nothing was done; and now, when in turn we are attacked by the enemy, the defence of the country rests on the people and on the States, almost unassisted by the aid of Government. In what quarter of the country does the Government afford efficient protection to the people? In most assailable places, the States are obliged to call out their militia upon their own responsibility, and the strength of their own resources; and here, at the heart of the nation, a force of five thousand men has routed and dispersed the Government, and scattered the ashes of the Capitol over the soil which claimed its peculiar and exclusive protection. He had said last session, and he repeated it now, that the Government had failed in the discharge of its first great duty—the main object of all Governments—the protection of the people.

He wished also the House and the country to consider how we stood with all the neutral Powers of Europe in relation to this war. It had been said by his honorable friend from New York (Mr. OAKLEY) that the ears of the European Courts were shut against us. He believed this to be perfectly true. The Administration itself knew better than any individual that it had not been able to excite the sympathies of a single Power in Europe, in its favor, on the subject of this war. The reason was obvious. The nations of Europe had seen the part this Government had acted. They had seen it come in, in the moment of European extremity and agony, and take part on the side of an always defeated and now fallen tyranny. Without discussing the question, of no importance to them, whether the measures of this Government grew out of a previous stipulation, signed and sealed, and interchanged with that of France, or whether in these measures it had acted gratuitously, and only followed the bent of its own inclination, they could not but take notice of the fact, that these measures were brought into play precisely at the moment when they were most likely to aid in the overthrow of the Governments, and the subjugation of the nations of Europe. It was difficult, he thought, to restrain one's indignation on this subject. If anything could make one ashamed of his country, it would be that its Government had been capable of acting such a part. How different would our situation be at this time, if the Government could say to England: "We have interfered in none of your European quarrels. We have sought to take no advantage of the pressure of your circumstances. A Republic, ourselves, and attached to the principles of political liberty, we have lent neither aid nor countenance to any projects formed against the general liberty or prosperity of Europe. We have held a course strictly and scrupulously impartial; and for proof of the correctness of our conduct in all these respects, we refer to the unbiassed judgment of neutral nations. We appeal to those who have been with you through the struggle which has now terminated, whether they suspect us of having had any leaning or partiality towards your "common enemy."

As to the negotiation and the terms of peace offered by England, Mr. W. said it would not be supposed that those who opposed the war as unnecessary and ruinous, were on that account to consent to any other than fair and honorable terms of peace. They held the Administration answerable for an honorable peace. The country's honor was unblemished, when they took the guardianship of its concerns, and it would be required at their hands equally unblemished. For one, he said, in no crisis, in no emergency, in no distress of national affairs, would he consent to a peace which should inflict a wound on the true honor or substantial interests of the country. But he did not affect to conceal his opinion; he wished, rather, on all proper occasions, to express it, that there was no chance of coercing England, or even of defending the country successfully, until the power and strength of the nation should be called forth, and guided

by different hands. He wished, at the same time, to express his regret, that the American Commissioners had not proposed *their* terms of peace. He wished they had stated explicitly, whether the Government of this country had or had not given up the grounds upon which it originally went to war. If the British Commissioners looked for extravagant terms to be proposed by ours, it was not very unnatural that they should set out with terms as extravagant themselves. It is to be lamented, that having found out what were the terms of England, our Ministers did not propose their own terms, to the end that the world might see the difference. It may be a question fit for casuists, which partakes least of a pacific temper and moderate views, to propose terms of peace, which are deemed inadmissible, as was done by England, or to propose no terms at all, as was done by ourselves. If the American Ministers were instructed to make peace on fair and reasonable terms, it cannot be too much regretted that they did not make those terms known; because, in order to put the enemy completely in the wrong, it is necessary to show, not only that his terms were extravagant, but that ours were not so.

The publication of the documents here is relied on to satisfy the people of this country of the equity and moderation of the views of the Cabinet. If it should answer that purpose, still it does not answer the other, of making known its equity and moderation to England. Because, until now, that they are published here, England had no means of knowing the instructions given to our Ministers. She could only know that if you insisted now, on what you demanded when you went to war, your terms, in her estimation, were as inadmissible as hers are in yours.

But will the publication of *parts* of these instructions satisfy the people of this country that the Government has made fair terms of peace? If anything was published, why not the whole? If the part concealed is not material, why conceal it? In cases of this sort, it is obvious, that whatever has been previously done, may be undone by something subsequent. It is not like a series of correspondence between different parties. Unless the Government publishes the whole in this case it may as well publish nothing.

Mr. W. said he did not underrate the difficulties of the present crisis. He was well aware of all these difficulties. But he would not say, because he did not think that they were at all insurmountable with a wise and able Administration of Government. But it did appear to him, that the country had committed itself into the hands of men not likely to make peace, nor competent to conduct the war. This, he thought, our greatest difficulty, and he believed the nation would come to the same opinion.

In the meantime he should not obstruct; he should only hold himself at liberty not to approve, without reason, the course pursued. It could not be said, then, that the Administration was asked to do its duty while the means are refused; means will not be refused so far as they

466   HISTORY OF CONGRESS.   468

OCTOBER, 1814.   The Ways and Means.   H. OF R.

depend on measures here. Its measures will be carried here, and as far as the aid of this House can go, it will have it. But he should not give his vote for the measures proposed, either by way of expressing his approbation of the past, or his expectations for the future. On the past he looked with mixed emotions of indignation and grief; on the future with fearful forebodings and apprehensions, relieved only by the hope that the immediate adoption of better counsels might lead to better times.

When Mr. W. had concluded, the House adjourned.

TUESDAY, October 25.

The House proceeded to consider the message from the Senate, notifying that they insist on their amendments to the resolutions expressive of the sense of Congress of the gallantry and good conduct with which the reputation of the arms of the United States has been sustained by Major General Brown, Major General Scott, and Brigadiers Ripley, Miller, Porter, Gaines, and Macomb," and asking a conference thereon: Whereupon,

Resolved, That this House agree to the conference asked by the Senate, and that Mr. TROUP, Mr. WRIGHT, and Mr. STUART, be the managers at the same on their part.

WAYS AND MEANS.

The House resumed the consideration of the unfinished business, being the report of the Committee of Ways and Means recommending the imposition of additional taxes; and the first resolution, for adding 100 per cent. to the present amount of the direct taxes, being on its passage—

Mr. RHEA, of Tennessee, spoke at length in support of the resolve, and in reply to Mr. WEBSTER's speech of yesterday.

Mr. CALHOUN said, he did not rise to consider whether the war was originally just and necessary; or whether the Administration had abandoned the original objects of the contest; much less, whether the Opposition, according to the very modest declaration of the member from New Hampshire, (Mr. WEBSTER,) possessed all of the talent and confidence of the country. His object was to call the attention of this House to the necessity of prompt and vigorous measures for the prosecution of the war. If ever a body of men held the destinies of a country in their hands, it was that which he was now addressing. You have for an enemy a Power the most implacable and formidable; who, now freed from any other contest, will, the very next campaign, direct the whole of his force against you. Besides his deep rooted enmity against this country, which will urge him to exertion, the enemy is aware of the necessity, on his part, to bring the contest to a speedy termination. He dreads its continuance; for he well knows, that should it be maintained by us with vigor, for only a few years, there will be other parties to the struggle, which may again involve him in a war with all Europe. He then will put forth, from spite and policy, the whole of his strength the very next Summer, to crush

us if possible by one mighty effort. To meet this state of things, the whole of the resources will have to be called into action; and, what is of equal importance, with such promptitude as to be ready to act as soon as the season will admit. What then are the duties which devolve on this House, and which must be performed in order that we may be in a state of desirable preparation to meet and maintain the struggle? This is the question which he proposed to consider, not indeed in detail, or with great accuracy, but generally, in order that we may be aware of the urgent necessity for despatch. First, then, it will be absolutely necessary to pass these resolutions, or some others of equal vigor, into laws. Our finances it is acknowledged are much deranged; and it is also admitted, on all sides, that they can only be restored by a vigorous system of taxes. Has any member estimated how much time this will consume. It is now the 25th of October, and we have not passed even the resolutions; at the same rate of proceeding, to settle all the complexity of the detail of bills, and pass them into laws, will require months. In the next place, it will be necessary (he presumed no member could doubt it) to take the state of the circulating medium into consideration; and to devise some measure to render it more safe, and adapted to the purposes of finance. The single fact, that we have no proper medium, commensurate in its circulation with the Union—that it is all local—is calculated to produce much embarrassment in the operation of the Treasury. But, sir, after we have passed the taxes and established an adequate circulating medium, which must of necessity, with the closest attention, consume much time, much still will remain to be done. The Army, to which the President has so strongly called our attention, has not yet claimed a moment of our time. He would not pretend to anticipate the plan which the Military Committee would doubtless submit to this House, but he would state what appeared to him indispensable to give the greatest effect, with the most economy, to our arms. He did not wish to be understood parsimony, but that which gave to the amount expended the greatest effect.

The enemy at present presses the war both on our seaboard and interior frontier. The nature of the war on either, will, if properly considered, indicate the mode, that it ought to be met and resisted. On the seaboard it must be strictly defensive. The enemy can make no permanent conquest of any importance there; but he hopes, by alarming and harassing the country, and putting us to an enormous expense in defending it, to break the spirit of the nation, and bring it to his own terms. The only remedy in our hand, without a marching force, is to fortify as strongly as possible the cities and exposed points, and to garrison them with a sufficient number of experienced regular troops. In case of an attack, they are to be aided by militia of the cities and adjacent country, called out on the occasion en masse which can be done without much vexation or expense. It is thus by having respectable garrisons of regular troops, aided as he has stated, and supported by strong works, we will afford more security, and will save millions of expense. The present militia force he supposed, in actual service, could not be much short of one hundred thousand. Less that half that number of regulars could be made abundantly adequate to the defence of our seaboard.

On the Canada frontier the war must assume an opposite character. If we wish to act with effect, it must there be wholly offensive. He did hope the miserably stale and absurd objections against offensive operations in Canada had ceased, till he heard yesterday the member from New Hampshire (Mr. Webster.) It was so obviously the cheapest and most effectual mode of operating on our enemy, that thinking men, he believed, with little exception, of all parties, had agreed in its expediency. For, suppose that we should have at the opening of the next campaign a sufficient force on the Canada frontier for its reduction; and what would then be the result? Either our enemy must call off the whole of his force to defend himself in that quarter, or he must permit it to fall into our possession. Either event would be desirable. If the enemy should adopt the former, as in all probability he would be compelled to do, our seaboard would be freed from danger and alarm, and we would have the further advantage of meeting him on equal terms. He would no longer be aided by his maritime superiority. If, however, he should not strengthen himself in Canada, but continue the war on the coast, it would be still more to our advantage. The reduction of his possessions, besides shedding a glory on our arms, and producing both here and in England the happiest effects in our favor, would enable us to maintain the struggle with half the expense in men and money. After so desirable an event our efforts might be almost exclusively directed to the defence of the seaboard, and the war would assume a new aspect highly favorable to this country.

To cause so desirable a state of things, a regular force of at least fifty thousand men ought to be ready to act against Canada by the first of May or June, at farthest. If they could be immediately raised and marched to their proper depots for training, they could in a few months be well trained for service. He was well assured that the brilliant battles of Bridgewater and Chippewa were won by men, three-fourths of whom had not been in the ranks more than four months. With skilful officers, and with the aptitude of the Americans to acquire the military art, the finest army in a few months might be formed. He said, he could not refrain from congratulating this House and country on the acquisition we had made, in so short a time, of military skill. It was wonderful, almost incredible, that in a year or two, with very little opportunity, such Generals should be found as have the last Summer led our Army to glory. No country, under all of these circumstances, ever in so short a time developed so much military talent. Put under their command without delay a sufficient force, well

appointed, and you will then find yourselves in the road to honor and secure peace. But, can this be done by idle debate, by discussing the origin of the war, and the relative talent and virtue of the two great parties in this country? Now is our time, not for debate, but action. Much is to be done. We have not a moment to lose. Time is to us everything, men, money, honor, glory, and peace. Should we consume it in debate, and let the moments for preparation glide away, our affairs must be irretrievably ruined. Compare what remains to be done with the time for action, and it is certain, that to act promptly is as important as to act at all. Under these impressions, he hoped that the House would pass this day on all the resolutions; and that they would be referred back to the Committee to report bills immediately; and that whatever was needful to our early and complete preparation, would be promptly despatched. The enemy is already arrived, and, as soon as permitted by the season, will strike with deadly intention; let us be ready to receive and return the blow with redoubled force. We are placed in circumstances the most urgent and imperious. Our supposed weakness has tempted the enemy to make his extraordinary demands. Who that bears the heart of an American can think of them without the most just indignation? Surrender the Lakes to his control; renounce the fisheries, that nursery for seamen; cede a part of Maine, and all beyond the Greenville line, and recognise the Indians as their allies, and under their protection. Such is his language. He relies not so much on his own strength as our weakness and disunion. Let it be our most serious business, by vigor and promptitude, to baffle and destroy his vain hopes. If we fail, it will not be for the want of means, but because we have not used them. We have generals and troops that have proved themselves an over match for the choicest of the enemy's battalions, commanded by her most boasted officers. To this evidence of skill and courage, superadd preparations on our part equal to our resources; by this means you will make him sensible of his presumption, and listen to terms of peace honorable to both nations. He has it in his power at all times to make such a peace. Every member who hears me, knows this to be the fact, notwithstanding the unjust and unfounded insinuations of the member from New Hampshire (Mr. Webster) to the contrary. He observed again, that England dreaded a continuance of the contest. The affairs of Europe are far from being settled. Her relation in a commercial point of view is calculated to raise up powerful enemies on the Continent. Should she be foiled and disgraced here, which she must be if we but do our duty, the opportunity so favorable to humble her will be seized. Of these facts she is sensible; and our very preparation for a vigorous war will make her dread the contest. But, suppose, instead of vigorous and prompt preparation, we consume our time in debate here, and permit our affairs to go on in the consequent slow and feeble way. Where is the man so blind as to believe that England will limit her views

469 HISTORY OF CONGRESS. 470

469   **HISTORY OF CONGRESS.**   470

OCTOBER, 1814.   *The Ways and Means.*   H. OF R.

by her present demands, as extravagant as they are? We are already told, that she will proportion her future demands to the relative situation of the two countries. She neither expected nor desired peace on the terms which were offered. Her bosom is repossessed with the ambition and projects that inspired her in the year '76. It is the war of the Revolution revived; we are again struggling for our liberty and independence. The enemy stands ready, and eagerly watches to seize any opportunity which our feebleness or division may present, to realize his gigantic schemes of conquest. In this struggle for existence, he must entreat the members of the Opposition, though they can reconcile it to their conscience to stand with folded arms and coldly look on, not to impede by idle and frivolous debate the efforts of those who are ready by every sacrifice to maintain the independence of the country. The subject is weighty; he felt himself pressed on all sides by the most interesting topics; but he would abstain from further observation, lest he who admonished against the consumption of the time of the House in long debate, should set an example of it in himself. The time is precious. He felt that he owed an apology for consuming so much as he had done.

Mr. WEBSTER, of New Hampshire, spoke briefly in explanation.

Mr. FISK, of Vermont, in his usual pointed manner assigned the reason which induced him to vote for the increased tax.

Mr. SHIPHERD addressed the Chair as follows:

Mr. Speaker, although we have been solemnly admonished, by a gentleman from South Carolina, (Mr. CALHOUN,) to waste no more time in idle debate, as he is pleased to call the arguments on the question before the House, you will pardon me if I venture yet to exercise the privilege of the Representative of a free people, and frankly express my reasons for the vote I shall give against the resolution before you. The question, sir, is a momentous one, and ought not to be hurried. To dash into a measure so interesting to our constituents without deliberation, would be rash and imprudent.

If the convictions of my mind would permit, I should most cordially vote in this case with the majority. Had their side of the question the least perceptible advantage, nothing would give me more pleasure than to add a vote to their number. For, sir, I declare most sincerely and truly, that any opposition of mine, is from no desire to give new asperity to party animosity. Fain would I hush its bickerings, and, if possible, drive the fiend from our country, and extinguish her torch.

No man, more than myself, can wish to conciliate, and, in the patriotic desire to save the country from ruin, lose forever those prejudices which have long been an evil deeply to be lamented. Fain would I, if possible, convince the majority by a cordial co-operation when they are right, and a dispassionate opposition when wrong, of a disposition, on our part, to seek and promote the welfare of the nation, and to support any discreet measure whether it shall come from this or that side of the House.

Sir, gentlemen ought not to resent opposition. The dearest and strongest convictions may impel the legislator zealously to resist what a majority may as sincerely think right. Members of the same party think and vote differently on particular questions, and yet it is productive of no resentments.

Such, sir, ought to be our charity towards those who oppose even our most favorite objects, especially if they are in the least doubtful, as to believe they act from a sense of duty, unless we have sufficient evidence of a different disposition. Indiscriminate condemnation of the motives of an antagonist is certainly no less than odious intolerance, which must be avoided, to perpetuate the blessings of freedom.

But, sir, however strong I may desire union and a perfect good understanding between the different sides of this House, an aberration from duty, or the abandonment of an opinion formed after a long and deliberate examination of the subject, would be a sacrifice too great, and therefore cannot be made. From such examination I have formed an opinion, and therefore proceed to give this House the view I have taken of the subject.

It is said by gentlemen on the other side, in substance, that the Treasury is without money, Government without credit, and the armies without men. That the Union is in danger, and, unless prompt and sufficient aids are furnished by the Legislature, we shall be ruined. To this statement of facts I subscribe. The evidences are too strong to be doubted; and, because such is the state of the nation, am I opposed to the resolution, and the reasons urged for an affirmative vote will induce me to give a negative. If we are ruined, who has been the despoiler? Surely it cannot be charged upon those who, for fourteen years, have been deprived of the means of doing good or evil to the Government; men who have been declared unworthy to participate in the administration of our public affairs. Sir, it must be charged to your public agents as having produced this mighty ruin.

There was a time, Mr. Speaker, when the Government was wisely administered, and the speedy fruits were fame, wealth, peace, and prosperity, to the Government and people.

The Union was a splendid luminary, whose light attracted the attention, and excited the admiration, of the civilized world. The surest earnest of permanency and stability seemed to be given, and we fondly thought that remote generations would partake of the blessings of our admired institutions.

When the power was wrested from the men of other times, the Treasury was full, our credit was high, and the revenue annually increasing. No calamities, no evils, either existed or threatened to impede the nation in the career of prosperity. Every class of citizens felt the happy influence of a free Government, administered with wisdom and benignity.

The glory of those times appears more conspicuous, contrasted with the gloom and misery of the present. And the wisdom which had framed the Government, and given it motion and direction, was so powerful and correct, that for years it endured the hard service of novel and ruinous experiment ; and, for aught we know, might have continued, had not the way of success been blocked up, and the Government jostled from its original course.

If, then, sir, the high officers of the nation have so managed our political concerns, as to sink us from a proud and lofty station to the very depths of poverty and disgrace, dry up the sources of revenue, load it with debt, and make us contemptible in our own and the eyes of the nations, it becomes us well to examine, and seriously to inquire whether it will be prudent to burden our constituents with oppressive taxes ; vainly hoping to retrieve our lost credit by replenishing our empty Treasury, to be laid out under the agency of the very men who have given us so many sad examples of a destitution of those qualities which only ought to invite confidence.

Where is our guarantee that the money forced from our suffering fellow-citizens, will be expended with less prodigality than the millions which have been squandered in unavailing experiments or lavished upon worthless men ? Will it be denied, that the country swarms with such, and that they have been too much the favorites of power for the interest of the grand community ? If a pledge of reformation can or is to be given, let us see it. Convince us that the Executive has become trustworthy, and obtain the united confidence of the House. But, sir, we are to have no such pledge, not even a promise; on the contrary, the same phantoms are to be chased, the same ruinous measures to be adopted, and this is openly avowed upon this floor. We, therefore, are not permitted to hope for a change, or even conjecture that new measures may produce a new and happy result. Nothing before us but an obstinate determination to persist in that course, the end of which is inevitable ruin.

Mr. Speaker, it is fair and correct to calculate from what has been, what will be the effect of the same causes, and therefore, from experience, ought we to judge of the fitness of any proposition, more especially when a nation's interests, a nation's salvation, is depending. It is high time to dismiss the dreams and visions that have bewildered and led us astray. From the past, let us, as we love our country, look to the future, and, guided by this sure index, determine. In the exercise of sober sense, ask ourselves whether we can, with a due regard to the interests of this much injured nation, call upon it so loudly. To me this subject appears big with importance. The consequences may yet be lamented.

It must require a faith not imposed, a charity which would savor more of weakness than piety, to believe or anticipate a renewing spirit hereafter to prevail in the management of our pecuniary concerns, so long as the managers remain unaltered. There is no demonstration more clear than that, under the charge of the men who have wasted the public finances and destroyed your credit, your country will sink deeper and deeper in ruin.

If the majority, sir, possessed any inclination to cheer the desponding hopes of the nation or brighten its prospects, and thereby invite the confidence and co-operation of the minority, their President would give some token that he had abandoned the old and ruinous course, and designed to seek one, new and more promising. He would even now have emptied his Cabinet of a group of deluded and deluding Ministers, by whom he has been misled, whose conduct has palpably proved a defect of head or heart, or both, and replenished it with the first choice of the States, regardless of party distinction. But, sir, he has seen the ship sinking, and retains, in despite of the most awful premonitions, the same pilot and helmsman. Permit me, sir, to enforce the observations already made, and those which may be made, by example, and then judge of the Chief of your Government.

The example remains a monument of disgrace to this metropolis. Look at the walls of your once magnificent Capitol. Where now is all its grandeur, its lofty arches and proud columns with the costly garnishing that delighted the eye, and afforded ease, convenience, and elegance, to the Representatives of the people?

They are gone, and what remains is a striking proof of the impotence, the folly, not to say cowardice, of the men, who, had they been as they ought to have been, would have abandoned, only with life or liberty, this ornament of your city to the torches of your enemy. But unresisted, undisturbed, the hated foe was permitted to destroy the very Hall where, but about two years before, this proud boast was vauntingly made, "My word for it, if you will declare war, in six months the Canadas will be ours." Yes, sir, to the disgrace of our country, the very Hall where the question of peace and war was debated, and the declaration of the latter was solemnly adopted, fell a sacrifice to the enemy who were so contemptibly thought of.

Permit me also, sir, to present you the palace of your President in flames, or, if you please, its yawning ruins, and the offices of State, and above all your navy yard, and the ashes of the frigate and sloop-of-war; and, lastly, your President, Secretary of War, of the Navy, the Commanding General, and seven thousand men, flying before a handful of marauding British, worn down with fatigue and melted with heat. And, sir, we are now asked with the most earnest importunity to intrust these men who gave up to certain destruction this immense property, without even an effort to save it, with twenty-one or two millions of dollars more. The destruction of the navy yard was such an act of imprudence that it indicated lunacy. Not content with the firebrand of the enemy, perhaps praying that his ruthless hand might spare some part of the public property, the high officer, whose duty it was to protect it, orders it all to be burned.

473 HISTORY OF CONGRESS. 474

October, 1814. *The Ways and Means.* H. of R.

Military gentlemen, Mr. Speaker, say all this vast property might have been defended, together with this city. Why burn the navy yard? Why the sloop-of-war, which had her guns on board and prepared for action, and might have been used to defend the place where she was built; and as a last resort could have been saved by choosing the middle or eastern shore of the Potomac?

But no, she must be burned. The frigate on the stocks, together with the immense property of the excellent establishment at the navy yard, must all be devoted to the indiscretion of the honorable Secretary. No one, sir, will pretend to say that this property could have been carried off or used by the enemy. Steam engines, forges, workshops, sawmills, and vessels, are not convenient for a knapsack, or even a baggage wagon. Why then burn this necessary and valuable property?

It is answered, it was burned to prevent the enemy from taking it. Supposing they had done so, it is certain they could have done no more than destroyed it; they might, it is true, have so done, and probably would, if no attempt was made to defend it. A few more heroic souls, however, like Barney and Miller, would unquestionably have taught your enemy, by experience sad and fatal to them, that the rights and property of the nation were not to be infringed with impunity.

But supposing the worst, that the enemy had done the same that was done in pursuance of the Secretary's peremptory order, and had burned this admirable establishment; in point of property, the loss to the nation would have been no greater; in point of character, infinitely better. And, after a faithful experiment, if we had failed, it was but to abandon it to the invaders to spare or destroy at their election. Hence, sir, it is most obvious that there was no necessity of committing this detestable suicide.

Here it may be asked, how this reasoning concerns the subject before the House? I will show you, sir, in a few words, that your Chief Magistrate in particular is responsible for this shameful transaction. He, his Secretary of War, and of the Navy, were on the field of battle, or rather of flight. Was it then by their orders or the order of either of them, that the metropolis was cowardly given up to be sacked by an enemy not one-third of the number of our troops? And whether this base desertion was caused by either the one or the other of the three, or the Commanding General, in either case your President, sir, is responsible to the nation for the loss and disgrace attached to the transaction. How? If it was by his order, then he is answerable directly. If by either of the pair of Secretaries, then it became him, indeed it was an indispensable duty, to have inquired, and dismissed from office the man whose examples proved him unworthy of his station. If it was from the mere motion of the Commanding General, he should have caused an immediate arrest, tried and punished him for disgracing his nation and office. A severe sentence was pronounced against General Hull for cowardice, and his surely was a venial transaction compared with the flight from Bladensburg.

I would not be understood as charging General Winder with unmilitary conduct. I had ever supposed him a brave and honorable man, and without more proof I wish still so to consider him; and for the sake of this argument it is immaterial whether he is guilty or innocent. In either case your President must be answerable. That some one is guilty cannot be doubted, and it behooved the President to seek redress for the nation who had entrusted him with the prerogatives of his exalted station. Now, sir, let us inquire what was done to satisfy the loud claims of an injured people; what to retrieve their lost honor? Nothing—just nothing. It is true a proclamation was issued, and the enemy *"vandalized"* with sufficient heat and asperity; but the Secretary of War, who had become so odious to the people that a universal murmur of discontent was heard in every direction, and whose infamy is attested with chalk and charcoal in rude prose and verse upon the solitary walls of your Capitol, was solicited, entreated by the President still to retain his office. He could not endure the thought of parting with his dear friend—this precious officer.

You have, sir, already been pointed to the destruction of the navy yard. It is presumed no one doubts that the Secretary of the Navy ordered this destruction; an indiscretion, to say the least, so extraordinary that not a single apologist can be found to excuse or justify the transaction. Well, sir, where is he; dismissed from office as not trustworthy? No, sir; but basking in the smiles of the President—not a whisper from his lips disapproving the act.

If the Commanding General was guilty, where is he? Still in favor without inquiry and without censure.

If it is the unyielding determination of the President to retain such men in office, to suffer the country to be disgraced without requiring satisfaction from, or inflicting punishment upon, the authors, what, sir, is there left to encourage the people to shed their blood or pay their money in a cause that affords not a ray of hope? The heart sinks with despondence at the prospect.

We are asked with emphasis, "Will you suffer the enemy to overrun the country without opposition, jeopardize the Union, and submit to recolonization? Will you unnerve the arm of Government by withholding men and money for defence?" Sir, could we believe that voting men and money would produce the promised effect there would be a sufficient inducement to the minority to afford every encouragement towards the support of the common cause. Had we but reasonable grounds to hope that the money would be expended to save the country, for one I should feel it a duty to contribute my feeble aid in furnishing the Administration with cash and character. The minority possess as ardent desires to serve and ennoble their country as can be felt on the other side; but examples—actions that speak louder than promises—demonstrate the certainty, if men and money should be voted, of a failure of the desired object. The regular armies are not intended by the men in power for defence, and the money will not be expended for that purpose. If the Capitol of the nation, the offices of State, indeed the palace of the President, were given up by the high officers, who were present, to ravage and conflagration, without an attempt to defend them, what reason have we to believe that other parts of the Union, less dear and interesting to the Cabinet, are to find in our armies a more prompt and effectual shield? Where, sir, is the benefit in building ships of war, if our own torches are to burn them before they leave the ways or harbors where they were launched? But our country must and will be defended, and to reason from facts, not by the armies under the control of your President, but by the militia of the States; not by the money we may here vote to levy upon our suffering fellow-citizens, but at the expense of the States. Look, sir, at the examples before you since the commencement of hostilities and see how many instances of defence can be found from regular troops. Detroit had regulars, but no defence at the Niagara frontier, Sackett's Harbor, the seaboard in the South, Baltimore. In the Eastern States the militia have almost alone opposed their breasts to an invading enemy; and at New London they not only defended the State, but your vessels of war.

At Plattsburg you have had a striking comment upon the text. While the enemy, sir, with a formidable army hovered upon the frontier line, General Izard, by whose order I know not, drew off about four thousand of the regulars, and left, says the official account, but fifteen hundred, to oppose Governor Prevost with fourteen thousand. A place where our fleet, if necessary, might have been protected, and where, when no enemy, a large regular army was stationed, was instantly abandoned when the enemy began to approach; and while the hosts of General Izard were marching South from the field of danger, the militia were marching North towards it; and while this regular army were enjoying the scene at Lake George, a place of fashionable resort, or admiring the stupendous scenery at Glenn's Falls, the militia were fighting the British upon the banks of Saranac; and this same General Izard and army passed through Sackett's Harbor, to give another opportunity to the militia, if invaded, to show how capable they were of defending their country. Add to all this, the General Government have refused to indemnify Massachusetts the expense of defence by her militia.

New York is garrisoned principally by militia, and the city has obtained by loan a million of dollars to defray the expenses. Whether the Government will ultimately reimburse them this large sum, remains to be known.

This, sir, is the state of the country. Such is the conduct of men who guide its destinies; therefore I beg to be forgiven if I withhold my confidence from them, and my vote to furnish

them with means not to be used for defence, but, for I know not what new and idle scheme that may strike the infatuated mind.

One of the first objects of the Union, was the more effectual protection of the States; and while they engaged to pour their wealth into the coffers of the General Government, the Government undertook to reciprocate the contribution, by affording the arms of the Union, in all its strength, for the security and protection of the commerce and soil of the United States.

The commerce is long since fallen a miserable sacrifice to the experiments of the Government; an enemy has been provoked to attack our soil. In the name of common justice permit me to ask, what right can you have to demand money of the States from which you withhold your promised protection? The moment, sir, that the contracted reciprocity is broken then you have violated the bond of union, and you deprive yourself of the right to ask for men or money. Indeed, sir, you absolve the States from their obligation to furnish you with either.

I deny, sir, that the compact on the part of Government has been fulfilled—it has ceased to do its duty—and there is too much reason to doubt the fidelity to place any confidence in the Government. Therefore, sir, if you divest the States of the means of defending themselves, by draughting away their men and taking away their money, you not only infringe the instrument, by virtue of which you claim the power, but you do an act of injustice—you grieve and oppress. Go on with the proposed plans of invasion, taxes, and perhaps conscriptions, and what will be the consequence? You will beggar the people, provoke the enemy of your own creating to invade the States, and then, after you have deprived them of the means of security, they will be left naked and ruined, to fall a prey to the power of an enemy enraged by your unsuccessful invasions.

It is said the Union is in danger, "and, unless we furnish the Government with prompt and effectual means, it will be too late." Sir, the Union, to all beneficial purposes, is already gone. Nothing but a name and shadow is left; a shadow intangible, empty, and evanescent. Inquire, sir, for it is worth your inquiry, what are the benefits contemplated by your Constitution that remain to the people? Can you vouch that there is one? It has been shown, that commerce and protection do not exist in any measure in the General Government. Its credit is gone, its strength is worn out, and pardon me when I say that the word Union cannot be applied to a people among whom nothing but a political bond exists, and that so worn and weakened that it binds to no beneficial purpose.

It has been also said, over the way, that "union is necessary to carry on the war, and give credit to the Government." It is much to be lamented that this consideration (which is by no means new) had not prevailed before the war was declared. Gentlemen will not deny that the warning voice of the minority told them the danger of declaring war against the feelings and wishes, if not of a majority, at least of a powerful minority of the people. Yes, sir, they were warned with a voice, solemn, argumentative, and prophetic, and the destructive result has proved with what accuracy the contemned expostulation of the minority were scorned. It is said that gentlemen are too late in calling for help. The Union is convulsed with those awful spasms that are the too certain precursors of dissolution.

An honorable gentleman from South Carolina (Mr. Calhoun) observed, that we must have fifty thousand men raised for the next campaign, to invade the Canadas. How, sir, can they be raised? The most extravagant bounties for soldiers have been offered, and to little purpose; few have been enlisted, and it is thought still fewer will enlist on a further attempt; and, could you raise a large army, Canada is strongly defended, and defies your power.

The flower of the American army have made an attempt; they have fought well; have richly earned thanks and praise for themselves, and medals for their Generals; they have conquered, and how far have they progressed into the enemy's country? Merely obtained a foothold; and, in so doing, the army is almost annihilated. A few more victories like those would leave us destitute of a soldier—would leave us glory and ruin.

The same gentleman also observed, that "the aspect of the war was changed, and had now become defensive." In fact, sir, this is correct. Our enemy have become more powerful by their victories, and the consequent peace in Europe. The face of our affairs has changed in another respect. When the war was declared we were to take the Canadas in six weeks, and, after three campaigns, we have much less of their country than they have of ours. The change of the aspect of the war, it seems, ought to admonish us to beware. If, when the enemy had Europe to fight, we were unable to invade them with success, from whence do we derive a hope that we can now succeed, when we are their only enemy? I beseech gentlemen to deceive themselves no longer, but to abandon those airy schemes which can never be realized; which serve only to sink and ruin their country.

I would ask the honorable gentleman how, if he had money, he will obtain men for the invasion? Surely he cannot be ignorant that men will not enlist for that purpose; and I beg of the majority to reflect well before they attempt to force men into the ranks. The free and brave men of the North and East will never submit to the attempt. They will resist to blood those who shall encroach upon their liberties, and lamented consequences might follow such an attempt. The aspect of the war in such a case would change and become purely defensive, but it would wear frowns more terrible to the invaders than America has ever witnessed.

When Mr. S. had concluded—

A division of the question having been called on the resolution respecting the direct tax, the first question put was on the following part: "Resolved, that it is expedient to continue the direct tax." On this question, the votes were—For the motion 104, against it 26, as follows:

Yeas—Messrs. Alexander, Alston, Anderson, Avery, Barbour, Bard, Barnett, Bowen, Bradley, Brown, Burwell, Butler, Caperton, Caldwell, Calhoun, Cannon, Chappell, Clark, Clopton, Comstock, Condict, Conard, Crawford, Creighton, Crouch, Culpeper, Cuthbert, Dana, Davis of Pennsylvania, Denoyelles, Desha, Duvall, Earle, Eppes, Evans, Farrow, Fisk of Vermont, Fisk of New York, Forney, Forsyth, Franklin, Gaston, Gholson, Glasgow, Goldsborough, Goodwyn, Griffin, Grosvenor, Hall, Hanson, Harris, Hasbrouck, Hawes, Hawkins, Hopkins of Kentucky, Humphreys, Hungerford, Ingham, Irving, Johnson of Virginia, Johnson of Kentucky, Kennedy, Kent of New York, Kent of Maryland, Kerr, Kershaw, Kilbourn, King of North Carolina, Lefferts, Lowndes, Lyle, Macon, McCoy, McKee, McLean, Montgomery, Moore, Nelson, Newton, Oakley, Ormsby, Pearson, Pickens, Pleasants, Rhea of Tennessee, Rich, Ringgold, Robertson, Sage, Schureman, Seybert, Sharp, Smith of New York, Smith of Virginia, Stanford, Strong, Tannehill, Taylor, Telfair, Troup, Udree, Ward of New Jersey, Wilson of Pennsylvania, and Yancey.

Nays—Messrs. Baylies of Massachusetts, Bradbury, Brigham, Davenport, Hale, Hulbert, Jackson of Rhode Island, King of Massachusetts, Lovett, Markell, Moffit, Pickering, Pitkin, Post, Potter, John Reed, Ruggles, Shipherd, Sturges, Taggart, Thompson, Vose, Ward of Massachusetts, Wheaton, White, and Wilcox.

The question was then taken on the remaining clause of the resolution, "and to increase the same 100 per cent."—and decided as follows:

Yeas—Messrs. Alexander, Anderson, Avery, Barbour, Bard, Barnett, Bowen, Brown, Burwell, Butler, Caldwell, Cannon, Chappell, Clark, Clopton, Comstock, Condict, Conard, Crawford, Creighton, Crouch, Cuthbert, Dana, Davis of Pennsylvania, Denoyelles, Desha, Duvall, Earle, Eppes, Evans, Farrow, Fisk of Vermont, Fisk of New York, Forney, Forsyth, Gholson, Glasgow, Goodwyn, Griffin, Hall, Hanson, Harris, Hawes, Hawkins, Hopkins of Kentucky, Humphreys, Hungerford, Ingham, Irving, Johnson of Virginia, Johnson of Kentucky, Kennedy, Kent of Maryland, Kerr, Kershaw, Kilbourn, King of North Carolina, Lefferts, Lowndes, Lyle, McCoy, McKee, McLean, Montgomery, Moore, Nelson, Newton, Oakley, Ormsby, Pickens, Pleasants, William Reed, Rhea of Tennessee, Rich, Ringgold, Robertson, Sage, Seybert, Sharp, Smith of Virginia, Strong, Tannehill, Taylor, Telfair, Troup, Udree, Ward of New Jersey, Wilson of Pennsylvania, and Yancey—89

Nays—Messrs. Baylies of Massachusetts, Bradbury, Brigham, Caperton, Cooper, Culpeper, Davenport, Franklin, Gaston, Goldsborough, Hale, Hulbert, Jackson of Rhode Island, King of Massachusetts, Lovett, Macon, Markell, Moffit, Pearson, Pickering, Pitkin, Post, Potter, John Reed, Ruggles, Schureman, Shipherd, Smith of New York, Stanford, Sturges, Taggart, Thompson, Vose, Ward of Massachusetts, Wheaton, White, and Wilcox—37

So it was determined to continue the present direct tax, and increase the same 100 per cent.

The second resolution, "to increase the duty on spirits distilled by an additional duty of twelve and a half cents per gallon," being under consideration, together with the amendment made in Committee of the Whole, going to increase the same to 15 cents per gallon—

Mr. FISK, of New York, renewed his motion to insert twenty-five instead of fifteen.

Mr. GASTON, of North Carolina, in the course of discussion, moved to lay on the table so much of the report of the Committee of the Whole as applies to the resolution; which motion was agreed to; and then the House adjourned.

WEDNESDAY, October 26.

Mr. INGERSOLL presented a petition of Stephen Girard, banker, of Philadelphia, setting forth that the provisions of the act laying duties on the notes of banks, bankers, and certain companies, which allows a composition, have been denied to him in his banking establishment, and praying that the provisions of said act may be extended to him.—Referred to the Committee of Ways and Means.

The SPEAKER laid before the House a letter from the Postmaster-General, stating that no official books or papers were lost, belonging to that Department, in consequence of the late incursion of the enemy.

WAYS AND MEANS.

The House resumed the consideration of the unfinished business, being the question on the motion of Mr. FISK, of New York, to strike out fifteen (the proposed increase of the tax) and insert twenty-five cents per gallon, in addition to the present duty on the capacity of the still.

Mr. WRIGHT, of Maryland, spoke in favor of an early decision of the question, on this and other parts of the report of the Committee of Ways and Means.

Mr. WILSON, of Pennsylvania, spoke in opposition to Mr. FISK's motion, at some length, for reasons of a practical nature.

The question on Mr. FISK's motion was then determined in the negative—yeas 67, nays 74, as follows:

YEAS—Messrs. Anderson, Avery, Baylies of Massachusetts, Bigelow, Boyd, Bradbury, Bradley, Butler, Chappell, Cilley, Comstock, Condict, Cooper, Davenport, Denoyelles, Ely, Evans, Fisk of Vermont, Fisk of New York, Forsyth, Gaston, Grosvenor, Hale, Hulbert, Ingersoll, Irving, Jackson of Rhode Island, Kennedy, Kent of New York, King of Massachusetts, Lovett, Lowndes, Markell, Moffit, Moseley, Nelson, Pickering, Pitkin Post, Potter, John Reed, William Reed, Rich, Robertson, Ruggles, Sage, Schureman, Seybert, Sherwood, Shipherd, Skinner, Smith of New York, Strong, Sturges, Taggart, Taylor, Telfair, Troup, Vose, Ward of Massachusetts, Ward of New Jersey, Webster, Wheaton, Wilcox, Wilson of Massachusetts, Winter, and Wright.

NAYS—Messrs. Alexander, Alston, Barbour, Bard, Barnett, Bowen, Brigham, Brown, Burwell, Caldwell, Calhoun, Cannon, Clark, Clopton, Conard, Crawford, Creighton, Crouch, Culpeper, Cuthbert, Davis of Pennsylvania, Desha, Duvall, Earle, Eppes, Farrow, Forney, Franklin, Geddes, Gholson, Glasgow, Goodwyn, Griffin, Hall, Harris, Hasbrouck, Hawes, Hawkins, Hubbard, Humphreys, Hungerford, Johnson of Virginia, Johnson

of Kentucky, Kent of Maryland, Kerr, Kershaw, Kilbourn, King of North Carolina, Law, Lefferts, Lewis, Lyle, Macon, McKee, McLean, Montgomery, Moore, Newton, Ormsby, Pickens, Piper, Pleasants, Rhea of Tennessee, Ringgold, Sevier, Sharp, Smith of Virginia, Stanford, Tannehill, Thompson, Udree, White, Wilson of Pennsylvania, and Yancey.

This motion having been negatived—Mr. FISK moved to amend the amendment of the Committee of the Whole by inserting twenty, instead of fifteen cents per gallon.

The question on this motion was decided as follows:

YEAS—Messrs. Anderson, Avery, Barnett, Baylies of Massachusetts, Bigelow, Boyd, Bradbury, Bradley, Brigham, Butler, Chappell, Cilley, Comstock, Condict, Conard, Cooper, Crouch, Dana, Davenport, Denoyelles, Ely, Evans, Fisk of Vermont, Fisk of New York, Forsyth, Gaston, Gholson, Grosvenor, Hale, Hawes, Hulbert, Ingersoll, Irving, Jackson of Rhode Island, Kennedy, Kent of New York, King of Massachusetts, King of North Carolina, Lefferts, Lovett, Lowndes, Markell, Moffit, Moore, Moseley, Nelson, Pickering, Pitkin, Post, Potter, John Reed, William Reed, Rich, Robertson, Ruggles, Sage, Seybert, Sherwood, Skinner, Smith of New York, Strong, Sturges, Taggart, Taylor, Telfair, Troup, Vose, Ward of Massachusetts, Ward of New Jersey, Webster, Wheaton, Wilcox, Wilson of Massachusetts, Winter, and Wright—75.

NAYS—Messrs. Alexander, Alston, Barbour, Bard, Bayly of Virginia, Bowen, Brown, Burwell, Caldwell, Calhoun, Cannon, Clark, Clopton, Crawford, Creighton, Culpeper, Cuthbert, Davis of Pennsylvania, Desha, Duvall, Earle, Eppes, Farrow, Forney, Franklin, Geddes, Glasgow, Goodwyn, Griffin, Hall, Harris, Hasbrouck, Hawkins, Hubbard, Humphreys, Hungerford, Ingham, Jackson of Virginia, Johnson of Virginia, Johnson of Kentucky, Kent of Maryland, Kerr, Kershaw, Kilbourn, Law, Lewis, Lyle, Macon, McCoy, McKee, McLean, Montgomery, Newton, Ormsby, Pearson, Pickens, Piper, Pleasants, Rhea of Tennessee, Ringgold, Sevier, Sharp, Smith of Virginia, Stanford, Thompson, Udree, White, Wilson of Pennsylvania, and Yancey—69.

So this amendment was carried.

And the amendment of the Committee of the Whole, as last amended, was decided as follows: Affirmative votes 70, negative 60.

So the amendment as amended (that is, to insert twenty, instead of twelve and a half cents per gallon, as the additional tax) was agreed to.

Mr. YANCEY, of North Carolina, then moved an amendment going to place a duty of —— cents on every gallon of spirits from domestic materials, instead of dividing it between the capacity and product of the still.

Mr. Y. spoke in support of his amendment, which he conceived necessary to do equal justice to all distillers. &c.

Mr. MACON, of North Carolina, spoke in support of the motion. He acknowledged the necessity of providing a revenue, and there was no better subject of taxation than spirits, provided it was not taxed higher than it could bear.

Mr. FARROW, of South Carolina, also spoke in favor of Mr. YANCEY's motion.

Mr. BAYLY, of Virginia, proposed to fill the blank in Mr. YANCEY's motion with twenty-five, and Mr. FISK, of New York, to fill it with thirty. But no motion was at present made on that head.

Mr. INGHAM, of Pennsylvania, opposed Mr. YANCEY's motion.

The question on Mr. YANCEY's motion was decided in the negative: For the amendment 55, against it 67, as follows:

YEAS—Messrs. Barbour, Barnett, Bayly of Virginia, Bowen, Burwell, Butler, Caperton, Caldwell, Cannon, Clark, Clopton, Crawford, Culpeper, Desha, Duvall, Farrow, Forney, Forsyth, Franklin, Gholson, Glasgow, Goodwyn, Hall, Harris, Hawkins, Hopkins of Kentucky, Humphreys, Hungerford, Johnson of Virginia, Johnson of Kentucky, Kennedy, Kerr, Kershaw, Kilbourn, King of North Carolina, Lewis, Lowndes, Lyle, Macon, McKee, McLean, Montgomery, Newton, Ormsby, Pearson, Pickens, Rhea of Tennessee, Sevier, Sharp, Skinner, Smith of Virginia, Stanford, Stuart, Telfair, and Yancey.

NAYS—Messrs. Alexander, Anderson, Avery, Bard, Baylies of Massachusetts, Bigelow, Boyd, Bradbury, Brown, Calhoun, Chappell, Cilley, Comstock, Condict, Conard, Creighton, Cuthbert, Dana, Davenport, Davis of Pennsylvania, Denoyelles, Ely, Eppes, Evans, Fisk of Vermont, Fisk of New York, Gaston, Geddes, Griffin, Hale, Hanson, Hawes, Ingersoll, Ingham, Irving, Jackson of Rhode Island, Kent of New York, Kent of Maryland, King of Massachusetts, Lefferts, Markell, McCoy, Moffit, Moseley, Nelson, Pickering, Pitkin, Pleasants, Post, John Reed, William Reed, Rich, Ruggles, Schureman, Seybert, Sherwood, Smith of New York, Strong, Sturges, Thompson, Udree, Ward of Massachusetts, Wheaton, White, Wilcox, Wilson of Pennsylvania, and Winter.

Mr. CANNON, of Tennessee, then moved to strike out the additional duty of twenty cents per gallon, and in lieu thereof proposed an additional duty of one hundred per cent. on the present duty on stills. This motion was negatived without a divison.

The question was then taken on the said second resolution, and carried in the affirmative by a large majority; when the direct-tax resolution adopted yesterday, and that just agreed to, were referred to the Committee of Ways and Means to report bills pursuant thereto.

And on motion the House adjourned until to-morrow.

THURSDAY, October 27.

The following resolution was submitted by Mr. TAYLOR for consideration:

Resolved, That the standing committees of this House, and also the select committees appointed on the 21st day of September last, on the Message of the President of the United States, have leave to report by bill or otherwise.

Ordered to lie on the table.

Mr. McKEE, from the Committee on the Public Lands, reported the bill from the Senate "further extending the time for locating Virginia military land warrants, and for returning the surveys thereon to the General Land Office,"

without amendment, and the bill was ordered to be read the third time to-morrow.

Mr. PLEASANTS, from the Committee on Naval Affairs, reported the resolution from the Senate "expressive of the sense of Congress relative to the capture of the British sloop Reindeer, by the American sloop Wasp;" and the resolution was ordered to be read the third time to-morrow.

A message from the Senate informed the House that the Senate have agreed to the modification proposed by the joint committee of conference, to the amendments proposed by the Senate to the resolutions "expressive of the sense of Congress of the gallantry and good conduct with which the reputation of the arms of the United States has been sustained by Major General Brown, Major General Scott, and Brigadiers Ripley, Miller, Porter, Gaines, and Macomb," and have modified the same accordingly.

WAR MEASURES.

Mr. TROUP, of Georgia, from the Military Committee, reported a bill making further provision for filling the ranks of the Regular Army by classifying the free male population of the United States.

[This bill proposes to provide for the division of the whole free male population of the United States, by the assessors, into classes of twenty-five men each; each class to be compelled, under a penalty of —— hundred dollars, to furnish, within —— days after the classification aforesaid, an able-bodied recruit for the service of the United States. The bill is of some length, and contains very full provisions for carrying itself into effect.]

Mr. TROUP also reported a bill "To authorize the President of the United States to accept the services of volunteers who may associate and organize themselves, and offer their services to object."]

Mr. TROUP also reported a bill "to provide for the further defence of the frontiers of the United States by authorizing the President to augment the present Military Establishment."

[This bill proposes to provide, that, "in addition to the present Military Establishment of 'the United States, there be immediately raised 'forty regiments, in such proportions of infantry, 'artillery, riflemen, and cavalry, as the President 'of the United States may deem proper, to be 'enlisted to serve during the war, unless sooner 'discharged, and limited as to service to the defence of the frontiers of the United States," &c.]

The three bills were severally twice read and referred to a Committee of the Whole.

Mr. TROUP also laid before the House the following letter from the Secretary at War to the Military Committee:

DEPARTMENT OF WAR, *October* 17, 1814.

SIR: The great importance of the subject, and the other duties of the Department, which could not fail to be very sensibly felt, at so interesting a period, by a person who had just taken charge of it, are my apology for not answering your letter of the 24th of September at an earlier day, on the defects of the present Military Establishment.

Due consideration has been bestowed on the subject-matter of that letter, and I have now the honor to submit to the committee the following report:

1. That the present Military Establishment, amounting to sixty-two thousand four hundred and forty-eight men, be preserved and made complete, and that the most efficient means authorized by the Constitution and consistent with the general rights of our fellow citizens be adopted, to fill the ranks, and with the least possible delay.

2. That a permanent force, consisting of at least forty thousand men, in addition to the present Military Establishment, be raised for the defence of our cities and frontiers, under an engagement by the Executive with such corps that it shall be employed in that service within certain specified limits, and that a proportional augmentation of general officers of each grade, and other staff, be provided for.

3. That the corps of engineers be enlarged.

4. That the ordnance department be amended.

Respecting the enlargement of the corps of engineers, I shall submit hereafter a more detailed communication.

For the proposed amendment of the Ordnance department, I submit a report from the senior officer of that department in this city, which is approved.

I shall be ready and happy to communicate such further remarks and details on these subjects as the committee may desire, and shall request permission to suggest hereafter the result of further attention to, and reflection on, our Military Establishment generally, should anything occur which may be deemed worthy its attention. I have the honor to be, &c.

JAMES MONROE.

Hon. G. M. Troup,
Chairman Military Committee.

Explanatory Observations accompanying the Letter from the Secretary of War to the Chairman of the Military Committee of the House of Representatives.

In providing a force necessary to bring this war to a happy termination, the nature of the crisis in which we are involved, and the extent of its dangers, claim particular attention. If the means are not fully adequate to the end, discomfiture must inevitably ensue.

It may be fairly presumed, that it is the object of the British Government, by striking at the principal sources of our prosperity, to diminish the importance, if not to destroy the political existence of the United States. If any doubt remained on this subject, it has been completely removed by the despatches from our Ministers at Ghent, which were lately laid before Congress.

A nation contending for its existence against an enemy powerful by land and sea, favored in a peculiar manner by extraordinary events, must make great exertions, and suffer great sacrifices. Forced to contend again for our liberties and independence, we are called on for a display of all the patriotism which distinguished our fellow-citizens in the first great struggle. It may be fairly concluded, that if the United States sacrifice any right, or make any dishonorable concession to the demands of the British Government, the spirit of the nation will be broken, and the foundations of their union and independence shaken. The United States must relinquish no right, or perish in the struggle. There is no intermediate ground to rest on. A concession on one point, leads directly to the surrender

of every other. The result of the contest cannot be doubtful. The highest confidence is entertained that the stronger the pressure, and the greater the danger, the more firm and vigorous will be the resistance, and the more successful and glorious the result.

It is the avowed purpose of the enemy to lay waste and destroy our cities and villages, and to desolate our coast, of which examples have already been afforded. It is evidently his intention to press the war along the whole extent of our seaboard, in the hope of exhausting equally the spirits of the people, and the national resources. There is also reason to presume, that it is the intention to press the war from Canada on the adjoining States, while attempts are made on the city of New York, and other important points, with a view to the vain project of dismemberment or subjugation. It may be inferred likewise to be a part of the scheme to continue to invade this part of the Union, while a separate force attacks the State of Louisiana, in the hope of taking possession of the city of New Orleans, and of the mouth of the Mississippi, that great inlet and key to the commerce of all that portion of the United States lying westward of the Alleghany mountains. The peace in Europe having given to the enemy a large disposable force, has essentially favored these objects.

The advantage which a great naval superiority gives to the enemy, by enabling him to move troops from one quarter to another, from Maine to the Mississippi, a coast of two thousand miles extent, is very considerable. Even a small force moved in this manner cannot fail to be sensibly felt, more especially by those who are most exposed to it. It is obvious, if the militia are to be relied on principally for the defence of our cities and coasts against their predatory and desolating incursions, wherever they may be made, that, by interfering with their ordinary pursuits of industry, it must be attended with serious interruption and loss to them, and injury to the public, while it greatly increases the expense. It is an object, therefore, of the highest importance, to provide a regular force, with the means of transporting it from one quarter to another along our coast, thereby following the movements of the enemy with the greatest possible rapidity, and repelling the attack wherever it may be made. These remarks are equally true as to the militia service generally under the present organization of the militia, and the short terms of service prescribed by law. It may be stated with confidence, that at least three times the force in militia has been employed at our principal cities along the coast, and on the frontier, in marching to and returning thence, that would have been necessary in regular troops; and that the expense attending it has been more than proportionably augmented, from the difficulty, if not the impossibility, of preserving the same degree of system in the militia as in the regular service.

But it will not be sufficient to repel these predatory and desolating incursions. To bring the war to an honorable termination, we must not be contented with defending ourselves. Different feelings must be touched, and apprehensions excited in the British Government. By pushing the war into Canada, we secure the friendship of the Indian tribes, and command their services, otherwise to be turned by the enemy against us; we relieve the coast from the desolation which is intended for it, and we keep in our hands a safe pledge for an honorable peace.

It follows, from this view of the subject, that it will be necessary to bring into the field, next campaign, not less than one hundred thousand regular troops. Such a force, aided, in extraordinary emergencies, by volunteers and militia, will place us above all inquietude as to the final result of this contest. It will fix, on a solid and imperishable foundation, our union and independence; on which the liberties and happiness of our fellow-citizens so essentially depend. It will secure to the United States an early and advantageous peace. It will arrest, in the further prosecution of the war, the desolation of our cities and our coast, by enabling us to retort on the enemy those calamities which our citizens have been already doomed to suffer; a resort which self-defence alone, and a sacred regard for the rights and honor of the nation, could induce the United States to adopt.

The return of the regular force now in service, laid before you, will show how many men will be necessary to fill the present corps; and the return of the numerical force of the present Military Establishment, will show how many are required to complete it to the number proposed. The next and most important inquiry is, how shall these men be raised? Under existing circumstances, it is evident that the most prompt and efficient mode that can be devised, consistent with the equal rights of every citizen, ought to be adopted. The following plans are respectfully submitted to the consideration of the committee. Being distinct in their nature, I will present each separately, with the considerations applicable to it.

First Plan.—Let the free male population of the United States, between eighteen and forty-five years, be formed into classes of one hundred men each, and let each class furnish —— men for the war, within thirty days after the classification, and replace them in the event of casualty.

The classification to be formed with a view to the equal distribution of property among the several classes. If any class fails to provide the men required of it, within the time specified, they shall be raised by draught on the whole class; any person thus draughted being allowed to furnish a substitute.

The present bounty in land to be allowed to each recruit, and the present bounty in money, which is paid to each recruit by the United States, to be paid to each draught by all the inhabitants within the precinct of the class, within which the draught may be made, equally, according to the value of the property which they may respectively possess; and if such bounty be not raised within —— days, the same to be levied on all the taxable property of the said inhabitants. And in like manner, the bounty, whatever it may be, which may be employed in raising a recruit, to avoid a draught, to be assessed on the taxable property of the whole precinct.

The recruits to be delivered over to the recruiting officer in each district, to be marched to such places of general rendezvous as may be designated by the Department of War.

That this plan will be efficient, cannot be doubted. It is evident that the men contemplated may soon be raised by it. Three modes occur by which it may be carried into effect. 1st. By placing the execution of it in the hands of the county courts throughout the United States. 2d. By relying on the militia officers in each county. 3d. By appointing particular persons in each county for that purpose. It is believed that either of these modes would be found adequate.

Nor does there appear to be any well-founded objection to the right in Congress to adopt this plan, or to its equality in its application to our fellow-citizens individually. Congress have a right, by the Constitution, to raise regular armies, and no restraint is imposed in the exercise of it, except in the provisions which are intended to guard generally against the abuse of power, with none of which does this plan interfere. It is proposed, that it shall operate on all alike, that none shall be exempted from it except the Chief Magistrate of the United States, and the Governors of the several States.

It would be absurd to suppose that Congress could not carry this power into effect, otherwise than by accepting the voluntary service of individuals. It might happen that an army could not be raised in that mode, whence the power would have been granted in vain. The safety of the State might depend on such an army. Long continued invasions, conducted by regular, well-disciplined troops, can best be repelled by troops kept constantly in the field, and, equally well disciplined. Courage in an army is in a great measure mechanical. A small body, well trained, accustomed to action, gallantly led on, often breaks three or four times the number of more respectable and more brave, but raw and undisciplined troops. The sense of danger is diminished by frequent exposure to it without harm; and confidence, even in the timid, is inspired by a knowledge that reliance may be placed on others, which can grow up only by service together. The grant to Congress to raise armies was made with a knowledge of all these circumstances, and with the intention that it should take effect. The framers of the Constitution, and the States who ratified it, knew the advantage which an enemy might have over us, by regular forces, and intended to place their country on an equal footing.

The idea that the United States cannot raise a regular army in any other mode than by accepting the voluntary service of individuals, is believed to be repugnant to the uniform construction of all grants of power, and equally so to the first principles and leading objects of the Federal compact. An unqualified grant of power gives the means necessary to carry it into effect. This is an axiom, which admits of no exception. Equally true is it, that the conservation of the State is a duty paramount to all others. The Commonwealth has a right to the service of all its citizens, or rather, the citizens composing the Commonweath have a right collectively and individually to the service of each other, to repel any danger which may be menaced. The manner in which the service is to be apportioned among the citizens, and rendered by them, are objects of legislation. All that is to be dreaded in such a case, is the abuse of power, and happily our Constitution has provided ample security against that evil.

In support of this right in Congress, the militia service affords a conclusive proof and striking example. The organization of the militia is an act of public authority, not a voluntary association. The service required must be performed by all, under penalties which delinquents pay, The generous and patriotic perform them cheerfully. In the alacrity with which the call of the Government has been obeyed, and the cheerfulness with which the service has been performed throughout the United States by the great body of the militia, there is abundant cause to rejoice in the strength of our Republican institutions, and in the virtue of the people.

The plan proposed is not more compulsive than the militia service, while it is free from most of the objections to it. The militia service calls from home, for long terms, whole districts of the country. None can elude the call. Few can avoid the service, and those who do, are compelled to pay great sums for substitutes. This plan fixes on no one personally, and opens to all who choose it a chance of declining the service. It is a principal object of this plan to engage in the defence of the State the unmarried and youthful, who can best defend it and best be spared, and to secure to those who render this important service, an adequate compensation from the voluntary contribution of the more wealthy in every class. Great confidence is entertained that such contribution will be made in time to avoid a draught. Indeed it is believed to be the necessary and inevitable tendency of this plan to produce that effect.

The limited power which the United States have in organizing the militia may be urged as an argument against their right to raise regular troops in the mode proposed. If any argument could be drawn from that circumstance, I should suppose that it would be in favor of an opposite conclusion. The power of the United States over the militia has been limited, and that for raising regular armies granted without limitation. There was, doubtless, some object in this arrangement. The fair inference seems to be, that it was made on due consideration; that the limitation in the first instance was intentional, the consequence of the unqualified grant of the second.

But it is said, that by drawing from the militia service into the regular army, and putting them under regular officers, you violate a principle of the Constitution which provides that the militia shall be commanded by their own officers. If this was the fact the conclusion would follow. But it is not the fact. The men are not drawn from the militia, but from the population of the country; when they enlist voluntarily, it is not as militiamen that they act, but as citizens. If they are draughted it must be in the same sense. In both instances they are enrolled in the Militia corps, but that, as is presumed, cannot prevent the voluntary act in the one instance, or the compulsive in the other. The whole population of the United States within certain ages belong to these corps. If the United States could not form regular armies from them they could raise none.

In proposing a draught as one of the modes of raising men in case of actual necessity in the present great emergency of the country, I have thought it my duty to examine such objections to it as occurred, particularly those of a Constitutional nature. It is from my sacred regard for the principles of our Constitution that I have ventured to trouble the Committee with any remarks on this part of the subject.

Should it appear that this mode of raising recruits was justly objectionable on account of the tax on property, from difficulties which may be apprehended in the execution, or from other causes, it may be advisable to decline the tax, and for the Government to pay the whole bounty.

In this case it is proposed that, in lieu of the present bounty, the sum of fifty dollars be allowed to each recruit or draught at the time of his engagement, and one hundred acres of land in addition to the present bounty in land, for every year that the war may continue.

It is impossible to state with mathematical accuracy the number which will be raised by the ratio of four to one hundred, or one to twenty-five, nor is it necessary. It is probable that it will be rather more than sufficient to fill the present corps. The extra number, in that case, may form a part of the local force in contemplation, a power to that effect being given to the President.

No radical change in the present Military Establishment is proposed. Should any modification be found necessary, on further consideration, it will form the subject of a separate communication. It is thought advisable, in general, to preserve the corps in their present form, and to fill them with new recruits in the manner stated. All these corps have already seen service, and many of them acquired in active scenes much experience and useful knowledge. By preserving them in their present form, and under their present officers, and filling them with new recruits, the improvement of the latter will be rapid. In two or three months it will be difficult to distinguish between the new and old levies.

The additional force to be provided amounts to forty thousand men. Of this it is proposed that local corps be raised, to consist partly of infantry, partly of mounted men, and partly of artillery. There is reason to believe that such corps may be raised in the principal cities, and even on the frontier, to serve for the war, under an engagement as to the limit beyond which they should not be carried. Every able-bodied citizen is willing and ready to fight for his home, his family, and his country when invaded. Of this we have seen, in the present year, the most honorable and gratifying proofs. It does not suit all, however, to go great distances from home. This generous and patriotic spirit may be taken advantage of, under proper arrangements, with the happiest effect to the country, and without essential inconvenience to the parties.

The officers who may be appointed to command these corps should be charged with recruiting them. Local defence being their sole object, it may be presumed that the corps will soon be raised. Patriotism alone will furnish a very powerful motive. It seems reasonable, however, that some recompense should be made to those who relieve others from the burden. One hundred acres of land and fifty dollars to each recruit will, it is presumed, be deemed sufficient.

It is proposed that this additional force shall form a part of any plan that may be adopted.

Second Plan.—This plan consists of a classification of the militia, and the extension of their terms of service.

Let the whole militia of the United States be divided into the following classes, viz:

All free male persons capable of service, between the ages of eighteen and twenty-five, into one class ; all those between the ages of twenty-five and thirty-two into another class ; and those between thirty-two and forty-five into a third class.

It is proposed, also, that the President shall have power to call into the service any portion of either of these classes, which, in his judgment, the exigencies of the country may require, to remain in service two years from the time each corps shall be assembled at the appointed place of rendezvous.

It is believed that a shorter term than two years would not give to these corps the efficiency in military operations that is desired, and deemed indispensable, nor avoid the evils that are so sensibly felt, and generally complained of, under the present arrangement.

It requires two campaigns to make a complete soldier, especially where the corps, officers and men, are alike raw and inexperienced. In the interim, the numbers must be multiplied to supply the defect of discipline. And it requires the extension of the term of service, to avoid the additional proportional augmentation of having so many in the field at the same time, in marching to the frontier and returning from it. The inconvenience to the parties, and loss to the community in other respects, need not be repeated. It is proper to add, only, that if substitutes are allowed in the service, it must put an end to the recruiting of men for the regular army, especially the old corps. Of the justice of this remark, what has occurred in the present year has furnished full proof. It follows that, if this plan is adopted, the militia must be relied on principally, if not altogether, in the further prosecution of the war.

The additional force for local service, amounting to forty thousand men, will likewise form a part, as already observed, of this plan.

Third Plan.—It is proposed to exempt every five men from militia service, who shall find one to serve for the war. It is probable that some recruits might be raised in this mode, in most or all the States. But it is apprehended that it would prevent recruiting in every other mode, by the high bounty which some of the wealthy might give. The consequence would probably be very injurious, as it is not believed that any great number could be raised in this mode.

Fourth Plan.—Should all the preceding plans be found objectionable, it remains that the present system of recruiting be adhered to, with an augmentation of the bounty in land. Should this be preferred, it is advised that, in addition to the one hundred and sixty acres of land now given, one hundred be allowed annually for every year while the war lasts.

These plans are thought more deserving the attention of the committee than any that have occurred. The first, for the reasons stated, is preferred. It is believed that it will be found more efficient against the enemy, less expensive to the public, and less burdensome on our fellow-citizens.

It has likewise the venerable sanction of our Revolution. In that great struggle, resort was had to this expedient for filling the ranks of our regular Army, and with decisive effect.

It is not intended by these remarks, should the first plan be adopted, to dispense altogether with the service of the militia. Although the principal burden of the war may thereby be taken from the militia, reliance must still be placed on them for important aids, especially in cases of sudden invasion. For this purpose, it will still be advisable that the men be classed according to age, and that their term of service be prolonged. Even should this plan be attended with all the advantages expected of it, such an arrangement could not fail to produce the happiest effect. The proof which it would afford of the impregnable strength of the country, of the patient virtue and invincible spirit of the people, would admonish the enemy how vain and fruitless his invasions must be, and might dispose him to a speedy, just, and honorable peace. Of the very important services already rendered by the militia, even under the present organization, too much cannot be said.

If the United States make the exertion which is proposed, it is probable that the contest will soon be at an end. It cannot be doubted that it is in their power to expel the British forces from this continent, should the British Government, by persevering in its unjust

demands, make that an object with the American people. Against our united and vigorous efforts, the resistance of the enemy will soon become light and feeble. Success in every fair and honorable claim, is within our easy grasp. And surely the United States have every possible inducement to make the effort necessary to secure it. I should insult the understanding and wound the feelings of the committee, if I touched on the calamities incident to defeat. Dangers which are remote, and can never be realized, excite no alarm with a gallant and generous people. But the advantages of success have a fair claim to their deliberate consideration. The effort we have already made has attracted the attention and extorted the praise of other nations. Already have most of the absurd theories and idle speculations on our system of government been refuted and put down. We are now felt and respected as a Power; and it is the dread which the enemy entertain of our resources and growing importance, that has induced him to push the war against us, after its professed objects had ceased. Success, by discomfiture of his schemes, and the attainment of an honorable peace, will place the United States on higher ground, in the opinion of the world, than they have held at any former period. In future wars, their commerce will be permitted to take its lawful range unmolested. Their remonstrances to foreign Governments will not again be put aside unheeded. Few will be presented, because there will seldom be occasion for them. Our Union, founded on interest and affection, will have acquired new strength by the proof it will have afforded of the important advantages attending it. Respected abroad and happy at home, the United States will have accomplished the great objects for which they have so long contended. As a nation, they will have little to dread; as a people, little to desire.

Extract from Marshall's Life of Washington, volume 4th, page 241.

"In general, the Assemblies (of the States) followed the example of Congress, and apportioned, on the several counties within the State, the quota to be furnished by each. This division of the State was again to be subdivided into classes, and each class was to furnish a man by contributions or taxes imposed on itself. In some instances, a draught was to be used in the last resort; in others, the man was to be recruited by persons appointed for that purpose, and the class to be taxed with the sum given for his bounty."

Extract from Ramsay's Life of Washington, volume 2d, page 248.

"When voluntary enlistments fell short of the proposed number, the deficiencies were, by the laws of several States, to be made up by draughts or lots from the militia. The towns in New England, and the counties in the Middle States, were respectively called on for a specified number of men. Such was the zeal of the people of New England, that neighbors would often club together to engage one of their number to go into the Army. Maryland directed her lieutenants of counties to class all the property in their respective counties into as many equal classes as there were men wanted; and each class was by law obliged, within ten days thereafter, to furnish an able-bodied recruit during the war; and, in case of their neglecting or refusing to do so, the county lieutenants were authorized to procure men at their expense, at any rate not exceeding fifteen pounds in every hundred pounds worth of property classed agreeably to law. Virginia likewise classed

491   HISTORY OF CONGRESS.   492

H. of R.   *The Ways and Means.*   October, 1814.

her citizens, and called upon the respective classes for every fifteenth man for public service. Pennsylvania concentrated the requisite power in the President, Mr. Reed, and authorized him to draw forth the resources of the State, under certain limitations, and if necessary to declare martial law over the State. The execution of these arrangements, although uncommonly vigorous, lagged far behind."

WAYS AND MEANS.

The House resumed the consideration of the report of the Committee of the Whole on the report of the Committee of Ways and Means.

The resolution for imposing an additional duty on postage being under consideration, together with the amendment going to increase the rates of postage one hundred instead of fifty of per cent. of their present amount, after considerable debate, the question on inserting "one hundred" instead of "fifty per cent." was decided in the affirmative: For one hundred 95, against it 45, as follows:

YEAS—Messrs. Alexander, Alston, Anderson, Avery, Barbour, Bard, Barnett, Bowen, Bradley, Brown, Burwell, Butler, Caldwell, Calhoun, Cannon, Chappell, Clopton, Comstock, Condict, Conard, Crawford, Creighton, Crouch, Cuthbert, Dana, Davis of Pennsylvania, Denoyelles, Desha, Duvall, Eppes, Evans, Farrow, Fisk of Vermont, Fisk of New York, Forney, Forsyth, Franklin, Gholson, Goodwyn, Griffin, Hall, Hanson, Harris, Hasbrouck, Hawes, Hawkins, Hopkins of Kentucky, Hubbard, Humphreys, Hungerford, Ingersoll, Ingham, Irving, Jackson of Virginia, Johnson of Virginia, Kennedy, Kent of Maryland, Kerr, Kershaw, Kilbourn, King of North Carolina, Lowndes, Lyle, Macon, McCoy, McKee, McKim, McLean, Montgomery, Moore, Nelson, Newton, Ormsby, Pearson, Pickens, Pleasants, Rich, Ringgold, Robertson, Sage, Sevier, Seybert, Sharp, Skinner, Smith of Virginia, Strong, Stuart, Tannehill, Taylor, Telfair, Troup, Udree, Ward of New Jersey, Wilson of Pennsylvania, and Wright.

NAYS—Messrs. Baylies of Massachusetts, Bigelow, Boyd, Bradbury, Brigham, Cooper, Culpeper, Davenport, Ely, Gaston, Geddes, Grosvenor, Hale, Hulbert, Jackson of Rhode Island, Kent of New York, Law, Lewis, Lovett, Markell, Moffit, Moseley, Oakley, Pickering, Pitkin, Post, Potter, John Reed, Rhea of Tennessee, Ruggles, Schureman, Sherwood, Shipherd, Smith of New York, Stanford, Sturges, Taggart, Thompson, Vose, Ward of Massachusetts, Webster, Wheaton, White, Wilcox, and Wilson of Massachusetts.

The question to adopt the resolution (as amended) to increase the present rates of postage, was then stated.

Mr. GASTON, of North Carolina, assigned, as the principal reason why he should vote against this tax, that this was not a subject, the revenue on which could be safely or properly pledged to the public creditor. The revenue therefrom accruing, in fact, he conceived to be exclusively pledged to the perfection of the Post Office Establishment.

The question was then taken on the resolution as amended, and carried: For the postage-tax 96, against it 47, as follows:

YEAS—Messrs. Alexander, Alston, Anderson, Avery, Barbour, Bard, Barnett, Bowen, Bradley, Brown, Burwell, Butler, Caldwell, Calhoun, Cannon, Chappell, Clopton, Comstock, Condict, Conard, Crawford, Creighton, Crouch, Cuthbert, Dana, Davis of Pennsylvania, Denoyelles, Desha, Duvall, Earle, Eppes, Evans, Farrow, Fisk of Vermont, Fisk of New York, Forney, Forsyth, Franklin, Gholson, Goodwyn, Griffin, Hall, Hanson, Harris, Hasbrouck, Hawes, Hawkins, Hopkins of Kentucky, Hubbard, Humphreys, Hungerford, Ingersoll, Ingham, Irving, Jackson of Virginia, Johnson of Virginia, Kennedy, Kent of Maryland, Kerr, Kershaw, Kilbourn, King of North Carolina, Lefferts, Lowndes, Lyle, Macon, McCoy, McKee, McKim, Montgomery, Moore, Nelson, Newton, Ormsby, Pearson, Pickens, Pleasants, Rhea of Tennessee, Rich, Ringgold, Robertson, Sage, Sevier, Seybert, Sharp, Skinner, Smith of Virginia, Strong, Stuart, Tannehill, Taylor, Telfair, Udree, Ward of New Jersey, Wilson of Pennsylvania, and Wright.

NAYS—Messrs. Baylies of Massachusetts, Bigelow, Boyd, Bradbury, Brigham, Caperton, Champion, Oilley, Cooper, Culpeper, Davenport, Ely, Gaston, Geddes, Grosvenor, Hale, Hulbert, Jackson of Rhode Island, Kent of New York, Law, Lewis, Lovett, Markell, Moffit, Moseley, Oakley, Pickering, Pitkin, Post, Potter, John Reed, Ruggles, Schureman, Sherwood, Shipherd, Smith of New York, Stanford, Sturges, Taggart, Thompson, Vose, Ward of Massachusetts, Webster, Wheaton, White, Wilcox, and Wilson of Massachusetts.

The next question for consideration presented itself in the following words: "*Resolved*, That it is expedient to add one hundred per cent. to the present duty on sales at auction;" and was agreed to without debate.

The next resolution was that embracing a tax, among other articles, on cotton yarn, and other manufactures, furniture, &c.

The questions to concur with the Committee of the Whole in striking out "cotton, yarn, and shoes." (that is, exempting them from taxation,) were decided in the affirmative without debate; as also was the proposition for taxing all manufactured paper at the rate of five per cent.

The amendments of the Committee of the Whole to this resolution, having been gone through—

Mr. OAKLEY, of New York, moved to strike out "tallow candles;" to which motion, Mr. J. REED proposed to add "spermaceti" candles. But, that motion not being in order, as an amendment to Mr. OAKLEY's motion, the question was taken by yeas and nays on striking out "tallow candles," and decided in the negative. For exempting "tallow candles" 59, against it 74, as follows:

YEAS—Messrs. Alexander, Baylies of Massachusetts, Bigelow, Boyd, Bradbury, Bradley, Brigham, Burwell, Butler, Caperton, Champion, Cilley, Comstock, Conard, Cooper, Crawford, Culpeper, Davenport, Davis of Pennsylvania, Denoyelles, Ely, Fisk of New York, Forsyth, Geddes, Hale, Ingham, Irving, Jackson of Rhode Island, Law, Lefferts, Lewis, Lovett, Markell, Moffit, Moseley, Oakley, Pickering, Pitkin, Post, Potter, John Reed, William Reed, Ruggles, Sage, Schureman, Seybert, Shipherd, Stuart, Sturges, Taggart, Taylor, Thompson, Vose, Ward of Massachusetts, Webster, Wheaton, White, Wilcox, and Winter.

NAYS—Messrs. Anderson, Avery, Barbour, Bard, Barnett, Bowen, Brown, Caldwell, Calhoun, Cannon,

Chappell, Clopton, Condict, Creighton, Dana, Desha, Duvall, Earle, Eppes, Evans, Farrow, Forney, Franklin, Gaston, Gholson, Goodwyn, Griffin, Hall, Harris, Hasbrouck, Hawes, Hawkins, Hopkins of Kentucky, Hungerford, Jackson of Virginia, Johnson of Virginia, Kennedy, Kent of New York, Kent of Maryland, Kerr, Kershaw, Kilbourn, King of North Carolina, Lowndes, Lyle, McCoy, McKee, McKim, McLean, Montgomery, Nelson, Newton, Ormsby, Pearson, Pickens, Pleasants, Rhea of Tennessee, Rich, Ringgold, Robertson, Sevier, Sharp, Sherwood, Skinner, Smith of N. York, Smith of Virginia, Stanford, Strong, Tannehill, Telfair, Troup, Udree, Ward of New Jersey, and Wilson of Pennsylvania.

Mr. J. REED then moved to strike out "spermaceti" candles, on account of the peculiarly oppressive operation of such a tax on the Island of Nantucket and town of New Bedford, in Massachusetts. After further debate, the question was put, and decided in the negative by yeas and nays. For striking out "spermaceti" 50, against it 73, as follows:

YEAS—Messrs. Baylies of Massachusetts, Bigelow, Boyd, Bradbury, Brigham, Butler, Caldwell, Champion, Cilley, Dana, Davenport, Duvall, Ely, Fisk of Vermont, Fisk of New York, Gaston, Hale, Irving, Jackson of Rhode Island, Kennedy, Kent of N. York, Law, Lefferts, Lovett, Markell, McKee, Moffit, Moseley, Oakley, Pickering, Pitkin, Post, John Reed, William Reed, Ruggles, Sage, Schureman, Sherwood, Skinner, Smith of New York, Strong, Sturges, Taggart, Taylor, Thompson, Vose, Ward of Massachusetts, Webster, Wheaton, and Wilcox.

NAYS—Messrs. Alexander, Anderson, Avery, Barbour, Barnett, Bowen, Bradley, Brown, Burwell, Calhoun, Cannon, Chappell, Clopton, Comstock, Condict, Conard, Crawford, Creighton, Davis of Pennsylvania, Denoyelles, Desha, Earle, Eppes, Farrow, Forney, Forsyth, Franklin, Gholson, Goodwyn, Griffin, Hall, Harris, Hasbrouck, Hawes, Hawkins, Hopkins of Kentucky, Hungerford, Ingham, Jackson of Virginia, Johnson of Virginia, Kent of Maryland, Kerr, Kershaw, Kilbourn, King of North Carolina, Lewis, Lowndes, Lyle, McCoy, McKim, McLean, Montgomery, Nelson, Newton, Ormsby, Pearson, Pickens, Pleasants, Rhea of Tennessee, Rich, Ringgold, Robertson, Seybert, Sharp, Smith of Virginia, Stanford, Tannehill, Telfair, Troup, Udree, Ward of New Jersey, Wilson of Pennsylvania, and Winter.

Mr. BIGELOW, of Massachusetts, then moved to strike out the word "leather," so as to exempt it from taxation; which motion, Mr. B. supported at some length. The motion was negatived by a considerable majority.

Mr. WHEATON, of Massachusetts, then moved to strike out the article "nails, manufactured by machinery." In support of which motion, he made some remarks, to which Mr. EPPES replied. And the motion was negatived without a division.

Mr. GASTON, of North Carolina, then moved to strike out so much of the resolution now under consideration as proposes to tax "furniture" above a certain value, (beds, bedding, kitchen furniture, and articles of domestic manufacture, excepted;) which motion was, without debate, decided in the negative. For the motion 43, against it 72, as follows:

YEAS—Messrs. Anderson, Baylies, Bigelow, Boyd, Bradbury, Bradley, Brigham, Caperton, Champion, Cilley, Cooper, Culpeper, Davenport, Ely, Farrow, Gaston, Hale, Hasbrouck, Jackson of Rhode Island, Johnson of Virginia, Kent of New York, Law, Lewis, Lovett, Markell, Moseley, Oakley, Pearson, Pickering, Post, Potter, John Reed, William Reed, Ruggles, Seybert, Sherwood, Sturges, Vose, Ward of Massachusetts, Ward of New Jersey, Wheaton, White, Wilcox.

NAYS—Messrs. Alexander, Avery, Barbour, Barnett, Bowen, Burwell, Butler, Caldwell, Calhoun, Cannon, Chappell, Clopton, Condict, Conard, Crawford, Creighton, Dana, Davis of Pennsylvania, Denoyelles, Desha, Duvall, Eppes, Fisk of Vermont, Fisk of New York, Forney, Forsyth, Franklin, Gholson, Goodwyn, Griffin, Hall, Harris, Hawes, Hawkins, Hopkins of Kentucky, Hungerford, Ingham, Irving, Jackson of Virg's, Kennedy, Kerr, Kershaw, Kilbourn, King of North Carolina, Lefferts, Lowndes, Lyle, McCoy, McKee, McKim, McLean, Montgomery, Nelson, Newton, Pickens, Pleasants, Rhea of Tennessee, Rich, Ringgold, Robertson, Sage, Sharp, Skinner, Smith of New York, Smith of Virginia, Stanford, Tannehill, Taylor, Telfair, Troup, Udree, and Wilson of Pennsylvania.

The question was then stated on the whole resolution, (which goes to tax sundry articles of manufacture, besides those mentioned in the foregoing.)

Mr. OAKLEY, of New York, stated that he was friendly to some and opposed to others of the taxes embraced in this resolve, and should therefore vote against the whole, reserving the right to vote for the bills for laying some of these taxes, when they should be brought in.

The question on the adoption of the whole of the resolution (as amended by striking out "cotton yarn" and "hats") was decided in the affirmative—yeas 76, nays 34, as follows:

YEAS—Messrs. Alexander, Anderson, Avery, Barbour, Barnett, Bowen, Bradley, Burwell, Butler, Caldwell, Calhoun, Cannon, Chappell, Clopton, Condict, Conard, Crawford, Creighton, Dana, Denoyelles, Desha, Duvall, Eppes, Farrow, Fisk of Vermont, Fisk of New York, Forney, Forsyth, Franklin, Gholson, Goodwyn, Griffin, Hall, Harris, Hasbrouck, Hawes, Hawkins, Hopkins of Kentucky, Hungerford, Ingham, Irving, Jackson of Virginia, Johnson of Virginia, Kennedy, Kent of Maryland, Kerr, Kershaw, Kilbourn, King of North Carolina, Lefferts, Lowndes, Lyle, McCoy, McKee, McLean, Montgomery, Nelson, Newton, Pickens, Pleasants, Rhea of Tennessee, Rich, Ringgold, Robertson, Sage, Sharp, Skinner, Smith of New York, Smith of Virginia, Tannehill, Taylor, Telfair, Troup, Udree, Ward of New Jersey, Wilson of Pennsylvania.

NAYS—Messrs. Baylies of Massachusetts, Bigelow, Boyd, Bradbury, Brigham, Caperton, Champion, Cilley, Cooper, Ely, Gaston, Hale, Jackson of Rhode Island, Law, Lewis, Lovett, Markell, Moseley, Oakley, Pearson, Pickering, Pitkin, John Reed, William Reed, Ruggles, Seybert, Sherwood, Stanford, Sturges, Vose, Ward of Massachusetts, Wheaton, White, and Wilcox.

The next resolution is, "That it is expedient to class the retailers of foreign merchandise, and add 50 per cent to the present duty thereon."—Agreed to.

The next resolution was, so to impose a duty on plated harness, combined with the tax on carriages, as to add to the present duty on carriages 100 per cent.

The eighth and last resolution. "That it is expedient to establish a National Bank, with branches in the several States," being under consideration—

On motion, the House adjourned.

FRIDAY, October 28.

Mr. TROUP, from the committee of conference on the disagreeing votes of the two Houses on the amendments proposed by the Senate to the resolutions expressive of the sense of Congress of the gallantry and good conduct with which the reputation of the arms of the United States has been sustained by Major General Brown, Major General Scott, and Brigadiers Ripley, Miller, Porter, Gaines, and Macomb, made a report; which was read: Whereupon,

Resolved, That this House do agree to the modification of the said amendments, as proposed by the committee of conference.

The bill from the Senate to give a further time for locating Virginia military land warrants was read a third time, and passed.

The resolution from the Senate expressive of the sense of Congress relative to the victory of the Wasp over the Reindeer, was read a third time, and passed unanimously.

Mr. DANA, of Massachusetts, laid before the House the petition of John Appleton, who being appointed Principal Assessor of the Tenth District of Massachusetts, performed all the duties of said office, when his nomination was rejected by the Senate, in consequence of which refusal to confirm his appointment, he loses the compensation due him; and praying that it may be directed to be paid to him.—Referred to the Secretary of the Treasury.

A Message was received from the President of the United States, transmitting the information requested by the House in relation to the retaliation prisoners; which was referred to the Committee on Foreign Relations.

Mr. WILLIAM REED, of Massachusetts, after remarking, that he had understood there was before the Senate a bill for the increase of the naval force of the United States, in order to acquire information necessary to enable the House to act understandingly on the subject, submitted a resolve for consideration, which, after undergoing some modification, presented itself in the following shape:

Resolved, That the Secretary of the Navy be, and he is hereby, directed to report to this House a statement of the number of armed vessels belonging to the United States, at the declaration of the existing war, designating the names and force of each, and their present condition; also, the number and rate of new vessels, authorized and directed by law, since that time; the progress made in execution of these laws, and, if not completed, the causes that have prevented their execution.

After some desultory conversation, as to the state of the information on this subject, the resolution was ordered to lie on the table.

WAYS AND MEANS.

The House resumed the consideration of the remaining part of the report of the Committee of the Whole—it being a resolution "that it is expedient to establish a National Bank with branches in the several States."

Mr. POST, of New York, hoped the chairman, or some member of the Committee of Ways and Means, would explain the reasons on which the proposition was founded.

Mr. CLOPTON, of Virginia, called upon gentlemen in favor of the proposition to show in what part of the Constitution was contained the power to establish a National Bank. Having always himself denied the Constitutional power, and the House having so decided six years ago, he could not see what had occurred to change the nature of the Constitutional question. Unless his objections on this head were removed, he must certainly vote against this proposition.

Mr. EPPES, of Virginia, said his sentiments in relation to this question were well known, and were not changed. However necessary he might believe the agency of such an institution at the present moment, he could not give his consent to a measure which he believed contrary to the Constitution. For the reasons in favor of the resolve which he had reported in obedience to the instructions of the committee, he referred to Mr. Dallas's report; and to the gentlemen of the committee who favored it.

Mr. WRIGHT, of Maryland, expressed himself decidedly in favor of the establishment of a bank, but, in order to obviate objections, some might conscientiously entertain on Constitutional grounds, he was of opinion that the bank ought to be located within this District. He therefore moved to amend the resolve by inserting therein the words "within the District of Columbia."

Mr. BURWELL, of Virginia, said he had no doubt of the power of Congress to establish a bank of the kind proposed, in the District of Columbia; but he should vote against the amendment, because he believed such a bank would not at all assist the finances of the Government. He was also entirely hostile to the establishment of a bank on the principles recommended in the Secretary's report as its basis, for reasons growing out of their general impracticability and inexpediency.

Mr. DUVALL, of Kentucky, said he was opposed to the proposed amendment, because it would destroy the utility of the bank, so far as regards its issuing a medium which should possess the general confidence, and he was opposed to it also because the adoption of it would virtually sanction the construction, which he denied, that it was not Constitutional to establish a bank with branches in the several States. Mr. D. was proceeding to argue in support of the Constitutionality of a bank—when

Mr. WRIGHT withdrew the amendment which he had proposed.

Mr. STANFORD, of North Carolina, moved to strike out of the resolve the following words: "with branches in the several States." Some gentlemen, he said, were of opinion a bank might be established adequate to all necessary purposes, having no branches, but arrangements with some one or more banks now existing in each State. He was in favor of leaving the question as broad as possible.

Mr. DUVALL resumed his argument on the Constitutional question, which he examined with no little ability and ingenuity. He chiefly rested his opinion of the power to incorporate a bank on that section of the Constitution which prohibits the States to coin money, or issue "bills of credit;" which negation of power, he apprehended, implied the existence of the power in Congress. If Congress had not power under the Constitution of the United States to establish a bank or banks, nearly or all the States had violated their own State constitutions as well as the Constitution of the United States, in authorizing the circulation of bank notes, which, call them what you will, are "bills of credit." Mr. D. went deeper still into this question, and concluded with expressing his decided hostility to the proposed amendment.

Mr. GROSVENOR, of New York, having no doubt of the constitutionality of a National Bank, entreated gentlemen to vote down the proposed amendment; because, if adopted, it would hold out fallacious ideas of the adequacy of a bank without branches, to be established within this District, which would no more relieve the embarrassment of our finances, than will the five and ten cents bills issued by the Corporation of this City and Georgetown. He should vote for the general proposition. As for the Secretary's proposition, it was a *felo de se*; and many of its features could not be sanctioned in this House.

Mr. HAWKINS, of Kentucky, said, that one of his earliest convictions on political topics, was, that this Government had no power to establish a National Bank; but, if it is to be established, he was clearly of opinion it ought to be on general principles. In order to give the question full and ample consideration on the widest national, just, and general objects, he should vote against the amendment, without intending in any way to sanction the idea that Congress has the power "to establish a National Bank with branches in the several States."

Mr. CLOPTON made a number of observations in reply to the argument of Mr. DUVALL. The true principle of construction of the Constitution being, that all powers not expressly delegated are reserved, he contended that Congress could by no forced construction, derive the power to establish a National Bank.

Mr. WILSON, of Pennsylvania, predicated his views in favor of the resolution, and against the amendment, on the statement of facts and reasoning of the Secretary of the Treasury, on this subject, which combined, he believed to be conclusive.

Mr. McKEE, of Kentucky, expressed surprise that the opposition to this measure, declared by the Secretary of the Treasury to be necessary not only to the maintenance but to the restoration of the public credit, proceeded from those who had, in every other respect, been the most zealous and inflexible in their pursuit of measures to sustain the operations of the Government. He had no doubt of the power of the Government to establish a National Bank as an instrument of finance, and entered into a train of reasoning with his usual acumen, as well to prove this, as to prove the injury which had resulted from the refusal to recharter the late Bank of the United States. As to establishing the bank within this District, for all present practical purposes, it might as well be established in Abyssinia. He was decidedly opposed to the motion now under consideration.

The question on Mr. STANFORD's motion to strike out the words, "with branches in the several States," was decided by yeas and nays in the negative. For the motion 14, against it 138, as follows:

YEAS—Messrs. Bard, Burwell, Clopton, Crawford, Gholson, Hall, Hungerford, Johnson of Virginia, Macon, Nelson, Newton, Pleasants, Smith of Virginia, and Stanford.

NAYS—Messrs. Alexander, Alston, Anderson, Archer, Avery, Barbour, Barnett, Baylies of Massachusetts, Bayly of Virginia, Bowen, Boyd, Bradbury, Brigham, Brown, Butler, Caperton, Caldwell, Calhoun, Cannon, Champion, Chappell, Cilley, Clark, Comstock, Condict, Conard, Cooper, Creighton, Crouch, Culpeper, Cuthbert, Dana, Davenport, Davis of Pennsylvania, Denoyelles, Desha, Duvall, Earle, Ely, Eppes, Evans, Farrow, Findley, Fisk of Vermont, Fisk of New York, Forney, Forsyth, Franklin, Gaston, Geddes, Glasgow, Goodwyn, Gourdin, Griffin, Grosvenor, Hale, Hanson, Harris, Hasbrouck, Hawes, Hawkins, Hopkins of Kentucky, Hubbard, Humphreys, Hulbert, Ingersoll, Ingham, Irving, Jackson of Rhode Island, Jackson of Virginia, Kennedy, Kent of New York, Kent of Maryland, Kerr, Kershaw, Kilbourn, King of Massachusetts, King of North Carolina, Law, Lefferts, Lewis, Lovett, Lowndes, Lyle, Markell, McCoy, McKee, McKim, McLean, Moffit, Montgomery, Moore, Moseley, Oakley, Ormsby, Pearson, Pickens, Piper, Pitkin, Post, Potter, John Reed, William Reed, Rea of Pennsylvania, Rhea of Tennessee, Rich, Ringgold, Robertson, Ruggles, Sage, Schureman, Sevier, Seybert, Sharp, Sherwood, Shipherd, Skinner, Smith of New York, Strong, Sturges, Taggart, Tannehill, Taylor, Telfair, Thompson, Troup, Udree, Vose, Ward of Massachusetts, Ward of New Jersey, Webster, Wheaton, Wilcox, Wilson of Massachusetts, Wilson of Pennsylvania, Winter, Wright, and Yancey.

The question being stated on the passage of the resolution—

Mr. POST, of New York, said, under present impressions, he should vote against it, because the idea it embraced was illusive, and its object impracticable at the present moment; to show which he made a number of remarks going to establish the insufficiency of such a measure to remedy the general want of confidence among individuals as well as in the banks, which at present prevailed.

The question on the adoption of the resolution was decided by the following vote:

YEAS—Messrs. Alexander, Alston, Anderson, Archer, Avery, Barnett, Bayly of Virginia, Bradley, Brown, Butler, Caperton, Caldwell, Calhoun, Cannon, Chappell, Clark, Comstock, Condict, Conard, Creighton, Crouch, Culpeper, Cuthbert, Dana, Davis of Pennsylvania, Denoyelles, Duvall, Earle, Farrow, Findley,

Fisk of New York, Forney, Forsyth, Gaston, Geddes, Gourdin, Griffin, Grosvenor, Hanson, Harris, Hasbrouck, Hawes, Hopkins of Kentucky, Hubbard, Hulbert, Ingersoll, Ingham, Irving, Kent of New York, Kent of Maryland, Kerr, Kershaw, Kilbourn, King of North Carolina, Lefferts, Lewis, Lovett, Lowndes, Lyle, Markell, McKee, McKim, McLean, Montgomery, Moore, Oakley, Ormsby, Parker, Pearson, Pickens, Piper, Rea of Pennsylvania, Rich, Robertson, Sage, Sevier, Sherwood, Shipherd, Skinner, Smith of New York, Strong, Sturges, Tannehill, Taylor, Telfair, Thompson, Udree, Ward of New Jersey, Webster, Wilson of Pennsylvania, Winter, Wright, and Yancey—93.

NAYS—Messrs. Barbour, Bard, Baylies of Massachusetts, Bowen, Boyd, Bradbury, Burwell, Champion, Cilley, Clopton, Crawford, Davenport, Desha, Ely, Eppes, Evans, Franklin, Gholson, Glasgow, Goodwyn, Hale, Hall, Hawkins, Humphreys, Hungerford, Jackson of Rhode Island, Jackson of Virginia, Johnson of Virginia, Kennedy, King of Massachusetts, Law, Macon, Moseley, Nelson, Newton, Pitkin, Pleasants, Post, Potter, John Reed, William Reed, Rhea of Tennessee, Ringgold, Ruggles, Schureman, Seybert, Sharp, Smith of Virginia, Stanford, Taggart, Vose, Wheaton, Wilcox, and Wilson of Massachusetts—54.

So the resolution was agreed to, and this, together with the other resolutions, were referred to the Committee of Ways and Means, to bring in bills accordingly.

SATURDAY, October 29.

The SPEAKER laid before the House a letter from the Secretary of the Navy, stating that the whole of the books, papers, trophies in his office, except the furniture, were preserved, and are now entire; and that all the books and papers in the Accountant's Office, except those papers relative to accounts settled and transmitted to the Treasury Department, have been preserved.

MR. YANCEY, from the Committee of Claims, made a report on the petition of Moses Alley; which was read, and the resolution therein contained was concurred in by the House. The report is as follows:

That, at the declaration of war against Great Britain, and for some time previous thereto, the petitioner was an inhabitant of Upper Canada; in the Summer or Autumn of the year 1812, he came to the United States and reported himself to General Dearborn, who then commanded on the Northern frontier. Being considered of suspicious character, he was arrested by military authority, and sent to Greenbush, in New York, for examination; at the time of his arrest, he had in his possession a sorrel stud-horse, which was, by directions of the officer who arrested him, placed in the possession of a Mr. Benjamin Van Vleck for safe-keeping, at the expense of the United States, until he should receive further orders how to dispose of him. He kept the horse until the 16th of April, 1813, when, having had his house and property consumed by fire, he delivered the horse over for safe-keeping to a Mr. Norton, of Lewis county. He kept him until September, 1813, when he sold him, at the price of twenty dollars, to pay for his keeping. It does not appear to the committee who was the purchaser; but, from the manner in which the account for keeping the horse is credited,

it is presumed that Norton himself was the purchaser. It appears, also, to the committee, from the certificate of Generals Wilkinson and Dearborn, that the charge against the petitioner was not well founded. He then received an order from General Wilkinson for his horse, to be delivered to him clear of the expense of keeping; but, upon application, found that he had been sold to pay that expense. The petitioner asks of Congress the value of the horse.

The committee are of opinion that the United States are under no legal obligation to pay for the horse; if the petitioner had a good title to the property, it is presumed he would be entitled to recover his value of the man in whose possession he was placed by the officer. Having been put in his possession upon conditions, and with instructions to keep him at public expense, it is believed he was not liable to be sold for that expense; they therefore recommend the following resolution:

Resolved, That the prayer of the petitioner ought not to be granted.

MR. CLOPTON, of Virginia, introduced into the House, with a few appropriate observations, the following resolution:

"It being a duty particularly incumbent, in a time of public calamity and war, humbly and devoutly to acknowledge our dependence on Almighty God, and to implore his aid and protection: Therefore,

"*Resolved, by the Senate and House of Representatives of the United States of America in Congress assembled*, That a joint committee of both Houses wait on the President of the United States, and request that he recommend a day of public humiliation, prayer, and fasting, to be observed by the people of the United States, with religious solemnity, and the offering of fervent supplications to Almighty God, for the safety of these States; his blessings on their arms, and a speedy restoration of peace."

The resolution was twice read, and referred to a Committee of the Whole.

The House resumed the consideration of a resolution offered a few days ago by Mr. TAYLOR of New York, which was agreed to in the following words:

Resolved, That the Standing Committees of this House, and also the select committees appointed on the 21st day of September last, on the Message of the President United States, have leave to report by bill or otherwise.

THE WAYS AND MEANS.

The House resolved itself into a Committee of the Whole, on the bill to authorize a loan not exceeding —— dollars.

MR. EPPES, of Virginia, moved to fill the blank for the amount to be borrowed, with three millions. The Secretary of the Treasury had recommended, in his letter, a larger sum to be borrowed; but since that letter had been written, it was ascertained that three of the six millions of stock proposed to be sent to Europe for sale had not yet left the country, and the President had determined to retain it. The retention of this stock from the market would, by so much as its amount, reduce the additional amount necessary to be authorized. It was therefore determined to ask only for three millions on this occasion.

The blank was filled accordingly.

Mr. GROSVENOR, of New York, moved to amend the bill by adding thereto the following proviso:

"*Provided, also,* That the making the loan authorized by this bill, the President shall in no case and in no way contract for a greater interest or premium than eight per cent. per annum."

Mr. GROSVENOR said, he had offered the amendment in the belief, nay, the certainty, that public credit and confidence would never be restored to any Government which supplied the treasury by loans, at the rate, and in the manner heretofore adopted by the President. To former bills similar amendments had been moved and rejected, and what had been the consequence? Let gentlemen cast their eyes upon the report of the Secretary of the Treasury at the commencement of the session. The Government had, under a bill just like the present, gone into the market for twenty-five millions. It first proposed for a part of that sum, to wit: ten millions. As it was well understood, by the influence of one man, a condition had been annexed to the ten millions then taken, of a most ruinous and extortionate character. That condition he need not state, because it was known to all; nor should he go over the calculations made the other day by his honorable friend from New York, (Mr. OAKLEY.) If that gentleman was correct, and no doubt existed that he was so, this very condition had forced the Government to take another portion of the loan, about two millions and a half, at more than fifty per cent. for the present year of its existence, and at six or seven per cent. forever thereafter. How could this condition operate differently? It made it the interest of every holder of the first part of the twenty-five million loan (and it was certain that, as far as possible, every moneyed man in the nation would be made a holder) to bear down upon the Government, and for them to give the most exorbitant premium for all that remained to be taken. This was early foretold by the men of reflection among us. But it was treated as a chimera, as the common story of opposition, by those whose business it is to defend every act of the Government. Now, the truth of what was foretold is absolutely certain. It stands on the official documents in this House, an eternal monument of the wild errors, and the fiscal incapacity of your Government. By it the people of these States have been subject to the most frightful extortion. Do I therefore accuse those who forced the Government to these terms? No; for to such a condition was the Government reduced in September, that even an open bankruptcy must have followed, but for the money then obtained. And if these money lenders had so pleased, you must have saved the nation by giving cent per cent for every dollar. Patriotism has nothing to do with this subject. It is a moneyed operation; and thus considered, perhaps you ought to thank the lenders that they accommodated you at all, rather than to curse them for the terms they demanded.

Mr. G. said, to a Government which had thus exhibited an utter disregard of the plainest rules of discretion and common sense—an entire ignorance of public policy—who had shown an incapacity for all fiscal operations, and had delivered themselves and their country, bound hand and foot, into the iron grasp of money lenders, he was totally unwilling, nay, he thought it madness, to trust unlimited powers as to further loans.

Sir, said Mr. G., you have rejected in Committee a proposition to render your taxes responsible for your loans, by pledging them specifically to the payment of the interest, and the gradual redemption of the principal. You are adopting the same old principles, and pursuing the same old course, which has produced the evils of the past year. You are again pledging the faith of the nation, instead of the wealth of the nation, to obtain loans. The Secretary of the Treasury has told you, and wisely told you, that this has been the cause of your failures—the principle which has destroyed your credit and ruined your finances. And he has told you that your system must be changed, or all your efforts are hopeless. Why will you disregard his admonition—an admonition enforced by the most disastrous experience? By this bill your President again appears in the money market, precisely as he appeared on the 31st of last August; can he get money on better terms now than he could then? Nay, is not the prospect darker and more desperate? And may he not, nay, will he not, pressed on by the public creditors and the public necessities, be induced to give almost any premium rather than fail? Unless his power be limited, he will again deliver the people as unresisting victims to the brokers and money lenders of the nation. Sir, to this I, as one, never will consent. Wishing, as I do, to preserve the remnant of public credit; anxious as I am to give my vote to provide for the defence of the soil, I cannot vote for this bill in its present shape. I cannot vote for it, because I am certain that by it you will obtain no money, but on terms extortionate, ruinous, and which will give the last blow to the expiring credit of the nation.

Mr. EPPES said he had no idea that a larger interest than eight per cent. would or ought to be given for this money, and he did not feel any great objection to the amendment. But he could see no reason, when this bill was merely intended to supply the amount sent to Europe for sale of the loan last authorized, why it should be granted in a different form from that.

Mr. JACKSON, of Virginia, said that gentlemen were mistaken in the calculation of the rate of interest given by the Government for the loans lately negotiated. They were obtained at seven and a half per cent. with a bonus, payable whenever the debt was extinguished, of twenty-five per cent. on the money loaned. This was demonstrable by a plain question in the rule of three. For example, the Government for eighty dollars issued a scrip for one hundred bearing six per cent. interest. If, therefore, eighty dollars gives six dollars of interest, one hundred dollars will give seven dollars and a half, or seven and a half per cent. As to the bonus, if it be divided on twelve and a half years it will make two per cent., if on twenty-five years one, and if a hundred, only one fourth per cent. The term of twelve years, specified in the contract, is a limitation of the right of the Government to redeem within that period; not an engagement to pay at the expiration of it. It was inserted at the instance and for the benefit of the stockholders, who being disposed to make an investiture in the funds, preferred a deferred payment to a speedy redemption, for the obvious reason that induces men of wealth to prefer a bank, or other moneyed institution, with an unlimited or extensive charter to any other, viz: that there will be no necessity for an early re-investiture, or a loss by the want of employment for their capital. No one will pretend to say that the Government is legally or morally bound to repay the capital advanced in twelve years, or in one hundred years, or a hundred centuries, provided it pays punctually the accruing interest. Such an obligation to pay in twelve years, would require the most oppressive system of taxation. It cannot be denied that the persons who loaned the last money to the Government made the most exorbitant exactions. The state of the country imperiously demanded money at any price; and they rose in proportion to the pressure. As we were not bound, he would not pay off the capital of that debt, until every other contracted upon better terms was extinguished, unless it was selling under par in the market, and they would, in that way, relinquish a portion of their spoils. This could be done by changing the mode of borrowing, and instead of a bonus, increase the rate of interest. Give, if necessary, eight per cent. as was done by a former Administration, for future loans, and it would be made the duty of Government to pay them off first, which was the practice in relation to the eight per cent. and six per cent. stock heretofore. It would be recollected (Mr. J. observed) that when the old debt was assumed, a large portion of it was deferred and three per cent. stock, and the Secretary of the Treasury had been authorized to pay off those three.per cent. at sixty-eight dollars per centum. This was never complained of; the holders were under no compulsion to take less than cent per cent., and if they receive their interest for ever, the contract of the Government was fulfilled. So, if the present six per cents fall below par, there would be immorality in employing agents to purchase them at a discount. If the principal were due, such a measure would be a breach of faith, but until it becomes payable there was no impropriety in buying the stock at market price; and it could not be pretended that a change of the mode as proposed would be derogatory to the spirit of the existing contracts. Among all the objections urged against the eight per cent. loans, no one ever suggested this; and hence it may be fairly asserted that it would be untenable. Whatever might be his opinion as to the conduct of the money lenders, Mr. J. declared he would faithfully perform the contract made with them by paying the interest on their loans quarter-yearly, even if it were necessary to quadruple the contemplated taxes; and he expressed some surprise at the pre-

tended solicitude which his remarks produced in a certain quarter, when the sentiment had been avowed by one of the leaders of Opposition, and applauded by them, that the Federal party would not be bound to pay the interest on the debt incurred by the Government, although they entertained no doubt of soon supplanting the men in power. Mr. J. said these remarks were merely incidental to the argument concerning the rate of interest given. He was of opinion that those disadvantageous contracts were in a great degree owing to the spirit of opposition, whereby the capitalists of the country were prevented from entering into competion with the men who contracted for the late loans, and not to the want of confidence in the good faith and ability of the nation. As to the pledge in the mode proposed, Mr. J. said, he had insuperable objections. The taxes designated were novel in this country; some of them were very high, and others were denounced by the gentlemen as oppressive. He would not entail these upon the people, and deprive the nation of the advantages which experience might afford to substitute others for them, or if the revenue were ample dispense with them altogether. It was urged, said Mr. J., that the money lenders require a more solid security than the pledge of the national faith; they prefer specific pledges, and the case of a mortgage by an individual was mentioned as analogous. Mr. J. said, that the obvious dissimilarity consisted in this: Where an individual executed a mortgage, he transferred all control over his property to a third party, and in default of payment, the courts of justice interposed and delivered over his property to the mortgagee or a purchaser. Not so with the Government; there was no physical control vested in an independent tribunal to coerce a compliance—it had only to repeal the law to defeat the security, and there was no restraint upon this power but the moral sense of the Government, which it was said cannot be relied on. Mr. J. said it was not necessary that the faith of the Government should be pledged, in terms, by any law or contract. The passage of a law vesting a right or conferring a power, was a pledge in fact that the right should be preserved and the power, when executed, was irrevocable and obligatory; but, inasmuch as that phraseology had been used he would not object to it. With these views Mr. J. said he could not imagine that a formal pledge of funds to meet the engagements of the Government was in any case necessary; inasmuch as the good faith of the nation was pledged to make good its engagements, and, having never been violated, it was not suspected by any. Yet, he added, as some gentlemen argued differently, and it might by possibility have an influence on the price of stock, he was willing to vote for an amendment whereby the taxes proposed should be pledged until an equivalent security was substituted for them.

The question on Mr. Grosvenor's amendment was decided affirmatively, as follows: For the amendment 59, against it 58.

Mr. Oakley, of New York, then moved a further amendment, viz: to strike out the general pledge of public faith to make good any deficiency in the funds for payment of the principal and interest of this loan, and insert in lieu thereof, a pledge of the proceeds of the direct tax and internal duties for that purpose : For the motion 41, against it 71.

The bill having been further immaterially amended, the Committee rose and reported the bill.

The House having confirmed the amount of three millions to be borrowed, the question offered itself on the concurrence with the Committee of the Whole, in agreeing to Mr. Grosvenor's amendment; on which question the yeas and nays were demanded by Mr. Grosvenor.

On this motion there arose a long and desultory debate, in the course of which the motion was opposed by Messrs. Lowndes, Gholson, Calhoun, Wright, and Kilbourn, and supported by the mover, and Messrs. Hulbert, Gaston, and Hanson.

On the one hand, it was argued, that such a limitation as was proposed was inexpedient because it was unusual ; because it would have the effect rather to increase than limit the rate at which the loan could be had ; and because, by a remote possibility, it might prevent the loans being had at all, and thus, as this loan was only necessary to meet the reimbursement of public debt during this quarter, produce consequences ruinous to the public credit. Occasion was taken to rebut the statements made by Mr. Oakley the other day in relation to the terms of the late loan, and to vindicate in the warmest terms the conduct of the Executive in this respect. Occasion was also taken to state several facts, among which were these : that the interest which this Administration had given for money was less than had been given by the Federal Administration under circumstances which afforded incomparably greater facility for loans ; that notwithstanding all the clamors against the credit of the nation, it is now better supported, by a sinking fund, &c., than it was in the days when those were in power who now decry it ; and that the refusal of a Boston bank lately to pay the interest of the public debt in specie, arose from no fault of the Government, which then had in the vaults of that bank three times the amount which was there due.

On the other hand, it was said, that the late improvidence of the Administration made it necessary to provide such a guard over their conduct. The consequence of what he called fiscal gambling, it was said by one speaker, (Mr. Hanson,) had been to throw the country into the arms of speculators ; to make the Government the victim of such men as Jacob Barker, who, it appeared by the documents had been unable to fulfil his engagements, and he believed that failure was the foundation of this loan. To insure the co-operation of those who spoke thus, and the confidence of the country, it was said to be necessary to give some pledge that the Government would change its course, and no longer trust itself in the hands of extortioners, &c.

Mr. Hanson's remarks were as follows :

Mr. H. observed, he now felt the same reluctance in presenting himself to the Chair which he always felt, condemning, as he did, the example of daily and constantly, upon all subjects, consuming the time, and trespassing upon the patience of the House.

As so much had been said about union and patriotism, he saw fit distinctly to notice these topics, at the same time that he reprobated the course about to be adopted to relieve the Treasury, somewhat, in its embarrassments. Mr. H. trusted that on this, as on all other occasions, his nature would show itself to be utterly irreconcilable, and his principles openly at war, with the meanness and duplicity which would act a part to gain a name for magnanimity, and attract vulgar and insincere applause for patriotism. Patriotism ! in the modern acceptation of the term, the very sound was hateful and grating to his ears. From the day of the first dawn of reason and philosophy in France, the loudest patriots in every country, visited by the revolutionary mania, had always been the boldest traitors. They were ever ready to sell, for their twenty pieces of silver, themselves or their country to the highest bidder. It was the brawling demagogues who drove the profitable trade of patriotism, and lived upon its avails, that had plunged the country into a wasteful, bloody, and calamitous war ; who had brought upon the country the sufferings and burdens which bowed it down to the very dust it was biting, and jeopardized its very political existence. Such men were the curse of every country that contained them. It had been well said, by a moral essayist, that patriotism had become the last refuge of a scoundrel. From the accusation of such patriotism he meant at least to deliver himself.

[Mr. H. was called to order by a member, who erroneously took to himself, particularly, the general denunciation of the great body of patriots in the country.]

Mr. H. would admit no man in the nation to be before him in an ardent desire to provide the means for defending the country. The proper course being taken to effectuate the object which all professed to have at heart, he was as anxious and as ready as any gentleman to co-operate in the necessary measures to restore and support public credit, and resuscitate the finances. Unless public credit was revived, and the Treasury relieved, it was idle to talk of defending the country. Money was the great sinew of war. Without it the invader could not be repelled, the country could not be defended. It was mockery to talk of defending the country, without providing the means, but that defence and protection must be extended equally to all parts of the Union. Mr. H. was as ready as any gentleman to expose his person and spill his blood in defence of his country ; could he, then, be disposed to withhold money for the same purpose ? Life and treasure were not to be weighed against each other. He would vote for the loan, provided gentlemen would not continue to disregard and set at naught the established maxims of all well regulated Governments.

If they would not set experience at defiance, and treat with contempt its lessons so dearly bought, but would follow the counsels of wisdom, his hearty support was already pledged. But if they persisted in a downward course of desperate fiscal gambling, subjecting themselves to be preyed upon by harpies, speculators, and usurers, it was impossible, without an abandonment of the most sacred duties, to give any countenance to their measures. The inevitable consequence of such a course was bankruptcy and ruin, for already was the credit of the Government no better than that of Jacob Barker's himself, with which it had been identified. It appeared by the late Secretary's report, with the accompanying documents, that there was a defalcation on the part of some one of the contractors for the ten million loan to an immense amount, and there was no doubt that the said Barker was the defaulter referred to, although the Secretary had not mentioned his name.

Mr. H. said he was placed in a most painful situation. Understanding that the system of finance, which had brought so much distress and disgrace upon the country, was to be abandoned, and that gentlemen had been at last brought to consent to resort to the fundamental maxims of finance, which forbid the creation of debt without providing and pledging the means of payment, he had voted for the highest rate of taxes. He had done so under the fullest persuasion, he might say an assurance, that the taxes were to be specifically appropriated for the payment of the interest, and the ultimate reimbursement of the principal of the public debt. He had done so under the belief that the sponge was to be applied to the system of finance hitherto relied on; that we were all prepared to rub out and begin anew, having the benefit of experience to steer us clear of the shoals and rocks upon which the vessel of State had been so near bilging.

Mr. H. hoped that the limitation of interest moved by his friend from New York, (Mr. GROSVENOR,) would be adopted. He had no doubt that the money could be had upon more advantageous terms if security was given, by pledging the public funds for the payment of the debt, but after the experience we had had of the profusion and profligacy introduced into the Treasury Department in the loan negotiations, there could be no reliance on the Administration to obtain loans upon better terms; they should, therefore, be restricted in the interest to be given. So extremely anxious was Mr. H. to place the country in the best possible posture of defence, in the hope that the nation might yet be saved, and to take from those who are responsible for its preservation and safety all pretexts for shifting the blame upon other shoulders, that he would still vote for the bill if the amendment failed, as it was pretty evident it would do. But although the rejection of that amendment did not present an insurmountable difficulty, should the House refuse to accept the amendment moved by his friend next to him, (Mr. OAKLEY,) in Committee, Mr. H. could not in his conscience vote for the bill. He could not bring himself to sanction a vicious, ruinous, system, which had been the cause of all our financial embarrassments and disgrace. Why, after the fatal experience we had had of the futility of all attempts to borrow money upon reasonable terms, without pledging something more substantial than the public faith for its repayment, and the punctual discharge of the interest, persist in the old plan of expedients, of living from hand to mouth, of squandering all to-day and letting to-morrow provide for itself. Why persist in a system which can eventuate in nothing but ruin? Was the mere pride of opinion to stand between the country and its defence—probably its salvation! He hazarded nothing in saying that the loan would fail, or be obtained upon the most ruinous terms, unless something more substantial than the moral sense of the nation was pledged as security. That moral sense was the reliance for the former loans, and it was now thirty per cent. below par; yes, the moral sense of the nation had depreciated 30 per cent. since the last session of Congress.

He, Mr. H., was the more surprised at the determination of gentlemen to go into the market to borrow three millions of dollars, without offering any new inducement, but, on the contrary, refusing to give security when they have 13 millions of the 25 million loan still on hand, and for which there had been no bid. His surprise was the more excited at the determination of gentlemen to adhere to the old plan of finance, when the honorable Chairman of the Committee of Ways and Means avowed that the money to be borrowed was to pay the interest of the public debt which fell due the present quarter. If such was the important and indispensable uses to which it was to be applied, how could gentlemen reconcile it to good conscience and duty to hesitate to give the pledge and security which would insure success, when, by refusing it, everything was put at hazard. Anxious as Mr. H. was to demonstrate, in every way, his ardent desire to revive and sustain public credit, which was inseparably connected with the national defence, he could not, in any way, countenance the system which it seemed was to be persisted in, let the consequence be what it might. The great object to be accomplished, was to restore confidence in the ability and efficiency of the national finances, which was only to be done by an adequate provision for the wants of Government, and pledging the public funds for the payment of the interest and redemption of the principal of the public debt. Public credit was a sentiment; like matters of faith, it was a thing not to be reasoned about. If gentlemen expected to restore public confidence, and thereby recover public credit, they must abandon at once, and forever, their old shifts and expedients adopted with a single view to their popularity.

He again reminded the House that the system they seemed disposed to persevere in, could result in nothing but disappointment and disgrace to themselves, and injury to the country. Was everything to be sacrificed, even our political existence, to the pride of opinion? It would not be amiss to embrace the present occasion to remind gentlemen, that the minority had ever protested against the system of finance which had induced the embarrassments the Treasury labored under.

They clearly foresaw, and distinctly and repeatedly foretold, its fatal consequence. They opposed the war in all its approaches, in all its parts, and in every stage of it. They had constantly held up to view the enormous expenditures to which it would subject the country. They had pointed out the manner in which the general measures of Government would destroy the revenue and resources of the country. They knew, and declared, whenever an opportunity occurred, that loans after loans must be resorted to, and that loans could not be had except upon the most ruinous terms, unless general confidence was produced in the ability and efficiency of the national finances, and that the finances could not have a solid basis without an efficient and permanent system of taxation. The Congress was conjured not to declare war. The most conspicuous men of the majority admitted that war ought not to be declared, unless gentlemen were prepared to enact such a system. The fatal step being taken, its authors were admonished, warned, not to reply upon loans to defray the expenses of the war, without laying a broad and solid foundation for the finances. The inevitable fatal consequences of such a reliance, were predicted. From your pen, and from your lips, sir, (said Mr. H., pointing to the Speaker,) proceeded the same admonitions and predictions. We, differently situated from you, sir, enjoying as you do, the rare and singular felicity of uniting the confidence of a majority of all parties, we did not escape suspicion and censure. We were accused of predicting what we secretly labored to realize, the greatest national calamity, an explosion of public credit. It is to be lamented that your advice and our predictions were regarded as worthy only of scoff and crimination. We were both supported at the time by the concurrent opinions of all the enlightened men of the country, and the subsequent expositions and advice of two successive Heads of the Treasury Department corroborate and establish the soundness of our opinions. But party prejudice and the pride of opinion is not to be affected by argument: There is but one school, the teacher in which is Experience, where the intellects of some men can be illuminated.

Mr. H. incidentally noticed the reference of Mr. EPPES to the difficulties which arose in relation to the payment of the interest of the public debt due in one section of the country. Mr. EPPES laid the blame of the defalcation to a Boston bank. Mr. H. said, the circumstances in relation to the default of the bank alluded to, were too well established and known to admit of any misunderstanding or delusion. In conformity to the settled system of favoritism, the Gerrymander State Bank had been selected by Government as most worthy of its confidence and patronage. If that bank, the circumstances attending the creation of which were so well known, was the only one in Boston unable to continue its payments in specie, there was no difficulty in properly attaching the blame of the failure to meet the public engagements.

Mr. H. reiterated the declaration of his readiness to co-operate in every practical and effectual effort to revive public credit. He had only to repeat his sincere regret that gentlemen in the majority had not brought their minds to adopt the only measure that could accomplish the all-important and desirable object. It was their refusal to come at once to the determination which they must at last come to, if public credit was ever to be recovered, that placed him in his present painful situation. After the pledge which he had given, by his vote for all the tax resolutions, he might appear inconsistent in voting against a loan which was declared to be indispensable for the public service, but it was impossible for him to sanction what he had always pronounced to be a system of desperate financial gambling. Suppose, said he, an individual reduced by extravagance, gaming and improvident speculations, to bankruptcy and ruin, were to call upon his family and friends to extricate him from his difficulties. Could they be expected to give him assistance unless he promised to forsake and renounce his ruinous courses, and no more pursue his pernicious practices? Could they be expected, without such a promise, and the more upon his positive refusal, to give such a promise—could they be expected to supply him with the means of continuing his dissolute and riotous course of life, and thus waste their own substance without affording any lasting relief to him? The mistaken zeal of friendship, and the blind excess of affection, sometimes betrayed individuals in private life into such acts of folly, and they have become partners in the ruin and sorrow of their friends and relatives. But public men, who had in charge the happiness and destiny of a people, must hush and subdue the feelings of weakness springing from the frail nature of man. Not generosity, but the fixed principles of right and justice they were bound to regard. When was it, said Mr. H., that the prodigal son was received again into the paternal mansion? It was when he had forsaken his evil ways, abandoned his riotous course of life, and returned to the paths of prudence and of duty.

If gentlemen were not sufficiently instructed in the school of experience, as to agree to abandon their political system generally, they had only to give up their vicious destructive system of finance, to insure a cordial concurrence in the necessary measures to build up the dilapidated credit of the nation upon a new and solid foundation. To do this, nothing more was required but to recur to the example, the principles and system of their predecessors in power. There were two roads leading to prosperity and adversity, one to the right the other to the left. We had travelled the wrong road for fourteen years, and had gone an immense distance, but the shortest way to get right was to go back to where we started. It was the only sure mode of arriving at the goal we all professed to aim for, the safety, honor, and prosperity of the nation.

The question on concurrence in the amendment was then decided in the negative—yeas 51, nays 97, as follows:

YEAS—Messrs. Baylies of Massachusetts, Bigelow, Boyd, Bradbury, Brigham, Butler, Caperton, Champion, Cilley, Cooper, Culpeper, Davenport, Ely, Gaston, Geddes, Grosvenor, Hale, Hanson, Hulbert, Jackson of Rhode Island, Kent of New York, King of Massachusetts, Law, Lewis, Lovett, Macon, Markell, Moseley, Oakley, Pearson, Pickering, Pitkin, John Reed, William Reed, Ruggles, Schureman, Sherwood, Shipherd, Smith of New York, Stanford, Sturges, Taggart, Thompson, Vose, Ward of Massachusetts, Webster, Wheaton, White Wilcox, Wilson of Massachusetts, and Winter.

NAYS—Messrs. Alexander, Alston, Anderson, Archer, Avery, Barbour, Bard, Barnett, Bowen, Bradley, Brown, Caldwell, Calhoun, Cannon, Chappell, Clark, Clopton, Comstock, Condict, Conard, Crawford, Creighton, Crouch, Cuthbert, Dana, Davis of Pennsylvania, Denoyelles, Desha, Duvall, Earle, Eppes, Farrow, Findley, Fisk of Vermont, Fisk of New York, Forney, Franklin, Gholson, Glasgow, Goodwyn, Gourdin, Griffin, Hall, Harris, Hasbrouck, Hawes, Hawkins, Hopkins of Kentucky, Hubbard, Humphreys, Hungerford, Ingham, Irving, Jackson of Virginia, Johnson of Virginia, Johnson of Kentucky, Kennedy, Kent of Maryland, Kerr, Kershaw, Kilbourn, King of North Carolina, Lefferts, Lowndes, Lyle, McCoy, McKee, McKim, McLean, Nelson, Newton, Parker, Pickens, Piper, Pleasants, Post, Potter, Rea of Pennsylvania, Rhea of Tennessee, Rich, Ringgold, Robertson, Sage, Sevier, Seybert, Sharp, Skinner, Smith of Virginia, Strong, Tannehill, Taylor, Telfair, Troup, Udree, Wilson of Pennsylvania, Wright, and Yancey.

So the amendment made in Committee of the Whole was rejected by the House.

Mr. OAKLEY, of New York, renewed the motion he had made in committee to pledge specifically the proceeds of the direct tax and internal duties for the redemption of the principal and interest of the loan.

On suggestion of Mr. SHARP, of Kentucky, Mr. OAKLEY so modified his motion as to embrace also a pledge of the duties on impost and tonnage.

This motion was opposed by Mr. EPPES, and Mr. HAWKINS, of Kentucky; and opposed by Messrs. HANSON, WRIGHT, FARROW, of South Carolina, and RICH, of Vermont.

Mr. RICH offered an amendment to the amendment of Mr. OAKLEY, the object of which was to extend the pledge to such part of the loan of twenty-five millions as remains uncontracted for.

Mr. OAKLEY objected to this amendment because it would have a retro-active operation, in consequence of the terms of the ten million loan, by which the contractors were to have the most advantageous terms which might be allowed to the lenders of the remainder of the twenty-five million loan.

The amendment moved by Mr. RICH was negatived.

The motion of Mr. OAKLEY was then further opposed by Mr. SHARP, of Kentucky, and Mr. JACKSON, of Virginia, and supported by Mr. GASTON, and the mover.

This motion was opposed on the ground that to adopt it would place this loan on a footing different from any other; that it was unnecessary, because the funds already established were abundantly sufficient to redeem the public debt, and because the Sinking Fund was about to be re-organized so as to be more active in its operation. In allusion to the argument of the mover of this motion, and his friends, on the question of the removal of the Seat of Government, it was said, rather jocosely than seriously, that it would be perfectly unimportant to establish such a pledge, because pledges by one Congress are not binding on another, being at any moment liable to be repealed.

The motion was warmly supported, on the ground that it was expedient to place the credit of the Government in future loans on such a broad, visible basis as should satisfy the most scrupulous lender of the security of his money; that it was the want of such a basis which had interposed a difficulty in the obtaining former loans; that the loans so obtained ought not to be placed on a par with future loans, obtained on terms more favorable to the Government; that the sponge ought to be applied to the old system of finance, and a new, better, and more durable system substituted for it, of which the provision proposed in this motion should constitute a feature.

Mr. OAKLEY's motion was negatived—for it 37, against it 87, as follows:

YEAS—Messrs. Archer, Bigelow, Boyd, Caperton, Champion, Chappell, Cilley, Duvall, Farrow, Gaston, Grosvenor, Hanson, Hawes, Hopkins of Kentucky, Ingham, Irving, Kent of New York, Kent of Maryland, Kerr, Lefferts, Lewis, Lovett, Markell, Moseley, Oakley, Pearson, William Reed, Rich, Ruggles, Seybert, Sherwood, Skinner, Sturges, Thompson, Vose, White, and Wright.

NAYS—Messrs. Alexander, Alston, Anderson, Avery, Barbour, Bard, Barnett, Baylies of Massachusetts, Bowen, Bradbury, Brown, Butler, Calhoun, Cannon, Clark, Clopton, Comstock, Condict, Conard, Crawford, Creighton, Crouch, Cuthbert, Dana, Davis of Pennsylvania, Denoyelles, Desha, Earle, Eppes, Fisk of Vermont, Fisk of New York, Forney, Franklin, Gholson, Glasgow, Goodwyn, Gourdin, Griffin, Hall, Harris, Hawkins, Hubbard, Humphreys, Hungerford, Hulbert, Jackson of Virginia, Johnson of Virginia, Johnson of Kentucky, Kennedy, Kershaw, Kilbourn, King of North Carolina, Lowndes, Lyle, Macon, McCoy, McKim, McLean, Nelson, Newton, Parker, Pickens, Piper, Pitkin, Pleasants, Potter, John Reed, Rea of Pennsylvania, Rhea of Tennessee, Ringgold, Robertson, Sage, Sharp, Smith of Virginia, Stanford, Strong, Tannehill, Taylor, Telfair, Udree, Ward of Massachusetts, Wilcox, Wilson of Massachusetts, Wilson of Pennsylvania, and Yancey.

The bill was ordered to be engrossed for a third reading.

MONDAY, October 31.

Another member, to wit: from Connecticut BENJAMIN TALLMADGE, appeared, and took his seat.

On motion of Mr. JOHNSON, of Kentucky,

Resolved, That the Committee on Pensions and Revolutionary Claims be directed to inquire into the expediency of allowing Captain Richard Taylor, senior, his claims for medical aid for his wounds received in the Revolution, commutation of half pay, and a pension from the United States, in addition to the one received from the State of Virginia.

Mr. EPPES, of Virginia, from the Committee of Ways and Means, reported a bill for authorizing the Secretary of State, during the continuance of the present war, to give additional compensation to masters of vessels for bringing home destitute and distressed American seamen from abroad; which was read, and committed.

Mr. E. also reported a bill for the relief of John Castille; which was twice read, and committed.

Mr. E. also made an unfavorable report on the petition of John H. Beasley and others; which was, on motion of Mr. FISK, of Vermont, recommitted to the Committee of Ways and Means for further examination.

The joint resolution, offered by Mr. CLOPTON, of Virginia, for the appointment of a committee to wait on the President, and request him to appoint a day of public humility, fasting, and prayer, was also ordered to be engrossed for a third reading, and to be read a third time to-morrow.

On motion of Mr. JOHNSON, of Kentucky, the Committee on Public Lands were directed to inquire into the expediency of granting to Anthony Shane, (a half-breed Indian who has performed eminent services to the United States,) the right of the United States to three hundred and twenty acres of land in the State of Ohio, at a place on St. Mary's river, known by the name of Shane's Crossing; and leave was given to them to report thereon by bill or otherwise.

The engrossed bill to authorize a loan for a sum not exceeding three millions of dollars, was read a third time, and passed without debate or division, though not without opposition.

The report of the Committee of Claims unfavorable to the petition of Joseph Forrest, passed through a Committee of the Whole, and was concurred in by the House.

A bill was received from the Senate, entitled "An act authorizing the President of the United States to cause to be built or purchased the vessels therein described." [The bill provides for the building or purchase and employment of any number not exceeding twenty vessels, to carry not less than eight nor more than fourteen guns.]

The bill was twice read, and referred to the Committee on Naval Affairs.

On motion of Mr. WILLIAM REED, the House proceeded to consider the resolution submitted by him on the 28th instant, and the same being again read, a motion was made by Mr. WILLIAM REED, to amend his said motion, by striking out from the word "war," to the end thereof, and to insert the following words:

"Which have since that time been commissioned for service, designating the names and force, with the number of officers and men attached to each, and the present condition of these vessels; and if any essential change has been made in any of them during that time; also, the number of vessels that have been added to the force on the Atlantic, under authority of the laws of 2d of January and 3d of March, 1813; and if those laws have not been fully executed, the progress that has been made, and the causes that have prevented their entire execution."

The adoption of this resolution was opposed by Mr. PLEASANTS of Virginia, and RHEA of Tennessee, and supported by the mover; but finally rejected by the following vote: For the motion 52, against it 68.

PETITION OF REBECCA HODGSON.

Mr. YANCEY, from the Committee of Claims, made a report on the petition of Rebecca Hodgson; which was read, and referred to a Committee of the Whole on Monday next.

The report is as follows:

That on the 14th day of August, 1800, Joseph Hodgson, then of the City of Washington, leased, by deed, for the term of eight months, to Samuel Dexter, as Secretary of War, a tenement in the said city, to be occupied for the term aforesaid, as the War Office. In consideration of which occupation and use, he was to give the sum of four hundred dollars, which has been paid and satisfied to the intestate of the petitioner. In the lease, Mr. Dexter covenants for himself and his successors in office, "that he or they shall and will, at all times during the said term, keep, or cause to be kept, in good and sufficient repair the said demised premises, inevitable casualties and ordinary decay excepted, and the same so well and sufficiently kept in repair, shall and will, at the end of the said term, yield and surrender up to him, the said Joseph Hodgson." Mr. Dexter immediately took possession of the tenement, under the contract, and occupied the same as the War Office, until the 8th of November, following, when, in the evening of that day, it was consumed by fire. The petitioner is the legal representative of Joseph Hodgson, and prays of Congress such compensation as the circumstances of her case merit.

In the investigation of the merits of this claim, the first question that presented itself to the committee was, in what manner was the fire communicated to the house? Was it by negligence or inattention to duty on the part of the officer or his servants, or was it from some other cause not within his or their control? It would seem, from the evidence of the petitioner, that she alleges the fire was communicated by design, with a criminal intention to destroy the house and the public papers contained in it, by some person employed by the War Department.

It is also alleged, that the fire was communicated from an adjoining building, belonging to, and then in possession of, a Mr. Jackson. It is not pretended by the petitioner that the house was burnt by any negligence or inattention on the part of the lessor, or his servants or clerks; indeed, the evidence is clear and satisfactory, that the room in which it is alleged by the petitioner the fire originated, had not been used, nor fire made in it, for several weeks previous to the destruction.

Your committee have diligently examined the circumstances offered in evidence, and are of opinion the fire was communicated from the fire-place of Jackson's house, and in this they concur in opinion with a committee appointed by the House of Representatives, in

February, 1801, to investigate the causes of the destruction of the War Office, and also with the committee to whom this petition was referred at the last session of Congress.

Assuming, then, as an established fact, that the fire was communicated from Jackson's house to the War Office, the question arises, was the destruction such as would exonerate the lessor from his undertaking to surrender the premises at the end of the term, according to the conditions of the contract? This question involves the meaning of the term "inevitable casualties." It is believed that writers upon law define it to be those accidents which happen by the act of God; such as destruction by lightning, tempest, or floods; or such as are produced by a public enemy; or such as happen without any design or negligence, and such as human foresight and prudence could not prevent or control. A fire which produces the destruction of a house, under circumstances like the present case, is said, by the distinguished author upon the law of bailments, to be an inevitable misfortune, an inevitable accident. It is therefore believed that, if the fact be considered as established, that the fire proceeded from the house of Jackson, the United States are not liable to the petitioner under the covenant.

It is not believed, however, by the committee, that the United States are liable, considering the claim of the petitioner upon the principle she places it. It is attempted to be shown by her that the fire originated by design, with a criminal intention to destroy the house and the public papers, either by some person employed in the office, or some other incendiary. If it was destroyed by the former, the Government cannot be considered liable; the principal who employs the agent is liable for injuries sustained by his negligence or omission of duty, but not for the commission of his crimes.

If an officer or agent of the Government, in his official capacity, does an injury to an individual, by neglecting to do that which a man ordinarily attentive to his own business would have done, it is believed the Government ought, perhaps, to be liable; but if one who happens to be in public employment commits acts felonious in themselves, in consequence of which an injury accrues to third persons, it is not believed the Government is liable. If the fire was communicated by the latter, the act itself would be highly criminal in the individual, and for which he might be punished by the criminal law of the country. But it is believed that the civil injury would be merged in the felony; and it is considered doubtful, at least, whether he, if discovered, would be liable for the civil injury; but there can be no doubt, that the Government would not.

Upon the whole, the committee are of opinion that, if an individual stood in the place of the Government in this case, the petitioner, from her own showing, would be without any remedy against him; and they conceive that the rule applicable to the case of individuals is the best to adopt between the Government and individuals; they are of opinion that sound principles of policy and justice require that the prayer of the petitioner be disallowed; they therefore recommend to the House the following resolution:

Resolved, That the prayer of the petitioner ought not to be granted.

SUSPENSION OF DIRECT TAX, &c.

Mr. Wilson, of Massachusetts, offered for consideration the following resolution:

Resolved, That the Committee of Ways and Means inquire into the expediency of suspending the collection of direct tax and internal duties in those districts of the State of Massachusetts, which are in possession of the enemy.

The House agreed, 62 to 47, now to consider the resolution.

Mr. Sharp, of Kentucky, who had voted for the consideration of the resolution, desired that the gentleman would state his object.

Mr. Wilson stated that the enemy, having possession of Eastport and Castine, thus possessed the command of territory which belonged to two collection districts; one of the collectors of which resided within the territory thus occupied, and the other just without it, although five-sixths of the territory attached to his district was in possession of the enemy. It was the duty of those collectors, according to law, to proceed in the collection of the duties. These duties, the British Governor, Sherbrooke, as gentlemen had, no doubt, seen in the public papers, had required the collectors to pay over to his officers established at Castine or Eastport; and with this requisition the collectors must comply, or suffer confiscation of their property; on the other hand, they would violate their duty, according to law, if they did not proceed in their collection. He wished to relieve them from this disagreeable alternative, and to put it out of the power of the British Government to tax the people through the intervention of American officers.

Mr. Wright, of Maryland, said, there was no novelty in this proposition, as precedents might be found for it in the Journals of the Old Congress. Whenever a district was in possession of the enemy, some provision of this kind ought to be interposed to relieve the people as well as the collectors. Mr. W. was for doing equal justice to all; for considering the people of all parts of the Union as one great family—and, in regard to this question, he was willing to begin with Massachusetts, anything in her denunciations of the General Government to the contrary notwithstanding.

After a few words of explanation from Mr. Wilson, the resolution was agreed to—79 to 42.

Tuesday, November 1.

The Speaker laid before the House a letter from the Secretary of the Treasury, transmitting a report of the papers lost or destroyed from the Treasury in consequence of the incursion of the enemy on the 24th day of August last; whereby it appears that no papers essential to the adjustment of pending accounts, or of material value, were lost or destroyed.

The resolution "requesting the President of the United States to recommend a day of public humiliation, fasting and prayer," was read a third time, and passed.

The bill to incorporate the Columbian Manufacturing Company of Alexandria, in the District of Columbia, being called up by Mr. Kent, of Maryland, passed through a Committee of the

Whole, and then, on motion of Mr. WEBSTER, of New Hampshire, was recommitted to the District Committee.

THE FLOTILLA MEN.

The House resumed the consideration of the bill for allowing compensation to Commodore Barney's officers and men, for the loss of their clothing, &c.

Mr. PLEASANTS, of Virginia, took occasion to read the following letter he had received from Commodore Barney since this subject was last under consideration:

BALTIMORE, *October* 30, 1814.

SIR: It was not until this morning that I saw a short sketch of the debate on the "flotilla bill." I was much surprised at what was said on that occasion; for it is well known when orders were given to blow up the flotilla, that the enemy were firing upon them from forty barges with cannon and rockets, and had landed a body of marines at Pig Point, within a mile of the flotilla. The orders from the Secretary of the Navy to me were, to keep the flotilla above the enemy, and if they attempted to march for Washington, to land my men, leaving sufficient to destroy the flotilla if attacked. On Sunday 21st of August, finding the enemy on the road to the Wood Yard, direct for Washington, I landed upwards of four hundred men, leaving only eight men in each barge to take care of them or destroy them as the case might be, but by no means to suffer them to fall into the hands of the enemy; most of the baggage and all the bedding of the men which were landed was left on board, not wishing to encumber my men with much baggage. On Monday morning the 22d, we joined the Army at the Wood Yard, where I found the marine corps and five pieces of heavy artillery, which the Secretary of the Navy had had the precaution to send forward from Washington and place under my command. I need not relate our services afterwards; but when the flotilla was blown up, we, and not the enemy, "were a day's march from it"—of course could not save the baggage. So far from being able to get "further up the river," as was said, the vessels were aground and blown up in that situation; and as to having time to save the baggage, so contrary is the truth, that several of the men were taken prisoners in the act of destroying the flotilla, and still remain so. Much more might be said on this subject, but the Winter coming on imperiously calls for some assistance to these unfortunate men.

I have the honor to be, &c.,

JOSHUA BARNEY.

Hon. Mr. PLEASANTS.

The amendment pending when this subject was last before the House, was agreed to.

On motion of Mr. J. G. JACKSON, the word "officers" was stricken out of the bill—53 to 47. His reason was, that it would set a bad precedent for remuneration of officers in other cases where they should lose baggage, which frequently occurred.

The bill thus amended, was ordered to be engrossed for a third reading on to-morrow.

WEDNESDAY, November 2.

A new member, to wit: from New Jersey, THOMAS BINES, elected in the place of Jacob Hufty, deceased, appeared, produced his credentials, was qualified. and took his seat.

Mr. FARROW, of South Carolina, presented the petition of sundry inhabitants of Chester district, South Carolina, remonstrating against the transportation and opening of the mail on the Sabbath, which they consider as injurious to the morals and civil welfare of the people.—Referred to the Committee of Post Offices and Post Roads, to whom like petitions from other quarters have been referred.

The bill for the relief of the petty officers and seamen under the command of Captain Joshua Barney, was read a third time, and passed.

BOUNTY TO PRIVATEERS.

Mr. ROBERTSON, of Louisiana, offered the following resolution:

Resolved, That the Committee on Naval Affairs be instructed to inquire into the expediency of giving a bounty to the owners, officers, and crews of privateers, for the vessels of the enemy destroyed at sea, and that they have leave to report by bill or otherwise.

Mr. R. stated his object, in moving this resolution, to be, in the first place, to operate on the commerce of the enemy; in the second, to preserve to our country the services of the seamen, who, by manning the prize vessels, were frequently captured by the enemy, and as far as possible retained by him in his possession, and withheld from exchange. There were other cogent reasons why such a measure ought to be adopted, viz: to give encouragement to a species of warfare which the enemy most sensibly felt, &c. Whatever were the general impressions of gentlemen in relation to privateering, this measure was peculiarly proper in relation to us, because at present the enemy has all the commerce of the world, and we have none.

The resolution was agreed to *nem. con.*

WAR MEASURES.

The House, according to the order of the day, resolved itself into a Committee of the Whole, on the bill to authorize the President of the United States to accept the services of volunteers who may associate and organize themselves, and offer their services to the Government of the United States.

The bill having been read through as far as the section which declares that, after having served out their nine months, they should not be held liable for a longer period—

Mr. LOWNDES, of South Carolina, expressed his regret at being called upon to vote partially on the system reported by the Military Committee, of which this was only a subordinate feature. But, in any view, he was desirous to know whether the provision immediately under consideration contemplated the exemption of such persons, in consequence of their nine months' service, from any classification or draught which might apply generally to all the people? Whilst on the one hand it could scarcely be expected to get volunteers unless they were in some degree exempted from militia service by volunteering, it would on

519   HISTORY OF CONGRESS.   520

H. OF R.   *War Measures.*   NOVEMBER, 1814.

the other hand be a fatal objection to this system, if, for nine months' voluntary service, they are to be exempted from all future service or draught. He repeated that it would be desirable to act on the whole system at once, and not first to act on the subsidiary force proposed by this bill, and afterwards on the foundation, the regular force.

Mr. TROUP repeated, that the Military Committee, convened for the purpose, this morning, of deciding whether it would be proper first to act on the two bills which accompanied this bill, had decided that it would be proper for the present to postpone taking up these bills. The reasons which produced this decision were, that the subject of raising men was a very difficult one, insomuch that it presented, at best, a choice of difficulties. They had understood, also, that there was a probability that, through some channel or other, another plan than that adopted and reported by the Military Committee would be presented to the House. It had been deemed proper to give the House an opportunity of seeing all the plans which could be offered, that they might select the best; that is, the one which should be subject to the fewest difficulties. With this view they had determined to postpone for a few days the consideration of the other bills. As to the section to which the gentleman objected, it had no reference whatever to an exemption from draught, and was perhaps in itself mere surplusage, its object being only to define more accurately the term of service of the proposed force, which was intended to substitute frequent requisitions of militia force, than which it was believed this would be a more efficient, and probably, from its protracted term of service, a much cheaper force. The subject of general or partial exemption from draught, would properly enter, if deemed expedient, into the general classification bill.

Mr. LOWNDES rejoined, that to the particular section under consideration, as explained by Mr. TROUP, he had no sort of objection.

Mr. TROUP moved to strike out nine months (the proposed term of service) and insert twelve.

Mr. DESHA, of Kentucky, opposed the motion, because he said nine months was enough for one campaign, and twelve months too little for two. If the time was extended, he should prefer eighteen months, which should embrace two campaigns.

Mr. JOHNSON, of Kentucky, assigned the reason why the Committee on Military Affairs had determined to propose to change the term of service from nine to twelve months. It was, that three months might be afforded for discipline and instruction in the evolutions necessary in the face of an enemy before they were called into the field; and the remaining nine months would cover a Summer and Fall campaign.

Mr. HOPKINS, of Kentucky, said he should vote against the proposed amendment, because he was desirous of inserting eighteen in lieu of twelve months. He believed that corps of this description might be as easily obtained for eighteen months or two years as for any other term; and the longer the period of their service the more useful they would certainly be.

Mr. TROUP said he should be glad if the gentlemen from the Western country would settle this question among themselves. They best knew what term of service would be most agreeable. The object was to get the men; and the period most agreeable to those disposed to enter the service would certainly be the best.

Mr. BARBOUR, of Virginia, stated that the Military Committee proposed the period of twelve months as the minimum of service—the men would, according to the bill, if amended as proposed, serve not less than twelve months—which period certainly embraced a longer term of service, if it should be found as easy to obtain the men under it.

The motion to strike out nine and insert twelve was agreed to—57 to 55.

The bill having been further amended and the blanks filled—

Mr. SHARP, of Kentucky, inquired, whether it had been the intention of the Military Committee that single regiments only should be raised of this description of force? If otherwise, whether any provision was intended to be made for general officers?

Mr. TROUP replied, that that was a point which the Committee had not taken under consideration; as the bill now stood, it only contemplated the acceptation of these volunteers by regiments, battalions, and companies, who would of course be placed, when necessary, from their numbers or the nature of the service, under regular general officers.

Mr. FORSYTH, of Georgia, moved to add as an amendment to the bill a new section in nearly the following words:

"*And be it further enacted,* That the officers, non-commissioned officers, and privates, whose services are accepted under the authority of this act, who shall serve for two years, shall be exempted from militia service during the present war."

Mr. TROUP suggested the propriety of deferring a motion of this kind until the bill for classification should be taken up, when it would be properly determined who should and who should not be exempt from its operation. What would be the effect of such a provision in this bill on any future act respecting the militia, he could not, nor could any person now determine. He therefore thought the subject would come more fairly and properly before the House, when the other bill should be taken up.

Mr. FORSYTH said it was impossible for him to say what would be done in relation to the bill his colleague had alluded to. Whether the bill would ever pass the House he could not say. The tendency of the proposition he had offered would be to increase the length of the term of service—to induce a great number to engage for two years instead of one. If he could be certain the bill in question would pass, and if it did pass, that such a provision as this would be attached to it, Mr. F. said he would withdraw his motion. But as these points were both doubtful, he must insist on his motion.

Mr. TROUP then said he would state candidly

the point of his objection to this motion. The bill now under consideration was not intended to substitute that particular kind of force which this House must rely mainly on for the prosecution of the war. If it was intended to substitute a volunteer force for a regular force, such a provision would be well worthy of consideration. But so long as he hoped no one entertained such an idea, he feared such an amendment as this would, at the same time that it would make the amount of volunteer force unnecessarily great, tend to diminish the amount of the regular force which might be raised by draught, &c.

Mr. Johnson, of Kentucky, said he was sorry to differ from the chairman of the Military Committee in relation to this amendment. He thought it a very proper one. It would afford a great inducement to persons to volunteer for two years; and it was his opinion, Mr. J. said, that volunteers for two years were as efficient a force as any we could have, and equal in every respect to regular force. If we had an army of an hundred thousand men of this description, we should not want a single regular soldier.

Mr. Forsyth said, in reply to the argument, that too many volunteers might be called forth by such a provision, that the President had the power to limit the number.

The amendment of Mr. Forsyth was adopted by the following vote, viz: For the amendment, 64; against it, 51.

On motion of Mr. Rich, of Vermont, the daily compensation of the volunteers was changed from twenty-six and two-third cents to thirty-three and one-third cents per day.

Mr. Kilbourn, of Ohio, moved to extend to privates killed during the service, the same provisions for the relief of their widows and children, as is provided in the bill for officers' families.

To this motion it was objected, by Mr. Troup, that to adopt this amendment would be to place privates in this corps on a different footing from privates in any other corps in the service of the United States, in regard to whom the Senate had uniformly rejected every provision of the kind proposed by this House.

The motion of Mr. Kilbourn was negatived—36 only rising in favor of it.

The Committee then rose and reported the bill. The several amendments made in Committee of the Whole were concurred in by the House.

On motion of Mr. Smith, of New York, the bill was further amended, in that part providing land bounty to accrue when discharged, so as to read " when honorably discharged."

Mr. Kilbourn renewed the motion he had unsuccessfully made in Committee of the Whole, remarking that he did not believe it had been understood by many gentlemen, and spoke in support of it.

The motion was now decided in the affirmative—yeas 88.

The bill having been further amended—

On the suggestion of Mr. McKee, of Kentucky, that he desired to propose an amendment going to place volunteers, during the war, on the same terms as to bounty in money and land as our other troops; which amendment he desired time to prepare; the bill was ordered to lie on the table till to-morrow.

. Thursday, November 3.

Another member, to wit: from Virginia, Daniel Sheffey, appeared and took his seat.

Mr. Pleasants, of Virginia, reported without amendment the bill from the Senate to authorize the President to cause to be purchased or built the vessels therein described; which was referred to a Committee of the Whole.

Mr. Kilbourn, of Ohio, said, having observed that there was much difficulty in filling the ranks of the Army, and believing that to attain that highly important object, nothing could more greatly conduce than a provision for the families of those who die in the service, he had been induced to offer the following resolution:

Resolved, That the Committee on Military Affairs be instructed to inquire into the expediency of providing, by law, for the relief of the widows and children of all such non-commissioned officers, musicians, and privates, as shall be killed, or die of wounds received in the public service, in any of the corps composing the Army of the United States.

After some conversation, in the course of which it appeared that a resolution embracing partially the objects of this motion, had been passed in the early part of the session—the resolution was ordered to lie on the table.

The House resumed the consideration of the volunteer bill; which was amended, on motion of Mr. Troup, so as to authorize the acceptance of volunteers for the war, to receive the same bounty and in other respects to be placed on the same footing as persons enlisted for the war. And, thus amended, the bill was ordered to be engrossed for a third reading.

PROVISION FOR COLLECTORS.

Mr. Ingersoll, of Pennsylvania, offered for consideration the following resolution:

" *Resolved*, That the Committee of Ways and Means be instructed to inquire into the expediency of making some provision for the support of such collectors and other officers of the customs, as are deprived of it by the war."

This motion was objected to by Mr. Yancey, of North Carolina, on the ground that this was an improper mode of proceeding; if the persons holding sub-offices cannot be satisfied with their emoluments, they had the option to resign; on the other hand, if the emoluments were too small it was for the Government to recommend their increase.

To this, Mr. Ingersoll replied, that, if the subject were inquired into, it would be found, that so far from affording a support, many of the offices of the revenue were a burden on those holding them, and a tax on their private resources. Such certainly was not the intention of Congress in constituting the offices, and it rested with the

523   HISTORY OF CONGRESS.   524

H. OF R.   *Judiciary System—The Investigation—Volunteer Bill.*   NOVEMBER, 1814.

House to say whether they would not examine into the subject.

The resolution was rejected by a large majority.

JUDICIARY SYSTEM.

Mr. FISK, of Vermont, called up the bill to amend the judiciary system, in which he was particularly interested, on account of a provision it contains respecting the further enforcing the revenue laws and strengthening the hands of those whose duty it is to prevent intercourse with the enemy.

Mr. INGERSOLL, of Pennsylvania, who reported the bill, was opposed to acting on it at present; because, on account of the importance of several features of that bill, he was desirous, before it was acted on, to consult the opinions of the judges of the Supreme Court and others, and if he could, to obtain their assistance and support to it, &c.

This order of the day was postponed; and no other business being brought forward, the House adjourned.

FRIDAY, November 4.

On motion of Mr. JENNINGS,

Resolved, That a Committee be appointed to inquire into the expediency of authorizing the Secretary for the Department of State to cause the Laws of the United States, passed or to be passed during the present or any future session of the Congress of the United States, to be printed in two of the public newspapers in each of the Territories of the United States, with leave to report by bill, or otherwise.

Mr. JENNINGS, Mr. KENNEDY, Mr. SHIPHERD, Mr. PICKENS, and Mr. FARROW, were appointed a committee.

Mr. LEWIS, of Virginia, presented the petition of an inhabitant of Fairfax county, Virginia, praying compensation for a horse belonging to him, forcibly taken from him during the late incursion of the enemy to this place by an officer of the United States; and also the petition of Thomas Ewell, manager and principal proprietor of the Anacosta bridge, (over the Anacosta or Eastern Branch,) praying indemnification for the loss sustained by the burning of that bridge by the Government officers.—Referred to Committee of Claims.

Mr. KENT, of Maryland, reported a bill "establishing the Bank of the Metropolis," (in this District;) which was twice read, and committed.

Mr. KILBOURN, of Ohio, called up the resolution offered by him yesterday, and then laid on the table, directing the Military Committee to consider the expediency of providing for the families of private soldiers slain in service.

Mr. K. modified his motion so as to embrace only regular soldiers and volunteers engaged in the service, excluding the case of militia, which has already been referred to the Military Committee; and, so modified, the motion was agreed to.

Mr. TROUP, of Georgia, gave notice that, if opportunity offered, he would to-morrow call up the bill for classifying the male population of the United States.

THE INVESTIGATION.

Mr. SMITH, of New York, called the attention of the House to the resolution appointing a committee to investigate the capture of this city. He had been, and yet was, very anxious to hear the report of that committee. The chairman of that committee (Mr. JOHNSON) had the other day assigned the reason why the report of that committee had been delayed, which was, that letters had been written to Generals Armstrong and Winder, to which answers had not yet been received. With submission to the committee, he knew not why application had been made to those sources for information. Did they expect those persons to furnish proofs of their own imbecility or misconduct?

[Mr. S. was proceeding, when the SPEAKER reminded him there was no motion before the House.]

Mr. S. then moved that the committee be requested to make a report on this subject as early as possible, notwithstanding they may not have received answers to all the letters they had written.

Whilst Mr. S. was reducing this motion to writing—

Mr. SHARP, of Kentucky, suggested to the gentleman the propriety of deferring his motion until the chairman of the committee of investigation should be in his seat, which he was not at present.

Mr. SMITH said he had no objection to defer his motion for the present; and, indeed, if the gentleman from Kentucky would be good enough to communicate his sentiments on this subject to his colleague, it might save the necessity of making the motion at all. The crisis to which our affairs had arrived required, he said, a prompt examination of such events as that which had occurred at this place.

THE VOLUNTEER BILL.

The bill to authorize the President to accept the services of volunteer corps, which shall associate and organize themselves, was announced for a third reading.

Mr. IRVING, of New York, for reasons which he assigned, moved to recommit this bill. His objections were principally to the clause which allowed a compensation of six cents and a quarter per day, or twenty-two dollars and eighty-one cents a year, or double that sum for two years, to such persons as should arm themselves, for the use of arms, inasmuch as the arms could be purchased by the United States and put into their hands for a less sum; and to the provision which allowed the volunteers a greater per diem compensation for their services than was now allowed to the regulars.

Mr. TROUP objected to the recommitment on these grounds; for, although he might not be wholly pleased with some features of the bill, he did not know that they would be improved by recommitment, which would consume much time. In reply to the objection to the compensation to those who arm themselves, he said it would have much more weight if the United States were able conveniently to furnish them; which, however, was not the fact, &c.

Mr. CALHOUN, of South Carolina, and Mr. WEBSTER, of New Hampshire, favored the re-commitment, on account of the section which exempts two years' volunteers from all further militia duty, to which they both had decided objections.

Mr. TROUP admitted in some degree the force of these objections to a provision, the insertion of which he had himself opposed. And, on the question being taken, the bill was recommitted to a Committee of the Whole.

A short time afterwards, the House resolved itself into a Committee of the Whole on said bill.

Mr. KILBOURN, of Ohio, moved to amend the bill, by striking out the clause authorizing the volunteers to be commissioned by the States, as well as by the Government of the United States. His object was to obtain uniformity in the service, and in the grades of commissions.

Mr. JOHNSON, of Kentucky, opposed the motion from various reasons; the principal of which were, that the Governors of States disposed to co-operate with the General Government, having better opportunities of information of personal character in their States, would better know how to dispose of commissions properly; that there were persons whose situation might be incompatible with holding commissions under the United States, who would not be precluded from accepting commissions from the States, &c. On the other hand, volunteers might be obtained in some States hostile to the General Government, and indisposed to commission the officers; for which case, it was proposed commissions should be given by the United States.

Mr. KILBOURN, yielding to the force of one or the other of Mr. JOHNSON'S reasons, withdrew his motion.

Mr. WEBSTER, of New Hampshire, renewed it. He did so, on the ground that there was no law or clause of the Constitution to authorize the commissioning of these volunteers by the States. The volunteers to be raised by this bill were not, and could not be considered as militia, but, so long as they were in service, as a part of the Army of the United States, under a peculiar organization.

This motion was debated at some length. The affirmative side of the question was maintained by Messrs. WEBSTER, GROSVENOR, of New York, and INGERSOLL, of Pennsylvania, and the negative by Messrs. JACKSON, of Virginia, and SHARP, of Kentucky.

This discussion turned principally on the distinction between militia and State corps, and soldiers, whether enlisted or voluntarily engaged, whether regulars or volunteers. On one hand, it was contended that the Governors had constitutionally no right to commission volunteers in the service of the States; and, on the other, that Congress could by law give them the power to commission them as militia volunteers, and then receive them into the service of the United States.

The motion to strike out the words " or by the

States," from that clause which directs the manner in which the officers shall be commissioned, was finally agreed to—ayes 89.

Mr. LOWNDES, of South Carolina, followed up this amendment by a motion to strike out so much of the bill as authorizes the volunteers to choose their own officers. Such an amendment, he said, would be merely formal, because the indication of the wishes of the volunteers, in this respect, would still doubtless regulate the appointments; but it appeared to him necessarily to follow the amendment already made.

Mr. JOHNSON expressed his fears of the effect of these amendments, particularly of the latter, in entirely defeating the intention of the bill. Besides spreading a host of officers over the country, without men to command, the effect of the amendment will be to tie up the will and energies of the people, which had never yet been fairly appealed to, and again to resort to inefficient measures. The amendment now proposed, he argued, would take the soul out of this bill, and destroy its utility.

Mr. LOWNDES, in reply to the objection to this amendment that it would create an army of officers, said there was no fear, certainly, that the President would commission officers before men were enrolled for their command.

This motion again gave rise to a considerable debate, in the course of which it was opposed with much warmth and force by Messrs. J. G. JACKSON, TROUP, and ROBERTSON, and advocated by Messrs. LOWNDES and PICKERING.

In addition to what is already stated, the principal argument in favor of one motion, was the alleged inability of Congress to place the power of appointing officers to command troops of the United States in any other hands than those of the Executive. To this argument, it was said in reply, that it might be allowed to have some weight, if the President had no election to accept or refuse the proffered services of volunteers thus organized; but, after the selection by the volunteers, the power of confirmation still remained with the Executive, and he was at liberty to accept or reject the corps so organized. Gentlemen opposed to the force contemplated to be raised by the bill, were entreated not to propose amendments to it which would entirely destroy any efficiency it might have according to the original plan.

Mr. LOWNDES'S motion having been rejected—

Mr. IRVING, of New York, moved to strike out thirty-three and a third cents, the daily compensation proposed to be allowed, and reinstate twenty-six and two-thirds, the rate originally contained in the bill.

This motion was opposed by Mr. RICH, of Vermont, and Mr. JACKSON, of Virginia, on the ground that, no bounty being allowed to these volunteers, their pay ought to be higher than that of the regulars.

The motion of Mr. IRVING was negatived by a large majority.

Mr. IRVING also moved to reduce the per diem allowance of six and a quarter cents to each man for use of the arms with which the volunteers shall supply themselves; this allowance he conceived to be now too great. This motion was, after some remarks of Messrs. TROUP and JACKSON in opposition to it, likewise negatived by a large majority.

Mr. CANNON, of Tennessee, made a motion going to require the volunteers to be uniformly armed; which motion, having been opposed by Mr. TROUP and Mr. JOHNSON as unnecessary and inexpedient, was negatived.

Other amendments were proposed and negatived.

Mr. CALHOUN, of South Carolina, then moved to strike out the section of the bill which proposes exemption from future militia service for all those who shall volunteer for two years. Mr. C. advocated the motion, on the grounds before stated in objection to it by Mr. WEBSTER and himself.

Mr. JOHNSON, of Kentucky, opposed this motion, but suggested a modification of the provision, so that the volunteer who has served for two years shall not be liable to militia draught until the whole body of the militia in his State have served for a like term.

Mr. HAWKINS, of Kentucky, moved an amendment, embodying the idea of his colleague, Mr. JOHNSON, which, however, was not in order until the pending question was decided.

Mr. FORSYTH, of Georgia, warmly opposed this motion, and replied to those who advocated it. Without this provision, the inducements held out in the bill were not sufficient to call forth any number of volunteers; and he denied the validity of any of the objections which had been brought against it.

Some further debate took place, when Mr. CALHOUN's motion was agreed to, and the committee agreed to strike out this section.

Mr. HAWKINS then renewed the motion he had before offered, which was agreed to.

Mr. GHOLSON, of Virginia, then proposed an amendment to the bill, the object of which was to authorize the President to receive into the service of the United States volunteer corps organized under the authority of the States.

On this motion, the Committee of the Whole being equally divided, the Chairman decided it in the negative.

The Committee rose, and reported the bill; and the House immediately adjourned.

SATURDAY, November 5.

Another member, to wit: from Massachusetts, SAMUEL DAVIS, appeared, and took his seat.

The SPEAKER laid before the House a letter from the Governor of the Indiana Territory, enclosing the credentials of JONATHAN JENNINGS, as the Delegate for that Territory in the Fourteenth Congress.

A message was received from the Senate informing the House that they had passed the three million loan bill, with amendments. On motion of Mr. JACKSON, of Virginia, (the chairman of the Committee of Ways and Means being absent

from indisposition,) the bill and amendments were referred to the Committee of Ways and Means.

TAX ON SALARIES, &c.

Mr. FARROW, of South Carolina, offered for consideration the following resolution:

Resolved, That the Committee of Ways and Means be instructed to inquire into the expediency of laying a duty on all salary officers, and on the professional income of lawyers, solicitors, and counsellors, and the legal proceedings of civil courts of justice.

Mr. F. said it appeared to him while Congress were engaged in devising taxes on every description of articles, there were a number of officers under high salaries, paying comparatively no taxes to the Government, whom he thought ought to be taxed in some way. While we are taxing the poor man who has but an hundred acres of land, and from that has besides to maintain a large family, where is the propriety, Mr. F. asked, of exempting a man who receives annual thousands, and, after maintaining his family, can lay up a large part of it? The object of Mr. F. was to lay a certain per centage on the salary. As to the income of lawyers, &c., he thought them equally worthy of taxation, &c.

The motion of Mr. FARROW was agreed to without a division.

THE INVESTIGATION.

Mr. JOHNSON, of Kentucky, said he understood that, in his absence from the House yesterday, an honorable member from New York had expressed some anxiety to know what progress had been made by the committee appointed to investigate the causes of the capture of this city by the enemy, in the execution of that duty. In obedience to the direction of the committee on that subject, who at all times were anxious and willing to satisfy any honorable member of the House in his reasonable inquiries, he now rose to state that they had not been idle in the discharge of the duties committed to them. But, on a subject so interesting and so important, it would have been improper in them to present an imperfect development of events which had been the foundation of so many different rumors. And to enable the House to judge of the labor imposed on this committee, he made the following statement of the papers before that committee, &c.

Communications received by the Committee of Investigation, viz:

1st. General Winder's report, accompanied with one hundred and twenty-three letters to Governors of States, regular and militia officers, &c., pp. 96.

2d. Report from the War Department, sheets 34.

3d. Reports from the Navy Department, accompanied by twenty-one letters to various officers and persons, pp. 32.

4th. Report of General Smith of District militia, accompanied with a few letters, pp. 23.

5th. General Armstrong's letter, accompanied by two or three letters, pp. 20.

6th. Richard Rush's report, pp. 21.

529   HISTORY OF CONGRESS.   530

NOVEMBER, 1814.   *Petition of Thomas Cutts—Volunteer Bill.*   H. OF R.

7th. Secretary of the Navy, in relation to the proceedings of the Cabinet, pp. 5.

8th, Report from the Corporation of Alexandria, accompanied with nineteen letters, pp. 16.

9th. Two reports from the Ordnance Department.

10th. Estimates of the value of public property destroyed, (excluding the Navy Yard.)

11th. Report from the superintending Surgeon, pp. 19.

12th. Thirty-five letters from various persons, (General Hungerford, Colonel Tayloe, Captain Caldwell, Captain Burch, &c.) upon subjects relating to the object of the inquiry, making together eleven reports, containing three hundred and fifty-nine pages, and two hundred and ten letters, besides daily and almost hourly interviews with persons upon the subject.

Letters and reports yet expected.

Letters from Colonel Monroe, Walter Jones, William Pinkney, General Van Ness, General Stansbury; an estimate of the public property destroyed at the Navy Yard; a letter from General Douglass; the proceedings of the court martial over Captain Dyson; a letter from John Law, &c.

This statement and enumeration, Mr. J. said he hoped would satisfy the gentleman from New York and the House that the committee have not unnecessarily delayed a report. They would make a report at as early a day as was consistent with a due discharge of their duty.

PETITION OF THOMAS CUTTS.

The House, on motion of Mr. YANCEY, of North Carolina, resumed the consideration of the report of the Committee of Claims on the petition of Thomas Cutts, of the District of Maine. Further evidence on the claim was read. Mr. YANCEY, of North Carolina, Mr. PICKENS, of the same State, Mr. ALEXANDER, of Ohio, and Mr. SHARP, of Kentucky, spoke in favor of the report of the committee, (unfavorable to the petitioner,) which was opposed by Mr. KING, of Massachusetts, Mr. FARROW, of South Carolina, Mr. JACKSON, of Virginia, Mr. HULBERT, of Massachusetts, Mr. HAWKINS, of Kentucky, and Mr. GROSVENOR, of New York.

This was strictly a legal discussion, and conducted with great ability on both sides, and at considerable length. The case is as follows: Mr. Cutts purchased at a marshal's sale certain property, of which he was dispossessed in due process of law by a third person. He prays of the United States reimbursement of money paid to their officer for the purchase aforesaid and interest thereon, together with costs incurred in defending the suit.

The question, on the amendment going to reverse the report of the committee, was at length decided in the negative. For the amendment 55, against it 79.

The question on concurring in the report of the committee was then decided in the affirmative by yeas and nays. For the report 81, against it 58, as follows:

YEAS—Messrs. Alexander, Alston, Anderson, Avery, Barbour, Bard, Barnett, Bines, Bowen, Bradley, Brown, Burwell, Caldwell, Calhoun, Cannon, Chappell, Clark, Comstock, Condict, Conard, Crawford, Crouch, Cuthbert, Davis of Pennsylvania, Denoyelles, Desha, Duvall, Earle, Findley, Forney, Forsyth, Gholson, Goodwyn, Gourdin, Griffin, Hall, Harris, Hasbrouck, Hawes, Hubbard, Humphreys, Hungerford, Ingersoll, Irving, Johnson of Virginia, Johnson of Kentucky, Kennedy, Kerr, Kershaw, Kilbourn, King of North Carolina, Lefferts, Lowndes, Lyle, Macon, McCoy, McKim, McLean, Moore, Newton, Ormsby, Parker, Pickens, Piper, Pleasants, Rea of Pennsylvania, Rhea of Tennessee, Rich, Ringgold, Robertson, Sage, Sharp, Skinner, Smith of Virginia, Stanford, Strong, Tannehill, Taylor, Telfair, Udree, and Yancey.

NAYS—Messrs. Baylies of Massachusetts, Bayly of Virginia, Bradbury, Brigham, Butler, Caperton, Cilley, Clopton, Cooper, Culpeper, Dana, Davenport, Ely, Farrow, Fisk of Vermont, Geddes, Grosvenor, Hale, Hawkins, Hopkins of Kentucky, Hulbert, Jackson of Rhode Island, Jackson of Virginia, Kent of New York, Kent of Maryland, King of Massachusetts, Law, Lewis, Lovett, Markell, McKee, Moseley, Nelson, Pearson, Pickering, Pitkin, John Reed, William Reed, Ruggles, Schureman, Sheffey, Shipherd, Smith of New York, Smith of Pennsylvania, Stuart, Sturges, Taggart, Tallmadge, Thompson, Vose, Ward of Massachusetts, Webster, Wheaton, Wilcox, Wilson of Massachusetts, Wilson of Pennsylvania, Winter, and Wright.

THE VOLUNTEER BILL.

The House resumed the consideration of the unfinished business of yesterday, being the amendments of the Committee of the Whole to the bill authorizing the President of the United States to accept the services of such volunteer corps as shall organize themselves and offer their services to the President of the United States.

The amendments having been all agreed to, until that came under consideration which goes to strike out the twelfth section, which is in the following words:

"*And be it further enacted,* That the officers, non-commissioned officers, and privates, accepted under this act, who shall serve two years in the Army of the United States, shall be exempted from militia duty during the present war."

On the question to strike out this section, to which he was decidedly opposed, Mr. HAWKINS required the yeas and nays.

Mr. FISK, of Vermont, opposed the erasure of this section. He deplored the errors of a false economy, which had pervaded the measures of Congress from the commencement of the war, and which he saw with regret in the determination to withhold this, the only inducement to volunteer under this bill. The section proposed to introduce no new principle; for exemptions were already recognised by law in particular cases, and in none more rightfully than this. If they went on by scanty means, as they had heretofore done, the war might continue not only two years, but ten times two, &c.

Mr. HAWKINS, of Kentucky, spoke at some length, and with much force in favor of retaining this section, which he believed vital to the utility of the bill. He addressed himself to the majority of the House; for, as to the minority, they were opposed to the Administration and to war, and could not be expected to go along with those who supported either. What, said he, do we now want? We want soldiers, and expect to obtain them under this bill, and under another of a more energetic character now before this House. Appeals to the patriotism of the country, to volunteers, said Mr. H., are beautiful in sound; they please the ear; but, when brought to the test, this species of patriotic spirit may be worn out by too severe a pressure. If Government rests its claims to the services of its citizens exclusively on the patriotism of the country, in the time of most need they will be found most wanting. In particular sections of the country, particular classes of men had borne the brunt of the war by voluntary contributions of service, as far as they could so bear it. There was scarcely a man of any standing in the Western country who had not contributed in some way his personal services in support of a war which he believed to be righteous and just. Let future calls on their patriotism be made in such manner as to convince them the Government does not wish to tax exclusively their patriotism. Mr. H. then examined the inducements of land bounty, and pay held out by this bill, which, he said, were no temptation to the hardy backwoodsman of the West, who by laboring one-fourth of his time can earn a subsistence for his family, &c. He then made a few remarks on the military services already rendered by the citizens of the Western States, where these men were expected to be had; that portion of the country was already exhausted by the services they had frequently and successively rendered. It was impossible, therefore, that any large force could be collected under this bill, even retaining the section which had been stricken out in Committee of the Whole. But if gentlemen persisted in calling upon men for a contribution of voluntary services, not to defend their homes, but to fight our battles, to march here and there, without appealing to other inducements than patriotism and bravery, they would only deceive themselves and the Government.

Mr. CALHOUN, of South Carolina, remarked that the military force by which we can operate consists of two descriptions; the regular force, whose general character is mercenary, the soldiers enlisting for the sake of the bounty and subsistence; draughted militia called into service under legal obligations; and volunteers, brought into the field by patriotic motives only. If volunteers were to be obtained only by the greatness of the inducements or the amount of compensation held out, why call for volunteers at all? Mr. C. said he would not consent to derogate from the motives of those who volunteer by supposing them to be altogether actuated by such motives. There were temptations of one kind held out to those who enlist in the regular Army, and of another to those who volunteer. Love of country is the boast, it is the jewel of the volunteer corps. They are unfit for the tug of war, for its drudgery and fatigue. They are peculiarly adapted to cases of emergency, of great personal danger, but not great fatigue. We must rely on regulars to be enlisted, and, if not to be had in sufficient numbers, on

those who shall be draughted from the whole body of the militia. These two constitute the bone and muscle of the Army. If great reliance had been placed on a volunteer force, why had another bill been reported by the Military Committee, with extraordinary provisions for filling the ranks of the Army? Certainly, the volunteers had only been considered a co-operating or subsidiary force, the regulars being the basis. A body of volunteers for instance, might individually and collectively, possess the same spirit as the little army under General Brown, but they could not be expected to render the same kind of services.

Mr. FISK, of Vermont, said that the argument of the gentleman from South Carolina, extended a little farther, would favor the denial of any compensation to volunteers for their service. The gentleman would then see, how many patriotism alone would induce to take the field for two years. Volunteers, Mr. F. said, were of the same materials as regulars, if not better. None of Brown's army had been in service two years, many of them not six months, and yet they have covered themselves with glory, and established the national character. Under the guidance of men who know how to bring into action the military spirit with which the country was universally inspired—under such men as Brown, volunteers would soon be fitted for the "tug of war."

Mr. BARNETT, of Georgia, said he was in favor of the war, and always had been, and yet he was in favor of striking out this section. In old times, he said, the patriotism of the people had burnt till its objects were answered; now it seems patriotism is to be burnt out in two years. He hoped, however, it never would be extinguished until we obtain the object of the war. He was in favor of the war, he said, and was in hopes we were to fight it out with ball and powder—we are now fighting it with words and wind, and never shall bring it to a conclusion if we spend so much time in talking about it. Mr. B. concluded by saying he was opposed to exemption in any way.

Mr. DUVALL, of Kentucky, asked whether, after faithfully serving his country for two years, a volunteer was to be told, his patriotism was not worth a rush because it had not carried him to the end of the war? Let gentlemen place themselves in the situation of the volunteer. Why not serve the nation here from motives of pure and unadulterated patriotism? If we have so much of it on our tongue, why not a little in practice? The members of this House, he presumed, were in general more wealthy than the volunteers. Let them begin with themselves, and then preach disinterested patriotism to others; their doctrines would then be much more attended to than now that they talked of patriotism, and pocketed the *per diem.* Patriotism will not feed a man; it is most of it air, and, however anxious to serve his country by fighting, a man must eat, and all the patriotism of the world will not enable him to dispense with it. The bill contained no temptations to the service, he said, save the section which is proposed to be stricken out. When a man, after two years' service, came home seamed with honorable scars, was he to be liable the next day to be again called into the field? This, he said, would be the monstrous effect of striking out the section. But this species of troops, it appeared, was not fit for the tug of war. This Mr. D. denied. They have given evidence of their ability to bear every hardship. In the campaign on the Wabash, in the depth of Winter, they had marched barefoot without complaining. From the severe battle of Massissiniway, how many had returned who were not frostbitten? The men who will volunteer have no idea of enlisting; you come at a species of force to be had in no other way, and as effective as any in any scene of action but in the open field, which must be contested by military art alone. He did not believe more than ten thousand at the utmost could be got by this bill; but if we had a hundred thousand such men, officered by such officers as Brown, Scott, and Gaines, divided into three armies, they would end the war in a single season, by conquering the whole of the enemy's adjacent provinces, the post of Quebec perhaps alone excepted. &c. He hoped therefore this section, the main inducement to volunteers, would not be stricken out.

Mr. GHOLSON, of Virginia, was clearly of opinion that, in consequence of their service, the volunteers ought to be entitled by law to some exemption from militia service, but not so far as this bill proposed to go. The section which had been substituted, in Committee of the Whole, for that now under consideration, (going to exempt them until all the other militia in their district shall have served an equal term,) he thought went far enough. But if the war continued, ten, fifteen, or twenty years, would gentlemen require the main body of the militia to do duty two, three, or four years, and continue the exemption in favor of those volunteers who shall have served only two years? Mr. G. said he could not agree to do so.

The question on striking out the section before recited, was then decided: For striking out 105, against it 43, as follows:

YEAS—Messrs. Archer, Avery, Barbour, Bard, Barnett, Baylies of Massachusetts, Bayly of Virginia, Bigelow, Bradbury, Bradley, Brigham, Brown, Burwell, Caperton, Calhoun, Cannon, Champion, Chappell, Cilley, Clark, Clopton, Cooper, Crawford, Crouch, Cuthbert, Dana, Davenport, Davis of Pennsylvania, Denoyelles, Earle, Ely, Gaston, Geddes, Gholson, Goodwyn, Gourdin, Grosvenor, Hale, Hasbrouck, Hawes, Hopkins of Kentucky, Hubbard, Humphreys, Hungerford, Hulbert, Ingham, Irving, Jackson of Rhode Island, Jackson of Virginia, Johnson of Virginia, Kennedy, Kent of New York, Kershaw, King of Massachusetts, King of North Carolina, Law, Lefferts, Lewis, Lovett, Lyle, Markell, McKim, Moore, Moseley, Newton, Oakley, Parker, Pearson, Pickering, Pitkin, Pleasants, William Reed, Rea of Pennsylvania, Rhea of Tennessee, Ringgold, Ruggles, Schureman, Seybert, Sheffey, Sherwood, Shipherd, Skinner, Smith of New York, Smith of Pennsylvania, Smith of Virginia, Stanford, Stuart, Sturges, Taggart, Tallmadge, Tannehill, Taylor, Thompson, Troup, Udree, Vose, Ward of Massachusetts, Ward of New Jersey, Webster, Wheaton, Wil-

cox, Wilson of Massachusetts, Wilson of Pennsylvania, Winter and Wright.

NAYS—Messrs. Alexander, Alston, Anderson, Bines, Bowen, Butler, Caldwell, Condict, Conard, Creighton, Desha, Duvall, Farrow, Findley, Fisk of Vermont, Fisk of New York, Forney, Forsyth, Griffin, Hall, Harris, Hawkins, Johnson of Kentucky, Kent of Maryland, Kerr, Kilbourn, Lowndes, McCoy, McKee, McLean, Montgomery, Nelson, Ormsby, Piper, John Reed, Rich, Robertson, Sage, Sevier, Sharp, Strong, Telfair, and Yancey.

This question having been carried, the section reported in lieu of it, going to exempt all volunteers who shall serve two years under this act from being in future called into military service until all other militiamen in their States or districts shall have served for two years, was read.

Mr. JACKSON, of Virginia, moved an amendment to this section, to strike out "two years" in each instance, and insert in lieu thereof "one year," or any longer term which the volunteers may engage to serve.

Mr. GHOLSON, of Virginia, embodied Mr. JACKSON's amendment in the following form, which Mr. J. accepted as his motion:

"That any volunteer whose service shall be accepted under this act shall be exempt from any military service until all the militia in any State or Territory in which he resides shall have served a tour of duty equal to that which the said volunteer shall have served."

After a short debate, this motion to amend was negatived—54 to 47.

On motion of Mr. FISK, of Vermont, the section reported by the Committee was amended by striking out those words which have the effect to exempt such volunteers from subsequent service, whenever the militia are called out *en masse.*

Mr. GROSVENOR, of New York, denying the Constitutional power of Congress, to preclude the States from making use of the militia for State purposes, moved an amendment to the section, going to make the volunteers therein mentioned liable still to State calls for militia.

Mr. JACKSON, of Virginia, called the attention of Mr. GROSVENOR to one of the earliest acts of the General Government, to exempt certain persons (public officers) from militia duty, which fact overturned the whole of the gentleman's arguments on this head.

This remark of Mr. JACKSON's was applied to others, who took side with Mr. GROSVENOR, and some debate took place on it.

On the question, Mr. GROSVENOR's amendment was agreed to by a majority of two or three votes.

The question being stated on the adoption of the new section reported by the Committee as amended, the yeas and nays thereon were required by Mr. WEBSTER.

At length a motion for adjournment was made and carried.

MONDAY, November 7.

Mr. FISK, of New York, from the Committee of Ways and Means, asked and obtained leave to

535   HISTORY OF CONGRESS.   536

H. of R.   *Petition of John Chalmers—Volunteer Bill.*   November, 1814.

report a bill to incorporate the subscribers to the Bank of the United States of America; which was twice read by its title, and referred to a Committee of the Whole.

PETITION OF JOHN CHALMERS.

Mr. YANCEY, of North Carolina, from the Committee of Claims, made a favorable report on the petition of John Chalmers, who asks of Congress reimbursement of certain expenditures made by him in manufacturing certain cordage for the United States, which, together with the rope-walk, were burnt at Baltimore on the approach of the enemy, by order of the Commanding General. The committee also reported a bill for the relief of John Chalmers, which was twice read, and, together with the report, referred to a Committee of the whole House.

The report is as follows:

That, on the 29th of March, 1814, the petitioner and the Secretary of the Navy entered into a contract for the manufacture of cordage for the United States' frigate Java, upon the following terms: the Navy Department was to furnish him at Baltimore with Russia hemp and Kentucky yarn in such quantities as might be found convenient, and he should require, which was to be manufactured in good navy cordage, sufficient for the complete equipment of the frigate. For every pound of hemp and yarn delivered to the petitioner he was to return a pound of cordage to the Navy agent, free from expense to the United States; so that his profit and compensation for his labor and art in manufacturing consisted in the difference in the weight of the hemp and yarns, increased by the quantity of tar used in the manufacture. It was also understood by the Secretary of the Navy and Mr. Chalmers, that the raw material, thus delivered, was to be at the risk of the United States, in the event of loss by fire.

The petitioner commenced manufacturing the cordage, and had prepared and delivered to the Navy agent at Baltimore upwards of nine tons, and had a considerable quantity ready to deliver, when, on the approach of the enemy towards Baltimore, in the month of September last, the rope-walks in which the cordage was manufacturing and then deposited, was set on fire by order of General Forman, who then commanded the Maryland militia at that place; in consequence of which the rope-walks were destroyed, and, with them, about thirty tons of Russia hemp, belonging to the Government, and all the labor and profit of the petitioner, except that part of the hemp which had been delivered. He asks of Congress to reimburse him to the amount of his actual expenditures, in the purchase of tar, and the money which he has paid to persons employed in the manufacture of the cordage.

The committee are not in possession of facts which would authorize them to determine whether the destruction of this property was necessary; if it was not, however much they might regret and deprecate that work, yet they are of opinion that, under the circumstances of this case, the individual who sustained the loss should at least be reimbursed by the Government to the amount of his claim. They, therefore, report by bill, and submit to the House the following resolution:

Resolved, That the prayer of the petition is reasonable, and ought to be allowed.

THE VOLUNTEER BILL.

The House resumed the consideration of the Volunteer bill.

The question depending at time of adjournment, viz: on the adoption of the section exempting the two years' volunteers "from draught or other militia duty" at the call of the United States, until all the militia within their States have served—having been again stated,

Mr. FISK, of Vermont, moved to amend it so as to read, that any volunteer who shall serve for two years, "shall not thereafter be enrolled in the militia or subject to draught or any other militia duty during the present war," unless when the militia shall be called out *en masse.*

The motion of Mr. FISK was opposed by Messrs. PITKIN, of Connecticut, BARNETT, of Georgia, and McKEE, of Kentucky, and advocated by the mover, and Messrs. WRIGHT, of Maryland, RHEA, of Tennessee, and BARBOUR.

Mr. DESHA, of Kentucky, said he hoped the amendment proposed by the gentleman from Vermont (Mr. FISK) would be adopted, which exempted volunteers who served the United States two years from military service, pending the war, except for the defence of the State, or when they were called out *en masse,* as it was the only inducement held out for volunteers to tender their services. He viewed them as a valuable description of force, particularly if they joined the service for eighteen months or two years. What was the object for introducing this bill? Certainly, to obtain speedily a formidable force, not to act as the body of your Army, but as an auxiliary to the regular force. No; I am for depending principally on regulars. What is the encouragement held out by the provisions of this bill for men to offer their services? Very inconsiderable, indeed. You give them no bounty in land, nor money; not even clothing for the first six months. You give them the poor pittance of the monthly pay. Can gentlemen calculate on obtaining a considerable number of volunteers on these terms? If they do, they will be most egregiously mistaken. Men cannot live on the wind; they must have something more substantial. They must have something to sustain their families on while they are fighting the battles of their country. The price of common labor is from thirteen to fifteen dollars per month; and can gentlemen expect that men, possessing the virtue, the integrity, and enterprise of your people, (I mean the yeomanry, of whom the volunteer corps must be composed,) will leave their peaceable homes and families to encounter the toils and difficulties incident to a military life, unless the necessary inducements are held out? Thus, all men who make their calculations for a living. You must meet their calculations, or you do not obtain them; particularly when they are to obtain no credit for patriotic exertions, which, I am to conclude, is the case from the manner in which some gentlemen have expressed themselves, by saying that they would not give anything for patriotism that would not last longer than two years' service. Gentlemen are doing their country a serious injury by such expressions, and acting parsimoniously. Be liberal in your encouragements, and, my word for it, you will succeed in obtaining a formidable volunteer force. Corps of this description must be formidable when they are composed of the best materials. But the gentleman from South Carolina (Mr. CALHOUN) tells you that this description of force cannot stand the tug of war, and appears, from the manner he has expressed himself on this bill, as if he had no confidence in them. And does the gentleman prove that they cannot stand the tug of war, by referring you to the volunteers under General Porter, who have, during this campaign, signalized themselves in the different conflicts with the enemy on the Niagara frontier—who stood and fought, side by side, with General Brown's regulars, and signalized themselves so nobly ? If they did not, Congress have acted very inconsistently in giving them their thanks for their bravery and activity, and awarding a medal to their General for his gallantry. Does the gentleman prove it by referring you to the Tennessee volunteers, who, under the gallant Jackson, endured almost incalculable difficulties and hardships, and surmounted all obstacles in the Creek war ? Or did the gentleman undertake to prove it by referring you to Governor Shelby's volunteers, who, to the amount of thirty-five hundred, met on a few days' notice, joined the standard of the brave and patriotic Shelby, and travelled three hundred miles to Lake Erie ? On the command of the General, they abandoned their horses, and crossed the Lake, where it was forty miles wide, principally in small brittle boats, pursued the enemy one hundred miles into the interior of their country and took them; and, with the aid of a regiment of volunteers commanded by my worthy colleague, killed and took prisoners the British army commanded by General Proctor, and defeated the Indians with considerable slaughter. They quartered eight or nine days on the enemy, living for that time on beef, without bread or salt; wading waters, in some instances nearly half a mile, up to the waist. All this was done by the volunteers, without tents to keep them from the storms, without Government advancing them a single cent of money, and done too without a murmur; and yet these are the description of forces, agreeably to the favorite phrase of the gentleman from South Carolina, that cannot stand the tug of war. Mr. D. said the volunteers had done everything of a decisive character that has been done from the time of the declaration of war until this campaign, and participated in it, but are to receive no credit for their patriotic exertions, agreeably to the declarations of the gentleman from Georgia, (Mr. FORSYTH) who has told you that it was not patriotic motives that induced the Kentuckians to volunteer and go into Canada, but from a principle of revenge. Mr. D. said this was not the fact; whoever undertakes to judge without knowing, is very apt to find himself in an error. If that gentleman had travelled through Kentucky; had made himself acquainted with the habits, dispositions, and principles of the people, he would know they were above the low, malignant principle of revenge. He would know that their exertions have arisen from the purest of motives, from a real love of country, the pure principle of patriotism, and not from the low principle of revenge. The truly brave are always humane; they soar above any grovelling motives, and that gentleman ought to have made himself better acquainted with the different sections of the country, before he undertook to speak so freely. Such expressions, I conceive, were not warranted by the occasion; they are calculated to do a serious injury. If men who have done their country signal services from pure patriotic motives, (for pay was scarcely a consideration with them,) are to be treated thus lightly, it will perhaps have the effect to make them withhold their services when they are wanting. Mr. D. said we must have men of some description or give up the contest, which no American ought to think of. Militia cannot be deemed an efficient force, and they were certainly the most expensive. The kind of economy, or rather the want of economy, pursued, of having hundreds of thousands of militia under arms at a time, would bankrupt the nation. He did not wish the volunteers contemplated to be raised under the provisions of this bill, to be entirely relied on; we must rely principally on regulars. But he was satisfied, that under proper regulations they might be made a formidable auxiliary force to co-operate with the regular Army. He wished the ranks of the regular Army immediately filled, but he saw but little prospect of it from the slow progress of business. We have been in session seven weeks, and what have we done ? Nothing. From the indecisive course, the indisposition manifested to despatch business, he thought there was but little prospect of anything of a decisive character being done shortly, calculated to meet the emergency; for that reason, he wished proper encouragement given to induce volunteer corps to tender their services, that they might be ready to act in case of an emergency. The bill as it now stands is scarcely worth preserving; you cannot succeed under it to any considerable extent; hence the necessity of adopting the amendment under consideration. Mr. D. said there was a necessity of doing something speedily. A powerful enemy was, as it were, at your doors. To act indecisively, under existing circumstances, was tantamount to acting criminally. At a time as perilous as the present, hesitation was almost inevitable destruction. You must lay aside your temporizing, theoretical, or visionary projects. They will not do any longer. If the Councils of the nation, at a time as perilous as the present, are to be conducted by theoretical characters, proposing and advocating visionary projects, I am afraid the Government will be ultimately conducted to ruin. You must pick up the old fashioned plain matter of fact, common sense; you must adopt energetic measures, and adopt them promptly, if you wish to preserve your rights and save the nation.

Mr. FORSYTH said, he apprehended there was not a member of the House who had misunderstood him, besides the gentleman from Kentucky. It was very far from his intention to cast the slightest imputation on the volunteers from Kentucky, or on any other of our citizens who had volunteered their services. He estimated the value of their services and the purity of their motives as highly as any gentleman in the House. He did say, and he was prepared to repeat, that patriotism was not the only leading inducement to their energetic conduct. But for the transactions on the river Raisin, he believed those volunteers would not have turned out in such numbers as they did. They were governed by motives of resentment against a savage and brutal foe. They were, as he had said on a former occasion. stimulated by revenge—not that dark passion the gentleman alludes to, but the revenge which governs noble minds. The character of that revenge displayed itself in their conduct. They did not stain their hands in the blood of their foe. Having conquered him in the field of battle, they took a noble revenge, and showed their superiority to their enemy by extending to him the hand of friendship.

Mr. Desha thought the sense in which the gentleman had explained his observations was different from that in which he had understood him to make them. As explained, he was satisfied with them.

Mr. Forsyth said he did not mean what he had said as an explanation.

The amendment proposed was finally negatived by the following vote: For the motion 52, against it 81.

The question recurring on the adoption of the new section, Mr. McKee proposed a substitute to it, nearly in the following words:

"That all volunteers who may enter the service of the United States under this act, and serve out the time stipulated, in all future calls for militia service under the authority of the United States, shall have credit for a term of service equal to the term served by them respectively."

On the question to agree to this substitute, it was decided in the affirmative—ayes 95.

After a few remarks of Mr. Fisk, of Vermont, in objection to this amendment, and Mr. McKee in reply, the question was taken on agreeing to the section as amended, and carried in the affirmative without a division.

Mr. King, of Massachusetts, then moved an amendment going to limit the number of volunteers to be accepted to ten thousand.

This motion was opposed by Messrs. McKee, Troup, and Wright, and advocated by the mover.

This proposed amendment having been amended by striking out ten thousand and inserting "fifty thousand," the amendment limiting the number, as amended, was negatived—37 only rising in the affirmative.

Mr. Gholson, of Virginia, then moved to amend the first section of the bill, by incorporating therein, after the clause authorizing the acceptance of volunteers, the following words: "who may be organized in companies, battalions, and regiments, under the authority of any State," &c.

This motion. and that which follows, were debated at considerable length. Messrs. Gholson, Wright, Sharp, and Fisk, of New York, advocated the amendment, and Messrs. Webster and Grosvenor opposed it.

This amendment was agreed to by the following vote: For the amendment 68, against it 55.

Mr. Gholson then moved an amendment in the following section, which he conceived to be consequent on this; the object of which was, as the reporter understood, to authorize the Executive to receive into the service of the United States, the volunteer corps so associated and organized under State authority.

On the proposed amendment, the debate was renewed with considerable zeal. It was supported by Messrs. Gholson, Fisk, of New York, Wright, and Rhea, of Tennessee, and opposed by Messrs. Webster, Grosvenor, and Macon.

The question thereon was decided by yeas and nays: For the motion 71, against it 76, as follows:

Yeas—Messrs. Alexander, Alston, Anderson, Archer, Avery, Barbour, Bard, Bines, Bowen, Burwell, Butler, Caldwell, Cannon, Chappell, Clopton, Comstock, Condit, Conard, Crawford, Creighton, Crouch, Davis of Pennsylvania, Desha, Evans, Findley, Fisk of New York, Forney, Gholson, Goodwyn, Gourdin, Griffin, Hall, Harris, Hasbrouck, Hawes, Hubbard, Humphreys, Hungerford, Ingham, Irving, Jackson of Virginia, Johnson of Virginia, Johnson of Kentucky, Kerr, Kershaw, Kilbourn, King of North Carolina, Lefferts, Lyle, McCoy, McLean, Moore, Newton, Ormsby, Parker, Pickens, Piper, Pleasants, Rea of Pennsylvania, Rhea of Tennessee, Rich, Ringgold, Sage, Sevier, Sharp, Smith of Pennsylvania, Smith of Virginia, Strong, Tannehill, and Wright.

Nays—Messrs. Barnett, Baylies of Massachusetts, Bayly of Virginia, Bigelow, Boyd, Bradbury, Bradley, Brigham, Caperton, Champion, Cilley, Clark, Cooper, Cox, Culpeper, Cuthbert, Dana, Davenport, Ely, Farrow, Forsyth, Franklin, Gaston, Geddes, Grosvenor, Hale, Hopkins, of Kentucky, Hulbert, Ingersoll, Jackson of Rhode Island, Kennedy, Kent of New York, Kent of Maryland, King of Massachusetts, Law, Lewis, Lovett, Macon, McKee, Montgomery, Moseley, Markell, Nelson, Oakley, Pearson, Pickering, Pitkin, John Reed, Wm. Reed, Robertson, Ruggles, Schureman, Sheffey, Sherwood, Shipherd, Skinner, Smith of New York, Stanford, Sturges, Taggart, Tallmadge, Taylor, Telfair, Thompson, Troup, Vose, Ward of Massachusetts, Ward of New Jersey, Webster, Wheaton, White, Wilcox, Wilson, of Massachusetts, Wilson of Pennsylvania, Winter, and Yancey.

So the motion was negatived.

Mr. Gholson took occasion to observe, that the rejection of this amendment, though consequent upon the first, was of little importance, as every purpose he had in view was answered by that already adopted.

This Mr. Grosvenor denied, because, he said, as the bill now stood, these volunteers, nominally under State authority, must be officered by the Executive of the United States, &c.

To this Mr. Gholson replied, that the words "organized under State authority," certainly embraced also the commissioning the officers by the States.

To put this question entirely out of doubt, as he said, Mr. INGERSOLL moved to insert, after the clause just recited, the words "Provided, the officers of the said volunteers shall be commissioned by the President of the United States." This motion he supported by a speech of some length, to which Mr. GHOLSON replied also at some length. Mr. RHEA made a few observations in opposition to it.

Mr. JOHNSON, of Kentucky, rose to move the postponement of the further consideration of this subject for the present. He thought it probable, when the House had acted on other measures of more importance than this, they would be better prepared to act on this subject. When the Committee on Military Affairs had determined to call up this bill before the other two they had reported, it was under the impression it would meet with little or no discussion or diversity of opinion. Disappointed in that expectation, and believing himself that the provisions of this bill were inconsistent with each other, and that those provisions were wanting that were necessary to give it efficiency, he moved to lay the bill on the table, which was agreed to.

TUESDAY, November 8.

Mr. McKIM, of Maryland, presented the memorial of sundry ship-owners and merchants of Baltimore, representing, that in consequence of the strict blockade of our bays and rivers, the private-armed service is much discouraged, &c., and submitting to Congress the expediency of authorizing a bounty to be given for the destruction of the enemy's vessels. They state their opinion of the high effect of this sort of warfare on the enemy's commerce, and say that they are ready to give the best pledge of their sincerity in this belief, if encouragement be afforded, by entering largely into the enterprises against the commerce of the enemy.—The memorial was read, and referred.

Mr. KENT, of Maryland, reported a bill to incorporate the subscribers to a bank, by the name and style of "The Farmers and Mechanics' Bank of Georgetown;" which was twice read, and committed.

On motion of Mr. CLOPTON, of Virginia, a committee was ordered to be appointed to wait on the President of the United States, with the joint resolution requesting him to appoint a day of fasting and prayer.

The bill for the relief of John Castille passed through a Committee of the Whole. [The case of the petitioner is nearly this, as stated by Mr. ROBERTSON: The petitioner was convicted, before the United States' Court, of having in his possession smuggled goods, and was therefor fined to the amount of fourteen or fifteen thousand dollars. From circumstances which appeared on the trial, he was recommended by the jury to the mercy of the Government. He has now been in prison eighteen months, and, unless relieved by Congress, must forever remain there. Whatever property he has or may acquire still remains liable for the fine.] The bill was ordered to a third reading.

SMALL ARMED VESSELS.

The House resolved itself into a Committee of the Whole on the bill to authorize the President of the United States to cause to be built or purchased the vessels therein described, viz: not more than twenty vessels, to carry not less than eight nor more than fourteen guns.

The bill having been read through—

Mr. PLEASANTS, of Virginia, (the Chairman of the Naval Committee,) said, the object of the bill was sufficiently explained by its contents. As to its expediency, the experience of the present war had amply demonstrated the utility of this species of force. He called upon the Committee for a moment to turn its attention to the cruises of those vessels, and compare their effects with those of the cruises of the larger vessels. The conquests achieved by our frigates, &c., would never be forgotten; they were great and important; but their depredations on the commerce of the enemy, during long cruises, had been comparatively unimportant. On reference to the cruises of private armed vessels, of the class contemplated by this bill, a very different result appeared. The effects of their enterprises against the commerce of the enemy had been great and important; such, indeed, as to give us every reason to believe that a class of small, swift-sailing vessels, of this description, would, in all probability, conduce to put a speedy end to the war, by the impression it would make on the enemy's commerce. He very much doubted whether the Government could expend a small sum of money in any way so efficiently as if appropriated to the particular purposes of this bill. He knew some of the best and most enlightened friends of the Navy were opposed to the bill; but he did not believe, taking into consideration all the circumstances of the present situation of the country, that they could assign sufficient objections to it. Our Navy had acquired a greater stock of glory, credit, and reputation, to themselves, and reflected it upon the country, than ever had been acquired in the same space of time by any military equipment, either by land or ocean, in any country. He had paid some little attention to the history of the British navy, and he believed the history of our Navy would stand a comparison with any other the world affords. But, in regard to depredation on the commerce of the enemy, he believed their efficiency could not be compared to that of vessels of a smaller class.

Mr. W. REED, of Massachusetts, rose to oppose the bill as it now stood. If he could persuade himself that the effects anticipated by the honorable Chairman of the Naval Committee could ever be realized, he should be the last man in the House to oppose the passage of the bill for a moment. He thought he could make it appear that the ground assumed by the gentleman from Virginia was wholly untenable. By the force proposed in this bill, Mr. R.

should leave a wider discretion with the Executive.

The question was then taken on Mr. REED's motion to amend the bill, and negatived—ayes only 40.

Mr. INGERSOLL then moved to amend the bill by striking out 14, the maximum, and inserting 22 guns, so as that the rate of the vessels shall not fall short of 8 nor exceed 22 guns.

This motion Mr. I. supported by a speech, in which he expressed his decided preference for the larger class of vessels. He reviewed the cruises of our frigates, pronouncing the capture of the Guerriere by the Constitution as having been more important, in its moral effect, than all the cruises of all our privateers put together; and certainly the most efficient cruise of any vessel, great or small, had been that of the Essex. If these vessels were intended merely to act as privateers, they had nothing to do but to take off the double duties on prize goods, and they would have no occasion to employ public vessels on that service.

Mr. PLEASANTS spoke in explanation. He had no objection to the amendment now proposed, going to extend the Executive discretion, but that it would interfere with the bill as it had been arranged with some care in the Senate, and passed that body. The idea of disgrace attaching to vessels from running from superior force, was more romantic than real. On what principles ought naval commanders, or even military commanders, to act? Every wise general, every prudent sea captain, will get out of the way of a force too heavy for him; a ship flies a frigate, a frigate a seventy-four, &c. This objection, he thought, had as little weight as any other which had been urged.

The question on the amendment proposed by Mr. INGERSOLL, was decided in the affirmative by a large majority.

Mr. WILLIAM REED moved to amend the bill so as to put it in execution, "as soon as mea-' sures are taken to equip for sea such of the larger ' vessels directed to be built by former laws, as are ' in such a state of forwardness as that they may ' be equipped during the ensuing winter."

This motion he supported by a speech of considerable length, in which he expressed a want of confidence in the head of the Navy Department, which prevented him from relying implicitly on him for the faithful execution of this trust, unless he were bound to it by a special provision like this. He adverted to the state of these vessels; the inactivity of preparation. Why they were left defenceless, and obliged to rely on the indulgence or generosity of the States for the cannon to protect them, he could not say, but he should be glad to know. He made a number of other remarks in this strain, and to show the advantages the United States would derive from sending these vessels out this Winter, which was not yet too late to be accomplished by a zealous, faithful, and active officer, &c. Though no friend to the war, he was disposed by active exertions to bring it to as speedy a close as possible, &c.

Mr. WRIGHT and Mr. PLEASANTS very decidedly opposed this motion, on the ground of the very unnecessary delay it would occasion to the execution of this bill, which ought to be carried into effect promptly, if at all. The two objects did not conflict, nor were they connected; and the amendment was therefore injudicious. The Government had, no doubt, made every exertion to get these vessels ready, compatible with other engagements, and the urgency of the case, &c. This motion was negatived—ayes only 25.

The Committee then rose and reported the bill to the House, who agreed to the amendment which had been made to it.

Mr. WILLIAM REED then moved to strike out eight, the minimum of force, and insert "eighteen;" which motion was negatived by yeas and nays—yeas 43, nays 98.

The bill was then ordered to be read a third time to-morrow.

WEDNESDAY, November 9.

Mr. KILBOURN, of Ohio, presented a memorial of seven hundred and twenty-nine persons, praying, for reasons therein stated, that certain public lands may be appropriated and sold at twelve and a half cents the acre to actual settlers. On the question to refer the same to the Committee on Public Lands, there were for the motion 48, against it 50. So the House refused to refer the said memorial, which falls on the table of course.

Mr. KENT, of Maryland, from the District Committee, reported a bill to incorporate the subscribers to a bank in Alexandria, by the name and style of the Union Bank of Alexandria; which bill was twice read, and committed.

The bill for the relief of John Castille, of the city of New Orleans, was read a third time.

The bill from the Senate "authorizing the President of the United States to cause to be built or purchased the vessels therein described," as amended in this House, was read a third time, and passed, without opposition.

On motion of Mr. EPPES, of Virginia, the House resolved itself into a Committee of the Whole on the bill authorizing the Secretary of State to make an additional allowance, during the present war, to masters of vessels for bringing home destitute and distressed American seamen to the United States.

Mr. EPPES quoted the letters received from the Secretary of State at the last session recommending the passage of the bill; from which it appears that no larger appropriation is asked for than that annually made, but the appropriation of a gross sum of the same amount is recommended, and also the repeal of the limitation now provided of ten dollars for each seaman so brought into the United States.

The Committee reported the bill without amendment, and it was ordered to be engrossed for a third reading to-morrow.

The bill directing the staff officers of the Army to comply with the requisitions of the naval and marine officers in certain cases, having been

549   HISTORY OF CONGRESS.   550

NOVEMBER, 1814.   *Ways and Means—Army Supplies and Discipline.*   H. OF R.

called over, was, on motion of Mr. PLEASANTS, of Virginia, postponed until to-morrow week.

WAYS AND MEANS.

Mr. EPPES, of Virginia, from the Committee of Ways and Means, reported a bill "to provide ad- 'ditional revenues for defraying the expenses of 'Government, and sustaining the public credit, by 'laying duties on spirits distilled within the Uni- 'ted States, and amending the act laying duties 'on licenses to distillers of spirituous liquors."

The bill contains twenty-seven sections, all of mere detail, conformable to the resolutions which have passed the House, except the following:

SEC. 25. *And be it further enacted,* That towards establishing an adequate revenue to provide for the payment of the expenses of Government, for the punctual payment of the public debt, principal and interest, contracted and to be contracted, according to the terms of the contracts respectively; and for creating an adequate sinking fund gradually to reduce, and eventually to extinguish the public debt, contracted, and to be contracted; the rates and duties laid and imposed by this act, and the duties laid and imposed upon licenses to distillers, in and by the said act, entitled "An act laying duties on licenses to distillers of spirituous liquors," shall continue to be laid, levied, and collected during the present war between us and Great Britain, and until the purposes aforesaid shall be completely accomplished, anything in the said act of Congress to the contrary thereof, in any wise, notwithstanding. And for the effectual application of the revenue to be raised by and from the said duties to the purposes aforesaid, in due form of law, the faith of the United States is hereby pledged: *Provided always,* That whenever Congress shall deem it expedient, to alter, reduce, or change the said duties or either of them, it shall be lawful so to do, upon providing and substituting by law, at the same time, and for the same purposes, other duties which shall be equally productive with the duties so altered, reduced, or changed: *And provided further,* That nothing in this act contained shall be deemed or construed in anywise to rescind or impair any specific appropriation of the said duties or either of them; but such appropriation shall remain and be carried into effect according to the true intent and meaning of the law and laws making the same, anything in this act to the contrary notwithstanding.

SEC. 26. *And be it further enacted,* That it shall be lawful for the President of the United States to authorize the Secretary of the Treasury to anticipate the collection and receipt of the duties laid and imposed by this act, and by the said act, entitled "An act laying duties on licenses to distillers of spirituous liquors," by obtaining a loan, upon the pledge of the said duties for the reimbursement thereof, to an amount not exceeding six millions of dollars, and at a rate of interest not exceeding six per centum per annum. And any bank or banks now incorporated, or which may hereafter be incorporated, under the authority of the United States, is, and are, hereby authorized to make such loan: *Provided always,* and it is expressly declared, That the money so obtained upon loan, shall be applied to the purposes aforesaid, to which the said duties so to be pledged are by this act applied and appropriated, and to no other purposes whatsoever.

The bill was committed.—And on motion, the House adjourned.

THURSDAY, November 10.

A message from the Senate informed the House that the Senate do not concur in the amendment proposed by this House to the bill "to authorize the President of the United States to cause to be built or purchased the vessels therein described."

A motion was then made by Mr. PLEASANTS, that this House do recede from their amendment to the bill, disagreed to by the Senate as aforesaid. And the question being taken, it was determined in the negative: Whereupon,

Resolved, That this House do insist on the said amendment, and ask a conference upon the subject-matter thereof.

Mr. PLEASANTS, Mr. WILLIAM REED, and Mr. INGERSOLL, were appointed the managers at the said conference on the part of the House.

A message from the Senate informed the House that the Senate adhere to their disagreement to the amendments of this House to the bill "to authorize the President of the United States to cause to be built or purchased the vessels therein described," and agree to the conference asked upon the subject-matter thereof, and have appointed managers on their part.

The bill to authorize the Secretary of State, during the present war, to make an additional allowance to masters of vessels for bringing home destitute and distressed American seamen, was read a third time, and passed.

The House resolved itself into a Committee of the Whole on the bill for the relief of John Chalmers, jr. The bill was discussed, and its object explained by the Chairman of the Committee of Claims (Mr. YANCEY) and by the reading of the report of the Committee, and then reported to the House.

After the bill was reported to the House, some discussion took place on the point, whether Mr. Chalmers did or did not receive timely notice of the intention to burn the building containing the yarn, &c., which was destroyed. The bill was eventually ordered to lie on the table, on motion of Mr. EPPES of Virginia.

On motion of Mr. KILBOURN, of Ohio, the petition which he presented yesterday, praying for the exposure of the public lands for sale at twelve and a half cents per acre to actual settlers, was taken up and referred.

ARMY SUPPLIES AND DISCIPLINE.

Mr. CALHOUN, of South Carolina, offered for consideration the following resolutions:

Resolved, That the Committee on Military Affairs be directed to inquire into the expediency of changing the present mode of supplying the Army by contracts, or some other better calculated for a state of war, and that they have leave to report by bill or otherwise.

Resolved, That the Secretary of War be directed to inform the House whether the Army of the United States is trained by any one uniform system of discipline; and, if not, what are the causes which have prevented it.

Mr. CALHOUN said, it was not necessary to state to the House, that next to having an army, to have it well supplied and well trained was an object of the greatest importance. He had been informed, from a source to be relied on, that the present mode of supplying the Army, whilst it subjected the public to speculations by the contractors, was frequently on great emergencies found wholly inefficient. One of the most important enterprises in the South would have failed in consequence of the deficiency of the contractor, had not the difficulty been overcome by the great energy of the Commanding General on that occasion. There was, he had also understood, a variance in the discipline of the Army, in consequence of five or six different systems employed in training of the Army. So great was this variance, that no large body of our Army, Brown's command perhaps excepted, could be properly exercised together.

The resolutions were agreed to

WAYS AND MEANS.

Mr. Eppes, by general consent, made a report from the Committee of Ways and Means, on the amendment proposed by the Senate to the three million loan bill. [This amendment proposes to pledge, to pay the interest and gradually redeem the principal of this particular loan, a portion of the internal duties now existing, or to be hereafter imposed.] The Committee of Ways and Means recommend a disagreement to the amendment of the Senate.

Mr. Eppes, of Virginia said, the Committee of Ways and Means had had under consideration the propriety of a general increase of the Sinking Fund. They considered it proper that any measure of this kind ought to apply to all the new stock, and not to a small portion of it. On this subject they had addressed a letter to the Secretary of the Treasury, requesting him to state those particulars of information which were necessary to enable the Committee to take up the whole subject, and place the new debt of the United States upon the same firm and solid basis that the old debt had previously been placed on. If the House were of opinion that it would be better to apply this principle to a fragment of the debt, than to make the general provision he had suggested, they would vote for the amendment of the Senate. If, however, it was their opinion that every public creditor ought to receive the same measure of justice, and that no line of discrimination ought to be drawn between them, the rule ought to be extended to all the new debt, if to any. The Committee had on these grounds determined to recommend a disagreement to the Senate's amendment. On this view of the subject, when the House reflected that they had already given the most substantial pledges to impose sufficient taxes; when a bill had been reported containing a provision for creating an adequate Sinking Fund, and paying the interest of the debt, and thus reviving the public credit, he hoped the House would think with him, that it would be more correct to take that course than to adopt the amendment of the Senate.

The question to disagree to the amendment of the Senate, was decided in the affirmative.

Friday, November 11.

Another member, to wit: from New York, Isaac Williams, jr., appeared and took his seat.

Mr. Lewis presented a petition of the President and Directors of the Bank of Alexandria, praying that their charter may be so amended as that they may be authorized to issue notes for any sum not less than one dollar.—Referred to the Committee for the District of Columbia.

Mr. Lewis presented a petition of sundry inhabitants of the counties of Augusta, Rockingham, and Shenandoah, in the State of Virginia, who profess themselves to be of that class of citizens called ancient German Baptists, Tunkards, and Menonists; and are conscientiously scrupulous of bearing arms, praying to be protected in the full enjoyment of their religious liberties, and liberty of conscience, according to the faith.—Referred to the Committee on Military Affairs.

Mr. Eppes, from the Committee of Ways and Means, reported a bill to authorize the Commissioner of the Revenue to cause a clerk in his office to aid him in signing licenses; which was read twice, and ordered to be engrossed, and read the third time to-day.

Mr. Eppes also reported a bill to provide additional revenues for defraying the expenses of Government and maintaining the public credit, by duties on sales at auction; on the postage of letters; on licenses to retail wines, spirituous liquors, and foreign merchandise; on carriages for the conveyance of persons; and on plated harness; which was read twice and committed.

Mr. Jennings, from the committee appointed on the 4th instant, reported a bill to authorize the publication of the laws of the United States within the Territories of the United States; which was read twice, and ordered to be engrossed, and read the third time to-morrow.

An engrossed bill to authorize the Commissioner of the Revenue to cause a clerk in his office to aid him in signing licenses was read the third time and passed.

On motion of Mr. Condict,

Resolved, That the report and documents submitted to the House, on the 9th of April last, by the committee appointed to inquire into the manner of making contracts for supplying the Army of the United States, be referred to the Committee on Public Expenditures, with instructions to inquire in what particular instances, if any, the public moneys advanced to quartermasters and army contractors have been misapplied; what losses, if any, are likely to be sustained, and what measures, if any, are taken for their recovery; and that said committee be further instructed to inquire and report to this House, in what particular instances, if any, the supplies of provisions and other necessaries, furnished by the contractors for the use of the militia, when in service, have been found to be either deficient in quantity or unfit for use, together with such amendments as the laws on these subjects may, in their opinion, require.

The Speaker laid before the House a report from the War Department, stating, that few or no material papers were lost, during the late incursion of the enemy.

A message was received from the Senate insisting on their amendment to the three million loan bill, and inviting a conference. On motion of Mr. EPPES, the House insisted on their disagreement, and accepted the invitation of the Senate to a conference.

The House, on motion of Mr. YANCEY of North Carolina, resumed the consideration of the bill for the relief of John Chalmers, jr. Further evidence in support of his claim was produced and read.

The motion depending on the former discussion of the bill, was to recommit the bill to the Committee of Claims.

The questions now presented by it were these: 1. Whether this was a class of cases, which, if clearly established, was entitled to the favorable attention of Congress? 2. Whether, if it was such a case, it would be proper to act singly on this case, without reference to others of a similar character? 3. Whether the statement of facts was supported by the evidence? On the two first of these points, the opinion appeared to be generally favorable to the claimant, considering his case entirely *sui generis.* On the last point, there was a difference of opinion, on the ground that the House had not before it as conclusive evidence on the subject as was within their reach.

In the end, however, the motion to recommit the bill was negatived, and the bill was ordered to be engrossed for a third reading.

Mr. FISK, of New York, called up the National Bank bill; but, on suggestion of Mr. GASTON of North Carolina that time had not been allowed since it was reported for the due consideration of its provisions, waived his motion, and gave notice that he should call it up on Monday.

The order of the day on the bill making further provision "for filling the ranks of the regular Army by classifying the free male population of the United States;" having been called over—

Mr. LOWNDES, of South Carolina, moved that the further consideration of this order of the day be postponed until Tuesday next. In support of this motion, he urged the impropriety of the two branches of the Legislature acting at the same time on two bills, with totally distinct provisions, having the same object in view. If both should pass, the interchange of the bills would place each House in an awkward predicament. In any view, no time could be saved by acting on this bill, pending the discussion of another bill on the same subject in the other branch of the Legislature.

The question on postponement was carried in the affirmative without a division.

PETITION OF WILLIAM ARNOLD.

Mr. CHAPPELL, from the Committee on Pensions and Revolutionary Claims, made a report on the petition of William Arnold; which was read, and committed to a Committee of the whole House on Monday next. The report is as follows:

That the petitioner states that he was possessed of a loan office certificate, issued from the loan office in Massachusetts, payable to Christopher Clark, or bearer, for $600, and dated the 25th October, 1777. That on the 27th December, 1787, his house was burnt, and, with it, this certificate, &c. He prays that another certificate of like value may be issued to him.

From the papers submitted to the committee, it appears that the house of the petitioner was destroyed by fire, as stated in the petition; that the said certificate had been in the possession of the petitioner; that the fact of its destruction was made known to two witnesses soon after it happened; and that notice of said destruction was given in one of the public papers of Boston, and also in the Newport *Herald.* These advertisements were not inserted, however until October, 1790, nearly three years after the destruction.

In December, 1790, the petitioner notified the commissioner of loans at Boston of the fact, and deposited with him the evidence thereof. That in November, 1791, he petitioned Congress on the subject, which was referred to the Secretary of the Treasury, who made his report in April, 1792. This report was referred to the committee who reported thereon, but the report was not further acted on.

From the above facts it appears that the petitioner has complied with the requisites of the resolve of Congress of the 10th of May, 1780, in every particular except as to the time in which notice should have been given of the destruction.

It also appears, by a letter received from the Auditor of the Treasury, that this claim was presented, and registered in his office on the 29th of May, 1795, which is within the time prescribed by the act of the 21st April, 1794; and that the reason why it was not recognised and settled was, that the advertisement of the destruction of the certificate was too late to entitle the claimant to relief.

From the foregoing facts, the committee feel satisfied that the claim is a just one; and they find no legal objection to its being allowed, except that the provision of the resolve of 1780, relative to the notice of the destruction of the certificate has not been complied with. They do not think this objection sufficient to bar the claim. . It may not be proper, on slight occasions, to forego the provisions of a law founded in wisdom, and thereby give precedents to sanction claims supported neither by law nor equity; but when to obtain justice it is necessary to do so, the committee feel not only willing, but bound to do it. They, therefore, recommend the adoption of the following resolution:

Resolved, That the prayer of the petitioner ought to be granted.

TREASURY DEPARTMENT,
Auditor's Office, October 28, 1814.

SIR: In answer to your letter of the 27th instant, I have the honor to state, that the claim of William Arnold for the renewal of a loan office certificate of the *nominal* value of six hundred dollars, under the act of the 21st April, 1794, was presented and registered at this office, on the 29th May, 1795; and that the papers in relation thereto (believed to be the same now offered in support of his petition) remained in my possession until the 5th of March, 1814, when they were withdrawn by Mr. Potter of the House of Representatives. The objection to the admission of this claim at the Treasury, as noted on a general statement furnished the chairman of the Committee of Claims, on the 8th of March, 1802, were in the following words: "The destruction appears to have taken place

555   HISTORY OF CONGRESS.   556

H. of R.   *Pay of the Troops—Small Armed Vessels.*   November, 1814.

on the 27th December, 1787, but was not advertised until the month of October, 1790, which was too late to entitle the claimant to the benefit of the act." The petition and documents are herewith returned.

I have the honor to be, with great respect, sir, your obedient humble servant,

R. HARRISON.

Hon. JOHN C. CHAPPELL,
Chairman of Committee on Pensions, &c.

PAY OF THE TROOPS.

Mr. HARRIS, of Tennessee, submitted for consideration the following resolution:

Resolved, That the Committee of Ways and Means be instructed to inquire into the expediency of providing by law that any kind of money which may be paid by the Government to the troops in the service of the United States, for military services, shall be receivable in payment from the people for their taxes.

Mr. H. said that the propriety of offering the resolution had suggested itself to his mind from the circumstance of the Tennessee troops having been paid for their services in the Creek war, with Chilicothe notes. It was true, he said, that some of the notes were made payable in Baltimore and Philadelphia, but many of them were payable at the Chilicothe Bank, in Ohio. These notes, he said, would not pass in Tennessee, without a discount of from ten to twenty-five per cent. and that the tax gatherers were not authorized to receive them in the payment of taxes. Mr. H. said that a provision like the one contemplated by the resolution, would prevent the paymasters from speculating upon the people. That it was now in the power of the paymasters to make arrangements so as to pay troops off with notes on the most distant and inconvenient banks, and afterwards to have them purchased up at a considerable discount. It was a fact, he said, that the Chilicothe notes would not be taken from the people in Tennessee, even by the merchants, without a discount of at least ten per cent. He said that the Tennessee troops who fought last Winter the Creek war, and returned covered with scars, received for their services these notes, which are not allowed to be taken in the payment of their taxes. For this evil he hoped the Committee of Ways and Means would be able to provide a remedy.

The motion was agreed to.

SMALL ARMED VESSELS.

Mr. PLEASANTS, of Virginia, from the committee of conference on the disagreeing votes of the two Houses relative to the bill authorizing the purchase or building of not more than twenty small armed vessels, made a report recommending the House to strike out the words "twenty-two" guns and insert "sixteen;" so as that the vessels to be built or purchased shall carry not less than eight nor more than sixteen guns.

Mr. P. stated, that on recurring to the letter of the Secretary of the Navy, recommending the authorization of those vessels, it appeared that they were intended to be schooners. It was pretty well understood that sixteen was the largest number of guns which the largest class of schoon-

ers carries. The vessels embraced by the bill were considered by the Naval Committee merely in the light of a temporary acquisition, not as a permanent addition to the Navy. Vessels of this description could be very readily obtained, prepared with great facility and sent to sea with expedition, (which was a great object,) and when there was no longer occasion for them, could be disposed of at their full value. All these considerations, combined, urged the adoption of the modification proposed by the committee.

Mr. W. REED, of Massachusetts not desiring to repeat arguments he had heretofore urged on this subject, said he rose only to remind the House of the abortion of former attempts to procure by purchase a temporary naval force. As to the disposal of them at the end of the war, Mr. R. said most probably the enemy would take care of them all before the end of the Winter.

The report of the committee of conference was then agreed to.

SATURDAY, November 12.

A message from the Senate informed the House that the Senate have passed a bill, "making further provision for filling the ranks of the Army of the United States;" in which they desire the concurrence of this House.

The bill was read twice, and committed to the Committee of the Whole, to whom is committed the bill making further provision for filling the ranks of the regular Army, by classifying the free male population of the United States.

An engrossed bill to authorize the publication of the Laws of the United States within the Territories of the United States, was read the third time, and passed.

An engrossed bill for the relief of John Chalmers, jun., was read the third time, and passed.

On motion of Mr. McKIM, the Committee of Ways and Means were directed to inquire into the expediency of imposing a duty on all goods and merchandise imported into the United States, that, under the existing laws, may be admitted to entry free of duty.

Mr. McKEE, from the Committee on the Public Lands, reported a bill giving the right of preemption on the purchase of lands to certain settlers in the Indiana Territory; which was read twice, and committed to a Committee of the Whole.

Mr. EPPES, of Virginia, made the following report from the committee of conference:

"The managers on the part of the Senate, and on the part of the House of Representatives, at the conference on the amendments of the Senate, disagreed to by the House of Representatives, to the bill entitled 'An act to authorize a loan for a sum not exceeding three millions of dollars,' report, that the Senate do recede from their amendments to the said bill, except so much thereof as strikes out the last clause of the 5th section, and do agree, as a substitute therefor, to the two following sections, &c.

"SEC. 6. *And be it further enacted,* That in addition to the annual sum of eight millions of dollars heretofore appropriated to the Sinking Fund, adequate and permanent funds shall, during the present session of Congress, be provided and appropriated for the payment of the interest, and reimbursement of the principal of said stock created by this act.

"SEC. 7, *And be it further enacted,* That an adequate and permanent sinking fund, gradually to reduce, and eventually to extinguish the public debt, contracted and to be contracted during the present war, shall also be established during the present session of Congress."

The report having been read, it was, on motion of Mr. EPPES, ordered to lie on the table, until the bill should be returned from the Senate. It was subsequently taken up, and the report agreed to.

TREASURY NOTES.

The following resolutions were submitted for consideration by Mr. HALL.

1. *Resolved,* That the Committee of Ways and Means be directed to inquire into the expediency of authorizing the Secretary of the Treasury to issue notes convenient for circulation, to the amount of —— millions of dollars, under such checks as may be thought best calculated to detect counterfeits, in which alone, and gold and silver, shall all taxes, duties, imposts, or debts due, or which hereafter become due to the United States, be paid.

2. *Resolved,* That the Treasury notes which may be issued as aforesaid, shall be a legal tender in all debts due, or which may hereafter become due, between the citizens of the United States, or between a citizen of the United States and a citizen or subject of any foreign State or Kingdom.

3. *Resolved,* That the Secretary of War, under the direction of the President, shall cause to be purchased, in each State and Territory, and in each collection district thereof, as nearly as circumstances will permit, supplies for the Army and Navy of the United States, to the amount of taxes to be collected in each State, Territory, and collection district.

4. *Resolved,* That any individual, or body corporate or politic, at the expiration of twelve months from the date of the Treasury notes, by them held, and annually thereafter at their option, may fund the same, and receive in lieu thereof six per cent. stock.

5. *Resolved,* That, after paying the annual amount of principal and interest of the existing public debt, and the interest which may accrue on the stock created, by funding the Treasury notes to be issued by the Secretary of the Treasury, the whole amount of taxes, duties, imposts, and sales of public lands, shall be pledged for the redemption of the notes which may remain in circulation.

Upon each of these resolutions Mr. H. made a number of remarks. He said they embraced, together, a system, he verily believed was the only one which would relieve the United States from their present difficulty, and support the public credit in future. The want of a circulating medium was generally felt; and, indeed, without it, the people in the interior would be unable to pay their taxes, deprived as they were of a market for their surplus produce. Bank paper of one section of the country was in a state of depreciation in another; and unless some medium of general credit was immediately established, incalculable evils would result, &c.

The question on consideration of these resolves was taken separately, at the instance of Mr. OAKLEY.

The House agreed to consider the 1st, 3d, 4th, and 5th, but refused to consider the 2d, by the following vote, as taken by yeas and nays—for considering it 42, against it 95, as follows:

YEAS—Messrs. Alexander, Alston, Anderson, Avery, Bard, Barnett, Bowen, Burwell, Butler, Cannon, Clark, Comstock, Condict, Conard, Crawford, Davis of Pennsylvania, Desha, Earle, Forney, Franklin, Gholson, Glasgow, Goodwyn, Gourdin, Griffin, Hall, Harris, Hubbard, Kerr, Kershaw, Kilbourn, Macon, McCoy, Parker, Pickens, Rea of Pennsylvania, Rhea of Tennessee, Roane, Robertson, Shipherd, Stanford, and Williams.

NAYS—Messrs. Archer, Baylies of Massachusetts, Bayly of Virginia, Bigelow, Boyd, Bradbury, Bradley, Brigham, Brown, Caperton, Caldwell, Calhoun, Champion, Chappell, Cilley, Clopton, Cooper, Cox, Creighton, Crouch, Culpeper, Cuthbert, Dana, Davenport, Duvall, Ely, Fisk of Vermont, Forsyth, Gaston, Geddes, Grosvenor, Hale, Hasbrouck, Hawes, Hawkins, Hopkins of Kentucky, Humphreys, Hungerford, Hulbert, Ingersoll, Irwin, Johnson of Virginia, Kennedy, Kent of New York, Kent of Maryland, King of Massachusetts, King of North Carolina, Law, Lewis, Lowndes, Lyle, Markell, McKee, McKim, McLean, Moore, Moseley, Newton, Oakley, Ormsby, Pearson, Piper, Pitkin, Pleasants, John Reed, William Reed, Rich, Ruggles, Sevier, Seybert, Sharp, Sheffey, Sherwood, Skinner, Smith of New York, Smith of Pennsylvania, Smith of Virginia, Stuart, Sturges, Taggart, Tallmadge, Taylor, Telfair, Thompson, Udree, Vose, Ward of Massachusetts, Webster, Wheaton, Wilcox, Wilson of Massachusetts, Wilson of Pennsylvania, Winter, Wright, and Yancey.

The question having been stated on agreeing to the other resolutions—

Mr. GASTON, of North Carolina, said, that, in the absence of the Chairman of the Committee of Ways and Means, he should assign reasons, which he hoped would appear satisfactory, for the motion he was about to make. The resolutions, so far as they were directory to the committee, enjoined on it no other duties than it had already performed. To establish a circulating medium, the Committee of Ways and Means had proposed, in their report, at an early day in the session, to issue Treasury notes, in many respects resembling the species of paper embraced in the motion of the gentleman from Georgia. Soon after the committee made this report, a correspondence had been opened through the chairman, between the committee and the new Secretary of the Treasury, which correspondence had been already laid before the House. The Secretary of the Treasury, believing that the emission of Treasury notes could only be made with advantage to a certain extent, had thought proper to suggest a proposition for supplying a circulating medium of general confidence, by establishing a National Bank. After receiving and reporting this correspondence, the Committee of Ways and Means had thought proper to report, in general terms, a resolution that it is expedient to establish a National Bank; which resolution had received the

559   HISTORY OF CONGRESS.   560

H. of R.   Bank of the United States.   November, 1814.

sanction of the House. A plan, in pursuance of that resolution, had been reported, and was now in possession of the House. The House were then in possession of two projects; the one first reported, for issuing Treasury notes, and that now reported for the establishment of a bank. The object of the resolutions now before the House, was to direct the committee to make an inquiry already made, and its result reported to the House. Treasury notes must be the alternative, if a National Bank be not established; and when the House should so decide, the committee would have pleasure in carrying the wishes of the House into effect. In the meantime, Mr. G. moved that these resolves should lie on the table.

Mr. HALL said, he was well aware of the first report made by the Committee of Ways and Means, and also of the second, which had been adopted by the House. This was the only reason which induced him to bring forward those resolutions; because he believed the system recommended by the Committee of Ways and Means to be totally inadequate to the occasion. It was proposed to establish a bank of fifty millions of dollars, with only six millions of specie. To him this appeared one of the most extraordinary propositions ever laid before a public body. It was time to lay aside these visionary projects, and come to a direct question on some practicable system. Establish your bank, said Mr. H., and what will be the consequence? It will be established at last only on the credit of the Government, because forty-four out of fifty millions of the capital are to be paid in stock. If the bills of the bank circulate, it will be on the credit of the Government, and not on the credit of the capital. As to the bank coming in aid of the Government, would gentlemen say that it could give aid to the Government? Could it lend the Government thirty millions of dollars? If it did, and the Northern and Eastern capitalists continue opposed to your measures, they will have it in their power within twelve months to arrest the operations of the bank, by accumulating in their hands its notes, which must circulate principally in the North and East. Such a system, therefore, he considered as improper, impolitic, and one of the most ruinous measures which could be adopted by the Government. Mr. H. was also averse to postponement, because he considered this the most important subject that could possibly be brought before the House; because, on its adoption depended entirely the future credit of the Government. The measures heretofore adopted by the Government in respect to the public revenue and credit, had, Mr. H. said, been the best calculated to defeat their object. The time was come when the nation ought to depend on its own means, and resort no more to theoretic expedients. He was sorry the House had refused to consider the second resolution, which he considered very material; but he hoped they would adopt the others.

The question on laying the resolutions on the table, was then decided in the affirmative by a large majority.

BANK OF THE UNITED STATES.

On motion of Mr. FISK, of New York, the House resolved itself into a Committee of the Whole, on the bill to incorporate the subscribers to the Bank of the United States of America.

After the reading of the bill through, to give it preference in the orders of the day, the Committee rose, reported progress, and the House adjourned.

MONDAY, November 14.

BENJAMIN STEPHENSON, returned to serve as a Delegate for the Territory of Illinois, in the place of Shadrack Bond, resigned, appeared, produced his credentials, was qualified, and took his seat.

Mr. YANCEY, from the Committee of Claims, reported on the petition of Joel Strawn, James Robey, George Cooper, Benjamin Smith, sundry inhabitants of Cincinnati who served in the army of General Hull; William Gates, and Thomas Reed, Elijah Browning, and Charles Gilkey, Thomas Weathers, Thomas Pace, Mary Deibler, and Asahel Schovil; as also, on a resolution of the 28th of September last, by a bill to authorize the payment of property lost, captured, or destroyed by the enemy, while in the military service of the United States; which was read twice, and committed to a Committee of the Whole on Thursday next.

Mr. TROUP, from the Committee on Military Affairs, reported a bill to authorize a donation in land to persons in the military and naval service of the enemy, who shall come within the limits of the United States, and claim the protection of the Government of the United States; which was read, and committed to a Committee of the Whole on Thursday next.

On motion of Mr. DESHA, the Committee of Claims were instructed to inquire into the expediency of authorizing the horses to be paid for that were lost by the mounted volunteers who served under Governor Shelby, in the expedition into Canada last Fall.

The following resolution was submitted by Mr. RHEA, of Tennessee; which was ordered to lie on the table.

Resolved, That the following rule be added to the rules and orders of this House:

When a bill is taken up for consideration, either in the House or in Committee of the Whole House, the House, or the Committee of the Whole House, shall continue in session until the bill is gone through.

The following resolution was submitted by Mr. PITKIN; which was ordered to lie on the table:

Resolved, That the Secretary of the Treasury be directed to lay before this House a statement of the amount of the public debt on the first day of October, 1814, distinguishing the several kinds of debt, as well as that contracted before and since the present war, together with the amount owned by foreigners; containing also the amount at that time owned by States, corporations, and individuals, and the amount at the Treasury, and in the loan offices in the several States.

BANK OF THE UNITED STATES.

The House then resolved into a Committee of the Whole, on the bill to incorporate the subscribers to the Bank of the United States of America.

The first section of the bill having been read, in the following words:

Be it enacted, &c., That a Bank of the United States shall be established, the capital stock of which shall be fifty millions of dollars, and no more, divided into one hundred thousand shares, of five hundred dollars each share, and that subscriptions towards constituting the said capital stock shall be opened on the first Monday of —— next, at the following places, viz: Boston, New York, Philadelphia, Baltimore, Richmond, Charleston, and Pittsburg, under the superintendence of the following persons, as commissioners to receive the same: at Boston, James Lloyd, Thomas Perkins, and William Gray; at New York, General John Smith, Isaac Bronson, Theron Rudd; at Philadelphia, Thomas M. Willing, Stephen Girard, Chandler Price; at Baltimore, Henry Payson, William Cooke, William Wilson; at Richmond, Benjamin Hatcher, John Brockenbrough, William Preston; at Charleston, John C. Faber, John Potter, James Carson; at Pittsburg, George Robinson, Samuel Robert, and Henry Baldwin; which subscriptions shall continue open every day from the time of opening the same, from ten o'clock in the forenoon until four o'clock in the afternoon, until the Saturday following, at four o'clock in the afternoon, when the same shall be closed; and immediately thereafter, the commissioners, or any two of them, at the respective places aforesaid, shall cause two transcripts or fair copies of such subscriptions to be made, one of which they shall send to the Secretary of the Treasury, one they shall retain, and the original subscriptions shall, within three days from the closing of the same, be by the said commissioners transmitted to the said commissioners at Philadelphia, or to one of them; and, on the receipt thereof, the said commissioners at Philadelphia, or any two of them, shall immediately thereafter convene, and proceed to take an account of the said subscriptions, and if more than the amount of the said capital stock of thirty millions of dollars shall have been subscribed, then the said last mentioned commissioners shall apportion the same among the several subscribers in a just and equal ratio, according to their several and respective subscriptions: *Provided, however,* That such commissioners shall, by such apportionment, allow and apportion to each subscriber at least one share; and in case the aggregate amount of the said subscriptions shall exceed thirty millions of dollars, the said commissioners, after having apportioned the same as aforesaid, shall cause lists of the apportioned subscriptions to be made out, including in each list the apportioned subscription for the place where the original subscription was made, one of which lists shall be transmitted to the commissioners, or to one of the commissioners, under whose superintendence such subscriptions were originally made, that the subscribers may ascertain from them the number of shares apportioned to such subscribers respectively.

Mr. FISK, of New York, stated the reasons which had influenced the Committee of Ways and Means in confining to a few cities and towns the books of subscription, which were, generally, that the Atlantic cities were the principal repositories of specie and superfluous wealth, and that the exigencies of the times required greater expedition than was consistent with a more diffused subscription. It had been deemed proper, however, to add more commissioners in two or three of the cities; and he was instructed to move accordingly. And, on motion of Mr. F., the following gentlemen were added: to the commission at Boston, William Eustis and Samuel Brown; to the commission at New York, Isaac Lawrence and John Hone; to the commission at Philadelphia, Jared Ingersoll and Anthony Taylor.

Mr. SHARP, of Kentucky, then said, he was not satisfied, by the reasons of the gentleman, for limiting to so few the places of subscription, and moved, for the convenience of the Western country, to insert Lexington, in Kentucky.

Mr. ROBERTSON, of Louisiana, proposed, also, New Orleans, and argued with much force in support of his suggestion; and other gentlemen proposed other places.

The motion of Mr. SHARP being the one immediately before the House, gave rise to considerable debate. The motion was supported by Messrs. SHARP, ROBERTSON, LEWIS, MACON, WRIGHT, PEARSON, HARRIS, HOPKINS of Kentucky, BURWELL, and BARNETT, and opposed by Messrs. FISK of New York, OAKLEY, CREIGHTON, and INGHAM.

On the one hand, various arguments were urged in favor of extending the subscription, founded on the equal rights of all sections of the country to participate in any general benefit; the expediency of collecting specie from every part of the country; the advantages of uniting in the subscription people of every quarter of the country, and thus uniting the people of all sections to the Union by the ties of interest, which are frequently stronger than those of legal or moral force. On the other hand it was said, besides the delay inseparable from such a course, that it was important that the bank should be put into operation speedily, if at all, and that its commencement would be greatly delayed by multiplying places of subscription. It was also said, that if this motion were withdrawn, an amendment might be devised by the Committee of Ways and Means, which would meet the views of all parties.

Mr. SHARP's motion at length prevailed. Lexington, Kentucky, was inserted, as one of the places at which subscriptions should be opened, and Messrs. Charles Wilkins, Lewis Sanders, and John H. Morton, designated as the commissioners.

On motion of Mr. ROBERTSON, New Orleans was then added, and commissioners named for that place.

On motion of Mr. HARRIS, Nashville was added, and Robert Weakley, Felix Grundy, and John R. Bedford, named as the commissioners.

On motion of Mr. LEWIS, Washington City was added, and Robert Brent, Walter Smith, and Thomas Swann, named as commissioners. [Mr. FISK, of New York, named John Mason, Daniel

Carroll, and John P. Van Ness; but Mr. Lewis's motion being the first made was agreed to.]

On motion of Mr. Macon, Raleigh, in North Carolina, was inserted, and Sherwood Haywood, Beverly Daniel, and William Peace, named as commissioners.

On motion of Mr. Forsyth, Savannah, in Georgia, was added, and John Bolton, Charles Harris, and James Johnson, named as commissioners.

On motion of Mr. Condict, New Brunswick, in New Jersey, was added, and James Vanderpool, John Gray, and Peter Gordon, named as commissioners.

Mr. Grosvenor moved to add Utica, in New York, and John C. Devereaux, Benjamin Walker, and Jeremiah Van Rensselaer, as commissioners; but the motion was negatived, after some objections by Mr. Ingham, and replication by Mr. Grosvenor.

On motion of Mr. Webster, Portsmouth, in New Hampshire, was added, and John Goddard, Nathaniel A. Haven, and Nathaniel Gilman, named as commissioners.

On motion of Mr. Kilbourn, Pittsburg was stricken out, Chilicothe, in Ohio, added, and Samuel Findley, Thomas James, and William McFarland, named as commissioners.

Mr. Lewis then made a motion, the object of which was to establish the principal bank at the City of Washington, in this District.

This motion was opposed by Mr. Fisk, of New York, who said that the Committee of Ways and Means had fixed on Philadelphia, in preference to New York and other places, to be the seat of the principal bank, as being a place of greater security and greater wealth, and as being more central to the commercial transactions and wealth of the country, &c.

Mr. Lewis said, he had no doubt that the gentleman from New York preferred Philadelphia to this place, as he had already given sufficient evidence of his candor in that respect. The Military School, the National Bank, and every institution of a national character, had been contemplated to be fixed at this place by those who located the Seat of Government here, &c., and so they ought to be, &c. Besides, there might be many gentlemen who would vote for a bank to be established at this place, who would, on Constitutional grounds, be opposed to its establishment elsewhere. He, therefore, hoped his motion would be agreed to.

Mr. Lewis's motion was negatived, about fifty members only rising in favor of it.

On motion of Mr. Fisk, of New York, an amendment was adopted, authorizing the Philadelphia commissioners, in case thirty individuals should not be subscribed and returned to them within the time allowed, to open the books at Philadelphia until the whole should be subscribed.

Mr. Gaston, of North Carolina, then said, before the Committee proceeded further in the bill, he wished to propose a material amendment to it,

and with a view to ascertain whether the House were disposed to hear him in support of his motion at that late hour of the day, he moved that the Committee now rise. This motion was negatived.

Mr. Gaston proceeded, in a speech of considerable ability, and more than an hour in length, to lay before the Committee his views in relation to this bill. He professed himself anxious for the establishment of a National Bank, which he had always favored when opportunity offered. But it was his decided conviction, he said, that a bill like that on the table would not answer the purposes of the nation or of the Government. This view of the subject he supported by various objections to different features of the bill, and particularly to the mode of subscription in stock of the United States; the operation of all which he contended would be to throw into circulation a quantity of paper, founded not on a specie capital, but on the credit of the United States stock, &c., which would therefore be of no greater value than any other paper which the United States should make receivable in taxes, though much more expensive to the United States than Treasury notes or bills of credit would be, &c. In support of this idea, Mr. G. adduced many illustrations, from writers on this subject, from our own history, and from analogy. He objected also to the proposed appointment of a part of the directors by the President, to the large portion of the stock to be held by the United States, &c. He wound up his argument on these and other points by observing, that as he was friendly in principle to the establishment of a National Bank, he should not consider himself as doing his duty, if, while he disapproved of this plan, he did not offer another as a substitute to it. Instead of a bank of a nominal capital of fifty millions, he would establish a bank whose capital should not, at farthest, exceed twenty millions. He considered it as by no means important to its success that the Government should subscribe a cent to its capital stock; but as that was a fashionable idea, he would say a portion of the capital, five millions, should be subscribed by the Government; that the remaining fifteen millions should be subscribed by individuals, five millions of it at least in specie, the remainder either in Treasury notes at par, or in six per cent. stock of future loans at par, or six per cent. stock of former loans at the price at which it was contracted for with the Government. So far from such stock being inalienable, as now proposed, he would permit the directors to manage and dispose of it as they pleased. They might lend money to the Government if they found it to their interest and convenience to do so. He would abolish from such a charter the idea that the fiat of the President should at any time suspend the payment of specie by the bank, &c. If any plan of a National Bank could succeed, it must be on something like the plan of which this was the outline. To try the principle of this bill, and whether the House were disposed to accept any amendment whatever to it, Mr. G. concluded his speech by moving to strike out fifty millions (the proposed capital stock of the bank) and insert in lieu thereof twenty millions.

On motion of Mr. HOPKINS, of Kentucky, the Committee then rose, and obtained leave to sit again.

TUESDAY, November 15.

Mr. JOHNSON, of Kentucky, offered for consideration the following resolution, in conformity to a representation of the Legislature of Kentucky at the last session:

"*Resolved*, That the Committee of Claims be instructed to inquire into the expediency of paying for wagons and horses lost in the campaign of the Northwestern Army, in that division of it commanded by General James Winchester."

Mr. YANCEY, of North Carolina, moved that the resolution lie on the table, alleging as a reason therefor, that a general bill on the subject of such claims had been reported by the Committee of Claims, and was now before the House.

The resolution was ordered to lie on the table accordingly.

Mr. EPPES, of Virginia, in introducing the following motion, remarked, that in the late calls of the militia from different parts of the United States, the persons composing most of the detachments had been compelled to leave their homes with that clothing suitable for the summer season, but unfit for that now approaching; and, in various instances, they were suffering for want of clothing fit for the season. They are unable to return for clothing, and in many instances are not able to procure it. To bring this subject before the House, Mr. E. moved

"That the Committee on Military Affairs be instructed to inquire into the expediency of authorizing the Secretary of War, on the application of the commanding officer of any detachment of the militia, to furnish the necessary clothing to such of the private soldiers of the militia as may require it, and to deduct the same from their pay."

The motion was agreed to.

On motion of Mr. BIGELOW, a resolution was twice read, and ordered to be engrossed for a third reading, directing a copy of the public documents to be furnished to the Historical or Antiquarian Society of Massachusetts.

Mr. BRADLEY, of Vermont, offered the following resolution for consideration:

"*Resolved*, That the Committee of Ways and Means be instructed to inquire into the expediency of allowing interest to the public creditors, whose balances have been stated at the Treasury."

Mr. EPPES inquired on what views this motion was grounded.

Mr. BRADLEY said he had understood that in some cases balances had been struck at the Treasury, in relation to army supplies particularly, and remained unpaid. He could not see why the United States should not pay the interest on such balances until they were paid.

Mr. EPPES said that in his report the Secretary of the Treasury had contemplated the issu-

ing of debentures to all those persons to whom balances appeared to be due by Government, which, from the insufficiency of appropriations, or from other causes, had not been paid. He thought, therefore, this motion had better lie on the table, until the House had acted on that suggestion, or at least until it could be ascertained what were the amount and character of those balances. For his part, Mr. E. said, he had no knowledge of their existence. There might be some such, but if there were, they were small in amount and few in number. Such as they were, they might have arisen from the deficiency in the authorized loans; but he believed means were in operation for meeting all the demands of the Government without the intervention of any provision of this kind. He, therefore, moved that the resolution should lie on the table.

The motion to lay the resolution on the table was agreed to.

On motion of Mr. INGHAM, of Pennsylvania, a resolution was adopted requesting the Secretary of State to cause the members of Congress to be furnished with the volumes of the new Digest of the Laws as they might be respectively finished.

NATIONAL BANK.

The House again resolved itself into a Committee of the Whole, on the bill to incorporate the subscribers to the Bank of the United States of America.

The motion of Mr. GASTON to make the capital of the bank *twenty* instead of *fifty* millions of dollars, being still under consideration—

Mr. FISK, of New York, spoke in reply to Mr. GASTON's speech, and in explanation of the views of the Committee. He declined replying to Mr. G.'s objections to various details of the bill, until those details should come immediately under the consideration of the House; but applied his observations particularly to Mr. G.'s objections to the amount and character of the proposed capital of the bank. The objects of the Committee of Ways and Means in proposing such an institution, ought ever to be kept in view in this discussion. They were, generally, the revival and support of the public credit. These objects could be best accomplished: 1. By raising the value of the public stocks; and, 2. By the establishment of a competent circulating medium. Mr. F. then entered into an argument to show that the plan now before the House was that which would best accomplish these objects. He referred to the history of the former Bank of the United States, established with similar objects, and under like circumstances, and from its efficiency argued what might be expected from this bank. The Committee, in inquiring as to the amount of circulating medium which could be now advantageously employed, had fixed on fifty millions, which amount had also received the sanction of the opinion of the Secretary of the Treasury. The present banking capital of the nation being estimated at an hundred millions, it was believed by the Committee that the addition of fifty millions would not be dangerous either to those institutions or to the community. Having thus determined on an increase of the circulating medium of the country, the next object was the appreciation of the value of the public stock. That stock had depreciated in value, not from any doubt of the ability or disposition of the Government to comply with its engagements to the public creditors, but from the quantity of the stock which it had been necessary to throw into market exceeding the means for purchasing it. A relief of the stock from its present depreciation was promised by the withdrawal of a part of it from the market; and with this view, it had been contemplated that twenty-four millions of the capital stock of the bank should be subscribed in Government securities. This, by taking so much stock out of the market, would raise the price of the stock, and make room for more which it might be necessary to create. It had been thought proper, too, that the United States should hold a part of the stock of the bank; to what amount, there had been some difference of opinion, and if the House thought too great a proportion was by this bill allowed to the United States, they would so decide. Mr. F. was willing, for himself, that the bank should be connected with the Government, and the Government with the bank, and that they should mutually support each other, &c. As to the share of the Government in the appointment of directors, while it could be no injury to the institution, it was necessary as well to guard the interest of the United States, as to take care of their interest in the security of the revenue in the various branches of the bank. Mr. F. took a comparative view of the situation of the nation now and in 1791, when the Bank of the United States was established, dwelling on the diminution of the public debt, and increase of the means of payment since that day; the increase of circulating medium, wealth, population, &c., from which he concluded there was ample employment for a bank of fifty millions now, as for a bank of fifty millions then. Of the ten millions capital of that bank, three-fourths of it was composed of public stock, as much depreciated at that day as public stock now is. The operation of that bank, he said, had been not only beneficial but wonderful, giving a spring to public credit, and raising the price of all public stock, as he believed this bank would, when once established. As to the specie capital, it was difficult, he remarked, to say how much specie would give confidence to the operations of the bank. The old Bank of the United States had commenced its operations on a specie capital of 400,000 dollars. He had no doubt, therefore, but this bank might safely commence its operations on a specie deposite of $1,200,000, which he believed there would be no difficulty in procuring. As to the confinement of the subscription to the stock created since the war, the Committee had deemed it proper to confine their object of raising the price of the public stock to such as was depreciated, viz: to that which had been created since the declaration of war, and

which had depreciated, perhaps, because not so well supported by specific pledges of revenue as the old six per cent. stock. These various features were, however, in the hands of the Committee of the Whole, and entirely at their disposal, &c. Mr. F. spoke nearly an hour.

Mr. GASTON said, it was the established usage, when an important bill was under consideration in a Committee of the whole House, for the gentleman who was especially charged with its management, to present a distinct and connected view of the objects which it was designed to effect, and of the process by which they were to be accomplished. The propriety of such a course was obvious. It could answer no purpose to receive an explanation in detail of the disconnected parts of a scheme, until you were first apprized of the general nature of the whole. He had presumed that the gentleman who acted on this occasion as Chairman of the Committee of Ways and Means, (Mr. FISK,) would have observed this approved practice, and on this vast and complicated project of the committee have come forward with a thorough statesman-like development of their plan. Nothing of the kind had been done. No exposition whatever had been given. This omission he particularly regretted, as it increased the difficulties of the undertaking in which he was about to engage.

As a member of the Committee of Ways and Means, he had conceived it his duty to examine with some attention the proposed scheme of a National Bank. The result of that examination he should now submit, without apology, to the Committee of the Whole. Although he had but small pretensions to skill, either in the science or practice of banking, he might have collected by patient industry some views of the subject which the Committee would be willing to receive.

A well regulated National Bank, was, with Mr. G., a favorite institution. At this session he had voted for the resolution, declaring it expedient that one should be established. At the last he had supported a proposition brought forward but a few weeks before its close, by a gentleman from Tennessee, not now a member of this House, (Mr. GRUNDY,) contemplating such an institution; and, as a member of the committee then raised in pursuance of that proposition, had contributed his efforts towards the success of the measure. He believed that this Government ought never to be destitute of the aids which a National Bank was calculated to afford. It was essential, as an instrument of finance, for the easy collection, the safe keeping, and the judicious expenditure of the public revenue. To the nation, as distinguished from the Government, it was eminently beneficial. It was the only basis on which could be securely established a circulating medium commanding credit and confidence in every part of the United States. It had another tendency, which he deemed of infinite value—a tendency to connect, by a common bond of interest, the different sections of this Confederacy. Should the centrifugal force of any of the bodies of our system become excessive, such an interest would be a countervailing power of attraction to cause them to revolve steadily in their orbits.

It was mortifying to recollect that we once had a National Bank, which after an experience of twenty years was found to realize every hope that had been formed by its friends, and disappoint every expectation which had been raised by its enemies. At the very moment when it was in the full vigour of successful operation, when the Government and the nation were deriving from it every advantage which ought to have been wished, and when it was in our power to increase these advantages in degree by giving to the bank an increased efficiency; at this very moment we utterly subverted the establishment. In vain did the ancient and fast friends of Federal institutions raise their united voice against the ruinous measure. In vain did others, breaking through the trammels of prejudice and party, describe in prophetic terms the fatal consequences of the work of destruction. All efforts to save the establishment were unavailing; and the oracular admonitions of wisdom were treated as the phantoms of a heated imagination. What was then prophecy is now history—what was then theory, ably demonstrated, is now fact, universally admitted. The Committee of Ways and Means tell you in their report at the commencement of this session, "the want of some medium which, rest-
' ing on a firm and solid basis, may unite public
' confidence, and have a general, instead of a lo-
' cal circulation, is now universally acknowledged.
' The stoppage of specie payments by the princi-
' pal banks of the Middle States, has embarrassed
' greatly the operations of the Treasury, and, by
' confining the circulation of notes to the limits
' of the States within which they are issued, has
' deprived the Government of all the facilities in
' the remittance of money which was afforded
' while public confidence gave to bank notes a
' general circulation." The head of the Treasury Department has officially declared, "that the con-
' dition of the circulating medium of the country
' presents a copious source of mischief and em-
' barrassment. It may in general be affirmed that
' there exists at this time no adequate circulating
' medium, common to the citizens of the United
' States. The moneyed transactions of private
' life are at a stand; and the fiscal operations of
' the Government labor with extreme inconve-
' nience. It is impossible that such a state of
' things should be long endured. The establish-
' ment of a national institution operating upon
' credit, combined with capital, and regulated by
' prudence and good faith, is, after all, the only
' efficient remedy for the condition of our circula-
' ting medium." Sore indeed must be the distress which can extort such self-reproving acknowledgments from a dominant party, who not four years ago overturned as useless to the Government and pernicious to the nation, precisely such an institution, thus operating and thus regulated. It is much to be feared that these skilful "architects of ruin" may not be able to rear such an establishment as that which they prostrated.

It must be admitted that the present is not a favorable moment for engaging in the undertaking. It is now neither easy to procure the fit materials for this establishment, nor so to combine them as to make the work stable and permanent. Commercial restrictions, war, and blockade, have played sad havoc with capital, and credit is so depressed that it will be difficult to find anything bearing its stamp which can be advantageously united with capital. While all is unsettled within and threatening without, it is an arduous task to command, for any new establishment, the public confidence. Mr. G. said that he felt these difficulties in all their force. But he did not thence infer, as he believed did some of his most valuable and intelligent friends, that the attempt should be therefore forborne. These very difficulties proved a state of things that emphatically demanded some institution which might relieve credit and increase capital; which would afford facilities to combat external danger, and the means to retrieve internal derangement. Such an institution, at all times useful, was at this juncture indispensable. It was indeed to be lamented, that its foundations had not been laid deep in the day of prosperity; but they must be laid, if practicable, even now in the night of adversity, for now it is that it is so eminently needed. There was one impression, however, which he hoped that these difficulties would make upon the minds of the Committee. He trusted that they would inspire a salutary circumspection and prudence in examining well every step they might take. With their best caution, and adopting the wisest plans, it was far from certain that their scheme would succeed. But it was morally certain, that unless it were carefully arranged in all its parts, it must fail. This circumspection was the more necessary because of the danger of error from the severity of that pressure which called on them to act. At a moment when the Treasury was without money, and the Government almost destitute of credit; when every day added to our necessities, while it diminished the scanty means of supply; we were to found a great national institution, the consequences of which, good or evil, must be widely spread, and permanently felt. There was imminent danger, lest, in the prosecution of this purpose, we should regard too much its immediate influence upon our present exigency, and too little its more remote, yet more important and lasting effects. The largest object when removed to a vast distance, makes an angle on the eye so acute as to render it invisible, while a mote may be brought so near as to cover the pupil. In the plan now under consideration, he thought it demonstrable that this error of disregarding remote consequences had been committed; nay, he believed, that the eagerness to meet the immediate exigency had defeated its own purposes, as well as neglected to provide for the durable interests of the nation and the Government.

Mr. G. begged that gentlemen would accompany him in the view of the great outlines of this plan. A National Bank was to be established with a capital of fifty millions. This capital was to consist in the first place, of twenty millions of six per cent. United States debt, which the Government were to subscribe, in payment for two-fifths of the stock of the bank, and which was to be redeemed only at their pleasure. The remaining thirty millions were to be subscribed by individuals in shares of five hundred dollars each. These shares were to be paid for in three instalments. The first instalment on each share was to consist of $20 in gold or silver, $50 in Treasury notes, and $150 in the war stock, (as it was usually termed,) at their nominal value. The second and third instalments were to be composed of $40 cash, $25 Treasury notes, and $75 of the stock above mentioned. The bank was to commence its operations immediately on the payment of the first instalment. The Treasury notes on being received into the bank were to be converted into six per cent debt, redeemable at the will of the Government; and no part of the public debt held by the bank, was to be aliened during the war, nor afterwards, for less than its nominal value. This institution with all its appendages was to be governed by twenty-five directors, twenty of whom should be elected by the stockholders and five appointed by the President of the United States. It was to be obliged to lend to the Government, at an interest of six per cent, thirty millions of dollars; and the President during the war, and for five years afterwards, was to have the power of liberating it from the obligation to pay specie for its notes. This institution was to continue twenty years, during which the United States were bound not to establish any other.

The great purposes contemplated by this splendid scheme, other than those of a mere temporary nature, are the creation of an adequate medium of general circulation, and the affording to the Government of the necessary facilities in the collection, keeping, and distribution of its revenue. These are indeed most important purposes. It must be self-evident that no banking establishment can effect either of them unless it command the confidence of the public. This confidence must be the life-giving principle of the bank—without this vital spark it is a dead mass—useless, nay, noxious to the community. Without a confidence that the institution is at every moment competent to meet its engagements, who will receive the evidence of its engagements as cash? The bank note becomes then, and then only, a fit medium of circulation when every one believes that he can obtain for it, whenever his necessities may require, the gold or silver which it represents. Such a belief suspends the notes of a bank in circulation, and prevents them from being returned for payment the moment they are issued. It enables the bank to perform very extensive business without the issue of notes, by communicating to a credit on its books the character of money, so that such a credit passes through a hundred hands by the means of checks, without drawing from the bank either a dollar or a note. It is this belief which induces individuals to deposite with a bank their stores of treasure; and, without such a confidence, it never can be a fit place for the custody of the public revenue.

Now, sir, said Mr. G., whether you regard the capital on which this bank is to be founded, or the government to which it is to be subjected, or the operations which it will be required to perform, it is visionary to hope that you can for a moment command for it the confidence of the public. All the elements of its formation are calculated to excite distrust. It has every ingredient in its composition which can attract suspicion.

What is the efficient capital of the bank? The Government will subscribe, in new stock, twenty millions; individuals are to pay, in the present depreciated public debt, eighteen millions; and in Treasury notes, which are to be converted into Government stock, six millions. Six millions, the bill directs to be paid in coin. But, this will not be done. The bank is to go into operation when the first instalment is paid. There will then be received, of gold or silver, but one million two hundred thousand dollars. Now, when the scarcity of specie is taken into consideration, there is little doubt but that the directors will take care to accommodate themselves and their brother stockholders with loans to the amount of the cash part of the second and third instalments. I am persuaded that I make a very liberal allowance, when I say, that, of the six millions of specie required by the bill, not more than two will be paid, and the other four represented by stock or accommodation notes. This vast capital is, then, to be composed of forty-four millions of public debt, inalienable by the bank, and redeemable only at the will of the Government; four millions of individual debt, designed not to be redeemed, but on long credit; and two millions of specie. The bank has an *efficient* capital of but two millions: for, that portion of its capital which cannot be converted into cash, whenever cash may be required to meet demands upon it, affords no basis on which to support an issue of paper.

In the direction of the bank is there full security that prudence, ability, and strict attention to its interest will be found? Here we are presented with a feature in the plan of a very odious kind—the appointment of five of the directors by the President of the United States will have a most injurious effect on the credit of the institution, while it is utterly useless to the Government. The Committee will pardon a quotation of some length from a report of the illustrious Hamilton on a National Bank, showing decisively the impolicy of any interference by the Government in the appointment of its directors—

"To attach full confidence to an institution of this nature, it appears to be an essential ingredient in its structure, that it shall be under a private not a public direction, under the guidance of individual interest not of public policy; which would be supposed to be, and in certain emergencies, under a feeble or too sanguine administration, would really be liable to being too much influenced by public necessity. The suspicion of this would continually corrode the vitals of the credit of the bank, and would be most likely to prove fatal in those situations, in which the public good would require that they should be most sound and vigorous. It would indeed be little less than a miracle, should

573   HISTORY OF CONGRESS.   574

NOVEMBER, 1814.   *Bank of the United States.*   H. OF R.

the credit of the bank be at the disposal of the Government, if, in a long series of time, there was not experienced a calamitous abuse of it. It is true that it would be the real interest of the Government not to abuse it; its genuine policy to husband and cherish it, with the most guarded circumspection, as an inestimable treasure. But what Government ever uniformly consulted its true interests in opposition to the temptations of momentary exigencies? What nation was ever blessed with a constant succession of upright and wise administrators?

"The keen, steady, and as it were magnetic sense, of their own interest as proprietors in the direction of a bank, pointing invariably to its true pole the prosperity of the institution, is the only security that can always be relied upon for a careful and prudent administration. It is therefore the only basis on which an enlightened, unqualified, and permanent confidence can be expected to be erected and maintained."

This great and practical statesman then proceeds to show, that a good Government has nothing more to wish for from a bank than that its concerns should be skilfully managed, and that such a Government always must have influence enough with the bank to procure a compliance with its reasonable desires. He then sums up the argument, and draws his conclusion: "It will ' not follow from what has been said that the ' State may not be the holder of a part of the ' stock of a bank, and consequently a sharer in the ' profits of it. It will only follow that it ought ' not to desire any participation in the direction ' of it." This hankering after a share in the administration of the bank has no adequate motive to justify it. The plausible and ordinary pretext is to secure the interest of the Government in the institution. But no such security is in fact afforded. On a former occasion an intelligent gentleman from Pennsylvania (Mr. SMYLIE) placed the fallacy of this expectation in a point of view which would be weakened by an adoption of other language than his own. Speaking of a proposed appointment of directors by the Government, when the question of renewing the charter of the former United States Bank was before this House, he asks, "Who will such directors gene- ' rally be? Certainly persons who need the aid ' of the bank, for none others would make appli- ' cation for the appointment. When they are ' appointed, they will be subservient to the views ' of such of the directors as are chosen by the ' stockholders; in their places they will lose sight ' of the public welfare; they will be interested by ' the accommodations which they may find ne- ' cessary for their purposes; to obtain these they ' will yield to their associates. Instead of being ' the guardians of the public treasure in case of dan- ' ger, they will remain silent until a spontaneous ' explosion of the bubble solves for the world the ' important secret of the insolvency of the insti- ' tution." Let it be added, what the magnani- mous soul of Hamilton could never have antici- pated, and what the gentleman from Pennsylvania forbore to state; let it be added in answer to the question, "Who will such directors be;" that, according to the fixed usage of the existing Ad- ministration, they must be devotees of the party

in power. The inquiry will not be, are they honest, or are they competent? but are they partisans staunch and true, and will their elevation promote the petty interests of faction? Such is the settled practice of the Executive in all civil appointments—I say civil appointments, for men of heterodox opinions are occasionally permitted to oppose themselves to the bullets of the enemy.

If in the capital, and in the administration of the bank, there is nothing found on which public confidence can fix itself, let us see whether its practical operations are likely to be such as may gradually attract this confidence. The first operation of the bank, after making the necessary discounts for enabling the directors and stockholders to pay for their shares, will be to loan to the Government thirty millions of dollars. Of this no one can doubt who knows our needs and has read this bill. This Government pays off these thirty millions of bank paper to its numerous creditors, and what then becomes of it? There is no confidence that the bank can be able to redeem it when presented, for it has not two millions of money. The Government indeed owes it seventy-four millions—fifteen per cent. more than its whole capital. But on this vast debt it cannot command a dollar, except the annual interest, and this will be paid to it in its own paper; it is not at liberty to require payment of any part of the principal, and it is forbidden to sell. Besides the little specie it may have, and the accommodation loans before spoken of, these seventy-four mil- lions of Government debt constitute all its effects.

Not only therefore is the bank without money to meet the fifteenth part of its issues, but its credits are not of a nature to be converted into money. The bank carries on no business by which an artificial circulation is given to this paper; and which like the wonderful process of nature that propels the blood through the arteries, and returns it through the veins to be propelled again with equal warmth and vigor, sends it forth in well-timed discounts to be brought back in periodical payments again to be issued. The con- sequence inevitably is, that the paper is brought directly to the bank for redemption, and the va- rious holders contend who shall be first in this race, till the President comes forth with his proc- lamation and frees the bank from the obligation to pay specie. Some exigency soon occurs to render an additional loan convenient to a needy Administration. The bank and the Executive are on the best possible terms—politically married— they "in one fate, their lives, their fortunes, and their beings blend." The bank lends as fast as the Executive can ask, and the Executive kindly protects the bank from the rude duns of saucy creditors. Thus there is thrown on the commu- nity an immense emission of paper which does not pretend to represent money, which is utterly worthless, except in consequence of a quality which the Government annexes to it, (and which it can give to any paper,) that of being receivable in payment of taxes. The great evil under which we labor, in relation to our circulating me- dium, is not a defect in its quantity, but in its value. We have paper enough, but we have little or no money. This deficiency of money, though no doubt produced by many causes, is in no small degree attributable to the superabundance of paper. Strange mistakes have prevailed upon this subject, where correct information might have been expected. It is perfectly ascertained in political economy, that no more paper of any kind can circulate in a country than is equal in value to the gold and silver, which would circulate there, if there was no paper. If more be thrown out than this circulation can employ, as there is no use for it at all, the surplus is returned upon the banks for gold and silver. When converted into this form an use is then found for it abroad, and it is exported, leaving the ordinary business of buying and selling within the country to be transacted through the agency of the paper circulation, which is adequate to the purpose. I have no doubt that in this way we are to account in a great measure for the scarcity of specie. And is this evil, and its concomitant, the depreciation of all bank paper, to be remedied by throwing more paper into market? Burke, with inimitable severity of humor, compares the reiterated issues of assignats by the Convention of France to the prescriptions of Moliere's candidate for the doctor's degree. The remedy is to be repeated as frequently as experience may prove its inefficacy. If the obstinate disease will not be cured, but becomes more and more exacerbated, why then, *"repurger, resaigner"*—"purge again, bleed again." Are you about to adopt the same course? Has an excessive issue of paper banished the precious metals from your country? Issue more paper. Is commercial intercourse destroyed; are the operations of the Treasury embarrassed; are all the moneyed institutions of the Middle and Southern States compelled to acts of bankruptcy, by the deluge of paper which has covered the country? Open the floodgates and pour forth a fresh inundation of paper. Assignats—assignats—more assignats!

And is it for the sake of an institution thus worthless, thus pernicious, that the solemn faith of the United States is to be pledged that no other bank shall be established for twenty years? The Government needs and the nation needs a bank founded on a solid basis, operating wisely, furnishing a circulation that will command universal confidence and credit, and capable of aiding the Administration in the management of its finances. Yet the possibility of making such an establishment is to be forbidden for twenty years, and this for the sake of a mere manufactory of paper! But this is not all. The Government binds itself to receive this paper in discharge of all public dues! Thus stipulating for its own bankruptcy, and rendering impracticable a compliance with its most solemn engagements. For, if it receive nothing but worthless paper, in what shall it pay its creditors—its domestic and foreign creditors? It will be unable to pay cash. It cannot dare to impose on them what is not the representative of cash.

If this view of the permanent consequences re-

sulting from the proposed bank be correct, it must be regarded as a most ruinous project. Instead of resorting to it as the only efficient remedy for the mischiefs and embarrassments that now exist, we should reject it as big with evils infinitely more fatal than any we have yet endured.

Mr. G. here remarked that he had heard the example of the Bank of England, after the suspension of its specie payments, urged as an authority for the usefulness of an institution which should not be compelled to redeem its paper. He had not the leisure, nor indeed the information, which would be required to go into a full refutation of such an inference. But he could not forbear from stating some prominent facts which would put an end to this supposed analogy. The Bank of England had been established more than a century. It was so firmly rooted in the public confidence, that "safe as the Bank of England" had become a proverb. Though not in form connected with the Government, yet a mutual interest and a variety of concurrent operations had produced such a connexion, in. fact, that the stability of one was a pledge for that of the other. All the private bankers in London transacted business on the credit of this bank; and these, by their connexion with the bankers throughout the Kingdom, sustained and everywhere extended this credit. Such were the ramifications through which the agency of this bank was spread, that there was not an individual in the Kingdom, possessing anything to lose, who directly or indirectly was not interested in its solidity. Yet with all these aids to uphold it—the most powerful (except the possession of cash to meet its engagements) that ever were or can be united to support any institution—thus sustained by ancient reverence, by universal interest, and by a stable Government, which determined to stand or fall with it—the interruption of specie payments gave it such a shock that it tottered to its base. Many of its friends feared, and most of our oracles predicted, its utter fall. The paper of the bank depreciated to a most alarming extent. And had not a prosperous commerce and the most fortunate political occurrences come in aid of the institution, it is difficult to conjecture how far such depreciation would have gone. Can a mere escape from destruction, by a suspension of specie payments, under all these singularly favorable circumstances, be viewed as an argument for the establishment of a bank, which is to begin by an issue of paper that it is known it cannot redeem? Because such a suspension did not utterly annihilate confidence in an ancient institution, does it follow that it will create confidence in a new one? There is nothing in the history of the Bank of England which can furnish an argument in favor of the proposed scheme.

But, sir, said Mr. G., I am perfectly aware that it is not so much the expectation of permanent benefit, as the hope of immediate succor from the proposed bank, that excites the zeal of its supporters. In a paroxysm of pain, the impatient sufferer often flies for relief to the empiric potion, although he knows that it is ultimately fatal.

"The Treasury is empty, and public credit at the
'lowest stage of depression. Something must be
'done, and done immediately, to help the finances.
'What can be effectual but the establishment of
'a great National Bank?" Such is the general
style of thought and expression among those who
are most earnest for the passage of this bill. It
cannot be denied, sir, that the fiscal concerns of
this nation are in a state alarmingly critical, and
emphatically require whatever of wisdom can be
found in the Government to snatch them from
ruin. But, let me conjure gentlemen not to be
led away by this sense of danger into a hasty
adoption of any measure which promises the disembarrassment of our finances. It is always at
such moments, in the history of nations, that
daring adventurers and visionary projectors obtain
a favorable reception of their desperate schemes.
With the magnificence of promise, and the enthusiasm of presumption, they dazzle the imagination, and seduce the judgment of the ardent,
the timid, the indolent, and the credulous. It was
at such a moment as this, in the history of French
finance, that the celebrated John Law came forward with his magnificent project. The old
fashioned mode of redeeming public credit by
economy, punctuality, and affording security to
the creditors, was thought too slow a process for
the exigencies of the time. A more rapid and
complete remedy was desired; and who could
fail to perceive such a remedy in his great Mississippi Bank? For a while it exceeded the expectations of the most credulous. Secured by the
farms of all the farmed revenues in France, holding a monopoly of the African and East Indian
commerce, and resting on a solid capital of the
fertile lands and golden mines of the Mississippi,
it gained the public confidence, and commanded
all the specie of the Kingdom. Its stock rose to
an enormous value, and the circulation of its
paper seemed to have no bounds. But, in practice, it was unable to meet its engagements and
to redeem its paper. In vain did Government
interpose to uphold the credit of the institution.
Confidence was withdrawn; circulation ceased;
the bubble burst; thousands were ruined, and
the finances degraded far below their former debasement. If the proposed plan is to afford relief
to our necessities, it cannot be difficult to discover
it. This is not a matter of faith, but of calculation. Whence is this relief, and what is the
amount of it? It will be said that the bank is to
accommodate the Government, at six per cent.,
with a loan of thirty millions of dollars. Such a
loan is absolutely necessary to our wants; perhaps can be no where else obtained, and certainly
not upon as moderate terms. Let this suggestion
be examined for a moment, and all that is plausible in it vanishes. In what does the bank make
this loan? Not in money, for it has it not; not
in the representative of money, for its issues are
made on a capital of irredeemable public debt;
not in paper that will command money, for the
bank, as we have seen, must be immediately relieved from the obligation to pay specie. In what
then is this loan made? In paper having no
13th CON. 3d SESS.—19

value except that it represents the engagements
of an institution whose only wealth consists in
the engagements of the Government, and answering no purpose of circulation except that the
Government has made it receivable in payment
of taxes. Is it not manifest that the direct engagements of the Government must have at least
equal value with that paper which ultimately
represents them; and that these engagements
may equally be made receivable in commutation
of taxes? Then the simple meaning of this transaction is to procure paper engagements of a suitable form and devices to be prepared for the Government, and to pay the manufacturers for their
trouble (at the rate of six per cent. on the nominal amount manufactured) one million eight hundred thousand dollars per annum. This is a very
expensive establishment, sir. You can surely
have your Treasury notes equally well struck,
and filled up, and signed, at a much less cost.
And none can doubt but that they will answer
every purpose of the Treasury bank notes. Unless swindling be designed, there is something
preposterous in the idea that A, who has capital,
cannot attempt a circulation of his own negotiable paper, but gives his bond to B, who has no
capital, and obtains B's notes in the expectation
that they will circulate freely on his [A's] promise to take them in payment of debts, as though
they were his own. But the idea approaches to
insanity when A regularly pays interest on the
bond to B for the use of these notes, which draw
no interest, and whose sole claim to credit is derived from their connexion with that bond, and
from his consent to treat them with respect. The
only quality which these bank notes can possess,
entitling them to confidence, or fitting them to
be the medium of circulation, is that which the
Government imparts to them—of being receivable in payment of taxes. If it annex this quality
to its own paper, and makes it as convenient for
receipts and payments as the notes of this paper
bank, an immense saving is made, and every beneficial purpose equally answered. It is idle to
imagine that the engagements of an institution,
whose capital is composed of Government debt,
can have any other credit than those of the Government itself. The whole foundation on which
either can rest, is the credit of the Government.
If you seek a further basis you but imitate the
Indian sage, who rested his world on the back of
an huge elephant, who stood on the back of an immense tortoise, who stood on he knew not what.
We are told one immediate benefit to result
from this institution is, that it will absorb twenty-
four millions of Government stock now in the
market, and make room for the Government to
throw more stock into it. This is surely a delusion. Six millions of Government securities in
the form of Treasury notes, and eighteen millions
in the form of six per cent. stock, will be made
to assume the form of United States Bank stock.
But this bank has a capital consisting almost exclusively of Government securities. Shares in
this capital are then, in fact, little else than evidences of an interest in these securities. These

twenty-four millions of Government stock are not actually removed from the market, but remain there under a different name. Instead of being transferred as Treasury notes, or as Government six per cents., they are assigned as bank stock. No burden is thereby taken from the market; no ability to loan is communicated to any one; no demand for Government paper created.

But the principal advantage which is boasted of, as resulting from this bank, is the revival of public credit by the appreciation of the public debt. This consideration is entitled to attention, both because it is somewhat plausible, and because it is much insisted on by the friends of the scheme. Public credit, at all times important to the nation, is now, when revenue is exhausted, and a war of immense expenditures pressing upon the Treasury with daily increasing demands, of incalculable value. This faculty, known to be exceedingly impaired by late occurrences, is to be renovated by imparting value to certain evidences of the public debt now much depreciated in the market. I am utterly unable to perceive how the result is to be produced. A high price of Government stock is often an indication of the healthful state of public credit. When every species of Government stock is at full price, not from the operation of accidental or temporary, but of permanent and regular causes, it may be regarded as an unequivocal evidence of sound public credit. But an artificial value communicated for a moment to a part of the public debt, not extending to the rest nor promising long continuance, is a proof of irregular excitement, indicating diseased, not vigorous, credit. To revive public credit by imparting an extraneous value to stock seems about as wise as to restore health by an artificial coloring of the cheek. Superficial observers may be cheated by the appearance; the credulous experimenter may for a moment delude himself, but the mistake of either cannot last long.

Let us examine a little more in detail the effect which this bank is to produce on the public stock and the public credit. There is now in market (I speak in round numbers) sixty millions of Government debt created since the war, which, at an average, may be said to be worth in specie seventy dollars in the hundred. By allowing twenty-four millions of this debt to be subscribed at its nominal price in payment for bank shares, it is supposed that you will create a demand for this stock, which will raise it to eighty-five or ninety. But, after the twenty-four millions are subscribed, the residue having no new value communicated to it, will preserve its former place in the market. Thus far nothing is seen but a mere stock-jobbing operation—an adventitious price given to public securities to enable the present holders to get rid of them at the expense of others in whose hands they are to depreciate. But the twenty-four millions subscribed are converted into bank stock; and, as it is presumed bank stock will be at par, these twenty-four millions are raised in value from sixteen millions eight hundred thousand dollars to their nominal amount. This may be a correct statement—and here there is a clear gain of seven millions two hundred thousand dollars; but, if I may be allowed a phrase of the gentleman near me, (Mr. Wright,) I would ask, *"Cui bono?"* to whom does this gain accrue? Eight millions distributed among the holders of certain favored stock may be a vast help to their financial operations, but I do not see how our finances are thereby aided, or our credit restored. The practical definition of credit is the ability to buy and borrow cheap—how this ability is increased by legislating fortunes to a few at the expense of the community is not very obvious. Do you expect that those whom you thus enrich will lend you from gratitude? They will remember the fate they have so narrowly escaped, and be careful how they again incur the risk of bankruptcy. Will others be eager to lend you from the hope of similar favors? You have put it out of your power to oblige, for you can make no more banks.

A very strange opinion prevails in relation to the holders of this war stock. It seems to be supposed that Government is under some obligation to raise its price. So far as its value is to be effected by a punctual, faithful, and liberal compliance with the engagements of the Government, no man more sincerely wishes its rise than myself. I have joined in the pledge to give it full security by an adequate sinking fund before the close of this session, and I certainly shall be ready to redeem my pledge. I will concur in any plan which may be requisite to provide for the faithful payment of the interests, and the honest reimbursement of their principal. Thus far I go, for thus far the Government is morally bound to go; but to do more than this, to make a bank for them, is to legislate, not for the nation, but for individuals.

From what I have said it is manifest that, whatever may be my predilection for a National Bank, it is impossible that I should sanction the plan which is now proposed. Its general and permanent effects I regard as most pernicious; its immediate consequences without adequate benefit to counteract its expense to Government, and wearing too much the appearance of a mere stock-jobbing operation. While I disapprove the scheme submitted, I owe it to candor to state what plan I would be ready to support. Let the capital of the bank be reduced to a manageable size. The Bank of England, the only incorporated institution of the kind within the Kingdom, has a capital less than twenty millions sterling, the paper of which is a sufficient medium for the collection of a revenue of eighty millions. Ours, surely, will be large enough if we make it equal to our revenue, twenty millions of dollars. I am not anxious that the Government should take an interest in it, especially as, at this moment, it is not advisable to contract more debts than are unavoidable. But, as this is a fashionable idea, I would consent that the United States should subscribe for five millions of this stock. Of the remaining fifteen millions, five millions, at least, should be paid, *actually* paid, in specie; and ten might be subscribed in Treasury notes, or stock hereafter to be created, at par. The appreciation of these notes, or of this stock, would be taken into consideration at the time of issuing them, and its benefit thus accrue directly to the Government. In favor of existing stock, I would agree that it might be received in lieu of new stock or Treasury notes, but at its original contract prices with Government. Either this would be a beneficial privilege, or it would not. If a privilege, and therefore embraced, the Government would derive a profit of the difference on all the subscribed stock between the contract and nominal price, by way of bonus for the charter; and if it should not be regarded as a privilege, there is no compulsion on the holder of the stock to subscribe. The direction of the bank should be confided solely to the officers selected by the stockholders. The institution should be left free to pursue its interest, and under no obligation to lend to the Government. It should be *compelled* to redeem all its issues by gold and silver, and, whenever it needed an addition of specie to its capital, it might sell any portion of its public debt to procure it. Such an establishment, honestly and prudently managed, would be a basis on which to support a circulating medium adequate to our wants and deserving of our confidence. Such an establishment would afford to the Government all the facilities it could wish for collecting, keeping, and disbursing its revenue. These great purposes answered, must essentially aid the public credit. Other aids it should have, which are not to be obtained through any bank. Giving full security to the public creditor, not by a pledge of faith, but of funds; provide competent revenue for paying him his interest, and be punctual in the payment; and, above all, put down all profusion, and extravagance, and waste —economy will save the necessity of immense loans. These things done, all will be accomplished which, while the war continues, is on your part practicable, and the issue must then be trusted to Providence.

To ascertain, sir, how far my opinions may be acceptable to the Committee, I move you to amend the first section of the bill. where it provides for the capital of this bank, by striking out the word "fifty," and inserting, in lieu thereof, "twenty."

Mr. FISK made some remarks by way of resisting the attack which he said the gentleman had to-day made from the same battery as he yesterday opened on the bill. He denied the applicability of some of his remarks, particularly of that in relation to LAW's scheme, which arose from that bank's having issued a vast amount of paper on its capital, founded on the fictitious value of certain land certificates, &c., an excess of folly into which no properly regulated bank was in any danger of falling, &c.

The question on Mr. GASTON's motion to strike out *fifty* and insert *twenty* millions, was then decided as follows: For the motion 47, against it 79.

So the motion was negatived.

On motion of Mr. PARKER, of Massachusetts, among the places at which subscription books should be opened, Hallowell in Maine was inserted, and three persons named as commissioners.

Mr. CONDICT, of New Jersey, said he thought it would be good policy to permit as large a portion of the agricultural community to contribute to the stock as possible. With this view he moved to increase the number of shares from one to five hundred thousand, and reduce the amount of each share to one instead of five hundred dollars.

Mr. FISK, of New York, opposed this motion. The shares, he conceived, were made sufficiently small to enable every one so disposed to participate in the bank; while a still further subdivision of the stock would produce great embarrassment, and a total derangement of the details of the bill, and much difficulty in apportioning the proportions of stock, Treasury notes, and specie, to be paid on each share.

The motion was rejected, yeas 32.

Mr. WRIGHT, of Maryland, proposed to substitute, for the provision respecting the manner of taking subscriptions for this stock, a provision for dividing its capital stock among the several States in proportion to their representation; so that all the members of the Union might equally participate in the benefits of such subscription. He had no doubt the subscriptions would be advantageous to the individuals, inasmuch as he believed the stock would be greatly above par as soon as the bank went into operation. Not having, however, had time to prepare an amendment to meet his wishes, he should waive his motion for the present, until the bill was gone through.

After making further verbal amendments to the first section, the second section of the bill was read, in the following words:

SEC. 2. *And be it further enacted,* That it shall be lawful for any person, copartnership, or body politic, to subscribe for so many shares of the said capital stock of the said bank, as he, she, or they, shall think fit, not exceeding one thousand shares; except as is hereinafter provided for the subscription on behalf of the United States; and the sums respectively subscribed, except on behalf of the United States, as is hereinafter provided, shall be payable in the manner following, that is to say: one-fifth part thereof in gold or silver coin of the United States; three-fifth parts thereof in gold or silver coin of the United States, or in the public debt of the United States, contracted by virtue of the act of Congress, entitled "An act authorizing a loan for a sum not exceeding eleven millions of dollars," passed the fourteenth day of March, one thousand eight hundred and twelve, or contracted by virtue of any subsequent act and acts of Congress, authorizing a loan, or loans; and one-fifth part thereof in gold or silver coin, or in Treasury notes, issued under the act of Congress, entitled "An act to authorize the issuing of Treasury notes;" passed the thirtieth day of June, one thousand eight hundred and twelve, or issued under the authority of any subsequent act or acts of Congress, authorizing Treasury notes to be issued. And the said payment shall be made and completed in the sums and at the times hereinafter declared, that is to say: at the time of subscribing, there shall be paid twenty dollars on each share, in gold or silver coin, and two hundred dollars more in gold or silver coin, or in the public debt and Treasury notes aforesaid, in the proportions aforesaid. At the expiration of four calendar months, after the time of subscribing, there shall be paid the further sum of forty dollars on each share, in gold or silver coin, and one hundred dollars in gold and silver coin, or in the public debt and Treasury notes aforesaid, in the proportions aforesaid. At the expiration of six calendar months, from the time of subscribing, there shall be paid the further sum of forty dollars, in gold or silver coin, and one hundred dollars in gold or silver coin, or in the public debt and Treasury notes aforesaid, in the proportions aforesaid. And the subscriptions in public stock and Treasury notes, as aforesaid, shall be taken and credited for the principal, and so much of the interest thereof, respectively, as shall have accrued on the day of subscribing the same.

Mr. HALL, of Georgia, moved to amend this section by adding thereto a proviso, in the following words:

"*Provided,* That no interest shall accrue on the Public Stock or Treasury notes paid by the subscribers as a part of the capital of the bank during the continuance of the charter."

The reason assigned by Mr. HALL was, that the bank would draw a double interest on the stock part of the capital, viz: six per cent. on the stock, and a per centage from the operations of the bank upon that stock.

Mr. FISK opposed this motion, and expressed much surprise at it. He thought the moral sense of the Government must revolt at its injustice: besides, that it would destroy all possibility of organizing a bank on the principles proposed by the bill.

The motion of Mr. HALL was negatived, very few voices only appearing in favor of it.

Mr. OAKLEY, of New York, moved so to amend the bill as to make it optional to subscribers to pay in the whole of their shares (except the specie part) in six per cent. stock, instead of compelling them to pay in a part of the subscription in Treasury notes.

This motion was opposed by Mr. FISK, of New York, and negatived, yeas only 43.

Mr. BRADBURY, of Massachusetts, made a motion, the object of which was, in the provision respecting the subscription of a certain proportion of the capital in stock of the loans created since the war, to substitute in lieu thereof the stock "in loans hereafter to be contracted by authority of any act of Congress, passed or to be passed during the present session."

Mr. B. said, that the bill, as it now stood, would afford no real advantage to the Government unless it were in the privilege of borrowing thirty millions of dollars from the bank. The intention of the charter proposed to be granted by the bill, was, to authorize the individuals associating to issue paper money—notes which would promise to pay nothing but paper—for, he contended, whether the provision authorizing the President, on certain occasions, to suspend payment of specie, were adopted or not, the institution would be nothing but a bank of paper money; and he

could see no advantage the Government could derive from borrowing thirty millions of paper money. If, however, this bank should be advantageous or profitable to stockholders, he could see no reason why those who had lent the Government money since the declaration of war, should have any advantage over any present or future stockholders. They had obtained, he conceived, sufficient discount beyond the six per cent. interest for the loans they had made—and yet, it appeared to him, from an examination of this bill, that its whole object was to benefit this description of persons. If this bank should go into operation, which he doubted—even should the bill pass, what, he asked, would be the consequence? Ignorant and unwary men would purchase the public stock, at par, from those who contracted for it and now hold it, and presently the bubble would burst, and these purchasers become the losers by the scheme. If the individuals who took the last loans had been permitted to devise a bill for their particular advantage, they could not have drawn one to suit them better.

Mr. WRIGHT, of Maryland, proposed to submit, in lieu of Mr. BRADBURY'S motion, an amendment which he had prepared. If the House meant to do perfect justice to themselves, to their country, and to the United States, he said they would be indisposed to put the public stock, redeemable at the will and pleasure of the Government, on the same footing as specie; and, if that stock were permitted to be subscribed, at the contract price, it would be a sufficient bonus to the stockholders that their stock was converted into bank capital, which would immediately rise to 50 or 60 per cent. above par. In such a provision as he proposed, there would be nothing coercive; the stockholder might or might not subscribe his stock; if he did, he would be placed on the same footing as the rest of the community. Mr. W. wished, therefore, to admit any stock to be subscribed at the past or future loans at the contract price.

Mr. BRADBURY declined assenting to this substitute to his motion, which, however, he modified by adding to the end of it the words, "at its par value," thus proposing to allow subscriptions to the bank in the stock of any future loan, at its par value.

Mr. FISK opposed Mr. BRADBURY'S motion with considerable warmth. If they could not aid the public credit, he said, he hoped Congress would refrain from doing anything which should injure it. The public creditor had generally gone to the extent of his means in purchasing the public stock now lying on his hands. But it never could have entered into his calculation that the Government would adopt any measure calculated directly to bear on him, as the creation of a new stock on different footing certainly would, by giving it the advantage in the market over him. Such a course pursued by a Government, of exercising its power to serve its own purposes, instead of pursuing a course of magnanimous policy, must, Mr. F. said, be repugnant to every sentiment of morality as well as justice, which ought to be observed by nations. It would be an iniquitous delusion practised on the community, inasmuch as the depreciation of public stock does not now arise so much from distrust of the Government as from inability of the people to lend, which ability could not be increased by giving this sort of privilege to the stock in any subsequent loans, &c. Such a discrimination as is proposed would so weaken the confidence in the public faith, that he did not believe, after adopting it, the Government would be able to obtain further loans on any terms.

Mr. HAWKINS, of Kentucky, in a very decided manner, reprobated the adoption of this amendment. It was pretty well understood, he said, that the Government had exhausted almost to the last cent the ability of the nation to obtain loans under the existing state of things. It was true, that while this House was recently debating on the three million loan bill, he had suggested, and it was the fact, that the Executive was negotiating a part of the six million loan. They had hopes, also, to obtain, under the bill last proposed, a loan to enable them to redeem the Treasury notes becoming due in this quarter. But, how could this body expect this Government should, in the hour of most need and difficulty, obtain those resources which are indispensable to the fulfilment of the public engagements, if gentlemen, first on one day and then on another, should persist in introducing motions and speeches in respect to the present creditors which must have an injurious effect on future loans? No doubt, the gentleman in this motion, thought he was advocating the interests of his country; but, unfortunately, by one and another proceeding, public credit was injured and the operations of Government retarded. Remarks had been made on this floor, and he alluded emphatically to those unfortunately made by a gentleman from Virginia, (Mr. JACKSON,) who he regretted was not now in his seat; which had a more deleterious effect on public credit than that gentleman could possibly have expected or wished. They were certainly not authorized by sound policy, and he would venture to say, so far as they respected the public credit, the redemption of the public debt, and payment of past and future loans, were not sanctioned by the Administration or any member of it. He would not support any men or Administration that supported such a doctrine; and, so far as the doctrine had been advocated by one of his political friends, he declared the opinions expressed were not his; that they were unworthy of any party, of any Government, of any Administration, or any member of it. As to this bill, he entertained Constitutional objections to the establishment of any bank; if they could be removed, he might vote for this bill. He did not rise to speak of its merits, but to protest against propositions calculated to weaken if not destroy all confidence in the public faith. It had been assigned as a reason for such a motion, that speculators had preyed on the public credit. This he denied. The Government had gone on, relying on the public credit alone to support its loans, until the terms on which they could be obtained had fallen from par to 88, from 86 to 80, &c. The Government had been

compelled to have money, and had bought it as low as they could. As to the terms of the ten million loan, on which so much had been said, Mr. H. said it was only an adaptation to that loan by Mr. Campbell of the terms on which Mr. Gallatin had, without censure, obtained the sixteen million loan, and in consequence of which last engagement the terms of the loan had been more than once varied, &c. Nay more, he said the terms allowed by Mr. Campbell were less advantageous to the contractors than those allowed by Mr. Gallatin; so that the blame thrown on him was imputable not to the terms of the late loan, but to the inability of the Government to borrow, &c. Mr. H. protested against the principle of this amendment. If the House resorted to invidious discriminations between the public creditors, he admonished them that they would paralyze their own arm, and arrest the future operations of the Government.

Mr. GHOLSON said he sincerely regretted that the animadversions of the honorable gentleman from Kentucky (Mr. HAWKINS) on the speech of the honorable gentleman from Virginia, (Mr. JACKSON,) on the loan bill, had not been made while that gentleman was present, so that he might have had an opportunity of vindicating himself before the Committee and the nation. Mr. G, observed that he did not recollect the remarks of his friend (Mr. JACKSON) with sufficient distinctness to attempt to state the substance of them to the Committee. He, however, did not understand them to be such as could be construed into an indisposition to pay the public debt. Mr. G. said he applauded the zeal which had been manifested by the honorable gentleman from Kentucky in favor of the public credit. With that gentleman, he ardently hoped that ample provision would be made at the present session for the punctual payment of the interest, and for the redemption within a reasonable time of the last cent of the principal of every description of the public debt.

Mr. CALHOUN, of South Carolina, said, they had arrived at that part of the bill, on which he presumed there would be the greatest diversity of opinion. The subject was highly important, and worthy of mature consideration. He therefore moved that the Committee now rise, to allow time for further reflection on it.

The Committee rose accordingly, reported progress, and obtained leave to sit again.

WEDNESDAY, November 16.

RUFUS EASTON, returned to serve as the Delegate from the Territory of Missouri, appeared, produced his credentials, was qualified, and took his seat.

The Committee on the Post Office and Post Roads were discharged from the several petitions referred to them, complaining of the conveyance of the mails on the Sabbath day, and they were referred to the Postmaster General.

Mr. TROUP, of Georgia, from the Committee on Military Affairs, reported a bill making provision for the widows and orphans of soldiers who die, or are killed in the service of the United States.

Mr. TROUP, of Georgia, from the Committee on Military Affairs, reported that there was no occasion for any provision in respect to the furnishing of militia with clothing, as contemplated by the resolve adopted yesterday—such a provision being already in existence.

The engrossed resolution for presenting a copy of the Public Documents to the Antiquarian Society of Massachusetts, was read a third time and passed.

The House resumed the consideration of Mr. RHEA's motion, requiring that every bill under discussion shall be gone through, before the adjournment, on the day it is taken up. This motion, on suggestion of Mr. BRADLEY and Mr. OAKLEY, was so modified as to require the question under discussion to be decided on the day on which it is made. Thus amended, the motion was opposed with wit and argument by Messrs. WRIGHT, PITKIN, DUVALL, GHOLSON, MACON, FORSYTH, and ALEXANDER, and supported by Messrs. RHEA, of Tennessee, and FISK, of New York. Mr. CONDICT moved to postpone it indefinitely. At length, to put an end to an unprofitable discussion, the House, on motion of Mr. LOWNDES, proceeded to the orders of the day.

BANK OF THE UNITED STATES.

The House resumed, in Committee of the Whole, the consideration of the bill to incorporate the subscribers to the Bank of the United States of America.

At the request of Mr. CALHOUN, of South Carolina, who desired to propose another amendment, Mr. BRADBURY, of Massachusetts, withdrew the amendment he offered yesterday. A great part of his object, he said, had been answered, by arresting the attention of the Committee on this subject.

Mr. CALHOUN then, in a very ingenious and elaborate speech, laid before the House his views on this subject, and the reasons why he should propose a total change in the features of the bill. The motion he now made was one of limited character, but such a one as he proposed to follow up by other amendments, or by distinct Legislative provisions, which should together embrace a plan of which the following is a brief outline: The capital of the bank remaining unchanged, at fifty millions, the payments of subscriptions to this capital stock to be made in the proportion of one-tenth in specie (which he afterwards varied to six-fiftieths) and the remainder in specie, or in Treasury notes to be hereafter issued; subscriptions to be opened monthly in the three last days of each month, beginning with January next, for certain proportions of the stock, until the whole is subscribed—payment to be made at the time of subscribing; the shares to consist of one hundred instead of five hundred dollars each; the United States to hold no stock in bank, nor any agency in its disposal, nor control over its operations, nor right to suspend specie payments. The amount

of Treasury notes to be subscribed, viz. forty-five millions, to be provided for by future acts of Congress, and to be disposed of in something like the following way, viz: fifteen millions of the amount to be placed in the hands of the agents, appointed for the purpose, or in the hands of the present Commissioners of the Sinking Fund, to go into the stock market, to convert the Treasury notes into stock; another sum, say five millions, to be applied to the redemption of the Treasury notes becoming due at the commencement of the ensuing year; the remaining twenty millions he proposed to throw into circulation as widely as possible. They might be issued in such proportions monthly as to be absorbed in the subscriptions to the bank at the end of each month, &c. This operation, he presumed, would raise the value of Treasury notes perhaps twenty or thirty per cent. above par, being the value of the privilege of taking the bank stock, and thus afford at the same time a bonus and an indirect loan to the Government; making unnecessary any loan by the bank until its extended circulation of paper shall enable it to make a loan which shall be advantageous to the United States. The Treasury notes so to be issued to be redeemable in stock at six per cent., disposable by the bank at its pleasure, and without the sanction of Government; to whom neither is the bank to be compelled to loan any money. This, it is believed, is, in a few words, a fair statement of the project of Mr. CALHOUN, which he supported by a variety of explanations of its operations, &c.; the notes of the bank, when in operation, to be received exclusively in the payment of all taxes, duties, and debts to the United States. The operation of this combined plan, Mr. C. conceived, would be to afford, 1. Relief from the immediate pressure on the Treasury; 2. A permanent elevation of the public credit; and, 3. A permanent and safe circulating medium of general credit. The bank should go into operation, he proposed, in April next. He concluded his exposition by a motion, the effect of which is to deprive the United States of any share in the stock of the bank, and to change the proportions of specie and paper in which it shall be payable to one-tenth in specie, and nine-tenths in Treasury notes.

This motion opened a wide and interesting scene of debate.

Mr. FISK attacked Mr. CALHOUN's proposition with considerable zeal, principally on two points: its failure to provide for the present absorption of United States stock, and the difficulty which would occur in the circulation and disposal of so immense a mass of Treasury notes. He drew a comparison between Mr. CALHOUN's *projet* and that of the Committee of Ways and Means, highly favorable to the latter.

Mr. FORSYTH, of Georgia, opposed the adoption of this proposition, and examined the features of the amendment proposed by Mr. CALHOUN, and the arguments advanced in favor of it. He was opposed to it in nearly all its features, and greatly preferred the plan reported by the Committee of Ways and Means. His arguments were principally in reply to those of Mr. CALHOUN, which he generally pronounced to be erroneous and delusive.

Mr. LOWNDES, of South Carolina, replied at considerable length to Mr. FORSYTH, and vindicated the proposition of Mr. CALHOUN, in an able argument on the principal points of objection urged by Mr. FORSYTH, and in illustration of the principles of the bill. He showed what he believed a decided superiority of the amendment over the original project of the Committee of Ways and Means.

When Mr. LOWNDES ended his speech, the debate on the main question terminated, and this day's sitting ended with the following skirmishing debate, during the whole of which the Chairman and the members of the House were endeavoring to limit the debate to the question before the House.

Mr. OAKLEY, of New York, after remarking on the very high importance of this subject, and the magnitude of the change which this amendment proposed to introduce into the principles of the bill, and the obvious necessity of further time for consideration of so important an amendment, moved that the Committee rise, report progress, and ask leave to sit again.

Mr. INGHAM, of Pennsylvania, with much warmth, opposed this motion. He feared, if the House were to adjourn without deciding on this motion, coming from the imposing quarter whence it did, and supported with so much ability from the gentleman from South Carolina, it would arrest the loan of three millions, and even the nine million loan, which were absolutely indispensable to support the Military Establishment and other departments of the Government. What, then, he asked, would become of the soldier who is now in a Northern climate, depending on the fate of these loans for his pay, clothing, and sustenance? Whoever, in the face of such considerations, should vote to rise without deciding on this proposition, possessed, he said, more courage and philosophy of temper than he would boast. He hoped the Committee would not rise without deciding on this motion.

Mr. GROSVENOR, of New York, said he hoped the Committee would rise. This was the very question, how money should be raised, whether by Treasury bills or by any other mode, which more than any other required the deliberate decision of Congress. It was not a question simply of paying the militia of the army now out, but of establishing a system which should enable the Government to discharge all the demands against it. It was all-important, on such a subject as this more than on any other, to vote considerately and after deliberation. The proposition of the gentleman from South Carolina he considered to be generally advantageous; but he had some objections to it, which he wished an opportunity to submit. He hoped, before deciding on a subject like this, the House would take due time to deliberate on a proposition to throw into circulation fifty millions of Treasury notes, trusting to the bank for their absorption.

Mr. SHARP, of Kentucky, said he hoped the Committee would not rise. He wished, before rising, that they would decide upon the proposition before them; not, however, for the reasons expressed by the gentleman from Pennsylvania. He did not, like that gentleman, conceive that the decision on this amendment could affect the loans; for one, he said, he protested against loans made, or to be made, on the expectation of the creation of a bank to give a bonus to the holders of the public stock, in addition to that which they have already contracted to receive from the Government. It was important that some decision on this subject should immediately take place, which had been already three days debated; and he knew of no plan which would be so operative as that now proposed by his friend from South Carolina, whose arguments, he said, together with those of his colleague, (Mr. LOWNDES,) were something like mathematical demonstration.

Mr. OAKLEY denied any weight to the remarks of the gentleman from Pennsylvania, and allowed almost as little to the argument of Mr. SHARP, that three days had been consumed in the discussion of this subject. He should, for his part, say that three weeks might be well employed in the discussion of a project for establishing a bank with a capital of fifty millions of dollars—a capital sufficiently large to influence the destinies of this nation to future ages. He was friendly to the main principles of Mr. CALHOUN's proposition; but he was not certain but there might be radical objections to some of them. He hoped some indulgence would be afforded to those who, like him, wished to deliver their opinion on this subject.

Mr. INGHAM remarked, that the House had been sitting here nine weeks, and not a single measure had been definitively adopted for the support of the public credit. Delay and procrastination had taken place day after day; and, if the House were to wait until every gentleman was satisfied as to every word and letter in a bill, it would never get through one. The very suggestion of such an amendment as that now under consideration would, he said, produce ill consequences. It ought to be determined, therefore, as early as possible. He did know, that a speech (Mr. JACKSON's) delivered in this House had depressed the price of stocks in Philadelphia full two and a half per cent. The proposition now before the House, he feared, would depress them still further; and, when the public stock was in a state of depression, going down, down, down, he was unwilling the House should take any course which should still further prostrate it.

Mr. FISK hoped the Committee would not be induced to rise, at the early hour of three o'clock, by the old plea of want of time for consideration. It was important now to act, and that the whole course of proceedings of the House should be reformed, and one of greater energy and promptitude substituted.

Mr. GROSVENOR said this was no ordinary subject, on which men could make up their minds in a moment; and, although some gentlemen might

591 HISTORY OF CONGRESS. 592

H. of R. Bank of the United States. November, 1814.

be prepared to vote on it, he hoped they would allow some time to those who desired to reflect before they voted on a question of so great moment.

The Committee then rose, reported progress, and obtained leave to sit again.

Thursday, November 17.

Mr. Pleasants, of Virginia, from the Committee on Naval Affairs, made a report unfavorable to the allowance of a bounty for the destruction of vessels of the enemy at sea. Ordered to lie on the table.

On motion of Mr. McKim, of Maryland,

Resolved, That the Judiciary Committee be directed to inquire into the expediency and necessity of providing by law for the punishment of persons voluntarily holding intercourse with the enemy without the permission of the Government.

A letter was received from the Acting Secretary of State, setting forth that all the material papers in that office were saved on the late incursion of the enemy into this District.

Mr. Wright moved that this report, together with all the other letters received from other Departments on the same subject, be entered on the Journal of the House. The motion was negatived.

BANK OF THE UNITED STATES.

The House again went into Committee of the Whole, on the bill to incorporate the subscribers to the Bank of the United States of America.

The amendment yesterday proposed by Mr. Calhoun to the bill being still under consideration, an amendment was moved thereto by Mr. Fisk, of New York, and accepted by the House, authorizing the receipt of foreign gold and silver coin (as well as gold and silver coin of the United States) in payment for the subscriptions to the stock of the Bank at certain rates expressed in the amendment.

Mr. Wright, of Maryland, in the course of a few remarks on the motion of Mr. Calhoun, expressed his approbation of the principle, and avowed a decided preference to the plan it embraces over that contained in the original bill.

Mr. Sharp, of Kentucky, moved to amend the bill so as to preclude anything but Treasury notes from being received in payment of the forty-four millions, which are now proposed to be payable in specie or in Treasury notes. His object was to prevent the latter payments into the bank from being made by the aid of accommodation from the bank after it goes into operation.

After some conversation, Mr. S. withdrew his amendment with a view of offering it in some future stage of the discussion.

Mr. Ingham.—Mr. Chairman, as the question on the amendment proposed by the gentleman from South Carolina (Mr. Calhoun) now recurs, I beg leave to submit a few observations before it is decided. No member of this Committee can be more sensible than I am of the disadvantages I shall have to contend with in entering the lists against either of the honorable gentlemen from South Carolina who have supported the amendment; and I am now fully conscious that I shall fail to communicate my ideas with that perspicuity which alone can give them their proper force and effect; yet I am emboldened by the importance of the occasion, and shall rely upon the intelligence of the Committee and the subject itself to supply all other deficiencies. The amendment under consideration, taken in connexion with the suggestions of the honorable mover, contemplates a radical change of all the principal features of the bill reported by the Committee of Ways and Means; it will, therefore, be necessary, in order to contrast the two plans, to notice that which has been proposed by the committee somewhat at large, though I shall endeavor to be as brief as the subject will possibly admit. It will be seen that the only important features of the bill are: First, the amount of the capital stock. Second, the character of it. Third, the loan to the Government of $30,000,000; and Fourth, a qualified power to suspend specie payments. To all these points objections have been urged, either by the gentleman from South Carolina or the gentleman from North Carolina, (Mr. Gaston,) and a particular examination of them becomes necessary as a preliminary to the examination of the amendment. First, with respect to the amount of capital. The bill proposes a capital of $50,000,000; it is sufficiently apparent that the establishment of the proposed bank is designed as an instrument in aid of other measures, to revive the public credit, and thereby enable the Government to procure the necessary resources to prosecute the war with such effect as to bring a speedy and honorable peace. But we find that, since the commencement of the war, the public stocks have suffered a gradual depression up to the present year, when it seems that loans on any terms are totally at an end. The reason of this is obvious; we have borrowed and attempted to borrow too much, and have not resorted, as we ought to have done, to a more enlarged system of internal revenue. It is unnecessary to go back farther. What is the present state of things? We find the market exhausted of the money and overloaded with the public debt. In addition to this misfortune, we find, literally, no circulating medium in the nation. What then is to be done? You cannot borrow; you cannot impose taxes to the extent of your demands, and even those which are laid, cannot be paid in money that will answer the purposes of the Government. The answer is plain. By withdrawing a portion of the encumbering mass of stock from the market, you relieve it from its pressure—a pressure which bids defiance to your efforts to penetrate it. But if by this process you can convert this weight of debt into an instrument of credit, not only for those interested in it, but for a great portion of the community, and also for the Government to an almost unlimited extent; and at the same time restore the circulation of the money medium to its accustomed action, you have accomplished great and essential purposes. It is for these purposes that this bill was reported, and the amount named in it fixed upon for the capital of a National Bank, that it might absorb such a mass of the encumbering stock as would relieve the market; raise the price of debt not taken up; give facilities to the obtaining of loans for the present year, and for each succeeding year. And here I would beg leave to remark, that an evident repugnance has been manifested by some gentlemen (which I will not, however, impute to the honorable gentleman from South Carolina) to doing anything to raise the price of public stock, lest those who have purchased at a low rate should be benefitted. Permit me to inquire of those who have no gratitude nor feeling for public creditors, who have loaned you their money in the time of your necessity; will you refrain from doing an act indispensably necessary for the credit of the Government, and to enable it to borrow more money, for fear you do a benefit, not to call it an act of justice, to your creditors? I would ask such gentlemen how they expect to go into the market and sell stock for eighty-eight, when that already sold is every day to be bought for eighty? It is humiliating to dwell upon a subject so plain and simple, and but for the strange declarations which I have heard, it would not have been noticed. Mr. Chairman, there is no consideration which every financier who is obliged to anticipate his resources by loans is more attentive to than that of supporting public credit; or, in other words, keeping up the price of stocks. The faithful payment of interest, though indispensable, is not always sufficient. Sinking funds have therefore been resorted to, but as your power of establishing sinking funds is limited, when we find by a repetition of loans we have overloaded the market, you must if possible withdraw that surplusage before you can recommence your loaning operations, and even then you must return to the market with that caution which experience has indicated, as necessary to your success. It is therefore, that we propose to take out of the market the eighteen millions of stock, and the six millions of Treasury notes; and, as the stocks are now selling at eighty, it was calculated that an advance of twenty-five per cent. upon $24,000,000, equalized as it would be upon the whole amount of the debt in which subscriptions to the bank could be made, (about eighty millions,) might be computed to advance the whole of these depressed stocks to about eighty-eight; the sum proposed to be absorbed, therefore, was the least amount that could, consistent with the plan, have been taken. But there is another reason why a large capital was determined upon; we prepare, for the sake of mutual benefits to the bank and the Government, to give it great facilities in the circulation of its notes. In fact, this will be almost the only medium which can be employed for the payment of taxes, or to carry on the ordinary commercial intercourse between people of different States, those of most of the State banks being now exclusively confined to a circumscribed atmosphere around the bank from which they issued. With these facilities, it is apparent that the bank may issue considerable

quantities of paper, and it was much safer to make the capital of the bank exceed the amount of notes which the demand for circulating medium would enable it to issue, than that it should have power to contract debts equal to its capital. And here it should be observed, that a bank with a small capital, possessing in all other respects the same facilities with a bank with a large capital—specie payments being suspended—will be able to issue nearly, if not exactly, the same quantity of paper. It therefore becomes necessary for the security of the creditors of such a bank that it should have a large capital. I heard the honorable gentleman from South Carolina, (Mr. CALHOUN,) with some degree of astonishment, yesterday state, that a bank of one million of dollars could with safety issue paper to the amount of two or three millions. I would ask him what would be the situation of an individual whose debts three times exceed his whole real and personal estate? He would be insolvent, and so would the bank. No bank conducted with integrity ever did issue notes to the amount of its capital; and no bank that has any regard to its reputation will ever dare to do it. The gentleman has probably confounded discounts and emission together; an error into which many others have been led before him. Although these operations are intimately connected, yet they are extremely different in their nature; the one constitutes the debts due to the bank while the other constitutes the debts due by the bank. The gentleman and every member of the Committee will see the distinction, and it will be unnecessary further to illustrate it. I think it has been sufficiently shown that a bank, with a capital much less than fifty millions, could not with safety issue upon the customary mode of bank operation notes to meet the present demands for a circulating medium and preserve an adequate security to its creditors. It is I believe unusual for the large State banks to issue in paper more than one third or, at most, one-half the amount of their capital, although they often loan or discount to the whole amount.

The next point which presents for consideration is the character of the capital; it is proposed to be constituted of twenty-four millions of public debt that have accrued since March, 1812, or that is now authorized to be created; $18,000,000 of this will be six per cent. stock, and $6,000,000 in Treasury notes now issued or to be issued in pursuance of existing laws; twenty millions to be subscribed by the Government and paid in six per cent. stock, and six millions in specie. The objections that have been urged to the character of this capital are worthy of some particular notice. We are told "that it is nothing more than a paper bank," that it is not entitled to credit;" that " its paper " will not circulate, having no security for its " solvency but the obligation of the Government to pay its debts." It is perhaps fortunate for the friends of this bill that they have the light of experience to justify their expectations and calculations on this subject. Is there not a strong resemblance between the character of this capital and that of the old United States

Bank? The amount and proportions are somewhat variant, but the essentials are precisely the same, and when was the validity of that paper questioned? It is true specie payments were not suspended, but everybody knew that while it was doing business upon a capital of ten millions of dollars, issuing notes to the amount of five to six millions, its specie capital only amounted to $2,500,000, and no difficulties were ever experienced for want of more specie that I have heard of. In ordinary times, there is very little occasion for specie in banking operations; none is wanted except for the payment of balances between the merchants of different cities, between different banks, and the small change required by retailers; and the amount of specie required for these purposes does not increase in proportion to the amount of banking capital employed in the country. As an evidence of this fact we may refer to the operations performed by the Bank of England. The amount of payments made every day by the different banks of London, is estimated to exceed four millions sterling; and in the year 1810, the whole amount of notes of the Bank of England, and private banks, in circulation amounted to seventy-nine millions sterling, while the specie only amounted to four millions. It may be fairly inferred that the credit of a bank does not depend upon the amount of specie in its vaults, no more than the credit of a merchant depends upon the amount of money he keeps in his desk; his visible estate, his income and his integrity are the foundation of his credit, and it is the same with the bank; the visible estate of which is the public debt and specie, its income is the interest arising therefrom, and from loans to Government and individuals; and the caution that will be exercised in the selection of directors, will no doubt, as has almost universally been the case, especially in the large banks, insure a faithful and judicious management of its affairs. But, we are told the only security for its paper is the obligation of the Government to pay its debts. And are we to be gravely told that this is no security? I never can for a moment believe that this security will be questioned, regarding, as every man in the nation does, the obligations of the Government to its creditors of so solemn and unchangeable a character that, let whatever may happen, they must be fulfilled in good faith. In addition to these considerations, the credit which the paper of the bank will receive in payment of taxes and customs, and the imperious necessity which exists for a circulating medium that will be co-extensive with the States, will insure the circulation of the paper, and there cannot exist a rational doubt of its credit being maintained without depreciation, answering all the valuable purposes that are expected from it both for the Government and the community. But here we are met by another objection, viz: that the enormous loan, as it has been called, of thirty millions, to be made to the Government, will produce a run on the bank that will exhaust all its specie and arrest its future operations. In the first place, it is not to be presumed that the

Government will do any act that will embarrass the bank, being as it always must be so deeply interested in it preservation. The loan will therefore be asked for according to the terms of the bill, in such sums and at such periods as may be made mutually convenient and consistent with the objects of the Government; and there is no doubt the Government would regard this resource as a reserve only to be used in time of particular necessity, when the depression of stocks should forbid them from going at large into the market. At any rate the amount would not be required, as it could not be wanted in large sums; and such of these as would be drawn out of the bank, would mostly find their way into it again before another payment would be demanded; a portion would return in taxes, and other portions in payment of debts due from the country to the city merchants, and a very considerable part of this loan would, like ordinary loans or discounts as they are called, to individuals, never get from the drawer of the bank, but merely pass from the credit to the debtor side of its books. Under this view of the subject, which exhibits the necessary and natural operations, it will be admitted that not so much danger exists from this loan as some gentlemen seem to apprehend; but should any unexpected difficulties menace the bank, there will be a resort to the power of suspending specie payments. But this provision has also been objected to, and almost in the same breath we are told that no bank can exist with the extensive operations designed for this, with an obligation to make specie payments—but objectors have not furnished us with an alternative. I do not apprehend any serious consequence will result from the temporary suspension of specie payments; the experiment was tried many years ago in England, and has been continued up to this time without injury to the commercial interests, and with essential benefit to the nation at large. It has also been tried here, and although bank paper is somewhat depreciated thereby, it is solely because it will not answer the purpose of paying balances between people of different States, for which specie had usually been employed. For example, the bank paper of this District will not enable you to trade east of Baltimore; yet every article to be purchased with it here is as cheap as it was twelve months ago. It may therefore be fairly inferred, that a paper which was receivable all over the United States, in taxes, and might be exchanged for notes of smaller or greater denomination or Treasury notes in each of the States, would, from its general convenience, continue to circulate without depreciation, even though a temporary suspension of specie payments should take place. It has already been shown that but a small quantity of specie is actually necessary, when the people have faith in the capital, the income, and the integrity of the bank, and in this case necessity would become an auxiliary to faith, and business would go on as usual. But further: is it not probable that most of the moneyed capitalists in the United States would vest a portion of their disposable funds in this bank, as also a number of the State banks, and will not all these be interested in the support of the credit of its paper? I do not believe it possible for any hostile combination to resist their influence in money transactions, when thus united and thus interested; and, from every view that can be taken of the subject, there does not appear any rational doubt of the success of the plan proposed by the committee in answering all the valuable purposes for which it was designed. But further: the plan has been for a considerable time before the public, and although some have objected to the amount of the specie called for by the bill, as being difficult to procure and unnecessary, it has met the approbation of the most intelligent men in this community, (as to money matters I mean;) to say nothing of the mature and deliberate consideration which has been given to it by the able and enlightened statesmen at the head of the Treasury Department, who, relying upon the support of Congress, has assumed the high responsibility of his station with a degree of energy and confidence that does no less honor to himself than it promises to do service to the country; to say nothing of the discussion and consideration which has been given to this subject by the Committee of Ways and Means, for whom although no more confidence should be claimed than for any like number of the members of the House, yet their duty, their great responsibility, could not fail to produce a laborious examination of the plan. But we are not without experience as to its influence. The stocks had began to advance, of course public credit was reviving, and some loans were actually negotiating for the relief of the present quarter, in anticipation of the success of this bill to carry into effect the general plan of finance submitted to Congress by the Secretary of the Treasury. Such was the progress of our fiscal operations, and we were emerging, as it were, from a dense cloud of difficulties and embarrassments that hung over the nation. A more extensive and efficient system of finance than any ever adopted in this country, was progressing to maturity as rapidly as circumstances would admit; and the bill under consideration, an indispensable instrument to carry it into effect, had progressed with a flattering prospect of success; and behold! at a crisis so eventful, we are met by a proposition which goes (to use the expression of the gentleman from South Carolina) to effect a radical change in the whole system of the bill reported by the Committee of Ways and Means. I shall say nothing farther as to the time and manner of this proposition; but I trust it will appear to have been suggested without due consideration, as it has been without concert or consultation; and, however plausible in theory, that it is impracticable in its details and will be injurious in its effects.

In attempting to investigate this new plan, we are subjected to considerable difficulties on the threshold, because it has neither assumed form nor shape. The plan can therefore only be collected from the suggestion of the honorable gentleman in his speech yesterday, except so far as it is found in the amendment on the table, which only appears to be a small patch of the scheme.

That the scheme is crude and undigested, there can be little doubt, when we recollect the changes that have been proposed or consented to by the mover since it made its appearance in the Committee yesterday; but I will proceed to examine it. The plan proposes to constitute the bank upon a basis of six millions of specie and forty-four millions of Treasury notes; these notes hereafter to be issued, and when subscribed to the bank to be exchanged for six per cent. stock at par; fifteen millions of the forty-four to be placed in the hands of the Commissioners of the Sinking Fund. And to carry the plan into effect, a law must be passed to authorize the issuing of the Treasury notes, and another law to dispose of the fifteen millions in the hands of the Commissioners of the Sinking Fund; and, as there may be a great difference of opinion as to these ulterior measures between the branches of Congress, the possibility of a failure to pass these laws presents a strong objection to the plan. We already find a difference of opinion between the two gentlemen from South Carolina who have supported the amendment; one of them (Mr. LOWNDES) altogether disapproves of placing fifteen millions of notes in the hands of the Commissioners of the Sinking Fund, to be exchanged for six per cent. stock and subscribed to the bank. I shall presently consider this part of the subject, with reference to both of their schemes, and in the mean time recur to the proposition to issue either the forty four or the twenty-nine millions of Treasury notes, for the purpose of being subscribed to the bank; and it may here be observed, that the Treasury notes are not, as some seem to think, calculated for a circulating medium, nor can they ever be made to supply its place; it is an evidence of debt bearing interest, in no essential particular different from the public stock, except that the former is made payable monthly at the end of a year, while the latter are redeemable at a longer period; the interest that accrues retards, instead of accelerating the circulation, and it must partake of all the essential qualities of capital. If, therefore, you issue a sum of Treasury notes, you make virtually a loan to that amount, and especially if they are not to be repaid, as in the present case, at the end of the year; the money market is as much exhausted by the operation as if six per cent. stock is sold to the same amount. It is therefore fair to consider this enormous emission of Treasury notes as a loan, which, by offering extraordinary inducements, you calculate to effect. Now, in order to judge of the propriety of this measure at this time, we must consider the state of the money market, and also what constitutes the capacity of a people to loan to their Government. It has already been observed that the market is overcharged with stocks, and each succeeding loan has (except in one instance) been obtained on more unfavorable terms than the former. It must be evident, therefore, that we have attempted to borrow, and that we have borrowed too much in proportion to the provisions that have been made to redeem, especially when we consider the stagnation of the medium. The stock market is glutted and overloaded, and you may buy stocks in it at a much cheaper rate than the Government ought to sell them. Is it then prudent or wise to force out at such a time, in one year, the enormous sum of forty-four millions of new stock to accumulate this now insupportable burden on the market? It should be recollected that the amount which the people can loan to their Government, within a given time, can never exceed the amount of their net profits for the same time; and in a country like this, where there are so many avenues to wealth by the reinvestment of the yearly profits in capital, either by enlarging existing establishments, or engaging in new employments, it cannot be expected that any very considerable portion of the annual profits can be borrowed, without giving a high premium for them. But at this particular time, owing to the interruption of all business by the stoppage of specie payments by the banks, and the consequent location of their paper to a very limited boundary, it cannot be expected that the habits of industry or means of loaning can be near as great as they will be when the circulating medium of the country shall resume its accustomed activity. If these premises are correct, the conclusion is inevitable, that it would not only be unwise and impolitic to press so great a loan as it were by force upon the market at this time, but that it would be much more safe and prudent to withdraw a part of the stocks from the market, and abstain if possible from pressing it again until it shall have become relieved by the income of the succeeding year. Hence it is that we propose to require the bank to loan money to the Government, a part of which would perhaps be required for the next year, and the remainder reserved for similar exigencies. But the honorable gentleman from South Carolina calculates to obviate all difficulties and embarrassments for two years, by the sale of the twenty-nine or the forty-four millions of Treasury notes, which he calculates will readily be sold at par, nay, even at a premium. Now, as the amendment stood when he delivered his speech, and as it now stands (although I am aware of the proposition of the honorable gentleman from Kentucky to require payment for the bank subscription to be made in Treasury notes only, to the amount of forty-four millions, which he had thought proper, however, on reflection to withdraw, and which upon more mature reflection, I am sure I will not renew)—as the amendment now stands, the payments may be made in Treasury notes or gold and silver. And how will Treasury notes be sold for specie or bank notes of equal value, at a premium or at par, when the specie can be paid directly into the bank? The thing is too absurd to dwell upon for a moment. But perhaps we shall be told that the subscriptions for the forty-four millions must be paid in Treasury notes only. I can hardly think it possible that the honorable gentleman, with all his courage, would venture upon such a measure to force his Treasury notes into the market; it would be little better than a tender law in principle, and in its operation most iniquitous, and injurious to the success of his plan. For instance, an individ-

ual being in possession of specie must be compelled to buy Treasury notes before he can subscribe to the bank—thus preventing specie from finding its way into bank, which must always continue its specie payments, and he must be subjected to the risk of not being able to secure the amount of his subscription to the bank; in which case there will no doubt be a loss upon the Treasury notes that are not absorbed, and of course the less inducement to buy them. But it does not appear to me that the Treasury notes can be sold to the amount proposed. How are they to be paid for? Specie cannot be found: will you sell them for bank notes? One-half of these, if the Treasury notes are distributed over the States for sale, as the gentleman proposes, will answer the Government no purpose. It has now near three millions of Southern notes, which cannot be applied to the payment of the interest on the public debt in Boston—nor can the notes of Baltimore be certainly applied to the payment of debts even in Philadelphia. How then can these forty-four millions of Treasury notes be sold for a valuable consideration in any State where the taxes exceed the disbursements of the Government, and in which the banks do not pay specie? The gentlemen of this House may, perhaps, take a few of their per diems home in Treasury notes, but it will be impossible to distribute them when the credit of the Government exceeds its debts, unless you give them away. But the gentleman proposes to reduce the denomination—and what will this avail his plan? A few of them may be picked up by hucksters and tin-pedlers, and there it will end. You cannot pay money where you do not owe it, nor sell Treasury notes to people who have no money to buy them with, or whose money answers you no purpose. I conclude, thus far, that the scheme is unwise, impolitic and impracticable.

But suppose it were possible to carry it into effect, what is its moral character and its effect upon public credit? I do not mean to impeach the motives or moral principles of the honorable gentlemen who have advocated this plan of a bank. I know they are utterly incapable of supporting any measure of which they entertain a doubt as to its strict moral propriety; but, thinking differently from them in this particular, I shall be excused for explaining my views of it. It has already been stated that the stocks are in a state of heavy depression; and, it may be added, that those who have given you one hundred dollars in specie for one hundred dollars in stock, cannot now sell the same for more than eighty dollars; so of those who have given you eighty-eight for one hundred. This depression is not the fault of the creditor; it is his misfortune; and when the Government can, without injury to itself, either do a benefit to its creditors thus circumstanced, or avoid doing them an injury, it is bound by every moral obligation so to do. But what will be the effect of the measure under consideration? We find the stock market glutted; the public creditor sinking under his burdens, and, without any occasion whatever, we accumulate an additional mass upon him and consummate his ruin. But, says the honorable gentleman from South Carolina, (Mr. CALHOUN,) fifteen million of Treasury notes shall be applied to purchase up the depressed stocks—that is, he will offer seventy-five or eighty dollars in Treasury notes for a certificate, which purports, on its face, to demand one hundred dollars in specie. But this is not all; by our own act we first depress the price and depreciate the value of our debt, and then, by the aid of some speculating scheme, we buy up that debt at its depreciated rates, just like some swindling traders in our cities, who, when their credit is exhausted, shut up shop, and send out runners to buy up their notes at forty or fifty per cent. discount. Such is, to my mind, the character of the transaction. But one honorable gentleman from South Carolina, (Mr. LOWNDES,) is opposed to this part of the plan; he will not employ any part of the intended capital of this bank to purchase up the depressed stocks. So much the worse. The public creditor would then have no remedy for even a part of his misfortunes, and the Government, in such a case, would act the part of a spendthrift whose land could not be sold for debt, and while he was giving usurious advantages to obtain new credit, he would defy his old ones, and mock at their complaints. I am aware that many plausible things may be said to show what are the obligations of the Government to its creditors, and that they may be fulfilled according to the terms of the contract without being noticed in this bill. Be it so; but I contend that you are attempting to effect by indirect means, what you would not venture to do by direct means—that is, to obtain from the public creditor your obligation for a less amount than you promise upon the face of it to pay him. He will not be satisfied with special pleadings and logic; he will realise his misfortunes and execrate his wrong-doers. When his children cry for bread, his answer will be, I loaned to my country; I confided in her justice; but, in an unlucky hour, her councils were guided by logicians, and I am ruined. But there is another feature in the new plan which constitutes an insuperable objection. Specie payments are to be made absolute. If we did not know that necessity sometimes requires a suspension of specie payments by banks both at home and abroad, and that it may be done without that terrible danger which some affect to apprehend, there would be some reason to refuse making any provision for the case; but with all this light, and the existing condition of the specie medium of the country in full view before us, it would seem to be a species of frantic enthusiasm not to provide for the case. If bank credit can be restored, and it has not been essentially impaired, there will be a better opportunity to do it under the power to suspend the specie payments, guarded as it is, than there would be in any other way. But suppose the balance of trade to continue strongly against us, and a high premium for specie to be given by our enemy. Your bank will become an instrument by which it will be driven from the country; and it may happen,

and probably will happen, that their specie payments cannot be discontinued—and what will then be the situation of the bank? Failing to fulfil the purposes designed, its credit is blighted, its operations are stopped, and its charter violated; and if this should take place before your Treasury notes are sold, the Government will scarce obtain a moment's relief; but if the Treasury notes have been forced out, will they not come back upon the Government for payment when it has no means to redeem them, instead of passing into the drawer of a broken bank?

The patience of the Committee is no doubt exhausted, and I will conclude by exhibiting the relative pecuniary value of the two plans, in a calculation that cannot be misunderstood.

By the scheme of the honorable gentleman from South Carolina, suppose that you succeed in issuing the forty-four millions of dollars in Treasury notes at par, whether to be vested in stock or for the purpose of a direct subscription into the bank, and suppose, too, that the fifteen millions of Treasury notes will purchase one hundred dollars of stock for eighty dollars of notes—the advance or profit obtained in the operation will be the difference between the present price that is paid for money and the rate thus obtained, viz: twenty-five per cent., which, upon forty-four millions, will be eleven millions. This is the utmost that can be claimed for his plan, if it succeeds.

Now, by the plan proposed by the bill, we have the same advance upon six millions of Treasury notes, viz: - - - - $1,500,000
Twenty-five per cent. upon a loan of thirty millions - - - 7,500,000
And, if we suppose our bank stock to advance twenty per cent. above par, it will make a disposable capital of $25,000,000, to obtain which we should be obliged at the present rates to pay a premium of $6,250,000 6,250,000
Which, together with the advance on the stock - - - - 5,000,000
Will make a net gain to the Government of - - - - 20,250,000
Making a difference in favor of the Government, by the bill as reported by the Committee of Ways and Means of - - - - $9,250,000

This is a plain arithmetical fact, that cannot be controverted. The figures will speak for themselves, and every member of the Committee may make the calculations for himself. But I can scarcely hope to convince the honorable gentleman from South Carolina. He appears to be so enthusiastically attached to his proposition, that he has called in the aid of his prophetic spirit to sustain him, and has painted in glowing colors the prospect of the blockade being raised, and the speedy restoration of our foreign commerce and coasting trade to their accustomed activity. But I cannot rely upon anticipations of this kind, though I have often listened with pleasure to them. I have heard of his prophecies before, and recollect listening with pleasure, though with some degree of scepticism, to a speech of his, highly colored with promising prospects, on a bill which has contributed to produce, more than any other cause, our present fiscal embarrassments. It does appear to me that the wisest course would be not to yield to visionary speculations, nor to adapt our measures to a state of things not likely to be realized. We have been trying expedients too long. Solid, substantial, and lasting measures are now indispensable. Such is the character of the proposition contained in the bill, while the amendment proposed totally changes its character as well as form. That which was designed as an agent to revive public credit, to supply the present exigence of the country, and give such facility in obtaining future loans as would enable us to prosecute this war with vigor and effect, is to be converted into a machine to squeeze a little depreciated money out of the people for the present—abandoning the other great and important objects, so indispensably necessary to be effected.

I beg pardon of the Committee for having trespassed so long upon their patience, and the only apology that can be offered is the importance of the subject.

Mr. Ingersoll said that he inserted himself into this debate with great reluctance; almost in despair—reluctance to take part in a discussion for which he had no inclination, and which he thought had better be left to the members of the committee who had reported the bill—in despair, because he had no hope of making any impression on an assembly but too studious of change, too fond of novelty, too apt to think that national wealth was most certainly to be found in individual impoverishment. Ever since this war was declared, and, indeed, since the session of Congress preceding it, the nation had been kept alive on sickly hopes of peace and the empirical sustenance of inadequate loans; and it was not till just now, when these flattering unctions were no longer applicable, that we had made up our minds to the solid food of heavy taxes, pledges of them in sinking funds, and a national banking institution. For his part, Mr. I. said, he had uniformly denied and deprecated the effects anticipated from the Russian mediation, as well as those of the negotiation subsequently translated from Gottenburg to Ghent. These always appeared to him to be the *beau ideal* of our Foreign Relations. He had never ceased to remonstrate against abstracting an eminent person from the head of the Treasury Department, to send him to make the grand tour of Europe in pursuit of peace. I have invariably thought and said, said Mr. I., that the only policy was that just indicated by my friend and colleague, who preceded me, (Mr. Ingham,) to look the difficulties manfully in the face, conceive them at their worst, and deal with them accordingly. We have at last come to this complexion, and I congratulate the country on the occasion. We never should have had peace until war was waged in earnest; and, perhaps, we are now much nearer to a ter-

mination of hostilities than we were while subsisting on pacific overtures.

The Treasury Department, in concert, and after long consideration with the Committee of Ways and Means, assuming the responsibility of their respective stations, have recommended to us the plan of a bank which is comprehended in the bill under discussion. In this Congress of Ambassadors (as I think it was the late President Adams, in his *Treatise on the Constitution*, very aptly denominates us,) rather than a Congress of the Representatives of different portions of the same people, it should always be the first preliminary to entering upon any subject, the *sine qua non*—since *sine qua nons* are so much the mode in modern Congresses—to agree, by mutual sacrifices of pride of opinion and the spirit of system, to endeavor to attain some practicable object and result. It is well known to every member that a National Bank, while nearly all acknowledge the imperious necessity of such an establishment, has to encounter the various obstacles and collisions which arise from various quarters of this House. In the first place, it will be opposed by the gentlemen on the opposite side, who, deeming the war unjust in its origin, deem it, moreover, a Constitutional and correct orbit of opposition to move indiscriminately against every measure calculated to act in furtherance of the war. I will not take upon myself to determine whether this is a proper view of the subject. We, at all events, know that it is one most steadfastly adhered to. In the next place, a bank is resisted by certain scruples respecting the Constitutional power of Congress to create one, which obtain with several gentlemen on this side of the House. And lastly, it cannot be doubted but that the most powerful, pervading, and indefatigable hostility out of doors will be organized by the innumerable State banking institutions, which comprehend within the sphere of their influence almost every man of property in the country, who may apprehend that a Bank of the United States would tend to curtail, to cripple, or to destroy their resources. As long, however, as the objections urged on this floor were confined to those which might have been expected, and which may be urged against all such establishments, I did not suppose it incumbent on any member to assist those gentlemen of the committee who have the particular conveyance of this bill through the House. I should not have presumed, therefore, to mingle in the debate in reply to such objections. Indeed, the grounds which were eloquently occupied by the gentleman from North Carolina (Mr. Gaston) seemed to me to be sufficiently answered by himself, for I really think that there were few of the difficulties which he recapitulated against the proposed plan that are not in equal force of resistance against the substitute he suggested. As to plans, indeed, I am not, myself, at all tenacious. Any plan will answer my purposes that promises to restore public credit and create a circulating medium. Nor can we, to be sure, complain of any deficiency of projects. Almost every gentleman has his own; and, if you happen to look into a newspaper, *ecce homo!* here is a daily column of most comfortable schemes, already printed for your perusal. [In allusion to a voluminous writer on these subjects in the *National Intelligencer*, who affixed the signature of "Homo" to his essays.] It affords me pleasure to bear testimony to the satisfaction with which I followed the gentleman from South Carolina (Mr. CALHOUN) in the development of his substitute for the system recommended by the Treasury Department. I must do that gentleman the justice to say that his views were exhibited in a clear, connected, and well-digested discourse on this abstruse and complicated subject, in which he unquestionably showed, at least, his own preparation and capacity for explaining and supporting any favorite project he may choose to introduce; and, while I declare my unequivocal opinion that his appears to me to be the most fantastic, impracticable, and, I will add, pernicious of all the plans we could adopt, calculated inevitably to destroy the public credit of this Government— to damn it to all eternity—yet, so anxious am I to provide for the crisis which presses on us, that I would rather fall in even with this alternative, at the expense of all your remaining public credit, in preference to not voting for some immediate means for meeting present embarrassments. If we must ruin our existing creditors in order to procure fresh supplies, and if that is the best manner of procuring them, I profess my readiness to proceed to so deplorable a resort, rather than to omit altogether the making of some provision for the exigency. But the gentleman from South Carolina (Mr. CALHOUN) has pointed out to us a stream of finance which positively is not navigable. We may trace its origin and follow its course—seemingly a fine volume of water, fertilizing as it flows—until we behold it emptying itself into the ocean; but when we come to try its usefulness, we find that, like the river Susquehannah, its navigation is doubtful, dangerous, and unsafe. It invites population to settle on its shores, but diseases and death infest them; and we are amazed to discover, on experiment, how fatally it disappoints the expectations that were at first encouraged of its beneficial properties. Nothing but a freshet will justify our venturing on this current; and that is precarious, uncertain, and alarming.

Let us examine this unexpected substitute. What do we find? Why, sir, in the outset, an insuperable difficulty, *in limine*, before we reach the body of the project. The gentleman from South Carolina, (Mr. CALHOUN,) who, no doubt, in the zeal of an ardent mind, let drop some rather inadmissible expressions by way of forestalling the objections he anticipated to his scheme, will excuse me for the similitude; but really it reminds me of the French veterinary surgeon, who killed the sick horse, in order that he might prove his skill by restoring him to life. Is it not so? Does not his plan demand, as its first postulate, a total prostration of the public means, an absolute vacuum in the Treasury, to be afterwards revived by filling it with forty millions of

Treasury notes? Does it not require that the twelve millions which are indispensable for the current quarter of this year, should be sacrificed, and that the Government should stop payment for the present, relying on this scheme for obtaining funds hereafter? Most assuredly the doors to which you look for loans will be locked up and double-bolted against your advances, if you enact a law, impregnated as this is now proposed to be with injustice to those who have hitherto sustained your credit by administering to your occasions. You are to forego the advantages of an approved and rational plan, you are to abandon the attempt to borrow what you stand most seriously in need of at the present moment, you are to stop payment, you are to become bankrupt, in order that new, untried, and impracticable efforts may afterwards be made to raise you from the grave. The thing is impossible; and if if it were not, the experiment, at all events, is rather too critical a one. You may, I believe that you must, perish under the operation. Of how nice and delicate a texture public credit is composed, we have had demonstrations but too painful during the present session. It is the very gossamer of political elements. The perpetual sunshine of confidence is necessary to its existence. Withhold this, and it languishes. Withdraw it, and it dies. And once dead, where is the magic, where the power, that can revive it? Let me caution gentlemen against even handling it too roughly. It is but too easily destroyed; and, whatever may be said in speculations here, depend upon it, sir, that there is no skill in either surgery or quackery that can call it back again to an animation once suspended.

Such, however, so imminent, so full of dissolution and decay, are the very foundations on which this new superstructure is to be built up. Let us now look a little further into its details. And here, at the very inside of the threshold, I am again struck with a general imperfection. Why not come at once to the rejected resolutions of my honest friend from Georgia? (Mr. HALL.) What use is there in such a mass of banking machinery to give circulation to some millions of Treasury notes? Why not issue them at once, without this unwieldy, this unnecessary medium? Do you surround them with it in order to pass them off with less embarrassment, supposing that the public will occupy themselves in examining the mill, without scrutinizing the material? If you do, disappointment will be the consequence; for those moneyed men whom you hitherto have looked to for support, though now you seem ready to discard them, are not to be so easily prevailed upon. They are a sharpsighted animal, who will pierce through your projects at a glance, however you may wrap and fold them up from common observation.

Again: If Treasury notes are to constitute the universal succedaneum, and you intend to deprive the Government of authority to prohibit the issue of specie even under peculiar circumstances and for short periods, what occasion have you for any specie capital at all? Do you imagine, sir, that your five or six millions will be suffered to remain quietly in circulation, going in and out of the vaults of this bank, without any guard whatever against its fraudulent evasion? I am quite mistaken if the whole sum would not migrate to Halifax within a fortnight after its deposite. I cannot pretend to speak with precision as to the amount of specie, now in retirement, belonging to the different banks of Philadelphia, and individuals who have secured portions of it in safe places, but I should imagine that it must be considerable, perhaps some millions. How long is it supposed it would continue in fair circulation if the banks were to pay it out for notes? It would infallibly and almost instantaneously disappear. I confess that I have my doubts as to the propriety of affording Government any number of the directors of the bank. But I cannot conceive a mode for dispensing with the inhibition by law of specie issues in certain cases, without referring this authority for its exercise to the directors themselves, who must endanger the charter by its enforcement. It is, therefore, best in other hands. But after all, sir, it was in behalf of the public creditors that I was mainly induced to address you. It was to bespeak your indulgence; to appeal to your faith; to indicate your policy, as regards the stockholders of the late loans that I have ventured to rise on this occasion. In order to understand and appreciate their relation to the Government, let us inquire how it came about. It is not two years since, when I first came to this House, I felt it my duty to assert their pretensions against attack from the other side. And now already, much sooner, I confess, than I expected, I am called upon to defend them from attacks on this side. Blessed encouragement this, to be sure, for those who may be disposed to lend their money to the public. And, pray, what are the circumstances that justify these aggressions? You first went into the market for a loan of eleven millions at six per cent., of which you obtained but about six. [Here some explanations took place between Mr. Eppes, Chairman of the Committee of Ways and Means, and Mr. Ingersoll, by which it appeared that Mr. I. was mistaken in supposing that the residue of this loan had been filled up by a diversion of the Sinking Fund for that purpose. Mr. E. pointedly denied that the Sinking Fund ever had been diverted from its true object.]

The explanation afforded by the gentleman from Virginia, (Mr. Eppes,) makes no change, (proceeded Mr. Ingersoll) in the aspect of my argument. I was about to show that your loan market was exhausted by a loan of six or seven millions, at the hundred for a hundred. Your next bargain was for sixteen millions at eighty-eight for the hundred. Afterwards, seven millions and a half at the same rate. And, finally, that portion of the twenty-five millions which has been negotiated at eighty, and perhaps less, for the hundred. And what inducements did you hold forth to those who advanced these sums? Of course the faith of Government for the punctual payment of the interest, and faithful redemp-

tion of the principal at the expiration of the stipulated term. But was this all? Was there no accessory, no additional inducement, besides the plighted faith of the nation? This House must well remember that there was. It cannot be forgotten that the Secretary of the Treasury was selected as one of the Commissioners to repair to Europe to treat for peace; and it is perfectly well known that both he and his colleague, at the time that some of these loans were under contract, were sanguine in their calculations on the prosperous result of their mission. Indeed, since we have become acquainted with their instructions, it cannot be matter of surprise that they should have entertained such a confidence. The fact, however, is, that subscribers to the loan at eighty-eight, were led to believe, and from the best authority, that their stock would enjoy all the benefits of peace within twelve months from the time of their subscription, and that instead of merely par for the eighty-eight which they loaned, they might reasonably calculate on a rise of ten or fifteen per cent. above the one hundred which they were promised for their money. It was, moreover, made a test of patriotism in the subscribers, and hundreds contributed in part on this principle. Gentlemen talk of these persons as if they were the veriest brokers and stockjobbers in the world; and as if, too, none but brokers and stockjobbers had subscribed. But no misconception could be more unfounded. Let such as imagine that some half a dozen usurious capitalists hold all the stock in question, attend on quarter day at the door of a bank in which dividends are payable, and examine there into the characters and conditions of the crowd of anxious expectants for their income. They will find the widow and the orphan, the aged and the infirm, as well as the wealthy and the competent, waiting for their shares—some of them for small sums, payable by way of annuity, (which was authorized by the loan laws,) and the only reliance of the poor people who have invested their funds in this stock. These are the persons whom you are proposing to cast aside. They did not seek you nor press themselves into your assistance. But, on the contrary, you went in search of them, and induced them, by strong and seductive promises, to part with their money for your necessities. They did so at your earnest instances. They paid it to you when they could have had gold and silver for their checks. But now, having bound them to your destiny, having exhausted their capacity to lend, you deny them (should the proposed amendment be adopted) any participation in your plans for the improvement of their funds. You leave them to their fate, vainly imagining that, after such crying injustice, you can substitute another class of creditors in their places. No moneyed institution can succeed which is to be founded on principles at war with the interests of the moneyed men of a community. You may rail at these persons if you will. But depend upon it, that to enlist their opposition to any plan for the restoration of public credit, is not the way to accomplish it.

The bank contemplated by the original bill on the table was to be laid on the liberal, the politic, and the natural endowments of public stock and specie in certain adequate proportions. That which is to be attempted, should the amendment succeed, would, for the first time in the history of such institutions, be founded on a vast basis of new paper or stock to be created, to the prejudice of those who now own the stocks and regulate the prices, in the market. Of these, there are between sixty and eighty millions (including Treasury notes) in existence. Instead of withdrawing a third of this amount and appropriating it to a bank, the gentleman from South Carolina (Mr. CALHOUN) would send in forty odd millions more, in the shape of Treasury notes, more heavily than ever to choke up and overdo the market. I do not pretend to be very conversant with these matters; but I must confess that I cannot perceive how such a scheme could possibly succeed in operation.

Of all models for a moneyed institution the late Bank of the United States affords one, the most worthy of imitation. And upon what was it founded? Public stock and specie capital. What public stock? Not new stock created for the purpose; but that which was funded at twenty shillings in the pound, though a great deal of it was purchased as low as one-and-sixpence. The Secretary of the Treasury would hear of no discrimination between the creditors. He well knew that public credit was to be created, not by looking forward to new auxiliaries, and discarding old ones, but by a punctilious and faithful, an indiscriminate and universal fulfilment of all former engagements. Paying old debts is the best mode of enabling a community to contract new ones. The Bank of England, the Bank of Genoa, most of the celebrated moneyed institutions in Europe, were established on similar recognitions and adoptions of the public stocks of their respective countries. The Bank of the United States therefore followed their example. Stockholders, who were known to have purchased their stock at a great discount, were nevertheless allowed to subscribe without discrimination, though it was well ascertained that the bank stock would immediately rise after the subscription, and though it did actually rise to one hundred and forty. Now, in all views of this subject, the late Bank of the United States affords a precedent to be consulted with the utmost consideration, and one not to be departed from without very sufficient causes. Broken up as that institution has been, and subjected to the severest tests of investigation, the wisdom, fidelity and punctuality of its transactions have been manifested in the strongest light; and I think it would be hazarding not a little to disregard them.

The gentlemen from South Carolina, both the honorable mover of this amendment (Mr. CALHOUN) and his colleague who supports him (Mr. LOWNDES,) deny that the creation of a new stock for the bank capital, would be either an injury or any injustice to the present stockholders. I understand that the stock was at eighty-one the day before yesterday in Baltimore, and looking up, in

13th CON. 3d SESS.—20

anticipation of its incorporation into the bank. No doubt it will fall again as soon as this proposition for excluding it goes abroad. What more infallible thermometer can we have of the effect of such a measure on the stock? There are between sixty and eighty millions of it in circulation. You propose to issue fifteen millions of Treasury notes for purchasing up such of it as is to be subscribed to the bank. The inevitable consequence must be, first a competition, a most unfair one, in the market, and then a depreciation of the stock. He who subscribed at eighty has twenty per cent. advantage over the more meritorious subscriber at one hundred or at eighty-eight, and no alternative is left for the latter but to sacrifice his stock at fifty or sixty, in order to reimburse himself by the profits of a subscription to the bank, or to hold his stock depreciated to one-half of what he gave for it. I am not disposed to repeat the epithets that were bestowed on such dealings by my friend and colleague, (Mr. INGHAM,) but really I must say that I should consider them most reprehensible proceedings. There is, too, a difference of from fifteen to twenty per cent. in the prices of stock at different places, at Baltimore and Boston, for instance, and the scandalous speculations to be authorized would therefore carry with them this additional aggravation. In fact, there is no stock market in this country; and, whenever the purchases in question are to be made, the holders of stock in different places must abide the effects of the variation in the prices accumulated on the other hardships of their case.

But why, we are asked, are these stockholders to be preferred? Why is an individual holding certificates of this stock to enjoy the advantages of a subscription to the Bank of the United States, in preference to any individual who does not happen to hold such certificates? The answer is, that they are not preferred any more than the few possessors of specie. Any person may buy the stock who chooses it, and thus become capacitated to subscribe it to the bank. There is no deficiency of it for sale in the market. We have taken care of that. And but too numerous, unfortunately, are they who are anxious to get rid of it.

As to taking it at the rate at which Government received their money, could anything be more unjust? The public faith was plighted to redeem eighty-eight with a hundred. The stockholders are consequently entitled, in the first place, to have one hundred for their eighty-eight; and then most assuredly they have a right, in common with all other subscribers, to all the profits to accrue, above par, on their subscription to the bank. In this they are not preferred to other subscribers; though perhaps it might be shown, without any great difficulty, that they are entitled to at least a highly favorable attention from the Government. We have got all their money. We took it when it was convertible into gold and silver. And it would be neither generous nor just now to postpone them to other members of the community.

These arguments, however, are controverted

by the gentlemen from South Carolina, both of whom deny that Government is bound to admit these stockholders into the bank, as well as that any injury will be done to them by the exclusion. But what facts have they advanced to sustain their theory? The rise and fall of the stock is, as I have shown, a very clear criterion of the state of the stockholders' interests; and really I cannot help saying, that when so much experience and fact is to be overthrown by a speculation, we should have something more than even the most respectable opinions in its favor. One of those gentlemen (Mr. CALHOUN) insists that no depreciation can be the consequence of his scheme, and the other (Mr. LOWNDES) expressed his conviction that the proposed amendment is preferable to the original bill. Those honorable gentlemen know, I am well persuaded, of the attention and pleasure with which I always listen to whatever falls from either of them. But I must be pardoned for withholding my consent to this conclusion of theirs, which really is only asserted, not proved, by the one, with, if I may so express it, his most respectable colleague's endorsement on the draft.

I was surprised, I confess, at the latter gentleman's (Mr. LOWNDES) repetition of a question which had been previously put by the gentleman from North Carolina, (Mr. GASTON.) Why, it is with seeming triumph demanded, why, if former and not new stock is to be part of the capital, do you exclude the old funded debt of the United States? Most obviously, it may be answered, because that account has long ago been settled; because a sinking fund has been many years operating the absorption of that debt; because it is not liable to the fluctuation of the market, as the late stock is, and because the holders of it do not desire you to meddle with it. [Mr. LOWNDES here inquired if Mr. INGERSOLL included the Louisiana stock, to which he answered that he did not.] The difference is very great indeed between the old six per cents., of which I am speaking, and the recent stocks created during the present war. After the experience public creditors have lately had of Congressional kindness and good will, they might well exclaim, like the French merchants to the economists: "*Laissez nous faire.* Let us alone. 'We do not stand in need of your assistance, nor 'desire your interposition. All that we ask is to 'be let alone.*" Very different indeed is the situation of the new stockholders, with all their money gone, their funds depreciated, and their Representatives in Congress inveighing against their contracts as usurious and iniquitous. They are bound to the public car by the ties they cannot break. They must continue to follow public fate. They cannot afford either to sell or to hold. After exhausting their credit at bank they are driven to the usurer for relief, who strips them of half their stock for the preservation of the residue—and that residue they must needs hold—to bequeath it to their children with curses on the Government which borrowed of them, on fair promises, to their last cent, and then left them to their ruin.

Mr. Chairman, we are debating this interesting subject under very peculiar circumstances. It is now two months since Congress have been in session, convened by the President under the pressure of great and weighty considerations. Since we assembled a most alarming temper has appeared in very decided indications among some of the Eastern States; and it is said to be intended, by the agitation of the Hartford Convention, to proceed deliberately to the disintegration of New England from the Union. For my part I cannot believe it. I cannot impute such designs to a people whose forecast, and orderly and general attachment to regular Government, have been so much vaunted, and, perhaps, not without reason. But what encouragement, if such be their object, are we not holding out to them? And what a rebuke the Hartford Convention may, in all probability, impose upon Congress! The fifteenth of December is advertised as the day of their meeting, scarcely more than three weeks from the moment when I address you—after having been two months in session, under every impulse to action and concert, without having yet achieved any one important act—without, in fact, being now as likely to agree as we were six weeks ago—still amusing ourselves with discordant projects and visionary speculations. The Hartford Convention will find disunion ready made to their occasions. Instead of taking steps to separate themselves from the other States, to delay or to defeat our measures, they will have, I fear, but too much opportunity for declaring that their Convention was rendered indispensable by our procrastination and idle controversy; that they met to save, not to destroy; not to deny the authority of Congress and prevent its proceedings, but to provide for our omissions; to raise an army to repel invasion; to create a navy; to establish adequate taxes and a circulating medium; to uphold the staggering credit of the country. We are disputing about details, while the nation is agonized with the pangs of dissolution. We must come to action, and that speedily, too, or the agony will be over. I hope, therefore, Mr. Chairman, that the amendment will be rejected, and that we shall endeavor to make some harmonious progress with the original bill on the table.

Mr. OAKLEY, of New York, in a powerful and impressive speech of an hour and a half, replied to the speeches of Messrs. INGHAM and INGERSOLL, and advocated the motion of Mr. CALHOUN. He began by deprecating a hasty decision on this subject, one of the most important that could ever come before a legislative body, being no less than the establishment of a charter for a moneyed institution of fifty millions, the features of which could not, when once settled by a solemn act of Congress, be changed, but must be as irrevocable, during the term of the charter, as the Constitution itself, &c. The National Bank, if necessary, was required by the public good alone. He, therefore, threw out of view, as wholly irrelative, the argument in relation to the effect of the proposed amendment on the holders of public stock, who had no right to demand any advantages from such an institution, and to whom no injustice would be done by precluding them from any other share in it than other citizens of the United States. He stated some things in relation to this bill to show that the facts of its having been reported by the Committee of Ways and Means was not an unanswerable argument against amendment; for, he stated, that the principal feature proposed to be changed by this amendment scarcely obtained a majority in the Committee of Ways and Means, &c. He then proceeded to examine, first, the details of the bill before the House, and next of the amendment proposed to be made to it; and concluded an elaborate and able view of the subject, by expressing his decided conviction of the superior practicability of Mr. CALHOUN's proposition over the bill as reported, &c.

When Mr. OAKLEY concluded, at a little past 4 o'clock, the question was taken on Mr. CALHOUN's motion to amend the bill, and decided in the affirmative by a majority of about sixty votes. The Committee then rose, reported progress, and obtained leave to sit again.

FRIDAY, November 18.
BANK OF THE UNITED STATES.

Mr. CALHOUN, of South Carolina, remarked, that he looked upon the decision of the House, yesterday, as indicating a disposition on the part of the House to change the whole nature of the bill, now before a Committee of the Whole, for incorporating the subscribers to the Bank of the United States of America. As many amendments in detail would be required, he thought the most proper way to act on the bill would be to recommit it, for amendment, to a select committee.

This motion was opposed by Mr. WRIGHT of Maryland, and Mr. LOWNDES of South Carolina, on the ground that there were parts of the plan of the gentleman, against which the House might decide, and which could as well be acted on in Committee of the Whole as by a select committee.

Mr. CALHOUN then withdrew his motion, reserving the right to offer it again, when further progress should have been made in the discussion of the bill.

On motion of Mr. FISK, of New York, the House again resolved itself into a Committee of the Whole on the said bill.

Mr. FORSYTH, of Georgia, moved an amendment to the second section of the bill, (as it has been amended,) the object of which was, to admit the forty-four millions of the capital to be paid in Treasury notes, as it now stands, or in public stock created since the war.

This motion was declared by the Chairman to be out of order, inasmuch as the Committee of the Whole had yesterday decided that no part of the payments of the subscriptions to the bank should be made in the manner proposed by the amendments.

Mr. FORSYTH was, in this decision, disposed for the present to waive his motion; but an appeal was taken by Mr. FISK, of New York, from the decision of the Chair on this point; which decision was affirmed by the Committee of the Whole, 75 to 39.

The House then proceeded to the consideration of the third section of the bill, which contemplates the subscription by the United States of twenty millions in six per cent. stock to the capital of the bank.

This section Mr. CALHOUN moved to strike out of the bill.

Mr. FORSYTH, of Georgia said, he hoped the section would not be struck out. He considered it important that the United States should hold a certain proportion of the stock of the bank, because he believed the privilege of so doing would be valuable to the Government. In the stock of the old Bank of the United States the Government had held a considerable portion of the stock, and the benefit derived from it had not been denied. It had been a matter of boast on the other side of the House, and the Republican Administration had enjoyed the advantages arising to the Government from it. He could not conceive any solid objection to this course. It might be said the bank would be injuriously affected by the shares the United States would hold in it, because they would subscribe nothing but stock. But, Mr. F. said, if the basis of the bank was to be public stock, its value would not be destroyed by a part of it being owned by the United States as well as by individuals. He hoped the motion would not prevail.

Mr. CALHOUN said, the principle of his motion had been decided by the amendment which had been made to the second section. Consistency required that the House, after deciding as they did yesterday, should now strike out this section.

Mr. WRIGHT said, he did not consider the decision of yesterday as at all interfering with this motion. If it did, he felt himself to be committed contrary to his intention. The discussion on yesterday had not turned on this point; and, he contended, even had the House inadvertently decided the principle yesterday, the decision to retain this section would control the provision in the said second section, inasmuch as offer in law posterior control prior provisions. The Government ought, he contended, to have a share in the stock and in the direction of the bank. The old Bank of the United States would yet have been in operation, he said, if a portion of the direction had been under the control of the Government, to have prevented it from being a perfect inquisition. He instanced the advantages which several of the States derive from holding a share in the stock and a direction of banks within their respective limits. Seven-eighths of the capital of the bank, had, he said, been held by foreigners; and every man who had any hand in the direction of its concerns was adverse to the politics of this Administration. Some of them were refugees from the country, who ought to have been hung during the Revolution. It could not, therefore, be expected that Congress would revive that institution or create any other, the whole weight of which would have been thrown in the opposite scale to that of the United States. Mr. W. was desirous not only that the

United States, but that the agricultural interest of the country should hold a due proportion in the stock of this bank, to keep it out of the exclusive control of the commercial class, which he intimated was generally in the British interest, and not a few actually connected in business with British houses. The landed and manufacturing interest, he agued, ought to be at least equally interested in the bank with the commercial. It was necessary the Government should hold both stock and direction in the bank, to guard the United States against the operation of any foreign influence, &c.

Mr. CALHOUN, finding, as he said, from the course of the debate, that the eyes of the Committee had been so entirely directed to the main object of the amendment adopted yesterday, that they had overlooked the part of it to which this section had reference, rose to explain the reasons of his present motion. Whether the provision now under consideration should be struck out or retained, he contended, depended on the situation of the nation. He was clearly of opinion, that, in the present situation of the nation, it ought to be struck out. One great object of this bank was to afford the means of relieving the nation from difficulties under which it now labored. By striking out this section, the Government would not, he said, lose the advantages it would derive from retaining it, inasmuch as the twenty millions, instead of being vested by the United States in stock, would assume the shape of Treasury notes, and in reality produce the effect, by their absorption in the bank, of an immediate loan to the Government. Which, he asked, does the United States now most want, a capital or the use of a capital? He said he should be glad, indeed, abstractedly, that the United States should possess a share in the capital of the bank; he should be glad the United States should possess a capital in the bank on which they could draw one, two, or three per cent. more interest than they had to pay for it. But we want still more the use of the capital. If any gentleman could conceive the situation of the country to be such that we could lock up instead of using these twenty millions of capital, he would vote against this amendment. The capital, he said, would not be lost to the United States, but would assume for them the most active and most efficient form, by means of the Treasury notes, which, being put into circulation and absorbed by the Government, would effect an immediate loan to the Government. But, it had been said, unless the United States held some share in the bank, it would fall into the hands of our enemies. Mr. C. said, he did not think so harshly as the gentleman from Maryland of the commercial interest; in the large, he believed, that great interest to be American, notwithstanding some exceptions might be found to that character. But even if such a disposition as was feared by the gentleman should exist, it would not be controlled by retaining the present provisions of the bill, because the twenty directors could always vote down the five proposed to be appointed by the Executive, if there should arise

a contest between the Government and the bank. But there was another means of protecting the Government against the bank, more potent and certain than any such provisions; let the United States retain the power over its deposites, and over the receipt of the bank notes in payment of duties and debts to the Government, and it would possess a sufficient control over the bank.

Mr. FORSYTH admitted an immediate loan would be an advantage to the Government; but was such a loan wanted, to the proposed amount, in addition to the taxes to be raised by the bills now before the House? He contended that it probably would not. But, if it would, he argued that part of the project was impracticable, because of the difficulty of throwing into market forty-four millions of dollars of Treasury notes; whereas, if twenty millions of that amount were subscribed in stock in behalf of the United States, the balance of twenty-four millions would be all disposed of, and would probably be sufficient for all the purposes of the Government. Even for the benefit of the gentleman's plan, therefore, this feature ought to be retained.

Mr. CALHOUN said, that if fifteen millions of the forty-four millions of Treasury notes were applied, as he had suggested, to the purchase of stock, and five millions to the redemption of Treasury notes falling due at the commencement of the next year, there would be no difficulty in disposing of the remainder of them. He said, to vest twenty millions in the capital stock of the bank would be acting like a man without a dollar in his pocket offering to lend out money at an interest lower than he has to pay for it for his use. If the demands of the Treasury during the next year did not require the whole of these notes, Mr. C. said, a part could be retained until the year after, and thus provision be made for two years. If the subscriptions were received monthly, in twelve instalments, there would never be out at one time more than two millions, much less than the amount of Treasury notes now in circulation. There would be no doubt, he thought, of their being sought for with avidity.

Mr. INGHAM, of Pennsylvania, said that, if the whole amount of Treasury notes now proposed to be issued should not be wanted in the course of the next year, it would unquestionably be more to the interest of the Government to invest twenty millions of the amount in stock in the bank, provided it would be an advantage to them to possess that stock. Allowing the stock of the bank to advance as it might be expected to do, it would afford a profit to the United States, in twelve months, of six millions of dollars; and the United States would, besides, dispose of the capital stock at its full value whenever they chose.

Mr. FORSYTH still questioned the ability to circulate so large an amount of Treasury notes; because they were not like bank paper, which could at any time command specie; nor would they circulate even as well as the present Treasury notes, because not payable at the end of the year, but to be funded in six per cent. stock. The fact that money is not to be paid for the proposed issue of Treasury notes, would be as well known to the people of the United States as this House. The circulation of Treasury notes at present was principally among those who have money on hand for which they have not immediate use, which they invest in Treasury notes in preference to this public stock; because, at the same time that they produce an interest, they are payable at a day certain. The Treasury notes to be issued will not suit such persons, and will therefore probably have a very limited circulation.

Mr. KILBOURN said he had voted for the amendment yesterday, without any idea that the other amendments indicated by its mover would necessarily follow. He hoped the section now under consideration would not be struck out. For, though he had ever believed the establishment of a National Bank one of the most important objects, yet, if this motion prevailed, he should greatly deprecate it. Was it true, he asked, that this nation was so embarrassed in its finances, was in such a critical situation, that to obtain money for a year it was necessary to establish a colossal moneyed institution, with a charter which it would be beyond the power of this Government to alter for twenty years; that might, in one year, if amended as proposed, fall entirely under the direction of the enemies of the Government? He trusted not. If, on the other hand, this stock was taken by the Government in the bank, it might be sold at any moment, if necessary, at twenty per cent. profit, or at least without a sacrifice, and thus furnish the United States with as much money as it would sell for.

Mr. LOWNDES supported the motion to strike out this section. The reservation of twenty millions for the United States, of the capital of the bank, would, he said, unquestionably be attended with some advantages. It could not be denied that it would, by the strength of this capital, or by selling it at an advance, afford the means of obtaining money for the service of the Government in the year 1816. But the course proposed by gentlemen was to lessen the security of the loan for 1815, in order, with remarkable foresight, to provide the ways and means for the year 1816. Mr. L. said, he differed from his colleague as to the application of fifteen millions of Treasury notes to the purchase of public debt, and five millions for the redemption of Treasury notes. The object of Mr. L. was nothing more than this—to induce the House to reduce the capital of the bank from its present proposed amount. It almost necessarily followed, from the main points of his colleague's plan, that the capital should be reduced. It was impossible every Treasury note thrown out should be absorbed in the bank at the times of subscription; and the amount to be issued must therefore, of necessity, exceed the amount to be paid in as a part of the capital stock of the bank. It was important, in giving additional value to the Treasury notes, that the bank stock should be made as valuable as it could. The success of the plan for immediately aiding Government by the means proposed, must depend on the value of the Treasury notes, which must de-

pend on the value of the shares in the bank. The less valuable the shares in the bank, as they would be by the retention of so large a capital stock, the less temptation would there be to purchase the notes or stock, which is the basis of the subscription. Mr. L. said he hoped, before this subject was finally acted on, the Committee would limit to thirty or thirty-five millions, to some moderate, some reasonable amount, the circulation of the bank, and thus guard against danger of the plan from the amount of capital, at the same time that it would increase the value of the Treasury notes. The plan of the gentleman before him, (Mr. FORSYTH,) he thought it obvious, provided for the demands of the public service in 1816, by rendering utterly hazardous, if not entirely defeating, the provision for 1815. He denied that the Treasury notes to be issued in pursuance of this plan would be less valuable than those now in circulation. It was impossible, he said, in the nature of things; but, in furnishing additional modes of application of them, the Committee would increase instead of diminishing the value of Treasury notes, &c.

After a few words from Mr. RHEA, of Tennessee, indicative of an impatience for the question, the Committee agreed to Mr. CALHOUN's motion by the following vote: For the motion 79, against it 53. So the third section was struck out.

The Committee then proceeded in further examination and amendment of the details of the bill; in the course of which considerable debate took place, involving generally the minor principles of the art or science of banking. Among the amendments agreed to were the following, viz: To strike out so much as gives the Government a share in the direction of the bank; so much as prohibits the bank from selling the United States stock, which may come into its possession; so much as binds the bank to loan thirty millions to the Government, &c.

A motion was made by Mr. LEWIS, of Virginia, and supported by Mr. PEARSON, to amend that part of the section authorizing the bank to establish offices of discount, deposite, and distribution, so as to require the bank, whenever the Government may direct it, to establish an office of discount and deposite at the City of Washington, with a capital (not less than five millions of dollars.) After striking out the latter clause within parentheses, the motion was negatived.

When the Committee rose for to-day, an amendment was under discussion affecting the manner in which the bank shall pay specie for its notes, whether at all its offices, or at the Mother Bank only. Immediately on the Committee's rising, the House adjourned.

SATURDAY, November 19.

A message from the Senate informed the House that the Senate have passed the bill "to authorize the Commissioner of the Revenue to cause a clerk in his office to aid him in signing licenses," with an amendment; in which they ask the concurrence of this House.

619   HISTORY OF CONGRESS.   620

H. of R.   *Renner and Heath—Bank of the United States.*   November, 1814.

PETITION OF RENNER AND HEATH.

Mr. Yancey, of North Carolina, from the Committee of Claims, made an unfavorable report on the petition of Renner & Heath, of the City of Washington. The report is as follows:

That the petitioners were owners of ropewalks in the City of Washington, in which were contained a large quantity of spun yarns and navy cordage, all of which was destroyed by the enemy in his late incursion into this city. On or about the 20th of July last, one of the petitioners, Mr. Heath, applied to Mr. Southerian, the owner of some long boats then lying in the Potomac, and engaged of him five of them to transport his cordage and yarns up the river, if the enemy should invade the city. On the 18th or 19th of August, it was deemed expedient, by General Winder, to impress the boats of Mr. Southerian, for the purpose of transporting the troops across the Potomac, which were kept in the employment of the Government until after the invasion of the city. On the 20th of August the petitioners applied for the boats, according to contract, for the purpose of removing their property, when they were informed that they were impressed. It also appears to the committee, that on the 22d of August the petitioners employed a wagon and nine or ten carts, for the purpose of removing the property, but the wagon and two or three of the carts were impressed by the officers of the departments, to remove the public papers and property; and that seven of the carts employed, after taking loads from the ropewalks out of the city, refused to return to haul any more for the petitioners, apprehending, if they did, they would be impressed into the employment of the Government. It is also stated, and believed, that, after that day, and before the enemy entered the city, carriages were not to be had in the city to remove the property. The loss of the petitioners, exclusive of the price of the ropewalks, is estimated at about thirty-four thousand eight hundred dollars; they ask of Congress to be reimbursed to the amount of their loss.

The committee are of opinion the Government is under no obligation to pay for the property. The destruction of private property by the enemy, in the progress of the war, is much to be regretted and highly deprecated; but when it does happen, it is to be considered, between the Government and its citizens, as one of the calamities of war. It may be presumed, that the circumstance of the boats, wagon, and carts being impressed by the Government to perform services valuable to it, may create some equitable considerations in favor of the petitioners. It is, however, believed by the committee, not to be sufficient to authorize them to allow the claim; they, therefore, recommend to the House the following resolution:

Resolved, That the prayer of the petitioners ought not to be granted.

Mr. Farrow, of South Carolina, for the reason that he thought the principles of the report questionable, and involving a case of great hardship against the petitioners, moved that the report should lie on the table.

This motion was also supported by Mr. Cooper, of Delaware, who desired further time to reflect on the subject.

Mr. Alexander, of Ohio, and Mr. Yancey, of North Carolina, opposed this motion, and further explained the circumstances of this case, which, though a case of hardship, was one in which the Congress were under no obligation, legal or equitable, to indemnify the petitioners.

The motion to lay the report on the table was negatived; and the yeas and nays thereon having been required by Mr. Hanson, of Maryland, the question on the adoption of the report was decided in the affirmative. For the report 80, against it 43, as follows:

Yeas—Messrs. Alexander, Alston, Anderson, Avery, Bard, Barnett, Bines, Bowen, Bradley, Brown, Burwell, Caldwell, Calhoun, Cannon, Cilley, Clark, Comstock, Condict, Conard, Crawford, Creighton, Crouch, Cuthbert, Davenport, Davis of Pennsylvania, Denoyelles, Desha, Earle, Findley, Fisk of New York, Forney, Forsyth, Franklin, Gaston, Geddes, Gholson, Goodwyn, Gourdin, Griffin, Hasbrouck, Hawes, Hopkins of Kentucky, Hubbard, Humphreys, Irving, Kennedy, Kent of Maryland, Kerr, Kershaw, Kilbourn, Lefferts, Lowndes, Lyle, Macon, McKee, McKim, McLean, Moore, Nelson, Parker, Piper, Rea of Pennsylvania, Rhea of Tennessee, Rich, Roane, Robertson, Sage, Sevier, Sharp, Skinner, Smith of Pennsylvania, Smith of Virginia, Stanford, Strong, Tannehill, Telfair, Udree, Vose, Williams, Wilson of Pennsylvania, Wright, and Yancey.

Nays—Messrs. Bayly of Virginia, Bigelow, Brigham, Butler, Caperton, Cox, Culpeper, Dana, Davis of Massachusetts, Duvall, Ely, Farrow, Fisk of Vermont, Hale, Hanson, Hawkins, Hungerford, Ingersoll, Johnson of Virginia, Kent of New York, King of Massachusetts, Law, Lewis, Lovett, Markell, Moseley, Pearson, Pickering, Potter, Ruggles, Sheffey, Sherwood, Shipherd, Sturges, Taggart, Taylor, Thompson, Troup, Ward of Massachusetts, Wheaton, Wilcox, and Winter.

BANK OF THE UNITED STATES.

The House again went into Committee of the Whole, on the bill to incorporate the subscribers to the Bank of the United States of America.

The question depending on yesterday's adjournment was, on a motion of Mr. Oakley, of New York, to strike out the 18th fundamental rule for the government of the bank, which is in the following words:

18. [During the continuance of the present war between the United States and Great Britain, all the votes of the said corporation, whether payable at the seat of the bank in Philadelphia, or elsewhere, shall be payable in other notes of the said corporation, in Treasury notes, or in gold and silver coin, at the bank in the city of Philadelphia, at the option of the applicant At all the offices of discount, deposite and distribution, and of deposite and distribution only, established as aforesaid, the notes of the said corporation, during the continuance of the said war, shall be payable in other notes of the said corporation, or in Treasury notes only. And] the said corporation shall, at all times, distribute among the offices and banks aforesaid, a sufficient sum in the various denominations of the notes of the said corporation, and in Treasury notes, to answer the demand therefor, and to establish a sufficient circulating medium throughout the United States and the Territories thereof.

On the suggestion of Mr. Lowndes, Mr. Oakley modified his motion so as to strike out that part only of the rule which is in brackets; and, after some remarks in opposition from Mr. FISK, the motion was agreed to—ayes 82.

Mr. LOWNDES then moved to amend the remainder of this rule, by adding after the words " Treasury notes," the words " which it may receive upon deposite of the Government." Agreed to.

The 19th rule having been read, in the following words:

19. The officer at the head of the Treasury Department of the United States shall be furnished from time to time, as often as he may require, not exceeding once a week, with statements of the amount of the capital stock of the said corporation, and of the debts due to the same; of the moneys deposited therein; of the notes in circulation, and of the cash in hand; and shall have a right to inspect such general accounts in the books of the bank as shall relate to the said statement: *Provided,* That this shall not be construed to imply a right of inspecting the account of any private individual or individuals with the bank.

Mr. FORSYTH moved to strike out this rule. If the Government had no interest in or control over the institution, he saw no reason or propriety in the United States having a right to inspect the proceedings or state of the bank.

To this Mr. CALHOUN replied, that there was an obvious propriety in the United States having the right to inspect the affairs of the bank, to ascertain whether its deposites, &c., would be safe in its hands.

The motion to strike out the rule was negatived.

The 10th section, making the notes of the bank receivable in all payments of the United States, having been read—

Mr. CALHOUN, of South Carolina, moved to strike it from the bill; assigning, as a reason for this motion, that as the United States were now, by the amendments which had taken place, divested of all control over the operations of the bank, it would be proper, in self-defence, for the Government to retain in its hands the power to make the notes of the bank receivable or not, to protect it against misconduct or attempt at control by the bank.

The motion was agreed to without a division.

On motion of Mr. CALHOUN, the section authorizing the suspension, on proclamation of the President, of specie payment, in certain cases and for certain periods, was stricken out without debate or division.

The 13th section of the bill, which pledges the faith of Congress, not to establish any other bank during the continuance of the charter—being read,

Mr. LEWIS, of Virginia, moved an amendment, the object of which was to except, from this prohibition, the Banking Associations existing within the District of Columbia, not at present incorporated.

Agreed to; and the bill having been gone through, the Committee recurred, on suggestion of Mr. LOWNDES, to the first section of the bill.

Mr. LOWNDES made a motion, which he supported, by a train of reasoning predicated on the impracticability and unwieldiness of so large a moneyed institution as this bank was proposed to be, to reduce the capital of the bank from fifty to thirty-five millions of dollars.

Mr. CALHOUN opposed the motion with much zeal, defending the proposed amount of capital on the ground of the proposed appropriation of fifteen millions of the Treasury notes for the purchase of existing stock, &c.

Mr. CUTHBERT and Mr. FORSYTH supported Mr. LOWNDES's motion, and Mr. CALHOUN replied to them.

The motion was, in the end, negatived as follows: For the motion 56, against it 75.

On motion of Mr. CALHOUN, an amendment was adopted to the first section of the bill, changing the time of subscription to conform it to the intimations he had before given.

On motion of the delegate from Missouri, the town of St. Louis was inserted as one of those at which subscriptions should be received, and J. B. C. Lucas, Alexander Stuart, and Bernard Pratt, named as Commissioners; and, on motion of Mr. FISK, of Vermont, Windsor in that State was also inserted, and Elias Lyman, William Levering, and Eleazer May named as Commissioners.

Various other amendments were proposed to the bill, some of which were adopted and some rejected. At length the Committee rose and reported the bill as amended.

The bill having been so interleaved and interlined with amendments made by the Committee of the Whole, that the Clerk himself could scarcely arrange them or the SPEAKER state them to the House, it was ordered to lie on the table, and be printed as amended.

MONDAY, November 21.

On motion of Mr. EASTON, the Committee on Military Affairs were instructed to inquire what provisions, by law, are necessary to be made for the defence of the Western and Northwestern frontiers.

On motion of Mr. HUMPHREYS,

Resolved, That the Committee on Military Affairs be instructed to inquire into the expediency of authorizing, by law, the payment of the officers lately under the command of Major General Andrew Jackson, and in the service of the United States, for transporting their baggage from Natchez to Nashville, in the year 1813; and also, for the transportation of their baggage from the said State to the Mississippi Territory, on the late campaign against the Creek Indians, and on their return from said Territory to the State of Tennessee.

TAX ON CARRIAGES.

Mr. EPPES, of Virginia, from the Committee of Ways and Means, reported a bill to provide additional revenue for defraying the expenses of the Government and maintaining public credit, by laying duties on carriages for the conveyance of persons, and the harness thereof; which was twice read, and committed.

Mr. EPPES also communicated the following letter from the Commissioner of the Revenue:

NOVEMBER 15, 1814.

SIR: No subject of internal taxation has, in its collection, been attended with so much difficulty, as the duty on carriages, either under the old or existing system, between which there is a close, though not an entire resemblance. This difficulty may be intrinsic, or may proceed from the incorrectness of the principle on which the duty is laid. After making a fair allowance for the first circumstance, I am, on a full consideration of the subject, satisfied that the principle of the existing act is incorrect. This conviction is corroborated by the abundant evidence on the files of the revenue office that the duty is extremely unequal. This is in so great a degree the case, that the small sum of two dollars is frequently paid on carriages of greater value than those which pay seven, and even ten dollars.

This inequality proceeds from the erroneous principle on which carriages are classed, the leading feature of which is the kind of springs on which they hang, which is rarely a true criterion of their value.

It seems to be universally admitted that the duty should be graduated according to the value of the carriage.

I feel a confidence in the opinion that no classification, founded on name or form, can equitably equalize the duty. This will be manifest from considering the ceaseless activity of human ingenuity in devising new forms, especially where the caprice of fashion rules, perhaps, more imperiously than reason, and novelty and ornament are more esteemed than utility.

The only remaining resort is, a classification according to the value, which, I think, presents the fewest difficulties, and which, besides the attainment of a just equality, will be attended with many other benefits. I have, accordingly, taken the liberty to form a bill on this principle.

If the proposed bill should not be accepted by the Committee of Ways and Means, a regard to the public interests calls for the expression of the opinion, that it will be indispensable to make three radical amendments in the existing act:

First. To lay the duty on all carriages not exclusively employed in husbandry or the transportation of goods. Under the present equivocal provision some abuses are practised, and much greater are expected, which may, perhaps, prove the act incapable of execution.

Second. To increase the penalty for not entering a carriage.

Third. To define what is meant by "iron springs," a substance which, according to the opinions of seventeen out of twenty-one respectable coachmakers, in different parts of the United States, now before me, cannot exist. Agreeably to this opinion, as it corresponds with my own, it will become my duty, unless the existing act be altered, to instruct the collectors to receive the lowest duty for the various classes of carriages, however expensive and elegant in their structure, which hang on iron jacks or bows, or any other iron substance. I am, with great respect,

S. H. SMITH.

Hon. SECRETARY OF THE TREASURY.

PUBLIC BUILDINGS.

Mr. LEWIS, of Virginia, from the committee on the subject, made the following report:

The committee to whom was referred a resolution directing them to inquire into the expediency of rebuild-ing or repairing the public buildings, &c., report that, among the first steps deemed necessary in discharge of the duties assigned them, they caused the Superintendent of the City to lay before them the reports of several architects and mechanics of reputed skill and character, who had, at his request, examined the remains of the public buildings, all of whom reported, as their opinion, that the walls generally had not been materially damaged, and were not rendered unsafe or insufficient to rebuild on, conformably either to the former plan, or to some variations suggested, or such as may be adopted as improvements in the rebuilding.

These reports were accompanied by estimates of various amounts, forming an average of $458,000. The whole first cost of these buildings appears to have ben $1,215,110 10.

With the view of better understanding the grounds, and probable accuracy of the reports and estimates, the committee attended personally at the Capitol, and examined the state of that building, where, after a conference, and making such inquiries of an architect on the spot, as were considered proper, they were induced to believe that the walls of both wings of the Capitol may be safely built on, and that the estimated expense of about $250,000 for repairing the same, was as nearly accurate, and as much to be relied on, as could be reasonably expected, or as circumstances either admitted or required.

With the foregoing information, the committee proceeded to a due and general consideration of the subject-matter referred to them, and readily came to the decision, that it was expedient, either to repair the late buildings, or to build others in their stead on different sites; but as it appeared that the latter could not be effected without incurring a great additional expense, so much greater, as the committee conceived, than would be counterbalanced by any "public interest or convenience," to be derived from a "change of sites," they were of opinion that it would be inexpedient to make such a change. Connected with this part of the duty prescribed by the committee, it may not be improper that they should state to the House the representations of sundry individuals, who allege, and offer to prove, that the designation of the present sites by President WASHINGTON, who possessed full power, having been always considered by him as part of the permanent plan of the city, they purchased at very advanced prices, and improved lots, on the faith of those designations near those sites, the supposed permanency whereof has ever since sustained the value of all adjacent and contiguous property; but that, if those sites were now to be altered without some equivalent public establishment being made thereon, they apprehended that this property would become comparatively valueless during the lifetime of the present holders at least. The committee, however, desire it to be understood that other views and considerations having induced their decision on this member of the resolution, under which their inquiries were directed, they did not enter into the discussion of, or give any opinion of the force or validity of these considerations.

From the suggestions of the architects consulted, and also from the observations of the committee, they are of opinion that parts of the walls, arches, and columns, of the late buildings, are in a state requiring a small expense for workmanship and materials, to preserve them from injury by the weather, and from falling down, thereby endangering the vaulting which supports some of the floors, and which at present is very little, if at all, weakened by the burning; but as there is no money applicable to the payment of such expense, inconsiderable as it may be, the committee beg leave to suggest the propriety of an appropriation for that object.

The committee think it not irrelative to the object of their inquiries, though it is not specifically enjoined, to state, also, that the several banks within the District of Columbia, desirous of facilitating an object so interesting to the District, have made a formal and binding offer, in writing, to advance on loan to the Government, upon reasonable terms, the sum of five hundred thousand dollars, to be applied exclusively to the purpose of rebuilding or repairing the President's house, Capitol, and public offices.

Conformably to the foregoing statement, the committee ask leave to report a bill.

Mr. LEWIS then reported a bill, making appropriations for repairing or rebuilding the public buildings in the City of Washington. [The bill proposes to authorize the President of the United States to cause to be forthwith rebuilt or repaired the public buildings, on their present sites; and, for this purpose exclusively, to borrow such sum as may be necessary for the purpose, from the banks or individuals within the District.] Twice read, and committed.

Mr. STANFORD offered, for consideration, the following resolution:

Resolved, That a committee be appointed, to join such committee as may be appointed on the part of the Senate, to inquire and report whether the present Chambers of the two Houses can be so altered, or otherwise improved, as to be rendered more convenient for their deliberations, or better rooms provided during the present session, within a convenient distance of the public offices.

Mr. LEWIS moved to strike out all the resolve, after the word "deliberations."—Negatived, 72 to 48.

Mr. FARROW, of South Carolina, moved to lay the resolve on the table.—Negatived.

Mr. LEWIS then moved to add, at the end of the resolve, the words "within the City of Washington."

Mr. GROSVENOR moved to amend the amendment, by adding, after those words, "in the District of Columbia."—Agreed to, 67 to 49.

The question was then taken on the amendment, as amended, and negatived.

The question recurring on the original motion of Mr. STANFORD, it was opposed by Messrs. LEWIS, PEARSON of North Carolina, FARROW of South Carolina; and supported by Messrs. STANFORD and GROSVENOR.

Mr. FARROW moved to postpone the further consideration of the resolution indefinitely, which motion was negatived.—For the postponement 60, against it 66.

After some appropriate objections by Mr. GHOLSON, of Virginia, the question on the adoption of the resolve was decided in the affirmative, as follows:—For the resolve 62, against it 60.

And Messrs. STANFORD, GROSVENOR, ROBERTSON, LEWIS, and PEARSON, were appointed the committee on the part of this House.

BANK OF THE UNITED STATES.

The House took up the amendments, reported by the Committee of the Whole, to the bill to incorporate the subscribers to the Bank of the United States of America.

The amendments to the first section having been taken up, and the question being about to be put generally; on motion, of Mr. FORSYTH, the question was divided, and first put on agreeing to such amendments as add places of subscription and names of Commissioners; and, with modifications, that class of amendments was agreed to.

The question was then stated on agreeing to the amendments, which go to change the times and mode of subscription, viz: to make the number of shares five hundred thousand, at one hundred dollars, instead of one hundred thousand, at five hundred dollars; to be subscribed and paid in on the two last days of January next, and the three last days of each succeeding month of the year 1815.

On this question, Mr. FORSYTH, of Georgia, said he had no idea of renewing, at this time, the debate on this subject, having already expressed his sentiments on this project. He wished it at the same time to be distinctly understood, that he was not prevented from doing so by any signs of impatience exhibited in the House; because he should never be deterred from doing his duty by any emotion which might be thereby excited. But he thought it fair, for the gentlemen who advocated the amendments made by the committee to this bill, to make it as perfect as they could; and reserved the right, when the bill should be perfected, to make such remarks as the subject should appear to him to call for. As, however, the House had not expressed their sense directly, on the subject of the change of the principles of the bill, he should call for the yeas and nays on the first question which should involve the principle of the main amendment.

The amendments to the first section were then all agreed to; and the section was further amended, on suggestion of various gentlemen.

Mr. BIGHAM moved to strike out *fifty*, and to insert *twenty-five* millions, as the capital of the bank. In support of this motion, he observed, that the professed objects of the bill were, to restore public credit, and establish a sufficient circulating medium. To effect these important objects, it is intended to authorize the issuing of forty-four millions of dollars in Treasury notes, and in such small denominations as shall be accommodated to the ordinary transactions of life. The whole of the Treasury notes are to be put into circulation in the course of the year, and become the circulating medium of the country. If it were possible to throw these notes into circulation in the term of twelve months, it would deluge the country with paper money, under the name of Treasury notes, and they would depreciate in proportion to the quantity you throw into the market. It is now pretty well ascertained, that this description of notes, now in circulation, have depreciated 20 per cent.; and if you obtain eighty cents only for the dollar, the Government in the first outset will, on the forty-four millions of dollars, make a sacrifice of eight millions eight hundred thousand. This will not restore public credit, nor secure the confidence of the people in the wisdom or ability of the Government, nor will it raise the price of public stock.

The whole capital stock of the bank is to consist of six millions of dollars in specie, and forty-four millions in Treasury notes; making, in the whole, a capital stock of fifty millions of dollars. The forty-four millions in these paper notes will not be the representative of specie or of wealth, but the representative of national poverty—of an enormous debt; and will be evidence, in the hands of every individual who shall hold them, of a public debt, which he or they must be taxed to pay.

Mr. B. said, that he did not believe there could be found six millions of dollars in specie within the limits of these United States, that would associate and keep company with forty-four millions of Treasury notes. And it was not reasonable to suppose that the capitalists of the country would, for the privilege of operating on six millions of specie, on banking principles, loan to the Government forty-four millions. Yet, this is the condition upon which the bank is to go into operation; for, the bank will not be authorized to operate on the six millions until they shall have purchased the forty-four millions of dollars in Treasury notes; and without this purchase the prime object of the bill will be defeated, and the exigencies of the Government in no part provided for or satisfied.

Sir, said Mr. B., if the capital stock of the bank is reduced from fifty to twenty-five millions of dollars, it may be within the purchase of the capitalists of the country, and possibly may, at some future period, be within the power and ability of the Government to redeem; but, the present circumstances of the country will not justify the establishment of a bank of fifty millions. If it is designed that the bank shall issue their paper upon that part of the capital stock which consists of Treasury notes, then, according to the ordinary principles of banking, the bank may issue one hundred millions of dollars in their bills, and every man knows that the bank will not, cannot, redeem this enormous sum of paper with six millions of specie only. Of course, the bank notes or bills issued under such circumstances, and in such profusion, will be of no more value than paper money, and must ruin thousands of our fellow-citizens, unless you make a tender law, and that will increase the mischiefs and distress the nation.

In the days of our national prosperity, it was supposed that the whole amount of specie within these United States exceeded thirty millions of dollars; and then there was no complaint for want of a sufficient circulating medium, nor was there complaint for want of specie capital in the United States' Bank, lately put down, whose capital stock consisted only of ten millions of dollars. But, now, in these times of public embarrassment, when there is not more than fifteen millions of dollars in specie within the limits of these United States, you propose to establish a bank, whose capital stock shall consist of fifty millions of dollars!

To pass this bill, and authorize the circulation of forty-four millions of paper dollars, in addition to the present circulating medium of the country, will surfeit the nation with paper, and will greatly impair, if not wholly destroy, the public credit.

It is proposed that fifteen millions of the forty-four of these Treasury notes shall be placed in the hands of the Commissioners of the Sinking Fund, to enable them to pay the same amount of the public debt. Whoever supposes that this provision will enable the Government, through the medium of the Commissioners of the Sinking Fund, to diminish the public debt, will be greatly deceived; for, if the fifteen millions of Treasury notes are sold in the market, as they have been—that is, at the rate of 20 per cent. discount—there will be a sacrifice of three millions of dollars. So, by this provision, instead of diminishing, you will increase the public debt; and, to make the best of this process, you will only change the name or plan, and keep the debt.

Mr. B. said, he did not believe that the bill, with its present provisions, was calculated to relieve the Government of its present embarrassments, or to promote the public interest or convenience, did he think this system to be practicable; and he hoped that the motion would prevail, and that the capital stock would be reduced.

Mr. CALHOUN replied to the argument of Mr. BRIGHAM, and explained the process by which the Treasury notes, which appeared to alarm the gentleman so much, would be absorbed.

Mr. LOWNDES, of South Carolina, explained, at some length and with much clearness, the objections he entertained to the present magnitude of the capital of the bank, founded on the disproportion of the paper to the specie to be subscribed, and the impracticability of the circulation and absorption of so much paper. He concluded his observations by intimating, that if the gentleman from Massachusetts would withdraw his motion, he (Mr. L.) would substitute "thirty" instead of "twenty-five" as the amount to which he desired the capital of the bank to be reduced.

Mr. BRIGHAM declined to vary his motion; but subsequently waived it until the House should have acted on all the amendments proposed.

The House then proceeded to the amendments to the second section, which embrace the principle of Mr. CALHOUN's amendment, and which put the second section in the following shape:

SEC. 2. *And be it further enacted,* That it shall be lawful for any person, copartnership, or body politic, to subscribe for so many shares of the said capital stock of the said bank, as he, she, or they, shall think fit; and the sums respectively subscribed shall be payable in the manner following, that is to say: *six millions of dollars* in gold or silver coin of the United States; or in gold coin of Spain, or the dominions of Spain, at the rate of one hundred cents for every twenty-eight grains and sixty-hundredths of a grain of the actual weight thereof, or in other foreign gold or silver coin, at the several rates prescribed by the first section of an act regulating the currency of foreign coins in the United States, passed tenth day of April, one thousand eight hundred and six; and *forty-four millions* of dollars thereof in such gold or silver coin as aforesaid, or in Treasury notes now authorized, or to be authorized, to be issued in the year one thousand eight hundred and fifteen.

Mr. FORSYTH moved to amend this section by adding the following clause to the end thereof—which motion would restore the principle embraced by the bill as first reported, viz:

"Or in the public debt of the United States, contracted by virtue of the act of Congress, entitled 'An act authorizing a loan for a sum not exceeding eleven millions of dollars,' passed the 14th day of March, 1812, or contracted by virtue of any subsequent act or acts of Congress authorizing a loan or loans."

This question was decided. without debate, by yeas and nays. For the motion 45, against it 94, as follows:

YEAS—Messrs. Anderson, Bines, Brigham, Brown, Champion, Comstock, Condict, Conard, Dana, Davis of Pennsylvania, Denoyelles, Farrow, Findley, Fisk of Vermont, Fisk of New York, Forsyth, Franklin, Gholson, Griffin, Grosvenor, Hall, Hawkins, Hopkins of Kentucky, Hubbard, Hungerford, Ingham, Lewis, Lyle, Macon, McCoy, McKim, Nelson, Newton, Parker, Rhea of Tennessee, Roane, Sage, Smith of Pennsylvania, Tannehill, Taylor, Telfair, Udree, Williams, and Wilson of Pennsylvania.

NAYS—Messrs. Alexander, Alston, Avery, Barbour, Bard, Baylies of Massachusetts, Bayly of Virginia, Bowen, Boyd, Bradley, Burwell, Butler, Caperton, Caldwell, Calhoun, Cannon, Cilley, Clark, Cooper, Cox, Crawford, Creighton, Crouch, Culpeper, Cuthbert, Davenport, Davis of Massachusetts, Desha, Duvall, Earle, Ely, Evans, Forney, Gaston, Glasgow, Goodwyn, Gourdin, Hale, Harris, Hasbrouck, Hawes, Hulbert, Irving, Jackson of Rhode Island, Johnson of Virginia, Kennedy, Kent of New York, Kent of Maryland, Kerr, Kershaw, Kilbourn, King of Massachusetts, King of North Carolina, Law, Lovett, Lowndes, Markell, McKee, McLean, Moore, Moseley, Oakley, Pearson, Pickering, Pickens, Piper, Pitkin, Pleasants, Potter, John Reed, William Reed, Rea of Pennsylvania, Rich, Robertson, Ruggles, Sharp, Shefley, Shipherd, Smith of New York, Smith of Virginia, Stanford, Stockton, Sturges, Tallmadge, Thompson, Vose, Ward of Massachusetts, Webster, Wheaton, White, Wilcox, Wilson of Massachusetts, Winter, and Yancey.

So the motion was negatived.

A motion of Mr. GASTON was more successful, being agreed to, to amend the bill by striking out the words in italic, and in lieu thereof insert, in the first place, the words "on each share twelve dollars," and in the second place the words "eighty-eight" — so that subscriptions shall be paid in the proportion of twelve dollars in specie and eighty-eight in Treasury notes, on each share of $100.

Mr. SHARP, of Kentucky, moved to strike out, in the latter part of this section, the words "in such gold or silver coin as aforesaid, or"—his object being to require Treasury notes, only, to be received in payment of the eighty-eight dollars on each share allowed to be paid in that way. The motion was negatived, 75 to 58.

Mr. HAWKINS, of Kentucky, then moved to add after the words "now authorized," in the latter clause of the above section, the words "to be issued," his object being to allow to be received in payment on the bank shares as well those Treasury notes now in circulation, or already authorized to be put in circulation, as those hereafter to be authorized, &c. The motion was negatived, yeas 26.

The question on the amended section having been divided. was, on the suggestion of Mr. KILBOURN, of Ohio, first taken on striking out so much of the original second section of the bill as limits the subscription of any individual or body politic (the United States excepted) to 1,000 shares.

This part of the amended section having been agreed to, the question recurred on the main principle of the section as amended.

Mr. GROSVENOR, of New York, requested the yeas and nays on the question of concurrence with the Committee of the Whole on agreeing to the amendment. He believed the plan embraced in the amendments to be fanciful and wholly impracticable, and such as would, in its failure, prove more ruinous in its consequences to the community than could be well anticipated. He, therefore, desired to record his vote against it.

Mr. FISK, of Vermont, opposed the amendment and conjured gentlemen on the same side with himself to oppose this amendment, embracing a system which, he said, he was confident would disappoint the hopes of its projectors, and prostrate the party now in power. If the House should determine to exclude the holders of the stock of the United States from any participation in the subscription, and should permit the bank to go into operation, as was proposed, whenever $13,200,000 should be subscribed, it would fall wholly into the hands of the opponents of the present Administration, who would never lend the United States a cent of the capital of the bank, but employ it as far as possible in opposing the measures of the Government. The very moment the subscription is opened, Mr. F. said, it would be filled by those who have modestly told you that they alone are competent to carry on the operations of the Government, and its influence be employed against the measures of the Government. Rather than follow such an *ignis fatuus* as this, Mr. F. said, he would take his hat, make his bow, and retire from the House at once. The bill did not contain a single provision to oblige a man to pay in his subscription in Treasury notes. The bill, he said, as proposed to be amended, would completely disappoint its projectors. In the first place it would shut out our friends, all the subscribers to the old stock who have exhausted their funds, and in the next place the only subscribers to the bank would be those who wish us, as they say, to retire as soon as possible, and who have not aided us very much in the prosecution of the war. They are under no obligation by this bill to loan money to the Government—and they would not do it until better times and better men being in the Government (according to their modest opinion of themselves) should authorize them in doing it.

Mr. F. said he was for taking a practical course in whatever he did, and, therefore, he would never agree to such a system as this.

Mr. CALHOUN said, in reply to these remarks, that it was a sound rule in legislation, not to act with a view to benefit one or another party, but with a view to promote the national good. If a bank was to be erected to prop up this or that party, Mr. C. said, it should not receive his sanction. In moving the amendment, he said, he had not been governed by views of so limited a character. He had regarded the nation as a nation, and not as divided into two political parties. The subscription was equally open to both parties; and although the moneyed class attached to the ruling party might be exhausted, the farming interest was not in so miserable a situation. Mr. C. was not willing to recognise the correctness of the picture which the gentleman had drawn of the great Republican party, as exhausted and moneyless. Although there was great capital on one side, so there was on the other; and it is our boast that the yeomanry, the substantial part of the population, are on that side of the question to which we belong. The very amendments proposed, and now objected to, present the opportunity to every capitalist, however inconsiderable, to share in the capital of the bank, &c., and to disseminate its benefits all over the country, &c. As to the control over the bank, Mr. C. contended that the amendments, retaining the power over deposites and of making the bills receivable for the revenue or otherwise, gave the Government a greater control than it before possessed over the operations of the bank, &c. Legislation on party principles, he said, must ever react on the party pursuing it. He would, therefore, not resort to it. No, said he; rather let us act on national, on great principles.

Mr. FISK rejoined, and defended with his usual point the ground he had taken.

Mr. INGHAM, of Pennsylvania, took occasion, in behalf of the Committee of Ways and Means, to disclaim the operation of any party feelings in recommending to the House the system advocated by the gentleman from Vermont—from whom, although he agreed with him in opposition to the present amendment, he differed as to the grounds of his opposition.

The question was then taken by yeas and nays on agreeing to the 2d section as amended, and decided in the affirmative. For the amendment, 87, against it 52, as follows:

YEAS—Messrs. Alexander, Alston, Barnett, Baylies of Massachusetts, Bayly of Virginia, Bigelow, Bines, Bowen, Bradbury, Bradley, Burwell, Butler, Caperton, Caldwell, Calhoun, Cannon, Chappell, Clark, Cox, Crawford, Creighton, Crouch, Culpeper, Cuthbert, Davenport, Davis of Massachusetts, Desha, Duvall, Earle, Ely, Forney, Gaston, Geddes, Goodwyn, Gourdin, Hale, Harris, Hasbrouck, Hawes, Hulbert, Irving, Irwin, Jackson of Rhode Island, Johnson of Virginia, Kent of New York, Kent of Maryland, Kerr, Kershaw, Kilbourn, King of Massachusetts, King of North Carolina, Lovett, Lowndes, Markell, McKee, McLean, Moore, Oakley, Ormsby, Pearson, Pickering,

Pitkin, Pleasants, Potter, John Reed, William Reed, Rea of Pennsylvania, Rich, Robertson, Ruggles, Sharp, Sheffey, Shipherd, Smith of Virginia, Stanford, Stockton, Sturges, Tallmadge, Thompson, Vose, Ward of Massachusetts, Webster, Wheaton, White, Wilcox, Wilson of Massachusetts, and Yancey.

NAYS—Messrs. Anderson, Brigham, Brown, Champion, Comstock, Condict, Conard, Dana, Davis of Pennsylvania, Denoyelles, Eppes, Farrow, Findley, Fisk of Vermont, Forsyth, Franklin, Gholson, Griffin, Grosvenor, Hall, Hanson, Hawkins, Hopkins of Kentucky, Hungerford, Ingersoll, Ingham, Johnson of Kentucky, Kennedy, Lefferts, Lewis, Lyle, Macon, McCoy, McKim, Moseley, Nelson, Newton, Parker, Pickens, Piper, Rhea of Tennessee, Roane, Sage, Smith of Pennsylvania, Strong, Tannehill, Taylor, Telfair, Udree, Williams, and Wilson of Pennsylvania.

And the House adjourned.

TUESDAY, November 22.

BANK OF THE UNITED STATES.

The House resumed the consideration of the remainder of the amendments of the Committee of the Whole to the bill to incorporate the Bank of the United States of America.

That amendment of the Committee of the Whole to strike out the third section of the original bill (authorizing the Government to subscribe twenty millions to the capital of the bank) was concurred in.

The amendment being under consideration which strikes out so much of the original bill as allows to the Government the appointment of five directors of the bank—

The amendment was opposed by Messrs. ROBERTSON, GHOLSON, and WRIGHT, and supported by Messrs. CALHOUN, GROSVENOR, and LEWIS.

[The advocates of this amendment contended that the power of appointment of five of the directors of the bank would be merely nominal as to any control over the operations of the institution, which control would be much better effected by the power of the Government to withhold its deposites, &c. On the other hand, it was said that a large majority of the directors would probably be, in future, as they have been heretofore, adverse to the politics of the Government, and, unless properly guarded, would be disposed to thwart its operations, and favor the views of its opponents, &c.]

The question on concurring with the Committee of the Whole in this amendment to the bill, was decided—for the amendment 86, against it 64, as follows:

YEAS—Messrs. Alston, Baylies of Massachusetts, Bayly of Virginia, Bigelow, Bradbury, Bradley, Brigham, Burwell, Butler, Caperton, Caldwell, Calhoun, Champion, Chappell, Cilley, Clark, Cooper, Cox, Crawford, Creighton, Crouch, Culpeper, Davenport, Davis of Massachusetts, Duvall, Earle, Ely, Evans, Findley, Forney, Gaston, Geddes, Glasgow, Grosvenor, Hale, Hanson, Hasbrouck, Hulbert, Ingersoll, Irwin, Jackson of Rhode Island, Kent of New York, Kent of Maryland, Kerr, Kershaw, King of Massachusetts, King of North Carolina, Law, Lewis, Lovett,

Lowndes, Markell, McKee, McKim, Miller, Moseley, Oakley, Ormsby, Pickering, Pitkin, Potter, John Reed, Rich, Ruggles, Seybert, Sheffey, Sherwood, Shipherd, Skinner, Smith of New York, Smith of Virginia, Stanford, Stockton, Sturges, Tallmadge, Taylor, Thompson, Vose, Ward of Massachusetts, Ward of New Jersey, Webster, Wheaton, White, Wilcox, Wilson of Massachusetts, and Winter.

NAYS—Messrs. Alexander, Anderson, Barbour, Bard, Barnett, Bines, Bowen, Brown, Cannon, Clopton, Comstock, Conard, Cuthbert, Dana, Davis of Pennsylvania, Denoyelles, Desha, Farrow, Fisk of Vermont, Fisk of New York, Forsyth, Franklin, Gholson, Goodwyn, Gourdin, Griffin, Hall, Harris, Hawes, Hopkins of Kentucky, Hubbard, Humphreys, Hungerford, Ingham, Johnson of Va., Kennedy, Kilbourn, Lefferts, Lyle, Macon, McCoy, McLean, Moore, Nelson, Newton, Parker, Pickens, Pleasants, Rea of Pennsylvania, Rhea of Tennessee, Roane, Robertson, Sage, Sevier, Sharp, Smith of Pennsylvania, Strong, Tannehill, Telfair, Udree, Williams, Wilson of Pennsylvania, Wright, and Yancey.

The House proceeded in the further consideration of the amendments to the bill.

When the House came to that amendment to the 10th rule for the government of the bank, which is expressed in the following words: "But the said corporation may sell any part of the public debt whereof its stock shall be composed:"

A motion was made by Mr. FORSYTH so to amend this amendment as to make it read as follows: "But the said corporation shall not sell any part of the public debt whereof its stock shall be composed, during the present war."

After a debate of considerable length and warmth, the question on the motion to amend the amendment was decided—for the motion 64, against the motion 73, as follows:

YEAS—Messrs. Alexander, Anderson, Barnett, Bines, Bowen, Chappell, Clopton, Comstock, Conard, Creighton, Cuthbert, Dana, Davis of Pennsylvania, Denoyelles, Desha, Duvall, Eppes, Evans, Farrow, Fisk of New York, Forsyth, Franklin, Gholson, Goodwyn, Griffin, Hall, Harris, Hawes, Hopkins of Kentucky, Hubbard, Humphreys, Hungerford, Ingersoll, Ingham, Irwin, Johnson of Virginia, Kennedy, Kershaw, Kilbourn, Lefferts, Lowndes, Lyle, Macon, McCoy, McKim, Nelson, Newton, Parker, Pickens, Piper, Pleasants, Rhea of Tennessee, Roane, Robertson, Sage, Sevier, Seybert, Smith of Pennsylvania, Tannehill, Telfair, Udree, Williams, Wilson of Pennsylvania, and Wright.

NAYS—Messrs. Alston, Avery, Barbour, Bard, Baylies of Massachusetts, Bigelow, Boyd, Bradley, Brigham, Burwell, Butler, Caperton, Caldwell, Calhoun, Cannon, Champion, Cilley, Clark, Crawford, Crouch, Culpeper, Davenport, Davis of Massachusetts, Ely, Forney, Gaston, Geddes, Grosvenor, Hale, Hasbrouck, Hulbert, Jackson of Rhode Island, Kent of Maryland, Kerr, King of Massachusetts, King of North Carolina, Law, Lewis, Markell, McKee, Moore, Moseley, Oakley, Ormsby, Pearson, Pickering, Potter, William Reed, Rea of Pennsylvania, Rich, Ruggles, Sharp, Sheffey, Sherwood, Shipherd, Skinner, Smith of New York, Smith of Virginia, Stanford, Sturges, Tallmadge, Taylor, Thompson, Troup, Vose, Ward of Massachusetts, Ward of New Jersey, Webster, Wheaton, White, Wilcox, Winter, and Yancey.

The motion of Mr. FORSYTH having been thus rejected—

The amendment reported by the Committee of the Whole, as first above stated, was amended by adding thereto the following, on motion of Mr. RICH:

"Provided, that, during the continuance of the present war, the said corporation shall not, without the consent of Congress, sell or dispose of their public debt to an amount above ten millions of dollars."

A motion was made by Mr. INGHAM, of Pennsylvania, further to amend the said amendment by adding to it as follows: "nor after the war any part thereof at a price less than its par value." This motion was negatived.

The amendment of the Committee of the Whole, as amended, was then agreed to.

Other amendments were then considered and agreed to.

The amendment to the 12th rule for the government of the bank is to strike out the following clause:

"But the said corporation shall be bound to loan to the Government of the United States thirty millions of dollars, at an interest not exceeding six per centum per annum, in such sums, and at such periods as, consistently with the objects of the Government, may be made mutually convenient to the Government and the corporation, whenever any law or laws shall authorize and require such loan or loans."

The question on concurring in this amendment was decided as follows:

YEAS—Messrs. Alston, Avery, Bard, Barnett, Baylies of Massachusetts, Bayly of Virginia, Bigelow, Boyd, Bradley, Brigham, Burwell, Butler, Caperton, Caldwell, Calhoun, Champion, Cilley, Clark, Crawford, Creighton, Crouch, Culpeper, Cuthbert, Davenport, Davis of Massachusetts, Duvall, Ely, Forney, Gaston, Geddes, Grosvenor, Hale, Hanson, Hasbrouck, Hulbert, Ingersoll, Jackson of Rhode Island, Kent of New York, Kent of Maryland, Kerr, King of Massachusetts, Law, Lewis, Lovett, Lowndes, Markell, McKee, McKim, McLean, Miller, Moore, Moseley, Oakley, Ormsby, Pearson, Pickering, Pitkin, Pleasants, Potter, John Reed, William Reed, Rea of Pennsylvania, Rich, Robertson, Ruggles, Sharp, Sheffey, Shipherd, Smith of New York, Smith of Virginia, Stanford, Stockton, Sturges, Tallmadge, Taylor, Thompson, Vose, Ward of Massachusetts, Ward of New Jersey, Webster, Wheaton, White, Wilcox, Wilson of Massachusetts, Winter, and Yancey—86.

NAYS—Messrs. Alexander, Anderson, Barbour, Bines, Bowen, Cannon, Chappell, Clopton, Comstock, Conard, Dana, Davis of Pennsylvania, Denoyelles, Desha, Earle, Eppes, Farrow, Findley, Fisk of New York, Forsyth, Franklin, Gholson, Goodwyn, Gourdin, Griffin, Hall, Harris, Hawes, Hopkins of Kentucky, Hubbard, Humphreys, Hungerford, Ingham, Irwin, Johnson of Virginia, Kennedy, Kershaw, Kilbourn, Lefferts, Lyle, Macon, McCoy, Nelson, Newton, Parker, Pickens, Piper, Rhea of Tennessee, Roane, Sage, Sevier, Seybert, Smith of Pennsylvania, Tannehill, Telfair, Udree, Wilson of Pennsylvania, and Wright—58.

So the amendment was concurred in.

The House having under consideration the new section added to the bill by the Committee of the Whole, giving the Congress power at any time to appoint a special committee to examine into the state of the bank, a motion was made by Mr. KILBOURN to amend the same by adding thereto the following:

"And if, upon full investigation, it shall appear that the said corporation have exceeded their powers, or violated any of the provisions or restrictions of this act, it shall be within the power of Congress to declare their charter void."

This motion was negatived, after debate, and the new section concurred in.

All the amendments made in Committee of the Whole having been agreed to, on motion of Mr. PICKENS, the House agreed to reconsider the disagreement to Mr. SHARP's motion to amend the bill by excluding other medium but Treasury notes being received in payment of that portion, of the subscription on each share, which is proposed to be paid in that way.

And the question being put on now agreeing to this amendment, after debate, the House adjourned.

WEDNESDAY, November 23.

A message from the Senate informed the House that the Senate have passed a bill "to authorize the President of the United States to call upon the several States and Territories thereof for their respective quotas of eighty thousand and four hundred and thirty militia, for the defence of the frontiers of the United States against invasion;" in which they ask the concurrence of this House.—The bill was read twice and committed to the Committee of the whole House on the bill making further provisions for filling the ranks of the regular Army by classifying the free male population of the United States.

BANKS OF NEW YORK.

Mr. IRVING presented the memorial of a committee appointed by five of the banks in the city of New York, to take into consideration all matters relating to the state of credit in that city, remonstrating against the proposed incorporation of the subscribers to the Bank of the United States of America; which was read, and ordered to lie on the table.

The memorial is as follows:

To the Senate and House of
     Representatives of the United States:

The memorial of the subscribers, committees appointed by five of the banks in the city of New York, to take into consideration all matters relating to the state of credit in the city, respectfully represents—

That your memorialists, with great deference to the wisdom of Congress, presume that it will not be considered as unbecoming in them to express their opinions on a subject which they have practically under their constant view.

That they see with great alarm the proposed incorporation of a Bank of the United States with a capital of fifty millions of dollars; not that they are insensible of the advantages of such an institution, but because they are persuaded, in their most deliberate view of the subject, that the present time is most inauspicious for the creation of such a bank, and that so far from aiding the fiscal operations of the Government, it will, in their opinion, tend to embarrass still more, than the adverse circumstances of the times have already done, all public as well as private credit.

Your memorialists firmly believe that the proposed capital will be found too large.

That six millions of dollars in specie cannot be obtained by any inducements which can be held out, and that a less sum will not afford a proper security to the public.

That, even if six millions could be procured, the payment of the notes in specie could only be continued for a short period, under the present circumstances of the country.

That if, by the exercise of the power proposed to be lodged in the President of the United States, the notes are not paid in specie, they will infallibly depreciate.

That, if they depreciate, no existing bank can possibly take them without the greatest injury to their stockholders.

That if the notes are not taken by the present banks throughout the United States, they cannot serve as a general medium of circulation.

A full discussion of this subject, your memorialists are well aware, would transgress the proper limits of this memorial; they will therefore confine themselves to a few of the reasons which have induced them to form these opinions. They think that the capital will be found too large, because the late Bank of the United States had only a capital of ten millions of dollars at the period of our greatest commercial prosperity, and, since the expiration of the charter of that bank, the amount of its capital has been much more than supplied by the incorporation of other banks. It is believed to have been the opinion of the part of the community best informed on that subject, that this amount was abundantly sufficient. Your memorialists therefore cannot but dread the effects which a new banking capital of fifty millions must have upon the paper circulation of the country, particularly when it is considered, that the proposed bank is to be pledged to lend to the Government thirty millions, which the public exigencies will probably very soon call for, without any power of refusal being left to those who are to manage the bank, even if convinced that the emission of so large a sum in notes must be ruinous to the bank itself.

It is well known that a great and constant drain of the precious metals from the United States has existed for a long time past, while supplies of them have been cut off by the war; and that the alarms necessarily existing during a war, have induced many timid and cautious persons to hoard specie, the consequence of which has been to render a suspension of specie payments necessary to the different banks in Baltimore, Philadelphia, New York, and in various other parts of the United States. Notwithstanding the utmost care has been taken to restrain the circulation of notes within moderate bounds, yet it has been found impossible to prevent a difference in value between specie and the notes of banks in the best credit. This difference is now, in the city of New York, from twelve to fifteen per cent., and in other places still greater. Your memorialists have therefore no hesitation in giving it as their opinion that six millions of specie cannot be procured; but they are persuaded also, that, if procured, that sum could not long supply specie payments, because, as the same causes are likely still to operate, and with increased effect, when the paper circulation is so much increased as it must be by the proposed loans to the Government, it is believed that as fast as the notes are issued they will be returned for specie; as they bear no interest, there will be no inducement for any person to hold them, to counteract the great advantage offered by the high price for specie, in sending them for payment.

If it should be found necessary to restrain the bank from paying specie, your memorialists are convinced the notes will depreciate. The Treasury notes which have been issued have done so, although in much less quantity, and under more favorable circumstances, because bearing interest and being payable at definite periods. While Treasury notes have these obvious advantages, it is not perceived that the notes of the proposed bank will have any to balance them, the security having been presumed the same in both cases. The expenses of the war must, in the first instance, be paid in these notes, and of course they will be, to a considerable extent, in the hands of persons who must, of necessity, dispose of them for what they will bring. The late Bank of the United States, while redeeming its notes in specie and possessing the entire support of the Government and the confidence of the public, never had, it is believed, more than six millions of notes in circulation. The banks in the city of New York, whose aggregate capital is about fifteen millions of dollars, have not, upon an average, had a circulation of more than five millions, although possessing all the advantages to be derived from the business and support of the Government in this city. Presuming that the proportion of circulation to capital is nearly the same in other parts of the United States, and taking into view that the circulation is probably as great at the present period as, under the circumstances of the country and the removal of the check of specie payments, it can safely be, can it be doubted what the effect of an additional emission even of twenty millions of paper will necessarily be?

As it appears evident to your memorialists that the notes of the proposed bank must depreciate, it appears equally so, that no existing bank can take them without the greatest injury to their stockholders. However disposed they may be to aid the fiscal operations of the Government, yet, from the moment the notes are depreciated, if they are taken either in payment or in deposites, all their debts will be paid in that description of paper, the circulation of their own notes will nearly cease, and they will be left in possession of notes redeemable at some future uncertain period and bearing no present interest. Can such a sacrifice of the interest of their constituents be called for or expected from the present institutions?

It has been supposed that the want of a medium of general circulation rendered a National Bank necessary; but your memorialists beg leave to observe, that while they admit the want of a medium, they are quite persuaded that bank notes will not answer the purpose, unless they can be exchanged at pleasure for specie, or taken generally by the banks throughout the United States. If your memorialists are right in the opinions already stated, it appears to follow, as a necessary consequence, that the notes of the proposed bank will not supply the place of a general medium.

As your memorialists are persuaded that the best interests of the United States require that the suspension of specie payments, which has unfortunately been found necessary, should be continued for as short a period as possible, they dread the increased difficulty which an additional paper circulation probably of thirty or forty millions will occasion; they fear it will approach to an insuperable bar to the resumption of specie payments;

while, on the other hand, a National Bank, founded upon proper principles, and at a more favorable period, when there was a reasonable prospect of continuing to pay specie, would offer the best remedy for the deranged state of the circulation, and a most powerful instrument to renovate the commercial credit of the United States.

Your memorialists beg the indulgence of Congress when they add, that they have no doubt that Treasury bills, issued nearly in the way proposed by the Committee of Ways and Means of the House of Representatives, would be found of more service to the Government, be much less dangerous to the public, and tend much more to supply the want of a general medium of circulation. They believe that Treasury notes, issued for various denominations, redeemable at the pleasure of the Government, but not at any definite periods, bearing interest while in circulation at the present rate, but fundable at the option of the holder at a higher rate of interest, would be less liable to depreciation than the notes of a bank bearing no interest, and the security being the same. The present interest on the Treasury notes would offer an inducement to keep them, and, whenever the market was overcharged, the power to fund them at a higher rate of interest would take off the redundance. In this way the issue of Treasury notes would probably operate, to a considerable amount, as a constant loan at a reduced rate of interest: nor should it be overlooked that the consequences of a depreciation, if it unfortunately should take place, would neither be so extensive nor so lasting as in the case of a Bank of the United States.

[Signed by the President and Cashiers of the Bank of New York, the Merchants' Bank, the Union Bank, and the Bank of America, and the New York Manufacturing Company.]

DISCIPLINE OF THE ARMY.

The following report was received from the Secretary of War:

WAR DEPARTMENT, *Nov.* 22, 1814.

The Secretary of War, to whom was referred the resolution of the House of Representatives of the 10th instant, requesting information whether the Army of the United States was trained by any uniform system of discipline, and, if not, what were the causes that have prevented it, and whether any legislative provision was necessary to effect the same, has the honor to report—

1. That no uniform system of discipline has heretofore been practised in training the Armies of the United States, either in line, by battalion, or company.

2. That, in the opinion of the Secretary of War, it would be advisable to institute a Board of General and Field Officers, to digest and report to this Department a system of discipline for the Army of the United States; which report, when approved by the President of the United States, should be carried into effect under the orders of this Department.

3. That the sanction of Congress, by a resolution of the Senate and House of Representatives, to this measure, if not absolutely necessary, in consideration of the powers already vested in this Department by law, would, nevertheless, have a very salutary effect.

JAMES MONROE.

Hon. SPEAKER, *House of Representatives.*

The report was, on motion of Mr. CALHOUN, referred to a select committee.

Two other reports were also received from the War Department, in relation to the burning of

639   HISTORY OF CONGRESS.   640

H. of R.   *Death of the Vice President—Remission of Forfeiture.*   November, 1814.

the Potomac and Eastern Branch bridges. Neither, nor any part of either, the Secretary reports, was destroyed under the orders of the War Department.

BANK OF THE UNITED STATES.

The House resumed the consideration of the bill to "incorporate the subscribers to the Bank of the United States of America."

The question depending yesterday, on Mr. Sharp's motion, was, after further debate, decided in the affirmative.

The bill having been further amended, a motion was made by Mr. Gaston further to amend the bill, by striking out "fifty millions," the proposed amount of the capital of the bank, and inserting "twenty" in lieu thereof.

This motion was supported by Mr. Webster, in a speech of considerable length; which he had not concluded when the Secretary of the Senate was announced, and, in becoming terms, informed the House of the decease of the Vice President of the United States, and the resolution the Senate had thereupon adopted.

On motion of Mr. Findley, of Pennsylvania, the business on hand was ordered to lie on the table.

On motion of Mr. William Reed,

Resolved, unanimously, That this House doth concur in the resolution of the Senate, for the appointment of a joint committee, "to consider and report measures proper to manifest the public respect for the memory of the deceased," and expressive of the deep regret of the Congress of the United States, for the loss of a citizen so highly respected and revered.

Mr. William Reed, Mr. Macon, Mr. Tallmadge, and Mr. Nelson, were appointed the committee on the part of this House.

Thursday, November 24.

DEATH OF THE VICE PRESIDENT.

The Journal of yesterday's proceedings having been read—

Mr. Macon, of North Carolina, rose and observed, that, after the melancholy event recorded in the Journal just read, it could scarcely be considered proper for the Speaker to call for petitions, or for the House to proceed to the orders of the day. The nation well knows what Congress ought to feel for the loss of the Vice President of the United States. In order to exhibit that feeling in a proper manner, Mr. Macon moved the following resolutions:

" *Resolved,* That, from an unfeigned respect to the late Elbridge Gerry, Vice President of the United States and President of the Senate, the Speaker's Chair be shrouded with black during the present session; and, as a further testimony of respect for the memory of the deceased, the members of this House go into mourning, by wearing crape on the left arm for thirty days.

" *Resolved,* That the members of this House will attend the funeral of Elbridge Gerry, late Vice President of the United States, to-day, at two o'clock."

The resolutions were unanimously adopted, and then the House adjourned.

Friday, November 25.

On motion of Mr. Bowen, of Tennessee,

Resolved, That the Committee of Claims be instructed to inquire into the expediency of paying for the horses lost or destroyed in the campaign, against the hostile Creek Indians, commanded by Major General Jackson.

Mr. Stevenson, of Illinois, presented for consideration the following resolution:

Resolved, That the Committee on Military Affairs be instructed to inquire into the expediency of providing for the defence of the frontiers of the United States, by continuing and increasing the number of rangers heretofore authorized; and that they have leave to report by bill or otherwise.

Mr. Sharp, of Kentucky, advocated the adoption of this motion; which, however, on the suggestion of Mr. Troup, that the Military Committee already had a similar proposition before them, and were about to act on it, was not agreed to.

On motion of Mr. Stevenson, of Illinois, supported by Mr. Easton, of Missouri. it was

Resolved, That the Committee on Public Lands be instructed to inquire whether any, and what, alterations or amendments are necessary by law to be made in the act confirming certain claims to lands in the Illinois Territory, and providing for their location, passed in April, 1814.

Resolved, That the Committee on Public Lands be instructed to inquire whether any, and if any, what, further provision by law is expedient to be made for giving the right of pre-emption to public lands to certain settlers in the Illinois Territory.

REMISSION OF FORFEITURE.

Mr. Eppes, from the Committee of Ways and Means, made a report on the petition of Justin and Elias Lyman; which was read, and referred to a Committee of the Whole House on Monday next. The report is as follows:

That the facts which are material to the decision on the prayer of the petition, are contained in a letter from the Secretary of the Treasury to the chairman of this committee, which accompanies this report. From this statement of facts it appears, 1st. That the unlawful importation was made by the express order of the agents of the petitioners; 2d. That the papers of the schooner and her cargo, exhibited on the entry at the custom-house at Newport, were false, colorable, and fraudulent; 3d. That the real facts of the case coming accidentally to the knowledge of the Collector, without any disclosure on the part of the petitioners, the schooner and cargo were seized and libelled as forfeited; and the late Secretary of the Treasury refused to remit the forfeitures incurred, "because it did not appear, to his satisfaction, that the said forfeitures and penalties were incurred without wilful negligence or any intention of fraud. On a review of the circumstances of the case, the committee concur in the opinion already pronounced by the Treasury Department, that the petitioners are not entitled to relief. The following resolution is, therefore, submitted:

Resolved, That the prayer of the petition ought not to be granted.

TREASURY DEPARTMENT, *Nov.* 21, 1814.

SIR: In answer to your inquiries, on behalf of the Committee of Ways and Means, I have the honor to state, that, on the 28th of June, 1814, the late Secretary of the Treasury decided not to remit the forfeitures and penalties incurred by the petitioners, because "it did not appear, to his satisfaction, that the said forfeitures and penalties were incurred, without any wilful negligence or intention of fraud." I cannot discover any reason to presume that the Secretary declined acting, at any time, on the ground that the general power to remit did not embrace the present case, and having, in fact, acted, his decision is final, unless the petitioners can entitle themselves, by the equitable circumstances of the case, to the favor of Congress.

The information to be collected in this Department, upon the merits of the case, appears to authorize the following general statement of facts:

That the petitioners, merchants of New York, in April or May, 1810, were holders of bills of exchange for £1,100 sterling, drawn in Berbice, on merchants in Glasgow, which they negotiated, but which they were afterwards obliged to pay, on being returned protested for non-payment. That, in the Spring of 1811, the petitioners sent the bills to Berbice, in order to recover the amount from the drawer, and their agents accepted a quantity of coffee in payment. That the coffee was shipped from Berbice to St. Andrew's, in Nova Scotia, where it arrived in the month of February or March, 1812, and was there landed and stored. That, upon the declaration of war, in June, 1812, the petitioners assigned the coffee, in trust, to Messrs. Murray and Sons, of New York, who were well known at St. Andrew's, and, particularly, to the consignees of the coffee. That, on the 26th of December, 1812, the petitioners applied to the Secretary of the Treasury (Mr. Gallatin) for permission to import the coffee into the United States, but were refused. That, early in the year 1813, the consignees requested Messrs. Murray and Sons to remove the coffee, expressing some doubts of its safety at St. Andrew's; and, thereupon, Messrs. Murray and Sons, at the instance of the petitioners, assigned the coffee, in trust, to a Portuguese, in order that it might be protected, as neutral property, from British capture, on its passage to the United States. That the coffee was afterwards (about the 2d of August, 1813) shipped on board of a Portuguese schooner, and brought to Newport, in Rhode Island, about the 24th of August, 1813, when the captain of the schooner reported that he had arrived from St. Bartholomew. That the captain delivered to the Collector of Newport sundry documents, and, particularly, 1st. Certificates, dated Gustavia, St. Bartholomew, June 26th and 28th, 1813, stating the cargo of coffee to be the growth and produce of Spanish settlements, and that it had been imported into that island; 2d. A clearance for the Portuguese schooner, dated at Gustavia, island of St. Bartholomew, June 26th, 1813, particularly specifying the cargo of coffee. That, upon these documents, the schooner was admitted to an entry, bonds were given for the duties, and the cargo was landed. That the real facts of the case coming accidentally to the knowledge of the Collector, without any disclosure on the part of the petitioners, the schooner and the coffee were seized and libelled as forfeited under the non-im-

13th CON. 3d SESS.—21

portation law; the petitioners applied, in due form, to the Secretary of the Treasury for a remission, and the Secretary decided not to remit.

Upon these general facts the District Attorney and the Collector of Newport have objected to a remission of the forfeiture; 1st. Because the unlawful importation was made by the express order of the agents of the petitioners; 2d. Because it did not appear that the petitioners informed their agent that the Secretary of the Treasury had refused to permit the importation of the coffee; 3d. That the papers of the schooner and her cargo, exhibited on the entry at the custom-house at Newport, were false, colorable, and fraudulent.

In answer to these objections the petitioners allege: 1st. That, by clothing the American property with a neutral cover, they meant to elude the British cruisers and privateers, not to violate the laws of this country; 2d. That the colorable documents, respecting the origin of the cargo, and the clearance of the vessel, were put on board by the agent of the petitioners, without their authority, and might have been designed to enable the schooner to escape capture by American privateers, until the vessel should arrive in a port of the United States, when an appeal could be made to the equity of the Government for relief against the forfeiture incurred by the importation; 3d. That the captain of the Portuguese schooner was ignorant of our language and laws; that he made an entry without instructions from the petitioners, and contrary to their intention; and that the colorable papers ought not to have been produced at the custom-house without an explanation of the facts; 4th. That the silence of the petitioners, on the impropriety of the entry upon false papers, was owing to their desire to avoid involving the Portuguese captain in the penalties of the law.

Under these circumstances, the case rests with the committee; and (returning the papers accompanying their reference) I have only to repeat the assurances of the sincere respect with which I am, sir,

Your most obedient servant,
A. J. DALLAS.

BANK OF THE UNITED STATES.

The House, on motion of Mr. CALHOUN, resumed the bill to incorporate the subscribers to the Bank of the United States of America.

The question under consideration being on Mr. GASTON's motion to substitute "twenty" for "fifty" millions of dollars, as the amount of the capital of the bank—

Mr. WEBSTER concluded the speech which he commenced on Wednesday, in opposition to the bill as it now stands. In the course of his remarks to-day, he indicated generally his views as to the sort of bank which ought to be established. He would have a bank of a limited amount, say twenty millions of capital; he would make it indispensable that it should pay specie, by a provision that all notes not paid in specie, when properly presented, should thenceforth bear a certain interest, and by inflicting a penalty on such directors as should, during the suspension of specie payment, consent to put the notes of the bank in circulation; he was willing the Government should, if others believed it necessary, hold some stock in the bank, but at the extent not to exceed one-half of the whole amount; the remaining half to be paid in specie, or, at the discretion of the directors, in notes of existing banks, on condition that such banks should agree to resume their specie payments within a given time; and, if it was thought desirable, the Government might, he said, retain the right to subscribe hereafter an additional five millions to the capital of the bank. This was, generally, his plan. Upon the whole, he concluded by saying, although there were many points in which the present bill was preferable to the bill first reported, still, with its present amount of capital, and the great proportion of stock to specie, it was wholly objectionable in his mind, and he could not vote for it.

When Mr. W. sat down—

Mr. LOWNDES, of South Carolina, said, if he conceived any advantage to the nation could result from permitting this discussion to progress, he should not make the motion he was about to offer; but, believing, from the difference of views entertained in different parts of the House, and from the variety of plans which had been offered, that longer discussion would merely consume time, without a prospect of the final passage of the bill; and believing, also, that, by a reference to a select committee, a concurrence of the views of all parties might be obtained in favor of one plan, he moved that this bill be referred to a select committee.

Mr. INGHAM, of Pennsylvania, said, he was in favor of the recommitment of the bill, because he believed that, in its present form, it would not pass the House; but that a bill might be devised that would meet the views of gentlemen on all sides of the House. It was possible, at least, a combination of the views of different gentlemen might be effected, which might produce great good, and could do no harm. He was, therefore, in favor of recommitment, as the only means of effecting this desirable object.

Mr. FISK, of New York, said, he merely rose to add his wish to that of his friend from Pennsylvania. It was as certain, as anything yet in suspense could be, that the bill would not pass the House in its present shape. That it might be kept in possession of the House, and not destroyed without an effort to preserve it, he hoped the House would agree to refer it to a select committee, for such modification as might appear to be calculated to meet the views of the House. The opinions of gentlemen on all sides had been so fully expressed, that the committee, being in possession of them, would be able to mould the bill accordingly.

Mr. CALHOUN, of South Carolina, said, it must be obvious, from the course of the debate, if it were not from the nature of the subject, that a great diversity of sentiment existed on this head. No question could exhibit a greater division of sentiment, confined neither to party or locality. As he was extremely anxious that the bank should be established, Mr. C. said he should be averse to throwing any obstacle in the way of the practicability of the measure, and would, therefore, heartily assent to the motion for recommitment.

The question was then taken on recommitment, and decided in the affirmative without a

division; and Mr. LOWNDES, Mr. FISK of New York, Mr. CALHOUN, Mr. INGHAM, Mr. FORSYTH, Mr. OAKLEY, and Mr. GASTON, were appointed the committee.

TAX ON DISTILLED LIQUORS, &c.

The House then, on motion of Mr. EPPES, resolved itself into a Committee of the Whole, on the several tax bills reported by the Committee of Ways and Means.

The bill for laying an additional duty on distilled spirituous liquors was first taken up, and discussed with much zeal. Various amendments were made to the bill and the blanks filled, in conformity to the previous determination of the House, and to the suggestion of the chairman of the Committee of Ways and Means.

Mr. McLEAN moved to amend the first section so as to repeal the present tax upon the capacity, and retain the duty of twenty cents per gallon upon the product of the still.

Mr. McLEAN said the motion he had now submitted, was the same in substance as the one made on a former occasion by an honorable member (Mr. YANCEY) from North Carolina. I am aware, said he, of the extreme difficulty in adopting a system of taxation that will be equal in its operation in every part of our extended country. The situation of our citizens is so various, their pursuits so diversified, that it is impossible perfectly to equalize any general system of taxation. The diversity of circumstances and pursuits arises from local causes, confined in their nature and effects. But if we cannot arrive at entire equality, we should at least aim at it. In taxing any one article, we should guard against an imposition that would discourage the manufacture of such article. My object, in submitting this amendment, is to guard against the evil, as well resulting from the extravagance of the tax, as from the complicated system proposed.

While the resolutions submitted by the Committee of Ways and Means were under discussion, I was surprised to hear several gentlemen contend that an internal revenue, apportioned amongst the several States in proportion to their population, was the most equitable and the most conformable to the principles of our Government. Never was an argument more fallacious. The direct tax, because it is apportioned among the several States according to their population, is the most unequal tax. This inequality was sufficiently shown by the honorable chairman of the Committee of Ways and Means. He instanced the States of New Jersey and Ohio, as being nearly equal in population; in the former, the lands are in a high state of cultivation and productive to the owners; in the latter, ninety hundredths are in a state of nature and unproductive to the owners. Nothing more can be necessary to show the unequal operation of this tax. The individual in New Jersey who owns five hundred acres of land, worth forty dollars per acre, has but little more tax to pay than the citizen in Ohio, who owns the same quantity of land, not worth more than four dollars per acre. The disproportion is here more than twelve to four.

In every country, except where despotism has left no rights to the people, a tax on the person has ever been viewed as the most odious tax. It has ever been odious, because of its inequality, exacting as much from the poor man as the rich man. The same inequality would exist if the internal revenue were apportioned among the several States according to their population. What had been the principal basis of taxation where any regard has been had to the rights of the citizen? Property; and, in the general, that kind of property which is productive to the owner. If a revenue is derived from it by the individual, something may be yielded to the Government. I do not make these observations in opposition to the direct tax; the imposition of that tax had my hearty concurrence, and its proposed increase meets equally with my assent. But my object is, to rebut the charge that has been made against the Western representation, because they resisted the argument that it would be equal and just to impose the internal duties according to the population of the respective States, that they therefore wished to exonerate their constituents from an equal burden of taxation. I make these observations to show that it would be the extreme of injustice to exact as much from the citizen of the West, who resides in a cabin and cultivates the field with his own hands for the support of his family, as from the wealthy citizen of the Eastern and Northern States. Some gentlemen have contended this would be just, inasmuch as the States are represented in the National Legislature in proportion to their numbers. What would such an argument lead to? The poor, it would be found, would be utterly unable to pay their proportion of the burden thus imposed; the certain consequence would be, that States would be represented in proportion to their wealth, and not their population. The argument used by gentlemen could lead to no other result. This might be pleasing to a few of the wealthy, who wish influence to be attached to property, but it would subvert one of the most inestimable principles of our Government, that of equality.

In proportion to the wealth of the Western country, there is a much greater quantity of domestic spirits manufactured than in the Eastern and Northern States. Notwithstanding, the imposition of this tax would not produce much inequality, if a market could be found in the Eastern States for the spirits manufactured in the West, but the transportation is impracticable, no market is open for this article in the West; it is therefore presumable, if this additional duty to the amount proposed be imposed, that no more will be manufactured in the Western country than is necessary for home consumption. No individual can afford to pay the enormous duty, and manufacture this commodity in anticipation of a future market. I am more than willing to tax domestic spirits to the utmost extent they will bear; but I am under the most certain conviction, from the operation of the present tax on the capacity, that the additional duty proposed will rather diminish than increase the public revenue. It may not have

this effect in some of the States. In New York, a market will be had for great quantities of spirit to the troops in the service of the United States who will occupy the Northern frontier. In that State, and perhaps a few others, the increased duty will yield more to the public revenue; but the principal sales being to the United States, they must necessarily pay the advanced price of the spirit; so that, although the receipts into the Treasury might be enhanced, yet the real advantage to the public revenue would be inconsiderable. The depression of the revenue in the West will equal the advance of it in other States from this source. Being willing to obtain to the public revenue the largest possible amount from this source, I would assent to a considerable addition to the present tax; I believe some addition would not depress the revenue in the West. If we can obtain the largest amount of revenue from this source, without producing an extreme pressure in any portion of the community, it is certainly most politic to do so. Gentlemen calculate on realizing an immense sum from this tax; their calculations are extravagant; they will be found illusive; they will find, when it may be too late, that they have been too anxious to fill the coffers of the Treasury from this source. Their reach has been eager, but they have grasped at a shadow that has eluded their grasp.

A gentleman from Maryland, (Mr. WRIGHT,) not now in his seat, who has taken a very active part in the imposition of this tax, stated as a fact, that distilled spirits from grain in his part of the country are worth one dollar and twenty-five cents per gallon; from this fact, he has drawn an argument in favor of the tax, and that it would operate most favorably to the Western country, as there the price of the same kind of spirit was not more than sixty-two and a half cents per gallon. What regulates the value of an article? The price it will bring in a market. If a gallon of domestic spirit will bring in Maryland one dollar and twenty-five cents, and will only sell in Ohio for sixty-two and a half cents, the tax will operate on the value of the article one hundred per cent. higher in Ohio than in Maryland; it is therefore unequal. However various my objections are to the inequality and amount of this tax, they are not less so to the manner in which it is to be imposed. A tax on the capacity and on the product of the still, will be found complicated and embarrassing. What are the evils this system is proposed to remedy? We are told it will guard against fraud; it will enable the collector to detect imposition. Sir, from this very source, I apprehend much odium will be excited against this tax and the Government. What criterion is afforded the collector to detect frauds? The most uncertain. We all know, from the ordinary concerns of life, that two men engaged in the same business, under the same advantages, will frequently produce very different results. Is it, indeed, a sufficient presumption of fraud, that one individual has not manufactured as large a quantity of spirits as his neighbor; and is this a ground on which to charge him with the commission of fraud, or to subject him to the inquisitorial powers of a collector? It ought to be on grounds more substantial, that we suspect the integrity of a citizen. In those States where taxable property has long been given in for taxation under oath, no complaints have arisen. In Ohio, a list of personal property is furnished the assessor without oath, and yet I never heard it alleged that an individual had defrauded the revenue by making an incorrect return; why, then, shall we distrust the virtue of the citizen in the collection of this tax? By this distrust we do him injustice, of which he would have a right to complain; and, while we give evidence of distrust, we afford the most uncertain means for detection. But, admitting this tax on the capacity would afford some security against fraud, is it necessary for this purpose to continue the tax? It is not probable that under the additional duty any (if any, very few) new distilleries will be erected. The tax on the capacity has been in operation the present year. All the distilleries that will be employed the ensuing year, are occupied the present year, and every means for the detection of fraud is thereby furnished to the collectors that the continuation of this tax will afford. Why, then, shall we continue it? The capacities of the distillers are known to the collectors; a tax on their capacities, therefore, cannot give any additional security to the public revenue. As this security is the only argument in favor of the continuation of the tax upon the capacity of the still, and as it must be evident that it can answer no valuable purpose, I trust it will be abandoned. Make it necessary, if any new distilleries should be erected, for the proprietor to enter the capacity of his stills with the collector under a heavy penalty.

This tax upon the capacity of the still operates the most unequally; it depresses the smaller establishments to the advantage of the larger ones. Although there is a provision in this bill somewhat favorable to the proprietor of a single still not exceeding one hundred gallons, it will be found of very little advantage. A gentleman from Pennsylvania, (Mr. INGHAM,) the other day, attempted to obviate this objection of inequality, by observing that the smaller stills manufacture much more in proportion than the larger ones. If the gentleman be correct, I am utterly at a loss to assign a reason why all large establishments prefer the largest stills. But if the gentleman be in part correct, when we advert to the increased price of license for a shorter term, we will find the advantage is greatly with the large establishments, who obtain licenses for the longest term. In the price of license, if my recollection serve me, there is a difference of more than one hundred per cent. between the longest and shortest terms. Those who own small establishments, from necessity, often obtain their license for the shortest term; they have not materials, nor can they obtain them, to justify their taking license for a longer period.

There is another objection against the tax on the capacity of the still, that is well worthy of consideration. When a license is obtained, al-

though by sickness, or a thousand contingencies, the individual may be prevented from occupying his establishment, the accident of fire, I believe, is the solitary exception which excuses him from the full payment of his bond; nor can he obtain relief by an extension of his license.

We are informed that, under the administration of Mr. Adams, the excise was odious, and that it was found necessary to change the tax from the product to the capacity of the still. Sir, it will be recollected, that the circumstances under which that tax was first imposed were extremely objectionable; the mode of its collection was still more obnoxious. When the tax was on the quantity distilled, the people were dissatisfied. When it was changed to the capacity of the still, their objections were not removed. They did not believe the situation of the country demanded the tax. But the argument, if it prove anything, proves too much; it would require us to lay the whole tax upon the capacity; this has been rejected by a large majority of this House. It appears to me, a tax upon the capacity of the still, and on the product, will subject us to the inconveniences of both systems, without any beneficial consequence resulting therefrom. I would again beg leave to repeat, that nothing is further from me than a wish to retrench, by my motion, the public revenue. I am altogether willing and anxious to obtain the utmost cent that can be obtained from this source. I believe domestic spirits is a proper object of taxation; but believing, as I do, that a more moderate addition to the present tax on the capacity would yield to the public Treasury a much larger sum; and having well-grounded apprehensions, from the operation of the present tax, that the proposed increase will rather lessen than advance the revenue in the Western country, I should act a most inconsistent part if I were not to favor a reduction of the tax. I have no fears that this or any other tax will meet with resistance in the Western country. However enormous the tax, the people of the West will submit in silence. They will find it ruinous to continue the distillation of domestic spirits; they will therefore permit their establishments to remain unoccupied without a murmur or complaint. They are sensible that the present crisis is eventful to their country; they believe sacrifices from the people are necessary; they are prepared to make them. Of this they have given evidence that is not equivocal.

Believing that it would conduce to the interest of the Government and the people to reduce the proposed tax, I cannot but hope that the motion I have submitted may obtain.

Before the bill was gone through, the House adjourned.

SATURDAY, November 26.

TAX ON DISTILLED LIQUORS, &c.

The House again resolved itself into a Committee of the Whole on the tax bills; and, after further discussion thereof, rose and reported the amendments they had made to the bill "to provide additional revenues for defraying the expenses of Government, and maintaining the public credit, by duties on spirits distilled within the United States, and by amending the act laying duties on licenses to distillers of spirituous liquors;" which amendments the House immediately proceeded to take into consideration.

Several of the amendments were agreed to without debate. Other questions of amendment were debated; among which were the following:

An amendment was made in Committee of the Whole to strike out twenty cents, the amount of duty to be paid on each gallon of spirits distilled, and insert fifteen. The question on concurring in this amendment was decided in the negative—yeas 72, nays 78, as follows:

YEAS—Messrs. Alexander, Anderson, Bard, Bayly of Virginia, Bines, Bowen, Brown, Burwell, Caldwell, Calhoun, Cannon, Clark, Clopton, Conard, Creighton, Culpeper, Cuthbert, Davis of Pennsylvania, Desha, Duvall, Earle, Eppes, Farrow, Findley, Forney, Franklin, Gholson, Glasgow, Goodwyn, Griffin, Hall, Harris, Hasbrouck, Hopkins of Kentucky, Hubbard, Humphreys, Hungerford, Ingham, Irwin, Johnson of Virginia, Johnson of Kentucky, Kent of Maryland, Kerr, Kershaw, Kilbourn, Lyle, Macon, McCoy, McKee, McLean, Newton, Ormsby, Pearson, Pickens, Piper, Pleasants, Rea of Pennsylvania, Rhea of Tennessee, Reane, Sevier, Sharp, Sheffey, Skinner, Smith of Pennsylvania, Smith of Virginia, Stanford, Tannehill, Thompson, Udree, White, Wilson of Pennsylvania, and Yancey.

NAYS—Messrs. Barnett, Baylies of Massachusetts, Bigelow, Boyd, Bradbury, Bradley, Brigham, Butler, Champion, Chappell, Cilley, Comstock, Condict, Cooper, Cox, Dana, Davenport, Davis of Massachusetts, Denoyelles, Ely, Fisk of Vermont, Fisk of New York, Forsyth, Gaston, Grosvenor, Hale, Hanson, Hawes, Hulbert, Ingersoll, Irving, Jackson of Rhode Island, Kennedy, Kent of New York, King of Massachusetts, King of North Carolina, Law, Lefferts, Lewis, Lovett, Lowndes, Markell, McKim, Miller, Moore, Moseley, Murfree, Nelson, Oakley, Parker, Pickering, Pitkin, Potter, John Reed, William Reed, Rich, Robertson, Ruggles, Sage, Seybert, Shipherd, Stockton, Strong, Sturges, Taggart, Tallmadge, Taylor, Telfair, Vose, Ward of Massachusetts, Ward of New Jersey, Webster, Wheaton, Wilcox, Williams, Wilson of Massachusetts, and Winter.

So the House disagreed to the amendment made in Committee.

A motion was made by Mr. WILLIAM REED to amend the bill by adding to it the following new section:

And be it further enacted, That if any of the said spirits (whereupon any of the duties imposed by this act shall have been paid or secured to be paid) shall, after the first day of January next, be exported from the United States to any foreign port or place, there shall be an allowance to the exporters thereof, by way of drawback, equal to the duties thereupon, according to the rates by this act imposed, deducting therefrom half a cent per gallon, and adding to the allowance upon spirits distilled within the United States, from molasses which shall be so exported, *ten cents per gallon as an equivalent for* the duty laid upon molasses; *Provided always*, That the said allowance shall not be made, unless the said exporter or export-

ers shall observe the regulations hereafter prescribed: *And provided further*, That nothing herein contained shall be construed to alter the provisions in any former acts, concerning drawbacks or allowances in nature thereof.

Mr. PICKERING moved to amend the proposed amendment by striking out the words in italic, and inserting in lieu thereof the words "a sum equivalent to."—Negatived.

The question on agreeing to the above proposed new section was decided in the negative. For the amendment 47, against it 99, as follows:

YEAS—Messrs. Baylies of Massachusetts, Bayly of Virginia, Bigelow, Bradbury, Brigham, Champion, Cooper, Culpeper, Davenport, Davis of Massachusetts, Ely, Farrow, Gaston, Geddes, Grosvenor, Hale, Hanson, Hungerford, Jackson of Rhode Island, Kent of New York, King of Massachusetts, Law, Lewis, Lovett, Macon, Markell, Miller, Moseley, Pearson, Pickering, Pitkin, Potter, John Reed, William Reed, Ruggles, Sheffey, Stanford, Stockton, Sturges, Taggart, Thompson, Vose, Ward of Massachusetts, Webster, White, Wilcox, and Wilson of Massachusetts.

NAYS—Messrs. Alexander, Alston, Anderson, Avery, Barbour, Bard, Barnett, Bines, Bowen, Bradley, Brown, Burwell, Butler, Caldwell, Calhoun, Cannon, Chappell, Clark, Clopton, Comstock, Condict, Conard, Creighton, Cuthbert, Dana, Davis of Pennsylvania, Denoyelles, Desha, Duvall, Earle, Eppes, Findley, Fisk of Vermont, Fisk of New York, Forney, Franklin, Gholson, Glasgow, Goodwyn, Gourdin, Griffin, Hall, Harris, Hasbrouck, Hawes, Hubbard, Humphreys, Hulbert, Ingersoll, Ingham, Irving, Irwin, Johnson of Virginia, Johnson of Kentucky, Kennedy, Kent of Maryland Kerr, Kershaw, Kilbourn, King of North Carolina, Lefferts, Lowndes, Lyle, McCoy, McKee, McKim, McLean, Moore, Murfree, Nelson, Newton, Ormsby, Parker, Pickens, Piper, Pleasants, Rea of Pennsylvania, Rhea of Tennessee, Rich, Roane, Robertson, Sage, Seybert, Sharp, Shipherd, Skinner, Smith of Pennsylvania, Smith of Virginia, Strong, Tannehill, Taylor, Telfair, Troup, Udree, Ward of New Jersey, Williams, Wilson of Pennsylvania, Winter, and Yancey.

The bill was then further amended.

Mr. PICKERING moved to amend that part of the 25th section of the bill which pledges Congress to substitute other duties equally productive, if it shall be deemed expedient to alter, reduce, or modify these, &c., by striking out the words "other duties," and in lieu thereof inserting "*other internal duties or taxes.*"

This motion was negatived. For the amendment 27, against it 107, as follows:

YEAS—Messrs. Bayly of Virginia, Bigelow, Bradbury, Champion, Cilley, Cooper, Cox, Davenport, Geddes, Grosvenor, Hale, Ingersoll, Kent of New York, Law, Lovett, Markell, Moseley, Pickering, Pitkin, Ruggles, Shipherd, Sturges, Thompson, Vose, Ward of Massachusetts, Wilson of Massachusetts, and Winter.

NAYS—Messrs. Alexander, Alston, Anderson, Avery, Barbour, Barnett, Bines, Bowen, Bradley, Brown, Burwell, Butler, Caldwell, Calhoun, Cannon, Chappell, Clark, Clopton, Comstock, Condict, Conard, Creighton, Culpeper, Cuthbert, Dana, Davis of Pennsylvania, Denoyelles, Desha, Duvall, Earle, Eppes, Farrow, Findley, Fisk of Vermont, Fisk of New York, Forney, Franklin, Gaston, Gholson, Goodwyn, Griffin,

Hall, Harris, Hasbrouck, Hawes, Hopkins of Kentucky, Hubbard, Humphreys, Hungerford, Hulbert, Ingham, Irving, Irwin, Jackson of Rhode Island, Johnson of Virginia, Johnson of Kentucky, Kennedy, Kent of Maryland, Kerr, Kershaw, Kilbourn, King of Massachusetts, King of North Carolina, Lefferts, Lowndes, Lyle, Macon, McCoy, McKee, McKim, McLean, Moore, Murfree, Nelson, Newton, Ormsby, Parker, Pickens, Piper, Pleasants, Potter, William Reed, Rea of Pennsylvania, Rhea of Tennessee, Rich, Roane, Robertson, Sage, Seybert, Sharp, Sheffey, Skinner, Smith of Pennsylvania, Smith of Virginia, Stanford, Stockton, Tannehill, Taylor, Telfair, Udree, Ward of New Jersey, White, Wilcox, Williams, Wilson of Pennsylvania, and Yancey.

The same section begins thus: " That towards establishing an adequate revenue *to provide for the payment of the expenses of Government,* for the punctual payment of the public debt," &c., (pledging the duties laid by this act, for these purposes.)

Mr. Pitkin moved to amend this section by striking out the words above stated in italic. For the motion 28, against it 80.

Mr. Culpeper then moved to amend the bill by striking out *twenty cents,* (the amount of duty on each gallon of spirits distilled,) and inserting in lieu thereof *twelve and a half cents.* Which motion also was negatived by the following vote: For the motion 41, against it 81. The bill was then ordered to be engrossed for a third reading.

Monday, November 28.

BANK OF THE UNITED STATES.

Mr. Lowndes, of South Carolina, from the select committee to whom was committed the bill to incorporate the subscribers to the Bank of the United States of America, reported, that the committee had had said bill under consideration, but not having been able to discover any means of uniting the conflicting opinions on the subject, had therefore directed him to report the bill without amendment. Mr. L. also laid before the House a letter obtained from the Secretary of the Treasury by the committee, on the subject of the amendments made to the bank bill.

The letter is as follows:

Washington, *November* 27, 1814.

Sir: The committee of the House of Representatives, to which the bank bill was recommitted on Friday last, have directed me to request you to communicate your opinion, in relation to the effect which a considerable issue of Treasury notes, (to which should be attached the quality of being receivable in subscriptions to the bank) might have upon the credit, and particularly upon the prospects of a loan for 1815. As the bill, as it was referred to the committee, provides for the subscription of forty-four millions of Treasury notes, to form, with six millions of specie, the capital of the bank; any information which you may think proper to give, either in relation to the practicability of getting them into circulation without depreciation, or in regard to their operation on any part of our fiscal system afterwards, will be very acceptable. I am, sir, &c.,
WILLIAM LOWNDES.

Hon. Secretary of the Treasury.

Treasury Department, *Nov.* 27, 1814.

Sir: I have the honor to acknowledge the receipt of your letter, requesting, for a committee of the House of Representatives, an opinion upon the following inquiries:

1. The effect which a considerable issue of Treasury notes, with the quality of being receivable in subscriptions to a National Bank, will have upon the credit of the Government; and, particularly, upon the prospects of a loan for 1815.

2. The practicability of getting forty-four millions of Treasury notes, forming, with six millions of specie, the capital for a National Bank, into circulation, without depreciation.

The inquiries of the committee cannot be satisfactorily answered, in the abstract, but must be considered in connexion with the state of our finances, and the state of the public credit.

When I arrived at Washington, the Treasury was suffering under every kind of embarrassment. The demands upon it were great in amount; while the means to satisfy them were comparatively small, precarious in the collection, and difficult in the application. The demands consisted of dividends upon old and new funded debt, of Treasury notes, and of Legislative appropriations for the Army, the Navy, and the current service; all urgent, and important. The means consisted, first, of the fragment of an authority to borrow money, when nobody was disposed to lend, and to issue Treasury notes, which none but necessitous creditors, or contractors, in distress, or commissaries, quartermasters, and navy agents, acting, as it were officially, seemed willing to accept: 2d. Of the amount of bank credits, scattered throughout the United States, and principally in the Southern and Western banks, which had been rendered, in a great degree, useless, by the stoppage of payments in specie, and the consequent impracticability of transferring the public funds from one place, to meet the public engagements in another place: 3d. Of the current supply of money from the import, from internal duties, and from the sales of public land; which ceased to be a foundation of any rational estimate, or reserve, to provide even for the dividends on the funded debt, when it was found that the Treasury notes, (only requiring, indeed, a cash payment at the distance of a year) to whomsoever they were issued at the Treasury, and almost as soon as they were issued, reached the hands of the collectors, in payment of debts, duties, and taxes; thus disappointing and defeating the only remaining expectations of productive revenue.

Under those circumstances, (which I had the honor to communicate to the Committee of Ways and Means,) it became the duty of this Department, to endeavor to remove the immediate pressure from the Treasury; to endeavor to restore the public credit; and to endeavor to provide for the expenses of the ensuing year. The only measures that occurred to my mind, for the accomplishment of such an important object, have been presented to the view of Congress. The act, authorizing the receipt of Treasury notes in payment of subscriptions to a public loan, was passed, I fear, too late to answer the purpose for which it was designed. It promises, at this time, little relief, either as an instrument to raise money, or to absorb the claims for the Treasury notes, which are daily becoming due. From this cause, and other obvious causes, the dividend on the funded debt has not been punctually paid; a large amount of Treasury notes has already been dishonored; and the hope of preventing further injury and reproach, in transacting business with the Treasury, is too visionary to afford a moment's consolation.

The actual condition of the Treasury, thus described, will serve to indicate the state of the public credit. Public credit depends, essentially, upon public opinion. The usual test of public credit is, indeed, the value of public debt. The faculty of borrowing money is not a test of public credit; for a faithless Government, like a desperate individual, has only to increase the premium, according to the exigency, in order to secure a loan. Thus, public opinion, manifested in every form and in every direction, hardly permits us, at the present juncture, to speak of the existence of public credit; and yet, it is not impossible that the Government, in the resources of its patronage and its pledges, might find the means of tempting the rich and the avaricious to supply its immediate wants. If it is now a charter of incorporation, it may then be a grant of land; but, after all, immeasurable tracts of the western wild would be exhausted in successive efforts to obtain pecuniary aids, and still leave the Government necessitous, unless the foundations of public credit were reestablished, and maintained. In the measures, therefore, which it has been my duty to suggest, I have endeavored to introduce a permanent plan for reviving the public credit; of which the facility of borrowing money, in anticipation of settled and productive revenues, is only an incident, although it is an incident as durable as the plan itself. The outline seemed to embrace whatever was requisite, to leave no doubt upon the power and the disposition of Government, in relation to its pecuniary engagements, to diminish, and not to augment the amount of public debts, in the hands of individuals, and to create general confidence, rather by the manner of treating the claims of the present class of creditors, than by the manner of conciliating the favor of a new class.

With these explanatory remarks, sir, I proceed to answer, specifically, the questions which you have proposed:

1. I am of opinion, that considerable issues of Treasury notes, with the quality of being receivable in subscriptions to a National Bank, will have an injurious effect upon the credit of the Government; and, also, upon the prospects of a loan for 1815.

Because, it will confer, gratuitously, an advantage upon a class of new creditors, over the present creditors, of the Government, standing on a footing of at least equal merit.

Because, it will excite general dissatisfaction among the present holders of the public debt; and, generally, distrust among the capitalists, who are accustomed to advance their money to the Government.

Because, a quality of subscribing to the National Bank, attached to Treasury notes, exclusively, will tend to depreciate the value of all public debt, not possessing that quality; and whatever depreciates the value of the public debt in this way, must necessarily impair the public credit.

Because, the specie capital of the citizens of the United States, so far as it may be deemed applicable to investments in the public stocks, has already, in a great measure, been so vested; the holders of the present debt will be unable to become subscribers to the bank, (if that object should, eventually, prove desirable,) without selling their stock at a depreciated rate, in order to procure the whole amount of their subscriptions in Treasury notes; and a general depression in the value of the public debt will inevitably ensue.

Because, the very proposition of making a considerable issue of Treasury notes, even with the quality of being subscribed to a National Bank, can only be regarded as an experiment, on which it seems dangerous to rely; the Treasury notes must be purchased at par, with money; a new set of creditors are to be created; it may, or it may not, be deemed an object of speculation, by the money holders, to subscribe to the bank; the result of the experiment cannot be ascertained, until it will be too late to provide a remedy, in the case of failure; while the credit of the Government will be affected by every circumstance which keeps the efficacy of its fiscal operations in suspense or doubt.

Because, the prospect of a loan, for the year 1815, without the aid of a bank, is faint and unpromising; except, perhaps, so far as the pledge of a specific tax may succeed; and then, it must be recollected, that a considerable supply of money will be required for the war, beyond the whole amount of the taxes to be levied.

Because, if the loan for the year 1815 be made to depend upon the issue of Treasury notes, subscribable to the National Bank, it will probably fail, for the reasons which have already been suggested; and, if the loan be independent of that operation, a considerable issue of Treasury notes, for the purpose of creating a bank capital, must, it is believed, deprive the Government of every chance of raising money in any other manner.

2. I am of opinion, that it will be extremely difficult, if not impracticable, to get forty-four millions of Treasury notes (forming, with six millions of specie, the capital of a National Bank) into circulation, with or without depreciation.

Because, if the subscription to the bank becomes an object of speculation, the Treasury notes will probably be purchased at the Treasury, and at the loan offices, and never pass into circulation at all.

Because, whatever portion of the Treasury notes might pass into circulation, would be speedily withdrawn, by the speculators in the subscription to the bank, after arts had been employed to depreciate their value.

Because, it is not believed, that, in the present state of the public credit, forty-four millions of Treasury notes, can be sent into circulation. The only difference between the Treasury notes now issued, and dishonored, and those proposed to be issued, consists in the subscribable quality; but reasons have already been assigned for an opinion, that this difference does not afford such confidence in the experiment, as seems requisite to justify a reliance upon it, for accomplishing some of the most interesting objects of the Government.

I must beg you, sir, to pardon the haste with which I have written these general answers to your inquiries. But, knowing the importance of time, and feeling a desire to avoid every appearance of contributing to the loss of a moment, I have chosen rather to rest upon the intelligence and candor of the committee, than to enter upon a more labored investigation of the subject referred to. I have the honor, &c.,

            A. J. DALLAS.

WILLIAM LOWNDES, Esq.

A motion was made by Mr. HANSON to print

the letter; which motion being objected to, was declared not to be in order at this time.

The House proceeded to the consideration of the bill.

The question depending when the bill was referred to a select committee, now recurred. It was on a motion of Mr. GASTON to strike out fifty millions, (the proposed capital of the bank,) and insert twenty.

This motion was immediately decided without debate—for the motion 54, against it 85, as follows:

YEAS—Messrs. Baylies of Massachusetts, Bigelow, Boyd, Bradbury, Brigham, Cilley, Cox, Culpeper, Davenport, Ely, Farrow, Gaston, Geddes, Gholson, Goodwyn, Gourdin, Grosvenor, Hale, Hanson, Hungerford, Hulbert, Kennedy, Kent of New York, King of Massachusetts, Law, Lewis, Lovett, Markell, McKee, Miller, Moseley, Oakley, Pearson, Pickering, Pitkin, Potter, John Reed, William Reed, Ruggles, Schureman, Seybert, Shaffey, Stanford, Stockton, Sturges, Taggart, Thompson, Vose, Webster, Wheaton, White, Wilcox, Wilson of Massachusetts, and Winter.

NAYS—Messrs. Alexander, Alston, Anderson, Avery, Barbour, Bard, Barnett, Bines, Bowen, Brown, Burwell, Butler, Caldwell, Calhoun, Cannon, Chappell, Clark, Clopton, Comstock, Condict, Conard, Crawford, Creighton, Crouch, Cuthbert, Dana, Davis of Pennsylvania, Demoyelles, Desha, Earle, Eppes, Evans, Findley, Fisk of Vermont, Fisk of New York, Forney, Forsyth, Franklin, Griffin, Hall, Harris, Hasbrouck, Hawes, Hopkins of Kentucky, Hubbard, Humphreys, Ingersoll, Ingham, Irving, Johnson of Virginia, Kershaw, Kilbourn, King of North Carolina, Lefferts, Lowndes, Lyle, McCoy, McLean, Moore, Murfree, Newton, Pickens, Piper, Pleasants, Rea of Pennsylvania, Rhea of Tennessee, Rich, Roane, Robertson, Sage, Sevier, Sharp, Shipherd, Skinner, Smith of Pennsylvania, Smith of Virginia, Strong, Tannehill, Telfair, Troup, Udree, Ward of New Jersey, Williams, Wilson of Pennsylvania, and Yancey.

Mr. LOWNDES then moved to amend the bill by striking out fifty and inserting thirty millions, which question was decided without debate. For the motion 77, against it 66, as follows:

YEAS—Messrs. Alexander, Barbour, Bard, Baylies of Massachusetts, Boyd, Bradbury, Brigham, Burwell, Cannon, Cilley, Cox, Culpeper, Cuthbert, Davenport, Davis of Massachusetts, Desha, Earle, Ely, Evans, Farrow, Fisk of Vermont, Gaston, Geddes, Gholson, Goodwyn, Gourdin, Hale, Hanson, Hungerford, Hulbert, Irving, Johnson of Virginia, Kennedy, Kent of New York, Kershaw, King of Massachusetts, Law, Lewis, Lovett, Lowndes, Macon, Markell, McKee, McKim, Miller, Moseley, Newton, Oakley, Pearson, Pickering, Piper, Pitkin, Pleasants, Potter, John Reed, William Reed, Rich, Robertson, Ruggles, Schureman, Seybert, Shaffey, Skinner, Stanford, Stockton, Sturges, Taggart, Thompson, Vose, Ward of Massachusetts, Ward of New Jersey, Webster, Wheaton, White, Wilcox, Wilson of Massachusetts, and Winter.

NAYS—Messrs. Alston, Anderson, Avery, Barnett, Bines, Bowen, Brown, Butler, Calhoun, Chappell, Clark, Clopton, Comstock, Condict, Conard, Crawford, Creighton, Crouch, Dana, Davis of Pennsylvania, Demoyelles, Eppes, Findley, Fisk of New York, Forney, Franklin, Griffin, Grosvenor, Hall, Harris, Hasbrouck, Hawes, Hopkins of Kentucky, Hubbard, Humphreys,

Ingersoll, Ingham, Kerr, Kilbourn, King of North Carolina, Lefferts, Lyle, McCoy, McLean, Moore, Murfree, Parker, Pickens, Rea of Pennsylvania, Rhea of Tennessee, Roane, Sage, Sevier, Sharp, Shipherd, Smith of Pennsylvania, Smith of Virginia, Strong, Tannehill, Taylor, Telfair, Troup, Udree, Williams, Wilson of Pennsylvania, and Yancey.

So the House determined to reduce the capital of the bank to thirty millions.

Mr. LOWNDES then suggested several amendments, to make other parts of the bill correspondent with the amendment just made; which were agreed to.

Mr. EASTON then moved an amendment to the bill, and spoke some time in support of it, the object of which was, to require the directors of the bank, at any time when one hundred thousand dollars should be subscribed and paid in, or held, by citizens of Missouri Territory, and when the same shall be required by three-fourths of such stockholders, to establish an office of discount and deposite at St. Louis in the Missouri Territory.

This motion was supported also in a cogent manner by Mr. McKEE, of Kentucky.

It was however negatived, 27 only rising in favor of it.

Mr. HANSON, of Maryland, then moved to strike out the first section of the bill.

Mr. H. said, he was not less alive to the critical and awful condition of the country, than the Secretary of the Treasury, whose letter had been just read by the Clerk. The picture he had painted of our financial affairs was not more frightful than the reality. In some features it fell short of the original. Not only had Government bills been dishonored, and the interest of the public debt remained unpaid, as stated by the Secretary of the Treasury, but facts were within the knowledge of Mr. H. still more disreputable and degrading to the Administration. So completely empty was the Treasury, and destitute of credit, that funds could not be obtained to defray the current ordinary expenses of the different Departments. Disgraceful, humiliating as the fact was, it ought not to be concealed from the nation, and he felt it his duty to state to the House, that the Department of State was so bare of money as to be unable to pay even its stationery bill. The Government was subsisting upon the drawings of unbartered banks in the District, who felt themselves compelled to contribute their means, lest the rod, in terrorem, which was held over them, should be applied, and an act of incorporation refused. Yes, it was well known to the citizens of the District, that the Treasury was obliged to borrow pitiful sums, which it would disgrace a merchant in tolerable credit to ask for.

Mr. H. mentioned the instance of an acceptance of $3,500, which the War Department was unable to pay, and persuaded a bank in Georgetown to pay for them. He mentioned several acceptances, which he himself had seen, for large amounts, which had been protested by the public notary. The Paymaster was unable to meet demands for paltry amounts—not even for $30, which was a well established fact. He spoke also of the failure to meet the public engagements at New York and Philadelphia. He said he was apprized, several days in advance, of the explosion which happened in the latter place, and had attempted to take the floor several days past, to prepare the House for the event, but he had not been so fortunate as to catch the Speaker's eye. In short, it was difficult to conceive a situation more critical and perilous, than that of the Government at this moment, without money, without credit, and destitute of the means of defending the country.

Under such circumstances, I agree, said Mr. H., with the Secretary of the Treasury, that not a moment should be lost in exerting the Constitutional power of Congress to its utmost energy, to check, or turn aside this evil current of events, which threatens to overwhelm the nation. Not a moment was to be lost in preventing, if possible, further mischief, and in repairing what was already done. But if an opinion was to be formed of the future, from the past proceedings of the House, there was little ground for hope. Congress was in the third month of its session; it had been convened under circumstances appealing to whatever of spirit and patriotism there was in the country, addressing themselves with peculiar force to the authors of our calamities—the party in power. What had been done towards discharging the interesting and sacred trust reposed in the representatives of the people—the guardians of the national honor and safety? The House was daily involved in useless wrangling debates, which from all appearance were likely to result in nothing but words, and abortive attempts at action. While the doctors are disputing, said Mr. H., about the medicines to be administered, the patient is rapidly approaching to its last breath. It cannot be said of me, sir, that I have thrown obstructions in the way of the ruling party. So far from it, I have abstained purposely from taking part in many interesting debates, in the hope that action would be substituted for words, and from an unwillingness to consume time, every moment of which I deemed precious to the country. Such is my ardent desire to economise time, as far as is consistent with intelligent legislation, that I would not now claim the attention of the House, but that my patience is exhausted. I have waited, and in vain, to see this pernicious measure consigned to the fate which evidently awaits it, and to see some other feasible plan, which the discretion and good sense of the House can sanction, introduced in its place. I can remain silent no longer. Its palpable deformity, its utter inadequacy to the ends proposed, and its destructive tendency, seem to be apparent to a large majority of the House, who are impatient to despatch it. A scheme so absurd and visionary, could have been looked for from no other quarter than that which produced it; and I am glad to see that gentlemen on the other side of the House have at last collected the courage, and manifested their determination to pursue what they call an *ignis fatuus* (Mr. CALHOUN) no further. An *ignis*

fatuus, truly, sir, and which, like other jack-o'-lanterns, engendered in the fens of party, will play about the surface of those stagnated pools until it sinks, and is extinguished. It was this same bold and false prophet who led us into Canada, to conquer free trade and sailors' rights; and such is the sanguine nature of the late chairman of the Committee of Foreign Relations, that I have not a doubt, even now, he would contract, if he could find security for the forfeiture, to capture, in six weeks, more or less, the whole British army, and deliver them, bound hand and foot, at the Capitol.

The SPEAKER called to order, conceiving the remarks to be personal.

Mr. HANSON said, that hitherto he had with pleasure paid the most scrupulous regard to the judgment of the Chair, and bowed cheerfully to its decisions, but on this occasion he must be allowed to suggest that the latitude usually indulged in such discussions was favorable to the course now taken in debate. Besides, the honorable Speaker would recollect, upon this very question, the liberty contended for had been enjoyed by the other side of the House in a degree and mode not now proposed to be transcended.

The SPEAKER said his anxiety to exclude every thing like personality from debate, and a conviction that the rule of the House supported his opinion, were sufficient reasons for his adhering to his decision. And it was due to the gentleman from Maryland to say, that he had always paid that respect to the Chair, which was so necessary in supporting its dignity, and that of the House.

Mr. HANSON acquiesced. He knew of nothing more visionary than the idea of the gentleman from South Carolina, that, in the present depreciated state of the public credit and finances, the enormous sum of forty-four millions of Treasury notes could be put in circulation. A scheme of a paper medium so stupendous, at a time so critical, destroyed every hope of extricating the country. If sanctioned by the House, so far from relieving the nation, it would plunge it into still deeper difficulties. He looked with horror and dismay at the project, and was most of all astonished that the House treated it with the respect of entertaining it one day in debate.

Sir, said Mr. H., my opposition to this gigantic, rickety, deformed project, cannot be ascribed to a sinister design to embarrass the Government, and prevent the relief necessary to be afforded, and speedily to be afforded, to its finances. I know, sir, the country cannot be defended, it will be out of the power of the Government to save it, if they are so disposed, unless the Treasury is relieved. My opposition to the bill proceeds from my extreme anxiety, to place it in the power of those who direct the Government, to defend and save the country. I will permit no man in this nation to take precedence of me, in straining every nerve, and stretching the Constitution to the utmost limit of liberal interpretation, to impart the power requisite to defend the country, and maintain its rights of sovereignty and soil;

but I will embark in no rash and desperate measures, which will put everything at hazard, and entail unnumbered woes upon posterity. "Desperate situations produce desperate councils and desperate measures!" But it is in such times that men of virtue, reflection, and wisdom, are especially called on to look with dispassionate calmness on the state of affairs, and to oppose with firmness all expedients which are calculated to increase, instead of diminishing the evils to be remedied. At a period like the present, when "men are as much blinded by the extremes of misery," as, in times past, they have been intoxicated with the extreme of prosperity, the corrective of sober judgment and wholesome inquiry is more necessary to prevent irremediable mischief than to guard against probable reverses. It has been said that "great distress never has hitherto taught, and, while the world lasts, never will teach lessons of wisdom to mankind." But, if wisdom in our councils cannot be assured by past calamities, we may at least avoid a pitfall which is visible to the dullest vision.

I say again, and again, sir, my undisguised, avowed object is, to defend the country, and, if it be not too late, under Providence, to preserve it by prompt, and wise, and vigorous Constitutional measures. I am not ignorant that the first and indispensable step towards defending the country, is the recovery of public credit, and the disembarrassment of the finances. But I do fear, without a united effort in this House and throughout this nation to restore confidence in the Treasury, every attempt to reinstate the finances will prove abortive. I entertain the opinion, formed after much reflection and a free interchange of sentiment with enlightened men, that, unless a general and generous effort is made by all parties to revive the expiring credit of the Treasury, it will continue to languish, daily to depreciate, until I would say the credit of Jacob Barker himself, if it were not attaching more importance to him than he merits, will be high, compared with that of the Government, in the money market. Under this strong conviction, and knowing, as every man in the nation must know, that the country cannot be defended without the ways and means, and, as far as depends on me, being resolved at every hazard and extremity consistently with civil liberty and the Constitution, to preserve, unimpaired, the rights and honor of the nation, I therefore shall co-operate in all measures to defend the country. This can only be done by reproducing and bracing the main sinew of war—money, public credit—without which, the nation will be delivered up, bound hand and foot, to the enemy, unless rescued by the energy of the respective State sovereignties. When things come to the worst, the States can and will defend themselves, I have no doubt; but my object is to defend the country under the Constitution, and to prevent a dissolution of the Union, which is inevitable, if the means are not provided to enable the General Government to defend the States. If the means are supplied, and they are still misapplied and wasted in fruitless attempts at conquest, the States must, of necessity, take their defence into their own hands. But the condition of the country is so critical, I see no choice but to take the chance of a correct application of means to be placed at the disposal of the Government. The charge never shall be brought against me, that I folded my arms and looked on an indifferent spectator, while the country was sinking. The men in power shall never be able to throw upon me any portion of the blame of not extricating the country from the difficulties into which their incompetency and folly have plunged it. It will be demanded of them to return the Government pure and undefiled, as they received it. Degrading terms of peace I will never agree to; and if our rights and honor are to be sacrificed, they shall never have it to say they were so sacrificed, because I, as one of the minority, withheld from them the means of preserving them. No; they shall have the means, as far as I can give them. I will bear my portion of the odium of their measures for defence, where they do not trench upon the Constitution. When they do so trench; when their measures go to prostrate civil liberty, and overthrow the Constitution, I will resist them, and recommend resistance to the people. I will draw the sword to put down and punish usurpation and tyranny at home, with the same alacrity that I would rush to the water's edge, to repel the invading foe. I now fear nothing from usurpation, because we are now free and able to resist it successfully. The attempt will prove that both the physical and numerical strength of the country lies where it ought to lie, because it will never be exerted except in defence of the country and the liberties of the people. Subjugation by a foreign Power can hardly be deemed an evil, compared with domestic despotism and slavery. The foreign yoke may be broken and thrown off, but the chains rivetted upon a people by their own tyrants, are difficult to be loosened and destroyed. It will be unavailing, and worse than unavailing, to put the country in a posture to meet the enemy without, if a more dangerous enemy within is permitted quietly, and at his leisure, to reduce this people to a state of ignominious bondage.

In coming to the determination to grant the supplies asked for to defend the country, I maintain I am neither inconsistent with myself, faithless to my friends, nor false to my country. The highest temporal obligations, according to my moral sense, and the soundest policy, according to my judgment, approve the course I have marked out for myself. The reason is obvious why I shall abstain from a particular discussion of the points of difference between me and some of my political friends. Either being wrong, I know it is for me to wait the award of an enlightened and virtuous community, having no other palliation to offer, than that, if I have erred, it is my firm conviction I have erred on the side of the best interests of my country. We, no doubt, aim at the same goal, but choose different routes to arrive at it. I am perfectly sure that we all prefer our country to ourselves, its good to our own gratification. That my political friends, in common with me, have a single eye to the safety and lasting happiness of the nation, cannot be doubted. We are alike anxious, and resolved, if possible, though we may differ in some respects about the means, to save the country. When I say country, I, of course, do not mean those fell destroyers of its rights, peace, safety, and honor, whose misdeeds have brought upon the people the suffering under which they smart, the burdens which force from them deep groans which are heard throughout the land. No man feels a more thorough sovereign contempt for the wicked authors of our afflictions than I do; and if it is said, in contributing to the relief and salvation of the country, I incidentally relieve them, I justify, by replying, even such men must be relieved in preference to certain national bankruptcy, and the overthrow of the freest form of Government known on the globe. Let the tempest-beaten vessel of State be first brought into port, I will then join gentlemen in throwing the treacherous pilot overboard. Now is not the time to put all at hazard by rash and untried acts of violence. The ship is sinking, I will give a hand to the pump. The temple is in flames, I will hand a bucket.

Such is the perilous situation of the country, visible to every eye, and plain to every understanding, that unless a combined effort is made to rescue us from the dangers which are seen on all sides, I do fear our case is desperate, our ruin irretrievable, that we are lost irrecoverably. But, sir, while there is yet life there is still hope. I will not, must not, *dare* not, abandon the country. If deserted by its true friends now, it will sink so low, that it cannot hereafter, under the guidance of other councils, be re-elevated to that pinnacle of honor, dignity, and glory, from which it has been dashed by heartless and corrupt men in their despicable contests for personal aggrandizement. If the country, two years hence, is to be governed by wiser and abler men, I see no reason to conceal the opinion that the sooner a good and sufficient system of revenue and a well regulated bank are organized the better. They will be necessary instruments for those who may succeed the authors of the burdens, which must constitute the basis of a system imparting efficiency and ability to the national finances. If we can save the vessel of State from being wholly wrecked, the easier it will be to repair and rig her out again. But most certain it is, if our affairs are suffered to go on in their present downward course, a few months hence, I might point to the naked, crumbling columns of your Capitol as a type or symbol of the Government.

Let, then, a united effort be made to save the country. But, at the same time, be it understood that we are not to withdraw our opposition to those unconstitutional measures, and that pernicious policy of Government, which are adopted with no other view than that the party in power may be more firmly seated in power, and the better enabled to persevere in their mischievous career. This we cannot do, without abandoning

our most sacred duties, without a base dereliction of those well tried principles which have stood every test and passed through every ordeal for a long series of years. No, sir, we cannot be expected to add fuel to the flame by which we ourselves are consumed; to feed the fever which is raging in our veins; to become the architects of our own ruin; to assist in forging chains for posterity, if not for ourselves.

I confess, sir, I have the less difficulty in voting supplies, and uniting to recover public credit, since the disclosures made to the House by the President in relation to the discussions at Ghent. Anterior to that communication, the resolution had been formed, as far as I might be supposed to be entitled to political consideration, to join in measures for defence. Although I believed the war was unjust and wicked in its origin, yet a state of things had arisen out of the revolution in Europe, the threats of devastation by the enemy, and his increased ability to execute his menaces, which rendered it necessary to unite in objects of defence, and to strengthen the arm of Government for that purpose. Although *declared*, the war is not now *continued* from motives and designs foreign to this people. On the contrary, the Administration has humbled itself, to a degree exciting commiseration, to obtain peace. Without violating "the injunction of secrecy," which locks up from the eye of the people the most interesting part of the despatches, I will advert merely to such parts as are public. I say, then, I have the less difficulty in voting supplies, because the Administration has changed its ground since the revolution in Europe, and come over to my opinion and views of the fair terms of peace. As the contest now stands the question of blockade no longer presents difficulties. That of impressment, ay, of *impressment*, is abandoned by the very authors themselves of the cabalistic words "free trade and sailors' rights!" The Napoleon notion of floating colonies is also discarded, since its author has himself been consigned to a state of colonial dependence, being struck from the list of continental potentates, though he preserves all the forms of royalty in his little kingdom, not so large as the possessions of some of our Southern dons, with their thousands of acres and battalions of blacks. The question of "free ships, free goods," is also put at rest. The right of visit and search is impliedly conceded, and the flag is not to cover the crew. It is not three months, sir, since I myself saw "free trade and sailors' rights," floating in proud defiance on your flag at the battery of the White-House. The mystic words were written on the star spangled banner, which our naval heroes carried into the very British Channel, where it waved in triumph. But, alas! your Hulls, Decaturs, Perrys, and McDonoughs, now know that the President is content to waive the question of sailors' rights, and to give the go-by to that of "the flag's covering the crew." They now know from what sources and what motives proceeded all the delusive, senseless uproar about sailors' rights, by the very men who have struggled in times past to degrade our Navy, and, in their own words, "would have gone further to see it consumed by fire than to extinguish the flames." Yes, sir, these heroes may now ask, for what have we fought glorious battles, achieved brilliant victories, spilt our blood, plucked the brightest gem from the British diadem, when cowardice "had torn down the flag which valor had nailed to the mast."

I may be complained of, sir, for these digressions, but, if we are to trace our difficulties to their source, we must mount higher than to this or that particular error and act of folly, which has characterized the vicious system of politics so long persevered in, to the disgrace and ruin of the country. The root of the evil is not this or that blunder, that or the other piece of deception and mischief, but it is the political system of Administration, not only in relation to the finances, but to the general policy of the Government. It has been tried, fatally tested, and has led, and can lead to nothing but disappointment, suffering, and disgrace. Let it, then, be abandoned at once and for ever, or all efforts to preserve the country will have but a temporary effect, and be productive only of increased difficulties hereafter.

Mr. Speaker, it once was the pride and happiness of the country—and I bring back the recollections of gentlemen to the period, with bitter feelings of regret—to flourish under the benign influence of a political system, which experience proved to be conducive to our fame and welfare. Preferring the people's good to the people's favor, the party now in the minority introduced and faithfully adhered to that system, which raised the nation to an unexampled state of prosperity and happiness. Its results are now matter of history. Unfortunately for the country, it was misunderstood, systematically misrepresented and decried by the demagogues of the day, and finally rejected by a majority of the people. Yes, sir, a false and erroneous understanding of it was imposed upon the minds of the deluded people, and it was discarded, because they knew not its value. Even after we were denied by the people, it continued our chief care—the principal object of our ambition—the sole motive to exertion—to preserve to the country what had been already gained. We betrayed no unwillingness that our successors should reap the glory and benefit of our institutions, provided, only, that they were preserved to the country. When, at the last, the infuriate passion of party, and the unrelenting spirit of persecution, succeeded in overthrowing and sweeping away most of those institutions, we should still have been content, if the great objects for which they were designed—the peace, honor, and safety of the country—could have been preserved. They have all been destroyed, and covered up in the same grave. Gentlemen now feel and acknowledge the loss of one of those noble institutions—the National Bank—and they would recall it, to relieve them from difficulties which cause distress and dismay throughout the land. That cannot be; it is too late; the dead cannot be restored to life. To use the language of the gentleman from South Carolina, (Mr. CALHOUN,)

they who legislate upon party principles must expect their measures to react upon themselves. Did it not involve the dearest interests and safety of the country, I should rejoice that retribution has at last overtaken the men who have inflicted such deep injuries upon us. Suffer, greatly suffer, they must; but, the country!—*we* suffer with them, the innocent and the guilty alike, except the consolation which a good conscience never fails to administer.

Mr. Speaker, when I reflect on what our country once was, and might still have been, and what it now is; when I think of the blessings thrown away, and the miseries induced; my indignation against the cool, remorseless, perverse plotter of our afflictions and perils, is ready to burst forth on this floor in disorderly exclamations. My heart almost overflows with mingled grief and indignation. Daily do I expect the happening of some great event—the coming of some awful public calamity—to be decisive of our fate. A war of wide-spread, cruel desolation, threatened by a powerful and exasperated foe; the Union shaken to its very centre, and tottering to a fall; with a Government bankrupt in fortune and in fame!—and, yet, where are we; what doing; what have we done? Where are we? Look around! seated on a barren heath, amidst ruin; surrounded by the loathsome objects of our dishonor; indebted to the Vandals for the roof that covers us; the Government itself paralyzed—chained down, as it were—by the drowsiness that precedes death! And, yet, gentlemen seem perfectly at their ease—tranquil as the undisturbed moonbeams that play upon the gently-waving billows. They repose in the delusive idea that there is no danger. The sentinel upon the watch-tower has told them "all's well." When the midnight robber has sallied forth from his covert, and prowls about the streets for prey; when the mercenary has clapped his torch, and the city is wrapt in flames; the perfidious watchman, "'twixt sleep and wake," cries from his box, *all's well!*

Sir, at this moment the cold, icy hand of death is on this people. The agony cannot be of long continuance; the crisis must soon be over. And, if we are doomed to fall, as a punishment for our sins as a nation, the day will have come when the blindest party zealot will acknowledge that but one man stood between his country and its salvation. God knows, sir, no one more devoutly and fervently wishes, than I do, that he may be inspired with the wisdom, virtue, and energy, to save the nation. But, all is dark and cheerless. I see no lambent ray of hope gilding the dreary prospect before us. The handwriting on the wall points to our fixed destiny. It is written in characters so glaring and so legible that he who runs may read. When, says the greatest moral philosopher of any age, did distress ever oblige a Prince to abdicate his authority? This bars up every avenue of escape.

Here, perhaps, I ought to stop; but I will not leave the country in so forlorn and desperate a condition. No, sir, I will address myself especially to this body, holding as it does now, with

665   **HISTORY OF CONGRESS.**   666

NOVEMBER, 1814.   *Bank of the United States.*   H. OF R.

the other branch, the destinies of the nation in its hands. Let them act with promptitude and vigor, and, in the language of the Secretary of the Treasury, resolve not to delay another moment in every Constitutional effort to save the country. If they attempt to violate the Constitution, they must sprinkle it with blood—with my blood;—for, I will not outlive the liberties of my country. Under the Constitution, the country can be saved, or let it fall. Consign this bill at once to the fate it merits. Adopt at once measures to revive public credit—to unite the people and fill your armies. *Nec gentium quies sine armis, nec arma sine stipendiis, nec stipendia sine tributis.*

My voice and arm are with you in every just and Constitutional measure for the defence of the country. Energy, wisdom, and virtue, will yet save the Republic. If we have them not; if we cannot bring ourselves, regardless of considerations of popularity, to discharge our sacred trust like men—like patriots; let us take the advice of the honorable member (Mr. FISK:) leave our seats, and render back our powers to the people.

When Mr. HANSON had concluded—

Mr. CALHOUN, of South Carolina, followed, in reply to some points of Mr. HANSON's speech, and in energetic defence of the bill.

[During the speeches of these gentlemen, both of them were called to order more than once by the SPEAKER, who earnestly endeavored to prevent the introduction of personal matter into the debate.]

Mr. GROSVENOR said he laid claim to no particular knowledge of the practical rules of banking. Like other gentlemen, he had studied the works of those who have been acknowledged the great masters of the science of political economy. But as many of their dogmas upon this subject had been refuted, and most of their rules had been exposed to doubt, if not to subversion, by the experience of modern times, he could not consent to detain the House with a repetition of them, however well they might subserve his purpose, or decorate his argument. Such a repetition would be the less excusable, as it was not necessary to his purpose; for it was not his intention to discuss the question as to the practicability of establishing, at this particular crisis, any bank which could aid the Government, and furnish a circulating medium for the nation.

This great question had, he said, been examined with much ability and eloquence by gentlemen on both sides of the House; and if he could concur in all the opinions, either of his friend from North Carolina, (Mr. GASTON,) or his colleague, (Mr. OAKLEY,) or his friend from New Hampshire, (Mr. WEBSTER,) he should certainly vote against any bank, however strongly founded, or artfully modelled.

They had, he said, with an energy of reasoning, and eloquence of language, distinct to be sure in the manner, but common to all of them, attempted to show, that in these times of peril and universal distrust, the project of a National Bank would be both dangerous and useless to the nation. To this conclusion, their arguments, however varied and dissimilar, clearly tended. In this conclusion he was not yet ready to concur with his honorable friends. I shall not, said Mr. G., attempt to conceal that many views of this subject which I had entertained, and many opinions which I held to be sound and correct, have been swept away by the reasoning and eloquence which have proceeded from them. Yet, sir, they have stopped far short of producing a conviction in my mind, that a bank may not now be framed, which, to a great extent, shall not furnish immediate relief to the Treasury, and a circulating medium to the nation. Whether this be practicable, however, or whether it be not, it is not my intention to examine. My objections to this bill cannot be affected by deciding this question; they rest on grounds totally distinct from any considerations so general, and so uncertain; they arise from the peculiar character of the bill itself; from the untempered materials of which it is constructed, and from the visionary character of its details.

To give the House full possession of his objections, Mr. G. said, it would be necessary to treat of topics, already much discussed, perhaps exhausted. As much brevity as was compatible with a clear view of them, he would promise.

A single glance, said Mr. G., at the miserable condition to which our unhappy country is reduced, must convince us all, that a vigorous and an immediate effort for her relief must be made, or she will surely perish.

With the authors of this mighty wreck and ruin, I will not talk of concert or union. I know them only as the spoilers of the choicest heritage with which the Almighty Father ever blessed a people. Were they only in jeopardy, I would raise my voice only to say, "sink, go to the bottom, and God speed your passage for the salvation of our country."

No, sir, I speak only for our country; for the country of our birth, where the bones of our fathers rest in the Lord, and where, in good time, we must sleep by their side. For that country, crying for succor, almost in the agonies of dissolution, I invite the aid of her worthiest sons.

I speak for the Union; that sacred temple which our fathers modelled into proportion, and delivered to us, only as a deposite for posterity. To this Union, rudely shaken by foreign war and intestine disorder, threatened with utter destruction by the weakness and madness of those very men appointed to guard and preserve it, I would ask the watchful care of all its friends.

I speak for the Constitution of our country, written and hallowed by the founders of our nation. To this Constitution, soiled as as it has been, by the boorish hands of ignorant politicians, deformed as it has been by the tinkering projects of sciolists, daily trampled on by the fiery zealots of party, I would, even yet, point as a *sacred thing*, and most earnestly ask, is is not worth preserving?

Sir, the Constitution, the Union, the country, cannot be saved, but by immediate and powerful exertion. What is in truth our condition?

In the third year of a war, declared in vain defiance, and with ignorant gasconade, you at length find all your means and all your efforts inadequate even for defence. In the nature of things, this war has become entirely defensive; and happy shall we be, happy beyond all our hopes, if by any exertion we shall be able to defend from invasion the very soil where, but forty years ago, the banner of independence first floated in the breeze. So far in the nature of things is conquest beyond our power, that, in the next Summer, all the means of the nation, all the bravery of the people, and all the energies of the Government, will be indispensable to preserve our cities from conflagration, our States from subjugation, our Government from dissolution.

As a first and indispensable requisite to these objects, we turn to the Treasury, and there the most appalling views are presented. We find it empty, approaching bankruptcy. All confidence in the promises of Government is gone; and public credit has become a spectre haunting the place where it once had flourished.

In this situation, any supply from any existing resource is utterly hopeless. Such in brief is the state of our finances; on the sombre picture I will not enlarge; the portrait is indeed disgusting. That it does not in any shade belie the original, I appeal to the faithful and forlorn sketch, presented in the letter of Mr. Secretary Dallas, this morning read to the House. Sir, it is folly to talk of defence, it is madness to hope the preservation of the Union, unless your credit can be revived, your finances restored, and your Treasury replenished.

The great object of the Federal Union was the "common defence." If you finally fail in this grand object, the *end* for which the Federal Government was established, is wholly abandoned. Can you wonder, then, if the States, forced to defend themselves, shall seize the first opportunity to dissolve a Government, efficient for the destruction of their peace and prosperity, but wholly unable to avert one evil which its weak or rash conduct has brought upon them?

Money is not only the sinew of war. In modern times, it is the mainspring of every machine of Government. It is the sinew of our Union; and if your Treasury shall become finally and irretrievably bankrupt, the grand ligament of the States is severed, and we are lost as a nation.

These, Mr. Speaker, are the honest convictions of my mind. Can I hesitate, then, to vote for any just and Constitutional plan, which, in my judgment, will provide a revenue so indispensable for the defence of my country? Can I hesitate to vote for any practical and Constitutional measures, which will fairly promise to revive credit, improve the public finances, and replenish the Treasury?

The *general plan* of the Secretary of the Treasury, in my judgment, embraces the only practical measures which afford a rational prospect of either temporary or permanent relief. He has proposed to revive and sustain public credit by the only means now within our reach. We

are to resort no longer to those popularity-hunting measures, those vicious expedients for revenue, which have produced the overthrow of our finances, and all but ruin to our country.

We are no longer to be satisfied with vain and fabulous statutes, with high-sounding titles, professing "the payment of the whole national debt," but proving in the end delusive and wicked. The "moral sense" of the nation—that worn out hack of our unfledged financiers—is not again dressed up to delude the nation, and insult its creditors. The ample resources of the country, its money and its capital, are now to constitute the pledge; a pledge which, in other countries, has proved an unbending and durable pillar of public credit; and which, if promptly made, and faithfully continuing, will, in our own, prove its restorer and abiding supporter.

These are the wise and only means to revive and sustain our credit recommended by the Secretary; and, entirely unknown as he is to me, I will not withhold from him the praise which I think he merits for the fidelity and intrepidity with which he has performed this unpopular, but great and indispensable duty. But, so roughly has public credit been treated by the financial quacks who preceded him, so long has it been the victim of patent nostrums and cancer doctors, that it has languished almost to the grave. With the most skilful treatment, its recovery to health and vigor must be slow and protracted. By the report from the Secretary, in unison with the report from his predecessor, it is certain, that to comply with your contracts during the present quarter, you have yet unprovided a supply of thirteen millions of dollars. This must be promptly obtained, or the operations of the Treasury are arrested, and your Government is dissolved.

How is this sum to be obtained? Not by loans, in the present condition of the stock market and of your credit. You have now in the market, at least, forty millions of stock, reduced in price to seventy-five or eighty per cent. While this stock continues in the market, at this depressed value, no loan can be contracted; or, if it can, upon no better terms than the market value of this stock. The only practical remedy is to remove this stock from the market, or, by some act of yours, to raise its value, and thus to deliver the Treasury from an insuperable bar to a new loan. The general measures for the revival of credit to which I have before alluded might finally accomplish this necessary work. But it is apparent they would accomplish it too late to afford any present relief to the Treasury. Hence, in anticipation of these measures, some plan, competent to obtain the object, seems to be indispensable.

For this purpose and to accomplish this object, it is presumed, was one of the views of the Secretary in the plan of a bank, which he has projected and recommended to the House. Is the plan so entirely chimerical, as has been represented? By authorizing a subscription of this depressed stock to such a bank, you would raise its value in the market, and thus relieve the Government, in contracting a new loan, from all competition with it. You would do more; you would relieve the capitalists and banks from the heavy load which now presses them to the earth, and you would inspire them with both the disposition and the ability to aid you in another loan. In the meantime your general plan of finance for the revival of your credit would be felt in the community. And if it should answer the hopes of all; if it should revive confidence, and restore the credit of the nation, you might then proceed to contract new loans to the extent of the ability of the country. It is in this way, in my apprehension, Mr. Speaker, that the bank proposed by the Secretary would afford the prompt relief so indispensable to the Treasury. I do not perceive in it those visionary qualities which have been so liberally ascribed to it. In every respect, I deem it preferable to its rival and substitute, now on your table. But, sir, we have been told that these are the mere visions of imagination. My friend from North Carolina (Mr. GASTON) has told us, that the war stock will still remain in the market; that its conversion into bank stock will be idle and illusory, because it will still press upon the country, and meet the Government in every attempt at another loan. Mr. Speaker, this objection is founded on the notion that the stock itself, and not the depressed price of it, is the obstruction to the Government; directly the reverse, I believe to be the state of the fact. I would ask my friend whether, if this stock, even in its present condition, could be elevated to its par value, there would be any difficulty in contracting another loan? He has not pretended there would be any. Surely, then, if the bank be of any value, the subscribable quality attached to the stock must raise its price, and although its character be only changed, and it remain as bank stock in the country, the object is accomplished, the road is clear to the Government for another loan, and the Treasury is relieved.

The gentleman from South Carolina, (Mr. CALHOUN,) perceiving this obvious conclusion, attempted to fortify the objection of my honorable friend. He declared that the surplus capital of the country was exhausted; therefore it was, and not because your credit was shaken, that the stocks already created found no purchasers; and their price, like that of any other commodity with which the market is surcharged, has fallen. And hence he contended that though, by the plan of the Secretary, the price of the stock would be raised, yet all efforts for another loan would be hopeless.

Mr. Speaker, if this opinion of the honorable gentleman be well founded, then indeed have we a prospect before us, dark in the extreme.

I will not detain the House to examine the position. Perhaps it is impossible, from the data we here possess, to arrive at any certain conclusion upon the subject. The honorable gentleman has not attempted to sustain it by facts or reasoning. He has advanced it as a mere hypothesis. I shall content myself with avowing my

firm belief, that it is an hypothesis without foundation. It is not that your loaning capital is exhausted, but that the confidence of the capitalist in your wisdom, integrity, and policy, is entirely departed. It is not that no surplus capital remains unemployed in the country, but, that your credit has sunk so low that they who hold it will not confide it to your faithless hands. That this is the fact, is proven by events daily presented to our view. The States have no difficulty in procuring loans to any extent which their exigencies demand. Even your towns and cities are intrusted with millions. At the very time that the Secretary of the Treasury was advertising the credit of the Government, and calling, in vain, for money upon terms and conditions the most extravagant and ruinous, your cities had but to open their subscriptions, and millions were at once obtained upon the ordinary and legal premiums. Do you want other proof, Mr. Speaker, that the hypothesis of the honorable gentleman is utterly unfounded, and therefore that his objection is entirely fanciful?

If I am mistaken in this, sir, then I admit the objection to be conclusive and fatal to the plan of the Secretary. But does not the honorable gentleman perceive that his objection is equally fatal to his own system? that he has presented a dilemma, on the horn of which, his own offspring must hang and surely perish?

If the capital of the country is exhausted; if the market is already saturated with public stock, will the gentleman tell me, what is to become of the Treasury notes which his plan is to pour forth in a stream of millions? Through what magical process is it, that after they have fluttered their hour on the public stage, they are to transmute themselves into six per cent. stock, and settle quietly into the vaults of his mammoth bank? If the surplus capital is exhausted, if all is already gone, the process is utterly impossible. Surely the remorseless hand of the parent has wrung the neck from his own bantling.

I stop not here, sir. If this hypothesis be correct, why are you contriving novel schemes for the revival of public credit? Why a sinking fund? Why a pledge of taxes? Abandon all this unwieldy apparatus of financial machinery. You have it seems mistaken the seat of the disorder. You are applying plasters to the head, when you should be administering tonics to the stomach; you are bleeding and blistering a body politic already exhausted. Quit at once all this quackery; take the opinion of this learned doctor. Your credit is in full health—it needs no physician; the capital of the nation alone languishes! Restore, then, to the nation her life blood, the vital principle of her prosperity; restore her commerce, her agriculture, her peace. This is your only remedy—the only prescription which can rescue her from dissolution and the grave.

Mr. Speaker, with my friend from New York, (Mr. OAKLEY,) I am ready to say that this is the only effectual remedy remaining in your hands. Peace, and peace alone, can staunch the deep and bleeding wounds of our country. But, until that blessed messenger shall arrive "with healing in his wings," we have nothing left but our own arm for defence and preservation. If the hypothesis of the gentleman be correct, that arm has become too feeble for any purpose of safety. Attempt not to stretch it forth; its form is destroyed; its strength is withered; its very sinews are blasted.

I have hitherto fondly hoped that this nation, even under her present Government, was amply competent to her own defence; that, palsied as she is by the councils of rashness and of folly, her own energies would burst spontaneously forth, and strike to the earth even the gigantic enemy who meditates her ruin. But if the hypothesis of the honorable gentleman is correct, my fond hopes are ended. If all your surplus capital is gone, this war must close on any terms, or the union of these States must follow it. For vain will be the attempt to wrest, by oppressive taxes, from the industry and the annual income of the people, those annual millions, which defence itself will annually consume. But, sir, I hope, and I believe better things of our condition. I believe we have capital still remaining to be loaned; and that nothing is necessary but the prompt and vigorous application of the means yet within our reach to bring that capital to the immediate relief of the Treasury.

Mr. Speaker—another, and the prime object of a bank, is to furnish a circulating medium for the nation. We have not, we never had a currency of gold and silver, which ever approached a sufficiency for the business of the country. Banks, incorporated by the States, have issued paper, which for twenty years has constituted the great mass of our circulating medium. By means of the National Bank, which three years ago was immolated at the shrine of party resentment, the General Government retained an indirect, though inadequate influence over this State paper. But from the period when that bank was dissolved, this country has exhibited the monstrous absurdity of a Government "charged with the care ' of the integrity and prosperity of the Empire, ' without any direct or indirect control over its ' currency." What has been the consequence? These State institutions, in no way responsible to you, have so managed as to render the currency of the nation suspected and uncertain, and thus have embarrassed all your fiscal measures.

No loan can be paid you, but in this State paper. On this side of New England, as has been demonstrated by my friend from New Hampshire, (Mr. Webster,) this paper has depreciated to an alarming extent. In the very inception of a loan you have the certainty of a loss to the full amount of this depreciation. From the loss of confidence in these State institutions, and from the limited circulation of the paper, you encounter almost insuperable embarrassments in its expenditure.

Paper issued from banks south of the Potomac, and west of the Alleghanies, is almost worthless north of the Delaware. The notes of Maryland and Pennsylvania produce to you enormous losses,

and even bank bills of the North must be paid out within a day's journey of the bank which issues them, or the same consequences follow. In this situation, it must be obvious, that a national currency, equal in value throughout the country, and founded on a competent capital, is a *sine qua non* to any system of loaning, which will not produce ruin to the country.

Whether the plan of the Secretary can furnish such a currency, is certainly problematical; perhaps the case is at present without remedy. In this country it is an untried experiment. But I have no hesitation in averring, that I think it to the full as likely to attain this great and desirable object, as the novel system on your table, which has become its substitute.

Mr. Speaker, when I speak of the plan of the Secretary, I would not be understood as embracing all its details. In relation to those details, I accord in opinion with my friend from North Carolina (Mr. Gaston;) I consider them erroneous in every view. The appointment of five directors by the President, the total prohibition of the sale of the stock, the compulsory loan of thirty millions to the Government, and the arbitrary power reposed in the President, to compel a suspension of specie payment, are in my opinion, features which deform the plan, and will prove the most inveterate enemies to its success. On this subject, I think, not a man can doubt, who attended to the conclusive reasoning of my honorable friend. It would but diminish its irresistible force, for me to attempt to fortify his eloquent argument. I rejoice, sir, that those details have been stricken from the bill; and as they are equally inconsistent with the principles and the successful operation of the former plan, as they are with that on the table, I most sincerely trust they will never be suffered to accompany any system which shall receive the sanction of this House.

Before I quit this part of the subject, I beg the attention of the House to a topic which I consider of no little importance, as it relates as well to the justice as the permanent fiscal policy of this Government. I mean, sir, the interests and claims of the holders of the stock, which the Secretary proposes to place in the bank.

Mr. Speaker; when I speak of these men, I speak of gentlemen, few of whom are known to me—I hold them, like all other men, "enemies in war, in peace friends."

In no way, am I partial to them. On the contrary, I have no doubt that the pecuniary aids, which they have furnished for the prosecution of this war, have proved most injurious to our country. If they had withheld their aid, the storm of war must have ceased to roll onward; and peace, an honorable and advantageous peace, would long since have blessed the nation. A peace, to which at this moment every member of the Administration would think it happiness to fly, from the evils which are accumulating on their guilty heads.

It is not wonderful, therefore, that the honorable friends who sit around me should regard the conduct of these gentlemen with disapprobation, and look to their claims with coldness, if not with antipathy. Yet, sir, they are the legal creditors of the nation, entitled to the same justice and equity with those who became creditors before them. And if I am sure of anything, depending on the judgment of man, it is this: that whatever may be the feelings of my honorable friends, those feelings will not for a moment be suffered to control their conduct, upon a question of such vital and permanent consequence to the nation.

But, sir, I would ask the authors and supporters of the war on this floor, how it consists with the plain principles of gratitude and honor for them to treat these creditors with reproach or their claims with indifference?

They relied on loans to keep in motion their whole machinery of Government and war. To procure these loans, all the arts of persuasion and remonstrance were played off upon the public; "lives and fortune and sacred honor" men stood aloof—the whole machinery of war was disordered, and about to run down.

In these critical moments, these men stepped forth and saved you from disgrace abroad, and indignation at home. They went to the very top of the market in their offers. True, the conditions were disgraceful to you and injurious to your country; but let them not be blamed for this, for prudent men even then believed, that, by giving you their property on any terms, they exhibited a lunacy or folly amply sufficient to consign them to the care of a guardian or conservator. Under these circumstances, is it for you to reproach them—you, to whose interests they have devoted their fortunes, all but their honor? Is such the Republican gratitude of modern times and of modern politicians?

When it has been stated that the bill on your table would, by the new and enormous issue of Treasury notes, produce the ruin of these men, it has been coolly answered—are we their guardians? Are we responsible for their ruin? Are we bound to more than a strict compliance with the terms of our contract? An honorable gentleman from South Carolina (Mr. LOWNDES,) with unusual ability and eloquence, has attempted to prove that this bill violates neither the justice or equity to which they are entitled.

With that honorable gentleman, so well qualified as he is to decide this question, not only by the strong powers of intellect, but by those lofty and honorable feelings which adorn his character, I am unwilling to disagree. I would yield much to his opinion.

Strict justice and equity, perhaps, require no more of us than a rigid compliance with the terms of our contract. But as we have not contracted to furnish a bank for the reception of stock, nor to refrain from an emission of Treasury notes, we may, perhaps, refuse the former, and perform the latter, without any violation of our faith. Certainly we may do so, if, upon a candid view of the whole ground, the safety of the State or the essential interests of the people shall require either at our hands.

But I would ask that honorable gentleman, if, in deciding on the course which the faith and interests of the country require, nothing else is to be taken into consideration than the mere terms of our contracts? Is it not the first dictate of justice and generosity, that you should pass beyond the legal forms of your contracts, and take especial care that those who have confided their fortunes to your faith, from which there can be no appeal, should not be ruined by any course of fiscal policy which you may resolve to pursue? If this be not so—yet, I would again ask the honorable gentleman, are there not considerations of higher import, and more durable consequence, which you must respect? I mean the permanent interests of the nation itself.

In modern times, loans are the great and only resources of Government in their wars. Without a resort to the system of loaning, in some form, not a Government of modern Europe would have survived the universal tempest which has shaken them all to their deepest foundations. To preserve such a resource to a Government, the course of her fiscal policy must regard the interests of her creditors, and speak undoubted security to those who possess the surplus capital of the country.

In this important science, it is not degrading to receive the lessons of experience, even from our enemy. The credit and the finances of England had languished for nearly a century, under the influence of a fiscal machine called a Sinking Fund, not unlike our own miserable institution, having the same name, for the last twelve years. In the year 1784, when Mr. Pitt became the financial minister of England, he found her finances in a state of rapid decline, not unlike our own at the present period. Her credit was impaired; her stocks consequently low; a debt of enormous amount, and daily increasing; without sufficient revenue to discharge the annual dividends as they became due to the creditors. Instantly, resolving to triumph over every difficulty, he risked his popularity and his place, that he might perform the great duties which he owed his country. He increased the taxes, funded the floating claims on the Treasury, and adopted safe and energetic rules for organizing the finances.

In the year 1786 he established a sinking fund, on principles which promised undoubted success. But, in the year 1792, upon the suggestion of his great rival, he introduced into his system that grand improvement in finance which will render his name as immortal as the fame of his country. Henceforward, under each loan, taxes were to be placed and inviolably pledged, sufficient annually to discharge the interest, and one per cent. upon its principal, until its entire extinction should be accomplished. By this improvement, not the slightest departure from which has ever been allowed, the creditors of England have become annuitants, and her loan annuities determinable, at periods more or less distant, according to the price of stocks in the market.

But this acknowledged chieftain of modern

financiers did not stop here. He knew that the capitalists of the country, who were also her creditors, were his only sure resource in times of national alarm. Their interests were cherished in all his fiscal policy; they were constantly consulted in the formation of all his plans; and his measures were arranged upon principles of an enlarged policy, embracing in its scope, what he considered inseparably connected, the interest of the creditor and the public credit of his country. Hence it was, that though the black cloud of destruction hovered over his island for twenty years; in the darkest hours of a long, eventful, and mortal struggle, in which his country was engaged for her existence; even in that day of despair, when the colossal tyrant of France arrayed his myriad of slaves, and threatened to pour them across the Channel, he never for a moment lost the confidence of the capitalists of his country, but was always able to elicit supplies equal to his wants, and on conditions moderate and advantageous.

Mr. Speaker, if you would preserve to your Government a similar resource, pursue the example of this great minister; and then, though this war should continue, and tenfold darkness should settle on your prospects, you will fasten to your interests a body of men able and willing to succor you in the day of your deepest distress.

But, sir, what a cold and sickening contrast does your policy present. Like "the Jew of Venice," you refer all to "your bond." Your "bond" becomes the substitute for your judgment—the rigid test of your justice and gratitude. When, standing on the very verge of ruin, your creditors cry to you for preservation; you point to the bond, and in cool triumph ask, "is it there written?" They show you that your policy is their total destruction, and invoke you to spare them; you point to your contract, and exclaim, "Here is our warrant. We have a right to a pound ' of flesh, and we will have it, though your heart's ' blood shall stream upon the knife."

Go on, Mr. Speaker: Perhaps, in these days of disorder, policy and justice are no more inseparable. It is possible that, in the vicissitudes of modern times, human nature has, also, been revolutionized. If so, your policy may be well adapted to the actual condition of things. Go on, sir; it may be that the mind of man is no longer influenced by the same motives—excited by the same objects, as in former days. It is possible that *experience* has become a mere idle babbler, and *history* an instrument of deception. If so, your course may prove triumphant. It is possible that, with the clamors of thousands whom you have ruined sounding in your ears, you may pass at once to the destruction of other thousands. But, sir, believe me, if "man is yet mad," with the destruction you will now work will end your power of mischief. Do not believe—be not mad—men enough to hope—that after you shall have coolly perpetrated the ruin of your present creditors, you will find others, idiots enough, to throw their fortunes within "the scope of your policy."

I turn now, sir, to a particular examination of the bill before you. The bank to be incorporated by this bill, is modelled on the novel plan of the honorable gentleman from South Carolina, (Mr. Calhoun;) and its objects are the same as were those, intended by that, for which it has become a substitute. Indeed, with the exception of the right of the Government to subscribe, which is stricken from this bill, the bank will present the same proportions of stock and specie, a capital of the same complexion and consistency, subject to the same objections, and in its operations opposed by the same obstacles which have been supposed conclusive against the success of the first project. The grand distinction between the two projects is this: The first plan relied on loans for the relief of Government, and was modelled for the purpose of rendering loans practicable. This plan renounces all hopes of future loans, and proposes, as a succedaneum, the issuing of twenty-four millions of Treasury notes. And on these notes alone is the Government to rely for present relief, and for all its supplies during the ensuing year. These Treasury notes are intended to range awhile through the country as a currency, pass into a solid mass of six per cent. stock, settle quietly and in full credit into the vaults of a bank; and, assuming there yet another shape, to flutter forth, and constitute another circulating medium. Sir, the process is captivating in theory, charming to the fancy; but, unless I am much mistaken, it is one of those splendid visions which the noble science of alchymy has often produced, to mortify the pride and disappoint the hopes of man. It has no practicable qualities, and the danger is, that while you are pursuing the unsubstantial vision, admiring its varied colors, and fanciful forms, the mighty bubble will burst, and leave you in the midst of mortification and despair.

It will be perceived, Mr. Speaker, that should these Treasury notes make their grand tour ever so brilliantly, before they arrive at the vaults of the bank they settle down into stock, just like the stock now existing, of no more value in itself, and combining no superior qualities. And therefore it was that I stated, when this bank shall have passed its periods of danger, and issue forth a full grown bank, it will be in no wise better calculated to aid the Government or furnish a national currency, than a bank formed of the stock already existing. In this respect, the two plans are upon a level. It is to the process, to which I have above alluded, that I object, as illusory, and highly dangerous to the country. Your Treasury notes never can be kept at par; they will probably never reach the bank at all; and if they do so, it will be after they have scourged the land by a dreadful depreciation, and through the ruin of thousands who shall hold them.

Let it not be forgotten, that the adoption of this plan precludes all hopes of contracting loans; indeed, it professes to become an entire substitute for the system of loaning. In three months from the passing this bill, the whole twenty-four millions must issue forth, like the locusts of Egypt,

677   **HISTORY OF CONGRESS.**   678

NOVEMBER, 1814.   *Bank of the United States.*   H. OF R.

to scourge the land. For the supplies even of the present quarter, your Treasury must obtain thirteen millions of dollars, or your contracts must all be violated. During the first quarter of the next year you can expect but little aid from taxes; yet your armies must be recruited and paid. Preparations of vast magnitude for the next Summer must be made; for then you must engage in a mortal struggle, upon the issue of which you have placed the existence of the country. The issuing of these notes will be your only resource. Loans, I repeat it, will be out of the question. You not only will have left the present stock a massive drug in the market, pressing to the earth the moneyed men of the country, but you will have added to its weight by masses of new stock in the form of Treasury notes. In the nature of things, therefore, you will be bound to issue all the notes in your power to put forth. Do you imagine that they can be circulated at par upon your credit alone? Those who believe so, have but little knowledge of the worthless state of public credit. They have not seen the contractors tremble, the merchants frown, the farmers scowl, and the speculators laugh, at the very name of public credit. Sir, such an expectation is utterly fallacious.

Of all paper, Government bills are the most unfit for a circulating medium. I might read from the pages of the great founder of your whole financial system, arguments conclusive, to show the wide difference between a paper medium, depending upon the faith of Government alone, and that which is founded on the capital of a private bank. The former has no bounds to its issue, but the discretion which generally becomes another name for the exigencies of the Government. It is always suspected, always received with doubt and hesitation, and, therefore, always depreciates. While the latter, founded on solid capital, always protected, regulated, and restrained by the honor and integrity of the directors, fortified by the interest of the stockholders and the existence of the bank, all of which are jeopardized by an over issue, comes to the public with the strongest title to their confidence, and is generally received and circulated. The works of the lamented Hamilton are now before me; I will not detain the House, but refer them to his argument upon this interesting subject.

If these objections in the general are well founded, it does appear to me, that the peculiar qualities of the paper contemplated by this bill, will render it a mere burlesque on the very name of a circulating medium. Experience has proved that it is essential, perhaps a *sine qua non*, to a circulating medium, that it should bear its value on its face. It cannot be clogged with qualities, which render calculations of its worth a pre-requisite to its daily circulation. But these notes are to bear an interest of five and three-quarters per cent.; their value will vary with each passing day. Can a currency thus encumbered pass freely along, through the illiterate classes of the community? No, sir, it is fit only for a nation of mathematicians; and if you issue them, every farmer must have at his elbow a Zerah Colbourn to carry on the ordinary transactions of society.

To surmount these difficulties, however, the honorable gentleman proposes a resort to the tricks of the Treasury. This paper, and this alone, shall be received in taxes. Mr. Speaker, this expedient may be ingenious, but in my opinion, like the rest of the machine, it is wholly impracticable. Your Treasury notes never will be sufficiently diffused to furnish the people with a medium in which to pay the taxes. Besides, sir, such a plan, if successful, would drive back to its vaults the notes of every State bank, and render their charters nearly worthless. Hence, sir, in self-defence, to preserve their existence, you would force the State banks into a combination to resist and defeat a measure which would produce their ruin. They would all refuse your notes. The great body of influential citizens, interested in the preservation of the State banks, would be arrayed against you. Your notes might pay taxes, but good care would be taken that they should pay nothing else. In such a struggle your defeat would be certain. Distraction would be introduced into your medium; its circulation would be impeded, and an indefinite depreciation would leave you to lament the injustice of your attempt.

Mr. Speaker, never was such a circulating medium issued and sustained at par, under similar circumstances, by any Government. I would appeal to the experience of European Governments; I would remind you of the assignats of France, at the mention of which, justice frowns and policy blushes—I would appeal to your own experience.

It might be improper to point to the close of our Revolution, to describe the mere spectre of public credit which survived, and the consequent destruction of the Government paper which filled the country. But look at the few Treasury notes which are now abroad; they are receivable in taxes; they are shortly due at the Treasury; yet you may purchase them in the market, from five to twenty per cent. under their par value. Let gentlemen read their errors in their own experience.

But, Mr. Speaker, the honorable gentleman did not much rely on these expedients to sustain his system. The bank was his grand and final reliance; the bank is the stay and staff of his plan. This bank is to act as a kind of alchymical engine, by which worthless paper is to be turned into gold, the sickly credit of the nation restored to health, and the mighty operations of the Government and of the war sustained and regulated. And this wonderful engine is to work in this wise: The books of the bank are to be opened, and the flood of paper, as it rushes from the Treasury, is to flow rapidly, and regularly, and monthly, into the reservoir, just as the deep and placid current of a mighty river flows to the bosom of the ocean. Suppose, Mr. Speaker, the river should meet some unsurmountable obstruction cast across its channel, its smooth course should be interrupted, and its flood should be beaten back towards its source. It would rush from its bed, roll over the fields which before it had nourished, and leave the country a stagnant pool, charged with pestilence and death. So, sir, if in the vicissitudes to which all mortal projects are exposed, this flood of paper should be obstructed in its course, it would settle down upon the community, full of the seeds of fiscal pestilence and ruin.

My honorable friend from New York, (Mr. OAKLEY,) perceiving this danger, and its obvious consequences, thinks there is a remedy within our reach. By legislative acts, he would have the Government so restricted that they should issue this paper no faster than it should be able to pass into the bank, and then the danger would be averted. Does not my honorable friend perceive, that the invention of such a provision would render the whole project a *felo de se?* When you have adopted this system, and voluntarily abandoned all hopes of loans, you will have no resort for supplies but to this Treasury paper; in truth, when you enter on this plan there is no retreat. "You set your life upon a throw, and you must stand the hazard of the die." According to the exigencies of the Government you must continue to issue your paper, and, if the bank fails to receive it, the evils I have described are inevitable. If there is reasonable doubt upon the subject, you ought to pause long, and reflect well, before you hazard the venture. What is it you put at hazard? Not your bank alone, but all the character and credit that remains to you; all preparation for the deadly struggle which awaits you. If there is much hazard in the game, you are made to place your life upon the issue. Should you lose, all is lost; the dissolution of the Union—the subjugation of the States are consummated. In solemn truth, Mr. Speaker, the chances are all against you; not one doubt of your loss remains in my mind.

May I ask, said Mr. G., how these bills are ever to escape from the Treasury into circulation? Think you that capitalists will buy them of you at anything like their par value? Will you put them forth as a currency under par; thus stamping them with the image of death before they issue from the womb? Nothing of this is practicable. No, sir, if they go forth at all, they must pass to your contractors, your commissaries, your soldiers, and your sailors—to any of your creditors who prefer your paper to your parol promise. Hence, it is possible they may pass to others, and thus obtain a partial circulation among the merchants, farmers, and mechanics.

But, sir, are we deluded enough to expect that these men will place them in the bank? All their active capital is necessary for their ordinary pursuits; essential to put in motion and extract profit from their own fixed property. To establish banks, is as far removed from all their views and objects as it is inimical to their pursuits and interests. Sometimes, when a bank has been long established, and has gained reputation for prudent management, this class of men do invest small sums in its stocks, both for profit and security; but never do you find them, to any material extent, risking their hard-earned fortunes in speculations novel and uncertain.

When I heard the honorable gentleman from South Carolina (Mr. CALHOUN) dilating upon the wide diffusion of these notes, whereby the farmers of the North and the South, and the East and the West, would be furnished with an opportunity to participate in this great national speculation, I could consider it in no other light than as a rhetorical flourish to attract favor to his project; I considered it as a mere "springe to catch woodcocks." And the House must have been amused to observe how suddenly the honorable delegate from Missouri (Mr. EASTON) was noosed. He actually prevailed on the House to open a subscription, somewhere in the forests of the West, near, as I am informed, the fur settlement on Columbia river.

Mr. Speaker, I could not but be diverted at the amusing little contest upon this subject, between the honorable gentleman from South Carolina and his friend from Vermont (Mr. FISK.) The latter gentleman did not hesitate to declare that he saw the ruin of this bill lurking in the provisions of this bill. "Why," said he, "the capital-'ists alone can buy the Treasury notes and form 'the bank. Those who belong to the Adminis-'tration are exhausted. The Federalists will 'therefore get the bank, and with it dash out the 'brains of the Administration." And he threatened to take his hat, make his bow, and bid good night to the Administration, sooner than to stay here and be blown up by this gunpowder institution.

The honorable gentleman from South Carolina rose to quiet the apprehensions of his friend. He seemed to agree that the capitalists attached to the Administration might have been somewhat surfeited with the paper potions they had too liberally swallowed; but he assured his friend that one sure resource remained to the party.— "Have we not," he exclaimed, "the rich yeo-'manry of the country on our side? Are they 'not the pride and boast of our party? And will 'not our yeomanry aid our loans, and assist in 'the establishment of our bank?"

And he seemed to conclude, that his friend might safely let his hat hang on its nail, and continue to sit and to vote, until something more substantial should "push him from his stool." The gentleman from Vermont, though evidently puzzled by this bold appeal, appeared to me not entirely satisfied. I saw a smile on his face, which seemed contemptuously to say: "Yes, yes, we have the rich yeomanry with us; and they have their cotton fields and their corn fields, but will they convert them into loans? They also have their pigs and their poultry, but will they place them in your bank?" Sir, the plain practical common sense of the gentleman from Vermont taught him, that all the talk about the wide diffusion of this Treasury paper, to afford opportunities to our farmers to subscribe to the bank, was the airy creation of inexperience and enthusiasm.

Does the gentleman from South Carolina, indeed, expect any material aid in establishing his bank from this worthy class of our citizens? The experience of this war should correct his error. Your late loans were authorized to support this just and necessary war; to prosecute your holy crusade against the Canadas. Of course, every motive of patriotism would impel "our yeomanry" to step forth with all their means. Your Government called loudly for the aid of its friends Was its voice heard by "our yeomanry?" Let the gentleman step to the Treasury, and see how much of the late loan has been taken by the plain farmers of Kentucky, the proud planters of Carolina, the lords of the soil of Virginia? He will find a beggarly account of pitiful subscriptions.

Even now, sir, when your Treasury contains not one dollar, when this honest and glorious war is about to expire, merely for want of nourishment, where are these patriotic supporters of Administration? You have loans unfilled—your Government in tones of deep anguish call for succor, and yet "our rich yeomanry," who are able to invest millions in bank stock, are nowhere to be found. They abandoned their leaders and their war in this their darkest and most perilous hour. Did I believe that these men were exclusively supporters of this war, and that they had the ability to furnish aid, I should view them as the most sordid of mankind. But believing directly the reverse, and not having a doubt that the surplus capital, which must create loans and bank stock, rests with them but in a very limited extent, they are subject to no reproach. It is their part, to perform their political duties with fidelity, and to wrestle morning and evening with their God, to deliver their country from its two most dreadful scourges, the war and the authors of the war.

Mr. Speaker, the capitalists of the country must convert the Treasury paper into bank stock, or it will remain unconverted. By capitalists, I mean those enterprising men who have accumulated masses of active and surplus capital, for the purpose of venturing it in great and advantageous speculations.

Have these men, at this time, the ability to perform the process? You have nothing to hope from New England. Her citizens have their money and their capital safe at home; and you will not find them idiots enough, in this tempestuous season, to venture it on the ocean, in any vessel that you can build and rig and navigate. From the capitalists south of the Hudson, and from them only, must you expect aid. It is a mistake to suppose the depressed war stock to be in few hands. The original contractors retain, comparatively, but trifling portions of the whole mass. It is widely diffused among these capitalists, and unless, by some act of yours, its market value is elevated, it will paralyze all their efforts to afford any aid to your project.

The banks, too, are groaning under the weight of this depressed stock. They have received it in pledges and in payment. It lies useless in their vaults, and clogs even their operations. I have not a doubt of the fact, that from this cause, more than any other, they have been forced to suspend their specie payments. And, I think, nothing is hazarded in saying, that they never will resume them, until this cause shall be removed.

But, Mr. Speaker, if we grant the ability, shall we find the disposition? What are the inducements for any man to purchase your notes at par, and place them in the bank? Is there any profit to justify the speculation? Sir, if the friends of this bank are at all accurate in their descriptions of it, instead of inviting, it will deter any prudent man from venturing money in it.

The gentleman from South Carolina thinks it will be at first a weak institution, capable of performing but little business; that it must slowly feel its way, discounting cautiously, and he hopes, by such a course, it may survive its infancy. My friend from New York (Mr. OAKLEY) says, it is strictly a six million bank, and to that capital must its business be limited. And my friend from New Hampshire (Mr. WEBSTER) has no doubt it will perish by the draining of its specie, if it should issue paper equal to one-half of its specie capital. If these gentlemen are near the truth, then it is indeed a poor bank—a very beggarly institution, well calculated to devour capital, but with a wretched capacity to return profit. To obtain dividends on six millions of capital, it is supposed that men of fortune will be so weak as to convert twenty-four millions of property into six per cent. stock, and lay it by in the vaults of the bank, safe to be sure, but almost wholly unproductive! Such fanciful hopes can never be realized.

But my friend from New York has remarked, that in this respect the two plans are on a precise level. If there would be no adequate inducement for moneyed men to invest their property in this bank, neither would there be for the holders of the present stock to invest it in the bank recommended by the Secretary. My honorable friend has not treated this subject with his usual sagacity.

The cases are entirely dissimilar. And so are the motives, which would excite to investments in the different banks. The present holders of the stocks are already committed. Their stock is now a drug in their hands. It threatens them with ruin. The motive they would have to comply with the terms of the bill, and obtain specie, would be, therefore, strong and irresistible—the elevation of the price of their stock, the rescue of themselves from ruin. In the present case there is no such motive. Here no risk is already incurred. The only motive is a profitable speculation—the only inducement, positive gain. It is apparent, that while on the Secretary's plan the present holders of stock would fly to the bank as a refuge from ruin, on the present plan, the nature of the institution might, and probably would, forbid any capitalist from approaching it.

If, in peaceful and prosperous times, this bank might present a fair speculation, and obtain ample subscriptions; yet, can it be hoped, that prudent men would venture their fortunes in it, in these times of dismay and peril? Look around, sir. From abroad, invasion is menaced of every part of your extended coast. Our cities, the great depositories of our surplus wealth, have but feeble assurance of safety. The storms of war are beating on our country from every quarter of the heavens. What is our condition at home? The foul spirit of party sits like a bloated incubus upon the Cabinet, and turns all its counsels to rashness and folly. Like the fabled Gorgon, this foul fiend daily mounts this very Capitol, and scattering the snakes of discord among the people, he calls them, in tones of fury, to civil commotion and bloody violence. The Constitution has received deep, perhaps mortal wounds. War, in his iron chariot, is rolling through the land, crushing, with its heavy wheels, our civil institutions, those bulwarks of civil liberty. The Government totters from untimely decrepitude. And the very temple of our Union, toppled from its base, is ready to be dashed to the earth, and to leave the country encumbered with its fragments. This country resembles the strong man filled with wine, his head full of delirious visions, and mad projects of ambition and vengeance, revolving vast projects, and deciding on prompt and vigorous exertion; but his limbs are palsied, his nerves are withered, and he lies, supine on the earth, huge, disgusting, and impotent.

To what fate we are destined is unknown to man. We have been borne along to our destruction almost with the rapidity of the lightning. And it is not for human foresight ever to conjecture whether the God of our fathers has finally forsaken us, and whether the end of our Republic is at hand. In such "crazy times," think you that men, who possess sane minds, will embark their fortunes in any vessel whose safety depends on such commanders, such pilots, and such a crew as you can furnish?

But, Mr. Speaker, suppose I am mistaken in all this. If there are men able and willing to purchase the Treasury paper and transmute it to bank stock—the very process of transmutation will be destructive to the country. Such men, if they exist at all, exist for the most part in our cities, and are closely connected by the strong band of common interest. In these moneyed operations, their interests lead them to act united and in concert. What will be their conduct in this business?

Finding your Treasury notes wholly unsupported, and beginning to descend, they will leave them to take their downward course. Nay, they will aid their descent, certain that they will remain at all times within the reach of their coin. The strong interests of these men will impel them to such a course, and they will surely pursue it. And thus the whole machinery becomes disordered by the very agents upon whom you rely to keep it in motion. Immediately, and of necessity, your paper will greatly depreciate. Will the Government, then, suffer me to repeat the question, Will the Government then stop its issues? It has no alternative—the gate must continue hoisted, and the stream must continue running.

The very period has now arrived so eloquently deprecated by my honorable friend from North Carolina (Mr. GASTON.) Your contractors are clamorous—give them "assignats."

Your sailors demand their wages—out with a new edition of Treasury notes.

Your armies clamor for arrearages. Dare you refuse them? Remember the tragedy at Newburgh—it may be attempted in your day. There are Armstrongs still alive to excite rebellion, but no WASHINGTON remains to parry its fury and save the country. A new swarm of "assignats" will be the dreadful and the only remedy.

Your paper will rapidly reach its lowest point of depression. And now it is that the remorseless speculator will begin to prowl for his prey.

The war-worn soldier, as he halts slowly and painfully from Canada, must surrender the price of his blood for half its value.

The widow and the orphan of him who in your battles has laid his bones amid the snows of the North, must sacrifice their little all for a lean subsistence. Some of you witnessed, we all have read and have wept, the fate of the ruined soldiers of the Revolution. The same picture will be now presented, only on a larger canvass, and with more tragical coloring.

I appeal to those who belong to the dominant party. Have you forgotten the history of those days when the debt of our independence was funded? Your party then, with the present Chief Magistrate at its head, professed to be the soldier's friend and champion; and the country rung with your clamors for a discrimination of the debt. So strongly did you then profess to feel for the soldier, that you were ready to violate the most solemn contracts to save him from the loss of depreciated money. What is now your conduct? You are about to adopt a system which will bring the soldiers of your present armies to the same loss and the same condition. You are not contented even with this. In this bill, you consummate the whole transaction; you not only frame the engine by which the soldier may be defrauded, but you provide an asylum to which the agents who shall defraud him may fly with their spoils and set at defiance all human justice and power. You do not intend this crying iniquity.

No, when the crisis shall arrive, when your paper shall sink to half its nominal value, when, like voracious sharks prowling the ocean, the speculators shall range through every village, seizing the miserable victims of their cupidity, then will you step boldly forth, and cheered by the approving voice of the people, which now would thunder indignation against the measure, you would consummate your goodly work, by that unpardonable political sin a tender law. This bill will lay the sure foundation for such a measure.

I appeal to the friends who sit around me. Are you ready to support a system which will press on to this consummation of ruin, with a step "steady as time, certain as death?"

The plan of the Secretary may be vicious.

But if that be hurtful in detail, this is the very essence of ruin in its principles. If that would injure the country, this is the very box of Pandora, from which will surely issue the most dreadful evils which ever scourged and cursed a people. Better that our Republic be struck at once from "the great firmament of nations," than that she should linger a few months of rayless existence, and then plunge into such an abyss of embarrassment and misery.

Mr. Speaker, I may be mistaken in all these forebodings of evil. If the bill shall pass, and prove beneficial, my country will owe me no thanks for the boon. But if it shall produce the evils I have anticipated, here, in the face of the nation, I wash my hands of all the consequences.

When Mr. GROSVENOR concluded—

Mr. JOHNSON, of Kentucky, assigning as a reason therefor his anxiety to expedite the public business, and proceed to the adoption of those measures which the times imperiously demand, required the previous question.

The call was sanctioned by a vote of 73 to 71; but some misapprehension of the question having taken place, a second count took place, after some little confusion, and there appeared to be 62 for the previous question, and 70 against it. So the call was not duly sanctioned.

After a few remarks from Mr. MACON and others, as to the effect of striking out the first section of the bill—which some appeared to think would have the effect to destroy the bill—

Mr. HANSON, to save difficulty in that respect, withdrew his motion to strike out the first section of the bill.

Mr. JOHNSON then renewed his demand of the previous question—which precludes all further amendment as well as debate—which demand was seconded by a vote of 62 to 59.

The previous question was then put in the following form, viz: "Shall the main question be now put?" and decided by yeas and nays. For the previous question 75, against it 67, as follows:

YEAS—Messrs. Alston, Anderson, Avery, Barbour, Bard, Barnett, Bines, Brown, Caldwell, Cannon, Chappell, Clark, Comstock, Condict, Conard, Crawford, Creighton, Crouch, Cuthbert, Davis of Pennsylvania, Denoyelles, Desha, Earle, Eppes, Evans, Findley, Fisk of Vermont, Forney, Franklin, Gholson, Goodwyn, Gourdin, Griffin, Humphreys, Ingersoll, Ingham, Irwin, Johnson of Virginia, Johnson of Kentucky, Kennedy, Kent of Maryland, Kerr, Kershaw, Kilbourn, King of North Carolina, Lefferts, Lowndes, Lyle, McCoy, McKee, McKim, McLean, Montgomery, Moore, Murfree, Nelson, Newton, Parker, Pickens, Piper, Rea of Pennsylvania, Rich, Roane, Sage, Sevier, Seybert, Skinner, Smith of Pennsylvania, Smith of Virginia, Strong, Tannehill, Udree, Ward of New Jersey, Williams, and Wilson of Pennsylvania.

NAYS—Messrs. Alexander, Baylies of Massachusetts, Bayly, of Virginia, Bigelow, Bowen, Boyd, Bradley, Brigham, Burwell, Calhoun, Cilley, Clopton, Cox, Dana, Davenport, Davis of Massachusetts, Duvall, Ely, Farrow, Fisk of New York, Forsyth, Gaston, Grosvenor, Hale, Harris, Hasbrouck, Hawes, Hopkins

of Kentucky, Hubbard, Hungerford, Hulbert, Irving, Jackson of Rhode Island, Kent of New York, King of Massachusetts, Law, Lewis, Macon, Markell, Miller, Moseley, Pearson, Pickering, Pitkin, Pleasants, Potter, John Reed, William Reed, Rhea of Tennessee, Robertson, Ruggles, Schureman, Sharp, Sheffey, Stanford, Sturges, Taylor, Telfair, Thompson, Vose, Ward of Massachusetts, Wheaton, White, Wilcox, Wilson of Massachusetts, Winter, and Yancey.

The requisite number having required the main question to be put, it was put on the engrossing the bill for a third reading; and was decided in the negative. For the motion 49, against it 104, as follows:

YEAS—Messrs. Alexander, Alston, Barnett, Bines, Bradley, Caldwell, Calhoun, Cannon, Chappell, Clark, Condict, Crawford, Creighton, Crouch, Culpeper, Cuthbert, Duvall, Earle, Findley, Forney, Gaston, Gourdin, Griffin, Harris, Hasbrouck, Irving, Kent of Maryland, Kerr, Kershaw, Kilbourn, King of North Carolina, Lowndes, McKee, McLean, Montgomery, Oakley, Pearson, Pickens, Rea of Pennsylvania, Rich, Robertson, Sevier, Sharp, Skinner, Smith of Virginia, Taylor, Ward of New Jersey, Winter, and Yancey.

NAYS—Messrs. Anderson, Avery, Barbour, Bard, Baylies of Massachusetts, Bayly of Virginia, Bigelow, Bowen, Boyd, Bradbury, Brigham, Brown, Burwell, Cilley, Clopton, Comstock, Conard, Cooper, Cox, Dana, Davenport, Davis of Massachusetts, Davis of Pennsylvania, Denoyelles, Desha, Ely, Eppes, Evans, Farrow, Fisk of Vermont, Fisk of New York, Forsyth, Franklin, Geddes, Gholson, Goodwyn, Grosvenor, Hale, Hanson, Hawes, Hopkins of Kentucky, Hubbard, Humphreys, Hungerford, Hulbert, Ingersoll, Ingham, Irwin, Jackson of Rhode Island, Johnson of Virginia, Johnson of Kentucky, Kennedy, Kent of New York, King of Massachusetts, Law, Lefferts, Lewis, Lovett, Lyle, Macon, Markell, McCoy, McKim, Miller, Moore, Moseley, Murfree, Nelson, Newton, Parker, Pickering, Piper, Pitkin, Pleasants, Potter, John Reed, William Reed, Rhea of Tennessee, Roane, Ruggles, Sage, Schureman, Seybert, Sheffey, Shipherd, Smith of Pennsylvania, Stanford, Stockton, Strong, Sturges, Taggart, Tannehill, Telfair, Thompson, Udree, Vose, Ward of Massachusetts, Webster, Wheaton, White, Wilcox, Williams, Wilson of Massachusetts, and Wilson of Pennsylvania.

So the House decided that the bill should not be read a third time—in other words, that it should be rejected.

Mr. FORSYTH, of Georgia, then rose, and said he had voted in the majority against the bill, and was, therefore, at liberty to move a reconsideration of the vote just taken. This motion he did make with a view to retain the bill still in possession of the House, in order to recommit it—that the House might not be deprived of an opportunity of passing a bank bill during the present session.

Mr. MILLER, of New York, observed, that he was opposed to the reconsideration of the vote which the House had just given. Gentlemen who favored the establishment of a National Bank, had urged a reconsideration, with a view to ascertain if they could not meet on some middle ground, and reconcile their conflicting opinions. Those who were in favor of a bank, but differed merely as to the details, might well vote for a re-consideration. Mr. M. said he was opposed to the establishment of any bank, and no shape could be given to it which could induce him to vote for it; and as the gentlemen who had spoken on the question had not taken a view of it, which precisely presented the ground on which his objections rested, he would beg leave to trespass one moment on the time of the House.

Mr. M. found no hesitation in saying, that he considered Congress had undoubted power to establish a bank; and he would say, too, in his judgment, that power had been discreetly exercised in the establishment of the old Bank of the United States. He said he had listened with much attention and instruction to the remarks which had fallen from the advocates of both the systems which had been presented in the discussion, and he did not think either of them free of objections; yet, had he been persuaded, that, under present circumstances, it would be proper to establish any bank, he might perhaps have agreed to one of the projects which had been presented. He doubted, however, the propriety of any more banks in the present alarming state of our country—paper money had depreciated, and suspicion was so much afloat, that he could not travel the credit of almost any bank, in three hours ride, on any post road. He doubted the propriety of adding to this flood of bank paper, and feared it would hasten the return of that singular spectacle, when "a debtor will be seen persecuting his creditor with unrelenting punctuality, and paying him without mercy." He could not but doubt the propriety of increasing the issue of paper money at this time.

But, Mr. M. said, his objections did not stop here; he had understood, throughout the whole debate, that this bank was part of a system of finance; he doubted the propriety of placing reliance on a bank, for bringing any considerable revenue into the Treasury; he thought the proper office of a bank was to facilitate the collection of revenue created in some other way. If, as had been avowed, the object was to create a revenue by means of the bank, he considered it competent for him to look beyond the means, and inquire what was the object to which these means were to be applied? He was free to confess his opinions had undergone a complete revolution on this subject. At the commencement of the session, he had felt no disposition to withhold supplies of men or money; he arrived at this conclusion, in the belief that the conquest of Canada had been abandoned, and that our resources would be directed to the defence of the country. His opinion in favor of granting men and money, had been fortified by the despatches from our Ministers at Ghent. Under these impressions, he had lately visited his constituents, (by permission of the House,) and, in free conversation with his friends, had told them he should vote, not only for the bank, but a full system of finance; and would moreover agree to the most efficient Constitutional measures which might be devised for filling the ranks of the Army. This was his de-termination when he left his district, and this determination was not altered till he read Mr. Monroe's letter, which came out in favor of conscription! Mr. M. feared that letter might be considered as expressing the sense of this House, as well as that of the Administration. He hoped he might be mistaken; but when he read the law of the Legislature of the State of New York, and understood that a similar law was in progress before the Virginia Legislature; when he saw before him the bill which had passed the Senate, and the one which had been laid on his table from the Military Committee of this House, he could not but consider them all as giving "dreadful note of preparation."

Mr. M. considered that he had a perfect right to discuss the question of conscription on the passage of this bill; he contended that on any bill which seeks to raise money, it was a legitimate inquiry to ask the object for which the money was wanted, and if it was for an improper object, the money ought not to be granted. But he did not intend, at this time, to enter into a discussion of this question of conscription; he had no doubt some occasion would shortly present, which would bring this question directly before the House; in that case he might, perhaps, trouble them with a few remarks. In the mean time he could not forbear to say that he had not been able to disguise from himself, and he had no wish to conceal from others, that he viewed this subject with horror and alarm. He was opposed to it in all its aspects, and would not give it any aid directly or indirectly.

Mr. M. said he had of late considered this bank as part of a system to raise money for the conquest of Canada, by means of a military conscription. He considered himself, therefore, bound by every motive of duty and of patriotism to oppose it; and he would oppose it. He should not only vote against the reconsideration of the question, but, once for all, he wished it to be understood, that, until the question of conscription was disposed of, he should on the same ground vote against any bills for men or money which could by any possibility be used for that object.

The motion was opposed by Mr. Fisk of Vermont, and advocated by Mr. Fisk of New York, and Mr. Farrow of North Carolina.

Mr. Forsyth then withdrew his motion for the present, intimating that he might renew it to-morrow.

Mr. Calhoun moved to print the Secretary of the Treasury's letter read this morning; when an adjournment was called for and took place just before sundown.

Tuesday, November 29.

A new member, to wit: from Pennsylvania, Samuel Henderson, appeared, produced his credentials, was qualified, and took his seat, in the place of Jonathan Roberts, appointed a Senator.

The bill from the Senate, "supplementary to an act laying duties on notes of banks, bankers, and certain companies; on notes, bonds, and obligations, discounted by banks, bankers, and certain companies; and on bills of exchange of certain descriptions;" was read twice, and committed to a Committee of the Whole.

A message was received from the Senate announcing the rejection of the joint resolution from this House for appointing a committee to inquire into the expediency of removing the sittings of Congress to some other building.

THE INVESTIGATION.

Mr. JOHNSON, of Kentucky, from the committee appointed to inquire into the causes of the success of the enemy, in his invasion into this District in August last, delivered in a report of very great length, together with a voluminous mass of documents. This report (principally of a narrative character) Mr. J. moved to be printed, together with the following documents, selected from the mass laid before the Committee, as tending to give an impartial view of the whole transaction:

1. A report of the Army, its number and distribution, previous to the 1st July, 1814.
2. Letter of Colonel Monroe, then Secretary of State.
3. Letter of General Armstrong, late Secretary of War.
4. Letter from the Hon. William Jones, Secretary of the Navy.
5. Letters from the Hon. Richard Rush, Attorney General.
6. Communication from the War Department, including the orders in relation to the 10th military district, the requisition of the 4th July, and the correspondence with the Governors of Pennsylvania, Virginia, and Maryland, and with General Winder.
7. The narrative of General Winder.
8. Reports of Generals Stansbury, Smith, Young, Douglass, and Hungerford; Colonels Sterrett, Minor, Taylos, Laval, and Beall; Major Pinkney; and Captains Burch and Caldwell.
9. Report from the Navy Department, including the official report of Commodore Barney.
10. Letters from General Van Ness, Doctor Catlett, and John Law.
11. Reports from the Ordnance department.
12. Sentence of the court martial in relation to Captain Dyson, and the correspondence between him and the Secretary of War.
13. Report from the Corporation of Alexandria, including the capitulation, and letter from General John Mason.
14. Report from the Superintendent of Public Buildings.
15. Letter from William Simmons.

Mr. GROSVENOR, of New York, observing the great volume of the report and documents, objected to the printing of these papers, lest the length of time it would occupy should delay a consideration of the report.

Mr. WEBSTER, of New Hampshire, (a member of the Committee of Investigation,) hoped the papers would be printed. He dissented altogether from the manner in which that report had been prepared, though he was willing to do justice to the assiduity of the chairman of the committee in maturing the report. As soon as the

documents should be properly in the possession of the House, Mr. W. said he should think it his duty to make some motion on the subject. The report itself had indeed been a product of great labor—it was a sort of chronicle—but, in his view, it answered no one purpose for which the committee who made it had been appointed. So far from clearing up the causes of the failure of our arms at this place, he thought it was calculated (though not intended) to cover up in a mass of prolixity and detail what he considered a most disgraceful transaction.

Mr. GROSVENOR withdrew his opposition to the printing of these papers.

Mr. JOHNSON said, the House would form its judgment of the manner in which the committee had discharged their duty, from the documents collected by it and presented to the House, and from the statements of facts, and the conclusions which they had drawn therefrom. The committee had deemed it their duty—and that duty they performed without favor or affection—to speak freely upon all subjects arising from the transaction, the development of which had been committed to them, except on the solitary question of military conduct. They had collected all the facts that had come to their knowledge in relation to the military movements, and had thought proper to leave for the decision of those equally qualified with themselves to judge what better might have been done. If the committee had erred in any of their opinions, those opinions were subject to the will of the House. In relation to the mere military question, whenever the proper opportunity presented itself, he was not disposed to withhold either censure or praise, when it should appear to him to be due. He would venture to say, whatever difference of opinion might arise on those points on which the committee had not expressed an opinion, on those on which it *had* expressed an opinion, its views would receive the sanction, not only of the House, but of the whole world. In relation to himself, Mr. J. said, he claimed no other merit than having toiled with the rest of the committee in making up an opinion on the subject, &c.

Mr. WEBSTER said, he should be sorry to be supposed to have found fault with the manner of execution of the principle adopted by the committee. He complained that the committee had not thought proper to express any decided opinion on the transactions submitted to their investigation. Although the fact was announced that the enemy had landed within fifty miles of this place, and that twelve hundred men of their army had overthrown all the force collected here with two months' notice, no opinion was expressed of these circumstances. Neither would it be seen in the report that the burning of the Navy Yard was justifiable, or whether it was not an act of infatuation.

[Here the SPEAKER interrupted Mr. W., and called his attention to the question.]

Mr. W. said he objected to the report, because it expressed no opinion, and served in no degree to lead the public sentiment in respect to this disaster, and it was therefore that he proposed to question its correctness, &c. He heartily concurred in the motion for printing the report.

Mr. JOHNSON moved to refer the report to a Committee of the Whole, and make it the order for the third Monday in December. This would leave the report open to discussion, in which, some when it would, he proposed to be in the front rank and not in the rear. On this, as on all other occasions, he should face his duty as became a man.

Mr. YANCEY, of North Carolina, suggested the propriety of the report's lying on the table until printed. When the House should be in full possession of its contents, they would be able to act on it more intelligently, &c. This suggestion, however, was overruled, and the reference and printing of the report, as moved, were both agreed to.

FISCAL AFFAIRS.

The House resumed the consideration of the unfinished business of yesterday, viz: the motion to print the letter of the Secretary of the Treasury, yesterday laid before the House by the bank committee.

Mr. EPPES, of Virginia, said he thought the best course to pursue in relation to this subject, would be to recommit the letter to the committee who reported it, or to the Committee of Ways and Means. Mr. E. said he understood the fact to be, that the failure on the part of the public to meet any payment of the public debt, had not arisen from any want of funds, but from the difficulty of transporting those funds. He had understood, for instance, that there were sufficient funds in Baltimore to meet the payments which it was necessary to make at Philadelphia. It was important for the public to know that the difficulties adverted to by the Secretary, in his letter, had proceeded from causes which materially affected the ability of individuals to meet their engagements, and not from want of foresight in the financial department, or from a disregard to the inviolability of the public engagements. Another reason induced him to believe that this letter ought to be referred to the Committee of Ways and Means. At the commencement of the session, that committee had reported their opinion that it was not the interest of the United States further to rely on loans; they had therefore reported to the House a plan to provide for the ways and means of the ensuing year, not bottomed on loans. While their report was before the House, and not acted on, the new Secretary of the Treasury arrived, and took his station at the head of that department. The committee, conceiving it due to him to give him an opportunity to express his views on the subject, had called on him to do so. In this letter to them, he had preferred a different system to that they had recommended for the relief of the immediate exigencies of the Government; and, instead of providing for a national circulating medium, had relied on the aid to be afforded by a National Bank. Mr. E. said he had no wish whatever to cast censure on the Sec-

retary of the Treasury, but to screen himself, and the committee to which he belonged, from censure for any alleged deficiency in the provision for the supplies for the present quarter. Every supply asked for by the Treasury had been granted by Congress—being merely a partial loan to supply the deficiency created by sending a part of the twenty-five million loan to Europe for sale. The idea of the Secretary was, that, with the aid of a National Bank, he could negotiate the balance of the loan within the present quarter, so as to meet the demands against the Treasury within that period. No blame, therefore, rested on the Committee of Ways and Means in this respect; they had acquitted themselves of their duty. There was another reason why he thought the letter ought to be committed as he proposed. If there was no adequate provision for the demands of the present quarter provision ought to be immediately made to enable our citizens having unsatisfied claims on the Government to fund the balances due to them, or receive interest on the amount of them. For another reason, he thought the letter ought to be referred. The circumstances stated by the Secretary of the Treasury required that some circulating medium should be forthwith established to prevent embarrassment to the Government from the recurrence of like difficulties.

Mr. FORSYTH, of Georgia, said he was opposed to the proposed reference of this letter to the Committee of Ways and Means, because there was no information contained in it, he presumed, which was not already in possession of the House; and because no scheme of finance was suggested in it which had not been already before that committee. It appeared to him the gentleman from Virginia had misapprehended a part of the letter altogether, when he considered it as personally concerning himself. Mr. F. said he could not see anything in the letter which threw a censure on the Committee of Ways and Means, or on any part of this House. He saw no general reason for the reference, and he could not see the force of the particular reason which the gentleman had assigned.

The question was then taken on reference, and carried; and also on printing, and likewise carried. [For the letter, see *ante* page 651.]

NATIONAL BANK.

Mr. KILBOURN, of Ohio, said he had ever considered it to be the interest of the United States that a National Bank should be established, for the convenient management of its finances. It was with satisfaction he found that to be the opinion of a great majority of the House, by the vote some time ago, on the proposition that it was expedient to establish a National Bank. The project before the House having been rejected, he held in his hand a resolution embracing a sketch of a plan which, if approved, might be put into the shape of a bill. Mr. K. then offered his resolution for consideration.

Resolved, That the Committee of Ways and Means be instructed to prepare, in due form, and report to this

House, a bill to establish a National Bank, of which the following shall be the principal, or prominent features, viz: It shall be called the National Bank of the United States. It shall be seated in the city of Philadelphia, but may have branches throughout the Union. The capital stock thereof shall be fifty millions of dollars, divided into five hundred thousand shares, of one hundred dollars each. Thirty millions of the capital may be subscribed by individuals, companies, and corporations; and twenty millions thereof shall be subscribed by the Secretary of the Treasury on behalf of the United States. The thirty millions, subscribed by individuals, companies, and corporations, shall be paid at proper periods, as follows, viz: six millions in specie, eighteen millions in stock created since the year 1811, and six millions in Treasury notes issued since the commencement of the war; that is to say, on each share twenty dollars in specie, sixty dollars in stock, and twenty dollars in Treasury notes. The twenty millions subscribed for the United States, shall be paid in Treasury notes hereafter to be issued, or in stock of the United States, to be hereafter created. For the management of the bank, there shall be fifteen directors, nine of whom shall be elected by the individual stockholders; and six shall be nominated by the Secretary of the Treasury, and appointed by the President of the United States. The board of directors shall appoint the president, and all other officers and servants of the principal bank and of the branches. The charter to continue twenty years, and no other bank charters to be granted by Congress during that time, except to the banking associations now formed within the District of Columbia. Subscriptions to be opened in one or more places in every State and Territory, and in the District of Columbia, under the care of proper superintendents. The bank shall go into operation, so soon as one million two hundred thousand dollars, [as intended *twelve* millions of dollars,] in due proportion of specie, stock, and Treasury notes, is paid in upon the subscriptions. The bank shall be authorized to receive, upon all loans it shall make, an interest at the rate of five per cent. per annum, and no more. When the subscriptions shall be filled to the amount of fifty millions, and the same be paid in, the bank may be required to loan to the Government twenty-five millions of dollars, and at any time prior to the completing of that amount of subscription, it may be required to loan to Government, in that proportion, to the amount actually subscribed and paid in. It shall be the right and duty of the Secretary of the Treasury to inspect all the books of the bank, and Congress may appoint committees for that purpose. And the President of the United States shall be empowered, in certain cases, and during certain limited periods, to authorize or direct the suspension of specie payments at the bank, or to substitute therefor certain Treasury notes; which suspension, or substitution, with the causes thereof, he shall make public by proclamation; and the same, in like manner, to recall and revoke, when the cause or causes shall cease to operate; or, in case of their continuance, to lay the same before Congress at the next session thereafter, that they may take such measures thereon as shall appear to them expedient.

[Had the foregoing been received and adopted by the House, Mr. K. intended to have added the following proposition, viz: Congress shall have power, when they shall deem it expedient, to extend the capital of the bank to $60,000,000, by authorizing a further subscription, on the part of the United States, of $10,000,-000, payable in six per cent. stock of the United States; and, in such case, there shall be appointed, as above, on behalf of the Government, three additional directors in the board.]

This motion the SPEAKER pronounced to be out of order, as, in substance and matter, the same as that already rejected by the House, and which, therefore, could not now be resumed, unless by a vote of reconsideration to-day.

Mr. KILBOURN remarked, that he had not understood that his motion would be considered by the Chair out of order, or he would not have proposed it. He the more readily withdrew it, because he understood that it was yet intended to move a reconsideration of the vote of yesterday.

On motion, of Mr. EPPES, the House then proceeded to the orders of the day.

TAX ON DISTILLED LIQUORS, &c.

The bill to provide an additional revenue for defraying the expenses of the Government, and for the payment of the public debt, by laying an additional duty on spirits distilled, and for amending the act, already in existence, for taxing that article, was read a third time. [The additional tax is fixed at twenty cents per gallon on the quantity distilled.]

Mr. CANNON, of Tennessee, moved to recommit the bill to the Committee of Ways and Means.

On this motion Mr. C. spoke as follows:

Mr. Speaker, I have two objections to the bill in its present shape, which I think probably the House will remedy, in the event this motion succeed. In the first place, I object to the amount of the additional duty on the article on which we are about to increase the tax; and in the second place, I also object to the mode in which this tax is about to be laid. The double mode of laying the tax now about to be adopted, is somewhat intricate and vexatious, and I think would be calculated to produce much difficulty to the persons who collect the revenue, as well as all those who may be engaged in making spirits. Sir, said he, by continuing the tax on the capacity of the stills, you subject all those persons engaged in this business, to all the trouble, difficulty, and inconvenience of going to the collectors from the different parts of the collection districts, and carrying with them their securities, and giving bonds to the collector for the tax on the capacity, that you otherwise would do, were the whole of the tax laid in that way; and now, in addition to all this, you are about to subject the owner of every distillery, who may think proper to use it under this law, to the additional trouble and inconvenience of keeping an exact account of every drop of spirits made in his distillery, and render the same to the collector of the revenue four times in each and every year; to be sworn to, either by himself or by the person or persons who may be employed in attending his distillery; this I think, sir, will produce much embarrassment and difficulty. It must be known to every member in this House, that in many parts of the United States—I know it is the case in the Western country—the owners of distilleries frequently have other persons employed to attend them; and sometimes in the course of two or three months they have two or three different persons in their employ, whom they would find it difficult and almost impossible to collect together, and have present at the time of rendering to the collector their different accounts of the amount of spirits distilled (during the time pointed out in this bill,) in which they are required to make said returns. Again, Mr. Speaker, a similar additional trouble and difficulty must be imposed on the collector. If this bill passes with its present provisions, he will certainly have to keep some kind of a separate book, containing the amount of spirits made by each person engaged in distilling spirits in his district, within the certain stated period, pointed out by this bill; he must certainly first know the precise amount of spirits made by each individual, before he can possibly know the amount of additional revenue to demand and collect from each distiller in his district. Thus, sir, I think I have clearly shown that a two-fold difficulty, trouble, and expense, will be imposed by this mode of laying the tax, both on the collectors of the revenue as well as those engaged in distilling spirits; and that, too, without the smallest possible benefit either to individuals or the Government. And although I would have preferred an increase of the tax on the capacity of the stills, to a certain extent, because I think it the most certain revenue; at the same time I think it better to lay the whole tax on the gallon, than to adopt the measure now before us. Either mode of laying the tax I think far preferable to this double mode of taxation. Either of the modes I have suggested for increasing the tax, I think far better than the one contemplated by the House; with only half the trouble and difficulty to encounter, it would produce precisely the same current of revenue.

The honorable gentleman from Virginia, who is chairman of the Committee of Ways and Means, has told us that the tax laid on the capacity of the stills, by the former act of Congress, produces a certain revenue which he could not consent to give up, because the other mode proposed, to lay the tax on the gallon, was more uncertain. This certainly would be a strong argument in favor of increasing the tax on the capacity of the stills, because, if you increase the tax in that way to a certain amount, you will still continue to have a certain revenue to anticipate. But, sir, as it is contemplated to be laid by this bill, you cannot know what your revenue will be, derived from that article, until you can ascertain the amount of spirits made and returned to the collectors under the provisions of the law. And in addition to all this, be assured, if the tax is increased to this amount and in the manner contemplated by the bill now under consideration, it will have a tendency, in a great degree, to depress the business of making domestic spirits throughout the United States. The price of this article consequently must be vastly increased; and all this increased price on the large quantities that must be purchased by the Government for the use of the Army, will

amount to the same, as respects the Government, as a reduction of the revenue derived from this article. Certainly it cannot be the intention of this House to lay such enormous duties on the distilling of spirits, as to prevent those persons owning distilleries from using them, nor can it at this time be the interest of the Government to impose such taxes on them as will in a very great degree diminish the quantity made, as, by doing this, the very object of the law will be defeated; instead of obtaining a larger amount of revenue, than that derived heretofore, I fear we would obtain less. Sir, I cannot see, for my own part, the policy of laying such heavy taxes on our infant manufactures, so useful in our country, and so indispensable to increase the wealth and prosperity of this nation. I would think it much better to bear as lightly on them as possible, and endeavor to give them every encouragement in our power.

But, Mr. Speaker, to return more immediately to the subject before you, I contend that the tax contemplated to be laid by this bill, is unjust and unequal. A distillery, the whole establishment of which would not cost more, perhaps, than five hundred or one thousand dollars, under this law the owner for using the same one year would probably have to pay a tax of seven hundred or one thousand dollars, being as much, or perhaps more than the property thus used would be worth. If you pass the bill in its present shape, what would be the situation of the poor man, owning a small distillery of this description, with but little property of any other description, when compared with that of a wealthy citizen owning vast property of a different description? Why, sir, the poor man thus owning a distillery, whose whole property including the same not amounting to more than seven or eight hundred dollars, would have to pay to the Government for using his distillery one year, an amount equal to the value of his whole property, while his wealthy neighbor would be secured in the enjoyment of property of perhaps ten times his amount, without paying half as much to the support of the Government. A law of this kind, I think, will certainly have an unjust as well as an unequal operation. I am willing to go as far as any member in this House in the adoption of such measures as will support the Government and revive the public credit, but at the same time I think we ought to endeavor to lay our taxes and increase our revenue in such way as will, as near as possible, have an equal bearing on all the people of the United States, and to call on each individual more in proportion to his wealth, and consequently his ability to pay. I am confident, if this bill passes without alteration, it will defeat the object we have in view—it will put down many of the distilleries in every part of the country, and, instead of increasing, may, perhaps, lessen the revenue. Sir, it is very far from being my object to throw obstacles in the way of any measures calculated to get the Government out of its present difficulties, nor would I have made this motion to recommit the bill for the purpose of changing it, and reducing the tax, had I believed it was the intention of the House to raise the taxes on any other property, or articles of any description, equal to the tax contemplated by this bill. But, believing no article or other property will be taxed equal to it, I cannot vote for this bill as it now stands. I believe it to be inconsistent with those grand principles of justice and equality that should at all times distinguish the conduct of this Legislative body. Were I to give this measure my support, I should believe I was supporting a measure, the operation of which would be unjust and unequal in its operation, not only as it respects the different States in the Union, but also between individuals who are citizens of the same State. The honorable gentleman from Maryland (Mr. McKim) as well as the gentleman from South Carolina (Mr. Farrow,) are both opposed to the recommitment of this bill, because they think the House has previously settled the question, as to the amount of the tax. But, sir, it must be recollected, when in Committee of the Whole, we did determine to reduce the additional tax to fifteen cents per gallon, which was afterwards disagreed to in the House; therefore I cannot but hope the motion I have submitted to the House for recommitting the bill for the objects I have stated will prevail.

Mr. Fisk, of Vermont, opposed the motion. This tax, he contended, would, in the result, exhibit as great a product from the Eastern as Western States, &c.

The motion for recommitment was supported by Mr. Humphreys, of Tennessee, in an argument of some length, the object of which was to demonstrate the unequal operation of this tax as affecting relatively the Eastern or Western States.

Mr. Grosvenor said, he hoped the bill would not be recommitted. If there were no better reasons to be offered for such a motion, than those which have transpired from the gentleman just sat down, the recommitment would, in his opinion, be worse than useless. The gentleman, Mr. G. said, moaned most piteously about the unequal pressure of the bill; it pressed the Western States to the earth, while the East and the North escape the pressure. How is this made out? Why, says the gentleman, the State of Connecticut has much more property than that of Tennessee; yet the land tax of the first is about one hundred and eighteen thousand dollars, while that of the latter is one hundred and ten thousand. Why, said Mr. G., has the gentleman forgotten that blessed principle in our Constitution which gives a representation of his slaves? And does he not know that the consequence was, that representation and direct taxation should jump together. Tennessee, with nearly fifty thousand less of free population, yet has a number of representatives equal to Connecticut. Hence it is, that the direct tax in the two States must be equal. The gentleman must thank the Southern patriots for this, and, if he dislikes it, join to amend the Constitution. But look at the indirect taxes; by the report of the Secretary, Connecticut has paid, of internal duties, more than fifty-eight thousand dollars, while in the same period, Tennessee has paid only eighteen thousand dollars. Thus, sir, it is apparent, the complaints of the West are wholly unfounded. The indirect taxes press harder upon the Northern and Eastern States, than upon the West. The gentleman has asked, if he should vote for this bill, what he should say to his constituents, when he should return home? I will relieve the gentleman from his difficulty; he may tell them, that three years ago this nation was basking in peace. All the revenues for the support of the Government were derived from commerce, and the country prospered while you were free from burdens. You became loud for war; you forced all your representatives on this floor to vote for war. Commerce was of course destroyed, and all our revenue vanished. To support this war, which was in part compelled by you, this bill is now indispensable; you must be content with deep taxation; you must "pay for the whistle which you have purchased." This may be the conclusive answer, said Mr. G., to any reproach which the gentleman may receive from his constituents.

Mr. Ingersoll, of Pennsylvania, opposed the recommitment. In the dispute between the Eastern and Western States, the intermediate ground was entirely overlooked; though he contended Pennsylvania would pay as large a proportion of the tax as any other State; and therefore he should vote for it, because he was desirous that State should, in the present crisis, contribute its full proportion. Among other things, speaking in support of the tax, Mr. I. said, he could not see why, whenever this whiskey tax came up, so many wry faces should be made upon it; and the amount of the tax could not be considered very oppressive, when, even after the tax was laid, a man might make himself dead drunk for sixpence.

Mr. Humphreys, in reply to Mr. Grosvenor, who remarked, that even if the tax did operate oppressively, the people of the West ought to bear it patiently, because made necessary by the war for which they had been so anxious—remarked, with much point, on the weakness of this argument. The people of Tennessee, he said, had advocated the war from their zeal in behalf of the rights and honor of the country, which they believed to demand it; and it would be hard indeed, if they were to be taxed higher than other sections of the Union, because more devoted to their country's rights.

Mr. Kilbourn, of Ohio, also advocated the recommitment of the bill, for the general reasons assigned by other gentlemen. The tax already in existence, he said, had suppressed or stopped perhaps one-half of the distilleries in his district, and the increase now proposed of four hundred per cent. on the present duty would, he conceived, rather reduce than increase the revenue, as he endeavored to demonstrate by a number of arguments.

Mr. Webster, of New Hampshire, asked for information of the gentleman from Ohio, what proportion of the direct tax within that State was paid by non-residents?

Mr. Kilbourn admitted, that more than one-half of the last direct tax in Ohio, had, in effect been paid by non-residents, though but a small part more; but that four-fifths of the soil was owned by non-residents; which disproportion in the amount of tax paid by the residents to the lands owned by them, he might have mentioned when up before, had he been so disposed, as one of the hardships under which the State labored.

Mr. McKim spoke against the recommitment of the bill, and in reply to the arguments of inequality and oppressiveness in its operation, both which he denied. The consumer paying the tax, independent of the general view of the taxes, he believed the Atlantic States would pay as large a portion of this particular tax as the Western.

Mr. Farrow, of South Carolina, opposed recommitment, on the ground that the question had already been amply discussed, and seriously settled as to the amount of the tax; though, he intimated, he should be opposed to the passage of the bill unless a provision should be introduced into it allowing a drawback on exportation, in order to avoid a violation of the Constitutional provision against a tax on exports.

Mr. Cannon again spoke in support of his motion. He said he could not vote for the bill as it now stood; if he did, he should believe he was voting for a measure whose operation would be unjust and unequal—not only as to the different States of the Union, but as to the citizens of the same State. As the House had already once changed its vote on this subject, he hoped it might in this instance yield to his wishes for a recommitment.

The question on a recommitment of the bill was then decided in the negative—for recommitment 44, against it 111, as follows:

Yeas—Messrs. Alexander, Alston, Bowen, Burwell, Caldwell, Cannon, Clark, Crawford, Creighton, Culpeper, Dana, Davis of Pennsylvania, Desha, Duvall, Findley, Forney, Franklin, Harris, Hopkins of Kentucky, Humphreys, Hungerford, Irwin, Kerr, Kilbourn, Lyle, Macon, McCoy, McKee, McLean, Montgomery, Murfree, Ormsby, Pearson, Pickens, Piper, Rea of Pennsylvania, Rhea of Tennessee, Sevier, Sharp, Smith of Virginia, Stanford, Stuart, Tannehill, and Yancey.

Nays—Messrs. Anderson, Avery, Barbour, Bard, Barnett, Baylies of Massachusetts, Bayly of Virginia, Bigelow, Bines, Boyd, Bradbury, Bradley, Brigham, Brown, Calhoun, Champion, Chappell, Cilley, Clopton, Comstock, Condict, Conard, Cooper, Cox, Crouch, Cuthbert, Davenport, Davis of Massachusetts, Denoyelles, Earle, Ely, Eppes, Evans, Farrow, Fisk of Vermont, Fisk of New York, Forsyth, Gaston, Geddes, Gholson, Goodwyn, Gourdin, Griffin, Grosvenor, Hale, Hall, Hanson, Hasbrouck, Hawes, Henderson, Hulbert, Ingersoll, Ingham, Irving, Jackson of Rhode Island, Johnson of Virginia, Johnson of Kentucky, Kennedy, Kent of New York, Kent of Maryland, Kershaw, King of Massachusetts, King of North Carolina, Law, Lefferts, Lewis, Lovett, Lowndes, Markell, McKim, Miller, Moore, Moseley, Nelson, Newton, Oakley, Parker, Pickering, Pitkin, Pleasants, Potter, John Reed, William Reed, Rich, Roane, Robertson, Ruggles, Sage, Schureman, Seybert, Sheffey, Shipherd, Smith of Pennsylvania, Stockton, Sturges, Taggart, Taylor, Telfair, Thompson, Troup, Udree, Vose, Ward of New Jersey, Webster, Wheaton, White, Wilcox, Williams, Wilson of Massachusetts, Wilson of Pennsylvania, and Winter.

The question then recurred on the passage of the bill, and was decided by the following vote:

Yeas—Messrs. Anderson, Avery, Barbour, Bard, Barnett, Bayly of Virginia, Bines, Bowen, Bradbury, Bradley, Brown, Calhoun, Chappell, Cilley, Clopton, Comstock, Condict, Conard, Cox, Crawford, Crouch, Cuthbert, Dana, Davenport, Davis of Massachusetts, Davis of Pennsylvania, Denoyelles, Earle, Eppes, Evans, Findley, Fisk of Vermont, Fisk of New York, Forsyth, Gaston, Gholson, Goodwyn, Gourdin, Griffin, Grosvenor, Hale, Hall, Hanson, Hasbrouck, Hawes, Henderson, Hopkins of Kentucky, Hulbert, Ingersoll, Ingham, Irving, Irwin, Johnson of Virginia, Johnson of Kentucky, Kennedy, Kent of New York, Kent of Maryland, Kershaw, Kilbourn, King of North Carolina, Lefferts, Lewis, Lovett, Lowndes, Macon, Markell, McCoy, McKim, Montgomery, Moore, Murfree, Nelson, Newton, Oakley, Ormsby, Parker, Pickens, Pleasants, John Reed, William Reed, Rhea of Tennessee, Rich, Roane, Robertson, Ruggles, Sage, Schureman, Seybert, Shipherd, Skinner, Smith of Pennsylvania, Stockton, Tannehill, Taylor, Telfair, Troup, Udree, Vose, Ward of New Jersey, Webster, White, Wilcox, Williams, Wilson of Massachusetts, Wilson of Pennsylvania, Winter, and Yancey—107.

Nays—Messrs. Alexander, Alston, Baylies of Massachusetts, Bigelow, Boyd, Brigham, Burwell, Caldwell, Cannon, Champion, Clark, Creighton, Culpeper, Desha, Duvall, Ely, Farrow, Forney, Franklin, Geddes, Harris, Humphreys, Hungerford, Jackson of Rhode Island, Kerr, King of Massachusetts, Law, Lyle, McKee, McLean, Moseley, Pearson, Pickering, Piper, Rea of Pennsylvania, Sevier, Sharp, Sheffey, Smith of Virginia, Stanford, Sturges, and Thompson—42.

So the bill was passed and sent to the Senate for concurrence.

On motion of Mr. Eppes, the House then resolved itself into a Committee of the Whole, on the two other tax bills. The bill first taken up was that for imposing additional taxes on pleasure carriages and the harness thereof.

The bill having been read through, Mr. Eppes stated in a very lucid manner, the grounds on which the committee had framed the provisions of this bill in the shape in which it was presented to the House.

This bill having been discussed and gone through, the other bill, for imposing a variety of miscellaneous taxes, was also taken up and gone through, and both bills were reported to the House.

Wednesday, November 30.

Another member, to wit: from New York, Nathaniel Howell, appeared, and took his seat.

The House resumed the consideration of the report of the Committee of the Whole on the two tax bills, and the amendments made thereto were taken up and considered. And the bills having been further discussed and amended, were ordered to be engrossed for a third reading.

The report of the Committee of Pensions and Revolutionary Claims, in favor of William Arnold, passed through a Committee of the Whole, and was concurred in by the House, and the Committee of Pensions and Revolutionary Claims directed to bring in a bill accordingly.

The bill extending the right of pre-emption to settlers in the Illinois Territory, passed through a Committee of the Whole, and underwent considerable discussion. When the bill was reported to the House, it was ordered to lie on the table.

The House then resolved itself into a Committee of the Whole on the bill from the Senate authorizing a draught of 80,000 militia for the defence of the frontier, and on the bill for filling the Regular Army by a classification of the free male population. The bills were no more than read through, when (the House being thin) the Committee rose, reported progress, and adjourned.

THURSDAY, December 1.

On motion of Mr. PLEASANTS, the Committee on the Judiciary Establishment were instructed to inquire into the propriety of authorizing the judges of the circuit Courts of the United States to call special courts, for the trials of appeals from the decisions of the district courts in admiralty, and especially in prize cases.

The following resolution was submitted by Mr. ROBERTSON, and was read, and ordered to lie on the table:

Resolved, That so much of the rules of this House which is supposed to prevent the re-examination of a subject which has been decided on, be suspended, so far as relates to the establishment of a National Bank.

The SPEAKER laid before the House a letter from the Secretary of the Navy, transmitting his report, made in obedience to a resolution of the House of the 3d March, 1813, upon the state and condition of the several navy yards belonging to the United States; which were read, and ordered to lie on the table,

The following Message was received from the PRESIDENT OF THE UNITED STATES:

To the Senate and House of
    Representatives of the United States:

I transmit, for the information of Congress, the communications last received from the Ministers Extraordinary and Plenipotentiary of the United States at Ghent, explaining the course and actual state of their negotiations with the Plenipotentiaries of Great Britain.

           JAMES MADISON.

DECEMBER 1, 1814.

The said Message and communications were read, and referred to the Committee on Foreign Relations; and 5,000 copies thereof ordered to be printed for the use of the members of this House.

PETITION OF JOHN APPLETON.

The SPEAKER laid before the House a report from the Secretary of the Treasury, on the petition of John Appleton; which was read, and ordered to lie on the table. The report is as follows:

TREASURY DEPARTMENT, *Nov.* 28, 1814.

SIR: I have the honor to transmit herewith a report, prepared in obedience to a resolution of the House of Representatives of the 28th day of October last.

I have the honor to be, very respectfully, sir, your most obedient servant,   A. J. DALLAS.

Hon. L. CHEVES, *Speaker, H. of R.*

TREASURY DEPARTMENT, *Nov.* 28, 1814.

In obedience to the order of the House of Representatives, dated the 28th October, 1814, referring the petition of John Appleton to the Secretary of the Treasury, the Secretary respectfully reports:

That the act of Congress for the assessment and collection of direct taxes and internal duties fixes the compensation of the principal assessor by the number of days employed in hearing appeals and making out lists, allowing, in that respect, two dollars each day; and by the number of taxable persons contained in the tax lists as delivered by the principal assessors to the collectors, allowing, in that respect, four dollars for every hundred taxable persons. But, the act requires the principal assessors to perform various other important services, in the division of assessment districts, in the appointment and direction of assistant assessors, in the preparation or holding appeals, and, generally, in carrying the instructions of the Secretary of the Treasury into effect, without providing any compensation for those services independent of the general provision, which has been stated, and which, it is seen, graduates the compensation, by reference only to services performed in the latter stages of official duty.

That, on the 27th November, 1813, the petitioner, John Appleton, was duly appointed by the President of the United States, in the recess of the Senate, to be principal assessor for the tenth Massachusetts district; and that the petitioner (as it is understood and believed at this Department) entered upon his official duties, and performed all the services required by the act of Congress, until the Senate rejected his nomination, at their next session, and until the rejection was made known to him, as well as the appointment of Samuel Hoar to be his successor, by a letter from the Secretary of the Treasury, dated the 26th March, 1814. That, at this period, however, the valuation and assessment of the direct tax had not been matured; no appeals had been heard, and no lists of taxable persons had been delivered to the collector; but the petitioner promptly and fairly delivered his official books and papers to his successor, reserving his right of compensation for the subsequent consideration of the proper department.

That the petitioner is entitled to some compensation for services rendered during a period of four months cannot be denied, consistently with the principles of justice; but it seems to have been the opinion of the late Secretary of the Treasury that the compensation prescribed by law could not be exceeded; that the whole was payable to the principal assessor in office, at the time of holding the appeals and delivering the tax lists to the collector; and that any apportionment of the compensation was a matter of private arrangement and agreement between the new and the old officer. The latter, however, has claimed the whole amount, upon the terms of the act of Congress; and his account has been stated and settled, accordingly, by the Auditor and Comptroller; but the warrant for payment has not yet been issued.

That, under these circumstances, the order of the House of Representatives has made it the duty of the Secretary of the Treasury to review the subject; and, with every proper deference for the judgment of his predecessor, he has been led to a result differing, in some measure, from the opinion expressed by that respectable gentleman.

He considers the designation of a principal assessor as the designation of an officer, and not of a person; and that the whole compensation is given for the performance of the whole of the duty of the office. Whether a change of the officer is produced by death, resignation, or removal, the office itself and the duties of the office equally remain entire and unchanged.

He considers the opposite construction of the words of the act as hostile to its spirit, leading to a contingent charge upon the public, which the Legislature did not contemplate, or to the oppression of an individual, which justice will not permit.

He considers the apportionment of the compensation, in this case, between the first and the second principal assessors, to be regularly within the province of the accounting officers of the Treasury; and that the materials for making it (if the parties should not prefer an amicable adjustment) may readily be obtained.

All which is respectfully submitted.

A. J. DALLAS.

TAX BILLS.

An engrossed bill to provide additional revenues for defraying the expenses of Government and maintaining the public credit, by duties on sales at auction; on the postage of letters; on licenses to retail wines, spirituous liquors, and foreign merchandise; on carriages for the conveyance of persons, and on plated harness; was read the third time. And, on the question that the same do pass, it passed in the affirmative—yeas 114. nays 35, as follows:

Yeas—Messrs. Alexander, Alston, Anderson, Avery, Barbour, Bard, Bayly of Virginia, Bines, Bowen, Bradley, Brown, Burwell, Butler, Caldwell, Calhoun, Cannon, Chappell, Clark, Clopton, Comstock, Condict, Conard, Coxe, Crawford, Creighton, Cuthbert, Dana, Davis of Pennsylvania, Denoyelles, Desha, Duvall, Earle, Eppes, Evans, Farrow, Fisk of Vermont, Forney, Forsyth, Franklin, Gaston, Geddes, Gholson, Glasgow, Goodwyn, Gourdin, Griffin, Grosvenor, Hall, Harris, Hasbrouck, Hawes, Hopkins of Kentucky, Howell, Hubbard, Humphreys, Hungerford, Ingersoll, Ingham, Irving, Irwin, Johnson of Virginia, Johnson of Kentucky, Kennedy, Kent of New York, Kent of Maryland, Kerr, Kershaw, Kilbourn, Lefferts, Lowndes, Lyle, Macon, McCoy, McKee, McKim, McLean, Montgomery, Moore, Murfree, Nelson, Newton, Oakley, Ormsby, Parker, Pearson, Piper, Pleasants, Rea of Pennsylvania, Rhea of Tennessee, Rich, Roane, Robertson, Sage, Seybert, Sharp, Sheffey, Skinner, Smith of New York, Smith of Pennsylvania, Smith of Virginia, Stanford, Stockton, Stuart, Tannehill, Taylor, Telfair, Troup, Udree, Ward of New Jersey, Williams, Wilson of Pennsylvania, Winter, and Yancey.

Nays—Messrs. Baylies of Massachusetts, Bigelow, Boyd, Bradbury, Champion, Cilley, Cooper, Davenport, Davis of Massachusetts, Ely, Hale, Henderson, Hulbert, Jackson of Rhode Island, King of Massachusetts, Law, Lewis, Lovett, Markell, Moseley, Pickering, Pitkin, John Reed, Ruggles, Schureman, Shipherd, Sturges, Taggart, Thompson, Vose, Ward of Massachusetts, Webster, Wheaton, and Wilcox.

Ordered, That the title be, "An act to provide additional revenues for defraying the expenses of Government and maintaining the public credit, by duties on sales at auction; on the postage of letters; on licenses to retail wines, spirituous liquors, and foreign merchandise."

An engrossed bill to provide additional revenues for defraying the expenses of Government and maintaining the public credit, by duties on carriages for the conveyance of persons, and the harness used therefor, was read the third time; and, on the question that the same do pass, it passed in the affirmative—yeas 120, nays 34, as follows:

Yeas—Messrs. Alexander, Alston, Anderson, Avery, Barbour, Bard, Barnett, Bines, Bowen, Bradley, Brown, Burwell, Butler, Caldwell, Calhoun, Cannon, Chappell, Clark, Comstock, Condict, Conard, Coxe, Crawford, Creighton, Crouch, Culpeper, Cuthbert, Dana, Davenport, Davis of Pennsylvania, Denoyelles, Desha, Duvall, Earle, Eppes, Evans, Farrow, Fisk of Vermont, Fisk of New York, Forney, Forsyth, Franklin, Gaston, Geddes, Gholson, Glasgow, Goodwyn, Gourdin, Griffin, Grosvenor, Hall, Harris, Hasbrouck, Hawes, Henderson, Hopkins of Kentucky, Howell, Hubbard, Humphreys, Hungerford, Ingersoll, Ingham, Irving, Irwin, Johnson of Virginia, Johnson of Kentucky, Kennedy, Kent of New York, Kent of Maryland, Kerr, Kershaw, Kilbourn, Lefferts, Lewis, Lowndes, Lyle, Macon, McCoy, McKee, McKim, McLean, Montgomery, Moore, Murfree, Nelson, Newton, Oakley, Ormsby, Parker, Piper, Pleasants, Rea of Pennsylvania, Rhea of Tennessee, Rich, Roane, Robertson, Sage, Sevier, Seybert, Sharp, Sheffey, Skinner, Smith of New York, Smith of Pennsylvania, Smith of Virginia, Stanford, Stockton, Strong, Stuart, Tannehill, Taylor, Telfair, Troup, Udree, Ward of New Jersey, White, Williams, Wilson of Pennsylvania, Winter, and Yancey.

Nays—Messrs. Baylies of Massachusetts, Bayly of Virginia, Bigelow, Boyd, Bradbury, Brigham, Champion, Cilley, Clopton, Davis of Massachusetts, Ely, Hale, Hulbert, Jackson of Rhode Island, King of Massachusetts, Law, Lovett, Markell, Moseley, Pickering, Pitkin, Potter, John Reed, Ruggles, Schureman, Shipherd, Sturges, Taggart, Thompson, Vose, Ward of Massachusetts, Webster, Wheaton, and Wilcox.

Ordered, That the title be, "An act to provide additional revenues for defraying the expenses of Government, and maintaining the public credit, by duties on carriages for the conveyance of persons and the harness used therefor."

Friday, December 2.

A message from the Senate informed the House that the Senate have passed a bill "to extend the time of Oliver Evans's patent for his improvement on steam engines;" in which they ask the concurrence of this House.

The House resumed the consideration of Mr. Robertson's motion, to suspend so much of the rule of the House as precludes the reconsideration of any subject on which the House has during the same session decided.

Some debate arose on the motion, which was supported by the mover and by Mr. Wilson of Pennsylvania, and opposed by Mr. Stanford, and others. In the course of the debate, it was mentioned that a bill on the subject of a National Bank was in preparation in the Senate. Mr.

WARD, of New Jersey, moved to lay the resolution on the table; which motion was negatived, 64 to 44.

The question was then taken on agreeing to the resolution, and negatived, as follows: For the motion 50, against it 65.

The SPEAKER laid before the House a letter from the Secretary of the Treasury, in reply to one from the Speaker requiring a warrant for money to defray the charges of this House, apprizing him that, the appropriation on this head being exhausted, a further provision therefor by law was necessary. The letter was ordered to lie on the table, on the intimation of Mr. INGHAM that the Committee of Ways and Means were about to act on the subject.

A report was received from the War Department on the petition of the President and Directors of the Eastern Branch Bridge. The report states that the bridge was destroyed at the instance of General Winder, but by the agency of the Navy Department, and under the immediate superintendence of Captain Creighton.

This report was, on motion of Mr. LEWIS of Virginia, referred to the Committee of Claims.

WAR MEASURES.

The House then, on motion of Mr. TROUP, resolved itself into a Committee of the Whole, on the several bills reported by the Military Committee of this House, as well as the two bills from the Senate on that subject. The bill first taken up, was the bill authorizing the President of the United States to call into service eighty thousand four hundred and thirty militia, to serve two years, for the defence of the frontiers of the United States.

Mr. TROUP said, that the bill before them being a bill from the Senate, which had not been referred to the Military Committee, but which had been taken up on the motion of the gentleman from South Carolina, (Mr. CALHOUN,) the Military Committee, as such, were strangers to its provisions. It was not to be expected, therefore, that he could give to the House an exposition of its principles and details. The gentleman from South Carolina was no doubt prepared to do so. For himself, Mr. T. said he was opposed to the measure of the Senate, and would therefore move to strike out the first section of the bill; it would try the principle. The measure of the Senate, he humbly conceived, was inadequate to the object. It proposed to give you a militia force, when you wanted not a militia but a regular force. He respectfully suggested to the House, in considering this subject, the propriety of endeavoring, in the first place, to establish the principle on which they would rest their military measures for the further prosecution of the war; whether it were the principle of classification and draught, or classification and penalty; whether the principle proposed by the Senate, or any other principle, they could not, he humbly conceived, arrive at any conclusion satisfactory to the country, or useful and honorable to the country, without adopting this mode of proceeding. Having established the principle, the

Committee of the Whole, or a select committee, might consider the details.

Mr. T. said he very well knew that mankind were governed by their hopes and fears; more by their hopes than their fears; and he was not insensible of the effect which the despatches received yesterday from our Ministers at Ghent might have on the measures under consideration. He should be very sorry if the effect would be to induce the Legislature to discontinue or relax the preparations necessary for a vigorous prosecution of the war. If such should be the effect, the enemy might have good reason to exult in the success of a diplomatic trick played off at Ghent, which, lulling us into a false security, would enable him to strike us at the opening of the next campaign, unarmed and unprepared. If he should be able to do so, he would begin to consider himself a match for the Yankees in cunning, and we would repent when it was too late. Mr. T. said he did not mean to say we would not have peace—politics were too uncertain to justify such a declaration—we may have peace in a few weeks. He only meant to say, that calculations founded on events which may happen at Ghent or at Vienna, and which would induce the Legislature to relax in the necessary preparations for the next campaign, ought not to be indulged; measures ought to be taken, not on a supposition of speedy peace, but of protracted war. If peace happened, the preparation for war would do no harm. If peace did not happen, the want of preparation would do much harm; it might lose the next campaign, and losing the next campaign might lose the objects of the war. I only suggest therefore, sir, that it is wise and prudent to act as if the negotiations at Ghent would certainly fail. In submitting, sir, to the Committee, the few observations with which I intend to trouble them on this motion, I will endeavor to satisfy them that the measure proposed by the Senate ought not to be taken, because it places our reliance for a successful prosecution of the war on irregular militia; whereas our reliance ought to be placed on disciplined troops, and that some other measure, therefore, ought to be resorted to—some measure calculated to fill the regular ranks and augment the regular establishment.

In making provision for the further prosecution of the war there would be but one object common to all—to bring the war to a speedy and honorable termination by all the means in the power of the Legislature. At least it would be an object common to every genuine American, because every American had an interest in it. The war was a war for the country, and the result of it, whatever it might be, whether glorious or inglorious, would determine the character of the country and Government. If glorious, every American, without distinction of party, would participate in that glory; if inglorious, every American, without distinction of party, would participate in the infamy of it. He knew very well that certain gentlemen had said the war was a party war, a war for the Administration—but gentlemen would find ere long their mistake.

They would find that Europe, the civilized world, who will alone be competent to pass judgment upon this subject. will not stop to inquire by what party in America this war was declared—by what party it was prosecuted—by what party brought to its termination. No, sir, they will look to the result, and to the result only, and as that result is glorious or inglorious for the country, so will they determine the character of this country and Government. Every American, therefore, is interested to bring the war to an honorable termination by all the means in his power. But how is this to be done? I answer, in the spirit and language of perfect simplicity, by endeavoring to create a motive in the enemy to discontinue the contest. But how is this to be effected? I answer, in the same spirit and language, by endeavoring to wound him where he is vulnerable. The enemy is vulnerable in two points; in his commerce on the ocean—in his territorial possessions neighboring to us. If by any possibility (which I do not admit) he should succeed so effectually to blockade our ports and harbors as to shut up completely our public and private armed vessels, he will cease to be vulnerable in his commerce; he will remain vulnerable in his territorial possessions only. There, sir, I would carry the war without hesitation; there I would endeavor to create a motive in him to discontinue the contest. In proportion as he values his territory, in the same proportion will he make sacrifices to preserve it; as you endanger the existence of his territory, in the same degree will be his motive to discontinue the war to preserve it. That he sets a high value on his territories you have the strongest evidence. He has already made great exertions to preserve them; he has been able to preserve them only because you have not made great efforts to conquer them. You never will conquer them by taking the measure of the Senate. Will any man believe we can induce the enemy to discontinue the war by manning the lines of our frontiers—standing on the defensive—receiving and repelling his blows as well as we can? No, sir, so far from inducing the enemy to abandon the contest, this mode of prosecuting the war would only increase his motive to continue it, whilst the motive on our part to discontinue it would be daily and hourly increasing. A dishonorable peace would terminate the contest—the surrender of our independence would terminate it—nothing else could. I would, therefore, carry the war into the enemy's country, and with a force enabling you to wound him there. But the military force of the enemy has been greatly augmented. It is unnecessary to speak of the events by which this augmentation has been brought about—it is sufficient that we know and feel it. Ordinary prudence requires that your own military force be augmented; not merely in the same proportion—in a much greater proportion. In a much greater proportion, because, all other things being equal, he has one decided advantage over you—an advantage which we can neither destroy nor remove—I mean the command of the ocean, by which he compels you

to stand upon the defensive on a line of frontier of 2,000 miles, and to defend that line with 100,000 men against 10,000 afloat. He comes, no man can tell when, no man can tell where; and, to be prepared at all, he compels you to be prepared at all points. I say, therefore, your augmentation ought to be in much greater proportion than his augmentation. But what description of our military force will you augment? Sir, if, after what has happened, I could for a moment believe there could be any doubt or hesitation upon this point, I would consider everything as lost; then, indeed, would there be an end of hope and of confidence—then, indeed, would there be nothing before us but gloom and despondency, and the horror of despair. But you will not doubt—you will place your reliance on a disciplined regular force; upon a regular disciplined force alone can you rely for success. It matters not whether you determine to conduct the war offensively or defensively; if you determine to prosecute it offensively, you ought to rely mainly on a regular force—because, to be successful, you must meet and beat in the open field the regular veteran troops of Europe. Not one step can you advance in the conquest of Canada until you are prepared to do this. This can only be done by regular disciplined troops. If you determine to prosecute the war defensively, you ought to rely mainly on regular troops; for you must expect to meet and to repel regular disciplined troops—and this can be done most effectually with regular disciplined troops. It will be done not only more effectually, but more economically; not only more economically, but more conveniently for the country. It will save the militia of the country, and in saving the militia it will save the active industry of the country—it will save of course the product of that industry; the product of that industry is national wealth—it will save the national wealth.

But not only do these considerations urge you, in my humble opinion, to resort to all the means within your power to fill the ranks and augment the regular establishment; other considerations call upon you to make the army as respectable in number as it is already in character—considerations growing out of that character. An army, little better than two years old, collected hastily from the plough, the loom, and the work shop—without discipline, without even the rudiments of the military science—the officer to be instructed, that he might be qualified to instruct the soldier—this army has performed deeds of heroism and of gallant daring that would have done honor to the best days of Greece and Rome, that will adorn the page of your own history. It is true, that this army has not from the beginning everywhere triumphed; it is true, it has not from the beginning carried everything before it: it had not strength, it had not numbers. But this much may be said of it, and with truth, that, from the beginning to this moment, it has in no one instance dishonored the standard which it bore; unless, indeed, a solitary instance may be appealed to as an exception—an instance as yet of doubtful and undecided character. More recently its triumphs have been more brilliant; in open field, man to man, it has vanquished the conquerors of the conquerors of Europe. Who can hesitate, therefore, (the war continuing,) to make this army as respectable in number as it is already in character, to enable it to continue these triumphs? The bill from the Senate, instead of proposing this, proposes to authorize the President to call upon the States for eighty thousand raw militia; and this is to be our reliance for the successful prosecution of the war. Take my word for it, sir, that if you do rely upon it (the military power of the enemy continuing undivided) defeat, disaster, and disgrace, must follow. As an auxiliary or secondary force the militia may be relied on; as principal, in a contest with regular troops, never. But the state of the army: Upon this part of the subject, sir, I will say nothing, because I can say nothing that you are not already in possession of. You have authorized a force of sixty odd thousand men; you have raised thirty odd thousand; you have a deficiency of twenty odd thousand to supply: these thirty odd thousand men, already raised, are distributed over a line of four thousand miles of frontier; is it any wonder then, Mr. Speaker, that Canada has not been conquered? No, sir, the wonder is not that Canada has not been conquered, the wonder is that this little army has been able to keep its ground; the enemy has been stronger in regular troops at all points from the beginning, and the very annunciation of this fact is enough to cover our little army with glory. You have a deficiency of twenty odd thousand to supply; how will you supply it? Assuredly the bill from the Senate will not supply it; will the mode heretofore resorted to supply it? Will the re-cruiting system supply it? No, sir, the recruiting system has failed, I mean it has failed to fill your ranks; what are the facts upon this subject? They are, that two millions of dollars have been applied since January last, and thirteen thousand men have been enlisted; this it may be said is doing very well. So it is; but what is the general result? The general result is, that our army is very little stronger now than it was this time last year; and in testing the operation of the system it is to the general result we must look. At the rate of thirteen thousand men per annum, it would take five years to raise the authorized force; the re-cruiting system therefore has failed, it has failed to fill our ranks. I do not mean to say, sir, that the recruiting system with the present high bounty and encouragement would not eventually fill our ranks; I am not disposed to say that it would not (provided the power of the enemy had continued broken and divided by the troubles of the Continent) have answered our purpose; but I do say, that under existing circumstances and for our present purpose, the recruiting system ought not to be relied on; it cannot be relied on to fill our ranks by the opening of the next campaign, and to risk the loss of the next campaign is to risk the loss of everything. But is there no mode to which you can resort for filling the ranks but voluntary enlistment? I would be extremely sorry if we

could not. I have always thought this Government, when administered in the true spirit of the Constitution, the strongest Government in the world, even for the purposes of war; but if the doctrine set up of late be true, this is the weakest and most contemptible Government on earth, it is neither fit for war nor peace, it has failed of all the ends for which Governments are established. It cannot be true that this Government, charged with the general defence, authorized to declare war and to raise armies, can have but one mode of raising armies, whilst every other Government that has ever existed has had an absolute power over the population of the country for this purpose, and has actually exercised it. But this question is not properly before the House, and I will not go into an argument to show that you can, like other Governments, resort to other modes of raising armies than that of voluntary enlistment; that you can resort to classification and draught, to classification and penalty, or any other mode which a sound discretion may in a particular state of the country dictate and justify. All I intend to say at present is, that you have an absolute power over the population of this country for this purpose, and that in the present state of the country it is wiser to resort to classification and draught, than to resort to the bill from the Senate; the one will give the men certainly and expeditiously, the other will not. But, sir, compare the measures of the Senate with the measures proposed by your own committee, and which are before you. The measure of the Senate proposes to authorize the President to call out eighty thousand militia for two years, and this is called a remedy for the evil of State. Now, sir, the evil of State, as I understand it, is not the want of a militia force, but the want of a regular force. The evil of which the country complains, of which the Government complains, of which the militia themselves complain most grievously, is the number of militia in service; the incessant harassment, vexation, and oppression of the militia, and the extraordinary and burdensome expense of that particular service. As a remedy for this grievance, the Senate propose to detach eighty thousand militia. The President has at command, and has always had at command, a million of militia; and in this extraordinary crisis of our affairs, when pressed by a formidable enemy, and surrounded with difficulties, the remedy proposed by the Senate is eighty thousand militia, which it must be admitted on all hands can be no better, for at least the next campaign, than raw militia called out in the ordinary way. But the bill proposes to furnish regular troops. How? by holding up *in terrorem* a militia classification and draught. Exempting every three classes which shall furnish two regular soldiers, from the liability to furnish three militiamen. Do the friends of this measure believe—will they with any degree of confidence assert, that it will have the effect, even partially, to fill the ranks? I think not. And suppose it should fail to furnish regular soldiers, what will be our condition in the months of July and August next? Much worse, sir, than our condition in the months of July and August last. The war continuing, the power of the enemy unbroken, our condition will be desperate. The regular force every day falling off, (for be it remembered these eighty thousand militia will be withdrawn from the operations of the recruiting service,) we shall have to oppose to the enemy a remnant of regular troops, and these eighty thousand raw militia—and who will answer for the consequences? In the months of August and September last, we had in the field the regular Army and upwards of one hundred thousand militia, and we nowhere found ourselves too strong. It is true the Senate propose to improve the recruiting system—an improvement which two years ago this House proposed to the Senate, but which the Senate then thought proper to reject. I mean the enlistment of young men between the ages of eighteen and twenty-one. But if these eighty thousand militia for two years should happen to be, as they are likely to be, that very description of population upon which this system would otherwise operate, what hope can be entertained that the recruiting system even with its improvements will be as productive the next year as the last. I humbly conceive, Mr. Speaker, that the measure of the Senate, proceeding from the best intentions, will fail in the accomplishment of our object. I conceive, with much deference to the House, that the measures reported by their own committee are much to be preferred. They propose—first, to augment the regular establishment to one hundred thousand men ; second, to authorize the President to accept under liberal encouragements the service of volunteer corps ; third, to authorize the President to receive into the service of the United States State troops, which may be raised to serve in lieu of the militia of such States. The principle of the system is, to substitute, as far as we are able, a regular force for a militia force, as more efficient, more economical, and, for the militia themselves, more convenient—and one hundred thousand regulars would take the place of two hundred thousand militia—two hundred thousand militia would cost as much as three hundred thousand regulars. If we can command an hundred thousand regular troops, it may, notwithstanding, be necessary, on particular emergencies, to resort to the militia. To enable the Government still further to spare the militia, volunteers are authorized. They also will be more efficient than ordinary militia. It is impossible to say to what extent these corps will offer themselves—to whatever extent the Government is enabled to avail itself of their services, to the same extent will the militia be saved. If Government should derive no aid from this source, it has another resource in State troops. They also will take the place of the militia. The militia will still continue the bulwark of the country. Whenever the existence of the country shall be endangered, it is the militia that must save it. The system proposes to relieve them from the constant harassment of which they complain, and justly complain. To raise the regular troops, you have the alternative proposed by the Secretary of War, or the com-

mittee. The plan of the Secretary of War is the only effectual one. If we have energy and spirit to take it, it will fill our ranks and augment our regular establishment certainly and expeditiously. The people will justify the measure, because they will feel that it is necessary to the maintenance of the honor, the character, and independence, of the country. The plan of the committee, though less efficient, is, in my humble opinion, better than that of the Senate. Where it fails to give you men it will give you money. It will be certain to give some men, and some money. I hope the House will agree to strike out the section.

Mr. Calhoun briefly replied to the call made upon him by Mr. Troup for the reasons why he preferred acting on the bill: that reason he thought was very obvious; that the bill, having met the approbation of the Senate, would, if it passed this House, immediately become a law. Policy appeared to him to require a preference of this bill to that reported by the committee of this House. If the Senate send us one bill, and we, instead of acting on it, send them another, it would place the two Houses in an awkward predicament. It seemed to him, he said, that the whole argument of the gentlemen against this bill was misplaced. This bill, as well as the gentleman's bill, would produce a certain number of recruits for the regular Army. Should the bill reported by the gentleman prevail, it would give us either regulars or money; if this bill should pass, we shall have regulars or good militia. Both bills were calculated to produce regulars, if they could be obtained by purchase. If absolute certainty was the object of the gentleman, it could be only obtained by resorting to a regular and fair system of conscription. To the result of any other system, whether that reported by the Military Committee of this House, or that now under consideration, some uncertainty must attach. The bill from the Senate promising as much certainty as that reported in this House, he hoped it would be gone through with and finally passed.

The question was then taken, without further debate, on the motion to strike out the first section of the bill, and decided as follows—for the motion 62, against it 64. So the motion to strike out the first section was negatived.

The following is the apportionment of the proposed draught of men among the several States and Territories:

From New Hampshire, two thousand five hundred eighty.

From Massachusetts, eight thousand six hundred five.

From Vermont, two thousand five hundred eighty.

From Rhode Island, eight hundred sixty.

From Connecticut, three thousand ten.

From New York, eleven thousand six hundred fifteen.

From New Jersey, two thousand five hundred eighty.

From Pennsylvania, nine thousand eight hundred ninety-five.

From Delaware, eight hundred sixty.

From Maryland, three thousand eight hundred seventy.

From Virginia, nine thousand eight hundred ninety-five.

From North Carolina, five thousand five hundred ninety.

From South Carolina, three thousand eight hundred seventy.

From Georgia, two thousand five hundred eighty.

From Kentucky, four thousand three hundred.

From Ohio, two thousand five hundred eighty.

From Tennessee, two thousand five hundred eighty.

From Louisiana, four hundred thirty.

From the Mississippi Territory, five hundred twenty-two.

From the Indiana Territory, five hundred forty-nine.

From the Illinois Territory, two hundred thirteen.

From the Michigan Territory, sixty.

From the Missouri Territory, three hundred seventy-six.

And from the Territory of Columbia, four hundred thirty.

Mr. JENNINGS moved to amend the apportionment for Indiana Territory, by striking out five hundred and forty-nine and inserting three hundred. The motion was opposed by Mr. RHEA of Tennessee, and negatived, 20 or 30 members only rising in favor of it.

Mr. LEWIS, of Virginia, moved to strike out the present apportionment of the District of Columbia, viz: four hundred and thirty, and insert eighty, which he said would be at the rate of every twenty-fifth man. This motion was opposed by Mr. RHEA. and negatived.

Mr. McKEE, of Kentucky, moved to strike out the 7th section of the bill, (which limits the services to be required of the draughted militia, to the bounds of their own and any adjoining State, with the exception of the Western States, who are, when required, to serve in Louisiana, and those of Pennsylvania and Virginia, in like manner, in the Michigan Territory, &c.) He could not see any possible benefit to arise from it, but he could see great inconvenience. It might frequently be important that the militia of one State should serve in a State which was not adjoining to theirs, and in some sections of the country might refuse their co-operation in such case, sheltering themselves under the provisions of this act. This motion was seconded by Mr. SHARP, of Kentucky, who thought this section calculated to excite feelings of dissention, and State and local prejudices. We ought to legislate as if for a nation, and not for State authorities. We ought to encourage national feeling, not sectional views. He should like to see that feeling diffused through the nation, which prevails in some parts of the Union, that would induce the citizens freely to march from one extreme to another to meet the enemy, rather than he should hold a foot of the soil. But when you recognise the principle that the militia of one State, say Massachusetts, shall not, on occasion, be liable to march for the defence of the shores of another, say Maryland or Virginia, or that the militia of the State of Kentucky or Tennessee should not, if necessary, march to the defence of Massachusetts, you sanction a local State feeling, which will be the bane of the prosperity of the nation. The States West of the mountains, and those East of the Potomac, were as much sister States, he said, as if they lay contiguous to each other. From the mode of legislation embraced in this section, Mr. S. feared the excitement of sentiments hostile to the grandeur of the character of this nation, as well as to its honor, both of which could only be attained by an amalgamation of national feeling.

Mr. CALHOUN remarked that, even were the section stricken out, it would not materially vary the nature of the service of these militia forces, which would be confined to their respective States, unless necessity required their service elsewhere; in which case such a limitation as is contained in the bill would be very inconvenient. He, therefore, concurred in the opinion that the section ought to be stricken out.

Mr. KILBOURN, of Ohio, supported the motion to strike out the 7th section. He conceived the militia service already sufficiently injured, if not dishonored, by the construction of the Constitution which had limited its utility. He hoped it would not be further restricted in such a provision as this. To show its injurious tendency, he instanced the case, which might happen, of the militia of New Jersey being called on to cross the Delaware, to aid in the defence of Pennsylvania or Delaware; the enemy retiring across an imaginary line into the State of Maryland, to regain their ships in the Chesapeake, the militia would, under this section, be precluded from pursuing them beyond the line, unless it suited their pleasure.

The question on striking out the 7th section was decided in the affirmative by a large majority.

Several other unimportant amendments were proposed, giving rise to desultory discussion, which were variously disposed of.

Mr. KING, of North Carolina, moved to amend the bill, so as not to confine the Governors of States, in the selection of the officers to command the militia to be draughted in pursuance of the bill, to the present militia officers.

This motion was supported by the mover, and by Messrs. FORSYTH of Georgia, FISK and SHEPHERD of New York, and GHOLSON of Virginia, on the ground of the expediency of allowing the widest field for the selection of officers qualified for command, without confining it to the militia officers now in commission, many of whom, though highly respectable men, were unfit for military command, having been selected in a time of peace, without reference to their military qualifications.

The motion was opposed by Messrs. CANNON and RHEA of Tennessee, PEARSON of North Carolina, and PICKERING of Massachusetts, on the ground of alleged injustice to the merits of our present militia, on Constitutional scruples, and on the difficulty which would be presented by the variance of the modes of appointment in the different States.

The motion was at last negatived—43 voting in favor of it.

Mr. LEWIS, of Virginia, moved to strike out two years, the proposed term of service of the militia to be draughted in pursuance of this bill

715   HISTORY OF CONGRESS.   716

H. of R.   *Income Tax—Moneys Receivable for Taxes.*   December, 1816.

and insert *six months.* The motion was negatived by the following vote: For the motion 45, against it 82.

On motion of Mr. Forsyth, the bill was so amended as to make the officers of the draughted militia eligible, according to the Constitution and laws of the several States.

This bill having been gone through, the House proceeded to the consideration of the bill from the Senate, "further to provide for filling the ranks of the Army of the United States."

[This is the bill that has occasioned so much debate in the Senate, and which authorizes the enlistment of minors.]

The bill having been read through, a motion was made by Mr. Pitkin, of Connecticut, to strike out so much of the bill as authorizes the enlistment of minors over eighteen years of age, without the consent of their parents or guardians; which motion he supported by a few pertinent remarks.

This motion was opposed by Mr. Hopkins, of Kentucky, in a short speech of much force and energy.

It was negatived by the following vote: For the motion 51, against it 83.

The House then proceeded to consider the bill, authorizing the President to accept the services of certain volunteer corps, (which bill was before the House some weeks ago for several days.) On motion of Mr. Johnson, of Kentucky, this bill was then so amended, as to reinstate it precisely in the form in which it stood before it underwent amendment by the House.

The Committee then rose, and reported to the House the three bills they had had under consideration.

The first of those bills, viz: the bill from the Senate, requiring a draught for two years of a body of militia, was, on motion of Mr. Johnson, of Kentucky, referred to a select committee for their consideration.

The second of the above bills being before the House, and the question being on the engrossing of the bill for a third reading—

The House adjourned without deciding thereon.

SATURDAY, December 3.

A message from the Senate informed the House that the Senate have passed a bill "to authorize the purchase of the library of Thomas Jefferson, late President of the United States;" in which they ask the concurrence of this House.

Mr. McKee reported a bill, giving further time to the purchasers of public lands to complete their payments; and a bill for the relief of the heirs of James Hynum; which were twice read and committed.

The bill to extend Oliver Evans's patent for steam engines, was twice read and committed.

INCOME TAX.

Mr. Eppes, from the Committee of Ways and Means, to whom was referred a resolution of the House of Representatives, instructing them to inquire into the "expediency of laying a duty on all salaried officers, and on the professional income of lawyers, solicitors, and counsellors, and on the legal proceedings of courts of justice," made the following report:

That a tax upon salaries can only be expedient and proper under arbitrary Governments, where pensions and places are bestowed without a just regard to the public interest. In the United States, according to the principles of our Government, no salary can be allowed, except as a compensation for public service; a tax operates as a deduction from the salary, and such a tax, so far as respects the officers of the United States, would be an admission on the part of the legislative body, that, in fixing the salaries of their public officers, the public interest had been disregarded, and more than a just compensation allowed. Without deciding whether in some instances this may not be the case, the committee are of opinion that, if the evil exists, the proper Constitutional remedy is not a tax, but a reduction of the salaries. The second member of the resolution embraces the income of lawyers, solicitors, and counsellors. The selection of a particular class of the community, which already pays, in common with others, a tax on property and on consumption, and imposing on it an income tax, from which every other class is exempted, would be a departure from that system of equal and exact justice, which ought to form the basis of legislation in a free country. The third member of the resolution proposes a tax on the legal proceedings of courts. This tax, if confined to the Courts of the United States, would be unproductive; if extended to the State Courts, difficult in the collection. It would fall principally on the necessitous and unfortunate, and produce collision with the State authorities. Upon the whole, it is considered inexpedient to resort to either of the proposed taxes. The following resolution is, therefore, submitted:

Resolved, That it is inexpedient to impose a duty on salaried officers, on the income of lawyers, or on the proceedings of courts at law.

The report was ordered to lie on the table.

MONEYS RECEIVABLE FOR TAXES.

Mr. Eppes, from the Committee of Ways and Means, to whom was referred a resolution of the House of Representatives, instructing them to inquire into the expediency of providing by law, that any kind of money paid by the Government to the troops in the service of the United States, for military services, shall be receivable from the people in payment of taxes, made the following report:

That, under the general power to regulate the collection of taxes, the Secretary of the Treasury is preparing instructions to the collectors, in which a uniform rule as to the receipt of bank notes will be prescribed. The committee consider that it would be unsafe to designate, by law, the notes in which taxes shall be received, and that a due regard for the public interest requires that this subject should be regulated, at present, by instructions issued, from time to time, from the Treasury Department; which may be so framed, as to unite the safety of the revenue with the accommodation of the individual citizens. A statement of the circumstances which produced the resolution drawn up by the Representatives of Tennessee, together with a letter from the Secretary of the Treasury, accompanies this report; and the committee submit the following resolution:

Resolved, That it is inexpedient to designate, by law, the bank notes which shall be receivable in payment of taxes.

TREASURY DEPARTMENT, *Nov.* 23, 1814.

SIR: I have the honor to acknowledge the receipt of your letter, dated the 21st instant, enclosing a resolution of the House of Representatives, passed the 11th instant, directing an inquiry "into the expediency of providing by law, that any kind of money which may be paid by the Government to the troops in the service of the United States, for military services, shall be receivable in payment from the people in taxes."

In the course of an endeavor to ascertain the grounds of the resolution, I have been favored with a communication from the Representatives of Tennessee in Congress, (of which a copy is annexed,) in addition to the general information possessed in this Department; and I believe that the facts of the case are briefly these: The Secretary of War, having occasion for money to pay the militia who marched from Tennessee against the Creek Indians, obtained a loan in bank notes, for that purpose, from the Bank of Chilicothe. Some of these notes have since been offered in the payment of taxes to the collectors of the internal duties in the State of Tennessee; but, as the banks of Tennessee (where the money collected for taxes is required to be deposited) refuse to receive them as cash deposites, the collectors, in their turn, refuse to receive them as cash for taxes. Owing to the causes suggested in the communication to which I have already referred, and, perhaps, to other causes, perfectly consistent with the general solvency of the Bank of Chilicothe, the notes circulating in Tennessee have suffered a considerable depreciation. They have already been, it is alleged, an object of speculation; those paid by the United States to the militia cannot now be distinguished from other notes issued by the Bank of Chilicothe; and any attempt to give the former a preference, in the payment of taxes, would probably increase the arts of speculation, as well as the other inconveniences of which the citizens of Tennessee complain.

Under these circumstances the case is, obviously, one of great delicacy. The Government has passed the notes at their nominal value; but it is equally true, that the Government is bound to pay for them to the bank according to their nominal value. The Government did not contract any engagement to support the credit of the notes, nor to accept them in payment of duties at any subsequent period; and all the persons who have accepted the notes, either in payment from the Government, or by transfer from the militia, have done so voluntarily, without any pretence of reliance upon any such engagement. If, therefore, it should be deemed proper to direct, by the legislative authority, that the notes of the Bank of Chilicothe shall be received in payment for duties, the principle of the direction will be equally applicable to every other case where the Government has paid its troops or creditors in bank notes, which have afterwards suffered (from whatever cause) a depreciation in credit or circulating value. The effect of such a law, upon the public revenues, need not be particularly stated.

Considering the subject, however, as a general subject, meriting the serious attention of the Treasury Department, I am preparing instructions to the collectors, to regulate their conduct in receiving bank notes for taxes. The design of the instructions will be, to unite the security of the revenue with the accommodation of the banks, as well as of individual citizens, during the disordered condition of the circulating medium of the country; and, in making this arrangement, I shall be highly gratified to find that the views of the mover of the resolution under consideration can be accomplished.

I have the honor to be, &c.

A. J. DALLAS.

J. W. EPPES, *Chairman, &c.*

CONGRESS HALL, *November,* 1814.

SIR: It may be satisfactory to you to be informed of the situation of the banks in the State of Tennessee. There are two banks in that State—one at Knoxville, and the other at Nashville; both of them of unquestionable credit and solvency. No suspension has taken place of specie payments, nor do we believe any suspension will take place.

With respect to the Bank of Chilicothe, in the notes of which most of the troops in the service of the United States, from the State of Tennessee, have been paid, we can only observe, that no doubt was entertained of its solvency and ability to discharge its respective engagements, so far as we have been informed; but the notes would not circulate without considerable discount. This, we think, was produced in consequence of the course of trade being from the Southwest, Eastwardly, and Northeast, and money was not wanted at Chilicothe by the citizens of the mercantile towns in Tennessee, and not by any doubt existing of the solvency of the bank.

As these notes do not suit the commercial relations existing between the citizens of Tennessee and the Eastern States, we do not wish them to be further used in the payment of troops there.

The refusal, by the Government, to receive them again in the payment of taxes, has necessarily produced considerable irritation, and it is believed, by some of the people there, to be an intentional attempt to impose on them.

The spirit of patriotism and military ardor, now existing in as high a degree as in any part of the United States, is sinking under the injustice of this measure.

We have the honor to be, &c.

P. W. HUMPHREYS,
JOHN H. BOWER,
THOS. K. HARRIS,
N. CANNON.

The report was ordered to lie on the table.

PETITION OF NOAH SHAW.

Mr. EPPES, from the Committee of Ways and Means, to whom was referred the petition of Noah Shaw, made the following report:

That the facts necessary for forming an opinion on the case, are stated in a letter from the Secretary of the Treasury, which accompanies this report. From this statement it appears that the petitioner is not entitled to relief under the special act of Congress, passed on the second day of January, 1813; and that the former Secretary refused, under the general law of the 3d of March, 1797, to remit the forfeiture incurred by the petitioner, on the ground, that it did not appear to his satisfaction that the forfeiture was incurred without wilful negligence, or any intention of fraud. On a review of the circumstances, the committee concur in opinion with the late Secretary of the Treasury, that the petitioner is not entitled to relief. The following resolution is therefore submitted.

Resolved, That the prayer of the petitioner ought not to be granted.

TREASURY DEPARTMENT,
November 4, 1814.

SIR: In answer to your letter of the 28th ultimo, I have the honor to state, from the documents which accompany the reference of the Committee of Ways and Means, and from the facts ascertained at the Treasury Department, that, in the 1813, Noah Shaw, on behalf of Samuel Salsbury and A. P. Cleaveland, of Boston, presented a petition to the judge of the district court for the district of Vermont, setting forth, that Salsbury and Cleaveland, on the 9th of June, 1811, had imported into the province of Upper Canada, from Liverpool, in England, certain goods, specified in the invoice annexed, which they afterwards, on the 5th of March, 1813, imported into Burlington, in the district of Vermont; that the goods being owned by citizens, were imported into Canada on board of a ship which departed from Liverpool between the 23d of June and the 15th of September, to wit: on the 1st of August, 1811; and that the goods were purchased in Great Britain before the war was there known to exist.

That, on the 20th of November, 1813, the district judge certified to the Secretary of the Treasury the petition and the proofs, but he made no statement of facts; and, on the 12th of July, 1814, the Secretary of the Treasury decided, in form, not to remit the forfeiture incurred by the importation of the goods into the United States.

That it appears by the petition which Noah Shaw has recently presented to Congress, that Salsbury and Cleaveland had sold the goods to B. and C. Adams, on the 23d of September, 1812, from whom they were purchased by Noah Shaw, on the 11th of January, 1813, with a view to the importation, which he effected in the ensuing month of March.

Upon these facts I take the liberty to offer the following observations, for the consideration of the committee:

1. That, from the terms of the petition to the district judge, it appears that Mr. Shaw intended to seek relief, as for Salsbury and Cleaveland, under the special act of the 2d of January, 1813, directing the remission of certain forfeitures; and the prayer of the petitioner is, therefore, for relief according to the law in such case made and provided. The case, however, was certainly not embraced by the special act; for the goods were not imported into the United States from the United Kingdom of Great Britain and Ireland; they were not shipped on board of a vessel which departed therefrom between the 23d of June and the 15th of September, 1812; and, so far as respects Mr. Shaw, the owner at the time of the importation, the purchase of the goods was made long after the war was known to exist at the place of purchase.

2. That, although the case was not embraced by the special act, it became, properly, a question, whether the Secretary of the Treasury was authorized to remit, or mitigate, the forfeiture, under the general law of the 3d of March, 1797, if, in his opinion, it was incurred without wilful negligence, or any intention of fraud. It does not appear that the late Secretary objected merely to an irregularity in the mode of exhibiting the facts, or of transmitting the documents; for,

then, he would not have decided the case, but he would have returned it to the district judge, to undergo the necessary revision and amendment in point of form. Nor does it appear, from any information within my reach, that the Secretary decided the case upon any doubt of his jurisdiction to remit the forfeiture. The case must therefore be deemed to have been decided on its merits; and the power of the Secretary of the Treasury being once executed, the department cannot afterwards modify, or rescind, or change, the decision.

It will remain, upon this general view of the subject, for the committee to decide, whether the petitioner ought to be recommended for relief to Congress. The danger of giving a sanction to speculations which involve an unauthorized intercourse with the enemy, and the tendency of such speculations to cover and countenance the worst kind of smuggling, will, no doubt, be duly considered. If, indeed, the case had been originally presented for my official interposition, I should have reflected well before I decided, that, in principle, and in circumstances, it was entitled to the equitable relief of the act of the 3d of March, 1797. That act was meant to provide for cases of mere accident or misfortune, and for cases uncontaminated by any fraudulent intention, when the necessary rigor of the general law would become, in the particular instance, an instrument of hardship and cruelty. But no man is ever permitted to obtain relief in the courts of justice, upon a claim founded in his own wilful violation of the law; and it would be an extraordinary, and, I presume, a novel application of the equitable powers of the Secretary of the Treasury, to legitimate a trade with the enemy, through the medium of remitting penalties and forfeitures incurred by a breach of the non-importation acts.

I have the honor to be, &c.
A. J. DALLAS.
Hon. J. W. EPPES, *Chairman, &c.*

The report was ordered to lie on the table.

ENLISTMENTS IN THE ARMY.

The House resumed the consideration of the bill "making further provision for filling the ranks of the Army of the United States."

Mr. PITKIN, of Connecticut, made a motion, the object of which was to strike out of the bill that part of it which makes binding the enlistment of all persons from eighteen to fifty years of age.

A long debate ensued, in which Messrs. KING, of Massachusetts, WARD, GROSVENOR, and WEBSTER, were the principal speakers against the bill; and Messrs. FISK, SHARP, and BARNETT, its principal defenders.

Mr. CYRUS KING, of Massachusetts, addressed the Chair as follows:

Mr. Speaker. I think it my duty to make to the House some observations on the bill now under discussion, in connexion with other military bills and some of the revenue bills, which have been reported, as I deem the whole of your war system either against the enemy or the people of this country. This mode of considering the subject will do justice to the Administration, and to their friends in the respective Houses of Congress. And this justice I am disposed to render to them, notwithstanding I believe that, by some of their past acts, they have proved themselves the very worst enemies of the American people. This view, sir, I wish to submit to the House, if it be possible steadily to look at this system of military conscription, and of oppressive taxation, and not startle at the destruction with which it threatens our country.

A sagacious political writer, in speaking of the errors and oppressions of rulers, has remarked, that the necessity of any Government is the greatest reflection upon the virtue of the people; but, sir, with all due deference, I never shall consider that as the greatest reflection, as long as a people can be found so degraded, so regardless of their own interest and importance, as to tolerate an Administration after they shall have failed to accomplish the very end of their institution, and shall have raised their parricidal arm against the very instrument by which they have their existence. That this is the case with the present Administration, a little more reflection, and some more suffering, if it be possible to add to it, will convince the American people.

Take, if you please, sir, the ordinary evidence of a well-administered Government, respect abroad and prosperity at home, and ask yourself if this Administration have continued these blessings to this nation. That our form of Government, when correctly administered agreeably to the Constitution, is capable of producing, and for a time continuing, these national blessings, we have the splendid example of the Administrations of Washington, and of Adams, before his fall. Are you now respected abroad? No, sir, there is not a nation, not a crowned head in Europe, that is friendly towards you. I ask pardon, sir, there is perhaps one—I mean the great Emperor of the little island of Elba; but even he is now said, like Milton's devil, to eye you askance, and to grin horribly at the destruction which he has brought upon you. How you alienated foreign nations from you is now matter of history; by constantly aiding the attempts of the late fell tyrant of Europe at universal empire, your destinies were united with his, and you must now expect to share with him the general detestation of mankind. But, sir, what will forever fix your character in Europe, and I think your doom at home, is your rash declaration of war at the time you did it;—thus, like willing slaves, binding yourselves to the then triumphal car of the enslaver of nations. Yes, sir, you courageously declared your war when you supposed the imperial tyrant had his victim bound at his feet, and the sword out and whetted that was to be plunged into her vitals. You then magnanimously expected to be in at the death and share the spoils. Sir, the rashness and folly of this Administration, on that occasion, forcibly reminds us of the fable of the madman, who undertook to shear a wolf. What, exclaimed his friends, shear a wolf! Have you considered the danger and difficulty of the undertaking, and the little profit you are likely to gain if you succeed? No, says the madman, I have considered nothing but the *right!* The Sovereign of the Universe has given to man dominion over the beasts of the forest and of the field; I, therefore, have the right, and will shear the wolf.

So this Administration, believing that the imperial robber of France had the royal bull of England by the horns, thought they had a right, this a favorable opportunity, and attempted to shear him; but, most unfortunately for them, the royal beast broke from the imperial robber, trod him under foot, and is now pushing, with full vigor, at poor Mr. Madison and his friends.

Have you, sir, been more fortunate at home, in continuing the prosperity of this country and of its citizens? The bankruptcy of your Treasury, and the misery and groans of the people, pronounce an awful negative to this question. Still, in this ruined state of the country, and impoverished situation of the people, you call upon them for more men and more money. For this purpose numerous tax bills and military bills have been reported. And with these facts staring him in the face, your new Secretary, the fresh hand at the Treasury bellows, who has labored so hard to blow up public credit, had the effrontery to declare, in his first report, that the resources of the nation remain almost untouched by the hand of the Government; because I suppose his hand had not before touched them. And this, sir, is one of the evils attendant on the perpetual fluctuation of officers in some of your departments. No sooner is one leech brushed from the veins of the people than a fresh one is fastened on them, to suck the last drop of their blood.

You attempt to raise a revenue in two ways—by direct and indirect taxes—though the genius of the Administration, I think, leads them to the indirect mode, that the hand of the Government should as seldom as possible be seen by the people while they are picking their pockets. The justice of this mode may well be questioned. When you impose a direct tax every citizen knows what he has to pay; but when you tax articles in the hand of the manufacturer, the retailer, or the merchant, they add what they please, certainly never less than the tax, for advance of money and interest; and thus the citizen is often obliged to pay more than double the amount of the tax. Though indeed, sir, in the present impoverished situation of the people, I can see but little other difference in the two modes of taxation than between petit larceny and robbery. The disposition that would induce an Administration, at a time like this, to adopt the indirect mode would urge an unfortunate being, in humble life, clandestinely to pick a pocket or rob a hen roost; and the evil genius that would impel the former to resort to the direct mode, would embolden the latter to attack the citizen, and demand his money at the point of the bayonet, or the muzzle of the pistol.

[Mr. KING was here cautioned by the honorable SPEAKER not to violate that order and decorum in debate which the rules of the House require. Thanking the honorable Speaker for the caution, Mr. K. replied: This, sir, is a subject which I never will debate but with the Constitution in my hand. I will boldly march to the extreme verge of its powers, and there be ready, at all times, to give to my political opponents a practical illustration of my ideas of the rights of a Representative and of the privilege of a member; I never will wantonly invade the territory of my adversary, nor, without a struggle, be driven from my own.]

On the subject of taxes, sir, your President, in his first Message at this session, says: "We have ' seen them (the people) everywhere paying their ' taxes, direct and indirect, with the greatest alac- ' rity." And the late Secretary, Mr. Campbell, taking his pitch from the President, celebrates in the same strain, "the promptitude and cheerful- ness with which the present taxes are paid." What reward, said Mr. K., do the people receive for all this patriotism and devotion to their coun- try? You double their burdens, and increase your exactions. You have resolved to double your land tax, making it six millions of dollars; to double the auction and carriage taxes; to add fifty per cent. to the taxes on the retailers, and on the postage of letters and newspapers; it is nat- ural, sir, that you should increase the latter tax; by taxing the press, many of the people will be compelled to give up their newspapers, and thus be less able to scrutinize the conduct of this Ad- ministration. On domestic distilled spirits, you have increased the tax four hundred per cent., lest the people should obtain a drop of comfort from that source. And, to crown the whole, you have resolved to add twenty-one new items to your list of taxable articles. Many of which, such as the taxes on hats, leather, nails, iron, &c., will fall peculiarly heavy on those who are poorly able to pay. If such be the reward of their pa- triotism, you will compel the people to try the effect of a manly resistance to such oppression. But happy, happy would it be for this dis- tressed, this devoted people, if after thus depriv- ing them of their property, in many cases of their last dollar, this Administration would be satisfied. No, but the people must then bestow their ser- vices, must surrender their bodies, and spill their blood for these ungrateful men, in carrying on this ruinous war. For this purpose sundry mili- tary bills have been reported; the three principal may be described as the conscription bill of the Senate; the conscription bill of the House; and that now under consideration, the minor conscrip- tion bill.

The great objection to all these bills is, that they confound the distinction made in the Con- stitution between the regular army and the mili- tia; a subject upon which no mistakes can be made except such as are wilful. How did your predecessors, and how ought you to exercise the Constitutional power of raising armies? By vol- untary enlistment of persons capable of contract- ing; for enlistment is only a contract. Congress has power " To provide for organizing, arming, ' and disciplining the militia, and for governing ' such part of them as may be employed in the ' service of the United States, reserving to the ' States respectively the appointment of the offi- ' cers, and the authority of training the militia

' according to the discipline prescribed by Con- ' gress." Also—" To provide for calling forth the ' militia to execute the laws of the Union, sup- ' press insurrections, and repel invasion." And when called into the actual service of the United States, the President shall be the Commander-in- Chief thereof. Now, sir, Congress has already passed laws for organizing the militia into divis- ions, brigades, regiments, battalions, and compa- nies, and they have been organized accordingly. Also, for arming the militia, and which you have partially executed; and for some of the other purposes. mentioned in the Constitution. They are then, sir, by your Constitution and laws, and they were such in most of the States before the Constitution was adopted, or your laws enacted, an independent, organized, armed, and disciplined corps, in the respective States, with an inde- pendent Commander-in-Chief over each. And, sir, Congress can now approach them in no other form, nor through any other channel than that of this independent commander; any law or laws of Congress to the contrary notwithstanding.

Now, sir, what do your first two bills contem- plate? That from the Senate, which is drawn with great art, and may be abused to the worst of purposes, does indeed call upon the Executives of the States for their respective quotas of the mili- tia required, but after that we hear no more of the State authority. The second section divides the whole militia into as many classes as there are soldiers required from each State, ordering each class to furnish one; the third section directs the commanders of companies what persons to enrol, and to make their returns to the Adjutant General of the United States; he is to send his orders to the commanders of brigades, and these again to the commanders of regiments, who are to issue their orders to commanders of companies, and they to see the draught made. And these State officers over whom you have no legal control, till called into your service, are to be fined, imprisoned, and cashiered, if they do not obey your illegal mandates: and all this without consulting their Constitutional Commanders-in-Chief. Now, sir, it is very certain, that if they do obey those man- dates, they will be liable to fine and imprison- ment, under the State laws; you therefore place them between two fires. And thus the poor mili- tia officers are to be put up, whether they obey or disobey.

But, sir, the conscription bill of the House is still more destructive of our militia; it goes, sir, to disband the whole; to melt it down to one common mass; and out of this chaos makes up little squads of twenty-five, each of which is, under severe penalties, to furnish a man during the war for the regular army. If, sir, you have a right thus to take a twenty-fifth, you may take the whole, and convert the whole militia into a standing or regular army, under the command of your President—thus completely annihilating the State sovereignties. The great mistake, is, sir, that you undertake to command the militia before they are, according to the Constitution, called into the actual service of the United States. To illustrate my meaning, suppose the case of two independent commanders under your laws, where one, in case of necessity, is required to support the other: take, if you please, the case of General Izard and General Brown. The latter has occasion for a thousand men from the command of the former; according to the bill from the Senate, Brown calls upon Izard for that number; but, lest Izard should not comply, he directs Izard's subordinate officers, without consulting their commander, to send him the number required, and threatens to cashier them if they do not instantly comply; or, according to the principle of the bill of the House, Brown goes to Izard's army, disbands the whole, cuts it up into twenty-fives, and takes one man from each. Do you suppose, sir, that such orders or such conduct would be submitted to? Are they not subversive of all military subordination, and destructive to our militia —the guardians of our rights and liberties? I again repeat, sir, that the militia of each State are an independent, organized, and armed corps, with an independent Commander-in-Chief over each; that you must approach them as such; and I will add, that if you attempt to do it in any other manner, you will be received at the point of the bayonet.

The necessity of considering the militia in this light is apparent, it is the physical force of the State to defend it against all aggressions, liable to be called upon at a moment's warning; but if the United States can thus interfere with it at pleasure, take such part as they please, and garble it to suit their purposes, they will ruin the system, and deprive the States of their only protection. A State suddenly invaded, and an instant call upon an adjoining State becomes necessary, what will you do without an organized militia, to fly to the relief of such State? Or what will you do for one, if your present plans are adopted? Besides, sir, is not the State commander of the militia the best judge from what part of his command, on a call, the troops can most safely be detached? But your plans go to take the militiamen indiscriminately from every part of the State, although a large proportion of them may be on duty, or a part of the State invaded. Such arbitrary plans can only be calculated to destroy the militia system, and of course the sovereignties of the States. The militia system of New England, sir, is almost coeval with its settlement, and I trust in God, and on the valor of her sons, that it will be co-extensive with her existence.

But, sir, the principle embraced in the minor conscription bill, is the most inhuman, immoral, and oppressive, that ever was attempted to be established by this, and, of course, by any other assembly, called deliberative. I mean, sir, the authority intended to be given to your recruiting officers to enlist minors, without the consent, or even against the will of the parent, master or guardian; in other words, and in effect, if carried, to steal the ward from the guardian, entice the apprentice from his master, and to seduce the child from his parent; and thus destroy, "all the charities of father, son, and brother." Where

were the feelings of the father, when the cold politician could recommend such a horrid principle; nay a father could not, a christian would not do it.

And, sir, besides outraging the best feelings of the heart, the principle violates several important provisions of the Constitution. Suppose, sir, an opposer of the Constitution had inquired of its friends, before its adoption, how the power to raise armies was to be exercised; his answer must have been by the voluntary and fair enlistment of persons capable of contracting; this would have satisfied the parent, master, and guardian, because they would have shown that their wards, apprentices, and children, under twenty-one, were incapable of forming such contract. Can you then, sir, against common law and common right, by any act of yours, confer a capacity to enlist, or contract, which did not exist at the information of the Constitution? Sir, the illustration so pointedly stated by my honorable friend and colleague (Mr. WARD) in a different manner, respecting married women, had occurred to me, in relation to their inability to contract. You have occasion, in your armies, for women to attend the sick, and to nurse some of your old generals; suppose you should, by law, attempt to authorize your officers to recruit some women for these necessary purposes, and as married women are generally most experienced, you should instruct your officers to contract with such, without the consent of their husbands. Do you suppose that such a law ought to be executed? Should you imagine it Constitutional? If not, neither is it so in regard of minors, for they no more than married women, can, by law, contract; nor can you any more confer the capacity upon the one, than upon the other.

Besides, sir, by the Constitution, "no State shall pass any law impairing the obligation of contracts;" you will not contend that this prohibition to the several States, confers the power on the United States; because, but for the prohibition, it would have been reserved to the States or people, though, I trust in God, never to have been exercised. But pass this law, and you not only impair, but dissolve a thousand solemn contracts, now authorized by law, between parents, masters, and guardians. You attempt to do more—impiously to sever that tie between parents and children, formed by the finger of God, in the heart of man.

It is no answer to say that the master is to receive part of the bribe, which is to entice his apprentice from him; for we deny your right thus to entice or enlist him. It is well that you do not thus insult the parent by offering him some of the pieces of silver, which are to betray his child from him—the price of blood. Though he too has a property in the service of the child till twenty-one, which you cannot take "for public use without just compensation."

Believe me, sir, as your laws now stand, this war has already introduced into private families, too much distress. On this very subject of enlisting minors, the most inhuman and distressing acts have been perpetrated by some of your recruiting officers. Minors have been often enlisted without the consent of their parents; and when these parents have demanded them of your officers, they have laughed them to scorn; and when they have called in the civil authority to enforce their demands, it has been resisted by force of arms; and the unhappy youth marched off, in the dead of night, and concealed from his parent. And when, driven by the severity of his officers, the suffering child has fled to his paternal mansion for protection, that mansion, the castle of his parent, has been surrounded at night by ruffian soldiers, its sanctity violated, its doors burst open, and the struggling child torn from the arms of his distracted mother. Another instance, I know, where a child, enticed away and enlisted, ran to the arms of his father for safety—the father and son were waylaid by armed soldiers in the woods, were attacked with swords and pistols, and the suffering child forcibly taken from the wounded parent.

If these cruelties are inflicted contrary to law, what accumulation of distress may we not anticipate, when they shall be authorized by law? I speak of facts which I do know, of distresses of daily occurrence, of crimes which have wrung the father's heart with anguish, and filled his house with misery and woe.

This act, sir, authorizes your recruiting officers to enlist into your army, any free, effective, able-bodied man, between the ages of eighteen and fifty. Now, sir, what kind of a free, able-bodied man, is a stripling of eighteen, under the authority of his parent, or bound to a master. I agree with the honorable gentleman from Kentucky, (Mr. Hopkins,) whose zeal and intelligence I have often admired, (they, I think, were misapplied here,) that the minor contemplated by this bill, is not

      " The infant
Mewling and puling in his nurse's arms."

Nor, sir, can, or ought he to be—a
      " Soldier,
Full of strange oaths, and bearded like the pard,
Jealous in honor, sudden and quick in quarrel,
Seeking the bubble reputation
Even in the cannon's mouth."

I would ask that honorable gentleman, what such a stripling would do in battle, opposed to his huge frame and nervous arm? Could he turn your bayonet, or stop the descending sword? Believe me, he could not. No, sir, boys of that age cannot bear the hardships of a camp, much less can they withstand the shock of battle, or breast the storm of war.

If what I have urged will not induce you to arrest the progress of this bill, I appeal to you—I beseech you, as friends of humanity, to spare the tears which the passage of this law will cause to flow; I appeal to you as fathers, by every endearing tie which binds you to your children, not to deprive the aged parent of the child of his youth, the support and solace of his declining years, lest you bring his gray hairs with sorrow to the grave.

I entreat you to make the case your own—suppose a darling child, an only son, snatched from you by the scourge of war—in the language of grief and of nature, you will then exclaim: "Would to God I had died for thee, O Absalom, my son, my son!"

James Madison, President of the United States, is the father of this system of conscription for America, as his unfortunate friend Bonaparte was of that of France; this he announced in his Message, before referred to, as follows:

"I earnestly renew, at the same time, a recommendation of such changes in the system of militia, as, by classing and disciplining for the most prompt and active service the portions most capable of it, will give to that great resource for the public safety all the requisite energy and efficiency."

His plans therefor, substantially embraced by these conscription bills, were afterwards submitted to Congress, by his Secretary of War, James Monroe, and by him attempted to be recommended to the American people, by the plea of necessity:

"So spake the fiend, and, with necessity,
The tyrant's plea, excus'd his devilish deeds."

Your President further says, in the same Message: "We see the people rushing with enthusi-
' asm to the scenes where danger and duty call.
' In offering their blood, they give the surest pledge
' that no other tribute will be withheld." If this be true, sir, where is the necessity of violating the Constitution to impose upon the people a military despotism and French conscription? That it is true, in one sense, the acknowledged and tried virtue and patriotism of the people are proof. But it is at the call of the State authorities (now our only efficient rulers) that they fly to arms, to defend the soil, and everything dear to them; this they are able, this they are ready, this they are determined to do, against all invaders—not, however, as a tribute to Nero, but as a sacred duty to themselves and their country.

As to the patriotism and devotion of the people to their country, we hear much said by gentlemen on both sides of the House; and comparisons, too often odious, have been made between the relative patriotism of the West and North; these sectional views I regret as much as any one, especially, when rendered necessary by the constant oppression, by the Administration, of particular sections of the country. The Governors of New England have been traduced, because they would not fall down and worship the idols of Democracy, while the gentlemen of the West have continually celebrated the devotion of their States to the powers that are. In the first and second session of the 13th Congress, we were almost deafened with their cry of patriotism and proffers of service; but, at this session, the tune appears to be a little changed; it is now said that the people must be encouraged; that it is wrong to expect them to save their country without a liberal compensation; in other words, no pay, no patriotism. Sir, I am disposed to do more than justice, if possible, to our brethren of the West; I most cordially acknowledge them as

729   HISTORY OF CONGRESS.   730

DECEMBER, 1814.   *Enlistments in the Army.*   H. OF R.

brethren; many of them are from New England; I know them to be hardy, bold, and enterprising. But, sir, it is a little unfortunate, for our poor country, that the stock of patriotism of the West and our national Treasury should both be exhausted at the same moment. I cannot say that there was any very intimate connexion between them, or that the one received its aliment from the other. I only mention facts which have been announced on this floor.

Pause for a moment, sir, and reflect upon the manner in which you have attempted to raise and recruit your Army, for carrying on this ruinous war. At first, you appealed to the patriotism of the people to support you in this rash measure, and expected to raise an army by offering the usual bounty and wages; disappointed in that expectation, you next attempted to buy soldiers, and authorized your recruiting officers to give for them in bounty, land, and wages, about the value of a prime slave in the South. And those who were tempted, by the price only, to sell themselves to you, except to save their families from starving, deserve to be slaves. Thus baffled in all your attempts to enlist the people on your side, in this war, you intend, by these conscription bills, sticking to the slave principles still, to kidnap the people, as you would slaves; and they will deserve this fate, if they tamely submit to such oppression.

We were gravely told, the other day, by an honorable gentleman, (Mr. BARNETT,) in debate, that this was the people's war; that they must and should come out and fight their own battles. It was, I think, sir, but a poor compliment to the people of this country, to call an act theirs, passed by so lean a majority of their Representatives. No, sir, you passed the act declaring war at your peril, as you pass every other law; if it be salutary, if it prove beneficial to the country, the people will support you; if not, the disgrace and ruin ought to fall upon your own heads. That honorable gentleman said further, that they had heretofore fed the people with soft corn; that is, treated them too kindly, rendered them too prosperous and happy. What, in the name of God, does the honorable gentleman mean by this? What species of distress, what complication of misery, have you failed to bring upon the people, in the last seven years? A whole apprenticeship of wretchedness. Have you not destroyed their commerce, paralyzed their industry, loaded them with taxes, (after depriving them of the ability to pay,) forced them into your ranks to support their wives and children, subjected them to frequent and harassing calls for militia service, often discharged them therefrom without clothing or pay, far from their families and friends, sick, distressed, and wounded? And what, let me ask, is the situation of a whole army in the North, so pathetically described by an honorable gentleman from Pennsylvania, (Mr. INGHAM,) at this inclement season of the year, in that severe, cold climate, destitute of clothes, with nothing to cover them but the heavens; no friendly mansion to receive their wounded bodies, unless the friendly earth, in compassion of their suffering, should open her bosom, and receive them and their miseries forever!

If this, sir, be to treat the people with soft corn, I pray that honorable gentleman to give it to his slaves, and not to freemen. But he further remarked, that they have been hitherto daubing the people with untempered mortar. There, sir, I perfectly agree with him. When the great Jefferson, (I mean great in theory, but little in fact, the author of the Declaration of Independence, and the hero of Carter's Mountain,) in his Inaugural Address, in honeyed, though deceitful accents, which never ought to be forgotten by his friend, or forgiven by the friends of our country, said, we are all Federalists, all Republicans—all white, all black—he daubed the people with untempered mortar. Mr. Madison (the destroyer of Washington, as he would be of every one that bore his name or revered his virtues) following the example of his great predecessor, has, in many of his Messages, and by many of his acts, daubed the people with untempered mortar; and you have attempted to build up your party with untempered mortar, until the political fabric, like the remains of the edifices around us, is tumbling into ruin.

We have, indeed, sir, fallen on evil times, and this is a strange Government under which we suffer. Our Constitution is beautiful in theory. In reading it we should suppose that the people were everything, and that it could not fail of rendering them prosperous and happy, as indeed it did, under the wise administration of WASHINGTON; but, since it has fallen into the hands of its enemies, it appears to be entirely changed. As now administered, we should suppose that the people were made for the Government, not the Government for the people, and, that the great duty of the people was to maintain a corrupt Administration, with its thousand dependants and hungry expectants, in idleness and dissipation. You tax the people, you deprive them of employment and property; you fight your battles with the people, and when your severity forces them to desert, you shoot them by dozens. And all this is done in the name and for the good of the people. "We, the people," stand first in the Constitution, and the last to receive any benefit from it.

When, sir, gentlemen on this side of the House have, in behalf of the people, accused Mr. Madison and some of his Cabinet of high crimes and misdemeanors, the friends of these men have referred them to the Constitution for their impeachment and punishment. Cruel insult and mockery! Impeachment? Who, in the name of God, are to vote and carry up—I ask pardon, sir, I should say down—everything in this strange Government is sadly turned topsy-turvy—who, I repeat, in the name of God, are to vote and carry down articles of impeachment against these high offenders? Is it not the majority on this floor; the fast friends of the Executive; the advisers and abettors of some of the most oppressive acts of which we complain? Will they vote articles of impeachment which go to criminate themselves? It is too much to expect of poor human nature, constituted as it is. If, however, returning to a sense of justice and of duty to the people—and I well know that I violate all probability by the supposition—the majority should be induced to perform this sacred office, after this Grand Inquest for the body of the nation, as it is sometimes called, have found a true bill, what is the body or petit jury which is to try it? Is it a packed jury? No, not so good; for then there would be a right of challenge; but the people must take them as they find them, unanointed, unannealed, with all their party and political sins about them. Yes, sir, when you approach the Senate of the United States you go one step nearer to the President, one step nearer the head of power, patronage, and corruption. The present majority in that body are the personal friends and advisers of the President; they are connected by official duties, confirm his nominations, extend the Executive patronage, whereby the offices of the people are made use of as instruments to debauch and corrupt them. Can you expect such a majority to find one of their friends guilty, when the same verdict would seal their own condemnation?

This consolidation of the different departments of Government, I must observe to you, sir, is one of the high crimes which this Administration has committed against the Constitution and the American people. For party and corrupt purposes, you have broken down the barriers interposed by the Constitution, for the safety of the people, between the several departments of power, whereby this Administration, including the majorities in both Houses of Congress, have become one unleavened lump of democracy and oppression. Not content with the Constitution, as you violently tore it from Washington and its other friends; not content with creeping under it, leaping over it, winding round it—now, sword in hand, attempting to pierce through it; you have so altered it, changed it, and mangled it, to suit your party views and purposes—to perpetuate your power and misrule—that the people no longer know or acknowledge it; no longer find under it protection for their property or safety for their lives. It is time then, sir, high time, for the people, in their turn, to look into this instrument; to see if they can heal the wounds which violence has inflicted on it—restore it to its pristine health and vigor; that they may, as at the beginning, find safety and protection under the shadow of the wings of the American Eagle.

If this Administration can, consistently with the provisions of the Constitution, ruin the country and oppress the people as they have done, that Constitution should, and must be changed. If, on the contrary, they have brought this ruin and oppression upon the country in open violation of that charter, once deemed sacred, then is this Administration, with James Madison at its head, a common nuisance, and ought to be abated by the people.

We still hear a feeble, though insidious cry of union. Union with whom? The present bankrupt, oppressive Administration? Believe me, gentlemen, you want no aid for that purpose; you are completing it as fast as time and your crimes will permit. You complain that avarice hoards, and that timidity locks up the money from you. No, gentlemen, you mistake; it is common sense and common prudence which keep it from the grasp of bankrupts and spendthrifts.

Sir, this country is in an alarming and awful situation. She is tottering on the brink of ruin. The people have, indeed, a difficult and painful labor and duty to perform, to protect themselves and their country against the desperate assaults of an oppressive and wicked Administration, and of an exasperated foreign enemy; but, with the blessing of Heaven on their exertions, they will triumph over all their enemies. It is now said, and I think with truth, that the salvation of this country depends upon the revival of its expiring credit. This the present men in power cannot accomplish. The Administration is bankrupt in means and resources, and they have ruined most of their friends who have loaned them money. In vain do they resort to the bubble of paper credit, which will burst with the very breath that blows it up; in vain do they turn their vacant stare on that huge spectre of a fifty million paper bank—that castle in the air, that baseless fabric of a vision, which must dissolve in thin air. No, sir; such visions will not meet or avert the dreadful calamity which surrounds us. There is but one mode, then, in which this nation can be saved. By placing, and that immediately, the nation in the hands and under the guardian care of men in whom the people have, and ought to have confidence; in the hands of men who, with Washington, before laid the foundation of public credit—which nothing but folly and wickedness could undermine; under the care of men who, with Washington at their head, and with his spirit and principles in their hearts, raised our Republic to glory and renown. But, mistake me not. No bribe can tempt, no office seduce, the true disciples of Washington to desert or betray their principles or their country. Nothing but the interest—nothing short of the salvation, of their country, could induce them to resume that authority, now so abused, which was insidiously wrested from them. Place such men in authority; put the destinies of the nation into their hands, and thousands of their friends will rally round their standard—not with empty professions of lives and fortunes, but with the free-will offering of their treasures and their blood.

Mr. GROSVENOR rose in reply to Mr. SHARP, of Kentucky.

Mr. G. said, that, impatient as the House appeared to be for the question, he could not suffer it to be taken without some animadversions upon the sentiments expressed by the honorable gentleman who had just sat down. Before he offered those, however, he would speak briefly to the propriety and Constitutionality of the provision under discussion. He confessed he had bestowed upon it no particular attention, as it had not been his purpose to take any part in the debate. He had thought that the reasoning of his honorable friend was conclusive against it upon Constitutional grounds; and he had hoped, that the distress which would be carried into domestic life, so eloquently described by the two gentlemen from Massachusetts, (Messrs. WARD and KING,) would reach the heart of every member, and compel him to reject the provision. But he was wholly mistaken. If, said Mr. G., anything could astonish me in this House, it would be the pertinacity with which this offensive provision is pressed upon us. The object to be obtained is so extremely trifling, as to render the ardor of pursuit as ridiculous as it is impolitic. I believe my friend from New Hampshire has gone to the very extent of the fact, when he has admitted that you might, possibly, by this provision, gain an accession of one thousand to your armies. Under the present law minors enlist. All that worthless description of young men, who have received their education in the tippling shops and the brothels, now go into your armies, and nobody reclaims them, because the camp is their proper element. Beyond this description, which you now have, if you gain an annual thousand you will exceed even your own expectation; and for this paltry gain you are about to adopt a principle, not only in the opinion of many unconstitutional, but, in practice, jeopardizing the good order of the community, violating contracts, disturbing the sacred rights of natural affection, and all the felicities of domestic life. My honorable friend from New Hampshire has characterized the proceeding as folly; I pronounce it a measure combining strong characters of weakness and violence, of folly and madness.

Is it Constitutional? The provision is, that all minors, of every condition, may, of their own mere will, contract to serve in your armies, and that such contract shall be conclusive and binding. By the laws of every State the age of minority is fixed, and no minor can make a valid and binding contract. Can you abrogate this State law? No, sir. To do so, was never delegated to you by the State or the people. All analogies from other Governments fail you. Yours is a Government, sovereign to be sure, but whose sovereignty is confined to particular subjects of legislation, and is limited by articles and sections. You have power to legislate upon no subjects, except such as are brought within your jurisdiction by the Constitution.

Sir, in what article or section of the Constitution do you find a power to enter the sanctuary of society, and frame municipal laws for this people? Where is your authority to give ability to the citizens to make contracts, which ability is forbidden by the municipal laws of the States? The ability to contract is the creature of municipal law; it is the subject of State legislation; it is exclusively reserved to the States, as sovereign States. And it is a direct subversion of the very frame of our Government to usurp that power, which exists not in the Constitution. Where will you stop? If you can,

in defiance of State law, declare that a minor may make a binding contract, can you not, on the same principle, extend the time of minority, and declare that any contract by a man over the age of minority, as fixed by State laws, shall not be binding? May you not interfere with any other subject of municipal law? Why may you not abolish the statutes of usury in any State? Why not new model the laws of descent, and declare that the brother or a stranger shall inherit in preference to the son? And why not interfere with your remedial laws and regulations? Your principle bears you through all these usurpations; and if it be correct you may, if you have the courage to attempt it, steal away all the powers of the States, and render their sovereignties ridiculous phantoms. Sir, the attempt is usurpation, and must experience the same fate with other usurpations, with all arbitrary efforts to destroy the Constitution.

My friend from New Hampshire (Mr. WEBSTER) has said, that if you can enlist apprentices in defiance of their masters, you may also deliver the slave from his servitude. Is he not literally correct? Why may you not enlist the slave? Because, by the municipal laws of the States, he has not the power to contract. The same reason, precisely, forbids the enlisting of minors and apprentices. If you can remove the incapacity from the latter, so you may from the former. Will you say that the master has a property in the services of his slave? How has he that property? Solely by a State law. By the same law the master has a property in the service of the apprentice—the father in the minority of his son. And if you may abrogate the law and violate the property in the one case, you may do it in the other. Nor is there any distinction arising from the duties of native allegiance. I have already stated that the sovereign powers of Government, in this country, are divided; part rests with the States, and part with the Union. With the latter, rest those powers delegated in the Constitution; all the remainder are in the States or the people. The natural allegiance of the people is due to the State sovereignties; and that allegiance only is due to the Federal Government which is promised by the Constitution. In that Constitution the minor has promised no military duty, but that which is to be performed in the militia. In the militia he may be forced into the service of the United States, "to execute the laws, suppress insurrection, and repel invasion;" beyond this you cannot force him into your service; nor can you entice him by any contract, not sanctioned by his father, guardian, or master. I will not pursue the Constitutional objection to the bill any further.

But your right to adopt this provision has been argued on precedent; and the law of 1798 has been cited. Sir, could a thousand precedents of the violation of the Constitution be produced in your statute book, they would have no weight with me. These are not times to be influenced by those precedents which arose in the agitations of any period, or by the opinions of others, perhaps lightly formed and hastily expressed. The

Constitution is now daily fooled to the very top of its bent. For purposes of unhallowed conquest, the Secretary of War, who seems to be at once the director general and organ of the Administration, has stretched all its limbs upon the rack of party, until it has spoken any and every language which its tormentor has dictated. This is not a moment for the sentinels of freedom to sleep, or to be deluded by idle opinion, or ill-advised precedent.

The provisions of the Constitution are before us. I will admit all the acknowledged rules of construction to obtain its legitimate meaning; but though precedents of its violation should be cited by the month, they should have no weight with me, however plausible or authoritative they may be deemed by others.

But even precedent is not to be found. What is the principle of the law of 1798? Citizens, "of able bodies and suitable age," might be enlisted "under the direction of the President." In point of fact, the President did direct that minors should not be enlisted. But suppose he had directed otherwise, and minors had been enlisted, their contracts were voidable under the State laws, and, on application, the State judges might, and frequently did, release them. If the enlisted minor had a parent, guardian, or master, either might, and frequently did, reclaim him from the service. How different is this act. Here you not only in express terms authorize the enlistment of minors, but you consider their contract of enlistment conclusive. You, in express terms, authorize the apprentice to violate the contract with his master; and you declare the master entirely without remedy. Have gentlemen considered the partial operation of this provision? Its effects will not be felt in the South, where manual labor is performed, not by hardy freemen but by slaves. It will not be felt in the South and the West, where manufactories, and consequently apprentices, are few; but it will fall with dreadful violence upon the North and the East, where the hardy owners of the soil rely upon their sons to till the earth; where manufactories of all descriptions, private and public, have suddenly multiplied beyond all parallel; and where the services of apprentices are all-important to their success. Certainly, if any act was ever justly odious, this will be most justly detested by the freemen of the North and East.

Here, perhaps, I ought to stop; but I hope the House will bear with me while I bestow a few moments attention upon the speech of the honorable gentleman from Kentucky, (Mr. Sharp.) That gentleman has given his fancy a latitude of party crimination beyond the ordinary field of debate.

An honorable gentleman from Massachusetts (Mr. Ward) had spoken of the domestic happiness, the social and maternal feelings, which this act would violate—of the heart-rending scenes that must occur, when the youth, who in a moment of feverish ambition, or giddy revelry, had enlisted, should be dragged from the embraces of his mother and sisters to the dangers of a Cana-

dian war. Gentlemen who favor the bill have all appeared to me to treat this subject with too much levity.

Sir, the best feelings of our natures, those strong family affections which form at once the ligaments and felicities of social life, cannot be violated by any Government with impunity; and those measures which cause the tears of a whole nation to flow, cannot comport with its interests, its honor, or its durable prosperity. But these, it seems, will be the tears of women.

The age of chivalry may have departed, but the nature and affections of man remain unchanged. And the annals of the world will prove, that when by oppression and injustice tears are wrung from female eyes, it never can be long before they mingle with the blood of man. Let no Legislature forget, that so closely are the social affections knit together—so well are all our feelings and interests woven in the very frame of society, that the arm of the strong can never long be wanting to avenge the wrongs and protect the rights of the weak. While on this subject, I would say a word upon the refined lesson which has just been read by the gentleman from Kentucky to his countrywomen. He has recited, for their imitation, the address of a Spartan mother to her son, as he was departing on a marauding expedition: "Bring back this shield, or be brought back upon it."

I trust I am not insensible to sentiments or actions of heroism; but, whenever I have read this address, an emotion very different from admiration has always been prevalent in my mind. Where were those claims of nature—those strong natural affections—which cling to the offspring with a force stronger than death? None of them resided in the bosom of that Spartan mother. Sir, I have often wondered, when I have heard the sentiments and conduct of the Spartan aristocracy cited for the imitation of a Christian Republic. They were a race, faithless, cruel, and barbarous; hateful and terrible to the rest of mankind. All their maxims were unjust and selfish, and all their institutions modelled on principles of immoral tendency; calculated only to extend the empire of ignorance, desolation, and revenge.

Why will not the honorable gentleman proceed, and cite, from the same polluted source, examples for the imitation of our youth? One great object of Spartan policy was to accomplish her youth in the *useful* science of thieving! It became a maxim, that to steal adroitly was meritorious; but, to be detected, was crime and ignominy. And no doubt many a Spartan mother has charged her son, upon the eve of some petty larceny expedition, Return successful and undetected, or return a corpse.

I have seen and have admired female heroism; but, that is not heroism which smothers in the female bosom those refined feelings—those fond attachments and divine affections—which constitute all there is of glory in woman, in her relations of daughter, wife, and mother. Give to the females of the Choctaw tribes the polished language of Greece, and they would turn you a sentence breathing the same spirit and feelings as that uttered by this Amazon of Sparta.

That our countrywomen should cherish the defenders of their country, is natural and noble. And when the defence of our rights is the sole question, even female timidity may assume defiance, and, with her own hand, arm the warrior for battle. But, no American mother can urge her son to the invasion of Canada—to carry misery to those whom the spirit of Christianity has made her sisters. If that dreadful work of desolation must go on, let the only agent be *man*; and, if he falls in the battle, deny not to his mother, his wife, or his sister, the holy office of mourning his fall, and bedewing his corse with her tears.

Mr. Speaker, the same honorable gentleman has complained of the assertion, so often made by us, that this war has produced ruin to our country, and stained with disgrace our national character. He has declared the charge unfounded. The *Navy* has preserved our drowning honor. The late campaign on the Niagara has covered a multitude of stains. Apart from these, he seemed to admit there had been disgrace; and he declared he would pour the whole torrent of his indignation upon those who had produced it. "But 'who (he asked) had produced it? Who were 'the authors of our misfortunes and our disgraces? 'Those who had declared and directed the war, 'or those who had opposed the declaration, and at 'all times remonstrated against its continuance?"

Sir, the question is important; let it be now decided. Who are the guilty authors of the disgrace on our name and all the misfortunes of our country? Are they the men who, before the war was declared, spoke of its dreadful impolicy; portrayed the defenceless condition of the country; pointed daily to the weakness of our means; warned you that your frontiers would be swept by savage desolation, and your cities destroyed; that your States would be exposed to subjugation, your Union to dissolution, and, almost in the agony of despair, invoked you to save your wives, your children, your country, from the sufferings and the evils of the conflict? Or, are they the men, who, forgetting all the sacred duties which bound them to peace; buoyed up by the transitory huzzas of a mob; vain with a little brief authority; hurried along by the fatal influence of party; without necessity, and without mercy, plunged their country, defenceless and naked, into that lake of blood where she is yet swimming? The men who resisted, even unto death, all your weak and wicked schemes of commercial coercion, which spread distress over the land, and conducted directly to this war? Or those who, day after day, and year after year, adopted a course of oppressive and ruinous policy—a succession of weak, yet suicidal measures, from which even war seemed almost a relief?

Who are the guilty authors of your ruin? Those who to the last moment, even on the brink of the bloody gulf, still pointed to the white flag of peace and prosperity, which WASHINGTON had erected? Or those who rudely tore it down, and hoisted the crimson banner in its stead?

13th CON. 3d SESS.—24

Who are the guilty authors of our disgraces? The men, who, when you had plunged into the gulf, still spoke to you of peace—still urged you to grasp the proffered hand of the enemy? Or, those who, having tasted blood, continued to cry for havoc, madly despising the only offer which could issue in a permanent pacification? The men who constantly invoked you to defend your towns and coasts—always protested against your unjust invasion of a neighboring province, and forewarned you that the frowns of a just God would cover with defeat and ignominy all your ambitious schemes of conquest? Or they who, abandoning their own soil and capital to ravage and desolation, in the very spirit of ignorance and gasconade, boasted the conquest of Canada in six weeks, and sent a Hull there, to surrender in thirty days? Who proudly proclaimed that the finger of Heaven pointed to Quebec—that her lofty ramparts were already trembling at their prowess—and sent a Wilkinson to be chased back, covered with the blackest disgrace? Who, for three years, have bent all their power to subjugate a province, poor, thinly populated, badly defended, and in every instance have been overthrown and discomfited? Upon whom, sir, shall the good genius of this country frown!

Review these acts, and tell me who in truth are the authors of this wide-spread ruin—this black disgrace which shrouds the American name?

Let me not be misunderstood. No doubt, our gallant frigates have gilded the national escutcheon with the brightest beams of glory. To the unbending spirit and gallant conduct of the American soldier no man is more sensible. Our armies in the North, during the past Summer, have fought with an heroic bravery worthy the best days of our Revolution. Their gallant leaders are entitled to every meed of applause. But all their resolution, and all their gallantry, but shrouds the Cabinet conductors of the war in tenfold darkness.

How have the bravery and the resolution of our armies been applied? To accomplish the unhallowed schemes of ambition; to carry desolation and death into a country, feeble and pacific, and always the friend of our Republic, until you forced her to become our enemy. And how, even in this work of unjust desolation, how have they been directed? In a manner, weak and foolish beyond example. Look to the Niagara. How has the life of man been made the sport of imbecility and ambition! What hecatombs of human victims have been sacrificed, in an unmeaning contest, for a Canadian fortress, of no use to our country, finally abandoned as worthless.

The fields of Chippewa, of Cornwall, of Bridgewater, and of Erie, are still smoking with human blood, crying to Heaven for vengeance.

O, sir, the authors of this war cannot be guiltless! I tell them, in the final day of retribution, when the rulers of nations shall be summoned to answer at the dread tribunal, the disgrace, the misery, the ruin, and the blood which now covers this land, will lie with the weight of a mountain on their souls.

And what is our guilt? We warned, we conjured you to shun the ruin of this unnecessary, this guilty war. When you despised all our remonstrances, and made the fatal plunge, we still invoked you to turn your thoughts on peace. But when we found all your armies sent on plans of conquest, we appealed to Heaven for our rectitude, and boldly took our stand; conscious that no fate could await our country more dreadful than the guilt of unjust invasion and an alliance with the French usurper. Could we unite in plans which we verily believed had such ends in view? Could we vote for measures to support a war of conquest, which in our souls we loathed, as unjust, dishonest, impolitic? We saw the monstrous tyrant of France standing like a Colossus in the midst of Europe, beating her liberties to the earth, and frowning upon all our free institutions, so hostile in their nature to his despotic soul and his views of universal empire. We saw the final struggle for the independence of mankind about commencing, and its issue involved in dreadful doubt.

Your war, however intended, must be the tyrant's gain. We knew it was better, far better, that all your invasions should be turned back upon you, than that your conquests should add one nerve to that iron arm which was beating down the independence of every nation. We could not aid in your schemes of ambition and conquest. As men, as patriots, as Christians, we could not voluntarily mingle in the unjust conflict.

Yet, sir, for defence we have been always ready; defence which could be separated from your invasion of Canada. This last is your sole property. The wreath of Canadian conquests, whether it be woven of the laurel or the cypress; whether it beam with justice and glory, or be dyed in the black and crimson hues of disgrace and guilt, shall decorate your brows alone. We have not, we never had, we never will have part, or lot, in that matter. But for the defence of our country, even from those dangers with which your madness alone has surrounded her, borne down, persecuted, slandered, as we are by the very Government which should protect us, here we stand, here we have always stood, prepared to furnish every aid, even to the last vital drop which warms our hearts. Such is the very front of our offending. With our opponents we are at the bar of Heaven.

The name of an honorable gentleman, formerly of this House, now a Commissioner at Ghent, has been introduced. A gentleman from Vermont, (Mr. Fisk,) alluding to the charge of the British commissioners, that the conquest of Canada was one object of this war, expressed some indignation at the Massachusetts remonstrance, which they had quoted in proof of their charge. My honorable friend from Massachusetts (Mr. Ward) remarked, in reply, that it was strange the British commissioners had wandered so far for testimony, inasmuch as a simple question to Mr. Clay, if truly answered, would have placed the subject beyond the power of doubt.

The honorable gentleman from Kentucky, after an eulogium upon the character of Mr. Clay, remarked, that although he might have mentioned an invasion of Canada, as a means of compelling the enemy to do us justice, yet he never contemplated a permanent conquest, and an annexation of a British province to the Union. Mr. Speaker, it is strange to me that any doubt exists on this subject. The permanent conquest of Canada has been often avowed within this House, and by gentlemen high in the confidence of the Government. And to me it is wholly unaccountable, that all the American Commissioners have ventured to deny it. The conquest of Canada, it is true, was not set forth in the manifesto, either of the President or of this House. It was not to be expected that an object so shameful would be officially avowed. But you find it avowed in all the gazettes in the confidence of the Government, in the speeches of those members of Congress who declared the war, in the proclamations of those Generals who have conducted the war. And never, to my knowledge, has it been disavowed by the Executive Government, unless the assertion of our Commissioners at Ghent may be deemed such a disavowal.

Sir, I have often heard it asserted on this floor. I have heard it avowed by Mr. Clay while a member of this House. I hold in my hand a speech of that gentleman delivered sometime before the war was declared. I was accidentally in the House; and to show that my friend from Massachusetts (Mr. Ward) was in nowise mistaken, I will read an extract from this speech. "I am not, sir, in favor of cherishing the pas- 'sion of conquest. But I must be permitted to ' conclude, by declaring my hope to see, ere long, ' the new United States (if you will allow me the ' expression) embracing not only the old thirteen ' States, but the entire country east of the Mis- ' sissippi, including East Florida, and some of the ' territories to the North of us also."

These latter "territories" are none other than the Canadas. Is not this the plain and palpable spirit of conquest? Was my friend from Massachusetts mistaken? At the time, the orator was the champion of the Administration in the Senate. He was transferred to this House, and afterwards, Mr. Speaker, occupied the place in which you have succeeded. It is well known he was the confidential friend of the President. I need not describe his standing in this House, nor state his powerful influence in plunging the country into war. Did he understand the views of the Government? Did he know the objects of the war? It may be now convenient to answer in the negative. Then of course his authority is nothing.

The honorable gentleman has also spoken of union. What are his notions of an useful and honorable union? Not a union of men, but of measures; not of council, but of action. Action! to what end? To save our country? Be it so. But the first step towards that object must be made by those who have dragged the country to the very verge of ruin. Yes, we are ready to act for the salvation of our country. But to what efficient purpose can men act with you, who believe that all your conduct still points to her destruction?

Would you save this country, you must become sensible of her perilous condition, of your own fatal errors. You must learn, that your menaces of conquest have become the mere bravados of rage and mortification; that your frequent party denunciations are the delirious ravings of disappointment and despair; that your hopes of succor from foreign wars are but the lunatic visions of political madness. You must bend all your thoughts on peace; and, until you obtain it, you must apply all your means solely to the defence of the country. Then you will obtain that general union in action which can alone produce any permanent good to the State. How widely different are your designs and your professed ostensible measures! You continue to talk of that miserable policy which has dragged you so heavily through the last three years, and elevated you to the pinnacle of disgrace which you now occupy. You still, in your daily dreams, menace the towers of Quebec, reckless that your cities may meet the same ignoble fate which has swept your Capitol. Party spirit still pollutes all the councils of the Cabinet, and impels it to hunt, with bloodhounds of persecution, the most independent, wise, and virtuous men of the nation. You well know that a course like this presents a wall of brass in the way of a general union. And yet you pursue it with untiring ardor. Where will it finally conduct this devoted country? Is not her fate written in glaring capitals upon the tombstone of every departed Republic?

With such conduct in the ruling power, what is the duty of those in the House, who, like myself, have no confidence in the wisdom of the Administration? I judge for myself alone. The cause is brought home to my conscience. This country must fall, unless every hand is stretched forth to her rescue. I fear there is no hope of safety but in a radical change of rulers. This cannot now be constitutionally effected. We must patiently wait until a whole people, roused from the stupor almost of the grave, shall interpose for our final rescue. In the meantime, the country must be defended.

As a member of this Government, I feel I have no choice remaining. Notwithstanding the continued frenzy of the Administration in relation to conquest, must not this war, in the nature of things and in spite of its authors, be entirely defensive? Where, and in what quarter, have not their errors compelled us to struggle for the very possession of our soil?

In the East, a whole province is torn from us; in the South, we are menaced with the loss of a State. On our Northern frontier, the disciplined hosts of the enemy are marshalled, and, having beaten back invasion, are ready, in their turn, to carry desolation into the bosom of our Union. The forests of the West are again disturbed by the war-shout of the savage. Our Capitol has disgracefully fallen, and all our coasts are open to ravage and conflagration.

When, in this condition of my country, I bow to the Constitution, and, by force of its provisions, am compelled, either to stand neuter, or to trust means of defence to men who may cast them away, or pervert them to conquest, do I therefore participate in their guilt?

But *can* those means be thus perverted? If even our present rulers are so lost to their country, as to wish to leave her a defenceless victim to the enemy, dare they venture on the suicidal measure? Where are our forces to meet and repel the mighty fleets and armies which threaten invasion? Where are our armies, even for defence?

The very means which must bring them into existence are still slumbering in your committee rooms. What if they should fail? Have we pictured to ourselves the consequence? What man who hears me will survive the bloody spasms, the social distractions, and civil and servile commotions which must ensue a violent termination of our Republic? When I view our own State, the great mart of her wealth, of easy access, and of difficult defence; the great lake extending to her interior, commanded by the enemy; her borders bristling with hostile bayonets, only waiting the Spring to be levelled at our citizens; and when I know the extreme distress, perhaps overthrow that must await her, if unaided in the struggle, my duty forbids me to hesitate. Our States must be defended from invasion; beyond that, is not possible for our means. For, sir, let those mortified and disgraced men, whose rashness and imbecility have combined to produce all our misfortunes, talk as they may, about their vain designs of future invasion and conquest, the wretched state of the Treasury, the melancholy condition of our armies, are no longer susceptible of concealment.

So far is invasion and conquest beyond their power that, in the next campaign, all the resources of the nation, all the spirit of the people, and, I fear, twice the wisdom of the Administration, will be indispensable, to preserve our cities from conflagration, our Union from dissolution, and some of our States from subjugation. In this firm belief, though faint, indeed, are my hopes of success under the influence of present auspices, I hold it as a sacred duty to keep nothing back which may aid in the defence of the country. Every measure applicable to this great object, whether for the supply of money or of men, which shall promise advantage, and which is sanctioned by the spirit of the Constitution, shall have all the aid in my power to furnish, my voice and my vote.

When Mr. GROSVENOR had concluded—

Mr. BARNETT said that the old saying of "one day older and two days worse," was not inapplicable, he thought, to the present state of some gentlemen's irritable faculties; for the nearer we are like to approach to a system calculated to give a manly and vigorous defence to the nation, and security to the blessings we enjoy, in a twofold proportion do they appear to be dispirited, and doubly loud the denunciations of the cruelty and wickedness of the measure. Mr. B. said he

in the months of July and August last. The war continuing, the power of the enemy unbroken, our condition will be desperate. The regular force every day falling off, (for be it remembered these eighty thousand militia will be withdrawn from the operations of the recruiting service,) we shall have to oppose to the enemy a remnant of regular troops, and these eighty thousand raw militia—and who will answer for the consequences? In the months of August and September last, we had in the field the regular Army and upwards of one hundred thousand militia, and we nowhere found ourselves too strong. It is true the Senate propose to improve the recruiting system—an improvement which two years ago this House proposed to the Senate, but which the Senate then thought proper to reject. I mean the enlistment of young men between the ages of eighteen and twenty-one. But if these eighty thousand militia for two years should happen to be, as they are likely to be, that very description of population upon which this system would otherwise operate, what hope can be entertained that the recruiting system even with its improvements will be as productive the next year as the last. I humbly conceive, Mr. Speaker, that the measure of the Senate, proceeding from the best intentions, will fail in the accomplishment of our object. I conceive, with much deference to the House, that the measures reported by their own committee are much to be preferred. They propose—first, to augment the regular establishment to one hundred thousand men; second, to authorize the President to accept under liberal encouragements the service of volunteer corps; third, to authorize the President to receive into the service of the United States State troops, which may be raised to serve in lieu of the militia of such States. The principle of the system is, to substitute, as far as we are able, a regular force for a militia force, as more efficient, more economical, and, for the militia themselves, more convenient—and one hundred thousand regulars would take the place of two hundred thousand militia—two hundred thousand militia would cost as much as three hundred thousand regulars. If we can command an hundred thousand regular troops, it may, notwithstanding, be necessary, on particular emergencies, to resort to the militia. To enable the Government still further to spare the militia, volunteers are authorized. They also will be more efficient than ordinary militia. It is impossible to say to what extent these corps will offer themselves—to whatever extent the Government is enabled to avail itself of their services, to the same extent will the militia be saved. If Government should derive no aid from this source, it has another resource in State troops. They also will take the place of the militia. The militia will still continue the bulwark of the country. Whenever the existence of the country shall be endangered, it is the militia that must save it. The system proposes to relieve them from the constant harassment of which they complain, and justly complain. To raise the regular troops, you have the alternative proposed by the Secretary of War, or the committee. The plan of the Secretary of War is the only effectual one. If we have energy and spirit to take it, it will fill our ranks and augment our regular establishment certainly and expeditiously. The people will justify the measure, because they will feel that it is necessary to the maintenance of the honor, the character, and independence, of the country. The plan of the committee, though less efficient, is, in my humble opinion, better than that of the Senate. Where it fails to give you men it will give you money. It will be certain to give some men, and some money. I hope the House will agree to strike out the section.

Mr. CALHOUN briefly replied to the call made upon him by Mr. TROUP for the reasons why he preferred acting on the bill: that reason he thought was very obvious; that the bill, having met the approbation of the Senate, would, if it passed this House, immediately become a law. Policy appeared to him to require a preference of this bill to that reported by the committee of this House. If the Senate send us one bill, and we, instead of acting on it, send them another, it would place the two Houses in an awkward predicament. It seemed to him, he said, that the whole argument of the gentleman against this bill was misplaced. This bill, as well as the gentleman's bill, would produce a certain number of recruits for the regular Army. Should the bill reported by the gentleman prevail, it would give us either regulars or money; if this bill should pass, we shall have regulars or good militia. Both bills were calculated to produce regulars, if they could be obtained by purchase. If absolute certainty was the object of the gentleman, it could be only obtained by resorting to a regular and fair system of conscription. To the result of any other system, whether that reported by the Military Committee of this House, or that now under consideration, some uncertainty must attach. The bill from the Senate promising as much certainty as that reported in this House, he hoped it would be gone through with and finally passed.

The question was then taken, without further debate, on the motion to strike out the first section of the bill, and decided as follows—for the motion 62, against it 64. So the motion to strike out the first section was negatived.

The following is the apportionment of the proposed draught of men among the several States and Territories:

From New Hampshire, two thousand five hundred eighty.

From Massachusetts, eight thousand six hundred five.

From Vermont, two thousand five hundred eighty.

From Rhode Island, eight hundred sixty.

From Connecticut, three thousand ten.

From New York, eleven thousand six hundred fifteen.

From New Jersey, two thousand five hundred eighty.

From Pennsylvania, nine thousand eight hundred ninety-five.

From Delaware, eight hundred sixty.

From Maryland, three thousand eight hundred seventy.

From Virginia, nine thousand eight hundred ninety-five.

From North Carolina, five thousand five hundred ninety.

From South Carolina, three thousand eight hundred seventy.

From Georgia, two thousand five hundred eighty.

From Kentucky, four thousand three hundred.

From Ohio, two thousand five hundred eighty.

From Tennessee, two thousand five hundred eighty.

From Louisiana, four hundred thirty.

From the Mississippi Territory, five hundred twenty-two.

From the Indiana Territory, five hundred forty-nine.

From the Illinois Territory, two hundred thirteen.

From the Michigan Territory, sixty.

From the Missouri Territory, three hundred seventy-six.

And from the Territory of Columbia, four hundred thirty.

Mr. JENNINGS moved to amend the apportionment for Indiana Territory, by striking out five hundred and forty-nine and inserting three hundred. The motion was opposed by Mr. RHEA of Tennessee, and negatived, 20 or 30 members only rising in favor of it.

Mr. LEWIS, of Virginia, moved to strike out the present apportionment of the District of Columbia, viz: four hundred and thirty, and insert eighty, which he said would be at the rate of every twenty-fifth man. This motion was opposed by Mr. RHEA and negatived.

Mr. McKEE, of Kentucky, moved to strike out the 7th section of the bill, (which limits the services to be required of the draughted militia, to the bounds of their own and any adjoining State, with the exception of the Western States, who are, when required, to serve in Louisiana, and those of Pennsylvania and Virginia, in like manner, in the Michigan Territory, &c.) He could not see any possible benefit to arise from it, but he could see great inconvenience. It might frequently be important that the militia of one State should serve in a State which was not adjoining to theirs, and in some sections of the country might refuse their co-operation in such case, sheltering themselves under the provisions of this act.

This motion was seconded by Mr. SHARP, of Kentucky, who thought this section calculated to excite feelings of dissention, and State and local prejudices. We ought to legislate as if for a nation, and not for State authorities. We ought to encourage national feeling, not sectional views. He should like to see that feeling diffused through the nation, which prevails in some parts of the Union, that would induce the citizens freely to march from one extreme to another to meet the enemy, rather than he should hold a foot of the soil. But when you recognise the principle that the militia of one State, say Massachusetts, shall not, on occasion, be liable to march for the defence of the shores of another, say Maryland or Virginia, or that the militia of the State of Kentucky or Tennessee should not, if necessary, march to the defence of Massachusetts, you sanction a local State feeling, which will be the bane of the prosperity of the nation. The States West of the mountains, and those East of the Potomac, were as much sister States, he said, as if they lay con-

tiguous to each other. From the mode of legislation embraced in this section, Mr. S. feared the excitement of sentiments hostile to the grandeur of the character of this nation, as well as to its honor, both of which could only be attained by an amalgamation of national feeling.

Mr. CALHOUN remarked that, even were the section stricken out, it would not materially vary the nature of the service of these militia forces, which would be confined to their respective States, unless necessity required their service elsewhere; in which case such a limitation as is contained in the bill would be very inconvenient. He, therefore, concurred in the opinion that the section ought to be stricken out.

Mr. KILBOURN, of Ohio, supported the motion to strike out the 7th section. He conceived the militia service already sufficiently injured, if not dishonored, by the construction of the Constitution which had limited its utility. He hoped it would not be further restricted in such a provision as this. To show its injurious tendency, he instanced the case, which might happen, of the militia of New Jersey being called on to cross the Delaware, to aid in the defence of Pennsylvania or Delaware; the enemy retiring across an imaginary line into the State of Maryland, to regain their ships in the Chesapeake, the militia would, under this section, be precluded from pursuing them beyond the line, unless it suited their pleasure.

The question on striking out the 7th section was decided in the affirmative by a large majority.

Several other unimportant amendments were proposed, giving rise to desultory discussion, which were variously disposed of.

Mr. KING, of North Carolina, moved to amend the bill, so as not to confine the Governors of States, in the selection of the officers to command the militia to be draughted in pursuance of the bill, to the present militia officers.

This motion was supported by the mover, and by Messrs. FORSYTH of Georgia, FISK and SHIPHERD of New York, and GHOLSON of Virginia, on the ground of the expediency of allowing the widest field for the selection of officers qualified for command, without confining it to the militia officers now in commission, many of whom, though highly respectable men, were unfit for military command, having been selected in a time of peace, without reference to their military qualifications.

The motion was opposed by Messrs. CANNON and RHEA of Tennessee, PEARSON of North Carolina, and PICKERING of Massachusetts, on the ground of alleged injustice to the merits of our present militia, on Constitutional scruples, and on the difficulty which would be presented by the variance of the modes of appointment in the different States.

The motion was at last negatived—43 voting in favor of it.

Mr. LEWIS, of Virginia, moved to strike out two years, the proposed term of service of the militia to be draughted in pursuance of this bill

715 **HISTORY OF CONGRESS.** 716

H. of R.　　　*Income Tax—Moneys Receivable for Taxes.*　　　December, 1816.

and insert six months. The motion was negatived by the following vote: For the motion 45, against it 82.

On motion of Mr. Forsyth, the bill was so amended as to make the officers of the draughted militia eligible, according to the Constitution and laws of the several States.

This bill having been gone through, the House proceeded to the consideration of the bill from the Senate, "further to provide for filling the ranks of the Army of the United States."

[This is the bill that has occasioned so much debate in the Senate, and which authorizes the enlistment of minors.]

The bill having been read through, a motion was made by Mr. Pitkin, of Connecticut, to strike out so much of the bill as authorizes the enlistment of minors over eighteen years of age, without the consent of their parents or guardians; which motion he supported by a few pertinent remarks.

This motion was opposed by Mr. Hopkins, of Kentucky, in a short speech of much force and energy.

It was negatived by the following vote: For the motion 51, against it 83.

The House then proceeded to consider the bill, authorizing the President to accept the services of certain volunteer corps, (which bill was before the House some weeks ago for several days.) On motion of Mr. Johnson, of Kentucky, this bill was then so amended, as to reinstate it precisely in the form in which it stood before it underwent amendment by the House.

The Committee then rose, and reported to the House the three bills they had had under consideration.

The first of those bills, viz: the bill from the Senate, requiring a draught for two years of a body of militia, was, on motion of Mr. Johnson, of Kentucky, referred to a select committee for their consideration.

The second of the above bills being before the House, and the question being on the engrossing of the bill for a third reading—

The House adjourned without deciding thereon.

Saturday, December 3.

A message from the Senate informed the House that the Senate have passed a bill "to authorize the purchase of the library of Thomas Jefferson, late President of the United States;" in which they ask the concurrence of this House.

Mr. McKee reported a bill, giving further time to the purchasers of public lands to complete their payments; and a bill for the relief of the heirs of James Hynum; which were twice read and committed.

The bill to extend Oliver Evans's patent for steam engines, was twice read and committed.

INCOME TAX.

Mr. Eppes, from the Committee of Ways and Means, to whom was referred a resolution of the House of Representatives, instructing them to inquire into the "expediency of laying a duty on all salaried officers, and on the professional income of lawyers, solicitors, and counsellors, and on the legal proceedings of courts of justice," made the following report:

That a tax upon salaries can only be expedient and proper under arbitrary Governments, where pensions and places are bestowed without a just regard to the public interest. In the United States, according to the principles of our Government, no salary can be allowed, except as a compensation for public service; a tax operates as a deduction from the salary, and such a tax, so far as respects the officers of the United States, would be an admission on the part of the legislative body, that, in fixing the salaries of their public officers, the public interest had been disregarded, and more than a just compensation allowed. Without deciding whether in some instances this may not be the case, the committee are of opinion that, if the evil exists, the proper Constitutional remedy is not a tax, but a reduction of the salaries. The second member of the resolution embraces the income of lawyers, solicitors, and counsellors. The selection of a particular class of the community, which already pays, in common with others, a tax on property and on consumption, and imposing on it an income tax, from which every other class is exempted, would be a departure from that system of equal and exact justice, which ought to form the basis of legislation in a free country. The third member of the resolution proposes a tax on the legal proceedings of courts. This tax, if confined to the Courts of the United States, would be unproductive; if extended to the State Courts, difficult in the collection. It would fall principally on the necessitous and unfortunate, and produce collision with the State authorities. Upon the whole, it is considered inexpedient to resort to either of the proposed taxes. The following resolution is, therefore, submitted:

Resolved, That it is inexpedient to impose a duty on salaried officers, on the income of lawyers, or on the proceedings of courts at law.

The report was ordered to lie on the table.

MONEYS RECEIVABLE FOR TAXES.

Mr. Eppes, from the Committee of Ways and Means, to whom was referred a resolution of the House of Representatives, instructing them to inquire into the expediency of providing by law, that any kind of money paid by the Government to the troops in the service of the United States, for military services, shall be receivable from the people in payment of taxes, made the following report:

That, under the general power to regulate the collection of taxes, the Secretary of the Treasury is preparing instructions to the collectors, in which a uniform rule as to the receipt of bank notes will be prescribed. The committee consider that it would be unsafe to designate, by law, the notes in which taxes shall be received, and that a due regard for the public interest requires that this subject should be regulated, at present, by instructions issued, from time to time, from the Treasury Department; which may be so framed, as to unite the safety of the revenue with the accommodation of the individual citizens. A statement of the circumstances which produced the resolution drawn up by the Representatives of Tennessee, together with a letter from the Secretary of the Treasury, accompanies this report; and the committee submit the following resolution:

Resolved, That it is inexpedient to designate, by law, the bank notes which shall be receivable in payment of taxes.

Treasury Department, *Nov. 23, 1814.*

Sir: I have the honor to acknowledge the receipt of your letter, dated the 21st instant, enclosing a resolution of the House of Representatives, passed the 11th instant, directing an inquiry "into the expediency of providing by law, that any kind of money which may be paid by the Government to the troops in the service of the United States, for military services, shall be receivable in payment from the people in taxes."

In the course of an endeavor to ascertain the grounds of the resolution, I have been favored with a communication from the Representatives of Tennessee in Congress, (of which a copy is annexed,) in addition to the general information possessed in this Department; and I believe that the facts of the case are briefly these: The Secretary of War, having occasion for money to pay the militia who marched from Tennessee against the Creek Indians, obtained a loan in bank notes, for that purpose, from the Bank of Chilicothe. Some of these notes have since been offered in the payment of taxes to the collectors of the internal duties in the State of Tennessee; but, as the banks of Tennessee (where the money collected for taxes is required to be deposited) refuse to receive them as cash deposites, the collectors, in their turn, refuse to receive them as cash for taxes. Owing to the causes suggested in the communication to which I have already referred, and, perhaps, to other causes, perfectly consistent with the general solvency of the Bank of Chilicothe, the notes circulating in Tennessee have suffered a considerable depreciation. They have already been, it is alleged, an object of speculation; these paid by the United States to the militia cannot now be distinguished from other notes issued by the Bank of Chilicothe; and any attempt to give the former a preference, in the payment of taxes, would probably increase the arts of speculation, as well as the other inconveniences of which the citizens of Tennessee complain.

Under these circumstances the case is, obviously, one of great delicacy. The Government has passed the notes at their nominal value; but it is equally true, that the Government is bound to pay for them to the bank according to their nominal value. The Government did not contract any engagement to support the credit of the notes, nor to accept them in payment of duties at any subsequent period; and all the persons who have accepted the notes, either in payment from the Government, or by transfer from the militia, have done so voluntarily, without any pretence of reliance upon any such engagement. If, therefore, it should be deemed proper to direct, by the legislative authority, that the notes of the Bank of Chilicothe shall be received in payment for duties, the principle of the direction will be equally applicable to every other case where the Government has paid its troops or creditors in bank notes, which have afterwards suffered (from whatever cause) a depreciation in credit or circulating value. The effect of such a law, upon the public revenues, need not be particularly stated.

Considering the subject, however, as a general subject, meriting the serious attention of the Treasury Department, I am preparing instructions to the collectors, to regulate their conduct in receiving bank notes for taxes. The design of the instructions will be, to unite the security of the revenue with the accommodation of the banks, as well as of individual citizens, during the disordered condition of the circulating medium of the country; and, in making this arrangement, I shall be highly gratified to find that the views of the mover of the resolution under consideration can be accomplished.

I have the honor to be, &c.

                 A. J. DALLAS.

J. W. Eppes, *Chairman, &c.*

Congress Hall, *November, 1814.*

Sir: It may be satisfactory to you to be informed of the situation of the banks in the State of Tennessee. There are two banks in that State—one at Knoxville, and the other at Nashville; both of them of unquestionable credit and solvency. No suspension has taken place of specie payments, nor do we believe any suspension will take place.

With respect to the Bank of Chilicothe, in the notes of which most of the troops in the service of the United States, from the State of Tennessee, have been paid, we can only observe, that no doubt was entertained of its solvency and ability to discharge its respective engagements, so far as we have been informed; but the notes would not circulate without considerable discount. This, we think, was produced in consequence of the course of trade being from the Southwest, Eastwardly, and Northeast, and money was not wanted at Chilicothe by the citizens of the mercantile towns in Tennessee, and not by any doubt existing of the solvency of the bank.

As these notes do not suit the commercial relations existing between the citizens of Tennessee and the Eastern States, we do not wish them to be further used in the payment of troops there.

The refusal, by the Government, to receive them again in the payment of taxes, has necessarily produced considerable irritation, and it is believed, by some of the people there, to be an intentional attempt to impose on them.

The spirit of patriotism and military ardor, now existing in as high a degree as in any part of the United States, is sinking under the injustice of this measure.

We have the honor to be, &c.

              P. W. HUMPHREYS,
              JOHN H. BOWER,
              THOS. K. HARRIS,
              N. CANNON.

The report was ordered to lie on the table.

PETITION OF NOAH SHAW.

Mr. Eppes, from the Committee of Ways and Means, to whom was referred the petition of Noah Shaw, made the following report:

That the facts necessary for forming an opinion on the case, are stated in a letter from the Secretary of the Treasury, which accompanies this report. From this statement it appears that the petitioner is not entitled to relief under the special act of Congress, passed on the second day of January, 1812; and that the former Secretary refused, under the general law of the 3d of March, 1797, to remit the forfeiture incurred by the petitioner, on the ground, that it did not appear to his satisfaction that the forfeiture was incurred without wilful negligence, or any intention of fraud. On a review of the circumstances, the committee concur in

751   HISTORY OF CONGRESS.   752

H. of R.   *Horses lost in Public Service—Indemnity for Ropewalks.*   December, 1814.

reported the same with amendments; which were read, and with the bill ordered to lie on the table.

The bill from the Senate, "to authorize the purchase of the library of Thomas Jefferson, late President of the United States," was read twice, and committed to a Committee of the Whole.

HORSES LOST IN THE PUBLIC SERVICE.

Mr. YANCEY, from the Committee of Claims, made a report on the resolutions of this House of the 14th and 25th of November last, instructing them to inquire into the expediency of making payment for horses lost or destroyed in the public service; which was read, and referred to the Committee of the whole House on the bill to authorize the payment for property lost, captured, or destroyed by the enemy, whilst in the military service of the United States.—The report is as follows:

That, from statements made to the committee, the correctness of which they cannot doubt, it appears that at the time the American troops crossed over Lake Erie, just before the battle of the Thames, the mounted volunteers were ordered by the Commanding General to leave their horses at Portage river, on the lake, with a guard and other persons sufficient to take care of them. The horses were put in a large wood, enclosed, for the purpose of keeping them safe; and it was intended and expected that they should live by grazing until the return of the troops. The troops were absent about five weeks, and upon their return the horses were found to be reduced in order, many of them injured, and some dead. It does not satisfactorily appear whether they died for the want of forage or from accident, or the peculiar difficulty and hardship of the service. If their loss is to be ascribed to the former, then the committee have heretofore reported to the House a bill which it is believed will include this case. If the horses died, or were lost or destroyed by accident or labor, then it is conceived that the United States are not liable.

By an act of Congress passed the 2d day of January, 1795, it is enacted, "that, in addition to the monthly pay, there shall be allowed to each officer, non-commissioned officer, musician, and private of the cavalry, for the use of his horse, arms, and accoutrements, and for the risk thereof, except of horses killed in action, forty cents per day; and to each non-commissioned officer, musician, and private, twenty-five cents per day, in lieu of rations and forage, when they shall provide the same."

Mounted volunteers, it is believed, are entitled to and receive the same pay as cavalry. By the above section of the act of Congress, they receive, "for the use of the horse, arms, and accoutrements, and for the risk thereof, except of horses killed in battle, forty cents;" which the committee are of opinion was intended and is a full compensation. They are, therefore, of opinion that for the loss or destruction of horses, except in battle, the United States are not liable. They, however, think that where horses have died while in the public service for want of forage, when it was the duty of the Government to furnish it, the owners ought to be paid their value; and they have accordingly reported a bill to the House for that purpose.

With respect to the horses lost or destroyed by the troops under Major General Jackson, it is stated to the committee that they were lost by accident or surprise,

while in the several battles with the Creek Indians. The committee entertain the same opinion of these claims that they do of the others. They therefore recommend to the House the following resolution:

Resolved, That it is inexpedient to authorize payment for the horses aforesaid, otherwise than according to the provisions of a bill already reported to the House for that purpose.

INDEMNITY FOR ROPE-WALKS, &c.

Mr. YANCEY, from the Committee of Claims, made a report on the petitions of Jacob Schinnich and Schultz and Vogeler, of Aesah Calef and Christian Chapman; which was read, when Mr. Y. reported a bill for the relief of Jacob Schinnick and Schultz and Vogeler, of Christian Chapman and the legal representative of John Calef, deceased; which was read twice, and committed to a Committee of the Whole.—The report is as follows:

That the petitioners were owners of rope-walks, near Baltimore, which contained a quantity of cordage and raw material, together with the necessary implements for the manufacture of the same; all of which were consumed by fire, on the approach of the enemy on Baltimore, on the 12th of September last, by order of Brigadier General Forman, of the Maryland militia.

The circumstances under which the property was destroyed, as well as the necessity of such destruction, will appear by the following certificates, which the committee offer as part of their report.

CAMP, HAMPSTEAD HILL,
September 19, 1814.

I hereby certify, that in consequence of discretionary power invested in me by Major General Samuel Smith, commanding officer at Baltimore, I ordered the rope-walks near my lines, in the possession of Jacob Shinnick, to be set on fire and consumed on the evening of the 12th instant. The rope-walks at the time contained the tools of the trade, some hemp, and some yarns. I also, at the same time, and under the same circumstances, directed a common frame stable in pasture of Mr. Shinnick to be set on fire and consumed.

T. M. FORMAN,
B. G. Md. Militia.

Two other certificates from the same officer, stating the fact of destruction, under similar circumstances, of the rope-walks of Chapman and Calef, were also before the committee.

BALTIMORE, *November* 16, 1814.

Although it was decidedly evident that the three rope-walks in front of my lines must be destroyed the moment the enemy appeared before them, yet I did not obtain Major General Smith's permission to burn them until Monday evening, the 12th September. It was then impossible to remove anything, and notice to the owners would have been useless. Indeed, from my knowledge of the demand for wagons and carts to remove the inhabitants after the enemy had landed at North Point, I do not think that teams could have been procured to remove bulky articles.

T. M. FORMAN,
B. G. Md. Militia.

WASHINGTON, *November* 22, 1814.

I do certify, that the rope-walk owned or occupied by Jacob Shinnick, was situated directly in front of the lines, and under a battery within the command assigned to Brigadier General Forman; that rope-walk

753   HISTORY OF CONGRESS.   754

H. of R.   *Enlistments in the Army.*   December, 1814.

and two others were so close to the works, that, had they remained, and an attack been made by the enemy, they would have afforded such a cover as would have enabled him to have approached close to the works undiscovered. It became necessary to destroy them; nor did I give the discretionary power to General Forman until the attack of the enemy appeared certain. Their destruction was postponed as long as prudence permitted, nor were they destroyed until it became absolutely and indispensably necessary.

S. SMITH,
Late Maj. Gen. comm'g at Baltimore.

The committee are of opinion, from the foregoing facts, that the destruction of the rope-walks was deemed by the commanding officer prudent and necessary, in the defence of the city of Baltimore, then threatened to be invaded by a merciless and vindictive enemy; they are, therefore, of opinion, that the public good, in his opinion, requiring their destruction, the owners of the property should be compensated to the amount of its value, and recommend to the House the following resolution, and report by bill:

Resolved, That the prayer of the petitioners is reasonable, and ought to be granted.

ENLISTMENTS IN THE ARMY.

The House resumed the consideration of the bill from the Senate, "making further provision for filling the ranks of the Army of the United States."

The question depending on Saturday, at the time of adjournment, to strike the word "surprise" out of the amendment proposed by Mr. OAKLEY, was again stated; on which Mr. O. withdrew his said amendment.

A motion was then made by Mr. TAYLOR, to amend the bill by inserting the following section, as the second thereof:

SEC. 2. *And be it further enacted,* That it shall not be lawful for any recruiting officer to pay or deliver to a recruit, under the age of twenty-one years, to be enlisted by virtue of this act, any bounty or clothing, until after the expiration of four days from the time of his enlistment; and it shall be lawful for the said recruit, at any time during the said four days, to reconsider and withdraw his enlistment, and thereupon he shall forthwith be discharged and exonerated from the same.

A motion was made by Mr. FISK, of Vermont, to strike out the word "four," in the said section, and to insert the word "two." And the question being taken, it was determined in the negative.

On motion of Mr. RICH, the said section was amended.

The question was then taken to agree to the said section, and passed in the affirmative—yeas 96, nays 60, as follows:

YEAS—Messrs. Bard, Baylies of Massachusetts, Bayly of Virginia, Bigelow, Boyd, Bradbury, Breckenridge, Brigham, Burwell, Butler, Caperton, Calhoun, Cannon, Champion, Cilley, Comstock, Conard, Cox, Crawford, Culpeper, Dana, Davenport, Davis of Massachusetts, Davis of Pennsylvania, Denoyelles, Desha, Duvall, Ely, Eppes, Evans, Farrow, Fisk of New York, Forsyth, Gaston, Geddes, Glasgow, Grosvenor, Hale, Hasbrouck, Henderson, Howell, Hulbert, Ingham, Irving, Irwin, Jackson of Rhode Island, Johnson of Virginia, Kennedy, Kent of New York, Kerr, King of

Massachusetts, Law, Lefferts, Lewis, Lovett, Lowndes, Macon, Markell, McKee, McLean, Miller, Montgomery, Moseley, Oakley, Pearson, Pickering, Pickens, Piper, Pitkin, Potter, John Reed, William Reed, Rich, Ruggles, Schureman, Seybert, Sheffey, Shipherd, Skinner, Smith of New York, Smith of Virginia, Stanford, Stockton, Sturges, Taggart, Taylor, Thompson, Vose, Ward of Massachusetts, Ward of New Jersey, Webster, Wheaton, White, Wilcox, Wilson of Massachusetts, and Winter.

NAYS—Messrs. Alexander, Alston, Anderson, Archer, Avery, Barbour, Barnett, Bines, Bowen, Bradley, Brown, Caldwell, Chappell, Clark, Clopton, Condict, Crouch, Cuthbert, Findley, Fisk of Vermont, Forney, Franklin, Gholson, Goodwyn, Gourdin, Griffin, Hall, Harris, Hawes, Hubbard, Humphreys, Ingersoll, Johnson of Kentucky, Kershaw, Kilbourn, King of North Carolina, Lyle, McCoy, McKim, Moore, Murfree, Nelson, Newton, Ormsby, Parker, Pleasants, Rea of Pennsylvania, Rhea of Tennessee, Roane, Robertson, Sevier, Sharp, Strong, Tannehill, Telfair, Troup, Udree, Williams, Wilson of Pennsylvania, and Yancey.

A motion was made by Mr. WEBSTER, to strike out the fourth section of the said bill.

On motion of Mr. CHAPPELL, the said section was amended. And a motion was made by Mr. OAKLEY, further to amend the said section by striking out these words, "and every recruit thus furnished shall be entitled to the bounty in land, in the same manner and upon the same conditions as the other recruits in the Army of the United States."

And the question being taken, it was determined in the negative.

A motion was made by Mr. FISK, of Vermont, further to amend the said section, by inserting, after the word "land," aforesaid, the words "and money." And the question being taken, it was determined in the negative.

The question was then taken on striking out the said fourth section, and determined in the negative—yeas 57, nays 90, as follows:

YEAS—Messrs. Baylies of Massachusetts, Bigelow, Bowen, Breckenridge, Brigham, Burwell, Caperton, Champion, Cilley, Cox, Culpeper, Davenport, Davis of Massachusetts, Ely, Fisk of Vermont, Gaston, Geddes, Grosvenor, Hale, Henderson, Hulbert, Jackson of Rhode Island, Kennedy, Kent of New York, King of Massachusetts, Law, Lewis, Lovett, Macon, Markell, Miller, Moseley, Oakley, Pearson, Pickering, Pitkin, Potter, John Reed, William Reed, Ruggles, Schureman, Sheffey, Shipherd, Smith of New York, Stockton, Strong, Sturges, Taggart, Thompson, Vose, Ward of Massachusetts, Webster, Wheaton, White, Wilcox, Wilson of Massachusetts, and Winter.

NAYS—Messrs. Alexander, Alston, Anderson, Archer, Avery, Barbour, Bard, Barnett, Bayly of Virginia, Bines, Boyd, Bradley, Butler, Caldwell, Calhoun, Cannon, Chappell, Clark, Clopton, Comstock, Condict, Conard, Crawford, Crouch, Cuthbert, Dana, Davis of Pennsylvania, Denoyelles, Desha, Duvall, Eppes, Evans, Findley, Fisk of New York, Forney, Forsyth, Franklin, Gholson, Glasgow, Goodwyn, Gourdin, Griffin, Hall, Harris, Hasbrouck, Hawes, Hopkins of Kentucky, Humphreys, Ingersoll, Ingham, Irving, Irwin, Johnson of Virginia, Johnson of Kentucky, Kerr, Kershaw, Kilbourn, King of North Carolina, Lefferts, McCoy, McKee, McKim, McLean, Montgomery,

Moore, Nelson, Newton, Ormsby, Parker, Pickens, Piper, Pleasants, Rea of Pennsylvania, Rhea of Tennessee, Rich, Roane, Sevier, Seybert, Sharp, Smith of Virginia, Stanford, Tannehill, Taylor, Telfair, Troup, Udree, Ward of New Jersey, Williams, Wilson of Pennsylvania, and Yancey.

The question was then taken that the amendments agreed to be engrossed, and the bill read the third time, and passed in the affirmative—yeas 91, nays 55, as follows:

YEAS—Messrs. Alexander, Alston, Anderson, Archer, Avery, Barbour, Bard, Barnett, Bines, Bowen, Bradley, Burwell, Caldwell, Calhoun, Cannon, Chappell, Clark, Clopton, Comstock, Condict, Conard, Crawford, Crouch, Cuthbert, Dana, Davis of Pennsylvania, Denoyelles, Desha, Duvall, Eppes, Fisk of New York, Forney, Forsyth, Franklin, Gholson, Goodwyn, Gourdin, Griffin, Hall, Harris, Hasbrouck, Hawes, Hopkins of Kentucky, Hubbard, Humphreys, Ingersoll, Ingham, Irving, Irwin, Johnson of Virginia, Johnson of Kentucky, Kennedy, Kerr, Kershaw, Kilbourn, King of North Carolina, Lefferts, Lowndes, Lyle, McCoy, McKee, McKim, McLean, Montgomery, Moore, Nelson, Newton, Ormsby, Parker, Pickens, Piper, Pleasants, Rea of Pennsylvania, Rhea of Tennessee, Rich, Roane, Robertson, Sevier, Seybert, Sharp, Skinner, Smith of Virginia, Tannehill, Taylor, Telfair, Troup, Udree, Ward of New Jersey, Williams, Wilson of Pennsylvania, and Yancey.

NAYS—Messrs. Baylies of Massachusetts, Bayly of Virginia, Bigelow, Boyd, Bradbury, Breckenridge, Brigham, Butler, Caperton, Cilley, Cox, Culpeper, Davenport, Davis of Massachusetts, Ely, Gaston, Geddes, Grosvenor, Hale, Henderson, Howell, Hulbert, Jackson of Rhode Island, Kent of New York, King of Massachusetts, Lewis, Lovett, Macon, Markell, Moseley, Oakley, Pearson, Pickering, Pitkin, Potter, John Reed, William Reed, Ruggles, Schureman, Sheffey, Shipherd, Smith of New York, Stanford, Stockton, Sturges, Taggart, Thompson, Vose, Ward of Massachusetts, Webster, Wheaton, White, Wilcox, Wilson of Massachusetts, and Winter.

Ordered, That the said bill be read the third time to-morrow.

And the House adjourned.

TUESDAY, December 6.

The House resumed the consideration of the bill to authorize the President of the United States to accept the service of volunteers who may associate and organize themselves and offer their services to the Government of the United States, and the amendments thereto having been agreed to, it was ordered to be engrossed for a third reading; and was accordingly afterwards read a third time, and passed.

The report of the Committee of Claims unfavorable to the petition of Rebecca Hodgson, passed through a Committee of the Whole, by whom it was concurred in, and was then ordered by the House to lie on the table.

The bill to provide for the widows and orphans of militia and volunteers who may die or be killed in the service of the United States, passed through a Committee of the Whole, and, having been amended, was ordered to be engrossed for a third reading.

The bill from the Senate supplementary to the act laying duties on the notes of certain banks, bankers, &c., passed through a Committee of the Whole, and was ordered to be engrossed for a third reading.

The report of the Committee of Claims unfavorable to the petition of sundry inhabitants of Knox county, Kentucky, passed through a Committee of the Whole, where it was widely debated, and at length disagreed to. The report having been also reversed by the House, the Committee of Claims were instructed to report a bill favorable to the petitioners.

ENLISTMENTS IN THE ARMY.

The bill from the Senate "making further provision for filling the ranks of the Army of the United States," was read a third time as amended.

A motion was made by Mr. FISK, of Vermont, to recommit the bill to a Committee of the Whole; which motion was negatived by yeas and nays, 95 to 51.

The bill was then passed. For the bill 95, against it 52, as follows:

YEAS—Messrs. Alexander, Alston, Anderson, Avery, Barbour, Bard, Barnett, Bines, Bowen, Bradley, Brown, Burwell, Caldwell, Calhoun, Cannon, Chappell, Clark, Clopton, Comstock, Condict, Conard, Crawford, Creighton, Crouch, Cuthbert, Dana, Davis of Pennsylvania, Denoyelles, Desha, Duvall, Eppes, Farrow, Findley, Fisk of New York, Forney, Forsyth, Franklin, Gholson, Glasgow, Goodwyn, Griffin, Hall, Harris, Hasbrouck, Hawes, Hopkins of Kentucky, Hubbard, Humphreys, Ingersoll, Ingham, Irving, Irwin, Johnson of Virginia, Johnson of Kentucky, Kennedy, Kent of Maryland, Kerr, Kershaw, Kilbourn, King of North Carolina, Lefferts, Lowndes, Lyle, McCoy, McKee, McLean, Montgomery, Moore, Nelson, Newton, Ormsby, Parker, Pickens, Piper, Pleasants, Rea of Pennsylvania, Rhea of Tennessee, Rich, Roane, Robertson, Sage, Sevier, Sharp, Skinner, Smith of Pennsylvania, Smith of Virginia, Strong, Tannehill, Taylor, Telfair, Troup, Udree, Ward of New Jersey, Williams, and Yancey.

NAYS—Messrs. Baylies of Massachusetts, Bayly of Virginia, Bigelow, Boyd, Bradbury, Brigham, Butler, Caperton, Champion, Cilley, Culpeper, Davis of Massachusetts, Ely, Fisk of Vermont, Gaston, Grosvenor, Hale, Henderson, Hulbert, Jackson of Rhode Island, Kent of New York, King of Massachusetts, Law, Lovett, Macon, Markell, Miller, Moseley, Oakley, Pearson, Pickering, Pitkin, Potter, John Reed, William Reed, Ruggles, Schureman, Sheffey, Shipherd, Smith of New York, Stanford, Stockton, Sturges, Taggart, Thompson, Vose, Ward of Massachusetts, Webster, Wheaton, White, Wilcox, and Winter.

The bill directing the staff officers of the Army to comply with the requisitions of marine and naval officers in certain cases, went through a Committee of the Whole, and was ordered to be engrossed for a third reading.

And the House adjourned.

WEDNESDAY, December 7.

On motion of Mr. JENNINGS, a call was ordered to be made on the Commissioner of the General Land Office, for an account accruing to the Treasury, in each collection district, for the sale of public lands, by forfeitures, and whether such forfeitures have occurred more frequently on limited or extended purchases.

The bill directing the staff officers of the Army to comply with the requisitions of naval and marine officers in certain cases; the bill to provide for the widows and orphans of volunteers or militia who may die or be killed in the service of the United States; and the bill authorizing a composition with private bankers in lieu of the stamp duty, were read a third time and passed.

Mr. INGERSOLL, of Pennsylvania, laid upon the table, without preface, the following resolutions:

Resolved, That the Committee on Military Affairs be instructed to report to this House a bill or bills for classifying the free male population of the United States, from the age of twenty-one years to the age of forty-five years, for the purpose of draughting therefrom a sufficient number, annually, to fill up the ranks of the regular Army.

2. *Resolved,* That the Committee on Naval Affairs be instructed to report to this House a bill or bills for the immediate, constant, and gradual augmentation of the Navy of the United States, by adding annually (with the least possible delay in the commencement and progress of the system) to the ships of the line, frigates, sloops of war, and other vessels now built or building.

The consideration of them not being required at this time, they lie on the table of course.

REVENUE LAWS.

Mr. EPPES, from the Committee of Ways and Means, to whom was referred a resolution for aiding and protecting the officers of the customs, and for preventing intercourse with the enemy, reported a bill to prohibit intercourse with the enemy, and for other purposes; which was read twice, and committed to a Committee of the whole House on Saturday next.

Mr. EPPES also communicated the following document.

TREASURY DEPARTMENT,
November 19, 1814.

SIR: I have the honor to acknowledge the receipt of your letter, requesting, on behalf of the Committee of Ways and Means, "any information which the Treasury Department can furnish, as to the defects of the present revenue laws, and the best mode of correcting the evils arising from an intercourse with the enemy."

Although the expediency of a general revision of the revenue laws, with the view contemplated by the committee, is acknowledged, I fear it will be impracticable, at this time, to undertake, and to execute, satisfactorily, so extensive a task. The pressure of the current business upon the department is severe, and precludes an application of the Secretary's time to any object which is not of immediate importance. The inconveniences that are suggested in the documents from Vermont, accompanying the reference of the Committee, require, however, an early attention, and the following views of the subject are respectfully submitted to your consideration:

I. The representations from Vermont present various causes of complaint:

1. That smuggling is extensively prosecuted, on the Northern frontier, by citizens of the United States, sometimes with, and sometimes without, the cover of a neutral character; in the course of which the enemy obtains important intelligence; he is furnished with cattle, and other essential supplies; and he is enabled to introduce his merchandise surreptitiously into our markets.

2. That the powers of the revenue officers are inadequate to the detection and prosecution of these offences, because the right of search is not extended to every vehicle that may be employed; because the prohibitory laws do not sufficiently define and enumerate the subjects of an illicit trade; because no efficient act of prevention is authorized to be performed, even upon the strongest ground of suspicion; and because there is no force, civil or military, provided to aid the revenue officers in the execution of their duty, when cases of violent opposition occur.

3. That, limited as the general powers of the revenue officers appear to be, they are rendered still more inadequate by the terror which the officers now feel, of being exposed to suits for damages, under the authority of recent decisions in the courts of law; for it has been adjudged in Vermont, that the inspectors of the customs are not authorized, in any case, to make seizures, and that actions may be maintained against them, to recover the whole value of the property seized, even when the property itself has been duly condemned, as forfeited by law.

II. The actual state of the laws, in relation to these subjects of complaint, may be sufficiently seen in the following analysis:

Of the power and privileges of Inspectors, and other officers of the customs.

1. The inspectors of the customs are persons employed by the collector, with the approbation of the principal officer of the Treasury Department, and their duties are entirely directed to guard against frauds upon the revenue, by smuggling, or any other kind of illicit trade. They are described and considered, throughout the acts of Congress, as officers of the customs, through not as chief officers.

2. On the arrival, or the approach, of ships or vessels, the inspectors, as well as the chief and other officers of the customs, are empowered to go on board, (whether in or out of their respective districts,) for the purpose of demanding manifests of their cargoes, and of examining and searching the ships and vessels. This act is to be performed, *ex officio,* by way of precaution, without any special deputation from a collector, naval officer, or a surveyor.—4 vol. 367, s. 64.

3. If, however, there be reason to suspect that any goods, subject to duty, are concealed in any ship or vessel, an inspector cannot enter such ship or vessel, to search for, seize, and secure such goods, without being specially appointed for that purpose by the collector, naval officer, or surveyor. And if there be cause to suspect a concealment of such goods, in any particular dwelling house, store, building, or other place, a search warrant must be obtained from a justice of the peace, to authorise a search and seizure. The cases here provided for, are cases of suspicion only, when probable information has been received of a concealment of goods, either on water, or on land, with a design to evade the payment of duties. The act to be performed is not in the ordinary course of an inspector's official duty; it is not an act of precaution, but of detection; it is not an act authorised for seizing goods

which are notoriously liable to seizure, but for entering a ship, or a house, in a doubtful case, to ascertain whether any goods liable to seizure are there concealed.—4 vol. 389, s. 68.

4. But any ship, or vessel, goods, wares, or merchandise, which are liable to seizure by virtue of any act respecting the revenue, it is the duty of the several officers of the customs (including, by general description, and practical construction, the inspectors of the customs) to seize and secure, as well without, as within their respective districts. The act to be performed, in this case, is founded on the fact, that the property is liable to seizure, but that it is not necessary to enter either a ship or a house, to ascertain whether such goods are so liable, and are there concealed.—4 vol. 390, s. 70.

5. In the performance of their duties, the inspectors, in common with the other officers of the customs, are protected by the law, when unjustly sued or molested, in actions for damages; and when any prosecution is commenced, on account of the seizure of any ship, or goods, in which judgment is given for the claimant, the inspectors are released from all responsibility, on showing that there was a reasonable cause of seizure. [4 vol. 391, s. 71 ; *Ibid* 429, s. 89.] This last provision, indeed, has been extended generally for the protection of any collector, or other officer, under any act of Congress authorising a seizure of any ship or vessel, goods, wares, or merchandise, where the seizure has been made on probable cause, although restitution should be decreed.—8 vol. 255, s. 1.

6. The "Act to prohibit any American from proceeding to, or trading with, the enemies of the United States, and for other purposes," declares, that " if any person shall transport, or attempt to transport, over land, or otherwise, in any wagon, cart, sleigh, boat, or otherwise, naval or military stores, arms, or the munitions of war, or any article of provision, from any place of the United States, to Upper or Lower Canada, Nova Scotia, or New Brunswick," certain forfeitures and penalties shall be incurred. And authority is given " to the collectors of the several ports of the United States, to seize and stop naval or military stores, arms, or the munitions of war, or any articles of provision, and ship or vessel, wagon, cart, sleigh, boat, or thing, by which any article, prohibited as aforesaid, is shipped or transported, or intended to be shipped or transported." It seems to be a strained and impracticable construction of the provision, to confine the exercise of the authority for stopping and seizing the contraband articles, to the personal agency of the collectors. A collector, in this case, as in every other case where a positive restriction is not imposed, must act through the vigilance and co-operation of the inspectors, and other officers of the customs.

Of the existing auxiliary means to execute the revenue laws, and the laws prohibiting trade and intercourse with the enemy.

1. In addition to the means which the preceding statements will suggest, the Judges of the Supreme Court, and of the several district courts of the United States, and all judges and justices of the courts of the several States, (having authority, by the laws of the United States, to take cognizance of offences against the Constitution and laws thereof,) have the like power to hold to security of the peace, and for good behaviour, in cases arising under the Constitution and laws of the United States, as may, or can be lawfully exercised,

by any judge or justice of the peace of the respective States, in cases cognizable before them.—4 vol. 231.

2. Whenever the laws of the United States are opposed, or the execution thereof obstructed, in any State, by combinations too powerful to be suppressed by the ordinary course of judicial proceedings, or the power of a marshal, the President is authorized to call forth a competent force of the militia, to cause the laws to be executed. [4 vol, 188, s. 2, 9.] And by a subsequent act, the President is authorised to employ the land or naval force of the United States, for the same purpose.—8 vol. 311.

3. A final judgment, or decree, in any suit, in the highest court of law or equity of a State, in which a decision of the suit could be had, where is drawn in question the validity of an authority, exercised under the United States, (as in the case of an officer of the customs,) and the decision is against the validity, may be re-examined, and reversed, or affirmed, in the Supreme Court of the United States, upon a writ of error ; but the matter in dispute must exceed the value of two thousand dollars, exclusive of costs.—Vol, 1. s. 61, 63.

III. From these views of the subject of complaint, and of the state of the law in relation to them, we are led to consider the best modes of amending the defects, and correcting the evils which exist.

1. An habitual respect for the judicial authority does not permit me to controvert, any further, the decisions of the courts of law in the State of Vermont, respecting the official character and powers of inspectors, and other officers of the customs. It is recommended, therefore, that the law should be so amended, as to place the inspector upon the footing of officers within the meaning of the revenue laws, and laws prohibiting trade and intercourse with the enemy ; and that the collectors should be authorized to employ a competent number of inspectors, with authority to stop, search, detain, and seize, all cattle, live stock, and other supplies; all goods and money, and, generally, all other articles whatsoever, howsoever carried and transported, by land or by water, on the way to, or from, the British provinces, subject to such regulations as will secure, with as little embarrassment as possible, the rights of a lawful and neutral trade.

2. The officers of the customs should be entitled, in proper cases, and on proper proofs, to obtain, from any magistrate, a warrant to search dwelling houses, and other buildings ; to demand the assistance of the marshal of the district, and his deputies, with the posse of the district, if necessary, for the execution of their duties; and to hold any person to security for his good behaviour, stating, on oath, that they have probable and just cause for believing that such person is carrying on an unlawful trade, or intercourse, with the enemy.

3. No citizen, or person usually residing within the United States, should be allowed to cross the frontier into the British provinces, without a passport from the Secretary of State, or from the Secretary of War, or from the officer commanding the military district in which such person usually resides. All persons coming from the British provinces into the United States, should be required to report themselves, within a reasonable time, to the military commander, or to the collector of the district within which they shall, respectively, first arrive. And any person hovering upon the frontier, at a distance from his usual place of residence, without any business requiring his attendance there, and without a passport, should be held to security for his good behaviour, as a person suspected, upon proba-

ble cause, to be engaged in an unlawful trade, or intercourse with the enemy.

4. The militia and army of the United States, on the frontier, should be authorized, under proper regulations, to co-operate with the civil magistrates, and officers of the customs, in seizing and securing persons engaged in an unlawful trade, or intercourse with the enemy, together with the articles and vehicles employed in such trade, or intercourse.

5. A more effectual provision should be made for transferring, from the State courts to the Federal courts, suits brought against persons exercising an authority under the United States, so that such suits may be transferred, as soon as conveniently may be, after they are commenced.

6. Treason being defined by the Constitution, and misprision of treason being an offence which is necessarily founded upon that definition, many practices, of a treasonable nature and effect, which cannot be constitutionally classed with treason, are unnoticed in our penal code. An act of Congress declaring such practices to be misdemeanors, and punishing them with fine and imprisonment, would, perhaps, be the most effectual mode of correcting the evils arising from an intercourse with the enemy.

The papers that were received from the committee, are now returned; and I embrace the opportunity to repeat the assurances of the sincere respect, with which I have the honor to be, sir, your most obedient servant,

A. J. DALLAS.

J. W. Eppes, Esq., *Chairman, &c.*

LOANS, TREASURY NOTES, &c.

The House, on motion of Mr. Eppes, of Virginia, resolved itself into a Committee of the Whole, on the bill supplemental to the act authorizing a loan for twenty five millions, and the act lately passed, authorizing a loan of three millions for the service of the current year.

[The *first* section of the bill authorises the Secretary of the Treasury, with the approbation of the President of the United States, to accept Treasury notes to be prepared, signed, and issued, for, and in lieu, of so much of the sum authorized to be borrowed on the credit of the United States, by the twenty-five million and three million loan acts, as has not been borrowed or otherwise employed in the issue of the Treasury notes according to law, provided the whole amount so to be issued shall not exceed $7,500,000, and applied to the same uses as the loans so authorized were intended to be applied.

The *second* section authorizes the issuing of Treasury notes in like manner for a further sum of three millions, to defray the expenses of the War Department for the remainder of this year, and one million for the Navy Department.

The *third, fourth, fifth,* and *sixth* sections provide these Treasury notes shall be in the same form and possess the same qualities as the Treasury notes already authorized, be redeemable in same manner, appropriates money therefor, &c., as well as for the expenses of issuing and distributing said notes and for punishing counterfeits thereof.]

The bill having been read through—

Mr. Eppes quoted extracts from the letter last received from the Secretary of the Treasury, which is given at length, viz:

Washington, *December* 2, 1814.

Sir: Your letter of the 27th of November has been referred to the Committee of Ways and Means, and I am instructed to ask for the amount of the payments to be made during the present quarter, on account of the public debt; the funds prepared to meet those payments, and any other information which may enable the committee to decide as to the necessity of adopting additional measures for meeting the public engagements during the present quarter of the year.

I have the honor to be, your most obedient,

JOHN W. EPPES.

Hon. Mr. Dallas, *Secretary of the Treasury.*

Treasury Department, *Dec.* 2, 1814.

Sir: I have the honor to acknowledge the receipt of your letter, dated this morning, stating that mine of the 27th of November, addressed to the committee on a national bank, has been referred to the Committee of Ways and Means.

In my communications to the committees of Congress, I have never been disposed to disguise the embarrassments of the Treasury. A frank and full development of existing evils will always, I hope, be best calculated to secure the attention and exertion of the public authorities; and, with legislative aid, I am still confident, that all the difficulties of a deficient revenue, a suspended circulating medium, and a depressed credit, may be speedily and completely overcome. My only apprehension arises from the lapse of time; as a remedy which would be effectual to-day, will, perhaps, only serve to increase the disorder to-morrow.

In answering the inquiries of your letter, permit me to state: 1st. The amount of the payments which were to be made during the whole of the present quarter on account of the public debt, and the funds prepared, or applicable to meet those payments; 2d. The payments that remain to be made, and the funds that remain to meet them, for the residue of the quarter; and, 3d. General information, in relation to additional measures for meeting the public engagements.

First Point.

It is respectfully stated, agreeably to an estimate which was formed on the 4th of October, 1814:

Dr.

1. That the quarter commencing the 1st of October, 1814, and ending the 1st of January, 1815, including both days, there was payable, for the principal and interest of Treasury notes, during the whole quarter, chiefly at Boston, New York, and Philadelphia, a sum of - - - $4,457,069 80

2. That, during the same period, there was payable, for the principal and interest of temporary loans, at Boston, Baltimore, and Charleston, the sum of - - - - - 771,125 00

3. That, during the same period, there was payable, in dividends upon the public funded debt, at the several loan offices, the sum of - - - 1,900,000 00

　　　　　　　　　　　　　　　 7,128,194 80

Cr.

1. That there were bank credits scattered throughout the United States, on the 1st of October, 1814, amounting, by estimate, to - - - $2,500,000 00

2. That there was receivable from the customs, during the whole quarter, the sum of - - - - $1,800,000 00

3. That there was receivable, on account of the sales of public lands, during the same period, a sum of - 160,000 00

4. That there was receivable, on account of internal duties and direct taxes, during the same period, a sum of about - - - - 900,000 00

5. That there was receivable, on account of loans, during the same period, a sum of - - - 1,700,000 00

6. That there might be obtained, upon an issue of Treasury notes, during the same period, a sum of about - 2,500,000 00

                      9,560,000 00

From which it results :

1. That the amount of the whole payments, for dividends of public debt, for temporary loans, and for Treasury notes, during the whole of the current quarter, was - - - $7,128,194 80

2. That the amount of the whole of the estimated receipts of the Treasury, was - - - - 9,560,000 00

Leaving a surplus of receipts of - 2,431,805 20

It is believed that this estimate, which is formed upon official facts and experience, would have been substantially realized in the event, if the banks had not suddenly determined to suspend their payments in specie. But for that occurrence, the dividend on the public debt would have been punctually paid to the individual creditors at Boston on the 1st of October last; the transfer of the public funds, from one place to another place, in order to meet the public engagements, would have continued easy and certain ; the credit and use of Treasury notes, (limited to the specified amount,) would, probably, have been preserved, and the revenue arising from duties and taxes would not have been materially intercepted, if at all, in its passage to the Treasury, by payments in Treasury notes.

Second Point.

Dr.

1. That, of the principal and interest of the Treasury notes, payable during the present quarter, and which have already fallen due, there remains, on this day, unpaid, at the places mentioned in the schedule A, the sum of - - - $1,902,686 80

2. That the principal and interest of the Treasury notes, which will become due on or before the 1st of January, 1815, at the places mentioned in the schedule B, amount to - 1,243,720 00

3. That the dividends on the public debt, payable on the 1st of January, 1815, at the places mentioned in schedule C, amount to the sum of 1,873,000 00

4. That the principal and interest of temporary loans, payable during the present quarter, and contracted at the Treasury, in part execution of the authority granted by the act of

Congress passed the 14th of March, 1812, and payable at Boston on the 15th and 31st of December, amount to - - - - 506,875 00

                  $5,526,275 80

Cr.

1. That, on the 28th ultimo, there were bank credits, in the banks specified in the schedule D, applicable to the payment of the public debt, during the present quarter, (deducting the amount of bank credits ($813,000) which, as it could not be transferred for the payment of public debt, has been recently applied to the appropriations for the War and Navy Departments,) amounting to - - $2,372,287 13

2. That the amount receivable during the remainder of the present year, on account of the loan of six millions, applicable, also, to the payment of the public debt, if no failure in payment occurs, will be about 450,000 00

3. That the estimated amount, receivable during the remainder of the present year, on account of customs, applicable, also, to the payment of the public debt, (subject, however, to various contingencies, such as the non-payment of bonds, the payment of bonds in Treasury notes, &c.) may be stated at - - - - 350,000 00

4. The estimated amount, receivable during the remainder of the present year, on account of the sales of public lands, subject, however, to contingent payment in Treasury notes, may be stated at - - - 150,000 00

5. The estimated amount, receivable during the remainder of the present year, for internal duties and direct tax, subject, however, to contingent payment in Treasury notes, may be stated at - - - 450,000 00

                  3,772,287 13

From this second view of the debit and credit of the account, limited merely to the payment of the public debt becoming due for the residue of the present quarter, it appears—

1. That the debt amounts to the sum of $5,526,275 80

2. That the resources to pay the debt, (excluding the sum applied to the Army and Navy Departments, as before stated, and excluding the possible proceeds of new loans, and new issues of Treasury notes, for the single purpose of paying public debt,) amount to - - - 3,772,287 13

                  1,753,988 67

The difference between the results of the statements, under the first and the second points, will be accounted for, by the unexpected effect of payments in Treasury notes, on account of duties, taxes, and land; by the total cessation of the use of Treasury notes, either to pay the public creditors or to raise money; and by an unavoidable variance in estimates, depending upon a variance in the state of information at the Treasury. A priority of payment may be justly claimed by the holders of the funded debt; and, therefore, it is proper to add—

1. That the amount of public credits, as estimated in the preceding statement, is the sum of - - - - - - - - - -$3,772,287 13

2. That the amount of the dividend, on the old and new funded debt, payable on the 1st of January, 1815, is the sum of - - - - - -   1,873,000 00

3. And that, consequently, the surplus of the resources, after satisfying that single object, is the sum of - -   1,899,287 13

It will be observed that these estimates do not include, as an item of the debt, the dividend on the funded debt, amounting to two hundred thousand dollars, which was not actually paid to the individual creditors at Boston on the 1st of October last. But it is omitted, because an adequate fund in the State bank was seasonably provided for the occasion, and the usual Treasury draft was issued in favor of the Commissioner of Loans, so as to deduct a corresponding amount from the bank credits of the Government. The State bank declined, for several reasons, (which it is unnecessary to repeat,) paying in coin, or in bank notes, and most of the public creditors refused to accept the Treasury notes, which the bank offered to them as an alternative payment. It is not considered that, under these circumstances, connected with the general state of the circulating medium, (which places the power of the Government to meet its engagements, on the same footing with the power of the most opulent of its citizens,) there can exist any just reproach upon the public credit, or resources. But, nevertheless, efforts have been anxiously made by this department, and are still in operation, to satisfy the public creditors, independent of the fund which was originally set apart, and which still remains on deposite at the State bank, by all the remaining means at the disposal of the Treasury.

Nor, on the other hand, have I included in the statement of our resources to pay the public debt, the unexecuted authority to borrow upon public loans, and to issue Treasury notes. I have only included the items of revenue, which, in ordinary times, would be deemed certain and effective; reserving any surplus of those items, with the loan and the Treasury notes, to meet the general appropriations for the public service

Third Point.

It is respectfully stated, that the non-payment of the Treasury notes, and the hazard of not being able to pay the dividend on the public debt, according to the respective contracts, was chiefly (I believe entirely) owing to the suspension of specie payments at the banks, and the consequent impracticability of transferring the public funds, from the place in which they were deposited to the place in which they were wanted. I have endeavored, therefore, to induce the banks, as an act of justice, not inconsistent with their interest or their policy, to assist in alleviating the fiscal embarrassments of the Government, which they have thus contributed to produce. The answers to my last proposition (of which a copy is annexed, in schedule E.) have not been received. But the danger of depending upon gratuitous aids (of depending, indeed, upon anything but the wisdom and the vigilance of Congress,) makes, with every day's experience, a deeper impression upon the mind. In speaking, therefore, of additional measures for meeting the public engagements during the present quarter of the year, I derive great satisfaction in reflecting upon the inevitable and immediate effect of the legislative sanction (even so far as it has already been given) to a settled and productive system of taxes, for defraying the expenses of Government and maintaining the proper credit. This policy, embracing in its course the introduction of a national circulating medium, and the proper facilities for anticipating, collecting, and distributing the public revenue, will at once enliven the public credit; and even the existing resources of the present quarter must ripen and expand under an influence so auspicious. But something may be conveniently and usefully added, for instance—

1. A discretionary authority may be given, by law, to issue Treasury notes for the amount of the sums now authorized to be raised by law.

2. An authority may be given, by law, to transfer bank credits from one place to another place, in order to meet the public engagements, allowing a reasonable rate of exchange.

3. Appropriations may be made, by law, to defray the extra expenses of the War and Navy Departments, during the present year; and a general authority may be given to borrow, or to issue Treasury notes, to supply any deficiencies in former appropriations for those Departments, and for the payment of the public debt, the Treasury notes, and the civil list.

The present opportunity enables me to assure you, sir, that I am preparing, with all possible diligence, to report to the Committee of Ways and Means upon the subjects which they have been pleased to confide to me—

1. The tax bills are numerous, new in some of their principles, and complicated in most of their details; nor are the best sources of information at hand. They will, however, be draughted, and sent to the committee in succession.

2. The plan for establishing a competent sinking fund is under consideration, and will, probably, be ready to be reported before the tax bills are passed.

3. The estimates for the expenses of 1815, the annual appropriation bill, and the bills to authorize a loan, and issue of Treasury notes for that year, are, also, objects of attention.

I have the honor to be, &c.

A. J. DALLAS.

John W. Eppes, Esq.,
   Chairman Com. of Ways and Means.

A.

Schedule of Treasury notes which have already fallen due, and remain unpaid, this 2d day of December, 1814.

Where payable.	When payable.	Principal.	Interest.	Total.
Philadelphia - -	1814, November 1 -	$269,000	$14,526 00	$283,526 00
Do. - - -	1814, December 1 -	366,200	19,774 80	385,974 80
New York - - -	- - - -	570,000	30,780 00	600,780 00
Boston - - -	- - - -	600,000	32,400 00	632,400 00
		$1,805,000	$97,480 80	$1,902,680 80

B.

Schedule of Treasury notes becoming due on or before the first of January, 1815.

Where payable.	When payable.	Principal.	Interest.	Total.
New York - - -	1814, December 11 -	$100,000	$5,400	$105,400
Philadelphia - -	- - - -	600,000	32,400	632,400
Boston - - -	1814, December 21 -	30,000	1,620	31,620
New York - - -	1815, January 1 -	400,000	21,600	421,600
Philadelphia - -	- - - -	50,000	2,700	52,700
		$1,180,000	$63,720	$1,243,720

C.

Estimated amount of the dividends on the domestic funded debt of the United States, payable on the first of January, 1815.

At Portsmouth, N. H. - - -	$12,000
Boston - - - - -	320,000
Providence - - - -	20,000
Hartford - - - -	37,000
New York - - - -	625,000
Trenton - - - -	8,000
Philadelphia, including stocks on Treasury books - - -	545,000
Wilmington, Delaware - -	1,000
Baltimore - - - -	125,000
Richmond - - - -	20,000
Raleigh - - - -	5,000
Charleston - - - -	85,000
Savannah - - - -	5,000
Treasury at Washington, exclusive of dividends payable at Philadelphia -	65,000
	$1,873,000

Note.—From the daily transfers of stock, from one loan office to another, it is impossible at this time to estimate, with precision, the amount which will be payable at each loan office on the first of January next. The above may be considered as near the sums which will be payable, unless the removal of stock should, in the meantime, be unusually large.

D.

Cash in the several banks, according to the state of the information at the Treasury, on the 28th of November, 1814, after deducting moneys in the Southern and Western banks, assigned to the Secretaries of the War and Navy Departments, in consequence of their being transferrable from the places of deposite to the places of payment of the public debt, amounting to eight hundred and thirteen thousand dollars.

Bath Bank - - - -	$9,723 13
Lincoln Bank, Bath - - -	5,750 00
Cumberland Bank, Portland -	24,317 79
Portland Bank - - - -	12,043 18
New Hampshire Union Bank -	12,807 39
Saco Bank - - - -	1,435 83
Merchants' Bank, Salem - -	34,376 82
Roger Williams's Bank - -	12,365 57
Newport Bank - - -	42,738 99
New Haven Bank - - -	15,081 12
New York State Bank, Albany -	40,730 17
Mechanics and Farmers' Bank, Albany	18,369 08
Manhattan Company - -	378,788 46
Branch Bank of do., Utica -	15,433 59
Mechanics' Bank, New York -	222,896 14
City Bank, New York - -	34,254 08
Bank of Pennsylvania - -	94,666 63
Farmers and Mechanics' Bank, Philad'a	376 67
Branch Bank, Pittsburg - -	910 59
Bank of Baltimore - - -	65,288 16
Commercial and Farmers' Bank, Balt.	18,212 19
Mechanics' Bank, Baltimore -	628,594 51
Washington - - - -	67,067 82
Metropolis - - - -	11,609 80
Columbia - - - -	241,974 36
Farmers and Mechanics' B'k, Georgetown - - - - -	596 48
Union Bank, Georgetown - -	37,561 45
Mechanics' Bank of Alexandria -	5,000 00
Bank of Potomac, Alexandria -	15,000 00
Bank of Virginia - - -	35,020 35

Branch of do., at Norfolk - - -	372	24
State Bank, Raleigh - - -	366	93
Branch of do., Salisbury - - -	6,263	86
Branch of do., Wilmington - -	5,502	33
Bank of Cape Fear - - -	1,697	26
Planters and Mechanics' B'k, Charlest'n	101,235	28
Bank of South Carolina - - -	22,712	50
Union Bank, South Carolina - -	14,028	47
Planters' Bank, Savannah - -	102	98
Bank of Kentucky - - -	9,174	70
Branch of do., at Russellville - -	1,247	61
Branch of do., at Louisville - -	699	01
Bank of Chilicothe - - -	9,366	08
Miami Exporting Company, Cincinnati	30,110	89
Louisiana Bank - - -	66,514	92
	$2,372,287	13

Schedule E.—[Circular.]

TREASURY DEPARTMENT, *Nov. 25, 1814.*

SIR: The sudden determination of most of the banks, in which the deposites of public money were made, to refuse payment of their notes and of drafts upon them, in specie, deprived the Government of the use of its gold and silver, without any act or assent on the part of the Treasury. The equally sudden determination of the banks of each State to refuse credit and circulation to the notes issued in other States, deprived the Government, without its participation, of the only means that were possessed for transferring its funds from the places in which they lay inactive to the places in which they were wanted, for the payment of the dividends on the funded debt, and the discharge of Treasury notes. It was the inevitable result of these transactions, that the bank credits of the Government should be soon exhausted in Boston, New York, Philadelphia, &c., where the principal loan offices for the payment of the public debt were established; and that the Government should be unable to satisfy its engagements in those cities, unless the public creditors would receive drafts on banks in other States, or would subscribe the amount of their claims to a public loan, or would accept a payment in Treasury notes. It was not unreasonable, indeed, to hope that the banks, whose conduct had produced the existing embarrassment, would cheerfully afford some alleviating accommodation to the Government; but every attempt to realize that hope has hitherto failed. Even, however, if the present application should also be unsuccessful, I think I may rely on the intelligence and candor of our fellow-citizens to vindicate the Government from any reproach, for the want of good faith, or of essential resources to maintain the public credit. The events which have occurred the Government could neither avert nor control.

Under these circumstances, I have deemed it a duty to the public, and to myself, to request the attention of the banks, which have acted as agents of the Treasury in the receipt and distribution of public money, to the following propositions:

1. That the banks shall assist the Government with the means of discharging the Treasury notes, and paying the dividends of public debt during the present quarter, at the loan office of their respective States. A great portion, both of the Treasury notes and public debt, belongs to the banks respectively; and, so far, nothing more than a protracted credit will be required.

The balance of the demand will be payable, of course, in the notes of the respective banks.

2. That, to secure and satisfy the advances thus to be made by the banks, respectively, the banks shall be admitted, on reasonable terms, to subscribe to the loan of three millions of dollars; or they shall receive Treasury notes, or they shall receive bank notes, or drafts upon banks in other States. If any bank should prefer accommodating the Treasury with a temporary loan, on a legal interest, this course may be pursued.

I will thank you, sir, for an early answer to this proposition, and, if it should be accepted, I will immediately make the necessary arrangements to carry it into effect.

I have the honor to be, &c.
A. J. DALLAS.

Mr. EPPES then explained the object of this bill, which was to carry into effect the Secretary's recommendations, except that part which relates to the transfer of funds from one quarter to another, which they had determined to postpone until the question relating to a National Bank should have been finally acted on, &c.

The blanks in the bill were then filled, on motion of Mr. EPPES, with seven and a half millions to supply the possible deficiency in the two loans, and with three millions for the deficiency in the provision for the military, and one million for the deficiency in the provision for the naval service for the remainder of the present year.

No debate took place on the principle of the bill. Some discussion and amendment took place on the section for punishing counterfeiters of the bills, in which Messrs. GASTON, WARD, and HOPKINS of Kentucky, took part.

The Committee at length rose and reported the bill; which, the amendments having been concurred in, was ordered to be engrossed for a third reading to-morrow.

APPROPRIATIONS.

The House then resolved itself into a Committee of the Whole, on motion of Mr. EPPES, on the bill making further appropriations for the support of the Government during the remainder of the year.

Mr. EPPES read a letter he had received from the Secretary of War, in relation to the deficiency of appropriations in that department; from which it appeared that though it was impossible to ascertain with precision at this time the number of militia in service during the past Summer, there was little doubt but their expenses would greatly exceed the appropriations made for those objects. On motion of Mr. EPPES, the blanks in this bill were then filled with three millions for the Military department, one million for the Naval department, and other sums for the expenses of Congress, &c.

And the Committee rose and reported the bill; which, as amended, was ordered to be engrossed for a third reading.

MILITIA DRAUGHTS.

The remainder of this day's sitting was occupied in Committee of the Whole, on the consideration of the bill authorizing the President to call into service 80,430 militia for the defence of the United States.

The first of the amendments reported by the select committee which came under consideration, was that authorizing the President, on failure of the Governors of the several States to comply with the requisition, to call directly on the officers of the militia to cause the draught to be made. This amendment was supported by Mr. Johnson, of Kentucky, Mr. Robertson, and Mr. Troup, and opposed by Mr. Pearson. It was agreed to, ayes 90.

The next amendment goes to change the whole rate of apportionment, so as to fix it on the principle of free population, as ascertained by the last census, instead of the principle of representation, as if it were a direct tax, on which principle the apportionment was fixed in the bill by the Senate.

This amendment was opposed, on opposite grounds, however, by Mr. Fisk, of New York, Mr. Calhoun, Mr. Ingersoll, and Mr. Forsyth, and advocated by Messrs. Gholson, Troup, and Pearson. This amendment was also agreed to. [The quota of the District of Columbia is hereby reduced to 263 instead of 430.] Other amendments were proposed, and further discussion took place.

The Committee rose, without having gone through the bill, and the House adjourned.

Thursday, December 8.

The Speaker laid before the House a letter from the Secretary of the State of Pennsylvania, enclosing copies of the returns for members of Congress for the district composed of the counties of Lancaster, Dauphin, and Lebanon, and for the district composed of the counties of Chester and Montgomery, in that State.—Laid on the table.

On motion of Mr. McLean, of Ohio,

Resolved, That the Committee on the Public Lands be instructed to inquire into the expediency of subdividing the quarter sections of the lands of the United States.

Resolved, That the said Committee inquire into the expediency of making provision, by law, for the sale of sections heretofore reserved for the future disposition of Congress, and not sold or otherwise disposed of in the State of Ohio, on the same terms and at the same price that other public lands are offered for sale at the respective land offices within the State.

Resolved, That the said Committee inquire into the expediency of attaching to the Canton District, in the State of Ohio, the tract of land extending one mile in width on each side of the rapids of the Miami of Lake Erie, and the Western line of the Connecticut Reserve, which, by a late treaty at Brownstown, in the Michigan Territory, with certain Indian tribes, was ceded to the United States.

An engrossed bill supplementary to the acts authorizing a loan for the several sums of twenty-five millions of dollars and three millions of dollars, was read the third time and passed.

An engrossed bill making additional appropria-

tions for the service of the year 1814, was read the third time and passed.

A message from the Senate informed the House that the Senate have passed a bill "for the relief of John C. Hurlburt, of Chatham, in the State of Connecticut," in which they ask the concurrence of this House. The Senate have also passed the bill "to provide additional revenues for defraying the expenses of Government, and maintaining the public credit, by laying duties on spirits distilled within the United States, and by amending the act laying duties on licenses to distillers of spirituous liquors," with amendments; in which they ask the concurrence of this House.

MILITIA DRAUGHTS.

The House resumed the consideration of the bill from the Senate "to authorize the President of the United States to call upon the several States and Territories thereof for their respective quotas of 80,430 militia, for the defence of the frontiers of the United States."

Mr. Lewis, of Virginia, rose and said: He wished to offer an amendment to the bill, which he deemed of the first importance. There existed throughout this country a class of industrious, respectable, and highly meritorious citizens, whose religion forbade them to engage in this trade of war. From the time when the Christian religion was promulged, however strange the fact might appear to those whose business is the destruction of our race, there have always existed thousands who held it a most sacred duty not to imbrue their hands in the blood of their brethren, simply because their rulers had been pleased to declare them enemies. The history of centuries would prove that this was no theory, no speculative vision. It was an article of Christian faith, deemed a command of the Most High; and thousands of these pacific Christians have attested the sincerity of their faith and their practice at the stake and on the scaffold. The bill on the table, Mr. L. said, made no exceptions as to these noiseless, though numerous, Christians. They were subject to be draughted into the ranks of death, there to continue for a year; and if they refused the call, they were subjected to all the rigorous penalties of the law. In most of the States, Mr. L. said, he believed those men were excused from any kind of militia duty whatever, by paying a certain annual tax deemed equivalent to their personal services. He believed, with the exception of Virginia, there was not a State in the Union that did not suffer these peaceful Christians, in some way, to be exempted from military service. The militia laws of Virginia exact the same personal services from them as from others. None are exempted on account of religious faith and conscientious scruples. Their fines and penalties for neglect or refusal are highly severe, and, in general, are rigorously executed.

The courts martial have, it is true, discretionary powers, as relates to fines; but that discretion is generally exercised rather to punish than protect all who cannot join in the ranks. There was a practice, founded on the law of the

State, so highly unjust and oppressive in its operation to these peaceful citizens, that he was astonished it should be endured in an enlightened community. When once draughted or called to service, in case of failure to obey, which must always happen to this people, a heavy fine is levied and collected. The delinquent is immediately placed on the next class for another draught, is again, of course, delinquent, and again heavily fined. This call, or draught, is sometimes repeatedly made in quick succession, and fines accumulate to an amount which reduce the most affluent to distress, and those of competent fortune to entire ruin.

It operates, too, most oppressively upon those of the militia who have no religious scruples as to bearing arms. The number draughted from any particular company is in proportion to the whole number of the company, although it is composed half of men whose consciences forbid military service, and who, of course, never do, and never will, serve; yet the whole number is called forth, and thus, while these Christians are ruined by accumulated penalties, the residue have a most oppressive share of personal service.

Mr. L. said, in the district he represented, this description of their condition had lately, to a great extent, been realized. The fines had accumulated to an amount which the property of those oppressed people could not satisfy. It, of course, must be sacrificed under the marshal's hammer; and, in case of deficiency, their persons committed to prison to expiate the sin of serving their God with perseverance and pure consciences. Mr. L. said, when he viewed the benevolent genius of the constitution of his native State, the liberal spirit of her general laws, and the magnanimous justice which she was in the habit of distributing to her sons, he could not but wonder that this stain on her policy and her justice was suffered to remain. It was in direct hostility to her own spirit, views, and declarations. In 1788, when ratifying the Constitution of the United States, her convention tendered a bill of rights to the Union; and this was the 19th article of that bill : "That any person religiously scrupu-'lous of bearing arms ought to be exempted, upon 'payment of an equivalent, and another employed 'in his stead." Mr. L. said, he cited from memory, but was sure that he was substantially correct. How different from this is the present practice ? The present law is most unequal in its operation; the mass of the militia, having no religious restraints, could perform their duty in person, or, at worst, by hiring a substitute; and a tour of duty, performed in either way, exonerated them from further calls, until every militiaman, of every class, had, in his turn, gone through the same process. These peaceful Christians could not, as they believed, under the penalties of eternal perdition, enter your ranks in arms, and they are not casuists enough to believe that they may innocently do that by substitute, which the Prince of Peace has forbidden them to perform in person. They cannot, therefore, deliver themselves from the constant harassing of marshals, and fines and imprisonment. In every class they are bound to take a chance for draught, and, if unsuccessful in every class and upon every draught, they are subjected to a round of suffering and oppression. He said it might be objected, that his amendment would interfere with State militia laws and regulations. He denied it; or, if it should, so did all the provisions of the bill. The bill contained principles in open violation of the State rights; it went not through the State executive, but directly to the ranks of the militia upon a certain contingency. It made direct requisitions upon those ranks, and annexed penalties and punishment to neglect or refusal to obey those requisitions. It was against this assumption of power he wished to protect these people. He said, if gentlemen would look at the bill, they would find that a power was assumed, from which no State exemption could deliver the citizen; you impose fines and penalties in a manner which the States alone have the Constitutional power to do. You make a call upon the militia, and you doom those who do not obey your call, without discrimination, to fine, imprisonment, and probable ruin. In this way you approach directly a class of citizens who you know would suffer crucifixion sooner than obey your requisition, and you leave them no refuge but in your penalties and punishments. Why is this done ? Not to fill your ranks! For you know these men will never be in your ranks, unless by ruffian force. It is to wring from them the little property which, by frugality, sobriety, and labor, they have collected to sustain their families, and smooth the pillow of old age. He said it was unjust, oppressive, and sinful. Mr. L. said, he did not mean to ask for those people any peculiar boon beyond what the true principles of toleration demanded. Of all the pecuniary burdens of the State, the property of those men must bear its share. He did not ask an exemption from the general weight and burdens of the State—there ought to be, there could be, no such exemption. But, as to personal service in arms, if any man conscientiously believed it was forbidden by the voice of God, no human tribunal had the right to force such a man to violate his religion and his conscience, and to stain his hands with human blood. A fair equivalent was all that any Government had the right to require from such a man, to be applied, not particularly to the work of war, but to the general purposes of Government; with this all ought to be satisfied. The equivalent ought not to be oppressive on the one hand, nor on the other ought it to be so reduced as to permit any but the really conscientious to take advantage of it for improper purposes. Mr. L. then offered the following section to the bill, which was adopted by a large majority:

SEC. 10. *And be it further enacted,* That every person who is a member of any religious sect or denomination of Christians, conscientiously scrupulous of bearing arms, shall be exempted from the performance of the duties required by this act, by paying his due proportion of the amount contracted to be paid by the class in which he is included, according to the provision of the fourth section of the act; or, in case there shall be a draught in such class, by paying to the person draughted such sum as shall be ascertained by the commanding officer of the company, so that the sum shall not exceed three months' pay; and the payment of such sum of money, in either case, shall be considered as entitling such person to an exemption from all the duties required by this act.

On motion of Mr. EPPES, of Virginia, the bill was amended so as to reduce the term of service of the militia proposed to be draughted, from two years to one year. The majority in favor of this motion was about twenty votes.

Mr. MILLER, of New York, observed that he thought the bill objectionable in principle; and with a view to try the sense of the Committee, he moved to strike out the first section of the bill. He begged the indulgence of the Committee, while he submitted some remarks in support of his motion.

Mr. Chairman, you have been correctly told by the honorable chairman of the Military Committee (Mr. TROUP) that, in discussing this bill, it will be proper to settle the principle, on which you intend to rely, for assisting your military force to carry on the war. With this object in view, it will be necessary to compare the provisions of this bill with the other military plans now on your table.

The honorable chairman (Mr. TROUP) has pursued that course; and without entering at large into a discussion of the question, has objected to this bill, because he considers it too inefficient in its provisions; and because the kind of force (militia) is not of that character required by the present situation of the country. He says " it ' cannot be true that this Government, charged ' with the general defence, authorized to declare ' war, and raise armies, can have but one mode ' of raising armies, whilst every other Govern- ' ment that has ever existed has had an absolute ' power over the population of the country for ' this purpose, and has actually exercised it. But ' this question is not properly before the House, ' and (he says) I will not go into an argument to ' show that you can, like other Governments, re- ' sort to other modes of raising armies than that ' of voluntary enlistment. That you can resort ' to classification and draught, to classification ' and penalty, or any other mode which a sound ' discretion may in a particular state of the coun- ' try dictate and justify. All I intend to say at ' present is, that you have an absolute power over ' the population of the country for this purpose, ' and that, in the present state of the country, it is ' wiser to resort to classification and draught, than ' to resort to this bill from the Senate." These are the positions taken by the honorable chairman of the Military Committee, (Mr. TROUP.)

I object, sir, to the whole system of force and coercion; and contend that under this Constitution you have no right to raise armies except by voluntary enlistment; and further, that if you had the right it would not be discreet to exercise it.

The plan which gentlemen wish adopted is conscription! They call it classification and penalty—classification and draught. Sir, there is poison in the dish; garnish it as you please, there is poison still. You call it classification! I stickle not for names—"a rose by any other name would smell as sweet." Is this classification ? " Disguise thyself as thou wilt, slavery, still thou art a bitter draught." The times demand that things should be called by their right names—this is conscription, and with features more hideous, than are to be found in the exploded system of our unfortunate cousin of Elba.

This system of conscription, I contemplate with a horror which I cannot express, and with an alarm, which it would be criminal to conceal. Other gentlemen think differently, and will of course act differently—he who views it as I do, but illy performs his duty to his conscience or his country, if he neglects to remonstrate against it, with a zeal proportioned to the enormity of the principle, and the extent of the evils involved in it.

For one, I cannot consent to be a mere spectator of a scene like this. I should consider myself as utterly unworthy the confidence of my constituents, if I did not oppose this high-handed attempt upon their rights and privileges. I would not dare to meet the indignant frowns which I should deservedly receive from them, if I did not oppose this system to the utmost of my power—I should consider that I insulted the ashes of my forefathers, who, during the struggle of the Revolution, in their humble station (and humble indeed it was) performed some little service to the State. I should be unjust to my own claims to personal freedom; I should be an unfaithful guardian to the interests of my children, if I did not oppose this system in all its forms and in all its aspects. The finger of scorn shall never be pointed to a son of mine, and say, that man's father, placed by the partiality of his friends in the councils of the nation, omitted to oppose this system by every means in his power. I seize this occasion to put myself upon the record, in characters too legible to be misunderstood. If the liberties of this country are now to be sacrificed, I wash my hands of any share of the crime. I may indeed be offered upon the altar of conscription, but if my voice and my strength do not fail me, I will this day make you my witnesses to prove that I was not a willing victim.

What are the plans by which you intend to fill your army ? I object to them all, as unconstitutional and inexpedient; they all look to force, and you have no right to raise an army except by voluntary enlistment. I have indeed heard that these were rival plans; for myself I consider them all as parts of a system of tyranny and oppression— they are all branches of this Bohun Upas which is to overshadow this country, and poison all the comforts of this people. If either bill passes, the principle of coercion is established; and the claim to "absolute power over the population of the country" will soon be asserted.

Your present military plans are all unconstitutional. In order to arrive at a just conclusion, as to the extent of your powers, it will be well to remember the structure of our Government, and the objects of its formation. This Constitution was formed by separate, free, and independent States, who mutually agreed to give up some of their rights of sovereignty for a common object. The States were jealous of their rights, and, with much care and circumspection, limited their grant to the General Government, for the objects defined. It was not a leading motive with the States to make this a great military nation. The objects are disclosed in the preamble to the Constitution, viz: "To form a more perfect union, establish ' justice, insure domestic tranquillity, provide for ' the common defence, promote the general welfare, ' and secure the blessings of liberty to ourselves ' and our posterity." These were the inducements which procured the adoption of this Constitution.

You are now unfortunately at war, and you wish to fill the ranks of your army. The bill before us discloses one of your plans; it seeks to raise eighty thousand men from the militia "by contract or draught." This bill, I am free to admit, is less objectionable than either of the other projects; but it is nevertheless unconstitutional. Congress have no power to "raise militia." You have only a right to provide for calling them out in the three cases mentioned in the Constitution. The title of the bill would seem to imply, that "the defence of the frontiers" was its object, but there is no provision in it which limits the service of the militia to defence, or to either of the cases enumerated in the Constitution. Indeed, gentlemen have avowed the intention to carry on the war by means of these militia. Sir, the Constitution gives you no such right. The militia may be used by the General Government in the emergencies stated, but the exigency must exist, or the right to call them out does not exist. A power to use the militia to carry on a war is not granted by the Constitution. You can employ them to "repel invasion," but not to carry on the war. By this bill you may take the militia to Quebec or to Halifax; and the same usurpation which permits you to push them beyond the St. Lawrence, will justify you also in pushing them to the Shannon or the Thames.

There is another argument which bears upon this question. Militia officers are appointed under the State authorities; these State authorities vibrate with parties. To day you have one description of officers, who are called out to carry on the war—to-morrow there is a change in the State government, the officers on duty are removed, and others are appointed. The inconvenience which would flow from such a state of things goes far to prove that you have no power to carry on a war by militia.

There is another feature of this bill which deserves some notice. You have introduced an amendment by which, in case the Governors refuse to comply with the requisition, the President may issue his order to other military officers of the States. The effect of this amendment will be, to encourage mutiny and insubordination in the militia; and thus, like all your other measures, tend to weaken the security of the States.

Connected with this system, is a bill we passed a day or two since, authorizing the enlistment of minors, without the consent of parents, masters, or guardians. This has been considered unconstitutional, and I think there can be no doubt that it is inexpedient. It subverts all order, it goes to the destruction of civil society. Under that law, you need not be surprised to see some philosophical recruiting sergeant, marching through your towns and villages, with this inscription on his standard: "If any children have undutiful parents, or if any servants have disobedient masters, let them come here and enlist."

But this project, bad as it is, is not by any means so objectionable as either the system contemplated by the bill from the Military Committee of this House, or that recommended by the Secretary at War in his letter of the 17th of October, 1814. The bill from the Military Committee proposes to divide the whole free male population of the country (without any exception) into classes of twenty-five; each class to furnish a recruit to serve during the war; and in case any class shall make default in furnishing the recruit, a direct tax is to be laid on the property within the territorial districts comprising the class. This is what has been called classification and penalty. The project of the Secretary of War is:—"Let the free male population of ' the United States between eighteen and forty- ' five years, be formed into classes of one hundred ' each, and let each class furnish four men for ' the war, within thirty days after the classifica- ' tion, and replace them in the event of casualty." From this system, there are to be no exempts, except the President of the United States, and the Governors of the States and Territories. This is called classification and draught; but is in fact, a system of military conscription more extensive than was ever before attempted by the ambition of tyrants.

Mr. Chairman: This plan violates the Constitution of your country; it invades the rights of the State governments; it is a direct infringement of their sovereignty; it concentrates all power in the General Government, and deprives the States of their "necessary security." It does away all claim to personal freedom; it is a daring attempt upon the rights and liberties of this people.

This conscription is unconstitutional. The Government of the United States is a Government of limited powers. You take by grant; your powers are special and delegated—they must be construed strictly. "All powers not delegated, are reserved to the States or the people." Your authority is defined—you take nothing by inference or application, except what may be "necessary and proper for carrying into execution" the powers expressly granted.

What then are the legitimate powers of this Government over the military force of the country? There are two kinds of military force mentioned in the Constitution, armies and militia, and your authority over each is set down with accuracy and precision. Congress have power to declare war, and with it the necessary power "to raise and support armies," and to "make rules for their government and regulation." Armies then are the forces of the United States, with which they are to carry on their wars; and are subject to their exclusive jurisdiction and control. But the militia are the State troops, which Congress have no power to raise. They are a force existing, known and acknowledged at the time of the adoption of this Constitution; existing without the aid or concurrence of the General Government. The general power over the militia resides in the States; a particular authority, for objects defined, was carved out of that general power, and granted to the United States. The militia are the security of the States against foreign or domestic foes. The States were not a little jealous of this right, and to prevent any encroachment upon it, they procured an "amendment" to the Constitution in these words: 2d. Amendment: "A well regulated militia being necessary ' to the security of a free State, the right of the ' people to keep and bear arms shall not be in- ' fringed." Thus this "necessary security" is not only recognised but guarded and protected. Congress has no power to raise militia, to appoint their officers, or to train them. The general power is in the States; out of this general power there is delegated to the United States a particular authority, in certain specified cases, and this authority is "to provide for calling forth the militia to execute the laws of the Union, suppress insurrection, and repel invasion." And with a view to give uniformity to their manœuvres, and make them more efficient, when their services should be required by the exigencies enumerated, it is permitted Congress to provide "for organ- ' izing, arming, and disciplining the militia; and ' for governing such part of them as may be em- ' ployed in the service of the United States."

Now, waiving all arguments against this plan, which may be derived from the genius of our Government, and the freedom of our institutions, I ask, whether under the naked power to "raise armies" you can adopt a plan which goes to alter the whole military system of the United States, and to destroy the militia of the States, thereby depriving them of their "necessary security?" The Secretary seems to be aware of this objection, and has labored to obviate it. He admits (let it be remembered) that it would be a violation of the Constitution to draw men from the militia service into the regular army: but, he says, by his plan "the men are not drawn from the militia, but from the population of the country." With all due deference and humility, this is a pitiful sophism. The militia of many of the States are now out on duty, and, if his plan is adopted, you will literally draw men from the "militia service." But it is not material whether the militia are on duty or not; you have no right to force a man from the militia into the regular army. If he offers voluntarily, you may take him, but you cannot compel him by force. You say you do not take him from the militia, but from the population of the country. Now I

should like to know, whether the military population of the country is not the militia of the States? If it is, then you have no right to force one of them into your service; and yet you claim a right to force them all. The classes are to replace the men who are lost by casualty, and the case may happen, that each individual of a particular class may thus be compelled to render personal service. I can see no escape from this argument. If you have a right to force one man from a particular class, you have a right to force all the men from that class; and if you have a right to force all the men of one class, you have a right to force all men of all the classes. The power to raise armies under this Constitution, can never be construed to extend to a plan which goes to alter the whole military system of the United States, and take from the States that "necessary security" so explicitly acknowledged and guarantied.

I now proceed to examine some of the other positions which the Secretary takes in support of his conscription. Congress have power to raise armies, and he says, "an unqualified grant of power gives the means necessary to carry it into effect." This is a position which I do not mean to controvert: but, I do say that the grant of power "to raise armies" is not an unqualified grant. It is qualified by the spirit of our Constitution; it should be exercised in the spirit of freedom, and in the manner usually and ordinarily pursued by free States: not by means arbitrary, vexatious, unusual, and oppressive. Besides, this "power to raise armies" is qualified by that authority and claim on the militia which was known and acknowledged to reside in the States; you have no right to raise armies in a way which must necessarily defeat all the security which the States have under the Constitution.

The Secretary says, "the militia service affords a conclusive proof and striking example" in support of the right which he claims for Congress, to raise armies by conscription. This I must deny—the cases are not parallel. The militia belong to the State governments, whose powers are more extensive than those of the General Government. Your powers are limited, and must be construed strictly. With respect to State governments, a different construction has obtained—the residuum of power is with the States or the people; and, in regard to State Legislatures, the general rule is, that all powers are granted, except those which are expressly denied. Indeed, so obvious and undoubted is this opinion, that respectable authority is not wanting to prove that as to State Legislatures, a power to legislate, in a case not forbidden, is not to be taken away by inference or implication. The example of the militia under the State laws is not to be drawn into precedent, to establish a right in the United States to raise armies by conscription. You have no such right; it violates the first principles of the Constitution.

There is another objection to the bill proposed by your Military Committee. By the Constitution direct taxes are to be apportioned among the several States according to representation, and this rule is palpably violated by this bill. The fourth section contains the principle which I contest. It provides that the class which fails to furnish a recruit shall forfeit four hundred dollars, to be collected on the property of every taxable person within the territorial division of such class. Sir, this is a direct tax not apportioned according to representation, and therefore unconstitutional. The slaveholding States have an unreasonable and an unjust advantage. Each one of their slaves, as to all purposes of political consequence, is three-fifths of a man; but, by this bill, he dwindles to nothing in the apportionment of the burdens of the war. The slaveholding States furnish less, and the other States more than their fair proportion of men, provided the classes furnish the men. Suppose the men are not furnished, then the slaveholding States pay a direct tax in no way proportioned to their representation.

Take as examples the States of Massachusetts and Virginia. The inequality is apparent. Massachusetts has twenty Representatives, and Virginia twenty-three. The free male population of Massachusetts, between the ages of eighteen and forty-five years amounts to 120,270, and that of Virginia to 93,750. Massachusetts will have 4,810 classes of twenty-five each, and Virginia 3,750 classes. If, then, each class provides a recruit, Massachusetts will furnish 1,060 recruits more than Virginia, whereas Virginia ought to furnish more men than Massachusetts in the proportion of twenty-three to twenty, the number of their Representatives. But suppose each State pays the penalty, then Massachusetts will pay $331,400 more, and Virginia the same sum $331,-400 less than the Constitution requires; and Massachusetts will pay $424,000 more than Virginia, whereas Virginia ought, by the Constitution, to pay $238,890 more than Massachusetts. The apportionment is unconstitutional.

Your conscription system, in any view of it, ought not to be adopted. The Secretary of War admits that the abuse of power in raising armies is to be dreaded; and he says, too, that "our Constitution has provided ample security against that evil." It has, sir; and if so, it forbids conscription. If the General Government has that "absolute power" which is contended for, I can see no security against the exercise of it. If to-day you can raise men by conscription, to-morrow some military despot may embody anticipated conscripts as the ministers of his vengeance. The guard which our Constitution has placed against the abuse of power in raising armies is this: you must raise them by voluntary enlistment. If you have a right to force the people of this country into your armies, then they have no right left worth preserving. Life and all its comforts are robbed of half their value.

The effect of this conscription will be to alter the whole character and genius of your people. Instead of pursuing the arts of peace you must become a military nation. This system will break up all our habits and all our pursuits. It is a daring violation of the rights of this people. It has been our boast that we lived in a land of freedom. How often have we proudly claimed pre-eminence in the rank of nations—a pre-eminence founded on the free spirit of our institutions? How often have the citizens of this Government fondly contrasted their situation with that of most European countries? We have said that while the wretched subjects of other Governments were compelled to fight the battles of their masters, we could pursue in quiet and in peace those arts and those avocations which best suited our taste and convenience. If this conscription system is adopted, farewell to all our claims to personal freedom—farewell to all our boast of civil liberty. By this system, the people of these United States will be instantly and forcibly transformed into soldiers; the ordinary pursuits of life must be abandoned for the peril and vexations of a camp; our peaceful occupations must be forsaken; the merchant must quit his counting-house; the farmer his plough; the mechanic his workshop; the professional man his pursuits—all, all must become soldiers! Our sons and our brothers, those who are to be the "future men" of this country, instead of laying the foundation for future usefulness, must be subjected to the moral and physical evils of a camp. All the habits of domestic life must be annihilated, and all its endearments outraged or disregarded. The husband must be torn from his wife and his children, and the child forcibly separated from the society and protection of his parents. I beseech gentlemen to pause before they venture upon a system like this.

The example of Rome has been quoted to justify a conscription. No argument can be drawn from ancient Rome in favor of this project. We live in another age, and in another country. Our people are different; the objects of our Government are entirely different. Our Government was formed by patriots, in peaceable times, and for peaceable objects. Rome was founded by a military chieftain, at the head of a daring and profligate band of freebooters—it was founded on fraud and on violence, on rapine and on rape. Romulus was not only an adventurous military leader; he was, also, a consummate legislator. He shaped his Government to suit the people he governed, and with a view to the situation of the surrounding nations. His object was to make a military Government. The Roman Government, in some of its features, was a Republic, but in regard to its military institutions it was despotic in the extreme. Let us be warned by her example. She could raise great armies, but those armies destroyed her liberty. She did, indeed, extend her conquests, but it ought not to be forgotten that Rome fell by her own weight.

Rome herself, arbitrary and despotic as was her military system, affords an example not more detestable than the one now recommended;—there were many *exempts* under her laws. Those who held offices, whether civil or sacred; those who had rendered important services to their country, including men of extraordinary merit, with many others, were exempted from military service. But our system is to include everybody. Besides, in Rome, military duty was considered a *personal* service, and none were called upon to perform it except those who possessed the necessary personal qualifications. So well settled was this principle, that draughts were not usually resorted to; the ordinary mode was for the Tribunes to select; and this selection was determined by the personal qualities and appearance of the soldier. But your system, like no other military system, except the French *Conscription*, disregards the personal disability of the recruit, and includes the lame, the halt, the diseased, and blind; all are swallowed up in the devouring vortex of your proposed conscription. The leading example of conscription is found in modern France. The future historian of this country will no doubt consider it not a little remarkable, that an American Congress was called to debate a project of conscription at the very instant that the crowned heads of Europe had, by unanimous consent, abandoned it as the most detestable remnant of despotism and usurpation. Sir, the iron system of Bonaparte was not so intolerable as yours. He included only those between twenty and twenty-five years; you propose to take all from eighteen to forty-five. By his plan the young men were called upon; those of twenty years first, and others were not demanded unless there was a deficiency; your merciful conscription will make all from eighteen to forty-five equally liable. Besides, the despotic power of Bonaparte enabled him to make discriminations in cases of peculiar hardship, and he did discriminate. But pass your law, and where is the power which can dispense with its provisions?

France has been a military nation; the idea of war and its dangers had become familiar to the young men of that country, and they prepared for it; here all our people are taken unprepared, and the total ruin of families must be the consequence. In France, the liability extended only to those from twenty to twenty-five years of age; here, all are included, from eighteen to forty-five, and all business arrangements must be interrupted or suspended for that period. In France, a call for anticipated conscripts was not unusual. It is long since they were anticipated for four years; the same thing may happen here. If the recruit furnished by the class is killed, dies, deserts, or his place becomes vacant by any casualty, it must be made good. I have authority for saying that in France the ninety-sixth man has been drawn from a class of one hundred; the same may happen here. I entreat you to try this ground well before you attempt to tread it. The same evils, the same desolation, and the same anguish which have followed this system in another country, must and will follow it here. It will be more severely felt by this people than by France. France was a military nation, accustomed to despotic power. We are a peaceful people, cradled in a land of liberty. "The apprehension of the good gives but a keener relish to the worse."

Faber, in his "*Sketches of the internal state of France,*" has marked the operation of this system of conscription in that devoted country. If

we adopt this system, so sure as the effect follows the cause, so sure shall we witness the deplorable consequences which there flowed from it. Hear the evidence of an eye-witness, and be warned by the example. I beg your attention while I read a few extracts. He says:

"The law admits of no exception or modification. It reaches even those who are recognised by the proper tribunals as unfit for service in consequence of physical infirmity. They are compelled to pay a fine, proportioned to the whole amount of the taxes, levied either upon them or their parents. No recruiting system ever before presented such a feature as this. Personal service has been everywhere considered as the sole object of such systems. The idea of exacting a pecuniary compensation from those who labor under a physical disability to serve, was never before entertained."

"No condition of life; no circumstances of position, however peculiar, give title to exemption. I have seen a conscript, the son of a blind mother, whom he supported by his labor, forced to march. I have known a hard-working mechanic, robbed of three sons, in three consecutive years, whom he had laboriously instructed in his trade, and upon whose assistance he relied for the support of his old age."

"The day fixed for the drawing of lots for the conscription, is one of public mourning and of anguish for every private family. Parents, both mothers and fathers, accompany their children to this horrid lottery, and display in their countenances, and by their accents, the most violent emotions of grief and despair. A gloomy silence prevails until the drawing commences, when the decisions of chance lead to demonstrations, either of joy or of sorrow, which equally shock or overpower the feelings of a spectator."

"The Prefect, the sub-Prefect, and the Mayors, preside on the occasion, and frequently see their own children among the number of the conscripts. I have remarked a Mayor, when his child approached to seek his destiny in the fatal urn; the faultering voice of the father, and the tears that rushed to his eye, showed how nature worked, in spite of the sense of imperious necessity which accompanies this transaction. I have noted the swellings of his heart, and the invincible oppression of his spirits when he undertook, as is enjoined upon him by law, to pronounce a discourse of encouragement and exhortation to the new soldier. When he expatiated on the beneficence of the Emperor, and gave the signal of ' *Vive Bonaparte !*' at the end of his speech."

"After the conscript sets out there is but little hope of his return. The term of service is limited only by the duration of hostilities. When the parent, therefore, takes into consideration the character of his Government, the evils, both moral and physical, to which his child is exposed in the armies, and the havoc of lives made in them, he must regard a summons to the conscription as a visitation upon the latter worse for all parties than that of death."

I appeal to honorable gentlemen who are parents, and entreat them not to adopt a system which deprives them of their children forever. Compared with conscription, death itself is mercy. I beg gentlemen to believe that I feel what I say. I have followed four children to the tomb. Under present circumstances ought I to repine their loss? When I see the attempt to fasten this conscription upon us, ought I to regret that they have gone to Heaven? My daughters, had they lived, might have been the mothers of conscripts; my sons might have been conscripts themselves. I have yet, (I am grateful for it,) I have yet, two lovely boys—lovely indeed, though they are, and inexpressibly dear to me, rather than see them the subjects of this conscription, I would, with resignation, follow them also to the tomb of their fathers. Gentlemen may say that my whole head is weak; I confess to them, that on this subject my whole heart is faint.

There is another consideration well worthy of notice. Already the war is carried on with much disadvantage on our part. The character of the enemy's troops—and the kind of force which we oppose to them—shows the contest to be much in his favor. The enemy brings against us the sweepings of Europe; good soldiers, no doubt, but good for nothing else. We oppose to them the bone and sinew of the country; our honest, respectable and industrious citizens, many of them with large families, are put into this contest of blood, against men without character, without occupation, and without homes. Your conscription system will add much to this disparity. There are certain evils of war which you can remedy. Your commerce may revive; your agriculture and your manufactures may be restored; the public edifices now in view may be refitted. You may rebuild a city that is sacked. Time and money may replace all these. But there are evils which you have no power to remedy. You cannot fill up the space which will be made at many a happy fireside—you cannot restore the husband to his wife and his family—you cannot bring back the son to the arms of his parents—you cannot rouse the sleeping warrior from his tomb—you have no cure for a wounded spirit—you cannot mend a broken heart! These are awful facts; I beg gentlemen to consider them.

This conscription is not only utterly incorrect and inadmissible in principle, but it will prove arbitrary, hard, and oppressive in practice. It will impose an intolerable burden on the poorer classes of society. Each class is to furnish a man; and the man may be designated by lot: in this way the poorest citizen runs an equal hazard with the most wealthy man in the community. If the rich man is drawn, he has the means and may perhaps hire a substitute, while the poor man must perform the service himself—he must quit his business and family, and leave them dependent for a precarious subsistence on the bounty of their neighbors and friends.

This system is the more intolerable, from the consideration that the recruit is to be placed under an officer of the United States. If he is called out as a militiaman, he goes for a definite object, with his own officers, and in the society of his friends and neighbors. Not so under this conscription; no one can calculate on what service he is to be employed; under what command he is to serve; or with whom he is to associate. I have no disposition to lessen the respectability of the regular Army; but I cannot look to the prac-

tical effects of this system, without remembering that armies are not usually composed of the most estimable portion of the population of a country. Much less can I forget that the Governor of New York, (who has lent himself to the Administration as the pioneer of conscription) did pardon a horse thief, on condition that he should enlist, and serve in the Army of the United States: a condition not left to doubt or uncertainty; I have seen it patent on the pardon. That Governor Tompkins is the friend of the war, I well believe; for, just before his last election, he descended from his elevated station, as Governor of New York, and acted as a sort of deputy paymaster, for your great men in this Administration. He is said also to be a friend to the Army. But it was an insult to the ranks of your Army to say this horse thief was a fit associate for your soldiers. What greater discouragement could be given to the recruiting service than this act of the Governor, which so expressly declares, that he considers the punishment of enlistment a sufficient commutation for the punishment due to the crimes of a convicted felon?

I must and will oppose this project, so humiliating, so oppressive, and so unjust. I tell you, sir, that my constituents are too respectable, and too valuable, for a service of this sort; and with my consent they never shall be compelled to associate on equal terms with Governor Tompkins' pardoned horse thief. If they choose to enlist, it is an affair of their own; but you shall not have my vote to coerce them. No, sir, this system should be adopted by none but tyrants, it should be submitted to by none but slaves. If you succeed, in common with others, my constituents will be forced into your Army. In spite of their reluctance to military life—in spite of their objections to this war of conquest and ambition—in spite of their families, and all the tender ties which bind them to their firesides, they must be "delivered over" to the recruiting officer, and dragged to a military rendezvous. They must go. If they refuse, they will be compelled by the same cruel and oppressive means which the French conscription authorized towards refractory conscripts.

Sir, I am alarmed and dismayed by the extent of the evils involved in this system. Rely upon it, conscription will never be submitted to in this country; it will be resisted. If your system is adopted, I may be called to take a near view of a picture, in the front ground of which will be seen Governor Tompkins (an exempt under the plan) "prancing over the field, his horse's hoofs wet" with that blood which must flow in opposition to these laws. On the one hand may be seen some of the most respectable citizens of New York, starting back with grief and indignation, at the rude approach of a hardened outcast, who has scarcely grace enough left to endeavor to conceal his crimes, by covering them with his pardon. On the other side may be seen, a group of American freemen, handcuffed and in chains, reluctantly marching on the road to Canada. Turning from this view, and looking for relief to some other parts of the canvass, you will observe "Free trade and sailors' rights," in large staring capitals. As you approach, you perceive a figure covered with a thin veil—on examination, it proves to be the hideous and menacing aspect of Despotism, holding the sword of conscription in her hand, while the Goddess of Liberty lies cold and breathless at her feet.

The honorable gentleman from Georgia (Mr. Troup) has told us, that this system is required by the situation of the country ; he has expressed his opinion, also, that the people will cheerfully acquiesce. I think he is mistaken ; the people of this country are not prepared for conscription—you have no right to impose it—you have no right to fasten chains upon the hands of freemen. They will prove to be the flaxen bands upon the arms of Sampson—he will rouse himself in his might and burst them. You say you will pass your law ; that you will fasten it with a gordian knot, which cannot be untied. The swords of freemen then will cut it !

Mr. Chairman, it has been the habit of certain gentlemen here, to omit no occasion to charge the British Government with being arbitrary and tyrannical. But she affords no example to justify your present project of conscription. As to her armies, she has no law or practice which in any way resembles it. Instead of recruiting her armies by force, she gets them by voluntary enlistment ; and so careful is she to prevent mischiefs from hasty and unadvised contracts, that the recruit under her practice, in all cases, has four days to revise his enlistment, and within that time the recruit must be discharged, on refunding the bounty money.

The only instance in which the practice of Great Britain can be claimed to justify the principle of conscription, is the practice of pressing sailors into their naval service. From my earliest infancy, I well remember to have heard this practice reprobated as an intolerable grievance ; and, so far as my observation has extended, it has been very generally considered by this nation as arbitrary, tyrannical, and unjust. Indeed, this Administration, in their late instructions to our Ministers at Ghent, expressly say, that, "impressment is not an American practice, but is repugnant to our Constitution and our laws." And yet the late Secretary of the Navy, in his letter to the President of the Senate, on the sixteenth November, proposes a naval conscription ; and says that he does not consider it "incompatible with the free spirit of our institutions, or with the rights of individuals."

It is not my intention to prove that the present Administration are the peculiar champions of "free trade and sailors' rights." Nor shall I stop to show the ardor and violence of that love which prompts them to the seize upon the persons of seamen against their consent. My object in noticing this subject, is merely to show the universality of your conscription project ; and incidentally to mark its resemblance to the practice of other nations.

The British practice of impressment, so far as it goes, corresponds in principle with your con-

scription ; but it is much less general in its operation. The British press-gangs are not permitted to take any but sailors. Your plan embraces all the population of the country. The British, in cases of emergency, press sailors, who have all their lives been accustomed to the sea—fitted for the service, and fitted for nothing else. But this is a grievance, and the hardship is, that they force their sailors from merchant vessels into their public ships ; and compel them to quit a service which is safe and profitable, for one more hazardous and less lucrative. But that your conscription plan is infinitely more oppressive than this, must be evident to everybody. Now, sir, let it be remembered, that the British practice of impressment, limited as it is to sailors, is not sanctioned by any statute—it is resorted to only in cases of emergency, and is justified on the ground of State necessity alone.

Perhaps some honorable gentleman here, who doubts the strict constitutionality of the conscription, may seek its justification in the necessities of the times. To such I would say, in the language of Jaffier to Pierre, " I tell thee, friend, if this your cause require, your cause is in a damned condition." On occasions much less important than this, I have heard on this floor, that, "in time of war the laws sleep." I am not now to learn, that cases may be imagined in which the necessities of the State must supersede the ordinary course of law, and in which private rights must be postponed to the safety of the nation. But the rule of " *silent leges inter arma,*" has been quoted in debate, as applicable to the ordinary wants of the public, or its agents, in the management of war. Against this principle, thus applied, I beg leave solemnly to protest. In a Government of laws, it is not to be endured, that every petty officer, at a recruiting rendezvous, or on his march through the country, shall decide on the State necessity, and violate private rights at his will and pleasure. This is tyranny and oppression of the worst sort. The people of this country have no rights worth preserving, provided they can be sported with at the whim and caprice of every epauletted upstart. Sir, it is not the law of the land.

Nor can this State necessity be called in aid of this conscription. What ! the leading measure for the permanent prosecution of the war, founded on usurpation ! Do our laws sleep ? I have been taught to believe that our laws never sleep. Has the operation of our laws been suspended ? Why then do you mock this people with a show of legislation ? Let us go home. Scatter the pages of your statute book to the winds of heaven. Your Constitution is the evidence of your rights, and the witness of your degradation—put it in the fire ; it is made of paper, and like your Capitol, it will burn. But are we, indeed, reduced to this humiliating condition ? Where is the author of our shame ? Let him be pointed out, and you may, perhaps, view another act " of doubtful ' public spirit, at which morality is perplexed, ' reason is staggered, and from which affrighted ' nature recoils." Name the usurper, who claims to place himself above the law, and trample on the rights and liberties of a free people. Perhaps some modern Brutus may be found, rising " refulgent from the stroke of Cæsar's fate, amidst a crowd of patriots."

Mr. Chairman, the object of this conscription is, to fill the ranks of your army. By it, you propose to abandon all your former systems. By your first plan, you appealed, in a good degree, to the patriotism of the nation. That did not succeed. Your second proposition made the same call on the patriotism, and addressed itself also to the cupidity of the people. You failed in that, and you now propose a direct resort to force. It is a rule of political wisdom, that leading measures of Government, when once adopted, should not be departed from on slight causes. The respectability of a nation, in a great degree, depends on the stability of its institutions, and that Administration which expects to be useful to the people it governs, or held in respect by other nations, must adopt wise measures, and pursue them with steadiness and perseverance.

If these remarks are true, even if you had a Constitutional right to raise an army by the means proposed, prudence would seem to dictate that you should not exercise that right, except in a case of urgent necessity. On your own principles, does this urgent necessity exist? The war, you have uniformly said, was popular. The people have always been admitted to be patriotic, and the war has been said to be successful. Why, then, force your patriotic people into this popular war, which has been crowned with such success?

Whence arises the necessity for this conscription? It is said the state of affairs in Europe has placed vast means in the power of the enemy; that he has avowed the intention to prosecute this war with the utmost rigor and barbarity; that we must defend ourselves; and hence it is said arises a necessity for the measure now under consideration. If this is a fair statement of the case, the bill is wanted for the defence of the country. If the defence of the country was the real object of our rulers, I should not consider myself at liberty to withhold my assent to any Constitutional mode which might be proposed to raise supplies of men or money. While I should hold the Administration responsible for the present alarming state of the country; while I should consider that those who declared the war had failed in their essential duty "to provide for the common defence," I should deem it the part of patriotism to unite in repelling the invaders of the country. If defence was the object, you should have my vote for a full system of finance, and for the most vigorous and effective military system which could be devised, consistent with the Constitution of the country. But the present system is one which, if adopted, must end in the destruction of this Government. Your affairs have been for some time in the inclined plane of ruin; do not, I beseech you, add to the weight by which they are descending. If you pass this law, you drive this country to destruction with accelerated velocity.

Conscription is not necessary for defensive measures, nor is the force to be raised by it intended for that object. Certainly, sir, you will not pay so poor a compliment to the patriotism of the people as to say, that you must resort to arbitrary and violent means to compel them to defend their country. So long as you continue to avow your weak and ambitious views of conquest, so long the recruiting service will not progress.

You want men and money, and you cannot expect to get men unless you have money. It is not to be expected that men will imbody for the defence of the nation for any considerable time, if you keep them on bad rations and no pay; but if you had money, and, under existing circumstances, would call on the nation for services limited to the defence of the nation, you could get men enough by voluntary enlistment. The great evil is, you have wasted the resources of the country—you have no money—the bills of your authorized and most confidential officers are every day dishonored. What is worse, you have no credit; you cannot borrow a dollar but at usurious interest; and the rate of interest must rise upon you, because the risk of the eventual repayment of the principal is every day increasing. What shall we do; pass this law? If you do, the Government is at an end; if you do not pass this law, I think there is too much reason to fear the affairs of the nation are irretrievable. You, who in June, 1812. declared the war, have neglected to provide the means for carrying it on. Without money you cannot meet your present engagements, much less can you raise another army. What, then, must be done; what can be done? My poor advice would be, to meet the crisis as it deserves. The crisis, indeed, is an awful one; and it becomes you, you, the majority, who now direct the destinies of the nation—it becomes you to breast yourselves to the storm which you see rising around you.

I know of but one way in which I think this country can be saved. Abandon the idle project of conquering a foreign territory; put yourselves on the defensive; deal honestly with the people; tell them that your plans for raising money have failed; tell them, what is true, that you are on the eve of bankruptcy. and throw yourselves on their magnanimity. Honorable gentlemen may lose their offices, but they may save their country. I do not think it possible for you to get money for conquest; you may, perhaps, raise it for defence. Having provided the money for supporting your army, use the means which the Constitution has put into your hands; raise men by voluntary enlistment; and, in cases of emergency, "call out the militia to repel invasion," and engage to pay them when you are able. It is not to be believed that the people of this country, under such circumstances, could be subjugated; but if you will send your regular armies to Canada, and leave the States defenceless, and refuse to pay the militia when called out by their proper officers, I will not answer for the result. The inevitable consequence of this course is, that the States must and will take care of themselves;

and they will preserve the resources of the States for the defence of the States. If you will pursue the plan which I have just suggested, the people, in defence of their families, their homes, and their institutions, will rally to the standard of their country. In such a conflict you may rely on their patriotism and their zeal; they will fulfil every duty with cheerfulness and alacrity. Do not force them into your ranks for conquest. If you require them for defence, they will be found where danger presses and where glory calls; and they will bring with them that heroic courage which will cover you with glory in the day of battle; they will bring with them that elevated sentiment which raises the common man to the hero, and that holy enthusiasm which makes an army irresistible. I cannot persuade myself that 'conscription is necessary for the defence of the country.

Nor is the force contemplated to be raised by it intended for defence. I see no provision in any of the bills, which goes to limit its application to the defence of the country; and if a proposition should be made so to limit it, I make no doubt it would share the fate of a similar attempt, on a former occasion—it would be instantly rejected, and that too without discussion. As the plans submitted to us contain no provision of this kind, we must look elsewhere for the objects to which this army is to be applied. Hitherto the defence of the country has not been the leading object of Administration: the war has been conducted as a war of conquest and ambition. Yes, sir, the efficient part of the Army was tilting in Canada, while the affrighted inhabitants in this vicinity, with the President at their head, were seeking refuge by the light which ascended from the hill of your Capitol! The proclamation of Hull avowed the intention of conquest. He said he came to give the inhabitants of Canada "the blessings of civil and religious liberty." The redoubted Alexander Smyth (a General by commission) proclaimed that he was about to enter a territory, which, at no distant period, would form a part of the United States. In this House, the conquest of Canada has been again and again distinctly urged as an object of the war. A gentleman from Tennessee, not now a member of the House, (Mr. GRUNDY,) and the gentleman from Pennsylvania, (Mr. INGERSOLL,) have both favored us with arguments on that subject, and I believe this has been a favorite plan on the war-side of the House. The Administration must, I think, be considered as committed by the proclamations of their Generals and the opinions of their friends.

But the letter of the Secretary of War ends all doubt on this subject. He proposes to bring into the field, for the next campaign, not less than one hundred thousand regular troops. Are these for the defence of the country? Are the services of the militia and volunteers to be dispensed with? No, sir; this force—the one hundred thousand regular troops—is to be "aided, in extraordinary exigencies, by volunteers and militia." And, again, he expressly says, that although the bur-

dens of the militia may be in some cases lightened, yet, "reliance must still be placed on them for important aids, especially in cases of sudden invasion." Thus, you see, resort is still to be had to the militia, in the only case in which you have a right to their services. You have no power over the militia, except in the cases specified; and the exigency must exist, or the right to call out the militia does not exist. Trifling, indeed, will be the relief which the militia can expect from the plan of the Secretary. According to his views, and in his own words, "it will not be sufficient to repel the predatory and desolating incursions" of the enemy. "We must not be contented with defending ourselves." His object can only be obtained "by pushing the war into Canada."

Now, sir, let us not be told that this conscription is intended for the *defence* of the nation. I had hoped that the Administration would have grown wiser by experience, and that this project would have been abandoned by common consent. The war against the provinces of Canada is a war without object, for it is not worth the conquest; it is at the present time a war without hope, for you cannot take it. I would as soon attempt literally "to pluck bright honor from the pale-faced moon," as to attempt the conquest of Canada in the present state of the country, and under the auspices of this Administration.

Sir, the conquest of Canada must be a hopeless project under the direction of this Administration: they are utterly incompetent. On a former occasion, when I so sensibly felt the indulgence of this House, I undertook to examine the two first campaigns, and thought I found evidence for a thorough conviction that their claim to military talent was unfounded. My opinion, at that time, was put upon the record; and I have seen no reason to alter that opinion, in the history of the last campaign.

The military operations in the South, I believe, have been generally considered as successful. I have not a sufficient knowledge of that country to venture upon an examination of them. I cannot, however, in this place, omit to express my admiration and respect for Colonel Pearson, of North Carolina, who conducted the expedition against the Indians, in a manner not less creditable to his military talents than to the excellence of his heart. The youthful soldier will look to this accomplished officer as a pattern well worthy of imitation; and the philanthropist will point to the scene of his glory, on the Alabama, not only to disprove the assertion that wars against Indians must be conducted on the principle of extermination, but also to discourage the atrocious conduct, which we have sometimes witnessed, in carrying that principle into effect.

My local situation has led me to observe the Northern campaign with some attention; and I feel justified in saying, it will not stand the test of military criticism. I pass over the want of attention to the supplies so necessary to the comforts of an army, nor will I dwell upon the shameful waste and prodigality, so apparent to every one in the vicinity of our camps, and the neglect to provide the necessary means of transportation, in all the marches and counter-marches which we have witnessed in that quarter. Time would fail me to notice the many departures from military rules, in other minor arrangements for the campaign. I pass over all these, and come to examine the operations on the Niagara River, and at Lake Champlain. These, I believe, are considered by the friends of Administration as affording ample evidence of a just claim to military talent.

In looking at the events of the war on the Northern frontier, I find cause to bestow almost unbounded praise on the officers who conducted and the brave men who executed the enterprises; but I can see little reason to admit the claim of Administration to prudence or forecast. Under the auspices of General Brown, the military character of the people has been retrieved, and the tone of the Army raised to no common pitch. I feel the full weight of the services of that General and his associates, and have not been backward in expressing these feelings. But no practical good has resulted from the operations there, except in raising the character of the Army. The officers and men employed on this service are not to blame for it, they did everything which men could do, with their means and under their circumstances. Acquitting the officers and the men, I must hold the Administration responsible for not furnishing the means necessary to effect the object contemplated. The means furnished were utterly disproportioned to the end. The object of General Brown was to seize the post of the enemy at Burlington Heights, and to press from thence to Kingston. Can any one say, that the means furnished were competent to either of these objects? No, sir. The first battle on the Niagara, in which our troops were successful, and where General Scott covered himself with glory —that battle settled the fate of the campaign. General Brown, from that instant, knew that his purpose of penetrating into Canada was frustrated; offensive operations, with a view to the possession of the country, were abandoned. Our army, as was right, fell back, and all the subsequent battles were fought, not in the expectation of driving the enemy from the peninsula, but, on the mere *point of honor,* whether our forces should or should not re-cross the Niagara river. This is apparent to every man who has attended to that campaign. In all the enterprises new lustre was added to our arms; in every instance we claimed the victory, and yet we did not attempt to penetrate into the country. The prudence of the General foresaw that such an attempt would have been idle and ruinous. He gained the *point of honor;* he retained his post till the end of the campaign, and the army has since gone into Winter quarters on this side of the Niagara. This, I believe, is a fair examination of that campaign. The Administration deserve no credit, but are justly censurable for the part they have acted.

One other fact ought to be noticed. The two

most important military posts which we had on the Western waters are Michilimackinac and Niagara. Both these are in the hands of the enemy, and held in proud defiance. Administration did set on foot an expedition to recover Michilimackinac, but, *according to custom,* the necessary means were not afforded, and the enterprise failed. As to Fort Niagara, it was not even attempted. And both these important posts yet remain in the possession of the enemy, the monuments of the folly and imbecility of our National Councils.

Let us now look towards Lake Champlain, and notice the events of the war in that quarter. We all remember, that, when our army made their escape across the St. Lawrence, about a year ago, they took post at French Mills, with a view to preserve their boats, and other necessary means, preparatory to a descent on Montreal. I well remember, too, that we were consoled for the loss and disgrace of the campaign, which had just closed, by assurances that our army should positively take Montreal in the Spring, before the enemy could be reinforced from beyond the Atlantic. Scarcely had the remnant of our gallant troops begun to be comfortable in their quarters at French Mills, before they were ordered to strike their tents. The boats were burnt; provisions and all the supplies usually found in a camp were ordered to be destroyed, for fear they might fall into the hands of the enemy; and so precipitate was the retreat, that very large quantities of military stores did actually fall into the hands of the British, who remained in quiet possession of the post which our army had abandoned, and leisurely removed everything which they considered of value. Under these circumstances, however, comforters were found, who had no doubt that it was all right to concentrate our forces, and that we should see wonders in the Spring. Well, the Spring at length arrived, and with it the expectation of a rich harvest of glory. The campaign opened with an attack on La Cole Mill. We know the result. The officer who conducted it is now once again on trial.

In the latter stages of our operations on Lake Champlain, with pleasure and with pride we can view the gallantry and good conduct of officers and men, both on the water and the land. And here—more fortunate than on the Niagara—we can look, with gratitude, to the practical good resulting from these services. But, the Administration deserves the severest censure. The officers at the head of both our naval and land forces, and their brave associates, have all deserved well of their country. The name of *Macdonough* shall live forever. The opportunity presented; on that instant—

" He snatch'd, to grace Columbia's infant name,
" Old Neptune's trident and Old England's fame."

I certainly do not intend to praise him; he is above all praise. The conduct of General Macomb deserved what it has received—the admiration and gratitude of his country. I scarcely know how to express my admiration of that daring gallantry which determined him to maintain his post against the fearful odds of the enemy. The skill and promptness with which the defences of the camp were formed, and the judicious distribution of the troops, all reflect the highest honor on that General. The situation of General Macomb was more critical and hazardous than that of any other officer during the war. More cannot be said in his favor, than to say his conduct was exactly the reverse of what was witnessed in the base, inglorious surrender of this city.

But how stands the conduct of the Administration? At the opening of the campaign, their object was to take Montreal; and the opinion of their friends excited a pretty general expectation of success. But, after the attempt on La Cole Mill, all reasonable hope of seizing Montreal appears to have vanished. No further demonstrations were made on Montreal; and the enemy, in turn, began to think of invading us. His project, to be sure, was gigantic, but if he had met with no more resistance than he did in this District, it might have been accomplished. What was the object of the enemy?

According to Governor Tompkins, it was "to 'penetrate with his Northern army by the waters 'of Lake Champlain and the Hudson; and by a 'simultaneous attack with his maritime force on 'New York, to form a junction to sever the com- 'munication of the States." In this view of the object of the enemy, it is manifest that the position of our army at Plattsburg was infinitely more important than that at Fort Erie. And what did this wise Administration do? Did they strengthen the post at Plattsburg? Did they collect all their disposable force and throw in relief? Exactly the reverse. At the very instant that Sir George Prevost was preparing to execute this plan, General Izard was ordered to withdraw the main body of the army, and General Macomb was left at Plattsburg, with scarce fifteen hundred regular troops to oppose fourteen thousand British veterans, led on by the Commander-in-Chief and all his ablest Generals. The folly of this arrangement is the more apparent, when it is remembered that General Brown was fighting merely for the point of honor. And besides, the order for General Izard to join the army on the Niagara was given at such an advanced stage of the season, that he did not reach there till the time for military operations had passed by. The campaign closed about the time General Izard arrived on the Niagara—the bird had flown. General Drummond went into Winter quarters at Kingston; and our troops have wisely blown up Fort Erie, and abandoned the Canada side of the Niagara. And all this took place at the very instant when every suggestion of prudence pointed directly to Plattsburg, as much the most important post.

Examine this subject, and you will see folly and infatuation written on every part of it. Instead of ordering General Izard to join General Brown, common sense required that General Brown should have been directed to join General Izard. Sound policy loudly declared against the removal of the army from Plattsburg; but, if they were removed at all, they should have remained at Sackett's Harbor, which they passed on their way to Niagara. This, sir, cannot be doubted; for General Izard had scarcely left the Harbor—the rations which he took from thence were scarcely expended—before Sackett's Harbor was menaced, and the militia of the country called out *en masse* to defend it; and after a severe tour of duty, on bad rations, they have returned to their homes without pay. And yet this Administration is well suited to manage the affairs of this nation!

As to the part the Administration took on the Niagara frontier, I think I have shown they deserved but little credit; and the view just given of their management on Lake Champlain must forever silence their claim to military skill. The honor and glory is due to those who conducted the enterprises; certainly not to those who planned the expeditions, and failed to provide the means necessary to carry them into effect. Too much cannot be said of the officers. Posterity will do justice to General Brown. The brow of General Scott is crowned with unfading laurels. And the historian, who shall speak of the situation and conduct of General Macomb at Plattsburg, will proudly mark the resemblance it bears to that of Leonidas at the straights of Thermopylæ. While the American people will fondly gaze at Macdonough by the side of Perry, the twin stars in the galaxy of our naval heroes, they will not fail to pronounce that the conduct of the Administration has been marked by folly and improvidence.

Depend upon it, sir, Canada is not to be taken by the present men in power. Under the circumstances of the country the project is hopeless. The people of this country, however ready and able to defend their firesides and their institutions, are opposed to the conquest of Canada. Your army is frittered to nothing—your Treasury exhibits a "beggarly account of empty boxes;" yet this Administration, with a perfect knowledge of the facts—with hearts yet panting from the affrighted plains of Bladensburg—in full view of the ruins of the Capitol—with the flames of the palace still crackling in their ears—will posterity believe it? That, under such circumstances, this Administration sat down quietly and philosophically to devise a plan for the conquest of Canada. Well may it be said, "*Quos Deus vult perdere, prius dementat.*" Did I not know that this Administration was composed of philosophers, I would swear to you, Mr. Chairman, they were mad, stark staring mad, and entitled to all the hellebore in Anticyra. I can view this project of conquering Canada, under present circumstances, in no other light than as the last desperate effort of expiring madness.

But Canada must be conquered, and by an army of American conscripts. The conquest of a neighboring province has frequently been followed by the loss of the liberties of the conquering nation. But we are called upon to surrender our liberties as preliminary to conquest. The army of conscripts, on its way to Canada, must, at every step, trample on the Constitution of the country. This is worse than was predicted. Experience, history, and the nature of man, had taught us to believe that the victorious army, which was to "dictate the terms of peace at Quebec, or at Halifax," might, on its return, be dangerous to the liberties of this country. But few indeed could have believed that our rulers would have required us to sacrifice the Constitution in order to raise an army for such a conquest. The freedom of other nations has fallen by the ambition of tyrants, at the head of conquering armies. But we are called to give up our's—to whom? Our fate is not less hard than that of other nations, but is to be much more humiliating and inglorious. Cæsar, returning from Gaul, at the head of his victorious cohorts, trampled on the laws of his country, passed the Rubicon, and marched to Rome. It was not until Cromwell had possessed himself of his infatuated army that he dared to take the Kingdom of Great Britain under his holy protection. And it was from the plains of Italy that Bonaparte brought his witnesses to the Crown of the ancient Kings of France. But we are called upon to surrender all that is sacred and dear to freemen—to whom? Not to some haughty chieftain, with his vassals at his heels; not to a dashing soldier of fortune, the glory of whose exploits might shed some lustre on our chains—but to whom? To Knights of the Spur, whose horses are scarce yet groomed from the races at Bladensburg. If the people of this country are prepared to receive chains from masters like these, I will only say they richly deserve such masters and such chains.

Gentlemen have often intimated, that the object of the minority was power and place rather than the good of the country. To that charge I plead not guilty. I am not competent to office; and if I had the talent, I have not the disposition to accept any. I look to the day which shall free me from my public duties here as one of the happiest of my life. As to my friends, I must admit they are ambitious; but their ambition seeks to save the country, not to rule it. We have a stake in this community equal to other gentlemen. To what should we be unfaithful? To that Constitution which we have sworn to support? To that land which gave us birth? Where are our families, our altars, and our firesides? Where are the bones of our children and the ashes of our ancestors? It is not to be believed that these duties and these privileges are to be abandoned for any motive of personal ambition.

If the object was merely to strip you of your robes of office, depend upon it my friends would not endeavor to arrest you in your present career. Be warned by experience. Look at the fate of the most remarkable man of this or any other time; he fell from the pinnacle of ambition, and by conscription. Mark the progress of this prodigy of the age—this wonder of the world! See him with daring hand seize the Crown which had lately fallen from the head of the amiable and unfortunate Louis. See him at the zenith of his glory—observe this Colossus, with one foot on Portugal and with the other planted on the territory of the Czars—with one hand controlling the destinies of the Baltic, and with the other pointing to his dependents on the Eastern verge of continental Europe. Mark the contrast! "How are the mighty fallen!" Where and what is he? A State prisoner in the Island of Elba—a pensioner on the bounty of the Bourbons.

     "The desolator, desolate,
     "The victor overthrown;
     "The arbiter of others' fate,
     "A suppliant for his own."

Take warning by this example. Bonaparte split on this rock of conscription; if you travel the same road you must share the same destiny. The needle by which you have directed your political course has been for some time trembling in the gale of experiments; it seems now to be settled, and points with unerring polarity to ruin.

There is another view of this subject which honorable gentlemen ought well to consider. The tendency of your whole system is to destroy the bond of union which connects us together. Let me not be charged with any wish to separate the States; I disclaim it. I have cherished the union of these States with an ardor, with an enthusiasm, not inferior to any other gentleman in or out of this House. But all your measures seem to point to separation. The defence of the States has not been a leading object of this war. The States, however, must be defended; if you will not protect them, if you refuse to pay the expense necessarily incurred for that object, they will take care of themselves. The natural consequence is, the States will preserve their own resources for their own defence; and the practical result will be a dissolution of the Union.

If you resort to conscription you will have a commentary upon it written in the blood of this country. I beg gentlemen to remember the days when York and Lancaster drew forth their battles. They appear to me to be fast returning. Serious discontents already exist in many parts of the United States. Causes already exist which are claimed to justify a dissolution of the Union; and, rather than submit to a military conscription, there are States who may consider themselves bound by duty and interest to withdraw from this Confederacy. You will say they have not justifiable cause. I entreat you not to afford them a plausible pretext. I am no alarmist; nor is this view of the subject taken for any purpose of threat or intimidation. I give it as my opinion, and you will, I dare say, receive it for as much as it is worth. I have carefully examined this conscription question, with all that seriousness and attention required by the solemnity of the occasion; I have exercised that small measure of talent which it has pleased the Almighty to bestow upon me, and I have arrived at this conclusion: the plan of conscription violates the Constitution; it trenches on the rights of the States, and takes from them their "necessary security;" it destroys all claim to personal freedom; it will poison all the comforts of this people. In this belief I can have no hesitation to say, that I think it will be resisted, and that it ought to be resisted.

Sir, I speak not particularly of this bill immediately before your committee—I allude to the conscription system as proposed by the Secretary of War. To use the language of a former member of this House, (Mr. Edward Livingston, of New York, on the alien bill in 1798,) who was a distinguished leader of the present majority, I ask, whether the people of this country are "base ' enough to be prepared for this? No, sir, they ' will, I repeat it, they will resist this tyrannic ' system. The people will oppose—the States ' will not submit to its operation—they ought not ' to acquiesce, and I pray to God they never may."

Mr. Chairman, the view I have taken of our public affairs has filled me with gloom and despondency. Life and all its enjoyments are with me much diminished in value. The plot of this political drama has been for some thickening; the catastrophe is at hand. We live in an age of wonders. It has been our lot to witness some of the most remarkable events which have ever taken place in the moral, political, or physical world. In common with others I have marked the signs of the times, and look to their development with the most awful forebodings. It is perhaps possible that this country may escape destruction; I hope it may. But when I see ruin and desolation staring us in the face, although I am not given to superstition, I cannot but remember that I have seen comets blaze, and the sun struggle under a total eclipse. I hope, sir, almost against all hope, that the freedom of our institutions may be preserved; but when I see this system of conscription about to be forced upon us, although I can scarcely bring myself to believe in omens, yet I feel an unusual emotion at the recollection that the Goddess of Liberty was burnt up in your Capitol.

If this military conscription becomes the law of the land, the freedom of this country is destroyed, and the union of the States is gone for ever!

When Mr. M. had concluded, the Committee rose, and had leave to sit again.

FRIDAY, December 9.

The amendments proposed by the Senate to the bill to provide additional revenues for defraying the expenses of the Government and maintaining the public credit, by laying duties on spirits distilled within the United States, and by amending the act laying duties on licenses to distillers of spirituous liquors," were read, and referred to the Committee of Ways and Means.

A message from the Senate informed the House that the Senate have passed a bill "to incorporate the subscribers to the Bank of the United States of America;" in which they desire the concurrence of this House.

Mr. EPPES, of Virginia, from the Committee of Ways and Means, reported a bill "to provide additional revenue for defraying the expenses of the Government and maintaining the public credit, by laying duties on various goods, wares and merchandise manufactured within the United States"—which bill was twice read and committed.

Mr. EPPES, also reported a bill "to provide additional revenue for defraying the expenses of the Government and maintaining the public credit, by laying duties on household furniture, on horses kept exclusively for the saddle or carriage, and on gold and silver watches."

The bill from the Senate for the relief of John C. Hurlburt, was twice read and committed.

MILITIA DRAUGHTS.

The House again resolved itself into a Committee of the Whole, on the bill authorizing the President of the United States to call into service 80,430 militia, for the defence of the frontiers of the United States.

The motion to strike out the first section being yet under consideration—

Mr. BARNETT, of Georgia, and Mr. RHEA, of Tennessee, opposed the motion to strike out.

Mr. WEBSTER, of New Hampshire, spoke in favor of the motion.

Mr. DUVALL, of Kentucky, spoke as follows:

Mr. Chairman: My desire to address the Committee on the present bill, does not arise from the hope of either fame or distinction. These can only belong to great talents and distinguished action. But, sir, I am impelled by my judgment and duty to protest against the opinions and doctrines which have been advanced by the honorable gentleman from New York, (Mr. MILLER,) on the various subjects which he has brought before this Committee—opinions and objections against the powers of Congress, which, if they unfortunately should be brought into practice, would overturn every principle of civil liberty, destroy all subordination and union, and rend into pieces the Constitution of the country. Before I proceed to examine the arguments of the gentleman from New York, (Mr. MILLER,) permit me to say, I am opposed to striking out any part of this bill, unless I can be persuaded, in an hour of alarm and peril, to surrender the rights and liberties of the nation. The provisions contained in this bill are not only proper, but absolutely necessary. The rejection of the measure would be to disarm the nation, and increase the calamities of war. I had hoped that, as the motion of the honorable gentleman from Virginia (Mr. EPPES) had prevailed, to reduce the term of militia service from two years to one, that all further objections on the part of the Opposition would vanish. I did not long remain in this error. All the clamor of party has been roused by this measure, and, by gentlemen in the opposition, is loudly denounced as odious, tyrannical, and unconstitutional. Sir, I had hoped that the stormy passions of party were in a great measure allayed by the perilous situation of the country. Opposed to a powerful and ambitious enemy, who is collecting all the deluge of war to pour on this devoted land, with a Treasury exhausted, and a gallant army reduced in numbers but not in spirit, I, indeed, had hoped that gentlemen in the opposition (under these circumstances) would have stood forward to defend their soil and sovereignty. In this hope I have not altogether been disappointed. Some gentlemen of high and distinguished talents, who now stand at the head of the Federal party, have declared their determination to vote the supplies for the Government, and, on several occasions, have nobly triumphed over their feelings, and placed themselves on American ground. This is the duty of every American; they owe it to themselves and their country. I ask not gentlemen to sacrifice their principles. Surely, when their aid is demanded to preserve our rights, let them expose the errors of the Administration; let them expose the policy which has been pursued by the dominant party; let them endeavor to convince the people that their confidence has been misplaced and abused; nay, let them exert all their powers to change the rulers of the nation, and call other men and measures into action. But, in the name of our common country, I call on them to prepare to meet an enemy as implacable as he is powerful. The member from New York (Mr. Miller) commenced his arguments against this bill, by gravely informing the Committee that he not only objected to this, but to all the military plans which had been offered, because, he says, they are coercive. Will the gentleman be so obliging as to inform us how long it has been since he made this important discovery? That the civil, criminal, and military laws of this country should be coercive on its citizens, is surely tyrannical. But, until the learned gentleman can point out to me a country whose laws have no penalties, and whose military code is not coercive, I must be permitted to believe this strange and visionary notion has been only drawn from Plato's ideal republic. Indeed, sir, this argument is an excellent specimen of the lengthy, and learned, and elaborate speech delivered by the gentleman on this subject; the whole of which was no doubt the offspring of much painful reflection and deep research. It was the most logical, historical, and tragical discourse, that ever was delivered in a legislative body. I was at a loss to determine, whether most to admire his powers as an historian, his clearness as a logician, or the refined excellence of his poetic fancy. It is rare that one individual excels in more than one science or accomplishment, but the honorable gentleman from New York is surely an exception. I feel half inclined to complain of the brilliancy of his fancy, for it threw such a dazzling flood of light around his subject and arguments, that I must own my mind was often so bewildered as not to comprehend all his nice and excellent deductions; but this was certainly my fault, or rather my misfortune, for the eye of real genius is always clearest and brightest in the blaze of science.

The Committee will pardon this digression; it was justly due to the gentleman. This bill has been called conscription, for the purpose of rendering it odious to the people. It is not the first

time that a measure has been denounced by some peculiar name, in order to produce opposition, or to defeat its object. Such a shallow artifice cannot deceive any but those who are willing to be deluded. The gentleman from New York (Mr. Miller) read to the Committee some pages of most pathetic declamation on the distressing scenes which conscription had produced in France; but he forgot to show the coincidence between the bill now before us and the conscription code of France. I say there is no coincidence; no, not even in the classification, and still less in any other feature. The conscription laws of France were first introduced by their Directory, and are in strict imitation of the Roman discipline, which compelled every citizen to become a soldier. They were adopted for the purpose of aggrandizement and conquest. All Frenchmen were classed between the ages of twenty and twenty-five only; in this particular it was oppressive and unjust. The conscripts were often treated with the utmost cruelty, and if they deserted their parents were made responsible for their appearance, or their fortunes paid an exorbitant fine. All this, too, was done to carry on foreign wars without their consent, to gratify an ambitious tyrant. The people of France were controlled by the iron rod of a military despot, who was only governed by his interest and glory. They made no laws—their voice was not heard in their councils. Day after day, and year after year, were they dragged unwilling victims to fight the wars of their master in every part of their continent. The young men saw no termination to their military toils but in the arms of death; and if they survived the period assigned for military service, they were but seldom rewarded for the scars which they bore, while unusual hardships and constant exposure entailed upon them poverty and premature old age. No wonder can then be excited when we are told that the people of France dreaded and execrated conscription.

Let us now examine this American bill, and compare it with the conscription of France. First, all the free male population of the United States, over the age of eighteen and under forty-five, are bound to render military service whenever they are legally draughted. The section which permits a class to exonerate itself by furnishing one recruit for the regular army, so far from being objectionable, is, in fact, an advantage to the whole body of militia. This difference, and the extension of the term of service six months longer than usual, are the only changes in the militia laws now in operation.

If this is conscription, it was practised during our Revolution. It has been the invariable practice during the present war, and must continue so long as we are governed by the Constitution. It is nothing more than the people of these States expected, when they instructed their Representatives in Congress to declare war with Great Britain. If this be called conscription by the Opposition, it is equally so to bring the militia into the field for six or three months; nay, even for a single day. But the member from New York, (Mr. MILLER,) and his friends, feeling that this argument was too weak to support them even for a moment, turned to the Constitution, and endeavored to base their reasonings on its sacred principles. Sir, in this they have failed, and their attempt has only more clearly exposed the error of their doctrines. The militia belong to the States, it is urged, and Congress have no right to call them into service, for they may be wanted for State defence.

I answer—the General Government is bound to provide for the weal and protection of every State in the Union. That the Constitution gives to Congress the power to provide for organizing, arming, and disciplining the militia, and for governing such part of them as may be employed in the service of the United States. That it also invests Congress with power to call forth the militia to execute the laws of the Union, suppress insurrections, and repel invasions. Will it be denied that our country is now invaded? No, this must be admitted by the most incredulous. Yet, possessing these powers, and under these circumstances, we are told that this bill is unconstitutional. I ask gentlemen if the very compact which they guard with so much watchfulness, does not recognise the militia as the bulwark of our liberties? And yet they say, in effect, that Congress cannot command their services. Before my mind can assent to this strange contradiction, and extraordinary opinion, gentlemen must prove to me that it is unconstitutional to call the militia into service for six or three months, or even for a day; for their reasons will apply as strong in every instance I have mentioned, as they can against this bill.

The member from New York (Mr. MILLER) with great emotion has declared that, were he to vote for this bill, he should disgrace the ashes of his fathers, that it violates the rights of the people, who ought to be suffered quietly to enjoy their own firesides. I will tell the gentleman that he can never disgrace the ashes of his fathers by defending his country; they have given to him an example that should awaken all his pride to emulate; they never refused to defend the soil and independence which their noble valor has since given to their posterity; could their pure and generous spirits witness these scenes, and hear such sentiments, they would weep angel tears over the degeneracy and ingratitude of their sons. But we should enjoy our firesides! What enjoyment, let me inquire, is to be found in this enviable situation, when war is striding over the people, breathing destruction on our borders? Can the member from New York (Mr. MILLER) feel, in times such as these, the quiet and enjoyment of which he speaks? No, in the interest which he has taken in our various campaigns, in the minute recital of our misfortunes, in the painful and melancholy feelings which he has illustrated by such frequent quotations of the poetic language of the great dramatist, it is disclosed that he reposes not in these times in quiet content by his own fireside; let us not talk of these enjoyments in the strife of war—this theme the American will reserve for the halcyon days of peace.

But the member from New York (Mr. MILLER) has said, that this nation can only be saved by reviving its credit, and recruiting its armies; yet he declares that his assent shall not be given to this end, although he has told us this, and this only, can save the nation. Is it possible that the honorable member is so lost to duty and love of country, that, under no situation in which he may be placed, will he give his aid to provide men or money for defence?

[Here Mr. MILLER rose, and said he was misunderstood by the gentleman from Kentucky; that he had said he would not give any supplies to the Government for the conquest of Canada; but that if our army was withdrawn from that country, and the project of conquest relinquished, he would go as far as any gentleman to raise men and money for defence.]

Mr. DUVALL regretted he had misunderstood the gentleman; that it was neither his object or inclination to misstate his arguments, and no gentleman would accuse him of so mean a subterfuge.

It was but the other day that the member from New York (Mr. MILLER) declared on this floor, that the Government had abandoned every object for which this war was commenced. I take him at his word, and the supposed conquest of Canada cannot now be an obstacle; but, to remove his fear of conquest, let me offer him proof which is undeniable, to dissipate the inquietude which he still feels on this subject. I mean the instructions given to our Ministers, and the offer to make peace on their part with the British commissioners, on terms of which they have no right to complain. How, then, can it be seriously urged that this is a war of conquest? Even the gentleman himself has said, that all the objects for which this war was declared are now abandoned. In one breath we are told it would be dangerous to the liberties of the people to place at the disposal, and under the control of the men in power, a great military force; in the next moment the same gentleman declares that the Administration have neither talents nor capacity to carry on the war; and that such is their imbecility, that were they to furnish the supplies they would be profusely and ineffectually expended. I leave such absurd contradictions to be reconciled by those who claim them as just and unanswerable arguments.

But, said the gentleman, (Mr. MILLER,) beware how you trample on the rights of your citizens, for remember justice never sleeps; I lament that his conduct has not proved the truth of his remark. Justice among the great body of the people I trust will never sleep, but with some in the opposition she even now slumbers unto death. Justice expired with the gentleman and some of his friends in the opposition, when they declared in this Hall, and in the face of the whole nation, that this war is wicked and unjust.

That the nation commenced the war before they were prepared, was, and is yet, my opinion. But that we had not ample cause to justify our resort to arms, I do deny. Was it wicked and unjust to resist the enemy in their illegal decrees and blockades? Was it wicked and unjust to resist the capture and confiscation of our vessels and cargoes? Was it wicked and unjust to resist the impressment of our seamen? If none of these contain the wickedness and injustice of which gentlemen complain, I ask in what does it exist? Let gentlemen no longer refuse their assistance; let them not sit calmly by and see the farms of their citizens pillaged, their habitations wrapped in flames; and when the voice of maddening distress shall assail them with petitions, coldly answer, we will not aid or protect you, for this war is wicked and unjust. When our territory is invaded by your enemy, and he bids defiance to your arms; when your citizens, no longer able to resist their iniquitous and rapacious demands, call on you for protection, which you have solemnly sworn under our Constitution to give, will you violate the high obligation, and answer, it cannot be given, for this war is wicked and unjust? Have you not heard the cries of distress arising from ruffian profanation? Have you not marked the spots where your cities and hamlets once stood, whose ashes have been slaked with the blood of your citizens? and, yet, are you calm and undisturbed, refusing to redress their sufferings, or to aid in the punishment of the incendiary myrmidons who have violated your people, because you say this war is wicked and unjust?

In vain may the citizens of your Indian frontier recite their sad and dreadful sufferings. The exterminating warfare of a merciless foe, whose joy in blood rises to madness, is suffered, with your consent, to rage with death and desolation on your borders. The rude children of the brave and daring hunter, and the family of the unoffending and peaceable emigrant, sink alike beneath the arm of their savage foe. Do they desire your protection? Yes; but you sternly bid them die, because you still say that this war is wicked and unjust.

I would ask, from what does this apathy, on the part of many in the opposition originate? I fear, from local distinctions and invidious remarks, which, with regret and pain, I have so often heard thrown out in the warmth of discussion. There is a class of politicians in this country who have, for years, with the most unwearied industry and artifice, endeavored to make the Eastern and Northern sections of this Union believe that the Southern and Western States are jealous of their increasing wealth and commercial importance. This opinion has been supported and encouraged by demagogues, for base and perfidious purposes. The good sense of the nation (it is the hope of every American) will soon correct so fatal an opinion. The happiness and interest of all the States are linked together by every tie that can bind society—speaking the same same language, living under the same general laws, connected by marriage, blood, and friendship, and worshipping the same great benevolent Being—how can stronger connexion exist? Is interest

more binding? Be it so. The North and East are commercial; the South and the West are engaged in agriculture; if commerce is impeded or suspended, the ships of our merchants are idle and decaying; the produce of the South and West remain on the planter's or farmer's hands, dead, wasting, and unproductive, or becomes spoiled, unfit for market, and is wholly lost. Nature intended that the Northern and Eastern States should produce the daring and enterprising mariners of the Union; to make them so, she has given to them fine bays, harbors, and rivers; she has placed the fisheries in their neighborhood as a nursery for their seamen; their climate is cold, and soil unsuited to the various productions of raw material necessary for their factories, which are found in abundance in the South and West. New England will not only possess the carrying trade of the South and West, but will, from her great and increasing population, necessarily become their manufacturer. All this is so obvious and certain, that the demagogues of either party cannot long deceive the people, by crying out that their interests are separate and distinct. Away, then, with invidious sectional distinctions; let us speak of ourselves as a nation, and not as separate hordes of wrangling and jealous savages. The bold and enterprising mariner of the North may proudly rank with the first in the nation. Yes, sir, these are the men who belong to your Navy, who have acquired more glory in two years for themselves and country, than ever England could boast in half a century; a gem which shall shine with undiminished splendor down the long annals of time. This nation should never, in peace, forget that a Navy is her right arm in war.

It was with pleasure I listened to the gentleman from New York while he praised the valor of our land and naval commanders, and I could not but deem it strange that he, who seemed so animated at his own recital of their gallant deeds, should yet refuse to follow their example in defending his country.

I did not hope to follow the gentleman from New York through all the various remarks which he pressed into this discussion; nor can I follow him in the sublime poetic effusions and numberless quotations from celebrated authors. Indeed, sir, it seemed to me that the gentleman's speech was not made for the present bill, but for the bill which has been reported to this House by the honorable chairman (Mr. TROUP) of the Military Committee; but, as it is probable it will not be acted on, the honorable member from New York has transferred his objection from that to the bill from the Senate. But nothing is impossible to great genius; no subject is too high or too low to escape its subtile attention. It delights to bring objects and things, radically different, together; and, like electricity, its course is brilliant, wild, and eccentric. Hence, we may account for the introduction of Governor Tompkins and his charger by the honorable member, to this Committee, caparisoned in all the pomp of war; and also for the rapid flight which he instantly took from the back of this war horse, as he said, "to pluck bright honor from the pale-faced moon," where, for the present, I leave the gentleman.

The attention of the Committee shall not be claimed much longer by me, for I throw by many remarks, which have been made in the course of debate, in order to call your reflections to a subject that has been too often agitated to escape reply. I mean the doctrine of rebellion, which has been trumpeted in our ears by more than one member of this body. It is time that gentlemen in the Opposition should allay the fury of passion by the exercise of reason and calm inquiry. Can one individual in this body be found who will advocate principles destructive of the happiness and Constitution of his country? Yes, this House has heard discord and rebellion encouraged and avowed from more than one quarter. The member from New York (Mr. MILLER) has declared that this militia system, or, as he terms it, *conscription*, will not be submitted to by the people; that they ought to resist such oppression, such infringements of their rights, and he hoped they would resist.

[Here Mr. MILLER rose to explain, and said that the language he had used, were the words of Mr. Livingston, a Democrat, and were delivered in a speech when he was opposed to Mr. Adams's Administration, and he (Mr. M.) now adopted them as his own.]

Mr. DUVALL said, he had so understood the gentleman, and although he claimed the benefit of the example introduced, it was not on that account the less mischievous and pernicious; that demagogues belonged to all parties, and were equally to be detested and condemned. Let gentlemen who are giving tone and encouragement to rebellion, beware of the consequences; for, I tell them, they are treading over a burning volcano that may burst upon them in dreadful ruin. Do they propose to better their conditions, or the condition of their country, by such dangerous and mad contention? If so, let me drive from them far the fatal delusion. Look to the French Revolution, and learn, in time, to avoid the bloody scenes which may and will be reacted in America. How many of all the numerous and daring revolutionists of France are now in existence? Few, indeed, compared to the many who have fallen before the power of that rebellion, which owed to them its spring and creation. All France did not produce, with her millions of men, a single individual who could snatch the helm and wield the sword of the nation. Such men are rare creations of nature—five centuries will not produce such another man as the Corsican, who braved the tempest of Revolution, and rode on surges of blood to the imperial throne of France.

Beware, in time, beware, of the fate that will attend your temerity; for, believe me when I tell you, you, who create, are not the men that can control the tide of rebellion; you, first of all, shall be overwhelmed by its resistless fury. Deceive not yourselves and friends with the vain and foolish hope that you can "mount the whirlwind and direct the storm," for you will be scattered before it "like chaff before the wind of heaven."

Mr. INGERSOLL, of Pennsylvania, addressed the Chair as follows:

Mr. Chairman, it seems to be the determination of gentlemen to debate all the military, and and all the national subjects too, on the present motion. I had hoped that discussion would have been reserved for the consideration of the resolutions I laid on the table the day before yesterday, and which it was my intention to have called up the moment the present business is disposed of. I never much liked this bill. It embraces the same principles without the powerful effects of the other plan, with a greater complication of machinery. It was, originally, but a weak, diluted measure, in my opinion, and a bad substitute for the direct classification and draught into the regular armies, which I hold to be the best, and indeed the only efficient system. I had resolved, however, to vote for the bill, because I do not perceive that it may not serve as an accessory to the classification; and even, eviscerated as it has been by the success of the motion of the gentleman from Virginia, (Mr. EPPES,) to reduce the term of service from two years to one, I do not yet say that I will withhold from it my support. Something must be done.

To be insensible to the extreme importance of time at this crisis is to be insensible to the crisis itself. This is the moment for action, not declamation; and gentlemen on both sides may rest assured that their controversies are, like a sea-fight, surrounded by a mass of destructive element infinitely more to be apprehended than their own ability to injure each other—an element of destruction, which, if neglected or provoked, will swallow up both the contending parties together, while they are vainly striving which shall overthrow the other. To change the illustration, we are in conflict. sir, as it were, in a vast place of interment, where eternity yawns upon us from ten thousand mouths, and where, whichever party brings his antagonist to the earth, can achieve no more enviable victory than that of being buried altogether in the same unhonored grave. Gentlemen seem to think, sir, that their constituents sent them here with no other purpose than to pull down one Administration and supplant it with another. They tell us, with one breath, that the present Administration was forced into this war, and with the next breath, they make the Administration answerable for all its misfortunes. They denounce that Administration as the most imbecile, indigent, and despicable in the world; and yet, with all the wealth, and all the talents, they have in vain withheld their wealth, in vain exercised their talents to thrust this miserable obstacle from their course. They possess, exclusively, all the physical resources, and all the patriotic attachments of the soil of the country—the bone, marrow, sinews, and vitals of the State—and they come here to reproach Administration for not having prevented or defeated a sudden inroad upon this Capital, while a portion of their own territory has been, for six months, in the undisputed occupation of the enemy—subdued without resistance, and held without an effort to regain it. We can all recollect, Mr. Chairman, how the gentleman from New Hampshire, (Mr. WEBSTER,) in particular, demonstrated to us, about this time last year, that our war was unpopular and unjust; how he entertained us with distinctions between war offensive and war defensive; between the mercenary spirit of extra-territorial conquest and aggrandizement on the one hand, and the generous ardor of repelling invasion on the other; how he proved our inability to conquer Canada without the cordial co-operation of New England; and how speedily Canada would be overrun and subdued if his immediate fellow-citizens could be enlisted into the cause, instead of the armies—and yet, now that the war has become defensive to them; now that it has pushed itself into their plantations; now that the conqueror rings the knell of a curfew every evening over their own firesides, not a note of preparation or resistance do we hear from their mountains or their seaboard, nor any other note but that of rejoicing in the happy exchange they have made of war without trade for trade without war. Nay, sir, they are more robust than ever in opposition to the war, now that nothing is left in dispute but a canton of their own soil; and they venture to threaten us with disunion for presuming to enact a militia law, when the enemy offers us a peace we can accede to at any moment, and leave that section which shakes the rod of dismemberment over our heads to fight out the battle with Great Britain. Sir, I do not belong to that slaveholding portion of these States to which such frequent and such angry allusions are made from another quarter, and, for particular reasons, I look with a degree of reverence and a strong regard towards the East. I listen, too, with pleasure, generally, to whatever falls from the gentleman from New Hampshire, (Mr. WEBSTER,) because, however I may disapprove the doctrine, it is, for the most part, supported by argument, as to-day it was by eloquence. But it was, if I may so express it, with a very painful pleasure that I attended to his pathetic threats this morning.

Mr. Chairman, a dissolution of this Confederacy is a national misfortune, upon which I never think without great pain. The political school in which I have made my inconsiderable acquisitions, abhors and deprecates so desperate a resort. I know of but one evil more to be dreaded. But there is one, and of that one I inform the gentleman from New Hampshire. It is the deterring those States who hold a legitimate ascendency in the Government from any measure whatever, by the threat of a dismemberment as the consequence of it. Whenever this is the case, the Union is virtually dissolved. The substance is gone, and nothing remains but the shadow—a cold and melancholy shade of authority—without warmth, without life—contemptible to our enemies, and formidable only to ourselves. Minorities have their rights, and I should be one of the last to infringe upon them. But majorities have duties too, and duties to be performed at every hazard.

Sir, we have been but too long threatened with dissolution, but too often deterred from proper and Constitutional purposes by such apprehensions. The same ground was taken in the same quarter against the embargo laws. The same threats. But there was no resistance to those very severe and unpalatable acts; and I trust there will be none to this militia bill. I do not believe that there will. But whether there will or not shall have no influence upon me. If I consider the thing just, I shall vote for it and maintain it, leaving results to themselves. Is there nothing, sir, from the Potomac to the Penobscot but one vast sea of Administration? Is there no country left to embark upon? Have we no wrongs to avenge? No rights to assert? No enemy to contend with? No home to feel for? Or do gentlemen consider their country (to adopt a figure of Mr. Burke's) a *carte blanche*, on which they may scribble what they please. For my part, I rise to-day, Mr. Chairman, the advocate of no administration. I have taken the floor to assert the cause of my country against its foreign enemy: and I think the conjuncture has well nigh arrived when both Administration and Opposition may give way to nobler views than those of reviling and destroying each other. It is a fact, at once mortifying and alarming, that England is waging hostilities, not against your Union and resources, but against your divisions and prejudices. Reserving all my animosity for her, and anxious to defend our common cause, permit me cursorily to inquire whether it is really so low and so wretched as seems to be imagined. I am not disposed, I think it would be out of date at this time of day, to inquire into the wisdom of the declaration of war, which is besieged with such pertinacious and preposterous denunciation by almost every member of this House, who rises to oppose any measure now necessary for sustaining the contest in which we are involved. But this I will say, that I have no doubt, whenever the parties and passions of the moment shall be mellowed and melted down by the lapse of years and change of circumstances, that declaration will be recorded by the historian as the wisest and most fortunate act in the annals of America. I had not the honor of voting for the declaration of war—I wish I had. With a full and a keen sense of all the dangers and difficulties it has brought upon us, I would vote for it now were it again in question. Yes, sir, were we now in June, 1812, and had I the faculty to pierce the veil of futurity and discover all that has happened since, I would not hesitate. The venerable patriot whose mortal remains we lately consigned to the earth, (the Vice President, Mr. GERRY,) with the obsequies that became his services and his station, does not bequeath to his posterity a richer inheritance of public gratitude for the vote he gave for independence on the 4th of July, 1776, than will descend upon his children from any member of this Congress, who, from pure and patriotic considerations, (and I can suppose none other,) voted for the war on the 18th of June, 1812. It is true that we have experienced since then a great variety of fortunes, and that we are now arrived at a conjuncture big with portentous events. But to appreciate our situation properly, we should inquire not what it is or may be, but what it would and must have been if war had not been resorted to. What then would have been our condition? We might indeed have slumbered on through 1812 and 1813 in the protracted torpor of an ignominious peace. We might have still clung to a sorry remnant of the rags of trade. We might have remained in morbid neutrality, watching the phases of the moon in Europe. We might have witnessed those astonishing transactions there, which, crowding the business of centuries into the space of months, have overthrown the Colossus of the Continent, and bestrode his fallen carcass with that of the Colossus of the Seas. We might have hailed the ascendant star of England with a joy unmixed with apprehension, unadulterated with hostility. We might still have amused ourselves with furious factions and the war of words. Restrictive systems, and other such political polemics, would have never failed to separate us into unrelenting parties, just as we are marked off now. As to making preparation for hostilities under such circumstances, it is absurd to talk about it. And when the Spring came for our reanimation from this torpid, creeping, odious, miserable state, to what sort of vernal pleasures should we have risen up? With all the original causes of complaint existing, and aggravated, between you and England—for not one of them would have disappeared but from your demonstrations of resistance—without an officer or a soldier, a fortification or an equipment, distracted at home, despised abroad, you would have been cast upon the tender mercies and the magnanimity of Great Britain. And what has been your experience of those mercies, of that magnanimity? What claims have you beyond the Dutch, the Irish, the East Indian, or the Portuguese, to the forbearance and the fondness of your mother country? Has your Revolution left no sting? Or has your subsequent prosperity inflicted no pang? Holland, annexed to England, in return for the Dutch emancipation from the yoke of France, is the volume in which you may read your own fate. I refer gentlemen to an extract from the Leyden Gazette, lately published in our newspapers, by which it appears that not a Dutch vessel is to sail without a British license. And what right have we to be preferred to the Dutch? Instead of a question whether the Canadas should be annexed to the United States, there would have been no question as to the annexation of the United States to the Canadas. If a lady is to be found in this reprobate region worthy to be united in marriage with one of the worthies of the illustrious house of Brunswick, we should have been wedded to our *ci-devant* mother, with all the blessings of the incestuous Union. This, sir, is but a faint outline of the destiny of America, but for the attitude, the character, and the means of self-preservation, for all of which we are indebted to this war.

It is true, to be sure, that we have been consigned, almost without a thought from nations whose battles we are fighting, (particularly that one which offered its mediation) to the bloody and ferocious visitation of those modern Buccaneers, who have carried their calicoes for sale throughout the world at the point of the bayonet, plunging the bayonet into every bosom that refused to cover itself with the calico—who have wrapped the four corners of the earth in flames for a monopoly of manufactures. We could not dress but in their broadcloths. We could not eat but with their hardwares. We could not sleep but in their blankets. They had reduced us to Lord Chatham's wish. Not a hob-nail but was English. They had us effectually recolonized, without bloodshed or expense. But this did not content them. They must act the farcical tragedy which France performed with Spain. America belonged to England, in effect, as much as France belonged to Spain. But the goose must be killed that laid the golden egg. To this we demurred—we resisted. After a series of endurance and procrastination, to which I never can recur without shame and sorrow, we finally resisted. If we had begun the contest with the cause of it, it would have ended long ago, and ended to our honor. But we deferred it till the eve of a fundamental revolution of things in Europe, which, instead of turning European politics to our account, has left us England single-handed on our hands. We have accordingly suffered all that the combination of British power and British perfidy could inflict; no inconsiderable matter, sir—for British power, for the purposes of distant maritime aggression, is the most formidable in the world; and I defy all history, ancient as well as modern, sacred and profane, for parallels with British perfidy. We have endured invasion, prosecuted avowedly in defiance of the laws of civilized warfare. After sacking our Capital, the enemy, for the first time, I believe, that Christendom ever witnessed such an act, has proclaimed his purpose to ravage and destroy beyond the precincts of humanity. We have had warriors to contend with, whose first reinforcement was from the savage of your borders—whose last appeal was to the pirate lurking on our shores. All this we have undergone—the overcharged eruption from the volcano of British aggression. But we survive. The white heat of the fiery ordeal has subsided; and we find ourselves breathing again; with our union, our spirit, our resources, our territory; unsubdued, except the strip on the Penobscot—slowly, it must be confessed, but too slowly making preparation for another campaign. Never was stratagem more hollow, more perfidious, more cruel, more base than the overture last Winter by the Bramble—a stratagem against which this House will do me the justice to recollect that I then admonished them. Never was warfare more barbarous, more inhuman, more brutal, more unmanly than that waged against us by the English, pending the negotiation for peace, to which they gave the invitation. It has excited against them but one unanimous spirit of hearty detestation. An honorable gentleman of the other House (Mr. KING,) for whose person and character I shall always cherish the most affectionate regard, however I may differ from him in politics; who has not been distinguished by his dislike to England, has, within these few days, pronounced his eloquent and severe reprobation of their remorseless and sanguinary hostilities. Never were preliminaries of peace laid down upon a broader basis of stupid ignorance and infatuated misconception than those proposed by the British Commissioners at Ghent. Never was inflexible or supercilious superiority so soon relaxed—never was a peremptory *sine qua non* so soon commuted for a paltry *uti possidetis*. When gentlemen therefore labor by the good hour to prove to us how disastrous our affairs have been, I beg leave to commend them to the enemy for a contradiction. I request them to inform me how it happened, that mighty England has so soon descended from her towering height, unless she has found reasons in her reverses here, to moderate her tone there. She knows, she feels her disappointment. She recognises it in acts too strong to be argued out of existence by all the rhetoric and all the logic of this House. While her fleets, without a single occasion for their presence in any other quarter, have in vain attempted to maintain the paper blockade of our coast, our privateers have enforced an actual and absolute blockade of the coasts of Great Britain. While British ships-of-the-line have degraded the naval character by every species of vile exaction and dastardly mischief upon these shores, the American corsair has visited the shores of England with examples of heroism and humanity. The privateer has taught the man-of-war the lesson of his art—how to conquer and how to be generous. There are some vestiges, it must be acknowledged, of British conquest, but they are nowhere to be seen without the bloody print of British vandalism too. Even this Capitol presents a diurnal spectacle of mutilated columns and demolished monuments. But the blood of martyrs is the seed of the church; and every capital in Europe, which has survived unhurt the occupation of a conqueror, resounds with execration against the British barbarians who one day laid in ashes the Capitol of America, and the next day fled to their ships, leaving their wounded to the mercy of those whom they had thus alienated from the feelings of humanity.

But Canada has not been conquered; and my friend from South Carolina (Mr. CALHOUN) has been reminded of his prediction, that it would be. To all the purposes of that prediction, Canada has been conquered. It was not that we desired to magnify our Republic by adding the Canadas to the Confederacy. If the inhabitants could be removed, I should not care, for my part, if Canada could be overflowed by the ocean. But as a means of obtaining peace, and not as the end of the war, the conquest of the Canadas has been almost achieved. And for this again I beg leave to refer to Ghent and England. We have performed

a campaign on Canadian ground which is worth the acquisition of ten thousand Canadas. We have accomplished officers, and that being done, England knows that we can create soldiers. The American in Europe need now no longer blush to be an American. The European who visits America—after traversing the ocean, every latitude of which is in a blaze with the naval glories of our glorious tars—and who repairs to the Falls of Niagara, as the most prodigious of nature's wonders, will find every species of classic recollection superadded to the natural prodigy of the scene. The grounds round the Falls of Niagara are all sanctified with romantic exploits and brilliant achievements—achievements which have plucked the military as well as the naval plume from British brows—which have been followed by the congratulations and applause of the whole American people. Whether the campaign has been well or ill conducted, on the part of the Administration, I cannot stop to inquire. Whether General Izard ought to have been here and General Brown there, or what share the Administration should have of credit or censure for these operations, I neither know nor care. It answers all my purposes that they redound to the honor of the country—that they enhance the American name at the expense of the enemy of America—the rest is matter of controversy with which I cannot disturb my feelings.

Our ministers in Europe may now with honest pride and independence declare to those potentates who shrunk from our assistance, though our cause was theirs, because they dared not aid us—We have triumphed without your reinforcement, ay, without even your countenance, we have vanquished the victors of your conquerors. We do not ask your alliance. We do not stand in need of it. With the blessing of God, and our means, we can do without it. All that we ask of you is, to cause your neutral rights to be respected as we have caused ours to be. Learn from our example how strong a good cause renders the weak against the mighty. Betrayed by inordinate love of peace and the infamous double dealing of England into but partial preparation for war, we were overtaken unawares by fearful odds. You thought, no doubt, that the chances were against us. But, after a whole campaign of our infernal enemy's utmost scope, not a wreath of laurel have we lost nor an inch of ground, excepting a small part which was not defended as it should have been. My life upon it, sir, the magnanimous Alexander will find that his esteem for us is greater than he supposed it; and Louis the Desired, in 1815, like his predecessor in 1778, will generously press in with his assistance, since he perceives that we can do without it.

But we must have armies, and we must have money. I venture to assert, that the mere enactment, by something like unanimity in this House, of a good military system, with indications of acquiescence in it out of doors, would secure us a peace forthwith, without the necessity of enforcing the system. I appeal to those gentlemen, who are so clamorous for peace, to coalesce for an object so desirable. That system, in my opinion, is a classification of the white male population of the country for the purpose of a draught into the regular armies. You may call it by what odious ugly name you will—conscription or what not—but it is the only sufficient, the only republican, the only fair, the only equal plan for applying the physical means to the end of common military defence and protection. Sir, vast improvements have taken place in the military art since the last twenty years. All Europe has in effect adopted these improvements; and this country will be left lamentably behind in the march of mankind, unless, like the rest, it adopts them too. What are they, sir? Simply a return to the great cardinal principles of republican Government—to the principles which maintained Rome for so many centuries on the ascendant, and again for so many centuries on the decline, before her mere declension disappeared in the darkness of the middle ages. The gentleman from New York (Mr. Miller) was mistaken in supposing that the *Militia Romanorum* admitted of either alternative or exemption. There was no such thing. Every citizen was in fact a soldier. Every citizen was compelled to serve his country under arms, and no citizen was permitted to be elevated to civil honor who had not served them in the military field. It is some time, sir, since I read Polybius; and Washington is not the best place on earth for reference to books. But unless I am quite wrong in my remembrance, the gentleman from New York will find, in the 7th book of that work, the Roman system as I have stated it. But it is somewhat scholastic to refer to such authorities. Let us come down to the later times. We all know the military tenures, the scutage, the knight service, &c., by which the vassal was bound to serve his lord, his lord the duke, and the duke his sovereign. We know the base and arriere law, which used to carry men into the field for short and insufficient terms of service. We read, at still more recent periods, of the Condottieri, the Hessians, the Walloons, the various mercenaries, which for the most part composed the armies of Europe. We know that the great Frederick fought his famous seven years' war with troops of this description. But these again may be thrown out of view, together with the Roman precedent. I invite gentlemen to accompany me to England for a conscription, and I pledge myself to find them one of the harshest and most unequal kind—not impressment for the sea, but conscription for the land service. I invite, particularly, the attention of the gentleman from New Hampshire (Mr. Webster) to the book I am about to read from—it is the English Statutes at Large—a treatise with which his pursuits ought to make him peculiarly conversant. Here, where there are no naughty assignats nor Napoleons; here, in this adorable land of liberty and wisdom, here we shall find conscription at full length.

[Mr. Ingersoll then read several sections of an act of Parliament for recruiting the regular army, enacted in 1756, and to be found in the 7th volume of the English Statutes at Large, page 625, 28 G., 2 c. 4; and from another act, enacted in 1757, to be found in the 8th volume of these Statutes, page 11, 30 G. 2, c. 8.]

Thus, sir, it appears that Lord Chatham planned and Wolfe executed a precedent for Bonaparte's conscriptive system. Here we find that all persons without employment are to be draughted into the King's service. For how long? Five years! From what ages? From seventeen to forty-five. For how much? For forty shillings a head. By what means? By seizing on their persons, and throwing them into confinement till the recruiting sergeant was ready to receive their translation to the ranks. And who were intended by her sons out of employment? The yeomanry of the country. How does this appear? Most conclusively from that section which excepts them in the time of harvest. It was not the lounger, the gentleman, the man of fortune, the cockney, that Lord Chatham laid hold of as a person without employment. Oh, no! his lordship knew better. He has left, to be sure, the impression of the energies of his character and administration upon this act of Parliament. But he had not the jacobin temerity to meddle with the privileged orders; that was reserved for the Corsican, who, with his own scymitar, cut his own way to a throne; and who, with all the vulgar prejudices of his former situation, devised and executed a scheme for making gentlemen serve their country just like common people. Oh, the monster! The yeoman, whom Lord Chatham forced into General Wolfe's army, had no friend at court. Like the ten thousand American seamen in British ships, he might have writhed in anguish till the flesh rotted from his bones, without an advocate to assert his claims, unless the merchant had become a sufferer too, and clamored his country into a war against Orders in Council. Lord Chatham violated only the sanctuary of the cottage. But Napoleon intruded on the palace.

And for what war, in particular, was it that this act of Parliament raised men by conscription? For the conquest of Canada. Chatham was the minister, and Wolfe the commander—names dear to England—illustrious and venerable names. I subscribe to the sentiments, and quote the language of a modern poet, that it is—

"Praise enough
To fill the ambition of a private man,
That Chatham's language was his mother tongue,
And Wolfe's great name compatriot with his own."

Thus it appears, Mr. Chairman, that Napoleon had a precedent, an English precedent, for his conscription. To argue the objections to this system, from its abuse by the late French Emperor, is a false mode of argument. He did abuse the engine, to the most extensive, and wanton, and abominable ends. But it does by no means follow, therefore, that the system itself is a bad one.

Have we no American great name associated with this system, which seems to excite at once all the Gog and Magog terrors, that one would think ought by this time to be banished to the

Island of Elba? We have, sir, a name never mentioned but with reverence; never uttered by the tongue without a glow of the heart. General Washington, after remonstrating for three or four years in vain against militia and short enlistments, was constrained at last to have recourse to classification and draught; and our liberties were ultimately gained by American conscripts. Not, indeed, until our towns were occupied and sacked. our shores in flames, and our prejudices subdued by our stronger feelings—a course of discipline which I am afraid will again be necessary. Our strong measures are almost always reserved for the next year after the occasion for them.

We have ascertained that neither militia nor voluntary enlistments are to be relied upon. The fatal doctrine of citizen-soldier (as we adhere to it) has cost us more money, more blood, more mourning, in six months, than a war of six years should or would cost under proper military organization. For proof of this, go to the camp at Ellicott's Mills, in this neighborhood; see every fourth man on his sick bed, or rather sick without a bed to lie upon; every day a funeral; count the cost; estimate the expense of actual disbursement and of loss of labor, and no rational, no feeling man can doubt as to the shocking inexpediency of such a system. I appeal to the honorable gentleman from Virginia (Mr. Breckenridge) for the correctness of what I say. With such dreadful scenes of preparation for service, let me refer the Committee to a still nearer and still more painful scene, for the inefficiency of militia. I mean the affair at Bladensburg. In making this reference, I beg leave to be understood as intending to blame nobody, from the General down to the private. It always has been, and always will be, impossible with militia to contend with regulars. It takes seven years apprenticeship to make a tinker or a tailor; and is it to be conceived that the military science is to be acquired by intuition?

Such are the militiamen, and what are they, obtained by what is termed voluntary enlistment? Go to the recruiting rendezvous for information. A poor ignorant creature is cajoled into the dramshop, and betrayed into intoxication; when his senses are gone, the Evangelists are put into his hands, and he is called upon to invoke the Almighty to witness his engagement to serve his country; a bounty is thrust into his pocket; a cap is put upon his head, and he becomes a soldier. When the fit of drunkenness goes off, he is informed of his enlistment; he denies it; he is manacled; he resists; he is confined, until finally he is subdued into voluntary enlistment. Let me not be asked why I support a war which involves these evils. I answer, that war is itself an evil, but a necessary one. Whereas these disgusting practices may be easily avoided. They are one of our English legacies. Recruiting is a brutal exercise of violence and fraud over mental alienation. It is an image of the bastard liberty of England. It is slavery called liberty.

The substitute for it is the most simple, the most republican, the most equal and unexception-able system in the world—that of militia classification and draught. That is, militia as it should be, not as it is. Of all countries in the world, this is the one best adapted to such a system. It is here, alone, that all men are treated as equals. By this, I do not mean any revolutionary equality. No; education, and even wealth, place their possessors above the illiterate and the indigent. In spite of all they do, fortune will make her own selections, and laws cannot control them. The most powerful and consistent argument extant in favor of republicanism, is to be found in the New Testament; but, at the same time, the most positive authority for the graduation of the social order. For, as the great republican poet has expressed it, "orders and degrees jar not with liberty, but well consist." But, then, it should be the constant endeavor of Government to maintain a perfect equality in all civil enjoyments and impositions; to burden the poor with nothing that does not fall likewise on the rich; to call upon the latter according to their opulence for pecuniary aid; and not to call upon the former for any personal services that are not exacted of all alike. Upon these principles emphatically does that military system rest, which, by whatever title denominated, classifies a population and compels them to serve without exemption or reservation.

As to the constitutionality of this measure, I refuse to argue it. I hold it to be too clear for argument. Independent of the explicit terms of the Constitution, this power is inherent in the nature of Government. Its exercise and extent must be referred for their regulation to a sound discretion. I adopt the sentiment of the chairman of the Military Committee, (Mr. Troup,) that the Constitution authorizes it, and that, if it does not, such a Constitution is not worth regarding or having.

That it would be popular, (I mean in the legitimate acceptation of popularity, agreeable to the people at large,) I have no doubt, because it calls upon them for no duty that is not necessary and common to all. And the people never murmur at such calls. In that portion of the country with which I have any acquaintance, I am sure it has been expected from Congress, and would be received with pleasure, as the best alternative for the oppressive militia functions. Whether it would be odious or resisted, as is threatened elsewhere, is not for me to determine. I can tell the gentleman from New Hampshire, (Mr. Webster,) however, that the glowing picture he has drawn of its effects is but faintly shadowed to that which this country will present, unless some energetic and adequate system be enforced. The late developments from Europe place us, sir, upon critical ground. On one side, all is peace, prosperity, renown, and respect. On the other, war interminable, disunion, devastation, disgrace, and irretrievable ruin. Dismemberment would be but a little misfortune, contrasted with what may be our lot, unless we rise up to the exigency. The dangers of despotism which are imagined, are alarming, it must be confessed; but they are not so awful as the degradation and misery which may result from a fear to do what our position demands. Convulsion is no more to be dreaded than paralysis. For myself, I see no peril but in our own divisions. The Republic is perfectly safe, if we pursue those energetic and powerful measures which alone can save us—which alone are consistent with our duty, and commensurate with the occasion.

Mr. SHIPHERD addressed the Chair as follows :

Mr. Chairman, should it be my good fortune to secure the attention of the Committee, I shall submit a few humble remarks upon the interesting question which is under consideration. One more so, has rarely, in my opinion, if ever occupied the deliberation of Congress. All that is dear to freedom, hangs upon the decision—in forming which we must say to our fellow-citizens, henceforth be ye slaves ; relinquish that blood-bought freedom for which your fathers fought, or still enjoy ye its blessings. We are to say, sir, whether they shall be dragged forth to die in the camp, or be slaughtered in the field, or still enjoy the comforts of domestic life with its pursuits and emoluments. Whether, in obedience to the awful mandate of despotic power, they must be forced from the protection of civil to the rigours of military law—marched from all the heart holds dear, this side the grave, to encounter the perils, hardships, and privations of war, or still reposing in security under the shadow of an unviolated Constitution, present the heartfelt offering of thanks to Heaven for liberty and protection.

On a question of such moment, we ought to proceed with the utmost caution, taking good care that we do not lose forever the most valued blessings of life, by the indulgence of a mistaken zeal to prosecute with effect an unhappy war. Yes, sir, before we adopt a measure so new and extraordinary, one which must strike at the vitals of civil liberty, we are admonished by every serious consideration to investigate with all our skill, and then say whether, by passing the bill before you, we do not overleap the bounds of our authority, and tread on forbidden ground. I believe, sir, we should do so, and therefore it is a sacred duty with me to protest against the measure. If you are determined to dig the grave of your country's freedom, when the awful deed is done, you shall not be left the excuse to say to an accusing conscience, " I was was not warned of the rash step before it was too late to retrieve it." No, sir, not even this slender consolation will be permitted us, if, in defiance of the soundest principles of the Government, we shall strip from our countrymen the shield of their liberties.

The member impressed with this belief, would prove a coward in his duty, if, in dread of the frowns of a majority, he should barter the rewards growing out of the exercise of honest convictions for indemnity against their resentments.

Much, sir, has been said, which related more to the measures of Administration generally, than the particular topic presented by the motion of my honorable friend and colleague (Mr. MILLER,) which in my mind is, first : whether Congress have a Constitutional right to pass the bill ? If so, then, secondly, whether the interest of the country demands the exercise of a power so extraordinary ? I propose, Mr. Chairman, to examine these two points.

The inquiry then, sir, is, first, does the Constitution delegate to Congress the right to make laws coercing the citizens of the Union into the armies thereof ? If it does not, our legislating on this subject must cease, for whatever may be the necessity of a measure which cannot be adopted without an usurpation of power, an infringement of the Constitution, that necessity must give place to the more imposing duty of keeping within its limits. In other words, unless the Constitution has expressly given the power to the Legislature to fill the ranks of our armies or create new armies by compulsion, it is useless to debate about the convenience, importance, or even necessity of the measure. For unless authority is expressly given or derived by fair implication, we have no right whatever to pass the bill. All the powers which are not expressly delegated to the General Government are expressly reserved to the States. What, then, sir, are expressly given to the General Government in relation to this subject : they are two—

1. To provide the calling out the militia.
2. To raise armies.

I had hoped, sir, that the honorable gentleman from Kentucky, (Mr. DUVALL,) whose talents I respect, and which certainly entitle him to a high stand in this House, would have shown us in what particular the Constitution gives us the authority contended for on this side of the question ; but hope was vain, " he passed by on the other side." Is it not fair, then, sir, to say, if talents such as his avoided the support of a favorite topic, that it cannot be supported ? He ingeniously led off the Committee by complaining of the eccentric course of my honorable friend, (Mr. MILLER,) and in order to surround him, as he pretended, took the liberty of a far more extensive route.

Another question, sir, has been debated between gentlemen on my left, and was it not that I hope to prove them both wrong, it would be passed without notice, because to me it is most evident that whether the one or the other is right they are both wrong. The question is, whether the troops to be called or rather forced out in pursuance of the bill before you are regulars or militia.

The gentleman from Virginia (Mr. GHOLSON) pronounced them of the former, and, therefore, he would infer that Congress have a right to work up citizens into regular soldiers. But his friend from South Carolina, (Mr. CALHOUN,) adhered to the title of the bill, and named them the latter, and thence inferred that we have power to compel them to serve as militiamen, whatever may be the time or conditions of service. Here, sir, you perceive we have different commentaries from gentlemen of the same creed upon the same text, and for the purpose of supporting the proposition laid down, that we have no Constitutional right to pass this bill, it is a point of no impor-

tance whether they are militia or regulars, the
consequence deduced by the gentlemen will not
follow, whether these or those are the premises.
I shall, therefore, leave the gentlemen to settle
the question and proceed, as mentioned, to show
them both wrong.

1st. Then, sir, admit the title of the bill to be
correct, which most certainly is not, for the sake
of the argument, I will search the Constitution
and endeavor to show that we have no power to
pass the bill.

The Constitution authorizes Congress to provide for calling out the militia; in what cases,
sir? Only for the purposes of—

1st. To execute the laws of the Union.
2d. To repel invasion; and
3d. To suppress insurrection.

If, therefore, Mr. Chairman, the bill on your
table is to accomplish either of these objects,
then no doubt can exist of a Constitutional right
to make it a law.

It is somewhere said the prosecuting an offensive or defensive war is executing the law, and
therefore the militia may be called out to aid in
the one or the other; but this must be an interpretation of meaning so weak and absurd that it
never can be adopted as sound.

The meaning is too obvious to be doubted;
that this power was given to the civil magistrate in executing the municipal law, carrying
into effect the sentences of courts of judicature,
and to aid in the civil or criminal process, in cases
of resistance, and has not the most distant allusion to raising an invading or opposing army.
If this be the true construction of this clause,
your laws, sir, are already sufficient, not only for
this, but the other two cases: namely, to suppress insurrection, and repel invasion. Congress
has already provided amply for the exigency of
the three cases, and there can be no necessity of
auxiliary laws.

But most evidently neither of these objects
was the motive which induced the framing this
monster. There is a design of horrid import
beyond this. No one has, no one will deny it.
And a specious purpose is avowed in the title of
the bill to conceal the occult object. Canada
must be taken, said a gentleman from Virginia,
(Mr. GHOLSON,) and to take Canada are these
militia, regulars, or mongrels, to be be dragged
to the camps, to battle and slaughter.

Sir, you may call out the militia to repel invasion. But you cannot call them out for two
years, or one, for a month, a day, or even an hour,
unless the country is invaded; you have no right
to anticipate the invasion, it must exist, in fact,
or the Constitution does not reach the case. Is
your country invaded? Be it so; then under
already existing laws, the President can call for
the militia; but I deny, sir, that Congress have a
right to make laws calling out the militia for a
definite period, however short.

It is most obvious from the wording of the
Constitution, the militia were designed as a specific for enumerated evils, and in no other case
has the General Government power to command

them. Will any honorable gentleman risk the
charge of absurdity by contending that the Government have a right to the remedy, although the
evil does not exist. And it seems equally absurd
to contend that they may be used as a remedy
for other evils than those enumerated. The
States had an exclusive right to the militia; and
in forming the compact and delegating powers to
the General Government, they say we will permit you to call for our militia in three cases,
namely, when your officers cannot execute your
laws; when any of your citizens rise in arms
against you, or when an enemy shall invade your
frontier. This is the utmost extent of the power
granted, and can it possibly follow from this
grant, that, in expectation of the enumerated
cases, the General Government have a right to
call the militia to camp in waiting for an event
which may or may not happen. If it does, the
limitation, or rather the enumeration of distinct
cases to define the authority of the General Government is ridiculous, because it must be useless;
and adopting this Constitution, we are to suppose the wise men who framed the Constitution
filled it up with unmeaning and useless sentences
to make it of sufficient length. For, if this is
the construction, your powers are not limited at
all; they are general, and it is only to say, we
expect a case mentioned. Therefore, we exercise
our prerogatives, and lead the militia to the
camp. For how long? as long as we please, for
months, years, or for life, at our election. This
would be the consequence of the doctrine; and
this, at one blow, might break down the State
sovereignties—rob them of their highest and
most valued prerogatives. If this right really
exists in Congress, the citizens and State governments have no shield against their power; it
will be only necessary to wave its rod, like a
magic wand, and the citizens, in greater or less
numbers, are instantly metamorphosed, and become soldiers. Absolute authority may be exercised over their liberties and occupations, and at
once they cease to be freemen, and become
slaves.

But, sir, if you adopt the construction contended for on this side, you are again free. You
at once perceive a meaning, a glorious object
congenial with, and a sure protector of liberty, in
the specification of cases for the General Government. It surrounds the citizen with an impregnable barrier against the encroachments of
ambition; it defines his rights and duties, and
marks the line between legitimate power and
despotism.

Destroy this limitation, and what becomes of
the State sovereignties? Impotent must be their
laws without the means of executing them. The
respect secured thereby must be held on the precarious tenure of the friendly disposition of the
General Government. A tenure at this time
precarious indeed. Sir, we should much dislike
a dependence of this kind; let us keep our State
governments on the old ground, "by the grace of
God free and independent." You will gain nothing by swallowing us; we shall disturb and

sicken you within, and compel you, like Jonah's whale, to throw us up.

This construction of the Constitution is suited to the notions entertained at its adoption. I mean the jealousies which were cherished by the States, and which were so strong towards the General Government as to threaten the rejection of that instrument. These jealousies not only exist in history, but in the recollection of thousands, indeed, in the very paper itself and its amendments. Why does it reserve to the States all powers which are not expressly delegated, but from the caution just mentioned? If the States were willing to intrust the Government of the Union with absolute dominion over their liberties, property, and other privileges, tell me why all those checks and restraints are imposed upon your National Legislature? Now, sir, if we find the Constitution framed with so much caution, avoiding any oppugnation of the essential principles of State sovereignty, can any discreet man believe that the States which had won their independence by the dint of their own sovereign arms, merely advised by Congress, and tremblingly alive to their interests, fearing lest the new Government should curtail their prerogatives, reserving all powers not delegated, should without any limitation give up to the absolute control of the General Government their whole militia, and at once divest themselves of their sovereignty? For only deprive a Government of armed force sufficient to carry into effect its laws, and what remains can neither command respect or enforce obedience.

If, sir, you are left without any Constitutional restraints in relation to this subject, or to be more explicit, if you have a right to pass this bill, the Government is a despotism. You may exercise absolute power over the liberty of the citizen, and whether exercised by one or many, does not alter its nature. The principles and not the number of men who make laws or pass edicts constitutes the free or despotic nature of the Government. One man may make a people free and happy, while an hundred may enslave them. You therefore perceive, sir, if we hold this power in our hands, we are intrusted with a dangerous power, totally irreconcileable with the idea of the freedom of our Government and habits; totally inconsistent with that security of the political blessings which has been boasted of, experienced, and appreciated—a power which the Mother Country, whose tyranny we could not endure, never pretended to possess, and dare not exercise.

It is true, sir, that this bill may be created without passing the limits of the Constitution. We had better tear in pieces an instrument which affords so little security to our citizens. Why shackle Congress with any restraints, if they are left free to trample on the most sacred rights of freemen? It only marks us with a name and shadow, while the substance is entirely the reverse.

If the power to pass this law is delegated to or exists in Congress, see, sir, what may be its fruits! It is not confined to a time of war; but in peace, as well as war, might your citizens be subjected to a military life. You might treat them as you do your slaves—compel them to toil and drudge at your pleasure. For, sir, if you take away the limitation which we say bounds your power, there is none left, and it is purely a matter of discretion in Congress whether our fellow-citizens may control their own pursuits, recreations, pleasures, enjoyments, and employments; or whether we (their masters) shall ease them of that trouble, and place them under military government, regimen, and discipline—subjugate them to the care of a sergeant or sabre of a subaltern. This, sir, would be the evil as it respects the right at any time, and all times, to control the citizen. But, this is not all. If it does exist, it enables Congress not only to call at any time, but on anybody. It may be as unrelenting as death, and like him take all ranks, ages, and classes, of men—the minister from the altar of his God; the judge from the bench of justice; the lawyer from the bar; the merchant from his counting-room; the physician from the sick-bed of his patient; the farmer from his field; and the mechanic from his workshop. Whenever you may please to exercise this high, dangerous, unlimited prerogative, you tear away whoever you please from their homes and employments, and, without exemption or distinction, devote them to the horrors, filth, and vermin, of a camp. This tremendous power would not be compelled to spare the decrepitude of old age or tenderness of youth. And do we live under such a Government, Mr. Chairman? If we do, let us instantly change it before our strength is taken away and our chains rivetted. Do you call that Government free, sir, that does not stand sentinel over the freedom of the ground; that places no limits but discretion to the power of the governors? It is said, this discretion will not be abused: the limitation, therefore, is unnecessary. Congress, governed by a just sense of the solemn duties imposed upon them, will never oppress the citizen.

Sir, Congress is composed of men liable to err, and fallible, like other men, whose passions may predominate over their reason; whose lust of power may control their love of justice.

If the militia, sir, are the mere creatures of the General Government, as contended for by gentlemen, why, let me ask, was the right to appoint their officers reserved to the States? It would be strange, if they were wholly devoted to the Union, that such an essential principle should have been reserved.

"Congress may provide for organizing and arming the militia." Yes, sir, but does it follow from this provision that they have a right to call them to the field? Certainly not. The object of this clause most evidently was to promote uniformity in their arms, exercise, and discipline; that if at any time they were called into the field, they could the better act in unison.

Having, Mr. Chairman, as far as I have been able, and to the unbiassed mind, I trust, sufficiently proved, that the General Government have no control over the militia of the Union, for the objects contemplated in this bill, I will make a few remarks to show their want of power to coerce the citizens of this country to become regular soldiers.

I am constrained to say, with the gentleman from Virginia, (Mr. GHOLSON,) that the army intended to be raised by virtue of this act would not be militia, but regular soldiers. Adopting this as true, can they, as such, be changed from citizens into soldiers? It really seems that some gentlemen think so, for attempts have been made to prove it by citing the clause of the Constitution which gives power to Congress to raise armies. This power is given without doubt. The only question remains to determine the mode; and as it respects that, the gentleman will find their Constitution to fail them. How shall they raise armies? is the inquiry. All is silent. It then follows most irresistibly, that they are to be raised agreeably to the usages of free countries, controlled by a scrupulous regard to the dearest interests of the nation, by and only by voluntary enlistment. Great Britain, whose tyranny we could not endure, raises her armies in this way. She neither dare to enact, nor could she execute, a law forcing the subject into the regular army. The employing men to become soldiers is done in the same way as the employing them to become laborers, by contract. Such must be the meaning of the Constitution—adopt any other meaning, and the charter of liberty becomes an instrument of tyranny; you give to it attributes which are inadmissible even in idea. The Constitution itself declares the Government therein described to be free. Such is its character; no construction therefore of any part of it ought ever to be tolerated for a moment, incompatible with freedom. I beseech gentlemen, therefore, not to indulge in experiments diametrically opposed to the most sacred principles of liberty.

It is most evident that such is the construction, and was so intended by the framers of that instrument. If not, see with what absurdity they must have acted. In the first place they limit the powers of the General Government over the citizen as a militiaman, and expose him to an unlimited power, when called by another name, to wit: a regular soldier; and the doctrine contended for goes still further. You have not only the ordinary powers over him after he has become such, but you have a right to make him a regular soldier; by a sort of magic process, to cause all ranks, employments, and ages of citizens to undergo the instantaneous and wonderful mutations of enchantment—transferring the judge if you please from his honorable seat to the glories derived from the regions of blasphemy, drunkenness, and pollution. If, sir, it was intended to surround the militia with a Constitutional guard, how much stronger was the reason for the like or more effectual guard for the citizen, to prevent his being forced to become a regular soldier! The reason is as much stronger in the latter than the former case, as the services and sufferings of the latter are more irksome and severe. The reasoning of the gentleman from Virginia (Mr.

GHOLSON) must be fallacious. The amount of it is, you, citizen, are exempted from involuntary service, unless in the three cases mentioned in the Constitution, as one enrolled in the militia; but the Government can get at you under another name, and doom you to any service they please.

This is, truly, a strange doctrine to advance, in giving meaning to the Constitution of a country. Giving the name all efficacy, and the object named none at all. What consolation will it be, sir, to the wretched man, torn by the ruthless hand of power from the bosom of a wife and family he adores, while his heart swims in the tears of anguish, to be told by the ruffian who comes to snatch him from all his soul values on earth, that his rights are not violated in the capacity of a militiaman, but as a regular soldier! In Governments it is the substance of things which ought, and with wise and good politicians does control their measures. Regardless of names they will look to effects, and not mock the sufferer by telling him this or that horrid and cruel measure is called by this and not that name. Will the victim of your oppressive measures, with heart bleeding and eyes weeping, feel the one staunched and the other dried, should you tell him. "comfort yourself my friend, you are not going to be butchered in the capacity of a militiaman, but only as a regular soldier?" Why, sir, was you to say so, you would soon see mingled with the tear of sorrow the smile of contempt, and low as he would feel himself sunk, in his soul he would despise the idiot whose contemptible intellects could stoop to a remark so mean and pitiful.

If this doctrine is correct, what are the benefits resulting from the limitations of power in Congress? Certainly none. It is shielding the limbs and leaving the vitals exposed to the darts of despotism; and can you, can any man believe that the people in their cool moments, deliberating with care, feeling no warmth but zeal for the best interests of their country, could have been guilty of such inconsistency, or weak enough to have overlooked it? Tell it not; believe it not. It cannot be so. Let us not thus slander the hearts or heads of the sainted men, who travailed with this precious instrument until a joyful reckoning was run, and the people hailed its birth as a millenial epoch. However we may act, whether consistently or otherwise, let us not reproach their memories or names.

Turn the subject over as often as you please, torture it to your purpose, it amounts to no more or less than this: "As a white man, the law protects A B—presume not to touch him; but if you call him an Indian, by the same law you have a perfect right to kill him."

I will now, Mr. Chairman, ask the attention of the Committee to the second point, which is the expediency of this measure, provided no Constitutional scruples existed. And it appears to me perfectly demonstrable, if the power existed in Congress, it would be inexpedient, indeed it would be hazardous, to attempt the exercise of it. Remember, sir, that your people have ever been, and ever will be free. Remember that they possess a keen, but laudable jealousy in respect to their rights; that the power is in their hands; they delegate it when and to whom they please, and they never will submit to any extensive encroachments upon their privileges. Wisdom, therefore, most unquestionably dictates to the legislator, that, while he legislates agreeable to his conscience, to please those whom he binds by his laws, is an object of no trifling importance. And, sir, there can be but little necessity of our adopting measures which the people will dislike; if there is, it must have originated in previous misconduct. The majority of the people may, and sometimes by falsehood have, been misled; but left to draw their own conclusions from correct information, they will be right. In the grand community there is much of the best of all sense, common; the best of all knowledge, practical; and by those standards they will condemn or approve, as bad or good measures shall be adopted. If I am correct, how stands your war? Do the people approve of it? We were told they do. That it is the people's war, that they declared it; if so, what necessity can there be of forcing the people into your armies? It must be strange that they approved, nay, declared the war, and yet nothing short of coercion will fill the ranks of your legions. "It is strange, passing strange," that the people will not support a measure of their own devising and creating unless whipped into their duty.

That they refuse, and have refused, is most manifest, for while with one breath we are told the war is popular, with the next we are also told that every attempt to awaken the patriotism or the cupidity of the people has fallen far behind the high expectations entertained before the experiments were made. Now, sir, it is most certain that if the gentleman from Kentucky (Mr. DUVALL) is correct, you can have no necessity of exercising powers so unusual, so abhorrent, and so unjust and dangerous, to accomplish your object. If they love your war, they will love to support it, and will devote their services and blood to the cause, and consequently there can be no need of force. And it will be inexpedient and imprudent to pass the bill, for if the people now love you, there is at least some risk of losing their affections by a measure not of the most inviting complexion. But suppose the honorable gentleman should be mistaken, which to me is most probable, can you be so credulous as to believe that an army forced from a comfortable home, with its delights and conveniences, to the miseries of a camp, will cheerfully expose their lives, and shed their blood in defence of a Government which had proved by its measures to be their greatest enemy? No; as they loved their liberty, as they loved that proud independence, won by the blood of their fathers, they would turn upon you to rend the sceptre of ill-gotten power from unworthy hands. Confide not, sir, in such an army; if you do, disappointment awaits you. Bear in mind that our countrymen are free Americans, not Frenchmen, and they will not submit to chains. If the people do not like your measures, I will not say what some gentlemen have boldly said, that they would resist, and they hoped they would, but I have a right to exercise a natural privilege; I have a right to guess, and I guess they will resist in all the majesty of insulted freedom; and if they do, like a mighty tornado, or overwhelming torrent, they will sweep away every opposing object. I therefore entreat gentlemen to beware what they do; to be cautious how they enkindle a flame they will not be able to extinguish.

Sir, I do not believe the war was ever popular; I verily believe the people detested it from the beginning, and the wretched manner in which it has been prosecuted has increased that detestation; it needs only the passage of this bill, and but an attempt to execute it, to give the finishing blow that will sever all honest hearts from the Government and its war.

Do you flatter yourself, sir, that the people will submit to the execution of a law which is composed of more baleful materials, more cursed ingredients, and may produce more miseries than all that have been felt in the aggregate, under the British Government and our own? Think you, sir, that the people will tamely behold the widowhood and orphanage of their friends and neighbors, the result of your law? I say so because the tracks are nearly all one way. If the father, the son, the husband, or brother, goes out in pursuance of this mandate, he probably goes to die; disease or battle gives him shortly a termination to his sufferings in this world.

But, Mr. Chairman, admit that you can carry this law into effect, and that, too, without opposition by force, are you willing to do so great injustice to your fellow-citizens? Surely, sir, you must feel some compassion for them, some sense of what is right. As an apology on this part of the subject, it was said by a gentleman, the citizen is not obliged to serve unless he pleases. He has only to pay the penalty and exonerate himself. Sir, need the honorable gentleman be told that a vast portion of the population of our country are altogether unable to satisfy the requisition of the law in this respect? To such a person there is no alternative. The lot falls on such a man—the father of a numerous family, whose patient labor gives them bread; he must go, and his family left wretched and forlorn. Now, sir, is all this right? Let me ask, with an emphasis, is it right? If you expect success to follow such measures; measures, which blight and wither our present joys and sicken all hopes of the future, you must have cherished a delusion, for nothing less could create expectations wholly destitute of foundation. If we are to be slaves, why are we told we must defend ourselves against an invading enemy? We were once the subjects of that enemy, and, as I have said, they never did, nor ever dared to pass a law as odious as the bill on your table; but I have no fancy to be conquered by that enemy. I know my brave countrymen, or that portion of them which have minds to devise, courage to dare, and strength to execute, what their rights require in the field, and speak it with pleasure, they are not to be conquered.

They have lived free, and will die so; and they will not thank you to violate the Constitution they love, and impugn the freedom they adore, under pretence of defending them. No, sir, do not take this rash step; better let them, if you cannot enlist men, defend themselves. Let them manage their own matters in their own way. This is the least you can do. Let the people alone; for this they might thank you, but not for exercising a usurped authority which threatens to enslave them.

The gentleman from Kentucky seemed to chide my honorable colleague (Mr. MILLER) for calling this measure a conscription. He says it is not so. Well, sir, although the name conscription "freezes the blood and chills the mortal frame," although it carries in the sound every horrible thought that can fix on the heart the cold shudderings of approaching death; yet no greater evils would follow in its train, had its title been "an act of conscription," than the present title, "to provide for calling out the militia." The name of this, as of all other measures, is but of little importance; and call this bill what you please, it still will retain all the odious provisions that it now does.

Again, sir, have we been solicited to unite with the majority, and as a motive, the melancholy state of our country has been pathetically described; this description is too true to be doubted, and it is an alarming truth. This great fabric seems nodding and tottering to its fall, and Heaven only knows how long before the mighty ruin will take place. But, sir, this state of things, so far from being a motive to induce a union, on the ground to which we are invited, loudly admonishes us to avoid it. The gentlemen have ruined the country by a class of measures, and now, to restore it, they invite us to join in continuing the same. No, sir, we should do injustice even to them to do so, as we certainly act the most friendly part to them and our country, when we oppose and are able to impede them in the career of ruin. If they wish to lay aside party, reason dictates, as they have acknowledged their inability to manage the political concerns of the nation, that they should abandon their ground, and take one which WASHINGTON explored—adopt his principles, and the gentlemen will not need to give us a second invitation to union. Most willingly, sir, would we receive with brotherly good-will, those who, sensible of error, expressed, by abandoning it, their dispositions to adopt another and a better course. That we are right, amounts to almost mathematical certainty; for, whatever opposes wrong is right, and we have been accused of systematic opposition to the men in power, to their measures; and who among them will venture to deny that those measures have been wrong? Should we, then, give up our justifiable opposition, we should only add to the number of hands employed in the total destruction of this once happy country? No, sir, excuse us, we cannot go over; we are a little band, it is true, but, like that little band who valiantly braved a formidable opposition at the straits of Thermopylæ, we still design to stand between the enemy and irretrievable ruin; and faint as are our hopes, yet we know nothing of abandoning our duty or principle; we hold out to the last, and fall when all fall.

Sir, I feel this to be a just boast, and the calamitous state of our country is more than a volume to prove the correctness of it. We always told you we were right and you wrong, and do not the fruits manifest that we judged correctly? "By their fruits shall ye know them," is an unerring rule; by that rule you are found wanting. Your fruits are not good, therefore we have a right, at least, to condemn the heads, if not the hearts, of those who love those fruits.

You took the country in a high state of prosperity, and you admit that it is now otherwise. You admit you are sinking, and call loudly upon us for help; and if we offer assistance, we discover you wish us to do that, or help you to do that, which has produced the evils under which we suffer. Most willingly would we help you, if you would accept of the services which could do you any good, but, should we do as you wished, we should only sink you still deeper.

A gentleman from Georgia (Mr. BARNETT) also called for union, and he used some expressions immensely calculated to promote an object he seemed most ardently to desire. He said he would administer hemp and confiscation, and also a new specific, which I had not before heard of—"Mohawk tea." The first is old, it has been spoken formerly by a zealous gentleman from Maryland, (Mr. WRIGHT.) For the first time, sir, we have no particular longing at the North, we should not take it kindly; and the latter, when explained, "powder and lead," may be equally unacceptable, used as the gentleman means. We should not like a dose of either, when administered, as was intended by him, or as was expressed by a colleague of that gentleman, (Mr. TROUP,) "to be shot like a dog." We, somehow, have an aversion to be forced to do what we dislike, and it will require, possibly, more force than can be raised on that side to accomplish the object of conciliation by hanging or shooting us.

Mr. MOSELEY said, he begged gentlemen who were anxious either for the question or the floor, not to be alarmed. He would detain them but a very short time. It was not his intention to go into a particular consideration of the merits of the bill. He was satisfied with the discussion it had already undergone. It had, in his opinion, been most clearly shown that the bill was unconstitutional in its principles; odious, tyrannical, and oppressive, in its provisions, and altogether unworthy the sanction of this House, as the legislators of a free and enlightened people.

His object in rising was principally to notice some of the remarks which had fallen from gentlemen in the course of this debate. It had been repeatedly stated and urged with much confidence that the war, in which we are engaged, has been as successful and well conducted as could rationally be expected. And that what little of misfortune had attended it, was to be ascribed chiefly to Federal opposition.

That gentlemen should predict favorably is not extraordinary. They have unfortunately been too much in the habit of doing this. But that they should, in the face of surrounding facts, boast of past success and good management, was really more than he should have believed.

Suppose, sir, said Mr. M., that at the time we were about declaring this war; when so many flattering predictions were made respecting it; and with others, the one so often mentioned, that in a very few weeks Canada would inevitably be conquered—for then it appeared to be within the scope of our vast designs, to conquer Canada; and he recollected to have heard gentlemen expatiate with great delight upon the incalculable advantage which must result from the annexation of these provinces to the United States;—suppose that some gentleman opposed to the war had then risen in his place and predicted, that you would not in the course of three campaigns, after expending millions of money, and sacrificing thousands of lives, be able to obtain one foot of Canada. That before you could conquer Canada or any part of it, your own capital would be in possession of the enemy, the splendid Hall you then occupied reduced to ashes, and your Administration, with the President at their head, be seen flying for safety before the British. Nay, more sir, that before you should have proceeded two years with this just and necessary war, every object for which it was declared should be abandoned, and that you would be unable even then to procure a peace upon terms so humiliating. Would not the man who should have made this prediction, which has been literally fulfilled, have been pronounced a madman or a traitor, unworthy the least regard or confidence? And yet the invasion of this city, with its consequent evils, are but items in the long list of calamities brought upon the country, by the war in which we are engaged.

And what are our future prospects? He said he felt no disposition to dwell upon the disasters which we have already experienced, or to magnify those to which we must be exposed in its further progress. But is it wise to shut our eyes against dangers which threaten us? Are our resources more ample than they have been? Or will they in the same hands be more ably and skilfully applied? Has the war grown more popular as it has progressed? Are the innumerable hosts of those who have pledged their lives, their fortunes, and their sacred honor, in support of this war, now found ready to step forward and redeem their pledges? One would have supposed from the professions of patriotic zeal and military ardor, which were formerly witnessed throughout the nation, that upon the slightest call the very pillars of the earth would have been shaken by the trampling of volunteers to Canada, or wherever their services might be needed, and for any term of time.

And what are we now told, not by those unfriendly to the war, who are charged with a disposition to embarrass every measure, and view everything through the darkest medium, but by gentlemen friendly to the war, and zealous for its support? Sir, has it not been said upon this floor, that men cannot now be induced by motives of patriotism, nor by the immense bounties in money and land offered, to enter the service, and that recourse must be had to coercive measures, to conscription, to fill up your ranks; that Congress had declared war, and the people had supported them in that declaration, and that they should now be compelled to fight whether they were willing or not; and in pursuance of this principle is the bill on your table. Sir, if it has come to this, if the Government have in the first place to conquer the people, in order to compel them to conquer a peace, their prospect of a speedy and honorable termination of this war is, to say the least, not very promising.

If the conscription system, even under the military despotism of Bonaparte, was attended with difficulties, he would leave gentlemen to judge of its probable result in a Government where, it is to be hoped, there remains some portion of that spirit by which their liberty and independence was achieved.

Mr. M. observed, that it was not his object, as he stated when he rose, to detain the House by repetition, for he could add nothing to the objections which had been so ably urged against the principles and provisions of this bill by gentlemen who had preceded him. And he would frankly declare that he should not vote for the bill were it ever so perfect. He had never voted for any bill to raise men for the prosecution of this war, and he should not begin with the present.

He knew it was said, that the character of the war was changed, and that it had now become the duty of all parties to unite in its support. But he could perceive no change in the character of the war or its authors, to justify a change of conduct in those who were originally opposed to it, and who have uniformly refused upon principle to give it their aid. Nor is their co-operation more necessary now, than it has ever been. The supplies requisite for the operations of Government do not depend on their votes. When, as was observed by an honorable gentleman from New Hampshire, (Mr. Webster,) "such a condition of things shall happen, it will bring its own rule of action along with it."

And gentlemen in vain attempt to ascribe their want of success in this war to any opposition either in or out of this House. There has been no opposition but what they were bound to expect.

Is not the majority in this House sufficient to control the minority; and to carry every measure when and how they please? He said *when*, because it was well known they possess and exercise the power of putting an immediate end to debate, when from any cause it becomes troublesome. They can instantly put to silence every argument of their opponents. Not by any intellectual efforts, not by any old-fashioned logical process, but by the magic power of the previous question, which proves at once—not what some speculative writers have attempted to show, that mind may become omnipotent over matter; but that matter may be made omnipotent over mind.

Having obtained this species of triumph, gentlemen, no doubt, felicitate themselves with the conclusive inference, that they must be right, when nothing can be said against them.

No sir: gentlemen, he remarked, must look to other causes than to the opposition of the minority for their want of better success in this war; for the deplorable state of their Treasury, and the wretched condition to which the country is reduced.

But he would venture to predict, if they were determined to prosecute the war by a recourse to such measures as are provided in the present bill, that they would have no occasion for future committees of investigation to inquire into the causes of the failure of their arms.

Mr. M. said he meant no improper menace to the House; but an allusion had been made to the late public proceedings in the State from which he was a Representative, and he was sorry to say, that he had heard some expressions of a threatening nature.

He would assure gentlemen, that there was no terror in their threats, to deter the people of that State from any course of duty, which they should deliberately prescribe to themselves. So long as the General Government shall respect their rights, and faithfully discharge its duties towards them, so long they would not be found wanting on their part. But the same principles, the same feelings, and, he would beg leave to say, the same intelligence, which would ever secure from them obedience when due, would prevent them at all hazards from yielding it when arbitrarily and unconstitutionally demanded.

After a short but animated speech of Mr. JOHNSON of Kentucky, in opposition to the motion, the question on striking out the first section of the bill was decided in the negative, ayes 44. And the Committee rose and reported the bill to the House; which immediately adjourned.

SATURDAY, December 10.

The bill from the Senate, "to incorporate the subscribers to the Bank of the United States of America," was read the first time, and, on motion, the said bill was read the second time, and referred to the Committee of Ways and Means.

A message from the Senate informed the House that the Senate have passed the bill "to provide additional revenues for defraying the expenses of Government, and maintaining the public credit, by laying duties on carriages for the conveyance of persons, and the harness used therefor," with amendments; in which they ask the concurrence of this House.

MILITIA DRAUGHTS.

The House resumed the consideration of the report of the Committee of the Whole on the Senate's bill, to authorize the President to call into service 80,430 militia, for the defence of the frontiers.

A motion was made by Mr. STOCKTON of New Jersey to postpone the bill indefinitely.

On this motion Mr. STOCKTON addressed the Chair as follows:

Mr. Speaker: I have moved for the indefinite postponement of this bill before the amendments made in the Committee of the whole House are disposed of—not with any wish to interpose artificial obstructions to its passage through the House, but to secure to myself, and to other gentlemen, the common privilege of expressing our opinions upon a great political subject; a precaution made the more necessary by the intimations thrown out yesterday of an intention of stopping further discussion by a resort to the previous question. I can assure you, sir, that I rise to advocate this motion in no spirit of party or of opposition; but because I feel myself constrained, by all the ties which bind me to my constituents and country, to make use of every exertion to prevent the passage of the bill. I know the difficulties which at this moment surround the Government and the nation. I know, and I feel, as sensibly as any member can feel, the crisis—the awful crisis, at which our public affairs have arrived. I know, sir, that we are engaged in a war with a powerful, irritated, and revengeful enemy. Since the late despatches from Europe have been submitted to us, I have been induced to believe that the Administration could not at this moment make a just and honorable peace if it were now really disposed so to do. I admit that there is too much ground to apprehend that if this war is continued for another campaign, it will require a great exertion to maintain the just rights and integrity of the United States. I know that our treasury is empty and must be filled—that our public credit is gone and must be restored—that the ranks of our army are thin and must be increased—all this I know—and, without stopping now to inquire why or wherefore these things are, I am ready to act accordingly. I am willing to accept the invitation of an honorable member from Kentucky, (Mr. DUVALL,) and to sacrifice for the good of the public. I am willing at this moment to forget all that I have ever thought and believed of this terrible war. I am willing to forget the folly, the political insanity, in which it was declared—the neglect, the culpable neglect, to provide the necessary means of carrying it on—the waste—the profuse and shameful waste of blood and treasure, which has marked its progress. Although every event since that fatal step was taken has confirmed me in these opinions, I am willing to forget them all, and to act as if they did not exist. I am willing to place them upon the altar of public safety, and there to immolate them. I am willing, for myself, to go further, and to refrain from all irritating expressions in reference to those who hold the reins of Government and control the destinies of the nation. I most sincerely pray that our gloomy forebodings as to the issue of affairs in their hands may not be realized—that they may be able to extricate the country from the dangers which surround it, and to make a speedy, lasting, and honorable peace. I have already acted in conformity with these professions, by voting during this session for every measure intended to increase your revenues or armies, which appeared to me to be Constitutional, and founded on principles of justice and equality, and I shall continue so to act. But, Mr. Speaker, there are bounds which every man of principle must observe. There are some limits which neither arguments, difficulties, nor dangers, can induce me to exceed. The limits which I have prescribed to myself in providing for the exigencies of the day are just and indispensable—they are, the Constitution; the general principles of political expediency; the eternal, immutable principles of justice, equal justice, to all the community. These principles I must and will adhere to at all hazards. To me, sir, public wants can afford no inducement to vote for an act which my best judgment informs me transcends the legitimate powers of Congress. To me, State necessity can be no plea for resorting to wild and visionary plans, which, though they may be honestly intended to redeem the public credit, I conscientiously believe will sink it deeper into ruin. Nor, sir, will necessity ever induce me in the imposition of taxes to violate the great principles of justice and equality. With these exceptions, I am willing to go as far as any other member in providing the proper means of defending the rights and interests of these United States. In regard to the bill now on the table, I have read it with attention, bestowing upon it all the consideration its importance demanded. I have endeavored to analyze its objects and provisions. I have listened with the most respectful attention to everything which has been said in its favor. The result is a solemn conviction that we have no Constitutional right to pass the bill in its present shape, and that it will be destructive of the best interests of this country to enact it. Will you listen to me, Mr. Speaker, whilst I state as concisely as I can the reasons which have induced me to form this opinion? In performing this task, I shall endeavor to adhere strictly to the bill. There are, indeed, other most important matters intimately connected with it, which, as parts of the same general plan, would be proper objects of remark; but from these I shall refrain at present—I allude particularly to the proposed draught of the militia to fill the ranks of the regular army. On this monstrous device I shall make no remarks now. That bill may never be called up. It is already damned in public estimation—I trust that it is sleeping the sleep of death, and that it will never be raised to affright and afflict us. Mr. Speaker, there are certain general principles which lie at the bottom of this subject. In a limited Government, such as that established by the Constitution of the United States, they may truly be called fundamental. By some they may be considered as familiar and true—and by others as scarcely worthy of attention in these enlightened days. But the great men to whom we are indebted for our independence and civil institutions, thought differently. They supposed that they were all-important. They believed that it was always

necessary to bear them in mind, and advisable frequently to recur to them, to keep this Government within its proper sphere, and to defend the rights and liberties of the people. One of these general principles is, that the militia of the several States belongs to the people and Government of the States, and not to the Government of the United States. I consider this, sir, as a proposition too clear to require illustration, or to admit of doubt. The militia consists of the whole people of a State, or rather of the whole male population capable of bearing arms; including all of every description, avocation, or age. Exemption from militia duty is a mere matter of grace. This militia, being the very people, belongs to the people or to the State governments, for their use and protection. It was theirs at the time of the Revolution, under the old Confederation, and when the present form of government was adopted. Neither the people nor their State governments have ever surrendered this their property in the militia to the General Government, but have carefully kept and preserved their general dominion or control, for their own use protection, and defence. They have, it is true, granted or lent (if I may use such an expression) to Congress a special concurrent authority or power over the militia in certain cases; which cases are particularly set down, guarded, limited, and restricted, as fully as the most scrupulous caution, and the use of the most apt and significant words our language affords, could limit and restrict them. The people have granted to Congress a right to call forth the militia in certain cases of necessity and emergency—a right to arm and organize them—and to prescribe a plan, upon which they shall be disciplined and trained. When they are called into the service of the United States (and they cannot be called, unless upon the happening of one of the contingencies enumerated) they are to be under the command of the President. Hence it follows that the general power, authority, or jurisdiction, remains in the State governments. A special, qualified, limited, and concurrent power is vested in Congress, to be exercised when the event happens, and in the manner pointed out, prescribed, and limited in the Constitution. And hence it also follows, that this delegated power cannot be executed upon any other occasion, nor in any other ways than those prescribed by the Constitution. There is another general rule or principle of construction to which I must allude. It is, that all particular, special, and limited powers, taken from or carved out of the general power, must be construed strictly. The general power remains in full force, unimpaired, except where it is expressly granted away, and the construction must be on the words of the grant, and not by recurring to the doctrine of analogy or parity of reason. This is a rule applicable to all grants of power, public or private, but it is particularly to be attended to in grants of public authority; and most of all in those solemn grants denominated constitutions. These grants, being from the people to their rulers, are always deliberately framed. They are penned with the utmost accuracy and precision of language. All powers intended to be granted, and those not included in the terms made use of, are withheld. This is not a mere technical rule of the schoolmen or the forum. It is founded in reason, good sense, and justice; and is all-important in the construction of constitutions. If the words of such grants are departed from, upon any pretence, what safety do they afford? If reasoning by analogy is once permitted, so that cases not enumerated, but supposed to stand upon a footing in point of reason and expediency, are, by liberal construction, held to be included in it, what security is there but the discretion of those who undertake to expound it? A constitution should be considered as a pillar of marble, not as a figure of wax; it must remain as it comes from the hand of the artist, and not be moulded by officious hands into a more convenient shape. The rule I have laid down, has been considered of sufficient importance to be engrafted into the Constitution itself. The tenth amendment, in ordaining that "all powers not delegated by the Constitution, nor prohibited by it to the States, are reserved to the States respectively and to the people," declares, in the spirit of the rule I have stated, that all powers not granted to the Congress by the Constitutional charter, remain with the people or the State governments.

Mr. Speaker, this special, limited, concurrent power over the militia, is given by the States to Congress only in three cases—"to enforce the laws, suppress insurrections, and repel invasion." I call it a special concurrent power, and it is clearly no more; for the States, notwithstanding this grant, retain the power to call forth their militia for the same or any other lawful purpose. There is, then, no grant of absolute power even in these cases; and the people and the State governments have not only the right of insisting upon a strict observance of the limitation, but the corresponding right to resist all encroachments upon what they have reserved unto themselves—for, as it is of the very essence of a limited government to be kept within its proper orbit, so it is the unquestionable right and duty of the people to oblige those who administer it to preserve this boundary, and to resist and repel illegal encroachments.

I consider these principles to be unquestionable. They will, I should hope, receive the assent of every gentleman of this House. Be this as it may, I flatter myself that they will stand the test of the severest scrutiny; and, being established, the only question must be, whether the act now under consideration is a proper execution of the limited authority vested in Congress, to "call forth the militia to repel invasion."

In examining this question, I shall not follow the example which has been set by some of the advocates for the bill; I shall spend no time in ransacking ancient and modern history for precedents or examples of governments asserting the right of making every man a soldier. In my opinion, it is nothing to the purpose to examine what was the law in Greece or Rome, or what has been the practice of George III. or of Bonaparte—the question is exclusively an American question. I shall keep it in mind that I am in the American Congress, considering an American act, to be tested by the American Constitution, and shall not trouble the House in going over matters so entirely useless and inapplicable.

The bill before us is curiously framed. There is little or no coincidence between the title and the provisions of the bill; between the pretended and the real objects. But its best friends can discover only two objects apparent on its face: First, to call out eighty thousand militia for the defence of the frontiers against invasion; or, secondly, to compel these eighty thousand militia to furnish forty thousand regular soldiers.

Supposing these to be the real objects, and that the provisions of the bill were adapted to them, it can be easily proved that they are unauthorized by the Constitution. Let me ask, sir, what section of the Constitution empowers Congress to call forth the militia to defend the frontiers from invasion? None can be produced—and it never was the intention of the people to grant such a power. A power to call forth the militia to "defend the frontiers against invasion," would be a general power to make use of the militia during a war; it would be destitute of all substantial limitation, and might be exercised without control. Such a power, not depending upon notorious fact, would include in it a right to order out the militia for the common purposes of war—when and where, and for as long a time as Congress should see fit. If Congress may call them forth for the general purpose of defence, who is to judge—who, but itself, can judge of the necessity and propriety of the call? Such a power would necessarily destroy those limitations so carefully provided, and place the whole militia of the United States under the control of the General Government for the general purposes of war. They might be marched from the seaboard to the northwestern frontier, and there be kept during a war, doing duty as garrison soldiers; or, in other words, as regular soldiers, under the pretext that they were called forth to defend the frontiers. Indeed, I can see no reason why, if this construction be correct, they may not be marched to those remote regions before the war is actually declared; or why they may not be kept there until it ended. If the power be that of employing the militia for the general purposes of defence, where is the necessity of waiting until the war is actually declared? Surely, a prudent Government would not wait until that event took place, before it provided the means of defence. A wise Government, intending to wage a war, would be so provident as at least to place its frontiers in a state of defence, before it drew the sword: and as the duty of defending the frontiers would exist as long as the war, it is manifest, if the militia could be called forth for this general purpose, they might be detained there as long as the occasion existed; or, in other words, during the war.

But no such power is given, or was intended

to be given. The power actually given to Congress is to call forth the militia to repel invasion—not to defend the frontiers from invasion. The power claimed by this bill is, that whenever Congress think an invasion probable, they may call forth the militia to guard against it.

The power granted by the Constitution is, that when an invasion takes place, Congress may call forth the militia to repel it.

The powers are not the same, but essentially and substantially different. The one is general, depending for its just exercise on will and discretion. The other is limited, guarded by express words, and defended against perversion, by the requirement of a notorious fact, of the existence of which the State governments are as competent to judge and decide, as the Government of the United States.

The power claimed, in its practical operation, places the militia of the States, without limitation as to number or time of service, in the power of Congress.

The power granted only authorizes calling them out on a particular emergency, which carries with it its own limitation, both as to numbers and time of service.

The power claimed subjects the militia to the general duty and service of the war. It makes them, in truth, regulars, though they are called militia; for the President may command them to perform every service without restriction, and at any place.

The power granted preserves the essential quality of being called out in aid of a regular army, upon the contemplated emergency happening, and of returning to their homes as soon as the emergency has ceased.

The power claimed subjects the citizen to be made a soldier without his consent, for any length of time. For whether he shall serve one year, or two, or ten, or during a war, is admitted to be only a matter of sound discretion.

The power granted leaves him all his rights as a citizen; guards and protects him in the service required; calls him to arms to repel an invader; and, as soon as he is repelled, returns the citizen to his family.

Mr. Speaker, I consider the claim now for the first time set up by the General Government to the personal service of every citizen—subjecting him to be made a soldier, under the pretence of defending against invasion, and binding him to military service whether it happens or not, and after the enemy is expelled, as entirely unwarranted, whether we regard the words of the Constitutional grant, or the manifest intention of its makers. The people have never vested such a power in Congress—they have reserved it to themselves, or it is deposited, together with the general mass of sovereignty, in the State Governments.

The noxious illegal character of this bill is not at all taken away or altered by the amendment made in Committee, requiring only a service of one year instead of two. It is true, that it alleviates its harshness: it will be less oppressive. It

may be more palatable, and, for that reason, it may be more dangerous. When the oppressor assumes the form of a giant, he creates alarm, and will be sure to meet with due opposition. When oppression comes like a mighty flood to overwhelm the privileges of the people, they will not fail to breast the torrent with firmness and spirit. But, when he assumes a reasonable shape—a common form;—when the measure carries with it the imposing pretence of public wants, or public defence; and, especially, when the original plan is softened and meliorated in its application; then we are apt to comfort ourselves that it is no worse, and and finally to disregard the dangerous principle that lurks beneath.

The amendment leaves the objection to the principle of the bill in full force. Congress have it not in their power to call forth the militia for a year, a month, or a day, except to repel invasion, execute the laws, and suppress insurrection.

It appears to me that the power now claimed, of using the militia of the several States, for the general purposes of war, under pretext of defending the frontier from invasion, is not only unfounded, in the fair interpretation of the Constitution, by the words and evident meaning of the granting clause, but that it is inconsistent with other parts of the charter; that it reverses the whole plan or scheme of Government; destroying its symmetry, and removing some of its most important balances and checks.

One principal and avowed object of the Federal Constitution was, to provide for the public defence, and to take that duty from the individual States, and impose it upon the General Government. Experience, during the war of the Revolution, had taught how little the State Governments were to be relied on to perform this important task. It had been found that acting without obligatory union, oftentimes under the influence of narrow, interested politics, they were not to be trusted for steady efforts, proportionate to relative ability, or to the interests which they had at stake. The people had become tired of a Government of requisitions, which could not be enforced. They called for one, which, acting immediately on the population, would possess the power of securing due respect to its own Constitutional demands. Hence they imposed the great duty of public defence on the General Government, and furnished it with most ample means to enable it to perform the service required. They endowed it, not only with the high powers of making war and peace, but with those also of raising regular armies, and of imposing taxes. Thus it became invested with the great powers of the sword and the purse, of raising men and money, without limitation, as to number or sum; having no bounds but the public wants, and the great principles of civil liberty. Having thus provided and vested in the Federal Government, all the means requisite to the great end in view, the State Governments are absolved from the general duty, and are merely required to furnish their militia to aid in repelling an invader. It is evident, then, to me, that the Constitution contemplated a regular army as the steady and proper means of public defence in time of war; the militia as a temporary auxiliary force, to be called in aid, on emergency or sudden onset. But the plan of this bill reverses everything. Instead of the Federal Government providing for the public defence, by the means surrendered to it; instead of raising armies, to defend the States, in a war declared by itself—it calls on the States to defend the Union. The militia of the particular States must be called forth to defend the United States. The militia is converted into the regular force, the regulars into the auxiliary!

The experience of the Revolution and the paternal warnings of their illustrious Chief had further taught the people, that militia were not to be relied on in a war with a foreign Power; that they were a most expensive and ineffectual force; that every principle of sound policy forbade their being called from their occupations and business, to be made soldiers; nevertheless, their usefulness in aiding a regular army, on sudden emergency, had oftentimes been experienced, and was well known. The plan, therefore, was to defend the country, in case of foreign war, by regulars, and to add the qualified authority, to call forth the militia, on the emergency contemplated. This was a wise and safe course, and it is folly and weakness in the extreme to attempt to alter it.

There was also a further reason for leaving the general authority over the militia in the State governments, and denying it to the General Government;—that it might be a check upon the great powers of war and peace, sword and purse, thus surrendered to the General Government. The Federal Government is not only a limited Government, but it is furnished with its balances and checks. It was framed upon the principle, that no set of men can be safely trusted with power, without some means left elsewhere to keep it within proper bounds. It was this proud principle of jealousy of power, wherever it might be deposited, that produced the Revolution. That great event was not so much brought about by actual oppression, as by the assertion of principles which were derogatory to the rights of freemen. So thought the great men who formed and adopted this Constitution. They were high-minded republicans in deed, and not merely in the name. Their political creed was, that no set of men were to be trusted with discretionary powers. They knew that paper limitations were useless, unless accompanied by the means. Hence they denied some powers to the General, and some to the State Governments. They limited others; and when they bestowed general powers on the Federal head, the means of a wholesome control was left with the people and the State Governments. But these salutary principles are now out of fashion. They are either unknown, forgotten, or disregarded. The plan of the Republican Administration has been evidently to accumulate power in the Executive branch of the Government, from the President down to the lowest collector, or tax gatherer. Scarcely is a bill reported upon any subject, relating either to war or revenue, which does not contain some covert attack

on the unquestionable rights of a free people. It is manifest to me that the Constitution contains no grant of the militia to the Federal Government for the general purpose of even defensive war. When this instrument was before the people, such a power as is now contended for was never attributed to it, either by its enemies or its friends. On the other hand, when the great and dangerous powers actually granted by it, such as those of making war and peace, raising armies, and imposing taxes, were objected to by honest and enlightened opposers, the answer was (and it is a sound one if the Constitution is executed in its true sense and spirit) that there was a sufficient security against abuses in the habits of the people, their aversion from war, and their spirit of liberty; but especially in the State Governments, and their militia. And I might, with perfect safety, hazard the assertion, that if the power, now contended for, to call forth the whole militia for the general purposes of war, without any regard to the Constitutional limitation, or to time or place of service, had been inserted in plain terms in the charter, it would have been rejected.

But, Mr. Speaker, perhaps it may be demanded of me whether the militia may not be called forth until an invasion actually takes place. It may be asked, must the Government wait until the enemy lands upon our shores, before it can resort to this force? Upon this point I would answer, that the act of Congress passed in 1795, to carry into effect that part of the Constitution now under consideration, places this subject on its proper footing. The act authorizes the President to call forth the militia in case of invasion, or imminent danger of invasion. This, in terms, is an extension of the provisions of the instrument, and it certainly goes to the very verge of the Constitutional limit; but I am disposed to think that it is a sound exposition of its true intent and meaning. The words of this law, not to be found in the Constitution, are these—"imminent danger of invasion," and they seem to have been carefully selected for their accuracy and precision. By imminent danger is meant—impending, threatening danger—danger at hand. It does not include danger only expected, or probable, resulting from a general state of war. For instance, it is no such emergency as is provided for in the Constitution, that we are engaged in a war with a powerful nation, and that there is a moral certainty that she will invade some part of our territory. This would induce a provident Administration to have a good army in the field, but does not authorize ordering the militia into actual service. But, if the President were now in possession of information, that a large expedition had been prepared for and was on its way to attack New Orleans, (as we have reason to believe he is,) he need not delay his call on the militia until the enemy shall arrive, but he may lawfully call on those of the contiguous States, to meet and repel that invasion, whenever the enemy shall make his appearance. So, if a fleet should arrive at Sandy Hook, or at the Capes of the Delaware; it might require a long time to enable them to get up and land their troops. Still the President need not wait until they have landed; because these are cases of invasion, or of imminent danger of invasion, within the fair meaning of the words of the Constitution.

This statute of 1795 asserts no power to call forth the militia for the general purposes of war, or to defend the frontiers; but only to repel invasion actually made or depending. Yet this statute was drawn with the utmost care, and was doubtless intended to occupy all the ground given to the General Government by the Constitution, as it was then understood. It is entitled to the utmost respect and weight, as a Legislative declaration how far this right extends, and what are its just limits.

It is unnecessary to detain the House in remarking on the circumstance that the enemy are in possession of some part of the territory of the United States, as that circumstance can afford no aid to this bill, and indeed does not seem to be much relied on. None of the provisions of this bill are adapted to that case. It is not designed to enable the President to call forth the militia to expel them. The existing laws are already fully competent to this end. He may call forth the militia to repel this invasion. But the object of this bill is to form a militia armament, not to expel those invaders, but to serve for one year. The enemy is left in quiet possession of what he has taken, and this army is to be raised to carry on the war as the President shall direct. It may be marched into Canada, leaving the invaders behind. But more of this hereafter.

As to the second object of this bill, which is to induce this corps of 80,000 militia to furnish 40,000 regulars; to be sure it does not figure in the title of the act; yet it has been avowed by many gentlemen to be the real object which this bill is to attain.

I cannot avoid remarking, how admirably the title of this act has been contrived, to give notice of a matter which is not to be found in the bill—that is, a plan to defend the frontiers against invasion, and to conceal what it does contain, an illegal device to compel the militia to furnish recruits for the regular army. But surely those gentlemen who excused themselves in voting for it, although they acknowledge that it is no militia bill, because it affords a prospect of supplying the ranks of the regular army; surely such gentlemen have not considered, that if Congress have no right to call for the militia as this bill does call for them, neither can it possess even a pretence of right to require them to furnish regulars, as the commutation proposed for the militia service. But if there is no right to require the principal duty there can be none to require the substitute. If the obligation to serve in the militia, as this bill requires, does not exist, the alternative ought not to exist. This need only be stated to receive the assent of every just man in the community. Then, to demand by law what we have no right to demand—to impose on the people a burden which we have no right to impose, and oblige them to perform it, or to provide a substitute, will at once give to the whole process the char-

acter of illegal compulsion. To class the militia for purposes, not within our control; to require of them a service, which they are not bound to perform; and then to excuse them if they will furnish half the number of regular soldiers—what is this but coercion? what is this but classing the militia, and draughting them to furnish recruits for the regular army? It becomes conscription; which is nothing more than obliging men to serve in the army, or to furnish others to serve, without their consent, and without the authority of Constitutional law. It is conscription of the most odious character. The form and shape given to it are the most offensive that could be proposed to a free people. It is concealed and covert—it is injustice perpetrated under the pretence and color of rightful authority.

The friends of the bill are then reduced to this dilemma. If the bill is really a militia bill, it is unconstitutional, and should be rejected. If it is not a militia bill, (as some of the majority have contended,) but the real object is to obtain regulars, this is still more objectionable, and should receive no countenance in this House.

Mr. Speaker, I shall now proceed to consider the provisions of this bill. My observations will be general. I shall not trouble the House with descending to particulars. And I cannot refrain from again remarking on the title of this bill—its deceptive form and character. It affects to inform the reader that he may within expect to find a plan for calling forth the militia to defend the frontiers against invasion, and yet there is not a single provision to be found in the enacting clauses adapted to such an object. The plan which the bill developes is, to class the militia, under the direction and authority of the President. They are then to be draughted. Those selected are to be organized into regiments and brigades, and are to pass at once into the United States service. There is no provision regulating the particular service upon which they are to be employed; there is nothing to confine the service to the Constitutional emergencies, to repel invasions, to execute the laws, or to suppress insurrections. But the men are put under martial law and must serve as they shall be ordered. The bill pursues no plan of a militia law heretofore passed. It has not a militia feature in it; but on the contrary prostrates at once all their rights and privileges. It may, sir, be laid down as a general proposition, that a bill professing to be a militia bill, but which disregards and destroys all the essential qualities of the militia armament, which deprives the militiaman of inherent fundamental rights, rights always acknowledged and possessed, cannot be consistent with the Constitutional powers of this Government. The rights of the militia were long known and universally acquiesced in, before this Government acquired its qualified jurisdiction over them. They claimed and exercised these rights during the war of the Revolution, and at the time of the adoption of the Constitution. Congress received the powers it possesses subject to these privileges. They are founded in justice, and in the intrinsic nature of a force composed of the whole body of the people. They are supported by prescription or constant usage. When I speak of militia rights, I mean these: to be called out for short periods of emergency; to be taken from places contiguous, and not to be compelled to serve elsewhere; to serve only in just rotation with others. An act which violates all these principles may be safely called no militia law, but an unconstitutional requisition.

When the bill came from the Senate, the term of service required by it was two years. We have reduced it to one. The principle however is not changed. The obligation to serve is absolute, peremptory, unconditional. There is no one provision limiting the service by any contingency. If the enemy, in one month after this force shall be organized, should be driven to the walls of Quebec, or besieged in Halifax, still the militiaman must be a soldier. What section of the Constitution, let me ask, authorizes this? What letter of that instrument enables Congress to fix any absolute time of service? The legal call is to repel invasion. It carries with it its own limitation. The obligation to serve lasts so long, and no longer, as the particular invasion for which the service is required exists. It is to be remarked, that the act of 1795, before alluded to, contains no provision ascertaining how long the militia called forth to serve in the cases stated in the Constitution, shall serve; it leaves it in this respect as it ought to be left, to the intrinsic limitation of the granting clause. But it ordains that they shall not be required to serve more than three months in any one year; thereby guarding and protecting this essential quality of militia service. This is a correct exposition of the limited Constitutional grant. The words of that charter carried with them the intended limitation, and therefore it was unnecessary to insert another. But as it might so happen, that invasion, or one of the other exigencies, might endure longer than a militiaman ought to be compelled to serve, care was taken that they should not on any pretence be required to serve for more than three months out of twelve.

There appears to me to exist no right to fix the time of service but for the purpose of establishing a day beyond which they shall not be required to serve. The period of service which the Government may rightfully demand, is quite another thing, and depends entirely on the exigency out of which the right to call them forth may arise. If the call is to enforce the laws, the right of service ceases when the empire of the laws are restored. If to suppress insurrections; when the insurgents are quelled. If to repel invasions; when the invader is driven back. If prudence—if reasons of State, or alleged necessity, require a long period of service, recourse must be had to the State Legislature. The State governments are absolute, except where they are controlled by their own constitutions. They may safely be trusted—they would co-operate with the General Government in all necessary measures of defence as long as that Government respected their rights, and performed its relative duties.

The next characteristic privilege of the militia is to be taken from a State contiguous to that where service is required; and how is this to be secured? There is but one method of effecting it—adhere to the Constitution; construe it according to its words and plain intent; confine the power of Congress to call forth the militia to the enumerated cases; do this, and this important privilege is secured. These are all the cases of emergency. If the militia cannot be called forth until the emergency exists, then they must necessarily be taken from the contiguous neighborhoods or States. But, as I have before stated, this bill contains no provision that the militia shall not be called into actual service until the exigencies occur; nor that they shall be called from the adjacent parts of the neighboring States; but they are left in these important respects altogether in the power of the President. The rules of martial law will oblige them to obey. They may be marched from Maine to Louisiana. There is no limitation in regard to the place where the service is to be performed. In the bill, as it came to us, there was a section restraining the right of service to the State from whence the militia came, or to the next adjoining; but this we have stricken out, thereby declaring our opinions to be that the power is unlimited in this particular, and they may rightfully be sent anywhere. As the bill now stands, under the specious pretext of defending the frontiers, the militia of New Jersey may be marched to Detroit or to Maine; acting on the favorite maxim of the Administration, that the United States must be defended in Canada, that the invasion of that country is a measure purely defensive, these troops may be ordered to Quebec or Montreal. And if they refuse to pass the frontiers they are called forth to defend, they may be shot as mutineers. It is nothing to the purpose to say, that the President will exercise a sound discretion, and will not order these men to serve at a great distance from their homes. If the Constitution has not subjected the militia to the discretion of the President, we have no right to do so by law. What a freeman may claim as an undoubted right, he ought not to be compelled to receive as a favor.

This bill also destroys the great principle of rotation, by which I mean the important privilege of every freeman, not to be subject to military service, but in a just proportion of time with other freemen of his vicinage. This appears to me to be a most important privilege. The militia consists of all the people—the entire male population. They have their rights, not only as between them and the Government, but as between each man and the residue. All cannot be called forth at a time, or the country would become a desert. Hence the right of each man is, that he shall only be called into actual service in just rotation with all others. To declare by law that one class shall absolutely serve for one, two, or ten years, is entirely unjust and illegal. Substantially, it makes them regular soldiers. Suppose the war should terminate with the year, then one class will have borne the whole burden. No such injustice takes place if we use them as militia ought to be used. If we require their services according to the intrinsic nature of the force, and as the rules of justice require, all will be right. They should be ordered out for short periods, and be often relieved during a campaign, so that no one class should be compelled to serve for a longer time than its equal tour of duty may demand. Let it not be urged that so short a service will prevent their improvement in the military art. The error is, in requiring of the militia a service to which they are incompetent, and for which they were never designed. The militia were not intended, and should never be relied on to fight pitched battles with a disciplined foe. They are only calculated to serve as an irregular auxiliary force, to harass and distress the enemy upon a sudden onset. The sooner they are brought into action after they leave their homes the better. They must have brave men to command, and be employed in the service suited to their nature and genius. In a service adapted to them they will render essential aid. Thus employed, they dare to follow wherever their officers dare to lead. In a camp they will learn little that is good; there perhaps you may discipline select corps composed of the flower of your youth, but the militia *en masse* will learn little else than bad habits, and to become disgusted with your service. Let us then abandon the vain expectation of compelling the militia to do the duty and supply the place of regulars. Let us respect their rights, and they will be more useful. If we trample their privileges under foot, they will be less dangerous to the enemy than to their oppressors.

It is most worthy of remark, that in the act of 1795, all these essential characteristics of the militia force are carefully preserved. That act provides that they shall be called from the parts most contiguous to the place of danger. That they shall not serve more than three months in any one year, and each man only in due rotation with every other able-bodied man of the battalion to which he belongs. This act is entitled, as I before remarked, to the most profound respect, as a correct exposition of the Constitutional powers of the Federal Government over the militia of the States, not only because it was enacted while WASHINGTON was President and Hamilton his Counsellor, but from other circumstances. It is a revised law, a former act, passed in 1792, had been found defective. It was enacted at a time when the Government would naturally be disposed to execute all the authority vested in it; directly after the formidable insurrection in the western counties of Pennsylvania was crushed, and when a foreign war had been recently expected. It is a precedent well worthy to be followed, but of late years its principles have been disregarded. The time of service has been doubled by acts already passed. Now we are to quadruple it. We have rejected or disregarded its other wholesome provisions and restraints; and boldly demand an entire authority and control over the male population of the country. But, Mr. Speaker, it is apparent to me that this bill not only destroys the characteristic principles of the militia force, but that it prostrates at once the important personal rights of our citizens, and also of our State governments.

This bill will deprive all the citizens who shall fall under the draughts of their dearest personal rights. You force them against their will to be soldiers for a whole year. You drag them from their wives, their children, their occupations, their professions and trades. You consign them to the camp, and to the hardships and toils of a common soldier. You ruin them. Take the farmer from his plough; the tradesman from his shop; the laborer from his employment, and what but ruin can await men of moderate means and large families, depending upon daily industry for maintenance and support? When they return, at the close of the year, they will find their farms unproductive and in ruins; their customers gone; their business passed away into other hands, and their families in want. What will become of men, with small means, dependent upon daily and steady exertions? What will become of tenants who cultivate the lands of other men? Of the mechanics or laborers on whom this lot may fall? They will, I repeat it, be ruined. Besides, while we thus injure and destroy their families, we at the same time make slaves of them. We deprive them for a year of the inestimable right of civil liberty; we place them under martial law; expose them to military tribunals—to ignominious punishment—perhaps to death itself, for asserting what they believe to be their inalienable right. You make them slaves to their officers, many of whom will be their inferiors in worth and standing in society; perhaps to beardless boys, who, having never been taught themselves to obey, are sure to be insolent and overbearing in command.

Such will be the inevitable fate of your militia soldiers, if they are to perform this cruel service.

And why are they thus to be imposed upon? Will it be answered that it is to save the country? There is no necessity to save the country by such means. The people do not require us—they will not permit us thus to save them. What consolation will it be to them to be saved at such a price? If this war continues, as it probably will, another year, one hundred thousand more must be provided. The whole country may be impoverished and ruined. We ought to remember that we are legislating for American freemen. We may assure ourselves, that our countrymen possess this honorable trait of character, that, while they will be ever ready to submit to us if we are in the right, they will be equally on the alert to resist if we are in the wrong.

This bill also attacks the right and sovereignty of the State governments. Congress is about to usurp their undoubted rights—to take from them their militia. By this bill we proclaim that we will have their men; as many as we please; when and where, and for as long a time as we see

HISTORY OF CONGRESS.

Militia Draughts.

fit, and for any service we see proper. Do gentlemen of the majority seriously believe that the people and the State governments will submit to this claim? Do they believe that all the States of this Union will submit to this usurpation? Have you attended to the solemn and almost unanimous declaration and protestation of the Legislature of Connecticut? Have you examined the cloud arising in the East? Do you yet perceive that it is black, alarming, portentous? Do you wish to put a match to it, and to plunge the country into discord and civil war? and when the enemy is at hand? No, you do not—you cannot mean to bring about such ills; you must see the necessity of union at such a time at this.

I speak not in the language of menace. But let me entreat you to desist from this course of measures. Give up, I entreat you, all the harsh features of this bill. Indeed you want no new act. The existing laws are sufficient for all fair purposes. Give up also, I conjure you, by the best interests of our common country—give up all the other acts you contemplate for raising armies by compulsion. Rely upon it, the people will not support you in such measures. Let me again ask you, as practical men, do you seriously believe that every State of this Union will submit to this compulsory system? Suppose that New England refuses, to what a condition do you reduce the Middle and Southern States, which may be disposed to submit! You will either invite them by their interests and feelings to join in the opposition, or you expose them to burdens to which the others successfully object. Thus they will be punished for their loyalty and devotion. Be reassured by me that these measures are not required to defend the country. You have no right to defend the country by such means. Such a defence will leave it not worth defending. It is not for me to offer any advice to this majority; but listen to me for a moment longer; hearken to my earnest entreaty; that you defend the country by Constitutional means; by such means as the people have been accustomed to, and which will command public confidence and approbation; give up, I again pray you, these cruel plans of compulsory service. Be warned, in season, that if you do not, you will convulse this Union to its very centre. Disguise them as you may, the people will discover the entering wedge of conscription. Let your defensive efforts be on our own soil; a few well disciplined regiments properly posted and commanded, aided by the militia, will perform wonders. Remember that recently less than fifteen hundred men have foiled and driven back with disgrace the best appointed and most numerous army that Britain has ever had in Canada. Raise armies by voluntary enlistment only. Be under no apprehension of failure. Employ trusty officers in the recruiting service; furnish them with money, and keep them constantly supplied. The efforts you hold out are abundantly sufficient to command men; if they are not, increase them. Encourage volunteer corps; arrange your militia under existing laws; arm them; but call them not from their homes until they are wanted. Respect their rights and interests; cultivate their good will by attending to their comfort and wants; leave them to their own commanders; interfere not with the State governments respecting their militia, but encourage them to make exertions for the common defence. Pass an act guaranteeing the pay of the militia which may be advanced by the States. Pursue a Constitutional and conciliatory course, and you may safely rely upon the strength, valor, and patriotism of the people.

Mr. SHEFFEY, of Virginia, next addressed the Chair as follows:

Mr. Speaker, I beg the attention of the House, while I submit a few observations on the subject under consideration. It is not my intention to investigate the details of the bill before you minutely, but to confine my remarks to some general principles, which have been brought into discussion. With the honorable member from New Jersey, (Mr. STOCKTON,) I am conscious of the awful crisis at which the affairs of this country have arrived; with him, I admit that ruin is staring us in the face on every side; with him, too, I feel it to be my duty to contribute my efforts to rescue this devoted nation from the impending calamities. Considering the revival of public credit, at present prostrate in the dust, and the security of the country from foreign danger of vital interest to us all, I shall most cordially co-operate in such measures as may be calculated to effect these great ends. I shall pursue this course, though I did not participate in the councils whose temerity and folly have precipitated us from the highest elevation of national prosperity, to the lowest abyss of suffering. But, with a sincere determination to go every reasonable length in the course thus marked out, I shall not consider myself bound to accord in every measure that may be proposed under the name of a remedy for existing evils. To obtain my approbation, there must be, according to my judgment, a natural connexion between the means and the end. The means, too, must be of a character suited to the spirit of free institutions, that the great principles of civil liberty, on which this Government is erected, shall not be violated.

Formidable and alarming as the dangers may be which threaten us from abroad, I shall not forget that the country has other interests at stake, of equal consideration with its independence, and as necessary to be preserved; that public liberty merits a full portion of our solicitude. It will be a paltry object to remain independent, unless we also remain free. Shall the shackles of domestic slavery be the only reward of this people for their toils and sufferings, in expelling from their soil a powerful enemy? For myself, sir, holding the opinion once entertained by some of the leading men now in power to be indubitably correct—that the liberties of a free people are most in danger at home, in time of foreign peril—I shall deem it my duty to look with a vigilant and jealous eye on the public measures. It will be an object of the first importance with me, that, when the valor and patriotism of the people shall have successfully resisted their external enemy, there may be left something worthy of their exertions; that there shall remain to them a country worth preserving.

The present period has given birth to doctrines more alarming than all the other dangers which surround us. On the part of those in power, claims have been set up, tending to subject the life and liberty of every member of the community to their arbitrary and unlimited control. Should they succeed in enforcing these claims by practical measures, the great principles of this Government must necessarily be subverted. Its character will no longer be free, or its powers limited. By one effort, they will alike prostrate the authority of the States and the liberties of the people.

The Secretary of War, the official author of these high-toned pretensions, recommends that we should raise a regular force of one hundred thousand men, to be employed in offensive operations in Canada. To obtain and keep up that number, he proposes, substantially, that the people shall be *coerced* into the ranks of the Army, if they will not, or cannot, procure the requisite number of recruits by contract. Aware that such a proposal would raise the indignant feelings of freemen, and that the power of this Government to adopt a measure so violent, would be seriously questioned, he submits to us a course of reasoning, which with him, and, from what we have heard on this floor, with others, seems to be conclusive. He informs us that "Congress have a right, by the Constitution, to raise regular armies, and no restraint is imposed on the exercise of it"—that "an unqualified grant of power gives the means to carry it into effect." This, he says, "is a universal maxim, which admits of no exception." Hence, the honorable Secretary infers, that you have the power to drag the citizen from the land of his birth, to be slaughtered on the plains of Canada. To force the father, the only support of a destitute family, and the son, the comfort of his aged parents, to undergo the miseries of a camp in a foreign country. I meet this bold pretension as I would every attempt at usurpation. I deny the right to convert a nation of freemen into slaves, under any pretence whatever. I take upon myself to assert, that no such power can be exercised by this Government, or by any other which maintains any respect for the liberties of its people.

That the authority of this Government in the execution of its power (where not expressly restricted) is sovereign, I am not disposed to controvert; but that it is despotic, I can never admit. Every free Government possesses sovereign power over the means necessary to the attainment of its legitimate objects. But, in the selection of those means, the security of life, liberty, and property, cannot be disregarded; because that security forms the great end for which all power was granted. This great principle can never be infringed, or the people are not free. Hence, the

opinion of some of the wisest and best men that ever lived, that laws violating this security, where the Government is not absolutely despotic, are void.

The objects for which the Government was instituted are not left to conjecture. The men who framed and those who adopted the present Constitution thought it necessary to transmit, to those who should live after them, the most conclusive evidence of the views with which they entered into this new political compact. Not content that they should be inferred from the limitations and restrictions of the powers granted, they declared them in terms thus express and unequivocal: "To form a more perfect union, es-'tablish justice, insure domestic tranquillity, pro-'vide for the common defence, promote the gen-'eral welfare, and secure to themselves and to 'their posterity the blessings of liberty." These were the ends for the accomplishment of which all the powers vested by the Constitution, in the United States, were granted; and now it is asserted that the powers *so* granted may be executed in a manner wholly regardless of the ends in view—that, to "raise armies," the Government have the right to adopt measures by which the people and their posterity shall be deprived of the "blessings of liberty."

Sir, I have said that, if the principles assumed should receive countenance in this country, not only the liberties of the people, but the authority of the States, would be alike annihilated. There is no act of tyranny which may not be perpetrated with as much plausibility as the measure demanded by the Administration at our hands. It has already been ably shown by a member from New Hampshire, (Mr. Webster,) that the same construction that authorizes you to drag the citizen by force into the ranks of your Army, will warrant you to enter into his dwelling and force from him his money. The analogy is unquestionably correct. The power to "borrow money" is as unrestrained as the power to "raise and support armies." Under the latter power you claim arbitrary dominion over the "life and liberty" of the citizen, because it contains no express restriction. Why, I ask, not over his money, when the power "to borrow" it is equally unrestrained? Is there any distinction in the nature and reason of the subject, that would make his money sacred, while his person is at your mercy? Will it be said that the poor man may be coerced in the field to meet misery and death, leaving a helpless family without support, and that his wealthier neighbor's money is not equally subject to your power? This cannot be asserted with the least shadow of reason. If there is power to compel the one to render his person, there is power to compel the other to render his money to your service. —

The analogy becomes still stronger as the subject is pursued. To justify the claim set up over the persons of the people, the Secretary of War tells us, that "the conservation of the State is a duty paramount to all others;" that, therefore, "the Commonwealth has a right to all the service of its citizens." Does "the conservation of the State" depend alone on "the service" of its citizens? Is money, justly termed the sinews of war, not equally necessary to render that "service" beneficial? Are the "citizens" to be coerced into the field to perish for want of subsistence, or to fall before the enemy for want of the necessary means of defence? If "the conservation of the State" will warrant you to coerce "the *service* of the citizens," when you are destitute of *men*, and cannot get the requisite number in any other way, it will surely warrant you to coerce their *money*, when the same necessity exists, as indispensable to the attainment of the same end.

We are further informed, from the same quarter, that "it would be absurd to suppose that Congress could not carry this power (to raise and support armies) into effect otherwise than by accepting the voluntary service of individuals." "It might happen that an army could not be raised in that mode, whence the power would have been granted in vain." The position here assumed, is, that all the means that will give effect to any of the delegated powers, of whatever character, are within the control of Congress, if, without the means proposed to be employed, the power could not be executed at the time, to the extent required by public exigencies, "real or pretended." Hence it clearly follows, that, whenever money cannot be obtained by voluntary loans, when the Government is hard pressed, the power "to borrow money" may be executed by compelling individuals to loan; otherwise, "the power would have been granted in vain." Apply this monstrous principle to the present state of things in this country. Your Treasury is exhausted. There is at this moment a deficit of many millions. Your soldiers are unpaid; your militia, in the inclement season of Winter, are discharged without money enough to defray their expenses to their homes. You have used every effort to borrow money, in the ordinary mode, "in vain." You have not been able to obtain sufficient to discharge the interest of the public debt, and save the Treasury notes falling due from being dishonored. In truth, the Government is on the verge of bankruptcy! Now, with this convenient power at your command, why not borrow money at the point of the bayonet? If you do not, the power to borrow has "been granted in vain." Nay, why not, if this mode should fail, take the people's property to "support your armies," or sell it under the hammer, and give the owner a certificate for the proceeds, as for so much money borrowed? Should you want precedents for such atrocious acts, you would find them in the history of the same despotic Governments whose examples have been cited by gentlemen on this floor to prove the right and propriety of coercing American freemen into the ranks of your army.

The honorable gentleman from New Hampshire (Mr. WEBSTER) has also most clearly demonstrated, that, if the construction given to the Constitution by the Secretary of War is correct, you have the power to take by violence the ships of your merchants, and convert them into ships of war, and man your Navy by impressment. The conclusion of the honorable gentleman is inevitable, admitting the Secretary's reasoning. The power "to provide and maintain a navy" is wholly unrestricted. "The conservation of the State" may, and in reality does, depend as much on a competent naval as on a land force; and, therefore, the same principle which sanctions coercion to raise an army, will bear you out in using the means stated "to provide a navy." Yet, the same person who has attempted to impose the doctrine upon this body, that every man in the nation can be coerced into the Army, has, on another occasion, denied that a single citizen could be impressed into the Navy. In the instructions to our Ministers, appointed to negotiate a treaty with Great Britain, which he composed as Secretary of State, he says, that "impressment is not an American practice, but utterly repugnant to our Constitution and laws." What must every impartial man think of such morality? When one object is sought to be effected, it is asserted that coercion is "utterly repugnant to our Constitution;" when another is desirable, we are told that "it would be absurd to doubt the right to employ it to every possible extent." Or, are seamen exempt from your power, and landsmen only subject to it? Surely no such absurdity as this will be insisted on.

The practice of impressment, as exercised over her seafaring subjects by Great Britain, has been for years a fruitful theme of declamation in this House and elsewhere. The incessant efforts that were made to irritate the people against this crying iniquity, as it was characterized, was not among the least of the causes which exasperated the public feeling, and prepared the country for hostilities. The sufferings of the incarcerated seamen in "the floating dungeons of England" haunted the imaginations of a certain class of politicians, and seemed to be the sole object of all their sympathies. Little did they suppose, that, in a very short time, it would become convenient for them to claim and execute this abhorred and despotic power over their own people. Gentlemen ought to take back the reproaches and denunciations against this practice, since they have become convinced that it is nothing more than a legitimate right, necessary to "the conservation of the State." Unless, indeed, there is a distinction between the sufferings of him who is torn from his family and friends, and immured in one of the "floating dungeons of England," and him who shall be taken by like violence, and under like circumstances, and confined in an American ship of war.

Sir, if in the execution of the powers expressly confided to this Government, you have the right to use arbitrary and despotic means to obtain the end, what will prevent you from imprisoning, for life, the man on whom you shall impose a capitation tax, which he is unable to pay? Or what will prevent you from selling him as a slave in the market, to obtain the money which you may levy on him, when his poverty denies you the means of enforcing payment in any other manner?

Congress are authorized, by the Constitution, to define and punish certain crimes. They have, moreover, the power to create offences and provide for their punishment, as necessary sanctions to their laws. In neither of these cases is their discretion expressly limited. But can they, therefore, direct that the accused shall be put to the rack, and that his confessions, extorted under the torture, shall be evidence to prove his guilt? If all these things can be done by this Government, without transcending its Constitutional limits, then has the blood of the Revolution flowed in vain—then was the manly and patriotic resistance made by the Father of American Independence, to the claims of Great Britain, worse than useless—then was the solicitude of the framers of our Constitution, to "secure to themselves and posterity the blessings of liberty," wholly unavailing.

What becomes of the authority of the States, if the omnipotent power ascribed to this Government properly belongs to it? It will be a mere shadow—an empty name. You have already given capacity to persons under age to enlist in your armies, against the consent of their parents, guardians, or masters, while under the laws of the States they are incapable of making any contract. What prevents you from giving the same capacity to slaves, that they may become soldiers? There is no distinction in principle, and certainly none in reason. The incapacity of infants and slaves depends alike on the municipal laws of the States. Those who authorized the son, in the giddy moments of youth and indiscretion, to be torn from the bosom of his parents, will surely not stickle for the rights of the master, to secure to him his property in his slave.

It is not only in these instances that the power of the States will be subverted, but the great principles of society, resting on municipal institutions, must be wholly overthrown. Let me state one or two examples. If you have the right to raise an army in any way which is calculated to attain the object, then you have the right to defeat the criminal justice of the States, by absolving from punishment those accused or convicted of crimes, on condition they enter your army. You may change the course of descents, and repeal the statutes of wills, by holding out the inducements to recruits that the sole inheritance of their ancestors' property shall belong to them, and that their right shall not be defeated by any testamentary disposition. Is there a man who, in the face of this people, dare assert that such powers belong to this Government? And yet they unquestionably do, if it is correct that the power "to raise an army" is subject to no restriction.

In relation to the militia, pretensions equally exorbitant have been advanced on the part of those in power. They are considered under the absolute control of this Government, to be called forth when it may think proper, in any number, to be employed in any service, and retained for any period. Nothing can be more incorrect in principle, and more dangerous in practice, to this community, than this assumption. It effectually prostrates the State sovereignties, and destroys the security of the people from oppressive military service. To me it seems evident that the general power over the militia was intended, by the authors of the Constitution, to remain with the States, while a special power, arising out of, and limited by, certain emergencies, was confided to this Government. This is obvious to my mind, from the nature of the subject, as well as the express provisions contained in that instrument. The enlightened men, on whose labors depended the fate of their country, understood the nature of man, his thirst for dominion, and the character and tendency of human institutions; they knew that political power, without physical means to secure it, and give it effect, was a mere mockery. Is it reasonable, therefore, to suppose that, while they transferred a portion only of the whole sovereignty to the United States, they intended to invest them with an absolute control over all the physical means of the community? What will be the condition of the States, should this construction obtain? They will be at the mercy of this Government. The most palpable infraction of their rights must be submitted to. Aggression will succeed aggression, until consolidation shall terminate even the appearance of State authority. Sir, very different opinions were entertained in this country at the time the Constitution was adopted. It was considered (as is evident from a work of high celebrity written at the time) that the States were independent political bodies, whose powers and means afforded the best security against the encroachments of the General Government, and who would employ force, if necessary to resist such encroachments, whenever they should be seriously attempted.[*] How, I ask, can the States resist usurpation, if we possess a supreme and general power over the militia? They may, indeed, call them to their aid to maintain the remnant of sovereignty; but such call will be nugatory. The United States (according to the doctrine of the day) may at any moment assume the control over them, and place them into their service, in which situation they are under the sole command of this Government, and subject to the rules and articles of war. Should any of them refuse to be employed, to further the projects of ambition, and to prostrate the authority

[*] The following is an extract from the forty-sixth number of the Federalist, written by Mr. Madison:

"But ambitious encroachments of the Federal Government, on the authority of the State governments, would not excite the opposition of a single State, or a few States only. They would be signals of general alarm. Every Government would espouse the common cause. A correspondence would be opened. Plans of resistance would be concerted. One spirit would animate and conduct the whole. The same combination, in short, would result from an apprehension of the Federal, as was produced by the dread of a foreign yoke; and unless the projected innovation should be voluntarily renounced, the same appeal to a trial of force would be made in the one case as was made in the other."

of their native State, punishment for mutiny awaits them. The minions of power will be ready to execute upon them the despotic provisions of military law.

There are other considerations which strongly tend to establish that the general power over the militia was deemed essential to the security of the State. They are prohibited in time of peace from keeping in their service any regular force; yet it is indispensable to their own existence that they should possess military means to maintain their own authority, to suppress conspiracies and insurrections, and to repel invasions when suddenly made, or when the United States have not provided a force competent to resist the invader. How, I ask, can these objects be effected, if the militia can, at the discretion of this Government, be withdrawn from their control?

What I have said hitherto on this part of the subject has arisen from the character of the American confederacy. My object was to show that as the whole sovereignty was divided between the States and the United States, so a division of the means to maintain each in its portion, would be a just inference deducible from those premises. That as the United States had general (and in time of peace exclusive) power to raise armies to effect the objects, it was rational to infer that a general power over the militia remained with the States, as necessary to the attainment of their ends. I will now beg leave to request your attention to the express provisions of the Constitution on this subject.

When that instrument was formed, it will be recollected that the sole power over the militia was vested in the States. By the Confederation they were enjoined "to keep up a well regulated militia;" but no authority to employ them was granted to the United States in any event. They were, in every sense of the term, "the militia of the States." In this situation of things, while the power of the States, in relation to this subject, was general and exclusive, the new Government came into existence. Its powers were composed of all powers vested in Congress under the Confederation, and a portion of those belonging to the States. To obviate the necessity of keeping up a large Military Establishment in ordinary times, the United States were empowered to call "the militia of the States" to their aid in certain sudden emergencies; to enable them to execute their laws, repel invasion, and to suppress insurrections. And as, in the performance of those duties, it was possible that the militia of different States might be brought to act together in one corps, it became important that there should be uniformity in their organization and discipline. Hence arose the power of Congress over those subjects, as necessary instruments to render the service of the militia, in the cases provided for, more effectual than could have been expected from the discordant regulations of the different States.

Thus it appears to me that the power granted to us to employ the militia is in its character qualified and contingent; always dormant and inactive, until the emergencies provided for in the Constitution give it life and vigor; while the power of the States is general and exclusive, except so far as the actual existence of these emergencies interfere. From this position it seems to me necessarily to follow, that the *qualified* cannot be exercised in such manner as to destroy the *general* power; that the proper State authorities have the unquestionable right to judge for themselves, whether the actual situation of the country demands the exercise of the qualified powers of this Government to call forth the militia. The principle is universal and applicable in all cases. Where a general right exists in one, and a qualified right in another, over the same subject, he who possesses the latter cannot be permitted to decide alone that his right attaches. If he could, his right, instead of being limited or contingent, would be absolute.

By the provisions of the bill before you, a general power over the militia is assumed. They are not to be called forth when any Constitutional emergency shall authorize their employment; but the call is immediate and peremptory; their service is not to be limited by the duration of any such emergency, but by a definite and distant period, or by the discretion of the Executive. Nor is that service to be confined to the objects designated in the Constitution, but to be used for the general purposes of war. And these provisions are adopted for the avowed purpose of compelling the militia, rather than submit to the hardships created by your law, to furnish recruits for your army. It is not necessary for me to show that you have no more right to exact this commutation, than you have to demand the service from the militia.

To give some plausibility to the high-handed measures proposed during the present session, attempts have been made to depreciate the value of the militia in the public estimation. The cry has been raised that they are wholly useless and incompetent to the defence of the country. It is observed by a celebrated writer of the last century, equally distinguished for his eloquence and his knowledge of public men, and public affairs, that those whose object it is to enslave the people, first endeavor to degrade them in their own eyes. Where is our security against the usurpation of those who command the public force, if the militia is thus inefficient? It is only necessary for the people to believe the libels so industriously circulated against them, and slavery must be their lot. Sir, I believe the militia more competent to the defence of the country against the predatory warfare of the enemy than any force you can obtain. Whenever the idea shall become general that you cannot rely on the militia, and some other force shall be substituted in their stead, it will beget the same indifference among the great body of the people which exists in other countries. If you once persuade them that their services, their privations, and their blood, are wholly unavailing, do you presume that they will feel disposed to make useless sacrifices? If it was possible for you to procure a regular force of 200,000 men, on whom alone, for all military purposes, our whole reliance should be placed in this war, I do not believe that to all essential purposes the country would be better defended than it is at present. That portion of the force which would be spared from the Canadian warfare, must be distributed along our extended maritime frontier, in such manner as to occupy the most prominent and important points only. All other places must be left wholly defenceless, consequently to the enemy having the command of the water assailable. In such a state of things, the enemy would have only to dread the force actually embodied in the neighborhood of his attack, and make his movements accordingly. At present he knows that every man in the country is one of its legitimate defenders, upon whose services it relies. That circumstance is calculated to inspire him with a proper portion of caution, and tends to limit the extent of his incursions.

If the object of the enemy had been the conquest of our country, and if that object depended on a few great and decisive actions in the field, I admit that the militia would not be the proper kind of force to oppose to him. In such actions, discipline and experience, which the militia, from the short periods and nature of their service, cannot possess, in an eminent degree, are generally essential to victory.

We are frequently told that we *oppose* everything coming from the majority, and that we *propose* nothing calculated to save the country from the perils which surround us. This is an old and a stale accusation. As long as gentlemen are determined to disregard our counsels, how can they ask us to submit to the repeated mortifications of having our propositions rejected? On the present, as on many other occasions, however, the assertion is not founded in fact. The honorable gentleman from New Jersey (Mr. STOCKTON) has marked out the course for you in detail; permit me to repeat his admonitions, in substance. Abandon the project which experience has stamped with folly, of conquering Canada. Manifest a determination to defend your country by Constitutional means. Banish from you all idea of conscription to fill the ranks of your army. Inspire confidence by a just, liberal, and conciliatory policy; and I hesitate not to say that the present dangers will pass away, and that the country will remain independent and free.

I know that the situation of gentlemen in the majority is different from my own. Having by an ill-judged and unfortunate course of policy brought this nation into a condition admitted on all sides to be extremely perilous and alarming, they feel the high responsibility that awaits them, should the country perish in their hands. In the anxiety which such a situation necessarily begets, the character of the means will not be very scrupulously examined, if there is hope that they will serve the end. Something is necessary to be done. I warn gentlemen against the influence of this sentiment. It has been the bane of this country. Ever since I have had the honor of a seat in this House, it has given birth to all the measures connected with your foreign policy. The commencement of every session brought with it a deep conviction that something was necessary to be done, but it did not bring with it the lights requisite to judge correctly what it ought to be. Hence it happened that we were plunged from one difficulty into another still greater, until, at last, we find ourselves in a condition almost hopeless.

Sir, it is not my intention to menace gentlemen with the prospect of forcible opposition to their projects of coercing freemen into the ranks of the Army, but I will take the liberty to offer my admonition. Permit me to say that a period like the present, when your Treasury is exhausted; when all your operations are almost at a stand for want of means to impel them, is not the season for violent measures. Every Government becomes imbecilitated when its finances become deranged; and in this Government, more than any other, money is the vital principle of action. The catastrophe which deprived Louis XVI of his life—that tremendous revolution which has been the cause of so much calamity to the whole community of civilized man—would never have happened had not France been bankrupt in her finances.

Mr. HOPKINS, of Kentucky, said:—The silence I have imposed upon myself in many discussions deemed of great importance to our country, would not now be broken, had not arguments have been used against the constitutionality and expediency of this bill. The old mournful song of "weakness and wickedness of the Administration," at the tail of the cry of "French influence," is still, sir, the fashionable ditty, and chanted in all, as prelude or finale of every subject. I mean not to enter into a vindication of others; believing it is incident to our nature to err, and believing that the best of our fellow-citizens, raised by the suffrages of our country into the most exalted and honorable stations, do not thereby "partake of the nature of angels," but still remain the "seed of Abraham," I feel disposed to admit those aberrations of the head, incident to our race; but I deny, nor can it be proved, that the hearts of this Administration can be truly assailed with any taint, or the want of honor, intrepidity, or patriotism. Their actions are tested by the applause and approbation of the great majority of our country, and prove their worth and excellence. Their virtue and talents, "fair as the moon, bright as the sun, and (to the enemies of our Union) terrible as an army with banners," need not my advocation. But I come to the questions. Are the provisions of this bill Constitutional? Are its exactments within the positive powers of Congress; and, if they are, is it expedient at this time?

On looking into the Constitution, I find a power given, in the eighth section, to " provide for the ' common defence of the United States, to raise ' and support armies, to provide for organizing the ' militia, and to make all laws necessary and proper ' for carrying into execution the foregoing powers."

Permit me to ask. Can words make power more ample? Can language increase its attributes? Neither time, place, or occasion, limits this power. 'Tis positive—the Congress possess it, and are alone responsible for abuse of it. If, indeed, it were necessary to add to this well-defined power, I might be pardoned for quoting a statute of much greater antiquity and much higher authority, as well as more positive; a statute registered in Heaven, and recorded in the great volume of animate being, entitled Self-preservation; teaching its lessons to brutes, and lecturing man, that whenever the occasion requires it, "it is meet that some should die for the people," to prevent the whole nation from perishing. If, sir, such authorities as these fail to show the constitutionality of this bill, I confess I have none greater, and should despair of seeing the honorable opponents to it convinced by "a decree from Heaven." Sir, it is not sufficient to oppose paradoxes, sophistry, and argument, to the veritable assertions here made. Could gentlemen "burst the cerements" of reason, logic, and syllogism, they would not be able to mar the features, extenuate or shroud the meaning of those authorities; their effects must be operative, and their force irresistible.

On the expediency and present necessity of raising men for this war, will it be pardonable to dilate? To say we are opposed by an enemy, ferocious, powerful, vindictive, actively employed at this moment, in burning, plundering, robbing and murdering our fellow-citizens on seventeen hundred miles of seacoast, would be repeating what we all know to be fact; to say that we expect this enemy will be greatly augmented early in the next year, would express our belief. That our business here is to provide, as effectually as we can obtain the means, for the safety of our nation, none will deny. Who then will question the necessity of this bill, or some other equally remedial?

But, Mr. Speaker, as we advance towards this desirable object, at every step we are told of conscription; at this cabalistic word, horrors, gorgons, and dire chimeras arise and follow in its train; the separation of father, mother, wife, and child, is grouped; the tender scenes of an everlasting parting are pencilled with a master's hand, and woe, woe, woe, is portrayed with the powers of the most enchanting eloquence. My feelings were (I am not ashamed to own) in sympathetic unison with the dulcet sounds of chastened sorrow flowing from the lips of the honorable gentleman from New Hampshire, in his tale of things yet to come, his group of apprehensions. When, alas! sir, the scene changed from fancy to reality, from the visionary idea of possibility, to the melancholy, mournful catastrophes of substantial misery. What busy scene-shifter of the brain drew the curtain, and presented the cold-blooded murders, burnt and mangled corses of Raisin, Rapids, and Brownstown, the conflagrations and sacking of Black Rock, Havre de Grace, Washington, and every assailable part of the Chesapeake and its tributary streams! Here, indeed,

we might rally, sir—the weeping mother, the orphan, the murdered or imprisoned father or son, the hoary head and green youth, robbed, plundered, imprisoned or murdered, by that infamous enemy who never spared when his avarice or violence were his dictators.

If this recital excites horror; if it would make the swords of freemen fly from their scabbards, to repress and chastise a foe so barbarous, let me ask what additional feeling would edge them? There is existing, sir, a tale, yet untold; the scenes were laid at Hampton, in Virginia, and St. Inigoes, in Maryland; a tale too horrid, too shocking, to bear expression here; a tale that would freeze your blood, excite your vengeance, and make you, like Hannibal, swear eternal enmity to the name of Briton; a tale that would make angels weep, and excite tender emotions from fiends; a tale, the truth of which is unquestionable, passing almost within sight and sound of your Capitol; a tale, repeated but the last week at Tappahannock, which plainly proves it the deliberate purpose of our enemy to persist. This tale, sir, will, I hope, reconcile gentlemen to the objects of this bill, and convince them of its expediency. Let them not be affrighted by the word *conscription;* it is older than the oldest man here; well do I remember it fifty-seven years ago. Then, sir, I saw and recollected the parting of husband and wife, father and son. The occasion required it; the savage was upon the borders, and must be repelled; none murmured. In the war of the Revolution, this same conscription, or draught, which are but words to designate the details for military duty, saved your country. After the reverses in '76, on Long and York Islands, Fort Washington, &c., had almost destroyed every appearance of resisting further the arms of the foe; at a time when even hope was only kept alive and cherished by the example of that exalted man who led the feeble resistance of his country; then, sir, at that hour of alarm and peril, the force raised by conscription saved us; and at every period through that eventful war, we know and feel its efficacy. Sir, when I hear it asserted here, that this law cannot be executed, the Eastern States will revolt, they will not submit to be detailed for the defence of this nation, of which they are a part, I feel astonished. Can you believe these assertions? What, sir! can it be credited that the sons, the offspring of those immortal bands who in 1775 first taught our enemy the might and prowess of freemen, and all America the true principles and value of liberty; who said to Britain, "the soil is our own, and you tread not on it but by permission," and who have gone down into the dust, mature in years and ripe in honors; will their descendants, pious, learned, industrious, and patriotic, wage war against their Government, because of the new exposition of a phrase, or definition of a word, in a law prescribing the means of safety, at this hour of extreme danger? Gentlemen must pardon me for not admitting conclusions so uncharitable (I had almost said) so invidious, from their premises; it is not possible.

Mr. Irving, of New York, spoke as follows:

Mr. Speaker, it appears to me, that the nice distinctions, that have heretofore been made, between a defensive and an offensive war, are no longer of any consequence. The ground on which the war commenced, can no longer, it is presumed, affect the question, whether hostilities shall be carried on with every efficient means within our power. The terms proposed by the British Commissioners have been communicated to this House; and the question now is, whether these terms are to be accepted, or, whether we are to employ the means Providence has placed within our reach in the expectation of procuring better?

Sir, I would ask any gentleman in this Assembly, whether he is willing to accept of these terms—to dismember the territory of the United States, to lop off the hands and arms of this country, and thus deliver her a prey to the enemy; or, at any rate, take from her every future hope of obtaining either satisfaction for injuries, or security against the exercise of oppression on the ocean? If he says he is willing to do this, it is well; he takes this stand, and we know what he means by opposing this measure. But if, on the other hand, by a feeling of generous indignation at these new and unwarrantable claims, that violate the integrity of this country, and outrage every principle of reciprocity, he answers, that he will not make peace on such ignoble terms; then, if he differs with me, it is only as to the expediency of this measure, or its capacity to answer the purpose for which it is intended. It is with a view of investigating these two points that I enter into this debate; for I do not believe there is any honorable gentleman in this House who would recommend a peace on the terms which have been offered. If there is, I should consider it idle to address myself to such a person. It is impossible to create a soul under the ribs of death—and I would consider it equally hopeless to reason against the want of certain feelings, or attempt to excite emotions in a breast steeled by insensibility.

I would, then, ask, are the present means of raising an army adequate to the exigencies of the present crisis? No, sir. The history of the war, and the experience of every day, are a sufficient answer to this question. What with the habits engendered by a long peace—the want of means to pay the enormous bounties, which are necessary to tempt the prosperous multitude of this country—and, most of all, the various and unjustifiable means that have been resorted to, for the purpose of impeding or discouraging enlistments, it is found totally impossible to fill the ranks of the Army. Are the militia ordered out? It is called oppression. Are they selected by lot? Gentlemen cry out conscription—as if there was any analogy between the temperate behests of the law, and the arbitrary will of a despot. Should any man be willing to enlist voluntarily, he is told, that his pay will be withheld, for that, in New England, several soldiers have sold their certificates at a loss of fifty per cent. And this fact, which, if it be true, was the result of a panic arising from the suggestions of some patriotic adviser,

or conscientious broker, who wished to take advantage of his credulity, is trumpeted from one end of the country to the other—hawked about in newspapers, and recorded in triumph by the friends of their country.

What then remains for us, sir? Are we to go on in this miserable ricketty mode of warfare to the end of time, and waste our resources by driblets, in this preposterous economy—this lady-like forbearance of using the means in our power? Or are we, by one manly and decisive effort, to do that at once, which we must do at last, or submit to a most dishonorable peace? This is not the land of Colchis—you cannot sow dragons' teeth and reap armed men; you must resort to human means—and all human means, hitherto tried, have failed; we must, therefore, find others, or we must crouch and cringe, and say to the enemy, in the debased and whining language of cowardice, "take all we have, but spare our lives."

Sir, as a means of raising an efficient army, I see nothing unconstitutional or illegal in the bill before us, nor, indeed, any very extraordinary hardship. If the country is worth defending, and I do trust some part of it, at least, will be considered so, there appears no very good reason why men should not be called upon to perform that duty. The framers of this Constitution thought so, and they invested the General Government with the power of calling out the militia, as a sufficient defence against any force that might be brought against us. If, sir, this resource is withheld by the delicate scruples of some State authorities—if pretence, or construction, or quibble is resorted to—or if men shelter themselves behind an ambiguity, are the country, the lakes, and our honor, to be sacrificed in consequence? I hope not—I trust not—I am sure not. I do believe there is spirit enough in this House to resist both foreign and domestic foes, and energy sufficient to surmount the imaginary barriers of the Constitution, which rather seem to invite the aggressions of the enemy than to afford safety to those whom this very Constitution was intended to protect.

I say imaginary barriers, because I see nothing in the Constitution which opposes this classification. It is true, sir, I am no lawyer, expert in legal subtleties, and equally expert in applying either end of the glass to an object, as it suits his purpose, to increase or diminish it. But there is one rule of law, to which I have not been inattentive, and that is, to consult the intention of the law which we are to expound. What was the intention of that section of the Constitution which provides for calling out the militia; in short, sir, what was the whole object of the Constitution itself? It was framed solely for the purpose of combining the people of the United States into a community for mutual defence. If, therefore, the usual resource of militia is insufficient, we resort to regular enlistment; and if that fails, what are we to do but try more efficient means, or surrender the honor, and barter the interests of the country for imaginary Constitutional scruples?

Sir, there is one political axiom that cannot be

controverted; the country must be defended; and whether this is done by drawing the enemy to a distance, or receiving him at our doors, is a matter of policy, and not of conscience. It does not alter the principle one single hair's breadth. For my part, sir, I cannot find in the Constitution any one principle that militates against classification any more than against a draught, or conscription, as some gentlemen call it. If there was, cases might occur, even then, to justify such a measure, as indispensable to self-defence, which, while that necessity lasts, supersedes all other laws but those of nature.

But it appears to me, that sometimes we "strain at a gnat and swallow a camel." There is a fundamental principle in the Constitution which requires the minority to submit to the will of the majority, constitutionally expressed—yet some in our country have forgotten that; there is another, that " no State shall enter into compact with another State"—some have quite forgotten that; and there is a sacred principle of union pervading every article of the Constitution—and some have quite forgotten that.

No! Mr. Speaker, having so glorious an inheritance, equal to that promised land that the Jews were forty years suffering in the wilderness in the hope of obtaining, is it not wonderful, that instead of devising ways and means for defending and securing the precious possession, we should be seeking for quibbles to render useless the means that God has provided for its defence?

Sir, we hear the Executive of the United States every day charged with incapacity in carrying on the war; but how could we have expected anything else, when we take into consideration the situation in which he has been placed? Instead of providing money by taxation, we chose to resort to the expedient of loans, and sent our Government out borrowing, until they returned penniless. The consequence has been, that instead of employing their time the Summer past in devising plans how they could most annoy the enemy, they have been scuffling with national penury—perplexed to know, from day to day, how they could employ to the best advantage their stinted means—how they could exist from hour to hour, with an exhausted Treasury, and a depreciated credit. It is in vain to expect a well-conducted war and an efficient Administration, unless we provide money and men to produce both.

Sir, gentlemen talk of this General Government as if it were a self-supported superior being; some abstract and independent power; some cloud-enthroned Hercules, on whom we are to depend for overcoming our difficulties, without any exertion of our own. What is the Government of the United States, but an aggregate of the physical power and wealth of the people at large? It is from those it derives its strength and its energy; and if those are withheld, I, for one, should like to know what means gentlemen would propose for the purpose of supplying that strength and energy. Sir, you might as well wither this arm by a powerful spell, and stop the current of blood that flows in these veins, and then, when the arm

13th CON. 3d SESS.—28

was rendered powerless, and the heart ceased to beat, deride the body for being inert and motionless.

There is but one way of giving energy to a free Government that I know of, and that is by being liberal, not reckless, of the public resources; and it is the special duty of this House, charged as it is with that distribution, to be careful, while it guards the public wealth from waste, and the people of this free country from oppression, to give to the Government the means of being strong and energetic.

If we refuse these means, the gentlemen on the other side, who, after having clamored for taxes as they did for war, and afterwards voted against both, may, if they please, charge the Administration with not being energetic; they may attempt to lift the load of responsibility from themselves, but it will cling to them with the pertinacity of some natural deformity; and, though they may perchance deceive themselves, those who trace effects right home to their true causes, will point to this House, which, with a most prodigal economy, refused to bestow, what it was content the Government should borrow, at a rate of interest beyond what any individual who was not desperate in fortune and reputation ever paid.

I came not here, sir, as the advocate of any Administration whatever, but as an agent from the part of the country I represent to promote, according to the best of my judgment, the public good. Still, I think it the part of every honest man to vindicate the rulers of his free choice, when he thinks they are unjustly calumniated. Neither do I impeach any man's motives in saying, that when gentlemen accuse the Executive with want of energy, they may as well go a little further, and accuse the body of not taking care of the limbs, when the limbs have refused to do their office.

It is this mistaken, this fatal economy, that accounts for the ill conduct of the war, of which gentlemen every day, and on all occasions, complain. No matter what may be the subject before us, we are condemned on every question to hear a repetition of the same arguments. The clock does not strike, or the sentinel walk his rounds, more regularly than some gentlemen go the singsong round of " unjust, unnecessary, and unnatural war." They are continually reminding us of the unfortunate cook, who, for want of a little genius to diversify his dinners, every day served up the same dull round of "three roasted pigs, three buttered apple pies." Whenever they are asked for men or money, they either fly out into a passion and scold the Administration roundly, or, they resort to as many excuses as a miser dunned for some miserable pittance. One gentleman will not give his money, because his section of the Union is not represented in the Committee of Ways and Means. Why, sir, this is the first time that I have ever heard the doctrine of the union of taxation and representation narrowed down to such miserable localities. If such a principle is to be introduced into this House, there is not a measure that may not be opposed on this ground. Every State must be represented in each committee; and the jostling of local interests, local prejudices, and local partialities, would in all probability most effectually prevent any well digested report from ever being made to this House.

Sir, it is here, on this floor, that the final decision on every report is made; and, so long as any member of this House can here freely deliver his sentiments and utter his objections in language that suits either the suavity or malignity of his own disposition, it does appear to me a matter of perfect indifference whether his section of the Union is represented in the committee or not.

Sir, I repeat again, it is this mistaken economy which, by withholding what is necessary, renders what it bestows almost useless, that accounts for the alleged bad conduct of the war, on which the gentlemen dwell with such wonderful and incessant pertinacity. Not having money, the Government could not procure men; and not having men, they could not undertake any extensive and splendid enterprise. And this, in my opinion, is all the bad conduct that can be properly charged upon the Administration. Even thus circumscribed by our jealous economy, what one advantage has the enemy gained, except the solitary one of injuring this capital? And that, in a national point of view, as affecting the spirit of the nation, has been rather a good than an evil. Something was necessary to rouse the dormant spirit of the nation, and this has effectually done it. But even this disaster is to be attributed to our own imprudence—not in expending but withholding the public resources. The want of money, so imperiously felt at the Treasury, which prevented the raising of men, prevented the possibility of having a sufficient force ready to repel the enemy at every avenue of attack; it prevented the erecting of necessary fortifications at every vulnerable point; and it prevented the doing anything, until the dangers of the moment called the attention of the Government to act.

Unable to obtain means for expenditures that were absolute in their demand, such as the subsistence of troops, the supplying arms, ammunition, ordnance, clothing, &c., for those already employed, and for erecting fortifications where it was conceived they were immediately wanted, those contingencies that were apparently remote were not taken into consideration; they were of necessity neglected; and hence the opportunity given to the enemy to make an incursion into this place; and here we are to look for the cause of the inefficiency of the present Administration. We did not provide in time the means to enable them to be efficient; and any Administration would have been inefficient under similar circumstances.

I urge these remarks on this House, considering it a thinking, reflecting, body; a co-ordinate branch of the Government; and equally bound with the Executive, in the laws that are framed, to consult the interests and promote the safety of the people. When, therefore, we accuse the Ex-

ecutive of not performing what we did not afford him the means to perform, we either treat him unjustly, or we virtually declare ourselves mere automatons, to be directed by his will, which is notoriously not the case. Sir, let us try to do better in future. Let us provide ample means to insure success, and then, and not till then, can we hold the Executive responsible for disaster and disgrace.

Sir, this is not a time to talk, but to act. When our Army is composed of a mere handful of men, and our Treasury empty, so that it cannot provide for this gallant handful; when an enemy, powerful and active, is beating against our shores like the strong wave of the ocean; when everything is at stake; when personal safety, property, and everything valuable, and everything dear to us, lie all exposed to the mercy of momentary events; and when, in the language of Scripture, we may emphatically say, "we know not what a day may bring forth," surely, such is not the moment for parsimonious feelings in raising taxes, or for forced constructions to defeat the means for raising men. If we are parsimonious now, the next year everything is to be done over again; the same expense is to be repeated, and the same result ensues. Sir, this is the way to exhaust a country without producing one single good. It renders her sacrifices of no avail; it is offering up victims without a hope that the offering will be accepted; it is bleeding a little every day, till the patient is exhausted, while the disease remains.

The motion was further opposed by Messrs. Forsyth, Troup and Bradley, and advocated by Mr. Grosvenor.

After refusing several times to adjourn, the question on the motion for indefinite postponement was decided as follows:

Yeas—Messrs. Baylies of Massachusetts, Bayly of Virginia, Bigelow, Boyd, Bradbury, Breckenridge, Brigham, Burwell, Caperton, Champion, Cilley, Cooper, Culpeper, Davenport, Davis of Massachusetts, Davis of Pennsylvania, Ely, Gaston, Grosvenor, Hale, Henderson, Jackson of Rhode Island, Kent of New York, King of Massachusetts, Law, Lewis, Lovett, Markell, Miller, Moseley, Oakley, Pearson, Pickering, Pitkin, Potter, John Reed, William Reed, Ruggles, Schureman, Sheffey, Shipherd, Skinner, Smith of New York, Stanford, Stockton, Sturges, Taggart, Thompson, Vose, Ward of Massachusetts, Webster, Wheaton, White, Wilcox, and Wilson of Massachusetts—55.

Nays—Messrs. Alexander, Alston, Anderson, Archer, Avery, Barbour, Bard, Barnett, Bines, Bowen, Bradley, Brown, Butler, Caldwell, Calhoun, Cannon, Chappell, Clark, Clopton, Comstock, Condict, Conard, Crawford, Creighton, Crouch, Cuthbert, Denoyelles, Desha, Duvall, Earle, Eppes, Fisk of Vermont, Fisk of New York, Forney, Forsyth, Franklin, Gholson, Goodwyn, Gourdin, Griffin, Harris, Hasbrouck, Hawes, Hopkins of Kentucky, Hubbard, Humphreys, Ingersoll, Ingham, Irving, Irwin, Johnson of Virginia, Johnson of Kentucky, Kennedy, Kent of Maryland, Kerr, Kershaw, Kilbourn, King of North Carolina, Lefferts, Lowndes, Lyle, Macon, McCoy, McKee, McKim, McLean, Moore, Murfree, Nelson, Newton, Ormsby, Parker, Pickens, Piper, Pleasants, Rhea of Pennsylvania, Rhea of Tennessee, Rich, Roane, Robertson, Sage, Seybert, Sharp, Smith of Pennsylvania, Smith of Virginia, Tannehill, Taylor, Telfair, Troup, Udree, Ward of New Jersey, Williams, Wilson of Pennsylvania, Wright, and Yancey—95.

Two or three ineffectual attempts were then made to adjourn.

The question being then stated on concurring in the first amendment to the bill, as agreed to in Committee of the Whole, which amendment authorizes the President to call directly on the officers of militia in case of the refusal of the Governors of the States to aid in the execution of the law—

Mr. WARD, of Massachusetts, spoke a short time in opposition to it.

The question was then taken on concurring in this amendment, and agreed to—For the amendment 87, against it 42, as follows:

YEAS—Messrs. Alexander, Alston, Anderson, Archer, Avery, Barbour, Bard, Barnett, Bines, Bowen, Brown, Butler, Caldwell, Calhoun, Chappell, Clark, Clopton, Comstock, Condict, Conard, Crawford, Creighton, Crouch, Cuthbert, Denoyelles, Desha, Earle, Eppes, Fisk of Vermont, Fisk of New York, Forney, Forsyth, Franklin, Gholson, Goodwyn, Gourdin, Griffin, Harris, Hasbrouck, Hawes, Hopkins of Kentucky, Hubbard, Humphreys, Ingersoll, Ingham, Irving, Irwin, Johnson of Virginia, Johnson of Kentucky, Kennedy, Kent of Maryland, Kerr, Kershaw, Kilbourn, King of North Carolina, Lefferts, Lowndes, Lyle, McCoy, McKim, McLean, Moore, Nelson, Newton, Ormsby, Parker, Pickens, Piper, Pleasants, Rea of Pennsylvania, Rhea of Tennessee, Roane, Robertson, Sage, Sharp, Skinner, Smith of Pennsylvania, Smith of Virginia, Tannehill, Taylor, Telfair, Udree, Ward of New Jersey, Williams, Wilson of Pennsylvania, and Yancey—87.

NAYS—Messrs. Baylies of Massachusetts, Bigelow, Boyd, Bradbury, Bradley, Breckenridge, Brigham, Caperton, Champion, Cooper, Culpeper, Davis of Massachusetts, Ely, Gaston, Grosvenor, Hale, Henderson, Jackson of Rhode Island, King of Massachusetts, Lewis, Lovett, Macon, Miller, Moseley, Pickering, Pitkin, John Reed, William Reed, Rich, Ruggles, Schureman, Sheffey, Stanford, Sturges, Thompson, Vose, Ward of Massachusetts, Webster, White, Wilcox, Wilson of Massachusetts, and Wright—42.

The question, on a motion of Mr. MILLER, to adjourn (at 6 o'clock) was then taken by yeas and nays—for the motion 53, against it 75.

Mr. LEWIS, of Virginia, then moved to postpone the bill and amendments to Monday.—Negatived.

The House then proceeded to consider and separately to agree to all the amendments reported by the Committee of the Whole. That amendment made in the Committee of the Whole, on motion of Mr. EPPES, to reduce the term of service of the militia to be draughted from two years to one year, was agreed to by the following vote:

YEAS—Messrs. Alexander, Alston, Barbour, Bard, Baylies of Massachusetts, Bradbury, Bradley, Breckenridge, Brigham, Burwell, Butler, Caperton, Cannon, Clopton, Culpeper, Cuthbert, Desha, Ely, Eppes, Fisk of Vermont, Franklin, Gaston, Gholson, Goodwyn, Grosvenor, Hale, Harris, Hawes, Henderson, Humphreys, Johnson of Virginia, Kennedy, Kent of Mary-

land, Kerr, King of Massachusetts, Lewis, Lovett, Lowndes, Macon, McCoy, McLean, Moore, Moseley, Piper, Pitkin, Pleasants, John Reed, Rich, Roane, Ruggles, Seybert, Sheffey, Skinner, Smith of Virginia, Stanford, Vose, Ward of Massachusetts, Ward of New Jersey, White, Wilcox, Wilson of Massachusetts, and Wright—62.

NAYS—Messrs. Anderson, Archer, Avery, Barnett, Bines, Bowen, Brown, Caldwell, Calhoun, Chappell, Clark, Comstock, Condict, Conard, Crawford, Creighton, Crouch, Denoyelles, Fisk of New York, Forney, Forsyth, Gourdin, Griffin, Hasbrouck, Hopkins of Kentucky, Hubbard, Ingersoll, Ingham, Irving, Irwin, Johnson of Kentucky, Kershaw, Kilbourn, King of North Carolina, Lefferts, Lyle, McKim, Nelson, Newton, Ormsby, Parker, Pickering, Pickens, Rea of Pennsylvania, Rhea of Tennessee, Robertson, Sage, Sharp, Smith of Pennsylvania, Tannehill, Taylor, Telfair, Udree, Webster, Williams, Wilson of Pennsylvania, and Yancey—57.

A motion was then made by Mr. MACON, further to amend the first section of the bill, by striking out the quotas assigned to each of the States, and, in lieu thereof, to insert:

From New Hampshire	3,100
From Massachusetts	10,036
From Rhode Island	1,100
From Connecticut	3,720
From Vermont	3,032
From New York	12,405
From New Jersey	3,087
From Pennsylvania	10,552
From Delaware	803
From Maryland	3,395
From Virginia	7,897
From North Carolina	5,217
From South Carolina	2,870
From Georgia	1,875
From Kentucky	4,025
From Tennessee	2,785
From Ohio	2,960
From Louisiana	428

And the yeas and nays having been required on this motion, the House at length adjourned, a little before 8 o'clock, after a sitting of nearly ten hours.

MONDAY, December 12.

A new member, to wit: from Pennsylvania, AMOS SLAYMAKER, appeared, produced his credentials, and took his seat, in the place of James Whitehill, resigned; the oath to support the Constitution of the United States being first administered to him.

Mr. TAYLOR, of New York, presented the petition of sundry merchants, and other citizens of New York, praying for the establishment of a general bankrupt law; which was read.

Mr. T. said, he had desired the reading of this memorial, for the purpose of calling the attention of the House more particularly to a subject of the utmost importance. Among the signatures to that petition were the names of persons who had contributed millions to the revenue, and of others who had, within a short time, bestowed thousands of dollars on charitable institutions; men than whom there were none more respectable in the

871   HISTORY OF CONGRESS.   872

H. of R.   *Distilled Spirits—Destruction of Public Books, &c.*   December, 1814.

nation. They look to Congress alone for relief from the difficulties into which they have been plunged by the recent embarrassments of commerce; by whom alone they can be relieved, if the recent decision of the circuit court of Pennsylvania be confirmed, &c. He, therefore, moved that the memorial be referred to the Committee on the Judiciary.—Agreed to.

Mr. EPPES, of Virginia, from the Committee of Ways and Means, reported a bill to provide additional revenue for defraying the expenses of the Government and maintaining the public credit, by laying a direct tax within the United States, and to provide for assessing and collecting the same; twice read, and committed.

The bill from the Senate for the relief of J. C. Hurlburt having been reported without amendment, was ordered to a third reading.

The House then took up for consideration the amendments of the Senate to the carriage duty bill; which were agreed to.

DISTILLED SPIRITS.

Mr. EPPES, from the Committee of Ways and Means, to whom was referred the amendments of the Senate to the bill laying a duty on distilled spirits, made a report thereon. Several of the amendments having been agreed to, the question was then stated on agreeing to that amendment of the Senate, which proposes to strike out the section allowing distillers to sell any quantity not less than one gallon of the liquor they distil.

[The section thus proposed to be struck out of the bill was originally inserted, in the House, at the suggestion of Mr. GHOLSON, of Virginia, who, with others, contended that the law, as it now stood, had a most inconvenient and even oppressive operation on the people in the particular part of the country in which he resided, many of whom did not distil to the quantity which they are by law allowed to dispose of, and who were now precluded from selling enough of the liquor they distil, to enable them to pay the tax on it.]

The proposition to strike out this section was opposed by Mr. GHOLSON and Mr. EPPES, Mr. McKEE of Kentucky. Mr. MACON of North Carolina, Mr. RHEA of Tennessee, Mr. PICKENS of North Carolina, and Mr. INGHAM of Pennsylvania; and supported by Mr. McKIM of Maryland, Mr. WARD and Mr. JOHN REED, of Massachusetts, Mr. FISK of New York, and Mr. POTTER.

The question on concurring in the amendment, which goes to strike out this section, was decided in the negative by yeas and nays, which exhibited the following result: For the amendment 71, against it 81, as follows:

YEAS—Messrs. Anderson, Archer, Avery, Baylies of Massachusetts, Bayly of Virginia, Bigelow, Bines, Boyd, Bradbury, Bradley, Breckenridge, Brigham, Butler, Champion, Cilley, Comstock, Cox, Crawford, Dana, Davenport, Davis of Massachusetts, Denoyelles, Ely, Fisk of New York, Geddes, Glasgow, Gourdin, Grosvenor, Hale, Hasbrouck, Henderson, Howell, Ingersoll, Kent of New York, King of Massachusetts, Law, Lewis, Lovett, Lowndes, Markell, McKim, Miller, Moore, Moseley, Oakley, Pickering, Potter, John

Reed, William Reed, Rich, Robertson, Ruggles, Schureman, Seybert, Shipherd, Smith of New York, Stockton, Sturges, Taggart, Taylor, Thompson, Vose, Ward of Massachusetts, Ward of New Jersey, Webster, Wheaton, Wilcox, Williams, Wilson of Massachusetts, Winter, and Wright.

NAYS—Messrs. Alexander, Alston, Barbour, Bard, Barnett, Bowen, Brown, Burwell, Caperton, Caldwell, Calhoun, Cannon, Chappell, Clark, Clopton, Conard, Creighton, Culpeper, Cuthbert, Davis of Pennsylvania, Desha, Duvall, Earle, Eppes, Evans, Farrow, Findley, Forney, Forsyth, Franklin, Gholson, Goodwyn, Griffin, Hall, Harris, Hawes, Hopkins of Kentucky, Hubbard, Humphreys, Ingham, Irwin, Johnson of Virginia, Johnson of Kentucky, Kennedy, Kerr, Kershaw, King of North Carolina, Lefferts, Lyle, Macon, McCoy, McKee, McLean, Montgomery, Murfree, Nelson, Newton, Ormsby, Parker, Pearson, Pickens, Piper, Pleasants, Rea of Pennsylvania, Rhea of Tennessee, Roane, Sage, Sevier, Sharp, Sheffey, Smith of Pennsylvania, Smith of Virginia, Stanford, Stuart, Tannehill, Telfair, Troup, Udree, White, Wilson of Pennsylvania, and Yancey.

All the amendments (this one excepted) were agreed to, and the bill returned to the Senate.

DESTRUCTION OF BOOKS AND PAPERS.

Mr. PEARSON, of North Carolina, from the select committee, to whom was referred the letter of Patrick Magruder, respecting the destruction of the library and papers belonging to the office of the Clerk of the House of Representatives, made a report thereon, exhibiting a detailed view of the circumstances attending the loss of the library, which the committee conceive might have been preserved in whole or in part, and the vouchers for the contingent expenditures of the House of Representatives; and concluding with a resolution, that he be credited with a certain sum, ascertained to have been expended by him between the 14th January, 1814, and the day on which the Capitol was destroyed by the enemy. The report was read by Mr. P. in his place, and ordered to be printed. It is as follows:

That the committee have satisfactory evidence that the library of Congress, consisting of volumes agreeably to the catalogue herewith submitted, was destroyed by the enemy on the 24th of August last; and, also, the manuscript records, papers, and secret journals of Congress, mentioned in the communication submitted to this committee. In addition to the ascertainment of those facts, the committee have considered it their duty to form and express some opinion as to the degree of diligence and precaution exercised by the Clerk, and those in his employ, to prevent the loss which has been sustained. In doing this they have taken into consideration the threatening aspect of the enemy in the Chesapeake, the Potomac, and the Patuxent, almost uniformly from the month of June to the period of their incursion on the city of Washington, and the apprehension which prevailed on this subject, as developed by the committee appointed to inquire into the "causes of the success of the enemy in his recent enterprises against this metropolis," &c. They have also referred to the several Heads of Departments, and obtained information as to the time and manner of their removing and securing the papers and effects belonging to their offices; which information the com-

873   HISTORY OF CONGRESS.   874

DECEMBER, 1814.   *Destruction of Public Books and Papers.*   H. OF R.

mittee herewith submit as part of their report, contained in the letters marked Nos. 1, 2, 3, and 4; from which it appears that measures, preparatory to a removal of the documents belonging to the several Departments, were taken as early as the 20th and 21st of August, and the removals all effected by the 22d; whereas no preparatory measures were taken to secure the library and papers appertaining to the office of the House of Representatives, or any efforts made to procure the means of transportation till the afternoon of the 22d of August; after which time the committee were convinced that the means of transportation were difficult to obtain, if not impracticable.

As to the absence of the Clerk on account of indisposition, as alleged, the committee have not examined as to the particular nature and extent of that indisposition. They will only say that it was, or ought to have been, serious and alarming, to have justified his absence under the circumstances which then existed. The committee are, therefore, constrained to express the opinion, that due precaution and diligence were not exercised to prevent the destruction and loss which has been sustained.

In relation to the remaining subject of inquiry submitted to the committee, viz: the amount of money paid on account of the contingent expenses of the House, since the first of January last, for which the Clerk ought to be credited, (the original vouchers having been destroyed in the conflagration of the Capitol,) the committee have no reason to disbelieve the statement of the Clerk, and his deputies, as to the destruction of the vouchers alluded to. They have, however, experienced much difficulty, delay, and embarrassment, in their endeavors to ascertain and adjust the accounts of the Clerk, so as to do justice between the public and the individual. This task was the more arduous and unpleasant, from the circumstance of the Clerk himself disavowing any knowledge of the pecuniary transactions of his office, and referring the committee to his chief clerk, Colonel George Magruder, who, on application, appeared equally unable or unwilling to enter into such a specification of the accounts and expenditures as would enable the committee to form any probable result. He presented a general statement, (herewith submitted, marked M,) by which it appeared that the Clerk of the House of Representatives stood charged on the books of the Treasury with the sum of $50,863 16,' and that he claimed credit for $48,000, for expenditures for contingent expenses of the House, from January, 1814, to 23d August of the same year; leaving a balance due the United States, on that day, of $2,863 16. The committee considering this alleged amount of expenditure as being very great and unprecedented, for the same length of time, and presuming, as the Clerk was able to state a particular sum expended, and a small amount remaining in his hands on the day his vouchers were destroyed, he might, from the same data which produced the results stated, by the aid of his recollection, the assistance of the clerks in his office, and the officers of the House, and especially by reference to the bank or banks in which his public deposites were kept, and individuals to whom the principal payments were made, furnish such specific statements as would have enabled the committee to form a reasonable opinion as to the correctness of the general statement which had been presented, they deemed it their duty to require a statement of the principal items of ordinary expenditure, and the names of persons who had furnished them; this information

was ultimately obtained by the admission of the chief clerk, the information of other officers of the House, and the knowledge which the committee themselves had of the most considerable objects of expenditure. All of which are stated in the account herewith presented, marked A. The Clerk was then requested to ascertain, from such sources as seem practicable, the sums paid on account of those several items of expenditure; some of which they know he could ascertain with certainty, and most of which with probable accuracy. In compliance with this request the committee were furnished with the statement marked B.; the principal items of which are—

To paying Messrs Way and Weightman, for printing and stationery   -   -   -   - $25,600 10
To paying messengers of the House -   2,584 50

The committee having obtained from the Treasury Department a copy of the last settlement made by the Clerk, on the 14th January, 1814, on account of the contingent expenses of the House of Representatives, and having examined the books of Messrs. Way and Weightman, as also the cashiers of the Bank of Washington and the Union Bank of Georgetown, are satisfied that the sum of $2,539 53 ought to be deducted from the $25,600 10, charged for printing and stationery in the account rendered by the clerks, and marked B, as aforesaid. The same having, in the opinion of the committee, been already allowed, and included in the settlement with the Treasury on the 14th of January, 1814; which settlement the committee herewith submit, marked T.

The charge in account B, for the pay of messengers for the House, is manifestly incorrect, and exceeds their proper allowance by the sum of $613 55.

The committee having allowed all other charges specified and claimed by the Clerk, and having, by every means in their power, ascertained the items with which the contingent fund is chargeable, and made the most liberal allowance for its expenditure, submit the statement, marked A, as the result of their inquiry.

From which it appears that, on settlement with the Treasury, on the 14th January, 1814, a balance remained in the hands of the Clerk of the House of Representatives, due the U. States, of $6,574 87
That, from the 14th of January, 1814, to the 18th April, 1814, the Clerk drew from the Treasury the sum of   -   -   44,288 29

Making the sum of   -   -   - $50,863 16
with which he now stands charged at the Treasury.

That his expenditures since the above settlement, and such as the committee presume were not included in it, on account of the contingent expenses of the House, to the 19th September, 1814, amount to the sum of   -   -   -   30,933 57½

Leaving a balance unaccounted for by the Clerk, and due the United States, of $19,929 58

The committee recommend the following resolution:
Resolved, That Patrick Magruder, Clerk of the House of Representatives, be credited at the proper office of the Treasury Department with the sum of $30,933 57½, for expenditures on account of the contingent expenses of the House of Representatives, from the date of his last settlement to the 19th September, 1814.

Treasury Department, *Nov.* 5, 1814.

Sir: Upon inquiry, I find that the books and papers appertaining to the Treasury were packed up on Sunday, the 21st of August, 1814, and sent off in the afternoon of the following day.

It is also stated to me that much difficulty was not experienced in procuring carriages to transport the books and papers; and that, in fact, two wagons, more than were eventually found necessary, were engaged by the Department.

I have the honor to be, very respectfully, sir, your most obedient servant,

A. J. DALLAS.

Joseph Pearson, Esq.

War Department, *Nov.* 21, 1814.

Sir: I have had the honor to receive your letter of the 21st instant, inquiring at what time the papers belonging to the Department of State were removed previous to the destruction of the public buildings in this city, and whether it was practicable for the Clerk of the House of Representatives to have obtained the means of removing the library and papers belonging to that House in the Capitol of the United States within the space of three days previous to that event.

Having left this city on the Thursday preceding the 24th of August for the neighborhood of Benedict, and having entered it afterwards, momentarily only, prior to the 24th, I have no knowledge, from personal observation, of the means which might have been obtained by the Clerk of the House of Representatives, for the removal of the library and documents of that branch of the Legislature.

Apprehending, when I left the city, that the documents belonging to the Department of State would be in danger, I gave orders that they should be packed up and in readiness to be moved on notice of the approach of the enemy. It was under this order, and on the subsequent notice, which was communicated, that they were removed to a place of safety on the 22d of August.

I have understood that the papers of the Department of War were likewise removed on the 22d of August.

I have the honor to be, with great respect, sir, your obedient servant, JAMES MONROE.

Hon. Joseph Pearson, *H. of Reps.*

Navy Department, *Nov.* 5, 1814.

Sir: In compliance with the request contained in your note of yesterday, requiring "such information as to the time when the papers of this Department were packed up and removed; and, finally, my opinion as to the practicability of obtaining the means of conveyance, for three days, immediately preceding the destruction of the Capitol by the enemy," I have the honor to represent that, having, on Saturday, the 20th August last, directed the Chief Clerk of this Department to prepare for the removal of the books, papers, and effects of the Navy Department, and to procure the necessary transportation, I now enclose his statement of the facts and circumstances attending the execution of my order, as conveying more correct information, in relation to the subject of your inquiry, than that which comes within my own knowledge.

I am, respectfully, sir, your obedient servant,

A. JONES.

Hon. Joseph Pearson, *Chairman, &c.*

Navy Department, *Nov.* 5, 1814.

In obedience to the instructions from the Secretary of the Navy, to prepare for the removal and safety of the public documents and archives of the Navy Department, on Saturday, the 20th day of August, 1814, and anticipating a difficulty in procuring wagons, he sanctioned the transportation by water, in boats up the Potomac river.

On Sunday three of the clerks were employed packing up, in boxes and trunks, all the books of record, papers, library, maps, charts, plans, stationery, trophies, various valuable instruments, paintings, prints, &c., ready for removal on the next day; and in the evening of Sunday, the 21st of August, two river boats, with their crews, were engaged for the purpose at the ordinary pay and wages.

On Monday, the 22d August, two of the city carts were engaged, and all the boxes and articles in the Navy Department, (heavy desks and furniture excepted,) were put on board a boat at the nearest wharf to the offices, and at 4 P. M. proceeded up the river as far as Georgetown.

In the forenoon of Monday, the 22d, two large wagons with drivers presented themselves at the Department for employ, and on account of the previous arrangement to transport by water, they were transferred to the Accountant of the Navy Department, who loaded them with the effects of his office.

On Tuesday, the 23d August, the Chief Clerk, with one of the clerks of the Department, proceeded up the river Potomac, and passed through the locks and canal to a place of safety.

There was no difficulty in procuring more boats and men enough to navigate them up the river above the falls. BENJAMIN HOMANS, *Clerk.*

Treasury Department,
General Land Office, November 5, 1814.

Sir; In the absence of the Commissioner I have the honor to reply to the questions in your letter of yesterday.

On the Sunday preceding the destruction of the public buildings, the records of this office were prepared for removal.

On Monday wagons were procured in the country, loaded in the evening, and the records removed the same night.

As to the practicability of obtaining the means of conveyance on other roads than that which I travelled I cannot form an opinion, but on that road I found no difficulty in procuring what I wanted for this office on that day. I am, very respectfully,

JOHN GARDINER, *Chief Clerk.*

Hon. J. Pearson.

[The tables, being voluminous, are omitted.]

MILITIA DRAUGHTS.

The House resumed the consideration of the bill from the Senate authorizing a draught of 80,430 militia, for the defence of the frontiers.

The motion of Mr. Macon, to place the apportionment of the draught on the basis of military strength (or free white population) instead of the basis of representation, on which it now stands, being under consideration—

Mr. Kennedy spoke as follows:

Mr. Speaker, I have generally contented myself with giving a silent vote on most of the subjects which have been presented to this House, after bestowing upon them the best consideration and the most mature reflection I was able to do, agreeably to the powers which it has been my lot to possess; but to remain silent on a question which involves the best interests of my constituents, as well as that of the whole Southern country, I think would be a wanton, if not a criminal neglect of duty, I must therefore beg to be excused for troubling the House with a few remarks.

Sir, I hope the amendment proposed by my honorable colleague (Mr. Macon) will prevail. In all coalitions or unions formed by independent sovereign Powers for the attainment of any object which required military requisitions or requisitions of money, those demands have always been made upon the principles of military strength, and the ability to pay, and not in proportion to political strength or political privileges; it is the usage and practice of the world, founded in eternal justice and plain common sense.

In the late coalition between Great Britain and the Continental Powers against the French Emperor, which resulted in the overthrow of that Monarch, why was it not required of Sweden, who possessed all the political privileges of a free and independent nation, to furnish as many troops for that object as Russia or Austria? The answer is obvious, because she was not able, her population was not equal to the task, without a great sacrifice; it could not be done without perhaps ruin and destruction to the State; justice therefore only required that the demand upon her should be made in proportion to her military strength, and in that ratio I presume her troops were furnished.

The same principle was recognised and practised by the Old Congress, under the Articles of Confederation; each State had the same political strength, as to any vote in that body, yet notwithstanding, whenever any requisition was made by them upon the States for men, it was always in proportion to the physical strength of the States respectively, and not in proportion to their political rights, as independent sovereign Powers, nor in proportion to their political strength in the General Government of the nation; and every requisition for money was made in proportion to their ability to pay, and not in any other ratio whatever.

But the gentleman from New York (Mr. Fisk) contends that a call for militia is a direct tax upon the people, and ought to be apportioned among the States, respectively, according to the number of their Representatives. In this opinion, I presume, he thinks he is warranted by the second section of the first article of the Constitution, which says—"Representatives and direct taxes ' shall be apportioned among the several States ' which may be included within this Union accord- ' ing to their respective numbers, which shall be ' determined by adding to the whole number of ' free persons, including those bound to service ' for a term of years, and excluding Indians not ' taxed, three-fifths of all other persons."

This strange and alarming doctrine I will now,

air, endeavor, to examine and refute. A call upon the States for militia is not a direct tax upon the people within the spirit and meaning of the Constitution, otherwise the tax would have to be collected, or rather, the duty would have to be performed according to representation, in the precise manner that it would be imposed; and in order to see the impropriety of the opinion contended for, we have only to look at the absurdity to which the doctrine would lead us if pursued. Suppose an attack is made by the enemy on New Orleans; according to this idea, the President would be bound to call out the whole draughted militia from every State and Territory within the Union, in order that the service should be performed in the proportion that it was imposed, although one half of the number might not be wanted for the object; or, if this plan should be considered too expensive and inconvenient to the nation, he will then be driven to the alternative of ordering out the precise number wanted for the expedition from all parts of the Union. But still it must be done according to this ratio of representation, the inevitable consequence of which would be, the place attacked would be destroyed before a sufficient force could be brought to relieve it.

If this reasoning be correct—and I presume it cannot be denied—then it must be plainly inferred, according to the doctrine contended for by that gentleman, that the President cannot with propriety order out the whole draughted militia from the States nearest to the place invaded; because, if there should be no occasion for ordering out the remainder of the requisition before a restoration of peace, the duty cannot be performed, according to representation. From which it is obvious, if this opinion is persisted in, the nation cannot be defended by the militia; and, in reality, it appears to me a vain and idle attempt, and beyond the power of man, be the events what they may in respect to invasion, considering the extent of our country and the difference in the distance each detachment has to march over, to apportion the actual service of the militia among the States according to representation, like direct taxes, or in any other precise proportion whatsoever. This subject, therefore, was, in my judgment, very properly left to the sound discretion of Congress, who, it is presumed, will lay this burden upon the States as nearly equal, upon principles of justice, as the circumstances of the country will permit; and no plan appears to me so consistent to those principles as the one which makes the apportionment according to the physical strength of each State, leaving the actual service to be controlled by future wants.

But, before I leave this point, I will take the liberty to add one more remark. Suppose the President, agreeably to his power under the act of 1795, upon a sudden and pressing emergency, calls out the whole militia en masse from one of the Northern States; I would ask any gentleman, in order to comply with this opinion, how are they to be called out in the slaveholding States, when the whole body of their militia if called upon in proportion to representation is not sufficient for the purpose. The idea really appears to me so absurd and preposterous that it will not even do to think about.

Some gentlemen, however, are of opinion that the great object of this bill is to raise forty thousand regular troops; that the militia part of it is only to coerce the people to raise the troops from the Government, and is in its spirit a direct tax upon them, and ought to be apportioned among the States according to representation. Sir, this burden, like most others, if gentlemen are disposed, may be compared to direct taxes, and although in its bearing and operation it may have the resemblance of such a tax, though not a direct tax in reality, yet it appears to me clear that if the spirit of the Constitution must be distorted for this purpose the utmost extent that gentlemen can go is to lay the additional burden upon the slaveholding States only in that proportion that the direct tax would bear to the whole revenue of the country; and I am of this opinion, because if the forty thousand troops were actually enlisted and paid by the Government, one-seventh part only of the money that would be required for that purpose would be raised from the people by direct taxes, agreeably to the system of taxation we are about to adopt the present session; then if the slaveholding States must have an extraordinary burden laid upon them, that excess of burden ought only to be one-seventh part of the difference between a calculation made upon the score of free population, and a calculation on the ground of representation, and not the whole of that difference, according to the provision of the bill which is moved to be stricken out.

But suppose in exercising the delegated power "to call forth the militia" it does not operate as a lever to the execution of another delegated power "to raise armies," in the manner as I presume was contemplated by some gentlemen, and the probability of its having that effect appears to be considerably lessened by the change the bill has undergone, in altering the term of service from two years to twelve months; then the bill will result in nothing but a plain, common militia bill, the impropriety of apportioning which among the States according to representation, under such a law, I think I have already sufficiently shown.

And I now contend, sir, that no part of this bill imposes a direct tax upon the people, within the letter, spirit, or meaning of the Constitution. I know that any inconvenience may figuratively be called a tax; but are we to impose burdens upon the people by tropes or figures, or are we bound by the principles contained in the Constitution of our country? I say that this is no direct tax; because the militia, when called into active service, receive a compensation for their trouble, and it never was known for the people to be reimbursed in a pecuniary manner by their Government for any tax imposed upon them: such an idea is totally inconsistent with the character of a direct tax.

And although a part, or the whole of the forty thousand regular troops should be raised by the provisions of the bill, it will not on that account operate as a direct tax upon the people, because they are not bound to raise them. It will be a mere voluntary act, and amounts to nothing more than a commutation with the Government for militia service—in other words, a purchase of exemption during the war, from that militia duty which, by the institutions of our country, every free man is liable to perform.

But why should we have recourse to argument to show what a direct tax is, when the Constitution itself furnishes a plain solution to the question? The 8th section of the 1st article says, "The Congress shall have power to lay and col-
' lect taxes, duties, imposts, and excises, to pay the
' debts and provide for the common defence and
' general welfare of the United States; but all
' duties, imposts, and excises, shall be uniform
' throughout the United States." From the plain import and meaning of these words, nothing properly can be understood, but a grant of power to raise money, and a specification of the purposes to which it should be applied. But, sir, if the idea of the gentleman from New York is a correct one, that a call of the militia is a direct tax upon the people, then it will follow, as a necessary consequence, that the debts of the United States might be paid in men; a doctrine too monstrous ever to be thought of in a free country.

Sir, the words "to pay the debts and provide for the common defence and general welfare of the United States," do not contain a separate and distinct delegation of power, agreeably to the idea advanced by the gentleman from Kentucky (Mr. Hopkins) yesterday on another occasion, but only relate to the application of money, arising out of taxes, duties, imposts, and excises imposed by Congress; and this is the old Republican and true doctrine. Then it must follow, if draughted militiamen, by any construction whatever, are taxes, those taxes are applicable to the payment of the public debts, the absurdity of which doctrine must be obvious to every person.

I think this part of my argument might be safely rested here, but, before I leave it, I will make one remark. If a call of the militia is a direct tax, then that part of the Constitution which authorizes Congress to lay taxes, contains in itself a power also to call out the militia; which, if correct, renders that provision in the Constitution which authorizes Congress to call out the militia for three purposes, altogether useless and nugatory. But the framers of that instrument most assuredly used the word taxes, for the purpose of raising money only; and when used in that sense, it became necessary to insert the other provision in relation to the militia.

Under these considerations I presume it must be apparent to every one that there is nothing in the Constitution which requires the apportionment to be made according to representation, and that every principle of justice and reason forbids it. Then I ask, in the name of Heaven, why are the slaveholding States, the weakest in the Union in proportion to their numbers, from the character of their population, to have this extraordinary and excessive burden thrown upon them?

The Constitution was formed in a mutual spirit of concession and compromise; it was agreed that three-fifths of the slaves should be represented in Congress, and, as an equivalent for that privilege, it was conceded that in imposing direct taxes, they might be apportioned among the States according to representation; but it never was expected that any other burden would be laid upon them for that privilege. Had this have been anticipated, is it possible that the Constitution would have been adopted by them? I rather think not.

Sir, this excessive burden cannot be laid upon the slaveholding States for this political privilege with any more propriety than you can lay an extraordinary burden upon the small States of Delaware and Rhode Island for the political privilege of having an equal representation in the Senate, and of course an equal vote there with the largest State in the Union—although they have not, respectively, one-twelfth part of the population. I am, therefore, clearly of opinion that every Representative of a slaveholding State ought to endeavor to arrest this principle in its progress, and never by their votes suffer it to be fixed upon them as an established practice, which, when once adopted, will probably never end but with the Constitution itself.

But the gentleman from South Carolina (Mr. CALHOUN) will vote for this provision of the bill as it now stands, upon the ground of liberality and generosity; that, as the Southern States had a considerable agency in the declaration of war, and bringing about the present state of things, he is willing to take hold of the laboring oar. If the gentleman, in giving his vote, would impose an extraordinary duty only upon himself and his constituents, I do not know that any others would have a right to murmur; but when that vote is not confined to his own district, but operates through the whole slaveholding country, and upon many who are not disposed to be thus generous, I think there is some cause of complaint. Nor, sir, do I approve of the ground of patriotism upon which the honorable gentleman from Georgia (Mr. TROUP) places his vote on this occasion. I have not the least doubt but both of those gentlemen feel the sentiments which they express, but they are high-sounding words, which we have long been used to in the southern country, and which we have always paid dearly for. If the slaveholding States bear an equal share of their country's burdens, it is all that can or ought, in justice, to be demanded of them; that far I believe they will always be willing to go, but not beyond.

I do now most earnestly beseech gentlemen who represent those States, that are equally concerned in producing the existing state of things with the slaveholding States, that they will, on the present occasion, act towards us with some degree of magnanimity and justice, and not ease themselves of a burden, by placing it upon the shoulders of others who are much less able to bear it; and I call upon the gentleman from New Jersey, (Mr. STOCKTON,) who has shown himself in the discussion of this bill, to be the able advocate of civil liberty, and the rights of the people under the Constitution, that he will not suffer the spirit of that instrument to be violated by this unjust provision. With these remarks I submit to the good sense of the House whether the proposed amendment ought not to prevail.

Other gentlemen spoke for and against the motion; which was at length decided in the negative by the following vote:

YEAS—Messrs. Alexander, Alston, Archer, Barbour, Bard, Barnett, Bayly of Virginia, Bines, Breckenridge, Burwell, Caperton, Caldwell, Chappell, Clark, Clopton, Conard, Crawford, Culpeper, Desha, Earle, Eppes, Evans, Findley, Forney, Franklin, Gaston, Gholson, Glasgow, Goodwyn, Hall, Hawes, Humphreys, Ingham, Johnson of Virginia, Johnson of Kentucky, Kennedy, Kent of Maryland, Kerr, Kershaw, King of North Carolina, Lewis, Macon, McCoy, McKim, Montgomery, Moore, Nelson, Newton, Ormsby, Pearson, Pickens, Pleasants, Roane, Robertson, Sevier, Sharp, Sheffey, Smith of Virginia, Stanford, Stuart, Tannehill, Telfair, White, Wilson of Pennsylvania, Wright, and Yancey—66.

NAYS—Messrs. Avery, Baylies of Massachusetts, Bigelow, Bowen, Boyd, Bradbury, Bradley, Brigham, Brown, Butler, Calhoun, Cannon, Champion, Cilley, Comstock, Condict, Cooper, Cox, Creighton, Crouch, Cuthbert, Dana, Davenport, Davis of Massachusetts, Davis of Pennsylvania, Denoyelles, Ely, Farrow, Fisk of New York, Forsyth, Geddes, Griffin, Grosvenor, Hale, Harris, Hasbrouck, Henderson, Hopkins of Kentucky, Hubbard, Ingersoll, Irving, Irwin, Jackson of Rhode Island, Kent of New York, Kilbourn, King of Massachusetts, Law, Lefferts, Lovett, Lowndes, Lyle, Markell, McKee, Miller, Moseley, Murfree, Oakley, Parker, Pickering, Piper, Pitkin, Potter, John Reed, William Reed, Rea of Pennsylvania, Rhea of Tennessee, Rich, Ruggles, Sage, Schureman, Seybert, Shipherd, Slaymaker, Smith of New York, Smith of Pennsylvania, Stockton, Sturges, Taggart, Taylor, Thompson, Troup, Udree, Vose, Ward of Massachusetts, Ward of New Jersey, Webster, Wheaton, Wilcox, Williams, Wilson of Massachusetts, and Winter—91.

The bill having been further amended—

A motion was made by Mr. WEBSTER, of New Hampshire, to amend the bill by striking out these words, as applied to the term of service of the draughted militia: "for the term of one year from the time of meeting at the place of rendezvous, unless sooner discharged," and to insert these words, "to serve for the term prescribed by existing laws;" that is, to serve for six months instead of one year.

On this motion a question of order arose, when the SPEAKER decided it to be in order; and his decision being appealed from, was confirmed by yeas and nays—129 to 29.

After some debate on this point, the question on Mr. WEBSTER'S motion was decided as follows:

YEAS—Messrs. Alexander, Avery, Baylies of Massachusetts, Bayly of Virginia, Bigelow, Boyd, Bradbury, Bradley, Breckenridge, Brigham, Burwell, Butler, Caperton, Champion, Cilley, Comstock, Cooper,

Cox, Culpeper, Davenport, Davis of Massachusetts, Davis of Pennsylvania, Denoyelles, Ely, Farrow, Gaston, Geddes, Gholson, Grosvenor, Hale, Harris, Henderson, Howell, Irwin, Jackson of Rhode Island, Kennedy, Kent of New York, Kerr, King of Massachusetts, Law, Lewis, Lovett, Macon, Markell, Miller, Moseley, Nelson, Oakley, Ormsby, Pearson, Pickering, Pitkin, Potter, John Reed, William Reed, Rich, Ruggles, Schureman, Sheffey, Shipherd, Skinner, Slaymaker, Smith of Virginia, Stanford, Stockton, Sturges, Taggart, Thompson, Vose, Ward of Massachusetts, Webster, Wheaton, White, Wilcox, Williams, Wilson of Massachusetts, Winter, and Wright—78.

NAYS—Messrs. Alston, Anderson, Archer, Barbour, Bard, Barnett, Bines, Bowen, Caldwell, Calhoun, Cannon, Chappell, Clark, Clopton, Condict, Conard, Crawford, Creighton, Crouch, Cuthbert, Dana, Desha, Duvall, Earle, Eppes, Findley, Fisk of Vermont, Fisk of New York, Forney, Forsyth, Franklin, Goodwyn, Gourdin, Griffin, Hall, Hasbrouck, Hawes, Hopkins of Kentucky, Hubbard, Humphreys, Ingersoll, Ingham, Irving, Johnson of Virginia, Johnson of Kentucky, Kent of Maryland, Kershaw, Kilbourn, King of North Carolina, Lowndes, Lyle, McCoy, McKee, McKim, McLean, Montgomery, Moore, Newton, Parker, Pickens, Piper, Pleasants, Rea of Pennsylvania, Rhea of Tennessee, Roane, Robertson, Sage, Sevier, Seybert, Sharp, Smith of Pennsylvania, Tannehill, Taylor, Telfair, Troup, Udree, Ward of New Jersey, Wilson of Pennsylvania, and Yancey—79.

So the motion was negatived by a majority of one vote.

A motion was then made by Mr. NELSON, of Virginia, to recommit the bill to a Committee of the Whole; which motion was negatived.

A motion was then made by Mr. WRIGHT, of Maryland, further to amend the first section of the bill by striking out the words, "to serve for the term of one year from the time of meeting at the place of rendezvous, unless sooner discharged," and to insert these words: "to serve a term not exceeding seven months after arriving at the place of rendezvous." And, before deciding on the motion, the House adjourned.

TUESDAY, December 13.

Mr. INGERSOLL, from the Committee on the Judiciary, reported a bill for the regulation of the courts of justice of Indiana; which was read twice, and ordered to be engrossed, and read the third time to-morrow.

The SPEAKER laid before the House a letter from the Commissioner of the General Land Office, transmitting, in obedience to a resolution of the 7th instant, a statement of forfeitures which have accrued to the United States on account of the purchase of public lands; which were read, and ordered to lie on the table.

A message from the Senate informed the House that the Senate have passed a bill "authorizing the appointment of certain naval officers therein named," in which they desire the concurrence of this House.

On motion of Mr. EPPES, of Virginia, the House resolved itself into a Committee of the Whole on the bill to provide additional revenues for defray-

ing the expenses of Government, and maintaining the public credit, by laying duties on various goods, wares, and merchandise; which bill having been read over, the Committee rose, reported progress, and obtained leave to sit again.

The following motion was submitted for consideration by Mr. WRIGHT:

Resolved, That the Committee of Ways and Means be instructed to inquire into the expediency of prohibiting the receipt of the paper of any bank in the United States for any debts due on demand of the United States, which said bank shall refuse to receive the Treasury notes of the United States, already issued or hereafter to be issued; and, also, into the expediency of issuing Treasury notes of small denominations.

The said motion lies on the table.

PETITION OF JAMES LINDSEY.

Mr. YANCEY, from the Committee of Claims, made a report on the petition of James Lindsey; which was read, and the resolution therein contained was concurred in by the House. The report is as follows:

That in the year 1802, Joseph Scott, the Marshal of Virginia, sold, for the direct tax due thereon, a tract of land estimated at about eight thousand acres, supposed to be the property of Levi Judson, and lying in the county of Harrison and State of Virginia. William Scott, of Trenton, in New Jersey, became the purchaser at the sale of the marshal, and has since sold the land in question to the petitioner. It is stated by the petitioner, that, since the purchase of the land from William Scott, he has discovered that the land did not belong to Judson, and was therefore improperly sold as his property. He complains of having sustained damages in consequence of the contract, and asks of Congress such relief as may be just and equitable.

Your committee are of opinion he is not entitled to relief from the United States:

1st. Because it does not appear the land did not belong to Judson; no judicial decision having been made thereon.

2dly. Because William Scott, who was the purchaser at the marshal's sale, sold to the petitioner, and who must be liable to him, if any person is.

3dly. Because, under these circumstances, the United States cannot be considered the warranter of the property sold.

The committee, therefore, recommend to the House the following resolution:

Resolved, That the prayer of the petitioner ought not to be granted.

MILITIA DRAUGHTS.

The House resumed the consideration of the bill from the Senate, authorizing the President to call into service eighty thousand four hundred and thirty militia, for the defence of the frontiers.

The motion of Mr. WRIGHT, to make the term of service seven months after arriving at the place of rendezvous, instead of one year as the bill now stands, being before the House—

Mr. WRIGHT supported this proposition by a few remarks, in the course of which, he decidedly expressed the opinion that no measure, except providing money, was necessary for filling the ranks of the Army.

Mr. HARRIS, of Tennessee, spoke as follows:

Mr. Speaker, presuming from the vote which was taken yesterday, upon a question similar to the one now under consideration, that I shall vote differently from the most of my colleagues on the proposed amendment, I beg the indulgence of the House while I submit the reasons which will influence my vote.

I shall vote for it, sir, because a whole year is too long to keep militia in the field, and because, if the bill passes in its present shape, I find many gentlemen are prepared to adopt it as a substitute for the more efficient measure recommended by the Secretary of War. But, while I am opposed to the bill in its present form, I wish it to be understood that I am not influenced by the reasons urged by gentlemen in the opposition. I do not believe with them that it is unconstitutional to draught militia for twelve months, nor am I induced to vote as I shall from their declamations against conscription.

Before I proceed to examine into the objects and merits of the bill now before the House, I will take the liberty of noticing some of the arguments of an honorable gentleman from New Jersey (Mr. STOCKTON) upon the constitutionality of its provisions. He says that the Government of the United States is composed of special and limited powers; that it is a Government of checks and balances, there being powers delegated and powers reserved; that such as have not been expressly delegated are reserved by the tenth amendment to the Constitution, which is founded on a principle of reason applicable in the construction of public as well as private powers; and, that as the Constitution only gives Congress the right to call forth the militia " to execute the laws of the Union, suppress insurrections, and repel invasions," the provisions of the bill are unconstitutional. He says that the power is granted to call out the militia to repel invasion when it happens, but that we abuse the power by calling them out to be ready to repel invasion when it happens.

I agree with the honorable gentleman that the General Government is composed of powers delegated by the people, which, in their nature, are special and limited; that is to say, they are limited as to the subjects upon which Congress shall legislate, and, in many cases, as to the extent to which Congress shall go in legislating on particular subjects. But there are some subjects upon which Congress have been vested with unlimited power to legislate.

It is true, also, that all powers which have not been expressly delegated, and which are not necessary and proper to be exercised in order to carry the powers expressly delegated into execution, are reserved; and this reservation of power is not founded alone upon the declaration in the tenth article of the amendments to the Constitution, but is founded upon a principle of reason and common sense. All sovereign power was originally vested in the people, and so much as they have not delegated, they must, of course, have retained. It is a principle universally applicable in the construction of all powers, whether of a public, municipal, or private character. But let us see whether the application of this principle will support the honorable gentleman in the position which he has taken. He admits that Congress may provide for calling out the militia to repel invasion, but contends that we have not the power to provide for calling them out before the happening of the invasion, in order to place them in a state of readiness to enable them to repel it when it does happen. The construction which the gentleman would give that provision of the Constitution, would render the power delegated perfectly nugatory; because, if the Government was compelled to wait until after the country was actually invaded, before the militia could be called out, the enemy could always burn and plunder our cities and villages, and retire without our limits, before opposition could be made to his incursions. Such a construction would be unreasonable, and would be calculated to take from the country its legitimate means of defence, and to place our seaboard at the mercy of the enemy. The power being expressly granted to Congress to provide for calling forth the militia to repel invasion, we have also the power necessary and proper to be exercised in order to enable the Government to make ready before hand, when its danger is threatened, to meet and repel it when it happens. But if the doctrine of the gentleman was correct, still the provisions of the bill would not be unconstitutional, because the country is already actually invaded, there being scarcely a day but that some inroads are made by the enemy upon our maritime or inland frontier.

The gentleman, however, in the course of his remarks, stated that the act of 1795, which provides for calling forth the militia, had put this question upon its true grounds—that is to say, " that whenever the United States shall be in- ' vaded, or be in imminent danger of invasion, it ' shall be lawful for the President of the United ' States to call forth the militia," &c. Now, to my mind, the arguments of the gentleman are entirely contradictory. At one time, he says that we abuse the power vested in Congress by providing for calling out the militia, to be ready to repel invasion when it happens; and, at another time, he admits that Congress possess the power to provide for calling out the militia in case of imminent danger of invasion.

What, sir, can the act of 1795 mean, unless it was intended that whenever invasion became seriously threatened, the militia should be called forth to be ready to repel it? It surely could not mean that the militia should not be called forth unless in case of actual invasion. But gentlemen say that it is conscription, and that it is equally unconstitutional with the measure for raising a regular army recommended by the Secretary of War. Sir, I have no doubt of the power of Congress to pass the law under consideration, nor have I any doubts as to our power to pass a law embracing the plan recommended for raising a regular army.

In order for us to ascertain whether Congress possess the power to raise regular armies otherwise than by voluntary enlistment, I consider it necessary that we should go back and see what practice was pursued for the purpose of raising armies in the time of the Revolutionary war, previous to the adoption of the Constitution. We should then examine the language of that part of the Constitution which we contend contains the delegation of unlimited power to raise armies, and afterwards notice the construction which was given to it early after its adoption, by persons eminently calculated to decide correctly upon it.

Previous to the adoption of the Constitution, while we were engaged in the Revolution, we find that we were compelled to resort, for the purpose of raising armies, to other more efficient measures than voluntary enlistment. The extracts which have been furnished us by Mr. Monroe, in his report to the chairman of your Military Committee, show the practice upon this subject at that day. We learn from them that when voluntary enlistments fell short of the proposed number, the deficiencies were, by the laws of several States, to be made up by draughts or lots from the militia. The towns in New England, and the counties in the Middle States, were respectively called on for a specified number of men. Such was the zeal of the people in New England, that neighbors would often club together to engage one of their number to go into the army. Maryland directed her lieutenants of counties to class all the property in their respective counties into as many equal classes as there were men wanted, and each class was by law obliged, within ten days thereafter, to furnish an able-bodied recruit during the war; and in case of their neglecting or refusing to do so, the county lieutenants were authorized to procure men at their expense, at any rate not exceeding fifteen pounds in every hundred pounds' worth of property classed agreeably to law. Virginia and Pennsylvania pursued plans equally as efficient.

This, then, having been the practice previous to the adoption of the Constitution, and the framers of that instrument having been intimately acquainted with it, if they had intended, while they were delegating to Congress the power to raise and support armies, that armies should not be raised otherwise than by voluntary enlistment, it is fair to presume that the power would have been given in terms limited to that extent.

But what is the language of the Constitution in relation to this subject? It is, that "Congress shall have power to raise and support armies; but no appropriation of money to that use shall be for a longer term than two years." As to the mode of raising regular armies, whether by voluntary enlistment, by draught, or by classification, there is no restriction in the power granted. The mode is reserved to be prescribed by the discretion of Congress. It is true that the abuse of the power thus vested is provided against, by prohibiting appropriations from being made for the support of regular armies for a longer term than two years. This was done for the purpose of enabling

the people at a subsequent election to put an end to the employment of armies unnecessarily raised, by electing persons to vote against additional supplies. But nothing can fairly be collected from any provision in the Constitution which will infer an intention on the part of the framers of it to prohibit regular armies from being raised otherwise than by voluntary enlistment. And can it be believed, sir, that the members of the Convention, who were so well acquainted with the practice pursued by the whole country in raising armies, would have given Congress a power embraced in terms so unlimited and unqualified, if they had intended to exclude every other mode of raising armies but by voluntary enlistment? Surely not. As regards the control of the militia, the power of Congress has been limited—they cannot be called forth but for three purposes. And this has been urged as an evidence that it was not intended to vest Congress with the power of raising armies in the way contended for. But to my mind the limited power in the one case affords no evidence of an intention to limit it in the other, where the power is granted without limitation. Under the power granted over the militia, it was intended that they might be called forth *en masse* if necessary, for any of the purposes mentioned. And as unlimited power was given to raise a regular force, competent for every purpose of the Government, it was no doubt deemed necessary to limit the occasions which justify the calling forth the militia.

But in order to settle all doubt as to the proper construction to be given to that provision of the Constitution, which authorizes Congress to raise armies, we need only to refer to the opinion of General Washington, given upon that subject at the second session of the first Congress, in the year 1790. And I would suppose, that a construction given to the instrument soon after its adoption by a person who should be presumed to have understood the intention of the framers of it (he being one of them) ought to have some influence, even with legal gentlemen.

We find, from a report made by General Knox, then Secretary of War, the principles of which were modified and sanctioned by General Washington, that a system for raising a regular army, in case the exigencies of the country should require it, by classification, similar to the plan now recommended to us by Mr. Monroe, was concluded upon and submitted to Congress.

But an honorable gentleman from New York (Mr. Grosvenor) has said, that the opinion of General Washington is not good authority upon a subject of this nature—that he was raised a soldier in the camp, and therefore it ought not to be presumed that he was capable of giving as correct a construction to the Constitution as the civilians of the present day are, Sir, I flatter myself that the honorable gentleman will never bring the people of this nation to think so lightly of the talents and judgment of that distinguished character, as to believe him to have been incapable of putting a proper construction upon the Constitution of his country, in the adoption of which he had acted so conspicuous a part.

Besides, at that day Gen. Hamilton was Secretary of the Treasury; and, as the Presidents have always been in the habit of consulting the members of their Cabinet upon all important subjects, it is but reasonable to conclude that the plan reported by the Secretary of War, modified and sanctioned by General WASHINGTON, was not without his approbation. It therefore, sir, appears to be manifest to my mind, that it is not only Constitutional for Congress to pass the bill now under consideration, but that we do possess the power to raise a regular army in the manner recommended by the Secretary of War. The mode of raising regular armies previous to the adoption of the Constitution, the unqualified grant of power upon the subject, and the construction given to it by such high authority, soon after it went into operation—all conspire to produce the confirmation of my opinion in the positions which I have taken.

But, sir, I am opposed to the extension of the time of service of the militia to twelve months, not because I think it unconstitutional, but because I think it entirely inexpedient, and well calculated to produce much mischief, if not ruin to the country. If this bill passes in its present shape, I understand from its friends that it is to be received and adopted as a substitute for the plan for raising a regular army recommended to us by the Secretary of War, the provisions of which are contained in the bill reported by the Military Committee of this House. And in that event, I presume it is contemplated to rest the fate of the next campaign on a militia force, and the few regulars that this bill and our other laws are calculated to produce.

I have witnessed, sir, with the deepest concern and regret, a disposition on the part of gentlemen in this House, to pursue a measure so feeble and inefficient, at a time when all the energies of the nation should be called forth to meet the danger with which the country is threatened.

With a view, sir, to show the inexpediency of relying upon the force to be raised by the provisions of this bill, I will examine: First—whether a course of policy will put the most speedy termination to the war, which provides that in the future prosecution of it, our arms shall be confined within our territorial limits? and, secondly, if it will not, whether the bill now under consideration is the best calculated to raise an efficient force to operate in the enemy's provinces?

As to the first point—it does appear to me, sir, that a little reflection ought to convince us of the danger and inexpediency of relying so entirely on defensive operations to put an end to this war. We find from experience, that, our maritime frontier being nearly two thousand miles in extent, the enemy has it in his power, with his means of transportation, to keep upwards of one hundred thousand of our militia continually in the field, with not more than eight or ten thousand British troops. If we fail to keep any vulnerable point properly defended by an immense militia force, it is immediately exposed to the mercy of the enemy, and the conflagration and plunder of our towns, and the ruin of our citizens, follow as consequences.

The British transport vessels are continually hovering upon our coast from Maine to New Orleans, with a view, as well to keep our militia in the field, that the expenses of the war may be increased, as to lay waste those places which they find undefended. We are thus going on with a defensive war, prosecuted almost alone by a militia force, which by far is the most expensive to the Government and oppressive to the people, while it is the least efficient that could be employed.

And can it be expected, sir, that England is entirely ignorant of the fact, that this course of policy is ruinous to this nation? No, sir—an examination of the measures adopted by that Government ought to convince us, that she is endeavoring to influence our deliberations, and to paralyze our preparations for the offensive prosecution of this war. They know well, from experience, that they can practise with success upon our credulity. It is their object and their interest to prevent us from providing a regular force at the present session. They know that such a force could be provided and employed in the next campaign with success on our part. And they also know, that if we can be prevented from adopting such an efficient plan, and can be induced to rely still longer upon a militia force and upon defensive measures, that it will be the means of increasing our public burden and of breaking down the spirit of the people, while it will facilitate, and give time to ripen into perfection, their schemes for our subjugation and ruin.

What course of policy does it appear that the British Government has been pursuing? We find that early in the month of August last, at a time when they expected that Congress would not be convened until December, the conditions offered our Ministers for the restoration of peace were disgraceful and humiliating. They claimed the surrender on our part of nearly one-third of the territorial limits of the United States. But as soon as they found that Congress was convened, they deemed it necessary to recede from their haughty demands, and to manifest an almost entire willingness to conclude a treaty upon terms acceptable to our Government. Still, however, they kept minor obstacles in the way of a final settlement of our differences, and procrastination was discovered by our Ministers to be their object. With a view further to prevent strong grounds from being taken by Congress, in the establishment of an efficient regular force, calculated at once to put a termination to the war, Lord Hill's expedition, with which we have been threatened, was at once suspended, and it was made known through the medium of the ministerial prints that the prospects of a rupture upon the continent of Europe rendered the suspension necessary. It should be expected that such measures will be pursued by the British Government in conducting the negotiation at Ghent, and in the management of their affairs at the Congress of Vienna, as will be best calculated to deceive us, and to relax the vigor of our measures at the present session. They well knew that the arrival of Lord Hill with his forces upon our coast, would have driven Congress into the adoption of more efficient and vigorous measures for the prosecution of the war. They therefore deemed it necessary to suspend his expedition, and to lower their tone towards our Ministers, with the hope that, in the anticipation of peace, the measures of Congress would be relaxed accordingly.

Sir, it is evident that the British Government never will make peace with us so long as they find that we continue to rely so exclusively upon defensive measures in the prosecution of the war. They see, most clearly, that it must ultimately terminate in their favor, unless the character of it is changed on our part. The support of the immense militia force which we have continually to keep up, is entailing upon this nation a public burden which, in a few years longer, will become truly oppressive upon the people; and so long as we continue this course of policy, there are no visible prospects of putting a termination to the war. The enemy knows our situation, and it would afford evidence of his weakness to make peace with us so long as we continue to pursue a policy so admirably calculated to make us conquer ourselves.

But, sir, there is a mode by which this war can be speedily terminated in a manner honorable to this nation. An overwhelming force should be thrown into Canada at the opening of the next campaign, calculated to extort from the enemy an acknowledgment of our rights, and reparation for our wrongs. If one hundred thousand men could be marched across the lines early in the next Summer, it would immediately give relief to the whole of our seaboard. The enemy would be compelled to concentrate his forces there to save his provinces, and we could there meet him, and beat him, and put an end to the war. I would conquer the enemy's provinces, not with the view of extending the territorial limits of the United States, for I am aware of the pernicious example of cherishing a thirst for foreign conquest, but I would conquer them to be again surrendered to him, upon being indemnified for the injuries which he has done us. I would rather they should remain British provinces, for they will always afford a safe and convenient pledge for the security of our commercial rights.

It must, I think, be agreed, that it is in the power of Congress to raise such an army, and it is acknowledged on all sides that it would put an end to the war. The question, then, ought to be, is the bill now under consideration the best calculated to produce such a force? I think not, sir. On the contrary, it does appear to me, that if the British Government had it in their power to control the deliberations of this body, they could not devise the adoption of a measure, of a military character, better calculated to subserve their purposes. If the bill passes in its present shape, it is very obvious that it will not produce the regular force contemplated by its friends, nor will the provisions of the bill secure to the members of each class any probable chance of raising the two militiamen, or the one regular, by contribution.

The militia, therefore, who have not served a tour of duty, will have to be draughted for twelve months instead of six; and the consequence will be, that we shall rest the fate of the next campaign, as we did the last, almost alone upon a militia force, the operations of which will be confined mostly, as it heretofore has been, within the limits of the United States. It is true that the bill contains a provision authorizing each class to raise, either by contract or by draught, the two militiamen to serve for twelve months; and it also exempts them from the draught, provided they will furnish one able-bodied recruit to serve for five years, if the war should so long continue. And upon the first view of the bill as it came from the Senate, and as it was reported by the select committee of this House, to whom it was afterwards referred to be amended, its provisions appeared to be fair, with the exception that no mode was pointed out by which to enable the members of each class to employ the men by contract, in case there should be a disinclination on the part of any to contribute according to property. It was believed, at first, that this defect could be remedied by an amendment, which was afterwards, however, introduced by an honorable gentleman from Ohio, (Mr. McLean,) and rejected. The amendment provided that a majority of each class should decide whether the men required of them to be furnished should be raised by contract or by draught; that where it was concluded to furnish them by contract, every person within the class, whether subject to militia duty or not, was to be compelled to contribute according to property; and provision was made for the ascertainment and collection of the sum to be paid by each to the draughts or the regular hired by the class. The principles contained in this amendment were considered to be fair, equitable, and just, because they were bottomed upon the rule that the wealth of the nation should furnish the army to defend it. But it was astonishing to me, when I discovered that the warmest friends of the bill were the first and most zealous in opposition to the amendment. They are willing that the bill should contain a provision allowing each class to furnish their men by contract; but they are opposed to the principle which would compel the members of the classes to contribute according to property. It follows, therefore, that they will not agree to compel the most wealthy man in a class to contribute more than the poorest. And what will be the operation of the bill throughout the nation? Sir, the wealthy will almost invariably refuse to join in a contribution according to property for the purpose of raising men by contract, because they would have much more to pay than the poorer members of the class. A few (perhaps not more than one, in many cases) of the most wealthy of a class will drive the balance into a draught, by which means they will stand the same chance to get clear as the poorest members of it. If it should fall upon the wealthy, their circumstances will enable them to hire substitutes; but if it falls upon the poor man, he has no alternative but to serve his tour of duty.

In opposition to that amendment, it has been contended by an honorable gentleman from Virginia, (Mr. Sheffey,) and the same argument has since been used by an honorable gentleman from South Carolina, (Mr. Lowndes,) that there are two kinds of service due from the people to their Government; that is to say, personal or military service, and service by pecuniary contribution; that the wealthy contribute to the support of Government by the way of taxes; and that when military services are wanting, they should be afforded by the militia without regard to property. And, in order to illustrate this doctrine, the gentleman from South Carolina told us the other day that he would state a case which would occur if the amendment was adopted, that he was sure would have prevented the introduction of the amendment by the gentleman from Ohio, if he had known of it. The case was, that an honorable colleague of his represented a district upon this floor, which, if the amendment was adopted, would have to pay, according to the plan of contribution proposed, a tax equal to its proportion of a tax upon the United States of eighty-five millions of dollars. Now, sir, the case put by the honorable gentleman was so far from convincing me of the impropriety and unjust operation of the amendment proposed by the gentleman from Ohio, that it manifested the necessity of its adoption still more clearly to me. The gentleman from South Carolina was willing to impose upon his colleague's district, by the passage of the bill in its present shape, the performance of military service to the value of a sum equal to its proportion of a tax upon the United States of an immense amount; and yet he was unwilling to afford to a majority of each class of the militia of that district the liberty of deciding whether the classes should furnish persons to perform the military service required of them by contract rather than by draught. He seems to suppose that, if the men were raised by a pecuniary contribution according to property, the service required of that district to the Government would be too great; whereas, if the same service was rendered by men to be draughted from each class, it would not be too great. I am aware, sir, that the principles of that amendment would not suit the owners of the large cotton plantations, and overgrown fortunes in the South, because, as members of their classes, they would have to contribute according to their wealth; but the provisions would be just in their operations upon the great body of the people of the nation. Sir, I cannot agree with gentlemen, that when military services are called for, that they shall be rendered by the militia without regard to property. This rule may be endured while the militia tours are short, but it ought not to be suffered, should it be so increased.

Sir, it is true, that the wealthy contribute to the support of Government in the payment of taxes, but it is equally true, that the poorer classes of the community have always been made to pay taxes also, in proportion to the value of their property. The direct taxes and internal duties imposed at the present session, will bear heavier upon the common people of the country than upon the wealthier portion of the community. The direct tax of six millions is paid as equally by all, according to property, as the Constitution will permit, but the internal duties are not; for the seven or eight million whiskey tax, which is the largest item in our system of taxation, will be paid mostly by that class of the community who render the most military service. We lay, then, a tax of six millions of dollars in money upon the people of the nation, to be collected according to property; and, allowing the military services of a militiaman to be worth two hundred dollars for twelve months, it is proposed by this bill to lay a tax of sixteen millions of dollars upon the militia of the nation, to be collected in personal services, without regard to property. It is unreasonable and unjust for the wealth of the nation to bear so small a proportion of the public burden.

It really does appear to me, sir, that since the amendment which was proposed by the gentleman from Ohio has been rejected, the bill is calculated to do much more mischief than good. The classes will not agree to raise regulars instead of the draughts, unless it could be done by a contribution according to property, and this contribution but seldom ever would be agreed to voluntarily by all the members of the classes. Perhaps there would be a few exceptions in some of the most patriotic quarters of the Union. But can it be believed that Massachusetts, and the rest of the New England States, would furnish any regulars? I think not, sir. They would stand the draught, and, as militia, they would claim to be kept within the limits of the United States. I shall not pretend to say whether this claim would be justified by the provisions of the Constitution or not, but it appears that the Senate entertained an opinion favorable to that pretension, by their having incorporated a provision in this bill, confining the operations of the militia within the United States. The militia draughts in the New England States would all have, by the provisions of the bill, to be called out; they would not march beyond the line, where alone they would be wanting, but they would remain in camp, within their own States, squandering the public revenue, while they would be entirely useless to the Government. And what would the militia of Tennessee have to do? Those who have not yet served a tour of duty, and who would not be enabled to hire substitutes, would be compelled to leave their families, and their farms, and march to Mobile and New Orleans, where they would have to remain in camp for a whole year, in the most sickly climate on the continent. This burden will be unequal and unjust in its operation, because many of the most wealthy persons in the community will be excluded from bearing any portion of it. And it will be borne with less fortitude by those whose duty it may become to perform this twelve months tour, when they recollect that this species of force, relied on again by Congress, is better fit for the purpose of increasing the public debt, and for producing greater distress in the country, than for putting a termination to the war.

The character of the militia of Tennessee, sir, is well known throughout the nation. They are known to be a brave, patriotic, and magnanimous people—always ready to bear, with the most distinguished cheerfulness, any burden imposed upon them by the Government, whether of a pecuniary or a military kind, which they may think in the least calculated to promote the common cause of their country. There are many thousands of them now marching through a wilderness of several hundred miles in extent to meet and repel the invasion of the enemy. And on this occasion, sir, I will beg leave to read a short extract from a paper published at Nashville, showing the alacrity with which the militia turned out upon a late emergency, when there was a call upon that State for five thousand men to march to the defence of the Louisiana country. It is in these words:

"TUESDAY, *November* 16, 1814.

"We must confess that we are not capable of describing the pleasure we have experienced for the last week, in viewing the alacrity with which our brother Tennesseeans have turned out in defence of their injured country; but for an evidence of their patriotism, the following may serve as a proof. In the past week there has been almost as many offering their services as substitutes, as there were men called for by the Government. And, one man offering his services to a youth, he was answered, that he (the youth) would not take twenty-five dollars for his place. We could add a number of like instances."

I have read this, sir, to show that the people of Tennessee are prepared to make any sacrifices to aid the Government in resisting the encroachments of the enemy, and in prosecuting this war, in a way calculated to put and to it, in a manner honorable to the country. But, sir, let me tell you, that while these people are thus prepared to make every sacrifice, and to meet every danger, they have a right to expect that Congress, at a time like the present, will at least do its part. They have expected that Congress, upon receiving the first despatches from our Ministers, would immediately determine to raise an efficient regular force, capable of putting an end to this war. But, sir, instead of doing this, we are about to adopt a measure of all others the very best calculated to prolong its duration. For the bill in its operation would not produce regulars, but would require a most oppressive kind of militia service. This kind of service answers alone for defensive operations, and I repeat again that it cannot put an end to this war. Believing, then, as I do, that the bill would fail to answer the expectations of its friends, in producing a regular force, I am in favor of the amendment of the gentleman from Maryland, (Mr. WRIGHT,) with the hope that its adoption will the means of rejecting the bill before us, and that we shall afterwards take up and adopt the more efficient measure contained in the bill reported by our Military Committee. The President is already authorized to order out any number of militia for six months, and I am

unwilling to extend the time of that kind of service to twelve months. But if this measure is persisted in, and the bill should pass as it now is, I think I plainly see the consequences that are to result from it. An overgrown public debt will be heaped upon us; the spirit of the people will be broken down by oppressive and ruinous twelve months tours of militia service, and the increased taxes which it will be necessary for them to pay. And in three or four years from now, after the nation is nearly ruined, we shall be driven to the necessity, before we can get rid of this war, of adopting the measure recommended by the Secretary of War and reported by our Military Committee.

But I have heard it suggested by gentlemen, friendly to draughting the militia for two years, with permission to each class to furnish a regular, that it would be unconstitutional to raise a regular force in the manner provided by the other military bill which lies upon the table. They are willing to pass the bill before us as it came from the Senate, for draughting the militia for two years, without the incorporation of the amendment proposed by the gentleman from Ohio, and yet they consider unconstitutional the provisions of the other bill which provides that every class of twenty-five militia shall furnish a recruit for during the war, by a contribution, from all within the class, according to property, whether subject to militia duty or not, under a penalty to be inflicted and collected from the class. Now, to my mind, sir, if the one is unconstitutional, the other must be so too. In the one case, each class of the militia must furnish a regular, without the principle of compelling every member of the class to contribute according to property, (without which it could not be done,) under the penalty of a draught of a two years' tour of service. In the other case, every class would be compelled to furnish a regular by contribution according to property (which would enable them to do it) or pay a penalty to be collected from the class. If you have a right to say that a class shall furnish a regular, without prescribing any rule by which it shall be done, or be subject to a two years' tour of duty, you would upon the same principle have the right to compel a class to furnish a regular, or be subject to a draught for a ten years' tour of duty. I have heard it said, sir, that the adoption of the measure recommended to us by the Secretary of War would afford a precedent, the abuse of which might be dangerous in future times. I am in favor of saving the country with the Constitutional means which appear to my mind to present themselves. Whenever the Congress of the United States shall become so corrupt as to determine upon the ruin of this Government, by the abuse of the power delegated to them, they will not be prevented from doing so alone by the want of precedents. If they should determine in future to raise regular armies when the necessities of the country should not need them, the plan, if adopted, which is now under consideration, would as well afford them a precedent by which they could do so, as the plan proposed by the Secretary of War. They could lay the militia of the nation off into classes, and compel every class to furnish a regular, under the penalty of being subject to a draught for a ten years' tour of duty.

I hope, sir, that the amendment of the gentleman from Maryland will be adopted, and that the bill will afterwards be rejected. We can then take up the other bill containing the more efficient measure, and provide a force for the next campaign competent for the protection of the nation. A force raised in that way will be less oppressive upon the people, and will better answer the purposes of the Government in putting a speedy termination to the war. By adopting that plan, we can be able to march a force into Canada at the opening of the next campaign, which would wring from the enemy an advantageous peace.

But, sir, if we do not adopt that measure, the country may be ruined by our neglect. The enemy is evidently making every preparation to strike a deadly blow at us in the commencement of the next campaign—and it is our duty to provide against it. Suppose we should neglect to provide an efficient regular force, and the enemy should invade the country in the early part of the next campaign with forty or fifty thousand regular troops, what would be the situation of the nation? Sir, I hope this feeble and inefficient measure will not be adopted. If it is not, we can take up the other bill, and we shall then see who are willing, at a time like the present, to take upon themselves the responsibility of voting against the only measure capable of affording protection to the country, and of putting the most speedy termination to the war.

After some explanatory remarks from Mr. LOWNDES in reply to Mr. HARRIS, and in rejoinder by him—

Mr. RHEA, of Tennessee, made a short speech in reply to Mr. HARRIS. He considered this as a bill for relieving the militia from frequent and harassing calls on them for occasional service.

The previous question was now required by Mr. YANCEY of North Carolina, but was not sanctioned by a sufficient number. The House was equally divided, 66 to 66, and the SPEAKER, voting in the negative, quashed the motion.

Mr. CANNON spoke briefly against the reduction of the term of service, as proposed, and expressed some doubts of the expediency of the bill, as well as of the necessity of any measure of this character to fill the ranks of the Army.

Mr. KILBOURN, of Ohio, opposed the motion to reduce the term of service, intending, if that motion was rejected, to move to increase the term of service to one year and eight months.

The question was then taken by yeas and nays, on Mr. WRIGHT's motion, and decided in the negative—for the motion 71, against it 84, as follows:

NAYS—Messrs. Alexander, Avery, Baylies of Massachusetts, Bigelow, Boyd, Bradbury, Bradley, Breckenridge, Brigham, Burwell, Butler, Caperton, Champion,

13th CON. 3d SESS.—29

Cilley, Cooper, Cox, Culpeper, Davenport, Davis of Massachusetts, Davis of Pennsylvania, Denoyelles, Ely, Gaston, Geddes, Gholson, Grosvenor, Hale, Harris, Henderson, Howell, Kennedy, Kent of New York, Kerr, King of Massachusetts, Law, Lewis, Lovett, Macon, Markell, Miller, Moseley, Oakley, Pearson, Pickering, Pitkin, Potter, John Reed, William Reed, Rich, Ruggles, Schureman, Sheffey, Shipherd, Slaymaker, Smith of New York, Smith of Virginia, Stanford, Stockton, Stuart, Sturges, Thompson, Vose, Ward of Massachusetts, Webster, Wheaton, White, Wilcox, Williams, Wilson of Massachusetts, Winter, and Wright.

YEAS—Messrs. Alston, Anderson, Archer, Barbour, Bard, Barnett, Bines, Bowen, Brown, Caldwell, Calhoun, Cannon, Chappell, Clark, Clopton, Comstock, Condict, Conard, Crawford, Creighton, Cuthbert, Dana, Desha, Duvall, Eppes, Evans, Findley, Fisk of Vermont, Fisk of New York, Forney, Forsyth, Franklin, Glasgow, Goodwyn, Gourdin, Griffin, Hall, Hasbrouck, Hawes, Hopkins of Kentucky, Hubbard, Humphreys, Ingersoll, Ingham, Irving, Irwin, Johnson of Va., Johnson of Kentucky, Kent of Maryland, Kershaw, Kilbourn, King of North Carolina, Lefferts, Lowndes, Lyle, McCoy, McKee, McKim, McLean, Moore, Murfree, Nelson, Newton, Ormsby, Parker, Pickens, Piper, Pleasants, Rea of Pennsylvania, Rhea of Tennessee, Roane, Robertson, Sage, Seybert, Sharp, Smith of Pennsylvania, Tannehill, Taylor, Telfair, Troup, Udree, Ward of New Jersey, Wilson of Pennsylvania, and Yancey.

So the House refused to reduce the term of service below one year.

Mr. BAYLIES, of Massachusetts, moved to amend the bill by adding thereto the following as a new section:

"*And be it further enacted,* That the militia called forth by virtue of this act shall not be liable to perform any service, except such as may be necessary to repel invasion, suppress insurrection, or execute the laws of the Union."

This motion was negatived, by yeas and nays—103 to 58, as follows:

YEAS—Messrs. Baylies of Massachusetts, Bayly of Virginia, Bigelow, Boyd, Bradbury, Breckenridge, Brigham, Caperton, Champion, Cilley, Cooper, Cox, Culpeper, Davenport, Davis of Massachusetts, Ely, Gaston, Geddes, Grosvenor, Hale, Hall, Henderson, Howell, Kennedy, Kent of New York, King of Massachusetts, Law, Lewis, Lovett, Markell, Miller, Moseley, Oakley, Pearson, Pickering, Pitkin, Potter, John Reed, William Reed, Ruggles, Schureman, Sheffey, Shipherd, Slaymaker, Smith of New York, Stockton, Stuart, Sturges, Taggart, Thompson, Vose, Ward of Massachusetts, Webster, Wheaton, White, Wilcox, Wilson of Massachusetts, and Winter—58.

NAYS—Messrs. Alexander, Alston, Anderson, Archer, Avery, Barbour, Bard, Barnett, Bines, Bowen, Bradley, Brown, Burwell, Butler, Caldwell, Calhoun, Cannon, Chappell, Clark, Clopton, Comstock, Condict, Conard, Crawford, Creighton, Cuthbert, Dana, Davis of Pennsylvania, Denoyelles, Desha, Duvall, Earle, Eppes, Evans, Farrow, Findley, Fisk of Vermont, Fisk of New York, Forney, Forsyth, Franklin, Gholson, Glasgow, Goodwyn, Gourdin, Griffin, Hall, Hasbrouck, Hawes, Hopkins of Kentucky, Hubbard, Humphreys, Ingersoll, Ingham, Irving, Irwin, Johnson of Virginia, Johnson of Kentucky, Kent of Mary-

899 HISTORY OF CONGRESS. 900

H. of R. *Militia Draughts.* December, 1814.

land, Kerr, Kershaw, Kilbourn, King of North Carolina, Lefferts, Lowndes, Lyle, Macon, McCoy, McKee, McKim, McLean, Montgomery, Moore, Murfree, Nelson, Newton, Ormsby, Parker, Pickens, Piper, Pleasants, Rea of Pennsylvania, Rhea of Tennessee, Rich, Roane, Robertson, Sage, Sevier, Seybert, Sharp, Skinner, Smith of Pennsylvania, Smith of Virginia, Stanford, Tannehill, Taylor, Telfair, Troup, Udree, Williams, Wilson of Pennsylvania, Wright, and Yancey—103.

Mr. McLean, of Ohio, renewed the motion he had unsuccessfully made in Committee of the Whole, to add to the bill the following section, by way of amendment:

And be it further enacted, That if any class shall neglect for five days after having been notified to furnish a recruit to the regular army, or two substitutes, agreeably to the provisions of this act, a majority of the individuals composing such class shall have power to bind the whole of the class for the payment of any sum that may be necessary to procure a recruit to the regular army, or two substitutes, as aforesaid; provided such sum shall not exceed three hundred dollars; and all persons residing within the district of such class, who are exempt from militia duty, shall be liable for the payment of such sum as shall be engaged to the recruit or substitutes aforesaid, equally with those who are liable to perform militia duty.

And be it further enacted, That when a recruit or substitutes shall be obtained, as aforesaid, the sum agreed to be given shall be certified by the class, or a majority of them, to the captain of the company in which they or a majority of them belong, who shall immediately ascertain how much each individual within the district must pay, apportioning the amount according to the real and personal property possessed; the amount of property to be ascertained by the valuation made under the laws of the United States, and of the individual State; but, where no such valuation shall have been made, the captain shall cause a valuation to be made by three disinterested and respectable freeholders under oath, who shall be paid by the class one dollar and fifty cents each per day for their services, to be assessed and collected with the appointment aforesaid.

And be it further enacted, That when the apportionment shall have been made as aforesaid by the captain, he shall advertise the same in the most public place within each class, particularly specifying the amount each individual is required to pay, and each individual, within the class aforesaid, shall pay or satisfy the same to the recruit or substitutes within ten days thereafter; and, in default thereof, the captain shall notify the commandant of the regiment in which he belongs, who shall order a court martial immediately to assemble, which court shall take into consideration the apportionment made as aforesaid, and on finding the same to have been made agreeably to the provisions of this act, shall proceed to assess the same as a fine on the delinquents, which shall be collected with costs as other fines are, and when collected shall be paid to the recruit or substitutes, or to his or their order.

And be it further enacted, That the court martial, called as aforesaid, shall have power to correct any errors or relieve against any inequality that may have taken place, either in the valuation of property or in the apportionment, by equalizing the amount amongst the citizens within the class.

This motion was pronounced by the Speaker to be out of order, in the present stage of the bill.

Mr. Kilbourn, of Ohio, then moved to amend the bill by adding eighteen months to the present proposed term of service, so as to make it one year and eight months.

Mr. King, of North Carolina, from a desire to preclude these motions, and to come to a decision on the bill at once, requested the previous question; but was not supported therein by a sufficient number, fifty-six members, who rose in support of it, not constituting a majority of the House.

The question on Mr. Kilbourn's motion was then taken, and decided in the negative. For the motion 63, against it 95, as follows:

Yeas—Messrs. Anderson, Archer, Avery, Bard, Barnett, Bines, Bowen, Brown, Caldwell, Calhoun, Chappell, Clark, Comstock, Condict, Conard, Crawford, Creighton, Denoyelles, Earle, Evans, Findley, Fisk of New York, Forney, Forsyth, Glasgow, Gourdin, Griffin, Hall, Hasbrouck, Hopkins of Kentucky, Hubbard, Ingersoll, Ingham, Irving, Irwin, Johnson of Kentucky, Kershaw, Kilbourn, King of North Carolina, Lefferts, Lyle, McKee, McKim, Murfree, Nelson, Newton, Ormsby, Parker, Pickens, Rea of Pennsylvania, Robertson, Sage, Sharp, Shipherd, Smith of Pennsylvania, Strong, Tannehill, Taylor, Telfair, Udree, Williams, Wilson of Pennsylvania, and Yancey.

Nays—Messrs. Alexander, Alston, Barbour, Baylies of Massachusetts, Bayly of Virginia, Boyd, Bradbury, Bradley, Breckenridge, Brigham, Burwell, Butler, Caperton, Cannon, Champion, Cilley, Clopton, Cooper, Cox, Culpeper, Cuthbert, Davenport, Davis of Massachusetts, Davis of Pennsylvania, Desha, Duvall, Ely, Eppes, Farrow, Fisk of Vermont, Franklin, Gaston, Geddes, Gholson, Goodwyn, Grosvenor, Hale, Harris, Hawes, Henderson, Howell, Humphreys, Jackson of Rhode Island, Johnson of Virginia, Kennedy, Kent of New York, Kent of Maryland, Kerr, King of Massachusetts, Law, Lewis, Lovett, Lowndes, Markell, Macon, McCoy, McLean, Moore, Moseley, Oakley, Pearson, Pickering, Piper, Pitkin, Pleasants, Potter, John Reed, William Reed, Rhea of Tennessee, Rich, Roane, Ruggles, Schureman, Seybert, Sheffey, Skinner, Slaymaker, Smith of New York, Smith of Virginia, Stanford, Stockton, Stuart, Sturges, Taggart, Thompson, Troup, Vose, Ward of Massachusetts, Webster, Wheaton, White, Wilcox, Wilson of Massachusetts, Winter, and Wright.

Mr. Fisk, of Vermont, with the express view of incorporating in the bill provisions which he deemed necessary to give it efficacy, moved to recommit the bill to the Committee on Military Affairs.

Mr. Johnson, of Kentucky, opposed this motion with much zeal, and contended for the efficacy of the bill as it then stood, either to afford a valuable militia force, or a body of recruits for the regular Army, which were much wanted. The bill was not as efficient as he wished, but, his opinion having been overruled as to the details of the bill, was no reason for him to reject the bill altogether. It was high time, he added, that Congress should rouse themselves from their lethargy, and at length proceed to act.

Mr. Ingersoll then, with a view to enable the

House to proceed without further delay to the consideration of other highly important bills on the table of the House, again required the previous question.

Many members supporting the demand, the previous question was propounded, in the usual form, "Shall the main question be now put?" and decided in the affirmative. For the question 101, against it 57, as follows:

YEAS—Messrs. Alexander, Alston, Anderson, Archer, Avery, Barbour, Bard, Barnett, Bines, Bowen, Brown, Burwell, Butler, Caldwell, Calhoun, Chappell, Clark, Comstock, Condict, Conard, Creighton, Cuthbert, Dana, Davis of Penn., Denoyelles, Desha, Duvall, Earle, Eppes, Evans, Farrow, Findley, Fisk of N. York, Forney, Forsyth, Franklin, Gholson, Goodwyn, Gourdin, Griffin, Hall, Harris, Hasbrouck, Glasgow, Hawes, Hopkins of Kentucky, Hubbard, Humphreys, Ingersoll, Ingham, Irving, Irwin, Johnson of Virginia, Johnson of Kentucky, Kennedy, Kent of Maryland, Kerr, Kershaw, Kilbourn, King of North Carolina, Lefferts, Lowndes, Lyle, McCoy, McKee, McKim, McLean, Moore, Murfree, Nelson, Newton, Ormsby, Parker, Pickens, Piper, Pleasants, Potter, Rea of Pennsylvania, Rhea of Tennessee, Rich, Roane, Robertson, Sage, Sevier, Seybert, Sharp, Shipherd, Skinner, Smith of Pennsylvania, Smith of Virginia, Stuart, Tannehill, Taylor, Telfair, Troup, Udree, Ward of New Jersey, Williams, Wilson of Pennsylvania, and Yancey.

NAYS—Messrs. Baylies of Massachusetts, Bayly of Virginia, Boyd, Bradbury, Breckenridge, Brigham, Caperton, Cannon, Champion, Cilley, Clopton, Cooper, Cox, Davenport, Davis of Massachusetts, Ely, Fisk of Vermont, Gaston, Geddes, Grosvenor, Hale, Henderson, Jackson of Rhode Island, Kent of New York, King of Massachusetts, Law, Lewis, Lovett, Macon, Markell, Miller, Moseley, Oakley, Pearson, Pickering, Pitkin, John Reed, William Reed, Ruggles, Schureman, Sheffey, Slaymaker, Smith of New York, Stanford, Stockton, Sturges, Taggart, Thompson, Vose, Ward of Massachusetts, Webster, Wheaton, White, Wilcox, Wilson of Massachusetts, Winter, Wright.

The main question, viz: on the engrossing of the amendments and ordering the bill to be read a third time, was decided in the affirmative—yeas 91, nays 71, as follows:

YEAS—Messrs. Alexander, Alston, Anderson, Archer, Avery, Barbour, Bard, Barnett, Bines, Bowen, Brown, Caldwell, Calhoun, Cannon, Chappell, Clark, Clopton, Comstock, Condict, Conard, Crawford, Creighton, Cuthbert, Davis of Pennsylvania, Denoyelles, Desha, Duvall, Earle, Eppes, Evans, Farrow, Findley, Fisk of New York, Forney, Forsyth, Franklin, Glasgow, Goodwyn, Gourdin, Griffin, Hall, Hasbrouck, Hawes, Hopkins, of Kentucky, Humphreys, Ingersoll, Ingham, Irving, Irwin, Johnson of Virginia, Johnson of Kentucky, Kent of Maryland, Kerr, Kershaw, Kilbourn, King of N. Carolina, Lefferts, Lowndes, Lyle, McCoy, McKim, McLean, Moore, Murfree, Nelson, Newton, Ormsby, Parker, Pickens, Piper, Pleasants, Rea of Pennsylvania, Rhea of Tennessee, Roane, Robertson, Sage, Sevier, Seybert, Sharp, Smith of Pennsylvania, Smith of Virginia, Tannehill, Taylor, Telfair, Troup, Udree, Ward of New Jersey, Williams, Wilson of Pennsylvania, and Yancey.

NAYS—Messrs. Baylies of Massachusetts, Bayly of Virginia, Bigelow, Boyd, Bradbury, Bradley, Breckenridge, Brigham, Burwell, Butler, Caperton, Champion, Cilley, Cooper, Cox, Culpeper, Dana, Daven-

port, Davis of Massachusetts, Ely, Fisk of Vermont, Gaston, Geddes, Gholson, Grosvenor, Hale, Harris, Henderson, Howell, Hubbard, Jackson of Rhode Island, Kennedy, Kent of New York, King of Massachusetts, Law, Lewis, Lovett, Macon, Markell, Miller, Moseley, Oakley, Pearson, Pickering, Pitkin, Potter, John Reed, William Reed, Rich, Ruggles, Schureman, Sheffey, Shipherd, Skinner, Slaymaker, Smith of New York, Stanford, Stockton, Stuart, Sturges, Taggart, Thompson, Vose, Ward of Massachusetts, Webster, Wheaton, White, Wilcox, Wilson, of Massachusetts, Winter, and Wright.

And the said bill was ordered to be read a third time to-morrow.

WEDNESDAY, December 14.

Mr. WEBSTER presented a petition of Jonathan Bradley Eastman, late paymaster to the troops in the district of the Lakes, stating that, by the surrender of Detroit, by the late General Hull, a large sum of public money, together with his accounts and vouchers, fell into the hands of the enemy, by which he is unable to settle with the War Department, and praying relief from Congress.—Referred to the Committee of Claims.

Mr. TAYLOR presented a petition of the President and Directors of the New York State Bank, and of the Mechanics and Farmers' Bank of Albany, recommending an issue of "national bills of credit," to a limited amount, having the quality of a legal tender in payment of all contracts.—Referred to the Committee of Ways and Means.

Mr. FISK, from the Committee of Ways and Means, reported the bill from the Senate, "to incorporate the subscribers to the Bank of the United States of America," with amendments; which were read, and, together with the bill, committed to a Committee of the Whole to-morrow.

A message from the Senate informed the House that the Senate insist on their amendments, disagreed to by this House, to the bill "to provide additional revenues for defraying the expenses of Government, and maintaining the public credit, by laying duties on spirits distilled within the United States, and by amending the act laying duties on licenses to distillers of spirituous liquors," and ask a conference upon the same; to which conference they have appointed managers on their part.

Mr. FARROW, from the committee appointed on the 25th ultimo, on the petition of John Motlow, made a report; which was read, and committed to a Committee of the Whole on Monday next.—The report is as follows:

It is represented that, in the month of October, 1781, the petitioner, with a number of others, were in a fort called Jamersons, in the State of South Carolina, that a party of Indians and tories took the fort by force, put to death a great number of those so garrisoned, and made prisoners of the balance, (among the slain were the father of the petitioner;) and carried off three negroes, the property of the petitioner and his intestate father, whose legal representative the petitioner is. It is further represented that repeated endeavors have been made by the petitioner, at very great expense, to recover the said negroes, but without success.

And it further appears, that the ninth article of the treaty of 1798, concluded with the Cherokees, by obliterating all prior aggressions, plunderings, and thefts, to that date, has finally changed the right of property, and made a legal and complete transfer of the same from the petitioner over to the said nation.

The following is a copy of the said article: "It is mutually agreed between the parties, that horses stolen, and not returned within ninety days, shall be paid for at the rate of sixty dollars each; if stolen by a white man, citizen of the United States, the Indian proprietor shall be paid in cash; and if stolen by an Indian from a citizen, to be deducted, as expressed in the fourth article of the treaty of Philadelphia. This article shall have retrospect to the commencement of the first conferences at this place in the present year, and no further; and all animosities, aggressions, thefts, and plunderings prior to this day, shall cease, and be no longer remembered or demanded on either side."

And it further appears, by the fourth article of the said treaty, that the United States received a large cession of territory from the said nation for considerations therein expressed.

From an attentive consideration of the facts of this case and the principles that govern the same, the committee are of opinion that the prayer of the petition is equitable and just, and submit the following resolution to the House:

Resolved, That the request of the petitioner ought to be granted.

On motion of Mr. McCoy, of Virginia, the Committee of Ways and Means were instructed to inquire into the expediency of amending the direct tax assessment law, so as that the county of Bath, now a part of the sixth collection district, may be added to, and made part of, the seventh collection district in the State of Virginia.

The bill from the Senate for the appointment of certain naval officers, was read twice and committed.

The bill from the Senate for the relief of John C. Hurlburt, of Chatham, in Connecticut, was read a third time; and, on motion of Mr. Fisk, of Vermont, supported by Mr. Bradley the bill was postponed to Monday week, to allow time to obtain further evidence on this case.

The engrossed bill for the regulation of the courts of Indiana, was read a third time. [The bill provides that the Legislature of Indiana may fix the place of sittings of the General Court; and that two judges shall be present to form a court.] Considerable conversation took place on a proposition by Mr. Eppes to postpone the bill, in the course of which Mr. Eppes, Mr. Lewis, and Mr. Robertson, expressed their doubts as to its expediency, and a desire to examine it further; and Mr. Ingersoll and Mr. Jennings explained its provisions, &c. At length, on motion of Mr. Robertson, the bill was referred to a Committee of the Whole.

COMPENSATION OF POSTMASTERS.

Mr. Eppes, of Virginia, offered for consideration the following resolution:

Resolved, That the Committee on Post Roads be instructed to inquire whether any, and if any, what, change ought to be made in the compensation allowed to Postmasters; and whether any, and if any, what, change ought to be made in the right of franking.

Some conversation took place on this resolution, between Mr. Rhea and Mr. Eppes, in respect to its object.

Mr. Rhea opposed the proposed reference, desiring the subject in the first instance to be referred to the Postmaster General; and, after his report, to be referred to the Committee of Ways and Means, who properly had charge of all subjects relating to revenue.

Mr. Eppes, in assigning reasons for his motion, stated, that the increase about to take place, of fifty per cent. on the present rates of postage, would operate as an increase of fifty per cent. on the present compensation of postmasters, which probably was not necessary. He had also understood that great abuses had grown out of the privilege of franking, insomuch that the office had been accepted in some instances as a sinecure, to save the expense of postage, by those who performed no duties of the office; and that the office had even, in one instance, been bestowed on a member of this House.

The motion of Mr. E. was agreed to finally, without opposition.

MILITIA DRAUGHTS.

The bill from the Senate, to call upon the several States and Territories for their respective quotas of 80,430 militia for the defence of the frontiers against invasion, was read a third time as amended.

Mr. Ward, of Massachusetts, rose and addressed the Chair as follows:

Mr. Speaker, the gentleman from Tennessee, who last addressed the House on the subject of the amendment proposed by the gentleman from Maryland, expressed a deliberate opinion that the bill on your table is not only unconstitutional, but, in point of energy and efficiency, in its principles and provisions, is not adequate to the public exigencies; and gave a decided preference to the one reported by the chairman of the Military Committee, on the part of this House, pursuant to the plan submitted by the Secretary at War. He farther said, that an act, embracing principles equally vigorous with those exhibited in the plan of the Secretary, ought to be passed; and those who should oppose it, if successful, would ruin the country.

Sir, in my mind, Congress have no right, by the Constitution, to exercise the powers considered as belonging to them in the Secretary's plan; and to pass an act comporting with them, will be a gross and outrageous violation of the personal rights of our citizens, inconsistent with the privileges of freemen, the principles of our Government, and will strike a deadly blow at American liberty; and, according to my apprehension, those who advocate the principles embraced in the Secretary's plan, and attempt to execute them, and not those who resist them, will ruin their country. That I am sincere in my opinion, and serious in my apprehensions, I call Heaven to witness. In passing such a law, it appears to me as clear as any legal or moral position, which was ever stated, that we overstep the bounds of the Constitution, and assume a power which we have no right to exercise. And where the Constitution ends, tyranny begins. If power can be assumed for one purpose, it may be for another. And if necessity, the tyrant's plea, can justify the exercise of unconstitutional power in one case, it will do it in all cases. It is in the nature of man to have an avidity of power, and to scramble for the possession of it, and to think it ever safe in his hands. This remark applies with justice to men of all parties. Gentlemen of the majority, whatever their opinions once might have been, now seem to have no objection to extreme power, provided it can be lodged in them, and exercised their own way.

The propensity on the part of the Executive, to grasp power by construction and otherwise; and the disposition on the part of the House, to assume power and surrender it, are truly alarming. If the citizens of the United States can be forced from their families and domestic enjoyments, and placed in the ranks of the regular Army, and marched out of the United States for foreign conquest, or, as the Secretary expresses it, "to push the war into Canada," while we are dreaming of liberty, we are all slaves—we hold our liberty upon a tenure which renders it unworthy of the name. If we can be marched to Quebec, we may be sent to Gibraltar, the West Indies, or any quarter of the globe. Our Government, instead of being free and republican, is a military despotism, and the right of expatriation, contended for by some gentlemen, is of more value than all the other rights which we possess.

The exigencies of the country, I agree, are pressing, and those who are influenced by an honest zeal to serve it, do not merit reproach. But every feeling of impatience at Constitutional restraint, and every propensity to assume unconstitutional power, are germs of tyranny, and ought to be destroyed in embryo. Those rules which are established by the mind and the judgment, uninfluenced by passion, for the security of the rights and the liberties of the people, ought to be held sacred in times of convulsion and tempest. To restrain the passions of men, and the aggressions of power, in such times, is the purpose for which Constitutional rules were made; and he who feels an impatience of them, has the seeds of tyranny springing up in his heart. With the spirit and disposition in which the President and Secretary at War now interpret the Constitution, give them the hundred thousand men, contemplated in the Secretary's plan, to help them explain it, in time to come; and, shocking as the thought may be, I will venture to predict, that our free institutions will not survive it, and that a second election of President will never take place.

Sir, I may be told that these powers can be exercised only in time of war; that war can be declared by the Legislature only, by the representatives of a free people; and that it will never be done, excepting in such a state of things as makes the public good unequivocally demand it. Sir, in theory it would seem that we have some security in the form of our Constitution, against the declaration of improvident, unjust and unnecessary wars; but, in practice, it has been proved we have none. We find, by experience, that a war, marked with as much folly and injustice, and coupled with as much hazard, as it respects the citizens of the country which declared it, as ever disgraced any despot on earth, can be declared by a Republican Government.

The war in which we are engaged was said to be declared in defence of sailors' rights. Those rights were violated on the Ocean, and do not admit of adequate defence elsewhere. The defenceless state of our seacoast, of two thousand miles extent, was well known by our Government; and to what it was exposed by the war, we may see by what some parts of it have already suffered. The views of the President, as to the comparative force of our country, and the country against which we declared war, and the means possessed of mutual annoyance, may be learned by recurring to the instructions which he gave to our Ambassadors at Ghent. Alluding to the remark contained in the declaration of the Prince Regent, that, in impressing British seamen from American vessels, Great Britain exercised no right which she was not willing to acknowledge as appertaining equally to the United States, with respect to American seamen, in British merchant ships, the President observes: "The semblance of equal-' ity, however, in this proposition, which strikes at ' first view, disappears on a fair examination. Im-' pressment is not an American practice, but ut-' terly repugnant to our Constitution and laws. ' The exercise of a right in common at sea by ' two nations, the one powerful, and the other ' comparatively weak, would be to put the latter ' completely at the mercy of the former. But, ' should the United States be permitted to make ' impressments from British vessels, the effect ' would be unequal. Great Britain has, perhaps, ' thirty ships of war at sea, to one of the United ' States, and would profit of the arrangement in ' that proportion." We here have the President's view of the comparative force and means of annoyance of our country, and the country with which we are at war.

The Founder of our Religion, "who spake as never man spake," when on earth, in a discourse designed to enforce on his hearers the importance of observing a due proportion between their means and their ends, their efforts and their objects, puts several interrogatories, which imply strong negative answers. Among other things he asks, "What king, going to make war against another ' king, sitteth not down first and consulteth whe-' ther he be able with ten thousand to meet him ' that cometh against him with twenty thousand?" The manner in which this question is put, implies an answer, that no king could be so lost to his own security, and the interest of his subjects. More than eighteen centuries have rolled away, since this interrogatory was put; and I believe history, before the commencement of the war in which we are engaged, does not furnish us with evidence of such an event. This deed of madness and folly, which mocked and set credulity at defiance, was reserved for the commission of a President of the United States and an American Congress, the Government of a free people!

The able and critical examination of my honorable friend from New Jersey (Mr. Stockton) of the details of the bill on your table, and of the powers of Congress to "call forth the militia," and his luminous and logical argument on these points, has superseded the necessity of any farther attention to these topics. He has exhausted the subject. Any auxiliary arguments which my humble efforts could furnish, in support of his positions, would be like *valets-de-chambre* in an army; they would add something to the number, but nothing to the strength. He has demonstrated, with a degree of clearness and perspicuity, which no unprejudiced mind can resist, that this bill provides for calling forth the militia *for* a purpose not contemplated by the Constitution; for retaining them, when called out, for a period not limited by either of the occasions, on which they can constitutionally be called out; and that the bill is a piece of machinery or instrument of torture, not warranted by the Constitution, to compel militiamen to enlist themselves or procure others to enlist into the regular Army. The attacks which have been made upon his arguments, may aptly be compared to the waves of the troubled sea, dashing against a mighty rock, and falling in gentle murmurs at its foot.

Though I bow with great respect to the argument of my honorable friend, upon the unconstitutionality of this bill, and agree with him in the facts which he has stated, with reference to the public Treasury, the ranks of the Army, the necessity of defending the country, and the impracticability of doing it without money, yet I do not accord with him in opinion as to the propriety or the practice of voting for all Constitutional laws, which have for their object the supplying the Government of the United States with men and money. That the Treasury is empty, I admit; that the ranks of the regular Army are thin, I believe to be true; and that our country must be defended, in all events, I not only admit, but affirm. But, sir, if all the parts of the United States are defended, of course the whole will be defended. If every State in the Union, with such aid as she can obtain from her neighbors, defends herself, our whole country will be defended. In my mind, the resources of the States will be applied with more economy, and with greater effect in defence of the country, under the State Governments, than under the Government of the United States. Besides, what assurances have we, if funds are placed in the hands of the present Administration, that they will be applied in defence of the country? None at all. The immense sums which have heretofore been drawn from the States, have been expended with unexampled profligacy, in wild, unsettled projects of foreign conquest; while the fairest and most important parts of our country have been left defenceless. The

views of the Administration are "to push the war into Canada." Shall we pass all the supply bills, beneath the weight of which your table groans, draw all the funds of the States from them, and then leave them, thus exhausted, to the mercy of the enemy? This, in my mind, is unjust, and against the duty which we owe to the States. Money is as necessary to their defence, as to that of the United States. Under these impressions, I have uniformly voted against granting supplies to the Government of the United States, and shall continue to do it, until I have probable grounds for believing they will be judiciously applied in defence of the country. The people of the several States ought not to be compelled to pay for protection, unless it is afforded them by the United States. Shall Massachusetts be compelled to contribute to the common stock, from which she is allowed to draw nothing? When she is denied a reimbursement of necessary expenses, incurred in securing that protection which the United States owes her and has refused to afford, ought she to exhaust her treasury, to fill that of the United States? Surely not.

Before the debate on this bill commenced, the plan of the Secretary at War, for filling the ranks of the regular Army, had been laid before this House, and a bill founded upon that plan had been reported by our Military Committee, and committed to the same Committee of the whole House to which this bill was committed; and gentlemen who have preceded me in the debate on this bill, seem to have considered everything which relates to calling forth the militia, or filling the ranks of the regular Army, as an issue; and the principles involved in the Secretary's plan have been advocated by some, and reprobated by others, according to their several opinions. I shall therefore make no apology for assuming the same latitude.

The gentlemen who attempt to support the constitutionality of this bill, and of the Secretary's plan, contend that Congress, by the Constitution, "have power to raise armies, without limitation as to the mode;" that the important and extensive duties of "providing for the common defence, promoting the general welfare, and securing the blessings of liberty," are assigned to Congress, and because these are made their duties, it is contended they must have powers commensurate with them.

Sir, I cannot suppress my astonishment, when I hear gentlemen quote the preamble of our Constitution, as an authority to exercise the powers contemplated in the Secretary's plan. It appears to me to make directly against them. Under a Constitution expressly formed for the purpose of securing the blessings of civil liberty, they claim the right of exercising a power inconsistent with the first principles of civil liberty, and repugnant to the genius and nature of our Government. If Congress have such a power, we are not freemen.

"To provide for the common defence, promote the general welfare, and secure the blessings of liberty," are mentioned in the preamble of the Constitution as objects and ends which the people had in view, in giving the powers which they did give, and not as a designation of powers which were to be given. They were expressed as an admonition to after legislators, how to exercise their powers, and to restrain them from passing laws founded upon such principles as are embraced in the Secretary's plan, and not to justify it. "The common defence, general welfare, and securing the blessings of liberty," are a pole star, or constellation, to direct Congress in their course, and in the application of the powers which are expressly given them by the Constitution. Sir, I do not know of any express provision in the Constitution, that Congress shall have power "to provide for the common defence, promote the general welfare, and secure the blessings of liberty." To say that Congress have all powers which they may deem necessary to accomplish these objects, and that they are not restrained by the powers expressly given, is, in effect, to say there is no limit to their powers; that our Constitution is a mere *carte blanche.* But, sir, if powers were given in the general terms before mentioned, (which, however, is not the case,) and afterwards particular powers were expressed, the general powers would be controlled and restrained by the special. This is an established rule in the construction of all instruments. If A gives to B a letter of attorney, in which he constitutes him his agent, to represent him in all courts, and to transact all his concerns, and then proceeds to give powers to do special acts, in a particular manner, the general powers are controlled and restrained by the special.

The true construction of the provision in the Constitution, that "Congress shall have power to raise and support armies," is, that Congress shall have authority, or it shall be lawful for them to do it; not that they may use power or force, to coerce or compel the citizens to enter the regular army. Congress have power to establish post offices and make post roads; but no person ever supposed that they could chain the citizens to wheelbarrows, and make them work against their will. The power of Congress to raise armies must be exercised in such a manner as is consistent with the people enjoying "the blessings of civil liberty."

Though the Government of the United States cannot claim any power by implication or construction; being prohibited from doing it by the Constitution, yet the same cannot be said of the State governments or the people. It is admissible and fair to infer what they meant to reserve in one case, by what they refuse to give in another. That the people and the States did not intend to give Congress power by force to compel the citizens, our fathers, brothers, and children, to enter the regular Army, destined for foreign conquest, under United States' officers, is clearly to be inferred, from their refusing to take the militia under United States' officers when forced into the service, even in case of invasion, the most pressing exigency that can possibly happen.

What powers the people and the several States

thought it was necessary to give to Congress, and what they did give, is to be learned from the spirit of the times in which the Constitution was formed, from the views and motives which induced the people to form it, and from a fair construction of the Constitution itself, taking it all together.

When the Constitution was formed and adopted, a jealousy of the military power of the United States, and a caution as to what they should part with, were predominant feelings in the people of all the States. A consolidated military Government was the object of fearful apprehensions. The State Governments had been tried, and were familiar to the people, and a more general confidence was placed in them than that of the United States, of which they had made no experiment. The "blessings of civil liberty" were thought much more secure, without giving to Congress an unlimited power of the sword, than they would be if that were the case. Let the people of Massachusetts have been told, that Congress, if the Constitution were adopted, would have power to raise regular armies, against the opinion of their State Legislature, for foreign conquest, or any other purpose, and that their parents, themselves, and their children, could be forced into the ranks, under the command of United States' officers, and be subject to martial law, and the discipline, severity, and the privations of a camp; and the Constitution, instead of being suffered to lie on the table for consideration, would have been thrown under it. They would have said, we have fought for "the blessings of civil liberty," and we will not adopt a Constitution which will seal our slavery. The people of Massachusetts would have said, on such an occasion, what the people of Virginia did on one less warrantable, "We will secede from the Union, 'and be left to the protection and government of 'a hundred thousand free independent citizens."

In the express provisions of the Constitution, a hedge was intended to be set about the citizens of the several States, to guard them against the incursions of the military powers of the United States. The wisdom of that precaution is now manifest. If the United States could command the military power of all the States, they would endanger and could easily destroy any individual State. This was foreseen, and the power withholden. Even the qualified authority which is given to Congress by the Constitution, "to provide for calling forth the militia to execute the laws, suppress insurrections, and repel invasions," requires that the soldiers should be placed under officers appointed by the States. This reservation was made by the States to guard their citizen soldiers against oppressive power, to secure to the State Governments the attachment of the officers, and guard the State against a misapplication of their military force, and prevent it from being turned against them. Can any one believe when the people, in case of invasion, the most trying emergency which can happen, gave the United States power to call forth the militia under State officers only, that they intended to put the whole people of the several States at the disposal of the Government of the United States, and expose them to be forced into the regular Army, under United States' officers, in whose appointment they had no agency, and under whose command they would find no mercy; and this for the purpose of foreign conquest? No, sir! It is a doctrine too absurd and inconsistent to find support in any unprejudiced mind. We may as well suppose that they would have trembled at the yelping of a lapdog, and felt no terrors at the roaring of lions; that they would have strained at a gnat and swallowed a camel.

All those who labor to support the right of Congress to exercise the powers contemplated in the Secretary's plan, in my mind, fall into one common error. Instead of considering the Government of the United States as a Government of limited jurisdiction, possessing such powers only as are expressly given, they consider it as a Government of general jurisdiction, and as having all powers which are not denied.

All powers not expressly given to Congress by the Constitution, are reserved to the States or to the people. If the powers given are not adequate to the public exigencies (which I do not admit to be the case,) it is not the fault of Congress, who are the mere agents of the people, and accountable to them for the fair and faithful exercise of such powers only as are given to them. To say that it is necessary, or highly convenient to the defence of the country, that Congress should have the powers contemplated in the Secretary's plan, and therefore, that they have them, is very illogical. It is like arguing from right to fact, or from fact to right, which is never admissible. Whether or not it would have been better, according to the ideas which the majority now seem to have, that the United States should have been consolidated, and the independence of the States annihilated, and Congress possess all power, even the power of acting immediately upon the people for all military and civil purposes, it is of no importance to inquire. We do not sit here to alter the Constitution, or make a new one, but to administer it, according to its form and effect, as the people, from whom all power proceeds, and for whose benefit it is to be exercised, have made it.

For the purposes of defence, the State Governments have a right to command the services of all their citizens who are able to render any; but no Government under heaven has a right to compel the citizens of our country to enter the regular Army, under United States' officers, for the purpose of "pushing the war into Canada," or for the purpose of any foreign conquest, whatever. Such a power is at war with the vital spirit of our Constitution, and the first principles of civil liberty.

Sir, according to the principles of the Secretary's plan, and the provisions of the bill, which have been attempted to be defended in the present debate, the soldiers may be wholly drawn from one section of the United States, and the officers appointed from another. The legislators, the judges, and the freemen of the Eastern States,

against their consent, may be placed under the command of minions and striplings from distant States. This may be thought to be a vision of fancy, a delusion of the mind; but, judging from appointments which have heretofore been made, we could not expect that more attention would be paid to our feelings or our interest, in a certain section of our country, than such a state of things would exhibit. As I am unwilling to be thought to make railing accusations, without evidence to support them, I shall trouble the House with the statement of a few facts, which fully maintain the suggestions which I have made.

Not to mention the embarrassments experienced by Massachusetts in defending against the enemy (which have been fully stated by my honorable friend, Mr. King) arising from the President's sending a General, in whom the Government of the United States had practically said they had no confidence, to command on one of the most important stations, the case of Colonel Loring ought not to pass unnoticed. Some few years since, he commanded a company of militia in the town of Boston. and was chargeable with many acts of insubordination and unmilitary conduct, for which he was arrested. As a military man, he was a common mover of sedition and disorder. A court martial was legally appointed, and consisted of officers of both political parties. By the unanimous voice of the court, he was found guilty, and by their sentence disqualified for holding any military office (if I mistake not) for five years; and the sentence was approved by the supreme Executive of Massachusetts. Before this disability was removed, he received a colonel's commission from the President, and was sent to exercise his command in the very section in which he had received his sentence of disqualification, and, as I have been informed, over one of the officers who sat on his trial. This was an affront and an insult to the constituted authorities of Massachusetts, and to power legally exercised; and while the President thus practises himself, he cannot expect that his authority and jurisdiction will be respected by others. The embarrassments which the appointments to which I allude occasioned to the Government of Massachusetts, in their late measures of defence, were much more than a counterbalance for any aid they have received from the Government of the United States.

The express provision in the Constitution, that the States shall appoint the officers of the militia, when called into actual service, is considered as a strong argument against the right of Congress to exercise the powers contemplated in the Secretary's plan, and the train of reasoning he has adopted to get over it is extraordinary indeed. He admits that if the mode of raising an army which he proposes, "draws men from the militia service and places them under regular officers, the principles of the Constitution are violated." In the execution of the Secretary's plan, men will be forcibly drawn from the militia and placed in the regular Army, under the United States' officers. This I hold to be indisputably the case. The grounds upon which it is contended that such will not be the operation of the Secretary's plan, are, that the men are drawn from the population of the country, and not from the militia.

Sir, does not the population of the country embrace the militia? Is it not a well settled maxim in philosophy, law, and common sense, that the greater contains the less, and that the whole embraces all the parts? If one part, and that from which military force would most probably be attempted to be drawn, is guarded and secured by the Constitution, can you take the whole without violating the provision whch secures the part? Certainly you cannot. The population of the country embraces the militia, and more also; and because the power proposed to be exercised is not limited to the militia, it is said to be Constitutional, though it is admitted that it would not be so if it were thus limited. If you cannot touch a part, unless it be *sub modo*, you cannot touch the whole, which includes that part, unless it be subject to the same limitation. But, sir, Congress have no power over the population, for military purposes, excepting it be "to organize them as militia, and arm and discipline them," and when thus organized, to call them forth for the purposes expressed by the Constitution, under officers appointed by the States.

If the bill on your table is unconstitutional, resistance is not only lawful, but it is a duty. To resist usurped power, is as high a duty as to submit to power lawfully exercised; and the freemen of the East will much sooner incur the penalties of an unconstitutional law, than the guilt of treachery to their country and posterity. We have heard much from some of the majority, "of the power of Government, of rebellion, and of crisis." Sir, far be it from me to do anything to invite or hasten crises, but if they are forced upon the citizens of this country, when they are defending "the blessings of civil liberty," they will be met with that fortitude which conscious integrity inspires, and the power of the Government, exerted in an unjust cause, will be found to be impotent.

From the language of some gentlemen, I should suppose they imagine, that persons in authority have a right to use any powers which they may deem necessary to accomplish lawful ends, and are not restrained or limited to Constitutional means, and that resistance, in all cases, would be rebellion.

"Whoever in authority," said the great Mr. Locke, "exceeds his powers, acts without authority, and may be opposed as any other man who invades rights." Upon its being observed, that "to tell the people they may oppose power when perverted or misapplied, will lead to rebellion," the same great man replied, "you may as well say, to tell honest men they may oppose robbers and pirates will lead to disorder and bloodshed." When the famous Selden was asked, "by what statutes resistance to tyranny could be justified," he answered: "It is to be justified by the custom and usage of England, which is the law of the land." "We are to support the Crown," says Bolingbroke, "with our lives and fortunes, while it keeps within bounds, and protects us, and no

longer." "This is so well settled," as he expresses it, "that conscience has no occasion to battle with the understanding." "A King," says Mr. Erskine, "has no more authority to exceed his power, than a constable." If Government usurp a power, not given by the Constitution, they are wrong doers, and responsible for the consequences.

In the Secretary's explanatory observations, it is said, that "Congress had a right, by the Constitution, to raise regular armies, and no restraint is imposed in the exercise of it;" that "it would be absurd to suppose that Congress could not carry this power into effect, otherwise than by accepting the voluntary services of individuals"— and that "it might happen that an army could not be raised in that mode, whence the power would have been granted in vain."

Sir, it will never happen in a country like ours, that a wise and provident Administration cannot raise an army, without resorting to force, when the interest of the nation requires that they should have one. In a war just, necessary, and expedient, and wisely conducted, one in which the feelings of the people are engaged, armies will be raised with great facility. In any other war the Government ought not to have an army. Our Government is a Government of the people, was made for the people, for the good of the many, and not to support the pride, the weak, or wicked policy, or the passions of the few. War never ought to be declared by a Government like ours, excepting for causes of such magnitude, and for injuries of such a nature, as to cause a general excitement. After having legislated for years upon principles hostile to the interests of the people, and destructive of their attachment to the Government, to expect that the people would rally round the Government, and fight with enthusiasm, betrays a want of knowledge of men, and of the nature of our free institutions.

The Secretary further observes, that "long 'continued invasions, conducted by well disci-'plined troops, can best be repelled by troops 'kept constantly in the field, and equally well 'disciplined;" that "the framers of the Consti-'tution, and the States who ratified it, knew the 'advantage which an enemy might have over 'us by regular forces, and intended to place their 'country on an equal footing;" and so he concludes the Government have a right to raise such troops by compulsion.

If our Government can adopt such reasoning as this, and reduce it to practice, our citizens will soon find themselves in chains of despotism. "The framers of the Constitution, and the States who adopted it," also well knew that an attack made upon our country by the energies and undivided efforts of a foreign despot, could most effectually be resisted by despotic and arbitrary power; and it may as fairly be contended that, in time of war, it was intended by "the framers of the Constitution," that the President, to whom the command of the Army and Navy is given, should have all the power of a Roman Dictator. No doubt if one individual wielded the whole physical force, and commanded the whole re-

915   HISTORY OF CONGRESS.   916

H. of R.   *Militia Draughts.*   December, 1814.

sources of the country, in time of war, we could more successfully invade foreign countries, and more promptly defend our own. "The pace of snail," in which the American Congress moves, is not well suited to the energies and quick-time step of military operations. But with power in the President, so well suited to war, what would become of us in peace? We might then be oppressed with as much facility as we could be defended in war. To guard against oppression, the powers of Government are wisely limited by the people, and every branch of the Government, at their peril, must keep within the bounds prescribed. If we have free institutions, and enjoy "the blessings of civil liberty," we cannot possess all the despotic energies in war. This our Government ought to have considered before war was declared.

The President, through his Ministry, declares to us "that the nature of the crisis in which we ' are involved, and the extent of our danger, re- ' quire particular attention; that we are contend- ' ing for existence, and must make great exer- ' tions, and suffer great sacrifices; that we are ' called upon for a display of all that patriotism ' which distinguished us in the first great strug- ' gle; that we must relinquish no right, or perish ' in the struggle."

Is this a true picture of the state of our country? Are we contending for existence? Are we called upon for a display of those spasms of patriotism exhibited in our great struggle? How came we in this situation? By whose agency, and for what causes, were we thus involved? The same Government, the same men, involved us in the war, which is the cause of all the evils and calamities which await us, who now tell us and the world, that the principle in support of which they said the war was declared is not worth a serious contest. The same men who now call upon us to surrender our lives, our personal liberty, our children, and everything which is dear to us, to extricate our country from the state of wretchedness in which they have involved us, now, in effect, admit, that after the revocation of the British Orders in Council there was no adequate cause for prosecuting the war. It is true, as is said, after the peace in Europe, the principles of impressment, for which our enemy contend, "will have no practical effect;" but what were we told when the war was declared? It was then resounded from one end of the continent to the other, that the war was a war for principle; that sailors' rights were to be established on a basis eternal. No man supposed, from the representations of the supporters of the war, that the blood and treasure which were expended were to avert the current sufferings by impressment during the war in Europe. Every one knew that the evils of one year of war would be greater than those of a century, resulting from impressment, in the manner in which it was practised when the war was declared. Gentlemen may disguise it as they will, still the passions, the feelings, and the motives which led to the war, will be rightly apprehended and fully

understood by our enlightened citizens. Sir, the causes of the war, the motives which influenced our Government when they declared it, the conquest of Canada, and everything relating to these subjects, have become to me extremely disgusting. I have no pleasure in entering upon them, even for the purpose of justly reproaching the authors of the war, though the baneful effects of it meet my eyes in every direction. But, sir, when I hear the gentleman from Pennsylvania say, "he had not the honor of voting for the war, not being a member when it was declared;" when I hear him speak of "a morbid neutrality," and hear him ask "what situation would our country have been in had war not been declared?" implying that he thinks the war a blessing; when I view the picture of the distresses of our country, as described by the Government; when I look around upon my fellow-citizens and neighbors, and contrast their present with their situation before the war; when I see persons and families who were then in flourishing and happy circumstances, moving over the earth in a step so light as scarcely to touch it—when I see the same persons, in consequence of disasters which have grown out of the war, now moving in the solemn step of a funeral procession, poor as death, and gloomy as the grave; when I behold the silence of midnight pervade our commercial cities, where the busy hum of industry was heard in every street, I cannot repress my feelings. Many tears of blood have been shed in consequence of the war, and scenes have been acted, which none but minds blinded by infatuation, and hearts impenetrable by pity, and insensible to feelings of remorse, can contemplate without horror. Those who think that the happiness of the people deserves more consideration than the pride of mistaken rulers will readily admit that it is much to be regretted that war was declared.*

---

*The following extracts from a letter of the celebrated patriot, Edmund Burke, to the sheriffs of Bristol, on American affairs, in 1777, needs no comment to show their application to the supporters and opposers of the present war:

"Indeed our affairs are in a bad condition. I do assure those gentlemen who have prayed for war, and obtained the blessing they have sought, that they are at this instant in very great straits.

"The events of this war are of so much greater magnitude than those who either wished or feared it, ever looked for, that this alone ought to fill every considerate mind with anxiety and diffidence. Wise men often tremble at the very things which fill the thoughtless with security. Whether you are yet wholly out of danger from them is more than I know, or than your rulers can divine; but even if I were certain of my safety, I could not easily forgive those who had brought me into the most dreadful perils, because by accidents, unforeseen by them or me, I have escaped. A conscientious man would be cautious how he dealt in blood; he would feel some apprehensions of being called to a tremendous account, for engaging in so deep a play, without any sort of knowledge of the game. I cannot conceive any existence under Heaven,

We are told " that the result of the contest cannot be doubtful." If further contest must take place, it is my wish that the prediction may prove true. But I want something more to rest my hopes upon than the prophecies of the present Administration, or their ability to conduct the war. Their predictions, heretofore, have proved illusory and vain ; and I believe history does not furnish an example of funds so extensive being expended, and means so extensive exhausted, and so little effect produced. If the Administration have the talents requisite for conducting the war, why has not more been done? It is said that this is a war of the nation, and not of a party ; that a great majority of the people, the substantial yeomanry, the physical strength of the country, are with the Government. All the laws have been passed for raising men and money, which the supporters of the war have required. If the war is popular, at least four millions of people, a greater number than the whole population of the country in the Revolutionary war, must be heart and hand with the Administration. The purses, even of the Opposition, have been open to the supporters of the war, as far as they would draw upon their own. If the statements of the majority are true, the results of three campaigns, and the existing state of things, most clearly show a want of talents in the Government to call forth and apply the resources of the country.

The President, through his Minister, says: " The United States must give up *no* right, or perish in the struggle."

These were not the sentiments of Alexander the Deliverer, at the Treaty of Tilsit ; and we have seen the fruits and effects of the wisdom of Romanzoff, in negotiating that treaty, wonderfully displayed in the battle of Borodino, and in the after events of Europe. No wise Government, despotic or republican, ever held such language, or practised upon such a principle. A mad adherence to this principle hurried Bonaparte from the government of the fairest part of Europe to that speck of creation, the island of Elba. What, yield nothing ! give up no right, however unimportant, even to quiet the reasonable fears of our enemy ! not even be at peace with " our red brethren," and suffer those children of nature to

(which in the depths of its wisdom tolerates all sorts of things,) that it is more truly odious and disgusting, than an impotent, helpless creature, without civil wisdom, or military skill, bloated with pride and arrogance, calling for battles which he is not to fight, contending for a dominion which he can never exercise, and satisfied to be himself mean and miserable, in order to render others wretched.

" If you and I find our talents not of the great and ruling kind, our conduct at least is conformable to our faculties. No man's life pays the forfeit of our rashness. No desolate widow weeps tears of blood over our arrogance.

" I know many have been taught to think that moderation in a case like this is a sort of treason, and that all arguments for it are sufficiently answered by charging all the present or future miseries which we may suffer on the resistance of our brethren. But I would wish them in this grave matter, and if peace is not wholly removed from their hearts, to consider seriously that to criminate and recriminate never yet was the road to reconciliation in any difference among men. If measures of peace are necessary, they must begin somewhere ; and a conciliatory temper must precede and prepare every plan of reconciliation. Nor do I conceive that we suffer anything by thus regulating our minds ; we are not disarmed by being disencumbered of our passions. This outrageous language which has been encouraged, and kept alive by every art, has already done incredible mischief.

" If I had not lived long enough to be little surprised at anything, I should have been in some degree astonished at the continued rage of several gentlemen, who, not satisfied with carrying fire and sword into another country, are animated nearly with the same fury against those neighbors of theirs, whose only crime it is that they have charitably and humanely wished them to entertain more reasonable sentiments, and not always to sacrifice their interest to their passion. All this rage against unresisting dissent, convinces me that at bottom they are far from satisfied they are in the right. For what is it they would have ? A war ! They certainly have, at this moment, the blessing of something that is very like one. Is it the force of the nation they call for ? they have it already ; and if they choose to fight their battles in their own persons nobody prevents their marching with the next expedition. Do they think the service is stinted for the want of liberal supplies ? Indeed they complain without reason. The table of the House will glut them, let their appetite for expense be ever so keen.

" In order to produce this favorite unanimity in delusion, and to prevent all possibility of a return to our ancient happy concord, arguments for our continuance in this course are drawn from the wretched situation itself into which we have been betrayed. It is said that, being at war, all the policy we have left is to strengthen the hand of Government. On the principle of this argument, the more mischiefs we suffer from Administration, the more our trust in it is to be confirmed.

" Let them but once get us into a war, and then their power is safe, and an act of oblivion passed for all their misconduct. Accordingly, the least resistance to power appears more inexcusable in their eyes than the great abuses of authority. All dread of a standing military force, is looked upon as a superstitious panic ; and we are taught to believe that a desire of domineering over our countrymen is love to our country.

" It is impossible that we should remain long in a situation which breeds such notions and dispositions without some great alteration in the national character. Many things have been long operating towards a gradual change in our principles ; but this war has done more in a few years than all the other causes could have effected in a century. It is, therefore, not on its own separate account, but because of its attendant circumstances, that I consider its continuance, or its ending in any way but that of an honorable and liberal accommodation, as the greatest evil that can befall us ; for that reason I entreat you, again and again, neither to be persuaded, shamed, or frighted out of the principles that have hitherto led so many of you to abhor the war."

enjoy undisturbed, a small portion of the lands which the God of nature gave them! The proudest Monarchs, in their proudest days, have often, for the sake of peace, given up rights not important to their security, to quiet the fears of a weaker neighbor. Louis XIV, when more powerful than any Monarch in Europe, for the sake of peace, and to quiet the fears of the English and Dutch, agreed to destroy his fortifications at Dunkirk. The English, when they were conquerors, to obtain peace, and quiet the fears of Spain, agreed to demolish their forts near the Bay of Honduras. No wise Government, to avoid a present contest, will surrender rights which will weaken itself essentially, or give an accession of power to its enemy which will operate a serious disadvantage in future contests. These general observations I have thought it not improper to make; as negotiation for peace is pending, I will not be more particular.

Sir, I am not a little surprised at the reproaches which have been cast upon the Government and people of Massachusetts, for suffering a part of her territory to be captured, and hitherto to remain in possession of the enemy. It is the more extraordinary, as the censure comes from members of a Government to whom she has paid the price of protection, and from whom she has a right to demand it. It is owing to the improvidence of the Government of the United States that the enemy now possesses the territory to which allusion is had. A small portion of the millions drawn from Massachusetts, and wasted by dishonest agents, or expended in mad projects, if it had been laid out in building fortifications, and placing garrisons in them, would have prevented even a temporary loss of this territory. If the United States declare to New England that they cannot protect them, and that all expectations of the General Government doing their duty are mere delusions, Massachusetts will use her means to better purposes than the United States have employed them. Since the adoption of the Constitution, more money has been received from Massachusetts by the United States than they have been able to beg or borrow, even at an enormous premium, of their partisans and supporters; in return for which, for twelve years past, she has received nothing but injuries. Moreover, the place invaded is nearly three hundred miles from Massachusetts proper, and her whole intermediate seacoast, three hundred miles in extent, has been left unprotected by the United States, whose duty it was to provide for their defence; and even her capital, daily in expectation of invasion, was wholly neglected by the General Government. In this situation it did not comport with the wisdom and sound policy of the supreme Executive of Massachusetts, to draw his troops from the capital of his State into the wilds of the District of Maine, to rescue a portion of its territory from a possession of the enemy, which, as it respects the most of it, is merely nominal, and leave the capital of the State to be sacked and destroyed by the enemy. Acts of folly and weakness of this description

are the exclusive right of another Executive. Sir, I desire, with suitable feelings and emotions, to thank my God, that the capital of Massachusetts has not been invaded. Had it been so ordered, even if we had been victorious, victory might have been purchased with blood, precious to me as my own. In the event of an invasion, which I pray God to avert, I believe that the rebellious people of Boston, and their brethren in the vicinity, would look at Bunker's Hill, and at their enemy, and that very different materials would be furnished for the pages of future history, from those furnished by the President of the United States, and his loyal subjects of this patriotic section, in the Hudibrastic victory which he obtained in the memorable battle of Bladensburg—

"When the fight becomes a chase,
"He wins the fight who wins the race."

Sir, I do not like to draw geographical lines, or make sectional comparisons. Discussions of this nature are never invited or commenced by me. But when gentlemen from other States question the prowess or patriotism of Massachusetts, I must be permitted to remind them of what the history of our country will prove, that a force, equal to that which overran whole States in the South, and chased Legislators from their seats into the mountains after the first gun was fired, were never able to penetrate into Massachusetts the distance of cannon shot from her shores.

Although I have already occupied the floor too long, I cannot quit it without expressing the high gratification which I felt in hearing the remarks of two of the gentlemen from Kentucky, (Mr. Hopkins and Mr. Duvall,) who preceded me in this debate. To hear the mutual interests, the mutual wants and mutual supplies of the Eastern and Western States, and the adaptation of one to the other, and the legitimate and proper defence of the whole, a navy, recognised and described, in language so lively and so just, excited in my breast very pleasing emotions. I have witnessed nothing like it since I have had the honor of a seat in this House. The feelings of friendship and respect which were expressed for the people of the Eastern States were of a new impression. One of the gentlemen (Mr. Duvall) mixed a little gall with his honey, and planted a few seeds of henbane and nightshade in his garden of spices; but upon that I shall not dwell.

When I consider the relative circumstances and situations of the Eastern, Southern, and Western States, and see how much of harmony and how little of opposition there is in their interests, and how happily they are calculated to relieve the mutual wants of each other, and to furnish mutual benefits, I am astonished at the seeds of bitterness which have sprung up among them. When inquiry is made how this happened, we may say, as it was said in Holy Writ, when the tares were found among the wheat, "an enemy hath done it." In my mind, a few prominent, influential men in our country, too ardent friends of one foreign nation, and too inveterate haters of another; enemies to commerce, to a navy, to the fisheries, and to everything excepting the *terra firma* of our country, whatever their views may have been, were the founders of the mistaken and ruinous policy of our Government, and of course sowed the seeds of the heartburnings and ill blood among our citizens, and of all the evils which await our country.*

If a reconciliation ever takes place between our citizens, and between the different sections of our country, it must commence somewhere, and most clearly it ought to commence with the majority. If a system of measures calculated to save our country, and not partaking of the spirit of party, should be proposed by them and rejected by the minority, the majority have the power of votes to enforce their own measures, and without mortification can say to the minority, we can do without you; whereas the minority, destitute of this power, must approach the majority in the style of petitioners; a style which the majority have no right to expect they will assume, considering the state in which the measures of the majority, against admonitions and remonstrances, have involved their country.

Mr. FARROW.—Mr. Speaker, I will not, on the question of the passage of the bill on your table, detain you with my opinion in respect of either the justice or policy of the war that you are now engaged in, nor with the wisdom of the measures in which it has been prosecuted. The day for examining the propriety of the war is passed by. It must now be enough for me to know that war was Constitutionally declared, and that it has been conducted by the constituted authority. As man must be fallible, it is his province to err; and I have no wish to live under a Government where he is not allowed that privilege. However great may have been the errors of your Administration, it is, nevertheless, my boast and pride that I am a citizen of your Government. I would not exchange it for any other. While I wish all nations well, my own is the most dear to me. Influenced by these impressions, I will give you every support in my power to enable you to prosecute the war, until you can obtain a just and equitable peace.

It is contended by several honorable gentlemen that the principles of the bill are unconstitutional. The honorable gentleman from New Jersey, (Mr. STOCKTON,) with great perspicuity, and with a strong discriminating mind, so contended. I subscribe to every principle that he contended for, and every position that he laid down; but he did not, nor cannot, apply them to the bill under consideration. When a case comes before you to

which they can be applied I will vote with that gentleman. It is in this case, Mr. Speaker, like all others, proper first to establish facts before you can properly apply principles. He states that the militia can only be called out by you, to either execute the laws of the Union, suppress insurrections, or repel invasions. That is also my opinion. As I told you, we agree on principles, but how he came to the conclusion that this bill is not to call out the militia for either of those purposes I cannot tell. The facts, as I will show, will not authorize such a conclusion. Let us now examine what are the facts. We all know that, at this time, the enemy has possession of the town of Castine, and a large country around there, within the State of Massachusetts. Some of the forts on your Northern and Northwestern frontiers, some of the islands in the Chesapeake and on your Northern coasts, the enemy holds possession of. Now, under these circumstances, what is your duty marked out by the eighth section of the first article of the Constitution of the United States?

[Here Mr. F. read from the said section: "To 'make rules for the government and regulation of 'the land and the naval forces; to provide for 'calling forth the militia to execute the laws of 'the Union, suppress insurrections, and repel in-'vasions."]

Having in view this part of the Constitution, indulge me while I read the first section of the bill before you. "That the President of the Uni-'ted States be, and he is hereby, authorized and 'required to call upon the Executives of the sev-'eral States and Territories thereof, for their re-'spective quotas of 80,000 militia, armed and 'equipped according to law, to serve for the term 'of one year, from the time of meeting at the 'place of rendezvous, unless sooner discharged." These are the principles of the bill; there is a provision in the bill, holding out an inducement to any man called out as a militiaman, to enlist and join the regular army. They may do so if they please; and so they may, whether this law is passed or not. If they go into the regular service, it must be by virtue of their voluntary contract. I did vote with those who wished to reduce the term of service, believing, as I do, that six months is as long as the militia ought to be called out from their homes and families. But a majority of this honorable body differs with me in opinion, and have fixed the term of service at twelve months. I will, therefore, vote for the bill, as I am not willing for the nation to strike her flag until the enemy will suffer you to rest in peace.

Mr. GASTON said, he hoped he might be indulged with the attention of the House for a few minutes. It was not his purpose to wander over the extensive field of controversy, which had been opened on this occasion, but briefly to notice one or two interesting topics, which had not received the attention due to them. The bill on the table was such a singular nondescript that it was difficult to define its character. Its friends were generally solicitous that it should be regarded as an

---

* Monsieur Genet, the first Minister from the French Republic to our Government, has recently said, that in the measures which he adopted towards the supreme Executive of our country, the character of which is known by every one, he had the advice and approbation of Mr. Jefferson, the late President.

ordinary militia bill. A majority of the House had viewed it in the light of a bill imposing a direct tax, while he believed, with his friends around him, that it was a disingenuous and unwarrantable contrivance for compelling the militia to find recruits for the regular army. If the bill were to be regarded, as its friends wished, as an ordinary militia bill, one objection alone was sufficient to insure its rejection. It was utterly inefficient for the purposes it professed to have in view. As to other parts of the country, he would not speak decisively; but in that with which he was best acquainted, he would venture to assert, that the quota required by this bill could not be brought into the field, in conformity to its provisions, in less than twelve months after the requisition. Let these provisions be examined a moment. After the President has made his requisition upon the Executive of a State, the captain of every infantry company within it is to be instructed and required to enroll on his muster list the names of all persons within the local limits of his company, liable to do military duty, whether members of his own or any other military corps. When this enrolment is completed, every captain is to make a return thereof, by mail or otherwise, to the brigade-inspector of his brigade. When this officer has received the returns from all the captains of his brigade, he is then to make out and forward a return to the Adjutant General of the State, setting forth in it the numbers belonging to each regiment, battalion, and company. The Adjutant General, on receiving the returns of all the brigade inspectors, is to ascertain the number of men which each brigade, regiment, battalion, and company, ought to furnish towards making up the quota required. Having performed this arithmetical labor, he is then to communicate the result to the brigadiers throughout the State, who will parcel out so much of the intelligence as may be necessary to the commandants of regiments, who, in their turn, will issue orders to the captains with whom this process began. This business happily concluded, the captains will then divide their companies into classes, equal to half the number of persons whom they are to furnish, taking especial care that these classes shall contain the same number of persons and the same quantity of wealth. Each class will then, by draught or contract, furnish two soldiers. Then is to be resumed the task of reporting to brigade inspectors, who, in their turn, report again to the Adjutant General. When this second routine of returns is completed, the men who are to form the quota are known, and are to be organized by companies, battalions, regiments, brigades, and divisions, and to have their appropriate officers selected and commissioned. When it is recollected that many of the officers whose agency is essentially necessary to set this complicated machine in motion, (men appointed in the piping days of peace,) are very little acquainted with military duties generally, and will not be apt soldiers in learning the new duties assigned them, that they are scattered over an extensive territory, live remote from post offices, and are not in the habit of correspondence by mail, it is scarcely possible to doubt that many casualties and failures must occur to interrupt the regular transmission and return of their official communications. This will take place with the best intentions. But if some should be disposed not to co-operate zealously in the plan, how will you detect culpable omissions on their part? How prove the regular receipt of orders, intrusted to a conveyance well known to be uncertain, and probably delivered privately, if delivered at all, and without the power afterwards of distinctly recollecting the fact? If the militia are to be resorted to for the defence of this country, the utmost promptitude and despatch are essential. The emergency is immediate; so should be the call. Yet all our legislative energy is to be compressed into a scheme which will prevent the forthcoming of militia, until the occasion for their services is past. As a militia bill, that now before us is worse than nugatory. It is ruinous, trifling with the most important interests of the country.

But, sir, said Mr. G., I rose principally for another purpose; for a purpose which must interest the best feelings of every man who loves Constitutional freedom, or respects the memory of the man, "first in war, first in peace, and first in the hearts of his countrymen." In the course of this discussion, the monstrous and detestable doctrine asserted by our Secretary of War, that the General Government has an uncontrolled power to force every American into the ranks of a regular army, has been maintained and combatted with equal zeal, though with unequal argument. To the reasoning of my honorable friends I presume not to add anything. The jury before whom this issue is tried, the enlightened freemen of this country, cannot hesitate as to the verdict they are to pronounce. They are ready to declare the claim which has been advanced, is arbitrary, unconstitutional, and fitted only for the region of slavery. But recourse has been had to authority, and the name of Washington has been brought forward in this House to give sanction to doctrines utterly subversive of the principles of civil liberty, as if he had left on record one act, heretofore undiscovered by friend or foe, sufficient to tarnish all the fame of his illustrious actions, and to strike off his name from the list of the benefactors of mankind. Mine be the task to rescue from this unmerited imputation the memory of the man, whom, from infancy, I was taught to love and revere.

The doctrine of the Secretary of War, stated in its mildest form, is, that the United States have a right to draught men out of the militia, to fill the ranks of the regular Army. This doctrine is said to be explicitly advanced in a report of General Knox, while Secretary of War, and to have been distinctly approved by General Washington, to whom that report was submitted. If either of these positions be unfounded, the pretence of the authority of Washington must be abandoned. Both are unfounded.

And first, sir, admitting for a moment that

General Knox's report intimates such a claim on the part of the General Government. on what evidence are we to pronounce that this claim obtained the sanction of General Washington?

It appears, that at the second session of the first Congress, under the present Constitution, when the head of the Executive Departments were presenting their respective plans upon the great subjects which came immediately under their view, when Hamilton was making his reports on public credit and a National Bank, Jefferson on the fisheries and other subjects, and Randolph upon the Judiciary Establishment, that General Knox, then Secretary of War, submitted his plan for the arrangement of the militia of the United States with a view to their effectual defence. This plan was presented to the President by Gen. Knox, with a letter, stating that it was substantially the same plan which had been prepared for the consideration of the late Congress, under whom he had also been Secretary of War, and had then been submitted to General Washington's examination. That the general principles of that plan having then met his approbation, with some exceptions, such modifications had been made as conformed to his suggestions.'

This plan and letter the President sent to Congress, with the following Message:

" *Gentlemen of the Senate*
and House of Representatives :

"'The Secretary of the Department of War has submitted to me certain principles, to serve as a plan for the general arrangement of the militia of the United States.

"Conceiving the subject to be of the greatest importance to the welfare of our country, and liable to be placed in various points of view, I have directed him to lay the plan before Congress for their information, that they may make such use thereof as they shall judge proper.

"GEORGE WASHINGTON.
"UNITED STATES, *Jan.* 21, 1790."

The Message and plan were referred by Congress to a Committee of the whole House, who did nothing in relation to it. Some months after it was laid before a select committee, who had been appointed to bring in a militia bill, and of its history I can discover no further trace.

It is obvious that General Knox's plan, from his own account of it, was constructed under the old Confederation, when the only authority of Congress to raise soldiers was by requisitions on the States, and when it could not therefore be contemplated to draught men into the regular Army, except by virtue of State authority, and through the medium of State regulations. In this plan, at the time it originated, General Washington had perceived military merit, and had suggested hints towards its further improvement. If afterwards, in attempting to accommodate this system to the purposes of the new Government, and to incorporate into it the former military suggestions of General Washington, Gen. Knox had unguardedly left in it any provision which would seem not suited to the powers of the new Government, it does not appear that such feature

was ever brought to the distinct notice of the President. He submitted it to Congress, merely as a report from the Head of the War Department of a plan for a system of military defence, with a well-founded confidence that Congress would extract from it such provisions as they might deem useful, and were not beyond the sphere of their Constitutional powers.

But, sir, the egregious fallacy of this argument will be detected by an examination of the report itself. I have examined it attentively, and I pronounce unhesitatingly, that it does not contain the principle said to be found in it. Although detached passages of the report might seem to countenance the doctrine, which it is now relied on to support, yet when they are examined in connexion with each other, and with the context, it is demonstrable, that it holds forth no claim to draught men from the militia of the States into the regular Army of the United States. In the letter of General Knox, accompanying the plan, it is recommended as a national system of " defence;" and in the introduction, it claimed to be "the most efficient system of defence which may be compatible with the interests of a free people." He notices the prejudice which the modern practice of Europe has created in favor of standing armies. He expressed his opinion, that "a small ' corps of well-disciplined and well-informed artil- ' lerists and engineers, and a legion for the protec- ' tion of the frontiers and the magazines and arse- ' nals, are all the Military Establishment which ' may be required for the present use of the United ' States; the privates of these corps to be enlisted, ' for a certain period, after the expiration of which ' to return to the mass of the citizens." He declares his conviction, that "an energetic national militia is to be regarded as the capital security of a free Republic." "If," in conformity to his recommendation, "it should be decided to reject ' a standing army, for the military branch of the ' Government, as possessing too fierce an aspect, ' and being hostile to the principles of liberty, it ' will follow that a well-constituted militia ought ' to be established." Then, taking as the principles of his plan these maxims which are applicable only to a militia defence, and declaring his purpose to be to carry into effect, not that power of the Government which relates to the raising of armies, but that which authorizes the United States "to provide for organizing and disciplining ' the militia, and for governing such parts of ' them as may be employed in the service of the ' United States; reserving to the States, respect- ' ively, the appointment of the officers and the ' authority of training the militia according to ' the discipline prescribed by Congress," he brings forward his scheme of a national defence by means of militia only, without a recurrence to a regular army. It is not necessary to call the attention of the House to a minute examination of this scheme, for it is immaterial to the present question whether it was practicable and convenient or otherwise. It was a bold plan of militia organization and discipline. I hazard no opinion as to its correctness or utility. Its prominent features were, a division of all the militia into three corps; an advanced, a main, and a reserved corps; composed of individuals of different ages; giving to all these corps the legionary form; and a sub-division into sections for the more ready and equal compliance with every proper requisition. The reserved corps, consisting of persons of advanced age, was set apart for the domestic defence of each State, and was not to be obliged to furnish men, except in cases of actual invasion or rebellion near home. The advanced corps "were designed not only as a school in which the ' youth of the United States were to be instructed ' in the art of war; but they were in all cases of ' exigence to serve as an actual defence to the ' community." And "in all cases of invasion or ' rebellion, were, on requisition of lawful author- ' ity, obliged to march to any place within the ' United States." And when in the service of the United States, were to be allowed the same pay, "subsistence, clothing, and other allowance, as should be made to Federal troops under the same circumstances." The main corps, forming the principal defence of the country, either united with the reserve corps for domestic purposes, or "on sudden occasions, to which the advanced corps was incompetent," furnished thereto an adequate portion of its force "by means of its sections." Thus, in the language of General Knox, for a sum less than four hundred thousand dollars annually, an energetic national militia was to be durably established, the invaluable princi- ples of liberty secured and perpetuated, and a dignified national fabric erected on the solid foun- dation of public virtue. Thus much for the ordi- nary organization of this national force, and for its application to those casual and fleeting pur- poses which might arise in a state of general tranquillity. But should any serious and perma- nent interruption of the public tranquillity, either from external or internal causes, require a more permanent and vigorous form to be given to this national force, this end was to be accomplished by requisitions on the States, which would be answered from the advanced and main corps by means of the sections. This, sir, is the obvious meaning of the clauses in this report, which have been relied on as warranting the doctrine of con- scription. The clauses are these—"All requisi- ' tions for men to form an army, either for State ' or Federal purposes, shall be furnished by the ' advanced and main corps, by means of the sec- ' tions." "The Executive government, or Com- ' mander-in-chief of the militia of each State, ' will assess the numbers required, on the respect- ' ive legions of these corps." The army here in- tended is an army of militia, not of regulars; not procured by recruiting, still less by forcing men into the ranks, under the authority of the General Government, but obtained by means of requisi- tions on the States, sanctioned by their respective Executives. The requisitions must be under- stood to be such as are recognised in the Consti- tution, to repel invasions, suppress insurrections, and execute the laws of the United States. The officers of this army were contemplated to be

militia officers, not Federal; for the report ex- plicitly declares that the constitutions of the indi- vidual and United States having prescribed the mode in which the officers of the militia should be appointed, no alteration can be made therein, "and expresses a solicitude that the wisdom of ' the States may be manifested by inducing indi- ' viduals, who had acquired military skill in our ' Revolutionary contest, to accept of these militia ' appointments, and thus render their dear bought ' knowledge useful to the nation."

The army of which General Knox speaks, in this report, is an army to be formed by "requisi- tions" on the States; to be employed only in the exigence of the Constitution, and to be com- manded by officers appointed by the State author- ities. It is clear, therefore, that he is speaking not of a regular, but of a militia army.

Let this report, sir, be examined from begin- ning to end, and every sentence criticised, and ingenuity may still be defied to point out a single clause, which, by fair construction, can be made to support the idea, that General Knox intended a draught from the militia into the ranks of the regular Army, under the authority of the Gen- eral Government. I am indebted to an intelli- gent gentleman for an idea, which very much corroborates my construction of the report.— General Knox proposes, with a view to maintain defence, a classification of seamen somewhat similar to that of militia. But, to carry this into operation, he declares it requisite that "efficient ' regulations should be established in the respect- ' ive States to register seamen, and to render ' those of a certain age amenable to the public ' for personal service, if demanded within a given ' period." Now, sir, why was it necessary to call in the aid of State laws to impose this obligation on the seamen of the United States? It must be because the Constitution of the United States had not conferred on the General Government a right to compel their services; yet that Consti- tution had given as unlimited a power to provide and maintain a navy, as it had to raise and sup- port an army. Could General Knox, while ad- mitting that the General Government had no compulsatory power, in the one case, be supposed to contend for it in the other. Sir, I will trouble the House no further. I trust I have proved to the satisfaction of every reflecting mind, that the documents so confidently produced afford no countenance to the doctrines they were meant to uphold. Whatever other names may be brought forward to sanction the doctrine of conscription, that of the great founder of our liberties cannot be pressed into the detestable service.

The previous question having been required by Mr. Rhea, of Tennessee, was then taken, and decided as follows: For the previous question 87, against it 63.

The main question on the passage of the bill was then taken, and decided in the affirmative: For the bill 84, against it 72, as follows:

Yeas—Messrs. Alston, Anderson, Archer, Avery, Barbour, Bard, Bines, Bowen, Brown, Calhoun, Chap- pell, Clark, Clopton, Comstock, Condict, Crawford,

Creighton, Cuthbert, Denoyelles, Desha, Duvall, Earle, Eppes, Evans, Farrow, Findley, Fisk of New York, Forney, Forsyth, Franklin, Goodwyn, Gourdin, Griffin, Hall, Hasbrouck, Hawes, Hawkins, Hopkins of Kentucky, Humphreys, Ingersoll, Ingham, Irving, Irwin, Johnson of Virginia, Johnson of Kentucky, Kent of Maryland, Kershaw, Kilbourn, King of North Carolina, Lefferts, Lowndes, Lyle, McCoy, McKee, McKim, McLean, Montgomery, Moore, Murfree, Nelson, Newton, Ormsby, Parker, Pickens, Piper, Pleasants, Rea of Pennsylvania, Rhea of Tennessee, Ringgold, Roane, Robertson, Sage, Seybert, Sharp, Smith of Pennsylvania, Smith of Virginia, Tannehill, Taylor, Telfair, Udree, Ward of New Jersey, Williams, Wilson of Pennsylvania, and Yancey.

Nays—Messrs. Alexander, Bayliss of Massachusetts, Bayly of Virginia, Bigelow, Boyd, Bradbury, Bradley, Breckenridge, Burwell, Butler, Caperton, Caldwell, Champion, Cilley, Cooper, Cox, Culpeper, Dana, Davenport, Davis of Mass., Davis of Pennsylvania, Ely, Fisk of Vermont, Gaston, Geddes, Gholson, Grosvenor, Hale, Harris, Henderson, Howell, Jackson of Rhode Island, Kennedy, Kent of New York, Kerr, King of Massachusetts, Law, Lewis, Lovett, Macon, Markell, Miller, Moseley, Oakley, Pearson, Pickering, Pitkin, Potter, John Reed, William Reed, Rich, Ruggles, Schureman, Sheffey, Shipherd, Skinner, Slaymaker, Smith of New York, Stanford, Stockton, Sturges, Taggart, Thompson, Vose, Ward of Massachusetts, Webster, Wheaton, White, Wilcox, Wilson of Massachusetts, Winter, and Wright.

A motion was then made by Mr. Wright, to amend the title of said bill, by inserting after the word "militia," the words "or forty thousand regulars, if they shall be furnished under the provisions of this bill." And the question being taken, it was determined in the negative.

A motion was made by Mr. Gaston to amend the title by striking out the words "for the defence of the frontiers of the United States against invasion." And the question being taken, it was determined in the negative.

Ordered, That the title be, "An act to authorize the President of the United States to call upon the several States and Territories thereof for their respective quotas of 80,000, militia, for the defence of the frontiers of the United States against invasion."

Thursday, December 15.

On motion of Mr. Gholson, the petition of Amey Dardin, presented on the 27th December, 1804, was referred to the Committee on Pensions and Revolutionary Claims.

Mr. Yancey reported a bill for the relief of James Doyle, which was read twice, and committed.

The House proceeded to consider the message from the Senate, asking a conference on the subject-matter of the disagreeing votes of the two Houses on the amendments of the Senate to the bill "to provide additional revenues for defraying the expenses of Government, and maintaining the public credit, by laying duties on spirits distilled within the United States, and by amending the act laying duties on licenses to distillers of spirituous liquors." Whereupon,

13th Con. 3d Sess.—30

Resolved, That this House do insist on their disagreement to the said amendments, and agree to the conference asked by the Senate thereon.

Ordered, That Mr. Eppes, Mr. Fisk of New York, and Mr. Gholson, be the managers at the said conference on the part of this House.

A message from the Senate informed the House that the Senate have passed the bill "to provide additional revenues for defraying the expenses of Government, and maintaining the public credit, by duties on sales at auction; on the postage of letters; on licenses to retail wines, spirituous liquors, and foreign merchandise," with amendments; in which they ask the concurrence of this House.

DUTIES ON MANUFACTURES.

The House, on motion of Mr. Eppes, of Virginia, resolved itself into a Committee of the Whole, on the bill "to provide additional revenues for defraying the expenses of Government, by laying duties on various goods, wares, and merchandise, manufactured within the United States."

[This bill proposes to lay on all manufactures the duties specified in the following extract from the bill:]

On pig iron, per ton, one dollar.

On castings of iron, per ton, one dollar and fifty cents.

On bar iron, per ton, one dollar.

On rolled or slit iron, per ton, one dollar.

On cut nails, brads, and sprigs, made wholly or in part by machinery, per pound, one cent.

On candles of spermaceti or white wax, per pound, ten cents.

On mould candles of tallow, or of wax, or other than white, or in part of each, per pound, three cents.

On dipped candles of tallow, or of wax, other than white, or in part of each, per pound, one cent.

On hats, caps of leather or fur, bonnets, except made entirely from wool, silk, cotton, or linen, or in part from each, or which, if made from other materials, shall not exceed in value one dollar and fifty cents, eight per centum ad valorem.

On paper, five per centum ad valorem.

On playing cards, fifty per centum ad valorem.

On saddles and bridles, six per centum ad valorem.

On boots and bootees, exceeding five dollars per pair in value, five per centum ad valorem.

On beer, ale, and porter, six per centum ad valorem.

On tobacco, cigars, and snuff, twenty per centum ad valorem.

On leather, including therein all hides and skins, whether tanned, tawed, dressed, or otherwise made, on the original manufacture thereof, ten per centum ad valorem.

Mr. Eppes assigned, at some length, the reasons why the committee had, on these manufactures, departed occasionally from the instructions of the House, and generally preferred an ad valorem to a specific duty; the principal of which was, the great variety in quality and denomination of these articles, which, while it would make specific duties vexatious, would render them liable to continual evasions. All the articles proposed to be dutied, he further said, pay a much higher duty when imported, and, whilst the last section of this bill limited the operation of the tax to the continuance of the double duties now imposed by law, no article had been selected for taxation which it was believed the United States could not manufacture in abundance for their consumption. In the present situation of the country, conceiving it unnecessary to say anything on the necessity of imposing additional taxes, he waived any remarks on that head.

Mr. BAYLIES, of Massachusetts, moved to strike out the following words in the above enumeration: "Cut nails, brads, and sprigs, made wholly or in part by machinery, one cent per pound."

Mr. B. supported this motion by a variety of arguments, to show the probable oppressive effects of this duty on the manufacture in question, particularly in the part of the country which he represented, where nails are manufactured entirely from imported iron. This description of manufacture, he said, already labored under great disadvantage, arising from the expense of erecting the necessary machinery, from the high premium paid to inventors for the use of their patent right, and from the increase of the cost of transportation and diminution of consumption occasioned by the war, &c. So high a duty would have the effect, he feared, of converting the manufacture by machinery to the manufacture by hand, to the prejudice of the morals and agriculture of the country. He said, he could not see why a discrimination was made between nails manufactured by the aid of machinery, and those made by hand. Mr. B. added, that this tax was not one of those recommended by the Secretary of the Treasury.

Mr. EPPES, in reply to one of Mr. B.'s suggestions, said, that the reason why wrought nails were exempted from taxation, was, that there was no other way in which nails made for domestic use, for shoeing horses, or such occasional purposes, could be exempted from taxation. No tax on nails, made by the hand, could be made to produce anything to the revenue without involving great oppression. It was, besides, however, not reasonable or equitable that a man who makes nails by a laborious operation by hand, should be placed on a level with him who cuts off a peck of nails at a single stroke or movement of a machine.

The motion of Mr. BAYLIES was negatived—ayes only 39.

This amendment having failed—

Mr. KING, of Massachusetts, moved to amend this clause so as to reduce the tax on nails from one cent to half a cent per pound, which he supported by a variety of observations.

The motion was opposed by Mr. FISK of Vermont, Mr. EPPES, and Mr. KILBOURN; and supported by Mr. WM. REED; and was negatived—ayes 34.

Various modifications of this clause were proposed, one only of which succeeded, viz: to insert, "or rolled," after the word "cut."

On motion of Mr. YANCEY, of North Carolina, the word "manufactured," was added to the word "tobacco," so as to define more clearly the nature of that tax.

Mr. FORNEY, of North Carolina, moved to amend the clause respecting pig iron, so as to reduce the duty from one dollar to fifty cents per ton.—Negatived.

Mr. F. then moved to strike out the words "castings of iron per ton, one dollar and fifty cents," and insert in lieu thereof, "hollow ware per ton one dollar, or open sand castings fifty cents per ton;" which motion he supported on the alleged inequality of value of the articles thus proposed to be taxed alike. The motion was negatived.

Mr. WHEATON moved to amend the clause for taxing "hats," by inserting, among the exceptions, such as are made of "straw;" in support of which motion he made a number of ingenious and pertinent remarks, arising from the domestic nature of this manufacture, principally carried on by young females in the Eastern States.

Mr. WRIGHT, of Maryland, in an equally good-humored manner, objected to the motion; deeming the elegant bonnets which adorn our ladies' heads, and their perpetually changing fashions, as fit subjects of taxation.

Mr. FISK, of New York, observed, that it was far from the Financial Committee's intention to include this branch of manufacture; and the motion of Mr. WHEATON was agreed to by a great majority.

Mr. BIGELOW, of Massachusetts, supported by his colleague, (Mr. BRIGHAM,) moved to strike out the tax on leather altogether. Negatived—ayes 42.

Mr. MACON, of North Carolina, moved to amend the clause relating to the tax on hats, by striking out "one dollar and fifty cents," and inserting in lieu thereof, "two dollars."—Agreed to.

Mr. WILSON, of Massachusetts, moved to amend the above extract, by striking out all the proposed taxes, except those on pig iron, castings, bar, and rolled, and slit iron, playing cards, beer, ale and porter, and tobacco, cigars, and snuff; and to insert in lieu thereof the following:

On flour, fifty cents per barrel.
On corn, five cents per bushel.
On rye, five cents per bushel.
On cotton, two cents per pound.
On hemp, two cents per pound.
On sugar, two cents per pound.
On rice, one cent per pound.
On tobacco, one cent per pound.

On copper and leaden ore, and coal of mines, ten per centum ad valorem.

On steam engines, if employed in factories, fifty dollars; if employed in propelling boats, one hundred dollars; and when an exclusive privilege shall be enjoyed by the person or persons chargeable therewith, two hundred dollars.

On offices, created by authority of the United States, whose emolument, by salary or perquisites, shall annually exceed fifteen hundred dollars, and not exceed five thousand, one per centum; and on those which exceed five thousand dollars, five per centum on such excess, except those offices whose emoluments are prohibited from diminution by the Constitution: *Pro-*

vided, That so much of each of the foregoing products, as shall be consumed by the owner, shall be exempted from taxation.

This motion Mr. WILSON supported by a train of reasoning on this basis: that the freeholders, who form the body of those who are represented on this floor, ought to pay a tax, if not higher, at least in some degree proportioned to the tax now proposed to be levied on the poor and industrious mechanics of the country. He made use of a number of arguments to show that the taxes he proposed were equitable in themselves, and more reasonable than those proposed by his motion to be exempted from taxation; and particularly the article of spermaceti candles, and some others, which will have an exclusively sectional operation. In this exposition he went much into detail.

The question on this motion was taken without debate, and decided in the negative—ayes only thirteen.

Mr. FISK, of New York, moved to amend the bill so as to exempt from the operation of the tax, all such castings as the Government may now have contracted for to be delivered at stipulated prices. This motion was opposed by Mr. EPPES, and negatived by a decided majority.

Mr. OAKLEY, of New York, moved to strike out the article of "dipped candles;" which motion was supported by Mr. EPPES, and decided in the affirmative by a large majority.

Mr. OAKLEY then moved to except from taxation altogether all mould candles of tallow.—Negatived by a large majority.

Mr. JOHN REED, of Massachusetts, moved to strike out "spermaceti" candles; and argued at some length in support of his motion, on the ground of the almost exclusive operation of this tax on the Island of Nantucket and town of New Bedford, &c., and therein diminished ability to pay; as, also, on the ground of its tendency to depress the whale fisheries.

The question on the motion being taken without debate, was decided in the affirmative, as follows: For the motion 54, against it 50.

Mr. UDREE, of Pennsylvania, moved to amend the clause for taxing iron castings, by adding thereto the following proviso:

"*Provided,* That all castings made use of in furnaces and forges, shall be exempted from paying the duty thereon."

The motion was opposed by Mr. EPPES, and negatived by a very large majority.

Mr. PITKIN, of Connecticut, moved to reduce the proposed tax on leather from ten to five per cent. ad valorem.

This motion, having been opposed by Mr. EPPES, was negatived.

Mr. PITKIN, considering, as he said, the tax on iron as out of all proportion, and impolitic in the mode of imposition, moved to strike out the proposed tax on pig iron, to try the principle of reducing the tax on iron manufactures.

In the course of his observations, Mr. P. called the attention of the Committee to objects of taxation more eligible than those selected by the Committee of Ways and Means, totally omitted in this bill, viz: manufactures of gold and silver, jewelry, glass wares, umbrellas, &c., and oil-mills. Mr. P.'s motion was negatived—ayes 32.

Mr. BAYLIES moved to strike out five per centum, the proposed tax on paper, and insert three in lieu thereof. This motion was supported by Mr. EPPES, and decided in the affirmative.

Mr. BRADBURY, of Massachusetts, then moved to except from the clause for taxing paper, such paper as is used for printing newspapers. He said it had ever been the policy of free Governments to encourage the diffusion of information, which this tax would have a tendency to check.

Mr. EPPES opposed this motion, not from any disposition to suppress newspapers, because he did not believe it would have this effect; but because he believed the proprietor of a newspaper who, by his business, made his four or five thousand dollars a year, was as fit a subject for taxation as the manufacturers, many of whom derived less profit from their business.

The motion was negatived by a large majority. The House proceeded in further discussion and amendment of the bill. And, about four o'clock, the Committee rose and reported their proceedings to the House, and the House adjourned.

FRIDAY, December 16.

Mr. McKEE of Kentucky, from the Committee on Public Lands, reported a bill giving further time for the location of certain confirmed claims to lands in the district of Vincennes. Twice read and ordered to be engrossed for a third reading.

The amendments of the Senate to the bill for laying additional duties on sales at auction, postage, and retailers' licenses, were taken up, and referred to the Committee of Ways and Means.

DUTIES ON MANUFACTURES.

The House resumed the consideration of the report of the Committee of the Whole on the bill to impose duties on certain goods, wares, and merchandise.

On concurring in the amendment to exempt spermaceti candles from the proposed tax of ten cents per pound, there were, for the motion 63, against it 50.

On the question of concurring in exempting dipped candles from taxation, there were 83 votes in the affirmative.

All the other amendments noted in the proceedings of yesterday were agreed to without a division.

The other amendments made to the details of the bill having been agreed to—

Mr. WRIGHT, of Maryland, moved to place visiting cards in the same clause of taxation as playing cards; which motion was agreed to by the following vote: For the motion 63, against it 29.

Mr. BAYLIES, of Massachusetts, renewed the motion he yesterday made to amend this bill, by striking out the clause for imposing a tax of one cent per pound on the manufacture of nails.

After some debate, this motion was negatived,

by yeas and nays—for the motion 39, against it 106, as follows:

YEAS—Messrs. Baylies of Massachusetts, Bigelow, Boyd, Bradbury, Caperton, Champion, Cilley, Cooper, Davenport, Davis of Massachusetts, Ely, Geddes, Grosvenor, Jackson of Rhode Island, King of Massachusetts, Law, Lewis, Lovett, Markell, Moseley, Pearson, Pitkin, Potter, John Reed, William Reed, Ruggles, Schureman, Sheffey, Sherwood, Shipherd, Stuart, Sturges, Taggart, Thompson, Vose, Ward of Massachusetts, Wheaton, Wilcox, and Wilson of Massachusetts.

NAYS—Messrs. Alexander, Alston, Anderson, Archer, Avery, Barbour, Bard, Barnett, Bayly of Virginia, Bines, Bowen, Breckenridge, Brown, Burwell, Caldwell, Calhoun, Cannon, Chappell, Clark, Clopton, Comstock, Condict, Conard, Crawford, Creighton, Culpeper, Cuthbert, Dana, Davis of Pennsylvania, Denoyelles, Desha, Duvall, Eppes, Farrow, Findley, Fisk of Vermont, Fisk of New York, Forney, Forsyth, Franklin, Gholson, Goodwyn, Gourdin, Griffin, Hall, Harris, Hasbrouck, Hawes, Hawkins, Henderson, Howell, Hubbard, Ingersoll, Ingham, Irving, Irwin, Johnson of Virginia, Johnson of Kentucky, Kent of New York, Kerr, Kershaw, Kilbourn, King of North Carolina, Lefferts, Lowndes, Lyle, Macon, McCoy, McKee, McKim, McLean, Moore, Murfree, Nelson, Oakley, Parker, Pickens, Piper, Pleasants, Rea of Pennsylvania, Rhea of Tennessee, Rich, Ringgold, Roane, Robertson, Sage, Seybert, Sharp, Skinner, Slaymaker, Smith of New York, Smith of Pennsylvania, Smith of Virginia, Stanford, Strong, Tannehill, Taylor, Telfair, Udree, Ward of New Jersey, Wheaton, Williams, Wilson of Pennsylvania, Winter, Wright, and Yancey.

Mr. BRIGHAM, of Massachusetts, moved to strike out from the clause for taxing nails, the words "made wholly or in part by machinery," which motion was negatived.

Mr. BIGELOW, of Massachusetts, then renewed the motion which he had made in Committee of the Whole, to strike out the tax on leather; which motion was decided in the negative, by yeas and nays: For the motion 57, against it 97, as follows:

YEAS—Messrs. Avery, Baylies of Massach'ts, Bigelow, Boyd, Bradbury, Breckenridge, Brigham, Burwell, Caperton, Champion, Cilley, Comstock, Cooper, Davenport, Davis of Massachusetts, Denoyelles, Ely, Forney, Grosvenor, Hale, Henderson, Hulbert, Jackson of Rhode Island, Kent of New York, King of Massachusetts, Law, Lewis, Lovett, Macon, Markell, Moseley, Oakley, Pearson, Pitkin, Potter, John Reed, Wm. Reed, Ruggles, Schureman, Sheffey, Sherwood, Shipherd, Slaymaker, Smith of Virginia, Stockton, Stuart, Sturges, Taggart, Thompson, Vose, Ward of Massachusetts, Ward of N. Jersey, Wheaton, White, Wilcox, Wilson of Massachusetts, and Winter.

NAYS—Messrs. Alexander, Alston, Anderson, Archer, Barbour, Bard, Barnett, Bayly of Virginia, Bines, Bowen, Bradley, Brown, Butler, Caldwell, Calhoun, Cannon, Chappell, Clark, Clopton, Condict, Conard, Crawford, Creighton, Cuthbert, Dana, Davis of Pennsylvania, Desha, Duvall, Earle, Eppes, Farrow, Findley, Fisk of Vermont, Fisk of New York, Forsyth, Franklin, Gholson, Goodwyn, Gourdin, Griffin, Hall, Harris, Hasbrouck, Hawes, Hawkins, Hopkins of Kentucky, Howell, Hubbard, Ingersoll, Ingham, Irving, Irwin, Johnson of Virginia, Johnson of Kentucky, Kennedy, Kerr, Kilbourn, King of N. Carolina, Lefferts,

Lowndes, Lyle, McCoy, McKee, McKim, McLean, Montgomery, Moore, Murfree, Nelson, Newton, Parker, Pickens, Piper, Pleasants, Rea of Pennsylvania, Rhea of Tennessee, Rich, Ringgold, Roane, Robertson, Sage, Seybert, Sharp, Skinner, Smith of New York, Smith of Pennsylvania, Stanford, Strong, Tannehill, Taylor, Telfair, Troup, Udree, Williams, Wilson of Pennsylvania, Wright, and Yancey.

A motion was made by Mr. KERR, of Virginia, to reduce the tax on manufactured tobacco, from twenty per cent. ad valorem to ten per cent., which motion was negatived, ayes only 34.

Mr. OAKLEY, of New York, moved to amend the first section of the bill so as to reduce the proposed tax on leather from ten to five per cent. ad valorem; which motion, after considerable debate, was agreed to. For the motion 104, against it 53, as follows:

YEAS—Messrs. Avery, Barnett, Baylies of Massachusetts, Bigelow, Bines, Bowen, Boyd, Bradbury, Breckenridge, Brigham, Brown, Burwell, Butler, Caperton, Cannon, Champion, Cilley, Comstock, Conard, Cooper, Crawford, Culpeper, Cuthbert, Dana, Davenport, Davis of Massachusetts, Davis of Pennsylvania, Denoyelles, Desha, Earle, Ely, Farrow, Findley, Fisk of Vermont, Fisk of New York, Forney, Geddes, Goodwyn, Gourdin, Grosvenor, Hale, Hasbrouck, Hawes, Henderson, Hulbert, Ingham, Jackson of R. Island, Kennedy, Kent of New York, Kent of Maryland, Kerr, Kilbourn, King of North Carolina, Law, Lefferts, Lewis, Lovett, Lyle, Macon, Markell, Moore, Moseley, Oakley, Parker, Pearson, Pickens, Piper, Pitkin, Pleasants, Potter, John Reed, William Reed, Rea of Pennsylvania, Rich, Ruggles, Sage, Schureman, Seybert, Sheffey, Sherwood, Shipherd, Skinner, Slaymaker, Smith of New York, Smith of Pennsylvania, Smith of Virginia, Stanford, Stockton, Stuart, Sturges, Taggart, Tannehill, Taylor, Thompson, Udree, Vose, Ward of Massachusetts, Ward of New Jersey, Wheaton, White, Wilcox, Williams, Wilson of Massachusetts, and Winter.

NAYS—Messrs. Alexander, Alston, Anderson, Archer, Barbour, Bard, Bayly of Virginia, Bradley, Caldwell, Calhoun, Chappell, Clark, Clopton, Condict, Creighton, Duvall, Eppes, Franklin, Gholson, Griffin, Hall, Harris, Hopkins of Kentucky, Hubbard, Humphreys, Ingersoll, Irving, Irwin, Johnson of Virginia, Johnson of Kentucky, Kershaw, King of North Carolina, Lowndes, McCoy, McKim, McLean, Montgomery, Murfree, Nelson, Newton, Ormsby, Rhea of Tennessee, Ringgold, Roane, Robertson, Sevier, Sharp, Strong, Telfair, Troup, Wilson of Pennsyl'a, Wright, and Yancey.

Mr. KILBOURN, of Ohio, then moved an amendment, the object of which was to tax candles of spermaceti, at the rate of three cents per pound; which motion prevailed, by the following vote: For the motion 74, against it 51.

Mr. WHEATON, of Massachusetts, moved to amend the bill by adding, after the clause for taxing cut nails, &c., the following words—"when sold." This motion was negatived.

Mr. SHIPHERD, of New York, moved to amend the bill so as to confine the proposed tax on paper to writing and letter paper; under the idea that those qualities of paper could best afford to pay a tax, and from a desire to exempt from taxation all printing paper, and such paper as is used in schools, and in common farmers and mechanics' books, &c.

Mr. INGHAM, of Pennsylvania, remarked, that the gentleman had unfortunately selected for taxation the two qualities of paper which could least bear it. He was himself opposed to any discrimination in the tax.

Mr. SHIPHERD's motion was negatived by a large majority.

Mr. PITKIN, of Connecticut, renewed his call upon the attention of the House to what he deemed the impolicy of the tax on pig iron. He dwelt upon the inexpediency of taxing the raw material of manufactures; and added, that there was not on this article, as on others, any duty on its importation, &c. It was imported, if at all, duty free.

The question on this motion was decided in the negative, by yeas and nays. For the motion 46, against it 97, as follows:

YEAS—Messrs. Baylies of Massachusetts, Bigelow, Boyd, Bradbury, Brigham, Caperton, Champion, Cilley, Cooper, Davenport, Davis of Massachusetts, Ely, Grosvenor, Hale, Howell, Jackson of Rhode Island, Kent of New York, Kershaw, King of Massachusetts, Law, Lovett, Moseley, Oakley, Pearson, Pickering, Pipe, Pitkin, Potter, John Reed, William Reed, Ruggles, Schureman, Seybert, Sheffey, Sherwood, Shipherd, Smith of New York, Stockton, Stuart, Sturges, Tannehill, Thompson, Udree, Vose, Ward of Massachusetts, Wheaton, Wilcox, and Wilson of Massachusetts.

NAYS—Messrs. Alexander, Alston, Anderson, Archer, Avery, Barbour, Bard, Barnett, Bayly of Virginia, Bines, Bowen, Bradley, Burwell, Butler, Caldwell, Calhoun, Cannon, Chappell, Clark, Clopton, Comstock, Condict, Conard, Creighton, Culpeper, Cuthbert, Dana, Denoyelles, Desha, Duvall, Earle, Eppes, Farrow, Findley, Fisk of Vermont, Fisk of New York, Forney, Forsyth, Franklin, Gholson, Goodwyn, Gourdin, Griffin, Hall, Harris, Hasbrouck, Hawes, Henderson, Hopkins of Kentucky, Hubbard, Humphreys, Ingersoll, Ingham, Irving, Irwin, Johnson of Virginia, Johnson of Kentucky, Kennedy, Kent of Maryland, Kerr, Kilbourn, King of North Carolina, Lefferts, Lowndes, Lyle, Macon, McCoy, McKee, McKim, McLean, Moore, Murfree, Nelson, Newton, Ormsby, Parker, Pickens, Pleasants, Rea of Pennsylvania, Rhea of Tennessee, Rich, Ringgold, Roane, Sage, Sevier, Sharp, Slaymaker, Smith of Virginia, Stanford, Strong, Taylor, Telfair, Ward of New Jersey, White, Williams, Wright, and Yancey.

Mr. FORNEY, of North Carolina, then moved to strike out the words "castings of iron, per ton, one dollar and fifty cents;" and to insert in lieu thereof "Hollow ware, one dollar per ton; all other castings seventy-five cents per ton;" which motion was negatived.

Mr. RUGGLES, of Massachusetts, made a motion to reduce the tax on candles of white wax from ten cents per pound to three cents per pound; which motion was negatived.

Mr. KING, of Massachusetts, then moved to reduce the duty on nails, sprigs, and brads, from one cent per pound to half a cent per pound; which motion was negatived.

Mr. PICKENS moved to amend the bill in the first section, and ninth line, by inserting the word "hollow," before the word castings;" and, after the word "cents," insert these words: "on all other kind of castings of iron, one dollar," which motion was determined in the negative.

Mr. BRADBURY, of Massachusetts, moved to amend the clause taxing paper, by inserting thereafter the words, "except such as shall be used in printing of bibles, testaments, and common school books;" which motion was negatived.

And the bill was then ordered to be engrossed for a third reading to-morrow; and on motion, the House adjourned.

SATURDAY, December 17.

The engrossed bill, "giving further time to locate certain claims to lands confirmed by an act of Congress, entitled "An act confirming certain claims to lands in the district of Vincennes," was read a third time, and passed.

Mr. EPPES, of Virginia, from the committee of conference on the disagreeing votes of the two Houses on the amendments to the bill for laying additional duties on distillation, made a report. The report recommends that the Senate recede from their determination to strike out the section which allows distilleries to sell liquor in any quantity not less than one gallon, and that the House agree to certain amendments to the details of the bill.

A message having been received from the Senate, announcing their agreement to the said report, the House also agreed to concur in the same.

The House spent some time in Committee of the Whole, on the bill for laying a direct tax on the United States; but, before making much progress, the Committee rose, and obtained leave to sit again.

Mr. EPPES, from the committee of conference on the amendments proposed by the Senate to the bill for laying duties on postage, sales at auction, and retailers' licenses, made a report, recommending an agreement to all the amendments of the Senate except one; which report was concurred in.

TAX BILLS.

The House resumed the consideration of the report of the Committee of the Whole, on the bill to provide additional revenues for defraying the expenses of Government and maintaining the public credit, by laying duties on household furniture, on horses kept exclusively for the saddle or the carriage, and on gold and silver watches; and the amendments made to the same in Committee of the Whole were read, and concurred in by the House.

[The following are the taxes included in this bill. On all household furniture, kept for use, the value of which, in any one family, with the exception of beds, bedding, kitchen furniture, and articles made in the family from domestic materials, shall exceed two hundred dollars in value a tax to be laid according to the following scale

If not exceeding $400	-	-	-	$1 00
Above $400 and not more than	$600	-	1 50
"	600	"	"	1,000	-	3 00
"	1,000	"	"	1,500	-	6 00
"	1,500	"	"	2,000	-	10 00
"	2,000	"	"	3,000	-	17 00
"	3,000	"	"	4,000	-	28 00
"	4,000	"	"	6,000	-	45 00
"	6,000	"	"	9,000	-	75 00
"	9,000	-	-	-	-	100 00

One dollar on every horse kept exclusively for the saddle; one dollar and fifty cents for every horse kept for use in a carriage liable to be taxed; and one dollar and fifty cents for every horse kept for the use of both saddle and carriage.

Two dollars on every gold watch, and one dollar on every silver watch, kept for use.]

Several unsuccessful attempts were made to amend the bill; amongst which was one by Mr. GASTON, to strike out so much of the bill as includes the tax on household furniture; which was decided by yeas and nays—For the motion 52, against it 99, as follows:

YEAS—Messrs. Baylies of Massachusetts, Bigelow, Boyd, Bradbury, Breckenridge, Brigham, Caperton, Cilley, Cooper, Culpeper, Davenport, Ely, Farrow, Gaston, Geddes, Grosvenor, Hale, Henderson, Jackson of Rhode Island, King of Massachusetts, Law, Lewis, Lovett, Markell, Miller, Moseley, Pearson, Pickering, Pitkin, Potter, John Reed, William Reed, Ruggles, Schureman, Seybert, Sheffey, Sherwood, Shipherd, Slaymaker, Stanford, Stockton, Sturges, Taggart, Vose, Ward of Massachusetts, Ward of New Jersey, Webster, Wheaton, White, Wilcox, Wilson of Massachusetts, and Winter.

NAYS—Messrs. Alexander, Alston, Anderson, Archer, Avery, Barbour, Barnett, Bayly of Virginia, Bines, Bowen, Brown, Burwell, Butler, Caldwell, Calhoun, Cannon, Clark, Clopton, Comstock, Condict, Conard, Creighton, Cuthbert, Dana, Davis of Pennsylvania, Denoyelles, Desha, Duvall, Earle, Eppes, Evans, Findley, Fisk of Vermont, Fisk of New York, Forney, Forsyth, Franklin, Gholson, Gourdin, Griffin, Hall, Harris, Hasbrouck, Hawes, Hopkins of Kentucky, Howell, Hubbard, Humphreys, Ingersoll, Ingham, Irving, Irwin, Johnson of Virginia, Johnson of Kentucky, Kennedy, Kerr, Kershaw, Kilbourn, King of North Carolina, Lefferts, Lowndes, Lyle, Macon, McCoy, McKim, McLean, Montgomery, Moore, Murfree, Nelson, Newton, Ormsby, Parker, Pickens, Piper, Pleasants, Rea of Pennsylvania, Rhea of Tennessee, Rich, Ringgold, Roane, Robertson, Sage, Sevier, Sharp, Skinner, Smith of New York, Smith of Pennsylvania, Smith of Virginia, Strong, Tannehill, Taylor, Telfair, Troup, Udree, Williams, Wilson of Pennsylvania, Wright, and Yancey.

Mr. LAW, of Connecticut, spoke as follows.

Mr. Speaker, as I have not hitherto retarded the despatch of the public business, by consuming the time of the House in debate, I trust I shall be indulged, while I make a few remarks in justification of the vote I intend to give, on the bill now under consideration. This bill proposes to lay a tax on the manufacture of iron, leather, candles, paper, and other articles which are indispensably necessary, for the people generally, and will be sensibly felt by the poorer classes of community. The bill grows out of the report of the Committee of Ways and Means, accepted by the House, and forms a branch of an extensive system of taxation, which will probably continue for years; and as my opposition arises from a conviction that the objects to which the money is to be applied will not warrant the levy, my remarks will go to the system generally, as well as to this particular bill.

The object is to continue the war in which we are engaged; and as an inducement to us, to unite in the measures proposed, many considerations, are urged. Little is of late said of the justice of the war, or the principles on which it was declared; indeed, this would be now idle, if not indecorous, inasmuch as the Administration themselves have relinquished and abandoned every principle on which the war was declared. And instead of fighting to gain, or secure any rights, the question now seems to be, how much we shall give up, to regain that peace we rashly threw away.

We are now called upon to unite in granting the means necessary to prosecute the war; because it is said its character is changed, it has now become a defensive war;—that as we are engaged in it, we must prosecute it with union, firmness, and vigor, or submit to terms which the nation ought not to brook; and that the credit of the nation will be irretrievably lost, unless speedily revived by making suitable and ample provision by taxes. And for these reasons we are required to unite, and this union is to be evidenced by our willingness to grant all the means the Administration demand in men and money. Let us, sir, examine these grounds, and calmly inquire, whether they impose any obligation, or furnish any new claim on those who, from the beginning, have been opposed to the war, among which number I have the consolation to be ranked.

That this nation is in a deplorable condition cannot be denied; but that the character of the war is changed I do deny. It is true, that the effects and operation of the war on this people have been different from what was expected or anticipated by its advocates; but not diverse from those predicted by its opposers. Instead of possessing the British provinces on the North and East in rapid succession, we daily tremble even here, and on the whole seacoast, watching the movements of the hostile fleets, which ride undisturbed in every bay and inlet bordering along the Atlantic; scarcely a spot is guarded against their encroachment; they assail us, put the country in commotion, burn, ravage, and destroy the dwellings of our citizens, and retire when they please. Still the character of the war is not changed; every thing else has changed, except the Administration and the character of the war, and this will remain the same, so long as they continue to guide and direct the affairs of this nation. Some of the causes which engendered and produced the war had been nurtured and cherished for years; nor was the act, in my opinion, so much the result of wise policy and sound judgment, as the effect of passion. Our grand object had been for years to cripple and injure Great Britain, then struggling for the liberties of the European world, as it is now proved and confessed. Hence, that long course of griping policy, which, under the pretence of regulating commerce, had been adopted in deadly succession, in unison with the views of the now fallen tyrant, and which was vainly believed would soon operate the destruction of that kingdom; the effects of which was only to impoverish ourselves, blast our prosperity, and check the vigor and enterprise of this once happy and active people; and which system was persevered in, until it brought down this nation from the proud eminence it once held, to abject poverty and ruin. Our trade was destroyed, our sailors dispersed and banished like our commerce, under the fostering care of the Government. Our stores and warehouses, which once teemed with merchandise of all climes, became vacant and solitary; our wharves and quays were deserted, or lined with empty and mouldering hulks; the hum of business which once enlivened our cities, changed to groans of poverty; industry, which once invigorated and supported thousands, driven for want of employment to idleness and beggary. And, to cap the climax of our calamities, at last came the declaration of war, and converted thousands, who, in better times, might have been employed in productive labor, into drones, consuming the substance of the nation, in the shape of soldiers, contractors, tax-gatherers, and sharpers, in the employment of the Administration, in endless varieties.

We, sir, struck the first blow, as it were, in the dark, against the defenceless provinces of Canada; they resisted and repelled our attacks; disgrace and mortification ensued. Our Administration were disappointed; they awoke from their delirium, and behold! the author and contriver of the evils we have suffered, and are suffering, retires from the nations of the earth—his kingdom taken from him. Our enemy increased in strength, having finished his work on the continent of Europe, is at liberty to succor his provinces, and send his ships on our coast, not in the small number of six or seven, which was once stated on this floor to be the extent he could maintain at any one time on our Atlantic frontier, but in fleets powerful and numerous; and powerful and numerous must they be to drive our gallant navy from the ocean, compel them to retire into rivers, or seek refuge under fortifications, to avoid the grasp of the enemy.

Sir, the great body of the people in this country were never heartily disposed to engage in this controversy. We perceive no national enthusiasm on the subject of the war; this appears pretty clear from the difficulty in recruiting the army, even with the artificial stimulus of great bounties and high wages, which have been held out to them. They saw nothing at the time of the declaration, different from what had existed for years; injuries they knew this country had experienced from Great Britain, but they were, and ever had been considered, as growing out of the peculiar relation the countries stood in to each other, and which required a remedy by negotiation rather than by force—an opinion now entertained by the present Administration. But the people never were disposed to contend for abstract principles, and fight for rights, which required subtlety to define and sophistry to support. Many indeed believed, as they had been told, that a halcyon period would follow after a very short struggle. They acquiesced, and some justified the war—others deploring the mad career which the Administration were pursuing, and the certain ruin to which their measures would lead, strove to arrest the downward course; they were stigmatized as traitors and enemies to the country, and even threatened with confiscation and hemp, because they opposed the war; their apprehensions are now realized, and their prediction verified.

This war, sir, was invited at a time when it was altogether unwise and unnecessary to declare it; no preparations had been previously made to meet the crisis, and we all remember with what hard and painful struggles it was produced; and Great Britain at that time had no wish to engage in the contest. I will not say that this disposition, on their part, proceeded from any regard to this country, or respect for our rights, which our policy had inspired, but because they had other engagements on hand, which required their whole energies and resources; it was to rescue the world from the dominion of a bloody despot. And I confess I was not a little surprised to notice in a late literary communication, from one who may be presumed to have some knowledge of the views, and perhaps some influence in the Cabinet, an insinuation that Great Britain, "suddenly withdrawn from a great war, full armed and full handed, taking advantage of this nation, whom they had recently forced into war unarmed and unprepared, to indulge themselves in acts of barbarism which do not belong to a civilized age;" representing, with no little art, that Great Britain first declared war against this country, at a moment unexpected, and solely for the purpose of indulging a fiend-like disposition! Now, sir, the world knows we first declared this war, and whatever consequences may flow from it, the blood will be required at our hands. We have none to reproach for the miseries we are now suffering but ourselves—our own rash folly produced them. We did expect Great Britain would be occupied for years in the war with France, as was suggested in the Message at the opening of the present session; we are disappointed—that struggle is at an end; we have lost the aid we expected, and we are now left with war, distress, and misery, while most other nations are reposing in the calm delights of peace. And so indignant is the enemy we have chosen, at the time and manner in which the war was declared, and so flushed and willing is that nation to continue the conflict in which we are engaged, that, although we have in the very ashes of humility and repentance, given up every principle, real or pretended, for which war was declared, we are now willing to make peace without securing anything but national poverty and ridicule. Yet Great Britain, not pitying, but mocking at our calamities, refuses to treat of peace, but on the most humiliating conditions.

Sir, what are our hopes by continuing the war? The Administration have had, so far as we could grant, all the means, in men and money, which their ambition and prodigality demanded; and, under the most auspicious circumstances, they have now wasted two years and a half, and what have they accomplished? Have they secured "Free Trade and Sailors' Rights," this darling national amulet? Both have been, on mature consideration, deliberately abandoned. Have they made any progress in the conquest of the Canadas? So far from progressing in this great work, that for a long time after the declaration of war no rays of that glory, which at one time seemed almost to intoxicate some gentlemen, darted in the Northern sky. And except the instances of Perry, Macdonough, and a few others, over whose heads the *Aurora Borealis* has shone resplendent, we have gained nothing; and our prospects in that quarter now are as gloomy and cheerless as the sterile regions we covet. We have lost much territory; our armies have been wasted; our money is exhausted, and our credit gone. If, after all this, we persevere in the original scheme of conquering the Canadas, thereby provoking the enemy to commit devastation and waste on the seaboard, how can it be said the character of the war is changed? It is still marked with its original hideous and deformed features.

And, sir, it is owing in no small degree to the weakness and incompetency of the Administration to execute their own projects, that the progress of the enemy has not been marked with more extended ruin; recollect the proclamation of the Governor of Canada, when he took ample vengeance on the wretched borderers, on Lake Erie, the last year; also the correspondence between Mr. Monroe and Admiral Cochrane in the months of August and September last, in which the Admiral says:

"Having been called upon by the Governor of the Canadas, to aid him in carrying into effect measures of retaliation against the inhabitants of the United States, for the wanton destruction committed by their army in Upper Canada, it has become imperiously my duty, conformably to the nature of the Governor General's application, to issue to the naval force under my command an order to destroy and lay waste such towns and districts upon the coast as may be found assailable."

And in reply to Mr. Monroe's argumentative answer, complaining of the above plan of desolating warfare, the Admiral says:

"As I have no authority from my Government to enter upon any kind of discussion relative to the points contained in your letter, I have only to regret that there does not appear to be any hope that I shall be authorised to recall my general order; which has been further sanctioned by a subsequent request from Lieutenant General Sir George Provost."

This order, sir, has been partially, but too fatally executed already. But should we grant the money required by this and other bills, and, in conformity with the plan of the Secretary of War, raise 100,000 men, and actually invade Canada the ensuing campaign, have we not reason to fear that, before the next 24th of August, many of our beautiful and most flourishing cities, towns, and villages, on the seacoast, will present the same melancholy spectacle which the capital of the nation now exhibits? And yet we are called on to furnish money to prosecute this war of conquest, regardless of all consequences. The passions which gave birth to the war have not yet subsided, nor will they be suffered to expire so long as the present Administration continue in power.

The character of the war is not changed, nor ought we to be deceived, and imagine it is altered essentially from an offensive to a defensive war; or believe that the people have become more in love with it, because thousands have volunteered without request, on well-founded hopes of reward from the General Government, to defend their soil and their homes. The Administration have one object in view, and the brave yeomanry of our country are actuated by totally different motives. The first are regardless of the duty of protection, and are eager for conquest and aggrandizement; the latter are influenced by the strong principle of self-defence. Men who detest the war, its authors, and the vain objects of ambition they are pursuing, are constrained to defend themselves against those dangers which Government have invited, but against which they have provided no protection. The States, feeling themselves abandoned by the General Government, have defended themselves; and while fighting for defence of their soil, they generally have been, and will be, meritorious, for they are animated in a just cause, which must be triumphant. But the Administration having started in this war upon wrong principles, and having pursued a course as unwise as it is difficult, have failed in all their plans—military, financial, and diplomatic. Indeed, such is the baneful influence which hangs about them, that, where they personally direct and control, even patriotism, and the stronger principles of self-defence, is benumbed and withered by their touch. Witness the disgraceful scene which took place where we now are, on the 24th of August last! when our troops were led to battle in one of the most honorable causes which could possibly occur; when everything dear and valuable, everything which could animate the breast or nerve the arm, should have prompted them to valorous resistance—their families, houses—the very ark and sanctuary of the nation was the prize of the conflict; yet under such leaders our troops retired before the enemy; they fled after the example of the Captain General and his sympathetic Secretaries, the guardians of this consecrated spot, and surrendered the pride of the nation to the spoilers, to be stamped with indelible disgrace in characters of vandalism! On that fatal day our mighty chieftains seemed to possess no power or energy, except to vie with the victorious vandals in destroying the costly works of taste and art; and skilful rivals they proved themselves to be, as the sad monuments of their destruction now within our view do testify. In most other cases, where the States have depended on themselves, and confided in the justice of their cause, and directed their energies merely to defend their soil, they have resisted manfully, and generally with success. This I know has been the fact in the State I have the honor to represent; there, although they were opposed to the war, neither believing in its justice, expediency, or policy, yet they are determined to defend and protect the soil which gave them birth, and is hallowed by the sepulchres of their fathers; but from this noble determination the Administration can derive no aid in their ulterior views.

It is further urged, as a reason why we should grant money to prosecute the war, that it appears by the communications containing the instructions and correspondence with our commissioners, that the terms proposed by Great Britain are such as cannot be accepted, consistent with the honor and dignity of this nation, and therefore we ought to unite in a vigorous prosecution of the war. I am willing to admit the terms, as contained in the Message of October last, taken in the extent they seem to imply, without any modification or qualification, are such as we ought not to accept. But, I am happy to say, the correspondence contained in the Message of the first of the present month, looks much more favorable, and the aspect is much more pacific now than was at first supposed. Yet suppose the terms of peace are as hard and unreasonable as they at first appeared, it would not necessarily follow that we must unite in carrying on our offensive war against the Canadas, and thereby add tenfold to the miseries and distresses of the country. It is by no means certain that, during the time the present Administration remain in power, with their present views of territorial aggrandizement, we shall be able to obtain better terms. Great Britain is now powerful and flourishing; war is the habit of that nation; they are flushed with their recent successes, and, by commanding the trade of the world, they possess great resources—men, and munitions of war—they may continue the war for years, without greatly impairing their strength, while we are daily wasting our vigor; being locked up within ourselves, all our resources must be derived from internal impositions. This bill is to reach the hard earnings of the mechanic; another on your table is to spread over the farming interest, with supplements adapted to the pockets of all. Further, sir, the war is at a distance from them, and conquering the provinces will not conquer that nation; but we have unwisely brought the war within our own bosom—they can retire and recruit when they please, we cannot—and a continuance of the contest will be certain destruction to us, even if we succeed in the conquest of Canada. It is also uncertain what the conditions of peace may eventually be; this may depend on our success, and, judging of the past, our future prospects are not very flattering. It may be here asked what we shall do;

we are in a sad dilemma, and must prosecute the war, or submit to degrading terms? My answer is, that notwithstanding our present prospects are dark and gloomy, yet I believe it is in the power of the Administration to obtain terms, which would be for the honor and interest of both nations to accept; and I indulge this opinion for the following reasons: I believe Great Britain probably would, under a change of circumstances, negotiate with us on principles of reciprocity. I say it is probable she would, because it appears by the documents before us that our Administration, while Bonaparte was on his throne, and when it was supposed we were strong and Great Britain weak, were as haughty and arrogant in their demands as Great Britain is now, when Bonaparte is confined at Elba, and when they believe themselve strong and us weak; yet our Administration did descend from the high and lofty pretensions they once set up, to a tone of humility and condescension, which not long since would have been considered no less than a sacrifice of national pride, honor, and independence. This appears from a variety of documents. I will advert to a few extracts only.

In the Message of the President, of November 4th, 1812, after stating the progress of the war, and the proud attitude the United States had assumed by the declaration, he says:

"To have shrunk, under such circumstances, from manly resistance, would have struck us from the high rank where the victories of our fathers had placed us, and have betrayed the magnificent legacy which we held in trust for future generations; it would have acknowledged that on the element which forms three-fourths of the globe we inhabit, and where all independent nations have equal and common rights, the American people were not an independent people, but vassals and colonists."

In the report of the Committee of Foreign Relations, to whom the above Message was referred, they say—

"To appeal to arms, in defence of a right, and to lay them down without securing it, or a satisfactory evidence of a good disposition in the opposite party to assure it, would be considered in no other light than a relinquishment of it; to attempt to negotiate afterwards for the security of our right, in expectation that any of the arguments which have been urged before the declaration of war and been rejected, would have more weight after that experiment had been made in vain, would be an act of folly, which would not fail to expose us to the scorn and derision of the British nation and the world."

Again, in the same report—

"War having been declared, and the case of impressment being necessarily included as one of the most important causes, it is evident that it must be provided for in the pacification; the omission of it in a treaty of peace would not leave it on its former ground; it would, in effect, be an absolute relinquishment—an idea at which the feelings of every American must revolt."

In the instructions to our Ministers, in the letter of the 15th April, 1813, Mr. Monroe says—

"You are authorized to conclude a peace, in case

you obtain a satisfactory stipulation against impressment; one which will secure, under the flag, protection to the crew. If this encroachment is not provided against, the United States have appealed to arms in vain. If your efforts to accomplish it should fail, all further negotiations will cease, and you will return home without delay. It is also important to obtain a definition of neutral rights, especially of blockade; but this is not to be made an indispensable condition of peace."

In the letter of January 23, 1814—

"On impressment, as to the right of the United States to be exempted from it, I have nothing to add. The sentiments of the President have undergone no change on this important subject. This degrading practice must cease. Our flag must protect the crew, or the United States cannot consider themselves an independent nation." And in the same letter, referring to former instructions, he says: "The principal object of this review has been to show that the sentiments of the President are the same in every instance; and the reasons for maintaining them have become more evident and strong since the date of those instructions."

In the letter of 25th June, 1814, he says:

"We think it probable that the late events in France may have had a tendency to increase the pretensions of the British Government." And again: "No reliance was placed on the good offices of France in bringing the war with Great Britain to a satisfactory conclusion." And in the same letter he adds: "On full consideration it has been decided, that in case no stipulation can be obtained from the British Government at this moment, when its pretensions may have been much heightened by recent events, and the state of Europe most favorable to them, either relinquishing the claim to impress from American vessels, or discontinuing the practice, even in consideration of the proposed exclusion from them of British seamen, you may concur in an article stipulating that the subject of impressment, together with that of commerce between the two countries, be referred to a separate negotiation."

In a letter of June 27, 1814, he says—

"On mature consideration it has been decided, that under all the circumstances above alluded to, incident to a prosecution of the war, you may omit any stipulation on the subject of impressment, if found indispensably necessary to terminate it."

Sir, the only apology for this magnanimous change in the sentiments of the Administration, was a change of circumstances; this apology, I believe, would have been satisfactory to the nation, if peace had followed; and many of the most ardent friends of the war would have acquiesced, and have preferred to witness the Administration condemn their own logic, and commit "an act of folly, which could not fail to expose them to the scorn and derision of the British nation and the world," rather than continue in this mad and headlong course.

Now, I believe Great Britain would treat with us fairly, if they had a similar apology—a change of circumstances; and this change, which would lead to so desirable an event, is in the power of the Administration to produce. And here I must mention certain things, not as much on account of their novelty as their importance in bringing

about this great desideratum. Let the Administration recall the troops from Canada, or rather the borders of Canada, and abandon the project of conquering those provinces; and it might not be an unwise preparatory step for them to recall such of the Ministers as are well known to possess sentiments and opinions better calculated to excite disgust and repulsion, rather than to conciliate a pacific disposition in the enemy, and if need be, appoint others in their stead, better qualified to reconcile the jarring interests of the countries. But, above all, it would be desirable to have the Cabinet formed of men who prefer the peace and prosperity of the nation to personal aggrandizement. This, I am sensible, might wound the pride, and perhaps defeat the ambitious views of some high in office, but if they possess as much patriotism and love of country as they profess, they cannot hesitate to make the sacrifice for the good of the country. This being done, Great Britain may then say, in the language of the instructions, they are enabled to give to these circumstances all the weight to which they are entitled, and on full consideration, agree to waive their arrogant demands, and treat on terms acceptable to both nations.

This experiment has not yet been tried. The Administration have been trying experiments for years, but this appears to me the only one which can effect the great object we so much desire. The course of the Administration has, hitherto, been rather to justify their own conduct, than honestly and sincerely to seek for peace. Their policy has been marked with duplicity and cunning, and they have lost confidence at home and abroad. Their whole system must be abandoned before we can hope for better times. A change of measures can only follow a change of men. I say, then, the experiment has not been fairly tried. I do not yet despair of peace, but until every attempt is made, and all reasonable hopes of peace are absolutely destroyed, I shall neither vote for men or money to prosecute this war; nor can I be considered hostile to the best interest of the country, by withholding my aid from this bill.

As to our duty to vote for the money bills on the ground that the national credit is sinking, and will be irretrievably lost unless speedily revived by making suitable and ample provision by taxes. It certainly is, sir, the duty of those who are the guardians of the public interest, and hold the purse-strings of the nation, to preserve its credit. This does not depend so much on making profuse grants of money, as by husbanding the resources of the nation and limiting its expenditures within its means. Neither of these have been attended to by those who have had the control for years past. They have systematically, and of set design, dried up the sources of national wealth, and by a long course of unwise policy conducted this nation to beggary and ruin. The millions which have been raised at immense sacrifice have been dissipated with prodigality, and squandered in this destructive war. Appropriations have been made, taxes laid, and other means provided to cover the enormous estimates which have been deemed necessary to answer the demands of Government, and yet there now remains a deficit of many millions.

Under such management the public credit cannot be supported—the ability of the nation cannot sustain it. No prudent and wise steps have been taken to preserve it. The credit of the country was solid and stable when the power came into the hands of those who now hold it, but they have destroyed both public and private credit. Is it, then, reasonable to require of those who have been uniformly opposed to the measures which have reduced the nation to its present degraded and deplorable condition, to unite in adding new and grievous burdens on their suffering constituents when they are satisfied the money will be dissipated, as formerly, and no substantial benefit result? I think not. The majority have the power, and on them must rest the responsibility.

Sir, I should be doing injustice to my constituents—I should betray the trust reposed in me, were I to consent to burden them with the enormous taxes proposed to be applied to the objects intended. I know full well their feelings and opinions on this subject. They have been opposed to this ruinous war from the beginning. They had suffered much before, but more since the declaration of war. They did believe they should receive protection from the General Government. Under this expectation they have yielded obedience to all their lawful requisitions, and have paid their direct and internal taxes with a punctuality and promptness beyond any State in the Union, as the return will show. The amount of taxes paid by them into the Treasury the last year, exceeds the whole amount of their State taxes for five years before the war. In addition to which, in consequence of your ships taking refuge in their waters, (and many of them are not without a jealousy they were ordered there by the Government to draw them into the war,) the people of that State have now for eighteen months been called into actual service, and are still obliged to maintain a large force for the defence of the State, abandoned and neglected by the General Government, and the expense thrown on the State without any reasonable prospect of remuneration. And, sir, permit to me say, while as good citizens they feel disposed to comply with all just and lawful requisitions of the General Government, they did believe, as a consideration for their obedience, you would "provide for the common defence, promote the general welfare, and secure to them and their posterity the blessings of liberty." But they have been disappointed; they perceive no regard to these sacred duties—the great objects of the Constitution. You have not provided for the common defence—at least they are left to defend themselves, or fall a prey to the enemy whom you have invited to their very threshold. They perceive no evidence that you seek to promote the general welfare, and they fear if certain bills become the law of the land they shall be robbed of the blessings of liberty. Yet, under all these discouragements they are determined, and, I trust, will defend themselves against the enemy who dare approach their shores—and as evidence of the spirit and determination of my constituents, I cannot, in justice to them, forbear here to mention the attack on the village of Stonington, the last Summer.

When Sir Thomas Hardy appeared before that town with a formidable squadron, consisting of a ship-of-the-line, a frigate. a sloop of war, a bomb ship, and a bomb brig, and came to anchor within dead shot of the town, and gave but a few hours to remove the women and children, declaring in the most peremptory manner that he not only could, but would destroy the place, they refused to abandon their homes. Being freemen, and freeholders, they resisted. Federalists and Democrats rallied side by side, and with the feeble means in their power, they became strong from the justice of their cause, and, after three days' severe conflict, they repulsed the insolent invader, and drove him back to report his disgrace and discomfiture to his master. I mention this exploit because it is considered one of the most brilliant and heroic which has been achieved this war; but as it was performed in defence of that neglected State, and not in the conquest of Canada, I presume you have neither thanks nor medals to bestow on the heroes.

Now, sir, under all these considerations, I cannot feel justified to increase the taxes on my constituents, to be expended for objects which they deem worse than useless, and which, if persisted in, must expose them to greater perils and dangers. They do not believe, with the late Secretary (Campbell) "that the very expenditure of the additional taxes will themselves have increased in the community the ability to discharge them."

Sir, we have acted with precipitation long enough. It may be wise to stop and consider the consequences which may flow from the measures we are pursuing if persisted in much longer. The people begin to feel their grievances. Overwhelmed with taxes and expenses, their resources cut off—their murmurs and complaints are now mild and plaintive; they will become louder and louder. If the Government perseveres in the course it is pursuing, it may shake the pillars which support the national dome. The pressure has already caused some of them to tremble. If they add to the weight in the manner proposed, it may fall—not like yonder Capitol, for that can be rebuilt.

Mr. LAW was replied to by Mr. EPPES and Mr. WRIGHT; and after considerable discussion of the various amendments proposed to the bill, it was ordered to a third reading.

The engrossed bill "to provide additional revenues for defraying the expenses of Government, and maintaining the public credit, by laying duties on various goods, wares, and merchandise, manufactured within the United States, was read a third time, and passed by the following vote:

YEAS—Messrs. Alexander, Alston, Anderson, Archer, Avery, Barbour, Barnett, Bayly of Virginia,

Bines, Bowen, Bradley, Brown, Burwell, Butler, Caldwell, Calhoun, Cannon, Chappell, Clark, Clopton, Comstock, Condict, Conard, Crawford, Creighton, Cuthbert, Dana, Davis of Pennsylvania, Denoyelles, Desha, Duvall, Eppes, Evans, Farrow, Findley, Fisk of Vermont, Fisk of New York, Forney, Forsyth, Franklin, Gholson, Glasgow, Goodwyn, Gourdin, Griffin, Hall, Harris, Hasbrouck, Hawes, Hopkins of Kentucky, Howell, Hubbard, Humphreys, Ingersoll, Ingham, Irving, Irwin, Johnson of Virginia, Johnson of Kentucky, Kennedy, Kerr, Kilbourn, King of North Carolina, Lefferts, Lyle, McCoy, McKee, McKim, McLean, Montgomery, Moore, Murfree, Nelson, Newton, Oakley, Ormsby, Parker, Pickens, Piper, Pleasants, Rea of Pennsylvania, Rhea of Tennessee, Rich, Ringgold, Roane, Sage, Sevier, Sharp, Skinner, Smith of New York, Smith of Pennsylvania, Smith of Virginia, Strong, Tannehill, Taylor, Telfair, Udree, Ward of New Jersey, Williams, Wilson of Pennsylvania, Wright, and Yancey—102.

NAYS—Messrs. Baylies of Massachusetts, Bigelow, Bradbury, Breckenridge, Brigham, Caperton, Champion, Cilley, Cooper, Culpeper, Davenport, Ely, Gaston, Geddes, Grosvenor, Hale, Henderson, Jackson of Rhode Island, King of Massachusetts, Law, Lewis, Lovett, Macon, Markell, Miller, Moseley, Pearson, Pickering, Pitkin, Potter, John Reed, William Reed, Ruggles, Schureman, Shaffey, Sherwood, Shipherd, Slaymaker, Stanford, Stockton, Stuart, Sturges, Taggart, Thompson, Vose, Ward of Massachusetts, Webster, Wheaton, White, Wilcox, Wilson of Massachusetts, and Winter—52.

MONDAY, December 19.

A message from the Senate informed the House that the Senate have passed a bill, "authorizing the payment to the widow of ELBRIDGE GERRY, deceased, late Vice President of the United States, of such salary as would have been payable to him during the residue of the term for which he was elected, had he so long lived; in which they ask the concurrence of this House." They have concurred in certain parts of the amendments proposed by this House to the bill "to authorize the President of the United States to call upon the several States and Territories thereof for their respective quotas of eighty thousand militia, for the defence of the frontiers of the United States against invasion;" and they have disagreed to other parts of the said amendments.

Mr. YANCEY, of North Carolina, reported a bill for the relief of William Robinson and others, (citizens of Knox county, Kentucky,) which was twice read and committed.

Mr. BURWELL, of Virginia, laid upon the table the following resolution:

Resolved, That the Committee on Military Affairs be instructed to report a bill directing the Secretary of War to reserve from the regular troops furnished by the militia of any State, in lieu of their own services, a sufficient number to perform garrison duty within each State.

The House, on motion of Mr. EPPES of Virginia, resolved itself into a Committee of the Whole, on the bill to provide additional revenue for defraying the expenses of the Government, and

for the maintenance of the public credit, by laying a direct tax upon the United States.

[This bill is of great length and minute in its details, proposed amendments to which occupied much time of the House in discussion. The amount of the direct tax is one hundred per cent. on the last year's tax, or six millions of dollars upon the whole United States.]

After the bill had been gone through, the committee rose, and reported to the House the amendments they had made.

PETITION OF W. H. WASHINGTON.

Mr. YANCEY made a report on the petition of William H. Washington; which was read; when, Mr. Y. reported a bill for the relief of William H. Washington; which was read twice and committed to a Committee of the Whole on Monday next. The report is as follows:

That the petitioner owned a small house, situated in Alexandria county, near the western end of the Potomac bridge; that, on the 24th of August last, a quantity of public stores was removed from Greenleaf's Point, by order of Colonel Wadsworth, and deposited in the house for safe keeping: a corporal and five men were stationed at the house to protect them from falling into the possession of the enemy. The command of the stores was given to Lieutenant Baden, who directed the corporal, in case of attack by the enemy, to blow up the stores and retire from the place.

It appears from the affidavit of the corporal, hereto attached, that he apprehended an attack by the enemy, and, under that impression, blew up the stores and destroyed the house. The petitioner claims the value of his house.

Whether the destruction of the house was necessary to prevent the public stores from falling into the hands of the enemy, is a matter of opinion, to be formed by the facts submitted to the House. The committee are of opinion that, inasmuch as the officer to whose care the public stores were committed thought it prudent and proper to destroy the house and stores, to prevent the latter coming to the possession of the enemy, the petitioner should be paid the value of his house. They therefore report by bill.

WASHINGTON COUNTY, *District of Columbia.*

Be it remembered, that on this third day of December, in the year of our Lord one thousand eight hundred and fourteen, before me, the subscriber, a justice of the peace for the county and district aforesaid, personally appeared Philip Boilie, corporal in the United States' Army, and, being sworn in due form, deposed and said: that, on the 24th August, he was stationed with five privates over a quantity of public stores which had been deposited in a frame house, said to belong to William H. Washington, at the foot of the Potomac bridge, in Alexandria county; that he was ordered to take care of the said stores by Lieutenant Baden, and to blow up the said stores, if the deponent was attacked by the enemy; that, on the 25th August, about three o'clock, P. M., as soon as the storm that day had ceased, the deponent saw a British officer, who came to the draw in the bridge, on the Virginia side, and soon after returned; that a number of British soldiers were, at the same time, at the toll-house on this side of the river; that the draws on the bridge had been raised the night before, and kept up, but were blown down during the storm, and the chains that raised them were broken; that, soon after the officers on the bridge returned, a cannon shot was fired at him, the deponent, from the Point; and this deponent thinking that the enemy intended an attack, and not having the means to prevent the enemy passing, as the draw was broken, blew up the stores with powder, and retired with the men to the hill near the place; that the explosion destroyed the house entirely, there being a quantity of ammunition and powder in the house.

his
PHILIP + BOILIA.
mark.

Subscribed and sworn to before me, this 3d day of December, 1814.   DANIEL RAPINE.

LETTER FROM THE CLERK.

The SPEAKER laid before the House a letter from Patrick Magruder, Clerk of the House, partly in explanation, and partly in refutation of the statements of the select committee appointed to take into consideration his former letter respecting the destruction of the public library, and certain papers belonging to his office, during the late incursion of the enemy; which letter was read and referred with the said report to a select committee. The letter is as follows:

OFFICE HOUSE OF REPRESENTATIVES, U. S.,
December 17, 1814.

SIR: The undersigned, Clerk of the House of Representatives, feels himself bound, from the respect due to the House and to himself, to state the situation in which he was previous to the destruction of his office and the Library of Congress. This is rendered indispensably necessary by the remarks contained in the report of the committee upon his accounts for disbursements of the contingent money of the House of Representatives.

It must be very distinctly recollected by every member of the committee, as well as by every member of the House, that I was laboring under a severe indisposition during the whole of the Fall, and the greater part of the Winter of 1813, and that I was unable to resume the discharge of my official duties until about the first of January, 1814. After the rising of Congress I was twice violently attacked with the same complaint, which assumed a serious appearance, and threatened my life. Under these circumstances, my physicians advised me to visit the Springs, as a measure necessary to restore my health. If the House shall deem it necessary, the certificates of the physicians will be procured and laid before them.

When I left this city I can say, without the fear of contradiction, that the enemy was not in any of the rivers leading to this place, or that their force was sufficient, either in the bay or on the coast, to justify an expectation of an attack on the Seat of Government. I believe that the Heads of the Departments did not, at that time, contemplate that any movement would be made by the enemy threatening the city of Washington. Under these circumstances and facts, the Clerk of the House of Representatives most respectfully asks leave to observe, that he is free from censure, because of his going to the Springs to recover his health, which was worn down by a constant and assiduous attention to his official duties.

With respect to that part of the report of the committee, which charges the Clerk and those in his employ with not using a proper degree of vigilance and precaution for the preservation of the papers appertaining to the office of the House and of the Library of Congress, he begs the House to refer to a statement for information upon this subject written by two of his clerks, who are known to be gentlemen of respectability and truth, and laid before the House on the 22d of September, a copy of which he herewith presents, marked No. 1.

The Clerk has further to observe upon this subject, that it will appear, by the certificate of Captain Burch, herewith accompanying, marked No. 2, that two of his clerks, Mr. Hamilton and Mr. Berry, were doing duty in his company of artillery from the 19th of August until after the destruction of the Capitol; that they could not leave the camp without a furlough from the Colonel or General, which was never granted them; that it will appear, by the statement of Captain Bestor, No. 3, that Mr. Burch, another of his clerks, and upon whom he placed much reliance, was marched from the city, and continued under his command until the afternoon of the 21st of August, when he was furloughed by General Smith, as will be seen by his General Order No. 4. Mr. Burch did not get into the city until nightfall of that day. Another of his clerks, Colonel George Magruder, who was the commander of one of the regiments then in the service, marched with his regiment, and continued with it, as was his duty, until after the destruction of the Capitol. There was then only one clerk left, Mr. Frost, who had just before been appointed in the office, and he also would have been taken away with the military, if he had not been over the age prescribed by law for militia service. From these facts it results that, of the clerks in my employ, those in the company of Captain Burch had no power whatever to interfere in the saving of the office and library from destruction; that Mr. Burch could not do anything for their preservation until Monday, the 22d, nor could Colonel Magruder, without deserting his duties in the field.

On the 22d Mr. Burch and Mr. Frost did commence the removal of the office, not in the afternoon, as is stated in the report of the committee, but actually in the forenoon. The means of transportation were limited for three days previous, and on that day the committee have admitted it was almost impossible to procure it at all.

The evidence which the committee have procured from the Departments, of the facility which they found in removing their papers, can have no bearing on the present case, as these Departments began to pack up on the 18th or 19th of the month, and, in fact, removed before the afternoon of the 22d; and, consequently, had all their means of transportation in readiness previous to the time it became so difficult to procure it.

The Clerk begs leave further to observe, that the Heads of Departments, being in the confidence of the Government, had much better means of procuring correct information of the movements of the enemy than the clerks in his office, whose only sources of information were the common reports to be heard in the streets; and it is notorious, that the public mind was in darkness and ignorance upon the subject of the strength and movements of the enemy; that the Heads of Departments gave orders to pack up their papers, as has been observed before, some on the 19th, and one even on the 18th of the month; and that, as many, if not a majority, of their clerks were over the age of forty-five years, they were not compelled to leave the offices. This accounts for their ability to pack up their papers, and, in some cases, actually to remove them,

955   **HISTORY OF CONGRESS.**   955

H. of R.   *Letter from the Clerk of the House.*   DECEMBER, 1814.

before it was in the power of my clerks to commence the business.

The Clerk must, therefore, be permitted to say, and he says it with confidence, that those in his employ were not guilty of negligence, or inattention in the preservation of the office, unless, indeed, the committee will prove that they were not in the military service; that they remained during the whole time in the city; and that they took no part or interest in its preservation.

With respect to the Library, he asks the House to refer to the letter of Mr. Frost, marked No. 5. This gentleman acted as under-librarian; the rest of the clerks in my office had no authority or control in that department.

In regard to the contingent expenses of the House, the vouchers for which were destroyed, the undersigned begs leave to state, that the Committee of Accounts have always had the sole control of the disbursements of the funds appropriated for this object, and have sanctioned all the payments which have been made out of it. Being, from the nature of the other duties of his office, unable to attend to this branch of the business, it was confided by the Clerk to Mr. George Magruder, his principal clerk. The amounts drawn at different times from the Treasury have always been so drawn under the direction of the Committee of Accounts, after they had received satisfactory information that the funds already drawn were expended. The Committee of Accounts have always kept a record of their accounts, as well as their chief clerk, and acted as a check upon him, the undersigned has had no further agency in the same, than to affix his signature to them when the forms of office required it. This is not a novel practice, but is, he believes, pursued in regard to the contingent expenses of every office under the Government of any extent; the chief clerks always disbursing the contingent fund, though the principal is responsible for the same. It is not, therefore, so very extraordinary, the undersigned would respectfully suggest, that he was not able to afford to the committee of inquiry a specification of expenditures, of which all the accounts and vouchers were so unfortunately destroyed. He greatly regrets that the chief clerk had kept no duplicate book or memorandum of the accounts paid, which could supply the deficiency of that destroyed, in consequence entirely of his absence on duty in the field of battle. Could the event of that day have been foreseen six hours before it happened, those papers had probably escaped the flames.

It must be obvious to the honorable House that, out of so large a mass of accounts of a miscellaneous character as are paid, in the course of seven months, out of the contingent fund of the House, it would be impossible for the person having paid it, to recollect more than a few items. It is true that the evidence of payment of such accounts may be collected, in a great degree, by the voluntary testimony of those to whom the money was paid, but it is no less true, that this must be a work, not of a day or a week, but of time and research. The undersigned has taken means, by a public advertisement, to accomplish this object, and will not fail to use due diligence in pursuit of it. Meanwhile, he most respectfully suggests that, to accuse him of deficiency and default in his accounts, because the particular items of disbursement are unascertained, could not enter the views of the honorable House or any member of it, because it would be unjust in itself, and would be to add cruelty to that pain which

the undersigned has already suffered from the loss sustained in his office.

After these general observations, the undersigned begs the attention of the House to a few remarks on that part of the report which implies an unjust statement as to two of the very few accounts which he or his chief clerk have been able to specify as having been paid. This is due to the House from its Clerk, as well as to his own conscious rectitude, and to a reputation which he hopes no man can justly impeach.

First. As to the account stated by the committee to be overcharged as paid to the messengers and servants of the House, nothing is capable of more satisfactory explanation. These persons were requested to furnish a statement of the amounts they had severally received. They made an error in their statements, which the honorable committee detected, but of which the chief clerk neither participated nor had information until it was reported to the House by the committee, and which neither he nor the persons who made it were afforded an opportunity to amend. That circumstance is more fully explained, and the undersigned hopes in a manner which will be entirely satisfactory to the House, in the accompanying letter from Mr. George Magruder, marked No. 7, and also by a statement of the principal messenger referred to in his letter.

Secondly. As to the amount which the committee appear to have been satisfied was overcharged, as having been paid to the printers, the undersigned in the absence of that documentary proof, which would have completely satisfied the House on this head, (but which was destroyed with other papers, not in his office, but in the Department of the Treasury,) begs leave to submit the following statement of facts, in order to refute, as publicly as it was made, the charge in this respect contained in the report of the committee. The abstract obtained from the Treasury bears date the 14th of January, 1814, as to its settlement at the Auditor's office. On the face of it, however, it is stated that the accounts settled at that time, were up to the seventh only of that month, and the probability is, they were not up to that by some days, as it is well known that papers are left for settlement at the Treasury frequently, and, indeed, always several days before they are acted upon. Application has been made by my order, two or three times, to ascertain the date of the deposite of that account at the Treasury, and have as often been answered, that the account itself, together with every accompanying voucher, is lying in ashes at the site of the former Treasury building. It is much to be regretted, and it is doing injustice to me, for the officers of the Treasury to be giving certificates, that means of transportation of public papers were everywhere to be had in abundance, when they suffered accounts and vouchers of such recent date to be burned. The papers marked Nos. 11 and 12, herewith submitted, will demonstrate, as far as evidence can be obtained, not only that these accounts were not included in the settlement of the 14th of January, 1814, but that the Clerk ought to have credit on that head for a sum of more than two thousand dollars than he claimed. The statement of Mr. Way, and the letter of Mr. Weightman, will exhibit how liable to error all estimates must be, collected in the unusual manner in which those of the committee were.

The schedule marked A, which accompanies this report, with vouchers from No. 11 to No. 17, obtained since the committee reported, will exhibit a further sum to be credited to the account of the Clerk, to the amount of about seven thousand dollars.

957   HISTORY OF CONGRESS.   958

DECEMBER, 1814.   *Tax on Personal Property—Direct Tax*   H. OF R.

These amounts combined, (nearly seven thousand dollars,) with cash in hand at the commencement of this session, as estimated by the chief clerk in his statement accompanying the report of the committee, will reduce the amount of expenditures, for which vouchers are not yet obtained, to about one-half of the amount of deficiency stated by your honorable committee.

Other vouchers of a like character will be duly obtained, and the undersigned does not despair, in a seasonable time, to be able to account to the satisfaction of the House for the whole amount of the expenditures from the contingent fund. All which he respectfully solicits the House to take into their consideration.

PATRICK MAGRUDER.

Hon. SPEAKER *of the House.*

TAX ON PERSONAL PROPERTY.

An engrossed bill to provide additional revenues for defraying the expenses of Government, and maintaining the public credit, by laying duties on household furniture, or horses kept exclusively for the saddle or carriage, and on gold and silver watches, was read the third time; and on the question, that the same do pass? it passed in the affirmative—yeas 102, nays 46, as follows:

YEAS—Messrs. Alexander, Alston, Anderson, Archer, Avery, Barbour, Barnett, Bines, Bowen, Brown, Burwell, Butler, Caldwell, Calhoun, Cannon, Chappell, Clark, Comstock, Condict, Conard, Crawford, Creighton, Culpeper, Cuthbert, Dana, Davis of Pennsylvania, Denoyelles, Desha, Duvall, Earle, Eppes, Farrow, Findley, Fisk of Vermont, Fisk of New York, Forney, Forsyth, Franklin, Gholson, Goodwyn, Gourdin, Griffin, Hall, Harris, Hasbrouck, Hawes, Hawkins, Hopkins of Kentucky, Howell, Hubbard, Humphreys, Hungerford, Ingersoll, Ingham, Irving, Irwin, Johnson of Virginia, Johnson of Kentucky, Kennedy, Kent of New York, Kerr, Kershaw, Kilbourn, King of North Carolina, Lefferts, Lowndes, Lyle, Macon, McCoy, McKee, McKim, McLean, Moore, Murfree, Nelson, Newton, Oakley, Parker, Pickens, Piper, Pleasants, Rea of Pennsylvania, Rhea of Tennessee, Rich, Sage, Sevier, Seybert, Sharp, Smith of Pennsylvania, Smith of Virginia, Strong, Tannehill, Taylor, Telfair, Troup, Udree, Ward of New Jersey, Williams, Wilson of Pennsylvania, Winter Wright, and Yancey.

NAYS—Messrs. Baylies of Massachusetts, Bigelow, Boyd, Bradbury, Breckenridge, Brigham, Caperton, Champion, Cilley, Cooper, Davenport, Ely, Geddes, Grosvenor, Hale, Henderson, Jackson of Rhode Island, King of Massachusetts, Law, Lewis, Lovett, Markell, Miller, Moseley, Pearson, Pickering, Pitkin, Potter, John Reed, Ruggles, Schureman, Sherwood, Shipherd, Slaymaker, Stanford, Stockton, Stuart, Sturges, Thompson, Vose, Ward of Massachusetts, Webster, Wheaton, Wilcox, and Wilson of Massachusetts.

TUESDAY, December 20.

The bill from the Senate, "authorizing payment to the widow of ELBRIDGE GERRY, deceased, late Vice President of the United States, of such salary as would have been payable to him during the residue of the term for which he was elected, had he so long lived," was read twice and committed to a Committee of the Whole.

The House proceeded to consider the message from the Senate in relation to the amendments proposed by this House to the bill from the Senate "to authorize the President of the United States to call upon the several States and Territories thereof for their respective quotas of eighty thousand militia, for the defence of the frontiers of the United States against invasion;" and the said message was read: Whereupon,

Ordered, That the bill and amendments do lie on the table.

The following resolution was submitted by Mr. STOCKTON:

Resolved, That the Committee of Ways and Means be instructed to inquire into the constitutionality and expediency of imposing a direct tax upon the District of Columbia and the several Territories of the United States.

Mr. PEARSON moved to amend the resolution by adding the following words: "and that the Committee be instructed to inquire into the propriety and expediency of authorizing the several corporations within the District to impose a direct tax on the public property therein."

Mr. EPPES moved that the resolution do lie on the table.—Negatived.

The question was then taken on the amendment proposed by Mr. PEARSON, and negatived.

The resolution was then agreed to by the House.

DIRECT TAX.

The House resumed the consideration of the report of the Committee of the whole House on the bill to provide additional revenues for defraying the expenses of Government, and maintaining the public credit, by laying a direct tax upon the United States, and providing for assessing and collecting the same; and the amendments reported by the Committee of the whole House being read, were, in part, concurred in, and in part disagreed to, by the House.

The said bill was further amended.

And a motion was made by Mr. SHARP further to amend the said bill by striking the words "annually" out of the following clause: "That a direct tax of six millions of dollars be hereby annually laid upon the United States."

And the question being taken, it was determined in the negative—yeas 50, nays 102, as follows:

YEAS—Messrs. Alston, Bard, Barnett, Baylies of Massachusetts, Bayly of Virginia, Bigelow, Bowen, Boyd, Bradbury, Breckenridge, Burwell, Butler, Caperton, Calhoun, Culpeper, Earle, Fisk of Vermont, Forney, Franklin, Gaston, Hale, Hall, Henderson, Humphreys, Hungerford, Kennedy, Kerr, King of Massachusetts, King of North Carolina, Law, Lewis, Macon, Moseley, Murfree, Pearson, Pickens, Pitkin, John Reed, Rhea of Tennessee, Sharp, Sheffey, Smith of Virginia, Stanford, Strong, Telfair, Wheaton, White, Wilcox, Wilson of Massachusetts, and Yancey.

NAYS—Messrs. Alexander, Anderson, Archer, Avery, Barbour, Bines, Bradley, Brown, Caldwell, Cannon, Champion, Chappell, Clark, Clopton, Comstock, Condict, Conard, Cooper, Cox, Crawford, Creighton, Cuthbert, Dana, Davenport, Davis of Massachusetts, Davis of Pennsylvania, Denoyelles, Desha, Duvall, Ely, Eppes, Farrow, Findley, Fisk of New York, Forsyth, Geddes, Gholson, Goodwyn, Gourdin, Griffin, Grosvenor, Hasbrouck, Hawes, Hawkins, Hopkins of New

York, Hubbard, Ingersoll, Ingham, Irving, Irwin, Jackson of Rhode Island, Johnson of Virginia, Johnson of Kentucky, Kent of New York, Kent of Maryland, Kershaw, Lefferts, Lovett, Lowndes, Lyle, Markell, McCoy, McKim, McLean, Montgomery, Moore, Nelson, Newton, Oakley, Ormsby, Parker, Pickering, Piper, Pleasants, Potter, William Reed, Rea of Pennsylvania, Rich, Ringgold, Robertson, Ruggles, Sage, Schureman, Seybert, Sherwood, Skinner, Slaymaker, Smith of New York, Smith of Pennsylvania, Stockton, Sturges, Tannehill, Taylor, Thompson, Udree, Vose, Ward of Massachusetts, Ward of New Jersey, Webster, Williams, Wilson of Pennsylvania, and Winter.

Mr. YANCEY moved further to amend the said bill by adding thereto the following section:

And be it further enacted, That this act shall continue to be in force for and during the war in which the United States are now engaged with the United Kingdom of Great Britain and Ireland, and the dependencies thereof, and until the expiration of the year in which the said war shall terminate, and no longer.

Mr. FISK, of New York, moved to amend the said section by striking out all thereof from the word "Ireland," and insert, "and for one year thereafter, and no longer." And the question being taken, it was determined in the negative.

The question was then taken on agreeing to the said section, and was determined in the negative—yeas 61, nays 78, as follows:

YEAS—Messrs. Alexander, Alston, Avery, Barbour, Bard, Barnett, Baylies of Massachusetts, Bines, Bowen, Breckenridge, Brigham, Burwell, Butler, Caldwell, Calhoun, Clark, Condict, Crawford, Creighton, Cuthbert, Davis of Pennsylvania, Denoyelles, Desha, Earle, Forney, Franklin, Gaston, Gholson, Goodwyn, Hale, Hall, Harris, Hawes, Henderson, Humphreys, Hungerford, Kennedy, Kent of Maryland, Kerr, Kershaw, King of Massachusetts, King of North Carolina, Lefferts, Lewis, Lowndes, Macon, McLean, Murfree, Pearson, Pickens, Piper, Rhea of Tennessee, Sharp, Skinner, Smith of Virginia, Stanford, Strong, Telfair, Wheaton, White, and Yancey.

NAYS—Messrs. Anderson, Archer, Bradley, Cannon, Champion, Chappell, Cilley, Clopton, Comstock, Conard, Cooper, Cox, Dana, Davenport, Davis of Massachusetts, Duvall, Eppes, Farrow, Findley, Fisk of New York, Forsyth, Gourdin, Griffin, Grosvenor, Hasbrouck, Hawkins, Hopkins of Kentucky, Hubbard, Ingersoll, Ingham, Irving, Irwin, Jackson of Rhode Island, Johnson of Virginia, Johnson of Kentucky, Kent of New York, Kilbourn, Lovett, Lyle, Markell, McCoy, McKim, Montgomery, Moore, Moseley, Nelson, Newton, Oakley, Ormsby, Parker, Pickering, Pitkin, Pleasants, Potter, Rea of Pennsylvania, Rich, Robertson, Ruggles, Sage, Schureman, Seybert, Sherwood, Slaymaker, Smith of New York, Smith of Pennsylvania, Stockton, Tannehill, Taylor, Thompson, Udree, Vose, Ward of Massachusetts, Ward of New Jersey, Webster, Wilcox, Wilson of Massachusetts, Wilson of Pennsylvania, and Winter.

WEDNESDAY, December 21.

Mr. McKEE, from the Committee on the Public Lands, made a report on the several petitions from inhabitants of the Mississippi Territory, relating to claims to lands derived from the British

Government; which was read, and Mr. McKEE reported a bill for quieting and adjusting claims to lands in the Mississippi Territory; which was read twice, and committed to a Committee of the whole House.

DIRECT TAX.

The House resumed the consideration of the bill for laying a direct tax of six millions of dollars upon the United States.

Mr. YANCEY, of North Carolina, moved to amend the bill by striking out therefrom the 41st section, which is as follows:

"SEC. 41. *And be it further enacted,* That, towards establishing an adequate revenue, to provide for the payment of the expenses of Government; for the punctual payment of the public debt, principal and interest, contracted, and to be contracted, according to the terms of the contracts respectively; and for creating an adequate sinking fund, gradually to reduce, and eventually to extinguish the public debt contracted, and to be contracted, the direct tax by this act laid shall continue to be laid, levied, and collected, during the present war between the United States and Great Britain, and until the purposes aforesaid shall be completely accomplished, anything in the said act of Congress to the contrary thereof in any wise notwithstanding. And for the effectual application of the revenue, to be raised by and from the said direct tax laid by this act, and also, by and from the direct tax laid by the said act of Congress, entitled "An act to lay and collect a direct tax within the United States," to the purposes aforesaid, in due form of law, the faith of the United States is hereby pledged: *Provided always,* That, whenever Congress shall deem it expedient to alter, reduce, or change, the said direct tax by this act laid, it shall be lawful so to do, upon providing and substituting by law, at the said time, and for the same purposes, other taxes or duties, which shall be equally productive with the direct tax so altered, reduced, or changed: *And provided further,* That nothing in this act contained shall be deemed or construed in any wise to rescind or impair any specific appropriation of the said direct taxes, or either of them; but such appropriation shall remain and be carried into effect, according to the true intent and meaning of the law and laws making the same; anything in this act to the contrary thereof in any wise notwithstanding."

On this motion a very interesting but desultory debate arose, in which Messrs. YANCEY, CALHOUN, RHEA, LOWNDES, and TELFAIR, advocated the motion, and Messrs. EPPES, INGERSOLL, POTTER, DUVALL, FINDLEY, GROSVENOR, HAWKINS, WEBSTER, PICKERING, NEWTON, and NELSON opposed it.

The advocates of the motion urged that they had no wish to defeat the passage of the bill, but that the spirit of the Constitution required that a direct tax should be laid only for one year, and continued no longer than imperious necessity required; that the Constitution having given to Congress the power to control the taxes, to part with it for a series of years, would be to surrender their Constitutional power, inasmuch as they could not, after giving the proposed pledge, withhold the taxes without the consent of the two other branches of the Government; that, whilst the pledge to be given might saddle the nation forever with a land tax, it was not necessary to the maintenance of the public credit, because a sufficient sum was pledged, by the bills already passed, for the annual payment of the interest and a portion of the principal of the public debt; that this discovery of supporting public credit by pledging an annual land tax, was of recent date—for, during the Administrations of WASHINGTON and ADAMS, when the Government would naturally be most solicitous for the establishment and invigoration of public credit, a direct tax had been imposed but one year, and was then pledged, as now proposed; it was flying too suddenly from one extreme to the other, after refusing to pledge anything, to pledge all the resources of the Government, of every description, to the public creditor. Various arguments were also urged against the pledge for the continuance of this tax, derived from its general character; it was a tax, it was said, unequal in its character on different sections of the Union, and unequal in its operation frequently when not unequal in its amount, owing to the local advantages and disadvantages of different sections of the nation, and the disbursements of the Government therein. It was, besides, argued that direct taxation was the principal resource of the State governments for revenue —because, from their nature and relative situation, they cannot resort to internal taxation; and, therefore, a direct tax ought not to be overcharged, nor too long persevered in.

The arguments in opposition to the motion were various, as they proceeded from one or the other side of the House. They were, in general, to this effect: The argument against parting with the power of taxation, it was said, would apply as well to the pledges contained in the internal tax bills (against which it had not been suggested) as to this; and was besides inconclusive if correct, inasmuch as the House, by withholding appropriations, over which it had an efficient check, could at any time coerce the other branches of the Government to repeal or modify existing taxes. That, though in ordinary times, the pledges already given of the internal taxes might be sufficient to maintain public credit, it was necessary now to resuscitate that credit—in the words of one gentleman, "to dig it from the grave;" that this was a duty peculiarly devolving on those who had declared and supported the war, and on whom devolved the responsibility for its success or failure. That it would be highly unjust and impartial, after pledging the taxes on the materials and labor of the artisan, mechanic, and poor retailer—after, in fact, pledging the taxes on the industry of the community—to refuse to pledge the tax on its solid wealth and landed property, &c. That this pledge of a land-tax, as a foundation for borrowing money, would be worth much more than all the internal taxes put together, because its product would be certain, whilst the products of the other taxes must be matter of estimate and conjecture. The argument that a sufficient amount of taxes was already pledged to sustain the public credit, was

denied any weight, because it made the eligibility of the taxes to be pledged depend on the priority of passage of several bills which were intended and calculated to form parts of a general system of taxation, &c.

Various other points were brought into discussion, as to the intention of the framers of the Constitution in regard to the frequency and permanency of a land tax, &c., and on the merits of the present and former systems of finance, which could not be here detailed with any justice to those who introduced them.

The question being at length taken on this motion, was decided in the negative—yeas 48, nays 105, as follows:

YEAS—Messrs. Alston, Bard, Barnett, Baylies of Massachusetts, Bowen, Boyd, Bradbury, Burwell, Butler, Calhoun, Clark, Crawford, Culpeper, Denoyelles, Desha, Earle, Forney, Franklin, Gaston, Glasgow, Goodwyn, Hale, Hall, Harris, Henderson, Humphreys, Hulbert, Kennedy, Kent of Maryland, Kerr, Kershaw, King of Massachusetts, King of North Carolina, Law, Lefferts, Lowndes, Macon, Pearson, Pickens, Rhea of Tennessee, Sharp, Smith of Virginia, Stanford, Strong, Telfair, Wheaton, Wilson of Massachusetts, and Yancey.

NAYS—Messrs. Alexander, Anderson, Archer, Avery, Bigelow, Bines, Bradley, Brigham, Brown, Caldwell, Cannon, Champion, Chappell, Cilley, Clopton, Comstock, Condict, Conard, Cooper, Coxe, Creighton, Cuthbert, Dana, Davenport, Davis of Massachusetts, Davis of Pennsylvania, Duvall, Ely, Eppes, Farrow, Findley, Fisk of New York, Forsyth, Geddes, Gholson, Gourdin, Griffin, Grosvenor, Hasbrouck, Hawes, Hawkins, Hopkins of Kentucky, Howell, Hubbard, Ingersoll, Ingham, Irving, Irwin, Jackson of Rhode Island, Johnson of Virginia, Johnson of Kentucky, Kent of New York, Lovett, Lyle, Markell, McCoy, McKee, McKim, McLean, Miller, Montgomery, Moore, Moseley, Nelson, Newton, Oakley, Ormsby, Parker, Pickering, Piper, Pleasants, Potter, John Reed, William Reed, Rea of Pennsylvania, Rich, Ringgold, Robertson, Ruggles, Sage, Schureman, Seybert, Sheffey, Sherwood, Shipherd, Skinner, Slaymaker, Smith of New York, Smith of Pennsylvania, Stockton, Sturges, Taggart, Tannehill, Taylor, Thompson, Troup, Udree, Vose, Ward of Massachusetts, Ward of New Jersey, Webster, Wilcox, Williams, Wilson of Pennsylvania, and Winter.

Mr. POTTER moved to amend the 26th section of the bill, by striking out these words: "Shall, within ten days after receiving his collection list from the principal assessors, respectively, as aforesaid;" and inserting the words, "upon receiving his collection lists, shall proceed to collect the same, under the directions of the Secretary of the Treasury, on such day as shall be fixed upon by him, which day shall be uniform in all the States."

And the question being taken, it was determined in the negative—yeas 52, nays 90, as follows:

YEAS—Messrs. Baylies of Massachusetts, Bigelow, Bradbury, Brigham, Champion, Cilley, Condict, Cooper, Cox, Culpeper, Dana, Davenport, Davis of Massachusetts, Ely, Gaston, Gourdin, Grosvenor, Hall, Henderson, Hulbert, Jackson of Rhode Island, Kent of New York, Law, Lovett, McKee, Miller, Moseley, Oakley, Pearson, Pickering, Pitkin, Potter, John Reed,

William Reed, Ruggles, Schureman, Sheffey, Sherwood, Shipherd, Slaymaker, Smith of New York, Stanford, Stockton, Sturges, Thompson, Vose, Ward of Massachusetts, Ward of New Jersey, Webster, Wheaton, Wilcox, and Winter.

NAYS—Messrs. Alexander, Alston, Archer, Avery, Bard, Barnett, Bines, Bowen, Brown, Burwell, Butler, Caldwell, Calhoun, Cannon, Chappell, Clark, Clopton, Comstock, Conard, Crawford, Creighton, Cuthbert, Davis of Pennsylvania, Denoyelles, Desha, Duvall, Earle, Eppes, Farrow, Fndley, Fisk of New York, Forney, Franklin, Gholson, Goodwyn, Griffin, Hall, Harris, Hasbrouck, Hawes, Hawkins, Hopkins of Kentucky, Hubbard, Humphreys, Ingersoll, Ingham, Irving, Irwin, Johnson of Virginia, Johnson of Kentucky, Kennedy, Kent of Maryland, Kerr, Kershaw, Kilbourn, King of Massachusetts, King of North Carolina, Lefferts, Lowndes, Lyle, Macon, Markell, McCoy, McKim, McLean, Moore, Nelson, Newton, Ormsby, Parker, Pickens, Piper, Pleasants, Rea of Pennsylvania, Rhea of Tennessee, Rich, Ringgold, Robertson, Sage, Seybert, Sharp, Smith of Pennsylvania, Tannehill, Taylor, Telfair, Udree, Williams, Wilson of Pennsylvania, and Yancey.

Mr. STANFORD moved to amend the said bill by inserting, after the word "districts," in the 30th line of the printed bill, the following words: "and also, a like certified copy for each county or district within the said collection districts, to be, by said collector, deposited with the clerk or prothonotary of the several counties or districts."

And the question being taken, it was determined in the negative.

Mr. POTTER moved to amend the bill by inserting the following as the 41st section:

SEC. 41. *And be it further enacted,* That every person who shall pay the full amount of his taxes on or before the first day of June, annually, shall be entitled to an abatement of twelve per centum on the amount of his taxes, to be allowed and deducted therefrom by the collector; and if not paid on said first day of June, but shall be paid on or before the first day of October, annually, he shall be allowed a deduction of six per cent. on the amount of his taxes, to be made in manner aforesaid; and every person who shall neglect to pay his taxes until after the said first day of October, shall pay interest at the rate of six per centum per annum, on the amount of his taxes, from said first day of October, until paid, to be collected together with such taxes due and payable as aforesaid.

And the question being taken, it was determined in the negative.

Mr. KENNEDY moved to amend the bill, by striking out the words "six millions of dollars," in the third line of the first section of the printed bill, and inserting the words "four millions five hundred thousand dollars."

And the question being taken, it was determined in the negative.

Mr. INGERSOLL moved to amend the bill by adding the following section:

SEC. 41. *And be it further enacted,* That every person who shall pay the full amount of his taxes on or before the first day of June, annually, shall be entitled to an abatement of twelve per cent. on the amount of his taxes, to be allowed and deducted therefrom by the collector; and if not paid on said first day of June, but shall be paid on or before the first day of October

annually, he shall be allowed a deduction of six per cent. on the amount of his taxes, to be made in manner aforesaid.

And the question being taken, it was determined in the negative.

Mr. WARD, of Massachusetts, moved to amend the said bill, by inserting, after the words "passage of this act," in the tenth line of the fifth section of the printed bill, the following words: "or specially exempted from taxation by the last tax act passed by such State."

And the question being taken, it was determined in the negative.

The bill was then ordered to be engrossed, and read the third time to-morrow.

THURSDAY, December 22.

A new member, to wit: from Ohio, DAVID CLENDENIN, elected to supply the vacancy occasioned by the resignation of Rezin Beall, appeared, produced his credentials, was qualified, and took his seat.

A message from the Senate informed the House that the Senate have passed the bill "supplemental to the acts authorizing a loan for the several sums of twenty-five millions of dollars, and three millions of dollars," with an amendment; in which they ask the concurrence of this House. The amendment was read, and concurred in by the House.

On motion of Mr. EASTON, of Missouri, so much of the report of the Committee of Revisal and Unfinished Business as relates to the bill permitting certain locations, and granting certain donations of land in the county of New Madrid, in the Missouri Territory, was referred to a committee to report thereon.

On motion of Mr. REED, of Massachusetts, the report recently received from the Navy Department, in answer to the resolution of the House of last session, was referred to the committee of investigation on that subject, which was appointed in March last.

DIRECT TAX.

The bill to provide additional revenues for defraying the expenses of the Government and maintaining the public credit, by laying a direct tax upon the United States, was read a third time.

Mr. BRIGHAM, of Massachusetts, spoke as follows: Mr. Speaker, taxing the people to raise money to enable the present Administration to perpetuate the war, has, in my opinion, no connexion with the welfare of the country, or the credit of the nation. And being opposed to the war, of course I am opposed to the passage of this bill for its support.

War is a great calamity, and blasts the happiness of those who are involved in it, and is now the occasion of the many embarrassments and distresses so sensibly felt in these United States.

Those rulers, whoever they be, and wherever they are, who hastily and unnecessarily involve a country in the horrors and mischiefs of war, are a scourge and abhorrence to any people. My anxiety for peace has been so ardent, that, at the commencement of the session, I indulged a sanguine hope that the present war, of waste and folly, was in one of its last struggles, and that its existence would soon terminate. I fear a disappointment. The Government, although unable to prosecute the war, do not seem to have ability and disposition to negotiate a peace. And in this situation, unable to do one thing or the other, tell us that they intend, if they can obtain money by taxing the people, to undertake to do what they have already found by experience that they are unable to accomplish.

To devise ways and means to raise men and money to carry on the war, were among the great and weighty matters alluded to by the President in his proclamation, and what induced him to convoke Congress, at so early a period, the present session. In obedience to his wishes and recommendations, Congress have been very industriously engaged in providing the means to enable the Administration to prosecute their schemes of misery, and have prepared a frightful increase of taxes and burdens for the citizens of the country. If the several laws which have been passed this session shall be carried into operation, they will be sensibly felt by this people, for you will take from them not only their money, but you take their personal liberty; you will take from them their children, and, in my opinion, you will take from them their Constitutional freedom. And although desperate cases may require desperate remedies, yet it does not appear to me that the present state of things, deplorable as it is, can justify the very extraordinary measures which have been adopted.

Sir, I consider this and the other revenue bills, and the army bills, component parts of one great war system, and preparatory to another Canadian campaign.

Canada is marked out by our rulers for the theatre where they intend again to exhibit their bravery and their blunders; and whoever shall see the result, will find the balance on the side of the latter; and to aid in this project, we are about to insult the miseries of the people by increasing their taxes.

This war, in my opinion, is one of the most unfortunate and distressing that ever any civilized nations voluntarily and of choice plunged themselves into. And although it is of our own choice, it is a very impolitic war; it is wrong *ab initio;* it was conceived in error; it was of premature birth, agonized into the world under very inauspicious circumstances, and without preparation for its support; it is like its father, of corrupt constitution, of feeble understanding, of violent passions, and not to be reasoned with; money has been its aliment, and like a vulture, it has preyed on the vitals of the country until its substance is devoured and its Treasury exhausted.

In this impoverished and distressed situation, the friends of the war say it is necessary that the people should be taxed, that the Administration may have millions more of money to prosecute the war. It does not however follow, because the Administration are destitute of money, that it is necessary or expedient that they should have more.

You would not say, in the case of a private individual, the father of a respectable and industrious family, who had neglected his social and paternal duties, wasted and expended his living and their earnings in profligacy, in rioting, and drunkenness, to their ruin and his own shame, that without any evidence of repentance or reformation, it would be necessary or expedient that he should have more money to feed his lusts and consummate their misery. So in the case before us, to say nothing of the waste of fifty thousand dollars paid to John Henry, it seems to be understood and admitted, that there has been great waste of public money in the War Department. And shall we tax the people, and raise money to put into the hands of the same agents, to be applied to the same purposes, without any evidence of reformation, or of more economy or discretion, and without any regard to the feelings and welfare of the great American family?

Common sense and common prudence forbid it; the circumstances of the people forbid it; nor do I conceive that the honor or the safety of the nation will justify it.

Mr. Speaker, the predicted embarrassments and distresses in our public affairs are before us.

We witness the loss of national prosperity; the loss of the public credit; and we witness the infirmities of our rulers, and the impolicy of their measures. And by the taxes, exactions, and impositions on the people, authorized by this and the other revenue bills already passed, we are to restore national prosperity and public credit.

I am sensible that money is wanted, and that our rulers have come to their *ne plus ultra;* they have worked up their stock, their Treasury notes, and their loans; they have expended their millions and tens of millions, and have accomplished no part of their object, the conquest of the Canadas.

And now in the fullness of their political wisdom, and with all the gravity of statesmen, they say that the salvation of the country depends on their having twenty or thirty millions of dollars to prosecute their system of measures and get possession of the Canadas.

The bill provides for six millions of the sum by a direct tax on the United States.

In times of difficulty like the present, it is natural to advert to the sources from whence the evils have originated.

The system of policy which was commenced in the year 1807, and which has since been in operation; whose character and objects were distinctly settled, and fully disclosed on the never to be forgotten 18th day of June, 1812, had in its rear a train of mischiefs and calamities incident to a hopeless and unnecessary war.

The country is now perplexed, the people are distressed, and the Government almost, if not altogether, bankrupt. And to restore national credit, we are by this bill to call on the people of these United States, including those of the State of Massachusetts, who are now standing on their defence against the enemy, without any support from the General Government, to advance their money, and to pay heavy taxes, to enable the Administration to prosecute a foreign war.

This nation has fallen from the elevated rank which it once held. The circumstances of the country are changed from affluence to indigence, and from glory to shame. It is humiliating when we compare the existing state of our public affairs and interest with the condition and circumstances of the nation under the Federal Administration. In the year 1801, when Mr. Jefferson came into office, he told the nation that he found their prosperity in the full tide of successful experiment. And toward the close of his Administration, he informed the people that the National Treasury was full and overflowing. How is it now? It is empty, and resembles more the exhausted receiver of an air pump than a National Treasury. Whence this mighty change from wealth to poverty? It certainly would be extraordinary that an orderly and well regulated people, under a faithful and wise Administration, should have fallen from a situation so prosperous to such a state of poverty and disgrace.

To what shall we attribute these misfortunes of the country? Our halcyon days seem to be past, and instead of peace and prosperity we have war and adversity.

The present state of things is truly alarming; there must be something rotten in the state of Denmark; and there is no rule of evidence so conclusive of the merit or demerit of an Administration as the happiness or misery of the people.

The people of these United States are depressed, but not subdued; nor will they quietly submit to be enslaved by the hands of tyranny, either foreign or domestic. They have in times past remonstrated against the oppressive measures of their own Government, but without success. And now they have nothing to expect but the increase of taxes.

It appears to me that those who now hold the destinies of this nation are as insensible of the distresses and deprivations occasioned by their measures as if they were locked up in the tomb of death.

The Administration say that they want money, and must have it. And they tell you, in language which cannot be misunderstood, that they intend to employ the money of the people and the courage of the poor to subdue the neighboring provinces. They seem to have a fatal passion for war, and with no better motive for its continuance than to revenge their own mortification.

I am ready to admit that money is the sinew of war, and I am sensible that the Government cannot carry it on without money; and am equally sensible that they cannot obtain money commensurate with their objects without oppressing the people—a people, too, who complain, and not without cause, of their public burdens; who are innocent and unoffending; who feel no interest in the success of this Canadian war, and who have not in the slightest degree been the authors of it.

I am aware that the Government are embarrassed, that money has been wasted, and that the Treasury is empty; but notwithstanding the state of our public funds, or rather no funds, I do not feel myself bound by any rule of duty, moral or political, in good conscience, or sound policy, to vote for this bill, or any other revenue bill, knowing the object to which the money is to be applied. Sir, I would sooner consent, were these taxes now assessed, collected, and the money in the hands of the Government, that it should suffer the same fate with the Navy Yard, and there be consumed, under the direction and superintendence of the President and the heads of the departments, than it should be applied to worse than waste—to the support of an offensive war.

The Government, for years, have been making experiments on the people, and, in my opinion, have been marching on in the broad road to destruction; they have expended millions of money, and are now destitute and unable to fulfil their promises or to execute their contracts. Shall they have more money to waste in the same useless manner? I say, no! Furnishing them with more money, to be applied to their schemes of aggrandizement, will seal the fate of these United States, and render their ruin more certain.

We have secured no important advantage by all the blood and treasure which have been expended for foreign conquest; we have gained nothing, either in reputation or territory, and have realized little else than disaster and suffering.

Is there not reason to call in question the moral as well as the political rectitude of the measure? And if we are fighting against Him, whose arm is omnipotent, we shall surely be defeated; we cannot succeed; we shall be disgraced, if not destroyed. I have been uniformly opposed to the present war, and do not feel sensible that I have, in my political conduct, been accessary to the deplorable situation in which the country now is; nor do I feel responsible for the present system of measures, nor for money, to enable the Administration to perpetuate the mischiefs which they have originated.

The granting of money and the laying of taxes to carry on the war against Canada, will not only increase the burdens, but the dangers of my constituents, for the character of the war I consider the same now as at its commencement.

I know it has been said by some gentlemen on the floor of this House, and denied by others, that the war has assumed a new character; that now it is a war of defence. I do not so consider it. The war of defence spoken of, is a war of the individual States, and they are forced into it by the measures of the General Government. It is a natural consequence—a result which was predicted at the time war was declared; and no man of sound understanding could imagine that the British Government, while ours were invading her provinces, would innocently float with her hundreds of ships on our extended and almost defenceless seacoast, and do nothing to divert the American forces from invading her territory.

In the original compact, provision was made for the protection and defence of the several individual States, and it was considered an important provision, and of some security. But several of the States, particularly Massachusetts, derive no benefit or advantage from this provision in the Constitution.

· The Administration are inattentive to their Constitutional duties; this will appear by the correspondence between Governor Strong and Mr. Monroe, Secretary of War; not only so, but the General Government have refused to indemnify Massachusetts for the expenses incurred in a war of defence, occasioned and made necessary by its own measures. An attack on Canada I consider a challenge to the enemy to molest our seaboard, and to annoy and interrupt the cities and seaport towns. And shall I, as one of the Representatives of Massachusetts, consent to load the citizens of that State with taxes to prosecute the war against Canada, and leave them to defend themselves at their own expense?

Sir, I trust that I shall never be so insensible of my duty, to the principles of justice, or so regardless of the rights and interest of my constituents. The principles of justice and of humanity, in my opinion, forbid the delegation of Massachusetts to vote for this or any other tax bill while the State is abandoned by the General Government, and that, too, in the time of peril and danger, and for no other cause than that the State declined putting her troops under the command of one of their cast-off Generals.

Though I have indirectly expressed an opinion of the duty of my colleagues, I am very sensible that they do not stand in need of my advice on this or any other subject; nor do I presume to pledge the part which they may act; I pledge no man, nor do I authorize any man to pledge me, or the part which I may act, without consultation or consent.

There is another serious objection to the imposition of these taxes. There does not appear to be any object to justify the further sacrifice of men or money. The causes of the war are removed; the Orders of Council, which were the principal ground on which the war was predicated and declared, were revoked before there was a single trespass committed; before even General Hull had issued his proclamation; before the inhabitants of Canada had been interrupted, or the laws of humanity and justice violated, and before that soil had been stained with the blood of native Americans.

· At that time the enemy seemed disposed to hold out the olive branch; they proposed an armistice, but without effect. The bosom of our Executive was then so swollen with Napoleon prospects and the glory of war, and so regardless was he of the rights and interest of the people, that he laughed at their calamities, and refused to restore the blessings of peace.

He said that the war was successful, and must be continued until the claims on the subject of impressment and seamen's rights were secured, or we had appealed to arms in vain, and could

no longer be considered an independent nation. Examine the subsequent documents and the letters of instructions given to the Commissioners at Ghent, and then decide on the soundness of his declaration. In the letters of instruction of the 25th and 27th of June, 1814, he authorizes the Commissioners to stipulate, that the subject of impressment, together with that of commerce, may be referred to a separate negotiation; nay, further, he instructs them that, on mature consideration, it had been decided that under all the circumstances incident to a prosecution of the war, they might omit any stipulation on the subject of impressment, and that the question might be so disposed of as to form no obstacle to a pacification.

In his letter of August the 11th, he says to the Commissioners, that the Government can go no further, because it will make no sacrifice of the rights or honor of the nation.

And hence it appears, from the President's own showing, that the war has been continued for more than two years, without having either the rights or honor of the nation for its object; which, in my mind, is highly reprehensible, and without excuse.

Another objection which I have to this bill, and the placing of more money in the hands of our rulers, is their incapacity to manage a war of defence, much less a war of offence.

For the correctness of this remark, I will turn you to the battle of Bladensburg; there you have a specimen of the military talents of our chieftain and his associates, all of whom were struck with terror at the first appearance of the British uniform. They were terrified at the sight of an enemy they had long affected to despise. Their passion for war seemed then to be suspended; they fled where none pursued; and, with the usual courage of vain boasters, made their escape, leaving their troops to their own discretion, and the inhabitants of the city to the mercy of an exasperated enemy; and the Commander-in-Chief of the American forces put spurs to his steed, and not venturing to look back, supposed the enemy perpetually at his heels, and fled to the mountains of Virginia.

The enemy having put our army to flight, marched unmolested into the City of Washington, and there destroyed what of the public property had escaped the *not less* destroying hand of our rulers. And where now is your magnificent Palace; where is yonder splendid Hall, with its drapery and trappings; where are your public offices? Why, they are like the cities of Sodom and Gomorrah, turned to ashes, and we are witnesses of the disgraceful catastrophe. Had the enemy with such advantages been under the command of a coward, no question but the whole city would have been laid in ruins. No sooner had the British retired, and our Commander-in-Chief been notified that he might return with perfect safety, than he, with his ordinary heroism and magnanimity, returned back into the city, calling on the nation manfully to chastise the

British for their vandalism, and for frightening and driving the American Captain-General from his domicil and duty.

This event I consider a blot on the escutcheon of the American character; and had General Hull been in the command, and fled under like circumstances with or without courage, he probably would have been arrested and tried for his life by a court martial—an evil which he has once suffered, and is now the living monument of the President's sparing mercy.

The condition of the country is every day becoming more and more alarming; and the only means in our power to correct the extravagance of our rulers, and to check them in their progress to ruin, is to withhold supplies, and to do this I consider both patriotic and Constitutional.

The advocates of the war, and those who are desirous to continue it, say there is no other course for them but to pursue the present system of measures, and ask what else can they do? I will answer: change the character of the war, abandon the mad project of conquering the Canadas, deal justly with your own citizens, and magnanimously with your enemy; recall your privateers, withdraw your troops from Canada, and make it notorious that the war is really, and in fact, a war of defence. If it shall then be continued, it will become the war of the enemy, and no longer the American war for conquest.

I am sensible we have a haughty and powerful enemy to contend with, who manifest a disposition to convince the American Government that it is not for their interest to quarrel with them.

Yet I apprehend our rulers might have peace, if they were really pacific, if they would undertake to negotiate a peace in the spirit of it, and would themselves cease to do wrong, and learn to do well.

With these impressions I am opposed to the passage of this and all other bills intended to raise either money or men for the purpose of pushing the war into Canada.

We need no addition to the skirts of our Northern territory; nor shall I ever consent to purchase misery and disgrace at the price of blood and treasure.

The question was then taken on the passage of the bill, and decided in the affirmative—yeas 106, nays 53, as follows:

YEAS—Messrs. Alexander, Anderson, Archer, Avery, Bard, Barnett, Bines, Bowen, Bradley, Brown, Burwell, Caldwell, Calhoun, Cannon, Chappell, Clark, Clendenin, Clopton, Comstock, Conard, Cox, Crawford, Creighton, Cuthbert, Dana, Davis of Pennsylvania, Denoyelles, Desha, Duvall, Earle, Eppes, Evans, Farrow, Findley, Fisk of Vermont, Fisk of New York, Forney, Forsyth, Franklin, Gholson, Goodwyn, Gourdin, Griffin, Grosvenor, Harris, Hasbrouck, Hawes, Hawkins, Hopkins of Kentucky, Howell, Hubbard, Humphreys, Ingersoll, Ingham, Irving, Irwin, Johnson of Virginia, Johnson of Kentucky, Kent of New York, Kent of Maryland, Kerr, Kershaw, Kilbourn, King of North Carolina, Lefferts, Lowndes, Lyle, McCoy, McKee, McKim McLean, Montgomery, Moore, Murfree, Nelson, Newton, Oakley, Ormsby, Parker, Pickens, Piper,

Pleasants, Rea of Pennsylvania, Rhea of Tennessee, Rich, Robertson, Sage, Sevier, Seybert, Sharp, Skinner, Smith of New York, Smith of Pennsylvania, Smith of Virg'a, Stockton, Tannehill, Taylor, Telfair, Troup, Udree, Ward of N. Jersey, Williams, Wilson of Pennsylvania, Winter, and Yancey.

NAYS—Messrs. Baylies of Massachusetts, Bayly of Virginia, Boyd, Bradbury, Breckenridge, Brigham, Butler, Caperton, Champion, Cilley, Cooper, Culpeper, Davis of Massachusetts, Ely, Gaston, Geddes, Hale, Hall, Henderson, Hulbert, Jackson of Rhode Island, Kennedy, King of Massachusetts, Law, Lewis, Lovett, Macon, Markell, Miller, Moseley, Pearson, Pickering, Pitkin, Potter, John Reed, William Reed, Ruggles, Schureman, Sheffey, Sherwood, Shipherd, Slaymaker, Stanford, Sturges, Taggart, Thompson, Vose, Ward of Massachusetts, Webster, Wheaton, White, Wilcox, and Wilson of Massachusetts.

So the bill was passed, and sent to the Senate for concurrence.

MILITIA DRAUGHTS.

The House took up the message of the Senate announcing their agreement to some and disagreement to others of the amendments made by the House to their bill for authorizing the President of the United States to call into service 80,000 militia.

[Amongst the amendments disagreed to by the Senate, was that reducing the term of service from two years to one year, and that authorizing the Executive to make requisitions on the militia officers directly, in case of the failure of the Governors to comply with the demand made on them for this object.]

Mr. LEWIS, of Virginia, moved the indefinite postponement of the bill, and the amendments thereto.

Mr. INGHAM, of Pennsylvania, moved to lay the subject on the table, (for the purpose of taking up a more urgent message from the Senate;) which motion was opposed by Mr. LEWIS, Mr. JOHNSON of Kentucky, and Mr. CALHOUN; and supported by Mr. INGHAM and Mr. FISK, and was negatived.

The question recurring on indefinite postponement, on which the yeas and nays were demanded, a short debate arose.

Mr. GASTON, of North Carolina, rose, he said, to call the attention of the House to a single fact: The bill—the indefinite postponement of which was now moved—it had been stated by the Chairman of the Committee of Ways and Means, would cost the United States twenty millions of dollars. Before encountering this vast expenditure, the House ought to feel a moral certainty that some benefit would result from it, in some degree commensurate with the magnitude of the expenditure. So far from this being the case, the strongest sentiment expressed in favor of the bill was a hope that some benefit would result from it. This amount of money, he thought, had better be expended in the old-fashioned way of procuring recruits. This bill, he added, had done more to impede the adoption of efficient measures by Congress and the Government than any bill which had been before them. The time employed on it would have been much better spent in devising means to fill the Treasury, &c., than on a bill which he believed would produce so little efficient good to the country. He trusted the House would now put an end to this project, and employ the money in the old-fashioned way of filling the ranks of the regular Army. Mr. G. purposely avoided renewing the discussion on the Constitutional question, on which he was persuaded enough had been said. ·

Mr. Troup, of Georgia, in reply to Mr. Gaston's objections, on the score of expense, said the gentleman was perhaps not aware that—the war continuing on its present footing; the undivided power of the enemy employed against us in time to come, as it had been in time past—the Government must incur an expense for defensive purposes, in the ensuing year, of not twenty merely, but of forty millions of dollars. This was a fact from which gentlemen must not at this moment shrink. Gentlemen must remember, that, if Congress are not either able or not willing to encounter this expense, the safety of the country will be jeopardized, its existence endangered.

Mr. Gaston observed, that his objection to the expense to be caused by this bill, was not that it was too much to be expended for the defence of the country. The gentleman had misapprehended him, if he supposed that he thought any expense too great to accomplish that object. His objection was, that the bill peremptorily demanded the expenditure of so much money, without any certainty that such an expenditure would be necessary. If this law were not to pass, there yet remained in existence an act authorizing the President to call into service the militia, to serve for six months. He therefore saw no necessity for passing a law compelling him, whether he deemed it necessary or not, to call into service so many militia, to serve for so long a term.

Mr. Hawkins, of Kentucky, remarked, that the statement, to which allusion had been made, that this bill would cause to the United States an expense of $20,000,000, was altogether hypothetical, and he could not, for his part, see on what data it had been founded. The bill had an object in view, viz: to obtain men to carry on the war. It offered to the militiamen to be draughted, the alternative of furnishing substitutes in the shape of recruits for the regular army. If it produced regulars, it would be of the good old-fashioned sort, which the gentleman from North Carolina so much desired, which were in the same way obtained during the Revolution. If so, the very benefit would result which the gentleman desired, of recruiting the army; and, whether it had this operation or not, the statement of the expense was altogether speculative.

Mr. Gholson, of Virginia said, no man would go further than him to raise a powerful regular army, in any way deemed most expedient. But he considered it his bounden duty, enjoined on him by the consideration of what he owed to his country and himself, not to give his assent to any such project as that embraced in the bill now before the House. He believed it would bring ruin on the country ; that it would prolong the war, by creating a dependence on a broken reed ; and he was unwilling, therefore, to squander the treasure of the nation on any such project. We shall be visited next Spring by one of the most powerful armies ever seen among any people. He asked gentlemen if they were willing such an army should be met by a raw, undisciplined militia? He meant no disrespect to the militia ; he acknowledged them brave and high spirited—but, if every man were as brave as Cæsar, without discipline, they would not be considered as competent to meet and contend with the veteran regulars of the enemy. As a militia bill, this would not be approved by the country ; and it was nothing but a militia bill at last. Let us not, said he, turn aside from the lessons of experience. From the time of Washington to this day, few men of military character, he said, had ever recommended the adoption of such a system as this.

Mr. Johnson, of Kentucky, said it was as painful to him, and no doubt to the House, to hear arguments advanced in relation to this subject, which ought not to have one moment's influence, as to take up a single moment of the House in deliberating on a question which had been bandied about the House for weeks. He would only say that this was the only proposition which had been offered for the defence of the country, and yet it was opposed, on one hand, because it was too energetic, and on the other because it was said to be feeble and inefficient. He would not dwell on the subject; but, rather than obtrude himself on the House in debating a question on which every man's mind was made up, he would only observe, that, if this bill was rejected, they would have no dependence for defence but on six months' militia, and on that point he confidently rested the issue of this question.

Mr. Calhoun, of South Carolina, made a few remarks, principally to show an error in the statement of the comparative utility of twenty millions as employed in the recruiting system, or in the defraying the expenses arising from the present bill. In the one case, he said, it would require another twenty millions to support for one year the troops to be recruited, and in the other, the twenty millions would suffice for one year's maintenance. The present bill would, he believed, produce a regular force; it might, however, produce a militia force, which, if such were the effect of the bill, would be of a quality superior, from their extended term of service, to ordinary militia.

The question of indefinite postponement was decided in the negative. For the motion 69, against it 83, as follows :

Yeas—Messrs. Baylies of Massachusetts, Bayly of Virginia, Bigelow, Boyd, Bradbury, Bradley, Breckenridge, Brigham, Burwell, Caperton, Champion, Cilley, Cooper, Cox, Culpeper, Dana, Davenport, Davis of Massachusetts, Davis of Pennsylvania, Ely, Gaston, Gholson, Grosvenor, Hale, Harris, Henderson, Howell, Hubbard, Hulbert, Jackson of Rhode Island, Kennedy, Kent of New York, Kerr, King of Massachusetts, Law, Lewis, Lovett, Macon, Markell, Miller, Moseley, Oakley, Pearson, Pickering, Pitkin, Potter, John Reed, William Reed, Rich, Ruggles, Schureman, Sheffey, Sherwood, Shipherd, Skinner, Slaymaker, Smith of New York, Stanford, Stockton, Sturges, Taggart, Thompson, Vose, Webster, Wheaton, White, Wilcox, Wilson of Massachusetts, and Winter.

NAYS—Messrs. Alexander, Anderson, Archer, Bard, Barnett, Bines, Bowen, Brown, Calhoun, Cannon, Chappell, Clendenin, Clopton, Comstock, Condict, Crawford, Creighton, Cuthbert, Denoyelles, Desha, Earle, Evans, Farrow, Findley, Fisk of Vermont, Fisk of New York, Forney, Forsyth, Franklin, Goodwyn, Gourdin, Griffin, Hall, Hasbrouck, Hawes, Hawkins, Hopkins of Ky., Humphreys, Ingham, Irving, Irwin, Johnson of Va., Johnson of Kentucky, Kent of Maryland, Kershaw, Kilbourn, King of North Carolina, Lefferts, Lowndes, Lyle, McCoy, McKee, McKim, McLean, Montgomery, Moore, Murfree, Nelson, Newton, Ormsby, Parker, Pickens, Piper, Pleasants, Rea of Pennsylvania, Rhea of Tennessee, Robertson, Sage, Sevier, Seybert, Sharp, Smith of Pennsylvania, Smith of Virginia, Strong, Tannehill, Taylor, Telfair, Troup, Udree, Ward of New Jersey, Williams, Wilson of Pennsylvania, and Yancey.

The SPEAKER then proceeded to state the amendments of this House, in which the Senate has refused to concur.

The first of these amendments was, that which proposes to strike out two years and insert one, as the term for which the draughts shall be held to service.

Mr. HAWKINS, of Kentucky, moved that the House recede from this amendment, so as to fix two years as the term of service.

The question on this motion was taken by yeas and nays, and decided in the negative—for the motion 59, against it 93, as follows:

YEAS—Messrs. Anderson, Archer, Bard, Barnett, Bines, Bowen, Brown, Caldwell, Calhoun, Chappell, Clendenin, Condict, Conard, Crawford, Creighton, Denoyelles, Evans, Findley, Fisk of New York, Forney, Forsyth, Gourdin, Griffin, Hall, Hasbrouck, Hawes, Hawkins, Hopkins of Kentucky, Hubbard, Ingersoll, Ingham, Irving, Johnson of Kentucky, Kershaw, Kilbourn, King of North Carolina, Lefferts, Lyle, McKim, Murfree, Nelson, Newton, Ormsby, Parker, Pickens, Rea of Pennsylvania, Robertson, Sage, Sharp, Smith of Pennsylvania, Strong, Tannehill, Taylor, Telfair, Troup, Udree, Williams, Wilson of Pennsylvania, and Yancey.

NAYS—Messrs. Alexander, Baylies of Massachusetts, Bayly of Virginia, Bigelow, Boyd, Bradbury, Bradley, Breckenridge, Brigham, Burwell, Caperton, Cannon, Champion, Cilley, Clopton, Cooper, Cox, Culpeper, Cuthbert, Dana, Davenport, Davis of Massachusetts, Davis of Pennsylvania, Desha, Duvall, Ely, Farrow, Fisk of Vermont, Franklin, Gaston, Geddes, Gholson, Goodwyn, Grosvenor, Hale, Harris, Henderson, Howell, Humphreys, Hulbert, Irwin, Jackson of Rhode Island, Johnson of Virginia, Kennedy, Kent of New York, Kent of Maryland, Kerr, King of Massachusetts, Law, Lewis, Lovett, Lowndes, Macon, Markell, McCoy, McKee, McLean, Miller, Moore, Moseley, Oakley, Pearson, Pickering, Pitkin, Pleasants, Potter, John Reed, William Reed, Rhea of Tennessee, Rich, Ruggles, Schureman, Sevier, Seybert, Sheffey, Sherwood, Shipherd, Skinner, Slaymaker,

Smith of Virginia, Stanford, Stockton, Sturges, Taggart, Thompson, Vose, Ward of New Jersey, Webster, Wheaton, White, Wilcox, Wilson of Massachusetts, and Winter.

So the term of service remains, at present, one year.

The House having refused to recede from this amendment, Mr. JOHNSON of Kentucky moved that the House insist on it; which motion was agreed to.

The House then proceeded, *separatim*, to insist on all its amendments to which the Senate had disagreed, and a committee of conference was appointed to join the committee of the Senate on that subject.

FRIDAY, December 23.

A message from the Senate informed the House that the Senate have passed the bill "giving further time to locate certain claims to lands confirmed by an act of Congress, entitled "An act confirming certain claims to lands in the district of Vincennes," with amendments; in which they ask the concurrence of this House.

Mr. TROUP, of Georgia, reported a bill to authorize the President of the United States to raise certain companies of rangers for the defence of the frontiers of the United States, and to repeal certain acts heretofore passed on this subject; which was twice read and committed.

BANK OF THE UNITED STATES.

On motion of Mr. FISK, of New York, the House resolved itself into a Committee of the Whole, on the bill from the Senate to incorporate the subscribers to the Bank of the United States of America.

The first section of the bill contains the leading principles of the bill, substantially as follows: The capital to consist of fifty millions of dollars, to be divided into an hundred thousand shares of five hundred dollars each; subscriptions for forty millions whereof to be opened on the third Monday in January next, at Boston, New York, Philadelphia, Richmond, Charleston, and Pittsburg. [The amendments proposed to this section by the Committee of Ways and Means contemplate an extension of the number of places of subscription, &c.] Before the question was stated on these amendments—

Mr. CLOPTON, of Virginia, moved to strike out the first section of the bill.

I have made this motion, Mr. Chairman, (said Mr. CLOPTON,) at this stage of the discussion, as being at the most proper time to try the general principle of the bill; because I cannot, under my present convictions, vote for this or any other bill to establish a bank, and therefore wish to state to this Committee the ground of Constitutional objection which I have to it. The objection is not one which admits a right to legislate on the subject proposed, but would prescribe the precise extent to which it might be exercised, and beyond which it ought not to be exercised; but it is an objection grounded on a thorough belief, the result of deliberate examination of the Constitution and reflection thereon, that there does not exist in this body any manner of right to legislate on the subject at all; that no sort of authority to do so is vested in it, either by express grant, or as incidental to any express grant.

I should, indeed, have been glad if some gentleman who patronises this scheme would have presented to us his views of the authority which he conceives the Constitution has given to pass such a bill as this; that, if I had been convinced of having been heretofore in error, I might have been left free to decide upon the measure, accordingly as it should appear to be expedient or otherwise; but, no gentleman having done so in the course of a long discussion of the bill on the same subject, which was before this body some time ago, when I was in a very low state of health, and expecting that the same silence in that respect will be observed upon this bill, I am left to presume altogether as to the ground on which the friends of the scheme rest for their authority; and, being left so to presume, I cannot conceive of any part of the Constitution on which they can rely for authority, other than the concluding clause of the eighth section of the first article of the Constitution, commonly called the sweeping clause, in the following words: "To make all laws which shall be necessary and proper for carrying into execution the foregoing powers," &c. Because there is no other part of the Constitution, that I know of, which can afford even a shadow of pretext for exercising such a power as is now proposed to be exercised by the bill before you. Because, upon every occasion which has heretofore occurred, when a right has been claimed to exercise a distinct power or powers, not expressly granted, for the avowed purpose of carrying into execution other powers that are so granted, that clause has been always resorted to; and, more especially, because the Secretary of the Treasury, the original parent of this scheme, in his letter to the chairman of the Committee of Ways and Means of the 17th of October last, after modestly suggesting the propriety of a change of opinion respecting the Constitution, to suit the "difference of times and circumstances," wound up his recommendation of the scheme with a declaration of his "opinion, that in these times it will not only 'be useful in promoting the general welfare, but ' that it is necessary and proper for carrying into ' execution some of the most important powers ' constitutionally vested in the Government;" thus using the most operative words of that clause, the words "necessary and proper for carrying into execution," &c., and evidently thereby inviting the attention of the members of this body to the clause, as being of singular importance in guiding their deliberations on the subject.

It would seem, sir, nevertheless, that even in the mind of the Secretary himself, there existed at least some doubt whether a power to establish the proposed bank is itself constitutionally vested in Congress; for he does not say that it is, but only that in his opinion "the establishment of a National Bank is necessary and proper for carry-ing into execution" some powers that are constitutionally vested in the Government, as if he intended to confine the actual Constitutional investiture to powers expressly granted. If he did intend so to confine it, he was thus far correct; for no power whatever is constitutionally vested in this body that is not expressly granted to it.

Let the opinion of the Secretary on this point be what it may, his letter will not, cannot, induce me to participate in the exercise of a power which I verily believe, is not in any manner whatever vested in this body. Even if the measure proposed should seem ever so expedient, which, however, is far from appearing to me to be the case with respect to the proposed institution; but, on the contrary, should it be established, I fear it may ultimately turn out to be a dangerous, a very dangerous political machine to this country, even if some temporary advantages should be derived from it; if some of the difficulties under which the Government is said to labor should, for the present, be obviated—difficulties, I am constrained to say, which might have been prevented by timely provisions, by other means not in any way conflicting with the Constitution—which might have precluded that great necessity, as it is represented to be, and now spoken of by some gentlemen, as in their opinion so imperiously calling for such an institution as the one proposed. But, sir, I am not prepared, nor am I willing, to admit that the Government is in such a desperate situation as to render the proposed bank necessary for its relief or accommodation, even if the right to establish the institution was unquestionable. I deny that such necessity does exist. On this occasion, therefore, as on others, I take the liberty to decide according to the dictates of my own judgment. If in this instance I judge upon mere visionary speculation in respect to the Constitution, let the observations I am about to offer to the Committee determine.

In tracing the features of the Federal Constitution, Mr. Chairman, I have always found that they present themselves to my mind as being rooted in one great fundamental principle, which is, that all the powers at the command of this Government are those only which are delegated to it. This principle is expressly recognised by an amendment to the Constitution, adopted at a very early period after the Constitution was carried into operation. The term "delegated," as used in that amendment, I consider to be a peculiar phrase of special, distinct, definite meaning, and, when applied to any particular power, not fairly susceptible of implication or involution of any distinct power, other than the power to which it is immediately and directly applied. In other words, sir, I understand the term to mean that the powers "delegated," are those only which are specifically designated by express grants. The delegation of the powers of this Government comprehends, then, no more than what are distinctly expressed in the delegation or series of positive grants.

A sort of powers, however, has been much and often spoken of, the true nature and extent of which, perhaps, have not been always distinctly and clearly understood—if, indeed, the existence of any powers at all under that denomination ought to be admitted. I allude to what are called incidental powers. The broadest latitudinarians, in relation to the powers of this body, have never, that I know of, extended their notions of its powers farther than to these two species—the powers strictly denominated "delegated" powers, or powers "expressly granted," and what they call "incidental" powers. This notion of incidental powers is deduced altogether from the same concluding clause of the 8th section of the first article of the Constitution, as being "necessary and proper" for carrying into execution the express powers specified in the preceding clauses of that section; and very much, if not the whole, of the diversity of opinion which has prevailed in relation to the powers constitutionally vested in Congress, has proceeded, perhaps, from the difference between the construction given to that clause by some, and the construction given to it by others.

According to my understanding of the word "incidental," I take it to be an adjective not only in point of grammar strictly, but that, if it can properly be applied to a power at all, it can be applied only to a power which is itself but the adjective or adjunct of another power to which it belongs, and has no existence separate from that power. In my opinion, then, what is commonly called incidental powers are not real, distinct powers, but rather modes of exercising the express powers to which they belong or are incident. Whence, sir, I consider myself perfectly justifiable in the declaration that the clause in the Constitution, which has been mentioned, and by which alone it is generally thought the exercise of those supposed incidental powers is authorized, does not embrace any distinct substantive power at all. The power now proposed to be exercised in passing the bill before you, I consider to be a distinct substantive power, as clearly as any power can be, and therefore not embraced in that clause. It is not expressly granted, as must be admitted by everybody; whence it is evident to my mind, that it is not in any manner whatever vested in this body, and therefore cannot be constitutionally exercised by this body.

Firmly, then, as the Secretary of the Treasury or other advocates of this bill may conceive the doctrine, they entertain in favor of it, to be supported by the clause in the Constitution which has been mentioned, I must beg leave to differ from them entirely in opinion. I consider it affording no solid, no substantial support at all to such a doctrine; and never in my opinion was an appellation more improperly bestowed upon anything than the appellation which has been bestowed upon that clause. On account, then, of the very extensive latitude of construction given to the clause, ascribing to it abundantly more force than it actually possesses, I have been inclined to think that it might have been better, perhaps, if the clause had never been inserted in the Constitution; or, at least, that part of it which relates to the several grants of power specified in

the preceding clauses of the section. For so far from sweeping, by which it would seem, is meant (if indeed the appellation is designed to mean anything,) a carrying along with it powers not specified in the enumeration of grants immediately preceding the clause, it carries along with it nothing at all. It imparts not a scintilla of power to Congress which the preceding enumeration does not grant. If then by the ascription to it of the sweeping quality be really meant that it imparts to Congress powers other than those enumerated in the preceding clause of the section, which are distinct from and additional to them, indefinite in number and extent, a little reflection. I should imagine, might convince any one that such construction must involve dangerous consequences—that such would be a sweeping quality indeed—that it might sweep away not only all the restrictions intended by the specification of those particular grants of power, but also every vestige of authority reserved to the States. Yes, sir, such must be its quality, such the extent of its force, if it be allowed that the clause conveys to Congress any real substantive powers not contained in the special grants enumerated; for if it be admitted that it conveys any such additional powers at all, since they are not defined, they would consequently be general as well as unlimited. To give to the clause, then, the full force which the appellation by which it has been distinguished, were it a proper application for it, would be in fact to give to Congress general, unlimited, discretionary powers. I presume, sir, that nothing would be hazarded by the declaration, were I to take upon myself to affirm that not a single member of this honorable body will admit that it contains a grant of such general, discretionary powers. Hence, sir, it is clear to my mind that those, who ascribe to the clause in question the quality which seems to have been ascribed to it, must be involved in the dilemma of either advocating so great an extent of power as existing in this body, as would render altogether useless and nugatory the special grants of power enumerated in the Constitution, and therefore much more power than they would really be willing to allow it to convey; or of admitting at last that it conveys none at all more than what the enumeration of itself grants without that clause. Hence too it is equally clear to me that, so far from conferring on this body any real powers additional to those described in the *preceding* enumeration, the clause is merely the recognition of a general principle, necessarily inherent in each grant of power, that Congress being invested with the power, may use or authorize by law a use of the natural appropriate means of carrying the power into execution, for which purpose alone such means can be used, the application of them depending entirely upon the exercise of the power granted, and without which right all the several grants expressed would be merely so many naked grants, and would convey to this body no such powers as the grants purport to convey.

Permit me, sir, to illustrate the position, I have

981   **HISTORY OF CONGRESS.**   982

DECEMBER, 1814.   *Bank of the United States.*   H. OF R.

now advanced, by a reference to one of the special grants of power enumerated; I say one of them, because it would be unnecessary to trouble the Committee with any more, although observations similar to these about to be made on the one selected might be made upon all, or nearly all of them, tending equally to establish the truth of the position, but which would require more time than perhaps it might be either convenient or agreeable to the Committee to be detained; and because it is believed that the observations on one of them may suffice for my purpose as amply as if I were to trouble the Committee with similar remarks on all of them. I will take the first grant enumerated in these words: "Congress shall have power to lay and collect taxes, duties, imposts, and excises," &c. To this grant let the clause in question be applied, and the recognition of the principle I have mentioned, may, I think, be clearly perceived. What is its operation? The words of the grant expressly confer on Congress a specific power to lay and collect taxes, duties, imposts, and excises. Now, sir, does this grant operate no further than merely to authorize Congress to provide by law that "taxes, duties," &c. on certain articles, at certain rates, or to certain amounts, shall be laid and collected, and to do no more? To confine its operation to this limit would be to ascribe no efficient meaning, to give no force at all to the words *lay* and *collect*. But they certainly have such meaning; they certainly have some force; and from the operation of the general principle, such as I have alluded to, which is necessarily inherent in the grant of "power to lay and collect taxes, duties," &c., Congress becomes vested with a right to authorize by law a use of the natural, appropriate means of causing taxes, duties, &c., to be laid and collected, which in fact is nothing more than an efficient exercise of the simple "power to lay and and collect taxes, duties," &c., such as to authorize by law the establishment of custom-houses; rules for the entrances and clearances of vessels; the employment of public armed vessels about the mouths of rivers or other inlets and on the coasts to prevent smuggling and evasions of duties directed by law to be laid on imports; the appointments of collectors, inspectors and other necessary officers for collection of the revenues arising therefrom and conveyance of them into the Treasury. So also in relation to the system of internal taxation lately established, and now enlarged, as appropriate means of carrying the system into effect, the appointments of a commissioner of that revenue, collectors, assessors and other necessary officers, and rules of proceeding in every case of taxation have been all authorized by law for the purposes of levying the taxes and bringing them into the use of the Government.

Now, sir, I beg leave to ask, would not Congress have had a Constitutional right to make laws authorizing all the several proceedings, I have just noticed, if the clause, which has been cited, had never been inserted at the end of the section which has been mentioned? Can there exist any doubt respecting its authority to have

done so? It seems to me that not a shadow of ground for doubting its authority would have existed, but that the words "shall have power to lay and collect taxes, duties, imposts, and excises," convey to this body the same extent of authority as the grant would, if it had been expressed that Congress shall have power to lay and collect taxes, duties, imposts, and excises, by making the necessary and proper laws for laying and collecting them. For a legislature cannot lay and collect taxes, duties, imposts, or excises, but by making some law or laws for laying and collecting them; that is to say, some law or laws appropriate to the purposes of laying and collecting them.

The "power to lay and collect taxes, duties, imposts, and excises" is the same, then, as a power to make laws which shall be "necessary and proper" to lay and collect taxes, duties, imposts and excises. But to make laws which shall be "necessary and proper" to lay and collect taxes, duties, &c., is the same as to make laws, which shall be "necessary and proper for carrying into execution" the power to lay and collect taxes, duties, &c. Hence, then, a power to make laws, which shall be "necessary and proper for carrying into execution" the power to lay and collect taxes, duties, imposts and excises, is the same as, and can be no more than, the simple power "to lay and collect taxes, duties, imposts and excises." It is evident, therefore, to my mind, sir, that what have been generally called powers incidental to express powers are not real, distinct powers, but nothing more than modes of exercising the express powers to which they belong, or using the natural, appropriate means of carrying them into execution, which are the only purposes, for which the means are required and to which only they can be applied; the objects, on which they can operate, being those only on which the express powers, to which they respectively belong, are exercised; that nothing more is comprehended within the meaning of the words "to make all laws, which shall be necessary and proper for carrying into execution the foregoing powers," &c., contained in the clause which has been characterized as the sweeping clause and to which so extensive a scope has been given.

Now, Mr. Chairman, if the words "to make all laws, which shall be necessary and proper," instead of having been inserted at the end of the section, had been inserted in the first grant between the word "power," and the words "to lay and collect taxes, duties," &c., so as to have made the clause read thus, "Congress shall have power to make all laws which shall be necessary and proper to lay and collect taxes, duties," &c., would any gentleman contend that Congress under this grant, so modified, would have a Constitutional right to exercise, as the means of laying and collecting taxes, duties, &c., a distinct substantive power, not expressed in the grant, and not necessarily belonging to the power of laying and collecting taxes, duties, &c., but which could be exercised independently of the exercise of that power, and operate on objects not at all connected

983   HISTORY OF CONGRESS.   984

H. of R.   Bank of the United States.   December, 1814.

with the exercise of it? Surely not; yet, it is the same thing to contend that those words of the clause at the end of the section, contain a grant of such power; for they apply to each special grant of power enumerated in the same manner, and only in the same manner, as if they had been incorporated into the body of each grant respectively. Nothing can be more clear and evident than that the words so apply, and so only. Nevertheless, sir, this famous clause has been so construed, and, I suppose, still is so construed, as to give to Congress separate, distinct, substantive powers, not expressed in the enumeration of grants. Expediency is made the basis of such construction; and from an opinion entertained by some gentlemen, that the proposed banking institution may afford a useful engine to the Government in its financial arrangements; though the correctness of that opinion is controverted by others, and is upon the whole extremely problematical: yet from their opinion merely of its expediency a right to establish the institution is claimed, and now in rapid exercise; although nothing can be more evident, than that to do so is to exercise a distinct, substantive power not contained in the enumeration—a power as distinct, and as substantive as any of those enumerated are with respect to the others on the list. This observation leads me, sir, and indeed almost irresistibly impels me, to bring to the notice of the Committee one particular grant of power enumerated, so extremely apt in my opinion, and well fitted is it for a further illustration of the principles I contend for—it is the power "to establish post offices and post roads."

Here, sir, is a power distinctly expressed in the enumeration of so much importance to the Government in affording ready, convenient and expeditious means of conveyance of intelligence, to and from every department, every branch and every individual member of every branch and department of the Government, as well as to and from the citizens of the United States at large, as to render it almost absolutely necessary for carrying on the affairs of the Government. Yet we see this power expressly designated in the enumeration. Why do we see it here expressly designated? For this very obvious and undeniable reason—that it is a power completely substantive in its nature, distinct and separate from, and independent of all others enumerated. Whence the framers of the Constitution, from a consideration of its great importance to the General Government, and the manifest propriety of vesting it in this Government, took care to insert it in the enumeration of express grants—well knowing that it could not by any possible just construction be considered as the incident of any of those express grants; and consequently that, however necessary and proper it might be for carrying on the affairs of the Government, such a power could not be constitutionally exercised, unless inserted among the express grants.

Now, Mr. Chairman, I will seriously, I will solemnly address myself to the members of this honorable body, and ask, Will any gentleman undertake to say that a power to establish such an institution as the one now proposed—an institution of such vast moment, involving interests so deep, so extensive, so fathomless, indeed, as almost to baffle the powers of human language to describe them; an institution, which, if established, as was said, and justly said, by a gentleman from New York (Mr. Oakley) some time ago in relation to the bill on the same subject then under discussion, will be likely to wield the destinies of this nation for ages to come—I say, sir, will any gentleman undertake to affirm that a power to establish such a monstrous institution as this, is not a power so completely substantive in its nature as the power to establish post offices, and to direct that the mails shall be carried on certain roads? Sir, is the sun shining in his meridian splendor clearer to the eye than it must be to every mind, high and low, wise and ignorant, that a power to create so terrific and stupendous an establishment as this, is no less a substantive power and no less distinct and separate from, and independent of, all other whatever, than is the power to establish post offices and post roads? Sir, this is too clear and too plain to need any illustration. It would be but an idle waste of time, indeed, to trouble the Committee with any observations upon it, with a view of attempting to prove more clearly that it is such a power; and if gentlemen are determined to assume the power, the exercise of it will be totally unconnected with that of any of the express powers enumerated in the Constitution, and its operation is independent of their operation as the power itself is independent of all those express powers. These are the characteristic properties of a distinct, substantive power. Strange, I think, must be the construction, then, which interprets it to be a power merely incidental to either of those express powers; and, since it is not itself one of them, my impressions are irresistible, that it is not in any matter vested in this body, and therefore cannot be constitutionally exercised by it.

Sir, if the doctrine, under which this power is assumed and exercised, should be generally tolerated and sanctioned—if this vast unlimited latitude of construction should become the established construction of the clause in the Constitution, which has been so often referred to, what will become of the great landmarks of the Constitution? Will they not in effect be all levelled with the ground? Will not the wide unbounded ocean of human affairs be then laid open to this restricted Federal Legislature, (as everybody, who pretends to know anything of the principles of the Constitution, acknowledges it to be,) to select from them such subjects as it may choose, as bases of its laws? Surely, sir, it will. All the restrictions contained in the Constitution, which have been marked out by the specification of particular powers, as limitations to Congress in legislating for these United States, will be swept away, will be annihilated; and there will be nothing to hinder a course of legislation from being pursued without restraint, without any limitation whatever but its own discretion, as to what it may determine upon as necessary or proper to be done. Sir, can a single object fall within the compass of the human imagination, which may not be also drawn within the scope of this boundless construction, and according to it be deemed a legitimate subject of Congressional legislation? Not one, sir. Every possible object of human legislation, not palpably repugnant to the first principles of our nature, of which the mind can conceive, under this very extensive construction may as well and as rightfully form a basis of legislation for this body, as the subject on which it is now acting. Admit this doctrine as correct, and in vain, sir, has your Constitution been framed upon the principles that, "the powers, not delegated to the United States by the Constitution, nor prohibited by it to the States, are reserved to the States respectively or the people." In vain has this hallowed principle been solemnly recognised and expressly incorporated into the Constitution by way of amendment. In vain have the people of these States confided in this great fundamental principle as a solemn and safe guarantee of their State sovereignties. There is not a single power heretofore considered as reserved, and heretofore deemed sacred to the States, which may not be as rightfully exercised by this body, as the power now proposed to be exercised by it; for I aver that not a single power is more completly reserved to the States, under the Constitution, than this power is—that, if this power is not reserved. no power whatever is reserved to them; and it would be preposterous indeed, to talk or think of reserved powers at all. But, sir, I undertake to aver that this power is not delegated to this body, either expressly or incidentally, and I do consider an exercise of it by this body as an unauthorized assumption, as an usurpation not only not warranted, but absolutely forbidden to it by the Constitution. I assert, then, that this monstrous construction operates no less than a complete reversal of the great and essential principle, which has been spoken of—introduces the fatal, destructive one, that all powers whatever are delegated to the United States which are not expressly reserved to the States; and, in effect, converts this Government of special, defined, express powers, into one entire consolidated Government, of general undefined powers.

Let this alarming doctrine be fully confirmed and established, what a fatal verification will it be of the presages of some of our venerable statesmen, whose mortal remains have been long since mouldering in the grave! At the ever memorable and important epoch when the people of these States were called upon to deliberate on the great and interesting question relating to the adoption of this Constitution, the minds of many were impressed with serious, with solemn, with awful apprehensions, mingled with no small degree of alarm that the very clause in the 8th section of the first article of the Constitution, which has been so often cited, might be resorted to as a ground for legislating to an extent never contemplated by the framers of the Constitution as being within the scope of its true and legitimate meaning. It was feared that the term "necessary"

contained in the clause, though qualified and restricted in its meaning by the addition of the term "proper," from the union and combination of which two qualities it was manifestly intended to apply the clause to the making of such laws only, as should have an immediate relation to, and a natural, intimate connexion with the enumerated express powers, as means or instruments of carrying them efficiently into execution, might nevertheless be so perverted as to have a construction given to the clause not confined to the limits embraced within that intention, but arbitrarily extended to laws having no manner of relation to, and no sort of natural connexion with any of those express powers—that such a principle of construction once established, the time might come when it would expand itself to the widest circuit of human discretion. The American people in general were satisfied, however, to receive the Constitution as proposed, with that clause in it, resting their hopes upon the principles and structure of it, that these were sufficiently clear and explicit to guard against the abuses and dangers so much apprehended by some.

Now, Mr. Chairman, will the thirteenth Congress of the United States, fatally to those hopes, fatally to the pleasing expectations then entertained by the people, who adopted this Constitution—will they so soon verify the presages which have been alluded to? Will they in the re-establishment of so dangerous a precedent, which was thought to have been happily demolished but three or four years ago by a refusal to recharter a similar institution—will they, I say at so early a period after that event, by a creation of the proposed huge mammoth institution, sufficiently capacious to swallow up four or five of the former establishments, thus hermetically seal and secure perhaps forever the groundwork of future assumptions of power, and this too by adopting a measure of itself fraught with inconceivable danger, the natural tendency of which will be gradually, at least, if not rapidly (and if such a sad misfortune must befall this country, I pray that it may be but gradual) to break down the barriers of the Constitution and sweep away the restrictions and limitations of power marked out by the specification of particular grants as designated in the Constitution? Sir, should such a state of things ever arrive—should such ever be the condition of this country—when this Legislature should so entirely change its true character—when it should no longer confine its proceedings to the limits of its "delegated" powers and the great leading principles of the Constitution—when these principles should be disregarded and cease to have any force, who could undertake to say how far an evil of such great magnitude might not progress? No man, I undertake to affirm, could prophetically explore the full extent of its progress.

It is not much to be wondered at, perhaps, that gentlemen should differ in opinion as to the extent in which a power, though expressly granted, ought to be exercised, when that power is in its nature limited, or qualified by the terms of the grant, to which different gentlemen may give different constructions, as on several recent occasions we have witnessed. But when a power is assumed which is not even mentioned in the Constitution, I must confess, sir, it appears to me as something much more extraordinary. If an erroneous construction in the first case should prevail at one time, the evil will be remedied, perhaps, by a more correct construction at another time, the express power being always a fixed, defined standard, to which the mind can resort; and therefore the precedent is not likely to be as durable and dangerous as in the latter case, where mere arbitrary interpretation, or opinion, having at any time prevailed, upon the general ground of necessity or expediency, without any such fixed, defined standard to judge by, one assumption is much more likely to form a durable precedent for future similar assumptions from time to time in succession, and consequently so much the more dangerous. If, therefore, it be not too late—if gentlemen have not irrevocably made up their minds upon this subject, I would beseech this honorable assembly to consider, to pause for a while, to meditate on a subject of such vast magnitude before they come to such irrevocable decision in favor of it, and not precipitately hurry into the adoption of a measure so big with momentous, incalculable consequences—consequences, the extent of which the keenest foresight of man cannot now discern—the baneful influences of the evils of which may be such as the most eagle-eyed statesman our country produces may not be able to trace, until they shall have extended themselves beyond the reach of any practicable remedy!

When Mr. CLOPTON had concluded—the question being about to be put on his motion without debate—

Mr. GASTON, of North Carolina, took the floor. Among the most alarming indications of the times, he remarked, was the apathy which pervaded the House on this occasion; an apathy resembling the numbness which generally precedes mortal dissolution, under the influence of which a question of such importance as this was about to be taken without debate and almost without deliberation. If the bill would produce that effect which its friends predicted, it would prove a beneficial and valuable institution; if fraught with the mischiefs which he saw in it, its passage would bring with it certain destruction to the nation. He took it for granted, from the course of proceedings which had taken place in the House when this subject was before under consideration, that all hope of obtaining a bank at all resembling what banks have heretofore been, must now cease; and that the institution embraced by this bill, if it passed, would be a mere paper bank, and nothing else, from which no benefit could result to the Government or the community. He examined the character of this bill, and particularly objecting to the extent of the capital; the limited proportion of specie to be employed in it; and the power to suspend specie payments. Upon a full view of all its features, he denied that it would restore public credit, or establish an adequate circulating medium, the

purposes which its friends hoped it would accomplish. It would, on the contrary, from the moment of its establishment, give birth to a monstrous scene of stock-jobbing and speculation, always detrimental to the public credit. By a system of rigid economy and carrying into effect the taxes agreed to by the House, he said. he had some hope that the Government would weather the storm with which it was assailed, without national bankruptcy; but, if Congress passed a bill of this kind, he conscientiously believed it would not be possible to avoid the evil; and that, if they passed this, they might as well at the same time pass a bill of national bankruptcy.

Mr. McKIM, of Maryland, said without saying how he should vote on the final question, he should vote against the motion to strike out the first section of the bill in the present stage of it, from motives of respect to the co-ordinate branch of the Legislature from which the bill came, and to those who advocated the bill in this House.

The motion to strike out the first section of the bill was then decided in the negative by the following vote: For striking it out 50, against it 71.

Mr. FISK then briefly explained the character of this bill, and in what respect the amendments proposed by the committee would change the features of it. The bill, as it came from the Senate, and as it now stands, proposes that the forty millions to be subscribed by individuals, shall be at the rate of twenty-seven millions of dollars in war stock, five millions in specie, and eight millions in Treasury notes; and that subscriptions shall be opened in Boston, Baltimore, New York, Philadelphia, Richmond, Charleston, and Pittsburg. The committee had recommended to reduce the proportion subscribable by individuals to thirty-five millions, of which twenty to be in public stock, five in specie, and ten in Treasury notes. The details of the bill being nearly the same as those of the bill originally reported in this House, were not proposed to be changed, except that the committee had recommended that books of subscription should be opened at one place in every State, in conformity with what appeared to be the sentiment of the House when the bill was before under consideration.

The amendments proposed by the Committee of Ways and Means to the bill were separately considered, and agreed to by a considerable majority.

The Committee proceeded in further consideration of the bill—rose, after 4 o'clock, reported progress, and obtained leave to sit again.

SATURDAY, December 24.

Mr. CALHOUN, from the committee to whom was referred, on the 23d ultimo, the report of the Secretary of War, relating to an uniform system of discipline for the Army of the United States, reported the following resolution:

Resolved, That the Secretary of War be directed to appoint a Board of Officers, to modify " the rules and regulations for the field exercise and manœuvres of the French Infantry," as translated by Macdonald, so as to make them correspond with the organization of the Army of the United States, and to make such additions and retrenchments as may be thought proper; and to lay the same, as soon as possible, before this House.

The resolution was read, and agreed to.

The amendments proposed by the Senate to the bill "giving farther time to locate certain claims to lands confirmed by an act of Congress, entitled "An act confirming certain claims to lands in the District of Vincennes," were read, and concurred in by the House.

BANK OF THE UNITED STATES.

On motion of Mr. FISK, of New York, the House again resolved itself into a Committee of the Whole, on the bill to incorporate the subscribers to the Bank of the United States of America.

The whole of the day was consumed in the discussion of the details and propositions to amend this bill, without giving birth to any material amendments.

The amendments made in the Committee were reported to the House, and agreed to, before the House adjourned.

As amended, the bill exhibits the following features, viz:

The capital to consist of fifty millions of dollars, divided into shares of five hundred dollars each; subscribable and payable as follows: by the Government, in stock to bear an interest of four per cent. per annum; fifteen millions, by individuals; the remaining thirty-five millions, payable as follows, viz: five millions in specie, ten millions in Treasury notes, and twenty millions in what is usually called the war-stock. The bank to commence its operations so soon as eleven million five hundred thousand dollars are paid in, in the proportions before mentioned, of specie, Treasury notes and stock.

Other amendments were proposed to the bill; when the House adjourned, without taking a question on the bill's going to a third reading.

MONDAY, December 26.

Mr. TROUP, from the managers appointed by this House to attend a conference with the managers on the part of the Senate, on the disagreeing votes of the two Houses on the amendments proposed by the House of Representatives to the bill from the Senate "to authorize the President of the United States to call upon the several States and Territories thereof for their respective quotas of eighty thousand militia, for the defence of the frontiers of the United States against invasion," made a report; which was read, and ordered to lie on the table.

MATTHEW GUY.

Mr. INGERSOLL, of Pennsylvania, rose to make a motion. He said there was now an individual in this town, by the name of Matthew Guy, a native of the town of Dumfries, who, by an extraordinary act of bravery and heroism, had himself captured a British officer and four British seamen. He was in an oyster boat in the neighborhood of Chippewanzie, into which he was pursued by a British vessel; and, after he got into the creek, a barge was sent after him with a midshipman and four men. This individual, finding he must be overtaken, went ashore in a small skiff, and concealed himself on the margin of the creek with his duck-gun, directing a mulatto man who was the only person in company with him, to pursue his way up the creek. The mulatto man accordingly steered up the creek, under a sharp fire from the barge which was in pursuit. When the barge passed within a convenient distance, Mr. Guy discharged his gun with such steady aim at it, as to wound four of the five men on board, who immediately cried for quarter; which being readily granted, they pushed ashore while Guy was loading his gun a second time. On finding the inferiority of force to which they had surrendered their arms, the prisoners were disposed to attempt a rescue; but their captor presented his piece a second time at them, and they deemed it proper to submit, the officer and three others being already wounded. The brave man who performed this exploit, delivered his prisoners up to the militia in St. Mary's county, by whom they had been brought to the city. Though this case did not come within the letter, he said it certainly did within the equity of the law, which allows a bounty of one hundred dollars on every prisoner taken by privateers; because this individual had redeemed from captivity one of our naval officers and four of our seamen by obtaining the means of their exchange; which was the principle on which the act in question was passed. He was desirous to extend the provision of that bill to this individual; and therefore moved the following resolution:

Resolved, That the Committee on Naval Affairs be instructed to inquire into the expediency of allowing a bounty to Matthew Guy, for five English prisoners captured by him.

The motion was agreed to without opposition.

BANK OF THE UNITED STATES.

The House proceeded to consider the report of the Committee of the Whole on the bill from the Senate "to incorporate the subscribers to the Bank of the United States of America;" and the amendments reported by the Committee of the Whole to the said bill being again read, were amended, and severally concurred in by the House, except the amendment which goes to add a new section to the bill.

The said section was further amended.

The question was then taken to concur with the Committee of the Whole in the said new section, which is as follows:

SEC. 14. *And be it further enacted*, That it shall at all times be lawful for a committee of either House of Congress, appointed for that purpose, to inspect the books, and to examine into the proceedings of the corporation hereby created; and to report whether the provisions of this charter have been by the same violated or not. And whenever any committee, as aforesaid, shall find and report, or the President of the United States shall have reason to believe, that the charter has been violated, it may be lawful for Congress to direct, or the President to order, a *scire facias* to be sued out of the Circuit Court for the District of Pennsylvania, in the name of the United States, (which shall be executed upon the President of the corporation for the time being, at least fifteen days before the commencement of the term of said court,) calling on the said corporation to show cause wherefore the charter hereby granted shall not be declared forfeited: And it shall be lawful for the said court, upon the return of the said *scire facias*, to examine into the truth of the alleged violation, and if such violation be made appear, then to pronounce and adjudge that the said charter is forfeited and annulled : *Provided, however*, Every issue of fact which may be joined between the United States and the corporation aforesaid, shall be tried by jury. And it shall be lawful for the court aforesaid to require the production of such of the books of the corporation as it may deem necessary for the ascertainment of the controverted facts, and the final judgment of the circuit court aforesaid shall be examinable in the Supreme Court of the United States by writ of error, and may be there reversed or affirmed, according to the usages of law.

The concurrence of the House in this amendment was opposed by Mr. INGHAM of Pennsylvania, Mr. FORSYTH of Georgia, and Mr. HAWKINS, of Kentucky ; and supported by Mr. GASTON of North Carolina, Mr. SHEFFEY of Virginia, Mr. OAKLEY of New York; and opposed and advocated by other gentlemen.

The question on concurrence therein was decided in the affirmative.—For concurrence 95, against it 36, as follows:

YEAS—Messrs. Bard, Baylies of Massachusetts, Bayly of Virginia, Bigelow, Bowen, Boyd, Bradbury, Breckenridge, Brigham, Caperton, Caldwell, Calhoun, Cannon, Champion, Cilley, Clark, Clendenin, Clopton, Cooper, Cox, Crawford, Culpeper, Davenport, Davis of Massachusetts, Desha, Earl, Ely, Evans, Farrow, Fisk of Vermont, Forney, Franklin, Gaston, Gholson, Gourdin, Hale, Hall, Hasbrouck, Hawes, Henderson, Humphreys, Hulbert, Irving, Jackson of Rhode Island, Johnson of Virginia, Kennedy, Kent of New York, Kent of Maryland, Kilbourn, King of North Carolina, Law, Lovett, Lowndes, Macon, Markell, McKee, McLean, Miller, Montgomery, Moseley, Nelson, Newton, Oakley, Parker, Pearson, Pickering, Pleasants, Potter, John Reed, William Reed, Rich, Ringgold, Robertson, Ruggles, Schureman, Seybert, Sharp, Sheffey, Sherwood, Shipherd, Slaymaker, Smith of Virginia, Stanford, Stockton, Taggart, Taylor, Thompson, Vose, Ward of Massachusetts, Ward of New Jersey, Wheaton, White, Wilcox, Wilson of Massachusetts, and Yancey.

NAYS—Messrs. Alexander, Anderson, Archer, Bines, Brown, Comstock, Conard, Creighton, Cuthbert, Dana, Davis of Pa., Findley, Forsyth, Griffin, Hawkins, Hopkins of Kentucky, Ingersoll, Ingham, Kerr, Kershaw, King of Massachusetts, Lefferts, Lyle, McCoy, Moore, Murfree, Rea of Pennsylvania, Rhea of Tennessee, Sage, Skinner, Smith of Pennsylvania, Strong, Tannehill, Telfair, Udree, and Wilson of Pennsylvania.

And on motion, the House adjourned until tomorrow.

TUESDAY, December 27.

The SPEAKER laid before the House a representation from James Monroe, acting Secretary of State; Alexander J. Dallas, Secretary of the Treasury ; and Richard Rush, Attorney General, Commissioners appointed by the act " providing for the indemnification of certain claimants of public lands in the Mississippi Territory," commonly called the Yazoo claims, passed on the 31st of March, 1814, representing their inability, owing to the multiplied and laborious *duties* which demand their attention in their respective departments, to discharge the *duties* enjoined upon them by the said act, and suggesting the propriety of appointing other Commissioners to execute the provisions of the act, whose attention shall not be engrossed by other public duties. The said representation was read, and referred to Messrs. OAKLEY, LOWNDES, and BAYLIES, of Massachusetts.

Mr. McKEE, from the Committee on Public Lands, reported a bill regulating the sale of certain reserved sections of land in the State of Ohio; which was read twice, and committed to a Committee of the Whole on Thursday next.

Mr. McKEE also reported a bill attaching to the Canton district, in the State of Ohio, the tract of land lying between the foot of the rapids of the Miami of Lake Erie and the Connecticut Western Reserve; which was read twice, and committed to the Committee of the Whole on the bill last mentioned.

MILITIA DRAUGHTS.

On motion of Mr. TROUP, of Georgia, the House proceeded to consider the report of the committee of conference on the disagreeing votes of the two Houses on the bill to authorize the President of the United States to call into service eighty thousand militia for the defence of the frontiers of the United States.

The first proposition of the committee relates to the term of service of the militia, and proposes that a compromise between the two Houses shall take place, the Senate receding six months and the House advancing six months in the service, so as to fix it at eighteen months.

Mr. TROUP explained that this report was the result of compromise between the two Houses; and Mr. STOCKTON stated that, though he had consented, as a member of the committee of conference, to the report being made, he was opposed to it, as was a majority of the conference committee of this House.

Mr. FARROW made a short speech in opposition to the report, the object of which was to explain the reason why he, who had voted in favor of the bill, should now vote against this report; it was, because he considered the militia character of the bill to be changed, and that, as proposed to be amended, it would possess the conscriptive character. He made a number of observations, principally drawn from our history, to show that the militia were, and always would be, under proper officers, an effective force.

The question, on agreeing to this part of the

report, was decided—for concurrence 64, against it 73, as follows:

YEAS—Messrs. Alston, Anderson, Archer, Avery, Bard, Barnett, Bines, Bowen, Brown, Caldwell, Calhoun, Chappell, Clark, Clendenin, Comstock, Conard, Crawford, Creighton, Denoyelles, Duvall, Earle, Evans, Findley, Forney, Forsyth, Glasgow, Gourdin, Griffin, Hall, Hasbrouck, Hawes, Hubbard, Humphreys, Ingersoll, Ingham, Irwin, Johnson of Virginia, Kilbourn, King of North Carolina, Lefferts, Lyle, Markell, McKee, McLean, Montgomery, Murfree, Nelson, Newton, Ormsby, Parker, Pleasants, Rea of Pennsylvania, Rhea of Tennessee, Robertson, Sage, Sharp, Smith of Pennsylvania, Strong, Tannehill, Taylor, Troup, Udree, Williams, Wilson of Pennsylvania, and Yancey.

NAYS—Messrs. Alexander, Baylies of Massachusetts, Bigelow, Boyd, Bradbury, Breckenridge, Caperton, Cannon, Champion, Cilley, Clopton, Cooper, Cox, Culpeper, Cuthbert, Dana, Davenport, Davis of Massachusetts, Davis of Pennsylvania, Desha, Ely, Farrow, Fisk of Vermont, Franklin, Gaston, Geddes, Gholson, Hale, Harris, Henderson, Howell, Jackson of Rhode Island, Kennedy, Kent of New York, Kent of Maryland, King of Massachusetts, Law, Lovett, Lowndes, Macon, Markell, McCoy, Miller, Moore, Moseley, Oakley, Pickering, Pitkin, Potter, John Reed, William Reed, Rich, Ruggles, Schureman, Seybert, Sheffey, Sherwood, Skinner, Slaymaker, Smith of New York, Smith of Virginia, Stanford, Stockton, Sturges, Taggart, Thompson, Vose, Ward of Massachusetts, Webster, Wheaton, White, Wilcox, and Wilson of Massachusetts.

So the House refused to concur in extending the term of service from twelve to eighteen months.

The second proposition of the committee of conference is, that the House shall recede from an amendment, the object of which is to authorize the Executive, in case of neglect or refusal of the Governors of the States to execute the provisions of the law, to call directly on the militia officers of the States to carry them into effect.

On the question to agree to this proposition, an interesting debate of considerable length took place, in the course of which, it was advocated by Messrs. TROUP, STOCKTON, PICKERING, KING of Massachusetts, SHIPHERD, and WEBSTER; and opposed by Messrs. ROBERTSON, HAWKINS, FORSYTH, GHOLSON, CUTHBERT, and FISK of Vermont.

The discussion ended in the refusal of the House to agree to the proposition of the committee of conference by the following vote:—For agreeing to it 69, against it 80.

YEAS—Messrs. Baylies of Massachusetts, Bigelow, Boyd, Bradbury, Bradley, Breckenridge, Brigham, Caperton, Cannon, Champion, Cilley, Clopton, Cooper, Cox, Culpeper, Davenport, Davis of Massachusetts, Ely, Farrow, Gaston, Geddes, Hale, Henderson, Howell, Hulbert, Jackson of Rhode Island, Kent of New York, King of Massachusetts, King of North Carolina, Law, Lovett, Macon, Markell, McKee, Miller, Montgomery, Moore, Moseley, Oakley, Pearson, Pickering, Pitkin, Potter, John Reed, William Reed, Rich, Ruggles, Schureman, Sheffey, Sherwood, Shipherd, Slaymaker, Smith of New York, Stanford, Stockton, Sturges, Taggart, Taylor, Thompson, Troup, Vose, Ward

13th CON. 3d SESS.—32

of Massachusetts, Ward of New Jersey, Webster, Wheaton, White, Wilcox, Wilson of Massachusetts, and Winter—69.

NAYS—Messrs. Alexander, Alston, Anderson, Archer, Bard, Barnett, Bines, Bowen, Brown, Caldwell, Calhoun, Chappell, Clark, Clendenin, Comstock, Conard, Crawford, Creighton, Cuthbert, Dana, Davis of Pa., Denoyelles, Desha, Duvall, Earle, Evans, Findley, Fisk of Verm't, Forney, Forsyth, Gholson, Glasgow, Gourdin, Griffin, Hall, Harris, Hasbrouck, Hawes, Hawkins, Hopkins of Kentucky, Hubbard, Humphreys, Ingersoll, Ingham, Irwin, Johnson of Virginia, Kennedy, Kent of Maryland, Kerr, Kershaw, Kilbourn, Lefferts, Lowndes, Lyle, McCoy, McLean, Murfree, Newton, Ormsby, Parker, Pickens, Pleasants, Rea of Pennsylvania, Rhea of Tennessee, Ringgold, Robertson, Sage, Sevier, Seybert, Sharp, Skinner, Smith of Pennsylvania, Smith of Virginia, Tannehill, Telfair, Udree, Williams, Wilson of Pennsylvania, and Yancey—80.

The House then agreed to the other propositions of the committee of conference; and,

On motion of Mr. TROUP, the House resolved to *insist* on the amendments from which it had just refused to recede; and a message was sent to the Senate to acquaint them of this determination.

BANK OF THE UNITED STATES.

The House then resumed the consideration of the bill to incorporate the subscribers to the Bank of the United States of America.

A motion was made by Mr. HALE to amend the bill, by striking out the thirteenth section of the bill, which authorizes occasional suspension of payments in specie by the bank: Whereupon,

Mr. INGERSOLL, of Pennsylvania, required the previous question, which precludes all further debate or amendment of the bill. This call being duly sustained, the previous question was taken, and decided—for taking the main question 72, against taking it 70.

YEAS—Messrs. Alexander, Alston, Anderson, Archer, Avery, Bard, Barnett, Bines, Brown, Caldwell, Cannon, Chappell, Clark, Clendenin, Comstock, Conard, Creighton, Cuthbert, Dana, Davis of Pennsylvania, Denoyelles, Evans, Findley, Fisk of Vermont, Forney, Forsyth, Gholson, Gourdin, Griffin, Hall, Harris, Hopkins of Kentucky, Hubbard, Humphreys, Ingersoll, Ingham, Irving, Irwin, Kennedy, Kent of Maryland, Kerr, Kershaw, Kilbourn, King of North Carolina, Lefferts, Lowndes, Lyle, McCoy, McLean, Moore, Murfree, Newton, Ormsby, Parker, Pleasants, Rea of Pennsylvania, Rhea of Tennessee, Rich, Ringgold, Sage, Seybert, Skinner, Smith of Pennsylvania, Smith of Virginia, Tannehill, Taylor, Telfair, Troup, Udree, Ward of New Jersey, Williams, Wilson of Pennsylvania, and Yancey.

NAYS—Messrs. Baylies of Massachusetts, Bigelow, Bowen, Boyd, Bradbury, Brigham, Caperton, Calhoun, Champion, Cilley, Clopton, Cooper, Cox, Crawford, Culpeper, Dana, Davenport, Davis of Mass., Desha, Duvall, Ely, Farrow, Franklin, Gaston, Hale, Hasbrouck, Hawes, Hawkins, Henderson, Howell, Hulbert, Jackson of Rhode Island, Johnson of Virginia, Kent of New York, King of Massachusetts, Law, Lovett, Macon, Markell, McKee, Miller, Montgomery, Moseley, Oakley, Pearson, Pickering, Pitkin, Potter, John Reed, William Reed, Robertson, Ruggles, Schureman,

Sharp, Shaffey, Sherwood, Shipherd, Slaymaker, Smith of New York, Stanford, Stockton, Thompson, Vose, Ward of Massachusetts, Webster, Wheaton, White, Wilcox, Wilson of Massachusetts, and Winter.

The previous question having thus been decided in the affirmative—a motion was made to lay the bill and amendments on the table.

The CHAIR decided (Mr. MACON, in the absence of Mr. CHEVES, occupying the Chair) that the motion was not in order, inasmuch as the House having decided that the main question shall be now put, no other motion can obtain, unless a motion to adjourn.

An appeal was taken from this decision of the Chair; which, after some debate, was confirmed by yeas and nays, by the following vote: In favor of the Chair 108, against it 36.

Mr. GASTON, of North Carolina, then took an appeal from the decision of the Chair, (Mr. MACON still occupying it,) that the *main question* was, that the bill should pass to a third reading. He contended that the *main* question was, that on the amendment under discussion when the previous question was called.

[The question has, more than once, been decided in the same manner by the present and late Speaker, and affirmed with much solemnity.]

After some debate, the decision of the Chair was affirmed by the following vote: In favor of the decision 91, against it 52.

The main question, viz: Shall the amendments be engrossed, and, together with the bill, be read a third time? was then put, and decided as follows:

YEAS—Messrs. Alexander, Alston, Anderson, Archer, Avery, Bard, Barnett, Bines, Bradley, Brown, Caldwell, Calhoun, Cannon, Chappell, Clark, Clendenin, Comstock, Conard, Creighton, Cuthbert, Dana, Davis of Pennsylvania, Denoyelles, Duvall, Earle, Farrow, Findley, Fisk of New York, Forney, Forsyth, Gourdin, Griffin, Harris, Hasbrouck, Hawes, Hawkins, Hopkins of Kentucky, Hubbard, Ingersoll, Ingham, Irving, Irwin, Kent of Maryland, Kerr, Kershaw, Kilbourn, King of North Carolina, Lefferts, Lowndes, Lyle, McCoy, McKee, McLean, Montgomery, Moore, Murfree, Nelson, Ormsby, Parker, Pickens, Pleasants, Rea of Pennsylvania, Rhea of Tennessee, Rich, Ringgold, Robertson, Sage, Sevier, Sharp, Skinner, Smith of Pennsylvania, Smith of Virginia, Strong, Tannehill, Taylor, Telfair, Udree, Ward of New Jersey, Williams, Wilson of Pennsylvania, and Yancey—81.

NAYS—Messrs. Baylies of Massachusetts, Bigelow, Bowen, Boyd, Bradbury, Brigham, Butler, Caperton, Champion, Cilley, Clopton, Cooper, Cox, Crawford, Davenport, Davis of Massachusetts, Desha, Ely, Evans, Franklin, Gaston, Gholson, Hale, Hall, Henderson, Humphreys, Jackson of Rhode Island, Johnson of Virginia, Kennedy, King of Massachusetts, Law, Lovett, Macon, Markell, Miller, Moseley, Newton, Oakley, Pearson, Pickering, Pitkin, Potter, John Reed, William Reed, Ruggles, Schureman. Seybert, Shaffey, Sherwood, Shipherd, Slaymaker, Stanford, Stockton, Thompson, Vose, Ward of Massachusetts, Webster, Wheaton, White, Wilcox, Wilson of Massachusetts, and Winter—62.

So the bill was ordered to be read a third time to-morrow; and the House adjourned.

On motion of Mr. PICKENS, the Committee on Military Affairs were instructed to inquire into the expediency of making a change in the organization of the corps of artillery and engineers, which may allow the officers thereof to be placed on a more favorable footing in regard to promotion.

On motion of Mr. KILBOURN,

Resolved, That so much of the report of the Committee of Revisal and Unfinished Business, made to this House on the 8th ultimo, and now lying upon the table, as relates to the "bill for the more effectual defence of the Northwestern frontier," be referred to a select committee, with leave to report by bill or otherwise.

Mr. KILBOURN, Mr. McKEE, Mr. CUTHBERT, Mr. HENDERSON, Mr. WILCOX, Mr. KENNEDY, and Mr. PARKER, were appointed the committee.

The bill from the Senate, "for the relief of John C. Hurlburt, of Chatham, in the State of Connecticut," was read the third time, and passed.

Mr. YANCEY, of North Carolina, from the Committee of Claims, made a report on the petition of Benjamin Wells, and others. The case of these persons is that of persons who suffered injury in their property and persons in the year 1794, and who pray remuneration therefor. The report was accompanied by a letter from the Secretary of the Treasury, recommending the authorizing of legal provision for the adjustment of their accounts. The report having been read—

Mr. YANCEY, of North Carolina. reported a bill for the relief of Benjamin Wells and others; which was twice read, and referred to a Committee of the Whole.

BANK OF THE UNITED STATES.

The bill to incorporate the subscribers to the Bank of the United States of America, was announced for its third reading.

Mr. GASTON, of North Carolina, moved to recommit the bill to the Committee of Ways and Means with instructions to report an amendment thereto, authorizing the twenty millions of dollars (therein directed to be paid in gold or silver coin, or in public stock created since the declaration of war) to be paid in gold or silver coin, or in any public debt contracted or to be contracted, which shall at the time of subscription bear an accruing interest of six per cent.

On suggestion of Mr. SHARP, of Kentucky, Mr. GASTON included in his motion the following further instruction to the committee: "And that ' the said committee be also instructed to extend ' the time for opening subscriptions at New Or- ' leans, Nashville, Lexington, and Chilicothe, ' (the time fixed in the bill being the third Mon- ' day in January)—and to strike out so much of ' the 18th fundamental rule as directs that all ' specie payments during the present war shall be ' made at Philadelphia."

The motion for the recommitment gave rise to a long and animated debate, in which Messrs. GASTON, OAKLEY, SHEFFEY, SHARP, McKEE,

KING of Massachusetts, and PICKERING, supported the motion; and Messrs. INGHAM, HOPKINS, FISK of Vermont, and FORSYTH, opposed it.

The debate turned principally on the question of the expediency of restricting the privilege of subscription to the bank to such stock of the United States, now in existence, as has been created since the war, and excluding all stock previously existing, and which may be hereafter created. Interwoven with this discussion, were some remarks on both sides, on the general question of establishing such a bank as that proposed by the bill, and particularly on the celerity with which the minority alleged it had been pushed through the House.

The recommitment was also advocated by one or two gentlemen friendly to the principle of the bill, on other grounds than that above stated; the principal of which was, a desire to extend the time for opening the subscriptions at distant places, for which it was argued that much too short a time was now allowed by the bill.

The question, on recommitment of the bill, was decided by yeas and nays—for recommitment 79, against it 76, as follows:

YEAS—Messrs. Bard, Baylies of Massachusetts, Bayly of Virginia, Bigelow, Bowen, Boyd, Bradbury, Breckenridge, Brigham, Caperton, Calhoun, Cannon, Champion, Cilley, Clopton, Cooper, Cox, Crawford, Culpeper, Davenport, Davis of Massachusetts, Desha, Ely, Evans, Farrow, Gaston, Geddes, Glasgow, Gourdin, Hale, Harris, Hawes, Henderson, Howell, Hulbert, Irving, Jackson of Rhode Island, Kennedy, Kent of New York, Law, Lovett, Macon, Markell, McKee, Miller, Montgomery, Moseley, Oakley, Pearson, Pickering, Pitkin, Potter, John Reed, William Reed, Robertson, Ruggles, Schureman, Sharp, Sheffey, Sherwood, Shipherd, Slaymaker, Smith of New York, Stanford, Stockton, Stuart, Sturges, Taggart, Thompson, Vose, Ward of Massachusetts, Ward of New Jersey, Webster, Wheaton, White, Wilcox, Wilson of Massachusetts, and Winter.

NAYS—Messrs. Alexander, Alston, Anderson, Archer, Avery, Barnett, Bines, Bradley, Brown Butler, Caldwell, Chappel, Clark, Clendenin, Comstock, Conard, Creighton, Cuthbert, Dana, Davis of Pennsylvania, Denoyelles, Duvall, Earle, Findley, Fisk of Vermont, Fisk of New York, Forney, Forsyth, Franklin, Gholson, Griffin, Hasbrouck, Hawkins, Hopkins of Kentucky, Hubbard, Humphreys, Ingersoll, Ingham, Irving, Johnson of Virginia, Kent of Maryland, Kerr, Kershaw, Kilbourn, King of North Carolina, Lefferts, Lowndes, Lyle, McCoy, McLean, Moore, Murfree, Nelson, Newton, Ormsby, Parker, Pickens, Pleasants, Rea of Pennsylvania, Rhea of Tennessee, Rich, Ringgold, Sage, Sevier, Seybert, Skinner, Smith of Pennsylvania, Smith of Virginia, Strong, Tannehill, Taylor, Telfair, Udree, Williams, Wilson of Pennsylvania, and Yancey.

THURSDAY, December 29.

Mr. SEYBERT presented a petition of the representatives of the religious society of friends (Quakers) in Pennsylvania, New Jersey, Delaware, and parts adjacent, praying that members of their society may be exempt from military duty, and that the National Legislature will consent, by a solemn act, to the rights of conscience.—Referred to the Committee on Military Affairs.

A message from the Senate informed the House that the Senate have passed a bill "to provide additional revenues for defraying the expenses of Government, and maintaining the public credit, by laying duties on various goods, wares, and merchandise, manufactured within the United States," with amendments. The Senate have also passed a bill "to provide for leasing certain lands reserved for the support of schools in the Mississippi Territory;" in which amendments and bill they ask the concurrence of this House. The Senate have also resolved that a committee of three members be appointed, who, jointly with such committee as the House of Representatives may appoint, shall be a committee to inquire into the expenses of stationery, printing, and binding, for both Houses of Congress, and into the expediency of establishing permanent rules for regulating and conducting the printing and binding, and for the supply of stationery for the Senate and House of Representatives; and Mr. DAGGETT, Mr. FROMENTIN, and Mr. MORROW, have been appointed the committee on the part of the Senate.

BANK OF THE UNITED STATES.

Mr. ARCHER, of Maryland, from the Committee of Ways and Means, to whom was referred for amendment the bill from the Senate to incorporate the subscribers to the Bank of the United States of America, reported three amendments thereto, in conformity to the instructions of the House.

The first amendment proposes to substitute the second Monday in February for the third Monday in January, as the day on which the books of subscription to the bank shall be opened.—Agreed to.

The second amendment proposes to strike out so much of the bill as describes the (war) stock which shall be subscribable to the bank, and in lieu thereof to insert "any public debt of the United States contracted, or to be contracted, which at the time of payment shall bear an accruing interest of six per centum per annum."

After a few words from Mr. GASTON and Mr. OAKLEY, expressive of a hope that this amendment would pass, and from Mr. INGHAM and Mr. DESHA to the contrary, the question on this amendment was decided without debate—For the amendment 72, against it 73, as follows:

YEAS—Messrs. Baylies of Massachusetts, Bayly of Virginia, Bigelow, Bowen, Boyd, Bradbury, Breckenridge, Brigham, Calhoun, Champion, Cilley, Clark, Clopton, Cooper, Cox, Culpeper, Davenport, Davis of Massachusetts, Ely, Gaston, Geddes, Glasgow, Hale, Henderson, Howell, Humphreys, Hulbert, Jackson of Rhode Island, Johnson of Virginia, Kennedy, Kent of New York, Kent of Maryland, King of Massachusetts, Law, Lovett, Macon, Markell, McKee, Miller, Montgomery, Moseley, Oakley, Pearson, Pickering, Pitkin, Potter, John Reed, William Reed, Rich, Ruggles, Schureman, Sharp, Sheffey, Sherwood, Shipherd, Slaymaker, Smith of New York, Stanford, Stockton, Stuart, Sturges, Taggart, Thompson, Vose, Ward of Massachusetts, Ward of New Jersey, Webster, Wheaton, White, Wilcox, Wilson of Massachusetts, and Winter.

NAYS—Messrs. Alexander, Alston, Anderson, Archer, Avery, Bard, Barnett, Bines, Bradley, Brown, Butler, Caldwell, Cannon, Chappell, Clendenin, Comstock, Conard, Crawford, Creighton, Cuthbert, Dana, Davis of Pennsylvania, Denoyelles, Desha, Duvall, Evans, Farrow, Findley, Fisk of Vermont, Fisk of New York, Forney, Forsyth, Franklin, Gholson, Griffin, Harris, Hasbrouck, Hawes, Hawkins, Hopkins of Kentucky, Hubbard, Ingersoll, Ingham, Irwin, Kerr, Kershaw, Kilbourn, Lefferts, Lyle, McCoy, McLean, Moore, Murfree, Nelson, Newton, Ormsby, Parker, Pleasants, Rea of Tennessee, Rhea of Tennessee, Ringgold, Robertson, Sage, Smith of Pennsylvania, Smith of Virginia, Strong, Tannehill, Taylor, Troup, Udree, Williams, Wilson of Pennsylvania, and Yancey.

So the House refused to accept this amendment.

The other amendment proposes to strike out that part of one of the fundamental rules which restricts the payment of the notes in specie to such as are presented at the principal bank.

The adoption of this amendment was opposed by Mr. ARCHER, Mr. FORSYTH, Mr. INGHAM, Mr. HAWKINS, and others, on the ground, generally, that the provision would not in fact be effectual, because it would be in the power of the bank, notwithstanding such provision, to issue notes payable at the principal bank; but, if it would be operative, its effect would be injurious in the highest degree, inasmuch as it would, in a very few days after the bank commenced operation, compel it to cease payment in specie, owing to its liability to pay it at so many points, and the great demand for specie now existing, and likely to continue during the war, to the end of which this proposition was limited.

The amendment was supported by Mr. SHARP, and Mr. OAKLEY, of New York, and others, on the ground, principally, that it would be infinitely better that the notes should bear on their face their actual value and place of payment, than that they should purport to be payable at places at which in fact they would not be payable in specie. If made payable at Philadelphia only, the persons receiving the paper would know its real value, and not under a deceptive aspect of being payable at any of the branches, where in fact no payment in specie was to be made, &c. It was also objected to the bill, as it now stands, that it would drain all the specie in the country to accumulate it at Philadelphia.

The question on the amendment resulted by yeas and nays—For the amendment 76, against it 75, as follows:

YEAS—Messrs. Bard, Bayles of Massachusetts, Bayly, of Virginia, Bigelow, Bowen, Boyd, Bradbury, Bradley, Breckenridge, Brigham, Butler, Caperton, Calhoun, Champion, Cilley, Clopton, Cooper, Cox, Crawford, Culpeper, Davenport, Davis of Massachusetts, Desha, Earle, Ely, Farrow, Gaston, Geddes, Glasgow, Hale, Hall, Henderson, Howell, Humphreys, Hulbert, Jackson of Rhode Island, Johnson of Virginia, Kennedy, Kent of New York, King of Massachusetts, Lovett, Lowndes, Markell, McKee, Miller, Moseley, Oakley, Pearson, Pickering, Pitkin, Potter, John Reed,

William Reed, Ruggles, Schureman, Sharp, Shefley, Sherwood, Shipherd, Slaymaker, Smith of New York, Smith of Virginia, Stanford, Stockton, Stuart, Sturges, Taggart, Thompson, Vose, Ward of Massachusetts, Ward of New Jersey, Webster, Wheaton, White, Wilcox, and Wilson of Massachusetts.

NAYS—Messrs. Alexander, Alston, Anderson, Archer, Avery, Barnett, Bines, Brown, Caldwell, Cannon, Chappell, Clendenin, Comstock, Conard, Creighton, Cuthbert, Dana, Davis of Pennsylvania, Denoyelles, Duvall, Evans, Findley, Fisk of New York, Forney, Forsyth, Franklin, Gholson, Gourdin, Griffin, Harris, Hasbrouck, Hawes, Hawkins, Hopkins of Kentucky, Hubbard, Ingersoll, Ingham, Irving, Irwin, Kent of Maryland, Kerr, Kershaw, Kilbourn, King of North Carolina, Lefferts, Lyle, Macon, McCoy, McLean, Montgomery, Moore, Murfree, Nelson, Newton, Ormsby, Parker, Pickens, Pleasants, Rea of Pennsylvania, Rhea of Tennessee, Rich, Ringgold, Robertson, Sage, Sevier, Seybert, Smith of Pennsylvania, Strong, Tannehill, Taylor, Telfair, Troup, Udree, Williams, Wilson of Pennsylvania, and Yancey.

The SPEAKER decided it in the affirmative by his casting vote.

Mr. FARROW then moved to amend the bill by striking out so much as describes the stock to be subscribable, and inserting in lieu thereof a provision limiting the privilege of subscription in the stock of the bank to such public debt as shall be hereafter contracted.

On this motion, Mr. FARROW addressed the Chair as follows:

Mr. Speaker, you have rejected the old revolutionary war stock, and on every principle of either consistency, policy, or honesty, you now ought to exclude the present war stock. You state that the stock that you have excluded was purchased up from the soldiery, who rendered the service at the rate of eight or ten dollars for one, and therefore the present holders have no equitable claim to come into the bank with their stock. The speculation on your soldiers was dishonest and dishonorable, indeed; and, what rendered it a little more infamous than ordinary, it extended from your Congress Hall. Yes, sir, some of your honorable members of that day were deeply engaged in it; they had their agents out purchasing up the indents, the soldier's claim; and, as soon as they purchased all that they could get, they then voted for the claims to be funded, which raised the stock immediately above par. Let us now leave this disgraceful transaction, after reminding you that it is a debt that you justly owe. And I will further remind you, that some of this stock is at this moment in the hands of those who fought your battles, and wear the scars of their bravery; some of it is in the hands of the widow, whose husband fell in your battle; some of it is held by the minor as a legacy from the ancestor. Those are the persons, among others, that you have shut the door of your bank against; with their demands, they cannot purchase the stock of your bank.

If you will now indulge me, I will examine what equitable claim those creditors have for whom alone you are about to establish this great institution. I believe them to be honest and honorable men. They have acted so with you. You wanted their money; they had a right to make the best bargain that they could obtain. They offered you eighty dollars for a hundred dollars of your stock; you took it. You stated to them the terms of payment, and the security that you would give them; they accepted of it. They have acted faithful (to themselves) over a few; you are now about to give them a bank, which will make them rulers over many. With this bank, I fear they will be able to govern the nation in their own way. Those creditors are entitled to strict justice from you, and nothing more. The true policy would be to reject this class of creditors as you have the other class who holds the old war stock, and only admit the stock of such debts as will accrue on subsequent loans. By this course, you can make your loans on better terms; you can obtain money at six per cent. In this way the advantage of the bank will be to the Government, in place of going to a few individuals who you are under no obligations to but to comply with the contract as made between you. I do insist that you ought to put all of your creditors on the same footing; either admit them all to come in, or keep them all out. I call on every honorable member, individually, to think for himself on the subject of this amendment. A man making himself acquainted with facts, and deliberately making up an opinion, will nine times out of ten determine on correct principles; but when he throws himself, soul and body, upon a party, he will nine times out of ten decide wrong, for it is but seldom that correct principles will answer party purposes. I do not know that the source from whence this plan came has been actuated from any but pure motives. I do not know who those stockholders are, nor where they are; but this I do know, that a more profitable project could not be planned, either by themselves or any other person in their favor, than what the bill on your table contemplates.

The principles of banking I am not acquainted with; and I find that this Hall is not a place to acquire any knowledge on the subject, for those who understand it best differ the most. I am in favor of a National Bank either in a time of peace or war. And if the bill before you cannot be altered for the better, Mr. Speaker, I am still not certain but what I will vote for it. I am not afraid that it will be altered for the worse. If I do vote for the bill in its present shape, I shall do so under the influence of a hope that it is possible it will afford some little relief to the Government. If you adopt the amendment that I have proposed, it will not then be such a bill as I would wish to see pass. I want the capital reduced; the specie capital raised; the sum to be loaned to the Government reduced; and that the bank should be compelled to pay specie for their bills whenever demanded. I want such a bank as will wear, at least, the complexion of a commercial bank on banking principles.

Mr. Ingham and Mr. Forsyth opposed and Mr. Gaston and Mr. Oakley supported the motion.

Mr. Potter, of Rhode Island, said he wished the motion to prevail, which would give the benefit of the bank to the nation, instead of a few individuals. He said, if this was a question of ordinary legislation, that could be modified or repealed whenever it should be thought expedient by a future Congress, he would have been satisfied with giving a silent vote, that its friends might find out, from experience, what its opposers had predicted. But when he considered if this charter, in its present form, was granted, that it was out of the reach of the Legislature for twenty years, and was granting an exclusive right to a particular description of creditors, to make paper money for the same time, almost without restraint in amount, and entirely without responsibility, he could not let it pass without entering his protest against it.

He said he would not vote for such a charter, under any Administration, at any time, or under any circumstances; but if this must be granted, he wished the capital, as far as it was to consist of paper, to be made of new stock and Treasury notes, which would be of some benefit to the nation. He said much time had been consumed, the preceding as well as on the present day, in discussing and comparing the merits and tender mercies of the speculators, who purchased up the debt of the Revolution, with those who hold the present war stock. He said he believed, if one description of them had succeeded better than the other in their speculations, it was more owing to their skill and opportunity than to any other cause; their disposition to make the most of their money was the same.

The gentleman from Pennsylvania, (Mr. Ingham,) being himself in favor of war-stock, thinks it strange that any other person should wish to include all the present and future stock, putting all the present creditors upon a par, and giving the nation the advantage in the sale of future stock, and says that the minority discouraged the loans for the purposes of the war, and predicted the fate of those who should loan their money to the Government for that purpose, and now wished to see their predictions verified. This, he said, was the reason of its depreciation.

Mr. P. said it was very easy to make those general charges against a party, even when they were without foundation; but, he said, it was not in the power of a minority to injure the credit of the Government, if they did their duty in fulfilling their engagements; but this they had not done. They had not provided ways and means to meet the exigencies of the Government; they had not collected from the people, in direct and internal taxes, since the war, but about five millions of dollars. Having neglected to provide ways and means to pay the interest, the principal must depreciate. Their political friends in New York and Pennsylvania had been the first to injure, and eventually to destroy the credit of bank paper; their friends in Boston the first to refuse to pay the draft of the Government with funds in their hands.

At the commencement of the war, public stock

was at par, and the interest punctually paid; bank paper was in good credit generally until the collector of the port of New York, maliciously and without any justifiable cause, seized and stopped a large sum of money belonging to the banks in Boston, under pretence that it was about to be sent out of the country to the enemy, when he must have known better, as bills could have then been bought in New York for twenty per cent. discount; but as he was in office, and, as he understood, a director of the bank from whence some of this money was taken, he must exercise his power to discourage similar applications. This was the first check to the credit of bank paper. The next shock it received was in Pennsylvania, which eventually compelled the banks in that State and New York to stop payment. The Government of the United States being in great want of money to help to prosecute this war, the banks in Philadelphia were induced to loan them large sums in their bills, which were put in general circulation. The Legislature of Pennsylvania knowing the situation of those banks, and professing great friendship for the present Administration, after having sent in the annual pledges of life, fortune, and honor, to aid them in the prosecution of the war, granted forty bank charters, interesting a great portion of her citizens, in every part of the State, in them, who set about collecting the bills of those banks who had loaned their money to the Government, in order to get specie out of the vaults of the new banks, in such sums that they were unable to meet all their bills, and immediately stopped payment. In this situation the directors of the banks had a meeting, and being desirous of being on good terms at the Treasury of the United States, and not willing to offend the State of Pennsylvania, on whom they depended for the renewal of their charters, instead of acknowledging that they had been imprudent in loaning so much of their money, or charging their misfortunes to the State, for granting so many bank charters at such a time, and being desirous of assigning some plausible reason to the public for the course they were about to pursue, in refusing to pay specie for their bills—in this situation, prevailed upon themselves to believe it to be patriotic to stop payment, pretending that the money was going out of the country, and stopped accordingly.

Mr. P. said he would next call their attention to their pretended friends in Boston. At this place, the Government owed about two hundred thousand dollars, for interest on its debt, and, in order to pay it, had placed in the State Bank in Boston, (owned and managed exclusively by the friends of Administration,) about six hundred thousand dollars, which the bank had received as a general deposite. The bank refused to pay, and the Government draft was dishonored, under a pretence that the deposite consisted of Treasury notes, and that, at some future day, the Government would owe them. If they had taken those notes in special deposite, they would have been accountable for those notes only; but as they had given credit for them generally, and had been

benefitted by the interest, they could have no excuse for not paying the money, the more especially, as he had been credibly informed that the banks in Boston, in order to sustain the credit of the Government, and bank paper generally, and to enable this bank to fulfill its engagements, offered to loan them four hundred thousand dollars, which was refused. From this bank, he said, the Government had a right to expect better things, as he had frequently heard it observed, that, in case of war, the Government might reasonably expect a loan from its president alone of two millions of dollars, to aid them in the prosecution of the present war.

Mr. P. said he could trace the same system of depreciating the credit of the Government to the Treasury Department, in this city, in respect to Treasury notes. He said, while we had been endeavoring to hire money, making great sacrifices to pay those notes, he had understood they could not be received in taxes, unless the individual, paying his tax, had a note of about the same sum; that he could not pay his neighbor's taxes and his own to the amount of his note, and there were none issued in less sums than twenty dollars.

Mr. P. said he was aware that it would be said of the minority, on this question, as it had been on many others, that they opposed everything, either in principle or detail. Be it so. They never were consulted on any subject; they had no opportunity to originate any measure; nor had they even a choice of evils; and whenever any project of the majority failed, and did not answer their expectations, its failure is generally charged to the minority. He said he would ask the majority to review their own conduct, going no further back than the commencement of the last session, and see if they had any reason to believe that we should be in any better condition respecting our finances than we are. We were then together about five months. Knowing the nakedness of the Treasury, and the exposed and defenceless situation of the country, and that we were contracting immense debts, and that our expenses were enormous; knowing all this, they did not devise ways and means, by taxes, to get money to pay their own expenses; and, after talking about a land and whiskey tax, separated without laying either, satisfying themselves with the repeal of the non-importation law, thus humbling ourselves to Great Britain in the face of the world, by giving up a system that had done us much injury, (put on to coerce them,) for the purpose of getting their goods into this country; not because we wanted them, but because we wanted to derive a revenue from them in an indirect way, rather than disturb the people with taxes—thus giving the English an opportunity to fill our country with their merchandise, to the relief of their manufactories and to the destruction of our own, while they drew the specie out of the country in payment for them; and this we did merely for the privilege of collecting a duty upon them from our own people. But the English, seeing our situation, and seeing that this was a revenue more than a commercial project, they immediately extended their blockade, and turned our favorite system of coercion upon ourselves, by way of chastisement, having it in her power to let vessels under neutral flags pass in and out of such ports as she pleases.

Mr. P. said that the great and weighty matters that induced the President to call Congress to meet at an earlier day than that to which they stood adjourned, was nothing more than to provide against the defalcation in the revenue expected in consequence of the repeal of the non-importation law. He said he supposed Congress, having seen where they had neglected to provide ways and means, to meet the exigencies of the country, the last session, would have proceeded immediately to have laid a land and whiskey tax as high as was prudent, and to have extended the stamp tax as far as was practicable, without taxing all the manufactories in the United States, and every article used by the poor. This, he said, would have done much to revive public credit. Mr. P. said, if they had then issued Treasury notes, in small sums, bearing an interest of six per cent., with the privilege of funding them at eight per cent. in sums of five hundred dollars, and made them receivable for all taxes and debts due to the Government; if the friends of the Administration and the war, who are by far more numerous and wealthy than the people of the United States who achieved the independence of this country, had returned home, and instead of finding fault, and laying all the misfortunes of the country, occasioned by their own mismanagement, to the minority, (who have no power to do anything, and are never noticed but to be reviled, and never called upon but to suffer or to pay their money,) and if they had shown them faith by their works, and taken up those notes to the amount of four or five per cent. on their capital, and funded them, it would have shown to the people generally, that they had confidence in one another, and in the Government. Thereby they would have induced others to have done the same thing. Many people of the United States, who would be able and willing to take up these notes to the amount of many thousand dollars and fund them, were not able to loan twenty-five thousand dollars, the least sum that could be subscribed to the loan, and who would not be concerned with speculators to make up that sum. Thus the demand for those notes, for funding and for paying debts and taxes, would have been very great, and would have created a general demand for them. These notes would then have relieved the Government, and answered a tolerable purpose as a currency, at any rate much better than the bills of the contemplated bank.

Mr. P. said this course would have been very simple and easy; would have answered a good purpose for the Government and people, and would neither injure other institutions, nor furnish an object for speculation.

Mr. P. said that this amendment brought up the question fairly between the present war stock and future stock, and Treasury notes. He said he thought that new stock and Treasury notes would make much the best stock for a bank, the opinion of the Secretary of the Treasury to the contrary notwithstanding.

Mr. P. said, if this bank was to be made for the exclusive benefit of speculators in war stock, it ought to remain as it was; but if it was for the benefit of the nation, the amendment ought to prevail. He said, it would seem from the letter of the Secretary of the Treasury to the chairman of a committee, to whom the business was referred, that he is in favor of a war stock exclusively; but, when he attempts to assign his reasons for his judgment, it would seem that he had mistaken his side. Upon being asked if Treasury notes, to a considerable amount, could be got into circulation, his answer is in the negative, and he assigns for reason, that they will be bought up at the offices, and, by that means, prevented from going into circulation. Admit it to be so, if the Government gets the money for them, it serves to establish their credit, and if they are absorbed in the stock of this bank, it creates a demand for more of them, that will get into circulation in aid of the Government.

But, Mr. P. said, that a war-stock bank that could issue as much paper almost as they pleased, without being under any obligations to pay their bills, seemed to be a *sine qua non* with the Secretary of the Treasury. Mr. P. said, whenever he thought of this bank, the names of certain speculators came into his mind at the same time, and when he asked why this bank was made exclusively for their benefit, without consulting the interest of the nation, or other stockholders, he was told that those who had loaned their money to Government to prosecute this war, were patriots, and ought to be preferred to other creditors. He said he should be glad to know what further claim those patriots have upon the Government whose credit they had depressed and taken advantage of. They took from us a war premium for a war risk. We owe them nothing; we never promised them a bank. They would not have returned any part of their exorbitant premium if the war had ceased.

In England, Mr. P. said, a public creditor does all he can to keep up the credit of the nation and its stocks, and, in doing this, he keeps up the value of his own stocks; but, in this country, it seems to be quite the reverse; it seems that our stock-jobbers and patriots, after making the best terms they could with our Treasury Department, induced them to agree, if they should be in greater distress, before they should procure all the money they wanted to hire, and any other person should take a greater advantage of them than they had, that they should make them an allowance to make up the difference, by which means those who first loaned their money, instead of having an interest in supporting the credit of the stocks, had an interest in depressing them. And he said he had understood that some of them had begun so soon to depreciate the price of stock in the market, to compel the Government to hire on less advantageous terms, and had done it so effectually, that they were unable to fulfil their own contracts,

Mr. P. said, he was opposed to this bank in its present form, because the Government lends its aid to induce the people to take its bills, without becoming themselves responsible for them, or without making any provision in the charter, to compel the bank to pay either principal or interest, or even to compel them to assign over the stock of the bank, if they would take it, on which they are receiving an interest from the Government, and because its capital is to be made of depreciated stock, and, he feared, managed by men in desperate circumstances and depreciated credit, who will have all the benefit of the bank, and the nation derives no advantages eventually from it. He said the people would be taxed to pay six per cent. interest for all the bills of this bank that the Government may hire of them, and when they shall have received them, having sold their property or rendered services for them, they can get neither principal nor interest, they therefore loan six per cent. more by holding them, besides the depreciation of them in their hands.

Mr. P. said, as soon as there should be paid into this bank about twelve millions of war stock, and something over one million of specie, it was to go into operation, and was obligated to loan to the Government thirty millions in its bills. He said such an amount of paper, of such a bank, put into circulation, if it should be possible, in addition to the present depreciated stock-bank paper, would effectually destroy the credit of the whole paper system, and stop its circulation.

Mr. P. said, it would appear from what had been said by the friends of this bill, that almost everything was to be expected from it; that it was to be a remedy for all the difficulties under which we labor; that it would infuse new life and vigor into the body politic. Its bills would answer as a circulating medium, revive the public credit, relieve the Government from its present embarrassments, and support the credit of bank paper generally. He said if he might be permitted to compare small things with great, when the reasons were the same, he should as soon expect a merchant who owned a large quantity of flour at Alexandria, that he could hardly sell at any price, owing to the quantity in market beyond the demand for it, to go to Baltimore and buy a quantity in the same situation, and take it to Alexandria in order to raise the price, and create a demand for that already there, as to attempt to raise the credit, and create a demand for bank paper already depreciated by the quantity in circulation, by increasing the quantity tenfold, and of an inferior quality.

Mr. P. said he was opposed to this bank, because a better substitute may be furnished for a circulating medium in Treasury notes, more honorable to the Government, and more safe to this people, as there was no person, he believed, but what would rather have a Treasury note on interest, having the faith of the Government pledged with the taxes, all the real and personal property of the United States for their payment, than the bills of such a bank, having no foundation.—

Without the aid of Government in making them receivable for debts and taxes due them, they would, he believed, hardly pass for enough to pay for their printing.

Mr. P. said he had heard much about the credit of bank paper, and it would seem that many thought there was a kind of magic in it; but he said that as soon as some of the banks refused to pay specie for their bills, and it was known that they were not the honest representatives of specie, they soon lost all their charms. And that they were now distrusted and suspected by all classes, no person could deny; until the refusal of those banks they had a general credit, and the public had confidence in them, and it was for the interest of all banks and all persons interested in them to keep up the credit of bank paper, until by the imprudence of some of them all became suspected, many lost their credit, and some nearly ruined.

Mr. P. said much had been said about the bank capital in this country, it was now said we had one hundred millions, and he supposed as soon as this charter should be granted, we should have fifty millions more, when no person he believed would pretend that we had more than fifteen millions of dollars in specie in the United States. Mr. P. said this nominal bank capital consisted of stockholders' notes, many of whom have always owed the bank the amount of their stock, and some of them much more, and that part actually paid in by those who had money, and had no use for it, has been loaned out by the bank; so that all this capital, at this time, consists of debts due to the bank from stockholders who never calculated to pay, and from others who have as much as they can do to pay the interest of their debts and their taxes. The Government, therefore, cannot derive much aid from this kind of capital.

Mr. P. said it was now very clearly ascertained, that our wealth and strength, for the purposes of offensive war, had been very much overrated by both parties. It was said by those in power, if we were unanimous in our measures, it would have a very great effect in putting an end to the war. This, he said, would appear well on paper, but it would not add a dollar to the wealth of the nation. It is frequently said by some of the minority, that we would do much better if we had a mixed instead of a party Administration. This, Mr. P. said would only increase our difficulties. The Administration ought not to admit a person in the Opposition into the Cabinet, and such a person ought not to accept an appointment, if he had the offer of it. Many suppose if we had an entire change of Administration, and had a national, instead of a party war, all would soon be well. Mr. P., said that such an Administration he believed could do much to get the nation out of this war, by making a speedy and honorable peace. As they had no hand in making the war, they would not have to justify all the measures that led to it ; but as to prosecuting the war in the present situation of the country, he believed they would do very little better than the present Administration. They would not make men or money; the fault had been in going to war unprepared after our revenue had been destroyed, and the spirit of the nation broken down, without taking early means to supply the Treasury and support the credit of the nation, which was now too far gone to be revived, by the paper of such a bank as the one proposed.

Mr. P. said, as the House were very anxious to decide this question, and the gentleman from Kentucky (Mr. Hopkins) had said the subject was perfectly well understood—as he knew but little about it himself, he should give them no further trouble, although, he said, he considered it a question of very great importance, as when this charter was granted, it would be granting an exclusive privilege to a few people, for twenty years. He therefore thought it a question that ought to be maturely considered and well understood. If then we have doubts as to the expediency of the measure, and of its answering the expected purpose in relieving the Government from its present embarrassments, he thought we ought to pause before we pass it. He said if the war lasted it would ruin many, who might take its bills, and if we had peace soon such a bank with such a capital, would be a dangerous political machine. Its stockholders and its debtors would make a numerous and powerful combination with those who may wish favors. He said, he believed, that such a bank, even in time of peace, when it would be in the hands of the real moneyed men of the nation, would have much influence in making Presidents, in supporting armies, and in controlling the future political destinies of this country.

He said it ought to be with a nation, as with an individual, who was surrounded with difficulties on all sides; when about to make a great effort to extricate himself (the failure of which would be likely to involve him in great difficulties, and perhaps ruin) he ought to be certain as to the correctness of the course he was about to pursue, that the object in view was attainable, with the means he was about to employ, and that, if successful, it would afford him the expected relief. If not, he ought to reflect, to pause, and to wait events.

The question on Mr. Farrow's motion was decided in the negative—yeas 65, nays 89, as follows:

Yeas—Messrs. Baylies of Massachusetts, Bayly of Virginia, Bigelow, Bowen, Boyd, Bradbury, Breckenridge, Brigham, Butler, Caperton, Champion, Cilley, Clopton, Cooper, Cox, Crawford, Culpeper, Davenport, Davis of Massachusetts, Ely, Farrow, Gaston, Geddes, Hale, Henderson, Howell, Hulbert, Jackson of Rhode Island, Johnson of Virginia, Kent of New York, King of Massachusetts, Law, Lovett, Macon, Markell, Miller, Moseley, Oakley, Pearson, Pickering, Pitkin, Potter, John Reed, William Reed, Ruggles, Schureman, Sheffey, Sherwood, Shipherd, Slaymaker, Smith of New York, Stanford, Stockton, Stuart, Sturges, Taggart, Thompson, Vose, Ward of Massachusetts, Webster, Wheaton, White, Wilcox, Wilson of Massachusetts, and Winter.

Nays—Messrs. Alexander, Alston, Anderson, Archer, Avery, Bard, Barnett, Bines, Bradley, Brown,

Caldwell, Calhoun, Cannon, Chappell, Clark, Clendenin, Comstock, Conard, Creighton, Cuthbert, Dana, Davis of Pennsylvania, Denoyelles, Duvall, Earle, Evans, Findley, Fisk of Vermont, Fisk of New York, Forney, Forsyth, Franklin, Gholson, Glasgow, Gourdin, Griffin, Hall, Harris, Hasbrouck, Hawes, Hawkins, Hopkins of Kentucky, Hubbard, Humphreys, Ingersoll, Ingham, Irving, Irwin, Kennedy, Kent of Maryland, Kerr, Kershaw, Kilbourn, King of North Carolina, Lefferts, Lowndes, Lyle, McCoy, McKee, McLean, Montgomery, Moore, Murfree, Nelson, Newton, Ormsby, Parker, Pickens, Pleasants, Rea of Pennsylvania, Rhea of Tennessee, Rich, Ringgold, Robertson, Sage, Sevier, Sharp, Smith of Pennsylvania, Smith of Virginia, Strong, Tannehill, Taylor, Telfair, Troup, Udree, Ward of New Jersey, Williams, Wilson of Pennsylvania, and Yancey.

Mr. Pitkin, of Connecticut, then proposed a further amendment to the bill, viz: to strike out the word "fifty," so as to leave the amount of the capital blank.

The previous question having been thereupon demanded by Mr. Harris, of Tennessee, and supported by a sufficient number, viz: 75 for it, 67 against it—

Mr. Webster, of New Hampshire, moved to lay the bill on the table; which motion was negatived, by yeas and nays—For the motion 85, against it 93, as follows:

Yeas—Messrs. Baylies of Massachusetts, Bigelow, Bowen, Boyd, Bradbury, Breckenridge, Brigham, Caperton, Champion, Cilley, Clopton, Cooper, Cox, Culpeper, Davenport, Davis of Massachusetts, Ely, Gaston, Geddes, Hale, Henderson, Howell, Hulbert, Jackson of Rhode Island, Kent of New York, King of Massachusetts, Law, Lovett, Markell, Miller, Moseley, Oakley, Pearson, Pickering, Pitkin, Potter, John Reed, William Reed, Ruggles, Schureman, Sheffey, Sherwood, Shipherd, Slaymaker, Stanford, Stockton, Sturges, Thompson, Vose, Ward of Massachusetts, Webster, Wheaton, White, Wilcox, Wilson of Massachusetts, and Winter.

Nays—Messrs. Alexander, Alston, Anderson, Archer, Avery, Bard, Barnett, Bines, Bradley, Brown, Caldwell, Calhoun, Cannon, Chappell, Clark, Clendenin, Comstock, Conard, Crawford, Creighton, Cuthbert, Dana, Davis of Pennsylvania, Denoyelles, Desha, Duvall, Earle, Evans, Farrow, Findley, Fisk of Vermont, Fisk of New York, Forney, Forsyth, Franklin, Gholson, Glasgow, Gourdin, Griffin, Hall, Harris, Hasbrouck, Hawes, Hawkins, Hopkins of Kentucky, Hubbard, Humphreys, Ingersoll, Ingham, Irving, Irwin, Johnson of Virginia, Kennedy, Kent of Maryland, Kerr, Kershaw, Kilbourn, King of North Carolina, Lefferts, Lowndes, Lyle, Macon, McCoy, McKee, McLean, Moore, Murfree, Nelson, Newton, Ormsby, Parker, Pleasants, Rea of Pennsylvania, Rhea of Tennessee, Rich, Ringgold, Robertson, Sage, Sevier, Seybert, Sharp, Smith of Pennsylvania, Smith of Virginia, Strong, Tannehill, Taylor, Telfair, Troup, Udree, Ward of New Jersey, Williams, Wilson of Pennsylvania, and Yancey.

Another motion was then made to adjourn, and negatived.

The previous question was then put in the usual form—"Shall the main question be now put?" and decided in the affirmative—For putting the main question 83, against it 63, as follows:

YEAS—Messrs. Alexander, Alston, Anderson, Archer, Avery, Bard, Barnett, Bines, Brown, Caldwell, Cannon, Chappell, Clark, Clendenin, Comstock, Conard, Crawford, Creighton, Cuthbert, Dana, Davis of Pennsylvania, Denoyelles, Desha, Earle, Evans, Findley, Fisk of Vermont, Fisk of New York, Forney, Forsyth, Franklin, Gholson, Glasgow, Gourdin, Griffin, Hall, Harris, Hasbrouck, Hawkins, Hopkins of Kentucky, Hubbard, Ingersoll, Ingham, Irving, Irwin, Kennedy, Kent of Maryland, Kerr, Kershaw, Kilbourn, King of North Carolina, Lefferts, Lyle, McCoy, McLean, Moore, Murfree, Nelson, Newton, Ormsby, Parker, Pickens, Pleasants, Rea of Pennsylvania, Rhea of Tennessee, Ringgold, Robertson, Sage, Sevier, Seybert, Sharp, Smith of Pennsylvania, Smith of Virginia, Strong, Tannehill, Taylor, Telfair, Troup, Udree, Ward of New Jersey, Williams, Wilson of Pennsylvania, and Yancey.

NAYS—Messrs. Baylies of Massachusetts, Bigelow, Bowen, Boyd, Bradbury, Bradley, Brigham, Calhoun, Champion, Cilley, Clopton, Cooper, Cox, Culpeper, Davenport, Davis of Massachusetts, Duvall, Ely, Farrow, Gaston, Geddes, Hale, Hawes, Henderson, Howell, Humphreys, Jackson of Rhode Island, Johnson of Virginia, Kent of New York, King of Massachusetts, Law, Lovett, Lowndes, Macon, Markell, McKee, Miller, Moseley, Oakley, Pearson, Pickering, Pitkin, Potter, John Reed, William Reed, Ruggles, Schureman, Sheffey, Sherwood, Shipherd, Slaymaker, Stanford, Stockton, Sturges, Thompson, Vose, Ward of Massachusetts, Webster, Wheaton, White, Wilcox, Wilson of Massachusetts, and Winter.

The question on ordering the bill to a third reading was then decided in the affirmative without a division.

On the question when the bill should be read a third time, *to-morrow* and *to day* were named. The question being taken on to-morrow, there were for to-morrow 57, against it 76.

The bill was then ordered to be read a third time to-day.

A motion was then made to adjourn, and negatived by a vote of 75 to 60.

The bill was then announced for a third reading.

Mr. BIGELOW raised a question of order, whether it was proper to read the bill a third time before the other orders of the day were disposed of. The SPEAKER having decided that bills on their third readings had preference in the order of the day, Mr. B. appealed from the decision of the Speaker, (Mr. MACON,) which was affirmed by the House.

Mr. WEBSTER, of New Hampshire, moved to recommit the bill with certain instructions, substantially as follows:

1. To reduce the capital to twenty-five millions of dollars, with liberty to the Government to subscribe five millions additional at any future time.

2. To strike out the provision allowing the bank to cease specie payment.

3. To strike out so much of the bill as makes it obligatory on the bank to lend money to the Government.

4. To introduce a provision, that if the bank shall not commence operations within —— months after the passage of the act, the charter shall be forfeited.

5. To allow an interest of —— per cent. per annum on any note, payment of which shall have been demanded of the bank, and refused.

6. To provide that of the twenty-five millions, five shall be payable in specie, and twenty in any United States six per cent. stock, or in Treasury notes.

7. To strike out that provision which restrains the bank from selling its stock.

Mr. W. supported his motion by a number of remarks, the general purport of which was, that he had resorted to this method to show to the world what sort of a bank he and his friends were willing to support.

Mr. GASTON followed in a short speech of much vehemence in favor of this motion, and with the zeal he has uniformly exhibited on this subject in opposition to the bill.

Mr. WILLIAM REED, of Massachusetts, next took the floor in decided opposition to this bill, of which he expressed the utmost abhorrence, and the greatest dread of its effects.

After the rejection of several motions to adjourn—

Mr. BIGELOW made a speech on the same *side* of the question as the two gentlemen who had preceded him in debate.

Before Mr. B. finished his speech, however, a motion to adjourn prevailed; and the House adjourned at 7 o'clock in the evening.

FRIDAY, December 30.

On motion of Mr. HALL,

Resolved, That the committee to whom was referred the letter from the Secretary of State, the Secretary of the Treasury, and the Attorney General, be directed to inquire into the expediency of providing, by law, for settling the claims of persons to public lands in the *Mississippi* Territory, derived from the purchase of certain companies under an act, or pretended act, of the State of Georgia, passed on the 7th day of January, 1795, whose claims have not been recorded in the office of the Department of State, agreeably to the provisions of the eighth section of an act of Congress, passed on the 3d day of March, 1803.

The following resolution was submitted by Mr. JENNINGS, and was read, and ordered to lie on the table:

Resolved, That a committee be appointed to inquire into the expediency of authorizing the Executive authorities of the several States and Territories of the United States, respectively, by law, to apprehend, secure, and deliver to the Governor, for the time being, of any Territory of the United States, or his agent, any fugitive or fugitives from justice, upon demand being made of the Executive authority of any such State or Territory, to which such fugitive or fugitives shall have fled, and upon producing an indictment found, or an affidavit made before a competent officer, charging the person so demanded with having committed treason, felony, or other crime, within the jurisdiction of the said Territory, from which he so fled, with leave to report by bill or otherwise.

The House resumed the consideration of the bill to incorporate the subscribers to the Bank of the United States of America; and the motion to recommit the bill with instructions being again stated, the bill was, on motion of Mr. PLEASANTS, ordered to lie on the table.

A message was received from the Senate announcing the death of RICHARD BRENT, a Senator of the United States from Virginia.

A motion was then made by Mr. FISK, of New York, that the House do again proceed to the consideration of the bank bill; which motion was decided in the affirmative by the following vote: For the motion 81, against it 70.

Mr. PICKERING commenced a speech in favor of recommitment, and in opposition to the bill; when, on motion of Mr. PLEASANTS, the bill was again ordered to lie on the table.

The SPEAKER laid before the House a letter from the committee of the Senate appointed to make arrangements for the burial of Mr. BRENT, announcing their determination to attend the funeral at 12 o'clock to-morrow; which letter having been read—

On motion of Mr. PLEASANTS,

Resolved, unanimously, That the House will attend the funeral of RICHARD BRENT, Esq., late a member of the Senate of the United States.

Resolved, unanimously, That this House will wear mourning on the left arm for the space of one month, in testimony of their respect for the memory of the deceased.

The House then immediately adjourned.

SATURDAY, December 31.

No business was transacted in the House this day, in consequence of the funeral of Mr. BRENT, of the Senate.

MONDAY, January 2, 1815.

A message from the Senate informed the House that the Senate have passed the bill "to provide additional revenues for defraying the expenses of Government, and maintaining the public credit, by laying duties on household furniture, on horses kept exclusively for the saddle or carriage, and on gold and silver watches," with amendments; in which they ask the concurrence of this House.

Mr. McKEE, of Kentucky, from the Committee of Public Lands, reported a bill for the relief of the inhabitants of the late county of New Madrid, in the Missouri Territory, who have suffered by earthquakes; which was twice read and committed.

Mr. JOHNSON, of Kentucky, laid before the House, on behalf of the committee of investigation, a letter from the late Secretary of the Treasury, on subjects connected with the capture of Washington by the enemy in August last; which was ordered to be printed.

The SPEAKER laid before the House a report from the acting Secretary of the Navy, on the memorial of Uriah Brown, respecting his invention for projecting liquid fire as a means of military or naval annoyance. The report is favor-able to the utility and practicability of the invention; and was referred to a select committee.

The resolution from the Senate for appointing a joint committee to inquire into the propriety of adopting fixed rules for conducting in future the printing, stationery, and binding, for both Houses of Congress, was taken up, read three times and concurred in.

The bill from the Senate authorizing the leasing of public lands, reserved for the use of schools, was twice read, and ordered to be read a third time to-morrow.

The amendments of the Senate to the bill laying duties on certain manufactures, were taken up. [The changes of duties proposed by the Senate in this bill, are principally to strike out pig iron and spermaceti candles, and to add umbrellas. There are other amendments to the detail of the bill.] The amendments were referred to the Committee of Ways and Means.

BANK OF THE UNITED STATES.

The House resumed the consideration of the bill from the Senate to incorporate the subscribers to the Bank of the United States of America. Mr. WEBSTER's motion to recommit the bill being still under consideration.

Mr. WEBSTER, of New Hampshire, spoke as follows:

Mr. Speaker, however the House may dispose of the motion before it, I do not regret that it has been made. One object intended by it at least, is accomplished. It presents a choice to the House, and it shows, that the opposition which exists to the bill in its present shape, is not an undistinguishing hostility to whatever may be proposed as a National Bank, but a hostility to an institution of such a useless and dangerous nature, as it is believed the existing provisions of the bill would establish.

If the bill should be recommitted and amended according to the instructions which I have moved, its principles will be materially changed. The capital of the proposed bank will be reduced from fifty to thirty millions; and composed of specie and stocks, in nearly the same proportion as the capital of the former Bank of the United States. The obligation to lend thirty millions of dollars to Government, an obligation which cannot be performed without committing an act of bankruptcy, will be struck out. The power to suspend the payment of its notes and bills will be abolished, and the prompt and faithful execution of its contract secured, as far as, from the nature of things, it can be secured. The restriction on the sale of its stocks will be removed, and, as it is a monopoly, provision will be made, that if it should not commence its operations in reasonable time, the grant shall be forfeited. Thus amended, the bill would establish an institution, not unlike the late Bank of the United States, in any particular which I deem material, excepting only the increased amount of the capital.

To a bank of this nature, I should at any time be willing to give my support, not as a measure of temporary policy, or an expedient to find means of relief from the present poverty of the Treasury; but as an institution of permanent interest and importance, useful to the Government and country at all times, and most useful in times of commerce and prosperity.

I am sure, sir, that the advantages which would at present result from any bank, are greatly overrated. To look to a bank, as a source capable not only of affording a circulating medium to the country but also of supplying the ways and means of carrying on the war, especially at a time when the country is without commerce, is to expect much more than will ever be obtained. Such high wrought hopes can end only in disappointment. The means of supporting an expensive war are not of quite so easy acquisition. Banks are not revenues. They cannot supply its place. They may afford facilities to its collection and distribution. They may furnish, with convenience, temporary loans to Government, in anticipation of its taxes, and render important assistance in divers ways to the general operations of finance. They are useful to the State, in their proper place and sphere; but they are not the sources of national income.

The fountains of revenue must be sunk deeper. The credit and circulation of bank paper are the effects, rather than the cause, of a profitable commerce and a well ordered system of finance. They are the proofs of national wealth and prosperity, not the foundations of them. Whoever shall attempt to restore the fallen credit of this country by the creating of new banks, merely that they may create new paper, and that Government may have a chance of borrowing, where it has not borrowed before, will find himself miserably deceived. It is under the influence of no such vain hopes, that I yield my assent to the establishment of a bank on safe and proper principles. The principal good I expect from it is rather future than present. I do not see, indeed, that it is likely to produce evil at any time. In times to come it will, I hope, be useful.

If it were only to be harmless, there would be sufficient reason why it should be supported, in preference to such a contrivance as is now in contemplation.

The bank, which will be created by the bill, if it should pass in its present form, is of a most extraordinary, and, as I think, alarming nature. Its capital is to be fifty million of dollars, five millions in gold and silver, twenty millions in the public debt, created since the war, ten millions in Treasury notes, and fifteen millions to be subscribed by Government in stock, to be created for that purpose. The ten millions in Treasury notes, when received in payment of subscriptions to the bank, are to be funded also into the United States stocks. The stocks subscribed by Government on its own account, and those in which the Treasury notes are to be funded, to be redeemable only at the pleasure of Government. The war stock will be redeemable according to the terms upon which the late loans have been negotiated.

The capital of the bank, then, will be five millions of specie, and forty-five millions of Government stocks. In other words, the bank will possess five millions of dollars, and the Government will owe it forty-five millions. This debt from Government, the bank is restrained from selling during the war, and Government is excused from paying until it shall see fit. The bank is also to be under obligation to loan Government thirty millions of dollars, on demand, to be repaid, not when the convenience or necessity of the bank may require, but when other debts due the bank from Government are paid; that is, when it shall be the good pleasure of Government. This sum of thirty millions is to supply the necessities of the Treasury, and supersede the occasion of other loans. This loan will doubtless be made on the first day of the existence of the bank, because the public wants can admit of no delay. Its condition then will be, that it has five millions of specie, if it has been able to obtain so much, and a debt of seventy-five millions, no part of which it can either sell or call in, due to it from Government.

The loan of thirty millions to Government can only be made by an immediate issue of bills to that amount. If these bills should return, the bank will not be able to pay them. This *is* certain; and to remedy this inconvenience, power is given to the directors, by the act, to suspend, at their own discretion, the payment of their notes, until the President of the United States shall otherwise order. The President will give no such order, because the necessities of Government will compel it to draw on the bank, till the bank becomes as necessitous as itself. Indeed, whatever orders may be either given or withheld, it will be utterly impossible for the bank to pay its notes. No such thing is expected of it. The first note it issues will be dishonored on its return, and yet it will continue to pour out its paper, so long as Government can apply it in any degree to its purposes.

What sort of an institution, sir, is this? It looks less like a bank than like a department of Government. It will be properly the paper money department. Its capital is Government debts; the amount of issues will depend on Government necessities; Government in effect absolves itself from its own debts to the bank, and by way of compensation, absolves the bank from its own contracts with others. This is, indeed, a wonderful scheme of finance. The Government is to grow rich, because it is to borrow, without the obligation of repaying, and is to borrow of a bank which issues paper without liability to redeem it. If this bank, like other institutions, which dull and plodding common sense has erected, were to pay its debts, it must have some limits to its issues of paper, and therefore there would be a point beyond which it could not make loans to Government. This would fall short of the wishes of the contrivers of this system. They provide for an unlimited issue of paper, in an entire exemption from payment. They found their bank, in the first place, on the discredit of Government; and then hope to enrich Government out of the insolvency of the bank. With them, poverty itself is the main source of supply, and bankruptcy a mine of inexhaustible treasure. They rely, not on the ability of the bank, but on its beggary; not on gold and silver collected in its vaults to pay its debts and fulfil its promises, but on the locks and bars provided by statute to fasten its doors against the solicitations and clamors of importunate creditors. Such an institution, they flatter themselves, will not only be able to sustain itself, but to buoy up the sinking credit of Government. A bank which does not pay, is to guarantee the engagements of a Government which does not pay. "John Doe is to become security for Richard Roe." Thus the empty vaults of the Treasury are to be filled from the equally empty vaults of the bank, and the ingenious invention of a partnership between insolvents is to restore and re-establish the credit of both.

Sir, I can view this only as a system of rank speculation, and enormous mischief. Nothing in our condition is worse, in my opinion, than the inclination of Government to throw itself upon such desperate courses. If we are to be saved, it is not to be by such means. If public credit is to be restored, this is not one of the measures that will help to restore it. If the Treasury is exhausted, this bank will not fill it with anything valuable. If a safe circulating medium be wanted for the community, it will not be found in the paper of such a corporation.

I wish, sir, that those who imagine that these objects, or any of them, will be effected by such a bank as this, would describe the manner in which they expect it to be done. What is the process which is to produce these results? If it is perceived, it can be described. The bank will not operate either by miracle or magic. Whoever expects any good from it, ought to be able to tell us in what way that good is to be produced. As yet we have had nothing but general ideas, and vague and loose expressions. An indefinite and indistinct notion is entertained, nobody here seems to know on what ground, that this bank is to reanimate public credit, fill the Treasury, and remove all the evils which have arisen from the depreciation of the paper of existing banks.

Some gentlemen, who do not profess themselves to be in all respects pleased with the provisions of the bill, seem to content themselves with an idea that nothing better can be obtained, and that it is necessary to do something.

A strong impression that something must be done, is the origin of many bad measures. It is easy, sir, to do something; but the object is to do something useful. It is better to do nothing, than to do mischief. It is much better, in my opinion, to make no bank, than to pass the bill as it now is.

The interests to be affected by this measure, the finances, the public credit, and the circulating medium of the country, are too important to be hazarded on schemes like this. If we wish to restore the public credit, and to re-establish the finances, we have the beaten road before us. All true analogy, all experience, all just knowledge of ourselves and our condition point one way. We can hardly mistake it, without wilful blindness. A wise and systematic economy, and a settled and substantial revenue are the means to be relied on; not excessive issues of bank notes, a forced circulation, and all the miserable contrivances to which political folly can resort, with the idle expectation of giving to mere paper the quality of money.

These are all inventions of a short-sighted policy, vexed and goaded by the necessities of the moment, and thinking less of a permanent remedy, than of shifts and expedients to avoid the present distress. They have been a thousand times exploded, as delusive and ruinous, as destructive of all solid revenue, and incompatible with the security of private property.

It is, sir, sufficiently obvious, that to produce any benefit, this bank must be so constituted as that its notes shall have credit with the public. The first inquiry, therefore, should be, whether the bills of a bank of this kind will not be immediately and greatly depreciated. I think they will. It would be wonderful if they should not. This effect will not be produced by that excessive issue of its paper, which the bank must make in its loan to Government. Whether its issues of paper are excessive, will depend, not on the nominal amount of its capital, but on its ability to redeem. This is the only safe criterion. Very special cases may perhaps furnish exceptions, but there is in general no security for the credit of paper, but the ability in those who emit to redeem it. Whenever bank notes are not convertible into gold or silver at the will of the holder, they become of less value than gold and silver. All experiments on this subject have come to the same result. It is so clear, and has been so universally admitted, that it would be waste of time to dwell upon it. The depreciation may not be sensibly perceived the first day or the first week it takes place. It will first be discerned in what is called the rise of specie; it will next be seen in the increased price of all commodities.

The circulating medium of a commercial community must be that which is also the circulating medium of other commercial communities, or must be capable of being converted into that medium without loss. It must be able, not only to pass in payments and receipts between individuals of the same society or nation, but to adjust and discharge the balance of exchanges between different nations. It must be something which has a value abroad, as well as at home, and by which foreign as well as domestic debts can be satisfied. The precious metals alone answer these purposes. They alone, therefore, are money, and whatever else is to perform the offices of money must be their representative, and capable of being turned into them at will. So long as bank paper retains this quality, it is a substitute for money; divested of this, nothing can give it that character.

No solidity of funds, no sufficiency of assets, no confidence in the solvency of banking institutions has ever enabled them to keep up their paper to the value of gold and silver, any longer than they paid gold and silver for it on demand. This will continue to be the case so long as those metals shall continue to be the standard of value and the general circulating medium among nations.

A striking illustration of this common principle is found in the early history of the Bank of England. In the year 1797, it had been so liberal in its loans, that it was compelled to suspend the payment of its notes. Its paper immediately fell to a discount of near twenty per cent. Yet such was the public opinion of the solidity of its funds, that its stock then sold for one hundred and ten per cent., although no more than sixty per cent. upon the subscriptions had been paid in.

The same fate, as is well known, attended the paper of the banks of Scotland, when they adopted the practice of inserting in their notes a clause, giving the banks an option of paying their notes on demand, or in six months after demand, with interest. Paper of this sort was not convertible into specie at the pleasure of the holder; and no conviction of the ability of the bank which issued it, could preserve it from depreciation.

The suspension of specie payments by the Bank of England in 1797, and the consequences which followed, afford no argument to overturn this general experience. If Bank of England notes were not immediately depreciated on that occasion, depreciation nevertheless did ensue. Very favorable causes existed to prevent their sudden depression. It was an old and rich institution. It was known to be under the most discreet and independent management. Government had no control over it, to force it to make loans against its interest or its will. On the contrary, it compelled the Government to pay, though with much inconvenience to itself, a very considerable sum which was due to it. The country enjoyed at that time an extensive commerce, and a revenue of three hundred millions of dollars was collected and distributed through the bank. Under all these advantages, however, the difference of price between bank notes and coin became so great as to threaten at one time the most dangerous consequences.

Suppose the condition of England to have been reversed. Suppose, that instead of a prosperous and increasing commerce, she had suffered the ruin of her trade; and that the product of her manufactures had lain upon her hands, as the product of our agriculture now perishes on ours. Does any one imagine that her circulating paper could have existed, and maintained any credit in such a change of her condition? What ought to surprise us is, not that her bank paper was depreciated, but that it was not depreciated sooner and lower than in fact it was. The reason can only be found in that extraordinary combination of favorable circumstances which never existed before, and is hardly to be expected again. Much less is it to be discovered in our condition at present.

But we have experience nearer home. The paper of all the banks south of New England has become depreciated to an alarming extent. This cannot be denied. All that is said of the existence of this depreciation only at places remote from the banks, is unfounded and idle. It exists everywhere, even at the very doors of the banks themselves. The rates of exchange, both foreign and domestic, put this point beyond controversy. If a bill of exchange on Europe can be purchased, as it may, twenty per cent. cheaper in Boston than in Baltimore, the reason must be, that it is paid for in Boston in money, and in Baltimore in something twenty per cent. less value than money.

Notwithstanding this depression of their paper, it is not probable that any general doubt is entertained of the sufficiency of the funds of the principal banks. Certainly no such doubt is the cause of the fall of their paper; because the depression of the paper of all the banks in any place, as far as I learn, is generally uniform and equal; whereas, if public opinion proceeded at all, upon the adequacy or inadequacy of their funds, it would necessarily come to different results, in different cases, as some of these institutions must be supposed to be richer than others.

Sir, something must be discovered, which has hitherto escaped the observation of mankind, before you can give paper, intended for circulation, the value of a metallic currency, any longer than it represents that currency, and is convertible into it, at the will of the holder.

The paper then, of this bank, if you make it, will be depreciated for the same reason that the paper of other banks which have gone before it, and of those which now exist around us, has been depreciated: because it is not to pay specie for its notes.

Other institutions, setting out perhaps on honest principles, have fallen into discredit through mismanagement or misfortune. But this bank is to begin with insolvency. It is to issue its bills to the amount of thirty millions at least, when everybody knows it cannot pay them. It is to commence its existence in dishonor. It is to draw its first breath in disgrace. The promise contained in the first note it sends forth, is to be a false promise and whoever receives the note, is to take it with the knowledge that it will not be paid, according to the terms of it.

But this, sir, is not all. The framers of this bill have not done their work by halves. They have put the depreciation of the notes of their bank beyond all doubt or uncertainty, by the manner in which the capital is constituted. They have made assurance doubly sure. In addition to excessive issue of paper, and the failure to make payments, both which they provide for by law, they make the capital of the bank to consist principally of public stock.

If this stock could be sold as in the former Bank of the United States, the evil would be less. But the bank has not the power to sell it, and for all purposes of enabling it to fulfil its engagements, its funds might as well be at the bottom of the ocean, as in Government stocks, of which it cannot enforce payment, and of which it cannot dispose.

The credit of this institution is to be founded on public funds, not on private property or commercial credit. It is to be a financial, not a commercial bank. Its credit, therefore, can hardly be better at any time, than the credit of the Government. If the stocks be depreciated, so of course must everything be which rests on the stocks.

It would require extraordinary ingenuity to show how a bank which is founded on the public debt, is to have any better reputation than the debt itself. It must be some very novel invention which makes the superstructure keep its place after the foundation has fallen. The argument seems to stand thus. The public funds, it is admitted, have little credit; the bank will have no credit which it does not borrow of the funds; but the bank will be in full credit.

If, sir, we were in a temper to learn wisdom from experience, the history of most of the banks on the continent of Europe might teach us the futility of all these contrivances. Those are, like this before us, established for purposes of finance, not purposes of commerce. The same fortune has happened to them all. Their credit has sunk. Their respective Governments go to them for money, when they can get it nowhere else; and the banks can relieve their wants only by new issues of their own paper. As this is not redeemed, the invariable consequence of depreciation follows; and this has sometimes led to the miserable and destructive expedient of a depreciation of the coin itself.

Such are the banks of Petersburg, Copenhagen, Vienna, and other cities of Europe. And while the paper of these Government banks has been thus depressed, that of other banks, existing in their near neighborhood, unconnected with Government, and conducting their business on the basis of commercial credit, has retained a value equivalent to that of coin.

Excessive issues of paper, and a close connexion with Government, are the two circumstances, which of all others are most certain to destroy the credit of bank paper. If there were no excessive issue, or in other words, if the bank paid its notes in specie on demand, its connexion with Government, and its interest in the funds, would not perhaps materially affect the circulation of its paper, although they would naturally diminish the value of its stock. But when these two circumstances exist in the condition of any bank; that it does not pay its notes, and that its funds are in public stocks, and all its operations intimately blended with the operations of Government, nothing further need be known, to be quite sure that its paper will not answer the purpose of a creditable circulating medium.

I look upon it, therefore, sir, as certain that a very considerable discount will attach itself to the notes of this bank, the first day of their appearance; that this discount will continue to increase, and unless Congress should be able to furnish some remedy, which is not certain, the paper in the end will be worth nothing. If this happens, not only will no one of the benefits proposed be obtained, but evils of the most alarming magnitude will follow. All the horrors of a paper money system are before us. If we venture on the present expedient, we shall hardly be able to avoid them. The ruin of public affairs and the wreck of private property will ensue.

I would ask, sir, whether the friends of this measure have well considered what effect it will produce on the revenue of the country? By the provisions of this bill, the notes of the bank are to be received in payment of all taxes and other dues to Government. They cannot be refused on account of the depreciation of their value. Government binds itself to receive them at par; although it should be obliged to pay them out immediately at a discount of a hundred per cent. It is certain, then, that a loss on the revenue will be sustained, equal to any depreciation which may take place in this paper; and when the paper shall come to nothing, the revenue of the country will come to nothing along with it. This has happened to other countries, where this wretched system has been adopted, and it will happen here.

The Austrian Government resorted to a similar experiment, in a very critical period of its affairs, in 1809, the year of the last campaign between that country and France, previous to the late coalition. Pressed by the necessities of the occasion, the Government caused a large quantity of paper to be issued, which was to be received in imposts and taxes. The paper immediately fell to a depreciation of four for one. The consequence was, that the Government lost its revenue, and with it the means of supplying its armies, and defending its Empire.

Is this Government, sir, now ready to put its resources all at hazard, by pursuing a similar course? Is it ready to sacrifice its whole substantial revenue, and permanent supplies, to an ill contrived, ill considered, dangerous and ruinous project, adopted only as the means of obtaining a little present and momentary relief?

It ought to be considered also, what effects this bank will produce on other banking institutions already existing, and on the paper which they have issued. The aggregate capital of these institutions is large. The amount of their notes is large, and these notes constitute at present, in a great portion of the country, the only circulating medium, if they can be called a circulating medium. Whatever affects this paper, either to raise it, or to depress it lower than it is, affects the interest of every man in the community.

It is sufficient, on this point to refer to the memorial from the banks of New York. That assures us that it must be the operation of such a bank as this bill would establish, to increase the difficulties and distress which the existing banks now experience, and to render it nearly impossible for them to resume the payment of their notes. This is what every man would naturally expect. Paper already depreciated will necessarily be sunk still lower when another flood of depreciated paper is forced into circulation.

Very recently, sir, this Government refused to extend the charter of the Bank of the United States, upon the ground that it was unconstitutional for Congress to create banks. Many of the State banks owe their existence to this decision. It was an invitation to the States to incorporate as much banking capital as would answer all the purposes of the country. Notwithstanding whatever we may now see and hear, it would then have been deemed a gross imputation on the consistency of Government if any man had expressed an expectation that in five years all these Constitutional scruples would be forgotten, all the danger to political liberty from moneyed institutions disregarded, and a bank proposed upon the most extraordinary principles, with an unprecedented amount of capital, and with no obligation to fulfil its contracts.

The State Banks have not forced themselves in the way of Government. They were established, many of them at least, when Government had declared its purpose to have no bank of its own. They deserve some regard on their own account, and on account of those particularly concerned in them; but they deserve much more consideration on account of the quantity of their paper which is in circulation, and the interest which the whole community has in it.

Let it be recollected, also, sir, that the present condition of the banks is principally owing to their advances to Government. The Treasury has borrowed of the banks, or of those who themselves borrowed of the banks, till the banks have become as poor, and almost as much discredited, as the Treasury itself. They have depreciated their paper, nearly ruined themselves, and brought the sorest distress on the country by doing that on a small scale, which this new bank is to perform on a scale vastly larger.

It is almost unpardonable in the conductors of these institutions not to have foreseen the consequences which have resulted from the course pursued by them. They were all plain and visible. If they have any apology, it is that they were no blinder than the Government, and that they yielded to those, who would take no denial. It will be altogether unpardonable in us, if with this, as well as all other experience before us, we continue to pursue a system which must inevitably lead us, through depreciation of currency, paper money, tender laws, and all the contemptible and miserable contrivances of disordered finance and national insolvency, to complete and entire bankruptcy in the end.

I hope the House will recommit the bill for amendment.

When Mr. WEBSTER had concluded, the motion for recommitment was supported by Messrs. PICKERING, SHIPHERD, and WHEATON, in speeches of considerable length, and opposed by Messrs. FORSYTH and RHEA.

The question on recommitment was at length decided in the negative by yeas and nays—yeas 66, nays 89, as follows:

YEAS—Messrs. Baylies of Massachusetts, Bayly of Virginia, Bigelow, Bowen, Boyd, Bradbury, Breckenridge, Brigham, Butler, Caperton, Calhoun, Champion, Cilley, Clopton, Cooper, Cox, Crawford, Culpeper, Davenport, Davis of Massachusetts, Ely, Evans, Farrow, Gaston, Geddes, Grosvenor, Hale, Henderson, Howell, Humphreys, Hulbert, Jackson of Rhode Island, Kent of New York, King of Massachusetts, Law, Lewis, Lovett, McKee, Miller, Moseley, Markell, Oakley, Pearson, Pickering, Pitkin, Potter, John Reed, William Reed, Ruggles, Schureman, Sheffey, Sherwood, Shipherd, Slaymaker, Smith of New York, Stan-

ford, Stockton, Sturges, Taggart, Thompson, Vose, Ward of Massachusetts, Webster, Wheaton, White, Wilcox, Wilson of Massachusetts, and Winter.

NAYS—Messrs. Alexander, Alston, Anderson, Archer, Avery, Barbour, Bard, Barnett, Bines, Burwell, Caldwell, Cannon, Chappell, Clark, Clendenin, Comstock, Conard, Creighton, Crouch, Cuthbert, Dana, Davis of Pennsylvania, Denoyelles, Desha, Duvall, Earle, Findley, Fisk of Vermont, Fisk of New York, Forney, Forsyth, Franklin, Gholson, Gourdin, Griffin, Hall, Harris, Hasbrouck, Hawes, Hawkins, Hopkins of Kentucky, Hubbard, Ingersoll, Ingham, Irving, Irwin, Jackson of Virginia, Johnson of Virginia, Johnson of Kentucky, Kennedy, Kent of Maryland, Kerr, Kershaw, Kilbourn, King of North Carolina, Lefferts, Lowndes, Lyle, Macon, McCoy, McKim, McLean, Montgomery, Moore, Murfree, Nelson, Newton, Ormsby, Parker, Pickens, Pleasants, Rhea of Pennsylvania, Rhea of Tennessee, Rich, Ringgold, Robertson, Sage, Sevier, Seybert, Sharp, Skinner, Smith of Pennsylvania, Tannehill, Taylor, Telfair, Ward of New Jersey, Williams, Wilson of Pennsylvania, and Yancey.

The bill was then read through, in the usual manner.

Mr. RHEA, of Tennessee, spoke a short time in explanation of the motives which would govern his vote in this case.

Mr. GROSVENOR, of New York, for the purpose of introducing a motion in aid of the rule, to prevent those members interested in the question from voting, moved to lay the bill on the table.

The motion was predicated on the fact that one member of the House (and perhaps others might be) was the proprietor of certain of the public stock, which is allowed to be paid in, in part, on account of shares to be subscribed to the bank.

This motion was opposed by Mr. FISK, of New York, and Mr. FINDLEY, of Pennsylvania; by whom it was contended that the rule of the House in this respect was sufficiently operative without this aid. It was supported by the mover, and by Mr. WARD, and Mr. FARROW.

The question on laying the bill on the table, was decided by yeas and nays—for laying the bill on the table 58, against it 104, as follows:

YEAS—Messrs. Baylies of Massachusetts, Bayly of Virginia, Bigelow, Boyd, Bradbury, Breckenridge, Brigham, Caperton, Champion, Cilley, Cooper, Coxe, Culpeper, Davenport, Davis of Massachusetts, Duvall, Ely, Farrow, Gaston, Grosvenor, Hale, Hanson, Henderson, Hulbert, Ingersoll, Jackson of Rhode Island, Kent of New York, Law, Lewis, Lovett, Markell, Miller, Moseley, Oakley, Pearson, Pickering, Pitkin, Potter, John Reed, William Reed, Ruggles, Schureman, Sheffey, Sherwood, Slaymaker, Stanford, Stockton, Stuart, Sturges, Thompson, Vose, Ward of Massachusetts, Webster, Wheaton, White, Wilcox, Wilson of Massachusetts, and Winter.

NAYS—Messrs. Alexander, Alston, Anderson, Archer, Avery, Bard, Barnett, Bines, Bowen, Bradley, Brown, Burwell, Butler, Caldwell, Calhoun, Cannon, Chappell, Clark, Clendenin, Clopton, Comstock, Conard, Crawford, Creighton, Crouch, Cuthbert, Dana, Davis of Pennsylvania, Denoyelles, Desha, Earle, Evans, Findley, Fisk of Vermont, Fisk of New York, Forney, Forsyth, Franklin, Geddes, Gholson, Glasgow, Gourdin, Griffin, Hall, Harris, Hasbrouck, Hawes, Hawkins, Hopkins of Kentucky, Howell, Hubbard,

Humphreys, Ingham, Irving, Irwin, Jackson of Virginia, Johnson of Virginia, Johnson of Kentucky, Kennedy, Kent of Maryland, Kerr, Kershaw, Kilbourn, King of Massachusetts, King of North Carolina, Lefferts, Lyle, Macon, McCoy, McKee, McKim, McLean, Montgomery, Moore, Murfree, Nelson, Newton, Ormsby, Parker, Pickens, Pleasants, Rea of Pennsylvania, Rhea of Tennessee, Rich, Ringgold, Robertson, Sage, Sevier, Seybert, Sharp, Shipherd, Skinner, Smith of Pennsylvania, Strong, Taggart, Tannehill, Taylor, Telfair, Troup, Udree, Ward of New Jersey, Williams, Wilson of Pennsylvania, and Yancey.

The question was then taken on the passage of the bill. The yeas and nays thereon stood—yeas 81, nays 80, as follows:

YEAS—Messrs. Alexander, Alston, Anderson, Archer, Avery, Barnett, Bines, Bradley, Brown, Caldwell, Cannon, Chappell, Clark, Clendenin, Comstock, Conard, Creighton, Crouch, Cuthbert, Dana, Davis of Pennsylvania, Denoyelles, Duvall, Earle, Farrow, Findley, Fisk of Vermont, Fisk of New York, Forney, Forsyth, Gholson, Gourdin, Griffin, Harris, Hasbrouck, Hawes, Hawkins, Hopkins of Kentucky, Hubbard, Ingersoll, Ingham, Irving, Irwin, Kent of Maryland, Kerr, Kershaw, Kilbourn, King of North Carolina, Lefferts, Lowndes, Lyle, McCoy, McKee, McLean, Montgomery, Moore, Murfree, Nelson, Ormsby, Parker, Pickens, Pleasants, Rea of Pennsylvania, Rhea of Tennessee, Rich, Ringgold, Robertson, Sage, Sevier, Sharp, Skinner, Smith of Pennsylvania, Strong, Tannehill, Taylor, Telfair, Udree, Ward of New Jersey, Williams, Wilson of Pennsylvania, and Yancey.

NAYS—Messrs. Bard, Baylies of Massachusetts, Bayly of Virginia, Bigelow, Bowen, Boyd, Bradbury, Breckenridge, Brigham, Burwell, Butler, Caperton, Calhoun, Champion, Cilley, Clopton, Cooper, Cox, Crawford, Culpeper, Davenport, Davis of Massachusetts, Desha, Ely, Evans, Franklin, Gaston, Geddes, Glasgow, Grosvenor, Hale, Hall, Hanson, Henderson, Howell, Humphreys, Hulbert, Jackson of Rhode Island, Johnson of Virginia, Johnson of Kentucky, Kennedy, Kent of New York, King of Massachusetts, Law, Lewis, Lovett, Macon, McKim, Miller, Moseley, Markell, Newton, Oakley, Pearson, Pickering, Pitkin, Potter, John Reed, William Reed, Ruggles, Schureman, Seybert, Sheffey, Sherwood, Shipherd, Slaymaker, Stanford, Stockton, Stuart, Sturges, Taggart, Thompson, Vose, Ward of Massachusetts, Webster, Wheaton, White, Wilcox, Wilson of Massachusetts, and Winter.

The state of the vote having been declared—

The SPEAKER (Mr. CHEVES, of South Carolina,) rose. After adverting to the rule of the House, which makes it the right and duty of the Speaker to vote in two cases, of which this was one, he proceeded to assign briefly the reasons which influenced him to vote against the bill. He noticed the opinions expressed on both sides of the House for and against the measure; and declared · his own conviction that the bill proposed a dangerous, unexampled, and, he might almost say, a desperate resort. He cursorily examined the three views in which the passage of the bill had been advocated, namely, as calculated to resuscitate public credit; to establish a circulating medium; and to afford the ways and means for the support of the Government. He delivered, with even more than his usual eloquence and impressiveness, his opinions of these several points, and concluded with

13th CON. 3d SESS.—33

expressing his solemn belief, that neither of these purposes would be answered by the bill. He denied that the passage of this bill was demanded by the safety of the nation; but intimated his opinion that a National Bank bill might be framed, by which the avowed objects of the present bill might be accomplished, which he had no doubt would unite a majority in its favor. Although the vote was painful to him to give, he was therefore obliged to vote in the negative.

The SPEAKER's vote having produced an equality of votes, he declared the decision of the House to be, that the bill should not pass.

So the bill is rejected.

Mr. HALL, of Georgia, who had voted against the bill, then moved a reconsideration of the vote just taken. He said he was opposed to this bill, and should be opposed to any bill for the establishment of a National Bank; but he was willing that his friends should have an opportunity of giving such a shape to a bill on that subject, as should unite the votes of all who were friendly on principle to the establishment of a National Bank.

The question for a reconsideration of the vote having been stated from the Chair—a motion was made to adjourn, and decided in the affirmative.

TUESDAY, January 3.

Another member, to wit: from Massachusetts, ABIEL WOOD, appeared and took his seat.

Mr. FISK, of New York, from the Committee of Ways and Means, to whom was referred the amendments of the Senate to the bill for taxing certain manufactures, reported in favor of an agreement to all the amendments of the Senate, except that one which proposed a tax of eight per cent. ad valorem on all umbrellas or parasols. This report was referred to a Committee of the Whole.

Mr. INGERSOLL, of Pennsylvania, from the Judiciary Committee, to whom was referred the petition of sundry citizens of New York on that subject, reported a bill to establish an uniform system of bankruptcy throughout the United States; which was twice read, and referred to a Committee of the whole House.

Mr. PLEASANTS, of Virginia, from the Naval Committee, to whom was referred the bill from the Senate, authorizing the appointment of certain naval officers therein named, reported the same without amendment; and it was referred to a Committee of the Whole.

A message was received from the President of the United States, transmitting a report of the Secretary of the Treasury, of the proceedings under the act for laying out the great western road—Referred to a select committee.

The amendments of the Senate to the furniture tax bill, were referred to the Committee of Ways and Means.

BANK OF THE UNITED STATES.

The House resumed the consideration of the unfinished business, being a motion to reconsider the vote to reject the bill to incorporate the subscribers to the Bank of the United States of America.

[On this motion there arose a desultory but very interesting debate, which occupied the House from 12 to about 5 o'clock. We must content ourselves with very briefly stating the several grounds taken by the gentlemen who spoke on the one side or the other.—*Editors.*]

Mr. HALL, of Georgia, commenced the debate by assigning the reasons which had influenced him to move a reconsideration of the question; which were, generally, that though he was and should continue to be opposed to any bank that could be established, unless within the District of Columbia, yet the state of the vote of last night gave him reason to believe that some plan might be adopted to meet the views of what was evidently a majority of the House on that subject. He therefore proposed, if the vote should be reconsidered, to call up the proposition laid upon the table by him some time ago, respecting an issue of Treasury notes, and to move its reference, together with this bill, to the Committee of Ways and Means; that, from a combination of the principles of both, some measure might be adopted which would subserve the public interest. He called upon gentlemen of the majority, in an impressive manner, to rally themselves around the public good, to sacrifice to each other a little of their own opinion, in order to serve the nation. Having to contend not only with a foreign enemy, but with internal traitors, it was high time, instead of putting themselves into the hands of merchants and men who are determined, if they could, to crush the present Administration, to draw on the real, solid resources of the nation, &c. Mr. H. took occasion to express his disgust at the attempt, twice repeated, which he had witnessed, to prevent an individual from voting, because he had lent money to the Government or held Government security (meaning Mr. INGERSOLL.) Such proceedings, he said, made his blood run cold. They required the friends of the Government to unite, to beware how they act, instead of aiding those whose only object was to defeat every act calculated for the defence of the country, &c.

Mr. ALEXANDER, of Ohio, made a few general remarks as to the readiness with which he should approach this question to reconsider what had been denounced as a rash, desperate, and destructive measure. His remarks were evidently intended to reflect on the observations with which the SPEAKER had on the preceding evening prefaced his vote. He should feel no pain, he said, when acting from his own choice, in giving a vote which was to destroy a ruinous measure; he should rather rejoice in the opportunity of giving such a vote, and not complain that he did it with pain, &c.

Mr. McKEE, of Kentucky, favored the reconsideration of the bill, in the hope that, when reconsidered, it would be recommitted, and its features changed. He had voted for it in its present shape with much reluctance; he had so voted, however, because he believed the taxes could not be paid by the people unless they were

aided by the establishment of a medium of general circulation, &c. He did not believe, in its present shape, that the bill would pass; but he did believe it might be so modified as to meet the views of a majority of the House.

Mr. INGERSOLL, of Pennsylvania, said he should vote for a reconsideration of the bill, because he was of the same opinion to-day that he was yesterday. He was not tenacious as to the plan of it, but a National Bank he believed to be indispensable, &c. He took occasion to remark, in allusion to the observation of Mr. HALL, that although he, with several other gentlemen of the House, possessed a small interest in the public stock, he had no idea that it could disqualify him or any one else from voting on this question, any more than on the tax or any other revenue or loan bills, &c.

Mr. MACON, of North Carolina, said he should vote against reconsideration; for, although he had of late uniformly entertained the opinion, that it would be convenient and expedient to establish a National Bank, he as firmly believed that there was no delegated power in Congress to establish such a bank. He had given such votes as he thought calculated to improve or perfect the various bills before the House, but he must eventually vote against any bank. Mr. M. concluded his examination of this question by expressing the opinion that Treasury notes would circulate and obtain as good a credit as the notes of the bank proposed to be established; and to those the nation must, he believed, at last resort, &c.

Mr. ROBERTSON, of Louisiana, was in favor of reconsideration, and made an animated appeal to those who were friendly to the establishment of a bank, and yet had opposed this bill because the details did not exactly meet their views. He called upon them to sacrifice their particular prejudices, and not prostrate the public interest at the shrine of their own pride or independence of opinion. Scarcely any subject, he said, could come before the House, in regard to which gentlemen might not urge that there were certain of the details which did not meet their approbation, and for which they could not vote. This bill had been called a desperate, a dangerous measure. It might be so, Mr. R. said; but, from the nettle danger we frequently pluck the flower safety. Nothing could be more dangerous than the very situation in which we now are; which could not be worsted even by the failure of the novel experiment which this bill had been pronounced to be, &c.

Mr. ALSTON, of North Carolina, said he should vote against reconsideration. Believing no good could result from further attempts to unite conflicting opinions on this subject; he was in favor of putting it to rest, and letting the responsibility rest on the shoulders of those who had twice already defeated the bill, &c.

Mr. DUVALL, of Kentucky, in advocating a reconsideration, called upon those who had refused to sacrifice their individual opinions, to remember the sacrifices made by those of their own party, and to exhibit that liberality and spirit of mutual concession, without which there could be no legislation. He believed there was a decided majority in the House in favor of a National Bank, and he entreated gentlemen to consent to recommitment, to make one last effort to save the sinking credit of the country, &c. He dwelt at some length on the absurdity of every man in a public body clinging to his own opinion as the standard of perfection. Unless men yield occasionally their particular opinions on minor points and mere matters of detail, no majority could ever be obtained in favor of any particular measure. He had thus yielded his opinions when he voted for this bill, and he hoped a sufficient number would now do so to obtain a reconsideration.

Mr. GHOLSON, of Virginia, conjured gentlemen to put an end to debate, and to act. While they were debating, the Army was suffering for the want of necessary supplies; the nation was suffering at every point. He entreated gentlemen to permit the question to be taken.

Mr. HAWKINS, of Kentucky, addressing himself to the majority of the House, exhorted them to unite, and no longer suffer themselves to be driven from ground to ground, from shift to shift, by the pertinacity of a minority who openly disavowed any responsibility for the failure of measures which they were frequently the means of thwarting. He adverted to the majority which a day or two ago had appeared in favor of this bill, who had been driven from their ground by the pertinacity of the minority, in violation of the usages and decorum of legislation, &c. He appealed also to the liberality of those opposed to this bill on mere points of detail, whether an opportunity ought not to be afforded to those who were friendly to the principle to try this question again. He dwelt with much emphasis on the weight of responsibility attaching to every one who voted on this question, and the propriety of allowing them to vote again, on a vote on which the House was equally divided, after having an opportunity since to reflect on it.

Mr. PEARSON expressed himself favorably towards a National Bank, but as strongly opposed to the bill now before the House, the vote on which he would not consent to reconsider, lest the bill might then pass, though he was willing to suspend the rule of the House forbidding a bill once rejected to be originated anew, so as to give an opportunity to obtain the establishment of a bank on proper banking principles, &c.

Mr. FISK, of New York, said the very importance of this bill was a reason why a question, decided as it had been, should be reconsidered; that, if a majority should not favor its passage in its present shape, it might be put in such a form as should insure it the support of a majority. The proposal of the gentleman who preceded him, to dispense with the rule, he considered as more objectionable by far, than the practice of reconsidering a vote.

Mr. FORSYTH, of Georgia, at some length, warmly contended for the reconsideration of the bill, avowing himself still friendly to it, in preference to any other plan which could be proposed.

Mr. CALHOUN was in favor of reconsideration of the bill, but on different grounds from Mr. FORSYTH. He was and should continue opposed to the present bill.

Mr. GASTON, Mr. CULPEPER, Mr. WEBSTER, and Mr. GROSVENOR, expressed themselves friendly to a National Bank on the principles they have heretofore advocated, but decidedly opposed to this, and therefore determined to vote against reconsidering it, though they were willing to suspend the rule forbidding future reconsideration.

Mr. WILSON, of Pennsylvania, advocated reconsideration of the bill, on the grounds of partiality to the form of the present bill, which he examined and supported by a train of argument going to exhibit its particular merits.

Mr. HALL then said he had made his motion with the hope of obtaining a compromise of conflicting opinions, and a modification of the present bill. But, finding its friends so wedded to it as to attempt to force it through the House, he withdrew his motion for a reconsideration.

Mr. WEBSTER took this opportunity to lay upon the table the following resolution:

Resolved, That the rule of the House which prevents a subject once acted upon from being acted upon again during the same session, be suspended until otherwise ordered.

Mr. McKIM renewed the motion to reconsider the vote on the Bank bill; not from any intention to change his vote, but from a disposition to accommodate his friends on a question of so much magnitude.

Mr. SHARP, of Kentucky, opposed, and Mr. NEWTON, of Virginia, advocated the reconsideration—the one, on grounds of unabated hostility to the present bill; the other from a disposition to afford the utmost latitude to the consideration of a subject so highly important to the nation.

The question on reconsideration was at length decided by yeas and nays.—For reconsideration 107, against it 54, as follows:

YEAS—Messrs. Alexander, Anderson, Archer, Avery, Bard, Burnett, Bines, Bowen, Brown, Burwell, Butler, Caldwell, Calhoun, Cannon, Chappell, Clark, Clendenin, Comstock, Conard, Crawford, Creighton, Crouch, Cuthbert, Dana, Davis of Pennsylvania, Desacyelles, Duvall, Earle, Farrow, Fisk of Vermont, Fisk of New York, Forney, Forsyth, Franklin, Geddes, Gholson, Glasgow, Gourdin, Griffin, Hanson, Harris, Hasbrouck, Hawes, Hawkins, Hopkins of Kentucky, Hubbard, Humphreys, Ingersoll, Ingham, Irving, Irwin, Jackson, of Virginia, Johnson of Kentucky, Kent of New York, Kent of Maryland, Kerr, Kershaw, Kilbourn, King of North Carolina, Lefferts, Lewis, Lovett, Lowndes, Lyle, Markell, McCoy, McKee, McKim, McLean, Montgomery, Moore, Murfree, Nelson, Newton, Oakley, Ormsby, Parker, Pickens, Pleasants, Rea of Pennsylvania, Rhea of Tennessee, Rich, Ringgold, Robertson, Sage, Sevier, Sharp, Sherwood, Shipherd, Skinner, Smith of New York, Smith of Pennsylvania, Stockton, Strong, Tannehill, Taylor, Telfair, Troup, Udree, Ward of New Jersey, White, Williams, Wilson of Pennsylvania, Winter, Wood, Wright, and Yancey.

NAYS—Messrs. Alston, Baylies of Massachusetts, Bayly of Virginia, Bigelow, Boyd, Bradbury, Breckenridge, Brigham, Caperton, Champion, Cilley, Clopton, Cooper, Cox, Culpeper, Davenport, Davis of Massachusetts, Ely, Gaston, Grosvenor, Hale, Hall, Henderson, Howell, Hulbert, Jackson of Rhode Island, Johnson of Virginia, Kennedy, King of Massachusetts, Law, Macon, Miller, Moseley, Pearson, Pickering, Pitkin, Potter, John Reed, William Reed, Ruggles, Schureman, Seybert, Sheffey, Slaymaker, Stanford, Sturges, Taggart, Thompson, Vose, Ward of Massachusetts, Webster, Wheaton, Wilcox, and Wilson of Massachusetts.

And the question being again stated—"Shall the bill pass?"—

Mr. McKee moved to recommit the bill to a select committee, and presented his view of the change which he conceived ought to be made in its provisions.

Mr. Butler, of Vermont, supported this motion, and in a speech of some length exhibited his views on the same subject.

Mr. Forsyth opposed the recommitment with much zeal and eloquence, on grounds of preference to the present bill.

Mr. King, of Massachusetts, expressed his opinions generally in hostility to the establishment of any bank at this time, and in opposition to any compromise.

Mr. Findley advocated the recommitment, principally on the ground of opposition to that feature of the bill which requires the bank to make a loan to Government—which he believed at once superfluous and inexpedient.

Mr. Oakley and Mr. Stockton advocated recommitment with earnestness and ability, in order to procure a modification of the details. If modified, as they believed it might be, they pledged themselves to vote for the bank bill, and expressed their opinion that in that vote they would be joined by a majority of their political friends.

The question on recommitment was decided by yeas and nays. For recommitment 89, against it 71, as follows:

Yeas—Messrs. Bard, Barnett, Baylies of Massachusetts, Bayly of Virginia, Bigelow, Bowen, Boyd, Bradbury, Breckenridge, Brigham, Butler, Caperton, Calhoun, Champion, Cilley, Clark, Clopton, Cooper, Cox, Crawford, Crouch, Culpeper, Dana, Davenport, Davis of Massachusetts, Duvall, Earle, Ely, Farrow, Findley, Forney, Franklin, Gaston, Geddes, Glasgow, Grosvenor, Hale, Hanson, Hasbrouck, Hawes, Henderson, Hopkins of Kentucky, Howell, Humphreys, Hulbert, Jackson of Rhode Island, Kent of New York, Kershaw, Law, Lewis, Lovett, Lowndes, Markell, McKee, Miller, Montgomery, Moseley, Oakley, Ormsby, Pearson, Pickering, Pitkin, Potter, John Reed, William Reed, Ruggles, Schureman, Seybert, Sharp, Sheffey, Sherwood, Shipherd, Slaymaker, Smith of New York, Stanford, Stockton, Sturges, Taggart, Thompson, Vose, Ward of Massachusetts, Ward of New Jersey, Webster, Wheaton, White, Wilcox, Wilson of Massachusetts, Winter, and Wood.

Nays—Messrs. Alexander, Alston, Anderson, Archer, Avary, Bines, Brown, Burwell, Caldwell, Cannon, Chappell, Clendenin, Comstock, Conard, Creighton, Cuthbert, Davis of Pennsylvania, Denoyelles, Desha, Fisk of Vermont, Fisk of New York, Forsyth, Gholson, Gourdin, Griffin, Hall, Harris, Hawkins, Hubbard, Ingersoll, Ing-

ham, Irving, Irwin, Johnson of Virginia, Johnson of Kentucky, Kennedy, Kent of Maryland, Kerr, Kilbourn, King of Massachusetts, King of North Carolina, Lefferts, Lyle, Macon, McCoy, McKim, McLean, Moore, Murfree, Nelson, Newton, Parker, Pickens, Pleasants, Rea of Pennsylvania, Rhea of Tennessee, Rich, Ringgold, Robertson, Sage, Sevier, Smith of Pennsylvania, Strong, Tannehill, Taylor, Telfair, Troup, Udree, Williams, Wilson of Pennsylvania, and Yancey.

And it was determined to recommit the bill to a select committee of seven members.

Messrs. McKee, Findley, Stockton, Pitkin, Taylor, Cuthbert, and Yancey, were appointed the committee.

WEDNESDAY, January 4.

On motion of Mr. Jennings, the House proceeded to consider the resolution submitted by him on the 30th ultimo, and the same being modified, was agreed to as follows:

Resolved, That the Committee on the Judiciary be directed to inquire into the expediency of authorizing the Executive authorities of the several States and Territories of the United States, respectively, by law, to apprehend, secure, and deliver to the Government, for the time being, of any Territory of the United States, or his agent, any fugitive or fugitives from justice, upon demand being made of the Executive authority of any such State or Territory, to which such fugitive or fugitives shall have fled, and upon producing an indictment found, or an affidavit made before a competent officer, charging the person so demanded with having committed treason, felony, or other crime, within the jurisdiction of the said Territory from which he so fled; and what amendments, if any, are necessary to the act or acts respecting persons escaping from the service of their masters.

A message from the Senate informed the House that the Senate insist on their amendments proposed to the bill "to provide additional revenues for defraying the expenses of Government, and maintaining the public credit, by laying duties on household furniture, on horses kept exclusively for the saddle or carriage, and on gold and silver watches;" The Senate recede from their first amendment proposed to the bill "to provide additional revenues for defraying the expenses of Government, and maintaining the public credit, by laying duties on various goods, wares, and merchandise, manufactured within the United States;" and they insist on that part of their fifth amendment to the said bill to which this House have disagreed.

Mr. Fisk, of New York, from the Committee of Ways and Means, to whom was referred the amendments of the Senate to the furniture tax bill, recommended a disagreement to the same; and the question being taken thereon, they were accordingly disagreed to.

Mr. Troup, of Georgia, from the Committee on Military Affairs, reported a bill for the better regulation of the Ordnance department; which was twice read, and committed.

1033   HISTORY OF CONGRESS.   1034

JANUARY, 1815.   *Intercourse with the Enemy.*   H. OF R.

The bill from the Senate, to provide for leasing lands reserved for the use of schools in the Mississippi Territory, was read a third time, and passed.

The amendments of the Senate to the bill for taxing certain manufactures, were considered in Committee of the Whole, and afterwards in the House. Those amendments which go to exempt "pig iron" from taxation, and add "umbrellas and parasols," were disagreed to, and the others were agreed to.

The House spent some time in Committee of the Whole on the bill to prohibit intercourse with the enemy, and for other purposes; which underwent a considerable discussion, until late in the day, when the Committee rose, reported progress and obtained leave to sit again.

THURSDAY, January 5.

A message was received from the Senate, announcing their recession from all their amendments to the bill laying duties on certain manufactures, except so much as proposes to lay a duty of eight per cent. on all umbrellas and parasols above the value of two dollars.

Mr. FISK, of New York, stated that the principal difficulty with the Committee of Ways and Means, in assenting to this amendment, had been a doubt of the Constitutional power of the Senate, to propose new taxes. As this was a question which he believed had never been decided; and as the tax was in itself unimportant, he moved that the House insist on its disagreement to this amendment. This motion was agreed to.

The House also determined to insist on disagreement to a part of of the amendments of the Senate, to the furniture tax bill, and to ask of the Senate a conference on that bill.

INTERCOURSE WITH THE ENEMY.

The House resumed the consideration of the report of the Committee of the Whole, on the bill for preventing intercourse with the enemy. [This is a bill containing ample and energetic provisions, for preventing the treasonable intercourse, which has recently prevailed to so great an extent on our northern borders, and elsewhere.] The few amendments made in Committee of the Whole having been agreed to—

Mr. GROSVENOR moved to strike out the fifth section of the bill; which is as follows:

SEC. 5. *And be it further enacted,* That every Collector of the Customs shall have authority to appoint, within his district, such number of inspectors of the customs as he shall judge necessary, who are hereby declared to be officers of the customs: *Provided, however,* That it shall be discretionary with the Secretary of the Treasury, what number of such inspectors shall be paid for their services by the respective collectors, out of the revenue of the United States; and the said inspectors, before they enter upon the duties of their offices, shall take and subscribe before the collectors appointing them, or before some magistrate within their respective districts, authorized by law to administer oaths, the following oath or affirmation, to wit: I, ——, having been appointed an inspector of the customs, within and for the district of ——, do solemnly, sincerely, and truly swear, or affirm, (as the case may be,) that I will diligently and faithfully execute the duties of the said office of inspector, and will use my best endeavors to prevent and detect frauds and violations against the laws of the United States; I further swear, or affirm, that I will support the Constitution of the United States.

This motion gave rise to an extended debate, in which many gentlemen partook, and was decided in the negative—for the motion 51, against it 85, as follows:

YEAS—Messrs. Baylies of Massachusetts, Bigelow, Boyd, Breckenridge, Caperton, Champion, Cilley, Clopton, Cooper, Cox, Culpeper, Davenport, Farrow, Gaston, Geddes, Grosvenor, Hale, Henderson, Howell, Hulbert, Jackson of Rhode Island, Kent of New York, King of Massachusetts, Law, Lewis, Lovett, Markell, Miller, Montgomery, Moseley, Pearson, Pickering, Pitkin, Potter, John Reed, William Reed, Ruggles, Sheffey, Sherwood, Slaymaker, Smith of New York, Stanford, Stockton, Stuart, Sturges, Thompson, Vose, Ward of Massachusetts, Wheaton, White, and Wilcox.

NAYS—Messrs. Alexander, Alston, Anderson, Archer, Avery, Barbour, Bard, Barnett, Bines, Bowen, Brown, Burwell, Butler, Caldwell, Calhoun, Cannon, Chappell, Clark, Clendenin, Comstock, Conard, Crawford, Creighton, Crouch, Dana, Davis of Pennsylvania, Denoyelles, Desha, Duvall, Earle, Evans, Fisk of Vermont, Fisk of New York, Forney, Forsyth, Franklin, Gholson, Gourdin, Griffin, Hall, Harris, Hasbrouck, Hawes, Hawkins, Hubbard, Humphreys, Ingersoll, Ingham, Irving, Johnson of Virginia, Johnson of Kentucky, Kent of Maryland, Kerr, Kershaw, Kilbourn, King of North Carolina, Lefferts, Lyle, Macon, McCoy, McKim, McLean, Moore, Murfree, Nelson, Newton, Ormsby, Parker, Pickens, Pleasants, Rea of Pennsylvania, Rhea of Tennessee, Rich, Ringgold, Sage, Sharp, Smith of Pennsylvania, Tannehill, Taylor, Telfair, Troup, Udree, Williams, Wilson of Pennsylvania; and Yancey.

Mr. KING, of Massachusetts, moved further to amend the bill by inserting, after the word "customs," in the 4th line of the 5th section, these words: "for whom, in the execution of their trust, such Collector shall be answerable;" which motion, after debate, was determined in the negative—yeas 62, nays 74, as follows:

YEAS—Messrs. Baylies of Massachusetts, Bayly of Virginia, Bigelow, Boyd, Breckenridge, Brigham, Caperton, Champion, Cilley, Cooper, Cox, Culpeper, Dana, Davenport, Davis of Massachusetts, Duvall, Ely, Farrow, Gaston, Geddes, Grosvenor, Hale, Hawes, Henderson, Howell, Hulbert, Johnson of Virginia, Kent of New York, King of Massachusetts, Law, Lewis, Lovett, Markell, Miller, Moseley, Nelson, Oakley, Ormsby, Pearson, Pickering, Pitkin, John Reed, William Reed, Ruggles, Sheffey, Sherwood, Slaymaker, Smith of New York, Stanford, Stockton, Stuart, Sturges, Taggart, Taylor, Thompson, Vose, Ward of Massachusetts, Wheaton, White, Wilcox, Wilson of Massachusetts, and Winter.

NAYS—Messrs. Alexander, Alston, Anderson, Archer, Avery, Barbour, Bard, Barnett, Bines, Bowen, Brown, Burwell, Caldwell, Calhoun, Cannon, Chappell, Clendenin, Clopton, Comstock, Conard, Crawford, Creighton, Crouch, Davis of Pennsylvania, Denoyelles, Desha, Earle, Evans, Findley, Fisk of Vermont

Fisk of New York, Forney, Franklin, Gholson, Glasgow, Gourdin, Griffin, Hall, Harris, Hasbrouck, Hubbard, Ingham, Irving, Kennedy, Kent of Maryland, Kerr, Kershaw, Kilbourn, King of North Carolina, Lefferts, Lyle, McCoy, McKim, Moore, Murfree, Newton, Parker, Pickens, Pleasants, Rea of Pennsylvania, Rhea of Tennessee, Rich, Ringgold, Sage, Seybert, Sharp, Smith of Pennsylvania, Tannehill, Telfair, Troup, Udree, Williams, Wilson of Pennsylvania, and Yancey.

Mr. KING, of Massachusetts, moved further to amend the said fifth section of the bill, by inserting, after the words "officers shall," the following words: "give bonds with securities to the satisfaction of the collectors appointing them, for the true and faithful execution of their office, and ;"—which motion was determined in the negative.

The sixth section of the bill is as follows:

SEC. 6. *And be it further enacted,* That any collector, naval officer, surveyor, or inspector, when proceeding to make any search or seizure, authorized by this act, be and is hereby empowered to command any person who shall be present, to aid and assist such officer in the discharge and performance of his duty therein; and if any person, being so commanded, shall neglect or refuse to aid and assist such officer in making such search or seizure, the person so neglecting or refusing shall forfeit and pay a sum not exceeding two hundred dollars, and not less than fifty dollars. And such officer may also demand, in cases where it may become necessary, the assistance of the marshal of the district, or any of his deputies, who shall call upon the posse of the district, if necessary, in his or their judgment, to render effectual the execution of this act; and all citizens or inhabitants of the district, above the age of eighteen years, and able to travel, who refuse or neglect, on proper notice from the marshal, or any of his deputies, to join such posse, shall be considered guilty of a misdemeanor, and be liable to be fined in any sum not exceeding three hundred dollars, and be imprisoned for any term not exceeding three months.

A motion was made by Mr. STOCKTON, to amend the said section, by inserting the word "if," after the words "enacted that;" by inserting after the word "inspector," where it first occurs, the words "shall be resisted or obstructed;" and by inserting after the word "act," where it occurs the first time, the words "he shall." This motion was determined in the negative—yeas 50, nays 78, as follows:

YEAS—Messrs. Baylies of Massachusetts, Bayly of Virginia, Boyd, Bradbury, Breckenridge, Brigham, Caperton, Champion, Cilley, Cooper, Cox, Culpeper, Davenport, Ely, Gaston, Geddes, Grosvenor, Hale, Henderson, Howell, Hulbert, Jackson of Rhode Island, Kent of New York, King of Massachusetts, Law, Lewis, Lovett, Markell, Miller, Moseley, Pickering, Pitkin, Potter, John Reed, Ruggles, Sheffey, Sherwood, Slaymaker, Smith of N. York, Stanford, Stockton, Sturges, Taggart, Thompson, Vose, Ward of Massachusetts, Wheaton, White, Wilcox, Wilson of Massachusetts.

NAYS—Messrs. Alexander, Alston, Anderson, Archer, Barbour, Bard, Barnett, Bowen, Brown, Burwell, Butler, Caldwell, Calhoun, Cannon, Chappell, Clendenin, Crawford, Creighton, Crouch, Cuthbert, Davis of Pennsylvania, Desha, Duvall, Earle, Evans, Farrow, Findley, Fisk of Vermont, Fisk of New York, Forney, Forsyth, Gholson, Glasgow, Gourdin, Griffin,

Hall, Hasbrouck, Hawes, Hubbard, Humphreys, Ingersoll, Irving, Johnson of Virginia, Johnson of Kentucky, Kennedy, Kent of Maryl'd, Kerr, Kershaw, Kilbourn, King of North Carolina, Lefferts, Lyle, Macon, McCoy, McKim, Moore, Murfree, Nelson, Newton, Ormsby, Parker, Pickens, Pleasants, Rea of Pennsylvania, Rhea of Tennessee, Rich, Ringgold, Robertson, Sage, Seybert, Sharp, Smith of Pensylvania, Tannehill, Telfair, Udree, Williams, Wilson of Pennsylvania, Yancey.

Mr. STOCKTON moved to amend the eighth section of the bill, by striking out these words: "try and determine the facts and the law in such action in the manner as if the same had been there originally commenced, the judgment in such case notwithstanding;" and to insert, "reverse or affirm the said judgment, according to law." Which motion was determined in the negative—yeas 52, nays 71, as follows:

YEAS—Messrs. Baylies of Massachusetts, Bigelow, Boyd, Bradbury, Breckenridge, Brigham, Caperton, Champion, Cilley, Clopton, Cooper, Cox, Culpeper, Davenport, Davis of Massachusetts, Ely, Gaston, Grosvenor, Hale, Henderson, Howell, Hulbert, Jackson of Rhode Island, Kennedy, Kent of New York, King of Massachusetts, Law, Lewis, Lovett, Markell, Miller, Moseley, Nelson, Oakley, Pickering, Pitkin, Potter, John Reed, Ruggles, Sheffey, Sherwood, Slaymaker, Stanford, Stockton, Sturges, Thompson, Vose, Ward of Massachusetts, Webster, Wheaton, Wilcox, and Wilson of Massachusetts.

NAYS—Messrs. Alexander, Alston, Anderson, Archer, Avery, Barbour, Barnett, Bines, Bowen, Brown, Burwell, Butler, Caldwell, Chappell, Clendenin, Conard, Crawford, Creighton, Crouch, Cuthbert, Dana, Davis of Pennsylvania, Desha, Evans, Farrow, Findley, Fisk of Vermont, Fisk of New York, Forney, Gholson, Gourdin, Griffin, Hall, Harris, Hawes, Hubbard, Humphreys, Irving, Jackson of Virginia, Johnson of Virginia, Johnson of Kentucky, Kent of Maryland, Kerr, Kershaw, Kilbourn, King of North Carolina, Lefferts, Lyle, McCoy, McKim, Moore, Newton, Ormsby, Parker, Pickens, Pleasants, Rea of Pennsylvania, Rhea of Tennessee, Rich, Ringgold, Roane, Robertson, Sage, Seybert, Sharp, Smith of Pennsylvania, Tannehill, Udree, Williams, Wilson of Pennsylvania, and Yancey.

A motion was made by Mr. KING, of Massachusetts, to strike out the ninth section of the bill, and, in lieu thereof, to insert the following:

And be it further enacted, That, if any officer or other person, executing or aiding or assisting in any seizure under this act, shall be sued or molested for anything done in virtue of the powers given by this act, or by virtue of a warrant granted by any judge or justice, pursuant to law, such officer or other person may plead the general issue; and if in such suit the plaintiff is nonsuited, or judgment passed against him, the defendant shall recover double costs. And when any prosecution shall be commenced on account of any seizure under this act, and judgment shall be given for the claimant or claimants, if it shall appear to the court before whom such prosecution shall be tried that there was reasonable cause of seizure, the said court shall cause a proper certificate of entry to be made thereof, and in such case the claimant or claimants shall not be entitled to costs, nor shall the person who made the seizure, or the prosecutor, be liable to action, suit, or judgment, on account of such seizure and prosecution: *Provided*, That the property or articles seized and held by the prosecutor or person making the seizure, be, after judgment, forthwith returned to such claimant or claimants, his, her, or their agent or agents: *And provided*, That no action or prosecution shall be maintained in any case under this act, unless the same shall have been commenced within one year next after the penalty or forfeiture was incurred.

And the question being taken, it was determined in the negative.

A motion was made by Mr. KING, of Massachusetts, to strike out the twelfth section of the said bill, which is as follows:

SEC. 12. *And be it further enacted*, That it shall be lawful for the President of the United States, or such other person as he shall have empowered for that purpose, to employ, under proper instructions to be by him given, such part of the land and naval forces of the United States, or of the militia thereof, as shall be judged necessary, for the purpose of aiding and co-operating with the officers of the customs, and all other civil magistrates, in seizing and securing persons engaged, or suspected from probable cause as aforesaid to be engaged, in unlawful trade or intercourse with the enemy as aforesaid, together with the articles or supplies, or vessels, boats, vehicles, or animals, employed as aforesaid, in such trade or intercourse.

And the question being taken, it was determined in the negative—yeas 37, nays 69, as follows:

YEAS—Messrs. Baylies of Massachusetts, Bigelow, Bradbury, Breckenridge, Brigham, Caperton, Champion, Cox, Culpeper, Davenport, Gaston, Grosvenor, Hale, Henderson, Hulbert, Jackson of Rhode Island, King of Massachusetts, Law, Lewis, Lovett, Miller, Moseley, Oakley, Pickering, Pitkin, Potter, John Reed, Ruggles, Sherwood, Slaymaker, Stanford, Stockton, Vose, Ward of Massachusetts, Webster, Wilcox, and Wilson of Massachusetts.

NAYS—Messrs. Alexander, Alston, Anderson, Archer, Avery, Barbour, Bines, Bowen, Brown, Butler, Caldwell, Calhoun, Cannon, Chappell, Clendenin, Clopton, Conard, Crawford, Creighton, Crouch, Davis of Pennsylvania, Desha, Findley, Fisk of Vermont, Fisk of New York, Forney, Gholson, Gourdin, Griffin, Hall, Harris, Hawes, Hubbard, Humphreys, Ingham, Irving, Johnson of Virginia, Johnson of Kentucky, Kent of Maryland, Kerr, Kershaw, Kilbourn, King of North Carolina, Lefferts, Lyle, McCoy, McKim, Moore, Nelson, Newton, Ormsby, Parker, Pickens, Pleasants, Rea of Pennsylvania, Rhea of Tennessee, Rich, Ringgold, Roane, Robertson, Sage, Seybert, Sharp, Smith of Pennsylvania, Strong, Tannehill, Udree, Wilson of Pennsylvania, and Yancey.

Mr. KING, of Massachusetts, moved to amend the bill as follows:

Section 1, line 8. After the word "duty," insert "the payment thereof intended to be evaded."

Section 3, lines 8 and 9. Strike out the words "or of which they may be in possession."

Section 4, line 22. After the word "building," insert "in day-time only."

Section 8, line 28. Strike out the words "now pending or."

And the question being taken on the said amendments, it was determined in the negative.

Mr. WILSON, of Massachusetts, moved to add

to the third section the following words: "or for the use of any citizen residing within the limits of the United States." Which motion was determined in the negative.

It appearing about this time, owing to the retirement of a number of the members of the House, that a quorum was not present, a motion was made for a call of the House.

Mr. GROSVENOR contended that one day's notice was necessary to a call of the House. The Chair decided such notice was not necessary. Mr. GROSVENOR appealed from this decision, which the House affirmed.

The call of the House then took place, when it appeared that the following members were present:

Messrs. Alexander, Alston, Anderson, Archer, Avery, Barbour, Bard, Barnett, Bines, Bowen, Brown, Butler, Caldwell, Calhoun, Cannon, Chappell, Clark, Clendenin, Clopton, Comstock, Conard, Crawford, Creighton, Crouch, Cuthbert, Dana, Davis of Pennsylvania, Desha, Duvall, Earle, Fisk of Vermont, Fisk of New York, Forney, Gholson, Gourdin, Griffin, Grosvenor, Hale, Hall, Harris, Hawes, Hawkins, Hopkins of Kentucky, Hubbard, Humphreys, Hulbert, Ingham, Irving, Jackson of Virginia, Johnson of Virginia, Johnson of Kentucky, Kent of Maryland, Kerr, Kershaw, Kilbourn, King of Massachusetts, King of North Carolina, Lefferts, Lovett, Lyle, McCoy, McKim, Miller, Moore, Nelson, Newton, Ormsby, Parker, Pickens, Pleasants, John Reed, Rea of Pennsylvania, Rhea of Tennessee, Ringgold, Roane, Robertson, Sage, Seybert, Sharp, Smith of Pennsylvania, Strong, Sturges, Tannehill, Taylor, Udree, Vose, Ward of New Jersey, Wilson of Massachusetts, Wilson of Pennsylvania, Wood, and Yancey—92.

The doors of the House were then closed, according to the rules of the House, and ingress and egress forbidden, but not before two or three other members had come in.

Some difficulty arose as to the course now proper to be pursued as to compelling the attendance of absentees, &c. At length, on motion of Mr. YANCEY, it was ordered that all further proceedings on the call be suspended; and the bill, which had been all day under debate, was then ordered to be engrossed for a third reading without a division—a sufficient number not rising to support the motion of Mr. MILLER, for the yeas and nays.

A message from the Senate informed the House that the Senate have passed a bill "for the relief of William Gamble," in which they ask the concurrence of this House: They have agreed to the conference asked by this House, on the disagreeing votes of the two Houses on the amendments depending on the bill "to provide additional revenues for defraying the expenses of Government, and maintaining the public credit, by laying duties on household furniture, on horses kept exclusively for the saddle or carriage, and on gold and silver watches," and have appointed managers on their part. They ask a conference on the disagreeing votes of the two Houses on the amendments depending between the two Houses to the bill "to provide additional revenues for defraying the expenses of Government, and maintaining the public credit, by laying duties on various goods, wares, and merchandise, manufactured within the United States," to which conference they have appointed managers on their part.

Friday, January 6.

A message from the Senate informed the House that the Senate have passed a bill "supplementary to the act, entitled "An act providing for the indemnification of certain claimants of public lands in the Mississippi Territory;" in which they ask the concurrence of this House.

The said bill was read twice, and referred to the committee appointed on the letter on the same subject from the acting Secretary of State, the Secretary of the Treasury, and the Attorney General.

Another message from the Senate informed the House that the Senate ask a conference on the disagreeing votes of the two Houses on the amendment depending to the bill "to provide additional revenues for defraying the expenses of Government, and maintaining the public credit, by laying duties on various goods, wares, and merchandise, manufactured within the United States;" to which conference they have appointed managers on their part.

Resolved, That this House agree to the conference asked by the Senate on the bill last mentioned, and that Mr. Eppes, Mr. Fisk of New York, and Mr. Oakley, be the managers at the said conference on the part of this House.

The bill from the Senate, "for the relief of William Gamble," was read twice, and referred to the Committee of Claims.

Mr. Fisk, from the managers appointed by the House to attend a conference with the managers appointed by the Senate, on the disagreeing votes of the two Houses on the amendments depending to the bill "to provide additional revenues for defraying the expenses of Government, and maintaining the public credit, by laying duties on household furniture, on horses kept exclusively for the saddle or carriage, and on gold and silver watches," made a report; which was read: Whereupon,

Resolved, That this House do recede from their disagreement to the amendments of the Senate, so far as the same relate to the duty on horses kept exclusively for the saddle or carriage, and that they also recede from their disagreement to the amendment to the fifth section, and that they do agree to the amendments therein specified.

BANK OF THE UNITED STATES.

Mr. McKee, from the select committee to whom was recommitted the bill from the Senate to incorporate the subscribers to the Bank of the United States of America, reported sundry amendments thereto; which were read.

A motion was then made by Mr. Robertson to lay the report on the table for one day, that it might be printed for the more particular information of the members; which motion was negatived, ayes 36.

Mr. McKee explained, briefly, the nature and amount of the amendments now proposed to the bill. The first principle introduced into the bill, he said, was a reduction of the capital stock from fifty to thirty millions; such capital to be composed of five millions in specie, fifteen millions in Treasury notes, ten millions in stock of the United States created since the declaration of the war. The capital to be subscribable in shares of one hundred instead of five hundred each. The payments of the subscription to be so apportioned that two-fifths of the amount of the capital should be paid in at the time of subscribing. This would bring at once into the bank, $1,666,000 in specie, and the residue in Treasury notes and stock, amounting to twelve millions in the whole. There was every reason to believe that this payment could be made, at the time of subscription, to the full amount proposed; if so, the bank could forthwith go into operation, and its capital would not remain inactive, as a part of it must do if a less amount were payable at the time of subscription. The principle requiring the bank to make a loan of thirty millions to the Government to be stricken out, and the provision respecting the suspension of payments in specie, which appeared to be inseparably connected with the compulsory loan, to be also stricken out. The immediate aid which the plan would afford to the Government, in addition to the establishment of a circulating medium of undoubted credit, would be in the issue and free circulation of fifteen millions of Treasury notes and the relief to the stock market by the abstraction from it of ten millions to be subscribed in the stock of the bank. The bank thus to be established was predicated on the idea of a specie bank, on which principle alone must forever rest a sound circulating medium. There was no danger, as had been frequently observed, but, without a requisition to that effect in its charter, the bank would, for its own interests, afford to the Government every assistance and accommodation in its power. A right was also reserved to the Government to subscribe on its own behalf and for its benefit, whenever Congress shall authorize it by law, five millions to the stock of the bank, payable in certificates of stock bearing an interest of four per centum. This stock it might sell at great advantage, even during the present year, if the bank went successfully into operation.

The amendments to the first section having been stated, and the question being proposed to the House on that amendment which reduces the proposed capital from fifty to thirty millions of dollars—

Mr. Telfair, of Georgia, being desirous of fixing the capital of the bank at forty millions, as a proper medium, said he should vote against this amendment, and briefly assigned his reasons for so doing.

Mr. Hawkins, of Kentucky, stated the reasons why he should vote against this amendment, though willing to make what he deemed reasonable concession to those who differed from him.

Mr. Rhea, of Tennessee, made a few observations, principally expressive of a hope that this question would be decided with as little debate as possible.

Mr. TAYLOR explained at some length the reasons, which had induced him, as a last effort to relieve the finances of the country by the establishment of a bank, to consent to this report, embracing a compromise of his own opinions. He spoke at some length in explanation of the provisions of this bill, and of the advantage which it held forth to the public interest, &c.

Mr. FORSYTH briefly stated the grounds on which he was opposed to the report of the committee, and preferred the bill in its present shape. If the amendments prevailed, he contended that the will of the majority would in fact be defeated, and a bill passed on a plan, of which the majority had already expressed their decided disapprobation.

Mr. McKEE spoke at some length in defence of the report, and to show its superiority to the present features of the bill.

Mr. INGERSOLL explained briefly why, although entertaining a decided preference for the bill, as it now stood, he should vote for the report of the committee in all its parts; because, being the result of a compromise, if it were not accepted, he feared no National Bank would be established—a measure which he deemed at this moment absolutely indispensable.

Mr. YANCEY said he should give the report his decided support, and regretted that any of his friends should act differently. He considered the proposed amendments highly expedient, and, withal, that, if they were not adopted, no bank could be established at this session.

Mr. PITKIN, in a speech of some length, explained the reasons why he had been induced to compromise a part of his own opinions, in agreeing to this report, to which he had acceded with some reluctance, and for the success of which he did not consider himself responsible. Being willing to lend his aid to extricate the Government from its present financial difficulties, he had agreed to this report, which however he believed embraced much too extensive a scale for the proposed institution. He went into an examination at some length of the principles of banking, principally to show that a forced loan would be destructive to the ability or prospects of any bank.

Mr. FORSYTH replied at some length to some of the objections which had been made to the bill as it now stands, and in vindication of his own opinion; and

Mr. PEARSON added a few words of explanation in reply to a part of Mr. FORSYTH's speech.

The question being taken, after nearly two hours debate, on the first amendment reported by the select committee, was decided as follows:

YEAS—Messrs. Alexander, Anderson, Archer, Barbour, Bard, Barnett, Baylies of Massachusetts, Bayly of Virginia, Bigelow, Bines, Bowen, Boyd, Bradbury, Breckenridge, Brigham, Burwell, Butler, Caperton, Calhoun, Cannon, Champion, Chappell, Cilley, Clark, Clendenin, Clopton, Comstock, Cox, Crawford, Creighton, Crouch, Culpeper, Cuthbert, Dana, Davenport, Davis of Massachusetts, Davis of Pennsylvania, Desha, Duvall, Earle, Ely, Evans, Farrow, Findley, Forney, Gaston, Geddes, Gholson, Grosvenor, Hanson, Harris, Hasbrouck, Hawes, Henderson, Howell, Humphreys, Hulbert, Ingersoll, Irving, Jackson of Rhode Island, Jackson of Virginia, Johnson of Virginia, Johnson of Kentucky, Kennedy, Kent of New York, Kent of Maryland, Kerr, Kershaw, King of Massachusetts, King of North Carolina, Law, Lovett, Lowndes, Markell, McKee, McKim, McLean, Miller, Montgomery, Moore, Moseley, Newton, Oakley, Ormsby, Pearson, Pickering, Pickens, Pitkin, Pleasants, Potter, John Reed, William Reed, Rea of Pennsylvania, Rhea of Tennessee, Rich, Robertson, Ruggles, Sage, Schureman, Seybert, Sharp, Shaffey, Sherwood, Shipherd, Slaymaker, Smith of New York, Smith of Pennsylvania, Stanford, Stockton, Stuart, Sturges, Taggart, Tannehill, Taylor, Thompson, Troup, Udree, Vose, Ward of Massachusetts, Ward of New Jersey, Webster, Wheaton, White, Wilcox, Williams, Wilson of Massachusetts, Winter, Wood and Yancey—129.

NAYS—Messrs. Alston, Brown, Caldwell, Conard, Denoyelles, Eppes, Fisk of Vermont, Fisk of New York, Forsyth, Franklin, Gourdin, Griffin, Hall, Hawkins, Hopkins of Kentucky, Hubbard, Ingham, Irwin, Kilbourn, Lefferts, Lyle, Macon, McCoy, Murfree, Nelson, Parker, Ringgold, Roane, Sevier, Telfair, and Wilson of Pennsylvania—31.

The other amendments, as indicated above in Mr. McKEE's remarks, were then all agreed to—among them being an amendment to postpone the opening of the books of subscription to the last instead of the second Monday in February.

A motion was made by Mr. GASTON further to amend the bill, by striking out that part of the amendment describing the (war) stock which shall be subscribable to the bank, and inserting in lieu thereof, " or in any of the public debt of the ' United States drawing an accruing interest of ' six per centum per annum, contracted or to be ' contracted by virtue of any act of Congress ;" which motion was negatived.

The bill as amended was then ordered, without a division, to be read a third time to-morrow.

SATURDAY, January 7.

Mr. FISK of New York, from the Committee of Ways and Means, reported a bill for the relief of John Brahany ; which was read, and committed to a Committee of the Whole.

Mr. OAKLEY, from the committee to whom was referred the bill from the Senate "supplementary to the act, entitled 'An act providing for the indemnification of certain claimants of public lands in the Mississippi Territory,'" reported the same with amendments; which were committed to a Committee of the Whole.

A message from the Senate informed the House that the Senate have passed the bill " to authorize the President of the United States to accept the services of volunteers who may organize themselves, and offer their services to the Government of the United States," with amendments ; in which they ask the concurrence of this House.

The engrossed bill to prevent intercourse with the enemy having been read through—

Mr. OAKLEY, of New York, moved to lay the

bill on the table, to take up the Bank bill, the passage of which he feared might be too long delayed by the discussion which might arise on the bill just read. This motion was supported by Mr. YANCEY and Mr. INGERSOLL.

The motion was opposed by Messrs. FISK of New York, FISK of Vermont, and RHEA, on the ground that the speedy passage of the bill just read, was required by the interest and honor of the nation, to arrest the supplies to the enemy, and the loss of duties on smuggled goods, which our revenue officers now could not, dare not, attempt to seize.

The motion to lay the bill on the table prevailed, ayes 83.

BANK OF THE UNITED STATES.

The engrossed amendments to the bill from the Senate "to incorporate the Bank of the United States of America," were then read, and the question stated, " Shall this bill pass, as amended ?" and the yeas and nays thereon having been required by Mr. STANFORD—

Mr. FISK, of New York, rose to assign the reasons which now influenced him to vote against this bill. His objections were, to the reduction of the capital, and to the omission of what had been miscalled the forced loan feature of the bill, which he considered one of the best. The bill, before it was amended, would, he said, have afforded to the Government a benefit to the amount of twenty millions, but now would not afford to it a greater bonus than three millions. He objected to the amendments which had taken from the bill the control which the Government ought to have over it, and would throw the Government and the moneyed resources of the nation into the power of its political adversaries. There were also other features of the bill to which he objected ; so strongly, upon the whole, that he would not vote for the bill.

Mr. HANSON, of Maryland, expressed his regret to see any impediment thrown in the way of the bill. He expressed all the satisfaction he felt at being able on this occasion to redeem his pledge to co-operate with the majority, in any measure which he could hope or believe would be beneficial to the nation. This bill, in its present shape, he remarked, was the result of a compromise produced by mutual and magnanimous concessions, and at a period like this, of bitter political animosity, concessions reflecting equal honor on both sides of the House.

Mr. GROSVENOR, of New York, assigned, at some length, the reason why he should vote against the bill. He expressed, in a feeling manner, his regret at being compelled to vote, on this occasion, against so many of those with whom he had heretofore acted in opposition to the measures of this Administration. His objections were more to the time when and purposes for which a bank is to be established, than to the features of this bill, to some of which he objected. He denied that it could be a specie bank, or that the bank would ever be able to get a million of its notes into circulation. The Government relying

upon it would be disappointed, and ruin soon stare them in the face. He denied the operation upon himself of the argument that this was a lesser evil than what might be substituted for it if it did not pass. He would not, he said, embrace this evil in order to avoid a greater which might not happen ; he would never, he said, adopt a principle looking towards that which imports that the end may justify the means.

Mr. TELFAIR, of Georgia, stated the reasons why, although he decidedly approved of the bill which had been first before the House, he should yet vote for this bill. He was seriously convinced, he said, that under the present embarrassment of our circulating medium, and of the fiscal concerns of the nation, that a bank was indispensable ; and, though the system now before the House was one, the details of which he could not approve, he would vote for it as a last resort. He frankly intimated his hope that the other House would propose some modification of the amendments of this House, that would render the compromise of opinion more equitable than as it now stood. Mr. T. went into a general examination of the principles and history of banking, principally to show that banks founded on the credit of Governments and on public stocks had not been as generally unsuccessful as had been contended ; and he then compared the present system with that which came from the Senate, to the latter of which he gave a decided preference.

Mr. INGHAM, of Pennsylvania, believed, he said, a National Bank to be essentially necessary to give relief to the present embarrassed state of things. Believing this bill would contribute in some degree to relieve the national wants, it would receive his vote, though reluctantly ; and he wished it to be distinctly understood, that instead of its being a preferred measure, be considered the first bill as more efficient and calculated to give the Government all it wanted. The vote of the House this day, he said, would be no test of the excellence of this system, or even of the approbation of it by the House—the question being whether the House would take this or no bank. Mr. I. made a statement of the comparative advantages and disadvantages of the two plans, giving the decided superiority to the original plan.

The question on the final passage of this bill was then decided—yeas 120, nays 38, as follows :

YEAS—Messrs. Alexander, Alston, Anderson, Barnett, Bayly of Virginia, Bigelow, Bines, Breckenridge, Brigham, Brown, Butler, Caperton, Caldwell, Calhoun, Cannon, Champion, Chappell, Cilley, Clark, Clendenin, Comstock, Conard, Cooper, Cox, Creighton, Crouch, Culpeper, Cuthbert, Dana, Davenport, Davis of Massachusetts, Davis of Pennsylvania, Duvall, Earle, Ely, Farrow, Findley, Fisk of Vermont, Forney, Forsyth, Gaston, Geddes, Gholson, Hale, Hanson, Harris, Hasbrouck, Hawes, Hawkins, Henderson, Hopkins of Kentucky, Howell, Hungerford, Hulbert, Ingersoll, Ingham, Irving, Jackson of Rhode Island, Kent of New York, Kent of Maryland, Kerr, Kershaw, Kilbourn, King of North Carolina, Lefferts, Lovett, Lowndes, Markell, McCoy, McKee, McKim, McLean, Montgomery, Moore, Moseley, Oakley, Ormsby, Pearson, Pickering, Pickens, Pitkin, Pleasants, Potter, John Reed, William Reed, Rea of Pennsylvania, Rhea of Tennessee, Rich, Ringgold, Robertson, Ruggles, Sage, Schureman, Sevier, Sharp, Sheffey, Sherwood, Shipherd, Slaymaker, Smith of New York, Smith of Pennsylvania, Stockton, Stuart, Sturges, Taggart, Tannehill, Taylor, Telfair, Thompson, Udree, Vose, Ward of Massachusetts, Ward of New Jersey, Webster, Wheaton, White, Williams, Winter, Wood, and Yancey.

NAYS—Messrs. Baylies of Massachusetts, Boyd, Bradbury, Burwell, Clopton, Crawford, Denoyelles, Desha, Eppes, Evans, Fisk of New York, Franklin, Gourdin, Griffin, Grosvenor, Hall, Hubbard, Humphreys, Irwin, Johnson of Virginia, Johnson of Kentucky, Kennedy, King of Massachusetts, Law, Lewis, Lyle, Macon, Murfree, Nelson, Newton, Parker, Reane, Seybert, Stanford, Strong, Wilcox, Wilson of Massachusetts, and Wilson of Pennsylvania.

So the bill was passed.

TREASURY NOTES.

Mr. LAW, of Connecticut, submitted the following resolution:

Resolved, That the Committee of Ways and Means be instructed to inquire into the expediency of extending the several laws authorizing the issuing of Treasury notes, in such manner as to make them receivable in payment in all cases of fines, forfeitures, penalties, and executions, which may accrue, be due or owing to the United States; and also, to extend the said laws so as to make Treasury notes receivable in payment for taxes due to the United States from any number of persons who may unite for that purpose, and report thereon.

Mr. EPPES, of Virginia, desired to know the object of this motion. It appeared to him, on the first view, that it would introduce a speculation in the Government paper, immoral in itself, and injurious to the public credit. Every individual was by existing laws authorized to pay his particular taxes in Treasury notes.

Mr. LAW said, his object was not to encourage speculation, but to enable the people to pay their taxes upon an equal footing. At present, if several persons having taxes to pay can make up the precise amount they owe in Treasury notes, the collectors will not receive them, alleging that they are so instructed by the Treasury Department. Treasury notes were not now issued of any denomination less than twenty dollars; and yet, if two persons owing ten dollars each, tendered such a note in payment, the collector would not receive it. The consequence of which is, that such persons have to procure specie to pay their taxes, nothing else being receivable. He had, therefore, thought it would be advisable that the Committee of Ways and Means should inquire into the subject.

Mr. BIGELOW, of Massachusetts, confirmed the statement of Mr. LAW, having received, as he said, several letters from his district of the same import. He had understood that the Secretary of the Treasury complained that all the taxes were paid in Treasury notes. He knew not how that could be, as he knew that most of the taxes, in his district at least, were paid in other money;

unless that the collectors receive the taxes in good money, and instead of paying it into the Treasury, make use of it to buy in Treasury notes at a discount to pay into the Treasury, and make a profit from the difference.

Mr. HAWKINS, of Kentucky, moved to amend the motion so as to strike out that part of it authorizing associations for paying taxes in Treasury notes. He stated his knowledge of the fact, that the Treasury Department had it in contemplation to issue notes of a smaller denomination than those now in circulation, which would obviate altogether the difficulty the gentleman desired to remedy.

This motion was opposed by Messrs. POTTER, BAYLIES, and LAW.

Mr. FISK, of New York, moved to lay the resolve on the table; which motion was supported by Mr. EPPES, and agreed to, 61 to 56.

MONDAY, January 9.

Mr. INGERSOLL presented a petition of the Chamber of Commerce of the city of Philadelphia, praying for the passage of a law establishing an uniform system of bankruptcy throughout the United States.—Referred to the Committee of the Whole on the bill to establish an uniform system of Bankruptcy throughout the United States.

Mr. LATTIMORE presented a petition of the Legislature of the Mississippi Territory, praying that a law may be passed authorizing the appointment of an additional Judge for that part of the Territory which lies east of Pearl river.—Referred to the Committee on the Judiciary.

On motion of Mr. EASTON,

Resolved, That the Committee on the Public Lands be instructed to inquire, if any, what, further provisions, by law, are expedient to be made for ratifying the unconfirmed claims to land in the Territory of Missouri, and to provide for their location.

Resolved, That the Committee on the Public Lands be instructed to inquire, if any, what, alterations or amendments are necessary to be made in the act, entitled "An act for the final adjustment of land titles in the State of Louisiana and Territory of Missouri."

On motion of Mr. FORSYTH,

Resolved, That the Committee of Revisal and Unfinished Business be, and they are hereby, instructed to report to this House a bill to continue in force the act "declaring the consent of Congress to an act of the Legislature of Georgia, passed on the 13th of December, 1804, establishing the fees of the harbor master and health officer of the ports of Savannah and St. Mary's," being a part of the unfinished business of the last session of Congress.

On motion of Mr. KILBOURN,

Resolved, That the resolution and petition of the Legislature of the Illinois Territory, relating to the protection of the Northwestern frontier, and sundry memorials of the citizens of the United States west of the Alleghany mountains, upon the same subject, which were presented to this House at the last session and referred, be again referred to the committee having that subject under consideration.

Mr. YANCEY reported a bill for the relief of Joseph Perkins; which was read twice and committed to a Committee of the Whole.

The amendments proposed by the Senate to the bill " to authorize the President of the United States to accept the services of volunteers who may associate and organize themselves, and offer their services to the Government of the United States," were read, and referred to the Committee on Military Affairs.

A message from the Senate informed the House that the Senate have passed a bill " authorizing the President of the United States to cause to be built, equipped, and employed, one or more floating batteries, for the defence of the waters of the United States;" in which they ask the concurrence of this House.

The bill for the relief of Schultz and Vogeler and others, passed through a Committee of the Whole, and was ordered to be engrossed for a third reading.

The bill for the relief of James Doyle; the bill for the relief of William H. Washington; and the bill for the relief of William Robinson and others, severally passed through Committees of the Whole and were ordered to be engrossed for a third reading.

A bill for quitting and adjusting claims to land in the Mississippi Territory occupied the remainder of the day; and the Committee obtained leave to sit again thereon.

THE NAVAL ESTABLISHMENT.

Mr. WILLIAM REED, from the committee appointed on the 18th of March last, to inquire whether any, and, if any what, means of retrenchment and economy, and of reform in the general management, and of extension and efficiency in the Naval Establishment, may be practicable and expedient, made a detailed report; which was read, and is as follows:

That, having considered the several important subjects referred to them, they do not deem it useful to exhibit to the House a detail of the various abuses which have prevailed in the Naval Establishment. Such a detail, though it might lead to the detection of individual delinquents, would not afford redress for former abuses or prevent their repetition; for it was obvious to your committee that these abuses were either sanctioned by the forms of law, or, for the want of adequate provisions and penalties in the law, must remain unpunished. After having examined and availed themselves of the labors of their predecessors in their investigations, made under the direction of this House, and referred to this committee, they have concluded that it is unnecessary and unprofitable further to extend that investigation, and that it would be more satisfactory to the House, and more promotive of the object of their appointment, to limit their efforts to " a reform in the general management of this establishment." Under a full conviction that the experience of this war has already satisfied the most scrupulous of the ability of this country to create

and equip a naval force, competent not only to the defence of our extensive maritime frontier, but also for the great annoyance of a foreign enemy; and that such a force is now equally demanded by every section of our country, as indispensable for its security; the committee have likewise deemed it unnecessary to go into an argument to show the propriety of bestowing upon this branch of our national force, that measure of increase and support which its brilliant exploits on the ocean and on the lakes, and its efficiency in annoying the trade of the enemy, during this war, under all the abuses to which it has been exposed, have shown, should only be limited by our means.

The opinion that has existed from the first establishment of this Department, and been declared successively by almost every Secretary, that the duties incumbent on them were greater and more diversified than the most capable and laborious could discharge, with honor to himself and justice to the nation, led the committee to an examination of the system as now established, and the abuses that resulted from it. In prosecution of this examination, especially on that part which applies to the detail of service, they have principally relied on the information derived from the intelligent and experienced officers of the Navy, whom they have always found ready and desirous of giving all the information in their power. By the information obtained from this and other sources, the committee are convinced that most, if not all the abuses complained of are attributable to three distinct causes:

First. The excessive and laborious duties of the Secretary.

Second. The want of sufficient checks upon, and the consequent irresponsibility of, subordinate agents.

Third. The great latitude allowed commanders in altering, repairing, and furnishing their ships.

It is presumed to be unnecessary to offer to the House any further evidence of this statement than is contained in the following extract from the report of the late Secretary of the Navy, made to the Senate of the United States on the 15th November last:

" But regulations, however correct and adequate to the end, become nugatory or worse, unless the authority and the means are co-extensive and competent to enforce the execution or punish the violation thereof. This may account for the non-existence of many wholesome regulations in the civil administration of the Navy of the United States, and for the imperfect execution of those which exist. Breaches of the latter too frequently escape with impunity, from the impossibility of the Head of the Department taking cognizance of all the multifarious concerns of the establishment."

Great and obvious as the defects in this establishment are by all confessed to be, the committee have felt no little anxiety as to the best mode of correcting them. Desirous equally of avoiding the opposite errors, of rashly changing from one system to another without an attempt to correct known abuses, or loading it with formal but inefficient appendages, which more frequently encumber than relieve, or give energy to its operations; and concurring in the opinion expressed by the late Secretary, in the report before referred to, that a board, composed of intelligent and experienced officers, in aid of the executive of this Department, would most effectually accomplish this object, and if properly organized, avoid the dangers from too great innovation on one hand and inefficiency on the other, they directed a copy of this report to be forwarded to every captain in the Navy of the United States, with the annexed circular, marked A. From the answers thereto, which invariably approve the general design, it was thought unnecessary to publish more than those which contained particular observations upon the plan submitted. These are annexed, numbered 1 to 8.

From these materials, collected from intelligent and practical sources, the committee have endeavored to digest a plan which, they unanimously believe, if adopted, will immediately correct many of the abuses complained of, and lay the foundation of an improved system for the management of this Department. They, therefore, beg leave to recommend the adoption of the two bills accompanying this report.

A.—[*Circular*.]

WASHINGTON, *Nov.* 17, 1814.

SIR: I am directed, by the committee appointed under a resolution of the House of Representatives, adopted on the 15th of March last, "authorizing and directing an inquiry into the expediency and practicability of reform in the Naval Department of the United States," to forward for your examination a letter from the Secretary of the Navy to the Senate of the United States" of the 18th, communicating his views and plans for effecting this object; and to request you to favor the committee with your opinion of the plan proposed by the Secretary, and to suggest such additions and alterations as shall appear to you necessary for attaining this desirable object.

With respect I am, sir, your very obedient servant.

No. 1.

Observations, submitted to the Naval Committee, on the report of the Secretary of the Navy to the Senate of the United States, dated the 18th November, 1814, relative to the better organization of the Navy of the United States.

I should, for the reasons which follow, recommend three instead of five Navy inspectors; that they be taken from the captains in the Navy; and that the officer of the oldest date of commission should preside.

1st. I believe that three inspectors are adequate to the performance of the duties contemplated, and this number will be sufficient to form a quorum. If it should be said, that, by confining the board to the number of three, it might be rendered incompetent by the death or disability of a member, it may be replied, that, while the President has the power of supplying the deficiency from the captains in the Navy, this objection can have no force. 2d. I recommend the appointment of Navy officers in preference to gentlemen out of the Navy, who may be skilled in naval affairs, because, in a science in which, of all others, experience has set theory at defiance, practical men only should be allowed to act; and I firmly believe the officers of the Navy, after many years of experience in the naval service and of constant reflection on the subject, are better qualified to execute the duties required than any other characters. 3d. The officer whose commission is of the oldest date should preside, because, by such an arrangement, no offence could be given to individual feeling, and that union and harmony would be preserved which are so necessary to insure a co-operation of mind and action.

2d. I should recommend the following alteration in the fourth section: Instead of the Secretary of the

Navy preparing the rules and regulations for conducting the business of the naval constructor's department, that that duty be assigned to the board of inspectors, who would always be professional men, and thereby judges of the matter. And it might happen that the Secretary of the Navy would not be a nautical character.

3d. The respective duties, designated in five classes, it appears to me would be much better conducted under the general direction of the board than could be done under the separate direction of the respective members, inasmuch as the greater part of the duties detailed therein are specified in the general duties of the board, and the whole are placed under its control; and more especially as a considerable part would require, for the public interest, the united talents of the board. And should it be found, from experience, that a select distribution of duties ought to be made among the members of the board, with due deference I suggest that the board would be enabled, from actual experiment, to recommend the best classification of duties for such inspector. A system so complicated and extensive as a perfect organization of the civil department of the navy cannot be expected, even under the direction of the best talents, to be the work of a day. But the want of some uniform system in the Naval Department of our country has evidently manifested itself; and the adoption of the general principles for such a system, as recommended by the honorable Secretary of the Navy, I doubt not would be attended with the most favorable result.

WM. BAINBRIDGE.

No. 2.

UNITED STATES' FRIGATE CONSTITUTION, *Boston Harbor, November* 26, 1814.

SIR: I received the honor of your circular letter of the 17th instant, enclosing a report of the honorable Secretary of the Navy to the honorable Senate of the United States, relating to the organization of the Navy Department. You express a desire that the committee may be possessed of my opinion of the plan proposed, and that I should suggest such additions and alterations as may appear to me necessary for attaining so desirable an object.

It appears to me, sir, and is my opinion, that the plan proposed by the report will contribute towards the desired end, but I do not think it calculated to obtain the whole object proposed by Congress. Viewing it as an auxiliary to the Navy Department, it will unquestionably facilitate the operations and relieve the officers of that Department from much of the detail duties, which all must be aware are too extensive and diversified for any one person to discharge with necessary and due attention. We must also be aware how difficult it is to change a system once begun, and whose basis is not established on the best foundation, though it should afterwards be found inadequate to the object.

If we compare this new and young nation, rising in the Western hemisphere, and progressing towards a zenith of greatness which may cast a shade over some of the oldest and most enlightened nations of the Eastern, to a young man commencing life, with the experience of his predecessors, whereby to regulate his conduct and economy, would not his error strike us forcibly, on observing him erecting temporary structure after structure, instead of raising on solid foundations the ground work of his future comfort and prosperity, which would bid defiance to time, and could only be shaken by the general wreck of things? Presuming the Legislature wish to establish the marine of this country on the best possible foundation, and calculated to be conducted with the greatest economy in all its various branches, I do apprehend the plan submitted will not be found to effect that object, and will fall far short of the end contemplated.

Of the first section, it will only be necessary to remark, that it would be injudicious to destroy the department, but highly essential to reorganize it.

The second section provides five inspectors of the Navy, to form a sort of navy board, which will contribute no further than to relieve the department from some of the detail service, and sharing with it certain portions of the responsibility. The principal objection to a board of inspectors constituted as I apprehend, arises from its not combining the variety and necessary practical knowledge and information among its members requisite on many important subjects that will come before them.

The assigning to individuals of the board of inspectors (as contemplated by the third section) distinct control over, and responsibility for, specific portions of the service, can and will answer no purpose whatever.

The provisions of the fourth section will be highly essential at all events.

Section the fifth may or may not be requisite; in the latter case the office could at any time be created.

Sections six and seven will only be requisite if the plan is adopted.

As the principal features in the plan of the bill proposed are contained in the section providing the board of inspectors, it will only be necessary to remark, in support of my objection above, that the duties contemplated to be assigned to this board would require, at least, one member in it conversant with each of the important branches of the establishment. The drawing up all the rules and regulations for each branch of the service; the examination of all the officers below the rank of masters commandant for appointments or promotion; the adopting models, for vessels of war to be created from; the planning and arranging their internal apartments; the external equipment and armament; the arranging the proper stores for a given time for each department; the regulating dock yards, navy yards, foundries, &c., demand the combined talents and professional experience of men conversant with the different professions. By referring to my letter of the 20th of January, 1818, to the honorable Langdon Cheves, you will observe by the plan of a board there proposed that I had those objects in view, and therefore constituted it of such characters and professions as are essential to give every subject submitted to them a fair and professional examination. The above duties comprise almost the whole economy of the establishment, and form a subject of the first importance to the nation.

With respect to the flotilla, it ought either to form a part of the navy, and be subject to its rules, regulations, and economy, and be under the superintendence and control generally of the Navy Department and Navy Board, or else be entirely separated therefrom.

One great source of expenditure and inconvenience to the naval service arises from the short enlistment of our seamen, ordinary seamen, and boys, and the principal cause which would defeat any particular object of expedition of our marine, more so than any imagined deficiency of seamen. During part of our war with Tripoli, the crews were enlisted only for one year; the consequence was, that a ship could scarcely arrive at her station, and have time to organize her crew, before she was obliged to return and discharge them. The term of enlistment now is two years; but such is the difficulty of getting men, for the small pay and bounty allowed, compared with what they can get in other service, and the ship is so long delayed in procuring her complement, that the times of one half expire before the crew is completed. The inducements given to fill the ranks of the Army being much greater than that of the Navy, many seamen have joined it; some, from necessity, have gone into foreign service, and are even navigating the commerce of the enemy; many are in the private armed ships and privateers, owing to the exclusive advantages given them over the Navy. By this means the glory and maritime reputation of the nation is made to yield to the inglorious warfare of plunder, which deeply affects some individuals of the enemy, but makes only a small impression on the nation at large; some are locked up in the prisons of our foe, who is aware of the short period of their enlistment, and is wary enough to detain them from exchange until their term of service expires, when our Government can no longer command their services. The frequency of changing men from the ship they select to cruise in, to another, or into different service, such as the lakes and flotilla, contributes much to impede the recruiting service. When the above causes are considered, it is only wonderful that any men can be procured for our ships of war. The registering and classing of the seamen of the United States would produce much good, but the compulsory command of their services would produce much evil, and should only be resorted to in the most extreme necessity. None will serve so well as those who serve voluntarily. To this account may be placed much of our superiority over the British, which has hitherto baffled all their boasted advantages of experience, skill, and long practice.

With respect to a naval academy, the best school for the instruction of youth in the profession is the deck of a ship, presuming that none would be offered or received into the service as midshipmen whose education had not been such as to fit them for officers, and calculated for gentlemen. To derive advantage from expenditure, and induce that corps of officers to pursue their profession, in time of peace, through private service, I would allow no half pay to midshipmen, except for such term as they can produce a journal of their voyages, and certificates of the master or owner of the vessel, countersigned by the collector of the port. By this means many will be induced to pursue that calling to acquire the essential knowledge of seamanship, the properties of different species of vessels, an acquaintance and familiarity with coasts, countries, and nations; a knowledge of their marine, commerce, and fortresses; the genius of the people, and their language; which would be essential to them as officers, and important to the nation. It would enable them to form a true estimate of the requisite force for the attack of any point, place, or object, and the seasons best calculated for expeditions and enterprises, with the least hazard to themselves, when they should be called to execute the object, or plant the standard of our Union over the humbled foe.

The love of country and patriotism of the seamen of the United States stand unrivalled, or only equalled by their intrepidity and perseverence in commercial pursuits, and their valor in naval combat. We see them encountering all the horrors of the enemy's prisons, the privation of liberty and comfortable support, in preference to bearing arms against their country: impressed (during a state of peace with us) on board the British ships of war, and, by oppression, compelled to serve them against other enemies, they submitted with patience to their misfortune; but, when they heard of the war with their own country, no inducement or force could prevail on them to take arms against her. Sir, the Navy looks up to the Government, with confidence, for its fostering care, and the nation trusts that they will place this important and essential national force on a systematic and solid foundation, that it may progress to maturity by gradual and regular augmentation. Although it may present to the enemies of our country a front too formidable for them to penetrate, it never can be rendered a machine to menace the Constitution or liberties of our country; it will at all times strengthen the arm of Government, bind the Union together, protect our coast and harbors from blockade, menace, or insult, our commerce from plunder, and our citizens from the slavery and dungeons of Barbary.

I have the honor to be, very respectfully, sir, your obedient humble servant,

         CHARLES STEWART.

No. 3.

NAVY YARD, PORTSMOUTH, *Nov.* 30, 1814.

SIR: I have had the honor to receive your letter of the 17th instant, covering a letter from the honorable the Secretary of the Navy to the Senate of the United States, dated the 17th instant, communicating his views and plan of effecting a reform in the management of the Naval Department, and requesting my opinion thereon.

I now beg leave to inform you that I have examined the letter, and am of opinion that the plans, generally, proposed by the honorable Secretary, are such as would, if carried into effect, go far towards effecting the object so much wished for, particularly as it respects the establishment of a Navy Board. It would be presumption in me to propose additions or alterations of a plan proposed by the honorable the Secretary of the Navy, with the knowledge he has of naval affairs, and the means he possesses of getting at the transactions of every branch of the establishment; I can, therefore, only say, in general terms, that I think the changes in the Navy Establishment, proposed by him, are such as will remedy many of the evils that now exist. If, however, it is not thought absolutely necessary to make the proposed changes immediately, (and it would not be thought presumption in me,) I beg leave to suggest the idea of appointing, this session, the gentlemen that are to compose the Navy Board, and let them enter immediately on the duties of that office. They, together with the honorable the Secretary of the Navy, would, before the next meeting of Congress, be able to lay before the Senate a complete system for the reform of the establishment, founded on observation and facts taken from these gentlemen collectively, that may not be known or inquired into as individuals. If I dare give an opinion, these would be my sentiments. The board would have time to examine particularly into the establishment as it now is. They would be able, some of them, to visit the different naval establishments, and inform themselves of what improvements are necessary, and how far it will be expedient to occupy all the navy yards we now have, or, rather, whether it will not be advisable to fix on some two or three establishments, as being important ones, and only improve the others for temporary purposes, such as repairing ships, or giving them an outfit when they fall in, and cannot, without risk, get to the larger establishment. In short, a board appointed immediately, and commencing on the duty of the office, would, in my opinion, as I have before stated, lay before the Government a system, with such rules and regulations for the better government of our establishment, as cannot fail to meet their approbation, and, I am sure, such as will save millions to the nation, if we are to have a navy of any magnitude.

I have the honor to be, most respectfully, sir, your obedient servant,

         ISAAC HULL.

Hon. WILLIAM REID,
    Chairman of the Naval Committee.

No. 4.

NEW YORK, *December* 3, 1814.

SIR: Circumstances have prevented me from replying, until now, to your letter accompanying the report of the Secretary of the Navy, on the subject of a new organization of that department. The objects of reform contemplated in that report being those on which I had heretofore communicated my ideas, I shall merely remark, in compliance with your request, upon the only subject which remains, namely, the organization of one board of inspectors, as recommended by the Secretary.

It appears to be the intention of that officer, that the board is to be so constituted as simply to exercise such powers as may be delegated to them by the Secretary of the Navy, and approved by the President of the United States, and that it is not to be located at the seat of Government.

After having maturely considered the subject in every point of view that presented itself to my mind, it appears to me that the object contemplated would be attained much more effectually, by so constituting this board, that the Secretary of the Navy should be its presiding officer, and the members his counsellors, with whom he might and would be expected to consult, in all those affairs which they would be supposed, from their professional experience, to be better acquainted with than himself: I say better acquainted, because it is presumed that the Secretary will not, generally, be a person thoroughly versed in the details of the service. The members of the board thus constituted, might, in addition to the duties of counsellors, exercise the respective powers contemplated in the report, and as effectually execute the duties of inspectors and comptrollers of abuses as if they formed a separate and distinct establishment, placed in a central part of the United States, and having their separate districts particularly defined.

By this arrangement, the Secretary of the Navy might, at all times, and at the instant, have the advice of one or more competent officers, responsible for their counsel and conduct, and with whom he could at all times consult, without incurring the delay which would result from placing the board at a distance from its head. There is always an advantage in hearing and comparing the different opinions of experienced men on every subject. Letters must, of necessity, be less particular and explanatory than verbal communications, and it is much more easy to come at the whole truth by the latter medium.

In short, sir, I can conceive no advantages that can result from placing this board in a central situation, that will counterbalance the probable disadvantages of the arrangement contemplated in the report of the Secretary. One principal object of this arrangement appears to me, ought to be to bring into the Department the experience and activity of a number of professional men, who should be at all times ready on the spot, to furnish either Congress or the Secretary with such information as either might call for, and which their professional experience enable them to communicate.

The board, with the exception of the Secretary of the Navy, should consist of naval officers exclusively, of a grade not inferior to Post Captains, and composed of not more than three in number, as that would, I think, be fully competent to the discharge of all the duties required. A greater number might tend rather to embarrass and retard, and would take from the navy officers that, on some occasions, could not be spared from the service; these officers to be selected by the President of the United States, and changed as he should find it expedient. The accountant and clerks of the Navy Department to remain, as heretofore, under the Secretary of the Navy, who should be the only disbursing officer of the board; the great duty of this board to consist in forming, arranging, and bringing into operation, a system of order and economy for the Navy, which would remedy the defects and abuses now existing in that Department. A board thus constituted would, I feel satisfied, reduce the expenses of the establishment at least one-fourth.

I am, with much respect, sir, &c.
         STEPHEN DECATUR.
The above accords entirely with our opinion.
         O. H. PERRY,
         D. PORTER,
         L. WARRINGTON.

No. 5.

NAVY YARD, BROOKLYN, *Dec.* 6, 1814.
SIR: In compliance with the request of the committee appointed by the House of Representatives to inquire "into the expediency and practicability of reform in the management of the Navy Department of the United States," I have examined attentively the letter from the Secretary of the Navy, which you did me the honor to transmit me; and my sentiments on the subjects it embraces, with such remarks as appear to me of weight, and applicable to those subjects, are respectfully submitted.

In examining the plan proposed by the Secretary, I am at a loss to discover clearly his views of the duties and powers that are to remain with the Secretary of the Navy, after the board he has recommended is in full operation. I assume it is admitted that the duties and powers of that office are loosely defined now, and I consider it very important, if the office is continued with a board, that the extent of its operations should be clearly marked; if this is done, I believe the officer holding must possess but a small share of power, and his duties be very limited, or he must combine in himself the authority to direct and control the board in all cases.

It will be considered scarcely worth while, I presume, to retain it for unimportant purposes; but if it be clothed with the extensive powers alluded to, it ap-

pears to me that ill consequences may easily arise from it, because the judgment of an individual, who it does not appear must necessarily be conversant with naval affairs, may, and might, frequently, be placed in competition with that of a board of five, who are selected expressly for their knowledge in those matters, and with power to reject, modify, or render useless their most important decisions. This power, I am persuaded, should be held by the President of the United States alone.

It is true, I believe, that with special and limited authority vested by an act of Congress, which would clearly define the powers and duties of the office, some benefit might be derived from it. I am decidedly of opinion that the Navy should be represented in the Cabinet, if I may use the expression, and the office would most probably be of advantage for that purpose; but then, if there is a board created as recommended, it appears to me that the Secretary of the Navy should be more the advocate of that board than the controller of it; he might also be serviceable as the organ of communication between the President of the United States and the board, and between the latter and Congress, but there I think his labors should cease.

He should have no absolute control, over either the civil or military department of the establishment. In the light, therefore, in which I view the subject, it is manifest to me that the benefits to be derived from the office, limited as above stated, would be of little importance, and could all be executed with equal advantage if it had no existence; but if it is to exist, with all the qualities of a directing and controlling power, I am of opinion that the service would be much benefitted by the alteration of the second section proposed, so as to constitute a board of three, to be selected from the Captains of the Navy, and located at the Seat of Government. These would, most probably, be competent to the discharge of all the duties that would devolve on a board of this nature, under any circumstances that could arise, until our navy is considerably increased, when, it is to be presumed, the number of members could be increased from the same materials.

I am averse to the introduction of gentlemen into a board of this description, that have lived principally in the merchants' service, who, however well they might be skilled in the duties devolving on mariners in general, cannot, I conceive, without distending the imagination, be supposed to be acquainted with the ramifications of a naval service, and who would, most probably, from these circumstances, rather retard and embarrass than be of advantage to it. If it is considered necessary to introduce other than naval officers in this board, I would greatly prefer their being selected from other classes of citizens, possessing sound judgment and extensive information, without regard to maritime qualifications. There are duties, perhaps, that would be allotted to a board of this nature, which gentlemen possessing those qualities could execute with advantage.

On the proposition to authorize the President to appoint a naval constructor, with assistants, I will only trouble the committee by observing, that an able naval architect could, I believe, be employed to advantage in the Department; but I am of opinion that more importance is proposed to be given to the office than is necessary or advisable, and this officer should be under the direction of the board.

The appointment of a paymaster, as proposed, would not, as far as I am enabled to judge, be attended with advantage to the service. It appears to me that a well regulated system to govern the pursers, which it should be the duties of the board to prescribe, and the accountant's office as it now exists, is all that is necessary on this subject.

The establishment of a naval academy, as recommended, would unquestionably be productive of great advantage to the service. A well regulated establishment of this nature I consider to be much wanted.

These comprise all the objects that the Secretary deems it necessary for the Legislature to provide. I am of opinion, however, that there would be advantages obtained by extending the law so as to define, as clearly as possible, the duties and powers of the board, and to designate the boundaries of the naval districts.

All the regulations recommended I believe to be necessary, and much wanted, but I am of opinion that the appointment of pursers had better be limited by law, and the distribution of the duties of the board would, most probably, be made with more advantage by the members of it.

Upon the whole, it is my opinion that the duties and powers of the Secretary of the Navy, as they now exist, and all the duties and powers that it is necessary should be invested in a Navy Department, would be most advantageously settled in a board, to consist of five members and a secretary; one to be selected by the President, for his abilities as a statesman, who should preside at the board, and the remaining four to be selected by the same authority from the officers of the Navy. This plan would, I believe, combine all the qualities that are wanting to compose a Navy Department, fundamentally efficient for the administration of a permanent and extensive naval establishment.

I have the honor to be, &c.
SAMUEL EVANS.

Hon. WILLIAM REED,
   Chairman, Naval Committee.

No. 6.

PORTSMOUTH, N. H., *Dec.* 9, 1814.

SIR: Your circular of November 17th, covering a letter from the Secretary of the Navy to the Senate of the United States, I had the honor to receive a few days since.

The appointment of a board for the assistance of the Secretary of the Navy has long been advocated by the different commanders in service, upon the presumption that, with their advice and assistance, the naval force might be rendered much more efficient, without an increased expense to the country. I should, however, suppose three persons sufficient, at this time, for the performance of all the duties of such a board. I cannot but think that part of the plan, authorizing the President to appoint the presiding officer, as unnecessary, or improper, since no other rule of precedence can be established among officers than that of rank. I should also presume, that the naval officers possess that information on general naval subjects, and the particular details of service, which render them more peculiarly qualified for the duties of this board than persons whose attention has been generally devoted to other subjects.

The different duties assigned to the particular members of the board, as classed by the Secretary, I should presume might be more advantageously distributed by the advice of the board itself, after its organization. The appointment of a naval constructor would be at-

13th CON. 3d SESS.—34

tended with many advantages. That of paymaster, I should think unnecessary at present.

Anxious for the establishment of a board, composed of men whose vigilance and professional talents would enable them to discover and correct abuses; to furnish all the information which might be required upon naval affairs; and to superintend the general police, and all those details of service which have hitherto necessarily interfered with the more important duties of the Secretary, I am particularly gratified that it has been officially recommended, at a time when the Legislature are endeavoring to discover and reform the existing abuses of the naval establishment. The advantages which will naturally result from it appear too obvious to require enumeration; but not the least important would be the information they could soon furnish the honorable committee of naval reform, upon the different subjects of their present inquiries.

With sincere respect, I have the honor, &c.
C. MORRIS.

Hon. WILLIAM REED,
   Chairman, Com. of Naval Reform, Washington.

No. 7.

FRIGATE UNITED STATES, *Dec.* 9, 1814.

SIR: A few days since I had the honor to receive your circular of the 17th ultimo, enclosing a letter from the Secretary of the Navy, transmitting a report relative to the better organization of the Department of the Navy of the United States.

From long experience, and so far as my knowledge extends of naval transactions, and to naval regulations, it has been but too obvious that many imperfections have existed in the civil administration of our establishment, and that the only and best method that can be devised to remove the evil, will be to select, by law, a naval board, to consist of three Post Captains, (or of a higher grade, if there should be such,) and that the Secretary of the Navy, where it may be deemed necessary, in joint council to be the presiding officer. This board of inspection, if well selected, I am perfectly satisfied will be enabled to give to our establishment a tone satisfactory in effect, and salutary in its operation. It will be to our navy its sheet anchor; all points of duty will be equally made explicit by its salutary and well-defined regulations, and all untoward and unnecessary expenses, which have but too long continued to exist in our establishment, will, in a great measure, be brought to a final determination. When that object be obtained, the navy cannot do otherwise than progress, under the fostering care which, it is hoped, the Executive of the country will feel disposed to appreciate agreeably to its consequences.

I have the honor to be, &c.
JOHN SHAW.

Hon. WILLIAM REED.

No. 8.

NAVY YARD, WASHINGTON, *Dec.* 10, 1814.

SIR: I have been honored with your letter of the 26th ultimo, as Chairman of a committee of the House of Representatives, for "inquiring into the expediency and practicability of a reform in the Naval Department of the United States; transmitting therewith a letter from the late "Secretary of the Navy, of 15th November, to the Senate, communicating his views and plans for effecting this object," and requesting my opinion, &c., of the plan proposed.

I have perused with attention the said "report" to the Senate, and now proceed to give you my opinion on the several parts thereof, as the nature of the subject appears to me to require.

It has been long evident to every experienced officer in our navy, and experience has made it known to the community at large, that no one man, (whatever his intellectual powers and endowments may be) is fully competent to execute the multiplicity of complex duties which have been incumbent on the Head of the Navy Department.

Thus, then, another branch of power in that Department appears to have become indispensably necessary, and none so appropriate, in my opinion, as a board of three or more experienced, practical, professional men.

Whether the appellation given to the board, in the report of Mr. Jones, is the most appropriate, it is considered unnecessary herein to discuss; but it is incontrovertibly demonstrable that such a board, with proper powers, under an act of the Legislature, will effect a saving of many thousand dollars annually, in the expenses of our Naval Establishment.

The Secretary having presented his report in the form of "a bill," it may, I conceive, be found convenient to the committee, as well as to myself, to follow its sections in their regular course, with such a fair and candid opinion thereon, as their propositions appear more or less forcible and conclusive on my mind.

The first section, being totally indefinite and prospective, appears to be susceptible of no comment.

In the adoption of the second section, for the organization of the board, I conceive particular care should be taken to avoid any probable cause for disunion in its members. I would, therefore, respectfully advise that the presiding member be designated by law, and not embarrass the President of the United States with the selection, which, from resignation, death, or other casualty, may very frequently occur; it appears to me more eligible, therefore, that the law should enact that the senior navy officer of the board should be the presiding member; and, being once so established, should continue so to act as long as he remains a member thereof, notwithstanding any changes that might thereafter take place by the supply of vacancies.

The board conjointly should have the power to nominate one or more persons qualified for the duties of the secretary thereof, and submit such nominations to the President of the United States for his selection and approval.

A quorum of the board, or at least the presiding member and its secretary, should reside at the Seat of Government of the United States, for the great convenience of frequent communications and conferences with the Secretary of the Navy, or with the President of the United States, in cases of particular importance. The board should hold its regular stated meetings in its office at the Seat of Government, unless, on emergency, or some important occasion, the Secretary of the Navy may deem it more eligible to be held elsewhere.

The duties of the secretary of the board are clearly and amply defined in the "report," as well as is also the powers of the board for the establishment of its rules, and the regulations of its proceedings, &c.

The third section appears to require some elucidation respecting the contemplated time or times for holding "each stated meeting" of the board; as this section states that an abstract of the transactions of each such meeting shall be "transmitted monthly to the Secretary of the Navy," &c. Now, the transmission of such "abstracts," monthly, would necessitate an almost perpetual session of the board, and perhaps such continued sitting of a quorum thereof might be found imperative, especially in time of war; but, otherwise, it is respectfully conceived that, after the first complete organization of the board, once in two or three months will be sufficient for general stated meetings, and transmission of the transactions thereof to the Secretary of the Navy, thus affording time for a part of the members to visit personally the several naval stations, which I conceive to be one of the most essential points of their duty. And if, as heretofore suggested, a quorum of the board, or at least the presiding member, and the secretary thereof, reside at and hold their office at the Seat of Government, the other members will be better enabled to inspect the proceedings at the different naval stations, or the equipment of any squadron or single ship, (if deemed necessary,) and report daily, or otherwise, as may appear requisite, by correspondence, to the president of the board, or those executing the duties of the board at the Seat of Government, who can immediately confer thereon with the Secretary of the Navy, or the President of the United States, if deemed essential, and thus a judgment may be formed whether or not it may be expedient for the presiding member to convene the board earlier than the next approaching general stated meeting, or at any other port or place than their permanent office. Thus, also, by this constant correspondence, the president of the board, with the aid of the secretary, will always have the business necessary for the consideration of the board methodically arranged, and ready to lay before them immediately on their meeting.

On the fourth section I would only observe that, in my opinion, it would be more eligible that the board, contemplated in the "report," should "prepare such rules and regulations, for conducting the business of the Constructor's department, as shall appear proper and necessary," and submit them for the approval of the President of the United States, through the Secretary of the Navy.

The fifth section, appointing a "paymaster" of the Navy, it is believed, will be productive of great saving in the appropriation to which that office applies, and lessen in a great degree the risk of misapplication or long retention of the moneys appertaining thereto.

The sixth section is believed to be very just and proper.

The seventh section is respectfully submitted to the wisdom and judgment of the committee. Its provisions are, however, considered as adequate and equitable, but it is nevertheless conceived that the travelling expenses of the members, while on duty, should be provided for.

It is firmly believed that a naval academy will have an amply beneficial effect on the Naval Establishment, and tend to preclude the probability of public ships and vessels falling under the management of incompetent uninformed men.

"The powers and duties of the board" are, I conceive, amply illustrated and defined in the "report," except that, immediately following the first general regulation, it might be proper and highly useful to add, that no officer, whatever his grade may be, shall in anywise alter the internal or external equipments or arrangements of the ship or vessel under his command, or to which he may be in any manner attached, under pain of ——; but, on perceiving that any eligible im-

1061 HISTORY OF CONGRESS. 1062

JANUARY, 1815. *Intercourse with the Enemy.* H. OF R.

provement may be made in any particular whatever, he shall, as speedily as practicable, submit his ideas of such improvement to the board, with his reasons therefor, for their decision.

The latitude that has been practised, in this respect, has cost the Naval Establishment many thousands of dollars.

In addition to the form of the bill, I would respectfully suggest the following:

And be it further enacted, &c., That, from and after the passing of this act, no person shall be commissioned as a lieutenant in the Navy of the United States, until he shall have attained the full age of ——— years, shall have been full five years in sea service, two of which at least he shall have served in the capacity of midshipman, master's mate, or sailing master, in the Navy of the United States; and shall have and produce a certificate of his abilities (after a full examination before a court of competent officers) to manage and conduct the duties of a ship-of-war, in ballasting and stowing the hold, masting, rigging, docking, careening, arming, and exercising the great guns and small arms; shall be capable of working a ship at sea, under all the forms and variety of sailing; making and taking in sail, anchoring, and getting under way; mooring and unmooring, and laying at single anchor in a tides-way, and in still water; shall be competently skilled in mathematical navigation, to conduct a ship to pilot water, on any known coast, island, bay, river, or harbor, in the world.

All which is respectfully submitted.

I have the honor to be, very respectfully, sir, your obedient servant,

THOMAS TINGEY.

Hon. WILLIAM REED,
 Chairman of the Committee, &c.

Mr. REED, then reported a bill to alter and amend the several acts for establishing a Navy Department, by adding thereto a Board of Commissioners; which was read twice, and committed to a Committee of the Whole.

Mr. REED, also reported a bill directing the manner of contracts and purchases in the Navy Department, and for promoting economy therein; which was read and committed to a Committee of the Whole.

INTERCOURSE WITH THE ENEMY.

The bill which was read a third time on Saturday, and then laid on the table, was taken up; and the question being stated—"Shall the bill pass?"

Mr. FARROW assigned, in a few words, the reasons which obliged him to vote against this bill, though he was in favor of its object. His principal objection was, to that part of the bill which gives power to collectors to appoint inspectors, to be considered as officers of the Government.

When Mr. F. sat down, the question was taken, without further debate, and decided in the affirmative, by the following vote:

YEAS—Messrs. Alexander, Alston, Anderson, Avery, Barbour, Bard, Barnett, Bayly of Virginia, Bines, Bowen, Brown, Burwell, Butler, Calhoun, Cannon, Clark, Clendenin, Crawford, Creighton, Couch, Cuthbert, Dana, Davis of Pennsylvania, Desha, Duvall, Eppes, Evans, Findley, Fisk of Vermont, Forney, Forsyth, Franklin, Ghelson, Griffin, Hall, Harris, Hasbrouck, Hawes, Hopkins of Kentucky, Hubbard, Humphreys, Hungerford, Ingersoll, Ingham, Irwin, Johnson of Kentucky, Kennedy, Kerr, Kershaw, Kilbourn, King of North Carolina, Lefferts, Lyle, Macon, McCoy, McKee, McKim, McLean, Montgomery, Nelson, Newton, Ormsby, Parker, Pickens, Pleasants, Rea of Pennsylvania, Rhea of Tennessee, Rich, Ringgold, Roane, Robertson, Sage, Sevier, Sharp, Smith of Pennsylvania, Tannehill, Troup, Udree, Williams, Wilson of Pennsylvania, Wright, and Yancey—82.

NAYS—Messrs. Baylies of Massachusetts, Boyd, Breckenridge, Brigham, Caperton, Champion, Cilley, Cooper, Cox, Culpeper, Davenport, Davis of Massachusetts, Ely, Farrow, Geddes, Grosvenor, Hale, Hanson, Hawkins, Henderson, Howell, Hulbert, Kent of New York, King of Massachusetts, Law, Lewis, Lovett, Miller, Markell, Moseley, Oakley, Pearson, Pickering, Pitkin, John Reed, William Reed, Ruggles, Schureman, Sherwood, Shipherd, Slaymaker, Smith of New York, Stanford, Stockton, Stuart, Sturges, Taggart, Thompson, Vose, Ward of Massachusetts, Wheaton, White, Wilcox, Winter, and Wood—55.

So the bill was passed.

TUESDAY, January 10.

Mr. EPPES, from the managers on the part of this House at the conference on the disagreeing votes on the amendments depending to the bill "to provide additional revenues for defraying the expenses of Government, and maintaining the public credit, by laying duties on various goods, wares, and merchandise, manufactured within the United States," made a report; which was read, and committed to a Committee of the Whole to-day.

The SPEAKER laid before the House a letter from the Secretary of the Treasury, transmitting the estimates of appropriations necessary for the service of the year. The letter was read, and, with the accompanying documents, referred to the Committee of Ways and Means.

The bill from the Senate to authorize the President of the United States to cause to be constructed certain floating batteries for the defence of the United States, was twice read, and referred to the Naval Committee. [This bill appropriates $500,000, in addition to the sum heretofore appropriated for that object.]

The engrossed bill for the relief of Jacob Shinnick, Schultz, and Vogeler, Christian Chapman, and the legal representatives of John Calef, deceased, (whose property was destroyed by our officers on the approach of the enemy to Baltimore in August last,) was read a third time, and passed.

The engrossed bill for the relief of James Doyle (compensating him for services rendered at the instance of a United States officer in North Carolina, in apprehending counterfeiters of the paper of the late Bank of the United States) was read a third time. This bill was opposed by Mr. FISK, of New York, and advocated by Mr. YANCEY, and Mr. KING, of Massachusetts. The division on the passage of the bill was, 62 yeas, 40 nays.

The engrossed bill for the relief of William

Robinson and others, was read a third time, and passed.

The engrossed bill for the relief of William H. Washington, was read a third time (making compensation for a house destroyed by the officers of the United States during the invasion of this district in August last,) which was read a third time and passed.

SUNDAY MAILS.

Mr. FARROW presented a petition from sundry inhabitants of Chester district, South Carolina, remonstrating against the transportation and opening the mail on the Sabbath, which he moved might be committed to the Committee on Post Offices and Post Roads.

Mr. F. said there had been eighty-five petitions on this subject before Congress this session, all of which had been referred to the Postmaster General. Since the first has been so referred, it has been about three months, on which there has been no report made to Congress. I am not, said Mr. F., about to charge that high officer with a neglect of duty, but have stated those facts for a very different purpose. It is for the purpose to inquire whether Congress have properly and Constitutionally discharged their duty in respect to those petitions. I contend that they ought to have been referred to the committee to which I have moved this, or to a select committee. To prove this position, I will first draw your attention to the first amendment of the Constitution, page twenty-five. Mr. F. read—"Congress shall make 'no law respecting an establishment of religion, 'or prohibiting the free exercise thereof; or abridg-'ing the freedom of speech, or of the press; or the 'right of the people peaceably to assemble, and 'to petition the Government for a redress of 'grievances."

The rule or order of the day, page 31, makes it the duty of the Speaker every morning to call on the members of the several States to present any petitions that they may be charged with. As the Constitution permits the people to petition you, and the order of the day is to hear them, this does imply an engagement on the part of Congress, that they will redress the complaints of the people or state to them the reason why you reject them. You are the body petitioned, not the Postmaster General, as you are their representatives, and not him. To prove to you that this petition ought to be referred to the Committee on Post Offices and Post Roads, I must bring to your view the standing rule of this House. [Here he read from page 37.] "It shall 'be the duty of the Committee on Post Offices and 'Post Roads to take into consideration all such 'petitions, and matters, or things, touching the 'post office and post roads, as shall be presented or 'may come in question, and be referred to them 'by the House, and to report their opinion thereon, 'together with such propositions relative thereto, 'as to them shall seem expedient." There is no rule that authorizes the House to send a petition of the description of the one before you, to the Postmaster General, notwithstanding you have

given that direction to eighty-five this session. I believe that they have been thus disposed of in order that the House may not be further troubled with them, which appears to be very well understood by the Postmaster General. Is it, Mr. Speaker, that the subject is not of sufficient importance that you refuse to give those petitions the ordinary and usual course of all other petitions addressed to you? I acknowledge that the scheme contemplated by those petitions is not sanctioned by any law or practice in this Government, or any country or State in Europe. You boast that this is the only free and happy nation—your petitioners wish to add another jewel in your crown, not less bright than the other—that yours is the only virtuous and Sabbath observing nation. You have set apart the day after to-morrow to be spent thoughout the Union in prayer. By your laws, and the rules of the Postmaster General to carry the same into execution, you command many thousands of your citizens, with their horses, to be laboriously employed each and every hour of the day on the next Sabbath, and to spend every Sabbath in the year in the same way. It appears to me that you might as well suspend either the one practice or the other, (stop praying or violating the Sabbath,) unless you are of the opinion that by those laws and rules that you have enacted, you have the power to repeal that decretal order of Heaven that commands you "to keep holy the Sabbath day." You are the best judge of your repealing powers on that subject. It is stated, and so contended, by the honorable gentleman from Rhode Island, (Mr. POTTER,) that it is the work of necessity to carry and open the mail on the Sabbath. He further observed, that if you prevented the opening of the mail on the Sabbath, it would occasion more sin to be committed, as the people would attend at the post offices, and while impatiently waiting there for their letters and papers, by being debarred from obtaining them. I should suppose that if you pass a law to prohibit the carrying or opening the mail on that day, that as your law would be public it would be known to all, therefore they would not go or send to the post offices on that day, as they would know that the mails could not be opened—the postmasters themselves would not attend. In favor of a long-established favorite, national, sinful practice, I know that many excuses and reasons can be given in favor of the continuance of it—but if none better can be given than what that learned gentleman assigned, the Lord have mercy on us!

On great national occurrences, it is now the practice, and properly so, to employ expresses; they are not carried by mails, and it is expedient that they should travel as well on the Sabbath as on other days. But, Mr. Speaker, I am not able to see the necessity for the transportation and opening the mails on the Sabbath; and conscious of my high responsibility to God, as well as to my country, for my public acts, I am not willing to take it on myself to fly in the face of divine law. I do, therefore, most solemnly disavow and condemn the practice of the transportation and opening the mails on that holy day, believing it to be unnecessary, inadmissible and wicked.

After the motion was negatived, and the petition referred to the Postmaster General, Mr. F. offered for consideration the following resolution:

"*Resolved,* That the Committee on the Post Offices and Post Roads be authorized and required to examine into the propriety of submitting to the consideration of this House a law prohibiting the Postmaster General from making any contracts, in future, for the transportation or opening of the mails on the Sabbath, and that they have leave to report by bill or otherwise."

Mr. F. observed, that if the subject-matter of the resolution was not of sufficient importance to arrest the attention of the House, that any observations he could make would prove ineffectual.

DUTIES ON MANUFACTURES.

The House resolved itself into a Committee of the Whole, on the report of the committee of conferees on the disagreeing votes on the manufacture tax bill. The conferees recommended that the House recede from its opposition to the tax proposed by the Senate on umbrellas. The Committee concurred in the report without debate, and reported accordingly to the House. The House took up the report.

A debate arose thereon, in which Messrs. EPPES, WRIGHT, BARBOUR, STOCKTON, and others, advocated the adoption of the report, and Messrs. OAKLEY, SHEFFEY, RHEA, FISK of New York, PICKERING, INGERSOLL of Pennsylvania, and others, opposed it.

The debate on this question turned not on the expediency of the tax, which we did not hear denied, but on the Constitutional power or right of the Senate to make such an amendment to a bill for raising revenue. The debate was able, and, being on a question never before believed to have been debated, was highly interesting. The provision of the Constitution is as follows: "All bills for raising revenue shall originate in the House of Representatives; but the Senate may propose or concur with amendments as on other bills." On the one hand it was contended that the Senate could not amend a bill by adding a new tax thereto, because to do so would be to originate a tax, which, it was urged, was forbidden by the spirit of the Constitution. In support of this doctrine, an argument was drawn from the practice under the British Government, where the House of Lords is not permitted to amend such a bill. On the other hand it was urged, that the power to amend being expressly given to the Senate, forbade analogy to the practice of any other Government, whose unwritten constitution contained no such provision; that, the power of the Senate to increase or diminish a tax not being denied, the power otherwise to modify a tax followed of course; and that in a bill imposing a tax on manufactures, the Senate had an undoubted right to add to the articles enumerated, any other article which they deemed a proper subject of taxation, &c.

The question on agreeing to the report was, after a long and ingenious debate on this point, decided in the affirmative. by yeas and nays—for the report 97, against it 53, as follows:

YEAS—Messrs. Alexander, Alston, Anderson, Avery, Barbour, Bard, Barnett, Bayly of Virginia, Bines, Bowen, Breckenridge, Brown, Burwell, Butler, Caldwell, Calhoun, Cannon, Chappell, Clark, Clendenin, Conard, Cox, Crawford, Creighton, Crouch, Culpeper, Dana, Denoyelles, Desha, Duvall, Eppes, Evans, Farrow, Findley, Forney, Franklin, Geddes, Gholson, Gourdin, Griffin, Grosvenor, Hall, Hanson, Harris, Hasbrouck, Hawes, Hawkins, Hopkins of Kentucky, Howell, Hubbard, Humphreys, Irwin, Johnson of Kentucky, Kennedy, Kent of New York, Kent of Maryland, Kerr, Kershaw, King of North Carolina, Lewis, Lyle, Macon, Markell, McCoy, McKim, McLean, Miller, Montgomery, Newton, Parker, Pickens, Pleasants, Rea of Pennsylvania, Rich, Ringgold, Roane, Sage, Schureman, Sevier, Seybert, Sharp, Sherwood, Slaymaker, Smith of New York, Smith of Pennsylvania, Stockton, Strong, Tannehill, Taylor, Troup, Udree, White, Williams, Wilson of Pennsylvania, Wood, Wright, and Yancey.

NAYS—Messrs. Baylies of Massachusetts, Bigelow, Boyd, Bradbury, Brigham, Caperton, Champion, Cilley, Clopton, Comstock, Cooper, Davenport, Davis of Pennsylvania, Ely, Fisk of New York, Forsyth, Hale, Henderson, Hungerford, Hulbert, Ingersoll, Ingham, Jackson of Rhode Island, King of Massachusetts, Law, Lovett, Lowndes, Moseley, Murfree, Nelson, Oakley, Ormsby, Pickering, Pitkin, Potter, William Reed, Rhea of Tennessee, Robertson, Ruggles, Sheffey, Stanford, Stuart, Sturges, Taggart, Taylor, Thompson, Vose, Ward of Massachusetts, Webster, Wheaton, Wilcox, Wilson of Massachusetts, and Winter.

WEDNESDAY, January 11.

Mr. RINGGOLD presented the petition of the President and Directors of the Potomac Company, praying an extension of the powers of their charter so as to allow them to dispose of mill-seats within the District of Columbia, in case the erection of mills on the same shall not be prejudicial to the navigation. The petition was referred to the Committee on the District of Columbia.

Mr. STANFORD, of North Carolina, reported a bill to revive and continue in force the act declaring the consent of Congress to the act of the Legislature of the State of Georgia, passed the 12th of December, 1814, establishing the fees of the harbor master and health officer of the ports of Savannah and St. Mary's; which was twice read, and committed.

Mr. TROUP, from the Committee on Military Affairs, to whom was referred the amendments of the Senate to the volunteer bill, reported sundry amendments to the said amendments; which were agreed to. On the question to agree to the amendments of the Senate as amended, it was determined in the affirmative.

On motion of Mr. McKIM, the House determined not to sit on to-morrow, it being a day assigned by the President as a day of national fasting, humiliation, and prayer.

Two Messages were received from the Presi-

1067   HISTORY OF CONGRESS.   1068

H. of R.   *Land Claims in Mississippi—Lost Certificates.*   JANUARY, 1815.

dent of the United States, the one transmitting an account of the contingent expenses of the Government for the year past; the other, transmitting the annual report of the Director of the Mint.

LAND CLAIMS IN MISSISSIPPI.

The House again resolved itself into a Committee of the Whole on the bill for quieting and adjusting claims to land in the Mississippi Territory; and, after some time spent therein, the Chairman reported that the Committee had made several amendments thereto.

Mr. McCoy moved that the said bill be postponed until the second Monday in March next; which motion was determined in the negative—yeas 63, nays 71, as follows:

YEAS—Messrs. Alexander, Alston, Anderson, Barbour, Bard, Barnett, Bowen, Brown, Butler, Caldwell, Calhoun, Cannon, Clark, Clendenin, Comstock, Conard, Crawford, Crouch, Cuthbert, Davis of Pennsylvania, Denoyelles, Desha, Eppes, Farrow, Findley, Forsyth, Franklin, Gholson, Gourdin, Griffin, Hall, Harris, Hawes, Hungerford, Ingham, Kennedy, Kerr, Kilbourn, King of Massachusetts, Lefferts, Lyle, McCoy, McKim, McLean, Parker, Pleasants, Rea of Pennsylvania, Rhea of Tennessee, Ringgold, Roane, Sage, Seybert, Smith of Virginia, Stanford, Strong, Tannehill, Taylor, Telfair, Troup, Udree, Wilson of Pennsylvania, Wright, and Yancey.

NAYS—Messrs. Baylies of Massachusetts, Bayly of Virginia, Boyd, Breckenridge, Brigham, Caperton, Champion, Cooper, Cox, Creighton, Culpeper, Davenport, Duvall, Ely, Forney, Gaston, Geddes, Grosvenor, Hale, Hasbrouck, Hawkins, Henderson, Hopkins of Kentucky, Howell, Humphreys, Irwin, Jackson of Rhode Island, Jackson of Virginia, Johnson of Kentucky, Kent of New York, Kent of Maryland, Kershaw, Law, Lovett, Lowndes, Macon, Markell, McKee, Miller, Montgomery, Moseley, Nelson, Oakley, Ormsby, Pickering, Pitkin, Potter, John Reed, William Reed, Rich, Robertson, Ruggles, Schureman, Sevier, Sharp, Sheffey, Sherwood, Shipherd, Slaymaker, Smith of New York, Smith of Pennsylvania, Stockton, Thompson, Vose, Ward of Massachusetts, Webster, Wheaton, White, Wilcox, Wilson of Massachusetts, and Wood.

The question was then taken to concur in the amendments made by the Committee of the Whole in the first section, and was determined in the negative. The question on concurring in the amendments to the second section was stated: when the House adjourned.

FRIDAY, January 13.

Mr. SEYBERT presented the petition of sundry merchants and traders of Philadelphia, praying for the passage of a law establishing an uniform system of bankruptcy throughout the United States.—Referred to the Committee of the Whole to whom the bill on that subject is referred.

Mr. CHAPPELL, from the Committee on Pensions and Revolutionary Claims, reported a bill for the relief of William Arnold; which was twice read, and committed.

Mr. PLEASANTS, from the Naval Committee, reported two bills for compensating individuals, not having commissions from the United States, for prisoners and property taken from the enemy by spirited enterprise, viz: a bill concerning Matthew Guy and others, and a bill concerning Weston Jenkins and others; which were read twice, and committed.

LOST CERTIFICATES.

Mr. CHAPPELL, from the Committee on Pensions and Revolutionary Claims, made a report on the petition of Farrington Barcalow, administrator of Mary Rapelyea; which was read; when Mr. C. reported a bill for the relief of Farrington Barcalow, administrator of Mary Rapeleya; which was read twice, and committed to a Committee of the Whole on Monday next. The report is as follows:

That the petitioner states that the said Mary Rapelya was possessed of two loan office certificates; that her house was consumed by fire, and with it the said certificates. He prays that they may be renewed, or some other compensation made for them.

It appears that there were issued to the said Mary Rappelya two certificates from the loan office of New Jersey: one, No. 1,594, dated June 8, 1778, for $600; the other, No. 204, dated the same day, for $560; and that the said certificates are still outstanding and unpaid. It also appears that she made known the fact of the destruction of the said certificates shortly after it happened, which was in March, 1787, but did not advertise it in the papers until February, 1792, near five years afterwards, which she has sworn was occasioned by her ignorance of its necessity. She petitioned Congress for redress in the case, in February, 1795, and a favorable report was made thereon, but it was not finally acted on. She died in the year 1807, and in 1811 the administration of her effects was committed to the petitioner.

From the foregoing facts it appears that the claim is a just one; but it is barred by the statute of limitation, it not appearing that the claim was presented at the Treasury on or before the 1st of June, 1795, which is required by law. It also appears that the requisites of the resolve of 1780 have not been complied with, so far as to advertise the destruction *immediately* after it happened. The committee feel satisfied, however, that as the destruction was advertised, and as a petition was presented to Congress, and not to the Treasury, before the limited time had expired, there has been a compliance with the *spirit*, although not with the letter of the laws. They are, therefore, of opinion that relief ought to be granted, and report a bill for that purpose.

LAND CLAIMS IN MISSISSIPPI.

The House resumed the consideration of the report of the Committee of the Whole on the bill for quieting and adjusting claims to land in the Mississippi Territory.

[This bill provides a mode of settlement of claims to lands in the Mississippi Territory, north of the 31st degree of latitude, derived from grants or patents issued by the British Government.]

Considerable debate took place on this bill to-day, as it had done on Wednesday, in which the bill was strenuously advocated by Mr. McKEE, Mr. ROBERTSON, Mr. LATTIMORE, and others, and as strenuously opposed by Mr. McCoy, Mr. WRIGHT, and others.

The question on the passage of the bill to a third reading, was decided in the negative, by a majority of one vote—For the engrossment 70, against it 71, as follows:

YEAS—Messrs. Baylies of Massachusetts, Bayly of Virginia, Boyd, Bradbury, Breckenridge, Brigham, Caperton, Champion, Cilley, Cooper, Cox, Creighton, Culpeper, Davenport, Duvall, Ely, Fisk of Vermont, Forney, Gaston, Geddes, Grosvenor, Hale, Hasbrouck, Hawkins, Henderson, Hopkins of Kentucky, Howell, Hulbert, Irwin, Johnson of Kentucky, Kent of New York, Kershaw, Kilbourn, King of Massachusetts, Law, Lewis, Lovett, Lowndes, Macon, Markell, McKee, Montgomery, Moseley, Oakley, Ormsby, Pickering, Pitkin, John Reed, William Reed, Rich, Robertson, Ruggles, Schureman, Sevier, Sharp, Sheffey, Sherwood, Slaymaker, Smith of New York, Stockton, Sturges, Taggart, Thompson, Vose, Ward of Massachusetts, White, Wilcox, Wilson of Massachusetts, Winter, and Wood.

NAYS—Messrs. Alexander, Alston, Anderson, Avery, Barbour, Bard, Barnett, Bowen, Brown, Burwell, Butler, Caldwell, Calhoun, Cannon, Clark, Clendenin, Comstock, Cenard, Crawford, Crouch, Cuthbert, Davis of Pennsylvania, Denoyelles, Desha, Eppes, Evans, Farrow, Findley, Fisk of New York, Forsyth, Franklin, Gholson, Gourdin, Griffin, Hall, Harris, Hawes, Hubbard, Hungerford, Ingham, Kennedy, Kerr, King of North Carolina, Lefferts, Lyle, McCoy, McKim, McLean, Nelson, Newton, Parker, Pickens, Piper, Pleasants, Rea of Pennsylvania, Ringgold, Roane, Sage, Smith of Pennsylvania, Smith of Virginia, Stanford, Strong, Tannehill, Taylor, Telfair, Troup, Udree, Williams, Wilson of Pennsylvania, Wright, and Yancey.

So the bill was rejected.

The following is a copy of the bill on the subject of the adjustment of these claims, in the shape in which it stood when the question was taken on engrossing the same for a third reading:

An Act for quieting and adjusting claims to land in the Mississippi Territory.

Be it enacted by the Senate and House of Representatives of the United States of America in Congress assembled, That every person or persons claiming lands in the Mississippi Territory, north of the thirty-first degree of latitude, by virtue of any grant or patent issued by the British Government, before the 4th day of July, 1776, be, and they are hereby, authorized to file with the Commissioner of the General Land Office, all the evidence of their claim or claims, on or before the first day of November, one thousand eight hundred and sixteen. And it shall be lawful for the claimants, by themselves or their agents, to withdraw the original title papers, and all evidence relating to such claims, from the registers of the land offices within the Territory aforesaid, and which may have been filed by the claimants according to law.

SEC. 2. *And be it further enacted,* That the Secretary of State, the Attorney General, and Commissioner of the General Land Office, be, and they are hereby authorized and empowered to examine such of the claims thus filed as extend over land granted by the United States, or actually possessed by persons whom the United States are in any manner bound to secure therein, and to decide therein according to law and equity. And it shall be the duty of the commissioners aforesaid, to proceed to examine and decide on the claims aforesaid, whenever it shall appear to them that claims to the amount of one hundred and fifty thousand acres shall have been filed with the Commissioner of the General Land Office, in pursuance of this act.

SEC. 3. *And be it further enacted,* That the act of filing the claims aforesaid, with the Commissioner of the General Land Office in pursuance of this act, shall be considered as conclusive evidence of the acceptance by the claimants of the provisions of this act; and the decisions of the commissioners aforesaid shall be final, and shall have all the effect in law of a decision of the Supreme Court of the United States.

SEC. 4. *And be it further enacted,* That, in all cases where the commissioners aforesaid shall decide in favor of the claimant, the Commissioner of the General Land Office shall issue to the claimant a certificate of confirmation, specifying the quantity of land confirmed by such decision; and it shall be the duty of the Commissioner of the General Land Office to deliver such certificate of confirmation to the claimant, his agent, or attorney, which shall be received in lieu of, and in full compensation for, the land so claimed.

SEC. 5. *And be it further enacted,* That the certificates of confirmation authorized by this act, shall be received at any of the land offices of the United States, in payment for any public lands of the United States, lying within the limits of the Mississippi Territory, at rates to be established by said commissioners in said certificates, but not to exceed two dollars per acre, for every acre contained in such certificate of confirmation: *Provided,* That such certificates shall not be received in payment for any lands sold before the date of such certificate; nor shall any discount be allowed for prompt payment in such certificates: *And provided, also,* That nothing in this act shall be so construed as to authorize any British grant or patent to be read as evidence in any court of the United States, which may not be filed with the Commissioner of the General Land Office, in pursuance of this act, and which may be barred by the provisions of any former law.

The House then resolved itself into a Committee of the Whole, on the bill to authorize the President of the United States to raise certain companies of rangers for the defence of the frontiers of the United States. After having made some progress therein, the Committee rose, reported progress, and obtained leave to sit again.

SATURDAY, January 14.

Another member, to wit: from Delaware, HENRY M. RIDGELY, appeared, and took his seat.

Mr. EPPES, from the Committee of Ways and Means, made a favorable report on the petition of Isaac Smith, and therewith a bill for the relief of Isaac Smith and G. Caldwell; which was twice read, and committed.

Mr. E. also reported a bill supplementary to the act laying duties on licenses to distillers, explanatory of the provision authorizing a remission of the duty in cases of stills being burnt; which was twice read, and ordered to be engrossed for a third reading.

Mr. E. also reported a bill to amend the act for laying taxes on household furniture, extending the time to which the first shall take effect, from the first day of February to the first of April, and

1071   HISTORY OF CONGRESS.   1072

H. of R.   *Petition of Ann Hodgkinson—Relief of New Madrid.*   January, 1815.

the time in which the other shall be carried into effect from February to May. The bill was ordered to be engrossed, and read a third time.

Mr. JACKSON, of Virginia, from the Militia Committee, reported a bill to amend the act more effectually to provide for the national defence, by establishing a uniform militia in the United States.

[This bill prescribes certain regulations for a general organization of the militia, to take place within one year from the date of its passage, under the direction of the several State Legislatures; among which is the arrangement of the militia of each State, where it has not already been done, into divisions, to consist of not less than two nor more than three brigades, having one Major General to each division; the divisions, when in field, to rank according to their numbers, the lowest number to be the highest in rank.] The bill was twice read, and committed.

Mr. KILBOURN, of Ohio, moved the following resolution:

Resolved, That the Committee on Public Lands be instructed to prepare and report to this House a bill to provide for the sale of lands of the United States, in that tract of country within the State of Ohio and district of Chilicothe, heretofore set apart for satisfying the claims of refugees from Canada and Nova Scotia.

The resolution having been modified, on the suggestion of Mr. KING, of Massachusetts, so as to authorize the committee to inquire into the expediency of such a measure, instead of making the provision peremptory, was agreed to.

On motion of Mr. CANNON,

Resolved, That the Committee on Military Affairs be instructed to inquire into the expediency of allowing to any person who shall take up a deserter from the service of the United States, and deliver him to any commissioned officer in said service, an exemption from a draught or six months tour of duty in the service aforesaid.

The House then resolved itself into a Committee of the Whole, on the bill to authorize the raising certain companies of mounted rangers for the defence of the frontier. The bill was reported to the House, without amendment, and ordered to be engrossed for a third reading.

On motion of Mr. McKEE, the House resolved itself into a Committee of the Whole, on the bill regulating the sale of certain reserved sections of land in Ohio, and the bill attaching to the Canton district, in the State of Ohio, the tract of land lying between the foot of the Rapids of Miami of Lake Erie and the Western line of the Connecticut reserve. These bills were reported to the House, and severally ordered to a third reading.

A message from the Senate informed the House that the Senate have agreed to the second and fourth of the amendments proposed by this House to their amendments to the bill " to authorize the President of the United States to accept the services of volunteers who may associate and organize themselves, and offer their services to the Government of the United States," and have disagreed to the residue of the said amendments.

The House resolved itself into a Committee of the Whole on the bill for the relief of Benjamin Wells, and others. The bill was reported with an amendment; which was read, and concurred in by the House. The bill was then laid on the table.

The message from the Senate notifying their disagreement to certain amendments of this House to the amendments of the Senate to the bill " to authorize the President of the United States to accept the services of volunteers who may associate and organize themselves, and offer their services to the Government of the United States," was read, and referred to the Committee on Military Affairs.

PETITION OF ANN HODGKINSON.

Mr. PLEASANTS, from the Committee on Naval Affairs, made a report on the petition of Ann Hodgkinson; which was read, and the resolution therein contained was concurred in by the House. The report is as follows:

That the memorialist represents that, after the declaration of war, her late husband entered on board a private armed vessel, the York of Baltimore, and was killed in an engagement with the enemy; that, after his death, she applied to the Secretary of the Navy to be placed on the pension list; her request was complied with, but only as much allowed her as is allowed the widows of common seamen in such cases. She prays that Congress would grant to her a further allowance, as her husband acted as prize-master on board the York; and states that, according to the constant usage of the privateer service, prize-masters rank with and receive the emoluments of first lieutenants. It appears that the late Secretary of the Navy gave as a reason for not allowing more to the widow, that prize-masters are unknown to the laws of the United States, and that he was not authorised to grant anything additional in consequence of that appointment. The committee are of opinion that the Secretary was correct; that the office of prize-master is generally conferred upon an experienced seaman, in whom confidence is placed, and is matter of private arrangement as to pay and emolument between the captain and such prize-master. The committee see no sufficient reason for Congress interfering in this particular case, and recommend the following resolution:

Resolved, That the prayer of the petitioner ought not to be granted.

RELIEF OF NEW MADRID.

The House resolved itself into a Committee of the Whole on the bill for the relief of the inhabitants of the late county of New Madrid, in the Missouri Territory, who suffered by earthquakes. The bill was reported with several amendments; which were read, and, except one, which was disagreed to, were concurred in by the House.

The bill was then further amended; and a motion was then made, by Mr. McKIM, further to amend the bill by adding thereto the following sections:

Be it further enacted, That it shall be lawful for the President of the United States to appoint two disinterested and skilful persons to inquire into and ascertain the damage which has been been done by the storm of wind, in the month of August last, to the houses and property of persons residing in the City of Washington. The persons so appointed shall return, under oath, to the President of the United States, a just estimate of the damage sustained in the cases aforesaid.

'*And be it further enacted,* That, for the injury sustained, and the estimates reported by the persons appointed as aforesaid, the sufferers shall receive public land, to be located as is heretofore provided by this act, at the rate of two dollars per acre, as a full compensation for the injuries done as aforesaid.

And the question being taken, it was determined in the negative; and the bill was ordered to be engrossed, and read the third time on Monday next.

MONDAY, January 16.

Mr. NELSON presented a petition of William Tatham, praying compensation for his services for nearly twenty-five years, in the accumulation of civil, military, topographical, and public economical materials, by order of President WASHINGTON, in the year 1799.—Referred to the Secretary of War.

Mr. KILBOURN, from the committee to whom was referred, on the 28th ultimo, so much of the report of the Committee of Revisal and Unfinished Business as relates to the bill for the more effectual defence of the Northwestern frontier, reported a bill for the more effectual protection of the Northwestern frontier, by granting donations of land to actual settlers, and for public purposes; which was read twice, and committed to a Committee of the Whole.

An engrossed bill to authorize the President to raise certain companies of rangers for the defence of the frontiers of the United States, and to repeal certain acts now in force for this purpose, was read the third time, and passed.

An engrossed bill regulating the sale of certain reserved sections of land in the State of Ohio was read the third time, and passed.

An engrossed bill attaching to the Canton district, in the State of Ohio, the tract of land lying between the foot of the rapids of the Miami of Lake Erie and the Connecticut Western reserve, was read the third time, and passed.

An engrossed bill for the relief of the inhabitants of the late county of New Madrid, in the Territory of Missouri, who suffered by earthquakes, was read the third time, and passed.

An engrossed bill supplementary to the act, entitled "An act laying duties on licenses to retailers of wines, spirituous liquors, and foreign merchandise, and for other purposes, was read the third time, and passed.

An engrossed bill to amend the act, entitled "An act to provide additional revenues for defraying the expenses of Government, and maintaining the public credit, by laying a direct tax upon the United States, and to provide for assessing and collecting the same;" and the act, entitled "An act to provide additional revenues for defraying the expenses of Government, and maintaining the public credit, by laying duties on household furniture, and on gold and silver watches," was read the third time, and passed.

A message from the Senate informed the House that the Senate have passed a bill "giving further time to complete the surveys and obtain the patents for the lands located under Virginia resolution warrants;" in which they ask the concurrence of this House. The bill was read twice and referred to the Committee on the Public Lands.

Mr. WARD, of Massachusetts, presented the petition of sundry citizens of Boston, in Massachusetts, praying for the passage of a law establishing an uniform system of bankruptcy; which was referred to the Committee of the Whole having that subject under consideration.

Mr. TROUP, of Georgia, from the Military Committee, reported a recommendation that the House insist on that amendment, proposed by them, to the volunteer bill, which provides that State corps (to be accepted in pursuance of this bill into the service of the United States,) shall be received in lieu of a like number of militia, which shall at any time be required from the State which offers them; and also on the amendment which varies or extends the descriptions of rifles which the volunteers may use.

And the House determined to insist thereon, accordingly.

Mr. PEARSON, of North Carolina, from the committee to whom was recommitted the report of the committee on the destruction of certain papers and vouchers in the office of the Clerk of the House of Representatives, together with the Clerk's second letter in relation thereto, made a further report, which was read and ordered to lie on the table.

The House then resolved itself into a Committee of the Whole on the bill giving further time to the purchasers of public lands to complete their payments. The bill was reported to the House, and ordered to be engrossed for a third reading.

The bill for the relief of the heirs of James Hynum next passed through a Committee of the Whole, and was ordered to be engrossed for a third reading.

The House then resolved itself into a Committee of the Whole on the bill supplementary to the act for the settlement of the Yazoo claims; which occasioned considerable discussion. The Committee rose, before having gone through the same, and obtained leave to sit again.

SUNDAY MAILS.

Mr. BRADBURY, Mr. PITKIN, of Connecticut, and Mr. COMSTOCK, of New York presented petitions from their respective districts, remonstrating against the transportation and opening of the mail on the Sabbath; which were referred to the Postmaster general.

Mr. HOWELL, of New York, presented a petition of the like nature, which he moved to refer to the Committee on Post Offices and Post Roads. He said he was not to be deterred from making this motion by the failure of a former attempt of the same character. It was a respect due to the petitioners, he conceived, that a report should be made on their petition, which it was not probable, having been so long delayed, would be received at the hands of the Postmaster General.

On this motion of Mr. HOWELL, there arose a smart debate, the motion being opposed and advocated by several gentlemen. The debate turned on the merits of these petitions, which were denied by Mr. RHEA, Mr. JOHNSON, of Kentucky, and Mr. WRIGHT, and upheld by Mr. HOWELL, Mr. COMSTOCK, Mr. HULBERT, and Mr. FINDLEY. In the course of the debate, it was stated by Mr. KILBOURN, that he knew that the Postmaster General did intend to report on this subject at an early day. On the one hand of this question, it was contended that this was an attempt to blend the affairs of Church and State, which had been systematically made, and industriously promoted by the circulation of petitions for signature all over the Union; and it was intimated that some political party considerations might have entered into the motives which produced them. On the other hand, it was urged that these petitions were signed by religious persons of all denominations, whose respectability, professions, and standing in life, equally entitled these petitions to a respectful hearing, &c.

The yeas and nays having been required by Mr. HOWELL on this motion, it was decided in the affirmative—for the reference proposed 81, against it 70.

Mr. CROUCH, of Pennsylvania, and Mr. KILBOURN, of Ohio, presented petitions of a like tenor with the above; which were referred.

TUESDAY, January 17.

An engrossed bill, giving further time to purchasers of public lands to complete their payments, was read the third time, and passed.

An engrossed bill for the relief of the heirs of James Hynum, was read the third time, and passed.

A message from the Senate informed the House that the Senate have agreed to a part of the amendments proposed by this House to their bill "to incorporate the subscribers to the Bank of the United States of America," with amendments, in which they ask the concurrence of this House; and the Senate have disagreed to the other part of the amendments proposed by this House to the said bill. The Senate insist on their disagreement to the amendments insisted on by this House to the amendments of the Senate to the bill "to authorize the President of the United States to accept the services of volunteers who may associate and organize themselves, and offer their services to the Government of the United States," and ask a conference on the said amendments; to which conference they have appointed managers on their part.

Mr. COOPER, of Delaware, laid upon the table the following resolution:

Resolved, That the Secretary of War be, and he hereby is, directed to state to this House the reason why he has not made a report to this House, as directed by their resolution of the 13th October last, (calling for a report relative to the advancing of moneys by States, &c.)

SUNDAY MAILS.

The SPEAKER laid before the House a report from the Postmaster General, on the several petitions which have been referred to him at the present session, remonstrating against the opening or conveyance of the mails on Sundays; which was read, and referred to the Committee on the Post Office and Post Roads.—It is as follows:

GENERAL POST OFFICE, *Jan. 16, 1815.*

SIR: The Postmaster General, to whom was referred sundry memorials against the usage of transporting and opening the mails on the Sabbath, has the honor to report the following facts and observations:

The usage of transporting the mails on the Sabbath, is coeval with the Constitution of the United States; and a prohibition of that usage will be first considered.

The mail passes every day in the week from Portsmouth, New Hampshire, to Savannah, in Georgia, and from Wiscasset, in Maine, to Scoodic Falls, without rest on the Sabbath. And the same practice prevails on the great route from Washington City to Ohio, Kentucky, and the Missouri Territory; and from that city to Tennessee, Mississippi Territory, and New Orleans; and from Charleston, South Carolina, to Tennessee and Kentucky; and on several other great chains of communication.

If the mail was not to move on Sunday, on the first mentioned route, it would be delayed from three to four days in passing from one extreme of the route to the other. From Washington City to St. Louis, Missouri Territory, the mail would be delayed two days. From Washington City to New Orleans, the mail would be delayed three days. From New Orleans to Boston it would be delayed from four to five days. And generally the mails would, on an average, be retarded equal to one-seventh part of the time now employed, if the mails do not move on the Sabbath.

On the smaller cross routes, the transporting of the mail has been avoided on the Sabbath, except when necessary to prevent great delays, and to preserve connexions with different routes.

In relation to opening the mails on the Sabbath, it may be noticed, that the ninth section of the "Act regulating the Post Office establishment," makes it the duty of the postmasters to attend to the duties of his office "every day" on which a mail shall arrive at his office, and at "all reasonable hours" on every day of the week. When a mail is conveyed on the Sabbath, it must be opened and exchanged at the offices which it may reach in the course of the day. This operation, at the smaller offices, occupies not more than ten or twelve minutes; in some of the larger offices, it occupies one hour; and, it is believed, does not very greatly interfere with religious exercises, as to the postmasters themselves.

The practice of "delivering" letters and newspapers on the Sabbath is of recent origin, and directed by the above quoted section, commencing in 1810. Prior to that period, no postmaster (except the postmaster at Washington City) was required to deliver letters and newspapers on the Sabbath. The "reasonable hours" were to be determined by the Postmaster General, who established the following regulations, now existing: "At post offices where the mail arrives on Sunday, the office is to be kept open, for the delivery of letters, &c., for one hour after the arrival and assorting of the mail; but in case that would interfere with the hours of public worship, then the office is to be kept open for one

1077   HISTORY OF CONGRESS.   1078

JANUARY, 1815.   *Yazoo Claims.*   H. OF R.

hour after the usual time of dissolving the meeting, for that purpose." Also, if the mail arrives at an office too late for the delivery of letters on Saturday night, the postmaster is instructed to deliver them on Sunday morning, at such early hour as not to entrench upon the hours devoted to public religious exercises. If these regulations are not strictly attended to, it must be impossible to the urgency of applicants, and the complaisance of postmasters.

After the preceding statement, it is to be observed, that public policy, pure morality, and undefiled religion, combine in favor of a due observance of the Sabbath. Nevertheless, a nation owes to itself an exercise of the means adapted to its own preservation, and for the continuance of those very blessings which flow from such observance; and the nation must sometimes operate, by a few of its agents, even on the Sabbath; and such operation may, as in time of war, become indispensable, so that the many may enjoy an uninterrupted exercise of religion in quietude and in safety. In the present state of the nation, it may be supposed necessary, daily, to convey Governmental orders, instructions, and regulations, and to communicate and receive information. If this daily carriage of the mail be, as relates to the safety of the nation, a matter of necessity, it also becomes a work of mercy. When peace shall arrive, the necessity will greatly diminish, and it will be, at all times, a pleasure to this Department to prevent any profanation of the Sabbath, as far as relates to its official authority.

The preceding statement of facts and observations are submitted, with much respect for the memorialists, and with great deference to yourself and the honorable the House of Representatives.

    RETURN J. MEIGS, JR.

Hon. SPEAKER
 Of the House of Representatives.

YAZOO CLAIMS.

The House then resolved itself into a Committee of the Whole on the bill supplemental to the act for the settlement of the Yazoo claims. The question yet depending on the motion of Mr. HALL, of Georgia, to add a new section to the bill, is substantially the same as that stated below.

The motion was opposed by Messrs. OAKLEY and WRIGHT, and advocated by Messrs. HALL and FORSYTH, but was finally negatived.

The Committee then rose, and reported the bill; and the amendments made thereto were agreed to. Among the amendments was one extending the time for filing releases, &c., to the second Monday in March.

Mr. HALL, of Georgia, renewed the motion he had made in Committee of the Whole, to add a new section to the bill, which he now varied to read as follows:

And be it further enacted, That the commissioners aforesaid, having decided upon the sufficiency of the releases and assignments of individual claimants, according to the true intent and meaning of the act, entitled "An act for the indemnification of certain claimants to public lands in the Mississippi Territory," shall, in their report to the President of the United States, certify such portion of the claims of each individual claimant, as in justice should and ought to be reserved for defraying their respective proportions of all just and reasonable expenses incurred by the trustees, guarantees, or agents of the companies to which they respectively belong, and for which, by agreement entered into in writing, they are bound; which said portion shall be delivered over to said trustees, agents, or guarantees, and certificates for the residue to the individual himself, his agent, or attorney, specially authorized to receive the same.

This motion was opposed by Messrs. OAKLEY and BARNETT, and supported by Messrs. HALL, TELFAIR, and FORSYTH. The question on the motion was decided in the negative, by yeas and nays—For the motion 61, against it 86, as follows:

YEAS—Messrs. Alexander, Alston, Anderson, Barbour, Bard, Bines, Bowen, Brown, Caldwell, Conard, Crawford, Creighton, Crouch, Cuthbert, Denoyelles, Desha, Earle, Eppes, Forney, Forsyth, Franklin, Gholson, Gourdin, Hall, Hawes, Hawkins, Humphreys, Hungerford, Ingersoll, Ingham, Irwin, Johnson of Virginia, Kennedy, Kent of Maryland, Kerr, Kershaw, Kilbourn, King of North Carolina, Lefferts, Lyle, McCoy, McKim, McLean, Moore, Murfree, Nelson, Newton, Piper, Pleasants, Rea of Pennsylvania, Ringgold, Roane, Sage, Sharp, Smith of Pennsylvania, Stanford, Strong, Tannehill, Telfair, Troup, and Udree.

NAYS—Messrs. Avery, Barnett, Baylies of Massachusetts, Bayly of Virginia, Bigelow, Boyd, Bradbury, Breckenridge, Brigham, Butler, Caperton, Cannon, Champion, Cilley, Clark, Clendenin, Cooper, Cox, Culpeper, Dana, Davenport, Davis of Massachusetts, Ely, Farrow, Fisk of Vermont, Fisk of New York, Geddes, Grosvenor, Hale, Hanson, Hasbrouck, Henderson, Howell, Hubbard, Hulbert, Irving, Jackson of Rhode Island, Jackson of Virginia, Kent of New York, King of Massachusetts, Law, Lewis, Lovett, Lowndes, Macon, Markell, McKee, Miller, Moseley, Oakley, Ormsby, Parker, Pickering, Pickens, Pitkin, Potter, John Reed, William Reed, Rich, Robertson, Ruggles, Schureman, Sherwood, Shipherd, Slaymaker, Smith of New York, Smith of Virginia, Stockton, Stuart, Sturges, Taggart, Taylor, Thompson, Vose, Ward of Massachusetts, Webster, Wheaton, White, Wilcox, Williams, Wilson of Massachusetts, Wilson of Pennsylvania, Winter, Wood, Wright, and Yancey.

The bill, after being slightly amended, was ordered to be read a third time.

A motion was then made by Mr. INGHAM, of Pennsylvania, that the remaining orders of the day be postponed until to-morrow, in order to take up the message this morning received from the Senate, respecting their decision on the amendments to the National Bank bill; which motion was negatived by the following vote—For the motion 71, against it 73.

After refusing to take up several orders of the day, which were called up—

Mr. GHOLSON renewed the motion to postpone the remaining orders of the day until to-morrow, in order to take up the Bank bill. Whereupon,

Mr. McKEE moved to adjourn, assigning as a reason for the motion that the hour was too late, and the House too much fatigued, to enter into a subject of so great moment.

The motion to adjourn prevailed.

WEDNESDAY, January 18.

Mr. IRVING, of New York, presented a petition from a number of merchants and others, praying for the establishment of an uniform system of bankruptcy.—Referred.

On motion of Mr. LATTIMORE,

Resolved, That a committee be appointed to inquire into the expediency of providing by law for repairing, and keeping in repair, so much of the road leading from Nashville, in Tennessee, to Natchez, in the Mississippi Territory, as is included within the boundaries of the Chickasaw and Choctaw nations of Indians; and also, of repairing, and keeping in repair, the road leading from Fort Hawkins, in the State of Georgia, to Fort St. Stephens, in the Territory aforesaid; and that the said committee have leave to report by bill or otherwise.

Messrs. LATTIMORE, ROBERTSON, GEDDES, WILSON of Pennsylvania, and CANNON, were appointed the said committee.

Mr. KILBOURN, of Ohio, offered for consideration the following resolutions:

Resolved, That the Committee of Ways and Means be instructed to inquire into the expediency of laying and collecting an income tax from such people of the United States as have capital vested in public or any kind of stock, or in private loans, or in any other way yielding profits to the owner; and on those who are engaged in professional or other employments, producing an annual income exceeding a certain amount which the said committee may think proper to fix; it being intended that this inquiry shall extend only to such capital or employments as are not taxed by any existing laws.

Resolved, That the said committee be instructed to inquire into the expediency of increasing the tax upon the income, or dividend, of the capital vested in the several banking institutions within the United States, on which a tax is now imposed by law of Congress.

On the question now to consider this resolution, the vote was as follows: For its consideration 60, against it 66.

Mr. JACKSON, of Virginia, moved that these resolutions be printed, with a view to calling them up at some future day. He could not see, he said, why a vast mass of property, more productive than any other, not now taxed at all, should not be taxed as well as all the land, and nearly all the industry of the nation.

This motion was opposed by Mr. SEYBERT, and advocated by Mr. KILBOURN, and negatived by the following vote: For printing 66, against it 63.

PETITION OF JOSHUA PENNY.

Mr. YANCEY, from the Committee of Claims, made a report on the petition of Joshua Penny; which was read, and the resolution therein contained was concurred in by the House.—The report is as follows:

That the petitioner states that, on the night of the 22d of August, 1813, a party of armed men, from the ship Ramilies, commanded by Commodore Hardy, forcibly entered his house, took him from his bed, and carried him by force, and entirely destitute of clothing, with the exception of his shirt, to that ship, then lying off Gardiner's bay, where he was immediately put in irons and close confinement; that he was then sent to Halifax, where he was imprisoned and badly treated

till the 20th of May, 1814; that he was at that time liberated from prison, and sent to Salem, in Massachusetts, in a cartel. It is also stated by the petitioner, that while he was confined on board the ship, he received nothing for subsistence but bread and water, and that his treatment was wanton and cruel. The only cause assigned for all his punishment was, that he had once been in the employment of Commodore Decatur, as a pilot to a torpedo. The petition is not accompanied with any documents to establish the facts, but the committee have no reason to disbelieve their correctness. The petitioner asks of Congress "some compensation on account of his great and uncommon sufferings."

In common with every friend of humanity, the committee sympathize with the petitioner, while they deprecate and abhor the conduct of the enemy in such cruel and unheard-of treatment towards a citizen, not in the military or naval employment of the Government; they cannot, however, adopt the principle, that for every such violation of the usages of civilized warfare, on the part of the enemy, the Government is bound to make compensation for the injury. They view the present as one of the multiplied examples, on the part of the enemy, during the present war, of outrage known only in the history of British aggression and British warfare. The principle upon which this opinion is founded has been established in a variety of cases during the present and last session of Congress. They recommend to the House the following resolution:

Resolved, That the prayer of the petition ought not to be granted.

BANK OF THE UNITED STATES.

The House then resumed the consideration of the message from the Senate announcing their amendments to the amendments of this House to the bill to incorporate the subscribers of the Bank of the United States of America.

The first amendment having been stated, which proposes to make the capital of the bank thirty-five millions instead of thirty millions—

Mr. McKEE, of Kentucky, expressed his hope that the amendment would not be agreed to, considering it as the keystone of all the amendments of the Senate. He could see no possible advantages to result from the addition of five millions of capital, particularly as connected with the section authorizing the stoppage of payment in specie. He could see no consequence to result from that clause, which was not disastrous and ruinous, and he therefore hoped it would not be agreed to.

Mr. HAWKINS, of Kentucky, denied the applicability of the remarks of Mr. McKEE to the amendments of the Senate. The only question, since the Senate had agreed to expunge the condition of a permanent loan to the Government was, whether the Senate should be accommodated by increasing the capital of the bank by the addition thereto of five millions; for, in fact, the retention of the clause authorizing the suspension of specie payment was immaterial, unless that it is more expedient to incorporate such a provision at once, than yield it to the importunity of the bank hereafter. For he had no doubt, if the war continued, the bank must sooner or later suspend specie payment; even the banks of Kentucky and Ohio (where specie abounded) had at length been compelled in self-defence to stop payment of specie. The advantage to Government in the proposed amendment, Mr. H. argued, would be found in the taking out of the market so much more of the war stock, &c. Something, he contended, was due to the Senate, in the spirit of accommodation which that body had exhibited in yielding so far to the wishes of the House, as to accept the greater part of the amendments; and particularly inasmuch as, in several cases of difference with that body, the House had exhibited much pertinacity in adhering to its peculiar opinions, &c. He treated as altogether ideal the argument of danger to the existence of the Republic from the refusal to incorporate a bank. He had, he said, higher opinions of the destinies of this Government, and of its durability and ability to overcome every difficulty; opinions which gained ground by every day's experience, &c.

Mr. STOCKTON, of New Jersey, rose to say, that he and those with whom he had acted, in the concessions they had made relative to the features of the bank bill, had gone as far as they could go, and further than they had originally intended, in order to conciliate with gentlemen on the other side of the House. After they had done this, it could not be expected, he said, that they should recede. He wished it, therefore, to be understood, that, while he should be happy to pay all due respect to the other branch of the Legislature, it could not be expected that they should yield up to them their honest convictions; and therefore that they could not yield their assent to the amendments of the Senate.

Mr. WRIGHT, of Maryland, made a speech of some length expressive of his hope that a spirit of accommodation would have induced the House at once to have acceded to the amendments of the Senate, which he deemed advantageous. He considered it particularly important that a provision should exist to prevent the agents or friends of the enemy from drawing all its specie from the vaults of the bank. The state of war he considered as changing essentially the usual state of mercantile operations, and requiring from the banks a suspension of payments in specie. He concluded his speech with the following quotations from legal authorities: "*Inter arma leges silent;*" "*Necessitas non habet legem.*"

Mr. GROSVENOR, of New York, after remarking that he felt not at all encumbered by the stipulations of compromise, inasmuch as he was not a party to it, having voted against the bill, proceeded to assign the reason why he should vote for this amendment. He found himself obliged to do so from a regard to his own consistency; for, though he doubted of the efficacy of any bank that could be established, he was pretty certain that the plan of the bank would be improved by the addition to its capital proposed by the Senate.

Mr. FORSYTH, of Georgia, advocated at some length the adoption of the amendments of the

Senate. He believed the addition of five millions to the capital of the bank would operate as a benefit to the Government, by taking so much of the stock out of the market, &c. He denied the necessity, or even the propriety of any part of the House sacrificing their views of the national interest in any ideas of compromise or conciliation. At least, he disclaimed, for himself, the operation of any such consideration on him.

Mr. CUTHBERT, of Georgia, made a speech of some length against the amendments of the Senate. He considered them as inseparably connected with each other, and being so, he was altogether opposed to them. To the amendment now under consideration he was particularly opposed, because by extending the quantity of war stock to be purchased, the ability to purchase Treasury notes would be so far diminished, and the immediate benefits to the Government so far curtailed. Mr. C. also dwelt with some emphasis on the propriety of carrying into effect in good faith the compromise, by the aid of which the bill had passed this House in the form in which it had been returned to the Senate, &c.

Mr. FORSYTH denied the operation on him of the compromises alleged to have taken place in regard to this question. He was no party to it, and was ignorant of its terms. If the agreement had been in writing, he should like to see the names signed to it; to know who it was that was willing to bind the solid interests of the country as a propitiatory sacrifice on the altar of conciliation.

Considerable further debate took place on this amendment, in the course of which Mr. HAWKINS, of Kentucky, Mr. TELFAIR, of Georgia, Mr. RHEA, of Tennessee, and Mr. ALSTON, of North Carolina, denied the authority of the compromise alleged to have taken place on a former occasion, which was on the other hand asserted by Mr. CUTHBERT and Mr. OAKLEY, and incidentally by Mr. McKEE. The first named gentlemen supported the amendment, and the latter opposed the amendment. Mr. HAWKINS, in the course of his speech, took occasion to pay a high tribute to the talents and independence of the present Secretary of the Treasury, of which he challenged a denial.

Mr. FORSYTH, in conclusion of the debate, by way of disproving the obligation of the Republican to conciliate the Federal side of the House on any question affecting the National Bank, quoted the yeas and nays on the question of reconsideration of the bill, (after it had been rejected by the casting vote of the Speaker,) from which it appeared that of the fifty-four who voted *against* reconsideration, but *six* belonged to the Republican side of the House.

The question on concurrence in the first amendment of the Senate was finally decided in the negative by yeas and nays. For the amendment 80, against it 87, as follows:

YEAS—Messrs. Alexander, Alston, Anderson, Avery, Barbour, Bines, Bowen, Brown, Burwell, Caldwell, Cannon, Chappell, Clendenin, Comstock, Con-

1068 HISTORY OF CONGRESS. 1084

H. of R. *Proceedings.* January, 1815.

dict, Conard, Creighton, Crouch, Davis of Pennsylvania, Denoyelles, Desha, Eppes, Findley, Fisk of Vermont, Fisk of New York, Forney, Forsyth, Franklin, Gholson, Gourdin, Griffin, Grosvenor, Hall, Harris, Hawes, Hawkins, Hopkins of Kentucky, Hubbard, Humphreys, Ingersoll, Ingham, Irwin, Jackson of Virginia, Johnson of Kentucky, Kerr, Kershaw, Kilbourn, King of North Carolina, Lefferts, Lewis, Lyle, Macon, McCoy, McLean, Montgomery, Moore, Murfree, Nelson, Newton, Ormsby, Parker, Pickens, Piper, Pleasants, Rea of Pennsylvania, Rhea of Tennessee, Rich, Ringgold, Roane, Sage, Sevier, Smith of Pennsylvania, Smith of Virginia, Strong, Taunehill, Telfair, Troup, Udree, Williams, Wilson of Pennsylvania, and Wright.

NAYS—Messrs. Bard, Barnett, Baylies of Massachusetts, Bayly of Virginia, Bigelow, Bowen, Boyd, Bradbury, Breckenridge, Brigham, Butler, Caperton, Calhoun, Champion, Cilley, Clark, Cooper, Cox, Crawford, Culpeper, Cuthbert, Dana, Davenport, Davis of Massachusetts, Duvall, Earle, Ely, Evans, Farrow, Gaston, Geddes, Hale, Hanson, Hasbrouck, Henderson, Howell, Hungerford, Hulbert, Jackson of Rhode Island, Johnson of Virginia, Kennedy, Kent of New York, Kent of Maryland, King of Massachusetts, Law, Lovett, Lowndes, Markell, McKee, Miller, Moseley, Oakley, Pearson, Pickering, Pitkin, Potter, John Reed, William Reed, Robertson, Ruggles, Schureman, Seybert, Sharp, Sheffey, Sherwood, Shipherd, Slaymaker, Smith of New York, Stanford, Stockton, Stuart, Sturges, Taggart, Taylor, Thompson, Vose, Ward of Massachusetts, Ward of New Jersey, Webster, Wheaton, White, Wilcox, Wilson of Massachusetts, Winter, Wood, and Yancey.

The other material amendments were also disagreed to, after debate.

Among others, was the amendment going to reinstate the payment in specie suspending section, on which the vote was—for reinstating 80, against it 85.

So the House refused to reinstate that section.

The House, after agreeing to some trivial amendments, determined to insist on those of their amendments to which the Senate had disagreed.

Thursday, January 19.

The House resumed the consideration of the bill for the relief of Benjamin Wells, and others ; and it was ordered to be engrossed, and read the third time to-morrow.

Mr. Chappell, from the Committee on Revolutionary Claims, to whom was referred the petition of Amy Dardin, made a detailed report thereon, accompanied by a bill for the relief of the legal representatives of the heirs of David Dardin, deceased; which was twice read and committed.

The bill from the Senate, supplementary to the act passed at the last session for the indemnification of certain claimants of public lands in the Mississippi Territory, was read the third time as amended, and passed.

The bill for the better regulation of the Ordnance department, and the bill for the relief of James Brahany, passed through the Committee of the Whole, and were ordered to be engrossed for a third reading.

The bill to alter and amend the several acts establishing a Navy Department, by adding thereto a Board of Commissioners, went through a Committee of the Whole; and, after being amended, was, on motion of Mr. Forsyth, postponed till to-morrow.

The House resumed the consideration of the report of the select committee on the letter of Patrick Magruder, Clerk of this House, touching the destruction, by the hands of the enemy, of the vouchers, for the contingent expenditures of his office ; and, after considerable debate, the resolution reported by the committee was amended so as to read as follows, and then agreed to by the House, viz :

Resolved, That Patrick Magruder, Clerk of the House of Representatives, be credited at the proper office in the Treasury Department for the sum of $39,668 78, and such further sums as he shall exhibit satisfactory evidence of having properly paid for expenditures on account of the contingent expenses of the House of Representatives since his last settlement ; and that a copy of this and the former report of the committee be filed in the Auditor's office.

Friday, January 20.

Mr. Rhea, from the Committee on Post Offices and Post Roads, to whom were referred sundry petitions and memorials remonstrating against the usage of transporting the mail on the Sabbath, and the report of the Postmaster General relating thereto, made a report; which was read, and committed to a Committee of the Whole on Monday next. The report is as follows:

" That they have had the same under consideration, and deeming it of great national importance, particularly in time of war, that no delay should attend the transportation of the mail, they deem it inexpedient to interfere with the present arrangements of the Post Office Establishment ; and, therefore, submit the following resolution :

" *Resolved,* That it is inexpedient to grant the prayer of the petitioners."

Mr. Rhea, from the same committee, reported a bill in addition to the act regulating the Post Office Establishment; which was read twice, and committed to a Committee of the Whole.

Mr. McKee, from the Committee on Public Lands, reported to the House the Senate's bill giving further time to complete the surveys, and obtain patents for lands located under Virginia Revolutionary land warrants ; which was twice read and committed.

Mr. Troup, from the committee of conference with the Senate on the disagreeing votes on the volunteer bill, made a report thereon, which was read, and ordered to lie on the table.

The House resumed the consideration of the bill to alter and amend the several acts for establishing a Navy Department by adding thereto a Board of Commissioners.

Mr. King, of Massachusetts, moved to amend the bill so as to limit its duration to the continuance of the present war, which motion was negatived ; and the bill was then ordered to be engrossed for a third reading.

The bill for the relief of B. Wells, and others; the bill for the better regulation of the Ordnance department; and the bill for the relief of James Brahany; were read a third time and passed.

The bill for the relief of Joseph Perkins; the bill to continue in force the act declaring the assent of Congress to a certain act of the Legislature of Georgia; the bill for the relief of William Arnold; the bill for the relief of Farrington Barcalow; the bill concerning Weston Jenkins, and others; and the bill concerning Matthew Guy and others, severally passed through Committees of the Whole, and were ordered to be engrossed for a third reading.

SATURDAY, January 21.

Mr. LATTIMORE presented a petition of the Legislature of the Mississippi Territory, praying that the amount of losses sustained by citizens of the said Territory, in the present war against the Creek Indians may be ascertained, in order that the sufferers may be indemnified in lands to be acquired from said Indians.—Referred.

Mr. LATTIMORE presented another petition of the Legislature of the Mississippi Territory, praying that the inhabitants of said Territory may be authorized to form a Convention for the adoption of a Constitution, and that the said Territory may be admitted into the Union as a State.

Ordered, That the said petitions be referred to the committee appointed on the 18th instant, to inquire into the expediency of making certain roads in the Mississippi Territory.

The following resolution was submitted by Mr. CLARK; which was read, and ordered to lie on the table.

Resolved, That Patrick Magruder, Clerk of the House of Representatives, be removed from office; that this House will, on Monday next, proceed to the election of a Clerk.

An engrossed bill to alter and amend the several acts for establishing a Navy Department, by adding thereto a Board of Commissioners, was read the third time and passed.

An engrossed bill directing the manner of contracts and purchases in the Navy Department, and for promoting economy therein, was read the third time, and passed.

An engrossed bill for the relief of Joseph Perkins was read the third time, and passed.

An engrossed bill concerning Matthew Guy, John Woodward, Samuel Tennison, and Wilfred Drury, was read the third time and passed.

An engrossed bill concerning Weston Jenkins and others, was read the third time, and passed.

An engrossed bill for the relief of William Arnold was read the third time, and passed.

The House resolved itself into a Committee of the Whole on the bill to amend the acts "more effectually to provide for the national defence, by establishing an uniform militia throughout the United States; and, after some time spent therein, the bill was reported with amendments, which were ordered to lie on the table.

On motion of Mr. JOHNSON, of Kentucky, *Ordered,* That General Winder have leave to withdraw the original documents, accompanying his communication to the committee appointed to inquire into the causes of the success of the enemy, in his recent enterprise against the City of Washington and the neighboring town of Alexandria, and reported by the committee of the House; the Clerk of the House first taking and retaining copies of such of them as have not been printed.

A message from the Senate informed the House that the Senate have agreed to the amendments proposed by this House to the bill "supplementary to the act, entitled 'An act providing for the indemnification of certain claimants of public lands in the Mississippi Territory," with amendment. The amendment was concurred in by the House.

Another message from the Senate informed the House that the Senate have adopted the modification proposed by the committee of conference on the disagreeing votes of the two Houses on the amendments depending to the bill "to authorize the President of the United States to accept the services of volunteers, who may associate and organize themselves, and offer their services to the Government of the United States," with an amendment.

The report of the committee of conference was read and agreed to by the House.

STATE OF THE TREASURY.

Mr. EPPES laid before the House a letter from the Secretary of the Treasury to the Chairman of the Committee of Ways and Means, exhibiting a view of the state of the Treasury of the United States at the close of the year 1814; which was read, and ordered to be printed.

The letter is as follows:

TREASURY DEPARTMENT, *Jan.* 17, 1815.

SIR: I have deemed it hitherto my duty to wait, with deference and respect, for a decision upon the measures which I had the honor to suggest to the Committee of Ways and Means on the 17th October last. But the rapid approach to the termination of the session of Congress induces me again to trespass upon your attention, earlier, perhaps, than is consistent with a satisfactory view of the situation of the Treasury, as some important plans are still under legislative discussion. I have now, however, the honor to submit to the consideration of the Committee of Ways and Means the following additional statements and propositions:

STATEMENTS.

I. Statement of the situation of the Treasury at the close of the year 1814.

1. *The charges on the Treasury for* 1814.

It appears, that at the close of the year 1813, there was a general balance of the appropriations for that year, remaining unsatisfied, and subject to be called for at the Treasury in the year 1814, amounting to about \$8,131,913 03, and composed of the following items:

Of the appropriations for the civil department, about - - - - \$390,499 07

Of the appropriation for the military department - - - - 2,666,230 33
Of the appropriation for naval department 3,611,240 75
Of the appropriation for the diplomatic department - - - - 253,846 62
Of the appropriation for miscellaneous services - - - - - 1,209,496 26

　　　　　　　　　　　　　　　$8,131,313 03

The annual appropriations for the year 1814, amounted to the sum of 38,003,691 28
The sum necessary to meet the engagements, in relation to the public debt, was about - - - 11,560,586 39

　　　　　　　　　　　　　　　49,563,277 67

The gross charge on the Treasury for the year 1814, was - - - - 57,694,590 70

2. *The Ways and Means of the Treasury for* 1814.

The gross charge upon the Treasury for the year 1814, amounting to $57,694,590 70, included, as above stated, the balance of the appropriations of 1813, remaining unsatisfied, at the close of that year. It is, therefore, proper to place to the credit of the Treasury, the outstanding revenue and resources, at the commencement of the year 1814, and these consisted of the following items:
Of cash in the Treasury on the 1st of January, 1814 - - - $5,196,482 00
Of revenue received at the Treasury in the first quarter of 1814 4,236,062 28
Of revenue received in the second quarter - - 2,822,106 05
Of revenue received in the third quarter - - 2,313,183 20
Of revenue received in the fourth quarter, by estimate - - - 1,920,000 00

　　　　　　　　　　　　　　11,311,353 53

Of the proceeds of loans contracted for in 1813, and paid in 1814 - 3,592,665 00
Of the proceeds of Treasury notes issued under the act of 1813, and received in 1814 - 1,070,000 00

　　　　　　　　　　　　　　　4,662,665 00

Of the amount of the loan authorized by the act of the 24th March, 1814 25,000,000 00
Of the amount of the loan authorized by the act of 15th November, 1814 - 3,000,000 00

　　　　　　　　　　　　　　28,000,000 00

Of the amount of Treasury notes authorized to be issued by the act of the 4th of March, 1814 5,000,000 00
Of the amount of Treasury notes authorized to be issued by the act of December 26, 1814 - 3,000,000 00

　　　　　　　　　　　　　　　8,000,000 00

　　　　　　　　　　　　　　$57,170,500 53

From this statement, therefore, it appears
That the charges on the Treasury for 1814 amounted to - - - 57,694,590 70
That the Ways and Means of the Treasury for 1814 amounted to - 57,170,500 53

　　　　　　　　　　　　　　　$524,090 17

And this excess of charges on the Treasury amounting to 524,090 17-100 dollars, beyond the ways and means, actually appropriated, will be payable out of the revenue, uncollected on the 31st of December, 1814. But, independent of the general view thus taken of the existing charges on the Treasury, and of the ways and means designated by law, for the service of 1814, it is necessary to present a statement of the actual receipts and disbursements for that year.

The *actual receipts* at the Treasury, during the year 1814, amounted to the sum of $40,007,661 53, and consisted of the following items:
The cash in the Treasury on the 1st of January, 1814, amounted, as above stated to - $5,196,482 00
The revenue received at the Treasury, during the year 1814, amounted, as above stated to - - - 11,311,353 53
The cash received at the Treasury, in the year 1814, on account of the loans and issues of Treasury notes authorized in 1813, amounted, as above stated, to - - - - - 4,662,665 00
The cash received at the Treasury on account of the loans authorized in 1814, amounted, in the second quarter, to - 6,087,014 00
In the third quarter, to - 2,815,060 00
In the fourth quarter, by estimate, to - - 2,707,810 00

　　　　　　　　　　　　　　11,609,881 00

The cash received at the Treasury on account of the issues of Treasury notes, authorized in 1814, amounted, in the second quarter, to 1,392,100 00
In the third quarter, to - 1,603,900 00
In the fourth quarter, to 4,231,280 00

　　　　　　　　　　　　　　　7,227,280 00

　　　　　　　　　　　　　　40,007,661 53

The actual disbursements at the Treasury, during 1814, (taking a part of the fourth quarter by estimate,) amounted to the sum of $38,273,619 28, and consisted of the following payments:
For the civil department - 933,327 97
For miscellaneous services - - - 1,207,492 30
For the diplomatic department - - 206,306 52
For the military department - 20,510,238 00
For the naval department 7,313,899 90
For the public debt - 8,103,354 59

　　　　　　　　　　　　　　38,273,619 28

The estimated balance of cash in the Treasury, on the 31st of December, 1814, being - - - - 1,734,042 25

To these views however, first, of the general charges

on the Treasury, and of the ways and means designated by law, for the service of 1814; and second, of the actual receipts and disbursements at the Treasury, during that year, it is proper to add a statement of the result, showing the condition of the Treasury at the end of 1814, in relation to the unsatisfied demands, and to the unexpended ways and means.

The *unsatisfied demands* on the Treasury at the close of 1814, amounted to $19,426,971 42, and consisted of the balances of appropriations for the following objects:

For the civil department	- -	$519,967 11
For miscellaneous services	-	1,285,682 36
For the diplomatic department	-	230,940 10
For the military department	-	9,458,896 33
For the naval department	- -	4,468,251 72
For the public debt	- -	3,457,231 60
		19,426,971 42

The *unexpended amount of the ways and means* provided for 1814, was the sum of $23,396,881 25, and consisted of the following items:

Cash in the Treasury on the 1st of January, 1814, estimated at	1,734,042 25
Revenue uncollected and outstanding, estimated at	4,500,000 00
Authority to borrow money and to issue Treasury Notes, not executed, or not yet productive, under acts of the 4th and 24th of March, 1814 -	8,162,839 00
Stock sent to Europe 3,000,000; under act of November 15, 1814, $3,000,000; under act of Decem. 26, 1814, $3,000,000 -	9,000,000 00
	23,396,881 25

The surplus of ways and means, in reference to the service of 1814, including revenue and the unexecuted authority to borrow, and to issue Treasury notes, is therefore - - - 3,975,909 83

The conclusion from this statement of the situation of the Treasury at the close of 1814, under the different views which have been presented, would seem to establish, that the ways and means provided for the service of that year were considerably more than the demands on the Treasury would require. But it must always be recollected that the demands are positive and urgent; while a great portion of the ways and means rests upon a precarious foundation. Thus:

The unsatisfied demands on the Treasury for the service of 1814, positive and urgent in their nature, amount to - - -	$19,420,971 42
The cash in the Treasury and the outstanding revenue only amount to - - - - -	6,234,042 25
	13,186,929 17

And, consequently, the payment of the difference, amounting to $13,186,929 17, for the service of 1814, must depend on the success of raising money by loan, or by issues of Treasury notes, under the unexecuted

authority, constituting the remaining ways and means designated for the same year.

II. Statement of the situation of the Treasury for the year 1815.

1. *The charges upon the Treasury for the year 1815, as already ascertained.*

The estimates for the annual appropriations amount to $40,538,889 39, consisting of the following items:

For civil, diplomatic, and miscellaneous expenses	-	$1,979,289 39
For the military department	-	30,342,238 00
For the naval department	-	8,217,362 00
		40,538,889 39

The public debt will call for a sum of $15,493,145 30, to answer the following claims:

For interest and reimbursement of stocks existing before the war, the sum of - -	-	3,462,775 46
For interest on the funded debt created since the war	-	2,922,816 72
For the interest on loans to be effected in 1815, by estimate -	-	1,500,000 00
For the principal and interest of the Treasury notes falling due in 1815, and on the 1st of January, 1816	-	7,617,553 12
		15,493,145 30
		56,032,034 69

From this view it appears, that ways and means must now be provided for an expenditure of the sum of $56,032,034 69, in the year 1815, independent of such additions as may arise from the contemplated establishment of a sinking fund, in relation to the public debt created since the war, and from any other new object of expense, which shall be authorized during the present year.

2. *The Ways and Means of the Treasury for 1815.*

The outstanding and uncollected revenue, at the commencement of 1815, has been considered as applicable to the payment of the unsatisfied balances of the appropriations for the preceding year; and, consequently, only such parts of the revenue as shall accrue, and be actually received at the Treasury, during 1815, can be embraced in the resources for the current service. But it also follows, from that view of the subject, that the Treasury is entitled to be credited in 1815, for the excess, in the provision of ways and means, to meet the expenditure of 1814.

This excess, consisting of cash, of outstanding revenue, and of an authority to borrow, or to issue Treasury notes, amounts, as above stated, to the sum of - - - - -	$3,975,909 83
The net sum receivable into the Treasury in the year 1815, for the duties on goods imported during that year, cannot be safely estimated at a greater sum than - - - - -	1,000,000 00
The direct tax will probably give to the Treasury, during the year 1815, a sum of - - - - -	2,000,000 00

The internal duties, old and new, and postage, on an estimate which is stated in the schedule A, will probably produce, in the year 1815, a sum of   -   -   -   - $7,050,000 00

The sales of public lands will probably produce, in the year 1815, a sum of   1,000,000 00

The amount of incidental receipts, from miscellaneous sources, will probably be   -   -   -   100,000 00

        15,125,909 83

But it appears that the single item of public debt will require, in the year 1815, a sum of— $15,493,145 30

And that the revenue (independent of the excess of the authority to borrow, &c., brought from the last year's ways and means) will only be   11,150,000 00

Leaving a deficiency, in that respect alone, of   -   -   -   -   4,343,145 30

In a more general view, however, it is to be stated, that the charges upon the Treasury for the year 1815, amount to the sum of -   - $56,032,034 69

That the existing sources of supply amount only to   -   -   15,125,909 83

And that ways and means must be provided to raise the deficit of   -   40,906,124 86

It will be readily seen that the estimates of the product of the direct tax, and of the new internal duties, are applicable only to the present year; and that, in every succeeding year, the amount will be greatly augmented.

It must also be repeated, that in the statements now presented, no provision is inserted for the contemplated sinking fund; nor for the payment of a considerable amount of unliquidated claims upon the Government for services and supplies; as these objects seem to require a distinct consideration.

Propositions.

I. It is respectfully proposed that provision be made to raise a sum of $40,906,124 86, in addition to the amount of the existing revenue, for the service of the year 1815—partly by taxes, partly by an issue of Treasury notes, and partly by an authority to procure money by loan.

II. It is respectfully proposed that an additional sum be raised by taxes, to the amount of $5,000,000; and that the following objects, or a selection from these objects of taxation, graduated in the amount to produce that sum, to be made equally productive, shall form the basis of the additional levy:

1. A tax upon inheritances and devises, to be paid by the heirs or devisees, may be made to produce   -   -   - $900,000

2. A tax upon bequests, legacies, and statutory distribution, to be paid by the legatees or legal representatives, may be made to produce   -   -   -   -   500,000

3. An auxiliary tax upon all testamentary instruments and letters of administration, to be paid by the executors or administrators, may be made to produce -   200,000

4. A tax upon legal process and proceedings in the courts of the United States,

to be paid by the parties at the time of taking out the process, or entering the proceedings, may be made to produce - $250,000

5. A tax upon conveyances, mortgages, and leases, to be paid by the grantees, mortgagees, and lessees, may be made to produce   -   -   -   -   300,000

6. A stamp tax upon bonds, penal bills, warrants of attorney, notarial instruments, policies of insurance, all negotiable notes, protests of bills of exchange and promissory notes, bills of sale, and hypothecations of vessels, bottomry and respondentia bonds, may be made to produce   -   -   -   -   400,000

7. A tax of one dollar upon every barrel of wheaten flour, to be paid by the miller, may be made to produce   -   -   3,500,000

8. A tax upon the dividends (other than the dividends of banks,) and upon the sale and transfer of the stocks of banks, insurance companies, and other corporations, operating for profit upon a money capital, may be made to produce   -   600,000

9. An income tax may easily be made to produce   -   -   -   -   3,000,000

III. It is respectfully proposed that the additional sum to be raised by the specified taxes shall be appropriated as follows:

1. Towards establishing a sinking fund, in relation to the public debt, created since the war   -   -   -   - $

2. Towards the payment of principal and interest of the Treasury notes, to be issued in the manner hereafter suggested -

3. Towards defraying the expenses of the present year   -   -   -   -

     Total   -   -   -   -   - $

IV. It is respectfully proposed that there shall be an emission of Treasury notes, for the service of the year 1815, to the amount of $15,000,000, on the following plan:

1. The denominations of the notes shall be such as the Secretary of the Treasury, with the approbation of the President, may direct.

2. The notes of the denomination of $100 and upwards shall be made payable to order, and shall bear an interest of 5 2-5 per cent. per annum.

3. The notes of a denomination less than $100, and not less than $20, shall be payable to order, and bear an interest at the same rate; or shall be payable to bearer, and bear no interest; as the Secretary of the Treasury, with the approbation of the President of the United States, shall direct.

4. The notes of a denomination under $20 shall be made payable to the bearer, and shall be circulated without interest.

5. The notes shall be issued, and be made payable to the Treasury only; but, any portion of them may be deposited with the loan officers of banks throughout the United States, for the purpose of being put into general circulation.

6. The holders of the Treasury notes not bearing an interest may at any time exchange them, *in sums* not less than $100, for certificates of public stock bearing an interest of 7 per cent. per annum, and irre-

deemable for twelve years from the date of the certificates respectively.

7. The notes shall be receivable in all payments of the United States, but in such cases they may be reissued.

8. The notes shall be payable by annual instalment, according to their dates, and in the manner to be notified by the Treasury, to wit:

In 1816, the sum of, (one-fifth)	-			$3,000,000
In 1817,	do.	do.	- -	3,000,000
In 1818,	do.	do.	- -	3,000,000
In 1819,	do.	do.	- -	3,000,000
In 1820,	do.	do.	- -	3,000,000
Total	-	- -	-	$15,000,000

9. The reimbursement of the notes shall be effected, according to the instalments, either by the payment of the principal and interest to the holders, or by taking out of circulation and destroying the amount of the instalment in notes which have been paid to the United States for duties, taxes, or other demands.

10. There shall be an appropriation of such a portion of the taxes, above specified, as will be adequate to the payment of the successive instalments of the notes; and the faith of the United States should be pledged to make good any deficiency.

11. There shall be no additional issue of Treasury notes, except upon a specific pledge of the same taxes, or of other competent taxes, to an amount equal to the reimbursement of the notes, according to the stipulated instalments.

V. It is respectfully proposed that authority should be given to the President to borrow the sum of $25,000,000, on the faith of the United States.

1. The loan to be accepted on the most advantageous terms that can be obtained.

2. The amount of the loan, for the payment and security of principal and interest, to be placed on the same footing as the rest of the funded debt created since the war.

If the propositions submitted to the consideration of the Committee of Ways and Means should be adopted, the Treasury will be placed on the following footing for the year 1815:

1. The ascertained demands upon the Treasury amount to	- -	$56,032,034 69
2. The existing sources of revenue and supply will produce	$11,150,000 00	
3. The excess of outstanding revenue, and of authority to borrow money and to issue Treasury notes for the service of 1814, beyond the demand, is estimated at	- -	3,975,909 83
4. The taxes now proposed are estimated to produce, for 1815	-	5,000,000 00
5. The issue of Treasury notes, for the service of 1815, will produce	- -	15,000,000 00
6. The authority to raise money by loan, for the service of 1815, extends to	- -	25,000,000 00
		60,125,909 83

The demands on the Treasury, as above, being deducted, amounting to - 56,032,034 69

Leave a surplus of ways and means of $4,093,875 14

The surplus of ways and means, for the year 1815, will be applicable to the establishment of the contemplated Sinking Fund, and to the payment of any additional expenses that Congress may authorize.

In making the present communication, I feel, sir, that I have performed my duty to the Legislature of the country; but when I perceive that more than forty millions of dollars must be raised, for the service of the year 1815, by an appeal to public credit, through the medium of Treasury notes and loans, I am not without sensations of extreme solicitude. The unpromising state of the public credit, and the obstructed state of the circulating medium, are sufficiently known. A liberal imposition of taxes, during the session, ought to raise the public credit, were it not for counteracting causes; but it can have no effect in restoring a national circulating medium. It remains, therefore, with the wisdom of Congress to decide, whether any other means can be applied to restore the public credit, to re-establish a national circulating medium, and to facilitate the necessary anticipations of the public revenue. The humble opinion of this Department on the subject has been respectfully, though frankly, expressed on former occasions, and it remains unchanged.

I have the honor to be, with great consideration, sir, your most obedient servant,

A. J. DALLAS.

J. W. EPPES, Esq., *Chairman, &c.*

Schedule A.

TREASURY DEPARTMENT,
REVENUE OFFICE, Dec. 16, 1814.

SIR: I have the honor, in compliance with your request, to submit the annexed estimates of the products of the existing internal duties, and of the additional duties proposed to be laid by the bills now before Congress; the first statement exhibiting the products for an entire year after the respective duties shall be in full operation, and the last statement showing the amounts that may be expected to be received from each duty during the year 1815. It may be proper to add, that the materials do not exist for forming estimates, with regard to the new duties, on which a perfect reliance should be reposed.

I am, very respectfully, your obedient servant,

S. H. SMITH,
Commissioner of the Revenue.

HON. SECRETARY *of the Treasury.*

No. 1.

Estimates of the products of the existing internal duties, and of the proposed additional duties for an entire year after they shall be in full operation.

Stamps	- - - - -	$510,000
Carriages	- - - -	300,000
Sales at auction	- - -	300,000
Refined sugar	- - -	150,000
Licenses to retailers	- - -	900,000
Licenses for stills, with the duty on spirits	4,000,000
Postage	- - - - -	250,000
Lotteries	- - - -	150,000
Furniture	- - - -	1,238,000
Horses for the saddle and carriage	70,000

Gold watches	60,000
Silver watches	170,000
Boots	75,000
Saddles and bridles	66,000
Paper	50,000
Candles	200,000
Playing cards	80,000
Tobacco and snuff	200,000
Hats	400,000
Iron	350,000
Nails	200,000
Beer, ale, and porter	60,000
Leather	600,000
	$10,379,800

No. 2.

Estimate of the amounts that may be expected to be received from the foregoing duties, during the year 1815.

Stamps	$510,000
Carriages	300,000
Sales at auction	210,000
Refined sugar	150,000
Licenses to retailers	875,000
Licenses for stills, with the duty on spirits	2,600,000
Postage	250,000
Lotteries	50,000
Furniture	1,238,000
Horses for the saddle and carriage	70,000
Gold watches	60,000
Silver watches	170,000
Boots	
Saddles and bridles	
Paper	
Candles	
Playing cards	
Tobacco and snuff	570,000
Hats	
Iron	
Nails	
Beer, ale, and porter	
Leather	
	$7,053,000

This estimate has been made on the supposition that the bills laying the new duties will be passed previously to the 1st of January next.

MONDAY, January 23.

Ordered, That the Committee of Ways and Means be discharged from the further consideration of the petitions of the tallow-chandlers in Philadelphia; the brewers in the city of New York; non-resident owners of lands lying in the State of Ohio; the Paper Manufacturing Society of Pennsylvania; inhabitants of the city of New York, praying for the establishment of a National Bank; F. F. Breman; Stephen Girard; as also, from the resolution of the 4th of October last, instructing them to inquire into the expediency of allowing the proprietors of spirituous liquors distilled from domestic materials of which they are themselves the growers, to sell, without license, any quantity thereof not less than one gallon.

Mr. McKEE, from the Committee on the Public Lands, reported a bill granting a donation of three hundred and twenty acres of land to Anthony Shane; which was read the first time, and, on motion, the said bill was read the second time, and committed to a Committee of the Whole House to-morrow.

Mr. INGHAM, of Pennsylvania, presented the petition of sundry inhabitants of Pennsylvania, praying for the establishment of an uniform system of bankruptcy.—Referred.

Mr. EPPES, from the Committee of Ways and Means, reported a bill to provide additional revenue for defraying the expenses of Government, and maintaining public credit, by laying a duty on lotteries; a bill for the relief of Saltus, Son, & Co., merchants, of the city of New York; and a bill to amend the act laying duties on retailers' licenses, for the relief of domestic manufacturers of wine, who themselves dispose of their product; the two first of which were committed, and the latter ordered to be engrossed for a third reading.

OPERATION OF THE DIRECT TAX.

Mr. EPPES, from the Committee of Ways and Means, made a report on the petitions of the inhabitants of the counties of Hickman and Dickson, in the State of Tennessee; which was read, and ordered to lie on the table. The report is as follows:

That the petitioners pray to be relieved from the unequal operation of the act imposing a direct tax. The —— section of the act authorised the several State Legislatures to vary the sums imposed on the respective counties. The Legislature of the State of Tennessee passed an act, requiring the assessors of the United States, after the valuations were completed, to equalize and apportion the tax on the several counties. The Congress of the United States passed a law declaring its assent to the act of the State of Tennessee, with a proviso, declaring, " that in case the assessors should, from any circumstance, fail to make the equalization and apportionment required by the act of the State of Tennessee, that then, and in that case, the tax should be levied and collected in the form prescribed by the law of the United States, imposing a direct tax." It appears that some of the assessors performed the duties required by the act of the State of Tennessee; the assessor from the county of Murry refused to discharge the duties required by the act; in consequence of which the counties of Hickman and Dickson were deprived of the advantages derived from the equalization and apportionment, and the tax was levied and collected in conformity with the provisions of the law of the United States, declaring the assent of Congress to the act of the State of Tennessee. The petitioners state, that the refusal of the assessor to act, has subjected the county of Hickman to a tax of fifty-four cents in the hundred dollars, and the county of Dickson to a tax of forty cents, while the county of Murry, the place of residence of the assessor, is subjected to a tax of only nineteen cents in the hundred dollars. The petitioners pray, either that the equalization may be now made, or that the counties of Hickman and Dickson may be allowed a credit for the sum with which, from the conduct of the assessor, they were made chargeable. It cannot be doubted but that the

1097   HISTORY OF CONGRESS.   1098

JANUARY, 1815.   *Duty on Stills—Direct Tax on the District of Columbia.*   H. OF R.

conduct of the assessor produced, as stated by the petitioners, inequality in the operation of the tax on the counties of Hickman and Dickson. As, however, the State of Tennessee alone had the benefit of a partial equalization by the assessors, all the counties in all the States might, with equal justice, claim an examination of the principles on which their respective portions of the State quota have been fixed. By the direct tax bill recently passed, provision is made for an equalization of the tax; this will afford ample relief for the counties of Hickman and Dickson, against the future operation of the inequality complained of. The tax having been paid in many of the States, and the collection having progressed in all, the committee consider that it would be inexpedient to recommend any measure which might bring into question the principles on which the tax was originally imposed. The following resolution is, therefore, submitted:

Resolved, That the prayer of the petitioners ought not to be granted.

DUTY ON STILLS.

Mr. EPPES, from the Committee of Ways and Means, made a report on the petition of sundry inhabitants of the State of Connecticut, owners of stills, referred on the 2d of November, 1814; which was read, and ordered to lie on the table. The report is as follows:

The Committee of Ways and Means, to whom was referred the petition of sundry proprietors of copper stills in the State of Connecticut, submit, as a part of their report, a letter from the Commissioner of the Revenue. On a view of the facts contained in the letter, the committee unite in opinion with the Commissioner of the Revenue, that the duty recently imposed on the gallon of spirits distilled will tend, in some degree, to remedy the inequality complained of, and that it is inexpedient, at present, to vary the proportion between the duty on stills and boilers.

TREASURY DEPARTMENT,
REVENUE OFFICE, Nov. 25, 1814.

SIR: I have the honor to acknowledge the receipt of your favor of the 23d instant, enclosing a petition from sundry inhabitants of the State of Connecticut, representing the unequal operation of the existing duty on stills and boilers.

The information in my possession does not enable me to form a decided opinion whether the present duty on stills is greater than it should be, compared with that on boilers. Several letters have been received, all of which state the advantages which the distillers will derive from recent improvements in the construction of boilers, and generally recommending an increased duty on them; but it does not satisfactorily appear that these advantages are peculiar to boilers, and that equal advantages do not attach to some stills over others, owing to the late improvements in their construction. Such is undoubtedly the variety in the forms and modes of operation of the several descriptions of vessels used in the United States for the purposes of distillation, in their productive powers, and in the expense with which they are worked, that the existing duty is relatively light on some, compared with other stills, and on some, compared with other boilers, as well as on some boilers compared with some stills. This effect, it will be perceived, is altogether independent of the duty, and is incident to the superior improvements of the one kind of vessel over the other. The boilers, it is to be added, being of recent introduction, possess, so far as applicable to them, all the improvements made in stills.

From an inspection of the whole number of licenses ascertained to have been granted in all the collection districts during the two first quarters of the present year, and in seventy districts for the third quarter, it appears that there have been granted 18,846 licenses for stills, and 542 for boilers; of which number there have been granted in the State of Connecticut, 425 for stills, and 26 for boilers.

It is certainly desirable that a just equality should characterise the duty on stills and boilers. A just equality cannot, however, require the imposition of such a duty as would tend in any way to disturb the relative benefits attendant on different descriptions of vessels which would be used independent of the existence of the duty, much less to deprive ingenuity of the stimulus to improvement which it reasonably finds in the profit that flows from such improvement.

Upon the whole, as the contemplated duty on the gallon of spirits distilled within the United States will, in some degree, overcome any inequality in the present duty, and as more experience of the operation of the present duty is required to ascertain the nature and extent of any existing inequalities, I am of the opinion that it would be inexpedient at this time to vary the proportion between the duty on stills and boilers.

I am, with great respect, &c.,

S. H. SMITH,
Commissioner of the Revenue.
Hon. JOHN W. EPPES, *Chairman, &c.*

DISTRICT OF COLUMBIA.

Mr. EPPES, from the Committee of Ways and Means, in pursuance of the resolution instructing them to inquire into the expediency of imposing a direct tax on the District of Columbia, and other Territories of the United States, and other revenue thereon, accompanied by a bill to provide additional revenue for defraying the expenses of Government, and maintaining the public credit, by laying a direct tax upon the District of Columbia; which was twice read, and committed.

The report is as follows:

That the sixteenth clause of the eighth section of the Constitution declares, that Congress shall have power to "exercise exclusive legislation, in all cases whatsoever, over such district of country, not exceeding ten miles square, as may, by cession of particular States and the acceptance of Congress, become the Seat of the Government of the United States." No doubt can be entertained but that this general grant of legislative powers, must include the right of imposing taxes, which is among the most common and ordinary objects of legislation. Nor is it believed that the exercise of this power, so far as it respects the District of Columbia, is either prohibited or limited by any clause of the Constitution. The third clause of the second section of the Constitution, which declares " that representatives and direct taxes shall be apportioned among the several States, which may be included within this Union, according to their respective numbers, which shall be determined by adding to the whole number of free persons, including those bound to service for a term of years, and excluding Indians not taxed, three-fifths of all other persons," is considered as applying exclusively to the States, and was evidently designed, so far as respects the imposition of taxes, as a substitute for the rule of apportionment fixed by the eighth Article of the Old Confederation, under which each State contributed for the common defence and general welfare, according to the value of its lands, buildings, and improvements, instead of the amount of its population. The right to tax the other Territories of the United States, appears equally clear. The fourth article of compact between the United States and the Territories, declares " the said territory and the States which may be formed therein, shall forever remain a part of this Confederacy of the United States of America, subject to the Articles of Confederation, and to such alterations therein as may be constitutionally made, and to all the acts and ordinances of the United States in Congress assembled, conformable thereto. The inhabitants and settlers in the said territory, shall be subject to pay a part of the federal debt, contracted or to be contracted, a proportional part of the expenses of Government, to be apportioned on them by Congress according to the same common rule and measure by which apportionments thereof shall be made on the other States."

On the other point referred to the committee, viz: the policy of imposing a direct tax, they have bestowed all the attention which its importance merits, from involving the principles of representation and taxation. It cannot be denied, that the imposition of taxes, by persons who owe complete responsibility to the people, is one of the best securities against the abuse of power. By the Constitution of the United States, this principle of representative responsibility was violated, so far as respects the District of Columbia, and the rights and interests of the people transferred to persons over whose election the inhabitants have no control. The only question is, whether their being placed in a peculiar situation by the Constitution, ought to operate as a permanent exemption from taxes. It is not believed that the right to tax, exercised by persons who owe no responsibility to those on whom their laws must operate, is in principle more exceptionable, than the exercise of powers which affect the personal rights, and even the life of the citizen. On these important questions, however, the Congress of the United States must legislate. No other power can, within the District of Columbia, prescribe the regulations necessary to protect the innocent and punish the guilty. In a free country, every portion of the community ought to contribute to the common defence and general welfare; nor is it believed that the framers of the Constitution intended to violate this principle, by exempting from taxes a district of country whose natural advantages are surpassed by no portion of the United States, and which derives peculiar benefits from the disbursement annually of large sums drawn from other portions of the Union.

The situation of the other Territories is materially different: at a distance from market, with a large portion of unimproved and unproductive land, they are still struggling with all the inconveniences attendant on infant settlements, surrounded by powerful tribes of hostile savages. While, therefore, no doubt can be entertained as to the Constitutional right to impose a direct tax on Territories, the committee deem it at present inexpedient, and submit a bill for imposing a direct tax on the District of Columbia.

CLERK OF THE HOUSE.

On motion of Mr. CLARK, of Kentucky, the further consideration of the orders of the day was postponed until to-morrow, in order to proceed to the consideration of the resolution for the removal of Patrick Magruder from the office of Clerk of the House of Representatives, and the appointment of a successor.

The House then proceeded to the consideration of the resolution offered on Saturday, by Mr. CLARK, on that subject.

A motion was made, by Mr. FISK, of Vermont, to postpone the further consideration of this motion to Monday next; which was opposed by Mr. DUVALL, and Mr. CLARK, and supported by Mr. FISK, Mr. FARROW, and Mr. HAWKINS, when Mr. FISK withdrew his motion.

The adoption of the resolve was then opposed by Mr. WRIGHT, in a speech of full two hours in length. It was also opposed by Mr. GHOLSON and Mr. McKIM, and supported by Mr. PEARSON, Mr. MACON, and Mr. CLARK.

Mr. McKIM moved to postpone the further consideration of the resolution to this day week.

This motion was opposed by Mr. CLARK, Mr. PEARSON, and Mr. OAKLEY, and supported by Mr. MOORE and Mr. EPPES.

The motion was finally decided at a late hour as follows: For postponement 71, against it 71.

The SPEAKER decided the question by an affirmative vote, and the further consideration of the resolution was therefore postponed to this day week.

[The foundation for this motion to oust Mr. MAGRUDER is briefly this: During the late incursion of the enemy, Mr. M. was, on account of ill-health, at the Springs, and, of course, absent from the city, leaving his office in charge of his clerks. The principal clerk being a colonel in the militia, and all the others except one called out in the militia, one of those so in service was, on the near approach of the enemy, permitted to return, and, with the remaining clerk, to attempt the salvation of the records. Many of them, and those the most valuable, were saved by being carried into the country; others, of less importance, were removed into the house formerly belonging to General Washington, which was wantonly destroyed by the enemy. Among the papers left in the Capitol were the vouchers of the contingent expenses of the past year, which, being in a small drawer, were overlooked, and irrecoverably lost in the general conflagration. Soon after the meeting of Congress, in consequence of a letter from Mr. Magruder narrating these circumstances, and inviting inquiry, a committee was appointed to investigate the matter, who reported unfavorably to the clerks as to the exertions made in saving the public papers; and also reported that, out of $50,000 received on account of contingent moneys, and all of which, except about $3,000, is alleged to have been expended, vouchers are produced for little more than $30,000 of the amount, which, or a great part of it, the committee infer has been improperly used. Whereupon, the House resolves that the Clerk shall have credit at the Treasury for all the ascertained expenditures, and such other amount as he shall produce or hereafter obtain vouchers for. It ought to be observed that the contingent fund has always been exclusively under the direction of Mr. Magruder's principal clerk, and it does not appear that Mr. M. himself had any knowledge of its disbursement, considering it as having been duly controlled by the Committee of Accounts. Under these circumstances a motion is made to remove him, on the ground of neglect in confiding these matters to his deputies; which is opposed on the ground of his unimpeachable character and general good conduct. This is believed to be an impartial statement of the case.]

The House adjourned at a late hour.

TUESDAY, January 24.

Mr. TROUP, from the Committee on Military Affairs, reported a bill making provision for subsisting the Army of the United States, by authorizing the appointment of commissaries of subsistence; which was read twice, and committed to a Committee of the whole House.

Mr. TROUP, from the same committee, reported a bill to authorize the purchase of a tract of land for the use of the United States; which was read twice, and ordered to be engrossed and read the third time to-morrow.

On motion of Mr. LOWNDES,

Ordered, That General Winder have leave to withdraw the papers mentioned in the Journal of the 21st instant, by his agreeing to furnish copies thereof for the use of the House.

The SPEAKER laid before the House a letter from the Secretary of the Navy, transmitting the annual report of the Commissioners of the Navy Pension Fund.

An engrossed bill to amend the act laying duties on licenses to retailers of wines, spirituous liquors, and foreign merchandise, was read the third time and passed.

On motion of Mr. INGHAM, the bill for the relief of Isaac Smith and Bratton Caldwell, passed the Committee of the Whole, and was ordered to be engrossed.

The order of the day, on Mr. JACKSON's proposition to amend the Constitution, so as to give to Congress power to establish a National Bank, &c. having been called over, on motion of Mr. JACKSON the further consideration thereof was postponed indefinitely.

The bill to extend the time of Oliver Evans's patent for his improvement on steam engines, underwent considerable discussion, in Committee of the Whole, and was, after a long debate, amended, and reported to the House.

Mr. LEWIS moved further to amend the bill, by adding thereto, the following proviso:

"*And provided also,* That the said Oliver Evans shall not be entitled to any of the privileges granted by this act, but upon the express condition that he shall permit any person or persons to use the improvements of the said Oliver Evans in the machinery of mills for the manufacture of flour during the continuance of his extended patent therefor, upon the same terms as were demanded by the said Oliver Evans before the extension of the said patent."

The motion was negatived, and the bill was ordered to be engrossed and read a time to-morrow.

WEDNESDAY, January 25.

Mr. McKEE, of Kentucky, from the Committee of Public Lands, reported a bill to amend and extend the provisions of the act of the 16th April, 1814, entitled "an act confirming certain claims to land in the Illinois Territory, and providing for their location;" which was twice read and committed.

The engrossed bill, declaring the assent of Congress to an act of the Legislature of the State of Georgia, establishing the fees of the health officer and harbor master of the ports of Savannah and St. Mary's, was read a third time.

Mr. TAYLOR moved that the further consideration of the bill be postponed until Monday next; which motion was negatived.

On motion of Mr. PITKIN, of Connecticut, the further consideration of the bill was, after debate, postponed indefinitely.

The engrossed bill to authorize the purchase of a certain tract of land for the use of the United States (in the vicinity of Plattsburg) was read a third time, and passed; and sent to the Senate for concurrence therein.

The engrossed bill for the relief of Isaac Smith and Bratton Caldwell, was read a third time, passed, and sent to the Senate.

The bill from the Senate to extend the time of Oliver Evans's patent, for his improvement in the steam engine, was read a third time.

Mr. FISK, of New York, moved to postpone indefinitely the further consideration of the bill; which motion was decided as follows by yeas and nays: For the motion 54, against it 79.

The bill was then passed, and the concurrence of the Senate requested in the amendments made by the House thereto.

MILITIA BILL.

The House then resumed the consideration of Mr. JACKSON's bill to amend the militia law, so as to conform the organization of the militia of the several States, as far as regards the officers thereof, to that of the military force of the United States.

A motion was made by Mr. WRIGHT, of Maryland, to strike out the second section of the bill.

That motion was superseded by a motion of Mr. TAYLOR, of New York, to postpone the further consideration of the bill indefinitely.

The object of the bill was advocated by Messrs. JACKSON, HAWKINS, CANNON, and others, and opposed by Messrs. WRIGHT, TAYLOR, PICKERING, WEBSTER, and others.

The arguments in favor of the bill were, generally, the dissonance arising from the dissimilarity of the provisions of the State laws for organizing the militia, to those of the laws directing the organization of the Army of the United States; and the confusion hence produced in the militia draughts, &c. The opponents of the bill contended that it would be highly inexpedient, on the other hand, to disturb the present organization of the militia, which, it was also said, was by many well-informed military men believed to be superior to the organization of the Army of the United States, &c.

The question on indefinite postponement was decided in the affirmative: For the postponement '94· against it 45, as follows:

YEAS—Messrs. Alexander, Archer, Avery, Baylies of Massachusetts, Bigelow, Boyd, Bradbury, Breckenridge, Brigham, Brown, Burwell, Butler, Caperton, Caldwell, Calhoun, Champion, Cilley, Comstock, Cooper, Cox, Crawford, Creighton, Culpeper, Davenport, Davis of Massachusetts, Ely, Farrow, Fisk of New York, Forney, Gholson, Goldsborough, Goodwyn, Grosvenor, Hale, Hasbrouck, Henderson, Hopkins of Kentucky, Hungerford, Hulbert, Irving, Jackson of Rhode Island, Kent of Maryland, King of Massachusetts, King of North Carolina, Law, Lefferts, Lewis, Lovett, Lowndes, Markell, McCoy, McKee, McKim, Miller, Montgomery, Moseley, Ormsby, Pearson, Pickering, Piper, Potter, John Reed, Rea of Pennsylvania, Rich, Roane, Ruggles, Schureman, Seybert, Sheffey, Sherwood, Shipherd, Slaymaker, Smith of New York, Smith of Pennsylvania, Smith of Virginia, Stanford, Stockton, Stuart, Sturges, Taggart, Taylor, Thompson, Troup, Vose, Ward of Massachusetts, Ward of New Jersey, Webster, Wheaton, Wilcox, Williams, Wilson of Massachusetts, Winter, Wright, and Yancey.

NAYS—Messrs. Alston, Anderson, Barbour, Bard, Bines, Cannon, Chappell, Clendenin, Desha, Duvall, Earle, Findley, Forsyth, Gourdin, Griffin, Harris, Hawes, Hawkins, Hubbard, Humphreys, Ingersoll, Ingham, Jackson of Virginia, Johnson of Kentucky, Kennedy, Kerr, Kilbourn, Lyle, Macon, McLean, Murfree, Nelson, Newton, Pickens, Pleasants, Rhea of Tennessee, Ridgely, Ringgold, Sevier, Sharp, Strong, Tannehill, Udree, and Wilson of Pennsylvania.

THURSDAY January 26.

Mr. YANCEY, from the Committee of Claims, made a report on the petition of the President and Directors of the Anacostia Bridge Company; which was read, when,

Mr. YANCEY reported a bill for the relief of the Anacostia Bridge Company; which was read twice and committed to a Committee of the Whole.

Mr. PLEASANTS, from the Committee on Naval Affairs, reported the bill from the Senate, "to authorize the President of the United States to cause to be built, equipped, and employed, one or more floating batteries for the defence of the waters of the United States," without amendment; and the bill was committed to a Committee of the Whole on Saturday next.

On motion of Mr. TAYLOR, the Committee of Military Affairs was instructed to inquire into the expediency of repealing or amending so much of the act for establishing rules and articles for the government of the armies of the United States, as relates to the infliction of corporal punishment.

On motion of the same gentleman, the Committee of Ways and Means were instructed to inquire into the expediency of imposing a duty on silver plate and jewelry manufactured for sale, in the hands of the manufacturer.

Mr. TAYLOR also submitted for consideration the following resolution:

Resolved, That the committee on so much of the Message of the President of the United States as relates to the militia, be instructed to inquire whether any, and, if any, what provision ought to be made by law for assessing, collecting, or remitting fines imposed on officers, non-commissioned officers and privates, by militia courts martial.

Mr. McCoy, of Virginia, moved to amend this motion by adding thereto the following: "And that they inquire into the expediency of increasing the fines on such officers, non-commissioned officers, and privates, for offences under the military laws;" which motion was negatived.

The motion of Mr. TAYLOR was then agreed to as moved by him.

The SPEAKER laid before the House a letter from the Secretary of the Treasury, transmitting the remainder of the copies ordered to be printed by the House of Representatives of the digest of the returns of the arts and manufactures of the United States.

The bill from the Senate for the relief of Henry Nimmo, was twice read, and committed.

PETITION OF GEORGE HITE.

Mr. CHAPPELL, from the Committee on Pensions and Revolutionary Claims, made a report on the petition of George Hite; which was read, and the resolution therein contained was concurred in by the House.

The report is as follows:

That the petitioner asks Congress to remunerate him for a number of negroes, horses, and cattle, which, he alleges, were the property of his father; and which were taken by the Cherokee Indians in the year 1776, from his father's residence, after having first killed the whole family, except himself; some of which negroes, he states, are now in the possession of the said Indians. The petitioner is so defective in his testimony that he does not make out such a claim as can be granted. He neither shows himself to be the heir of the person, whose property is said to have been taken, nor does he show, satisfactorily, the value of the property taken, or that any was taken. But, if all these points were established, the committee still think he has no claim upon Congress. He bottoms his claim on the treaties made by the United States with these Indians in 1785 and 1795; by the first of which the Indians were bound to deliver up and restore all the property belonging to the citizens of the United States which they had taken; and by the latter they were allowed to retain all such property as still remained in their possession. There is no satisfactory evidence that any proper efforts were ever made to recover this property between the dates of these two treaties. The neglect of the petitioner to do this certainly cannot create an obligation on the Government to remunerate him. Every person who had lost a horse or a cow, by the depredations of these Indians, has an equal claim on the Government with the petitioner, and, by obtaining the remuneration asked for, would find in the Government a convenient warrantor for all their losses. This, it is believed, would not be considered good policy at this day. If there ever were an obligation created, on the part of the Government, by the neglect of the petitioner it has been destroyed; therefore,

Resolved, That the prayer of the petitioner ought not to be granted.

MR. JEFFERSON'S LIBRARY.

The House proceeded to the consideration of the bill from the Senate authorizing the purchase of the library of Thomas Jefferson.

A motion was made by Mr. LEWIS, that the same be postponed indefinitely. For the motion 69, against it 73.

A motion was then made by Mr. COOPER, of Delaware, to postpone the further consideration of the bill to the 4th day of March next. For the motion 68, against it 74.

The question was then stated on the passage of the bill.

Mr. KING, of Massachusetts, moved to recommit the bill with instructions to a select committee to report a new section, authorizing the selection of such of the books belonging to said library as might be necessary or useful to Congress in their deliberations, and to dispose of the remainder at public sale. This motion was negatived—yeas 56.

Mr. KING afterwards moved to recommit the bill to a select committee, with instructions to report a new section authorizing the Library Committee, as soon as said library shall be received at Washington, to select therefrom all books of an atheistical, irreligious, and immoral tendency, if any such there be, and send the same back to Mr. Jefferson without any expense to him. This motion Mr. K. thought proper afterwards to withdraw.

This subject, and the various motions relative thereto, gave rise to a debate which lasted till the hour of adjournment; which, though it afforded much amusement to the auditors, would not interest the feelings or judgment of any reader. Those who supported the bill in debate were Messrs. WRIGHT, FISK of Vermont, RHEA of Tennessee, and HULBERT; and those who opposed it were Messrs. KING of Massachusetts, FARROW, CANNON, HANSON, GROSVENOR, PICKERING, and WEBSTER.

Those who opposed the bill, did so on account of the scarcity of money, and the necessity of appropriating it to purposes more indispensable than the purchase of a library; the probable insecurity of such a library placed here; the high price to be given for this collection; its miscellaneous and almost exclusively literary (instead of legal and historical) character, &c.

To those arguments, enforced with zeal and vehemence, the friends of the bill replied with fact, wit, and argument, to show that the purchase, to be made on terms of long credit, could not affect the present resources of the United States; that the price was moderate, the library more valuable from the scarcity of many of its books, and altogether a most admirable substratum for a National Library.

The final question on the passage of the bill was decided in the affirmative. For the passage of the bill 81, against it 71, as follows:

YEAS—Messrs. Alexander, Alston, Anderson, Barbour, Bines, Bowen, Brown, Butler, Calhoun, Chappell, Conard, Crawford, Creighton, Crouch, Cuthbert, Desha, Duvall, Earle, Evans, Findley, Fisk of Vermont, Fisk of New York, Forney, Forsyth, Franklin, Gholson, Goodwyn, Gourdin, Griffin, Hall, Harris, Hasbrouck, Hawes, Hawkins, Hopkins of Kentucky, Hubbard, Hulbert, Ingersoll, Ingham, Irving, Jackson of Virginia, Johnson of Kentucky, Kennedy, Kent of Maryland, Kerr, Kershaw, Kilbourn, Lefferts, Lowndes, Lyle, McCoy, McKim, McLean, Murfree, Nelson, Newton, Ormsby, Pickens, Piper, Pleasants, Rea of Pennsylvania, Rhea of Tennessee, Rich, Ringgold, Roane, Robertson, Sage, Sevier, Seybert, Sharp, Smith of Pennsylvania, Smith of Virginia, Taylor, Telfair, Troup, Udree, Ward of New Jersey, Williams, Wilson of Pennsylvania, Wright, and Yancey.

NAYS—Messrs. Archer, Avery, Baylies of Massachusetts, Bayly of Virginia, Bigelow, Boyd, Bradbury, Breckenridge, Brigham, Caldwell, Cannon, Champion, Cilley, Clendenin, Comstock, Cooper, Cox, Culpeper, Davenport, Davis of Massachusetts, Davis of Pennsylvania, Ely, Farrow, Geddes, Goldsborough, Grosvenor, Hale, Hanson, Henderson, Howell, Hungerford, Jackson of Rhode Island, Kent of New York, King of Massachusetts, Law, Lewis, Lovett, Macon, Markell, Montgomery, Moseley, Oakley, Pearson, Pickering, Pitkin, Potter, John Reed, William Reed, Ridgely, Ruggles, Schureman, Sheffey, Sherwood, Shipherd, Slaymaker, Stanford, Stockton, Strong, Stuart, Sturges, Taggart, Tannehill, Thompson, Vose, Ward of Massachusetts, Webster, Wheaton, White, Wilcox, Winter, and Wood.

FRIDAY, January 27.

Mr. McKIM presented a petition of sundry merchants and other inhabitants of Baltimore, praying for the establishment of an uniform system of bankruptcy throughout the United States. —Referred.

Mr. GASTON presented a petition of the President and Directors of the College of Georgetown, praying to be invested with authority and power to confer the usual academical honors on those who, by their proficiency in the liberal arts, may be judged deserving of such distinctions.—Referred to the Committee on the District of Columbia.

Mr. PLEASANTS, of Virginia, from the Naval Committee, to whom was referred the report of the acting Secretary of the Navy on the petition of Uriah Brown, made a report unfavorable to the Government's making any experiment on this invention at the present time; which was read, and ordered to lie on the table.

The House then proceeded to the consideration of the bill giving the right of pre-emption in the purchase of public lands to certain settlers in the Indiana Territory; which was ordered to be engrossed and read a third time to-morrow.

The remainder of the day was spent on the bill, reported by the Committee of Claims, to authorize payment for property lost, captured, or destroyed by the enemy whilst in the military service of the United States, to which sundry amendments were made in Committee of the Whole, and reported to the House.

After employing the day wholly on this bill, the House adjourned without having gone through the same.

SATURDAY, January 28.

Mr. EPPES, from the Committee of Ways and Means, reported a bill making appropriations for the support of Government for the year 1815; which was read the first time, and, on motion, the said bill was read the second time, and committed to a Committee of the Whole House on Monday next.

A message from the Senate informed the House that the Senate have passed the bill "supplementary to the act, entitled 'An act laying duties on licenses to retailers of wines, spirituous liquors, and foreign merchandise, and for other purposes," with an amendment, in which they ask the concurrence of this House. The Senate have also passed a bill "concerning field officers of the militia;" in which bill they ask the concurrence of the House.

CLERK OF THE HOUSE.

The SPEAKER laid before the House a letter from PATRICK MAGRUDER, the Clerk to the House, resigning his situation as such; which was laid on the table.

The letter is as follows:

To the honorable SPEAKER

of the House of Representatives:

             CLERK'S OFFICE, *Jan.* 28, 1815.

SIR: It is with a reluctance I cannot well express, that I find it necessary again to throw myself on your politeness as the medium of communication to the House, on a subject no less painful to me than it must be to them. This is imposed upon me as a duty, as well by the arguments derived from those inimical to me, (as I learn,) from silence in regard to the last report of the committee, appointed at my request to investigate the situation of the office under my charge, as by the indications afforded by the recent vote of the House. In regard to the accounts of my office, the correctness of which has been arraigned by a committee of the House, I have nothing to add to what I have said on a former occasion on this subject, except to reassert my entire innocence and ignorance of any misapplication of the public moneys, and to express my conscientious belief that the public money has been faithfully disbursed by my principal clerk, to whom it was confided, and that he will be able to account for it at the Treasury; and would have been able to do so at this day, had not the unfortunate conflagration of the Capitol destroyed his accounts, and subjected his conduct to a scrutiny, in which the fact of a deficiency of the vouchers destroyed has been adduced as evidence against him.

Could I presume so far, it might be an easy task to exhibit errors of great importance in that part of the report of the committee on my conduct, which relates to the account of the contingent fund. It is in my belief demonstrable, that its errors are not limited to hundreds, or to any moderate number of thousands of dollars. Still easier would it be to dissipate almost every argument used in debate on that report, tending by assertion or implication to prejudice the House against me personally; but, sir, he who is put upon his trial without opportunity to defend himself from accusations adduced against him, can expect no benefit from an after appeal to those who have already pronounced judgment against him.

Little, sir, did I ever expect to have to answer to this House, on charges affecting my character, at this advanced period of my life. Since I passed the age of eighteen years, have I been in public life. By those who knew me best, I have been selected to fill various public stations, judicial as well as legislative, under both State and General Governments, and no man has ever before appeared to impute to me malfaisance in the duties of my station. In every situation in which it has pleased my country to place me, I have endeavored to sustain a character more dear to me than wealth; and the attempt to rob me of a jewel more precious than life, to deprive me of that honest fame which I had acquired by a long course of public service, however it may temporarily succeed in this body, cannot eventually depress my character or standing in the eyes of the American people. Truth is great, and will prevail. I court its light, and shrink not from its test. The office of Clerk of this House, arduous and trying as are the duties to be performed during the sessions of Congress, has never been considered by me, in a pecuniary point of view, an object. Two years since I should have resigned it, but for the dissuasions of my friends. I was too proud of the honor conferred by the flattering suffrage I had received from the honorable House. I retained my seat; and how cruelly I am treated for that determination let recent events decide.

But, sir, it is not my intention to weary you or the House by reiterating unavailing regrets which force themselves on my bosom. It is probable, sir, I might, by resorting to humiliating solicitation, reinstate myself in my former footing in the House; but there is implanted within my bosom a principle much more powerful than the love of popularity or of office. It is the sense of honor which forbids solicitation from, or even association with, those who entertain a suspicion derogatory to my fair fame. That there are such among those whom I have once been proud to call my political friends, the motion now pending in the House, and the manner in which it has been supported, sufficiently indicate. After a struggle between contending feelings, I have therefore determined to resign the office I now hold, to permit those by whom I am persecuted to attain, with greater ease, an object to which they have been willing to sacrifice, not only my family but my reputation. I beg the Speaker and House to accept of this my resignation of the office of Clerk of the House of Representatives. I take this last opportunity to offer to yourself, and the House, the homage of my unfeigned respect, and to those who have stood forth to befriend an injured man, and resisted the accusations against me, the assurances of my eternal gratitude. To my successor in office, let him be whom he may, I wish an easier and happier time in the discharge of his duties than I have had.

I am, sir, with respect,

            PATRICK MAGRUDER.

PAYMENT FOR PROPERTY LOST, &c.

The House resumed the consideration of the bill authorizing payment for the property lost, captured, or destroyed, while employed in the military service of the United States: When,

Mr. STANFORD moved that the bill do lie on the table.—Negatived.

Mr. BIGELOW moved that the bill be recommitted to the Committee of Claims; which was determined in the negative.

The amendment made by the Committee of the

Whole House to the second section was then again read, and concurred in by the House.

A motion was made by Mr. HARRIS further to amend the bill, by inserting therein the following section, as the 4th section thereof:

SEC. 4. *And be it further enacted,* That every person whose rifle or other firearm may heretofore have been impressed into the service of the United States, by the order of any officer therein employed, and which shall not have been returned or otherwise accounted for, shall be entitled to pay for the same.

Which was determined in the negative.

Mr. KING, of Massachusetts, moved further to amend the bill by striking out the following words, contained in the 5th and 6th lines of the 2d section, to wit: "either by impressment or contract;" which was determined in the negative.

The bill was further amended; and a motion was made by Mr. KILBOURN, further to amend the bill by inserting, between the 11th and 12th lines of the 1st section, the following words: "or who shall have lost any horse or horses while in service as aforesaid, in consequence of the owner being killed or wounded, or his obedience to the orders of the officer commanding any expedition."

Which motion was determined in the negative.

Mr. DESHA moved further to amend the bill by adding thereto the following section:

And be it further enacted, That the mounted volunteers who served in the Northwestern expedition in the Fall of the year 1813, or in the Southern campaign against the hostile Creek Indians, commanded by Major General Jackson and General Floyd, and who lost their horses by death, or otherwise, in consequence of being dismounted and separated from their horses by the orders of the Commanding General, without the default or negligence of the owner, shall be entitled to compensation therefor.

And the question thereon being taken, it was determined in the negative—yeas 62, nays 65, as follows:

YEAS—Messrs. Alexander, Anderson, Avery, Bard, Bines, Bowen, Butler, Caldwell, Cannon, Clendenin, Comstock, Conard, Creighton, Davis of Pennsylvania, Desha, Duvall, Earle, Evans, Farrow, Forney, Gholson, Gourdin, Griffin, Hall, Harris, Humphreys, Hungerford, Ingham, Irving, Jackson of Virginia, Johnson of Kentucky, Kerr, Kershaw, Kilbourn, Lefferts, Lowndes, Lyle, McKee, McKim, McLean, Montgomery, Moore, Nelson, Newton, Ormsby, Rea of Pennsylvania, Rich, Roane, Robertson, Sevier, Sharp, Sheffey, Slaymaker, Smith of Pennsylvania, Smith of Virginia, Strong, Tannehill, Telfair, Williams, Wilson of Pennsylvania, Winter, and Wright.

NAYS—Messrs. Archer, Barbour, Barnett, Baylies of Massachusetts, Bigelow, Boyd, Bradbury, Breckenridge, Burwell, Champion, Cilley, Cox, Culpeper, Cuthbert, Davenport, Franklin, Gaston, Geddes, Goldsborough, Goodwyn, Grosvenor, Hale, Hanson, Hasbrouck, Hawes, Henderson, Hulbert, Jackson of Rhode Island, Kennedy, Kent of New York, Kent of Maryland, King of Massachusetts, King of North Carolina, Law, Lewis, Lovett, Macon, Markell, Moseley, Oakley, Pickering, Pickens, Pitkin, Potter, John Reed, William Reed, Ruggles, Schureman, Sherwood, Shipherd, Stanford, Sturges, Taggart, Taylor, Thompson, Troup, Vose, Ward of Massachusetts, Webster, Wheaton, White, Wilcox, Wilson of Massachusetts, and Yancey.

Mr. JACKSON, of Virginia, moved further to amend the said bill by inserting the following section:

And be it further enacted, That mounted men who have been, or shall hereafter be, employed in the service of the United States, and who have lost, or shall hereafter lose, their horses, by death or otherwise, without their default or negligence, in consequence of their being dismounted and separated from their horses by the orders of the commanding officer, shall be allowed and paid the value thereof.

Which was determined in the negative.

Mr. McLEAN moved further to amend the bill by inserting, after the words "United States," in the 10th line of the 1st section, the following words: "or where any horse or horses may have been surrendered to the enemy and lost to the owner by capitulation;" which was determined in the negative.

Mr. KING, of Massachusetts, moved further to amend the first section of the bill, by adding thereto the following words: "deducting therefrom the amount which may have accrued to the claimant for the use and risk of his horse;" which was determined in the negative.

Mr. KING, of Massachusetts, moved further to amend the first section, as follows:

Line 5, after the word "damage," insert "without any fault or neglect on his part."

Line 4, strike out the word "has," and insert "have."

Line 6, after the word "or," strike out the word "by," and insert "which have died, or shall hereafter die of."

And the question being taken on the said amendments, it was determined in the negative.

On motion of Mr. KING, of Massachusetts, the bill was further amended; and it was ordered to be engrossed, and read a third time on Monday next.

MONDAY, January 30.

The amendments proposed by the Senate to the bill, supplementary to the act entitled "An act laying duties on licenses to retailers of wines, spirituous liquors, and foreign merchandise, and for other purposes," were read, and concurred in by the House.

On motion of Mr. McKEE,

Resolved, That the Committee of Accounts be instructed to inquire into the expediency of compelling the Clerk of this House to give bond for the faithful application and disbursement of the contingent fund of this House.

The bill from the Senate, "concerning field officers of the militia," was read a second time, and referred to a Committee of the Whole.

The engrossed bill, giving a right of pre-emption in the purchase of public lands to certain settlers in the Indiana Territory, was read a third time, passed, and sent to the Senate.

The engrossed bill to authorize payment for property lost, captured, or destroyed, whilst in the military service of the United States, was read a third time and passed.

The bill to authorize the President of the United States to receive into the service of the United States certain corps which may be raised and organized in any State to serve in lieu of the militia thereof, passed through a Committee of the Whole, and was ordered to be engrossed and read a third time.

Mr. LEWIS called up the bill for repairing or rebuilding the public buildings in this city, which the House refused to take up, 60 to 49; and also the bill to incorporate the Farmers and Mechanics' Bank of Georgetown; and also the bill establishing the Bank of the Metropolis; all which the House refused to take up.

The bill for the regulation of the courts of justice in the Territory of Indiana was then taken up in Committee of the Whole, on the motion of Mr. JENNINGS. After some discussion on this bill, it was ordered to be engrossed for a third reading.

The House resolved itself into a Committee of the Whole, on the bill in addition to the act regulating the Post Office Establishment; the bill was reported to the House, and made the order of the day for Monday next.

Mr. EPPES, from the Committee of Ways and Means, reported a bill to authorize the issuing of Treasury notes for the service of the year 1815; which was read twice, and committed to a Committee of the Whole.

A message from the Senate informed the House that the Senate have passed a bill, "in addition to the act to regulate the laying out and making a road from Cumberland, in the State of Maryland, to the State of Ohio;" in which they ask the concurrence of this House. The Senate have also passed the bill "to prohibit intercourse with the enemy, and for other purposes," with an amendment, in which they request the concurrence of this House.

On motion of Mr. CANNON,

Resolved, That the committee on that part of the President's Message which relates to the militia, be instructed to inquire into the expediency of amending the act supplementary to an act, entitled "An act to provide for calling forth the militia to execute the laws of the Union, suppress insurrections, and repel invasions, and to repeal the act now in force for those purposes, and to increase the pay of volunteer and militia corps," passed February the 2d, 1813, so as to allow to the militia, in addition to the pay and emoluments allowed by the before recited act, who now are, or may hereafter be, in the service of the United States, the same amount of clothing, in proportion to the time they are in said service, as is allowed to the regular army; and in all cases where the said militia shall furnish themselves with clothing, while in service as aforesaid, to allow them the amount of the United States' price in money in lieu thereof.

The following resolution was submitted by Mr. KILBOURN:

Resolved, That provision ought to be made, by law, for payment to the mounted volunteers and draughted militia, who have served in the Northwestern army, or against the Creek Indians, under the command of Generals Jackson and Floyd, of the value of the horses lost by them in the service of the United States, in either of their several expeditions, in consequence of the men being dismounted and separated from their horses, by order of their respective commanding officers, and without the fault or neglect of the owner, or in consequence of the rider or riders being killed or wounded in battle; and that the Committee of Claims be instructed to prepare and report to this House a bill accordingly.

The question was taken to consider the said resolution, and determined in the negative—yeas 43.

Mr. RUGGLES offered for consideration the following resolution:

"*Resolved*, That the Committee of Ways and Means be instructed to inquire into the expediency of reducing the tax laid on stills or boilers used solely in the rectification of spirituous liquors, or on spirits rectified therein."

The House agreed to consider the resolution—54 votes to 52.

Mr. RUGGLES stated his reasons for this motion, viz: that the duty was now so high as to effectually suppress such distillation, as he was informed by letters from his district.

The question was then taken on the adoption of the resolution, and decided in the negative—ayes 45.

The following amendment to the standing rules and orders of the House was submitted by Mr. FORSYTH; which was read, and ordered to lie on the table:

"After reports from select and standing committees have been called for and disposed of, motions for the reconsideration of any decision of the preceding day shall be in order, and have precedence of all other business."

"All bills, resolutions, orders, or other propositions, adopted by the House, shall be retained in its possession until the time limited for motions for reconsideration shall have expired, unless otherwise specially directed."

JOSEPH G. ROBERTS.

Mr. PLEASANTS, from the Committee on Naval Affairs, made a report on the petition of Joseph G. Roberts; which was read, and ordered to lie on the table. It is as follows:

The petitioner states that he is a surgeon in the Navy of the United States, and as such was attached to the squadron on Lake Erie, commanded by Commodore Perry; that whilst the squadron lay in port, the men becoming sickly, a hospital was established on shore, and the petitioner placed over it as surgeon; that whilst discharging his duty on shore the action on the lake took place, on the 10th of September, 1813, in which the whole of the enemy's squadron was captured; that some of the wounded seamen were sent to the hospital after the action; that, in dividing the prize money, such a construction has been given to the law as to exclude the petitioner from any part thereof; under which construction the whole of said prize money has been distributed among the officers and crew; the petitioner prays that Congress would

1113　　　　　HISTORY OF CONGRESS.　　　　　1114

JANUARY, 1815.　　　Petition of Thomas Riddels—Election of Clerk.　　　H. of R.

grant him such a sum as will be equal to what his proportion of the said prize money would have been, had it been determined that he was entitled to a proportion thereof.

The committee are of opinion that the construction given to the law in the case stated is a correct one, and conformable to naval usage in similar cases. Prize money is allowed as a stimulus to courage and exertion in action, and a reward for valor, danger, and victory. They, therefore, recommend to the House the following resolution:

Resolved, That the prayer of the petitioner ought not to be granted.

THOMAS RIDDELS.

The SPEAKER laid before the House a report from the Secretary of the Navy, on the petition of Thomas Riddels; which was read, and ordered to lie on the table. It is as follows:

NAVY DEPARTMENT, *Jan.* 28, 1815.

SIR: In reply to an order of the honorable the House of Representatives, of the third inst., referring the petition of Thomas Riddels, of Philadelphia, to the Commissioners of the Navy Pension Fund, I have the honor to state that Thomas Riddels was regularly shipped in the United States' service at six dollars per month wages, and was stationed on board gunboat No. 121, commanded by Sailingmaster Wm. Sheed; that, on the 29th day of July, 1813, in an action with the enemy, which took place near the entrance of the Delaware bay, the said Thomas Riddels lost his leg. After recovering from amputation, he was employed at the navy yard, Philadelphia, and on the 30th May, 1813, a pension was granted to him of three dollars per month, being the highest rate authorized by law.

There are many cases of peculiar hardship similar to this, particularly in the corps of marines, in which a man, for the greatest degree of disability, can receive no more than half his monthly pay, which heretofore has been only six dollars.

As the pension granted to this boy, Thomas Riddels, is for life, he might be bound apprentice to some profitable sedentary trade, and the accumulation of his pension, under guardianship, and proper management, may enable him to be usefully employed both for himself and the country.

All which is respectfully submitted.

B. W. CROWNINSHIELD.

The Hon. the SPEAKER
Of the House of Representatives.

ELECTION OF CLERK.

Mr. JACKSON, of Virginia, moved the following resolution:

Resolved, That this House will proceed on ——— at ——— o'clock, to the appointment of a Clerk, in the room of Patrick Magruder, who has resigned that office.

The question on filling the first blank with the word to-morrow was decided in the negative—60 to 55.

Mr. PEARSON then moved to lay the resolution on the table, with a view to introduce a motion to postpone the appointment of a Clerk until the next session, and in the meantime to appoint a Clerk temporarily. He desired time to make a selection from such candidates as should present themselves for this important office.

To this it was objected, that the office of Clerk was in itself temporary, and would require re-election at the commencement of next session.

The motion to lay the resolution on the table was decided in the negative.

Mr. FISK, of Vermont, moved to fill the blank with the word Wednesday; which was negatived—ayes 43.

The blanks were then filled with the words, "this day, at two o'clock."

The motion, as amended, was then agreed to.

The House afterwards proceeded to ballot for a Clerk. Messrs. Thomas Dougherty, Thomas L. McKenney, O. B. Brown, Samuel Burch, and N. B. Van Zandt, were severally nominated. On the first balloting there were—

For Mr. Dougherty	80
McKenney	35
Burch	19
Brown	13
Van Zandt	4
Scattering	6

On the second ballot Mr. Dougherty had 83 votes, and Mr. McKenney 73, and four scattering; so Mr. DOUGHERTY was elected.

TUESDAY, January 31.

THOMAS DOUGHERTY, who was, on yesterday, elected Clerk of this House, gave his attendance, and took the oath of office prescribed by the act, entitled "An act to regulate the time and manner of administering certain oaths."

Mr. EASTON presented a memorial of the Legislature of the Territory of Missouri, setting forth the defenceless situation of that Territory, and praying that such number of troops may be stationed in said Territory as will be sufficient, not only to repel aggression, but to carry on active warfare in the heart of the enemy's country. Laid on the table.

The Committee of Ways and Means were discharged from a further consideration of a resolution of the 12th of November last, relative to the importation of certain goods free of duty, and it was referred to the Committee of Commerce and Manufactures.

On motion of Mr. INGERSOLL, the Committee on the Judiciary were discharged from the further consideration of the memorial of the Legislature of the Mississippi Territory, presented on the 9th instant; and from the further consideration of the petition of the Legislature of the Territory of Illinois, presented on the 18th instant; as also, from the further consideration of the resolution of the 4th instant, relative to fugitives from justice, and to persons escaping from the service of their masters; and the said memorials and resolutions were referred to Messrs. SHARP, TAYLOR, LAW, SHERWOOD, KING, of North Carolina, WOOD, and JENNINGS.

The bill from the Senate, "in addition to the act to regulate the laying out and making a road from Cumberland, in the State of Maryland, to the State of Ohio," was read twice, and committed to a Committee of the Whole.

Mr. EPPES, of Virginia, reported a bill to fix

1115   HISTORY OF CONGRESS.   1116

H. of R.   *Appropriation Bill—Sureties of a Collector.*   February, 1815.

the compensation and increase the accountability of collectors of the direct tax; which was twice read, and committed.

The bill sent from the House to prohibit intercourse with the enemy, was returned to the House with sundry amendments; which occasioned considerable discussion, but were all concurred in eventually.

APPROPRIATION BILL.

The House resolved itself into a Committee of the Whole, on the bill making appropriations for the support of the Government for 1815.—[The civil list bill.]

Bills of this description are generally considered as little more than mere matter of form, as designating moneys to be applied to purposes already authorized by law; and, therefore, seldom give rise to discussion. One clause of this bill, however, gave rise to a wide and rather animated debate of a desultory character.

Mr. McKee, of Kentucky, moved to strike out the clause which appropriates, for the salary of the Superintendent General of Military Supplies, and clerks and messenger employed in his office, ten thousand dollars. This motion he predicated on the idea that this office was in itself unimportant, and its utility by no means commensurate with its cost to the Government.

This motion was supported, in debate, by the mover and Messrs. Pitkin, Sheffey, Gaston, Farrow, Hanson, and Grosvenor; and opposed by Messrs. Eppes, Hawkins, Wright, and Fisk, of New York.

On the one hand, it was alleged that no man could assign the uses of this office to the Government, or at least any adequate to its cost, which could not as well be performed by a single clerk in the office of the Accountant of the War Department, &c.; and, if useless, that it would be a proper course to strike out that item of this bill, and postpone it till the bill making appropriations for the Military department should come under consideration, in which it might be conveniently inserted, if then deemed expedient to be continued.

On the other hand it was argued, that this office was one of great importance to the proper distribution and accountability for military supplies, of which a proper account and checks thereon could in no way, probably, be so well supplied. If, however, the continuance of this office were not indispensable, of which most of the gentlemen on either side professed themselves unqualified to judge, this was not the proper way to get at the office for the purpose of abolishing it. The office now existed by law, and it was as proper and necessary to appropriate money for its support as for that of any office under the Government.

When the question was taken, there appeared to be, for striking out the clause 59, against it, 54.

The bill as amended was reported to the House, but the House adjourned before deciding on the amendments made in Committee.

WEDNESDAY, February 1.

Mr. Moore presented a petition of the Committee of Vigilance and Safety of the city and precincts of Baltimore, representing the defenceless situation of that city, and praying that a force may be provided adequate to their defence, during the next campaign.—Referred to the Committee on Military Affairs.

Mr. Jennings presented a petition of sundry inhabitants of the Indiana Territory, praying that the said Territory may be erected into a separate and independent State.—Laid on the table.

Mr. Newton, from the Committee of Commerce and Manufactures, reported a bill for the relief of Thomas and John Clifford, of Philadelphia; which was read twice, and committed to a Committee of the Whole.

Mr. Kershaw, from the Committee of Accounts, reported a bill to compel the Clerk of the House of Representatives in the Congress of the United States, to give security for the faithful application and disbursement of the contingent fund of the said House; which was read twice, and committed to a Committee of the Whole.

Mr. Pleasants, from the Committee on Naval Affairs, reported a bill for the relief of Uriah Coolidge and James Burnham; which was read twice, and committed to a Committee of the Whole.

Mr. Yancey, from the Committee of Claims, reported a bill for the relief of George S. Wise; which was read twice, and committed to a Committee of the Whole.

Mr. Yancey, from the same committee, to whom was referred the bill from the Senate "for the relief of William Gamble," made a report thereon; which was read, and, together with the bill, ordered to lie on the table.

Mr. Eppes, from the Committee of Ways and Means, reported a bill to provide additional revenues for defraying the expenses of Government, and maintaining the public credit, by laying a duty on gold, silver, and plated ware, and jewelry, and paste work, manufactured within the United States; which was read twice, and committed to the Committee of the Whole on the bill laying a direct tax upon the District of Columbia.

SURETIES OF A COLLECTOR.

Mr. Eppes, from the Committee of Ways and Means, made a report on the petition of Solomon Frazer and Mary Eccleston; which was read, and referred to a Committee of the whole House on Saturday next. The report is as follows:

That the following is the statement of facts which must govern the opinion of the House in this case:

James Frazer was appointed collector of the port of Vienna, in Maryland, about the 1st day of April, 1795; and Solomon Frazer and Charles Eccleston (the latter now deceased, of whom the petitioner, Mary Eccleston, is the personal representative,) became his sureties in a bond to the United States in the penal sum of two thousand dollars. At the end of the year 1795, James Frazer was in arrear, on rendering his accounts to the Government, in the sum of $350 82; which balance against him continued to increase from year to year, until the month of June, 1805, about which time James Frazer went out of office, when the sum due from him to the United States was $3,924 86. No measures were taken by the United States to enforce the payment of the arrears due from James Frazer until June, 1785, (after he was out of office,) when a suit was commenced against him and his sureties. The writ against James Frazer was returned, served at September term, 1807, and judgment was obtained against him at September term, 1808, for the balance of his account. Execution was taken out on this judgment, on the 29th day of June, 1810, by virtue of which James Frazer was imprisoned; and on the 3d day of July thereafter was discharged from his imprisonment, by an order of the Secretary of the Treasury, on the ground of his insolvency. This order of the Secretary was irregular, being granted by him under a mistaken supposition that James Frazer was imprisoned on a judgment obtained on a revenue bond; the law empowering the Secretary to discharge from imprisonment in certain cases not extending to the case of collectors.

It does not appear when the insolvency of James Frazer took place; but it appears that, in February, 1804, he sustained a considerable loss by fire; and that he had property to the amount of two or three thousand dollars about the end of the year 1808.

It also appears that a judgment was obtained against Solomon Frazer for the sum of $2,000, (the penalty of the bond,) before the year 1808, which is still in force. It does not appear that any judgment has been obtained against Charles Eccleston or his personal representative.

On this statement of facts the committee are of opinion that the petitioners are entitled to the relief they ask for; and, therefore, submit the following resolution:

Resolved, That the prayer of the petitions of Solomon Frazer and Mary Eccleston is reasonable, and ought to be granted.

APPROPRIATION BILL.

The House resumed the consideration of the report of the amendments reported by the Committee of the Whole to the bill making appropriations for the support of Government for the year 1815; and the said amendments being again read, were concurred in by the House, except the following, to wit:

"Strike out the following items:

"For compensation to the Superintendent General of Military Supplies, clerks, and persons employed in his office, ——;"

"For contingent expenses in the office of the Superintendent General of Military Supplies, ——."

After much debate, the question was taken to concur with the Committee of the House in striking out the said items, and was determined in the negative—yeas 61, nays 86, as follows:

YEAS—Messrs. Baylies of Massachusetts, Bigelow, Boyd, Bradbury, Breckenridge, Brigham, Champion, Cilley, Cox, Culpeper, Davenport, Davis of Massachusetts, Ely, Farrow, Gaston, Geddes, Goldsborough, Grosvenor, Hanson, Henderson, Hungerford, Hulbert, Jackson of Rhode Island, Kent of New York, Kent of Maryland, King of Massachusetts, Law, Lewis, Lovett, Macon, Markell, McKee, Montgomery, Moseley, Oak-

ley, Pearson, Pickering, Pitkin, Potter, John Reed, William Reed, Ruggles, Schureman, Sheffey, Sherwood, Shipherd, Slaymaker, Stanford, Stockton, Stuart, Sturges, Taggart, Thompson, Vose, Ward of Massachusetts, Ward of New Jersey, Webster, Wheaton, Wilcox, Wilson of Massachusetts, and Winter.

NAYS—Messrs. Alexander, Anderson, Archer, Avery, Barbour, Bard, Barnett, Bines, Bowen, Brown, Burwell, Butler, Caldwell, Calhoun, Cannon, Comstock, Condict, Conard, Crawford, Creighton, Crouch, Cuthbert, Davis of Pennsylvania, Desha, Duvall, Earle, Eppes, Findley, Fisk of Vermont, Fisk of New York, Forney, Franklin, Gholson, Goodwyn, Griffin, Hall, Harris, Hasbrouck, Hawes, Hopkins of Kentucky, Hubbard, Humphreys, Ingersoll, Ingham, Irwin, Johnson of Virginia, Johnson of Kentucky, Kennedy, Kerr, Kershaw, Kilbourn, King of North Carolina, Lefferts, Lowndes, Lyle, McCoy, McLean, Moore, Murfree, Nelson, Newton, Ormsby, Pickens, Piper, Pleasants, Rea of Pennsylvania, Rhea of Tennessee, Rich, Ringgold, Roane, Robertson, Sage, Sevier, Sharp, Smith of Pennsylvania, Smith of Virginia, Tannehill, Taylor, Telfair, Troup, Udree, Williams, Wilson of Pennsylvania, Wood, Wright, and Yancey.

The bill was then further amended, and ordered to be engrossed, and read the third time to-morrow.

THURSDAY, February 2.

Mr. EPPES, from the Committee of Ways and Means, reported a bill for the relief of Edward Hallowell; which was read twice, and committed.

Mr. BRIGHAM submitted the following resolution; which was read, and ordered to lie on the table:

Resolved, That the Committee on Military Affairs be directed to inquire into the propriety and expediency of reducing the national expenses, by abolishing any of the offices in the Military or War Department, or by discharging any of the officers of the United States, whose continuance in office may not be necessary for the public service.

Mr. RHEA, of Tennessee, submitted the following resolution; which was read, considered, and rejected by the House:

Resolved, That the committee appointed on so much of the President's Message of the 20th of September last, as relates to the classing and disciplining of the militia, be instructed to inquire into the expediency of making provision, by law, to make all white male persons, between the ages of eighteen and forty-five years, residing on lands to which the Indian title is not extinguished, liable to do militia duty.

On motion of Mr. NELSON,

Resolved, That the memorial of William Lambert, accompanied with astronomical calculations relative to the establishment of a first meridian for the United States, at the seat of their Government, presented on the 27th of December, 1809; also, the reports of two committees of this House, and a report of the Secretary of State on that subject, made the 28th of March, 1810, the 20th of January, 1813, and the 3d of July, 1812, be referred to a select committee, to inquire into the expediency of Congress adopting such measures as may be proper to carry into effect the objects proposed in the said memorial and reports, with leave to report by bill or otherwise.

Messrs. NELSON, LOWNDES, WEBSTER, KENT, of New York, and BOWEN, were appointed the committee.

An engrossed bill making appropriations for the support of Government for the year 1815, was read the third time, and passed.

An engrossed bill to authorize the President of the United States to receive into the service of the United States, certain corps which may be raised and organized by any State, to serve in lieu of the militia thereof, was read the third time, and passed.

An engrossed bill for the regulation of the courts of justice of Indians, was read the third time, and passed.

The House resolved itself into a Committee of the Whole on the bill for the relief of Saltus, Son, and Company, merchants, of the city of New York; which was ordered to be engrossed, and read a third time to-morrow.

The House resolved itself into a Committee of the Whole on the bill to amend and extend the provisions of the act of the 16th of April, 1814, entitled "An act confirming certain claims to land in the Illinois Territory, and providing for their location. The bill was reported with amendments; which were concurred in by the House, and the bill ordered to be engrossed, and read a third time to morrow.

The House resolved itself into a Committee of the Whole on the bill to provide additional revenues for defraying the expenses of Government, and maintaining the public credit, by laying a direct tax upon the District of Columbia; also, on the bill to provide additional revenues for defraying the expenses of Government, and maintaining the public credit, by laying a duty on lotteries; and on the bill to provide additional revenues for defraying the expenses of Government, and maintaining the public credit, by laying a duty on gold, silver, and plated ware, and jewelry, and paste work, manufactured within the United States; and, after some time spent therein, the Committee reported the second mentioned bill with amendments, and had leave to sit again on the remaining bills.

PAYMENT FOR HORSES LOST, &c.

The following resolution was submitted by Mr. KILBOURN:

Resolved, That the Committee of Claims be instructed to inquire into the expediency of providing, by law, for paying to the mounted volunteers and draughted militia, who have served in the Northwestern army, under the command of Generals Jackson and Floyd, against the Creek Indians, or to their heirs or assigns, the value of the horses by them lost in said service, in consequence of the men being dismounted or separated from their horses, by order of their respective commanding officers, on any expedition, or in consequence of the riders being killed or wounded in battle, or who have lost their horse or horses while in the service of the United States, by any unavoidable accident, deducting from the original value of such horses, respectively, as were received into the service, the amount which may have been paid for the use thereof, in any of the cases, prior to the loss of the same as aforesaid.

The House proceeded to consider the said resolution; and, the same being amended, on the question to agree to the same, it passed in the affirmative—yeas 67, nays 49, as follows:

YEAS—Messrs. Alexander, Anderson, Barbour, Bard, Barnett, Bines, Bowen, Burwell, Butler, Caldwell, Cannon, Chappell, Clendenin, Condict, Crawford, Crouch, Davis of Pennsylvania, Desha, Eppes, Evans, Findley, Forney, Forsyth, Franklin, Gholson, Goodwyn, Griffin, Hall, Hawes, Hubbard, Humphreys, Hungerford, Jackson of Virginia, Johnson of Virginia, Kennedy, Kent of Maryland, Kerr, Kilbourn, King of North Carolina, Lefferts, Lowndes, Lyle, Macon, McKee, McLean, Montgomery, Moore, Nelson, Newton, Pickens, Piper, Pleasants, Rea of Pennsylvania, Rhea of Tennessee, Rich, Robertson, Sage, Sevier, Sharp, Sheffey, Smith of Virginia, Strong, Stuart, Tannehill, Udree, Wilson of Pennsylvania, and Yancey.

NAYS—Messrs. Baylies of Massachusetts, Bayly of Virginia, Bigelow, Boyd, Breckenridge, Brigham, Champion, Cilley, Cooper, Cox, Culpeper, Davenport, Davis of Massachusetts, Ely, Goldsborough, Grosvenor, Hale, Hasbrouck, Henderson, Hulbert, Jackson of Rhode Island, King of Massachusetts, Law, Lewis, Lovett, Markell, Moseley, Pearson, Pitkin, John Reed, William Reed, Ruggles, Schureman, Sherwood, Shipherd, Slaymaker, Smith of New York, Stanford, Stockton, Sturges, Taggart, Taylor, Thompson, Troup, Vose, Ward of Massachusetts, White, Wilcox, and Wilson of Massachusetts.

FRIDAY, February 3.

Mr. RHEA, from the Committee on the Post Office and Post Roads, reported a bill to alter and establish certain post roads; which was read, and committed to a Committee of the Whole.

A message from the Senate informed the House that the Senate proceeded to the reconsideration of the bill, entitled "An act to incorporate the subscribers to the Bank of the United States of America," which was returned by the President of the United States, on the 30th day of January, 1815, with objections; and have resolved that the said bill do not pass, two-thirds of the Senate not agreeing thereto.

The House resumed the consideration of the bill for taxing lotteries; and it was ordered to be engrossed for a third reading.

The engrossed bill for the relief of Saltus, Son & Co., was read a third time and passed.

The engrossed bill to amend and extend the provisions of the act of the 16th April, 1814, entitled "An act confirming certain claims to lands in the Illinois Territory, and providing for their location," was read a third time and passed.

The bill to provide additional revenues for defraying the expenses of Government, and maintaining the public credit, by laying a duty on all gold and silver plate, jewelry, and pastework, in the hands of the manufacturer, passed through a Committee of the Whole, and was, without objection, ordered to be engrossed for a third reading on to-morrow.

VIRGINIA MILITARY LAND CLAIMS.

The House resolved itself into a Committee of the Whole, on the report of the Committee of Claims on the petition of Sarah Easton and Dorothy Storer, representatives of Colonel Robert H. Harrison, of Virginia, deceased, who pray for permission to locate a land warrant granted to them by the State of Virginia in consideration of the revolutionary services of the deceased, on the public lands, a portion of which rightfully belongs, as it is contended, to Virginia for the satisfaction of claims of this character.

[The circumstances of this case are nearly these: Colonel Harrison was one of the best and most approved officers of the Continental army, until after the siege of Yorktown, in the Revolutionary war, in the capacity of aid and secretary to General Washington, whose representatives did not, until 1813, obtain from the State of Virginia a grant of land in consideration of his services; which grant, however, owing to the cession of her land by Virginia to the United States, without sufficient reservation for the satisfaction of military claims, (though such reservation was intended,) is of no present use to them; and they therefore pray permission to locate this warrant on any unappropriated lands of the United States, and also pray compensation from the United States for the services of their deceased father. The committee to whom the petition was referred report, that this case cannot be distinguished from a mass of other claims, barred by the statute of limitations, and therefore ought not to be granted.]

This report was warmly and eloquently opposed by Mr. SMITH, of New York, Mr. JACKSON, Mr. SHEFFEY, and Mr. NELSON, of Virginia, and Mr. MCKEE, of Kentucky, and advocated by Mr. BOWEN, of Tennessee, Mr. WRIGHT, of Maryland, and Mr. CHAPPELL, of South Carolina.

The debate on the report spread over the whole field of the equitable right of the State of Virginia to claim of the United States the location of her military land warrants on the lands of the United States, seeing that she only of all the States had accepted the invitation of the General Government to cede to them all her public land, reserving only a portion thereof for the satisfaction of claims and donations for military services, which portion had been too small for that object. Those who opposed the report advocated this right; those who supported the report denied the legal or equitable claim of Virginia. Other topics intermingled in the debate, arising in a degree from State feelings, but not from any denial of the merits of Colonel Harrison, except by the assertion that there were persons in other States, of equal merit, to whom, or to whose representatives, no compensation had been granted for their military services, comparable to that now proposed to be too generously bestowed on the representatives of Colonel Harrison, in preference to the satisfaction of other claimants for Revolutionary services, whose claims were rigorously barred by the statute of limitations. On the other hand, the location of the land warrant granted by Virginia, was claimed as a right growing out

13th CON. 3d SESS.—36

of the cession by Virginia to the General Government, with a reservation of a certain tract of land (which had proved insufficient) for the satisfaction of her military land warrants.

The debate resulted in a disagreement to the resolution reported by the Committee of Pensions and Revolutionary Claims, and the adoption of the following in lieu of it:

"*Resolved*, That so much of the said petition as prays compensation for the extraordinary and valuable revolutionary services of the ancestors of the petitioners, be rejected; and, that so much thereof as prays that a law may pass authorizing them to locate, on the lands of the United States, a warrant lately issued to them by the State of Virginia, for the services aforesaid, is reasonable and ought to be granted."

This resolve having been reported to the House, they adjourned without coming to a decision thereon.

SATURDAY, February 4.

Mr. EPPES, from the Committee of Ways and Means, reported the bill from the Senate, "for the relief of Henry Nimmo," without amendment, and it was committed to a Committee of the Whole.

On motion of Mr. JOHNSON, of Kentucky, the order of the day on the report of the committee appointed on the 23d of September last, to inquire into the cause of the success of the enemy in his recent enterprises against this city and the neighboring town of Alexandria, was postponed indefinitely.

A message from the Senate informed the House that the Senate have passed the bill "to alter and amend the several acts for establishing a Navy Department, by adding thereto a Board of Commissioners;" also, the bill "for the better regulation of the Ordnance department;" with amendments to each, in which they ask the concurrence of this House. The Senate have passed a bill "making appropriations for repairing or rebuilding the public buildings in the City of Washington;" in which bill they ask the concurrence of this House.

Mr. KENT, from the Committee on the District of Columbia, reported a bill concerning the College in Georgetown, in the District of Columbia; and Mr. EPPES reported a bill for the relief of Joshua Sands. The first bill was read three times and passed, and the latter was twice read and committed.

The House resumed the consideration of the report of the Committee of Claims on the petition of Sarah Easton and Dorothy Storer; which was ordered to lie on the table.

The engrossed bills for taxing lotteries, and for laying a duty on gold, silver, and plated ware and jewelry, were each read a third time and passed.

The bill for the relief of the Anacostia Bridge Company passed through a Committee of the Whole, was amended, and ordered to be engrossed for a third reading.

The amendments of the Senate to the bill to

1123　　　　　　　HISTORY OF CONGRESS.　　　　　1124

H. of R.　　　　　　*Amy Dardin—Battle of New Orleans.*　　　　FEBRUARY, 1815.

amend the act establishing the Navy Department, by adding thereto a Board of Commissioners, were read and concurred in.

The amendments of the same body to the bill for the better regulation of the Ordnance department, were also read and committed.

The bill from the Senate making appropriations for repairing or rebuilding the public buildings, in the City of Washington, was twice read and committed.

The SPEAKER laid before the House a letter from the Secretary of the Treasury, transmitting sundry statements, which have usually been presented to the view of Congress in the annual report on the state of the finances, and are intended to accompany the report upon that subject, made on the 23d day of September last.

AMY DARDIN.

The bill for the relief of Amy Dardin, the representative of David Dardin, deceased, passed through a Committee of the Whole, was widely debated, and at last (for perhaps the twentieth time in one or other branch of the Legislature) ordered to be engrossed for a third reading.—For the bill 69, against it 59, as follows:

YEAS—Messrs. Alston, Anderson, Barbour, Bard, Bowen, Breckenridge, Brigham, Cannon, Conard, Creighton, Culpeper, Davis of Massachusetts, Duvall, Eppes, Gholson, Goldsborough, Goodwyn, Gourdin, Griffin, Grosvenor, Harris, Hawes, Hopkins of Kentucky, Humphreys, Hungerford, Ingersoll, Jackson of Rhode Island, Jackson of Virginia, Johnson of Virginia, Johnson of Ky., Kennedy, Kent of Md., Kerr, Kershaw, King of North Carolina, Lowndes, McKee, McLean, Montgomery, Murfree, Nelson, Newton, Oakley, Ormsby, Pearson, Pleasants, Rea of Pennsylvania, Ringgold, Robertson, Ruggles, Sevier, Seybert, Sharp, Shefley, Shipherd, Smith of New York, Smith of Pennsylvania, Smith of Virginia, Stanford, Taggart, Telfair, Thompson, Troup, White, Wilcox, Wilson of Pennsylvania, Winter, Wood, and Wright.

NAYS—Messrs. Alexander, Archer, Barnett, Baylies of Massachusetts, Boyd, Bradbury, Butler, Champion, Cilley, Clendenin, Condict, Cox, Crawford, Davis of Pennsylvania, Ely, Fisk of New York, Franklin, Gaston, Geddes, Hale, Hall, Hasbrouck, Henderson, Ingham, Kent of New York, King of Massachusetts, Law, Lefferts, Lovett, Lyle, Macon, Markell, McCoy, McKim, Moore, Moseley, Pickering, Piper, Pitkin, John Reed, William Reed, Rhea of Tennessee, Sage, Schureman, Sherwood, Stockton, Strong, Sturges, Tannehill, Taylor, Udree, Vose, Ward of Massachusetts, Ward of New Jersey, Webster, Wheaton, Williams, Wilson of Massachusetts, and Yancey.

MONDAY, February 6.

An engrossed bill for the relief of the Anacostia Bridge Company was read the third time and passed.

An engrossed bill for the relief of the legal representatives of David Dardin was read the third time; and a motion was made, by Mr. TAYLOR, that the said bill be recommitted to the Committee on Pensions and Revolutionary Claims, with instructions to inquire into the expediency of admitting to payment at the Treasury, all just

claims against the United States, which have been liquidated and barred by any resolve or statute of limitations.

And the question being taken thereon, it was determined in the negative.

The question was then taken, Shall the bill pass? and passed in the affirmative.

The SPEAKER laid before the House, a memorial from Thomas Ewell, of this District; in which, after describing the advantages of such institutions, he prays a law may be passed, authorizing landed proprietors of the United States, to issue notes payable six months after date, &c., (in the manner of the notes Mr. E. himself had issued,) which was read by the Clerk, and laid on the table.

Mr. SHARP, of Kentucky, from a select committee, reported a bill declaratory of the powers of the Legislature of Illinois Territory, (giving it power to fix the time and places at which the Judges of the Territory shall hold the courts therein.) The bill was twice read and committed.

On motion of Mr. EPPES, the bill authorizing the issue of Treasury notes for the year 1815, were recommitted to the Committee of Ways and Means.

The bill to compel the Clerk of the House of Representatives to give bond, having passed through a Committee of the Whole, was recommitted to the Committee of Accounts.

The bill for the relief of George S. Wise passed through a Committee of the Whole, and was ordered to lie on the table.

The bill for subsisting the Army of the United States, by authorizing the appointment of Commissioners of Subsistence, passed through a Committee of the whole House, and was ordered to be engrossed for a third reading.

BATTLE OF NEW ORLEANS.

Mr. TROUP, of Georgia, from the Committee on Military Affairs, made a report recommending the adoption of the following resolve:

Resolved, by the Senate and House of Representatives of the United States of America in Congress assembled, That the thanks of Congress be and they are hereby presented to Major General Jackson, and through him to the officers and men under his command, for their gallantry and good conduct, in defeating the enemy before the city of New Orleans, in successive battles fought on the 23d of December, 1814, and 1st and 8th of January, 1815; in which a British veteran army, formidable in number as in discipline, commanded by renowned Generals, was thrice beaten and driven back with great loss, and in the battle of the 8th of January, with immense slaughter, by a militia force hastily collected to the defence of that city, aided by a small body of regular troops; thus illustrating the patriotic defence of the country with brilliant achievement, and signalizing the Americans by steady perseverance, incessant vigilance, patient suffering, undaunted firmness, and in victory moderation and clemency: And that the President of the United States be requested to cause a gold medal to be struck, with suitable emblems and devices, and presented to Major General Jackson, in testimony of the high sense entertained by Congress of events so memorable, and of services so eminent.

The resolution was twice read, and referred to a Committee of the Whole.

CLASSIFICATION OF MILITIA.

Mr. RICH, of Vermont, having caught the SPEAKER's eye, spoke nearly as follows:

Sir: Impressed as I am with the importance of the crisis to which our country is approaching, and anxious as I feel to contribute the utmost of my feeble efforts to insure success to the contest in which it is engaged, I deem it unnecessary that I should offer an apology for troubling the House with the propositions I am about to submit. Surely, sir, if the present contest shall terminate ingloriously, the cause of it must and will be charged upon this Congress; and, I may be permitted to add, that nothing can ever be urged as an apology for us. For it can never be said, that the country which has produced a Brown, a Scott, and a Jackson, with the Spartan bands which have fought by their sides, and which contains near two millions of men equally capable of bearing arms, together with all the means of supplying armies and subsisting its inhabitants, can be unsuccessful in a contest with any nation whatever, except for want of a proper application of the means within the power of the Government. With a knowledge, however, of the difficulty we have experienced in uniting the House in any important measures, I ought, perhaps, to forbear making an attempt at a new project at this late period of the session, and content myself with trusting the defence of our country to what regular forces may obtained by the ordinary mode of enlistment, relying on volunteers and militia for the balance. But, sir, when I consider the dangers with which our country is threatened, and the unequal burdens which are imposed upon the people by draughts from the militia, as well as the enormous expense attending them, I feel it my duty, late as it is, to make one effort to accomplish that which shall better comport with what I believe to be a duty we owe to the community.

Mr. R. then submitted the following resolutions:

Resolved, That the Committee on Military Affairs be instructed to inquire into the expediency of providing, by law, for arranging the citizens subject to the direct tax, into classes, in such manner that each shall, as far as may be practicable, consist of persons residing contiguous to each other, and from which together —— hundred dollars shall be due; and of permitting each class to furnish one man for the regular Army, within a given number of days, in lieu of said tax.

Resolved, That the said committee be instructed to inquire into the expediency of augmenting the direct tax for the present year, so as that it may be sufficient to procure —— thousand men at —— hundred dollars each.

The House having agreed to consider these resolutions, Mr. R. again rose and addressed the House as follows:

Having submitted the propositions before you, it is due to myself and to the House, that I should give a brief explanation of my views as to the details of the proposed measure. I propose, sir, that it shall be made the duty of the principal assessors in the several States, as soon as the tax lists shall be made out, to furnish each assistant assessor with a list comprehending the taxable persons in the assessment districts respectively, and that the assistant assessors shall be required to arrange them into classes in such manner that each class shall, as far as may be practicable, consist of persons residing contiguous to each other, and from whom, in the whole, two hundred dollars of the tax shall be due; requiring of the said assessors that they should make a return of the classification to the collector, designing the classes by numbers, or in some other manner which shall be sufficiently descriptive, and that the citizens of each assessment district should be notified of the class to which they may severally belong, and of the tax due from each, by the posting up of class lists, at a suitable number of the most public places in each district. I propose that each class should be allowed to exonerate itself from the tax by furnishing a man (within a given number of days) to engage for the war, without the bounty in money from the Government; but to be entitled to the land bounty, and that a class on furnishing a recruit should be entitled to a certificate from the officer authorized to receive the recruits, which being presented to the collector should be good payment for the tax of the class. And in the absence of such certificate, for a given number of days, the collector should proceed in the collection. It is not improbable that in arranging the classes it might be expedient in some cases, and perhaps in all, to include in a class those whose tax together should amount to four, or six, or perhaps eight hundred dollars, and provide that it should exonerate itself from the tax by furnishing a corresponding number of men. I feel no difficulty, sir, in hazarding an opinion, that most of the classes would furnish the men, and I believe they would do so, because thereby they would make a saving to themselves in money, and not only would they make a saving in amount, but in most cases they would pay a recruit in the necessary supplies for a family, and in various other ways, in which they would compensate him, with more convenience than to raise the same amount in money at a given period. And in aid of this plan, we should enlist, not only all the feelings which result from a wish to see the country properly defended, but those of pecuniary interest. Every taxable citizen would in a degree voluntarily become a recruiting officer, and, among the whole, there can be little doubt but a sufficient number of recruits would be found. If, however, it should be believed, that to allow two hundred dollars of the tax for a recruit would be a sum insufficient to insure the obtaining of them, let the sum be augmented, and, if necessary, increase the tax accordingly; to which I can see no objection, as, whatever the nominal amount of the tax may be, no other burden would be imposed on the people, than the smallest sum necessary to procure the men; and sure I am, that at a time when the people in every direction are crying aloud to the Government to provide an army for the defence of everything dear to them, they will not complain of the imposition of the burdens necessary to that object, particularly if no more money is required of them, than what they shall find necessary, they having the sole direction of the application of it. I am not insensible, that to raise any given number of men in the manner I propose, may nominally cost the Government something more than to raise them in the ordinary mode; but I believe it would cost the people much less. Indeed, I very much doubt whether our soldiers do not now cost two hundred dollars each, taking into consideration the bounty, premiums, pay, and rations, to recruiting officers, loss of money in the hands of some of them, and other incidental expenses. I am not able to anticipate any Constitutional objections which can be urged against the plan I have proposed, even by the most scrupulous. Nor can I presume that it will be subject to the term of "conscription," a word which to some is so alarming. The present direct tax of six millions of dollars, if applied in the manner proposed, allowing two hundred dollars for each recruit, would raise thirty thousand men; but it cannot be calculated that the whole tax will be thus applied, even if the citizens should in no part of the country find any difficulty in procuring a sufficient number of men, because there will in all of the States be more or less property owned by non-residents, to which the classification would not be applicable. It might therefore be fair to calculate that, from the cause I have just mentioned, and other incidental causes, not more than twenty or twenty-five thousand would be obtained, while the balance of the tax would be paid in money.

I will not at present hazard an opinion as to the number which we ought to calculate on raising, provided the plan is adopted—that being a subject which more properly belongs to others. But, presuming that it might be expedient to increase the tax for the present year, with a view of enlarging the number of men beyond what the six millions would raise. I have proposed by the second resolution an inquiry on that subject.

I may perhaps be told, that, in consequence of the pledges contained in the direct tax bill, and the engagements of the Government founded on them, there is an insurmountable difficulty in the way of adopting the plan I have suggested, and such may be the fact, though I am myself inclined to a different opinion.

If, however, there be no other way of getting over the supposed difficulties, I should be in favor of substituting other new taxes, or of so increasing the present direct tax, as to make it sufficient to procure a proper number of men, leaving the present six millions to find their way into the Treasury. Gentlemen perhaps will say, that, to substitute other indirect taxes for the present direct tax, or to increase the direct tax in the manner I have proposed, will be to impose burdens upon the people heavier than can be borne. I admit they will be heavy; but, sir, the people of this country had rather support their rights at any expense than surrender them, and I am altogether mistaken as to public opinion, or it is clamorous from every quarter, for the Government to adopt strong, energetic measures, such as, with common prudence and exertion, will insure success. I have not the vanity to suppose that the propositions I have submitted, are free from objections. But, unless something can be offered less liable to them, I hope they may be adopted, for sure I am that we ought to do something, and that without delay. Should it be objected that too great delay will attend the plan I have submitted, I ask of gentlemen to present one which shall be practicable, and which will be attended with less, and assure them that I will give my aid in adopting it. But I beg of gentlemen that we may not let this session pass by without doing something which will have a tendency to relieve our citizens from their fearful apprehension.

Mr. WEBSTER opposed these resolves, and demanded the yeas and nays on their adoption. He objected to the consideration, at this late hour, of new projects, which, though they would seriously obstruct the recruiting service, could produce no good. The present direct tax, he observed, was pledged to specific purposes; and an addition to the direct tax was not practicable, that tax being already as heavy as could be borne. The true interest of the country, he believed, indicated a reliance on voluntary enlistments for filling the ranks of the Army, &c.

Mr. GOLDSBOROUGH appeared to be inclined to see this subject referred to a Committee of the Whole, for a full and mature consideration.

Mr. WRIGHT expressed his regret at seeing such a proposition introduced at this time, for, sure he was, it would produce no good; but, besides consuming public time, the very publication of the motion would have a tendency to check the recruiting service. He had information which authorized him to say that there was a perfect confidence the Army would be filled in good time by the ordinary process of recruiting; and, if we had been able to obtain money at the commencement of the session, he had no doubt but the Army would now have presented a very numerical front, indeed. He adverted to the high bounties now paid, compared to those paid during the Revolution, which would soon produce a good army, and an army of wealthy men, too, each entitled, by virtue of his enlistment, to three hundred and twenty acres of land. The States, too, were raising troops, of which the State of Maryland had magnanimously voted to raise five thousand. These new projects, Mr. W. feared, would defeat the only one on which reliance could be placed, viz: the recruiting service.

Mr. GROSVENOR said, he was totally opposed to this motion in principle, which was, besides, impracticable. The assumption of the direct tax, by some of the States, interposed, of itself, an insuperable difficulty in the way of this wild project.

Mr. GHOLSON said, he did believe that the subject of providing for filling the ranks of the regular army and of providing the ways and means, ought, until they were entirely arranged, to occupy the attention of Congress, to the exclusion of all other business. That the mode now proposed was the proper one for filling the ranks, he did not say; but, as it introduced this subject of inquiry, he hoped the resolution would be adopted. That the country was capable of bringing at once a regular army into the field, no man acquainted with its resources could deny, if they were properly applied. The only question, then, was whether such an army was wanting? Of that, he thought there could be no doubt; and he therefore hoped the 'House would seriously enter on this subject.

Mr. FISK, of Vermont, opposed a proposed postponement of this motion, not that he approved it entirely, but because it was susceptible of modification, and that, in his opinion, it would become Congress, before they parted, to take some efficient and certain measures to fill the ranks of the regular army. A combination of this proposition with that made with the War Department, at the commencement of the session, would produce such a system as he should approve; and such, as he believed, from the want of money, the Government would at last be compelled to resort to. What answer, he asked, could they give to their constituents, if they returned home and left the country comparatively defenceless? It was time, he said, that they should act, and act efficiently.

Mr. STANFORD made a motion to lay the resolves on the table; which was negatived.

Mr. LOWNDES objected to the inquiry into the propriety of diverting the direct tax already laid, or a part of it, to the purposes of raising men. After that tax had been solemnly pledged by law to a specific purpose, to enter into a discussion of the propriety of diverting it to any other purpose, while it would be impracticable for any useful end, might be seriously injurious to the finances and credit of the country. He had no objections, however, to inquire into the propriety of increasing the direct tax to this end.

Mr. TROUP (the chairman of the Military Committee) said that, being a member of the committee to whom it was proposed to refer this subject, it did not become him to express any decided opinion on it. All he hoped was, that the House would not instruct the committee on this head, unless determined to perfect the proposition into the shape of a law; inasmuch as the committee, in its ministerial capacity, had already cognizance over this subject, and could report on it without instruction, if deemed by them expedient. With respect to the military subjects of the present session, the House could not fail to recollect that the report of the Secretary of War had stated what force we had, and what addition to it was desirable for the further defence of the country. It had been proposed to Congress to augment the regular force to one hundred thousand men, for which purpose it was proposed to resort to the most energetic means. It was necessary for the committee of this House, said Mr. T., to endeavor to ascertain the opinion of both branches of the Legislature, as to the different modes of raising men. We did so; and found that no efficacious measure, calculated certainly and promptly to fill the regular army, could be effectually resorted to. Measures were matured and proposed by the committee, but were not pressed on the House from the solemn conviction that there was no disposition in the Legislature to act finally on the subject. This being ascertained, other measures were adopted, to improve the recruiting service, to authorize the acceptance into the service of volunteers and State troops in the nature of regulars. If the whole number authorized of the two latter could be commanded, together with the sixty thousand regulars, (supposing the ranks to be filled,) it would give an effective force of one hundred and forty thousand men, and might be reasonably expected to produce one hundred thousand; as great a number, perhaps, as, under present circumstances, the finances of the country would bear. Even at this late day of the session, however, Mr. T. said, he was willing to resort to the only certain and effectual mode of augmenting the regular army to a hundred thousand men, to the support of which the finances of the country might, before the adjournment, be made adequate. He hoped, at least, the House would so decide on this question, as to make the vote on it decisive of their real views in regard to it.

Mr. ALSTON remarked, in reply to the objection derived from the existing pledge of the direct tax, that that pledge applied only to the continuance of that tax until a certain part of the principal and interest of the debt should be redeemed; but the proceeds of the tax might be applied to this or any other purpose the Government should see fit.

Mr. MACON was of opinion that the motion proposed no violation of the public faith. If the army could be filled by the regular mode of enlistment, as was now said, how happened it that so many projects of this nature were offered? The reliance on volunteers and State troops was uncertain; and Congress ought to devise some mode by which the ranks of the army could be positively filled. If it could be done without violating the public faith, Mr. M. said it was his opinion, that the direct tax could be more easily paid in this way than in money, and he should therefore favor the plan.

At length, after some other desultory debate, the resolves were, on motion of Mr. FISK, of Vermont, believing, he said, they would not pass in their present shape, referred to a Committee of the whole House—63 to 57—and ordered to be printed, 59 to 39.

TUESDAY, February 7.

The SPEAKER laid before the House the annual report of the Commissioners of the Sinking Fund, detailing their proceedings since their last report, made on the 5th of February, 1814; which was read.

On motion of Mr. EASTON, a committee was

1131   HISTORY OF CONGRESS.   1132

H. of R.   *Pay of the Members—Public Buildings.*   FEBRUARY, 1815.

appointed to inquire into the expediency of better regulating, by law, the working and leasing the public lead mines in the Territory of Missouri, in such manner as to secure the lessees in the quiet enjoyment of their leases, and to enable the Government to collect its rents; and that the committee have leave to report by bill, or otherwise.

Messrs. EASTON, SHEFFEY, and MONTGOMERY, were appointed the committee.

The engrossed bill making provision for subsisting the armies of the United States, by authorizing the appointment of Commissioners of Subsistence, was read a third time, and passed.

PAY OF THE MEMBERS.

Mr. SHIPHERD, of New York, submitted for consideration the following resolution:

Resolved, That a committee be appointed to inquire into the expediency of providing for the making a reasonable compensation to the members of both Houses of Congress for travelling to and from Congress, and attendance thereon, respectively; that they report thereon by bill or otherwise; and that the committee embrace in such inquiry the present session.

Mr. PEARSON inquired the object of this motion, and the grounds for it.

Mr. SHIPHERD said he should have supposed his honorable friend understood his own interest sufficiently not to have required any explanation on this head. Congress having the right to regulate their own pay, in the same manner as the compensation of other officers of the Government, they ought to render to themselves that justice which they feel bound to do other officers of the Government. He need not, he said, tell the House that the pay now received by the members was not half what its value was when that pay was fixed; more particularly when it was considered that the paper with which the members were paid, was full twenty-five per cent. below par or the value of specie. His object was so to augment the pay of the members as to make it equal to six dollars of that medium in which members formerly received their pay.

Mr. RHEA, of Tennessee, said he did not conceive this the proper time to enter into the consideration of this subject. He thought gentlemen should let the nation get through the war before they increased their pay.

Mr. FARROW was opposed to the motion throughout, on principle, and denied the alleged depreciation of money, which he said was very gladly received in payment, in dealings of any sort, in the District.

Mr. SHIPHERD, in support of his first observation, said, that it was as obvious that all our paper was depreciated, as that the Continental money was depreciated. He had no fastidious delicacy about him, which would prevent him from doing justice to himself. If payment could be obtained in specie, it would be a good argument against the proposed motion; but it was notorious that for specie they must pay a discount of twenty-five per cent. on the paper which they received for their pay.

Mr. RHEA said that every member knew, when he was chosen, what compensation he was to expect, and had no right to complain of it. He required the yeas and nays, that he might at least record his vote against the motion.

Mr. HALL, of Georgia, observed, if the object of the gentleman was, as he had avowed, to give to the members a compensation adequate to their services, he would recommend to him to depreciate their pay instead of increasing it, *for he was confident* the acts of Congress had depreciated as much as the paper of which the gentleman had spoken.

The question on the adoption of the motion was decided in the negative, by yeas and nays, as follows: For the motion 8, against it 99.

[Those who voted in the affirmative were Messrs. BOYD, DAVIS of Massachusetts, FISK of Vermont, GROSVENOR, HOPKINS of Kentucky, SHIPHERD, STURGES, and THOMPSON.]

PUBLIC BUILDINGS.

The House then, on motion of Mr. LEWIS, resolved itself into a Committee of the Whole on the bill from the Senate making an appropriation of five hundred thousand dollars, for repairing or rebuilding the public buildings in the City of Washington. [The money is to be borrowed of banks or individuals within the District, at six per cent. interest, for rebuilding or repairing the Capitol, President's House, and public offices, on their present sites.]

A debate arose on this bill which occupied the remainder of the day's sitting.

The advocates of the main object of the bill were, Messrs. LEWIS, FISK of Vermont, RHEA of Tennessee, INGERSOLL, WRIGHT, GROSVENOR, DUVAL, BOWEN, McKIM, SHIPHERD, HAWKINS, and PEARSON; its opponents, Messrs. ALSTON, FARROW, and WEBSTER. Of those who advocated the bill, there were several (Messrs. INGERSOLL, GROSVENOR, DUVALL, and SHIPHERD) who have been in favor of a removal of the Seat of Government; but, considering the question as settled by the votes in both Houses, desired now to see the city rebuilt and beautified.

The debate was not so much on the expediency of rebuilding or repairing the public buildings, as on the mode of doing it.

Mr. GOLDSBOROUGH moved to strike out from the bill the "President's House," so as to confine the repairs to the Capitol and public offices, with a view to leave the repair of the President's House to times of more leisure and tranquillity than the present, and also with a view to a future concentration of the public buildings.

This motion, after debate, was negatived by a large majority.

Mr. GROSVENOR then moved an amendment, the object of which was, to cause the public offices to be removed to the public grounds on Capitol Hill, near the Capitol. This motion, after debate, was agreed to, 66 to 56.

The Committee then rose and reported the amendments to the House; and the House forthwith adjourned.

1133   HISTORY OF CONGRESS.   1134

FEBRUARY, 1815.   *The Reward of Valor—Public Buildings.*   H. OF R.

WEDNESDAY, February 8.

Mr. EPPES, from the Committee of Ways and Means, reported sundry amendments to the bill authorizing the issue of Treasury notes for 1815; which were referred to a Committee of the Whole.

Mr. JACKSON, of Virginia, from the Military Committee, reported without amendment a bill from the Senate concerning field officers in the militia.

[This bill provides that, after the first day of March next, there shall be to each regiment, instead of the present field officers, one colonel, one lieutenant colonel, and two majors.]

The question being stated, "Shall the bill be read a third time?"

Mr. TAYLOR, of New York, moved to refer it to a Committee of the Whole.

Mr. SMITH, of New York, supported the motion for reference or postponement, with a view to proposing amendments for the better organization of the militia in other respects, and for providing the manner in which future detachments of the militia shall be regulated.

The motion was opposed by Mr. JACKSON, of Virginia, but was decided in the affirmative—54 to 41.

Mr. JACKSON, from the same committee, reported a bill making provision for clothing the militia called into the service of the United States.

[The bill proposes to provide that, in addition to the pay and emoluments now provided by law, the non-commissioned officers and privates in the militia, when called into service for a tour of six months, shall be entitled to one suit of clothes.]

The bill was twice read, and committed.

THE REWARD OF VALOR.

Mr. TROUP, from the Committee on Military Affairs, reported the following resolutions, the adoption of which is recommended by the said committee, viz:

Resolved, by the Senate and House of Representatives of the United States of America in Congress assembled, That the President of the United States be, and he is hereby, requested to cause a monument to be erected at a suitable place, and with a suitable inscription, in testimony of the high sense entertained by Congress of the military virtues of the late Brigadier General Pike, who, gallantly leading a column to the attack of York, in Upper Canada, fell, in the arms of victory, on the 27th April, 1812, terminating gloriously a life devoted to his country, and leaving behind him an honorable example of enterprise, perseverance, and contempt of death, for the imitation of the American soldier.

2. *Resolved,* That the thanks of Congress be, and they are hereby, presented to Major General Harrison and to Governor Shelby, and through them to the officers and men under their command, for their gallantry and good conduct in defeating the combined British and Indian forces under Major General Proctor, on the Thames, in Upper Canada, the 5th of October, 1813, capturing the entire British army, with their baggage, camp equipage, and artillery; and that the President of the United States be requested to cause gold medals

to be struck, emblematical of this triumph, and presented to General Harrison and Governor Shelby.

3. *Resolved,* That Congress entertain a high sense of the gallantry and good conduct of Lieutenant Colonel Beatty, and the officers and men under his command, in repulsing, with inferior numbers, the combined attack of a British land and naval force on Craney Island, on the 22d of June, 1813; and that the President of the United States be requested to present an elegant sword to Lieutenant Colonel Beatty.

4. *Resolved,* That Congress entertain a high sense of the merit of Colonel Croghan, and the officers and men under his command, for the gallant defence of Fort Stephenson, on the Lower Sandusky, on the 1st and 2d of August, 1813, repelling with great slaughter the assault of a British and Indian army much superior in number; and that the President be requested to present an elegant sword to Colonel Croghan.

5. *Resolved,* That the President of the United States be requested to cause a monument to be erected, at a suitable place and with a suitable inscription, to the memory of Brigadier General Covington, who, gallantly leading up his troops to a successful charge, fell in the battle of Williamsburg, in Upper Canada, on the 11th November, 1813.

6. *Resolved,* That the thanks of Congress be, and they are hereby, presented to Major General Jackson, and to Brigadier Generals Floyd and Coffee, and through them to the officers and men under their command, for their gallantry and good conduct in the campaign against the Creek Nation of Indians in the Winter of 1813-'14, defeating formidable tribes of savages in successive battles, fought with great obstinacy, and finally subduing them to terms of peace; and that the President of the United States be requested to cause gold medals to be struck, with suitable emblems and devices, and presented to Major General Jackson, and Brigadiers Floyd and Coffee.

7. *Resolved,* That Congress entertain a high sense of the merit of Lieutenant Colonel Armistead, and the officers and men under his command, in their late gallant and successful defence of Fort McHenry against the attack of a formidable British squadron; and that the President of the United States be requested to present an elegant sword to Lieutenant Colonel Armistead.

8. *Resolved,* That Congress entertain a high sense of the merit of Major Lawrence, and the officers and men under his command, in their late gallant defence of Fort Bowyer, repelling with inferior numbers, and with great slaughter, the combined attack of a British land and naval force, aided by a body of savages; and that the President of the United States be requested to present an elegant sword to Major Lawrence.

The resolutions were twice read, and referred to a Committee of the Whole.

PUBLIC BUILDINGS.

The House resumed the consideration of the report of the Committee of the Whole, on the bill for making appropriations for repairing or rebuilding the public buildings in the city of Washington.

That amendment being under consideration which requires the public offices to be built on Capitol Hill—

Mr. LEWIS, of Virginia, rose and said, that he hoped the House would not concur in the amendment made in Committee of the Whole. After the lengthy discussion of this subject yesterday, it was with extreme reluctance that he again obtruded himself upon the patience of the House; but the deep stake which the State he had the honor to represent, in part, had in its decision, he trusted would be a sufficient apology.

Mr. L. said, that since yesterday, he had been enabled to fortify the opinions he had advanced in opposition to the amendment, by an authority which ought to be revered by all. He had obtained the correspondence between General Washington, then President of the United States, and Mr. Adams his successor, and the commissioners for the city, upon the subject of the location of the public offices, which he would take the liberty of reading. He then read a letter from Mr. White, one of the commissioners, who stated "that in a 'conversation with General Washington, upon the 'subject of the location of the public buildings, the '. General was decidedly of opinion, that the offices ' of the different departments should be as conve-'nient to the President as possible, and that it was ' unnecessary, for any public convenience, that they ' should be contiguous to the Legislative Hall; in-'deed, that the officers had complained to him, ' when in Philadelphia, that it was impossible to at-'tend to their public duties from the constant calls ' of the members, and that they were obliged to ' deny themselves." He also read a letter from the commissioners of the city, to General Washington, at Mount Vernon, requesting him to fix on the sites for the public offices, and his answer, fixing a day for that purpose—and a letter from Mr. Adams, ratifying and confirming the acts of the commissioners in fixing the sites of the public offices under the direction of General Washington.

Thus then, said Mr. L., we have not only the opinion of that illustrious man, as to the most proper sites for the public offices, but we have evidence that ought to satisfy the most incredulous, that he actually came upon the ground, and marked the very spots upon which the buildings were to be placed, and these acts were officially confirmed by his successor, Mr. Adams. But my honorable friend from New York (Mr. Grosvenor) has said, that General Washington had been teased and importuned by those interested, into the location he had made. Sir, said Mr. L., my honorable friend can know little of the character of that great man, if he believes there existed a being who dared approach him in that way. No, sir, as soon would he attempt to grasp the forked lightning, as to intimate a wish that he would swerve from his public duty.

There were many considerations, said Mr. L., why no changes ought to be made in the present plan of the city, or of the sites for the public buildings; and that which operated most irresistibly with him was, that it was a plan sanctioned by that great and good man, whose name it bears. Sir, said Mr. L., what that man has done, let no mortal attempt to undo. His ways are not to be mended by man. This House is not competent to do it. He considered the two public edifices, the foundation stones of which our ever to be revered hero, statesman, and patriot, laid, as permanently fixed, by public faith; particularly as maps were distributed throughout Europe, with the sanction of President Washington, designating the sites of the Capitol, President's House, and other public buildings, and that foreigners had been induced to purchase property, judging of its value from its contiguity to some one of the public edifices as marked upon the map. Change the situation of your city, and they are deceived and injured; hereafter they will have no confidence in your acts. We have been told, that large quantities of our public stock have been lately sent to Holland for sale. Is it to be believed, sir, with a knowledge of what we are about to do, (for it is in that country that our city lots have been sold, and held as security for money borrowed,) that they will trust us for a cent, when everything which they deemed sacred is thus violated? No, sir, they will not, and I will say, they ought not to trust us. But, sir, if we have no regard to our plighted faith to foreigners, let us at least save our own people. Do not, by this act, ruin thousands of honest, industrious mechanics, who have at very advanced prices purchased and improved lots near the present sites, under an assurance and firm belief in their permanency. Let us not do an act which will excite distrust abroad and contempt at home.

But, why are gentlemen desirous of removing the offices from their present sites near the President's House, to the Capitol square? It had been shown, he hoped satisfactorily, that their appropriate place was near the President's House, and not the Capitol. The President must necessarily have considerable intercourse with the offices; but he was unable to see the necessity of any personal intercourse between the members of the Legislature and the offices. It is known that all public business between Congress or its members, and the public offices, is done by a resolution of the House, or by letter from any individual member, which is conveyed by a messenger of Congress paid for that purpose.

In addition to the reasons given for a preference of the old sites, there would be a saving of more than one half of the expense. The committee, to whom this subject was confided, attended personally at the Capitol, and examined the state of that building, when, after a conference, and making such inquiries of an architect on the spot, as was considered proper, they were induced to believe that the walls of both wings of the Capitol might be safely built on, and that the estimated expense of about $250,000 for repairing the same, was as nearly accurate, as could be reasonably expected. The President's House and the offices were not so particularly examined, but it was the opinion of the committee, that the whole might be repaired for about $500,000, which would be $715,110 less than the first cost of those buildings. But, Mr. L. said there was another objection which would be, with him, an insuperable one; and that was, that he would not be compelled by an act of the enemy to abandon, or change in the smallest degree, any of the plans of the public edifices they had destroyed.

1137   HISTORY OF CONGRESS.   1138

FEBRUARY, 1815.   *Public Buildings.*   H. OF R.

He would rebuild them precisely on the same ground; not a stone or brick should be changed, but they should be finished in a style of increased magnificence and grandeur. It never should be said, because the enemy had destroyed our Capitol, that Congress were afraid to rebuild it, lest it might again be destroyed. No, let us have another trial, and if we cannot then defend our Capitol, it will be time to put an end to the war in the best way we can. My friend from North Carolina (Mr. GASTON) objects to an appropriation of so much money at a time like this, when the Treasury is bankrupt, our soldiers unpaid, &c., for repairing the public buildings; but he has no objection to double the sum for the purpose of rebuilding on new sites. How inconsistent! The gentleman from North Carolina ought to recollect, that not a cent of this appropriation would come out of the Treasury. The banks of the District had generously and magnanimously come forward and offered to loan the amount wanted upon reasonable terms, for the accomplishment of an object so interesting to the District; and it was probable that the sales of lots belonging to the public in the city, would furnish money enough to reimburse the loan before it became due. Reject this amendment—pass this bill, which will restore public confidence, and there will be no difficulty in selling, at good prices, the property of the public, which is now worthless. My friend from New Hampshire (Mr. WEBSTER) says, he does not think this a proper time to make an appropriation for building up the Capitol, and recommends that some trifling alterations be made in the present room, which will then answer very well until we have peace. Mr. L. said, he congratulated his friend upon the sudden change of his feelings. It was but a few days since, the gentleman could not exist in this confined, inconvenient, and unwholesome room, and nothing but the pure atmosphere of Philadelphia would satisfy him; but now it seems, when it is ascertained he cannot get to Philadelphia, that he is perfectly reconciled with the present room, and thinks it good enough for war times. The gentleman from New Hampshire also complains, that this city is deficient in population, in wealth and commerce, and therefore an improper place for the seat of Government. If it be true that it is thus deficient, to what, I ask, is it to be ascribed? Let those who, like the gentleman from New Hampshire, are desirous of removing the seat of Government, answer. It is to the repeated efforts to remove, to retrocede, and to concentrate, which have been alternately made for the last twelve years in Congress, that the population and wealth of Washington have not equalled any other town on the continent of its age. What prudent man, I ask, would risk his fortune in making improvements in a place, that was every year threatened with destruction, by the very power who ought to foster and protect it? If inconveniences have been felt from the dispersed population of the city and the want of accommodations, those alone are accountable who by their own acts have produced both. The people of this District are political or-

phans. They have been abandoned by their legitimate parents, and claim protection of us, who are constitutionally bound to protect them; but, instead of extending to them the parental hand of affection and assistance, we cruelly abandon them to their fate. If they ask us for bread, we give them a stone. If they even ask us for justice, we tell them they are rudely importunate. Instead of extending to them the parental hand of affection, we do all in our power to blight and destroy their fair prospects. If we are not disposed to be their guardians and friends, let us at least do nothing to injure them; let them pursue undisturbed their own way, and you will not have to complain of the want of population, wealth, or accommodations in the city. There are few places in the United States possessing greater commercial advantages than Washington; placed at the head of an excellent navigation, supported by an extensive and wealthy back country in Virginia and Maryland, and in a climate extremely healthy; if it has but fair play it will soon rival many of the most important towns in the Union, in wealth and population.

The public are greatly interested in promoting the welfare of the city, as it would make very valuable a large property given by the proprietors of the land on which the city stands, which at present is worth nothing. The proprietors of the city gave the land to the public, with an understanding that the sites for the public buildings should remain unchanged; therefore the present alteration would be unjust as to them. The States of Virginia and Maryland have both a deep stake in the permanency of the seat of Government. Virginia made a donation of $120,000, and a cession of a moiety of ten miles square of her territory, including a town which was the pride of the State. Maryland made a donation of $75,000 and a cession of a moiety of ten miles square of her territory, including a town, second to one only in the State; and these States will not view with complacency any act which may have a tendency to jeopardize the Seat of Government.

All the country within fifty miles of the seat of Government, both in Virginia and Maryland, are greatly interested in the welfare of the city, and representing, as I do, an adjoining district, whose property would diminish at least 50 per cent. in value, if the Government is removed, I trust I shall be excused for the solicitude I have manifested, and the time I have occupied in the discussion.

The amendment was also opposed by Messrs. MASON, FORSYTH, and others, and advocated by Messrs. GROSVENOR and WRIGHT.

The question having been taken after much debate, by yeas and nays, was decided—For the amendment 55, against it 77; as follows:

YEAS—Messrs. Anderson, Baylies of Massachusetts, Bigelow, Boyd, Bradbury, Brigham, Cannon, Cilley, Condict, Cooper, Cox, Culpeper, Davenport, Davis of Massachusetts, Davis of Pennsylvania, Desha, Duvall, Ely, Farrow, Findley, Goldsborough, Grosvenor, Henderson, Hulbert, Ingham, Irwin, Kennedy, King of Massachusetts, Law, Lovett, Markell, Pickering, Pitkin,

Potter, John Reed, William Reed, Ruggles, Schureman, Slaymaker, Smith of New York, Stanford, Stockton, Stuart, Taggart, Taylor, Thompson, Voss, Ward of Massachusetts, Ward of New Jersey, Webster, Wheaton, Wilcox, Wilson of Pennsylvania, Winter, and Wright.

NAYS—Messrs. Alexander, Alston, Avery, Barbour, Bard, Barnett, Bayly of Virginia, Bines, Bowen, Breckenridge, Brown, Burwell, Butler, Champion, Clendenin, Comstock, Conard, Crawford, Crouch, Evans, Fisk of Vermont, Fisk of New York, Forney, Forsyth, Franklin, Geddes, Gholson, Goodwyn, Gourdin, Griffin, Hall, Harris, Hasbrouck, Hawes, Hawkins, Hubbard, Humphreys, Hungerford, Jackson of Rhode Island, Jackson of Virginia, Johnson of Kentucky, Kent of Maryland, Kerr, Kershaw, Kilbourn, King of North Carolina, Lefferts, Lewis, Lyle, Macon, McCoy, McKim, McLean, Moore, Nelson, Newton, Ormsby, Pearson, Piper, Pleasants, Rea of Pennsylvania, Rhea of Tennessee, Ringgold, Roane, Sage, Sevier, Sharp, Sheffey, Smith of Pennsylvania, Smith of Virginia, Strong, Sturges, Troup, Udree, White, Williams, and Yancey.

The effect of this decision is, that the public offices shall be rebuilt on their old sites.

Mr. BIGELOW moved to amend the bill so as to require the President, previously to expending the money to be appropriated, to cause to be laid before Congress a plan and estimates for the buildings; by which, he believed, one-half of the expense might be saved.

This motion was opposed as unnecessary, by Mr. LEWIS, and negatived—ayes 39.

Mr. FARROW assigned the reasons why he should vote against the bill; not because he was against rebuilding, but because of the great scarcity of money in the Treasury.

Mr. STANFORD moved to recommit the bill, with instructions to make some report as to concentration, and the manner and method of executing the provisions of the bill.

This motion was opposed by Mr. LEWIS, and negatived—ayes 44.

The question on ordering the bill to be read a third time, was then decided as follows:

YEAS—Messrs. Alexander, Avery, Barbour, Bard, Barnett, Bayly of Virginia, Bines, Bowen, Breckenridge, Burwell, Calhoun, Champion, Cox, Crawford, Creighton, Culpeper, Duvall, Evans, Findley, Fisk of Vermont, Fisk of New York, Forney, Forsyth, Franklin, Gholson, Goodwyn, Gourdin, Griffin, Harris, Hasbrouck, Hawes, Hawkins, Hubbard, Hungerford, Johnson of Kentucky, Kennedy, Kent of Maryland, Kershaw, Kilbourn, Lefferts, Lewis, Macon, McCoy, McKim, McLean, Moore, Newton, Ormsby, Pearson, Pickens, Pleasants, Rhea of Tennessee, Rich, Ringgold, Roane, Sage, Sevier, Sharp, Sheffey, Smith of Pennsylvania, Smith of Virginia, Stuart, Sturges, Telfair, Troup, White, and Yancey—67.

NAYS—Messrs. Alston, Baylies of Massachusetts, Bigelow, Boyd, Bradbury, Brigham, Brown, Cilley, Conard, Cooper, Crouch, Davis of Massachusetts, Davis of Pennsylvania, Ely, Eppes, Farrow, Gaston, Geddes, Goldsborough, Henderson, Humphreys, Hulbert, Ingham, Kerr, King of Massachusetts, Law, Lovett, Markell, Murfree, Pickering, Piper, Potter, John Reed, William Reed, Rea of Pennsylvania, Ruggles, Schureman, Slaymaker, Smith of New York, Stanford, Stockon Strong, Taggart, Taylor, Thompson, Udree, Vose,

Ward of Massachusetts, Ward of New Jersey, Webster, Wheaton, Wilcox, Williams, Wilson of Pennsylvania, and Winter—55.

THURSDAY, February 9.

Mr. FISK, of New York, submitted the following resolution; which was read, and ordered to lie on the table:

Resolved, That the rules of this House be so amended, that officers who have received, or shall hereafter receive, the thanks of Congress for their gallantry and good conduct, displayed in the service of their country, shall be admitted to seats within the walls of this House.

On motion of Mr. JOHNSON, of Kentucky, the Committee of Ways and Means were instructed to inquire into the expediency of establishing, in the State of Kentucky, a loan office, and in such other States in which no such office is established.

A message from the Senate informed the House that the Senate have passed a bill "to allow a drawback of duties on spirits distilled, and certain goods, wares, and merchandise, manufactured within the United States, on the exportation thereof to any foreign port or place." They have also passed the bill from this House "for the relief of Benjamin Wells and others," with amendments; in which bill and amendments they request the concurrence of this House.

An engrossed bill in addition to the act regulating the Post Office Establishment was read a third time; and the further consideration postponed till to-morrow.

PUBLIC ROADS.

Mr. LATTIMORE, from the committee appointed to inquire into the expediency of repairing and keeping in repair the road from Nashville to Natchez, as also the road from Fort Hawkins in Georgia, to St. Stephen's in the Mississippi Territory, delivered in a report, accompanied by a bill making an appropriation for repairing the road from Nashville to Natchez; which was read twice and committed. The report is as follows:

It appears, by a treaty concluded with the Choctaws on the 25th October, 1801, and another with the Choctaws on the 17th December in the same year, that the consent of these Indians was obtained to the opening of a wagon road through their respective lands; and by an act of Congress of the 21st April, 1806, that six thousand dollars was appropriated to this purpose; which was effected, as provided by those treaties and this act, under the direction of the President of the United States. It appears also by a treaty with the Creek Indians, concluded on the 14th November, 1805, that the United States have a right to a horse-path through their lands; and, by the act above-mentioned, that six thousand dollars was appropriated for the purpose of opening a road from the frontier of Georgia, on the route from Athens to New Orleans, as far as the thirty-first degree of north latitude; which was likewise effected, as provided, under the direction of the President of the United States.

Although the country through which these roads respectively pass is, naturally, as convenient for the purposes of transportation and intercourse as any other parts of the United States, yet, considering its great extent, it is not presumed that the appropriations heretofore made could have been considered as adequate to any other object than that of merely opening the roads. The necessary bridges over the streams, and the necessary causeways through the swamps on these extensive routes, would in the opinion of your committee require of themselves larger sums than those mentioned above.

Your committee deem it wholly unnecessary to offer any general remarks to show the great national advantages of an easy and certain intercourse between distant parts of the United States. The sense of Congress on this subject is already well ascertained, from the large and liberal appropriations bestowed on the great Western road from the Potomac to the Ohio river. Without entering into comparisons as to which parts of the Union most require the provident attention of Government, in relation to this subject, it appears to your committee that the improvement of the roads in question, under the direction and at the expense of the National Government, is at all times recommended by a consideration of the importance of the country to which they lead, as well as the want of both authority and means to make it in the territory through which they pass. At this time the subject is rendered unusually interesting, from the efforts of the enemy to seize upon the emporium of an immense country, as well as other positions in the same quarter of less, though great, importance to the United States. So long as the war continues, New Orleans and other adjacent parts will be liable to invasion, and will of course require no inconsiderable force for their defence. During such a state of things, it is highly desirable—indeed necessary—that good roads should facilitate the transmission of intelligence, as well as the march of troops and the transportation of supplies, when a passage by water may be too hardy or wholly impracticable.

The improvements of these roads being deemed expedient by your committee, the next inquiry is, in what way can this end be best obtained? How far it might be proper to effect this purpose by the incorporation of a turnpike company, your committee are not prepared to say. Several objections have presented themselves in considering such a plan; but whether, under other circumstances, it would be advisable or not, its slow execution would necessarily defer the advantages which, in the present state of affairs, it is desirable promptly to enjoy. As the immediate interest of the public is the particular consideration which induces your committee to recommend the improvement of these roads, and as they believe that it cannot be so well promoted in any other way as by a special appropriation, they have prepared a bill for the purpose of improving the road from Nashville to Natchez, which they ask leave to report.

PUBLIC BUILDINGS.

The bill from the Senate making an appropriation for rebuilding or repairing the public buildings in the City of Washington was read a third time.

Mr. PICKERING spoke against the bill, on the general ground of opposition to the permanency of the seat of Government.

A motion was made by Mr. WEBSTER, that the said bill be recommitted to a select committee, with instructions so to alter the bill as to appropriate twenty thousand dollars to the preservation of the public buildings in the City of Washington, and to the improvement and repairs of the building in which Congress now sit, for its better accommodation therein—said sum to be paid out of any moneys in the Treasury not otherwise appropriated—and to strike out of the bill the appropriation of the sum of five hundred thousand dollars.

This motion was advocated by the mover, and by Messrs. GROSVENOR, GASTON, WRIGHT, and ALSTON; and opposed by Messrs. LEWIS, FISK of New York, RHEA of Tennessee, and McKIM. The debate was long and warmly contested by the affirmative side of the House.

The question being taken thereon, it was determined in the negative—yeas 67, nays 79, as follows:

YEAS—Messrs. Alston, Baylies of Massachusetts, Bigelow, Boyd, Bradbury, Brigham, Brown, Butler, Cannon, Cilley, Condict, Cooper, Cox, Davenport, Davis of Massachusetts, Davis of Pennsylvania, Desha, Duvall, Ely, Eppes, Farrow, Gaston, Geddes, Goldsborough, Grosvenor, Henderson, Humphreys, Hulbert, Ingham, Irving, Jackson of Rhode Island, Kent of New York, King of Massachusetts, Law, Lovett, Markell, Moseley, Murfree, Pickering, Piper, Pitkin, Potter, John Reed, William Reed, Rea of Pennsylvania, Ruggles, Schureman, Sherwood, Slaymaker, Smith of New York, Stanford, Stockton, Strong, Taggart, Taylor, Thompson, Udree, Vose, Ward of Massachusetts, Ward of New Jersey, Webster, Wheaton, Wilcox, Wilson of Massachusetts, Wilson of Pennsylvania, Winter, and Wright.

NAYS—Messrs. Alexander, Anderson, Avery, Barbour, Bard, Barnett, Bayly of Virginia, Bines, Bowen, Breckenridge, Calhoun, Champion, Clendenin, Conard, Crawford, Creighton, Crouch, Culpeper, Cuthbert, Earle, Evans, Findley, Fisk of Vermont, Fisk of New York, Forsyth, Franklin, Gholson, Goodwyn, Griffin, Hall, Harris, Hawes, Hawkins, Hopkins of Kentucky, Hubbard, Hungerford, Ingersoll, Jackson of Virginia, Johnson of Kentucky, Kennedy, Kent of Maryland, Kerr, Kershaw, Kilbourn, King of North Carolina, Lefferts, Lewis, Lyle, Macon, McCoy, McKim, McLean, Moore, Nelson, Ormsby, Pearson, Pickens, Pleasants, Rhea of Tennessee, Rich, Ringgold, Roane, Sage, Sevier, Seybert, Sharp, Sheffey, Shipherd, Smith of Pennsylvania, Smith of Virginia, Stuart, Sturges, Telfair, Troup, White, Williams, Wood, and Yancey.

Mr. TAYLOR moved that the said bill be recommitted to the Committee for the District of Columbia, with instructions to prepare and report to this House amendments for concentrating the public buildings, to be erected in the City of Washington, for the accommodation of the Government.

And the question being taken thereon, it was determined in the negative—yeas 65, nays 78, as follows:

YEAS—Messrs. Alston, Baylies of Massachusetts, Bigelow, Boyd, Bradbury, Brigham, Cannon, Cilley, Cooper, Cox, Culpeper, Davenport, Davis of Massachusetts, Davis of Pennsylvania, Desha, Duvall, Ely, Eppes, Farrow, Gaston, Geddes, Goldsborough, Grosvenor, Hawes, Henderson, Hulbert, Ingham, Kent of New York, Kerr, King of Massachusetts, Law, Lovett, Markell, Montgomery, Moseley, Pickering, Piper, Potter, John Reed, William Reed, Rea of Pennsylvania, Rich, Ruggles, Schureman, Sharp, Sherwood, Shipherd, Slaymaker, Smith of New York, Stanford,

Stockton, Strong, Taggart, Taylor, Thompson, Vose, Ward of Massachusetts, Ward of New Jersey, Webster, Wheaton, Wilcox, Wilson of Massachusetts, Wilson of Pennsylvania, and Wright.

NAYS—Messrs. Alexander, Anderson, Avery, Barbour, Bard, Barnett, Bayly of Virginia, Bines, Bowen, Breckenridge, Brown, Burwell, Calhoun, Champion, Crawford, Creighton, Crouch, Cuthbert, Earle, Evans, Findley, Fisk of Vermont, Fisk of New York, Forsyth, Franklin, Gholson, Goodwyn, Gourdin, Griffin, Hall, Harris, Hawkins, Hopkins of Kentucky, Hubbard, Humphreys, Hungerford, Ingersoll, Irwin, Jackson of Rhode Island, Johnson of Virginia, Johnson of Kentucky, Kennedy, Kent of Maryland, Kerr, Kershaw, Kilbourn, King of North Carolina, Lefferts, Lewis, Lyle, Macon, McCoy, McKim, McLean, Moore, Nelson, Newton, Ormsby, Pearson, Pickens, Pleasants, Rhea of Tennessee, Ringgold, Roane, Sage, Sevier, Sheffey, Smith of Pennsylvania, Smith of Virginia, Stuart, Sturges, Telfair, Troup, Udree, White, Williams, Wood, and Yancey.

After much zealous debate, the question was then taken, Shall the bill pass? and passed in the affirmative—yeas 78, nays 63, as follows:

YEAS—Messrs. Alexander, Anderson, Archer, Avery, Barbour, Bard, Barnett, Bayly of Virginia, Bines, Bowen, Breckenridge, Burwell, Calhoun, Champion, Clendenin, Crawford, Creighton, Culpeper, Cuthbert, Duvall, Earle, Evans, Findley, Fisk of Vermont, Fisk of New York, Forsyth, Franklin, Gholson, Goodwyn, Gourdin, Hall, Harris, Hasbrouck, Hawes, Hawkins, Hopkins, Hubbard, Hungerford, Ingersoll, Jackson of Virginia, Johnson of Kentucky, Kennedy, Kent of Maryland, Kershaw, Kilbourn, King of North Carolina, Lefferts, Lewis, Lowndes, Lyle, Macon, McCoy, McKim, McKee, Moore, Nelson, Newton, Ormsby, Pearson, Pickens, Pleasants, Rhea of Tennessee, Rich, Ringgold, Roane, Sage, Sevier, Seybert, Sharp, Shipherd, Smith of Pennsylvania, Smith of Virginia, Stuart, Sturges, Telfair, Troup, White, Wood, and Yancey.

NAYS—Messrs. Alston, Baylies of Massachusetts, Bigelow, Boyd, Bradbury, Brigham, Brown, Butler, Cannon, Cilley, Cox, Crouch, Davenport, Davis of Mass., Desha, Ely, Eppes, Farrow, Gaston, Goldsborough, Greevenor, Henderson, Humphreys, Hulbert, Ingham, Irwin, Jackson of Rhode Island, Kent of New York, Kerr, King of Massachusetts, Law, Lovett, Markell, Moseley, Oakley, Pickering, Piper, Potter, John Reed, William Reed, Rea of Pennsylvania, Ruggles, Schureman, Slaymaker, Smith of New York, Stanford, Strong, Taggart, Taylor, Thompson, Udree, Vose, Ward of Massachusetts, Ward of New Jersey, Webster, Wheaton, Wilcox, Williams, Wilson of Massachusetts, Wilson of Pennsylvania, Winter, and Wright.

FRIDAY, February 10.

Mr. EPPES, from the Committee of Ways and Means, reported a bill making appropriations for the support of the Navy of the United States for the year 1815; which was read twice, and committed to a Committee of the Whole.

Mr. EPPES, from the same committee, also reported a bill making appropriations for the support of the Military Establishment for the year 1815; which was read twice, and committed to a Committee of the Whole.

Mr. YANCEY, from the Committee of Claims,
reported a bill for the relief of Charles Todd; which was read twice, and committed to a Committee of the Whole.

Mr. YANCEY, from the same committee, reported a bill to authorize the payment for horses lost in the public service in the Northwestern army, or in the campaigns under Generals Jackson and Floyd, in the present war; which was read twice, and committed to a Committee of the Whole.

Mr. WOOD, from the committee to whom was referred the petition of John McMaster, reported a bill for the relief of John McMaster; which was read twice, and committed to a Committee of the Whole.

On motion of Mr. FISK, of New York, the House proceeded to consider the resolution submitted by him yesterday, to amend the standing rules and orders of the House, and the same being again read and amended was agreed to, as follows, to wit:

Resolved, That the rules of this House be so amended, that officers who, by name, have received, or shall hereafter receive, the thanks of Congress for their gallantry and good conduct displayed in the service of their country, shall be admitted to seats within the hall of this House.

The amendments proposed by the Senate to the bill "for the relief of Benjamin Wells and others," were read, and concurred in by the House.

The bill from the Senate, "to allow a drawback of duties on spirits distilled, and certain goods, wares, and merchandise, manufactured within the United States, on the exportation thereof to any foreign port of place," was read twice, and referred to the Committee of Ways and Means.

An engrossed bill in addition to the act regulating the Post Office Establishment was read the third time and passed.

The House then, on motion of Mr. JACKSON of Virginia, resolved itself into a Committee of the Whole, on the bill making provision for clothing the militia, called into the service of the United States; and, after some debate thereon, the Committee rose, reported progress, and obtained leave to sit again.

MONEY LOST BY A PAYMASTER.

Mr. YANCEY, from the Committee of Claims, made a report on the petition of John Palmer Cox, which was read, and referred to a Committee of the Whole on Monday next. The report is as follows:

That the petitioner is a paymaster to a regiment of New York militia commanded by Colonel Anthony D. Lameter, and which, in the month of August last, was stationed at Harlem Heights, in the city of New York; that he had received of the United States several thousand dollars, to pay off the militia, which he had deposited in a small trunk about eighteen inches in length, and which he usually kept locked up in a closet in his bed-chamber, until, by indisposition, he was confined to his bed, when he had the same brought and placed on the floor of the room, near the side of his bed; that, on the evening of the 31st of October last, the petitioner, and some other officers who lived in the room with him, went to a neighboring house to take tea, leaving the trunk in the room; and, when they returned, it was gone.

It appears from the depositions of Maria and Sophia Grensebeck, which were referred to the committee, that, on the 24th of December last they saw the trunk lying in the bushes, some distance from their father's house on Harlem Heights; and that, as soon as they saw it, they knew it at a distance to be the trunk of the petitioner.

They gave information to their father, who carried the trunk to his house, and sent for a Mr. Henry Post to come and open it, and view its contents. He opened the trunk, and found it contained $137 37½, and many papers belonging to the petitioner.

The petitioner states that he had in the trunk, at the time it was stolen, $2,587. One deponent swears that he verily believes that sum was in the trunk when it was taken; and another states that, on the evening the trunk was stolen, he saw the petitioner count the money, and, from the appearance of the bundles of the bills, he believes there was that amount. The petitioner asks relief of Congress.

The committee are of opinion that to the prayer of the petitioner there are several objections:

1. That the loss of the money, and the amount thereof, are not clearly and satisfactorily shown.

2. That the loss, if it actually did take place, was under such circumstances as would constitute negligence on the part of the petitioner.

3. That if the money actually was stolen from the petitioner, without any negligence on his part, the United States would not be liable for it. It is believed they should not be considered the insurers of money in cases of this description; the same principle has often been established at the present and last session of Congress. They therefore recommend to the House the following resolution:

Resolved, That the prayer of the petitioner ought not to be allowed.

TREASURY NOTES.

The House, on motion of Mr. EPPES, resolved itself into a Committee of the Whole, Mr. BRECKENRIDGE in the Chair, on the bill to authorize the issuing of Treasury notes, for 1815.

The bill was, on motion of Mr. EPPES, so amended as to provide for issuing Treasury notes to an amount not exceeding twenty-five millions of dollars; such of the notes as are of less amount than one hundred dollars, to be transferrable by delivery, (without endorsement,) and all notes of one hundred dollars or upwards, to bear an interest of five and two-fifths per cent.; the notes of the first description, in amounts of one hundred dollars and upwards, to be payable or redeemable in public stock to bear an interest of eight per cent.; those of the latter description to be payable or redeemable in public stock to bear an interest of seven per cent.

The bill, as first reported, proposed an issue of fifteen millions of notes, redeemable in five annual instalments of three millions each, as proposed by the Secretary of the Treasury, for which the land tax was pledged. Connected with this plan, was the intention to propose a loan of twenty-five millions of dollars. The amendments last reported by the financial committee, are connect-

ed with a proposed loan of fifteen millions, thus reversing the proportion of loan and Treasury notes first proposed.

It was stated by Mr. EPPES, that the committee had, on further consideration, deemed a loan to so large an amount as of questionable practicability, and had therefore determined to increase the issue of Treasury notes, and proportionably reduce the loan, and therefore proposed the amendments which were now made to the bill.

The amendments having been reported to the House, were agreed to without debate or opposition; and the bill was ordered to be engrossed for a third reading to-morrow.

SUNDAY MAILS.

The House resolved itself into a Committee of the Whole, on the report of the Committee on Post Offices and Post Roads, that it is *inexpedient* to make any alteration in the present regulations respecting the transportation and opening the mails on the Sabbath.

Mr. FARROW moved to amend the report so as to declare it *expedient,* instead of *inexpedient,* to grant the prayer of the petitioners. This motion was negatived without debate, and the Committee rose and reported the resolution unamended to the House.

Mr. KING, of Massachusetts, moved to lay the report on the table; which motion, after debate, was negatived.

Mr. KING then moved to add to the end of the resolution the words, "during the present war," so as to confine the resolve to the inexpediency of acting on the subject during the present war.

This motion was superseded by a motion of Mr. JACKSON, to postpone the further consideration of the resolution indefinitely, with a view to end the discussion of this subject for the present.

This motion was opposed by Mr. RHEA of Tennessee, Mr. McKIM, and others, and subsequently withdrawn by the mover.

The question on Mr. KING's motion was decided in the negative. For the motion 52, against it 60, as follows:

YEAS—Messrs. Baylies of Massachusetts, Bigelow, Boyd, Bradbury, Breckenridge, Brigham, Butler, Champion, Cilley, Condict, Cox, Culpeper, Davenport, Davis of Pennsylvania, Duvall, Ely, Farrow, Findley, Fisk of Vermont, Forsyth, Hale, Henderson, Hopkins of Kentucky, Hulbert, Jackson of Virginia, Kent of New York, King of Massachusetts, Law, Lewis, Lovett, Lyle, Markell, Montgomery, Moseley, Nelson, Ruggles, Schureman, Sherwood, Shipherd, Slaymaker, Smith of New York, Smith of Pennsylvania, Stanford, Stockton, Stuart, Sturges, Thompson, Vose, Ward of Massachusetts, Wheaton, White, and Wood.

NAYS—Messrs. Alexander, Alston, Avery, Barbour, Barnett, Bines, Brown, Cannon, Comstock, Conard, Crawford, Creighton, Crouch, Cuthbert, Desha, Fisk of New York, Forney, Gholson, Glasgow, Gourdin, Griffin, Hall, Hawes, Hubbard, Humphreys, Hungerford, Ingham, Jackson of Rhode Island, Johnson of Kentucky, Kennedy, Kerr, Kershaw, Kilbourn, King of North Carolina, Lefferts, Macon, McCoy, McKim, McLean, Moore, Murfree, Newton, Ormsby, Pickens, Pleasants, Potter, Rea of Pennsylvania, Rhea of Tennesses, Rich, Ringgold, Roane, Sage, Sevier, Sharp, Smith of Virginia, Tannehill, Taylor, Udree, Williams, and Winter.

Mr. STANFORD then moved to amend the resolution by adding thereto the following: "so far ' as respects the progress of the mail and the issu-' ing of letters on the Sabbath; but that the issuing ' of newspapers under the proper restrictions may ' be prohibited;" which motion was negatived.

The question on concurring in the resolution reported by the committee, was then decided by yeas and nays. For the report 81, against it 41, as follows:

YEAS—Messrs. Alston, Avery, Barbour, Barnett, Bines, Brown, Cannon, Cilley, Clendenin, Comstock, Conard, Crawford, Creighton, Crouch, Desha, Duvall, Eppes, Findley, Fisk of Vermont, Fisk of New York, Forney, Forsyth, Gholson, Goodwyn, Gourdin, Griffin, Hall, Harris, Hasbrouck, Hawes, Hopkins of Kentucky, Hubbard, Humphreys, Hungerford, Ingham, Jackson of Rhode Island, Jackson of Virginia, Johnson of Kentucky, Kennedy, Kent of Maryland, Kerr, Kershaw, Kilbourn, King of North Carolina, Lefferts, Lyle, Macon, McCoy, McKim, McLean, Montgomery, Moore, Murfree, Nelson, Newton, Ormsby, Pickens, Piper, Pleasants, Potter, Rea of Pennsylvania, Rhea of Tennessee, Rich, Ringgold, Roane, Sage, Sevier, Seybert, Sharp, Sherwood, Smith of New York, Smith of Tennessee, Smith of Virginia, Tannehill, Taylor, Telfair, Troup, Udree, Ward of New Jersey, Williams, and Yancey.

NAYS—Messrs. Baylies of Massachusetts, Bigelow, Boyd, Bradbury, Brigham, Butler, Champion, Condict, Cooper, Cox, Culpeper, Davenport, Davis of Massachusetts, Davis of Pennsylvania, Ely, Farrow, Geddes, Hale, Henderson, Hulbert, King of Massachusetts, Law, Lewis, Lovett, Markell, Moseley, John Reed, Ruggles, Schureman, Shipherd, Slaymaker, Stanford, Stockton, Sturges, Taggart, Thompson, Vose, Ward of Massachusetts, Webster, Wharton, and Wilcox.

So it was resolved that it is inexpedient to grant the prayer of the petitioners.

SATURDAY, February 11.

Mr. YANCEY, from the Committee of Claims, reported a bill for the relief of the Eastern Branch Bridge Company; which was read twice, and committed to a Committee of the Whole.

Mr. EPPES, from the Committee of Ways and Means, to whom was referred two resolutions of the House, instructing them to inquire into the expediency of changing certain collection districts, and a petition of sundry inhabitants of the county of Cumberland, in the State of Pennsylvania, made a report; which was read, and ordered to lie on the table.

Mr. JOHN REED, from the Committee of Accounts, to whom was recommitted the bill to compel the Clerk of the House of Representatives, in the Congress of the United States, to give security for the faithful application and disbursement of the contingent fund of the said House, reported the same with an amendment; which was read, and concurred in; and the bill was ordered to be engrossed, and read a third time on Monday next.

Mr. EASTON, from the committee appointed on the 7th instant, reported a bill concerning the lead mines in the county of Washington, in the Territory of Missouri; which was twice read, and committed to a Committee of the Whole.

Ordered, That Mr. CALHOUN be appointed of the Committee on Foreign Relations, in the place of Mr. CLARK, who is absent on leave.

On motion of Mr. WRIGHT, the Committee on Military Affairs were instructed to inquire whether any regulations in the Army are necessary to their better accommodation and comfort.

The House resumed the consideration of Mr. JACKSON'S bill providing for clothing the militia in the service of the United States; which was amended, and then ordered to be engrossed for a third reading.

The engrossed bill to authorize the issuing of Treasury notes for the service of the year 1815, was read a third time, and passed.

Ordered, That the Committee of the Whole be discharged from the consideration of the bill from the Senate "giving further time to complete the surveys and obtain the patents for lands located under Virginia resolution warrants."

A message from the Senate informed the House that the Senate have passed a bill "to incorporate the subscribers to the Bank of the *United States of America*," in which they ask the concurrence of this House.

INDEMNITY TO COLLECTORS.

Mr. EPPES, from the Committee of Ways and Means, to whom was referred the petition of Jeremiah Hill, made the following report:

That the said Hill was indebted to the United States when he left the office of collector at Biddeford. He had officially obtained a judgment against certain persons, for breaches of the act of Congress laying an embargo, and claimed one moiety of the amount as collector. Before any money had been received on the judgment, he insisted on a right of set-off, and refused to pay the balance due from him into the Treasury. The Comptroller directed a suit to be instituted against him. It appears that the marshal had previously levied a part of the amount of the judgment claimed as an off-set by Hill; and that, pending the suit against him, lands were sold by the marshal to satisfy the residue. When the whole amount was received at the Treasury, Mr. Hill was allowed credit for his portion of the judgment, and the Comptroller directed a discontinuance of the suit against him, on the payment of costs. The petitioner claims—

1. The costs incurred in prosecuting the suit against the persons who committed the breach of the embargo law.

2. Reimbursement in the costs of the suit against himself.

3. Compensation for his trouble and expenses in attending to the two suits.

The defendants in the suit brought for the breach of the embargo law were liable for the legal costs of that suit; the petitioner was liable for the costs of the suit brought against himself, the United States not being bound to wait for the receipt of the amount of the judgment which he had obtained against others, before they instituted suit against him for money received as collector; and it appears to the committee that the personal services of the petitioners were amply remunerated by his moiety of the penalty incurred. The following resolution is therefore submitted:

Resolved, That the prayer of the petition ought not to be granted.

PUBLIC ROADS.

The bill from the Senate "in addition to the act to regulate the laying out and making a road from Cumberland, in the State of Maryland, to the State of Ohio," passed through a Committee of the Whole, where it was amended by striking out "one hundred thousand dollars" (the additional sum appropriated) and inserting "twenty thousand."

The question, on concurring in this amendment, was decided by yeas and nays, and stood—for the amendment 62, against it 70, as follows:

YEAS—Messrs. Barnett, Baylies of Massachusetts, Bigelow, Bradbury, Breckenridge, Brigham, Brown, Butler, Cannon, Cilley, Cooper, Crawford, Crouch, Culpeper, Davenport, Davis of Massachusetts, Davis of Pennsylvania, Ely, Farrow, Forney, Franklin, Gaston, Geddes, Goldsborough, Henderson, Hulbert, Jackson of Rhode Island, Kennedy, Kent of New York, Kerr, King of Massachusetts, Law, Lefferts, Lovett, Markell, Moseley, Oakley, Pickering, Piper, Pitkin Potter, John Reed, William Reed, Ruggles, Schureman, Sherwood, Shipherd, Slaymaker, Stanford, Stockton, Strong, Stuart, Taggart, Taylor, Thompson, Vose, Ward of Massachusetts, Wheaton, Wilcox, Wilson of Massachusetts, and Yancey.

NAYS—Messrs. Alexander, Alston, Anderson, Avery, Barbour, Bard, Bayly of Virginia, Bowen, Calhoun, Clendenin, Comstock, Condict, Conard, Cox, Creighton, Cuthbert, Desha, Duvall, Eppes, Findley, Fisk of New York, Gholson, Goodwyn, Gourdin, Griffin, Grosvenor, Hanson, Harris, Hasbrouck, Hawes, Hawkins, Hopkins of Kentucky, Hubbard, Hungerford, Jackson of Virginia, Johnson of Kentucky, Kent of Maryland, Kershaw, Kilbourn, Lewis, Lowndes, Lyle, McCoy, McKee, McKim, McLean, Montgomery, Moore, Murfree, Nelson, Ormsby, Pearson, Pickens, Pleasants, Rea of Pennsylvania, Rhea of Tennessee, Rich, Ringgold, Roane, Sage, Sevier, Seybert, Smith of Virginia, Telfair, Troup, Udree, White, Wilson of Pennsylvania, Winter, and Wright.

So the amendment was rejected; and the bill was ordered to a third reading; and was then read a third time, and passed.

MONDAY, February 13.

A message from the Senate informed the House that the Senate have passed the bill "making appropriations for the support of Government, for the year 1815," with amendments; in which they ask the concurrence of this House.

Mr. INGERSOLL, from the Judiciary Committee, to whom was referred the inquiry into the expediency of increasing the salary of the District Judge of the State of Massachusetts, made a report unfavorable to an increase in this case, separate from the general class of such salaries; which was ordered to lie on the table.

BANK OF THE UNITED STATES.

A message from the Senate announcing the passage of a bill to incorporate the subscribers to the Bank of the United States of America, was brought up, and the bill read a first and second time.

Mr. GASTON moved to refer the bill to the Committee of Ways and Means, with a view to the amendment of its details, which he pronounced to be incorrect and in many respects impracticable.

This motion was opposed by Mr. FORSYTH, and Mr. FISK of New York, who argued in favor of the correctness of the details of the bill, and denied that any other object but delay would be answered by the proposed reference.

The motion was negatived, yeas 59, nays 70.

Mr. SHARP them moved to refer the bill to a select committee, with the following instructions:

1. To strike out all that part of the bill that allows fifteen millions of dollars of the capital of said Bank to be paid in six per cent. stock of the United States heretofore created and now in the hands of stockholders; and then amend the bill so as to allow the Government to take the said fifteen millions on their account.

2. That all the Government subscriptions shall be paid at five per cent. interest.

3. That the Government shall have a number of Directors in the said Bank equal to the proportion it may have of the capital of the Bank; who shall be appointed by the President of the United States.

4. That so long as the Bank shall not be required to pay specie for its notes or bills, or after having commenced paying of specie, shall from any cause stop the payment of the same, the Government shall not be required to pay to the Bank a higher rate of interest on any loans to Government, either as permanent loans or in anticipation of taxes, than four per cent.

5. That the Bank shall not be allowed to sell or transfer any part of the Government stock that it may acquire by permanent loans to Government, until the end of one year after the war.

In support of this motion, Mr. S. made a speech of nearly an hour in length.

Mr. FORSYTH replied to the principal points of this speech at considerable length.

Mr. SHARP explained.

Mr. OAKLEY expressed himself, in a speech of some length, as favorable to some of the objects of the motion of Mr. SHARP, and as preferring them generally to the present provisions of the bill.

Mr. CALHOUN, in a pithy speech of moderate length, expressed himself in favor of commitment, though friendly only to two of the proposed instructions, viz: the reduction of the interest on loans to the Government, and striking out the old stock. He assigned the reasons also why the plan of a bank now before the House did not meet his approbation.

Messrs. HAWKINS, WRIGHT, RHEA, and FORSYTH, further opposed the commitment, and Messrs. OAKLEY, BOWEN, and GASTON, advocated it.

The question on Mr. SHARP's motion having been divided, the question on reference to a select committee was taken separately from the instructions proposed to be given to the committee; and—

On the question of commitment, the vote stood, by yeas and nays, for commitment 75, against it 80, as follows:

YEAS—Messrs. Bard, Baylies of Massachusetts, Bayly of Virginia, Bigelow, Bowen, Boyd, Bradbury, Breckenridge, Brigham, Butler, Calhoun, Champion, Cilley, Cooper, Cox, Crawford, Culpeper, Cuthbert, Davenport, Davis of Massachusetts, Duvall, Ely, Farrow, Gaston, Geddes, Goldsborough, Grosvenor, Hale, Hanson, Hasbrouck, Henderson, Hulbert, Jackson of Rhode Island, Kent of New York, King of Mass., Law, Lewis, Lovett, Lowndes, Markell, McKee, Montgomery, Moseley, Oakley, Pearson, Pickering, Pitkin, Potter, John Reed, William Reed, Ruggles, Schureman, Seybert, Sharp, Shefley, Sherwood, Shipherd, Slaymaker, Smith of New York, Stanford, Stockton, Stuart, Sturges, Taggart, Thompson, Vose, Ward of Massachusetts, Ward of New Jersey, Webster, Wheaton, White, Wilcox, Wilson of Massachusetts, Winter, and Yancey.

NAYS—Messrs. Alexander, Alston, Anderson, Avery, Barbour, Bines, Brown, Caldwell, Cannon, Clendenin, Comstock, Condict, Conard, Creighton, Crouch, Davis of Pennsylvania, Desha, Earle, Eppes, Findley, Fisk of Vermont, Fisk of New York, Forney, Forsyth, Franklin, Gholson, Gourdin, Griffin, Harris, Hawes, Hawkins, Hopkins of Kentucky, Hubbard, Humphreys, Hungerford, Ingersoll, Ingham, Irwin, Jackson of Virginia, Johnson of Kentucky, Kennedy, Kent of Maryland, Kerr, Kershaw, Kilbourn, King of North Carolina, Lefferts, Lyle, Macon, McCoy, McKim, McLean, Moore, Murfree, Nelson, Newton, Ormsby, Parker, Pickens, Piper, Pleasants, Rhea of Tennessee, Rich, Ringgold, Roane, Sage, Sevier, Smith of Pennsylvania, Smith of Virginia, Strong, Tannehill, Taylor, Telfair, Troup, Udree, Williams, Wilson of Pennsylvania, and Wright.

Mr. GASTON then moved to refer the bill to a Committee of the Whole; which motion was decided as follows: For the motion 70, against it 84.

Mr. SHARP then moved to amend the bill by striking out so much as allows the subscription of stock heretofore created.

This motion was supported by Mr. DUVALL, and opposed by Messrs. WRIGHT and HUMPHREYS; and was negatived by yeas and nays. For the motion 72, against it 82, as follows:

YEAS—Messrs. Bard, Barnett, Baylies of Massachusetts, Bayly, of Virginia, Bigelow, Bowen, Boyd, Bradbury, Breckenridge, Brigham, Butler, Calhoun, Champion, Cilley, Cooper, Cox, Crawford, Culpeper, Cuthbert, Davenport, Davis of Massachusetts, Duvall, Ely, Farrow, Gaston, Geddes, Grosvenor, Hale, Hanson, Hasbrouck, Henderson, Hulbert, Jackson of Rhode Island, Kent of New York, King of Massachusetts, Law, Lovett, Lowndes, Markell, McKee, Moseley, Oakley, Pearson, Pickering, Pitkin, Potter, John Reed, William Reed, Ruggles, Schureman, Seybert, Sharp, Shefley, Sherwood, Shipherd, Slaymaker, Smith of New York, Stanford, Stockton, Stuart, Sturges, Thompson, Vose, Ward of Massachusetts, Ward of New Jersey, Webster, Wheaton, White, Wilcox, Wilson of Massachusetts, Winter, and Yancey.

NAYS—Messrs. Alexander, Alston, Anderson, Avery, Barbour, Bines, Brown, Caldwell, Cannon, Clendenin, Comstock, Condict, Conard, Creighton, Crouch, Davis of Pennsylvania, Desha, Eppes, Findley, Fisk of Vt., Fisk

of New York, Forney, Forsyth, Franklin, Gholson, Goldsborough, Goodwyn, Gourdin, Griffin, Hall, Harris, Hawes, Hawkins, Hopkins of Kentucky, Hubbard, Humphreys, Hungerford, Ingersoll, Ingham, Irwin, Jackson of Virginia, Johnson of Kentucky, Kennedy, Kent of Maryland, Kerr, Kershaw, Kilbourn, King of North Carolina, Lefferts, Lewis, Lyle, Macon, McCoy, McKim, McLean, Moore, Murfree, Nelson, Newton, Ormsby, Parker, Pickens, Piper, Pleasants, Rea of Pennsylvania, Rhea of Tennessee, Rich, Ringgold, Roane, Sage, Sevier, Smith of Pennsylvania, Smith of Virginia, Strong, Tannehill, Taylor, Telfair, Udree, Williams, Wilson of Pennsylvania, Wood, and Wright.

Mr. SHARP further moved to amend the said bill by striking out of the 4th line of the 12th rule for the regulation of that institution, the word "six," and inserting in lieu thereof the word "four," being the maximum rate per centum per annum, at which the said institution may charge the Government upon loans.

And the question being taken thereon, it was also determined in the negative—yeas 74, nays 77, as follows:

YEAS—Messrs. Bard, Barnett, Baylies of Massachusetts, Bayly of Virginia, Bigelow, Bowen, Boyd, Bradbury, Breckenridge, Brigham, Butler, Calhoun, Champion, Cilley, Cooper, Cox, Crawford, Culpeper, Davenport, Davis of Pennsylvania, Ely, Farrow, Gaston, Geddes, Goldsborough, Grosvenor, Hale, Hanson, Henderson, Hulbert, Jackson of Rhode Island, Kennedy, Kent of New York, King of Massachusetts, Law, Lewis, Lovett, Macon, Markell, McKee, Moseley, Nelson, Oakley, Pearson, Pickering, Pitkin, Potter, John Reed, William Reed, Ruggles, Schureman, Seybert, Sharp, Shefley, Sherwood, Shipherd, Slaymaker, Smith of New York, Stanford, Stockton, Stuart, Sturges, Taggart, Thompson, Vose, Ward of Massachusetts, Ward of New Jersey, Webster, Wheaton, White, Wilcox, Wilson of Massachusetts, Winter, and Yancey.

NAYS—Messrs. Alexander, Alston, Anderson, Avery, Barbour, Bines, Brown, Caldwell, Calhoun, Clendenin, Comstock, Condict, Conard, Creighton, Cuthbert, Davis of Pennsylvania, Eppes, Findley, Fisk of Vermont, Fisk of New York, Forney, Forsyth, Franklin, Gholson, Gourdin, Griffin, Harris, Hasbrouck, Hawes, Hawkins, Hopkins of Kentucky, Hubbard, Humphreys, Hungerford, Ingersoll, Ingham, Irving, Jackson of Virginia, Johnson of Kentucky, Kent of Maryland, Kerr, Kershaw, Kilbourn, King of North Carolina, Lefferts, Lowndes, Lyle, McCoy, McKim, McLean, Moore, Murfree, Newton, Ormsby, Parker, Pickens, Piper, Pleasants, Rea of Pennsylvania, Rhea of Tennessee, Rich, Ringgold, Roane, Sage, Sevier, Smith of Pennsylvania, Smith of Virginia, Strong, Tannehill, Taylor, Telfair, Udree, Williams, Wilson of Pennsylvania, Wood, and Wright.

TUESDAY, February 14.

Mr. NELSON, from the committee to whom was referred a report of the Secretary of War, on the petition of William Tatham, reported a bill to authorize the Secretary of the War Department to purchase, for the use of the United States, the topographical materials of William Tatham; which was read twice, and committed to a Committee of the Whole.

The House resumed the consideration of the bill from the Senate "to incorporate the subscribers to the Bank of the United States of America;" Whereupon, the bill was ordered to lie on the table.

An engrossed bill requiring the Secretary of the Senate and Clerk of the House of Representatives, in the Congress of the United States, to give security for the faithful application and disbursement of the contingent funds of the Senate and House of Representatives, was read the third time, and passed.

The bill making provision for clothing the militia of the United States when called into the actual service of the United States, was read a third time and passed, by the following vote, by yeas and nays: For the bill 145, against it none.

So the bill was unanimously passed, and sent to the Senate for concurrence.

The amendments of the Senate to the civil list and miscellaneous appropriation bill, were read and agreed to.

The bill for the relief of Uriah Coolidge and others, was passed through a Committee of the Whole, and ordered to be engrossed for a third reading.

The House resolved itself into a Committee of the Whole on the bill granting a donation of three hundred and twenty acres of land to Anthony Shane. The bill was reported without amendment, and ordered to be engrossed, and read the third time to-morrow.

A message from the Senate informed the House that the Senate have passed the bill "for the relief of the inhabitants of the late county of New Madrid, in the Missouri Territory, who suffered by earthquakes," with amendments; in which they ask the concurrence of this House.

WEDNESDAY, February 15.

Mr. WRIGHT, of Maryland, rose to make a motion. Believing, he said, that the war was about to receive a termination, he felt it a duty to those brave patriots who, by their exertions, had placed the character of the country so high that we should never again be disturbed by any foreign Power, unless unhappily intestine division should afford an opportunity to an enemy, to move the following resolution, with a view to redeem the national pledge to those who had enlisted under the banners of their country to defend its soil and enforce its rights. He therefore moved—

"That a committee be appointed to inquire into the expediency of laying off as much of the public lands as shall be necessary to satisfy the claims of the Army of the United States, and of fixing the location thereof."

Mr. W. said he should not press the consideration of this motion to-day, but call for it on some future day.

Mr. NEWTON, of Virginia, offered for consideration the following resolution, which, he said, would speak for itself, and preclude the necessity of any elucidatory remarks:

Resolved, That the President of the United States be requested to cause to be laid before this House such

13th Con. 3d Sess.—37

information as he shall deem necessary to be communicated, touching the state of the relations existing between the United States and the Barbary Powers."

The resolution was agreed to *nem. con.*, and a committee appointed to lay it before the President.

The report of the Committee of Ways and Means, favorable to the petition of Solomon Frazer and Mary Eccleston, was agreed to in Committee of the Whole, and referred to the Committee of Ways and Means to report a bill.

The bill for laying a direct tax on the District of Columbia, was agreed to in Committee of the Whole, and ordered to be engrossed for a third reading.

Mr. YANCEY, from the Committee of Claims, reported a bill for the relief of Thomas Spriggs; which was read twice, and committed to a Committee of the Whole.

Mr. YANCEY, from the same committee, reported a bill for the relief of James Savage and others; which was read twice, and committed to a Committee of the Whole.

Mr. LAW, from the committee appointed on the petition of Anthony B. Ross, reported a bill authorizing the release of Anthony B. Ross from imprisonment; which was read twice, and committed to a Committee of the Whole.

The amendment proposed by the Senate to the bill "for the relief of the inhabitants of the late county of New Madrid, in the Missouri Territory," was read, and concurred in by the House.

Ordered, That the engrossed bill granting a donation of three hundred and twenty acres of land to Anthony Shane, be committed to Messrs. PICKERING, McKEE, and McKIM.

An engrossed bill for the relief of Uriah Coolidge and James Burnham, was read the third time and passed.

Ordered, That the bill from the Senate, "giving further time to complete the surveys and obtain the patents for lands located under Virginia resolution warrants" be read the third time to-morrow.

Ordered, That the Committee of the Whole be discharged from the bill making further provision for filling the ranks of the regular Army by classifying the free male population of the United States, and that the said bill be postponed indefinitely.

A message from the Senate informed the House that the Senate have passed a bill "for the relief of Bowie and Kurtz, and others;" in which they ask the concurrence of this House.

A message from the Senate informed the House that the Senate have passed resolutions of the following titles:

"Expressive of the thanks of Congress to Major General Jackson, and the troops under his command, for their gallantry and good conduct in the defence of New Orleans;"

"Expressive of the high sense entertained by Congress of the gallantry and good conduct of Commodore D. T. Patterson, and Major D. Carmick, and of the officers, seamen, and marines, under their command, in the defence of New Orleans;" and

" Expressive of the high sense entertained by Congress of the patriotism and good conduct of the people of Louisiana and of New Orleans, during the late military operations before that city;" in which several resolutions they ask the concurrence of this House.

The remainder of the day was spent in Committee of the Whole, on the bill to fix the compensations and increase the responsibility of the collectors of the direct tax and internal duties, and for other purposes connected with the collection thereof. The bill was reported to the House; and the House adjourned.

Tuesday, February 16.

The bill from the Senate for the relief of Bowie and Kurtz, and others, late of the ship Alleghany, was read twice, and referred to the Committee of Claims.

The resolutions from the Senate expressive of the high sense of Congress of the gallantry and good conduct of Commodore D. T. Patterson and Major Carmick, and the officers and men under their command in the defence of New Orleans, were twice read, and ordered to a third reading.

A resolution was received from the Senate for the appointment of a joint committee to inquire into the expediency of causing the Chambers, at present occupied by the two Houses of Congress or others in the same building, to be altered and fitted up for their better accommodation.

DEFENCE OF NEW ORLEANS.

The resolutions from the Senate expressive of the thanks of Congress to General Jackson and the troops under his command, for their gallantry in defence of New Orleans, were twice read and amended.

On the question of ordering these and the subsequent resolves to a third reading—

Mr. Troup, of Georgia, said, that he congratulated the House on the return of peace; if the peace be honorable, he might be permitted to congratulate the House on the glorious termination of the war. He might be permitted to congratulate them on the glorious termination of the most glorious war ever waged by any people. To the glory of it General Jackson and his gallant army have contributed not a little. I cannot, sir, perhaps language cannot, do justice to the merits of General Jackson, and the troops under his command, or to the sensibility of the House, I will therefore forbear to trouble the House with the usual prefatory remarks; it is a fit subject for the genius of Homer. But there was a spectacle connected with this subject upon which the human mind would delight to dwell—upon which the human mind could not fail to dwell with peculiar pride and exultation. It was the yeomen of the country marching to the defence of the city of Orleans, leaving their wives, and children, and firesides, at a moment's warning. On the one side, committing themselves to the bosom of the mother of rivers; on the other, taking the route of the trackless and savage wilderness for hundreds of miles. Meeting at the place

of rendezvous—seeking, attacking, and beating the enemy in a pitched battle—repulsing three desperate assaults with great loss to him—killing, wounding, and capturing more than four thousand of his force—and finally compelling him to fly, precipitately, the country he had boldly invaded. The farmers of the country triumphantly victorious over the conquerors of the conquerors of Europe. " I came, I saw, I conquered," says the American husbandman, fresh from his plough. The proud veteran who triumphed in Spain, and carried terror into the warlike population of France, was humbled beneath the power of my arm. The God of Battles and of Righteousness took part with the defenders of their country, and the foe was scattered before us as chaff before the wind. It is, indeed, a fit subject for the genius of Homer, of Ossian, or Milton.

That militia should be beaten by militia is of natural and ordinary occurrence; that regular troops should be beaten by militia is not without example; the examples are as numerous, or more numerous, in our own country, than in any other; but that regular troops, the best disciplined and most veteran of Europe, should be beaten by undisciplined militia with the disproportionate loss of a hundred to one, is, to use the language of the commanding General, almost incredible. The disparity of the loss, the equality of force, the difference in the character of the force, all combine to render the battle of the eighth of January at once the most brilliant and extraordinary of modern times. Nothing can account for it but the rare merits of the commanding General, and the rare patriotism and military ardor of the troops under his command.

Glorious, sir, as are these events to the American arms, honorable as they are to the American character, they are not more glorious and honorable than are the immediate consequences full of usefulness to the country. If the war had continued, the men of the country would have been inspired with a noble ardor and a generous emulation in defence of the country; they would have struck terror into the invader, and given confidence to the invaded. Europe has seen that, to be formidable on the ocean, we need but will it. Europe will see that, to be invincible on land, it is only necessary that we judiciously employ the means which God and Nature have bountifully placed at our disposal. The men of Europe, bred in camps, trained to war, with all the science and all the experience of modern war, are not a match for the men of America taken from the closet, the bar, the court-house, and the plough. If, sir, it be pardonable at any time to indulge these sentiments and feelings, it may be deemed pardonable on the present occasion.

I think the resolution of the Senate defective; it does not record the prominent fact which, more than any other, contributes to the brilliancy of General Jackson's triumph—the fact that the triumph was the triumph of militia over regular troops; on the contrary, it is so worded that strangers or posterity, deriving their knowledge from the record itself, would be led to believe that the regular troops constituted the principal force, and that the militia was only auxiliary. If the House should consider the defect as important, I would move to amend the resolution.

Mr. ROBERTSON spoke as follows:

Mr. Speaker, representing alone on this floor an interesting part of our country, saved by heroism unmatched from horrors which cannot be described, I shall be excused for expressing my admiration of General Jackson, his great achievements, and the splendid battles which we now commemorate.

Permit me too, sir, to avail myself of this occasion to pour forth the gratitude with which I am impressed, not only for the protection of Louisiana, but for the opportunity which has been afforded her citizens of displaying a zeal, a patriotism, and an unanimity, which command the applause of an admiring nation.

Scarce three months are past, since a mighty armada, with troops accustomed to victory, the well fleshed myrmidons of sanguinary European wars, with others collected in the West India Islands, from their description intended to produce terror, led on by chiefs whose fame had filled the universe, directed its course across the Atlantic with a view to desolate a distant portion of our country. They calculated on an easy conquest; never were hopes more confident—never were hopes more effectually blasted.

Pursuing their insidious system, they issued proclamations and sent forth emissaries, to corrupt the unwary, and excite disaffection. They offered to those who should be weak enough to confide in their perfidious promises, protection and liberty under a British constitution. Insolent thought! To whom were those offers addressed? To Americans, who themselves, or whose fathers had once before chased them from their shores covered with disgrace and overwhelmed with dismay. To whom were they addressed? To the natives of Louisiana—to Frenchmen, and their descendants. The English dared to speak to them of peace and fraternity, holding in their hand a sword reeking, as it had reeked for centuries, with the blood of Frenchmen.

Hasty levies of half-armed undisciplined militia, from the interior of our vast continent, from the banks of the Tennessee, the Cumberland, and the Ohio, traversing wide and trackless regions, precipitate themselves to the scene of conflict, resolute to defend their distant brethren from the dangers with which they were menaced. There the hardy sons of the West, with the yeomanry of the adjacent territory and the invaded State, with a handful of regulars and a few armed vessels, constituted that force from which the tremendous armament of our enemy was to experience the most signal overthrow the world has ever witnessed. But Jackson was their leader, and though inexpert in scientific warfare, they were animated by something more valuable than discipline, more irresistible than all the energy which mere machinery can display; they were animated by patriotism—by that holy enthusiasm which surmounts all difficulties and points the way to triumph. Happy if a parallel to their conduct may be found, it must be looked for in the achievements of those who like themselves fought for the liberties of their country. History records, to the consolation of freemen, that the Poles, unarmed and ignorant of tactics, beat the veteran troops of Frederick and Catharine in many pitched battles, never less than three times their numbers—but their leader was Kosciusko. In the early stages of the revolution, the peasantry of France, under Custine and Dumourier, repulsed from their soil the disciplined thousands of the Duke of Brunswick; but it was not the Poles, nor the Frenchmen—it was love of country—it was the cause.

Foiled in their attempt to disseminate distrust and treachery, they now prepared to take by force what fraud had failed to secure.

The defence of Fort Bowyer, the battle of their hundred well manned barges, with five of our gunboats, were a foretaste of what they were further to expect. But, flushed with thoughts of the full fruition of their hopes, they pushed forward to seize the prize just presented to their grasp. They passed unseen through narrow defiles and deep morasses; evaded the natural defence of the State, and found themselves quietly posted on the fertile banks of the Mississippi, in full view of the alluring metropolis of Louisiana, where they had been promised plunder without check and riot without restraint.

Among the wonderful occurrences of that eventful period, the simultaneous arrival at the same distant point of the brave defenders of their country and the daring invader, cannot be considered less miraculous. Confident in its strength, and contemptuous of its foe, the veteran army was unprepared for the reception that awaited it. Suddenly and fiercely attacked, panic struck at the unlooked for blow, they were defeated by half their number of raw American troops. This was conclusive. Their subsequent conduct exhibited little else than a tissue of blunders and misfortunes, or of courageous efforts which recoiled with ruin on themselves.

At length the time arrived which was to witness the most extraordinary event recorded in military annals. On the 8th of January, a day destined to form an era in history, this army of invincibles, led on by gallant chiefs, advanced to the charge with firm step, according to methods most approved—trenches hastily thrown up, defended by what they considered a mob, a vagabond militia, promised an enterprise destitute alike of hazard and of honor. They were met by an incessant and murderous discharge of musketry and artillery, the whole line was a continued sheet of fire; intrepidity stood appalled—their General slain—the ditch filled—the field strewed with the dying and the dead—a miserable remnant of their thousands fled back to their entrenchments. The battle closed, a battle whose character, from the nature of the troops engaged and the disparity of loss, is the most wonderful, whose effects are as important as any that was ever fought. And now we are invited to the contemplation of a scene which reflects immortal honor on the inhabitants of New Orleans, and, by contrast, eternal shame on the enemy.

The dead were interred, the agonies of the dying assuaged, the wounded relieved; that property which was to have been given up to plunder was willingly yielded to their wants, and the very individuals, the marked victims of their licentiousness, vied with each other in extending to them every proof of tenderness and humanity.

It was my intention, Mr. Speaker, to have adverted to the manner in which the English have carried on their war, particularly to their views in regard to New Orleans, but peace is this moment announced; I do not wish to mar the feelings which belong to it; if I cannot forget their atrocities, I disdain to triumph over a disgraced and fallen foe. Whilst resuming my seat I take much satisfaction in doing justice to the indefatigable exertions of the Secretary of War. From the time of his taking charge of that Department, and of being apprized of the danger which threatened Louisiana, no efforts were spared, no applications unattended to, which had for their object the protection of that State.

Mr. Ingersoll said: Mr. Speaker, I regret that these resolutions require any amendment. I am persuaded, however, that their final passage will be unanimous. The House will excuse me, I hope, if I indulge myself in a few observations on this occasion. I speak impromptu, sir, without premeditation—I have found it impossible to think—I have been able only to feel these last three days. The unexpected, the grateful termination of the glorious struggle we have just concluded, is calculated to excite emotions such as can be understood by those only who can feel them. For the first time during this long, arduous and trying session, we can all feel alike—we are all of one mind—all hearts leap to the embraces of each other. Such a spectacle as that now exhibited by the Senate and House of Representatives of the United States of America was never presented to the world before. While the Senate are ratifying a treaty of peace, the House of Representatives are voting heartfelt thanks to those noble patriots, those gallant citizen soldiers who have crowned that peace with imperishable lustre. The terms of the treaty are yet unknown to us. But the victory at Orleans has rendered them glorious and honorable, be they what they may. They must be honorable under such a termination of the war. Those Commissioners who have afforded us such signal credentials of their firmness heretofore, cannot possibly have swerved. The Government has not betrayed its trust. The nation now cannot be discredited. It has done its duty, and is above disgrace. Within five and thirty years of our national existence, we have achieved a second acknowledgment of our national sovereignty. In the war of the Revolution we had allies—in arms—reinforcements from abroad on our own soil—and the wishes of all Europe on our side. But in this late conflict we stood single-handed. Not an auxiliary to support us—not a bosom in Europe that dared beat in our behalf—not one but what was constrained to stifle

its hopes, if it entertained any in our favor. The treaty signed at Paris on the 30th of last May placed us in a situation of the utmost emergency. England had triumphed over France—and she turned upon us with her hands full of the implements of destruction—her heart almost bursting with vengeance and fury—malediction in her manifestoes, subjugation on her sword. We have already voted thanks to those heroes of the North who, in Canada, faced and broke the spell of English invincibility. From the North the tempest rolled on to this neighborhood: And it was in the midst of the ruins—the cinders—of this Capital, which became the momentary prize of a successful incursion—it was at a period the most awful, under difficulties the most appalling, that preparations were made to meet the final, the concentrated onset at New Orleans—the most remote, the weakest point of our territories—the most vulnerable—the hardest to hold, and the hardest to regain, if once lost. For the capture of that city a most formidable force was embodied. All the disposable troops to be spared by England from Europe, the detachments scattered along our coasts, all the garrisons and troops that could be collected from the West India Islands, were concentrated for this last and grand object. The gallant and generous inhabitants of the West flew to arms. It was not their firesides they had to defend. It was in many cases more than a thousand, in all more than five hundred miles from home they were to seek the scene of their exploits. They went with an immortalizing alacrity of patriotism. Every man of them is entitled to a panegyric. There is no distinction but that of rank to be made between them and their wary, their consummate commander. Hardly arrived in New Orleans when the enemy appeared, they instantly attacked him—and in the night time. The result of this immediate intrepidity was their *striking* a salutary respect into the invaders. The conquerors of Europe sent the flower of their armies, under the most eminent of their commanders, on this expedition. On the 28th December and the 1st of January, attempts were made to carry the American lines—but without success, without impression. Finding that their men had learned a reluctance to attack from these experiments, the British officers, on the memorable 8th, threw themselves into the front and led on to the charge. It is this that alone can account for the enormous effusion of officers' blood. Not *relying* on the example thus set, they added moreover those enticements which, at Badajoz and St. Sebastians, had seduced the soldiers to success. They offered beauty and booty—in other words, rape and rapine, as the reward of victory. Thus led and thus invited, the British army made its storm. Their discomfiture is without example. Never was there such a disparity of loss. With the tidings of this triumph from the South, to have peace from the East, is such a fullness of gratification as must overflow all hearts with gratitude to the Giver of all good—to that Being who has saved us from the enemy, who has saved us from all harms. Not to be grateful would be impious—

not to triumph, cold and churlish indeed. England has conquered Europe. In the midst of her conquests she is discontented and unhappy. Europe, relieved from French dominion, is already enslaved afresh, cruelly enslaved. Poland, the richest, finest country on that Continent, with a population romantically free and patriotic, is unnexed to Russia. After fighting the battles of France for the pay of emancipation, Poland falls under the Russian yoke. Saxony, one of the most ancient and repectable of the sovereignties of Europe, is subjoined as a province to Prussia, the most recent, the most despicable of all the European powers—a Kingdom which found a transient consequence in the genius of the great Frederick, which never can be considerable without such a genius to sustain it. The Italians are torn from their homes to serve in Austrian armies. Norway dislocated from Denmark to be forced into the arms of Sweden—France is unsettled—Spain convulsed—Holland swelled into an ephemeral magnitude. What a contrast with this happy, thriving, blessed country! Who does not rejoice that he is not an European! Who is not proud to feel himself an American—our wrongs revenged—our rights recognised! For I repeat, that no matter what the terms of the treaty may be, the effects of this war must be permanently prosperous and honorable. The catastrophe at Orleans has fixed an impress, has sealed, has consecrated the compact beyond the powers of parchment and diplomacy. At sea a tide of triumphs—by land a Continent on which the enemy could gain no foothold. Your Navy transcendent in achievements—your Army at length equalling your Navy. Mr. Speaker, for the richest Kingdom in Europe I would not exchange my American citizenship—for the most opulent endowment I would not surrender the delight which I derive from the feelings of this moment. Let us then pass, let us vote by acclamation, the thanks of Congress to General Jackson and his companions in victory.

I cannot resume my seat, sir, without a word of merited eulogium on an individual not comprehended in these resolutions, but to whom the nation is greatly indebted for his success. I mean the present Secretary at War. From the monumental dilapidations of this Capital, with enemies to provide against on all quarters, those arrangements were made and those aids afforded by the Government which mainly contributed to the glorious result at Orleans. Jackson, to be sure, and his cohort banded together from all regions by his powerful ascendency, were the executors—but the able and honest statesman, who now holds the War Department, was the author and originator of the preparations. Let us therefore—I hope all will agree to it—let us consider him too in our applause.

The resolutions from the Senate expressive of the high sense entertained by Congress of the patriotism and good conduct of the people of Louisiana and New Orleans during the late military operations before that city, were twice read, and ordered to a third reading.

Mr. ROBERTSON said he was prevented from taking any part in regard to them, by feelings that would be properly appreciated. He would content himself with expressing the high sense he entertained of the very complimentary terms in which his constituents were mentioned. If suspicions had heretofore been indulged in, derogatory to the history of Louisiana, they would no longer exist. If cold calculations had been made of her value and importance in the Union, they would no more be heard.

COMPENSATION TO COLLECTORS.

The House proceeded to consider the amendments reported by the Committee of the whole House to the bill to fix the compensations and increase the responsibility of the collectors of the direct tax and internal duties, and for other purposes connected with the collection thereof.

The said amendments being read, and that to the first section being under consideration, Mr. EPPES moved to amend the same, by striking out the word "three," being the rate per centum of the compensation to collectors, upon all moneys not exceeding $50,000 accounted for, and paid into the Treasury, between the first day of July, 1815, and the first day of January, 1816, and inserting the words four and a half."

And the question being taken thereon, it was passed in the affirmative—yeas 81, nays 62, as follows:

YEAS—Messrs. Alexander, Alston, Anderson, Avery, Barbour, Bard, Barnett, Bines, Brown, Butler, Caperton, Calhoun, Clopton, Comstock, Condict, Conard, Crawford, Creighton, Crouch, Cuthbert, Desha, Duvall, Earle, Eppes, Findley, Fisk of Vermont, Fisk of New-York, Forney, Forsyth, Franklin, Gholson, Glasgow, Goodwyn, Gourdin, Griffin, Hall, Hanson, Harris, Hasbrouck, Hawkins, Hopkins of Kentucky, Hubbard, Humphreys, Ingham, Jackson of Virginia, Johnson of Kentucky, Kennedy, Kent of Maryland, Kerr, Kershaw, Kilbourn, Lefferts, Lowndes, Lyle, McCoy, McLean, Montgomery, Moore, Newton, Ormsby, Parker, Pickens, Pleasants, Rea of Pennsylvania, Rhea of Tennessee, Rich, Ringgold, Roane, Robertson, Sage, Seybert, Sharp, Smith of Pennsylvania, Smith of Virginia, Tannehill, Taylor, Telfair, Troup, Wilson of Pennsylvania, Wright, and Yancey.

NAYS—Messrs. Baylies of Massachusetts, Bigelow, Boyd, Bradbury, Brigham, Cannon, Champion, Cilley, Clendenin, Cooper, Cox, Culpeper, Davenport, Ely, Farrow, Gaston, Geddes, Goldsborough, Grosvenor, Hale, Hawes, Henderson, Hungerford, Hulbert, Kent of New York, King of Massachusetts, King of North Carolina, Law, Lewis, Lovett, Macon, Markell, McKee, Moseley, Nelson, Oakley, Pearson, Pickering, Potter, John Reed, Ruggles, Schureman, Sevier, Sheffey, Sherwood, Shipherd, Slaymaker, Smith of New York, Stanford, Stockton, Stuart, Sturges, Taggart, Thompson, Vose, Ward of Massachusetts, Ward of New Jersey, Wheaton, White, Wilcox, and Wilson of Massachusetts.

Mr. STANFORD then moved to amend the said amendment to the first section, by adding thereto the following proviso:

Provided, That no collector in any city shall receive a greater compensation than $5,000, nor any collector in the country more than $3,500.

Mr. FISK, of New York, moved to amend the said proviso, by striking out the word "five," in the maximum of the compensation to a city collector, and inserting, in lieu thereof, the word "eight." And the question being taken thereon, it was determined in the negative—yeas 2, nays 131, as follows:

YEAS—Messrs. Fisk of New York, and Ingham.

NAYS—Messrs. Alexander, Alston, Anderson, Avery, Barbour, Barnett, Baylies of Massachusetts, Bigelow, Bines, Bowen, Boyd, Bradbury, Breckenridge, Brigham, Butler, Caperton, Calhoun, Cannon, Cilley, Clendenin, Clopton, Comstock, Conard, Cooper, Cox, Crawford, Culpeper, Cuthbert, Davenport, Davis of Pennsylvania, Desha, Duvall, Earle, Ely, Eppes, Evans, Farrow, Findley, Forney, Franklin, Gaston, Geddes, Gholson, Glasgow, Goldsborough, Goodwyn, Gourdin, Griffin, Grosvenor, Hale, Hall, Hanson, Harris, Hasbrouck, Hawes, Hawkins, Henderson, Hopkins of Kentucky, Humphreys, Hungerford, Hulbert, Jackson of Virginia, Johnson of Kentucky, Kennedy, Kent of New York, Kent of Maryland, Kerr, Kilbourn, King of Massachusetts, King of North Carolina, Law, Lefferts, Lewis, Lovett, Lowndes, Lyle, Macon, Markell, McKee, McKim, Moore, Moseley, Nelson, Newton, Oakley, Ormsby, Pearson, Pickering, Pickens, Piper, Pitkin, Pleasants, Potter, John Reed, Rea of Pennsylvania, Rhea of Tennessee, Rich, Ringgold, Roane, Robertson, Ruggles, Sage, Schureman, Sevier, Seybert, Sharp, Sherwood, Shipherd, Slaymaker, Smith of Pennsylvania, Smith of Virginia, Stanford, Sturges, Taggart, Tannehill, Taylor, Telfair, Thompson, Troup, Udree, Voss, Ward of Massachusetts, Ward of New Jersey, Wheaton, White, Wilcox, Wilson of Massachusetts, Wilson of Pennsylvania, Wood, Wright, and Yancey.

Much debate occurring on the proposition, it was withdrawn by Mr. STANFORD; and the House adjourned.

FRIDAY, February 17.

Mr. McKEE, from the Committee on the Public Lands, reported a bill supplemental to the act, entitled "An act for the final adjustment of land titles in the State of Louisiana, and Territory of Missouri," approved the 12th of April, 1814; which was read, and committed to a Committee of the Whole.

Mr. PICKERING, from the committee to whom was committed the bill granting a donation of three hundred and twenty acres of land to Anthony Shane, reported the same with an amendment; which was read and agreed to by the House, and the bill ordered to be engrossed, and read the third time to-morrow.

The bill from the Senate to give further time to complete surveys and locate patents for lands granted under Virginia resolution warrants, was read a third time and passed.

The engrossed bill to lay a direct tax on the District of Columbia, was read a third time, without debate, and passed.

On motion of Mr. TAYLOR, the Committee on the Judiciary were instructed to inquire into the expediency of authorizing the appointment of a district attorney and marshal for the Northern District of the State of New York.

The resolution from the Senate for the appointment of a joint committee to inquire into the expediency of causing the Chambers at present occupied by the two Houses of Congress, or others in the same building, to be altered and fitted up for their better accommodation, was read, and agreed to by the House; and Mr. LEWIS, Mr. MACON, and Mr. KENT, of Maryland, were appointed the committee on the part of the House.

The House resolved itself into a Committee of the Whole on the bill for the relief of Edward Hallowell. The bill was reported without amendment, and ordered to be engrossed, and read a third time to-morrow.

THE ARMY AND NAVY.

Mr. JACKSON, of Virginia, submitted the following resolutions for consideration:

1. *Resolved*, That the Committee on Military Affairs be instructed to inquire and report to what extent the Military Establishment of the United States can be reduced consistently with the public interest.

2. *Resolved*, That the said Committee be further instructed to inquire whether any, and, if any, what, provision ought to be made, by law, for allowing months' extra pay and a donation in land to the officers of the Army who may be disbanded.

3. *Resolved*, That the said Committee be instructed to inquire into the expediency of establishing one or more additional military schools.

4. *Resolved*, That the Naval Committee be instructed to inquire and report to what extent the Navy of the United States on the Lakes can be reduced consistently with the public interest.

5. *Resolved*, That the said Committee be further instructed to inquire into the expediency of establishing one or more naval academies.

6. *Resolved*, That the Committee on Foreign Relations be instructed to ascertain and report whether any, and, if any, what, modification of existing laws are necessary to adapt them to the State of our relations with foreign nations.

The House having agreed to consider these resolutions,

Mr. JACKSON, of Virginia, made a few remarks in respect to each of these resolutions, the whole of which the reporter was not fortunate enough to hear. They were of an explanatory nature.

Mr. INGERSOLL moved that these resolutions should lie on the table. The consummation of the peace, he said, had not taken place, and it appeared to him, therefore, improper now to enter into a discussion of them.

Mr. CANNON also considered them premature. It would certainly be time enough for the House to act on them when they found the ratification had actually taken place. Before that time, he was opposed to any discussion of the subjects embraced in the resolutions.

Mr. GROSVENOR said, sensible as he was of the force of the motive, which has prompted the motion, viz: the brevity of the remainder of the session, yet he considered the motion entirely premature. As individuals, the members of the House knew the fact of a ratification of a treaty of peace; but the nature of the treaty was not known, nor was the fact officially before the House.

Mr. JACKSON, of Virginia, said he could not see any strong objections to laying the resolutions on the table; though he could see no objections to acting on them on the score of a regard to the dignity of the House. Could any evil grow out of an inquiry into the subject? There was no danger of precipitation in acting on this or any other subject; for even now, at the close of the session, at this interesting moment, the House had employed two days in debating what compensation should be allowed to the collectors of the taxes. True dignity, Mr. G. said, always consists in doing what you intend to do, promptly, and with a good grace.

Mr. FISK, of New York, desired to see added to these resolves another, contemplating provision for the widows and orphans of officers who have fallen in the war.

Mr. RHEA, of Tennessee, thought the agitation of these questions ought to be delayed until the House had, from the proper authority, official information of the peace. In their capacity of representatives, Mr. R. said, they knew nothing of what had taken place, whatever they might have individually heard. The treaty, when communicated, would probably be attended with other information, properly relative to the subject, and which the House ought to take into consideration.

Mr HANSON said there could not be a doubt but it would be improper to act on this subject till official information was received, which the House now had not. It was almost a maxim, he said, that precipitancy is always unjustifiable. How did they know that the Executive had made up his mind to ratify the treaty? Mr. H. went on to repeat what were reported to be the characteristics of the treaty; but, on the suggestion that this debate was not strictly applicable at this time, refrained from pursuing the topic. He said, however, that he thought the House ought not to act on the subject as if it was pre-determined to accept the treaty, be it good or bad. To act on these resolutions now, would have an undignified appearance.

The resolutions were ordered to lie on the table.

On the question to print them, there were for printing them 57, against it 58.

DEFENCE OF NEW ORLEANS.

The resolutions expressive of the thanks of Congress to Major General Andrew Jackson, and the troops under his command, for their gallantry and good conduct in the defence of New Orleans, were read a third time.

The resolution expressive of the high sense entertained by Congress of the patriotism and good conduct of the people of Louisiana and New Orleans, was also read a third time.

Mr. ROBERTSON, of Louisiana, expressed in a feeling manner his high sense of the complimentary manner in which his constituents were mentioned in this resolve; and flattered himself they would never forfeit, at any time, the high character they had now acquired.

Mr. SHARP then rose, and addressed the House as follows: Mr. Speaker, the subject those res-

olutions present for our consideration, is the most interesting occurrence in the history of our country.

The people of Louisiana, approached by an enemy who suspected their fidelity to their newly adopted Government, and who held out every allurement that could be presented to seduce them from the Union, at this very moment whilst assailed by the blandishments of the enemy, with open arms they received their fellow-citizens who came to their aid, and, by voluntary contributions, furnished everything necessary to their comfort, while exposed in the open field in defence of their city. Yet their patriotism and humanity are surpassed by their bravery. On the 23d of December, it was a company of Louisianians that penetrated the very centre of the enemy's camp, and made good their retreat, and brought off a number of prisoners. On the 8th of January, the Louisianians aided in defending the breastworks on the right, and when the enemy got possession of one of our bastions, they were among the foremost who met them; and, amidst the clash of swords and bayonets, grappled with them on the ramparts, and bore them into the ditch.

If we compare the conduct of Louisiana with any other part of the nation—even the oldest and best established in their political institutions—so far from losing anything in the comparison, it is on their part splendid and honorable, and must effectually put down all those feelings of distrust and jealousy that have been entertained in some parts of the Union in relation to their adoption into our Republic.

In another point of view this subject is still more interesting. There is, perhaps, no epoch to be found on the historic page, none in the history of America in which we have been called upon to present the thanks of the American people to a whole State. Louisiana, the youngest daughter of the Union, composed of a population most of whom had tasted of liberty but yesterday; it had not been their birthright, but such are the charms of liberty to a people who have felt its blessings and known its value, that, on the approaching of a foe to enslave them, the whole population of Louisiana are bristling with the bayonet; the old men, the exempts, are clad in mail, and rushing to meet the foe..

> " If humanity shows to the God of the world,
>   A sight for his fatherly eye,
> It is when a people, with banner unfurl'd,
>   Resolve for their freedom to die."

Such a spectacle was presented by the State of Louisiana. As we are ever to expect, in so just a cause, they received the benedictions of Heaven, and, under its benign influence, aided by their fellow-citizens in arms, they not only triumphed over but almost exterminated their enemy.

Can there be an American, whose bosom does not beat high with joy to call Louisiana a legitimate daughter of the Union, and hail her citizens as brothers?

Is there any part of the American empire that could hesitate ever hereafter to hold Louisiana in the maternal embrace of the nation; to extend to her our care and protection?

The resolutions were then unanimously passed.

The resolution expressive of the high sense entertained by Congress of the merits of Commodore D. T. Patterson, Major Daniel Carmick, and the officers and men under their command, were read a third time. and passed, with *one* negative, (Mr. McKEE, of Kentucky.)

BANK OF THE UNITED STATES.

The House resumed the consideration of the bill from the Senate, "to incorporate the subscribers to the Bank of the United States of America."

Mr. FORSYTH moved to refer the bill to a select committee.

Mr. LOWNDES superseded this motion, by a motion to postpone the bill indefinitely. He made this motion, not from any hostility to a National Bank, wishing, as the gentleman did, that a National Bank should be established, but because he wished it to be done at a time and under circumstances which would give the House ability to decide correctly on the subject. He believed, he said, and he was not alone in that opinion, that the present moment was a most unfavorable one for the establishment of a bank. It must be known that, long as the subject of a bank had been agitated, there had been important differences of sentiment as to the principles of such an institution, which had been suppressed because of the pressure of the times. Among other objections to acting on this subject at present, he said, it was no trifling one that the suspension of specie payments by the State banks, which every one considered an evil, would unquestionably be prolonged by it. In the fragment of the session which now remains, there would not be time to enter into a consideration of these points; and, if there were full time, the mere circumstance of the new and almost insuperable difficulties arising from a new state of things which now present themselves, ought to suggest a reason for postponement. Congress could not now establish a bank half so eligible, or half so durable, as they could at a future session.

Mr. FORSYTH said, he was perfectly aware that the subject of a National Bank was attended with great difficulty at this or any other session; but his opinion was, that this was the best time for an attempt of this kind. The subject had been so much discussed, that he apprehended every gentleman was prepared to decide on it without much further discussion. It was from a hope that all sides of the House could now come to some understanding, and agree on the establishment of such an institution as should be not only valuable to the United States, but satisfactory to all parties, that he had now moved to commit the bill, which he hoped would not be indefinitely postponed.

Mr. GASTON conceived there would be less difficulty in acting on this subject at the present session than was anticipated by the gentleman from South Carolina. The subject has been so repeatedly discussed, that he thought it could be acted on more advantageously in the small remnant of the present session than in the first session of a new Congress, bringing together individuals not acquainted with each others' views, and not having the advantage of hearing the subject frequently discussed. Having always been friendly to such an institution, and believing it as important in peace as in war, he hoped an experiment would be made by referring this subject to a committee, which, whether successful or not, would not consume much time of the House.

Messrs. GROSVENOR, PICKERING, and FARROW, also advocated the postponement; and Messrs. KILBOURN, FISK of Vermont, CALHOUN, and TALFAIR, opposed it.

On the question of postponement, which was decided by yeas and nays, the vote stood—yeas 74, nays 73. as follows:

YEAS—Messrs. Avery, Barbour, Bard, Barnett, Baylies of Massachusetts, Bigelow, Boyd, Bradbury, Brigham, Champion, Cilley, Clopton, Cooper, Crawford, Cuthbert, Davenport, Desha, Ely, Eppes, Farrow, Franklin, Geddes, Glasgow, Goodwyn, Grosvenor, Hale, Hall, Hasbrouck, Hawes, Henderson, Hulbert, Jackson of Rhode Island, Johnson of Kentucky, Kennedy, Kent of New York, King of Massachusetts, Law, Lowndes, Macon, Markell, McKee, Montgomery, Moseley, Nelson, Ormsby, Pickering, Pitkin, Potter, John Reed, Wm. Reed, Roane, Ruggles, Schureman, Seybert, Sheffey, Shipherd, Slaymaker, Smith of New York, Stanford, Stockton, Stuart, Taggart, Thompson, Troup, Vose, Ward of Massachusetts, Ward of New Jersey, Wheaton, White, Wilcox, Williams, Wilson of Massachusetts, Winter, and Wright.

NAYS—Messrs. Alston, Anderson, Bayly of Virginia, Bines, Bowen, Breckenridge, Brown, Butler, Caperton, Calhoun, Cannon, Clendenin, Comstock, Conard, Cox, Creighton, Crouch, Culpeper, Duvall, Earle, Findley, Fisk of Vermont, Fisk of New York, Forney, Forsyth, Gaston, Gholson, Gourdin, Griffin, Hanson, Hawkins, Hubbard, Hungerford, Ingersoll, Ingham, Jackson of Virginia, Kent of Maryland, Kerr, Kershaw, Kilbourn, Lefferts, Lewis, Lovett, Lyle, McCoy, McLean, Moore, Murfree, Newton, Parker, Pearson, Pickens, Piper, Pleasants, Rea of Pennsylvania, Rhea of Tennessee, Rich, Ringgold, Robertson, Sage, Sevier, Sharp, Smith of Virginia, Strong, Sturges, Tannehill, Taylor, Telfair, Udree, Wilson of Pennsylvania, Wood, and Yancey.

So the bill was indefinitely postponed.

Some time was spent in Committee of the Whole on the bill respecting the compensation of collectors of taxes, &c., and some material amendments having been moved to its details, it was ordered to lie on the table.

The remainder of the day was spent in Committee on the bill respecting post offices.

SATURDAY, February 18.

Mr. EPPES, from the Committee of Ways and Means, reported the bill from the Senate, "to allow a drawback of duties on spirits distilled, and certain goods, wares, and merchandise, manufactured within the United States, on the exportation thereof to any foreign port or place," without amendment; and the bill was committed to a Committee of the Whole.

Mr. E., from the same committee, reported a bill for the relief of Solomon Frazer, and the representatives of Charles Eccleston; which was read, and committed to a Committee of the Whole.

Mr. E. also reported a bill for the relief of William P. Bennett, of the State of New York; which was read, and committed to a Committee of the Whole.

Mr. CULPEPER submitted the following preamble and resolution; which was read, and ordered to lie on the table:

It being a duty peculiarly incumbent, in a time of public calamity and war, humbly and devoutly to acknowledge our dependence on Almighty God, and to implore his aid and protection; and, in times of deliverance and prosperity, to manifest our deep and undissembled gratitude to the Almighty Sovereign of the Universe: Therefore,

Resolved by the Senate and House of Representatives of the United States of America, in Congress assembled, That a joint committee of both Houses wait on the President of the United States, and request that he recommend a day of *thanksgiving,* to be observed by the people of the United States with religious solemnity, and the offering of devout acknowledgments to God for his mercies, and in prayer for the continuance of his blessings.

An engrossed bill granting a donation of three hundred and twenty acres of land to Anthony Shane, was read the third time, and passed.

An engrossed bill for the relief of Edward Hallowell was read the third time, and passed.

Ordered, That the bill to authorize a donation of land to persons employed in the military service of the enemy, who shall come within the United States and claim the protection of the Government thereof, and the bill to provide for the further defence of the frontiers of the United States by authorizing the President to augment the Military Establishment, be postponed indefinitely.

Ordered, That the resolution expressive of the sense of Congress of the gallantry and good conduct with which the reputation of the arms of the United States has been sustained by Major General Jackson, and the officers and men under his command, be postponed indefinitely.

The House resolved itself into a Committee of the Whole on the bill for the relief of Joshua Sands. The bill was reported with an amendment; which was concurred in by the House, and the bill ordered to be engrossed, and read the third time on Monday next.

The bill to alter and establish certain post roads, passed through a Committee of the Whole, and was ordered to be engrossed for a third reading.

The bill for the relief of Henry Nimmo, passed through a Committee of the Whole, was ordered to a third reading, and read a third time, and passed accordingly.

A message from the Senate informed the House that the Senate have passed the bill "for the re-lief of Isaac Smith and Bratton Caldwell." And they have passed a bill "to authorize the settlement and payment of certain claims for the services of the militia;" in which they ask the concurrence of this House.

NATIONAL OBSERVATORY.

Mr. NELSON, from the committee to whom was referred, on the second instant, the petition of William Lambert, and other documents relating to the establishment of a first meridian for the United States, made a report; which was read, and the resolution therein contained was amended, and concurred in by the House.

The report is as follows:

That the reasons detailed in the said reports appearing to be well founded, your committee have no hesitation in declaring their full assent to them. It is also the opinion of the committee that the plan proposed by the memorialist ought to be carried into complete effect, whenever attention to objects of a pressing nature and more immediate importance to the welfare of our country will permit, by the erection of a national observatory, and providing suitable instruments and apparatus at the public expense, to enable skilful persons to determine the places of the moon, planets, and other heavenly bodies with sufficient accuracy, by repeated and careful observations of the times of their transit over the meridian of the place.

It further appears that the memorialist has made calculations, in addition to those presented to this House in the month of December, 1809, from data afforded by the occultations of two fixed stars by the moon, which happened in January, 1793, and January, 1813; also, from the external and internal contacts of the sun and moon, in an annular solar eclipse on the 17th of September, 1811, which have all been referred to the Capitol, in the City of Washington; and that the mean result of the longitude is found to be nearly $76°\ 55'\ 45''$, or five hours seven minutes and forty-three seconds in time west of Greenwich observatory, in England.

It has been represented that astronomical calculations subsequent to the close of the year 1812, can be depended upon with greater assurance of the accuracy of their results than before that period, in consequence of the publication and introduction into use of improved solar and lunar tables, constructed by M. de Lambre, of Paris, in France, and introduction into use of improved solar and lunar tables, constructed by M. de Lambre, of Paris, in France, and M. Burg, of Vienna, in Germany. This circumstance will suggest the propriety of authorizing additional experiments to be made, by approved methods of computation, to test the accuracy of the result found by William Lambert. Under this impression, the committee submit to the House the following resolution:

Resolved, That the President of the United States be requested to cause such further observations to be made by competent persons residing at the seat of the National Government as may be deemed most proper to determine the longitude of the Capitol, in the City of Washington, with the greatest practicable degree of exactness, and that the data, with abstracts of the calculations, and the results founded thereon, be laid before Congress at their next session.

The remainder of the day was spent in the discussion of the bill declaratory of the powers of the Legislature of the Indiana Territory; several propositions to amend and postpone it were rejected, but, before getting through the bill, the House adjourned.

MONDAY, February 20.

Mr. WRIGHT presented a petition of William Thornton, Superintendent of the Patent Office, praying for an increase of compensation, and that letters and communications to and from that office may not be charged with postage.

Ordered, That the said petition be referred to the Committee of Claims.

Mr. INGERSOLL, from the Committee on the Judiciary, reported a bill supplementary to an act, entitled "An act for the better organization of the Courts of the United States within the State of New York ;" which was read twice, and ordered to be engrossed, and read the third time to-morrow.

Mr. BOWEN, from the Committee on Pensions and Revolutionary Claims, reported a bill concerning invalid pensioners; which was read twice, and committed to a Committee of the Whole.

The bill from the Senate, "to authorize the settlement and payment of certain claims for the services of the militia," was read the first time, and, on motion, the said bill was read the second time, and referred to the Committee of Ways and Means.

The House resumed the consideration of the bill declaratory of the powers of the Legislature of the Territory of Illinois: whereupon, the bill was ordered to lie on the table.

An engrossed bill to alter and establish certain post roads was read the third time, and passed.

An engrossed bill for the relief of Joshua Sands was read the third time, and passed.

The order of the day on Mr. RICH's resolution for classifying persons liable to the direct tax, and allowing them to furnish soldiers in lieu of the same, was, on motion of its author, indefinitely postponed.

A message was received from the President of the United States, transmitting copies of the Treaty of Peace and Amity between the United States and His Britannic Majesty, which was signed by the Commissioners of both parties at Ghent, on the 24th December, 1814, and the ratifications of which have been duly exchanged.— The Message was read, and 5,000 copies of the Message and Treaty ordered to be printed. [See Senate proceedings, *ante,* p. 255, for the Message.]

A message from the Senate informed the House that the Senate have passed the bill "to amend the act, entitled "An act to provide additional revenues for defraying the expenses of Government, and maintaining the public credit, by laying a direct tax upon the United States, and to provide for assessing and collecting the same ;" and the act, entitled "An act to provide additional revenues for defraying the expenses of Government, and maintaining the public credit, by laying duties on household furniture, and on gold and silver watches," with amendments ; and they have passed a bill, "increasing the compensation allowed to the Sergeant-at-Arms of the Senate ;" in which amendments and bill they ask the concurrence of this House.

MILITARY AND CREEK LANDS.

Mr. HARRIS moved the adoption of the following resolution :

Resolved, That the Committee on the Public Lands be instructed to report a bill with provisions for having the boundary lines of the lands ceded to the United States by the Creek Treaty, recently ratified, run and marked, and having the same laid off into sections and quarter-sections, preparatory to the sale thereof, and for making an appropriation for defraying the expenses incident thereto.

Mr. HUMPHREYS remarked, that there was already in existence a general law authorizing the laying off of lands, &c., and that so much of this resolve as embraced that object was unnecessary; an appropriation of money only was necessary to enable the President to carry the law into effect.

Mr. HARRIS said, that, although there might be such a law as his colleague had described, it was proper that the land in question should be immediately laid off; and used a number of arguments to show that the people of Tennessee, who had conquered these lands for the United States, should, as soon as possible, have access to the waters of Mobile, which could only be obtained by a sale and settlement of the lands recently acquired, &c.

Mr. McKEE said, that, as soon as the treaty with the Indians was proclaimed, the Committee on the Public Lands had turned their attention to this subject, and, on examination, had found that no legal provision was necessary to the laying off, and surveying of these lands, and that an appropriation of money only was necessary for the purpose. In answer to a letter addressed to the Commissioner of the General Land Office on the subject, Mr. McK. said he had been informed it was first necessary that the boundaries of the Indian lands, and those of the United States, should be first surveyed and marked, before the lands were laid off. To enable the Government to proceed in it, an appropriation of money only was necessary.

Mr. HUMPHREYS said, that, as respected the settlement of the Creek territory, it was important not only to the people of Tennessee, but to the United States, in order to facilitate the intercourse between the United States and Louisiana, and to give security to the frontier, and cut off the influence of the Spanish Government and British traders over that country. But, as nothing more than an appropriation for the expenses of survey was necessary to that object, he moved to amend Mr. HARRIS's motion, so as to read as follows :

Resolved, That the Committee of Ways and Means be instructed to inquire into the necessity and expediency of making an appropriation of money to meet the expenses of surveying and laying off the military bounty lands, and the lands lately ceded by the Creek Indians to the United States, in the Treaty of Fort Jackson, in order to the settlement thereof by the citizens of the United States.

This motion was opposed by Mr. HARRIS. He contended for the propriety of a special law on the subject, which should define the duty of the Executive, in this respect, beyond doubt. The President now possessed authority to act on the subject. it was true, but he might not conceive the law obligatory as to these lands, unless Congress gave special direction in regard to them. The importance of the object was such, that he was not willing to leave anything to construction or uncertainty.

Mr. McKEE again contended that no further provision than an appropriation was necessary, unless it was intended to impose a penalty on the Executive for a failure to exercise the authority in this respect vested in him by a general law.

Mr. HUMPHREYS' amendment prevailed ; and, as amended, the motion was agreed to.

WIDOW OF ELBRIDGE GERRY.

The order of the day having been called for by Mr. FISK, of New York, on the bill from the Senate, "authorizing payment to the widow of Elbridge Gerry, late Vice President of the United States, of such salary as would have been payable to him during the remainder of his term of service, had he so long lived,"

A motion was made, by Mr. EPPES, to postpone the further consideration thereof indefinitely.

This motion gave rise to a debate, in which Messrs. EPPES, CANNON, POTTER, TAYLOR, GROSVENOR, SHEFFEY, and PICKERING, advocated the postponement; and Messrs. FISK of New York, McKIM, FISK of Vermont, JACKSON of Virginia, HULBERT, WRIGHT, and OAKLEY, opposed it.

The debate was one of some interest. The general principle asserted by those opposed to the bill, was the impropriety of setting a precedent of pensions for civil services, which would entail on the United States the evils so grievously felt in despotic Governments, from the same source. The bill was advocated on the ground of respect for the services of the deceased patriot and public servant, whose family was by his decease placed in a state of absolute dependence.

The question on postponement was at length decided by yeas and nays—for postponement 86, against it 44, as follows:

YEAS—Messrs. Alston, Anderson, Avery, Barnett, Brown, Capeston, Cannon, Champion, Cilley, Clendenin, Clopton, Comstock, Condict, Conard, Cooper, Crawford, Crouch, Culpeper, Davenport, Desha, Duvall, Ely, Eppes, Franklin, Gaston, Geddes, Gholson, Glasgow, Goldsborough, Goodwyn, Grosvenor, Hale, Hall, Harris, Hawes, Henderson, Humphreys, Hungerford, Irwin, Kennedy, Kilbourn, King of Massachusetts, King of North Carolina, Law, Lefferts, Lewis, Lovett, Lyle, Macon, Markell, McLean, Montgomery, Moseley, Nelson, Ormsby, Pearson, Pickering, Piper, Pitkin, Potter, Rea of Pennsylvania, Rhea of Tennessee, Rich, Sage, Schureman, Seybert, Sheffey, Sherwood, Shipherd, Slaymaker, Stanford, Stockton, Strong, Sturges, Taggart, Tannehill, Taylor, Troup, Udree, Voss, Wheaton, White, Wilcox, Williams, Winter, and Yancey.

NAYS—Messrs. Alexander, Bard, Baylies of Massachusetts, Bigelow, Bines, Boyd, Bradbury, Brigham, Cox, Creighton, Farrow, Fisk of Vermont, Fisk of New York, Gourdin, Hanson, Hasbrouck, Hopkins of Kentucky, Hubbard, Hulbert, Ingersoll, Jackson of Rhode Island, Jackson of Virginia, Kent of New York, Kent of Maryland, Kershaw, McKim, Moore, Murfree, Oakley, Parker, Pleasants, Ringgold, Roane, Robertson, Sevier, Smith of New York, Smith of Penn., Smith of Virginia, Stuart, Thompson, Wilson of Massachusetts, Wilson of Pennsylvania, Wood, and Wright.

So the bill was indefinitely postponed—in other words, rejected.

The remainder of the sitting was occupied on Mr. KILBOURN's bill to provide, by encouraging actual settlement, for the protection of the Northwestern frontier; which was, in the end, indefinitely postponed.

TUESDAY, February 21.

The amendments proposed by the Senate to the bill "to amend the act, entitled "An act to provide additional revenues for defraying the expenses of Government, and maintaining the public credit, by laying a direct tax upon the United States, and to provide for assessing and collecting the same ;" and, "the act, entitled 'An act to provide additional revenues for defraying the expenses of Government, and maintaining the public credit, by laying duties on household furniture, and on gold and silver watches ;" were read, and referred to the Committee of Ways and Means.

A message from the Senate informed the House that the Senate disagree to the amendment of this House to the "resolution expressive of the thanks of Congress to Major General Jackson, and the troops under his command, for their gallantry and good conduct in the defence of New Orleans;" except so much thereof as strikes out the word "immediate," in the third line of the first resolution.

The House proceeded to consider the said message: Whereupon, it was resolved, that this House insist on that part of their amendment to the resolutions aforesaid, to which the Senate have disagreed.

Ordered, That the Clerk do acquaint the Senate therewith.

A message from the Senate informed the House that the Senate have passed the bill "to authorize the issuing of Treasury notes for the service of the year 1815," with amendments, in which they ask the concurrence of this House. They adhere to their disagreement to that part of the amendment of this House to the "resolutions expressive of the thanks of Congress to Major General Jackson and the troops under his command, for their gallantry and good conduct in the defence of New Orleans," to which they disagreed. and which have been insisted upon by this House.

The amendments to the bill "to authorize the issuing of Treasury notes for the service of the year 1815," were read, and referred to the Committee of Ways and Means.

Mr. TROUP, from the Military Committee, reported sundry resolutions expressive of the sense

1175   HISTORY OF CONGRESS.   1176

H. of R.   *Thanksgiving—British and Indian Depredations.*   FEBRUARY, 1815.

entertained by Congress of the gallantry and good conduct, with which the reputation of the arms of the United States have been sustained during the late war by certain officers therein named—(including many militia officers, and several field officers who have fallen in the service.) The resolutions were twice read, and referred to the same committee, to whom resolutions of a similar character, reported by that committee, have been referred.

The bill supplementary to the act for the better organization of the courts of the United States within the State of New York, was read a third time, passed, and sent to the Senate.

The bill from the Senate to increase the compensation of the Sergeant-at-Arms of the Senate, was twice read, and committed.

The House proceeded to the consideration of the bill declaratory of the powers of the Legislature of Illinois Territory, which, after the proposition of other amendments thereto, was ordered to lie on the table, and made the order of the day for to-morrow.

The bill fixing the compensation, &c., of collectors of the direct tax and internal duties, was further debated and amended, and then ordered to be engrossed for a third reading.

DAY OF THANKSGIVING.

On motion of Mr. CULPEPER, the House proceeded to the consideration of the resolution submitted by him a day or two ago, which is in the following words:

"It being a duty peculiarly incumbent *in a time of public calamity and war, humbly and devoutly to acknowledge our dependence on Almighty God, and to implore his aid and protection ; and,* in times of deliverance and prosperity, to manifest our deep and undissembled gratitude to the Almighty Sovereign of the Universe:

"*Resolved, by the Senate and House of Representatives of the United States of America in Congress assembled,* That a joint committee of both Houses wait upon the President of the United States, and request that he recommend a day of thanksgiving, to be observed by the people of the United States with religious solemnity and the offering of devout acknowledgments to God for his mercies, and in prayers to him for a continuance of his blessings."

On motion of Mr. REEA, the resolution was amended in its preamble, by striking out the words in *italic,* and thus amended, the resolution was, after some conversation as to the preamble, ordered to be engrossed for a third reading; and, being accordingly subsequently read a third time, was ordered to be referred to a select committee to consider and report thereon.

BRITISH AND INDIAN DEPREDATIONS.

Mr. LATTIMORE, from the committee to whom was referred, on the 21st ultimo, the memorial of the Legislature of the Mississippi Territory, relative to Indian depredations, made a report; which was read, as follows:

The memorialists state, that, in the eastern part of the above-mentioned Territory, great losses have been sustained from the wanton and unwarranted depreda-

tions of the Creeks; for which they conceive reparation is due to the sufferers out of the lands which have been ceded by the treaty lately concluded with that nation of Indians to the United States, and pray that a board of commissioners may be instituted for the purpose of ascertaining such losses, and with a view to such reparation.

Your committee have no doubt that the losses sustained by the inhabitants of this section of the country are great, and that their sufferings have been severe; but, conceiving that other cases may furnish claims to reparation, they are of opinion that any proceeding on the subject should not be partial in its object or effect. Abstaining from all remarks as to the important and extensive principle which this subject involves, your committee believe that it would be proper to ascertain, without unnecessary delay, all such losses, whether from English or Indian depredations, as may hereafter claim the attention of Congress, when the general question of indemnity may come before them ; and in this view of the subject, and also with due regard to the particular case presented by the memorialists, they offer the following resolution to the consideration of the House:

Resolved, That the President of the United States be requested to take such measures as may be convenient for the purpose of obtaining satisfactory evidence of all losses of property which have been sustained in consequence of the depredations of the British or Indians, or of the troops of the United States, during the late war; and that the memorial above considered be transmitted to him for his information on the subject to which it relates.

On the question of concurrence in said resolution, a desultory debate took place, which ended in laying the report on the table—the principal argument for this course being the propriety of so amending it as to limit it to depredations contrary to the laws and usages of war, which, it appeared to be admitted, ought to be a subject of amicable discussion and settlement between the two Governments.

WEDNESDAY, February 22.

A message from the Senate informed the House that the Senate have passed bills from this House with the following titles: "An act for the regulation of the courts of justice of Indiana;" and "An act giving the right of pre-emption in the purchase of lands to certain settlers in the Indiana Territory," with amendments. And they have passed bills of the following titles: "An act authorizing the discharge of Edward Martin from imprisonment ;" "An act for the better temporary accommodation of the two Houses of Congress ;" and "An act to repeal certain acts therein mentioned ;" in which amendments and bills they ask the concurrence of this House.

The House resolved itself into a Committee of the Whole on the bill for the relief of Thomas Sprigg; which passed through a Committee of the Whole, and was ordered to be engrossed, and read the third time to-morrow.

The House resolved itself into a Committee of the Whole on the bill for the relief of James

1177   HISTORY OF CONGRESS.   1178

FEBRUARY, 1815.   *Military Peace Establishment—Estimated Revenue.*   H. OF R.

Savage and others. The bill was reported to the House and ordered to be engrossed, and read the third time to-morrow.

Mr. McKEE, of Kentucky, reported a bill authorizing the sale of lands which may hereafter be forfeited within the Jefferson Land District at the land office for said district (merely declaring the place where such sales shall take place.) The bill was twice read, and ordered to be engrossed for a third reading.

The act to fix the compensation and increase the responsibility of the collectors of the direct tax, &c., and for other purposes connected therewith, was announced for a third reading. On motion of Mr. FISK of New York, supported by Mr. JACKSON of Virginia, the bill was recommitted to the Committee of Ways and Means.

The order of the day on the bill from the Senate authorizing the President of the United States to cause to be built one or more floating batteries for the defence of the waters of the United States, was indefinitely postponed.

The bill authorizing the discharge of A. B. Ross from his imprisonment passed through a Committee of the Whole, and was ordered to be engrossed for a third reading.

The bill supplementary to the act for the final adjustment of land titles in the State of Louisiana and Territory of Missouri, passed through a Committee of the Whole, and was ordered to be engrossed for a third reading; as also did the bill for the relief of William T. Bennett, of the State of New York.

The bill for the relief of Solomon Frazer, and the representatives of Charles Eccleston, passed through a Committee of the Whole, and was ordered to be engrossed for a third reading.

The bill from the Senate, "concerning the field officers of the militia," was postponed indefinitely.

TREASURY NOTES.

Mr. EPPES, from the Committee of Ways and Means, made a report recommending an agreement to the amendments of the Senate to the Treasury note bill.

The bill, as it went from this House, provided that those Treasury notes to be issued bearing no interest should be fundable at eight per cent., and those bearing interest at seven per cent. The Senate propose to amend the bill so as that the notes bearing no interest shall be fundable at seven per cent., and those bearing interest shall be fundable at six per cent.

Mr. E. said, that as the state of war had ceased since the bill passed this House, and the state of peace would probably appreciate the value of the public securities, it was supposed the interest proposed by the Senate would be sufficient.

The amendments were agreed to.

MILITARY PEACE ESTABLISHMENT.

Mr. TROUP, from the Committee on Military Affairs, reported a bill fixing the Military Peace Establishment of the United States.

[The bill provides that the Military Peace Establishment shall consist of such proportions of artillery, infantry, and riflemen, not exceeding in the whole ten thousand men, as the President shall think proper; the corps of engineers to be retained. The general officers to consist of two Major Generals and four Brigadier Generals. The President to cause selections to be made of officers from the existing force, and to cause the supernumerary officers to be discharged as soon as circumstances shall permit. Three months pay to be given to each officer, &c., so honorably discharged, and, in addition, to each officer a donation of land; two thousand five hundred acres to a Major General, &c.; six hundred and forty to a Captain, four hundred and eighty to a subaltern. To each private, also, an additional donation of one hundred and sixty acres of land, provided the whole quantity of land such private receives shall not exceed three hundred and twenty acres. The bill also proposes to regulate the future organization of the Army.]

The bill was twice read, and referred to a Committee of the Whole.

ESTIMATED REVENUE.

Mr. EPPES laid on the table the following letter from the Secretary of the Treasury:

TREASURY DEPARTMENT, *Feb.* 20, 1815.

SIR: I have the honor to acknowledge the receipt of your letter, dated the 15th instant, which, in consequence of the termination of the war, requests, in behalf of the Committee of Ways and Means, "a view of the probable receipts from imports and tonnage during the year 1815, and any other information that may enable the committee to decide on the measures necessary to meet the unexpected and fortunate change which peace must produce in the resources of the United States." It has hitherto been my arduous and painful employment, to suggest to your consideration measures for relieving the embarrassments of the Treasury, with a view to the expenditures of a protracted war; and you will readily believe that, on every account, personal as well as public, I join you most sincerely in rejoicing at an event which brings with it an immediate alleviation of the pressure upon the Department, as well as a general assurance of national honor and prosperity.

The objects which claimed the attention of the committee in my former communication, were, 1st. The state of the public credit; 2d. The state of the circulating medium; and, 3d. The ways and means to defray the various expenses of the Government.

1. The public credit was depressed during the war, owing to several causes that must now cease to operate. All the circumstances, internal and external, which were calculated to excite doubt as to the duration, or as to the issue of the contest, in the minds of the cautious and the timid, have passed away, and, in their place, the proofs of confidence begin already to appear, with practical advantage. While it was doubtful to what extent the public exigencies would require the aid of loans, those persons who retained the means of lending either feared, or affected to fear, the eventual security of the Government; and even the exemplary display of the national resources, which has been made during the present session of Congress, for the benefit of the public creditors, was curtailed of its natural effect in the resuscitation of public credit, by the countervailing influence of causes which it is unnecessary

to specify. But when the whole amount of the public debt incurred during the war is fixed and ascertained; when it is known that ample provision is made for the punctual payment of the interest, and for the gradual extinguishment of the principal of the debt; and when, above all, it is seen that Congress is inflexible in its adherence to the faith and policy of the Legislative pledges, the public credit of the United States will stand upon a basis the most durable and the most honorable.

2. The difficulties of the national circulating medium remain, however, to be encountered, under circumstances which the Government cannot control. The effects of the peace will certainly restore a metallic medium; but, until that result be produced, the only resource for all the pecuniary transactions of the Treasury, as well as of individuals, will be the issue of Treasury notes, and the notes of the State banks. If, indeed, the State banks were soon to resume their payments in specie; or if they were again to give credit and circulation to the notes of each other throughout the United States; and if they were, moreover, able and willing to accommodate the fiscal views of the Government, (which I do not permit myself for a moment to doubt,) a total dependence upon those institutions, however impolitic in the abstract, would be practically safe and beneficial. But if, on the other hand, the notes of the State banks shall continue limited, in circulation and use, to the city, the town, or the State, in which they are issued, it must be obvious that they cannot answer the purposes of a national medium; and that the receipt of such notes, in payments for duties of import, or national duties, will convert the public revenue, which is destined for general uses abroad as well as at home, into a local fund, that may not be wanted where it exists, and cannot be applied where it is wanted. It is, nevertheless, in the power of Congress to obviate, in a considerable degree, this difficulty, by authorizing the payment of a reasonable rate of exchange, upon the transfer of its revenue, from the places of collection and deposite to the places of demand and employment; and I respectfully recommend the expedient to the consideration of the Committee of Ways and Means.

The alternative, or concurrent resource of Treasury notes, for a national circulating medium, has, on other occasions, been considered. The security of the Government must always, upon every reasonable and candid estimate, be deemed superior to the security of any private corporation; and so far as Treasury notes bear an interest, and are receivable in the payment of duties and taxes, they are evidently more valuable than bank notes, which do not possess these characteristics. But the machinery of a bank is calculated to give an impulse and direction to its issues of paper which cannot be imparted by the forms of the Treasury, or any merely official institution, to the paper of the Government. In the operations of a bank, too, the facilities of bank credit supply the place, in a very important degree, of the issues of notes; so that a bank loan of thirty millions of dollars, for instance, would, probably, require no greater issue than six millions of dollars in notes. On the contrary, the whole amount of whatever sum is to be raised by an issue of Treasury notes, must be actually sent, in the form of Treasury notes, into the market, through the various channels of credit or demand. It is, however, to be admitted, that an issue of Treasury notes not greatly exceeding in amount the demand created for them by the duties and taxes, for which they are receivable, can be annually sustained;

but if the amount exceeds, or even equals, the amount of that demand, the revenue will generally be absorbed by the notes before it reaches the Treasury. The holder of the Treasury notes being thus paid in preference, and often to the exclusion of every other public creditor, and the other branches of the public service being thus deprived of the contemplated means for their support.

It is proper here to observe, that the actual issue of Treasury notes on this day, (including those due and unpaid, those which are daily becoming due, and those which have been ordered, but are not yet signed,) amounts to the sum of $18,637,436 80, and the amount will be constantly augmenting. If, therefore, the revenue for the year 1815, enriched by the duty on imports, and by the other beneficial effects of the peace, should amount to $20,000,000, it is still evident that the whole of the revenue might be expended in the single purpose of paying the Treasury note debt; leaving every other object of the Government to be provided for by loans, or by new issues of Treasury notes.

Having suggested the difficulty and the danger, I cannot presume to dwell upon any expedient for relief, which Congress has already refused to adopt; but I take the liberty, with deference and respect, to renew the recommendation of the plan that was submitted to your consideration in my letter of the 17th January last, under the belief that, considering the outstanding amount of Treasury notes, any new issue should be made to rest upon a basis that will enable the Government to employ it, both as a circulating medium, and as the means of raising money in aid of the revenue. How far a power, given to fund the Treasury notes upon an advanced interest, or to pass them in payment of taxes and duties, will be sufficient for the purposes contemplated, without providing other means of payment by regular instalments, I must submit to the judgment of the committee.

3. The ways and means to defray the various expenses of Government for 1815, will consist of the revenue which will be actually received at the Treasury during that year. It is not intended, on the one hand, to take into view the balances due upon the appropriations of preceding years; nor, on the other hand, to take into view the revenue which will accrue in the present year, but which will not be payable until the year 1816.

The direct amelioration of the resources of the country, in consequence of the peace, applies principally to the item of the duties on imports and tonnage. The effect, however, must be confined, with immaterial exceptions, for 1815, to two-thirds, or the eight concluding months of the year. The West India trade will produce little, and the European trade nothing, by way of revenue, before the first of May next. Some outstanding adventures beyond the Cape of Good Hope will hardly be brought home, upon the intelligence of peace, before the present year has expired. Considering, therefore, that a credit of eight, ten, and twelve months, is allowed for the duties on merchandise imported from Europe, and that a credit of three and six months is allowed for the duties on merchandise imported from the West Indies, it is evident, that whatever may be the amount accruing on merchandise imported from Europe for the year 1815, the actual receipts at the Treasury cannot be great; that the whole of the duties accruing on merchandise imported from the West Indies before the first of July, will be actually received at the Treasury in the year 1815; and that one moiety of the amount of the duties on merchandise imported from the West Indies, between the first of July and the first of October, will also be received at the Treasury in the year 1815.

The average of the net revenue of the customs which accrued for the three years, 1806, 1807, and 1808, was more than $14,000,000 for each year; and a similar average for the three succeeding years, 1809, 1810, and 1811, was about nine millions of dollars for each year. But the first period was one of uncommon commercial prosperity, when the United States were the only neutral nation, and cannot be taken as the basis of an estimate for the present time, when the other nations of the world are also at peace. The second period was embarrassed by commercial restrictions; but, probably, the effect of these embarrassments upon the revenue were counterbalanced by the advantages of our neutrality. It is thought, therefore, upon the whole, that, in a state of general peace, the customs, operating upon the single duties, would not have produced, before the American war, more than a sum between nine and ten millions of dollars annually. But the comparatively small quantity of foreign merchandise at present in the American market, would, probably, give rise to an extraordinary amount of importations during the first year of peace, equal at least to the supply of two years; if the fact, that the double duties are limited in their continuance to a year after the termination of the war, did not operate as a check upon importations, beyond what may be requisite for the consumption of the present year. These counteracting causes may, therefore, be reasonably supposed to neutralize the force of each other, and, consequently, to refer and confine any estimate of the double duties upon merchandise imported in the year 1815, to the amount of the importations for the consumption of a single year.

Under these views it is estimated that the produce of the customs, during the first twelve months of peace, will amount, with double duties, to a sum between eighteen and twenty millions of dollars. Of that period ten months occur in the year 1815; but as the importations can only partially commence for the space of two months, and cannot reach their average extent for three or four months, the fair proportion of time to form the ground of an estimate, will be (as already suggested) eight months of the year 1815. Upon this scale of computation the product of the customs, which will accrue from the 1st of May to the 31st of December, 1815, will probably be $13,500,000; but there must be added to that sum the estimated amount of customs accruing, independent of the effects produced by the peace, from the 1st of January to the 1st of May, to wit, $1,500,000; making the aggregate of the revenue of the customs, accruing in the year 1815, about $15,000,000.

It remains, however, to present an estimate of the amount of the customs which will not only accrue, but which will be actually received at the Treasury in the year 1815. The extent of the commerce, which is expected to be opened, and the effects of the credits which are allowed for the payment of duties for the year 1815, have been already explained. The estimate, therefore, assumes the following form:

1. The total revenue of the customs, accruing in the year 1815, being, as above stated   - $15,000,000

It is estimated that, of that sum, there will become payable, and will actually be received into the Treasury, in the

year 1815, in the manner exhibited in the annexed schedule marked A, about   3,500,000

2. That on account of custom-house bonds outstanding at the end of the year 1814, which, in the letter from this Department, dated the 17th of January, 1815, was reserved to meet the unsatisfied appropriations of that year, there will be received during the year 1815, near   -   -   -   3,000,000

Making the total amount of the actual receipts into the Treasury, from the customs, for the year 1815   - $6,500,000

The ways and means of the Treasury for 1815, provided and payable during the year, may now be presented in a view essentially different from that which was necessarily taken in the letter from this Department, dated the 17th of January last, while contemplating a continuance of the war.

1. The duties on imports and tonnage will, probably, produce a sum, inclusive of that receivable for duties which accrued prior to the present year, of about   -   -   -   -   - $6,500,000

2. The direct tax, instead of a sum of $2,000,000, will probably give to the Treasury, in the year 1815, in consequence of the facilities of the peace, a sum of about   -   -   -   -   -   2,500,000

3. The internal duties, old and new, and postage, instead of a sum of $7,050,000, will probably give to the Treasury, in the year 1815, in consequence of the facilities of the peace, a sum of about   8,000,000

4. The sales of the public lands will probably produce, in the year 1815   -   1,000,000

5. The amount of incidental receipts, from miscellaneous sources, will, probably, be about   -   -   -   -   200,000

$18,200,000

While the revenue is thus materially augmented, the charges upon the Treasury will be considerably reduced. It is not in the power of this Department, at the present time, to advert to the estimates of the expenses of the peace establishment for the War and Navy Departments; but with the aid of the public credit, and the legislative sanction for the measures which will be proposed, it is believed that the Treasury will be competent, in that respect, to meet the most liberal views of the Government. Independent, therefore, of the estimates of the War and Navy Departments, the charges on the Treasury for the year 1815 will consist of the following items:

1. Civil, diplomatic, and miscellaneous expenses, as stated in the general estimates for one thousand eight hundred and fifteen   -   - $1,979,289 39

2. The public debt will call for a sum of $14,723,808 56, to answer the following claims:

For interest and reimbursement of the funded debt created before the war, (the amount of principal unredeemed on the 31st of December, 1814, being about $39,905,183 dollars 60 cents,) $3,452,775 46.

1183   HISTORY OF CONGRESS.   1184

H. OF R.   *Tax Bills—Defence of New Orleans.*   FEBRUARY, 1815.

For interest of the funded debt created since the war, (the amount of principal on December 31, 1814, being $48,580,812 26, to which little has been since added,) about— $3,000,000 00

For the principal and interest of Treasury notes falling due in 1815, and the first January, 1816, including $620,000 of notes issued under the act of February 25, 1813, falling due within this period   8,271,033 12

          14,723,606 58

          $16,703,097 97

It is to be observed, however, that the preceding estimate does not include a sum of $2,799,200, being the principal of the Treasury notes which became due in 1814, and remain unpaid, because the unexecuted authority to raise money by loan for that year is sufficient to cover the amount, if a loan can be obtained, independent of the custom-house debt ($3,000,000) which accrued in 1814, but is payable in 1815, and which is now considered as part of the excess of $3,975,909 83, stated in the letter of the 17th of January, 1815, for the purpose of being specifically transferred, in the present estimates, from the ways and means of last year to the credit of the ways and means for the present year.

Upon the whole, then, it appears that the revenue for the year 1815 will probably amount to $18,200,000, and that ways and means are now to be devised to provide for the difference between that sum and the aggregate amount of the demands for the service of the year 1815; which will be ascertained by adding the amount of the estimates for the peace establishment of the War and Navy Departments to the amount of the demands for the expenses of Government and the public debt, being, as above stated, the sum of $16,703,097 97.

It only remains to suggest some additional measures, which appear to be required at this time for the support of the public credit, and the supply of the Treasury.

1. It is respectfully suggested that all the holders of the Treasury notes, issued or to be issued under the authority of any existing law, should be allowed to fund them at an interest of seven per cent.; and that interest be allowed on all Treasury notes which have not been punctually paid, until the day of funding, or of payment.

2. It is respectfully suggested that a new issue of Treasury notes should be authorized upon the principles suggested in the letter from this Department, dated the 17th of January, 1815.

3. It is respectfully suggested that a loan should be authorized to the amount necessary, upon a view of all the estimates, to complete the ways and means for the year 1815.

4. It is respectfully suggested, that the exportation of specie should be prohibited for a limited period.

I am, very respectfully, sir, your most obedient servant,   A. J. DALLAS.

J. W. EPPES, Esq.,

TAX BILLS.

The amendments of the Senate to the bill amendatory of the direct tax and furniture tax bill, were before the House, and partly agreed and partly disagreed to. Among the amendments, was one repealing the section allowing annual assumption by the States of their respective quotas of the direct tax, and allowing a deduction of fifteen per cent. on the amount so assumed. The Committee of Ways and Means recommended a disagreement to this amendment. This recommendation was supported by Messrs. EPPES, LOWNDES, FISK of Vermont, BARBOUR, JACKSON of Virginia, FARROW, MACON, and TAYLOR, and opposed by Messrs. PITKIN, and SHEFFEY.

In favor of the amendment, it was urged, by the latter gentlemen, that, although in time of war there might be good reasons for authorizing the anticipation of the revenue by allowing assumption of the direct tax by the States, yet, as a permanent tax, the direct tax and all other taxes ought to be collected by the United States' officers; and, besides, that the discount of fifteen per centum on such assumption was too great. Mr. SHEFFEY contended that this mode of laying direct tax was unconstitutional, inasmuch as the taxes ought to be laid on the people, and not on the States. Against the amendment was opposed the greater convenience to the people of allowing this mode of assumption, and the obvious advantages to the United States from that mode of collection, which, it was alleged, was also more economical than any other, inasmuch as it obviated the difficulties and delays unavoidably interposing in the way of the collection of the direct tax, and insured greater security to the revenue.

This amendment of the Senate was eventually disagreed to.

DEFENCE OF NEW ORLEANS.

An unfortunate disagreement having arisen between the two Houses as to the terms of the resolution bestowing thanks on General Jackson, a message was received from the Senate announcing its adherence to its disagreement to the amendments proposed by the House thereto. This left to the House the alternative only, it was believed, to adhere to or recede from its amendments.

Mr. TROUP proposed to adhere, in which course he was supported by Messrs. ROBERTSON, RHEA, and HUMPHREYS; on the other hand, Messrs. HAWKINS, WRIGHT, and MACON, were desirous of receding, if a conference could not be agreed on.

The point of difference is, that the House proposes to ascribe the merit of the great achievements on the banks of the Mississippi, principally to the militia volunteer force; whilst the Senate has given the merit generally to the regulars, volunteers, and militia, in language admitting the inference, it is contended, that our force was principally a regular force.

It was, therefore, argued, in favor of adherence, that the resolution of this House was a veritable history of the facts as they occurred, giving honor to those to whom honor was due, and that the resolution had better be lost altogether than to enter upon record a vote which would convey an erroneous impression, as it was contended the resolution of the Senate did. In favor of receding, it was argued, that history would narrate, in conspicuous characters, the facts as they exist, and that the light in which they would be viewed by posterity, would not depend on the terms of the vote of Congress on this occasion. The object of such a vote was not to afford materials for history, but to express the gratitude of the nation to its defenders. In the course of the debate, Mr. MACON took occasion to pass a very high eulogium on the character of Major General Jackson, whom he said he had long personally known, and he did not believe there existed a more honorable or highminded man.

In the end, the House determined, before a final decision, to request a conference with the Senate on the subject.

DISTRICT BANKS.

Mr. KENT, of Maryland having called up the order of the day on the bill to incorporate the Farmers and Mechanics' Bank of Georgetown—

Mr. YANCEY proposed to postpone this order of the day indefinitely, under the impression that Congress would not act upon it at the present session.

The motion was opposed by Mr. JACKSON of Virginia, and Mr. KENT, but was decided in the affirmative.

The bill to incorporate the Bank of the Metropolis being called up by Mr. KENT of Maryland, the House refused to go into a Committee of the Whole on that bill.

Mr. GROSVENOR then moved to postpone the further consideration of the motion indefinitely.

Which motion was opposed by Mr. JOHNSON, and Mr. SHARP of Kentucky, and supported by Mr. GOLDSBOROUGH of Maryland.

In support of the motion, it was alleged, generally, that all the applications of this character ought to share the same fate. Against it, it was argued that Washington had not been hitherto equally favored by Congress, it being notorious that there was greatly less incorporated bank capital in Washington than in either Georgetown or Alexandria.

The question on indefinite postponement was decided in the affirmative.

THURSDAY, February 23.

The amendments proposed by the Senate to the bill "giving the right of pre-emption in the purchase of lands to certain settlers in the Indiana Territory" were read, and concurred in by the House.

The amendments proposed by the Senate to the bill "for the regulation of the courts of justice of Indiana," were read, and concurred in by the House.

The bill from the Senate, "authorizing the discharge of Edward Martin from imprisonment,"

13th CON. 3d SESS.—38

was read twice, and committed to a Committee of the Whole.

The bill from the Senate, "for the better temporary accommodation of the two Houses of Congress," was read twice and committed to a Committee of the Whole.

The bill from the Senate, "to repeal certain acts therein mentioned," was read twice, and ordered to be read a third time to-day.

Mr. EPPES, from the Committee of Ways and Means, reported back to the House the bill to authorize the settlement and payment of certain claims for the services of the militia, sent from the Senate, without amendment; and it was committed to a Committee of the Whole.

Mr. EPPES, under the direction of the same committee, moved,

"That the Secretary of the Treasury be directed to report at the next session a general tariff of duties proposed to be imposed upon imported goods, wares, and merchandise."

The motion was agreed to, *nem. con.*

On motion of Mr. SEYBERT, the Committee on Naval Affairs were instructed to inquire into the expediency of providing by law for the purchase of the vessels captured by Commodore Macdonough on Lake Champlain in the month of September last, with leave to report by bill or otherwise.

On motion of Mr. SHERWOOD, the Committee of Ways and Means were instructed to inquire whether any, and, if any, what alterations ought to be made in the laws relative to duties imposed on stills, employed solely in the rectification of spirituous liquors.

A message from the Senate informed the House that the Senate have passed the bill entitled "An act to authorize the President to raise certain companies of rangers for the defence of the frontiers of the United States, and to repeal certain acts now in force for this purpose," with amendments. They have passed bills of the following titles: "An act to repeal so much of the several acts imposing duties on the tonnage of ships and vessels, and on goods, wares, and merchandise, imported into the United States, as imposes a discriminating duty on tonnage between foreign vessels and vessels of the United States, and between goods imported into the United States in foreign vessels and vessels of the United States;" "An act further supplementary to an act, entitled 'An act providing for the indemnification of certain claimants of public lands in the Mississippi Territory;'" "An act to provide a library room, and for transporting the library lately purchased;" and "An act to repeal certain acts concerning the flotilla service, and for other purposes;" in which amendments and bills they ask the concurrence of this House. They agree to the amendment to the act, entitled "An act to provide additional revenues for defraying the expenses of Government, and maintaining the public credit, by laying duties on household furniture, and on gold and silver watches," and insist on their fifth amendment disagreed to by this House.

The bill from the Senate, "to repeal certain

acts therein mentioned," was read the third time, and passed.

Two or three Messages were received from the President of the United States, one of which it appeared was of a confidential nature; and the doors were closed and galleries cleared, and, after so remaining for a short time, were again opened; when the following Message, being of a public nature, was read:

To the Senate and House of
    Representatives of the United States:

I lay before Congress copies of two ratified treaties which were entered into on the part of the United States, one on the 22d day of July, 1814, with the several tribes of Indians, called the Wyandotts, Delawares, Shawanees, Senacas, and Miamies; the other on the 9th day of August, 1814, with the Creek nation of Indians.

It is referred to the consideration of Congress, how far Legislative provisions may be necessary for carrying any part of those stipulations into effect.

JAMES MADISON.

February 22, 1815.

The Message and treaties were referred to the Committee of Ways and Means.

The engrossed bill, authorizing the sale of the public lands, which may hereafter be forfeited within the Jeffersonville district, to be exposed for sale at the land office within the same; the engrossed bill to authorize the discharge of A. B. Ross from his imprisonment; the engrossed bill for the relief of Thomas Spriggs; the engrossed bill for the relief of James Savage and others; the engrossed bill for the relief of Solomon Frazer, and the representatives of Charles Eccleston; the engrossed bill for the relief of William P. Bennet; and the engrossed bill supplementary to the act "for the final adjustment of land titles in the State of Louisiana and Territory of Missouri," were severally read a third time, and passed.

MISSISSIPPI TERRITORY.

Mr. LATTIMORE, from the select committee on the memorial of the Legislature of the Mississippi Territory, praying admission into the Union, made a report favorable thereto, accompanied by a bill authorizing the people of the Territory of Mississippi to call a convention for the purpose of forming a Constitution and State Government preparatory to admission into the Union. The report was read, and, with the bill, on the motion of Mr. L., ordered to lie on the table.

The report is as follows:

By the articles of cession and agreement between the United States and the State of Georgia, it is provided that the Territory aforesaid shall form a State, and be admitted as such into the Union, as soon as it shall contain sixty thousand free inhabitants, or at an earlier period, if Congress shall think it expedient. Agreeably to the last general census, the population of this Territory, of all descriptions, amounted to forty thousand three hundred and fifty-two souls. Since this was taken, the amount has considerably increased by the annexation of that part of West Florida which lies east of Pearl river, and also, as your committee are informed, by emigrations to the eastern settlements of the Territory from several of the States.

Your committee are in possession of no data from which they can form an estimate of the number to which these accessions of population may amount; but they deem it not an unreasonable presumption that the return of peace, by renewing inducements to emigration, may produce an increase to the amount required by the agreement with Georgia, by the time the usual preparatory steps can be taken towards the actual admission of the Territory into the Union as a State. It would seem, therefore, as if what is now solicited would be obtained, of course, in a few years at most.

The question, then, is, is it expedient to provide for the adoption of this Territory into the Union as a favor, or was its admission of right?

The expediency of anticipating the admission of this community to the rights of an independent State involves in its consideration as well the particular interest of the Territory as the general interest of the United States. In relation to the former, it is to be presumed that the people themselves, who are best acquainted with their own local condition, can best judge of their ability to bear the additional expense of self-government, and weigh other consequences which may ensue from the change. As it respects the latter, your committee possess no facts which would add to the information, and can offer no reasons which would influence the opinion of the House on this point. Their mere opinion is all they have to submit; and it is, that there would be no impropriety in principle, and no injury in effect, to the interest of the nation, in providing, without further delay, for the admission of the Territory in question into the union of the States.

This Territory has been, as your committee believe, a longer time under the restraints of political minority than any other Territory of the United States; and they can perceive no good reason why its enlargement should still be deferred, merely on account of its present deficiency of numbers, since a like deficiency did not prevent others, or one other at least, from the enjoyment of a similar boon.

Hitherto your committee have considered this subject as though the admission solicited were desired by all the inhabitants of the Territory without delay, but they cannot undertake to state that such is the fact. While it is true, that it has been prayed for and urged with much interest and zeal at several successive sessions, it is also true that at the last one at which the subject was brought before Congress there were counter-petitions, praying that it might be postponed. How far a union of sentiment and wishes may be inferred from the absence of any counter-petition at the present session, when it was known that the memorial under consideration had been forwarded, your committee are not prepared to say. They can, however, judge and act from only what is before them; and it is to be presumed that the representatives of the people express the will of their constituents, unless the contrary appears. To which consideration it may be added, that the extinguishment of the Yazoo claims having removed what was perhaps the most general objection to admission, it is probable that many who were opposed to it are now in favor of it; and, since peace is restored, it is probable, also, that many others will desire to exchange the restrictions of a Territory for the rights of a State. If, however, from local considerations, other than those suggested, a difference of opinion in relation to the expediency of this object should still exist, your committee conceive that the question cannot be more fairly settled than by a convention, which should first decide whether it should form a constitution or not, and which might be chosen with a reference to the respective sentiments of the members on this particular point.

Believing it expedient, therefore, that the people of the Mississippi Territory should be authorized to elect a convention, with powers to form a constitution, as prayed for by the memorialists, your committee have prepared a bill for this purpose, which they ask leave to report.

MILITIA BOUNTY.

The following resolutions were submitted by Mr. EASTON:

1. *Resolved*, That the Committee on Military Affairs be instructed to inquire into the expediency of allowing to each non-commissioned officer and private of the militia of the Missouri Territory, who have performed a tour of duty by order of the Government of the United States, a donation in lands, as a compensation for their services.

2. *Resolved*, That the said committee be instructed to inquire into the expediency of granting donations of land to the frontier inhabitants of said Territory, who have been forced by the enemies of the United States to abandon their plantations or dwellings, and who have not abandoned or removed out of the said Territory.

The House proceeded to consider the said resolutions, and the same were amended to read as follows:

1. *Resolved*, That the committee appointed on that part of the President's Message, at the commencement of the session, which relates to the militia, be instructed to inquire into the expediency of allowing to each non-commissioned officer and private of the militia of the United States, and Territories thereof, who have performed a tour of duty by the order of the Government of the United States, a donation in lands, as a compensation for their services.

2. *Resolved*, That the said committee be instructed to inquire into the expediency of granting donations of lands to the frontier inhabitants of said States and Territories, who have been forced by the enemies of the United States to abandon their plantations and dwellings, and who have not abandoned or removed out of the said States or Territories.

And on the question to agree to the said resolutions, it was determined in the negative.

PAY OF MEMBERS.

Mr. FISK, of Vermont, offered for consideration the following resolution:

Resolved, That the Committee of Ways and Means be instructed to inquire into the expediency of making provision by law for paying the members of this House in money current in the States to which they respectively belong.

This motion gave rise to some debate.

Mr. FISK grounded his motion on the discount the Eastern members were obliged to pay for Eastern notes, and the alleged impropriety of members of Congress travelling from shop to shop selling their wages, or bartering off the notes they receive in payment for such as shall be current in their States, &c.

Mr. RHEA moved to amend the resolution, by striking out the latter part of it, and inserting in lieu thereof, the words "Treasury notes or bank notes."

The object of the whole motion was supported by Mr. WRIGHT, Mr. FISK, and Mr. POTTER, and opposed by Mr. RHEA, Mr. NEWTON. Mr. FARROW, Mr. EPPES, Mr. INGHAM, Mr. McKIM, and Mr. HAWKINS, who denied both its necessity and expediency.

A motion of Mr. EPPES, to lay the resolution on the table, was negatived.

Mr. HAWKINS moved an indefinite postponement of the whole subject, on the general and very obvious ground of the injustice of members of Congress discriminating between themselves and other public creditors, who have at least equally high claims on the Government.

Several unsuccessful motions were made to get rid of this question, by proceeding to the orders of the day, or laying it on the table. The question on indefinite postponement, was at length decided by yeas and nays—for the postponement 82, against it 50, as follows:

YEAS—Messrs. Alexander, Alston, Anderson, Avery, Barbour, Bard, Bines, Bowen, Brown, Caperton, Calhoun, Cannon, Clopton, Comstock, Cox, Crawford, Creighton, Cuthbert, Davis of Pennsylvania, Desha, Duvall, Eppes, Farrow, Findley, Fisk of New York, Forsyth, Franklin, Geddes, Gholson, Goodwyn, Gourdin, Griffin, Hall, Harris, Hawes, Hawkins, Humphreys, Hungerford, Ingersoll, Ingham, Jackson of Virginia, Johnson of Kentucky, Kennedy, Kent of Maryland, Kerr, Lefferts, Lewis, Lovett, Lowndes, Lyle, Macon, McCoy, McKee, McKim, McLean, Montgomery, Moore, Newton, Ormsby, Pearson, Piper, Pleasants, Rhea of Pennsylvania, Rhea of Tennessee, Rich, Ridgely, Ringgold, Roane, Robertson, Sage, Sevier, Seybert, Sharp, Smith of Virginia, Tannehill, Taylor, Telfair, Troup, Udree, Ward of New Jersey, Williams, and Yancey.

NAYS—Messrs. Baylies of Massachusetts, Bigelow, Boyd, Bradbury, Brigham, Butler, Champion, Cooper, Culpeper, Davenport, Ely, Fisk of Vermont, Gaston, Goldsborough, Grosvenor, Hale, Hasbrouck, Henderson, Hopkins of Kentucky, Hubbard, Hulbert, Kent of New York, King of Massachusetts, Moseley, Nelson, Oakley, Parker, Pickering, Potter, John Reed, William Reed, Ruggles, Schureman, Sherwood, Slaymaker, Smith of New York, Stanford, Stuart, Sturges, Taggart, Thompson, Vose, Wheaton, White, Wilcox, Wilson of Massachusetts, Wilson of Pennsylvania, Winter, Wood, and Wright.

So the resolve was indefinitely postponed.

The House resumed the consideration of the bill declaratory of the powers of the Legislature of the Territory of Illinois. And debate arising on the amendment proposed by Mr. McLEAN, on the 21st instant, the House adjourned.

FRIDAY, February 24.

The House proceeded to reconsider their disagreement to the fifth amendment proposed by the Senate to the bill "to amend the act to provide additional revenues for defraying the expenses of Government, and maintaining the public credit, by laying a direct tax upon the United States, and

1191   HISTORY OF CONGRESS.   1192

H. OF R.   *Tax Collectors—Relations with Algiers.*   FEBRUARY, 1815.

to provide for assessing and collecting the same;" and the act "to provide additional revenues for defraying the expenses of Government, and maintaining the public credit, by laying a duty on household furniture, and on gold and silver watches." Whereupon,

Resolved, That this House insist on their disagreement to the said fifth amendment, and ask a conference with the Senate upon the subject-matter thereof.

Ordered, That Messrs. EPPES, LOWNDES, and OAKLEY, be the managers at the said conference on the part of this House.

The amendments proposed by the Senate to the bill "to authorize the President to raise certain companies of rangers for the defence of the frontiers of the United States, and to repeal certain acts now in force for that purpose," were read, and, together with the bill, ordered to lie on the table.

The bill from the Senate "further supplementary to an act, entitled 'An act providing for the indemnification of certain claimants of public lands in the Mississippi Territory,'" was read twice, and committed to a Committee of the Whole.

The bill from the Senate, "to repeal so much of the several acts imposing duties on the tonnage of ships and vessels, and on goods, wares, and merchandise, imported into the United States, as imposes a discriminating duty on tonnage between foreign vessels and vessels of the United States, and between goods imported into the United States in foreign vessels and vessels of the United States," was read twice, and committed to the Committee of Ways and Means.

The bill from the Senate, "to provide a library room, and for transporting the library lately purchased," was read twice, and committed to a Committee of the Whole.

The bill from the Senate, "to repeal certain acts concerning the flotilla service, and for other purposes," was read twice, and referred to the Committee on Naval Affairs.

Mr. TROUP, from the committee of conference on the disagreeing votes of the two Houses in regard to the resolution of Congress expressive of their sense of General Jackson's great achievement, made a report, recommending a modification thereof, which was agreed to on the part of this House.

Mr. FISK, of New York, from the committee to whom was referred Mr. CULPEPER'S motion for a thanksgiving day, reported the same with amendments; which having been agreed to, the resolution as amended was ordered to a third reading.

TAX COLLECTORS.

Mr. FISK, of New York, from the Committee of Ways and Means, to whom was recommitted the engrossed bill to fix the compensations and increase the responsibility of the collectors of the direct tax and internal duties, and for other purposes connected with the collection thereof, reported the same with amendments; which were

read, and the first thereof was concurred in by the House.

The question was then taken to concur in the second amendment, which proposes to strike out the following words contained in the 8th section of the bill, to wit:

"And it shall further be the duty of the said collectors, by themselves, or their deputies, to attend at the court-house of each of the counties or districts composing their respective collection districts, on the first and second days of each term of the court of the county or common pleas in said county or district, if the court continue in session so long."

And passed in the affirmative—yeas 76, nays 49, as follows:

YEAS—Messrs. Alexander, Alston, Anderson, Avery, Barbour, Bard, Bigelow, Bines, Bowen, Boyd, Bradbury, Brown, Butler, Calhoun, Comstock, Condict, Crawford, Creighton, Crouch, Cuthbert, Davis of Pennsylvania, Desha, Duvall, Ely, Eppes, Findley, Fisk of New York, Forsyth, Goodwyn, Griffin, Hall, Hasbrouck, Hopkins of Kentucky, Humphreys, Ingersoll, Ingham, Jackson of Rhode Island, Jackson of Virginia, Johnson of Kentucky, Law, Lefferts, Lowndes, Lyle, McCoy, McKim, McLean, Moore, Moseley, Newton, Ormsby, Pickering, Piper, Pitkin, William Reed, Rea of Pennsylvania, Rhea of Tennessee, Rich, Ringgold, Roane, Sage, Sharp, Smith of Pennsylvania, Smith of Virginia, Strong, Sturges, Taggart, Tannehill, Taylor, Telfair, Troup, Udree, Wheaton, Williams, Wilson of Massachusetts, Winter, and Wright.

NAYS—Messrs. Brigham, Caperton, Cannon, Champion, Clopton, Cooper, Culpeper, Farrow, Fisk of Vermont, Franklin, Gaston, Gholson, Goldsborough, Grosvenor, Hale, Harris, Hawes, Henderson, Hubbard, Hungerford, Hulbert, Irwin, Kennedy, Kent of New York, Kerr, King of Massachusetts, Lovett, Macon, Markell, Montgomery, Nelson, Pickens, Pleasants, Ruggles, Schureman, Sevier, Sherwood, Shipherd, Slaymaker, Stanford, Stockton, Stuart, Thompson, Vose, Ward of Massachusetts, White, Wilcox, Wilson of Massachusetts, and Yancey.

Ordered, That the said bill be re-engrossed, and read the third time to-morrow.

RELATIONS WITH ALGIERS.

The following report, yesterday transmitted to the House by the PRESIDENT OF THE UNITED STATES, was read:

DEPARTMENT OF STATE, *Feb.* 20, 1815.

The acting Secretary of State, to whom was referred the resolution of the House of Representatives of the 15th instant, requesting the President of the United States to cause to be laid before that House such information as he shall deem necessary to be communicated, touching the state of relations existing between the United States and the Barbary Powers, has the honor to state, that, according to the latest accounts from Morocco, Tunis, and Tripoli, our relations with those Powers remained upon their former footing; nor is there any particular reason to believe that any change has since taken place.

It will appear, by the documents accompanying the Message of the President to Congress on the 17th November, 1812, that the Dey of Algiers had, violently and without just cause, obliged the Consul of the United States, and all American citizens then in Algiers, to leave that place in a manner highly offensive to their country and injurious to themselves, and in violation of the treaty then subsisting between the two nations. It appears, moreover, that he exacted from the Consul, under pain of immediate imprisonment, a large sum of money, to which he had no claim but what originated in his own injustice.

These acts of violence and outrage have been followed by the capture of at least one American vessel, and by the seizure of an American citizen on board a neutral vessel. The unfortunate persons thus captured, are yet held in captivity, with the exception of two of them, who have been ransomed. Every effort to obtain the release of the others has proved abortive; and there is some reason to believe that they are held by the Dey as a means by which he calculates to extort from the United States a degrading treaty.

JAMES MONROE.

The galleries were then cleared, and the doors of the House closed, and so remained until near five o'clock, when the House adjourned.

SATURDAY, February 25.

Mr. EPPES, from the Committee of Ways and Means, reported a bill to authorize a loan for a sum not exceeding —— dollars; which was read twice, and committed to a Committee of the Whole.

Mr. EPPES also reported a bill to prohibit the exportation of specie, gold or silver coins, or bullion; which was read twice, and committed to a Committee of the Whole.

Mr. YANCEY, from the Committee of Claims, reported a bill for the relief of Thomas B. Farish; which was read twice, and committed to a Committee of the Whole.

On motion of Mr. YANCEY, the Committee of Claims were discharged from the further consideration of the petition of William Thornton, and it was referred to the Secretary of State.

Mr. PLEASANTS, from the Committee on Naval Affairs, reported a bill authorizing the purchase of the vessels captured on Lake Champlain; which was read twice, and committed to a Committee of the Whole.

Mr. PLEASANTS, also from the Naval Committee, to whom was referred the bill for repealing certain acts relative to the flotilla service, reported an amendment thereto, the object of which was to authorize the President to cause to be sold such of the gunboats now in service as he shall deem it unnecessary to retain. And this amendment being agreed to, the bill was ordered to be read a third time, and was accordingly subsequently read a third time, passed, and the concurrence of the Senate desired in the amendment.

On motion of Mr. NEWTON,

Ordered, That the digest of the manufactures of the United States, made in pursuance of an order of this House, under the direction of the Secretary of the Treasury, be distributed amongst the members of the House of Representatives and of the Senate of the United States, and Executive authorities of the States and Territories.

A message from the Senate informed the House that the Senate have passed the bill from this House, entitled "An act to amend and extend the provisions of the act of the 16th of April, 1814, entitled 'An act confirming certain claims to land in the Illinois Territory, and providing for their location,'" with amendments. The amendments were read, and concurred in by the House.

The House resumed the consideration of the bill declaratory of the powers of the Legislature of the Territory of Illinois; and the amendment proposed by Mr. McLEAN, on the 21st instant, was concurred in by the House, and the bill ordered to be engrossed, and read a third time on Monday next.

An engrossed bill to fix the compensations and increase the responsibility of the collectors of the direct tax and internal duties, and for other purposes, connected with the collection thereof, was read the third time and passed.

An engrossed resolution for the appointment of a joint committee to wait upon the President and request that he recommend a day of thanksgiving to Almighty God for his goodness in restoring to these United States the blessings of peace, was read the third time and passed.

The bill from the Senate, "to repeal certain acts concerning the flotilla service, and for other purposes," was read the third time, as amended, and passed.

A Message was received from the President of the United States recommending the navigation of American vessels exclusively by American seamen, either natives, or such as are already naturalized.—Referred to the Committee on Foreign Relations.

Mr. FISK, of New York, offered for consideration the following resolution:

Resolved, That a committee be appointed to inquire into the expediency, of providing by law, for the meeting of the next Congress.

Mr. F. said, he was not prepared to say that it was necessary to pass such a law; but he was prepared to say that the state of the nation was such as to make it expedient to inquire into the subject, and ascertain whether an extra session might not be necessary, or, if not, at an earlier session than will take place otherwise.

The resolution was agreed to.

A message from the Senate informed the House that the Senate unanimously agree to the amendment to the resolution "expressive of the thanks of Congress to Major General Jackson, and the troops under his command, for their gallantry and good conduct in the defence of New Orleans," modified agreeably to the report of the committee of conference. They agree to the conference upon the disagreeing vote of the two Houses upon the subject-matter of the fifth amendment to the bill "to amend the act, entitled "An act to provide additional revenue for defraying the expenses of Government, and maintaining the public credit, by laying a direct tax upon the United States, and to provide for assessing and collecting the same," and the act, entitled "An act to provide additional revenues for defraying the expenses of Government, and maintaining the public credit, by laying duties on household furniture and on gold and silver watches;"

to which conference they have appointed managers on their part. They have passed the bill from the House, entitled "An act to alter and establish post roads," with amendments. And they have passed bills of the following titles: "An act making further provision for completing the public buildings at West Point, for the accommodation of the Military Academy ;" and "An act to continue in force, for a limited time, the act, entitled 'An act for establishing trading houses with the Indian tribes ;" in which amendments and bills they ask the concurrence of this House.

PROTECTION TO MANUFACTURES.

Mr. Seybert presented a petition of sundry manufacturers residing in the city and county of Philadelphia, and State of Pennsylvania, praying for the adoption of such measures as will afford to the manufacturers of the country that protection and support necessary to bring them to maturity.—The memorial is as follows:

To the honorable the Senate and House of Representatives of the United States in Congress met, the memorial of the manufacturers of the city and county of Philadelphia respectfully showeth :

That your memorialists, while filled with joy and exultation for the inestimable blessing of honorable peace to their country, cannot divest themselves of anxiety and dread for the fate of the infant manufactures, whose existence and prosperity are unquestionably of vital importance to the whole community. That, trusting to Providence, to the wisdom and protection of your honorable body, and to their own industry, they look forward, with hope, to the permanent establishment of such manufactures as shall render the United States independent on foreign nations for the necessaries and comforts of life.

That, confiding implicitly in the wisdom and patriotism of your honorable body, your memorialists will not presume to suggest any particular measure, but will content themselves with observing, that every civilised nation has thought proper, by legislative acts, to afford to the industry of their respective countries that protection and support necessary to bring forth to maturity the establishment of manufactures necessary to their existence and prosperity. The intimate connexion of the agricultural with the manufacturing interest, and the extreme importance of a competent supply, in times of war, for the Army and Navy of the United States, without dependance on foreign aid, will be so obvious to your honorable body as to require no comment on the part of your memorialists.

But your memorialists respectfully beg leave to call the attention of your honorable body to the existence and correction of an abuse, which is, at the same time, destructive of the revenues of the United States, highly injurious to the honest merchant, and, if persisted in, will render entirely useless any law enacting protecting duties. This abuse is the introduction, through the custom-houses of our country, of merchandise subject to ad valorem duties, at from one-fourth to one-half of their value. This enormity, practised in various shapes, cannot be checked by any provision of the present revenue laws, and it is to the wisdom of your honorable body, alone, that your memorialists and the country can look for a competent remedy. This remedy may probably be found in the substitution of specific for ad

valorem duties, or in the establishment of a board, at each custom-house, possessing the requisite power; which board might be composed of the collector and naval officer, and one respectable competent individual capable of deciding on the value of merchandise imported. The extraordinary expense to be borne by the merchandise imported.

Your memorialists respectfully add, that, in making the above suggestion, they resign themselves, with perfect confidence, to the better judgment of your honorable body. And for the welfare of your honorable body your memorialists will ever sincerely pray.

THOMAS GILPIN, *and others.*

The memorial was referred to the Committee of Ways and Means.

PROTESTED BILLS OF EXCHANGE.

Mr. Hawkins moved the adoption of the following resolution :

Resolved, That the Committee of Ways and Means, be instructed to inquire into the expediency of refunding to individuals the amount of damages, or loss of interest sustained in consequence of the protest of any bills of exchange, drawn on the Government by any individuals, within the last last twelve months.

In reply to an inquiry by Mr. McKim, for facts on which this motion was predicated—

Mr. Hawkins stated, that there had been a few instances in which individuals had procured bills of exchange on the Government, and, in consequence of inability to pay them, had been compelled to pay damages thereon. There was only one case within his own knowledge, and that was one in which an individual had paid for a draft on the Government $14,000, which draft had been sold by him to the Bank of Kentucky, by it to the Bank of Pennsylvania, by whom, through the Bank of Washington, it had been presented to the Government, protested for want of funds, and returned. The laws of Kentucky authorizing ten per cent. damages on protested bills, paid over to third persons, that allowance had been claimed by the banks, and the individuals compelled to pay it. The bill had since been presented by him (Mr. Hawkins) to the Treasury, and paid in Treasury notes, on which the person before named was compelled to pay six and a half per cent. discount.

Mr. Farrow opposed the motion at some length, and moved to amend it by adding to the end thereof, the following words: "And also Treasury notes which have been paid by the Government to fair creditors, and necessarily sold by said creditors at a discount."

This amendment, after some conversation, having been agreed to by a small majority—

On motion of Mr. Hawkins, the motion as amended was ordered to lie on the table.

MILITARY PEACE ESTABLISHMENT.

The House went into Committee of the Whole, on the bill for fixing the Military Peace Establishment; and the first section of the bill having been read, which proposes to fix it at ten thousand men—

Mr. Troup said the Military Establishment had just been perfected—the Army had just been made one of the finest in the world, when it became necessary to reduce it. It was the less to be regretted, however, as the cause of it was a subject of sincere and universal congratulation—it was proper to reduce the Army. The only questions for the House were, 1st. The extent of the reduction. 2dly. The mode of reduction.

With respect to the first, (the extent of reduction) he presumed that three objects ought to claim the attention of the House. 1st. The security of the country; 2dly. The interest of the country; and 3dly. The just claims of the Army.

In considering the security of the country, it was only necessary to advert to the actual state of the country. The war had this moment terminated and left us surrounded with the fleets and armies—the formidable fleets and armies of our late enemy. What security had we that those fleets and armies would be withdrawn? At least we had no other security than the good faith of the nation with whom we had concluded the peace. Admitting that faith to be what it ought to be, he submitted with much deference to the House, whether the security of any country ought to be made to depend upon the good faith of any other country. He presumed that a respectable military force would be a much safer dependence. So said the policy and practice of all civilized nations—so said the policy and practice of all the nations of Europe. There the practice was to disband or withdraw *pari passu*—the one Power withdrawing as the other withdrew—the one Power reducing as the other reduced. He did not know an instance in European history of two nations terminating a war, by an honorable peace, where the one instantaneously reduced its military force to a Peace Establishment, leaving the other to maintain its force on a War Establishment upon its frontier. Such, however, would be precisely our case if we determined on a sudden and great reduction of the army.

The treaty of peace had stipulated the surrender of posts and the restoration of certain property—both were important, and yet what security had we that either stipulation would be fulfilled if we suddenly stripped ourselves of our military power? We would have no reliance left but on the good faith of our late enemy. If the posts were not surrendered or the property restored, he presumed we would begin to reorganize and restore our Army; he thought it therefore more wise and more prudent, on the ground of security, to make our reduction moderate, limited, and gradual.

But, 2dly. The interest of the country. The interest of the country, in one sense of the word, required not merely the reduction but the annihilation of the Army. It was the interest of the country to relieve the Government and country from the burden of the whole military expense; but this could only be done by the entire destruction of the military force. Why, therefore, was it not proposed to put down the Army altogether? Only because the security of the country forbade it. Here, then, was a consideration of interest connected with the consideration of security. But

there was an interest distinct and independent; it was that which would look with a steady eye to what were considered great and important rights and principles, not settled by the treaty of peace. The treaty of peace was a treaty of peace merely—it was properly such—it proposed little more than to put an end to the war. Much more remained to be settled; rights, principles and interests, considered essential to the prosperity of commerce, navigation and fisheries, remained to be settled. This was to be done in the only way in which it ought to be done—by a treaty of commerce. Nations negotiate with more weight and influence with arms in their hands than without them, and a large army would carry into a negotiation more weight and influence than a small one; he submitted therefore to the House, whether a great and sudden reduction of the Army would not prejudice those rights and interests, and whether the interest of the United States did not, on this account, require for the present the exhibition of a respectable military force.

But, 3dly. The just claims of the Army. Whether the reduction were great or small, instantaneous or eventual, the just claims of the Army could not fail to be a subject of consideration with the House. By the just claims of the Army he did not mean to be understood as speaking of absolute right on the one side and correspondent absolute obligation on the other; all he meant was, a just and equitable claim to liberal provision from the generosity of the Legislature. The officers and soldiers to be disbanded were entitled to a liberal provision, not because they had embarked in the regular service—not because they had exposed their lives in defence of their country—not because very many of them had been wounded and disabled—not because very many of them had fallen, leaving their wives and children dependent on the charities of the world—not because these brave men were still willing further to expose their lives—not because their skill and valor had greatly contributed to the restoration of the blessings of peace—not for all these—but because they had entered into the service for years, perhaps forever; abandoning the pursuits of civil life by which they subsisted and betaking themselves to arms as a profession. This profession was not by their own act, but by the act of Government suddenly and unexpectedly taken from them, and they were turned upon the world without occupation, many of them penniless and in debt. It was right, it was just, that a provision should be made which would enable them to subsist until they could find employment, it was the more so in a country where there was no pension list, no hotel of invalids; it was on this principle that all Governments had made liberal and generous provision for disbanded officers; it was on this principle that the Old Congress had made provision for the disbanded officers of the Revolution. The provision proposed was far from a liberal provision, but it was better than nothing; it was a provision in land and not in money; it was believed to be more convenient to the Government to give land than money. He hoped that the House would never think of disbanding the Army without making some provision.

Secondly. The mode of reduction. There were three modes of reducing the Army; the first was, by retaining in service all the regiments, reducing both officers and men—the skeletons of regiments being preserved, it would only be necessary on any emergency compelling a resort to arms, to fill up and supply; the second mode was, by reducing the number of regiments one-half or one-third, and reducing at the same time both officers and men of each regiment, but so reducing the officers as to retain a sufficient number of field, and company, and staff officers to enable the Government on the recurrence of war to double the number of regiments, giving to each regiment an experienced officer of the various grades; the third mode was, the consolidation and reduction proposed by the bill, the effect of which was, to reduce the Army to the old Peace Establishment. It was hoped that the House would consider the reduction to ten thousand as the lowest possible reduction; it would reduce the expense of the Military Establishment to a mere trifle compared with the war expenditure. He would give the estimate, which would show that the annual expense would be less than three millions:

10,000 men, at $200 each	- -	$2,000,000
2 major generals and aids	-	12,900
4 brigadier generals and aids	-	14,500
8 colonels	- -	13,000
14 lieutenant colonels	-	20,000
128 captains	- -	84,000
128 first lieutenants	-	78,000
128 second lieutenants	-	70,000
48 third lieutenants (artillery,)	-	23,600
128 ensigns	- -	60,764
		2,376,764
Staff	- - - -	100,000
Camp equipage	- -	60,000
Medicine and hospital stores	- -	30,000
Quartermaster's stores, fuel, stationery, straw, and transportation	- -	100,000
		$2,666,764

Making an aggregate expense of two millions six hundred thousand dollars. The actual expenditure would, he was convinced, fall short of the estimate; the war cost of a soldier, completely equipped and furnished, was three hundred and eight dollars per annum; the peace cost was only one hundred and ninety dollars per annum, but he had set it down at two hundred dollars per man; besides, the estimate supposed that the corps would always be full, which would seldom or never happen, and the quantity of camp equipage, hospital stores, and quartermaster's stores on hand, would, for the first year or two, make a considerable deduction from those items. With these observations he would submit the subject for the decision of the House.

Mr. PICKERING, said, he should be glad to know how this force was to be disposed of; where it was to be stationed, and how employed. He should be glad to hear the reasons why so large a number of men were to be employed, as, he said, the reasons in favor of so large a force had not been such as to satisfy him. If any detailed statement on these points were afforded, he said, the House would be better able to judge of the propriety of the course proposed.

Mr. TROUP said, the committee had no such detailed statement; but, there could be no doubt the troops would be stationed at the various posts and garrisons in the United States, and wherever their services would appear to be best applied.

Mr. DESHA said, duty impelled him to make a motion to try the sense of the Committee, as to the number of the Army necessary to be kept up for a Peace Establishment. Although he had always been in favor of the greatest number proposed in time of war, because he thought it prudent to relieve the militia from being harassed by draughts, yet he was not in favor of a large Peace Establishment. He therefore moved to strike out the word *ten* and insert *six.* He believed six thousand to be sufficient for all purposes in time of peace; we have no use for a regular army in time of peace, but for the purpose of keeping up the frontier garrisons, and to take care of the arms, &c.—then how many garrisons will it be necessary to keep up? not exceeding twenty-five or thirty. Indeed he believed thirty to be the extent of the number we have, and will not one hundred be sufficient, on an average, to each garrison? He said some would require perhaps more than a hundred, but others would not require more than twenty-five or thirty men—then supposing the average to be one hundred and the number of garrisons thirty, which will be the extent, you will require but three thousand for garrison purpose; then, admitting the amendment succeeds, you will have three thousand to go on, supposing the number always to be complete, but which is not to be presumed. Then where is the necessity of keeping up ten thousand? Gentlemen tell you it is necessary as a security against imposition from foreign Powers. Mr. D. said we have a better security than ten, or even fifty, thousand regulars. The yeomanry of the country is the great security; and circumstances have proven in this war that the militia and volunteers of the country, when well officered and managed, are able for the best veteran troops of Britain, which is, I confess, a subject of pride, because it proves that there is no necessity of keeping up a large standing army in time of peace. He said the people had suffered privations of every description since the declaration of war, and would have borne as much more if it had been necessary. They have acted generally worthy of freemen. But if all the taxes are to be rivetted on them for the purpose of keeping up large standing armies in time of peace, what have they gained by their patriotic exertions? Very little but the satisfaction of having decently drubbed the enemy in many instances. We have gotten through the war—peace is concluded—the first consideration in my estimation is to curtail our expenses, and by which ameliorate the condition of the people. It is proven that the militia of the country are capable at all times at least of defensive operations, consequently will not be willing to pay heavy taxes, for the purpose of keeping large standing armies. We have boasted that a well organized militia was the bulwark of our liberty, and recent circumstances have proved it to be a fact; then where is the necessity of going into a measure that is inconsistent with the nature of our Government? But it is said that ten thousand regular forces are necessary to keep the hostile Indians of the West in check. Mr. D. said regulars were not the kind of force the best adapted to Indian warfare; the Western riflemen were the best calculated to chastise the insolence of the Indians. There will be no difficulty, if it becomes necessary, to obtain a sufficiency of volunteer riflemen from the West to keep the Indians in check. They are the kind of force that the Indians are afraid of; they care very little for your regular musketry. But it is said to be imprudent to reduce the regular Army much till the British give up our garrisons. Sir, we have possession of, and have garrisons on their territory; we have also possession of two of the lakes. It is presumed that the garrisons on each side will be given up simultaneously. He said he believed there was no danger but they would give up the garrisons and be glad to be off so. They will not run the risk of having their veteran troops again chastised by the militia. Mr. D. said, the best security was, that the enemy know that we have nearly a million of militia, composed of the yeomanry of the country, who are willing at all times to protect their rights as becomes freemen.

Mr. Wʀɪɢʜᴛ said he hoped that the motion of his friend from Kentucky would not obtain. To reduce the Army at this time to six thousand, said he, appears to me to be premature, while the forces of Great Britain are yet in our neighborhood, and hovering on our coast. I think it should not be reduced to less than ten thousand, the number reported by the committee, and indeed, sir, a larger number would meet my approbation. It will be recollected, that there are several executory articles, the delivery of posts, &c., and in this posture of our affairs we ought to move with caution. The Kings and Emperors of Europe, it will be recollected, are now at Vienna distributing the spoils of their confederation, the petty dominions of the Continent, and may not do it so as to effect a general peace. They too have yet large armies. We ought not to forget the Treaty of Amiens, and the immediate breach of it, although I have little doubt of the sincerity of Great Britain in the peace, and hope it may be permanent. But, had she been insincere at the time, I am confident that the disaster her troops have sustained at New Orleans would be a perfect panacea of her war spirit against the United States. I hope my friend will withdraw his motion, upon its being considered that ten thousand men was the Peace Establishment in 1808, and then met the approbation of Congress, and that the Administration at this time have advised a much larger number. The Indians may not feel disposed to be at peace with us, although I have

the strongest grounds to hope they will, as I have always believed that they were pressed into the war by the British, and that, as they were now at peace with us, they would cease their excitements of the Indians to hostility against us, and that the effect will cease with the cause.

Mr. Dᴇsʜᴀ declined withdrawing his motion.

Mr. Sʜᴀʀᴘ said, he should have been gratified had the Military Committee given the House some statement of what number of troops would be necessary to keep up the garrisons at the different posts. He should like to know the number estimated by the Executive, as necessary for that purpose. If ten thousand men were necessary for that purpose, he would vote them; but he was unwilling to vote a single man for any other purpose. For the purposes of war a standing army of ten thousand men was nothing—for a Peace Establishment, five thousand were enough. The way to support the military character, and to propagate and preserve military science, he conceived, was by a liberal establishment of military schools, &c. Education makes soldiers. Our old army, the officers of which had generally been so long in service, had, he said, made no considerable figure during the late war; its officers had been generally eclipsed by those of later appointment. The officers of a Peace Establishment were by their habits fitted to command on garrison duty, but were frequently mere drones; it was in times of exigency, that talents and intrepidity were called to the standard of their country, and not in time of peace, when there was so little in the military life attractive to a man of spirit and enterprise. Mr. S. said, unless it should be proved to him, that ten thousand men were necessary for garrison duty, he should vote in favor of five thousand, which he believed to be sufficient. In time of peace, he believed no gentleman would employ our soldiers in opening roads, or making canals, as the Romans did theirs; they could therefore perform no labor or service, unless it was in building forts, repairing garrisons, or mere military parade. As to what might be the disposition of our late enemy, five, ten or fifteen thousand men more or less would not put us in a better situation to enforce our rights in the negotiation of a treaty of commerce, than we are now in. A decided course on the part of those who administer the Government, a proper use of their resources of men and money, would put them in a very short time in a condition to wage war, if it ever again became necessary, and would secure them the respect of those Powers disposed to invade our rights. Meanwhile, as things now stand, we ought to curtail our expenses, and husband our resources. This is a Government of the people, and, to carry them with you, the burdens you impose on them should be made as light as possible. Mr. S. said he felt as much as any one the value of the services rendered by our army; he admired as much as any one the brilliant achievements by the talents of our officers and the bravery of the soldiers. That character had been principally acquired since the commencement of the war, and was not to be supported by the extent of the

Peace Establishment beyond its necessary force, but rather by the establishment of proper military academical institutions throughout the country, &c.

Mr. Troup stated that the Military Committee had received from the War Department, yesterday, a communication, which, in its material parts, was a confidential communication, and improper to be exposed to the world at large, though it might without impropriety be read by every member of the House; and, if the House thought it of sufficient importance to go into secret session on the subject, they might do so, and it could be read. The communication, he said, expressed in as decided terms as could be used, the opinion that a certain amount of military force ought to be retained. Mr. T. then quoted a part of the Message recommending the retention of twenty thousand men on the Military Establishment.

Mr. Potter said he hoped the motion now pending to reduce the Army to six thousand would prevail, and wished that the gentleman had moved to reduce the Army to two thousand men. Ten thousand men, he said, were nothing for the purposes of war, but quite enough to garrison the posts on the seaboard during a time of peace. We did not want more for the latter object in peace than it seemed we had wanted in war; and, as regarded the State he represented, he wanted none of them. As to the points to be settled by a treaty of commerce, to-day was the first time he had ever heard it was necessary to keep up an army, to induce a nation to make a good bargain with you. We stand on equal ground in relation to a commercial treaty; and if Great Britain should not see fit to make one, he would not agree to fight her for it. If the objects for which we went to war are not attained, and, instead of settling them in a treaty of peace, they are reserved to quarrel about in a treaty of commerce, we have gone to war for nothing, and made peace in vain. He hoped and believed it was the mutual interest of the two nations to be at peace, and to have a good commercial treaty. It had been said that twenty thousand men would cost less than six millions. We have, Mr. P. said, talked so long about millions and millions, that we have almost lost all idea of the value of money. But, if the people, who are taxed to pay these six millions, were told it was only for the purpose of supporting a little standing army, they would think it a matter of some consequence. It was of more importance, Mr. P. said, to reduce the burdens on the people than to keep up a small army for the purpose of continuing the present taxation on the people. This nation would have more influence with the British or any other nation, if it had plenty of money, without an army, than it would have if it were pressed for money and had a standing army. We had derived some experience from the war just closed, which had been begun without money and without men. The re-establishment of the credit of the nation would be of much more importance to the nation should it again be involved in war, than the support of a standing army in the interval of peace.

To keep up an army of ten thousand men would, he said, be an useless and unnecessary expense.

The question on reducing the number from ten to six thousand, was then taken and decided in the affirmative.

One section of the bill, provides that "from and after the first day of April next, or as soon thereafter as circumstances may permit," this act shall take effect, and the supernumerary officers and men be discharged:

A motion was made to substitute for the above quoted words, the words "as soon as the necessary arrangements can be made."

Mr. Lowndes opposed the motion. He suggested that it would be extremely imprudent to direct that as soon as the mere mechanical arrangements could be made, the whole army should be disbanded. It would be the first time, he believed, any such arrangement had been made by a nation on the instant of a conclusion of a peace. Suppose any difficulty should occur in the evacuation of the posts held by the late enemy on our territory—there is no man who would not say a discretion to retain the army in being in such a case ought not to be left with the Executive. He would not wish the Government so imperiously bound by law, that, no matter what unexpected emergency might arise, it would be compelled to drop this force from its hands. He therefore thought there was an obvious impropriety in the proposed amendment.

The motion above stated was then withdrawn by the mover.

Mr. Pickering said, if this discretion was left in the bill, its provisions would be nearly nugatory. When will circumstances admit of disbanding the Army, according to the ideas of the gentleman from South Carolina? Something had been said of the unsettled state of Europe. But, suppose war to arise in Europe—shall we not thereby be more than ever secured against war on our shores? Surely no gentleman in the House could believe there was any danger of a renewal of the war we had just terminated; and, if not, why not reduce the Army so soon as arrangements for that purpose can be made? If the latitude proposed be left, then the whole army may be retained in service for six months longer, or even until the next session of Congress. Why should the nation, burdened as it is with taxes, groaning under the weight of taxes necessary to pay the war debt, be still further burdened by unnecessarily keeping this force in service?

Mr. P. Barbour said, as a member of the Military Committee, he had accorded in opinion with the report. All things considered, he had preferred the number of ten thousand men for the Peace Establishment. That number had been to-day reduced by the House. Mr. B. said he was as desirous as any one could be to curtail the expenses of the nation; and if he believed one thousand men sufficient for the Peace Establishment, he would vote to reduce it to that number; but in the present state of things, and in the actual situation of the country, the suggestion of the gentleman from South Carolina was entitled to much weight. To leave a discretion with the Executive, may do the nation much good, and cannot do it much harm. Have we, said Mr. B., confidence in the Executive that he will do his duty; that he will, if the discretion be confided to him, do what is right? I have no hesitation in saying, he will. How then will the case stand? On this obvious and correct ground: If the circumstances of the country warrant the disbandment, it will take place. If not, the reduction will not and ought not to take place. With regard to the European conflict, that, Mr. B. apprehended, the Executive would not take into the inquiry as to the expediency of disbanding the Army; but, there were, by the treaty, posts mutually to be restored. There was an army of the British Government now in Canada from twenty-five to thirty or thirty-five thousand strong, which he hoped would be withdrawn from our lines, as well as the blockading squadrons from our coast. He hoped that all the articles of the treaty would be faithfully executed on the part of the British Government, as he knew they would be on the part of the American. But we have had experience on the conclusion of the former war, which teaches us that these expectations may be disappointed. We know that the posts on the frontier were not delivered up, and other articles were not complied with of a treaty entered into with as much solemnity as this; that, from 1783 to 1794, one of our posts was not delivered up. Mr. B. said, he was anxious to pare down the expenses of the Government to the least possible sum, compatible with the interest and security of the Government; but, in the present situation of the country, peace having terminated with a nation with whom we once before made a treaty, portions of which treaty (about which there could be no difficulty of construction) had not been complied with for from four to eleven years, there could not be any possible objection to vesting a discretionary power in the Executive in regard to a disbandment of the Army. On this simple proposition, truth and propriety were stamped on its face; if the situation of the country justifies disbandment, it will take place; if it does not, the Army will not, because it ought not to be disbanded.

Mr. JACKSON, of Virginia, having moved to amend the clause above stated, by striking out the words "from and after the first day of April"—

Mr. EPPES said, he was certainly as much disposed as any other man to repose confidence in the present Executive; but he was unwilling to repose in any Executive a power to decide absolutely so important a question as that of the disbandment of an army. As the bill was reported, a fair limit was given to the discretion of the Executive, by enacting that, as soon as practicable after a given day, the Army should be disbanded: but, were the amendment adopted, it would be left to the discretion of the Executive, whether the Army should be disbanded at all. Mr. E. said, it was that to which he objected. If the arguments of his colleague (Mr. BARBOUR)

were correct, we ought to keep up the Army for another year, because, before the late enemy gives up the territory in his possession, the boundary lines must be ascertained and run by commissioners. Mr. E. said, he was opposed to committing the reduction of the Army entirely to the Executive, for very obvious reasons; because the House already knew what was the opinion of the Executive. A part of a paper had been read from that department of the Government, expressing the opinion that we ought to keep up the skeleton of an army, consisting of twenty thousand men. Can the Executive then, consistently with the opinion that we ought to retain a force of twenty thousand men, reduce the Army to six thousand, if the matter be, as proposed, entirely submitted to his discretion? If the amendment does not prevail, the President will,be compelled, on the first day of April next, unless some new circumstance occurs, to disband all the Army except six thousand men. Whilst upon this subject, Mr. E. said, he would state to the Committee that he believed it of great importance that the Military Establishment should be confined within narrow limits. Whilst the war continued, he was as willing as any member to make every exertion to support the contest in which we were engaged. But the war having now terminated, gloriously as he thought to the American character, we ought at once to reduce our expenses as low as possible, consistently with the public interest, and to prepare to relieve the people from the burdens imposed upon them. If, during the present session, Congress did not reduce the Military Establishment within reasonable limits, the people would in vain look for a reduction or repeal of the taxes in the next year. Nothing but an immediate reduction of the Army could insure that object. Every dollar for the support of the Military Naval Establishment, must, during the present year, be borrowed. To show the correctness of this position, Mr. E. made the following statement:

Receipts into the Treasury for the year 1815.

From customs - - - - -	$6,500,000
Direct tax - - - - -	2,500,000
Internal duties, old and new, and postage - - - -	8,000,000
Sales on public lands - - - -	1,000,000
Incidental receipts - - - -	200,000
	$18,200,000

Expenditures for 1815.

Civil list - - - - -	$1,949,285 54
Interest and reimbursement of the old debt, unredeemed, which amounted on the 31st December, 1814, to 39,905,183 60 - - - -	3,753,811 46
Interest on the funded debt since the present war, on the 31st December, 1814, amounted to $48,580,812 -	3,000,000 00
Treasury notes falling due within the year 1814, and on the first January, 1816 - - - - -	8,000,000 00
	$16,703,097 00

Which, taken from $18,200,000, the amount of the receipts, will leave the sum of $1,496,902, being the surplus of the revenue after paying the civil list, the debt, and Treasury notes due in 1815 and 1816—everything appropriated for the Army and Navy must of course in some form or other be borrowed.

From this statement it appears that the whole receipts for the year 1815 exceed the expenditure for the civil list, and the payment of the debt, including the Treasury notes reimburseable during the present year, and on the first of January, 1816, by the sum of $1,496,902, which is not more than ought to be left in the Treasury. Everything, therefore, appropriated for the war and Navy must be borrowed. If the Army is reduced to ten thousand, the expenses, including the fortifications commenced, will probably amount to $4,600,000; to which add $2,000,000, a sum necessary for advancing three months' pay to the officers and soldiers, and making the sum necessary for the Military Establishment during the present year, $6,600,000—and supposing the naval expenditures to be reduced one-half, viz: $4,000,000, there will be a saving on the military and naval expenditures of $2,000,000. The chairman of the Military Committee has, I think, estimated the expenditure of the Military department too low—three hundred dollars per man is as low as it ever has been, even in the most favorable period of peace. Mr. E. said, he would have been satisfied at the present moment, until our affairs were settled, to keep the old Peace Establishment, ten thousand. As, however, a majority had pronounced in favor of six thousand, he thought it would save $1,200,000, and afford additional security for taking off the taxes at the next session of Congress.

The revenue from commerce during 1816, will probably yield $16,000,000—and supposing the expenditures during that year to be the same for the civil list and the debt as during the present year, and that there will be reimbursed during that period $10,000,000 of Treasury notes, the expenditures for the next year will exceed the revenue from commerce, exclusive of the military and naval expenditure, by a sum of $2,000,000. This statement shows the necessity of an immediate reduction of our expenditures, unless we mean to perpetuate a system of taxes on the people. Mr. E. said, he was decidedly in favor of reducing the expenditures within such limits as to enable us to take off the taxes during the next session of Congress.

Mr. Jackson, of Virginia, quoted the laws, passed in 1800, for disbanding the army then authorized by law, with a view to show, that although Congress then intended that Mr. Adams should discharge the army, the terrors of French invasion having subsided, yet they used the terms "authorize and empower," which necessarily implied a discretion in the Executive. He did not intend, by his amendment, to enlarge that discretion; but if it were practicable to discharge some of the soldiers before the first of April, now at the places where they were recruited, and

who, by the terms of their enlistment, were entitled to a discharge at the end of the war, he wished it might be done, as he could not see the necessity of marching them one or two hundred miles, at the public expense, to the places of rendezvous, there to discharge them. He concurred entirely with his friend (Mr. Eppes) in the opinion, that there was no necessity for keeping up so large a Peace Establishment as the bill originally contemplated. Gentlemen referred *to the* state of the world, to the force of the British on our borders, and to the unadjusted territorial and commercial claims of the United States and Great Britain, as affording an argument in favor of a larger number. No species of reasoning, he said, was more plausible or more fallacious; it was the doctrine of those who favored large standing armies, and which had enslaved one-half of the world. If we kept up an army until the affairs of Europe were adjusted, he contended we would have a standing army rivetted upon us forever. They have not been settled for the last hundred years, and may not be for the hundred to come. He had no idea of an armed neutrality; of maintaining an army during peace, as was the practice, and perhaps the duty, of the continental States, whose dominions were separated only by mathematical lines, or small rivers, over which bridges might easily be thrown. He thanked God no nation could bridge the Atlantic, to reach our shores. He would rather rely on the militia to repel sudden invasion than keep up a force enervated by the inactivity of a camp in time of peace—a moth on the public Treasury, eating out the substance of the people, and requiring the payment of heavy taxes. Six thousand men, he believed to be as many as were necessary for a peace establishment; and while he would not, by a peremptory provision, require the President, without reference to circumstances, to disband the Army, neither would he keep up a large military force, to insure a due respect to our rights or interests, as likely to be affected by a treaty of commerce. Such a treaty, he remarked, is in its very nature a matter of contract—of reciprocal concession and advantage—and, he believed, we had more to give than to ask. On the basis of interest, therefore, we might rest that subject. It was true, the British force in our vicinity was considerable; but he contended, that keeping up our own, and predicating that act upon the fact of their having a large force, would have the effect of retaining theirs for a longer period. For it might be retorted by them, if we will not confide in the good faith with which they ratified the treaty, neither will they confide in ours; that those who distrust the motives of others, generally, are actuated by unworthy ones themselves, and therefore we are not to be trusted.

Mr. J. said, he did believe there were not ten thousand men of the present army (perhaps not six thousand) whom the Government could retain by the terms of their enlistment beyond the time necessary for their regular discharge, they having been generally enlisted to serve during the war only; for, in proportion as the prospects of peace brightened, the ranks of the Army had been filled, many men having enlisted as a matter of speculation to obtain the bounties of land and money. Mr. J. said, however, as there was a difference of opinion as to the effect of the amendment, he would withdraw it; and he did so.

On motion of Mr. PEARSON, the word "thereafter" was struck out of the clause above recited.

Mr. WRIGHT moved to add cavalry to the quality of force proposed to be retained; which motion was opposed by Messrs. TROUP and STUART, and negatived.

Mr. JACKSON, of Virginia, moved to amend the section enumerating the officers of each regiment, by inserting one lieutenant colonel and two majors, in lieu of one colonel, one lieutenant colonel, and one major; which motion was opposed by Mr. TROUP, and negatived.

On motion of Mr. CANNON, in consequence of the reduction of the amount of force proposed to be retained, the general officers were also reduced, from two major-generals and four brigadier generals, to one major general and two brigadiers.

Other discussion took place on amendments, some of which were adopted, and others negatived.

The bill was reported to the House, and the House adjourned.

MONDAY, January 24.

Mr. McKIM and Mr. HAWES presented petitions from sundry distillers, praying for a diminution of the duty on spirits distilled, and an increase of the duty on distilled spirits imported; which were referred to the Committee of Ways and Means.

Mr. SHARP reported without amendment the bill from the Senate for the relief of Bowie and Kurtz, and the bill was referred to a Committee of the Whole.

On motion of Mr. YANCEY, the Committee of Claims were discharged from the further consideration of all the subjects which have been referred to them at the present session, yet unacted on.

On motion of Mr. FORSYTH, the Committee of Foreign Relations were discharged from the consideration of sundry papers which had been referred to them during the present session, which, in consequence of peace, they had thought it unnecessary to act on.

The bill from the Senate making appropriations for completing the public building for the Military Academy at West Point, was twice read and committed.

The bill from the Senate to continue in force for a limited time the bill to establish trading houses with the Indian tribes, was twice read and ordered to a third reading.

The amendments proposed by the Senate to the bill "to alter and establish certain post roads," were read, and concurred in by the House.

A message from the Senate informed the House that the Senate have passed "An act to provide for exploring the Chesapeake bay and its waters, for the purposes therein mentioned;" "An act to pro-

vide for the ascertaining and surveying of the boundary lines fixed by the treaty with the Creek Indians, and for other purposes;" and "An act to repeal certain acts therein mentioned;" in which they ask the concurrence of this House.

Mr. EPPES, from the Committee of Ways and Means, reported a bill "to place more effectually in the State Courts and District Courts of the United States the jurisdiction in the cases therein mentioned"—(in cases arising under the internal revenue laws)—which was twice read and committed.

Mr. EPPES, from the Committee of Ways and Means, to whom was referred the bill from the Senate to repeal (in certain events) the discriminating duties now imposed on foreign tonnage, and on goods, wares, and merchandise, imported into the United States, reported the same without amendment, and moved that it pass to a third reading.

Mr. SEYBERT said this was a subject of great importance, in which his constituents, as much as any people of the United States, were interested; that it came into the House at too late a period of the session to be fully discussed and maturely considered; that, when heretofore the subject had been brought before the Congress, it had been opposed by petitions from various quarters, which would not now appear, because no such measure was expected to have been agitated at this session. He therefore moved that the bill be postponed indefinitely.

Mr. EPPES hoped this motion would not prevail. It was true, on former occasions, when this subject had been before the House, it had excited some sensibility among the merchants; but this was a very different proposition from any which had before been agitated. The bill proposed to take off these countervailing duties when other nations shall adopt corresponding regulations. For his part, Mr. E. said, he believed we were capable of building vessels as cheaply, perhaps more cheaply, than any country on earth, and such a regulation as was proposed, if reciprocal, would prove highly advantageous to our navigation, &c.

Mr. SEYBERT interrupted Mr. EPPES by a withdrawal of his motion to postpone the bill, and it was, on motion of Mr. EPPES, committed to a Committee of the Whole.

MILITARY PEACE ESTABLISHMENT.

The House resumed the consideration of the report of the Committee of the Whole on the bill fixing the Military Peace Establishment of the United States.

On the question to concur in reducing the force to be retained, from ten to six thousand men, there arose an animated and deeply interesting debate.

Mr. HOPKINS rose to oppose the proposed reduction. We had just emerged from a war of no ordinary magnitude, characterized by many sanguinary scenes. If the word peace, written on a piece of paper, in its practical operation, was what its signification imports, he agreed that

6,600 men would be quite enough for the Peace Establishment. But, if we take into view the present situation of the nation, promising ourselves all the benefits which naturally spring from peace, let us look into the circumstances which generally secure its continuance, and see whether, in so greatly reducing our Military Establishment, we shall not be acting with a precipitation we may hereafter be sorry for. The enemy, Mr. H. said, was yet all around us. A narrow strait only separates our lately hostile forces. You are about to disperse your force to their homes ; the late enemy keeps his in existence. We cannot expect to prescribe to those who have been our enemy what they shall keep on their own ground. But would it not be premature in us to take the ground proposed and agreed to in Committee? Are the British now not in possession of some of our most important posts? Is there anything magical in the word peace to bind them in good faith to fulfil their engagement to deliver them up? What does the history of former times inform us? In 1783, when the word peace was spoken, it was received with as much avidity, and as much relied upon as it is now; but not until 1793, were those who were hostile to us removed from our country, and not until a treaty upon the subject relieved us from them. West of your mountains, they retained some of our strongest posts. Look at the records and see the rivers of blood, and count the millions of dollars it cost you to drive the savages from your frontier who were fed and supported from those posts. Is the possession of Fort Erie nothing? Of Michilimackinac, the Gibraltar of America, nothing? Are our fleets and posts on the Lakes to be deserted, or left with only an hundred men each for their protection? When the British shall withdraw from our posts; when they shall reduce their forces in our neighborhood ; if, when all this is done, our Peace Establishment be too large, it can be reduced. It is always in the power of Congress to reduce it. If we do divest ourselves of all our force before we see this peace going into absolute effect, will it not be premature ; will it not, in fact, be an invitation to aggression? There was another consideration of a more general nature opposed to this reduction of the Army. What is a force of ten thousand men to this vast continent? Look at the belt which surrounds you by ocean and land, and answer how, with less than ten thousand men, even in time of profound tranquillity, we can garrison the necessary posts. His honorable colleague had remarked, he said, that if the Indians were affronted, the Western riflemen would subdue them. Though they can do so, their blood and the National treasure must first freely flow; for they are a brave enemy. Besides, they are fellow men; and Christianity teaches us to use the means to prevent their hostility, rather than to be obliged to punish it by extermination hereafter. Our Spanish neighbors, Mr. H. demanded, were they to be entirely trusted at this moment? Did gentlemen recollect how distant from our shores was Havana, one of their

strongest holds, and where they keep the strongest military force? Did they recollect the contiguity of Vera Cruz? That Kingdom, in a state of distraction at this moment, may eventually become hostile to the United States. Ought we not to graduate the Peace Establishment to events which might befall us in a year? The Creek Indians, too, Mr. H. said, were yet sore with the beatings they had received. If the Spaniards were hostile, would they not command all that country? Would gentlemen, to guard against all these contingencies, and to meet them when they occurred, rely on taking their fellow-citizens from their farms and firesides to fight our battles, and disband men already in service, who would be very glad to remain in it? New Orleans itself would require for its constant guard one-sixth of the whole force now proposed to be retained. Would gentlemen abandon Plaquemine; keep no force at Coquille? How long was it since a party of pirates lodged themselves in the sea islands, in the vicinity of Orleans, and committed enormities which men shudder to relate, until expelled by our gallant tars? Mr. H. said he believed the people would much rather agree to support an army commensurate to his wishes, than be subject to be harassed and troubled, called away from their fields and firesides on every petty occasion. Our Western country, he said, would always be, for some years to come, in a state of trouble. Russia, he had heard it said, considered herself at peace, when there were not more than thirty or forty thousand men fighting on each side on her borders. So in our Western country, even in time of peace, the moment you enter a sparse settlement you are on hostile ground. Scatter your garrisons along Prairie du Chien, Michilimackinac, the key of the Lakes, and by the time you get to Plattsburg, and have placed in safety and secured your invaluable stores in that direction, you will find your six thousand men dwindling into that sort of insignificance, that, if a foe you have, he will laugh in your face. Our force ought to be ten thousand at least. Common sense and common prudence, Mr. H. appeared to think, would place it much higher. But as the bill had been reported for ten thousand, he would be contented with that, though he was sensible it was bad policy to reduce it so low. Let gentlemen, he said, lay to their hearts the considerations he had urged. When gentlemen objected to keeping up an adequate force, lest it should degenerate into a standing army, he begged them to reflect that they were creating a military host by resorting to militia, and that danger to our civil institutions was much more likely to arise from making every man in the country a soldier, than from keeping up an efficient Peace Establishment. Let us not, said he, by a kind of impetuous haste destroy the benefits we expect from a peace. It is because I wish to see a peace efficient in all its parts, that I would keep up, at least until the next session of Congress, an efficient military force. Our safety requires it, and prudence demands it of us.

Mr. Forsyth said he was opposed to reducing

the military force to be retained to six thousand men; and was desirous of increasing it to at least fifteen thousand men. Time had been, he said, when the recommendations of the Executive of the United States, and persons to whom the Executive offices were committed, had some weight in this House; when the opinions of persons who had examined, in all their details, subjects on which they must be best informed, were considered of some force and authority. I fear, sir, said Mr. F., this time is now passed. The President, in communicating to Congress the Treaty of Peace, called to their recollection the important question of the reduction of our expenditures, and accompanied it with important and rational remarks, adverse to the policy of immediately and inconsiderately disarming ourselves. The Secretary of War had also informed the House, through the Military Committee, that, in the present exigency, at least twenty thousand men ought to be retained in service. And yet, with this rational recommendation of the President of the United States, this recommendation of the officer presiding at the head of the War Department, a proposition has prevailed to reduce the Army to six thousand men! He begged gentlemen to pause, and reflect whether this was an adequate military force. For what was it adequate? It was not sufficient to man our fortifications; it was scarcely sufficient to take care of the arms of the United States. He called the attention of the House to the variety of points necessary to be preserved in a state of defence from New Orleans to Maine; to the chain of posts in the West necessary to prevent Indian excitement. These alone would require more than six thousand men. Were there not also other considerations which forbid the great reduction of the Army which was proposed? What, Mr. F., asked, was our situation in regard to the European Powers? Are not our affairs with Spain wholly unsettled? The territory west of the Perdido was still a subject of dispute. With the knowledge we have of the character of the present King of Spain, would it be prudent to disband all our forces without knowing what were his sentiments in regard to that territory? In regard to Great Britain, it is true we have a Treaty of Peace. But what is it? Nothing but a suspension of hostilities; it does not bind her for her future abstinence from practices which produced the war. Shall we believe, said he, that she will not, on the first moment, avail herself of the opportunity to repeat them? The only obligations on her on this subject are, the wounds her pride and interest have received during this contest. Even her wounded pride may stimulate her to redeem the honor she has lost, by a renewal of hostility. Gentlemen may imagine, and unfortunately there are too many who do imagine, that the justice of Great Britain is such as to induce her to observe with scrupulous fidelity the treaty which has been made. Make it her interest, and she will not violate it. Does not every gentleman recollect how our posts were held by her after the Treaty of 1783, and retained until it became her interest to release them? An

honorable gentleman has said, too, that we hold British posts, and the delivery will be reciprocal. But, after we have disbanded our force, she may do in that respect as she pleases. Let us take into view another consideration, said Mr. F., the public sentiment in Great Britain after the news from New Orleans. The public expectation there will have been on tiptoe; the Ministers full of hope and joy at the idea of having struck a blow which would be felt an hundred years thereafter. May we not calculate on some hostility from the deep mortification they will feel on hearing the reality? It may drive the Ministry to a renewal of hostilities against us; or it may drive them from their seats. And who will be their successors? Not the friends of peace with us; not those who will cultivate a good understanding with us; but the Cannings and the Castlereaghs; those who wish us punished for our ingratitude to Great Britain, for "assisting the great destroyer of Europe!" Mr. F. concluded by saying he hoped the reduction to take place would at least be partial, not total, until these questions were settled, until we had not only a peace in name, but a peace in reality.

Mr. SHEFFEY, repeating the observation of Mr. FORSYTH, that the period in our history when Executive recommendations had influence had passed away, said he wished to God it had passed away, and that the time had arrived when such recommendations had no more influence than they merited; for himself, Mr. S. said, he could not bend to Executive recommendations, what he believed the good of his constituents. When he looked at the calamities of the people, and the pressures upon them, he could not bend his opinion to that of the Executive to continue them. If the doctrine of the gentleman was correct, instead of diminishing, we ought to increase our Military Establishment; he having given it as his opinion that the peace was but a truce, a suspension of hostilities, and that we ought to expect a renewal of the war. Had it not been a complaint during the whole of the war that the whole of our military force was not adequate; and was there not now on the table a recommendation to draw out by force the free people of the country into the ranks of the regular army? If we are yet to expect war; if this be but a cessation of hostilities, one of two things follows: either that the recommendation on the table was preposterous, or we ought now to increase the Army. Instead of telling the people that their calamities have ceased, we must commence a system of vigor to obtain an army. Mr. S. said he did not believe six thousand men of our present army would remain, after discharging all those men who were enlisted during the war; and, if the establishment was fixed at ten thousand men, the recruiting officers might at once be sent out to get men. He did not understand the doctrines of the gentleman from Georgia, when he argued that Britain's having been beaten would induce her to renew the war. If we have been thus successful in the contest, and she is thus smarting under the lash, we may reasonably expect some security, that some time will elapse before she engages in a contest on such unequal terms. Nothing but folly worse than madness could induce her to engage in hostilities again. For his part, Mr. S. was for settling the Peace Establishment at six thousand men; if it were larger, the recruiting officers must be again set to work. Of this he had no idea, nor had the people. The time had arrived when these notions would not be borne, and must be abandoned.

Mr. FISK, of Vermont, said, he was not a little surprised to see the course taken by some gentlemen on this question. It had been well stated that the enemy was yet in our neighborhood, and was yet in possession of many of our posts. What was now proposed? To reduce the Army to rather less than the last Peace Establishment. Experience ought to dictate a contrary course. Who could recollect the disasters of Harmar, the defeat of St. Clair, and not fear similar results of similar circumstances? Some of the best blood of the nation was spilt because we had not a force to awe the savages and compel the fulfilment of the treaty. Men change with times; there is nothing truer. Examine the Journals of 1805–6 and we shall find sentiments very different from those now uttered from the Federal side of the House. It was then contended, and the Journals will show it, that our Military Establishment was too small, that ten thousand men would be too few for a time of perfect apparent peace. We shall find the votes of these gentlemen at that day to increase the Military Establishment. Now, it seems, with our posts multiplied, our frontier extended, the powerful armies of a nation with whom we have just concluded a peace yet on our frontier, we are to reduce our Army to six thousand men. Have gentlemen become converts to the doctrine they once thought so hostile to the public interest? Would they agree to disarm the nation in the face of an enemy who holds some of our most important posts? He hoped not. He trusted we should at least keep up a force of ten thousand men for the present. The next Congress could reduce it, if the then state of things would authorize them to do so; if our posts were delivered up. When our late enemy reduces his army in our neighborhood, we may more safely do it. Do it now, and we shall invite another war with a nation whose pride is stung by her defeats, and encourage the hostility of another Government with whom we have a serious dispute as to the boundary lines of our territory.

Mr. CALHOUN said, it appeared to him, that, on fixing the Military Peace Establishment, the House were acting rather in the dark, having before them neither the estimates nor the facts on which they were founded. In determining the amount of the Military Establishment, he said, the House ought to take into view three objects, and graduate the force to be retained accordingly— the proper maintenance and garrison of our military posts and fortresses; the retention of so large a force as would keep alive military science, and serve as a seminary for that purpose; and the adaptation of our military force to the policy of the enemy in regard to this country. As regarded either of these objects, it appeared to him the House was not in possession of information to enable it to act understandingly. What force should be necessary to guard our seaports—to protect our northwestern and western frontiers from Indian hostility? Of this there was no estimate, but everything was left to conjecture. As to the second point, practical military men ought to be consulted, whether it would be proper to keep up a military force to maintain military science. The next question was the most important: Have we a sufficient knowledge of the force and policy of the enemy to authorize a reduction of our military force? He contended we had not. What would be the feelings of England on receiving intelligence of the late events, he did not know. Whether the soreness of her recent defeat would produce a disposition to remain at peace, or to retaliate, no gentleman could say. If there was any doubt on the subject, we ought to act with caution in reducing our Military Establishment. What course the enemy will pursue, we cannot determine; whether he will keep up a small peace establishment, or a large military force, we do not know. It ought to be recollected, that he has abundance of military means, and that *living is as cheap in Canada as in England.* If the enemy should keep up a force on our borders, of thirty or forty thousand men, instead of reducing it to four or five thousand, would it be wise for us wholly to disarm? It would not. Mr. C. said he deprecated such a state of things; but, if the enemy should retain a large force in service, in our vicinity, it would be highly impolitic for us to reduce ours as low as is proposed. The gentleman from Virginia (Mr. JACKSON) had, on a former day, remarked that our situation was particularly felicitous, in having no enemy immediately in our neighborhood. But, it ought to be borne in mind that the most powerful nation in Europe possessed provinces adjoining our territory, into which she could readily pour an armed force. He hoped that nation never would, but it might do so. Suppose, with forty thousand men, he chose, without notice, to make a hostile movement against our territory; every strong position on the Niagara frontier would fall at once into his hands, and the very expense we wish to avoid must be quadrupled, to enable us to regain them. Having neither estimates nor facts, as he had before remarked, the House ought to act cautiously. It is easier to keep soldiers than to get them—to have officers of skill and renown in your possession, than to make them. Let us wait awhile before we reduce our Army to a mere Peace Establishment.

Mr. GOLDSBOROUGH said, that one argument which had been urged in favor of a large Military Establishment, appeared to him to cut both ways. It was contended that it was our duty to keep up a large military force until our late enemy reduces his. Suppose our late enemy, in the same way, should keep up his force, because we keep up ours; we shall maintain our present military forever; and this argument, therefore, goes too far.

It appeared to him, Mr. G. said, that gentlemen holding the affirmative of the question of reduction of the Army to six thousand men, need resort for its support only to the general policy of the country—to the duty of every member of the House, to relieve his constituents from the heavy burdens which must be imposed on them for its support. This argument is sufficiently solid to repel all the arguments he had heard in favor of a larger Military Establishment than six thousand men. The advocates of a larger force had dwelt on the apprehension of a war with Spain, and of a renewal of the war with Britain. Were gentlemen serious? Did they mean to alarm the country by such language? Did they mean to express a wish for a Spanish war? He hoped not. Our complaint against Spain (if any) is, that she has been accessory to the acts of a principal aggressor on our rights. Having released the principal, (France,) he hoped we should not make war upon a secondary Power. As to West Florida, we have possession; and it may be a good reason to raise an army to defend it, whenever we shall have reason to believe it will be attacked, but not before. As to the renewal of war with Great Britain, he had no sort of fear of it. The difficulties which arose in carrying into effect the Treaty of 1783 afforded no argument in favor of the expectation of a similar course now. Britain then complained that we had not complied with some of our stipulations in that treaty, and particularly that which secured to British citizens the debts due to them before the war; and we complained that she did not deliver up some of the Western posts; and both parties were unquestionably to blame. It had been said, that six thousand men would be a smaller Peace Establishment than we had before the war. This, Mr. G. denied. Our Peace Establishment in 1805, about the time our collision with Great Britain broke out, was short of three thousand men; and it was not until this unlucky war, from which we are fortunately freed, was expected to take place, that our Military Establishment was nominally increased to ten thousand men. At this time, he could not see any necessity for preparing for war; he could not think Congress would be justified in maintaining any further burden on the people than was necessary to garrison the various posts in the United States. They would not, he thought, do their duty to their country, if they went beyond six thousand men.

Mr. PICKERING said, he held in his hand the Message of the President of the United States, transmitting to the Congress a Treaty of Peace and Amity with Great Britain. He had supposed this an authentic document; that we really had been at peace; that we had been rejoicing and illuminating for peace. But were he or any other person to form his opinions on the words used by the gentleman from South Carolina, (Mr. CALHOUN,) he should conclude that we were still at war. That gentleman had urged, as a conclusive reason, why we should not reduce the Army below ten thousand men, that we did not yet know the disposition of the enemy! The

13th CON. 3d SESS.—39

President's recommendation for the maintenance of an adequate regular force having been read by one gentleman, Mr. P. begged the attention of the House to another passage, which he read, expressing the sanguine hope and belief that the Treaty of Peace would be a lasting foundation of the most friendly intercourse. The sentiments now expressed on one side of the House appeared to him to be of a character directly opposed to this; and would have a tendency to stir up all the sentiments which had existed, and should only exist in a state of war. If we have peace in fact; if we are desirous of renewing friendly intercourse with Great Britain, we should lay aside all enmity, and forbear any expressions calculated to keep alive that irritability which has existed in time past, against the nation with whom we are now at peace. If we desire a renewal of friendly intercourse, we ought to lay aside unfounded suspicions, and act upon the state of things declared and established by the treaty. There was one argument that had been so often repeated, he could not omit noticing it, though he had been substantially anticipated by the gentleman from Maryland. In the Treaty of 1783, there was a stipulation that neither nation should throw any impediment in the way of the recovery of debts due from citizens of one nation to citizens of the other. It was a notorious fact, that such impediments were thrown in the way by some of the States, the consequence of which was, that Great Britain kept possession of the posts she was to have given up to us. The surrender of the posts, and the removal of legal impediments to the collection of old British debts, took place at one and the same time; and, unquestionably, as the gentleman who last spoke had observed, on both sides there was blame. Mr. P. said he was well aware that he could neither speak or write, if he had any reference to Great Britain in any way, but it was said that he was a British advocate. His conduct throughout the war of the Revolution, and since, ought to contradict the insinuation. I am, said he, an American citizen, and know no other predilection. But he might add, that after the Treaty of 1794, the Board of Commissioners under that treaty were broken up, and no measures were taken for the payment of those British debts; and it was not until the Administration of Mr. Jefferson, that a treaty was entered into, and ratified by him, whereby the United States were pledged to pay those debts, computed at a certain sum. Without waiting for that payment, Britain did surrender the posts. But, it had been said, we ought to keep up a large force if Great Britain did. Great Britain, remote as she is from her provinces, has much stronger reason for keeping up a large force than the United States could have for maintaining a corresponding force. The continuing to harbor such suspicions, Mr. P. said, would, more than all other things, tend to produce another war. But could any gentleman seriously apprehend another war after what had taken place at the close of this? It had been said that the pride of Great Britain would be wounded by the events at New Orleans. To this Mr. P. answered, she had made peace without knowing the result of that expedition. Why did she make peace? Some supposed, on account of the aspect of affairs in Europe. Mr. P. rather attributed it to the state of things in Great Britain. The sentiments of the opposition in both Houses, we know to have been favorable to peace. The sense of the people of England on that head, may be gathered also from the vast number of petitions for peace with the United States. It may also be attributed to the conviction experience had taught, of its being clearly the interest of Great Britain to be at peace with us. She wants a vent for her manufactures. Her merchants had supposed, when the whole Continent was open to her, there would be an insatiable market for her commodities. There was an error in that speculation, and many of her merchants were injured, if not ruined, by engaging in it. The Continent was inundated by British manufactures; the people of the Continent were unable, or not inclined to purchase, and the goods remained in consequence in the hands of the exporters. The British nation, therefore, so large a portion of whose people are manufacturers, were anxious for peace with the United States, that this better market than any other should be open to them. This is the great reason why they desired peace with us. Mr. P. adverted to the recent disaster of the British army before New Orleans. If it had only happened to those who were on our coast before, during the last Summer; to Admiral Cochrane and his command, (whose lust for plunder was well known,) the effect would have been very different on the British nation, though, had the attempt succeeded, it would have made fortunes for him and all his officers. But the expedition was fitted out with the approbation and under the eyes of the British Ministry, by whom it was provided with an immense number of troops and vast equipments, destined expressly for the subjugation of New Orleans. Before the issue of that expedition was known, from which complete success must have been anticipated, the same Ministry concluded a peace. When the result of that expedition is known in England, the Ministry, he said, must be disgraced, and probably driven from their seats. Who will succeed them? The Cannings, as the gentleman from Georgia supposes? No. Mr. Canning himself is now a Minister, appointed by the present Ministry, to represent that Government in Portugal. Their successors will be those very members of opposition in both Houses of Parliament who have clamored for a peace with America. But, the gentleman from South Carolina says, Great Britain has a great army in Canada, and may attack us if we disarm ourselves. What motive can she have to do so? If they made peace when they were in possession of very important posts on our frontier, and expected New Orleans to fall, how can we expect they will attack us for the purpose of conquest? [Mr. Calhoun explained, that he had not asserted that such would be the case, but only put

a case to show the policy of keeping up a respectable military force. The loss of Detroit, at the commencement of the war just closed, for the want of adequate officers and force, had occasioned more than half the whole expense of the war.] Mr. Pickering resumed. Instead of our maintaining a vast military force, at an expense which will require a continuance of the present oppressive taxation on the people, he said we ought to reduce the Army and relieve the people from a load of taxes, by which they were almost crushed. We ought to husband our means instead of exhausting them, because it is possible a war may take place, God knows when. Great Britain may maintain a considerable force in Canada, but, if she does, it ought to give no umbrage to the United States. Why will she probably keep up a large force in Canada? From the apprehension of such a sudden incursion from the United States as took place three years ago. So far from expecting invasion, Mr. P. said he would be willing to raze to the foundation all our posts on the frontier. Great Britain was smarting, he remarked, under the effects of more than twenty years' war; the nation sighed for repose, and assuredly would not suffer the Ministry to engage in a new war with the United States. One gentleman, Mr. P. said, had referred to the Spaniards, and intimated that, as we had some differences with them, we therefore ought not to disband our army. We very well know, and certainly do not fear, the military strength of Spain. The feebleness of that Government, especially with its present head, leaves us nothing to fear in that quarter. After the signal defeat of a very large British force at New Orleans, what motive can Spain have to enter into a war with us? The effect of that defeat will be felt not only in Great Britain, but in Spain. She is weak; in her provinces bordering on the United States peculiarly weak. Her internal distraction forbade the possibility almost, certainly the probability, of her thinking of war with the United States. These were briefly the reasons, Mr. P. said, which satisfied him that the force of our Military Establishment ought to be reduced at least as low as had been voted in Committee of the Whole. He should, for his own part, be satisfied with that number. Running along the whole frontier, he believed that six thousand men would be abundantly sufficient for all the purposes of defence and security. Very small garrisons would be sufficient in most of our seaports to keep the fortifications in repair. Except New York, he did not know one that would require more than two hundred men, many not more than fifty, and some not more than twenty-five.

Mr. Troup rose for the purpose of correcting some erroneous statements which had been made, greatly exaggerating the amount of expenditure necessary for a Military Peace Establishment. If the Army was to be destroyed, he added, let it be by fair argument, and not by erroneous calculations of the cost.

Mr. Grosvenor rose to assign the reasons why he should, in his vote on the present occasion,

1221　　　　HISTORY OF CONGRESS.　　　　1222

FEBRUARY, 1815.　　　Military Peace Establishment.　　　H. OF R.

differ from most of his friends. He considered this a totally distinct question from fixing and voting a Peace Establishment. He did not believe this was the time, or that the House had the necessary information on which to fix the Military Peace Establishment; and this was the real question presented to the House. It had been said, and truly, that the British nation have on our soil ports of the utmost importance yet unrelinquished. It is a fact, that many tribes of the Indian nations are yet in a state of disturbance, with whom we have no treaty, no peace, or security for a peace. This House did not yet know the manner and spirit in which the Treaty of Peace had been concluded. He regretted that the President had not laid before Congress the correspondence in regard to this very treaty. To have done so would have been no violation of principle, because the President had on a former occasion adopted that course. To this treaty, Mr. G. said, was opposed in England perhaps the strongest party in that country; and, whatever gentlemen might think, this treaty was not very cordially received in this country, notwithstanding all our illuminations and rejoicings. He thought he had already seen symptoms of dissatisfaction at it in debate. Mr. G. said, he had been early taught to respect the wisdom of the maxim, that to be sure of peace you must be prepared for war. If ever this maxim had application or point, it applied to the very circumstances in which we are placed; to this state of things, wherein the enemy has possession of so much of our soil, and several of our strongest posts, of the redemption of which we have no certainty but the reliance on her faith. In this unsettled state of things, the maxim to which he had referred had made a deep impression on him. He did not know, but, in the opinion of many gentlemen, the faith of the English nation might be relied on. Mr. G. inclined to think it might; but upon this occasion he would be guarded at all points; he would rely on established maxims of policy, instead of relying on the faith of any nation. We have tried a great number of experiments, but there is yet another, it appears. Was it ever before heard of, that on the bare signature of peace, its late antagonist remaining on its soil and borders, that a nation disarmed itself altogether? To be sure, it will occasion some additional expense to retain our force in existence, but to disband our forces at once and entirely, would have a bad influence, and the world would have a right to say, we had escaped from the contest so completely worn down by its pressure that we could not even act up to the ordinary rules of prudence. If this force should be disbanded, and an unfortunate collision should again arise, what expenses and losses may we have to encounter hereafter, in order to save a comparatively trifling expense now? What would be the expense of supporting four or five thousand men for a few months, when put into the balance against those evils which may grow out of a different course? In all these matters, Mr. G. said, it appeared to him that a nation acts wisely when it acts according to maxims established by prudence, and sanctioned by experience. The history of the world, he boldly pronounced, did not afford an instance in which any nation had completely disarmed itself in the circumstances in which this nation was placed.

Mr. GHOLSON said, that, for his part, he should not act on the presumption of the inexecution of the Treaty of Peace; if he did, he should feel himself bound to retain the Military Establishment on its present footing. On the contrary, however, he should act on the principles of the President's Message; on the hope that Great Britain would carry the treaty into effect; because, from the events of the war just terminated, he believed it to be as little her interest as ours to renew the war. But, while freely and frankly avowing this sentiment, he could not, under other views of the subject, agree to the rapid reduction of the Army, which was proposed. Was there anything in the present situation of the country which required a smaller force than we had had for several years before the declaration of war? We have an extent of three or four thousand miles of frontier, on which are a number of points requiring garrisons; we are in hostility with a great many Indian tribes, and our affairs with Spain are yet unsettled. Everything considered, he thought the Army ought not to be reduced below ten thousand men. No man in the House was more solicitous than himself to reduce the public expenditures; and he entertained a strong hope that they would be so reduced by the reduction of the Army, &c., that the next Congress might repeal nearly all the taxes that have been laid.

Mr. DESHA said, that he did not regret that he had brought this subject forward, for it was necessary for the nation to know, whether they were to be saddled with a large standing army in time of peace, or a moderate Peace Establishment. But he regretted that the question should take up so much time in debate at this late period of the session, notwithstanding there has been so much eloquence displayed. The question on this amendment was, on Saturday, carried in the Committee of the whole House by a majority of nineteen votes, where I did hope it was sufficiently discussed, and where I did believe it was sufficiently understood; but gentlemen have come forward with a new string of arguments against the proposition. Do they suppose that the House do not understand the subject, or do they suppose that, by this great flow of eloquence, they can make the substantial part of the House change their opinions in so short a time? When I speak of the substantial part of the House, I mean those who think much and speak but little; who make common sense their guide, and not theoretical or visionary projects. Mr. D. said he should not have arisen to trouble the House with a single remark, but for that positive statement made by the gentleman from Georgia, (Mr. FORSYTH,) who stated, in a very positive manner, that six thousand men were not sufficient to garrison the outposts. How does the gentleman know this?

What data does he judge from? If he has any correct data on which he bottoms his calculations, he ought to give them to the House. But I shall take for granted that he has none; that it is a mere guess, notwithstanding the positive manner in which it has been asserted. I have made some calculations, and, as I observed on yesterday, there is not more than twenty-five or thirty forts in all, which, it is presumed, are not all necessary to be kept up in a time of peace. I much question if it is necessary to keep up more than twenty. Will not one hundred men, on an average, be sufficient to man each fort? It is true, some may perhaps require two hundred, but others will not require more than twenty-five or thirty men. Then, sir, you will have upwards of one-half of the 6,000, as contemplated by the amendment, for other purposes. But some gentlemen advocate 10,000, and others 20,000, of a standing army. The policy is easy to be seen through; the advocates of a perpetual system of taxation discover that, if they cannot retain a considerable standing army, they will have no good plea for rivetting the present taxes on the people. I was an advocate for taxes when taxes were necessary in support of the war, but as soon as it can be done, consistent with propriety, I shall be in favor of removing the heaviest of them. Commerce brought us into the war, and I am for making commerce pay the principal part of the debt incurred by the war, and not suffer the people to be ground down to dust by heavy taxation. Mr. D. said, if the argument of his colleague (Mr. Hopkins) proved anything, it proved too much; it proved, that while there was the least speck in the political horizon abroad, that was not favorable to us, we must keep up large standing armies to guard against possible difficulties. This is a kind of doctrine inconsistent with the peaceful habits of republics, and calculated to oppress the people by heavy burdens, instead of ameliorating their condition. The gentleman tells us that we have been menaced by the Spaniards, and, therefore, ought to keep a force in pay sufficient to repel any attempt on their part. But he has defeated his purpose by his own remarks, by saying, the Spaniards are in an unsettled state; that they are in a state of internal distraction, and, therefore, it is uncertain what moment they may pounce upon us. Sir, a moment's recurrence to common sense would be sufficient to discover the fallacy of these remarks. Is it to be presumed, while they are in a state of internal distraction, that we have anything to apprehend from them? certainly not. They will have enough to do to settle their own affairs—to keep their own Government from being overturned—without turning their eye to foreign wars, even if they had any just cause of complaint against us, which I deny. And would it be wise to keep up large standing armies in time of peace, to the oppression of our own people, because there is a distant possibility of being attacked by the Spaniards? Mr. D. said, we are either at war or we have peace; if we are at war, not a single man ought to be discharged; if we are at peace, it would be inexpedient to keep more regulars than was sufficient to garrison our outposts and secure our frontiers. He thought that six thousand were sufficient for these purposes, and therefore hoped the amendment would be adopted. One word in relation to other remarks made by the gentleman from Georgia. He laments that more respect is not paid to recommendations from the Executive. Mr. D. said, there was no man in the nation had a higher opinion of the goodness and purity of the intentions of the Executive than he had, and such recommendations always had due weight with him, and would continue to create a preponderance in all cases of a doubtful character; but as man is fallible, and liable to err, as a Representative of a free people he should take the liberty on this, as well as on all cases, where no doubt existed, of exercising his own judgment, holding himself responsible for his conduct to those whom he had the honor to represent.

Mr. Rhea, of Tennessee, said, he heartily coincided in sentiment with that part of the President's Message which had been quoted by the gentleman from Massachusetts. He meant, he said, to endeavor, as much as lay in his power, to cultivate peace and friendship with Great Britain. If that nation would let us alone, he was willing to forget what had passed. He had no inclination to renew hostilities with her, and he hoped that all the members of this body corresponded with him in the feeling; but, to disarm ourselves altogether, would be just as wise as, when a warm day comes, to throw off all our clothes, expecting winter was over. Although the President had expressed in his Message pacific purposes, he also expressed an opinion, in which Mr. R. fully concurred, adverse to a sudden or total reduction of our military force. Taking into view the present state of the world, and the probability that the calm in Europe is nothing but the precursor of a violent storm, though he sincerely *desired it* might be otherwise, Mr. R. conceived it would be highly imprudent to part with so great a proportion of our army as was proposed. The President had expressed sentiments in direct opposition to those of the gentleman from Massachusetts, who had quoted another part of the Message. [Mr. R. here quoted the part of the Message recommending the retention of a respectable military force.] This, he said, was a very plain talk, and far from coinciding with the inferences drawn from that part of the Message recommending the cultivation of friendly sentiments towards Great Britain. The best writing, even the Holy Book itself, might be distorted from its meaning and general intent, by quoting detached sentences of it. The recommendation of the Executive is, in effect, that the Military Establishment be not so reduced, as that other nations may take advantage of its diminution. Mr. R. said he respected the gentleman from New York for the opinions he had just delivered; *they* were manly and noble; he highly approved them. Suppose the Military Establishment to be reduced to six, four, or three thousand men; we know, said Mr. R., who have been obliged to bear the responsibility of the war, and who have disavowed any responsibility. If there should be any encroachments on us on account of our weakness, the very majority of this House would be accused of want of foresight and wisdom in disbanding the Army. Mr. R. said he had no inclination to subject himself to this condition. Unless there should be a correspondent reduction of force by our late enemy, he would not consent to reduce the Army so greatly as was proposed. It had been said we ought to rely wholly on militia for defence. Militia generally, he said, would do their duty, and that manfully, when called on; but we know that our late enemy have been permitted to hold on a large portion of our territory, without molestation from the militia. He would not consent to subject the United States to a continuation or repetition of that disgrace, by a total disbandment of the Army.

Mr. STOCKTON said, that the subject of reducing the Army was very important—the pressure of the late war had already borne heavily upon the people, and would soon be more distinctly felt in the form of taxes by every man and in every family. He had, upon due consideration, determined to vote in favor of the amendment made in Committee, reducing the Peace Establishment to six thousand men. Nothing, however, would have induced him to take any part in the debate, but the alarming course of argument pursued on the other side of the House. The strange suggestions to which he alluded, coming as they did from a gentleman of standing—the Chairman of the Committee of Foreign Relations—and similar sentiments expressed by other gentlemen, had really alarmed him. He feared that all was not right. He was apprehensive, that there was some mystery in the present views of the Government, which was judged unfit to be communicated either to the people or their representatives. He feared that some design which could not be avowed, was maturing, to keep up a large standing army in time of peace; or that the peace lately negotiated, which had been hailed with so much enthusiasm, was deceptive; that the people had been amused, and would be deceived in their expectation of permanent peace and increasing prosperity. He could not but be alarmed to find that the Secretary of War had recommended the keeping up a regular army of 20,000 —to hear that this plan met the approbation of the Administration, and to see that it found advocates in that House. Mr. S. said that it appeared to him as if gentlemen had forgotten not only the first principles of our Government, but had determined to renounce all the sentiments which their friends had formerly avowed.

Mr. S. said, that if there was any one principle which might be called fundamental to our civil institutions, and which above all others had received the decided approbation of the friends of civil liberty in the United States without distinction of party, it was this—that a standing army was not to be tolerated in time of peace. It formed a prominent cause of complaint in the vindication of independence, and was denounced in many of the State constitutions—it was directly in opposition to the uniform opinion of our sages and patriots. Yet the plan seemed to have made many new friends. All the common-place reasons in favor of such a measure (and none other had been urged) had been resorted to—reasons which always had been and always would be pressed into such a service. Such as, the unsettled state of the world; large armies kept up by rival Powers; the unruly disposition of savage tribes; the necessity of always being prepared for war to preserve peace. This and the like species of drapery always had and ever would be held up to conceal the real motives of political action. The same arguments had been used for more than a century to support the same measure, and served only to prove a solemn truth, that an army was always in favor of those in power. Mr. S. said, that he imputed nothing remarkable to the Government for cherishing such a means of patronage and power, but thought it became the representatives of the people to discourage and restrain it. For his own part he would not vote for a man more than was absolutely necessary for common garrison duty. He was, however, more alarmed at the sentiments expressed in regard to the peace. The honorable gentleman had urged as a reason against reducing the Army, that we had no security for the duration of the peace; that the British Government had not relinquished its pretensions; and that if the same causes of war should occur again, the peace would also have an end. And the gentleman also added, that our condition was only that of a free or suspended hostility. Mr. S. said, that this was alarming information indeed; and his only consolation was derived from a conviction, that it was wholly unfounded. He asked if it could be possible that the treaty lately negotiated was mere deception? He hoped and believed that it was not, but that it had been produced by the dear-bought experience, that nothing was to be gained by the war. The error into which the gentleman had fallen was this: he supposed that, as the British Government had not relinquished its pretensions, the causes of war still existed, and might again produce hostility, if again resorted to by that Government. But Mr. S. said, that this opinion was not correct; the honorable gentleman seemed to have forgotten that we had declared the war, and were the complainants, and that, going to war for specific causes, when we made a general peace without providing for them, we must be considered as having abandoned them. There existed no necessity for the British to give up their pretensions, unless they intended so to do; so far from it, by the acknowledged laws of nations, every cause of war not provided for by the treaty is considered as given up, and can never be again made the foundation of hostility, without a breach of public faith. This rule was general, and had received the unqualified approbation of the most approved writers upon the law of nations. A treaty of peace not only puts an end to the war, but abolishes the cause of it. The party who made the war, and then the peace, can never again recommence hostilities for the same causes;

hence, in modern treaties, there will always be found a leading provision, that the peace shall be firm or perpetual, or universal, or of the like import, the meaning of which is, not that there shall be no future war, but that peace is to be perpetual, as far as respects the former points of difference. *

Mr. S. said, that the operation of this principle of national law upon the subject, was obvious. We had gone to war ostensibly on account of the Orders in Council; we had continued it because of impressments from American merchant vessels; we complained, as occasion required, about blockades and other subordinate matters. As to the Orders in Council, the treaty did not operate upon that subject, because they had been repealed at the beginning of the war, and did not constitute a matter in dispute when the treaty was signed—therefore that subject was not touched by the treaty. If they should again be renewed, we should have the same right to go to war on that account as we had before, and no more; but he thought that there was not the remotest probability that the British Government, after having voluntarily abandoned them, would ever again resort to such an experiment. But the causes for which the war had been continued after the repeal of these orders, and after the offer of an an armistice and pacific arrangement, stood upon a different footing, and were expressly within the principle. At the head of the list was the point of impressment. We claimed that our flag should cover and protect all persons on board our merchantmen. We continued the war because of the right claimed and exercised by the British to search, and to take away their own subjects; and because of the abuse of that right in often taking real American citizens under pretence that they were subjects. Yet the treaty is silent upon the matter; not a letter is to be found in it impairing or even regulating the exercise of the claim. We can never, therefore, maintain that our flag shall cover the persons on board our merchant ships. Nor, if we act with good faith, can we ever again go to war for the common abuses heretofore practised—for these were the causes of the war, which this peace has ended; all that can be left to us, acting *bona fide*, is to endeavor by amicable arrangements to provide against abuses of that claim, which this treaty has converted into an acknowledged right. The same might be said of blockades and the rest of our maritime pretensions.

* *Vattel, lib. 4, chap. 2. sect. 19*—"The effect of a treaty of peace, is to put an end to the war, and to abolish the subject of it. It leaves the contracting parties without any rights of committing hostility either for the subject which kindled the war, or for what has passed in the course of it; it is therefore no longer permitted to take up arms for the same cause; accordingly in these treaties the parties reciprocally oblige themselves to a perpetual peace, which is not to be understood as if the contracting parties promised never to make war on each other, for any cause whatever. Peace relates to the war which it terminates, and 'as it forbids the revival of the same war, by taking up arms for the cause which at first kindled it, is in reality perpetual."

The treaty was silent—the enemy would not suffer them to be named—they are all given up—we have ourselves abandoned the new doctrine of "Free Trade and Sailors' Rights," and can never again rightfully draw the sword on those pretensions.

Mr. S. said that he did not state this by way of reproach against the Government, for concluding such a peace—he had predicted and rejoiced at the event. It had saved the country, which was enough for him. He should not venture even to give a character to the peace, nor insinuate that it was not such as it ought to have been. He only wished that the people might understand it —that it might pass for what it was worth, and no more. Mr. S. said that the general principle of public law, which he had laid down, was not only just in itself, but its application to our case had been anticipated and recognised by the Administration; were it not for such a principle, war would be interminable. Peace would indeed be nothing more than a truce. What nation would make peace with its enemy merely to afford time for better preparation, if the war might be recommenced on the old grounds when he was inclined so to do? When he said that the Administration had recognised this principle of public law, he spoke from documents which could not err. In the instructions from the Department of State to our Ministers at Ghent, bearing date April 15th, 1812, Mr. Monroe says—"I have to repeat, 'that the great object which you have to secure, in 'regard to impressment, is, that the flag shall pro-'tect the crew. Your first duty is to conclude a 'peace with Great Britain, and you are authorized 'to do it, in case you can obtain a satisfactory stip-'ulation against impressment; one which will se-'cure under our flag protection to the crew." "If this encroachment is not provided for, the 'United States have appealed to arms in vain. If 'your efforts to accomplish it should fail, you will 'return home without delay."

In the instructions of the 28th January 1814, these words will be found: "On impressment, 'as to the right of the United States to be exempt 'from it, I have nothing new to add—the senti-'ments of the President have undergone no change 'on this important subject. This degrading prac-'tice must cease; our flag must protect the crew, 'or the United States cannot consider themselves 'as an independent nation."

In a report of the Committee of Foreign Relations, on the subject of impressment, of 29th January 1813, it is said: "To appeal to arms, and 'to lay them down without securing it, would be 'considered in no other light than a relinquish-'ment of it."

But the most important public document upon the point, was the instructions to our Ministers of the 27th June, 1814, because these were sent after the peace in Europe was known to this Government. In that despatch is the following sentence: "As it is not the intention of the United States, 'in suffering the treaty to be silent on the sub-'ject of impressment, to admit the British claim 'thereon, or to relinquish that of the United States, 'it is highly important that any such inference 'should be entirely preeluded by a declaration, or 'protest, in some form or other, that the omission 'is not to have such a tendency."

Mr. S. asked whether the treaty contained any such declaration, or protest—whether any other instrument of protest had been communicated to the British Ministers before the treaty was signed? No such paper has been communicated, and none existed. Suppose, instead of such a protest, distinct propositions had been made by our Ministers on the point of impressment, and had been instantly rejected, would not this put the point beyond doubt? If such was not the fact, why had not all the papers accompanying the treaty been laid before the House? For these reasons, Mr. S. said, he saw no cause to fear that the war would be renewed if the United States acted with good faith. He looked for a durable peace, in the interest which both parties had in maintaining it. But if the enemy should so act as to bring about war again, without fault of our's, the country would yet be safe. We could soon have as good an army as that now to be disbanded. And until we had, the people could defend themselves. We want no mercenary army to defend the country on sudden emergencies.

Our safety lies in the spirit, bravery, and patriotism of the people. Did we want proof of this? Let us cast our eyes to Sackett's Harbour, Plattsburg, and particularly to New Orleans, where the brave militia of the country, aided by their Western brethren, with no other aid than two skeleton regiments, had repulsed the enemy with signal slaughter. This had taught the world a lesson, how freemen would defend their homes. Why then, Mr. S. asked, should we keep up this army at the expense of many millions of dollars? For one, he would not consent to it. The taxes imposed on the people were enormous; they could not be dispensed with until our finances and credit were restored. We should retrench as much as possible. Lop off every unnecessary article of expense, and commence a system of rigid economy. Upon the whole, he trusted that the amendment made in Committee would be confirmed in the House by a decided majority.

Mr. MACON said, he would not take up the treaty or its merits, nor discuss the subject of Executive recommendations; but he should confine himself to the question of what it would be proper for the United States to do in the present state of things. Six or ten thousand men were nothing as a war establishment. If the treaty was only a truce, we ought not to stop at ten thousand men; instead of disbanding our forces, we ought to go on recruiting them, to be prepared for the state of things which will take place when the truce expires. But, Mr. M. said, he took the treaty for a covenant of peace, and he was willing, in good faith, to carry it into effect. There was a mistake, on the part of some gentlemen, in regard to what had been the original Peace Establishment. During all the trouble between this country and Spain and Britain, no addition had been authorized to the old Peace Establishment,

until after the attack upon the Chesapeake, and when the law then passed there was great dispute about the title of it, that the additional force might not be considered a part of the Military Peace Establishment. The old Peace Establishment consisted of one brigade only. With that force we had taken possession of Louisiana; with that force we had maintained it, besides keeping garrisons in most of our present forts. The Indians, he thought, might be safely left to themselves; our forts would not now be increased, and all the force that appeared to him necessary, was so much as should be sufficient to keep our works in repair. The true way to make our militia efficient, is to let them know that the safety of the nation depends on them, and to take nothing more from the products of their labor to support regular soldiers, than is absolutely necessary. In proportion as men live easily and comfortably, in proportion as they are free from the burdens of taxation, they will be attached to the Government in which they live. For his part, Mr. M. said, he should be willing to reduce the Army to the old Peace Establishment, of three thousand men.

As to the Indian hostilities, Mr. M. apprehended we should now hear very little of them. The Northwestern Company are at the bottom of the Indian wars; and it was now their interest to end them. So long as the British Ministry were on an amicable footing with this Government, so long the Indians will remain at peace. It was no matter what men composed the British Ministry, and therefore immaterial in this debate; whether they are the Cannings, Castlereaghs, or Wellesleys, it is our duty to consider them all as devoted to the British interests.

As to Spain, Mr. M. said, he considered the question settled as to the territory west of the Perdido. The people of Tennessee and Georgia had settled that question. If he had been so inclined, would Ferdinand of Spain have missed the favorable opportunity afforded by the double war in which we were engaged, to have made an attempt on the country? Once settle that country, said he, and you will want no garrisons there. The late enemy had calculated much from the operation of its army against Orleans. If they were satisfied with the treaty under a belief of that army being victorious, and the key of the whole Western country being in their possession, would they be dissatisfied with it now, when that army was ascertained to be destroyed, and the design of conquest totally defeated? The events in that quarter might be urged in England as a reason for putting the Ministers out of power, but not as a reason for violating the treaty. Mr. M. said he should be glad to see a reduction of the Army now. His experience had shown him that, if there was a difficulty in raising men and laying taxes, there was a greater difficulty in getting rid of both. He had heard strong arguments zealously urged why taxes should not be repealed when they were not necessary, and he was certain they would not be repealed if they were made necessary by keeping up a large military force. The security of this nation reposes not on a large military force, but on the happiness and freedom of the people. It is much cheaper to carry on a war with regulars than militia, but a regular army ought not to be kept up in time of peace. What enabled the people to stand the pressure of the restrictive system, but the lightness with which they were borne upon by taxes? History almost universally proves, that in proportion as you rely on regulars, militia lose their efficacy and utility. You must let the militiaman know, he must feel, that on him, and others like him, the safety of the nation rests, and not on a standing army. He hoped the House would concur in reducing the number of men to six thousand; though he should like it well if it were reduced still lower.

Mr. McKIM said, he was opposed to the amendment for reducing the force of the Army as low as six thousand men. He was not thus opposed to it from any apprehension of insincerity in the peace between the United States and Great Britain; but he was in favor of proceeding on the common rules of prudence and caution. The late enemy had at this time a large force on our coasts and borders, say thirty five thousand men; and with Great Britain, as a rival nation, holding so powerful a force in our neighborhood, it was not, in his opinion, compatible with prudence to reduce the Military Establishment. In his dealings in social life, he said, when he paid money to any man, of ever so great and unquestionable integrity, he took a receipt for the money; and if such a person owed him money, he took his bond or note for it; and, with these documents, he could, if necessary, defend his right before a legal tribunal. But it was not so between nations, whose last and best appeal was force. It became the duty of nations, therefore, not indiscreetly to disarm themselves. He said he was friendly to a small Military Establishment, and was willing to reduce ours in moderation. In the existing state of society, without indulging in ungenerous suspicions, it would be most wise and prudent never to put ourselves in the power of other nations.

Mr. WRIGHT said he rose, not to speak to the reduction of the Army, having already expressed his opinion on that subject, but briefly to reply to the gentleman from New Jersey, (Mr. STOCKTON,) who had just told the House that we went to war for "free trade and sailors' rights," illegal blockades and apoliations; that he will not speak of the *character* of the peace, and yet, in the same breath, tells us that the right of impressment has been given up, the right of blockade has been given up, and our claim for spoliation has been given up. I should be glad to know, said Mr. W., how he could more pointedly have given a character to the peace, or, indeed, more incorrectly have given that character. Sir, after the advice of the President to cultivate harmony in every section of the Union, and, indeed, when remarks tending to irritate Great Britain have been rebuked on this floor, I had hoped that remarks calculated to stir up the angry passions among our-

selves would have been forborne. I, for one, was prepared to act on the principle of amnesty—to drop the curtain of oblivion on the past, and to cultivate union, so necessary for the harmony and prosperity of the nation. Sir, the war was declared to arrest the *practice* of impressment and illegal blockades under the Orders in Council, and to obtain satisfaction for spoliations; objects admitted on all sides to justify the war. But the gentleman has told us that they have all, by the treaty, been given up. He has *forgotten* his own remarks on former occasions—that Britain never claimed the right of the impressment of our seamen, but to take her own. He has forgotten that he pressed us to put a stop to the further progress of the war, as the Orders in Council were revoked; and yet he says, the right of impressment has been given up; that the right of blockade has been given up, and no compensation for spoliation has been obtained. Sir, it will be recollected by all, that Great Britain never claimed the right of impressment of American seamen, and, of course, that the right would not have been among the causes of the war; but that she claimed the right to take British seamen sailing under the flag of the United States, and, under pretence of that claim, impressed our seamen. Sir, the Orders in Council imposing illegal blockades were revoked almost contemporaneously with the declaration of war, and before she knew it was declared, but I never had a doubt that our preparations for the war of which she was informed, at the revocation of the Orders in Council, was the cause of that revocation;—of course these Orders in Council and illegal blockades were abandoned long before the treaty, and, of course, it could not be necessary, by treaty to effect what had been done without, by the war. The practice of impressment was also, by the war, determined, and we can never forget that the Opposition contended that they had very few seamen impressed, fewer by far than we are taught were given up and restored to liberty, but kept as prisoners of war, although captured in time of peace, as their friends called it. I ask, then, if the right of impressment of American seamen, never claimed, has been given up? or the right of blockade, given up without treaty, has been revived by its not being inserted in the treaty? And I also ask, if the claim of Great Britain to take her own seamen has not been agreed to by the treaty, if she has not, upon the gentleman's principles, abandoned it? So much, sir, as to impressment and blockades. Now, upon the subject of spoliations. I humbly ask, if they have not been remunerated? They took nine hundred and seventeen ships in time of peace; we endeavored to regain them by replevin, but they were eloigned, or rather purloined, and we obtained a *capias in withernam*, whereby we have legally taken two thousand of her ships, richly laden, of double the value of ours so purloined. I then ask, if this be not perfect satisfaction, and if it would be lawful to release the ships they took *after* being thus remunerated by a condemnation on our *capias in withernam?* Sir, I am sorry to hear that gentlemen condemn their friends in the Senate, where the treaty was unanimously ratified. Would they have ratified a treaty giving up the right of impressment? Would they have given up the right of blockade, or any other right? Would they have unanimously ratified so dishonorable a treaty? It would be as foul a calumny on their patriotism as it would be on their understanding, to give such a construction to the treaty Sir, I trust the whole American people will be satisfied with the peace, and will consider the war as a demonstration of the strength of Republican Governments, founded on the affection of a free people, not like those Governments of slaves, executed by force or fear, and I have no doubt will demonstrate to Great Britain our strength; that we have not only the power but the will, anything in the Federal Opposition to the contrary notwithstanding, and convince her that America, united, is invincible.

Mr. FARROW was in favor of a small Peace Establishment. We had gone to war, he said, with a very small regular force, and, after the conclusion of a peace, we ought at least to reduce the Army to the amount of force we had at a time when war was daily expected. If ever we again go to war, he said, we shall act on the defensive only, and our militia, in every quarter of the country, are prepared to defend the soil. From the experience of the past war we shall derive immunity from aggression, because our citizen soldiers have shown themselves capable of defending the soil. They now know, if they ever before doubted it, that it will be in vain to invade us. If you want Canada, said he, entice the British Government, if you can, to attack you, and the militia will soon follow an enemy over the lines. Foreign nations, he believed, however, would in future have too much wisdom, if not too much goodness, to attack us; and there was no occasion to keep up a regular military force for defensive purposes. He was in favor of increasing the Navy, to a certain extent, but opposed to a large military force.

Mr. CUTHBERT said, there could be no doubt, he thought, that in the regulation of our Military Establishment, there should be some mean number to which it ought to be reduced. To reduce it as low as was proposed, would be as unwise, in his view, as not to reduce it at all. The reasons in favor of the proposed reduction, were not strong enough to balance the objections against it. In the first place, he argued, it was extremely important to know what the determination and spirit of the enemy is. In going into and coming out of a contest, it is all-important to know what is the spirit of your antagonist. Are you willing, said he, to tell your late enemy, you rejoice extremely in the peace, and are willing to rush at once into extreme tranquillity? If you persuade him that the people were so anxious for the return of peace, that they would therefore sacrifice everything, you encourage him to commit future aggressions. He adverted to the influence of such precipitation on our own people, and deprecated it as declaring peace and tranquillity too much,

and relaxing their spirits so greatly, that it would be with great difficulty, in case of future wars being forced on us, they could be induced to make the necessary sacrifices. Militia, he said, however to be depended on, were not calculated for garrison duty, which they abhorred and revolted from, and which could only properly be performed by regular troops. Neither were militia fit to contest a regular campaign, with an enemy in a fixed seat of war—such a campaign, for instance, as that of the last Summer on the Canadian frontier. Would you, said he, for such a service depend on militia force, serving for six months, and continually changing at the end of that term, or on a regular force, competent to meet in the open field, and to manœuvre against a regular army? While no one more highly than him appreciated the enthusiasm which militia had displayed in occasional service, he denied their capacity to sustain an equal conflict with regular troops in a regular campaign. On the other hand, Mr. C. said, he would by no means go into a large Military Establishment, in time of peace. The party to which he belonged had always been averse to heaping unnecessary burdens on the people; and the lightness of the burdens imposed on them, was what had induced them always to adhere to and support the Government as they had done throughout the war. He would not weaken that attachment, which, in the moment of danger, became a principle of energy and action. Ten thousand men, he said, for a time of trouble, were not too few, and for the present time, he thought, would be a proper force. In time of actual war, they would serve as a foundation, and a foundation only did we ever want, for a good army.

Mr. STUART said he had intended to have given a silent vote in favor of the largest number of men proposed; and, notwithstanding the arguments urged against the number of ten thousand men, he still adhered to his own opinion, that ten thousand men would not be too many. It was much easier to disband than to raise an army; and, while we have some of the best troops in the world, let us not disband too many of them. The difference of expense between six and ten thousand men for a few months, would be trifling. At the next session, if we had peace with every nation on that firm basis he hoped we should have, he would join with gentlemen in reducing the Army still lower. Ten thousand men, he said, he wished to retain, neither as a Peace or War Establishment, but as constituting such a force as the times required. He voted for this number, not entirely because a large force had been recommended by the Executive, but on his own opinion, deliberately and maturely formed; and, although the gentleman who had moved in the Committee to strike out ten thousand, appeared to hope it would be carried by a large majority, Mr. S. said he hoped the contrary. Mr. S. said he would pin his faith on no man's sleeve, in or out of this House; but he thought we had no right to expect to keep entirely clear of all hostility, and under present circumstances he could not consent to reduce the Army as low as was proposed.

Mr. Potter said he had been in hopes, until the debate of to-day, that we had made peace in the spirit of peace, and that the Army would have been reduced to the Peace Establishment. The people of the United States had suffered very great privations, and it was time they should be relieved. Mr. P. said he had some little knowledge of different Administrations for twenty years past, and so far as he knew them, it had always been a good time to continue or increase the burdens on the people and to multiply offices; but, under no Administration did he ever know it a good and proper time to begin the reduction of expenses and abolition of offices. He had been in hopes, he said, that gentlemen who have the management of the affairs of Administration, and had professed great Republicanism, would have shown a willingness, when they had the power, to practice what they had preached. The argument that we must support an army because the British have men in Canada, is entitled to no weight. If we are to support thirty thousand men on that ground, we need no war to destroy the Administration and beggar the people; we had better be in war, indeed, than in such a peace as that. Another gentleman was afraid of reducing the Army lest Britain should suppose we were heartily tired of the war and could not bear the burdens of it. This argument he treated as absurd—punishing ourselves to no purpose. In regard to the different calculations as to the expense of a military force, he said it was probable they were all underrated; that the calculation of the expense of an army was something like that of building a house; when you have made your estimate, you ought to double the estimate, which will then fall short of the actual expense. By all the direct and internal taxes, he said, the Government had not yet collected from the people five millions of dollars. The army proposed to be retained would cost more per year than had been actually collected from the people during the late war. We ought, he said, now to look forward, and not to look back; there had been more irritation and talking about "the enemy" to-day than there had been for almost a year during the war. Mr. P. made a few other remarks, going to show that the burdens on the people ought to be reduced as soon as possible, which would only be accomplished by an adequate reduction of the Army.

Mr. Calhoun was more and more convinced of the inexpediency of breaking up at once our whole Military Establishment. Had they before them, he asked, or could they have at this session, the necessary estimates whereon to fix the Peace Establishment? If they had, there would probably be little difference of opinion on the subject; but they had not. Gentlemen had said, that to retain so great a force would imply a suspicion of the good faith of Great Britain in regard to the peace. His reply to that argument was, that, if the largest number now proposed be agreed to, we shall reduce our army to one-sixth of the amount of our War Establishment; that is to say, from sixty to ten thousand men, and ultimately perhaps

from ten thousand to six. He rose now, however, principally to reply to the argument that our ratification of the Treaty of Peace amounted to an abandonment to Great Britain of the right of impressment, &c.; to an abandonment of "free trade and sailors' rights." In the first place, he denied the position that this country had ever set up a claim to the immunity of the flag. We had always been ready to make any arrangement by which our own seamen should be protected. Although the Government perhaps ought to have done so, it never made it a point, that the flag should protect everything under it. It had said, however, that unless the flag did protect all sailing under it, it would be difficult to remedy the abuse of the search for persons. We offered the rule that the flag should protect the seamen, as one subject to modification. This Government had always been willing to make such reciprocal regulations as should in this respect secure to each nation its rights. The celebrated seamen's bill, as it was generally called, was the result of a disposition of this sort. We have denied the right of Great Britain to take any other than her own seamen; and have we made any stipulation, express or implied, by which we yielded the right of our citizens to exemption from impressment by her authority? On the contrary, said Mr. C., I maintain that that right is substantially and forever fixed. We have exhibited, during this war, a power and an energy of character which will prevent any Power from hereafter finding it expedient to take our or any other seamen from our decks.

Mr. C. added, he had no doubt but Great Britain would be willing to guard against future collision on that subject, to enter into reciprocal arrangements which shall preclude hereafter any necessity or pretence for searching our merchant vessels for her seamen. There is no abandonment on our part, by the treaty, of any right. He had seen assertions to the contrary in newspapers; but he never expected to have heard it gravely said on this floor, that it would be something like a violation of the treaty if we should hereafter resist the practice of impressment of our seamen. The war, Mr. C. said, had effected all its great objects. The British claim of impressment, which we resisted, ended with the European war. It was a claim resulting from a state of war. That state ceasing, the operation of the claim ceased, and there was no necessity for a treaty stipulation against a claim which was extinct. If war should again break out in Europe, and that claim be revived, (which he believed it would not,) we shall be in a better condition than ever to assert the rights of our citizens; though, he believed, we have made such an impression on the British nation, that it will never feel the same disposition hereafter that it has formerly evinced to encroach on our rights, which are now better secured than by paper or parchment stipulations. They are secured and settled by the vigor and energy of the American people, who will again be ready to draw the sword if Britain again encroaches on our dearest rights.

1287   HISTORY OF CONGRESS.   1288

FEBRUARY, 1815.   *Military Peace Establishment.*   H. OF R.

Mr. HANSON, of Maryland, addressed the Chair as follows:

Mr. Speaker, it is because I am unwilling to consume much of the precious time of the House, at this late period of the session, that I rise with reluctance to reply to the honorable gentleman from South Carolina, (Mr. CALHOUN.) The Constitutional day for terminating the deliberations of this body is at hand; and a discussion, involving a question of such magnitude as the Treaty of Peace, cannot be disposed of in the manner which all parties would desire.

The reluctance I have expressed, is not meant as mere matter of form, by way of exordium. It is sincerely felt. But in avowing it, I must not be suspected of any disposition, from personal or political motives, to avoid a discussion, which the honorable gentleman appears to seek. I rejoiced with all my heart at the restoration of peace, and I should now rejoice at such a discussion of the provisions of the treaty as sooner or later must take place. Could I have my choice, I would choose this day for the discussion. I feel every disposition to communicate to my constituents the reflections naturally arising out of the new state of things which exists. When the proper moment does arrive, and the House consents to take up this question for full discussion, I shall hold myself in readiness to engage in it with the solemnity it requires, and to the extent of which I may be capable. It will still depend very much upon the prudence and discretion of gentlemen in the majority, whether the few remaining days of the session will be consumed in a debate, which by no means promises to be a very profitable one to them.

Already has the gentleman from South Carolina said enough to justify the few remarks I propose to offer in reply to his extraordinary assertions, and the strange and unexpected positions he has ventured to lay down.

Before I enter upon the execution of the task I have assigned myself, it will be proper to notice, as first in order, the particular question of reducing the Military Establishment to the standard proposed, six thousand men. On this subject, I entirely concur in the opinion expressed by my friend next to me, (Mr. GROSVENOR.) I agree with him, that it would be contrary to the dictates of prudence, and the best maxims of wisdom, regarded by all provident and well regulated Governments, to disarm the country in the present state of its affairs. I agree in the statesmanlike view he has concisely and eloquently taken of this subject. It would undoubtedly be impolitic and unsafe to cut down our Military Establishment to the peace standard, before Great Britain had complied with the provisions of the treaty, and restored the important military posts she now occupies within our territory. I am happy to find that opinion confirmed and corroborated by my experienced and worthy colleague who sits near me, (Mr. STUART.) He has given his opinion also, to the House, in the language of a soldier and a statesman, uninfluenced by those little party feelings which sometimes sway the most independent minds, and warp the strongest judgments.

In the vote I am prepared to give upon the proposed reduction of the Army, I am governed not at all by an apprehension that Great Britain is disposed to violate the treaty, or in bad faith to create any difficulties or delay in withdrawing her troops from our territory. But is it the part of a prudent and wise Government to repose entirely for its safety upon the honor and good faith of nations? While an inch of our territory is occupied by foreign troops, I can never consent to lay down our arms. It would be taking upon myself a responsibility which I could neither justify to my own conscience, my constituents, or my country. Certainly, I do not contemplate imposing upon the people the burden of a Military War Establishment in a time of peace. I know my duty, and understand the feelings of the people too well to contract the danger of a political error so unpardonable. I entertain no such design. All I ask is, that Fort Niagara be restored, that Castine be evacuated, before I will give my vote to reduce the Army below ten thousand men. The present War Establishment, authorized by law, exceeds sixty thousand men. I am ready at once to lop off five-sixths of the Army. I join gentlemen in voting to-day to dismiss fifty thousand; but further I cannot go consistently with my ideas of prudence, and a just sense of the obligations imposed upon me by my situation. On our Northern border, the late enemy presents a formidable force. From the best information, he is twenty thousand strong, with at least five thousand well disciplined militia co-operating with this powerful veteran army. Will the people agree, would it comport with the dignity and character of a Government deserving the respect of foreign nations, and the confidence of its own people, entirely to disarm itself immediately upon the ratification of a treaty, and under circumstances known to exist in this country? We first catch at the treaty with the ravenous avidity of a condemned malefactor accepting a reprieve with a halter around his neck. It is ratified almost without deliberation, as though it were predetermined to take it, "sight unseen," to its provisions ever so humiliating and derogatory to an independent nation. Then we disband our Army, strip ourselves of all defence, while foreign troops are still in the occupation of important military posts. Is this the conduct to be looked for from an exalted Government, intrusted with the conservatory power of a free and high minded-people? What can be more unwise, more undignified? What better calculated to draw down on both the contempt and derision of foreign nations? Our national character may already be sunk extremely low, but the popular course, as it is deemed, proposed now to be pursued, will sink it still lower—lower than the bitterest enemy of the Administration can desire to see it sunk.

I stand not here, sir, the supporter of large standing armies in time of peace. But unpopular as the vote may be considered, I am ready to encounter the odium of preserving a commanding attitude, until the relations of peace are perfectly restored, and each party reassumes its posture before the war. I will not allow myself to doubt, for a moment, what would be the determination of the minority if the reins of Government were in their hands, and they were responsible for the character and safety of the country. I have only to refer to their known principles, and the political maxims by which they have always been governed, to pronounce the policy which would prevail at such a moment and under existing circumstances.

My honorable friend before me, (Mr. Stockton,) upon whose opinion I am in the habit of relying almost implicitly, from his known strength of judgment, purity, and disinterestedness, acknowledges himself to be influenced by the threatening declarations of some gentlemen over the way, who look to a renewal of hostilities with England. He says, he is alarmed by declarations of the kind, proceeding from such high authority. For my part, sir, I am influenced by no such feelings. There is nothing in these warlike menaces which at all disturbs my mind. The honorable gentleman attaches too much importance to the airy, inconsiderate, idle declarations that proceed from some gentlemen, who fancy themselves as filling, on this floor, the stations of Lords Castlereagh and Liverpool, or the Chancellor in the British Parliament. So far from seeing in this vaporing declamation real cause of alarm, to use a vulgar figure, I should just as soon expect a scalded cat to jump into a cauldron of boiling water as to suspect this Administration of a design to plunge the country into another war with England. The gentleman from New Jersey may rest assured the intentions of the majority are quite as innocent as their declarations. An individual who has got disgracefully out of a quarrel, may, in charity, be allowed the consolation and relief to be derived from a courageous threat to renew the conflict. In private life, these instances are quite common, and they generally end with the threat. I will abstain from the remarks which belong to this subject, and proceed to reply to the gentleman from South Carolina.

I begin, sir, by acknowledging myself to be entirely at a loss for the proper language in which to express my amazement at the principles he has laid down, and the positions he has taken. In these, not all the gentleman's ingenuity, great as it is known and admitted to be, can sustain him.

He says, we have neither abandoned nor impaired any claim for which the war was declared, by accepting a treaty which is silent as to those claims. He contends that the question of impressment, as a claim, remains where it was before the war. With his accustomed confidence and boldness, he asserts that the claim of this Government was the protection of its own seamen; and he denies, unequivocally, that we ever contended for "the immunity of our flag," while the British set up the right to impress our seamen.

The gentleman's first position involves an important principle of public law. If there were any variance among the most approved writers on the law of nations on this point, still it is in my power to refer to the high authority of the gentleman himself to settle the question between us.

The position I contend for is this: Impressment being assigned as a principal cause of war, both in the Message of the President recommending war, and the celebrated manifesto promulgated by the Committee of Foreign Relations, and a Treaty of Peace having been ratified, in which no provision whatever is made for this claim, it is *ipso facto* abandoned, and war cannot be renewed for the same cause. The broad principle laid down by Vattel, and controverted by no public writer, supports my position. "A Treaty of Peace," says this writer, "abolishes the subject 'of the war, and prohibits the taking up arms 'again for the same cause." As far, then, as impressment was a cause of war, it is abolished by the Treaty of Peace, and we are precluded by our own act from taking up arms again for the same cause. But the gentleman repels this principle of public law with disdain. He is still resolved never to relinquish the claim of impressment. He will cling to it because of its justice, and because the law is on his side.

Upon the question of law, the gentleman's opinion has undergone a material change *since* the year 1813. I have fortunately found, on the records of the House, the gentleman's opinion in writing, drawn up after mature deliberation, and gravely pronounced by him in a report, as chairman of the Committee on Foreign Relations. The position assumed in this report was recognised and adopted by the House, being laid on the table and ordered to be printed. It is now matter of record; and, from that record, the passage I propose to read is in the following words:

"The impressment of our seamen being deservedly considered a principal cause of the war, the war ought to be prosecuted until that cause is removed. To appeal to arms in defence of a right, and to lay them down without securing it, or a satisfactory evidence of a good disposition in the opposite party to secure it, would be considered in no other light than a relinquishment of it. To attempt to negotiate afterwards for the security of such right, in the expectation that any of the arguments that had been urged before the declaration of war, and been rejected, would have more weight after that experiment had been made in vain, would be an act of folly, which would expose us to the scorn and derision of the British nation and the whole world."

In defence of their pretension upon *this* question of impressment, the party in power appealed to arms; and I call on them to deny, if they can, that they have laid down their arms without securing the right contended for. According to their own view of the subject, as set forth in the report of their committee, have they not relinquished the claim? It is not a circumstance too trivial to remark, that the gentleman who now finds it convenient to deny and combat the doctrines and principles contained in the report of the committee, was himself chairman of that committee. Unless, as is frequently the case with these chairman of standing committees, he acted as the mere amanuensis or scribe of the Executive, the report proceeded from his own pen. It is at least excusable, therefore, thus to brush up the gentleman's recollection, by referring to his former opinions. His memory must be exceedingly treacherous, to require any correction upon a point so material, and on which he had so lately given a grave opinion.

Does the gentleman deny that he was the chairman of the Committee of Foreign Relations when this report was made to the House? From his silence, we must infer this point at least is conceded. If it were not, the Journal of the House is at hand, and would as readily settle this difference as the report itself settled the other point in dispute. Nor does the gentleman deny that the extract read contains the opinion entertained by him, at the time the report was made. The difficulty and embarrassment of the gentleman's situation must occur to him, as it is certainly obvious to the House. Is it not manifest that he was guilty, at the time of making the famous war report, of imposing false principles of public law upon the credulity of his supporters; or he now renounces and abjures his own sound doctrines because it is convenient, party purposes requiring it? The gentleman's situation is by no means enviable. Take which alternative he may, there stands the difficulty staring him in the face. Turn which way he will, his difficulty fronts him. It is his own fault, not mine, that his embarrassment is such as I have described.

I contend, sir, that the gentleman's opinion, as deliberately formed, and gravely expressed, in 1813, is more to be respected than a contradictory opinion now hastily pronounced in debate, when he finds himself rather closely pressed in argument, and is disposed to extricate himself in the readiest way he can. A denial or a round assertion is the usual recourse of some gentlemen, when reduced to such straights. Custom may familiarize the practice, and make it venial in the vulgar estimate, but I neither choose to be guilty of it myself, nor overlook it when resorted to by others.

I trust, sir, the gentleman's first position is disposed of to the satisfaction of the House. I proceed to notice his second, to wit, "that we did not take up arms to secure the immunity of our flag, but to defend our own seamen." Here again I have occasion to correct the gentleman's memory. I must refer him to an extract or two, from the public documents, which I have fortunately laid my hands on since the gentleman took the floor. In the letter of instructions sent to our Ministers, appointed to negotiate under the mediation of Russia, dated April 15th, 1813, he may find this passage: "I have to repeat, that the great object you have to secure, in regard to impressment, is that the flag shall protect the crew."

What other meaning can the ingenious gentleman attach to this instruction, than the securing the immunity of our flag, as relates to the crew? The flag was to protect all the crew, consist it of British subjects, deserters, or who not. Our claim then went beyond the protection of our own sea-

men. It extended to the whole crew, whether enemies or British deserters. The gentleman will concede this point, unless his own authority is considered higher than the Secretary of State's.

The same instruction referred to is still more explicit, in another part of it, upon the same point. Mr. Monroe continues, "your first duty is 'to conclude a peace with Great Britain; and 'you are authorized to do it, in case you obtain a 'satisfactory stipulation against impressment— 'one which will secure, under our flag, protection 'to the crew."

Language cannot be plainer. Provided a stipulation can be obtained by which the crew of our merchant vessels, of whatever description, shall be protected from impressment, you may conclude a peace, but not otherwise. To say nothing of making our claim upon the subject of impressment a *sine qua non*, and then abandoning it, (for it is not my present purpose to take that view of the question,) what other meaning can be given to this instruction, but that our flag should be free and inviolate as regarded the crew.

In a subsequent instruction to our Ministers at Gottenburg, of 28th January, 1814, Mr. Monroe says: "On impressment, as to the right of the 'United States to be exempted from it, I have 'nothing new to add. The sentiments of the 'President have undergone no change on that 'important subject. This degrading practice must 'cease. Our flag must protect the crew, or the 'United States cannot consider themselves an 'independent nation."

Yet the gentleman says, we went not to war for the immunity of our flag; all we contended for, was the protection under our flag of American seamen. It would really appear as if the gentleman was totally ignorant of the correspondence with our Ministers abroad, and with foreign Governments, or if he ever read the public documents, that he has entirely forgotten them. It is impossible, otherwise he would have ventured on such an assertion, being aware of the facility with which he could be answered.

To place in a still clearer light, if possible, the claim of our Government, I must refer again to documentary evidence. In a letter to Lord Castlereagh, dated 24th August, 1812, Mr. Russell states his authority to stipulate an armistice with Great Britain, "on condition that the Orders in 'Council be repealed, and no illegal blockades be 'substituted to them, and that orders be imme- 'diately given to discontinue the impressment of 'persons from American vessels, and to restore 'the citizens of the United States already im- 'pressed."

In other words, the United States is to be exempted from impressment. All "persons," enemies of the belligerent, British deserters, fugitives from justice, traitors, or no matter who, all persons were to be protected by our flag. The flag was to cover the crew.

The same ground is taken, in rejecting the armistice made by Governor Prevost and General Dearborn. The same ground is taken in refusing to make an armistice with Admiral Warren; and, until to-day, I never heard it denied that the pretension set up by this Administration and its supporters was what I have proved it to be. To do full justice to the subject, it would be necessary to consult the documents as far back as the negotiation between Mr. Monroe and Lords Auckland and Holland.

The gentleman has also contended, that the British claim of impressment was to take American seamen, and that the resistance of this usurpation and outrage constituted the strength and justice of our cause. I deny, sir, that any such claim was ever set up by Great Britain; and I do not propose to meet the assertion by a bare denial on my own part, or on the part of Great Britain, who has repeatedly disclaimed any such pretension. I propose to meet it with an authority which this House will consider much higher than either. In a letter from Colonel Monroe to Admiral Warren, October 27th, 1812, I have found this passage, "The claim of the British Government is to take from the merchant vessels of other countries British subjects."

Without disgracing his office, and implicating the character of his Government for veracity, the Secretary of State could not allege that any other claim had ever been set up by Great Britain, but to seize her own subjects when found on board neutral vessels. That, in the exercise of this right of impressing her own subjects, great, shameful, and unsufferable abuses were frequently committed, is not disputed and was never denied.* But what I aim to establish is, that the British claim never went beyond the impressment of the subjects of Great Britain. Our claim was to protect British subjects sailing under our flag. We identified the dearest rights of the people and the national independence with this claim. "The flag must protect the crew, or the United States cannot consider themselves an independent nation." Our very independence is staked for the protection of foreign fugitives. The issue was predicted. It is now matter of history.

I flatter myself it has been shown, from authority to which the honorable gentleman will bow, that his notions about the opposite claims of the two countries are altogether fanciful and erroneous. I have before established, upon his own authority, that a Treaty of Peace which does not secure the right for which the war was declared, operates its abandonment, or to use his own words, its "relinquishment."

Knowing the general desire of the House to postpone to the next session an inquiry into the loss and gain by the war, and the provisions of the Treaty of Peace, I shall not cross its wishes by commencing the discussion. The extraordinary course taken in debate by the honorable gentleman from South Carolina, required at least as much as I have said. I would have him know, that I am not desirous of avoiding a full discussion of the treaty and all the topics connected with it. If there are but few on either side of the House who think the discussion should be brought on this session, and gone through thoroughly, I am one of the few who thought from

the first, and still think, it should take place if possible. The people look for it; they have a right to expect it. I am anxious to gratify them. For allow me to say on this question, the Executive is vulnerable at every point. An inveterate opponent of the Administration would select this as the choicest opportunity to gratify the most splenetic resentment against them. Therefore, on this side of the House no suspicion will be cast, certainly, by the gentleman, of an unwillingness to meet the question in any shape and at any time.

Before I sit down, sir, I beg leave to express the deep concern I feel at differing with so large a majority of my political friends. Conscious rectitude, and a perfect conviction of the correctness of the view which mature reflection has given the subject to my mind, has left me no choice but to separate in the present vote. The more I examine the question, the more confirmed am I in the opinion that it would be undignified, unwise, and unsafe to disarm the country before the foreign troops are withdrawn from our territory. Instead of presuming entirely upon the good faith of any nation, it is the part of a provident, wise, and well regulated Government to act upon the contrary presumption. I agree with gentlemen, the country is much exhausted, and a system of rigid economy and frugality will be necessary to recover and invigorate its resources. Our means have been squandered, shamefully wasted, to a degree exciting very just anxiety and alarm, but I still hope we are not reduced so low that a respectable force cannot be maintained for a few months more, until our territory shall have been cleared of foreign troops, and the military posts in his possession restored. Not, sir, that I seriously apprehend any difficulty in the fulfilment in good faith, by both parties, of all the provisions of the treaty; but I am compelled to vote in the present case as I would were my friends in power, and responsible for the due administration of the Government, and the safety of the country. I consider the majority, in this instance, as acting according to the wisest political maxims, and upon Federal principles. I will not, therefore, vote against the measure because it is their measure. I will not enter the lists in a race for popularity, in opposition to what may be the best interests of the country. My friends will engage in no such contest. It is to be feared, however, that the votes of many of the majority, who have declared in favor of disarming the country at once, are influenced by a desire to propitiate popular favor. But it must be the better opinion, that the wise and reflecting portion of the people will prefer our preserving a respectable state of defence until all danger has disappeared. They will consider the slight additional expense of maintaining a few thousand troops, more than necessary in a time of peace, as nothing compared with the enormous burdens which a continuance or a renewal of the war would render necessary. In the other branch of the Legislature, I learn with pleasure there prevails an unusual unanimity in favor of the course I have presumed to defend. I

entertain a hope it will be the course adopted—
It has prudence and dignity on its side; it has
the example of all nations on its side. For there
never was an instance of a wise and well regulated Government laying down its arms immediately on the ratification of a Treaty of Peace,
under the circumstances described and known to
exist in the present case. I hope the blank will
be filled with at least ten thousand men.

Mr. CALHOUN again rose. Nothing, he said,
was more easy, than by taking detached parts of
papers, and omitting to take circumstances into
view, entirely to misrepresent any question. If
the gentleman last up, who had quoted a part of
the instructions to our Ministers, had read a little
more of that report, he would have perceived the
gross error of the construction he had put upon
it; for he would have found that our Ministers
were authorized to have made a treaty, containing a stipulation respecting impressment, to terminate at the conclusion of a peace in Europe;
the object being to guard against the possible
continuance of the practice of impressment during the war in Europe. He would have further seen, that the necessity for such a stipulation ceased. What, said Mr. C., was the injury
which we complained of, and what was the claim
of the enemy? The claim of the enemy was, that
he had a right, in time of war, to enter on board
American (neutral) vessels, and to judge who
were American and who British seamen, and to
take therefrom whomsoever he thought proper.
What was the ground of complaint on our side?
That the enemy, in the exercise of this pretended
right, frequently took American seamen, to the
detriment of the commerce, and deprivation of
the personal liberty of American citizens. At
the time those instructions were expedited to our
Ministers there was a war raging in Europe, which
no gentleman then pretended to think would
come to a termination in many years. It appeared to be a contest which would endure for a series
of years, having already, with little intermission,
lasted twenty years. Those statements, and those
instructions, a part of which had been quoted,
were then given, respecting the question of impressment, as springing out of a state of war; and
it was at that time the report was made to this
House, proclaiming the necessity of unceasing
resistance of so grievous an injury. That state
of war, Mr. C. continued, having ceased, and with
it the evil of impressment, there was no necessity
to continue the war on that account; and, had we
continued the war on that account, what then
would have been the language of the gentleman
and his friends? That statesmen go to war for
practical injuries; that, as Great Britain never
impresses in time of peace in Europe, in the present state of things to have continued the war on
that ground, would have been fighting to resist a
speculative claim, on the part of the British Government, which in practice had ceased. To have
done so would have been unwise, and would have
met the severest reprobation of the gentlemen on
that side of the House. Everybody who heard
him knew, Mr. C. said, that such would have been

the clamor rung from one end of the country to
the other. Any one who adverted to the very
document, of which the gentleman had read a
part, would find his whole argument answered
by it, (taking in connexion with it the circumstances of the world,) as completely and demon-
strably as any proposition in Euclid. The idea
that we had relinquished our right in this respect,
because it was not recited in the Treaty, was, in
his opinion, preposterous. It could not be maintained by the semblance of an argument. It is
not at all affected by it, unless that it is fortified
by the events of the present war, and the spirit
with which it has been waged, which will probably make foreign Powers more careful of invading our rights. The benefit of the claim to Britain can never compensate for the injury she might
sustain by provoking us to war in resistance of it,
and in defence of the personal liberty of the citizens. In the late war this nation has acquired a
character which will secure respect to its rights.
If ever an American citizen should be forcibly
impressed, Mr. C. said, he should be ready again
to draw the sword in his defence; and no Government could prosper that would, with impunity, permit such a damnable violation of the personal rights of its citizens. Government itself is
only protection; and they cannot be separated.
I feel pleasure and pride, said Mr. C., in being
able to say, that I am of a party which drew the
sword on this question, and succeeded in the contest; for, to all practical purposes, we have
achieved complete success.

Mr. KING, of Massachusetts, spoke as follows:

Mr. Speaker, I regret to consume, on this subject, even a few moments of the remainder of the
session; so pressing and important is the business
which ought to engage our attention. But it
does appear to me, that in the wide range which
gentlemen have taken, they have lost sight of the
object and provisions of the bill. It is to fix the
Military Peace Establishment of the United
States, and has no relation to our connexion with
foreign nations, or even to the position and intentions of our late enemy. All arguments, therefore, drawn from these considerations, or sources,
are entirely out of place. But suppose further
danger was to be apprehended from your late
enemy, or from Spain, or any other Power, does
not the fifth section of the bill leave it discretionary with the President, whether to disband
your regular army, on the first day of April next,
or not? Should circumstances render it necessary, in his opinion, you give him the power,
however improperly, to retain the whole of your
present army. And there can be no doubt of his
disposition to do it, whether warranted by circumstances or not. The power of wielding sixty
thousand swords, or of turning sixty thousand
bayonets against his foreign or domestic foes,
possesses infinite charms for him, and the patronage which they confer is all-important, the vital
principle, to him, and most profitable to his
friends.

Sir, when I came to the House this morning
and saw a flock of Executive birds, of ill omen,

fluttering round the Hall, I expected a war breeze—I expected that Executive influence would be extended to the utmost to fix your Peace Establishment as high as possible. These ominous, ill-fated birds, are never on the wing but a storm, destructive of some important interest of the people, immediately follows. A regular force of six thousand men, nearly double the number of your former Peace Establishment, are as many as ought to be retained, for any and every beneficial purpose; indeed are more than can be intrusted with the present abusers of power, with safety to the people.

Mr. Speaker, on the subject of the peace, and the events and progress of the late war, relative to which so much has here been said, I would observe, that neither foreign nations, nor our own, will judge thereof by your harangues here, or even by the deceptive Message of your President. No, sir, they have read in your declaration of war the alleged causes thereof, and will look into the Treaty of Peace to see what you have gained—they will there see that not one of the objects for which you went to war, has been secured or obtained. That even the point of honor rests with your late enemy, with the possession of Moose Island. Your own Envoys having very wisely submitted to commissioners, whether a part of your own territory and inhabitants belong to you or not.

Administration should not deceive themselves by the enthusiastic expression of unbounded joy, on the return of the blessing of peace—a joy which has spread like lightning through our country, electrifying our citizens, and is echoed, and re-echoed, and echoed again, from Maine to Louisiana. Its peals are still heard, like remote thunder, in the extremes of our nation. It implies the severest censures on, and I devoutly hope and believe, will seal the doom of this worthless Administration. It is not in commendation of the terms of peace; because it burst forth spontaneously, before those terms were known. Yes, sir, it implies an utter detestation and abhorrence of your war; and of war men and war measures. Yes, sir, an abhorrence of a war, from which the survivors rejoice to have escaped with their lives, and with the miserable remnants of their property, before you had completed the ruin of your country.

But mistake me not, sir, most cordially do I unite with honorable gentlemen on this floor, and with all my fellow-citizens, in mutual congratulations on the return of peace; already our beloved country is saved from further danger and desolation—most cordially do I join with honorable gentlemen here, in voting thanks, and monuments, and swords, and medals, to the brave defenders of the country by sea or land; in wreathing for them the laurels of immortality; and in every other testimonial of national gratitude to those who have preserved America from the power and strength of our late enemy, and from the wickedness and folly of our rulers. But, sir, in all this, there is nothing to console the wicked Administration; unless, like the foolish bird, they decorate their disgraced body with the plumage of others. Notwithstanding the truth, others might presume from the language of gentlemen this day, that they had beaten their late enemy at all points, had indeed conquered him in the cabinet, and in the field, and had emerged from the horrors of this war, covered with glory. Yes, sir, that glory, like the all-extended mantle of charity, had covered the multitude of their political sins. But where are we to look for this glory? Is it mounted on the shoulders of your officers (who swarm our streets) in the pretty form of epaulettes, right and left; or in the ruins of your Capitol? In the heroic attacks of our warriors; or in the precipitate and disgraceful flight of your President, your Constitutional Commander-in-Chief, from the unfought field at Bladensburg? In the numerous and splendid victories of our gallant "ocean warriors;" or in the wreck of public credit, and in the loss of thirty thousand brave Americans, and of one hundred and fifty million of treasure, sacrificed in your late ruinous war. In these scenes we find no glory for the Administration.

Accompany me next, to the cottages of the poor, and to the palaces of those who once were rich, for your war, like pale Death, as described by the elegant Latin poet, "æquo pulsat pede pauperum tabernas regumque turres." Yes, sir, war,

> "With impartial fate,
> Knocks at the cottage and the palace gate."

Enter with me these dwellings of wretchedness; inquire of the ten thousand widows made such by your war, there found, if glory will compensate for the loss of everything dear to their hearts; ask the twice ten thousand fatherless children orphaned by your war, if glory will give them bread, when they cry therefor, or clothes when naked, or instruction or restore to them the endearing relation of father! No, sir, no; they are thrown destitute and helpless upon "the mercy of a rude world, which must forever hide them," and will be taught to lisp in curses, the name of Madison, and Madison's war. Follow me to your various encampments, visit with me your numerous fields of battle, and of blood, and cry glory, glory, over the mouldering remains of thirty thousand slaughtered, murdered American citizens, victims to your ambition and folly; and see if it will re-animate, and restore them to their country and their friends. No, sir, no—their accusing spirits have ascended to their God, and their blood will be required at your hands. Cry, glory, glory, to your destroyed public creditors, and see if it will drown their clamors, or satisfy their demands, or fill the empty vaults of your Treasury. If your glory can do none of these things, it is of no national importance, "'tis air, a mere 'scutcheon;" when weighed against our loss—the mere dust of the balance.

Sir, as to this peace—I fervently pray God, it may be perpetual! As to the treaty, whatever may be its terms, and I grant they are humiliating—since it is ratified—fulfil it with the most scrupulous good faith, extend to your late enemy a generous confidence, in advance; you will lose nothing by your magnanimity, though you may everything by your enmity and distrust; reduce your army immediately to the lowest Peace Establishment—the American people will not maintain a standing army, to gratify the pride and ambition of any man; curtail your enormous expenses, by the most rigid economy, and thus relieve the people from some of the grievous burdens, which your war, and your madness, and your folly, have imposed upon them. As to the fears pretended to be entertained by some of the majority, of further hostile designs, meditated by your late enemy, or by any other nation; they are in vain; against them, I will point to the brave yeomanry of our country, and be silent.

Mr. FORSYTH explained a remark which had not been correctly understood by the gentleman from New Jersey (Mr. STOCKTON.) In calling the Treaty of Peace a suspension of hostilities, he had no allusion to the disposition or wishes of the American Government. This Government desires nothing but the peaceful enjoyment of its rights, and there is no danger of a resort to hostilities on our part if these are not invaded. It was in reference to the probable policy and intention of Great Britain, as indicated by the pretensions with which the negotiations at Ghent were commenced—the ungracious manner in which it was conducted, and its extraordinary termination, connected with the then recent expedition to the Mississippi. There was one circumstance, not yet brought into view, which deserved notice, as another proof of the spirit of that Government to this country: the choice of the Secretary of Legation at Ghent, and the bearing of the olive branch to the United States. The man of all others in the Empire of Britain, who was chosen to perform this office, was one who had smuggled himself out of the United States, in consequence of a criminal prosecution commenced, or about to be commenced against him for violating the laws of the country, by whose hospitality he was protected. No man can calmly examine all the circumstances under which it was made, without feeling that the coals of hostility are still red beneath this treaty. A single breath of pride, interest, or ambition, will rekindle the smothered fire, and this instrument will be reduced to ashes by its ascending flame. It is to guard against the possible, the probable danger, that he was opposed to this reduction, at least until the season of danger is past; it was to deprive pride, interest, and ambition, of the hope of gratification, that he wished the armor of defence and offence to be for a short time retained. Is the danger imaginary? Have these powerful incentives to human action ceased to produce their wonted effects? Pride and interest are still the master-springs of the movements of Britain. Her ambition is an adder always coiled, whose fiery eye is eternally fixed upon its object; who watches with incessant anxiety for the moment of fatal security, when she can strike her poisoned tooth into the bosom of the victim. The porcupine can live in security in community with the serpent; the unarmed stag dies by its venomed

bite. To the course he wished pursued, he had heard but one objection—the expense; the necessity of lessening the public burdens, of diminishing the taxes, by which the people were ground to the earth. And this objection is urged before the taxes were felt or complained of. The people do not wish a diminution of these burdens, if it cannot be effected without endangering their country. They have been at all times more willing to pay the price of security and honor than we have been to ask it at their hands. He had hoped that the spirit of narrow calculation, *falsely styled economy*, whose contracted view was fixed upon present expense, and was incapable of enlarging it to permanent and eventual advantage, had been laid forever by the powerful exorcisms of reason and experience. It would seem, however, that it had been only lulled by the presence of a more powerful demon. Since the potent spell of necessity had been broken, the troubled spirit of petty calculation was again awakened to vex the counsels and destroy the best hopes of the country.

Mr. PICKERING made a few additional remarks. In regard to the inference drawn from the selection of the bearer of the treaty, he said that he was unacquainted with the fact to which the gentleman referred. Mr. Baker appeared to have been the sole Secretary of the Commissioners at Ghent; one of the several secretaries attached to our commission was selected to bring the treaty, and the secretary of that commission was very naturally selected by the British Government to bring the treaty, without particular reference to him personally. So that no argument whatever would fairly be drawn from that appointment.

Mr. JACKSON, of Virginia, said that no one estimated more highly the value of time at this moment, and none more regretted than he did that the honorable gentleman from New Jersey (Mr. STOCKTON) had thought proper to throw the firebrand of discord into the House on this question; but Mr. J. said he could not, consistently with a sense of duty, refrain from answering some of the remarks which had been made. Mr. J. proceeded to reply to some of the arguments drawn from the documents; and expressed his astonishment that those should now object to the peace, because the treaty contained no stipulation against a renewal of the practice of impressment, who had been willing to withdraw the declaration of war before the practice had ceased. In regard to the treaty, he said, it could not be expected that a Treaty of Peace could contain all the stipulations necessary to be entered into between nations who had just terminated a war. The treaty of Mr. Jay, for instance, was little more than a supplement, not a substitute to the Treaty of Peace of 1783. In the case of the late peace in Europe, the Treaty of Paris contained merely a provision that there should be peace, and other questions of territory and right were reserved for further negotiation; which negotiation was in train at Vienna, where questions of the highest importance were now agitated between those nations who had been parties to the peace. If our treaty is silent on the subject of the fisheries, it is also silent on a question equally important to Britain as the fisheries are to us—the right to a free intercourse with our Indian tribes. The right of searching our vessels, to which is charged against the treaty that it contains no limitation, is a belligerent power merely; and in time of peace no pretension is set up to it on the part of the British. It had been said it was too late now to talk about blockades; nor was it necessary, Mr. J. said, when the practice of blockade had ceased; and no one pretended that the practice was justifiable on the ground of right or public law. Mr. J. demonstrated by facts and reasoning, that the United States had at all times been willing to conclude a treaty when the practice of impressment should cease on the part of the British. No right is yet ceded by the treaty; and every assertion to the contrary is incorrect. Mr. J. spoke at some length, and would have gone more fully into the subject but for the lateness of the hour.

Mr. Stockton spoke in explanation, and in support of his position, that the rights asserted by us, and not recognised in the treaty, were thereby yielded.

Mr. Eppes rose to reply to the position which had been laid down by Mr. Stockton, in regard to the common law, respecting treaties. If the war in Europe continued, and the practice of impressment also continued, at the time the treaty was concluded, the argument of the gentleman from New Jersey would have been irresistible. But the facts are the very reverse. Before the conclusion of the treaty the practice had ceased; it no longer had existence. The abandonment by the United States can in no way be construed to embrace any other practices and claims than those that are actually in existence. If the gentleman's position was correct, it applied with equal force to the opposite side of the question; and the gentleman would hardly contend that Britain has forever abandoned her right to blockade an enemy's port, or impress her own citizens during war. What, in fact, are the circumstances? Great Britain claimed a right to impress our seamen, and to establish illimitable blockades. We resisted both pretensions. In the mean time, before a peace, circumstances occur which make them both useless to her, and both are withdrawn by Great Britain. As the war was commenced by us to resist, and by Great Britain to enforce those pretensions, the conclusion, if any, irresistibly follows, that *that* and not *this* Government had abandoned its claims.

Mr. Grosvenor said, *en passant,* that either he or the gentleman from Virginia had totally mistaken the principles of national law.

The question on the reduction was then taken, and decided in the affirmative, as follows:

Yeas—Messrs. Alston, Avery, Baylies of Massachusetts, Bigelow, Bowen, Boyd, Bradbury, Brigham, Brown, Burwell, Caperton, Cannon, Champion, Cilley, Clopton, Cox, Crouch, Culpeper, Davenport, Davis of Pennsylvania, Desha, Ely, Eppes, Farrow, Findley, Franklin, Gaston, Geddes, Goldsborough, Hale, Harris,

Henderson, Hungerford, Hulbert, Jackson of Rhode Island, Jackson of Virginia, Johnson of Kentucky, Kennedy, Kent of New York, Kent of Maryland, King of Massachusetts, Law, Lewis, Lovett, Lyle, Macon, Montgomery, Moseley, Ormsby, Pearson, Pickering, Piper, Pitkin, Potter, John Reed, Roane, Ruggles, Schureman, Sharp, Sheffey, Sherwood, Slaymaker, Stanford, Stockton, Strong, Sturges, Taggart, Thompson, Vose, Ward of Massachusetts, Wheaton, White, Wilcox, Williams, and Wilson of Massachusetts—75.

Nays—Messrs. Alexander, Anderson, Barbour, Bard, Barnett, Bines, Butler, Calhoun, Comstock, Condict, Crawford, Creighton, Cuthbert, Duvall, Fisk of Vermont, Fisk of New York, Forsyth, Gholson, Goodwyn, Gourdin, Grosvenor, Hall, Hanson, Hasbrouck, Hawes, Hawkins, Hopkins of Kentucky, Hubbard, Humphreys, Irwin, Kerr, Kershaw, Lefferts, Lowndes, McCoy, McKim, Moore, Nelson, Newton, Oakley, Parker, Pickens, Pleasants, William Reed, Rea of Pennsylvania, Rhea of Tennessee, Rich, Ringgold, Robertson, Sage, Sevier, Seybert, Smith of New York, Smith of Virginia, Stuart, Tannehill, Taylor, Telfair, Troup, Udree, Wilson of Pennsylvania, Winter, Wright, and Yancey—65.

The residue of the said amendments of the Committee of the Whole were then again read, and concurred in by the House.

Mr. Pickering moved further to amend the said bill, by inserting, after the word "that," where it first occurs in the second *section, the* words "such part of;" and, after the word "artillery," where it also first occurs in the said section, the words "as shall be retained in service;" which was determined in the negative.

A motion was then made by Mr. Cannon, further to amend the said bill by striking from the sixth section, the following words:

"And that there shall, moreover, be allowed and granted to every such officer, in consideration of services during the late war, the following donations in land, viz: to a Major General, 2,560 acres; to a Brigadier General, 1,920 acres; to each Colonel and Lieutenant Colonel, 1,280 acres; to each Major, 960 acres; to each Captain, 640 acres; to each Subaltern, 480 acres; and to the representatives of such officers as shall have fallen or died in the service, during the late war, the number of acres according to the rank they held respectively, at the time of their decease; to be designated, surveyed, and laid off, at the public expense."

And the question being taken thereon, it passed in the affirmative—yeas 54, nays 50, as follows:

Yeas—Messrs. Alston, Baylies of Massachusetts, Bigelow, Boyd, Bradbury, Brigham, Caperton, Cannon, Champion, Cilley, Cox, Crawford, Culpeper, Ely, Farrow, Gaston, Geddes, Goldsborough, Hale, Hall, Henderson, Hulbert, Jackson of Rhode Island, Kennedy, Kent of New York, King of Massachusetts, Law, Lewis, Lovett, Macon, Moseley, Oakley, Pickering, Piper, Pitkin, John Reed, William Reed, Ruggles, Schureman, Sheffey, Sherwood, Slaymaker, Stanford, Stockton, Sturges, Taggart, Taylor, Thompson, Vose, Ward of Massachusetts, Wheaton, White, Wilcox, and Wilson of Massachusetts.

Nays—Messrs. Barbour, Bowen, Butler, Calhoun, Clopton, Condict, Creighton, Crouch, Cuthbert, Eppes, Fisk of Vermont, Fisk of New York, Franklin, Gholson, Goodwyn, Gourdin, Grosvenor, Harris, Hasbrouck, Hawkins, Hopkins of Kentucky, Hubbard, Humphreys, Hungerford, Jackson of Virginia, Johnson of Kentucky, Kent of Maryland, Kerr, Kershaw, Lefferts, Lowndes, McCoy, Moore, Nelson, Newton, Ormsby, Pleasants, Rea of Pennsylvania, Rhea of Tennessee, Rich, Roane, Robertson, Sage, Sharp, Smith of Virginia, Troup, Udree, Wilson of Pennsylvania, Wood, and Yancey.

So the land bounty was stricken out.

Mr. CANNON then moved to strike out the seventh section, which proposes to make a similar allowance to staff officers deranged in virtue of the act.

On this motion a warm debate commenced, and the House adjourned, after a sitting of nearly seven hours.

TUESDAY, February 28.

Mr. FISK, of New York, from the committee appointed on the subject, reported a bill to alter the time for the next meeting of Congress, (fixing it for the fourth Monday in May next.) The bill was twice read and committed.

The bill from the Senate to provide for exploring the Chesapeake Bay and its waters, for the purposes therein mentioned, was twice read and committed.

The bill from the Senate to provide for ascertaining and surveying the boundary lines fixed by the treaty with the Creek Indians, and for other purposes, was twice read and committed.

The bill from the Senate to repeal certain acts therein mentioned, was twice read, and referred to the Committee on Foreign Relations.

The galleries of the House were then cleared, and its doors closed, and remained so for more than four hours. When the doors were again open, the House resumed the consideration of the bill fixing the

MILITARY PEACE ESTABLISHMENT.

Mr. CANNON withdrew his motion, which was under consideration when the House yesterday adjourned.

A motion was made by Mr. ALSTON, to reconsider the vote for striking out the donation in land to officers who shall be discharged from service in consequence of this act, or to the representatives of such as have fallen.

After debate, the question of reconsideration was decided in the affirmative. For the consideration 64, against it 50, as follows:

YEAS—Messrs. Alexander, Alston, Anderson, Barbour, Bines, Bowen, Calhoun, Clopton, Comstock, Condict, Creighton, Cuthbert, Desha, Duvall, Eppes, Findley, Fisk of Vermont, Fisk of New York, Forsyth, Franklin, Gholson, Goodwyn, Gourdin, Grosvenor, Harris, Hasbrouck, Hawes, Hawkins, Hopkins of Kentucky, Hubbard, Humphreys, Hungerford, Jackson of Virginia, Johnson of Kentucky, Kennedy, Kent of Maryland, Kerr, Kershaw, Kilbourn, Lefferts, Lowndes, McCoy, Moore, Nelson, Ormsby, Pickens, Piper, Pleasants, Rea of Pennsylvania, Rhea of Tennessee, Rich, Ringgold, Roane, Robertson, Sage, Sevier, Sharp, Smith of Virginia, Stewart, Tannehill, Telfair, Troup, Udree, Wilson of Pennsylvania, and Yancey.

NAYS—Messrs. Barnett, Baylies of Massachusetts, Bigelow, Bradbury, Brigham, Burwell, Caperton, Cannon, Champion, Cilley, Cox, Culpeper, Davenport, Ely, Farrow, Gaston, Goldsborough, Hale, Hanson, Henderson, Hulbert, Kent of New York, King of Massachusetts, Law, Lovett, Macon, Montgomery, Moseley, Oakley, Pearson, Pickering, Pitkin, Potter, John Reed, Ruggles, Schureman, Sheffey, Sherwood, Slaymaker, Stanford, Stockton, Strong, Taylor, Thompson, Vose, Ward of Massachusetts, Wheaton, White, Wilcox, and Wilson of Massachusetts.

The question recurring on striking out the same part of the bill—

Mr. GASTON moved to amend the said sixth section so as to limit the donation to such of the discharged officers as have by name been thanked by Congress, or have been brevetted, or have been wounded during the war.—Negatived.

On motion of Mr. MACON, the donation to field officers was reduced—the Major Generals to 1280, Brigadiers General to 1120, Colonels to 960, and Majors to 800 acres each.

And the question to strike out the donation clause, thus amended, was negatived.

The bill was then ordered to be engrossed for a third reading, and the House adjourned at sundown, after a session of more than seven hours.

WEDNESDAY, March 1.

A message from the Senate informed the House that the Senate have passed the bill, entitled "An act supplementary to an act, entitled 'An act for the better organization of the courts of the United States, within the State of New York;" with amendments. And that they have passed "a resolution directing the manner of providing stationery, and procuring printing for the Senate and House of Representatives;" in which amendments and resolution, they ask the concurrence of this House.

On motion of Mr. JOHNSON, of Kentucky,

Resolved, That the following named persons, employed by the Doorkeeper to aid him in the execution of the duties of his office, to wit: Elextius Spalding, George N. Thomas, Isaac Phillips, Oswald Dunn, and George Cooper, be, and they are hereby, allowed two dollars per day during the present session, and four days thereafter, and Charles Brooks two dollars per day for his services.

Mr. MACON, from the Committee on Public Expenditures, made a report, stating their inability to investigate the subject to their satisfaction during the present session, the general business of which has been so urgent, and recommending the appointment of a committee on the subject, to sit during the recess.

The engrossed bill "to fix the Military Peace Establishment of the United States," was read a third time and passed; as also was the bill to vest more effectually in the State courts, and in the district courts of the United States, jurisdiction in the cases therein mentioned.

Mr. Gaston submitted for consideration the following resolution:

Resolved, That the Postmaster General be directed to report to the next Congress a plan for establishing, with the co-operation of the States, a national road from Maine to Georgia, and from Milledgeville to New Orleans, inclusive, passing through the City of Washington, and, as far as may be practicable, through the seats of government, or principal towns in the Atlantic States.

A motion was made by Mr. Rhea, of Tennessee, to amend the same by adding to the end thereof the following:

"And from the City of Washington to the respective seats of government of the States of Kentucky, Tennessee, and Ohio."

This motion was negatived, and the resolution agreed to as originally proposed.

On motion of Mr. Jennings,

Resolved, That the Secretary for the Department of War be directed to lay before this House, at its next session, a statement of the amounts of merchandise and other articles furnished the Indians, under the superintendency of William Henry Harrison, late the Superintendent of Indian Affairs for the Territory of Indiana, from the 1st day of January, 1801, to the 1st day of January, 1813, distinguishing the different dates of purchase, of whom purchased, and for what tribe or tribes of Indians.

The bill from the Senate to repeal certain acts therein mentioned (prohibitory and non-importation acts) having been reported by Mr. Forsyth, of the Committee of Foreign Relations, without amendment, was ordered to a third reading, and was subsequently read a third time and passed.

Mr. Forsyth also made the following report:

"The Committee of Foreign Relations, to whom was referred the Message of the President of the United States recommending the passage of a law to exclude foreign seamen from employment in American vessels, report, that the present session of Congress necessarily terminating on the third day of March, there is not sufficient time to give this subject the deliberate examination its importance demands. They therefore recommend the following resolution:

"*Resolved*, That the further consideration of the Message of the President of the United States respecting the exclusion of foreign seamen from employment in American vessels be postponed until the next session of Congress."

The report was read and concurred in.

The amendments of the Senate to the bill supplementary to the act for the better organization of the Courts of the United States, were read and concurred in.

The bill from the Senate to continue in force the act for establishing trading houses with the Indian tribes, was read a third time and passed.

The engrossed bill "regulating and defining the duties of the United States' Judge for the Illinois Territory," was read a third time and passed.

The bill making appropriations for the support of the Navy of the United States, was read a third time and passed.

The bill concerning invalid pensioners (the annual bill on the subject) passed through a Committee of the Whole, and after occupying considerable time of the House on proposed amendments thereto, was ordered to be engrossed for a third reading.

The resolution from the Senate, "directing the manner of providing stationery and procuring printing for the Senate and House of Representatives," was read the first time, and, on motion, the said resolution was read the second time, and ordered to be read a third time to-day.

A message from the Senate informed the House that the Senate have passed a bill "concerning the Naval Establishment;" and "resolutions relative to the distribution of the laws of the United States;" in which bill and resolutions they ask the concurrence of this House.

The resolutions from the Senate "relative to the distribution of the laws of the United States," were read the third time and passed.

The bill from the Senate, "concerning the Naval Establishment," was read twice and committed to a Committee of the Whole to-day.

MILITARY PEACE ESTABLISHMENT.

The House resolved itself into a Committee of the Whole on the bill making appropriations for the support of the Military Establishment of the United States for the year 1815, and, after some time spent therein, the bill was reported with amendments; which were read, and concurred in by the House.

On motion of Mr. Eppes, the bill was recommitted to a Committee of the Whole, and the House again went into Committee of the Whole on the bill. The Committee rose and reported an additional amendment thereto, as follow:

"For purchasing horses for artillery, one hundred thousand dollars."

A motion was made by Mr. Pickering, to amend the said amendment by striking out "one hundred thousand dollars," and inserting "fifty thousand dollars;" which was determined in the negative—yeas 49, nays 57, as follows:

Yeas—Messrs. Bard, Barnett, Bigelow, Bradbury, Brigham, Caperton, Cannon, Champion, Clopton, Cox, Crawford, Crouch, Culpeper, Davenport, Ely, Farrow, Geddes, Goldsborough, Grosvenor, Hale, Hawes, Hungerford, Hulbert, Jackson of Rhode Island, King of Massachusetts, Law, Lovett, Lyle, Moseley, Oakley, Ormsby, Pearson, Pickering, Pitkin, Potter, John Reed, William Reed, Rea of Pennsylvania, Ruggles, Sage, Sherwood, Slaymaker, Smith of Pennsylvania, Stanford, Strong, Vose, Ward of Massachusetts, Wilcox, and Winter.

Nays—Messrs. Alexander, Avery, Alston, Anderson, Barbour, Bines, Bowen, Brown, Calhoun, Comstock, Condict, Creighton, Cuthbert, Eppes, Findley, Fisk of Vermont, Fisk of New York, Forsyth, Gholson, Goodwyn, Gourdin, Griffin, Hall, Harris, Hasbrouck, Hawkins, Hopkins of Kentucky, Hubbard, Humphreys, Jackson of Virginia, Johnson of Kentucky, Kent of Maryland, Kerr, Kershaw, Kilbourn, Lefferts, Lowndes, Macon, McCoy, McKim, Montgomery, Newton, Pleasants, Rhea of Tennessee, Rich, Robertson, Sevier, Seybert, Smith of New York, Smith of Virginia, Tannehill, Taylor, Udree, Williams, Wilson of Pennsylvania, Wright, and Yancey.

The amendment was then concurred in by the House; and the bill ordered to be engrossed and read a third time to-morrow.

THURSDAY, March 2.

Mr. EPPES, from the Committee of Ways and Means, to whom was referred a resolution instructing them to inquire into the expediency of making an appropriation for surveying certain lands designated in the resolution, made a report; which was read, and concurred in by the House, to wit: "That no appropriation is necessary."

Mr. EPPES from the same committee, reported a bill making additional appropriation for the service of the year 1815; which was read twice, and committed to a Committee of the Whole to-day.

On motion of Mr. EPPES, the Committee of Ways and Means were discharged from the consideration of all the matters and things referred to them during the present session, and upon which they have not reported.

The following resolution was submitted by Mr. JOHNSON, of Kentucky; which was ordered to lie on the table:

Resolved, That the messenger and office-keeper in the office of the Clerk of this House be allowed the same pay per day, during the sessions of Congress, and for four days thereafter, as is allowed to the messengers employed by the Doorkeeper, and that he be allowed at the rate of thirty dollars a month during a recess.

On motion of Mr. RHEA, the committee appointed on the 17th of March last, to inquire whether any, and, if any, what, means of retrenchment and economy of reform in the general management, and of extension and efficiency in the Naval Establishment, may be practicable and expedient, were discharged from the reports and documents submitted to them, and the said reports and documents were referred to the Board of Navy Commissioners.

On motion of Mr. CREIGHTON,

Resolved, That there be allowed and paid, out of the contingent fund, to the person employed by the Doorkeeper of this House to superintend the post office kept for the use of the House, in addition to the allowance already made him, the sum of one dollar per day during the sessions of Congress, and for twenty days after an adjournment of Congress, and that the said allowance commence from the first day of the present session.

On motion of Mr. JACKSON, of Virginia, the committee appointed on that part of the Message from the President of the United States, at the commencement of the present session, which relates to the militia, were discharged from a further consideration of the several matters referred to them, and upon which they have not reported.

An engrossed bill, making appropriations for the support of the Military Establishment for the year 1815, was read the third time, and passed.

Ordered, That Mr. FISK, of New York, and Mr. CULPEPER, be the committee on the part of this House to wait upon the President of the United States, and request that he recommend a day of thanksgiving to Almighty God for restoring to these United States the blessings of peace.

A message from the Senate informed the House that the Senate concur in the amendments of this House to the bill "to increase the compensation of the Sergeant-at-Arms to the Senate and House of Representatives, and of the Doorkeeper and Assistant Doorkeeper of the House of Representatives," with amendments; in which they ask the concurrence of this House.

Another message from the Senate informed the House that the Senate have passed the bill from this House, "to fix the compensations and increase the responsibility of the collectors of the direct tax and internal duties, and for other purposes connected with the collection thereof;" with amendments. They have also passed bills of the following titles: "An act for the relief of sundry persons in the service of the United States, in consequence of the destruction of their tools by fire at the Navy Yard;" and "An act further to provide for the collection of duties on imports and tonnage;" in which amendments and bills they ask the concurrence of this House.

The bill to authorize the discharge of Edward Martin from his imprisonment, passed through a Committee of the Whole, was subsequently read a third time, and passed.

The bill from the Senate further supplementary to the act for the settlement of the Yazoo claims, passed through a Committee of the Whole, was ordered to a third reading, and was read a third time and passed.

The House then sat a short time in conclave, and before the doors were opened, removed the injunction of secrecy from their proceedings.

The bill from the Senate for the relief of the mechanics who lost their tools by the destruction of the Navy Yard, was twice read and committed.

The amendment of the Senate, to the bill to define the duties, and fix the compensation of the collectors of the direct tax and internal duties, was agreed to, yeas 75. It goes to leave undefined the compensation after the first of January next, fixing it up to that time only.

PUBLIC DEBT.

Mr. EPPES laid before the House a letter addressed to him, as chairman of the Committee of Ways and Means, by the Secretary of the Treasury, submitting to their consideration a proposition to provide for paying the interest and gradually reducing the stock debt which has been created during the late war; which was read, and ordered to be printed. The letter is as follows:

TREASURY DEPARTMENT, *Feb.* 24, 1815.

SIR: I have the honor to submit to the consideration of the Committee of Ways and Means, a proposition to provide for paying the interest and gradually reducing the stock debt which has been created during the late war. It was my intention to have accompanied this communication with tables, illustrating, in detail, the operation of the Sinking Fund, as well as the effect of the present proposition; but various causes render the performance of this task impracticable be-

1259   HISTORY OF CONGRESS.   1260

H. OF R.   *Public Debt.*   MARCH, 1815.

fore the adjournment of Congress, and I cannot do better than to refer to the report which was made by the Treasury Department to the House of Representatives on the 9th of April, 1808, exhibiting explanatory statements and notes of the public debt, its increase or decrease, from the 1st of January, 1791, to the 1st of January, 1808. I shall, therefore, confine my views to—First. The general state of the public debt before the war; Second. The general state of the public debt contracted since the war; and, Third. The particular provision to be now made for the last description of the public debt.

I. On the 31st December, 1814, the amount of the public debt created before the war may be estimated at $39,905,183 66, and it consisted of the following particulars:

1. Old six per cent. stock, the nominal amount being $17,250,871 09
Of which there had been reimbursed 12,879,283 78

Leaving due on the 31st day of December, 1814 - - - $4,371,587 31
2. Deferred six per centum stock, the nominal amount of which is $9,358,320 35
Of which there had been reimbursed - 3,971,148 36

Leaving due on the 31st day of December, 1814 - - - $5,387,171 99
3. Three per cent. stock - - 16,158,177 34
4. Exchanged six per cent. stock under the act of 1812 - - 2,984,746 72
5. Six per cent. stock of 1796 - 80,000 00
6. Louisiana six per cent. stock 10,923,500 00

Estimated amount of the whole of the public debt, contracted before the war, due on 31st December, 1814 - $39,905,183 66

Upon the principles and estimates of the Treasury Report of the 9th of April, 1808, it was computed:
1. That on the 1st of January, 1808, the public debt amounted to - - $64,700,000 00
2. If, therefore, the amount of the public debt computed to be due on the 31st December, 1814, be deducted, to wit: - - - 39,905,183 66

The amount redeemed between the 1st of January, 1808, and the 31st day of December, 1814, may be estimated at - - - $24,794,816 34

The establishment of a Sinking Fund to redeem the principal of the public debt was coeval with the funding system of 1790, but the payment of the interest of the debt was not charged upon that fund until 1802. The amount of the public debt was increased during several of the years that intervened between January, 1791, and January, 1803, and the Sinking Fund was enriched at various periods by the assignment of additional revenues. The acts of the 8th of May, 1792, the 3d of March, 1795, the 29th of April, 1802, and the 10th of November, 1803, form, however, the principal basis of the present Sinking Fund, providing for the annual payment of the interest, as well as for the gradual redemption of the debt.

Under the authority of these acts of Congress, the Sinking Fund amounts to the sum of $8,000,000 annually, which at this time is supplied from the following sources:
1. From the interest on such parts of the public debt as have been reimbursed or paid off, and which, at present, amounts to the sum of - $1,969,577 64
2. From the net proceeds of the sales of public lands (exclusive of lands sold in the Mississippi Territory, which, as yet, belong to the State of Georgia,) estimated annually at the sum of - - - - 800,000 00
3. From the proceeds of duties on imports and tonnage, to make the annual sum of $8,000,000 estimated at about - - - - 5,230,422 36

          $8,000,000 00

II. On the 31st December, 1814, the amount of the public debt created since the war, (independent of temporary loans and issues of Treasury notes,) may be estimated at - - $49,780,322 13

And it consisted of the following particulars:
1. Six per cent. stock of 1812, being the eleven million loan - - - 7,710,000 00
2. Six per cent. stock of 1813, being the sixteen million loan - 18,109,377 51
3. Six per cent. stock of 1813, being the sixteen million five hundred thousand loan - - 8,498,583 56
4. Six per cent. stock of 1814, being the loan of ten millions, (part of the loan authorized for twenty-five millions) - - - 9,190,476 25
5. Six per cent. stock of 1814, being the loan of six millions, (part of the loan authorized for twenty-five millions) - - - 4,342,875 00

          $48,560,312 26

But it is proper to bring into view here, the additional six per cent. stock, which will be created in consequence of contracts depending on the 31st of December, 1814, to be completed in 1815, to wit:
1. The committee of defence of Philadelphia contracted to loan $100,000, to fortify the island in the river Delaware called the Pea Patch, for six per cent. stock at par, which will be issued under the act of March, 1812 - - $100,000 00
2. The corporation of New York contracted to advance money for fortifications, supplies, &c., at New York, on the terms of the six million loan, and the amount being liquidated, six per cent. stock has been ordered for - - 1,100,009 87

          1,200,009 87

          $49,560,322 13

There are, however, other contracts for loans, made through the medium of the War Department, which have been recognised at the Treasury to be paid in six per cent. stock, but which have not been so liquidated as to furnish a ground to estimate their amount.

The six per cent. stock, which was issued under the act of the 24th of March, 1814, amounting to $3,000,000, and sent to Europe, has not been, and probably will not be sold. It is, therefore, omitted in the present estimates.

Besides the funded debt above stated, there have been contracted debts to the amount of $19,002,800, upon temporary loans, and upon the issues of Treasury notes, consisting of the following particulars:

1. Temporary loans have been obtained under the act of March, 1812, (of which the sum of $500,000 became due in December, 1814, and remains unpaid; and of which $50,000 will be payable in the year 1817,) for - - - - - $550,000 00

2. Treasury notes had been issued or ordered on the 20th February, 1815

(1.) Payable on or before the 1st January, 1815, due and unpaid principal - - - 2,799,200

(2.) Payable since the 1st of January, 1815, due and unpaid - 620,00

(3.) Payable almost daily, from the 11th of March, to and including January 1, 1816   7,227,280

(4.) Payable from the 11th of January, to and including the 1st March, 1816 - - 7,806,320
      18,452,800 00

Making floating public debt in temporary loans and issues of Treasury notes - - - - -   19,002,800 00

To which add the amount of funded debt - - - - -   49,780,322 13

And the whole ascertained amount of debt created during the war, is the sum of - - - - - $68,783,122 13

The general claims for militia services and supplies, arising under the authority of the individual States, as well as of the United States, have been partially exhibited; but neither the principle of settlement, nor the amount of the claims, can at this time be stated.

III. In suggesting provisions to pay the interest and gradually to reduce the principal of the public debt, contracted since the declaration of war, the inconvenience, which has been introduced, by making the payment of the principal and interest of the Treasury notes a charge upon the Sinking Fund, is greatly to be lamented. The Treasury notes were in their design, and ought to be in their use, a species of circulating medium; but it is evident that a sinking fund of $8,000,000, could never supply the means of paying the prior claims, and, also, of discharging punctually the whole of the principal, as well as the interest, of annual issues of Treasury notes, amounting to eight or ten millions of dollars. It is indispensable, therefore, to the free and beneficial operation of the Sinking Fund, that it should be disengaged, as soon as possible, from this burden. The means of disengaging it are, 1st, by

the payment of the Treasury notes out of the current revenue; or, 2d, by funding them upon reasonable terms, under the act by which it is proposed to authorise a loan for the service of the year 1815; and these means, it is believed, will be effectual.

The Sinking Fund, being thus emancipated from the Treasury note debt, would be sufficient, in 1815, for the interest and reimbursement of the stock created before the war; for the interest of the stock created since the war; and for the interest of the loan to be raised for the present year, either in money, or by converting the Treasury note debt into stock debt. Thus,

1. The Sinking Fund amounts to - $8,000,060 00

2. The interest and reimbursement of stocks created before the war, will require a sum of - - 3,452,775 46

3. The interest of the stocks created since the war (computed on the above sum of $49,780,322 13,) and including $7,968, payable for annuities, will require a sum of - - 2,994,787 32

4. The interest on the loan for 1815 (computed to average a half year's interest on the sum of $11,500,000 being the estimated amount of the Treasury notes, which may be converted into stocks) will require a sum of - 345,000 00

5. But there must be added, the interest and principal of the temporary loans due and unpaid, which were obtained under the authority to borrow, granted by the act of the —— March, 1812, amounting for 1815, to the sum of - 533,000 00
      7,325,562 78

And would leave a surplus of - - - - $674,437 22

It appears, on this view of the Sinking Fund, (independent of the operation of the past year) that there will be a surplus of $674,437 22, to be further applied to the reduction of the principal, both of the old and the new public debt. But this can only now be done by purchases in the market.

The proposition to be, at this time, submitted to the consideration of the Committee of Ways and Means, in relation to the stock debt created since the war, involves the following points:

1. That provision be made for the payment, or for the funding, of the Treasury note debt, so as to relieve the Sinking Fund from that charge.

2. That the Sinking Fund be applied, in the first place, to the interest and reimbursement of the old six per cent. stock, according to the existing laws.

3. That the Sinking Fund be applied, in the second place, to the payment of the principal and interest of the temporary loans, obtained under the act of March, 1812.

1263   HISTORY OF CONGRESS.   1264

H. of R.   *Loan Bill—Militia Claims.*   March, 1815.

4. That the Sinking Fund be applied, in the third place, to the payment of the interest accruing upon the stock debt created since the war.

5. That the annual surplus of the Sinking Fund, after satisfying the above objects, be applied to the purchase of the stock created since the war; and that the interest upon the stock annually purchased, be added, from time to time, to that appropriation, for the purpose of making new purchases.

After the present year, there is reason to presume, that the public revenue will considerably exceed the public expenditure, and, consequently, that the necessity of borrowing will cease. At that period, a more satisfactory view may be taken of the subject, than can be taken while the amount of the public debt remains, in some measure, unascertained; the operation and product of the new taxes, as well as of the impost upon the revival of commerce, are conjectural, and the legislative intentions, respecting a Peace Establishment, have not been declared.

Since, therefore, the existing Sinking Fund (being relieved, in the manner before intimated, from the encumbrance of the Treasury note debt) is already charged with the payment of the interest on the stock created since the war, and will be sufficient for that purpose, besides paying the interest, and the annual reimbursement of the stock created before the war, I respectfully propose, that no further step be taken during the present session of Congress, than to authorize the subscription of Treasury notes to the loan which is now under Legislative consideration, and to direct the surplus of the Sinking Fund to be applied to purchases of the stock created since the war, for the emolument of the fund. But it will be proper to confine the benefit of subscribing to the loan to such Treasury notes only as have been, or may be issued under the acts which render them a charge upon the Sinking Fund, namely, the acts of the 30th of June, 1812; of the 25th of February, 1813; and of the 4th of March, 1814; and the Secretary of the Treasury should be authorized to designate the notes to be received in subscription, from time to time, according to the date of the issues.

I have the honor to be, very respectfully, sir, your most obedient servant,

       A. J. DALLAS.

J. W. Eppes, Esq., *Chairman, &c.*

LOAN BILL.

The House went into Committee of the Whole, on the bill authorizing a loan for the service of 1815; on the question to fill the blank for the amount of the loan.

Mr. Eppes expressed his regret that this bill had been delayed to so late a period of the session; a delay which had not arisen, however, from any neglect on the part of the Committee of Ways and Means, but from the pressure of other business. The loan necessary for the present year, was for the purpose of redeeming Treasury notes, charged on the Sinking Fund. Of these notes there would fall due, in the year 1815, eight millions and upwards, and in the month of March 1815, ten millions of dollars, being the whole amount now in circulation, viz: $18,452,000. The loan might be confined to the amount of notes payable within the present year, but as the notes due in 1816 may return to the Treasury as a part of the receipts for the present year, being receivable in payment of all debts due the United States, it had been thought better to authorize the loan for the whole amount. He therefore moved to fill the blank with the sum of $18,452,000. And the motion was agreed to.

On motion of Mr. Eppes, two new sections were added to the bill, one to authorize the Secretary of the Treasury to accept in payment of any loan such Treasury notes as have been actually issued and are by law chargeable on the Sinking Fund; the other to enable the Secretary of the Treasury to cause to be paid interest on Treasury notes which have fallen due and have not been paid for the want of funds, interest whereon has not of course since accrued.

The bill was reported to the House, and ordered to be engrossed for a third reading; and was subsequently read a third time, and passed.

OFFICERS OF THE HOUSE.

The bill from the Senate to increase the compensation of the Sergeant-at-Arms of the Senate, being before a Committee of the Whole—

Mr. Gaston moved to amend the bill by inserting, also, the Sergeant-at-Arms of the House of Representatives.

Mr. Seybert moved to add, the Doorkeeper of the House of Representatives.

Mr. Culpeper moved to add, the Assistant Doorkeeper of the same body.

All these motions were agreed to, and the bill was reported as amended. On proceeding to consider the report of the Committee—

Mr. Barnett moved to postpone the bill indefinitely; but subsequently withdrew the motion.

Some discussion took place on the amendments, which were all adopted; and the bill, thus amended, was ordered to a third reading, and was passed.

MILITIA CLAIMS.

The order of the day being called for on the bill from the Senate to "authorize settlement and payment of certain claims for the services of the militia"—

Mr. Fisk, of Vermont, moved to postpone the consideration thereof indefinitely.

This motion gave rise to a very animated and rather acrimonious debate, embracing, beside the real question, the merits of the conduct of the Governors of Massachusetts and Connecticut, their doctrines as to the militia, and the general conduct of the Eastern States opposed to the Government. The debate lasted perhaps two hours; and the question on indefinite postponement being taken, was decided in the negative—yeas 63, nays 69, as follows:

Yeas—Messrs. Alexander, Alston, Anderson, Avery, Bard, Barnett, Bines, Bowen, Brown, Calhoun, Cannon, Comstock, Condict, Crawford, Creighton, Crouch, Cuthbert, Desha, Duvall, Findley, Fisk of New York, Forsyth, Franklin, Gourdin, Griffin, Hall, Harris, Hasbrouck, Hubbard, Humphreys, Johnson of Kentucky, Kent of Maryland, Kershaw, King of North Carolina, Lefferts, Lowndes, Lyle, Macon, McKim, Moore, Ormsby, Parker, Pickens, Piper, Rea of Pennsylvania, Rhea of Tennessee, Rich, Ringgold, Roane, Robertson, Sage, Seybert, Sharp, Smith of Pennsylvania, Smith of Virginia, Tannehill, Taylor, Telfair, Troup, Udree, Williams, Wilson of Pennsylvania, and Yancey.

NAYS—Messrs. Barbour, Baylies of Massachusetts, Bigelow, Bradbury, Brigham, Burwell, Caperton, Champion, Cilley, Clopton, Cooper, Cox, Culpeper, Davenport, Ely, Eppes, Farrow, Gaston, Gholson, Goldsborough, Goodwyn, Grosvenor, Hale, Hanson, Hawes, Hopkins of Kentucky, Hungerford, Hulbert, Jackson of Rhode Island, Jackson of Virginia, Kennedy, Kerr, King of Massachusetts, Law, Lovett, McCoy, Montgomery, Moseley, Nelson, Newton, Oakley, Pearson, Pickering, Pitkin, Pleasants, Potter, John Reed, William Reed, Ridgely, Ruggles, Schureman, Sevier, Sheffey, Sherwood, Slaymaker, Stanford, Stockton, Stuart, Sturges, Taggart, Thompson, Vose, Ward of Massachusetts, Wheaton, White, Wilcox, Wilson of Massachusetts, Winter, and Wright.

On motion of Mr. FISK, of New York, the further consideration of the bill was postponed until to-morrow.

DUTIES ON TONNAGE &c.

The bill from the Senate, "further to provide for the collection of the duties on imports and tonnage," was read a first and second time. [This bill contains a number of provisions, applicable to violations of the revenue law, resembling the provisions of the bill lately passed for preventing intercourse with the enemy.]

Mr. FISK, of Vermont, moved that the bill be read a third time.

Mr. STOCKTON moved that the bill be indefinitely postponed.

This motion gave rise to a warm debate in the course of which Messrs. STOCKTON, WILLIAM REED, GROSVENOR, and SHEFFEY, advocated the motion, and Messrs. FISK of Vermont, RHEA, WRIGHT, EPPES, ALSTON, and NEWTON, opposed it.

At this stage of the debate—on motion of Mr. JOHNSON, of Kentucky, the bill was ordered to lie on the table, with a view to take up the bill fixing the Military Peace Establishment.

MILITARY PEACE ESTABLISHMENT.

The amendments proposed by the Senate to the bill "fixing the Military Peace Establishment of the United States," were read.

The first section of the said bill, as passed by this House, is as follows:

Be it enacted, &c., That the Military Peace Establishment of the United States shall consist of such proportions of artillery, infantry, and riflemen, not exceeding in the whole *six* thousand men, as the President of the United States shall judge proper, and that the Corps of Engineers, as at present established, be retained.

The Senate propose to amend the said first section by striking out the word "peace," and by striking out the word "six," and inserting the word "fifteen."

A division of the question on the said amendments was called for, when the question was taken on that part of the said amendments which proposes to strike out the word "peace," and was determined in the negative—yeas 33, nays 86, as follows:

YEAS—Messrs. Anderson, Bard, Calhoun, Crawford, Creighton, Duvall, Findley, Fisk of Vermont, Fisk of New York, Forsyth, Gourdin, Griffin, Grosvenor, Hanson, Hasbrouck, Hawkins, Humphreys, Irwin, Kershaw, Lowndes, McCoy, Moore, Newton, Oakley, Pleasants, Rich, Ringgold, Seybert, Taylor, Telfair, Wilson of Pennsylvania, Winter, and Yancey.

NAYS—Messrs. Alexander, Alston, Avery, Barbour, Barnett, Baylies of Massachusetts, Bigelow, Bines, Bradbury, Brigham, Brown, Caperton, Cannon, Champion, Cilley, Clopton, Comstock, Condict, Cooper, Crouch, Culpeper, Cuthbert, Dana, Ely, Eppes, Farrow, Franklin, Geddes, Gholson, Goldsborough, Goodwyn, Hale, Hall, Harris, Hawes, Hubbard, Hungerford, Hulbert, Jackson of Rhode Island, Jackson of Virginia, Johnson of Kentucky, Kennedy, Kent of New York, Kent of Maryland, Kerr, King of Massachusetts, Law, Lefferts, Lovett, Lyle, Macon, Moseley, Nelson, Ormsby, Pickering, Piper, Pitkin, John Reed, William Reed, Rea of Pennsylvania, Rhea of Tennessee, Roane, Robertson, Ruggles, Sage, Schureman, Sheffey, Sherwood, Slaymaker, Smith of Pennsylvania, Stanford, Stockton, Strong, Sturges, Taggart, Tannehill, Udree, Vose, Ward of Massachusetts, Wheaton, White, Wilcox, Williams, Wilson of Massachusetts, and Wright.

The question was then taken on concurring in that part of the said amendments which proposes to strike out the word "six," and to insert in lieu thereof the word "fifteen," and was also determined in the negative—yeas 18, nays 100, as follows:

YEAS—Messrs. Anderson, Bard, Duvall, Findley, Fisk of New York, Forsyth, Gourdin, Griffin, Grosvenor, Hanson, Hawkins, Irwin, Kershaw, Newton, Oakley, Ringgold, Seybert, and Wilson of Pennsylvania.

NAYS—Messrs. Alexander, Alston, Avery, Barbour, Barnett, Baylies of Massachusetts, Bigelow, Bines, Bradbury, Brigham, Brown, Caperton, Calhoun, Cannon, Champion, Cilley, Clopton, Comstock, Condict, Cooper, Cox, Crawford, Creighton, Crouch, Culpeper, Cuthbert, Dana, Ely, Eppes, Farrow, Fisk of Vermont, Franklin, Geddes, Gholson, Goldsborough, Goodwyn, Hale, Hall, Harris, Hasbrouck, Hawes, Hubbard, Humphreys, Hungerford, Hulbert, Jackson of Rhode Island, Jackson of Virginia, Johnson of Kentucky, Kennedy, Kent of New York, Kent of Maryland, Kerr, King of Massachusetts, Law, Lefferts, Lovett, Lyle, Macon, McCoy, Moore, Moseley, Nelson, Ormsby, Pickering, Piper, Pitkin, Pleasants, John Reed, William Reed, Rea of Pennsylvania, Rhea of Tennessee, Rich, Roane, Robertson, Ruggles, Sage, Schureman, Sheffey, Sherwood, Slaymaker, Stanford, Stockton, Strong, Sturges, Tannehill, Taylor, Telfair, Udree, Vose, Ward of Massachusetts, Wheaton, White, Wilcox, Williams, Wilson of Massachusetts, Winter, Wright, and Yancey.

The residue of the amendments of the Senate to the said bill were then again read, and disagreed to by the House.

FRIDAY, March 3.

On motion of Mr. HUMPHREYS, the Committee on the Public Lands were discharged from the further consideration of all matters and things referred to them during the present session, upon which they have not reported.

A message from the Senate informed the House that the Senate insist on their amendments disagreed to by this House, to the bill fixing the Military Peace Establishment of the United States."

The House proceeded to consider the message from the Senate, notifying that they insist on their amendments to the bill fixing the Military Peace Establishment of the United States: whereupon—

Resolved, That this House insist on their disagreement to the said amendments, and ask a conference upon the subject-matter thereof.

Ordered, That Mr. TROUP, Mr. JOHNSON of Kentucky, and Mr. STUART, be the managers at the said conference, on the part of this House.

The House resolved itself into a Committee of the Whole, on the bill from the Senate "to provide a library room, and for transporting the library lately purchased." The bill was reported to the House, read the third time, and passed.

The House went into a Committee of the Whole on the bill making additional appropriations for the service of the year 1815. The bill was reported with an amendment thereto, which was concurred in by the House; and the bill was read the third time, and passed.

A message from the Senate informed the House that the Senate have passed the bill, entitled "An act concerning invalid pensioners," with amendments. The amendments, were read, and concurred in by the House.

The bill to authorize the payment for horses lost in the public service in the Northwestern army, and in the campaigns under Generals Jackson and Floyd, in the present war, was postponed indefinitely.

The bill from the Senate, "to allow a drawback on duties on spirits distilled, and on certain goods, wares, and merchandise, manufactured, within the United States, on the exportation thereof to any foreign port or place," was postponed indefinitely.

The bill to authorize the purchase of the vessels captured on Lake Champlain, passed through a Committee of the Whole, and was ordered to be engrossed for a third reading; and was subsequently read a third time, and passed.

The bill for the relief of Bowie and Kurtz, and others, having been called up—

Mr. YANCEY moved to postpone the further consideration of the bill indefinitely, on the ground of want of time duly to act on the subject.

The motion was opposed by Mr. GOLDSBOROUGH and Mr. PITKIN, but was decided in the affirmative.

The bill from the Senate to repeal the discriminating duties on imports and tonnage, on condition that reciprocal measures are adopted by foreign Governments, passed through a Committee of the Whole without debate, and was reported to the House, and ordered to a third reading, and was read a third time, passed by unanimous vote, and returned to the Senate.

The bill to authorize the Board of Commissioners of the Navy to appoint clerks, passed through a Committee of the Whole, was ordered to be engrossed for a third reading, and was accordingly read a third time, and passed.

The bill to provide for ascertaining and surveying the boundary lines fixed by the treaty with the Creek Indians, and for other purposes; the bill concerning the Navy Establishment; the bill for the relief of Charles Todd; the bill for the relief of the Eastern Branch Bridge Company, passed through Committees of the Whole, and were severally read a third time, and passed.

The bill to alter the time for the next meeting of Congress having been called for—

Mr. NELSON moved that the further consideration of the bill be postponed indefinitely.

This motion was opposed by Mr. FISK, of New York, who enumerated the advantages to arise from an early session, and the propriety of Congress fixing the day, rather than that they should be called together by the Executive.

Mr. JACKSON, of Virginia, spoke in support of the motion, and stated his belief that an extra session would not in any event be necessary. He expressed his hope that Congress, as well as the people, might be permitted to enjoy a little peace.

Mr. NELSON supported his motion on the grounds of the total absence of a necessity for an extra session, and that their constituents *ought* not to be taxed for such an object *unnecessarily.*

Other gentlemen also spoke against as well as in favor of the motion for postponement; which was decided in the affirmative, and the bill indefinitely postponed.

WEST POINT ACADEMY.

The bill from the Senate authorizing an appropriation for completing the public buildings at West Point for the Military Academy, being before a Committee of the Whole—

Mr. TROUP moved to add thereto two other sections, to stand as first and second sections, contemplating the establishment of two corps of engineers, precisely of the same character, number, &c., as the present corps of engineers, each of which to be stationed at points to be designated by the President for the location of two military academies.

Mr. FISK, of New York, opposed the amendment as being too important to be decided at this late period of the session, and because not necessarily connected with the present bill. He stated several objections to the amendment, which at once occurred to him.

To these objections Mr. TROUP replied, and enforced the expediency of the amendment; and he contended that a more favorable opportunity for the attainment of such an object could not again occur.

Mr. YANCEY opposed the amendment, and expressed no great friendship for the bill. His principal objection was not to the establishment of other schools, but that Congress ought to fix the location of these other schools.

Mr. TAYLOR also opposed the amendment,

1269   HISTORY OF CONGRESS.   1270

MARCH, 1815.   *Thanks to the Speaker—Collection of Duties.*   H. OF R.

which, he said, instead of putting a graft upon a tree, was putting a tree upon the graft. He was only opposed to the amendment from the difficulty which would attend the adoption of such a provision in both Houses at this period of the session.

The amendment was negatived by a large majority; and the Committee rose and reported the bill without amendment.

Mr. YANCEY moved to postpone indefinitely the further consideration of the bill; which motion was opposed by Mr. FISK, of New York, and supported by Mr. ALSTON, but was negatived by a large majority.

The bill was then ordered to be read a third time, and was accordingly read a third time, and passed.

THANKS TO THE SPEAKER.

Mr. FINDLEY moved the following resolution:

Resolved, That the thanks of this House be presented to LANGDON CHEVES, in testimony of their approbation of his conduct in discharge of the arduous and important duties assigned him whilst in the Chair.

The motion was unanimously agreed to; and this vote having been announced, the SPEAKER addressed the House as follows:

"GENTLEMEN: I am very sensible of the honor you have done me by your vote; but I am much more deeply affected by the kindness of which it is an evidence—a kindness which has been uniform, and which alone could have sustained me in times and under circumstances of such unusual difficulty and embarrassment as those in which we have acted together. Almost the only qualification with which I took the Chair was a determination faithfully, impartially, and independently to do my duty; almost the only merit which I have been authorized to claim, while in it, has been that of a zealous endeavor to execute that determination. But you, in the partiality of your kindness, have bestowed on these poor pretensions the highest excellence. Real gratitude, gentlemen, is not eloquent; I can only say I thank you—affectionately and unfeignedly I thank you! May God bless you all, and restore you speedily and happily to your families and your homes!"

AMENDMENTS TO THE CONSTITUTION.

Mr. PICKERING submitted the following propositions of amendment to the Constitution of the United States; which were read, and ordered to lie on the table.

Resolved, by the Senate and House of Representatives of the United States of America in Congress assembled, two-thirds of both Houses concurring therein, That the following articles be proposed to the Legislatures of the several States, as amendments to the Constitution of the United States, each of which, when ratified by the Legislatures of three-fourths of the several States, shall be valid to all intents and purposes as part of the said Constitution:

ARTICLE 1. Representatives and direct taxes shall be apportioned among the several States, which may be included within this Union, according to their respective number of free persons, including those bound to serve for a term of years, and excluding Indians not taxed, and all other persons.

ART. 2. No new State shall be admitted into the Union by Congress, in virtue of the power granted by the Constitution, without the concurrence of two-thirds of both Houses.

ART. 3. Congress shall not have power to lay any embargo on the ships or vessels of the citizens of the United States in the ports or harbors thereof, for more than sixty days.

ART. 4. Congress shall not have power, without the concurrence of two-thirds of both Houses, to interdict the commercial intercourse between the United States and any foreign nation, or the dependencies thereof.

ART. 5. Congress shall not make or declare war, or authorize acts of hostility, against any foreign nation, without the concurrence of two-thirds of both Houses, except such acts of hostility be in defence of the Territories of the United States, when actually invaded.

ART. 6. No person who shall hereafter be naturalized shall be eligible as a member of the Senate or House of Representatives of the United States, nor capable of holding any civil office under the authority of the United States.

ART. 7. The same person shall not be elected President of the United States a second time; nor shall the President be elected from the same State two terms in succession.

COLLECTION OF DUTIES.

Mr. FISK, of Vermont, moved to proceed to the consideration of the bill for the further security of the collection of duties on imports and tonnage.

Mr. PITKIN moved that the House now proceed to the orders of the day. Negatived—55 to 40.

The question to postpone the said bill indefinitely being then again stated—

The motion was supported be Mr. WILLIAM REED, of Massachusetts, to whom Mr. FISK, of New York replied.

Mr. BARNETT then observing that this was the last day of the session, and that he found gentlemen were again commencing discussion on this question, required the previous question.

This call was supported by the House, by a vote of 57 to 42.

The SPEAKER being about to put the previous question in the usual form—

Mr. SHEFFEY moved that the bill lie on the table, and thereon required the yeas and nays; which motion was decided in the negative—For laying it on the table 47, against it 65, as follows:

YEAS—Messrs. Baylies of Massachusetts, Bigelow, Brigham, Caperton, Cilley, Clopton, Cox, Culpeper, Davenport, Ely, Farrow, Gaston, Geddes, Grosvenor, Hale, Hungerford, Hulbert, Kent of Maryland, King of Massachusetts, Law, Lovett, Moseley, Nelson, Oakley, Pearson, Pickering, Pitkin, Potter, William Reed, Ridgely, Ruggles, Schureman, Sheffey, Sherwood, Slaymaker, Smith of New York, Stanford, Stockton, Stuart, Sturges, Taggart, Vose, Ward of Massachusetts, Wheaton, White, Wilcox, and Winter.

NAYS—Messrs. Alexander, Alston, Anderson, Avery, Barnett, Bines, Brown, Burwell, Cannon, Clendenin, Comstock, Condict, Crawford, Creighton, Crouch, Cuthbert, Davis of Pennsylv'a, Desha, Duvall, Eppes, Fisk of Vermont, Fisk of New York, Gholson, Goodwyn, Gourdin, Griffin, Harris, Hasbrouck, Hawes, Hopkins of Kentucky, Hubbard, Humphreys, Irwin,

Johnson of Kentucky, Kennedy, Kerr, Kilbourn, Lefferts, Lowndes, Lyle, McCoy, McKim, Moore, Newton, Ormsby, Parker, Pickens, Piper, Pleasants, Rhea of Tennessee, Rich, Roane, Robertson, Sage, Sevier, Seybert, Smith of Pennsylvania, Smith of Virginia, Strong, Tannehill, Taylor, Troup, Udree, Wilson of Pennsylvania, and Yancey.

The previous question was then taken, in the usual form, to wit: Shall the main question be now put? and passed in the affirmative—yeas 66, nays 43.

The said main question was then taken, to wit: Shall the bill be read a third time? and passed in the affirmative—yeas 66, nays 48, as follows:

YEAS—Messrs. Alexander, Alston, Anderson, Avery, Barnett, Bines, Brown, Burwell, Butler, Calhoun, Clendenin, Comstock, Condict, Crawford, Creighton, Crouch, Cuthbert, Davis of Pennsylvania, Desha, Duvall, Eppes, Fisk of Vermont, Fisk of N. Y., Gholson, Goodwyn, Gourdin, Griffin, Hall, Harris, Hasbrouck, Hawes, Hubbard, Humphreys, Irwin, Johnson of Kentucky, Kennedy, Kent of Maryland, Kerr, Kershaw, Lefferts, Lyle, McCoy, McKim, Montgomery, Moore, Murfree, Ormsby, Parker, Pickens, Piper, Pleasants, Rhea of Tennessee, Rich, Roane, Robertson, Sage, Sevier, Seybert, Smith of Pennsylvania, Smith of Virginia, Strong, Tannehill, Taylor, Troup, Udree, Wilson of Pennsylvania, and Yancey.

NAYS—Messrs. Baylies of Massachusetts, Bigelow, Bradbury, Brigham, Caperton, Cilley, Clopton, Cox, Culpeper, Davenport, Ely, Farrow, Gaston, Geddes, Grosvenor, Hale, Hopkins of Kentucky, Hungerford, Hulbert, King of Massachusetts, Law, Lovett, Moseley, Nelson, Oakley, Pearson, Pickering, Pitkin, Potter, William Reed, Ridgely, Ruggles, Schureman, Sheffey, Sherwood, Slaymaker, Smith of New York, Stanford, Stockton, Stuart, Sturges, Taggart, Vose, Ward of Massachusetts, Wheaton, White, Wilcox, and Winter.

The said bill was then read the third time, when a motion was made by Mr. KING, of Massachusetts, to recommit the bill for amendment, which was negatived. The question was then taken, Shall the bill pass? and decided in the affirmative.

MILITARY PEACE ESTABLISHMENT.

Mr. TROUP, from the managers appointed on the part of this House, at the conference, on the disagreeing votes of the two Houses on the amendments depending to the bill "fixing the Military Peace Establishment of the United States," reported the following modifications:

That the Senate recede from the first amendment proposed to the bill;

That in lieu of the second amendment proposed, the Senate agree to substitute the word "ten," for the word "fifteen;"

That the House of Representatives recede from their disagreement to all the other amendments proposed by the Senate.

The House proceeded to consider the said modifications.

Mr. ROBERTSON said, that he hoped the report of the committee of conference would be agreed to. He had voted against the reduction of the Army to six thousand. He was now prepared to sanction a much larger force. Circumstances had occurred which produced considerable effect on his opinions. A report had been alluded to in debate, which merited much consideration. It is said that the Floridas had been ceded by Spain to Britain. Britain had very formally protested against our taking possession of a part of the country denominated West Florida. He had no doubt, from information recently received, that an attack was about to be made on Mobile. The enemy were building barges on board their fleet, evidently with a view to continue the conflict. He had no apprehension of their again visiting New Orleans; they would not soon, they would never, make another attempt upon that city. He believed Mobile was the object; they would be desirous of doing something to break their fall; to retrieve the expedition from utter disgrace. It is by no means clear, that a knowledge of the treaty would arrest their designs. He had no confidence in the good faith of England. He believed that war still raged in the South. He had said, that notwithstanding the treaty, it was probable an effort would be made to seize on West Florida. He entertained another opinion which he would express; he believed, that, had the English succeeded in getting possession of New Orleans, they would not have given it up; but they would have found out some pretext for holding it. Why was the acquisition of Louisiana introduced into discussion at Ghent? What connexion had that subject with any question of controversy between the United States and England? It had reached us through various channels, that all officers necessary for the civil government of the country had accompanied the grand expedition. Perhaps it might turn out, on explanation, that many important steps with a view to conquest and permanent occupation, had been taken after the determination to sign the treaty had been formed.

Under present circumstances, though hostile to a large army in time of peace, he was himself disposed to retain a larger force than ten thousand men; but he most earnestly hoped it would not be reduced below that number.

The question was taken to concur in the second modification, to wit: That the Military Peace Establishment shall consist of "ten" thousand men, instead of "fifteen" thousand, as proposed by the Senate; and it passed in the affirmative—yeas 70, nays 38, as follows:

YEAS—Messrs. Alexander, Alston, Anderson, Avery, Barnett, Bines, Bowen, Calhoun, Clendenin, Clopton, Comstock, Crawford, Creighton, Culpeper, Cuthbert, Duvall, Eppes, Findley, Fisk of Vermont, Fisk of New York, Forsyth, Franklin, Gholson, Goodwyn, Gourdin, Griffin, Grosvenor, Hall, Hawes, Hawkins, Hopkins of Kentucky, Hubbard, Humphreys, Jackson of Virginia, Johnson of Kentucky, Kennedy, Kent of Maryland, Kerr, Kershaw, King of North Carolina, Lefferts, Lowndes, Lyle, McCoy, McKim, Montgomery, Moore, Nelson, Newton, Pickens, Piper, Pleasants, Rhea of Tennessee, Rich, Ringgold, Roane, Robertson, Sage, Seybert, Smith of Pennsylvania, Smith of Virginia, Strong, Stuart, Tannehill, Taylor, Telfair, Troup, Wilson of Pennsylvania, Winter, and Yancey.

NAYS—Messrs. Baylies of Massachusetts, Bradbury, Brigham, Burwell, Caperton, Cannon, Cilley, Cox, Davenport, Desha, Ely, Farrow, Gaston, Geddes, Harris, Hungerford, King of Massachusetts, Lovett, Macon, Ormsby, Pearson, Pickering, Pitkin, John Reed, Ruggles, Schureman, Sharp, Sheffey, Sherwood, Stanford, Stockton, Sturges, Taggart, Vose, Ward of Massachusetts, White, Wilcox, and Wilson of Massachusetts.

The question was then taken, that the House recede from their disagreement to so much of the amendments of the Senate as proposes to strike out a part of the 6th and the whole of the 7th and 8th sections of the bill, being that part thereof which allows donations in land to disbanded officers and soldiers, as is proposed in the third modification recommended by the conferees; and passed in the affirmative—yeas 57, nays 55, as follows:

YEAS—Messrs. Alexander, Alston, Barnett, Baylies of Massachusetts, Bigelow, Bines, Bradbury, Brigham, Burwell, Caperton, Cannon, Champion, Cilley, Clopton, Cox, Crawford, Cuthbert, Ely, Gaston, Geddes, Griffin, Hale, Hall, Hopkins of Kentucky, Hubbard, Humphreys, Hulbert, King of Massachusetts, Law, Lovett, McCoy, Montgomery, Moseley, Ormsby, Pearson, Pickering, Pipes, Pitkin, John Reed, Ruggles, Schureman, Sheffey, Sherwood, Stanford, Stockton, Sturges, Taggart, Tannehill, Taylor, Vose, Ward of Massachusetts, Wheaton, White, Wilcox, Wilson of Massachusetts, Winter, and Yancey.

NAYS—Messrs. Anderson, Avery, Bowen, Calhoun, Comstock, Creighton, Culpeper, Davis of Pennsylvania, Desha, Duvall, Eppes, Farrow, Findley, Fisk of Vermont, Fisk of New York, Franklin, Gholson, Goodwyn, Gourdin, Grosvenor, Harris, Hawes, Hawkins, Hungerford, Jackson of Virginia, Johnson of Kentucky, Kennedy, Kent of Maryland, Kerr, Kershaw, King of North Carolina, Lefferts, Lowndes, Macon, McKim, Moore, Nelson, Newton, Pickens, Pleasants, Rhea of Tennessee, Rich, Ringgold, Roane, Robertson, Sage, Sharp, Smith of Pennsylvania, Smith of Virginia, Strong, Telfair, Troup, Udree, and Wilson of Pennsylvania.

The question was then taken to recede from their disagreement to the residue of the amendments of the Senate, as proposed in the third modification recommended by the conferees; and passed in the affirmative.

CLOSING BUSINESS.

A message from the Senate informed the House that the Senate have passed the bill " to vest more effectually in the State Courts and in the District Courts of the United States jurisdiction in the cases therein mentioned," with an amendment; in which they ask the concurrence of this House.

The amendment was concurred in by the House.

A message from the Senate informed the House that the Senate have passed the bill entitled "An act to authorize the payment for property lost, captured, or destroyed, by the enemy, while in the military service of the United States," with amendments.

The amendments were read; and a motion was made by Mr. FISK, of New York, that the bill be postponed indefinitely; which was determined in the negative.

The amendments were then in part concurred in, and in part disagreed to by the House.

The House went into Committee of the Whole on the bill from the Senate "for the relief of sundry persons in the service of the United States, in consequence of the destruction of their tools by fire at the Navy Yard." The bill was reported without amendment, read the third time, and passed.

A message from the Senate informed the House that the Senate have passed the bill "making appropriations for the support of the Military Establishment for the year 1815," with amendments; in which they ask the concurrence of this House.

The said amendments were read, and committed to a Committee of the Whole.

The House then went into Committee on the said amendments, agreed to the same; and they were concurred in by the House.

The order of the day on the bill from the Senate, " to authorize the settlement and payment of certain claims for the services of the militia," being called, Mr. FORSYTH moved to discharge the Committee of the Whole from the said bill, and to refer the same to the Secretary of War, with instructions to report at the next session of Congress the amount and description of claims for which it provides, and the grounds upon which payment has been refused by the United States.

A division of the question on this said motion was called for; when the question was taken on discharging the Committee of the Whole, and passed in the affirmative; and, on motion of Mr. RHEA, of Tennessee, the bill, together with the remaining member of the motion made by Mr. FORSYTH, was ordered to lie on the table.

On motion of Mr. SHARP, a committee was appointed, jointly, with a committee to be appointed by the Senate, to wait upon the President of the United States, and inform him that the two Houses are now ready to adjourn, and desire to know whether he has any further communication to make to them during the present session.

Mr. SHARP, from the joint committee appointed to wait upon the President of the United States, and inform him of the approaching recess of Congress, reported that they had performed that duty, and that the President answered that he had no further communication to make to Congress at the present session.

A message from the Senate informed the House that the Senate, having completed the Legislative business before them, are now ready to adjourn.

Ordered, That a message be sent to the Senate, to inform them that this House, having completed the business before them, are also ready to adjourn; and that the Clerk do go with the said message.

The Clerk having went with the said message, and being returned, the SPEAKER adjourned the House *sine die.*

SUPPLEMENTAL JOURNAL

Of such proceedings of the House of Representatives, at the Third Session of the Thirteenth Congress, as, pending their consideration, were ordered to be kept secret, but, respecting which, the injunction of secrecy was afterwards taken off by order of the House.

THURSDAY, February 23, 1815.

The confidential Message of the PRESIDENT of THE UNITED STATES, communicated on this day, was then taken up, and read, as follows, viz:

To the Senate and House of
    Representatives of the United States:

Congress will have seen, by the communication from the Consul General of the United States, at Algiers, laid before them on the 17th of November, 1812, the hostile proceedings of the Dey against that functionary. These have been followed by acts of more overt and direct warfare against the citizens of the United States trading in the Mediterranean; some of whom are still detained in captivity, notwithstanding the attempts which have been made to ransom them, and are treated with the rigor usual on the coast of Barbary.

The considerations which rendered it unnecessary and unimportant to commence hostile operations on the part of the United States, being now terminated by the peace with Great Britain, which opens the prospect of an active and valuable trade of their citizens within the range of the Algerine cruisers, I recommend to Congress the expediency of an act declaring the existence of a state of war between the United States and the Dey of Algiers; and of such provisions as may be requisite for a vigorous prosecution of it to a successful issue.

                        JAMES MADISON.
WASHINGTON, *Feb.* 23, 1815.

Ordered, That the said communication be referred to the Committee on Foreign Relations.

Mr. WRIGHT then submitted the following resolution:

Resolved, That the Committee on Foreign Relations be instructed to inquire of the President the reasons assigned by the Dey of Algiers for his conduct towards the United States.

And the question being taken, "Will the House now consider the resolution?" it was determined in the negative.

FRIDAY, February 24.

Mr. FORSYTH, from the Committee on Foreign Relations, to whom was referred the President's Message of yesterday, reported "a bill for the protection of the commerce of the United States against the Algerine cruisers;" which was twice read.

Mr. GASTON then moved to commit the bill to the Committee on Foreign Relations, with instructions "to inquire into and report, in detail, the facts upon which the measure contemplated by the bill is predicated."

Mr. HALL then moved to postpone the bill indefinitely; and, the question being taken thereon, it was determined in the negative—yeas 31, nays 108, as follows:

YEAS—Messrs. Alston, Avery, Butler, Comstock, Crawford, Crouch, Davis of Pennsylvania, Griffin, Hall, Johnson of Kentucky, Lyle, Pearson, Piper, Rea of Pennsylvania, Smith of Pennsylvania, Stanford, Strong, Tannehill, Wheaton, Williams, and Wilson of Pennsylvania.

NAYS—Messrs. Alexander, Anderson, Barbour, Baylies of Massachusetts, Bigelow, Bines, Bowen, Boyd, Bradbury, Brigham, Caperton, Calhoun, Cannon, Champion, Cilley, Clopton, Condict, Cooper, Creighton, Culpeper, Cuthbert, Davenport, Desha, Duvall, Eppes, Farrow, Findley, Fisk of Vermont, Fisk of New York, Forsyth, Franklin, Gaston, Geddes, Gholson, Goldsborough, Gourdin, Grosvenor, Hale, Harris, Hasbrouck, Hawes, Hawkins, Henderson, Hopkins of Kentucky, Hubbard, Humphreys, Hungerford, Hulbert, Jackson of Rhode Island, Jackson of Virginia, Kennedy, Kent of Maryland, Kerr, King of Massachusetts, Law, Lefferts, Lovett, Lowndes, Macon, Markell, McCoy, McKim, McLean, Moore, Moseley, Nelson, Newton, Ormsby, Pickering, Pickens, Pitkin, Pleasants, John Reed, William Reed, Rhea of Tennessee, Rich, Ringgold, Roane, Robertson, Ruggles, Sage, Schureman, Sevier, Sharp, Sheffey, Sherwood, Shipherd, Slaymaker, Smith of Virginia, Stockton, Sturges, Taggart, Taylor, Telfair, Thompson, Troup, Udree, Vose, Ward of Massachusetts, White, Wilcox, Wilson of Massachusetts, Winter, Wood, Wright, and Yancey.

Mr. HALL then moved to amend the motion of Mr. GASTON, by striking out the words "the Committee on Foreign Relations," and inserting, in lieu thereof, the words "a select committee;" and, the question being taken thereon, it passed in the affirmative.

Mr. HAWKINS then moved to postpone the further consideration of the bill until Monday next; which was determined in the negative.

The question was then taken on agreeing to Mr. GASTON's motion, as amended, and passed in the affirmative—yeas 79, nays 42, as follows:

YEAS—Messrs. Alston, Baylies of Massachusetts, Bigelow, Bowen, Boyd, Bradbury, Brigham, Butler, Caperton, Cannon, Champion, Cilley, Clopton, Condict, Cooper, Creighton, Culpeper, Davenport, Desha, Duvall, Ely, Eppes, Farrow, Findley, Fisk of Vermont, Fisk of New York, Gaston, Goldsborough, Grosvenor, Hale, Hall, Harris, Hasbrouck, Henderson, Hungerford, Hulbert, Jackson of Rhode Island, Kent of Maryland, Kerr, King of Massachusetts, Law, Lefferts, Lovett, Macon, Markell, McKim, Moore, Moseley, Ormsby, Pearson, Pickering, Pickens, Pitkin, John Reed, William Reed, Rich, Ruggles, Sevier, Seybert, Sheffey, Sherwood, Shipherd, Slaymaker, Stanford, Stockton, Sturges, Taylor, Vose, Ward of Massachusetts, Wheaton, White, Wilcox, Williams, Wilson of Massachusetts, Wilson of Pennsylvania, Winter, Wood, and Wright.

NAYS—Messrs. Alexander, Anderson, Avery, Barbour, Bines, Calhoun, Comstock, Crouch, Cuthbert, Forsyth, Franklin, Gholson, Goodwyn, Hawes, Hawkins, Hubbard, Humphreys, Ingersoll, Ingham, Jackson of Virginia, Johnson of Ky., Kennedy, Lowndes, McCoy, McLean, Nelson, Newton, Piper, Pleasants, Rea of Pennsylvania, Rhea of Tennessee, Ringgold, Roane,

Robertson, Sage, Sharp, Smith of Virginia, Strong, Tannehill, Telfair, Udree, and Yancey.

Ordered, That Messrs. GASTON, FORSYTH, WARD of Massachusetts, GROSVENOR, SEYBERT, McKIM, and NEWTON, be the said committee.

TUESDAY, February 28.

Mr. GASTON, from the select committee, to whom was referred, on the 24th instant, the bill for "the protection of the commerce of the United States against the Algerine cruisers," with instructions to inquire into, and report in detail, the facts upon which the measure contemplated by the bill is predicated," made a report thereupon ; which was read. The report is as follows:

The committee to whom has been referred the bill "for the protection of the commerce of the United States against the Algerine cruisers," with instructions to inquire and report, in detail, the facts upon which the measure contemplated by the bill is predicated, report :

That, in the month of July, 1812, the Dey of Algiers taking offence, or pretending to take offence, at the quantity and quality of a shipment of military stores, made by the United States in pursuance of the stipulation in the Treaty of 1795, and refusing to receive the stores, extorted from the American Consul General at Algiers, by threats of personal imprisonment, and of reducing to slavery all Americans in his power, a sum of money claimed as arrearages of treaty stipulations, and denied by the United States to be due ; and then compelled the Consul, and all citizens of the United States at Algiers, abruptly to quit his dominions.

It further appears to the committee, that, on the 25th of August following, the American brig Edwin, of Salem, owned by Nathaniel Silsbee of that place, while on a voyage from Malta to Gibraltar, was taken by an Algerine corsair, and carried into Algiers as prize. The commander of the brig, Captain George Campbell Smith, and the crew, ten in number, have ever since been detained in captivity, with the exception of two of them, whose release has been affected under circumstances not indicating any change of hostile temper on the part of the Dey. It also appears that a vessel, sailing under the Spanish flag, has been condemned in Algiers as laying a false claim to that flag, and concealing her true American character. In this vessel was taken a Mr. Pollard, who claims to be an American citizen, and is believed to be of Norfolk, Virginia, and who, as an American citizen, is kept in captivity. The Government, justly solicitous to relieve these unfortunate captives, caused an agent (whose connexion with the Government was not disclosed) to be sent to Algiers, with the means, and with instructions to effect their ransom, if it could be done at a price not exceeding three thousand dollars per man. The effort did not succeed, because of the Dey's avowed policy to increase the number of his American slaves, in order to be able to compel a renewal of his Treaty with the United States on terms suited to his rapacity. Captain Smith, Mr. Pollard, and the master of the Edwin, are not confined, nor kept at hard labor; but the rest of the captives are subjected to the well known horrors of Algerine slavery. The committee have not been apprised of any other specific outrages upon the persons or property of American citizens, besides those stated ; and they apprehend that the fewness of these is attributable to the want of opportunity, and not of inclination in the Dey, to prey upon our commerce, and to enslave our citizens. The war with Britain has hitherto shut the Mediterranean against American vessels, which it may be presumed will now shortly venture upon it.

The committee are all of opinion, upon the evidence which has been laid before them, that the Dey of Algiers considers his Treaty with the United States as at an end, and is waging war against them. The evidence upon which this opinion is founded, and from which are extracted the facts above stated, accompanies this report, and with it is respectfully submitted.

The said bill being then amended, by prefixing the following preamble—

"Whereas the Dey of Algiers, on the coast of Barbary, has commenced a predatory warfare against the United States,"

Mr. GOLDSBOROUGH moved further to amend the bill by inserting, after the word "aforesaid," in the 4th line of the second section, the following words :

"If the Dey of Algiers shall not, on demand by an accredited agent of the United States, duly authorized for that purpose, deliver up, without delay, all American citizens who may be detained by him as prisoners or slaves, and return to a state of amity with the United States, by a treaty of peace."

And the question being taken thereon, it was determined in the negative—yeas 47, nays 92, as follows :

YEAS—Messrs. Baylies of Massachusetts, Bigelow, Boyd, Bradbury, Brigham, Caperton, Champion, Cilley, Condict, Cooper, Davenport, Ely, Geddes, Goldsborough, Goodwyn, Hale, Hasbrouck, Henderson, Hungerford, Jackson of Rhode Island, Kent of New York, Kent of Maryland, Kerr, King of Massachusetts, Law, Lovett, Moseley, Pearson, Pickering, Pitkin, Potter, John Reed, Ruggles, Sheffey, Slaymaker, Stanford, Strong, Stuart, Sturges, Taggart, Thompson, Vose, Wheaton, White, Wilcox, Wilson of Massachusetts, and Winter.

NAYS—Messrs. Alexander, Alston, Anderson, Avery, Barbour, Bard, Barnett, Bines, Bowen, Brown, Burwell, Calhoun, Cannon, Clopton, Comstock, Cox, Creighton, Crouch, Culpeper, Cuthbert, Davis of Pennsylvania, Desha, Duvall, Eppes, Farrow, Findley, Fisk of Vermont, Fisk of New York, Forsyth, Franklin, Gaston, Gholson, Gourdin, Griffin, Grosvenor, Hall, Hanson, Harris, Hawes, Hawkins, Hopkins of Kentucky, Hubbard, Humphreys, Hulbert, Irwin, Jackson of Virginia, Johnson of Kentucky, Kennedy, Kershaw, Kilbourn, King of North Carolina, Lefferts, Lowndes, Macon, McCoy, McKim, Montgomery, Moore, Nelson, Newton, Oakley, Ormsby, Pickens, Piper, Pleasants, William Reed, Rea of Pennsylvania, Rhea of Tennessee, Rich, Ringgold, Roane, Robertson, Sage, Schureman, Sevier, Seybert, Sharp, Sherwood, Smith of New York, Smith of Pennsylvania, Smith of Virginia, Stockton, Tannehill, Taylor, Telfair, Troup, Udree, Ward of Massachusetts, Williams, Wilson of Pennsylvania, Wright, and Yancey.

Mr. STANFORD then moved to amend the same section, by inserting, after the word "into," in the 7th line, the word "some," and after the word "port," in the same line, the words "of the United States;" which motion was determined in the negative.

Mr. S. then moved to amend the same section, by inserting, after the word "of," in the tenth line, the word "maritime;" which was also determined in the negative.

The question was taken on engrossing the bill, and reading it a third time, and passed in the affirmative—yeas 94, nays 32, as follows:

YEAS—Messrs. Alexander, Anderson, Barbour, Baylies of Massachusetts, Bines, Bowen, Bradbury, Burwell, Calhoun, Cannon, Champion, Clopton, Condict, Cox, Creighton, Cuthbert, Desha, Duvall, Eppes, Farrow, Findley, Fisk of Vermont, Fisk of New York, Forsyth, Franklin, Gaston, Gholson, Goodwyn, Gourdin, Grosvenor, Hale, Hall, Harris, Hasbrouck, Hawes, Hawkins, Hopkins of Kentucky, Hubbard, Humphreys, Hungerford, Hulbert, Irwin, Jackson of Virginia, Johnson of Kentucky, Kennedy, Kent of New York, Kent of Maryland, Kerr, Kershaw, Kilbourn, King of North Carolina, Lefferts, Lowndes, Macon, McCoy, Montgomery, Moore, Nelson, Newton, Oakley, Ormsby, Pickens, Pleasants, Potter, John Reed, Wm. Reed, Rea of Pennsylvania, Rhea of Tennessee, Rich, Ringgold, Roane, Robertson, Ruggles, Sage, Schureman, Sevier, Seybert, Sharp, Shaffey, Sherwood, Smith of New York, Smith of Virginia, Stockton, Stuart, Tannehill, Taylor, Telfair, Troup, Udree, Ward of Massachusetts, Wilson of Pennsylvania, Winter, and Yancey.

NAYS—Messrs. Bard, Bigelow, Brigham, Brown, Caperton, Cilley, Constock, Crouch, Davenport, Davis of Pennsylvania, Ely, Goldsborough, Henderson, King, of Massachusetts, Law, Lovett, Pearson, Pickering, Piper, Pitkin, Slaymaker, Smith of Pennsylvania, Stanford, Strong, Sturges, Taggart, Thompson, Vose, Wheaton, White, Wilcox, and Wilson of Massachusetts.

And the bill having been engrossed, was read a third time, and sent to the Senate by the hands of Mr. GASTON and Mr. FORSYTH.

THURSDAY, March 2.

The bill "for the protection of the commerce of the United States against the Algerine cruisers," was returned from the Senate, they having passed it without amendment. And the injunction of secrecy was removed.

APPENDIX

TO THE HISTORY OF THE THIRTEENTH CONGRESS.

[THIRD SESSION.]

COMPRISING THE MOST IMPORTANT DOCUMENTS ORIGINATING DURING THAT CONGRESS, AND THE PUBLIC ACTS PASSED BY IT.

GREAT BRITAIN—RETALIATION.

[Communicated to Congress, the 26th day of September, 1814.]

To the Senate and House of
Representatives of the United States:

I transmit to Congress, for their information, copies of a letter from Admiral Cochrane, commanding His Britannic Majesty's naval forces on the American station, to the Secretary of State, with his answer, and a reply from Admiral Cochrane.

JAMES MADISON.

SEPTEMBER 26, 1814.

Vice Admiral Sir Alexander Cochrane to Mr. Monroe.

HIS BRITANNIC MAJESTY'S SHIP THE
TONNANT, PATUXENT RIVER,
August 18, 1814.

SIR: Having been called upon by the Governor General of the Canadas to aid him in carrying into effect measures of retaliation against the inhabitants of the United States for the wanton destruction committed by their army in Upper Canada, it has become imperiously my duty, conformably with the nature of the Governor General's application, to issue to the naval force under my command, an order to destroy and lay waste such towns and districts upon the coast as may be found assailable.

I had hoped that this contest would have terminated without my being obliged to resort to severities which are contrary to the usage of civilized warfare, and as it has been with extreme reluctance and concern that I have found myself compelled to adopt this system of devastation, I shall be equally gratified if the conduct of the Executive of the United States will authorize my staying such proceedings, by making reparation to the suffering inhabitants of Upper Canada, thereby manifesting that, if the destructive measures pursued by their army were ever sanctioned, they will no longer be permitted by the Government. I have the honor to be, &c.

ALEX. COCHRANE,
Vice Admiral, Commander, &c.

HON. JAMES MONROE.

13th CON. 3d SESS.—41

Mr. Monroe to Sir Alexander Cochrane, Vice Admiral, &c.

DEPARTMENT OF STATE,
September 6, 1814.

SIR: I have had the honor of receiving your letter of the 18th of August, stating that, having been called on by the Governor General of the Canadas, to aid him in carrying into effect measures of retaliation against the inhabitants of the United States for the wanton desolation committed by their army in Upper Canada, it has become your duty, conformably with the nature of the Governor General's application, to issue to the naval force under your command an order to destroy and lay waste such towns and districts upon the coast as may be found assailable.

It is seen, with the greatest surprise, that this system of devastation, which has been practised by the British forces, so manifestly contrary to the usage of civilized warfare, is placed by you on the ground of retaliation. No sooner were the United States compelled to resort to war against Great Britain, than they resolved to wage it in a manner most consonant to the principles of humanity, and to those friendly relations which it was desirable to preserve between the two nations after the restoration of peace. They perceived, however, with the deepest regret, that a spirit, alike just and humane, was neither cherished nor acted on by your Government. Such an assertion would not be hazarded if it was not supported by facts, the proof of which has, perhaps, already carried the same conviction to other nations that it has to the people of these States. Without dwelling on the deplorable cruelties committed by the savages in the British ranks, and in British pay, at the river Raisin, which, to this day, has never been disavowed or atoned for, I refer, as more immediately connected with the subject of your letter, to the wanton desolation that was committed at Havre-de-Grace and at Georgetown, early in the Spring of 1813. These villages were burnt and ravaged by the naval forces of Great Britain, to the ruin of their unarmed inhabitants, who saw, with astonishment, that they derived no protection to their property from the laws of war. During the same season, scenes of invasion and pillage, carried on under the same authority, were witnessed all along the waters of the Chesapeake, to an extent inflicting the most serious private distress, and under circumstances that justified the suspicion that revenge and cupidity, rather than the manly motives that should dictate the hostility of a high-minded foe, led to their perpetration. The late destruction of the houses of the Government in this city is another act which comes necessarily into view. In the wars of modern Europe, no example of the kind, even among nations the most hostile to each other, can be traced. In the course of ten years past, the capitals of the principal Powers of the continent of Europe have been conquered, and occupied alternately by the victorious armies of each other, and no instance of such wanton and unjustifiable destruction has been seen. We must go back to distant and barbarous ages to find a parallel for the acts of which I complain.

Although these acts of desolation invited, if they did not impose on the Government the necessity of retaliation, yet in no instance has it been authorized.

The burning of the village of Newark in Upper Canada, posterior to the early outrages above enumerated, was not executed on that principle. The village of Newark adjoined Fort George, and its destruction was justified by the officers who ordered it, on the ground that it became necessary in the military operations there. The act, however, was disavowed by the Government. The burning which took place at Long Point was unauthorized by the Government, and the conduct of the officer subjected to the investigation of a military tribunal. For the burning at St. David's, committed by stragglers, the officer who commanded in that quarter was dismissed, without a trial, for not preventing it.

I am commanded by the President distinctly to state, that it as little comports with any orders which have been issued to the military and naval commanders of the United States, as it does with the established and known humanity of the American nation, to pursue a system which it appears you have adopted. This Government owes it to itself, to the principles which it has ever held sacred,'to disavow, as justly chargeable to it, any such wanton, cruel, and unjustifiable warfare.

Whatever unauthorized irregularities may have been committed by any of its troops, it would have been ready, acting on these principles of sacred and eternal obligation, to disavow, and, as far as might be practicable, to repair. But, in the plan of desolating warfare which your letter so explicitly makes known, and which is attempted to be excused on a plea so utterly groundless, the President perceives a spirit of deep-rooted hostility, which, without the evidence of such facts, he could not have believed existed, or would have been carried to such an extremity.

For the reparation of injuries, of whatever nature they may be, not sanctioned by the law of nations, which the military and naval force of

either Power may have committed against the other, this Government will always be ready to enter into reciprocal arrangements. It is presumed that your Government will neither expect nor propose any which are not reciprocal.

Should your Government adhere to a system of desolation. so contrary to the views and practice of the United States, so revolting to humanity, and repugnant to the sentiments and usages of the civilized world, whilst it will be seen with the deepest regret, it must and will be met with a determination and constancy becoming a free people contending in a just cause for their essential rights and dearest interests.

I have the honor to be, &c.
                    JAMES MONROE.
Sir ALEXANDER COCHRANE,
    Vice Admiral, Commander, &c.

Vice Admiral Sir Alexander Cochrane to Mr. Monroe.

HIS BRITANNIC MAJESTY'S SHIP
    TONNANT, IN THE CHESAPEAKE,
                    September 19, 1814.

SIR: I have had the honor to receive your letter of the 6th instant this morning, in reply to the one which I addressed to you from the Patuxent.

As I have no authority from my Government to enter upon any kind of discussion relative to the points contained in your letter, I have only to regret that there does not appear to be any hope that I shall be authorized to recall my general order; which has been further sanctioned by a subsequent request from Lieutenant General Sir George Prevost.

A copy of your letter will this day be forwarded by me to England, and, until I receive instructions from my Government, the measures which I have adopted must be persisted in, unless remuneration be made to the inhabitants of the Canadas for the injuries they have sustained from the outrages committed by the troops of the United States.

I have the honor to be, yours, &c.
                    ALEX. COCHRANE,
    Vice Admiral, Commander, &c.
Hon. JAMES MONROE.

GREAT BRITAIN.

[Communicated to Congress, October 10th and 14th, and December 1, 1814.]

To the Senate and House of
    Representatives of the United States:

I lay before Congress communications just received from the Plenipotentiaries of the United States charged with negotiating peace with Great Britain, showing the conditions on which alone that Government is willing to put an end to the war.

The instructions to those Plenipotentiaries, disclosing the grounds on which they were authorized to negotiate and conclude a treaty of peace, will be the subject of another communication.

JAMES MADISON.
WASHINGTON, *October* 10, 1814.

To the Senate and House of
Representatives of the United States:

I now transmit to Congress copies of the instructions to the Plenipotentiaries of the United States charged with negotiating a peace with Great Britain, as referred to in my message of the 10th instant.

JAMES MADISON.
WASHINGTON, *October* 14, 1814.

To the Senate and House of
Representatives of the United States:

I transmit for the information of Congress the communications last received from the Ministers Extraordinary and Plenipotentiary of the United States at Ghent, explaining the course and actual state of their negotiations with the Plenipotentiaries of Great Britain.

JAMES MADISON.
DECEMBER 1, 1814.

Mr. Monroe, Secretary of State, to the Plenipotentiaries of the United States for treating of peace with Great Britain.

DEPARTMENT OF STATE, *April* 15, 1813.

GENTLEMEN : I had the honor, on the —— ultimo, to receive from Mr. Adams two letters, one bearing date 30th September, the other on the 17th October last, communicating the overture of the Emperor of Russia to promote peace by his friendly mediation between the United States and Great Britain. On the day following, Mr. Daschkoff, the Russian Minister, made a similar communication to this Department. The subject has, in consequence, been duly considered, and I have now to make known to you the result. The President has not hesitated to accept the mediation of Russia, and he indulges a strong hope that it will produce the desired effect. It is not known that Great Britain has acceded to the proposition, but it is presumed that she will not decline it. The President thought it improper to postpone his decision until he should hear of that of the British Government. Sincerely desirous of peace, he has been willing to avail himself of every opportunity which might tend to promote it, on just and honorable conditions, and in accepting this overture he has been particularly gratified to evince, by the manner of it, the distinguished consideration which the United States entertain for the Emperor Alexander. Should the British Government accept the mediation, the negotiation to which it leads will be held at St. Petersburg. The President commits it to you, for which a commission is enclosed, and he has appointed Mr. Harris secretary of the mission.

The impressment of our seamen and illegal blockades, as exemplified more particularly in the Orders in Council, were the principal causes of the war. Had not Great Britain persevered obstinately in the violation of these important rights, the war would not have been declared. It will cease as soon as these rights are respected. The proposition made by Mr. Russell to the British Government immediately after the war, and the answer given by this Department to Admiral Warren's letter since, show the ground on which the United States were willing to adjust the controversy relative to impressment.

This has been further evinced by a report of the Committee of Foreign Relations of the House of Representatives, and an act of Congress passed in consequence of that report. By these documents you will see that, to accommodate this important difference, the United States are disposed to exclude British seamen altogether from the American service. This being effectually done, the British Government can have no pretext for the practice. How shall it be done? By restraints to be imposed by each nation on the naturalization of the seamen of the other, excluding, at the same time, all others not naturalized ? Or shall the right of each nation to naturalize the seamen of the other be prohibited, and each exclude from its service the natives of the other ? Whatever the rule is, it ought to be reciprocal. If Great Britain is allowed to naturalize American seamen, the United States should enjoy the same privilege. If it is demanded that the United States shall exclude from their service all native British subjects, a like exclusion of American citizens from the British service ought to be reciprocated. The mode also should be common to both countries. Each should be at liberty to give the same facilities, or be bound to impose the same restraints that the other does. The President is willing to agree to either alternative, and to carry it into effect by the most eligible regulations that can be devised.

If the first alternative is adopted, the extent of the proposed exclusion will depend on the impediments to naturalization, on the efficacy of the regulations to prevent imposition, and the fidelity of their execution. The greater the difficulty in acquiring the right of citizenship, the easier will it be to avoid imposition, and the more complete the desired exclusion. The law of the last session of Congress relative to seamen proves how sincerely desirous the Legislative as well as Executive branch of our Government is, to adjust this controversy, on conditions which may be satisfactory to Great Britain. By that law it is made indispensable for every British subject who may hereafter become a citizen, to reside five years, without intermission, within the United States, and so many guards are imposed to prevent frauds, that it seems to be impossible that they should be eluded. No British subject can be employed in a public or private ship of the United States, unless he produces to the commander, in the one instance, and to the collector, in the other, a certified copy of the act by which he became naturalized. A list of the crew, in the case of a private ship, must be taken, certified and recorded by the collector, and the consuls or commercial agents of Great Britain may object to any seamen, and attend the investigation. The commander of a public ship receiving a person not duly qualified, shall forfeit a thousand dollars, and the commander or owner of a private ship, knowing thereof, five hundred dollars, to be recovered in any action of debt, one-half to the informer, and one-half to the United States. It is also made penal, punishable as a felony by imprisonment and labor from three to five years, or by fine from five hundred to one thousand dollars, for any person to forge or counterfeit, or to pass or use any forged or counterfeited certificate of citizenship, or to sell or dispose of one.

It may fairly be presumed, that, if this law should be carried into effect, it would exclude all British seamen from our service.

By requiring five years continued residence in the United States, as the condition of citizenship, few if any British seamen would ever take advantage of it. Such as had left Great Britain, and had resided five years in this country, would be likely to abandon the sea forever. And by making it the duty of the commanders of our public, and of the collectors in the case of private ships, to require an authenticated copy from the clerk of the court, before which a British subject, who offered his service, had been naturalized, as indispensable to his admission, and highly penal in either to take a person not duly qualified, and by allowing also British agents to object to any one offering his service, and to prosecute by suit the commander or collector, as the case might be, for receiving an improper person, it seems to be impossible that such should be received.

If the second alternative is adopted, that is, if all native British subjects are to be hereafter excluded from our service, it is important that the stipulation providing for it should operate so as not to affect those who have been already naturalized. By our law, all the rights of natives are given to naturalized citizens. It is contended by some that these complete rights do not extend beyond the limits of the United States; that, in naturalizing a foreigner, no State can absolve him from the obligation which he owes to his former Government, and that he becomes a citizen in a qualified sense only. This doctrine, if true in any case, is less applicable to the United States than to any other Power. Expatriation seems to be a natural right, and, by the original character of our institutions, founded by compact on principle, and particularly by the unqualified investment of the adopted citizen with the full rights of the native, all that the United States could do, to place him on the same footing, has been done. In point of interest, the object is of little importance to either party. The number to be affected by the stipulation is inconsiderable; nor can that be a cause of surprise, when the character of that class of men is considered. It rarely happens that a seaman, who settles on a farm, or engages in a trade, and pursues it for any length of time, returns to sea. His youthful days are exhausted in his first occupation. He

leaves it with regret, and adopts another, either in consequence of marriage, of disease, or as an asylum for old age.

To a stipulation which shall operate prospectively only, the same objection does not apply. In naturalizing foreigners, the United States may prescribe the limit to which their privileges shall extend. If it is made a condition that no native British subject, who may hereafter become a citizen, shall be employed in our public or private ships, their exclusion will violate no right. Those who might become citizens afterwards would acquire the right, subject to that condition, and would be bound by it. To such a stipulation, the President is willing to assent, although he would much prefer the alternative of restraints on naturalization; and, to prevent frauds, and to carry the same fully into effect, you are authorized to apply all the restraints and checks, with the necessary modifications, to suit the cases that are provided in the act above recited, relative to seamen, for the purposes of that act.

In requiring that the stipulation to exclude British seamen from our service, with the regulations for carrying it into effect, be made reciprocal, the President desires that you make a provision, authorizing the United States, if they should be so disposed, to dispense with the obligations imposed by it on American citizens. The liberal spirit of our Government and laws is unfriendly to restraints on our citizens, such at least, as are imposed on British subjects, from becoming members of other societies. This has been shown in the law of the last session, relative to seamen, to which your particular attention has been already drawn. This provision may likewise be reciprocated if desired.

The President is not particularly solicitous that either of these alternatives (making the proposed reservation in case the latter be) *should be* preferred. To secure the United States *against* impressment he is willing to adopt either. He expects in return, that a clear and distinct provision shall be made against the practice. The precise form in which it may be done is not insisted on, provided the import is explicit. All that is required is, that, in consideration of the act to be performed on the part of the United States, the British Government shall stipulate in some adequate manner, to terminate or forbear the practice of impressment from American vessels.

It has been suggested, as an expedient made for the adjustment of this controversy, that British cruisers should have a right to search our vessels for British seamen, but that the commanders thereof should be subjected to penalties in case they made mistakes, and took from them American citizens. By this the British Government would acquire the right of search for seamen, with that of impressing from our vessels the subjects of all other Powers. It will not escape your attention that, by admitting the right, in any case, we give up the principle, and leave the door open to every kind of abuse. The same objection is applicable to any and every other arrangement which withholds the respect due to our flag, by not allowing it to protect the crew sailing under it.

If the first alternative should be adopted, it will follow that none of the British seamen who may be in the United States at the time the treaty takes effect, and who shall not have become citizens, will be admitted into our service until they acquire that right.

If the second is adopted, the number of native British seamen, who have been naturalized, and will be admissible into our service, will not, it is believed, exceed a few hundred; all others who may be in the United States at the time the treaty takes effect, or who may arrive afterwards, will be excluded.

As a necessary incident to an adjustment on the principle of either alternative, it is expected that all American seamen, who have been impressed, will be discharged, and that those who have been naturalized, under the British laws, by compulsive service, will be permitted to withdraw.

I have to repeat that the great object which you have to secure, in regard to impressment, is, that our flag shall protect the crew, and, providing for this in a satisfactory manner, that you are authorized to secure Great Britain effectually against the employment of her seamen in the service of the United States. This, it is believed, would be done by the adoption of either the above alternatives, and the application to that which may be adopted, of the checks contained in the law of the last session, relative to seamen; in aid of which it will always be in the power of Great Britain to make regulations operating in her own ports with a view to the same effect. To terminate, however, this controversy, in a manner satisfactory to both parties, the President is willing, should other checks be suggested as likely to be more effectual, consistent with the spirit of our Constitution, that you should adopt them. The strong feature of the first alternative, which authorizes the naturalization of seamen, requires their continued residence in the United States for five years, as indispensable to the attainment of that right. In case this alternative be adopted, the President is willing, for example, to secure a compliance with that condition, to make it the duty of each alien, who may be desirous to become a citizen, to appear in court every year, for the term of five years, until his right shall be completed. This example is given, not as a limitation, but as an illustration of your power; for to the exclusion of British seamen from our service no repugnance is felt. To such exclusion the amicable adjustment of this controversy with Great Britain affords a strong motive, but not the only one. It is a growing sentiment in the United States that they ought to depend on their own population for the supply of their ships of war and merchant service. Experience has shown that it is an abundant resource. In expressing this sentiment you will do it in a manner to inspire more fully a confidence that the arrangement which you may enter into will be carried faithfully into effect, without derogating, however, from the conciliatory spirit of the accommodation.

A strong desire has heretofore been expressed by the British Government to obtain of the United States an arrangement to prevent the desertion of British seamen when in our ports, and it cannot be doubted that a stipulation to that effect would be highly satisfactory as well as useful to Great Britain. It is fairly to be presumed that it, alone, would afford to the British Government a strong inducement to enter into a satisfactory arrangement of the difference relating to impressment. The claim is not inadmissible, especially as the United States have a reciprocal interest in the restoration of deserters from American vessels in British ports; you may, therefore, agree to an article, such as has been heretofore authorized by the United States, which shall make it the duty of each party to deliver them up.

Of the right of the United States to be exempted from the degrading practice of impressment, so much has been already said, and with such ability, that it would be useless, especially to you, who are otherwise so well acquainted with it, to dilate on its merits. I must observe, however, that the practice is utterly repugnant to the law of nations; that it is supported by no treaty with any nation; that it was never acquiesced in by any; and that a submission to it by the United States would be the abandonment, in favor of Great Britain, of all claim to neutral rights, and of all other rights on the ocean.

This practice is not founded on any belligerent right. The greatest extent to which the belligerent claim has been carried, over the vessels of neutral nations, is, to board and see from them persons in the land and sea service of an enemy, contraband of war, and enemy's property. All nations agree respecting the two first articles, but there has been and still exists a diversity of opinion as to the last. On that and other questions of considerable importance, disputes have arisen which are yet unsettled. The Empress Catherine, of Russia, a distinguished advocate of just principles, placed herself, in 1780, at the head of neutral nations, in favor of a liberal construction of their rights, and her successors have generally followed her example. In all the discussions on these topics, we find nothing of the British claim to impressment; no acknowledgment of it in any treaty, or proof of submission to it by any Power. If instances have occurred in which British cruisers have taken British seamen from the vessels of other nations, they were, as it is presumed, in cases either not acquiesced in, or of an extraordinary nature only, affording no countenance to their practice and pretension in relation to the United States. Cases of this kind, if such there be, afford no proof of a systematic claim in the British Government to impressment, or of submission to it by other Powers. This claim has been set up against the United States only, who have, in consequence thereof, been compelled to discuss its merits.

The claim is, in fact, traced to another source,

Relations with Great Britain.

the allegiance due by British subjects to their Sovereign, and his right, by virtue thereof, to their service. This has been distinctly stated in a late declaration by the Prince Regent. Knowing the nature of the claim, we know also the extent of the right and obligations incident to it. Allegiance is a political relation between a sovereign and his people. It is the obligation which binds the latter in return for the protection which they receive. These reciprocal duties have the same limit. They are confined to the dominions of the sovereign, beyond which he has no rights, can afford no protection, and of course can claim no allegiance. A citizen or subject of one Power, entering the dominions of another, owes allegiance to the latter in return for the protection he receives. Whether a sovereign has a right to claim the service of such of his subjects as have left his own dominions, is a question respecting which also a difference of opinion may exist. It is certain that no sovereign has a right to pursue his subjects into the territories of another, be the motive for it what it may. Such an entry, without the consent of the other Power, would be a violation of its territory, and an act of hostility. Offenders, even conspirators, cannot be pursued by one Power into the territory of another, nor are they delivered up by the latter, except in compliance with treaties, or by favor. That the vessels of a nation are considered a part of its territory, with the exception of the belligerent right only, is a principle too well established to be brought into discussion. Each State has exclusive jurisdiction over its own vessels. Its laws govern in them, and offences against those laws are punishable by its tribunals only. The flag of a nation protects everything sailing under it in time of peace, and in time of war likewise, with the exception of the belligerent rights growing out of the war. An entry on board the vessels of one Power by the cruisers of another, in any other case, and the exercise of any other authority over them, is a violation of right, and an act of hostility.

The British Government, aware of the truth of this doctrine, has endeavored to avoid its consequences in the late declaration of the Prince Regent. It has not contended that British cruisers have a right to pursue and search our vessels for British seamen. It asserts only that they have a right to search them for other objects, and being on board for a lawful cause, and finding British seamen there, that they have a right to impress and bring them away, under the claim of allegiance. When we see a systematic pursuit of our vessels by British cruisers, and the impressment of seamen from them, not at a port of the enemy, where a regular blockade has been instituted, and by the blockading squadron, but in every part of the ocean, on our coast, and even in our harbors, it is difficult to believe that impressment is not the real motive, and the other the pretext for it. But, to place this argument of the British Government on the strongest ground, let it be admitted that the entry was lawful, is it so to commit an act not warranted by the pur-

pose for which the entry was made? There is a levity in this argument which neither suits the parties nor the subject. The British Government founds its right of impressment from our ships on that of allegiance, which is a permanent right, equally applicable to peace and war. The right of impressment, therefore, from the vessels of other Powers must likewise be permanent, and equally applicable to peace and war. It would not, however, take this broad ground, lest the injustice and extravagance of the pretension might excite the astonishment and indignation of other Powers, to whom it would be equally applicable. To claim it as a belligerent right would have been equally unjust and absurd, as no trace of it could be found in the belligerent code. The British Government was therefore reduced to a very embarrassing dilemma. To acknowledge that it could not support the claim on either principle would be to relinquish it, and yet it could rely on neither. It endeavored to draw some aid from both. A state of war exists which brings the parties together, Great Britain as a belligerent, and the United States as a neutral Power. British officers have now a right to board and search American vessels, but for what? Persons in the service of an enemy, contraband of war, or enemy's property? This would not accomplish the end. It is, however, the utmost limit of the belligerent right. Allegiance, which is an attribute of sovereignty, comes to her aid and communicates all the necessary power. The national character of the neutral vessel ceases. The complete right of sovereignty and jurisdiction over it is transferred to Great Britain. It is on this foundation that the British Government has raised this monstrous superstructure. It is with this kind of argument that it attempts to justify its practice of impressment from our vessels.

The remark contained in the declaration of the Prince Regent, that, in impressing *British* seamen from American vessels, Great Britain exercised no right which she was not willing to acknowledge as appertaining equally to the Government of the United States, with respect to American seamen in British merchant ships, proves only that the British Government is conscious of the justice of the claim, and desirous of giving to it such aid as may be derived from a plausible argument. The semblance of equality, however, in this proposition, which strikes at first view, disappears on a fair examination. It is unfair, first, because it is impossible for the *United* States to take advantage of it. Impressment is not an American practice, but utterly repugnant to our Constitution and laws. In offering to reciprocate it nothing was offered, as the British Government well knew. It is unfair, secondly, because if impressment was allowable, a reciprocation of the practice would be no equivalent to the United States. The exercise of a right in common, at sea, by two nations, each over the vessels of the other, the one powerful and the other comparatively weak, would be to put the latter completely at the mercy of the former. Great Britain, with her vast navy, would soon be the only party which made impressment. The United States would be compelled to abstain from it, and either to submit to the British rule, with all the abuses incident to power, or to resist it. But should the United States be permitted to make impressment from British vessels, the effect would be unequal. Great Britain has, perhaps, thirty ships of war at sea to one of the United States, and would profit of the arrangement in that proportion. Besides, impressment is a practice incident to war—in which view, likewise, the inequality is not less glaring, she being at least thirty years at war to one of the United States. Other considerations prove that the British Government made this acknowledgment merely as a pretext to justify its practice of impressment, without intending that the right or practice should ever be reciprocated. What would be the effect of its adoption by American ships of war with British merchant vessels? An American officer boards a British merchant vessel, and claims, as American citizens, whom he pleases. How many British seamen would disclaim a title which would take them to the United States, and secure them there all the advantages of citizenship? The rule of evidence, as the ground of impressment in every instance, must likewise be reciprocated between the two Governments. The acknowledgment of the men would surely be a better proof of their national character than the decision of a British officer who boarded an American vessel, however impartial he might be, and strong his power of discrimination, when opposed by the voluntary and solemn declaration of the party. In this way we might draw from the British service the greater part, if not all their seamen. I might further ask, why was this acknowledgment made at this late period, for the first time only, after the declaration of war, and when, on that account, it could produce no effect? In the various discussions of this subject, in many of which it has been demanded whether the British Government would tolerate such a practice from American ships of war, no such intimation was ever given.

If Great Britain had found the employment of her seamen in our service injurious to her, and been disposed to respect our rights, the regular course of proceeding would have been for her Government to have complained to the Government of the United States of the injury, and to have proposed a remedy. Had this been done, and no reasonable remedy been adopted, sound in principle and reciprocal in its operation, the British Government might have had some cause of complaint, and some plea for taking the remedy into its own hands. Such a procedure would, at least, have given to its claim of impressment the greatest plausibility. We know that such complaint was never made, except in defence of the practice of impressment, and that, in the meantime, the practice has gone on, and grown into a usage, which, with all its abuses and resistance been longer delayed, might have become a law. The origin and progress of this usurpation afford strong illustrations of the British

policy. The practice and the claim began together, soon after the close of our Revolutionary war, and were applicable to deserters only. They extended next to all British seamen; then to all British subjects, including, as in the case of emigrants from Ireland, persons who would not have been subject to impressment in British ports, not being seafaring men; and, finally, to Swedes, Danes, and others, known to be not British subjects, and by their protections appearing to be naturalized citizens of the United States.

Other views may be taken of the subject, to show the unlawfulness and absurdity of the British claim. If British cruisers have a right to take British seamen from our vessels, without regarding the abuses inseparable from the practice, they may take from them, on the same principle, and with much greater reason, every species of property to which the British Government has any kind of claim. Allegiance cannot give to a sovereign a better right to take his subjects than ownership to take his property. There would be no limit to this pretension or its consequences. All property forfeited by exportation, contrary to the laws of Great Britain, every article to which her sovereignty, jurisdiction, or ownership would extend, in British vessels, would be liable to seizure in those of the United States. The laws of England would be executory in them. Instead of being a part of the American, they would become a part of the British territory.

It might naturally be expected that Great Britain would have given, by her conduct, some support to her pretensions; that, if she had not disclaimed altogether the principle of naturalization, she would at least have excluded from her service foreign seamen. Her conduct, however, has been altogether at variance with her precepts. She has given great facility to naturalization, in all instances where it could advance her interest, and peculiar encouragement to that of foreign seamen. She naturalizes by special act of Parliament; she naturalizes all persons who reside a certain term of years in British colonies, all those who are born of British subjects in foreign dominions, and all seamen who have served a certain short term in the British service, and would doubtless protect all such as British subjects, if required by them so to do. Her Governors of neighboring provinces are, at this time, compelling emigrants thither from the United States to bear arms against the United States.

The mediation offered by Russia presents to Great Britain, as well as to the United States, a fair opportunity of accommodating this controversy with honor. The interposition of so obliging a Power, friendly to both parties, could not be declined by either, on just ground, especially by Great Britain, between whom and Russia there exists at this time a very interesting relation. When the British Ministers are made acquainted at St. Petersburg, with the conditions on which you are authorized to adjust this difference, it seems as if it would be impossible for Great Britain to decline them. Should she do it, still adhering to her former pretensions, her motive could not be misunderstood. The cause of the United States would thenceforward become the common cause of nations. A concession by them would operate to the disadvantage of every other Power. They would all find, in the conduct of Great Britain, an unequivocal determination to destroy the rights of other flags, and to usurp the absolute dominion of the ocean. It is to be presumed that the British Government will find it neither for the honor nor interest of Great Britain to push things to that extremity, but will have accepted this mediation, and have sent a Minister or Ministers to St. Petersburg with full powers to adjust the controversy on fair and just conditions.

Should improper impressions have been taken of the probable consequences of the war, you will have ample means to remove them. It is certain, that from its prosecution Great Britain can promise to herself no advantage, while she exposes herself to great expenses and to the danger of still greater losses. The people of the United States, accustomed to the indulgence of a long peace, roused by the causes and the progress of the war, are rapidly acquiring military habits and becoming a military people. Our knowledge in naval tactics has increased, as has our maritime strength. The gallantry and success of our little Navy have formed an epoch in naval history. The laurels which these brave men have gained, not for themselves, but for their country, from an enemy pre-eminent in naval exploits, for ages past, are among the proudest boasts of their grateful and affectionate fellow-citizens. Our manufactures have taken an astounding growth. In short, in every circumstance, in which the war is felt, its pressure tends evidently to unite our people, to draw out our resources, to invigorate our means, and to make us more truly an independent nation, and, as far as may be necessary, a great maritime Power.

If the British Government accepts the mediation of Russia, with a sincere desire to restore a good intelligence between the two countries, it may be presumed that a fair opportunity will be afforded for the arrangement of many other important interests, with advantage to both parties. The adjustment of the controversy relating to impressment only, though very important, would leave much unfinished. Almost every neutral right has been violated; and its violation persisted in to the moment that war was declared. The President sincerely desires, and it is doubtless for the interest of Great Britain, to prevent the like in future. The interposition of the Emperor of Russia to promote an accommodation of these differences is deemed particularly auspicious.

[Confidential paragraph No. 1, omitted.]

A strong hope is, therefore, entertained that full powers will be given to the British Commissioners to arrange all these grounds of controversy in a satisfactory manner. In entering on this interesting part of your duty, the first object which will claim your attention is that of blockade. The violation of our neutral right by illegal blockades, carried to an enormous extent, by Orders in Council, was a principal cause of the war. These orders, however, and with them the blockade of May, 1806, and, as is understood, all other illegal blockades, have been repealed, so that that cause of war has been removed. All that is now expected is, that the British Government will unite in a more precise definition of blockade, and in this no difficulty is anticipated, for having declared that no blockade would be legal, which was not supported by an adequate force, and that the blockades which it might institute should be supported by an adequate force, there appears to be, according to the just interpretation of these terms, no difference of opinion on the subject.

The British Government has recently, in two formal acts, given definitions of blockade, either of which would be satisfactory. The first is to be seen in the communication from Mr. Merry to this Department, bearing date on the 12th of April, 1804. The following are the circumstances attending it. Commodore Hood, the commander of a British squadron in the West Indies, in 1803, having declared the islands of Martinique and Guadaloupe in a state of blockade, without applying an adequate force to maintain it, the Secretary of State remonstrated against the illegality of the measure, which remonstrance was laid before the Lords Commissioners of the Admiralty, in England, who replied that they had sent "orders not to consider any blockade of those islands as existing unless in respect of particular ports, which might be actually invested, and then not to capture vessels, bound to such ports, unless they shall previously have been warned not to enter them." The second definition is to be found in a convention between Great Britain and Russia, in June, 1801, fourth section, third article, which declares, " that, in order to determine what characterizes a blockaded port, that denomination is given only to a port where there is, by the disposition of the Power which attacks it, with ships stationary or sufficiently near, an evident danger in entering." The President is willing for you to adopt either of these definitions; but prefers the first, as much more precise and determinate ; and when it is considered that it was made the criterion by so formal an act, between the two Governments, it cannot be presumed that the British Government will object to the renewal of it. Nothing is more natural, after the difference which have taken place between the two countries, on this and other subjects, and the departure from this criterion by Great Britain, for reasons which are admitted by her no longer to exist, than that they should, on the restoration of a good understanding, recur to it again. Such a recurrence would be the more satisfactory to the President, as it would afford a proof of a disposition in the British Government, not simply to compromise a difference, but to re-establish sincere friendship between the two nations.

An interference with our commerce between enemy colonies and their parent country, was among the first violations of our neutral rights, committed by Great Britain in her present war with France. It took place in 1805, did extensive injury and produced universal excitement. In securing us against a repetition of it, you will attend to an article of the convention between Russia and Great Britain, entered into on the —— day of ——, 1801, to the eleventh article of the project of a treaty with Great Britain that was signed by Mr. Monroe and Mr. Pinkney, on the 31st December, 1806, and to the instructions from this Department relating to that article. of the 20th May, 1807. The capture, by Great Britain, of almost all the islands of her enemies, diminishes the importance of any regulation of this subject; but, as they may be restored by a treaty of peace, it merits particular attention. It being understood, however, that unless such a trade can be obtained, in a proper extent, and without a relinquishment of the principle contended for by the United States, it will be best that the treaty be silent on the subject.

A disposition has been shown by the British Government to extend this principle so far as to inhibit a trade to neutrals, even between a Power at peace with Great Britain and her enemy; as, for example, between China and France. The absurdity of this pretension may prevent its being hereafter advanced. It will not, however, be unworthy of your attention.

By an order of the British Government in 1803, British cruisers were authorized to take neutral vessels, laden with innocent articles, on their return from an enemy's port, on the pretence that they had carried to such port contraband of war. This order is directly repugnant to the law of nations, as the circumstance of having contraband articles on board, bound to an enemy's port, is the only legal ground of seizure. The claim was relinquished by the British Government, in the ninth article of the project above recited. You will endeavor in like manner to provide against it. It is the practice of British cruisers to compel the commanders of neutral vessels which they meet at sea, either to board them in person with their papers, or to send their papers on board in their own boat by an officer. The injustice and irregularity of this procedure need not be mentioned. You will endeavor to suppress it in the manner proposed in the third article of a project communicated to Mr. Monroe at London, in his instructions of the 5th of January, 1804. You will endeavor likewise to restrict contraband of war, as much as is in your power, to the list contained in the fourth article of that project.

The pretensions of Great Britain to interdict the passage of neutral vessels, with their cargoes, from one port to another port of the enemy, is illegal and very injurious to the commerce of neutral Powers. Still more unjustifiable is the attempt to interdict their passage from one port of one independent nation to that of another, on the pretence that they are both enemies. You will endeavor to obtain, in both instances, a security for the neutral right.

Upon the whole subject I have to observe, that your first duty will be to conclude a peace with Great Britain, and that you are authorized to do it, in case you obtain a satisfactory stipulation against impressments, one which shall secure,

under our flag, protection to the crew. The manner in which it may be done has been already stated, with the reciprocal stipulations which you may enter into to secure Great Britain against the injury of which she complains. If this encroachment of Great Britain is not provided against, the United States have appealed to arms in vain. If your efforts to accomplish it should fail, all further negotiations will cease, and you will return home without delay. It is possible that some difficulty may occur in arranging this article respecting its duration. To obviate this, the President is willing that it be limited to the present war in Europe. Resting, as the United States do, on the solid ground of right, it is not presumable that Great Britain, especially after the advantage she may derive from the arrangement proposed, would ever revive her pretension. In forming any stipulation on this subject, you will be careful not to impair by it the right of the United States, or to sanction the principle of the British claim.

It is deemed highly important, also, to obtain a definition of the neutral rights which I have brought to your view, especially of blockade, and in the manner suggested; but it is not to be made an indispensable condition of peace. After the repeal of the Orders in Council, and other illegal blockades, and the explanations attending it, it is not presumable that Great Britain will revive them. Should she do it, the United States will always have a corresponding resort in their own hands. You will observe, in every case in which you may not be able to obtain a satisfactory definition of the neutral right, that you enter into none respecting it.

Indemnity for losses seems to be a fair claim on the part of the United States, and the British Government, if desirous to strengthen the relations of friendship, may be willing to make it. In bringing the claim into view, you will not let it defeat the primary objects intrusted to you. It is not perceived on what ground Great Britain can resist this claim, at least in the cases in favor of which she stands pledged. Of these a note will be added.

[Confidential paragraph No. 2, omitted.]

You are at liberty to stipulate in the proposed treaty the same advantages, in the ports of the United States, in favor of British ships of war, that may be allowed to those of the most favored nations. This stipulation must be reciprocal.

[Confidential paragraph No. 3, omitted.]

No difficulty can arise from the case of the non-importation act, which will doubtless be terminated in consequence of the pacification. Should any stipulation to that effect be required, or found advantageous, you are at liberty to enter into it. Should peace be made, you may, in fixing the periods to which it shall take effect in different latitudes and distances, take for the provisional articles of the Treaty of Peace with Great Britain in 1782, with such alterations as may appear to be just and reasonable.

In discharging the duties of the trust committed to you, the President desires that you will manifest the highest degree of respect for the Emperor of Russia, and confidence in the integrity and impartiality of his views. In arranging the question of impressment, and every question of neutral right, you will explain to his Government, without reserve, the claims of the United States, with the ground on which they severally rest. It is not doubted that from a conduct so frank and honorable the most beneficial effect will result.

[Confidential paragraph No. 4, omitted.]

I shall conclude by remarking that a strong hope is entertained that this friendly mediation of the Emperor Alexander will form an epoch in the relations between the United States and Russia, which will be extensively felt, and be long and eminently distinguished by the happy consequences attending it. Since 1780, Russia has been the pivot on which all questions of neutral right have essentially turned. Most of the wars which have disturbed the world in modern times have originated with Great Britain and France. These wars have affected distant countries, especially in their character as neutrals, and very materially the United States, who took no part in promoting them, and had no interest in the great objects of either Power.

[Confidential paragraph No. 5, omitted.]

I have the honor to be, &c.

JAMES MONROE.

Extract of a letter from the Secretary of State to the Commissioners of the United States for treating of peace with Great Britain, dated

DEPARTMENT OF STATE, *June* 23, 1813.

An opportunity offering, I avail myself of it to explain more fully the views of the President on certain subjects already treated on in your instructions, and to communicate his sentiments on some others, not adverted to in them.

The British Government having repealed the Orders in Council and the blockade of May, 1806, and all other illegal blockades, and having declared that it would institute no blockade which should not be supported by an adequate force, it was thought better to leave that question on that ground, than to continue the war, to obtain a more precise definition of blockade, after the other essential cause of the war, that of impressment, should be removed. But when it is considered that a stipulated definition of blockade will cost Great Britain nothing, after having thus recognised the principle, and that such definition is calculated to give additional confidence in the future security of our commerce, it is expected that she will agree to it. It is true, this cause of war being removed, the United States are under no obligation to continue it for the want of such stipulated definition, more especially as they retain in their hands the remedy against any new violation of their rights, whenever made. The same remark is applicable to the case of impressment; for, if the British Government had issued orders to its cruisers not to impress seamen from our vessels, and notified the same to this Government, that

cause of war would also have been removed. In making peace, it is better for both nations that the controversy respecting blockade should be arranged by treaty, as well as that respecting impressment. The omission to arrange it may be productive of injury. Without a precise definition of blockade, improper pretensions might be set up on each side respecting their rights, which might possibly hazard the future good understanding between the two countries.

Should a restitution of territory be agreed on, it will be proper to make a provision for settling the boundary between the United States and Great Britain, on the St. Lawrence and the Lakes, from the point at which the line between them strikes the St. Lawrence to the northwest corner of the Lake of the Woods, according to the principles of the Treaty of Peace. The settlement of this boundary is important, from the circumstance that there are several islands in the river, and lakes of some extent and great value, the dominion over which is claimed by both parties. It may be an advisable course to appoint commissioners on each side, with full powers to adjust, on fair and equitable considerations, this boundary. To enable you to adopt a suitable provision for the purpose, it will be proper for you to recur to the instructions heretofore given on the subject, published in the documents in your possession.

Mr. Monroe, Secretary of State, to the Plenipotentiaries of the United States at St. Petersburg.

DEPARTMENT OF STATE, *Jan.* 1, 1814.

GENTLEMEN: I have not received a letter from you since your appointment to meet Ministers from Great Britain at St. Petersburg, to negotiate a Treaty of Peace under the mediation of the Emperor of Russia. This is doubtless owing to the miscarriage of your despatches.

The Message of the President, of which I have the honor to transmit to you a copy, will make you acquainted with the progress of the war with Great Britain to that period, and the other documents which are forwarded will communicate what has since occurred.

Among the advantages attending our success in Upper Canada, was the important one of making capture of General Proctor's baggage, with all the public documents belonging to the British Government in his possession. It is probable that these documents will be laid before Congress, as they are of a nature highly interesting to the public. You will understand their true character by extracts of two letters from Governor Cass, which are enclosed to you. By these, it appears, that the British Government has exercised its influence over the Indian tribes within our limits as well as elsewhere in peace, for hostile purposes towards the United States; and that the Indian barbarities since the war were, in many instances, known to and sanctioned by the British Government.

I have the honor to be, &c.

JAMES MONROE.

Mr. Monroe, Secretary of State, to the Plenipotentiaries of the United States at St. Petersburg.

DEPARTMENT OF STATE, *Jan.* 8, 1814.

GENTLEMEN: I have the honor to transmit to you a copy of a letter from Lord Castlereagh to this Department, and of a note from Lord Cathcart to the Russian Government, with my reply to the communication.

The arrangement of a negotiation to be held at Gottenburg, directly between the United States and Great Britain, without the aid of the Russian mediation, makes it necessary that new commissions should be issued correspondent with it, and, for this purpose, that a new nomination should be made to the Senate. The President instructs me to inform you that you will both be included in it; and that he wishes you to repair, immediately on the receipt of this, to the appointed rendezvous. It is possible that the business may not be limited to yourselves, on account of the great interests involved in the result. The commissions and instructions will be duly forwarded to you, as soon as the arrangements shall be finally made.

In taking leave of the Russian Government, you will be careful to make known to it the sensibility of the President to the friendly disposition of the Emperor, manifested by the offer of his mediation; the regret felt at its rejection by the British Government; and a desire that in future the greatest confidence and, cordiality, and the best understanding, may prevail between the two Governments.

I have the honor to be, &c.
JAMES MONROE.

Mr. Monroe, Secretary of State, to the American Plenipotentiaries at Gottenburg.

DEPARTMENT OF STATE, *Jan.* 28, 1814.

GENTLEMEN: The British Government having declined the Russian mediation, and proposed to treat directly with the United States, the President has, on due consideration, thought proper to accept the overture. To give effect to this arrangement, it was necessary that a new commission should be formed, and, for that purpose, that a new nomination should be made to the Senate, by whose advice and consent this important trust is committed to you.

You will consider the instructions given to the commission to treat under the mediation of Russia as applicable to the negotiation with which you are now charged, except as they may be modified by this letter.

I shall call your attention to the most important grounds of the controversy with Great Britain only, and make such remarks on each, and on the whole subject, as have occurred since the date of the former instructions, and are deemed applicable to the present juncture, taking into view the negotiation in which you are now about to engage.

On impressment—as to the right of the United States to be exempted from it—I have nothing new to add. The sentiments of the President have undergone no change on that important subject. This degrading practice must cease; our flag must protect the crew, or the United States cannot consider themselves an independent nation. To settle this difference amicably, the President is willing, as you are already informed by the former instructions, to remove all pretext for it to the British Government, by excluding all British seamen from our vessels; and even to extend the exclusion to all British subjects, if necessary, excepting only the few already naturalized; and to stipulate, likewise, the surrender of all British seamen deserting in our ports in future from British vessels, public or private. It was presumed by all dispassionate persons, that the late law of Congress relative to seamen would effectually accomplish the object. But the President is willing, as you find, to prevent a possibility of failure, to go further.

Should a treaty be made, it is proper, and it would have a conciliatory effect, that all our impressed seamen who may be discharged under it should be paid for their services by the British Government, for the time of their detention, the wages which they might have obtained in the merchant service of their own country.

Blockade is the subject next in point of importance, which you will have to arrange. In the instructions bearing date on the 15th of April, 1813, it was remarked that, as the British Government had revoked its Orders in Council, and agreed that no blockade could be legal which was not supported by an adequate force, and that such adequate force should be applied to any blockade which it might thereafter institute, this cause of controversy seemed to be removed. Further reflection, however, has added great force to the expediency and importance of a precise definition of the public law on this subject. There is much cause to presume that, if the repeal of the Orders in Council had taken place in time to have been known here before the declaration of war, and had had the effect of preventing the declaration, not only that no provision would have been obtained against impressment, but that, under the name of blockade, the same extent of coast would have been covered by proclamation as had been covered by the Orders in Council. The war, which these abuses and impressment contributed so much to produce, might possibly prevent that consequence. But it would be more satisfactory, if not more safe, to guard against it by a formal definition in the treaty. It is true, should the British Government violate again the legitimate principles of blockade, in whatever terms or under whatever pretext it might be done, the United States would have in their hands a correspondent resort; but a principal object in making peace is to prevent, by the justice and reciprocity of the conditions, a recurrence again to war for the same cause. If the British Government sincerely wishes to make a durable peace with the United States, it can have no reasonable objection to a just definition of blockade, especially as the two Governments have agreed, in their correspondence,, in all its essential features. The instructions of the 15th of April, 1813, have stated in what manner the President is willing to arrange this difference.

On the other neutral rights enumerated in the former instructions, I shall remark only that the catalogue is limited in a manner to evince a spirit of accommodation; that the arrangement proposed in each instance is just in itself; that it corresponds with the general spirit of treaties between commercial Powers; and that Great Britain has sanctioned it in many treaties, and gone beyond it in some.

[Confidential paragraph No. 1, omitted.]

On the claim to indemnity for spoliations, I have only to refer you to what was said in the former instructions. I have to add, that should a treaty be formed, it is just in itself, and would have a happy effect on the future relations of the two countries, if indemnity should be stipulated on each side for the destruction of all unfortified towns, and other private property, contrary to the laws and usages of war. It is equally proper that the negroes taken from the Southern States should be returned to their owners, or paid for at their full value. It is known that a shameful traffic has been carried on in the West Indies, by the sale of these persons there, by those who professed to be their deliverers. Of this fact, the proof which has reached this Department shall be furnished you. If these slaves are considered as non-combatants, they ought to be restored; if as property, they ought to be paid for. The Treaty of Peace contains an article which recognises this principle.

In the view which I have taken of the conditions on which you are to insist in the proposed negotiation, you will find, on a comparison of them with those stated in the former instructions, that there is no material difference between them, the two last mentioned claims to indemnity excepted, which have originated since the date of those instructions. The principal object of this review has been to show that the sentiments of the President are the same in every instance, and that the reasons for maintaining them have become more evident and strong since the date of those instructions.

In accepting the overture of the British Government to treat independently of the Russian mediation, the United States have acted on principles which have governed them in every transaction relating to peace since the war. Had the British Government accepted the Russian mediation, the United States would have treated for themselves, independently of any other Power; and had Great Britain met them on just conditions, peace would have been the immediate result. Had she refused to accede to such conditions, and attempted to dictate others, a knowledge of the views of other Powers on those points might have been useful to the United States. In agreeing to treat directly with Great Britain, not only is no concession contemplated on any point in controversy, but the same desire is cherished to preserve a good understanding with Russia and the other Baltic Powers, as if the negotiation had taken place under the mediation of Russia.

[Confidential paragraph No. 2, omitted.]

It is probable that the British Government may have declined the Russian mediation from the apprehension of an understanding between the United States and Russia for very different purposes from those which have been contemplated, in the hope that a much better treaty might be obtained of the United States, in a direct negotiation, than could be obtained under the Russian mediation, and with a view to profit of the concessions which might thus be made by the United States in future negotiations with the Baltic Powers. If this was the object of the British Government, (and it is not easy to conceive any other,) it clearly proves the advantage to be derived, in the proposed negotiation, from the aid of those Powers, in securing from the British Government such conditions as would be satisfactory to all parties. It would be highly honorable as well as advantageous to the United States, if the negotiation with which you are charged should terminate in such a treaty.

[Confidential paragraph No. 3, omitted.]

I have the honor to be, &c.

JAMES MONROE.

Mr. Monroe, Secretary of State, to the Plenipotentiaries of the United States at Gottenburg.

DEPARTMENT OF STATE, *Jan.* 30, 1814.

GENTLEMEN: In addition to the claims to indemnity, stated in your preceding instructions, I have to request your attention to the following, to which, it is presumed, there can be no objection:

On the declaration of war by the United States, there happened to be, in the ordinary course of commerce, several American vessels and cargoes in the ports of Great Britain, which were seized and condemned; and, in one instance, an American ship which fled from Algiers, in consequence of the declaration of war by the Dey, to Gibraltar, with the American Consul and some public stores on board, shared a like fate.

After the declaration of war, Congress passed an act allowing to British subjects six months, from the date of the declaration, to remove their property out of the United States, in consequence of which many vessels were removed, with their cargoes. I add, with confidence, that, on a liberal construction of the spirit of the law, some vessels were permitted to depart, even after the expiration of the term specified in the law. I will endeavor to put in your possession a list of these cases. A general reciprocal provision, however, will be best adapted to the object in view.

I have the honor to be, &c.

JAMES MONROE.

From the Secretary of State to the Commissioners of the United States for treating with Great Britain.

DEPARTMENT OF STATE, *Feb.* 10 1814.

GENTLEMEN: Should you conclude a treaty, and not obtain a satisfactory arrangement of neutral rights, it will be proper for you to provide that the United States shall have advantage of any stipulations more favorable to neutral nations, that may be established between Great Britain and other Powers. A precedent for such a provision is found in a declaratory article between Great Britain and Russia, bearing date on the 8th October, 1801, explanatory of the second section third article of a convention concluded between them on the 5th of June of the same year.

I have the honor to be, &c.

JAMES MONROE.

Extract—The Secretary of State to the Commissioners of the United States for treating with Great Britain.

DEPARTMENT OF STATE, *Feb.* 14, 1814.

I received last night your letter of the 15th October, with extracts of letters from Mr. Adams and Mr. Harris of the 22d and 23d of November.

It appears that you had no knowledge, at the date even of the last letter, of the answer of the British Government to the offer which had been made to it a second time of the Russian mediation. Hence it is to be inferred that the proposition made to this Government, by the Bramble, was made not only without your knowledge, but without the sanction, if not without the knowledge, of the Emperor. Intelligence from other sources strengthens this inference. If this view of the conduct of the British Government is well founded, the motive for it cannot be mistaken. It may fairly be presumed that it was to prevent a good understanding and concert between the United States and Russia and Sweden, on the subject of neutral rights, in the hope that by drawing the negotiation to England, and depriving you of an opportunity of free communication with those Powers, a treaty less favorable to the United States might be obtained, which might afterwards be used with advantage by Great Britain in her negotiations with those Powers.

By an article in the former instructions, you were authorized, in making a treaty to prevent impressment from our vessels, to stipulate, provided a certain term could not be agreed on, that it might continue in force for the present war in Europe only. At that time it seemed probable that the war might last many years. Recent appearances, however, indicate the contrary. Should peace be made in Europe, as the practical evil of which we complain, in regard to impressment, would cease, it is presumed that the British Government would have less objection to a stipulation to forbear that practice for a specified term, than it would have should the war continue. In concluding a peace with Great Britain, even in case of a previous general peace in Europe, it is important to the United States to obtain such a stipulation.

Mr. Monroe, Secretary of State, to the Plenipotentiaries of the United States at Gottenburg.

DEPARTMENT OF STATE, *March* 21, 1814.

GENTLEMEN: By the cartel Chauncey you will receive this, with duplicates of the commission

to treat with Great Britain, and of the instructions and other documents that were forwarded by the John Adams. This vessel is sent to guard against any accident which might attend the other.

[Confidential paragraph omitted.]

If a satisfactory arrangement can be concluded with Great Britain, the sooner it is accomplished the happier for both countries. If such an arrangement cannot be obtained, it is important to the United States to be acquainted with it without delay. I hope, therefore, to receive from you an account of the state of the negotiation and its prospects, as soon as you may be able to communicate anything of an interesting nature respecting them.

I have the honor to be, &c.

JAMES MONROE.

Mr. Monroe to the Envoys Extraordinary and Ministers Plenipotentiary of the United States.

DEPARTMENT OF STATE, *June* 25, 1814.

GENTLEMEN: No communication has been received from the joint mission which was appointed to meet the Commissioners of the British Government at Gottenburg. A letter from Mr. Bayard at Amsterdam, of the 18th of March, was the last from either of our Commissioners. It was inferred from that letter, and other communications, that Mr. Bayard, Mr. Gallatin, and Mr. Adams, would be in Gottenburg; and it has been understood from other sources that Mr. Clay and Mr. Russell had arrived there about the 15th of April. It is, therefore, expected that a meeting will have taken place in May, and that we shall soon be made acquainted with your sentiments of the probable result of the negotiation.

It is impossible, with the lights which have reached us, to ascertain the present disposition of the British Government towards an accommodation with the United States. We think it probable that the late events in France may have had a tendency to increase its pretensions.

At war with Great Britain, and injured by France, the United States have sustained the attitude founded on those relations. No reliance was placed on the good offices of France in bringing the war with Great Britain to a satisfactory conclusion. Looking steadily to an honorable peace, and the ultimate attainment of justice from both Powers, the President has endeavored, by a consistent and honorable policy, to take advantage of every circumstance that might promote that result. He, nevertheless, knew that France held a place in the political system of Europe and of the world, which, as a check on England, could not fail to be useful to us. What effect the late events may have had, in these respects, is the important circumstance of which you are, doubtless, better informed than we can be.

The President accepted the mediation of Russia from a respect for the character of the Emperor, and a belief that our cause, in all the points in controversy, would gain strength by being made known to him. On the same principle he preferred (in accepting the British overture to treat independently of the Russian mediation) to open the negotiation on the Continent rather than at London.

It was inferred fom the general policy of Russia, and the friendly sentiments and interposition of the Emperor, that a respect for both would have much influence with the British Cabinet in promoting a pacific policy towards us. The manner, however, in which it is understood that a general pacification is taking place; the influence Great Britain may have in modifying the arrangements involved in it; the resources she may be able to employ exclusively against the United States; and the uncertainty of the precise course which Russia may pursue in relation to the war between the United States and Great Britain, naturally claim attention, and raise the important question in reference to the subject of impressment, on which it is presumed your negotiations will essentially turn, whether your powers ought not to be enlarged so as to enable you to give to those circumstances all the weight to which they may be entitled. On full consideration it has been decided, that, in case no stipulation can be obtained from the British Government at this moment, when its pretensions may have been much heightened by recent events, and the state of Europe be most favorable to them, either relinquishing the claim to impress from American vessels, or discontinuing the practice, even in consideration of the proposed exclusion from them of British seamen, you may concur in an article stipulating that the subject of impressment, together with that of commerce between the two countries, be referred to a separate negotiation, to be undertaken without delay, at such place as you may be able to agree on, preferring this city if to be obtained. I annex at the close of this letter a project of an article expressing more distinctly the idea which it is intended to communicate, not meaning thereby to restrain you in any respect as to the form. Commerce and seamen, the objects of impressment, may, with great propriety, be arranged in the same instrument. By stipulating that Commissioners shall forthwith be appointed for the purpose, and that all rights on this subject shall, in the meantime, be reserved, the faith of the British Government will be pledged to a fair experiment in an amicable mode, and the honor and rights of the United States secured. The United States having resisted by war the practice of impressment, and continued the war until that practice had ceased by a peace in Europe, their object has been essentially obtained for the present. It may reasonably be expected that the arrangement contemplated and provided for, will take effect before a new war in Europe shall furnish an occasion for reviving the practice. Should this arrangement, however, fail, and the practice be again revived, the United States will again be at liberty to repel it by war, and that they will do so cannot be doubted; for after the proof which they have already given of a firm resistance in that mode, persevered in until the practice had ceased, under circumstances the most favorable, it cannot be presumed that the practice will ever be tolerated again. Certain it is, that every day will render it more ineligible in Great Britain to make the attempt.

In contemplating the appointment of Commissioners, to be made after the ratification of the present treaty, to negotiate and conclude a treaty to regulate commerce, and provide against impressment, it is meant only to show the extent to which you may go, in a spirit of accommodation, if necessary. Should the British Government be willing to take the subject up immediately with you, it would be much preferred, in which case the proposed article would, of course, be adapted to the purpose.

Information has been received, from a quarter deserving attention, that the late events in France have produced such an effect on the British Government as to make it probable that a demand will be made at Gottenburg to surrender our right to the fisheries; to abandon all trade beyond the Cape of Good Hope; and to cede Louisiana to Spain. We cannot believe that such a demand will be made. Should it be, you will of course treat it as it deserves. These rights must not be brought into discussion. If insisted on, your negotiations will cease.

I have the honor to be, with great respect, gentlemen, your most obedient servant,

JAMES MONROE.

Whereas, by the peace in Europe, the essential causes of the war between the United States, and Great Britain, and particularly the practice of impressment, have ceased, and a sincere desire exists to arrange, in a manner satisfactory to both parties, all questions concerning seamen, and it is also their desire and intention to arrange, in a like satisfactory manner, the commerce between the two countries, it is therefore agreed that Commissioners shall forthwith be appointed on each side, to meet at ——, with full power to negotiate and conclude a treaty, as soon as may be practicable, for the arrangement of those important interests. It is, nevertheless, understood, that, until such treaty be formed, each party shall retain all its rights, and that all American citizens who have been impressed into the British service shall be forthwith discharged.

Extract of a letter from Mr. Monroe, Secretary of State, to the joint Commissioners of the United States for treating of peace with Great Britain, dated,

DEPARTMENT OF STATE, June 27, 1814.

The omission to send Ministers to Gottenburg, without a previous and official notification of the appointment and arrival there of those of the United States, a formality, which, if due from either party, might have been expected from that making the overture, rather than that accepting it, is a proof of a dilatory policy, and would, in other respects, justify animadversions, if there was less disposition here to overlook circumstances of form, when interfering with more substantial objects.

By my letter of the 25th instant, which goes with this, you will find that the subject had al-

Relations with Great Britain.

ready been acted on under similar impressions with those which Mr. Bayard and Mr. Gallatin's letter could not fail to produce. The view, however, presented by them is much stronger, and entitled to much greater attention. The President has taken the subject into consideration again, and given to their suggestions all the weight to which they are justly entitled.

On mature consideration, it has been decided, that, under all the circumstances alluded to, incident to a prosecution of the war, you may omit any stipulation on the subject of impressment, if found indispensably necessary to terminate it. You will, of course, not recur to this expedient until all your efforts to adjust the controversy in a more satisfactory manner have failed. As it is not the intention of the United States, in suffering the treaty to be silent on the subject of impressment, to admit the British claim thereon, or to relinquish that of the United States, it is highly important that any such inference be entirely precluded, by a declaration or protest, in some form or other, that the omission is not to have any such effect or tendency. Any modification of the practice, to prevent abuses, being an acknowledgment of the right in Great Britain, is utterly inadmissible.

Although Gottenburg was contemplated at the time your commission was made out, as the seat of the negotiation, yet your commission itself does not confine you to it. You are at liberty, therefore, to transfer the negotiation to any other place made more eligible by a change of circumstances. Amsterdam and the Hague readily present themselves as preferable to any place in England. If, however, you should be of opinion that, under all circumstances, the negotiation in that country will be attended with advantages outweighing the objections to it, you are at liberty to transfer it there.

Extract of a letter from the Secretary of State to the Commissioners of the United States for treating of peace with Great Britain, dated

DEPARTMENT OF STATE,
August 11, 1814.

I had the honor to receive, on the 3d of this month, a letter from Mr. Bayard and Mr. Gallatin, of the 23d of May, and one from Mr. Gallatin of the 2d of June.

The President approves the arrangement communicated by those gentlemen for transferring the negotiation with the British Government from Gottenburg to Ghent. It is presumed, from Mr. Gallatin's letter, that the meeting took place towards the latter end of June, and that we shall soon hear from you what will be its probable result.

By my letters of the 25th and 27th of June, of which another copy is now forwarded, the sentiments of the President, as to the conditions on which it will be proper for you to conclude a treaty of peace, are made known to you. It is presumed that either in the mode suggested in my letter of the 25th of June, which is much

preferred, or by permitting the treaty to be silent on the subject, as is authorized in the letter of the 27th of June, the question of impressment may be so disposed of as to form no obstacle to a pacification. This Government can go no further, because it will make no sacrifice of the rights or honor of the nation.

If Great Britain does not terminate the war on the conditions which you are authorized to adopt, she has other objects in it than those for which she has hitherto professed to contend. That such are entertained, there is much reason to presume. These, whatever they may be, must and will be resisted by the United States. The conflict may be severe, but it will be borne with firmness, and, as we confidently believe, be attended with success.

From the Commissioners Extraordinary and Plenipotentiary of the United States for treating of peace with Great Britain, to the Secretary of State, dated

GHENT, *August* 12, 1814.

SIR : We have the honor to inform you that the British Commissioners, Lord Gambier, Henry Goulburn, Esq., and William Adams, Esq., arrived in this city on Saturday evening, the 6th instant. The day after their arrival, Mr. Baker, their secretary, called upon us to give us notice of the fact, and to propose a meeting at a certain hour on the ensuing day. The place having been agreed upon, we accordingly met at one o'clock on Monday, the 8th instant.

We enclose, herewith, a copy of the full powers exhibited by the British Commissioners at that conference, which was opened, on their part, by an expression of the sincere and earnest desire of their Government that the negotiation might result in a solid peace, honorable to both parties. They, at the same time, declared that no events which had occurred since the first proposal for this negotiation had altered the pacific disposition of their Government, or varied its views as to the terms upon which it was willing to conclude the peace.

We answered, that we heard these declarations with great satisfaction, and that our Government had acceded to the proposal of negotiation, with the most sincere desire to put an end to the differences which divided the two countries, and to lay, upon just and liberal grounds, the foundation of a peace which, securing the rights and interests of both nations, should unite them by lasting bonds of amity.

The British Commissioners then stated the following subjects as those upon which it appeared to them that the discussions would be likely to turn, and on which they were instructed :

1st. The forcible seizure of mariners on board of merchant vessels, and, in connexion with it, the claim of His Britannic Majesty to the allegiance of all the native subjects of Great Britain.

We understood them to intimate that the British Government did not propose this point as one which they were particularly desirous of discussing ; but that, as it had occupied so prominent

Relations with Great Britain.

a place in the dispute between the two countries, it necessarily attracted notice, and was considered as a subject which would come under discussion.

2d. The Indian allies of Great Britain to be included in the pacification, and a definite boundary to be settled for their territory.

The British Commissioners stated that an arrangement upon this point was a *sine qua non ;* that they were not authorized to conclude a treaty of peace which did not embrace the Indians as allies of His Britannic Majesty; and that the establishment of a definite boundary of the Indian territory was necessary to secure a permanent peace, not only with the Indians, but also between the United States and Great Britain.

3d. A revision of the boundary line between the United States and the adjacent British colonies.

With respect to this point, they expressly disclaimed any intention, on the part of their Government, to acquire an increase of territory, and represented the proposed revision as intended merely for the purpose of preventing uncertainty and dispute.

After having stated these three points as subjects of discussion, the British Commissioners added, that before they desired any answer from us, they felt it incumbent upon them to declare, that the British Government did not deny the right of the Americans to the fisheries generally, or in the open seas; but that the privileges formerly granted by treaty to the United States, of fishing within the limits of the British jurisdiction, and of landing and drying fish on the shores of the British territories, would not be renewed without an equivalent.

The extent of what was considered by them as waters peculiarly British, was not stated. From the manner in which they brought this subject into view, they seemed to wish us to understand that they were not anxious that it should be discussed, and that they only intended to give us notice that these privileges had ceased to exist, and would not be again granted without an equivalent, nor unless we thought proper to provide expressly in the treaty of peace for their renewal.

The British Commissioners having stated that these were all the subjects which they intended to bring forward, or to suggest, requested to be informed whether we were instructed to enter into negotiation on these several points, and whether there was any among these which we thought it unnecessary to bring into the negotiation ? and they desired us to state, on our part, such other subjects as we might intend to propose for discussion in the course of the negotiation. The meeting was then adjourned to the next day, in order to afford us the opportunity of a consultation among ourselves, before we gave an answer.

In the course of the evening of the same day, we received your letters of the 25th and 27th of June.

There could be no hesitation on our part in informing the British Commissioners that we were not instructed on the subjects of Indian pacification or boundary, and of fisheries; nor did it seem probable, although neither of these points had been stated with sufficient precision in the first verbal conference, that they could be admitted in any shape. We did not wish, however, to prejudge the result, or, by any hasty proceeding, abruptly to break off the negotiation. It was not impossible that, on the subject of the Indians, the British Government had received erroneous impressions from the Indian traders in Canada, which our representations might remove. And it appeared, at all events, important to ascertain distinctly the precise intentions of Great Britain on both points. We, therefore, thought it advisable to invite the British Commissioners to a general conversation on all the points; stating to them, at the same time, our want of instructions on two of them, and holding out no expectation of the probability of our agreeing to any article respecting these.

At our meeting on the evening day, we informed the British Commissioners that, upon the first and third points proposed by them, we were provided with instructions; and we presented as further subjects considered by our Government as suitable for discussion—

1st. A definition of blockade, and, as far as might be mutually agreed, of other neutral and belligerent rights.

2d. Claims of indemnity in certain cases of capture and seizure.

We then stated that the two subjects, first, of Indian pacification and boundary; second, of fisheries, were not embraced by our instructions. We observed, that as these points had not been heretofore the grounds of any controversy between the Government of Great Britain and that of the United States, and had not been alluded to by Lord Castlereagh in his letter proposing the negotiation, it could not be expected that they should have been anticipated and made the subject of instructions by our Government. That it was natural to be supposed that our instructions were confined to those subjects upon which differences between the two countries were known to exist; and that the proposition to define, in the treaty between the United States and Great Britain the boundary of the Indian possessions within our own territories, was new and without example. No such provision had been inserted in the Treaty of Peace in 1783, nor in any other treaty between the two countries. No such provision had, to our knowledge, ever been inserted in any treaty made by Great Britain, or any other European Power, in relation to the same description of people, existing under like circumstances. We would say, however, that it could not be doubted that peace with the Indians would certainly follow a peace with Great Britain; that we had information that commissioners had already been appointed to treat with them; that a treaty to that effect might, perhaps, have been already concluded; and that the United States, having so interest nor any motive to continue a separate war against the Indians, there could never be a moment when our Government would not be disposed to make peace with them.

We then expressed our wish to receive from the British Commissioners a statement of the views and objects of Great Britain upon all the points, and our willingness to discuss them all, in order that, even if no arrangement could be agreed on upon the points not included in our instructions, the Government of the United States might be possessed of the entire and precise intentions of that of Great Britain respecting these points; and that the British Government might be fully informed of the objections, on the part of the United States, to any such arrangement.

In answer to our remark, that these points had not been alluded to by Lord Castlereagh in his letter proposing the negotiation, it was said that it could not be expected that, in a letter merely intended to invite a negotiation, he should enumerate the topics of discussion, or state the pretensions of his Government, since these would depend upon ulterior events, and might arise out of a subsequent state of things.

In reply to our observation, that the proposed stipulation of an Indian boundary was without example in the practice of European nations, it was asserted that the Indians must in some sort be considered as an independent people, since treaties were made with them both by Great Britain and by the United States; upon which we pointed out the obvious and important difference between the treaties we might make with Indians living in our territory and such a treaty as was proposed to be made respecting them with a foreign Power, who had solemnly acknowledged the territory on which they resided to be part of the United States.

We were then asked by the British Commissioners, whether, in case they should enter further upon the discussion of the several points which had been stated, we could expect that it would terminate by some provisional arrangement on the points on which we had no instructions, particularly on that respecting the Indians, which arrangement would be subject to the ratification of our Government.

We answered, that before the subjects were distinctly understood, and the objects in view more precisely disclosed, we could not decide whether it would be possible to form any satisfactory article on the subject, nor pledge ourselves as to the exercise of a discretion under our powers, even with respect to a provisional agreement. We added, that, as we should deeply deplore a rupture of the negotiation on any point, it was our anxious desire to employ all possible means to avert an event so serious in its consequences; and that we had not been without hopes that a discussion might correct the effect of any erroneous information which the British Government might have received on the subject which they had proposed as a preliminary basis.

We took this opportunity to remark, that no nation observed a policy more liberal and humane towards the Indians than that pursued by the United States; that our object had been, by all practicable means, to introduce civilization among them; that their possessions were secured to them

by well-defined boundaries; that their persons, lands, and other property, were now more effectually protected against violence or frauds, from any quarter, than they had been under any former Government; that even our citizens were not allowed to purchase their lands; that when they gave up their title to any portion of their country to the United States, it was by voluntary treaty with our Government, who gave them a satisfactory equivalent; and that through these means the United States had succeeded in preserving, since the Treaty of Greenville of 1795, an uninterrupted peace of sixteen years with all the Indian tribes—a period of tranquillity much longer than they were known to have enjoyed heretofore.

It was then expressly stated on our part, that the proposition respecting the Indians was not distinctly understood. We asked whether the pacification and the settlement of a boundary for them were both made a *sine qua non?* which was answered in the affirmative. The question was then asked the British Commissioners, whether the proposed Indian boundary was intended to preclude the United States from the right of purchasing by treaty from the Indians, without the consent of Great Britain, lands lying beyond that boundary, and as a restriction upon the Indians from selling, by amicable treaties, lands to the United States, as had been hitherto practised?

To this question it was first answered, by one of the Commissioners, that the Indians would not be restricted from selling their lands, but that the United States would be restricted from purchasing them; and, on reflection, another of the Commissioners stated that it was intended that the Indian territories should be a barrier between the British dominions and those of the United States; that both Great Britain and the United States should be restricted from purchasing their lands; but that the Indians might sell them to a third party.

The proposition respecting Indian boundaries, thus explained, and connected with the right of sovereignty ascribed to the Indians over the country, amounted to nothing less than a demand of the absolute cession of the rights both of sovereignty and of soil. We cannot abstain from remarking to you, that the subject of Indian boundary was indistinctly stated when first proposed, and that the explanations were at first obscure, and always given with reluctance; and it was declared, from the first moment, to be a *sine qua non,* rendering any discussion unprofitable until it was admitted as a basis. Knowing that we had no power to cede to the Indians any part of our territory, we thought it unnecessary to ask, what probably would not have been answered till the principle was admitted, where the line of demarcation of the Indian country was proposed to be established.

The British Commissioners, after having repeated that their instructions on the subject of the Indians were peremptory, stated that, unless we could give some assurance that our powers would allow us to make at least a provisional ar-

Relations with Great Britain.

not be misunderstood. The cause of the United States would thenceforward become the common cause of nations. A concession by them would operate to the disadvantage of every other Power. They would all find, in the conduct of Great Britain, an unequivocal determination to destroy the rights of other flags, and to usurp the absolute dominion of the ocean. It is to be presumed that the British Government will find it neither for the honor nor interest of Great Britain to push things to that extremity, but will have accepted this mediation, and have sent a Minister or Ministers to St. Petersburg with full powers to adjust the controversy on fair and just conditions.

Should improper impressions have been taken of the probable consequences of the war, you will have ample means to remove them. It is certain, that from its prosecution Great Britain can promise to herself no advantage, while she exposes herself to great expenses and to the danger of still greater losses. The people of the United States, accustomed to the indulgence of a long peace, roused by the causes and the progress of the war, are rapidly acquiring military habits and becoming a military people. Our knowledge in naval tactics has increased, as has our maritime strength. The gallantry and success of our little Navy have formed an epoch in naval history. The laurels which these brave men have gained, not for themselves, but for their country, from an enemy pre-eminent in naval exploits, for ages past, are among the proudest boasts of their grateful and affectionate fellow-citizens. Our manufactures have taken an astounding growth. In short, in every circumstance, in which the war is felt, its pressure tends evidently to unite our people, to draw out our resources, to invigorate our means, and to make us more truly an independent nation, and, as far as may be necessary, a great maritime Power.

If the British Government accepts the mediation of Russia, with a sincere desire to restore a good intelligence between the two countries, it may be presumed that a fair opportunity will be afforded for the arrangement of many other important interests, with advantage to both parties. The adjustment of the controversy relating to impressment only, though very important, would leave much unfinished. Almost every neutral right has been violated; and its violation persisted in to the moment that war was declared. The President sincerely desires, and it is doubtless for the interest of Great Britain, to prevent the like in future. The interposition of the Emperor of Russia to promote an accommodation of these differences is deemed particularly auspicious.

[Confidential paragraph No. 1, omitted.]

A strong hope is, therefore, entertained that full powers will be given to the British Commissioners to arrange all these grounds of controversy in a satisfactory manner. In entering on this interesting part of your duty, the first object which will claim your attention is that of blockade. The violation of our neutral right by illegal blockades, carried to an enormous extent, by Orders in Council, was a principal cause of the war. These

orders, however, and with them the blockade of May, 1806, and, as is understood, all other illegal blockades, have been repealed, so that that cause of war has been removed. All that is now expected is, that the British Government will unite in a more precise definition of blockade, and in this no difficulty is anticipated, for having declared that no blockade would be legal, which was not supported by an adequate force, and that the blockades which it might institute should be supported by an adequate force, there appears to be, according to the just interpretation of these terms, no difference of opinion on the subject.

The British Government has recently, in two formal acts, given definitions of blockade, either of which would be satisfactory. The first is to be seen in the communication from Mr. Merry to this Department, bearing date on the 12th of April, 1804. The following are the circumstances attending it. Commodore Hood, the commander of a British squadron in the West Indies, in 1803, having declared the islands of Martinique and Guadaloupe in a state of blockade, without applying an adequate force to maintain it, the Secretary of State remonstrated against the illegality of the measure, which remonstrance was laid before the Lords Commissioners of the Admiralty, in England, who replied that they had sent "orders not to consider any blockade of those islands as existing unless in respect of particular ports, which might be actually invested, and then not to capture vessels, bound to such ports, unless they shall previously have been warned not to enter them." The second definition is to be found in a convention between Great Britain and Russia, in June, 1801, fourth section, third article, which declares, "that, in order to determine what characterizes a blockaded port, that denomination is given only to a port where there is, by the disposition of the Power which attacks it, with ships stationary or sufficiently near, an evident danger in entering." The President is willing for you to adopt either of these definitions; but prefers the first, as much more precise and determinate; and when it is considered that it was made the criterion by so formal an act, between the two Governments, it cannot be presumed that the British Government will object to the renewal of it. Nothing is more natural, after the differences which have taken place between the two countries, on this and other subjects, and the departure from this criterion by Great Britain, for reasons which are admitted by her no longer to exist, than that they should, on the restoration of a good understanding, recur to it again. Such a recurrence would be the more satisfactory to the President, as it would afford a proof of a disposition in the British Government, not simply to compromise a difference, but to re-establish sincere friendship between the two nations.

An interference with our commerce between enemy colonies and their parent country, was among the first violations of our neutral rights, committed by Great Britain in her present war with France. It took place in 1805, did extensive injury and produced universal excitement. In securing us against a repetition of it, you will attend to an article of the convention between Russia and Great Britain, entered into on the —— day of ——, 1801, to the eleventh article of the project of a treaty with Great Britain that was signed by Mr. Monroe and Mr. Pinkney, on the 31st December, 1806, and to the instructions from this Department relating to that article. of the 20th May, 1807. The capture, by Great Britain, of almost all the islands of her enemies, diminishes the importance of any regulation of this subject; but, as they may be restored by a treaty of peace, it merits particular attention. It being understood, however, that unless such a trade can be obtained, in a proper extent, and without a relinquishment of the principle contended for by the United States, it will be best that the treaty be silent on the subject.

A disposition has been shown by the British Government to extend this principle so far as to inhibit a trade to neutrals, even between a Power at peace with Great Britain and her enemy; as, for example, between China and France. The absurdity of this pretension may prevent its being hereafter advanced. It will not, however, be unworthy of your attention.

By an order of the British Government in 1803, British cruisers were authorized to take neutral vessels, laden with innocent articles, on their return from an enemy's port, on the pretence that they had carried to such port contraband of war. This order is directly repugnant to the law of nations, as the circumstance of having contraband articles on board, bound to an enemy's port, is the only legal ground of seizure. The claim was relinquished by the British Government, in the ninth article of the project above recited. You will endeavor in like manner to provide against it. It is the practice of British cruisers to compel the commanders of neutral vessels which they meet at sea, either to board them in person with their papers, or to send their papers on board in their own boat by an officer. The injustice and irregularity of this procedure need not be mentioned. You will endeavor to suppress it in the manner proposed in the third article of a project communicated to Mr. Monroe at London, in his instructions of the 5th of January, 1804. You will endeavor likewise to restrict contraband of war, as much as is in your power, to the list contained in the fourth article of that project.

The pretensions of Great Britain to interdict the passage of neutral vessels, with their cargoes, from one port to another port of the enemy, is illegal and very injurious to the commerce of neutral Powers. Still more unjustifiable is the attempt to interdict their passage from one port of one independent nation to that of another, on the pretence that they are both enemies. You will endeavor to obtain, in both instances, a security for the neutral right.

Upon the whole subject I have to observe, that your first duty will be to conclude a peace with Great Britain, and that you are authorized to do it, in case you obtain a satisfactory stipulation against impressments, one which shall secure, under our flag, protection to the crew. The manner in which it may be done has been already stated, with the reciprocal stipulations which you may enter into to secure Great Britain against the injury of which she complains. If this encroachment of Great Britain is not provided against, the United States have appealed to arms in vain. If your efforts to accomplish it should fail, all further negotiations will cease, and you will return home without delay. It is possible that some difficulty may occur in arranging this article respecting its duration. To obviate this, the President is willing that it be limited to the present war in Europe. Resting, as the United States do, on the solid ground of right, it is not presumable that Great Britain, especially after the advantage she may derive from the arrangement proposed, would ever revive her pretension. In forming any stipulation on this subject, you will be careful not to impair by it the right of the United States, or to sanction the principle of the British claim.

It is deemed highly important, also, to obtain a definition of the neutral rights which I have brought to your view, especially of blockade, and in the manner suggested; but it is not to be made an indispensable condition of peace. After the repeal of the Orders in Council, and other illegal blockades, and the explanations attending it, it is not presumable that Great Britain will revive them. Should she do it, the United States will always have a corresponding resort in their own hands. You will observe, in every case in which you may not be able to obtain a satisfactory definition of the neutral right, that you enter into none respecting it.

Indemnity for losses seems to be a fair claim on the part of the United States, and the British Government, if desirous to strengthen the relations of friendship, may be willing to make it. In bringing the claim into view, you will not let it defeat the primary objects intrusted to you. It is not perceived on what ground Great Britain can resist this claim, at least in the cases in favor of which she stands pledged. Of these a note will be added.

[Confidential paragraph No. 2, omitted.]

You are at liberty to stipulate in the proposed treaty the same advantages, in the ports of the United States, in favor of British ships of war, that may be allowed to those of the most favored nations. This stipulation must be reciprocal.

[Confidential paragraph No. 3, omitted.]

No difficulty can arise from the case of the non-importation act, which will doubtless be terminated in consequence of the pacification. Should any stipulation to that effect be required, or found advantageous, you are at liberty to enter into it. Should peace be made, you may, in fixing the periods to which it shall take effect in different latitudes and distances, take for the basis the provisional articles of the Treaty of Peace with Great Britain in 1782, with such alterations as may appear to be just and reasonable.

In discharging the duties of the trust committed to you, the President desires that you will manifest the highest degree of respect for the Emperor of Russia, and confidence in the integrity and impartiality of his views. In arranging the question of impressment, and every question of neutral right, you will explain to his Government, without reserve, the claims of the United States, with the ground on which they severally rest. It is not doubted that from a conduct so frank and honorable the most beneficial effect will result.

[Confidential paragraph No. 4, omitted.]

I shall conclude by remarking that a strong hope is entertained that this friendly mediation of the Emperor Alexander will form an epoch in the relations between the United States and Russia, which will be extensively felt, and be long and eminently distinguished by the happy consequences attending it. Since 1790, Russia has been the pivot on which all questions of neutral right have essentially turned. Most of the wars which have disturbed the world in modern times have originated with Great Britain and France. These wars have affected distant countries, especially in their character as neutrals, and very materially the United States, who took no part in promoting them, and had no interest in the great objects of either Power.

[Confidential paragraph No. 5, omitted.]

I have the honor to be, &c.

JAMES MONROE.

Extract of a letter from the Secretary of State to the Commissioners of the United States for treating of peace with Great Britain, dated

DEPARTMENT OF STATE, *June* 23, 1813.

An opportunity offering, I avail myself of it to explain more fully the views of the President on certain subjects already treated on in your instructions, and to communicate his sentiments on some others, not adverted to in them.

The British Government having repealed the Orders in Council and the blockade of May, 1806, and all other illegal blockades, and having declared that it would institute no blockade which should not be supported by an adequate force, it was thought better to leave that question on that ground, than to continue the war, to obtain a more precise definition of blockade, after the other essential cause of the war, that of impressment, should be removed. But when it is considered that a stipulated definition of blockade will cost Great Britain nothing, after having thus recognised the principle, and that such definition is calculated to give additional confidence in the future security of our commerce, it is expected that she will agree to it. It is true, this cause of war being removed, the United States are under no obligation to continue it for the want of such stipulated definition, more especially as they retain in their hands the remedy against any new violation of their rights, whenever made. The same remark is applicable to the case of impressment; for, if the British Government had issued orders to its cruisers not to impress seamen from our vessels, and notified the same to this Government, that

cause of war would also have been removed. In making peace, it is better for both nations that the controversy respecting blockade should be arranged by treaty, as well as that respecting impressment. The omission to arrange it may be productive of injury. Without a precise definition of blockade, improper pretensions might be set up on each side respecting their rights, which might possibly hazard the future good understanding between the two countries.

Should a restitution of territory be agreed on, it will be proper to make a provision for settling the boundary between the United States and Great Britain, on the St. Lawrence and the Lakes, from the point at which the line between them strikes the St. Lawrence to the northwest corner of the Lake of the Woods, according to the principles of the Treaty of Peace. The settlement of this boundary is important, from the circumstance that there are several islands in the river, and lakes of some extent and great value, the dominion over which is claimed by both parties. It may be an advisable course to appoint commissioners on each side, with full powers to adjust, on fair and equitable considerations, this boundary. To enable you to adopt a suitable provision for the purpose, it will be proper for you to recur to the instructions heretofore given on the subject, published in the documents in your possession.

Mr. Monroe, Secretary of State, to the Plenipotentiaries of the United States at St. Petersburg.

DEPARTMENT OF STATE, *Jan.* 1, 1814.

GENTLEMEN: I have not received a letter from you since your appointment to meet Ministers from Great Britain at St. Petersburg, to negotiate a Treaty of Peace under the mediation of the Emperor of Russia. This is doubtless owing to the miscarriage of your despatches.

The Message of the President, of which I have the honor to transmit to you a copy, will make you acquainted with the progress of the war with Great Britain to that period, and the other documents which are forwarded will communicate what has since occurred.

Among the advantages attending our success in Upper Canada, was the important one of making capture of General Proctor's baggage, with all the public documents belonging to the British Government in his possession. It is probable that these documents will be laid before Congress, as they are of a nature highly interesting to the public. You will understand their true character by extracts of two letters from Governor Cass, which are enclosed to you. By these, it appears, that the British Government has exercised its influence over the Indian tribes within our limits as well as elsewhere in peace, for hostile purposes towards the United States; and that the Indian barbarities since the war were, in many instances, known to and sanctioned by the British Government.

I have the honor to be, &c.

JAMES MONROE.

Relations with Great Britain.

Mr. Monroe, Secretary of State, to the Plenipotentiaries of the United States at St. Petersburg.

DEPARTMENT OF STATE, *Jan.* 8, 1814.

GENTLEMEN : I have the honor to transmit to you a copy of a letter from Lord Castlereagh to this Department, and of a note from Lord Cathcart to the Russian Government, with my reply to the communication.

The arrangement of a negotiation to be held at Gottenburg, directly between the United States and Great Britain, without the aid of the Russian mediation, makes it necessary that new commissions should be issued correspondent with it, and, for this purpose, that a new nomination should be made to the Senate. The President instructs me to inform you that you will both be included in it; and that he wishes you to repair, immediately on the receipt of this, to the appointed rendezvous. It is possible that the business may not be limited to yourselves, on account of the great interests involved in the result. The commissions and instructions will be duly forwarded to you, as soon as the arrangements shall be finally made.

In taking leave of the Russian Government, you will be careful to make known to it the sensibility of the President to the friendly disposition of the Emperor, manifested by the offer of his mediation ; the regret felt at its rejection by the British Government ; and a desire that in future the greatest confidence and, cordiality, and the best understanding, may prevail between the two Governments.

I have the honor to be, &c.

JAMES MONROE.

Mr. Monroe, Secretary of State, to the American Plenipotentiaries at Gottenburg.

DEPARTMENT OF STATE, *Jan.* 28, 1814.

GENTLEMEN: The British Government having declined the Russian mediation, and proposed to treat directly with the United States, the President has, on due consideration, thought proper to accept the overture. To give effect to this arrangement, it was necessary that a new commission should be formed, and, for that purpose, that a new nomination should be made to the Senate, by whose advice and consent this important trust is committed to you.

You will consider the instructions given to the commission to treat under the mediation of Russia as applicable to the negotiation with which you are now charged, except as they may be modified by this letter.

I shall call your attention to the most important grounds of the controversy with Great Britain only, and make such remarks on each, and on the whole subject, as have occurred since the date of the former instructions, and are deemed applicable to the present juncture, taking into view the negotiation in which you are now about to engage.

On impressment—as to the right of the United States to be exempted from it—I have nothing new to add. The sentiments of the President have undergone no change on that important subject. This degrading practice must cease; our flag must protect the crew, or the United States cannot consider themselves an independent nation. To settle this difference amicably, the President is willing, as you are already informed by the former instructions, to remove all pretext for it to the British Government, by excluding all British seamen from our vessels; and even to extend the exclusion to all British subjects, if necessary, excepting only the few already naturalized ; and to stipulate, likewise, the surrender of all British seamen deserting in our ports in future from British vessels, public or private. It was presumed by all dispassionate persons, that the late law of Congress relative to seamen would effectually accomplish the object. But the President is willing, as you find, to prevent a possibility of failure, to go further.

Should a treaty be made, it is proper, and it would have a conciliatory effect, that all our impressed seamen who may be discharged under it should be paid for their services by the British Government, for the time of their detention, the wages which they might have obtained in the merchant service of their own country.

Blockade is the subject next in point of importance, which you will have to arrange. In the instructions bearing date on the 15th of April, 1813, it was remarked that, as the British Government had revoked its Orders in Council, and agreed that no blockade could be legal which was not supported by an adequate force, and that such adequate force should be applied to any blockade which it might thereafter institute, this cause of controversy seemed to be removed. Further reflection, however, has added great force to the expediency and importance of a precise definition of the public law on this subject. There is much cause to presume that, if the repeal of the Orders in Council had taken place in time to have been known here before the declaration of war, and had had the effect of preventing the declaration, not only that no provision would have been obtained against impressment, but that, under the name of blockade, the same extent of coast would have been covered by proclamation as had been covered by the Orders in Council. The war, which these abuses and impressment contributed so much to produce, might possibly prevent that consequence. But it would be more satisfactory, if not more safe, to guard against it by a formal definition in the treaty. It is true, should the British Government violate again the legitimate principles of blockade, in whatever terms or under whatever pretext it might be done, the United States would have in their hands a correspondent resort; but a principal object in making peace is to prevent, by the justice and reciprocity of the conditions, a recurrence again to war for the same cause. If the British Government sincerely wishes to make a durable peace with the United States, it can have no reasonable objection to a just definition of blockade, especially as the two Governments have agreed, in their correspondence, in all its essential featives. The instructions of the 15th of April, 1813, have stated in what manner the President is willing to arrange this difference.

On the other neutral rights enumerated in the former instructions, I shall remark only that the catalogue is limited in a manner to evince a spirit of accommodation ; that the arrangement proposed in each instance is just in itself; that it corresponds with the general spirit of treaties between commercial Powers ; and that Great Britain has sanctioned it in many treaties, and gone beyond it in some.

[Confidential paragraph No. 1, omitted.]

On the claim to indemnity for spoliations, I have only to refer you to what was said in the former instructions. I have to add, that should a treaty be formed, it is just in itself, and would have a happy effect on the future relations of the two countries, if indemnity should be stipulated on each side for the destruction of all unfortified towns, and other private property, contrary to the laws and usages of war. It is equally proper that the negroes taken from the Southern States should be returned to their owners, or paid for at their full value. It is known that a shameful traffic has been carried on in the West Indies, by the sale of these persons there, by those who professed to be their deliverers. Of this fact, the proof which has reached this Department shall be furnished you. If these slaves are considered as noncombatants, they ought to be restored ; if as property, they ought to be paid for. The Treaty of Peace contains an article which recognises this principle.

In the view which I have taken of the conditions on which you are to insist in the proposed negotiation, you will find, on a comparison of them with those stated in the former instructions, that there is no material difference between them, the two last mentioned claims to indemnity excepted, which have originated since the date of those instructions. The principal object of this review has been to show that the sentiments of the President are the same in every instance, and that the reasons for maintaining them have become more evident and strong since the date of those instructions.

In accepting the overture of the British Government to treat independently of the Russian mediation, the United States have acted on principles which have governed them in every transaction relating to peace since the war. Had the British Government accepted the Russian mediation, the United States would have treated for themselves, independently of any other Power ; and had Great Britain met them on just conditions, peace would have been the immediate result. Had she refused to accede to such conditions, and attempted to dictate others, a knowledge of the views of other Powers on those points might have been useful to the United States. In agreeing to treat directly with Great Britain, not only is no concession contemplated on any point in controversy, but the same desire is cherished to preserve a good understanding with Russia and the other Baltic Powers, as if the negotiation had taken place under the mediation of Russia.

[Confidential paragraph No. 2, omitted.]

It is probable that the British Government may have declined the Russian mediation from the apprehension of an understanding between the United States and Russia for very different purposes from those which have been contemplated, in the hope that a much better treaty might be obtained of the United States, in a direct negotiation, than could be obtained under the Russian mediation, and with a view to profit of the concessions which might thus be made by the United States in future negotiations with the Baltic Powers. If this was the object of the British Government, (and it is not easy to conceive any other,) it clearly proves the advantage to be derived, in the proposed negotiation, from the aid of those Powers, in securing from the British Government such conditions as would be satisfactory to all parties. It would be highly honorable as well as advantageous to the United States, if the negotiation with which you are charged should terminate in such a treaty.

[Confidential paragraph No. 3, omitted.]

I have the honor to be, &c.

JAMES MONROE.

Mr. Monroe, Secretary of State, to the Plenipotentiaries of the United States at Gottenburg.

DEPARTMENT OF STATE, *Jan.* 30, 1814.

GENTLEMEN : In addition to the claims to indemnity, stated in your preceding instructions, I have to request your attention to the following, to which, it is presumed, there can be no objection :

On the declaration of war by the United States, there happened to be, in the ordinary course of commerce, several American vessels and cargoes in the ports of Great Britain, which were seized and condemned ; and, in one instance, an American ship which fled from Algiers, in consequence of the declaration of war by the Dey, to Gibraltar, with the American Consul and some public stores on board, shared a like fate.

After the declaration of war, Congress passed an act allowing to British subjects six months, from the date of the declaration, to remove their property out of the United States, in consequence of which many vessels were removed, with their cargoes. I add, with confidence, that, on a liberal construction of the spirit of the law, some vessels were permitted to depart, even after the expiration of the term specified in the law. I will endeavor to put in your possession a list of these cases. A general reciprocal provision, however, will be best adapted to the object in view.

I have the honor to be, &c.

JAMES MONROE.

From the Secretary of State to the Commissioners of the United States for treating with Great Britain.

DEPARTMENT OF STATE, *Feb.* 10 1814.

GENTLEMEN : Should you conclude a treaty, and not obtain a satisfactory arrangement of neutral rights, it will be proper for you to provide

Relations with Great Britain.

that the United States shall have advantage of any stipulations more favorable to neutral nations, that may be established between Great Britain and other Powers. A precedent for such a provision is found in a declaratory article between Great Britain and Russia, bearing date on the 8th October, 1801, explanatory of the second section third article of a convention concluded between them on the 5th of June of the same year.

I have the honor to be, &c.
JAMES MONROE.

Extract—The Secretary of State to the Commissioners of the United States for treating with Great Britain.

DEPARTMENT OF STATE, *Feb.* 14, 1814.
I received last night your letter of the 15th October, with extracts of letters from Mr. Adams and Mr. Harris of the 22d and 23d of November.

It appears that you had no knowledge, at the date even of the last letter, of the answer of the British Government to the offer which had been made to it a second time of the Russian mediation. Hence it is to be inferred that the proposition made to this Government, by the Bramble, was made not only without your knowledge, but without the sanction, if not without the knowledge, of the Emperor. Intelligence from other sources strengthens this inference. If this view of the conduct of the British Government is well founded, the motive for it cannot be mistaken. It may fairly be presumed that it was to prevent a good understanding and concert between the United States and Russia and Sweden, on the subject of neutral rights, in the hope that by drawing the negotiation to England, and depriving you of an opportunity of free communication with those Powers, a treaty less favorable to the United States might be obtained, which might afterwards be used with advantage by Great Britain in her negotiations with those Powers.

By an article in the former instructions, you were authorized, in making a treaty to prevent impressment from our vessels, to stipulate, provided a certain term could not be agreed on, that it might continue in force for the present war in Europe only. At that time it seemed probable that the war might last many years. Recent appearances, however, indicate the contrary. Should peace be made in Europe, as the practical evil of which we complain, in regard to impressment, would cease, it is presumed that the British Government would have less objection to a stipulation to forbear that practice for a specified term, than it would have should the war continue. In concluding a peace with Great Britain, even in case of a previous general peace in Europe, it is important to the United States to obtain such a stipulation.

Mr. Monroe, Secretary of State, to the Plenipotentiaries of the United States at Gottenburg.

DEPARTMENT OF STATE, *March* 21, 1814.
GENTLEMEN : By the cartel Chauncey you will receive this, with duplicates of the commission to treat with Great Britain, and of the instructions and other documents that were forwarded by the John Adams. This vessel is sent to guard against any accident which might attend the other.

[Confidential paragraph omitted.]

If a satisfactory arrangement can be concluded with Great Britain, the sooner it is accomplished the happier for both countries. If such an arrangement cannot be obtained, it is important to the United States to be acquainted with it without delay. I hope, therefore, to receive from you an account of the state of the negotiation and its prospects, as soon as you may be able to communicate anything of an interesting nature respecting them.

I have the honor to be, &c.
JAMES MONROE.

Mr. Monroe to the Envoys Extraordinary and Ministers Plenipotentiary of the United States.

DEPARTMENT OF STATE, *June* 25, 1814.
GENTLEMEN : No communication has been received from the joint mission which was appointed to meet the Commissioners of the British Government at Gottenburg. A letter from Mr. Bayard at Amsterdam, of the 18th of March, was the last from either of our Commissioners. It was inferred from that letter, and other communications, that Mr. Bayard, Mr. Gallatin, and Mr. Adams, would be in Gottenburg ; and it has been understood from other sources that Mr. Clay and Mr. Russell had arrived there about the 15th of April. It is, therefore, expected that a meeting will have taken place in May, and that we shall soon be made acquainted with your sentiments of the probable result of the negotiation.

It is impossible, with the lights which have reached us, to ascertain the present disposition of the British Government towards an accommodation with the United States. We think it probable that the late events in France may have had a tendency to increase its pretensions.

At war with Great Britain, and injured by France, the United States have sustained the attitude founded on those relations. No reliance was placed on the good offices of France in bringing the war with Great Britain to a satisfactory conclusion. Looking steadily to an honorable peace, and the ultimate attainment of justice from both Powers, the President has endeavored, by a consistent and honorable policy, to take advantage of every circumstance that might promote that result. He, nevertheless, knew that France held a place in the political system of Europe and of the world, which, as a check on England, could not fail to be useful to us. What effect the late events may have had, in these respects, is the important circumstance of which you are, doubtless, better informed than we can be.

The President accepted the mediation of Russia from a respect for the character of the Emperor, and a belief that our cause, in all the points in controversy, would gain strength by being made known to him. On the same principle he preferred (in accepting the British overture to

Relations with Great Britain.

treat independently of the Russian mediation) to open the negotiation on the Continent rather than at London.

It was inferred fom the general policy of Russia, and the friendly sentiments and interposition of the Emperor, that a respect for both would have much influence with the British Cabinet in promoting a pacific policy towards us. The manner, however, in which it is understood that a general pacification is taking place; the influence Great Britain may have in modifying the arrangements involved in it; the resources she may be able to employ exclusively against the United States; and the uncertainty of the precise course which Russia may pursue in relation to the war between the United States and Great Britain, naturally claim attention, and raise the important question in reference to the subject of impressment, on which it is presumed your negotiations will essentially turn, whether your powers ought not to be enlarged so as to enable you to give to those circumstances all the weight to which they may be entitled. On full consideration it has been decided, that, in case no stipulation can be obtained from the British Government at this moment, when its pretensions may have been much heightened by recent events, and the state of Europe be most favorable to them, either relinquishing the claim to impress from American vessels, or discontinuing the practice, even in consideration of the proposed exclusion from them of British seamen, you may concur in an article stipulating that the subject of impressment, together with that of commerce between the two countries, be referred to a separate negotiation, to be undertaken without delay, at such place as you may be able to agree on, preferring this city if to be obtained. I annex at the close of this letter a project of an article expressing more distinctly the idea which it is intended to communicate, not meaning thereby to restrain you in any respect as to the form. Commerce and seamen, the objects of impressment, may, with great propriety, be arranged in the same instrument. By stipulating that Commissioners shall forthwith be appointed for the purpose, and that all rights on this subject shall, in the meantime, be reserved, the faith of the British Government will be pledged to a fair experiment in an amicable mode, and the honor and rights of the United States secured. The United States having resisted by war the practice of impressment, and continued the war until that practice had ceased by a peace in Europe, their object has been essentially obtained for the present. It may reasonably be expected that the arrangement contemplated and provided for, will take effect before a new war in Europe shall furnish an occasion for reviving the practice. Should this arrangement, however, fail, and the practice be again revived, the United States will again be at liberty to repel it by war, and that they will do so cannot be doubted; for after the proof which they have already given of a firm resistance in that mode, persevered in until the practice had ceased, under circumstances the most favorable, it cannot be presumed that

the practice will ever be tolerated again. Certain it is, that every day will render it more ineligible in Great Britain to make the attempt.

In contemplating the appointment of Commissioners, to be made after the ratification of the present treaty, to negotiate and conclude a treaty to regulate commerce, and provide against impressment, it is meant only to show the extent to which you may go, in a spirit of accommodation, if necessary. Should the British Government be willing to take the subject up immediately with you, it would be much preferred, in which case the proposed article would, of course, be adapted to the purpose.

Information has been received, from a quarter deserving attention, that the late events in France have produced such an effect on the British Government as to make it probable that a demand will be made at Gottenburg to surrender our right to the fisheries; to abandon all trade beyond the Cape of Good Hope; and to cede Louisiana to Spain. We cannot believe that such a demand will be made. Should it be, you will of course treat it as it deserves. These rights must not be brought into discussion. If insisted on, your negotiations will cease.

I have the honor to be, with great respect, gentlemen, your most obedient servant,

JAMES MONROE.

Whereas, by the peace in Europe, the essential causes of the war between the United States, and Great Britain, and particularly the practice of impressment, have ceased, and a sincere desire exists to arrange, in a manner satisfactory to both parties, all questions concerning seamen, and it is also their desire and intention to arrange, in a like satisfactory manner, the commerce between the two countries, it is therefore agreed that Commissioners shall forthwith be appointed on each side, to meet at ——, with full power to negotiate and conclude a treaty, as soon as may be practicable, for the arrangement of those important interests. It is, nevertheless, understood, that, until such treaty be formed, each party shall retain all its rights, and that all American citizens who have been impressed into the British service shall be forthwith discharged.

Extract of a letter from Mr. Monroe, Secretary of State, to the joint Commissioners of the United States for treating of peace with Great Britain, dated,

DEPARTMENT OF STATE, *June 27, 1814.*

The omission to send Ministers to Gottenburg, without a previous and official notification of the appointment and arrival there of those of the United States, a formality, which, if due from either party, might have been expected from that making the overture, rather than that accepting it, *is* a proof of a dilatory policy, and would, in other respects, justify animadversions, if there was less disposition here to overlook circumstances of form, when interfering with more substantial objects.

By my letter of the 25th instant, which goes with this, you will find that the subject had al-

Relations with Great Britain.

ready been acted on under similar impressions with those which Mr. Bayard and Mr. Gallatin's letter could not fail to produce. The view, however, presented by them is much stronger, and entitled to much greater attention. The President has taken the subject into consideration again, and given to their suggestions all the weight to which they are justly entitled.

On mature consideration, it has been decided, that, under all the circumstances alluded to, incident to a prosecution of the war, you may omit any stipulation on the subject of impressment, if found indispensably necessary to terminate it. You will, of course, not recur to this expedient until all your efforts to adjust the controversy in a more satisfactory manner have failed. As it is not the intention of the United States, in suffering the treaty to be silent on the subject of impressment, to admit the British claim thereon, or to relinquish that of the United States, it is highly important that any such inference be entirely precluded, by a declaration or protest, in some form or other, that the omission is not to have any such effect or tendency. Any modification of the practice, to prevent abuses, being an acknowledgment of the right in Great Britain, is utterly inadmissible.

Although Gottenburg was contemplated at the time your commission was made out, as the seat of the negotiation, yet your commission itself does not confine you to it. You are at liberty, therefore, to transfer the negotiation to any other place made more eligible by a change of circumstances. Amsterdam and the Hague readily present themselves as preferable to any place in England. If, however, you should be of opinion that, under all circumstances, the negotiation in that country will be attended with advantages outweighing the objections to it, you are at liberty to transfer it there.

Extract of a letter from the Secretary of State to the Commissioners of the United States for treating of peace with Great Britain, dated

DEPARTMENT OF STATE,
August 11, 1814.

I had the honor to receive, on the 3d of this month, a letter from Mr. Bayard and Mr. Gallatin, of the 23d of May, and one from Mr. Gallatin of the 2d of June.

The President approves the arrangement communicated by those gentlemen for transferring the negotiation with the British Government from Gottenburg to Ghent. It is presumed, from Mr. Gallatin's letter, that the meeting took place towards the latter end of June, and that we shall soon hear from you what will be its probable result.

By my letters of the 25th and 27th of June, of which another copy is now forwarded, the sentiments of the President, as to the conditions on which it will be proper for you to conclude a treaty of peace, are made known to you. It is presumed that either in the mode suggested in my letter of the 25th of June, which is much

preferred, or by permitting the treaty to be silent on the subject, as is authorized in the letter of the 27th of June, the question of impressment may be so disposed of as to form no obstacle to a pacification. This Government can go no further, because it will make no sacrifice of the rights or honor of the nation.

If Great Britain does not terminate the war on the conditions which you are authorized to adopt, she has other objects in it than those for which she has hitherto professed to contend. That such are entertained, there is much reason to presume. These, whatever they may be, must and will be resisted by the United States. The conflict may be severe, but it will be borne with firmness, and, as we confidently believe, be attended with success.

From the Commissioners Extraordinary and Plenipotentiary of the United States for treating of peace with Great Britain, to the Secretary of State, dated

GHENT, *August* 12, 1814.

SIR: We have the honor to inform you that the British Commissioners, Lord Gambier, Henry Goulburn, Esq., and William Adams, Esq., arrived in this city on Saturday evening, the 6th instant. The day after their arrival, Mr. Baker, their secretary, called upon us to give us notice of the fact, and to propose a meeting at a certain hour on the ensuing day. The place having been agreed upon, we accordingly met at one o'clock on Monday, the 8th instant.

We enclose, herewith, a copy of the full powers exhibited by the British Commissioners at that conference, which was opened, on their part, by an expression of the sincere and earnest desire of their Government that the negotiation might result in a solid peace, honorable to both parties. They, at the same time, declared that no events which had occurred since the first proposal for this negotiation had altered the pacific disposition of their Government, or varied its views as to the terms upon which it was willing to conclude the peace.

We answered, that we heard these declarations with great satisfaction, and that our Government had acceded to the proposal of negotiation, with the most sincere desire to put an end to the differences which divided the two countries, and to lay, upon just and liberal grounds, the foundation of a peace which, securing the rights and interests of both nations, should unite them by lasting bonds of amity.

The British Commissioners then stated the following subjects as those upon which it appeared to them that the discussions would be likely to turn, and on which they were instructed:

1st. The forcible seizure of mariners on board of merchant vessels, and, in connexion with it, the claim of His Britannic Majesty to the allegiance of all the native subjects of Great Britain.

We understood them to intimate that the British Government did not propose this point as one which they were particularly desirous of discussing; but that, as it had occupied so prominent a place in the dispute between the two countries, it necessarily attracted notice, and was considered as a subject which would come under discussion.

2d. The Indian allies of Great Britain to be included in the pacification, and a definite boundary to be settled for their territory.

The British Commissioners stated that an arrangement upon this point was a *sine qua non*; that they were not authorized to conclude a treaty of peace which did not embrace the Indians as allies of His Britannic Majesty; and that the establishment of a definite boundary of the Indian territory was necessary to secure a permanent peace, not only with the Indians, but also between the United States and Great Britain.

3d. A revision of the boundary line between the United States and the adjacent British colonies.

With respect to this point, they expressly disclaimed any intention, on the part of their Government, to acquire an increase of territory, and represented the proposed revision as intended merely for the purpose of preventing uncertainty and dispute.

After having stated these three points as subjects of discussion, the British Commissioners added, that before they desired any answer from us, they felt it incumbent upon them to declare, that the British Government did not deny the right of the Americans to the fisheries generally, or in the open seas; but that the privileges formerly granted by treaty to the United States, of fishing within the limits of the British jurisdiction, and of landing and drying fish on the shores of the British territories, would not be renewed without an equivalent.

The extent of what was considered by them as waters peculiarly British, was not stated. From the manner in which they brought this subject into view, they seemed to wish us to understand that they were not anxious that it should be discussed, and that they only intended to give us notice that these privileges had ceased to exist, and would not be again granted without an equivalent, nor unless we thought proper to provide expressly in the treaty of peace for their renewal.

The British Commissioners having stated that these were all the subjects which they intended to bring forward, or to suggest, requested to be informed whether we were instructed to enter into negotiation on these several points, and whether there was any among these which we thought it unnecessary to bring into the negotiation? and they desired us to state, on our part, such other subjects as we might intend to propose for discussion in the course of the negotiation. The meeting was then adjourned to the next day, in order to afford us the opportunity of a consultation among ourselves, before we gave an answer.

In the course of the evening of the same day, we received your letters of the 25th and 27th of June.

There could be no hesitation on our part in informing the British Commissioners that we were not instructed on the subjects of Indian pacification or boundary, and of fisheries; nor did it seem probable, although neither of these points had been stated with sufficient precision in the first verbal conference, that they could be admitted in any shape. We did not wish, however, to prejudge the result, or, by any hasty proceeding, abruptly to break off the negotiation. It was not impossible that, on the subject of the Indians, the British Government had received erroneous impressions from the Indian traders in Canada, which our representations might remove. And it appeared, at all events, important to ascertain distinctly the precise intentions of Great Britain on both points. We, therefore, thought it advisable to invite the British Commissioners to a general conversation on all the points; stating to them, at the same time, our want of instructions on two of them, and holding out no expectation of the probability of our agreeing to any article respecting these.

At our meeting on the ensuing day, we informed the British Commissioners that, upon the first and third points proposed by them, we were provided with instructions; and we presented as further subjects considered by our Government as suitable for discussion—

1st. A definition of blockade, and, as far as might be mutually agreed, of other neutral and belligerent rights.

2d. Claims of indemnity in certain cases of capture and seizure.

We then stated that the two subjects, first, of Indian pacification and boundary; second, of fisheries, were not embraced by our instructions. We observed, that as these points had not been heretofore the grounds of any controversy between the Government of Great Britain and that of the United States, and had not been alluded to by Lord Castlereagh in his letter proposing the negotiation, it could not be expected that they should have been anticipated and made the subject of instructions by our Government. That it was natural to be supposed that our instructions were confined to those subjects upon which differences between the two countries were known to exist; and that the proposition to define, in the treaty between the United States and Great Britain the boundary of the Indian possessions within our own territories, was new and without example. No such provision had been inserted in the Treaty of Peace in 1783, nor in any other treaty between the two countries. No such provision had, to our knowledge, ever been inserted in any treaty made by Great Britain, or any other European Power, in relation to the same description of people, existing under like circumstances. We would say, however, that it could not be doubted that peace with the Indians would certainly follow a peace with Great Britain; that we had information that commissioners had already been appointed to treat with them; that a treaty to that effect might, perhaps, have been already concluded; and that the United States, having so interest nor any motive to continue a separate war against the Indians, there could never be a moment when our Government would not be disposed to make peace with them.

We then expressed our wish to receive from the British Commissioners a statement of the views and objects of Great Britain upon all the points, and our willingness to discuss them all, in order that, even if no arrangement could be agreed on upon the points not included in our instructions, the Government of the United States might be possessed of the entire and precise intentions of that of Great Britain respecting these points; and that the British Government might be fully informed of the objections, on the part of the United States, to any such arrangement.

In answer to our remark, that these points had not been alluded to by Lord Castlereagh in his letter proposing the negotiation, it was said that it could not be expected that, in a letter merely intended to invite a negotiation, he should enumerate the topics of discussion, or state the pretensions of his Government, since these would depend upon ulterior events, and might arise out of a subsequent state of things.

In reply to our observation, that the proposed stipulation of an Indian boundary was without example in the practice of European nations, it was asserted that the Indians must in some sort be considered as an independent people, since treaties were made with them both by Great Britain and by the United States; upon which we pointed out the obvious and important difference between the treaties we might make with Indians living in our territory and such a treaty as was proposed to be made respecting them with a foreign Power, who had solemnly acknowledged the territory on which they resided to be part of the United States.

We were then asked by the British Commissioners, whether, in case they should enter further upon the discussion of the several points which had been stated, we could expect that it would terminate by some provisional arrangement on the points on which we had no instructions, particularly on that respecting the Indians, which arrangement would be subject to the ratification of our Government.

We answered, that before the subjects were distinctly understood, and the objects in view more precisely disclosed, we could not decide whether it would be possible to form any satisfactory article on the subject, nor pledge ourselves as to the exercise of a discretion under our powers, even with respect to a provisional agreement. We added, that, as we should deeply deplore a rupture of the negotiation on any point, it was our anxious desire to employ all possible means to avert an event so serious in its consequences; and that we had not been without hopes that a discussion might correct the effect of any erroneous information which the British Government might have received on the subject which they had proposed as a preliminary basis.

We took this opportunity to remark, that no nation observed a policy more liberal and humane towards the Indians than that pursued by the United States; that our object had been, by all practicable means, to introduce civilization among them; that their possessions were secured to them

by well-defined boundaries; that their persons, lands, and other property, were now more effectually protected against violence or frauds, from any quarter, than they had been under any former Government; that even our citizens were not allowed to purchase their lands; that when they gave up their title to any portion of their country to the United States, it was by voluntary treaty with our Government, who gave them a satisfactory equivalent; and that through these means the United States had succeeded in preserving, since the Treaty of Greenville of 1795, an uninterrupted peace of sixteen years with all the Indian tribes—a period of tranquillity much longer than they were known to have enjoyed heretofore.

It was then expressly stated on our part, that the proposition respecting the Indians was not distinctly understood. We asked whether the pacification and the settlement of a boundary for them were both made a *sine qua non?* which was answered in the affirmative. The question was then asked the British Commissioners, whether the proposed Indian boundary was intended to preclude the United States from the right of purchasing by treaty from the Indians, without the consent of Great Britain, lands lying beyond that boundary, and as a restriction upon the Indians from selling, by amicable treaties, lands to the United States, as had been hitherto practised?

To this question it was first answered, by one of the Commissioners, that the Indians would not be restricted from selling their lands, but that the United States would be restricted from purchasing them; and, on reflection, another of the Commissioners stated that it was intended that the Indian territories should be a barrier between the British dominions and those of the United States; that both Great Britain and the United States should be restricted from purchasing their lands; but that the Indians might sell them to a third party.

The proposition respecting Indian boundaries, thus explained, and connected with the right of sovereignty ascribed to the Indians over the country, amounted to nothing less than a demand of the absolute cession of the rights both of sovereignty and of soil. We cannot abstain from remarking to you, that the subject of Indian boundary was indistinctly stated when first proposed, and that the explanations were at first obscure, and always given with reluctance; and it was declared, from the first moment, to be a *sine qua non*, rendering any discussion unprofitable until it was admitted as a basis. Knowing that we had no power to cede to the Indians any part of our territory, we thought it unnecessary to ask, what probably would not have been answered till the principle was admitted, where the line of demarcation of the Indian country was proposed to be established.

The British Commissioners, after having repeated that their instructions on the subject of the Indians were peremptory, stated that, unless we could give some assurance that our powers would allow us to make at least a provisional arrangement on the subject, any further discussion would be fruitless; and that they must consult their own Government on this state of things. They proposed, accordingly, a suspension of the conferences until they should have received an answer; it being understood that each party might call a meeting whenever they had any propositions to submit. They despatched a special messenger the same evening, and we are now waiting for the result.

Before the proposed adjournment took place, it was agreed that there should be a protocol of the conferences; that a statement should, for that purpose, be drawn up by each party; and that we should meet the next day to compare the statements. We accordingly met again on Wednesday, the 10th instant, and ultimately agreed on what should constitute the protocol of the conferences. A copy of this instrument we have the honor to transmit with this despatch; and we also enclose a copy of the statement originally drawn up on our part, for the purpose of making known to you the passages to which the British Commissioners objected.

Their objection to some of the passages was, that they appeared to be argumentative, and that the object of the protocol was to contain a mere statement of facts. They, however, objected to the insertion of the answer which they had given to our question respecting the effect of the proposed Indian boundary; but they agreed to an alteration of their original proposition on that subject, which renders it much more explicit than as stated, either in the first conference or in their proposed draught of the protocol. They also objected to the insertion of the fact, that they had proposed to adjourn the conferences until they could obtain further instructions from their Government. The return of their messenger may, perhaps, disclose the motive of their reluctance in that respect.

We have the honor to be, very respectfully, your obedient servants,

JOHN QUINCY ADAMS,
J. A. BAYARD,
HENRY CLAY,
JONATHAN RUSSELL.

Draught of original Protocol, made by the American Ministers, of the two first conferences held with the British Commissioners.

At a meeting between the Commissioners of His Britannic Majesty and those of the United States of America, for negotiating and concluding a peace, held at Ghent, 8th August, 1814, the following points were presented, by the Commissioners on the part of Great Britain, as subjects for discussion:

1. The forcible seizure of mariners on board of merchant vessels, and the claim of allegiance of His Britannic Majesty upon all the native born subjects of Great Britain.

2. The Indian allies of Great Britain to be included in the pacification, and a boundary to be settled between the dominions of the Indians and those of the United States. Both parts of this point are considered by the British Government as a *sine qua non* to the conclusion of the treaty.

3. The revision of the boundary line between the territories of the United States and those of Great Britain adjoining them, in North America.

4. The fisheries, respecting which the British Government will not allow the people of the United States the privilege of landing and drying fish, within the territorial jurisdiction of Great Britain, without an equivalent.

The American Commissioners were requested to say whether their instructions from their Government authorized them to treat upon these several points; and to state, on their part, such other points as they might be further instructed to propose for discussion.

The meeting was adjourned to Tuesday, the 9th August, on which day the Commissioners met again.

The American Commissioners, at this meeting, stated that, upon the first and third points proposed by the British Commissioners, they were provided with instructions from their Government; and that on the second and fourth of these points, there not having existed heretofore any differences between the two Governments, they had not been anticipated by the Government of the United States, and were, therefore, not provided for in their instructions. That, in relation to an Indian pacification, they knew that the Government of the United States had appointed commissioners to treat of peace with the Indians; and that it was not improbable that peace had been made with them.

The American Commissioners presented, as further points [subjects] considered by the Government of the United States as suitable for discussion—

1. A definition of blockade, and, as far as may be agreed, of other neutral and belligerent rights.

2. Certain claims of indemnity to individuals for captures and seizures preceding and subsequent to the war.

3. They further stated that there were various other points, to which their instructions extended, which might, with propriety, be objects of discussion, either in the negotiation of the peace or in that of a treaty of commerce, which, in the case of a propitious termination of the present conferences, they were likewise authorized to conclude. That, for the purpose of facilitating the first and most essential object of peace, they had discarded every subject which was not considered peculiarly connected with that, and presented only those points which appeared to be immediately relevant to this negotiation.

The American Commissioners expressed their wish to receive from the British Commissioners a statement of the views and objects of Great Britain upon all the points, and their willingness to discuss them all, in order that, if no arrangement could be agreed to upon the points not in their instructions, which would come within the scope of the powers committed to their discretion, the Government of the United States might be put in possession of the entire and precise intentions of that of Great Britain with regard to such points; and that the British Government might be fully informed of the objections, on the part of the United States, to any such arrangement.

They, the American Commissioners, were asked whether, if those of Great Britain should enter further upon the discussion, particularly respecting the Indian boundary, the American Commissioners could expect that it would terminate by some provisional arrangement, which they could conclude, subject to the ratification of their Government?

They answered that, as any arrangement to which they could agree upon the subject must be without specific authority from their Government, it was not possible for them, previous to discussion, to decide whether an article on the subject could be formed which would be mutually satisfactory, and to which they should think themselves, under their discretionary powers, justified in acceding.

The British Commissioners declined entering upon the discussion, unless the American Commissioners would say that they considered it within their discretion to make a provisional arrangement on the subject, conformable to the view of it prescribed by the British Government, and proposed to adjourn the conferences for the purpose of consulting their own Government on this state of things.

The British Commissioners were asked whether it was understood, as an effect of the proposed boundary for the Indians, that the United States would be precluded from the right of purchasing territory from the Indians within that boundary, by amicable treaty with the Indians themselves, without the consent of Great Britain? And whether it was understood to operate as a restriction upon the Indians for selling, by such amicable treaties, lands to the United States, as has been hitherto practised?

They answered, that it was understood that the Indian territories should be a barrier between the British possessions and those of the United States; that the United States and Great Britain should both be restricted from such purchases of lands; but that the Indians would not be restricted from selling them to any third party.

The meeting was then adjourned to Wednesday, 10th August.

C. HUGHES, Jr.,
Secretary to the Mission Extraordinary.

Protocol of Conference, August 8, 1814.

The British and American Commissioners having met, their full powers were respectively produced, which were found satisfactory, and copies thereof were exchanged.

The British Commissioners stated the following subjects, as those upon which it appeared to them that the discussions between themselves and the American Commissioners would be likely to turn:

1st. The forcible seizure of mariners from on board merchant ships on the high seas, and, in connexion with it, the right of the King of Great Britain to the allegiance of all his native subjects.

2d. That the peace be extended to the Indian allies of Great Britain, and that the boundary of their territory be definitively marked out as a permanent barrier between the dominions of Great Britain and the United States. An arrangement on this subject to be a *sine qua non* of a Treaty of Peace.

3d. A revision of the boundary line between the British and American Territories, with the view to prevent future uncertainty and dispute.

The British Commissioners requested information whether the American Commissioners were instructed to enter into negotiation on the above points. But, before they desired any answer, they felt it right to communicate the intentions of their Government as to the North American fisheries, viz: that the British Government did not intend to grant to the United States, gratuitously, the privileges formerly granted by treaty to them, of fishing within the limits of the British sovereignty, and of using the shores of the British territories for purposes connected with the fisheries.

AUGUST 9.

The meeting being adjourned to the 9th August, the Commissioners met again on that day.

The American Commissioners at this meeting stated that, upon the first and third points proposed by the British Commissioners, they were provided with instructions from their Government; and that the second and fourth of these points were not provided for in their instructions. That, in relation to an Indian pacification, they knew that the Government of the United States had appointed Commissioners to treat of peace with the Indians, and that it was not improbable peace had been made with them.

The American Commissioners presented, as further subjects considered by the Government of the United States as suitable for discussion—

1st. A definition of blockade, and, as far as may be agreed, of other neutral and belligerent rights.

2d. Certain claims of indemnity to individuals for captures and seizures preceding and subsequent to the war.

3d. They further stated that there were various other points to which their instructions extended, which might, with propriety, be objects of discussion, either in the negotiation of the peace, or in that of a treaty of commerce, which, in the case of a propitious termination of the present conferences, they were likewise authorized to conclude. That, for the purpose of facilitating the first and most essential object of peace, they had discarded every subject which was not considered as peculiarly connected with that, and presented only those points which appeared to be immediately relevant to this negotiation.

The American Commissioners expressed their wish to receive from the British Commissioners a statement of the views and objects of Great Britain upon all the points, and their willingness to discuss them all.

They, the American Commissioners, were asked whether, if those of Great Britain should enter further upon this discussion, particularly respecting the Indian boundary, the American Commissioners could expect that it would terminate by some provisional arrangement which they could conclude, subject to the ratification of their Government.

They answered that, as any arrangement to which they could agree upon the subject must be without specific authority from their Government, it was not possible for them, previous to the discussion, to decide whether any article on the subject could be formed which would be mutually satisfactory, and to which they should think themselves, under their discretionary powers, justified in acceding.

The meeting was adjourned.

True copy:

           C. HUGHES, Jr.,
           Secretary of Legation.

Messrs. Adams, Bayard, Clay, Russell, and Gallatin, to Mr. Monroe, Secretary of State.

GHENT, *August* 19, 1814.

SIR: Mr. Baker, secretary to the British mission, called upon us to-day at one o'clock, and invited us to a conference to be held at three. This was agreed to; and the British Commissioners opened it by saying that they had received their further instructions this morning, and had not lost a moment in requesting a meeting for the purpose of communicating the decision of their Government. It is proper to notice that Lord Castlereagh had arrived last night in this city, whence, it is said, he will depart to-morrow, on his way to Brussels and Vienna.

The British Commissioners stated that their Government had felt some surprise that we were not instructed respecting the Indians, as it could not have been expected that they would leave their allies in their comparatively weak situation, exposed to our resentment. Great Britain might justly have supposed that the American Government would have furnished us with instructions, authorizing us to agree to a positive article on the subject; but the least she could demand was, that we should sign a provisional article, admitting the principle, subject to the ratification of our Government, so that if it should be ratified the treaty should take effect; and if not, that it should be null and void. On our assent or refusal to admit such an article, would depend the continuance or suspension of the negotiation.

As we had represented that the proposition made by them on that subject was not sufficiently explicit, their Government had directed them to give us every necessary explanation, and to state distinctly the basis which must be considered as an indispensable preliminary.

It was a *sine qua non* that the Indians should be included in the pacification, and, as incident thereto, that the boundaries of their territory should be permanently established. Peace with the Indians was a subject so simple as to require

no comment. With respect to the boundaries which were to divide their territory *from that* of the United States, the object of the British Government was, that the Indians should remain as a permanent barrier between our western settlements and the adjacent British provinces, to prevent them from being conterminous to each other; and that neither the United States nor Great Britain should ever hereafter have the right to purchase or acquire any part of the territory thus recognised as belonging to the Indians. With regard to the extent of the Indian territory and the boundary line, the British Government would propose the lines of the Greenville Treaty as a proper basis, subject, however, to discussion and modifications.

We stated that the Indian territory, according to these lines, would comprehend a great number of American citizens; not less, perhaps, than a hundred thousand; and asked what was the intention of the British Government respecting them, and under whose Government they would fall? It was answered that those settlements would be taken into consideration when the line became a subject of discussion; but that such of the inhabitants as would ultimately be *included* within the Indian Territory must make *their own* arrangements, and provide for themselves.

The British Commissioners here said that, considering the importance of the question we had to decide, (that of agreeing to a provisional article) their Government had thought that we should also be fully informed of its views with respect to the proposed revision of the boundary line between the dominions of Great Britain and the United States.

1st. Experience had proved that the joint possession of the Lakes, and a right common to both nations to keep up a naval force on them, necessarily produced collisions, and rendered peace insecure. As Great Britain could not be supposed to expect to make conquests in that quarter, and as that province was essentially weaker than the United States, and exposed to invasion, it was necessary for its security that Great Britain should require that the United States should hereafter keep no armed naval force on the western lakes from Lake Ontario to Lake Superior, both inclusive; that they should not erect any fortified or military post or establishment on the shores of those lakes; and that they should not maintain those which were already existing. This *must*, they said, be considered as a moderate demand, since Great Britain, if she had not disclaimed the intention of any increase of territory might, with propriety, have asked a cession of the adjacent American shores. The commercial navigation and intercourse would be left on the same footing as heretofore. It was expressly stated (in answer to a question we asked) that Great Britain was to retain the right of having an armed naval force on those lakes, and of holding military posts and establishments on their shores.

2d. The boundary line west of Lake Superior, and thence to the Mississippi, to be revised; and the treaty-right of Great Britain to the naviga-

Relations with Great Britain.

tion of the Mississippi to be continued. When asked whether they did not mean the line from the Lake of the Woods to the Mississippi? the British Commissioners repeated, that they meant the line from Lake Superior to that river.

3d. A direct communication from Halifax, and the Province of New Brunswick, to Quebec, to be secured to Great Britain. In answer to our question, in what manner this was to be effected, we were told that it must be done by a cession to Great Britain of that portion of the District of Maine, in the State of Massachusetts, which intervenes between New Brunswick and Quebec, and prevents the direct communication.

Reverting to the proposed provisional article respecting the Indian pacification and boundary, the British Commissioners concluded by stating to us, that if the conferences should be suspended by our refusal to agree to such an article, without having obtained further instructions from our Government, Great Britain would not consider herself bound to abide by the terms which she now offered, but would be at liberty to vary and regulate her demands according to subsequent events, and in such manner as the state of the war, at the time of renewing the negotiations, might warrant.

We asked whether the statement made respecting the proposed revision of the boundary line between the United States and the dominions of Great Britain embraced all the objects she meant to bring forward for discussion, and what were particularly her views with respect to Moose Island, and such other islands in the bay of Passamaquoddy as had been in our possession till the present war, but had been lately captured? We were answered that those islands, belonging of right to Great Britain (as much so, one of the Commissioners said, as Northamptonshire,) they would certainly be kept by her, and were not even supposed to be an object of discussion.

From the forcible manner in which the demand that the United States should keep no naval armed force on the Lakes, nor any military posts on their shores, had been brought forward, we were induced to inquire whether this condition was also meant as a *sine qua non?* To this the British Commissioners declined giving a positive answer. They said that they had been sufficiently explicit; that they had given us one *sine qua non,* and, when we had disposed of that, it would be time enough to give us an answer to another.

We then stated that, considering the nature and importance of the communication made this day, we wished the British Commissioners to reduce their proposals to writing before we gave them an answer. This they agreed to, and promised to send us an official note without delay.

We need hardly say, that the demands of Great Britain will receive from us an unanimous and decided negative. We do not deem it necessary to detain the John Adams for the purpose of transmitting to you the official notes which may pass on the subject and close the negotiation. And we have felt it our duty immediately to apprize you, by this hasty but correct sketch of our last conference, that there is not, at present, any hope of peace.

We have the honor to be, sir, with perfect respect, your obedient servants,

JOHN QUINCY ADAMS,
J. A. BAYARD,
H. CLAY,
JONATHAN RUSSELL,
ALBERT GALLATIN.

P. S. August 20, 1814.—We have this moment received the note of the British Commissioners, which had been promised to us, bearing date yesterday, a copy of which we have the honor to enclose.

Note of the British Commissioners.

GHENT, *August* 19, 1814.

The undersigned Plenipotentiaries of His Britannic Majesty do themselves the honor of acquainting the Plenipotentiaries of the United States, that they have communicated to their Court the result of the conference which they had the honor of holding with them upon the 9th instant, in which they stated that they were unprovided with any specific instructions as to comprehending the Indian nations in a treaty of peace to be made with Great Britain, and as to defining a boundary to the Indian territory.

The undersigned are instructed to acquaint the Plenipotentiaries of the United States, that His Majesty's Government having, at the outset of the negotiation, with a view to the speedy restoration of peace, reduced, as far as possible, the number of points to be discussed, and having professed themselves willing to forego, on some important topics, any stipulation to the advantage of Great Britain, cannot but feel some surprise that the Government of the United States should not have furnished their Plenipotentiaries with instructions upon those points which could hardly fail to come under discussion.

Under the inability of the American Plenipotentiaries to conclude any article upon the subject of Indian pacification and Indian boundary, which shall bind the Government of the United States, His Majesty's Government conceive that they cannot give a better proof of their sincere desire for the restoration of peace than by professing their willingness to accept a provisional article upon those heads, in the event of the American Plenipotentiaries considering themselves authorized to accede to the general principles upon which such an article ought to be founded. With a view to enable the American Plenipotentiaries to decide how far the conclusion of such an article is within the limit of their general discretion, the undersigned are directed to state fully and distinctly the basis upon which alone Great Britain sees any prospect of advantage in the continuance of the negotiation at the present time.

The undersigned have already had the honor of stating to the American Plenipotentiaries that, in considering the points above referred to as a *sine qua non* of any treaty of peace, the view of the British Government is the permanent tranquillity and security of the Indian nations, and the prevention of those jealousies and irritations to which the frequent alteration of the Indian limits has heretofore given rise. For this purpose it is indispensably necessary that the Indian nations who have been, during the war, in alliance with Great Britain, should, at the termination of the war, be included in the pacification.

It is equally necessary that a definite boundary should be assigned to the Indians, and that the contracting parties should guarantee the integrity of their territory by a mutual stipulation not to acquire, by purchase or otherwise, any territory within the special limits. The British Government are willing to take as the basis of an article on this subject those stipulations of the Treaty of Greenville, subject to modifications, which relate to a boundary line.

As the undersigned are desirous of stating every point in connexion with the subject which may reasonably influence the decision of the American Plenipotentiaries in the exercise of their discretion, they avail themselves of this opportunity to repeat what they have already stated, Great Britain desires the revision of the frontier between her North American dominions and those of the United States, not with any view to an acquisition of territory, as such, but for the purpose of securing her possessions and preventing future disputes.

The British Government consider the lakes from Lake Ontario to Lake Superior, both inclusive, to be the natural military frontier of the British possessions in North America. As the weaker Power on the North American continent, the least capable of acting offensively, and the most exposed to sudden invasion, Great Britain considers the military occupation of these lakes as necessary to the security of her dominions. A boundary line equally dividing these waters, with a right in each nation to arm, both upon the lakes and upon their shores, is calculated to create a contest for naval ascendency in peace as well as in war. The Power which occupies these lakes should, as a necessary result, have the military occupation of both shores. In furtherance of this object, the British Government is prepared to propose a boundary. But as this might be misconstrued as an intention to extend their possessions to the southward of the lakes, (which is by no means the object they have in view,) they are disposed to leave the territorial limits undisturbed, and as incident to them, the free commercial navigation of the lakes, provided that the American Government will stipulate not to maintain or construct any fortifications upon, or within, a limited distance of the shores, or maintain or construct any armed vessels upon the lakes in question, or in the rivers which empty themselves into the same.

If this can be adjusted, there will then remain for discussion the arrangement of the Northwestern boundary between Lake Superior and the Mississippi, the free navigation of that river, and such a variation of the line of frontier as may secure a direct communication between Quebec and Halifax.

The undersigned trust that the full statement which they have made of the views and objects of the British Government, in requiring the pacification of the Indian nations, and a permanent limit to their territories, will enable the American Plenipotentiaries to conclude a provisional article upon the basis above stated. Should they feel it necessary to refer to the Government of the United States for further instructions, the undersigned feel it incumbent upon them to acquaint the American Plenipotentiaries that their Government cannot be precluded by anything that has passed, from varying the terms at present proposed, in such a manner as the state of the war, at the time of resuming the conferences, may, in their judgment, render advisable.

The undersigned avail themselves of this occasion to renew to the Plenipotentiaries of the United States the assurance of their high consideration.

GAMBIER,
HENRY GOULBURN,
WILLIAM ADAMS.

The Plenipotentiaries of the United States to the Secretary of State.

GHENT, *October 25, 1814.*

SIR: We have the honor of transmitting herewith copies of all our correspondence with the British Plenipotentiaries, since the departure of Mr. Dallas. Although the negotiation has not terminated so abruptly as we expected at that period that it would, we have no reason to retract the opinion which we then expressed, that no hopes of peace, as likely to result from it, could be entertained. It is true, that the terms which the British Government had so peremptorily prescribed at that time have been apparently abandoned, and that the *sine qua non* then required as a preliminary to all discussion upon other topics has been reduced to an article securing merely an Indian pacification, which we have agreed to accept, subject to the ratification or rejection of our Government. But you will perceive that our request for the exchange of a project of a treaty has been eluded, and that, in their last note, the British Plenipotentiaries have advanced a demand not only new and inadmissible, but totally incompatible with their uniform previous declarations that Great Britain had no view in this negotiation to any acquisition of territory. It will be perceived that this new pretension was brought forward immediately after the accounts had been received that a British force had taken possession of all that part of the State of Massachusetts situate east of Penobscot river. The British Plenipotentiaries have invariably referred to their Government every note received from us, and waited the return of their messenger before they have transmitted to us their answer, and the whole tenor of the correspondence, as well as the manner in which it has been conducted on the part of the British Government, have concurred to convince us that their object has been delay; their motives for this policy we presume to have been to keep the alternative of peace, or of a protracted war in their own hands, until the general arrangement of European affairs should be accomplished at the Congress of Vienna, and until they could avail themselves of the advantages which they have anticipated from the success of their arms during the present campaign in America.

Although the Sovereigns who had determined to be present at the Congress of Vienna have been already several weeks assembled there, it does not appear by the last advices from that place that the Congress has been formally opened. On the contrary, by a declaration from the plenipotentiaries of the Powers, who were parties to the peace of Paris of 30th of May last, the opening of the Congress appears to have been postponed to the 1st of November. A memorial is said to have been presented by the French Ambassador, Talleyrand, in which it is declared that France, having returned to her boundaries in 1792, can recognise none of the aggrandizements of the other great Powers of Europe since that period, although not intending to oppose them by war.

These circumstances indicate that the new basis for the political system of Europe will not be so speedily settled as had been expected. The principle thus assumed by France is very extensive in its effects, and opens a field for negotiation much wider than had been anticipated. We think it does not promise an aspect of immediate tranquillity to this Continent, and that it will disconcert particularly the measures which Great Britain has been taking with regard to the future destination of this country, among others, and to which she has attached apparently much importance.

We have the honor to be, with great respect, sir, your very humble servants,

JOHN QUINCY ADAMS,
J. A. BAYARD,
HENRY CLAY,
JONATHAN RUSSELL,
ALBERT GALLATIN.

Hon. JAMES MONROE,
    Secretary of State.

[Referred to in the despatch of October 25, 1814.]
The American to the British Ministers.

GHENT, *August* 24, 1814.

The undersigned Ministers Plenipotentiary and Extraordinary, from the United States of America, have given to the official note which they have had the honor of receiving from His Britannic Majesty's Plenipotentiaries, the deliberate attention which the importance of its contents required, and have now that of transmitting to them their answer on the several points to which it refers.

They would present to the consideration of the British Plenipotentiaries that Lord Castlereagh, in his letter of the 4th November, 1813, to the American Secretary of State, pledges the faith of the British Government, that "they were willing to enter into discussion with the Government of America for the conciliatory adjustment of

the differences subsisting between the two States, with an earnest desire on their part to bring them to a favorable issue, upon principles of perfect reciprocity, not inconsistent with the established maxims of public law, and with the maritime rights of the British empire." This fact alone might suffice to show, that it ought not to have been expected that the American Government, in acceding to this proposition, should have exceeded its terms, and furnished the undersigned with instructions authorizing them to treat with the British Plenipotentiaries respecting the Indians situated within the boundaries of the United States. That such expectation was not entertained by the British Government might also have been inferred from the explicit assurances which the British Plenipotentiaries gave on the part of their Government, at the first conference which the undersigned had the honor of holding with them, that no events subsequent to the first proposals for this negotiation had, in any manner, varied either the disposition of the British Government, that it might terminate in a peace honorable to both parties, or the terms upon which they would be willing to conclude it.

It is well known that the differences which unhappily subsisted between Great Britain and the United States, and which ultimately led to the present war, were wholly of a maritime nature, arising principally from the British Orders in Council in relation to blockades, and from the impressment of mariners on board of American vessels. The boundary of the Indian territory had never been a subject of difference between the two countries. Neither the principles of reciprocity, the maxims of public law, nor the maritime rights of the British empire, could require the permanent establishment of such boundary. The novel pretensions now advanced could no more have been anticipated by the Government of the United States, in forming instructions for this negotiation, than they seem to have been contemplated by that of Great Britain in November last in proposing it. Lord Castlereagh's note makes the termination of the war to depend on a conciliatory adjustment of the differences then subsisting between the two States, and on no other condition whatever.

Nor could the American Government have foreseen that Great Britain, in order to obtain peace for the Indians residing within the dominions of the United States, whom she had induced to take part with her in the war, would demand that they should be made parties to the treaty between the two nations; or that the boundaries of their lands should be permanently and irrevocably fixed by that treaty. Such a proposition is contrary to the acknowledged principles of public law, and to the practice of all civilized nations, particularly of Great Britain and of the United States. It is not founded on reciprocity; it is unnecessary for the attainment of the object which it professes to have in view.

No maxim of public law has hitherto been more universally established among the Powers of Europe possessing territories in America, and

The British Plenipotentiaries consider the undersigned as having declared "that the United States will admit of no line of boundary between their territory and that of the Indian nations, because the natural growth and population of the United States would be thereby arrested." The undersigned, on the contrary, expressly stated in their last note, "that the lands inhabited by the Indians were secured to them by boundaries defined in amicable treaties between them and the United States;" but they did refuse to assign, in a treaty of peace with Great Britain, a definitive and permanent boundary to the Indians living within the limits of the United States. On this subject the undersigned have no hesitation in avowing that the United States, while intending never to acquire lands from the Indians otherwise than peaceably, and with their free consent, are fully determined, in that manner, progressively, and in proportion as their growing population may require, to reclaim from that state of nature, and to bring into cultivation every portion of the territory contained within their acknowledged boundaries. In thus providing for the support of millions of civilized beings, they will not violate any dictate of justice or of humanity; for they will not only give to the few thousand savages scattered over that territory an ample equivalent for any right they may surrender, but will always leave them the possession of lands more than they can cultivate, and more than adequate to their subsistence, comfort, and enjoyment, by cultivation. If this be a spirit of aggrandizement, the undersigned are prepared to admit, in that sense, its existence; but they must deny that it affords the slightest proof of an intention not to respect the boundaries between them and European nations, or of a desire to encroach upon the territories of Great Britain. If, in the progress of their increasing population, the American people must grow in strength proportioned to their number, the undersigned will hope that Great Britain, far from repining at the prospect, will contemplate it with satisfaction. They will not suppose that that Government will avow, as the basis of their policy towards the United States, the system of arresting their natural growth within their own territories, for the sake of preserving a perpetual desert for savages. If Great Britain has made sacrifices to give repose to the civilized world in Europe, no sacrifice is required from her by the United States to complete the work of general pacification. This negotiation at least evinces on their part no disposition to claim any other right than that of preserving their independence entire, and of governing their own territories without foreign interference.

Of the two proclamations, purported copies of which the British Plenipotentiaries have thought proper to enclose with their last note, the undersigned might content themselves with remarking that neither of them is the act of the American Government. They are enabled, however, to add, with perfect confidence, that neither of them was authorized or approved by the Government. The undersigned are not disposed to consider as the act of the British Government the proclamation of Admiral Cochrane, herewith enclosed, exciting a portion of the population of the United States, under the promise of military employment, or of free settlement in the West Indies, to treachery and rebellion. The undersigned very sincerely regret to be obliged to say, that an irresistible mass of evidence, consisting principally of the correspondence of British officers and agents, part only of which has already been published in America, establishes beyond all rational doubt the fact that a constant system of excitement to those hostilities was pursued by the British traders and agents, who had access to the Indians, not only without being discountenanced, but with frequent encouragement by the British authorities; and that, if they ever dissuaded the Indians from commencing hostilities, it was only by urging them, as in prudence, to suspend their attacks until Great Britain could recognise them as her allies in the war.

When, in the conference of the 9th ultimo, the undersigned invited discussion upon the proposal of Indian pacification and boundary, as well as upon all the subjects presented by the British Plenipotentiaries for discussion, they expressly stated their motives to be—1st, to ascertain, by discussion, whether an article on the subject could be formed, to which they could subscribe, and which would be satisfactory to the British Plenipotentiaries; and, 2dly, that, if no such article could be formed, the American Government might be informed of the views of Great Britain upon that point, and the British Government of the objections, on the part of the United States, to any such arrangement. The undersigned have, in fact, already proposed no less than three articles on the subject, all of which they view as better calculated to secure peace and tranquillity to the Indians, than any of the proposals for that purpose made by the British Plenipotentiaries.

The undersigned had repeated their assurances to the British Plenipotentiaries that peace, so far as it depended on the United States, would immediately follow a peace with Great Britain; and added, that the Indians would thereby be reinstated in the same situation in which they stood before the commencement of hostilities. The British Plenipotentiaries insist, in their last note, that the Indian nations shall be included in the Treaty of Peace between Great Britain and the United States, and be restored to all the rights, privileges, and territories which they enjoyed in the year 1811, previous to their commencement of the war, by virtue of the Treaty of Greenville, and the treaties subsequently concluded between them and the United States. Setting aside the subject of boundary, which is presented as for discussion only, there is no apparent difference with respect to the object in view, the pacification and tranquillity of the Indians, and placing them in the same situation in which they stood before the war; all which will be equally obtained in the manner proposed by the undersigned. And the only point of real difference is, the British Plenipotentiaries insist that it should be done by including the Indians, as allies of Great Britain, in the Treaty of Peace between her and the United States.

The United States cannot consent that Indians residing within their boundaries, as acknowledged by Great Britain, shall be included in the Treaty of Peace in any manner which will recognise them as independent nations, whom Great Britain, having obtained this recognition, would hereafter have the right to consider in every respect as such. Thus, to recognise those Indians as independent and sovereign nations would take from the United States, and transfer to those Indians, all the rights of soil and sovereignty over the territory which they inhabit; and this being accomplished, through the agency of Great Britain, would place them effectually and exclusively under her protection, instead of being, as heretofore, under that of the United States. It is not perceived in what respect such a provision would differ from an absolute cession by the United States of the extensive territory in question.

The British Plenipotentiaries have repeated the assertion that the treaty by which the Indians placed themselves under the protection of the United States was abrogated by the war; and thence infer, that they are no longer to be considered as under the protection of the United States, whatever may be the import of the term, and that the right of Great Britain to interfere in their behalf in the negotiation for peace can only be denied on the ground that they are regarded as subjects. In point of fact, several of the tribes, parties to the Treaty of Greenville, have constantly been, and still are, at peace with the United States. Whether that treaty be or be not abrogated, is a question not necessary now to be discussed. The right of the United States to the protection of the Indians within their boundaries was not acquired by that treaty; it was a necessary consequence of the sovereignty and independence of the United States. Previous to that time, the Indians living within the same territory were under the protection of His Britannic Majesty, as its Sovereign. The undersigned may refer the British Plenipotentiaries to all the acts of their own Government relative to the subject, for proof that it has always considered this right of protection as one of the rights of sovereignty which it needed no Indian treaty to confer, and which the abrogation of no Indian treaty could divest. They will particularly bring to their recollection, that when a similar proposition was made of considering Indian tribes as independent nations, to serve as a barrier between the French and English territories, was made by France to England, it was immediately rejected by a Minister to whom the British nation is accustomed to look back with veneration, and rejected on the express ground that the King would not renounce his right of protection over the Indians within his dominions. But whatever the relation of the Indians to the United States may be, and whether under their protection or not, Great Britain having, by the treaty of 1783, recognised the sovereignty of the United States,

and agreed to certain limits as their boundaries, has no right to consider any persons or communities, whether Indians or others, residing within those boundaries, as nations independent of the United States.

The United States claim, of right, with respect to all European nations, and particularly with respect to Great Britain, the entire sovereignty over the whole territory, and all the persons embraced within the boundaries of their dominions; Great Britain has no right to take cognizance of the relations subsisting between the several communities or persons living therein; they form, as to her, only parts of the dominions of the United States, and it is altogether immaterial whether, or how far, under their political institutions and policy, these communities or persons are independent States, allies, or subjects. With respect to her, and all other foreign nations, they are parts of a whole, of which the United States are the sole and absolute sovereigns.

The allegation of the British Plenipotentiaries that it is inconsistent with the practice or principles of Great Britain to abandon, in her negotiations for peace, those who have co-operated with her in war, is not applicable to the Indians, but on the erroneous assumption of their independence, which, so far as she is concerned, has been fully disproved. And although no power from these tribes to the British Government, to treat in their behalf, would, for the same reason, be admitted by the undersigned, they may nevertheless observe that the British Plenipotentiaries having produced no such powers, having no authority to bind the Indians, to engage for their assent to the pacification, or to secure the continuance of peace on their part, whilst speaking of them as allies, do really propose to treat for them, not as if they were independent nations, but as if they were the subjects of Great Britain. The undersigned, so far from asking that, in relation to the Indians, Great Britain should pursue a course inconsistent with her former practice and principles, only desire that she would follow her own example respecting them, in her former treaties with other European nations, and with the United States. No provision for the Indians is found in the treaty of 1763, by which France ceded Canada to Great Britain, although almost all the Indians living within the territory ceded, or acknowledged to belong to Great Britain, had taken part with France in the war. No such provision was inserted in the Treaty of Peace of 1783, between Great Britain and the United States, although almost all the Indians tribes living within the territory recognised by the treaty to belong to the United States, had, during the war, co-operated with Great Britain, and might have been considered as her allies more justly than on the present occasion. So far as concerns the relations between Great Britain and the United States, these Indians can be treated for only on the principles by which amnesties are stipulated in favor of disaffected persons, who, in times of war and invasion, co-operate with the enemy of the nation to which they belong. To go as far as possible

whole note, so little proof of any disposition on the part of the Government of the United States to enter into an amicable discussion of the several points submitted by the undersigned in their former communication. The undersigned are perfectly aware that, in bringing forward those points for consideration, and stating with so much frankness as they did, the views with which they were proposed, they departed from the usual course of negotiations, by disclosing all the objects of their Government while those which the American Government had in view were withheld; but in so doing they were principally actuated by a sincere desire of bringing the negotiation as soon as possible to a favorable termination, and in some measure, by their willingness to comply with the wishes expressed by the American Plenipotentiaries themselves.

It is perfectly true that the war between His Majesty and the United States was declared by the latter Power, upon the pretence of maritime rights, alleged to be asserted by Great Britain, and disputed by the United States.

If the war thus declared by the United States had been carried on by them for objects purely of a maritime nature, or if the attack which has been made on Canada had been made for the purpose of diversion, or in the way of defence against the British forces in that quarter, any question as to the boundaries of Canada might have been considered as unnecessary; but it is notorious to the whole world that the conquest of Canada, and its permanent annexation to the United States, was the declared object of the American Government. If, in consequence of a different course of events on the continent of Europe His Majesty's Government had been unable to reinforce the British armies in Canada, and the United States had obtained a decided superiority in that quarter, is there any person who doubts that they would have availed themselves of their situation to obtain on the side of Canada important cessions of territory, if not the entire abandonment of the country by Great Britain? Is the American Government to be allowed to pursue, so far as its means will enable it, a system of acquisition and aggrandizement to the extent of annexing entire provinces to their dominions, and is His Majesty to be precluded from availing himself of his means, so far as they will enable him, to retain those points which the valor of British arms may have placed in his power, because they happen to be situated within the territories allotted under former treaties to the Government of the United States?

Such a principle of negotiation was never avowed at any period antecedent to that of the revolutionary Government of France.

If the policy of the United States had been essentially pacific, as the American Plenipotentiaries assert it ought to be, from their political institutions, from the habits of their citizens, and from their physical situation, it might not have been necessary to propose the precautionary provisions now under discussion. That, of late years at least, the American Government have been

influenced by a very different policy, by a spirit of aggrandizement not necessary to their own security, but increasing with the extent of their empire, has been too clearly manifested by their progressive occupation of the Indian territories, by the acquisition of Louisiana, by the more recent attempt to wrest by force of arms from a nation in amity the two Floridas, and, lastly, by the avowed intention of permanently annexing the Canadas to the United States.

If, then, the security of the British North American dominions requires any sacrifices on the part of the United States, they must be ascribed to the declared policy of that Government in making the war not one of self-defence, nor for the redress of grievances, real or pretended, but a part of a system of conquest and aggrandizement.

The British Government, in its present situation, is bound in duty to endeavor to secure its North American dominions against those attempts at conquest which the American Government have avowed to be a principle of their policy, and which, as such, will undoubtedly be renewed whenever any succeeding war shall afford a prospect of renewing them with success.

The British Plenipotentiaries proposed that the military possession of the lakes from Lake Ontario to Lake Superior should be secured to Great Britain, because the command of those lakes would afford to the American Government the means of commencing a war in the heart of Canada, and because the command of them, on the part of Great Britain, has been shown, by experience, to be attended with no insecurity to the United States.

When the relative strength of the two Powers in North America is considered, it should be recollected that the British dominions in that quarter do not contain a population of five hundred thousand souls, whereas the territory of the United States contains a population of more than seven millions; that the naval resources of the United States are at hand for attack, and the naval resources of Great Britain are on the other side of the Atlantic.

The military possession of those lakes is not, therefore, necessary for the protection of the United States.

The proposal for allowing the territories on the southern banks of the lakes above mentioned to remain in the possession of the Government of the United States, provided no fortifications should be erected on the shores, and no armament permitted on the waters, has been made for the purpose of manifesting that security, and not acquisition of territory, is the object of the British Government, and that they have no desire to throw obstacles in the way of any commerce which the people of the United States may be desirous of carrying on upon the Lakes, in time of peace.

The undersigned, with the anxious wish to rectify all misunderstanding, have thus more fully explained the grounds upon which they brought forward the propositions contained in their former note, respecting the boundaries of the British dominions in North America.

They do not wish to insist upon them beyond what the circumstances may fairly require. They are ready amicably to discuss the details of them, with a view to the adoption of any modifications which the American Plenipotentiaries, or their Government, may have to suggest, if they are not incompatible with the object itself.

With respect to the boundary of the District of Maine, and that of the Northwestern frontier of the United States, the undersigned were not prepared to anticipate the objections contained in the note of the American Plenipotentiaries, "that they were instructed to treat for the revision of their boundary lines," with the statement which they have subsequently made, that they had no authority to cede any part, however insignificant, of the territory of the United States; although the proposal left it open to them to demand an equivalent for such cession, either in frontier or otherwise.

The American Plenipotentiaries must be aware that the boundary of the District of Maine has never been correctly ascertained; that the one asserted at present by the American Government, by which the direct communication between Halifax and Quebec becomes interrupted, was not in contemplation of the British Plenipotentiaries who concluded the treaty of 1783; and that the greater part of the territory in question is actually unoccupied.

The undersigned are persuaded that an arrangement on this point might be easily made, if entered into with the spirit of conciliation, without any prejudice to the interests of the district in question.

As the necessity for fixing some boundary for the Northwestern frontier has been mutually acknowledged, a proposal for a discussion on that subject cannot be considered as a demand for a cession of territory, unless the United States are prepared to assert that there is no limit to their territory in that direction, and, that availing themselves of the geographical error upon which that part of the treaty of 1783 was formed, they will acknowledge no boundary whatever; then, unquestionably, any proposition to fix one, be it what it may, must be considered as demanding a large cession of territory from the United States.

Is the American Government prepared to assert such an unlimited right, so contrary to the evident intention of the treaty itself? Or, is His Majesty's Government to understand that the American Plenipotentiaries are willing to acknowledge the boundary from the Lake of the Woods to the Mississippi, (the arrangement made by a convention in 1803, but not ratified,) as that by which their Government is ready to abide?

The British Plenipotentiaries are instructed to accept favorably such a proposition, or to discuss any other line of boundary which may be submitted for consideration.

It is with equal astonishment and regret the undersigned find that the American Plenipotentiaries have not only declined signing any provisional article by which the Indian nations who have taken part with Great Britain in the present contest may be included in the peace, and may have a boundary assigned to them, but have also thought proper to express surprise at any proposition on the subject having been advanced.

The American Plenipotentiaries state that their Government could not have expected such a discussion, and appear resolved at once to reject any proposition on this head, representing it as a demand contrary to the acknowledged principles of public law, tantamount to a cession of one-third of the territorial dominions of the United States, and required to be admitted without discussion.

The proposition which is thus represented is, that the Indian nations which have been, during the war, in alliance with Great Britain, should, at its termination, be included in the pacification, and with a view to their permanent tranquillity and security, that the British Government is willing to take as a basis of an article on the subject of a boundary for those nations, the stipulations which the American Government contracted in 1795, subject, however, to modifications.

After the declaration publicly made to these Indian nations by the Governor General of Canada, that Great Britain would not desert them, could the American Government really persuade itself that no proposition relating to those nations would be advanced; and did Lord Castlereagh's note of the 4th of November, 1813, imply so great a sacrifice of honor, or exclude from discussion every subject excepting what immediately related to the maritime questions referred to in it?

When the undersigned assured the American Plenipotentiaries of the anxious wish of the British Government that the negotiation might terminate in a peace honorable to both parties, it could not have been imagined that the American Plenipotentiaries would thence conclude that His Majesty's Government was prepared to abandon the Indian nations to their fate; nor could it have been foreseen that the American Government would have considered it as derogatory to its honor to admit a proposition by which the tranquillity of those nations might be secured.

The British Plenipotentiaries have yet to learn that it is contrary to the acknowledged principles of public law to include allies in a negotiation for peace, or that it is contrary to the practice of all civilized nations to propose that a provision should be made for their future security.

The Treaty of Greenville established the boundaries between the United States and the Indian nations. The American Plenipotentiaries must be aware that the war, which has since broken out, has abrogated that treaty. Is it contrary to the established principles of public law for the British Government to propose, on behalf of its allies, that this treaty shall, on the pacification, be considered subject to such modifications as the case may render necessary? Or is it unreasonable to propose that this stipulation should be amended; and that, on that foundation, some arrangement should be made which would provide for the existence of a neutral Power between

Great Britain and the United States, calculated to secure to both a longer continuance of the blessings of peace?

So far was that specific proposition respecting the Indian boundaries from being insisted upon in the note, or in the conference which preceded it, as one to be admitted without discussion, that it would have been difficult to use terms of greater latitude, or which appeared more adapted not only not to preclude but to invite discussion.

If the basis proposed could convey away one-third of the territory of the United States, the American Government itself must have conveyed it away by the Greenville Treaty of 1795.

It is impossible to read that treaty without remarking how inconsistent the present pretensions of the American Government are with its preamble and provisions. The boundary lines between the lands of the United States and that of the Indian nations are therein expressly defined. The general character of the treaty is that of a treaty with independent nations; and the very stipulation which the American Plenipotentiaries refer to, that the Indian nations should sell their lands only to the United States, tends to prove that, but for that stipulation, the Indians had a general right to dispose of them. The American Government has now, for the first time, in effect declared that all Indian nations within its line of demarcation are its subjects, living there upon sufferance on lands which it also claims the exclusive right of acquiring, thereby menacing the final extinction of those nations.

Against such a system the undersigned must formally protest. The undersigned repeat, that the terms on which the proposition has been made for assigning to the Indian nations some boundary, manifest no unwillingness to discuss any other proposition directed to the same object, or even a modification of that which is offered. Great Britain is ready to enter into the same engagements with respect to the Indians living within her line of demarcation, as that which is proposed to the United States. It can, therefore, only be from a complete misapprehension of the proposition that it can be represented as being not reciprocal. Neither can it, with any truth, be represented as contrary to the acknowledged principles of public law, as derogatory to the honor, or inconsistent with the rights of the American Government, nor as a demand required to be admitted without discussion.

After this full exposition of the sentiments of His Majesty's Government on the points above stated, it will be for the American Plenipotentiaries to determine whether they are ready now to continue the negotiations, whether they are disposed to refer to their Government for further instructions, or, lastly, whether they will take upon themselves the responsibility of breaking off the negotiation altogether.

The undersigned request the American Plenipotentiaries to accept the assurance of their high consideration.
         GAMBIER,
         HENRY GOULBURN,
         WILLIAM ADAMS.

From the American to the British Ministers.

GHENT, *September 9, 1814.*

The undersigned have had the honor to receive the note of His Britannic Majesty's Plenipotentiaries, dated the 4th instant. If, in the tone or substance of the former note of the undersigned, the British Commissioners have perceived little proof of any disposition, on the part of the American Government, for a discussion of some of the propositions advanced in the first note, which the undersigned had the honor of receiving from them, they will ascribe it to the nature of the propositions themselves; to their apparent incompatibility with the assurances in Lord Castlereagh's letter to the American Secretary of State, proposing this negotiation, and with the solemn assurances of the British Plenipotentiaries themselves, to the undersigned, at their first conferences with them.

The undersigned, in reference to an observation of the British Plenipotentiaries, must be allowed to say that the objects which the Government of the United States had in view have not been withheld.

The subjects considered as suitable for discussion were fairly brought forward in the conference of the 9th ultimo, and the terms on which the United States were willing to conclude the peace were frankly and expressly declared in the note of the undersigned dated the 24th ultimo. It had been confidently hoped that the nature of those terms, so evidently framed in a sincere spirit of conciliation, would have induced Great Britain to adopt them as the basis of a treaty; and it is with deep regret that the undersigned, if they have rightly understood the meaning of the last note of the British Plenipotentiaries, perceive that they still insist on the exclusive military possession of the Lakes, and on a permanent boundary and independent territory for the Indians residing within the dominions of the United States.

The first demand is grounded on the supposition that the American Government has manifested, by its proceedings towards Spain, by the acquisition of Louisiana, by purchases of Indian lands, and by an avowed intention of permanently annexing the Canadas to the United States, a spirit of aggrandizement and conquest which justifies the demand of extraordinary sacrifices from them to provide for the security of the British possessions in America.

In the observations which the undersigned felt it their duty to make on the new demands of the British Government, they confined their animadversions to the nature of the demands themselves; they did not seek for illustrations of the policy of Great Britain in her conduct, in various quarters of the globe, towards other nations, for she was not accountable to the United States. Yet, the undersigned will say that their Government has ever been ready to arrange, in the most amicable manner with Spain, the questions respecting the boundaries of Louisiana and Florida, and that of indemnities acknowledged by Spain due to American citizens. How the peaceable acquisition of

Louisiana. or the purchase of lands within the acknowledged territories of the United States, both made by fair and voluntary treaties for satisfactory equivalents, can be ascribed to a spirit of conquest dangerous to their neighbors, the undersigned are altogether at a loss to understand.

Nor has the conquest of Canada, and its permanent annexation to the United States, been the declared object of their Government. From the commencement of the war to the present time the American Government has been always willing to make peace, without obtaining any cession of territory, and on the sole condition that the maritime questions might be satisfactorily arranged. Such was their disposition in the month of July, 1812, when they instructed Mr. Russell to make the proposal of an armistice; in the month of October of the same year, when Mr. Monroe answered Admiral Warren's proposal to the same effect; in April, 1813, when instructions were given to three of the undersigned, then appointed to treat of peace, under the mediation of Russia; and in January, 1814, when the instructions, under which the undersigned are now acting, were prepared.

The proposition of the British Plenipotentiaries is, that, in order to secure the frontier of Canada against attack, the United States should leave their own without defence; and it seems to be forgotten, that if their superior population and the proximity of their resources give them any advantage in that quarter, it is balanced by the great difference between the Military Establishments of the two nations. No sudden invasion of Canada by the United States could be made, without leaving on their Atlantic shores and on the ocean, exposed to the great superiority of British force, a mass of American property more valuable than Canada. In her relative superior force to that of the United States, in every other quarter, Great Britain may find a pledge much more efficacious for the safety of a single vulnerable point than in stipulations ruinous to the interests and degrading to the honor of America. The best security for the possessions of both countries will, however, be found in an equal and solid peace, in a mutual respect for the rights of each other, and in the cultivation of a friendly understanding between them. If there be any source of jealousy in relation to Canada itself, it will be found to exist solely in the undue interference of traders and agents, which may be easily removed by proper restraints.

The only American forts on the Lakes known to have been, at the commencement of the negotiation, held by British force, are Michilimackinac and Niagara. As the United States were at the same time in possession of Amherstburg and the adjacent country, it is not perceived that the mere occupation of these two forts could give any claim to His Britannic Majesty to large concessions of territory, founded upon the right of conquest; and the undersigned may be permitted to add, that, even if the chances of war should yield to the British arms a momentary possession of other parts of the territories of the United States,

such events would not alter their views with regard to the terms of peace to which they would give their consent. Without recurring to examples drawn from the revolutionary Governments of France, or to a more recent and illustrious triumph of fortitude in adversity, they have been taught by their own history that the occupation of their principal cities should produce no despondency, nor induce their submission to the dismemberment of their empire, or to the abandonment of any one of the rights which constitute a part of their national independence.

The general position that it was consistent with the principles of public law, and with the practice of civilized nations, to include allies in a treaty of peace, and to provide for their security, never was called in question by the undersigned. But they have denied the right of Great Britain, according to those principles and to her own practice, to interfere in any manner with Indian tribes residing within the territories of the United States, as acknowledged by herself, to consider such tribes as her allies, or to treat for them with the United States. They will not repeat the facts and arguments already brought forward by them in support of this position, and which remain unanswered. The observations made by the British Plenipotentiaries on the Treaty of Greenville, and their assertion that the United States now, for the first time, deny the absolute independence of the Indian tribes, and claim the exclusive right of purchasing their lands, require however some notice.

If the United States had now asserted that the Indians within their boundaries, who have acknowledged the United States as their only protectors, were their subjects, living only at sufferance on their lands, far from being the first in making that assertion, they would only have followed the example of the principles uniformly and invariably asserted in substance, and frequently avowed in express terms, by the British Government itself. What was the meaning of all the colonial charters granted by the British monarchs, from that of Virginia, by Elizabeth, to that of Georgia, by the immediate predecessor of the present King, if the Indians were the sovereigns and proprietors of the lands bestowed by those charters? What was the meaning of that article in the Treaty of Utrecht, by which the Five Nations were described in terms as subject to the dominion of Great Britain? Or that of the treaty with the Cherokees, by which it was declared that the King of Great Britain granted them the privilege to live where they pleased, if those subjects were independent sovereigns, and if these tenants, at the license of the British King, were the rightful lords of the land where he granted them permission to live? What was the meaning of that proclamation of his present Britannic Majesty, issued in 1763, declaring all purchases of lands from the Indians null and void, unless made by treaties held under the sanction of His Majesty's Government, if the Indians had the right to sell their lands to whom they pleased? What was the meaning of boundary lines of

American territories, in all the treaties of Great Britain with other European Powers having American possessions, particularly in the treaty of 1763, by which she acquired from France the sovereignty and possession of the Canadas; in her Treaty of Peace with the United States of 1783; nay, what is the meaning of the Northwestern boundary line now proposed by the British Commissioners themselves, if it is the rightful possession and sovereignty of independent Indians of which these boundaries dispose? Is it, indeed, necessary to ask whether Great Britain ever has permitted, or would permit, any foreign nation, or, without her consent, any of her subjects, to acquire lands from the Indians, in the territories of the Hudson's Bay Company, or in Canada? In formally protesting against this system, it is not against a novel pretension of the American Government, it is against the most solemn acts of their own Sovereigns, against the royal proclamations, charters, and treaties of Great Britain for more than two centuries, from the first settlement of North America to the present day, that the British Plenipotentiaries protest.

From the rigor of this system, however, as practised by Great Britain and all the other European Powers in America, the humane and liberal policy of the United States has voluntarily relaxed. A celebrated writer on the law of nations, to whose authority British jurists have taken particular satisfaction in appealing, after stating, in the most explicit manner, the legitimacy of colonial settlements in America, to the exclusion of all rights of uncivilized Indian tribes, has taken occasion to praise the first settlers of New England, and the founder of Pennsylvania, in having purchased of the Indians the lands they resolved to cultivate, notwithstanding their being furnished with a charter from their Sovereign. It is this example which the United States, since they became by their independence the sovereigns of the territory, have adopted and organized into a political system. Under that system the Indians residing within the United States are so far independent that they live under their own customs, and not under the laws of the United States; that their rights upon the lands where they inhabit or hunt, are secured to them by boundaries defined in amicable treaties between the United States and themselves; and that whenever those boundaries are varied, it is also by amicable and voluntary treaties, by which they receive from the United States ample compensation for every right they have to the lands ceded by them. They are so far dependent as not to have the right to dispose of their lands to any private persons, nor to any Power other than the United States, and to be under their protection alone, and not under that of any other Power. Whether called subjects, or by whatever name designated, such is the relation between them and the United States. That relation is neither asserted now for the first time, nor did it originate with the Treaty of Greenville. These principles have been uniformly recognised by the Indians themselves, not only by that treaty, but in all the other previous as well

as subsequent treaties between them and the United States.

The Treaty of Greenville neither took from the Indians the right, which they had not, of *selling* lands within the jurisdiction of the United States to foreign Governments or subjects, nor ceded to them the right of exercising exclusive jurisdiction within the boundary line assigned. It was merely declaratory of the public law, in relation to the parties, founded on principles previously and universally recognised. If left to the United States, the rights of exercising sovereignty and of acquiring soil bears no analogy to the proposition of Great Britain, which requires the abandonment of both.

The British Plenipotentiaries state, in their last note, that Great Britain is ready to enter into the same engagements, with respect to the Indians living within her line of demarcation, as that which is proposed to the United States. The undersigned will not dwell on the immense inequality of value between the two territories, which, under such an arrangement, would be assigned by each nation respectively to the Indians, and which alone would make the reciprocity merely nominal. The condition which would be thus imposed on Great Britain, not to acquire lands in Canada from the Indians, would be *productive* of no advantage to the United States, and is, therefore, no equivalent for the sacrifice required of them. They do not consider that it belongs to the United States in any respect to interfere with the concerns of Great Britain in her American possessions, or with her towards the Indians residing there; and they cannot consent to any interference on the part of Great Britain with their own concerns, and particularly with the Indians living within their territories. It may be the interest of Great Britain to limit her settlements in Canada to their present extent, and to leave the country to the West a perpetual wilderness, to be forever inhabited by scattered tribes of hunters; but it would inflict a vital injury on the United States to have a line run through their territory, beyond which their settlements should forever be precluded from extending; thereby arresting the natural growth of their population and strength; placing the Indians substantially, by virtue of the proposed guarantee, under the protection of Great Britain; dooming them to perpetual barbarism, and leaving an extensive frontier forever exposed to their savage incursions.

With respect to the mere question of peace with the Indians, the undersigned have already explicitly assured the British Plenipotentiaries that, so far as it depended on the United States, it would immediately and necessarily follow a peace with Great Britain. If this be her sole object, no provision in the treaty to that effect is necessary. Provided the Indians will now consent to it, peace will immediately be made with them, and they will be reinstated in the same situation in which they stood before the commencement of hostilities. Should a continuance of the war compel the United States to alter their policy towards the Indians who may still take the part of Great Britain, they alone must be responsible for the consequences of her own act, in having induced them to withdraw themselves from the protection of the United States. The employment of savages, whose known rule of warfare is the indiscriminate torture and butchery of women, children, and prisoners, is itself a departure from the principles of humanity observed between all civilized and Christian nations, even in war. The United States have constantly protested, and still protest, against it, as an unjustifiable aggravation of the calamities and horrors of war. Of the peculiar atrocities of Indian warfare, the allies of Great Britain, in whose behalf she now demands sacrifices of the United States, have during the present war shown many deplorable examples. Among them, the massacre in cold blood of wounded prisoners, and the refusal of the rites of burial to the dead, under the eyes of British officers, who could only plead their inability to control these savage auxiliaries, have been repeated, and are notorious to the world. The United States might at all times have employed the same kind of force against Great Britain, and to a greater extent than it was in her power to employ it against them;. but, from their reluctance to resort to means so abhorrent to the natural feelings of humanity, they abstained from the use of them until compelled to the alternative of employing themselves Indians, who would otherwise have been drawn into the ranks of their enemies. The undersigned, suggesting to the British Plenipotentiaries the propriety of an article by which Great Britain and the United States should reciprocally stipulate never hereafter, if they should be again at war, to employ savages in it, believe that it would be infinitely more honorable to the humanity and Christian temper of both parties, more advantageous to the Indians themselves, and better adapted to secure their permanent peace, tranquillity, and progressive civilization, than the boundary proposed by the British Plenipotentiaries.

With regard to the cession of a part of the District of Maine, as to which the British Plenipotentiaries are unable to reconcile the objections made by the undersigned with their previous declaration, they have the honor to observe, that, at the conference of the 8th ultimo, the British Plenipotentiaries stated, as one of the subjects suitable for discussion, a revision of the boundary line between the British and American territories, with a view to prevent uncertainty and dispute; and that it was on the point thus stated that the undersigned declared that they were provided with instructions from their Government; a declaration which did not imply that they were instructed to make any cession of territory in any quarter, or to agree to a revision of the line, or to any exchange of territory, where no uncertainty or dispute existed.

The undersigned perceive no uncertainty or matter of doubt in the treaty of 1783, with respect to that part of the boundary of the District of Maine which would be affected by the proposal of Great Britain on that subject. They never have understood that the British Plenipotentiaries who signed that treaty had contemplated a boundary different from that fixed by the treaty, and which requires nothing more, in order to be definitely ascertained, than to be surveyed in conformity with its provisions. This subject not having been a matter of uncertainty or dispute, the undersigned are not instructed upon it; and have no authority to cede any part of the State of Massachusetts even for what the British Government might consider a fair equivalent.

In regard to the boundary of the northwestern frontier, so soon as the proposition of Indian boundary is disposed of, the undersigned have no objection, with the explanation given by the British Plenipotentiaries in their last note, to discuss the subject.

The undersigned, in their former note, stated with frankness, and will now repeat, that the two propositions—first, of assigning in the proposed treaty of peace a definite boundary to the Indians living within the limits of the United States, beyond which boundary they should stipulate not to acquire, by purchase or otherwise, any territory; secondly, of securing the exclusive military possession of the lakes of Great Britain—are both inadmissible; and that they cannot subscribe to, and would deem it useless to refer to their Government, any arrangement, even provisional, containing either of those propositions. With this understanding, the undersigned are now ready to continue the negotiations, and, as they have already expressed, to discuss all the points of difference, or which might hereafter tend in any degree to interrupt the harmony of the two countries.

The undersigned request the British Plenipotentiaries to accept the assurance of their high consideration.

JOHN QUINCY ADAMS,
J. A. BAYARD,
HENRY CLAY,
JONATHAN RUSSELL,
A. GALLATIN.

From the British to the American Ministers.

Ghent, *Sept.* 19, 1814.

The undersigned have the honor to acknowledge the receipt of the note addressed to them by the American Plenipotentiaries on the 9th instant.

On the greater part of that note the undersigned have no intention to make comments, having proposed to themselves throughout the negotiation to avoid all unnecessary discussions, more especially when tending to create irritation.

On the question of the Northwestern frontiers, they are happy to find that no material difficulty is likely to arise.

With respect to the boundary of the District of Maine, the undersigned observe, with regret, that, although the American Plenipotentiaries have acknowledged themselves to be instructed to discuss a revision of the boundary line with a view to prevent uncertainty and disputes, yet, by assuming an exclusive right at once to decide what

Relations with Great Britain.

is, or is not, a subject of uncertainty and dispute, they have rendered their powers nugatory, or inadmissibly partial in their operation.

After the declaration made by the American Plenipotentiaries that the United States will admit of no line of boundary between their territory and that of the Indian nations, because the natural growth and population of the United States would be thereby arrested, it becomes necessary further to insist on the proof of a spirit of aggrandizement afforded by the purchase of Louisiana from France, against the known conditions on which it had been ceded by Spain to that country, or the hostile seizure of a great part of the Floridas under the pretence of a dispute respecting the boundary.

The reason given by the American Plenipotentiaries for this declaration equally applies to the assignment of a boundary to the United States on any side, with whatever view proposed; and the unlimited nature of the pretension would alone have justified Great Britain in seeking more effectual securities against its application to Canada, than any which the undersigned have had the honor to propose.

Had the American Plenipotentiaries been instructed on the subject of Canada, they would not have asserted that its permanent annexation had not been the declared object of their Government. It has been distinctly avowed to be such at different times, particularly by two American Generals, on their respective invasions of Canada. If the declaration first made had been disapproved, it would not have been repeated. The declarations here referred to are to be found in the proclamation of General Hull in July, 1812, and of General Smith in November, 1812, copies of which are hereunto annexed.

It must be also from the want of instructions that the American Plenipotentiaries have been led to assert that Great Britain has induced the Indians to withdraw from the protection of the United States. The Government of the United States cannot have forgotten that Great Britain, so far from inducing the Indians to withdraw themselves from the protection of the United States, gave the earliest information of the intention of those nations to invade the United States, and exerted herself, though without success, to prevent and appease their hostility. The Indian nations, however, having experienced, as they thought, oppression, instead of protection, from the United States, declared war against them previously to the declaration of war by that country against Great Britain. The treaty by which the Indians placed themselves under the protection of the United States is now abrogated, and the American Government cannot now be entitled to claim as a right the renewal of an article in a treaty which has no longer any existence. The Indian nations are, therefore, no longer to be considered as under the protection of the United States—whatever may be the import of that term—and it can only be on the ground that they are regarded as subjects, that the American Plenipotentiaries can be authorized to deny the right of

Great Britain to interfere on their behalf in the negotiation for peace. To any such claim, it is repeated, that the treaties concluded with them, and particularly that of Greenville, are in direct opposition.

It is not necessary to recur to the manner in which the territory of the United States was at first settled, in order to decide whether the Indian nations, the original inhabitants of America, shall have some spot assigned to them, where they may may be permitted to live in tranquillity; nor whether their tranquillity can be secured without preventing an uninterrupted system of encroachment upon them under the pretence of purchases.

If the American Plenipotentiaries are authorized peremptorily to deny the right of the British Government to interfere with the pacification of the Indian nations, and for that reason refuse all negotiation on the subject, the undersigned are at a loss to understand upon what principle it was that, at the conference of the 9th ultimo, the American Plenipotentiaries invited discussion on the subject, and added, that it was not possible for them to decide, without discussion, whether an article could be framed which should be mutually satisfactory, and to which they should think themselves, under their discretionary powers, warranted in acceding.

The undersigned must further observe that, if the American Government has not furnished their Plenipotentiaries with any instructions since January last, when the general pacification of Europe could have been immediately in contemplation, this subsequent silence, after an event so calculated (even in the view which the American Plenipotentiaries have taken of it, in their note of the 24th ultimo,) to influence the negotiation, is, to say the least, no proof of a sincere desire to bring it to a favorable conclusion. The British Government has entered into the negotiation with an anxious wish to effect an amicable arrangement. After convulsions, unexampled in their nature, extent, and duration, the civilized world has need of repose. To obtain this in Europe, Great Britain has made considerable sacrifices. To complete the work of general pacification, it is her earnest wish to establish a peace with the United States, and, in her endeavors to accomplish this object, to manifest the same principles of moderation and forbearance; but it is utterly inconsistent with her practice and her principles ever to abandon, in her negotiation for peace, those who have co-operated with her in war.

The undersigned, therefore, repeat that the British Government is willing to sign a Treaty of Peace with the United States on terms honorable to both parties. It has not offered any terms which the United States can justly represent as derogatory to their honor, nor can it be induced to accede to any which are injurious to its own. It is on this ground that the undersigned are authorized distinctly to declare that they are instructed not to sign a Treaty of Peace with the Plenipotentiaries of the United States, unless the Indian nations are included in it, and restored to all the rights, privileges, and territories which they enjoyed in the year 1811, previous to the commencement of the war, by virtue of the Treaty of Greenville, and the treaties subsequently concluded between them and the United States. From this point the British Plenipotentiaries cannot depart.

They are further instructed to offer for discussion an article by which the contracting parties shall reciprocally bind themselves, according to boundaries to be agreed upon, not to purchase the lands occupied by the Indians within their respective lines of demarcation. By making this engagement subject to revision at the expiration of the given period, it is hoped that the objection to the establishment of a boundary, beyond which the settlements of the United States should be forever excluded, may be effectually obviated.

The undersigned have never stated that the exclusive military possession of the lakes, however conducive they are satisfied it would be to a good understanding between the two countries, without endangering the security of the United States, was to be considered as a *sine qua non* in the negotiation. Whenever the question relative to the pacification of the Indian nations (which, subject to the explanations already given, is a *sine qua non*,) shall be adjusted, the undersigned will be authorized to make a final proposition on the subject of Canadian boundaries, so entirely founded on principles of moderation and justice, that they feel confident it cannot be rejected. This proposition will be distinctly stated by the undersigned, upon receiving an assurance from the American Plenipotentiaries that they consider themselves authorized to conclude a provisional article on the subject, and upon their previously consenting to include the Indian nations in the treaty, in the manner above described.

The undersigned avail themselves of this opportunity of renewing to the American Plenipotentiaries the assurance of their high consideration.

    GAMBIER,
    HENRY GOULBURN,
    WILLIAM ADAMS.

From the American to the British Ministers.

GHENT, *September 26,* 1814.

In replying to the note which the undersigned have had the honor of receiving from His Britannic Majesty's Plenipotentiaries, dated on the 19th instant, they are happy to concur with them in the sentiment of avoiding unnecessary discussions, especially such as may have a tendency to create irritation. They had hoped that, in the same spirit, the British Plenipotentiaries would not have thought allusions again necessary to transactions foreign to this negotiation, relating to the United States and other independent nations, and not suitable for discussion between the United States and Great Britain. The observation made with respect to Louisiana is the more extraordinary, as the cession of that province to the United States was, at the time, communicated to the British Government, who expressed their

entire satisfaction with it, and as it has subsequently received the solemn sanction of Spain herself.

The undersigned will further say, that, whenever the transactions of the United States in relation to the boundaries of Louisiana and Florida shall be a proper subject of discussion, they will be found not only susceptible of complete justification, but will demonstrate the moderation and forbearance of the American Government, and their undeviating respect for the rights of their neighbors.

The undersigned are far from assuming the exclusive right to decide what is, or is not, a subject of uncertainty and dispute with regard to the boundary of the District of Maine. But until the British Plenipotentiaries shall have shown in what respect the part of that boundary which would be affected by their proposal is such a subject, the undersigned may be permitted to assert that it is not.

The treaty of 1783 described the boundary as a line to be drawn along the middle of the river St. Croix, from its mouth, in the bay of Fundy, to its source, and from its source directly north to the Highlands, which divide the rivers that fall into the Atlantic Ocean from those which fall into the river St. Lawrence; and thence, along the said Highlands, to the northwestern-most head of Connecticut river.

Doubts having arisen as to the St. Croix, designated in the treaty of 1783, a provision was made by that of 1794 for ascertaining it; and it may be fairly inferred, from the limitation of the article to that sole object, that, even in the judgment of Great Britain, no other subject of controversy existed in relation to the extension of the boundary line from the source of that river. That river and its source having been accordingly ascertained, the undersigned are prepared to propose the appointment of Commissioners by the two Governments to extend the line to the Highlands, conformably to the treaty of 1783. The proposal, however, of the British Plenipotentiaries was not to ascertain, but to vary, those lines, in such manner as to secure a direct communication between Quebec and Halifax; an alteration which could not be effected without a cession by the United States to Great Britain of all that portion of the State of Massachusetts intervening between the provinces of New Brunswick and Quebec, although unquestionably included within the boundary lines fixed by that treaty. Whether it was contemplated on the part of Great Britain to obtain the cession, with or without an equivalent, in frontier or otherwise, the undersigned, in stating that they were not instructed or authorized to treat on the subject of cession, have not declined to discuss any matter of uncertainty or dispute which the British Plenipotentiaries may point out to exist respecting the boundaries in that or in any other quarter, and are, therefore, not liable to the imputation of having rendered their powers on the subject nugatory or inadmissibly partial in their operation.

13th CON. 3d SESS.—43

The British Plenipotentiaries consider the undersigned as having declared " that the United States will admit of no line of boundary between their territory and that of the Indian nations, because the natural growth and population of the United States would be thereby arrested." The undersigned, on the contrary, expressly stated in their last note, " that the lands inhabited by the Indians were secured to them by boundaries defined in amicable treaties between them and the United States ;" but they did refuse to assign, in a treaty of peace with Great Britain, a definitive and permanent boundary to the Indians living within the limits of the United States. On this subject the undersigned have no hesitation in avowing that the United States, while intending never to acquire lands from the Indians otherwise than peaceably, and with their free consent, are fully determined, in that manner, progressively, and in proportion as their growing population may require, to reclaim from that state of nature, and to bring into cultivation every portion of the territory contained within their acknowledged boundaries. In thus providing for the support of millions of civilized beings, they will not violate any dictate of justice or of humanity ; for they will not only give to the few thousand savages scattered over that territory an ample equivalent for any right they may surrender, but will always leave them the possession of lands more than they can cultivate, and more than adequate to their subsistence, comfort, and enjoyment, by cultivation. If this be a spirit of aggrandizement, the undersigned are prepared to admit, in that sense, its existence ; but they must deny that it affords the slightest proof of an intention not to respect the boundaries between them and European nations, or of a desire to encroach upon the territories of Great Britain. If, in the progress of their increasing population, the American people must grow in strength proportioned to their number, the undersigned will hope that Great Britain, far from repining at the prospect, will contemplate it with satisfaction. They will not suppose that that Government will avow, as the basis of their policy towards the United States, the system of arresting their natural growth within their own territories, for the sake of preserving a perpetual desert for savages. If Great Britain has made sacrifices to give repose to the civilized world in Europe, no sacrifice is required from her by the United States to complete the work of general pacification. This negotiation at least evinces on their part no disposition to claim any other right than that of preserving their independence entire, and of governing their own territories without foreign interference.

Of the two proclamations, purported copies of which the British Plenipotentiaries have thought proper to enclose with their last note, the undersigned might content themselves with remarking that neither of them is the act of the American Government. They are enabled, however, to add, with perfect confidence, that neither of them was authorized or approved by the Government. The undersigned are not disposed to consider as the act of the British Government the proclamation of Admiral Cochrane, herewith enclosed, exciting a portion of the population of the United States, under the promise of military employment, or of free settlement in the West Indies, to treachery and rebellion. The undersigned very sincerely regret to be obliged to say, that an irresistible mass of evidence, consisting principally of the correspondence of British officers and agents, part only of which has already been published in America, establishes beyond all rational doubt the fact that a constant system of excitement to those hostilities was pursued by the British traders and agents, who had access to the Indians, not only without being discountenanced, but with frequent encouragement by the British authorities ; and that, if they ever dissuaded the Indians from commencing hostilities, it was only by urging them, as in prudence, to suspend their attacks until Great Britain could recognise them as her allies in the war.

When, in the conference of the 9th ultimo, the undersigned invited discussion upon the proposal of Indian pacification and boundary, as well as upon all the subjects presented by the British Plenipotentiaries for discussion, they expressly stated their motives to be—1st, to ascertain, by discussion, whether an article on the subject could be formed, to which they could subscribe, and which would be satisfactory to the British Plenipotentiaries ; and, 2dly, that, if no such article could be formed, the American Government might be informed of the views of Great Britain upon that point, and the British Government of the objections, on the part of the United States, to any such arrangement. The undersigned have, in fact, already proposed no less than three articles on the subject, all of which they view as better calculated to secure peace and tranquillity to the Indians, than any of the proposals for that purpose made by the British Plenipotentiaries.

The undersigned had repeated their assurances to the British Plenipotentiaries that peace, so far as it depended on the United States, would immediately follow a peace with Great Britain ; and added, that the Indians would thereby be reinstated in the same situation in which they stood before the commencement of hostilities. The British Plenipotentiaries insist, in their last note, that the Indian nations shall be included in the Treaty of Peace between Great Britain and the United States, and be restored to all the rights, privileges, and territories which they enjoyed in the year 1811, previous to their commencement of the war, by virtue of the Treaty of Greenville, and the treaties subsequently concluded between them and the United States. Setting aside the subject of boundary, which is presented as for discussion only, there is no apparent difference with respect to the object in view, the pacification and tranquillity of the Indians, and placing them in the same situation in which they stood before the war ; all which will be equally obtained in the manner proposed by the undersigned. And the only point of real difference is, the British Plenipotentiaries insist that it should be done by

Relations with Great Britain.

including the Indians, as allies of Great Britain, in the Treaty of Peace between her and the United Sates.

The United States cannot consent that Indians residing within their boundaries, as acknowledged by Great Britain, shall be included in the Treaty of Peace in any manner which will recognise them as independent nations, whom Great Britain, having obtained this recognition, would hereafter have the right to consider in every respect as such. Thus, to recognise those Indians as independent and sovereign nations would take from the United States, and transfer to those Indians, all the rights of soil and sovereignty over the territory which they inhabit; and this being accomplished, through the agency of Great Britain, would place them effectually and exclusively under her protection, instead of being, as heretofore, under that of the United States. It is not perceived in what respect such a provision would differ from an absolute cession by the United States of the extensive territory in question.

The British Plenipotentiaries have repeated the assertion that the treaty by which the Indians placed themselves under the protection of the United States was abrogated by the war; and thence infer, that they are no longer to be considered as under the protection of the United States, whatever may be the import of the term, and that the right of Great Britain to interfere in their behalf in the negotiation for peace can only be denied on the ground that they are regarded as subjects. In point of fact, several of the tribes, parties to the Treaty of Greenville, have constantly been, and still are, at peace with the United States. Whether that treaty be or be not abrogated, is a question not necessary now to be discussed. The right of the United States to the protection of the Indians within their boundaries was not acquired by that treaty; it was a necessary consequence of the sovereignty and independence of the United States. Previous to that time, the Indians living within the same territory were under the protection of His Britannic Majesty, as its Sovereign. The undersigned may refer the British Plenipotentiaries to all the acts of their own Government relative to the subject, for proof that it has always considered this right of protection as one of the rights of sovereignty which it needed no Indian treaty to confer, and which the abrogation of no Indian treaty could divest. They will particularly bring to their recollection, that when a similar proposition was made of considering Indian tribes, as independent nations, to serve as a barrier between the French and English territories, was made by France to England, it was immediately rejected by a Minister to whom the British nation is accustomed to look back with veneration, and rejected on the express ground that the King would not renounce his right of protection over the Indians within his dominions. But whatever the relation of the Indians to the United States may be, and whether under their protection or not, Great Britain having, by the treaty of 1783, recognised the sovereignty of the United States,

and agreed to certain limits as their boundaries, has no right to consider any persons or communities, whether Indians or others, residing within those boundaries, as nations independent of the United States.

The United States claim, of right, with respect to all European nations, and particularly with respect to Great Britain, the entire sovereignty over the whole territory, and all the persons embraced within the boundaries of their dominions; Great Britain has no right to take cognizance of the relations subsisting between the several communities or persons living therein; they form, as to her, only parts of the dominions of the United States, and it is altogether immaterial whether, or how far, under their political institutions and policy, these communities or persons are independent States, allies, or subjects. With respect to her, and all other foreign nations, they are parts of a whole, of which the United States are the sole and absolute sovereigns.

The allegation of the British Plenipotentiaries that it is inconsistent with the practice or principles of Great Britain to abandon, in her negotiations for peace, those who have co-operated with her in war, is not applicable to the Indians, but on the erroneous assumption of their independence, which, so far as she is concerned, has been fully disproved. And although no power from these tribes to the British Government, to treat in their behalf, would, for the same reason, be admitted by the undersigned, they may nevertheless observe that the British Plenipotentiaries having produced no such powers, having no authority to bind the Indians, to engage for their assent to the pacification, or to secure the continuance of peace on their part, whilst speaking of them as allies, do really propose to treat for them, not as if they were independent nations, but as if they were the subjects of Great Britain. The undersigned, so far from asking that, in relation to the Indians, Great Britain should pursue a course inconsistent with her former practice and principles, only desire that she would follow her own example respecting them, in her former treaties with other European nations, and with the United States. No provision for the Indians is found in the treaty of 1763, by which France ceded Canada to Great Britain, although almost all the Indians living within the territory ceded, or acknowledged to belong to Great Britain, had taken part with France in the war. No such provision was inserted in the Treaty of Peace of 1783, between Great Britain and the United States, although almost all the Indians tribes living within the territory recognised by the treaty to belong to the United States, had, during the war, co-operated with Great Britain, and might have been considered as her allies more justly than on the present occasion. So far as concerns the relations between Great Britain and the United States, these Indians can be treated for only on the principles by which amnesties are stipulated in favor of disaffected persons, who, in times of war and invasion, co-operate with the enemy of the nation to which they belong. To go as far as possible in securing the benefit of the peace to the Indians, now the only object professed by the British Government in their present *sine qua non*, the undersigned offer a stipulation in general terms: that no person or persons, whether subjects, citizens, or Indians, residing within the dominions of either party, shall be molested or annoyed, either in their persons or their property, for any part they may have taken in the war between the United States and Great Britain; but shall retain all the rights, privileges, and possessions which they respectively had at the commencement of the war; they, on their part, demeaning themselves peaceably and conformably to their duties to the respective Governments. This, the undersigned have no doubt will effectually secure to the Indians peace, if they themselves will observe it, and they will not suppose that Great Britain would wish them included in the peace, but upon that condition.

The undersigned have never intimated that their Government had not furnished them with any instructions since January last. On the contrary, they distinctly told the British Plenipotentiaries in conference, though it appears to have escaped their recollection, that instructions had been received by the undersigned, dated at the close of the month of June. The undersigned will now add, that those instructions were drawn with a full knowledge of the general pacification in Europe, and with so liberal a consideration of its necessary bearing upon all the differences that had been until then subsisting between Great Britain and the United States, that the undersigned cannot doubt that peace would long since have been concluded, had not an insuperable bar against it then raised by the new and unprecedented demands of the British Government.

With respect to the proposition which the British Plenipotentiaries inform them they will be prepared to make, in relation to the Canadian boundaries, which appears to them so entirely founded on principles of moderation and justice, but the nature of which they think proper, at present, to withhold, the undersigned can only pledge themselves to meet any proposition from the British Plenipotentiaries characterized by moderation and justice, not only with a perfect reciprocity of those sentiments, but with a sincere and earnest desire to contribute to the restoration of peace, by every compliance with the wishes of Great Britain compatible with their duty to their country.

The undersigned have the honor of tendering to the British Plenipotentiaries the renewed assurance of their high consideration.

JOHN QUINCY ADAMS,
JAMES A. BAYARD,
HENRY CLAY,
JONA. RUSSELL,
A. GALLATIN.

From the British to the American Ministers.

GHENT, *October* 8, 1814.

The undersigned have the honor to acknowledge the receipt of the note of the Plenipoten-

tiaries of the United States dated on the 26th ultimo.

As the continuance of the negotiation exclusively depends upon the question relating to *the* pacification and rights of the Indian nations, the undersigned are unwilling to extend their observations to the other subjects brought forward in the note of the American Plenipotentiaries further than may be required for the necessary explanation.

In adverting for this purpose to the acquisition of Louisiana, the undersigned must observe that the instrument by which the consent of His Catholic Majesty is alleged to have been given to the cession of it has never been made public. His Catholic Majesty was no party to the treaty by which the cession was made, and if any sanction has been subsequently obtained from him, it must have been, like other contemporaneous acts of that monarch, involuntary, and, as such, cannot alter the character of the transaction. The Marquis of Yrujo, the Minister of His Catholic Majesty at Washington, in a letter addressed to the President of the United States, formally protested against the cession, and the right of France to make it; yet, in the face of this *protestation*, so strongly evincing the decided opinion of *Spain* as to the illegality of the proceeding, the President of the United States ratified the treaty. Can it be contended that the annexation of Louisiana, under such circumstances, did not mark a spirit of territorial aggrandizement?

His Britannic Majesty did certainly express satisfaction when the American Government communicated the event that Louisiana, a valuable colony in the possession of France, with whom the war had just been renewed, instead of remaining in the hands of his enemy, had been ceded to the United States, at that time professing the most friendly disposition towards Great Britain, and an intention of providing for her interest in the acquisition. But the conditions under which France had acquired Louisiana from Spain were not communicated; the refusal of Spain to consent to its alienation was not known; the protest of her Ambassador had not been made; and many other circumstances attending the transaction, on which it is now unnecessary to dilate, were, as there is good reason to believe, industriously concealed.

The proof of a spirit of aggrandizement which the undersigned had deduced from the hostile seizure of a great part of the Floridas, under the most frivolous pretences, remains unrefuted; and the undersigned are convinced that the occasion and circumstances under which that unwarrantable act of aggression took place have given rise throughout Europe to but one sentiment as to the character of the transaction.

After the previous communication which the undersigned have had the honor of receiving from the American Plenipotentiaries, they could not but feel much surprise at the information contained in their last note, of their having received instructions dated subsequently to January, 1814. The undersigned have no recollection whatever

Relations with Great Britain.

of the American Plenipotentiaries having communicated to them, either collectively or individually, at a conference or otherwise, the receipt of instructions from the Government of the United States dated at the close of the month of June; and they must remind the American Plenipotentiaries that their note of the 9th ultimo distinctly stated that the instructions of January, 1814, were those under which they were acting. If, therefore, the American Plenipotentiaries received instructions drawn up at the close of the month of June, with a liberal consideration of the late events in Europe, the undersigned have a right to complain that, while the American Government justly considered those events as having a necessary bearing on the existing differences between the two countries, the American Plenipotentiaries should nevertheless have preferred acting under instructions which, from their date, must have been framed without the contemplation of such events.

The British Government never required that all that portion of the State of Massachusetts intervening between the province of New Brunswick and Quebec should be ceded to Great Britain, but only that small portion of unsettled country which intercepts the communication between Halifax and Quebec; there being much doubt whether it does not already belong to Great Britain.

The undersigned are at a loss to understand how Vice Admiral Cochrane's proclamation illustrates any topic connected with the present negotiation, or bears upon the conclusion which they contended was to be drawn from the two proclamations of the American Generals. These proclamations, distinctly avowing the intention of the American Government permanently to annex the Canadas to the United States, were adduced not as matter of complaint, but simply for the purpose of proving what had been denied as a fact, viz: that such had been the declared intention of the American Government.

The undersigned observe that, although the American Plenipotentiaries have taken upon themselves generally to deny that the proclamations were authorized or approved by their Government, without stating in what mode that disapprobation was expressed, yet they avoid stating that the part of these proclamations containing the declaration in question had not been so authorized or approved. It is, indeed, impossible to imagine that, if the American Government had intimated any disapprobation of that part of General Hull's proclamation, the same declaration would have been as confidently repeated four months after by General Smyth.

His Majesty's Government have other and ample means of knowing that the conquest of the Canadas, and their annexation to the United States, was the object and policy of the American Government. For the present, the undersigned will content themselves with referring to the remonstrance of the Legislature of Massachusetts in June, 1813, in which this intention is announced as matter of notoriety.

The undersigned deny that the American Government has proved, or can prove, that, previous to the declaration of war by the United States, persons authorized by the British Government endeavored to excite the Indian nations against the United States; or that endeavors of that kind, if made by private persons, (which the undersigned have no reason to believe,) ever received the countenance or encouragement of His Majesty's Government.

The American Plenipotentiaries have not denied that the Indian nations had been engaged in war against the United States before the war with Great Britain had commenced; and they have reluctantly confessed -that, so far from His Majesty's having induced the Indian nations to begin the war, as charged against Great Britain in the notes of the 24th of August and 9th ultimo, the British Government actually exerted their endeavors to dissuade the Indians from commencing it.

As to the unworthy motive assigned by the American Plenipotentiaries to this interference so amicably made on the part of Great Britain, its utter improbability is sufficiently apparent from considering by which party the war was declared. The undersigned, therefore, can only consider it as an additional indication of that hostile disposition which has led to the present unhappy war between the two countries. So long as that disposition continues, it cannot but render any effort on the part of Great Britain to terminate this contest utterly unavailing.

The American Plenipotentiaries appear unprepared to state the precise ground upon which they resist the right of His Majesty to negotiate with the United States on behalf of the Indian nations, whose co-operation in the war His Majesty has found it expedient to accept.

The Treaty of Greenville, to the words, stipulations, and spirit of which the undersigned have so frequently appealed, and all the treaties previously and subsequently made between the United States and the Indian nations, show beyond the possibility of doubt that the United States have been in the habit of treating with these tribes as independent nations, capable of maintaining the relations of peace and war, and exercising territorial rights.

If this be so, it will be difficult to point out the peculiar circumstances in the condition of these nations which should either exclude them from a treaty of general pacification, or prevent Great Britain, with whom they have co-operated as allies in the war, from proposing stipulations in their behalf at the peace. Unless the American Plenipotentiaries are prepared to maintain what they have in effect advanced, that, although the Indian nations may be independent in their relations with the United States, yet the circumstance of living within the boundary of the United States disables them from forming such conditions of alliance with a foreign Power, as shall entitle that Power to negotiate for them in a Treaty of Peace.

The principle upon which this proposition is

Relations with Great Britain.

founded was advanced, but successfully resisted, so far back as the Treaty of Munster. An attempt was then made to preclude France from negotiating in behalf of certain States and cities in Germany which had co-operated with her in the war, because, although those States and cities might be considered as independent for certain purposes, yet, being within the boundary of the German Empire, they ought not to be allowed to become parties in the general pacification with the Emperor of Germany, nor ought France to be permitted in that negotiation to mix their rights and interests with her own.

The American Plenipotentiaries, probably aware that the notion of such a qualified independence, for certain purposes and not for others, could not be maintained either by argument or precedent, have been compelled to advance the novel and alarming pretension that all the Indian nations living within the boundary of the United States must in effect be considered as their subjects, and consequently, if engaged in war against the United States, become liable to be treated as rebels or disaffected persons. They have further stated, that all the territory which these Indian nations occupy is at the disposal of the United States; that the United States have a right to dispossess them of it; to exercise that right whenever their policy or interests may seem to them to require it; and to confine them to such spots as may be selected, not by the Indian nations, but by the American Government. Pretensions such as these Great Britain can never recognise. However reluctant His Royal Highness the Prince Regent may be to continue the war, that evil must be preferred if peace can only be obtained on such conditions.

To support those pretensions, and at the same time to show that the present conduct of Great Britain is inconsistent with the former practice and principles, the American Plenipotentiaries have referred to the Treaty of Peace of 1783, to that of 1763, and to the negotiations of 1761, during the administration of a Minister whom the American Plenipotentiaries have stated, and truly stated, to be high in the estimation of his country.

The omission to provide, in the treaty of 1783, for the pacification of the Indian nations which were to be included within the proposed boundary of the United States, cannot preclude Great Britain from now negotiating in behalf of such tribes or nations, unless it be assumed that the occasional non-exercise of a right is an abandonment of it. Nor can the right of protection, which the American Plenipotentiaries have failed in showing to have been unclaimed by Great Britain, as incident to sovereignty, have been transferred by Great Britain to the United States, by a treaty to which the Indian nations were not parties.

In the peace of 1763, it was not necessary for Great Britain to treat for the pacification of the Indian nations, and the maintenance of their rights and privileges, because there had been no Indian nations living without the British boundaries who had co-operated with Great Britain in the war against France.

With respect to the negotiations of 1761, between Great Britain and France, on which the American Plenipotentiaries more particularly rely, they appear, in the judgment of the undersigned, to have much misunderstood the whole course of that negotiation.

It is very true that the French Government brought forward, at one period of the negotiation, a proposition by which a certain territory lying between the dominions of the two contracting parties was to have been allotted to the Indian nations. But it does not appear that this formed a part of their ultimatums, and it is clear that Mr. Pitt, in his answer, did not object to the proposition. He objected, indeed, to the proposed line of demarcation between the countries belonging to the two contracting parties, upon two grounds: first, that the proposed Northern line would have given to France what the French themselves had acknowledged to be part of Canada, the whole of which, as enjoyed by His Most Christian Majesty, it had been stipulated was to be ceded entirely to Great Britain. Secondly, that the Southern part of the proposed line of demarcation would have included within the boundary of Louisiana the Cherokees, the Creeks, the Chickasaws, the Choctaws, and another nation who occupied territories which had never been included within the boundary of that settlement. So far was Mr. Pitt from rejecting, as alleged by the American Plenipotentiaries, the proposition of considering Indian nations as a barrier, that, at one period of the negotiation, he complained that there was no provision for such a barrier; and he thus energetically urges his objection in his letter to Mr. Stanley, the British Plenipotentiary at Paris, dated on the 26th of June, 1761. " As to the fixation of new limits to Canada towards the Ohio, it is captious and insidious, thrown out in hope, if agreed to, to shorten thereby the extent of Canada, and to lengthen the boundaries of Louisiana, and in the view to establish, what must be not admitted, namely, that all which is not Canada is Louisiana, whereby all the intermediate nations and countries, the true barrier to each province, would be given up to France."

The undersigned confidently expect that the American Plenipotentiaries will not again reproach the British Government with acting inconsistently with its former practice and principles, or repeat the assertion made in a former note, that a definition of Indian boundary, with a view to a neutral barrier, was a new and unprecedented demand by any European Power, and, most of all, by Great Britain. The very instance selected by the American Plenipotentiaries undeniably proves, that such a proposition had been entertained both by Great Britain and France, and that Mr. Pitt, on the part of Great Britain, had more particularly enforced it.

It remains only to notice two objections, which the American Plenipotentiaries have urged against the proposal of Indian pacification, advanced by the undersigned; first, that it is not reciprocal; secondly, that, as the United States could have no security that the Indian nations would conclude a peace on the terms proposed, the objection would be, in effect, unilateral.

The article now proposed by the undersigned, and herewith enclosed, is free from both objections, and appears to them so characterized by a spirit of moderation and peace, that they earnestly anticipate the concurrence of the American Plenipotentiaries.

In making a last effort in this stage of the war, the undersigned are not apprehensive that the motives which have influenced His Royal Highness the Prince Regent to direct a renewal of the proposition, with its present modifications, can be misunderstood or misrepresented.

Whatever may be the result of the proposition thus offered, the undersigned deliver it as their ultimatum, and now await with anxiety the answer of the American Plenipotentiaries, on which their continuance in this place will depend.

The undersigned avail themselves of this opportunity of renewing to the American Plenipotentiaries the assurance of their high consideration.

GAMBIER,
HENRY GOULBURN,
WILLIAM ADAMS.

The United States of America engage to put an end, immediately after the ratification of the present treaty, to hostilities with all the tribes or nations of Indians with whom they may be at war at the time of such ratification, and forthwith to restore to such tribes or nations, respectively, all the possessions, rights, and privileges, which they may have enjoyed, or been entitled to, in 1811, previous to such hostilities.

Provided, always, That such tribes or nations shall agree to desist from all hostilities against the United States of America, their citizens and subjects, upon the ratification of the present treaty being notified to such tribes or nations, and shall so desist accordingly.

And His Britannic Majesty engages, on his part, to put an end, immediately after the ratification of the present treaty, to hostilities with all the tribes or nations of Indians with whom he may be at war at the time of such ratification, and forthwith to restore to such tribes or nations respectively, all the possessions, rights, and privileges, which they may have enjoyed, or been entitled to, in 1811, previous to such hostilities.

Provided, always, That such tribes or nations shall agree to desist from all hostilities against His Britannic Majesty and his subjects, upon the ratification of the present treaty being notified to such tribes or nations, and shall so desist accordingly.

From the American to the British Ministers.

GHENT, *October* 13, 1814.

The undersigned have the honor to acknowledge the receipt of the note of the Plenipotentiaries of His Britannic Majesty, dated on the 8th instant.

Satisfied of the impossibility of persuading the world that the Government of the United States was liable to any well grounded imputation of a spirit of conquest, or of injustice towards other nations, the undersigned, in affording explanations on several of the topics adverted to by the British Plenipotentiaries during this negotiation, were actuated by the sole motive of removing erroneous impressions.

Still influenced by the same motive, they will now add, that at the time when the Spanish Minister was remonstrating at Washington against the transfer of Louisiana, orders were given by his Government for its delivery to France; that it was, in fact, delivered a short time after that remonstrance; and that, if the treaty by which the United States acquired it had not been ratified, it would have become of course a French colony. The undersigned believe that the evidence of the assent of Spain to that transfer has been promulgated. They neither admit the alleged disability of the Spanish monarch, nor the inference which the British Plenipotentiaries would seem to deduce from it; on the contrary, the assent was voluntarily given in the year 1804, by the same King, who, about the same time, ceded Trinidad to Great Britain, and prior to the time when he was again engaged in a war with her. The cession by France was immediately communicated to Great Britain, no circumstance affecting it, and then within the knowledge of the United States, being intentionally concealed from her. She expressed her satisfaction with it, and if in any possible state of the case, she would have had a right to question the transaction, it does not appear to the undersigned that she is now authorized to do so.

After stating, generally, that the proclamations of Generals Hull and Smyth were neither authorized nor approved by their Government, the undersigned could not have expected that the British Plenipotentiaries would suppose that their statement did not embrace the only part of the proclamations which was a subject of consideration.

The undersigned had, indeed, hoped that, by stating in their note of the 9th ultimo that the Government of the United States, from the commencement of the war, had been disposed to make peace without obtaining any cession of territory, and by referring to their knowledge of that disposition, and to instructions accordingly given from July, 1812, to January, 1814, they would effectually remove the impression that the annexation of Canada to the United States was the declared object of their Government. Not only have the undersigned been disappointed in this expectation, but the only inference which the British Plenipotentiaries have thought proper to draw from this explicit statement has been that, either the American Government, by not giving instructions subsequent to the pacification of Europe, or the undersigned, by not acting under such instructions, gave no proof of a sincere desire to bring the present negotiations to a favorable conclusion. The undersigned did not allude, in reference to the alleged intention to annex Canada to the United States, to any instructions given by their Government subsequent to January last, because asking at this time for no accession of territory, it was only of its previous disposition that it appeared necessary to adduce any proof. So erroneous was the inference drawn by the British Plenipotentiaries in both respects, that it was in virtue of the instructions of June last, that the undersigned were enabled, in their note of the 24th of August, to state that the causes of the war between the United States and Great Britain having disappeared by the maritime pacification of Europe, they had been authorized to agree to its termination upon a mutual restoration of territory, and without making the conclusion of peace to depend on a successful arrangement of those points on which differences had existed.

Considering the present state of the negotiation, the undersigned will abstain, at this time, from adducing any evidence or remarks upon the influence which has been exerted over the Indian tribes inhabiting the territories of the United States, and the nature of those excitements which have been employed by British traders and agents.

The arguments and facts already brought forward by the undersigned respecting the political condition of those tribes render it unnecessary for them to make many observations on those of the British Plenipotentiaries on that subject. The treaties of 1763, and of 1783, were those principally alluded to by the undersigned to illustrate the practice of Great Britain. She did not admit in the first, nor require in the last, any stipulations respecting the Indians who, in one case, had been her enemies, and in the other her allies, and who, in both instances, fell by the peace within the dominions of that Power against whom they had been engaged in the preceding war.

The negotiation of 1761, was quoted for the purpose of proving what appears to be fully established by the answer of England to the ultimatum of France, delivered on the 1st of September of that year, that His Britannic Majesty would not renounce his right of protection over the Indian nations reputed to be within his dominions, that is to say, between the British settlements and the Mississippi. Mr. Pitt's letter, cited by the British Plenipotentiaries, far from contradicting that position, goes still further. It states that "the fixation of the new limits to Canada, as proposed by France, is intended to shorten the extent of Canada, which was to be ceded to England, and to lengthen the boundaries of Louisiana, which France was to keep, and in the view to establish what must be not admitted, namely, that all which is not Canada is Louisiana, whereby all the intermediate nations and countries, the true barrier to each province, would be given up to France." This is precisely the principle uniformly supported by the undersigned, to wit, that the recognition of a boundary gives up to the nation in whose behalf it is made, all the Indian tribes and countries within that boundary. It was on this principle that the undersigned have confidently relied on the treaty of 1783, which fixes and recognises the boundary of the United States without making any reservation respecting Indian tribes.

But the British Plenipotentiaries, unable to produce a solitary precedent of one European Power treating for the savages inhabiting within the dominions of another, have been compelled, in support of their principle, to refer to the German Empire, a body consisting of several independent States, recognised as such by the whole world, and separately maintaining, with foreign Powers, the relations belonging to such a condition. Can it be necessary to prove that there is no sort of analogy between the political situation of these civilized communities and that of the wandering tribes of North American savages?

In referring to what the British Plenipotentiaries represent as alarming and novel pretensions, which Great Britain can never authorize, the undersigned might complain that these alleged pretensions have not been stated, either in terms or in substance, as expressed by themselves. This, however, is the less material as any further recognition of them by Great Britain is not necessary nor required. On the other hand, they can never admit nor recognise the principles or pretensions asserted in the course of this correspondence by the British Plenipotentiaries, and which to them appear novel and alarming.

The article proposed by the British Plenipotentiaries in their last note, not including the Indian tribes as parties in the peace, and leaving the United States free to effect its object in the mode consonant with the relations which they have constantly maintained with those tribes; partaking, also, of the nature of an amnesty, and being at the same time reciprocal, is not liable to that objection, and accords with the views uniformly professed by the undersigned of placing those tribes precisely, and in every respect in the same situation as that in which they stood before the commencement of hostilities. This article, thus proposing only what the undersigned have so often assured the British Plenipotentiaries would necessarily follow, if, indeed, it has not already, as is highly probable, preceded, a peace between Great Britain and the United States, the undersigned agree to admit it in substance as a provisional article, subject, in the manner originally proposed by the British Government, to the approbation or rejection of the Government of the United States, which, having given no instructions to the undersigned on this point, cannot be bound by any article they may admit on the subject.

It will, of course, be understood that if, unhappily, peace should not be the result of the present negotiation, the article thus conditionally agreed to shall be of no effect, and shall not, in any future negotiation, be brought forward by either party by way of argument or precedent.

This article having been presented as an indispensable preliminary, and being now accepted, the undersigned request the British Plenipotentiaries to communicate to them a project of a treaty embracing all the points deemed material by Great Britain; the undersigned engaging on their part, to deliver, immediately after, a counter project with respect to all the articles to which

Relations with Great Britain.

they may not agree, and on the subjects deemed material by the United States, and which may be admitted in the British project.

> JOHN QUINCY ADAMS,
> JAMES A. BAYARD,
> HENRY CLAY,
> JONATHAN RUSSELL,
> ALBERT GALLATIN.

From the British to the American Ministers

Ghent, *October* 21, 1814.

The undersigned have had the honor of receiving the note of the American Plenipotentiaries of the 13th instant, communicating their acceptance of the article which the undersigned had proposed on the subject of the pacification and rights of the Indian nations.

The undersigned are happy in being thus relieved from the necessity of recurring to several topics which, though they arose in the course of their discussions, have only an incidental connexion with the differences remaining to be adjusted between the two countries.

With a view to this adjustment the undersigned, preferring in the present state of the negotiation a general statement to the formal arrangement of articles, are willing so far to comply with the request of the American Plenipotentiaries contained in their last note, as to waive the advantage to which they think they were fairly entitled, of requiring from them the first *projet* of a treaty.

The undersigned having stated, at the first conference, the points upon which His Majesty's Government considered the discussions between the two countries as likely to turn, cannot better satisfy the request of the American Plenipotentiaries, than by referring them to that conference for a statement of the points which, in the opinion of His Majesty's Government, yet remain to be adjusted.

With respect to the forcible seizure of mariners from on board merchant vessels on the high seas, and the rights of the King of Great Britain to the allegiance of all his native subjects, and with respect to the maritime rights of the British empire, the undersigned conceive that, after the pretensions asserted by the Government of the United States, a more satisfactory proof of the conciliatory spirit of His Majesty's Government cannot be given than by not requiring any stipulation on those subjects, which, though most important in themselves, so longer, in consequence of the maritime pacification of Europe, produce the same practical results.

On the subject of the fisheries the undersigned expressed, with so much frankness, at the conference already referred to, the views of their Government, that they consider any further observations on that topic as unnecessary at the present time.

On the question of the boundary between the dominions of His Majesty and those of the United States, the undersigned are led to expect, from the discussion which this subject has already undergone, that the Northwestern boundary, from the Lake of the Woods to the Mississippi, (the intended arrangement of 1803,) will be admitted without objection.

In regard to other boundaries, the American Plenipotentiaries, in their note of August 24th, appeared in some measure to object to the propositions then made by the undersigned, as not being on the basis of *uti possidetis*. The undersigned are willing to treat on that basis, subject to such modifications as mutual convenience may be found to require; and they trust that the American Plenipotentiaries will show, by their ready acceptance of this basis, that they duly appreciate the moderation of His Majesty's Government, in so far consulting the honor and fair pretensions of the United States as, in the relative situation of the two countries, to authorize such a proposition.

The undersigned avail themselves of this opportunity to renew to the American Plenipotentiaries the assurance of their high consideration.

> GAMBIER,
> HENRY GOULBURN,
> WILLIAM ADAMS.

From the American to the British Ministers.

Ghent, *October* 24, 1814.

The undersigned have the honor to acknowledge the receipt of the note of the British Plenipotentiaries, of the 21st instant.

Amongst the general observations which the undersigned, in their note of the 24th August, made on the propositions then brought forward on the part of the British Government, they remarked, that those propositions were founded neither on the basis of *uti possidetis* nor on that of *status ante bellum*. But so far were they from suggesting the *uti possidetis* as the basis on which they were disposed to treat, that, in the same note, they expressly stated that they had been instructed to conclude a peace on the principle of both parties restoring whatever territory they might have taken. The undersigned also declared in that note, that they had no authority to cede any part of the territory of the United States; and that no stipulation to that effect would they subscribe. And in the note of the 9th September, after having shown that the basis of *uti possidetis*, such as it was known to exist at the commencement of the negotiation, gave no claim to His Britannic Majesty to cessions of territory founded upon the right of conquest, they added that, even if the chances of war should give to the British arms a momentary possession of other parts of the territory of the United States, such events would not alter their views with regard to the terms of peace, to which they would give their consent.

The undersigned can now only repeat those declarations, and decline treating upon the basis of *uti possidetis*, or upon any other principle involving a cession of any part of the territory of the United States. As they have uniformly stated, they can treat only upon the principle of a mutual restoration of whatever territory may have been taken by either party. From this principle they cannot recede; and the undersigned, after the repeated declarations of the British Plenipotentiaries, that Great Britain had no view to acquisition of territory in this negotiation, deem it necessary to add, that the utility of its continuance depends on their adherence to this principle.

The undersigned having declared in their note of the 24th of August, that, although instructed and prepared to enter into an amicable discussion of all the points on which differences or uncertainty had existed, and which might hereafter tend to interrupt the harmony of the two countries, they would not make the conclusion of the peace at all depend upon a successful result of the discussion; and having since agreed to the preliminary article proposed by the British Government, had believed that the negotiations, already so long protracted, could not be brought to an early conclusion, otherwise than by a communication of a project, embracing all the other specific propositions which Great Britain intended to offer. They repeat their request in that respect, and will have no objection to a simultaneous exchange of the project of both parties. This course will bring fairly into discussion the other topics embraced in the last note of the British Plenipotentiaries, to which the undersigned have thought it unnecessary to advert at the present time.

The undersigned renew to the British Plenipotentiaries the assurance of their high consideration.

JOHN QUINCY ADAMS,
JAMES A. BAYARD,
HENRY CLAY,
JONATHAN RUSSELL,
A. GALLATIN.

To the PLENIPOTENTIARIES
  of His Britannic Majesty, &c.

The American Plenipotentiaries to the Secretary of State.

GHENT, *October* 31, 1814.

SIR: The detention of the Chauncey at Ostend enables us to send you the enclosed note from the British Plenipotentiaries, which we have just received.

We have the honor to be, with perfect respect, your obedient servants,

JOHN QUINCY ADAMS,
J. A. BAYARD,
H. CLAY,
JONATHAN RUSSELL,
ALBERT GALLATIN.

Hon. J. MONROE, *Sec'ry of State.*

From the British to the American Ministers.

GHENT, *October* 31, 1814.

The undersigned have the honor to acknowledge the receipt of the note addressed to them by the American Plenipotentiaries on the 24th instant, in which they object to the basis of *uti*

possidetis, proposed by the undersigned as that on which they were willing to treat, in regard to part of the boundaries between the dominions of His Majesty and those of the United States.

The American Plenipotentiaries, in their note of the 13th instant, requested the undersigned to communicate to them the *projet* of a treaty embracing all the points insisted on by Great Britain, engaging, on their part, to deliver immediately after a *contre-projet,* as to all the articles to which they might not agree, and as to all the subjects deemed material by the United States, and omitted in the *projet* of the undersigned.

The undersigned were accordingly instructed to waive the question of etiquette, and the advantage which might result from receiving the first communication, and, confiding in the engagement of the American Plenipotentiaries, communicated in their note of the 21st instant, all the points upon which they were instructed to insist.

The American Plenipotentiaries have objected to one essential part of the *projet* thus communicated; but before the undersigned can enter into the discussion of this objection, they must require from the American Plenipotentiaries that, pursuant to their engagement, they will *deliver* a *contre-projet,* containing all their objections *to the* points submitted by the undersigned, together with a statement of such further *points* as the Government of the United States consider to be material.

The undersigned are authorized to state distinctly that the article as to the pacification and right of the Indian nations having been accepted, they have brought forward in their note of the 21st instant all the propositions which they have to offer. They have no further demands to make, no other stipulations on which they are instructed to insist, and they are empowered to sign a Treaty of Peace forthwith, in conformity with those stated in their former note.

The undersigned trust, therefore, that the American Plenipotentiaries will no longer hesitate to bring forward, in the form of articles, or otherwise, as they may prefer, those specific propositions upon which they are empowered to sign a Treaty of Peace between the two countries.

The undersigned avail themselves of the present opportunity to renew to the Plenipotentiaries of the United States the assurance of their high consideration.

GAMBIER,
HENRY GOULBURN,
WILLIAM ADAMS.

GREAT BRITAIN—PRISONERS OF WAR.

[Communicated to Congress, October 28, 1814.]

To the House of Representatives
  of the United States:

I transmit to the House of Representatives a report from the Department of State, complying with their resolution of the 15th instant.

JAMES MADISON.

OCTOBER 28, 1814.

Great Britain—Prisoners of War.

DEPARTMENT OF STATE, *Oct.* 27, 1814.

The acting Secretary of State, to whom was referred the resolution of the House of Representatives of the 15th instant, has the honor of submitting to the President the accompanying papers marked Nos. 1, 2, 3, and 4, as containing the information which is presumed to be called for by the said resolution.

Respectfully submitted.

      JAMES MONROE.

PRESIDENT *of the United States.*

No. 1.

Extract of a letter from Reuben G. Beasley, Esq., to the Commissary General of Prisoners.

LONDON, *March* 18, 1814.

Having had several conversations on the subject of retaliation, previous to the receipt of your letters of the 6th and 9th of January, I took the earliest occasion to communicate the information they contained. On the 9th ultimo, I addressed a letter to the Transport Board on the subject, a copy of which I have now the honor to enclose. Although I have received no reply to this letter, I have the satisfaction to inform you that I have been assured by the Secretary of the Board, and have found the fact confirmed by my own observation, that the treatment of the individuals sent to this country for trial has in no respect been different from that of the other prisoners of war.

[Enclosed in the preceding.]

Mr. Beasley to the Secretary of the Transport Board.

HARLEY STREET, *Feb.* 19, 1814.

SIR: In consequence of the wish which you verbally expressed to me yesterday, I now present to the Board, in the form in which it has been communicated to me by the Commissary General of Prisoners of the United States, a statement of the various measures of retaliation which have been forced on the American Government by the unwarrantable acts of British officers. I the more readily comply with this wish, because it will lead to a proper understanding on the subject, and I persuade myself it will be followed by measures on the part of the British Government which will not only relieve the suffering individuals but put an end to the proceedings, the very idea of which is so painful to every generous and humane feeling. I begin in the order in which they occurred. [Here follows the statement extracted from General Mason's letter of the 6th January] 1814.*

To the foregoing I have to add, that information has been received by the Commissary General that the British commanding officer at Halifax had confined there sixty-four American officers, with intention to make the number ninety-two, in retaliation for the forty-six British officers confined by the American Government. As soon

* This statement contained the substance of the cases to be found in the report of the Secretary of State of the 14th April, 1814, printed by order of the Senate.

as this should be officially communicated to the Government, a correspondent and effectual measure would be adopted in the United States.

In this statement, and the documents which accompany it, will be found the disposition and sentiments of the American Government. It will be seen that the system was not begun by the United States. Prompt in the discharge of the duty they owe to their citizens, they have constantly lamented the necessity of the measures imposed on them, and have on every occasion shown, as you will see exemplified in the first, second, third, and fourth acts, above recited, that the moment the necessity of detention ceased to exist, the persons confined have been released.

The British agent in the United States, who has been regularly informed of every circumstance relative to this unpleasant subject, will no doubt have done the American Government the justice to say, that the sufferings of the individuals concerned have at all times been as little as the nature of the case would admit.

It has been thought extraordinary that, contrary to the stipulations of the cartel, American prisoners have been sent to this country from Canada. This measure was strongly remonstrated against to Colonel Barclay some time ago; but so far from having produced the desired effect, it has been continued under circumstances of the greatest hardship and suffering. About four hundred of these persons, many of whom had never before been at sea, were hurried on board ship, without the least previous notice to provide themselves with necessaries, and in that situation exposed to a boisterous Winter passage. The Government of the United States has sought in vain for a legitimate motive for this conduct, which will necessarily lead to a corresponding measure of severity, if not satisfactorily explained.

I am instructed to make inquiry relative to the situation of all the prisoners who have from time to time been sent to this country; and to give information of places of confinement and treatment of those who were sent here for trial.

I have to remark, that, while the British prisoners in the United States have been treated in exact conformity to the stipulations contained in the cartel, no change whatever has been made in the treatment of American prisoners in close confinement, nor has any satisfactory reason been given why they have not been placed on the same footing.

The situation of the British officers who are held in the United States as hostages to answer in their persons for the safety and proper treatment of the American prisoners, will be found described in the extract of a letter herewith transmitted, dated 13th December, 1813, and it will continue the same while it is understood that American officers, in the hands of the British Government, meet with similar treatment.

I am, sir, most respectfully, your obedient servant,

      R. G. BEASLEY.

ALEXANDER MCLEAY, Esq., &c.

No. 2.

Extracts of a letter of instructions from the Secretary of State to Colonel Tobias Lear.

WASHINGTON, *June* 27, 1814.

On the subject of hostages, if any are retained on either side, it cannot be admitted that a number of prisoners shall be left in the hands of the enemy in that state, or in any other, different from the ordinary state of prisoners of war, greater than shall be held by us to answer for their proper treatment and safety.

You are not unacquainted with the cause which induced the Government to designate certain persons prisoners of war, in our possession, to abide the fate of such American prisoners of war as the enemy had thought proper to separate from their comrades, and to transport, under severe and ignominious confinement, to England, for trial as traitors. While this treatment continued, and while there was a probability of the threatened trial and punishment, this Government could not, and would not, have relaxed in the measures it had adopted. Information, however, having been recently received from Mr. Beasley, American agent for prisoners at London, dated on the 18th of March last, by which it is known that he had received assurances, and that he was satisfied of the fact, that the treatment of the individuals sent to that country, avowedly for trial, has been in no respect different from that of other prisoners of war, the President has been induced to hope, from this circumstance, as well as from the length of time which has elapsed since these persons have been in England, without having been brought to trial, that it is not the intention of the British Government to take a step which would inevitably involve consequences shocking to humanity; and sincerely desirous of lessening, as much as possible, the sufferings of individuals on both sides, he has determined that, reserving to the Government the full right of replacing the hostages, who may have been designated here, and retaining the power to do so, such of the prisoners taken from the command of Sir George Prevost, as have been so designated, may be now exchanged. You are accordingly authorized to stipulate that the proposed release and exchange shall be without distinction of hostages, taking care that it shall be reciprocal, and that a special reservation be made of the right, which may be common, to replace them, whenever it is deemed proper to do so.

No. 3.

Extracts of such parts of a convention for the exchange of prisoners of war, proposed on the 15th of April, 1814, and of the instrument by which it was modified, and finally agreed upon, on the 16th of July following, between agents duly authorized by the Secretary of State of the United States, on the one part, and Sir George Prevost, Commander-in-Chief of the British forces in the Canadas, on the other, as relates to those who had been, on either side, confined under the system of retaliation.

Extracts of the Convention of the 15th of April.

ARTICLE 1. It is mutually stipulated and agreed, that all the persons belonging to the army, navy, or militia, of the United Kingdom of Great Britain and Ireland, or the provinces or dependencies thereof, under the command, authority, and jurisdiction of his excellency Sir George Prevost, or any subjects or residents thereof, within the same command, authority, and jurisdiction, who may have been captives during the present war, under and by the command and authority of the Government of the United States, and also all persons belonging to the navy, army, or militia of the United States, or any of them, or the *territories* thereof, or citizens or residents of the same, or any of them, who may have been made captives during the present war, by and under the command and authority of Sir George Prevost, aforesaid; and which said persons, so respectively captured, are now held in confinement by the said respective parties either as prisoners of war, hostages, or otherwise, shall be mutually and respectively forthwith released from confinement, and sent, or permitted to proceed, to the United States or Canada, respectively, in the manner hereinafter pointed out, with as little delay as may be, saving and excepting always the first three-and-twenty men first put into confinement on principles of retaliation, as hostages, by the United States, and the officers and non-commissioned officers put into confinement by his *excellency* Sir George Prevost, in retaliation for the confinement of the said twenty-three men, private soldiers.

ART. 9. It is further mutually agreed, that all the persons thus released, and sent or permitted to return to their respective countries, who are now in Lower Canada, or on the eastern side of the Alleghany mountains in the United States, and also all prisoners of war who are now on parole, or otherwise in their respective countries, be, and the same are hereby declared to be exchanged, and that they, and every of them, from and after the 15th of May next, shall be perfectly and entirely free to enter and engage in the military, naval, or other service of their repective countries, as if they never had been prisoners of war and hostages; and, in like manner, all the said persons who are on the western side of the Alleghany mountains, in the United States, and those who are in or near Halifax or in Nova Scotia, and who were captured by and under the command of Sir George Prevost, shall be, and are hereby, declared exchanged, and at liberty to enter into the naval, military, or other service of their respective countries, as if they had never been made prisoners of war and hostages.

ART. 12. It is further mutually agreed and expressly understood, that nothing herein contained is intended or shall in any manner prevent or hinder either party from resorting to retaliation, or replacing said hostages, whenever either may deem it proper, for the past or any future act or conduct of the opposite party.

Extracts of the instrument of modification and ratification of the 16th of July.

PREAMBLE.—The following modifications of the said Convention of the 15th of April last have

Great Britain--Prisoners of War.

been agreed to; in consequence of which the same is hereby ratified and confirmed, on the part of the United States, in virtue of the full powers given to the aforesaid Tobias Lear, the same having been before ratified by his excellency Sir George Prevost, &c.

ARTICLE 1. The twenty-three British soldiers put into confinement as hostages by the United States, and the forty-six American commissioned and non-commissioned officers put in confinement by his excellency Sir George Prevost, in retaliation for the confinement of the said twenty-three soldiers, as mentioned in the 1st article of the aforesaid Convention, are to be immediately released and exchanged, in the same manner as other prisoners of war mentioned in said article.

ART. 2. All accounts of exchange, relative to prisoners of war, officers and non-commissioned officers, and privates, of the army, navy, and militia, of the Government of Great Britain, and of the United States of America, and of all other persons, subjects or residents of the one, or citizens or residents of the other, captured by the forces under the command of Sir George Prevost, or from his command or authority, during the present war between Great Britain and the United States, prior to the 15th of April last, and for the release and exchange of whom it is stipulated by the 9th article of the aforesaid Convention of the 15th of April aforesaid, and the twenty-three and forty-six hostages, before mentioned, are by this present modification definitely liquidated and settled, without either party having any pretension or right to any claim therein hereafter.

No. 4.

Extract of a letter from Colonel Thomas Barclay to the Commissary General of Prisoners, dated

BLADENSBURG, *June* 14, 1814.

Should there be any British prisoners of war remaining in these States from New York eastward, permit me to recommend their being released, and sent in the Matilda (cartel) lately arrived at Salem, with American prisoners. In the number I hope you will include all those now held as hostages, and beg leave to assure you, I have recommended to the Admiral and General the release of all Americans held on similar principles, to the state of ordinary prisoners; and that Mr. Mitchell be informed he is at liberty to select them to be sent to these States, in return for British prisoners received.

Extract of a letter from the Commissary General of Prisoners to Colonel Thomas Barclay, dated

JUNE 21, 1812.

On the subject of hostages, I will cheerfully direct to be released and sent to Halifax any such as we now hold on the maritime frontier of Massachusetts, if you will engage that the persons at Halifax, on whose account they were confined, shall be immediately released and returned to the United States. I believe there are but sixteen of that description, whose names are enclosed. The few then remaining, with the desire to meet the relaxation proposed by you, I will direct to be confined, with other non-paroled prisoners, on board the prison-ship at Salem.

Colonel Thomas Barclay to General Mason.

BLADENSBURG, *June* 21, 1814.

SIR: I had hoped, in consequence of my having acquainted you I had recommended the naval and military commanders at Halifax to release to the state of ordinary prisoners all the Americans then held on retaliatory principles, that this Government would have been induced to adopt a similar conciliatory measure, and thereby relieve the unfortunate men who have been so unpleasantly situated. You will, by a reperusal of my late letters on this subject, perceive the unpleasant consequences to which His Majesty's Government will be driven, if the acts above mentioned on the part of His Majesty do not meet a corresponding conduct on the part of this Government.

Mr. Prince, the Marshal of Massachusetts, has informed Mr. Simpeon. that you have directed him to retain eighteen British prisoners as hostages for a like number of men, part of the one hundred and one American prisoners sent last Autumn to England.

On the 14th instant I requested you to inform me whether you would consent that all the British prisoners who might remain in the Eastern States after the departure of the Perseverance cartel to Halifax, should be sent in the Matilda cartel for Halifax, for whom I would order an equivalent to be returned. A measure of this nature must prove equally advantageous to both nations. Permit me to request your answer, and if it is the determination of this Government to hold any British subjects as hostages, that you will favor me with a list of their names, the persons they are held for, and the places of confinement.

I have the honor to be, sir, your obedient servant,

THOMAS BARCLAY.

General MASON, &c.

Extract of a letter from Colonel Thomas Barclay to the Commissary General of Prisoners, dated

BLADENSBURG, *June* 22, 1814.

SIR: I am this moment honored with your letter of yesterday.

I am pleased with your consenting to send all the British prisoners remaining in the Eastern States to Halifax, and that the hostages are to be included. I have repeatedly informed you, that I had requested every American prisoner, held as a hostage at Halifax, should be released to the state of ordinary prisoners, and that Mr. Mitchell should be at liberty to select whom he pleased in making up the equivalent to be sent from Halifax. I will be answerable that the above is carried into effect, and that an equivalent, under Mr. Mitchell's election, is immediately sent from Halifax to Salem, in return for the men whom the Matilda carries from Salem.

Extract of a letter from the Commissary General of Prisoners to Colonel Thomas Barclay, dated

WASHINGTON, *June* 22, 1814.

I have received your letters of this date, and of the 21st instant. I shall, in consequence of your engagement in that of the 22d instant, and in compliance with the terms of mine of yesterday, by the mail made up to-day, instruct Mr. Prince to collect all the prisoners he can, in a reasonable time, and send by the cartel Matilda, and such hostages as have been designated in retaliation against American prisoners confined at Halifax.

The other hostages designated for American prisoners sent to England will be placed in the ordinary state of non-paroled prisoners, and those at Fort Sewall removed to the prison-ship at Salem for that purpose.

Colonel Thomas Barclay to General Mason.

BLADENSBURG, *August* 9, 1814.

SIR: I had hoped, in consequence of my several letters to you on the subject of retaliation and the release of all the American prisoners held as hostages in His Majesty's dominions under retaliatory orders, of which I have given you notice, that this Government would have been induced to follow the example, and place in the ordinary state of prisoners, ready for release and exchange, the few British prisoners named at the foot of this letter, who are still held in confinement as hostages.

I request you will be pleased to inform me, whether it is the intention of this Government to continue these unfortunate men in prison as hostages, and to withhold their release and exchange; and I beg leave to add, that, if this is the case, double the number of American prisoners will once more be placed in a similar state of confinement in retaliation for these men.

I have the honor to be, sir, your most obedient servant,

THOMAS BARCLAY.

General MASON, &c.

List of prisoners referred to in the preceding letter.

In Massachusetts—John Price, R. Robertson, John Anderson, John Egan, James Dawson, Henry Beddingfield, William Kitts.

In Rhode Island—William Lincoln.

Extract of a letter from the Commissary General of Prisoners, to Colonel Barclay, dated

AUGUST 12, 1814.

SIR: In reply to your letter of the 9th instant, I shall pass over the terms in which you have thought proper to convey part of that letter, with the remark, that after the manner in which the subject of hostages had been treated in your letter of the 14th of June, and mine of the 21st and 22d of the same month, considering the information I had given you in my letter of the 30th of May, of the relaxation which had taken place in the condition of the twenty-three hostages in our power at Greenbush, and the cause of it, and the communication I had made you as late as the 28th ultimo, of the Convention concluded with Sir George Prevost, by which these and all other hostages appertaining to the class of prisoners captured by or from his command, were released and finally exchanged, it could not have been expected, when you thought proper to make further inquiry as to the situation of those persons yet remaining in our possession, who had been hostages, and the intention of the Government toward them, you should have then resorted to the same declaration of consequences, conveyed in terms amounting to a threat, which you had been informed in a letter I addressed to you on the 11th of June, on a former occasion, was unavailing, and had been considered exceptionable.

In my letter of the 22d of June, I informed you, that those who had been hostages, and not sent for exchange by the cartel then in port, should be restored to the ordinary state of prisoners. Why, then, unless you were well assured that this had not been done, do you say in yours of the 9th instant, you had hoped that the American Government would have been induced to follow the example of your Government? The fact is, at this time, there is no British prisoner in this country in any other situation. The order to that effect went from this office on the 22d of June, as to the prisoners in Massachusetts; and on the 19th of July, as to one William Lincoln, in Rhode Island. The copy of my letter to the Marshal of that State, now sent, will explain the cause of his confinement being thus much lengthened; namely, his attempt to escape.

The reasons which determined this Government to relax in the mode of treatment towards hostages are detailed in that letter, and were the same which induced it to accept a proposition, on the part of Sir George Prevost, to include all hostages on both sides in the general exchange of prisoners made with him, with the reservation of the right to replace them with others, should it, from any change of circumstances, be deemed necessary. These reasons, to wit: information from our agent in London that the American prisoners, sent to England for trial, were not then confined or treated otherwise than ordinary prisoners, operating generally, so soon as they had been acted on in the exchange of part of the hostages held by us in the quarter just mentioned, produced instructions from this office to put on the same footing "the persons heretofore designated as hostages of the maritime class, and to hold them ready for exchange." They are accordingly now so held.

I have the honor to be, sir, your most obedient servant.

GREAT BRITAIN.

[Communicated to the Senate, by the Messages of February 15, 16, and 20, 1815.]

To the Senate of the United States:

I have received from the American Commissioners a Treaty of Peace and Amity between His Britannic Majesty and the United States of America, signed by those Commissioners and by the Commissioners of His Britannic Majesty at Ghent on the 24th December, 1814. The termination of hostilities depends upon the time of the ratification of the treaty by both parties. I lose no time, therefore, in submitting the treaty to the Senate for their advice and approbation.

I transmit, also, a letter from the American Commissioners which accompanied the treaty.

JAMES MADISON.

FEBRUARY 15, 1815.

To the Senate of the United States:

I transmit to the Senate a report of the acting Secretary of State, complying with their resolution of yesterday.

JAMES MADISON.

FEBRUARY 16, 1815.

[Report of the Secretary of State, referred to in the preceding Message.]

DEPARTMENT OF STATE,
February 16, 1815.

The acting Secretary of State, to whom was referred the resolution of the Senate of the 15th instant, requesting the "President of the United States to cause to be laid before the Senate all instructions given to the Envoys at Ghent, the correspondence between the said Envoys and the Department of State, and the correspondence and protocols of conference between the said Envoys and the Ministers of His Britannic Majesty, during the negotiation at Ghent, which have not before been communicated to the Senate," has the honor to state that the instructions to the Envoys at Ghent have heretofore been communicated to the Senate, except those of which the accompanying papers marked A and B are copies.

The correspondence and protocols of conferences between the said Envoys and the Ministers of His Britannic Majesty which have been received at this Department, and which have not heretofore been communicated to the Senate will be found in the accompanying papers marked 1, 2, 3, 4, 5, 6, 7, 8, and 9.

All which is respectfully submitted.

JAMES MONROE.

To the Senate and House of
Representatives of the United States:

I lay before Congress copies of the Treaty of Peace and Amity between the United States and His Britannic Majesty, which was signed by the Commissioners of both parties, at Ghent, on the 24th of December, 1814, and the ratifications of which have been duly exchanged.

While performing this act, I congratulate you and our constituents upon an event which is highly honorable to the nation, and terminates, with peculiar felicity, a campaign signalized by the most brilliant successes.

The late war, although reluctantly declared by Congress, had become a necessary resort to assert the rights and independence of the nation. It has been waged with a success which is the natural result of the wisdom of the Legislative Councils, of the patriotism of the people, of the public spirit of the militia, and of the valor of the military and naval forces of the country. Peace, at all times a blessing, is peculiarly welcome, therefore, at a period when the causes for the war have ceased to operate; when the Government has demonstrated the efficiency of its powers of defence; and when the nation can review its conduct without regret and without reproach.

I recommend to your care and beneficence the gallant men, whose achievements in every department of military service, on the land and on the water, have so essentially contributed to the honor of the American name, and to the restoration of peace. The feelings of conscious patriotism and worth will animate such men under every change of fortune and pursuit; but their country performs a duty to itself, when it bestows those testimonials of approbation and applause which are at once the reward and the incentive to great actions.

The reduction of the public expenditure to the demands of a Peace Establishment, will doubtless engage the immediate attention of Congress. There are, however, important considerations which forbid a sudden and general revocation of the measures that have been produced by the war. Experience has taught us that neither the pacific dispositions of the American people, nor the pacific character of their political institutions, can altogether exempt them from that strife which appears, beyond the ordinary lot of nations, to be incident to the actual period of the world; and the same faithful monitor demonstrates that a certain degree of preparation for war is not only indispensable to avert disaster in the onset, but affords also the best security for the continuance of peace. The wisdom of Congress will, therefore, I am confident, provide for the maintenance of an adequate regular force; for the gradual advance of the Naval Establishment; for improving all the means of harbor defence; for adding discipline to the distinguished bravery of the militia; and for cultivating the military art, in its essential branches, under the liberal patronage of the Government.

The resources of our country were at all times competent to the attainment of every national object; but they will now be enriched and invigorated by the activity which peace will introduce into all the scenes of domestic enterprise and labor. The provision that has been made for the public creditors, during the present session of Congress, must have a decisive effect in the establishment of the public credit, both at home and abroad.

The reviving interests of commerce will claim the legislative attention at the earliest opportunity, and such regulations will, I trust, be seasonably devised, as shall secure to the United States their just proportion of the navigation of the world. The most liberal policy towards other nations, if met by corresponding dispositions, will, in this respect, be found the most beneficial policy towards ourselves. But there is no subject that can enter with greater force and merit into the deliberations of Congress, than a consideration of the means to preserve and promote the manufactures which have sprung into existence, and attained an unparalleled maturity throughout the United States during the period of the European wars. This source of national independence and wealth I anxiously recommend to the prompt and constant guardianship of Congress.

The termination of the legislative sessions will soon separate you, fellow-citizens, from each other, and restore you to your constituents. I pray you to bear with you the expressions of my sanguine hope that the peace which has been just declared, will not only be the foundation of the most friendly intercourse between the United States and Great Britain, but that it will also be productive of happiness and harmony in every section of our beloved country. The influence of your precept and example must be everywhere powerful, and while we accord in grateful acknowledgments for the protection which Providence has bestowed upon us, let us never cease to inculcate obedience to the laws, and fidelity to the Union, as constituting the palladium of the national independence and prosperity.

JAMES MADISON.

Washington, *February* 18, 1815.

A.

The Secretary of State to the American Plenipotentiaries.

Department of State,
March 22, 1814.

Gentlemen: Should a treaty be concluded with Great Britain, and a reciprocal restitution of territory be agreed on, you will have it in recollection that the United States had in their possession, at the commencement of the war, a post at the mouth of the river Columbia, which commanded the river, which ought to be comprised in the stipulation, should the possession have been wrested from us during the war. On no pretext can the British Government set up a claim to territory south of the northern boundary of the United States. It is not believed that they have any claim whatever to territory on the Pacific ocean. You will, however, be careful, should a definition of boundary be attempted, not to countenance, in any manner, or in any quarter, a pretension in the British Government to territory south of that line.

I have the honor to be, your obedient servant,
JAMES MONROE.
Secretary of State.

B.

The Secretary of State to the American Commissioners at Ghent.

Department of State, *Oct.* 19. 1814.

Gentlemen: I have the honor to inform you that your despatches by the John Adams have been received, and that your determination to reject the terms proposed by the British Commissioners is entirely approved by the President.

The importance of these despatches, and the great probability of your negotiation having been brought to a close, induced the President to determine on laying them before Congress immediately. This has been done, and there is every reason to believe that they are producing the best effect, in uniting all parties in a determined resistance to the extravagant pretensions of the enemy. It has also been judged proper to communicate to Congress so much of the instructions given to you by this Department as would show the terms on which you were authorized to make peace.

These, as well as your communications, have been printed, and several copies are now forwarded to you, as it is believed they may be usefully disposed of in Europe.

Should any circumstance have unexpectedly prolonged the negotiation, which it is *inferred* from your despatches will have been *finally closed*, and you find the British Commissioners *disposed* to agree to the *status ante bellum*, you will understand that you are authorized to make it the basis of a treaty.

I have the honor to be, with great respect, gentlemen, your obedient servant,
JAMES MONROE.

The American Plenipotentiaries to the Secretary of State.

Ghent, *December* 25, 1814.

Sir: We have the honor of transmitting herewith one of the three copies of the Treaty of Peace between Great Britain and the United States, signed last evening by the Plenipotentiaries of His Britannic Majesty and by us.

The papers, of which copies are likewise now forwarded, will exhibit to you so fully the progress of the negotiation since the departure of the Chauncey, that few additional remarks from us will be necessary. It may be proper for us, however, to state that, in the interval between the time when our first project of a treaty was sent to the British Plenipotentiaries and that when they communicated to us the answer to it, the despatches which we had sent by Mr. Dallas, and the instructions to us, which had been published in the United States, were republished in England. In declining to insist on the articles respecting impressment and indemnities, we made a formal declaration that the rights of both parties on the subject of seamen and the claims to indemnities for losses and damages sustained prior to the commencement of the war should not be affected or impaired by the omission in the treaty of a specific provision on these two subjects.

Relations with Great Britain.

From the time when the *projet* of the treaty presented by us was returned with the proposed alterations, it was apparent that, unless new pretensions on the part of Great Britain should be advanced, the only important differences remaining to be discussed were those relating to the mutual restoration of territory taken during the war, to the navigation of the Mississippi by British subjects, and to the right of the people of the United States to the fisheries within the British jurisdiction. Instead of a general restitution of captured territory, which we had proposed, the British Government at first wished to confine it to the territory taken by either party belonging to the other. On our objecting that this would make each party the judge whether territory taken did or did not belong to the other, and thereby occasion new disputes, they acknowledged it to be their object that each party should, until a decision had taken place with respect to the title, retain possession of all the territory claimed by both parties, which might have been taken by such party during the war. They proposed, however, to limit the exception from mutual restitution to the islands in the Bay of Passamaquoddy. As it had been on both sides admitted that the title to these islands was disputed, and as a method of settling amicably those disputes was provided for in the treaty, we had not expected that the British Government would adhere to the demand of retaining the temporary possession of those islands. We insisted, therefore, on their being included in the general restoration, until we had reason to believe that our further perseverance would have hazarded the conclusion of the peace itself. We finally consented, as an alternative preferable to the continuance of the war, to this exception, upon condition that it should not be understood as impairing in any manner the right of the United States to these islands. We also urged for a stipulation requiring an ultimate decision upon the title within a limited time; but to this we also found opposed an insuperable objection, and we were finally induced to accept in its stead a declaration of the British Plenipotentiaries, that no unnecessary delay of the decision should be interposed on the part of Great Britain.

At the first conference, on the 8th of August, the British Plenipotentiaries had notified to us that the British Government did not intend henceforth to allow to the people of the United States, without an equivalent, the liberties to fish and to dry and cure fish within the exclusive British jurisdiction, stipulated in their favor by the latter part of the third article of the Treaty of Peace of 1783. And in their note of the 19th of August, the British Plenipotentiaries had demanded a new stipulation, to secure to British subjects the right of navigating the Mississippi; a demand which, unless warranted by another article of that same treaty of 1783, we could not perceive that Great Britain had any colorable pretence for making. Our instructions had forbidden us to suffer our right to the fisheries to be brought into discussion, and had not authorized us to make any distinction in the several provisions of the third article

of the treaty of 1783, or between that article and any other of the same treaty. We had no equivalent to offer for a new recognition of our right to any part of the fisheries, and we had no power to grant any equivalent which might be asked for it by the British Government. We contended that the whole treaty of 1783 must be considered as one entire and permanent compact, not liable, like ordinary treaties, to be abrogated by a subsequent war between the parties to it; as an instrument recognising the rights and liberties enjoyed by the people of the United States as an independent nation, and containing the terms and conditions on which the two parts of one empire had mutually agreed, thenceforth. to constitute two distinct and separate nations. In consenting, by that treaty, that a part of the North American continent should remain subject to the British jurisdiction, the people of the United States had reserved to themselves the liberty, which they had ever before enjoyed, of fishing upon that part of its coasts, and of drying and curing fish upon the shores, and this reservation had been agreed to by the other contracting party. We saw not why this liberty, then no new grant, but the mere recognition of a prior right always enjoyed, should be forfeited by war, any more than any other of the rights of our national independence; or why we should need a new stipulation for its enjoyment more than we needed a new article to declare that the King of Great Britain treated with us as free, sovereign, and independent States. We stated this principle in general terms to the British Plenipotentiaries, in the note which we sent to them with our *projet* of the treaty, and we alleged it as the ground upon which no new stipulation was deemed by our Government necessary to secure to the people of the United States all the rights and liberties stipulated in their favor by the treaty of 1783. No reply to that part of our note was given by the British Plenipotentiaries, but, in returning our *projet* of a treaty, they added a clause to one of the articles, stipulating a right for British subjects to navigate the Mississippi. Without adverting to the ground of prior and immemorial usage, if the principle were just that the treaty of 1783, from its peculiar character, remained in force in all its parts, notwithstanding the war, no new stipulation was necessary to secure to the subjects of Great Britain the right of navigating the Mississippi, so far as that right was secured by the treaty of 1783, as, on the other hand, no stipulation was necessary to secure to the people of the United States the liberty to fish, and to dry and cure fish, within the exclusive jurisdiction of Great Britain. If they asked the navigation of the Mississippi as a new claim, they could not expect we should grant it without an equivalent; if they asked it because it had been granted in 1783, they must recognise the claim of the people of the United States to the liberty to fish and to dry and cure fish, in question. To place both points beyond all future controversy, a majority of us determined to offer to admit an article confirming both the rights, or we offered at the same time to be silent in the treaty upon both, and to leave out altogether the article defining the boundary from the Lake of the Woods westward. They finally agreed to this last proposal, but not until they had proposed an article stipulating for a future negotiation for an equivalent to be given by Great Britain for the navigation of the Mississippi, and by the United States for the liberty as to the fisheries within British jurisdiction. This article was unnecessary with regard to its professed object, since both Governments had it in their power, without it, to negotiate upon these subjects if they pleased. We rejected it, although its adoption would have secured the boundary of the forty-ninth degree of latitude west of the Lake of the Woods, because it would have been a formal abandonment, on our part, of our claim to the liberty as to the fisheries, recognised by the treaty of 1783.

You will perceive by the correspondence, that the ninth article was offered us as a *sine qua non* and an ultimatum. We accepted it, not without much hesitation, as the only alternative to a rupture of the negotiation, and with a perfect understanding that our Government was free to reject it, as we were not authorized to subscribe to it.

To guard against any accident which might happen in the transmission of a single copy of the treaty to the United States, the British Plenipotentiaries have consented to execute it in triplicate; and as the treaty with the British ratification may be exposed to the same danger, the times for the cessation of hostilities, the restoration of captures at sea, and the release of prisoners, have been fixed, not from the exchange of ratifications, but from the ratification on both sides, without alteration by either of the contracting parties. We consented to the introduction of this latter provision at the desire of the British Plenipotentiaries, who were willing to take a full, but were unwilling to incur the risk of a partial ratification, as the period from which the peace should be considered as concluded.

We are informed by them that Mr. Baker, their secretary, is to go out to America with the British ratification.

We have the honor to be, yours, &c.
JOHN QUINCY ADAMS,
J. A. BAYARD,
H. CLAY,
JONATHAN RUSSELL,
ALBERT GALLATIN.
The SECRETARY OF STATE
of the United States.

No. 1.

The American to the British Plenipotentiaries.
GHENT, *November* 10, 1814.

The undersigned have the honor to acknowledge the receipt of the note addressed to them by His Britannic Majesty's Plenipotentiaries on the 31st ultimo.

The undersigned had considered an interchange of the *projet* of a treaty as the course best calculated to exclude useless and desultory discussion, to confine the attention of both parties to the precise objects to be adjusted between the two nations, and to hasten the conclusion of the peace so desirable to both. Finding in the note of the British Plenipotentiaries of the 21st ultimo a mere reference to the points proposed by them in the first conference, with the offer of assuming the basis of *uti possidetis*, on which the undersigned had, in substance, already declined to treat, they did not consider it as the *projet* of a treaty, presented in compliance with their request. They proposed, in their note of the 24th ultimo, that the exchange of the two *projets* should be made at the same time. And it is not without some surprise that the undersigned observe in the note to which they now have the honor of replying, that the British Plenipotentiaries consider their note of the 21st ultimo as containing the *projet* of a treaty, to which the undersigned are supposed to be pledged to return a *contre projet*.

Believing that where both parties are sincerely desirous of bringing a negotiation to a happy termination, the advantage of giving or of receiving the first draught is not of a magnitude to be made a subject of controversy, and convinced that their Government is too sincerely desirous of that auspicious result to approve of its being delayed for a moment upon any question of *etiquette*, the undersigned have the honor to enclose herewith the *projet* of a treaty, accompanied with some observations upon several of the articles, which may more fully elucidate their objects in proposing them.

The British Plenipotentiaries stated in their last note that they had no other propositions to offer, nor other demands to make, than those contained in their note of the 21st ultimo, which, with the reference to their former declaration respecting the fisheries, contains only two propositions, viz: that of fixing the boundary from the Lake of the Woods to the Mississippi; and that of adopting, with respect to the other boundaries, the basis of *uti possidetis.*

In answer to the declaration made by the British Plenipotentiaries respecting the fisheries, the undersigned, referring to what passed in the conference of the 9th of August, can only state that they are not authorized to bring into discussion any of the rights or liberties which the United States have heretofore enjoyed in relation thereto. From their nature, and from the peculiar character of the treaty of 1783, by which they were recognised, no further stipulation has been deemed necessary by the Government of the United States to entitle them to the full enjoyment of all of them.

The undersigned have already, in their last note, explicitly declined treating on the basis of *uti possidetis.* They cannot agree to any other principle than that of a mutual restoration of territory, and have accordingly prepared an article founded on that basis. They are willing even to extend the same principle to the other objects in dispute between the two nations; and in proposing all the other articles included in this *projet*, they wish to be distinctly understood that they are ready to sign a treaty placing the two countries, in respect to all the subjects of difference between them, in the same state they were in at the commencement of the present war; reserving to each party all its rights, and leaving whatever may remain of controversy between them for future and pacific negotiation.

The British Plenipotentiaries having, in their note of the 4th of September, communicated the disposition of their Government to receive favorably a proposition which should acknowledge the boundary from the Lake of the Woods to the Mississippi, or to discuss any other line of boundary which might be submitted for consideration, the undersigned answered, that, as soon as the proposition of Indian boundary should be disposed of, they would have no objection, with the explanation given by the British Plenipotentiaries, to discuss the subject.

The Government of the United States had, prior to the acquisition of Louisiana, been disposed to agree to the boundary from the Lake of the Woods to the Mississippi, from a wish, not only to arrange that subject, but also to settle, in a definitive manner, the differences respecting the boundary and islands in the bay of Passamaquoddy; and its assent to the proposed stipulation of that boundary was refused, on account of the acquisition of Louisiana, the boundaries of which might have been affected by it. The undersigned cannot agree to fix the boundary in that quarter, unless that of Louisiana be also provided for in the arrangement. They accordingly submit for consideration the article on that subject, which appears to have been agreed on between the British and American Commissioners in the *projet* of convention of the year 1807.

In respect to the intended revision of the other boundaries between the British and American territories, with the view to prevent future uncertainty and dispute, the undersigned propose the reference of the whole subject to Commissioners; and they present, accordingly, five articles, drawn on the principle formerly adopted by the two Powers for settling the question respecting the river St. Croix.

The article already agreed on respecting the Indian pacification is included in the *projet* of the undersigned. In conformity with their former suggestions, they offer another, intended to restrain the hostilities, and to prevent the employment of the savages in war, and one reciprocally granting a general amnesty. The only other subjects which had been presented by the undersigned, as suitable for discussion, were those respecting seamen, blockades, and indemnities.

Keeping in view the declarations made by Lord Castlereagh, in his note of the 20th of August, 1812, to Mr. Russell, and in his letter of the 4th of November, 1813, to Mr. Monroe, the undersigned propose only a temporary article, intended, without affecting the rights or pretensions of either country, to attempt to accomplish, by means less liable to vexation, the object for which impressment has hitherto been thought necessary by Great Britain. The proposed agreement be-

ing purely conditional, and limited in duration, each party will be bound only so far and so long as the other shall fulfil its conditions, and at the end of the term fixed for the duration of the article, or whenever either party may fail to perform his engagement, the rights of both will be as valid and entire as they were before the agreement.

The article respecting blockades is believed to be in perfect conformity with the principles of the law of nations, as acknowledged by both nations. The definition is borrowed from the treaty of 1801, between Great Britain and Russia, and the residue of the article from the unratified treaty of 1806, between Great Britain and the United States.

That relating to indemnities consists of two parts; the first for irregular seizures, captures, and condemnations, of American property, contrary to the established laws and usages of nations, previous to the commencement of the war; and the second, for similar irregularities, committed during the war, and contrary to the known and established usages of war between civilized nations. The cases of the first apply exclusively to claims of the citizens of the United States, because the causes for such claims were then confined, by the relative situation of the parties, to one side. It is presumed that the British Government will itself be sensible of the justice of making indemnity for injuries committed by its officers, in violation of principles avowed and recognised by itself, particularly in the letter from Lord Hawkesbury to Mr. King of the 11th of April, 1801; and in that from Mr. Merry to Mr. Madison of the 12th of April, 1804; and that the same justice will be admitted in cases where the territorial jurisdiction of the United States was violated; and where the injury was occasioned by the retrospective effects of the British Orders in Council of June, 1803, as to the return from contraband voyages, and of the Orders in Council of January 7, 1807.

With regard to the Orders in Council of November, 1803, and of April, 1809, the undersigned will observe, that these orders having been issued solely on the ground of retaliation against France, and their object having altogether ceased, it is just to indemnify the citizens of the United States for losses now experienced by the effect of measures intended to operate against the enemy of Great Britain, and which fell almost exclusively on a country which was no party to the war. The United States have never ceased, and at this time continue to demand from France, indemnity for the losses they have experienced by the effect of the decrees of her Government, in violation of the law of nations.

The cases of the second part of this article apply equally to both belligerent parties. They have been, during the war, subjects of crimination on both sides. The American Government can give no stronger and more signal proof of its disapprobation of every departure, under color of its authority, from the established usages of legitimate warfare between civilized nations, than by the offer of mutual reparation.

Relations with Great Britain.

The article fixing a limitation for captures at sea does not seem to require any comment.

The undersigned present their entire *projet* in this specific form, with the full expectation of receiving from the British Plenipotentiaries their explicit answer respecting all the *articles* embraced in it, and a *projet* also reduced to specific propositions and embracing all the objects *which* they intend to bring forward.

The undersigned renew to the British Plenipotentiaries the assurances of their high consideration.

JOHN QUINCY ADAMS,
J. A. BAYARD,
H. CLAY,
JONATHAN RUSSELL,
ALBERT GALLATIN.

To the PLENIPOTENTIARIES *of His Britannic Majesty, &c.*

No. 2.

Copy of a projet of a Treaty of Peace submitted by the American to the British Plenipotentiaries at Ghent, on the 10th day of November, 1814, and of the alterations and propositions made by the latter in the margin of the said projet, returned by them to the American Plenipotentiaries.

TREATY OF PEACE AND AMITY BETWEEN HIS BRITANNIC MAJESTY AND THE UNITED STATES OF AMERICA.

His Britannic Majesty and the United States of America, desirous of terminating the war which has unhappily subsisted between the two countries, and of restoring, upon principles of perfect reciprocity, peace, friendship, and good understanding between them, have, for that purpose, appointed their respective plenipotentiaries, that is to say, His Britannic Majesty, on his part, has appointed the Right Honorable James Lord Gambier, Admiral of the White Squadron of His Majesty's fleet; Henry Goulburn, Esq., a member of the Imperial Parliament, and Under Secretary of State, and William Adams, Esquire, Doctor of Civil Laws; and the President of the United States, by and with the advice and consent of the Senate thereof, has appointed John Quincy Adams, James A. Bayard, Henry Clay, Jonathan Russell, and Albert Gallatin, citizens of the United States, who, after a reciprocal communication of their respective full powers, have agreed upon the following articles:

ARTICLE 1.

There shall be a firm and universal peace between His Britannic Majesty and the United States, and between their respective countries, territories, cities, towns, and people, of every degree, without exception of (1) persons or *places*. All hostilities, both by sea and land, shall *immediately* cease; (2) *all prisoners on both sides shall be set at liberty.* All territory, places, and possessions, without exception, *taken by* (3) either party *from* (4) the other during the war, or which may be taken after the signing of this treaty, shall be restored without delay and without causing any destruction, or carrying away any artillery or other public property, or any slaves (5) or other private property; (6) and all archives, records, deeds, and papers, either of a public nature or belonging to private persons, which, in the course of the war, may have fallen into the hands of the officers of either party, shall be (7) forthwith restored, and delivered to the proper authorities and persons to whom they respectively belong.

ARTICLE 2.

Immediately after the respective ratifications of this treaty, (2) orders shall be sent to the armies, squadrons, officers, subjects, and citizens of the two Powers, to cease from all hostilities; and to prevent all causes of complaint which might arise on account of the

British Alterations.

The following marginal remarks and alterations were made and proposed by the British Plenipotentiaries.

Note.—It is proposed to omit altogether the words that are underlined.

(1) Places or
(2) after the exchange of the ratifications as hereafter mentioned.

° It is thought more advisable that the provision respecting prisoners of war should be the subject of a separate article. The draught of an article on this subject is subjoined.

(3) belonging to
(4) and taken by
(5) of the
(6) originally captured in the said forts or places, and which shall remain therein upon the exchange of the ratifications of this treaty.
(7) as far as may be practicable.

(2) shall be exchanged.

prizes which may be taken at sea, after the (3) signing of this treaty, it is reciprocally agreed that the vessels and effects which may be taken in the channel, and in the North seas after the space of ——, from (1) that of the signature hereof, shall be restored on each side; that the term shall be ——, from the channel and the North seas to the Canary islands inclusively, (2) whether in the ocean or the Mediterranean, of —— from the said Canary islands to the equinoctial line, or Equator, and of —— in all other parts of the world without exception.

ARTICLE 3.

Whereas that portion of the boundary between the dominions of His Britannic Majesty in North America and those of the United States, from the mouth of the river St. Croix (as the said mouth was ascertained by the Commissioners appointed for that purpose,) to the Bay of Fundy, has not yet been regulated and determined; and whereas the respective rights and claims of His Britannic Majesty and of the United States to the several islands in the Bay of Passamaquoddy and to the island of Grand Menan, have never been finally adjusted and determined, the said islands being claimed on the part of the United States as lying within twenty leagues of their shores, and south of a line drawn due east from the mouth of the river St. Croix: and on the part of His Britannic Majesty as having been, at or before the former treaty of peace between the two countries, within the limits of the province of Nova Scotia. In order, therefore, finally to decide these several questions, it is agreed that they shall be referred to three Commissioners, to be appointed in the following manner, viz: one Commissioner shall be appointed by His Britannic Majesty, and one by the President of the United States, by and with the advice and consent of the Senate thereof, and the said two Commissioners shall have power to choose a third; and, if they cannot agree, they shall each propose one person; and of the two names so proposed one shall be drawn by lot, in the presence of the two original Commissioners. And the three Commissioners so appointed shall be sworn impartially to examine and decide the said questions, according to such evidence as shall respectively be laid before them, on the part of the British Government and of the United States. The said Commissioners shall meet at ——, and shall have power to adjourn to such other place or places as they shall think fit. The said Commissioners, or a majority of them, shall, by a declaration under their hands and seals, determine the boundary aforesaid, from the mouth of the river St. Croix to the Bay of Fundy, and decide to which of the two contracting parties the several islands aforesaid do respectively belong, in conformity with the true intent of the former treaty of peace. And both parties agree to consider such decision as final and conclusive.

(3) exchange of ratifications.

(1) the period of the exchange of the ratifications.

(2) The same term of —— for all parts of the Mediterranean.

ARTICLE 3.

Whereas it was stipulated by the second article in the Treaty of Peace of 1783, between His Britannic Majesty and the United States of America, that the boundary of the United States should comprehend "all islands within twenty leagues of any part of the shores of the United States, and lying between lines to be drawn due east from the points where the aforesaid boundaries, between Nova Scotia on the one part and East Florida on the other, shall respectively touch the Bay of Fundy and the Atlantic ocean, excepting such islands as now or heretofore have been within the limits of Nova Scotia." And whereas claims have been made by the Government of the United States to certain islands in the Bay of Fundy, which said islands are claimed as belonging to His Britannic Majesty, as having been at the time and previous to the aforesaid Treaty of 1783, within the limits of the province of Nova Scotia. In order, therefore, finally to decide upon these claims, it is agreed that they shall be referred to two Commissioners to be appointed in the following manner, viz: one Commissioner shall be appointed by His Britannic Majesty, and one by the President of the United States, by and with the advice and consent of the Senate thereof, and the said two Commissioners so appointed shall be sworn impartially to examine and decide upon the said claims, according to such evidence as shall be laid before them on the part of His Britannic Majesty and of the United States, respectively. The said Commissioners shall meet at ——, and shall have power to adjourn to such other place or places as they shall think fit. The said Commissioners shall, by a declaration or report under their hands and seals, decide to which of the two contracting parties the several islands aforesaid do respectively belong, in conformity with the true intent of the said Treaty of Peace of 1783; and if the said Commissioners shall agree in their decision, both parties shall consider such decision final and conclusive.

It is further agreed that, in the event of the two Commissioners differing upon all or any of the matters so referred to them, or in the event of both or either of the said Commissioners refusing or declining, or wilfully omitting to act as such, they shall make, jointly or separately, a report or reports, as well to the Government of His Britannic Majesty as to that of the United States, stating in detail the points on which they differ, and the grounds upon which their respective opinions have been formed, or the grounds upon which they, or either of them, have so refused, declined, or omitted to act. And His Britannic Majesty and the Government of the United States hereby agree to refer the report or reports of the said Commissioners to some friendly Sovereign or State, to be then named for that purpose, and who shall be requested to decide on the differences which may be stated in the said report or reports, or upon the report of one Commissioner, together with the grounds upon which the other Commissioner shall have so refused, declined, or omitted to act, as the case may be. And if the Commissioner so refusing, declining, or omitting to act, shall also wilfully omit to state the grounds upon which he has so done, in such manner that the said statement may be referred to such friendly Sovereign or State, together with the report of such other Commissioner, then such Sovereign or State shall decide ex *parte* upon the said report alone, and His Britannic Majesty and the Government of the United States engage to consider the decision of such friendly Sovereign or State to be final and conclusive on all the matters so referred.

ARTICLE 4.

Whereas, neither that point of the Highlands, lying due north from the source of the river St. Croix, and designated in the former treaty of peace between the two Powers, as the northwest angle of Nova Scotia, nor the northwesternmost head of Connecticut river, has yet been ascertained ; and whereas that part of the boundary line between the dominions of the two Powers, which extends from the source of the river St. Croix, directly, north to the above-mentioned northwest angle of Nova Scotia, thence along the said Highlands which divide those rivers that empty themselves into the river St. Lawrence from those which fall into the Atlantic ocean, to the northwesternmost head of Connecticut river, thence down along the middle of that river to the forty-fifth degree of north latitude, thence by a line due west on said latitude, until it strikes the river Iroquois, or Cataraquy, has not yet been surveyed ; it is agreed that for these several purposes (1) *three* Commissioners shall be appointed, sworn, (*mutatis mutandis*,) and authorized to act exactly in the manner directed, with respect to those mentioned in the next preceding article. (2) The said Commissioners shall meet at ——, and shall have power to adjourn to such other place or places as they shall think fit. The said Commissioners, or a majority of them, shall have power to ascertain and determine the points abovementioned, in conformity with the provisions of the said treaty of peace, (3) and shall cause the boundary aforesaid, from the source of the river St. Croix to the river Iroquois, or Cataraquy, to be surveyed and marked according to the said provisions. The said Commissioners, or a majority of them, shall make a map of the said boundary, and annex to it a declaration under their hands and seals, certifying it to be the true map of the said boundary, and particularizing the latitude and longitude of the northwest angle of Nova Scotia, of the northwesternmost head of Connecticut river, and of such other points of the said boundary as they may deem proper. And both parties agree to consider such map and declaration as finally and conclusively fixing the said boundary, (4)

ARTICLE 5.

Whereas, by the former Treaty of Peace, that portion of the boundary of the United States, from the point where the forty-fifth degree of north latitude strikes the river Iroquois, or Cataraquy, to the Lake Superior was declared to be, " Along the middle of said river into Lake Ontario, through the middle of said lake until it strikes the communication by water between that lake and Lake Erie ; thence, along the middle of said communication, into Lake Erie, through the middle of said

ARTICLE 4.

(1) Two

(2) unless otherwise specified in the present article.

(3) 1783

(4) And in the event of the said two Commissioners differing, or both or either of them refusing, declining, or wilfully omitting to act, such reports, declarations, or statements, shall be made by them, or either of them, and such reference to a friendly Sovereign or State, shall be made in all respects as in the latter part of the third article is contained, and in as full a manner as if the same was herein repeated.

ARTICLE 5.

Relations with Great Britain.

lake, until it arrives at the water communication into the Lake Huron; thence, through the middle of said lake to the water communication between that lake and Lake Superior." And whereas doubts have arisen what was the middle of said river, lakes, and water communications, and whether certain islands lying in the same were within the dominions of His Britannic Majesty or of the United States: In order, therefore, finally to decide these *questions,* (1) they shall be referred to (2) *three* Commissioners, to be appointed, sworn, (*mutatis mutandis*) and authorized to act, exactly in the manner directed with respect to these mentioned in the next preceding article. (3) The said Commissioners shall meet, in the first instance, at ——, and shall have power to adjourn to such other place or places as they shall think fit. The said Commissioners, or a majority of them, shall, by a (4) declaration, under their hands and seals, designate the boundary through the said river, lakes, and water communications, and decide to which of the two contracting parties the several islands lying within the said rivers, lakes, and water communications, do respectively belong, in conformity with the true intent of the (5) *former Treaty of Peace.* And both parties agree to consider such (6) decision as final and conclusive. (7)

(1) doubts   (2) two

(3) unless otherwise specified in this present article.

(4) report or
(5) said treaty of 1783.
(6) designation and
(7) And in the event of the said two Commissioners differing, or both, or either of them, refusing, declining, or wilfully omitting to act, such reports, declarations, or statements shall be made by them, or either of them, and such reference to a friendly Sovereign or State shall be made, in all respects, as in the latter part of the third article is contained, and in as full a manner as if the same was herein repeated.

ARTICLE 6.

It is further agreed, that the said (1) last mentioned Commissioners, after they shall have executed the duties assigned to them in the preceding article, shall be, and they, or a majority of them, are hereby, authorised, upon their oaths, impartially to fix and determine, according to the true intent of the said *former* (2) Treaty of Peace, that part of the boundary between the dominions of the two Powers, which extends from the water communication between Lake Huron and Lake Superior to the most northwestern point of the Lake of the Woods; to decide to which of the two parties the several islands lying in the lakes, water communications, and rivers, forming the said boundary, do respectively belong, in conformity with the true intent of the said *former* Treaty of Peace, (3) and to cause such parts of the said boundary as require it to be surveyed and marked. The said Commissioners, or a majority of them, shall, by a (4) declaration under their hands and seals, designate the boundary aforesaid, state their decisions on the (5) *questions* thus referred to them, and particularize the latitude and longitude of the most northwestern point of the Lake of the Woods, and of such other (6) *points on* the said boundary as they may deem proper. And both parties agree to consider such (7) decision as final and conclusive. (8)

ARTICLE 6.

(1) two

(2) of 1783

(3) of 1783
(4) report or
(5) points
(6) parts of
(7) designation and
(8) And in the event of the said two Commissioners differing, or both, or either of them, refusing, declining, or wilfully omitting to act, such reports, declarations, or statements shall be made by them, or either of them, and such reference to a friendly Sovereign or State shall be made, in all respects, as in the latter part of the third article is contained, and in as full a manner as if the same was herein repeated.

ARTICLE 7.

The several Boards of (1) Commissioners mentioned in the four preceding articles shall, respectively, have power to appoint a secretary, and to employ such surveyors or other persons as they shall judge necessary. Duplicates of (2) their respective (3) declarations (4) and decisions *of the statement* (5) of their accounts and of the journal of their proceedings, shall be delivered by them to the agents of His Britannic Majesty, and the agents of the United States, who may be respectively appointed and authorized to manage the business on behalf of their respective Governments. The said Commissioners shall be respectively paid in such manner as shall be agreed between the two (6) parties, such

ARTICLE 7.

(1) two

(2) all   (3) reports   (4) statements
(5) and

(6) contracting

Relations with Great Britain.

agreement being to be settled at the time of the exchange of the ratifications of this treaty. And all other expenses attending the said commissions shall be defrayed (7) *jointly* by the two parties, *the same being previously ascertained and allowed by the majority of the Commissioners.* And in the case of death, sickness, resignation, or necessary absence, the place of every such Commissioner, respectively, shall be supplied in the same manner as such Commissioner was first appointed; and the new Commissioner shall take the same oath or affirmation, and do the same duties.

It is further agreed between the two (8) parties, that in case any of the islands mentioned in any of the preceding articles which were in the possession of one of the parties prior to the commencement of the present war between the two countries, should, by the decision of any of the Boards of Commissioners aforesaid, (9) fall within the dominions of the other party, all grants of land made previous to that time by the party having had such possession, shall be as valid as if such island or islands had, by such decision or decisions, been adjudged to be within the dominions of the party having had such possession.

(7) equally

(8) contracting

(9) or of the Sovereign or State so referred to, as in many of the preceding articles contained.

ARTICLE 8.

It is agreed that a line drawn due north or south, (as the case may be,) from the most northwestern point of the Lake of the Woods, until it shall intersect the forty-ninth parallel of north latitude, and from the point of such intersection, due west along and with the said parallel, shall be the dividing line between His Majesty's territories and those of the United States to the westward of the said lake, as far as the said respective territories extend in that quarter, and that the said line shall to that extent form the southern boundary of His Majesty's said territories, and the northern boundary of the said territories of the United States: Provided, that nothing in the present article shall be construed to extend to the northwest coast of America, or to the territories belonging to, or claimed by, either party on the continent of America to the westward of the Stony Mountains.

ARTICLE 8.

It is agreed that a line drawn due west from the Lake of the Woods, along forty-ninth parallel of north latitude, shall be the line of demarcation between His Britannic Majesty's territories and those of the United States to the westward of the said lake, so far as the territories of the United States extend in that quarter; and the said line shall, to that extent, form the southern boundary of His Britannic Majesty's territories, and the northern boundary of the territories of the United States. It being always distinctly understood, that nothing in the present article shall be construed to extend to the northwest coast of America, or to territories belonging to, or claimed by, either party on the continent of America westward of the Stony Mountains; (and it is further agreed the subjects of His Britannic Majesty shall at all times have access) from His Britannic Majesty's territories, by land or inland navigation, into the aforesaid territories of the United States to the river Mississippi, with their goods, effects, and merchandise, and that His Britannic Majesty's subjects shall have and enjoy the free navigation of the said river.

ARTICLE 9.

The United States of America engage to put an end, immediately after the ratification of the present treaty, to hostilities with all the tribes or nations of Indians with whom they may be at war at the time of such ratification, and forthwith to restore to such tribes or nations respectively all the possessions, rights, and privileges, which they may have enjoyed or been entitled to, in 1811, previous to such hostilities.

Provided, alwaye, That such tribes or nations shall agree to desist from all hostilities against the United States of America, their citizens and subjects, upon the ratification of the present treaty being notified to such tribes or nations, and shall so desist accordingly.

And His Britannic Majesty engages on his part to put an end, immediately after the ratification of the present treaty, to hostilities with all the tribes or nations of Indians with whom he may be at war at the time of such ratification, and forthwith to restore to such tribes or nations respectively all the possessions,

ARTICLE 9.

Approved.

rights, and privileges, which they may have enjoyed or been entitled to in 1811, previous to such hostilities.

Provided, always, That such tribes or nations shall agree to desist from all hostilities against His Britannic Majesty and his subjects, upon the ratification of the present treaty being notified to such tribes or nations, and shall so desist accordingly.

Article 10.

His Britannic Majesty and the United States shall, by all the means in their power, restrain the Indians living within their respective dominions from committing hostilities against the territory, citizens, or subjects of the other party. And both Powers also agree, and mutually pledge themselves, if at any time war should unhappily break out between them, not to employ any Indians, nor to admit of their aid and co-operation in the prosecution of the war against the other party.

Article 11.

Each party shall effectually exclude from its naval and commercial service all seamen, seafaring or other persons, subjects or citizens of the other party, not naturalized by the respective Governments of the two parties before the ——— day of ———.

Seamen or other persons, subjects of either party, who shall desert from public or private ships or vessels, shall, when found within the jurisdiction of either party, be surrendered, provided they be demanded within ——— from the time of their desertion.

No person whatever shall, upon the high seas, and without the jurisdiction of either party, be demanded or taken out of any ship or vessel belonging to the subjects or citizens of one of the parties, by the public or private armed ships or vessels belonging to, or in the service of the other, unless such person be at the time in the actual employment of an enemy of such other party.

This article shall continue in force for the term of ——— years. Nothing in this article contained shall be construed thereafter to affect or impair the rights of either party.

Article 12.

If either of the contracting parties shall hereafter be engaged in war against any third Power, to which war the other of the parties shall remain neutral, it is agreed that every vessel of the neutral party, sailing for a port or place belonging to the enemy of the belligerent, without knowing that the same is besieged, blockaded, or invested, may be turned away from such port or place, but shall not be detained, nor her cargo, if not contraband, be confiscated, unless, after such notice, she shall again attempt to enter; but she shall be permitted to go to any other port or place she may think proper. Nor shall any vessel or goods of either party, that may have entered into such port or place before the same was besieged, blockaded, or invested by the other, and be found therein after the reduction or surrender of such place, be liable to confiscation, but shall be restored to the proprietors thereof; and in order to determine what characterizes a blockaded port, that denomination is given only to a port where there is, by the disposition of the Power which attacks it with ships stationary or sufficiently near, an evident danger in entering.

Article 13.

It is agreed that indemnity shall be made by His Britannic Majesty to the citizens of the United States

---

Article 10.

Inadmissible.

Article 11.

Inadmissible.

Article 12.

Inadmissible.

Article 13.

for all losses and damage sustained by them during the late war, between Great Britain and France, and prior to the commencement of the present war, by reason of irregular or illegal captures, seizures, or condemnations of vessels and other property, under color of authority, contrary to the known and established rules of the law of nations.

And it is also agreed, that indemnity shall be made by each of the contracting parties to the subjects or citizens of the other party, for all losses and damages sustained subsequent to the commencement of the present war, by reason of the seizure or condemnation of the vessels or cargoes belonging to the subjects or citizens of the one party, which, in the ordinary course of commerce, happened, at the commencement of hostilities, to be in the ports of the other party, and by reason of the destruction of unfortified towns, and the pillage or destruction of private property, and the enticement and carrying away of negroes, contrary to the known and established rules and usages of war between civilized nations.

It is agreed that, for the purpose of determining the indemnities due by each contracting party, in conformity with the provisions of this article, Commissioners shall be appointed in the following manner, viz: one Commissioner shall be named by His Britannic Majesty, and one by the President of the United States, by and with the advice and consent of the Senate thereof, and the said two Commissioners shall agree in the choice of a third; or, if they cannot agree, they shall each propose one person, and of the two names so proposed one shall be taken by lot, in the presence of the two original Commissioners, and the three Commissioners thus appointed shall be sworn, and authorized, and empowered, impartially to examine into all such claims and complaints, and to determine the indemnities which may be justly due for the same.

The said Commissioners shall meet at ——, and shall have power to adjourn to such other place or places as they shall think fit; they shall also have power to appoint a secretary, swear and examine witnesses, and have all assistance and facilities necessary to effect the object of their appointment.

The award of the said Commissioners, or a majority of them, shall in all cases be final and conclusive, both as to the justice of the claim, and as to the amount of the sum to be paid to the claimant and claimants.

And His Britannic Majesty and the United States agree and undertake to cause the sums so awarded to be due by them respectively, to be paid in specie to such claimant and claimants without deduction, and at such place or places, time or times, as shall be awarded by the Commissioners.

ARTICLE 14.

It is also agreed, that no person or persons residing within the dominions of one of the parties, who may have taken part with the other party in the war between Great Britain and the United States, shall, on that account, be prosecuted, molested, or annoyed, either in his person or property, and that all such persons disposed to remove into the dominions of the other party, shall be allowed the term of —— months freely to sell their property, of every nature and description whatever, and to remove accordingly

Inadmissible.

ARTICLE 14.

Inadmissible.

ARTICLE 15.

This Treaty, when the same shall have been ratified on both sides, and the *respective* ratifications mutually exchanged, shall be binding on both parties, and the ratifications shall be exchanged at (1) ——— in the space of —— months from this day, or sooner if *possible.*(2)

In faith whereof, we, the respective Plenipotentiaries, have signed this Treaty, and have thereunto affixed our seals.

Done at Ghent, this —— day of ——, one thousand eight hundred and fourteen.

Draught of article to be inserted immediately after article 2 of the American projet.

All prisoners of war, taken on either side, as well by land as by sea, shall be restored as soon as practicable after the ratifications of this Treaty shall have been exchanged, on their paying the debts which they may have contracted during their captivity. The two contracting parties respectively engage to discharge in specie the advances which may have been made by the other, for the sustenance and maintenance of such prisoners.

True copy of the *projet* submitted by the American to the British Ministers; and also of the marginal changes, propositions, and remarks, made by the latter on returning their answer to the American Ministers' note communicating said *projet* of a Treaty.

CHRISTOPHER HUGHES, Jr.,
Secretary of American Mission Extraordinary.

ARTICLE 15.

(1) Washington, with all practicable despatch.

(2) Practicable.

No. 3.
The British to the American Ministers.

GHENT, *November 26*, 1814.

The undersigned have had the honor to receive the note and *projet* of a Treaty of Peace, presented by the American Plenipotentiaries on the 10th instant.

The undersigned are of opinion that the most convenient course for them to adopt will be to return this *projet*, with their marginal alterations and suggestions on the several articles of which it is composed. The existing differences between the two Governments will thus be brought more immediately in view, and it is hoped that, by confining the discussions to one *projet*, the negotiations may sooner be brought to a favorable conclusion. The first part of the tenth article appears to be unnecessary, and the stipulation contained in the whole of it altogether inadmissible. Though His Majesty's Government sincerely hopes that a renewal of the war between His Majesty and the United States may be far distant, yet the undersigned cannot consent to enter into any engagement as to what shall be the conduct of their Government if such a war should unfortunately occur.

With respect to the eleventh and twelfth articles, His Majesty's Government has strongly manifested its sincere disposition to the speedy restoration of peace, by agreeing, under all the present circumstances, to conclude the treaty without any stipulation on the points to which these articles relate. No advantage can arise from entering into discussions, upon a successful result of which the American Plenipotentiaries have stated more than once that they will not make the conclusion of the peace at all to depend.

With respect to the thirteenth article, the indemnifications proposed by it, as applied to the actual circumstances of the war, are so unprecedented and objectionable, that any further perseverance of the American Plenipotentiaries in requiring them is not anticipated by the undersigned: if, however, contrary to expectation, indemnifications of this kind should be required, all hope of bringing the negotiations to a favorable issue must prove abortive. The undersigned are instructed explicitly to declare that as their Government makes no claim on account of losses sustained by British subjects arising out of a war declared by the United States, so neither can their Government agree to make compensation for losses sustained in such a war by the American people.

The undersigned are, however, willing to agree to a stipulation by which it shall be provided that the courts of justice in each country shall be open to the just demands of the respective people, and that no obstruction be thrown in the way of their recovery of the rights, claims, or debts of any kind, respectively due or belonging to them.

With respect to the fourteenth article, the undersigned do not concur in the necessity for any such stipulation as is there proposed.

The undersigned think proper to add that, with respect to the particular alterations suggested by them in various articles of the *projet*, they are ready to enter into such explanations as may be required of them, with the sincere desire of endeavoring to reconcile the pretensions brought forward on the part of their respective Governments.

The undersigned have forborne to insist upon the basis of *uti possidetis*, to the advantage of which they consider their country fully entitled. But should this negotiation terminate in a way contrary to their hopes and just expectations, they must protest against any claim or demand being urged by the American Government in any future negotiation, in consequence of the facilities which His Majesty's Government have now shown themselves willing to afford to the speedy restoration of peace.

The undersigned avail themselves of the present opportunity to renew to the Plenipotentiaries of the United States the assurances of their high consideration.

GAMBIER,
HENRY GOULBURN,
WILLIAM ADAMS.

No. 4.

The American to the British Ministers.

GHENT, *November* 30, 1814.

The undersigned have had the honor to receive the note of the British Plenipotentiaries of the 26th instant, together with their marginal alterations and suggestions on the several articles of the *projet* of a treaty of peace proposed by the undersigned.

The undersigned consent that the day of the exchange of the ratifications be substituted to that of the signature of the treaty at the time for the cessation of hostilities, and for regulating the periods after which prizes at sea shall be restored: it being understood that measures shall be adopted for a speedy exchange of ratifications, and that the periods in the second article shall be fixed in a manner corresponding with this alteration.

The undersigned will also agree to the new article respecting prisoners, and to the mode of reference proposed by the British Plenipotentiaries in the third, fourth, fifth, sixth, and seventh articles, instead of that which had been proposed by the undersigned. But in order to prevent delay, they will suggest that a time be fixed within which the Commissioners shall make their decisions and reports.

They will decline insisting upon the tenth, twelfth, and fourteenth articles, and upon so much of the thirteenth article as relates to indemnities for losses and damages sustained subsequent to the commencement of the present war. They wish to discuss the cases of vessels and property in port when war was declared or known; and have the honor to enclose a copy of the provision made in that respect by the United States. They will also waive the residue of that (the thirteenth) article, and the eleventh article, it being understood that the rights of both Powers on the subject of seamen, and the claims of the citizens and subjects of the two contracting parties to indemnities for losses and damages sustained prior to the commencement of the war, shall not be affected or impaired by the omission in the treaty of

any specific provision with respect to those two subjects.

In forbearing to insist upon the discussion of subjects deeply involving interests important to their country, and upon which the undersigned view the proposals offered by them for consideration as founded on principles the most moderate and conciliatory, they give the strongest evidence of the anxious wish of their Government that the negotiation should be brought to a happy issue.

Sincerely participating in the desire expressed by the British Plenipotentiaries of endeavoring to reconcile the pretensions of both Governments, on the few subjects remaining for discussion, the undersigned have also assented to most of the alterations proposed by the British Plenipotentiaries to those parts of the *projet* which they have not entirely rejected. To some of these alterations the undersigned are compelled, by their duty, to object. They have already stated, and now repeat, that, whilst requiring of Great Britain no sacrifice whatever, the Government of the United States has not authorized the undersigned to agree to any stipulation involving any cession of territory, or the dereliction of any of the essential rights of the people of the United States.

The objections of the undersigned are to one of the alterations suggested by the *British* Plenipotentiaries in the first article; to some parts of the preamble of the third article, and to the eighth article; and they have also some other verbal alterations to suggest. They request a conference, at such time and place as may suit the British Plenipotentiaries, for the purpose of discussing those points, and of agreeing on the places and time left in blank in several of the articles.

The undersigned renew to the British Plenipotentiaries the assurance of their high consideration.

JOHN QUINCY ADAMS,
JAMES A. BAYARD,
HENRY CLAY,
JONATHAN RUSSELL,
ALBERT GALLATIN.

Extract of a law of the United States, passed July 6, 1812.

SEC. 6. *And be it further enacted*, That the President of the United States be, and he is hereby, authorized to give, at any time within six months after the passage of this act, passports for the safe transportation of any ship, or other property belonging to British subjects, and which is *now* within the limits of the United States.

No. 5.

The British to the American Ministers.

GHENT, *November* 30, 1814.

The undersigned have the honor to acknowledge the receipt of the note addressed to them by the American Plenipotentiaries, and, in compliance with their request for a conference, shall be happy to receive them at the Chartreux to-morrow at 12 o'clock.

The undersigned request the American Plenipotentiaries to accept the assurance of their high consideration.

GAMBIER,
HENRY GOULBURN,
WILLIAM ADAMS.

No. 6.

Protocol of a Conference held the 1st December, 1814, at Ghent.

At a conference held this day, the American Plenipotentiaries proposed the following alterations in their *projet*, as amended by the British Plenipotentiaries.

1st. In article 1, strike out the alteration consisting of the words " belonging to," and " taken by," and preserve the original reading, viz ; " taken by either party from the other."

This alteration was objected to by the British Plenipotentiaries, and, after some discussion, reserved by them for the consideration of their Government.

2d. Transpose alteration consisting of the words " originally captured in the said ports or places, and which shall remain therein upon the exchange of the ratifications of this treaty," after the words " public property." Agreed to by the British Plenipotentiaries.

3d. Article 2d. The term to be fifteen days in the Channel, in the North seas, in all parts of the Atlantic ocean to the equinoctial line or equator, and in all parts of the Mediterranean. Two months in the Atlantic ocean to the latitude of Cape of Good Hope, and three months in all other parts of the world.

In lieu of this alteration, the British Plenipotentiaries proposed the following, viz : " That all vessels and effects, which may be taken after the space of twelve days from the period of the exchange of the said ratifications, and all parts of the coasts of North America, from the latitude of twenty-three degrees north, to the latitude of forty-seven degrees north, and as far eastward in the Atlantic ocean as the sixty-third degree of west longitude from the meridian of Greenwich, shall be restored on each side. That the time shall be thirty days in all other parts of the Atlantic ocean, as far eastward as the entrance of the British channel, and southward, as far as the equinoctial line or equator, and the same time for the Gulf of Mexico and all parts of the West Indies. Forty days for the British channel and the North seas. The same time for all parts of the Mediterranean, and one hundred and fifty days for all other parts of the world without exception." Which was reserved by the American Plenipotentiaries for consideration.

4th. Article 3d. After the words " all islands within twenty leagues of," insert " any part of," and substitute " points" for " point" after the words " to be drawn due east from the." Agreed to by the British Plenipotentiaries.

5th. Article 3. Strike out the words " whereas claims have been made by the Government of the United States to certain islands in the Bay of Fundy," and insert, " whereas the several islands in the Bay of Passamaquoddy, which is part of the Bay of Fundy, and the island of Great Menan, in the said Bay of Fundy, are claimed by the United States as being comprehended within their aforesaid boundaries." Agreed to by the British Plenipotentiaries.

6th. Article 7th. In the alteration consisting of the words " or of the Sovereign or State so referred, to as in many of the preceding articles contained," substitute " any" to " many."

Not insisted on, the British Plenipotentiaries consenting to substitute the words, " the four next," for the marginal words, " many of the."

7th. Articles 3, 4, 5, and 6, provide that the decision of the Commissioners shall be made within a limited time. Objected to by the British Plenipotentiaries.

8th. Article 8th. Substitute after the words " to the westward of the said lake so far as," the words " their said respective territories," instead of the words " the territories of the United States." Agreed to by the British Plenipotentiaries.

9th. Article 8th. Strike out from the words " and it is further agreed" to the end. Reserved by the British Plenipotentiaries for the consideration of their Government.

10th. The American Plenipotentiaries also proposed the following amendment to article 8th, viz : " The inhabitants of the United States shall continue to enjoy the liberty to take, dry, and cure fish in places within the exclusive jurisdiction of Great Britain, as secured by the former treaty of peace ; and the navigation of the river Mississippi within the exclusive jurisdiction of the United States shall remain free and open to the subjects of Great Britain, in the manner secured by the said treaty ; and it is further agreed, that the subjects of His Britannic Majesty shall, at all times, have access from such place as may be selected for that purpose in His Britannic Majesty's aforesaid territories, west, and within three hundred miles of the Lake of the Woods, in the aforesaid territories of the United States, to the river Mississippi, in order to enjoy the benefit of the navigation of that river with their goods, effects, and merchandise, whose importation into the said States shall not be entirely prohibited, on the payment of the same duties as would be payable on the importation of the same into the Atlantic ports of the said States, and on conforming with the usual custom-house regulations."

This amendment was left with the British Plenipotentiaries for consideration.

The American Plenipotentiaries also intimated their willingness to omit article 8th altogether, if that course should appear more advisable to the British Plenipotentiaries.

The American Plenipotentiaries further proposed, in conformity with their note of November 30, indemnification for ships detained in British ports on the breaking out of the war, and afterwards condemned ; which was resisted by the British Plenipotentiaries.

After much discussion on this point, the conference was adjourned.

CHRISTOPHER HUGHES, Jun.

Relations with Great Britain.

Protocol of Conference on December 10, 1814.

The protocol of the preceding conference held on the 1st instant was settled.

The British Plenipotentiaries stated that their Government could not consent or omit the words in article 1st, "belonging to either party and taken by the other," unless some modification should be introduced, either by excepting from mutual restitution all those territories which are made by any articles of the treaty the subject of reference to Commissioners, or by excepting the Passamaquoddy islands alone.—Received by the American Plenipotentiaries for consideration.

The British Plenipotentiaries then stated that, with respect to the 8th article, their Government offered in lieu of the American proposals to retain the amended article as far as the words, "Stony mountains," and insert the following stipulation:

"His Britannic Majesty agrees to enter into negotiation with the United States of America, respecting the terms, conditions, and regulations under which the inhabitants of the said United States shall have the liberty of taking fish on certain parts of the coast of Newfoundland, and other of His Britannic Majesty's dominions in North America, and of drying and curing fish, in the unsettled bays, harbors, and creeks of Nova Scotia, Magdalen islands, and Labrador; as stipulated in the latter part of the third article of the treaty of 1783, in consideration of a fair equivalent to be agreed upon between His Majesty and the said United States, and granted by the said United States, for such liberty as aforesaid."

"The United States of America agree to enter into negotiation with His Britannic Majesty respecting the terms, conditions, and regulations under which the navigation of the river Mississippi from its source to the ocean, as stipulated in the eighth article of the treaty of 1783, shall remain free and open to the subjects of Great Britain, in consideration of a fair equivalent, to be agreed upon between His Majesty and the United States, and granted by His Majesty."—Received by the American Plenipotentiaries for consideration.

In the 7th article the British Plenipotentiaries proposed after the words "all grants of land made previous to," to omit the words "to that time," and insert "previous to the commencement of the war;" so that the line would read, "all grants of land made previous to the commencement of the war."—Agreed to.

The British Plenipotentiaries proposed the insertion of the following article relative to the slave trade:

"Whereas the traffic in slaves is irreconcilable with the principles of humanity and justice, and whereas both His Majesty and the United States are desirous of continuing their efforts to promote its entire abolition, it is hereby agreed, that both the contracting parties shall exert every means in their power to accomplish so desirable an object."—Received for consideration.

The British Plenipotentiaries proposed the following provision:

"That the citizens or subjects of each of the contracting parties may reciprocally sue in the courts of the other, and shall meet with no impediment to the recovery of all such estates, rights, properties or securities as may be due to them by the laws of the country in whose courts they shall sue."—Received for consideration.

The British Plenipotentiaries proposed in the preamble to the *projet* of the treaty, to omit the words "Admiral of the White squadron," and insert "late Admiral of the White, now Admiral of the Red" in lieu of them. Agreed to.

The American Plenipotentiaries stated that possibly doubts might arise as to the geographical accuracy of the words at the beginning of the eighth article, "a line drawn due west from the Lake of the Woods, along the forty-ninth parallel of north latitude."

It was agreed that an alteration should be made to guard against such possible inaccuracy.

The American Plenipotentiaries proposed the following alteration in the draught delivered to them by the British Plenipotentiaries, relative to the manner of filling up the blanks in article 2d; "extend the term of twelve days to fifty-six degrees north latitude, and to the thirty-sixth west longitude."

"Include the British and Irish channels in the term of thirty days. Include the *Baltic* in the term of forty days. Instead of the term one hundred and fifty days, insert sixty days for the Atlantic as far as the latitude of Cape of Good Hope; ninety days for every other part of the world south of the equator; one hundred and twenty days for all other parts of the world."

The conference then ended.

CHRISTOPHER HUGHES, Jr.,
Secretary of American Mission.

Protocol of Conference on December 12, 1814.

The protocol of the preceding conference held on the 10th instant was settled.

After much discussion relative to the first and eighth articles, the conference ended by the American Plenipotentiaries undertaking to return an answer in writing to the propositions brought forward by the British Plenipotentiaries at the last conference.

C. HUGHES, Jr.
Secretary of American Mission.

No. 7.

American Note, written after the Conference of the 12th December.

GHENT, *December* 14, 1814.

The undersigned having considered the propositions offered in the conference of the 10th instant by the British Plenipotentiaries on the few subjects which remain to be adjusted, now have the honor of making the communication which they promised.

The first of them relates to the mutual restoration of the territory taken by either party from the other during the war. In admitting this principle, which the undersigned had repeatedly declared to be the only one upon which they were authorized to treat, the British Plenipotentiaries

Relations with Great Britain.

had at first proposed an alteration in the article offered by the undersigned, limiting the stipulation of restoring territory taken during the war to territory belonging to the party from which it was taken. The objection of the undersigned to this alteration was, that a part of the territory thus taken being claimed by both parties, and made a subject of reference by the treaty, the alteration would leave it in the power of one party to judge whether any portion of territory taken by him during the war did or did not belong to the other party, laying thereby in the very instrument of pacification the foundation of an immediate understanding the moment that instrument should be carried into execution.

The British Plenipotentiaries have now proposed to omit the words originally offered by them, provided that the Passamaquoddy islands should alone be excepted from the mutual restitution of territory.

The consent of the undersigned to this solitary exception, if founded on the alleged right of Great Britain to those islands, might be construed as an implied admission of a better title on her part than on that of the United States, and would necessarily affect their claim. The only ground for the exception consists in the allegation of the British Plenipotentiaries, that Great Britain had, during some period subsequent to the treaty of peace of 1783, exercised jurisdiction over those islands, and that the United States had subsequently occupied them contrary to the remonstrances of the British Government, and before the question of title had been adjusted.

Under these considerations the undersigned, unwilling to prevent the conclusion of the Treaty of Peace, will take upon themselves the responsibility of agreeing to the exception proposed, with a provision that the claim of the United States shall not thereby in any manner be affected. The undersigned have accordingly prepared a clause to that effect, and which provides, also, that the temporary possession may not be converted into permanent occupancy. They had agreed to the alteration proposed by the British Plenipotentiaries in the mode of reference of the several boundaries and country in dispute, under the expectation that the proposed exception to a general restoration would not be insisted on; and they will add that the objection to the temporary possession by Great Britain of the Passamaquoddy islands would be considerably lessened by adopting a mode of reference, which would insure a speedy and certain decision.

To the stipulation now proposed by the British Plenipotentiaries as a substitute for the last paragraph of the eighth article, the undersigned cannot accede.

The proposition made respecting the navigation of the Mississippi, in the alteration first proposed by the British Plenipotentiaries to that article, was unexpected. In their note of the 31st of October they had stated that they had brought forward, in their note of the 21st of the same month, all the propositions which they had to offer; and that subject was not mentioned either in this last men-

tioned note, or in the first conference to which it referred. In order to obviate any difficulty arising from a presumed connexion between that subject and that of the boundary proposed by the eighth article, the undersigned expressed their willingness to omit the article altogether. For the purpose of meeting what they believed to be the wishes of the British Government, they proposed the insertion of an article which should recognise the right of Great Britain to the navigation of that river, and that of the United States to a liberty in certain fisheries, which the British Government considered as abrogated by the war. To such an article, which they viewed as merely declaratory, the undersigned had no objection, and have offered to accede. They do not, however, want any new article on either of those subjects; they have offered to be silent with regard to both. To the stipulation now proposed, or any other, abandoning, or implying the abandonment of any right in the fisheries claimed by the United States, they cannot subscribe. As a stipulation merely that the parties will hereafter negotiate concerning the subjects in question, it appears also unnecessary. Yet to an engagement, couched in general terms, so as to embrace all the subjects of difference not yet adjusted, or so expressed as to imply in no manner whatever an abandonment of any right claimed by the United States, the undersigned are ready to agree.

Since neither of the two additional articles proposed by the British Plenipotentiaries were included amongst, or is connected with, the subjects previously brought forward by them, it is presumed they are offered only for consideration, as embracing objects of common and equal interest to both parties. The undersigned will accede to the substance of the article to promote the abolition of the slave trade. They cannot admit the other article, which appears to them unnecessary; the courts of the United States will without it be equally open to the claims of British subjects, and they rely that without it the British courts will be equally open to the claims of the citizens of the United States.

The undersigned renew to the British Plenipotentiaries the assurance of their high consideration.

    JOHN QUINCY ADAMS,
    JAMES A. BAYARD,
    HENRY CLAY,
    JONATHAN RUSSELL,
    ALBERT GALLATIN.

To the PLENIPOTENTIARIES
   of His Britannic Majesty, &c.

Such of the islands in the Bay of Passamaquoddy as are claimed by both parties, shall remain in the possession of the party in whose occupation they may be at the time of the exchange of the ratifications of this treaty, until the decision respecting the title to the said islands shall have been made in conformity with the ——— article of this treaty. But if such decision shall not have taken place within ——— years after the exchange of the ratifications of this treaty, such islands shall be restored to, and, until such decision may take place, shall be retained by, the party who had possession of the same at the commencement of the war. No disposition made by this treaty of the intermediate possession of the islands and territories claimed by both parties shall, in any manner whatever, be construed to affect the right of either.

No. 8.

The British to the American Ministers.

GHENT, *December 22*, 1814.

The undersigned have had the honor to receive the note of the American Plenipotentiaries, dated on the 14th instant, stating their consent to except the Passamaquoddy islands from the mutual restitution of territory captured during the war, provided the claim of the United States shall not be in any manner affected thereby.

To the article proposed by the American Plenipotentiaries, so far as it is adapted to this object, the undersigned are willing to agree; but they object, as before intimated by them, to that part of the proposed article which would make it imperative on the Commissioners to decide the question within any fixed time, trusting that, on this head, the American Plenipotentiaries will be satisfied with their declaration, that it is the intention of His Majesty's Government to do all that belongs to them to obtain a decision without loss of time. The *projet* of the article subjoined will be found to omit the clause intended to enforce a decision within some limited time, and to contain a slight alteration in the third clause by substituting in the place of the words "intermediate possession" the words "as to such possession."

So far as regards the substitution proposed by the undersigned for the last clause of the eighth article, as it was offered solely with the hope of attaining the object of the amendment tendered by the American Plenipotentiaries at the conference of the 1st instant, no difficulty will be made in withdrawing it.

The undersigned, returning to the declaration made by them at the conference of the 8th August, that the privileges of fishing within the limits of the British sovereignty, and of using the British territories for purposes connected with the fisheries, were what Great Britain did not intend to grant without equivalent, are not desirous of introducing any article upon the subject.

With a view of removing what they consider as the only objection to the immediate conclusion of the treaty, the undersigned agree to adopt the proposal made by the American Plenipotentiaries at the conference of the 1st instant, and repeated in their last note, of omitting the eighth article altogether.

The undersigned avail themselves of the opportunity to renew to the Plenipotentiaries of the United States the assurance of their high consideration..

GAMBIER,
HENRY GOULBURN,
WILLIAM ADAMS.

[Referred to in the preceding note from the British Ministers.]

Such of the islands in the Bay of Passamaquoddy as are claimed by both parties shall remain *in* the possession of the party in whose occupation they may be at the time of the exchange of the ratifications of this treaty, until the decision respecting the title to the said islands shall have been made in conformity with the fourth article of this treaty.

No disposition made by this treaty as *to* such possession of the islands and territories claimed by both parties shall, in any manner whatever, be construed to affect the right of either.

No. 9.

Protocol of Conference.

GHENT, *December 23*, 1814.

At a conference held this day, the protocol of the preceding conference was settled.

The American Plenipotentiaries intimated their readiness to accede to the propositions contained in the note of the British Plenipotentiaries of the 22d instant.

The following alterations were then agreed to:

In the first article, after the word "*cease*," omit the words "after the exchange of the ratifications," and insert "as soon as the treaty shall have been ratified by both parties." Substitute the word "whatsoever" for the words "without exception." Restore the words "taken by either party from the other," in the room of the words "belonging to either party and taken by." After the words "signing of this treaty," insert the words "excepting only the islands hereinafter mentioned;" after the words "respectively belong," insert *verbatim* the words of the amendment enclosed in the note of the British Plenipotentiaries of the 23d instant, filling up the blank with the word "fourth."

The second article was altered, so as to read as follows:

ART. 2. Immediately after the ratification of this treaty by both parties, as hereinafter mentioned, orders shall be sent to the armies, squadrons, officers, subjects, and citizens of the two Powers, to cease from all hostilities, and so prevent all causes of complaint which might arise on account of the prizes which may be taken at sea, after the said ratifications of this treaty. It is reciprocally agreed, that all vessels and effects, which may be taken after the space of twelve days from the said ratifications upon all parts of the coast of North America, from the latitude of twenty-three degrees north to the latitude of fifty degrees north, and as far eastward in the Atlantic ocean as the thirty-sixth degree of west longitude, from the meridian of Greenwich, shall be restored on each side: that the time shall be thirty days in all other parts of the Atlantic ocean north of the equinoctial line or equator, and the same time for the British and Irish channels, for the Gulf of Mexico, and all parts of the West Indies; forty days for the North seas, for the Baltic, and for all parts of the Mediterranean; sixty days for the Atlantic ocean, south of the equator, as far as the Cape of Good Hope; ninety days for every other part of the world, south of the equator, and one hundred and twenty days for all other parts of the world, without exception.

It was agreed that the article respecting prisoners of war, should be the third article, and that the words "as hereinafter mentioned," should be substituted for the words "shall have been exchanged."

The articles numbered in the original *projet* 3, 4, 5, 6, 7, to be respectively numbered 4, 5, 6, 7, 8.

In the fourth article, it was agreed that the blank should be filled up with the words "St. Andrews, in the province of New Brunswick."

In the fifth article, it was agreed that the blank should be filled up with the words "St. Andrews, in the province of New Brunswick."

Near the end of the fifth article, substitute the word "fourth" for "third."

In the sixth article, it was agreed to fill up the blank with the words "Albany, in the State of New York," and to substitute the word "fourth" for "third," in the concluding paragraph.

In the seventh article, substitute the word "fourth" for "third," in the last paragraph.

It was agreed that the article respecting the African slave trade, should be the tenth article, and that the words "use their best endeavors" should be substituted for the words "exert every means in their power."

The fifteenth article of the *projet* to be numbered 11: it was agreed to insert in it, after the words "on both sides," the words "without alteration by either of the contracting parties."

Omit the words "with all practicable despatch;" fill up the blank with the word "four;" insert after the word "done" the words "in triplicate." The British Plenipotentiaries urged the article formally proposed by them, as to suits of law to be prosecuted by the citizens or subjects of one nation in the courts of justice of the other.

Resisted by the American Plenipotentiaries.

The conference was adjourned to the 24th instant, for the purpose of signing the treaty.

Treaty of Peace and Amity between His Britannic Majesty and the United States of America.

His Britannic Majesty and the United States of America, desirous of terminating the war which has unhappily subsisted between the two countries, and of restoring, upon principles of perfect reciprocity, peace, friendship, and good understanding between them, have for that purpose appointed their respective Plenipotentiaries; that is to say, His Britannic Majesty, on his part, has appointed the right honorable James Lord Gambier, late Admiral of the White, now Admiral of the Red squadron of His Majesty's fleet, Henry Goulburn, Esq., a member of the Imperial Parliament and under Secretary of State, and Wm. Adams, Esq., Doctor of Civil Laws: and the President of the United States, by and with the advice and consent of the Senate thereof, has appointed

13th Con. 3d Sess.—45

John Quincy Adams, James A. Bayard, Henry Clay, Jonathan Russell, and Albert Gallatin, citizens of the United States, who, after a reciprocal communication of their respective full powers, have agreed upon the following articles:

Article 1. There shall be a firm and universal peace between His Britannic Majesty and the United States, and between their respective countries, territories, cities, towns, and people of every degree, without exception of places or persons. All hostilities, both by sea and land, shall cease as soon as this treaty shall have been ratified by both parties, as hereinafter mentioned. All territory, places, and possessions, whatsoever, taken by either party from the other during the war, or which may be taken after the signing of this treaty, excepting only the islands hereinafter mentioned, shall be restored without delay, and without causing any destruction or carrying away any of the artillery or other public property originally captured in the said ports or places, and which shall remain therein upon the exchange of the ratifications of this treaty, or any slaves or other private property. And all archives, records, deeds, and papers, either of a public nature or belonging to private persons, which in the course of the war may have fallen into the hands of the officers of either party, shall be, as far as may be practicable, forthwith restored and delivered to the proper authorities and persons to whom they respectively belong. Such of the islands in the Bay of Passamaquoddy as are claimed by both parties shall remain in the possession of the party in whose occupation they may be at the time of the exchange of the ratifications of this treaty, until the decision respecting the title to the said islands shall have been made, in conformity with the fourth article of this treaty. No disposition made by this treaty, as to such possession of the lands and territories claimed by both parties, shall in any manner whatever be construed to affect the right of either.

Art. 2. Immediately after the ratifications of this treaty by both parties, as hereinafter mentioned, orders shall be sent to the armies, squadrons, officers, subjects, and citizens of the two Powers, to cease from hostilities; and, to prevent all causes of complaint which might arise on account of the prizes which may be taken at sea after the said ratifications of this treaty, it is reciprocally agreed that all vessels and effects which may be taken after the space of twelve days from the said ratifications, upon all parts of the coast of North America, from the latitude of twenty-three degrees north to the latitude of fifty degrees north, and as far eastward in the Atlantic ocean as the thirty-sixth degree of west longitude from the meridian of Greenwich, shall be restored on each side; that the time shall be thirty days in all other parts of the Atlantic ocean north of the equinoctial line or equator, and the same time for the British and Irish channels, for the Gulf of Mexico, and all parts of the West Indies; forty days for the North seas, for the Baltic, and for all parts of the Mediterranean; sixty days for the Atlantic ocean, south of the equator, as far as the latitude of the Cape of Good Hope; ninety days for every part of the world south of the equator; and one hundred and twenty days for all other parts of the world, without exception.

ART. 3. All prisoners of war taken on either side, as well by land as by sea, shall be restored as soon as practicable after the ratifications of this treaty, as hereinafter mentioned, on their paying the debts which they may have contracted during their captivity. The two contracting parties engage to discharge, in specie, the advances which may have been made by the other for the sustenance and maintenance of such prisoners.

ART. 4. Whereas it was stipulated by the second article in the Treaty of Peace of one thousand seven hundred and eighty-three, between His Britannic Majesty and the United States of America, that the boundary of the United States should comprehend all islands within twenty leagues of any part of the shores of the United States, and lying between lines to be drawn due east from the points where the aforesaid boundaries between Nova Scotia on the one part, and East Florida on the other, shall respectively touch the Bay of Fundy and the Atlantic ocean, excepting such islands as now are, or heretofore have been, within the limits of Nova Scotia; and whereas several islands in the Bay of Passamaquoddy, which is part of the Bay of Fundy, and the island of Grand Menan, in the said Bay of Fundy, are claimed by the United States as being comprehended within their aforesaid boundaries, which said islands are claimed as belonging to His Britannic Majesty, as having been, at the time of, and previous to, the aforesaid treaty of one thousand seven hundred and eighty-three within the limits of the province of Nova Scotia: in order, therefore, finally to decide upon these claims, it is agreed that they shall be referred to two Commissioners, to be appointed in the following manner, viz: One Commissioner shall be appointed by His Britannic Majesty, and one by the President of the United States, by and with the advice and consent of the Senate thereof; and the said two Commissioners so appointed shall be sworn impartially to examine and decide upon the said claims according to such evidence as shall be laid before them, on the part of His Britannic Majesty and of the United States, respectively. The said Commissioners shall meet at St. Andrew's, in the province of New Brunswick, and shall have power to adjourn to such other place or places as they shall think fit. The said Commissioners shall, by a declaration or report under their hands and seals, decide to which of the two contracting parties the several islands aforesaid do respectively belong, in conformity with the true intent of the said Treaty of Peace of one thousand seven hundred and eighty-three; and if the said Commissioners shall agree in their decision, both parties shall consider such decision as final and conclusive. It is further agreed, that in the event of the two Commissioners differing upon all or any of the matters so referred to them, or in the event of both or either of the said Commissioners refusing, or declining, or wilfully omitting to act as such, they shall make, jointly or separately, a report or reports, as well to the Government of His Britannic Majesty as to that of the United States, stating in detail the points on which they differ, and the grounds upon which their respective opinions have been formed, or the grounds upon which they, or either of them, have so refused, declined, or omitted to act. And His Britannic Majesty and the Government of the United States hereby agree to refer the report or reports of the said Commissioners to some friendly Sovereign or State, to be then named for that purpose, and who shall be requested to decide on the differences which may be stated in the said report or reports, or upon the report of one Commissioner, together with the grounds upon which the other Commissioner shall have refused, declined, or omitted to act, as the case may be; and if the Commissioner so refusing, declining, or omitting to act, shall also wilfully omit to state the grounds upon which he has so done, in such manner that the said statement may be referred to such friendly Sovereign or State, together with the report of such other Commissioner, then such Sovereign or State shall decide *ex parte* upon the said report alone. And His Britannic Majesty and the Government of the United States engage to consider the decision of some friendly Power or State to be final and conclusive on all the matters so referred.

ART. 5. Whereas neither that point of the highlands lying due north from the source of the river St. Croix, and designated in the former Treaty of Peace between the two Powers as the northwest angle of Nova Scotia, nor the northwesternmost head of Connecticut river, has yet been ascertained; and whereas that part of the boundary line between the dominions of the two Powers which extends from the source of the river St. Croix, directly north, to the above-mentioned northwest angle of Nova Scotia; thence along the said highlands which divide those rivers that empty themselves into the river St. Lawrence from those which fall into the Atlantic ocean, to the northwesternmost head of Connecticut river; thence down along the middle of that river to the forty-fifth degree of north latitude; thence by a line due west on said latitude, until it strikes the river Iroquois or Cataraguy, which has not yet been surveyed: it is agreed that, for these several purposes, two Commissioners shall be appointed, sworn, and authorized to act exactly in the manner directed with respect to those mentioned in the next preceding article, unless otherwise specified in the present article. The said Commissioners shall meet at St. Andrews, in the province of New Brunswick, and shall have power to adjourn to such other place or places, as they shall think fit. The said Commissioners shall have power to ascertain and determine the points above-mentioned, in conformity with the provisions of the said Treaty of Peace of one thousand seven hundred and eighty-three, and shall cause the boundary aforesaid, from the source of the river St. Croix to the river Iroquois or Cataraguy,

Relations with Great Britain.

to be surveyed and marked, according to the said provisions. The said Commissioners shall make a map of the said boundary, and annex to it a declaration under their hands and seals, certifying it to be the true map of the said boundary, and particularizing the latitude and longitude of the northwest angle of Nova Scotia, of the northwesternmost head of Connecticut river, and of such other points of the said boundary as they may deem proper. And both parties agree to consider such map and declaration as finally and conclusively fixing the said boundary. And in the event of the said two Commissioners differing, or both, or either of them refusing, declining, or wilfully omitting to act, such reports, declarations, or statements, shall be made by them, or either of them, and such reference to a friendly Sovereign or State shall be made, in all respects, as in the latter part of the fourth article is contained, and in as full a manner as if the same was herein repeated.

ART. 6. Whereas by the former Treaty of Peace that portion of the boundary of the United States, from the point where the forty-fifth degree of north latitude strikes the river Iroquois or Cataraguy to the Lake Superior, was declared to be "along the middle of said river into Lake Ontario; through the middle of said lake until it strikes the communication by water between that lake and Lake Erie; thence along the middle of said communication into Lake Erie; through the middle of said lake until it arrives at the water communication into the Lake Huron; thence through the middle of said lake to the water communication between that lake and Lake Superior." And whereas doubts have arisen what was the middle of the said river, lakes, and water communications, and whether certain islands lying in the same were within the dominions of His Britannic Majesty or of the United States: In order, therefore, finally to decide these doubts, they shall be referred to two Commissioners, to be appointed, sworn, and authorized to act exactly in the manner directed, with respect to those mentioned in the next preceding article, unless otherwise specified in this present article. The said Commissioners shall meet, in the first instance, at Albany, in the State of New York, and shall have power to adjourn to such other place or places as they shall think fit: the said Commissioners shall, by a report or declaration, under their hands and seals, designate the boundary through the said river, lakes, and water communications, and decide to which of the two contracting parties the several islands lying within the said river, lakes, and water communications, do respectively belong, in conformity with the true intent of the said treaty of one thousand seven hundred and eighty-three. And both parties agree to consider such designation and decision as final and conclusive. And in the event of the said two Commissioners differing, or both, or either of them, refusing, declining, or wilfully omitting to act, such reports, declarations, or statements, shall be made by them, or either of them, and such reference to a friendly Sovereign

or State shall be made in all respects as in the latter part of the fourth article is contained, and in as full a manner as if the same was herein repeated.

ART. 7. It is further agreed that the said two last mentioned Commissioners, after they shall have executed the duties assigned to them in the preceding article, shall be, and they are hereby authorized, upon their oaths, impartially to fix and determine, according to the true intent of the said Treaty of Peace of one thousand seven hundred and eighty-three, that part of the boundary between the dominions of the two Powers, which extends from the water communication between Lake Huron and Lake Superior to the most northwestern point of the Lake of the Woods, to decide to which of the two parties the several islands lying in the lakes, water communications, and rivers, forming the said boundary, do respectively belong, in conformity with the true intent of the said Treaty of Peace of one thousand seven hundred and eighty-three; and to cause such parts of the said boundary as require it to be surveyed and marked. The said Commissioners shall, by a report or declaration under their hands and seals, designate the boundary aforesaid, state their decision on the points thus referred to them, and particularize the latitude and longitude of the most northwestern point of the Lake of the Woods, and of such other parts of the said boundary as they may deem proper. And both parties agree to consider such designation and decision as final and conclusive. And in the event of the said two Commissioners differing, or both, or either of them, refusing, declining, or wilfully omitting to act, such reports, declarations, or statements shall be made by them, or either of them, and such reference to a friendly Sovereign or State shall be made in all respects as in the latter part of the fourth article is contained, and in as full a manner as if the same was herein repeated.

ART. 8. The several boards of two Commissioners mentioned in the four preceding articles, shall respectively have power to appoint a secretary, and to employ such surveyors, or other persons, as they shall judge necessary. Duplicates of all their respective reports, declarations, statements, and decisions, and of their accounts, and of the journal of their proceedings, shall be delivered by them to the agents of His Britannic Majesty, and to the agents of the United States, who may be respectively appointed and authorized to manage the business on behalf of their respective Governments. The said Commissioners shall be respectively paid in such manner as shall be agreed between the two contracting parties—such agreement being to be settled at the time of the exchange of the ratifications of this treaty. And all other expenses attending the said Commissioners, shall be defrayed equally by the two parties. And in the case of death, sickness, resignation, or necessary absence, the place of every such Commissioner respectively shall be supplied in the same manner as such Commissioner was first appointed, and the new Commissioner shall take the same oath or affirmation, and do the same duties. It is further agreed between the two contracting parties, that in case any of the islands mentioned in any of the preceding articles which were in the possession of one of the parties prior to the commencement of the present war between the two countries, should, by the decision of any of the Boards of Commissioners aforesaid, or of the Sovereign or State so referred to, as in the four next preceding articles contained, fall within the dominions of the other party, all grants of land made previous to the commencement of the war by the party having had such possession, shall be as valid as if such island or islands had by such decision or decisions been adjudged to be within the dominions of the party having had such possession.

Art. 9. The United States of America engage to put an end, immediately after the ratification of the present treaty, to hostilities with all the tribes or nations of Indians with whom they may be at war at the time of such ratification; and forthwith to restore to such tribes or nations, respectively, all the possessions, rights, and privileges, which they may have enjoyed or been entitled to in 1811, previous to such hostilities: *Provided always,* That such tribes or nations shall agree to desist from all hostilities against the United States of America, their citizens and subjects, upon the ratification of the present treaty being notified to such tribes or nations, and shall so desist accordingly. And His Britannic Majesty engages, on his part, to put an end, immediately after the ratification of the present treaty, to hostilities with all the tribes or nations of Indians with whom he may be at war at the time of such ratification; and forthwith to restore to such tribes or nations, respectively, all the possessions, rights, and privileges, which they may have enjoyed or been entitled to in 1811, previous to such hostilities: *Provided always,* That such tribes or nations shall agree to desist from all hostilities against His Britannic Majesty, and his subjects, upon the ratification of the present treaty being notified to such tribes or nations, and shall so desist accordingly.

Art. 10. Whereas the traffic in slaves is irreconcilable with the principles of humanity and justice: and whereas both His Majesty and the United States are desirous of continuing their efforts to promote its entire abolition, it is hereby agreed that both the contracting parties shall use their best endeavors to accomplish so desirable an object.

Art. 11. This treaty, when the same shall have been ratified on both sides, without alteration by either of the contracting parties, and the ratifications mutually exchanged, shall be binding on both parties, and the ratifications shall be exchanged at Washington, in the space of four months from this day, or sooner, if practicable.

In faith whereof, we, the respective Plenipotentiaries, have signed this treaty, and have hereunto affixed our seals.

Done, in triplicate, at Ghent, the twenty-fourth day of December, one thousand eight hundred and fourteen.

[L. S.]   GAMBIER,
[L. S.]   HENRY GOULBURN,
[L. S.]   WILLIAM ADAMS,
[L. S.]   JOHN QUINCY ADAMS,
[L. S.]   J. A. BAYARD,
[L. S.]   H. CLAY,
[L. S.]   JONATHAN RUSSELL,
[L. S.]   ALBERT GALLATIN.

AN EXPOSITION OF THE CAUSES AND CHARACTER OF THE WAR.

[Note.—This Exposition of the Causes and Character of the War was prepared and committed to the press, before any account had been received in the United States of the signature of a Treaty of Peace, by the American and the British negotiators; and it would have been difficult, even if it were desirable, to withhold the exposition from the public.

But the charges which have been solemnly exhibited against the American Government, in the face of the world, render an exposition of its conduct necessary, in peace as much as in war, for the honor of the United States, and the unsullied reputation of their arms; lest those charges should obtain credit with the present generation, or pass, for truth, into the history of the times, upon the evidence of a silent acquiescence.]

Whatever may be the termination of the negotiations at Ghent, the despatches of the American Commissioners, which have been communicated by the President of the United States to the Congress, during the present session, will distinctly unfold, to the attentive and impartial of all nations, the objects and dispositions of the parties to the present war.

The United States, relieved by the *general* pacification of the Treaty of Paris from the *danger* of actual sufferance under the evils which had compelled them to resort to arms, have avowed their readiness to resume the relations of peace and amity with Great Britain, upon the simple and single condition of preserving their territory and their sovereignty, entire and unimpaired. Their desire of peace, indeed, "upon terms of reciprocity, consistent with the rights of both parties, as sovereign and independent nations,"[*] has not at any time been influenced by the provocations of an unprecedented course of *hostilities*; by the incitements of a successful *campaign*; or by the agitations which have seemed again to threaten the tranquillity of Europe.

But the British Government, after inviting "a discussion with the Government of America, for the conciliatory adjustment of the differences subsisting between the two States, with an earnest desire on their part (as it was alleged) to bring them to a favorable issue, upon principles of a perfect reciprocity, not inconsistent with the established maxims of public law, and with the

[*]See Mr. Monroe's letter to Lord Castlereagh, dated January, 1814.

Causes and Character of the War.

maritime rights of the British empire;"* and after "expressly disclaiming any intention to acquire an increase of territory,"† have peremptorily demanded, as the price of peace, concessions calculated merely for their own aggrandizement, and for the humiliation of their adversary. At one time, they proposed, as their *sine qua non,* a stipulation that the Indians, inhabiting the country of the United States, within the limits established by the Treaty of 1783, should be included, as the allies of Great Britain, (a party to that treaty,) in the projected pacification; and that definite boundaries should be settled for the Indian territory, upon a basis which would have operated to surrender to a number of Indians, not probably exceeding a few thousands, the rights of sovereignty, as well as of soil, over nearly one-third of the territorial dominions of the United States, inhabited by more than one hundred thousand of their citizens.‡ And, more recently, (withdrawing, in effect, that proposition,) they have offered to treat, on the basis of the *uti possidetis;* when, by the operations of the war, they had obtained the military possession of an important part of the State of Massachusetts, which, it was known, could never be the subject of a cession, consistently with the honor and faith of the American Government.‖ Thus, it is obvious, that Great Britain, neither regarding "the principles of a perfect reciprocity," nor the rule of her own practice and professions, has indulged pretensions which could only be heard in order to be rejected. The alternative, either vindictively to protract the war or honorably to end it, has been fairly given to her option; but she wants the magnanimity to decide, while her apprehensions are awakened for the result of the Congress at Vienna, and her hopes are flattered by the schemes of conquest in America.

There are periods in the transactions of every country, as well as in the life of every individual, when self-examination becomes a duty of the highest moral obligation; when the Government

of a free people, driven from the path of peace, and baffled in every effort to regain it, may resort, for consolation, to the conscious rectitude of its measures; and when an appeal to mankind, founded upon truth and justice, cannot fail to engage those sympathies, by which even nations are led to participate in the fame and fortunes of each other. The United States, under these impressions, are neither insensible to the advantages nor to the duties of their peculiar situation. They have but recently, as it were, established their independence; and the volume of their national history lies open, at a glance, to every eye. The policy of their Government, therefore, whatever it has been, in their foreign as well as in their domestic relations, it is impossible to conceal; and it must be difficult to mistake. If the assertion, that it has been a policy to preserve peace and amity with all the nations of the world, be doubted, the proofs are at hand. If the assertion, that it has been a policy to maintain the rights of the United States, but, at the same time, to respect the rights of every other nation, be doubted, the proofs will be exhibited. If the assertion, that it has been a policy to act impartially towards the belligerent Powers of Europe, be doubted, the proofs will be found on record, even in the archives of England and of France. And if, in fine, the assertion, that it has been a policy, by all honorable means, to cultivate with Great Britain those sentiments of mutual good will, which naturally belong to nations connected by the ties of a common ancestry, an identity of language, and a similarity of manners, be doubted, the proofs will be found in that patient forbearance, under the pressure of accumulating wrongs, which marks the period of almost thirty years, that elapsed between the peace of 1783 and the rupture of 1812.

The United States had just recovered, under the auspices of their present Constitution, from the debility which their Revolutionary struggle had produced, when the convulsive movements of France excited throughout the civilized world the mingled sensations of hope and fear—of admiration and alarm. The interest which those movements would, in themselves, have excited, was incalculably increased, however, as soon as Great Britain became a party to the first memorable coalition against France, and assumed the character of a belligerent Power; for, it was obvious, that the distance of the scene would no longer exempt the United States from the influence, and the evils, of the European conflict. On the one hand, their Government was connected with France, by treaties of alliance and commerce; and the services which that nation had rendered to the cause of American independence, had made such impressions upon the public mind, as no virtuous statesman could rigidly condemn, and the most rigorous statesman would have sought in vain to efface. On the other hand, Great Britain, leaving the Treaty of 1783 unexecuted, forcibly retained the American posts upon the Northern frontier; and, slighting every overture to place the diplomatic and commercial relations of the two countries, upon a fair and

---

* See Lord Castlereagh's letter to Mr. Monroe, dated the 4th of November, 1813.

† See the American despatch, dated the 12th of August, 1814.

‡ See the American despatches, dated the 12th and 19th of August, 1814; the note of the British Commissioners, dated the 19th of August, 1814; the note of the American Commissioners, dated the 21st of August, 1814; the note of the British Commissioners, dated the 4th of September, 1814; the note of the American Commissioners of the 9th of September, 1814; the note of the British Commissioners, dated the 19th of September, 1814; the note of the American Commissioners, dated the 26th of September, 1814; the note of the British Commissioners, dated the 8th of October, 1814; and the note of the American Commissioners, of the 13th of October, 1814.

‖ See the note of the British Commissioners, dated the 21st of October, 1814; the note of the American Commissioners, dated the 24th of October, 1814; and the note of the British Commissioners, dated the 31st of October, 1814.

friendly foundation,* seemed to contemplate the success of the American Revolution, in a spirit of unextinguishable animosity. Her voice had, indeed, been heard from Quebec and Montreal, instigating the savages to war.† Her invisible arm was felt, in the defeats of General Harmar,‡ and General St. Clair,‖ and even the victory of General Wayne§ was achieved in the presence of a fort which she had erected, far within the territorial boundaries of the United States, to stimulate and countenance the barbarities of the Indian warrior.¶ Yet, the American Government, neither yielding to popular feeling, nor acting upon the impulse of national resentment, hastened to adopt the policy of a strict and steady neutrality; and solemnly announced that policy to the citizens at home, and the nations abroad, by the proclamation of the 22d of April, 1793. Whatever may have been the trials of its pride and of its fortitude; whatever may have been the imputations upon its fidelity and its honor; it will be demonstrated, in the sequel, that the American Government, throughout the European contest, and amidst all the changes of the objects, and the parties, that have been involved in that contest, has inflexibly adhered to the principles which were thus, authoritatively, established, to regulate the conduct of the United States.

It was reasonable to expect, that a proclamation of neutrality, issued under the circumstances which have been described, would command the confidence and respect of Great Britain, however offensive it might prove to France, as contravening, essentially, the exposition which she was anxious to bestow upon the treaties of commerce and alliance. But experience has shown that the confidence and respect of Great Britain are not to be acquired by such acts of impartiality and independence. Under every Administration of the American Government, the experiment has been made, and the experiment has been equally unsuccessful; for, it was not more effectually ascertained in the year 1812, than at antecedent periods, that an exemption from the maritime usurpation, and the commercial monopoly, of Great Britain, could only be obtained upon the condition of becoming an associate in her enmities and her wars. While the proclamation of neutrality was still in the view of the British Minister, an order of the 8th of June, 1793, issued from the Cabinet, by virtue of which, " all vessels loaded wholly, or in part, with corn, flour, or meal, bound to any port in France, or any port occupied by the armies of France," were required to be carried, forcibly, into England; and the cargoes were either to be sold there, or security was to

be given that they should only be sold in the ports of a country in amity with his Britannic Majesty.* The moral character of an avowed design to inflict famine upon the whole of the French people, was, at that time, properly estimated throughout the civilized world; and so glaring an infraction of neutral rights, as the British order was calculated to produce, did not escape the severities of diplomatic animadversion and remonstrance. But this aggression was soon followed by another of a more hostile cast. In the war of 1756, Great Britain had endeavored to establish the rule, that neutral nations were not entitled to enjoy the benefits of a trade with the colonies of a belligerent Power, from which, in the season of peace, they were excluded by the parent State. The rule stands without positive support from any general authority on public law. If it be true that some treaties contain stipulations, by which the parties expressly exclude each other from the commerce of their respective colonies; and if it be true, that the ordinances of a particular State often provide for the exclusive enjoyment of its colonial commerce, still Great Britain cannot be authorized to deduce the rule of the war of 1756, by implication, *from such treaties* and such ordinances; while *it is not true* that the rule forms a part of the *law of nations*, nor that it has been adopted by any other Government; nor that even Great Britain herself has uniformly practised upon the rule; since its application was unknown from the war of 1756, until the French war of 1792, including the entire period of the American war. Let it be, argumentatively, allowed, however, that Great Britain possessed the right, as well as the power, to revive and enforce the rule; yet, the time and the manner of exercising the power, would afford ample cause for reproach. The citizens of the United States had openly engaged in an extensive trade with the French islands, in the *West Indies*, ignorant of the alleged existence of the rule of the war of 1756, or unapprized of any intention to call it into action, when the order of the 6th of November, 1793, was silently circulated among the British cruisers, consigning to legal adjudication, " all vessels loaden with goods, the produce of any colony of France, or carrying provisions or supplies, for the use of any such colony."† A great portion of the commerce of the United States was thus annihilated at a blow; the amicable dispositions of the Government were again disregarded and contemned; the sensibility of the nation was excited to a high degree of resentment, by the apparent treachery of the British order; and a recourse to reprisals, or to war, for indemnity and redress, seemed to be unavoidable. But the love of justice had established the law of neutrality; and the love of peace taught a lesson of forbearance. The American Government, therefore, rising superior to the provocations and the passions of the day, instituted a special mis-

*See Mr. Adams's correspondence.
†See the speeches of Lord Dorchester.
‡On the waters of the Miami of the Lake, on the 21st of October, 1790.
‖At Fort Recovery, on the 4th of November, 1791.
§On the Miami of the Lake, in August, 1794.
¶See the correspondence between Mr. Randolph, the American Secretary of State, and Mr. Hammond, the British Plenipotentiary, dated May and June, 1794.

*See the Order in Council of the 8th of June, 1793, and the remonstrance of the American Government.
†See the British order of the 6th of November, 1793.

Causes and Character of the War.

sion to represent at the Court of London the injuries and the indignities which it had suffered; "to vindicate its rights with firmness, and to cultivate peace with sincerity."* The immediate result of this mission was a treaty of amity, commerce, and navigation, between the United States and Great Britain, which was signed by the negotiators on the 19th of November, 1794, and finally ratified, with the consent of the Senate, in the year 1795. But both the mission and its result, serve, also, to display the independence and the impartiality of the American Government, in asserting its rights and performing its duties, equally unawed and unbiassed by the instruments of belligerent power or persuasion.

On the foundation of this treaty the United States, in a pure spirit of good faith and confidence, raised the hope and the expectation, that the maritime usurpations of Great Britain would cease to annoy them; that all doubtful claims of jurisdiction would be suspended; and that even the exercise of an incontestable right would be so modified, as to present neither insult, nor outrage, nor inconvenience, to their flag or to their commerce; but the hope and the expectation of the United States have been fatally disappointed. Some relaxation in the rigor, without any alteration in the principle, of the Order in Council of the 6th of November, 1793, was introduced by the subsequent Orders of the 8th of January, 1794, and the 25th of January, 1798; but from the ratification of the Treaty of 1794, until the short respite afforded by the Treaty of Amiens, in 1802, the commerce of the United States continued to be the prey of British cruisers and privateers, under the adjudicating patronage of the British tribunals. Another grievance, however, assumed at this epoch a form and magnitude which cast a shade over the social happiness, as well as the political independence of the nation. The merchant vessels of the United States were arrested on the high seas, while in the prosecution of distant voyages; considerable numbers of their crews were impressed into the naval service of Great Britain; the commercial adventures of the owners were often, consequently, defeated; and the loss of property, the embarrassments of trade and navigation, and the scene of domestic affliction, became intolerable. This grievance (which constitutes an important surviving cause of the American declaration of war) was early, and has been incessantly, urged upon the attention of the British Government. Even in the year 1792, they were told of "the irritation that it had excited, and of the difficulty of avoiding to make immediate reprisals on their seamen in the United States."† They were told "that so many instances of the kind had happened, that it was quite necessary they should explain themselves on the

subject, and be led to disavow and punish such violence, which had never been experienced from any other nation."* And they were told " of the inconvenience of such conduct, and of the impossibility of letting it go on, so that the British Ministry should be made sensible of the necessity of punishing the past, and preventing the future."† But after the Treaty of Amity, Commerce, and Navigation, had been ratified, the nature and the extent of the grievance became still more manifest; and it was clearly and firmly presented to the view of the British Government, as leading unavoidably to discord and war between the two nations. They were told, " that unless they would come to some accommodation which might insure the American seamen against this oppression, measures would be taken to cause the inconvenience to be equally felt on both sides."‡ They were told, " that the impressment of American citizens, to serve on board of British armed vessels, was not only an injury to the unfortunate individuals, but it naturally excited certain emotions in the breasts of the nation to whom they belonged, and of the just and humane of every country; and that an expectation was indulged that orders would be given that the Americans, so circumstanced, should be immediately liberated, and that the British officers should, in future, abstain from similar violences."|| They were told, " that the subject was of much greater importance than had been supposed; and that, instead of a few, and those in many instances equivocal cases, the American Minister at the Court of London had, in nine months (part of the years 1796 and 1797) made applications for the discharge of two hundred and seventy-one seamen, who had, in most cases, exhibited such evidence as to satisfy him that they were real Americans, forced into the British service, and persevering, generally, in refusing pay and bounty."§ They were told, " that if the British Government had any regard to the rights of the United States, any respect for the nation, and placed any value on their friendship, it would facilitate the means of relieving their oppressed citizens."¶ They were told, " that the British naval officers often impressed Swedes, Danes, and other foreigners, from the vessels of the United States; that they might, with as much reason, rob American vessels of property or merchandise of Swedes, Danes, and Portuguese, as seize and detain in their ser-

* See the President's Message to the Senate, of the 16th of April, 1794, nominating Mr. Jay as Envoy Extraordinary to his Britannic Majesty.
† See the letter of Mr. Jefferson, Secretary of State, to Mr. Pinkney, Minister at London, dated the 11th of June, 1792.

* See the letter from Mr. Jefferson to Mr. Pinkney, dated the 12th of October, 1792.
† See the letter from the same to the same, dated the 6th of November, 1792.
‡ See the letter from Mr. Pinkney, Minister at London, to the Secretary of State, dated the 13th of March, 1793.
|| See the note of Mr. Jay, Envoy Extraordinary, to Lord Grenville, dated the 30th of July, 1794.
§ See the letter of Mr. King, Minister at London, to the Secretary of State, dated the 13th of April, 1797.
¶ See the letter from Mr. Pickering, Secretary of State, to Mr. King, Minister at London, dated the 10th of September, 1796.

vice the subjects of those nations found on board of American vessels; and that the President was extremely anxious to have this business of impressing placed on a reasonable footing."[*] And they were told, "that the impressment of American seamen was an injury of very serious magnitude, which deeply affected the feelings and honor of the nation; that no right had been asserted to impress the natives of America, yet, that they were impressed; they were dragged on board British ships of war, with the evidence of citizenship in their hands, and forced by violence there to serve until conclusive testimonials of their birth could be obtained; that many must perish unrelieved, and all were detained a considerable time in lawless and injurious confinement; that the continuance of the practice must inevitably produce discord between two nations, which ought to be the friends of each other; and that it was more advisable to desist from, and to take effectual measures to prevent an acknowledged wrong, than, by perseverance in that wrong, to excite against themselves the well-founded resentments of America, and force the Government into measures which may possibly terminate in an open rupture."[†]

Such were the feelings and the sentiments of the American Government, under every change of its administration, in relation to the British practice of impressment; and such the remonstrances addressed to the justice of Great Britain. It is obvious, therefore, that this cause, independent of every other, has been uniformly deemed a just and certain cause of war; yet, the characteristic policy of the United States still prevailed: remonstrance was only succeeded by negotiation, and every assertion of American rights was accompanied with an overture to secure, in any practicable form, the rights of Great Britain.[‡] Time seemed, however, to render it more and more difficult to ascertain and fix the standard of the British rights, according to the succession of the British claims. The right of entering and searching an American merchant ship, for the purpose of impressment, was, for awhile, confined to the case of British deserters; and even so late as the month of February, 1800, the Minister of His Britannic Majesty, then at Philadelphia, urged the American Government "to take into consideration, as the only means of drying up every source of complaint and irritation upon that head, a proposal which he had made two years before, in the name of His Majesty's Government, for the reciprocal restitution of deserters."[||] But

this project of a treaty was then deemed inadmissible, by the President of the United States, and the chief officers of the Executive departments of the Government, whom he consulted for the same reason, specifically, which, at a subsequent period, induced the President of the United States to withhold his approbation from the treaty negotiated by the American Ministers at London in the year 1806, namely: "that it did not sufficiently provide against the impressment of American seamen;"[*] and "that it is better to have no article, and to meet the consequences, than not to enumerate merchant vessels on the high seas, among the things not to be forcibly entered in search of deserters."[†] But the British claim, expanding with singular elasticity, was soon found to include a right to enter American vessels on the high seas, in order to search for and seize all British seamen; it next embraced the case of every British subject, and finally, in its practical enforcement, it has been extended to every mariner who could not prove, upon the spot, that he was a citizen of the United States.

While the nature of the British claim was thus ambiguous and fluctuating, the principle to which it was referred, for justice and support, appeared to be at once arbitrary and illusory. It was not recorded in any positive code of the law of nations; it was not displayed in the elementary works of the civilian, nor had it ever been exemplified in the maritime usages of any other country, in any other age. In truth, it was the offspring of the municipal law of Great Britain alone, equally operative in a time of peace and in a time of war; and, under all circumstances, inflicting a coercive jurisdiction upon the commerce and navigation of the world.

For the legitimate rights of the belligerent Powers, the United States had felt and evinced a sincere and open respect. Although they had marked a diversity of doctrine among the most celebrated jurists, upon many of the litigated points of the late war; although they had formerly espoused, with the example of the most powerful Government of Europe, the principles of the armed neutrality, which were established in the year 1780, upon the basis of the memorable declaration of the Empress of all the Russias; and although the principles of that declaration have been incorporated into all their public treaties, except in the instance of the Treaty of 1794, yet the United States, still faithful to the pacific and impartial policy which they professed, did not hesitate, even at the commencement of the French revolutionary war, to accept and allow the exposition of the law of nations, as it was then maintained by Great Britain; and conse-

---

[*] See the letter from Mr. Pickering to Mr. King, dated the 26th of October, 1796.

[†] See the letter from Mr. Marshall, Secretary of State, (now Chief Justice of the United States,) to Mr. King, Minister at London, dated the 20th of September, 1800.

[‡] See particularly Mr. King's propositions to Lord Grenville, and Lord Hawkesbury, of the 13th of April, 1797, the 15th of March, 1799, the 25th of February, 1801, and in July, 1813.

[||] See Mr. Liston's note to Mr. Pickering, the Secretary of State, dated the 4th of February, 1800.

[*] See the opinion of Mr. Pickering, Secretary of State, enclosing a plan of a treaty, dated the 3d of May, 1800, and the opinion of Mr. Wolcott, Secretary of the Treasury, dated the 14th of April, 1800.

[†] See the opinion of Mr. Stoddert, Secretary of the Navy, dated the 22d of April, 1800, and the opinions of Mr. Lee, Attorney General, dated the 26th of February, and the 30th of April, 1800.

sequently, to admit, upon a much contested point, that the property of her enemy, in their vessels might be lawfully captured as prize of war.[*] It was also freely admitted, that a belligerent Power had a right, with proper cautions, to enter and search American vessels for the goods of an enemy, and for articles contraband of war; that, if upon a search such goods or articles were found, or if, in the course of the search, persons in the military service of the enemy were discovered, a belligerent had a right of transhipment and removal; that a belligerent had a right, in doubtful cases, to carry American vessels to a convenient station for further examination, and that a belligerent had a right to exclude American vessels from ports and places, under the blockade of an adequate naval force. These rights the law of nations might reasonably be deemed to sanction, nor has a fair exercise of the powers necessary for the enjoyment of these rights been, at any time, controverted or opposed by the American Government.

But it must be again remarked, that the claim of Great Britain was not to be satisfied by the most ample and explicit recognition of the law of war; for, the law of war treats only of the relations of a belligerent to his enemy, while the claim of Great Britain embraced, also, the relations between a Sovereign and his subjects. It was said, that every British subject was bound by a tie of allegiance to his Sovereign, which no lapse of time, no change of place, no exigency of life, could possibly weaken or dissolve. It was said, that the British Sovereign was entitled, at all periods, and on all occasions, to the services of his subjects. And it was said, that the British vessels of war upon the high seas, might lawfully and forcibly enter the merchant vessels of every other nation (for the theory of these pretensions is not limited to the case of the United States, although that case has been, almost exclusively, affected by their practical operation) for the purpose of discovering and impressing British subjects.[†] The United States presume not to discuss the forms, or the principles, of the governments established in other countries. Enjoying the right and the blessing of self-government, they leave, implicitly, to every foreign nation, the choice of its social and political institutions. But whatever may be the form or the principle of government, it is an universal axiom of public law, that every nation is bound so to use and enjoy its own rights as not to injure or destroy the rights of any other nation. Say then, that the tie of allegiance cannot be severed, or relaxed, as respects the sovereign and the subject; and say, that the sovereign is, at all times, entitled to the services

---

[*] See the correspondence of the year 1792, between Mr. Jefferson, Secretary of State, and the Ministers of Great Britain, and France. See also Mr. Jefferson's letter to the American Minister at Paris, of the same year, requesting the recall of Mr. Genet.

[†] See the British declaration of the 10th of January, 1813.

---

of the subject; still, there is nothing gained, in support of the British claim, unless it can, also, be said, that the British Sovereign has a right to seek and seize his subject, while actually within the dominion or under the special protection of another Sovereign State. This will not surely be denominated a process of the law of nations, for the purpose of enforcing the rights of war; and if it shall be tolerated as a process of the municipal law of Great Britain, for the purpose of enforcing the right of the Sovereign to the service of his subjects, there is no principle of discrimination which can prevent its being employed in peace or in war, with all the attendant abuses of force and fraud, to justify the seizure of British subjects for crimes or for debts; and the seizure of British property, for any cause that shall be arbitrarily assigned. The introduction of these degrading novelties into the maritime code of nations, it has been the arduous task of the American Government, in the onset, to oppose; and it rests with all other Governments to decide, how far their honor and their interests must be eventually implicated, by a tacit acquiescence, in the successive usurpations of the British flag. If the right claimed by Great Britain be, indeed, common to all Governments, the ocean will exhibit, in addition to its many other perils, a scene of everlasting strife and contention; but what other Government has ever claimed or exercised the right? If the right shall be exclusively established as a trophy of the naval superiority of Great Britain, the ocean, which has been sometimes emphatically denominated, "the highway of nations," will be identified, in occupancy and use, with the dominions of the British Crown; and every other nation must enjoy the liberty of passage, upon the payment of a tribute, or the indulgence of a license; but what nation is prepared for this sacrifice of its honor and its interests? And if, after all, the right be now asserted (as experience too plainly indicates) for the purpose of imposing upon the United States, to accommodate the British maritime policy, a new and odious limitation of the sovereignty and independence which were acquired by the glorious Revolution of 1776, it is not for the American Government to calculate the duration of a war that shall be waged, in resistance of the active attempts of Great Britain to accomplish her project; for, where is the American citizen who would tolerate a day's submission to the vassalage of such a condition?

But the American Government has seen, with some surprise, the gloss which the Prince Regent of Great Britain, in his declaration of the 10th of January, 1813, has condescended to bestow upon the British claim of a right to impress men, on board of the merchant vessels of other nations; and the retort, which he has ventured to make, upon the conduct of the United States, relative to the controverted doctrines of expatriation. The American Government, like every other civilized Government, avows the principle, and indulges the practice, of naturalizing foreigners. In Great Britain, and throughout the Continent of Europe, the laws and regulations upon the subject are not materially dissimilar, when compared with the laws and regulations of the United States. The effect, however, of such naturalization, upon the connexion, which previously subsisted, between the naturalized person and the Government of the country of his birth, has been differently considered, at different times, and in different places. Still, there are many respects in which a diversity of opinion does not exist, and cannot arise. It is agreed, on all hands, that an act of naturalization is not a violation of the law of nations; and that, in particular, it is not, in itself, an offence against the Government whose subject is naturalized. It is agreed, that an act of naturalization creates, between the parties, the reciprocal obligations of allegiance and protection. It is agreed, that while a naturalized citizen continues within the territory and jurisdiction of his adoptive Government, he cannot be pursued, or seized, or restrained, by his Sovereign. It is agreed, that a naturalized citizen, whatever may be thought of the claims of the Sovereign of his native country, cannot lawfully be withdrawn from the obligations of his contract of naturalization, by the force, or the seduction, of a third Power. And it is agreed, that no Sovereign can lawfully interfere, to take from the service, or the employment, of another Sovereign, persons who are not the subjects of either of the Sovereigns engaged in the transaction. Beyond the principles of these accorded propositions, what have the United States done to justify the imputation of "harboring British seamen, and exercising an assumed right, to transfer the allegiance of British subjects?"[*] The United States have, indeed, insisted upon the right of navigating the ocean in peace and safety, protecting all that is covered by their flag, as on a place of equal and common jurisdiction to all nations; save where the law of war interposes the exceptions of visitation, search, and capture; but, in doing this, they have done no wrong. The United States in perfect consistency, it is believed, with the practice of all belligerent nations, not even excepting Great Britain herself, have, indeed, announced a determination, since the declaration of hostilities, to afford protection, as well to the naturalized, as to the native citizen, who, giving the strongest proofs of fidelity, should be taken in arms by the enemy; and the British cabinet well know, that this determination could have no influence upon those councils of their Sovereign, which preceded and produced the war. It was not, then, to "harbor British seamen," nor to "transfer the allegiance of British subjects;" nor to "cancel the jurisdiction of their legitimate Sovereign;" nor to vindicate "the pretension that acts of naturalization, and certificates of citizenship, were as valid out of their own territory as within it;"[†] that the United States have asserted

[*] See the British declaration of the 10th of January, 1813.

[†] See these passages in the British declaration of the 10th of January, 1813.

the honor and the privilege of their flag, by the force of reason and of arms. But it was to resist a systematic scheme of maritime aggrandizement, which, prescribing to every other nation the *limits* of a territorial boundary, claimed for Great Britain the exclusive dominion of the seas; and which, spurning the settled principles of the law of war, condemned the ships and mariners of the United States to suffer, upon the high seas and virtually within the jurisdiction of their flag, the most rigorous dispensations of the British municipal code, inflicted by the coarse and licentious hand of a British press-gang.

The injustice of the British claim, and the cruelty of the British practice, have tested, for a series of years, the pride and the patience of the American Government; but, still, every experiment was anxiously made to avoid the last resort of nations. The claim of Great Britain, in its theory, was limited to the right of seeking and impressing its own subjects, on board of the merchant vessels of the United States, although, in fatal experience, it has been extended (as already appears) to the seizure of the subjects of every other Power, sailing under a voluntary contract with the American merchant; to the seizure of the naturalized citizens of the United States, sailing, also, under voluntary contracts, which every foreigner, independent of any act of naturalization, is at liberty to form in every country; and even to the seizure of the native citizens of the United States, sailing on board the ships of their own nation, in the prosecution of a lawful commerce. The excuse, for what has been unfeelingly termed, "partial mistakes, and occasional abuse,"[*] when the right of impressment was practised towards vessels of the United States, is, in the words of the Prince Regent's declaration, "a similarity of language and manners;" but was it not known, when this excuse was offered to the world, that the Russian, the Swede, the Dane, and the German; that the Frenchman, the Spaniard, and the Portuguese; nay, that the African and the Asiatic; between whom and the people of Great Britain there exists no similarity of language, manners, or complexion; had been, equally with the American citizen and the British subject, the victims of the impress tyranny?[†] If, however, the excuse be sincere; if the real object of the impressment be merely to secure to Great Britain the naval services of her own subjects, and not to man her fleets, in every practicable mode of enlistment, by right or by wrong; and if a just and generous Government, professing mutual friendship and respect, may be presumed to prefer the accomplishment even of a legitimate purpose, by means the least afflicting and injurious to others, why have the overtures of the United States, offering other means as effectual as impressment,

[*] See the British declaration of the 10th of January, 1813.

[†] See the letter of Mr. Pickering, Secretary of State, to Mr. King, Minister at London, of the 20th of October, 1796; and the letter of Mr. Marshall, Secretary of State, to Mr. King, of the 20th of September, 1800.

for the purpose avowed, to the consideration and acceptance of Great Britain, been forever eluded or rejected? It has been offered, that the number of men to be protected by an American vessel, should be limited by her tonnage; that British officers should be permitted, in British ports, to enter the vessel, in order to ascertain the number of men on board; and that, in case of an addition to her crew, the British subjects enlisted should be liable to impressment.* It was offered in the solemn form of a law, that American seamen should be registered; that they should be provided with certificates of citizenship;† and that the roll of the crew of every vessel should be formally authenticated.‡ It was offered, that no refuge or protection should be given to deserters; but that, on the contrary, they should be surrendered.‖ It was "again and again offered, to concur in a convention, which it was thought practicable to be formed and which should settle the questions of impressment, in a manner that would be safe for England, and satisfactory to the United States."§ It was offered, that each party should prohibit its citizens or subjects, from clandestinely concealing or carrying away, from the territories or colonies of the other, any seaman belonging to the other party.¶ And, conclusively, it has been offered and declared by law, that "after the termination of the present war, it should not be lawful to employ on board of any of the public or private vessels of the United States, any persons, except citizens of the United States; and that no foreigner should be admitted to become a citizen hereafter, who had not, for the continued term of five years, resided within the United States, without being, at any time, during the five years, out of the territory of the United States."**

It is manifest then, that such provision might be made by law; and that such provision has been repeatedly and urgently proposed; as would, in all future times, exclude from the maritime service of the United States, both in public and in private vessels, every person, who could, possibly, be claimed by Great Britain, as a native subject, whether he had, or had not, been natural-

ized in America.* Enforced by the same sanctions and securities, which are employed to enforce the penal code of Great Britain, as well as the penal code of the United States, the provision would afford the strongest evidence, that no British subject could be found in service on board of an American vessel; and, consequently, whatever might be the British right of impressment, in the abstract, there would remain no justifiable motive, there could hardly be invented a plausible pretext, to exercise it, at the expense of the American right of lawful commerce. If, too, as it has sometimes been insinuated, there would, nevertheless, be room for frauds and evasions, it is sufficient to observe, that the American Government would always be ready to bear, and to redress, every just complaint; or, if redress were sought and refused, (a preliminary course, that ought never to have been omitted, but which Great Britain has never pursued,) it would still be in the power of the British Government to resort to its own force, by acts equivalent to war, for the reparation of its wrongs. But Great Britain has, unhappily, perceived in the acceptance of the overtures, of the American Government, consequences injurious to her maritime policy; and, therefore, withholds it, at the expense of her justice. She perceives, perhaps, a loss of the American nursery for her seamen, while she is at peace; a loss of the service of American crews, while she is at war; and a loss of many of those opportunities, which have enabled her to enrich her navy, by the spoils of the American commerce, without exposing her own commerce to the risk of retaliation or reprisals. Thus, were the United States, in a season of reputed peace, involved in the evils of a state of war; and thus was the American flag annoyed by a nation still professing to cherish the sentiments of mutual friendship and respect, which had been recently vouched, by the faith of a solemn treaty. But the American Government even yet abstained from vindicating its rights, and from avenging its wrongs, by an appeal to arms. It was not an insensibility to those wrongs; nor a dread of British power; nor a subserviency to British interests, that prevailed, at that period, in the Councils of the United States; but, under all trials, the American Government abstained from the appeal to arms then, as it has, repeatedly since done, in its collisions with France, as well as with Great Britain, from the purest love of peace, while peace could be rendered compatible with the honor and independence of the nation.

During the period which has hitherto been more particularly contemplated, (from the declaration of hostilities between Great Britain and France in the year 1793, until the short-lived pacification of the Treaty of Amiens in 1802,) there were not wanting occasions, to test the consistency and the impartiality of the American Government, by a comparison of its conduct to-

---

* See the letter of Mr. Jefferson, Secretary of State, to Mr. Pinkney, Minister at London, dated the 11th of June, 1792, and the letter of Mr. Pickering, Secretary of State, to Mr. King, Minister at London, dated the 8th of June, 1796.

† See the act of Congress, passed the 28th of May, 1796.

‡ See the letter of Mr. Pickering, Secretary of State to Mr. King, Minister at London, dated the 8th of June, 1796.

‖ See the project of a treaty on the subject, between Mr. Pickering, Secretary of State, and Mr. Liston, the British Minister, at Philadelphia, in the year 1800.

§ See the letter of Mr. King, Minister at London, to the Secretary of State, dated the 15th of March, 1799.

¶ See the letter of Mr. King, to the Secretary of State, dated in July, 1803.

** See the act of Congress, passed on the 3d of March, 1813.

---

* See the letter of instructions from Mr. Monroe, Secretary of State, to the Plenipotentiaries for treating of peace with Great Britain, under the mediation of the Emperor Alexander, dated the 15th of April, 1813.

wards Great Britain, with its conduct towards other nations. The manifestations of the extreme jealousy of the French Government, and of the intemperate zeal of its Ministers near the United States, were coeval with the proclamation of neutrality; but after the ratification of the Treaty of London, the scene of violence, spoliation, and contumely, opened by France, upon the United States, became such, as to admit, perhaps, of no parallel, except in the contemperaneous scenes which were exhibited by the injustice of her great competitor. The American Government acted, in both cases, on the same pacific policy; in the same spirit of patience and forbearance; but with the same determination, also, to assert the honor and independence of the nation. When, therefore, every conciliatory effort had failed, and when two successive missions of peace had been contemptuously repulsed, the American Government, in the year 1798, annulled its treaties with France, and waged a maritime war against the nation, for the defence of its citizens, and of its commerce, passing on the high seas. But as soon as the hope was conceived, of a satisfactory change in the dispositions of the French Government, the American Government hastened to send another mission to France; and a convention, signed in the year 1800, terminated the subsisting differences between the two countries.

Nor were the United States able, during the same period, to avoid a collision with the Government of Spain, upon many important and critical questions of boundary and commerce; of Indian warfare, and maritime spoliation. Preserving, however, their system of moderation, in the assertion of their rights, a course of amicable discussion and explanation, produced mutual satisfaction; and a Treaty of Friendship, Limits, and Navigation, was formed in the year 1795, by which the citizens of the United States acquired a right, for the space of three years, to deposite their merchandises and effects in the port of New Orleans; with a promise, either that the enjoyment of that right should be indefinitely continued, or that another part of the banks of the Mississippi should be assigned for an equivalent establishment. But, when, in the year 1802, the port of New Orleans was abruptly closed against the citizens of the United States, without an assignment of any other equivalent place of deposite, the harmony of the two countries was again most seriously endangered, until the Spanish Government, yielding to the remonstrances of the United States, disavowed the act of the Intendant of New Orleans, and ordered the right of deposite to be reinstated, on the terms of the Treaty of 1795.

The effects produced, even by a temporary suspension of the right of deposite at New Orleans, upon the interests and feelings of the nation, naturally suggested to the American Government the expediency of guarding against their concurrence, by the acquisition of a permanent property in the Province of Louisiana. The Minister of the United States, at Madrid, was, accordingly,

instructed to apply to the Government of Spain upon the subject; and, on the the 4th of May, 1803, he received an answer, stating, that " by the retrocession made to France of Louisiana, that Power regained the province, with the limits it had, saving the rights acquired by other Powers; and that the United States could address themselves to the French Government, to negotiate the acquisition of territories, which might suit their interest."* But, before this reference, official information of the same fact had been received by Mr. Pinkney from the Court of Spain, in the month of March preceding, and the American Government, having instituted a special mission to negotiate the purchase of Louisiana from France, or from Spain, whichever should be its sovereign, the purchase was accordingly accomplished, for a valuable consideration, (that was punctually paid) by the Treaty concluded at Paris, on the 30th of April, 1803.

The American Government has not seen, without some sensibility, that a transaction, accompanied by such circumstances of general publicity and of scrupulous good faith, has been denounced by the Prince Regent, in his declaration of the 10th of January, 1813, as a proof of the "ungenerous conduct" of the United States towards Spain.† In amplification of the Royal charge, the British negotiators at Ghent have presumed to impute "the acquisition of Louisiana, by the United States, to a spirit of aggrandizement, not necessary to their own security;" and to maintain "that the purchase was made against the known conditions on which it had been ceded by Spain to France;‡ that "in the face of the protestation of the Minister of His Catholic Majesty at Washington, the President of the United States ratified the Treaty of Purchase;"‖ and that "there was good reason to believe that many circumstances attending the transaction were industriously concealed."§ The American Government cannot condescend to retort aspersions so unjust, in language so opprobrious; and peremptorily rejects the pretension of Great Britain to interfere in the business of the United States and Spain; but it owes, nevertheless, to the claims of truth, a distinct statement of the facts which have been thus misrepresented. When the special mission was appointed to negotiate the purchase of Louisiana from France, in the manner already mentioned, the American Minister at London was instructed to explain the object of the mission; and having made the

---
*See the letter from Don Pedro Cevallos, the Minister of Spain, to Mr. C. Pinkney, the Minister of the United States, dated the 4th of May, 1803, from which the passage cited is literally translated.

† See the Prince Regent's declaration of the 10th of January, 1813.

‡ See the note of the British Commissioners, dated the 4th of September, 1814.

‖ See the note of the British Commissioners, dated the 19th of September, 1814.

§ See the note of the British Commissioners, dated the 8th of October, 1814.

explanation, he was assured by the British Government, "that the communication was received in good part; no doubt was suggested of the right of the United States to pursue, separately and alone, the objects they aimed at; but the British Government appeared to be satisfied with the President's views on this important subject."[*] As soon, too, as the Treaty of Purchase was concluded, before hostilities were again actually commenced between Great Britain and France, and previously, indeed, to the departure of the French Ambassador from London, the American Minister openly notified to the British Government, that a treaty had been signed, "by which the complete sovereignty of the town and territory of New Orleans, as well as of all Louisiana, as the same was heretofore possessed by Spain, had been acquired by the United States of America; and, that in drawing up the treaty, care had been taken so to frame the same as not to infringe any right of Great Britain, in the navigation of the river Mississippi."[†] In the answer of the British Government, it was explicitly declared by Lord Hawkesbury, "that he received His Majesty's commands to express the pleasure with which His Majesty had received the intelligence; and to add, that His Majesty regarded the care which had been taken so to frame the treaty as not to infringe any right of Great Britain in the navigation of the Mississippi, as the most satisfactory evidence of a disposition on the part of the Government of the United States, correspondent with that which His Majesty entertained, to promote and improve that harmony which so happily subsisted between the two countries, and which was so conducive to their mutual benefit."[‡] The world will judge, whether, under such circumstances, the British Government had any cause, on its own account, to arraign the conduct of the United States in making the purchase of Louisiana; and certainly no greater cause will be found for the arraignment on account of Spain. The Spanish Government was apprized of the intention of the United States to negotiate for the purchase of that province; its Ambassador witnessed the progress of the negotiation at Paris, and the conclusion of the Treaty on the 30th of April, 1803, was promptly known and understood at Madrid—yet, the Spanish Government interposed no objection, no protestation, against the transaction in Europe; and it was not until the month of September, 1803, that the American Government heard with surprise, from the Minister of Spain at Washington, that His Catholic Majesty was dissatisfied with the cession of Louisiana to the United States. Notwithstanding this diplomatic remonstrance, however, the Spanish Government proceeded to deliver the possession of Louisiana to France, in execution of the Treaty of Ildefonso; saw France, by an almost simultaneous act, transfer the possession to the United States, in execution of the Treaty of Purchase; and, finally instructed the Marquis de Casa Yrujo to present to the American Government the declaration of the 15th of May, 1804, acting "by the special order of his Sovereign," "that the explanations, which the Government of France had given to His Catholic Majesty concerning the sale of Louisiana to the United States, and the amicable dispositions on the part of the King his master, towards these States, had determined him to abandon the opposition, which at a prior period, and with the most substantial motives, he had manifested against the transaction."[*]

But after this amicable and decisive arrangement of all differences, in relation to the validity of the Louisiana purchase, a question of some embarrassment remained in relation to the boundaries of the ceded territory. This question, however, the American Government always has been, and always will be, willing to discuss, in the most candid manner, and to settle upon the most liberal basis with the Government of Spain. It was not, therefore, a fair topic with which to inflame the Prince Regent's declaration, or to embellish the diplomatic notes of the British negotiators at Ghent.[†] The period has arrived when Spain, relieved from her European labors, may be expected to bestow her attention more effectually upon the state of the colonies; and, acting with wisdom, justice, and magnanimity, of which she has given frequent examples, she will find no difficulty in meeting the recent advances of the American Government, for an honorable adjustment of every point in controversy between the two countries, without seeking the aid of British mediation, or adopting the animosity of British Councils.

But still the United States, feeling a constant interest in the opinion of enlightened and impartial nations, cannot hesitate to embrace the opportunity for representing, in the simplicity of truth, the events by which they have been led to take possession of a part of the Floridas, notwithstanding the claim of Spain to the sovereignty of the same territory. In the acceptation and understanding of the United States, the cession of Louisiana embraced the country south of the Mississippi Territory, and eastward of the river Mississippi, and extending to the river Perdido; but "their conciliatory views, and their confidence in the justice of their cause, and in the success of a candid discussion and amicable negotiation with a just and friendly Power, induced them to acquiesce in the temporary continuance of that

---

[*] See the letter from the Secretary of State to Mr. King, the American Minister at London, dated the 29th of January, 1808; and Mr. King's letter to the Secretary of State, dated the 28th of April, 1803.

[†] See the letter of Mr. King, to Lord Hawkesbury, dated the 15th of May, 1803.

[‡] See the letter of Lord Hawkesbury, to Mr. King, dated the 19th of May, 1803.

[*] See the letter of the Marquis de Casa Yrujo, to the American Secretary of State, dated the 15th of May, 1804.

[†] See the Prince Regent's declaration of the 10th of January, 1813. See the notes of the British Commissioners, dated 19th September, 8th October, 1814.

territory, under the Spanish authority."* When, however, the adjustment of the boundaries of Louisiana, as well as a reasonable indemnification, on account of maritime spoliations, and the suspension of the right of deposite at New Orleans, seemed to be indefinitely postponed, on the part of Spain, by events which the United States had not contributed to produce, and could not control; when a crisis had arrived subversive of the order of things under the Spanish authorities, contravening the views of both parties, and endangering the tranquillity and security of the adjoining territories, by the intrusive establishment of a Government independent of Spain, as well as of the United States; and when, at a later period, there was reason to believe that Great Britain herself designed to occupy the Floridas, (and she has, indeed, actually occupied Pensacola for hostile purposes,) the American Government, without departing from its respect for the rights of Spain, and even consulting the honor of that State, unequal as she then was to the task of suppressing the intrusive establishment, was impelled by the paramount principle of self-preservation, to rescue its own rights from the impending danger. Hence, the United States in the year 1810, proceeding, step by step, according to the growing exigencies of the time, took possession of the country, in which the standard of independence had been displayed, excepting such places as were held by a Spanish force. In the year 1811, they authorized their President, by law, provisionally to accept of the possession of East Florida from the local authorities, or to pre-occupy it against the attempt of a foreign Power to seize it. In 1813, they obtained the possession of Mobile, the only place then held by a Spanish force in West Florida; with a view to their own immediate security, but without varying the questions depending between them and Spain, in relation to that province. And, in the year 1814, the American commander, acting under the sanction of the law of nations, but unauthorized by the orders of his Government, drove from Pensacola the British troops, who, in violation of the neutral territory of Spain, (a violation which Spain, it is believed, must herself resent, and would have resisted, if the opportunity had occurred,) seized and fortified that station, to aid in military operations against the United States. But all these measures of safety and necessity were frankly explained, as they occurred, to the Government of Spain, and even to the Government of Great Britain, antecedently to the declaration of war, with the sincerest assurances that the possession of the territory thus acquired "should not cease to be a subject of fair and friendly negotiation and adjustment."†

* See the proclamation of the President of the United States, authorizing Governor Claiborne to take possession of the territory, dated the 27th of October, 1810.

† See the letter from the Secretary of State, to Governor Claiborne, and the President's proclamation, dated the 27th of October, 1810.

The present review of the conduct of the United States towards the belligerent Powers of Europe, will be regarded by every candid mind as a necessary medium to vindicate their national character from the unmerited imputations of the Prince Regent's declaration of the 10th of January, 1813; and not a medium voluntarily assumed, according to the insinuations of that declaration, for the revival of unworthy prejudices or vindictive passions, in reference to transactions that are past. The Treaty of Amiens, which seemed to terminate the war in Europe, seemed also to terminate the neutral sufferings of America; but the hope of repose was, in both respects, delusive and transient. The hostilities which were renewed between Great Britain and France, in the year 1803, were immediately followed by a renewal of the aggressions of the belligerent Powers, upon the commercial rights and political independence of the United States. There was scarcely, therefore, an interval separating the aggressions of the first war from the aggressions of the second war; and although, in nature, the aggressions continued to be the same, in extent, they became incalculably more destructive. It will be seen, however, that the American Government inflexibly maintained its neutral and pacific policy in every extremity of the latter trial, with the same good faith and forbearance that, in the former trial, had distinguished its conduct; until it was compelled to choose from the alternative, of national degradation or national resistance. And, if Great Britain alone then became the object of the American declaration of war, it will be seen that Great Britain alone had obstinately closed the door of amicable negotiation.

The American Minister at London, anticipating the rupture between Great Britain and France, had obtained assurances from the British Government, "that, in the event of war, the instruc-'tions given to their naval officers *should be* 'drawn up with plainness and precision; and, in 'general, that the rights of belligerents should be 'exercised in moderation, and with due respect for 'those of neutrals."* And in relation to the important subject of impressment, he had actually prepared for signature, with the assent of Lord Hawkesbury and Lord St. Vincent, a convention to continue during five years, declaring, that "no 'seaman, nor seafaring person, should, upon the 'high seas, and without the jurisdiction of either 'party, be demanded or taken out of any ship,

See the proceedings of the Convention of Florida, transmitted to the Secretary of State, by the Governor of the Mississippi Territory, in his letter of the 17th of October, 1810; and the answer of the Secretary of State, dated the 15th of November, 1810.

See the letter of Mr. Morier, British Chargé d'Affaires, to the Secretary of State, dated the 15th of December, 1810; and the Secretary's answer.

See the correspondence between Mr. Monroe and Mr. Foster, the British Minister, in the months of July, September, and November, 1811.

* See the letter of Mr. King to the Secretary of State, dated the 16th of May, 1806.

Causes and Character of the War.

' or vessel, belonging to the citizens or subjects of one of the parties, by the public or private armed ships, or men of war, belonging to, or in the service of, the other party; and that strict orders should be given for the due observance of the engagement."* This convention, which explicitly relinquished impressments from American vessels, on the high seas, and to which the British Ministers had at first agreed, Lord St. Vincent was desirous afterwards to modify, "stating, that on further reflection, he was of opinion that the narrow seas should be expressly excepted, they having been, as his Lordship remarked, immemorially considered to be within the dominion of Great Britain." The American Minister, however, "having supposed, from the tenor of his conversations with Lord St. Vincent, that the doctrine of *mare clausum* would not be revived against the United States on this occasion, but that England would be content, with the limited jurisdiction, or dominion, over the seas adjacent to her territories, which is assigned by the law of nations to other States, was disappointed, on receiving Lord St. Vincent's communication; and chose rather to abandon the negotiation than to acquiesce in the doctrine it proposed to establish."† But it was still some satisfaction to receive a formal declaration from the British Government, communicated by its Minister at Washington, after the recommencement of the war in Europe, which promised, in effect, to reinstate the practice of naval blockades, upon the principles of the law of nations; so that no blockade should be considered as existing, "unless in respect of particular ports, which might be actually invested; and, then, that the vessels bound to such ports should not be captured, unless they had previously been warned not to enter them."‡

All the precautions of the American Government were, nevertheless, ineffectual; and the assurances of the British Government were, in no instance, verified. The outrage of impressment was again, indiscriminately, perpetrated upon the crew of every American vessel, and on every sea. The enormity of blockades, established by an Order in Council, without a legitimate object, and maintained by an Order in Council, without the application of a competent force, was, more and more, developed. The rule, denominated "the rule of the war of 1756," was revived, in an affected style of moderation, but in a spirit of more rigorous execution. ‖ The lives, the liberty, the fortunes, and the happiness, of the citi-

zens of the United States, engaged in the pursuits of navigation and commerce, were once more subjected to the violence and cupidity of the British cruisers. And, in brief, so grievous, so intolerable, had the afflictions of the nation become, that the people, with one mind and one voice, called loudly upon their Government for redress and protection;* the Congress of the United States, participating in the feelings and resentments of the time, urged upon the Executive Magistrate the necessity of an immediate demand of reparation from Great Britain;† while the same patriotic spirit, which had opposed British usurpation in 1793, and encountered French hostility in 1798, was again pledged, in every variety of form, to the maintenance of the national honor and independence during the more arduous trial that arose in 1805.

Amidst these scenes of injustice on the one hand, and of reclamation on the other, the American Government preserved its equanimity and its firmness. It beheld much in the conduct of France, and of her ally, (Spain,) to provoke reprisals. It beheld more in the conduct of Great Britain, that led unavoidably, as had often been avowed, to the last resort of arms. It beheld in the temper of the nation all that was requisite to justify an immediate selection of Great Britain as the object of a declaration of war. And it could not but behold in the policy of France the strongest motive to acquire the United States, as an associate in the existing conflict. Yet, these considerations did not then, more than at any former crisis, subdue the fortitude or mislead the judgment of the American Government; but, in perfect consistency with its neutral, as well as its pacific system, it demanded atonement by remonstrances with France and Spain, and it sought the preservation of peace by negotiation with Great Britain.

It has been shown, that a treaty proposed emphatically by the British Minister, resident at Philadelphia, "as the means of drying up every source of complaint and irritation upon the head of impressment," was "deemed utterly inadmissible" by the American Government, because it did not sufficiently provide for that object.‡ It has also been shown, that another treaty proposed by the American Minister at London was laid aside because the British Government, while it was willing to relinquish expressly impressments from American vessels on the high seas, insisted upon an exception in reference to the narrow seas, claimed as a part of the British dominion. And experience demonstrated, that, although the spe-

---

* See the letter of Mr. King to the Secretary of State, dated July, 1803.

† See the letter of Mr. King to the Secretary of State, dated July, 1803.

‡ See the letter of Mr. Merry to the Secretary of State, dated the 12th of April, 1804, and the enclosed copy of a letter from Mr. Nepean, the Secretary of the Admiralty, to Mr. Hammond, the British under Secretary of State for foreign Affairs, dated January 5, 1804.

‖ See the Orders in Council of the 24th of June, 1803, and the 17th of August, 1805.

* See the memorials of Boston, New York, Philadelphia, Baltimore, &c., presented to Congress in the end of the year 1805, and the beginning of the year 1806.

† See the resolutions of the Senate of the United States, of the 10th and 14th of February, 1806; and the resolution of the House of Representatives.

‡ See Mr. Liston's letter to the Secretary of State, dated the 4th February, 1800; and the letter of Mr. Pickering, Secretary of State, to the President of the United States, dated the 20th February, 1800.

Causes and Character of the War.

liations committed upon the American commerce might admit of reparation by the payment of a pecuniary equivalent; yet, consulting the honor and the feelings of the nation, it was impossible to receive satisfaction for the cruelties of impressment by any other means than by an entire discontinuance of the practice. When, therefore, the Envoys Extraordinary were appointed in the year 1806 to negotiate with the British Government, every authority was given for the purposes of conciliation; nay, an act of Congress prohibiting the importation of certain articles of British manufacture into the United States was suspended, in proof of a friendly disposition.* But, it was declared that "the suppression of impressment and the definition of blockades were absolutely indispensable;" and that, "without a provision against impressments, no treaty should be concluded." The American Envoys, accordingly, took care to communicate to the British Commissioners the limitations of their powers. Influenced, at the same time, by a sincere desire to terminate the differences between the two nations; knowing the solicitude of their Government to relieve its seafaring citizens from actual sufferance; listening with confidence to assurances and explanations of the British Commissioners, in a sense favorable to their wishes; and, judging from a state of information that gave no immediate cause to doubt the sufficiency of those assurances and explanations;—the Envoys, rather than terminate the negotiation without any arrangement, were willing to rely upon the efficacy of a substitute for a positive article in the treaty, to be submitted to the consideration of their Government, as this, according to the declaration of the British Commissioners, was the only arrangement they were permitted at that time to propose or to allow. The substitute was presented in the form of a note from the British Commissioners to the American Envoys, and contained a pledge "that instructions had been given, and should be repeated and enforced, for the observance of the greatest caution in the impressing of British seamen; that the strictest care should be taken to preserve the citizens of the United States from any molestation or injury; and that immediate and prompt redress should be afforded, upon any representation of injury sustained by them."†

Inasmuch, however, as the treaty contained no provision against impressment, and it was seen by the Government, when the treaty was under consideration for ratification, that the pledge contained in the substitute was not complied with, but, on the contrary, that the impressments were continued with undiminished violence in the American seas, so long after the alleged date of the instructions which were to arrest them, that the practical inefficacy of the substitute could not be doubted by the Government here, the ratification of the

treaty was necessarily declined; and it has since appeared, that, after a change in the British Ministry had taken place, it was declared by the Secretary of Foreign Affairs that no engagements were entered into, on the part of His Majesty, as connected with the treaty, except such as appear upon the face of it.*

The American Government, however, with unabating solicitude for peace, urged an immediate renewal of the negotiations on the basis of the abortive treaty, until this course was peremptorily declared, by the British Government, to be "wholly inadmissible."†

But, independent of the silence of the proposed treaty, upon the great topic of American complaint, and of the view which has been taken of the projected substitute; the contemporaneous declaration of the British Commissioners, delivered by the command of their Sovereign, and to which the American Envoys refused to make themselves a party, or to give the slightest degree of sanction, was regarded by the American Government, as ample cause of rejection. In reference to the French decree, which had been issued at Berlin, on the 21st of November, 1806, it was declared, that if France should carry the threats of that decree into execution, and "*if neutral nations*, contrary to all expectation, should acquiesce in such usurpations, His Majesty *might*, probably, be compelled, however *reluctantly*, to retaliate, in his just defence, and to adopt, in regard to the commerce of neutral nations with his enemies, the same measures which those nations should have permitted to be enforced against their commerce with his subjects;" "that His Majesty could not enter into the stipulations of the present treaty, without an explanation from the United States of their intentions, or a reservation on the part of His Majesty, in the case above mentioned, if it should ever occur;" and "that, without a formal abandonment, or tacit relinquishment, of the unjust pretensions of France, or without such conduct and assurance on the part of the United States, as should give security to His Majesty, that they would not submit to the French innovations, in the established system of maritime law, His Majesty would not consider himself bound, by the present signature of his Commissioners, to ratify the treaty, or precluded from adopting such measures as might seem necessary for counteracting the designs of the enemy." ‡

The reservation of a power to invalidate a solemn treaty, at the pleasure of one of the *parties*, and the menace of inflicting punishment upon the United States, for the offences of another nation, proved, in the event, a prelude to the scenes of violence which Great Britain was then about to display, and which it would have been improper for the American negotiators to anticipate.

---

* See the act of Congress, passed the 18th of April, 1806; and the act suspending it, passed the 19th of December, 1806.

† See the note of the British Commissioners, dated the 8th November, 1806.

* See Mr. Canning's letter to the American Envoys, dated the 27th October, 1807.

† See the same letter.

‡ See the note of the British Commissioners, dated the 31st of December, 1806. See, also, the answer of Messrs. Monroe and Pinkney, to that note.

Causes and Character of the War.

For, if a commentary were wanting to explain the real design of such conduct, it would be found in the fact, that within eight days from the date of the treaty, and before it was possible for the British Government to have known the effect of the Berlin decree on the American Government; nay, even before the Government had itself heard of that decree, the destruction of American commerce was commenced by the Order in Council of the 7th of January, 1807, which announced, "that no vessel should be permitted to trade from one port to another, both which ports should belong to, or be in possession of, France, or her allies; or should be so far under their control, as that British vessels might not trade freely thereat."[*]

During the whole period of this negotiation, which did not finally close until the British Government declared, in the month of October, 1807, that negotiation was no longer admissible, the course pursued by the British squadron, stationed more immediately on the American coast, was, in the extreme, vexatious, predatory, and hostile. The territorial jurisdiction of the United States, extending, upon the principles of the law of nations, at least a league over the adjacent ocean, was totally disregarded and contemned. Vessels employed in the coasting trade, or in the business of the pilot and the fisherman, were objects of incessant violence; their petty cargoes were plundered, and some of their scanty crews were often either impressed, or wounded, or killed, by the force of British frigates. British ships of war hovered, in warlike display, upon the coast; blockaded the ports of the United States, so that no vessel could enter, or depart, in safety; penetrated the bays and rivers, and even anchored in the harbors, of the United States, to exercise a jurisdiction of impressment; threatened the towns and villages with conflagration; and wantonly discharged musketry, as well as cannon, upon the inhabitants of an open and unprotected country. The neutrality of the American territory was violated on every occasion; and, at last, the American Government was doomed to suffer the greatest indignity which could be offered to a sovereign and independent nation, in the ever memorable attack of a British fifty gun ship, under the countenance of the British squadron, anchored within the waters of the United States, upon the frigate Chesapeake, peaceably prosecuting a distant voyage. The British Government affected, from time to time, to disapprove and condemn these outrages; but the officers who perpetrated them were generally applauded; if tried, they were acquitted; if removed from the American station, it was only to be promoted in another station; and if atonement were offered, as in the flagrant instance of the frigate Chesapeake, the atonement was so ungracious in the manner, and so tardy in the result, as to betray the want of that conciliatory spirit which ought to have characterized it.[†]

But the American Government, soothing the exasperated spirit of the people, by a proclamation, which interdicted the entrance of all British armed vessels, into the harbors and waters of the United States,[*] neither commenced hostilities against Great Britain, nor sought a defensive alliance with France, nor relaxed in its firm but conciliatory efforts to enforce the claims of justice upon the honor of both nations.

The rival ambition of Great Britain and France, now, however, approached the consummation, which, involving the destruction of all neutral rights, upon an avowed principle of action, could not fail to render an actual state of war, comparatively, more safe and more prosperous than the imaginary state of peace, to which neutrals were reduced. The just and impartial conduct of a neutral nation ceased to be its shield and its safeguard, when the conduct of the belligerent Powers towards each other became the only criterion of the law of war. The wrong committed by one of the belligerent Powers, was thus made the signal for the perpetration of a greater wrong by the other; and if the American Government complained to both Powers, their answer, although it never denied the cause of complaint, invariably retorted an idle and offensive inquiry into the priority of their respective aggressions; or each demanded a course of resistance, against its antagonist, which was calculated to prostrate the American right of self-government, and to coerce the United States, against their interest and their policy, into becoming an associate in the war. But the American Government never did, and never can, admit, that a belligerent Power, "in taking steps to restrain the violence of its enemy, and to retort upon them the evils of their own injustice,"[†] is entitled to disturb and to destroy the rights of a neutral Power, as recognised and established by the law of nations. It was impossible, indeed, that the real features of the miscalled retaliatory system, should be long masked from the world; when Great Britain, even in her acts of professed retaliation, declared that France was unable to execute the hostile denunciations of her decrees;[‡] and when Great Britain herself, unblushingly, entered into the same commerce with her enemy (through the medium of forgeries, perjuries, and licenses,) from which she had interdicted unoffending neutrals. The pride of naval superiority, and the cravings of commercial monopoly, gave, after all, the impulse and direction to the councils of the British Cabinet;

---

gress in November, 1806. See the documents respecting Captain Love, of the Driver; Captain Whitby, of the Leander, &c.

See also, the correspondence respecting the frigate Chesapeake, with Mr. Canning at London; with Mr. Rose, at Washington; and with Mr. Erskine, at Washington.

[*] See the proclamation of the 2d of July, 1807.

[†] See the Orders in Council of the 7th of January, 1807.

[‡] See the Orders in Council of the 7th of January, 1807.

---

[*] See the Order in Council of January 7, 1807.

[†] See the evidence of these facts reported to Con-

while the vast, although visionary projects of France, furnished occasions and pretexts for accomplishing the objects of those councils.

The British Minister, resident at Washington, in the year 1804, having distinctly recognised, in the name of his Sovereign, the legitimate principles of blockade, the American Government received, with some surprise and solicitude, the successive notifications of the 9th of August, 1804, the 8th of April, 1806, and more particularly of the 16th of May, 1806, announcing, by the last notification, "a blockade of the coast, rivers, and ports, from the river Elbe to the port of Brest, both inclusive."[*] In none of the notified instances of blockade, were the principles, that had been recognised in 1804, adopted and pursued; and it will be recollected by all Europe, that neither at the time of the notification of the 16th of May, 1806, nor at the time of excepting the Elbe and Ems from the operation of that notification,[†] nor at any time during the continuance of the French war, was there an adequate naval force, actually applied by Great Britain, for the purpose of maintaining a blockade from the river Elbe to the port of Brest. It was then, in the language of the day, "a mere paper blockade;" a manifest infraction of the law of nations; and an act of peculiar injustice to the United States, as the only neutral Power against which it could practically operate. But, whatever may have been the sense of the American Government on the occasion, and whatever might be the disposition to avoid making this the ground of an open rupture with Great Britain, the case assumed a character of the highest interest, when, independent of its own injurious consequences, France, in the Berlin decree of the 21st of November, 1806, recited, as a chief cause for placing the British islands in a state of blockade, "that Great Britain declares blockaded places before which she has not a single vessel of war; and even places, which her united forces would be incapable of blockading; such as entire coasts, and a whole empire: an unequalled abuse of the right of blockade, that had no other object, than to interrupt the communications of different nations; and to extend the commerce and industry of England, upon the ruin of those nations."[‡] The American Government aims not, and never has aimed, at the justification, either of Great Britain or of France in their career of crimination and recrimination; but it is of some importance to observe, that, if the blockade of May, 1806, was an unlawful blockade, and if the right of retaliation arose with the first unlawful attack, made by a belligerent Power upon neutral rights, Great Britain has yet to answer to mankind, according to the rule of her own acknowledgment, for all the calamities of

the retaliatory warfare. France, whether right or wrong, made the British system of blockade the foundation of the Berlin decree; and France had an equal right with Great Britain to demand from the United States an opposition to every encroachment upon the privileges of the neutral character. It is enough, however, on the present occasion, for the American Government to observe that it possessed no power to prevent the framing of the Berlin decree, and to disclaim any approbation of its principles or acquiescence in its operation: for, it neither belonged to Great Britain nor to France to prescribe to the American Government the time or the mode, or the degree of resistance, to the indignities and the outrages with which each of those nations in its turn assailed the United States.

But it has been shown that, after the British Government possessed a knowledge of the existence of the Berlin decree, it authorized the conclusion of the Treaty with the United States, which was signed at London, on the 31st of December, 1806, reserving to itself a power of annulling the treaty, if France did not revoke, or if the United States, as a neutral Power, did not resist the obnoxious measure. It has also been shown, that before Great Britain could possibly ascertain the determination of the United States in relation to the Berlin decree, the Orders in Council of the 7th of January, 1807, were issued, professing to be a retaliation against France, "at a time when the fleets of France and her allies were themselves confined within their own ports, by the superior valor and discipline of the British navy," but operating in fact against the United States, as a neutral Power, to prohibit their trade "from one port to another, both which ports should belong to, or be in the possession of France or her allies, or should be so far under their control, as that British vessels might not trade freely thereat."[*] It remains, however, to be stated, that it was not until the 12th of March, 1807, that the British Minister, then residing at Washington, communicated to the American Government, in the name of his Sovereign, the Orders in Council of January, 1807, with an intimation that stronger measures would be pursued, unless the United States should resist the operations of the Berlin decree.[†] At the moment the British Government was reminded "that within the period of those great events which continued to agitate Europe, instances had occurred in which the commerce of neutral nations, more especially of the United States, had experienced the severest distresses from its own orders and measures, manifestly unauthorized by the law of nations;" assurances were given "that no culpable acquiescence on the part of the United States would render them accessary to the proceedings of one belligerent nation, through their rights of neutrality, against

---

[*] See Lord Harrowby's note to Mr. Monroe, dated the 9th of August, 1804; and Mr. Fox's notes to Mr. Monroe, dated respectively the 8th of April and the 16th of May, 1806.

[†] See Lord Howick's note to Mr. Monroe, dated the 25th of September, 1806.

[‡] See the Berlin decree of the 21st November, 1806.

[*] See the Order in Council of the 7th of January, 1807.

[†] See Mr. Erskine's letter to the Secretary of State, dated the 12th of March, 1807.

Cause and Character of the War.

the commerce of its adversary;" and the right of Great Britain to issue such orders unless as orders of blockade, to be enforced according to the law of nations, was utterly denied.*

This candid and explicit avowal of the sentiments of the American Government, upon an occasion so novel and important in the history of nations, did not, however, make its just impression upon the British Cabinet; for, without assigning any new provocation on the part of France, and complaining merely, that neutral Powers had not been induced to interpose with effect, to obtain a revocation of the Berlin decree, (which, however, Great Britain herself had affirmed to be a decree nominal and inoperative,) the Orders in Council of the 11th of November, 1807, were issued, declaring " that all the ports and places of France and her allies, or of any other country at war with His Majesty and all other ports or places in Europe, from which, although not at war with His Majesty, the British flag was excluded, and all ports or places in the colonies belonging to His Majesty's enemies, should from thenceforth be subject to the same restrictions in point of trade and navigation, as if the same were actually blockaded by His Majesty's naval forces, in the most strict and rigorous manner;" that "all trade in articles which were the produce or manufacture of the said countries or colonies, should be deemed and considered to be unlawful," but that neutral vessels should still be permitted to trade with France from certain free ports, or through ports and places of the British dominions.† To accept the lawful enjoyment of a right as the grant of a superior, to prosecute a lawful commerce under the forms of favor and indulgence, and to pay a tribute to Great Britain for the privileges of a lawful transit on the ocean, were concessions which Great Britain was disposed insidiously to exact, by an appeal to the cupidity of individuals, but which the United States could never yield, consistently with the independence and the sovereignty of the nation. The Orders in Council were therefore altered, in this respect, at a subsequent period;‡ but the general interdict of neutral commerce, applying more especially to American commerce, was obstinately maintained, against all the force of reason, of remonstrance, and of protestation, employed by the American Government, when the subject was presented to its consideration by the British Minister residing at Washington. The fact assumed as the basis of the Orders in Council was unequivocally disowned; and it was demonstrated that, so far from its being true, " that the United States had acquiesced in an illegal operation of the Berlin decree, it was not even true, that at the date of the British Orders of the 11th of November, 1807, a single ap-

plication of that decree to the commerce of the United States on the high seas, could have been known to the British Government;" while the British Government had been officially informed by the American Minister at London, " that explanations, uncontradicted by any overt act, had been given to the American Minister at Paris, which justified a reliance that the French decree would not be put in force against the United States.*

The British orders of the 11th of November, 1807, were quickly followed by the French decree of Milan, dated the 17th of December, 1807, " which was said to be resorted to only in just retaliation of the barbarous system adopted by England," and in which the denationalizing tendency of the orders is made the foundation of a declaration in the decree, " that every ship, to whatever nation it might belong, that should have submitted to be searched by an English ship, or to a voyage to England, or should have paid any tax whatsoever to the English Government, was thereby, and for that alone, declared to be denationalized, to have forfeited the protection of its Sovereign, and to have become English property, subject to capture, as good and lawful prize; that the British islands were placed in a state of blockade, both by sea and land; and every ship, of whatever nation, or whatever the nature of its cargo might be, that sails from the ports of England, or those of the English colonies, and of the countries occupied by English troops, and proceeding to England, or to the English colonies, or to countries occupied by English troops, should be good and lawful prize; but that the provisions of the decree should be abrogated and null, in fact, as soon as the English should abide again by the principles of the law of nations, which are also the principles of justice and honor."† In opposition, however, to the Milan decree, as well as to the Berlin decree, the American Government strenuously and unceasingly employed every instrument, except the instruments of war. It acted precisely towards France as it acted towards Great Britain, on similar occasions; but France remained, for a time, as insensible to the claims of justice and honor as Great Britain; each imitating the other in extravagance of pretension, and in obstinacy of purpose.

When the American Government received intelligence that the orders of the 11th of November, 1807, had been under the consideration of the British Cabinet, and were actually prepared for promulgation, it was anticipated that France, in a zealous prosecution of the retaliatory warfare, would soon produce an act of at least equal injustice and hostility. The crisis existed, therefore, at which the United States were compelled to decide, either to withdraw their seafaring citizens and their commercial wealth from the ocean, or to leave the interests of the mariner and the

---

* See the Secretary of State's letter to Mr. Erskine, dated the 20th of March, 1807.

† See the Orders in Council of the 11th of November, 1807.

‡ See Mr. Canning's letter to Mr. Pinkney, 23d February, 1808.

* See Mr. Erskine's letter to the Secretary of State, dated the 22d of February, 1808, and the answer of the Secretary of State, dated the 25th of March, 1808.

† See the Milan decree of the 17th of Dec., 1807.

merchant exposed to certain destruction; or to engage in open and active war for the protection and defence of those interests. The principles and the habits of the American Government were still disposed to neutrality and peace. In weighing the nature and the amount of the aggressions which had been perpetrated, or which were threatened, if there were any preponderance to determine the balance against one of the belligerent Powers rather than the other, as the object of a declaration of war, it was against Great Britain, at least upon the vital interest of impressment, and the obvious superiority of her naval means of annoyance. The French decrees were, indeed, as obnoxious in their formation and design as the British orders; but the Government of France claimed and exercised no right of impressment; and the maritime spoliations of France were comparatively restricted, not only by her own weakness on the ocean, but by the constant and pervading vigilance of the fleets of her enemy. The difficulty of selection, the indiscretion of encountering at once both of the offending Powers, and, above all, the hope of an early return of justice, under the dispensations of the ancient public law, prevailed in the councils of the American Government; and it was resolved to attempt the preservation of its neutrality and its peace, of its citizens and its resources, by a voluntary suspension of the commerce and navigation of the United States. It is true, that for the minor outrages committed, under the pretext of the rule of war of 1756, the citizens of every denomination had demanded from their Government, in the year 1805, protection and redress; it is true, that for the unparalleled enormities of the year 1807, the citizens of every denomination again demanded from their Government protection and redress; but it is also a truth, conclusively established by every manifestation of the sense of the American people, as well as of their Government, that any honorable means of protection and redress were preferred to the last resort of arms. The American Government might honorably retire, for a time, from the scene of conflict and collision; but it could no longer, with honor, permit its flag to be insulted, its citizens to be enslaved, and its property to be plundered, on the highway of nations.

Under these impressions, the restrictive system of the United States was introduced. In December, 1807, an embargo was imposed upon all American vessels and merchandise;* on principles similar to those which originated and regulated the embargo law, authorized to be laid by the President of the United States, in the year 1794; but soon afterwards, in the genuine spirit of the policy that prescribed the measure, it was declared by law, "that in the event of such peace, or suspension of hostilities, between the belligerent Powers of Europe, or such changes in their measures affecting neutral commerce, as might render that of the United States safe, in the judgment of the President of the United States, he was

authorized to suspend the embargo, in whole or in part."* The pressure of the embargo was thought however, so severe upon every part of the community, that the American Government, notwithstanding the neutral character of the measure, determined upon some relaxation; and, accordingly, the embargo being raised, as to all other nations, a system of non-intercourse and non-importation was substituted in March, 1809, as to Great Britain and France, which prohibited all voyages to the British or French dominions, and all trade in articles of British or French product or manufacture.† But still adhering to the neutral and pacific policy of the Government, it was declared, " that the President of the United States should be authorized, in case either France or Great Britain should so revoke or modify her edicts, as that they should cease to violate the neutral commerce of the United States, to declare the same by proclamation; after which the trade of the United States might be renewed with the nation so doing."‡ These appeals to the justice and the interests of the belligerent Powers proving ineffectual, and the necessities of the country increasing, it was finally resolved, by the American Government, to take the hazards of a war; to revoke its restrictive system; and to exclude British and French armed vessels from the harbors and waters of the United States; but, again, emphatically to announce, "that in case either Great Britain or France should, before the 3d of March, 1811, so revoke, or modify, her edicts, as that they should cease to violate the neutral commerce of the United States; and if the other nation should not, within three months thereafter, so revoke, or modify, her edicts, in like manner," the provisions of the non-intercourse and non-importation law should, at the expiration of three months, be revived against the nation *refusing* or neglecting to revoke or modify its edicts.§

In the course which the American Government had hitherto pursued, relative to the belligerent orders and decrees, the candid foreigner, as well as the patriotic citizen, may perceive an extreme solicitude for the preservation of peace; but, in the publicity and impartiality of the overture, that was thus spread before the belligerent Powers, it is impossible that any indication should be found of foreign influence or control. The overture was urged upon both nations for acceptance at the same time, and in the same manner; nor was an intimation withheld, from either of them, that " it might be regarded by the belligerent first accepting it, as a promise to itself, and a warning to its enemy."§ Each of the nations, from the

* See the act of Congress, passed the 22d of December, 1807.

* See the act of Congress, passed the 22d of April, 1808.

† See the act of Congress, passed the first day of March, 1809.

‡ See the 11th section of the last cited act of Congress.

§ See the act of Congress, passed May 1, 1810.

§ See the correspondence between the Secretary of State, and the American Ministers at London and Paris.

commencement of the retaliatory system, acknowledged that its measures were violations of public law; and each pledged itself to retract them, whenever the other should set the example.* Although the American Government, therefore, persisted in its remonstrances against the original transgressions, without regard to the question of their priority, it embraced, with eagerness, every hope of reconciling the interests of the rival Powers, with a performance of the duty which they owed to the neutral character of the United States; and when the British Minister, residing at Washington, in the year 1809, affirmed, in terms as plain and as positive as language could supply, " that he was authorized to declare, that His Britannic Majesty's Orders in Council of January and November, 1807. will have been withdrawn, as respects the United States, on the 10th day of June, 1809," the President of the United States hastened, with approved liberality, to accept the declaration as conclusive, that the promised fact would exist, at the stipulated period; and, by an immediate proclamation, he announced, " that after the 10th day of June next, the trade of the United States with Great Britain, as suspended by the non-intercourse law, and by the acts of Congress laying and enforcing an embargo, might be renewed."† The American Government neither asked nor received, from the British Minister, an exemplification of his powers, an inspection of his instructions, nor the solemnity of an Order in Council; but executed the compact, on the part of the United States, in all the sincerity of its own intentions and in all the confidence which the official act of the representative of His Britannic Majesty was calculated to inspire. The act, and the authority for the act, were, however, disavowed by Great Britain; and an attempt was made, by the successor of Mr. Erskine, through the aid of insinuations, which were indignantly repulsed, to justify the British rejection of the Treaty of 1809, by referring to the American rejection of the Treaty of 1806; forgetful of the essential points of difference, that the British Government, on the former occasion, had been explicitly apprized by the American negotiators of their defect of power; and that the execution of the projected treaty had not, on either side, been commenced.‡

After this abortive attempt to obtain a just and honorable revocation of the British Orders in Council, the United States were again invited to indulge the hope of safety and tranquillity, when the Minister of France announced to the American Minister at Paris, that, in consideration of the act of the first of May, 1809, by which the Congress of the United States " engaged to oppose itself to that one of the belligerent Powers,

which should refuse to acknowledge the rights of neutrals, he was authorized to declare, that the decrees of Berlin and Milan were revoked, and that after the first of November, 1810, they would cease to have effect, it being understood, that in consequence of that declaration, the English should revoke their Orders in Council, and renounce the new principles of blockade, which they had wished to establish; or that the United States, conformably to the act of Congress, should cause their rights to be respected by the English."* This declaration, delivered by the official organ of the Government of France, and in the presence, as it were, of the French Sovereign, was of the highest authority, according to all the rules of diplomatic intercourse; and, certainly, far surpassed any claim of credence which was possessed by the British Minister, residing at Washington, when the arrangement of the year 1809 was accepted and executed by the American Government. The President of the United States, therefore, owed to the consistency of his own character, and to the dictates of a sincere impartiality, a prompt acceptance of the French overture: and, accordingly, the authoritative promise, that the fact should exist, at the stipulated period, being again admitted as conclusive evidence of its existence, a proclamation was issued on the 2d of November, 1810, announcing, " that the edicts of France had been so revoked, as that they ceased, on the first day of the same month, to violate the neutral commerce of the United States; and that all the restrictions imposed by the act of Congress should then cease and be discontinued, in relation to France and her dependencies."† That France, from this epoch, refrained from all aggressions, on the high seas, or even in her own ports, upon the persons and the property of the citizens of the United States, never was asserted; but, on the contrary, her violence and her spoliations have been unceasing causes of complaint. These subsequent injuries, constituting a part of the existing reclamations of the United States, were always, however, disavowed by the French Government; while the repeal of the Berlin and Milan decree has, on every occasion, been affirmed; insomuch that Great Britain herself was, at last, compelled to yield to the evidence of the fact.

On the expiration of three months from the date of the President's proclamation, the non-intercourse and non importation law was, of course, to be revived against Great Britain, unless, during that period, her Orders in Council should be revoked. The subject was, therefore, most anxiously, and most steadily, pressed upon the justice and the magnanimity of the British Government; and even when the hope of success expired, by the lapse of the period prescribed in one act of Congress, the United States opened the door of reconciliation by another act, which,

---

* See the documents laid before Congress from time to time, by the President, and printed.

† See the correspondence between Mr. Erskine, the British Minister, and the Secretary of State, on the 17th, 18th, and 19th of April, 1809; and the President's proclamation of the last date.

‡ See the correspondence between the Secretary of State, and Mr. Jackson, the British Minister.

---

* See the Duke de Cadore's letter to Mr. Armstrong, dated the 5th of August, 1810.

† See the President's proclamation of the 2d of November, 1810.

in the year 1811, again provided, that, in case, at any time, "Great Britain should so revoke or modify her edicts, as that they shall cease to violate the neutral commerce of the United States, the President of the United States should declare the fact by proclamation; and that the restrictions, previously imposed, should, from the date of such proclamation, cease and be discontinued."* But, unhappily, every appeal to the justice and magnanimity of Great Britain was now, as heretofore, fruitless and forlorn. She had, at this epoch, impressed from the crews of American merchant vessels, peaceably navigating the high seas, not less than six thousand mariners, who claimed to be citizens of the United States, and who were denied all opportunity to verify their claims. She had seized and confiscated the commercial property of American citizens to an incalculable amount. She had united in the enormities of France, to declare a great proportion of the terraqueous globe in a state of blockade; chasing the American merchant flag effectually from the ocean. She had contemptuously disregarded the neutrality of the American territory, and the jurisdiction of the American laws, within the waters and harbors of the United States. She was enjoying the emoluments of a surreptitious trade, stained with every species of fraud and corruption, which gave to the belligerent Powers the advantages of peace, while the neutral Powers were involved in the evils of war. She had, in short, usurped and exercised, on the water, a tyranny similar to that which her great antagonist had usurped and exercised upon the land. And, amidst all these proofs of ambition and avarice, she demanded that the victims of her usurpations and her violence should revere her as the sole defender of the rights and liberties of mankind.

When, therefore, Great Britain, in manifest violation of her solemn promises, refused to follow the example of France, by the repeal of her Orders in Council, the American Government was compelled to contemplate a resort to arms, as the only remaining course to be pursued for its honor, its independence, and its safety. Whatever depended upon the United States themselves, the United States had performed for the preservation of peace, in resistance of the French decrees as well as of the British orders. What had been required from France, in its relation to the neutral character of the United States, France had performed, by the revocation of its Berlin and Milan decrees. But what depended upon Great Britain, for the purposes of justice, in the repeal of her Orders in Council, was withheld, and new evasions were sought when the old were exhausted. It was, at one time, alleged, that satisfactory proof was not afforded that France had repealed her decrees against the commerce of the United States; as if such proof alone were wanting to insure the performance of the British promise.†

At another time it was insisted that the repeal of the French decrees, in their operation against the United States, in order to authorize a demand for the performance of the British promise, must be total, applying equally to their internal and their external effects, as if the United States had either the right or the power to impose upon France the law of her domestic institutions.* And it was finally insisted, in a despatch from Lord Castlereagh to the British Minister residing at Washington, in the year 1812, which was *officially* communicated to the American Government, "that the decrees of Berlin and Milan must not be repealed singly and specially in relation to the United States, but must be repealed also as to all other neutral nations, and that in no less extent of a repeal of the French decrees, had the British Government ever pledged itself to repeal the Orders in Council;"† as if it were incumbent on the United States, not only to assert her own rights, but to become the coadjutor of the British Government in a gratuitous assertion of the rights of all other nations.

The Congress of the United States could pause no longer, under a deep and afflicting sense of the national wrongs. While they "*postponed* definitive measures with respect to *France, in the* expectation that the result of unclosed discussions between the American Minister at Paris and the French Government, would speedily enable them to decide, with greater advantage, on the course due to the rights, the interests, and the honor of the country;"‡ they pronounced a deliberate and solemn declaration of war, between Great Britain and the United States, on the 18th of June, 1812. But it is in the face of all the facts which have been displayed in the present narrative, that the Prince Regent, by his declaration of January, 1813, describes the United States as the aggressor in the war. If the act of declaring war constitutes, in all cases, the act of original *aggression*, the United States must submit to the severity of the reproach; but if the act of declaring war may be more truly considered as the result of long suffering, and necessary self-defence, the American Government will stand acquitted, in the sight of Heaven and of the world. Have the United States, then, enslaved the subjects, confiscated the property, prostrated the commerce, insulted the flag, or violated the territorial sovereignty of Great Britain? No; but in all these respects the United States had suffered, for a long period of years previous to the declaration of war, the contumely and outrage of the British Government. It has been said, too, as an aggravation of the imputed aggression, that the United States chose a period for the declaration of war when Great Britain was struggling for her own existence,

---

* See the act of Congress passed March 2, 1811.
  † See the correspondence between Mr. Pinkney and the British Government.

* See the letters of Mr. Erskine.
  † See the correspondence between the Secretary of State and Mr. Foster, the British Minister, in June, 1812.
  ‡ See the President's Message of the 1st of June, 1812, and the report of the Committee of Foreign Relations, to whom the Message was referred.

against a power which threatened to overthrow the independence of all Europe; but it might be more truly said that the United States, not acting upon choice, but upon compulsion, delayed the declaration of war, until the persecutions of Great Britain had rendered further delay destructive and disgraceful. Great Britain had converted the commercial scenes of American opulence and prosperity, into scenes of comparative poverty and distress; she had brought the existence of the United States, as an independent nation, into question; and surely it must have been indifferent to the United States whether they ceased to exist as an independent nation, by her conduct while she professed friendship, or by her conduct when she avowed enmity and revenge. Nor is it true that the existence of Great Britain was in danger at the epoch of the declaration of war. The American Government uniformly entertained an opposite opinion, and at all times saw more to apprehend for the United States, from her maritime power, than from the territorial power of her enemy. The event has justified the opinion and the apprehension. But what the United States asked, as essential to their welfare, and even as beneficial to the allies of Great Britain in the European war, Great Britain, it is manifest, might have granted, without impairing the resources of her own strength, or the splendor of her own sovereignty; for her Orders in Council have been since revoked, not, it is true, as the performance of her promise to follow in this respect the example of France, since she finally rested the obligation of that promise upon a repeal of the French decrees as to all nations, and the repeal was only as to the United States; nor as an act of national justice towards the United States, but simply as an act of domestic policy, for the special advantage of her own people.

The British Government has also described the war as a war of aggrandizement and conquest on the part of the United States; but where is the foundation for the charge? While the American Government employed every means to dissuade the Indians, even those who lived within the territory, and were supplied by the bounty of the United States from taking any part in the war,* the proofs were irresistible that the enemy pursued a very different course,† and that every precaution would be necessary to prevent the effects of an offensive alliance between the British troops and the savages throughout the northern frontier of the United States. The military occupation of Upper Canada was, therefore, deemed indispensable to the safety of that frontier in the earliest movements of the war, independent of all views of extending the territorial boundary of the United States. But when war was declared, in

resentment for injuries which had been suffered upon the Atlantic, what principle of public law, what modification of civilized warfare, imposed upon the United States the duty of abstaining from the invasion of the Canadas? It was there alone that the United States could place themselves upon an equal footing of military force with Great Britain; and it was there that they might reasonably encourage the hope of being able, in the prosecution of a lawful retaliation, "to restrain the violence of the enemy, and to retort upon him the evils of his own injustice." The proclamations issued by the American commanders, on entering Upper Canada, have, however, been adduced by the British negotiators at Ghent as the proofs of a spirit of ambition and aggrandizement on the part of their Government. In truth, the proclamations were not only unauthorized and disapproved, but were infractions of the positive instructions which had been given for the conduct of the war in Canada. When the General commanding the Northwestern Army of the United States received, on the 24th of June, 1812, his first authority to commence offensive operations, he was especially told that "he must not consider himself authorized to pledge the Government to the inhabitants of Canada, further than assurances of protection in their persons, property, and rights." And on the ensuing 1st of August it was emphatically declared to him, "that it had become necessary that he should not lose sight of the instructions of the 24th of June, as any pledge beyond that was incompatible with the views of the Government."* Such was the nature of the charge of American ambition and aggrandizement, and such the evidence to support it.

The Prince Regent has, however, endeavored to add to these unfounded accusations a stigma at which the pride of the American Government revolts. Listening to the fabrications of British emissaries; gathering scandals from the abuses of a free press; and misled, perhaps, by the asperities of a party spirit, common to all free Governments, he affects to trace the origin of the war to "a marked partiality in palliating and assisting the aggressive tyranny of France," and "to the prevalence of such councils as associated the United States in policy with the Government of that nation."† The conduct of the American Government is now open to every scrutiny, and its vindication is inseparable from a knowledge of the facts. All the world must be sensible, indeed, that neither in the general policy of the late ruler of France, nor in his particular treatment of the United States, could there exist any political or rational foundation for the sympathies and associations, overt or clandestine, which have been rudely and unfairly suggested. It is equally obvious that nothing short of the aggressive

---

* See the proceedings at the councils, held with the Indians during the expedition under Brigadier General Hull, and the talk delivered by the President of the United States to the Six Nations, at Washington, on the 8th of April, 1813.

† See the documents laid before Congress on the 13th June, 1812.

* See the letter from the Secretary of the War Department, to Brigadier General Hull, dated the 24th of June, and the 1st of August, 1812.

† See the British Declaration, of the 10th of January, 1813.

tyranny exercised by Great Britain towards the United States, could have counteracted and controlled those tendencies to peace and amity which derived their impulse from natural and social causes combining the affections and interests of the two nations. The American Government, faithful to that principle of public law which acknowledges the authority of all Governments established *de facto*, and conforming its practice in this respect to the example of Europe, has never contested the validity of the Governments successively established in France; nor refrained from that intercourse with either of them, which the just interests of the United States required. But the British Cabinet is challenged to produce, from the recesses of its secret, or of its public, archives, a single instance of unworthy concession, or political alliance and combination, throughout the intercourse of the United States, with the revolutionary rulers of France. Was it the influence of French councils, that induced the American Government to resist the pretensions of France, in 1793, and to encounter her hostilities in 1798? that led to the ratification of the British Treaty in 1795; to the British negotiation in 1805, and to the Convention with the British Minister in 1809? that dictated the impartial overtures, which were made to Great Britain, as well as to France, during the whole period of the restrictive system? that produced the determination to avoid making any treaty, even a treaty of commerce with France, until the outrage of the Rambouillet decree was repaired?* that sanctioned the repeated and urgent efforts of the American Government, to put an end to the war, almost as soon as it was declared? or that, finally, prompted the explicit communication, which, in pursuance of instructions, was made by the American Minister, at St. Petersburgh, to the Court of Russia, stating, "that the principal subjects of discussion, which had long been subsisting between the United States and France, remained unsettled; that there was no immediate prospect that there would be a satisfactory settlement of them; but that, whatever the event, in that respect, might be, it was not the intention of the Government of the United States to enter into any more intimate connexions with France; that the Government of the United States did not anticipate any event whatever, that could produce that effect; and that the American Minister was the more happy to find himself authorized by his Government to avow this intention, as different representations of their views had been widely circulated, as well in Europe as in America."† But, while every act of the American Government thus falsifies the charge of a subserviency to the policy of France, it may be justly remarked, that of all the Governments maintaining a necessary relation and intercourse with that nation,

* See the instructions from the Secretary of State to the American Minister at Paris, dated May 29, 1813.
† See Mr. Monroe's letter to Mr. Adams, dated the 1st of July, 1812, and Mr. Adams' letter to Mr. Monroe, dated the 11th of December, 1812.

from the commencement to the recent termination of the revolutionary establishments, it has happened, that the Government of the United States has least exhibited marks of condescension and concession to the successive rulers. It is for Great Britain, more particularly, as an accuser, to examine and explain the consistency of the reproaches, which she has uttered against the United States, with the course of her own conduct; with her repeated negotiations, during the republican, as well as during the imperial, sway of France; with her solicitude to make and to propose treaties; with her interchange of commercial benefits, so irreconcilable to a state of war; with the almost triumphant entry of a French ambassador into her capital, amidst the acclamations of the populace; and with the prosecution, instituted, by the orders of the King of Great Britain himself, in the highest court of criminal jurisdiction in his Kingdom, to punish the printer of a gazette, for publishing a libel on the conduct and character of the late Ruler of France! Whatever may be the source of these symptoms, however they may indicate a subservient policy, such symptoms have never occurred in the United States, throughout the imperial Government of France.

The conduct of the United States, *from* the moment of declaring the war, *will serve, as well* as their previous conduct, to rescue them from the unjust reproaches of Great Britain. When war was declared, the Orders in Council had been maintained, with inexorable hostility, until a thousand American vessels and their cargoes had been seized and confiscated under their operation; the British Minister at Washington had, with peculiar solemnity, announced that the orders would not be repealed, but upon conditions, which the American Government had not the right, nor the power to fulfil; and the European war, which had raged, with little intermission, for twenty years, threatened an indefinite continuance. Under these circumstances, a repeal of the orders, and a cessation of the injuries which they produced, were events beyond all rational anticipation. It appears, however, that the orders, under the influence of a parliamentary inquiry into their effects upon the trade and manufactures of Great Britain, were provisionally repealed on the 23d of June, 1812, a few days subsequent to the American declaration of war. If this repeal had been made known to the United States, before *their* resort to arms, the repeal would have *arrested it;* and that cause of war being removed, the *other* essential cause, the practice of impressment, would have been the subject of renewed negotiation, under the auspicious influence of a partial, yet important, act of reconciliation. But the declaration of war having announced the practice of impressment as a principal cause, peace *could* only be the result of an express abandonment of the practice; of a suspension of the practice, for the purposes of negotiation; or of a cessation of actual sufferance, in consequence of a pacification in Europe, which would deprive Great Britain of every motive for continuing the practice.

Causes and Character of the War.

Hence, when early intimations were given from Halifax and from Canada, of a disposition, on the part of the local authorities, to enter into an armistice, the power of those authorities was so doubtful, the objects of the armistice were so limited, and the immediate advantages of the measure were so entirely on the side of the enemy, that the American Government could not, consistently with its duty, embrace the propositions.* But some hope of an amicable adjustment was inspired, when a communication was received from Admiral Warren, in September, 1812, stating that he was commanded by his Government to propose, on the one hand, " that the Government of the United States should instantly recall their letters of marque and reprisal against British ships, together with all orders and instructions for any acts of hostility whatever against the territories of His Majesty, or the persons or property of his subjects;" and to promise, on the other hand, if the American Government acquiesced in the preceding proposition, that instructions should be issued to the British squadrons, to discontinue hostilities against the United States and their citizens. This overture, however, was subject to a further qualification, " that, should the American Government accede to the proposal for terminating hostilities, the British Admiral was authorized to arrange with the American Government, as to the revocation of the laws which interdict the commerce and ships of war of Great Britain from the harbors and waters of the United States; but that, in default of such revocation within the reasonable period to be agreed upon, the orders in Council would be revived."* The American Government at once expressed a disposition to embrace the general proposition for a cessation of hostilities, with a view to negotiation; declared that no peace could be durable, unless the essential object of impressment was adjusted; and offered, as a basis of the adjustment, to prohibit the employment of British subjects in the naval or commercial service of the United States; but adhering to its determination of obtaining a relief from actual sufferance, the suspension of the practice of impressment pending the proposed armistice, was deemed a necessary consequence; for " it could not be presumed, while the parties were engaged in a negotiation to adjust amicably this important difference, that the United States would admit the right, or acquiesce in the practice of the opposite party; or that Great Britain would be unwilling to restrain her cruisers from a practice which would have the strongest effect

to defeat the negotiation."* So just, so reasonable, so indispensable a preliminary, without which the citizens of the United States, navigating the high seas, would not be placed, by the armistice, on an equal footing with the subjects of Great Britain, Admiral Warren was not authorized to accept; and the effort at an amicable adjustment, through that channel, was necessarily abortive.

But long before the overture of the British Admiral was made, (a few days, indeed, after the declaration of war,) the reluctance with which the United States had resorted to arms was manifested by the steps taken to arrest the progress of hostilities, and to hasten a restoration of peace. On the 26th day of June, 1812, the American Chargé d'Affaires, at London, was instructed to make the proposal of an armistice to the British Government which might lead to an adjustment of all differences, on the single condition, in the event of the Orders in Council being repealed, that instructions should be issued, suspending the practice of impressment during the armistice. This proposal was soon followed by another, admitting, instead of positive instructions, an informal understanding between the two Governments on the subject.† But both of these proposals were, unhappily, rejected.‡ And when a third, which seemed to leave no plea for hesitation, as it required no other preliminary, than that the American Minister, at London, should find in the British Government a sincere disposition to accommodate the difference relative to impressment, on fair conditions, was evaded, it was obvious, that neither a desire of peace, nor a spirit of conciliation, influenced the councils of Great Britain.

Under these circumstances, the American Government had no choice but to invigorate the war; and yet it has never lost sight of the object of all just wars, a just peace. The Emperor of Russia having offered his mediation, to accomplish that object, it was instantly and cordially accepted by the American Government ;§ but it was peremptorily rejected by the British Government. The Emperor, in his benevolence, repeated his invitation; the British Government again rejected it. At last, however, Great Britain, sensible of the reproach to which such conduct would expose her throughout Europe, offered to the American Government a direct negotiation for peace, and the offer was promptly embraced; with perfect confidence that the British Government would be equally prompt in giving effect to its own pro-

---

* See the letters from the Department of State to Mr. Russell, dated the 9th and 10th of August, 1812, and Mr. Graham's memorandum of a conversation with Mr. Baker, the British secretary of legation, enclosed in the last letter.

See, also, Mr. Monroe's letter to Mr. Russell, dated the 21st of August, 1812.

See the letters of Admiral Warren to the Secretary of State, dated at Halifax, the 30th of September, 1812.

* See the letter of Mr. Monroe to Admiral Warren, dated the 20th of October, 1812.

† See the letters from the Secretary of State to Mr. Russell, dated the 26th of June and 27th of July, 1812.

‡ See the correspondence between Mr. Russell and Lord Castlereagh, dated August and September, 1812; and Mr. Russell's letters to the Secretary of State, dated September, 1812.

§ See the correspondence between Mr. Monroe and Mr. Daschkoff, in March, 1813.

Causes and Character of the War.

posal. But such was not the design, or the course, of that Government. The American Envoys were immediately appointed, and arrived at Gottenburg, the destined scene of negotiation, on the 11th of April, 1814, as soon as the season admitted. The British Government, though regularly informed that no time would be lost on the part of the United States, suspended the appointment of its Envoys, until the actual arrival of the American Envoys should be formally communicated. This pretension, however novel and inauspicious, was not permitted to obstruct the path to peace. The British Government next proposed to transfer the negotiation from Gottenburg to Ghent. This change, also, notwithstanding the necessary delay, was allowed. The American Envoys, arriving at Ghent on the 24th of June, remained in a mortifying state of suspense and expectation, for the arrival of the British Envoys, until the 6th of August. And from the period of opening the negotiations, to the date of the last despatch of the 31st of October, it has been seen, that the whole of the diplomatic skill of the British Government has consisted in consuming time, without approaching any conclusion. The pacification of Paris had suddenly and unexpectedly placed at the disposal of the British Government, a great naval and military force; the pride and passions of the nation were artfully excited against the United States; and a war of desperate and barbarous character was planned, at the very moment that the American Government, finding its maritime citizens relieved, by the course of events, from actual sufferance, under the practice of impressment, had authorized its Envoys to waive those stipulations upon the subject, which might, otherwise, have been indispensable precautions.

Hitherto, the American Government has shown the justice of its cause, its respect for the rights of other nations, and its inherent love of peace. But the scenes of the war, will, also, exhibit a striking contrast, between the conduct of the United States and the conduct of Great Britain. The same insidious policy, which taught the Prince Regent to describe the American Government as the aggressor in the war, has induced the British Government (clouding the daylight truth of the transaction) to call the atrocities of the British fleets and armies, a retaliation upon the example of the American troops in Canada. The United States tender a solemn appeal to the civilized world, against the fabrication of such a charge; and they vouch, in support of their appeal, the known morals, habits, and pursuits of their people; the character of their civil and political institutions; and the whole career of their navy and their army, as humane, as it is brave. Upon what pretext did the British Admiral, on the 18th of August, 1814, announce his determination, "to destroy and lay waste such towns and districts, upon the coast, as might be found assailable?"*

* See Admiral Cochrane's letter to Mr. Monroe, dated the 18th of August, 1814; and Mr. Monroe's answer of the 6th September, 1814.

It was the pretext of a request from the Governor General of the Canadas, for aid to carry *into* effect measures of retaliation; while, in fact, the barbarous nature of the war had been deliberately settled and prescribed by the British Cabinet. What could have been the foundation of such a request? The outrages, and the irregularities, which too often occur during a state of national hostilities, in violation of the laws of civilized warfare, are always to be lamented, disavowed, and repaired, by a just and honorable Government; but if disavowal be made, and if reparation be offered, there is no foundation for retaliatory violence. "Whatever unauthorized irregularity may have been committed by any of the troops of the United States, the American Government has been ready, upon principles of sacred and eternal obligation, to disavow, and, as far as it might be practicable, to repair."* In every known instance (and they are few) the offenders have been subjected to the regular investigation of a military tribunal; and an officer commanding a party of stragglers, who were guilty of unworthy excesses, was immediately dismissed without the form of a trial for not preventing those excesses. The destruction of the village of Newark, *adjacent* to Fort George, on the 10th of *December*, 1813, was long subsequent to the *pillage* and conflagration committed on the shores of the Chesapeake, throughout the Summer of the same year; and might fairly have been alleged as a retaliation for those outrages; but, in fact, it was justified by the American commander who ordered it, on the ground that it became necessary to the military operations at that place;† while the American Government, as soon as it heard of the act, on the 6th of January, 1814, instructed the General commanding the Northern army, "to disavow the conduct of the officer who committed it; and to transmit to Governor Prevost a copy of the order under color of which that officer had acted."‡ This disavowal was accordingly communicated; and on the 10th of February, 1814, Governor Prevost answered, "that it had been with great satisfaction he had received the assurance, that the perpetration of the burning of the town of Newark was both unauthorized by the American Government, and abhorrent to every American feeling; that if any outrages had ensued the wanton and unjustifiable destruction of Newark, passing the bounds of just retaliation, they were to be attributed to the influence of irritated *passions* on the part of the unfortunate *sufferers by* that event, which, in a state of active *warfare*, it has not been possible altogether to restrain; and that it was as little congenial to the disposition of His Majesty's Government as it was to that of the Government of the United States, deliberately to adopt any plan of policy which had for

* See the letter from the Secretary at War to Brigadier General McClure, dated the 4th of October, 1813.
† General McClure's letters to the Secretary at War, dated December 10 and 13, 1813.
‡ See the letter from the Secretary at War, to Major General Wilkinson, dated the 26th of January, 1814.

Causes and Character of the War.

its object the devastation of private property."[*] But the disavowal of the American Government was not the only expiation of the offence committed by its officer; for the British Government assumed the province of redress in the indulgence of its own vengeance. A few days after the burning of Newark, the British and Indian troops crossed the Niagara for this purpose; they surprised and seized Fort Niagara, and put its garrison to the sword; they burnt the villages of Lewistown, Manchester, Tuscarora, Buffalo, and Black Rock; slaughtering and abusing the unarmed inhabitants; until, in short, they had laid waste the whole of the Niagara frontier, levelling every house and every hut, and dispersing beyond the means of shelter, in the extremity of the winter, the male and the female, the old and the young. Sir George Prevost himself appears to have been sated with the ruin and the havoc which had been thus inflicted. In his proclamation of the 12th of January, 1814, he emphatically declared, that for the burning of Newark, "the opportunity of punishment had occurred, and a full measure of retaliation had taken place;" and "that it was not his intention to pursue further a system of warfare so revolting to his own feelings and so little congenial to the British character unless the future measures of the enemy should compel him again to resort to it."[†] Nay, with his answer to the American General, already mentioned, he transmitted "a copy of that proclamation as expressive of the determination as to his future line of conduct;" and added, "that he was happy to learn that there was no probability that any measures on the part of the American Government would oblige him to depart from it."[‡] Where, then, shall we search for the foundation of the call upon the British Admiral, to aid the Governor of Canada in measures of retaliation? Great Britain forgot the principle of retaliation when her Orders in Council were issued against the unoffending neutral, in resentment of outrages committed by her enemy; and surely she had again forgotten the same principle when she threatened an unceasing violation of the laws of civilized warfare in retaliation for injuries which never existed, or which the American Government had explicitly disavowed, or which had been already avenged by her own arms, in a manner and a degree cruel and unparalleled. The American Government, after all, has not hesitated to declare, that "for the reparation of injuries, of whatever nature they may be, not sanctioned by the law of nations, which the military or naval force of either Power might have committed against the other, it would al-

ways be ready to enter into reciprocal arrangements; presuming that the British Government would neither expect nor propose any which were not reciprocal.[*]

It is now, however, proper to examine the character of the warfare which Great Britain has waged against the United States. In Europe, it has already been marked with astonishment and indignation, as a warfare of the tomahawk, the scalping knife, and the torch; as a warfare incompatible with the usages of civized nations; as a warfare, that, disclaiming all moral influence, inflicts an outrage upon social order, and gives a shock to the very elements of humanity. All belligerent nations can form alliances with the savage, the African, and the bloodhound; but what civilized nation has selected these auxiliaries, in its hostilities? It does not require the fleets and armies of Great Britain to lay waste an open country; to burn unfortified towns, or unprotected villages; nor to plunder the merchant, the farmer, and the planter, of his stores: these exploits may easily be achieved by a single cruiser, or a petty privateer; but when have such exploits been performed on the coasts of the continent of Europe, or of the British islands, by the naval and military force of any belligerent Power; or when have they been tolerated by any honorable Government, as the predatory enterprise of armed individuals? Nor is the destruction of the public edifices, which adorn the metropolis of a country, and serve to commemorate the taste and science of the age, beyond the sphere of action of the vilest incendiary, as well as of the most triumphant conqueror. It cannot be forgotten, indeed, that in the course of ten years past, the capitals of the principal Powers of Europe have been conquered, and occupied alternately, by the victorious armies of each other; [†] and yet there has been no instance of a conflagration of the palaces, the temples, or the halls of justice. No; such examples have proceeded from Great Britain alone; a nation so elevated in its pride, so awful in its power, and so affected in its tenderness for the liberties of mankind! The charge is severe, but let the facts be adduced.

1. Great Britain has violated the principles of social law, by insidious attempts to excite the citizens of the United States into acts of contumacy, treason, and revolt, against their Government. For instance:

No sooner had the American Government imposed the restrictive system upon its citizens, to escape from the rage and depredation of the belligerent Powers, than the British Government, then professing amity towards the United States, issued an order, which was, in effect, an invitation to the American citizens to break the laws of their country, under a public promise of the British protection and patronage, "to all vessels which should

---

[*] See the letter of Major General Wilkinson, to Sir George Prevost, dated the 28th of January, 1814, and the answer of Sir George Prevost, dated the 10th of February, 1814.

[†] See Sir George Prevost's proclamation, dated at Quebec, the 12th of January, 1814.

[‡] See the letter of Sir George Prevost to General Wilkinson, dated the 10th of February, 1814; and the British General Orders of the 22d of February, 1814.

[*] See Mr. Monroe's letter to Admiral Cochrane, dated the 6th of September, 1814.

[†] See Mr. Monroe's letter to Admiral Cochrane, dated the 6th of September 1814.

engage in an illicit trade, without bearing the customary ship's document and papers."*

Again: During a period of peace between the United States and Great Britain, in the year 1809, the Governor General of the Canadas employed an agent (who had previously been engaged, in a similar service, with the knowledge and approbation of the British Cabinet) " on a secret and confidential mission," into the United States, declaring, " that there was no doubt that his able execution of such a mission, would give him a claim, not only on the Governor General, but on His Majesty's Ministers." The object of the mission was, to ascertain whether there existed a disposition in any portion of the citizens, " to bring about a separation of the Eastern States from the general Union; and how far, in such an event, they would look up to England for assistance, or be disposed to enter into a connexion with her." The agent was instructed " to insinuate, that if any of the citizens should wish to enter into a communication with the British Government, through the Governor General, he was authorized to receive such communication; and that he would safely transmit it to the Governor General."† He was accredited by a formal instrument, under the seal and signature of the Governor General, to be produced. " if he saw good ground for expecting that the doing so might lead to a more confidential communication than he could otherwise look for;" and he was furnished with a cipher, "for carrying on the secret correspondence. ‡ The virtue and patriotism of the citizens of the United States, were superior to the arts and corruption, employed in this secret and confidential mission, if it ever was disclosed to any of them; and the mission itself terminated as soon as the arrangement with Mr. Erskine was announced.§ But, in the act of recalling the secret emissary, he was informed, " that the whole of his letters were transcribing to be sent home, where they could not fail of doing him great credit, and it was hoped they might eventually contribute to his permanent advantage."§ To endeavor to realize that hope, the emissary proceeded to London; all the circumstances of his mission were made known to the British Minister; his services were approved and acknowledged; and he was sent to Canada for a reward, with a recommendatory letter from Lord Liverpool to Sir George Prevost, "stating his Lordship's opinion of the ability and judgment which Mr. Henry had manifested on the occasions mentioned in his memorial, (his secret and confidential missions,) and of the benefit

the public service might derive from his active employment in any public situation, in which Sir George Prevost might think proper to place him."* The world will judge upon these facts, and the rejection of a Parliamentary call, for the production of the papers relating to them, what credit is due to the Prince Regent's assertion, "that Mr. Henry's mission was undertaken without the authority or even knowledge of His Majesty's Government." The first mission was certainly known to the British Government, at the time it occurred; for the Secretary of the Governor General expressly states, " that the information and political observations, heretofore received from Mr. Henry, were transmitted by his Excellency to the Secretary of State, who had expressed his particular approbation of them."† The second mission was approved when it was known; and it remains for the British Government to explain, upon any established principles of morality and justice, the essential difference between ordering the offensive acts to be done, and reaping the fruit of those acts, without either expressly or tacitly condemning them.

Again: These hostile attempts upon the peace and union of the United States, preceding the declaration of war, have been followed by similar machinations, subsequent to that event. The Governor General of the Canadas has endeavored, occasionally, in his proclamations, and general orders, to dissuade the militia of the United States from the performance of the duty which they owed to their injured country; and the efforts. at Quebec and Halifax, to kindle the flame of civil war, have been as incessant as they have been insidious and abortive. Nay, the Governor of the island of Barbadoes, totally forgetful of the boasted article of the British magna charta, in favor of foreign merchants, found within the British dominions upon the breaking out of hostilities, resolved that every American merchant, within his jurisdiction at the declaration of war, should at once be treated as a prisoner of war; because every citizen of the United States was enrolled in the militia; because the militia of the United States were required to serve their country, beyond the limits of the State to which they particularly belonged; and because the militia of " all the States, which had acceded to this measure, were, in the view of Sir George Beckwith, acting as a French conscription."‡

Again: Nor was this course of conduct confined to the colonial authorities. On the 26th of October, 1812, the British Government issued an Order in Council, authorizing the Governors of the British West India islands to grant licenses to American vessels, for the importation and exportation of certain articles, enumerated in the order; but, in the instructions, which accompanied the order, it was expressly provided, that " whatever importations were proposed to be made, from the United States of America, should, be by licenses, confined to the ports in the eastern States exclusively, unless there was reason to suppose, that the object of the order would not be fulfilled, if licenses were not granted, for importations from the other ports in the United States."[*]

The President of the United States has not hesitated to place before the nation, with expressions of a just indignation, "the policy of Great Britain thus proclaimed to the world; introducing into her modes of warfare, a system equally distinguished by the deformity of its features, and the depravity of its character; and having for its object to dissolve the ties of allegiance and the sentiments of loyalty in the adversary nation; and to seduce and separate its component parts, the one from the other."[†]

2. Great Britain has violated the laws of humanity and honor, by seeking alliances, in the prosecution of the war, with savages, pirates, and slaves.

The British agency, in exciting the Indians at all times to commit hostilities upon the frontier of the United States, is too notorious to admit of a direct and general denial. It has sometimes, however, been said, that such conduct was unauthorized by the British Government; and the Prince Regent, seizing the single instance of an intimation, alleged to be given on the part of Sir James Craig, the Governor of the Canadas, that an attack was meditated by the Indians, has affirmed, that "the charge of exciting the Indians to offensive measures against the United States, was void of foundation; that, before the war began, a policy the most opposite had been uniformly pursued; and that proof of this was tendered by Mr. Foster to the American Government."[‡] But is it not known in Europe, as well as in America, that the British Northwest Company maintain a constant intercourse of trade and council with the Indians; that their interests are often in direct collision with the interests of the inhabitants of the United States, and that by means of the inimical dispositions, and the active agencies of the company (seen, understood, and tacitly sanctioned by the local authorities of Canada) all the evils of an Indian war may be shed upon the United States, without the authority of a formal order emanating immediately from the British Government? Hence, the American Government,

in answer to the evasive protestations of the British Minister, residing at Washington, frankly communicated the evidence of British agency, which had been received at different periods, since the year 1807; and observed, "that whatever may have been the disposition of the British Government, the conduct of its subordinate agents had tended to excite the hostility of the Indian tribes towards the United States; and that in estimating the comparative evidence on the subject, it was impossible not to recollect the communication lately made, respecting the conduct of Sir James Craig, in another important transaction (the employment of Mr. Henry, as an accredited agent, to alienate and detach the citizens of a particular section of the Union, from their Government) which, it appeared, was approved by Lord Liverpool."[**]

The proof, however, that the British agents and military officers were guilty of the charge thus exhibited, become conclusive when, subsequent to the communication which was made to the British Minister, the defeat and flight of General Proctor's army, on the —— of ——, placed in the possession of the American commander the correspondence and papers of the British officers. Selected from the documents which were obtained upon that occasion, the contents of a few letters will serve to characterize the whole of the mass. In these letters, written by Mr. McKee, the British agent, to Colonel England, the commander of the British troops, superscribed, "on His Majesty's service," and dated during the months of July and August, 1794, the period of General Wayne's successful expedition against the Indians, it appears that the scalps taken by the Indians were sent to the British establishment at the rapids of the Miami;[†] that the hostile operations of the Indians were concerted with the British agents and officers;[‡] that when certain tribes of Indians, "having completed the belts they carried with scalps and prisoners, and being without provisions, resolved on going home, it was lamented that His Majesty's posts would derive no security from the late great influx of Indians into that part of the country should they persist in their resolution of returning so soon;"[‖] that "the British agents were immediately to hold a council at the Glaize, in order to try if they could prevail on the Lake Indians to remain; but that, without provisions and ammunition being sent to that place, it was conceived to be extremely difficult to keep them together;"[§] and that "Colonel England was making great exertions to supply the Indians with provisions."[¶] But the language of the correspondence becomes, at length, so plain

---

* See the proclamation of the Governor of Bermuda, dated the 14th of January, 1814; and the instructions from the British Secretary for Foreign Affairs, dated November 9, 1812.

† See the Message from the President to Congress, dated the 24th of February, 1813.

‡ See the Prince Regent's declaration of the 10th of January, 1813.

See, also, Mr. Foster's letters to Mr. Monroe, dated the 28th of December, 1811, and the 7th and 8th of June, 1812; and Mr. Monroe's answer, dated the 9th of January, 1812, and the 10th of June, 1812; and the documents, which accompanied the correspondence.

* See Mr. Monroe's letter to Mr. Foster, dated the 10th of June, 1812.

† See the letter from Mr. McKee to Colonel England, dated the 2d of July, 1794.

‡ See the letter from the same to the same, dated the 5th of July, 1794.

‖ See the same letter.

§ See the same letter.

¶ See the same letter.

Causes and Character of the War.

and direct, that it seems impossible to avoid the conclusion of a Governmental agency on the part of Great Britain, in advising, aiding and conducting the Indian war, while she professed friendship and peace towards the United States. "Scouts are sent (says Mr. McKee to Colonel England) to view the situation of the American army; and we now muster one thousand Indians. All the Lake Indians, from Sugana downwards, should not lose one moment in joining their brethren, as every accession of strength is an addition to their spirits."* And again: "I have been employed several days in endeavoring to fix the Indians, who have been driven from their villages and corn-fields, between the fort and the bay. Swan creek is generally agreed upon, and will be a very convenient place for the delivery of provisions," &c.† Whether, under the various proofs of the British agency, in exciting Indian hostilities against the United States in a time of peace, presented in the course of the present narrative, the Prince Regent's declaration, that, "before the war began, a policy the most opposite had been uniformly pursued by the British Government,‡ is to be ascribed to a want of information or a want of candor, the American Government is not disposed more particularly to investigate.

But, independent of these causes of just complaint, arising in a time of peace, it will be found that when the war was declared, the alliance of the British Government with the Indians was avowed upon principles the most novel, producing consequences the most dreadful. The savages were brought into the war upon the ordinary footing of allies, without regard to the inhuman character of their warfare, which neither spares age nor sex, and which is more desperate towards the captive at the stake, than even towards the combatant in the field. It seemed to be a stipulation of the compact between the allies that the British might imitate, but should not control the ferocity of the savages. While the British troops behold without compunction, the tomahawk and the scalping knife brandished against prisoners, old men and children, and even against pregnant women, and while they exultingly accept the bloody scalps of the slaughtered Americans;|| the Indian exploits in battle are recounted and applauded by the British general orders. Rank and station are assigned to them in the military movements of the British army; and the unhallowed league was ratified with appropriate emblems, by

intertwining an American scalp with the decorations of the mace, which the commander of the Northern army of the United States found in the Legislative chamber of York, the capital of Upper Canada.

In the single scene that succeeded the battle of Frenchtown, near the river Raisin, where the American troops were defeated by the allies under the command of General Proctor, there will be found, concentrated upon indisputable proof, an illustration of the horrors of the warfare which Great Britain has pursued, and still pursues, in co-operation with the savages of the South, as well as with the savages of the North. The American army capitulated on the 22d of January, 1813; yet, after the faith of the British commander had been pledged in the terms of the capitulation, and while the British officers and soldiers silently and exultingly contemplated the scene, some of the American prisoners of war were tomahawked, some were shot, and some were burnt. Many of the unarmed inhabitants of the Michigan Territory were massacred; their property was plundered, and their houses were destroyed.* The dead bodies of the mangled Americans were exposed, unburied, to be devoured by dogs and swine; "because, as the British officers declared, the Indians would not permit the interment;"† and some of the Americans who survived the carnage had been extricated from danger, only by being purchased at a price, as a part of the booty belonging to the Indians. But, to complete this dreadful view of human depravity and human wretchedness, it is only necessary to add, that an American physician who was despatched with a flag of truce to ascertain the situation of his wounded brethren, and two persons, his companions, were intercepted by the Indians, in their humane mission; the privilege of the flag was disregarded by the British officers; the physician, after being wounded, and one of his companions were made prisoners, and the third person of the party was killed.‡

But the savage who had never known the restraints of civilized life, and the pirate who had broken the bonds of society, were alike the objects of British conciliation and alliance for the purposes of an unparalleled warfare. A horde of pirates and outlaws had formed a confederacy and establishment on the island of Barrataria, near the mouth of the river Mississippi. Will Europe believe that the commander of the British forces addressed the leader of the confederacy, from the neutral territory of Pensacola, "calling upon him, with his brave followers, to enter into

---

* See the letter from Mr. McKee to Colonel England, dated the 13th of August, 1794.

† See the letter from the same to the same, dated the 30th of August, 1794.

‡ See the Prince Regent's declaration of the 10th of January, 1813.

|| See the letter from the American General Harrison, to the British General Proctor.

See a letter from the British Major Muir, Indian agent, to Colonel Proctor, dated the 26th September, 1812, and a letter from Colonel St. George to Colonel Proctor, dated the 28th of October, 1812, found among Colonel Proctor's papers.

---

*See the report of the committee of the House of Representatives, on the 31st of July, 1813, and the depositions and documents accompanying it.

†See the official report of Mr. Baker, the agent for the prisoners, to Brigadier General Winchester, dated the 26th of February, 1813.

‡In addition to this description of savage warfare under British auspices, see the facts contained in the correspondence between General Harrison and General Drummond.

the service of Great Britain, in which he should have the rank of captain; promising that lands should be given to them all, in proportion to their respective ranks, on a peace taking place; assuring them that their property should be guarantied, and their persons protected; and asking, in return, that they would cease all hostilities against Spain, or the allies of Great Britain, and place their ships and vessels under the British commanding officer on the station, until the commander-in-chief's pleasure should be known, with a guarantee of their fair value at all events?"[*] There wanted only to exemplify the debasement of such an act, the occurrence, that the pirate should spurn the proffered alliance; and, accordingly, Lafitte's answer was indignantly given, by a delivery of the letter containing the British proposition, to the American Governor of Louisiana.

There were other sources, however, of support, which Great Britain was prompted by her vengeance to employ, in opposition to the plainest dictates of her own colonial policy. The events which have extirpated or dispersed the white population of St. Domingo, are in the recollection of all men. Although British humanity might not shrink from the infliction of similar calamities upon the Southern States of America, the danger of that course, either as an incitement to a revolt of the slaves in the British islands, or as a cause for retaliation on the part of the United States, ought to have admonished her against its adoption. Yet, in a formal proclamation, issued by the Commander-in-Chief of His Britannic Majesty's squadrons upon the American station, the slaves of the American planters were invited to join the British standard, in a covert phraseology, that afforded but a slight veil for the real design. Thus, Admiral Cochrane, reciting "that it had been represented to him that many persons now resident in the United States had expressed a desire to withdraw therefrom, with a view of entering into His Majesty's service, or of being received as free settlers into some of His Majesty's colonies," proclaimed that "all those who might be disposed to emigrate from the United States would, with their families, be received on board of His Majesty's ships or vessels of war, or at the military posts that might be established upon or near the coast of the United States, when they would have their choice of either entering into His Majesty's sea or land forces, or of being sent as free settlers to the British possessions in North America, or the West Indies, where they would meet with all due encouragement."[†] But even the negroes seem, in contempt or disgust, to have resisted the solicitation; no rebellion or massacre ensued; and the allegation, often repeated, that, in relation to those who were seduced or forced from the service of their masters, instances have occurred of some being afterwards transported to the British West India islands, and there sold into slavery for the benefit of the captors, remains without contradiction. So complicated an act of injustice would demand the reprobation of mankind. And let the British Government, which professes a just abhorrence of the African slave trade, which endeavors to impose, in that respect, restraints upon the domestic policy of France, Spain, and Portugal, answer, if it can, the solemn charge against their faith and their humanity.

3. Great Britain has violated the laws of civilized warfare, by plundering private property; by outraging female honor; by burning unprotected cities, towns, villages, and houses; and by laying waste whole districts of an unresisting country.

The menace and the practice of the British naval and military force " to destroy and lay waste such towns and districts upon the American coast as might be found assailable," have been excused upon the pretext of retaliation, for the wanton destruction committed by the American army in Upper Canada;"[*] but the fallacy of the pretext has already been exposed. It will be recollected, however, that the act of burning Newark was instantaneously disavowed by the American Government; that it occurred in December, 1813; and that Sir George Prevost himself acknowledged, on the 10th of February, 1814, that the measure of retaliation, for all the previously imputed misconduct of the American troops, was then full and complete.[†] Between the month of February, 1814, when that acknowledgment was made, and the month of August, 1814, when the British Admiral's denunciation was issued, what are the outrages upon the part of the American troops in Canada to justify a call for retaliation? No; it was the system not the incident of the war. And intelligence of the system had been received at Washington, from the American agents in Europe, with reference to the operations of Admiral Warren upon the shores of the Chesapeake, long before Admiral Cochrane had succeeded to the command of the British fleet on the American station.

As an appropriate introduction to the kind of war which Great Britain intended to wage against the inhabitants of the United States, transactions occurred in England, under the avowed direction of the Government itself, that could not fail to wound the moral sense of every candid and generous spectator. All the officers and mariners of the American merchant ships, who, having lost their vessels in other places, had gone to England on the way to America; or who had been employed in British merchant ships, but were desirous of returning home; or who had been detained, in consequence of the condemnation of their vessels under the British Orders in Council; or who had arrived in England, through any of

---

[*] See the letter addressed by Edward Nichols, Lieutenant Colonel, commanding His Britannic Majesty's forces in the Floridas, to Monsieur Lafitte, or the commandant at Barrataria, dated the 31st of August, 1814.

[†] See Admiral Cochrane's proclamation, dated at Bermuda, the 2d of April, 1814.

---

[*] See Admiral Cochrane's letter to Mr. Monroe, dated August 18, 1814.

[†] See Sir George Prevost's letter to General Wilkinson, dated the 10th of February, 1814.

Causes and Character of the War.

the other casualties of the seafaring life, were condemned to be treated as prisoners of war; nay, some of them were actually impressed while soliciting their passports, although not one of their number had been in any way engaged in hostilities against Great Britain; and although the American Government had afforded every facility to the departure of the same class, as well as of every other class of British subjects, from the United States, for a reasonable period after the declaration of war.* But this act of injustice, for which even the pretext of retaliation has not been advanced, was accompanied by another of still greater cruelty and oppression. The American seamen, who had been enlisted or impressed into the naval service of Great Britain, were long retained, and many of them are yet retained, on board of British ships of war, where they are compelled to combat against their country and their friends; and even when the British Government tardily and reluctantly recognised the citizenship of impressed Americans to a number exceeding one thousand at a single naval station, and dismissed them from its service on the water, it was only to immure them as prisoners of war on the shore. These unfortunate persons, who had passed into the power of the British Government by a violation of their own rights and inclinations, as well as of the rights of their country, and who could only be regarded as the spoils of unlawful violence, were nevertheless treated as the fruits of lawful war. Such was the indemnification which Great Britain offered for the wrongs that she had inflicted, and such the reward which she bestowed for services that she had received.†

Nor has the spirit of British warfare been confined to violations of the usages of civilized nations, in relation to the United States. The system of blockade, by Orders in Council, has been revived; and the American coast, from Maine to Louisiana, has been declared, by the proclamation of a British Admiral, to be in a state of blockade, which every day's observation proves to be practically ineffectual, and which, indeed, the whole of the British navy would be unable to enforce and maintain.‡ Neither the Orders in Council, acknowledged to be generally unlawful, and declared to be merely retaliatory upon France, nor the Berlin and Milan decrees, which placed the British islands in a state of blockade without the force of a single squadron to maintain it, were, in principle, more injurious to the rights of neutral commerce than the existing blockade of the United States. The revival, therefore, of the system, without the retaliatory pretext, must de-

monstrate to the world a determination, on the part of Great Britain, to acquire a commercial monopoly, by every demonstration of her naval power. The trade of the United States with Russia, and with other northern Powers, by whose Governments no edicts violating neutral rights had been issued, was cut off by the operation of the British Orders in Council of the year 1807, as effectually as their trade with France and her allies, although the retaliatory principle was totally inapplicable to the case. And the blockade of the year 1814 is an attempt to destroy the trade of those nations, and, indeed, of all the other nations of Europe, with the United States; while Great Britain herself, with the same policy and ardor that marked her illicit trade with France, when France was her enemy, encourages a clandestine traffic between her subjects and the American citizens, wherever her possessions come in contact with the territory of the United States.

But, approaching nearer to the scenes of plunder and violence, of cruelty and conflagration, which the British warfare exhibits on the coast of the United States, it must be again asked what acts of the American Government, of its ships of war, or of its armies, had occurred, or were even alleged as a pretext, for the perpetration of this series of outrages? It will not be asserted that they were sanctioned by the usages of modern war, because the sense of all Europe would revolt at the assertion. It will not be said that they were the unauthorized excesses of the British troops, because scarcely an act of plunder and violence, of cruelty and conflagration, had been committed, except in the immediate presence, under the positive orders, and with the personal agency of British officers. It must not be again insinuated that they were provoked by the American example, because it has been demonstrated that all such insinuations are without color and without proof. And, after all, the dreadful and disgraceful progress of the British arms will be traced, as the effect of that animosity, arising out of recollections connected with the American Revolution, which has already been noticed; or, as the effect of that jealousy which the commercial enterprise and native resources of the United States are calculated to excite in the councils of a nation aiming at universal dominion upon the ocean.

In the month of April, 1813, the inhabitants of Poplar Island, in the Bay of Chesapeake, were pillaged, and the cattle and other live stock of the farmers, beyond what the enemy could remove, were wantonly killed.*

In the same month of April, the wharf, the stores, and the fishery, at Frenchtown Landing, were destroyed, and the private stores and storehouses in the village of Frenchtown were burnt.†

In the same month of April the enemy landed repeatedly on Sharp's Island, and made a general

---

* See Mr. Beasley's correspondence with the British Government, in October, November, and December, 1812. See, also, the act of Congress, passed the 6th of July, 1812.

† See the letter from Mr. Beasley to Mr. McLeay, dated the 13th of March, 1815.

‡ See the successive blockades announced by the British Government, and the successive naval commanders on the American station.

---

* See the deposition of William Sears.

† See the depositions of Frisby Anderson and Cordelia Pennington.

sweep of the stock, affecting however to pay for a part of it.*

On the 3d of May, 1813, the town of Havre-de-Grace was pillaged and burnt by a force under the command of Admiral Cockburn. The British officers being admonished "that, with civilized nations at war, private property had always been respected," hastily replied, "that, as the Americans wanted war, they should now feel its effects, and that the town should be laid in ashes." They broke the windows of the church; they purloined the houses of the furniture; they stripped women and children of their clothes; and when an unfortunate female complained that she could not leave her house with her little children, she was unfeelingly told, "that her house should be burnt with herself and her children in it."†

On the 6th of May, 1813, Fredericktown and Georgetown, situated on Sassafras river, in the State of Maryland, were pillaged and burnt, and the adjacent country was laid waste, by a force under the command of Admiral Cockburn, and the officers were the most active on the occasion.‡

On the 22d of June, 1813, the British forces made an attack upon Craney Island, with a view to obtain possession of Norfolk, which the commanding officers had promised, in case of success, to give up to the plunder of the troops.| The British were repulsed; but, enraged by defeat and disappointment, their course was directed to Hampton, which they entered on the — of June. The scene that ensued exceeds all power of description, and a detail of facts would be offensive to the feelings of decorum as well as of humanity. "A defenceless and unresisting town was given up to indiscriminate pillage, though civilized war tolerates this only as to fortified places carried by assault, and after summons. Individuals, male and female, were stripped naked; a sick man was stabbed twice in the hospital; another sick man shot in his bed, and in the arms of his wife, who was also wounded, long after the retreat of the American troops; and females, the married and the single, suffered the extremity of personal abuse from the troops of the enemy, and from the infatuated negroes, at their instigation."§

* See Jacob Gibson's deposition.

† See the deposition of William T. Killpatrick, James Wood, Rosanna Moore, and R. Mansfield.

‡ See the depositions of John Stavely, William Spencer, Joshua Wood, James Scanlan, Richard Barnaby, F. B. Chandlear, Jonathan Greenwood, John Allen, T. Robertson, M. N. Cannon, and J. T. Vearey.

| See General Taylor's letter to the Secretary of War, dated the 2d of July, 1813.

§ See the letters from General Taylor to Admiral Warren, dated the 29th of June, 1813; to General Sir Sidney Beckwith, dated the 4th and 5th of July, 1813; to the Secretary of War, dated the 2d of July, 1813; and to Captain Myers, of the last date. See also the letter from Major Crutchfield to Governor Barbour, dated the 20th of June, 1813; the letters from Captain Cooper to Lieutenant Governor Mallory, dated in July, 1813; the report of Messrs. Griffin and Lively to Major Crutchfield, dated the 4th of July, 1813; and Colonel Parker's publication in the Enquirer.

The fact that these atrocities were committed, the commander of the British fleet, Admiral Warren, and the commander of the British troops, Sir Sidney Beckwith, admitted, without hesitation;* but they resorted, as on other occasions, to the unworthy and unavailing pretext of a justifiable retaliation. It was said, by the British General, "that the excesses at Hampton were occasioned by an occurrence at the recent attempt upon Craney Island, when the British troops in a barge, sunk by the American guns, clung to the wreck of the boat, but several Americans waded off from the island, fired upon, and shot these men." The truth of the assertion was denied; the act, if it had been perpetrated by the American troops, was promptly disavowed by their commander, and a board of officers appointed to investigate the facts, after stating the evidence, reported "an unbiassed opinion, that the charge against the American troops was unsupported, and that the character of the American soldiery for humanity and magnanimity had not been committed, but, on the contrary, confirmed."† The result of this inquiry was communicated to the British General; reparation was demanded; but it was soon perceived that, whatever might personally be the liberal dispositions of that officer, no adequate reparation could be made, as the conduct of his troops was directed and sanctioned by his Government.‡

During the period of these transactions, the village of Lewistown, near the capes of the Delaware, inhabited chiefly by fishermen and pilots, and the village of Stonington, seated upon the shores of Connecticut, were unsuccessfully bombarded. Armed parties, led by officers of rank, landed daily from the British squadron, making predatory incursions into the open country; rifling and burning the houses and cottages of peaceable and retired families; pillaging the produce of the planter and farmer, (their tobacco, their grain, and their cattle;) committing violence on the persons of the unprotected inhabitants; seizing upon slaves, wherever they could be found, as booty of war; and breaking open the coffins of the dead, in search of plunder, or committing robbery on the altars of the church at Chaptico, St. Inigoes, and Tappahannock, with a sacrilegious rage.

But the consummation of British outrage yet remains to be stated from the awful and imperishable memorials of the Capitol at Washington. It has been already observed, that the massacre of the American prisoners, at the river Raisin, occurred in January, 1813; that throughout the

* See Admiral Warren's letter to General Taylor, dated the 29th of June, 1813; Sir Sidney Beckwith's letter to General Taylor, dated on the same day; and the report of Captain Myers to General Taylor, of July 2, 1813.

† See the report of the proceedings of the board of officers appointed by the general order of the 1st of July, 1813.

‡ See General Taylor's letter to Sir Sidney Beckwith, dated the 5th of July, 1813, and the answer of the following day.

Causes and Character of the War.

same year, the desolating warfare of Great Britain, without once alleging a retaliatory excuse, made the shores of the Chesapeake, and of its tributary rivers, a general scene of ruin and distress; and that in the month of February, 1814, Sir George Prevost himself acknowledged, that the measures of retaliation for the unauthorized burning of Newark, in December, 1813, and for all the excesses which had been imputed to the American Army, was, at that time, full and complete. The United States, indeed, regarding what was due to their own character, rather than what was due to the conduct of their enemy, had forborne to authorize a just retribution, and even disdained to place the destruction of Newark to retaliatory account for the general pillage and conflagration which had been previously perpetrated. It was not without astonishment, therefore, that, after more than a year of patient suffering, they heard it announced in August, 1814, that the towns and districts upon their coast were to be destroyed and laid waste, in revenge for unspecified and unknown acts of destruction which were charged against the American troops in Upper Canada. The letter of Admiral Cochrane was dated on the 18th, but it was not received until the 31st of August, 1814. In the intermediate time, the enemy debarked a body of about five or six thousand troops at Benedict, on the Patuxent, and by a sudden and steady march through Bladensburg approached the City of Washington. This city had been selected for the Seat of the American Government, but the number of its houses does not exceed nine hundred, spread over an extensive site; the whole number of its inhabitants does not exceed eight thousand; and the adjacent country is thinly populated. Although the necessary precautions had been ordered to assemble the militia for the defence of the city, a variety of causes combined to render the defence unsuccessful; and the enemy took possession of Washington on the evening of the 24th of August, 1814. The commanders of the British force held, at that time, Admiral Cochrane's desolating order, although it was then unknown to the Government and the people of the United States; but, conscious of the danger of so distant a separation from the British fleet, and desirous, by every plausible artifice, to deter the citizens from flying to arms against the invaders, they disavowed all design of injuring private persons and property, and gave assurances of protection wherever there was submission. General Ross and Admiral Cockburn then proceeded in person to direct and superintend the business of conflagration in a place which had yielded to their arms, which was unfortified, and by which no hostility was threatened. They set fire to the Capitol, within whose walls were contained the halls of the Congress of the United States, the hall of their highest tribunal for the administration of justice, the archives of the Legislature, and the National Library. They set fire to the edifice which the United States had erected for the residence of their Chief Magistrate; and they set fire to the costly and extensive buildings erected for the accommodation of the

principal officers of the Government in the transaction of the public business. These magnificent monuments of the progress of the arts, which America had borrowed from her parent Europe, with all the testimonials of taste and literature which they contained, were, on the memorable night of the 24th of August, consigned to the flames, while British officers of high rank and command united with their troops in riotous carousals by the light of the burning pile.

But the character of the incendiary had so entirely superseded the character of the soldier on this unparalleled expedition, that a great portion of the munitions of war which had not been consumed when the Navy Yard was ordered to be destroyed upon the approach of the British troops, were left untouched; and an extensive foundry of cannon, adjoining the City of Washington, was left uninjured; when, in the night of the 25th of August, the army suddenly decamped, and returning, with evident marks of precipitation and alarm, to their ships, left the interment of their dead, and the care of their wounded, to the enemy whom they had thus injured and insulted, in violation of the laws of civilized war.

The counterpart to the scene exhibited by the British army was next exhibited by the *British* navy. Soon after the midnight flight of General Ross from Washington, a squadron of British ships of war ascended the Potomac, and reached the town of Alexandria on the 27th of August, 1814. The magistrates, presuming that the general destruction of the town was intended, asked on what terms it might be saved. The naval commander declared, "that the only conditions in his power to offer were such as not only required a surrender of all naval and ordnance stores, (public and private,) but of all the shipping, and of all the merchandise in the city, as well as such as had been removed since the 19th of August." The conditions, therefore, amounted to the entire plunder of Alexandria, an unfortified and unresisting town, in order to save the buildings from destruction. The capitulation was made, and the enemy bore away the fruits of his predatory enterprise in triumph.

But, even while this narrative is passing from the press, a new retaliatory pretext has been formed, to cover the disgrace of the scene which was transacted at Washington. In the address of the Governor-in-Chief to the Provincial Parliament of Canada, on the 24th of January, 1815, it is asserted, in ambiguous language, "that, as a just retribution, the proud Capitol at Washington has experienced a similar fate to that inflicted by an American force on the Seat of Government in Upper Canada." The town of York, in Upper Canada, was taken by the American Army under the command of General Dearborn, on the 27th of April, 1813;[*] and it was evacuated on the succeeding 1st of May; although it was again visited for a day, by an American squadron, under the command of Commodore Chauncey, on the 4th of

* See the letters of General Dearborn to the Secretary of War, dated the 27th and 28th of April, 1813.

Causes and Character of the War.

August.* At the time of the capture, the enemy, on his retreat, set fire to his magazine, and the injury produced by the explosion was great and extensive; but neither then, nor on the visit of Commodore Chauncey, was any edifice, which had been erected for civil uses, destroyed by the authority of the military or the naval commander; and the destruction of such edifices, by any part of their force, would have been a direct violation of the positive orders which they had issued. On both occasions, indeed, the public stores of the enemy were authorized to be seized, and his public storehouses to be burnt; but it is known that private persons, houses, and property, were left uninjured. If, therefore, Sir George Prevost deems such acts inflicted on "the Seat of Government in Upper Canada" similar to the acts which were perpetrated at Washington, he has yet to perform the task of tracing the features of similarity; since at Washington the public edifices, which had been erected for civil uses, were alone destroyed, while the munitions of war and the foundries of cannon remained untouched.

If, however, it be meant to affirm, that the public edifices, occupied by the Legislature, by the Chief Magistrate, by the courts of justice, and by the civil functionaries of the Province of Upper Canada, with the Provincial library, were destroyed by the American force, it is an occurrence which has never before been presented to the view of the American Government, by its own officers, as matter of information; nor by any of the military or civil authorities of Canada as matter of complaint; it is an occurrence which no American had in any degree authorized or approved; and it is an occurrence which the American Government would have censured, and repaired with equal promptitude and liberality.

But a tale told thus out of date, for a special purpose, cannot command the confidence of the intelligent and the candid auditor; for, even if the fact of conflagration be true, suspicion must attend the cause for so long a concealment, with motives so strong for an immediate disclosure. When Sir George Prevost, in February, 1814, acknowledged that the measure of retaliation was full and complete for all the preceding misconduct imputed to the American troops, was he not apprized of every fact which had occurred at York, the capital of Upper Canada, in the months of April and August, 1813? Yet neither then, nor at any antecedent period, nor until the 24th January, 1815, was the slightest intimation given of the retaliatory pretext which is now offered. When the Admirals Warren and Cochrane were employed in pillaging and burning the villages on the shores of the Chesapeake, were not all the retaliatory pretexts for the barbarous warfare known to those commanders? And yet, "the fate inflicted by an American force on the Seat of Government in Upper Canada," was never suggested in justification or excuse! And finally, when the expedition was formed in August, 1814,

for the destruction of the public edifices at Washington, was not the "similar fate which had been inflicted by an American force on the Seat of Government in Upper Canada," known to Admiral Cochrane, as well as to Sir George Prevost, who called upon the Admiral (it is alleged) to carry into effect measures of retaliation against the inhabitants of the United States? And yet, both the call and the compliance are founded (not upon the destruction of the public edifices at York, but) upon the wanton destruction committed by the American Army in Upper Canada, upon the inhabitants of the Province, for whom alone reparation was demanded.

An obscurity, then, dwells upon the fact alleged by Sir George Prevost, which has not been dissipated by inquiry. Whether any public edifice was improperly destroyed at York, or at what period the injury was done, if done at all, and by what hand it was inflicted, are points that ought to have been stated when the charge was made; surely it is enough, on the part of the American Government, to repeat, that the fact alleged was never before brought to its knowledge for investigation, disavowal, or reparation. The silence of the military and civil officers of the Provincial Government of Canada, indicates, too, a sense of shame, or a conviction of the injustice of the present reproach. It is known that there could have been no other public edifice for civil uses destroyed in Upper Canada, than the House of the Provincial Legislature, a building of so little cost and ornament as hardly to merit consideration, and certainly affording neither parallel nor apology for the conflagration of the splendid structures which adorned the Metropolis of the United States. If, however, that House was indeed destroyed, may it not have been an accidental consequence of the confusion in which the explosion of the magazine involved the town? Or, perhaps, it was hastily perpetrated by some of the enraged troops, in the moment of anguish for the loss of a beloved commander, and their companions, who had been killed by that explosion, kindled as it was by a defeated enemy for the sanguinary and unavailing purpose. Or, in fine, some suffering individual, remembering the slaughter of his brethren at the river Raisin, and exasperated by the spectacle of a human scalp suspended in the Legislative Chamber, over the seat of the Speaker, may, in the paroxysm of his vengeance, have applied, unauthorized and unseen, the torch of vengeance and destruction.

Many other flagrant instances of British violence, pillage, and conflagration, in defiance of the laws of civilized hostilities, might be added to the catalogue which has been exhibited; but the enumeration would be superfluous, and it is time to close so painful an exposition of the causes and character of the war. The exposition had become necessary to repel and refute the charges of the Prince Regent, when, by his declaration of January, 1813, he unjustly states the United States to be the aggressors in the war; and insultingly ascribes the conduct of the American Government to the influence of French counsels. It was, also,

---

* See the letter from Commodore Chauncey, to the Secretary of the Navy, dated the 4th of August, 1813.

necessary to vindicate the course of the United States in the prosecution of the war; and to expose to the view of the world the barbarous system of hostilities which the British Government has pursued. Having accomplished these purposes, the American Government recurs with pleasure to a contemplation of its early and continued efforts for the restoration of peace. Notwithstanding the pressure of the recent wrongs, and the unfriendly and illiberal disposition which Great Britain has at all times manifested towards them, the United States have never indulged sentiments incompatible with the reciprocity of good will, and an intercourse of mutual benefit and advantage. They can never repine at seeing the British nation great, prosperous, and happy; safe in its maritime rights, and powerful in its means of maintaining them; but, at the same time, they can never cease to desire that the councils of Great Britain should be guided by justice, and a respect for the equal rights of other nations. Her maritime power may extend to all the legitimate objects of her sovereignty and her commerce, without endangering the independence and peace of every other Government. A balance of power, in this respect, is as necessary on the ocean as on the land; and the control that it gives to the nations of the world over the actions of each other, is as salutary in its operation to the individual Government which feels it, as to all the Governments by which, on the just principles of mutual support and defence, it may be exercised. On fair, and equal, and honorable terms, therefore, peace is at the choice of Great Britain; but if she still determine upon war, the United States, reposing upon the justness of their cause; upon the patriotism of their citizens; upon the distinguished valor of their land and naval forces; and, above all, upon the dispensations of a beneficent Providence; are ready to maintain the contest for the preservation of the national independence, with the same energy and fortitude which were displayed in acquiring it.

WASHINGTON, *February* 10, 1815.

STATE OF THE FINANCES.

[Communicated to the Senate, September 26, 1814.]

The Secretary of the Treasury, in obedience to the act "supplementary to the act, entitled "An act to establish the Treasury Department," has the honor respectfully to submit to Congress the following report and estimates:

The sums authorized by Congress to be expended during the year 1814, and for which appropriations have been made, are as follows:

1. For civil, diplomatic and miscellaneous expenses: $1,245,355 59

To this sum is to be added, the amount which may be payable on the following accounts, viz: 1. The amount of fines, penalties, and forfeitures actually received into the Treasury, which is appropriated for defraying the expenses of courts of the United States. 2. The sums received by the collectors of the customs for the marine hospital fund, and privateer pension fund, which are paid into the Treasury with the other moneys derived from the customs, but are exclusively applicable to the two objects here mentioned, respectively. 3. The moneys received into the Treasury for the United States' moiety of prizes captured by public vessels, which belong exclusively to the Navy pension fund. These items are contingent and uncertain, until the accounts for the year are made up, and their amounts ascertained. As they appear among the receipts into the Treasury, they must also be placed among its expenditures. They may be estimated for the year 1814, at $200,000 00

2. Military expenses, including the Indian Department, and the permanent appropriation of $200,000 annually, for arming and equipping the whole body of the militia of the United States   24,502,906 00

3. Naval expenses, including $200,000 for the purchase of timber, appropriated by the act of March 30, 1812   3,168,910 87

4. For the public debt, such sum as the public engagements may require; and which, during the year 1814, may be estimated as follows:

Interest on the public debt existing previously to the present war - $1,980,000 00

Interest on debt contracted during the present war, including the loans of the present year and the Treasury notes   2,950,000 00

Reimbursement of the principal, consisting of the annual reimbursement of the old six per cent. and deferred stocks, temporary loans payable during this year, and the Treasury notes to be reimbursed during the same period   7,572,000 00

         12,502,000 00

But for these purposes there had been advanced by the Treasury during the year 1813, to sundry commissioners of loans, beyond the demands upon them for the year 1813, and to the Treasurer of the United States, as the

State of the Finances.

agent for Commissioners of the Sinking Fund, about -   350,000 00

Leaving payable during the year 1814   12,152,000 00

             $47,270,172 46

The means by which this sum was to be provided, were the following :

1. Moneys receivable on account of the public revenue, and which were estimated thus :

From the customs	- $6,500,000 00	
Sales of public lands	- 600,000 00	
Direct tax and internal duties	- - 3,800,000 00	
Postage, and incidental receipts	- 50,000 00	
		10,950,000 00

2. Moneys receivable for the proceeds of loans, and for Treasury notes, to be issued as follows :

Amount payable into the Treasury during the year 1814, of the loan of seven and a half millions, made under the act of 2d August, 1813 - - $3,592,665 00

Amount authorized to be borrowed by act of March 24, 1814   25,000,000 00

Amount authorized by the act of March 4, 1814, to be issued in Treasury notes - 5,000,000 00

         33,592,665 00

And it was estimated that, out of the balance of cash remaining in the Treasury on the 1st day of January, 1814, which amounted to $5,196,482 00, there might be applied a sum sufficient to cover the whole amount of the authorised expenditures, and which would be - - - -   2,727,507 46

         $47,270,172 46

The accounts of the Treasury have as yet been made up only for the two first quarters of the year 1814, or to the 30th of June of that year. The annexed statement, marked A., shows the receipts and expenditures at the Treasury for the fourth quarter of the year 1813, which have not before been communicated to Congress, and separately, those of the two first quarters of the year 1814.

By this statement, it appears that the payments from the Treasury during the first half of the present year, have been

For civil, diplomatic, and miscellaneous expenses	- 1,444,062 60
Military expenses	- 11,210,238 00
Naval expenses	- 4,012,899 90
Public debt	- 3,026,580 77
	19,693,781 27

And would leave payable during the remainder of the year, on those several accounts, the following sums :

For civil, diplomatic, and miscellaneous expenses - - $1,001,292 99

Military expenses	- 13,292,668 00	
Naval expenses -	- 4,157,010 97	
Public debt	- 9,125,419 23	
		27,576,291 19
		$47,270,172 46

The receipts into the Treasury during the first half of the present year have been as follows :

For the proceeds of the customs	- $4,162,088 25	
Public lands, (including those in the Mississippi Territory, the proceeds of which are now payable to the State of Georgia) - - -	540,065 68	
Internal duties and direct taxes	2,189,272 40	
Postage and incidental expenses	166,744 00	
	7,078,170 33	

Loan of seven and a half millions, under the act of Aug. 2, '13   3,592,665

Loan of ten millions, (part of 25 millions,) under the act of March 24, 1814   6,087,011

       9,679,676

Treasury notes, issued under the act of February 25, 1813   1,070,000

Treas'y notes, issued under act of March 4, '14   1,392,100

       2,462,100

         12,141,776 00

         19,219,946 33

And there remained cash in the Treasury, on the 1st of July, 1814 - -   4,722,639 32

         $23,942,585 65

To make up the sum, therefore, which will be wanted to meet the expenditures as above estimated, there must be obtained during the 3d and 4th quarters of the present year -   23,327,586 81

         $47,270,172 46

And the further sum of $1,500,000, which is the least that ought at any time during a state of war to be left in the Treasury, making   - $24,827,586 81

Of this amount it is estimated that there will be derived from the various sources of existing revenue the following sums, viz :

From the customs - - $2,820,000 00

It has not been practicable to prepare the statements of this and of the other branches of the revenue in the usual official form, to be communicated to Congress at this time. Some of these statements have been heretofore regularly given for periods terminating on the 30th of September ; and, to preserve the series unimpaired, their preparation is postponed until they can be made out terminating with that day. They will hereafter be laid before Congress in the proper form.

The amount of the custom-house duties which accrued during the year 1813, was $7,070,000. During the two first quarters of the present year they amounted to about $3,000,000; but, during the two last quarters will not, probably, exceed $1,000,000. The amount receivable into the Treasury, during the year 1814, from bonds outstanding at the commencement of the year, and from the duties accruing, and which will become payable during that year, is estimated at $7,000,000; which was $500,000 more than was heretofore estimated. Of this sum, $4,162,096 25 was paid during the first half of the year, and will leave payable, during the remainder of the year, the sum here stated.

Sales of Public Lands.—The proceeds of the sales of public lands sold in the Mississippi Territory, which are now payable to the State of Georgia, are brought into the Treasury in the same manner as the moneys derived from the sales of other public lands. As the amount, when paid out of the Treasury to the State of Georgia, appears among the public expenditures, it is proper that these moneys should be placed upon the receipts of the Treasury. Including the proceeds of the lands in the Mississippi Territory, the receipts during the year 1814 are estimated at $900,000; of which $549,965 68 having been received during the two first quarters of the year, there will be receivable during the two last quarters - - - - **$350,000 00**

Internal Duties and Direct Tax.— The receipts into the Treasury, from these sources during the present year, will fully equal the estimate heretofore made. These taxes are paid readily and cheerfully. The direct tax is in collection in more than three-fourths of the districts, and will shortly be in the same state in all the districts, except two or three, where the difficulty of obtaining competent persons to act as assessors has produced some delay. In several of the districts the collection is already nearly completed. The amount estimated as receivable from these two sources, was $3,800,000; of this sum there was received, prior to the 1st of July last, $2,189,372 40, and leaves to be received during the remainder of the year - **1,610,000 00**

Postage and Incidental Receipts.— These were estimated, for the whole year, at $50,000. Including repayments, prize money, and the arrearages of the former direct tax and internal duties, there was received, on these accounts, during the first half of the year, $166,744. These re-

ceipts are so casual and uncertain, that it is difficult to make any estimate of their amount. During the remainder of the year they may, perhaps, be expected to produce - **30,000 00**

Total am't receivable for revenue   **$4,840,000 00**

Under the act of the 24th of March, 1814, by which the President was authorized to borrow twenty-five millions of dollars, a loan was opened on the 2d of May for ten millions of dollars, in part of that sum. A loan for ten millions of dollars was considered as more likely to prove successful, than if an attempt were made to obtain the whole amount of twenty-five millions at once. The sums offered for this loan amounted to $11,900,806; of which $2,671,750 were at rates less than 88 per cent., and $1,183,400 at rates less than 85 per cent. Of the sum of $9,229,656, which were offered at 88 per cent., or at rates more favorable to the United States, five millions were offered, with the condition annexed, that if terms more favorable to the lenders should be allowed for any part of the twenty-five millions authorized to be borrowed for the present year, the same terms should be extended to those holding the stock of the ten million loan. Taking into consideration the expectation then entertained, of an early return of peace, and the importance of maintaining unimpaired the public credit, by sustaining the price of stock in the meantime; and also considering the measure was sanctioned by precedent, it was agreed to accept the loan with that condition. Had the sum to which the condition was annexed, been rejected, the consequence would have been to reduce the amount obtained to less than five millions, a sum altogether inadequate to the public demands; or, by depressing the stock to 85 per cent., to have obtained only a little more than six millions, which would still have been insufficient to answer the purposes of Government. Offers were subsequently made to this loan, of sums amounting to $566,000, which were accepted on the same terms as the original offers, and augmented the amount of the loan which was taken to $9,795,056.

The papers annexed, under the letter B, exhibit the particulars relating to this loan.

There was paid into the Treasury, on account of the loan of ten millions, prior to the 1st of July, $6,087,011; leaving to be paid, after that day, $3,708,045. Of this sum a failure of payment, on the days fixed by the terms of the loan, of about $1,900,000, has taken place; and it is doubtful whether the payment will be effected. No more, therefore, can be relied on towards the supply necessary for the third and fourth quarters of the year 1814, than what has already been paid, and amounting to about $1,800,000.

Proposals were again invited on the 22d of August, for a loan of six millions of dollars, in further execution of the power contained in the act of the 24th of March, for borrowing twenty-five millions. The whole amount offered was $2,823,300, of which $100,000 were at rates less

State of the Finances.

than 80 per cent., and $2,913,000 were at the rate of eighty dollars in money for one hundred dollars of six per cent. stock. The remaining sum of $510,300 was offered at various rates, from 80 to 88. Notwithstanding the reduced rate at which the greater part of the above sum was proposed, yet, as the market price of stock hardly exceeded 80 per cent.; as there was no prospect of obtaining the money on better terms; and as it was indispensable for the public service, it was deemed advisable to accept the sums offered at that rate. Including the sums offered at rates more favorable to the United States than that here stated, the whole amount of the proposals accepted was $2,723,300, and a further sum of $207,000 has been accepted at the same rate; making the whole amount taken of this loan, $2,930,300.

The annexed papers, under the letter C, relate to this loan.

Some of the persons who originally made proposals for this loan, which were accepted, have since given notice that they could not carry their proposals into execution. The sums, in relation to which this failure has taken place, amount to $410,000; and there can, therefore, be relied on for the proceeds of this loan only $2,520,300.

Moneys having heretofore been obtained by the United States on loan in Europe upon favorable terms, and the punctuality and fidelity with which they were repaid having established their credit there on a firm and respectable footing, it was determined, in consequence of the difficulties experienced in obtaining at home the sums requisite for the public service, to try the market in that quarter. To effect this purpose, the requisite powers and instructions have been given for negotiating a loan for six millions of dollars, as a further part of the loan of twenty-five millions authorized by the act of the 24th of March last; and, in order to facilitate this object, six per cent. stock to that amount has been constituted and transmitted, with directions for its sale, if that shall be found the most advantageous mode for obtaining the money. The result, however, of this experiment is not certain; and the proceeds, in case it should be successful, will not, probably, come into the Treasury in the course of the present year; they cannot, therefore, be placed among the resources of this year. But as this sum forms a part of that which was authorized to be borrowed, and which will be necessary for the service of the present year, further authority will be required from Congress for obtaining this sum, by loan or otherwise; in which case the proceeds of the negotiation undertaken in Europe will be applicable to the service of the ensuing year. With a view to avoid the inconvenient increase of stock in the market, and its consequent depreciation, an effort was made to obtain temporary loans from the banks by special contracts, but the attempt was not attended with success.

The amount of Treasury notes issued prior to the 1st of July last, under the act of the 4th of March, 1814, was $1,392,100; those since issued amount to $1,512,300. The annexed statement, marked E, shows the particulars relating to these notes; and, in the paper marked D, an account is given of those Treasury notes issued under the act of the 25th of February, 1813, which have not been heretofore reported to Congress.

There are now in circulation near eight millions of dollars in Treasury notes; of which, during the fourth quarter of the present year, notes for more than four millions of dollars will become reimbursable. A part of them may, perhaps, be replaced by new notes, but it is not believed that, upon their present footing, more than two millions and a half of dollars can thus be replaced. This would still leave more than six millions of dollars of notes in circulation; which the experience of two years has shown to be nearly as large a sum, while the other circulating paper medium of the country remained unembarrassed, and maintained itself in the public confidence, as can, in their present shape, be freely and easily circulated. Notes of a smaller denomination than those heretofore issued have been prepared, and will, probably, by passing into a more numerous and extensive class of the money transactions of individuals, carry a greater quantity into circulation, there having been already issued, since the 1st of July, Treasury notes amounting to $1,500,000, and it being estimated that a further sum of $2,500,000 may be put in circulation previously to the end of the present year, the amount estimated to be derived from this source during the third and fourth quarters of the year will be $4,000,000.

The means, then, for meeting the demands upon the Treasury during the last half of the present year, as now ascertained, are estimated as follows:

From the revenue - - -		$4,640,000
Loans under the twenty-five million act:		
Loan of ten millions -	$1,800,000	
Loan of six millions -	2,520,000	
		4,320,000
		9,160,000
Treasury notes - - -		4,000,000
		13,160,000
And still leave to be obtained		11,660,000
		$24,820,000

The difficulties already experienced in obtaining loans, and the terms on which it has been found necessary to accept them, sufficiently show the propriety of Congress adopting effective measures for procuring the sums still required for the service of the residue of the present, as well as for that of the ensuing year.

The suspension of payments in specie, by many of the most considerable banks in the United States, and of those most important in the money operations of the Treasury, has produced, and will continue to cause difficulties and embarrassments in those operations. The circulating medium of the country, which has consisted principally of bank notes, is placed upon a new and uncertain

State of the Finances.

footing; and those difficulties and embarrassments will extend, in a greater or less degree, into the pecuniary operations of the citizens in general. The powers of Congress, so far as they extend, will be required to be exerted in providing a remedy for these evils, and in placing, if practicable, the currency of the country on a more uniform, certain, and stable footing.

If further reliance must be had on loans, it is respectfully suggested that additional inducements should be offered to capitalists to advance their money, by affording an ample and unequivocal security for the regular payment of the interest, and reimbursement of the principal of such loans as may be obtained. This may be effected by establishing an adequate revenue, and pledging the same specifically for that purpose.

It is also submitted, for the consideration of Congress, whether Treasury notes might not, by augmenting the rate of interest they now bear, and securing its payment, as well as their eventual reimbursement, by an adequate revenue pledged for that purpose, be placed on a footing better calculated than at present to sustain their credit, encourage their circulation, and answer with more certainty the purposes of Government.

The estimates for the service of the year 1815 have not yet been prepared. It is certain, however, if the war continues, that a sum will be required at least equal to that demanded for the present year; and, under the head of Public Debt, an additional sum, sufficient for the payment of the interest on the loans made in the meantime. By the plan of finance which was adopted at the commencement of the present war, this additional sum would be all that would be required to be raised, by new taxes, during the year 1815, except what might be necessary to make good a deficiency in any of the existing revenues. According to that plan of finance, the expenditures to be covered by the revenue during the year 1815, would be as follows:

Expense of the Peace Establishment		$7,000,000
Interest on the debt existing prior to the war	$1,900,000	
Interest on the debt contracted since the war, including Treasury notes, and including the interest which will become payable during the year 1815, on the debt contracted within that year	4,600,000	
		6,500,000
Total		$13,500,000

The revenues, as now established, are estimated to produce, during the year 1815, the following sums, viz:

Customs.—While the whole navy of the enemy is disposable for the interruption of our trade, this source of revenue cannot be very productive. From bonds which will be outstanding at the commencement of the year 1815, and from the duties which will accrue during that year, it is estimated that there will be received into the Treasury - - $4,000,000
Sales of public lands - - - - 800,000

Internal duties:—These will all bring their full amounts into the Treasury during the year 1815, and will, it is believed, produce a net sum of - - - - 2,700,000
Arrears of direct tax of 1814, which will be received in 1815 - - - 600,000
Postage, and other incidental receipts - 100,000

Total amount		$8,200,000
And leaving to be provided		5,300,000
Aggregate		$13,500,000

Towards making up this sum of $5,300,000, a continuance of the direct tax will, it is believed be necessary; but at its present rate it will not produce, net to the Treasury, more than $2,600,000.

In order to provide the remaining sum of $2,700,000, as well as such other sums as may be deemed requisite for the objects hereinbefore suggested, it will be for Congress to consider how far it would be expedient to increase this tax, as well as the present internal duties; and also what new objects of taxation may, for that purpose, be most advantageously resorted to.

But, the plan of finance above referred to assumed, as one of the grounds upon which it depended, that loans might be annually obtained during the continuance of the war, for the amount of the extraordinary expenses occasioned by it. The experience of the present year furnishes ground to doubt whether this be practicable, at least in the shape in which loans have been hitherto attempted. Nor is it even certain that the establishing and pledging of revenues adequate to the punctual payment of the interest and eventual reimbursement of the principal of the sums which will be required for the service of the year 1815, would enable the Treasury to obtain them through the medium of loans effected in the ordinary way.

With this view of the subject, it is respectfully submitted whether it would not be expedient to extend the provisions to be made for the service of the ensuing year beyond those contemplated in this plan of finance, hitherto pursued for carrying on the war, so as to provide, by means other than loans, for at least a portion of the extraordinary expenditures occasioned thereby. This would have a tendency to insure public confidence, and preserve and confirm the public credit.

The present state of our country, growing out of the unjust policy of the enemy, as well as the unusual manner in which he prosecutes the war, call for new and extraordinary exertions on the part of the nation; and the means requisite to meet the expenditures which these may occasion ought to be provided.

The resources of the nation are not exhausted; they are ample, and the occasion requires they should be brought into full activity.

The very expenditures which render necessary the imposition of additional taxes, will themselves have increased in the community the ability to discharge them.

The promptitude and cheerfulness with which

State of the Finances.

the present taxes are paid, afford the best pledges of the spirit with which the people will meet such demands as the interest and safety of the country may require. A people who have not only tasted, but enjoyed in their full extent, the blessings of liberty and independence, for more than thirty years, cannot consider any sacrifices too great, which are found indispensable to preserve them inviolate.

Those sacrifices, however, which may be demanded by the present crisis in our affairs, will be of a temporary nature only; for, while we may fairly calculate, that, with the termination of the present contest, the duration of which will be shortened in proportion to the vigor and unanimity with which it is sustained on our part, will cease the expenditures consequent on a state of war, and render no longer necessary a continuance of those extraordinary revenues established to provide the supplies requisite for that object, we may with equal confidence rely that the growing revenue arising from the commerce of a few prosperous years of peace will be found sufficient to redeem the pledges which may have been made to the public creditors, and thus relieve the people from these burdens which times of danger and difficulties rendered indispensable.

All which is respectfully submitted.

    G. W. CAMPBELL.

TREASURY DEPARTMENT, *Sept.* 23, 1814.

A.

Statement of Receipts and Payments at the Treasury of the United States, from the 1st October to the 31st December, 1813.

RECEIPTS.

Cash in the Treasury, subject to warrant, 1st October, 1813		$6,978,752 43
Received for the proceeds of the customs	$3,236,043 56	
Arrears of internal revenues	380 68	
Fees on patents	1,470 00	
Postage of letters	35,000 00	
Net proceeds of prizes captured	129,456 06	
Rent of the United States' saline	6,350 00	
Fines, penalties, and forfeitures	1,003 75	
Sales of public lands	263,049 06	
Repayments	3,810 13	
		3,678,565 26
Loan of $16,000,000, per act of 8th Feb'ry, 1813	1,511,875 00	
Loan of $7,500,000, per act of 2d August, 1813	3,907,335 00	
Treasury notes, per act of 30th June, 1812	101,700 00	
Treasury notes, per act of 25th February, 1813	3,677,000 00	
		9,197,910 00
Aggregate		$19,855,227 69

PAYMENTS.

Civil and Miscellaneous Expenses, both Foreign and Domestic.

Civil department, proper	$125,478 66
Grants and miscellaneous claims	23,552 03
Military pensions	675 34
Light-house establishment	7,104 15
Marine hospital establishment	12,869 58
Public buildings in Washington, and furniture for the President's House	7,000 00
Prisoners of war	54,000 00
Road from Cumberland to the Ohio	11,880 03
Prize money	112,668 25
Mint Establishment	4,516 41
Trading houses with the Indians	1,125 00
Ascertaining land titles in Louisiana	1,785 00
Surveys of public lands	12,176 62
Diplomatic department	19,017 91
Relief and protection of American seamen	31,017 50
Treaties with Mediterranean Powers	10,000 00
Total	$434,866 38

Military Expenses, viz:

Military department	5,887,747 00

Naval Expenses, viz:

Naval department, marine corps, &c.	1,248,145 10

Public Debt, viz:

Interest and charges	$1,563,762 35	
Reimbursement of principal	5,524,232 60	
		7,087,994 95
Balance in the Treasury, subject to warrant, 31st December, 1813		5,196,474 26
Aggregate		$19,855,227 69

Statement of Receipts and Payments at the Treasury of the United States, from the 1st January to the 30th June, 1814.

RECEIPTS

Cash in the Treasury, subject to warrant, 1st January, 1814		$5,196,474 26
Received for the proceeds of the customs	$4,182,088 25	
Arrears of internal revenues and direct taxes	4,505 32	
New internal revenue and direct tax	2,189,272 40	
Fees on patents	3,720 00	
Postage of letters	45,000 00	
Net proceeds of prizes captured	83,261 79	
Fines, penalties, and forfeitures	1,230 97	
Net proceeds of property seized, supposed to belong to A. Burr	448 00	
Sales of public lands	540,065 68	
Repayments	26,577 92	
		7,078,170 33
Loan of seven and a half millions, per act of 2d August, 1813	$3,592,665 00	
Loan of ten millions, per act of 24th Mar., 1814	6,087,011 00	

State of the Finances.

Treasury notes, per act of 28th February, 1813	1,070,000 00	
Treasury notes, per act of 4th March, 1814	1,398,100 00	
		12,141,776 00
Aggregate		$34,416,420 59

PAYMENTS.
Civil and Miscellaneous Expenses, both Foreign and Domestic.

Civil department, proper	$571,706 91
Grants and miscellaneous claims	144,194 99
Military pensions	47,424 27
Light-house establishment	66,469 12
Marine hospital establishment	24,697 89
Furniture for the President's House	2,000 00
Prisoners of war	199,000 00
Road from Cumberland to the Ohio	26,924 57
Prize money	108,069 50
Mint establishment	8,125 44
Trading houses with the Indians	8,044 86
Ascertaining land titles in Louisiana	2,757 67
Surveys of public lands	6,167 07
Survey of the coast of the United States	3,127 50
Payment to Georgia for Mississippi lands	96,222 94
Bounty to the owners, &c., of private armed vessels	4,300 00
Privateer pension fund	50,000 00
Diplomatic department	37,149 26
Relief and protection of American seamen	14,015 26
Treaties with Mediterranean Powers	8,300 00
Contingent expenses of foreign intercourse	12,720 35
Claims on France	2,635 00
Total	$1,444,062 60

Military Expenses, viz:

Military department	11,210,238 00

Naval Expenses, viz:

Naval Department, marine corps, &c.	4,012,899 90

Public Debt, &c.

Interest and charges	1,539,080 09	
Reimbursement of principal	1,487,500 68	
		3,026,580 77
Balance in the Treasury, subject to warrant, 30th June, 1814		4,722,639 32
		$34,416,420 59

B.
TREASURY DEPARTMENT,
April 4, 1814.

Whereas, by an act of Congress, passed on the 24th day of March, 1814, the President of the United States is authorized to borrow, on the credit of the United States, a sum not exceeding twenty-five millions of dollars; and, whereas, the President of the United States did, by an act or commission, under his hand, dated the 20th day of March, 1814, authorize and empower the Secretary of the Treasury to borrow, on behalf of the United States, the aforesaid sum of twenty-five millions of dollars, or any part thereof, pursuant to the act of Congress above recited:

Notice is therefore hereby given, that proposals will be received by the Secretary of the Treasury, until the 2d day of May next, from any person or persons, body or bodies corporate, who may offer, for themselves or others, to loan to the United States, on account and in part of the aforesaid sum of twenty-five millions of dollars, the sum of ten millions of dollars, or any part thereof, not less than twenty-five thousand dollars.

The stock to be issued for the money loaned, will bear an interest of six per cent. per annum, payable quarter yearly; and the proposals must distinctly state the amount of money offered to be loaned, and the rate at which the aforesaid stock will be received for the same.

The amount loaned is to be paid into a bank or banks authorized by the Treasury, in instalments, in the following manner, viz:

One-fourth part, or twenty-five dollars on each hundred dollars, on the twenty-fifth day of May next.

And one-fourth part on the 25th day of each of the ensuing months of June, July, and August next.

On the day fixed for the payment of any instalment after the first, all the remaining instalments may be paid.

The sum loaned is to be paid into such bank or banks as may be mutually convenient to the lender and to the Government, in the State where the lender resides, if desired by him. The proposals must state the bank or banks into which the lender may desire to make the payments.

If proposals, differing in terms from one another, should be accepted, the option will be allowed to any persons whose proposals may be accepted, of taking the terms allowed to any other person whose proposals may be accepted.

No proposals will be received for a sum less than twenty-five thousand dollars; but a commission of one-fourth of one per cent. will be allowed to any person collecting subscriptions for the purpose of incorporating them in one proposal, to the amount of twenty-five thousand dollars, or upwards, provided such proposal shall be accepted.

If proposals shall be made, amounting together to a greater sum than that required, the preference will, on equal terms, be given to those made by persons who were subscribers to the loan of eleven millions, in the year 1812.

On failure of payment of any instalment, the next preceding instalment to be forfeited.

Scrip certificates will be issued by the cashiers of the banks where the payments shall be made, to the persons making the payments; and the said cashiers will endorse on the certificates the payments of the several instalments, when made.

The scrip certificates will be assignable by endorsement and delivery; and will be funded after the completion of the payments, upon presentation by the proprietor, to the Commissioner of

Loans for the State where the payments have been made.

The funded stock to be thus issued, will be irredeemable until the 31st day of December, 1826; will be transferable in the same manner as the other funded stock of the United States; and will be charged for the regular and quarterly payment of its interest, and for the ultimate reimbursement of its principal, upon the annual fund of eight millions of dollars, appropriated for the payment of the principal and interest of the debt of the United States, in the manner pointed out in the aforesaid act of the 24th of March. 1814.

       GEO. W. CAMPBELL,
          Secretary of the Treasury.

Ba.

WASHINGTON, 4th mo. 30th, 1814.

RESPECTED FRIEND: I will loan to the Government of the United States five millions of dollars, receiving one hundred dollars six per cent. stock for each eighty-eight dollars paid; and will pay the money in the proportions, and at the periods, mentioned in thy advertisement of the 4th of April, to their credit, in such banks in the United States as may be agreeable to thee.

On the payment of each instalment, and satisfactory assurances for the payment of the others, funded stock to be issued. It being understood and agreed that, if terms more favorable to the loaners be allowed for any part of the twenty-five millions authorized to be borrowed the present year, the same terms are to be extended to this contract.

The commission of one quarter of one per cent. mentioned in thy advertisement, to be allowed me on the amount loaned.

With great respect and esteem, I am thy assured friend,

       JACOB BARKER.

The Hon. G. W. CAMPBELL,
     Secretary of the Treasury.

Bb.

TREASURY DEPARTMENT,
         May 2, 1814.

SIR: The terms upon which the loan has been concluded, are as follows, viz:

Eighty-eight dollars in money for each hundred dollars in stock; and the United States engage, if any part of the sum of twenty-five millions of dollars, authorized to be borrowed by the act of the 24th of March, 1814, is borrowed upon terms more favorable to the lenders, the benefit of the same terms shall be extended to the persons who may then hold the stock, or any part of it, issued for the present loan of ten millions.

Your proposal of the 30th of April, 1814, for $5,000,000 of the loan, having been at the above rate, or at a rate more favorable than the above to the United States, has been accepted; and you will please to pay, or cause to be paid, on the 25th day of the present month, into the bank or banks you have named, or into such as you shall name

to the Secretary of the Treasury, on the receipt of this letter, twenty-five per cent., or one-fourth part of the sum above stated, pursuant to the notification from this department, of the 4th of April last, and the remaining instalments on the days fixed in the said notification. You will be pleased, also, on or before the 25th of May, to furnish the cashier or cashiers of the bank or banks where the payments under your proposal are to be made, with the names of the persons in whose behalf the proposal has been made, and the sums payable by each.

The commission of one-fourth of one per cent. will be paid from the Treasury after the payment of the first instalment, on the 25th day of the present month.

    I am, respectfully, yours, &c.
       G. W. CAMPBELL,
         Secretary of the Treasury.

JACOB BARKER, Esq., New York.

A similar letter was addressed to the persons undermentioned, who made proposals for the sums set against their names, respectively:

Peleg Tallman, Bath, Maine	$25,000
Levi Cutter, Portland do.	94,000
John Woodman, do.	50,000
Henry S. Langdon, Portsmouth, New Hampshire	40,000
John W. Treadwell, Salem, Massachusetts	416,156
Thomas Perkins, Salem, Massachusetts	25,000
William Gray, Boston	197,000
Samuel Dana, do.	25,000
Jesse Putnam, do.	67,999
Amos Binney, do.	85,000
Nathan Waterman, jr., Providence, Rhode Island	35,300
James D'Wolf, Bristol	100,000
John R. Shearman, Newport	35,000
Elisha Tracy, Norwich, Connecticut	30,000
Michael Shepherd, Hartford do.	25,000
Abraham Bishop, New Haven do.	25,000
John Taylor, Albany	150,000
Alamon Douglas, Troy	50,000
Smith and Nicoll, New York	80,000
Harmon Hendricks, do.	42,000
G. B. Vroom, do.	500,000
Samuel Flewwelling do.	257,300
Jacob Barker do.	5,000,000
Whitehead Fish do.	250,000
Guy Bryan, Philadelphia	50,000
Thomas Newman, do.	108,000
Samuel Carswell, do.	25,000
Paul Beck, jr., do.	50,000
Wm. Patterson & Sons, Baltimore	50,000
George T. Dunbar, do.	191,800
James Cox, do.	71,900
Dennis A. Smith, do.	200,000
Samuel Eliot, jr., Washington	100,000
Alexander Kerr, do.	33,000
W. Jones, for Navy and Privateer Pension Funds, Washington	200,000
William Whann, Washington	42,000
Anthony C. Cazenove, Alexandria	30,000
Charles B. Cochran, Charleston, South Carolina	250,000

State of the Finances.

David Alexander, Charleston, South Carolina - - - - - -	60,000
John Lukins, Charleston, South Carolina,	70,000
Thomas W. Bacot, do. do. -	115,000
James Taylor, Newport, Kentucky -	25,000
	$9,239,056

There was subsequently offered, and accepted, proposals by the undermentioned persons, for the following sums, viz:

William Whann, Washington - -	$190,000
Do. do. - -	200,000
Robert C. Jennings, Richmond, Virginia -	176,000
	$566,000

C.

TREASURY DEPARTMENT.
July 25, 1814.

Notice is hereby given, that proposals will be received by the Secretary of the Treasury, until the 22d day of August next, for loaning to the United States the sum of *six millions* of dollars, or any part thereof, not less than twenty-five millions of dollars, the same being in part of the sum of twenty-five millions of dollars authorized to be borrowed by the act of Congress of the 24th day of March last.

The stock to be issued for the money loaned, will bear an interest of six per cent. per annum, payable quarter yearly; and the proposals must distinctly state the amount of money offered to be loaned, and the rate at which the aforesaid stock will be received for the same.

The amount loaned is to be paid into a bank or banks authorized by the Treasury, in instalments in the following manner, viz:

One-fourth part, or twenty-five dollars on each hundred dollars, on the tenth day of September next.

And one-fourth part on the tenth day of each of the ensuing months, of October, November, and December next.

On the day fixed for the payment of the first, or any other instalment, all the remaining instalments may be paid at the option of the lender.

The proposals must state the banks into which the lender may desire to make his payments; and he will be allowed to make them according to his wishes, thus expressed, in all cases where the convenience of the Treasury will permit.

The same terms will be allowed to all whose proposals are accepted.

No proposals will be received for a sum less than twenty-five thousand dollars; but a commission of one-fourth of one per cent. will be allowed to any person collecting subscriptions for the purpose of incorporating them in one proposal to the amount of twenty-five thousand dollars, or upwards, provided such proposal shall be accepted.

On failure of payment of any instalment, the next preceding instalment to be forfeited.

All the instalments must be paid at the same bank as that at which the first instalment shall be paid.

Scrip certificates will be issued by the cashiers of the banks where the payments shall be made, to the persons making the payments; and the said cashiers will endorse on these certificates the payments of the several instalments when made.

The scrip certificates will be assignable by endorsement and delivery, and will be funded after the completion of the payments, upon presentation to the Commissioners of Loans for the State where the payments have been made.

Certificates of funded stock will also be issued, if the holders of scrip certificates shall desire it, for the amount of any instalment paid, after the payment of the next succeeding instalment.

The funded stock to be thus issued will be irredeemable till after the 31st day of December, 1826; will be transferable in the same manner as the other funded stock of the United States; and will be charged for the regular and quarterly payment of its interest, and for the ultimate reimbursement of its principal, upon the annual fund of eight millions of dollars appropriated for the payment of the principal and interest of the debt of the United States in the manner pointed out in the aforesaid act of the 24th of March, 1814.

G. W. CAMPBELL,
Secretary of the Treasury.

Ca.

BALTIMORE, *August 22, 1814.*

SIR: I will take eighteen hundred thousand dollars of the six millions loan, at the rate of eighty per cent. The periods of payment to be in conformity with your advertisement for proposals; and the banks into which the payments shall be made, are the Bank of Pennsylvania and the Mechanics' Bank of Baltimore.

I am, sir, with great respect, your obedient servant,

D. A. SMITH.
G. W. CAMPBELL, Esq., Sec'ry Treas'y.

Cb.

TREASURY DEPARTMENT,
August 31, 1814.

SIR: That part of the loan of six millions of dollars for which the proposals were accepted, has been taken at the rate of eighty dollars, in money, for one hundred dollars in stock. Your proposal for —— dollars being at that rate, or at one more favorable for the United States, has been accepted, and you will be pleased to make your payments into the bank or banks specified in your proposal, in the manner, and at the times stated in the public notification. But as some delay, the cause of which is doubtless known to you, has unavoidably taken place in advising you of the acceptance of your proposal, the first payment may, if your convenience shall require it, be made on the 20th instead of the 10th of September, as required by the public notification. This, however, will not affect the subsequent instalments, which are, nevertheless, to be paid on the days already fixed, viz: the 10th day of the months of October, November and December.

The same causes which have occasioned a delay in advising you of the acceptance of your proposal, will perhaps render it impossible to place the scrip certificates in the hands of cashiers of the banks where the payments are to be made, by the time at which the first instalment will be payable. If this should be the case, you will please to receive from the cashier his receipt for the amount which you may pay, to be subsequently exchanged for a scrip certificate, when those papers shall be ready for delivery.

I am, respectfully, sir, your obedient servant,

G. W. CAMPBELL,
Secretary of the Treasury.

The above letter was addressed to the following persons, who made proposals for the sums affixed to their names respectively, viz:

William Rice, Portsmouth New Hampshire	$43,000
Henry S. Langdon, do. -	35,000
Amasa Stetson, Boston -	37,000
Jesse Putnam, do. -	15,000
Nathan Waterman, jr., Providence Rhode Island	10,000
John S. Shearman, Newport, do. -	25,000
John Savage, Philadelphia -	240,000
William W. Smith, do. -	100,000
William Patterson and Sons, Baltimore -	70,000
Dennis A. Smith, do. -	1,800,000
James L. Hawkins, do. -	15,000
John P. Van Ness, and others, Washington	201,000
David English, Georgetown -	35,000
John Lukens, Charleston -	47,300
George M. Deaderick, Nashville -	50,000
	$2,723,300

There has been subsequently offered, and accepted, proposals from the undermentioned persons, for the following sums, viz:

George T. Dunbar, Baltimore -	120,000
Clement Smith, Georgetown -	87,000
	$207,000

Of the persons who originally made proposals, the following have given notice that they could not carry them into effect:

John Savage, Philadelphia -	$240,000
William W. Smith, do. -	100,000
William Patterson and Sons, Baltimore -	70,000
	$410,000

SINKING FUND.

[Communicated to the Senate, February 6, 1815.]

The Commissioners of the Sinking Fund respectfully report to Congress as follows:

That the measures which have been authorized by the Board, subsequent to their last report, of the 5th of February, 1814, so far as the same have been completed, are fully detailed in the report of the Secretary of the Treasury to this Board, dated the sixth day of the present month, and in the statements therein referred to, which are herewith transmitted, and prayed to be received as part of this report.

JOHN GAILLARD,
President of the Senate, pro tem.
JAMES MONROE,
Acting Secretary of State.
A. J. DALLAS,
Secretary of the Treasury.

WASHINGTON, *February 6, 1815.*

The Secretary of the Treasury respectfully reports to the Commissioners of the Sinking Fund—

That the balance of moneys advanced on account of the public debt, remaining unexpended at the end of the year 1812, and applicable to payments falling due after that year, which balance, as appears by the statement B, annexed to the last annual report, amounted to	$335,826 04	
Together with sums disbursed from the Treasury during the year 1813, on account of the principal and interest of the public debt, which sums, as appears by the statement C, annexed to the last annual report, amounted to	11,110,117 43	
Together with a further sum arising from profit in exchange on remittances from America to Europe, during the year 1813, amounting, as appears by the statement D, annexed to the last annual report, to	$98,452 06	
From which is to be deducted, as explained in the note to the statement B, annexed to this report, the sum of	6,202 20	92,249 86
And with a further sum, being the difference between the principal of stock purchased during the year 1813, and the money paid for the same, of		1,902 34
And amounting, together, to -		$11,540,095 67

Have been accounted for in in the following manner, viz:

I. There was repaid into the Treasury, during the year 1813, on account of the principal of moneys heretofore advanced for the payment of the public debt, as appears by the statement E, annexed to the last annual report, the sum of - - - $2,002 43

II. The sums actually applied during the year 1813, to the payment of the principal and interest of the public debt, as ascertained by accounts rendered to the Treasury Department, amounted, as will appear by the annexed statement A, to ten millions seven hundred and seventy-six thousand eight hundred and eighty-seven dollars forty-nine cents, viz:

State of the Sinking Fund.

1. In reimbursement of the principal of the public debt	$7,177,432 27	
2. On account of the interest and charges on the same	3,599,455 22	
		10,776,887 49

III. The balance remaining unexpended, at the close of the year 1813, and applicable to payments falling due after that year, as ascertained by accounts rendered to the Treasury Department, amounted, as will appear by the annexed statement B, to - - - - -   761,205 75

                   $11,540,095 67

That, during the year 1814, the following disbursements were made out of the Treasury, on account of the principal and interest of the public debt, viz:

1. On account of the interest and reimbursement of the funded domestic debt	$4,937,451 33	
2. On account of the principal and interest of temporary loans, viz:		
Reimbursement of principal	250,000 00	
Payment of interest	57,798 90	
		307,798 90
3. On account of the principal and interest of Treasury notes		2,979,783 40
4. On account of the interest on Louisiana stock, payable in Europe		161,847 06

Amounting, together, as will appear by the annexed list of warrants, marked C, to - - - - -   **$8,386,880 59**

Which disbursements were made out of the following funds, viz:

I. From the balance of the annual appropriation of eight millions of dollars for the year 1813, remaining unexpended at the end of that year, which balance amounted, as stated in the last annual report, to - - - -   442,964 11

II. From the funds constituting the annual appropriation of eight millions of dollars for the year 1814, viz:

From the fund arising from the interest on the debt transferred to the Commissioners of the Sinking Fund, as per statement, I	$3,062,495 54	
From the fund arising from the net proceeds of the sales of public lands, being the amount received into the Treasury from the 1st of October, 1813, to the 30th of September, 1814, as per statement K,	1,091,958 19	
From the proceeds of duties on goods, wares, and merchandise, imported, and		

on the tonnage of vessels - - -	4,633,736 10	
		$7,658,289 83
Which sum of -	$7,658,289 83	
Being deducted from the annual appropriation of -	8,000,000 00	

Leaves an undrawn balance, to be applied in addition to the appropriation for the year 1815, of -   341,710 17

III. From repayments into the Treasury, on account of moneys heretofore advanced for the payment of interest on the Louisiana stock in Europe, and for the payment of the principal and interest of Treasury notes, as will appear by the annexed statement E - - -   286,336 65

               8,386,880 59

That the disbursements above mentioned, together with the balance above stated, which remained unexpended at the end of the year 1813, of -   761,205 75

Together with a further sum arising from profit in exchange, on remittances from America to Europe, made in the year 1814, and amounting, as appears by the annexed statement D, to   19,827 61

Making together - - -   **$9,167,913 95**

Will be accounted for in the next annual report, in conformity with the accounts which shall then have been rendered to the Treasury Department.

That, in the meantime, the manner in which the said sum has been applied is estimated as follows, viz:

I. The repayments into the Treasury on account of the principal of moneys advanced for the payment of interest on the Louisiana stock in Europe, and for the payment of principal and interest of Treasury notes, have amounted, during the year 1814, as by the above-mentioned statement E, to - - - -   286,336 65

II. The sums actually applied, during the year 1814, to the principal and interest of the public debt, are estimated as follows:

1. Paid in reimbursement of the principal of public debt	$4,283,735 90	
2. Paid on account of interest and charges on the same -	4,586,948 54	

As will appear by the annexed statement F - - -   8,870,684 44

III. The balance which remained unexpended at the end of the year 1814, and applicable to payments falling due after that year, is estimated, per annexed statement G, at -   11,492 86

              $9,167,913 95

That, agreeably to the terms of the contracts by which certain temporary loans had heretofore been obtained, under the authority of the act of the 14th of March, 1812, the instalments of the following loans, which became payable in the year 1814, were duly paid at the times when they respectively became payable, viz:

To the Bank of Baltimore, on the 16th November, 1814 - - -	$100,000 00
To the State Bank, at Charleston, on the 1st December, 1814 - -	150,000 00
	$250,000 00

Two instalments of $250,000 each, which became payable on the 16th and 31st December, 1814, to the State Bank, Boston, were not paid, it having been impracticable, in consequence of the general suspension of payments in specie, by the banks, to transfer the amount from those banks in which the moneys of the Treasury were deposited, to Boston, where the payment was to be made, and equally impracticable to obtain the money on the spot for that purpose.

That, during the year 1814, and on the 1st of January, 1815, Treasury notes became payable (in addition to those payable in the months of January and February, 1814, for the payment of which money was advanced in the year 1813, as stated in the annual report of February, 1814) amounting to $5,357,300. Of these, there was paid, or money advanced from the Treasury for their payment, notes amounting to $2,558,100, at the times and places stated in the annexed statement, marked L. From the same causes as those above stated, which prevented the reimbursement of the temporary loans payable to the State Bank, Boston, it was impracticable to provide at the Treasury for the payment of the remainder of the above mentioned notes; and they remain unpaid, amounting to $2,799,200. The times when, and the places at which, they became payable, are exhibited in the annexed statement, marked M.

For the payment of the dividend on the domestic funded debt, payable at the Loan Office in Massachusetts, on the 1st day of October, 1814, the Commissioner of Loans was furnished with a draft of the Treasury of the United States, on the State Bank, Boston, he having at that time a much larger sum than was necessary for this object, deposited to his credit in that bank. The draft was, nevertheless, refused payment by the bank, except upon the condition of paying the public creditors, whose dividends amounted to one hundred dollars, or upwards, in Treasury notes; and the payment to such of the creditors, as have been paid, is understood to have been made in that way.

For the payment of the dividend, payable at the same Loan Office, on the 1st day of January 1815, the Treasury was unable, from the causes above stated, to make any other provision than that of Treasury notes; and such of the public creditors, as have received their dividends payable that day, at that Loan office, have been paid in those notes.

A statement marked H, is annexed, exhibiting the amount of stock transferred to the Commissioners of the Sinking Fund, and standing to their credit on the books of the Treasury, on the 31st December, 1814.

All which is respectfully submitted,

A. J. DALLAS,
Secretary of the Treasury.

FEBRUARY 6, 1815.

[The tabular statements are omitted.]

IMPROVEMENT AND INCREASE OF THE MILITARY ESTABLISHMENT.

[Communicated to the Senate, November 5, 1814.]

SENATE'S COMMITTEE CHAMBER,
September 23, 1814.

SIR: In obedience to instructions from the committee, appointed to take into consideration the accompanying resolution, I do myself the honor to ask information from you upon the following points:

1st. What are the defects in the present Military Establishment?

2d. What further provisions, by law, are deemed necessary to remedy such defects?

Be pleased, sir, to accept assurances of my high consideration.

WM. B. GILES, *Chairman.*
The Hon. JAMES MONROE,
Acting Secretary of War.

COMMITTEE CHAMBER, *Sept.* 24, 1814.

SIR: In obedience to instructions from the Committee on Military Affairs, I now do myself the honor of enclosing, for your consideration, a resolution of the Senate of the 23d instant,[*] and of requesting that, in replying to the inquiries made by the committee on yesterday, you will give such information, and in such manner, in relation to the objects of the said resolution, as you may judge advisable.

Be pleased, sir, to accept assurances of my high consideration.

WM. B. GILES, *Chairman.*
The Hon. JAMES MONROE,
Acting Secretary of War.

DEPARTMENT OF WAR,
October 17, 1814.

SIR: The great importance of the subject, and the other duties of the Department, which could not fail to be very sensibly felt, at so interesting a period, by a person who had just taken charge of it, are my apology for not answering your letter of the 23d of September, at an earlier day, on the defects of the present Military Establishment.

* *Resolved*, That the Committee on Military Affairs be instructed to inquire into the state of preparations for the defence of the City of Washington, and whether any further provisions, by law, be necessary for that object.

Due consideration has been bestowed on the subject-matter of that letter, and I have now the honor to submit to the committee the following report:

1. That the present Military Establishment, amounting to 62,448 men, be preserved and made complete, and that the most efficient means authorized by the Constitution, and consistent with the equal rights of our fellow-citizens, be adopted to fill the ranks, and with the least possible delay.

2. That a permanent force, consisting of not less than 40,000 men, in addition to the present Military Establishment, be raised, for the defence of our cities and frontiers, under an engagement by the Executive with each corps that it shall be employed in that service within certain specified limits. And that a proportional augmentation of general officers of each grade, and other staff, be provided for.

3. That the corps of engineers be enlarged.

4. That the ordnance department be amended.

Respecting the enlargement of the corps of engineers, I shall submit hereafter a more detailed communication.

For the proposed amendment of the ordnance department, I submit a report from the senior officer in that department, now in this city, which is approved.

I shall be ready and happy to communicate such further remarks and details on these subjects as the committee may desire, and shall request permission to suggest, hereafter, the result of further attention to, and reflection on, our Military Establishment generally, should anything occur which may be deemed worthy its attention.

I have the honor to be, with great respect, your very obedient servant,

JAMES MONROE.

Hon. WILLIAM B. GILES,
Chairman Committee on Military Affairs.

Explanatory Observations.

In providing a force necessary to bring this war to a happy termination, the nature of the crisis in which we are involved, and the extent of its dangers, claim particular attention. If the means are not fully adequate to the end, discomfiture must inevitably ensue.

It may fairly be presumed that it is the object of the British Government, by striking at the principal sources of our prosperity, to diminish the importance, if not to destroy the political existence of the United States. If any doubt remained on this subject, it has been completely removed by the despatches from our Ministers at Ghent, which were lately laid before Congress.

A nation contending for its existence against an enemy powerful by land and sea, favored, in a peculiar manner, by extraordinary events, must make great exertions, and suffer great sacrifices. Forced to contend again for our liberties and independence, we are called on for a display of all the patriotism which distinguished our fellow-citizens in the first great struggle. It may be fairly concluded that if the United States sacrifice any right, or make any dishonorable concession to the demands of the British Government, the spirit of the nation will be broken, and the foundations of their union and independence shaken. The United States must relinquish no right or perish in the struggle. There is no intermediate ground to rest on. A concession on one point leads directly to the surrender of every other. The result of the contest cannot be doubtful. The highest confidence is entertained that the stronger the pressure, and the greater the danger, the more firm and vigorous will be the resistance, and the more successful and glorious the result.

It is the avowed purpose of the enemy to lay waste and destroy our cities and villages, and to desolate our coast, of which examples have already been afforded. It is evidently his intention to press the war along the whole extent of our seaboard, in the hope of exhausting equally the spirits of the people and the national resources. There is also reason to presume that it is the intention to press the war from Canada on the adjoining States, while attempts are made on the city of New York, and other important points, with a view to the vain project of dismemberment or subjugation. It may be inferred likewise, to be a part of the scheme, to continue to invade this part of the Union, while a separate force attacks the State of Louisiana, in the hope of taking possession of the city of New Orleans, and of the mouth of the Mississippi, that great inlet and key to the commerce of all that portion of the United States lying westward of the Alleghany mountains. The peace in Europe having given to the enemy a large disposable force, has essentially favored these objects.

The advantage which a great naval superiority gives to the enemy, by enabling him to move troops from one quarter to another, from Maine to the Mississippi, a coast of two thousand miles extent, is very considerable. Even a small force, moved in this manner, for the purposes avowed by the British commanders, cannot fail to be sensibly felt; more especially by those who are most exposed to it. It is obvious that, if the militia are to be relied on, principally, for the defence of our cities and coast against these predatory and desolating incursions, wherever they may be made, that, by interfering with their ordinary pursuits of industry, it must be attended with serious interruption and loss to them, and an injury to the public, while it greatly increases the expense. It is an object, therefore, of the highest importance, to provide a regular force with the means of transporting it from one quarter to another, along our coast, thereby following the movements of the enemy, with the greatest possible rapidity, and repelling the attack wherever it may be made. These remarks are equally true as to the militia service generally, under the present organization of the militia, and the short terms of service prescribed by law. It may be stated with confidence, that at least three times the force, in militia, has been employed at our principal cities, along the coast and on the frontier, in marching to, and returning thence, that would have been

Increase of the Military Establishment.

necessary in regular troops; and that the expense attending it has been more than proportionably augmented, from the difficulty, if not the impossibility of preserving the same degree of system in the militia as in the regular service.

But it will not be sufficient to repel these predatory and desolating incursions. To bring the war to an honorable termination, we must not be contented with defending ourselves. Different feelings must be touched, and apprehensions excited, in the British Government. By pushing the war into Canada, we secure the friendship of the Indian tribes, and command their services, otherwise to be turned by the enemy against us; we relieve the coast from the desolation which is intended for it, and we keep in our hands a safe pledge for an honorable peace.

It follows, from this view of the subject, that it will be necessary to bring into the field, next campaign, not less than one hundred thousand regular troops. Such a force, aided, in extraordinary emergencies, by volunteers and the militia, will place us above all inquietude as to the final result of this contest. It will fix on a solid and imperishable foundation, our Union and independence, on which the liberties and happiness of our fellow-citizens so essentially depend. It will secure to the United States an early and advantageous peace. It will arrest, in the further prosecution of the war, the desolation of our cities and our coast, by enabling us to retort on the enemy those calamities which our citizens have been already doomed to suffer—a resort which self defence alone, and a sacred regard for the rights and honor of the nation, could induce the United States to adopt.

The return of the regular force now in service, laid before you, will show how many men will be necessary to fill the present corps; and the return of the numerical force of the present Military Establishment will show how many are required to complete it to the number proposed. The next and most important inquiry is, how shall these men be raised? Under existing circumstances, it is evident that the most prompt and efficient mode that can be devised, consistent with the equal rights of every citizen, ought to be adopted. The following plans are respectfully submitted to the consideration of the committee. Being distinct in their nature, I will present each separately, with the considerations applicable to it.

First Plan.

Let the free male population of the United States, between eighteen and forty-five years, be formed into classes of one hundred men each, and let each class furnish four men for the war, within thirty days after the classification, and replace them in the event of casualty.

The classification to be formed with a view to the equal distribution of property among the several classes.

If any class fails to provide the men required of it, within the time specified, they shall be raised by draught on the whole class, any person

thus draughted being allowed to furnish a substitute.

The present bounty in land to be allowed to each recruit, and the present bounty in money, which is paid to each recruit by the United States, to be paid to each draught by all the inhabitants within the precinct of the class within which the draught may be made, equally, according to the value of the property which they may respectively possess; and if such bounty be not paid within —— days, the same to be levied on all the taxable property of the said inhabitants; and, in like manner, the bounty, whatever it may be, which may be employed in raising a recruit, to avoid a draught, to be assessed on the taxable property of the whole precinct.

The recruits to be delivered over to the recruiting officer in each district, to be marched to such places of general rendezvous as may be designated by the Department of War.

That this plan will be efficient cannot be doubted. It is evident that the men contemplated may soon be raised by it. Three modes occur by which it may be carried into effect: 1st. By placing the execution of it in the hands of the county courts throughout the United States: 2d. By relying on the militia officers in each county: 3d. By appointing particular persons for that purpose in every county. It is believed that either of these modes would be found adequate.

Nor does there appear to be any well founded objection to the right in Congress to adopt this plan, or to its equality in its application to our fellow-citizens individually. Congress have a right, by the Constitution, to raise regular armies, and no restraint is imposed on the exercise of it, except in the provisions which are intended to guard generally against the abuse of power; with none of which does this plan interfere. It is proposed that it shall operate on all alike; that none shall be exempted from it except the Chief Magistrate of the United States, and the Governors of the several States.

It would be absurd to suppose that Congress could not carry this power into effect, otherwise than by accepting the voluntary service of individuals. It might happen that an army could not be raised in that mode, whence the power would have been granted in vain. The safety of the State might depend on such an army. Long-continued invasions, conducted by regular, well disciplined troops, can best be repelled by troops kept constantly in the field, and equally well disciplined. Courage in an army is, in a great measure, mechanical. A small body, well trained, accustomed to action, gallantly led on, often breaks three or four times the number of more respectable and more brave, but raw and undisciplined troops. The sense of danger is diminished by frequent exposure to it, without harm; and confidence, even in the timid, is inspired by a knowledge that reliance may be placed on others, which can grow up only by service together. The grant to Congress to raise armies, was made with a knowledge of all these circumstances, and with an intention that it should take effect. The

Increase of the Military Establishment.

framers of the Constitution, and the States who ratified it, knew the advantage which an enemy might have over us, by regular forces, and intended to place their country on an equal footing.

The idea that the United States cannot raise a regular army in any other mode than by accepting the voluntary service of individuals, is believed to be repugnant to the uniform construction of all grants of power, and equally so to the first principles and leading objects of the Federal compact. An unqualified grant of power gives the means necessary to carry it into effect. This is an universal maxim, which admits of no exception. Equally true is it, that the conservation of the State is a duty paramount to all others. The commonwealth has a right to the service of all its citizens; or, rather, the citizens composing the commonwealth have a right, collectively and individually, to the service of each other, to repel any danger which may be menaced. The manner in which the service is to be apportioned among the citizens, and rendered by them, are objects of legislation. All that is to be dreaded in such case, is, the abuse of power; and, happily, our Constitution has provided ample security against that evil.

In support of this right in Congress, the militia service affords a conclusive proof and striking example. The organization of the militia is an act of public authority, not a voluntary association. The service required must be performed by all, under penalties, which delinquents pay. The generous and patriotic perform them cheerfully. In the alacrity with which the call of the Government has been obeyed, and the cheerfulness with which the service has been performed throughout the United States, there is abundant cause to rejoice in the strength of our Republican institutions, and in the virtue of the people.

The plan proposed is not more compulsive than the militia service, while it is free from most of the objections to it. The militia service calls from home, for long terms, whole districts of country. None can elude the call. Few can avoid the service; and those who do are compelled to pay great sums for substitutes. This plan fixes on no one personally, and opens to all who choose it a chance of declining the service. It is a principal object of this plan to engage in the defence of the State the unmarried and youthful, who can best defend it, and best be spared, and to secure to those who render this important service an adequate compensation from the voluntary contributions of the more wealthy, in every class. Great confidence is entertained that such contribution will be made in time to avoid a draught. Indeed, it is believed to be the necessary and inevitable tendency of this plan to produce that effect.

The limited powers which the United States have in organizing the militia may be urged as an argument against their right to raise regular troops in the mode proposed. If any argument could be drawn from that circumstance, I should suppose that it would be in favor of an opposite conclusion. The power of the United States over the militia has been limited, and that for raising regular armies granted without limitation. There was doubtless some object in this arrangement. The fair inference seems to be, that it was made on great consideration; that the limitation, in the first instance, was intentional, the consequence of the unqualified grant in the second. But it is said, that, by drawing the men from the militia service into the regular army, and putting them under regular officers, you violate a principle of the Constitution, which provides that the militia shall be commanded by their own officers. If this was the fact, the conclusion would follow. But it is not the fact. The men are not drawn from the militia, but from the population of the country. When they enlist voluntarily, it is not as militiamen that they act, but as citizens. If they are draughted, it must be in the same sense. In both instances, they are enrolled in the militia corps; but that, as is presumed, cannot prevent the voluntary act in the one instance or the compulsive in the other. The whole population of the United States, within certain ages, belong to these corps. If the United States could not form regular armies from them, they could raise none.

In proposing a draught as one of the modes of raising men, in case of actual necessity, in the present great emergency of the country, I have thought it my duty to examine such objections to it as occurred, particularly those of a *Constitutional* nature. It is from my sacred regard for the principles of our Constitution, that I have ventured to trouble the committee with any remarks on this part of the subject.

Should it appear that this mode of raising recruits was justly objectionable, on account of the tax on property, from difficulties which may be apprehended in the execution, or from other causes, it may be advisable to decline the tax, and for the Government to pay the whole bounty. In this case, it is proposed that, in lieu of the present bounty, the sum of fifty dollars be allowed to each recruit or draught, at the time of his engagement, and one hundred acres of land in addition to the present bounty in land, for every year that the war may continue.

It is impossible to state, with mathematical accuracy, the number which will be raised by the ratio of 4 to 100, or 1 to 25, nor is it necessary. It is probable that it will be rather more than sufficient to fill the present corps. The extra number, in that case, may form a part of *the local* force in contemplation, a power to that effect being given to the President.

No radical change in the present Military Establishment is proposed. Should any modification be found necessary, on further consideration, it will form the subject of a separate communication. It is thought advisable, in general, to preserve the corps in their present form, and to fill them with new recruits, in the manner stated. All these corps have already seen service, and many of them acquired in active scenes much experience and useful knowledge. By preserving them in their present form, and under their pre-

Increase of the Military Establishment.

ent officers, and filling them with new recruits, the improvement of the latter will be rapid. In two or three months, it will be difficult to distinguish between the new and old levies.

The additional force to be provided amounts to forty thousand men. Of this it is proposed that local corps be raised, to consist partly of infantry, partly of mounted men, and partly of artillery. There is reason to believe that such corps may be raised in the principal cities, and even on the frontiers, to serve for the war, under an engagement as to the limit beyond which they should not be carried. Every able-bodied citizen is willing and ready to fight for his home, his family, and his country, when invaded. Of this we have seen in the present year the most honorable and gratifying proofs. It does not suit all, however, to go great distances from home. This generous and patriotic spirit may be taken advantage of, under proper arrangements, with the happiest effects to the country, and without essential inconvenience to the parties.

The officers who may be appointed to command these corps should be charged with recruiting them. Local defence being their sole object, it may be presumed that the corps will soon be raised. Patriotism alone will furnish a very powerful motive. It seems reasonable, however, that some recompense should be made to those who relieve others from the burden; one hundred acres of land and fifty dollars to each recruit will, it is presumed, be deemed sufficient.

It is proposed that this additional force shall form a part of any plan that may be adopted.

Second Plan.

This plan consists of a classification of the militia, and the extension of their terms of service.

Let the whole militia of the United States be divided into the following classes, viz.:

All free male persons, capable of service, between the ages of 18 and 25, into one class; all those between the ages of 25 and 32, into another class; and those between 32 and 45, into a third class.

It is proposed, also, that the President shall have power to call into service any portion of either of these classes which, in his judgment, the exigencies of the country may require, to remain in service two years from the time each corps shall be assembled at the appointed place of rendezvous.

It is believed that a shorter term than two years would not give to these corps the efficiency in military operations that is desired, and deemed indispensable; nor avoid the evils that are so sensibly felt, and generally complained of, under the present arrangement. It requires two campaigns to make a complete soldier, especially where the corps, officers, and men, are alike raw and inexperienced. In the interim, the numbers must be multiplied, to supply the defect of discipline; and it requires the extension of the term of service, to avoid the additional proportional augmentation of having so many in the field at the same time, in marching to the frontier, and returning from it. The inconvenience to the parties, and

loss to the community, in other respects, need not be repeated. It is proper to add, only, that, if substitutes are allowed in this service, it must put an end to the recruiting of men for the regular Army, especially the old corps. Of the justice of this remark what has occurred in the present year has furnished full proof. It follows that, if this plan is adopted, the militia must be relied on principally, if not altogether, in the farther prosecution of the war.

The additional force for local service, amounting to forty thousand men, will likewise form a part, as already observed, of this plan.

Third Plan.

It is proposed by this plan to exempt every five men from militia service, who shall find one to serve for the war. It is probable that some recruits might be raised in this mode, in most or all of the States. But it is apprehended that it would prevent recruiting in every other mode, by the high bounty which some of the wealthy might give. The consequence would probably be very injurious, as it is not believed that any great number could be raised in this mode.

Fourth Plan.

Should all the preceding plans be found objectionable, it remains that the present system of recruiting be adhered to, with an augmentation of the bounty in land. Should this be preferred, it is advised that, in addition to the 160 acres of land now given, 100 be allowed annually for every year while the war lasts.

These plans are thought more deserving the attention of the committee than any that have ocurred. The first, for the reasons stated, is preferred. It is believed that it will be found more efficient against the enemy, less expensive to the public, and less burdensome on our fellow-citizens.

It has likewise the venerable sanction of our Revolution. In that great struggle, resort was had to this expedient for filling the ranks of our regular army, with decisive effect.

It is not intended by these remarks, should the first plan be adopted, to dispense altogether with the service of the militia. Although the principal burden of the war may thereby be taken from the militia, reliance must still be placed on them for important aids, especially in cases of sudden invasion. For this purpose it will still be advisable that the men be classed according to age, and that their term of service be prolonged. Even should this plan be attended with all the advantages expected of it, such an arrangement could not fail to produce the happiest effect. The proof which it would afford of the impregnable strength of the country, of the patient virtue and invincible spirit of the people, would admonish the enemy how vain and fruitless his invasions must be, and might dispose him to a speedy, just, and honorable peace.

Of the very important services already rendered by the militia, even under the present organization, too much cannot be said. If the United States make the exertion which is proposed, it is probable that the contest will soon be at an end

Increase of the Military Establishment.

It cannot be doubted that it is in their power to expel the British forces from this continent, should the British Government, by persevering in its unjust demands, make that an object with the American people. Against our united and vigorous efforts, the resistance of the enemy will soon become light and feeble. Success in every fair and honorable claim is within our easy grasp. And surely the United States have every possible inducement to make the effort necessary to secure it. I should insult the understanding, and wound the feelings of the committee, if I touched on the calamities incident to defeat. Dangers which are remote, and can never be realized, excite no alarm with a gallant and generous people. But the advantages of success have a fair claim to their deliberate consideration. The effort which we have already made has attracted the attention and extorted the praise of other nations. Already have most of the absurd theories and idle speculations on our system of Government been refuted and put down. We are now felt and respected as a Power, and it is the dread which the enemy entertains of our vast resources and growing importance, that has induced him to push the war against us, after its professed objects had ceased. Success by the discomfiture of his schemes, and the attainment of an honorable peace, will place the United States on higher ground, in the opinion of the world, than they have held at any former period. In future wars, their commerce will be permitted to take its lawful range unmolested. Their remonstrances to foreign Governments will not again be put aside unheeded. Few will be presented, because there will seldom be occasion for them. Our Union, founded on interest and affection, will have acquired new strength by the proof it will have afforded of the important advantages attending it. Respected abroad, and happy at home, the United States will have accomplished the great objects for which they have so long contended. As a nation, they will have little to dread; as a people, little to desire.

Extract from Marshall's Life of Washington volume 4th, page 241.

"In general, the Assemblies of the States followed the example of Congress, and apportioned on the several counties or towns, within the State, the quota to be furnished by each. This division of the State was again to be subdivided into classes, and each was to furnish a man by contributions or taxes on itself. In some instances, a draught was to be used in the last resort, in others the man was to be recruited by persons appointed for that purpose, and the class to be taxed with the sum given for his bounty."

Extract from Ramsey's Life of Washington, 2d volume, page 246.

"Where voluntary enlistments fell short of the proposed number, the deficiencies were, by the laws of several States, to be made up by draught on lots from the militia. The towns in New England, and the counties in the Middle States, were respectively called on for a specified number of men. Such was the zeal of the people in New England, that neighbors would often elect together to engage one of their number to go into the Army. Maryland directed her Lieutenants of counties to class all the property in their respective counties into as many equal classes as there were men wanted, and each class was by law obliged, within ten days thereafter, to furnish an able-bodied recruit during the war; and in case of their neglecting or refusing to do so, the county Lieutenants were authorized to procure men at their expense, at any rate not exceeding fifteen pounds in every hundred pounds' worth of property classed agreeably to law. Virginia also classed her citizens, and called upon the respective classes for every fifteenth man for public service. Pennsylvania concentrated the requisite power in the President, Mr. Reed, and authorized him to decree forth the resources of the State, under certain limitations, and, if necessary, to declare martial law over the State. The execution of these arrangements, although uncommonly vigorous, lagged far behind."

SENATE'S COMMITTEE CHAMBER.
October 19, 1814.

SIR: I lost not a moment in laying before the Committee of the Senate on Military Affairs the report you did me the honor to address to me on the 17th, and received on the 18th instant, in reply to a former communication; and, after the most respectful consideration of that report, I am instructed by the Committee to ask from you further information upon the following points:

1st. Whether any defects have been heretofore discovered in the existing provisions for filling the ranks of the regular Army? If so, what are the defects?

2d. In what mode, in the opinion of the War Department, could such defects be best remedied by legislative provisions?

3d. The Committee also request an outline of the plan for raising the forty thousand men proposed by your report, and particularly how far limitations are proposed to be imposed by law upon the President of the United States, in the application of that force?

I have the honor to be, sir, with great respect, your obedient servant,

WM. B. GILES, *Chairman.*
Hon. JAMES MONROE, *Secretary of War.*

WAR DEPARTMENT, *Oct. 21, 1814.*

SIR: In reply to your letter of yesterday, I have to state that I shall have the honor of an interview with the Committee of the Senate on Military Affairs, at half after nine o'clock to-morrow morning, at the house in which Congress holds its session. I shall then be happy to communicate to the Committee the views of this Department on the subjects adverted to in your letter.

I have the honor to be, with great respect, sir, your obedient servant,

JAMES MONROE.
Hon. W. B. GILES, *Senate, U. S.*

Increase of the Military Establishment.

SENATE'S COMMITTEE CHAMBER,
October 21, 1814.

SIR: I have this moment received your letter of the same date herewith, probably by mistake; and immediately submitted its contents to the Committee on Military Affairs, by whom I am instructed to inform you that the committee will be happy to receive your personal attendance to-morrow morning, at the time and for the objects mentioned in your letter.

I have the honor to be, with great respect, sir, your obedient servant,

W. B. GILES, *Chairman.*

Hon. JAMES MONROE, *Secretary of War.*

ADJ'T AND INSPECTOR GEN'S OFFICE,
Washington, October 22, 1814.

SIR: By direction of the Secretary of WAR, I have the honor to enclose herewith an abstract of the general return of the Army of the United States, to October 1st, 1814. Should the committee require a more general return, similar to the one furnished the Military Committee of the House, it could be furnished in the course of the next week. I am, sir, yours respectfully,

JOHN R. BELL,
Assistant Inspector General.

Hon. Mr. GILES, *Senate Washington.*

Return of the whole number of Recruits enlisted, agreeably to the act of Congress, passed 27th of January, 1814, for the several Corps and Regiments of the Army, from the 1st of February to the 20th of September, 1814, inclusive; agreeably to the returns received at this office.

Regiment light artillery	-	-	-	-	-	342
Regiment light dragoons	-	-	-	-	-	174
Corps of artillery	-	-	-	-	-	345
1st regiment infantry	-	-	-	-	-	91
2d	do	-	-	-	-	46
3d	do	-	-	-	-	5
4th	do	-	-	-	-	156
5th	do	-	-	-	-	215
6th	do	-	-	-	-	180
7th	do	-	-	-	-	143
8th	do	-	-	-	-	210
9th	do	-	-	-	-	215
10th	do	-	-	-	-	205
11th	do	-	-	-	-	194
12th	do	-	-	-	-	159
13th	do	-	-	-	-	330
14th	do	-	-	-	-	180
15th	do	-	-	-	-	213
16th	do	-	-	-	-	262
17th	do	-	-	-	-	262
18th	do	-	-	-	-	82
19th	do	-	-	-	-	346
20th	do	-	-	-	-	153
21st	do	-	-	-	-	198
22d	do	-	-	-	-	162
23d	do	-	-	-	-	323
24th	do	-	-	-	-	108
25th	do	-	-	-	-	310
26th	do	-	-	-	-	165
27th	do	-	-	-	-	550
28th	do	-	-	-	-	146

29th regiment of infantry		-	-	-	-	502
30th	do	-	-	-	-	274
31st	do	-	-	-	-	161
32d	do	-	-	-	-	28
33d	do	-	-	-	-	181
34th	do	-	-	-	-	441
35th	do	-	-	-	-	362
36th	do	-	-	-	-	136
37th	do	-	-	-	-	330
38th	do	-	-	-	-	206
39th	do	-	-	-	-	192
40th	do.					
41st	do	-	-	-	-	223
42d	do	-	-	-	-	188
43d	do	-	-	-	-	122
44th	do	-	-	-	-	292
45th	do	-	-	-	-	344
46th	do.					
1st rifle regiment	-	-	-	-	-	146
2d	do	-	-	-	-	172
3d	do	-	-	-	-	124
4th	do	-	-	-	-	97
			Total	-	-	-	9,991

It will be perceived that, from two of the above regiments, no return of recruits has been received; from many of them the returns for September have not been received. The whole number of recruits made since the passage of the law above referred to, to the present time, may be estimated at one thousand five hundred more than the above return.

ADJ'T AND INSPECTOR GEN'S OFFICE,
October 26, 1814.

JOHN R. BELL,
Assistant Inspector General.

SENATE'S COMMITTEE CHAMBER,
October 24, 1814.

SIR: The Committee of the Senate on Military Affairs being extremely anxious to come to a final determination upon the object of its appointment, and deeming some further information from your Department essential to enable it to determine correctly, has instructed me to ask for information on the following points:

1st. To what causes is the failure in the recruiting service, heretofore, properly attributable?

2. Has such failure arisen from any failure to place the requisite sums of money in the hands of the recruiting officers; or, has it arisen from the indisposition of the citizens to enlist?

Any other information within your Department, tending to throw light upon this subject, would be particularly acceptable to the Committee.

I am, sir, with great respect, your obedient servant, WM. B. GILES, *Chairman.*

Hon JAMES MONROE, *Sec'ry of War.*

WAR DEPARTMENT, *Oct.* 26, 1814.

SIR: In reply to the letter which I received from you of the 24th, I have the honor to transmit to you a report of the Paymaster General, of

Return of Enlistments.

the sums of money advanced on account of the recruiting service, since the 27th of January last. I also transmit a return of the number of men recruited within that time. A more detailed return, showing how many have been recruited in each month, in each regiment, shall be furnished as soon as it can be prepared.

By these returns it appears that more money has been advanced on account of the recruiting service than was sufficient to raise a much greater number of men than has been recruited. A considerable sum remains to be accounted for by the recruiting officers. Whether any of them failed in their duty, is an object of inquiry for this Department, which will not be neglected. I have been too short a time in it to make myself thoroughly acquainted with their conduct in this respect. By these returns, it would follow that the failure in the recruiting service was not owing to the want of money, if it was certain that the recruiting officers had in all instances done their duty; and that the money had been distributed in those quarters of our country where it would have been most easy to obtain recruits. How far the failure ought to be attributed to either of these causes, it is not in my power to state.

From the view which I have taken of the subject, founded on the best information I have been able to collect, I am led to believe that the failure of the recruiting service has been owing, in most of the States, principally to the high bounty given for substitutes by the detached militia.

Many of the militia detached for six months have given a greater sum for substitutes than the bounty allowed by the United States for a recruit to serve for the war.

I have the honor to be, with great respect, sir, your obedient servant,

JAMES MONROE.
Hon. WM. B. GILES, *Chairman, &c.*

———

ARMY PAY OFFICE, WASHINGTON,
October 26, 1814.

The Paymaster of the Army of the United States, to whom has been referred the letter from the honorable the Chairman of the Committee of the Senate on Military Affairs to the Secretary of War, under date of October 24th, 1814, has the honor to report:

1st. That the books of this office exhibit the disbursement of two millions and twelve thousand four hundred and thirty-nine dollars and thirty-three cents, on account of bounties and premiums for recruits, between the 27th of January, 1814, the date of the passage of the law increasing the bounty, and the date hereof: the distribution of this sum, as nearly as can well be ascertained, has been as follows, viz:

To Massachusetts, including the District of Maine - - - -	$237,400 00
To New Hampshire - - - -	37,800 00
To Vermont - - - -	109,300 00
To Connecticut - - - -	76,922 00
To Rhode Island - - - -	1,000 00
To New York - - - -	495,320 00

To New Jersey - - - -	15,000 00
To Pennsylvania - - - -	190,900 00
To Delaware - - - -	10,000 00
To Maryland, including the District of Columbia - - - -	95,002 35
To Virginia - - - -	160,982 98
To North Carolina - - - -	60,000 00
To South Carolina - - - -	72,800 00
To Georgia - - - -	34,000 00
To Tennessee - - - -	98,500 00
To Kentucky - - - -	106,800 00
To Ohio - - - -	98,000 00
To Louisiana - - - -	82,530 00
To the Michigan Territory - - -	20,000 00
To the Mississippi Territory - - -	4,000 00
To the Indiana Territory - - -	2,000 00
To the Missouri Territory - - -	1,492 00
Total - - - -	$2,012,439 33

2d. That pressing calls for very considerable sums of money for the recruiting service had been made on him for about three months past, which he has been able but partially to supply.

Respectfully, ROBERT BRENT,
Paymaster, U. S. A.

Hon. JAMES MONROE,
Secretary of War.

———

WAR DEPARTMENT, *Oct. 29, 1814.*

SIR: Enclosed is an abstract of the law establishing the Ordnance Department, and also of the bill now prepared for the new organization of that Department, which will give you a view of the contemplated changes in, and enlargements of the duties and powers of that Department.

I have the honor to be, sir, your obedient servant, JAMES MONROE.
Hon. WM. B. GILES, *Chairman, &c.*

———

RETURN OF ENLISTMENTS.

[Communicated to the Senate, November 10, 1814.]
WAR DEPARTMENT, *Nov. 10, 1814.*

SIR: Since I had the honor to enclose you a statement of the number of men who have been recruited in the Army of the United States during the present year, I have received a further statement from the Assistant Inspector General, attached to this Department.

This report shows more satisfactorily the expenditure of the money which has been advanced on that account, and number of men raised. The same data cannot, however, be adopted in estimating the future progress in recruiting, a considerable number of those who were recruited having been re-enlisted from the old corps. That resource has been exhausted. To form an estimate of the probable future success, we must take into consideration only those who were raised from the country, which is probably the number included in this return.

I have the honor to be, with great respect, sir, your obedient servant, J. MONROE.
Hon. Mr. GILES, *Chairman, &c.*

Capture of the City of Washington.

ADJ'T AND INSPECTOR GEN'S OFFICE,
WASHINGTON, *Nov.* 2, 1814.

SIR: The deranged state of the papers in this office by the late removals rendered it impracticable for me, when I submitted the hasty estimate on the 26th October, to have recourse to all the documents of the recruits made within the present year. On a further examination, the enclosed is submitted.

It may be necessary, with a view to your better information, to accompany the return I now have the honor to transmit, with some explanatory observations. The difficulty under which this office has labored for want of regular recruiting returns has been considerable, and necessarily occasions the general return to be inaccurate and unsatisfactory. No pains, however, have been spared to render the accompanying document as accurate as it can be made from the data which the files of this office afford.

In January last, large sums of money were put into the hands of commanders of regiments and corps, for the purpose of re-enlisting the men whose terms of service were about to expire. These were the soldiers enlisted for the additional army of 1808, and those of 1812, enlisted for twelve and eighteen months. This money was distributed among the officers commanding companies, who employed it to its fullest extent in the re-enlistment of their men, who, at the next muster, were returned on the muster rolls as re-enlisted. Satisfied as the officers seem to have been with this species of return, they made no special one to this office of those they had thus re-enlisted.

Indeed, the entire want of some returns, and the irregularity and defectiveness of others, render it extremely difficult to form a correct idea of the manner in which the public money has been expended. By way of illustration, I would refer you to the 46th regiment, of which no recruiting returns whatever have yet been made, when it is known by the Army returns that this regiment contains two hundred and thirty men, and to the 32d regiment, of which there is a return of only forty-two men, when it is known, through the same channel, that it now contains more than three hundred. From this, the difficulty of ascertaining, immediately, to what amount, if any, officers intrusted with public money have been guilty of defalcation, must be evident. On this subject, however, it may be proper to remark, that there exist no grounds for suspecting any defalcations; for, although the returns do not show all the recruits enlisted, and by whom, yet the general return, exhibiting the strength of armies and corps, compared with that of last year, shows plainly that the number of men raised corresponds with sufficient exactness with the money issued for that purpose.

The Paymaster of the Army has issued, up to the 27th October, on account of bounties and premiums, $2,012,439, which, supposing three thousand men to have received the second moiety of their bounty, (an estimate, it is believed, sufficiently moderate) would raise thirty thousand and twenty-three men. By the return communicated to the committee in a letter from the Secretary of War of the 1st January last, the effective force of the Army was then eight thousand and twelve. But, by the general return of the 30th of September, which embraces no return of a later date than August, it appears the strength of the Army was then thirty-four thousand and twenty-nine; from which it is evident that twenty-six thousand and seventeen men, at least, must have been raised since January last. I say at least, because the casualties of deaths, desertions, and discharges, during the campaign, are not included. This number would require the sum of $1,613,054. Now, estimating the casualties during the campaign at three thousand men, which, to raise them, would require $186,000, and adding to this the second moiety, which is presumed to have been paid to three thousand men, viz: $150,000, it is clear that, to raise the men borne on the return, it was necessary to expend $1,949,054. This will leave $63,385 in the hands of the recruiting officers, nearly the whole of which must have been since expended in the recruiting service.

With much respect, I have the honor to be, sir, your obedient servant,
JOHN R. BELL, *Insp'r General.*

CAPTURE OF THE CITY OF WASHINGTON

[Communicated to the House, November 29, 1814.]

IN THE HOUSE OF REPRESENTATIVES,
September 23, 1814.

Resolved, That a committee be appointed to inquire into the causes of the success of the enemy in his recent enterprises against this metropolis, and the neighboring town of Alexandria; and into the manner in which the public buildings and property were destroyed, and the amount thereof, and that they have power to send for persons and papers.

Mr. Johnson of Kentucky, Mr. Lowndes, Mr. Stockton, Mr. Miller, Mr. Goldsborough, Mr. Barbour, and Mr. Pickens, were appointed the said committee.

Mr. R. M. JOHNSON made the following report:

The committee charged with an inquiry so intimately concerning the character of Administration, the sensibility of the nation, and the honor of its arms, as the causes of success of the enemy in his recent enterprises against this metropolis, &c., have endeavored to combine despatch with effect, in the manner in which they have collected the facts and views presented in the following statement:

Proceedings of the Cabinet of 7th June, 1814.

Previous to the 2d of July, this city composed a part of military district No. 5. Early in June last, the Secretary of War furnished the President, at his request, with a general report of the strength of the regular troops and militia then in the service of the United States, and their distribution; which was submitted to the Heads of Departments, by the President, on the 7th of June. The Secretary of the Navy had furnished the President with a similar estimate of our naval forces: that which was applicable to the limits of military district No. 10, will hereafter appear. By a reference to the estimate of the land forces, it appears, that the aggregate number of troops stationed in district No. 5, on the 7th of June, amounted to two thousand two hundred and eight, of which, there were two thousand one hundred and fifty-four effectives, stationed as follows: At Norfolk, two hundred and twenty-four artillerists; the 20th, 35th, and 1st battalion of the 38th regiment of infantry, amounting to nine hundred and twelve; at Baltimore, one hundred and eleven artillerists; 2d battalion of the 38th infantry, amounting to three hundred and sixteen: sea fencibles, one hundred and seventy-three; at Annapolis, forty artillerists; at Fort Washington, eighty-two artillerists; St. Mary's, 36th regiment of infantry, three hundred and fifty. The meeting of the Cabinet on the 7th, and the estimates of land and naval forces, had no particular relation to the defence of any part of military district No. 5; but for measures generally, and particularly in regard to the campaign on our territorial frontiers in the North and Northwest. Nor does it appear that this city had excited more than ordinary attention at this time.

Proceedings of the Cabinet of the 1st of July.

But, soon after, certain intelligence being received of the complete success of the allies in the subjugation of France, the President believed that the enemy had the inclination and power to increase his military and naval forces against the United States; and, in that event, he believed that a variety of considerations would present this city as one of the prominent objects of attack. On the 26th of June, despatches were received from Mr. Gallatin and Mr. Bayard, confirming the views of the President, which induced him to convene the Heads of Departments on the 1st of July; at which time he presented a plan of a force immediately to be called into the field, and an additional force to be kept in readiness to march, without delay, in case of necessity. It seemed to be his object that some position should be taken between the Eastern Branch and Patuxent, with two or three thousand men, and that an additional force of ten or twelve thousand militia and volunteers should be held in readiness in the neighboring States, including the militia of the District of Columbia, and that convenient depots of arms and military equipments should be established. The measures suggested were approved by the Heads of Departments; or, in other words, it does not appear that any dissent was expressed.

Correspondence of the Secretary of War and General Winder.

The next day, July the 2d, by a general order of the War Department, the 10th military district was created, to embrace the State of Maryland, the District of Columbia, and that part of Virginia lying between the Rappahannock and Potomac, under the command of Brigadier General Winder, who, being then in Baltimore, was advised of the fact by a letter from the Secretary of War of the same date. On the 4th of July, a requisition was made on certain States for a corps of ninety-three thousand five hundred men, designating the quota of each, with a request to the Executive of each State to detach, and *hold in readiness for immediate service, their respective* detachments, recommending the *expediency of* fixing the places of rendezvous, with a due regard to points, the importance or exposure of which would most likely attract the views of the enemy. Of that requisition, two thousand effectives from the quota of Virginia; five thousand from that of Pennsylvania; six thousand, the whole quota of Maryland: and two thousand, the estimated number of the militia of the District of Columbia, were put at the disposition of the Commanding General, as hereafter appears, making the aggregate number of fifteen thousand, exclusive of the regular troops, viz: the 36th regiment, one battalion of the 38th, *two troops* of dragoons, two companies of the 10th *infantry,* one company of the 12th, and two *companies of* sea fencibles, supposed to amount *to one thousand* men, besides the artillerists *composing* the garrisons of *Forts* McHenry and Washington.

On the 9th of July, General Winder, in a letter to the Secretary of War, on the subject of the duties which devolved upon him as commander of the 10th military district, a previous conversation is alluded to as having taken place between them, in consequence of the request of the Secretary in his letter of the 2d of July. General Winder appears to have understood the intention of the Secretary of War to be, that the militia force proposed *for the 10th* military district should be draughted and designated, but that no part of it should be called into the field until the hostile squadron in the Chesapeake should be reinforced to such an extent as to render it probable that a serious attack was contemplated; states the difficulty of collecting a force, in an emergency, sufficient to retard the advance of the enemy; and suggests the expediency of calling out four thousand of the militia, with a view to station them, in equal proportions, between South river and Washington, and in *the* vicinity of Baltimore.

On the 12th of July, the Secretary of War, in a letter to General Winder, encloses a circular, addressed to the Governors of certain States, requiring a body of militia to be organized, equipped, and held in readiness for future service, and authorizes him, in case of actual or menaced invasion of the district under his command, to call for a part or the whole of the quota assigned to the State of Maryland; and in another, of the 17th July, the Secretary authorizes General Winder to draw from Virginia two thousand men; from Pennsylvania, five thousand men; and informs him that the whole of the militia of the District of Columbia, amounting to about two thousand, was in a disposable state, and subject to his orders; making, together with the six thousand from Maryland, the estimate of fifteen thousand militia. On the 15th of July, the Secretary of War advised General Winder that General Porter had communicated the fact of the arrival of the van of Cochrane's fleet at Lynhaven Bay, and that the agent at Point Lookout had represented that two seventy-fours, two frigates, an armed sloop and brig, ascended the bay at half past five, post meridian, on the 14th; that he considered it proper to call into service the brigade of militia which had been for some time held in readiness at Baltimore, and not knowing whether General Winder was at Baltimore or Annapolis, he had instructed the Major General, under whose orders they were organized, to call them out.

General Winder, in a letter of the 16th of July, to the Secretary of War, among other things expresses his embarrassment in relation to the situation of Annapolis, and gives it as his opinion that a large force and many additional works would be necessary to defend it against a serious attack by land and water; states its importance to the enemy, and the ease with which it might be maintained by them with the command by water, and an entrenchment of seven or eight hundred yards, protected by batteries; represents Fort Madison as exposed, and unhealthy in the months of August and September, provided with two fifty pound columbiads, two twenty-fours, two eighteens, one twelve, and one tom, which might be turned with success against Fort Severn; that these guns should be removed, and arrangements made to blow up the fort; and represents the importance of defending the town if the means could be obtained; states the Governor of Maryland and Council had taken the necessary steps to comply immediately with the requisition of the General Government. On the 17th of July a letter from General Winder to the Secretary of War states that information, that he deemed credible, was received, that the enemy was ascending the river in considerable force; that he had ordered the detachment of regulars to Nottingham, had sent out the alarm to assemble a militia force, and suggests the propriety of sending to that place the marine corps, and all the militia that could be procured from the District of Columbia. The Secretary, on the same day, acknowledges the receipt of the above letter, and states that the marine corps was not under his command; but had sent the request to the President, and as the authority to call the militia was vested in the Commanding General, he had transmitted his requisition upon the District to General Van Ness; he also reminds him that the two regiments near Baltimore had been called into actual service, and expresses the wish of the President that not less than two nor more than three thousand of the draughts, under the requisition of the fourth of July, should be embodied and encamped at some middle point between Baltimore and this city.

From the letter of General Winder, of the 20th of July, it appears the enemy proceeded up the Patuxent to Hunting creek, landed, and committed some depredations in Calvert county, and returned down the river. Three companies of city volunteers had marched from this District, in obedience to the call of General Winder, which he had halted at the Woodyard, and the detachments of the 36th and 38th regiments at Upper Marlborough; while he proceeded to Annapolis, to arrange with the Governor the calling out of the Maryland militia; which, he states, will be immediately attended to by the Governor. He states that he had called for the largest number directed by the President, viz: three thousand, expecting thereby to get two thousand, the lowest number; that he forebore to dismantle Fort Madison, as it might alarm the people, and produce disagreeable sensations; preferring rather to risk it in case of attack. On the 23d of July, General Winder informs the Secretary of War that the Governor of Maryland had issued his order for calling out three thousand of the draughts under the requisition of the 4th of July, and had appointed Bladensburg as the place of rendezvous according to his suggestion. In another letter of the same date, General Winder informs the Secretary of War that he had deemed it expedient to direct Captain Davidson, with the city volunteers, to return to the City of Washington; from the two-fold consideration that the facility with which they could turn out and proceed to any point, rendered them nearly as effective as if kept in the field, and the importance to them individually of attending to their private concerns. That the rifles used by Captain Doughty's company were very defective, and that Captain Burch's artillery were without swords. He recommends that the camp equipage should be left in charge of the company officers to facilitate their march. On the 25th of July, General Winder, in a letter to the Secretary of War, dated at Warburton, near Fort Washington, represents that fort, in several respects, to be incomplete in its preparation for defence; encloses a representation of Lieutenant Edwards on the subject; makes a requisition of ammunition, and requests that Colonel Wadsworth may cause the platform to be enlarged, so as to make the battery more effectual. The report of Lieutenant Edwards speaks of the necessity of mounting heavy artillery in the block-house; states that the eighteen pound columbiads were not mounted, and that the garrison wanted means to mount them, being destitute of gin and tackle; represents the width of the platform, which ought to be twenty-one feet, to be only fourteen, and that the heavy guns, at their first discharge, would recoil to the hartoirs, and on being heated would run over it; that five excellent long eighteens were mounted on the water battery, which would be very useful in case of attack; but there was not a single pound of ammunition for them, and that some of the gun carriages in the fort were quite out of order.

This statement of Lieutenant Edwards was referred, upon its receipt, to Colonel Wadsworth, with orders to supply what was wanting at the

Capture of the City of Washington.

fort, of which the Secretary advised General Winder, bearing date 28th July; and Colonel Wadsworth, in a representation, about the same date, states that two hands had been ordered from Greenleaf's Point, on the Monday previous, to execute the necessary repairs of the gun carriages; that the platform, as well as the parapet, was too narrow, but not so narrow as Lieutenant Edwards had stated, for it was directed to be made twenty or twenty-two feet wide; and that the disadvantage of too narrow a platform could be obviated with no great difficulty, by means of an elastic handspike introduced between the spokes of the wheels, which would prevent them from turning, and thus check the recoil of the piece. Further states, that two hundred rounds of shot and cartridges for the eighteens could be sent down if ordered; that he had long since directed some grape shot to be prepared for the eighteen-pound columbiads; that a tackle and fall to mount the guns in the block-house should be prepared; that Captain Marsteller had just informed him that a good tackle and fall were at the fort when he left it; and that the platform was upwards of twenty feet wide. General Winder, in a letter of the 26th of July, from Piscataway, advises the Secretary of War that the enemy had descended both the Potomac and Patuxent rivers; that he expected him up the bay; and should not be surprised to find Annapolis his object; which he feared would fall before five hundred men; and that he should return to Marlborough as soon as he could ascertain the movements of the enemy. On the 27th of July, General Winder, in two letters to the Secretary of War, from Piscataway, states the force under General Stewart at eight hundred; Colonel Beall's regiment, at Port Tobacco, from three hundred to three hundred and fifty infantry, and forty dragoons; Colonel Bowen's regiment, at Nottingham, at three hundred; and the detachment of regulars, under command of Lieutenant Colonel Scott, was also at Nottingham; and from General Winder's letter to the Secretary of War, of the first of August, from Port Tobacco, it appears that he had the detachment under Lieutenant Colonel Scott at Piscataway.

Correspondence of General Winder with the Governor of Pennsylvania.

In relation to the quota of Pennsylvania, under the requisition of the 4th of July, and more especially as it regards the five thousand men subject to the call of General Winder, and assigned to his command, it appears that General Winder wrote to the Governor of Pennsylvania, on the 6th of August, advising him that the Secretary of War had destined a part of that quota to act under his command, in defending the country, embraced in the 10th military district, and requesting that he might be informed of the place, or places, of rendezvous, which would be fixed for such troops, and recommending places most contiguous to the cities of Washington and Baltimore. On the 8th of August, General Winder writes again to the Governor of Pennsylvania,

stating that, since his first communication, he had read a letter from the Secretary of War, dated July the 17th, which had not reached him at an earlier period, in consequence of his having been in constant motion since that time; which informed him that, of the quota of militia of Pennsylvania, under the requisition of the 4th of July, five thousand were destined for the 10th military district, subject to his call as commanding officer, and requested that as great a proportion of the detachment as possible should be riflemen.

On the 11th of August, Secretary Boileau, under the direction of the Governor of Pennsylvania, in answer to General Winder, states that, in consequence of the deranged state of the militia system, great difficulties occurred to the Executive, in relation to the quota required to be held in readiness for the service of the United States. The only effort that could be made towards a compliance with the requisition, was to have ordered a designation for the service of the requisite troops, under the militia law of 1807, and before the expiration of that law; which order had been issued by the Governor, and was in a course of execution; that the militia law of 1807 expired on the first of August, and that all commissions under it became void, except of such officers as might be in service on that day; and that, by an oversight in the Legislature, no complete organization of the militia could be legally made in Pennsylvania, until the fourth Monday in October, when a classification was to take place.

On the 17th of August, General Winder makes a requisition on the Governor of Pennsylvania for one regiment, to march forthwith to the City of Washington; and, on the day following, in consequence of large reinforcements of the enemy in the mouth of the Patuxent, he calls for the whole five thousand Pennsylvania militia, by virtue of his previous authority. The five thousand were ordered out, to rendezvous at York, Pennsylvania, on the fifth of September; of course, not in time to give any aid on the occasion for which they were called; nor was General Winder's letter of the 18th received by the Governor of Pennsylvania until the evening of the twenty-third.

Correspondence of the Secretary of War and General Winder.

On the 13th of August, General Winder, in a letter to the Secretary of War, states that, in consequence of the acceptance of the 2d regiment draughted from General Smith's division, under the requisition of April, for part of the requisition of the 4th of July, the impracticability, besides impropriety, of calling any portion of the draughted militia from the Eastern Shore of Maryland, and the necessity of leaving all the men, immediately upon the bay, and low down on the rivers of the Western Shore, for local defence; the remaining portion of the Maryland draughts to be assembled at Bladensburg, instead of being three thousand, would not much exceed as many hundred; yet, he would require the Governor to order out all the draughts that could possibly be spared from the three lower brigades, on the Western Shore; but as the whole number draughted on the Western Shore, exclusive of the brigade drawn from General Smith's division, did not amount to fifteen hundred men, he did not expect more than one thousand under the second order of the Government, that of the 4th of July. The most immediate and convenient resource to supply this deficiency was to take the militia drawn out under the State authority, and assembled at Annapolis, to the amount of one thousand, into the service of the United States, and to call on Pennsylvania for one regiment, which would make his militia between two and three thousand men, besides two regiments from General Smith's division.

In answer to this letter, the Secretary of War, in a letter of the 16th of August, authorizes General Winder to take into the service of the United States the Maryland militia, then at Annapolis, or elsewhere, that had been called out under the State authority, as part of the quota required by the order of the 4th of July.

Correspondence of the Secretary of War with the Governors of Maryland, Pennsylvania, and Virginia.

On the 27th of July the Governor of Maryland states, in a letter to the Secretary of War, that, in conformity to the request of the President of the United States, communicated in the requisition of the fourth, a detachment of 5,500 infantry and six hundred artillery was directed to be organized and held in readiness to move at the shortest notice; and, in order to comply with the requisition of General Winder, for calling into the field three thousand draughts of the Maryland militia, by direction of the President, the whole of the draughts from the Western Shore, about three thousand five hundred infantry, had been ordered to embody. He speaks of the exposed situation of the Western Shore, bordering upon the bay, and presumes that the draughts from that section of the country would not be drawn away, and expects Baltimore will be unwilling to have any force withdrawn from that place, by which any aid might be expected. These considerations had induced the order for the three thousand five hundred men; this force was to be embodied, and moved on the shortest route to Bladensburg; that the artillery of the State was about nine hundred men, two-thirds in Baltimore; it would create uneasiness to take from that place four hundred, the proportion, and he had suspended that order until General Smith should have some communication with the Secretary of War. In a letter of the 20th of July, General Winder made the requisition on the Governor of Maryland for the three thousand militia, urging the necessity of having them assembled and in service with the least possible delay; and, on the 5th of August, the Governor of Maryland informed General Winder, by letter, that his demand for three thousand draughts could not be complied with without the brigade in service at Baltimore, from General Smith's divisions; that

the draughts from one brigade alone were under marching orders; the orders for the march of those lying on the Chesapeake and Potomac having been suspended.

On the 14th of July Mr. Boileau, Secretary of State for Pennsylvania, acknowledges the receipt of the communication from the War Department, containing the requisition of the 14th of July, for fourteen thousand Pennsylvania militia, which was forwarded by express to the Governor, who was absent; at Selin's Grove, with assurances that the Governor would execute, with promptness, the requisition of the General Government. On the 25th the Governor of Pennsylvania directs the Secretary Boileau to inform the Secretary of War that general orders had been issued in compliance with the requisition of the 4th of July; explains, as before, the difficulties resulting from the militia laws of Pennsylvania, and relies on the patriotism and voluntary services of the people.

On the 14th of July the Deputy Adjutant General of Virginia acknowledged the receipt of the communication from the War Department, containing the requisition of the 4th, and enclosed to the Secretary of War the general orders issued by the Governor of Virginia, on the 22d of June, placing in readiness a provisional force of fifteen thousand men and upwards, to repel sudden invasions, and for the purpose of defence, and the points of rendezvous designated, but not organized upon the Military Establishment of the United States, nor for a longer term than three months; which, with other considerations, prevented the acceptance of any part of those State troops, as a compliance with the requisition of the General Government. The Secretary of War was apprized in this letter, also, that the whole of the Virginia troops, then held in readiness, would be furnished with arms and ammunition by the State of Virginia; and on the 18th, the Secretary of War informs the Governor of Virginia that two thousand of the requisition upon the Virginia militia would be placed at the disposition of General Winder, as commander of the 10th military district.

Having presented a condensed view of the measures of the Cabinet; the correspondence between the Commanding officer and the War Department, the Governors of Pennsylvania and Maryland, and the Commanding General; the correspondence with the Governors of Pennsylvania, Maryland, and Virginia, and the Secretary of War, in regard to the requisition of the 4th of July; it will now be proper to present some facts connected with the movements and arrangements of the Commanding General up to the revocation of his command.

Towards the close of the month of June, the Secretary of War gave to General Winder the first intimation that it was in contemplation to constitute a new military district, embracing the country now composing the 10th military district, and that the President intended to invest him with its command. On the 4th or 5th July, he received notice of his appointment to the 10th military district, and the order creating it; proceeded to Washington, and called on the Secretary of War, who enumerated the regular force, as before supposed, to amount to one thousand or one thousand two hundred; the residue of his command to be composed of militia to be draughted, and was shown the circular to certain States making the requisition of the 4th. He then returned to Baltimore, and after writing the letter of the 9th, proceeded to Annapolis, to examine it, and to explore the 10th military district generally. The letter of the 12th, from the Secretary of War, was not received until he went to Annapolis, to Upper Marlborough, and back to Annapolis. On the 17th, at Nottingham, received intelligence that the enemy was proceeding up the Patuxent; wrote to the Secretary of War, and to General West, advising him to call out the militia of the county. The detachment of the 36th and 38th regiments was ordered from South River to Nottingham, and three companies of city militia were despatched to him promptly. On the 25th, visited Fort Washington; and on the 1st of August, fixed his permanent headquarters at the City of Washington; viewed and inspected the District militia. The people of St. Mary's and Charles had become importunate for aid and protection, and in obedience to the wish of the President, the 36th and 38th were ordered down to unite with General Stewart; but the enemy having retired, this detachment was encamped at Piscataway. He understood by letters from General Smith, of Baltimore, and the Governor of Maryland, that Stansbury's brigade, upon application of General Smith, had been accepted by the Secretary of War as part of the quota of Maryland militia, under requisition of the 4th of July. On the morning of the 18th of August, Thursday, intelligence was received from the observatory at Point Lookout, that on the morning of the 17th, the enemy's fleet off that place had been reinforced by a formidable squadron of ships and vessels of various sizes. The Commanding General immediately made requisitions on the Governors of Pennsylvania and Maryland; various officers of militia, and the militia of the District of Columbia, were ordered out *en masse.*

On the 19th, General Winder, in a letter to the Secretary of War, submitted several propositions to the President: 1st. Would it be expedient, under the direction of the Navy Department, to have vessels ready to be sunk in the Potomac, at Fort Washington, or other points, at a moment's warning, to obstruct the navigation? 2d. Would it not be proper to put all the boats which can be propelled by oars that are at the City of Washington, under the control of the navy at Fort Washington, to transport troops as events may require? 3d. Would it not be convenient to put the marine corps into service? at all events, to cause them to be in readiness to reinforce Fort Washington at a moment's notice, or to be applied, as events require, to any point of defence? 4th. That the force under Commodore Barney may co-operate with the Commanding General, in case of the abandonment of the flotilla. On the same day, the Secretary of War

in a letter states, that the propositions had been submitted to the President, and General Winder is referred to the Navy Department on the subject of the propositions relating to the means in that department. General Winder's call upon the militia *en masse* is approved; and, on the same day, the Secretary of War, in a letter to General Winder, advises that the cavalry be pushed into the neighborhood of the enemy without delay, if he indicated an attack upon the City of Washington, for the purpose of driving off all horses and cattle, and all supplies of forage, &c., in their route. Not a moment was to be lost. Colonel Monroe, with Captain Thornton's troop of horse, proceeded to find and reconnoitre the enemy on Friday, the 19th; on the same day the militia of Georgetown and the City of Washington, under General Smith, were mustered. On Saturday, the 20th, this and some other forces commenced their line of march towards Benedict, about 1 o'clock, and encamped that night about four miles from the Eastern Branch bridge, on the road to Upper Marlborough. On this day Colonel Monroe communicated the intelligence of the arrival of the enemy at Benedict in force. Same day, Colonel Tilghman and Captain Caldwell, with their commands of horse, were ordered and despatched to annoy the enemy, *impede his* march, to remove and destroy forage and provisions before the enemy.

On Sunday morning, the 21st, the troops were mustered, and the articles of war read to them. At 12 o'clock, the marines under Captain Miller joined the army; the regulars of the 36th and 38th also joined at the Woodyard, seven miles in advance, to which the main body of our troops were marched and encamped on Sunday night. Two letters from Colonel Monroe, on the 21st, one stating that he had viewed the enemy near Benedict, enumerated twenty-seven square rigged vessels, some bay craft and barges; the other dated from Nottingham, stating the advance of the enemy upon that place by land and water, and recommending the Commanding General to despatch five hundred or six hundred men to fall upon the enemy. Colonel Monroe and Colonel Beall both joined the army at night, and gave an account that the enemy had been viewed by them. Colonel Beall calculated that he had seen four thousand, without supposing he had seen all. Colonel Monroe estimated the enemy at about six thousand; Captain Herbert joins with *his* troop; Colonel Lavall had joined with two companies of cavalry on the day previous; the enemy remained at Nottingham, except an advance detachment about three miles from town. Monday, the 22d, early in the morning, a light detachment was ordered to meet the enemy, composed of the 36th and 38th—Lieutenant Colonel Scott, Colonel Lavall's cavalry, and three companies from the brigade of General Smith, under command of Major Peter, viz: his own company of artillery, Captain Stull's rifle corps, and Captain Davidson's light infantry. This detachment marched on the road to Nottingham, about 9 o'clock; the remainder of the army marched about one mile

Capture of the City of Washington.

in advance, to an elevated position; the Commanding General with his staff, accompanied by Colonel Monroe, proceeded in advance to reconnoitre the march of the enemy. Commodore Barney had joined the army with his flotilla men, besides the marines under Captain Miller; the horse preceded the advance detachment of our forces, met the enemy, and retired before them. This induced the advance corps to take a position to impede the march of the enemy; but the advance detachment was ordered to retrograde and join the main body of the army that had remained some hours in line of battle, expecting the enemy to come that route to the city, but who took the road to Upper Marlborough, turning to his right after having come within a few miles of our forces; upon which the Commanding General fell back with his whole forces to the Battalion Old Fields, about eight miles from Marlborough, and the same distance from the City of Washington. At this time heavy explosions in the direction of Marlborough announced the destruction of the flotilla under command of Commodore Barney. The enemy arrived at Upper Marlborough about 2 o'clock, and remained there until late next day, to be joined, it is presumed, by the detachment of the enemy which had been sent against the flotilla.

The Commanding General proceeded to Marlborough and found the enemy encamped; several prisoners taken; gave information that the enemy would remain in that position until next day; and after making observations of the enemy till the close of the day, General Winder returned to the army. Late in the evening of this day, the President, with the Secretaries of War and Navy, and the Attorney General, joined General Winder at the Battalion Old Fields, and remained with him till the evening of the 23d. In the morning the troops were drawn up and reviewed by the President. The most contradictory reports prevailed as to the movements and force of the enemy, and it was doubtful in camp whether Annapolis, Fort Washington—with a view to co-operate with his naval forces—or the City of Washington, was his object. As to numbers, rumors vibrated from four thousand to twelve thousand; the best opinion was from five to seven thousand. Our forces at this time at the Old Fields are variously estimated, with no material difference, at about three thousand men, in the following corps: About four hundred horse, under the command of the following officers: Lieutenant Colonel Lavall, Colonel Tilghman, Captains Caldwell, Thornton, Herbert, Williams, &c.; four hundred regular troops, under the command of Lieutenant Colonel Scott, viz: 36th, 38th, and Captain Morgan's company of the 12th infantry; six hundred marines and flotilla men under Commodore Barney and Captain Miller, with five pieces of heavy artillery, two eighteen pounders, and three twelve pounders; one thousand eight hundred militia and volunteers, Gen. Smith's brigade of Georgetown and city militia, and Maryland militia under Colonel Kramer; of which there were two companies of artillery

under Captain Burch and Major Peter, with six six-pounders each, making an aggregate of three thousand two hundred, with seventeen pieces of artillery. The enemy was without cavalry, and had two small field pieces and one howitzer, drawn by men; and the whole country well calculated for defence, skirmishing, and to impede the march of an enemy.

The enemy remained at Upper Marlborough till after 12 o'clock, about which time General Winder again ordered the detachment under Lieutenant Colonel Scott and Major Peter to advance and meet the enemy if he should be found advancing, or to attack his positions.—About this time, 12 o'clock, some prisoners were taken, and from the information given by them, and the observations of the videttes, General Winder was induced to believe that the enemy intended to remain stationary for the day, which induced him to think of uniting with him the forces at Bladensburg, and he despatched orders to General Stansbury, and other corps at Bladensburg, to move direct for Upper Marlborough, and proceeded himself towards Bladensburg to meet and hurry on the forces to form a junction. When General Winder left the command with General Smith, and proceeded towards Bladensburg with several troops of cavalry, he left orders that the advance corps should march upon the enemy, and annoy him by all possible means if in march, or if not, then in his positions; and if he advanced upon Bladensburg, General Smith, with the main body, should fall upon his flank, or be governed by circumstances in other movements.

Captain Caldwell joined the advance corps at 2 o'clock, P. M. An express brought intelligence that the enemy had left Upper Marlborough; that our advance had met the enemy about six miles in advance of our forces, and after a skirmish, in which Captain Stull's company had about four or five rounds, was compelled to retreat, and that the enemy was advancing. One of the Aids of General Smith was despatched for General Winder; the whole army was placed in a favorable attitude of defence, in which position it continued until about sunset, when General Winder, who had arrived some time previous, ordered the army to march to the City of Washington. The enemy was about three miles distant, and remained there that night. Having remained till the going down of the sun, the retreat to the city was induced by several considerations, stated by the Commanding General. 1st. To effect a union of his whole forces. 2d. The fear of a night attack, from the superiority of the enemy, and want of discipline in his troops. And, 3d. In a night attack his superiority in artillery could not be used. The march of our army to the city was extremely rapid and precipitate, and orders occasionally given to captains of companies to hurry on the men, who were extremely fatigued and exhausted before the camping ground was reached, near the Eastern Branch bridge, within the District of Columbia.

General Stansbury had arrived at Bladensburg

Capture of the City of Washington.

on the 22d, and the 5th Baltimore regiment, including the artillery and rifle corps, on the evening of the 23d; and, at 12 o'clock at night, Colonel Monroe, in passing through Bladensburg to the City of Washington, advised General Stansbury to fall upon the rear of the enemy forthwith, as it was understood that he was in motion for the city. General Stansbury having been ordered to take post at Bladensburg, did not think he was at liberty to leave it; but, independent of this consideration, the fatigue of the troops under Colonel Sterret made it impracticable.

It is here proper to state, that, on the 22d, the Secretary of War, in a letter to General Winder, which closes their written communications previous to the 24th, except a short note of that morning, states that he had ordered Gen. Douglas to march with his command to the District, without seeking a rendezvous with General Hungerford; that a detachment of the 12th infantry had arrived; that it should be armed, equipped, and march to the Woodyard; that the Baltimore brigade would arrive at Bladensburg that day, and suggests the propriety of throwing Barney's seamen and some other troops on the right of Nottingham—a demonstration which would menace the rear of the enemy, and his communication with his shipping, which would, if not stop, much retard his progress. On the morning of the 24th, in a short note to the Secretary of War, General Winder says, the information up the river is threatening; Barney, or some other force, should occupy the batteries at Greenleaf's Point and Navy Yard, and wishes counsel from the Government or the Secretary of War. Upon this note there is an endorsement in the handwriting of General Armstrong to this effect: "Went to General Winder, saw no necessity for ordering Barney to Greenleaf's Point or Navy Yard, advised the Commodore to join the army at Bladensburg, and ordered Minor's regiment to that place."

On the 21st, late at night, Colonel Tayloe arrived in the city from the Northern Neck, where he had been charged with orders in relation to the Virginia draughts, and reported himself to General Armstrong, who issued the following general order:

"WAR DEPARTMENT,
August 22, 1814.——12 o'clock.
" General Order:

"General Douglass will assemble his brigade at Alexandria, and hold it there subject to orders.
"JOHN ARMSTRONG."

Colonel Tayloe executed this order, and Tuesday night, the 23d, again reported himself to General Armstrong, who issued the following orders:

" General Order: "WAR DEPARTMENT.

"Lieutenant Colonel Minor will repair to Washington, with the regiment under his command, with the utmost despatch. He will report on his arrival to Colonel Carbery of the 36th regiment, and make a requisition for arms and ammunition.   "JOHN ARMSTRONG."

"WAR DEPARTMENT, *Aug.* 23, 1814.
" General Order:

"All the militia now in and marching to Alexandria, besides Colonel Minor, will march immediately to Washington. These orders will be communicated by Colonel Tayloe.
"JOHN ARMSTRONG."

On the 18th of August, General Van Ness ordered General Young to call out, *en masse*, the brigade under his command, including the Alexandria militia; the same day, two troops of cavalry, attached to the brigade, were ordered to rendezvous at Bladensburg; on the 19th, at four o'clock in the morning, to accompany Colonel Monroe, Secretary of State, and to be subject to his order. On the 20th, in the afternoon, Gen. Young's brigade was ordered by General Winder to cross the Potomac, opposite Alexandria, and encamp in the best position, and wait further orders, which was effected—the brigade consisting of four hundred and fifty-four men, two brass six-pounders and one brass four-pounder. On the 22d, early, General Young, by order of General Winder, marched his brigade and took a position on a height near the head of Piscataway creek, about three miles in the rear of Fort Washington, where the ground was favorable for a small detachment to defend the country against a much greater force, and remained in this position until the morning of the 24th, when several orders were given to him; first, to march towards the Eastern Branch bridge; second, to cross the Potomac to the Virginia side, &c. This brigade was intended, in its dispositions, to aid Fort Washington, the town of Alexandria, and to be in a situation to join General Winder.

On the morning of the 24th, General Winder established his headquarters near the Eastern Branch bridge; detachments of horse were out in various directions as videttes, and reconnoitering parties, and arrangements made to destroy the Eastern Branch bridge. Colonel George Minor, with his regiment of Virginia militia, composed of six hundred infantry and one hundred cavalry, arrived at the City of Washington in the twilight of the evening of the 23d: he called on the President, who referred him to the Secretary of War for orders; the Secretary informed him that arms could not be had that night, but gave orders to report himself to Colonel Carbery early in the morning, who would furnish him with arms and ammunition, as he was charged with that duty by General Winder. From early in the morning till late in the forenoon Colonel Minor sought Colonel Carbery diligently, but he could not be found. He rode to headquarters and obtained an order from General Winder upon the arsenal for arms, &c., marched to the place with his regiment, and its care he found committed to a young man, whose caution in giving out arms, &c., very much delayed the arming and supplying this regiment. As instance is here given, when the flints were counted out by the officers of the regiment, to expedite business at this crisis, the young man would count them over before they could be obtained. Colonel Carbery arrived at this moment, apologized for his absence, and informed Col. Minor that he had the evening previous ridden out to his country seat. Colonel Minor was again delayed some small length of time, in having to remain to sign receipts, &c. His men were ordered to Capitol Hill. In the meantime, various reports were brought into headquarters, as to the movements and intentions of the enemy. The President and Heads of Departments collected at headquarters in the following order: The President, next Secretary of State, next the Attorney General, next the Secretary of the Navy, and last the Secretary of War and Treasury together. Colonel Monroe had left headquarters, upon a rumor, that gained ground, that the enemy was marching upon the city by way of Bladensburg, with a view of joining General Stansbury, advising him of the rumor, and to aid him in the formation of a line of battle to meet the enemy. General Stansbury, for reasons given in his report, had marched from his position in advance of Bladensburg, and occupied the ground west of that village, on the banks of the Eastern Branch. Here the front line of battle was formed by General Stansbury and his officers, with the aid of Colonel Monroe, on the presumption that General Stansbury's brigade and the command of Colonel Sterret included the command of Major Pinkney and Baltimore artillery.

There is a bridge over the Eastern Branch at Bladensburg, and a large turnpike road leading direct to the City of Washington. About four hundred yards from this bridge, some small distance to the left of the road, the Baltimore artillery, six pieces of six pounders, occupied a temporary breast-work of earth, well calculated to command the pass over the bridge. Part of the battalion of riflemen, under Major William Pinkney, and one other company, took position on the right of the artillery, partially protected by a fence and brush; and on the left of the battery, leading to the rear of a barn, two companies, from the regiment under Colonel Shutz, and the other part of the riflemen from Baltimore. Colonel Ragan was posted in the rear of Major Pinkney, his right resting on the road; Colonel Shutz, continuing the line on the left, with a small vacancy in the centre of the two regiments; and Colonel Sterret formed the extreme left flank of the infantry. At this moment, Colonels Beall and Hood entered Bladensburg, with the Maryland militia from Annapolis, crossed the bridge, and took a position on a most commanding height, on the right of the turnpike, about three hundred yards from the road, to secure the right flank. In the meantime, (about eleven o'clock) certain intelligence was received at headquarters, that the enemy was in full march towards Bladensburg; which induced General Winder to put in motion his whole force, except a few men and a piece of artillery left at the Eastern Branch bridge, to destroy it. The day was hot, and the road was dusty—the march was rapid to Bladensburg. The cavalry and

mounted men arrived, and were placed on the left flank, and some small distance in its rear. General Winder now arrived, and told General Stansbury and Colonel Monroe that his whole force was marching for Bladensburg, and approved the dispositions which had been made of the troops; at which moment, it had become impracticable, in the opinion of the officers, to make any essential change: for the two armies were now coming to the battle ground, in opposite directions; and the enemy appeared on the opposite heights at Bladensburg, about a mile distant, and halted fifteen or twenty minutes. This was about twelve o'clock. The troops from the city were disposed of as they arrived. Captain Burch, with three pieces of artillery, was stationed on the extreme left of the infantry of the first line; and a rifle company, armed with muskets, near the battery, to support it. About this time the Secretary of War arrived, and in a few moments after, the President and the Attorney General, and proceeded to examine the disposition of the troops. In the meantime, as the enemy advanced into Bladensburg, the officers were forming rapidly the second line. The command of Commodore Barney came up in a trot; and formed his men on the right of the main road, in a line with the command under Colonels Beall and Hood, with a considerable vacancy, owing to the ground. The heavy artillery, Commodore Barney planted in the road; the three twelve pounders to the right, under Captain Miller, who commanded the flotilla men and marines, as infantry, to support the artillery. Lieutenant Colonel Kramer, with a battalion of Maryland militia, was posted in the wood, in advance of the marines and Colonels Beall and Hood's command. The regiment under command of Colonel Magruder, was stationed on the left of Commodore Barney, and in a line with him and Colonel Beall. The regiment under command of Colonel Brent, and Major Warring's battalion, and some other small detachments, formed the left flank of this second line, and in the rear of Major Peter's battery; and Lieutenant Colonel Scott, with the regulars, was placed in advance of Colonel Magruder, and to the left, forming a line towards Major Peter's battery, but in such a manner as not to mask it; other small detachments in various directions.

About half-past twelve o'clock, while the second line was thus forming, the enemy approached, and the battle commenced. The Baltimore artillery opened a fire and dispersed the enemy's light troops now advancing along the street of the village, who took a temporary cover behind the houses and trees, in loose order, and presented objects only occasionally for the fire of the cannon. The enemy commenced throwing his rockets, and his light troops began to concentrate near the bridge, and to press across it and the river, which was fordable above. The battalion of riflemen, under Major Pinkney, now united gallantly with the fire from the battery. For some minutes the fire was continued with considerable effect; the enemy's column was not only dispersed while in the street, but while approaching the bridge they were thrown into some confusion, and the British officers were seen exerting themselves to press the soldiers on. Having now gained the bridge, it was passed rapidly, and as the enemy crossed, flanked, formed a line, and advanced steadily on, which compelled the artillery and battalion of riflemen to give way, after which Major Pinkney was severely wounded. He exerted himself to rally his men, and succeeded, at a small distance in the rear of his first position, and united with the fifth Baltimore regiment.

It appears from reports of several officers, Stansbury, Pinkney, Law. Sterret, &c., that the command of General Stansbury was three .or four hundred yards in the rear of the battery, and Major Pinkney's riflemen and some other small corps to the left of the battery; of course this small party had to fight with the whole force of the enemy until they retired, and the enemy occupied the ground they left without any considerable resistance, as the enemy marched on without halting after the bridge was passed. Captain Burch and Colonel Sterret were about the same distance, when Colonel Sterret was ordered to advance to support the first line. One of the pieces of artillery was abandoned, but spiked previously. The enemy soon took advantage of the trees of an orchard, which was occupied or held by the force which had just retreated, and kept up a galling fire on part of our line. Captain Burch's artillery, and a small detachment near it, now opened a cross fire upon the enemy. Colonel Sterret, with the fifth Baltimore regiment, was ordered to advance, and made a prompt movement, until ordered to halt, as at this moment the rockets assuming a more horizontal direction, and passing near the heads of Colonel Shutz and Ragan's regiments, the right gave way, which was followed in a few minutes by a general flight of the two regiments, in defiance of all the exertions of General Winder, Stansbury, and other officers. Burch's artillery and the 5th regiment remained with firmness; the orchard obstructed their fire; but notwithstanding the enemy's light troops were, for a moment, driven back by them, the enemy having gained the right flank of the fifth, which exposed it, Burch's artillery and Colonel Sterret, who commanded the fifth, were ordered by General Winder to retreat, with a view of forming at a small distance in the rear; but instead of retiring in order, the fifth, like the two other regiments under General Stansbury, in a very few minutes were retreating in disorder and confusion, notwithstanding the exertions of Colonel Sterret to prevent it. From reports of various officers, exertions were made to rally the men and to bring them again to the battle, which partly succeeded in the first instance, but ultimately, and in a short time, all attempts were vain, and the forces routed; and the first line, together with the horse, were totally routed, and retreated in a road which forked in three directions; one branch led by Rock Creek Church, to Tenleytown and Montgomery Court-house, another led to Georgetown, and a third to the City of Washington. It does not appear that any movement was made or attempted

by the cavalry or horsemen, although the enemy to the left were in open and scattered order, as they pursued or pressed upon our lines, and a most fortunate moment presented itself for a charge of cavalry and horsemen.

It may be proper here to observe that General Winder states his exertions to direct the retreating line to the Capitol, with a view of rallying. This intention is corroborated by Colonel Sterret; but it appears as if this determination was not generally understood by the officers or men. Colonel Kramer, posted on the right of the road, and in advance of Commodore Barney, was next drawn from his position, after having maintained his ground with considerable injury to the enemy, and retreated upon the command of Colonels Beall and Hood, on a commanding eminence to the right. After the retreat of the militia under Colonel Kramer, from his first position, the enemy's column in the road was exposed to an animated discharge from Major Peter's artillery, which continued until they came into contact with Commodore Barney; here the enemy met the greatest resistance, and sustained the greatest loss, advancing upon our retreating line. When the enemy came in full view, and in a heavy column in the main road, Commodore Barney ordered an eighteen pounder to be opened upon them, which completely cleared the road, scattered, and repulsed the enemy for a moment. In several attempts to rally and advance, the enemy was repulsed, which induced him to flank to the right of our lines in an open field. Here Captain Miller opened upon him with the three twelve pounders, and the flotilla men, acting as infantry, with considerable effect. The enemy continued flanking to the right, and pressed upon the command of Colonels Beall and Hood, who gave way, after three or four rounds of ineffectual fire, at a considerable distance from the enemy, while Colonel Beall and other officers attempted to rally the men on this high position. The enemy very soon gained the flank and even the rear of the right of the second line. Commodore Barney, Captain Miller, and some other officers of his command, being wounded, his ammunition wagons having gone off in the disorder, and that which the marines and flotilla men had being exhausted; in this situation, a retreat was ordered by Commodore Barney, who fell himself into the hands of the enemy.

The second line was not exactly connected, but posted in advantageous positions in connexion with and supporting each other. The command of General Smith, including the Georgetown and city militia, still remained in order, and firm, without any part of them having given way, as well as the command of Lieutenant Colonel Scott of the regulars, and some other corps. The enemy's light troops had, in the meantime, advanced on the left of the road, and had gained a line parallel with Smith's command, and, in endeavoring to turn the flank, Colonel Brent was placed in a position calculated to prevent it; the enemy also advanced and came within long shot of part of Colonel Magruder's command, which opened a partial fire, but without much effect; and, at this moment, and in this situation, General Winder ordered the whole of the troops, then stationary, to retreat, which was effected with as much order as the nature of the ground and the occasion would permit; these troops, after retreating five or six hundred paces, were halted and formed, but were again ordered to retreat by General Winder. General Winder then gave orders to collect and form the troops on the heights west of the turnpike gate, about a mile and a half from the Capitol, which order was in part executed, and the forces formed by General Smith and the other officers, when Colonel George Minor came up with his regiment of Virginia volunteers, and united his forces with General Smith's command, having been detained, as before stated, in obtaining arms, ammunition, &c.; but, while in the act of forming, General Winder gave orders to retire to the Capitol, with the expectation of being united with the troops of the first line. Colonel Minor was ordered to take a certain position and disposition, and cover the retreat of all the forces by remaining until all had marched for the Capitol. The troops were again halted at the Capitol while General Winder was in conference with Colonel Monroe and General Armstrong.

The first line and cavalry, except one troop of Colonel Lavall's, had taken a route which did not bring them to the Capitol; the most of them had proceeded north of the District of Columbia, and others dispersed and returned home, and sought refreshment in the country. The Commanding General represented the diminution of his force, the dispersion of a large portion of it, the want of discipline, the great fatigue of the troops, and believed that it would be impossible to make effectual resistance to the invasion of the city; nor did he think it would be proper to attempt to defend the Capitol, the troops being without provisions, and which would leave every other part of the city to the mercy of the enemy, and the prospect of losing his army. In this consultation, the Secretaries of State and War, it appears, concurred in their views with General Winder, and advised him to retire and rally the troops upon the heights of Georgetown; this produced an order for the whole force to retreat from Capitol Hill through Georgetown. On receiving this order, the troops evinced the deepest anguish, and that order which had been previously maintained was destroyed. General Smith in his report uses this language: "when the order for a retreat from Capitol Hill was received, the troops evinced an anguish beyond the power of language to express." The troops were halted at Tenleytown, and an attempt was made to collect them together, which only partially succeeded. Some returned home, some went in pursuit of refreshments, and those that halted gave themselves up to the uncontrolled feelings which fatigue, exhaustion, privation, and disappointment, produced. The force thus collected were marched about five miles up the Potomac, and, early in the morning, Thursday the 25th, orders were given to assemble the troops at Montgomery Courthouse. General Winder seems to have taken this position with a view to collect

his forces, and to interpose for the protection of Baltimore, in case the enemy marched upon it as was anticipated by him. On the 23d, General Winder despatched an order to the commanding officer at Fort Washington to place patrols on every road leading to the garrison; and, upon the event of his being taken in the rear of the fort, to blow it up and retire across the river. On the 26th, the army at Montgomery took up the line of march about ten o'clock towards Baltimore: General Winder proceeded on to Baltimore. On the 27th, General Smith's brigade marched to this District.

The distance from Benedict to the City of Washington, by Bladensburg, is upwards of fifty miles. The enemy was without baggage wagons or means of transportation; his troops much exhausted with fatigue; many compelled to quit the ranks, and extraordinary exertions used to keep others in motion; and, as if unable to pursue our forces, remained on the battle ground; the enemy's advance reached the city about eight o'clock in the evening, the battle having ended about two o'clock, or before. The main body of the enemy remained on the heights west of the turnpike gate.

Doctor Catlett, the superintending surgeon, who was admitted to attend upon the wounded, and who passed through the enemy's camp, and remained at Bladensburg until the city was evacuated, had the best opportunity of estimating the loss on both sides, as well as a good opportunity to ascertain the number and force of the enemy. His estimate is as follows:

Of the enemy.—On Capitol Hill, seven hundred; Turnpike Hill, two thousand; wounded at Bladensburg, three hundred; attendants, three hundred; wounded and attendants in the City of Washington, sixty; killed at Bladensburg and the city, one hundred and eighty; total force, three thousand five hundred and forty. This statement is corroborated by all the information in his power, besides his own observations. Mr. Law estimated the enemy, on its march, at five thousand; but, from the best information, his estimate would be about four thousand five hundred. Colonel Monroe, who viewed the enemy on his march, estimated the number at about six thousand. General Winder states that the best opinion at the Woodyard made the enemy from five to seven thousand. Our forces are variously estimated; and, indeed, from the manner of collecting them, and their dispersion, makes it difficult to ascertain the number with perfect accuracy. General Stansbury represents Colonel Ragan's regiment at five hundred and fifty; Colonel Shutz's regiment at eight hundred; Colonels Beall's and Hood's at eight hundred; Colonel Sterret's regiment at five hundred; Major Pinkney's command, including two companies of artillery, three hundred; making two thousand nine hundred and fifty-three; but General Winder estimates Colonel Beall six or seven hundred; deduct one hundred, this leaves two thousand eight hundred and fifty-three; to which add the command of General Smith, and militia that united with him at the Woodyard, Battalion Old Fields, &c., the regulars under Lieutenant Colonel Scott, Barney's command, the cavalry, &c., three thousand two hundred; making an aggregate number of six thousand and fifty-three. Besides this force, several detachments are spoken of by General Winder's officers, not known, amounting to several hundred. But as a small detachment was left at the Eastern Branch bridge, others, particularly some of the cavalry, were on detachment, reconnoitering, &c., the number of forces, may be estimated at least at six thousand, including about twenty pieces of artillery, two eighteen pounders, three twelves, and the balance six pounders. Our loss on the field of battle, killed, is estimated by the superintending surgeon at ten or twelve, and the wounded, some of whom died, at about thirty. General Winder's official report estimates our loss at about thirty killed and fifty wounded.

The probable estimate of British forces on the 24th of August, total four thousand five hundred; killed at Bladensburg and in the city, one hundred and fifty; wounded at both places, three hundred. American forces, six thousand; killed, twenty, wounded forty; besides the regiment under command of Colonel Minor, six hundred infantry and one hundred horse, which met the retreat on the west of the turnpike gate; and General Young's brigade about five hundred, which was ordered to remain on the banks of the Potomac, about twelve miles from the City of Washington, until the evening of the 24th, when he crossed over to Alexandria, and proceeded to Montgomery Courthouse, to join the main army.

The enemy, on the evening of the 25th, made the greatest exertions to leave the City of Washington. They had about forty indifferent looking horses, ten or twelve carts and wagons, one ox cart, one coach, and several gigs; these were sent to Bladensburg to move off the wounded: a drove of sixty or seventy cattle preceded this party. Arriving at Bladensburg, the British surgeon was ordered to select the wounded who could walk; the forty horses were mounted by those who could ride; the carts and wagons loaded, and upwards of ninety wounded left behind. About twelve o'clock at night the British army passed through Bladensburg, and parties continued until morning, and stragglers until after mid-day. The retreat of the enemy to his shipping was precipitate, and apparently under an alarm, and, it is supposed, that it was known to him that our forces had marched to Montgomery Court-house.

The Hon. Richard Rush, General Stansbury, Major William Pinkney, Dr. Catlett, and Mr. Law, all remark, that General Winder was active and zealous, encouraged the men, and exposed himself, and acted as a man of firmness during the engagement, and endeavored to rally, with other officers, the lines, as they gave way.

There seems to be a general concurrence of statement, that our forces were much fatigued and worn down with marching, counter-marching, and their strength much exhausted, during their service, by remaining under arms much of the night, as well as the day, by false alarms, and otherwise. Nor does it appear that it was generally known among the officers and men of the first line, that the forces from the city were formed behind in the second line, to meet the enemy and support them. This statement is made by General Stansbury, Major William Pinkney, and some other officers of the first line.

Recapitulation.

This statement of facts has brought the committee to a recapitulation of some of the prominent circumstances in this part of the transaction. Without entering into the consideration of the means in the power of the Administration, and the equal claims of every part of the extensive maritime and territorial frontier of the United States, in proportion to its importance and exposure, to defensive measures, the committee are of opinion that the means authorized for the security of the 10th military district, by the President of the United States, in a Cabinet Council of the 1st of July, were ample and sufficient as to the extent of the force, and seasonable as to the time when the measures were authorized. On the 2d of July the 10th military district was constituted, and the command given to General Winder. On the 4th of July the requisition upon the States for ninety-three thousand five hundred men was made. On the 14th of July the Governors of Pennsylvania and Virginia acknowledged the receipt of the requisition of the 4th, and promised promptitude. About the 10th of July the Governor of Maryland was served with the requisition, and took measures to designate a corps of six thousand men, the whole quota from that State. On the 12th of July General Winder was authorized, in case of menaced or actual invasion, to call into service the whole quota of Maryland. On the 17th General Winder was authorized to call into actual service not less than two, nor more than three thousand of the draughts assigned to his command, to form a permanent force, to be stationed in some central position between Baltimore and the City of Washington. On the same day, 17th of July, General Winder was authorized to call on the State of Pennsylvania for five thousand men; on Virginia, two thousand; on the militia of the District of Columbia, in a disposable state, two thousand; together with the six thousand from Maryland: making an aggregate force of fifteen thousand draughted militia, three thousand of which authorized to be called into actual service, the residue in case of actual or menaced invasion, besides the regular troops, estimated at one thousand—making sixteen thousand, independent of marines and flotilla men. This was the measure of defence contemplated for the military district No. 10, and the measures taken by the War Department up to the 17th of July in execution of it.

In relation to the collection of this force, several unfortunate circumstances intervened to produce a great and manifest failure.

1st. On the 7th of July General Winder was authorized, in consequence of his own suggestions, and in conformity to the wishes of the President, to call into actual service as many as three thousand, and not less than two thousand of the draughts, under the requisition of the 4th of July, assigned for the operations of his district, as a permanent corps and rallying point with his other forces, in a central position as before stated, to protect Baltimore, the City of Washington, &c. in case of invasion. General Winder, upon the receipt of his authority, proceeded direct to Annapolis, and made this requisition upon the Governor of Maryland for the actual service of three thousand men; and on the 23d of July, thirty-two days previous to the battle at Bladensburg, General Winder informs the Secretary of War that the arrangements for this force had been made, orders had issued, and Bladensburg fixed as the place of rendezvous; and encourages expectation that the collection of the force would be prompt and certain.

On the 27th the Governor of Maryland informs the Secretary of War that measures had been taken to comply with the requisition of the 4th of July, and his orders had issued, calling into actual service three thousand five hundred men, to rendezvous at Bladensburg, to comply with the demand of General Winder, in conformity to the wishes of the President. In the meantime, Stansbury's brigade had been called into service at Baltimore, on account of the alarm about the 15th of July, by the Secretary of War; and although this force constituted a part of the Maryland quota of six thousand, by the consent of the Secretary of War it was to make no part of the three thousand to be called into actual service for the purposes mentioned.

To form a correct estimate of this failure, which did not bring as many hundred men into the field, in the words of General Winder, it may be proper to state, that at all times the marines, flotilla men, and regular troops, including the different garrisons, amounted to upwards of one thousand men. The militia of the District of Columbia amounted to two thousand men. These were always in a disposable state, and acknowledged by General Winder, in his letter of the 23d, to be almost as efficient as if in actual service, and the event proved this to be correct. The disposable force at Baltimore, including Stansbury's brigade, amounted to upwards of two thousand men, as the event proved, making an efficient force of at least eight thousand men, if the call for three thousand had been complied with. To this add the designated force assigned to the 10th military district, and the force to be raised on the spur of the occasion by calls upon the militia and population of the country en masse, and whose disposition is always operated upon more or less in proportion to the prospect of success. On the 13th of August, twenty-one days after the Secretary of War was informed that this arrangement had been made, General Winder advises him that there would be almost a total failure in relation to the call for the three thousand men, and, as a temporary remedy, proposes the acceptance of certain State troops, supposed to be about one thousand, under Colonels Beall and Hood, then in service at An-

napolis, which was authorized; and these troops came to the battle ground, as before stated, about one half an hour before the action on the 24th of August. The reasons which operated to produce this failure have been detailed, and there can be no object in having them repeated, as the committee do not consider it a duty to discuss the merit of those considerations.

2dly. On the 17th of July, the Secretary of War, by letter, authorized the Commanding General to call on Pennsylvania for five thousand men; on Virginia for two thousand men, &c., as before stated. This letter was not received by General Winder until about the 8th of August, as appears by his correspondence with the Governor of Pennsylvania, after a lapse of about twenty-three days. In explaining the delay in the receipt of this letter, General Winder says it originated from his being in constant motion, in traversing and examining the situation and various military positions of his command, and the letter had gone the circuit with him without having received it. It is impossible for the committee to say what particular influence this circumstance had upon the collection of the troops: and it may be proper here to state, that the difficulties explained in relation to the militia laws of Pennsylvania had no bearing upon the failure of our arms, as no specific call was made upon that State till the 17th of August, when one regiment was demanded, and on the 18th, the whole five thousand were demanded; but this requisition was not received by the Governor of Pennsylvania until the evening of the 23d, at which time the Pennsylvania detachment had been designated under the requisition of the 4th, and ready for the call which was made upon it.

3dly. The unfortunate circumstances which delayed the arming of a Virginia regiment under Colonel George Minor, consisting of six hundred infantry and one hundred horse, who arrived in the City of Washington late on the evening of the 23d. Colonel Minor called on the Secretary of War, after early candle-light, for orders. Colonel Carbery had been charged with supplying the various corps with arms, ammunition, &c. Colonel Minor was directed to report himself to Colonel Carbery early next morning, who would furnish him. Colonel Minor was in pursuit of Colonel Carbery from very early in the morning until very late in the forenoon, without finding him, and, after obtaining an order from General Winder, marched his regiment to Greenleaf's Point to the arsenal and magazine, where he again met with difficulties as before stated, which delayed his march and prevented him from being in the action. Having made this recapitulation of facts, the military question is presented for consideration; and having furnished the most ample means to the House to form correct opinions on this part of the inquiry, and as most of the communications from military characters enter more or less into this military view, the committee take it for granted that they have discharged their duty by the view they have taken, and submit this question to the consideration of the House.

The Navy Department.

As it regards the part taken by the Secretary of the Navy, including the destruction of the Navy Yard, &c., the solicitude of the President, in anticipation of the probable designs of the enemy against this city and the adjacent country, induced the Secretary of the Navy to cause three twelve pounders to be mounted on field carriages, and completely furnished for field service, in the month of May last, and the marines trained to act as infantry or artillery. Previous to the reinforcement of the enemy in the Patuxent, he caused to be mounted two long eighteen pounders on field carriages, and prepared for field service, to be given to Commodore Barney, in case of emergency, to co-operate with the land forces; and Commodore Barney was instructed to prepare for this eventual service in case he had to abandon his flotilla. On the 18th of August the Secretary received the first intelligence of the reinforcement of the enemy; the day on which they landed at Benedict. Commodore Barney was ordered to destroy his flotilla whenever it appeared certain that it would otherwise be captured, and to unite and co-operate with the forces under command of General Winder. Letters were despatched to Commodore Rodgers and Captain Porter, with orders to repair with their forces to the City of Washington with the utmost expedition. With every exertion, Commodore Rodgers was unable to reach the city by the 24th. The enemy entered our waters on the 16th; it was known in this city on the 18th; marched from Benedict on the 20th; and entered this city on the 24th; and left it precipitately on the evening of the 25th. The Secretary of the Navy called on General Winder on the 20th; pointed out the volunteer mechanics of the Navy Yard, then in his army, who were good axe-men, and would act with effect as pioneers. It was understood that a large squadron of the enemy's fleet had passed the principal obstacle in the navigation of the Potomac, and was ascending to co-operate with their land forces. The Secretary of the Navy expressed solicitude for Fort Washington, and proposed to throw into that fort the marines and part of the seamen for its defence: the Commanding General did not think it expedient to lessen his force by the abstraction of a part so efficient as the marines and seamen.

The Secretary of the Navy visited the Navy Yard on the 21st; inquired the means of transportation and the assistance left in the yard. The mechanics of the yard had been with the army from the first alarm: four officers and a few of the ordinary, chiefly blacks, remained: two of the old gunboats, the only craft for transportation. The wagons of this district had been pressed for the army; and the blacks usually in the market for hire, were employed at the works at Bladensburg. Orders were given for every means of transportation to be used. The public vessels afloat were, the new sloop of war Argus, the new schooner Lynx, three barges, and two gunboats. On the slip, the frigate Columbia, of the largest class, nearly ready for launching; her equipments generally made and ready, or in great forwardness. Besides the buildings, engines, fixtures, shop furniture, of the several mechanical branches in the Navy Yard, there were about one hundred tons of cordage, some canvass, considerable quantity of saltpetre, copper, iron, lead, block tin, naval and military stores, implements, and fixed ammunition, with a variety of manufactured articles in all the branches; seventeen hundred and forty-three barrels of beef and pork, two hundred and seventy nine barrels of whiskey, some plank and timber.

The Secretary states that he had no means left to transport the sloop Argus, nor place of safety, in his opinion, if the enemy took possession of the city. He ordered the barges to the Little Falls. On the morning of the 24th the Secretary visited the headquarters of General Winder, near the Eastern Branch bridge. The President and some of the Heads of Departments were present. The Secretary of the Navy presented to the President the consideration of the Navy Yard, in the presence of the Secretaries of War and Treasury. The public vessels and public property were described; the importance of the supplies and shipping to the enemy; and no doubt seemed to be entertained of the union of the squadron and the land forces, should the enemy succeed in the capture of the City of Washington, General Winder having distinctly stated that morning that Fort Washington could not be defended. In this event, nothing could be more clear than the plunder and destruction of the public buildings and property of the Navy Yard; and whether a junction was formed, or the land forces alone took the city, the loss of the Navy Yard and public property was certain. Upon this representation, the Secretary of the Navy, in his report, says, it was distinctly understood, as the result of the conversation, that the public shipping, naval and military stores and provisions at the Navy Yard, should be destroyed in the event of the enemy's obtaining possession of the city. It appears that the articles to be destroyed were in store, and could not be separated from those establishments which might have been left; one of the barges was sent to Alexandria, and remained there until taken by the enemy; one gunboat, with salt provisions, has been recovered, the other was laden with provisions and gunpowder, but run aground, and was plundered by the inhabitants about the Navy Yard. The powder and part of the provisions have been recovered. The new schooner Lynx escaped the flames, and remains without much injury. The metallic articles are chiefly all saved, and the timber in dock, and that which is partially consumed, will be useful. The machinery of the steam engine is not much injured; the boiler is perfect. The buildings, with the exception of the house of the commandant, the lieutenant of the guards, the guard houses, the gateway, and one other building, are all destroyed; the walls of some appear entire. The monument to perpetuate the memory of the naval heroes who fell in the attack upon Tripoli, is a little defaced. The issuing store of the yard and

Capture of the City of Washington.

its contents, which escaped the original conflagration, were destroyed by the enemy on the 25th.

The following estimate of the public property and buildings is the most accurate that the committee have been able to obtain, and, which to them is as satisfactory and as accurate as the nature of the inquiry would admit, viz:

The Capitol, from its foundation to its destruction, including original cost, alterations, repairs, &c.	$787,163 28
The President's house, including all costs,	334,334 00
Public offices, Treasury, State, War, and Navy	93,613 82
	$1,215,111 10

The buildings have been examined by order of a committee of the Senate. The walls of the Capitol and President's house are good, and require repairs only. The walls of the public

offices are not sufficient. It is supposed that the sum of four hundred and sixty thousand dollars will be sufficient to place the buildings in the situation they were in previous to their destruction

destruction	$460,000 00
Loss sustained at the Navy Yard—	
In moveable property	417,745 51
In buildings and fixtures	91,425 53
	$969,171 04

To this sum must be added the Library, estimated at

An estimate of the expense of rebuilding, in a plain and substantial manner, the Navy Yard, so as to carry on all the public works with as much advantage and convenience as previous to its destruction - - - - $62,370 00

RECAPITULATION.

Nos.	Public Property.	Original Value.	Value Recovered.	Real Loss.
1	Frigate Columbia -	$116,123 05	$10,432 00	$105,691 05
2	Sloop of war Argus	75,000 00	10,186 55	64,813 45
3	One large rowgalley	4,500 00	1,477 47	3,022 53
4	Two small do.	6,000 00	722 80	5,277 20
5	One armed scow	1,610 54	956 09	654 45
6	One do.	1,096 29	586 67	509 60
7	Gunboats, rowboats, &c.	6,553 84	5,773 34	780 00
8	Boatbuilder's shop	2,962 96	–	2,962 96
9	Blacksmith's and plumber's shop	4,539 60	1,996 50	2,563 30
10	Cooper's shop	7,689 75	2,854 04	4,835 71
11	Gun carriage shop, &c.	525 00	–	525 00
12	Painter's shop	969 97	15 00	954 97
13	Blockmaker's shop	1,610 00	–	1,610 00
14	Medical store	2,679 84	–	2,679 84
15	Ordnance store, &c.	18,769 90	–	18,769 90
16	Naval stores, cordage, &c.	78,262 25	–	78,262 25
17	Copper, iron, lead, &c.	49,965 27	42,522 40	7,442 87
18	Navy storekeeper's stores	20,431 77	2,921 89	17,509 88
19	Ordnance, small arms	173,284 97	162,926 22	10,358 75
20	Provisions and contingencies	48,962 04	4,071 44	42,890 60
21	Timber, plank, knees, &c.	45,000 00	–	45,000 00
22	Anchors	12,400 94	12,400 94	
23	Miscellaneous articles	1,380 13	648 85	731 18
		$678,210 71	$260,465 20	$417,745 51

Capture of Alexandria.

In relation to the conduct of the corporation of Alexandria, and its capture by the enemy in his recent enterprise, the committee have been furnished with various documents and information, and to which the committee refer; but, in justice to the town and to the public, a brief retrospect may not be deemed improper, as connecting certain events with the surrender of the town, on the 29th of August. October, 1812, a volunteer company was raised in Alexandria, amounting to about seventy, including officers, clothed by

voluntary aid and donation from the citizens of Alexandria, intended for the lines, but stationed at Fort Washington; remained in garrison till December; ordered to Annapolis, and there discharged. March, 1813, Captain Marsteller's company of artillery, stationed at Fort Washington for upwards of three months. 21st of March, 1813, corporation, by committee, called on the Secretary of War for arms, &c. for the defence of Alexandria. 8th of May, corporation, by committee, waited upon the President to apprize him of the defenceless state of the town. President acknowledged that attention was due to the representations of respectable men, and the proper attention should be given; and, at the same time, apprized the committee of the impossibility, in the nature of things, to give complete protection to every assailable point of the country. 11th of May, committee of vigilance appointed to co-operate with the committees of Georgetown and City of Washington: a deputation from the three committees waited upon General Armstrong, and represented the necessity of additional fortifications at Fort Washington. Colonel Wadsworth was ordered to attend the committee, examine, and report upon their suggestions. The examination was made, and Colonel Wadsworth reported that the battery at Fort Washington was in such a state, and it so effectually commanded the channel of the Potomac, that it was not to be apprehended that the enemy would attempt to pass it while its present defences remained entire. Its elevated situation should prevent dread of a cannonading from ships; that, in case of designs against the District of Columbia, an assault by land was most probable. To guard against this, some inconsiderable work on the land was recommended; an additional fort, in the same neighborhood, was considered unnecessary. On the 5th and 13th of August, 1814, the corporation loaned to the United States thirty-five thousand dollars, upon condition that it should be expended south of Alexandria. After the defeat of General Winder, at Bladensburg, the corporation, by committee, waited upon the British commander, at this city, to know what treatment was to be expected, provided Alexandria should fall into his hands. Admiral Cockburn assured the deputation that private property would be respected; that probably some fresh provisions and flour might be wanted, but they should be paid for. Without firing a gun, on the 27th, Fort Washington was blown up and abandoned by the commanding officer, Captain Dyson, who has been dismissed from the service of the United States, by the sentence of a court martial, in consequence of it.

On the 28th, after the enemy's squadron passed the fort, the corporation, by deputation, proceeded to the ship commanded by Captain Gordon, and requested to know his intentions in regard to Alexandria; which he proposed to communicate when he should come opposite the town, but promised that the persons, houses, and furniture, of the citizens, should be unmolested, if he met with no opposition. Next day, the 29th, the British squadron was drawn up in line of battle so as to command the whole town. There were two frigates, the Seahorse, thirty-eight guns, and Euryalus, thirty-six guns, two rocket ships of eighteen guns each, two bomb ships of eight guns each, and a schooner of two guns, arranged along the town. The committee will not attempt to condense the correspondence and terms of surrender, but refer to it as a part of the report. One hour was allowed the corporation to decide. It was stated to the British officer that the Common Council had no power to compel the return of merchandise carried to the country, nor to compel the citizens to aid in raising the sunken vessels: these two points were yielded by the enemy. The enemy was requested to explain what was included in the term merchandise, which was to be taken; and, in answer, it was stated that it would embrace such as was intended for exportation, such as tobacco, cotton, flour, bale goods, &c. The plunder of the enemy was indiscriminate, and not confined to any particular class of individuals, and included alike non-residents and inhabitants. The plunder of the enemy was confined principally to flour, cotton, and tobacco.

Estimate of the loss.—Three ships, three brigs, several bay and river craft, some vessels burned, sixteen thousand barrels of flour taken, one thousand hogsheads of tobacco, one hundred and fifty bales of cotton, five thousand dollars' worth of wines, sugar, &c. In relation to a letter written by Admiral Codrington to Captain Gordon, the committee will refer to the entire letter of General John Mason, who gives a satisfactory history of this transaction; and, to complete this part of the subject, reference is had to the statement of General Hungerford, giving the movements of his troops, and explains the interviews he had with the deputation from Alexandria, on his march to the City of Washington.

Conclusion.

In the inquiry into the causes of the success of the enemy, in his recent enterprises against this metropolis, the neighboring town of Alexandria, &c., the committee consulted a mode of investigation least embarrassing to themselves and to others. They determined that, as it was indispensable to resort to some of the parties for information not derivable from other sources, it would be equally their duty to hear, as far as practicable, those who were deeply concerned as to character and reputation, from the agency they had in this unfortunate transaction, with a determination that, in the event of any contradictions in material circumstances, to resort to impartial sources for explanation or correction. In the meantime, the committee called upon those who may be considered as impartial observers, for statements, that a just comparison might be made of different allegations and representations. If, therefore, the committee have failed to call upon persons in possession of any additional facts and views not submitted, it has not been through a want of inclination to receive all that could be important, but from a want of a knowledge of such persons and such facts. It was a question with the committee, at its earliest meeting, whether personal examinations before the committee should be adopted, or whether resort should be had, in the first instance, to call for written communications to views and interrogatories submitted by the committee, and best calculated to extract every important fact. Several considerations induced the adoption of the latter mode.

It gave the committee command of part of their time to attend to other public duties equally imperious and obligatory. It incurred no expense to Government or individuals, who were not interrupted in either their private concerns or public duties. The committee knew the anxiety of the House to have this inquiry closed as soon as possible, and which, by a different course, would have taken up the whole of the session, and encumbered with more useless and irrelevant matter and views than will be found in the communications. The committee feel therefore confident, that the House will be satisfied with the manner in which the subject has been developed; and to correct any possible error, and to receive any important fact or additional matter, although it is not very probable that much can remain, the committee will ask leave to report, with a reservation of a right to make any other communication that may be found necessary to an impartial examination of this subject.

APPENDIX.

In addition to the report of the committee, in order to give a more satisfactory view and detail upon the main subjects of inquiry, and a variety of incidental matter which has arisen from the investigation, the following communications are referred to as an appendix:

1. In relation to the measures adopted by Administration, and the part taken by the President and the Heads of Departments, the committee refer to the letters from the Secretaries of State, War, Navy, and the Attorney General: one is also expected from the Secretary of the Treasury, which shall be communicated when received.

2. In relation to the steps taken and measures adopted by the Secretary of War, the committee refer to the correspondence with the Commanding General, the Governors of Pennsylvania, Maryland, and Virginia, the letters of Colonel Tayloe, two reports from the ordnance office, as to arms, military stores, &c.

3. The conduct of the Commanding General, the collection and dispositions of the forces, and the conduct and movements of different corps, the committee refer to the narrative of General Winder, his correspondence with the States of Pennsylvania, Maryland, and Virginia, the War Department, and various officers, the reports of General Smith, General Young, General Stansbury, Colonel Sterret, Major William Pinkney, General Douglas, Colonel Minor, Colonel Beall, and Commodore Barney's official letter.

4. In relation to the measures and arrangements and acts of the Navy Department, including the destruction of the Navy Yard and the public property, as well as the destruction of the public buildings in the city, the committee refer to a report from the Secretary of the Navy, a report from Commodore Tingey, and a report from Mr. Munroe, Superintendent of the Public Buildings.

5. In relation to the capture and capitulation of Alexandria, the committee refer to the proceedings of the court martial upon Captain Dyson, the correspondence between him and the Secretary of War, as to the abandonment of the fort, the report of the corporation of Alexandria, including the terms of surrender, &c., and the letter from General Mason, relating to a letter from Admiral Codrington.

6. In relation to general information and incidental topics, the committee refer to Mr. Law, General Van Ness, and Doctor Catlett.

A LIST OF THE DOCUMENTS.

1. A report of the Army, its strength and distribution, previous to the first of July, 1814.

2. Letter of Colonel Monroe, then Secretary of State.

3. Letter of General Armstrong, late Secretary of War.

4. Letter from the honorable William Jones, Secretary of the Navy.

5. Letters from the honorable Richard Rush, Attorney General.

6. Communication from the War Department, including the orders in relation to the tenth military district, the requisition of the fourth of July, and the correspondence with the Governors of Pennsylvania, Virginia, and Maryland, and with General Winder.

7. The narrative of General Winder.

8. Reports of Generals Stansbury, Douglas, Smith, Young, and Hungerford; Colonels Sterret, Minot, Tayloe, Lavall, and Beall; Major Pinkney, and Captains Burch and Caldwell.

9. Report from the Navy Department, including the official report of Commodore Barney.

10. Letters from General Van Ness, Doctor Catlett, and John Law, Esq.

11. Reports from the Ordnance Department.

12. Sentence of the court martial in relation to Captain Dyson, and the correspondence between him and the Secretary of War.

13. Report from the corporation of Alexandria, including the capitulation, and letter from General John Mason.

14. Report from the Superintendent of the Public Buildings.

15. William Simmons's letter.

Capture of the City of Washington.

No. 1.

A Report of the Army, its strength and distribution, previous to the 1st of July, 1814.

DISTRICTS.	Effectives.	Aggregate.	STATION.
District No. 1.			
40th Regiment Infantry - - -	352	379	Boston, Portsmouth, Portland, and
Artillerists - - - -	363	276	Eastport.
Total - - - -	615	655	
District No. 2.			
Artillerists - - - -	127	149	New London.
37th Regiment Infantry - • -	490	565	Ditto.
Total - - - -	617	714	
District No. 3.			
Artillerists - - - -	378	370	
32d Regiment Infantry - -	335	602	
41st do. - -	628	692	New York.
42d do. - -	331	374	
Sea Fencibles - - - -	77	78	
Total - - - -	1,849	2,116	
District No. 4.			
Artillerists - - - -	108	108	Fort Mifflin, recruiting rendezvous.
Dragoons - - - -	200	200	
Total - - - -	308	308	
District No. 5.			
Artillerists - - - -	210	224	
20th Regiment Infantry - -			Norfolk.
25th do. - -	873	912	
38th do. 1st bat. - -			
Artillerists - - - -	65	111	
38th Regiment, 2d battalion - -	300	316	Baltimore.
Sea Fencibles - - - -	167	173	
Artillerists - - - -	40	40	Annapolis.
Do. - - - -	79	82	Fort Washington.
36th Regiment Infantry - -	320	350	St. Mary's.
Total - - - -	2,154	2,208	
District No. 6.			
Dragoons - - - -	135	141	
Artillerists - - -	413	430	
8th Regiment Infantry - -	688	728	
18th do. - -	443	482	North and South Carolina and
43d do. - -	261	269	Georgia.
1st Rifle Regiment, 1st Company -	87	92	
Sea Fencibles - - - -	100	102	
Total - - - -	2,127	2,244	
District No. 7.			
Artillerists - - - -	339	351	
2d Regiment Infantry - - -	408	422	New Orleans, Mobile, and the Creek
3d do. - - -	400	420	nation.
7th do. - - -	670	694	

Capture of the City of Washington.

No. 1—Continued.

DISTRICTS.	Effectives.	Aggregate.	STATION.
District No. 7—continued.			
39th Regiment Infantry - - -	379	394	} New Orleans, Mobile, and the Creek
44th do. - - -	89	97	} nation.
Total - - - -	2,276	2,378	
District No. 8.			
Artillerists - - - -	142	179	}
17th Infantry - - -			
19th do. - - -			
24th do. - - -	1,591	762	} Detroit, Sandwich, Sandusky, &c.
28th do. - - -			
Rangers - - - -	317	423	
Do. - - - -	71	108	}
Total - - - -	2,121	2,472	
District No. 9.			
Light Artillery - - -	458	610	}
Dragoons - - -	97	102	
Artillerists - - -	181	195	
4th Regiment Infantry - -	655	751	
5th do. - - -	275	407	
6th do. - - -	250	518	
10th do. - - -	254	327	
12th do. - - -	482	752	
13th do. - - -	194	381	
14th do. - - -	137	262	} 1st, or division of the right.
15th do. - - -	317	549	
16th do. - - -	299	434	
29th* do. - - -	364	515	
30th* do. - - -	274	354	
31st* do. - - -	90	99	
32d* do. - - -	165	236	
34th* do. - - -	183	240	
1st Rifle Regiment, 2d battalion -	223	276	}
Total - - - -	4,908	7,108	
The recruits of the above regiments, the 46th Infantry, three hundred dragoons, and two hundred and sixty-four light artillerists, under orders to join this division, will amount to - - - - -	4,687	4,687	
Total - - - -	9,595	11,795	
Light Artillery - - -	60	66	}
Dragoons, (troops mounted) -	443	557	
Artillerists - - - -	624	687	
9th Regiment Infantry - -	227	501	} Buffalo, Oswego, and Sackett's Harbor.
11th do. - - -	492	628	
21st do. - - -	456	664	
25th do. - - -	392	606	
1st Rifle Regiment, 1st battalion -	345	345	}
Total - - - -	3,041	4,074	

* Year's men re-enlisting.

Capture of the City of Washington.

No. 1—Continued.

DISTRICT.	Effectives.	Aggregate.	STATION.
Under orders to join this division:			
Artillerists - - - - -	248	248	
1st Regiment Infantry - - -	200	214	
22d do. - - -	359	517	
23d do. - - -	600	650	
The recruits of the 1st, 9th, 11th, 21st, and 25th, under orders to join, amount to - - - - -	910	910	
Total - - - - -	5,348	6,613	

ABSTRACTS OF TOTALS.

Districts.	Effectives.	Aggregate.
District No. 1 - - - - - - - - - - -	615	655
District No. 2 - - - - - - - - - - -	617	714
District No. 3 - - - - - - - - - - -	1,849	2,116
District No. 4 - - - - - - - - - - -	308	308
District No. 5 - - - - - - - - - - -	2,154	2,208
District No. 6 - - - - - - - - - - -	2,127	2,944
District No. 7 - - - - - - - - - - -	2,276	2,378
District No. 8 - - - - - - - - - - -	2,121	2,472
District No. 9 - - - - - - - - - - -	9,595	11,795
Miscellaneous - - - - - - - - - - -	5,348	6,613
	27,010	31,503

No. 2.

Letters of Colonel Monroe, then Secretary of State.

WASHINGTON CITY, *Nov.* 13, 1814.

The events in France having greatly augmented the disposable force of the enemy, and his disposition to employ it against the United States being well known, the safety of this Metropolis was thought to require particular attention.

On or about the first of July last, the President convened the Heads of Departments and the Attorney General, to consult them on the measures which it would be proper to adopt for the safety of this city and District. He appeared to have digested a plan of the force to be called immediately into the field; the additional force to be kept under orders to march at a moment's notice; its composition, and necessary equipment. It seemed to be his object, that some position should be taken between the Eastern Branch and the Patuxent, with two or three thousand men, and that an additional force of ten or twelve thousand, including the militia of the District, should be held in readiness, in the neighboring States, to march when called on. The whole force to be put under the command of an officer of the regular Army.

The measures suggested by the President were approved by all the members of the Administration. The Secretaries of War and Navy gave the information required of them, incident to their respective departments. The former stated the regular force which he could draw together at an early day, infantry and cavalry ; the amount of the militia of the District ; and the States from which he should draw the remaining force in contemplation, and in what proportions. The latter stated the aid which he could afford, from the officers and seamen of the flotilla on the Patuxent, and the marines at the navy yard, on the Eastern Branch. The result of the meeting promised prompt and efficacious measures for carrying these objects into execution. The command of this whole force, with that of the district No. 5, was given to Brigadier General Winder.

On the 5th of July I went to Virginia, whence I returned on or about the 25th. After my return, I was much engaged in the affairs of my own department.

Calling on the President on the morning of the

18th of August, he informed me that the enemy had entered the Patuxent in considerable force, and were landing at Benedict. I remarked that this city was their object. He concurred in the opinion. I offered to proceed immediately to Benedict, with a troop of horse, to observe their force, report it, with my opinion of their objects, and, should they advance on this city, to retire before them, communicating regularly their movements to the Government. This proposal was acceded to. Captain Thornton, of Alexandria, was ordered to accompany me, with a detachment of twenty-five or thirty of the dragoons of the District. I set out at about 1 P. M. on the 19th, and arrived at 10 next morning in sight of the enemy's squadron, lying before Benedict, and continued to be a spectator of their movements until after the action at Bladensburg on the 24th.

The annexed notes contain information which I communicated to the Government, of the force and designs of the enemy.

In retiring from Nottingham, late in the evening of the 21st, after writing a note to the President, I observed a column of the enemy in the rear of the town, which I concluded had passed from Benedict by a road near the river, moving in concert with the barges. The number I could not ascertain, having seen its head only. I went immediately to Mr. Oden's, where I met Colonel Beall, whom I had before seen at Nottingham. He had taken a view of the enemy's column from a commanding height contiguous to the town. From his statement we both concluded that it must have amounted to between four and five thousand men. The force in the barges was supposed to exceed one thousand; so that the whole force of the enemy might be estimated at about six thousand. Hearing that General Winder was at the Woodyard, I hastened to him. He had there about two thousand two hundred men, consisting of the marines, Colonel Lavall's cavalry, and the city and Georgetown militia. I understood that he either then gave orders, or repeated those he had before given, to a part of the militia at Baltimore, and to Colonel Beall, who commanded six or seven hundred at Annapolis, to move towards Bladensburg to his support.

On the morning of the 22d, General Winder put his force in motion from the Woodyard towards Nottingham. At 5, Lavall's cavalry met the enemy a mile in advance of Mr. Oden's. They were in full march, as was inferred, for Washington, with intention to attack General Winder. Our cavalry retired before the enemy, and General Winder, after reconnoitering his force as well as the nature of the ground would admit, retired the head of his column towards the Woodyard, with intention to concentrate his force and form it in line. It was soon perceived that the enemy had taken a road to his right, in a direction to Upper Marlborough, at which place they arrived about 2 P. M. on that day. General Winder retired by the Woodyard to a place called the Old Fields, which covered equally Bladensburg, the bridges on the Eastern Branch, and Fort Washington. Commodore Barney joined

him there with the flotilla men, amounting to about five hundred.

Late on the evening of the 22d, the President, with the Secretaries of War, Navy, and Attorney General, joined General Winder at the Old Fields, and remained with him until the afternoon of the 23d.

After mid-day on the 23d, General Winder detached Major Peter with some field pieces, and Captains Davidson and Stull's companies, to skirmish with the enemy near Marlborough, who advanced on him, and took a position near the camp at the Old Fields, menacing it with attack, either that night or early the next morning. General Winder retired, and passed the Eastern Branch into the city that night. Colonel Tilghman, with his cavalry, remained on the road between Marlborough and Bladensburg.

General Stansbury, with a part of his brigade, arrived at Bladensburg on the evening of the 22d, and the remainder arrived there on the evening of the 23d. This brigade amounted to between two thousand two hundred and two thousand three hundred men.

In the afternoon of the 23d, the President, with the Secretaries of War and Navy, returned to Washington. The Attorney General, and several respectable friends from the city, proceeded with me to the road leading from Marlborough to Bladensburg. Late that evening, I heard of the advance of the enemy on the party under Major Peter, and against General Winder.

Not knowing the result, I hastened to General Stansbury's quarters at Bladensburg, and found him encamped on the height beyond the village on the road leading to Marlborough. He had just heard of the enemy's movement, but was likewise unacquainted with the result. I had the pleasure to meet there Colonel Sterret and Major Pinkney. I advised the General to fall forthwith on the enemy's rear, although it was then 12 o'clock at night. He observed, that he had been ordered to take post at Bladensburg, and did not think himself at liberty to leave it; but, had it been otherwise, as a considerable portion of his force had just arrived, after a very fatiguing march, that it would not be in his power to march that night. I proceeded to the city, where I heard that General Winder had crossed the Eastern Branch, and taken post near the Navy Yard.

In the morning of the 24th, I met the President at General Winder's quarters. Among other rumors of the enemy's movements, the General had just heard that he was marching towards Bladensburg. I asked if General Stansbury was apprized of it. He presumed that he was. I offered to join him. The President and General Winder both expressed a wish that I would. I lost not a moment in complying with their desire. Between 11 and 12 I joined General Stansbury, who had moved his brigade on this side of the Eastern Branch, near the bridge. I inquired where were the enemy? He replied, advancing, not more than three miles distant. I advised the General to form his troops to receive them, which he immediately commenced. The order of battle

Capture of the City of Washington.

was formed on the presumption that his brigade would alone have to meet the enemy in the first instance. Major Pinkney, with a battalion of riflemen, was placed to the right of the battery to support it; another corps was placed on the left, for the same purpose, and the fifth Baltimore regiment in the rear. On forming the line on the brow of the hill, and extending the right to cover the road leading to Washington, it was found that the left would be much exposed, as it scarcely extended to the rear of the battery. If the battery should be forced, which seemed probable, the enemy's column would turn our left, and, ascending the heights and commanding the most advantageous grounds, force us towards the city. This induced, at a late period, the removal of the fifth Baltimore regiment from the rear of the battery to the left of the line, a measure taken with reluctance, and in haste. Colonel Beall's corps had entered Bladensburg from another route, and was at that moment approaching the bridge. Captain Thornton was sent to lead it to the height to the right of the road, which commanded the whole of the ground held by General Stansbury's brigade. It was deemed important to occupy that height to protect the line to the left, and likewise to impede the enemy's movement by the road towards the city. The cavalry were placed to the left, somewhat in the rear of the line. After General Stansbury had made this disposition, Mr. Walter Jones, junior, set out, at my request, for the city, to communicate it to the President, the Secretary of War, and General Winder, with the near approach of the enemy.

Immediately after this General Winder arrived, and informed us that his whole force was in full march to Bladensburg. On taking a view of the order which had been formed, he approved of it. This was the more satisfactory, because it had then become impossible to make any essential change. The General proceeded promptly, for the enemy were getting in sight, to make a disposition of each of his troops as had arrived. He placed one corps near the battery, to support it, and some pieces of artillery on the left of General Stansbury's line. We then passed to the right along the line. Near the road, leading from Bladensburg to Washington, we met the Secretary of War, and immediately afterwards, at the road, I met the President and Mr. Rush, who had just arrived, and who, joining with me, the Secretary of War, and General Winder, proceeded together towards the left of the line. Mr. Rush informed me that the President intended, when every arrangement should be completed, to take a position with the members of the Administration in the rear of the line, that, looking to all the functions of the Government, he might be able to act with their counsel according to circumstances. Shortly afterwards the President gave me the same intimation. The action may be said to have commenced, when we had arrived in the rear of the battery near the bridge. The enemy had saluted us with rockets, and, attempting to pass the bridge, our little batteries had begun to play on them. After some pause, the President remarked to the

Secretary of War and myself, that it would now be proper for us to retire in the rear, leaving the military movement to military men, which we did. The Attorney General followed us. After our little batteries were carried, and the left of our line broken, the President, with the members of the Administration present, retired along the eminence on which the left of the line had been formed, viewing the progress of the action to the right. On, or near the summit of this ground, I separated from the President, and the other gentlemen of the Administration with him; they continuing to move slowly towards the city, I remaining to view the enemy's progress. At this moment I fell in again with Mr. W. Jones, jun., who had been charged, as already mentioned, after the line was formed, with a communication to the President, the Secretary of War, and to General Winder. Hearing on the road that the General had passed him, he had immediately returned, and delivered to him the message in my presence, and afterwards remained with the Baltimore troops during the action. Inclining to the left, we hastened to the Capitol, where we met the Secretary of War and General Winder. The General consulted the Secretary of War and me, on the propriety of making an attempt to rally the troops on the Capitol Hill. We both advised him to rally and form them on the heights above Georgetown, believing, as I did, that much would be hazarded by an attempt near the Capitol. I knew that a column of the enemy had advanced from the high ground which had been held by our troops, and meeting, as they would, with no opposition, might take possession of the heights above the city, and thus force our troops, in case of a new disaster, to the plain between the Capitol, the Eastern Branch, and the Potomac; whereas, by occupying the heights above Georgetown, the enemy must either attack us to disadvantage, or, entering the city, expose his right flank and rear to an attack from us.

                  JAMES MONROE.

Copy of a letter from James Monroe to the President of the United States, dated

     AQUASCO MILLS, 7 miles from Benedict, Aug. 20, 1814, 1 o'clock, P. M.

DEAR SIR: I arrived here this morning at eight o'clock, and have been since within four miles of Benedict, at Butler's mill, where it was reported the enemy, on their march, had arrived. The report was unfounded. The enemy landed yesterday at Benedict, and had advanced their pickets within a mile and a half of that mill, for security. From a height between that mill and the Patuxent, I had a view of their shipping; but being at the distance of three miles, and having no glass, we could not count them. We shall take better views in the course of the evening, and should anything be seen material, I will immediately advise you of it. The general idea is, that they are still debarking their troops, the number of which I have not obtained any satisfactory information of. The general idea also is, that

Capture of the City of Washington.

Washington is their object; but of this I can form no opinion at this time. The best security against this attempt is an adequate preparation to repel it.

Respectfully, your friend and servant,

JAMES MONROE.

Copy of a letter from James Monroe to the President of the United States, dated

HORSE HEAD, *August* 21, 1814.

DEAR SIR: I quartered last night near Charlotte Hall, and took a view this morning, at eight o'clock, from a commanding height below Benedict creek, of all the enemy's shipping near the town and down the river, to the distance at least of eight or ten miles. I counted twenty-three square-rigged vessels; few others were to be seen, and very few barges. I inferred, from the latter circumstance, that the enemy had moved up the river, either against Commodore Barney's flotilla at Nottingham, confining their views to that object, or taking that in their way, and aiming at the city, in combination with the force on the Potomac, of which I have no correct information. I had, when I left Aquasco mills last night, intended to have passed over to the Potomac, after giving you an account of their vessels from the height below Benedict; but, observing the very tranquil scene which I have mentioned, I was led, by the inference I drew from it, to hasten back to take a view of the enemy's movements in this quarter, which it might be more important for the Government to be made acquainted with. I am now on the main road from Washington to Benedict, twelve miles from the latter, and find that no troops have passed in this direction. The reports make it probable that a force by land and water has been sent against the flotilla. I shall proceed with Captain Thornton's troop immediately to Nottingham, and write thence whatever may be deserving of notice.

The enemy have plundered the country, to the distance of three or four miles, of all their stock, &c.

The intelligence of the enemy's force in the Potomac varies here as much as in Washington. I have no means of forming a correct estimate of it.

JAMES MONROE.

Copy of a letter from James Monroe to Brigadier General Winder, dated

NOTTINGHAM, *August* 21, 1814.

SIR: The enemy are now within four hundred yards of the shore. There are but three barges at hand, and the force in view is not considerable. If you send five or six hundred men, if you could not save the town, you may perhaps cut off their retreat or rear. JAMES MONROE.

P. S. Ten or twelve more barges in view. There are but two muskets in town, and a few scattering militia.

Five o'clock. Thirty or forty barges in view.

J. M.

Copy of a letter from James Monroe to the President of the United States.

The enemy are advanced six miles on the road to the Woodyard, and our troops retiring. Our troops were on the march to meet them, but in too small a body to engage. General Winder proposes to retire till he can collect them in a body. The enemy are in full march for Washington. Have the materials prepared to destroy the bridges.

J. MONROE.

Monday, nine o'clock. You had better remove the records.

No. 3.

Letter of General Armstrong, late Secretary of War.

LABBAGORIE, *October* 17, 1814.

SIR: An occasional absence from the place of my usual residence prevented me from receiving the letter you did me the honor to write to me on the third instant, until this morning. I now hasten to fulfil the injunctions of the committee, in giving to them "such information, views, and remarks, as are deemed pertinent to the subject of their inquiry, and best calculated for an impartial investigation of the causes of the success of the enemy in his recent enterprise against the Metropolis, and the neighboring town of Alexandria."

"Of the manner in which the public buildings, and other property, were destroyed, and of the amount thereof," I know nothing personally, nor have I recourse to any documents which would enable me to make a satisfactory communication on these points.

The enemy's success in his late enterprise against the City of Washington, &c., must necessarily be traced to one of two causes: the incompetency of the means projected and employed to repel his attack, or, the mismanagement or misconduct of these.

Under the first head may be noticed, What was the force contemplated and ordered by the Government as competent? What was that actually assembled and employed? And what other, or additional means were at the disposal of the Government?

The second head would furnish an inquiry strictly military, viz: Whether all was done, that was necessary and practicable, by the Commanding General and the troops under his direction? For such an inquiry I am not prepared, and what, under either head, I may be able to offer, will but be a detail of facts coming within my official cognizance, without any admixture of opinions.

Early in the month of June last, a call was made on the War Department for a general report of the numbers of regular troops and militia employed by the United States, and the distribution which had been made of these for the service of the present campaign. This statement was promptly rendered, and submitted by the President to the Heads of Departments. It is not recollected that any alteration of the provisions exhibited by this document was either made or suggested. A reference to it will show what was the force then deemed competent for the defence of military district No. 5. of which the City of Washington made part.[*]

The better to secure the Seat of Government, &c., from the attacks of the enemy, and to relieve the War Department from details, not making part of its regular duties, and incident to district No. 5, as then constituted, a military district, comprehending that portion of country lying between the Rappahannock and Potomac rivers, the District of Columbia, and the State of Maryland, was created on the 2d July last, and placed under the command of Brigadier General Winder, who had been specially assigned by the President to that service.

In an interview with this officer, soon after his appointment, his attention was invited to the state of the existing defences within the limits of his command; to an examination of the different routes by which the enemy might approach the capital; to the selection of points best calculated to retard and to stop his movements, if directed thereto; and to the indication of such new defences, field or permanent, as he might deem necessary or practicable. The better to enable him to discharge these and other duties, a military staff, composed of an Assistant Adjutant General, an Assistant Inspector General, and two Assistant Topographical Engineers, were assigned to the district.

On the 1st July a consultation of the Heads of Departments was had. The questions proposed for discussion were two:

1. By what means can the Seat of Government and Baltimore be defended, in case the enemy should make these cities objects of attack?

2. Should he select the former, will his approach be made by way of the Potomac, or by that of the Patuxent?

On these questions, I took the liberty of offering the following statements and opinions:

1. That the principal defence to be relied upon, for either place, was militia; that, besides the artillerists composing the garrisons of Forts McHenry and Washington, about one thousand regular troops only could be collected, viz: the thirty-sixth regiment, one battalion of the thirty-eighth, two troops of dragoons, two companies of the tenth, ordered from North Carolina, and believed to be on their march, one company of the twelfth, and two companies of sea fencibles; that the number of militia called into service should be proportioned to the known or probable strength of the enemy, and be taken from the States of Virginia, Maryland, and Pennsylvania: that it is not believed that the enemy will hazard a blow at either place with a force less than five thousand men; that, to repel one of this extent, we should require at least double that number of militia; that these should be assembled at some intermediate point between Baltimore and the District of Columbia, leaving the sedentary or undraughted militia of both places an auxiliary force at the disposition of the Commanding General, and that arms and ammunition were in depot and ready for their supply.

[Under this head, the Secretary of the Navy stated, that the removal or destruction of the flotilla would put at his disposition between six and eight hundred seamen, and that the marines then in barracks exceeded one hundred.]

2. That the navigation of the Potomac is long and sinuous, and, if not doubtful as to practicability by large ships, is at least uncertain in relation to the time its ascent may occupy; while that of the Patuxent is short and safe, and may be calculated with sufficient precision for military purposes; that, should the enemy ascend the former, his object is unmasked—he at once declares his destination—and of course leaves us at liberty to concentrate our whole force against him; that, on the other hand, should he ascend the Patuxent, (or South river,) his object is uncertain—it may be the flotilla, or Baltimore, or Washington; and that, as long as his point of attack is unknown, so long must our force remain divided; that these considerations suggest the preference he will probably give to the Patuxent, but that this route is not without objections; that a separation from his fleet, and a land march of twenty miles through a country covered with wood, and offering at every step strong positions for defence, becomes inevitable; that, if these circumstances be turned to proper account against him, if he be not absolutely stopped, his march will be much retarded; that this state of things, on which every wise General will calculate, renders necessary a provision train, or the establishment of small intermediate posts, to keep open his communication with his shipping; that the loss of these would make his situation perilous; and that, should the main battle be given near Washington, and be to him disastrous, or even doubtful, his destruction is complete; that, after all, believing he will not hazard the movement but with a very superior force, or one he thinks such, it is also believed that he will prefer this route.

Conformably to these opinions, an order was taken to assemble a corps and form a camp at such point between the City of Washington and Baltimore as might be selected by the Commanding General.

On the 4th of July the militia requisition of that date was issued, and of that requisition two thousand effectives from the quota of Virginia; five thousand from that of Pennsylvania; six thousand, the whole quota of Maryland; and two thousand, the estimated number of the militia of the District, were put at the disposition of the Commanding General. General Stewart's brigade was already in service, under the authority of the State, and had been supplied with arms, ammunition, tents, &c., by the War Department.

At a later period, when discovered that the draughts could not be brought together, but slowly, and with difficulty, and a call upon the militia, en masse, was suggested by the General, and immediately authorized.

---

[*] This document is in possession of the President. No copy of it was retained by me.

Capture of the City of Washington.

Of the force actually assembled and employed I cannot speak with precision, as no return of these troops had been made to the War Department during my connexion with it. In the letter of the Commanding General, of the 27th of August, he states the whole force assembled at Bladensburg, on the 24th of that month, at five thousand men; a number less by two-thirds than that which had been required. This amazing deficiency is thus accounted for by him: "The slow progress of draught, and the imperfect organization, with the ineffectiveness of the laws to compel them to turn out, rendered it impossible to procure more. The militia of this State, and of the contiguous parts of Virginia and Pennsylvania, were called *en masse;* but the former militia law of Pennsylvania had expired on the 1st of June or July, and the one adopted in its place is not to take effect, in organizing the militia, before October. No aid, therefore, has been received from that State."

The third and last point of inquiry under this head is, what other or additional means of defence were within the reach of Government?

Of naval means I am not a competent judge, nor do I know what, of this description, were actually employed, nor what it was possible to have superadded; but of those strictly military, I know none within the view of this question that were omitted. It may be supposed that permanent fortifications should have been multiplied; yet, of works of this character, but one was suggested from any quarter entitled to respect, and this was a committee of bankers, who thought a new work on the Potomac, and below Fort Washington, desirable. To this suggestion it was answered, that a small work would be unavailing, and that, to erect one of sufficient size and strength, was impracticable, for want of money. An offer was then made to supply that want by loaning to the United States $200,000, on condition that this sum should be devoted to the special object of defending the District. An agreement to this effect was made, and the money promised to be paid into the Treasury on the 24th of August. The events of that day put an end to the business, and at the same time furnished evidence of the fallibility of the plan, had it even been executed, by showing that no works on the Potomac will, of themselves, be a sufficient defence for the Seat of Government. The considerations which governed my own opinion on this subject, and which may have governed that of others, were, that to put Washington *hors d'insulte*, by means of fortifications, would, from physical causes, among which is the remoteness from each other of the several points to be defended, have exhausted the Treasury; that bayonets are known to form the most efficient barriers; and that there was no reason, in this case, to doubt beforehand the willingness of the country to defend it.

In this brief statement you are presented with a view of the force contemplated and ordered by the Government; of the means taken to assemble that force through the usual medium of the Commanding General;[*] of that actually assembled and employed; and lastly, of my impressions in relation to any other or additional means of defence.

I now proceed to the second subject of inquiry, the employment of the means we had, and the conduct of the troops.

On the —— day of August was received the first notice of the arrival of Admiral Cochrane in the bay; and on the same day advices were brought, that he was entering and ascending the Patuxent. These facts were communicated to the General, and he was instructed to take a position near the enemy. On the 22d he was advised to hang on their rear and flank a heavy corps, while he opposed to them another in their front. My reasons for thus advising him were three: if Baltimore was the object of the enemy, this disposition interposed a corps between them and that city; if they aimed at Washington, it menaced their communication with their fleet, and the security of their return, and was, therefore, most likely to hold them in check; and lastly, it did not forbid a concentration of force in their front, at a later period and by a forced march. On the evening of the 22d I repaired to the army, and found it at the Old Fields, six or eight miles distant from the enemy. A part of the corps contemplated for the service mentioned in the preceding article had joined General Winder, and of the other part (under General Stansbury) no correct account could be given. I took this occasion to urge the necessity of a speedy concentration of our force, and of the usefulness of pushing our pickets frequently and freely upon those of the enemy, as the best means of circumscribing his supplies; of gaining a knowledge of his strength, (of which the accounts were various,) and of preventing a stolen march, which was to be suspected. I was glad to find the General entertained similar views, and that they were in a train of execution. In the afternoon of the 23d I returned to Washington, and during the night of that day the President transmitted to me the letter, of which that which follows is a copy:

"The PRESIDENT *of the United States:*

"The enemy are advanced six miles on the road to the Woodyard, and our troops retiring. Our troops were on the march to meet them, but in too small a body to engage. General Winder proposes to retire till he can collect them in a body. The enemy are in full march for Washington. Have the materials prepared to destroy the bridges.

             "JAMES MONROE.

"Tuesday, 9 o'clock. You had better remove the records."

On the morning of the 24th I received a note from General Winder, informing me of his re-

---

[*] His exertions were occasionally aided, and his authority enforced, by the War Department. See Col. Taylor's letter enclosed; and let me pray that this gentleman may be examined on the subject of it by the committee.

treat and the approach of the enemy, and "asking counsel from me, or from the Government." This letter was late in reaching me. It had been opened, and passed through other hands. The moment I received it I hastened, with the late Secretary of the Treasury, to the General's quarters. We found there the President, the Secretary of the Navy, and the Attorney General. General Winder was on the point of joining the troops, at Bladensburg, whither, it was now understood, the enemy was also marching. I took for granted that he had received the counsel he required; for, to me, he neither stated doubt nor difficulty, nor plan of attack or of defence. This state of things gave occasion to a conversation, principally conducted by the President and the Secretary of the Treasury, which terminated in understanding that I should repair to the troops, and give such directions as were required by the urgency of the case. I lost not a moment in fulfilling this intention, and had barely time to reconnoitre the march of the enemy, and to inform myself of our own arrangements, when I again met the President, who told me that he had come to a new determination, and that the military functionaries should be left to the discharge of their own duties, on their own responsibilities. I now became, of course, a mere spectator of the combat.

If our field combinations were not the most scientific, it ought to be recollected that many of our troops were incapable of receiving those of the best form,* and that circumstances had rendered the order of battle, on our part, nearly fortuitous. "Much of the largest portion of our force," says the General, in his letter of the 27th of August, "arrived on the ground when the enemy was in sight, and were disposed of to support, in the best manner, the position which General Stansbury had taken. They had barely reached the ground before the action commenced.

These facts may also explain why we had no guns in battery over the head of the bridge over which the enemy passed? why a brick house, which enfiladed that bridge, and was partially fortified, should not have been unroofed and occupied? and why a frame storehouse should have been left to cover the head of the enemy's column, and its subsequent display? &c.

If, also, the most efficient corps of the army was left out of the original arrangement, and but got into the line when other parts of it "were retreating, and apparently in much disorder," it will not be forgotten that this corps was distinct and independent, and that the General had no authority, of right, to command it. I witnessed the disquietude of the gallant officer who led this corps, at having been assigned to a duty which, in his own strong language, "but required a corporal and six men." The lateness with which

* Upon my inquiring why the dragoons had not been imbodied, masked, and made to charge the right flank of the enemy, the General replied, that an officer of that corps assured him that his men could not be brought to a charge.

he got into a post of more distinction, I consider as one of the causes of the disasters of the day; but, without all doubt, the determining *cause* of these is to be found in that love of life which, in many of the corps, predominated over a love of country and of honor. In illustration of this fact, I refer to the official reports of General Winder and of Commodore Barney, and shall close this letter by adopting the opinion of the former, "that the contest was not maintained as obstinately as could have been desired, but was, by *parts of the* troops, sustained with great spirit and *prodigious* effect; and, had the whole of our force been equally firm, I am induced to believe that the enemy would have been repulsed, notwithstanding all the disadvantages under which we fought."

I have the honor to be, sir, with very great respect, your most obedient servant,

JOHN ARMSTRONG.

P. S. On what may particularly relate to Alexandria, I beg leave to refer to my official letter to General Young, of the 24th of August, and to my note to Captain Dyson, and his reply of the 29th. It may be that no copy of the first was kept; in which case the original may be called for.   J. A.

Hon. Col. Johnson, *Chairman, &c.*

No. 4.

Letter from the honorable William Jones, Secretary of the Navy.

NAVY DEPARTMENT, *Oct.* 31, 1814.

SIR: In compliance with the request contained in your letter of the 24th instant, to state to the committee of inquiry "anything that may be within my knowledge, as to the measures taken and adopted by the Administration, and more especially those proposed and adopted at the Cabinet Council on the first of July last, in relation to the defence of the District of Columbia, with such other views and things as may be deemed, in my estimation, pertinent to an inquiry," I have the honor to reply, that, as the information required involves the confidential proceedings of a Cabinet Council, I deemed it expedient and respectful to ascertain, from the proper source, whether any obstacles existed to the development of what passed on that question; and, being freed from all restraint upon that occasion, I proceed to state briefly, from memory, my general recollections upon the subject of the inquiry.

The serious apprehensions of invasion and devastation, which succeeded the knowledge of those extraordinary events, which liberated the powerful naval and military forces of the enemy from European hostility, and the temper of the British nation, as displayed in the language of its journals and conduct of its Government, in relation to the pacific mission which it had invited, were deeply felt, and frequently discussed, in occasional conversations between the individual members of the Administration, prior to the Cabinet meeting on the first of July last, in which the probable points of attack were variously com-

Capture of the City of Washington.

sidered. My own impressions inclined to the opinion that there were some points more exposed, less difficult of access, and more inviting to the enemy, upon the system of warfare he had adopted, than the metropolis; the only important objects which it presented, according to my view, being the naval depot and public shipping.

I recollect, on one of those occasions, that the President expressed very great solicitude for the safety of the metropolis; his belief that the enemy would attempt its invasion, and urged the expediency of immediate defensive preparations, with all the disposable force that could be conveniently collected. I accorded in the expediency of preparation, but must confess I was not equally impressed with the apprehension of immediate danger, as well from the reasons I have before assigned, as from the then existing fact, that the force of the enemy, in the waters of the Chesapeake, was entirely naval, and apparently very satisfactorily engaged in conflagrating farm houses, and depredating upon slaves and tobacco, on the shores of the Patuxent. In this sentiment I was not alone.

On the 30th day of June the members of the Cabinet were invited to attend a meeting at the President's mansion, on the following day at noon. At or near the time appointed, the Secretaries of State, Treasury, War, and Navy, and the Attorney General, assembled.

The President stated the object of the meeting to be the consideration of the menacing aspect of things, in consequence of the augmented power of the enemy by the great political changes which had taken place in Europe, and the disposition manifested by the Government and people of Great Britain, to prosecute the war with the most vindictive and devastating spirit; represented the motives and inducements which, he conceived, the enemy had to prefer the invasion of the capital rather than any other immediate enterprise, and urged the necessity of speedy and efficient preparation for the defence of the District and capital; inquired into the existing state of its military and naval defences, and the extent of the disposable force which it would be practicable to concentrate in the District.

The Secretary of War estimated the disposable regular force, applicable to the intended purpose, to the best of my recollection, about twelve hundred, including about two hundred cavalry at Carlisle, Pennsylvania, who, I think he said, were not all mounted, but would probably be so in a short time. He brought into view the volunteer corps of the City and District, the particulars of which I do not recollect, and estimated the depot at Harper's Ferry, I think, to contain at that time about thirty-six thousand stand of arms.

The Secretary of the Navy enumerated the naval force, within immediate reach, as follows: The marines at headquarters, about - - 120
The force attached to the flotilla under the command of Commodore Barney, on the Patuxent, about - - - - - 500
                                     620

To the regular force the President proposed to add ten thousand militia, to be designated and held in readiness in such neighboring districts as should be found most convenient. He also suggested the propriety of depositing, at a suitable place contiguous to the metropolis, a supply of arms, ammunition, and camp equipage.

These propositions produced very little discussion, the propriety and expediency of the measures appeared to be admitted, though no formal question was taken, nor any dissent expressed.

The meeting separated, with an understanding, on my part, that the measures proposed were to be carried into effect; but what order took place thereon, other than in the Department of the Navy, I know not; nor do I know any thing further material to the inquiry, except what is embraced in the communication which I had the honor to make to the committee on the 3d inst.

The officers of the Navy Yard are closely engaged in making out the estimates of the loss sustained by the conflagration at that establishment, but the loss of books and papers has retarded their operations. It shall be completed as soon as possible, and transmitted without delay.

I have the honor to be, sir, with great respect, your obedient servant,

                   W. JONES,
                 Secretary of the Navy.

Hon. RICHARD M. JOHNSON,
     Chairman Com. of Inquiry, H. of R.

NAVY DEPARTMENT, *Nov.* 12, 1814.

SIR: I have the honor to transmit the reports and statements of the Commandant of the Navy Yard, showing the actual loss of public property by the conflagration of the Navy Yard on the 24th of August last.

Exhibit A shows the loss sustained in moveable property, viz: the estimated value previous to the fire; the value preserved or recovered; and the actual loss sustained; as condensed in the recapitulation on the last page.
Net loss - - - - - $417,745 51

Exhibit B shows the loss sustained in buildings and fixtures, in like manner showing the estimated cost and real loss sustained. Net - 91,425, 53

     Total loss - - - - $509,171 04

To which is annexed an estimate (believed to be founded upon such data as may be relied upon) of the "expenses of rebuilding in a plain substantial manner," so as to carry on all the public work with as much advantage and convenience as before the fire; amount - - $62,370 14

I am, very respectfully, sir, your obedient servant,

                   W. JONES,
                 Secretary of the Navy.

Hon. R. M. JOHNSON,
     Chairman Com. Inquiry.

Capture of the City of Washington.

No. 5.

Letters from the honorable Richard Rush, Attorney General.

Narrative by Richard Rush, Attorney General of the United States, of such facts and circumstances as are within his knowledge, relative to the capture of Washington on the 24th of August, 1814; and of measures adopted by the Government in relation to that event, previous to, or on that day; delivered on the requisition of a Committee of the House of Representatives, appointed to investigate the causes which led to the capture.

WASHINGTON CITY, *Oct.* 15, 1814.

As my official place in the Government embraces no connexion with the duties of either of the four Departments, farther than as I am liable to be consulted on legal questions growing out of the business of either of them, it is not to be expected that I can give information relative to the subject-matter of the committee's inquiries, except—

1st. Such as I may have derived from being present at the deliberations of the Cabinet, when thereto summoned by the Executive, supposing any to be derivable from that source; or,

2dly. Such as I may have derived from my personal presence at Washington, and the opportunities thence furnished of becoming acquainted with acts or measures of Government, or other events transpiring at its seat.

In regard to the former capacity, I would beg leave to premise, that, as these deliberations imply an intercourse of confidence amongst those who participate in them, I hope I do not misapprehend the true nature of the connexion between the Executive and those whom he may invite to his consultations, or fail in my respect to the committee, when I state that I do not hold myself bound to make a public disclosure of matters which may, in this mode, have been the subject of Executive advisement or consideration. The exceptions belonging to such a rule, if any do belong to it, I forbear to advert to, inasmuch as I would be understood to have waived upon this occasion the objections which might otherwise be interposed against the development of transactions from this peculiar source of information. Upon a subject of such delicacy, and one involving future rights, I would beg to be further understood, that, in waiving all objection, I act under the full belief that it is not desired to restrain the freedom of such a course on my part, by any prohibitory injunctions from the quarter whence they could issue.

As introductory, then, to what I may have to disclose under this head, and to meet, as far as in my power, the inquiry made as to my knowledge of any preparatory measures adopted for the defence of the metropolis, I proceed to state—

That, in the month of June, of the past Summer, when the momentous changes in Europe had become revealed to us, I had the honor of holding, individually, occasional interviews with the President. In dwelling upon our public affairs, he expressed his strong belief of the inauspicious results which these changes held out every likelihood of superinducing upon them. That the entire liberation of British military power from European conflicts, created a corresponding probability that portions of it, unexpectedly formidable, would be thrown upon our shores. In one, at least, of the conversations, he also dwelt upon the probability of an attack upon Washington; enforcing his opinion on the grounds, among others, of its own weakness, and the *eclat that* would attend a successful inroad upon the capital, beyond the intrinsic magnitude of the achievement. He spoke of the immediate necessity of preparing for its defence. His impressions of the danger appeared to acquire new force from the 26th of the month, upon which day despatches were received from two of our Ministers abroad, Mr. Gallatin and Mr. Bayard, dated early in May. Upon the 30th of June, the Heads of Departments were desired to meet at the President's House on the following day at 12 o'clock.

They accordingly assembled. All were present. I also, in pursuance of the President's request, attended. Our public affairs were brought into discussion; their altered, and more menacing character; the probable reluctance of the *Northern* Powers of Europe to regard favorably, at such a moment of European homage to *the British* name, the just rights for which we were contending; the fierce aspect which British military power now had the means, and probably would not want the disposition to put on towards us; the parts of our country most vulnerable to its immediate irruptions, as well as the general trials before us, were brought into view. The President mentioned what I had heard him, individually, express before, relative to Washington; stating his impression, unequivocally, to be, that, if it fell within the plans of the enemy to send out troops for operations upon the Atlantic frontier this season, he thought the Capital would be marked as the most inviting object of a speedy attack. That it would be right, forthwith, to put in train measures of precaution and defence. He then declared that, to him, it appeared that a force of ten thousand men should be got in readiness for the city and District. That it would be desirable to have as large a portion of it as practicable regular troops; but that, at the least, there should be a thousand of this description, and more if more could be obtained. That the residue should be made up of the volunteers and militia of the District of Columbia, combined with that from the parts nearest adjacent of the States of Virginia, Maryland, and Pennsylvania. That convenient depots of arms and military equipage should also be established. No dissent was expressed to these opinions of the President. The Secretary of War made some verbal estimate of the regiments, or parts of regiments, near at hand. By this, it appeared that either with, or independent of, the marines at the Navy Yard, (for of this I am not certain) the portion of regular force mentioned could readily be had. I recollect nothing farther to have passed at the meeting about the defence of Washington. What measures were subsequently taken; how far those proposed were carried into effect; or by what causes they have been retarded or frustrated I have not had the means of knowing with any certainty, and therefore cannot speak. In regard to what I have said, I am disposed to entertain the less distrust of its general accuracy from the habit of keeping occasional written memorandums connected with our public history, and from having refreshed my memory by a reference to some, in the present instance, made at the time.

As it appears to come within the scope of the committee's inquiries that I should also disclose such facts as I may possess a knowledge of, relative to any participation, by the Government, in the immediate events of the 24th of August, I have to state that my knowledge herein is merely incidental. As far as it extends, or may appear to have any bearing upon the interrogatories of the committee, I will proceed to unfold it.

On the morning of that day, probably at about 9 o'clock, I called at the lodgings of the Secretary of War to ask him for his latest intelligence respecting the enemy's movements. He was good enough to hand me a note he had received from General Winder, written from headquarters, then established within the city limits, near the Eastern Branch bridge. It was dated, I think, the same morning. It was short, and stated the accounts from the river below to be more and more serious. It also expressed a wish to receive counsel either from the Secretary individually, or the Executive, as to the operations proper to be adopted in an emergency so critical. Other things may have been in it, but, reading it hastily, I would not be understood to speak with accuracy of its contents. Leaving the Secretary of War, I proceeded to the President's. Arriving there, I learned that the President had gone to the headquarters of General Winder. Thither I also next went. I there found the President, General Winder, Commodore Tingey, and two or three military officers. The Secretary of State, I understood, had previously been there, but had gone on to Bladensburg. The Secretary of the Navy came into the room not long afterwards. Of Commodore Tingey's presence I am not certain. The conversation turned upon the route by which it was thought most likely the enemy would make his approach. It was interrupted by dragoons, who had been on scouts, coming in every few minutes with their reports. The preponderance of opinion, at this period, I took to be that he would be most likely to move in a direction towards the Potomac, with a view to possess himself of Fort Warburton in the first instance. By this course, he would secure the passage of his ships, then supposed to be in the river below, and thus their ulterior co-operation, whether in the attack or retreat of his land troops. This way of thinking induced, as I supposed, General Winder to retain a large portion of his force in the neighborhood of the Eastern Branch bridge, in preference to moving it on, under the existing state of intelligence, towards Bladens-

burg. In anticipation of success to the enemy's attempts by water or land, or both, some conversation was had as to the proper precautions for blowing up, or otherwise rendering useless, the vessels and public property of the Navy Yard. After the lapse of probably an hour from the time I reached headquarters, an express arrived from General Stansbury, commanding the Baltimore troops, at Bladensburg, rendering it at length certain that the British army was advancing in that direction. General Winder immediately put his troops in motion, and marched off with them for Bladensburg.

When he had left the house, the Secretary of War, in company with the Secretary of the Treasury, arrived there. The President mentioned to the former the information which had just been received, at the same time asking him whether, as it was probable a battle would soon be brought on, he had any advice or plan to offer upon the occasion. He replied that he had not. He added, that, as it was to be between regulars and militia, the latter would be beaten. All who were in the house then came out; the Secretary of War getting on his horse to go to Bladensburg, and the Secretary of the Navy going to the marine barracks close by. Commodore Barney, with his seamen and marines, who were still remaining in or near the barracks, were ordered to push on with all despatch to Bladensburg, an order their anxiety stood anticipating. The President first went to the barracks, inviting me to accompany him. He then observed that he would ride to Bladensburg, with a view to join the two Heads of Departments, already gone there, and be of any use in his power. I proceeded on with him. Before we could reach the town, the forces of the enemy had possession of it. General Winder, as it struck my eye in riding along, had formed the troops he marched out with him on each side of the road, stretching a mile from Bladensburg, in such way as the few moments left him would allow. But, according to what particular plan they were drawn up, or by whose order, I cannot say. The President met with the Secretary of War and the Secretary of State upon the field near the front ranks. The former had arrived just before him. When the President arrived, the arrangement for the battle, whatever it may have been, was apparently made. It commenced in a very few minutes, and, in not many more, some of our troops began to break. The President and two Secretaries, at about this period, retired together. I joined them very shortly afterwards, and rode into Washington with the President.

It does not, at present, occur to me that I can state anything further relevant to the inquiries of the committee. I shall be ready to answer any questions it may think fit to propound, with a view to recall any explanatory or additional circumstances or facts, not collected above, or which I have not deemed it material to state.

             RICHARD RUSH.

Hon. R. M. Johnson,
    Chairman Committee of Inquiry.

WASHINGTON, *November* 3, 1814.

SIR: I have had the honor to receive your note, of the 29th of last month, requesting of me such information as I may possess relative to a report made early in June, from the War Department, to the President, of the amount of regular and militia force, and its distribution throughout the country; which report was submitted by the President to the Heads of Departments; and requesting, also, that I will add any further matter to my former narrative, which may have since occurred to my recollection, that I may deem material, particularly as to the part taken by the President, or any of the members of the Government, on the day of the battle of Bladensburg.

With the same reservation which I before took the liberty to make, of the privilege of being at my option as to the disclosure of facts of which I may have derived the knowledge through any confidential medium whilst engaged in public duties, I have to state—

That, at a meeting which took place of the Heads of Departments, at the President's, on the 7th of June, at which I also was present, I do remember that a paper was read by the President, which had been furnished by the Secretary of War, containing an estimate of all our land force, as well as its distribution. A similar one was exhibited of the naval force, prepared by the Secretary of the Navy. This, too, was read by the President. I remember the aggregate amount of the land force, but not the portions of it as then distributed through the respective military districts; or, at least, not that falling within district No. 5. The meeting was called, and the estimate of force submitted, for purposes quite distinct from the defence of district No. 5. The latter object being excluded, renders it, I presume, unnecessary that I should trouble the committee with any detail of the deliberations or resolutions that were had upon the occasion.

As regards the other branch of inquiry, I feel at some loss. I am not sure that I do remember any supplemental facts, which the committee might think material to be stated, relative to what took place on the day of the battle. Upon this subject I would, with the most entire deference, beg leave to suggest, that perhaps the most eligible course would be for me to answer (as I should ever be ready to do) to such interrogatories as the committee might find it in their discretion or convenience to put, rather than leave in my own hands the choice of topics. I venture upon the freedom of the remark from the fear that I may omit or introduce matter, which, in other eyes, might wear a different aspect of relationship to the investigation, to what it had done in mine. When the President expressed his intention of going to Bladensburg, he observed, while on the road, that one motive with him was, that, as the Secretary of War, who had just gone on, might be able to render useful assistance towards arrangements in the field, it would be best that the requisite sanction to it should be at hand, preventing thereby, at a moment so important, any possible embarrassment, arising from the claims or duties of the Commanding General. But when we reached the field we found the troops formed, and waiting, in their stations, the onset of the battle. The British army was already in full sight, and advancing in full march, through Bladensburg. At this juncture the President joined the Secretary of State and the Secretary of War, and all approached to the spot where General Winder was. Some words of conversation seemed to pass between the President and the two latter. I was not near enough to overhear it. General Winder rode forward a few yards, exhorting the troops to be firm. The firing began almost immediately afterwards. Results took place that are known. It had been the wish of the President, as signified to me, on the ride out, that, after every military arrangement for the battle had been made, on the best advice attainable, the civil functionaries should join him, and retire to the rear of the army, with a view to any ulterior deliberations which events might render necessary. I took it to be in conformity with this wish that the Secretary of State, the Secretary of War, and himself, retired at the time, and in the manner, I have stated, and it was in pursuance of it that I accompanied them. Whilst still on the field, encompassed by part of our troops, I think I understood the two Secretaries to unite in opinion, that the mode in which they had been drawn up was judicious as the time and circumstances allowed. But of this I do not speak with confidence, as my situation was partly taken up in viewing, from hill to hill, the contending movements. To me it appeared plain that entire ranks of our men, in front, were dispersed by the shock of the enemy, before any order for retreat was given by the Commanding General.

I have the honor to be, with great respect, your obedient servant,   RICHARD RUSH.

Hon R. M. JOHNSON,
    Chairman Com. of Inquiry.

No. 6.

Communication from the War Department, including the orders in relation to the tenth military district, the requisition of the 4th of July, and the correspondence with the Governors of Pennsylvania, Virginia, and Maryland, and with General Winder.

BALTIMORE, *July* 9, 1814.

SIR: The objects of the command which has been conferred upon me have consequently, since I received it, occupied my serious consideration.

The utmost regular force which it is probable can, in the present state of affairs, be placed at my command, including the force necessary for garrisoning the several forts, will not exceed one thousand men, and some weeks will necessarily elapse before the detachments from Virginia and Carlisle will reach my district; the detachments of the 36th and 38th are, therefore, the only troops that I can expect to have in the field in the mean time; and when those other detachments join, the utmost field force will be seven to eight hundred.

In conversation with you at Washington, I understood the idea, at present entertained, relative to the auxiliary militia force proposed for the District, to be, that it shall be draughted and designated, but that no part of it is to be called into the field until the hostile force, now in the Chesapeake, shall be reinforced to such an extent as to render it probable that a serious attack is contemplated.

The enemy's fleet has now spent more than a twelvemonth in the waters of the Chesapeake, and, during that time, has visited almost every river falling into the bay; and must be presumed to have such accurate information, that, whatever expedition may be destined to these waters will have a definite object, to the execution of which, on its arrival, it will proceed with the utmost promptitude and despatch. Should Washington, Baltimore, or Annapolis, be their object, what possible chance will there be of collecting a force, after the arrival of the enemy, to interpose between them and either of those places? They can proceed, without dropping anchor, to within three hours' rowing and marching of Baltimore; within less of Annapolis; and upon arriving off South river, can debark, and be in Washington in a day and a half. This celerity of movement, on their part, is not probable, owing to adverse weather and other causes; but if the enemy has been active, while in our waters, to acquire a knowledge of our country, of which there can be no doubt, and should be favored with weather, on the arrival of reinforcements, he can be in Washington, Baltimore, or Annapolis, in four days from entering the Capes. But allowing, liberally, for all causes of detention, he can be in either of those places in ten days from his arrival. What time will this allow us to hear of his arrival, to disseminate through the intricate and winding channels the various orders to the militia, for them to assemble, have their officers designated, their arms, accoutrements, and ammunition, delivered, the necessary supplies provided, or for the commanding officer to learn the different corps and detachments, so as to issue orders with the promptitude and certainty so necessary in active operations? If the enemy's force should be strong, which, if it come at all, it will be, sufficient numbers of militia could not be warned and run together, even as a disorderly crowd, without arms, ammunition, or organization, before the enemy would already have given his blow.

Would it not then be expedient to increase the force of my command, by immediately calling out a portion of militia; so that, by previously selecting the best positions for defence, and increasing, as far as possible, the natural advantages of these positions, the advance of the enemy might be retarded, his force crippled, and time and opportunity thus gained for drawing together whatever other resources of defence might be competent to resist the enemy? The small force of regulars will be incompetent to accomplish any material works at favorable positions, for strengthening the defences, and to supply the various vidette parties, which it will be necessary to station,

on the prominent points of the bay, to watch the enemy, and communicate his movements with the greatest possible despatch.

Allow me, sir, respectfully to propose that four thousand militia be called out without delay. I propose to station these in equal proportions, in the most eligible positions between South river and Washington, and in the vicinity of Baltimore. Baltimore could not be aided by a force stationed between South river and Washington, unless a force were on the spot to retard the advance of the enemy until it could arrive, and so with respect to the force at Baltimore, in co-operating with that intended to defend Washington. Each could assist the other if of this magnitude, and it appears to me that, with materially less means actually in the field and ready for instant action, no hope can be entertained of opposing the enemy in assailing either of those places.

I shall proceed to Annapolis to-morrow, and have but little doubt that the Executive of Maryland will cordially co-operate in affording such means as it may be deemed advisable to call for; and I beg you will permit me to procure this, or such other militia force as the President may think proper immediately to be called out.

I sent an order from Washington for the detachments of the 36th and 39th to move up to the head of South river, where I propose to meet them, and fix upon the most eligible spot for the camp intended to defend Washington.

You will please, therefore, to direct any communications to me, to Annapolis, which will enable me to make the requisite arrangements with the Executive of Maryland at once.

I have the honor to be, with great respect, sir, your obedient servant,

W. H. WINDER,
Brig. Gen. 10th Military Dist.

Hon. J. ARMSTRONG, *Sec'y of War.*

UPPER MARLBOROUGH, *July* 16, 1814.

SIR: I reached this place last evening, in my tour of examining the country. From what I have seen and learned, it appears to me that there cannot be found a place of tolerable convenience with reference to the objects of defence, for an encampment, except in this neighborhood. Two places near here offer many conveniences: the one, two and a half miles on the Western branch and the road to Bladensburg, which I have seen; the other, about five miles on the road to Washington and Piscataway, near the Woodyard, which I shall examine to-day. The former is represented as unhealthy during August and September, but possesses all other requisites; the latter is said to be healthy, and unless there should be some considerable deficiency towards the comfort and convenience of a camp, I presume will be preferable; and if, upon examination, I shall find it eligible, I shall order the 36th and 39th immediately to proceed thither. I am much embarrassed about the situation of Annapolis: it cannot be defended against a serious attack by land and water, without a large force and many additional works; and yet it appears to me that, should the enemy contemplate serious operations in this quarter, with any considerable force, it will be of the utmost importance to him to occupy it. With the command of the water, an entrenchment of seven or eight hundred yards, properly protected by batteries, renders it secure against any attack by land. It furnishes a position in every respect desirable and useful to him for making enterprises against any other point, and a safe retreat against every calamity; in short, it appears to me to be the door to Washington, and it is not possible for us to shut it with our present means. Fort Madison, besides its exposed and defenceless situation, except from an approach direct by water, is so very unhealthy during the months of August and September, that it is not possible to keep a garrison in it. It is provided with two fifty pound columbiads, two twenty-four pounders, two eighteen pounders, one twelve and one six pounder. These guns will be exposed to certain capture if they are left there, and will be turned against the town and Fort Severn, with decisive effect, unless we can find the means of making a substantial defence of the place.

It appears to me that these guns should be removed, and the post mined, ready to be blown up whenever an attack of the town may be contemplated. I cannot, however, but again remark that the importance of the place to the enemy, in every point of view, renders it of the last importance to be defended, if the means can be obtained. But a considerable force ought to be instantly sent there to prepare the works necessary to give a chance of successful defence. On my arrival here last evening, I learned that an express had passed through this place to the Governor of Maryland, who stated that he was the bearer of information that two seventy-fours, with a number of small vessels, had made their appearance near the mouth of the Potomac. It is of importance that I obtain the earliest intelligence, if this be true; and I beg, if you have any intelligence worthy of attention, that you would communicate it to me here without delay. By the return of the express to Point Lookout, I shall write to the person employed there to give intelligence, and direct him to transmit me by express, intelligence of all the movements of the enemy. I shall also establish express lines from all the prominent points of observation on the bay, unless these may be already established, of which I beg you to inform me. The Governor and Council of Maryland have taken steps immediately to comply with the requisition of the General Government; but I fear, from my recent experience, it will be in vain to look for any efficient aid upon a sudden call upon the militia.

W. H. WINDER.

Hon. J. ARMSTRONG, *Sec'y of War.*

NOTTINGHAM, *July* 17, 1814.

SIR: We have information, deemed credible here, that the enemy are advancing up this river in considerable force. I have called the detachment of regulars to this place, who will be here to-morrow. The alarm is going out to assemble what militia force can be collected; and I take the liberty of suggesting the propriety of sending to this point, with the utmost expedition, the marine corps, and all the militia force that can be procured from the District.

Yours, respectfully,
W. H. WINDER,
Brig. Gen., 10th *Military Dist.*

Hon. SECRETARY OF WAR.

ANNAPOLIS, *July* 20, 1814.

SIR: Your letter of the 17th reached me on the 18th. The enemy proceeded no further up the Patuxent than Hunting creek, where he landed and committed some depredations in Calvert county. He has since returned down the river, leaving us in doubt where he will next appear. I, in consequence, halted the three companies of city volunteers at the Woodyard, and the detachments of the 36th and 38th at Upper Marlborough, until some further indication shall be made by the enemy.

I have seized this moment to proceed to this place to arrange the calling of the Maryland militia, demanded by the requisition of the fourth instant. This will be immediately attended to by the Governor of this State. I have deemed it advisable to call for the highest number directed by the President, supposing that, by this means, we might possibly get the lowest.

I shall immediately proceed to Baltimore, to see and understand the means of defence there, to make the necessary arrangements and orders. I shall leave this to-morrow afternoon, or next day morning at farthest, (unless some movement of the enemy renders it unnecessary) and proceed to the country between Potomac and Patuxent.

I am, very respectfully, sir, your most obedient servant,

W. H. WINDER,
Brig. Gen., 10th *Military Dist.*

Hon. J. ARMSTRONG, *Sec'y of War.*

N. B.—The Governor informs me that it will not be in his power to supply the arms, camp equipage, &c., to the quota. The requisitions already made and expected for local defence have exhausted the State arsenal.

"I have delayed dismantling Fort Madison, only because it will excite greater sensation and clamor, and by that means proclaim to the enemy that it was not to be, or could not be, defended, and thus invite him to take possession of it. It would be impossible to dismantle it without making it public; and I have deemed it more expedient to risk the loss of the guns there, than, by removing them, invite the enemy to take the place, which he may possibly abstain from while he supposes the place will be defended.

W. H. W.

Capture of the City of Washington.

UPPER MARLBOROUGH, *July* 23, 1814.

SIR: I availed myself of a suspension of the enemy's movements to proceed to Annapolis and Baltimore, to attend to the militia calls on Maryland. I returned here yesterday at two o'clock. The Governor has issued orders for calling out three thousand of the draughts, under the requisition of the fourth of July; and, at my suggestion, has appointed Bladensburg as the place of rendezvous. I preferred this place, because it was near the proposed line of defence, and contiguous to the supplies which Washington can afford. It will be necessary that arms, ammunition, accoutrements, tents, and camp equipage, be deposited there for them. I have no knowledge where these articles are in store, nearest that point, nor under whose charge they are. I must pray you give the necessary orders for having the requisite deposites made at that place. I have notified the contractor.

The two thousand militia from General Smith's division, and who are to rendezvous near Baltimore, will, I believe, need no supplies but provision and ammunition from the United States. Upon these points I have taken orders. I fear some time will elapse before either of these requisitions can be complied with, in having the men assembled, especially the former, the draught being yet to be made. Major Marsteller, if not too much occupied at Washington, ought to be with me in the field; but his duties will call him, probably, to so many different points, that it appears to me he will require an assistant. The enemy's force is divided between the Potomac and Patuxent. The accounts which ought most to be credited, give five hundred as having landed from the Patuxent squadron, and from one thousand to fifteen hundred from the Potomac squadron; and although, from repeated experience, we are forbid to rely on this intelligence, yet, as it is the only direct intelligence we have, and comes from respectable people having had opportunities of observation, it cannot be wholly disregarded. I shall, therefore, for the present, still retain the city volunteers, and keep them and the regulars in a post of observation and readiness. I shall myself proceed nearer the enemy, for the purpose of better information and observation.

As I do not know whether only the quota of the District militia is to be draughted and placed at my disposal, or whether, on occasion, they are all considered as liable to requisition, I would thank you for information on that subject. As that part of the Pennsylvania militia, assigned for my district, are remote, and could not be called out upon emergency, might it not be expedient to draw from remotest points, leaving that portion of the militia nearest the probable scene of action, to be called out on the spur of the occasion? A deserter from the British, whose examination I have seen, says they talk of attacking Annapolis. If they know their own interest and our weakness, in fact incapacity, to defend that point, they certainly will possess it.

I have the honor to be, &c.

          W. H. WINDER.

WOODYARD, *July* 23, 1814.

SIR: Since I wrote you this morning, I have, under all circumstances, deemed it expedient to direct Captain Davidson to return to Washington with his detachment of volunteers.

The facility with which they can turn out and proceed to any point, renders them nearly as effective as if actually kept in the field; and the importance to them individually of attending to their private affairs, decides me, even in the doubt of the enemy's probable movement, to give this order.

I take the liberty of suggesting, upon the information of Captain Doughty, that the rifles they have are very defective for service; and it would be useful, especially at the present moment, if they could be supplied with better. Captain Burch's artillery are also without swords. Whether both those articles are supplied to the militia of the District by the Government, I know not; but if they are and can be, the probable demand for the services of the militia of the District, and their importance in the scale of our force, would render it desirable they should be supplied.

I beg leave also to suggest, upon the information of the commanding officers of companies, that, if the tents and camp equipage were respectively left under their charge, it would enable them to march when called upon with much greater promptitude.

I have the honor to be, with very great respect, sir, your obedient servant,

          W. H. WINDER,
        Brig. Gen., 10th Military Dist.

Hon. J. ARMSTRONG, *Sec'y of War.*

WARBURTON, NEAR FORT WASHINGTON,
           July 25, 1814.

SIR: From the enclosed representation of Lieutenant Edwards, and my own observation in confirmation thereof, Fort Washington is, in several respects, incomplete in its state of preparation for defence. If the eighteen pound columbiads are not mounted even in the block-house, ammunition ought to be sent down for them and the eighteen pounders on the water battery. Lieutenant Edwards will send a requisition for the quantity and kind of ammunition necessary. Can Colonel Wadsworth, or the proper department at Washington, have the platform enlarged, which will be necessary to render the battery of the fort effectual?

I shall proceed down as far as Port Tobacco to-day.

I am, with great respect, &c.,

          W. H. WINDER,
        Brig. Gen., 10th Military Dist.

Hon. J. ARMSTRONG, *Sec'y of War.*

Report of Lieutenant Edwards.

FORT WASHINGTON, *July* 25, 1814.

SIR: I deem it my duty to report to you the defenceless situation of this post. The necessity of mounting heavy artillery in the block-house is apparent to every military character who is acquainted with the ground adjacent to the works. It is true a few eighteen pound columbiads have been sent here, but there are no means to enable us to mount them: we are destitute of a gin and tackle. The width of the platform in the fort is another subject upon which frequent representations (I understand) were made to General Bloomfield, but without effect. The depth of platforms for heavy pieces is generally from three to four toises, but seldom less than three. The width of this is but fourteen feet, very little more than two toises. At the first discharge of our heavy guns, I have known them to recoil to the hurtoirs. When they are heated they would undoubtedly run over it, and thus be rendered useless for a time.

On the water battery there are mounted five excellent long eighteen pounders, (ship guns,) but there is not a pound of ammunition for them. In case of an attack by water, the utility of these guns would soon be discovered. In defending ourselves against maritime attacks, it is of the first importance to have a battery near the level of the water, so as to strike the hull of the ship in a horizontal line; for the chance of hitting the object is much greater than when firing from an elevation; when it is only an intersection of the line of fire by the line of the surface that the ball can strike a ship's hull. In the first case the gunner has only to move his piece horizontally; in the other he must combine his direction with those of his elevation and the progress of the ship.

Some of the gun carriages in the fort are in bad order, but not so much so as to render them unserviceable. You will perceive by this morning's report, which I enclose, what is the strength of my force: those reported sick are invalids; those on extra duty, are men employed in the bake-house, garden, &c., and who are from bodily defects incapable of guard duty, but would be serviceable in the action.

I have the honor to be, &c.,
JAMES L. EDWARDS,
Lieutenant, comm'g Fort Washington.

Colonel Wadsworth's Report.

A couple of hands were ordered from Greenleaf's Point on Monday, to execute the necessary repairs of the gun carriages at Fort Washington. The platform is undoubtedly too narrow, as well as the parapet, but I think Lieutenant Edwards is mistaken in representing it to be but fourteen feet. It was directed to be made twenty or twenty-two feet, if I do not misrecollect. The disadvantage of too narrow a platform may be obviated with no great difficulty, by checking the recoil of the piece by means of an elastic handspike introduced between the spokes of the wheels to prevent them from turning. The defect of an insufficient parapet is not so easily obviated. It would be advisable I think, at a proper time, to make a new wall in front, fifteen or twelve feet in advance of the present, which

would give sufficient extent, as well for the platform as parapet, without disturbing the magazine, &c. The whole original design was bad, and it is therefore impossible to make a perfect work of it by any alterations.

Two hundred rounds of shot and cartridges for eighteen pounders can be sent down, if thought proper. I directed some grape shot for the eighteen pound columbiads to be prepared long ago. A tackle and fall, to mount those guns in the block-house, will be provided.

Captain Marsteller, whom I have just seen, informs me there was a good tackle and fall at Fort Washington when he left. He says the platform was made above twenty feet wide.

D. WADSWORTH.

PORT TOBACCO, *July 26, 1814.*

SIR: From the uniform train of information yesterday, the enemy are descending both the Potomac and the Patuxent. I cannot, however, rely implicitly on the intelligence. I expect more certain intelligence this morning. I expect the enemy will move up the bay next, and I shall not be surprised to find Annapolis his object, which I fear would fall before five hundred men. As soon as I am certain of the movements of the enemy, I shall return to Marlborough, and thence as circumstances may require.

What prospect of the cavalry from Carlisle, and the detachment from Virginia? I have received intelligence of neither.

I am, very respectfully, &c.,
W. H. WINDER,
Brig. Gen., 10th Military Dist.

Hon. J. ARMSTRONG, Sec'y of War.

PISCATAWAY, *July 27, 1814.*

SIR: I returned to this place from Port Tobacco this morning.

One of the enemy's frigates, the Loire, it is said passed through the Kettle Bottoms, but returned the day before yesterday to Clement's bay, where two seventy-fours still remain. I have not obtained information where the remainder of the fleet are. If there are any of their vessels in the Patuxent, they are at or near the mouth of the river. I expect to hear of them next up the bay. I shall go on immediately to Marlborough, where, or near it, I shall remain until the movements of the enemy may call me away.

General Stewart has a very considerable force at or near Cedar Point; Colonel Beall has his regiment and a troop of cavalry at Port Tobacco; and Colonel Bowie with his regiment is at Nottingham; the regulars under my command are at Marlborough, between the enemy and any possible approach to Washington. The Governor is exerting himself to collect a force at Annapolis.

I have employed myself without intermission in examining the country, and have acquired a knowledge of its topography, which will be extremely useful to me.

I should have proceeded lower down had the enemy's force been up the rivers Potomac or Patuxent; but the retrograde movements on both the rivers induces me to suppose they will proceed to some other point, and I return to Marlborough to be ready whenever he may appear.

I have heard nothing as yet of the dragoons from Carlisle, or the detachment of infantry from Virginia. Are there not enough recruits of the thirty-sixth and thirty-eighth to form a company each? If either have fifty men, would it not be advisable to organize and order them to join?

This will be delivered you by Major Stewart, who goes by the way of Washington, will join me at Marlborough, and take any commands you may have for me.

I am, with great respect, &c.,
W. H. WINDER,
Brig. Gen., 10th Military Dist.
Hon. J. ARMSTRONG, *Sec'y of War.*

PISCATAWAY, *July 27, 1814.*

SIR: In the third paragraph of my letter, just finished, and which will accompany this, I have used general expressions relative to the force, in order that, should it be deemed advisable to use any information I have communicated to tranquillize the morbid sensibility of the people of the District, no injurious disclosure may be made; and I add a more specific account of the force in a separate letter for your information.

General Stewart states his force at eight hundred; Colonel Beall has three hundred to three hundred and fifty, and forty dragoons; Colonel Bowie has, I presume, three hundred. The Governor has been, in vain, endeavoring to assemble the neighboring militia at Annapolis; he had called on Frederick county, and some militia were coming in from thence, when I last was at Annapolis. All this force is, however, called out by the authority of the State laws, and is not under my command. But they do and will cooperate toward the general defence. I am, &c.,
W. H. WINDER,
Brigadier General.
Hon. J. ARMSTRONG, *Sec'y of War.*

PORT TOBACCO, *August 1, 1814.*

SIR: I learn this morning, in a manner which leaves me no doubt of the fact, that the enemy have retired down near to the mouth of the river, if he has not left it, with all his ships. A rumor, not so well authenticated, but very probable, states the force in the Patuxent to be increased and ascending that river.

I have halted the detachment under Lieutenant Colonel Scott at Piscataway, where they will wait until some ascertained movement of the enemy shall render it necessary for them to move to some other point.

I shall see General Stewart, of the militia, this morning, and then be able to speak more decidedly.

I am, sir, with great respect, your most obedient servant,
W. H. WINDER,
Brigadier General commanding.
Hon. J. ARMSTRONG, *Sec'y of War.*

BALTIMORE, *August 13, 1814.*

SIR: In consequence of the two regiments which were draughted from General Smith's division, under the requisition of April last, being accepted as part of the quota of Maryland, under the requisition of the 4th of July last, of the impracticability, besides impropriety of calling any portion of those draughted from the Eastern Shore, and the necessity of leaving all the men immediately upon the bay, and low down upon the rivers, for local defence on the Western Shore, the remaining portion of the Maryland draughts to be assembled at Bladensburg, instead of being three thousand, will not much exceed as many hundred. I shall require the Governor to order out all the draughts that can possibly be spared from the three lower brigades on the Western Shore; but since the whole number draughted on the Western Shore, exclusive of those drawn from General Smith's division, do not amount to fifteen hundred, I apprehend that, after all shall be assembled, under this second order from the Governor of Maryland, they will not exceed one thousand men. The most convenient and immediate resource to supply this deficiency, which occurs to me, will be to take the militia drawn out under the State authority, and now assembled at Annapolis, to the amount of one thousand men, into the service of the United States, and to call on the Governor of Pennsylvania for one regiment. This would make the militia force (independent of the two regiments near this place) under my command between two and three thousand men, and would complete the views of the President in the order communicated to me by you, to call for not more than three, nor less than two thousand over and above the two regiments here.

The objects for which the militia were called to Annapolis, were such as to make it proper that the force should be under the direction of the commander of the 10th military district. Some force ought and must be kept at Annapolis, and if it should be deemed proper to authorize me to accept them, I should leave them there until some necessity occurred requiring them elsewhere; and the trouble and expense of advancing a detachment there, would be avoided.

These men are only called out for sixty days, which may, perhaps, be long enough, and will, at all events, afford sufficient time to ascertain whether a further force will be necessary. They are already in the field, equipped in all respects, and organized. A saving of their equipments will be gained by the United States, and all the time and trouble of calling a force in their place.

I shall proceed for Bladensburg and Washington to-morrow, or the day following.

I have the honor to be, sir, with great respect, your most obedient servant,

W. H. WINDER,
Brig. Gen., 10th Military Dist.

Hon. J. ARMSTRONG, *Sec'ry of War.*

WAR DEPARTMENT, *Aug. 22, 1814.*

DEAR GENERAL: Your letter of the 21st is received.

Of the force in the Potomac we do not know as much as we ought. Their fleet is said to consist of six frigates, one of which had got aground on the Kettle Bottoms. They have on board some troops or marines which had been previously encamped on St. George's Island. General Parker is observing them on the Virginia side of the river, at the head of a small brigade of militia, about fourteen or fifteen hundred.

Enclosed is a letter from General Douglas, of Loudoun. I have ordered him to come on directly, without seeking a rendezvous with General Hungerford. A detachment of the 12th infantry (recruits) arrived here yesterday. They shall be armed, equipped, and marched to the Woodyard this morning. The Baltimore brigade will be at Bladensburg to day. Would it not be well to throw Barney's seamen (six hundred) and some other troops on the right of Nottingham? A demonstration which shall menace the rear of the enemy and their communication with the shipping, will, if it does not actually stop, at least very much retard their progress.

I am, sir, with great respect, your most obedient servant,

JOHN ARMSTRONG.

Brig. General WINDER,
Prince George's county, Md.

WASHINGTON CITY, *Aug. 19, 1814.*

SIR: I beg leave to suggest, through you, for the consideration of the President, the following propositions:

Would it be expedient, under the direction of the Navy Department, to have vessels ready to be sunk in the Potomac, at Fort Washington, or other proper point, at a moment's warning, to obstruct the navigation?

Would it not be proper to put all the boats, which can be propelled by oars, that are at this place, under the control of the Navy Department, at Fort Washington, to transport troops across the river from either side, as circumstances may require?

Would it not be expedient, in our present destitute condition of military force, to put the marine corps into service, or, at all events, to cause them to reinforce Fort Washington at a moment's notice, or to be applied, as circumstances require, to any point of defence?

From the great and overwhelming force of the enemy on water, it is no longer useful to keep the flotilla armed in the Patuxent; might not that force be applied to some stationary point of defence on land, or be subjected in some way to co-operate in the general arrangements which the commander of the district may make?

Serious difficulties have already arisen from collision, in the Patapsco, with the command of Fort McHenry and the flotilla, in performing the duty of guard and look-out, the flotilla boat having stopped and kept in custody all night the look-out boat of the fort.

Would it be advisable for the commander of the district, or any other public authority, to make an appeal to the patriotism of the country, at the present moment, for volunteers, without regard to their legal obligations as militia men? A large force very useful might be obtained, probably, in this way, which would cost only provision and ammunition. In fine, would it not be advisable, without regard to forms, too slow for the emergency, to invite and call in every man that can be found? This is, perhaps, more expedient, because I have received official information that the Pennsylvania militia are not in a state to be called out legally; the former law having expired the 1st of July, and the law of last session not taking effect as to organization until October next. I take this occasion to state that I have called for the militia of the District of Columbia, en masse; for General West's brigade in Prince George's county, and General Williams's, of Anne Arundel, also en masse; and the Baltimore brigades, also en masse. I shall forward by express, immediately, demands for five hundred men each, from all the brigades on the Western Shore of Maryland, and the counties which border the Potomac on the Virginia side. General Hungerford, Northern Neck, has a force in the field which I have called on him to march, without delay, to this place. The result of all these operations will be certainly slow, and extremely doubtful as to the extent of force produced.

I am, sir, most respectfully, your obedient servant,

W. H. WINDER,
Brig. Gen., 10th Military Dist.

Hon. SECRETARY OF WAR.

WASHINGTON, *August 21, 1814.*

SIR: The calls which have been made upon the militia officers, and the appeals to the people to turn out, is likely to produce, in haste, an uncertain force in its amount and armament; probably, very considerable in numbers. I beg leave therefore, to suggest the propriety of augmenting the quantity of arms immediately at this place or its vicinity; perhaps Foxall's work, would be a good and safe depot, and sufficiently convenient. They can be drawn, by immediate exertions, in sufficient time. All the fints that the utmost efforts can produce, ought to be collected here without delay.

I am, sir, most respectfully, your obedient servant,

W. H. WINDER.

Hon. J. ARMSTRONG,
Secretary of War.

Capture of the City of Washington.

HEADQUARTERS, COMBS'S, NEAR
EASTERN BRANCH BRIDGE,
Wednesday, August 24, 1814.

SIR: I have found it necessary to establish my headquarters here, the most advanced position convenient to the troops, and nearest information. I shall remain stationary as much as possible, that I may be the more readily found, to issue orders, and collect together the various detachments of militia, and give them as rapid a consolidation and organization as possible.

With great respect, yours, &c.
WM. H. WINDER,
Brig. Gen., 10th *Military Dist.*
Hon. SECRETARY OF WAR.

P. S. The news up the river is very threatening. Barney's, or some other force, should occupy the batteries at Greenleaf's Point and the Navy Yard. I should be glad of the assistance of counsel from yourself and the Government. If more convenient, I should make an exertion to go to you the first opportunity.

NOTE.—The following memorandum was endorsed on the back of the foregoing letter, in the hand-writing of Secretary Armstrong:

"Went to General Winder; found there the President; Mr. Monroe had also been there, but had set out to Bladensburg to arrange the troops, and give them an order of battle, as I understood; saw no necessity for ordering Barney to Greenleaf's Point or Navy Yard. Advised the Commodore to join the army at Bladensburg, and ordered Minor's regiment to that place. Advised General Winder to leave Barney and the Baltimore brigade upon the enemy's rear and right flank, while he put himself in front with all the rest of his force. Repeated this idea in my letter to him of the 22d."

BALTIMORE, *August 27, 1814.*

SIR: When the enemy arrived at the mouth of the Potomac, of all the militia which I had been authorized to assemble, there were but about one thousand seven hundred in the field; from thirteen to fourteen hundred under General Stansbury, near this place, and about two hundred and fifty at Bladensburg, under Lieut. Colonel Kramer; the slow progress of draught, and the imperfect organization, with the ineffectiveness of the laws to compel them to turn out, rendered it impossible to have procured more.

The militia of this State, and of the contiguous parts of Virginia and Pennsylvania, were called on en masse, but the former militia law of Pennsylvania had expired on the first of June or July, and the one adopted in its place is not to take effect in organizing the militia, before October. No aid, therefore, has been received from that State.

After all the force that could be put at my disposal in that short time, and making such dispositions as I deemed best calculated to present the most respectable force at whatever point the enemy might strike, I was enabled, by the most ac-

tive and harassing movements of the troops, to interpose before the enemy at Bladensburg about five thousand men, including three hundred and fifty regulars and Commodore Barney's command. Much the largest portion of this force arrived on the ground when the enemy were in sight, and were disposed to support, in the best manner, the position which General Stansbury had taken. They had barely reached the ground before the action commenced, which was about one o'clock, P. M. of the 24th instant, and continued about an hour.

The contest was not so obstinately maintained as could have been desired, but was by parts of the troops sustained with great spirit, and with prodigious effect; and had the whole of our force been equally firm, I am induced to believe that the enemy would have been repulsed, notwithstanding all the disadvantages under which we fought. The artillery from Baltimore, supported by Major Pinkney's rifle battalion, and a part of Captain Doughty's from the Navy Yard, were in advance to command the pass of the bridge at Bladensburg, and played upon the enemy, as I have since learned, with very destructive effect; but the rifle troops were obliged, after some time, to retire, and, of course, the artillery. Superior numbers, however, rushed upon them, and made their retreat necessary, not, however, without great loss on the part of the enemy. Major Pinkney received a severe wound in his right arm, after he had retired to the left flank of Stansbury's brigade. The right and centre of Stansbury's brigade, consisting of Lieutenant Colonel Ragan's and Shutz's regiments, generally gave way very soon afterwards, with the exception of about forty rallied by Colonel Ragan, after having lost his horse, and a whole or a part of Captain Trower's company, both of whom General Stansbury represents to have made, even thus deserted, a gallant stand. The fall which Lieutenant Colonel Ragan received from his horse, together with his great efforts to sustain his position, rendered him unable to follow the retreat; we have therefore to lament that this gallant and excellent officer has been taken prisoner; he has, however, been paroled, and I met him here recovering from the bruises occasioned by his fall. The loss of his services at this moment is serious. The fifth Baltimore regiment, under Lieutenant Colonel Sterret, being the left of Brigadier General Stansbury's brigade, still, however, stood their ground, and, except for a moment, when part of them recoiled a few steps, remained firm, and stood until ordered to retreat with a view to prevent them from being outflanked.

The reserve under Brigadier General Smith, of the District of Columbia, with the militia of the city and Georgetown, with the regulars, and some detachments of Maryland militia, flanked on their right by Commodore Barney and his brave fellows, and Lieutenant Colonel Beall, still were to the right on the hill, and maintained the contest for some time with great effect.

It is not with me to report the conduct of Commodore Barney and his command, nor can I speak from observation, being too remote; but the concurrent testimony of all who did observe them, does them the highest justice for their brave resistance, and the destructive effect they produced on the enemy. Commodore Barney, after having lost his horse, took post near one of his guns, and there, unfortunately, received a severe wound in the thigh, and also fell into the hands of the enemy.

Captain Miller, of Marines, was wounded in the arm, fighting bravely. From the best intelligence, there remains but little doubt that the enemy lost at least four hundred killed and wounded, and of these a very unusual portion killed. Our loss cannot, I think, be estimated at more than from thirty to forty killed, and fifty or sixty wounded.

You will readily understand that it is impossible for me to speak minutely of the merit or demerit of particular troops so little known to me from their recent and hasty assemblage. My subsequent movements, for the purpose of preserving as much of my force as possible, gaining reinforcements, and protecting this place, you already know.

I am, with very great respect, &c.
WM. H. WINDER,
Brig. Gen., 10th Military Dist.
Hon. J. Armstrong, *Sec'ry of War.*

P. S. We have to lament that Captain Sterret, of the 5th Baltimore regiment, has also been wounded, but is doing well; other officers, no doubt, deserve notice, but I am as yet unable to particularize.

General Order erecting the Tenth Military District, and letters from the Secretary of War to General Winder.

War Department,
Adjutant and Inspector General's Office,
July 2, 1814.
General Orders:

The State of Maryland, the District of Columbia, and that part of Virginia lying between the Rappahannock and Potomac rivers, will constitute a separate military district (No. 10) under the command of Brigadier General Winder.
By order:　　　JOHN R. BELL,
Assistant Inspector General.

War Department, *July 2, 1814.*
Sir: Your letters of the 30th instant have been received.

Enclosed is an order constituting a new military district, and assigning you to the command thereof. Major Stewart has permission to serve in your staff. It would be desirable to see you here as soon as it may be convenient for you to come.

I am, very respectfully, sir, your obedient servant,
JOHN ARMSTRONG.
Brig. Gen. Wm. H. Winder, *Baltimore.*

War Department, *July 18, 1814.*
Sir: In addition to my circular letter of the 4th instant, which subjects to your call the quota of Maryland militia, you are also authorized to draw, from that of Virginia, two thousand men, and from the quota of Pennsylvania, five thousand. The whole of the militia of the District of Columbia, amounting to about two thousand, is kept in a disposable state, and subject to your orders.

Note.—The detached militia of Maryland amounted to six thousand.

I am, very respectfully, sir, your obedient servant,
JOHN ARMSTRONG.
Brig. Gen. Winder.

War Department, *July 28, 1814.*
Sir: I have the honor to acknowledge the receipt of your letters of the 25th and 27th instant. Lieutenant Edwards's representation is referred to Colonel Wadsworth, with orders to supply what may be wanting at Fort Washington. Lieutenant Colonel Lavall states that he is waiting the arrival of horses. The detachment of the 10th is in march, and the recruits of the 36th and 38th ordered to join their corps. They, I fear, are very few.

I am, very respectfully, your obedient servant,
JOHN ARMSTRONG.
Brig. Gen. Winder,
Comd'g 10th Military District.

War Department, *Aug. 19, 1814.*
Sir: Your letter of this date has been received, and submitted to the President. On the two first subjects, you are referred to the Navy Department. The marines are ordered to move. Orders have been given to Commodore Barney.

You will adjust, with the Secretary of the Navy, what relates to guard and vidette duty at Baltimore.

The call you propose making on volunteers is approved. It will be so worded as to guard against interfering with the legal draught, and putting it in the election of the militia to fulfil, or not to fulfil, their public engagments.

The calls you have actually made are also approved.

I am, very respectfully, your obedient servant,
JOHN ARMSTRONG.
Brig. Gen. Winder.

War Department, *Aug. 19, 1814.*
Sir: If the enemy's movements indicate an attack on this place, means should be taken to drive off all horses and cattle, and remove all supplies of forage, &c., on their route; a moment is not to be lost in doing both. For this purpose the whole of your cavalry may be pushed into the neighborhood of the enemy without delay.

Colonel McLean could be usefully employed with them. Lavall will be at Montgomery

Capture of the City of Washington.

Court-house to-day. He has with him one hundred and thirty mounted dragoons, under excellent officers.

I am, very respectfully, your obedient servant,

JOHN ARMSTRONG.

Brig. Gen. WINDER.

Correspondence with the Governors of Pennsylvania, Maryland, and Virginia.

Circular to the Governors of States.

WAR DEPARTMENT, *July* 4, 1814.

SIR: The late pacification in Europe offers to the enemy a large disposable force, both naval and military, and with it the means of giving to the war here a character of new and increased activity and extent.

Without knowing with certainty that such will be its application, and still less that any particular point or points will become objects of attack, the President has deemed it advisable, as a measure of precaution, to strengthen ourselves on the line of the Atlantic, and (as the principal means of doing this will be found in the militia) to invite the Executives of certain States to organize, and hold in readiness, for immediate service, a corps of ninety-three thousand five hundred men, under the laws of the 28th of February, 1795, and 18th of April, 1814.

The enclosed detail will show your Excellency what, under this requisition, will be the quota of ——. As far as volunteer uniform companies can be found they will be preferred.

The expediency of regarding (as well in the designations of the militia as of their places of rendezvous) the points, the importance or exposure of which will be most likely to attract the views of the enemy, need but be suggested.

A report of the organization of your quota, when completed, and of its place or places of rendezvous, will be acceptable.

I have the honor to be, with very great respect, your Excellency's most obedient and very humble servant.

His Exc'y the GOVERNOR OF ——.

Capture of the City of Washington.

Detail for Militia Service, under the requisition of July 4, 1814.

States.	Number and kind of troops.	Total number.	Number of Regiments.	General Staff.
New Hampshire	350 artillery 3,150 infantry	3,500	3 regiments and one battalion	One Major General, two Brigadier Generals, one Deputy Quartermaster General, one Assistant Adjutant General.
Massachusetts	1,000 artillery 9,000 infantry	10,000	10 regiments	Two Major Generals, four Brigadier Generals, one Deputy Quartermaster General, three Assistant Deputy Quartermaster Generals, and two Assistant Adjutant Generals.
Rhode Island	50 artillery 450 infantry	500	1 battalion.	
Connecticut	300 artillery 2,700 infantry	8,000	3 regiments	One Major General, one Brigadier General, one Deputy Quartermaster General, one Assistant Adjutant General.
New York	1,350 artillery 12,150 infantry	13,500	13 regiments and one battalion	Three Major Generals, seven Brigadier Generals, one Deputy Quartermaster General, and three Assistant Adjutant Generals, six Assistant Deputy Quartermaster Generals.
New Jersey	500 artillery 4,500 infantry	5,000	5 regiments	One Major General, two Brigadier Generals, one Deputy Quartermaster General, one Assistant Adjutant General.
Pennsylvania	1,400 artillery 12,600 infantry	14,000	14 regiments	Three Major Generals, seven Brigadier Generals, one Deputy Quartermaster General, six Assistant Deputy Quartermaster Generals, and three Assistant Adjutant Generals.
Delaware	100 artillery 900 infantry	1,000	1 regiment.	One Major General, two Brigadier Generals, one Deputy Quartermaster General, and one Assistant Adjutant General.
Maryland	600 artillery 5,400 infantry	6,000	6 regiments	One Major General, three Brigadier Generals, one Deputy Quartermaster General, and one Assistant Adjutant General.
Virginia	1,200 artillery 10,800 infantry	12,000	12 regiments	Three Major Generals, six Brigadier Generals, one Deputy Quartermaster General, and three Assistant Adjutant Generals, five Assistant Deputy Quartermaster Generals.
North Carolina	700 artillery 6,300 infantry	7,000	7 regiments	One Major General, three Brigadier Generals, one Deputy Quartermaster General, and one Assistant Adjutant General.
South Carolina	500 artillery 4,500 infantry	5,000	5 regiments	One Major General, two Brigadier Generals, one Deputy Quartermaster General, and one Assistant Adjutant General.
Georgia	350 artillery 3,150 infantry	3,500	3 regiments and one battalion	One Major General, two Brigadier Generals, one Deputy Quartermaster General, one Assistant Adjutant General.
Kentucky	5,500 infantry	5,500	5 regiments and one battalion	One Major General, two Brigadier Generals, one Deputy Quartermaster General, and one Assistant Adjutant General.
Tennessee	2,500 infantry	2,500	2 regiments and one battalion	One Major General, two Brigadier Generals, one Deputy Quartermaster General, and one Assistant Adjutant General, one Assistant Deputy Quartermaster General, one Assistant Adjutant General.
Louisiana, Mississippi Territory,	1,000 infantry 500 infantry	1,000 500	1 regiment 1 battalion	Louisiana and Mississippi, one Brigadier General, and one Assistant Deputy Quartermaster General.

Capture of the City of Washington.

SECRETARY's OFFICE, *July* 14, 1814.

Sir: In the absence of the Governor, I deem it my duty to inform you, that your communication containing a requisition for a detachment of fourteen thousand Pennsylvania militia came to the office this morning, and was immediately forwarded by express to the Governor, at Selin's Grove. Be assured the requisition will be met with all the promptness the circumstances possibly will permit.

With high considerations of respect, I am, sir, your obedient servant,

N. B. BOILEAU, *Secretary.*

J. ARMSTRONG, Esq., *Sec'y of War.*

SECRETARY's OFFICE, *July* 25, 1814.

SIR: The Governor has directed me to enclose to you copies of general orders issued by him in compliance with a late requisition for a military force from Pennsylvania, by the President, communicated by yours under date of the 4th instant. He has not, as you will perceive, designated places of rendezvous. He thinks it will be in time to do so in subsequent orders, which must be issued before the troops can march. The threatened point of attack by the enemy will, it is probable, then be better ascertained, and a more prudent selection of place can be made. The repeal of our militia law of 1807, and its several supplements, on the 1st of August next; the disannulling of all militia commissions on that day, by a new law of the last session, granted under the old law, except the commissions of such officers as may then be in actual service; the ordering by the new law; the holding of elections of officers by the militia, after the said 1st of August; the notice of election; returns to be made; and the protracting to the 4th Monday of October next, the classification of the militia; causes an almost total disorganization of our militia system, between the 1st of August and the 4th of October, and presents difficulties, in yielding perfect compliance with the requisition of the President, insurmountable. It is hoped, however, that the patriotism of the people will obviate the difficulty, by a voluntary tender of services, which the Governor has invited, growing out of the unaccountable oversight of the Legislature. It is strongly doubted whether any orders can be enforced under the present state of things.

The requisition refers to the act of Congress, passed 28th February, 1795, under which militia can be held in service three months only; and to the law of 1814, which authorized the President to keep them six months in service. The law of Pennsylvania, passed at the last session of its Legislature, requires the Governor to mention, in general orders, the period for which any militia ordered into service is to remain on duty. It is desirable, therefore, to know whether the requisition is intended for three or six months' service. The offices of Deputy Quartermaster General, and Assistants, and Assistant Adjutant Generals, are not recognised by our State laws.

I have taken the liberty of enclosing to you a copy of the militia law of this State, passed at the last session of the Legislature, from a perusal of which you will perceive the difficulties under which the Executive at present labors, in attempting to comply with the requisition.

With high considerations of respect, sir, your obedient servant,

N. B. BOILEAU, *Secretary.*

J. ARMSTRONG, Esq., *Secr'y of War.*

SECRETARY's OFFICE, *Aug.* 27, 1814.

SIR: I am directed by the Governor to enclose to you a copy of general orders, issued yesterday. The letter of General Winder, containing the requisition, under date of the 18th instant, was not received until the evening of the twenty-third. The deranged state of our militia system prevented a more prompt compliance with the demand. To obviate as far as practicable the inconvenience of delay, the Governor has directed the flank and volunteer companies to push on as rapidly as possible, without any regard to the time fixed on for the general rendezvous of the ordinary draughts. The commanding officers of the companies or detachments are instructed to report themselves, and the number of their men, to General Winder, as the officer who may have command of the troops in the service of the United States, in the 10th military district.

The tents, camp equipage, as well as arms and accoutrements, belonging to the State, being insufficient to accommodate the troops called into service, the Governor relies on the deficiency being supplied by the United States as promptly as practicable, to render the men comfortable and efficient.

With high respect and esteem, sir your obedient servant,

N. B. BOILEAU, *Secretary.*

J. ARMSTRONG, Esq. *Sec'ry of War.*

ANNAPOLIS, *July* 29, 1814.

SIR: In conformity to the request of the President of the United States, signified in your communication of the 4th instant, a detachment of five thousand four hundred infantry, and six hundred artillery, was directed to be organized and held in readiness to march at the shortest notice, and in consequence of General Winder having, by direction of the President, requested three thousand of the draughts of the militia of this State may be called into the field, and in order to comply as fully as practicable with the request, the whole of the draughts of the militia from the Western Shore, being about three thousand five hundred infantry, have been ordered to be embodied. You will observe by the map and line drawn from Washington to Baltimore (not far east of which I presume these men will be encamped) will have a very considerable portion of the militia between that line and the bay shore; and consequently, I presume the draughts from this section of the country would not be drawn back from that part most exposed. Baltimore, I fear, will be unwilling that any part of that force from which they expected to derive aid, should be withdrawn from them. Under these circumstances, it was thought most prudent to order the whole. They have been directed to be embodied in their several brigade districts, and move on the shortest route to Bladensburg, where, I presume, on the receipt of this information, arrangements will be made (under your directions) for their accommodation. What number will arrive there in any given time, I am not yet advised of. The whole artillery of the State does not amount to more than nine hundred; and more than two-thirds of that number are in Baltimore; consequently the proportion from thence would be more than four hundred. So great a proportion, or anything like it, being taken from what is their most efficient force, would create great uneasiness. The order, therefore, with respect to them, is suspended, until General Smith can have some communication with you.

I am, sir, with great respect, yours, &c.
LEVIN WINDER.

Hon. Secretary of War.

ADJUTANT GENERAL'S OFFICE,
RICHMOND, *July* 14, 1814.

SIR: Your requisition on the militia of this State, bearing date the 4th instant, has been received.

Apprehending that the object of this measure is to have in readiness a provisional force to repel a sudden invasion, I have enclosed the general orders from this department, of the 22d ultimo, placing in a state of preparation for such an event upwards of fifteen thousand men. They are not organized, other than on the plan of the militia generally; but you will perceive that the points of rendezvous are designated. In addition to this force, the 8th, and a greater part of the 9th brigade, (amounting to seven thousand, and all convenient to Norfolk,) are placed in the same situation, and directed to co-operate with General Porter in resisting an attack on Norfolk.

Arms, ammunition, &c., will be placed in the hands of the whole. Should these arrangements meet your views, it will be necessary to make a detail on all the regiments in the State for the twelve thousand called for; unless it is desirable that this number be set apart to perform a regular tour of duty. But, as the troops now in readiness are adequate to the emergency contemplated, and the requisitions for those that are to perform regular duty will be made in future in time for every preparation to be made, it is believed that the object of your requisition has been anticipated. If this is the fact, his Excellency the Governor is desirous that the regiments now held in requisition, and subject to be called out *en masse*, be considered by you as a provisional force only, and not subject to perform service beyond the continuance of the emergency which may call them into the field.

As concert in the measures of the General and State Governments is all important, permit me earnestly to solicit your earliest attention to this subject. In the meantime, arrangements will be made to take our quota from the militia, generally, as that measure cannot be avoided, under existing circumstances, unless the force required be provisional. Rest assured, sir, that nothing will be wanting on the part of this State to co-operate cordially and effectually with the General Government.

I have the honor to be, very respectfully, your obedient servant,
CLAIBORNE W. GOOCH,
Deputy Adjutant General.

J. ARMSTRONG, Esq., *Sec'y of War.*

WAR DEPARTMENT, *July* 18, 1814.

SIR: A letter of the 14th instant, from Deputy Adjutant General Gooch, enclosing a copy of your general orders of the 22d ultimo, and requesting to know whether the corps put into requisition by these orders would not supply the call of the 4th instant, made through this Department on the State of Virginia, has been received and submitted to the President. In reply thereto, I am instructed to state, that inasmuch as the service of the militia required by your Excellency is declared to be provisional, limited, in point of time, to the emergency that calls it forth, and, in point of place, to the State of Virginia, and not subjected to the direction of an officer of the United States, it cannot be considered as fulfilling the views of the President.

Permit me to take this occasion to state to your Excellency that two thousand of the quota of Virginia will be put at the disposition of General Winder, as commanding officer of this District.

I have the honor to be, your Excellency's most obedient servant,
JOHN ARMSTRONG.

His Exc'y the GOVERNOR OF VIRGINIA.

No. 7.
Narrative of General Winder.

O'NEALE's, *September* 26, 1814.

SIR: The readiest mode in which I can meet the inquiries which you have made, on behalf of the committee of which you are the chairman, will be to give a narrative of my agency as commander of the 10th military district, and to accompany it with the correspondence which I have had, by letter, with the General and State Governments, and their respective offices, while in that command.

Within the few last days of June, and before it was known that my exchange was perfect, although intelligence to that effect was anxiously expected, I was at the City of Washington, and the Secretary of War informed me that it was in contemplation to create another military district, to embrace the country from the Rappahannock northward, to include the State of Maryland, and that the President intended to vest me with the command of it.

On my return to Baltimore I addressed to the Secretary of War copies of the letters herewith transmitted, marked "1 A," "2 A."

About the 4th or 5th of July, I received a letter, a copy of which, marked 1 B, accompanies this, which enclosed an order constituting the 10th military district, a copy of which is annexed to the letter above referred to.

In obedience to the requisition of the letter, I immediately went to Washington, and waited on the Secretary of War. He stated to me that, in addition to the garrisons of the several forts within my district, and the detachments of the 36th and 38th infantry, then at Benedict, it was contemplated to order a detachment of cavalry, then at Carlisle, under orders to be mounted, amounting to about one hundred and fifty, a company of the 12th, and from one or two companies of the 10th regular infantry, which would be ordered to be collected from their several recruiting rendezvous and to march to the City of Washington, and that the whole regular force, thus to be collected, might amount to one thousand or twelve hundred, and that the balance of my command would be composed of militia. That a requisition was about to be made upon certain States for upwards of ninety thousand militia, intended for the defence of the maritime frontier of the country, and showed me a blank circular which had been printed but not filled up, nor sent to the respective Governors of the States.

I took the liberty of suggesting to the Secretary of War, at that time, my idea of the propriety of calling immediately into the field at least a portion of the militia intended for my district, and encamping them in the best positions for protecting the probable points at which the enemy would strike if he should invade the district of my command. The Secretary was of opinion that the most advantageous mode of using militia was upon the spur of the occasion, and to bring them to fight as soon as called out. I returned within a day or two to Baltimore, to prepare myself for visiting the different parts of my district, and to explore it generally, and particularly those parts of it which might be considered as the approaches to the three principal points of it, to wit: Washington, Baltimore, and Annapolis.

My impressions of the necessity of having a respectable force immediately called into the field were strengthened instead of diminished by subsequent reflection, and I, in consequence, on the 9th of July, addressed the letter to the Secretary of War, a copy of which is herewith sent, marked 3 A.

Agreeably to the suggestion contained in that letter, I proceeded to Annapolis to visit the military posts there, and to be ready on the spot, when the Governor should receive the requisition, and myself such instructions as might be thought proper to be given me, to take the most immediate steps to accomplish them.

The Governor received the requisition, and immediately issued the necessary orders to have the quota required draughted.

On the 12th July, the Secretary addressed me

a letter, (the copy of which is herewith marked 2 B,) but which, being directed to Baltimore, did not reach me until after I had been to Upper Marlborough and again returned to Annapolis, where it followed me. I proceeded from Annapolis to Upper Marlborough, and on the 16th addressed two letters to the Secretary of War, of which copies are sent, marked 4 A, 5 A.

The apprehension that the enemy would proceed up the Patuxent and attack the flotilla at Nottingham, in consequence of the reinforcement he had just received, gaining strength, I proceeded immediately to Nottingham, instead of going to the Woodyard, as I intended. During the 16th we received no information of a movement of the enemy up the river, but on the 17th, about 9 o'clock, Mr. Fitzhugh arrived, express from the mouth of the Patuxent, and stated that about twenty barges, several frigates, and some small armed vessels, were proceeding up the river. I, in consequence, wrote a letter to the Secretary of War, a copy of which is herewith sent, marked 6 A; and wrote a note to Brigadier General West, of the Maryland militia, advising him to call out the militia of the county.

I ordered the detachments of the 36th and 38th to hasten from the head of South river, by forced marches, to Nottingham. Three companies of the city militia were promptly despatched, in consequence of my letter of the 17th. But, by the time these latter had reached the Woodyard, and the regulars Marlborough, the enemy had entered Hunting creek, on the Calvert side of the river, had proceeded to Huntingtown, burned the tobacco warehouse, after having taken off the principal part of the tobacco, and were retiring down the river. I halted the city regulars at the Woodyard, and the regulars at Marlborough.

In answer to my letter of the 17th from Nottingham, I received the following answer from the Secretary of War, marked 3 B. As soon, therefore, as I ascertained that the enemy had retired to the mouth of the Patuxent, I proceeded to Annapolis, to make the requisition upon the Governor, as directed by the Secretary of War; and thence to Baltimore, to lend my aid and power to draw out the force authorized there.

While at Annapolis, I addressed to the Secretary of War the letter dated 20th of July, a copy of which is sent, marked 7 A, and at the same time made the requisition on the Governor, herewith sent, marked 1 C. After remaining at Baltimore a day, and leaving orders to Brigadier General Stansbury, who had been called on to command the militia to be assembled there relative to their muster and inspection, under the laws of Congress, I returned to Marlborough, to fix upon an encampment for the militia I had required from the Governor, and to be more at hand to be informed of the enemy's movements. From Upper Marlborough, on the 23d of July, I wrote the Secretary of War the accompanying letter, marked 8 A; and then proceeded to the Woodyard, from whence, on the same day, I wrote to the Secretary of War the following letter, marked 9 A.

The enemy still remaining inactive, or rather confining himself to depredations upon the lower parts of the rivers Patuxent and Potomac, I seized the opportunity of visiting Fort Washington, and on the 25th required from Lieutenant Edwards, the commanding officer, a representation of what he deemed necessary to complete the equipment of the fort, with its then works, and received from him a representation, which I enclosed in a letter to the Secretary of War on the 25th, of which copies are sent, marked 10 A. A copy of his answer, marked 4 B, is herewith sent.

Learning that some of the enemy's ships were proceeding up the Potomac, I proceeded down to Port Tobacco with a view of ascertaining more precisely his views, and of informing myself of the country; and on the 26th wrote the Secretary of War the following letter, marked 11 A.

Having ascertained the next morning that the enemy's ships had descended the river, I returned to Marlborough, and availed myself of the first opportunity I had to review and inspect the detachment of the 36th and 38th; and thence proceeded to Washington City, where I established permanent headquarters of the district, on the 1st of August. I availed myself of a day, at this time, to review and inspect the two brigades of District militia, in Alexandria and this place, and reported the result to Major General Van Ness, commanding the District militia, in the letter herewith, marked No. 1.

The people of St. Mary's and Charles's had become extremely sore under the harassing service to which they had been subjected, and the devastation and plunder which the enemy had been so long committing on their shores; and the remonstrances of Brigadier General Stewart, commanding the militia there, under the State authority, had become extremely importunate with both the Secretary of War and the President, to receive aid and protection from the General Government. The danger of throwing a force so far down into that neck of land, which exposed them to the danger of being cut off, besides that they would be lost for the defence of Washington, Baltimore, or Annapolis, had hitherto prevented me from pushing any part of my command so low down. But the President, in conversation, told me that their situation required aid, and directed me to move the detachments of the 36th and 38th down to unite with, and aid, General Stewart. I accordingly ordered Lieutenant Colonel Scott to move from Marlborough to Piscataway, and I proceeded directly down myself on the 3d. On the morning of the 4th of August I wrote the following letter from Port Tobacco, marked 13 A, to the Secretary of War, and agreeably to the intention therein expressed, proceeded twelve miles below, to General Stewart's camp. I there learned, beyond doubt, that the enemy had returned down the river; and after assuring the General of support, if they again advanced up the river, I returned back again to the City of Washington, directing Lieutenant Colonel Scott, commanding the regulars, to take

up his encampment at a very convenient place, two miles from Piscataway, on the road to the Woodyard and Marlborough.

On my arrival at Washington I found that the requisition made upon the Governor of Maryland for three thousand men, to be assembled at Bladensburg, had brought to that place only one company; but I learned that other detachments were about marching to that place, and, in order that no delay might occur in organizing and equipping them, I ordered Major Keyser, of the 38th regular infantry, to proceed to Bladensburg, to muster, inspect, and drill the detachments as they came in.

I thence proceeded to Baltimore to ascertain more precisely the effect of the requisition made on Major Smith for two thousand from his division; when arrived, I found about one thousand two hundred only assembled. I reviewed and inspected them, and gave Brigadier General Stansbury orders to endeavor by the most speedy means, to get in the delinquents and absentees.

I had just learned, by a letter from the Governor of Maryland, and also from General Smith, that, upon General Smith's application to the Secretary of War, he had determined that the two thousand men, now called to Baltimore, and which had been detached, under a requisition of the Secretary of War, directly on General Smith, of the 20th of April, were to be considered as part of the quota of Maryland, under the requisition of the 4th of July. I had drawn a different conclusion, and had so informed both the Governor and General Smith, in the visits I made to Annapolis and Baltimore, about the 20th of July, immediately after receiving the letter from the Secretary of War of the 17th of July, above exhibited. In order to supply the deficit in my calculation upon this force, I addressed the letter of the 13th of August to the Secretary of War, of which a copy, marked 14 A, is here presented; proceeded the same or the following day to Washington, by the way of Annapolis, and on the 17th, at Washington, the day following my arrival, received the letter from the Secretary of War, of which a copy, marked 5 B, is sent.

I should have stated that, two days after my return to the City of Washington, about the 6th of August, I received two letters from the Secretary of War, the one dated the 15th, the other the 17th of July, which, having been addressed to me at Baltimore, had followed me backward and forward from place to place, and unfortunately only reached me at this late period; copies of them are herewith sent, marked 6 B and 7 B.

I had, in the meantime, addressed the letter of the 6th of August to the Governor of Pennsylvania, a copy of which is sent, marked 1 D, and upon the 8th, on receiving the letter of the Secretary of War of the 15th, I wrote another letter to the Governor of Pennsylvania, of which, from haste or much occupation, I did not take a copy, or have mislaid it; it substantially, however, informed him of the number of militia I was authorized to call from him, requesting him to hasten their draughting and organization, and

Capture of the City of Washington.

to transmit a list of the officers, from brigadiers down, who would command. Should this letter be deemed material, a copy can be obtained from the Governor, and I have written to procure it.

I addressed, on the 16th, also, a similar letter to the Governor of Virginia. On the 16th or 17th of August, I received from the Secretary of State of Pennsylvania an answer, dated the 11th, of which a copy, marked 2 D, is herewith sent; and from the Adjutant General of Virginia, the answer and enclosures herewith sent, marked E.

On the morning of Thursday the 18th intelligence was received, from the observatory on Point Lookout, that, on the morning of the 17th, the enemy's fleet off that place had been reinforced by a formidable squadron of ships and vessels of various sizes.

I immediately made requisitions upon the Governors of Maryland and Pennsylvania, and to various militia officers, copies of which are herewith sent, marked as follows: to the Governor of Pennsylvania, 3 D; to the Governor of Maryland, 2 C; to Major General Smith of Baltimore, 1 F; to Brigadier General West, of Prince George's, Maryland, No. 18; to Major General Van Ness, No. 4; to Brigadier General Hungerford, Virginia, No. 14; to Brigadier General Douglas and Colonel Chilton, of Virginia, and Brigadier Generals Ringgold, Swearingen, Barrack, and Foreman, of Maryland, No. 5. Besides the letters and correspondence here referred to particularly, a mass of correspondence occurred with various persons relative to my command, and which, as far as I suppose they can have any influence on the investigation, are herewith sent.

That with the Governor of Maryland will be found in bundle C, and numbered, in addition to those already mentioned, from 3 C to 11 C, both inclusive. That with General Smith in bundle F, and that with other persons, not before referred to, with the numbers before referred to, are exhibited from No. 1 to number 53, inclusive. Much other correspondence, necessary to be carried on, and which occupied much time, took place; which, however, is not sent, as I deemed them not calculated to illustrate the inquiry, and only calculated uselessly to encumber and embarrass the inquiry. They will be furnished if thought requisite. I will state as nearly as possible the forces which were in the field under these various demands and requisitions, the time of their assembling, their condition, and subsequent movements. The returns first made when I came into command, gave me—

Fort McHenry, under the command of Major Armistead, non-commissioned officers, musicians, and privates, for duty - - - 194

At Annapolis, in Forts Severn and Madison, under Lieutenant Fay - - - - 39

At Fort Washington, under Lieutenant Edwards - - - - - 49

The detachments of the 36th and 38th. and a small detachment of artillery under Lieutenant Colonel Scott - - - 330

These corps received no addition, but were gradually diminishing by the ordinary causes which always operate to this effect.

The two thousand Maryland militia, who were ordered to assemble at Baltimore, had been draughted in pursuance of a requisition made by the Secretary of War on General Smith, of the 26th of April, and, as full time had been allowed to make the draught deliberately, they were, as far as practicable, ready to come without delay; notwithstanding Brigadier General Stansbury was unable to bring to Bladensburg more than one thousand four hundred, including officers, and arrived at Bladensburg on the evening of the 22d of August.

From General Stricker's brigade in the city of Baltimore, which had been called out en masse, I required a regiment of infantry, the battalion of riflemen, and two companies of artillery—not deeming it practicable to reconcile the people of Baltimore to march a greater number, and leave it without any force, and being strongly persuaded that the exigency would have drawn in time a greater force from the adjacent country. The detachment from Stricker's brigade, under Colonel Sterret, arrived at Bladensburg in the night of the 23d of August, and the total amount was nine hundred and fifty-six.

The detachment which had been stationed at Annapolis, under Colonel Hood, and which had been at the moment transferred by the Governor of Maryland to my command, arrived at the bridge at Bladensburg about fifteen minutes before the enemy appeared, and I suppose was six to seven hundred strong. I have never had any return of it.

The brigade of General Smith, consisting of the militia of the District of Columbia on this side the Potomac, were called out on Thursday, the 18th of August; on Friday were assembled, and on Saturday, the 20th, they crossed the Eastern Branch bridge, and advanced about five miles towards the Woodyard. They amounted, I suppose, to about twelve hundred; a return was never had before they separated from my command, as there was not an interval of sufficient rest to have obtained one.

General Young's brigade, from Alexandria, between five and six hundred strong, crossed the Potomac, Saturday or Sunday, the 19th or 20th, and took post near Piscataway.

The call for three thousand militia, under the requisition of the 4th July, had produced only two hundred and fifty men at the moment the enemy landed at Benedict. In addition to the causes herein beforementioned, the inefficacy of this call is to be attributed to the incredulity of the people on the danger of invasion; the perplexed, broken, and harassed state of the militia in St. Mary's, Calvert, Charles, Prince George's, and a part of Ann Arundel counties, which had rendered it impossible to make the draught in some of them, or to call them from those exposed situations where they had been on duty two months, under the local calls for Maryland.

Several other small detachments of Maryland

Capture of the City of Washington.

militia, either as volunteers, or under the calls on the brigadiers, joined about the day before the action, whose numbers or commanding officers I did not know. They may have amounted to some four or five hundred.

Lieutenant Colonel Tilghman, of the Maryland cavalry, under an order of the Governor of Maryland, with about eighty dragoons, arrived at the City of Washington on the 16th of August, on his way to join General Stewart, in the lower part of Charles or St. Mary's county.

Under the permission I just then received, to accept all the militia then in the field, under the State of Maryland, I informed Colonel Tilghman that I had no doubt of the Governor's sanction, for which I had applied, and recommended him to halt here. He agreed not only to this, but, by the consent of General Stewart, who happened then to be in the city, sick, agreed to take my orders.

Lieutenant Colonel Lavall, of the United States' Light Dragoons, with a small squadron of about one hundred and twenty, who had been mounted at Carlisle the preceding Monday, arrived at Montgomery Courthouse on the evening of the 19th of August, reported himself to the War Office, and received orders to report to me. He moved on the next morning and crossed the Eastern Branch.

Captain Morgan, with a company of about eighty of the 12th United States' infantry, joined at the Long Old Fields on the evening of the 22d.

Colonel Minor, from Virginia, arrived at the city on the evening of the 23d, with about five hundred men, wholly unarmed and without equipments. Under the direction of Colonel Carbery, who had been charged with this subject, they received arms, ammunition, &c., next morning, but not until after the action at Bladensburg. No part of the 10th had yet arrived.

There had been no Adjutant or Inspector General attached to my command from its commencement. Major Hite, Assistant Adjutant General, joined me, on the 16th of August, at Washington, and Major Smith, Assistant Inspector General, on the 19th.

This was the situation, condition, and amount of my force and command.

It will be observed that this detail is continued up to the moment of the battle of Bladensburg; but, as the time at which the different corps respectively joined is stated, it will be readily seen what troops were concerned in the different movements which will now be detailed.

The innumerably multiplied orders, letters, consultations, and demands, which crowded upon me at the moment of such an alarm, can more easily be conceived than described, and occupied me nearly day and night, from Thursday, the 18th of August, till Sunday, the 21st, and had nearly broken down myself and assistants in preparing, dispensing, and attending to them.

On Thursday evening, Colonel Monroe proposed, if I would detach a troop of cavalry with him, to proceed in the most probable direction to find the enemy and reconnoitre him. Captain Thornton's troop, from Alexandria, was detailed on this service, and, on Friday morning, the Colonel departed with them. At this time it was supposed the enemy intended up the bay, as one of his ships was already in view from Annapolis, and his boats were sounding South river. It was Colonel Monroe's intention to have proceeded direct to Annapolis; but, before he had got without the city, he received intelligence that the enemy had proceeded up the Patuxent, and were debarking at Benedict. He, therefore, bent his course to that place. By his first letter, on Saturday, which reached the President that evening, he was unable to give any precise intelligence, except that the enemy were at Benedict in force.

On Saturday, Lieutenant Colonel Tilghman, with his squadron of dragoons, was despatched by way of the Woodyard to fall down upon the enemy, to annoy, harass, and impede their march, by every possible means, to remove or destroy forage and provision from before the enemy, and gain intelligence. Captain Caldwell, with his troop of city cavalry, was despatched with the same views towards Benedict, by Piscataway, it being wholly uncertain what route the enemy would take, if it was his intention to come to Washington.

On Sunday, I crossed the Eastern Branch, and joined Brigadier General Smith, at the Woodyard, where Lieutenant Colonel Scott, with the 36th and 38th, and Lieutenant Colonel Kramer, with the militia from Bladensburg, had arrived by previous orders. On the road to the Woodyard, I received a letter from Colonel Monroe, of which a copy is sent, marked ——; and, at about eight o'clock in the evening, I received another letter from him, of which a copy is sent, marked ——; and, in a very short time after, he arrived himself, and, immediately after, Colonel Beall, who had seen a body of the enemy, which he estimated at four thousand, (without supposing he had seen the whole) enter Nottingham, on Sunday evening. Colonel Monroe, being much exhausted, retired to rest. I gave Colonel Beall, on account of his experience, orders to proceed and join Colonel Hood on his march from Annapolis, and take command of the detachment. I occupied the night in writing letters and orders to various officers and persons, and, at day-light, ordered a light detachment from General Smith's brigade, under Major Peter, the regulars under Lieutenant Colonel Scott, and Lavall's cavalry, to proceed immediately towards Nottingham, to meet the enemy.

I proceeded immediately in advance myself, accompanied by Colonel Monroe and the gentlemen of my staff. I had learned that Colonel Tilghman with his cavalry on the advance of the enemy had fallen back upon Marlborough the evening before, and had during the night sent him an order to proceed upon the road from Marlborough to Nottingham, and meet me at the Chapel. Having got considerably in advance of Lieutenant Colonel Scott's and Major Peter's detachments, and also to obtain intelligence, I halted at Mr. Oden's, within half a mile of the junction of the roads from Marlborough and the Woodyard to Nottingham, directing Lavall to gain the Marlborough road, post himself at the Chapel, and push forward patrols upon all the roads towards Nottingham. In less than half an hour, and before the detachments of Scott and Peter had come up, intelligence was brought that the enemy was moving from Nottingham in force towards the Chapel. I immediately proceeded, with the gentlemen who were with me, to gain an observation of the enemy, and came within view of the enemy's advance about two miles below the Chapel. The observation was continued until the enemy reached the Chapel, and Scott and Peter being then near two miles distant from that point, and it being therefore impossible for them to reach the junction of the Marlborough and Woodyard road before the enemy, I sent orders for them to post themselves in the most advantageous position, and wait for me with the body of the cavalry. I turned into the road to the Woodyard and detached a small party under Adjutant General Hite on the Marlborough road to watch the enemy's movements on that road and give information. Upon arriving at Oden's, himself or some other person of the neighborhood whom I knew, and on whom I could rely, informed me that there was a more direct road, but not so much frequented, leading from Nottingham to the Woodyard, and joining that on which I then was, two miles nearer to the Woodyard.

A doubt at that time was not entertained by anybody of the intention of the enemy to proceed direct to Washington, and the advantage of dividing their force and proceeding on two roads running so near each other to the same point was so obvious, that I gave orders to Scott and Peter to retire, and occupy the first eligible position between the junction of that road and the one we were on and the Woodyard; despatched a patrol of cavalry to observe that road, and give the earliest notice of the advance of the enemy upon it. I still continued the observation of the enemy myself, and he turned a part of his column into the road to the Woodyard, and penetrated a skirt of wood which hid the junction of the Marlborough and Woodyard road from view, and there halted it within a quarter of a mile of Oden's house. I hesitated for some time whether to attribute his delay to a view which he may have had of Scott's and Peter's detachment, or to a design to conceal his movement towards Marlborough, the road to that place being concealed by woods from any point of observation which could be gained.

It appeared afterwards that his whole force halted here for an hour or upwards, and thus continued in an uncertainty as to his intended route. I had in the meantime rode back and assisted Peter and Scott to post their detachments in a favorable position, from whence I entertained a hope to have given the enemy a serious check, without much risk to this detachment. Orders had been previously sent to General Smith to post his whole detachment in conjunction with Com-

modore Barney, who had by this time joined him from Marlborough, with about four hundred sailors and marines, and had taken also command of the marines, under Captain Miller, who had arrived from the city the night before. I presumed, from the appearance of his force, it was about one hundred or one hundred and twenty. As soon as I had satisfied myself as to the position and disposition of Scott's and Peter's detachments, I advanced again towards the enemy to ascertain his situation and intentions. It had now become certain that he had taken the road to Marlborough; and Colonel Monroe crossed over to that place, to join Lieutenant Colonel Tilghman, and observe his movements.

I sent an order immediately to Scott and Peter, to retire back to General Smith, and the latter to take post at the points where the roads from Washington City and the Woodyard, to Marlborough, unite. This order was incorrectly delivered, or misunderstood, and he took post, instead, at the point where the roads from the Woodyard and Marlborough, to the City of Washington, unite. The mistake, however, produced no inconvenience, but, on the contrary, was perhaps better than the position to which I had directed; because it threw my forces more between Marlborough and Bladensburg, and also in command of the road by which the enemy did finally advance, which the other position would not have done. Its inconvenience was, that it left open the road to Fort Washington, and rendered General Young's junction, if it should become proper to advance him, hazardous on the road. It further became necessary to retire still further back, and the only position where the troops could be tolerably accommodated, or posted to advantage, was at Dunlap's, or, as it is generally called, the Long, or the Battalion Old Fields.

General Smith was therefore ordered to retire to that point, with the whole of the troops, except the cavalry. Lieutenant Colonel Tilghman and Captain Herbert were charged with hovering upon the enemy on all the roads leading from Bladensburg, from the North, and from Annapolis to Marlborough. With Lavall's cavalry, I advanced to the nearest and most convenient positions between the Woodyard and Marlborough, and found the enemy quietly halted at Marlborough. Tilghman's cavalry picked up one or two prisoners, who had straggled beyond the enemy's pickets, and my examination of them confirmed me that the enemy did not contemplate leaving Marlborough that day.

After remaining near Marlborough, in observation, till towards the latter part of the afternoon, I returned to General Smith, where I arrived towards the close of the day. About dark I learned that the President and Heads of Departments had arrived at a house about a mile in the rear of the camp. I detached a captain's guard to his quarters; advanced the cavalry of Lavall on the roads towards Marlborough, with orders to patrol as close upon the enemy as possible during the course of the night; and after having waded through the infinite applications, consulta-

Capture of the City of Washington.

tions, and calls, necessarily arising from a body of two thousand five hundred men, not three days from their homes, without organization, or any practical knowledge of service on the part of their officers, and being obliged to listen to the officious but well intended information and advice of the crowd, who, at such a time, would be full of both, I lay down to snatch a moment of rest.

A causeless alarm from one of the sentinels placed the whole force under arms about three o'clock in the morning. A short time after sunrise, I rode over to the quarters of the President, to inform him and the Secretary of War of the state of things. Upon my return, rumors prevailed that the enemy had taken the road to Queen Ann, which was directly leading to Annapolis. I could not, however, suppose that Lieutenant Colonel Tilghman and Captain Herbert would fail to advise me if the fact were so. The rumor, however, gained ground; and just at this time, Mr. Luffborough, of this city, with some fifteen or twenty mounted men, offered himself ready to perform any duties on which I could employ them. I immediately despatched him to ascertain the truth of this report, by penetrating to that road, and also to obtain whatever information he could relative to the enemy. About twelve o'clock he sent me decisive information that the enemy were not on the Annapolis road.

I received constant intelligence that the enemy still remained in Marlborough; and, therefore, felt no doubt that, if he intended to take the road to Annapolis, any movement upon that road was only an advance party for observation, and preparatory to a general movement; and as the morning advanced, the information brought still confirmed the impression that the enemy intended no movement from Upper Marlborough, I resolved to endeavor to concentrate the force (which I hoped had now considerably accumulated within my reach) down upon the enemy's lines near Marlborough.

I accordingly ordered a light detachment to be sent forward by General Smith, under Major Peter, and having also learned by Major Woodyear, of General Stansbury's staff, that he had arrived the evening before at Bladensburg, I sent orders to him to advance toward Marlborough, and to take post at the point where the Old Fields to Queen Ann crosses the road from Bladensburg to Marlborough, which brought him within four miles of the Old Fields, and within from six to eight of the enemy. I was anxiously waiting to hear of Lieutenant Colonel Beall's progress with the detachment for Annapolis, and of Lieutenant Colonel Sterret's from Baltimore.

The President and Heads of Department had been upon the field since about eight o'clock. I communicated my views and intentions, as above detailed, and informed them that I proposed myself to pass over the road from Bladensburg to Marlborough to meet General Stansbury; to make closer observations upon the road direct from the enemy to Bladensburg, and to establish more thoroughly a concert between Stansbury and Smith's command; to be also nearer to Beall, to give him

also a direction towards the enemy on the road leading into Marlborough from the North, if my intelligence should continue to justify it, and to draw down Lieutenant Colonel Sterret, with his force, as soon as I should ascertain where it was. I accordingly, with a troop of Lavall's cavalry, proceeded about twelve o'clock: upon arriving at the Bladensburg road I halted, and pushed a patrol of cavalry down towards Marlborough.

In a few minutes after, three of Captain Herbert's troop, who were observing down the same road, arrived with two prisoners, who they had just seized in a very bold and dexterous manner. The information of these prisoners confirmed the impression that the enemy did not intend to move from Marlborough that day; and as it was now one o'clock, I felt little doubt of it. After remaining some time for intelligence from the United States' dragoons that I had sent down with orders to press down as closely as possible upon the enemy, a slight firing was heard in the direction of the enemy, which I concluded was from the enemy's picket upon this party. A few moments confirmed this conjecture, by the return of a dragoon with this intelligence. A more considerable firing was then however heard, which I concluded to be a skirmishing by Peter's detachment with the enemy, put upon the alert and advance by the firing at the dragoons.

The firing soon after ceased, and after having sent for the purpose of ascertaining the fact, with directions to follow with intelligence on towards Bladensburg, in which direction I proceeded with the expectation of meeting General Stansbury, and with the intention to halt him until my intelligence should decide my further proceedings.

I had proceeded within four or five miles of Bladensburg without meeting General Stansbury, when I was overtaken by Major McKenney, a volunteer aid with General Smith, who informed me that Peter had skirmished with the advancing enemy, who had driven him back on General Smith, and that the enemy had halted within three miles of the Old Fields; that, agreeably to my directions upon the probability of an attack, General Smith had sent off the baggage across the Eastern Branch; and that himself and Commodore Barney had drawn up the forces ready to receive the enemy, should he advance. On my way towards Bladensburg I had left orders with Lieutenant Colonel Tilghman's cavalry to continue their observation on the Bladensburg and Marlborough roads, and, in case the enemy should move on that road, to give General Stansbury immediate notice, and fall back on him. In proceeding to the Old Fields, I met Lieutenant Colonel Tilghman himself, and renewed these directions. Captain Herbert was also between General Stansbury and the enemy, with the same instructions.

When Major McKenney gave me the intelligence of the advance of the enemy, I despatched an aid to General Stansbury, with directions to him to fall back and take the best position in advance of Bladensburg, and unite Lieutenant Colonel Sterret, with him should he arrive at Bladensburg, as I expected, that evening; and should he be attacked, to resist as long as possible; and if obliged to retire, to retreat towards the city.

I reached the Old Fields about five o'clock in the afternoon, and found General Smith and Commodore Barney had judiciously posted their men in expectation of the enemy, and were expecting his approach. The head of the enemy's column was about three miles from our position, and five miles from Marlborough. He must have reached that point by or before one o'clock, and his halt there at that period of the day, so short a distance from Marlborough, and apparently only drawn out by my parties pressing upon him, and at the point from whence he could take the road to Bladensburg, to the Eastern Branch bridge, or Fort Washington, indifferently, or it might be to cover his march upon Annapolis; to which place he had strong temptations to proceed. His force was very imperfectly known, the opinions and representations varying from four to twelve thousand: the better opinion fixed it from five to seven thousand. If he supposed his force insufficient to proceed to Washington, and further reinforcements were expected, which all information concurred to state, the natural conclusion was, that he would seek some place where he could in security refresh his men, and place them in comfortable quarters, near a convenient port for his ships, and whence, upon receiving reinforcements, he would be ready to act against the important points of the country. Having, therefore, already accomplished one great object of the expedition—the destruction of Commodore Barney's flotilla—if he was not in a condition to proceed further into the country, Annapolis offered him a place in all respects such as he would desire. It brought him to a fine port, where his ships could lie in safety; it afforded abundant and comfortable quarters for his men; magazines and store-houses for all his stores and munitions of every description; was capable, with very little labor, of being rendered impregnable by land, and commanded the water; it was the nearest point of debarkation to the City of Washington, without entering a narrow river, liable to great uncertainty in its navigation from adverse winds; and was at hand to Baltimore; equally threatening those two great points, and rendering it absolutely necessary to keep a force doubly sufficient to resist him—one for the protection of Washington, the other for Baltimore. The squadron which was ascending the Potomac, and had now passed the Kettle Bottoms, the only obstruction in the navigation of the river, might be only a feint, the more effectually to conceal their intentions against Annapolis; or, what was more probable, was intended to unite with the land force, and co-operate in a joint attack on Washington. It was, therefore, strongly believed, that the land force was destined to proceed and take Fort Washington in the rear, where it was wholly defenceless, while it was capable of offering a very formidable resistance to the ascent of ships up the river, and, imperfect as it was, perhaps capable of repulsing them altogether. And it was therefore that I

sent to General Young, when the force under General Smith fell back to the Old Fields, to take a position so as to protect Fort Washington, and avoid being taken in the rear by the enemy.

If the object of the enemy was to proceed direct to Washington, the road by Bladensburg offered fewer obstructions than that over the Eastern Branch bridge, although it was six miles further; and yet, if I had retired toward Bladensburg, I should have been removed so much further from annoying or impeding the enemy if he proceeded to Fort Washington; and I should have left the road to Washington City, by the Eastern Branch bridge, open to him, which, although I had, as I supposed, left a secure arrangement for its destruction, yet the importance of leaving that bridge as long as possible, on account of its great value to us, and the danger that, in the multitude of business which was accumulated on every person during such alarm, confusion, and disorder, arising at such a moment, with such raw, undisciplined, inexperienced, and unknown officers and men, rendered it hazardous to trust this direct and important pass unguarded.

It was under all these circumstances, that, after waiting for the enemy at Old Fields till sundown, that I determined to retire over the Eastern Branch bridge, in which Commodore Barney concurred, and his force with mine proceeded accordingly.

My reasons for not remaining at the Old Fields during the night was, if an attack should be made in the night, our own superiority, which lay in artillery, was lost, and the inexperience of the troops would subject them to certain, infallible, and irremediable disorder, and probably destruction, and thereby occasion the loss of a full half of the force which I could hope to oppose, under more favorable circumstances, to the enemy.

The reasons for retiring by the Eastern Branch bridge, were, the absolute security it gave to that pass, the greater facility of joining General Young, and aiding in the protection of Fort Washington, the greater facility of pursuing the enemy should he recede and proceed to Annapolis, and the certainty that I could draw General Stansbury and Lieutenant Colonel Sterret to me if the enemy advanced too rapidly for me to advance and unite to support them.

Under the harassing and perplexing embarrassments, arising from having a mass of men suddenly assembled, without organization, discipline, or officers of any, the least, knowledge of service, except in the case of Major Peter, or, if possessing it, unknown to me as such, and the wearied and exhausted state in which incessant application and exertion, for nearly five uninterrupted days and nights, had left me, these views offered themselves to my mind, and determined me to fall back, on Tuesday evening, to the bridge, instead of Bladensburg. Since the event has passed, and if a movement to Bladensburg, had it been made, would not have induced the enemy to pursue another course, it is easy to determine that a retreat to Bladensburg might have been better; but those who undertake to pass a judgment, should place themselves back to the moment and situation I was in when I formed the resolution, and it will be very difficult to find it an error; or if one, it is of that sort which is supported, when viewed in perspective, by stronger reasons than those which oppose it; and is only found to be an error by the experience which so often confounds all reason and calculation.

Upon arriving at the bridge, about eight o'clock, I directed General Smith to halt his men in the most convenient position near the bridge, on this side; and I passed over and rode directly to the President's, and informed him of the then state of things. I had expected that I should probably have found the Secretary of War and other Heads of Departments there, but they had respectively retired to their homes. I returned to the bridge, leaving at McKeowin's hotel the borrowed horse on which I rode. Both those I had with me being exhausted and worn down, and as I knew no one who had a horse in a different situation, I proceeded on foot to the camp. General Smith was not at the moment there. I proceeded on to the bridge, where I found about thirty men with axes, for the purpose of cutting the bridge down, and no other preparation for destroying it made. I proceeded again to the camp; detached a party of volunteers to burn the upper bridge at once; detached a party of regular infantry across the bridge, in advance toward the enemy about half a mile, to prevent him from seizing it by surprise, and posted Burch's artillery to command the pass of the bridge on this side. I learned at the bridge that some persons from the Navy Yard had been to the bridge to take some steps for destroying it, and knowing that this was the nearest, and the only place, indeed, from whence I could draw the powder, boats, and combustibles, for the purpose of rendering its destruction sure at any moment, I proceeded, accompanied by Major Cox, of Georgetown, to ascertain what preparations had been made. I arrived there about twelve or one o'clock, saw Colonel Wharton, who referred me to Commodore Tingey, to whom I then proceeded and roused him from bed. He informed me that several casks of powder were ready in boats to be sent from the Navy Yard to blow up the bridge when necessary. I begged him to increase the quantity of powder, to furnish a quantity of combustibles also to be laid upon the bridge, that its destruction, when necessary, in one way or other, might be put beyond doubt. Commodore Tingey undertook to have what I requested provided, and sent without delay to the bridge. I returned to the bridge to see that the different detachments which I had stationed there were upon the alert, and understood the objects for which they were detached. And I thence returned to the camp, between three and four o'clock, much exhausted, and considerably hurt in the right arm and ancle from a severe fall which I had into a gulley or ditch on my way to the Navy Yard. I snatched about an hour or two of sleep, rose, and proceeded to gather my attend-

ants and horses, much exhausted and worn down by the incessant action of the three preceding days, and proceeded to establish my headquarters at a house near the bridge.

My patrols and videttes not having yet brought me any intelligence of a movement of the enemy, and being still doubtful whether he might not move upon Annapolis, Fort Warburton, or toward the bridge, rather than Bladensburg, I held the position near the bridge as that which, under all circumstances, would enable me best to act against the enemy in any alternative. I learned about this time, with considerable mortification, that General Stansbury, from misunderstanding or some other cause, instead of holding a position during the night in advance of Bladensburg, had taken one about a mile in its rear; and that his men, from a causeless alarm, had been under arms the greater part of the night, and moved once or twice, and that he was at that moment on his march into the city. I instantly sent him an order to resume his position at Bladensburg; to post himself to the best advantage; make the utmost resistance, and rely upon my supporting him if the enemy should move upon that road. I had, at a very early hour in the morning, detached Captain Graham, with his troop of Virginia cavalry, to proceed, by Bladensburg, down upon the road toward the enemy, and insure, by that means, timely notice to General Stansbury and myself, should the enemy turn that way. With this addition to the cavalry already on those roads, it became impossible for the enemy to take any steps unobserved. Additional cavalry patrols and videttes were also detached upon all the roads across the bridge, to insure the certainty of intelligence, let the enemy move as he might.

Colonel Minor had also arrived in the city the evening before, with five or six hundred militia from Virginia, but they were without arms, accoutrements, or ammunition. I urged him to hasten his equipment, which I learn was delayed by some difficulty in finding Colonel Carbery, charged with that business; and he had not received his arms, &c., when, about 10 o'clock, I received intelligence that the enemy had turned the head of his column towards Bladensburg. Commodore Barney had, upon my suggestion, posted his artillery to command the bridge early in the morning.

As soon as I learned the enemy were moving towards Bladensburg, I ordered General Smith, with the whole of the troops, to move immediately to that point.

The necessary detention arising from orders to issue, interrogations, and applications to be answered from all points being past, I proceeded on to Bladensburg, leaving the President and some of the Heads of Departments at my quarters, where they had been for an hour or more. I arrived at the bridge at Bladensburg about twelve o'clock, where I found Lieutenant Colonel Beall had at that moment passed with his command, having just arrived from Annapolis. I had passed the line of Stansbury's brigade, formed in the field upon the left of the road, at about a quarter

Capture of the City of Washington.

of a mile in the rear of the bridge; and on the road, a short distance in the rear of Stansbury's line, I met several gentlemen, and, among the others, I think Mr. Francis Key, of Georgetown, who informed me that he had thought that the troops coming from the city could be most advantageously posted on the right and left of the road near that point. General Smith being present, Mr. Key undertook, I believe, being sent for that purpose, to show the positions proposed. I left General Smith to make a disposition of these troops, and proceeded to the bridge, where I found Lieutenant Colonel Beall as before stated.* I inquired whether he had any directions as to his position; he replied, he had been shown a high hill upon the right of the road, ranging with the proposed second line. It being a commanding position, and necessary to be occupied by some corps, I directed him to proceed agreeably to the instructions he had received. I then rode up to a battery which had been thrown up to command the street which entered Bladensburg from the side of the enemy and the bridge, where I found the Baltimore artillery posted, with the Baltimore riflemen to support them. Upon inquiry, I learned that General Stansbury was on a rising ground upon the left of his line. I rode immediately thither, and found him and Colonel Monroe together. The latter gentleman informed me that he had been aiding General Stansbury to post his line, and wished me to proceed to examine it with them, to see how far I approved of it. We were just proceeding with this view, when some person rode up and stated that news had just been received of a signal victory obtained by General Izard over the enemy, in which one thousand of the enemy were slain and many prisoners taken. I ordered the news to be immediately communicated to the troops, for the purpose of giving additional impulse to their spirits and courage. The column of the enemy at this moment appeared in view, about a mile distant, moving up the Eastern Branch, parallel to our position. From the left, where I was, I perceived that, if the position of the advanced artillery were forced, that two or three pieces on the left of Stansbury would be necessary to scour an orchard which lay between his line and his artillery, and for another rifle company to increase the support of this artillery. These were promptly sent forward by General Smith, and posted as hastily as possible; and it was barely accomplished before I was obliged to give orders to the advanced artillery to open upon the enemy, who was descending the street toward the bridge. All further examination or move-

---

* Since writing the above I have seen General Smith, who informs me that Mr. Key had been examining the grounds with him, and that it was his views that Mr. Key had been stating. He came up at the moment Mr. Key had given me the information. I have been under the impression, till thus corrected, that it was the suggestion of Colonel Monroe and General Stansbury that had suggested that position. This circumstance is immaterial, except for the purpose of literal accuracy when necessary.

ment was now impossible, and the position where I then was, immediately in rear of the left of Stansbury's line, being the most advanced position from which I could have any commanding view, I remained there. The fire of our advanced artillery occasioned the enemy, who were advancing, and who were light troops, to leave the street, and they crept down, under the cover of houses and trees, in loose order, so as not to expose them to risk from the shot; it was, therefore, only occasionally that an object presented at which the artillery could fire.

In this sort of suspension the enemy began to throw his rockets, and his light troops began to accumulate down in the lower parts of the town, and near the bridge, but principally covered from view by the houses. Their light troops, however, soon began to issue out and press across the creek, which was everywhere fordable, and in most places lined with bushes and trees, which were sufficient, however, to conceal the movements of light troops, who act in the manner of theirs, singly. The advanced riflemen now began to fire, and continued it for a half a dozen rounds, when I observed them to run back to the skirts of the orchard on the left, where they became visible, the boughs of the orchard trees concealing their original position, as also that of the artillery, from view. A retreat of twenty or thirty yards from their original position toward the left brought them in view on the edge of the orchard; they halted there, and seemed for a moment returning to their position, but in a few minutes entirely broke, and retired to the left of Stansbury's line. I immediately ordered the fifth Baltimore regiment, Lieutenant Colonel Sterret, being the left of Stansbury's line, to advance and sustain the artillery. They promptly commenced this movement, but the rockets, which had for the first three or four passed very high above the heads of the line, now received a more horizontal direction, and passed very close above the heads of Shutz's and Ragan's regiments, composing the centre and left of Stansbury's line. A universal flight of these two regiments was the consequence. This leaving the right of the fifth wholly unsupported, I ordered it to halt; rode swiftly across the field toward those who had so shamefully fled; and exerted my voice to the utmost to arrest them. They halted, began to collect, and seemed to be returning to their places. An ill-founded reliance that their officers would succeed in rallying them, when I had thus succeeded in stopping the greatest part of them, induced me immediately to return to the fifth, the situation of which was likely to become very critical, and that position gave me the best command of view. To my astonishment and mortification, however, when I had regained my position, I found the whole of these regiments (except a few of Ragan's, not more than forty, rallied by himself, and as many perhaps of Shutz's rallied, I learn by Captain Shower and Captain ———, whose name I do not recollect) were flying in the utmost precipitation and disorder.

The advanced artillery had immediately followed the riflemen, and retired by the left of the fifth. I directed them to take post on a rising ground which I pointed out in the rear. The fifth, and the artillery on its left, still remained, and I hoped that their fire, notwithstanding the obstruction of the boughs of the orchard, which, being below, covered the enemy, would have been enabled to scour this approach and prevent his advance. The enemy's light troops, by single men, showed themselves on the lower edge of the left of the orchard, and received the fire of this artillery and the fifth, which made them draw back. The cover to them was, however, so complete, that they were enabled to advance singly, and take positions from which their fire annoyed the fifth considerably, without either that regiment or the artillery being able to return the fire with any probability of effect. In this situation I had actually given an order to the fifth and artillery to retire up to the hill, toward a wood more to the left and a little in the rear, for the purpose of drawing them further from the orchard, and out of reach of the enemy's fire, while he was sheltered by the orchard. An aversion, however, to retire before the necessity became stronger, and the hope that the enemy would issue in a body from the left of the orchard, and enable us to act upon him on terms of equality, and a fear that a movement of retreat might, in raw troops, produce some confusion and lose us this chance, induced me instantly to countermand the order, and direct the artillery to fire into a wooden barn on the lower end of the orchard, behind which I supposed the enemy might be sheltered in considerable numbers. The fire of the enemy now began, however, to annoy the fifth still more in wounding several of them, and a strong column of the enemy having passed up the road as high as the right of the fifth, and beginning to deploy into the field to take them in flank, I directed the artillery to retire to the hill, to which I had directed the Baltimore artillery to proceed and halt, and ordered the fifth regiment also to retire. This corps, which had heretofore acted so firmly, evinced the usual incapacity of raw troops to make orderly movements in the face of the enemy, and their retreat in a very few moments became a flight of absolute and total disorder.

The direct line of retreat to the whole of this first line, being to the hill on which I had directed the artillery to halt, and immediately in connexion with the positions of General Smith's corps, which were not arrayed in line, but posted on advantageous positions in connexion with and supporting each other, according as the nature of the ground admitted and required, I had not for a moment, dispersed and disordered as was the whole of Stansbury's command, supposed that their retreat would have taken a different direction. But it soon became apparent that the whole mass were throwing themselves off to the right on the retreat toward Montgomery Court-house, and flying wide of this point; the whole of the cavalry, probably from the pressure of the infantry that way, were also thrown wide of the line of retreat toward the right. After making every effort to turn the current more towards General Smith's command and the city, in vain, and finding that it was impossible to collect any force to support the artillery which I had directed to halt, and finding also that the enemy's light troops were extending themselves in that direction, and pressing the pursuit, I directed the artillery to continue their retreat, on the road they then were, toward the Capitol, it being impossible for them to get across to the turnpike road, or unite with General Smith's brigade.

The hope of again forming the first line at this point, and there renewing the retreat, or, at all events, of being able to rally them between the Capitol and that point, and renewing the contest, induced me, at the moment I directed the fifth regiment to retreat, to request Mr. Riggs, of Georgetown, to proceed to the President and inform him that we had been driven back, but that it was my hope and intention to form and renew the contest between that place and the Capitol.

As soon as I found it vain longer to endeavor to turn the tide of retreat toward the left, I turned toward the position occupied by Lieutenant Colonel Beall, Commodore Barney, and General Smith. By this time the enemy had advanced up the road, had driven back Lieutenant Colonel Kramer's command, posted on the right of the road, and in advance of Commodore Barney, after having well maintained his position and much hurt the enemy, and also continued to fire during his retreat. He had come under the destructive fire of Commodore Barney, which had turned him up the hill towards Lieutenant Colonel Beall, whose detachment gave one or two ineffective fires and fled. Their position was known to me, was very conspicuous, and the extreme right. The enemy, therefore, had gained this commanding position, and was passing our right flank; his force pursuing on the left, had also advanced into line with our left, and there was nothing there to oppose him. To preserve Smith's command from being pressed in front by fresh troops of the enemy, who were coming on at the same time, while they were under the certainty of being assailed on both flanks and rear by the enemy, who respectively gained them, in which circumstances their destruction or surrender would have been inevitable, I sent (my horse being unable to move with the rapidity I wished) to General Smith a retreat. I am not acquainted with the relative position of the different corps composing his command, and cannot therefore determine what then engaged the enemy, nor could I see how they acted; but when I arrived in succession at his different corps, which I did as soon as practicable, I do not recollect to have found any of them that were not in order, and retreating with as little confusion as could have been expected. When I reached the road I found Commodore Barney's men also retiring on the road, he having been overpowered by those who drove off Beall's regiment, about the time I sent the order to retreat.

I still had no doubt but that Stansbury's command, and the cavalry, would have fallen down upon the Capitol, by the roads which enter that

Capture of the City of Washington.

part of the city from the North, and still solaced myself with the persuasion that I should be able there to rally them, upon the city and Georgetown troops, who were retiring in order, and make another effort in advance, of the Capitol to repulse the enemy.

After accompanying the retreating army within two miles of the Capitol, I rode forward for the purpose of selecting a position, and endeavoring to collect those whom I supposed, from the rapidity of their flight, might have reached that point. A half a mile in advance of the Capitol I met Colonel Minor with his detachment, and directed him to form his men, wait until the retreating army passed, and protect them if necessary.

When I arrived at the Capitol I found not a man had passed that way; and, notwithstanding the commanding view which is there afforded to the North, I could see no appearance of the troops. I despatched an order to call in the cavalry to me there.

In a few moments the Secretary of State and the Secretary of War joined me, besides that they had been witnesses to the dispersion of the troops and the exhaustion of those just halted by me. I stated the diminution of my force, and the extent of the positions which rendered it impossible to place the force I then had in such a position as to prevent the enemy from taking me on the flank as well as front, and that no reasonable hope could be entertained, that we had any troops who could be relied on to make a resistance as desperate as necessary, in an isolated building which could not be supported by a sufficiency of troops without; indeed it would have taken nearly the whole of the troops to have sufficiently filled the two wings, which would have left the enemy masters of every other part of the city, and given him the opportunity, without risk, in twenty-four hours, to have starved them into a surrender. The same objection equally applied to the occupation of any particular part of the city.

Both these gentlemen concurred that it would subject the whole of my force to certain capture or destruction; and in its reduced and exhausted condition it was wise and proper to retire through Georgetown, and take post in the rear of it, on the heights, to collect my force. I accordingly pursued this course, and halted at Tenleytown, two miles north of Georgetown, on the Frederick road. Here was evinced one of the great defects of all undisciplined and unorganized troops; no effort could rouse the men to the exertion necessary to place themselves in such a state of comfort and security as is attainable, even under very disadvantageous circumstances. Such of them as could be halted, instead of making those efforts, gave themselves up to the uncontrolled feelings which fatigue, exhaustion, and privation produced, and many hundreds, in spite of all precautions and efforts, passed on and pursued their way, either towards home or in search of refreshments and quarters. After waiting in this position until I supposed I collected all the force that could be gathered, I proceeded about five miles further on

the river road, which leads a little wide to the left of Montgomery Court-house, and in the morning gave orders for the whole to assemble at Montgomery Court-house.

This positon promised us shelter from the rain that began to fall an hour before day; was the most probable place for the supply of provisions, which the troops very much needed; and was a position from which we could best interpose between the enemy and Baltimore, and to which place, at that time, nobody doubted he intended to go by land from Washington.

In pursuance of this view, among the first acts after my arrival at Montgomery Court-house, was, to direct a letter to General Stricker, who commanded at Baltimore, informing him that it was my intention to gather my force together there, receive what reinforcements I could, show myself to the enemy as strong as possible, hang on his flank, should he move to Baltimore, intimidate and harass him as much as possible in his movements, and endeavor always to preserve the power of interposing between him and Baltimore; directing him to re-establish the dispersed command of Lieutenant Colonel Sterret, multiplying his means as much as possible, stop all reinforcements of militia from Maryland, Pennsylvania, or elsewhere, and present himself to the enemy at the crossing of the Patapsco, in as imposing a form as possible.

This letter I sent by Captain Aisquith, whom I found at Montgomery, with fifteen or twenty others, the only part of the Baltimore detachment which had not returned home.

The first object was, in the absence of quartermaster and contractor, to make efforts to provide quarters and refreshments for my men; a few provisions were found there, belonging to the contractor, and a person temporarily appointed to issue, and the most active men of the place called upon and authorized to get in provisions.

The next object was to obtain a return of the different corps, which, from causes that can easily be understood, among undisciplined men and unskilful officers, proved abortive before we moved next day. The arrival of several detachments of reinforcements, the reports of officers bringing on detachments who wanted orders and instructions, and the multiplied complaints and wants of men and officers, crowded together in small quarters, or entirely out of doors in a rainy, tempestuous day; the calculations and arrangements necessary for ulterior operations, and to meet the demands and wants of the great force which my calls were likely to produce, may be supposed to have been as much as could be borne by the attention and efforts of one man, which he was obliged to encounter, for the want of a skilful, or even organized staff of any kind.

No regular details for service of any kind could be performed, and all the duties of this description were necessarily performed by the voluntary zeal of those corps who could not be borne down or discouraged by difficulties. My efforts were devoted to endeavor to prepare the detachment to move down toward the city, and hang upon and strike at the enemy whenever an opportunity occurred. The next morning, however, before a return of the corps could be had, and their situation known, I received intelligence that the enemy had moved from Washington the preceding night, and was in full march for Baltimore. I instantly put my command under arms, multiplied and strengthened my patrols to gain intelligence, and advanced as rapidly as was practicable to Baltimore. When the forces arrived at Snell's bridge, on the upper branch of the Patuxent, I had concluded that, if the enemy was, as we had had still reason to believe, proceeding to Baltimore, that it would be most advisable for me to proceed directly thither, to lend the whole force of my power, as commander of the district, to call out and bring into activity the resources of the place, and also because it was likely to become the most important station of the command. I accordingly left the command with General Stansbury, senior brigadier, and proceeded that night to Baltimore. On the road I met an express from Major General S. Smith, who delivered me a letter, in which he informed me he had been called out into service, and had assumed the command, according to his rank; and by the time I reached Baltimore, I also learned that the enemy was proceeding to Marlborough, and not toward Baltimore.

If I had had longer time, or to repeat the action of Bladensburg, I could correct several errors which might materially have affected the issue of that battle. The advanced force ought to have been nearer to the creek along the edge of the low ground, where they would have been skirted with bushes, and have avoided the inconvenience of the cover which the orchard afforded the enemy. The edge of the low grounds on the right of the road ought to have been lined with musketry, and a battery of cannon also planted in the field, on the right of the road, directly fronting the bridge; and if Commodore Barney's heavy artillery, with his more expert artillerists, had occupied the position which the advanced artillerists did, and these posts been obstinately defended, the enemy would not have crossed the river at that point, but would have been obliged to make a circuit round to his right, and have crossed above, and at the upper end of the town; or, if the whole force had been posted at the position of the second line, with all the advantage which it afforded, and have acted with tolerable firmness and courage, the event might have been different; but no advantage of position is proof against groundless panic and a total want of discipline, skill, and experience.

On the night of my retreat to the city, I sent Assistant Adjutant General Hite down to General Young, to inform him of the movement, and to direct him to take the best position to secure Fort Washington, and his junction with me; or, in case the enemy should interpose between him and me, to have his boats ready to transport his men across the river; or, if he could not do that, to fall down the river, and unite with General Stewart, and harass the enemy in the rear; and, above all, to be alert, and keep a vigilant guard upon every avenue of approach, to prevent a surprise. I also sent, by Major Hite, directions to the commanding officer of Fort Washington, to advance a guard up to the main road, upon all the roads leading to the fort; and, in the event of his being taken in the rear of the fort by the enemy, to blow up the fort, and retire across the river.

The distance of General Young, and the necessity of retaining a position near the fort as long as the designs of the enemy remained uncertain, rendered it impossible to have the assistance of his force at Bladensburg.

There was not a bridge on the road which the enemy pursued, from his debarkation to Washington, the destruction of which would have retarded his advance ten minutes. I believe, in fact, that the bridge at Bladensburg is the only one, and the facility with which that stream is everywhere fordable above the bridge rendered useless the destroying it. Indeed, I believe that, had artillery been posted as advantageously as it might have been, and well served, the bridge would have acted as a decoy to the enemy to lead him into danger, and have been useful to us.

Those who have that happy intrepidity of assurance in their own capacity to see with certainty, in all cases, the means by which they could have avoided the errors of others, and by which past calamities might always have been averted, will find my condemnation easy. Those who are disposed to measure difficulties by the limits of human capacity, and who will impartially place themselves in my situation, will find it difficult to decide that any errors have been committed which might not have been equalled or surpassed by any other commander, or that the calamities which have followed could have been averted or mitigated.

This narrative is accompanied by a map, with explanations, which will facilitate the understanding of it.

No. 8.

Reports of Generals Stansbury, Smith, Young, Douglas, and Hungerford; Colonels Sterett, Minor, Taylor, Lavall, and Beall; Major Pinkney, and Captains Burch and Caldwell.

General Stansbury's Report.

BALTIMORE, *November* 15, 1814.

By general orders from the War Department, of the 20th April, 1814, Major General S. Smith was directed to draught from his division and hold in readiness to march at a moment's warning, two thousand men, officers included.

By Major General Smith's division orders, of the 29th of April, I was directed to furnish, by draught, from my brigade, as its quota, one thousand of this requisition, and hold them in readiness to march, at a moment's warning, to Baltimore, for its defence. The first of May these orders were complied with, agreeably to a detail accompanying said orders.

On the 18th of July, Major General Smith issued division orders, requiring the quota from my brigade, the 11th, and from the 3d and 9th, a

Capture of the City of Washington.

march, and rendezvous at Baltimore. My orders were issued on the 19th; the troops began to assemble on the 24th, and were encamped about one and a half miles northward of the city, at a place called Camp Fairfield.

On the 21st of July, by Major General Smith, I was directed to take charge of this brigade, and commenced preparing for their reception. Early in August, General Winder, being vested with the command of the tenth military district, superseded General Smith in the command.

On Saturday, August the 20th, about one o'clock P. M., I received, by express, letter No. 1, directing me to move down with my whole force for Washington.

By this morning's regimental reports, the force of my brigade, then in camp, appeared as follows : The first regiment, under Lieutenant Colonel Ragan, officers included, 550; second regiment, under Colonel Shutz, officers also included, fit for duty, 803.

I immediately issued orders for wagons to be procured, provisions served out, tents struck, and everything prepared to march that evening. But the difficulty of obtaining wagons to transport tents and camp equipage prevented my moving more than part of the brigade this evening. The residue followed on the morning of the 21st. The advance party encamped at the Stag Tavern ; the rear three miles short of it, on the evening of the 21st.

About ten o'clock P. M. I received from General Winder, by express, letter No. 2, dated the 21st directing me to halt until further orders.

August 22, at ten o'clock A. M. received from General Winder letter No. 3, dated at the Woodyard, the 21st, ten o'clock P. M., directing me to advance with all speed to Bladensburg. In consequence thereof, the line of march was taken up immediately, and at seven P. M. we arrived at Bladensburg. The first regiment encamped on the hill southeast, the second, on the northeast of the town; and, on Tuesday morning, the 23d, joined the first regiment on Lowndes' Hill, near Bladensburg. About ten o'clock A. M. received from General Winder letter No. 4, dated at Headquarters, Battalion Old Fields, August 22, containing orders to march my brigade (with the troops under Colonel Sterret, if they had joined me) slowly towards Marlborough, and take a position on the road not far from that place, and that he would join me some time that day.

The troops under the command of Lieutenant Colonel Sterret had not joined me, nor was I certain at what time they would arrive. The brigade was instantly put in motion, and the march commenced towards Marlborough, with a view of complying with General Winder's orders. I immediately despatched my aid-de-camp, Major Woodyear, to General Winder, to communicate all the information which he might require as to my force; to receive particular orders as to the position I should take in the vicinity of Marlborough ; and to obtain a knowledge of the country, and of the situation of the enemy. After proceeding about one mile on the road to Marlbo-

rough, I met Captain Moses Tabbs riding express to inform me that the enemy, with their whole force, had left Marlborough, and were on their march toward me, distant about six miles. This information made me determine to avail myself of the high grounds I occupied in the morning, to which I immediately returned, and made the necessary preparations to receive the enemy. I directed Captain Tabbs to return and reconnoitre the enemy, and give me every information. About four o'clock P. M. he returned, and informed me that the enemy, on leaving Marlborough, had taken a different route. Soon after, my aid-de-camp, Major Woodyear, returned from General Winder, and informed me that the intelligence I had received of the movements of the enemy were, in part, incorrect, and that General Winder wished me to encamp on the direct road from Bladensburg to Marlborough, at about seven miles distant from the latter place. The Assistant Adjutant General, Major Hite, accompanied Major Woodyear. By letter No. 4, I was first informed that Lieutenant Colonel Sterret's detachment, consisting of the fifth regiment, about five hundred strong; Major Pinkney's rifle battalion, about one hundred and fifty ; and Captain Myers's and Magruder's companies of artillery, about one hundred and fifty, were attached to my command. These troops had not joined me, but were on their march. I despatched an express with this letter to Lieutenant Colonel Sterret, as soon as received, requesting him to move on with all possible expedition.

About sunset, on the 23d, he arrived with his command, and encamped near my brigade. The fatigued situation of his troops induced me to halt for the night, on the hill near Bladensburg, with the intention of moving towards Marlborough at reveille, on the 24th. At about eight o'clock P. M. a militia captain, who resided near Bladensburg, came into camp attended by one of my sentinels, and informed me he was from General Winder's camp, at the Battalion Old Fields; that General Winder was not in camp when he left it ; and that it was apprehended he had been taken prisoner; as he had gone out to reconnoitre the enemy, and had not returned: that a detachment from the army had skirmished that day with the British ; and that Brigadier General Smith, of the District of Columbia, had taken the command of the army, and would certainly join me in the course of the night. At about eleven o'clock P. M., the Secretary of State, Colonel Monroe, with several gentlemen, came to my tent ; and, as well as I recollect, Colonel Monroe observed that he was from Washington ; that he had been at, or heard from, the camp of General Winder ; that there was an alarming silence with respect to General Winder, who had gone out to reconnoitre the enemy, and had not been heard of ; and it was feared he was taken: that General Smith had, by persuasion, taken the command ; and that they would move towards, and join him before morning, he expected, from the Battalion Old Fields ; and advised vigilance to prevent surprise. Soon after the departure of Colonel Monroe, the advance pickets, on the road by which we expect-

Capture of the City of Washington.

ed the enemy, and which was the direct one from Marlborough. fired ; and, in a few moments, my whole command was under arms, and prepared for action. The cavalry, under Colonel Tilghman, who had come into town a little after dark for refreshments, were ordered down the Marlborough road, except Captain Herbert, with his troop, who was directed to push down the road, toward the Battalion Old Fields, until he should fall in with General Winder's army, which I was confident would join me that night.

The troops were under arms until after two o'clock A. M. of the 24th, when, being advised by the cavalry that the enemy were not near, I ordered them to retire to their tents, but to be ready to turn out at a moment's warning ; and strong pickets guards were placed on the road in every direction. Supposing my right and rear covered by General Winder's force, I felt no apprehensions of surprise there; and no expectation that the enemy, without first beating General Winder, could approach me, either by the Battalion or river road. But, about half after two o'clock A. M., Major Bates, Assistant Adjutant General of militia, came to me from Washington, with a message from General Winder, informing me that General Winder had retreated from the Battalion Old Fields into the City of Washington, across the bridge; which he had ordered to be burnt; and that the General expected I would resist the enemy as long as possible, should he move against me in that direction. Thus was my expectation of security from the Battalion and river roads cut off, my right flank and rear uncovered, and liable to be attacked and turned, without the possibility of securing it, in the position I then lay.

I instantly sent for Lieutenant Colonel Sterret, of the 5th, Major Pinkney, of the rifle corps, and Lieutenant Colonel Ragan, Lieutenant Colonel Shutz being present, officers in whom I placed the highest confidence, and stated to them the information and orders I had just received from General Winder, and our situation with respect to the enemy ; they were unanimous in opinion that our situation on that hill could not be defended with the force then under my command, worn down with hunger and fatigue as they were, and that it was indispensably necessary, for the security of the army, that we should immediately retire across the bridge of Bladensburg, and take a position on the road between Bladensburg and the city, which we could defend. Colonel Tilghman of the cavalry observed he thought we had no time to lose. In this opinion I perfectly coincided. Orders were instantly given to strike tents, and prepare to march, and in about thirty minutes, without noise or confusion, the whole were in motion, and, about half past three o'clock in the morning, passed the bridge at Bladensburg leading to the City of Washington. Securing our rear from surprise, we halted in the road until the approach of day, with a view of finding some place where water could be had, in order that the men might cook their provisions, and refresh themselves for a few moments. The provisions consisted of salt beef of an inferior quality, the flour old and musty. At daylight, I moved on to the foot of a hill near a brickyard, and there ordered the troops to refresh themselves. This was about one and a half miles from Bladensburg.

Early in the morning, I had despatched Major Woodyear to Washington, to inform General Winder of my movements and situation; of the exhausted state of the troops, and the impracticability of their meeting the enemy, in their present fatigued state, with any prospect of success, unless reinforced. I rode to the top of the hill to examine the country. On my descending it again, a note was presented to me, by an express from General Winder, dated at Washington. (written I presume without a knowledge of my movements,) directing me to oppose the enemy, as long as I could, should he attempt a passage by the way of Bladensburg. This note I have mislaid.

I called a council of war, consisting of Lieutenant Colonels Sterret and Ragan, and Major Pinkney. I laid the letter before them. Colonel Sterret observed, that he marched from Baltimore with a determination to defend the city ; that his men, the day before, by a forced march from the Back tavern, or Snowden's, reached Bladensburg without halting to cook ; that they had been under arms nearly the whole of the night, without any sleep or food ; that Major Pinkney's riflemen, and the two companies of artillery, were in the same situation ; and that they were so completely worn down and exhausted, that he should consider it a sacrifice of both officers and men, to seek the enemy at any considerable distance from General Winder's force, as no good could result therefrom. Major Pinkney and Colonel Ragan expressed themselves to the same effect; and, with Colonel Sterret, urged the propriety of moving further on the road towards the city, with a view of taking a stand on some more favorable ground for defence, with a better prospect of being joined by the forces under General Winder; and expressed their willingness to give their opinions in writing. I could not but admit the correctness of their views, and ordered the wagons to move on slowly towards the city; intending to follow on with the troops.

At this moment, Major Woodyear returned from Washington, with positive orders from General Winder to give the enemy battle at Bladensburg, should he move that way, and that he would join me if necessary.

I immediately ordered the troops to retrace their steps to Bladensburg, determined to maintain, if possible, the ground, at all hazards.

On arriving in the orchard near the mill, I directed the artillery to post themselves behind a small breastwork of dirt, that lately had been thrown up by Colonel Wadsworth. This battery commanded the pass into Bladensburg and the bridge southwesterly of the town. Our artillery consisted of six six-pounders; Major Pinkney's battalion of riflemen on their right, under cover of the town and bushes, also commanding the pass by the bridge; two companies from Lieutenant Colonel Shutz's regiment, under the command of Captains Ducker and Gorsuch, acting as riflemen, although principally armed with muskets, on the left of the artillery, near and protected by the barn, intended to defend the road leading by the mill on the left of the battery into the field; Colonel Sterret's regiment was halted in the orchard, on the right and in the rear, and the regiments of Colonels Ragan and Shutz were also halted in the orchard in the rear, and on the left flank near the creek. My intentions were, that they should remain here to refresh themselves as long as possible, and as soon as the enemy appeared, to form Colonel Sterret's regiment (in whom I placed great confidence) on the right, their left resting on and supporting the right of Major Pinkney's riflemen, in view of the bridge, and fronting the road, along which ran a fence, and act as occasion should require. Colonels Ragan's and Shutz's regiments were to be drawn up in echellon, their right resting on the left of Captains Ducker's and Gorsuch's rifle companies, in order to prevent the enemy from pressing and turning our left, hoping that General Winder would join me before the battle would commence, and occupy the ground in my rear, as a second line.

About eleven o'clock, A. M., I was informed by a dragoon from Lieutenant Colonel Beall, that he was on the road from Annapolis to Bladensburg, with about eight hundred men, distant from me about five miles, and wished to know the distance and situation of the enemy. I directed the dragoon to return and inform him that I had that moment received information that the British, with their whole force, were approaching Bladensburg by the river road, and that they were only three and a half miles distant; and advised the Colonel to file off to his right, and cross above Bladensburg, to fall into an old road, which I understood led to our left towards Washington; and take a position on the high grounds, north and northwest of Bladensburg, which would completely protect my left by preventing the enemy from out-flanking us that way, and force their main body across the bridge, in the face of my artillery and riflemen on the main road, and expose them to the fire of the fifth regiment, under Colonel Sterret, who would be protected by the fence.

This advice it appeared Colonel Beall only took in part, I presume from an anxious wish to place himself between the enemy and the city. He sent his baggage off to the right, and with his troops passed the bridge at Bladensburg, about thirty minutes before the enemy appeared on Mr. Lowndes' hill, and took his station on the hill, as I was informed, near the brick kiln where we halted in the morning, about one and a half miles in my rear, and on the left of the road leading to the city. About meridian, the enemy could clearly be seen making towards us by the river road.

While I was giving some directions to the artillery, I found Lieutenant Colonels Ragan's and Shutz's regiments had been moved from the place where I had stationed them, and marched out of the orchard up the hill, and formed in order of battle about two hundred and fifty yards above the orchard, and upwards of five hundred yards in the rear of the artillery and riflemen. Thus uncovered by the trees of the orchard, their situation and numbers were clearly seen by the enemy from Lowndes' hill, and the flanks of the artillery and riflemen unprotected, and laid liable to be turned, our main body being placed too far off to render them any aid. On riding up the hill to know who had ordered this movement, I was informed that General Winder was on the ground. At this time I met with Brigadier General Smith, of the District of Columbia, and some conversation took place between us respecting the order of battle and seniority; the particulars I do not recollect. I immediately rode to the mill, where I understood General Winder was, and found him reconnoitering the position of the enemy. While in conversation with him, the fifth regiment was taken out of the orchard, marched up the hill, and stationed on the left of Colonel Shutz's regiment, that of Colonel Ragan's being on the right, its right resting on the main road; but, as I before observed, the whole at so great a distance from the artillery and riflemen, that they had to contend with the whole British force, and so much exposed, that it has been a cause of astonishment they preserved their ground so long, and ultimately succeeded in retreating. Whose plan this was, I know not; it was not mine; nor did it meet with my approbation; but finding a superior officer on the ground, I concluded he had ordered it, consequently did not interfere. General Winder asked me where I meant to take my station? I answered, about the centre of my brigade. He said he would take his on the left of the fifth regiment. General Winder was extremely active in giving directions and in encouraging the men. I took my station in the centre of Colonels Ragan's and Shutz's regiments, but occasionally rode along the line, encouraging the men, and giving orders to the officers. Major Weedyear I directed to keep with the left of Colonel Shutz's regiment, to cheer up the men, and assist the officers. Major Randall rode with me. Soon after, the action commenced by the artillery and riflemen at the battery. The fire of the artillery had great effect, and evidently produced confusion in the ranks of the enemy, who took shelter behind a warehouse, from whence they fired rockets; but a few well directed shots drove them from this position. A flanking party, concealed by the banks and bushes, pushed up the river to turn our left, whilst a strong force attempted the bridge; but the incessant and well directed fire from our artillery and riflemen at the battery occasioned evident confusion amongst their ranks, so much so, that their officers could be seen actively engaged preventing their retreating, and pushing them on to the bridge; and here I think the enemy suffered considerably. At length they succeeded in passing the bridge in small parties, at full speed, which formed after crossing. I had ordered forty horsemen with axes, to cut away this bridge before the near approach of the enemy, and saw them with their axes.

Why this order was not executed, I never could learn. It is certain the enemy could have forded the stream above; but I considered it would, in some degree, impede their progress, and give our artillery and riflemen more time and opportunity to act with effect against them.

The artillery under the command of Captain Myer and Magruder, and the riflemen, the whole under the command of Major Pinkney, behaved in the most gallant manner; (this gallant officer in the course of the action was severely wounded) but the superior force of the enemy, and the rapidity with which he moved, compelled them to retire; but one of the pieces was lost, and this was rendered harmless before it was abandoned.

The enemy took every advantage of the cover afforded them by the trees of the orchard, and their light troops from thence kept up a galling fire on our line. On this party, when advanced nearer, the fifth regiment, under Colonel Sterret, opened a steady and well directed fire, which was followed by the fire from the right, and ultimately from our centre, when the firing on both sides became general. After a few rounds, the troops on the right began to break. I rode along the line, and gave orders to the officers to cut down those who attempted to fly, and suffer no man to leave the lines. On arriving at the left of the centre regiment, I found Lieutenant Colonel Shutz's and Ragan's regiments fled in disorder, notwithstanding the extraordinary exertions of their officers to prevent it. On the left, I soon after discovered a part of the fifth regiment giving way, and that excellent officer Lieutenant Colonel Sterret, with those under him, most actively engaged forming them again. Soon after, the retreat became general, and all attempts to rally them, and make a second stand, were fruitless. With a body of United States' cavalry, I endeavored to protect the rear and right of the retreating men, so as to prevent their falling into the enemy's possession.

The men under my command were worn down and nearly exhausted from long and forced marches, want of food, and watching. They had been, with very little intermission, under arms and marching from the time of their departure from Baltimore, with but little sleep, bad provisions, and but little opportunity to cook. They certainly were not in a situation to go into battle; but my orders were positive, and I was determined to obey them.

Before and during the action, I did not see any of the force I was led to expect would support me. I understood since, they were on their way to my assistance, and I presume exertions were made to bring them up.

Before and during the retreat, I heard the thunder of Commodore Barney's artillery; but till then I did not know he was near. I believe there were few if any other troops in the field when the action commenced, than the three regiments of infantry, under Lieutenant Colonels Sterret, Ragan, and Shutz, Major Pinkney's battalion of riflemen, Captains Myer's and Magruder's companies of artillery, amounting to about two thousand one hundred and fifty, exclusive of two regiments of cavalry, who did not act.

General Winder, on the field of battle, displayed all possible zeal, activity, and personal bravery, in encouraging the men to fight, and after they broke, in his exertions to rally them.

I saw the President and some of the Heads of Departments in the field, but did not perceive that any of them took any part in the arrangement made for battle. Colonel Monroe, the then Secretary of State, appeared extremely active in his efforts to aid the officers in the discharge of their duties, and exposed himself to much danger.

To my aid-de-camp, Major Edward G. Woolyear, and my acting Brigade Major, Major Beall Randall, I am much indebted for their unremitting exertions in encouraging the men before and during the action, and the zeal displayed by them in their attempts to keep the ranks unbroken, and to rally the men, in which they in some degree succeeded; for the company of Captain Galloway, and part of Shower's and Randall's were rallied, and were among the last troops who left the field, and did not retreat until directed; some of them were killed, and several severely wounded.

On arriving at the city, with part of Colonel Lavall's United States' cavalry covering the retreat, and collecting the rear of our scattered troops, I found General Winder's command had passed through it towards Georgetown. I proceeded there, and then followed to a village a few miles beyond it, where I overtook him with troops collecting under his command, and some of those of my brigade. The army thence proceeded to Montgomery Courthouse on the 25th of August, where it was hourly reinforced by those who fled from the field.

As there had been no place assigned by the Commanding General, previous to the action, to which the men should retreat in case of a defeat, many of those under my immediate command had fled from the field towards Baltimore.

On the 25th I directed my aid, Major Woolyear, to push on from Montgomery Courthouse to that place, organize the draughted men, and bring them on to any point that General Winder should direct.

On Friday, August 26th, at about 10 o'clock A. M., we took up the line of march from Montgomery Courthouse, on the road leading to Baltimore, with the United States' infantry, under Lieutenant Colonel Scott; Major Peter's corps of artillery; General Smith's brigade of District troops; the regiment of militia from Annapolis and Ann Arundel county, commanded by Lieutenant Colonels Beall and Hood; some riflemen from Frederick, Alleghany, and other places; a large body of cavalry, and part of my brigade of draughted militia—a force respectable as to numbers and appearance—and that night encamped about half way between Montgomery Courthouse and Ellicott's upper mills. General Winder having received some information respecting the enemy, indicating intentions of moving against Baltimore, concluded his presence there was in-

Capture of the City of Washington.

dispensable. He set out for that place, leaving me in command of the army, with directions to follow him in the morning. Colonel Monroe was with us.

During this night several expresses arrived from the City of Washington, by whom I was informed of the retreat of the enemy, said to be in such haste and confusion that many of their soldiers were straggling about in every direction; that the main army, after reaching Bladensburg, had taken the road to Marlborough, leaving their wounded. I ordered the cavalry to follow them, harass their rear, and pick up the stragglers. Reports from Georgetown and the city reached me, that the arms of many of the enemy had fallen into the hands of the blacks, and it was apprehended that they would take advantage of the absence of the men to insult the females, and complete the work of destruction commenced by the enemy; and at the earnest solicitation of Brigadier General Smith and Major Peter, who expressed much anxiety respecting their families, and considering it all important to prevent further injury to the city, I ordered the troops of the District of Columbia to move thither for its protection.

Having ascertained that the enemy had retreated to their shipping, I ordered the Prince George's troops down to Bladensburg, and those under the command of Lieutenant Colonels Beall and Hood to remain encamped on the ground then occupied, until they had orders from General Winder; and in the morning of the 27th, with the United States' infantry, my brigade, and part of Colonel Lavall's cavalry, marched for Baltimore in a very heavy rain. On my arrival there in the evening, I waited on General Winder, and detailed to him what I had done since he left me, with which he appeared well pleased.

Before I conclude, I must observe that Major Pinkney, with most of his battalion, and part of the two companies of artillery, retired from their advanced position to the left of the fifth regiment, and with that regiment continued to behave with that gallantry which had distinguished them in the onset, and only retired when pressed by superior numbers, and then, as I am informed, by orders from the Commanding General.

TOBIAS E. STANSBURY.

Hon. R. M. Johnson, *Chairman, &c.*

General W. Smith's Statement.

Camp, Washington, *October* 6, 1814.

Sir: In compliance with the request contained in your favor of the 28th ultimo, enclosing a copy of a resolution of the honorable the House of Representatives of the United States, appointing a committee to investigate the causes which led to the success of the enemy, in his late enterprise against this city, I have the honor respectfully to submit, for the consideration of the committee, the following detailed report, as connected with the inquiry, and embracing, as you wish, a view of the numbers, the movements, the conduct, and

13th Con. 3d Sess.—52

disposition of the troops of Washington and Georgetown, under my command, from the period they were called into service, until the 24th of August, the disastrous day of battle at Bladensburg, together with such facts and circumstances relative to the subject as present themselves.

Late at night on the 18th August, I received orders to call out the whole of the brigade under my command, to rendezvous on the evening of the following day on the banks of the Tiber, in Washington, and to report to General Winder. The troops assembled according to orders, but being deficient in many essential supplies for actual service, were, after an inspection, dismissed until the ensuing morning, the 20th, when every exertion on the part of the officers being made to perfect their equipment, they moved off from the Capitol about 3 P. M., crossed the Eastern Branch, and halted four miles therefrom, on the road leading to Nottingham. They were here overtaken by the baggage, when it was ascertained there was a great deficiency of necessary camp equipage, the public stores being exhausted; many of the troops were compelled to lay out in the open field; and of the essential article of flints, upon a requisition of one thousand, only two hundred could be had. Means were immediately adopted to supply the latter defect from private resources; the former was never accomplished. On the following morning, the 21st, the militia companies deficient in numbers were consolidated, and the supernumerary officers detached to bring up delinquents. The force on the ground amounted to about one thousand and seventy, comprised into two regiments, commanded by Colonels Magruder and Brent, and consisting of the following description of troops: two companies of artillery, twelve six pounders, and two hundred and ten men; two companies of riflemen, nominally, but armed with muskets, the Secretary of War having declined or refused to furnish rifles, one hundred and seventy men; one company of grenadiers, forty men; and five companies of light infantry, about two hundred and fifty men, in all about six hundred and seventy of volunteers, the residue common militia. Having here done all that could be done for the organization of the troops, and to enable them to move with celerity, they were, according to previous orders from General Winder, put in motion, and after a hot and fatiguing march, encamped that evening after dusk near the Woodyard. At this place I found the United States' 36th regiment, Lieutenant Colonel Scott, about three hundred and fifty strong, and a squadron of cavalry, under the command of Lieutenant Colonel Tilghman; the latter soon after moved off to reconnoitre on the different roads between the Woodyard, Marlborough, and Nottingham. While the troops were occupying the ground, I received a message from General Winder, then at the Woodyard, requesting an interview at his quarters; after which I returned to camp at 9 o'clock, and again, at his request, joined him at 12, where Colonel Monroe soon after arrived with the intelligence of the arrival at Nottingham, (distant about twelve miles) of the enemy, in considerable force, both by land and water. I received orders immediately to return to camp and hold the troops in readiness to march at the shortest notice, and was instructed by General Winder to direct, Lieutenant Colonel Scott, of the 36th United States' regiment, to get his men immediately under arms, and to march according to orders previously given him. I reached the camp about two o'clock, A. M.; the troops were roused, the tents struck, the baggage wagons loaded, and the men got immediately under arms, and so remained until sunrise the 22d, when General Winder arrived and directed an advanced corps to be formed and march immediately, to consist of about three hundred men, artillerists and infantry. This was promptly done, and placed under the direction of Major Peter, consisting of his own artillery, Captain Davidson's light infantry, and Captain Stull's rifle corps, armed with muskets. They moved immediately on the road to Nottingham, and were soon after followed by the main body to support them. Major Peter with the advance corps moved on for four or five miles, when he fell in with Colonel Lavall's cavalry, a part of Colonel Tilghman's, and the 36th United States' regiment, retiring. The troops were halted, and a position taken to repel the enemy, now rapidly approaching. General Winder here joined our troops, and soon after, orders were given to fall back, which was done. The main body had meanwhile arrived at a position within two miles of the advance, where they found the marine corps, under the command of Captain Miller, with five pieces of heavy artillery, judiciously posted.

This position not being deemed favorable for the infantry, they were directed to rest on their arms, whilst I rode briskly forward to discover one more adapted to them; but none presented, except for light troops, a body of which was thrown in advance into the woods, and the residue of the troops disposed of to act according to circumstances. Here we received advice, about 11 o'clock, of the advance of the enemy and of the retiring of our troops, and immediately after, orders from General Winder to send off the baggage from where it had been left in the morning, to the "Long Old Fields," and for the troops to retire slowly upon the same road. About this time, successive heavy explosions from the direction of Marlborough, announced the destruction of Commodore Barney's flotilla, which was known to be in that vicinity, and also that this course would be adopted, should the enemy approach in such force, by land and water, as to render the resistance unavailing. It was hence inferred, that the enemy had ascended the Patuxent in force, that a column of troops had co-operated, by taking the road in that direction, which was soon afterwards confirmed; and with the advices subsequently, that the whole of their army had filed off on that road, and taken possession of Marlborough. Our troops halted, and assembled at the fork of the roads, on this side of the Woodyard, one of which leads to Marlborough, the other to this place.

We here fell in with Commodore Barney and his sailors, and after a short rest the whole moved on, and about 4 P. M. arrived at the Long Old Fields. Here, pursuant to directions from General Winder, I assumed the command of the assembled forces, those of Commodore Barney excepted, consisting now of the following troops, viz: District volunteers and militia, one thousand and seventy; Lieutenant Colonel Scott's 36th United States' regiment, three hundred and fifty; Lieutenant Colonel Kramer's battalion of draughted militia, two hundred and forty; and Major Waring's battalion of Prince George's militia, about one hundred and fifty; total about eighteen hundred men. An encampment was formed for the night, and such positions taken as were best calculated to resist a night attack; the cavalry being already stationed in advance, in the different roads leading to Marlborough, with orders to keep patrolling parties constantly upon the enemy's quarters, and to advise of all his movements. The troops being greatly fatigued, sought in sleep that repose they so much wanted; in this they were disappointed: an alarm gun aroused them about 2 o'clock in the morning of the 23d; they were quickly formed in front of their encampment, and dispositions made to meet and repel the expected attack, but in a short time it was ascertained to be a false alarm, and the troops were dismissed, but with orders to hold themselves ready for their posts at a moment's warning. At daylight General Winder gave orders to have the tents struck, and the baggage wagons loaded, and that the whole should be ready to move in one hour. Those orders were complied with, with all possible expedition. Shortly after, the troops were got under arms, and were joined by another small detachment of Prince George's militia, under the command of Major Maynard, about one hundred and fifty. The whole were held ready to move according to orders. About this time I received directions from General Winder to have formed an advance corps, constructed as the one of the preceding day, and to be prepared to move as his subsequent orders should designate. Peter's, Davidson's, and Stull's companies were again selected for this purpose, and formed accordingly. The President of the United States, accompanied by the Secretary of War, and others of his Cabinet, now came upon the ground and reviewed the troops. About 10 o'clock, General Winder left the camp, accompanied by, and having under his command or direction, several troops of cavalry, intending to reconnoitre on the road leading from Marlborough to Bladensburg, as well as to be situated in a position where he might more conveniently communicate with the troops expected from Baltimore, leaving directions that I should report to him at the Cross Roads, it being the intersection of a road, proceeding from the Old Fields, and crossing the before mentioned road, about five miles distant. His orders were, that the advance troops should move forward in the direction of Marlborough, reconnoitre the enemy, approach him as near as possible, without running too much risk, and to annoy him, either in his position or in his movements, by all the means in their power, and that I should remain with the main body at the Old Fields, and act according to the intelligence I should receive of the movements of the enemy. If they moved upon Bladensburg, by the road before mentioned, that I should approach them by the intersecting road from the Old Fields, and attack their left flank, or, if upon the road we now occupied, that we should make the best possible dispositions in our power, and receive him there, unless circumstances imperiously forbade; otherwise, to retire by a road in our rear to Bladensburg or to Washington, as, at the time, should seem most advisable. In conformity with this arrangement, Major Peter, with the advance corps, and with Capt. Caldwell's cavalry, which had joined us, marched about 11 o'clock. About a quarter of a mile in front of our then camp, the road forks, both leading to Marlborough, one, on the main stage road, by which the distance was about eight miles, the other turning to the left, a more direct route, but not so good a road, about six miles. This last mentioned road was taken by our advancing troops. The commander was instructed to report every hour. The residue of our troops were dismissed to refresh. From this period until 2 o'clock, several deserters and prisoners were brought into camp, and I was engaged in examining them, when intelligence was received from Major Peter that the enemy had left Marlborough, and were advancing rapidly upon the road which we then occupied, in great force; that, according to his estimation of their column, and the best information he could obtain, their force was not less than six thousand men; that he had had a skirmish with them, in which they had endeavored to outflank him; and that he was then retiring before them. A part of Colonel Lavall's cavalry having then joined us, were immediately detached to cover the retreat, and the whole of our troops ordered under arms. Conferring with Commodore Barney on the subject, I proposed making a stand in our then position, with which, with his characteristic gallantry, he promptly acquiesced, professing his willingness to co-operate in any measures that might be deemed most advisable. The troops were immediately formed in order of battle, extending nearly a quarter of a mile on each side of the road; those of Commodore Barney, with his heavy artillery, the marines under Captain Miller, and the 36th United States' regiment, being posted on the right of the road; the District troops, and the residue of those attached to them, on the left—our advanced troops, as they arrived, taking their stations in the line, and the artillery, in which it was ascertained we were greatly their superior, and for which the ground was admirably adapted, so posted, as to have the best effect; indeed, so strong did we deem our position in front, that we were apprehensive that the enemy, upon viewing us, would forbear to assail us by daylight, or that, availing of his numbers, he would endeavor to outflank us. To guard against this last, parties of light troops and cavalry were detached to cover both flanks. We remained thus, two or three hours,

calmly awaiting the approach of the enemy, our vedettes successfully announcing his continued progress. About 5 P. M., General Winder, who had been apprized of the approach of the enemy arrived in camp. He examined the different positions, and approved of them, but the day being now nearly spent, and it being ascertained that the enemy had not arrived within a distance in which he would now, probably, be able to make his attack, while it lasted, and it being deemed unadvisable to receive a night attack there, when our advantage of artillery would be unavailing, he gave the orders to retire about sunset, and the whole of the troops, much wearied and exhausted, encamped, late in the night, within this city.

Thus terminated the four days of service of the troops of this District, preceding the affair at Bladensburg. They had been under arms, with but little intermission, the whole of the time, both night and day; had traversed, during their different marches in advance and retreat, a considerable tract of country, exposed to the burning heat of a sultry sun by day, and many of them to the cold dews of the night, uncovered. They had, in this period, drawn but two rations, the requisition therefor, in the first instance, having been but partially complied with, and it being afterwards almost impossible to procure the means of transportation, the wagons employed by our quartermaster for that purpose being constantly impressed by the Government agents, for the purpose of removing the public records, when the enemy's approach was known, and some of them thus seized while proceeding to take in provisions for the army.

Those hardships and privations could not but be severely distressing to men, the greater part of whom possessed and enjoyed at home the means of comfortable living, and from their usual habits and pursuits in life but ill qualified to endure them. They, however, submitted without murmuring, evincing by their patience, their zeal, and the promptitude with which they obeyed every order, a magnanimity highly honorable to their character. Great as was their merit in this respect, it was no less so in the spirit manifested whenever an order was given to march to meet the foe; and, at the "Long Old Fields," where his attack was momently expected in overwhelming force, they displayed, in presence of many spectators, although scarce any of them had ever been in action, a firmness, a resolution, and an intrepidity, which, whatever might have been the result, did honor to their country.

On Wednesday morning, the 24th August, at 11 A. M., I received orders from General Winder to detach one piece of artillery and one company of infantry, to repair to the Eastern Branch bridge, and there report to Colonel Wadsworth; and to proceed with the residue of the troops to Bladensburg, and take a position to support General Stansbury. This order was put in immediate execution, and the troops for Bladensburg moved off with all the expedition of which they were capable. Having put them in motion I passed on ahead, in order that I might select my position against their arrival. I found General Stansbury posted on the west side of the Eastern Branch, his right resting on the main road, distant from the bridge at Bladensburg five or six hundred yards, and extending northeastwardly, his left approaching nearer to the creek. An extensive apple orchard was in his front, and one hundred to two hundred yards in advance, a work thrown up, commanding the bridge, occupied by a corps of artillerists, with five or six pieces, and appeared to be supported by some rifle and light companies. In his rear, on the right, was a thick undergrowth of wood, and directly behind that a deep hollow or ravine, open or cleared, of about sixty yards in width, which the main road crosses. The ravine terminates on the left in a bold acclivity, about two hundred yards from the road; the rest of the ground in his rear was open, unbroken, and gradually ascending fields. Having hastily examined the grounds, and concluded on the dispositions I should make, I apprized General Stansbury of my view, as to the troops under my command, suggesting, that if his line should be forced, and he could again form on my left, that the nature of the ground there would be favorable for a renewal of the action, which might then become general. By this time we received advice that the enemy were near Bladensburg, and I left him, to hasten the arrival of my troops. They moved rapidly on, notwithstanding the excessive heat of the day, covered with clouds of dust, and were promptly disposed of as follows:

Lieutenant Colonel Scott, with the 36th United States' regiment, was posted in a field on the left of the road, his right resting upon it, and commanding the road descending into the ravine before mentioned, in the rear of General Stansbury's right, and the rest of his line commanding the ascent from the ravine. This position was about one hundred and fifty yards in the rear of the front line, but extending to the right. In the same field, about one hundred yards in the rear of the 36th regiment, Colonel Magruder was posted with a part of the 1st regiment of District militia, his right also resting upon the road, the left advanced, presenting a front obliquely to the road, and situated to cover and co-operate with the 36th regiment; Major Peter with his artillery, six six-pounders; Captain Davidson's light infantry, and Captain Stull's rifle corps, armed with muskets, all of the same regiment, were ordered to take possession of the abrupt acclivity before mentioned, terminating the ravine. This was deemed a desirable position, because it commanded completely the ravine and the road crossing it, and a considerable extent of the ground over which the front line would necessarily retire if forced back; but, after a short space of time, report was made to me, that broken grounds interrupted the approach to it with artillery, but by a circuitous route that would consume much time, and that, in case of retreat, the ground in the rear was such as might endanger the safety of the guns. It was mentioned, at the same time, that near to it was a commanding position for artillery, and easy of access from and to the road. I yielded with re-

luctance to the abandonment of the position first ordered, but time did not admit of hesitation. Meanwhile I had posted Lieutenant Colonel Kramer, with his battalion of Maryland draughted militia, in the woods, on the right of the road, and commanding the ravine which continued in that direction, with orders that, if forced, he should retire by his right, through a body of woods in that direction, and rally and form with the troops stationed in the rear, on the extreme right. Upon examining the position taken by Major Peter's battery, it was found that the range of his guns was principally through that part of the field occupied by the 36th regiment. To remove one or the other became necessary, and the difficulty of the ground for moving artillery, and the exigency of the movement, left no alternative. The 36th fell back about one hundred yards, losing, in some measure, the advantage of its elevated ground, and leaving the road. The position of the 31st regiment District militia, from this circumstance, was also necessarily changed. It fell back about the same distance, its right still resting on the road, and now formed, nearly in line with the 36th. Of the 2d regiment District militia, two pieces of artillery and one company of riflemen, armed with muskets, were, by directions of General Winder, sent on to the front; with those he flanked the extreme left of the front line; two pieces more of artillery were posted in the road near the bridge at Bladensburg; the residue of that regiment, about three hundred and fifty strong, under the command of Colonel Brent, was formed as a reserve a short distance in the rear of Major Peter's battery, and so disposed as to act on the right, or left, or in front, as occasion might require. Near them was posted, in the same manner, Major Waring's Prince George's battalion of militia, about one hundred and fifty. Colonel William D. Beall, with a regiment of troops from Annapolis, passed through Bladensburg as our troops arrived, and took a position on the right of the road and nearly fronting it, a distance of about two hundred and fifty yards. Previous to the arrival of the troops on the ground, General Winder came up from the city, and being made acquainted with the intended dispositions of the troops, as well as the ground reserved for Commodore Barney and the marines, approved of and confirmed them.

About half past twelve o'clock, and whilst the troops were taking their different positions, innumerable rockets thrown from the heights of Bladensburg announced the arrival of the enemy then; and, at this period, Commodore Barney's sailors and marines, in quick march, arrived, and took possession of the ground previously assigned them, his artillery being posted in and near the road upon its right, commanding the road and open field in front, and his infantry, together with the marines under Captain Miller, extending to the right; thus occupying the interval of ground between Colonel Magruder's first regiment District militia, and Colonel Beall's Maryland regiment.

The firing of artillery in front soon commenced, and immediately after, that of musketry, in quick

Capture of the City of Washington.

and rapid succession. In a few minutes the whole right and centre of the front line, with some small exceptions, were seen retiring in disorder and confusion. The firing still continued on the extreme left; shortly after, it also broke, and although it retired in more order, yet none could be rallied so as to renew the action with effect, and also soon entirely quitted the field.

Meanwhile the left of the enemy, in heavy column, passed along the road crossing the ravine. They were here encountered by the troops of Colonel Kramer, posted in the woods on the edge of the ravine. These, after a short conflict, were compelled to retire; which they did principally under cover of the adjacent woods, and formed with the troops of Colonel Beall on the right. The enemy's column now displayed in the field, on the right of the road. They here became exposed to the oblique fire of Major Peter's battery, which was kept up with great animation. Still pressing on to the front of our right, they came in contact with the heavy artillery of Commodore Barney, and of the troops posted there. Here the firing became tremendous. They were repulsed, again returned to the charge, succeeded in forcing the troops on the right, and finally carried the position of Commodore Barney.

The dispersion of the front line caused a dangerous opening on our left, of which the enemy in that quarter promptly availed. He advanced rapidly, then, wheeling on his left, soon gained, and was turning our left flank. To oppose this alarming movement, I directed Colonel Brent, with the second regiment of District militia, to take a position still more to the left; and he was proceeding in the execution of this order, when orders came from General Winder for the whole of the troops to retreat. The efforts of the enemy had hitherto been directed principally against the right and left of our whole line of battle. The troops of this District, and a part of those attached to them, occupying positions mostly in the centre, and some of them difficult of access, were consequently but partially engaged, and this principally with light troops and skirmishers, now pressing forward, supported by a column of infantry.

I here beg leave to refer to the reports of Colonels Brent and Thompson, Nos. 1 and 2, showing the positions, and the part taken by their respective commands during the action.

The order to retreat was executed by regiments and corps, as they had been formed, and with as much order as the nature of the ground would permit. The first and second regiment halted and formed, after retreating five or six hundred paces, but were again ordered by General Winder to retire. At this moment I fell in with General Winder, and, after a short conference with him was directed to move on, and collect the troops, and prepare to make a stand on the heights westward of the turnpike gate. This was done as fast as the troops came up. A front was again presented towards the enemy, consisting principally of the troops of this District, a part of those who had been attached to them in the action, and a Virginia regiment of about four hundred men,

under Colonel Minor, which met us at this place. Whilst the line was yet forming, I received orders from General Winder to fall back to the Capitol, and there form for battle. I took the liberty of suggesting my impression of the preferable situation we then occupied; but expecting that he might be joined there by some of the dispersed troops of the front line, he chose to make the stand there. Approaching the Capitol, I halted the troops, and requested his orders as to the formation of the line. We found no auxiliaries there. He then conferred for a few moments with General Armstrong, who was a short distance from us, and then gave orders that the whole should retreat through Washington and Georgetown. It is impossible to do justice to the anguish evinced by the troops of Washington and Georgetown on the receiving of this order. The idea of leaving their families, their houses, and their homes, at the mercy of an enraged enemy, was insupportable. To preserve that order which was maintained during the retreat, was now no longer practicable. As they retired through Washington and Georgetown, numbers were obtaining and taking leave to visit their homes, and again rejoining; and with ranks thus broken and scattered, they halted at night on the heights near Tenleytown, and, on the ensuing day, assembled at Montgomery Court-house.

I have thus, sir, given a detailed, and what will, I apprehend, in many respects, be deemed too minute an account, of the short tour of service of the District troops under my command, which preceded the capture of this capital. I fear its length may trespass too much on the patience of your honorable committee. I thought it, however, due to the occasion, and conformable to the spirit and purport of your inquiries. I had another object. The troops of Washington and Georgetown have been assailed, in the public prints, and elsewhere, with calumnies as unmerited as they are cruel and wanton. They have heard of them with indignant astonishment. Conscious that in no instance have they been wanting in the duty they owed to their country or to themselves, but, on the contrary, in obedience to the call of their Government, have, with alacrity, obeyed its orders, and intrepidly fronted an enemy vastly their superior in force, and never yielding the ground to him, but by orders emanating from superior authority, they cannot restrain the feelings excited by such manifest, such unprovoked injustice. They have seen with satisfaction the resolution of Congress to inquire into this subject; and persuaded of the justice and impartiality of your honorable committee, entertain a confident assurance that the result of your investigation will afford relief to their injured feelings. Connected with this subject, I beg leave to refer to a letter of General Winder, No. 3, in answer to an inquiry made of him, as to the general conduct of the brigade whilst under his command. I have, &c.

         W. SMITH, *Brig. General,*
             First Columbian Brigade.

Hon. R. M. JOHNSON.

P. S. I ought to have mentioned that parts of two companies of the United States' twelfth and thirty-eighth regiments were attached to the thirty-sixth regiment, under Lieutenant Colonel Scott. Previous to the march to Bladensburg, eighty men of his command had been stationed near the Eastern Branch bridge, and did not join until after the action. His force then was less than three hundred men.   **W. S.**

Brigadier General Robert Young's Statement.
    ALEXANDRIA, *Oct.* 3, 1814.

SIR: In compliance with your letter of the 28th of September, written in pursuance of a resolution adopted by the House of Representatives of the United States, requiring such information as may be in my power to give, more especially the part assigned my command, my numbers, orders, movements, and dispositions, previous and subsequent to the 24th of August last, and on that day; as also the conduct of my officers and men, their ideas upon the subject of the enemy's numbers, their confidence in success, and whether anything like a panic prevailed; with such other views as it may be in my power to communicate, pertinent to an impartial investigation of the subject: I have the honor respectfully to report, that, since the declaration of war, I am enabled, with great truth, to say, that the officers and a great portion of the privates of my command have manifested to me every disposition to defend the District of Columbia from the approach of the enemy; and this disposition has been communicated to the Secretary of War, requesting to be furnished with the necessary means of enabling the militia under my command to do so with effect.

On or about the 25th of July, 1814, General Winder visited the town of Alexandria, and was made acquainted with most of the officers of my brigade, and at that interview mentioned his intention of having a general inspection of the brigade. The men were accordingly assembled, on the first day of August, under an order of General Van Ness, when General Winder attended, and inspected the brigade, minutely, in person. And I beg leave here to remark, that, on General Winder's first visit to the town of Alexandria, he was furnished, by an officer of my brigade, with a topographical sketch of the Potomac, from a place called Indian Head, about twenty-three miles below Alexandria, containing the course of the river, the depth of the water, width of the channel at particular places, and pointing out Indian Head as the first proper point of defence against the approach of the enemy by water; the White House as the second point of defence; and suggesting a plan of increasing the defence at Fort Warburton. This was done with an understanding that General Winder would receive any communication upon that subject, in writing, from any of the inhabitants of Alexandria.

On the 18th day of August last, I received orders from General Van Ness to order out immediately the whole of my brigade, to encamp at some convenient place, and report myself to General Winder; which order was obeyed. See No. 1.

On the same day I received orders from the same officer, to detach two troops of cavalry attached to my brigade, to rendezvous at Bladensburg the next day, at four o'clock in the morning, to attend Colonel Monroe, Secretary of State, and be subject to his particular orders; which was complied with, as will appear by document No. 2.

On the twentieth of August I was directed by General Winder to hold my brigade ready to move at a moment's warning, with ammunition, and a supply of three days provision, as will appear by No 3; and, on the same day, about four o'clock, P. M., I received orders from the same officer to cross the Potomac, without delay, at Rozier's ferry, and take a position on the most convenient spot adjacent thereto, encamp, and there await further orders. See No. 4.

I accordingly the same evening took up my line of march, with the remaining part of my brigade, containing, in the whole, officers and privates included, four hundred and fifty four strong. I had with me two brass six pounders, one brass four pounder, and attempted to take two long twelve pounders, belonging to the corporation of Alexandria, but found them too unwieldy to move, with our means, across the river, and returned them. I was, at first, accompanied by a company of marine artillery, composed of volunteers from the seafaring persons in Alexandria, but the difficulty of transporting the twelve pounders occasioned several of them to retreat; the others remained with a brass four pounder, and joined the artillery commanded by Captain Griffith. On the twenty-first of August I received orders to move with my detachment, at reveille next morning, and pitch my tents at the most convenient spot nigh Piscataway, between that place and the Woodyard, and there await further orders, which was complied with. See No. 5.

On the twenty-second of August I received orders to fall back with my detachment, and take the most convenient position on the road from Piscataway to Washington, to defend the approach from below to Fort Warburton. This order was complied with, see No. 6; and here we received information of the approach of the fleet coming up the Potomac, and of their having passed the Kettle Bottoms. I accordingly took a strong position on a height called Hatton's Hill near the head of Piscataway creek, about three miles in the rear of Fort Warburton, removed the ground of the fort, which is favorable for a small number to defend against a greater, and made a disposition of the brigade in case of an attack, and communicated the information, and marked the ground, and made known to the troops their respective posts in the line, in case of an attack, in doing which both officers and privates exhibited to me the strongest and most determined resolution to make a proper and successful resistance. I saw no wavering or want of confidence, nor any symptoms of panic.

On the twenty-third of August, I received in-

Capture of the City of Washington.

formation from Colonel Tayloe, of the cavalry, that he had in charge to inform me, that General Smith's brigade was retreating to Washington, and the enemy pursuing rapidly. and, in case we were compelled to retreat, the Mayor of Alexandria would send every boat that could be had to Fort Washington, or Rozier's ferry, for the purpose of transporting the troops across the Potomac. See No. 7.

On receipt of this letter I addressed one to General Winder, by my Brigade Major, informing him of its contents, and observed, that as Colonel Tayloe did not say from whom he had the charge, I requested that he would please give Major Triplett his orders on the subject. See No. 8. On the morning of the 24th August I received a message from General Winder, by Assistant Adjutant General Hite, directing me to take up my line of march, and move on the road from Piscataway to the Eastern Branch bridge, and take a position at the Cross Roads, and send out videttes towards Marlborough and the city, to watch the movements of the enemy, then on their march, about —— miles on our flank. Our position was on Oxen Hill, where Major Hite again visited us, on his return from Fort Warburton.

On our march, and when the brigade had advanced about three miles, Major Triplett returned with orders from General Winder, directing the brigade to cross the Virginia shore, in the boats which were directed to be left at the fort, for the purpose of crossing troops, and if the boats were not there to retire on to Washington; but, in case we could cross up the river, to fall into the road through which the Virginia troops would pass, and co-operate with them, unless the advance of the enemy up the river should make it necessary to retire on Alexandria; and if there should be no Virginia troops retiring, to fall back immediately to Alexandria, and act in the best manner for the defence of that place, or, retreating to Washington, if necessary; and leaving a latitude, in case of events, to pursue such measures as would best secure us from disaster. See No. 9. Soon after the receipt of this letter, we were advised of the approach of the enemy up the river, above Port Tobacco, and I was also advised that the enemy were, that morning, advanced of Marlborough about five miles; and, without perceiving any want of steadiness in my men, I determined, in obedience to orders, to cross the Potomac to the town of Alexandria, at Rozier's ferry, and sent for the boats left at the fort, and also for the boats from Alexandria, which were immediately sent in great abundance; and, after some part of the brigade had embarked and left the shore, I received orders from General Armstrong, dated the 24th of August, but whether written before or subsequent to that of General Winder I was unable to ascertain, informing me that the most the enemy did the day before, was to move about two miles in advance of Marlborough, and that the ships in the Potomac had no troops; and directing me to hold my present post until assured that the enemy was in force and about to attack me, or until I should receive

further orders, and keep my videttes well posted on every road. See No. 10.

I accordingly recalled the troops embarked, and resumed my position back of Oxen Hill, on the road leading to the Eastern Branch bridge, and near its junction with the road leading to Marlborough, and sent out my videttes on each road. We were at this moment apprized of the enemy's being on his march to Bladensburg, and soon after. by the commencement of the action, which was distinctly heard; the videttes soon returned, and gave me information of the Eastern Branch bridge being blown up, and others, of the retreat of our troops through Washington. I had, in this interval, despatched the trooper who brought me General Armstrong's letter, with an answer, informing him that I had, in obedience to his letter, returned to my position on the heights back of Oxen Hill, and should there wait further orders.

The trooper, with great despatch, returned, and informed me that he could not see General Armstrong, but had inquired of the President and General Winder, both of whom he met with the army, retreating through Washington City, and they being unable to give any information of him, General Winder despatched the same trooper back, with verbal orders for my brigade to cross the Potomac, and form a junction with his army in Montgomery county, Maryland. I accordingly crossed the troops over to Alexandria, on the night of the twenty-fourth of August, and took a position a small distance in the rear of Alexandria, and during the night and next morning crossed my artillery and baggage. I had sent a vidette into the City of Washington, and learnt that the enemy were in possession, and were firing the public buildings. I took up my line of march for Conn' ferry, a small distance above the Great Falls of the Potomac, and immediately opposite Montgomery Court-house, where I was informed General Winder's army then were. The troops were, on the twenty-sixth, delayed on their march, near Carper's mills, opposite the Great Falls of the Potomac, by an alarm of a domestic nature, which I was credulous enough to give credence to, from the respectability of the country people who came to me for protection, and I accordingly halted my brigade, and sent out my light troops, and one troop of cavalry, which had joined me from Fauquier, to ascertain the fact, which finally proved erroneous. See letter No. 12, from the Mayor of Alexandria.

On my passing the road which led to the Little Falls bridge, I was apprized by a vidette that the enemy's pickets were still in view from Georgetown, and by several persons from the city, that I was in danger of being cut off, should the enemy make a sally out across the Little Falls bridge, which determined me to pursue my original intention, and not pass the bridge.

On the evening of the twenty-seventh of August I crossed my troops over the Potomac, at Conn' ferry, and the river being rocky, and but one boat, and owing to high winds, I was unable to pass the artillery and baggage across until late in the evening of the twenty-eighth of August, when I immediately despatched a vidette to General Winder, informing him of my movements, and that I should continue my march to reach his camp, unless otherwise ordered. See No. 12.

About one o'clock of the night of the twenty-eighth, I received an order from Colonel Monroe, Secretary of State, informing me that the British squadron had passed the fort, and was approaching the city; that the fort surrendered without opposition; and that the President of the United States desired that I should move with all possible despatch for Georgetown, to be in a situation to aid either Alexandria or the city, as circumstances might require. See No. 13. I soon after took up my line of march, and reached Georgetown, distant about twenty miles, at half past twelve o'clock, and then marched to the city, and encamped near the President's house, in full view of the enemy's fleet lying at the town of Alexandria.

On the thirty-first of August I was ordered to march across the Potomac, and join General Hungerford, from whence the brigade was marched to the White House. See No. 14. It may be proper for me here to remark, that, on my route to Conns' ferry, I gave directions for moving two twelve pounders, belonging to the corporation of Alexandria, out of the enemy's reach, and on my march to the White House I carried them with me, and caused to be removed from the gunhouse in Alexandria, and while it was in possession of the enemy, the crews, sponges, rammers, and apparatus, belonging to the guns, as also the powder from the powder-house, and, as facts are better than opinions, permit me to bring in view the artillery so handsomely mentioned by Captain Porter. Two of the infantry killed, and two wounded, that had been detailed under the command of Captain Janney, show the materials of the brigade from which they were drawn; the rifle corps were also on the flank of battery, and did their duty, and more to their honor, from knowing that their arms had previously been condemned. Whilst the troops lay at the White House, some opportunity was afforded me during the bombardment of that fort, as well as on the day the enemy's fleet passed it, from the quantity of large and grape shot and rockets which fell among them, of forming a correct judgment of their firmness, as well as from the circumstance of the defence of a particular spot having been previously assigned to me and my command, to which, on the first notice of the action, the remainder of the brigade repaired, with a cheerful serenity of mind free from the agitation or appearance of panic, which warranted the highest expectations from them: and, considering that the brigade was called into service en masse, drawing persons from all situations in life, on so short a notice, I am happy to say that they endured fatigue and privation without a murmur; and I most sincerely lament, both for them and myself, that so fair an opportunity should have passed by;—an opportunity above all others which could have presented itself to the mind of an American freeman, the most desirable; that such an opportunity, from circumstances beyond their control, should have passed, without all the officers and privates of the brigade being brought to a more earnest test of their professions and dispositions, both for the honor of their town, themselves, and beloved country.

I have the honor to be, &c.,
ROBERT YOUNG,
Brig. Gen. 2d brigade M. D. C.

Hon. R. M. JOHNSON, *Chairman, &c.*

NOTE.—Fort Warburton and Fort Washington is the same place, it being differently called in the different despatches received.

Brigadier General Hugh Douglas's Statement.

ELLICOTT'S MILLS, *Nov.* 20, 1814.

DEAR SIR: In answer to the inquiry contained in your letter of the fifteenth, I hasten to inform you, that I received the order calling me to Alexandria, and thence to the City of Washington, on the Monday immediately preceding the destruction of the public buildings. This was on the twenty-second of August. It directed me to march my brigade immediately to Washington. In pursuance of these orders, my brigade, or rather the greater part of it, marched on the next day; the twenty-third; the residue overtook them on their march.

In relation to the arms, I will add, that the Loudoun regiments under my command brought on some arms from Virginia, which were partly deposited at Ellicott's Mills, and partly delivered up, to be brought to this place from Baltimore, the troops having met with Harper's Ferry arms, with which those were supplied whose muskets were out of order.

The Fairfax regiment, under Colonel Minor's command, was armed at Washington, when he was detached from me. From him you may learn when he arrived in Washington; at what hour after his arrival he applied for arms; how long he was delayed, and what were the causes of delay.

It is not in my power to give further information that I deem material; but, as the committee have demanded of me all the information I possess, I feel it my duty to refer them to Colonel Minor, whose information, in relation to the arming the regiment under his command, and the delays attending it, may be perhaps important.

I have the honor to be, dear sir, &c.,
HUGH DOUGLAS,
Brig. Gen. 6th brigade, V. M.

Lieutenant Colonel Joseph Sterret's Statement.

BALTIMORE, *November* 22, 1814.

SIR: I have the honor to acknowledge the receipt of your letter of the 11th instant, and will, with pleasure give such information as I possess relative to the unfortunate affair of Bladensburg.

On the 19th of August last, the 3d brigade of Maryland militia was called into the service of the United States. On the 20th, the 5th regiment, the rifle battalion, under Major Pinkney, and two companies of artillery, under Captains Myer and Magruder, making, together, about eight hundred men, were ordered by General Stricker to proceed to Bladensburg, under my command, where I was to report myself to General Winder. On the 21st, the whole took up the line of march. At Elk Ridge Landing, I received a communication from General Winder, directing me to proceed to Snowden's by convenient marches, and there await his further orders. As the detachment set out without being completely equipped, I halted at the landing, to give an opportunity for the further supplies to come up. However, on Monday, the 22d, about 2 o'clock, P. M., I received an order from General Winder, by express, to advance by forced marches to Bladensburg. The whole of my detachment instantly struck their tents; and, with the greatest alacrity, took up the line of march. We arrived at the Buck, or Snowden's, at a late hour, and encamped for the night. Early the next morning we were in motion, and that evening arrived at Bladensburg, where, by order of Gen. Winder, I was placed under the command of General Stansbury. The whole encampment was alarmed about nine o'clock that night, soon after my detachment had pitched their tents, and before the men could refresh themselves. They, however, formed with cheerfulness and alacrity, and remained under arms until about one o'clock. We were scarcely dismissed before we were again called to arms, and about two o'clock were ordered to strike our tents; and, finally, before daylight, we marched, and crossed the bridge at Bladensburg, and took the road to Washington. We were occasionally halted and advanced, until about 11 o'clock, when we were countermarched, and formed in the orchard on the west side of Bladensburg bridge, to await the enemy, who, we were informed, was advancing in full force. I knew nothing of any second line or reserve being formed to support us, and no man of any judgment, acquainted with the fatigued, undisciplined, and inexperienced troops, under the command of General Stansbury, could, for a moment, suppose them capable of making a successful resistance to a superior, brave, and veteran enemy, conducted by officers of great experience and high reputation. In this situation I concurred in opinion with Colonel Ragan and Major Pinkney, that we ought to fall back, and, by uniting with the other troops under General Winder, which were supposed to be between us and Washington, enable the General to make a better disposition of his whole force; and so advised General Stansbury, who, in reply, observed that the order was positive; that he must make his stand where he was; to which, of course, we submitted.

The two companies of artillery and the riflemen, under Major Pinkney, were detached from me, and stationed near the bridge at Bladensburg. The fifth was formed under the directions of Colonel Monroe, the present Secretary of War, on the left, and in line with General Stansbury's brigade, from which period my attention was principally confined to this regiment. The men beheld the gradually approaching dangers of battle with a firm and undaunted countenance. The action commenced about one, by an attack on the redoubt, where the riflemen and artillery were placed. These soon retired, and the fifth covered their retreat, and kept up a lively fire, and supported their place in line with firmness, until the enemy had gained both flanks, and the order to retreat was given by General Winder himself. I was directed to take a road to the right, as we retired, leading to the City of Washington; but we were so annoyed by the enemy's flankers, followed by his whole force, and finding no reserve to support us, or upon which to form, it became impossible for me, though ably assisted by my field and other officers, to preserve order. On my arrival at Washington, I was informed that General Winder had passed through Georgetown, and taken the Fredericktown road. We followed, and came up with him about three miles from Georgetown, and reported ourselves. By this time it was nearly dark. General Winder here informed me that he should retire upon Montgomery Court-house. I obtained his permission to seek for refreshment and quarters, and discretionary orders to endeavor to turn the course of the retreat towards him. This night I had the mortification of witnessing the conflagration of the City of Washington, being only distant about four miles. Early the next morning, with my field officers, I crossed the country to the Baltimore road, with a view of turning the troops we might meet or overtake towards Montgomery. We soon fell in with numbers of General Stansbury's brigade, and those who marched from Baltimore under my command. But our exertions were again ineffectual, from the knowledge all possessed of the destruction of the public buildings in the city, and that our baggage wagons had passed into Virginia. In fine, I concluded that it would be impossible to collect any force short of this place, and so came on. General Winder soon after arrived here, and seemed satisfied with what I had done.

I ought to notice, that the first line, formed on the battle ground, was changed under the direction of Colonel Monroe. On this occasion he observed to me, "Although you see that I am active, you will please to bear in mind that this is not my plan," or words to this effect.

The fall of the capital must be ascribed chiefly to the insufficiency in point of numbers, and total inadequacy in point of discipline of the troops assembled for its defence. No General, however great his talents or exertions, with such means, against such a foe, could have saved it. The imposing front of the enemy was never disconcerted by the fire of the artillery or riflemen; and the brigade of General Stansbury was seen to fly as soon as the action became serious. No second line or reserve appeared to advance or support us, and we were outflanked and defeated in as short a time as such an operation could well be performed.

I have the honor to be, sir, your most obedient servant,

JOSEPH STERRET,
Lieut. Col. 5th Regiment Md. M.

Hon. R. M. JOHNSON,
in Congress, Washington.

Colonel George Minor's Statement.

In answer to the several interrogatories made by Colonel R. M. Johnson, chairman of the committee of inquiry into the causes of the destruction of the public buildings in the City of Washington, as hereunto annexed, I state as follows, viz:

On Friday, the 19th of August last, was informed (not officially) of the collecting of the enemy's forces in our waters, namely, the Potomac and Patuxent. Immediately issued orders for the regiment under my command to assemble at Wren's tavern on the Tuesday following, it being the nearest point of the county of Fairfax to the city; and, on Sunday the 21st, received orders, through Brigadier General Douglas, to repair with a detachment of ninety men, that had been previously placed in detail, to march at a moment's warning to the aid of General Hungerford, whose headquarters were either in the counties of Westmoreland, King George, or Northumberland; and to make one other requisition of one hundred and forty men, exclusive of officers, and order them to the aid of Gen. Winder, City of Washington. And on Monday evening, the 22d, received a verbal message from the President, by Mr. John Graham, to hasten on the troops which had been ordered from my regiment, which will more fully appear by said Graham's letter to General Winder, to which I beg leave to refer the committee; and, after informing Mr. Graham the purport of the orders I had received, we both concluded it would be proper for him to return to Washington, and have the orders, first alluded to, countermanded, so as to justify me in marching with my whole force to the city; which consisted, as well as I can recollect, of six hundred infantry and about one hundred cavalry; and the said Graham returned to Wren's tavern on Tuesday evening, the 23d, with General Winder's orders, written on the same letter to which I have referred the committee. On the receipt of which I took up my line of march immediately, and arrived at the Capitol between sunset and dark, and immediately made my way to the President and reported my arrival, when he referred me to General Armstrong, to whom I repaired, and informed him as to the strength of the troops, as well as to the want of arms, ammunition, &c., which made it as late as early candle light, when I was informed by that gentleman the arms, &c., could not be had that night, and directed me to report myself next morning to Colonel Carbery, who would furnish me with arms, &c.; which gentleman, from early next morning, I diligently sought for, until a late hour of the forenoon, without being able to find him, and then went in search of General Winder, whom I found near the Eastern Branch; when

he gave an order to the armorer for the munitions wanting, with orders to return to the Capitol, there to await further orders.

On my arrival at the armory, found that department in the care of a very young man, who dealt out the stores cautiously, which went greatly to consume time; as, for instance, when flints were once counted by my officers, who showed every disposition to expedite the furnishing the men, the young man had to count them over again, before they could be obtained, and at which place I met with Colonel Carbery, who introduced himself to me, and apologized for not being found when I was in search of him, stating he had left town the evening before, and had gone to his seat in the country. After getting the men equipped, I ordered them on to the Capitol, and waited myself to sign the receipts for the munitions furnished; and, on my arrival, was informed by Major Hunter, who commanded in my absence, orders had been given to march to Bladensburg, when we took up our march for that place, and met the retreating army on the side the turnpike gate, and was ordered by said General Winder's aids to form the line of battle on a height near that place, and was soon after ordered by the General in person to throw back my regiment from that position, into sections, and to wait until the retreating army had passed, and cover their retreat; and immediately after sent his aid to direct me to countermarch immediately, and come on to the Capitol.

After returning there, halted the troops, to wait further orders, until General Winder directed me to march them on, without telling me where; of course I marched with the other troops until I came to the Six Buildings, where I took the left hand road, leading to the foundry, and there occupied the nearest height to that place, and sent the adjutant to find where the General had made his rallying point, and was informed at Tenleytown, where I marched that evening, and found the troops moving off to encamp at some convenient place on the river road, where I followed on until I saw two barns, where I made to, and rested for the night. Next morning sought for General Winder; met him on the road leading from Tenleytown, to where my troops lay, when he ordered me to Montgomery Court-house, and from thence to Baltimore. Given under my hand, City of Washington, 30th of October, 1814.

GEORGE MINOR,
Colonel 80th Regt. V. Milit.

Lieutenant Colonel John Taylor's Statement.

FRANKLIN HOUSE, WASHINGTON,
November 4, 1814.

SIR: In obedience to your request, as chairman of the committee of investigation, &c., I have the honor to make to you the following statement; on my return from the Northern Neck army, commanded by Major General Parker, of the Virginia militia, which I left on the 20th August, with despatches from that officer, in reply to a communication I had been charged with, concerning the Virginia draughts, I arrived at Washington on Sunday night late, (the 21st,) and reported myself early the next morning to General Armstrong, who ordered me to meet him at the War Office at 12 o'clock, from whom I received the following order:

> " WAR DEPARTMENT,
> *August 22, 1814.—12 o'clock.*
>
> " *General Orders.*
>
> "General Douglas will assemble his brigade at Alexandria, and hold it there, subject to orders.
> "J. ARMSTRONG."

I immediately proceeded with all speed, and executed the above order. Having received Douglas's communication, I hastened to Washington, and handed it to General Armstrong on Tuesday night, the 23d; when he instantly sent me back to Virginia, charged with the following orders, and with verbal directions to forward on the Virginia draughts *with all possible speed :*

> " WAR DEPARTMENT, *Aug. 23, 1814.*
>
> " *General Order :*
>
> "Lieutenant Colonel Minor will repair to Washington, with the regiment under his command, with the utmost despatch. He will report, on his arrival at Washington, to Colonel Carbery, of the 36th regiment of United States' infantry, and make a requisition for arms and ammunition.
> "J ARMSTRONG."

> " WAR DEPARTMENT, *Aug. 23, 1814.*
>
> " *General Order :*
>
> "All militia now in and marching to Alexandria (besides that of Colonel Minor) will march immediately to Washington.
> "J. ARMSTRONG."

> " These orders will be communicated by Colonel Tayloe."

For the purpose of executing these orders without loss of time, and after communicating by a dragoon with Colonel Minor, I proceeded down the Northern Neck to General Hungerford's brigade, then encamped at Camp Selden, near Potomac creek. On the 27th August I moved from the brigade at Occoquan, on its march to Washington, and came on with a despatch from the General to Colonel Monroe, which I delivered at two o'clock in the morning at Washington.

General Armstrong manifested much zeal and earnest solicitation for the defence of Washington, and instructed me to use my best exertions in hastening the troops for the attainment of that desirable object.

I have thus made you acquainted with the orders I received from the late Secretary of War, previous to the capture of Washington by the enemy, and stated to you as concisely and accurately as I can recollect, at this distant period, the manner in which these orders were executed.

I am, sir, very respectfully, your most obedient servant,

JOHN TAYLOE,
Lieut. Col. Cavalry, M. D. C.

Lieutenant Colonel J. Lavall's Statement.

WASHINGTON CITY, *Oct.* 31, 1814.

SIR: I have been honored with your letter of the 26th instant, in behalf of the committee appointed to inquire into the causes which gave success to the enemy in his late enterprise against this city, desiring to know the part taken by my command; my orders, positions, and duties; the number of cavalry under my command, and the different corps of cavalry, &c.; in answer to which, I have the honor to inform you as follows:

It is necessary, first, I should beg leave to commence my narrative from Carlisle, the place which had been assigned me by the Secretary of War, to collect, equip, mount, and instruct, the dragoons, for whom that place was selected as a depot, and at which I received my orders for this city. This is the more necessary, as it is highly important to me to exhibit the true state in which I set off, and thus redress the erroneous opinion the public had formed of my command, both in point of strength and capacity as dragoons.

I took command early in March last of the depot at Carlisle, and as fast as the recruits arrived they were instructed in the sword exercise, marched through the drilling movements, and received all other instructions that could be given them without horses, having none then. After a few months one troop was completed, mounted, equipped, and trained, but it was ordered to Buffalo, under command of Captain Hopkins, who carried with him all the horses, except the lame and sick. Thus I had to begin again, and wait for men arriving from the different rendezvous, and patiently wait also for horses, which came on slowly, until about the 25th of July, when I received the following orders from the War Department, to which letter I must call your particular attention, it being an essential document to prove the state I was in, and the condition in which I left Carlisle to meet the enemy, as it happened in ten days:

> "ADJ'T AND INSPECTOR GEN's OFFICE,
> *Washington, July 20, 1814.*
>
> "SIR: As soon as you have assembled the recruits for the Light Dragoons, arrange them into two troops, with the requisite number of officers, if within your command, and as soon as Lieutenant Darrah has furnished you with a sufficient number of horses to mount them, you will, without delay, move to Montgomery Courthouse, Maryland, taking the nearest and best road to that place, &c.
>
> "The equipment, complete, cannot probably be furnished in time at Carlisle; you will, in that case, order them to Baltimore.
>
> "On your arrival at Montgomery you will report to Brigadier General Winder for orders.
> "By order of the Secretary of War.
> "JOHN R. BELL,
> "*Assistant Inspector General.*
> "Lt. Col. LAVALL, *Light Dragoons.*"

The above orders were executed with the utmost activity and punctuality. I despatched

Capture of the City of Washington.

immediately, an express to the officer mentioned, as purchaser of the horses, (Lieutenant Darrah,) who was then at Pittsburg, upwards of two hundred miles from Carlisle. I enclosed the tenor of my orders, in return of which, as soon as practicable, he sent what horses he had, being about twenty, and came himself some time after, with about the same number: and then, with all reasonable despatch, purchased what was wanted to mount what number of men, fit for duty, I then had, being about one hundred and forty, arranged as directed, into two troops, the one commanded by Captain Burd and two lieutenants, and the other by Captain Littlejohn and two lieutenants. The purchase of horses was completed on Saturday, the 13th of August, and I marched off with the squadron the Monday following, 15th. I arrived at Montgomery on Thursday, the 18th. On Friday, the 19th, I came to Washington for orders, and returned to Montgomery same day. And on Saturday, the 20th, about ten o'clock in the morning, I marched my troops through the city. I crossed, according to orders, the Eastern Branch bridge, and encamped nearly opposite the Navy Yard. There we remained until Sunday afternoon, 21st, when we were ordered to the Woodyard, between which place and Nottingham, and Marlborough, and the Old Fields, we were kept on constant duty in reconnoitering, in patrolling, in escorting, furnishing videttes, to and fro, until Tuesday, the 23d, when we recrossed the Eastern Branch bridge, about eleven o'clock at night, both men and horses hungry, and harassed with fatigue. We remained in that situation until about ten o'clock in the morning, Wednesday, 24th. A stack of hay had just been discovered and directed to be purchased, when I received the following order, to wit:

"HEADQUARTERS, WASHINGTON,
August 24.

"Lieutenant Colonel Lavall will proceed immediately with his detachment to Bladensburg, and report to Brigadier General Stansbury.
"WM. H. WINDER, *Brig. Gen., &c.*"

The men, extremely anxious to feed their horses, were in the act of fetching the hay on their heads, and it was with much difficulty they could be persuaded to drop it before they reached their horses. The trumpet sounded, the men ran to their horses, and in a few minutes I was under way for Bladensburg. A number of the horses were unable to proceed; several of the men sick; and from other casualties my command was reduced to about one hundred and twenty-five. This, sir, was the total amount of dragoons under my command. The report which has circulated of my having on that day from four to five hundred dragoons is erroneous. There were several other troops of volunteer cavalry, but, sir, I had no command nor control over them. What might have been their orders I know not; they did not join me, nor did I receive at any time any orders to take command of them, or any of them.

I have, in compliance with your request, sir, procured the names and probable strength of each troop, which, as near as I have been able to obtain, is herewith subjoined.

I proceeded to Bladensburg; I had never been there before; the enemy was in sight; my orders were to report to General Stansbury; I stopped my troops in the road near the river; I looked for the General; I could not come up with him; he was visiting his troops. Our horses being much in want of water, we marched to the river. The enemy was then advancing rapidly towards it; I retired without having met the General, whom I had never seen. On my retiring from the river, I was met by Colonel Monroe, (then Secretary of State.) I informed him I was in want of orders; and being totally unacquainted with the place, I was indebted to him for the place he pointed out, which I occupied immediately with the squadron. At the moment of my entering the ravine, General Stansbury passed by and approved of it. I was then satisfied that the General knew my position. The action began immediately; and the front of the ravine being too high for me to observe the movements of the enemy, I advanced in front with one of my officers (Lieutenant Brakin) to judge better of the opportunity which might offer. Our being elevated, and in a conspicuous situation, the balls and rockets soon showered around us. I had no other chance to form any idea, having never been at the place before. We were too late to form any judicious arrangements, not knowing how the troops and batteries were disposed in Bladensburg; and we arrived too much before our own troops from Washington to know the disposal of them in the rear.

The engagement was but short. I will not enter into the details of it, as you have no doubt, sir, been furnished by a better authority; nor is it your desire. I will only state what leads to my reference to my share. All of a sudden our Army seemed routed; a confused retreat appeared to be about in every corner of the battle ground, and the place we were occupying seemed to have been the one by which it was to be effected. They poured in torrents by us. My right wing being outside of the ravine, covered unfortunately, a part which it appeared was much wanted. An artillery company drove through before we could clear it; several of my men were crushed down, horses and all, and myself narrowly escaped having my thigh broken by one of the wheels, which nearly took me off my horse. All this created much confusion in the right wing of the squadron; they however soon got in order, and the steam of the running phalanx considerably abated.

In the midst of a confusion, the like of which I had never seen in a field of battle, one of my troops was carried off the field, either through some mistake or improper orders, as it was not known to me, who ought to have been first directed or consulted. The moment that such an important point of discipline is trampled upon, a commanding officer loses all responsibility as well as credit, and risks his honor for the sake of having a command.

Captain Burd's troop, which then did not com-sist of more than fifty-five men, was all the command I was then left with—hardly half of a captain's command. Yet, it has been wondered at why I did not cut to pieces four or five thousand of the British veteran troops with fifty-five men, all recruits, and upon raw horses. The most of them had not yet been purchased two weeks. The consequences are so obvious that I did not think myself justifiable to make so certain, so inevitable a sacrifice, without a hope of doing any good. There is a distinction between madness and bravery.

Regular troops never act or retreat without orders; I had no other orders than those I have stated above, I therefore remained as long as I could. I consulted with Captain Burd before we left the field, who had no more desire to leave it than I had; but it was high time; when we saw all going, I could no longer doubt of the order being general; I could not account for its not being more generally communicated. The enemy was then advancing rapidly under a shower of fire, besides a column of about seven or eight hundred which had gained considerably on our right; we then, and only then, sir, marched off on a walk between the flanking column and our disordered army. We continued in that order, walking our horses as slow as horses could walk, when we were again met by Colonel Monroe, who walked his horse with us better than a mile, until he was satisfied that the enemy on our right required to be kept in observation. He left us and advised to proceed in the order we then were, and we did so.

The pleasing hope to meet all our forces collected at Washington, and that there we would be better able to receive the enemy, from various motives and resources which we could not have had at Bladensburg, filled my mind with anxiety, and helped to comfort me in our retreat; for it was not in the power of imagination to have indulged itself with a moment of doubt, whether we should fight or not at Washington, and defend the Capitol to the last man. I have not met a man who was not of the same opinion with me on that score; by what fatality we were made to pass through the city and leave it unprotected I know not, nor is it within the reach of my comprehension.

Having arrived at the Capitol, I formed my troop. It had been rumored, or ordered, (I do not remember which,) that we were all to form near it; but, after remaining there half an hour, I saw no troops in the neighborhood. I was then informed that the President's house was the place before which the army was to be formed. I then marched through the avenue, and soon arrived before the President's house, but saw no army nor symptoms of any, which would indicate a probability of resistance. After remaining in that situation for about three quarters of an hour, I could not, nor would not, believe that the city was to be given up without a fight. When I received orders to follow the army, which it appeared had passed through Georgetown two hours before us, I then, sir, with a heart full of

sorrow, grief, and indignation, ordered my troop to follow the army, and met it about three or four miles above Georgetown. What follows that period, I presume, sir, is of little importance to you and the committee of inquiry; I, therefore, will close by saying that, from that day to this, I have not ceased to lament the event, without being able to penetrate into the cause.

I have now given you, sir, all the information in my power, relative to the several points, the subject of your request in the letter you have honored me with in behalf of the committee, of whom I have the honor to be, &c.

J. LAVALL,
Col. Com. Squadron U. S. L. D.

Hon. R. M. JOHNSON,

Strength and names of the several Mounted Volunteer Corps on the ground at Bladensburg.

Lieutenant Colonel Tilghman, about	70
Major Ridgely	110
Captain Graham	35
Lieutenant Williams	20
Captain Herber	25
Total	260

Colonel William D. Beall's Statement.

GEORGETOWN, *Nov.* 22, 1814.

SIR: I have the honor to reply to your request, directed by the honorable committee "appointed to inquire into the causes of the success of the enemy in his recent enterprises against this city," &c., that, on my march to Bladensburg, on the 24th of August, I received General Winder's order, in reply to a letter I had written him the day before, to join General Stansbury at Bladensburg; that, on my arrival at the mill, I was met by a gentleman, (General Winder's aid. I supposed,) who informed me my ground was Veitch's Hill; he conducted me to the ground, where I formed and received the enemy, after he had done with the army below the hill. On our retreat, at Capitol Hill, I received an order to march through Georgetown to the heights above it; but we reached Tenleytown, and, from thence, about twelve o'clock at night, were ordered to move on the river road, no point designated; the next day, we arrived at Montgomery Courthouse; the next day we encamped at Gaither's heights, thence to Ellicott's Mills, thence to the two mile stone towards Baltimore.

I have been informed by a gentleman, who acted as one of General Winder's aids, that he brought me an order to retreat; but I do not remember it.

This is as short a statement as I can make, to comprehend the design of the committee.

I have the honor to be, &c.

WM. D. BEALL.

N. B. Having marched about sixteen miles that morning, before the battle, my men were fatigued and exhausted. Although it is not my impres-

... that my command gave way as early as is .... is .... I must acknowledge that the .... of .... the enemy was not of a character .... in defending the ...... of the C.. of S.ates, and there.ore, made ...... .g.e .... if .... r .. be men, and partially suc- .... .t .... wa.e.. gate way, in despi.e of .... .he o....r troops. My command .... of about seven or eight hundred men.

Major William Pinkney's Statement.

BALTIMORE, *Nov.* 16, 1814.

SIR: I have the honor to make the following communication, in compliance with the request contained in your letter of the 17th of last month.

The detachment, of which my battalion of riflemen (or rather three companies of it) formed a part, marched from Baltimore on the 21st of August, under the command of Lieutenant Colonel Sterret of the 5th regiment, and arrived at Bladensburg about sun-set on the 23d, where it encamped below, and at a short distance from, the brigade of General Stansbury, who had fixed his encampment on Lowndes' Hill, by the side of the road from Marlborough, and between that road and the river road. The detachment was wholly from the third brigade of Maryland militia, and consisted of the 5th regiment, between four and five hundred strong; of two companies of artillery, (with six six pounders,) commanded by Captains Myer and Magruder, amounting to about one hundred and fifty men; and of three companies of my battalion, commanded by Captains Dyer, Aisquith, and Baden, amounting to about one hundred and eighty rank and file.

In the night of the 23d, (about eleven o'clock,) we were called to arms by several discharges of single muskets in quick succession, by General Stansbury's pickets. Our detachment, of which only I had much opportunity to observe the conduct, turned out with alacrity, and exhibited, during the alarm, great spirit and firmness. The dispositions made by General Stansbury to meet the enemy, who was supposed to be advancing by the upper road, appeared to be prompt and judicious. It was a false alarm, however, and, after a few hours, we were permitted to return to quarters.

We had scarcely reached our encampment, before Colonel Sterret and myself were summoned to the tent of General Stansbury, where we found his principal officers assembled. The General stated to us that he had just received intelligence from General Winder that he had retired upon Washington, across the Eastern Branch; and he asked our advice as to the course which, in consequence of that movement, it was proper for him to pursue, apprizing us at the same time, as I think, that General Winder expected him to fight the enemy, if he should take the route of Bladensburg. It appeared to be certain that the enemy would take that route, without loss of time, and that General Stansbury's force, fatigued and exhausted as a portion of it was, consisting altogether of militia unused to service, amounting to little more

than two thousand men, and deprived of all prospect of support from any quarter, was in no condition to withstand nearly three ts number of regular troops, in a position which presented ..... peculiar facilities for defence, espec.... whet. was considered that *General Winder's* .... numerous than *General Stansbury's*, ... partial of regulars, high in character a. .. .. furnished with more and heavier. ... and with a powerful body of horse, had ... ... compelled to pause t .. Eastern Branch .. ... at and those troops. ... these, and other reasons, the officers present, were of opinion that General Stansbury ought immediately to break up his encampment, and, by drawing nearer to Washington, commit the safety of the force under his command, and put it in a situation to co-operate ..... that of General Winder, and to receive and execute the orders of that General, whatever ... might be, far as the protection of the Capital, in conformity with it, we retired across the br... in good order, to a high ground, on the other the main road, about a mile and a half from Bladensburg, fr.. m whence the enemy come ... connoitered, if he should advance, as he... anticipated. We halted at this place and rise on the 24th, after General Stansbury ... he informed me, despatched his Aid-de-Camp (Major Woodyear) to General Winder, ... notice of this march, and take some ... ... it. While he remained here, General ... mentioned, or showed to me, (I forget whe... letter just received by him from Gener. W... der, written, I believe, before General ... knew of his late march, from which it ..... that General Winder still calculated in ... gaging the enemy, if he should attempt .... proach by Bladensburg. I was still of opinion .. so expressed myself to General Stansbury. ... although it seemed to be his duty to prepare ... troops to dispute, alone, and to the ut .... the enemy's passage to the city, and I was ... ble the military views of his superiors r .... pose such an undertaking upon him, ... not, unless his orders were peremptory, ... were not yet understood to be .... enemy at a distance from General Winder ... out whose immediate aid he could not ... ... rifice his men, already broken by .... fasting, and want of sleep, and .... the destruction of the Capital; that Major ... year would soon return with precise .... General Winder, founded upon a .... his situation and the designs of the .... ; ... that, even if Major Woodyear's return should ... unexpectedly retarded, and a .... actual position should become necessary ... ... be far more prudent that General .... should proceed to occupy one of the .... yet nearer to Washington, with .... abounded, where he might not .... the enemy to advantage, but ready to .... by the Commander-in-Chief, than .... go back to his old encampment, or .... hood, while General Winder's co-operation ....

tinued to be precarious. I believe that Colonel Sterret and Colonel Ragan gave to General Stansbury the same opinion, in substance, and that General Stansbury concurred in it. He did not, however, move nearer to Washington, for Major Woodyear shortly afterwards (about nine o'clock) brought him verbal orders from General Winder to retrace his steps, and contest with the enemy the pass at Bladensburg, together with an assurance that he would join him without delay. These orders were immediately obeyed, and, between ten and eleven o'clock, A. M., the troops were halted in a field, where there is an orchard, on the left of the road as you approach Bladensburg from Washington, not far from the bridge. The passage at Bladensburg may be effected, as I comprehend, by two routes: by the bridge and deep ford just above it, and by the more shallow ford in the old Baltimore road, a little above the fork made by the Northeast and Northwest branches; which ford is reached from Bladensburg, by first crossing the Northeast branch in the present Baltimore road, and then turning to the left; and we halted at the point from which a passage by either or both of these routes might be opposed.

While the enemy was expected, a cloud of dust announced the advance of a body of troops upon the upper road, and they soon showed themselves upon Lowndes' Hill, which they descended rapidly. As General Winder had not yet appeared, preparations were made to receive them by General Stansbury, assisted by Colonel Monroe. At the bottom of the field, between four and five hundred yards from the bridge, as I conjecture, was a sort of a battery, *en barbette*, which had been hastily constructed for heavy artillery, under the direction of Colonel Wadsworth. The Baltimore companies had been employed, from their first arrival in the field, (with such tools as they could get,) in cutting embrasures through the parapet, which was much too lofty for their six pounders, and which there was not time to reduce through its whole extent, and in masking them with brush wood. In this battery they were now stationed. I was ordered to place my companies in ambush on its right, with a view to afford protection to it, and to annoy the enemy in his approach, if he should succeed in crossing the bridge, or in fording the stream in its neighborhood. I conducted my battalion accordingly to the place prescribed, and there distributed them behind a fence and among the bushes, upon the slope of the bank which terminates the field, and also beyond the slope, as near to the bridge and ford as was practicable, taking my own station some yards in the rear, (with the Adjutant and Sergeant Major,) on the top of the bank in the field, where there was nothing to interrupt my view of an advancing enemy. The fifth regiment was posted about fifty yards in our rear, (outstretching us of course,) and gave confidence to my companies and the artillery. Two companies of General Stansbury's brigade (acting as riflemen, but principally armed with muskets) were posted near the barn, behind the battery, at a small distance from us. The residue of the brigade

was, I think, stationed to the left of the battery, near to and beyond the road which flanks it, called the Mill road, to watch, as I suppose, that road and the upper ford, and to march, or to supply detachments, as occasion might require, to sustain the other parts of our force. A few horse paraded on the main road, sometimes as far as the bridge. Such appeared to be our means of resistance, and such the distribution of them. It was soon ascertained, however, that the troops, whom we had believed to be foes, were a regiment of Maryland militia, under the command of Lieutenant Colonel Beall; and my battalion was consequently withdrawn into the field, where it rested upon its arms. The newly arrived regiment passed on to the rear, and took post out of my view, and, as I have since heard, on the opposite side of the main road, where we had halted in the morning, as before stated. It is but justice to the men, under my command to observe, in this place, that they went to their posts with cheerfulness, although they were about to contend, as they supposed, with veteran troops, greatly superior in numbers.

Soon after the arrival of Col. Beall's regiment, the enemy was discovered in full march for Bladensburg, along the river road, and we, once more, prepared for battle. I had now, from General Winder, (who had recently come upon the field,) the same orders I had before received for the employment of my men; with this difference only, that General Winder's orders imported, that it might be proper to place a portion of them upon the left of the battery, which it was undoubtedly of great importance to protect, and which the new order of battle, hereinafter in part explained, seemed to leave without protection, unless a detachment from my battalion should be so applied. In consequence, I detached Captain Aisquith, with the whole of his company, with directions to take, and maintain as long as possible, the most advantageous position there, for the objects indicated by General Winder's orders. I remanded the other two companies to their former stations amongst the bushes; and, after visiting the battery, and remaining there until the first and second shots were fired from it, I resumed my own station (with the battalion officers before mentioned) upon the top of the bank, in the field. A company of militia, under the command of Capt. Doughty, (having muskets only, but acting as riflemen) placed itself, at my instance, on our right, near to the main road, under cover of some bushes and a fence. The fifth regiment, which had been moved from its first position, (where it might have contributed to repulse the enemy in his attempts to leave the vicinity of the bridge) had now, to the great discouragement of my companies and of the artillery, been made to retire to a hill several hundred yards in our rear, but visible, nevertheless, to the enemy, where it could do little more than display its gallantry. The two companies of General Stansbury's brigade, acting as riflemen, had changed their station, so that I no longer perceived them; but I have heard that they still continued at no great distance from their old ground, although concealed from me by the barn or by trees; my impression, however, is, that they did not, and could not, come into action there. The residue of General Stansbury's brigade had been moved from the left, and made to take ground (invisible to us by reason of the intervening orchard) on the right of the fifth regiment, with its own right resting upon the main road, and disclosed to the enemy. A small body of troops (but under whose command I am uninformed) were drawn up in advance of the left flank of the fifth regiment, and nearly at right angles with it, but, on account of the barn, I did not see it until the two companies of my battalion, which were stationed on the right of the battery, retreated, as will hereafter be mentioned. Of Colonel Beall's very distant station, I have already spoken from hearsay, but, at the time of the action, I knew only that it must be considerably in the rear. Of some artillery in the rear of our right, I had no knowledge, until, during the engagement, I heard its fire, apparently well maintained.

I did not know that Brigadier General Smith's brigade was in or near the field, until the action had ceased; nor was I aware that the artillery of Commodore Barney, Major Peter, Captain Burch, and others, (which, if it had been brought up in time to act upon the bridge, and the road at each of its ends, could not well have failed to insure a triumph over the enemy, especially if supported by a part of the infantry, of which no use was made, and if sufficient care had also been taken to observe the upper ford, to which, perhaps, the enemy might have had recourse, if beaten at the bridge,) was at any time near to us. In a word, I was ignorant of any reinforcements which either preceded, accompanied, or followed General Winder, except only, that I supposed that Captain Doughty's company, and the few troops in advance of the left flank of the fifth regiment, (just before mentioned) and a large body of horse, which was kept idle, had come from Washington.

The enemy having reached Bladensburg, descended the hill, about twelve o'clock, in a very fine style, and soon showed his intention to force his way by the bridge. Assisted by some discharges of rockets, (which were afterwards industriously continued,) he made an effort to throw across the bridge a strong body of infantry, but he was driven back at the very commencement of it, with evident loss, by the artillery in the battery, which principally acted upon the street or road near the bridge, and he literally disappeared behind the houses. The effort was not immediately repeated; but the artillery continued its fire, with a view, as it seemed, to interrupt the discharge of rockets, as in some degree it did, and otherwise to check the enemy's operations.

After a long pause, during which I conjectured (erroneously, as I have since been told) that the enemy, less confident than before of the passage of the bridge, detached a corps of some strength to make its way by the ford, in the old Baltimore road, a second attempt was made to cross the bridge, with increased numbers and greater celerity of movement. This, too, was encountered by the artillery in the battery, but not with its former success, although it was served with great spirit, and commanded by officers of acknowledged skill and courage. In consequence, a large column of the enemy, which was every moment reinforced, either by the way of the bridge or by the ford immediately above it, was able to form on the Washington side, and to menace the battery, and the inadequate force by which it was to be supported. While the enemy was yet at a distance, the company on our right (commanded by Captain Doughty) discharged their pieces and fled, although he appeared to do all in his power to restrain them, as I myself did. My two companies were now (without other known aid than the other company on the left) to protect the artillery, and to receive the whole force of the enemy, which was rapidly accumulating. Following the example which had been set them by the company on their right, they too began to fire somewhat too soon; but in its progress, their fire was manifestly destructive, and for a short time seemed to produce disorder and hesitation in the enemy's ranks. The enemy, however, soon pressed forward again, and was close at hand when the artillery discontinued its fire. Its danger had become imminent, and it was apparent that it could do nothing more in its actual station to retard the enemy's progress. His advance, which threatened the right of my position, and had almost reached it, was probably out of the line of any fire which the half formed embrasures of the battery would admit; and I should presume that it would have been difficult, if not impracticable, to depress the guns in those embrasures (the ground of the battery being considerably elevated) so as to touch the enemy after his near approach.

My companies were now in that condition that their right was on the point of being turned; and, as the battery was evidently about to be evacuated, and Captain Aisquith's company was too weak to keep the enemy in check on the left, it followed that they were in that quarter exposed to the same peril. Our small force, moreover, (somewhat more than one hundred men) could not hope to make an effectual stand against the enemy, even if he should attack it only in front, where there was very little in the shape of natural obstructions to break his column or impede his march. The line of our retreat, too, to the fifth regiment, (the nearest visible rallying point was, of necessity, across the open field in our rear, and only one of my companies had bayonets. Under these circumstances of urgent peril, both companies began, at the same instant, to move towards the artillery, now in the act of limbering its guns. The retreat of my men and of the artillery appeared to be simultaneous. The whole fell back upon the fifth regiment, (on the left flank of which a great part of my two companies were halted, and formed by Captain [Dver] by the adjutant, and sergeant-major,) and the enemy succeeded instantly to their place. I followed in the rear of this retreat, narrowly escaping capture, and found my men in the situation above described, ready once more to act against the enemy. It is here my duty to say, that, although the predicament in which my two companies were placed, when they moved from the right of the battery, was almost as desperate as it could be, I had given no orders to retire, and did not at that moment intend to do so. I cannot, and certainly do not, blame them for anticipating such orders, when they saw their desolate condition, and discovered that the artillery, with which they had been connected as a supporting force, could not continue its fire, or hope to maintain its ground. My justification for withholding my orders to retreat is, that I had none myself, and further, that having found that the enemy had neither artillery nor cavalry, I thought we might venture upon another fire, which could not be otherwise than deadly, now that the enemy was at a small distance from our muzzles. I have this other justification, (which I hope I shall be pardoned for mentioning,) that, as I was myself on foot, and had no horse near me, I incurred my full share of the hazard of too long a delay. It is not improbable, however, that I was wrong, and that I owed it to these brave men to withdraw them, even at an earlier period, from a post where, beyond all question, if they had remained much longer, they must have been taken prisoners or cut to pieces; at any rate, I take pride in bearing my testimony to their bravery and skill, of which I had many proofs during the severe trial to which they were exposed on that most disastrous occasion, amidst such privations, discouragements, and hardships, as might have subdued the spirit, and beaten down the strength of veteran soldiers.

The fifth regiment had now to receive the enemy; and, with slight exceptions, it kept its ground with exemplary steadiness, and maintained a regular and spirited fire, until after it was ordered by General Winder to retreat, and after the necessity of retreat was perfectly obvious. My men adhered to its left, and did their duty there, and finally retired with it, the whole in considerable disorder. The troops of which I have spoken, (in advance of its left,) appeared to behave well, but were soon withdrawn or driven from their station, which the enemy could, indeed, reach with his shot without being seen by them.

Nothing could be more critical than the situation of the fifth regiment when it began to retire. Its right had been thrown open to the enemy by the precipitate retreat of the greater part, if not the whole of General Stansbury's brigade. Its left had nothing to protect it; and, even if the enemy had sent no force by the ford, on the old Baltimore road, to gain its rear, that which he had pushed on by the mill road, and the ground adjacent, was sufficiently formidable. Its front was singularly liable to be galled with impunity from the orchard, from the barn, and from other covers, within striking distance of which it had been posted, while itself was not covered by anything, and could hardly act upon anything. I speak with the more confidence of the good be-

13th CON. 3d SESS.—53

haviour of this regiment, because I was constantly with my men while they acted with it, except only for two or three minutes, when I was employed in going to and returning from the mill road, immediately on their left, from whence I expected an attack. I was, during all this time, too, on horseback, (having obtained a horse after we were driven from our first position,) and had thus the best opportunities of observation. During a part of this time I saw General Winder zealously engaged in the discharge of his very anxious and arduous duties, and manifesting the courage which becomes a gentleman and a soldier.

Of the conduct of Captain Aisquith's company I know no more than he and others have told me. I feel assured that it did well, and that the enemy felt the effect of the activity and resolution which distinguished it. My battalion sustained some small loss in wounded; and Captain Baden was made prisoner.

A wound inflicted in the field, (from which the 5th regiment and my men retreated, as above stated,) by a musket ball, which struck my right arm in front, a little above the elbow, and passing through it broke the bone, disabled me from further service, and made it necessary that I should not long delay to obtain surgical assistance. In this state I left the field, with (or a little after) the last of our friends, about five or six in number, among whom, I believe, was Mr. Meredith of the 5th. The enemy was then very close, and his fire was incessant but inaccurate. I have no further knowledge of the transaction to which your letter relates.

I have the honor to be, &c.

WM. PINKNEY.

HON. R. M. JOHNSON, &c.

Captain Burch's Statement.

CITY OF WASHINGTON, *Oct.* 12, 1814.

SIR: In answer to your request, I make the following statement:

On the 19th of August last, early in the day, I was ordered to call out my company for actual service, being, at the time, informed that the whole body of the militia were ordered into actual service, as it was ascertained that the enemy had landed near Benedict, and were about to proceed to this city. In the evening of that day, the first brigade was paraded, and about one o'clock, P. M., on the 20th, we marched from the city in the direction of Benedict, and encamped for that night about three miles beyond the Eastern Branch, when General Winder took the command. On Saturday, the 21st, we marched on, and encamped that night at the Woodyard, about fourteen miles from this place. On Monday morning it was understood in camp, that the enemy had, by rapid marches, got within a short distance of our encampment; upon which the Commanding General detached Major Peter, with his company of artillery. Captain Davidson's infantry, and Captain Stull's riflemen, as an advanced party, to reconnoitre and hold the enemy in check. They advanced some distance, and were soon after followed by

Capture of the City of Washington.

the brigade, for two miles, when it was halted, and partially formed in order of battle. Major Peter met the enemy, who immediately fled off on the left, and took the road to Upper Marlborough. Major Peter having returned with his command, the whole of the troops were immediately marched back to the Old Fields, where we encamped that night. On Tuesday morning, the same party, under the command of Major Peter, was again sent out to reconnoitre and skirmish with the enemy; and between four and five o'clock of that evening, we learned that they were actually engaged with the British forces. The line of battle was then formed without delay, and we remained so until Major Peter came up and took his position in the line. In a few minutes orders were carried through the line, for an immediate retreat to Washington, as it was said the enemy was too strong for us. I received orders to remain on the ground upon which we were formed, until all the troops had marched, and then, every fifteen minutes, to send off two of my pieces with the proper number of men, until I had despatched all six of them. That, if the enemy appeared in the meantime, (and his appearance was every moment expected,) to open my battery upon him, and continue to fire as long as I could do so in safety, and then retreat as fast as possible, and join the main body. Just as I had despatched the second division of my guns, the aid-de-camp of Brigadier Smith, of the District militia, gave me orders to move off with the whole as fast as possible. As the main body had, by this time, got a considerable distance ahead, I was unable to get up with the rear until they arrived at the Eastern Branch bridge, when my men were so greatly fatigued, that they could scarcely stand by their guns. After we had crossed the bridge into the city, and pitched our tents, between twelve and one o'clock at night, General Winder came to my tent and called me out; he observed that he knew my men were worn down with fatigue and from the loss of rest; but that, in all probability, one of the last good acts which it might ever be in my power to do for my country, would be that night. He wished me to take thirty of my men, with three of my guns, and defend the passage of the lower Eastern Branch bridge, as he had reason to believe the enemy would attempt the passage of it that night. General Winder further observed, that he had some time before left directions at the Navy Yard for a boat to be sent to the bridge, with combustibles to blow it up, in case it became necessary, but that his orders had not been attended to, and that he should not go to rest until he had sent me the boat. I took my thirty men and three guns, and proceeded to the foot of the bridge, with orders to open upon the enemy, if he appeared, as soon as our rear guard had come over, and that if the enemy succeeded in getting upon the bridge, to set fire to the boat and blow it up, and then to resume my position and recommence my fire. A little before daybreak the boat arrived, and was placed under the arch next the draw. I kept this position without rest or refreshment until ten o'clock on Wednesday morning, the 24th, when I was relieved by Commodore Barney. I was then ordered to leave one of my pieces and fifteen men at the bridge, under the direction of Colonel Wadsworth, and proceed on with the balance immediately to Bladensburg. I did so, and when I arrived near the latter place, I was again ordered to leave two of my guns and a party of men in the main road, and push on with the remaining three and the residue of my men, and to report myself at Bladensburg to General Winder. I proceeded until I arrived within a short distance of Bladensburg, when I found much difficulty in finding the General. I rode up and down the whole line in search of him, and when I returned, I found that my guns had been moved off to the left; I followed on and overtook them just as they were formed in battery near the extreme left of the line. I then discovered the General, and applied to him for directions; he replied, "Captain, there is the enemy, (pointing to the British who were then in plain view,) take charge of your pieces." I dismounted, and took charge of my pieces, and in a few moments we opened our fire, which proved to be very galling to the enemy, and after firing about fifteen rounds, the fifth regiment of Baltimore advanced and commenced their fire. By the advance of this regiment one of my guns was masked, which rendered it useless; the other two continued the fire with much effect. The infantry, who were posted on my right as a protection to my pieces, having given way, General Winder, in person, ordered me to limber and retreat. I did not do so immediately, but fired two or three rounds, when the General repeated his order in a peremptory manner. We retreated a few yards, when he observed to me that he thought I might venture to unlimber one of my pieces and give them another fire. I was in the act of doing so, but as the enemy advanced so rapidly he countermanded it, and again ordered me off. I saw no more of the General that day: the men were, that after retreating a mile or two, I was so exhausted from fatigue, fasting and heat, I was unable to keep up with my guns, and fell behind them some yards. I fainted by the side of a fence unobserved by my men. After coming to, they supposed I had been taken prisoner. When I came to my recollection, I found myself in a fever, notwithstanding which, I procured a horse, and found and joined my company on the route from Montgomery Courthouse to Baltimore, and marched with them to Snell's bridge, where we were halted, and afterwards countermarched to this place.

BENJAMIN BURCH.
Captain Washington Artillery.

Hon. R. M. JOHNSON.

Captain Caldwell's Statement.

The following is believed to be nearly a correct estimate of the cavalry on the ground, at the battle of Bladensburg, 24th August last:

Col. Lavall's United States' troops, about · 130

Capture of the City of Washington.

A squadron of Colonel Tilghman's regim't,
M. M., about - - - - -   75
A squadron, command of Major Ridgely,
M. M., about - - - - -   100
Captain Herbert's troop, M. M., about -   40
Captain Graham's troop, Virginia, about -   40

        Total   -   -   -   375

The Alexandria troop, under Captain Thornton, and the Georgetown troop, under Lieutenant Williams, (both small,) accompanied Colonel Monroe on the first day of the alarm to reconnoitre the enemy, and had so many detached on different duties as left but a few scattering ones on the field.

Part of the Washington troop were attached to General Winder, and had been generally detached in carrying expresses or conveying orders; the remainder were on vidette duty. On the morning of the 24th they were sent to patrol the road between the Eastern Branch bridge and the enemy, and did not leave the rear of the enemy in time to cross the bridge and join the army, till the army was on the retreat, except three or four, who were employed in conveying orders, &c., or wherever they could be useful.

                 E. B. CALDWELL.

Statement of General Hungerford.

On the 23d of July was called on by the Executive of Virginia, to take command of the militia in the Northern Neck; after which General Madison was called into service, and Major General Parker, to take the command of the two brigades under Hungerford and Madison. On the eighteenth of August General Winder wrote to General Hungerford to march with expedition to the city, with the forces under his command. This letter was received on the 21st, at camp Nominy Hall, in the Northern Neck, about one hundred and twenty-five miles from Washington. His force consisted of three regiments, under Colonels Boyd, Branham, and Parker. About fourteen hundred men, effectives, marched on towards the city, and Colonels Downey and Chawning, who were in the counties of Northumberland and Lancaster, were directed to follow with their regiments.

A letter was received from Colonel John Tayloe on the 24th, dated the 23d, stating that the Secretary of War required despatch, and directed the troops to march on by regiments, or even companies, if necessary. On Sunday, the 28th, was at Neabeco, about twenty-four miles from Alexandria; was waited upon by a committee from Alexandria about two o'clock, who delivered a communication from the corporation of Alexandria, stating that the town had no artillery or military force to protect it, and they intended to surrender at discretion to the enemy; and that the town being under the command of the civil authority, it would be injurious to the town for any military forces to march to Alexandria. General Hungerford informed the commit-

tee that he should move on, and be governed by circumstances. He received a line on the same day from Colonel Monroe, directing him to march with all possible despatch to Alexandria, and if the enemy had passed Alexandria to march on to the city.

On the morning of the 29th, about ten miles from Alexandria, another deputation waited on General Hungerford, with a printed order of the corporation, amounting to a request that he should not proceed on to Alexandria, and interrupt the arrangement made with the enemy. To this communication General Hungerford replied, that he was acting under the orders of the Government, and should execute those orders, and accordingly proceeded on his march. When within three miles of Alexandria he was met by Walter Jones, Esq., who informed him that the President and Colonel Monroe desired him to station his forces in the rear of Alexandria; detach five hundred men to the height just below Mason's Island, and send one hundred and fifty or two hundred to Aquia, to co-operate against the enemy. A written order was received from Colonel Monroe to the same effect that evening. General Hungerford arrived with the three first regiments in the rear of Alexandria on the 29th, about five o'clock in the evening, where he remained till the first day of September. He was then ordered to the White House, with a part of his forces, to co-operate with the naval forces under Commodore Porter.

No. 9.
Report from the Navy Department, including the official report of Commodore Barney.

Navy Department, Oct. 3, 1814.

Sir: In compliance with your letter of the 26th instant, as chairman of the committee appointed by the honorable House of Representatives, "to inquire into the causes of the success of the enemy in his enterprises against this metropolis, and the neighboring town of Alexandria; and into the manner in which the public buildings and property were destroyed, and the amount thereof;" and with your request "for such information on the subject as may be in my power, and more particularly in relation to the destruction of the Navy Yard, and the amount of public property destroyed," I have the honor to present the following report of the measures adopted by this Department, and of the facts within my knowledge, in relation to the objects of this inquiry:

In obedience to the general instructions and early solicitude of the President, in anticipation of the probable designs of the enemy to harass the country in this vicinity, and to attempt the invasion of this metropolis, I directed, in the month of May last, three twelve-pounders to be mounted on field carriages, by the mechanics of the Navy Yard, and completely equipped and furnished for field service. To these the marines at headquarters were trained, under the command of Captain Miller, and prepared to act either as artillerists or infantry, as the service might require. A short time previous to the reinforcement of the enemy in the Patuxent, I caused two long eighteen pounders to be mounted on field carriages, and prepared in like manner for field service, ready to be attached to the command of Commodore Barney, should the enemy at any time compel him to abandon the flotilla under his command on the Patuxent, and the emergency call for the aid of his force in defence of the capital or of Baltimore.

For this eventual service that officer was instructed to prepare; and by his zeal and activity his men acquired the expert use of their muskets, and a capacity, as well as an ardent disposition to be useful to their country on either element.

On the 26th of July, in consequence of the menacing movements of the enemy near the Kettle Bottoms, in the Potomac, which it was said they were sounding and buoying off, the letter A was written; but, on account of information received on the same day, the letter B, countermanding the former, was written.

The enemy in the Patuxent was occupied in depredating upon its shores, until large reinforcements arrived at the mouth of that river on the 18th of August, the account of which was communicated on the 19th to the Department, by Commodore Barney, in the letter C, with a list of the naval force of the enemy annexed.

On the morning of the 19th, information was received at the Department from Captain Gordon, commanding the United States' naval force at Norfolk, that, on the morning of the 16th came in from sea, and proceeded up the bay, twenty-two sail of enemy's vessels, viz: two seventy-fours, one sixty-four, one razee, seven frigates, seven transports, and two or three brigs or schooners, which, it appears by letter C, joined the force at the mouth of the Patuxent on the 18th; the whole of which ascended the Patuxent near to Benedict, on the 18th and 19th, and commenced debarking the troops. The letter marked D was immediately written to Commodore Barney; and the letter E to Commodore Rogers; and the letter F to Captain Porter; urging the two latter to repair with their forces towards this city with the utmost expedition.

Commodore Rodgers had previously made the most judicious arrangements to transport, with celerity, the marines and the principal part of the seamen under his command on the Delaware station, to the head-waters of the Chesapeake, or to Baltimore, upon any sudden emergency; and had organized and disciplined his men with a view to such service. It appears, however, by his letters G and H, that, with every possible exertion, he did not reach Baltimore until the 25th, consequently too late to participate in the defence of the metropolis, against a force, the greater part of which came in from sea on the 16th, was first known to the Department to have arrived on the 19th, marched from Benedict on the 20th, and entered the capital on the 24th.

Having sent to General Winder on the 19th a copy of letter C, on the 20th I called on him at

his quarters, at McKeowin's, to show him the letter I had just received from Commodore Barney, and my order to that officer to join and co-operate with the force under his command, (see letter K,) also to point out those volunteer corps in his army that comprised the mechanics of the Navy Yard, who, being excellent axemen, would act with great effect as pioneers. As it was understood that a strong squadron of the enemy's ships, in co-operation with his land force, had passed the principal obstacle in the Potomac, and was only retarded in its ascent by contrary winds, against which it was warping with great exertion, I expressed to him my solicitude for the defence of Fort Washington, and proposed to throw the marines, who had been trained to artillery exercise, and a part of the seamen, into that fort, for its defence.

The General did not conceive the state of his force such as to warrant the abstraction of so sufficient a part as that of the marines and seamen from the main body, which was to oppose the direct advance of the enemy's army on the city; and, indeed, his objection appeared to have weight. He did not, however, consider Fort Washington as tenable.

On the 21st the letter L was received from Commodore Barney, and a detachment of about one hundred and ten marines, with three twelves and two eighteen pounders, under the command of Captain Miller, marched from the headquarters to join Commodore Barney, and reached the Woodyard that evening.

In the course of this day and the following I visited the Navy Yard, and inquired of the commandant what were the means of transportation, and what assistance he had in the yard. He stated that all the mechanics of the fleet were, and had been, with the army from the first alarm; that no persons remained but the officers or the yard, three besides himself, and a very few of the ordinary, chiefly blacks; that two of the old gunboats were the only craft for transportation; that all the wagons in the District had been hired or impressed for the army; and that those blacks who were usually to be had for hire, were employed on the works at Bladensburg.

I directed him to employ all the means he had or could procure, to load the gunboats with provision and powder, and send them up to the Little Falls; employ as many wagons as could be either hired or impressed, and convey as much of the navy powder as possible from the magazine on the Eastern Branch, to Mr. Dulany's seat, on the Virginia side of the Potomac, about ten miles above the city; to direct Messrs. Grymes, Stull, and Williams, to transport the public works from their works to the same place; and to continue transporting the most valuable and portable articles from the yard to any place of safety, within the means he could command.

The public vessels afloat at the Navy Yard were the new sloop of war Argus, with her guns mounted, her topmasts launched, and her sails and detached equipments complete, at a short in store; the new schooner Lynx and three new barges, one of the first and two of the second class, completely equipped, with the two gunboats before mentioned.

On the slip was the new frigate Columbia, of the largest class, caulked, ready for coppering, and nearly so for launching. Her masts, spars, tops, &c., almost finished in the mast-house; gun carriages nearly completed; her sails made, and in the loft; her rigging fitted; blocks all made; and her equipments, generally, in great forwardness.

Besides the buildings, engines, fixtures, and shop furniture, of the several mechanical branches in the Navy Yard, there were about one hundred tons of cordage, some canvass, a considerable quantity of saltpetre, copper, iron, lead, block tin, blocks, ship chandlery, naval and ordnance stores, implements, and fixed ammunition, with a variety of manufactured articles in all the branches; seventeen hundred and forty-three barrels of beef and pork; two hundred and seventy-nine barrels of whiskey, and a moderate stock of plank and timber.

Had there been a prospect of transporting the sloop of war Argus to a place of safety, the representations of the commandant will show that he had not the means of transporting her, and there appeared to be no situation in which she could be placed, in which she would not fall into the hands of the enemy, in the event of his getting possession of the city. It, therefore, only remained to endeavor to save all the stores that could be transported, and the small vessels, particularly the barges, if practicable, by running them up to the Little Falls. This was directed to be done.

On the 22d the letter M was received from Commodore Barney. In the evening of that day I accompanied the President to General Winder's camp at the Old Fields, and passed the night in Commodore Barney's tent; the army of the enemy at Upper Marlborough, eight miles distant. On the morning of the 23d reviewed the seamen and marines, whose appearance and preparations for battle promised all that could be expected from cool intrepidity, and a high state of discipline.

In the hope that Commodore Rodgers might arrive that evening at Baltimore, and not doubting that the enemy would be retarded on his march by obstacles and annoyance, until the seamen from Baltimore could reach Bladensburg, I wrote to Commodore Rodgers the letter marked N, and sent it by a vidette.

About two o'clock P. M. I accompanied the President on his return to the city, and, in the course of the evening, was informed of the sudden retreat of our army from the Old Fields to the city, over the Eastern Branch bridge.

On the morning of the 24th I proceeded to General Winder's quarters, at Doctor Hunter's house, near the Eastern Branch bridge, where the President, and the Secretaries of War, State, and Treasury, soon after arrived.

I found Commodore Barney employed, by order of the General, in planting his battery on the hill, near the head of the bridge. He was charged to defend that pass, and to destroy the bridge on the approach of the enemy; for which purpose scows and boats, with combustible materials, were placed under the bridge, ready to explode. At this time the enemy was apparently advancing on the road to the bridge; but shortly after, advice was received that he had turned off on the road towards Bladensburg, about six miles from that place. General Winder set off for Bladensburg, leaving Commodore Barney, with his seamen and marines, in charge of the bridge.

It was soon observed that a very efficient part of the force had been left to destroy the Eastern Branch bridge, which could as well be done by half a dozen men as by five hundred. The subject was discussed by the President, Heads of Departments, and Commodore Barney, which resulted in the order for his immediate and rapid march, to join the army near Bladensburg, which he reached just in time to form his men for battle. Captain Creighton was left in charge of the bridge, to destroy it on the near approach of the enemy.

I here presented, for consideration, the subject of the Navy Yard, to the view of the President and Secretary of War, in the presence of the Secretaries of State and of the Treasury. I described the situation of the public vessels, and the nature of the public property at that establishment; the vast importance of the supplies, and of the shipping, to the enemy, particularly as there appeared to be no doubt of his squadron forming a junction with his army, should it succeed in the conquest of the capital, (General Winder having distinctly stated on the same morning that Fort Washington could not be defended;) and as, in this event, nothing could be more clear than that he would first plunder and then destroy the buildings and improvements, or, if unable to carry off the plunder and the shipping, he would destroy the whole; and if the junction should be formed, it would a strong inducement to the enemy to remain, in order to launch the new frigate, which the force at his command would accomplish in four or five days. He would then carry off the whole of the public stores and shipping, and destroy the establishment, and, in the meantime, greatly extend the field of his plunder and devastation. Thus, in either case, whether the junction was formed, or whether the army alone entered the city, the loss or destruction of the whole of the public property at the Navy Yard was certain.

It was therefore, distinctly agreed and determined, as the result of this consultation, that the public shipping, and naval and military stores, and provisions at the Navy Yard, should be destroyed, in the event of the enemy's obtaining possession of the city.

I went to the Navy Yard about two o'clock, and ordered the commandant to prepare the necessary trains for the destruction of the public shipping, and of the naval and military stores, and provisions, in the Navy Yard, and to destroy the same, so soon as he should ascertain that the enemy had taken possession of the city; first removing such articles of most value, as might be found practicable, particularly the new barges, if possible, and then retire in his gig.

Subsequent events prove the justness of these conclusions, if, indeed, further evidence had been at all wanting.

The only legitimate objects of the enterprise of the enemy to this place, were the public shipping and the naval and military establishments; and none can believe that these would have escaped the torch of the destroyer of our civil edifices, of private rope-walks, and everything in the most remote degree connected with navigation; but, above all, with the American Navy.

The order for the destruction of the public shipping and property at the Navy Yard was not issued without serious deliberation and great pain by him, under whose auspices and direction those noble ships had been constructed, and a degree of activity, usefulness, and reputation, imparted to the establishment, which it had never known before. It was given under the strongest obligations of duty. It is conceived that no military maxim is better established, nor duty better understood, than that which enjoins the destruction of public ships, arsenals, naval and military stores, and provisions, when they can be no longer defended, or prevented from falling into the hands of the enemy; and that this duty becomes the more imperative, as the ratio of the value of the objects is enhanced to the enemy. To defend the shipping or Navy Yard was out of the question; all the mechanics and laborers of the yard, as well as all the seamen and marines in the District, were with the army.

The Commandant of the Navy Yard is a captain in the Navy; the vessels and property were under his charge and command; and if no special order from the Department had been issued, and he had suffered the public shipping and property to have fallen into the hands of the enemy, he would have committed a high military crime, for which he would have been amenable before a court martial. The objects which it was proper to destroy, in order to prevent their falling into the hands of the enemy, could not be separated from those which might have been left for his destruction. They were in store, or in the midst of other combustible materials, and the fire from one would necessarily communicate to the other. Indeed, the whole surface of the yard was covered with ships, timber, pitch, tar, and other combustible matter, so that to set fire to any one object, must produce the successive conflagration of the whole.

On returning from the Navy Yard, towards the western part of the city, I learned that our army had retreated by the road to Tenleytown, and that of the enemy was rapidly advancing towards the city. I soon after received a message from the President, by Mr. Tench Ringgold, at Mr. Charles Carroll's, informing me that he had proceeded to cross the river, and requested that I would follow and meet him on the other side.

I returned to the city on the morning of the 28th, immediately on hearing of the retreat of the enemy, and wrote the letter O to Commodore Rodgers.

The paper P is a copy of the detailed report of the Commandant of the Navy Yard, of the manner in which he carried into execution the order I had given.

The barge he states to have been saved was sent to Alexandria, and, it appears, remained there until the enemy took possession of her.

One gunboat was sunk near Foxall's, laden with salted provisions, and has since been recovered. The other was laden with provisions and gunpowder, but ran aground in the Eastern Branch, in attempting to transport her to the Little Falls, and was plundered by the inhabitants near the Navy Yard; the powder and part of the provisions have since been recovered.

The new schooner Lynx escaped the flames in an extraordinary manner, and remains entire.

The metallic articles have nearly all been saved, including a vast quantity of iron work, which, with little labor, will answer the original purpose.

The timber that was in the dock is saved; and a great deal of that which was partially consumed, will be useful.

Almost the whole of the machinery of the steam engine is reported to be in good condition; the boiler is perfect.

The buildings, with the exception of the houses of the commandant and lieutenant of the yard, the guard houses, and gateway, and one other building, have been destroyed. The walls of some appear to be entire, and but little injured; of others they are destroyed.

The monument was but slightly injured.

Paper Q is a list of the cannon remaining perfect in the yard, and of those which were injured by the enemy.

The issuing store of the yard, and its contents, which had escaped the original conflagration, were totally destroyed by the enemy.

Orders have been issued to the officers of the yard to prepare their statements and estimates of the value of public property destroyed, which shall be furnished as soon as possible.

With the circumstances attending the abandonment and destruction of Fort Washington, and the fate of Alexandria, I am no otherwise acquainted than by the accounts which have been published.

After the capitulation of Alexandria, to the enemy's squadron, a considerable force, in seamen, was ordered from Baltimore, (See letter R,) under the command of Commodore Rodgers, with Captains Porter, Perry, and Creighton. The former attacked and annoyed the enemy in his rear, in boats and with fire vessels, whilst the other commanders planted their batteries on White House Point and Indian Head.

Those measures precipitated the departure of the enemy, and greatly annoyed him in descending the river; but there was not time sufficient to prepare the means to render that annoyance effectual. All that the limited means employed could possibly effect, was accomplished, by the gallantry, skill, and patriotism, of those distinguished officers, and the brave seamen, marines, and volunteers, under their command.

The measures pursued by this Department, in order to co-operate in the defence of the Metropolis, were not, in their nature, strictly sanctioned by the regulations and usages of the naval service, but were adopted with an ardent desire that they might prove effectual; with a certain knowledge that the zeal and patriotism of the naval corps would induce them to seek the enemy, with equal vigor and cheerfulness, in the field as on the main; and a conviction that the emergency fully justified any step which could contribute to the defence of the National Capitol.

Whether more or less has been done than duty required, is cheerfully and respectfully submitted.

I have the honor to be, &c.

W. JONES.

Hon. R. M. JOHNSON, *Chairman, &c.*

NAVY YARD, WASHINGTON,
October 18, 1814.

SIR: On a review of the consequences which emanated from the retreat of our army, and the entrance of that of the enemy into this city, on the twenty-fourth of August last, so far as relates to this establishment, I respectfully submit the following general statement:

After receiving repeated contradictory reports, relative to the strength and position of the enemy, during the afternoon and evening of that day, at twenty minutes past eight, P. M., I received incontestable proof (by Captain Creighton, and Mr. M. Booth, my clerk, both of whom had been voluntarily active to obtain me positive information) that the enemy was in complete possession of the city, having themselves been within the range of, and exposed to, the fire of his musketry.

The boats for our conveyance from the yard being stationed according to order, we immediately repaired down the yard, applying fire to the trains leading to the storehouses, the principal of which were almost instantly in irresistible flames.

Advancing towards the boats, those to the new frigate Essex,* and to the sloop of war Argus, were touched, and they also immediately enveloped in a sheet of inextinguishable fire.

From a momentary impulse, and faint hope of recovering the late schooner Lynx, I directed her not to be fired, and have the satisfaction to say, that, by an almost miraculous escape, she is still "ours."

The frigate Essex's hull, in the shipwright's department, was very near complete, her bottom ready for coppering, and she could have been launched in ten days; her masts and spars were nearly finished, with timber sufficient on the wharf to complete them; all her blocks, dead-eyes, and the major part of her gun carriages, ready; two suits of her heavy sails, and nearly the same

quantity of her others, were finished in the sail loft, ready for bending; her standing rigging, &c., fitted in the rigging loft, and sufficient running rigging in store for her complete equipment; her largest boats nearly ready for launching; all her water casks, and every material of cooper's work, ready to go on board.

The sloop of war Argus lay at the wharf, with all her armament and equipment on board, except her sails, which were in the sail loft, and her provisions in the stores, and therein consumed; and except her powder, which had not been shipped.

A large quantity of timber, plank, knees, &c., were in different parts of the yard, and the seventy-four gun ship timber, stored in the appropriate sheds, all fell a prey to the devouring element; also one large and one smaller row galley, both armed, rigged, and prepared for service; and three heavy armed scows, with their guns, &c. on board also ready.

The buildings destroyed by the fire from the frigate, &c., were, the mast shed and timber shed; the joiners' and boat builders' shops, and mould loft; all the offices; the medical store; the plumbers' and smiths' shops, and blockmakers' shop; the saw mill and block mill, with their whole apparatus, tools, and machinery; the building for the steam engines, and all the combustible parts of its machinery and materials; the rigging loft; the apartments for the master and the boatswain of the yard, with all their furniture; the gun-carriage makers' and painters' shops, with all the materials and tools therein at the time; also, the hulls of the old frigates Boston, New York, and General Greene.

The storehouses first fired were the provision stores, gunner's and ordnance store, cordage store, and sail loft; which, with all their perishable contents, were consumed.

The navy storekeeper's detail issuing store, containing in its different departments a large quantity of new canvass, twine, lines, bunting, and colors; together with all our stocks of mathematical instruments, and nautical apparatus, appertaining to navigation; ship chandlery, tools, nails, oils, paints, &c., had escaped through the night the effect of the fire, but was fired by the enemy on the succeeding morning, the twenty-fifth, and entirely consumed, with all its contents; as were also the coopers' shop, two small frame timber sheds, and that in which our tar, pitch, rosin, &c., were deposited.

The general loss of our papers prevents the possibility of forming a just estimate of the loss in the mechanical departments heretofore enumerated. Of that relative to the stores on hand, in the navy storekeeper's peculiar charge, it is presumed a tolerable accurate estimate may be formed, and will be the subject of a future communication, which shall be transmitted as soon as it is possible to effect.

On my return to the yard on the twenty-sixth, I had the mortification to observe, that the provisions which had been laded on board the old gun-boat, No. 140, (and with which she had grounded in endeavoring to get out of the Branch, on the

---

* The Columbia, as designated in my report of the third instant, but called the Essex, by the Commandant, upon the presumption that her name was to have been changed.

Capture of the City of Washington.

twenty-fourth) had become a prey to numerous unauthorized persons, some of whom, however, instantly offered to deliver up all in their possession, which was subsequently done, but several barrels are yet to be accounted for.

A subject of still greater regret is the loss of upwards of two hundred barrels of powder, which were wantonly and unauthorizedly taken out of the magazine, and chiefly thrown into the water, the cause of which, however, being under investigation by a court martial, on the corporal of the marine guard then there, I forbear to enlarge on the subject as my feelings would dictate.

I have the honor to be, &c.

THOMAS TINGEY.

Hon. WILLIAM JONES.

NAVY YARD, WASHINGTON,
August 27, 1814.

SIR: After receiving your orders of the twenty-fourth, directing the public shipping, stores, &c., at this establishment, to be destroyed, in case of the success of the enemy over our army, no time was lost in making the necessary arrangements for firing the whole, and preparing boats for departing from the yard, as you had suggested.

About four P. M., I received a message by an officer, from the Secretary of War, with information that he "could protect me no longer." Soon after this I was informed that the conflagration of the Eastern Branch bridge had commenced; and, in a few minutes, the explosion announced the blowing up of that part near the "draw," as had been arranged in the morning.

It had been promulgated, as much as in my power, among the inhabitants of the vicinity, the intended fate of the yard, in order that they might take every possible precaution for the safety of themselves, families, and property.

Immediately several individuals came, in succession, endeavoring to prevail on me to deviate from my instructions, which they were invariably informed was unavailing, unless they could bring me your instructions in writing, countermanding those previously given. A deputation also of the most respectable women came on the same errand, when I found myself painfully necessitated to inform them, that any further importunities would cause the matches to be instantly applied to the trains; with assurance, however, that, if left at peace, I would delay the execution of the orders as long as I could feel the least shadow of justification. Captain Creighton's arrival at the yard, with the men who had been with him at the bridge, (probably about five o'clock,) would have justified me in instant operation, but he also was strenuous in the desire to obviate the intended destruction, and volunteered to ride out and gain me positive information as to the position of the enemy, under the hope that our army might have rallied and repulsed them. I was myself, indeed, desirous of delay, for the reason that the wind was then blowing fresh from the south-southwest, which would most probably have caused the destruction of all the private

property north and east of the yard, in its neighborhood. I was of opinion, also, that the close of the evening would bring with its calm, in which happily we were not disappointed. Other gentlemen, well mounted, volunteered, as Captain Creighton had done, to go out and bring me positive intelligence of the enemy's situation, if possible to obtain it.

The evening came, and I waited with much anxiety the return of Captain Creighton, having almost continual information that the enemy were in the neighborhood of the marine barracks; at the Capitol Hill; and that their "advance" was near Georgetown. I therefore determined to wait only until half past eight o'clock, to commence the execution of my orders, becoming apprehensive that Captain Creighton had, from his long stay, fallen into the hands of the enemy. During this delay I ordered a few marines, and other persons who were then near me, to put off in one of the small galleys, which was done, and the boat is saved. Colonel Wharton had been furnished with a light boat, with which he left the yard probably between seven and eight o'clock. At twenty minutes past eight Captain Creighton returned; he was still extremely averse to the destruction of the property, but having informed him that your orders to me were imperative, the proper disposition of the boats being made, the matches were applied, and in a few moments the whole was in a state of irretrievable conflagration. When about leaving the wharf I observed the fire had also commenced at the works at Greenleaf's Point, and in the way out of the Branch we observed the Capitol on fire. It had been my intention not to leave the vicinity of the Navy Yard with my boat during the night; but, having Captain Creighton and other gentlemen with me, she was too much encumbered and overladen to render that determination proper. We, therefore, proceeded to Alexandria, in the vicinity of which I rested till the morning of the 25th, when, having also refreshed the gig's crew, we left Alexandria at half past seven o'clock, and proceeded again up to the yard, where I landed, unmolested, about a quarter before nine.

The schooner Lynx had laid along side the burning wharf still unhurt; hoping, therefore, to save her, we hauled her to the quarter of the hulk of the New York, which had also escaped the ravages of the flames. The detail-saving store of the Navy Storekeeper had remained safe from the fire during the night, which the men, (being in force in the yard,) about eight o'clock, set fire to, and it was speedily consumed.

It appeared that they had left the yard about half an hour when we arrived. I found my dwelling-house, and that of Lieutenant Haraden, untouched by fire; but some of the people of the neighborhood had commenced plundering them; therefore, hastily collecting a few persons known to me, I got some of my most valuable articles moved to neighbors' houses out of the yard, and tendered them their offers to receive them, the enemy's officer having declared private property sacred. Could I have staid another hour, I had

Capture of the City of Washington.

probably saved all my furniture and stores; but being advised by some friends that I was not safe, they believing that the Admiral was, by that time, or would very speedily be, informed of my being in the yard; he having expressed an anxious desire to make me captive; but had said that the officers' dwellings in the yard should not be destroyed.

I, therefore, again embarked in the gig, taking along, out of the Branch, one of the new launches, which lay safe, although alongside of a floating stage enveloped in flames. I had no sooner gone than such a scene of devastation and plunder took place, in the houses, (by the people of the neighborhood,) as is disgraceful to relate; not a moveable article from the cellars to the garrets has been left us, and even some of the fixtures, and the locks of the doors, have been shamefully pillaged. Some of the perpetrators, however, have been made known to me.

From the number and movements of the enemy it would have appeared rash temerity to have attempted returning again that day, though my inclination strongly urged it; therefore, reconnoitering their motions, as well as could be effected at a convenient distance, in the gig, until evening, I again proceeded to Alexandria for the night.

Yesterday morning, the 26th, it was impossible to form (from the various and contradictory reports at Alexandria) any sort of probable conjecture, either of the proceedings or situation of our army, or that of the enemy.

Determining, therefore, to have a positive knowledge of some part thereof, from ocular demonstration, I again embarked in the gig, proceeding with due caution to the yard, where I learned with chagrin the devastation and pillage before mentioned, and found, also, to my surprise, that the old gunboat, which had been loaded with provisions, and grounded in endeavoring to get out of the Branch, on the evening of the 24th, was nearly discharged of her cargo by a number of our people, without connexion with each other.

Having landed in the yard I soon ascertained that the enemy had left the city, excepting only a sergeant's guard, for the security of the sick and wounded. Finding it impracticable to stop the scene of plunder that had commenced, I determined instantly on repossessing the yard, with all the force at my command; repairing, therefore, immediately to Alexandria, Lieutenant Haradan, the ordinary men, and a few marines there, were ordered directly up, following myself, and got full possession again at evening.

I am now collecting the scattered purloined provisions, ready for your orders, presuming they will now become very scarce indeed; the quantity saved, you shall be informed of, when known to me.

The Lynx is safe, except her foremast being carried away, in the storm of the 25th, about four P. M. We have also another of the gunboats, with about one hundred barrels of powder, and one of the large yard cutters, nearly full with the filled cylinders, for our different guns, previously mounted. The powder of those, however, is probably much wetted by the storm. I would most willingly have an interview with you, but deem it improper to leave my station without some justifiable cause, or in pursuance of your instructions, under which I am ready to proceed wherever my services may be thought useful.

I have the honor to be. &c.

THOMAS TINGEY.

Hon. W. Jones.

P. S. *Sunday morning, 28th.*—After terminating the foregoing, last evening, I had scarcely laid down my pen when a smart cannonading commenced at, or from, Fort Washington; which continued from heavy cannon, until after seven o'clock, during which it appeared as if two or three severe explosions had taken place. No doubt that it was between the enemy's frigates and the fort; but as to the result I am entirely without information; nor have I at command the means of obtaining it; the wind blowing too fresh up the river for a light boat to make any progress down. I shall hire sufficient hands, as soon as practicable, and collect all the materials unhurt by the fire; which shall be suitably deposited and protected.   T. T.

FARM AT ELK RIDGE,
August 29, 1814.

SIR: This is the first moment I have had it in my power to make a report of the proceedings of the forces under my command since I had the honor of seeing you at the camp at the "Old Fields." On the afternoon of that day we were informed that the enemy was advancing upon us. The army was put under arms, and our positions taken; my forces on the right, flanked by the two battalions of the 36th and 38th, where we remained some hours; the enemy did not make his appearance. A little before sunset General Winder came to me, and recommended that the heavy artillery should be withdrawn, with the exception of one twelve-pounder to cover the retreat. We took up our line of march; and, in the night, entered Washington by the Eastern Branch bridge. I marched my men, &c., to the Marine barracks, and took up quarters for the night, myself sleeping at Commodore Tingey's, in the Navy Yard. About two o'clock General Winder came to my quarters, and we made some arrangements for the morning. In the morning I received a note from General Winder, and waited upon him. He requested me to take command, and place my artillery to defend the passage of the bridge on the Eastern Branch, as the enemy was approaching the city in that direction. I immediately put my guns in position, leaving the marines and the rest of my men at the barracks to wait further orders. I was in this situation when I had the honor to meet you, with the President and Heads of Departments, when it was determined I should draw off my guns and men, and proceed towards Bladensburg, which was immediately put into execution. On

Capture of the City of Washington.

our way I was informed the enemy was within a mile of Bladensburg; we hurried on. The day was hot, and my men very much crippled from the severe marches we had experienced the days before, many of them being without shoes, which I had replaced that morning. I preceded the men, and when I arrived at the line, which separates the District from Maryland, the battle began. I sent an officer back to hurry on my men; they came up in a *trot;* we took our position on the rising ground; put the pieces in battery; posted the marines under Captain Miller; and the flotilla men, who were to act as infantry, under their own officers, on my right, to support the pieces, and waited the approach of the enemy. During this period the engagement continued, and the enemy advancing, our own army retreating before them apparently in much disorder. At length the enemy made his appearance on the main road, in force, and in front of my battery, and, on seeing us, made a halt. I reserved our fire. In a few minutes the enemy again advanced, when I ordered an eighteen-pounder to be fired, which completely cleared the road; shortly after a second and a third attempt was made, by the enemy, to come forward, but all were destroyed. They then crossed over into an open field, and attempted to flank our right; he was there met by three twelve-pounders, the marines under Captain Miller, and my men, acting as infantry; and again was totally cut up. By this time not a vestige of the American army remained, except a body of five or six hundred, posted on a height, on my right, from whom I expected much support from their fine situation.

The enemy, from this period, never appeared in force in front of us; they pushed forward their sharp shooters, one of which shot my horse under me; who fell dead between two of my guns. The enemy, who had been kept in check by our fire, for nearly half an hour, now began to outflank us on the right; our guns were turned that way; he pushed up the hill, about two or three hundred, towards the corps of Americans stationed as above described; who, to my great mortification, made no resistance, giving a fire or two, and retired. In this situation we had the whole army of the enemy to contend with. Our ammunition was expended, and, unfortunately, the drivers of my ammunition wagons had gone off in the general panic. At this time I received a severe wound in my thigh; Captain Miller was wounded; Sailingmaster Warner killed; Acting Sailingmaster Martin killed, and Sailingmaster Martin wounded; but, to the honor of my officers and men, as fast as their companions and messmates fell at the guns, they were instantly replaced from the infantry.

Finding the enemy now completely in our rear, and no means of defence, I gave orders to my officers and men to retire. Three of my officers assisted me to get off a short distance, but the great loss of blood occasioned such a weakness that I was compelled to lie down. I requested my officers to leave me, which they obstinately refused; but, upon being ordered, they obeyed; one only remained. In a short time I observed a British soldier, and had him called and directed him to seek an officer; in a few minutes an officer came, and, on learning who I was, brought General Ross and Admiral Cockburn to me. Those officers behaved to me with the most marked attention, respect, and politeness; had a surgeon brought and my wound dressed immediately. After a few minutes' conversation, the General informed me (after paying me a handsome compliment) that I was paroled, and at liberty to proceed to Washington or Bladensburg; as, also, Mr. Huffington, who had remained with me, offering me every assistance in his power, giving orders for a litter to be brought, in which I was carried to Bladensburg. Captain Wainwright, first captain to Admiral Cockburn, remained with me, and behaved to me as if I was a brother. During the stay of the enemy at Bladensburg, I received every marked attention possible from the officers of the navy and army.

My wound is deep, but I flatter myself not dangerous; the ball is not yet extracted. I firmly hope a few weeks will restore me to health, and that an exchange will take place, that I may resume my command, or any other that you and the President may think proper to honor me with. Yours, respectfully,

JOSHUA BARNEY.

Hon. W. Jones.

No. 10.

Letters from General Van Ness, Doctor Catlett, and John Law, Esquire.

General Van Ness's Statement.

WASHINGTON, Nov. 23, 1814.

SIR: To your request to me to "report to the committee appointed to inquire into the causes which led to the success of the enemy against this city, &c., such information, facts, and views, as are in my power," I would have answered sooner, making such report, but for a very severe and protracted nervous attack, and a consequent considerable accumulation of indispensable private business. In the narrative which I have now the honor to transmit you, I shall, from the very nature of the case, be drawn into an egotism, which, I trust, the committee will be good enough to excuse.

In the campaign of 1813 we had a call from the War Department, produced by the approach of the enemy in the Potomac, for a part of the militia of the District of Columbia, which was promptly attended to on our part; but owing to the great want of preparation by the Government in respect to arms, ammunition, camp equipage, provisions, and the consequent delays and confusion, the troops would have been inadequate to an efficient resistance, until after they had been out some days—that fact, and those circumstances, were then evident to all. The incompetency of Fort Washington, on the east arm of the river, a few miles below Alexandria, and the necessity of its improvement, were then seen, and

Capture of the City of Washington.

freely spoken of by Secretary Armstrong. Indeed, the importance and necessity of erecting a new fortification or battery at some one of the several favorable sites on the river, so as completely to shut out from the upper part of it, or repel a hostile fleet, was strongly and repeatedly suggested and admitted by the Secretary. He frequently told me, then and afterwards, substantially, that he had "such a project, and was about to execute it; that he was only balancing between several different points which had been proposed or presented to his view, and he believed he must go down himself to reconnoitre and select." After the lapse of some time, not seeing or hearing of any step towards the execution of this project, I several times reminded him of it, and he, as often, still encouraged me, by words, to expect it, while he, generally otherwise, appeared rather indifferent, and expressed an opinion that the enemy would not come, or even seriously attempt to come to this District.

About the opening of the present campaign, I pressed again upon the Secretary the subject generally of our defence, suggesting, in addition to the occlusion of the river, the convenience and importance of a central camp, intermediate between Baltimore, Annapolis, Washington, Alexandria, Georgetown, and the neighboring towns and country. And, in frequent interviews, (in number, to be sure, very much increased by the importunate applications and solicitations to me, of both the civil and the military branches of the community, whose confidence in the Secretary appeared, at an early period, at best wavering, if not declining,) sometimes official, at other times not so, which I had with him, as the campaign progressed, I did not fail to repeat the suggestion. I still received assurances, generally verbally, favorable, accompanied by an otherwise apparent indifference, and confidence in our security. In April last, Colonel Clinch, with about one hundred men, (I believe recruits,) arrived in this city, where he, with those troops, together with a few hundred who had been garrisoned through the Winter at Greenleaf's Point, remained encamped for a few weeks. This was the only force of a regular character, excepting a small marine corps attached to the Navy Yard, which I recollect had been at all stationary in the place, and even the greater part of that was here only at a season when there was no actual danger, or even apprehension of it, and the whole was presently sent to the Northern frontiers.

Sometime in June last, the enemy appearing in or about the mouth of the Patuxent, the Secretary of War called on me for a detachment of militia. Several companies of light troops were immediately, in conformity with his instructions, ordered and marched to that river. After a short period of service, and the departure of the enemy, they were discharged.

Thus had the campaign progressed, without any visible steps towards works of defence, either permanent or temporary, either on the land or the water side, (I never having heard of a spade or an axe being struck in any such operation,) or towards forming a rendezvous or camp of regular troops in the neighborhood, to the great anxiety, inquietude, and alarm of the District and surrounding country; the Secretary generally treating with indifference, at least, if not with levity, the idea of an attack by the enemy.

When the conclusion of European hostilities, and the rumors and accounts of expeditions fitting out for this country by England, excited apprehensions more general and more serious than before, I again renewed the subject of our defence, and it was still treated by him as before. I had occasionally, though seldom, introduced it personally to the President himself, who, without going much into particulars, referred me, generally, on that subject, to the War Department, on which he seemed fully to rely for the proper arrangements. In my anxiety and solicitude I also occasionally mentioned this business to Secretary Monroe, who always appeared to take a warm interest in it, and gave me strong assurances that he would do "everything that he could with propriety do." At length, nothing visible having yet been done, and the danger being supposed constantly to increase, about the latter end of June, or beginning of July last, I inquired of Secretary Monroe whether it was the intention of Government to abandon and sacrifice the District or not, adding, that if it were so, it would be well for us, at least, to know it. He answered me, that, so far from it, every inch of ground about it was determined to be contested, and the last drop of blood to be spilt in its defence. He said it was decided (I then understood or inferred that there had been a recent Cabinet consultation on the subject) to form a camp of regular troops, say between two and three thousand, at a central position, such as I have before spoken of; who, together with the local troops, would constitute an adequate defence for the surrounding points, to either of which they might be promptly and conveniently drawn. When I saw Secretary Armstrong again soon afterwards, I expressed my satisfaction at what I had thus understood. He confirmed the information, and added that there would also be drawn from Carlisle about two hundred cavalry, commanded by Colonel Lavall. In answer to my inquiry, when we might expect them, he said the troops were ordered on, and would begin to assemble in a few days' time, and that orders had been given to procure horses for those of the cavalry corps who were not yet mounted. This period, however, elapsed without the arrival of any of them. There appeared not to be taken into the calculation a small detachment or fragment or two, of a regiment or two of the regular army, who were in some part of the neighboring country, and who, at best, were supposed to be very inefficient. I afterwards, several times, reminded Secretary Armstrong of our disappointment, considering the strong assurances given us, &c.; and I suggested the utility and propriety of ordering out our militia in successive or alternate detachments. I further informed him (which I was authorized to do, by the pressing, voluntary offers

Capture of the City of Washington.

of many of my fellow-citizens) that both the citizens and troops of the District of Columbia were ready and anxious to be made use of, in any way that the Government might prescribe or direct for the public good. He continued to tell me that the troops would soon be on. To my inquiries about the cavalry, more than once, he replied that he had sent orders for purchasing horses to mount the corps, and that it would soon be here. Colonel Lavall did not, however, arrive here until a day or two after the enemy had landed at Benedict.*

Some time in July last, the Secretary of War told me that General Winder (who was in the neighborhood of the Patuxent) had informed him that the enemy were ascending that river in force, and that he (General Winder) required as many of the militia of the District of Columbia as could be procured should be immediately sent to him; and the Secretary directed me to order out three companies to satisfy this call, which was immediately done. After having been in service nine days, they were discharged.

A few weeks before the incursion of the enemy here, a project was originated among the banks, generally, of the District, to offer the Government a loan for its defence. The Secretary was informed of it in its progress, and appeared to approve it, observing that the arrangement must be made with the Treasury Department. Although, owing to the necessity of some formalities at the offices, and the tedious delays in collecting the general sentiment of the different banks, as to certain arrangements and terms among themselves, this project was not matured until about a week before the capture of the city, the Secretary of War was informed that the money would certainly be raised. This was done without any intimation or suggestion from any branch of the Government, of the want of means for an adequate defence, although I recollect the Secretary of War had, some time before, in a conversation I introduced relative to the purchase of some more ground about Fort Washington for an extension of the works, observed, substantially, that the proprietor asked too much for it, considering how poor the Government was, and that, if we found it was really wanted in any pressing emergency, it would, of course, be taken and used.

At length, in August last, when the increased and reinforced fleet, with the troops, ascended the Chesapeake, and were known, from authentic information, to have entered the Patuxent, I called on Secretary Armstrong again, and expressed, as usual, my apprehensions, arising from want of means and preparations, adding that, from the known naval and reputed land force of the enemy,

he probably meant to strike a serious blow. His reply was, "oh yes! by G—d, they would not come with such a fleet without meaning to strike somewhere, but they certainly will not come here; what the d—l will they do here," &c. After remarking that I differed very much from him, as to the probable interest they felt in destroying or capturing our Seat of Government, and that I believed a visit to this place would, for several reasons, be a favorite object with them, he observed, "no, no! Baltimore is the place, sir; that is of so much more consequence."

The public confidence in the Secretary of War had, for some time, been evidently rapidly declining, and the frequent and unreserved expressions by individuals to that effect, sometimes temperate, and sometimes otherwise, were really disagreeable and troublesome to me. The President must, I presume, have been aware of the fact of this want or decline of confidence, as well from the ordinary sources of information, as from that which I have understood (from one of the members themselves) he received from a joint committee or deputation of the municipal authorities of the city of Georgetown, who had, sometime before, a formal interview with him, relative to the general state of the District.

On the 18th of August last, I furnished Secretary Monroe, at his request, and by instructions of Secretary Armstrong, with two small troops of horse, to accompany him to the Patuxent. On the same day, General Winder (after a conference with me, in which he was hesitating and undecided as to the force he might want from the District of Columbia, and in which I advised him, unequivocally, to call for all its militia) required my whole division of troops. They were accordingly immediately ordered out. Beginning to suspect, from circumstances, that some difficulty might arise between General Winder and myself, on the score of command, and not meaning to create any not absolutely necessary, I determined not to raise the point until it should become certain that my troops were to go into actual operation. It soon became so, by the near and direct approach of the enemy to the city. I then called on General Winder, and, after observing to him that, all my troops being in service, I considered myself so also, (as I was part of, or inseparably connected with, the division,) I informed him that I should, of course, expect to take the command the law had assigned to me, of the whole which I was prepared to do. He replied that I would certainly be entitled to the command if I were really in service; and that he would, in such case, yield it to me cheerfully, and without hesitation: but he said he did not consider me necessarily in service, because the two brigades (which composed the whole) of my division had been required, and were in the field; and, inasmuch as this military district had been committed to him, he was compelled to retain the command; and he should be regularly notified by the Government that an officer of superior rank was actually in service within the district. General Winder, in a conversation of some minutes between us,

---

* Colonel Lavall has since informed me that no effectual means were taken to mount his men, notwithstanding his frequent applications to the War Department for that purpose; and that, learning that the enemy was actually approaching us, he, on his own responsibility, adopted means for procuring horses, on the spur of the occasion, or he could not have been on at all for the particular service.

made a distinction (which I could not comprehend) between calling or having the two brigades of my division in service, and calling or having the division itself, which consisted wholly of those two brigades. In support of this claim to the command of my division, he instanced the case of General Smith, of Baltimore, who, although a considerable part of his troops were in requisition and service, had not claimed the command, although he said he had, at first, made some intimation to that effect. I observed, that General Smith's conduct might be explained by the circumstance of his whole division not being in service. I concluded my interview with General Winder by informing him that I would immediately apply to the Secretary of War to determine the principal fact on which the case rested, whether I was or was not in service, and thus to decide the question between us, in which he appeared cordially to concur. Had there been as little confidence then in that gentleman's generalship as there is now, my course would have been different. I accordingly instantly called on the Secretary of War, who expressly declared it was "an embarrassing case;" and, after some minutes' general and indecisive conversation on the subject, concluded by assuring me that he would immediately state it to the President for his decision, and would, without delay, advise me of the result. This was early in the morning of (I think) Saturday, immediately preceding the Wednesday of the affair at Bladensburg.

After leaving Secretary Armstrong, dissatisfied as I was with the general tenor of his language and conduct, relative to the business, during the interview, I also called on the President, stating to him substantially the case, and adding, as I had before done to both the other gentlemen, that, if it were the particular wish and determination of the Executive (which I began to think not improbable) that General Winder should have the principal command, in meeting the column of the enemy marching directly on the city from the Patuxent, that probably some separate station or command might be assigned me, as there were said to be other menaces and approaches. The President declined a decision until after the Secretary of War should have been consulted. I returned to my house, where I waited impatiently with my aids, Majors Brent and M'Kenney, who were ready and anxious to accompany me to camp, until half past twelve o'clock; and, although, upon reflecting on what had passed between the Secretary, General Winder, and myself, I was suspicious it was predetermined, and arranged or understood between them, that I was not to have the command, or, at least, that an attempt should be made to withhold it from me, still, not hearing from the Secretary, I sent a messenger to him requesting a decision. After detaining the servant about two hours, he sent me, by him, a written communication, giving me to understand that I was not considered in command or service. I determined not to attempt to create any discordance or schism at a moment of imminent peril, and when the cordial co-operation of

all was so important; and, at the same time whilst I held my commission of Major General, not being able to serve under General Winder, I instantly sent my resignation to the Secretary, taking an early opportunity of assuring General Winder that, although I felt the injury done me, there was nothing personal in my motives, and, further, offering and pledging myself to him for any service in my power, either civil or military, which the public exigencies might require.* I continued to see General Winder occasionally, as before, and to be astonished at the apparent sluggishness or procrastination in the preparation for the reception of the enemy, who was on his advance. I recollect well that, even after he had, according to authentic and undoubted information, ascended to the head of the ship navigation of the Patuxent, and had, for about twenty-four hours, been debarking on the hither bank of that river, and marching his troops to their encampment on the heights of Benedict, (about forty miles from this, on the usual route,) General Winder, in answer to an inquiry of mine, whether he had ordered on any troops from Baltimore, and whether he thought they would be here in time, said that they were ordered on, and that all his fear was, that they would be here too soon. Expressing to him my astonishment at the apprehension, he said he thought it very probable that the enemy would suddenly turn about, and make a blow at Baltimore. Having been surprised, for several days, at not having seen or heard of any actual attempt or movement towards throwing up works, of any description, in this vicinity, from behind which the enemy might be resisted with great advantage and effect, I proposed, at a meeting of our citizens, on the Saturday evening (after I had resigned) next preceding the day of the affair at Bladensburg, that a committee should be appointed to wait on General Winder, and suggest to him the importance of some such works at Bladensburg, through which village the enemy would certainly pass; and, in case the General should approve the proposition, to request him to assign an engineer or officer to prescribe or superintend the work, the citizens furnishing the laborers, &c., gratis. A committee accordingly waited on him: he approved the idea, assigned or procured Colonel Wadsworth, of the ordnance department, to locate, superintend, &c., and, according to that officer's project and directions, (after having reconnoitered nearly a day, an operation, in which, at his request, I accompanied him,) were the works completed by the citizens, although, to the universal astonishment, not a man occupied, during the action, the principal one; and most advantageous parts of the ground, also, which had been reconnoitered, (and where the enemy might have been cut up and slain by hundreds,) were not even occupied by our troops! Owing to accident and misinformation, I was not in the commencement of the action; but the whole scene,

* Annexed are copies of my resignation, a subsequent letter from the War Department, and my answer thereto.

during my advance towards the right front, where Commodore Barney, with his men and the marine corps, did themselves so much honor, whilst I continued there, and afterwards, in retiring from one point to another as far as Georgetown, contained disgusting and inglorious circumstances. How what was called the first line of our troops, on their left, generally, was formed, I do not know. In that part of the field on which I moved, and afterwards, during the retreat, I could discover or learn nothing like a system or an order of battle. of retreat, or of rallying, or re-forming; and several of the officers of the militia of the city and Georgetown, (General W. Smith's brigade,) whom I met with in the course of the affair (and who, with his men, were generally in good order, and deeply regretted the want of opportunity to act efficiently) appeared. in this respect, to be in the same predicament with myself.

A cardinal error in this whole business was, in my opinion, that the great body or mass of the Baltimore force * was not ordered on this wayho soon as the direction of the enemy's movement was ascertained, with instructions, whilst they (the Baltimore force) were advancing, always to keep themselves between Baltimore and the enemy, so that they might, and would, have been ready, as the two branches of our army and the enemy approached each other, always to co-operate, either before or after a junction, with the troops assembling here, (who would, of course, have followed the enemy had he wheeled towards Baltimore,) in case of an attempt either on this place or Baltimore; and thus an overwhelming and operative force would have been collected. Another very great error, I think, was, that the enemy were suffered undisturbedly to encamp on the heights of Benedict, where the local circumstances are well calculated for resistance, and to advance from thence to Bladensburg, without having been harassed or annoyed in their progress; this was probably, in part, and perhaps principally, owing to the want of a central camp, and, generally, of means and preparations, on our part, when the enemy landed.

Another error was, that our men were, for a short period before the action, unnecessarily harassed and worn down by fatiguing and ill-timed marches; which, in addition to the fatigues many of them underwent from running, as it were, from their homes (from which they were hurried and dragged at the moment, instead of having been ordered out in proper season) to this city, almost exhausted them. Another, a want of attention and promptness in having the reinforcements, as they arrived in the city, supplied with arms, ammunition, provisions, &c., and in accustoming them to the familiar use of the former. Another, that the enemy were suffered to advance too far, even at Bladensburg, before they were met; owing, doubtless, to the absence of our troops, who had been encamped the preceding night within about three or four miles only of the field of battle. Another, a want of the most advantageous order or arrangement in

the battle itself; one of the causes of which doubtless was, that the enemy were allowed really to anticipate us in the occupation of the ground intended for ourselves. Another, the evident want of a concerted plan of retreat to, or rallying at, some one or more of the advantageous positions between the battle ground and the Capitol. Another, a premature order (as generally understood) of retreat. Another, that a respectable body of apparently excellent troops, (the Fairfax regiment of militia,) who had been in the city since a late period of the preceding day, were not in the action. I understand, from a gentleman who was present, that, early in the evening of the preceding day, after the arrival of those troops in the city, their commander made application to the Secretary of War, for arms and ammunition for them; and that, owing to the objections made by the Secretary, he did not obtain them until the morning, which probably was a principal cause of his detention from the engagement. Another error, I think, was, that General Young's brigade of Alexandria, which was encamped at the east side of the Potomac, opposite to Alexandria, within a few miles of the Eastern Branch bridge, was not sent for immediately (if not before) when it was ascertained that the enemy was rapidly approaching Bladensburg. If this had been done, General Young might either have marched towards that place by the road south of the Eastern Branch, where he might have detained and annoyed the enemy in flank or rear, or he might, (crossing the Eastern branch bridge,) if he could not have reached the field of battle, have met our retreating troops at some point in the city, and might thus have been very instrumental in restoring the fortune of the day; and in either case, he might, in a few hours' time, have returned to his former station: whereas, he remained at the distance to an order (as he has himself informed me) that day given by the Secretary of War, at his position, not an enemy near him, or a sight, whilst his men distinctly heard the firing at Bladensburg, and were mortified at their absence from it. Another error was, that the woods, fences, ravines, &c., by the sides of the turnpike road were not lined with our light troops, to annoy the enemy in his advance from the battle ground. At all events, on the rising ground south east of the turnpike gate, if not before, our troops ought to have made another stand. By the extraordinary exertions of private gentlemen, or volunteer officers, and by the opportune arrival of a favorable spot of the Fairfax troops, (I think about six hundred,) who had not yet been opposed, a body of about ten or twelve hundred men, was already formed, including several pieces of artillery, well planted, and their number was rapidly increasing, by the rallying of fugitives, the arrival of fresh troops, &c.; and I am confident that had they remained there, (in a position as well commanding the Navy Yard as the city generally, the British would not have advanced that day, being at least two or three miles off, wearied and partially, severely handled; and, by the morning, such advantages of system, arrangement, and, in

---

* A part only of the Baltimore force came this way.

Capture of the City of Washington.

erease of numbers, confidence, &c., might have been improved by us, as would have led to the discomfiture and defeat of the enemy; but, unfortunately, even from here those troops were ordered to retreat towards the Capitol square; and thence to a more distant place; against both of which movements I took the liberty, at the time, of remonstrating to General Winder. Another unfortunate error was, that our troops, after it was determined to abandon the city itself, were not halted on some of the commanding heights around it, from which they might constantly have operated with effect, either by detachment, or otherwise, on the enemy, during his continuance here; and from which, if it had become necessary to retire, we might, at all times, have retired with safety. Another error was, that a considerable and unnecessary number of wagons and carts were in the field, or its immediate vicinity, from which, at an early period of the engagement, they fled, and in their flight contributed much to the dismay and confusion of the day. Another error was, that the enemy was not pursued and annoyed, in his precipitate departure to his ships. Many of these errors, doubtless, arose from the want of correct information relative to the enemy; which, in itself, was an extraordinary circumstance, as, for some days before they (the enemy) entered the city, there were several hundred cavalry among our troops. Many of the evils of the day also, unquestionably, arose from the rawness of a considerable part of our militia force; indeed, considering what the description of the great mass of our troops was, and that they had to contend with about an equal number of veterans, nothing but judicious and skilful management, added to our decided superiority of artillery and cavalry, the native valor of our men, fighting for all they held dear, and the local advantages within our reach, could have authorized the expectation of success.

Although I cannot think the means we had on the spot were used to the best advantage, still I think General Winder was by no means furnished with sufficient or timely means; which I always considered it the special duty of the War Department to have attended to.

From a certain degree of delicacy, sir, in my situation, as regards both the late Secretary of War and General Winder, it is not without some reluctance that I have given the committee the above view; but, considering your call as imperative, and having always been of opinion that it was due to the American people that the facts and circumstances connected with the fall of the capital should be fully developed, I transmit it to you, after having necessarily prepared it in great haste. Possibly other circumstances relative to the subject may hereafter occur to me; should that be the case, I will take the liberty of communicating them. I presume, also, that I shall have the privilege hereafter of correcting any errors, either in form or substance, that may have crept into the statement.

JOHN P. VAN NESS.
Hon. R. M. Johnson, &c.

CITY OF WASHINGTON, Aug. 20, 1814.

SIR: Give me leave hereby to resign the command which I have for some time past had the honor to hold, as Major General of the militia of the District of Columbia. My commission would have been enclosed, had I been able to lay my hands upon it. A principal regret which I feel upon this occasion is, that my resignation occurs at a moment when I would have been happy to have been permitted to participate in the defence of my country, and particularly of the District.

I have the honor to be, &c.
JOHN P. VAN NESS.
Hon. John Armstrong,
    Secretary of War.

WAR DEPARTMENT, Nov. 12, 1814.

SIR: I am instructed to state, that your resignation of the command of the militia of this District, as Major General, has not been accepted, and that it would be satisfactory to the President that you should resume it.

That you were not called into service with the troops of the District, did not proceed from a want of respect for your merit, which is acknowledged, but from the impossibility of doing it, at the time, without displeasing the commander of the district, from which the most serious injury was apprehended, the enemy having landed at Benedict, and being on his march for this city. Great confidence is entertained in your patriotism, zeal in support of the cause of your country, and fitness for the trust, regarding your comparative experience, with that of others of our fellow-citizens, in active service. I add, with pleasure, that your conduct, after presenting your resignation, and particularly at Bladensburg, after joining our troops as a volunteer on the preceding day, has increased these favorable impressions.

I have the honor to be, &c.
JAMES MONROE.
Maj. Gen. J. P. Van Ness,
    City of Washington.

WASHINGTON, November 14, 1814.

SIR: On my return to the city, after a few days' absence, I had the honor of receiving your communication of the twelfth instant, advising me that my resignation of the command of the militia of this District, offered some time since, has not been accepted, and that it would be satisfactory to the President that I should resume it.

Injured as I felt by the treatment I received, in relation to my military command, I adopted, as a proper expression of that feeling, what I considered the only course which, whilst it was just to myself, was not inconsistent with the public service—a course which I am gratified that my friends, both public and private, have universally approved. At the same time, sir, without at present hazarding an opinion, or going into any argument as to the sufficiency of the reason for disregarding my claim to the command, or to service, on the approach of the enemy to the Metropolis, permit me to state, that I am perfectly satisfied that the President was actuated solely by a regard for the public good.

For the general politeness of your letter, for acknowledging the correctness of my conduct subsequent to my resignation, and particularly in the unfortunate affair at Bladensburg, although I have due sensibility, and fully appreciate the honor done me by the intimation of the President's wishes, it is out of my power to comply with them upon this occasion; which, I presume, cannot be regretted, inasmuch as other gentlemen, better qualified for the purpose, must be within the view of the Government.

I have the honor to be, &c.
            JOHN P. VAN NESS.
Hon. Jas. Monroe,
     Secretary of War.

Doctor Catlett's Statement.

Sir: In compliance with your request, I will endeavor to make as concise and correct a statement of the circumstances, which came within my view, of the late campaign in this neighborhood, as is in my power.

On the evening of the 21st, (being attached to the suite of General Winder as staff surgeon,) we were met by Colonel Monroe at the Woodyard, who had left Nottingham about sunset, where he saw the advance of the enemy with their barges and small vessels. Next morning Colonel Monroe, General Winder, and suite, proceeded down and met them within three or four miles of Nottingham. After taking such positions as would afford the best view of the enemy, and remaining under cover of the woods until they advanced within three or four hundred yards of us, those gentlemen retired with Colonel Lavall's troop, which was also in advance, until we met an advanced detachment of our troops, about four or five hundred, which were immediately ordered to retreat to the main body at the Woodyard. Major Hite had been ordered to remain near the forks of the road, to observe whether the enemy took that leading to Marlborough, or the other we were on to the Woodyard. The country here, from the heights and fields, was admirably calculated to afford observations of the enemy. Their entire want of cavalry was observable, from there being none with their advance, to which we had been so near. Videttes were placed in our rear. General Winder proceeded towards the Woodyard; Colonel Monroe took a direction across the country towards Marlborough; I accompanied him. We soon (about twelve o'clock) began to hear the explosion and see the smoke from the flotilla. We were overtaken by some of the videttes, who stated that there were fifteen or twenty horsemen on our left, supposed to be of the enemy, attempting to cut us off. We immediately shaped our course towards the Woodyard; met General Winder, who returned; passed a number of our troops, and, arriving at the Woodyard, found the main body moving off towards the Long Old Fields, where the army encamped in the evening.

Next morning, 23d, the President and all the Heads of Departments were in camp, having (I understood) come down that night. The President reviewed the troops, supposed about three thousand five hundred, having been joined at the Woodyard by Commodore Barney's men, and other corps, at this place. About two thousand five hundred Baltimore troops were at Bladensburg. This day an advanced detachment, I believe under the command of Major Peter, met the advance of the enemy in the neighborhood of Marlborough, some firing took place, and our troops retreated. General Winder was some miles over to the left, observing on the direct road from Marlborough to Bladensburg. Towards evening we returned to the Old Fields, and found our army advantageously posted to receive the enemy. A retreat was soon after ordered to the city, leaving some flour and whiskey destroyed on the camping ground. This night I slept within a mile of the field, and at daylight sent a man over in that direction to learn whether the enemy were there. He reported in the negative, and I went directly into the road and came on to the city, before eight o'clock, believing that the enemy could not reach Bladensburg until late in the day. The upper bridge was on fire, and the other prepared to be blown up as I crossed it. The first news I heard on entering the city, was that the enemy were within two and a half miles, coming towards the bridge, and there appeared to be a continual succession and industrious circulation of false reports and false alarms. The enemy were pertinaciously represented to be at least nine thousand, and many were disposed to believe their number greater, although several prisoners taken yesterday could only enumerate four regiments, and name but one General, and one Colonel, acting as Brigadier. I examined several myself, with all the address I could, and would certainly have risked my life upon their almost entire want of artillery and cavalry. There appeared to be an impression with our troops, generally, that the enemy were much more formidable than appearances could justify. About 11 o'clock the main body of our troops moved off from near the Eastern Branch bridge toward Bladensburg, and, by a necessarily extraordinary effort, for men immediately from ship board, the British reached the opposite side of the village nearly at the same time with our troops, about 1 o'clock. They halted in front about twenty minutes, until their rear got up. Some officers were seen observing us from the heights. The two armies were about three-fourths of a mile apart, pretty much in view of each other. The position of our troops will be better described to you by others. A few minutes before the action commenced, by request of General Winder I delivered an order to Major Pinkney, in front, to take the most judicious position with his riflemen to protect the artillery at the battery, within two hundred yards of the Bladensburg bridge and three or four hundred in advance of our first line. The enemy were now coming down a street in the village in thick column. This battery, of

Capture of the City of Washington.

about seven pieces, commenced a destructive fire upon them, which immediately threw their advance out of the street, among the houses, but they were very soon crossing the bridge in great numbers, notwithstanding an additional cross fire from several pieces from our right. They advanced with great steadiness towards the battery. The artillery retreated; the rifles received them handsomely, but soon retreated also. They began by firing a few rockets about the time that our fire commenced, which passed a considerable distance over our first line, immediately in the rear of which were the President, and several other gentlemen of the Cabinet. It was suggested to them, I think by General Winder, to take a more respectful distance, and they did so. General Winder rode along the line, encouraging the men to disregard the rockets. The enemy having carried the battery in front of us, began to flank irregularly, but a considerable number, also, advancing directly upon this line, (through an orchard,) which soon commenced a fire upon them, from an elevated position, and too soon after, before they came within point blank shot, retreated. They were, however, a number of them, easily rallied by another officer and myself; but on part of the line giving way, which had stood fast, further on the left, they all broke off again. The fire now became very hot in the centre, from our musketry and artillery; the musketry too distant, although with great advantage of position, but the artillery evidently with great execution. The musketry continually and successively (without being rallied) retreating as the enemy advanced upon them; and as soon as they closed up with Commodore Barney's command, a general retreat took place, before they had reached a considerable portion of our infantry. Being in the rear, I observed that the enemy seemed to halt, when the firing ceased, about a mile and a half on this side of Bladensburg; there was nothing like pursuit. When I got to Capitol Hill, there were no troops formed there. As I passed through the city, it was reported that the enemy were coming in from towards the race ground. I observed that it was false, and only intended to produce panic. The few citizens I saw at their houses, appeared as if resigned to meet an awful fate. The main body of our army were now retreating through Georgetown, where I met a deputation, the Mayor and several others, going out to meet the enemy. They can best tell, but I do not think it probable that the enemy were advancing, or knew the extent of our retreat before this deputation met them, for I had seen them halting; and the next day, when I came in with a flag to attend our wounded, I learned from some of their officers that they suspected our troops were still on the heights above Georgetown, though they were at Montgomery Courthouse, from which place General Winder had ordered me back to Bladensburg, with permission of the British commander, for the purpose mentioned. I met the advance of the British army on Capitol Hill, supposed to be about seven hundred, and passed their main body, supposed about

two thousand, on the hill this side the turnpike. They appeared to be preparing to move; had about forty miserable looking horses haltered up, ten or twelve carts and wagons, one ox cart, one coachee, and several gigs, which the officers were industriously assisting to tackle up, and which were immediately sent on to Bladensburg, to move off their wounded. A drove of sixty or seventy cattle preceded this cavalcade. On our arrival at Bladensburg, the surgeons were ordered to select all the wounded who could walk, (those with broken arms and the like,) and send them off immediately. The forty horses were mounted with such as could ride, the carts and wagons loaded, and ninety odd wounded left behind. I estimated their wounded at three or four hundred, besides forty or fifty left in this city. One of the British surgeons informed me they had buried that day about one hundred on the field; and the men who were sent out next day after the retreat of the enemy, to bury three or four Americans, reported that they also buried fifty or sixty red-coats, or British. I found at Bladensburg Commodore Barney, Captain Miller, of marines, and seventeen other Americans, badly wounded. I estimate our whole loss at ten or twelve killed on the field, and thirty odd wounded; though others, who had less opportunity of judging, estimate it at more than double. About midnight (being up all night) I heard the sound of a bugle, and was informed that the whole British army were passing through the lower end of the village. In the morning, early, I saw them still going off in small squads, and some stragglers were moving off till noon, about which time we learned that their main body were halted about eight miles on the road to Marlborough. About sunset Captain Burd came down from Montgomery Courthouse, and informed Commodore Barney and myself that our troops were marching on to Baltimore, and about the same time we were informed by several persons that the British were within a few miles of Marlborough. The Commodore expressed a wish that General Winder could be immediately informed of the certainty and manner of their retreat; and, not being able to find any one else, to be depended on, to go for one hundred dollars, having engaged Doctors Martin and McCulloch to attend to our wounded until my return, with the advice of Commodore Barney, I set out, about dark, with one dragoon, and reached our camp, beyond Snell's bridge, twenty-eight miles, about one o'clock. The troops were intended, about this hour, to march on to Baltimore. General Winder was gone on; Generals Smith, Stansbury, and others, held a council on my information, and it was determined to send off (I think) the principal part of the cavalry in pursuit of the enemy, immediately; the troops to remain until daylight, and the militia of the District of Columbia to return to the District. I have never been able to learn what cavalry were actually sent off, or the success of their enterprises. After this I was, and have ever since been, confined to the attendance of a hospital, and can relate little further from my own observation.

I have the honor to be, sir, with great respect, your obedient servant,

HANSON CATLETT,
Surgeon 1st Regiment Infantry.

Respecting the condition of the enemy's troops, I was informed by several of the British officers, that just previous to their reaching Bladensburg, (with excessive fatigue or entire exhaustion) they were dropping off in considerable numbers; that, in the action, it was only by the most extraordinary exertions that the main body could be goaded on. Although I observed some of their flankers at times advance on the run a small distance, these were said to be only the most active of their light companies of, and attached to, their 85th regiment, commanded by Lieutenant Colonel Thornton, acting as Brigadier; they appeared to me to halt, as if exhausted with fatigue, at or near the place where the firing ceased on our part, about a mile and a half on this side of Bladensburg, about two o'clock, P. M. Their advance, however, reached the Capitol about dark or eight o'clock; the main body, I am informed, never came further than the height on this side the turnpike. You ask further for information as to their numbers. Although I had a better opportunity of observation after the battle than any other of our officers, I cannot pretend to state, with any degree of confidence, on this subject: but my estimate was, on Capitol Square, 700; Turnpike Hill, 2,000; wounded at Bladensburg, 300; attendants and guard, 300; wounded and attendants in the city, 60; and, from information, killed at Bladensburg and city, 180; total, 3,540. However incorrect these estimates may be in detail, they are corroborated, in the aggregate, by the best information I could get from the surgeons, sergeants, and men left in hospital.

Respectfully, **H. CATLETT.**

Mr. John Law's Statement.

WASHINGTON, *November* 10, 1814.

Sir: In compliance with your request, I beg leave to submit to you the following statement of the movements and operations of the troops to whom I was attached, from the period of their march against the enemy, who had landed at Benedict, until their return on the 27th of August.

On Friday, the 19th of August, the militia of this county were mustered near Mr. Ringgold's rope-walk, and, on being dismissed, were ordered to equip and hold themselves in readiness to march the next morning. The second regiment, under Colonel Brent, accordingly assembled near the Capitol; and, by nine o'clock, A. M., were prepared to take up the line of march. About one o'clock, the first regiment, under Colonel Magruder, arrived at the Capitol Hill. Shortly after, the whole force, collected from this county, commenced its march; and, after proceeding about five miles from the Eastern Branch bridge, encamped that night on the road to Upper Marlborough. The next morning the troops were again mustered, and the articles of war read to them. About twelve o'clock, the detachment of

marines, under the command of Captain Miller, passed our encampment with five pieces of artillery, and shortly after, our two regiments of militia again took up the line of march, and, after advancing about seven miles, encamped on a field belonging to the Woodyard estate. We here joined the regulars of 36th and 38th regiments. The main body of the enemy stayed that night at or near Nottingham, having an advance party stationed at a church about three miles this side of that town. About one o'clock the same night, our troops were beat up and ordered to strike their tents; although the principal part of the force did not move until nine or ten o'clock the next morning. About sunrise the regulars, together with a small detachment of about three hundred men, consisting of Captain Peter's company of artillery, Captain Stull's rifle corps, and Captain Davidson's light infantry, were sent in advance on the road to Nottingham. About nine or ten o'clock the same day, the remainder of our force marched about a mile, to an elevated position near the dwelling house of Mrs. West, and remained there about two hours, under the expectation that the enemy would take that road on his way from Nottingham to Washington. It was, however, ascertained that the enemy had taken the road to Upper Marlborough, and that the detachment of our troops, who had been sent that morning in advance, were retreating. All the troops were then ordered to retreat; and, instead of being marched towards Upper Marlborough, where the enemy remained that night, (waiting, it is presumed, to be joined by the detachment which had been sent against Commodore Barney's flotilla,) we were marched to the Battalion Old Fields, about eight miles distant from Upper Marlborough, and about the same distance from Washington. The same day we were joined by the crews of Commodore Barney's flotilla. On Tuesday, the 23d of August, the troops were drawn up in three or four lines, and reviewed by the President of the United States. The most contradictory reports prevailed at this time in our camp, respecting the strength and movements of the enemy. Our force at this place, from the best information I could collect, consisted of about four hundred horse, the flotilla men amounting to about five hundred and fifty, one hundred and ten marines, about four hundred regulars of the 36th and 38th regiments, and about eighteen hundred militia from Maryland and the county of Washington. The militia of Alexandria county were with us. About twelve o'clock the same day, the detachment of three hundred militia, which had been sent on the day before, were again ordered to advance towards the enemy. They met him on his march, about six miles in advance of our encampment, but with so great a disparity of force, that it was impossible for them to make a stand. After Captain Stull's rifle company had fired about four rounds, the detachment was compelled to retreat, to prevent being surrounded by the enemy. About five o'clock, P. M. after having remained some time in line of battle, we were ordered to retreat to Washington, and, at

Capture of the City of Washington.

though our march on the retreat was extremely rapid, yet orders were occasionally given to the captains of companies to hurry on their men. The march, therefore, literally became a run of eight miles, and the propriety of this rapid movement, which unnecessarily fatigued and dispirited the men, may be tested by the fact, that the main body of the enemy *bivouacked* that night on the Melwood estate, more than than three miles distant from the ground that we left.

On our arrival at the city, we encamped about half a mile from the Eastern Branch bridge. About midnight, a detachment of Captain Burch's company, to which I was attached, was called up and ordered to move with three pieces of artillery to an eminence near the bridge, which was done. During the night, a boat, containing eight barrels of powder, was stationed underneath the bridge, under the charge of Mr. Forrest, of the Navy, with orders to blow it up on the approach of the enemy. About sunrise, the remainder of our company joined us. We were shortly after ordered to pull down the rails of a neighboring fence, and place them on the bridge, in order that it might be effectually burnt, in case the explosion of gunpowder should not succeed in preventing the enemy from passing it. For the same purpose, the toll-house was ordered to be pulled down, and the planks placed on the bridge. About ten o'clock the same day, our company was ordered to give up its position to Commodore Barney, who had a number of heavier guns with him, and who immediately after took possession of the eminence we had occupied. About eleven o'clock, we were ordered to march, and on arriving at the boundary line of the city, we halted a short time, until we were joined by the remainder of the troops, when we continued our march to Bladensburg. At the distance of about a mile and a quarter from that town, the troops were halted, and shortly after, Captain Burch, with three of his pieces of artillery, was ordered to advance and report himself to General Winder. Captain Burch immediately advanced with three of his pieces; and, on reaching the left of the line of Baltimore militia, he halted the men in the road, in order that he might look for General Winder and receive his orders. At this time the advance of the British was just entering the outskirts of Bladensburg, and the arms of a large body of them were seen glittering in the sun, about a mile from the town. Finding that Captain Burch did not return as soon as might have been reasonably expected, and hearing that General Winder was a short distance from us, I marched our detachment of artillery towards the spot where he was, and, on coming up to him, inquired what position I should take with our artillery. He addressed me as Captain, and ordered me to place our pieces in battery on the left of the Baltimore line of infantry, which was immediately done. Shortly after, he came up to us, and, again addressing me, said, "When you retreat, take notice you must retreat by the Georgetown road;" at the same time he pointed to a road which led from Digges's mill into the country,

and passed near the position we had taken. Captain Burch soon after joined us. The time occupied in taking our position was sufficient to have enabled us, and also the troops that marched from the city, to take any position on the fields this side of Bladensburg. About a quarter of an hour after we had taken our position, the Baltimore artillery, which was posted in advance near the mill, (and shortly after, the Baltimore riflemen) commenced firing on the enemy. The artillery fired about ten rounds, as far as I could judge, and then retreated, with some of the Baltimore riflemen, towards our left. A few scattering British soldiers were soon after visible in the orchard before us, and they appeared to be forming behind a barn, which was about three hundred and fifty yards from our guns. We immediately commenced our fire upon them; and, shortly after, General Winder came behind our guns, and ordered us to direct our shot at the barn. We had scarcely fired three rounds, when the line of the Baltimore militia began to break; several of the 5th Baltimore regiment also fled. After we had fired about five rounds from our pieces, General Winder ordered us to retreat, in consequence, I presume, of the flight of the militia on our right. The British column had just then began to advance from the barn. Not a man of our company had been touched by the fire of the enemy, and I thought that the battle was only then seriously commencing. After retreating about a hundred yards, we were again ordered to unlimber our pieces; but this order was immediately after countermanded, and we were directed to continue our retreat. Our pieces were never after ordered into action; nor were we, at any time, told where to rally. The road, by which we had been directed to retreat, and by which the principal part of the Baltimore troops also retreated, forked, some miles from the battle ground, in three directions; one branch led by Rock Creek Church to Tenleytown and Montgomery Courthouse; another branch led to Georgetown; and the third to the City of Washington. Each individual, on the retreat, took the road that suited his inclination. For myself, having been separated, together with several of Captain Burch's company, from our guns, which were before us, and presuming that the principal part of the force had gone to Washington, I took the road leading to this place. On arriving at the Capitol, I understood that the city had been abandoned by our troops, without further struggle, to the enemy. Our forces encamped that night at Tenlytown, about three miles back of Georgetown. The next day they marched to Montgomery Courthouse; and, on the 26th of August, to Snell's bridge, on the road to Baltimore, where I joined them, having never had it in my power before to do so. On Saturday, the 27th, the troops belonging to this District returned here. The enemy left the city on the night of the 25th.

From what I could discern of the line of the enemy's march on his entrance into Bladensburg, before the battle, I conjectured that his force amounted to about five thousand men. I afterwards collected, from conversations with British prisoners; and from comparing together the several accounts they gave me, that it did not exceed four thousand four hundred men, including about one hundred or one hundred and fifty sailors, who were armed only with cutlasses. The enemy's artillery consisted of one howitzer, and two small pieces, drawn by men; and his whole force actually engaged in the battle did not exceed twelve hundred men, as I was informed by two British officers and some prisoners. Our force, on the other hand, consisted of the troops that were with us on the Battalion Old Fields, amounting, in my opinion, to about three thousand one hundred and sixty men, together with about two thousand troops from Baltimore, and about five hundred militia under Colonel Beall, who joined us on the field of battle. Our artillery consisted of eighteen six pounders, under Captains Peter, Burch, and Magruder, and two eighteen pounders and three twelves under Commodore Barney. The enumeration which I have given of our troops may, in some instances, be incorrect, as it is merely the result of general observation and inquiry. I would beg leave further to state, that the distance between Benedict and Washington, by the way of Bladensburg, is at least fifty miles, and that the whole of the intervening country is admirably calculated for every species of military operation. I shall refrain, sir, from expressing any opinion on the manner in which our force was conducted and employed; but, in justice to General Winder, I will add, that he evinced no deficiency of personal courage or military coolness during the action.

With respect, I am, &c.

             JOHN LAW.

No. 11.

Reports from the Ordnance Department.

U. S. ORDNANCE DEPARTMENT,
Washington, Nov. 28, 1814.

SIR: In addition to the information which I have had the honor to give to the committee of investigation upon the subject of the late invasion of the District by the enemy, I have to state:

That I have perused letters recently written by Colonel D. Wadsworth to Daniel Carroll, Esq., of this District, respecting the burning of the Potomac bridge, and the destruction of the military stores deposited on the Virginia side thereof; which in substance contain a specific denial of either circumstance having taken place by his orders or advice. He explicitly states, that the latter was occasioned by the corporal or non-commissioned officer commanding the guard, who, on the draws of the bridge having been broken by a violent tornado, and perceiving a body of the British ready to pass over, concluded the surest and best measure to prevent it, was to destroy, by fire, that end and part where he was posted; and that the other end, on the Washington side, was fired by the enemy.

The military stores which had been placed at the end of the bridge were destroyed by the event of firing that end.

I beg leave to take this occasion to repeat what I had the honor to state to you verbally, that, having been personally conversant with Colonel Wadsworth on the evening of the day of the battle of Bladensburg, and on the subsequent invasion of the city, the colonel at no time suggested to me (though the next officer in command) the necessity or expediency of firing the Potomac bridge; and I have, consequently, no belief that such was his intention or order.

Lieutenant Baden, who was directed to post the guard at the Virginia end of the bridge, and for the protection of the military stores, unequivocally and explicitly denies having given any similar order.

I beg leave to transmit here a more particular account of the stores furnished to Fort Washington: rendered, however, by the late decision of a court martial, less necessary than before.

I have the honor to be, &c.,

             JOHN MORTON,
      Captain and Deputy Commissary.

Hon. Col. R. M. JOHNSON.

ORDNANCE DEPARTMENT,
Washington, Oct. 21, 1814.

SIR: In the absence of the Commissary General, I have the honor to acknowledge the receipt of your letter to this department, of the 15th current, requesting, in behalf of the committee of which you are chairman, "all the information in its power on the subject of their inquiry; more especially to state what was the quantity and situation of the munitions of war within the District of Columbia, previous to, and at the time of, the invasion of the enemy in his recent enterprises against this metropolis."

The hurry with which many of those munitions were distributed, previous to, and at the time of, the invasion, and the dispersion and loss of some papers which gave some details thereof, necessarily render the reports from the several persons having charge of them somewhat imperfect, and will render it difficult to give from this department more than (as follows) a general statement. This statement, however, will be substantially correct; and will, perhaps, tend to answer or satisfy the committee on the leading objects of the inquiry made of this office.

Presuming that the expression, "munitions of war," was intended to include the ordnance within the District, I shall commence therewith, by stating, that there were, at the period alluded to, the following mounted cannon, viz:

Eight 24 pounders, cannon, mounted on garrison carriages, and forming the battery, Greenleaf's Point.

One 50 pounder, columbiad, mounted on garrison carriage, and forming the battery, Greenleaf's Point.

One 18 pounder, columbiad, mounted on garrison carriage, and forming the battery, Greenleaf's Point.

Two 18 pounders, cannon, complete for the field, on travelling carriages.

Five 12 pounders, cannon, complete for the field, on travelling carriages.

Six 6 pounders, cannon, complete for the field, on travelling carriages.

Three 24 howitzers, cannon, complete for the field, on travelling carriages.

These last were in charge at the United States' Arsenal, Greenleaf's Point; but occasionally distributed previous to the actual invasion of the city, as ordered; for instance, two eighteen pounders, on travelling carriages, were placed in front of the Capitol, for its defence; two twelve pounders in front of the President's house, and two near the General Post Office, for the same purposes.

In addition to the foregoing, there were twelve six pounders, field artillery, furnished by the order of the late Secretary of War, to, and in the service of, the District corps of artillery; and two twelve pounders loaned to the marine corps of the United States.

The number of field artillery attached to the brigade of Alexandria is not known to me; but it is presumed to have been four or six pieces.

Of ordnance stores, there were on hand at the United States' laboratory, exclusive, of course, of what had before been distributed, viz:

  140 bbls. (14,000 lbs.) gunpowder of different kinds.

  5 tons of lead.

  7,180 cannon cartridges, filled and empty (the empty are soon filled.)

  8,650 rounds of round grape and canister shot.

  150 ten inch shells, with other stores of ordinary consumption, or expenditure, too numerous to detail.

In the military store and laboratory, viz:

Stands of arms complete	2,993
Cartridge boxes and belts	1,595
Bayonet scabbards and belts	2,584
Flints	13,700
Musket cartridges of different kinds (single ball and ball and buck shot)	271,000

The foregoing were on hand immediately preceding the invasion, after considerable distributions had been occasionally made to the regular troops and the militia, employed in different situations or parts of this section of the country; and equal, it is believed by me, to all their requisitions.

Of rifles it was impossible, though every exertion was made by this department, to procure a seasonable supply.

What is here offered to the honorable committee embraces, perhaps, all which is expected from this department; but, if any additional objects of inquiry should occur, the undersigned will hold himself in readiness to furnish, either personally or in writing, whatsoever may be required and remain further within his means of information.

I have the honor to be, sir, with great respect, your obedient servant,

        JOHN MORTON,
    Deputy Commissary U. S. Ordnance.

Hon. Col. R. M. Johnson.

ORDNANCE DEPARTMENT, *Nov.* 4, 1814.

SIR: In compliance with your verbal request, I have the honor to state to you that, by an ordnance return, bearing date the 30th June, ultimo, received at this office, there were at Fort Washington, on the Potomac—

  Two 32 pounders on fixed carriages (cannon,)

  Eight 24 pounders   do.   do.

  Two 50 pounders (columbiads) on fixed carriages, cannon.

  Three 6 pounders on travelling carriages, cannon.

Of ordnance stores there were—

  132 rounds, 32 pounders, round shot.

  432 rounds, 24 pounders, round shot.

    564 round shot.

  99 flannel cartridges, 32 pounders, filled.

  86 flannel cartridges, 24 pounders, filled.

  88 flannel cartridges, 32 pounders, empty.

  405 flannel cartridges, 24 pounders, soon filled.

  44 paper cartridges, 32 pounders, empty.

  177 paper cartridges, 24 pounders, empty.

    899 cartridges, filled and empty.

  3,100 pounds cannon powder.

  246 pounds musket powder.

  100 musket cartridges.

  291 pounds lead.

  200 pounds junk.

  137 musket balls.

  31 stand small arms.

From the 30th June to August 27, there were furnished at Fort Washington the following:

  Four 18 pounders (columbiads) July 16.

  Forty-eight stands of arms, complete.

  One hundred and seventeen rounds ammunition for 18 pounders, columbiads.

  Two hundred and five rounds ammunition for 18 pounders, cannon.

  Forty-eight rounds ammunition for 18 pounders, grape shot.

  Two hundred rounds ammunition for 18 pounders, round shot.

  Two hundred and forty rounds ammunition for 6 pounders, strapped shot.

  Sixty rounds ammunition for 6 pounders, case shot.

  Forty-eight rounds ammunition for 18 pounders, case shot.

  Two hundred and thirty-two tubes.

  Thirty-four portfires.

  Thirty-three pounds slow match.

The number of men stationed at Fort Washington is not precisely known at this office, but it is supposed by me not to have exceeded sixty.

I regret that circumstances have delayed your receipt of this communication; but, as your former written request confined my report to the District, more time has been required to ascertain the facts here stated, (particularly the supplies since the 30th June,) than would otherwise have occurred.

I have the honor to be, sir, with great respect, your obedient servant,

JNO. MORTON,
Captain, and Dep. Com. U. S. Ordnance.

Hon. Colonel JOHNSON.

Return of fixed Ammunition and Ordnance Stores delivered to Fort Washington, in the month of August, 1814, previous to the 24th of that month.

Two hundred 18 pound round shot.

Forty-eight 18 pound grape.

One hundred and seventeen flannel cartridges, filled for 18 pound columbiads.

Two hundred and five 18 pound cannon cartridges, flannel bottoms, filled.

One hundred and forty 6 pound strapped shot, fixed.

Sixty 6 pound case shot, fixed.

Forty-eight 18 pound case shot, filled.

Two hundred and thirty-two tubes filled.

Thirty-four portfires.

Thirty-three pounds slow match.

Eight thousand one hundred and twenty-six musket cartridges, buck and ball.

Twenty-two thousand and fifty musket cartridges, single ball.

Nineteen ammunition boxes.

Forty-three kegs.

Seventeen barrels.

N. BADEN, *Lieut. Com.*

GREENLEAF's POINT, *Nov. 9, 1814.*

No. 12.

Sentence of the Court Martial in relation to Captain Dyson, and the correspondence between him and the Secretary of War.

WAR DEPARTMENT, *Aug. 29, 1814.*

SIR: I send Captain Manigault with orders to receive your written or verbal report of the causes under which you left the post committed to your charge. In this you will state the orders under which you acted, and from whom received.

I have the honor to be, &c.,

JOHN ARMSTRONG.

Capt. DYSON, *Corps of Artillery.*

CAMP AT MASON'S ISLAND,
August 29, 1814.

SIR: I had the honor to receive your communication of the 29th instant. The orders received from Brigadier General Winder, through Major Hite, verbally, on the 24th instant, were, in case I was oppressed by, or heard of, an enemy in my rear, to spike our guns, and make my escape over the river. The enemy approached by water on the 27th, and we had learnt on that day, through several channels, that the enemy had been reinforced at Benedict two thousand strong, and that they were on their march to co-operate with the fleet, in addition to the force which left the city. Under all these circumstances, the officers under my command were consulted, and agreed it was best to abandon the fort, and effect a retreat. The force under my command was thought not equal to a defence of the place.

I have the honor to be, &c.,

SAM. T. DYSON,
Captain Corps of Artillery.

Hon. J. ARMSTRONG,
Secretary of War, Washington.

General Orders.

HEADQUARTERS, 10TH MILITARY DIS,
Baltimore, Nov. 17, 1814.

At a general court martial, whereof Brigadier General Smith, of the militia of the District of Columbia, was president, which met at Washington City, and continued its sittings, by divers adjournments, until the 12th instant, Captain Samuel T. Dyson, of the United States' corps of artillery, was tried on the following charges and specifications:

Charge First.—Violating the fifty-second article of the rules and articles for the government of the armies of the United States.

Specification First.—In that the said Samuel T. Dyson, being commanding officer of the United States' Fort Washington, did, on or about the 27th of August, 1814, when an enemy was approaching said fort, misbehave himself before the enemy, run away, and shamefully abandon the fort, post, and guard, which he then and there commanded, and which it was his bounden duty to defend, and speak words inducing others to do the like.

Specification Second.—In that the said Samuel T. Dyson did, on or about the 27th day of August, aforesaid, at the post called Fort Washington, aforesaid, cast away and destroy his arms and ammunition, contrary to the said fifty-second article of the rules and articles of war, aforesaid, and to his duty as commanding officer.

Charge Second.—Conduct unbecoming an officer and a gentleman.

Specification First.—In that the said Captain Samuel T. Dyson, being commanding officer of the United States' fort and garrison, at a place called Fort Washington, did, on or about the 27th day of August, 1814, misbehave himself by dismantling and destroying said fort, which it was his bounden duty to preserve and defend.

Specification Second.—In that the said Captain Samuel T. Dyson did, on or about the 27th day of August aforesaid, quit his post, called Fort Washington, without any attempt to defend the same; and, without any necessity therefor, from the presence of an enemy, did march off the garrison of the same, in violation of his duty, and contrary to orders.

Specification Third.—In that the said Captain Samuel T. Dyson, on or about the 27th day of August, 1814, being commanding officer of the garrison at Fort Washington, and an enemy being then in his vicinity, was so drunk and intoxicated while on duty, that he abandoned and destroyed the fort which had been intrusted to his defence, and suffered the garrison of the same to disperse, without being pressed to the measure for the safety of himself and the garrison aforesaid.

                R. H. WINDER,
              Army Judge Advocate.

The court having heard all the evidence adduced, whether on the part of the prosecution or the defence, and after due deliberation thereon, pronounce the following sentence:

On the first specification of the first charge, the court find that Captain Samuel T. Dyson, of the United States' corps of artillery, being commanding officer of the United States' fort, Fort Washington, did, on or about the 27th day of August, 1814, when an enemy was approaching said fort, misbehave himself before the enemy, and shamefully abandon the fort and post which he then and there commanded, and which it was his bounden duty to defend.

The court find the said Captain Dyson guilty of the second specification of the first charge.

The court find the said Captain Dyson guilty of the first charge.

In like full and deliberate manner, the court took into consideration the second charge, and the three specifications attached to the charge.

The court find the said Captain Dyson guilty of the first specification of the second charge.

The court find the said Captain Dyson guilty of the second specification of the second charge.

The court acquit the said Captain Samuel T. Dyson, of the third specification of the second charge.

On the second charge the court find the said Captain Samuel T. Dyson guilty of conduct unbecoming an officer, but do not find him guilty of conduct unbecoming a gentleman.

The court do sentence Captain Samuel T. Dyson to be dismissed the service of the United States.

The Major General commanding the district approves of the proceedings and sentence of the general court martial in the foregoing case, and accordingly pronounces Samuel T. Dyson dismissed the service of the United States.

The general court martial, whereof Brigadier General Smith is President, is hereby dissolved.

By command: W. SCOTT.
      FRANCIS S. BELTON,
      Ass't Adj't Gen., 10th Mil'y Dist.

No. 13.
Report from the Corporation of Alexandria, including the capitulation, and letter from General John Mason.

         ALEXANDRIA, *Sept.* 28, 1814.

SIR : I had the honor of receiving your letter of the 26th instant, by this day's mail, and hasten to comply with your request therein contained. The enclosed printed statement is an official act of the Common Council of Alexandria, and contains a full and true account of the occupation of this town by the enemy, and of the circumstances connected with that event, and a copy of the terms imposed by Captain Gordon, the commander of the British squadron on the town of Alexandria.

There was no correspondence between the Common Council and the enemy, other than that mentioned in the statement.

As you request a statement of any other proceedings of the town of Alexandria, in a corporate capacity, touching the inquiry embraced in the resolution enclosed in your letter, I think it proper to state that, on the 8th of May, 1813, the Common Council appointed a deputation to wait on the President of the United States, and apprize him of the defenceless state of the town of Alexandria ; accordingly, the persons appointed waited on the President, and represented to him the defenceless state of the town, and the fears of the citizens that the Navy Yard, public buildings, and cannon foundry, would tempt the enemy to make an attack on the District. He observed, that the representation of any respectable body of men was entitled to attention ; and that the subject should be taken under consideration, or words to that effect.

On the 11th of May, in the same year, the Common Council appointed a committee to confer and co-operate with committees appointed by the constituted authorities of the City of Washington and Georgetown relative to the defence of the District. Those several committees soon afterwards met in the City of Washington, and appointed a sub-committee to wait on the Secretary of War, and on the Secretary of the Navy, and to solicit them to take measures for the defence of the District, and application on that subject was accordingly made to them by the sub-committees. The Common Council of Alexandria has appointed a committee to attend the committee of Congress appointed to inquire into the causes of the success of the enemy in his recent enterprises against the Metropolis and Alexandria, who will give every information which may be required of the proceedings of the Common Council, and of the citizens of Alexandria, in relation to the enemy. I have the honor to be, &c.

            CHARLES SIMMS.

A Report of the Committee of Council on the late occupation of Alexandria, by a British squadron, under the command of Captain James A. Gordon.

         IN COUNCIL, *Sept.* 7, 1814.

Present : Thomas Herbert, President ; John Gird, Andrew Fleming, Henry Nicholson, J. B. Paton, John Cohagen, James Milan, John Hunter, Reuben Johnston, R. I. Taylor, William Veitch, Anthony Rhodes.

The following narrative of the occupation of this town by the enemy, and of the circumstances connected with that unfortunate transaction, having been submitted to Council, and duly considered and examined, the Council do unanimously concur therein ; and it is thereupon ordered, that it be published in both of the papers printed in this town.   T. HERBERT, *Pres't.*

At a meeting of the Committee of Vigilance, this 7th of September, 1814,

Present : Charles Simms, Mayor ; Joseph Dean,

Matthew Robinson, Jonah Thompson, William Herbert, Thomas Vowell, Edmund I. Lee.

The following narrative of the occupation of the town of Alexandria by the British squadron, was submitted to the committee, who, upon examining the same, unanimously concur in it.

CHARLES SIMMS.
Chairman.

THOMAS VOWELL, *Secretary.*

A respect for the opinions of others, and a due regard for the character of the citizens of Alexandria, have induced the municipal authorities of the town to exhibit to the public a faithful narrative of the occupation of Alexandria by the British squadron under the command of Captain Gordon, together with the causes which led to that distressing event.

To those who are unacquainted with the situation and condition of Alexandria, in regard to its means of defence, it will be proper to state that it is situate in the District of Columbia, upon the west bank of the river Potomac, about six miles below the City of Washington, the depth of water admitting large frigates to come to the very wharves of the town.

It is totally destitute of fortifications of any kind, and its protection against invasion by water depended entirely upon a fort about six miles below the town, commonly known by the name of Fort Warburton, which was exclusively under the control of the Government of the United States.

About the month of July last, it was announced that General Winder was appointed to the command of the tenth military district of the United States, comprehending the District of Columbia, and a portion of the adjoining States of Virginia and Maryland, including the city of Baltimore.

In consequence of reports that the enemy contemplated an attack upon the City of Washington, the municipal authority of Alexandria thought it advisable to appoint a committee of vigilance, for the purpose of procuring information of the approaches of the enemy, and of obtaining assistance and advice as to the measures which it might be proper to pursue for protection and defence. As soon as this committee was appointed, they caused representations to be made to General Winder of the defenceless condition of the town, and earnestly entreated that some measures should be taken for its protection. General Winder was called on, because it had been distinctly understood that the Secretary of War would receive our communications through this channel only. From General Winder every assurance was made that could have been wished, that everything in his power should be done for the protection of the town. His means, however, were very inconsiderable; he had no money to expend in fortifications, or even in the erection of batteries; and unless some defence of this sort could be obtained, the town would be exposed to the mercy of the enemy, if he should approach by water, and should succeed in passing the fort. The committee of vigilance was duly impressed with the necessity of providing some adequate defence against an attack by water; and some of its members, under the authority of the committee, had repeated interviews with General Winder on this subject. In one of them, the President of the United States was present, and he was distinctly given to understand that, unless there was provided an adequate defence for the town, it would be at the mercy of the enemy, and would be compelled to make the best terms in its power. These representations and requests produced no other effect than the repetition of the assurance of an earnest desire on the part of General Winder to afford every assistance in his power.

On the 19th of August, a levy en masse was made of the militia of the town and county of Alexandria, and on the 20th and 21st they were ordered to cross the Potomac, and stationed between Piscataway and Fort Warburton. They took with them all the artillery which had been mounted at the expense of the corporation, except two twelve-pounders, which were left without ammunition, and nearly all the arms belonging to the town. They left no men but the exempt from age and other causes, and a few who had not reported themselves, or had found substitutes; and it is not believed that, after their departure, one hundred effective armed men could have been mustered in town. The two iron twelve-pounders remained until the 25th, when Alexandria being open to the enemy, then in full possession of Washington, they were removed some distance from the town, by orders received from General Young.

On the night of the 24th, the Alexandria militia were ordered to recross the Potomac; they did so, and were marched through the town, without halting, into the country, and without giving information to the authorities or inhabitants of the place of their destination; and on the evening of the 27th, when the fleet approached, the municipal authorities of the town knew not where they were. It has since appeared, that they were then stationed about nineteen miles from town, by the orders of General Winder. It is here proper to state that General Winder, on the morning of the 24th, informed the members of the committee of vigilance, who waited on him, that he could send no part of the forces with him to Alexandria, but that he had ordered General Young to cross over to Alexandria, if practicable, if not, to fall down the river. The committee of vigilance, on receiving this information, sent boats over to the Maryland shore, sufficient in number to bring over the whole of General Young's force at once, but when the boats reached him, he had received orders from the Secretary of War to keep his position, as General Young, in a communication to the Mayor, stated.

The committee of vigilance, despairing of obtaining any assistance from the General Government, and having information of the rapid approach of the enemy towards the Capitol by land, and that their squadron was approaching Alexandria by water, deemed it their duty to recommend to the Common Council a resolution to the following effect: "That, in case of British vessels should pass the fort, or the forces

Capture of the City of Washington.

approach the town by land, and there should be no sufficient force, on our part to oppose them, with any reasonable prospect of success, they should appoint a committee to carry a flag to the officer commanding the enemy's force, about to attack the town, and to procure the best terms for the safety of persons, houses, and property, in their power." This recommendation was made on the day of the battle at Bladensburg, and, on the same day, was unanimously adopted by the Common Council.

The battle of Bladensburg having terminated in the defeat of our troops, and General Winder having been obliged to retreat from the capital towards Montgomery Courthouse, about fifteen miles to the west of it, the City of Washington was left in the entire possession of the enemy. The citizens of Alexandria saw nothing to impede the march of the British to their town—saw nothing to restrain them from committing the most brutal outrages upon the female portion of the society, having neither arms nor men to make defence with. The President of the United States and the Heads of the Departments were absent, and it was not known where they were to be found; no military commander or officer of the General Government was present to direct or advise.

In this state of things, it was considered by the Common Council as their duty to send a flag to the British commander at Washington, to know what treatment might be expected from him, in case his troops should approach Alexandria, and should succeed in obtaining possession of the town. Admiral Cockburn, to whom the communication was made, assured the very respectable gentlemen who bore that flag, that private property, of all descriptions, should be respected; that it was probable that fresh provisions and some flour might be wanted, but that, whatever they did take, should be paid for.

While these things were going on in the City of Washington, the British squadron had been gradually ascending the Potomac, and on the 27th of August, three days after the battle at Bladensburg, it reached Fort Warburton. No change had taken place in relation to the means of the defence of the town of Alexandria. Upon the fort did the safety of Alexandria now entirely depend. The citizens looked with great anxiety to this point for protection; but, to their great surprise and mortification, and without the concurrence or the wish of the municipal authority of the town, or of any member of it, the fort was abandoned, and the magazine blown up, by the United States' garrison, on the evening of the 27th, without firing a single gun. The following correspondence between the Secretary of War and the commander at the fort, shows by what authority he acted:

Copy of a letter from the Secretary of War to Captain Dyson, dated

AUGUST 29, 1814.

SIR: I send Captain Manigault with orders to receive your written or verbal report of the causes under which you left the post committed to your charge. In this you will state the orders under which you acted, and from whom received.

I am, sir, your most obedient servant,

J. ARMSTRONG.

Capt. DYSON, *Corps of Artillery.*

CAMP AT MASON'S ISLAND,
August 29, 1814.

SIR: I had the honor to receive your communication of the 29th instant. The orders received from Brigadier General Winder, through Major Hite, verbally, on the 24th instant, were, in case I was pressed by or heard of an enemy in my rear, to spike our guns, and make my escape over the river. The enemy approached by water on the 27th, and we had learned that day, through several channels, that the enemy had been reinforced at Benedict two thousand strong, and that they were on their march to co-operate with the fleet, in addition to the force which left the city. Under all these circumstances the officers under my command were consulted, and agreed it was best to abandon the fort and effect a retreat. The force under my command was thought not equal to a defence of the place.

I have the honor to be, with great consideration, your obedient servant,

SAM. T. DYSON,
Capt. corps Artillery.

Hon. JOHN ARMSTRONG,
Secretary of War.

This relinquishment of the fort decided the fate of Alexandria. Nothing was left to oppose the progress of the squadron, and on the morning of the 28th it passed the ruins of the fort on its way to the town; their barges had sounded a considerable distance above. About ten o'clock of the morning of the 28th, after the squadron was above the fort, the committee appointed by the Council to bear the flag to the enemy, in case they should pass the fort, set out upon their mission, and proceeded to the ship commanded by Captain Gordon. They requested to know what his intentions were in regard to the town of Alexandria. They were informed by Captain Gordon that he would communicate his terms when he came opposite the town. But he assured them that, in the meantime, if the squadron was not molested by the inhabitants, the persons, houses, and furniture of the citizens, should not be injured. One of the gentlemen who attended the flag was the Mayor. Upon his return from the squadron he was informed that a small detachment of cavalry, from the army of General Hungerford, had been in town, probably for the purpose of reconnoitering the enemy; that it had remained but a short time. Upon inquiry, it was understood that the army of General Hungerford was at that time about sixteen miles from Alexandria, on its march to that place, having followed the British squadron along the shores of the Potomac a great part of its way up. The force of General Hungerford was composed of infantry and cavalry, with two or three small pieces of artillery, not calculated to afford any protection to the town.

The municipal authority of the town had received no advice of the approach of this army; and after the return of the flag it was too late to enter into any arrangement with General Hungerford for defence: he was too distant to afford relief.

The squadron having suspended its approach o the town, did not reach it until the evening of this day. On the morning of the next day, to wit, the 29th of August, it arranged itself along the town, so as to command it from one extremity to the other. The force consisted of two frigates, to wit, the Seahorse, rating thirty-eight guns, and Euryalus, rating thirty-six guns; two rocket ships, of eighteen guns each; two bomb ships, of eight guns each; and a schooner of two guns, which were but a few hundred yards from the wharves, and the houses so situated that they might have been laid in ashes in a few minutes. About ten o'clock in the morning of the 29th, Captain Gordon sent to the Mayor the following terms:

HIS MAJESTY'S SHIP SEAHORSE,
Off Alexandria, Aug. 29, 1814.

GENTLEMEN: In consequence of a deputation yesterday received from the city of Alexandria, requesting favorable terms for the safety of the city, the undermentioned are the only conditions in my power to offer:

The town of Alexandria, with the exception of public works, shall not be destroyed, unless hostilities are commenced on the part of the Americans; nor shall the inhabitants be molested in any manner whatever, or their dwelling houses entered, if the following articles are complied with:

Article 1. All naval and ordnance stores, public and private, must be immediately delivered up.

Article 2. Possession will be immediately taken of all the shipping, and their furniture must be sent on board by the owners, without delay.

Article 3. The vessels that have been sunk must be delivered up in the state they were in on the 19th of August, the day of the squadron passing the Kettle Bottoms.

Article 4. Merchandise of every description must be instantly delivered up; and, to prevent any irregularities that might be committed in its embarcation, the merchants have it in their option to load the vessels generally employed for that purpose, when they will be towed off by us.

Article 5. All merchandise that has been removed from Alexandria, since the 19th instant, is to be included in the above articles.

Article 6. Refreshments of every description to be supplied the ships, and paid for at the market price by bills on the British Government.

Article 7. Officers will be appointed to see that the articles Nos. 2, 3, 4, and 5, are strictly complied with; and any deviation or non-compliance, on the part of the inhabitants of Alexandria, will render this treaty null and void. I have, &c.

JAMES A. GORDON,
Capt. of His Majesty's ship Seahorse, &c.
To the COUNCIL *of the town of Alexandria.*

Upon the Mayor's receiving them, he sent for the members of the Committee of Vigilance. These terms were borne by one of the officers of Captain Gordon's frigate, who stated that but one hour was allowed him to wait for a reply to them. Upon their being read by the Mayor and the committee, it was observed to the officer, by the Mayor and one of the committee, that it would be impossible that the Common Council could accede to several of them; that the municipal authority of the town had no power to recall the merchandise that had been sent out subsequent to the 19th of August. The reply of the officer was, in that case it would not be expected.

He was further informed, that it would not be in the power of the Common Council to compel the citizens to assist in getting up the sunken vessels. The officer answered, that their sailors would then do it. He was required to explain what was intended by the term merchandise, as used in the fourth article. He answered, that it was intended to embrace that species of merchandise only that was intended for exportation, such as tobacco, flour, cotton, bale goods, &c.

The Mayor, and one of the committee, requested to know whether the Commodore intended to require a delivery of any more of the merchandise than he could take away with them. He answered, it would not be required. This explanation was afterwards recognised by Captain Gordon. With these verbal explanations the preceding terms were submitted to the Common Council. It will be here proper to remark, that, when these terms were proposed and submitted to the Common Council, General Hungerford had not arrived with his army, nor did it reach the suburbs of the town until the night of that day. The town was still without any means of defence, and it was evident that no defence could avail, but that species of force which would be calculated to drive the ships from their moorings. No communication had been received from the officers of the General Government, and the town appeared to be abandoned to its fate. Under these circumstances the Common Council could have no hesitation as to the course to be pursued. The citizens of the town, of all descriptions, with an immense value of property, were entirely in the power of the enemy, whose naval commander, according to the proclamation of the President of the United States, dated on the first of September, has declared his "purpose to be to employ the force under his direction in destroying and laying waste such towns and districts upon the coast as may be found assailable." A similar declaration had been made by Captain Gordon to the committee who bore the flag. Against the attack of such an enemy was the town of Alexandria, without any means of defence whatever. The people of the town were at his mercy, and compelled to yield to such terms as the "victor" might think fit to prescribe. If the members of the municipal authority, and citizens of the town, had given loose to the feelings of indignation which the occasion had excited, and had sacrificed the town, and exposed their wives and daughters to the wanton insults of an unrestrained enemy, they would have betrayed their trusts, and have deplored the consequences.

The Common Council, therefore, were obliged to yield submission to the terms as explained, and did, thereupon, pass and publish the following resolution:

"*Resolved*, That the Common Council of Alexandria, in assenting to the conditions offered by the commander of the British squadron now off the town, has acted from the impulse of irresistible necessity, and solely from a regard to the welfare of the town; that it considers the assent by it given as only formal, inasmuch as the enemy had it already in their power to enforce a compliance with their demand by a seizure of the property required from us; and believing the safety of the persons of the inhabitants, of their dwellings, and of such property as is not comprehended within the requisition, to depend entirely on the observance of the terms of it, the Common Council recommends to the inhabitants an acquiescence, at the same time that it does expressly disclaim the power of doing any act on its part to enforce compliance, its authority, in this particular, being limited to recommendation only."

In the execution of the terms proposed by the enemy it is proper to state, that the verbal explanations made by the officer to the Mayor, were generally adhered to. No merchandise was required to be brought back to the town; no assistance was required of, or offered by the citizens, in getting up the sunken vessels. The depredations of the enemy, with a few exceptions, were confined to flour, cotton, and tobacco, which they carried off in some of the vessels then at the town. Only one vessel was burnt; no private dwelling was visited or entered in a rude or hostile manner, nor were citizens personally exposed to insult.

The loss sustained from the enemy, it is believed, will not exceed the following: three ships, three brigs, several bay and river craft, the number of which has not been ascertained; all of which were carried away, and one ship burnt. The quantity of flour carried away, it is believed, will not exceed sixteen thousand barrels; about one thousand hogsheads of tobacco, and one hundred and fifty bales of cotton; and of wine, sugar, and other articles, not more than five thousand dollars' worth.

I, Israel P. Thompson, Clerk of the Common Council of Alexandria, do certify, that the above is a true copy from the original.

ISRAEL P. THOMPSON, *C. C.*

OCTOBER 6, 1814.

ALEXANDRIA, *Oct.* 7, 1814.

SIR: In pursuance of the enclosed resolutions of the Common Council of Alexandria, dated the 27th September, 1814, marked A, appointing us a committee, on the part of the town, for the purpose therein mentioned, we beg leave to lay before the committee of Congress the following statement and accompanying documents:

Misrepresentations of the conduct of the citizens of Alexandria, when the British squadron approached this place, having been circulated through the Union, the Common Council have deemed it their duty to lay before Congress a true history of the steps which the citizens have, from time to time, taken, in order to guard against that misfortune which has come upon them—a misfortune they deplore as much on the national, as on their own individual account. The citizens of Alexandria rejoice that an opportunity has been afforded them to lay before Congress a faithful narrative of the proceedings which self-preservation compelled them to adopt. It will show that they did all in their power to avert the blow.

In the month of October, 1812, a volunteer company was raised in Alexandria, and stationed at Fort Washington, in the manner stated in the letter of Captain McGuire, marked B. In the month of March, 1813, the artillery company of Alexandria, then commanded by Captain Marsteller, was stationed at Fort Washington. See Captain Griffith's certificate, marked C. On the 21st March, 1813, the Common Council appointed the Mayor of the town, and the President of the Council, to wait upon the Secretary of War; in company with the Colonel of the second legion, to request a supply of arms and ammunition for the use of the militia in the defence of the town. See document D. On the 8th of May, 1813, the Common Council appointed four respectable citizens to wait upon the President of the United States, and apprize him of the defenceless state of the town; which order is marked E. That committee, in compliance with the wishes of the Corporation, did wait on the President; the result of the interview they had with him will be found in the paper marked F. On the 8th of May, 1813, the Council appropriated $1,500, out of the funds of the Corporation, for mounting the cannon belonging to the town. See document marked D. On the 11th May, 1813, the Common Council appointed a committee of vigilance, to confer and co-operate with the committees of Washington and Georgetown, in requiring assistance from Government, for the general defence of the District of Columbia. See document E. A deputation from the committees of the three towns waited upon General Armstrong; the result of their conference was such as is stated in the certificate of Colonel George Deneale, one of the persons who waited upon the Secretary of War. See his certificate, marked G.

The Secretary of War did send an engineer, as he promised, who made a report to him, a copy of which is hereto annexed, and is marked H. The Common Council, on the 23d of July, 1814, passed two resolutions, and appointed a committee of vigilance, for the purposes in said resolutions expressed. See E. In pursuance of these last resolutions, the committee of vigilance proceeded to take such measures as they could, towards complying with the object of their appointment; they passed the resolutions which are marked I. In pursuance of the first resolution of the committee of vigilance General Winder was waited upon, and a few days after he visited Alexandria, had an interview with some of the committee of vigilance and Colonel Deneale, as will appear by the certificate of Colonel Deneale, marked K.

The banks of Alexandria and Potomac, on the 6th and 13th of August, loaned to the General Government, the one ten thousand, and the other twenty-five thousand dollars, upon the conditions that the same should be applied to the erection of fortifications for the District of Columbia, south of Alexandria. See the letters of the presidents of those banks, marked L and M. The Corporation, on the fifteenth of September, 1814, appropriated out of the funds of the town twelve hundred dollars, for the purpose of paying the expenses of laborers and carts to be employed in the erection of fortifications for the defence of the District. See document D.

The committee having laid before you the documents which exhibit the efforts of the citizens of Alexandria to have the town defended from invasion, beg leave to lay before the committee a report of the Common Council and committee of vigilance, dated on the 7th of September last, of the conduct of the citizens when the British squadron approached Alexandria. See document marked N. When the first attempt was made, on the 25th of August, to blow up the south end of the Potomac bridge, six hundred stand of arms were blown up, about two hundred of which, remained uninjured and fit for use; these were collected together by Mr. Joseph Dean, one of the committee of vigilance, and sent to the Little Falls of Potomac for safety. When General Hungerford's army arrived in the neighborhood of Alexandria, these arms were ordered to be delivered to General Hungerford. See Mr. Dean's certificate, O. On the 30th of August the Mayor apprized General Hungerford where two twelve-pounders, which had been by the order of General Young removed from town, could be found. See the Mayor's letter, marked P, and the reply of General Hungerford, signed by James Mercer, his aid, marked Q.

The day on which the enemy left Alexandria, a letter, purporting to be from Admiral Codrington, dated 28th August, 1814, addressed to the commanding officer of the British squadron in the Potomac, with the cover which now encloses it, was handed from the post office in this place to Mr. Joseph Dean, one of the committee of vigilance; how it got into the post office we know not; we can refer the committee to Mr. Thomas P. Gilpen, the deputy postmaster here, and to Mr. Basil Spalding, of Maryland, who, we have reason to believe, can give some account of the route the letter came to Alexandria; this document is marked R. If the committee should require any further information, or explanation, we shall be ready, at all times, to give it as far as we can.

We are, with great respect, &c.

WM. NEWTON,
EDM. I. LEE,
JOSEPH DEAN,
G. DENEALE.

ALEXANDRIA, *Nov. 20, 1814.*

SIR: From the appearance of the enemy's squadron in sight of Alexandria, in the evening of the 27th August last, until its departure on the 3d of September, I remained in town, with the exception of an absence of a few hours on the day last mentioned.

Among the many base calumnies propagated respecting our unfortunate town, by men more profligate than the enemy who plundered it, there is none more cruel and unfounded than the charge of the inhabitants having surrendered the property of strangers to procure safety for their own.

The printed narrative of the Common Council contains all the material facts connected with the capture of the town, and it is not in my power to add anything of importance. The charge above mentioned, which you have particularly noticed in your letter of the 19th instant, I can assure you, is totally destitute of truth. The people of Alexandria did not afford the enemy any assistance in removing or shipping the plundered property; nor did any instance, to my knowledge, occur of any individual having attempted to save his own property by turning the attention of the enemy towards that of another. In respect to persons, the plunder was indiscriminate. The enemy not having the aid of horses or carriages for the removal of the property, from a regard to their own convenience, and not the suggestions of others, confined their depredations to the warehouses on the water, in which large quantities of produce were contained, belonging to the inhabitants as well as to strangers; the sufferers alike.

After the Common Council had passed their resolution of the 29th of August, declaring their want of authority to require the observance of the terms to which they had been compelled to accede, and recommending submission, they did no other act at all connected with the seizure or surrender of property.

I remain, with respect, &c.

R. I. TAYLOR.

The Hon. R. M. JOHNSON.

To the honorable the Senate and House of Representatives of the United States of America in Congress assembled, the memorial of the subscribers, citizens of the town of Alexandria, respectfully represent

That the late capture by the British army of their town has afforded a pretext to certain defamers to brand the citizens of Alexandria with every epithet of ignominy and disgrace. Not content with proclaiming their slanders through the papers of the day, some have been so unprincipled as to whisper in the ears of some of the honorable members of your body, the most several accusations; one of which is, that the property of the citizens, taken from them by the violence of the invading enemy, had been voluntarily parted with by the inhabitants, and as plunder, received for it; a charge totally unfounded in fact, and without the smallest ground of truth

Capture of the City of Washington.

for its support; as your memorialists can venture to assert that not a solitary instance of the kind can be produced. When, therefore, your memorialists find the reputation of the town assailed in public and private, by those dark and restless spirits, whose delight it is to devour reputation, every virtuous and honorable-mind must feel it a solemn duty to solicit, as a right, from their Constitutional governors, a strict and just investigation into the whole of their conduct. The citizens of Alexandria, in the aggregate, can fear the result of no inquiry which may be made into their conduct on the occasion alluded to. They know their motives have been pure, and that the course they took can be justified by those immutable principles of self-preservation, for the exercise of which no just Government will condemn them, and the surrender of which cannot, of right, be demanded. Your memorialists cannot forbear, on this occasion, to express their indignant surprise to find their town traduced for a conduct which every citizen in the nation would have pursued had they been abandoned, as Alexandria was, to the mercy of a victorious and powerful enemy. In this situation, what alternative had we but to tell the enemy we could not resist, because we had not the means? This is all we did. We yielded to superior power. Our weakness has been our crime. Our reliance upon the protection of our Government has been our misfortune. For this misfortune have the citizens of Alexandria been publicly charged as traitors to their country. To submit to calumny of this nature without a murmur is more than could be calculated upon. To ask an investigation is what ought to be expected from the virtuous and innocent. This request is the more reasonable when it is recollected that the President of the United States has deemed it proper, in his public proclamation, to state that Alexandria had, in yielding to the terms imposed upon them, "inconsiderately" surrendered to the enemy. Your memorialists deem it a duty which they owe to the reputation of the town, concisely to state what have been the efforts, at different times, of the citizens, to obtain an adequate defence of the town and District.

In the month of October, in the year 1812, a few months after the declaration of war, a company of about seventy volunteers was raised in Alexandria, and equipped at the expense of some of the citizens. This company was under the orders of the General Government, who had them stationed at Fort Washington, where they continued for some months, and from thence removed to Annapolis, at which place they were disbanded.

In the month of March, in the year 1813, the artillery company, forming a part of the militia of the town, consisting of about seventy men, rank and file, was stationed for about three months at Fort Washington. The municipal authority of the town, conscious of its unprotected state, and justly considering it the duty of the General Government to defend every portion of that territory which was placed under its exclusive authority,

on the 21st of March, 1813, appointed the Chief Magistrate of the town, the President of the Common Council, together with the commanding officer of the second legion of the militia of the District, to wait upon the Secretary of War, and request a supply of arms and ammunition for the use of the militia in the defence of the town. Your memorialists have reason to believe that arms were furnished a short time after this request.

In the month of May, 1813, the Common Council sent four respectable citizens to the President of the United-States, to apprize him of the then defenceless state of the town. These gentlemen did wait upon and communicate to him what was the condition of Alexandria as to the means of defence; that the citizens felt great anxiety on account of the dangers with which they were threatened from the vicinity of the enemy in our waters, and the defenceless state of the District, and requested him to have some measures of defence and protection adopted as speedily as possible. To this request the President stated, that every portion of the community was entitled to the protection of the Government, and that representations of any respectable body of men had a claim upon its attention, and gave the gentlemen who waited upon him to understand that their representation would be properly attended to; he also stated it was impossible to extend protection to every assailable point of the country. The committee urged upon him the various circumstances which would invite the attack of the enemy upon the City of Washington in particular, which would of course involve the whole District in its dangers. The committee, at the same time, assured him of the perfect readiness of the citizens of Alexandria to co-operate, by their personal services, or in any other way, with the Government, in any measure of defence which it might adopt for the security of the District.

The Common Council, solicitous to provide for the defence of their town and District, as far as their limited powers and means would permit, did, in the month of May, 1813, appropriate, out of the funds of the corporation, fifteen hundred dollars, to pay for mounting some cannon which were in the town, and had been in the use of the militia while under the State government. In the month of May, 1813, a deputation from Alexandria, Washington, and Georgetown, had an interview with the Secretrry of War, relative to the defenceless situation of the District. This committee did urge that a more efficient defence might be afforded for the District than then existed. It was particularly urged upon the Secretary that the fortifications at Fort Washington, commonly known by the name of Fort Warburton, should be increased. In consequence of this representation, the Government sent an engineer to examine the fort, who, on the 28th of May, 1813, reported to the War Department, as the result of his examination, that "an additional number of heavy guns at Fort Warburton, and an additional fort in the neighborhood, are both to be considered unnecessary." Notwithstanding

Capture of the City of Washington.

the repeated solicitations of the citizens of Alexandria, in the year 1813, nothing was done towards its defence, except sending an engineer to examine the fort. In silence did Alexandria submit to this neglect of their safety, until the month of July, 1814, when the Common Council again endeavored to procure an adequate defence. Gentlemen, acting under the authority of the Corporation, in the month of July, waited on the military commander of the tenth district, with the view of ascertaining what measures of defence had been taken, or were intended to be adopted, for the defence of the town of Alexandria and District. The General, who seemed to be anxious to do his duty, as far as the means within his control would enable him, stated to those gentlemen the number of militia he expected would join him, and which seemed to be all the defence he calculated upon. This was a species of defence which certainly could be of no use against an attack by water. It is too obvious, that the town of Alexandria could not be defended in any other manner than by a proper fort or forts below it, with a competent garrison. The General commanding the tenth military district visted Alexandria. The mode of defending it from a water attack was pointed out to him. To adopt it, required money; this he was not furnished with. This difficulty, however, was removed by the offer of three of the banks in Alexandria to loan the Government fifty thousand dollars, for the purpose of erecting proper defences for the District: which loan was accepted, and the money paid to the Government. No steps were taken towards securing the town from attack by water, but it was left to be defended at the fort by a garrison not exceeding eighty men, rank and file. On the 24th of August, a few hours before the battle at Bladensburg, the Commanding General and President of the United States were, by the authority of the committee of vigilance of Alexandria, reminded of the destitute state of the town as to the means of defence, and informed what would be the deplorable alternative the citizens would be reduced to if the British squadron, which was approaching the town, and was then from twenty to thirty miles below, should find their town unprotected as it was at that time. In the afternoon of the 27th of August the squadron arrived at the fort, (the magazine having been blown up, and it abandoned by the few troops of the United States which had been stationed there) without opposition. On the morning of the 28th, after the fort had been destroyed by the enemy, and after their vessels had passed it, and were in full view of the town, and not before, no officer, military or civil, of the United States, being, on this emergency, in the town or District to defend or direct, (the military of the town having been previously marched off, *en masse*, by public authority,) the municipal authority of the town were, from extreme necessity, compelled to take such steps as were best calculated to save the town from conflagration. They authorized a flag to meet the advancing foe. The result of that interview was, that the

town, and a certain part of the property, was saved from destruction and plunder, upon condition that the enemy, during their continuance before the town, should not be molested. It is due to the citizens of Alexandria, who were in it, during that distressing period, to state, that no aid or assistance was offered by them to the enemy. They remained passive but indignant spectators of that plunder which they had not the means of preventing. In support of the various allegations, stated in the *preceding part* of this memorial, your memorialists beg leave to refer to documents laid before the committee of the House of Representatives, upon the subject of the capture of Alexandria and Washington. Your memorialists feel it their duty, more particularly, to call the attention of Congress to a subject connected with the capture of Alexandria, and which is enveloped in a mystery, that can be dissipated only by the power of your honorable body.

On the 29th of August, the British squadron commenced taking off from the warehouses the flour and tobacco. They continued until Friday morning, the 2d of September, when the last loaded vessel was sent down the river. The post office in Alexandria had, during *the time the fleet* lay opposite the town, been *removed into the* country some miles. On Friday, *the second* of September, the Postmaster found in the letter-box of the house which had been used as the post office, the following letter, to wit:

"*Iphigenia, 28th August*, 1814.

"The object of the expedition being accomplished, and the inhabitants of the country upon the banks of the Potomac being alarmed for their property, on account of the presence of the British squadron in that river, the Commander-in-Chief has directed me to forward openly, by the hands of one of the inhabitants, this *order, for the* ships in the Potomac to retire and *rejoin his* flag.

    "EDWARD CODRINGTON.
      "*Rear Admiral and Capt. of Fleet.*"

This letter is directed as follows:

"On H. B. M. *service, to the commanding officer* of H. B. M. *ships in the river Potomac.*"

The preceding letter was found in the post office, enclosed in a letter without name, date, or post mark, addressed "to the committee of vigilance or safety of the town of Alexandria,' which is in the following words:

"GENTLEMEN: Motives of a personal nature prevent my delivering the enclosure. You will best judge of the propriety of doing it in your official character, *without loss of time.*"

The above did not come to the knowledge of the committee of vigilance until after the squadron had left the town with their plunder. Your memorialists have been enabled to ascertain, that the letter from Admiral Codrington was in the Office of State, early in the morning of the 31st of August, and that it was there read. Among those who saw it there was a member of your honorable body.

How or when it was sent from the Department of State, or why it was sent in the manner it was, or by whom it was deposited in the deserted post office at Alexandria, your memorialists have not been able to ascertain, nor is it in their power to do so. Your memorialists have deemed it their duty to lay the transaction, so far as it has come to their knowledge, before your honorable body. It remains for Congress to take such further steps for the development of the transaction as in their wisdom shall seem to be proper, and which justice to the citizens of Alexandria demands.

All which is most respectfully submitted.

Jacob Hoffman,
Bathurst Daingerfield,
John Roberts,
George Coleman,
W. Veitch,
R. F. Degge,
A. Faw,
Thomas Steel,
James Keith,
Thomas Moore,
Charles Simms,
Ephraim Gilman,
William S. Moore,
William Newton,
Charles J. Catlett,
John Hooff,
Henry T. Compton,
John Muncaster,
John Gird,
John B. Paton,
John Potter,
Ch. Whiting,
Jonathan Ross,
Barnard Crook,
Philip G. Marsteller,
Thomas Preston,
Alexander McKenzie,
J. Laurason,
William Fowle,
John Lloyd,
John Harper,
Townshend Waugh,
Matthias Snyder,
Isaac Entwisle,
Samuel Harper,
Thomas M. Davis,
William Harper,
Joseph Harris,
S. Snowden,
Henry Bayne,
Thomas Jacobs,
Thomas Vowell,
Thomas Herbert,
William Smith,
Jacob Leap,
Ebenezer Vowell,
Anthony Rhodes,
Matthew Robinson,
Bryan Hampson,
James Kennedy, sen.
Silas Reed,
Guy Atkinson,
Benjamin Baden,

Joseph Smith,
Thomas Laurason,
Nehemiah Carson,
C. P. Thompson,
Isaac Gibson,
John D. Brown,
William N. Mills,
William H. Brown,
Grafton Cawood,
Joseph Rowen,
Sanford Reid,
Henry B. Deager,
Mark Butts,
Robert N. Windsor,
Jno. Plummer,
Peter Saunders,
Thomas Neill,
John Violett,
Gerrard Plummer,
Jacob Curtis,
William Bartleman,
William Tilham,
Thomas F. Herbert,
J. D. Simms,
J. B. Nickolls,
C. T. Chapman,
Samuel Smith,
Charles McKnight,
Israel P. Thompson,
William Herbert,
James Campbell,
James Fleming,
Robert Anderson,
William Harper, jr.
Thos. Janney & Co.
Samuel Mark,
Thomas Brookbus,
Jacob Morgan,
William Gregory,
Thomas K. Beall,
Andrew Fleming,
John H. Phillips,
Henry Nicholson,
John D. Longdon,
Daniel McClean,
Frederick Koons,
David Koons,
Charles Bennett,
James Shethar,
John H. Crease,
Joseph Cowing,
Newton Keene,
William Fox,

Joseph Mandeville,
Samuel B. Larmour,
Joseph Fowler, jr.
A. Newton,
N. Herbert,
John Jackson.

Thomas White.
W. Ramsay, of D.
John Ross,
John F. Smith,
James Allison.

GEORGETOWN, *October* 31, 1814.

SIR: In reply to your letter of the 28th instant, requesting, on the part of the Committee of Investigation, "all the information I have on the subject of a letter from Admiral Codrington to Captain Gordon," I have the honor to state that, on the morning of the 31st of August, some hours before day, I was called up by a dragoon, express from one of our camps below, who delivered a packet addressed to me by Admiral Cochrane; while I was opening and examining the despatch, the dragoon, who seemed to be an intelligent man, remarked to me that the British ships before Alexandria had been ordered down the river by the Admiral in the Patuxent. On questioning him, he stated that an open note to that effect, addressed to the British commander at Alexandria, had been brought to the camp from which he came, by the same messenger who had charge of the despatch I had just received from him; that he had understood both had been put into the hands of a countryman, on the shores of the Patuxent, by the enemy, from which countryman they had been taken by an American officer, and conveyed to the camp; that he heard the officer who gave him charge of the packet for me, speak of the manner in which they came, and mention the contents of the open note to other officers then near him; that the officers, as he heard them say, intended to send the note across the country, and have it put on board the British fleet by a citizen.

The letter addressed to me by Admiral Cochrane was dated on the 29th August. Under the same envelope he should receive this without delay, I immediately, although not yet day, called on Colonel Monroe, then acting as Secretary of War, delivered the letter, and informed him of what the dragoon had reported to me relative to the open note, said to be on its way to the enemy's fleet before Alexandria. This, I am confident, was the first information received at Washington of the note in question. During the latter part of the same day, being at Colonel Monroe's quarters, (I think about one o'clock,) he told me that the open note of which I had apprized him in the morning had now found its way to him, having been brought up by one of our officers from the camp, at which the dragoon had stated he had left it, and he showed it to me. I have no recollection of its date. I remember that it was addressed to Captain Gordon, and signed by Codrington, I think, as captain of the fleet, and by order of Admiral Cochrane. The substance, I well recollect, was to direct Captain Gordon to descend the Potomac, lest alarm for their property should be given to the inhabitants by the presence of his squadron.

Capture of the City of Washington.

The contents of this note, as well as the manner chosen by the enemy for its conveyance, if it did come from him, were thought not a little singular and suspicious. The communication by water was open to him; and to express his anxiety for the fears of the inhabitants about the safety of their property from a force which had been for two years in the constant habit of burning, and carrying it off in every direction on these waters, and which was at that moment emptying the stores of Alexandria of private property to an immense amount, could hardly be considered earnest; and particularly when this expression was contrasted with his determination to destroy and lay waste every district of country within his power, made known by the letter of Admiral Cochrane to the Secretary of State, of the 18th August, (since published,) which was the letter delivered by me that morning, and with which this note was understood to have come from Admiral Cochrane's fleet. Colonel Monroe took this view of the subject, and expressed his suspicions that the note was a forgery, and the possibility, if it was genuine, that, by previous concert, it might be intended to convey something different from, perhaps the very reverse of, what appeared on its face. Under these circumstances, and in the then same state of things—a preparation going on to intercept the British ships below Alexandria—some doubts were entertained of the propriety of permitting it to pass to them. He however determined that it should be disposed of in such a way as to let the citizens of Alexandria have the benefit of it, if benefit there was, and at the same time to keep the enemy in ignorance that the Government had any knowledge of it. He requested me to take charge of the note, to deliver it to a gentleman of Alexandria, and to ask of him to give it such a course immediately. I did accordingly, in about an hour after, put it into the hands of a highly respectable citizen of that town, accompanied by the request enjoined on me. He undertook the charge with great cheerfulness, and suggested, as the best mode of answering the purpose intended, that he would place it in the post office at Alexandria, under cover, addressed to one of the acting committees of the town, remarking that it would reach them in that way almost as speedily as if he were to deliver it himself; and that by this means the committee and himself would be relieved from embarrassment, if the committee were called upon to answer by the officers of the enemy, in whose power they were, as to the channel through which it had been received. I thought his reasons good, and approved of the mode he proposed to adopt. That he did so deposite the note, in the course of the same afternoon, I was informed by him on the next day; and I have no question of the fact.

Whether the enemy received this note, or when, and, if received, what influence it may have had on his conduct, I have never learned; but there is one fact notorious on this subject—that he ceased to levy contributions on the town of Alexandria about the middle of the day on which Commodore Porter's battery reached the White House,

(the position below Alexandria, selected from which to annoy him in his descent,) and that he immediately after began to draw off his ships from the station he had taken before the town. This was on the 1st day of September. Commodore Porter's artillerists and General Young's brigade crossed the ferry at Georgetown, on the expedition, at the commencement of the night of the 31st August. That this movement was known to the enemy on the next day, and instantly arrested his devastations at Alexandria, I have never had the slightest doubt. As to the time and circumstance of the movement, I cannot be mistaken, as I was with both the corps during that night, one at their encampment, and the other on their march.

In relation to the remaining part of your letter, there are no particular facts within my knowledge, that I am aware of, pertinent to the inquiry of the honorable committee into the cause of the success of the enemy in his recent enterprise against Washington and Alexandria.

With very great respect, &c.

J. MASON.

Hon. RICHARD M. JOHNSON.

No. 14.

Report from the Superintendent of the Public Buildings.

OFFICE OF SUPERINTENDENT, *Washington,* Oct. 29, 1814.

SIR: In answer to the inquiries you made of me yesterday, I have the honor to state that the whole cost of the under-mentioned public buildings, from the commencement to the burning by the enemy, appears as follows:

North wing of the Capitol, including the foundation walls of both wings, and of the centre or main building; and of alterations and repairs	$457,388 39
South wing of the Capitol	325,074 92
President's House	334,334 00½
Public Offices	93,613 68
	$1,215,111 23½

At the instance of a committee of the Senate, the remains of those buildings have been examined by architects and master builders, of whom report it as their opinions, that the walls of the President's House, and both wings of the Capitol, with some inconsiderable repairs, are safe and sufficient to rebuild on. The walls of the two offices, particularly of the upper stories, are deemed insufficient to bear new roofs, and will require taking down and renewing, as far as shall be found necessary. The amount of the estimates for repairing and rebuilding the edifices, making the offices fire proof, with some other improvements suggested, are from one hundred and fifty thousand dollars to upwards of six hundred thousand dollars. The larger estimate, however, embraces an expense of considerable amount, for completing the west part of the north wing for a library, which none of the lower estimates includes. The average amount estimated, of putting all the buildings in the state the enemy found them, appears, by dividing the aggregate amount of the estimates by the number of them, to be about four hundred and sixty thousand dollars, allowing for the materials of the burnt buildings, which may be used in rebuilding.

I have the honor to be, &c.

THOMAS MUNROE.

Hon. R. M. JOHNSON.

No. 15.

William Simmons's Letter.

WASHINGTON CITY, *Nov.* 28, 1814.

SIR: In answer to your note of to-day, I have to state, that, on the morning of the 24th August last, when the alarm was given that the enemy were on their march to this city, and it was expected that they would come by the way of the Eastern Branch bridge, being myself well armed, and mounted on horseback, I rode there under the wish to render all the service in my power to oppose them. When I arrived near the Eastern Branch, I found a few of the city and Georgetown uniform companies there, laying upon their arms, and understood that the President, the Secretary of War, and other officers, were at the house of a Mr. Minnifee, (where I observed their horses at the door,) and that they were holding council. I then rode down to the bridge, where there were a few sailors, with a piece or two of cannon in front of the bridge, who, I understood, were to destroy the bridge in case the enemy approached. After but little delay, I rode back to the uniform troops, who I found were getting in motion to march to Bladensburg, to which way it was then said that the enemy were coming. I immediately rode on towards Bladensburg with all expedition. When I arrived upon the hill, on this side of the Bladensburg bridge, I observed Colonel Monroe, the then Secretary of State, just in the rear of our troops, which were posted on both sides of the road, between there and Bladensburg; there was, that the enemy were coming, but no person appeared to be able to give any correct account of them. I then observed to Mr. Monroe, that I would go on and see the enemy, and would let them know when they were coming. I accordingly rode into Bladensburg, and halted a few minutes at Ross's tavern, where there were a few militiamen, from whom I could get no other information than that the enemy were coming on the river road. I then proceeded to a height, a little west of Ross's tavern, called Lowndes' Hill, which had a commanding prospect of the river road for a considerable distance, and which was almost fronting the hill. After remaining there for some time, I observed, at a considerable distance, a great cloud of dust rise to a great degree, which satisfied me that they were coming in great force. Sometime after, I observed a few horsemen, not in uniform, on the road, who appeared to be reconnoi-

13th CON. 3d SESS.—55

tering, and were soon followed by troops that filled the road. They appeared to march very slow, and in close order, not less than twenty-four or thirty abreast in front, and the horsemen before spoken of, sometimes in front, and at other times a little to the right of the front; which position they marched in until they nearly approached the foot of the hill, and not more than a gunshot from me, where I was sitting on my horse, and the road in full sight for near a mile, and that filled with British troops, and still approaching. At this time there was not a person in sight of me, other than the enemy, except one dragoon, who appeared to have been posted there a little to my left, upon the same hill, where I left him, and have since understood he was taken by the advance party of the enemy. When they approached to the foot of the hill, and I expected they might attempt to cut off my retreat to the bridge, I fell back, and descended the hill in the front of Mr. Lowndes' house; and, immediately after I crossed the bridge, I looked back, and found that the advance party of horse had got into the Annapolis road, to the east of Lowndes' house, about twenty-four of them went up a lane in Bladensburg, towards the Baltimore road, leaving six or eight at the entrance of the lane.

I then was proceeding to our troops, to give information, when I met the President, General Armstrong, Colonel Monroe, and Mr. Rush, the Attorney General, considerably in advance of all our troops, going immediately into Bladensburg. I observed, on meeting them, "Mr. Madison, the enemy are now in Bladensburg." He exclaimed, with surprise, "the enemy in Bladensburg!" and, at the same moment, they all turned their horses and rode towards our troops with considerable speed. I called out aloud, "Mr. Madison, if you will stop I will show them to you; they are now in sight." He paid no attention. They all rode off very fast, except Mr. Rush, who halted; and I observed to him that there are part of the enemy stopping at that lane; he said that cannot be the enemy, they are not in uniform. I told him that they were a part of the advance party, that the others had gone up the lane, and that not any of them were in uniform. At this moment the red-coats began to heave in sight, in two sections, some in the rear, and others in the front, of Lowndes's house, and were forming in the Annapolis road. Mr. Rush, on seeing them, observed, "I am satisfied;" and turned his horse very suddenly to ride away, when his hat fell off, and he rode some distance without it, when I called out to him "Mr. Rush, come back and take up your hat;" which he did, and then pursued his company with all speed. Our troops, before I could get up to them, began to fire, from the left of the line, with cannon and small arms, into the town of Bladensburg. I supposed, at the time, it was from the information communicated by Mr. Madison from me, as I was the last person from Bladensburg. I immediately rode up the hill, expecting to find some of the Heads of Departments, to endeavor to get them to stop the firing, until it could be more effectual. I could not see the President or any of the gentlemen that were with him when I gave him the information. But I observed General Winder in the rear of the line, who I found to be the commanding officer. I immediately addressed him, and informed him that I was just from Bladensburg, and that there was but a very small party of the enemy in the town; that they had commenced firing too early; and that, if they would reserve their fire for a few minutes, the British troops were then coming down the hill, and were about to form on the Annapolis road, when they would be able to do some execution; for they were then heaving their fire away. I found that General Winder appeared to pay but little attention to what I had said. I remained upon the battle ground for some time, and until the retreat was ordered, and everything and every body appeared to be in the greatest confusion, no point fixed for rallying, or bringing the enemy to action, and the greater part of our troops were retreating in the greatest disorder. I returned to the city, and stopped at the President's House, which I found entirely abandoned, excepting one white servant, who informed me that the President had returned from the battle ground, and that he had gone out of the city. I observed at the President's door two pieces of cannon, well mounted on travelling carriages, which had been fixed there for the defence of the house, under a guard of soldiers, for some time, which was also abandoned. This being late in the day, and the most of the retreating soldiers having passed by, there was, however, still some coming on, very much fatigued, and worn down with hunger and thirst. I stopped a number of them, and plied them with plenty of brandy, which I got the President's servant to bring forward from the house. I then prevailed upon the soldiery to remove the cannon, by hand, towards Georgetown, where they were saved from falling into the hands of the enemy, who took possession of the house soon after. This now being near night, and not seeing a single military man in the city, I retired a few miles in the country, where I soon was a spectator to the conflagration of the Capitol, President's House, &c.

I remained in the vicinity of the city until after the enemy had abandoned it, when I returned; and in a day or two after, when stopping at the door of Colonel Monroe, who was present, as well as Mr. Madison, Mr. Rush, and several other gentlemen, Mr. Rush observed to me, Sir, we consider ourselves under obligations to you for preventing our falling into the hands of the enemy at Bladensburg; observing, at the same time, that they were going immediately into Bladensburg, understanding that General Winder's troops were there, and that they should have supposed the advance part of the enemy, not in uniform, were a part of Winder's troops. The foregoing is as correct a narrative of facts as I can at this time recollect.

I am, sir, with great respect, &c.,
WM. SIMMONS.

Hon. R. M. Johnson, &c.

SUPPLEMENTARY DOCUMENTS.

Georgetown, Dec. 16, 1814.

Sir: I had the honor to receive yours of yesterday. My statement shall be concise as possible. On perusing, in the National Intelligencer, of the 10th instant, the report of the committee of which you are chairman, the following passage arrested my attention: "From early in the morning till late in the afternoon, Colonel Minor sought Colonel Carbery diligently, but he could not be found. He rode to headquarters and obtained an order from General Winder upon the arsenal, for arms, &c.—marched to the place with his regiment. Colonel Carbery arrived at the moment, and apologised for his absence, and informed Colonel Minor that he had, the evening before, ridden out to his country seat."

Without adverting to the information on which the committee may have thought proper to rely, for what is stated in the above extract, I shall merely proceed to state some facts, supported by respectable testimony, which, it is believed, will in the opinion of the committee, completely invalidate what is there set forth.

1. It will appear that, on the night of the 23d of August, between the hours of nine and eleven, I was seen between Capitol Hill and the camp. See the certificate of Major Manstelle, Deputy Quartermaster General, No. 1. That, late at night of the 23d, I arrived at Mr. Semmes' hotel, in Georgetown; that I lodged there that night; was seen about sunrise next morning, near McLeod's hotel, on the Pennsylvania avenue; and that afterwards I returned to my quarters in Georgetown and breakfasted. See Nos. 3 and 4 given by Mr. Semmes, my landlord, and Captain Cassin, of the District militia. That, on the morning of 24th August, between seven and nine, I signed requisitions for arms, &c., for Colonel Minor, and gave them to the surgeon of his regiment. See Lieutenant Hobbs, No. 2. That Doctor Jones, who was with our troops when the action commenced, returning to his hospital to attend to his duties there, saw Colonel Minor's troops halted on Capitol Hill, and think they were getting their dinners. See his certificate, No. 5. That, in the opinion of Lieutenant Boden, of the ordnance department, Colonel Minor's troops, from the time they arrived at the arsenal, had sufficient time to have got their arms, &c. and have marched to the battle ground before the action commenced. See his certificate, No. 6.

These certificates being in your hand are easily be referred to.

I have the honor to be, with great respect, sir, your obedient servant,

HENRY CARBERY,
Colonel 36th U. S. Infantry.

Hon. R. M. Johnson,
Chairman of a Committee of Congress.

George W. Campbell's Letter.

Nashville, (Ten.) Dec. —, 1814.

Sir: I have had the honor to receive your letter of the 29th October last. You request that I

Capture of the City of Washington.

should give the committee, of which you are chairman, such facts and views as may be in my power respecting the proceedings of a Cabinet Council on the 1st of July last, in relation to the defence of military district No. 10; and on the subject of a conversation that took place between the President and myself, on the 24th of August, respecting the part General Armstrong was to take at Bladensburg; and also any other facts and views that may be thought pertinent to a fair and impartial inquiry into the causes of the fall of the Capital of the United States.

The information requested by the committee shall be given without reserve, so far as my recollection and state of health will enable me. I deem it, however, proper, previously, to state, that, according to the views I entertain of the relations existing between the Executive and the other members of the Government, usually called on to assist in council, I should not consider myself bound, on such application as the present, to disclose, in all cases, the proceedings which may have taken place at such council, or what may have passed at a conversation held with the President individually, such as that above referred to, as such disclosure might justly be considered as restrained; in the former case, on the ground of official, and in the latter, on that of personal confidence; and, without taking into consideration the effect of the restraint that would naturally be imposed on such deliberations and interchange of sentiments, by establishing the precedent that they were liable to public disclosure whenever called for, there might be cases in which the public interest would be compromitted by such development. I do not, however, consider the present such a case; and I have no motive for withholding the information required on account of any bearing it might be supposed to have on my own conduct on that occasion, or on that of any other member of the Government, as I am perfectly satisfied it is the desire of the Executive, and presume it is so also of the other members, that every circumstance calculated to throw light on the subject before the committee, and develope the real causes which led to the late events at the Seat of Government, should be disclosed without reserve. Under these impressions, therefore, I act, in giving the information before.

At the Cabinet Council referred to, held on the 1st of July, by the members of the Government, convened by request of the President, I was present. Despatches had been received, a few days previously thereto, from two of our Ministers (Messrs. Gallatin and Bayard) in Europe, the consideration of which, according to my present impressions, was the principal object of the conference. They were accordingly taken up for deliberation, and the changed aspect of affairs in Europe, as unfolded by them, as well as by information derived from other sources, was brought into view. The subject of our foreign relations, generally, was taken into consideration, and the effect the late great events on the Continent would be likely to produce upon them was freely spoken of. It was stated as probable, first, I believe, by

the President, that England, considering her own relative power and influence greatly increased, would be disposed to employ a considerable portion of her military and naval forces, lately disengaged from the great European contest, in prosecuting the war against this country; that she might be expected to strengthen herself in Canada, and carry on her depredations against our Atlantic coast on a scale more extended than heretofore. Some general remarks were also made on the propriety of adapting our measures to that state of things an increase of the enemy's forces would produce; and there appeared a concurrence of opinion among the members as to the importance of providing the means, and making the requisite arrangements, for defending not only district No. 10, including the Seat of Government, but, as far as practicable, every other portion of the Union, against which an attack might reasonably be expected; but I do not at present recollect any specific proposition, made while I was present, in relation to the defence of that district, or any other place in particular. I cannot, however, undertake to state in detail all the proceedings that took place in relation to this subject on that occasion. The state of my health was very imperfect, and some official duty, according to my present recollection, requiring to be attended to at a certain hour, occasioned me to withdraw before the subject of the defence of the Seat of Government was formally taken up for decision; nor do I now recollect of being present when the question on that subject was decided. The President, either on my return the same day, or shortly after, informed me it had been determined to call forth and organize a force deemed sufficient for the defence of the district, and particularly the Seat of Government, of which measure I approved; and, from the Secretary of War, I afterwards understood the number to be called on for that purpose was fifteen thousand men, which appeared to me amply sufficient. Nothing further occurs to me, at present, in relation to what passed at that conference, while I was present, on the subject of the defence of the Seat of Government. I recollect that, about this time, the President, in conversation, stated his impressions to be, on the fullest consideration he had been able to give the state of affairs in Europe, in connexion with the disposition of Great Britain, as far as it could be ascertained from the late despatches of our Ministers, as well as from other sources of information, that we ought to calculate she would direct a considerable portion of her numerous forces, liberated from the late great conflicts on the Continent, and left entirely at her disposal, against this country, either to produce a favorable effect on the pending negotiation, and, if disposed to peace, close the war with some brilliant achievement calculated to give her arms the air of eclat; or, if not so disposed, for the purpose of prosecuting the war more vindictively, and possibly with a view to other more ambitious objects; and that, whatever might be her ulterior views, we ought to expect that Washington City, being the Seat of the National Government, and, from its local situation, more accessible, as well as less capable of defence, than most other places, would be among the first objects of her attack, and that we ought, therefore, to make the requisite preparations to meet such event. With this view, I understood, General Winder was appointed to the command of the District, and orders given for concentrating, in the neighborhood of the city, such force, to consist of regulars and militia, as was deemed sufficient for its defence.

The conversation between the President and myself, on the 24th August, respecting which the committee requests information, having taken place incidentally, and under peculiar circumstances, it will not be expected that I should recapitulate it at length; and it may be difficult to communicate its substance with precision, or the causes that led to it, without going more into detail than would be acceptable to the committee, or accord with my own inclination.

When it was known, on the evening of the 23d of August, that the troops under General Winder had retired across the Eastern Branch, and encamped in the city, it occasioned, as may be readily supposed, considerable agitation in the minds of the citizens. It appeared to have been expected, that, in case our force was not considered sufficient to meet and repulse the enemy on his landing, his advance would be opposed, and his progress, at least, retarded as far as practicable, by harassing him on his march, erecting defensive works at suitable positions, and throwing such other obstructions in his way as was best calculated to check his movements; for all which operations the nature of the country through which he must pass was said to be very favorable; when, therefore, it was stated that he was near the city, without such means having been either at all, or but partially resorted to, it produced some surprise, as well as inquiry into the causes that led to such a result. Falling in conversation with the Secretary of War, on this subject, I expressed my apprehensions that suffering the enemy to approach so near (if his progress could by any possible means have been checked) as to make the fate of the city depend on a single battle, to be maintained, on our part, principally by raw, inexperienced troops, was hazarding too much. He appeared to concur in this opinion. And when I inquired whether the late movements of the troops were made pursuant to his advice, or with his approbation; and what plan of operations was determined on to oppose the further progress of the enemy; and, also, whether our army would have the benefit of his suggestions and advice, in directing its future movements; he gave me to understand that the movements which had taken place were not in pursuance of any plan or advice given by him; that General Winder, having been appointed to the command of the district, including the city, and the means assigned for its defence placed at his disposal, was considered as having the direction of their application; and it was to be presumed he had formed such plans for defending the city as he deemed best suited to the emergency and the

means he possessed; and that interposing his opinion might be considered indelicate, and perhaps improper, unless he had the approbation of the Executive for so doing; in which case, any assistance that his suggestions or advice could render should be afforded.

It appeared to me an occasion so highly important and critical demanded the united efforts of all the military skill and ability within the reach of the Government; and that feelings of delicacy, if their cause could be removed, should not be allowed to come in collision with the public interest; and, I believe, I so expressed myself to General Armstrong.

On the following morning I set out with the Secretary of War for General Winder's headquarters, then near the bridge on the Eastern Branch. When we proceeded as far as the President's house, we learned he had gone on before. Some other company joining us, I proceeded in advance, and arrived there before the Secretary; where I found, with General Winder, the President, the Secretary of the Navy, and, I believe, the Attorney General of the United States, with some military officers. Some conversation took place in relation to the route the enemy would be most likely to pursue in approaching the city; when a messenger arrived, bringing the Commanding General information, considered by him decisive, that they would advance by Bladensburg, and he immediately proceeded with the troops to that place. At this time the Secretary of War had arrived. All the members of the Government that were present left the house. Falling in conversation with the President, I took occasion to state to him the impression of the Secretary of War, as to the line of conduct his duty required him to observe on that occasion; and added, in substance, according to my present recollection, that the very critical situation of affairs appeared to me to require all the aid that military skill and ability could afford; that, on so important an occasion, considerations of delicacy, as to conflicting authority, should not, I presumed, be allowed to jeopardise, in any degree, the public interest; that I regretted the reserve apparently observed by the Secretary of War; but understood from him, he acted on the ground that, as General Winder was appointed to the command of the district, and the means designed for its defence placed at his disposal, he was considered as possessing the right to direct the manner of their application; and that, in interposing his opinion, without Executive approbation, might be considered indelicate, and perhaps an improper interference with the Commanding General's authority; but that, if it was known to be the President's pleasure, he would afford any aid in his power, by his presence and advice; and I believe I also stated that, considering the extraordinary and menacing aspect of our affairs, I thought it my duty to make him this communication, in case he should think proper, the president which the Secretary acted might be amended. The President replied, as I understood him, that General Armstrong might have known it proper order given by him would readily meet with the Executive sanction ; and there was no doubt any suggestions from him would be duly attended to by General Winder. Upon my remarking I had reason to believe, without his approbation, the Secretary would not interpose his opinion, or take any part in the business of the day, the President observed, he would speak to him on the subject. The President, the Secretary of War, and myself, were then on horseback. The President joined the Secretary, and some conversation took place between them, the purport of which I did not hear.

The President, after parting from the Secretary, observed to me he had spoken to General Armstrong on the subject I had named to him, and that no difficulty, he presumed would occur in the case ; that any suggestions, made by the Secretary, would, without doubt, receive due attention from the Commanding General ; and, should any objection be made on the ground of authority, the matter might readily be adjusted, as he would not himself be far distant; and the Secretary's order, (I presume it was meant in writing,) given on the field, if necessary, would be considered as carrying with it the Executive sanction.

The foregoing is, according to the best of my recollection, the substance of what the President communicated to me after conversing with General Armstrong. It, however, occurred in the midst of much bustle, and where various other subjects presented themselves for consideration ; it is therefore possible I may not have understood him correctly, or may not now recollect all that passed.

Some general conversation took place about this time respecting the probable force, movements, and objects, of the enemy ; also respecting the direction to be given to certain portions of our own troops, particularly those under Commodore Barney, who had not been put in motion, and whom the Commodore appeared very desirous should be permitted, with himself, to take a share in the expected battle. Mention was also made of the precautionary measures proper to be taken, in the possible event of the enemy's success against the city, respecting the public property at the Navy Yard, &c.; also, the propriety, suggested in such case, of the members of the Government convening at some suitable place, to determine on ulterior arrangements; and Fredericktown was agreed on as best calculated for that purpose.

After parting with the President. I joined the Secretary of War, then on his way to Bladensburg ; he observed the President had spoken to him respecting the operations of the day ; that he would proceed to the scene of action; and, if there should be occasion, would suggest to the Commanding General whatever occurred to him as likely to be useful ; and, should it become necessary, he would, on the field, give a written order that would carry with it, of course, official authority. He did not, however, state to me the particulars of the conversation that passed between the President and himself. Near the turnpike gate I parted with the Secretary; the state of my health required that I should return to my lodging.

The foregoing contains all that occurs to me at present, in relation to the specific inquiries of the committee.

On the subject of their general inquiry, respecting the causes of the capture of the Seat of Government, it is not probable I can add anything to the information they already possess, derived from other sources. A combination of circumstances, not easily accounted for, some of which could not probably have been anticipated, and others against which it might have been difficult to provide by any precautions that could have been adopted, led, It is believed, to that event.

The sudden advance of the enemy, after his arrival on our coast, so considerable a distance into the country ; destitute as he was known to be of cavalry, and, in a great degree, of artillery, as well as of the means of transporting provisions; without delaying to establish garrisons, or otherwise to provide for keeping open his communication with his shipping and supplies; was a measure that could not, it is presumed, be justified on any military principle, and may not, therefore, have been anticipated in time to provide effectually against its consequences. On the other hand, the tardy movements of the militia, called on from the neighboring States for the defence of the city, and their consequent failure to arrive in time, at the scene of action, whatever may have occasioned it, may undoubtedly be considered as the principal cause of the catastrophe that followed.

How far the troops who had arrived, and were present, might, under the guidance of different management, have succeeded in retarding the enemy, and, with the aid of the reinforcements hourly expected, in finally repulsing him, it is not for me to decide: and it is a question on which even military men may not perhaps agree.

I have the honor to be, &c.

G. W. CAMPBELL.

Hon. R. M. Johnson, &c.

SUBSISTING THE ARMY.

—

[Communicated to the House, January 25, 1815.]

House of Representatives,
November, 12, 1814.

Sir : I am instructed by the Committee on Military Affairs to ask information on the following points:

1. What is the present mode of subsisting the army ?

2. If by contracts, what are the defects, if any, and the remedy ?

3. Whether any other mode can be adopted, combining, in a greater degree, certainty and promptitude with economy and responsibility ?

4. Whether the alternative offered by law, of substituting commissaries to contractors, has been

adopted; and if yes, what has been the general result?

I have the honor to be, with high consideration and respect,

G. M. TROUP.

WAR DEPARTMENT, *Dec.* 23, 1814.

SIR: Not wishing to rely altogether on my own judgment in replying to your inquiries relating to the best mode of subsisting the troops of the United States, I have consulted the officers of greatest experience who were within my reach, on the presumption that I should best promote the views of the committee, by collecting all the light that I could on the subject. I have the honor now to submit to you a letter from General Scott, one from General Gaines, and one from Colonel Fenwick, which meet fully those inquiries in every circumstance. These officers give a decided preference to the system of supply by commissaries, in preference to that by contractors; and I have reason to believe that the officers generally concur with them in that preference. It has my unqualified assent.

Should the proposed plan be adopted, it will readily occur to the committee that the commissaries to be appointed should be placed on a very respectable footing; so high a trust should be committed to such of our citizens only as are most distinguished for their abilities, their patriotism, and integrity. I shall be happy to furnish details on this subject, should the honorable committee desire it.

I have the honor to be, with great respect, sir, your obedient servant,

JAMES MONROE.

Hon. Mr. TROUP.

General Scott's Remarks.

Observations on the mode of subsisting an Army by Contract and by Commissariat.

The first method is believed to be impolitic, and is vicious in time of war; also liable to many objections in a state of peace. In time of war, contractors may betray an army; they are not confidential and responsible agents, appointed by the Government. The principal only is known to the War Office, and therefore may be supposed to be free from this objection; but his deputies and issuing agents are appointed without the concurrence or knowledge of the General or the Government. The deputies or issuing agents are necessarily as well acquainted with the numerical strength of the army to which they are attached, as the Adjutant General himself. For a bribe they may communicate this intelligence to the enemy, or fail to make issues at some critical moment, and thus defeat the best views and hopes of the Commander-in-chief. The movements of an army are necessarily subordinate to its means of subsistence; or, as Marshal Saxe expresses it, to considerations connected with the belly. The present mode of subsisting our armies, puts the contractors above the Gen-

eral. If a contractor corresponds with the enemy, he can only be tried by the civil courts of the United States, as in the case of other persons charged with treason; (courts martial having decided that contractors do not come within the meaning of the 60th article of the rules and articles of war;) and if a contractor fails to make issues, he can only be punished by civil actions. I speak of cases arising within the limits of the United States. In the enemy's country. I suppose, a General, who knows his duty, would not fail to hang a contractor who should, by guilty neglect or corruption, bring any serious disaster upon the army. A sudden event frequently obliges a General to order troops to a distant and new station; notice is given to this contractor to supply, &c.; but the latter, finding that prompt arrangements will diminish his profits, pleads a want of reasonable notice. This term is indefinite, and if the General and contractor differ, it can only be settled by a court of common law. It is no reply to his objection to say, that, on a sudden emergency, like that supposed, the General may appoint a special agent to supply the troops, by purchases on account of the United States. This would only show the superiority of a commissariat.

The interests of the contractor are in precise opposition to those of the troops. The checks provided by the contract may be sufficient to prevent abuse, if the officers are vigilant and have leisure to resort to those checks; but when the army is on a forced march, or is manœuvring in the face of the enemy, the contractor has it in his power to practise many impositions with impunity, as in the case of an army or detachment ordered to march on short notice, to take with it subsistence for a given time. In such case, there is no time for a formal survey or minute inspection of the rations offered by the contractor, according to the mode pointed out in the contract. The contractor avails himself of the hurry of the moment, and issues provisions deficient in quantity and quality. Unless the rations, before they are received by the regimental quartermaster, are surveyed and condemned, there is no remedy except by a civil action on the case, as between citizen and citizen. Contractors, as before observed, are not amenable to courts martial. Every option given to the contractor under the contract, operates to the prejudice of the troops, and frequently embarrasses the General: as in the case of bread or flour, either of which the contractor may issue at pleasure. Eighteen ounces of flour will yield twenty-seven of bread; therefore, when the soldier finds it convenient to bake his own bread, or to commute his flour for twenty or twenty-one ounces of bread, the contractor will not choose to issue flour, because he too finds the inconvenience, and reserves to himself the profit. [Under other circumstances, when both the soldier and contractor find it inconvenient or impossible to bake bread, the latter avails himself of his option, and issues flour. Under this uncertainty, it is impossible for the General to calculate any march with precision. When the troops receive

Subsisting of the Army.

flour instead of bread, more time must be allowed for cooking. It is this option which prevents the General from obliging the contractor to provide magazines of hard bread for prompt movements and expeditions, in which bread wagons cannot follow the troops. Hard bread occupies, comparatively, but little space. To attain an important object, every soldier may very well carry in his haversack five or six days' bread (without meat) and thus march more than one hundred miles independent of ovens, wagons, or contractors. Our armies have sometimes been supplied with hard bread in the following manner: The contractor delivers flour, and has credit for so many rations of that article as are contained in the barrels delivered at once. The Quartermaster General causes the flour to be converted into hard bread, at the expense of the United States. The bread is then turned over to the contractor, who issues it to the troops, receiving a certain per centage for his trouble. Nothing can more clearly demonstrate the necessity of appointing commissariats to supply the army in the place of contractors. It is almost impossible for the General to compel the contractor to supply the troops regularly with soap and vinegar (component parts of the rations) because the trouble of procuring them generally exceeds the contract prices of these articles; and yet, nothing can be more essential to the cleanliness and health of troops. The contractor generally endeavors to give whiskey in the way of commutation, which costs the officers much exertion to prevent. If the contract system is continued, I would recommend diminishing the allowance for whiskey, and the reverse for vinegar, soap, and candles.

It would be endless to trace the petty villanies which contractors are daily tempted to commit, to the prejudice of the troops, arising out of this opposition of interests before noticed. The interests of the contractor put him perpetually on the alert. The vigilance of the officer is sometimes necessarily relaxed. There is no such opposition between duty and interest in the case of commissariats, who purchase and issue on account of Government. A commissary, if destitute of character, might be disposed to charge the Government more for a barrel of whiskey, or a bullock, or flour, than the article cost him; but it can never be his interest to impose unsound provisions on the troops. It is presumed that, if a commissariat be resorted to, the officers composing it will be appointed on the usual evidences of character, and subjected to martial law. It will not be necessary to give them rank, except as it respects each other, as Commissary General, Deputy and Assistant Commissary General. Such is the practice in the French and English armies.

W. SCOTT.

General Gaines's remarks on Contracts for Provisions, &c.

Sir: I regret to be under the necessity of troubling you with complaints, but my own exertions to enforce the contract, and insure regular supplies of rations, having failed, I am compelled to resort to this mode of seeking a remedy.

The sub-contractor at Wilmington has not furnished a day's rations for near two weeks past. The sub-contractor at Billingsport, New Jersey, as well as the one at Marcus Hook, our principal encampment, have, in defiance of my frequent orders and threats, and contrary to their contract, contrived to palm upon the troops the coarsest and cheapest provisions, and such as are often damaged. To effect this criminal species of speculation, they keep in store little more, and often not as much, as is necessary to meet the returns from day to day; hence the troops are often compelled to draw damaged provisions, or draw none at all. This conduct, on the part of the sub-contractors, occasioned yesterday, at Marcus Hook, such serious disorders in some of the corps, that it became necessary to confine two young officers, and some twenty men; and I this evening received a report from Billingsport, that the troops there have been all day without provisions, the rations offered for issue in the morning being so much damaged as to require their condemnation. I have just now purchased and forwarded a supply. The New Jersey militia are very orderly.

I have uniformly given the best attention in my power, ever since the commencement of the war, to the supply of rations, and the conduct of contractors; and if I were called before Heaven to answer whether we have not lost more men by the badness of provisions than by the fire of the enemy, I should give it as my opinion that we had. And if asked what causes have tended most to retard our military operations, and repress that high spirit of enterprise for which the American soldiers are pre-eminently distinguished, and the indulgence of which would not fail to veteranize our troops by the annoyance and destruction of the enemy, I should say, the irregularity in the supply, and badness of the rations, have been the principal causes.

Original contractors seem to be a privileged order of men, who, by virtue of the profits of the contract, are elevated above the drudgery which a common-sense view of the contract would seem to impose on them. They take care to secure to themselves at least one cent per ration, leaving a second and sometimes a third order of miserable under-contractors to perform the duties, and each of these must calculate on making money. Thus the contract, after being duly entered into at Washington, is bid off, until it falls into the hands of men who are forced to bear certain loss and ultimate ruin, or commit frauds by furnishing damaged provisions. They generally choose the latter, though it should tend to destroy the Army. I know the opinion of no officer on this subject who does not think with me.

It is true, that, in most cases where purchases have been ordered by the General, on the failures of the contractor, the provisions have cost more than the ordinary contract price. But this proves nothing in favor of the contract system; but, on the contrary, proves that the contractor, when unable to purchase below the contract price, with-draws himself from the service, and leaves the troops to suffer, or be supplied by order of the General, with little or no previous notice, so that the purchasing officer is obliged to take what can be got, at the highest prices. And these failures generally take place when near the enemy, and where regular supplies are most wanted. The purchases are ordered by the General, and made by the officers when their time is most precious, and their attention constantly called to their regular duties. Under these circumstances, it is in vain to expect purchases at very low prices. But if, instead of a contractor, a commissioned officer should be authorized to supply the rations at the original cost of the provisions, and should be allowed a little time to look out for the best markets, and be enabled by punctual payments to support the public credit, I have no doubt that the supplies would not only be good and regular, but even lower than they can be under any contract system. Commissioned officers only should be employed in this duty—men who stand most solemnly pledged to serve the United States honestly and faithfully, and to obey orders—men who may be cashiered or capitally punished by military law, for neglect of duty, or for fraudulent practices.

I feel persuaded that I could, with the assistance of one of the general staff, and the regimental quartermasters, supply the troops altogether and completely, without being more frequently called from my other duties than the neglects in the contractor's department have usually called me. If you should deem an experiment desirable, I will most cheerfully undertake it, and pledge myself that the rations shall not cost more than eighteen cents, and probably not so much.

I have the honor to be, most respectfully, sir, your obedient servant,

E. P. GAINES.

Hon. James Monroe, Sec'ry of War.

Colonel Fenwick's remarks on supplying the Army with provisions.

WASHINGTON, Dec. 23, 1814.

In conformity with your commands, I have the honor of reporting to you the present means of victualling our Army by contract, the impositions and danger attending such a mode of supply, and the necessity of destroying the evil by substituting a commissariat.

Contracts are never fulfilled to the letter, and never will be so long as avarice exists. And, where so many opportunities present themselves to the military contractor for imposition and fraud, we must expect he will avail himself of them. That his fortune may be made with too great rapidity for the comfort and health of the soldier, every expedient is resorted to to increase his profits. Bread half baked, sour flour, damaged meat, are amongst the many resources they employ. More than half the issues are made without the smaller parts of the rations. Vinegar, soap, and candles, are retained under the most frivolous excuses;

and you are, sir, sensible how conducive to the soldier's health must be both soap and vinegar. These evils I have witnessed in every part of the country. Seldom could the wrong be redressed, because the commanding officer had neither means; the abuse could not be punished; the contractor was beyond his control. Discontent was excited amongst the men, but complaint is often found unprofitable; for, if the provisions are condemned, the agent is so dilatory in replacing them, that the men get no food for the greater part if not the whole of that day.[*] These are the causes of complaint with the Army, and the ill-planned operations may be frustrated by the penury or tardy contractor, or his dishonest agent, who if base enough to defraud the soldier, would be equally so in communicating with the enemy. The history of all the wars in Europe is big with treachery, whenever a Power depended for its supplies on contractors. Numerous are the instances of failures of expeditions in the wars of Marlborough and Frederick. Contractors or their agents were the principals in the mischief. In our own campaigns† we have already experienced this evil. Many other reasons might be adduced, how and why supplies will fail, if this system of contract is continued. It does not exist in any army in Europe. It has proven itself ruinous and expensive in a high degree. Even the British, riveted as they are to old habits, have been compelled to abandon it, and assume the commissariat of the Continent. Lord Wellington speaks of the impossibility of supplying his army in Spain by any other means. There is not an officer or soldier in the Army who would not petition you to do away this destructive system, and substitute commissaries, who would be actuated by feeling, honor, and the fear of disgrace.

I have the honor to be, sir, with very great respect and consideration, your obedient servant,

JOHN R. FENWICK.

RELATIVE POWERS OF THE GENERAL AND STATE GOVERNMENTS OVER THE MILITIA.

[Communicated to the Senate, February 16, 1815.]

Mr. GILES made the following report:

The Committee of the Senate on Military Affairs, understanding that serious difference of opinion existed between the Executive authority of the United States and the authorities of some of the individual States, respecting the relative powers of the General and State Governments over the militia, deemed it an incumbent duty on them to call for information upon that highly interesting subject, with a view of interposing, if found practicable, some legislative provisions for the mutual accommodation of such differences. For this purpose, on the 7th January last, in virtue of instructions from the committee, I asked

---

* Occurred at New York.
† At Black Creek, Upper Canada.

The Militia.

was addressed to the honorable Secretary for the Department of War, a copy of which accompanies this report; and, in reply thereto, the committee received from him the letter and documents which also accompany this report.

Although the return of peace has, for the present, relieved the committee from the necessity of providing a legislative remedy for these unfortunate differences, yet the committee conceive that the points in question are of vital importance to the essential rights and powers of the Government of the United States, and that the pretensions of the authorities of the States of Massachusetts, Connecticut, and Rhode Island, set up in opposition thereto, if now acquiesced in, might be resumed by the State authorities in the event of a future war, and thus deprive the Government of the United States of some of its most efficient legitimate means of prosecuting such war with vigor and effect; the committee have therefore thought proper to present the papers concerning this subject to the Senate, for consideration.

Whilst the committee will refrain from entering into arguments to fortify the grounds taken by the Executive Government on this subject, and explained in the letter of the Secretary for the Department of War, they feel themselves impelled by a sense of justice to express a decided approbation of its conduct, in supporting and preserving the Constitution of the United States against the effects of the pretensions of the State authorities aforesaid, which, after full consideration, the committee believe not warranted by the Constitution, nor deducible from any fair and just interpretation of its principles and objects. The direct and inevitable tendencies of these pretensions, in the opinion of the committee, would be, to deprive the Government of the United States of powers essentially necessary to insure the common defence, one of the great objects committed to its charge; to introduce discordant and contradictory counsels into the national deliberations, upon a point, too, of all others, most requiring union of thought and of action; to change the fundamental character of the Constitution itself, and thus eventually to produce its destruction, by debilitating the Government, and rendering it incompetent to the great objects of its institution; and to substitute in its stead the dismemberment of these United States, with all the horrible consequences respectively resulting from disunion.

COMMITTEE CHAMBER, *Jan.* 7, 1815.

SIR : The Committee of the Senate on Military Affairs having observed that differences exist between the authorities of the United States and of some of the individual States, respecting the relative command of the officers of the regular army and of the militia, when called to act together in certain cases, has instructed me to ask for such information upon that subject as may be in possession of your Department; and to inquire whether, in your judgment, some legislative provisions might not be adopted, which would tend to heal such differences, to prevent the recurrence of others from the same cause, and to facilitate the operations of your Department in that respect ?

Be pleased, sir, to accept assurances of my high consideration, &c.

WM. B. GILES,
Chairman.

Hon. JAS. MONROE,
    Secretary of War.

DEPARTMENT OF WAR, *Feb.* 11, 1815.

SIR : I have had the honor to receive your letter of the 7th ultimo, stating that the Military Committee of the Senate had observed that difficulties had arisen between the authorities of the United States and some of the individual States, respecting the relative command of the officers of the regular army and of the militia, when called to act together, and were desirous of such information on the subject as this Department might possess, and of its opinion whether some legislative provisions might not be adopted which would tend to heal such differences, to prevent the recurrence of the like for the same causes, and to facilitate the operations of the Department in other respects.

My late indisposition will, I trust, explain satisfactorily to the committee the cause of the delay of my answer, which I have much regretted.

In complying with the request of the committee, it has appeared to me advisable to communicate all the documents in this Department relating to the objects of its inquiry. By a detailed view of the several measures which have been adopted by the President, since the war, for the defence of the country, in discharge of the duties imposed on him by the Constitution and laws of the United States; of the objections to those measures by the Executives of some of the States; and of the correspondence between this Department and the military authorities acting under it, with the Executives of such States, the committee will see the grounds of the differences which have attracted attention, and be enabled to judge how far any legislative interposition may be useful or proper.

The paper A contains a copy of the letters of the Secretary of War to the Governors of the several States, detailing their respective quotas of militia, under the acts of Congress.

B is a copy of a report of the Secretary of War to the Military Committees of the Senate and House of Representatives, bearing date on the 21st day of December, 1812, communicating a division of the United States into military districts, then contemplated by the Department of War, with the reasons for it; which division, with certain modifications, was afterwards adopted. This report treats on some subjects not immediately within the scope of the call of the committee, yet, treating in all its parts on the important subject of defence, and thereby intimately connected with the object of the call, I have thought that a view of the whole paper, at this time, would not be unacceptable.

The Militia.

C is a copy of the answers of the Governors of several of the States to the Department of War, on the requisitions made for parts of their quotas of militia under the several acts of Congress, and of the correspondence which passed between them and the Department of War, and commanders of the military districts, acting under it, within which those States were.

D is a copy of the correspondence between the Governor of New Jersey and the Department of War, relating to the appointment of the Governor of New York to the command of the military district No. 3; a copy of this correspondence is presented, to communicate to the committee every circumstance that has occurred relating to the command of the militia in the service of the United States.

It appears by these documents, that the Governors of Massachusetts, Connecticut, and Rhode Island, have objected to the requisitions made on their several States, for parts of their respective quotas of militia, on the following grounds: 1st. That the President has no power to make a requisition for any portion of the militia, for either of the purposes specified by the Constitution, unless the Executive of the State, on whose militia such call is made, admits that the case alleged exists, and approves the call. 2d. That, when the militia of a State should be called into the service of the United States, no officer of the regular army had a right to command them, or other person, not an officer of the militia, except the President of the United States in person. These being the only difficulties which have arisen between the Executive of the United States and the Executives of any of the individual States, relative to the command of the militia, known to this Department, are, it is presumed, those respecting which the committee has asked information.

By these documents it is also shown, that certain portions of the militia were called out by the Executives of these States, and a part of them put into the service of the United States. These doctrines were nevertheless adhered to. I do not go into a detail on these points, deeming it unnecessary, as all the facts will be found in the documents.

Respecting, as I do, and always have done, the rights of the individual States, and believing that the preservation of those rights, in their full extent, according to a just construction of the principles of our Constitution, is necessary to the existence of our Union, and of free government in these States, I take a deep interest in every question which involves such high considerations. I have no hesitation, however, in declaring it as my opinion, that the construction given to the Constitution, by the Executives of these States, is repugnant to its principles, and of dangerous tendency.

By the Constitution, Congress has power to provide for calling forth the militia to execute the laws of the Union, suppress insurrections, and repel invasions; to provide for organizing, arming, and disciplining the militia, and for governing such part of them as may be employed in the service of the United States, reserving to the States, respectively, the appointment of the officers, and the authority of training the militia according to the discipline prescribed by Congress.

The President is likewise made Commander-in-Chief of the Army and Navy of the United States, and of the militia of the several States, when called into the actual service of the United States.

The power which is thus given to Congress by the people of the United States, to provide for calling forth the militia, for the purposes specified in the Constitution, is unconditional. It is a complete power, vested in the National Government, extending to all these purposes. If it was dependent on the assent of the Executives of the individual States, it might be entirely frustrated. The character of the Government would undergo an entire and radical change. The State Executives might deny that the case had occurred which justified the call, and withhold the militia from the service of the General Government.

It was obviously the intention of the framers of the Constitution, that these powers, vested in the General Government, should be independent of the States' authorities, and adequate to the ends proposed. Terms more comprehensive than those which have been used cannot well be conceived. Congress shall have power to provide for calling forth the militia to execute the laws of the Union. What laws! All laws which may be constitutionally made. Whatever laws are adopted for that purpose, within the just scope of that power, which do not violate the restraints provided in favor of the great fundamental principles of liberty, are Constitutional, and ought to be obeyed. They have a right to provide for calling forth the militia to suppress insurrections. This right is also unqualified. It extends to every case of insurrection against the legitimate authority of the United States. It may be said that the Government may abuse its authority, and force the people into insurrection, in defence of their rights. I do not think that this is a probable danger under our system; or that it is the mode of redress, even if such abuse should be practised, which a free people, jealous of their rights, ought to resort to. The right which they have to change their representatives in the Legislative and Executive branches of the Government, at short intervals, and, therefore, the whole system of measures, if they should think proper, is an ample security against abuse, and a remedy for it, if it should ever occur. Congress have also a right to provide for calling forth the militia to repel invasions. This right, by fair construction, is, in my judgment, an amplification of the power over the militia, to enable the Government to prosecute the war with effect, and not the limitation of it, by strict construction, to the special case of a declared war, the enemy on any particular part of our territory. War exists; the enemy is powerful; preparations are extensive; we may expect his attacks in many quarters. Shall we remain the active spectators of the dangers which surround

The Militia.

us, without making the arrangements suggested by an ordinary instinctive foresight, for our defence? A regular army, in sufficient extent, may not exist. The militia is the principal resource. Is it possible that a free people would thus intentionally trammel a Government which they had created for the purpose of sustaining them in their just rank, and in the enjoyment of all their rights, as a nation, against the encroachments of other Powers, more especially after they had experienced that reliance could not be placed on the States individually, and that, without a General Government, thus endowed, their best interests would be sacrificed, and even their independence insecure? A necessary consequence of so complete and absolute a restraint on the power of the General Government over the militia, would be to force the United States to resort to standing armies for all national purposes. A policy so fraught with mischief, and so absurd, ought not to be imputed to a free people in this enlightened age. It ought not, more especially, to be imputed to the good people of these States. Such a construction of the Constitution is, in my opinion, repugnant to their highest interests, to the unequivocal intention of its framers, and to the just and obvious import of the instrument itself.

The construction given to the Constitution, by the Executive is sanctioned by legislative authority, by the practice of the Government, and by the assent and acquiescence of all the States, since the adoption of the Constitution, to the period of the late unhappy differences, respecting which the committee has desired to be informed. By the law of 1795, the President is authorized to call forth the militia, for the purposes mentioned in the Constitution, by a direct application to the militia officers, without any communication with, or reference to, the Executives of the individual States, and penalties are prescribed for carrying the law into effect, should resort to them be necessary. It merits attention, in regard to the question under consideration, that the power given to the President to call forth the militia, not made dependent, by this law, on the fact of an invasion having actually occurred, but takes effect in case of imminent danger of it. In the year 1795, the President of the United States, on the certificate of a Judge of the Supreme Court, that an insurrection existed in the western parts of Pennsylvania, called out the militia of the several States including the militia of Pennsylvania, to suppress it; which call was obeyed. In this instance, the assent of the Governor of Pennsylvania to the existence of an insurrection was not asked. General Washington, who then held the office of Chief Magistrate, relied exclusively on the powers of the General Government for the purpose. The opinion of the same Chief Magistrate, of the power of the General Government over the militia, was also made known by another distinguished act of his Administration. By a report of General Knox, the then Secretary of War, to Congress, this doctrine is maintained to the utmost extent, and exemplifications of it insisted on, which prove that, from the nature of our population, the militia was the force which, in his judgment, ought principally to be relied on for all national purposes.

In the instances under consideration, powers are granted to Congress for specified purposes, in distinct terms. A right to carry powers, thus granted, into effect, follows of course. The Government to whom they are granted must judge of the means necessary for the purpose, subject to the checks provided by the system. It adopts a measure authorized, supervises its execution, and sees the impediments to it. It has a right to amend the law to carry the power into effect. If any doubt existed on this point, in any case, on general principles, and I see cause for none, it cannot in the present—a power having been explicitly granted to Congress, by the Constitution, to pass all necessary and proper laws for carrying into execution the powers which are vested in the General Government.

Equally unfounded, in my opinion, is the other objection of the Executives of the States abovementioned, that when the militia of a State are called into the service of the United States, no officer of the regular army, or other person, not a militia officer, except the President of the United States, in person, has a right to command them.

When the militia are called into the service of the United States, all State authority over them ceases. They constitute a part of the national force, for the time, as essentially as do the troops of the regular army. Like the regular troops, they are paid by the nation. Like them, their operations are directed by the same Government. The circumstance, that the officers of the militia are appointed by, and trained under, the authority of the State, individually, (which must, however, be done according to the discipline prescribed by Congress,) produces no effect on the great character of our political institutions, or on the character and duties of the militia, when called into the service of the United States.

That the President, alone, has a right to command the militia in person when called into the service of the United States, and that no officer of the regular army can take the command in his absence, is a construction for which I can see nothing in the Constitution to afford the slightest pretext. Is it inferred from the circumstance, that he is appointed Commander-in-Chief of the militia when called into the service of the United States? The same clause appoints him Commander-in-Chief of the land and naval forces of the United States. In construction of law he is Commander-in-Chief, though not present. His presence is not contemplated in either case. Equally necessary is it in the one as in the other. What has been the practice under the Constitution, commencing with the first Chief Magistrate, and pursuing it under his successors, to the present time? Has any President ever commanded, in person, either the land and naval forces, or the militia? Is it not known that the power to do it is vested in him, principally, for the purpose of giving him the control over the military and naval opera-

The Militia.

C is a copy of the answers of the Governors of several of the States to the Department of War, on the requisitions made for parts of their quotas of militia under the several acts of Congress, and of the correspondence which passed between them and the Department of War, and commanders of the military districts, acting under it, within which those States were.

D is a copy of the correspondence between the Governor of New Jersey and the Department of War, relating to the appointment of the Governor of New York to the command of the military district No. 3; a copy of this correspondence is presented, to communicate to the committee every circumstance that has occurred relating to the command of the militia in the service of the United States.

It appears by these documents, that the Governors of Massachusetts, Connecticut, and Rhode Island, have objected to the requisitions made on their several States, for parts of their respective quotas of militia, on the following grounds: 1st. That the President has no power to make a requisition for any portion of the militia, for either of the purposes specified by the Constitution, unless the Executive of the State, on whose militia such call is made, admits that the case alleged exists, and approves the call. 2d. That, when the militia of a State should be called into the service of the United States, no officer of the regular army had a right to command them, or other person, not an officer of the militia, except the President of the United States in person. These being the only difficulties which have arisen between the Executive of the United States and the Executives of any of the individual States, relative to the command of the militia, known to this Department, are, it is presumed, those respecting which the committee has asked information.

By these documents it is also shown, that certain portions of the militia were called out by the Executives of these States, and a part of them put into the service of the United States. These doctrines were nevertheless adhered to. I do not go into a detail on these points, deeming it unnecessary, as all the facts will be found in the documents.

Respecting, as I do, and always have done, the rights of the individual States, and believing that the preservation of those rights, in their full extent, according to a just construction of the principles of our Constitution, is necessary to the existence of our Union, and of free government in these States, I take a deep interest in every question which involves such high considerations. I have no hesitation, however, in declaring it as my opinion, that the construction given to the Constitution, by the Executives of these States, is repugnant to its principles, and of dangerous tendency.

By the Constitution, Congress has power to provide for calling forth the militia to execute the laws of the Union, suppress insurrections, and repel invasions; to provide for organizing, arming, and disciplining the militia, and for governing such part of them as may be employed in the service of the United States, reserving to the States, respectively, the appointment of the officers, and the authority of training the militia according to the discipline prescribed by Congress.

The President is likewise made Commander-in-Chief of the Army and Navy of the United States, and of the militia of the several States when called into the actual service of the United States.

The power which is thus given to Congress by the people of the United States, to provide for calling forth the militia, for the purposes specified in the Constitution, is unconditional. It is a complete power, vested in the National Government, extending to all these purposes. It is in no wise dependent on the assent of the Executives of the individual States, it might be entirely frustrate. The character of the Government would undergo an entire and radical change. The State Executives might deny that the case had occurred which justified the call, and withhold the militia from the service of the General Government.

It was obviously the intention of the framers of the Constitution, that these powers, vested in the General Government, should be independent of the States' authorities, and adequate to the ends proposed. Terms more comprehensive than those which have been used cannot well be conceived. Congress shall have power to provide for calling forth the militia to execute the laws of the Union. What laws? All laws which may be constitutionally made. Whatever laws are adopted for that purpose, within the just scope of that power, which do not violate the restraints provided in favor of the great fundamental principles of liberty, are Constitutional and ought to be obeyed. They have a right to provide for calling forth the militia to suppress insurrections. This right is also unqualified. It extends to every case of insurrection against the legitimate authority of the United States. It may be said that the Government may time its authority, and force the people into surrender, in defence of their rights. I do not think that this is a probable danger under our system; or that it is the mode of redress, even if such abuse should be practised, which a free people, jealous of their rights, ought to resort to. The right which they have to change their representatives in the Legislative and Executive branches of the Government, at short intervals, and, indeed, the whole system of measures, if they shall think proper, is an ample security against abuse, and a remedy for it, if it should ever exist. Congress have also a right to provide by raising forth the militia to repel invasions. The right by fair construction, is, in my judgment in the amplification of the power over the militia, to enable the Government to prosecute the war with effect, and not the limitation of it, by any construction, to the special case of a devoted the enemy on any particular part of our territory. War exists; the enemy is powerful; preparations are extensive; we may expect attacks in many quarters. Shall we and the active spectators of the dangers which surround us, without making the arrangements suggested by an ordinary instinctive foresight, for our defence? A regular army, in sufficient extent, may not exist. The militia is the principal resource. Is it possible that a free people would thus intentionally trammel a Government which they had created for the purpose of sustaining them in their just rank, and in the enjoyment of all their rights, as a nation, against the encroachments of other Powers, more especially after they had experienced that reliance could not be placed on the States individually, and that, without a General Government, thus endowed, their best interests would be sacrificed, and even their independence insecure? A necessary consequence of so complete and absolute a restraint on the power of the General Government over the militia, would be to force the United States to resort to standing armies for all national purposes. A policy so fraught with mischief, and so absurd, ought not to be imputed to a free people in this enlightened age. It ought not, more especially, to be imputed to the good people of these States. Such a construction of the Constitution is, in my opinion, repugnant to their highest interests, to the unequivocal intention of its framers, and to the just and obvious import of the instrument itself.

The construction given to the Constitution, by the Executive is sanctioned by legislative authority, by the practice of the Government, and by the assent and acquiescence of all the States, since the adoption of the Constitution, to the period of the late unhappy differences, respecting which the committee has desired to be informed. By the law of 1795, the President is authorized to call forth the militia, for the purposes mentioned in the Constitution, by a direct application to the militia officers, without any communication with, or reference to, the Executives of the individual States, and penalties are prescribed for carrying the law into effect, should resort to them be necessary. It merits attention, in regard to the question under consideration, that the power given to the President to call forth the militia is not made dependent, by this law, on the fact of an invasion having actually occurred, but takes effect in case of imminent danger of it. In the year 1795, the President of the United States, on the certificate of a Judge of the Supreme Court, that an insurrection existed in the western parts of Pennsylvania, called out the militia of the several States including the militia of Pennsylvania, to suppress it; which call was obeyed. In this instance, the assent of the Governor of Pennsylvania to the existence of an insurrection was not asked. General Washington, who then held the office of Chief Magistrate, relied exclusively on the powers of the General Government for the purpose. The opinion of the same Chief Magistrate, of the power of the General Government over the militia, was also made known by another distinguished act of his Administration. By a report of General Knox, the then Secretary of War, to Congress, this doctrine is maintained to the utmost extent, and exemplifications of it insisted on, which

prove that, from the nature of our population, the militia was the force which, in his judgment, ought principally to be relied on for all national purposes.

In the instances under consideration, powers are granted to Congress for specified purposes, in distinct terms. A right to carry powers, thus granted, into effect, follows of course. The Government to whom they are granted must judge of the means necessary for the purpose, subject to the checks provided by the system. It adopts a measure authorized, supervises its execution, and sees the impediments to it. It has a right to amend the law to carry the power into effect. If any doubt existed on this point, in any case, on general principles, and I see cause for none, it cannot in the present—a power having been explicitly granted to Congress, by the Constitution, to pass all necessary and proper laws for carrying into execution the powers which are vested in the General Government.

Equally unfounded, in my opinion, is the other objection of the Executives of the States abovementioned, that when the militia of a State are called into the service of the United States, no officer of the regular army, or other person, not a militia officer, except the President of the United States, in person, has a right to command them.

When the militia are called into the service of the United States, all State authority over them ceases. They constitute a part of the national force, for the time, as essentially as do the troops of the regular army. Like the regular troops, they are paid by the nation. Like them, their operations are directed by the same Government. The circumstance, that the officers of the militia are appointed by, and trained under, the authority of the State, individually, (which must, however, be done according to the discipline prescribed by Congress,) produces no effect on the great character of our political institutions, or on the character and duties of the militia, when called into the service of the United States.

That the President, alone, has a right to command the militia in person when called into the service of the United States, and that no officer of the regular army can take the command in his absence, is a construction for which I can see nothing in the Constitution to afford the slightest pretext. Is it inferred from the circumstance, that he is appointed Commander-in-Chief of the militia when called into the service of the United States? The same clause appoints him Commander-in-Chief of the land and naval forces of the United States. In construction of law he is Commander-in-Chief, though not present. His presence is not contemplated in either case. Equally necessary is it in the one as in the other. What has been the practice under the Constitution, commencing with the first Chief Magistrate, and pursuing it under his successors, to the present time? Has any President ever commanded, in person, either the land and naval forces, or the militia? Is it not known that the power to do it is vested in him, principally, for the purpose of giving him the control over the military and naval operations, being a necessary attribute of the executive branch of the Government? That, although he might take the command of all the forces under it, no President has ever done it? That a provision for the actual command is an object of legislative regulation, and the selection of the person to whom committed of executive discretion.

Under the commander, all officers of every species of service and corps, regular and militia, acting together, take rank with common consent, and perfect harmony, according to an article of war, sanctioned by the Constitution. By this article, the officers of the regular army take rank of those of the militia of the same grade, without regard to the dates of their commissions, and officers of any and every grade of the militia take rank of all officers of inferior grade of the regular army. When these troops serve together they constitute but one national force. They are governed by the same articles of war. The details for detachment, guard, or any other service, are made from them equally. They are, in truth, blended together, as much as are the troops of the regular army when acting by themselves only.

The idea advanced by the honorable Judges of Massachusetts, that, where the regular troops and militia act together, and are commanded in person by the President, who withdraws, there can be no chief commander, of right, of either species of force, over the whole, but that the regulars and militia, as implied, may even be considered as allied forces, is a consequence of the construction for which they contend. It pushes the doctrine of State rights further than I have ever known it to be carried in any other instance. It is only in the case of Powers who are completely independent of each other, and who maintain armies, and prosecute war, against a common enemy, for objects equally distinct and independent, that this doctrine can apply. It does not apply to the case of one independent Power who takes into its service the troops of another: for then the command is always at the disposal of the Power making war, and employing such troops, whether regular or militia. How much less does it apply to the case under consideration, where there is but one Power, and one Government, and the troops, whether regular or militia, though distinguished by shades of character, constitute but one people, and are, in fact, countrymen, friends, and brethren.

The President is in himself no bond of union in that respect. He holds his station as Commander-in-Chief of the land and naval forces, and militia, under a Constitution which binds us together as one people, for that and many other important purposes. His absence would not dissolve the bond. It would not revive discordant latent claims, or become a signal for disorganization.

The judicious selection of the chief commander, for any expedition or important station, is an object of high interest to the nation. Success often depends on it. The right to do this appears to me to have been explicitly vested in the Presi-

dent, by the authority given to Congress to provide for calling forth the militia, for organizing, arming, disciplining, and governing them, when employed in the service of the United States, and by the powers vested in him as Chief Executive of the United States. The rights of that highly respectable and virtuous body of our fellow-citizens, are, I am persuaded, completely secured, when the militia officers commanding corps are retained in their command—a Major General over his division, a Brigadier over his brigade, a Colonel over his regiment, and the inferior officers in their respective station. These rights are not injured or affected by the exercise of the right of the Chief Magistrate; a right incident to the Executive power, equally applicable to every species of force, and of high importance to the public, to appoint a commander over them, of the regular army, when employed in the service of the United States, if he should deem it expedient. The rights of the militia officers and those of the General Government are strictly compatible with each other. There is no collision between them. To displace militia officers for the employment of regulars, or to multiply commands of a separate character, especially of small bodies, for that purpose, would be improper.

In dividing the United States into military districts, and placing a General of the regular army in command in each, with such a portion of the regular force, artillery, and infantry, as could be spared from other service, it was the object of the President to afford the best protection to every part of the Union that circumstances would admit of, with the least burden which might be possible to the people. These commanders were specially charged with the defence of their respective districts. It was enjoined on them to watch the movements of the enemy, to communicate them to the Government, and to execute its orders in summoning to the field, in case of invasion, such portions of the quotas of the militia of each State, within their respective districts, as had been provided for by act of Congress, and detailed by this Department, as were thought necessary.

When this arrangement was entered into it will be observed that there was no menace of immediate invasion, and but few militia in the field. It was intended as a measure of precaution, to guard against possible, but, as was hoped and presumed, distant dangers. The Executive had no alternative between that arrangement or any other. The militia officers of rank could not. They were at home; for the Executive has no power, under existing laws, to call them into the field, without a command of men sufficient to their rank; and, even when thus called forth, the term of service must expire with that of the men whom they command. These facts show that nothing was more remote from the intention of the Government than to disregard the just claims of our fellow-citizens of the militia. They are, also, how difficult it is to provide, by any arrangement which can be adopted, for a general and permanent defence of our principal cities and seaboard, without employing officers who are always in service, in the principal commands at least, for the purpose.

It is admitted that, by the increased pressure of the war, in consequence of which much larger bodies of militia have been called into service, and with them many General officers of experience and merit, these difficulties have proportionably diminished. Of these officers several have been already advanced to distinguished commands, with great satisfaction to their fellow-citizens, and advantage to their country. The committee may be assured that opportunities of this kind, regarding the obligation of a just responsibility, will be seized by the Executive with pleasure.

How far these differences may be healed, or the recurrence of the like in future be prevented, by legislative provisions, the committee, on a full view of these documents, and on a due consideration of the whole subject, will be able to decide. It is proper, however, to remark, that the divisions of the country into military districts, so far as relates to that special object, requires no legislative sanction, if, indeed it admits of one. The definition of boundary was intended for the purpose of prescribing a limit to the civil duties, if they may be so called, rather than the military, of the commander of each district; rather to the period preceding an invasion, with a view to the necessary preparatory measures for repelling it, than after it should take place. An invasion by a large force would probably require the concentration of all our troops along the seacoast, who might be brought to act in it. In such an event, all limitations of boundary to the several commanders would cease. The march of the enemy would regulate that of our armies, who would from every quarter be directed against them.

I have the honor to be, with great respect, your most obedient and very humble servant,

JAMES MONROE.

A.

Copy of a letter from William Eustis, Secretary of War, to the Governors of States, dated

WAR DEPARTMENT, *April* 15, 1812.

I am instructed by the President of the United States to call upon the Executives of the several States to take effectual measures to organize, arm, and equip, according to law, and hold in readiness, to march at a moment's warning, their respective proportions of one hundred thousand militia, officers included, by virtue of an act of Congress passed the 10th instant, entitled "An act to authorize a detachment from the militia of the United States."

This, therefore, is to require your Excellency to take effectual measures for having —— of the militia of —— (being her quota) detached and duly organized in companies, battalions, regiments, brigades, and divisions, within the shortest periods that circumstances will permit, and as nearly as possible in the following proportions of artillery, cavalry, and infantry, viz: one-twentieth part of artillery, one-twentieth part of cavalry, and the residue infantry.

There will, however, be no objection, on the part of the President of the United States, to the admission of a proportion of riflemen, duly organized in distinct corps, and not exceeding one-tenth part of the whole quota of the States, respectively. Each corps should be properly armed and equipped for actual service.

When the detachment and organization shall have been effected, the respective corps will be exercised under the officers set over them; but will not remain embodied, or be considered as in actual service, until, by subsequent orders, they shall be directed to take the field.

Your Excellency will please to direct that correct muster-rolls and inspection returns be made of the several corps, and that copies thereof be transmitted to this Department as early as possible.

Copy of a letter from William Eustis, Esq., Secretary of War, to the Governor of Massachusetts, dated

WAR DEPARTMENT, *June* 12, 1812.

SIR: I am directed by the President to request your Excellency to order into the service of the United States, on the requisition of Major General Dearborn, such part of the quota of the militia of Massachusetts, detached conformably to the act of the 10th April, 1812, as he may deem necessary for the defence of the seacoast.

I am, &c.

NOTE.—A similar letter, addressed to the Governors of Connecticut, Rhode Island, and New Hampshire.

Copy of a letter from William Eustis, Secretary of War, to his Excellency Caleb Strong, Governor of Massachusetts, dated

JULY 21, 1812.

SIR: By information received from Major General Dearborn, it appears that the detachment from the militia of Massachusetts, for the defence of the maritime frontier, required by him under the authority of the President, by virtue of the act of the 10th April, 1812, have not been marched to the several stations assigned them.

Inasmuch as long delay may be followed with distress to a certain portion of our fellow-citizens, and with injurious consequences to our country, I am commanded by the President to inform your Excellency that this arrangement of the militia was preparatory to the march of the regular troops to the northern frontier. The exigencies of the service have required, and orders have accordingly been given to Major General Dearborn to move the regular troops to that frontier, leaving a sufficient number to man the guns in the garrisons on the seaboard. The execution of this order increases, as your Excellency cannot fail to observe, the necessity of hastening the detached militia to their several posts, as assigned by General Dearborn; in which case they will, of course, be considered in the actual service and pay of the United States.

The danger of invasion, which existed at the

time of issuing the order of the President, increases, and I am specially directed by the President to urge this consideration on your Excellency, as requiring the necessary order to be given for the immediate march of the several detachments, specified by General Dearborn, to their respective posts.

I have the honor to be, &c.

Extract of a letter from John Armstrong, Secretary of War, to the Governor of Connecticut, dated

AUGUST 9, 1813.

Whenever militia are called out, the contractor or his agent should be required to supply according to the contract.

Circular letter from John Armstrong, Secretary of War, to the Governors of the respective States, dated

JULY 4, 1814.

SIR: The late pacification in Europe offers to the enemy a large disposable force, both naval and military, and with it the means of giving to the war here a character of new and increased activity and extent.

Without knowing, with certainty, that such will be its application, and still less that any particular point or points will become objects of attack, the President has deemed it advisable, as a measure of precaution, to strengthen ourselves on the line of the Atlantic, and (as the principal means of doing this will be found in the militia) to invite the Executives of certain States to organize and hold in readiness, for immediate service, a corps of ninety-three thousand five hundred men, under the laws of the 28th of February, 1795, and 18th of April, 1814.

The enclosed detail will show your Excellency what, under this requisition, will be the quota of ——. As far as volunteer uniform companies can be found, they will be preferred.

The expediency of regarding (as well in the designations of the militia as of their places of rendezvous) the points, the importance or exposure of which will be most likely to attract the views of the enemy, need but be suggested.

A report of the organization of your quota, when completed, and of its place or places of rendezvous, will be acceptable.

I have the honor to be, &c.

Extract of a letter from John Armstrong, Secretary of War, to Nathaniel Searle, Jun., Adjutant General of Militia, State of Rhode Island, dated

JULY 9, 1814.

I have the honor to acknowledge the receipt of your letter of the 8th instant, accompanied by sundry documents in relation to the defence of the Alantic frontier of the State of Rhode Island.

The State troops, if considered part of the militia, or as substitutes therefor, will be taken into the service of the United States as the quota of Rhode Island, under the requisition of the 4th instant, and will be designated for the defence of that State.

B.

Copy of a letter from James Monroe, Acting Secretary of War, to the Chairman of the Military Committee, dated

DEPARTMENT OF WAR,
December 23, 1812.

I have had the honor to receive your letter of the 21st instant, requesting such information as this Department may possess respecting the defects in the organization of the General Staff of the Army, and in the laws relating to volunteers; and requesting, also, the opinion of this Department as to the propriety of augmenting the present military force, and, in case of augmentation, of what description of troops it ought to consist.

The committee of each House of Congress having called on the Department of War for information on the same points, I shall have the honor to make to each committee the same report. The enclosed remarks go to several of the inquiries suggested in your letter, and contain the views of the Department on the several subjects to which they relate. The pressure of business has forced me to give them a shape rather informal. A copy of them I have sent to-day to the committee of the House of Representatives, and hasten to forward a like copy to you.

EXPLANATORY OBSERVATIONS.

To make this war effectual as to its just objects, so much of the physical force of the country must be brought into activity as will be adequate. The force exists in an abundant degree, and it is only necessary to call it forth and make a proper use of it. This force must be employed alike in defensive and offensive operations. The exposed parts of our own country claim a primary attention. After providing for their defence, the remaining force may be employed in offensive operations. I will begin with that part which requires protection.

Defence of the Coast.

The whole coast, from our northern limit to St. Mary's, should be divided into military districts.

Boston, including New Hampshire and Massachusetts, to constitute one.

Newport, including Rhode Island and Connecticut, another.

New York, including the State of New York and Jersey, a third.

Philadelphia, including Pennsylvania and Delaware, a fourth.

Norfolk, including Maryland and Virginia, a fifth.

Charleston, including North and South Carolina and Georgia, a sixth.

At Boston, and at each of the other posts, a company of artillery, or more than one, according to circumstances, of the regular army, and a proportion of its infantry, be stationed. Let the whole placed under the command of a Brigadier; the following manner, and let him have attached to him an engineer. This force will join the nucleus of a little army, to be formed in case of

The Militia.

invasion, of the militia, volunteers, or such other local force, as may be specially organized for the purpose.

This apportionment is intended to give an idea. It would be carried into detail by the Executive. At Boston, including a suitable proportion of artillery, and at Eastport, and other ports eastward - - - - - 600
At Newport, with a company of artillery - 350
At New York, with a suitable proportion of artillery - - - - - - 1,000
At Philadelphia, with a company of artillery - - - - - - 200
Norfolk, with a company of artillery at Annapolis. - - - - - 300
North Carolina, one company of artillery 100
Charleston, with a company of artillery - 300

By placing a General officer of the regular army, with some experience, in command, at each of these stations, charged with the protection of the country, to his right and left, to a certain extent, suitable provision will be made for the whole. The country will have confidence, and, by degrees, a system of defence suited to any emergency, may be prepared for the whole coast. This may be done by the local force with economy, and, what is also of great importance, without drawing at any time for greater aid on the regular force of the nation, which may be employed in offensive operations elsewhere. There should be some flying artillery at each station, ready mounted, and prepared to move in any direction which may be necessary. An engineer will be useful, to plan and execute any works which may appear proper for the defence of the principal station, or any other within each military district.

It may be said, that it is not probable that the enemy will attempt an invasion of any part of the coast described, with a view to retain it, and even so for the purpose of desolation. It is nevertheless possible, and, being so, provision ought to be made against the danger. An unprotected coast may invite attacks which would not otherwise be thought of. It is believed that the arrangement proposed will be adequate, and that one can be devised, to be so, which would prove more economical.

For Savannah and East Florida, special provision must be made. Whether East Florida is left in possession of Spain, or taken immediate possession of by the United States, in either case, menaces the United States with danger to their local interests. While it is held by Spain, it will be used as a British province, for annoying us in every mode in which it may be made instrumental to that end. The ascendency which the British Government has over the Spanish regency, secures to Great Britain that advantage while the war lasts. We find that, at present, the Creek Indians are excited against us, and an aid can afforded to the slaves of the Southern States too seek it there. To guard the United States against the attempts of the British Government, in that vulnerable quarter, the province remaining in the hands of the Spanish authorities, a force

of about two thousand regular troops will be requisite. It will require no more to hold it, should possession be taken by the United States.

For New Orleans and Natchitoches, including the Mobile and West Florida, about two thousand five hundred men will be necessary. A local force may be organized in that quarter in aid of it, which, it is believed, will be adequate to any emergency.

The next object is Detroit and Malden, including the protection of the whole of our Western frontier. For these, it is believed that two thousand regular troops, with such aids as may be drawn from the States of Kentucky and Ohio, will be amply sufficient.

The following, then, is the regular force requisite for the defence of those places:

Boston - - - - -		600
Newport, Rhode Island - - -		350
New York - - - - -		1,000
Philadelphia - - - -		200
Norfolk - - - - -		300
North Carolina - - - -		100
Charleston - - - - -		300
Savannah and East Florida - -		2,000
New Orleans, Mobile, &c. - -		2,500
Detroit, Malden, &c. - - -		2,000
		9,350

This leaves a force of about twenty-six thousand regular troops, consisting of infantry, artillery, and cavalry, provided the whole force contemplated by law is raised and kept in the field, to be employed in offensive operations against Niagara, Kingston, Montreal, and all Lower Canada, and likewise against Halifax. This whole force, however, even if raised, cannot be counted on as effective. The difference between the force on the muster rolls, and the effective force in the field, through a campaign, is generally estimated at a deficiency in the latter of one-fourth, with troops who have already seen service. With young troops, it may be placed at one-third. Take from the nominal force ten thousand, and it would leave about sixteen thousand for these latter purposes.

Will this force be sufficient? This will depend of course on the number of the British force which may be opposed to us. It is believed that the British force at Niagara, and its neighborhood, at Kingston, Montreal, Quebec, and in all Lower Canada, ought to be estimated at twelve thousand regulars, and several thousand militia; say, in all, sixteen or eighteen thousand, and at Halifax, at three thousand.

To demolish the British force, from Niagara to Quebec, would require, to make the thing secure, an efficient regular army of twenty thousand men, with an army of reserve of ten thousand. The commander ought to have power to dispose of them as he thought fit. The movement against Niagara and Lower Canada ought to be in concert, and of course under the control of the same commander, who, alone could be a competent judge of the suitable time and manner. A corps of reserve is indispensable to guard against casualties, especially with raw troops. Nothing should be left to hazard. The expedition should be of a character to inspire a certainty of success, from which the best consequences would result. Our troops would be more undaunted, and those of the enemy proportionably more dismayed. In the interior, on both sides, the effect would be equally salutary; with us it would aid in filling our ranks with regular troops, and drawing to the field such others as occasion might require; with the enemy, the effect would be equally in our favor. It would soon drive from the field the Canadian militia, and, by depressing the spirits of the people, interrupt and lessen the supplies to the British army.

If the conquest of Canada should prove to be easy, a part of this force might be directed against Halifax; but for that purpose a force should be specially provided, to consist of not less than six thousand men. Before this time next year, the honor and interest of the United States require that the British forces be driven into Quebec and Halifax, and be taken there, if possible. They must, at all events, be excluded from every foot of territory beyond the reach of their cannon. This may be done, if timely and suitable measures are adopted for the purpose, and they be executed with vigor and skill.

If the Government could raise and keep in the field thirty-five thousand regular troops, the legal complement of the present establishment, the deficiency to be supplied, even to authorize an expedition against Halifax, would be inconsiderable. Ten thousand men would be amply sufficient; but there is danger of not being able to raise that force, and to keep it at that standard. The estimate, therefore, of the force to be raised for the next campaign, in addition to the legal complement, should cover any probable deficiency in it, as well as the addition which ought to be made to it. My idea is, that provision ought to be made for raising twenty thousand men in addition to the present establishment. How shall these men be raised? Shall new regiments be added to the standing army to constitute a part of it; the volunteer acts be relied on; or any other expedient adopted?

The first question to be answered is, can more than the force contemplated by the present Military Establishment be raised in time for the next campaign, and that force be kept in the field by new recruits to supply losses produced by the casualties of war? Will the state of our population, the character and circumstances of the people who compose it, justify a reliance on such a resource alone?

The experiments heretofore made, even under the additional encouragement given by the acts passed at the last session of Congress, and the excitement produced by the war, though great, forbid it. Abundant and noble proofs of patriotism have been exhibited by our citizens in those quarters where the approach and pressure of the enemy have been most felt. Many thousands have rallied to the standard of their country; but it has been to render voluntary service, and that for short terms. The increase of the regular army has been slow, and the amount raised, compared with the number sought, inconsiderable. Additional encouragement may produce a more important result; but still there is cause to fear that it will not be in the degree called for by the present emergency. If, then, there is cause to doubt success, that doubt is a sufficient motive for the Legislature to act on, and to appeal, in aid of the existing resource, to another, not likely to fail.

In rejecting a reliance on the regular Military Establishment alone, for the force necessary to give effect to the next campaign, the alternative is too obvious to be mistaken by any one. The occurrences of the present year designate it in the most satisfactory manner. The additional force must be raised for a short term, under every encouragement to the patriotism of the people which can be given consistently with the circumstances of the country, and without interfering with enlistments into the old corps. The volunteer acts of the last session may be the basis on which this force may be raised; but those acts must be radically altered to enable the President to raise the force. Experience has not been less instructive on this very important point. Although whole sections of our country, and among them many of our most distinguished and estimable citizens, have risen in arms and volunteered their services, and marched in the ranks, it has not been done under the volunteer acts. Those acts contemplate a beginning at the wrong end, and require too long an engagement to produce the desired effect. They contemplate a movement in no particular quarter, and by no particular person; they require that the people shall raise the affair up of their own accord, enrol themselves into companies, and then recommend their officers to the President; and that the President shall not appoint the field officers until a sufficient number of companies are formed to constitute a regiment. Thus it may happen that companies from different States, all strangers to each other, may be thrown into a regiment, and that the field officers appointed to command them may be strangers alike to all the company, officers and men. They contemplate, also, an enrolment for three years, with a service only of one; conditions which, in themselves, could not fail to defeat the object, as they enlist on their inherent motive to action. The patriot citizen, most truly wished to serve his country, would spurn the restraint imposed on him of two years of inactivity out of three, and enter the regular army, where he would find active employment for the whole term of his enlistment. And the farmer, the merchant, and the artist, willing to make a sacrifice of a certain portion of their time to the urgent calls of their country, would find a check to all impulse by the obligation they must enter into for so long a term; and by allowing no bounty, no pecuniary inducement nor aid to enable a man to leave home is offered. It is impossible that

The Militia.

such a project should succeed on an extensive scale. The ardent patriotism of a few, in detached circles of our country, may surmount these obstacles; but such examples will be rare.

To give effect to such a measure, the President alone should have the appointment of all the officers under the rank of Colonel, and it should be made in the following manner: He should first select such prominent men as had merited, and acquired, by a virtuous conduct, the confidence of their fellow-citizens, and confer on them, with the advice and consent of the Senate, the rank of Colonel, and then confide to them the selection and recommendation of all their officers, to be approved by the President. These men would go to their homes, look around the country where they were known, and where they know every one, select the prominent men there, such as enjoyed the esteem and confidence of their fellow-citizens, and recommend them, according to their respective pretensions, as field officers, captains, and subalterns under them. Thus the service would be truly voluntary, as every man would act under officers to whose appointment he had essentially contributed. The several corps would consist of neighbors, friends, and brothers; example would animate to action; generous motives would be excited; patriotism roused; and the ties of kindred would unite with the love of country and of free government to call our young men to the field.

The first object is to complete the regular establishment to its legal complement, and to keep it there. The pay of the soldiers has already been raised during the present session of Congress; but this, it is feared, will not afford a sufficient inducement to fill the ranks within the requisite time. Let the bounty be raised to the sum of forty dollars to each recruit, and let the officers receive the sum of five dollars per man for all whom they may recruit. These additional encouragements will, it is presumed, secure the desired success. When filled, how keep the regiments full? The presence of all the officers will be necessary, in that state, for their command; none could be spared to recruit. Different expedients have occurred to supply supernumerary officers for the recruiting business. It has, for example, been proposed to add a certain number of regiments, from fifteen to twenty, to the present Military Establishment; but this would be to rely on that establishment alone; which, as is presumed, it would be highly improper to do. This plan is further objectionable, on account of the expense attending it; and likewise, as it would create delay in the organization of the corps and appointment of the officers. The same objections are applicable to the addition of a company to each battalion, not to mention others. On much consideration, the following expedient has occurred as most eligible. Let one field officer, a major, be added to each regiment, and a third lieutenant to each company. This will allow a field officer and ten company officers from each regiment, for the recruiting service, which would be sufficient.

13th Con. 3d Sess.—56

The additional force proposed for one year is intended to supply the probable deficiencies in the present Military Establishment. This force being to be raised for a shorter term, and for a special purpose, it is presumed that much aid may be drawn from that source, and with great despatch, for the purposes of the next campaign. It is probable, also, that it may be done without essentially interfering with enlistments into the old corps, as most of the men who may enter into this, might not be willing to engage in them.

If a lingering war is maintained, the annual disbursements will be enormous. Economy requires that it be brought to a termination with the least possible delay. If a strong army is led to the field early in the Spring, the British power on this Continent must sink before it; and when once broken down, it will never rise again. The re-conquest of Canada will become, in the opinion of all enlightened men, and of the whole British nation, a chimerical attempt. It will therefore be abandoned; but if delay takes place, reinforcements may be expected, and the war be prolonged. It is to save the public money, and the lives of our people, and the honor of the nation, that high bounties, and premiums, and the most vigorous exertions in other respects, are advised. The prolongation of the war, for a single campaign, would exceed these expenditures more than tenfold.

C.

Boston, *August* 5, 1812.

Sir: I received your letter of the 21st of July, when at Northampton, and the next day came to Boston. The people of this State appear to be under no apprehension of an invasion. Several towns, indeed, on the seacoast, soon after the declaration of war, applied to the Governor and Council for arms and ammunition, similar to the articles of that kind which had been delivered to them by the State in the course of the last war, and in some instances they were supplied accordingly. But they expressed no desire that any part of the militia should be called out for their defence; and, in some cases, we were assured that such a measure would be disagreeable to them.

You observe, in your last letter, that the danger of invasion, which existed at the time of issuing the orders of the President, increases.

It would be difficult to infer, from this expression, that, in your opinion, that danger is now very considerable; as the President's order must have been issued before war was declared, your former letter being dated the 12th of June, and General Dearborn's, who was then at Boston, on the 22d of that month; besides, it can hardly be supposed that, if this State had been in great danger of invasion, the troops would have been called from hence to carry on offensive operations in a distant province; however, as it was understood that the Governor of Nova Scotia had, by proclamation, forbid any incursions or depredations upon our territories, and as an opinion generally prevailed that the Governor had no au-

The Militia.

thority to call the militia into actual service, unless one of the exigencies contemplated by the Constitution exists, I thought it expedient to call the Council together, and having laid before them your letter, and those I had received from General Dearborn, I requested their advice on the subject of them.

The Council advised, " That they are unable, from a view of the Constitution of the United States, and the letters aforesaid, to perceive that any exigency exists which can render it advisable to comply with the said requisition ; but as, upon important questions of law, and upon solemn occasions, the Governor and Council have authority to require the opinion of the Justices of the Supreme Judicial Court, it is advisable to request the opinion of the Supreme Court upon the following questions, viz :

" 1st. Whether the Commanders-in-chief of the militia of the several States have a right to determine whether any of the exigencies contemplated by the Constitution of the United States exist, so as to require them to place the militia, or any part of it, in the service of the United States, at the request of the President, to be commanded by him pursuant to acts of Congress.

" 2d. Whether, when either of the exigencies exist, authorizing the employing the militia in the service of the United States, the militia, thus employed, can be lawfully commanded by any officer but of the militia, except by the President of the United States."

I enclose a copy of the answers given by the judges to these questions.

Since the Council were called, a person deputed by the towns of Eastport and Robinston, on our eastern boundary, at Passamaquoddy, applied to me, representing that they had no apprehensions of invasion by an authorized British force, but that there were many lawless people on the borders, from whom they were in danger of predatory incursions, and requesting that they might be furnished with some arms and ammunition, and that three companies of militia might be called out for their protection. The Council advised that they should be supplied with such arms and ammunition as were necessary for their present defence, which has been ordered. They also advised me to call into the service of the United States, three companies of the detached militia, for the purpose abovementioned. I have this day issued an order for calling out three companies of the detached militia, to be marched forthwith to Passamaquoddy, and to be commanded by a major; two of the companies will be stationed at Eastport, and one company at Robinston, until the President shall otherwise direct.

I have no intention officially to interfere in the measures of the General Government; but, if the President was fully acquainted with the situation of this State, I think he would have no wish to call our militia into service in the manner proposed by General Dearborn.

It is well known that the enemy will find it difficult to spare troops sufficient for the defence

of their own territory, and predatory incursions are not likely to take place in this State ; for, at every point, except Passamaquoddy, which can present an object to those incursions, the people are too numerous to be attacked by such parties as generally engage in expeditions of that kind.

General Dearborn proposed that the detached militia should be stationed at only a few of the ports and places on the east; from the rest, a part of their militia were to be called away. This circumstance would increase their danger; it would invite the aggressions of the enemy, and diminish their power of resistance.

The whole coast of Cape Cod is exposed as much as any part of the State to depredations; part of the militia must, according to this leading order, be marched from their houses; and yet no place in the old colony of Plymouth is assigned to be the rendezvous of any of the detached militia.

Every harbor or port within the State has a compact settlement, and, generally, the country around the harbors is populous. The places contemplated in General Dearborn's specification, as the rendezvous of the detached militia, excepting in one or two instances, contain more of the militia than the portion of the detached militia assigned to them. The militia are well organized, and would undoubtedly prefer to defend their firesides, in company with their friends, under their own officers, rather than be marched to some distant place, while strangers might be introduced to take their places at home.

In Boston the militia is well disciplined, and could be mustered in an hour upon any signal of an approaching enemy; and in six hours the neighboring towns would pour in a greater force than any invading enemy will bring against it.

The same remark applies to Salem, Marblehead, and Newburyport; places where harbors render an invasion next to impossible. In all of them there are, in addition to the common militia, independent corps of infantry and artillery, well disciplined and equipped, and ready, both in disposition and means, to repair to any place where invasion may be threatened, and able to repel it, except it should be made by a fleet of heavy ships; against which, nothing perhaps but strong fortifications, garrisoned by regular troops, would prove any defence until the enemy should land, when the entire militia would be prepared to meet them.

Kennebunk is unassailable by any thing but boats, which the numerous armed population is competent to resist. Portland has a numerous and independent corps, sufficiently numerous for its defence; and the same is the case with Wiscasset and Castine.

Against predatory incursions the militia of each place would be able to defend their property, and in a very short time they would be able, if necessary, by the militia of the surrounding country. In case of a more serious attack, whole brigades or divisions could be assembled seasonably for defence. Indeed, considering the state of the militia in this Commonwealth, I

The Militia.

think there can be no doubt that, detaching a part of it, and distributing it into small portions, will tend to impair the defensive power.

I have thus freely expressed to you my own sentiments, and, so far as I have heard, they are the sentiments of the best informed men. I am fully disposed to afford all the aid to the measures of the National Government which the Constitution requires of me; but, I presume, it will not be expected or desired that I shall fail in the duty which I owe to the people of this State, who have confided their interests to my care.

I am, sir, with respect, your most obedient and humble servant,

CALEB STRONG.

Hon. Wm. Eustis,
     Secretary of War.

To his Excellency the Governor and the Honorable the Council of the Commonwealth of Massachusetts, the undersigned, Justices of the Supreme Judicial Court, have considered the questions proposed by your Excellency and Honors for their opinion.

By the Constitution of this State, the authority of commanding the militia of the Commonwealth is vested exclusively in the Governor, who has all the power incident to the office of Commander-in-Chief, and is to exercise them personally, or by subordinate officers under his command, agreeably to the rules and regulations of the Constitution and the laws of the land.

While the Governor of the Commonwealth remained in the exercise of these powers, the Federal Constitution was ratified; by which was vested in the Congress a power to provide for calling forth the militia to execute the laws of the Union, suppress insurrections, and repel invasions, and to provide for governing such part of them as may be employed in the service of the United States, reserving to the States, respectively, the appointment of the officers.

The Federal Constitution further provides, that the President shall be Commander-in-Chief of the Army of the United States, and of the militia of the several States when called into the actual service of the United States.

On the construction of the Federal and State constitutions must depend the answers to the several questions proposed. As the militia of the several States may be employed in the service of the United States, for the three specific purposes of executing the laws of the Union, of suppressing insurrections, and of repelling invasions, the opinion of the judges is requested, whether the Commanders-in-Chief of the militia of the several States have a right to determine whether any of the exigencies aforesaid exist, so as to require them to place the militia, or any part of it, in the service of the United States, at the request of the President, to be commanded by him, pursuant to acts of Congress.

It is the opinion of the undersigned that this right is vested in the Commanders-in-Chief of the militia of the several States.

The Federal Constitution provides that, whenever either of those exigencies exist, the militia may be employed pursuant to some act of Congress, in the service of the United States; but no power is given, either to the President or to Congress, to determine that either of the said exigencies do in fact exist. As this power is not delegated to the United States by the Federal Constitution, nor prohibited by it to the States, it is reserved to the States, respectively; and from the nature of the power, it must be exercised by those with whom the States have respectively intrusted the chief command of the militia.

It is the duty of these commanders to execute this important trust, agreeably to the laws of their several States, respectively, without reference to the laws or officers of the United States, in all cases except those specially provided in the Federal Constitution. They must, therefore, determine when either of the special cases exist, obliging them to relinquish the execution of this trust, and to render themselves and the militia subject to the command of the President. A different construction, giving to Congress the right to determine when these special cases exist, authorizing them to call forth the whole of the militia, and taking them from the Commanders-in-Chief of the several States, and subjecting them to the command of the President, would place all the militia, in effect, at the will of Congress, and produce a military consolidation of the States, without any Constitutional remedy, against the intentions of the people when ratifying the Constitution. Indeed, since passing the act of Congress of February 28th, 1795, chapter 101, vesting in the President the power of calling forth the militia, when the exigencies mentioned in the Constitution shall exist, if the President has the power of determining when those exigencies exist, the militia of the several States is, in effect, at his command, and subject to his control.

No inconveniences can reasonably be presumed to result from the construction which vests in the Commanders-in-Chief of the militia in the several States, the right of determining when the exigencies exist, obliging them to place the militia in the service of the United States. These exigencies are of such a nature that the existence of them can be easily ascertained by, or made known to, the Commanders-in-Chief of the militia; and when ascertained, the public interest will produce prompt obedience to the acts of Congress.

Another question proposed to the consideration of the judges is, whether, when either of the exigencies exist, authorizing the employing of the militia in the service of the United States, the militia thus employed can be lawfully commanded by any officer but of the militia, except by the President of the United States?

The Federal Constitution declares, that the President shall be Commander-in-Chief of the Army of the United States. He may, undoubtedly, exercise this command by officers of the Army of the United States, by him commissioned according to law. The President is also declared to be the Commander-in-Chief of the militia of the several States, when called into the actual service of the United States. The officers of the militia are to be appointed by the States, and the President may exercise his command of the militia by officers of the militia duly appointed; but we know of no Constitutional provision, authorizing any officer of the Army of the United States to command the militia, or authorizing any officer of the militia to command the Army of the United States. The Congress may provide laws for the government of the militia when in actual service; but to extend this power to the placing them under the command of an officer, not of the militia, except the President, would render nugatory the provision, that the militia are to have officers appointed by the States.

The union of the militia in the actual service of the United States, with troops of the United States, so far as to form one army, seems to be a case not provided for, or contemplated in the Constitution. It is, therefore, not within our department to determine on whom the command would devolve, on such an emergency, in the absence of the President. Whether one officer, either of the militia or of the army of the United States, to be settled according to military rank, should command the whole; whether the corps must be commanded by their respective officers, acting in concert, as allied forces; or what other expedient should be adopted, are questions to be answered by others.

The undersigned regret that the distance of the other justices of the Supreme Judicial Court renders it impracticable to obtain their opinions seasonably upon the questions submitted.

THEOPHILUS PARSONS,
SAMUEL SEWALL,
ISAAC PARKER.

Extract of a letter from General Dearborn to the Secretary of War, dated

Mil. Dist., No. 1, Headquarters.
Boston, July 14, 1814.

Sir: From the exposed and unprotected situation of the military posts in this harbor, and the seaboard of this State generally, and the threats and daily depredations of the enemy, I have concluded it my duty to exercise the authority vested in me by the President of the United States, by requesting the Governor to order out a detachment of artillery and infantry.

A copy of my letter to Governor Strong, and of his answer, are enclosed.

Copy of a letter from General Dearborn to His Excellency Caleb Strong, Governor of the State of Massachusetts, dated

Mil. Dist., No. 1, Headquarters,
Boston, July 8, 1814.

Sir: The existing state of alarm on the seaboard of this Commonwealth, arising from the daily depredations committed by the enemy on our coast, renders it desirable to afford some additional protection to the citizens generally on the seacoast, and especially to the principal towns and villages; and by virtue of authority derived from the President of the United States, I deem it my duty, at this time, to request that your Excellency will be pleased to give the necessary orders for having detached, as early as circumstances will permit, armed, and equipped as required by law, one major of artillery, *two* captains, eight lieutenants, thirteen sergeants, eleven corporals, six musicians, and two hundred *privates*; and one lieutenant colonel of infantry, two majors, ten captains, thirty subalterns, one adjutant, one quartermaster, one paymaster, one sergeant major, one quartermaster sergeant, two principal musicians, fifty sergeants, fifty corporals, twenty musicians, and nine hundred privates, to remain in the service of the United States for the term of three months, unless sooner discharged by order of the President of the United States. As it will be necessary to have the artillery and infantry placed at the different posts on the seaboard of this State, it would be desirable that, as far as practicable, they would be detached from the vicinity of the respective posts. The intended distribution of the detachment will be communicated to the Adjutant General of the State previous to his issuing the necessary orders. The proportion of officers, non-commissioned officers, musicians, and privates, is in conformity with the present regulations of the Department of War, from which I am not authorized to admit of any material deviation.

Copy of a letter from his Excellency Caleb Strong, Governor of the State of Massachusetts, to General Dearborn, dated

NORTHAMPTON, *July 12, 1814.*
Sir: This morning I received your *letter* of the eighth instant. As you propose to communicate to General Brooks your views concerning the particular destination of the militia to be called out for the defence of the towns on the seacoast of this State, I have written to him on the subject.

Your suggestion that the men should be detached, as far as may be, from the vicinity of the respective posts, I think is perfectly proper, and I have no doubt you will be able to make *such* arrangements with General Brooks as *will be* satisfactory.

Extract of a letter from General Dearborn to the Secretary of War, dated

Mil. Dist., No. 1, Headquarters,
Boston, Sept. 5, 1814.

Sir: Having received such information *as is* entitled to full credit, that the enemy, with a formidable naval and land force, has arrived in Penobscot Bay; and taken possession of Castine; and presuming his force, after forming a place of arms at Castine, will, with such reinforcements as he may receive from Halifax, in addition to

The Militia.

the naval force now in Boston Bay, attempt the destruction of the public ships, and other public and private property on the seaboard, I have deemed it necessary to request the Governors of this State and New Hampshire to order out, for the defence of Boston harbor, Portsmouth, Portland, and that part of the District of Maine between Kennebec river and Penobscot, five thousand two hundred infantry and five hundred and fifty artillery, for the term of three months, unless sooner discharged.

Extract of a letter from H. Dearborn to the Secretary of War, dated

HEADQUARTERS, DISTRICT No. 1,
Boston, October 15, 1814.

SIR: In obedience to the direction in your letter, of the 27th ultimo, on the 2d instant I made a formal requisition on Governor Strong for three hundred militia, to guard the prisoners at Pittsfield, and I enclosed to him a copy of your letter, for the purpose of showing him the necessity of his compliance. Having waited until yesterday morning without any answer from his Excellency, I directed one of my aids to call on the Adjutant General of the State, to ascertain whether he had received any order for making out the detachment for Pittsfield. The answer was, that no direction had been received from the Governor to make such detachment.

Copy of a letter from his Excellency Caleb Strong, Governor of the State of Massachusetts, to the Secretary of War, dated

BOSTON, September 7, 1814.

The troops of the United States which, at different periods, were stationed on the seacoast of this State, have been afterwards ordered to join the army on the Western frontiers, so that very few have remained in the State. We have, therefore, found it necessary, in the course of the last and present year, to call out small bodies of the militia, as guards to the towns most exposed. As the danger has increased, the number of detached militia has been augmented, and I have now issued the enclosed general order for the protection of Boston, and the towns and property in its neighborhood, and shall immediately issue an order of a similar kind for the security of the District of Maine.

A few weeks since, agreeably to the request of General Dearborn, I detached eleven hundred militia, for three months, for the defence of our seacoast, and placed them under his command as superintendent of this military district; but such objections and inconveniences have arisen from that measure, that it cannot now be repeated. The militia called out on this occasion will be placed under the immediate command of a Major General of the militia.

I will thank you, sir, to consult with the President, and inform me whether the expenses thus necessarily incurred for our protection will be ultimately reimbursed to this State by the General Government; and I shall be particularly obliged if you will favor me with an answer soon as may be, as the Legislature of the State will meet on the 6th of the next month.

Commonwealth of Massachusetts.

HEADQUARTERS, BOSTON,
September 6, 1814.

General Orders:

The war between the United States and Great Britain having lately become more destructive, in consequence of violations of our territory by the forces of the enemy, which continue to menace our cities and villages, the shipping in our harbors, and private property on shore, his Excellency the Commander-in-Chief orders the whole of the militia to hold themselves in readiness to march at a moment's warning, with arms, ammunition, and accoutrements, as the laws of the United States and of this State require. Every man must likewise be provided with a good knapsack and blanket. Captains of companies must realize it to be one of their most solemn and imperious duties to see the law respecting arms and equipments efficaciously executed; but the Commander-in-Chief relies on the concurring aid of all the general and field officers, in encouraging the company officers in the discharge of their duty. The Major Generals and commanding officers of divisions will give the necessary orders for an immediate inspection of their several regiments by companies. Every instance of deficiency of arms or equipments should be forthwith supplied by the delinquent individual, or by the town to which he may belong, agreeably to the requirements of the militia law.

The officers commanding regiments, battalions, and companies of artillery, will pay special attention, at this interesting moment, to the state of their field pieces, their carriages, and tumbrils, and see that everything appertaining to them is in the most perfect order for marching and for action, and particularly that suitable horses are always engaged, and ready at any moment to be attached to their pieces, that they may be moved to any point required with celerity. All the companies of artillery now to be called into immediate service, besides the requisite supplies of fixed and other ammunition, will be furnished by the Quartermaster General, with prolonges and briooles. The Legislature of this State, always proud of its militia, has been particularly liberal in its artillery establishment; and the Commander-in-Chief promises himself, that, emulating the brilliant example of Knox and his heroic associates in the artillery of the Revolution, they will be equally distinguished for their discipline as soldiers, and for their gallantry in the field.

Under possible events, the cavalry of the several divisions may be in requisition. Every motive, therefore, of love of country, of honor, and sympathy for their fellow-citizens who may be suffering the perils of war, will prompt them to maintain the most perfect state of preparation, and to move, when called to the scene of action, with all the rapidity of which cavalry is susceptible. The general officers, and the field officers of cavalry, as well as the company officers, will direct their attention to the quality of the horses, and suffer no man to be mounted but upon a horse sound and fit for actual service. A few bad horses may occasion irretrievable disaster.

The Commander-in-Chief having thus called the attention of all officers and soldiers of the militia to the observance of their several duties, at this eventful crisis, the more effectually to meet impending danger orders that all the flank companies, whether of light infantry, grenadiers, or riflemen, of the 1st and 2d brigades of the 1st division; two companies, viz: the one at Andover, and the other at Haverhill, of the 2d division; all the companies of the 3d division, excepting the two companies in Charlestown; four companies of the 4th division; five companies of the 5th division; eight companies of the 7th division; and two companies of the 9th division, do immediately march to the town of Boston, unless (in the meantime) otherwise directed. Each company will march to its place of destination by itself, without waiting for any other corps.

These companies, when assembled, will be arranged into regiments, or otherwise, as circumstances may dictate; and, with the addition of twelve companies of artillery, will form the elite, or advance corps of the Massachusetts militia. The field officers to command the regiments, and a general officer to command the whole, will hereafter be designated in general orders. The several companies of artillery, to be annexed to the advance corps, will be furnished by the following divisions, viz: two companies from the first brigade, and one company from the 2d brigade of the 3d division; four companies from the 4th division; one company from the 5th division; and four companies from the 7th division.

Besides the abovementioned companies, the Commander-in-Chief orders a detachment of sixteen companies of infantry to be immediately made from the fourth division, properly officered, and arranged into two regiments, which will march to Boston without the least unnecessary delay. Major General Mattoon is charged with the arrangement of the regiments.

From the 9th division, the Commander-in-Chief orders eight companies of infantry to be detached, properly officered, formed into a regiment, and marched to Boston. Major Generals Mattoon and Whiton will assign field officers for the troops to be detached from their respective divisions; and the Commander-in-Chief relies on their experience and zeal to carry this order into the most prompt and energetic effect. As soon as the troops shall commence their march, each Major General will give notice of it to the Adjutant General.

All the troops must be well armed, accoutred, and equipped, and provided with ammunition, provisions, knapsacks, and blankets, as the law requires. The men will be supplied with rations when they arrive at the place of destination, and will receive pay from the time of their being embodied.

The security of the town and harbor of Boston being an object of primary importance, the Commander-in-Chief, while he wishes to direct the principal energies of the State to the attainment of this end, is solicitous to render the militia of Boston itself as efficient as possible. With this view he orders the infantry of the 2d brigade of the 1st division, commanded by Brigadier General Welles, to be called out by regiments in rotation, two days successively, for the purpose of improving their discipline, already respectable, and of enabling them to practise the higher tactics of the field. This order is committed to Brigadier General Welles, whose knowledge in tactics, and animated zeal in the service of his country, are a sure to his exertions the highest effect. The order will be continued in operation until revoked. The flank companies of this brigade will be reserved for other service.

The troops called into actual service by this order, will serve three months after they arrive at their ultimate rendezvous, unless sooner discharged. By his Excellency's command.

—— ——, *Adjutant General.*

Copy of a letter from James Monroe, Secretary of War, to his Excellency Caleb Strong, Governor of Massachusetts, dated

SEPTEMBER 17, 1814.

SIR: I have had the honor to receive your Excellency's letter of the 7th instant.

The attack of the enemy on Baltimore, and probable eventual attack on other places, with the heavy duties incident thereto, pressing on this Department, have prevented my answering it at an earlier day.

It may be satisfactory to your Excellency for me to explain the views and principles on which this Government has acted, in regard to the defence of our Eastern frontier.

It was anticipated, soon after the commencement of the war, that, while it lasted, every part of the Union, especially the sea board, would be exposed to some degree of danger, greater or less, according to the spirit with which the war might be waged. It was the duty of the Government to make the best provision against that danger which might be practicable, and it was proper that the provision should continue while a cause existed.

The arrangement of the United States into military districts, with a certain portion of the regular force, artillery, and infantry, under an officer of the regular army, of experience and high rank, in each district, with power to call for the militia as circumstances might require, was adopted, with a view to afford the best protection to every part that circumstances would admit.

It was presumed that the establishment of a small force of the kind stated, constituting the first elements of an army, in each district to be aided by the militia, in case of an emergency,

The Militia.

would be adequate to its defence. Such a force of infantry and artillery might repel small predatory parties, and form a rallying point for the militia at the more exposed and important stations, in case of more formidable invasion. A regular officer, of experience, stationed in the district, acting under the authority, and pushing the will, of the Government, might digest plans for its defence; select proper points for works, and superintend the erection of them; call for supplies of ordnance, for tents, and camp equipage; for small arms, and other munitions of war; call for the militia, and dispose of the whole force. These duties, it was believed, could not be performed with equal advantage by the officers of the militia, who, being called into service for short terms, would not have it in their power, however well qualified they might be in other respects, to digest plans, and preserve that chain of connexion and system in the whole business which seemed indispensable. On great consideration, this arrangement was deemed the most eligible that could be adopted under the authority of the United States; indeed, none other occurred that could be placed in competition with it. In this mode the National Government acts, by its proper organs, over whom it has control, and for whose engagements it is responsible.

The measures which may be adopted by a State Government for the defence of a State must be considered as its own measures, and not those of the United States. The expenses attending them are chargeable to the State, and not to the United States.

Your Excellency will perceive that a different construction would lead into the most important, and, as is believed, into the most pernicious consequences. If a State could call out the militia, and subject the United States to the expense of supporting them, at its pleasure, the national authority would cease, as to that important object, and the nation be charged with expenses, in the measures producing which the National Government had no agency, and over which it could have no control. This, however, though a serious objection to such a construction, is not the most weighty. By taking the defence of the State into its own hands, and out of those of the General Government, a policy is introduced, on the tendency of which I forbear to comment. I shall remark, only, that, if a close union of the States, and a harmonious co-operation between them and the General Government, are, at any time, necessary for the preservation of their independence, and of those inestimable liberties which were achieved by the valor and blood of our ancestors, that period may be considered as having arrived.

It follows, from this view of the subject, that, if the force which has been put into service by your Excellency has been required by Major General Dearborn, or received by him and put under his command, the expenses attending it will be defrayed by the United States. It follows, likewise, as a necessary consequence, that, if this force has been called into service by the authority of the State, independently of Major General Dearborn, and be not placed under him, as commander of the district, that the State of Massachusetts is chargeable with the expense, and not the United States. Any claim which the State may have to reimbursement must be judged of hereafter, by the competent authority, on a full view of all the circumstances attending it. It is a question which lies beyond the authority of the Executive.

Your Excellency will perceive that this Government has no other alternative than to adhere to a system of defence, which was adopted, on great consideration, with the best view to the general welfare, or to abandon it, and with it a principle held sacred, thereby shrinking from its duty, at a moment of great peril, weakening the guards deemed necessary for the public safety, and opening the door to other consequences not less dangerous.

By these remarks it is not intended to convey the idea that a militia officer, of superior grade, regularly called into service, shall not command an officer of the regular army of inferior grade, when acting together. No such idea is entertained by the Government. The militia are relied on essentially for the defence of the country: in their hands everything is safe. It is the object of the Government to impose on them no burdens which it may be possible to avoid, and to protect them, in the discharge of their duties, in the enjoyment of all their rights.

The various points which are attacked and menaced by the enemy, especially in this quarter, where they are waging, in considerable force, a predatory and desolating warfare, make it difficult to provide immediately for all the necessary expenditures. Any aid which the State of Massachusetts may afford to the United States to meet those expenditures, will be cheerfully received, and applied to the payment and support of the militia of that State in the service of the United States.

It will be proper that the money thus advanced should be deposited in some bank in Boston, that the disbursement of it may be made under the authority of the Government of the United States, as in similar cases elsewhere. Credit will be given to the State for such advances, and the amount be considered a loan to the United States.

I have the honor to be, &c.

[A similar letter was written to the Governor of Connecticut.]

SHARON, (CONN.,) *July* 2, 1812.

SIR: His Excellency Governor Griswold has received from Major General Henry Dearborn a letter, under date of the 22d of last month, requesting that five companies of the militia of this State, detached conformably to the act of Congress, of April 10, 1812, may be ordered into the service of the United States, to wit: two companies of artillery, and two companies of infantry, to be placed under the command of the commanding officer at Fort Trumbull, near New London; and one company of artillery, to be stationed at the battery at the entrance of the harbor of New Haven.

Impressed with the deep importance of the requisition, and the serious consideration it involves, his Excellency deemed it expedient to convene the Council, at Hartford, on Monday, the 29th ultimo. He has taken their advice upon this interesting subject, and has formed his own deliberate opinion; but, as he is under the necessity of leaving the State on a journey, for the recovery of his health, it becomes my duty, as Lieutenant Governor, to communicate to you the result. The assurance contained in the Governor's letter of the 17th June last, in answer to yours of the 12th of the same month, was necessarily given in full confidence that no demand would be made by General Dearborn, but in strict conformity to the Constitution and laws of the United States. His Excellency regrets to perceive that the present requisition is supported by neither.

The Constitution of the United States has ordained that Congress may "provide for calling forth the militia to execute the laws of the Union, suppress insurrections, and repel invasions." Accordingly the acts of Congress, of February, 1795, and of April, 1812, do provide for calling forth the militia in the exigencies abovementioned.

The Governor is not informed of any declaration, made by the President of the United States, or of notice by him given, that the militia are required "to execute the laws of the Union, suppress insurrections, or repel invasions," or that "the United States are in imminent danger of invasion." As, therefore, none of the contingencies enumerated in the Constitution, and recognised by the laws, are known to have taken place, his Excellency considers that no portion of the militia of this State can, under existing circumstances, be withdrawn from his authority.

Further, if the call had been justified by either of the Constitutional exigencies already cited, still, in the view of his Excellency, an insuperable objection presents itself against placing the men under the immediate command of an officer or officers of the Army of the United States. The appointment of the officers of the militia is, by the Constitution, expressly reserved "to the States, respectively." In the event of their being called into the actual service of the United States, in the cases before specified, the laws of the United States provide for their being called forth as militia, furnished with proper officers by the State. And, sir, it will not escape your recollection, that the detachment from the militia of this State, under the act of Congress of the 10th of April last, is regularly organized into a division, consisting of brigades, regiments, battalions, and companies, and supplied, conformably to law, with all the necessary officers. His Excellency conceives, then, that an order to detach a number of companies, sufficient for the command of a battalion officer, and place them under the command of an officer of the United States, cannot with propriety be executed, unless we were also prepared to admit that the privates may be separated from their company officers, and transferred into the Army of the United States; thus leaving the officers of the militia without any command, but in name, and in effect impairing, if not annihilating, the militia itself, so sacredly guarantied by the Constitution to the several States.

Under these impressions the Governor has thought proper, by and with the advice of the Council, to refuse a compliance with the requisition of Major General Dearborn.

His Excellency is sincerely disposed to comply promptly with all the Constitutional *requests of* the National Executive—a disposition *which has* ever been manifested by the Government of this State; and he laments the occasion which thus compels him to yield obedience to the paramount authority of the Constitution and laws of the United States. He trusts the General Government will speedily provide an adequate force for the security and protection of the seacoast. In the meantime his Excellency has issued the necessary orders to the General officers commanding the militia in that quarter, to be in readiness to repel any invasion which may be attempted upon that portion of the State; and to co-operate with such part of the National forces as shall be employed for the same purpose.

With great respect, I am, &c.
JOHN COTTON SMITH.

Hon. WILLIAM EUSTIS,
    Secretary of War.

Extract of a letter from his Excellency John Cotton Smith, to the Secretary of War, dated

NEW LONDON, *June* 7, 1813.

I arrived at this place on the 5th instant, and found about six hundred of the militia of this State stationed on the two sides of the river, who had been assembled under the circumstances mentioned in my letter from Hartford, of the 2d inst.

I shall not disband any part of the militia *until* a communication is received from Commodore Decatur, being heartily disposed to assist his views in affording all possible protection to the squadron and harbor. I will address you again before my departure from this place, and, in the meantime, am desirous of receiving the instructions of the President as to the course proper to be pursued.

Extract of a letter from his Excellency John Cotton Smith, to the Secretary of War, dated

NEW LONDON, *June* 12, 1813.

On a consultation with Commodore Decatur, as proposed in my last, it was concluded to retain the whole of the militia then assembled, until their places could be supplied by two regiments drawn from the neighborhood. Orders were issued accordingly.

But, on the arrival of the two regiments, information was received that a bomb ketch had been added to the enemy's squadron, and that preparations were evidently making for an attack. At the instance of Commodore Decatur, who knows best his own capacity of meeting the exigency,

The Militia.

and on whose opinion, therefore, I must greatly rely, the whole force was directed to remain, excepting such individuals as were under a pressing necessity of returning to their homes. The number of militia now here is about fifteen hundred, including officers.

Extract of a letter from his Excellency John Cotton Smith, to the Secretary of War, dated

NEW LONDON, *June* 16, 1812.

Your favor of the 12th instant is received, and has afforded me much pleasure.

The details in my letter of the 12th instant, I trust, will fully justify, in the view of the President, the additional force it was then thought necessary to employ. After closing my despatches on that day, the hostile fleet got under sail, approached the harbor, and fired several shots at the guards, and, to all appearance, were meditating an attack.

Whether the display of so respectable a body of troops, or some other cause, discouraged them from the attempt is not known. The enterprise was for that time abandoned, and on the 14th two of their ships passed eastward, out of the Sound.

As soon as information of this diminution of the squadron was received, orders were issued to disband the two regiments that were first brought into the field, and a further reduction of the troops is this day made, to the number mentioned in your letter.

Extract of a letter from his Excellency John Cotton Smith, to the Secretary of War, dated

STATE OF CONNECTICUT,
Sharon, August 1, 1814.

Your letter of the 4th July last reached me on the 16th of the same month.

Although there appears to be no act of Congress expressly authorizing a detachment from the militia, for the purpose mentioned in your communication, yet the respect due to a recommendation from the President, having for its object the defence of the country, induced me, without unnecessary delay, to convene the Council of the State, and to submit the proposition to their consideration.

That honorable body having advised the Executive to detach the number of militia suggested, as the proportion of Connecticut, orders were immediately issued to that effect, and you will be speedily informed, by the proper officer, of their execution.

Copy of a letter from General Cushing to his Excellency Governor Smith, dated

MIL. DIST., No. 2, HEADQUARTERS,
New London, Aug. 1, 1814.

SIR: I have been notified by the Secretary of War that, on the 4th day of July last, a requisition was made on the Executive of the State of Connecticut for a body of militia, to be organized and held in readiness for immediate service; and I am instructed by him, "in case of actual or menaced invasion of the district under my command, to call for a part or the whole of the quotas assigned to the States of Connecticut and Rhode Island, which shall have been organized and equipped under the aforesaid requisition." But in the performance of this duty I am charged "to avoid all unnecessary calls; to proportion the calls to the exigency; and to have inspected, without delay, all corps entering on the service, to the end that men who, from any cause, are unfit therefor, be promptly discharged, and that a due proportion, in all cases, be maintained between officers and privates."

It is not deemed necessary to call any part of the quota of Connecticut into the service of the United States at this time; but it is desirable that the draught be made, and the men held in readiness for immediate service, whenever circumstances may indicate an intention on the part of the enemy to invade any part of the State. And I have, therefore, to request your Excellency to inform me whether the quota of militia required of this State by the aforesaid requisition has been, or will be "organized and held in readiness for immediate service?" whether, on my requisition, the whole or any part of the said militia will be ordered into the service of the United States in the first instance, or to such General and field officers as may have been detailed for this service? and, generally, that your Excellency would be pleased to favor me with such information and opinions, in relation to the objects and designs of the enemy, and to the defence of this State, as you may think proper to communicate.

I have only to add that, as commanding officer of this military district, it will be my constant endeavor to preserve the strictest harmony and good will between the National troops and the militia; and that the rights of the latter, as secured by the Constitution and laws of our country, shall be duly respected by every officer and soldier under my command.

Extracts of a letter from John C. Smith to General Cushing, dated

STATE OF CONNECTICUT,
Sharon, August 4, 1814.

"I have the pleasure to acknowledge the receipt of your letter of the 1st instant.

"The Adjutant General is directed to send you a transcript of the General Orders, issued on the 28th ultimo, for organizing and holding in readiness a body of militia, pursuant to a recommendation from the President of the United States. To that document I must refer you for answers to most of your inquiries."

"The militia, whenever their services are required, will expect to march under orders received from their Commander-in-Chief; and such orders as the exigency demand, you may rest assured, shall be promptly given."

The Militia.

STATE OF CONNECTICUT,
Hartford, July 28, 1814.
General Orders:.

The Commander-in-Chief has received a communication from the President of the United States, inviting the Executives of certain States to organize, and hold in readiness for immediate service, a corps of ninety-three thousand five hundred men, "as a measure of precaution to strengthen ourselves on the line of the Atlantic," and assigning, as the quota of Connecticut, three hundred artillery, and two thousand seven hundred infantry, with a detail of General and Staff officers.

The Commander-in-Chief having thought proper, by advice of the Council, to comply with the recommendation, directs that dispositions be immediately made for carrying the same into effect.

Accordingly the number of artillery and infantry abovementioned, including the regimental officers, will be detached from the militia of the State, exempting from the draught such as have, either in person or by substitute, performed a tour of duty the present season. Volunteer uniform companies will be accepted. The whole to be formed into four regiments, and duly officered. Their places of rendezvous as follows, to wit: for the first regiment, Hartford; for the second, New Haven; for the third, Norwich; and for the fourth, Fairfield. One Major General and one Brigadier General will be detailed in the usual manner; also one Deputy Quartermaster General; and, instead of an Assistant Adjutant General, (there being no such officer in the militia of this State,) there shall be detailed one Division Inspector.

The troops thus detached are to be completely armed and equipped according to law, and, until otherwise directed, will be held in readiness to march at a moment's warning, for the purpose of repelling invasions of the enemy, under such orders as they shall receive from the Commander-in-Chief.

Notwithstanding this arrangement, it is confidently expected that the whole body of militia, and every other description of military force, will bear in mind the general orders issued on the 19th of April last, and will stand in complete readiness for the defence of the State, at this unusual period of difficulty and danger.

E. HUNTINGTON, *Adj. Gen.*

NORWICH, *August* 11, 1814.

SIR: By desire of his Excellency Governor Smith, I have forwarded a copy of his general order, of 28th July, for your information, on some points of inquiry made to him. I am, &c.,
E. HUNTINGTON, *Adj. Gen.*
Brigadier General CUSHING.

Copy of a letter from General Cushing to the Governor of Connecticut, dated
MIL. DIST., No. 2, HEADQUARTERS,
New London, August 10, 1814.

SIR: By Major General Williams's communication of this date, your Excellency will be fully informed of the state of things in this quarter; and by the enclosed district order, that the militia ordered out by him, at my request, are to form a brigade, in the service of the United States, under the command of Brigadier General Isham.

Your Excellency's communication of the 4th instant was received this morning, since which General Williams has furnished me with your general order of the 28th of July; but I have heard nothing from the Adjutant General on this subject.

It is my opinion that the safety of this State requires that fifteen hundred infantry, and two companies of artillery, duly officered, and to be commanded by a Brigadier General of this State's quota of ninety-three thousand five hundred men, required by the President of the United States "to be organized and held in readiness for immediate service," should be immediately detached from the said quota, and ordered to this place, for the purpose of relieving the militia now on duty here, if circumstances should justify the measure, or to increase our means of defence, in the event of more formidable and vigorous operations on the part of the enemy. And I have the honor to request your Excellency to make and place the said detachment under my command. It is desirable that the Brigadier General to be detached on this service should be instructed by your Excellency to report himself to me, by letter, immediately after he shall have been so detached, to inform me of his route to this place, and the probable time of his arrival; and to receive and obey any orders he may receive from me while on his march.

I have the honor to be, &c.,
T. H. CUSHING.
Hon. J. C. SMITH,
Governor of Connecticut.

Copy of Adjutant General P. P. Schuyler's orders, dated
MIL. DIST., No. 2, HEADQUARTERS,
New London, August 10, 1814.

District Orders:

The militia of this State, ordered into service yesterday by Major General Williams, at the request of the Commanding General of the district, are to be considered in the service of the United States, and will form a brigade, under the command of Brigadier General Isham, who will furnish a return, by regiments, to the Adjutant General of the district the soonest possible.

Until the proper returns of General Isham's brigade can be obtained, the contractor will issue provisions on the requisitions of Major Goddard, countersigned by the Commanding General; and the Major will be held responsible for the proper application of all provisions so received, and which must be covered by regular returns, as soon as the strength of the brigade can be ascertained.

By order of the Commanding General.
P. P. SCHUYLER,
Adjutant General.

Extract of a letter from Brigadier General T. H. Cushing to the Secretary of War, dated

MIL. DIST., No. 2, HEADQUARTERS,
New London, Aug. 12, 1814, 10 o'clock, P. M.

"By the letter of the 11th instant, from Governor Smith, of which I enclose a copy, you will see that he has ordered the militia called for on the 10th; but, for the reasons therein stated, claims the right of placing a Major General at their head. I shall endeavor to satisfy him that, with the number of men called for, a Major General cannot be received; but, if he should persist, how is the difficulty to be gotten over?"

Extract of a letter from John Cotton Smith to General Cushing, dated

STATE OF CONNECTICUT, SHARON,
August 11, 1814, 9 o'clock, A. M.

"Your communication, by express, is this moment received.

"Major General Williams is directed to retain the militia now on duty until they shall be relieved by the force ordered out, conformably to your request, or unless circumstances shall justify an earlier dismission.

"It is probable the draught for the new detachment is not completed; but Brigadier General Lusk, detailed under the orders of the 28th ultimo, is instructed, by the return of the express, to hasten it as fast as possible, and to march, without a moment's delay, with the first and third regiments, whose places of rendezvous are Hartford and Norwich. Their numbers will make the complement you require, including artillery.

"As the force requested by you will constitute a majority of the detachment, there is an evident propriety that it should be commanded by the Major General detailed pursuant to the recommendation of the President. He will accordingly be directed to enter the service as soon as the necessary arrangements will permit. In the meantime Brigadier General Lusk is ordered to report himself to you agreeably to your desire."

Extract of a letter from Brigadier General T. H. Cushing to the Secretary of War, dated

MIL. DIST., No. 2, HEADQUARTERS,
New London, August 29, 1814.

"I deem it proper, at this time, to lay before you a copy of my correspondence with Governor Smith, from the 14th to the 28th, inclusive. Unwilling to relinquish his project for introducing a Major General of militia into the service of the United States, the Governor has attempted to prevail on me to accept a command of six hundred men, to be posted at New Haven, under the command of Major General Taylor, who, it appears, must be provided for.

"I have agreed to accept the men, if properly officered, because it will enable me to discharge an equal number, which must otherwise be marched from this neighborhood; but I have pointedly refused to recognise the Major General, or to have the men mustered and supplied, on any other consideration but that of their being subject to my orders."

Extract of a letter from Brigadier General Cushing to his Excellency John Cotton Smith, Governor of the State of Connecticut, dated

MIL. DIST., No. 2, HEADQUARTERS,
New London, August 14, 1814.

"A brigade in the army of the United States should consist of two thousand men, and the detachment of militia required of your Excellency, by my letter of the 10th instant, does not exceed one thousand seven hundred, which is probably less than any brigade of militia in the State of Connecticut. In asking for a Brigadier General to command this force, I have certainly gone as far as I am authorized by my instructions from the War Department; which are, "that a due proportion, in all cases, be maintained between officers and privates;" and I trust that, on reflection, your Excellency will relinquish the idea of ordering a Major General to assume the command of less than a complete brigade.

"Should circumstances require a further call for men, to an extent equal to a Major General's command, including the one thousand seven hundred, I shall not fail to include that officer in my requisition."

Copy of a letter from Brigadier General Cushing to his Excellency John Cotton Smith, Governor of the State of Connecticut, dated

MIL. DIST., No. 2, HEADQUARTERS,
New London, August 24, 1814.

A copy of your Excellency's letter to me of the 11th instant has been transmitted to the Secretary of War, and I have the honor to enclose an extract of a letter from him on the subject of militia draughts, and a copy of the rules referred to in his letter.

In acting on the late requisition of the President, for three thousand men, to be organized for the service of the United States, I had presumed that your Excellency would have pursued the course suggested by that requisition, and formed the State's quota into three regiments, of one thousand men each; and, under that impression, in my letter of the 10th instant, I did not express the number of privates, non-commissioned and commissioned officers, required. It now appears that a different course has been adopted, and the quota of the State formed into four regiments; but, although, in point of form, there is considerable difference between the three thousand men, as organized by your Excellency, and the same number, as organized in the Army of the United States, yet, as a due proportion between officers and privates will be maintained, and no additional expense incurred, I shall consider the spirit and intention of the rule as having been fully complied with, by the organization which your Excellency has been pleased to direct.

The Militia.

Extract of a letter from his Excellency John Cotton Smith, Governor of the State of Connecticut, to Brigadier General Cushing, dated

HARTFORD, *August* 25, 1814.

" As you seem, sir, not to have understood, correctly, the views of this Government, with respect to the late detachment, it is fit that I state them to you distinctly.

" The communication from the War Department, under date of the 4th July last, relative to a detachment from the militia, for the purpose therein mentioned, did not assume the style of a 'requisition,' and for the obvious reason, that there existed no law to authorize it. The invitation (for such was its purport) was accepted by the Executive of this State, from a desire to co-operate in what appeared to the President a proper measure of defence for the Atlantic coast. The terms of compliance are contained in the general orders issued on the 28th July, a transcript of which you have received. In organizing the regiment, I conformed as nearly as possible to the act of Congress, passed the 8th May, 1792. I am not informed that there is now in operation any other act of the National Legislature on that subject. If your instructions from the War Department materially interfere with the requirements of this act, it is indeed a subject of regret, but not of doubt, as to the authority which ought, in such case, to prevail.

" I am happy, however, to perceive, that you do not consider the difference as essentially varying the result."

Extract of a letter from Brigadier General Cushing to his Excellency John Cotton Smith, Governor of the State of Connecticut, dated

MIL. DIST., No. 2, HEADQUARTERS, *August* 28, 1814.

" Your Excellency's letter of the 25th instant was received last evening, and shall be submitted to the Secretary of War by the next mail.

" Not having the communication from the War Department, under date of the 4th July, before me, when my letter to your Excellency, of the 24th instant, was written, I inadvertently used the term requisition, when I should have employed that of invitation; and I beg leave to assure your Excellency that this was done without any intention or desire of giving to the invitation of the President, or the acceptance of your Excellency, a different understanding from that originally intended."

Extract of a letter from Brigadier General T. H. Cushing to the Secretary of War, dated

MIL. DIST., No. 2, HEADQUARTERS, *New London, Sept.* 2, 1814.

" I have the honor to enclose a copy of a letter from Governor Smith, of the 30th of August, with my reply of this date.

" It is now pretty evident that the Governor and Council have determined that their militia shall not be commanded by an officer of the United States; and it is possible an attempt may be made to withdraw the brigade now in service. I am, however, of opinion, that this will not be done before the meeting of the Legislature."

Copy of a letter from his Excellency John C. Smith to Brigadier General Cushing, dated

HARTFORD, *August* 30, 1814.

SIR : Colonel Wald has delivered me your letter of the 28th instant.

In referring you to the views of this Government respecting the detachment lately organised, it was my design not to criticise your language, but to point your attention to the precise conditions upon which that detachment was formed. The right of command, you will perceive, is expressly reserved. The detachment thus constituted is accepted ; and with a knowledge of the reservation just mentioned, you requested a large portion of the troops for public service. Whatever sentiments, therefore, may be entertained as to the right of the Executive of the State to direct its military force, when ordinarily employed in the national service, it surely cannot be questioned in the present instance. If, at your particular desire, Brigadier General Lusk was ordered to report himself to you, in the manner suggested in my letter of the 11th instant, I trust it evinces a spirit of accommodation which will be duly appreciated.

I think, sir, you will be satisfied, upon reflection, that you should have requested the Major General, when you called for a majority of the detachment; especially if you consider that another brigade of militia was at that time on duty; and, from appearances, the services of both might become necessary. That a Brigadier General of the regular army, with no troops in the field, should insist on the command of two entire brigades of militia, whose Brigadier Generals held senior commissions, would have produced a case which neither precedent nor principle could justify. To avoid so unusual and embarrassing a state of things, it became my duty to order the Major General into service. Having been properly detailed, no casual diminution of numbers can affect his right of command.

I enclose you the opinion of the Council in relation as well to this point as to the employment of a larger force at New Haven and Bridgeport. Their opinion is in perfect accordance with my own, and, therefore, will be carried into effect. The troops destined for these posts will arrive at New Haven on the 8th, and at Bridgeport on the 13th of September next. If no officer of the United States appears to muster them, that duty will be performed by an officer of the militia, agreeably to the late act of Congress. If supplies are withheld by your order, they will be furnished by the proper officers of the State, and charged over to the United States.

It is hoped the services of the third regiment may be dispensed with for the present.

From the harmony with which the service was conducted the last season, under an arrangement

The Militia.

not essentially dissimilar, I flattered myself that a temper equally conciliatory would distinguish the present campaign. Whilst I lament that any difference of opinion should exist as to the particular mode of defending our country, at a moment when its dearest interests are in jeopardy, I cannot lose sight of the high duties which I am solemnly bound to discharge.

Extract from the proceedings of the Governor and Council, at a meeting held at Hartford, the 24th day of August, A. D. 1814.

His Excellency the Governor laid before the Council a correspondence between him and Brigadier General Cushing, in regard to the command of two regiments of the militia of this State, now in service, and requested the advice of the Council thereon.

The Council, on mature deliberation, cannot doubt the right or expediency, under existing circumstances, of having in service, from this State, a Major General, authorized to command such portions of the military force as is, or may be, in service for its defence.

Extract of a letter from General Cushing to John C. Smith, Governor of Connecticut, dated

MIL. DIST., No. 2, HEADQUARTERS,
New London, Sept. 2, 1814.

Your Excellency's letter of the 30th of August was received this morning by the Southern mail.

Whether I have understood " the views of the Government, (Connecticut) respecting the detachment lately organized," or not, is, in my estimation, a question of no importance at this time, since, by referring to my letter of the 10th of August, your Excellency will there find the conditions on which the draughted militia, now in service, were asked for, and have been received into the service of the United States. If these conditions did not accord with the " views of this Government," it is not for me to assign the motive which induced your Excellency to make the detachment; but, while I regret that any misunderstanding should exist on this subject, I feel confident that my communications have been too explicit to leave a doubt as to the course authorized and enjoined by the Government of the United States.

Extract of a letter from his Excellency John Cotton Smith to the Secretary of War, dated

STATE OF CONNECTICUT,
Hartford, Sept. 3, 1814.

In consequence of the exposed and defenceless situation of the town of New Haven, and borough of Bridgeport, I have thought proper, by the advice of the Council, to order into service six hundred men, for the protection of these places.

The general officer of the United States, located at New London, has been advised of this procedure, and has also been requested to cause the troops to be duly mustered and supplied.

He admits the propriety of the measure, but,

as I understand, refuses to comply with the request, and on grounds which, in my view, are wholly inadmissible.

It is my duty, sir, to inform you of these circumstances, and to express the assurance I feel that you will order the requisite supplies to be immediately furnished.

Extract of a letter from his Excellency John Cotton Smith to the Secretary of War, dated

STATE OF CONNECTICUT,
Hartford, Sept. 14, 1814.

I am informed the agent of the United States, at New London, has refused any further subsistence to the militia now on duty in that vicinity, upon the unfounded pretext, that they are withdrawn from service by my authority. Unwilling to hazard the safety of those posts, and the national property in the river, by disbanding the troops, I have directed the Commissary General of the State to provide for them, until the pleasure of the President shall be known.

You will perceive the importance, sir, of apprizing me, without delay, whether the agent is to be countenanced in the course he has thought proper to adopt; and, also, how far I am to rely on the General Government for assistance, in the necessary defence of the State.

[NOTE.—A letter was written to the Governor of Connecticut, in reply to these letters to the Department of War, to the same effect with that to the Governor of Massachusetts, of September 14, 1814.]

Copy of a letter from James Monroe, Secretary of War, to his Excellency John C. Smith, Governor of Connecticut, dated

OCTOBER 17, 1814.

SIR: I have had the honor to receive your Excellency's communication of ——. The letters mentioned in it had been before received.

The regulations of this Department, in conformity to the laws of the United States, having designated commands for different grades of general officers of the militia—two thousand men for a Brigadier General—and General Cushing not having called for more than two thousand men at any time, and there not being more than that number of militia in the field, it was thought that the command of them ought not to be committed to a Major General of the militia.

The tendency of such an arrangement would be to take the force assembled for the defence of the military district, No. 2, out of the hands of the officer to whom the President had intrusted it. It was on this principle that my letter to your Excellency, of the 17th of September, was addressed, and with intention to explain the principles on which the arrangements of this Government were made, for the defence of every part of the United States; which explanation I gave on a belief that it would be satisfactory, and that it was particularly my duty to give it at this very important crisis of our affairs.

The Militia.

It is, however, distinctly to be understood that, if the whole quota assigned to Connecticut had been called into service, it would have been proper to have committed the command to a Major General of the militia. who, in cases where he and a Brigadier General of the Army of the United States acted together, would take the command of him. I have the honor to be, &c.

Copy of a letter from T. H. Cushing, Brigadier General, to the Secretary of War, dated

MIL. DIST., No. 2, HEADQUARTERS,
New London, September 12, 1814.

SIR: The enclosed copies, marked (a) (b) (c) and (d) will show you the situation in which I am placed, with respect to the militia in the State of Connecticut, and that it will be impossible for me to repel any attack of the enemy within its limits, not directed against the forts in this harbor, or the very small and inconsiderable battery in the neighborhood of New Haven.

The letter of Governor Smith was delivered to me yesterday morning, by the Aid of Major General Taylor. I inquired whether his General had been ordered into service by the Government of the United States, and assured him, if this was the case, I would, most cheerfully, resign to him, not only the command of the draughted militia, but of this military district. He replied that General Taylor had no such orders; but that he had been ordered by Governor Smith to take command of the draughted militia of Connecticut, in the service of the United States, and would immediately assume the command, and issue his orders agreeably to the Governor's instructions.

Finding that the usual report of the brigade was not furnished by Brigadier General Lusk, I sent for him to inquire the reason for this neglect, and to admonish him of the consequences which would ensue, in the event of his failing to discharge the duties of his station, as an officer in the service of the United States, and, as such, not accountable to Governor Smith, or any of his militia Generals.

The Brigadier requested a short time to make up his mind, as to the course he should pursue; and I heard nothing more from him until two o'clock this day, when his answer to my note was received, and the enclosed district order immediately issued.

I understand that General Taylor is making arrangements for the supply of Lusk's brigade at this place, and in its neighborhood; and it will readily occur to you that the power to call militia into service, vested in me by the President's proclamation, cannot be exercised to any beneficial result; since, the moment such militia shall have assembled, in pursuance of my requisition, they will be taken from me by State authorities.

I have the honor to be, sir, your most obedient servant,

T. H. CUSHING.

The Hon. JAMES MONROE,
Secretary of War.

(a.)

Copy of a letter from his Excellency John Cotton Smith, Governor of the State of Connecticut, to Brigadier General Cushing, dated

HARTFORD, *Sept.* 1, 1814.

SIR: Conformably to the original arrangement, Major General Taylor now goes to take the command of the militia on duty at New London and its vicinity.

He will retain or reduce their present number, according to existing circumstances. Upon this and other subjects, connected with the safety of those posts, he is instructed, and will be disposed to confer with you freely, and to promote, by all means in his power, that concert of operation on which the success of the service must essentially depend.

(b.)

Extract of a letter from Brigadier General Cushing to Brigadier General Lusk, commanding militia, dated

MIL. DIST., No. 2, HEADQUARTERS,
New London, Sept. 12, 1814.

SIR: The usual reports of the brigade of draughted militia under your command, in the service of the United States, were not delivered to the Adjutant General of the district yesterday, and report says that you have received, and are acting under, the orders of a militia officer, not in the service of the United States.

It has, therefore, become necessary that you assign a reason, in writing, for withholding your reports, and contradict or admit the fact of your having received, and actually executing, the orders of an officer not in the service of the United States.

(c.)

Copy of a letter from Brigadier General Lusk, of the militia, to Brigadier General Cushing, dated

NEW LONDON, *Sept.* 12, 1814.

SIR: I have the honor to acknowledge the receipt of your note of this morning. The following is an extract of the order of his Excellency the Captain General, dated the 28th of July, 1814:

" The troops thus detached, are to be completely armed and equipped according to law, and until otherwise directed, will be held in readiness to march at a moment's warning, for the purpose of repelling invasions of the enemy, under such orders as they shall receive from the Commander-in-Chief."

The following is an extract of a letter of instruction to me, from Governor Smith, dated Sharon, 11th August, 1814:

" You will inform General Cushing, by letter, of your state of readiness, and take his directions as to the route, and place or places of destination, and to conform to his instructions, until the arrival of Major General Taylor, who will take the command as soon as his health and the necessary arrangements will permit."

In addition to the above, Major General Taylor issued his orders to me, under date of the 11th of September, 1814, directing me to discontinue calling at the office of the Commanding General of the district for orders, and to obey no orders excepting such as shall be issued under the authority of this State.

He has also required of me regularly to make report to him of the forces under my command.

From a perusal of the foregoing extracts, you will readily infer the only answer to your interrogations which I have the power to make.

(d.)

Copy of District Orders, dated
MIL. DIST., No. 2, HEADQUARTERS,
     New London, Sept. 12, 1814.

The brigade of draughted militia from the State of Connecticut having been withdrawn from the service of the United States by his Excellency Governor Smith; and Brigadier General Lusk, the commanding officer of the said brigade, having refused to receive and obey the orders of the Brigadier General commanding this military district, no further supplies of any description are to be delivered to him, or his brigade, for and on account of the United States, without an express written order from the Brigadier General commanding, or from his superior officer, actually in the service of the United States.

By order of the Commanding General.
     P. P. SCHUYLER,
         Adjutant General.

Copy of a letter from his Excellency William Jones to the Secretary of War, dated
     PROVIDENCE, *April* 22, 1812.

SIR: I have had the honor to receive your letter, under date of the 15th instant, requiring me to take effectual measures to detach five hundred of the militia of Rhode Island, and that they be armed and equipped for actual service within the shortest period that circumstances will permit.

The General Assembly of this State will be in session in a few days, when I shall embrace the earliest opportunity to lay the request before them.

Copy of a letter from his Excellency William Jones to the Secretary of War, dated
     PROVIDENCE, *June* 18, 1812.

SIR: Your communication of the 12th instant came to hand by last evening's mail; and, in reply, permit me to state that, for the quota of militia required by the act of Congress of April 10, 1812, the General Assembly of this State, at their session, in May last, ordered a return of our militia made on or before the 4th of July next, and that therefrom a draught of the number required will be made, as soon as practicable, and ready for service.

Extract of a letter from his Excellency William Jones to the Secretary of War, dated
     PROVIDENCE, *Aug.* 22, 1812.

I have not been able to obtain an entire return of the men draughted, as this State's quota of militia, alluded to in my last, until the 11th instant. It is now done, and the detachment organized, as per enclosed roll, and will be held in readiness to act, when, *in my opinion,* any of the exigencies provided for by the Constitution, and referred to by the late act of Congress, under which they are detached, exists, agreeably to the opinion and advice of the Council of this State, given me on the occasion.

Extract of a letter from his Excellency William Jones, Governor of the State of Rhode Island, to the President of the United States, dated
     PROVIDENCE, *June* 29, 1814.

The views of the General Assembly, the Council of War, and myself, will be discovered from the act of Assembly. passed at their late session, a copy of which Mr. Searle will present to you, with whom I request you will make all the necessary arrangements for carrying it into full effect.

He will discuss the subject of his mission fully, and, I trust, to your satisfaction, so that the State will, by the assistance of the United States, be placed in a posture of defence, at least, against the predatory incursions of the enemy.

Extract of a letter from Nathaniel Searle, jr., to the President of the United States, dated
     WASHINGTON CITY, *July* 6, 1814.

The views of the General Assembly, of the Council of War, and of the Governor, will be clearly discovered, in relation to this subject, from an act of the Assembly, passed at their late June session, a copy of which I herewith present.

I beg leave, therefore, in behalf of the State by whose authority I am deputed, to solicit the peculiar attention of the President to her perilous and calamitous situation; to request of him a reimbursement of the expenditures already made, and the prompt provision of a military force for her protection; or that he will furnish, herewith, pecuniary means by which she can place herself in an attitude of defence.

State of Rhode Island and Providence Plantations.

IN GENERAL ASSEMBLY,
     June Session, A. D. 1814.

An Act providing for the defence of the State.

Be it enacted by the General Assembly, and by the authority thereof it is enacted, That his Excellency, the Governor, by and with the advice and consent of the Council of War, be and he is hereby authorized and requested to order into immediate service, according to the provisions of the Constitution, and of the laws of the United States, such portion of the militia and chartered companies of this State *as he may* think necessary for the defence of the most exposed parts thereof.

SEC. 2. *And be it further enacted,* That his Excellency, the Governor, may draught or detach the said militia, and chartered companies *as he may* think expedient; and that any private soldier of the militia, draughted or detached, may furnish an able-bodied man as a substitute.

Sec. 3. *And be it further enacted*, That each and every non-commissioned officer and private soldier shall receive two dollars per month, out of the general treasury, in addition to the pay allowed by the United States.

Sec. 4. *And be it further enacted*, That his Excellency, the Governor, be and he is hereby requested to cause the draughted or detached militia and chartered companies to be relieved as often as the nature of the service will permit.

Sec. 5. *And be it further enacted*, That all process, for the recovery of debt or taxes, against the non-commissioned officers and private soldiers, draughted or detached as aforesaid, shall be stayed during the time they are in service.

Sec. 6. *And be it further enacted*, That his Excellency, the Governor, be authorized and empowered to raise a State corps, and to appoint officers therefor, as soon as the President of the United States consents to receive them into service for the defence of this State; and that the officers appointed as aforesaid be commissioned by his Excellency, the Governor, in the usual manner.

Sec. 7. *And be it further enacted*, That his Excellency, the Governor, and Council of War, be authorized and requested to furnish to the towns most exposed, such ordnance, on travelling carriages, and such equipments and ammunition, as they shall think proper; and to furnish the militia with tumbrils for transporting their ammunition.

Sec. 8. *And be it further enacted*, That his Excellency, the Governor, be authorized to draw on the general treasury for any sum not exceeding ten thousand dollars, for the purpose of carrying this act into effect.

A true copy.

Witness: SAMUEL EDDY,
               Secretary.

Extract of a letter from Brigadier General T. H. Cushing to the Secretary of War, dated

MIL. DIST., No. 2, HEADQUARTERS,
       Providence, July 21, 1814.

. Your letter of the 11th instant, with enclosures, reached me at this place on the evening of the 15th, and on the next morning I had an interview with Governor Jones, who is, at this time, deliberating with his Council as to the mode of selecting the State's quota of five hundred men, which he assures me shall be raised, either by enlistment or draught, in a very few days.

Extract of a letter from his Excellency William Jones, Governor of the State of Rhode Island, to the Secretary of War, dated

PROVIDENCE, *August* 15, 1814.
Since the arrangement was entered into with you, relative to raising a State corps, rendezvous

have been opened in different parts of the State, officers appointed, and the recruiting service progresses in a manner and with a rapidity that promises success,

Should we be disappointed, however, in raising the number proposed by enlistment, the militia will be detached to make up the deficiency, for the defence of the State, according to the *invitation* of the President of the United States of the 4th of July last.

Extract of a letter from his Excellency William Jones, Governor of the State of Rhode Island, to the Secretary of War, dated

PROVIDENCE, *Sept.* 8, 1814.
SIR: I am ready, as I have by letter and through the Adjutant General, Colonel Searle, repeatedly expressed to your department, to call out the militia, and particularly the five hundred men ordered by the President, on the 4th day of July last, as our quota of the ninety-three thousand five hundred men; but we are destitute of almost every necessary for the comfort and subsistence of those men, and for making them effective as soldiers. We are without tents, equipage, and provisions, and have a very inadequate supply of cannon, muskets, and ammunition. I have attempted to raise a corps of five hundred men, to be accepted as substitutes for our quota of the militia. In this I have not yet succeeded, having been able to enlist only about one hundred and fifty men, notwithstanding a bounty was offered by the State. I have also detached four companies of militia for the defence of Newport, who have been called into actual service, one company at a time, and who were agreed to be mustered under the authority of the United States, as appears by the letter of General Armstrong, dated July 9, 1814 Five companies of militia were also called out by General Stanton, of Washington county, to assist in the defence of Stonington, in Connecticut. In the actual state of affairs, the militia must be draughted or detached to make up the five hundred men; and it may very probably be necessary to call out a much larger force; but you must be perfectly sensible of the inefficiency of any force, without further supplies of the munitions of war.

D.

Copy of a letter from his Excellency, William Pennington, Governor of the State of New Jersey, to the Secretary of War, dated

TRENTON, *October* 28, 1814.
SIR: I am informed that Governor Tompkins, as Governor of the State of New York, has taken command of the third military district of the United States; this district comprehends the principal part of New Jersey, and between two and three thousand Jersey militia are now in actual service in this district, at Sandy Hook, in the State of New Jersey. It might certainly appear, on first view, novel, at least, that a Governor of a State, as such, should have the command of the

militia of a neighboring State, within the actual territory of that State. I am far from entertaining a disposition, especially in the present state of our country, to throw the least obstruction in the way of the operations of the General Government in any measure of defence which it may think proper to adopt, but I conceive it my duty to inquire as to the fact, and the views of the War Department on the subject.

Copy of a letter from James Monroe, Secretary of War, to his Excellency William Pennington, Governor of New Jersey, dated

NOVEMBER 22, 1814.

SIR: I have had the honor to receive your Excellency's letter of the 29th ultimo, requiring information whether Governor Tompkins, as Governor of the State of New York, has been appointed commander of the third military district, comprehending a part of the State of New Jersey. Your Excellency seems to doubt whether the Governor of one State can have command of the militia of another State, within the limits of the latter; and it is to ascertain the views of the General Government on that point that the inquiry has been made.

The patriotic and national sentiments which you have expressed on this subject have afforded much satisfaction to the President, who desires that all the information which you have sought should be fully communicated.

Governor Tompkins has been appointed commander of the military district of the United States, No. 3, by virtue of which his command extends to that part of the State of New Jersey, and to such of her militia, as have been called into the service of the United States within that limit.

The city of New York being menaced by the enemy with a formidable invasion, and the United States not having a regular force to repel it, a large body of the militia were called into their service for the purpose. It was this circumstance which led to the appointment of Governor Tompkins to the command of the military district No. 3, he being, in the opinion of the President, well qualified for the trust.

It is a well established principle, that, when any portion of the militia are called into the service of the United States, the officers commanding it ought to retain their command, and enter with it into that service: a Colonel with his regiment; a Brigadier with his brigade; a Major General with his division. On the same principle, when several divisions of the militia of any State are called into the service of the United States, the Governor of the State may be authorized to take the command of them, he being the highest officer of the militia in the State. In such a case the Governor of a State is viewed in his military character only. He becomes, it is true, the military commander, by virtue of his office as Governor; but every other feature of that character is lost in the service of the United States. They relate to his civil functions, in which the State

13th CON. 3d SESS.—57

alone is interested. The militia of one State, when called into the service of the United States, may be marched into another State. We have seen the militia of Pennsylvania and Virginia serving in Maryland, and of North Carolina in Virginia, with many other examples of a like kind. In all these instances, the militia officers go with their respective corps, and, as such, no discrimination can be made to the exclusion of the Governor of a State, commanding the militia of a State; like other militia officers, he may march with the troops of his State into another State, and retain there his appropriate command, either as commander of the district, or acting under another Governor, to whom the President has already given the command.

Your Excellency will find these principles fully illustrated, and more than fully established, by an example which took place soon after the adoption of the present Constitution. In the year 1794, when President WASHINGTON thought it proper, on the certificate of a judge that an insurrection existed in the western parts of Pennsylvania, to order the militia of other States there, to aid the militia of that State in suppressing it, he committed the command of the whole force to the Governor of a neighboring State, who commanded the Governor of Pennsylvania. The relative rank and command of the Governor employed in the service was settled by the President himself.

In general, it is not desirable to impose on the Governors of States the duty of commanding the militia of their respective States, when called into the service of the United States, where they supersede the officer of the latter, commanding the military district in which such State is, because, as Governors, they have other duties to perform, which might interfere, if they did not conflict, with those incident to such command. A Governor, for example, under the influence of local feeling, might think the danger more imminent than it really was, and call into the service of the United States a greater force than would be necessary. He might even set on foot expeditions which the General Government could not approve. It would be improper that the charges incident thereto should be defrayed by the United States. The Constitution contemplates the exercise of the national authority, in contradistinction to that of the State, whenever the militia of a State are called into the service of the United States. The call must be made by the President, or by his authority, to be obligatory on the nation. If made by the Governor of a State it is the act of the State, and obligatory on, it only. These objections, however, to the union of both trusts in the same person, did not apply to the employment of the Governor of New York. All the force necessary for the defence of that State had already been called for, by order of this Government, and put into the service of the United States; and although the Governor is authorized to dismiss a part of the militia, in certain cases, he is instructed not to call out any without a special sanction from this department.

Your Excellency will observe, that the objec-

Capture of the British Fleet on Lake Champlain.

tion to the command of the militia of a State by its Governor, when called into the service of the United States, does not apply except to cases in which the command of the military district of the United States is superseded. In every other case, even in those having that effect, under similar circumstances with that under consideration, such active, patriotic service, by persons so highly intrusted by their country, will be seen by the President with great interest and satisfaction. Its example could not fail to produce the happiest effect.

I have the honor to be, &c.
JAMES MONROE.
Hon, W. Pennington.

CAPTURE OF THE BRITISH FLEET ON LAKE CHAMPLAIN.

[Communicated to the Senate, October 6, 1814.]
Navy Department, *Oct.* 3, 1814.

Sir: In compliance with your request I have now the honor to enclose copies of all the documents ,received from Captain Macdonough, in relation to the brilliant and extraordinary victory achieved by the United States' squadron under his command, over that of the enemy, in Plattsburg Bay, on Lake Champlain.

This action, like that of its prototype on Lake Erie, cannot be portrayed in language corresponding with the universal and just admiration inspired by the exalted prowess, consummate skill, and cool persevering intrepidity, which will ever distinguish this splendid and memorable event.

This, like those brilliant naval victories which preceded it, has its peculiar features, which mark it with a distinct character: It was fought at anchor. The firm, compact, and well-formed line, the preparations for all the evolutions of which the situation was susceptible, and the adroitness and decisive effect with which they were performed in the heat of battle, mark no less the judgment which planned than the valor and skill displayed in the execution.

All these are heightened by the contemplation of a vigorous and greatly superior force moving down upon this line, in his own time, selecting his position, and choosing his distance, animated by the proximity of a powerful army, in co-operation, and stimulated by the settled confidence of victory.

To view it in the abstract, it is not surpassed by any naval victory oh record; to appreciate its results, it is perhaps, one of the most important events in the history of our country.

That it will be justly estimated, and the victors duly honored by the Councils of the nation, the justice and liberality hitherto displayed, on similar occasions, is a sufficient pledge.

I have the honor to be, very respectfully, sir, your obedient servant,
W. JONES.

Hon. Charles Tait.
Chairman Naval Committee.

U. S. ship Saratoga,
off Plattsburg, Sept. 11, 1814.

Sir: The Almighty has been pleased to grant us a signal victory on Lake Champlain, in the capture of one frigate, one brig, and two sloops of war, of the enemy.

I have the honor to be, very respectfully, sir, your obedient servant,
T. MACDONOUGH,
Commanding.

Hon. William Jones,
Secretary of the Navy.

U. S. ship Saratoga,
At anchor off Plattsburg, Sept. 13, 1814.

Sir: By Lieutenant Commandant Cassin I have the honor to convey to you the flags of His Britannic Majesty's late squadron, captured, on the 11th instant, by the United States' squadron under my command. Also, my despatches relating to that occurrence, which would have been in your possession at an earlier period but for the difficulty in arranging the different statements.

The squadron under my command now lies at Plattsburg: it will bear a considerable diminution, and leave a force sufficient to repel any attempt of the enemy in this quarter. I shall wait your order what to do with the whole or any part thereof; and, should it be consistent, I beg you will favor me with permission to leave the lake, and place me under the command of Commodore Decatur, at New York. My health, (being some time on the lake,) together with the almost certain inactivity of future naval operations here are among the causes of this request for my removal.

I have the honor to be, sir, with much respect your most obedient servant,
T. MACDONOUGH.

Hon. William Jones,
Secretary of the Navy.

U. S. ship Saratoga,
Plattsburg Bay, Sept. 13, 1814.

Sir: I have the honor to give you the particulars of the action which took place on the 11th instant on this lake.

For several days the enemy were on their way to Plattsburg by land and water, and it being understood that an attack would be made at the same time by their land and naval forces, I determined to await at anchor the approach of the latter.

At 8 A. M. the lookout boat announced the approach of the enemy. At 9, he anchored in line ahead, at about three hundred yards distant from my line; his ship opposed to the Saratoga his brig to the Eagle, Captain Robert Henley his galleys, thirteen in number, to the schooner, sloop, and a division of our galleys; one of his sloops assisting their ship and brig, the other assisting their galleys; our remaining galley with the Saratoga and Eagle. In this situation, the whole force, on both sides, became engaged, the

Saratoga suffering much from the heavy fire of the Confiance. I could perceive, at the same time, however, that our fire was very destructive to her. The Ticonderoga, Lieutenant Commandant Cassin, gallantly sustained her full share of the action. At half past ten o'clock, the Eagle, not being able to bring her guns to bear, cut her cable, and anchored in a more eligible position, between my ship and the Ticonderoga, where she very much annoyed the enemy, but unfortunately leaving me exposed to a galling fire from the enemy's brig. Our guns on the starboard side being nearly all dismounted or not manageable, a stern anchor was let go, the bower cable cut, and the ship winded, with a fresh broadside on the enemy's ship, which soon after surrendered. Our broadside was then sprung to bear on the brig, which surrendered in about fifteen minutes after.

The sloop that was opposed to the Eagle had struck some time before, and drifted down the line; the sloop which was with their galleys having struck also; three of their galleys are said to be sunk, the others pulled off. Our galleys were about obeying, with alacrity, the signal to follow them, when all the vessels were reported to me to be in a sinking state; it then became necessary to annul the signal to the galleys, and order their men to the pumps.

I could only look at the enemy's galleys going off in a shattered condition, for there was not a mast in either squadron that could stand to make sail on; the lower rigging, being nearly all shot away, hung down as though it had been just placed over the mast heads.

The Saratoga had fifty-five round shot in her hull; the Confiance one hundred and five. The enemy's shot passed principally just over our heads, as there were not twenty whole hammocks in the nettings at the close of the action, which lasted, without intermission, two hours and twenty minutes.

The absence and sickness of Lieutenant Raymond Perry, left me without the services of that excellent officer. Much ought fairly to be attributed to him for his great care and attention in disciplining the ship's crew, as her first lieutenant. His place was filled by a gallant young officer, Lieutenant Peter Gamble, who, I regret to inform you, was killed early in the action. Acting Lieutenant Vallette worked the first and second divisions of guns, with able effect. Sailingmaster Brum's attention to the springs, and in the execution of the order to wind the ship, and occasionally at the guns, meets with my entire approbation; also Captain Young's, commanding the acting marines, who took his men to the guns. Mr. Beale, purser, was of great service at the guns, and in carrying my orders throughout the ship, with Midshipman Montgomery. Master's Mate Joshua Justin had command of the third division; his conduct during the action was that of a brave and correct officer. Midshipmen Monteath, Graham, Williamson, Platt, Twing, and acting midshipman Baldwin, all behaved well, and gave evidence of their making valuable officers.

The Saratoga was twice set on fire by hot shot from the enemy's ship.

I close, sir, this communication with feelings of gratitude for the able support I received from every officer and man attached to the squadron which I have the honor to command.

I have the honor to be, with great respect, sir, your most obedient servant,

T. MACDONOUGH.

Hon. WILLIAM JONES,
    Secretary of the Navy.

P. S. Accompanying this is a list of killed and wounded, a list of prisoners, and a precise statement of both forces engaged. Also letters from Captain Henley and Lieutenant Commandant Cassin.

U. S. SHIP SARATOGA, *Sept.* 13, 1814.

SIR: I have the honor to enclose you a list of the killed and wounded on board the different vessels of the squadron under your command in the action of the 11th instant.

It is impossible to ascertain correctly the loss of the enemy. From the best information received from the British officers, from my own observation, and from various lists found on board the Confiance, I calculate the number of men on board of that ship, at the commencement of the action, at two hundred and seventy, of whom one hundred and eighty at least were killed and wounded, and on board the other captured vessels at least eighty more, making, in the whole, killed and wounded, two hundred and sixty. This is, doubtless, short of the real number, as many were thrown overboard from the Confiance during the engagement.

The muster books must have been thrown overboard, or otherwise, disposed of, as they are not to be found.

I am, sir, respectfully, your obedient servant,
    GEO. BEALE, Jr., *Purser.*

THOMAS MACDONOUGH, Esq.,
    Commanding U. S. squadron
        on Lake Champlain.

Return of killed and wounded on board the United States squadron on Lake Champlain, in the engagement with the British fleet, on the 11th of September, 1814.

SHIP SARATOGA.

Killed—Peter Gamble, lieutenant; Thomas Butler, quarter gunner; James Norberry, boatswain's mate; Abraham Davis, quartermaster; William Wyer, sailmaker; William Brickell, seaman; Peter Johnson, ditto; John Coleman, ditto; Benjamin Burrill, ordinary seaman; Andrew Parmlee, ditto; Peter Post seaman; David Bennett, ditto; Ebenezer Johnson, ditto; Joseph Couch, landsman; Thomas Stephens, seaman; John White, ordinary seaman; Randall McDonald, ditto; Samuel Smith, seaman; Thomas Malony, ordinary seaman; Andrew Nelson, seaman; John Sellack, ditto; Peter Hanson, ditto; Jacob Laraway, ditto; Edward Moore, ditto; Jerome

Capture of the British Fleet on Lake Champlain.

Williams, ordinary seaman; James Carlisle, marine; John Smart, seaman.

Wounded—James M. Baldwin, acting midshipman; Joseph Barron, pilot; Robert Gary, quarter-gunner; George Cassin, quartermaster; John Hollingsworth, seaman; Purnall Smith, ditto; Thomas Robinson, ditto; John Ottiwell, ditto; John Thompson, ordinary seaman; William Tabee, ditto; William Williams, ditto; John Roberson, seaman; John Towns, landsman; John Shays, seaman; John S. Hammond, ditto; James Barlow, ditto; James Nagle, ordinary seaman, John Lanman, seaman; Peter Colberg, ditto; William Newton, ordinary seaman; Neil J. Heidmont, seaman, James Steward ditto; John Adams, landsman; Charles Ratche, seaman; Benjamin Jackson, marine; Jesse Vanhorn, ditto; Joseph Ketter, ditto; Samuel Pearson, ditto.

BRIG EAGLE.

Killed—Peter Vandermere, master's mate; Jno. Ribero, seaman; Jacob Lindman, ditto; Perkins Moore, ordinary seaman; James Winship, ditto; Thomas Anwright, ditto; Nace Wilson, ditto; Thomas Lewis, boy; John Wallace, marine; Joseph Heaton, ditto; Robert Stratton, ditto; James M. Hale musician; John Wood, ditto.

Wounded—Joseph Smith, lieutenant; William A. Spencer, acting lieutenant; Francis Breeze, master's mate; Abraham Waters, pilot; William C. Allen, quartermaster; James Duick, quarter-gunner; Andrew McEwen, seaman; Zebediah Concklin, ditto; Joseph Valentine, ditto; John Hartley, ditto; John Mielin, ditto; Robert Buckley, ditto; Purnell Boice, ordinary seaman; Aaron Fitzgerald, boy; John N. Craig, seaman; John McKenney, ditto; Matthew Scriver, marine; George Mainwaring, ditto; Henry Jones, ditto; John McCarty, ditto.

SCHOONER TICONDEROGA.

Killed—John Stansbury, lieutenant; John Fisher, boatswain's mate; John Atkinson, ditto; Henry Johnson, seaman; Deodorick Think, marine; John Sharp, ditto.

Wounded—Patrick Cassin, seaman; Ezekiel Goud, ditto; Samuel Sawyer, ditto; William Le Count, ditto; Henry Collins, ditto; John Condon, marine.

SLOOP PREBLE.

Killed—Rogers Carter, acting sailingmaster; Joseph Rowe, boatswain's mate.
Wounded—None.

GUNBOAT BORER.

Killed—Arthur W. Smith, purser's steward; Thomas Gill, boy; James Day, marine.
Wounded—Ebenezer Cobb, corporal marines.

GUNBOAT CENTIPEDE.

Wounded—James Taylor, landsman.

GUNBOAT WILMER.

Wounded—Peter Frank, seamen.

GUNBOATS.

Nettle, Allen, Viper, Burrows, Ludlow, Aylwyn, Ballard.—*None killed or wounded.*

RECAPITULATION.

					Killed	Wounded
Saratoga	-	-	-	-	28	29
Eagle	-	-	-	-	13	20
Ticonderoga	-	-	-	-	6	6
Preble	-	-	-	-	2	00
Borer	-	-	-	-	3	1
Centipede	-	-	-	-	00	1
Wilmer	-	-	-	-	00	1
Total	-	-	-	-	52	58

GEORGE BEALE, Jr. *Purr.*

Approved : T. MACDONOUGH.

List of Prisoners captured on the 11th September, and sent to Greenbush.

OFFICERS—Daniel Pring*, Captain; Creswick, Lieutenant; Robinson, ditto; Drew, ditto; McGhie, ditto; Hornby, ditto; Childs, ditto, marines; Fitzpatrick, ditto, 39th regiment; Bryden, sailingmaster; Clark, master's mate; Simmonds, ditto; Todd, surgeon; Giles, purser; Guy, captain's clerk; Dowell, midshipman; Aire, ditto; Bondell, ditto; Toorke, ditto; Kewstra, ditto; Davidson, boatswain; Elvin, gunner; Mickell ditto; Cox, carpenter; Parker, purser; Martin, surgeon; Mc Cabe, assistant surgeon.

Three hundred and forty seamen.

Forty-seven wounded men paroled.

Statement of the American Forces engaged on the 11th September, 1814.

Saratoga, long 24 pounders	8		
42 pound carronades	6		
32 ditto ditto	12		
	— Total guns	26	
Eagle, 12 32 pound carronades, and 8 long 18 pounders		-	20
Ticonderoga, long 12 pounders	8		
do. 18 do.	4		
32 pound carronades	- 5		
		17	
Preble, long 9 pounders	-	-	7
Ten galleys, viz :			
Allen, one long twenty-four pounder, and one eighteen pound columbiad	-	-	2
Burrows, one long twenty-four pounder, and one eighteen pound columbiad	-	-	2
Borer, one long twenty-four pounder, and one eighteen pound columbiad	-	-	2
Nettle, one long twenty-four pounder, and one eighteen pound columbiad	-	-	2
Viper, one long twenty-four pounder, and one eighteen pound columbiad	-	-	2
Centipede, one long twenty-four pounder, and one eighteen pound columbiad	-	-	2
Ludlow, one long twelve pounder, and one eighteen pound columbiad	-	-	1
Wilmer, one long twelve pounder, and one eighteen pound columbiad	-	-	1

*On parole.

Aylwyn, one long twelve pounder, and one eighteen pound columbiad - - - 1

Ballard, one long twelve pounder, and one eighteen pound columbiad - - - 1

Guns - - - 86

RECAPITULATION.

Long twenty-four pounders - - 14
Forty-two pound carronades - - 6
Thirty-two pound carronades - - 29
Long eighteen pounders - - 12
Long twelve pounders - - 12
Long nine pounders - - 7
Eighteen pound columbiads - - 6

Total guns - - - 86

Statement of the Enemy's Force engaged on the 11th September, 1814.

Frigate Confiance, long 24 pounders - - - 27
32 pound carronades - - 4
24 do. - - 6
long 18 pounders on berth deck - - - 2
          Total guns 39

Brig Linnet, long 12 pounders - - 16
†Sloop Chub, 18 pound carronades - - 10
long 6 pounder - - 1
          39

†Sloop Finch, 18 pound carronades - - 6
18 pound columbiad - - 1
long 6 pounders - - 4
          11

Thirteen galleys, viz:
Sir James Yeo, one long twenty-four pounder, and one thirty-two pound carronade - 2
Sir George Prevost, one long twenty-four pounder, and one thirty-two pound carronade - 2
Sir Sidney Beckwith, one long twenty-four pounder, and one thirty-two pound carronade - 2
Broke, one long eighteen pounder, and one thirty-two pound carronade - 2
Murray, one long eighteen pounder, and one eighteen pound carronade - 2
Wellington, one long eighteen pounder - 1
Tecumseh, one long eighteen pounder - 1
Name unknown, one long eighteen pounder - 1
Drummond, one thirty-two pound carronade 1
Simcoe, one thirty-two pound carronade 1
Unknown, one thirty-two pound carronade 1
Unknown, one thirty-two pound carronade 1
Unknown, one thirty-two pound carronade 1

Total - - - - 95

† These sloops were formerly the United States' Growler and Eagle.

RECAPITULATION.

Long twenty-four pounders - - 30
Long eighteen pounders - - 7
Long twelve pounders - - 16
Long six pounders - - 5
Thirty-two pound carronades - - 13
Twenty-pound carronades - - 6
Eighteen pound carronades - - 17
Eighteen pound columbiad - - 1

Total guns - - - 95

THOMAS MACDONOUGH.

UNITED STATES' BRIG EAGLE,
Plattsburg, Sept. 12, 1814.

SIR: I am happy to inform you that all my officers and men acted bravely, and did their duty in the battle of yesterday with the enemy.

I shall have the pleasure of making a more particular representation of the respective merits of my gallant officers to the honorable the Secretary of the Navy.

I have the honor to be, respectfully, sir, your most obedient servant,

ROBERT HENLEY.

P. S.—We had thirty-nine round shot in our hull, (mostly twenty-four pounders,) four in our lower masts, and we were well peppered with grape.

I enclose my boatswain's report.   R. H.

U. S. SCHOONER TICONDEROGA,
Plattsburg Bay, Sept. 12, 1814.

SIR: It is with pleasure I state that every officer and man under my command did their duty yesterday. Yours, respectfully,

STEPHEN CASSIN, *Lt. Comdt.*

Com. T. MACDONOUGH.

U. S. SHIP SARATOGA,
Off Plattsburg, Sept. 15, 1814.

SIR: As Providence has given into my command the squadron on Lake Champlain, of which you were (after the fall of Captain Downie) the commanding officer, I beg you will, after the able conflict you sustained, and evidence of determined valor you evinced, on board His Britannic Majesty's brig Linnet, until the necessity of her surrender, accept of your enclosed parole, not to serve against the United States, or their dependencies, until regularly exchanged. I am, &c.

THOMAS MACDONOUGH.

Captain PRING, *Royal Navy.*

CAPTURE OF THE EPERVIER.

[Communicated to the Senate, on the 10th of October 1814.]

NAVY DEPARTMENT, *October* 3, 1814.

SIR: Agreeably to your request I have the honor to enclose copies of the official account and other papers relating to the capture of the enemy's sloop of war Epervier, on the 29th April last, by the United States sloop of war Peacock, commanded by Captain Warrington.

If the relative force, and comparative effect of the fire of the combatants, and the speedy termination of the contest, though protracted by the early loss of the Peacock's fore yard, be taken as the criterion, then does it display a steady valor and superior skill on the part of the commander, officers, and crew, of the Peacock, which may fairly challenge any single action on record.

I have the honor to be, very respectfully, sir, your obedient servant,

W. JONES.

Hon. CHARLES TAIT,
　Chairman Naval Committee.

U. S. SLOOP PEACOCK, AT SEA.
Lat. 27° 47,' Lang. 80° 9,' April 29, 1814.

SIR: I have the honor to inform you that we have this morning captured, after an action of forty-two minutes, His Britannic Majesty's brig Epervier, rating and mounting eighteen thirty-two pound carronades, with one hundred and twenty-eight men, of whom eight were killed and fifteen wounded, (according to the best information we could obtain.) Among the latter is her first lieutenant, who has lost an arm and received a severe splinter wound on the hip. Not a man in the Peacock was killed, and only two wounded, neither dangerously so.

The fate of the Epervier would have been determined in much less time but for the circumstance of our fore yard being totally disabled by two round shot, in the starboard quarter, from her first broadside, which entirely deprived us of the use of our fore and fore-topsails, and compelled us to keep the ship large throughout the remainder of the action. This, with a few topmast and topgallant back-stays cut away, and a few shot through our sails, is the only injury the Peacock has sustained. Not a round shot touched our hull; our masts and spars are as sound as ever. When the enemy struck, he had five feet water in his hold, his main topmast was over the side, his main boom shot away, his foremast cut nearly in two, and tottering, his fore rigging and stays shot away, his bowsprit badly wounded, and forty-five shot holes in his hull, twenty of which were within a foot of his water line above and below. By great exertions, we got her in sailing order just as dark came on.

In fifteen minutes after the enemy struck, the Peacock was ready for another action, in every respect but her fore-yard, which was sent down, fished, and had the fore-sail set again in forty-five minutes. Such was the spirit and activity of our gallant crew.

The Epervier had under her convoy an English hermaphrodite brig, a Russian and Spanish brig; which all hauled their wind, and stood to the E. N. E. I had determined upon pursuing the former, but found that it would not answer to leave our prize in her then crippled state, and the

more particularly so, as we found she had one hundred and twenty thousand dollars in specie, which we soon transferred to this sloop. Every officer, seaman, and marine, did his duty, which is the highest compliment I can pay them.

I am, respectfully,
　L. WARRINGTON.

SAVANNAH, *May 4, 1814.*

SIR: I have great satisfaction in being able to report to you the arrival of the Peacock at this anchorage to-day, and also the arrival of the Epervier on Monday last.

I have now to detail to you the reason of our separation. We made sail, as mentioned in my last, on the evening of the 29th. The next afternoon we were, at half past five, abreast the centre of Amelia island, with the vessel in sight over the land, when two large ships, which had been some time previous a little to the northward of the island, were clearly ascertained to be frigates, and in chase of us. In this situation, at the suggestion of Lieutenant Nicholson, I took out all but himself and sixteen officers and men, and stood to the southward along shore on a wind, leaving him to make the best of his way for St. Mary's; which place I felt confident he would reach, as the weather frigate was in chase of the Peacock, and the other was too far to leeward to fetch him. At nine we lost sight of the chaser, but continued standing all night to the southward, in hopes to get entirely clear of him. At daylight we shortened sail and stood to the northward, and again made the frigate ahead, who gave chase a second time, which he continued until two P. M., when, finding, he could not come up, he desisted. In the evening we resumed our course, and saw nothing until daylight on Tuesday morning, when a large ship (supposed to be the same) was again seen in chase of us, and was again run out of sight.

This morning, at half past three, we made Tybee light, and at half past eight anchored near the United States' ship Adams. As the enemy is hovering close to St. Mary's, I concluded that he had received information of, and was waiting to intercept us. Accordingly we steered for this place, where we received intelligence of the Epervier's arrival, after frightening off a launch which was sent from the enemy's ship to leeward, on Saturday evening, to cut him off from the land.

From the 1st of April to the 24th, we saw but one neutral and two privateers, both of which we chased without overhauling, although we ran one amongst the shoals of Cape Canaveral and followed him into four fathoms water. We have been to the southward as far as the Great Isaacs and have cruised from thence to Matanilla reef and along the Florida shore to Cape Canaveral. Not a single running vessel has been through the Gulf in all this time. The fleet sails from Jamaica under the convoy of a seventy-four, two frigates, and two sloops, from the 1st to the 8th May. They are so much afraid of our cruisers that several ships in the Havana, ready for sea, which intended to run it, (as it is called,) were forced to wait the arrival of the convoy from Jamaica.

The Epervier and her convoy were the first English vessels we had seen.

We shall proceed in the further execution of your instructions as soon as we can get a foreyard, provisions, and water.

The Epervier is one of their finest brigs and is well calculated for our service. She sails extremely fast, and will require but little to send her to sea, as her armament and stores are complete.

I enclose you a list of the brig's crew, as accurately as we can get it. I am, respectfully,
         L. WARRINGTON.

Hon. Secretary *of the Navy.*

UNITED STATES SHIP PEACOCK,
         Savannah, May 5, 1814.

SIR: As my letter of yesterday was too late for the mail, I address you again, in the performance of a duty which is pleasing and gratifying to me in a high degree, and is but doing justice to the merits of the deserving officers under my command, of whom I have hitherto refrained from speaking, as I considered it most correct to make it the subject of a particular communication.

To the unwearied and indefatigable attention of Lieutenant Nicholson, (first,) in organizing and training the crew, the success of this action is, in a great measure, to be attributed. I have confided greatly in him, and have never found my confidence misplaced; for judgment, coolness, and decision, in times of difficulty, few can surpass him. This is the second action in which he has been engaged this war, and in both he has been successful. His greatest pride is to earn a commander's position, by fighting for instead of heiring it.

From Lieutenant Henley, (second,) and Lieutenant Voorhees, (acting third, who has also been twice successfully engaged,) I received every assistance that zeal, ardor, and experience, could afford.

The fire from their two divisions was terrible, and directed with the greatest precision and coolness. In Sailingmaster Percival, whose great wish and pride it is to obtain a lieutenant's commission, and whose unremitting and constant attention to duty, added to his professional knowledge, entitles him to it, in my opinion, I found an able as well as willing assistant. He handled the ship as if he had been working her into a roadstead. Mr. David Cole, acting carpenter, I have also found such an able and valuable man in his occupation, that I must request, in the most earnest manner, that he may receive a warrant: or I feel confident that, to his uncommon exertion, we, in a great measure, owe the getting of our prize into port. From 11 A. M. until 6 P. M. he was over her side, stopping shot holes, on a graing; and when the ordinary resources failed of success, his skill soon supplied him with efficient ones. Mr. Philip Myers, master's mate, has also conducted himself in such a manner as to warrant my recommendation of him as a master; he is a seaman, navigator, and officer, his family in New York is respectable, and he would prove an acquisition to the service. My clerk, Mr. J. S. Townsend, is anxious to obtain, through my means, a midshipman's warrant, and has taken pains to qualify himself for it, by volunteering, and constantly performing a midshipman's duty; indeed I have but little use for a clerk, and he is as great a proficient as any of the young midshipmen; the whole of whom behaved in a manner that was pleasing to me, and must be gratifying to you, as it gives an earnest of what they will make in time. Three only have been to sea before, and one only in a man of war, yet were they as much at home, and as much disposed to exert themselves, as any officer of the ship. Lieutenant Nicholson speaks in high terms of the conduct of Messrs. Greeves and Rodgers, midshipmen, who were in the prize with him.

I have the honor to be, sir, respectfully, your obedient servant,   L. WARRINGTON.

Hon. WILLIAM JONES,
     Secretary of the Navy.

CAPTURE OF THE REINDEER AND OTHER VESSELS, BY THE WASP.

[Communicated to the Senate, October 17, 1814.]
     COMMITTEE ROOM, *Oct.* 13, 1814.

SIR: In order that Congress may proceed in the agreeable duty of bestowing suitable honors and rewards on those gallant men whose noble achievements have already so signally distinguished themselves and their country during this war, I am directed by the Committee on Naval Affairs, on the part of the Senate of the United States, to request that you will transmit all the information in possession of the Navy Department, relating to the capture of the British sloop of war Reindeer by the American sloop of war Wasp.

I have the honor to be, &c.
         C. TAIT, *Chairman.*

Hon. WM, JONES,
     Secretary of the Navy.

NAVY DEPARTMENT, *Oct.* 15, 1814.

SIR: I have the honor to enclose copies of the documents received at this Department from the Commander of the United States sloop of war Wasp, relative to the capture and destruction of the enemy's sloop of war Reindeer, on the 28th of June last, after a brilliant action of nineteen minutes, which was terminated by boarding, in gallant and decisive style, having repulsed the enemy in repeated and vigorous attempts to board the Wasp. All that skill and valor could do was done quickly, and less it was certain would not be done. I am, very respectfully, &c.
         W. JONES.

Hon. CHARLES TAIT,
     Chairman Naval Committee.

Capture of the Reindeer and other Vessels.

UNITED STATES' SHIP WASP,
L'Orient, July 8, 1814.

SIR: I have the honor to announce to you the arrival of this ship to day at this place. By the pilot who carried us out of Portsmouth, N. H., I had the satisfaction to make you acquainted with our having left that place, and again had the pleasure of addressing you by the French national brig Olive, and which was the first vessel we had spoken since our departure from the United States. From the time of our sailing I continued to follow the route pointed out in your instructions until our arrival at this place, during which we have been so fortunate as to make several captures, a list of which will accompany this. These, with their cargoes, were wholly destroyed, with one exception; this was the galliot Henrietta, which was permitted to return with the prisoners, thirty-eight in number, after throwing overboard the greater part of her cargo, leaving only a sufficiency to ballast her. When arrived on our cruising ground, I found it impossible to maintain anything like a station, and was led in chase farther up the English Channel than was intended. After arriving on soundings, the number of neutrals which are now passing us kept us almost constantly in pursuit. It gives me much pleasure to state to you the very healthy condition of the crew of the Wasp during the cruise; sometimes without one on the sick list, and at no time any who remained there more than a few days. Great praise is due to Dr. Clark for his skill and attention at all times, but particularly after the action with the Reindeer; his unwearied assiduity to the necessities of the wounded was highly conspicuous.

The ship is at present under quarantine, but we expect to be released from it to-morrow, when the wounded will be sent to the hospital, and every exertion made to prepare the Wasp for sea.

I have the honor to be, &c.
J. BLAKELEY.

Hon. WILLIAM JONES.

UNITED STATES SHIP WASP,
L'Orient, July 8, 1814.

SIR: On Tuesday, the 28th ultimo, being in latitude 48° 36' North and longitude 11° 15' West, we fell in with, engaged, and after an action of nineteen minutes captured, His Britannic Majesty's sloop of war the Reindeer, William Manners, Esq., commander. Annexed are the minutes of our proceedings on that day, prior to, and during the continuance of, the action.

Where all did their duty, and each appeared anxious to excel, it is very difficult to discriminate. It is, however, only rendering them their merited due, when it is declared of Lieutenant Reilly and Barry, first and third of this vessel, and whose names will be found among those of the conquerors of the Guerriere and the Java, and of Mr. Tillinghast, second Lieutenant, who was greatly instrumental in the capture of the Boxer, that their conduct and courage, on this occasion, fulfilled the highest expectation, and gratified every wish. Sailingmaster Carr is also entitled to great credit for the zeal and ability with which he discharged his various duties.

The cool and patient conduct of every officer and man, while exposed to the fire of the shifting gun of the enemy, and without an opportunity of returning it, could alone be equalled by the animation and ardor exhibited when actually engaged, or by the promptitude and firmness with which every attempt of the enemy to board was met and successfully repelled. Such conduct may be seen; but cannot well be described.

The Reindeer mounted sixteen twenty-four pound carronades, two long six or nine pounders, and a shifting twelve pound carronade; with a complement on board of one hundred and eighteen men; her crew were said to be the pride of Plymouth.

Our loss in men has been severe, owing, in part, to the proximity of the two vessels, and the extreme smoothness of the sea, but chiefly in repelling boarders. That of the enemy, however, was infinitely more so, as will be seen by the list of killed and wounded on both sides.

Six round shot struck our hull, and many grape, which did not penetrate far. The foremast received a twenty-four pound shot, which passed through its centre, and our rigging and sails were a good deal injured.

The Reindeer was literally cut to pieces, in a line with her ports; her upper works, boats, and spare spars, were one complete wreck. A breeze springing up next afternoon, her foremast went by the board.

Having received all the prisoners on board, which, from the number of the wounded, occupied much time, together with their baggage, the Reindeer was, on the evening of the 29th, set on fire, and in a few hours blew up.

I have the honor to be, very respectfully, your most obedient servant,

J. BLAKELEY.

Hon. WILLIAM JONES,
Secretary of the Navy.

Minutes of the action between the United States ship Wasp and His Britannic Majesty's ship Reindeer, on the 28th June, 1814. Latitude 48° 36' North, Longitude 11° 15' West.

At four A. M. light breezes and cloudy. At a quarter after four discovered two sail, two points before the lee beam; kept away in chase; they after discovered one sail on the weather bow, altered the course, and hauled by the wind in chase of the sail to windward. At eight the sail to windward bore E. N. E., wind very unsteady; at ten the strange sail, bearing E. by N., hoisted an English ensign and pennant, and displayed a signal at the main (blue and yellow diagonally) Meridian, light airs and cloudy; at a quarter past twelve P. M. the enemy showed a blue and white flag, diagonally, at the fore, and fired a gun; at one hour fifteen minutes called all hands to quarters, and prepared for action; one hour twenty-two minutes, believing we could weather the enemy tacked ship, and stood for him; one hour fifty minutes, the enemy tacked ship and stood from us; one hour fifty-six minutes hoisted our colors, and fired a gun to windward, which was answered by the enemy with another to windward; two hours twenty minutes, the enemy still standing from us, set the royals; two hours twenty-five minutes set the flying jib; two hours twenty-nine minutes set the upper staysails; two hours thirty-two minutes, the enemy having tacked for us, took in the staysails; two hours forty-seven minutes furled the royals; two hours fifty-one minutes, seeing that the enemy would be able to weather us, tacked ship; three hours three minutes the enemy hoisted his flying jib; brailed up our mizzen; three hours fifteen minutes the enemy on our weather quarter, distant about sixty yards, fired his shifting gun, a twelve pound carronade, at us, loaded with round and grape shot, from his top-gallant forecastle; three hours seventeen minutes fired the same gun a second time; three hours nineteen minutes fired it a third time; three hours twenty-one minutes fired a fourth time; three hours twenty-four minutes a fifth shot, all from the same gun. Finding the enemy did not get sufficiently on the beam to enable us to bring our guns to bear, put the helm a lee, and at twenty-six minutes after three commenced the action with the after carronade, on the starboard side, and fired in succession; three hours thirty-five minutes hauled up the mainsail; three hours forty minutes, the enemy having his larboard bow in contact with our larboard quarter, endeavored to board us, but was repulsed in every attempt; at three hours forty-four minutes orders were given to board in turn, which were promptly executed, when all resistance immediately ceased; and at three hours forty-five minutes the enemy hauled down his flag.

            J. BLAKELEY.

UNITED STATES SHIP WASP,
L'Orient, July 10, 1814.

SIR: After the capture of His Britannic Majesty's sloop of war the Reindeer, it was my wish to have continued the cruise, as directed by you. I was, however, necessitated to relinquish this desire, after a few days, from a consideration for the wounded of our crew, whose wounds had, at this season, become offensive and aggravated, by the number of prisoners on board at the time, being seventy-seven in number. Fearing, from the crowded state of the Wasp, that some valuable lives might be lost if retained on board, I was compelled, though with reluctance, to make the first neutral port. Those belonging to the Reindeer, who were dangerously wounded, were put on board a Portuguese brig, bound to England, three days after the action, and from the winds which prevailed arrived, probably, in two or three days after their departure. Their surgeon, the Captain's clerk, with the Captain's and officers' servants, with the crew of the Orange Boven, were put on board the same vessel, to attend upon them. Since our arrival at this place we have experienced every civility from the public authorities; our quarantine was only for a few hours; and our wounded, fourteen in number, were yesterday carried to the hospital, where they are very comfortably situated. Our foremast, though badly wounded, can be repaired, and will be taken on shore as soon as possible. All the other damages sustained can be repaired by ourselves.

I have the honor to be, very respectfully, your most obedient servant,

            J. BLAKELEY.

Hon. WILLIAM JONES,
       Secretary of the Navy.

List of Killed and Wounded on board His Britannic Majesty's sloop of war the Reindeer, in action with the United States' sloop of war the Wasp, on the 28th June, 1814.

Killed.—William Manners, Esq., commander; John Thomas Barton, purser; James Humphreys, quartermaster; John Elly, armorer; Chas. Price, ropemaker; George Gibson, captain mast; Zenas Swift, seaman; George Sorlic, seaman; Samuel Laver, seaman; Bartholomew Johnson, seaman; Thomas Bassett, ordinary seaman; John Isles, ordinary seaman; Robert Smith, ordinary seaman; James Foreman, ordinary seaman; Patrick Sherry, landsman; John Maguire, landsman; William Lee, landsman; Collisters Glynn, boy, 2d class; Samuel Probert, boy, 2d class; Patrick Sharkey, boy, 2d class; Edward McGrath, boy, 3d class; John Roomer, private; James Allen, private; Thomas Musto, private; John Guest, private.

Wounded.—*Thomas Chambers, first lieutenant, severely; *Richard Johns, master, dangerously; *Ferguson Mason, quartermaster, severely; *Joshua Carson, captain forecastle, severely; *Thomas Williams, captain forecastle, dangerously; *James Candy, landsman, severely; *John Williamson, carpenter's crew, severely; *Thos. Clements, seaman, severely; *Richard Shippard, ordinary seaman, severely; *Joseph Waller, seaman, dangerously; *Robert Tole, seaman, dangerously; *Thomas Horne, seaman, severely; *James Wallace, ordinary seaman, dangerously; *David Livingston, seaman, severely; *Alexander Stupo, ordinary seaman, dangerously; *Thos. Bell, first, ordinary seaman, severely; *Nicholas Birmingham, ordinary seaman, dangerously; *William Williams, boy, second class, dangerously; *John Watley, private, severely; *William Wyley, corporal, severely; *Wm. Gurarty, private, severely; *William Watkins, private, severely; *Thos. Mitchell, boy, third class, severely; *Daniel Byrne, private, severely; *Thomas Marsh, sergeant, not very badly wounded, but permitted to proceed in consequence of the representation, and by the request, of the surgeon of the Reindeer; Matthew Mitchell, master's mate, slightly; Henry Hardiman, midshipman, slightly; James Legg, boatswain, slightly; John Stimson, quartermaster's mate, slightly; William Clark, cook, slightly; John Johnson, carpenter's crew, slightly;

Destruction of Public Books and Papers.

William Bruce, ordinary seaman, slightly; Benjamin Rufus, captain foretop, slightly; John Bramble, seaman, slightly; William Townholm, seaman, slightly; William Caldwell, seaman, dangerously, (since dead;) Archibald Adams, ordinary seaman, dangerously, (since dead;) Richard Hornby, seaman, slightly; Daniel Hart, boy, first class, slightly; William Ratclift, private, slightly; Thomas Major, private, severely; Richard Butler, captain after guard, slightly.

Killed.—25.

Wounded—Dangerously 10; severely 17; and slightly 15.

NOTE.—Those marked thus (*) were, in consequence of the severity and extent of their wounds, put on board a Portuguese brig, called the Lisbon Packet, on the third day after the action, to wit, the 1st of July, bound to Plymouth, England.

List of killed and wounded on board the United States' sloop of war the Wasp, Johnston Blakeley, Esq., commander, in action with His Britannic Majesty's sloop-of-war the Reindeer, on the 28th June, 1814.

Killed.—Timothy Stevens, seaman; Thomas Knight, ordinary seaman; Thomas R. Teel, seaman; John Brown, second, ordinary seaman; Joseph Vorse, ordinary seaman.

Wounded.—Henry S. Langdon, midshipman, dangerously; Frank Toscan, midshipman, dangerously; John Sweet, master's mate, slightly; William Thompson, boatswain's mate, severely; John Dick, quartermaster, severely; Nathaniel Scammon, seaman, severely; Jotham Perkins, seaman, dangerously, (since dead;) William Preston, seaman, slightly; Charles Green, dangerously, (since dead;) Charles Clinton, seaman, slightly; Andrew Passenger, seaman, severely; John Rowe, seaman, slightly; Joseph Atkins, seaman, dangerously, (since dead;) Robert Lowther, seaman, slightly; Merrel Roberts, seaman, slightly; Robert Jarvis, ordinary seaman, severely; Henry Herbert, ordinary seaman, dangerously; Simon Cassalis, ordinary seaman, severely; John C. Thurston, ordinary seaman, dangerously; Caleb Wheeden, ordinary seaman, severely; John Ball, boy, dangerously, (since dead.)

Killed—5.

Wounded—Dangerously 8; severely 7; slightly 6—21.

BOOKS AND PAPERS DESTROYED BY THE CONFLAGRATION IN 1814.

[Communicated to the House, October 26, 29, November 1, 11, and 17, 1814.]

GENERAL POST OFFICE,
October 25, 1814.

SIR: In compliance with the resolution of the House of Representatives, on the subject of information relative to the destruction of official books and papers belonging to the General Post Office, in consequence of the late incursion of the enemy, you are informed that no official books and papers are lost, belonging to the Department, in consequence of the late incursion.

I have the honor to be, your obedient servant,
R. J. MEIGS, Jr.
Postmaster General.

Hon. the SPEAKER
of the House of Representatives.

NAVY DEPARTMENT, *Oct. 27, 1814.*
SIR: In obedience to the resolution of the honorable House of Representatives, passed on the 24th instant, I have the honor to report.

That the whole of the official books, papers, trophies, and effects, in the office of the Secretary of the Navy, except the furniture of the office, were preserved from loss or injury by the late incursion of the enemy, and are now entire; and that all the official books and papers, in the office of the Accountant of the Navy, have been preserved, except those official papers relative to accounts settled and transmitted to the Treasury Department, referred to in the letter of which the enclosed is a copy.

I have the honor to be, very respectfully, sir, your obedient servant,
W. JONES.

Hon. the SPEAKER
of the House of Representatives.

NAVY DEPARTMENT,
Accountant's Office, Oct. 26, 1814.

SIR: In reply to your letter of this date, relative to the resolution of the House of Representatives on the subject of the destruction of the official books and papers in the respective departments, in consequence of the incursion of the enemy in the month of August, 1814, I have the honor to state that it is believed that all the official books and papers in this office were saved. I have no knowledge of the loss of a single book or paper of consequence; but I have understood that many of our official papers, relative to accounts settled and transmitted to the Treasury Department, were destroyed. What effect the loss may have on future adjustments, it is impossible for me to say.

With great respect, I have the honor to be, your obedient servant,
THOMAS TURNER.

Hon. WILLIAM JONES.

TREASURY DEPARTMENT.
October 3, 1814.
In obedience to the resolution of the House of Representatives, of the 24th instant, the Secretary of the Treasury respectfully reports:

That, with the exception of some old letters from the collectors of the customs and commissioners of loans, and other unimportant documents, no loss of official books or papers was sustained in his particular office by reason of the incursion of the enemy in the month of August, 1814.

Destruction of Public Books and Papers.

That the documents herewith transmitted, and marked A, B, C, D, E, and F, contain all the information furnished by the heads of the several offices attached to this Department, in relation to the object of the said resolution, and are prayed to be received as part of this report.

All which is respectfully submitted by

A. J. DALLAS,
Secretary of the Treasury.

A.

Treasury Department,
Comptroller's Office, Oct. 28, 1814.

Sir: To enable you to comply with a resolution of the House of Representatives, of the 24th instant, in relation to the destruction of official books and papers in the Treasury Department, I have to state, that all the official books and papers which were in this office on the 24th of August last, the day of the incursion of the enemy into this city, were packed up and removed from the Treasury, and have all since been returned, except a box containing brief entries of accounts, and another containing part of the accounts entered on the new books of the Accountant of the War Department, for the fourth quarter of 1813, and part of the accounts entered on the old books for the three last quarters of the same year.

These boxes, it is supposed, have, by some means, become mixed with others belonging to some other of the departments; and although diligent search has been made for them without effect, I do not yet despair of their being found.

I am, sir, with great respect, your obedient servant,

NATHAN LUFFBOROUGH,
Acting Comptroller.

Hon. A. J. Dallas,
Secretary of the Treasury.

B.

Treasury Department,
Auditor's Office, October 27, 1814.

Sir: In compliance with your request, accompanying a resolution of the House of Representatives, of the 24th instant, I have the honor to state, that of the official books and papers in the immediate charge of this office, none are known to have been destroyed or lost "in consequence of the incursion of the enemy in the month of August, 1814," excepting only a set of the printed journals and reports of the two Houses of Congress.

I have the honor to be, &c.

R. HARRISON.

Hon. Secretary of Treasury.

C.

Information respecting the books and papers of the Treasurer's office, required by a resolution of the House of Representatives, passed October 24, 1814.

Treasurer's Office, *Oct. 27, 1814.*

Legers, journals, remittance, bank, draft, and other books generally in use since the year 1810,

have been preserved, and many from the first establishment of the Treasury, particularly all the payments and receipts on account of the Treasury, War, and Navy Departments from their commencements. All the warrants, vouchers, and unsettled accounts of every kind, were preserved, except a few accounts and warrants which had been paid in July last, on account of the Privateer Pension Fund, and one on account of the seventh article of the British treaty. These can easily be replaced, the vouchers for the payments being preserved.

Many of the books and papers destroyed were brought from Philadelphia, and very few would ever have been wanted, as all the accounts of this office are adjusted at the end of every quarter, and the documents accompany the accounts to the accounting officers of the Treasury Department, and are afterwards deposited with the Register.

T. T. TUCKER,
Treasurer of the United States.

D.

Treasury Department,
Revenue Office, October 26, 1814.

Sir: I have the honor of stating, in compliance with your request, that no official books or papers belonging to this office were destroyed in consequence of the incursion of the enemy, in the month of August, 1814.

I am, with great respect,

S. SMITH,
Comm'r of the Revenue.

Hon. Secretary of Treasury.

E.

Treasury Department,
Register's Office, October 28, 1814.

The Register, in pursuance of the instructions from the Secretary of the Treasury, has the honor to represent, that the loss of books and papers in relation to the records of the Treasury, has, in a great degree, been limited to those of minor importance; and that, upon the late incursion of the enemy, all the essential books of the Treasury were removed to a place of safety.

That to comply more especially, by giving a description of the books and papers which were lost on that occasion, he begs leave to avail himself, by referring to certain papers herewith subjoined, being statements made by the clerks, respectively, having the charge of the principal books and records, and to which he submits the following remarks.

On the statements A and B, in relation to the principal books and records of the revenues of the United States:

The receipts and expenditures of public moneys, the accounts of individual collectors of the revenue, and of all public agents and persons accountable for moneys advanced or otherwise, were preserved; and that such as were lost (the very bulky and numerous settled accounts of the

Destruction of Public Books and Papers.

War and Navy Departments excepted,) were considered unimportant, compared with the books and records which were, on the emergency, removed, and which claimed the first attention of the Register with the few remaining clerks, who were not in the field in actual military service.

Statement C, in relation to the public debt:

In this branch of the public records, nothing has been lost that it is presumed can, in the most remote degree, affect the interests of the individual creditors, or the United States.

There arise two descriptions of records, from the mode adopted at the Treasury, of a quarter-yearly settlement of the legers, in which every individual creditor on the books of the Treasury is exhibited; the first of these are old legers closed, and put away as finished; the other, those which are operative, and contain the names of existing creditors, the sums due to each, and periods of interest. The journals and legers of the first description only were lost.

On the loss of the books in which were placed numerically the old cancelled loan-office certificates; the cancelled army certificates; the cancelled final settlement certificates; the Register respectfully remarks, that an official register of certificates of the aforegoing character outstanding, and which remained outstanding under each class, has been preserved; and that to this register of outstanding certificates reference has frequently been had in cases where petitions for payment have been presented to Congress; so that it is presumed no material inconvenience will arise from the destruction of those which have been brought in and satisfied.

On the marine records lost:

The records arising under the laws in relation to the registering, enrolling, and licensing ships and vessels of the United States, being duplicates transmitted to the Treasury by the district collectors, from the passing of those acts in the year 1792, bound up in volumes decriptive of their contents; together with the cancelled registers, enrolments, and licenses, placed numerically in books for, their reception; although they were destroyed, yet their loss, it is presumed, may be supplied in each port, by a reference to the corresponding records in the office of each collector; a mode which it is presumed has been resorted to, from the circumstance that, comparatively to their extent, few applications have been made for certified copies of such records at the Treasury.

Respectfully submitted, by your most obedient and most humble servant,

JOS. NOURSE, *Register.*
Hon. A. J. DALLAS, *Sec'ry of the Treas'y.*

A.

Schedule of the loss sustained by the destruction of the Treasury Department, in that branch of the Register's office where the books and accounts in relation to the impost and tonnage duties, the internal revenue, and direct tax, are kept, viz:

The legers, journals, and auxiliary books connected with the imports, tonnage, and internal revenues, from the commencement to the year 1810, inclusive.

The export books, from the commencement to the year 1803, inclusive.

The vouchers and documents relative to the settlement of the accounts of the collectors of the customs, and supervisors of the internal revenue and direct tax, from the commencement to the year 1811, inclusive.

It is to be observed, however, that the general results of the accounts of every individual collector and supervisor throughout the Union, as settled at the Treasury, being exhibited in the usual printed statements of the public accounts, the loss above enumerated cannot be considered as essential to, or in any way likely to affect the settlement of future accounts, arising from the statement of revenue before stated; and, further, that all the auditor's reports and statements of the accounts of the collectors of the customs, the internal revenue, and direct tax, from their commencement to the present period, have been saved.

JOS. DAWSON.

B.

Of the books and papers relative to the receipts and expenditures.

REGISTER'S OFFICE, *Oct. 26, 1814.*

The principal legers and journals, from the commencement of the present Government to the year 1798, were destroyed. The legers since that period, as well as the complete set of day books from the commencement of the Government, have been preserved.

The vouchers and reports on settled accounts, which were contained in upwards of one hundred large cases and chests in the fire-proof building, were destroyed. The Treasury statements and accounts from the commencement of the present Government have, in general, been preserved.

Upon the whole, it is conceived but little inconvenience will be incurred in the settlement of accounts from the destruction of books and papers in relation to this branch of the office.

JOS. STRETCH.

C.

Of the books and records in relation to the accounts of the public debt, the following were destroyed.

REGISTER'S OFFICE, *Oct. 25, 1814.*

1. Several old journals and legers, the accounts in which had been closed.

Books containing receipts for certificates of funded debt delivered at the Treasury previous to the year 1800. The receipts taken since have been preserved.

2. Cancelled certificates or evidences of the Revolutionary funded debt, numerically arranged and bound up in books, which were numerous and bulky; they contained,

1. Loan Office certificates.
2. Army certificates.
3. Final settlement certificates issued by the commissioners of the staff department.

Destruction of Public Books and Papers.

4. Final settlement certificates issued by commissioners in the several States.

5. Final settlement certificates issued in the marine department.

The whole were destroyed; an official list, however, exhibiting the certificates which remain outstanding was preserved, by which the equity of claims for certificates of either description may be ascertained with precision.

3. Receipts for dividends of principal and interest on the funded debt paid at the several loan offices, from the commencement of the Government to the 31st December, 1812, were lost; also, receipts for dividends declared at the Treasury to the 31st December, 1810.

Dividends returned unclaimed from the loan offices for payment at the Treasury; the transcripts of these dividends, however, which were made in this office, in books prepared with columns for receipts, and which were preserved, exhibit not only the amount paid thereon, but also every sum now due to individual creditors.

Transfers or cancelled certificates of the funded debt previous to the year 1811. All the powers of attorney for transferring stock were preserved.

MICHAEL NOURSE.

F.

GENERAL LAND OFFICE,
October 26, 1814.

SIR: All the maps of this office, and all the books and papers necessary to the settlement of accounts, were saved from destruction.

The papers destroyed were files of military warrants, which had been located and patented; files of final certificates, and other papers relative to purchased lands which had been patented; a few files of monthly returns from land offices, which files had been posted into the legers; the loss of these papers will not affect the public interest. I have, &c.

JOHN GARDINER,
Chief Clerk.

Hon. A. J. DALLAS,
Secretary of the Treasury.

WAR DEPARTMENT, *Nov. 9, 1814.*

SIR: Conformably to a resolution of the House of Representatives, of October 24, requiring of this Department a report relative to the destruction of books and papers in consequence of the incursion of the enemy in the month of August, 1814, I have the honor to report, that all the books of record belonging to this office were saved, and that no papers of any kind were lost, except recommendations for appointments in the Army, and letters received more than seven years previous; of all these, however, there is a record in the office, viz: the names of applicants, and a brief of the substance of all other letters which were not preserved.

All the standards and colors taken from the enemy during the Revolution, as well as those of the present war, which had been deposited in the War Office, were also saved.

In relation to the books and papers of several offices attached to this Department, I take the liberty to enclose the reports which have been made to me by the principal officer of each.

I have the honor to be, with great respect, your obedient servant,   J. MONROE.

Hon. the SPEAKER,
of the House of Representatives.

Adjutant's Report.

DEPARTMENT OF WAR,
Accountant's Office, Oct. 27, 1814.

SIR: In compliance with the resolution of the House of Representatives, of the 24th instant, this day transmitted to me from your office, directing the Secretaries of the several Departments, and the Postmaster General, to communicate to the House such information as may be in their power, in relation to the destruction of official books and papers in their respective Departments, in consequence of the incursion of the enemy, in the month of August, 1814, &c., I have the honor to state, that the books and papers belonging to this office were removed at the time above mentioned, and are now in a state of safety, excepting a part of the papers and army accounts appertaining to the Revolutionary war, which had been saved from the flames on the burning of the house occupied by the War Department in 1800. When the books and papers of this office were removed, as before mentioned, it was not practicable to obtain conveyance for all; it was, therefore, determined to leave the old papers and army accounts, as the loss of those (if any loss should happen) would be attended with less inconvenience than that of any other papers. They were in the fire-proof room of the office at the time of the incursion of the enemy, and when that building was burnt they remained uninjured by the flames; but the room having been entered by some persons soon after the building was destroyed, the papers were deranged, and many of them undoubtedly destroyed or carried away at that time; but it is not possible to identify those which may have been thus destroyed. When the public papers were brought back to the City of Washington, the remainder of those papers (by far the larger part of the whole) were removed to the house now occupied as the Accountant's office.

It is not probable that the loss of those papers can have any effect in the adjustment of the unsettled accounts of the United States, as the claims (if any) which might arise under them have been barred by acts of limitation.

With very great respect, I have the honor to be, sir, your most obedient servant,

TOBIAS LEAR.

Hon. SECRETARY OF WAR.

Paymaster's Report.

ARMY PAY OFFICE, *Oct. 29, 1814.*

The Paymaster of the Army of the United States, in obedience to a resolution of the House

Destruction of Public Books and Papers.

of Representatives, under date October the 24th, 1814, has the honor to report:

That, by great exertions all the books, accounts, rolls, and papers of his office, which were of any considerable importance, were saved from the destructive incursion of the enemy at this place, in the month of August, 1814; but agreeably to the tenor of the resolution he proceeds to mention, as nearly as can be well ascertained, those which were not saved, and the probable effect which will result from their loss. They are as follows, namely:

Part of the copies of the statements of such re-cruiting and other accounts as had been adjusted and settled in this office, with old duplicate vouchers, the originals of which were sent up to the other offices of the Government to be finally deposited in the Treasury Department. No inconvenience will result to the Government from this loss; (provided the originals are preserved;) the only inconvenience which will be felt is in this office, where, instead of referring to our copies for information, we shall have to resort to the originals at the Treasury Department.

The accounts and vouchers of Lieutenant Samuel Scott, as paymaster of the twenty-fourth regiment of infantry. The instructions of the Paymaster of the Army to all sub-paymasters, direct them to keep duplicates of their accounts and vouchers, and Lieutenant Scott has been called on for the duplicates of his; when they are received the loss will be made good.

A small book containing a record of certain stoppages from the pay of non-commissioned officers, musicians, artificers, and privates; a book of minor importance, and as the stoppages had all been directed, and many of them actually made and done, the loss of it is considered of very little consequence.

The recruiting account and vouchers (in part) of the late Major Timothy Dix, of the 14th regiment of infantry, deceased. If the legal representative of Major Dix produces the duplicates, which it is expected are among the papers of the deceased, the loss will be retrieved.

It is possible that some few other papers might have been lost, which cannot now be recollected or ascertained. It is believed, however, that they could not have been of much magnitude or importance.

Respectfully,　　　　R. BRENT,
　　　　　　　　Paymaster U. S. Army.
Hon. JAMES MONROE,
　　　Secretary of War.

Report of the Superintendent General of Military Supplies.

WASHINGTON, *October* 24, 1814.

SIR: In compliance with the resolution of the House of Representatives, of the 24th instant, I have the honor to state, that none of the books or papers belonging to the office of the Superintendent General of Military Supplies have been lost or otherwise destroyed, in consequence of the incursion of the enemy in the month of August last.

I have the honor to be, very respectfully, at your obedient servant,

　　　　　　RICHARD CUTTS,
　　　Supt. Gen. Military Supplies.
Hon. JAMES MONROE,
　　　Secretary of War.

Adjutant and Inspector General's Report.

ADJ. AND INS. GENERAL'S OFFICE,
　　　Washington, Oct. 28, 1814.

SIR: In conformity to your order, and with a view to meet a resolution of the House of Representatives, of the 24th instant, calling for information relative to the destruction of official books and papers by the enemy, on the 24th of August last, I have the honor to inform you that the papers which belonged to this office, and what were destroyed by the conflagration of the enemy, were files of muster-rolls, inspection, generals monthly and recruiting returns, up to the year 1813, inclusive. In addition to this, several copies of Stoddard's Artillery, and a few copies of a System of Drum Beating for the use of the Army, which had not been distributed, were also lost. The whole loss, however, is of no material consequence.

I have the honor, to be, very respectfully, at your obedient humble servant,

　　　　　　JOHN R. BELL,
　　　Assistant Inspector General.
Hon. JAMES MONROE,
　　　Secretary of War.

ORDNANCE OFFICE, WASHINGTON,
　　　October 27, 1814.

SIR: In obedience to a request from your Department, I have the honor to state that, in the late invasion and conflagration of the enemy at this city, no valuable books or papers stacked or belonging to this office sustained any loss or injury. A few printed books, of inconsiderable value, and some loose papers of no intrinsic importance, with a small quantity of furniture, stationery, &c., formed the only articles which were destroyed.

Very respectfully, I have the honor to be, at your obedient servant,

　　　　　　JOHN MORTON,
　　　Deputy Commissary
Hon. SECRETARY *of War.*

DEPARTMENT OF STATE,
　　　November 14, 1814.

The acting Secretary of State, in compliance with the resolution of the House of Representatives, of the 24th ultimo, requesting such information as may be in the power of the several Departments to afford, in relation to the destruction of the official books and papers in their Departments, respectively, in consequence of the incursion of the enemy in the month of August 1814, has the honor to report:

That, when it became apparent from the move-

Intercourse with the Enemy.

ments of the enemy, after his debarkation at Benedict, that his destination was the seat of Government, every exertion was made, and every means employed, for the removal of the books and papers of this office, to a place of safety; and, notwithstanding the extreme difficulty in obtaining the means of conveyance, it is believed that every paper and manuscript book of the office, of any importance, including those of the old Government, and all in relation to accounts, were placed in a state of security. That it was not found practicable, however, to preserve in like manner, the volumes of laws reserved by Congress for future disposition; many of the books belonging to the library of the Department, as well as some letters on file of minor importance from individuals on business mostly disposed of, which were unavoidably left, and shared the fate, it is presumed, of the building in which they were deposited.

All of which is respectfully submitted.
JAMES MONROE.

INTERCOURSE WITH THE ENEMY.

—

The Attorney General of the United States to the District Attorney of the United States for Massachusetts.

WASHINGTON, *July* 28, 1814.

DEAR SIR: I have had the honor to receive your letter of the 16th of this month. I perfectly agree with you that the intercourse which, in general terms, you describe as taking place on the part of our citizens with the enemy's ships upon the coast, is altogether incompatible with a state of war. Whatever of necessary business, growing out of the belligerent state, is to be transacted with the enemy, should be transacted with the knowledge and under the sanction of the Government. Any other doctrine might lead to consequences too palpably mischievous to be countenanced by any sound views of the public safety. To the highest powers of Government alone does it belong to make war. To the Government alone does it belong to carry it on. To its exclusive authority is negotiation committed, whatever character it may assume, whether involving the highest interests of the nation at large, or merely those matters of subordinate individual concern which spring up as unavoidably concomitant to a state of national hostility. The legal operation of the act declaring war was to put the subjects and citizens of the two countries in the condition of enemies towards each other. The slightest intercourse of trade between them is hence forbidden. All property detected as the subject of such trade is forfeitable under the general law resulting at all times and to all nations from a state of war, and which this nation appropriated to itself when it became belligerent, as indispensable to its operations, its duties, and its safety.

Much more subversive of these ends might it prove if our citizens be suffered to hold, without the license of public authority, personal intercourse with the enemy; to visit, at pleasure, their fleets, while actually invading our waters and threatening our towns. Such conduct constitutes an encroachment upon the attributes delegated to Government, and which, under the theory of our Constitution, should be exercised only by the Executive branch as a necessary incident to Executive authority. The Government that passively and promiscuously permits this encroachment must agree to surrender its power of self-preservation. The citizen who imagines himself at liberty to embark in it must have a limited and erroneous sense of the obligations that should bind him. The forecast of the former cannot fail to perceive that it too obviously confers the means of doing mischief to suffer it to stand excused by any subsequent allegations of an unexceptionable or laudable motive, and should cut off remote and probable dangers by a strict inhibition of every species of such intercourse, under whatever pretences attempted. The latter should hesitate at taking a step so susceptible of abuse, which might open a door to pernicious imitation; and which, whatever its genuine or harmless complexion in his particular instance, is calculated to beget suspicions unfavorable to his intentions and hazardous to his fame. By the act of spontaneously repairing to the hostile ships, he separates himself from his country; identifies himself, for the time being, with its foe, and by exhibiting himself upon their decks without the stamp of national permission, is liable, under first impressions, to be viewed by both the one and the other, as in a garb of doubtful innocence. He goes unshielded and unknown. If any one citizen may rightfully repair to the enemy for any purpose which he chooses either sincerely to avow, or fictitiously to set up, all must be allowed to claim a participation in the same indulgence. Thus, an evil-disposed person, veiling a malignant and treacherous intention under cover of these excursions, with no limit to their number, and left to his own choice of circumstances and time, may become the bearer of information and plans, to gratify his own turbulent designs and work the ruin of his country. These remarks are conceived to be founded upon principles intrinsically sound, because inseparable from the safeguard of the Commonwealth, and that must hold out the strongest titles to assent in every dispassionate mind. The policy of other nations has adopted the method of a flag of truce from the Government or its known agents, when intercourse is to take place with an enemy, which serves as an universal symbol, that it is under public permission, and for lawful and necessary purposes. That the citizens of the United States, during a war, should be all at once absolved from this ancient, cautionary usage; that they should be freely allowed to substitute their own will for that of the Government; passing to the enemy's lines or to the enemy's ships, for objects innocent or fatal, at their own loose discretion, seems as irreconcilable to reason as it is opposed to the maxims of prudence that have heretofore regulated the conduct of contending nations.

In reply to your request for my opinion as to what course it might be proper to pursue towards persons who go on board the enemy's ships hovering upon our shores, without any previous license derived from public authority, I beg leave to state—

That I think such intercourse should, in every case, be regarded as importing a strong, *prima facie* intention of guilt. It raises a presumption of designs adverse to the country, and favoring the enemy, which should not be passed over without a scrupulous inquiry on the part of those functionaries who are charged with the punishing justice of the laws; and it behooves good citizens to be assistant to the magistrates upon all such occasions. If there be reason to think that, under the guise of some specious or inoffensive purpose, any improper information has been conveyed by direct or indirect, but intelligible, means of communication, or any supplies been furnished, and the competent evidence of such fact or facts can be obtained, it is obvious that the party stands embraced by the Constitutional definition of treason, in giving aid to the enemy, and should be proceeded against accordingly.

If no evidence exist, or be discoverable to this effect, it may be asked, is the bare act of thus going on board punishable by indictment under our existing laws?

I am not prepared to answer this question in the affirmative. Good men may, undoubtedly, be found going on board for ends that are innocent; however, in the view of a wise and safe policy, independent of any law, its impropriety could scarcely fail to strike every mind intelligent while it was patriotic. But there may possibly be room for fearing, and if there be, it is deeply to be regretted, that those who slight the unsophisticated verdict of the public feeling, in making these voluntary visits, may have been looking with a more anxious discernment into the presumed defects of our existing jurisprudence, than consulting, under enlarged and unbiassed estimates of duty, their own paramount obligations as members of the social body. It is true, indeed, that, under my views of the subject, no statute has yet been passed by Congress, looking particularly to this kind of conduct, or establishing it by specific definition as an independent crime. I do not think that the act of the 3d of January, 1799, entitled an act for the punishment of certain crimes therein specified, or the more recent one of the 6th of July, 1812, for the prohibition of trade with the enemy, can be considered as having contemplated the particular species of intercourse with the armed enemy, of which we are speaking; or that, under the safe rules applicable to the interpretation of penal laws, they could now be made to embrace it. At the same time I imagine it will be conceded that there exists full power to prohibit and punish specifically such intercourse as an integral, primary offence. The high exercise of legislative authority which made the United States a belligerent, necessarily invested the body corporate of their Government with the resulting powers incident to a state of war; which powers, I cannot doubt, may be called into activity in detail and positive acts of legislation, at the direction of the same authority, and made co-extensive with the exigencies and duration of the war itself.

In what manner this kind of intercourse with a public enemy may be punished at mere common law, it is not necessary that I should inquire. Upon this point, if I must express an opinion, premising that it is of no more value than that of any other individual, I must declare that I do not think the common law applicable in such a case to the Government of the United States. I should feel regret at supposing that any official functions of which I may recognise the obligations, implied the necessity of my withholding the expression of this opinion. I do not think that a Federal Republic like ours, resting upon, as its only pillars, the limited political concessions of distinct and independent sovereign States, drew to itself, by any just implication, at the moment of its circumscribed structure, the whole common law of England, with all or any portion of its dark catalogue of crimes and punishments; a code which the more liberal and humane wisdom of a later day—the labors of the Romillys and the Benthams, following the more ancient structures of a Blackstone and a Hale—has been uniting, ever since, to free of its fierce and sanguinary features; a code which, among the vast variety of actions that, in a complicated community, human frailty may be betrayed into, denounces, upon scarcely less than two hundred, capital infliction; thereby, as the regular and melancholy fruit of such a system, and as authentic lights assure us, imprinting more of human blood upon the public than is known to the same extent of population in any other portion of Europe. Against the incorporation of such a code, even with the limitations that might be implied, upon the jurisprudence of the Union, I perceive serious and insurmountable objections. I believe, also, that this opinion has been adopted, partially at least, by the highest judicial tribunal known to the Constitution,[*] although I observe that you speak doubtfully upon this point, considering it as yet ultimately at rest. In order, therefore, to warrant proceedings against a party, under the systematic and regular course of a criminal prosecution by indictment, I confess it does appear to me that the act for which he is to be indicted, should be marked down, and the penalty affixed by some statute of Congress.

If no punishment can be superinduced through the medium of an indictment, it may next be asked, is there no other mode in which this person can be rendered obnoxious to legal animadversion? Is he to run no further risk than that of being made captive by trusting himself at a

---

[*] In the case of the United States against John and Goodwin; Supreme Court United States February, 1813.

Intercourse with the Enemy.

enemy's power; a risk which, on the pre-supposition of his intending to favor the enemy, it is idle to advert to ? Is an act, the abstract and universal impropriety of which must exist, as it would seem, in the convictions of every unclouded understanding, and, as we would also think, be traced in characters as legible upon every heart; is such an act to be passed over without any notice from the magistracy; thereby, in the absence of all correction, inviting its endless repetition; to the disparagement of that fidelity which should bind in its transcendent ties, the citizen to the public, to the signal disrepute of our citizens themselves, in derision of all law, and to the manifest danger of the State?

To these more important questions, I feel happy in not being obliged to give a negative answer. I think that every private individual who is seen to throw himself upon the armed and invading foe, without the knowledge and permission of his Government, should be arrested and taken before the proper judge or court. That if this cannot be done with a view to prosecute him by indictment, it at least may be with a view to lay the foundation of a charge on which he may be bound in sufficient sureties to his good behaviour; for such intercourse with the enemy puts him under a suspicion so strong, that the law should be awake with all its vigilance and activity. It lies on the direct road to treason; seems an approximation to it, opening at once every facility to its commission by taking the first and natural step. If no crime, in the moral scale, has in fact been perpetrated, such verisimilitude of criminal intention is held out, as should put the party upon his excuse. And this, as I apprehend, not by his own mere voluntary asseverations, of an inoffensive motive, but under the solemnities of a judicial scrutiny and sanction. If he can make out, by unexceptionable testimony, his innocence; that is, if he can show that, during all the while he was in communion with the enemy, he did nothing or uttered nothing that would bring him within the pale of treason; or if he can show that some invincible necessity compelled his going, the judges, as the law now stands, might probably exercise a discretion in directing his discharge. On the other hand, if there be no such repellent proof, I should presume that the bare going on board being fixed upon him, would authorize his being held to his good behaviour. The amount of security to be demanded, would, of course, regulate itself, under judicial discretion, by the previous habits and standing of the party, which might serve to give cause of greater or less suspicion. It will be seen that, in this course; no departure is implied from the rule of law, which requires the proof always to follow up the allegation; since proof of the substantive act, which must always, in the first instance, be adduced of going at mere private instigation to the enemy while in armed array, is to be the standard of enforcing against the accused this species of preventive justice. Nor, in the language of the books, can he reasonably complain of being laid under this restraint, when, by his own impru-

13th Con. 3d Sess.—58

dence, he has given such cause to suspect that he will perpetrate a crime.

It may perhaps be said that, as this binding over to good behaviour is a process at common law, to pursue it would be to recognise the authority of that system as the source of the remedy. It appears to me that such an objection is susceptible of an obvious answer. The right to bind over, is the necessary adjunct to the right to indict and punish the principal crime. It is, as it were, the accident inherent in the substance. Treason itself being forbidden and punishable by indictment, it becomes necessary that a step which, until fully explained away, verges so closely upon treason, should be followed up by this incipient restraint, so strictly comprehended within, and related to the power of final punishment. The voluntarily rushing into the enemy's camp, is to be considered in the light of a first probable commencement of that train, the entire series of which is, in sound construction, already declared to be a crime by the Constitution and the law. To wait its consummation, or the progressive stages of its development, might be to render the parent statute itself little less than a dead letter. Its existence may surely be anticipated where violent presumptions are afforded, and the arm of the statute be reached out, in indispensable extension of its efficacy to ward off, to check, to extinguish, the first movements towards the criminal deed. The power to punish, by established and known means, must draw after it the power to prevent, by derivative and kindred means. The less must be comprehended within the greater of its own quality and its own kind. Any other principles of construction would be over-scrupulous, would be against just reasoning upon judiciary powers, and might be in danger of paring down the statute of treason itself to a few abortive words.

The doctrine which goes to exclude the common law of England, taken as a general system, from the criminal jurisprudence of our country, has never denied it a prevalence and force *sub modo.* It has been adopted in universal practice, as the incidental guide and handmaid to our acts of positive legislation. The very institution of a court by Congress, necessarily implies its investiture with certain powers known at common law, fundamental to the discharge of its functions. How far is the aid of parts of this auxiliary code, incorporeal by inference and deduction upon our own statutes; how else could the statute of treason; how could any other statute of Congress which creates an offence and authorizes punishment, be executed? The shaping of the indictment; its caption; the form and body of phraseology; the legal idea of the offence; the rules of evidence on the trial; those applicable to the jury, to the carrying into effect the sentence upon conviction; these, and various other powers, are taken to be implied the moment that we are furnished by Congress with a statutory definition and punishment of a crime. Upon this foundation have the courts of the United States acted as soon as an offence has been thrown upon their general cognizance, without waiting for acts of

Proclamations by the President.

after-legislation, as their warrant for the observance and enforcement of these collateral attributes to the chief jurisdiction. But then such jurisdiction in chief must first have have been conferred, and in this I take it lies the true distinction. In like manner, the right to bind over to the peace or good behaviour, is an anterior attribute of juridical authority, applicable to all offences known to the English code. Whenever, therefore, our own statutory code recognises and punishes an offence, it must adopt such anterior attribute as it has done all others that are merely collateral, the statute of Congress when once passed, taking to itself every incident that ought to move within its principal orbit, and which is necessary to its complete effect. Care, indeed, must be taken, that where the power to bind over is drawn forth, the cause of suspicion must have direct and fair relation to some offence which our own statutes actually forbid. In no other way can there be laid a just groundwork for its exercise. If, for example, a citizen by menaces, by laying in wait, or by any other indications, had given probable cause to suspect that he meditated violence upon the person of a foreign ambassador, he ought, I think, to be restrained by this previous interposition of the law—the offence itself being punishable by a statute of the United States. But if he had barely given cause to think that he designed to introduce popery into the country, his hands could not be thus tied up, the silence of our own laws viewing this as altogether harmless, however it may be treated by those of England. It would be easy to multiply illustrations under this head, but I fear I have already dwelt unnecessarily upon what must seem so plainly an incident to every court clothed by Congress with powers to try and punish crimes.

I am informed that this power of binding over, has had, as matter of undisputed authority under our code, the sanction of the Chief Justice of the United States. That in a case which recently occurred before him in the district of Virginia, of a charge of treason, the proof being insufficient as to the overt acts, he dismissed the defendant without any recognizance to appear and stand his trial; but was nevertheless of opinion that circumstances justified his being held to his good behaviour; and, bail not being at hand, committed him to prison. In this case the party had been on board the British ships in the Chesapeake.

In no part of any of the foregoing observations, already I fear in danger of extending to too much length, have I introduced the question, how far a grand jury would be strictly called upon in every case to find a bill for treason against a citizen, founded upon the simple fact of his going of his own accord on board an enemy's ship while invading our waters; and considering this mere fact as proof quite sufficient of such an overt act, as to put him upon his trial and defence. Perhaps, however, if the proof stopped here without advancing any further, the petit jury might hesitate at a verdict which would fix upon the party the heavy penalties of treason. I abstain from enlarging upon this point; though, surely, than

the contumacious and unexplained repetition of such suspicious visits, more violent presumptions of the guilt of treason could scarcely be laid before the judgments and consciences of jurors. If the mere fact of going on board without permission from the Government, no matter in what way attempted to be justified or palliated, were made in every case a misdemeanor, punishable by fine and imprisonment, it would perhaps be most effectual towards putting an end to a species of intercourse so dangerous and reprehensible. But this is a subject for Congress alone to regulate. I will here just-remark, that if at any time a boat should be seen to put off from an enemy's ship invading our waters, and be making towards our shores, without the exhibition of a known symbol of truce from our own Government, or from the enemy, I do not see what is to prevent our land or naval officers in the vicinity firing upon it, considering it as a hostile boat; and, until the appearance be explained, incorporated with the force and intentions of the enemy. This I presume is a hazard which the party making the private visit, agrees not to take upon himself.

I have taken the liberty to express my opinions in the course of this letter with less reserve, under the satisfactory consciousness, that, if ever any of them should be thought worthy to be acted upon, whatever errors they contain will be corrected by the superior and authoritative learning of those Judges and Courts, who confer such dignity upon the judgment-seats of the Union; and to the controlling wisdom of whose decisions I shall ever be found amongst the foremost to pay reverence and submission.

I have the honor to be, with great respect, your obedient servant,

         RICHARD RUSH,
       Attorney General United States.

U. S. DISTRICT ATTORNEY
     for Massachusetts.

PROCLAMATION.

By the President of the United States of America.

The two Houses of the National Legislature having, by a joint resolution, expressed their desire that, in the present time of public calamity and war, a day may be recommended to be observed by the people of the United States as a day of public humiliation, and fasting, and of prayer to Almighty God, for the safety and welfare of these States, his blessings on their arms, and a speedy restoration of peace—I have deemed it proper, by this Proclamation, to recommend that *Thursday, the twelfth of January next,* be set apart as a day on which all may have an opportunity of voluntarily offering, at the same time, in their respective religious assemblies, their humble adorations to the Great Sovereign of the Universe, of confessing their sins and transgressions, and of strengthening their vows of repentance and amendment. They will be invited by the same solemn occasion, to call to mind the distinguished favors conferred on the

Proclamations by the President.

American people, in the general health which has been enjoyed; in the abundant fruits of the season; in the progress of the arts instrumental to their comfort, their prosperity, and their security; and in the victories which have so powerfully contributed to the defence and protection of our country—a devout thankfulness for all which ought to be mingled with their supplications to the Beneficent Parent of the human race, that he would be graciously pleased to pardon all their offences against Him; to support and animate them in the discharge of their respective duties; to continue to them the precious advantages flowing from political institutions so auspicious to their safety against dangers from abroad, to their tranquillity at home, and to their liberties, civil and religious; and that he would, in a special manner, preside over the nation, in its public councils and constituted authorities, giving wisdom to its measures, and success to its arms in maintaining its rights, and in overcoming all hostile designs and attempts against it; and finally, that by inspiring the enemy with dispositions favorable to a just and reasonable peace, its blessings may be speedily and happily restored.

Given under my hand, at the City of Washington, the sixteenth day of November, one thousand eight hundred and fourteen, and of the independence of the United States, the thirty-eighth.

JAMES MADISON.

By the President,
JAMES MONROE.
Acting Secretary of State.

PROCLAMATION.

By the President of the United States of America.

Among the many evils produced by the wars, which, with little intermission, have afflicted Europe, and extended their ravages into other quarters of the globe, for a period exceeding twenty years, the dispersion of a considerable portion of the inhabitants of different countries, in sorrow and in want, has not been the least injurious to human happiness, nor the least severe in the trial of human virtue.

It had been long ascertained, that many foreigners flying from the dangers of their own home, and some citizens, forgetful of their duty, had co-operated in forming an establishment on the Island of Barrataria, near the mouth of the river Mississippi, for the purpose of a clandestine and lawless trade. The Government of the United States caused the establishment to be broken up and destroyed: and, having obtained the means of designating the offenders of every description, it only remained to answer the demands of justice, by inflicting an exemplary punishment.

But it has been represented, that the offenders have manifested a sincere penitence; that they have abandoned the prosecution of the worst cause for the support of the best; and, particularly, that they have exhibited, in the defence of

New Orleans, unequivocal traits of courage and fidelity. Offenders, who have refused to become the associates of the enemy in the war, upon the most seducing terms of invitation; and who have aided to repel his hostile invasion of the territory of the United States; can no longer be considered as objects of punishment, but as objects of generous forgiveness.

It has, therefore, been seen, with great satisfaction, that the General Assembly of the State of Louisiana earnestly recommend these offenders to the benefit of a full pardon: And in compliance with that recommendation, as well as in consideration of all the other extraordinary circumstances of the case, I, JAMES MADISON, President of the United States of America, do issue this Proclamation, hereby granting, publishing, and declaring, a free and full pardon of all offences committed in violation of any act or acts of the Congress of the said United States, touching the revenue, trade, and navigation thereof, or touching the intercourse and commerce of the United States with foreign nations, at any time before the eighth day of January, in the present year one thousand eight hundred and fifteen, by any person or persons whatsoever, being inhabitants of New Orleans and the adjacent country, or being inhabitants of the said Island of Barrataria, and the places adjacent: *Provided,* That every person, claiming the benefit of this full pardon, in order to entitle himself thereto, shall produce a certificate in writing from the Governor of the State of Louisiana, stating that such person has aided in the defence of New Orleans, and the adjacent country, during the invasion thereof, as aforesaid.

And I do hereby further authorize and direct all suits, indictments, and prosecutions, for fines, penalties, and forfeitures, against any person or persons, who shall be entitled to the benefit of this full pardon, forthwith to be stayed, discontinued, and released: And all civil officers are hereby required, according to the duties of their respective stations, to carry this Proclamation into immediate and faithful execution.

Done at the City of Washington, the sixth day of February, in the year one thousand eight hundred and fifteen, and of the independence of the United States the thirty-ninth.

JAMES MADISON.

PROCLAMATION.

By the President of the United States of America.

The Senate and House of Representatives of the United States have, by a joint resolution, signified their desire, that a day may be recommended, to be observed by the people of the United States with religious solemnity, as a day of thanksgiving and of devout acknowledgments to Almighty God, for his great goodness, manifested in restoring to them the blessing of peace.

No people ought to feel greater obligations to celebrate the goodness of the Great Disposer of

Proclamations by the President.

events, and of the destiny of nations, than the people of the United States. His kind Providence originally conducted them, to one of the best portions of the dwelling place, allowed for the great family of the human race. He protected and cherished them, under all the difficulties and trials to which they were exposed in their early days. Under his fostering care, their habits, their sentiments and their pursuits, prepared them for a transition in due time for a state of independence and of self-government. In the arduous struggle by which it was attained, they were distinguished by multiplied tokens of his benign interposition. During the interval which succeeded, he reared them into the strength, and endowed them with the resources, which have enabled them to assert their national rights, and to enhance their national character, in another arduous conflict, which is now happily terminated, by a peace and reconciliation with those who have been our enemies. And to the same Divine Author of every good and perfect gift, we are indebted for all those privileges and advantages, religious as well as civil, which are so richly enjoyed in this favored land.

It is for blessings, such as these, and more especially for the restoration of the blessing of peace, that I now recommend that the second *Thursday in April* next be set apart, as a day on which the people, of every religious denomination, may, in their solemn assemblies, unite their hearts and their voices, in a free-will offering to their Heavenly Benefactor, of their homage of thanksgiving, and of their songs of praise.

Given at the City of Washington on the fourth day of March, in the year of our Lord one thousand eight hundred and fifteen, and of the independence of the United States the thirty-ninth.

JAMES MADISON.

PUBLIC ACTS OF CONGRESS;

An Act further to extend the right of suffrage, and to increase the number of members of the Legislative Council, in the Mississippi Territory.

Be it enacted by the Senate and House of Representatives of the United States of America, in Congress assembled, That each and every free white male person, being a citizen of the United States, who shall have attained the age of twenty-one years, and who shall have paid a county or Territorial tax, and who also shall have resided one year in said Territory previous to any general election, and be, at the time of any such election, a resident thereof, shall be entitled to vote for members of the House of Representatives, and a delegate to Congress; for the Territory aforesaid: anything in the ordinance or in any act relative to the government of said Territory to the contrary notwithstanding.

SEC. 2. *And be it further enacted,* That the House of Representatives of the Territory aforesaid be, and they hereby are, authorized to nominate eight persons, being citizens of the United States, to the President of the United States, four of whom shall be appointed members of the Legislative Council for said Territory, in addition to the number already provided, any act or ordinance to the contrary notwithstanding.

E. GERRY,
Vice President of the United States.
LANGDON CHEVES,
Speaker of the House of Representatives.
Approved, October 25, 1814.
JAMES MADISON.

An Act further extending the time for locating Virginia military land warrants, and for returning the surveys thereon to the General Land Office.

Be it enacted, &c., That the officers and soldiers of the Virginia line, on Continental Establishment, their heirs or assigns, entitled to bounty lands within the tract reserved by Virginia, between the Little Miami and Sciota rivers, for satisfying the legal bounties to her officers and soldiers upon Continental Establishment, shall be allowed a further term of three years, from and after the passage of this act, to obtain warrants and complete their locations, and a further term of five years, from and after the passage of this act as aforesaid, to return their surveys and warrants, or certified copies of warrants, to the General Land Office, anything in any former act to the contrary notwithstanding: *Provided,* That no locations, as aforesaid, within the above-mentioned tract, shall, after the passing of this act, be made on tracts of land for which patents had previously been issued, or which had been previously surveyed; and any patent which may, nevertheless, be obtained for land located contrary to the provisions of this act, shall be considered as null and void.

Approved, November 3, 1814.

An Act authorizing the President of the United States to cause to be built or purchased the vessels therein described.

Be it enacted, &c., That, in addition to the present Naval Establishment, the President of the United States be, and he is hereby, authorized to cause to be built or purchased, manned, equipped, and officered, any number of vessels, not exceeding twenty, which, in his opinion, the public service may require, to carry not less than eight, nor more than sixteen, guns each.

SEC. 2. *And be it further enacted,* That, for the building, or purchase, and equipping, of these vessels, the sum of six hundred thousand dollars be, and the same is hereby, appropriated, to be paid out of any money in the Treasury, not otherwise appropriated.

Approved, November 15, 1814.

An Act to authorize a loan for a sum not exceeding three millions of dollars.

Be it enacted, &c., That the President of the United States be, and he is hereby, authorized to borrow, on the credit of the United States, a sum not exceeding three millions of dollars, to be applied, in addition to the moneys now in the Treasury, or which may be received from other sources, to defray any expenses which may have been, or, during the present year, may be, authorized by law, and for which appropriations have been, or, during the present year, may be, made by law: *Provided,* That no engagement or contract shall be entered into, which shall preclude the United States from reimbursing any sum or sums thus borrowed, at any time after the expiration of twelve years from the last day of December next.

SEC. 2. *And be it further enacted,* That the Secretary of the Treasury, with the approbation of the President of the United States, be, and he is hereby, authorized to cause to be constituted certificates of stock, signed by the Register of the Treasury, or by a Commissioner of Loans, for the sum to be borrowed by this act, or for any part thereof, and the same to be sold. And the Secretary of the Treasury shall lay before Congress an account of all the moneys obtained by the sale of the certificates of stock in manner aforesaid, together with a statement of the rate at which the same may have been sold.

Sec. 3. *And be it further enacted,* That the Secretary of the Treasury be, and he is hereby, authorized, with the approbation of the President of the United States, to employ an agent or agents, for the purpose of obtaining subscriptions to the loan authorized by this act, or of selling any part of the stock to be created by virtue thereof. A commission, not exceeding one-quarter of one per cent. on the amount thus sold, or for which subscriptions shall have been thus obtained, may, by the Secretary of the Treasury, be allowed to such agent or agents; and a sum not exceeding nine thousand dollars, to be paid out of any moneys in the Treasury, not otherwise appropriated, is hereby appropriated for paying the amount of such commission or commissions as may be thus allowed, and also for defraying the expenses of printing, and issuing the subscription certificates and certificates of stock, and other expenses incident to the completing of the loan authorized by this act.

Sec. 4. *And be it further enacted,* That it shall be lawful to receive in payment of any loan obtained under this act, or under any other act of Congress authorizing a loan, Treasury notes which have been issued according to law, and which shall become due and payable on or before the first day of January next, at the par value of such Treasury notes, together with the interest thereon accrued, at the time of the payment on account of the loan.

Sec. 5. *And be it further enacted,* That so much of the funds constituting the annual appropriation of eight millions of dollars, for the payment of the principal and interest of the public debt of the United States, as may be wanted for that purpose, after satisfying the sums necessary for the payment of the interest and such part of the principal of said debt, as the United States are now pledged annually to pay or reimburse, is hereby pledged and appropriated for the payment of the interest, and for the reimbursement of the principal, of the stock which may be created by virtue of this act. It shall, accordingly, be the duty of the Commissioners of the Sinking Fund to cause to be applied and paid, out of the said fund, yearly, such sum and sums as may be annually wanted to discharge the interest accruing on the said stock, and to reimburse the principal, as the same shall become due, and may be discharged, in conformity with the terms of the loan; and they are further authorized to apply, from time to time, such sum or sums, out of the said fund, as they may think proper, towards redeeming, by purchase, and at a price not above

par, the principal of the said stock, or any part thereof.

Sec. 6. *And be it further enacted,* That, in addition to the annual sum of eight millions of dollars, heretofore appropriated to the sinking fund, adequate and permanent funds shall, during the present session of Congress, be provided and appropriated, for the payment of the interest and reimbursement of the principal of said stock created by this act.

Sec. 7. *And be it further enacted,* That an adequate and permanent sinking fund, *gradually to* reduce, and eventually to extinguish, the public debt, contracted, and to be contracted, during the present war, shall also be established during the present session of Congress.

Sec. 8. *And be it further enacted,* That it shall be lawful for any of the banks in the District of Columbia to lend any part of the sum authorized to be borrowed by virtue of this act, anything in any of their charters to the contrary notwithstanding.

Approved, November 15, 1814.

An Act to authorize the publication of the laws of the United States within the Territories of the United States. :

Be it enacted, &c., That the Secretary for the Department of State be, and he is hereby, authorized to cause the laws of the United States, passed, or to be passed, during the present or any future session of Congress, to be published in two of the public newspapers within each and every Territory of the United States : *Provided,* In his opinion, it shall become necessary and expedient.

Approved, November 21, 1814.

An Act authorizing the Secretary of the Treasury to appoint a Clerk in the office of the Commissioner of the Revenue, with power to sign licenses.

Be it enacted, &c., That the Head of the Treasury Department shall be, and he is hereby, authorized, from time to time, as may be requisite, to designate a clerk in the office of the Commissioner of the Revenue, to assist in the signing of the licenses issuing from that office; and the clerk so designated shall have power to sign his own name to such licenses; which signature shall be as valid as that of the said Commissioner of the Revenue.

Approved, November 22, 1814.

An Act authorizing the Secretary of State, during the continuance of the present war, to make an additional allowance to the owners and masters of vessels, for bringing back to the United States destitute and distressed American seamen.

Be it enacted, &c., That during the continuance of the present war, the Secretary of State be, and he is hereby, authorized, in *addition to* the sum of ten dollars, at present allowed by law for returning destitute American seamen to the United States, to allow such additional compensation as he may deem reasonable, to be paid out of the sum annually appropriated for the relief of destitute American seamen.

SEC. 2. *And be it further enacted,* That the Secretary of State be, and he is hereby, authorized to adjust and settle such claims as may have been exhibited at the Department of State, for returning destitute American seamen to the United States, and to allow, in addition to the ten dollars at present allowed by law, such additional compensation as he may deem reasonable, and to pay the same out of the fund appropriated for the relief of destitute American seamen.

SEC. 3. *And be it further enacted,* That this act shall continue and be in force during the continuance of the present war between the United States and Great Britain, and for one year thereafter.

Approved, December 1, 1814.

An Act making further provision for filling the ranks of the Army of the United States.

Be it enacted, &c., That, from and after the passing of this act, each and every commissioned officer who shall be employed in the recruiting service, shall be, and he hereby is, authorized to enlist into the Army of the United States, any free, effective, able-bodied man, between the ages of eighteen and fifty years; which enlistment shall be absolute and binding upon all persons under the age of twenty-one years, as well as upon persons of full age, such recruiting officer having complied with all the requisitions of the laws regulating the recruiting service.

SEC. 2. *And be it further enacted,* That it shall not be lawful for any recruiting officer to pay or deliver to a recruit under the age of twenty-one years, to be enlisted by virtue of this act, any bounty or clothing, or in any manner restrain him of his liberty, until after the expiration of four days from the time of his enlistment; and it shall be lawful for the said recruit, at any time during the said four days, to reconsider and withdraw his enlistment, and thereupon he shall forthwith be discharged and exonerated from the same.

SEC. 3. *And be it further enacted,* That so much of the fifth section of the act, passed the twentieth day of January, one thousand eight hundred and thirteen, entitled "An act supplementary to the act, entitled 'An act for the more perfect organization of the Army of the United States," as requires the consent, in writing, of the parent, guardian, or master, to authorize the enlistment of persons under the age of twenty-one years, shall be, and the same is hereby, repealed : *Provided, however,* That, in case of the enlistment of any person held to service as an apprentice, under the provisions of this act, whenever such person, at the time of his enlistment, shall be held by his indenture to serve for any term between two and three years, his master shall be entitled to receive one-half of the money bounty; if held, in like manner, to serve between one and two years, the master shall be entitled to receive one-third of the money bounty as aforesaid ; and if held, in like manner, to serve one year or less,

the master shall be entitled to receive one-fourth of the money bounty as aforesaid.

SEC. 4. *And be it further enacted,* That, in lieu of the bounty of one hundred and sixty acres of land, now allowed by law, there shall be allowed to each non-commissioned officer and soldier hereafter enlisted, when discharged from service, who shall have obtained from the commanding officer of his company, battalion, or regiment, a certificate that he had faithfully performed his duty whilst in service, three hundred and twenty acres of land, to be surveyed, laid off, and granted, under the same regulations, and, in every respect, in the manner now prescribed by law: and the widow and children, and, if there be no widow nor child, the parents of every non-commissioned officer and soldier enlisted according to law, who may be killed or die in the service of the United States, shall be entitled to receive the three hundred and twenty acres of land as aforesaid; but the same shall not pass to collateral relations, any law heretofore passed to the contrary notwithstanding.

SEC. 5. *And be it further enacted,* That any person subject to militia duty, who shall, according to law, furnish a recruit for the Army of the United States, at his own expense, to serve during the war, shall thereafter be exempt from militia duty during the war; and every recruit, thus furnished, shall be delivered to some recruiting officer of the United States, who shall immediately grant his receipt for such recruit, to the person furnishing him, and shall forthwith report the same to the Department of War, and shall specify in the report the name of such person, and his place of residence, as well as the name and description of the recruit; whereupon it shall be the duty of the Secretary for the Department of War to grant to the person furnishing such recruit a certificate of exemption from militia duty during the war, upon calls made upon the authority of the United States; which certificate shall be good and available to all intents and purposes for that object. And every recruit thus furnished shall be entitled to the bounty in land, in the same manner, and upon the same conditions, as the other recruits in the Army of the United States.

Approved, December 10, 1814.

An Act supplementary to an act; laying duties on notes of banks, bankers, and certain companies, on notes, bonds, and obligations, discounted by banks, bankers, and certain companies, and on bills of exchange of certain descriptions.

Be it enacted, &c., That, in respect to the stamp duties of any of the notes of private bankers which are subject by law to such duties, it shall be lawful for the Secretary of the Treasury to agree to an annual composition in lieu thereof, with any of the said private bankers, at the rate of one and a half per centum on the amount of the annual profit made by such private bankers, respectively, upon the capital employed in the business of their respective banks, to be ascertained as is hereinafter provided.

SEC. 2. *And be it further enacted,* That every private banker, who shall be desirous to enter into the composition aforesaid, shall, at the time of proposing the same, transmit to the Secretary of the Treasury a statement, verified by his own oath or affirmation, and that of his cashier or principal clerk, of the amount of the capital employed, or to be employed, in his bank, and the charges and expenses of conducting the business thereof, in such detail as shall be satisfactory to the Secretary of the Treasury. And every private banker, after entering into such composition, shall keep a weekly account of his discounts, issues of bank notes and deposites, and shall, once in every month, transmit to the Secretary of the Treasury a transcript thereof, verified by oath or affirmation, as aforesaid; and he shall also, half yearly, make and transmit to the Secretary of the Treasury a statement of the profits of his bank for the preceding half year, verified as aforesaid.

SEC. 3. *And be it further enacted,* That, for the purpose of carrying such compositions into effect, the Secretary of the Treasury may, from time to time, estimate the profits of the said private bankers, respectively, either according to the amount of the capital by them respectively stated to be employed in the business of their respective banks, as aforesaid, and the half yearly profits by them respectively stated to be actually made thereon, as aforesaid, or according to the amount of the capital which, upon the general principle and practice of banking, would be requisite and proper for conducting the business of a bank, to the extent appearing upon the said monthly returns of the said private bankers, respectively, and the usual profits made upon such capital. And the said private bankers, respectively, shall pay to the collector of internal duties, for the district wherein their banks, respectively, are established, for the use of the United States, a composition in lieu of the said stamp duties, at the rate of one and a half per centum on the profits of their respective banks, estimated and ascertained in either of the modes aforesaid.

Approved, December 10, 1814.

An Act to provide additional revenues for defraying the expenses of Government, and maintaining the public credit, by duties on carriages, and the harness used therefor.

Be it enacted, &c., That, from the last day of December instant, there shall be paid the following yearly rates and duties upon every carriage, with the harness used therefor, kept for use, which shall not be exclusively employed in husbandry, or for the transportation of goods, according to the following valuations, to wit:

If not exceeding fifty dollars, one dollar.

If above fifty, and not exceeding one hundred dollars, two dollars.

If above one hundred, and not exceeding two hundred dollars, four dollars.

If above two hundred, and not exceeding three hundred, seven dollars.

If above three hundred, and not exceeding four hundred, eleven dollars.

If above four hundred, and not exceeding five hundred, sixteen dollars.

If above five hundred, and not exceeding six hundred, twenty-two dollars.

If above six hundred dollars, and not exceeding eight hundred dollars, thirty dollars.

If above eight hundred dollars, and not exceeding one thousand dollars, forty dollars.

If above one thousand dollars, fifty dollars.

Which valuations shall be made agreeably to the existing condition of the carriage and harness at the time of making the first entry thereof, in conformity to the provisions of this act, and shall not be changed in relation to any carriage and harness, while subject to the duties imposed by this act.

SEC. 2. *And be it further enacted,* That every person having or keeping such carriage, shall yearly, in the month of January, make and subscribe a true and exact entry thereof, describing the same, and stating its denomination and the number of its wheels, together with its value, and that of the harness used therefor, as aforesaid; which entry shall be lodged with the collector appointed by virtue of the act, entitled "An act for the assessment and collection of direct taxes and internal duties," for the district in which the person liable for the payment of such duty may reside. And it shall be the duty of the collectors aforesaid to attend within the month of January, in each year, at three or more of the most public and convenient places in each county, within their respective districts, and to give public notice, at least ten days previous to such day, of the time and place of such attendance, and to receive such entry, made in the manner before directed, at such place, or at any other where they may happen to be within the said month of January, within which said month the duties shall be paid agreeably thereto, and, on the payment thereof, to grant a certificate for each carriage mentioned in such entry, therein specifying the name of the owner, the description and denomination of the carriage, and the sum paid, with the time when, and the period for which such duty shall be so paid; and the forms of the certificates to be so granted, shall be prescribed by the Treasury Department; and such certificates, or the acknowledgments of the collector aforesaid, by a credit in his public accounts, shall be the only evidence to be exhibited and admitted, that any duty imposed by this act has been discharged : *Provided, nevertheless,* That no certificate shall be deemed of validity any longer than while the carriage for which the said certificate was granted is owned by the person mentioned in such certificate, unless such certificate shall be produced to a collector, and an entry shall be thereon made by him, specifying the name of the then owner of such carriage, and the time when he or she became possessed of the same.

SEC. 3. *And be it further enacted,* That *e*̄ person who, after the month of December, *in* year, shall commence the having or keep*ing of* any carriage subject to duty, shall and *may,* at any time during thirty days after he *shall so* commence the having or keeping of such carriage, make like entry and payment in manner before prescribed; and on payment of such proportion of the duty laid by this act on such carriage, and the harness used therefor, as the time, from which he shall commence the keeping of such carriage to the end of the month of December then next ensuing, shall bear to the whole year, shall be entitled to, and may demand like certificates; subject, nevertheless, to the conditions before and hereinafter provided.

Sec. 4. *And be it further enacted,* That any person having or keeping any carriage subject to duty, who shall make an untrue or defective entry, to evade the whole or any part of the duty justly and truly payable according to this act, shall lose the sum paid pursuant to such untrue or defective entry; and where such untrue or defective entry hath been made, or where no entry shall be made, or where there shall be a neglect of payment at any time thereafter, on personal application and demand at the house, dwelling, or usual place of abode of such person, by the proper collector, be liable and shall pay the duty by this act imposed, with a further sum, double the amount thereof; one moiety of which last sum shall be to the use of the United States, and the other moiety thereof to the use of the person who, if a collector, shall first discover, if other than a collector shall first inform in such case; which duty, with the said addition, shall be collected by distress and sale of the goods and chattels of the person by whom the same shall be due. And in every case where the owner of a carriage shall fail to enter the same in conformity to the provisions of this act, the collector shall have power, and he is hereby authorized, to determine the class to which such carriage belongs, and to fix the duty payable on the same.

Sec. 5. *And be it further enacted,* That in all cases where any duty shall be collected pursuant to this act, whether by distress or otherwise, certificates shall be granted for each carriage, in manner as before prescribed.

Sec. 6. *And be it further enacted,* That in case a question shall arise, in the execution of this act, whether a carriage is exclusively employed in husbandry, or for the transportation of goods, such carriage shall be deemed not to be so employed, unless proof to the contrary be adduced by the owner or keeper thereof.

Sec. 7. *And be it further enacted,* That in case any entry of a carriage may have been made under the "Act laying duties on carriages for the conveyance of persons," passed July twenty-fourth, one thousand eight hundred and thirteen, for a period extending beyond the first day of January next, it shall be the duty of the owner or keeper thereof, notwithstanding, to render the entry required by the second section of this act to the proper collector, and to pay him such sum as, with any duty previously paid, shall amount to the whole duty payable, according to this act, on such carriage and the harness used therefor, subject, in case of neglect or failure, to a proportionate part of the penalty imposed in the fourth

section of this act; which payment shall be endorsed on any certificate which may have been granted.

Sec. 8. *And be it further enacted,* That whenever, hereafter, there shall be a general assessment made throughout the United States, it shall be the duty of the principal assessor in each collection district, agreeably to instructions to be given by the Secretary of the Treasury, to cause a list of carriages liable to duty, with the valuations thereof, as fixed in this act, to be made out and delivered to the collector for such district, according to which valuations, as far as the same may apply, the duties hereby imposed shall be thereafter assessed and collected: *Provided,* That the owner or keeper of a carriage liable to duty, shall not be thereby released from the obligation to make the entry hereby required to be made: *And provided, further,* That carriages that are not contained in said list shall be also liable to duty.

Sec. 9. *And be it further enacted,* That the several provisions of "An act making further provision for the collection of internal duties, and for the appointment and compensation of assessors," passed the second day of August, one thousand eight hundred and thirteen, shall, and are hereby declared to apply in full force to the duties laid by and to be collected under this act, the same as if such duties and this act were recognised therein; which said duties shall be collected by the same collectors, in the same manner, for the same commissions, and under the same directions, as are thereby established in relation to the other internal duties; and all the obligations, duties, and penalties thereby imposed upon collectors, are hereby imposed upon the collectors of the duties laid by this act.

Sec. 10. *And be it further enacted,* That towards establishing an adequate revenue to provide for the payment of the expenses of Government, for the punctual payment of the public debt, principal and interest, contracted and to be contracted, according to the terms of the contracts, respectively, and for creating an adequate sinking fund gradually to reduce, and eventually to extinguish the public debt, contracted and to be contracted, the internal duties laid and imposed by this act, (and those laid and imposed by the "Act laying duties on carriages for the conveyance of persons," passed twenty-fourth July, one thousand eight hundred and thirteen, so far as the same are not hereby abolished,) shall be laid, levied, and collected, during the present war between the United States and Great Britain, and until the purposes aforesaid shall be completely accomplished, anything in any act of Congress to the contrary thereof in anywise notwithstanding. And for effectual application of the revenue to be raised by and from the said internal duties to the purposes aforesaid, in due form of law, the faith of the United States is hereby pledged: *Provided always,* That whenever Congress shall deem it expedient to alter, reduce, or change, the said internal duties, or any or either of them, it shall be lawful so to do, upon providing and substituting by law, at the same time, and for the same purposes other duties, which shall be equally productive with the duties so altered, reduced, or changed: *And provided. further*, That nothing in this act contained shall be deemed or construed in anywise to rescind or impair any specific appropriation of the said duties, or any or either of them heretofore made by law, but such appropriation shall remain, and be carried into effect according to the true intent and meaning of the laws making the same; anything in this act to the contrary thereof in anywise notwithstanding.¶

SEC. 11. *And be it further enacted*, That the "Act laying duties on carriages for the conveyance of persons," passed July twenty-fourth, one thousand eight hundred and thirteen, shall cease after the thirty-first day of December, one thousand eight hundred and fourteen, except so far as the same may apply to the collection of duties which may have previously accrued, and except so far as entries may have been made or duties paid under the same, as contemplated in the seventh section of this act: *Provided*, That all fines, penalties, and forfeitures, which have been, or may be, incurred under the said act, shall be recovered and distributed, and may be mitigated or remitted, in like manner as if the said act had continued in full force and virtue.

Approved, December 15, 1814.

An Act making additional appropriations for the service of the year one thousand eight hundred and fourteen.

Be it enacted, &c., That, for defraying the expenses of the military establishment during the year eighteen hundred and fourteen, in addition to the sums heretofore appropriated by law to that object, the following sums be, and they are hereby, appropriated; that is to say:

For the pay of the army, five hundred thousand dollars.

For the subsistence of the army, one million of dollars.

For the quartermaster's department, five hundred thousand dollars.

For the ordnance department, five hundred thousand dollars.

For clothing, five hundred thousand dollars.

SEC. 2. *And be it further enacted*, That the following sums be appropriated for the purposes herein recited; that is to say:

For defraying the compensation granted by law to the members of the Senate and House of Representatives, their officers and attendants, during the year one thousand eight hundred and fourteen, in addition to the sum heretofore appropriated for that purpose, the sum of fifty thousand dollars.

For defraying the contingent expenses of the Senate of the United States, during the year one thousand eight hundred and fourteen, the sum of five thousand dollars, in addition to the sum heretofore appropriated.

For defraying the contingent expenses of the House of Representatives, during the year one

thousand eight hundred and fourteen, the sum of ten thousand dollars, in addition to the sum heretofore appropriated.

SEC. 3. *And be it further enacted*, That the several appropriations hereinbefore made, shall be paid and discharged out of any money in the Treasury, not otherwise appropriated.

Approved, December 15, 1814.

An Act directing the Staff Officers of the Army to comply with the requisitions of naval and marine officers, in certain cases.

Be it enacted, &c., That it shall be the duty of the several officers of the staff of the Army of the United States, to provide the officers, seamen, and marines, of the Navy of the United States, when acting, or proceeding to act, on shore, in co-operation with the land troops, upon the requisition of the commanding naval or marine officer of any such detachment of seamen or marines, under orders to act as aforesaid, with rations, also the officers and seamen with camp equipage, according to the relative rank and station of each, and the military regulations in like cases, together with the necessary transportation, as well for the men as for their baggage, provisions, and cannon: *Provided, nevertheless*, That the contract price of the rations which may be furnished shall be reimbursed out of the appropriations for the support of the navy.

SEC. 2. *And be it further enacted*, That the respective quartermasters of the army shall, upon the requisition of the commanding naval officer of any such detachment of seamen or marines, furnish the said officer and his necessary aids with horses, accoutrements, and forage, during the time they may be employed in co-operating with the land troops as aforesaid.

Approved, December 15, 1814.

An Act to provide additional revenues for defraying the expenses of Government, and maintaining the public credit, by laying duties on spirits distilled within the United States, and Territories thereof, and by amending the act laying duties on licenses to distillers of spirituous liquors.

Be it enacted, &c., That, from and after the first day of February next, there shall be paid upon all spirits, unless hereinafter specially excepted which, after the said day, shall be distilled within the United States, or Territories thereof, in any still or still, or in any other vessel, or by the aid of any boiler, as defined in the act, entitled "An act laying duties on licenses to distillers of spirituous liquors," in addition to the duties payable for licenses therefor, the duties following; that is to say: for every gallon of such spirits distilled wholly or in part from foreign materials, twenty cents; and for every gallon of such spirits distilled from domestic materials, twenty cents; which said duties shall be paid by the owner, agent, or superintendent of the still or other vessel, in which the said spirits shall have been distilled; the amount thereof payable by any one person, at any one time, if not exceeding ten dollars, shall, and if exceeding

Public Acts of Congress.

ten dollars may, be paid in money, with a deduction of two per centum, at the time of rendering the accounts of spirits so chargeable with duty, required to be rendered by the second section of this act, or without deduction at the next subsequent time prescribed for rendering such accounts.

SEC. 2. *And be it further enacted*, That every person who, on the first day of February next, shall be the owner of any still or boiler, or other vessel, used or intended to be used for the purpose of distilling spirituous liquors, or who shall have such still or boiler, or other vessel, under his superintendence, either as agent for the owner or on his own account, shall, before the said day, and every person who, after the said day, shall use or intend to use any still or boiler, or other vessel, as aforesaid, either as owner, agent, or otherwise, shall, before he shall begin so to use or cause the same so to be used, give bond in such sum as shall be prescribed by the Treasury Department, with at least two sureties, to the satisfaction of the collector of internal duties for the district in which the same shall be situate, in a sum not less than the computed duties for one year, nor less than one thousand dollars, that he will, before using or causing the same to be used, make true and exact entry and report, in writing, to the said collector, of every such still or boiler, or other vessel, owned or superintended by him, with the capacity thereof, the names of the owner, agent, and superintendent, the place where situate, and whether intended to be employed on foreign or domestic materials, with the quantity of domestic spirits, in gallons, which he may have on hand ; that he will thereafter, before using or causing the same to be used, make like entry and report of any other still or boiler, or other vessel, used, or intended to be used, for distillation, that he may own, or have the agency or superintendence of, with the capacity thereof, the names of the owner, agent, and superintendent, the place where situate, and whether intended to be employed on foreign or domestic materials, with information from time to time, of any change in the form, capacity, agency, ownership, or superintendence, which all or either of the said stills or boilers, or other vessels, may undergo; that he will, from day to day, enter, or cause to be entered, in a book to be kept by him for that purpose, and which shall be open at all times, between the rising and setting of the sun, for the inspection of the said collector, who may take any minutes, memorandums, or transcripts thereof, the number of gallons of spirits distilled, keeping separate accounts of the spirits distilled from foreign and domestic materials; and will render to the said collector, on the first day of January, April, July, and October, in each year, or within ten days thereafter, a general account in writing, taken from his books, of the number of gallons of each kind of spirits distilled for three months preceding said days, or for such portion thereof as may have elapsed from the date of said entry and report, to the said day which shall next ensue; that he will, at the said times, deliver to the said collector the

original book of entries, which book shall be retained by said officer ; that he will verify or cause to be verified, the said entries, reports, books, and general accounts, on oath or affirmation, to be taken before the collector, or some officer authorized by the laws of the State to administer the same, according to the form required by this act, where the same is prescribed ; and that he will pay to the said collector the duties which by this act ought to be paid on the spirits so distilled, and in the said account mentioned, if not exceeding ten dollars, at the time of rendering an account thereof, with a deduction of two per centum, and if exceeding ten dollars, either at said time, with a like deduction, or at the next subsequent time, prescribed for rendering such accounts, without deduction: and the said bond may, from time to time, at the discretion of the collector, be renewed or changed in regard to the sureties and penalties thereof.

SEC. 3. *And be it further enacted*, That the entries made in the books of the distiller, required to be kept by the second section of this act, shall, on the said first day of January, April, July, and October, or within ten days thereafter, be verified by the oath or affirmation; to be taken as aforesaid, of the person or persons by whom such entries shall have been made, which qualification shall be certified at the end of such entries by the collector, or officer administering the same, and shall be in substance as follows : " I do swear, (or affirm,) that the foregoing entries were made by me on the respective days specified, and that they state, according to the best of my knowledge and belief, the whole quantity of spirits distilled at the distillery, owned by —— in the county of —— amounting to —— gallons, distilled from domestic materials, and —— gallons, distilled from foreign materials."

SEC. 4. *And be it further enacted*, That the owner, agent, or superintendent aforesaid, shall, in case the original entries required to be made in his books by the second section of this act shall not be made by himself, subjoin to the oath or affirmation of the person by whom they were made, the following oath or affirmation, to be taken as aforesaid : " I do swear, (or affirm,) that, to the best of my knowledge and belief, the foregoing entries are just and true, and that I have taken all the means in my power to make them so."

SEC. 5. *And be it further enacted*, That in all cases in which the duties aforesaid, payable on spirits, shall not be duly paid, the person or persons chargeable therewith shall pay in addition ten per cent. on the amount thereof; and in case such duties, with said addition, shall not be paid within three months from the time the said duties ought to be paid, the collector for the district shall make a personal demand of the same from such person or persons, or by notice in writing, left at his or her dwelling, if within the collection district, and if not, at the distillery owned or superintended by such person or persons; and in case of refusal or neglect to pay the said duties, with the addition, within ten days after such demand or notice, the amount thereof shall be recovered by distress and

Public Acts of Congress.

sale of the goods, chattels, and effects, of the delinquent; and in case of such distress, it shall be the duty of the officer charged with the collection, to make, or cause to be made, an account of the goods or chattels which may be distrained, a copy of which, signed by the officers making such distress, shall be left with the owner or possessor of such goods, chattels, or effects, or at his or her dwelling, with a note of the sum demanded, and the time and place of sale; and the said officer shall, forthwith, cause a notification to be publicly posted up, at two of the taverns nearest to the residence of the person whose property shall be distrained, or at the court-house of the same county, if not more than ten miles distant, which notice shall specify the articles distrained, and the time or place proposed for the sale thereof, which time shall not be less than ten days from the date of such notification, and the place proposed for sale not more than five miles distant from the place of making such distress: *Provided.* That in any case of distress for the payment of the duties aforesaid. the goods, chattels, or effects, so distrained, shall and may be restored to the owner or possessor, if, prior to the sale thereof. payment. or tender thereof, shall be made to the proper officer charged with the collection, of the full amount demanded, together with such fee for levying, and such sum for the necessary and reasonable expenses of removing and keeping the goods, chattels, or effects, so distrained, as may be allowed in like cases by the laws or practice of the State or Territory wherein the distress shall have been made; but in case of non-payment, or tender, as aforesaid, the said officer shall proceed to sell the said goods, chattels, or effects, at public auction, and shall and may retain, from the proceeds of such sales, the amount demandable for the use of the United States, with the said necessary and reasonable expenses of distress and sale, as aforesaid, and a commission of five per centum thereon for his own use, rendering the overplus, if any there be, to the person whose goods, chattels, or effects, shall have been distrained: *Provided,* That it shall not be lawful to make distress of the tools or implements of a trade or profession, beasts of the plough necessary for the cultivation of improved lands, arms, or necessary household furniture, and apparel for a family.

SEC. 6. *And be it further enacted,* That all spirits which shall be distilled within the United States, or Territories thereof, the duties on which shall not have been duly paid or secured, according to the true intent and meaning of this act, shall be forfeited, and may be seized as forfeited, by any collector of the internal duties: *Provided always,* That such spirits shall not be liable to seizure and forfeiture in the hands of a *bona fide* purchaser without notice of the duties not being paid, or secured to be paid.

SEC. 7. *And be it further enacted,* That the owner, agent, or superintendent, of any still, boiler, or other vessel used in the distillation of spirits, who shall neglect or refuse to make true and exact entry and report of the same, or to do, or cause to be done, any of the things by this act required to

be done as aforesaid, excepting to pay the duties hereby laid in cases where the bond required by the second section of this act has been given, shall forfeit, for every such neglect or refusal, all the spirits distilled by or for him, and the stills, boilers, and other vessels used in distillation, together with the sum of one thousand dollars, to be recovered, with costs of suit; which said spirits, with the vessels containing the same, and stills, boilers, and other vessels used in distillation, may be seized by any collector of the internal duties and held by him until a decision shall be had thereon, according to law: *Provided,* Such seizure be made within three months after the cause for the same may have occurred, and that a prosecution or notification thereupon shall have been commenced by such collector, within twenty days after the seizure thereof.

SEC. 8. *And be it further enacted,* That in case the duties aforesaid shall not be paid or recovered agreeably to the provisions of this act, or in case any acts shall be done contrary to, or any act omitted that are required to be done by, the law, to be given as aforesaid, or the penalties incurred thereby shall not be recovered, the said bond shall be deemed forfeited, and shall be put in suit by the collector, for the recovery of the amount of the said duties, with the addition thereon, penalties, and costs, or either, as the case may be; and judgment thereon shall and may be taken at the return term, on motion to be made in open court, unless sufficient cause to the contrary be shown to, and allowed by, the court: *Provided,* That the writ of process in such case shall have been executed at least fourteen days before the return day thereof.

SEC. 9. *And be it further enacted,* That if any person shall forcibly obstruct or hinder a collector in the execution of this act, or of any of the powers or authorities hereby vested in him, or shall forcibly rescue, or cause to be rescued, any spirits, still, boiler, or other vessel, after the same shall have been seized by him, or shall attempt or endeavor so to do, the person so offending shall, for every such offence, forfeit and pay the sum of five hundred dollars.

SEC. 10. *And be it further enacted,* That a collector shall be authorized to enter, at any time between the rising and setting of the sun, any distillery or place where any stills, boilers, or other vessels used in distillation, are kept, within his collection district, for the purpose of examining and measuring the same, and the other vessels therein, or of inspecting the accounts of spirits from time to time distilled. And every owner of such distillery, or stills, or boilers, or other vessels, or persons having the agency or superintendence of the same, who shall refuse to admit such officer, or to suffer him to examine and measure the same, or to inspect said accounts, etc. for every such refusal, forfeit and pay the sum of five hundred dollars.

SEC. 11. *And be it further enacted,* That if any person who shall be convicted of wilfully taking a false oath or affirmation, in any of the cases in which an oath or affirmation is required by this

taken in virtue of this act, shall be liable to the pains and penalties to which persons are liable for wilful and corrupt perjury, and shall, moreover, forfeit the sum of five hundred dollars.

SEC. 12. *And be it further enacted,* That no person who shall have refused or neglected to comply with the provisions of this act, shall be entitled, while such refusal or neglect continues, to receive a license for employing, in distillation, any still, or boiler, or other vessel, or shall be entitled to credit for any duties on spirits that may have accrued.

SEC. 13. *And be it further enacted,* That every collector shall give receipts for all sums by him collected under this act.

SEC. 14. *And be it further enacted,* That if it shall appear to the satisfaction of the collector for the district, that any owner, agent, or superintendent, of a still, boiler, or other vessel used in distillation, who shall have given bond agreeably to the second section of this act, and shall have ceased to use the same for one year, and made oath or affirmation thereof, to be lodged with said collector, hath acted agreeably to the condition of such bond, the collector shall cause such bond to be delivered to said owner, agent, or superintendent.

SEC. 15. *And be it further enacted,* That all the provisions of this act, as well as of the "Act laying duties on licenses to distillers of spirituous liquors," passed the twenty-fourth day of July, one thousand eight hundred and thirteen, shall be deemed to apply to any still, or boiler, or other vessel used in distillation, which shall be employed in the rectification of spirituous liquors, and to spirits rectified therein, or with the aid thereof.

SEC. 16. *And be it further enacted,* That any license heretofore or hereafter granted for employing a still, boiler, or other vessel, in distilling spirits from foreign materials, shall authorize the distilling spirits from domestic materials also.

SEC. 17. *And be it further enacted,* That the "Act laying duties on licenses to distillers of spirituous liquors," passed the twenty-fourth of July, one thousand eight hundred and thirteen, shall be deemed to remain in full force, except as to the alterations thereof contained in this act, and that the several provisions of "An act making further provision for the collection of internal duties, and for the appointment and compensation of assessors," passed the second day of August, one thousand eight hundred and thirteen, shall, and are hereby declared to, apply in full force to the duties laid by, and to be collected under, this act, the same as if such duties and this act were recognised therein, which said duties shall be collected by the same collectors, in the same manner, for the same commissions, and under the same directions, as are hereby established in relation to the other internal duties; and all the obligations, duties, and penalties, thereby imposed upon the collectors, are hereby imposed upon the collectors of the duties laid by this act: *Provided,* That if any person to whom a license shall have been granted, according to the provisions of the act, entitled "An act laying duties on licenses to distillers of spirituous liquors," and who shall have given bonds for the payment of the duties therein mentioned, shall, on or before the first day of February next, discontinue the use of any still or stills, for the use of which the said license shall have been granted, and shall give notice thereof to the collector of internal duties for the district in which the same shall be situate, such license shall thereupon cease to be in force, and such person shall be holden to pay the same duties, and the same proceedings shall be had upon the bonds aforesaid, as in case the said license had been originally granted for the term during which it shall have been in force as aforesaid.

SEC. 18. *And be it further enacted,* That, in addition to the licenses authorized and directed to be granted by the "Act laying duties on licenses to distillers of spirituous liquors," passed on the twenty-fourth day of July, one thousand eight hundred and thirteen, there may and shall be granted like licenses for a still or stills, and for a boiler or boilers, for the term or period of one week, on payment, or securing of payment, of the following duties, for each gallon of the capacity, thereof.

For a still or stills, employed in distilling spirits from domestic materials, five cents.

For a boiler, or boilers, as defined in the said act, employed in distilling spirits from domestic materials, ten cents.

One-half only of which rates of duty shall be paid for a still or stills, and boiler or boilers, employed wholly in the distillation of roots.

Which said duties shall be collected in the same manner, and subject to the same provisions, as the duties imposed by the said act.

SEC. 19. *And be it further enacted,* That a deduction, at the rate of eight per centum per annum, shall be made from the duty payable for a license to distil spirituous liquors, on the payment thereof at the time of obtaining the same.

SEC. 20. *And be it further enacted,* That every person who may be the owner, agent, or superintendent, of one still only, whose capacity shall not exceed one hundred gallons, or of one boiler only, whose capacity shall not exceed fifty gallons, and each of which shall be wholly employed in distilling spirits from domestic materials, shall have the option of complying with the foregoing provisions of this act, and of the "Act laying duties on licenses to distillers of spirituous liquors," passed the twenty-fourth day of July, one thousand eight hundred and thirteen, or of paying, agreeably to the provisions of this act, twenty-five cents for every gallon of spirits distilled in such still or boiler: *Provided,* That, to entitle such person to the benefits of the latter alternative, he shall deliver a written statement of his desire to the collector of the district in which such still or boiler may be situate, specifying the contents of the same, previously to the times of using such still or boiler in every year. And any person so accepting the latter alternative, who shall fail to comply with the condition on which the same is hereby allowed, shall forfeit and pay the sum of five hundred dollars; which said forfeiture shall in no wise affect or impair any other penalty which would otherwise attach to such failure.

SEC. 21. *And be it further enacted*, That it shall be the duty of the collectors aforesaid, in their respective districts, and they are hereby authorized, to collect the duties imposed by this act, and to prosecute for the recovery of the same, and for the recovery of any sum or sums which may be forfeited by virtue of this act: And all fines, penalties, and forfeitures, which shall be incurred by force of this act, shall and may be sued for, and recovered, in the name of the United States, or of the collector within whose district any such fine, penalty, or forfeiture, shall have been incurred, by bill, plaint, or information, one moiety thereof to the use of the United States, and the other moiety thereof to the use of the person who, if a collector, shall first discover, if other than a collector, shall first inform, of the cause, matter, or thing, whereby any such fine, penalty, or forfeiture, shall have been incurred; and where the cause of action or complaint shall arise or accrue more than fifty miles distant from the nearest place by law established for the holding of a district court, within the district in which the same shall arise or accrue, such suit and recovery may be had before any court of the State, holden within the said district, having jurisdiction in like cases.

SEC. 22. *And be it further enacted*, That the collector shall furnish to each distiller within the collection district, an abstract of this act, and of the "Act laying duties on licenses to distillers of spirituous liquors," and of such provisions of the "Act to amend the act, laying duties on licenses to retailers of wines, spirituous liquors, and foreign merchandise, and for other purposes," as regards distillers; which abstract shall be prepared and furnished to the collectors, under the direction of the Secretary of the Treasury.

SEC. 23. *And be it further enacted*, That towards establishing an adequate revenue, to provide for the payment of the expenses of Government; for the punctual payment of the public debt, principal and interest, contracted and to be contracted, according to the terms of the contracts, respectively; and for creating an adequate sinking fund, gradually to reduce, and eventually to extinguish, the public debt, contracted, and to be contracted; the rates and duties laid and imposed by this act, and the duties laid and imposed upon licenses to distillers, in and by the said act, entitled "An act laying duties on licenses to distillers of spirituous liquors," shall continue to be laid, levied, and collected, during the present war between the United States and Great Britain, and until the purposes aforesaid shall be completely accomplished, anything in the said act of Congress to the contrary thereof in any wise notwithstanding. And, for the effectual application of the revenue to be raised by and from the said duties, to the purposes aforesaid, in due form of law, the faith of the United States is hereby pledged: *Provided always*, That whenever Congress shall deem it expedient to alter, reduce, or change, the said duties, or either of them, it shall

be lawful so to do, upon providing and authorizing, by law, at the same time, and for the same purposes, other duties, which shall be equally productive with the duties so altered, reduced, or changed: *And provided further*, That nothing in this act contained shall be deemed or construed in any wise to rescind or impair any specific appropriation of the said duties, or either of them; but such appropriation shall remain and be carried into effect, according to the true intent and meaning of the law and laws making the same, anything in this act to the contrary thereof in any wise notwithstanding.

SEC. 24. *And be it further enacted*, That in future it shall be lawful for the distiller or finisher of domestic spirits, and all persons from whose materials such spirits shall be distilled, to sell, without license, any quantity thereof not less than one gallon.

SEC. 25. *And be it further enacted*, That it shall be lawful for the President of the United States to authorize the Secretary of the Treasury to anticipate the collection and receipt of the duties laid and imposed by this act, and by the said act entitled "An act laying duties on licenses to distillers of spirituous liquors," by obtaining a loan upon the pledge of the said duties for the reimbursement thereof, to an amount not exceeding six millions of dollars, and at a rate of interest not exceeding six per centum per annum. And any bank or banks, now incorporated, or which may hereafter be incorporated, under the authority of the United States, is and are hereby authorized to make such loan: *Provided always*, and it is expressly declared, That the money so obtained upon loan, shall be applied to the purposes aforesaid, to which the said duties, so to be pledged, are by this act applied and appropriated, and to no other purposes whatsoever.

Approved, December 21, 1814.

An Act to provide additional revenue for defraying the expenses of Government, and maintaining the public credit, by duties on sales at auction, and on licenses to retail wines, spirituous liquors, and foreign merchandise, and for increasing the rate of postage.

Be it enacted, &c., That, from and after the first day of February next, there shall be had, levied and collected, for the use of the United States, a sum of one hundred per centum upon, and in addition to, the amount of the rates and duties respectively laid upon sales by way of auction, as prescribed by the act of Congress, entitled "An act laying duties on sales at auction of merchandise, and ships and vessels," passed on the twenty-fourth day of July, in the year eighteen hundred and thirteen. And the said additional duty of a hundred per centum shall be levied, collected, paid, and accounted for, in like manner, by the same officers, subject, in all respects, to the same regulations and provisions, and with the same penalties, forfeitures, and remedies, from and under of the law, as the said act of Congress and the act to amend the said act, passed on the twenty-

Public Acts of Congress.

fourth day of March, in the year eighteen hundred and fourteen, declare and establish for levying, collecting, and paying, the original duties to which the said duty of one hundred per centum is hereby added and attached. And it shall be the duty of every auctioneer, who shall have given bond under the said acts, to give like bond under this act, subject to the same penalties prescribed in the said act, passed on the twenty-fourth day of July, one thousand eight hundred and thirteen. And all sales at auction of any part, or parcel, of any merchandise, with the design and effect to ascertain and fix a price for the whole, or for any other part, of such merchandise, without exposing the whole, or such other part, to public sale, shall be deemed and taken to be sales at auction within the meaning of this act, and of the said act of Congress, to the whole amount of the merchandise whereof the sale is so effected, whether the same is afterwards conducted and effected by the auctioneer, or by any person or persons acting as a commission merchant, factor, or agent, or by the owner and owners of the merchandise. And it shall be the duty of the auctioneers, respectively, to specify, in their quarterly accounts, upon oath or affirmation, all sales by them respectively made of a part or parcel of any merchandise as aforesaid, with the design and effect aforesaid, for whom and to whom such sales, respectively, were made, and the amount of the commissions or other compensation to them, respectively, paid, or payable, by reason of such sales, as well with respect to the part or parcel of the merchandise actually exposed to sale, as with respect to the whole, or any other part, of such merchandise, the sale whereof is designed and effected as aforesaid. And the neglect or refusal so to do, shall be deemed to be a breach of the bond of the auctioneer, so neglecting and refusing, who shall, also, in that behalf, forfeit and pay such other penalties as the said act of Congress prescribes in case of the non-performance of any other duty required from auctioneers, to be performed in taking out licenses, giving bonds, and keeping and rendering accounts.

Sec. 2. *And be it further enacted,* That, from and after the first day of February next, there shall be added to the rates of postage, as at present established by law, a sum equal to fifty per centum upon the amount of such rates, respectively, for the use of the United States. And the said additional sum of fifty per centum shall be charged, collected, paid, and accounted for, in like manner, by the same officers, subject, in all respects, to the same regulations and provisions, and with the like fines, penalties, forfeitures, and remedies for breaches of the law, as are provided for charging, collecting, and paying, the original rates of postage to which the said sum of fifty per centum is hereby added and attached.

Sec. 3. *And be it further enacted,* That, from and after the first day of February next, there shall be laid, levied, collected, and paid, for the use of the United States, a sum of fifty per cent. upon, and in addition to, the duties laid on licenses, granted in pursuance of the act of Congress, entitled "An act laying duties on licenses to retailers of wines, spirituous liquors, and foreign merchandise," passed the second day of August, in the year eighteen hundred and thirteen. And the said additional sum of fifty per centum shall be charged, paid, collected, and accounted for, in like manner, by the same officers, subject, in all respects, to the same regulations and provisions, and with the same fines, penalties, forfeitures, and remedies, for breaches of the law, as in and by the said last mentioned act of Congress, and the act, entitled "An act to amend the act laying duties on licenses to retailers of wines, spirituous liquors, and foreign merchandise, and for other purposes," passed on the eighteenth day of April, in the year eighteen hundred and fourteen, are provided for charging, paying, and collecting, the original duties on the said licenses, respectively, to which the said sum of fifty per centum is hereby added and attached. And in case any license for carrying on the business of selling by retail, shall have been granted under the said act "laying duties on licenses to retailers of wines, spirituous liquors, and foreign merchandise," for a period extending beyond the first day of February next, the person to whom the same may have been granted, or transferred, shall, previous to the first day of May thereafter, make the like application required therein, which shall further specify such period, and shall pay to the proper collector a sum equal to such proportion of fifty per centum on the original duty imposed on such license, as said period bears to a year, the payment of which sum shall be endorsed on the license previously granted. And if any person shall, after the last mentioned day, deal in the selling of wines, distilled spirituous liquors, or merchandise, by retail, as defined in the said act, without having made such payment, such person shall, in addition to the payment of the additional duty hereby imposed, forfeit and pay the sum of one hundred and fifty dollars, to be recovered with cost of suit: *Provided,* That if any person to whom a license shall have been granted, according to the provisions of the act, entitled "An act laying duties on licenses to retailers of wines, spirituous liquors, and foreign merchandise," and who shall have paid for the same, or shall have given bond for the payment of the same, shall, on or before the commencement of the operation of this act, discontinue the use of the privileges by said license granted, and shall give due notice thereof, to the collector of the internal revenue of the district in which such license shall have been granted, such license shall cease to be of force, and such person shall be holden to pay a sum proportionate to the time which shall have run from the time of granting said license to the first day of February next. And in case of actual payment for a term subsequent to the last mentioned day, shall be entitled to receive back, from the Treasury of the United States, such sum so paid for such subsequent time, from the day last mentioned.

Sec. 4. *And be it further enacted,* That the act of Congress, entitled "An act making further

Public Acts of Congress.

provision for the collection of internal duties, and for the appointment and compensation of assessors," passed on the second day of August, in the year one thousand eight hundred and thirteen, shall be and remain in force, and shall, in all its provisions, be applied for the purpose of laying, collecting, and securing, the duties by this act added or imposed, except as regards the rates of postage, as well with respect to the persons respectively liable to the payment thereof, as with respect to the officers employed in collecting and accounting for the same.

SEC. 5. *And be it further enacted,* That, towards establishing an adequate revenue to provide for the payment of the expenses of Government, for the punctual payment of the public debt, principal and interest, contracted and to be contracted, according to the terms of the contracts, respectively, and for creating an adequate sinking fund, gradually to reduce, and eventually to extinguish, the public debt, contracted and to be contracted; the internal rates and duties added, laid, and imposed by this act, and the internal rates and duties laid and imposed by the said several acts of Congress, entitled, respectively, "An act laying duties on sales at auction of merchandise, and ships and vessels;" "An act regulating the Post Office Establishment;" and "An act laying duties on licenses to retailers of wines, spirituous liquors, and foreign merchandise;" shall continue to be laid, levied, and collected, during the present war between the United States and Great Britain, and until the purposes aforesaid shall be completely accomplished, anything in the said acts of Congress to the contrary thereof, in anywise, notwithstanding. And for the effectual application of the revenue, to be raised by and from the said internal duties, to the purposes aforesaid, in due form of law, the faith of the United States is hereby pledged: *Provided always,* That whenever Congress shall deem it expedient to alter, reduce, or change, the said internal duties, or any or either of them, it shall be lawful so to do, upon providing and substituting, by law, at the same time, and for the same purposes, other duties which shall be equally productive with the duties so altered, reduced, or changed: *And provided further,* That nothing in this act contained shall be deemed or construed in anywise to rescind or impair any specific appropriation of the said duties, or any or either of them, heretofore made by law; but such appropriation shall remain and be carried into effect, according to the true intent and meaning of the law and laws making the same, anything in this act to the contrary thereof, in anywise, notwithstanding.

Approved, December 23, 1814.

An Act supplemental to the acts authorizing a loan for the several sums of twenty-five millions of dollars and three millions of dollars.

Be it enacted, &c., That the Secretary of the Treasury be and he is hereby authorized, with the approbation of the President of the United States, to cause Treasury notes to be prepared, signed, and issued, for and in lieu of so much of the sum authorized to be borrowed on the credit of the United States, by the act of Congress, entitled "An act to authorize a loan for a sum not exceeding twenty-five millions of dollars," passed on the twenty-fourth day of March, in the year one thousand eight hundred and fourteen, and also for and in lieu of so much of the sum authorized to be borrowed on the credit of the United States, by the act of Congress, entitled "An act authorizing a loan for the sum of three millions of dollars," passed on the fifteenth day of November, in the year one thousand eight hundred and fourteen, as has not been borrowed, or otherwise employed in the issue of Treasury notes, according to law: *Provided always,* That the whole amount of Treasury notes issued by virtue of this act, for and in lieu of the residue of the said two sums as aforesaid, shall not exceed the sum of seven millions five hundred thousand dollars: and further, that the Treasury notes so issued shall be applied to the same uses to which the said two loans, authorized as aforesaid, were, respectively, by law made applicable.

SEC. 2. *And be it further enacted,* That the Secretary of the Treasury be and he is hereby authorized, with the approbation of the President of the United States, to cause Treasury notes to be prepared, signed, and issued, for a further sum of three millions of dollars, to defray the expenses of the War Department, for the year one thousand eight hundred and fourteen, in addition to the sums heretofore appropriated by law for those purposes, respectively.

SEC. 3. *And be it further enacted,* That the Treasury notes to be issued by virtue of this act shall be prepared, signed, and issued, in the like form and manner, shall be reimbursable at the same places, and in the like periods, shall bear the same rate of interest; shall, in the like manner, be transferrable, and shall be equally receivable in payments to the United States for duties, taxes, and sales of public lands, as the Treasury notes issued by virtue of the act of Congress, entitled "An act to authorize the issuing of Treasury notes for the service of the year one thousand eight hundred and fourteen," passed on the fourth day of March, in the year aforesaid. And the Secretary of the Treasury, with the approbation of the President of the United States, shall have the like powers, in all respects, to prepare, issue, sell, pay, and distribute, the Treasury notes authorized to be issued by this act, or to borrow money on the pledge thereof, and to employ and pay an agent or agents for the purpose of making sale thereof, as were vested in him by the said last mentioned act of Congress, in relation to the Treasury notes therein and thereby authorized to be issued; and the forms and course of proceeding, in all respects, for paying, receiving, and accounting for, the Treasury notes issued by virtue of this act, shall be similar to those prescribed in and by the said last mentioned act of Congress in relation to the Treasury notes therein and thereby authorized to be issued.

SEC. 4. *And be it further enacted,* That a sum equal to the whole amount of the Treasury notes issued by virtue of this act, to be paid out of any money in the Treasury, not otherwise appropriated, shall be, and the same is hereby appropriated for the payment and reimbursement of the principal and interest of such Treasury notes, according to contract; and the faith of the United States is hereby pledged to provide adequate funds for any deficiency in the appropriation hereby made.

SEC. 5. *And be it further enacted,* That a sum of forty thousand dollars, to be paid out of any money in the Treasury, not otherwise appropriated, be, and the same is hereby, appropriated for defraying the expense of preparing, printing, engraving, and signing, the said Treasury notes; the expense of employing agents to make sale thereof; and all other expenses incident to issuing the Treasury notes, as authorized by this act.

SEC. 6. *And be it further enacted,* That, if any person shall, with intent to injure or defraud the United States, or any person or corporation, falsely make, forge, or counterfeit, or cause or procure to be falsely made, forged, or counterfeited, or willingly aid or assist in falsely making, forging, or counterfeiting, any note, in imitation of, or purporting to be, a Treasury note, or shall falsely alter, or cause or procure to be falsely altered, or wilfully aid or assist in falsely altering, any Treasury note, issued by virtue of this act, or shall pass, utter or publish, or attempt to pass, utter, or publish, as true, any false, forged, or counterfeited note, purporting to be a Treasury note as aforesaid, knowing the same to be falsely made, forged, or counterfeited; or shall pass, utter, or publish, or attempt to pass, utter, or publish, as true, any falsely altered Treasury note, issued as aforesaid, knowing the same to be falsely altered; every such person shall be deemed and adjudged guilty of felony, and being thereof convicted by due course of law, shall be sentenced to be imprisoned for a period not less than three years, nor more than ten years, or imprisoned and kept to hard labor for a period not less than three years, nor more than ten years, and, in either case, be fined in a sum not exceeding five thousand dollars.

Approved, December 26, 1814.

An Act giving further time to locate certain claims to lands confirmed by an act of Congress, entitled "An act confirming certain claims to lands in the District of Vincennes."

Be it enacted, &c., That the several persons whose claims were confirmed by the act of Congress, entitled "An act confirming certain claims to lands in the district of Vincennes," approved the thirteenth day of February, one thousand eight hundred and thirteen, and which have not been located, are hereby authorized to enter their locations with the register of the land office at Vincennes, on any part of the tract set apart for that purpose in said district, by virtue of an act, entitled "An act respecting claims to lands in the

Indiana Territory and State of Ohio," and in conformity to the provisions of that act; and shall be entitled to receive their certificates and patents in the manner provided by the first mentioned act: *Provided,* That such locations shall be made prior to the first day of July next.

Approved, December 26, 1814.

An Act to provide for leasing certain lands reserved for the support of schools in the Mississippi Territory.

Be it enacted, &c., That the county court in each county in the Mississippi Territory shall be and is hereby authorized to appoint a number of agents, not exceeding five, who shall have power to let out, on lease, for the purpose of improving the same, the sections of land reserved by Congress for the support of schools, lying within the county for which the agents respectively are appointed, or to let them out at an annual rent, as they shall judge proper. And it shall be the duty of the said agents, under the direction of the county courts respectively, to apply with impartiality the proceeds arising from the rents of each section as aforesaid to the purposes of education, and to no other use whatsoever, within the particular township of six miles square, or fractional township, wherein such section is situated, in such manner that all the citizens residing therein may partake of the benefit thereof, according to the true intent of the reservation made by Congress.

SEC. 2. *And be it further enacted,* That, for the purpose of forming the aforesaid sections into convenient forms, the said agents shall have power to lay off the same into lots of not less than one hundred and six acres, nor more than three hundred and twenty acres, except in case of fractional sections; and in every case, whether of leases for the improvement of the lots, or for an annual rent, the lessee shall be bound, in a suitable penalty, not to commit waste on the premises by destroying of timber or removing stone, or any other injury to the lands whatever.

SEC. 3. *And be it further enacted,* That the said agents shall have full power within their respective counties, when and so often as they think proper, by legal process, to remove any person or persons from the possession of any of the aforesaid reserved sections, when such person or persons have not taken a lease, and refuse or neglect to take the same. And it shall, moreover, be the duty of the said agents to inspect and inquire into any waste or trespass committed on any of the reserved sections aforesaid, by cutting and carrying off timber or stone, or any other damage that may be done to the same, whether by persons residing thereon or others. And the said agents are hereby authorized, when waste or trespass shall be committed, to proceed against the person or persons committing the same, according to the laws in such case made and provided; and actions in the cases aforesaid shall be sustained by the agents, and the damages recovered shall be one-half to the use of such agents, and the other half to be applied to the same purpose as the pro-

Public Acts of Congress.

ceeds of rents from the land on which the damage was sustained.

SEC. 4. *And be it further enacted,* That, for each lease executed by the agents, they shall be entitled to receive the sum of two dollars, to be paid by the lessees, respectively.

SEC. 5. *And be it further enacted,* That every lease which may be granted in virtue of this act shall be limited to the period of the termination of the Territorial form of government in the said Territory, and shall cease to have any force or effect after the first day of January next succeeding the establishment of a State government therein: *Provided,* That outstanding rents may be collected, and damages for waste or trespass may be recovered, in the same manner as if the leases continued in full force.

Approved, January 9, 1815.

An Act to provide additional revenues for defraying the expenses of Government, and maintaining the public credit, by laying a direct tax upon the United States, and to provide for assessing and collecting the same.

Be it enacted, &c., That a direct tax of six millions of dollars be and is hereby annually laid upon the United States; and the same shall be and is hereby apportioned to the States, respectively, in manner following:

To the State of New Hampshire, one hundred and ninety-three thousand five hundred and eighty-six dollars and seventy-four cents.

To the State of Massachusetts, six hundred and thirty-two thousand five hundred and forty-one dollars and ninety-six cents.

To the State of Rhode Island, sixty-nine thousand four hundred and four dollars and thirty-six cents.

To the State of Connecticut, two hundred and thirty-six thousand three hundred and forty-five dollars and forty-two cents.

To the State of Vermont, one hundred and ninety-six thousand six hundred and eighty-seven dollars and forty-two cents.

To the State of New York, eight hundred and sixty thousand two hundred and eighty-three dollars and twenty-four cents.

To the State of New Jersey, two hundred and seventeen thousand seven hundred and forty-three dollars and sixty-six cents.

To the State of Pennsylvania, seven hundred and thirty thousand nine hundred and fifty-eight dollars and thirty-two cents.

To the State of Delaware, sixty-four thousand ninety-two dollars and fifty cents.

To the State of Maryland, three hundred and three thousand two hundred and forty-seven dollars and eighty-eight cents.

To the State of Virginia, seven hundred and thirty-eight thousand thirty-six dollars and eighty-eight cents.

To the State of Kentucky, three hundred and thirty-seven thousand eight hundred and fifty-seven dollars and fifty-two cents.

To the State of Ohio, two hundred and eight

thousand three hundred dollars and twenty-eight cents.

To the State of North Carolina, four hundred and forty thousand four hundred and seventy-six dollars and fifty-six cents.

To the State of Tennessee, two hundred and twenty thousand, one hundred and seventy-one dollars and ten cents.

To the State of South Carolina, three hundred and three thousand eight hundred and ten dollars and ninety-six cents.

To the State of Georgia, one hundred and eighty-nine thousand eight hundred and seventy-two dollars and ninety-eight cents. And,

To the State of Louisiana, fifty-six thousand five hundred and ninety dollars and twenty-two cents.

SEC. 2. *And be it further enacted,* That, from and after the passage of this act, the act of Congress, entitled "An act for the assessment and collection of direct taxes and internal duties," passed on the twenty-second day of July, one thousand eight hundred and thirteen, shall be and the same is hereby repealed, except so far as the same respects the collection districts therein and thereby established and defined, so far as the same respects internal duties, and so far as the same respects the appointment and qualifications of the collectors and principal assessors therein and thereby authorized and required; in all which respects, so excepted, as aforesaid, the said act shall be and continue in force for the purposes of this act: *Provided always,* That, for making and completing the assessment and collection of the direct tax laid by virtue of the act of Congress, entitled "An act to lay and collect a direct tax within the United States," passed on the second day of August one thousand eight hundred and thirteen, the said first-mentioned act of Congress shall be and continue in full force, anything in this act to the contrary thereof in any wise notwithstanding.

SEC. 3. *And be it further enacted,* That each of the principal assessors heretofore appointed, or hereafter appointed, shall divide his district into a convenient number of districts, within each of which he shall appoint one respectable freeholder to be assistant assessor: *Provided,* That the Secretary of the Treasury shall be and is hereby authorized to reduce the number of assessment districts, in any collection district, in any State if the number shall appear to him to be too great. And the principal assessors, respectively, and each assistant assessor, so appointed and accepting the appointment, shall, before he enters on the duty of his appointment under this act, take and subscribe before some competent magistrate, or the collector of the direct tax and internal duties (who is hereby empowered to administer the same,) the following oath or affirmation, to wit: "I, ———, do swear (or affirm, as the case may be) that I will, to the best of my knowledge, skill, and judgment, diligently and faithfully execute the office and duties of principal assessor (or assistant assessor, as the case may be) for (naming the district,) without favor or partiality; and will do equal right and justice in every case in which shall act as principal assessor (or assistant assessor, as the case may be.") And a certificate of such oath or affirmation shall be delivered to the collector of the district for which such assessor shall be appointed; and every principal or assistant assessor acting in the said office, without having taken the said oath or affirmation, shall forfeit and pay one hundred dollars—one moiety to the use of the United States, and the other to him who shall first sue for the same—to be recovered, with costs of suit, in any court having competent jurisdiction.

SEC. 4. *And be it further enacted,* That the Secretary of the Treasury shall establish regulations suitable and necessary for carrying this act into effect; which regulations shall be binding on each principal assessor and his assistants, in the performance of the duties enjoined by or under this act; and shall also frame instructions for the said principal assessors and their assistants; pursuant to which instructions the said principal assessors shall, on the first day of February next, direct and cause the several assistant assessors in the district to inquire after and concerning all lands, lots of ground, with their improvements, dwelling-houses, and slaves, made liable to taxation under this act, by reference as well to any lists of assessment or collection taken under the laws of the respective States, as to any other records or documents, and by all other ways and means, and to value and enumerate the said objects of taxation, in the manner prescribed by this act, and in conformity with the regulations and instructions above-mentioned. And it shall be further lawful for the Secretary of the Treasury to direct all errors committed in the assessment, valuation, and tax lists, or in the collection thereof, heretofore or hereafter made in the valuation, assessment, and tax lists, of the direct tax, laid by virtue of the said act of Congress, entitled "An act to lay and collect a direct tax within the United States," and also, all such errors as may, from time to time, be committed in the assessment, valuation, and tax lists, or in the collection thereof, as may hereafter be made in the assessment of the direct tax by this act laid, to be corrected, in such form, and upon such evidence, as the said Secretary shall prescribe and approve.

SEC. 5. *And be it further enacted,* That the said direct tax, laid by this act, shall be assessed and laid on the value of all lands and lots of ground, with their improvements, dwelling-houses, and slaves; which several articles, subject to taxation, shall be enumerated and valued by the respective assessors at the rate each of them is worth in money: *Provided, however,* That all property, of whatever kind, coming within any of the foregoing descriptions, and belonging to the United States, or any State, or permanently or specially exempted from taxation by the laws of the State wherein the same may be situated, existing at the time of the passage of this act, shall be exempted from the aforesaid enumeration and valuation, and from the direct tax aforesaid: *And provided, also,* That nothing

herein contained shall be construed to exempt from enumeration and valuation, and the payment of the direct tax, any public lands which heretofore have been, or hereafter may be, sold in the States of Ohio and Louisiana, under any law of the United States, the compact between the United States and the said States to the contrary notwithstanding.

SEC. 6. *And be it further enacted,* That the respective assistant assessors shall, immediately after being required, as aforesaid, by the principal assessors, proceed through every part of their respective districts, and shall require all persons owning, possessing, or having the care or management of, any lands, lots of ground, dwelling-houses, or slaves, lying and being within the collection district where they reside, and liable to a direct tax as aforesaid, to deliver written lists of the same, which lists shall be made in such manner as may be directed by the principal assessor, and, as far as practicable, conformably to those which may be required for the same purpose under the authority of the respective States: *Provided always, nevertheless, and it is hereby further enacted and declared,* That the valuations and assessments heretofore made and completed, or to be made and completed, by virtue of the said act of Congress, entitled "An act for the assessment and collection of direct taxes and internal duties," and the said act of Congress, entitled "An act to lay and collect a direct tax within the United States," in relation to the several States wherein the same has been assessed or is assessing, shall be and remain the valuations and assessments for the said States, respectively, subject only to the revision, equalization, and apportionment, among the several counties and State districts, by the board of principal assessors hereinafter constituted, to be made as is hereinafter directed, for the purpose of levying and collecting annually the direct tax by this act laid, in the manner hereinafter provided, until provision shall be made by law for altering, modifying, or abolishing, the same. And the principal assessors, in the said several States wherein a direct tax has heretofore been assessed as aforesaid, shall, at the time and times herein and hereby prescribed for making the valuation and assessment in the States wherein a direct tax has not heretofore been assessed, (in consequence of the legislative assumption of the quotas of the direct tax by such States, respectively,) proceed to revise, and shall revise, their several and respective valuations, assessments, and tax lists, correcting therein all errors, and supplying all omissions, which have been or shall be therein discovered and ascertained. And in making the said revisal as aforesaid, it shall be the duty of the said principal assessors to inquire and ascertain what transfers and changes of property in lands, lots of ground, dwelling-houses, and slaves, have been made and effected, since the time of the original valuation and assessment aforesaid; and also what changes of residents and non-residents have occurred; and also what slaves have been born, or have died, or have runaway, or become otherwise useless;

and also what houses, or other improvements of real estate, have been burned or otherwise destroyed; and thereupon to make such changes, additions, or reductions, in the said valuations and assessments, respectively, as truth and justice shall require. And, for the purpose of making the said revisal as aforesaid, of the said valuations, assessments, and tax lists, the principal assessors shall take and pursue all lawful measures, by the examination of records, by the information of the parties in writing, or by any other satisfactory evidence or proof. And, in case of any alteration made upon such revisal, affecting the property or interests of any person, so as to charge such person with any greater amount of tax, or to transfer the charge of the tax from one person to another person, there shall be the like proceedings as is herein provided in the case of appeals upon an original assessment. And the principal assessors, after hearing such appeals, shall proceed to make out and to deliver revised lists of their valuations and assessments, respectively, to the board of principal assessors, to be constituted as is hereinafter mentioned. And thereupon, the said board of principal assessors shall proceed in the like manner as is hereinafter provided in the case of an original assessment, submitted to the said board of principal assessors, for the purpose of an equalization and apportionment of the direct tax by this act laid to and among the counties and State districts of the States, respectively.

Sec. 7. *And be it further enacted,* That if any person owning, possessing, or having the care or management of, property liable to a direct tax, as aforesaid, shall not be prepared to exhibit a written list when required as aforesaid, and shall consent to disclose the particulars of any and all the land and lots of ground, with their improvements, dwelling-houses, and slaves, taxable as aforesaid, then and in that case it shall be the duty of the officer to make such list, which, being distinctly read and consented to, shall be received as the list of such person.

Sec. 8. *And be it further enacted,* That if any such person shall deliver or disclose to any assessor appointed in pursuance of this act, and requiring a list or lists, as aforesaid, any false or fraudulent list, with intent to defeat or evade the valuation or enumeration hereby intended to be made, such person so offending, and being thereof convicted, before any court having competent jurisdiction, shall be fined in a sum not exceeding five hundred dollars, at the discretion of the court, and shall pay all costs and charges of prosecution; and the valuation and enumeration required by this act, shall, in all such cases, be made as aforesaid, upon lists according to the form above described, to be made out by the assessors, respectively, which lists the said assessors are hereby authorized and required to make, according to the best information they can obtain; and for the purpose of making which they are hereby authorized to enter into and upon all and singular the premises, respectively, and from the valuation and enumeration so made there shall be no appeal.

Sec. 9. *And be it further enacted,* That, in case any person shall be absent from his place of residence at the time an assessor shall call to receive the list of such person, it shall be the duty of such assessor to leave, at the house or place of residence of such person, a written note or memorandum, requiring him to present to such assessor the list or lists required by this act, within ten days from the date of such note or memorandum.

Sec. 10. *And be it further enacted,* That if any person, on being notified or required as aforesaid, shall refuse or neglect to give such list within as aforesaid, within the time required by this act, it shall be the duty of the assessor for the assessment district within which such person shall reside, and he is hereby authorized and required to enter into and upon the lands, dwelling-houses, and premises, if it be necessary, of such persons so refusing or neglecting, and to make, according to the best information which he can obtain, and on his own view and information, such lists of the lands and lots of ground, with their improvements, dwelling-houses, and slaves, owned or possessed, or under the care or management of such person, as are required by this act; which lists, so made and subscribed by such assessor, shall be taken and reputed as good and sufficient lists of the persons and property for which such person is to be taxed for the purposes of this act: and the person so failing or neglecting, unless in case of sickness or absence from home, shall, moreover, forfeit and pay the sum of one hundred dollars, to be recovered, for the use of the United States, with costs of suit, in any court having competent jurisdiction.

Sec. 11. *And be it further enacted,* That whenever there shall be, in any assessment district, any property, lands, and lots of ground, dwelling-houses or slaves, not owned or possessed by, or under the care or management of, any person or persons within such district, and liable to be taxed as aforesaid, and no list of which shall be transmitted to the principal assessor in the manner provided by this act, it shall be the duty of the assessor for such district, and he is hereby authorized and required, to enter into and upon the real estate, if it be necessary, and take such view thereof, and of the slaves, of which lists are required, and to make lists of the same, according to the form prescribed by this act; which lists, being subscribed by the said assessor, shall be taken and reputed as good and sufficient lists of such property under and for the purposes of this act.

Sec. 12. *And be it further enacted,* That the owners, possessors, or persons, having the care or management of the lands, lots of ground, dwelling houses, and slaves, not lying or being within the assessment district in which they reside, shall be permitted to make out and deliver the lists thereof required by this act, provided the assessment district in which the said objects of taxation are, be, is therein distinctly stated, at the time and in the manner prescribed, to the assessor of the assessment district wherein such person resides. And it shall be the duty of the assistant assessor in all such cases, to transmit such lists, at the time and in the manner prescribed for the transmission of the lists of the objects of taxation lying and being within their respective assessment districts, to the principal assessor of their collection district, whose duty it shall be to transmit them to the principal assessor of the collection district wherein the said objects of taxation shall lie or be, immediately after the receipt thereof, and the said lists shall be valid and sufficient for the purposes of this act; and on the delivery of every such list, the person making and delivering the same shall pay to the assistant assessor one dollar; one-half whereof he shall retain to his own use, and the other half thereof he shall pay over to the principal assessor of the district, for the use of such principal assessor.

SEC. 13. *And be it further enacted,* That the lists aforesaid shall be taken with reference to the day fixed for that purpose by this act as aforesaid; and the assistant assessors, respectively, after collecting the said lists, shall proceed to arrange the same, and to make two general lists; the first of which shall exhibit, in alphabetical order, the names of all persons liable to pay a tax under this act, residing within the assessment district, together with the value and assessment of the objects liable to taxation within such district, for which each such person is liable, and, whenever so required by the principal assessor, the amount of direct tax payable by each person, on such objects, under the State laws imposing direct taxes; and the second list shall exhibit, in alphabetical order, the names of all persons residing out of the collection district, owners of property within the district, together with the value and assessment thereof, or the amount of direct tax due thereon, as aforesaid. The forms of the said general lists shall be devised and prescribed by the principal assessor; and lists taken according to such form shall be made out by the assistant assessors, and delivered to the principal assessor, within sixty days after the day fixed by this act, as aforesaid, requiring lists from individuals. And if any assistant assessor shall fail to perform any duty assigned by this act, within the time prescribed by his precept, warrant, or other legal instructions, not being prevented therefrom by sickness, or other unavoidable accident, every such assessor shall be discharged from office; and shall, moreover, forfeit and pay two hundred dollars, to be recovered, for the use of the United States, in any court having competent jurisdiction, with cost of suit.

SEC. 14. *And be it further enacted,* That, immediately after the valuations and enumerations shall have been completed, as aforesaid, the principal assessor in each collection district shall, by advertisement in some public newspaper, if any there be in such district, and by written notifications, to be publicly posted up, in at least four of the most public places, in each assessment district, advertise all persons concerned, of the place where the said lists, valuations, and enumerations may be seen and examined; and that, during twenty-five days after the publication of the noti-

fications as aforesaid, appeals will be received and determined by him, relative to any erroneous or excessive valuations or enumerations by the assessor. And it shall be the duty of the principal assessor in each collection district, during twenty-five days after the date of publication, to be made as aforesaid, to submit the proceedings of the assessors, and the lists by them received, or taken as aforesaid, to the inspection of any and all persons who shall apply for that purpose; and the said principal assessors are hereby authorized to receive, hear, and determine, in a summary way, according to law and right, upon any and all appeals which may be exhibited against the proceedings of the said assessors: *Provided, always,* That it shall be the duty of said principal assessors to advertise and attend two successive days of the said twenty-five, at the court-house of each county within his assessment district, there to receive and determine upon the appeals aforesaid: *And provided, always,* That the question to be determined by the principal assessor, on an appeal respecting the valuation of property, shall be, whether the valuation complained of be, or be not, in a just relation or proportion to other valuations in the same assessment district. And all appeals to the principal assessors, as aforesaid, shall be made in writing, and shall specify the particular cause, matter, or thing, respecting which a decision is requested, and shall, moreover, state the ground or principle of inequality or error complained of. And the principal assessor shall have power to re-examine and equalize the valuations, as shall appear just and equitable; but no valuation shall be increased, without a previous notice of at least five days to the party interested, to appear and object to the same, if he judge proper; which notice shall be given by a note in writing, to be left at the dwelling-house of the party, by such assessor as the principal assessor shall designate for that purpose.

SEC. 15. *And be it further enacted,* That whenever a county or State district shall contain more than one assessment district, the principal assessor shall have power, on examination of the lists rendered by the assistant assessors, according to the provisions of this act, to revise, adjust, and equalize the valuation of lands and lots of ground, with their improvements, dwelling-houses, and slaves, between such assessment districts, by deducting from, or adding to, either, such a rate per centum as shall appear just and equitable.

SEC. 16. *And be it further enacted,* That the principal assessor shall, immediately after the expiration of the time for hearing and deciding appeals, make out correct lists of the valuation and enumeration in each assessment district, and deliver the same to the board of principal assessors hereinafter constituted, in and for the States, respectively. And it shall be the duty of the principal assessors, in each State, to convene, in general meeting, at such time and place as shall be appointed and directed by the Secretary of the Treasury. And the said principal assessors, or a majority of them, so convened, shall constitute, and they are hereby constituted, a board of prin-

Public Acts of Congress.

cipal assessors for the purposes of this act, and shall make and establish such rules and regulations as to them shall appear necessary for carrying such purposes into effect, not being inconsistent with this act, or the laws of the United States.

SEC. 17. *And be it further enacted,* That the said board of principal assessors, convened and organized as aforesaid, shall and may appoint a suitable person or persons, to be their clerk or clerks, who shall hold his or their office, or offices, at the pleasure of the said board of principal assessors, and whose duty it shall be to receive, record, and preserve all tax lists, returns, and other documents, delivered and made to the said board of principal assessors, and who shall take an oath or affirmation, (if conscientiously scrupulous of taking an oath,) faithfully to discharge his or their trust; and in default of taking such oath or affirmation, previous to entering on the duties of such appointment, or on failure to perform any part of the duties enjoined on him or them, respectively, by this act, he or they shall, respectively, forfeit and pay the sum of two hundred dollars, for the use of the United States, to be recovered in any court having competent jurisdiction, and shall also be removed from office.

SEC. 18. *And be it further enacted,* That it shall be the duty of the said clerks to record the proceedings of the said board of principal assessors, and to enter on the record the names of such of the principal assessors as shall attend any general meeting of the board of principal assessors for the purposes of this act. And if any principal assessor shall fail to attend such general meeting, his absence shall be noted on the said record, and he shall, for every day he may be absent therefrom, forfeit and pay the sum of ten dollars, for the use of the United States. And if any principal assessor shall fail or neglect to furnish the said board of principal assessors, with the lists of valuation and enumeration of each assessment district within his collection district, within three days after the time appointed, as aforesaid, for such general meeting of the said board of principal assessors, he shall forfeit and pay the sum of five hundred dollars, for the use of the United States, and moreover shall forfeit his compensation as principal assessor. And it shall be the duty of the clerks of the said board of principal assessors to certify, to the Secretary of the Treasury, an extract of the minutes of the board, showing such failures or neglect, which shall be sufficient evidence of the forfeiture of such compensation. to all intents and purposes: *Provided, always,* That it shall be in the power of the Secretary of the Treasury to exonerate such principal assessor or assessors from the forfeiture of the said compensation, in whole or in part, as to him shall appear just and equitable.

SEC. 19. *And be it further enacted,* That if the said board of principal assessors shall not, within three days after the first meeting thereof, as aforesaid, be furnished with all the lists of valuation of the several counties and State districts of any State or States, they shall, nevertheless, proceed to make out the equalization and apportionment by this act directed, and they shall assign to such counties and State districts, the valuation lists of which shall not have been furnished, such valuation as they shall deem just and right; and the valuation thus made to such counties and State districts, by the board of principal assessors. shall be final, and the proper quota of direct tax shall be, and is hereby declared to be, imposed thereon accordingly.

SEC. 20. *And be it further enacted,* That it shall be the duty of the said board of principal assessors, diligently and carefully to consider and examine the said lists of valuation, as well in relation to the States which have been heretofore assessed, as in relation to the States which have not been heretofore assessed, for the direct tax for the year one thousand eight hundred and fourteen, and they shall have power to revise, adjust, and equalize the valuation of property in any county or State district, by adding thereto, or deducting therefrom, such a rate per centum as shall render the valuation of the several counties and State districts just and equitable: *Provided,* The relative valuation of property in the same county shall not be changed, unless manifest error or imperfection shall appear in any of the lists of valuation, in which case the said board of principal assessors shall have power to correct the same, as to them shall appear just and right. And if, in consequence of any revisal, change, and alteration of the said valuation, any inequality shall be produced in the apportionment of the said direct tax to the several States, as aforesaid, it shall be the duty of the Secretary of the Treasury to report the same to Congress, to the intent that provision may be made by law for rectifying such inequality.

SEC. 21. *And be it further enacted,* That, as soon as the said board of principal assessors shall have completed the adjustment and equalization of the valuation aforesaid, they shall proceed to apportion to each county and State district its proper quota of direct tax, and they shall lay the same upon all the subjects of direct taxation herein prescribed, within their respective counties and State districts, according to the provisions of this act, so as to raise upon each county or State district, a quota of taxes bearing the same proportion to the whole direct tax imposed on the State, as the valuation of such county or State district bears to the valuation of the State. And the said board of principal assessors shall, within twenty days after the time appointed by the Secretary of the Treasury for their first meeting, complete the said apportionment, and shall record the same; they shall thereupon further deliver to each principal assessor a certificate of such apportionment, together with the general lists by the principal assessors respectively presented to the board as aforesaid, and transmit to the Secretary of the Treasury a certificate of the apportionment of them made as aforesaid; and the principal assessors, respectively, shall thereupon proceed to revise their respective lists, and alter and make the same in all respects conformable to the apportionment aforesaid by the said board of principal assessors; and the said principal assessors, respectively, shall make out lists containing the sums payable, according to the provisions of this act, upon every object of taxation in and for each collection district; which lists shall contain the name of each person residing within the said district, owning, or having the care or superintendence of, property lying within the said district, which is liable to the said tax, when such person or persons are known, together with the sums payable by each; and where there is any property within any collection district, liable to the payment of the said tax, not owned or occupied by or under the superintendence of any person resident therein, there shall be a separate list of such property, specifying the sum payable, and the names of the respective proprietors, where known. And the said principal assessors shall furnish, to the collector of the several collection districts respectively, within thirty-five days after the apportionment is completed as aforesaid, a certified copy of such list or lists for their proper collection districts. And in default of performance of the duties enjoined on the board of assessors and principal assessors, respectively, by this section, they shall, severally and individually, forfeit and pay the sum of five hundred dollars, to the use of the United States, to be recovered in any court having competent jurisdiction: *And it is hereby enacted and declared*, That the valuation, assessment, equalization, and apportionment, made by the said board of principal assessors, as aforesaid, shall be and remain in full force and operation for laying, levying, and collecting, yearly and every year, the annual direct tax by this act laid and imposed, until altered, modified, or abolished by law.

SEC. 22. *And be it further enacted*, That each collector, on receiving a list as aforesaid, from the said principal assessors, respectively, shall subscribe three receipts, one of which shall be given on a full and correct copy of such list, which list shall be delivered by him to, and shall remain with, the principal assessor of his collection district, and shall be open to the inspection of any person who may apply to inspect the same, and the other two receipts shall be given on aggregate statements of the lists aforesaid, exhibiting the gross amount of taxes to be collected in each county or State district contained in the collection district, one of which aggregate statements and receipts shall be transmitted to the Secretary, and the other to the Comptroller, of the Treasury.

SEC. 23. *And be it further enacted*, That each collector, before receiving any list, as aforesaid, for collection, shall give bond, with one or more good and sufficient sureties, to be approved by the Comptroller of the Treasury, in the amount of the taxes assessed in the collection district, for which he has been or may be appointed, which bond shall be payable to the United States, with condition for the true and faithful discharge of the duties of his office, according to law, and particularly for the due collection and payment of all moneys assessed upon such district; and the said bond shall be transmitted to, and deposited in, the office of the Comptroller of the Treasury: *Provided always*, That nothing herein contained shall be deemed to annul, or in anywise to impair, the obligation of the bond heretofore given by any collector; but the same shall be and remain in full force and virtue, anything in this act to the contrary thereof, in any wise, notwithstanding.

SEC. 24. *And be it further enacted*, That the annual amount of taxes so assessed, shall be and remain a lien upon all lands and other real estate, and all slaves, of the individuals who may be assessed for the same, during two years after the time it shall annually become due and payable; and the said lien shall extend to each and every part of all tracts or lots of land, or dwelling-houses, notwithstanding the same may have been divided or alienated in part.

SEC. 25. *And be it further enacted*, That each collector shall be authorized to appoint, by an instrument of writing under his hand and seal, as many deputies as he may think proper, assigning to each deputy, by that instrument of writing, such portion of his collection district as he may think proper, and also to revoke the powers of any deputy, giving public notice thereof in that portion of the district assigned to such deputy; and such deputy shall have the like authority, in every respect, to collect the direct tax, so assessed within the portion of the district assigned to him; which is by this act vested in the collector himself; but each collector shall, in every respect, be responsible, both to the United States and to individuals, as the case may be, for all moneys collected, and for every act done, as deputy collector, by any of his deputies, whilst acting as such: *Provided*, That nothing herein contained shall prevent any collector from collecting, himself, the whole, or any part, of the tax so assessed, and payable in his district.

SEC. 26. *And be it further enacted*, That each of the said collectors, or his deputies, shall, within ten days after receiving his collection list from the principal assessors, respectively, as aforesaid, and, annually, within ten days after he shall be so required by the Secretary of the Treasury, advertise, in one newspaper printed in his collection district, if any there be, and by notifications to be posted up in at least four public places in his collection district, that the said tax has become due and payable, and state the times and places at which he or they will attend to receive the same, which shall be within twenty days after such notification; and, with respect to persons who shall not attend, according to such notifications, it shall be the duty of each collector, in person or by deputy, to apply once, at their respective dwellings, within such district, and there demand the taxes payable by such persons, which application shall be made within sixty days after the receipt of the collection lists, as aforesaid, or after the receipt of the requisition of the Secretary of the Treasury, as aforesaid, by the collectors; and if the said taxes shall not be then paid, or within twenty days thereafter, it shall be lawful for such collector, or his deputies, to proceed to collect the said taxes by distress and sale of the goods, chattels, or effects, of the persons delinquent, as aforesaid. And, in case of such distress, it shall be the duty of the officer charged with the collection, to make, or cause to be made, an account of the goods or chattels which may be distrained, a copy of which, signed by the officer making such distress, shall be left with the owner or possessor of such goods, chattels, or effects, or at his or her dwelling, with a note of the sum demanded, and the time and place of sale; and the said officer shall forthwith cause a notification to be publicly posted up at two of the taverns nearest the residence of the person whose property shall be distrained, or at the court-house of the same county, if not more than ten miles distant, which notice shall specify the articles distrained, and the time and place proposed for the sale thereof, which time shall not be less than ten days from the date of such notification, and the place proposed for sale not more than five miles distant from the place of making such distress: *Provided,* That, in any case of distress, for the payment of the duties aforesaid, the goods, chattels, or effects, so distrained, shall and may be restored to the owner or possessor, if, prior to the sale thereof, payment, or tender thereof, shall be made to the proper officer charged with the collection, of the full amount demanded, together with such fee for levying, and such sum for the necessary and reasonable expense of removing and keeping the goods, chattels, or effects, so distrained, as may be allowed in like cases by the laws or practice of the State wherein the distress shall have been made; but, in case of non-payment or tender as aforesaid, the said officer shall proceed to sell the said goods, chattels, or effects, at public auction, and shall and may retain from the proceeds of such sale, the amount demandable for the use of the United States, with the necessary and reasonable expenses of distress and sale, and a commission of five per centum thereon, for his own use, rendering the overplus, if any there be, to the person whose goods, chattels, or effects, shall have been distrained: *Provided,* That it shall not be lawful to make distress of the tools or implements of a trade or profession, beasts of the plough necessary for the cultivation of improved lands, arms, or household furniture, or apparel necessary for a family.

Sec. 27. *And be it further enacted,* That whenever goods, chattels, or effects, sufficient to satisfy any tax upon dwelling-houses or lands, and their improvements, owned, occupied, or superintended, by persons known or residing within the same collection district, cannot be found, the collector having first advertised the same for thirty days in a newspaper printed within the collection district, if such there be, and having posted up, in at least ten public places within the same, a notification of the intended sale, thirty days previous thereto, shall proceed to sell, at public sale, so much of the said property as may be necessary to satisfy the taxes due thereon, together with an addition of twenty per centum to the said taxes.

But in all cases where the property liable to a direct tax under this act, or the said act of Congress, entitled "An act to lay and collect a direct tax within the United States," shall not be divisible, so as to enable the collector, by a sale of part thereof, to raise the whole amount of the tax, with all costs, charges, and commissions, the whole of such property shall be sold, and the surplus of the proceeds of the sale, after satisfying the tax, costs, charges, and commissions, shall be paid to the owner of the property, or his legal representatives, or if he or they cannot be found, or refuse to receive the same, then such surplus shall be deposited in the Treasury of the United States, to be there held for the use of the owner, or his legal representatives, until he or they shall make application therefor to the Secretary of the Treasury, who, upon such application, shall, by warrant on the Treasurer, cause the same to be paid to the applicant. And if the property advertised for sale as aforesaid, cannot be sold for the amount of the tax due thereon, with the said additional twenty per centum thereto, the collector shall purchase the same in behalf of the United States for the amount aforesaid: *Provided,* That the owner or superintendent of the property aforesaid, after the same shall have been as aforesaid advertised for sale, and before it shall have been actually sold, shall be allowed to pay the amount of the tax thereon, with an addition of ten per centum on the same, on the payment of which the sale of the said property shall not take place: *Provided also,* That the owners, their heirs, executors, or administrators, or any person on their behalf, shall have liberty to redeem the lands and other property sold as aforesaid, within two years from the time of sale, upon payment to the collector, for the use of the purchaser, his heirs, or assigns, of the amount paid by such purchaser, with interest for the same, at the rate of twenty per centum per annum; and no deed shall be given in pursuance of such sale, until the time of redemption shall have expired. And the collector shall render a distinct account of the charges incurred in offering and advertising for sale such property, and shall pay into the Treasury the surplus, if any there be, of the aforesaid addition of twenty per centum, or ten per centum, as the case may be, after defraying the charges. And in every case of the sale of real estate, which has been made under the said act of Congress for the assessment and collection of direct taxes and internal duties, or which shall be made under the authority of this act, by the collectors or marshals, respectively, or their lawful deputies, respectively, or by any other person or persons, the deeds for the estate so sold shall be prepared, made, executed and proved, or acknowledged, at the time and times prescribed, in this act, by the collectors, respectively, within whose collection district said real estate shall be situated, in such form of law as shall be authorized and required by the law of the United States, or by the law of the State in which such real estate lies, for making, executing, proving, and acknowledging, deeds of bargain and sale, or other conveyances for the transfer and conveyance of real estate. And for every deed, so prepared, made, executed, proved, and acknowledged, the purchaser or grantee shall pay to the collector the sum of five dollars for the use of the collector, marshal, or other person, effecting the sale of the real estate thereby conveyed.

Sec. 28. *And be it further enacted,* That, with respect to the property lying within any collection district, not owned, or occupied, or superintended, by some person residing in such collection district, and on which the tax shall not have been paid to the collector within ninety days after the day on which he shall have received the collection list from the said principal assessors, respectively, as aforesaid, or the requisition of the Secretary of the Treasury, as aforesaid, the collector shall transmit lists of the same to one of the collectors within the same State, to be designated for that purpose by the Secretary of the Treasury: and the collector, who shall have been thus designated by the Secretary of the Treasury, shall transmit receipts for all the lists received, as aforesaid, to the collector transmitting the same. And the collectors thus designated in each State by the Secretary of the Treasury, shall cause notifications of the taxes due as aforesaid, and contained in the lists thus transmitted to them, to be published, for sixty days, in at least one of the newspapers published in the State; and the owners of the property on which such taxes may be due, shall be permitted to pay to such collector the said tax, with an addition of ten per centum thereon: *Provided,* That such payment is made within one year after the day on which the collector of the district where such property lies, had notified that the tax had become due on the same.

Sec. 29. *And be it further enacted,* That when any tax, as aforesaid, shall have remained unpaid for the term of one year, as aforesaid, the collector in the State where the property lies, and who shall have been designated by the Secretary of the Treasury as aforesaid, having first advertised the same for sixty days, in at least one newspaper in the State, shall proceed to sell, at public sale, so much of the said property as may be necessary to satisfy the taxes due thereon, together with an addition of twenty per centum thereon; or if such property is not divisible, as aforesaid, the whole thereof shall be sold and accounted for in manner hereinbefore provided. If the property advertised for sale cannot be sold for the amount of the tax due thereon, with the said addition thereon, the collector shall purchase the same in behalf of the United States, for such amount and addition. And the collector shall render a distinct account of the charges incurred in offering and advertising for sale such property, and pay into the Treasury the surplus, if any, of the aforesaid addition of ten or twenty per centum, as the case may be, after defraying the said charges.

Sec. 30. *And be it further enacted,* That the collectors, designated, as aforesaid, by the Secretary of the Treasury, shall deposite with the clerks of the district court of the United States, in the respective States, and within which district the property lies, correct lists of the tracts of land, or other real property, sold by virtue of this act for non-payment of taxes, together with the names of the owners, or presumed owners, or the purchasers, of the same, at the public sales aforesaid, and of the amount paid by such purchasers for the same; the owners, their heirs, executors, or administrators, or any person in their behalf, shall have liberty to redeem the lands or other property sold as aforesaid, within two years from the time of sale, upon payment, to the clerk aforesaid, for the use of the purchaser, his heirs, or assigns, of the amount paid by such purchaser for the said land, or other real property, with interest for the same, at the rate of twenty per centum per annum, and of a commission of five per centum on such payment, for the use of the clerk aforesaid. The clerk shall, on application, pay to the purchasers the money thus paid for their use; and the collectors, respectively, shall give deeds for the lands or property aforesaid, to the purchasers entitled to the same, in all cases where the same shall not have been redeemed within two years, as aforesaid, by the original owners thereof, or their legal representatives. And the said clerks shall be entitled to receive from the purchaser, for his own use, the sum of one dollar, in addition to the sum hereinbefore made payable to the collector, for every such deed, to be paid on the delivery thereof to such purchasers. And in all cases where lands may be sold under this act for the payment of taxes, belonging to infants, persons of insane mind, married women, or persons beyond sea, such persons shall have the term of two years, after their respective disabilities shall have been removed, or their return to the United States, to redeem lands thus sold, on their paying into the clerk's office aforesaid the amount paid by the purchaser, together with ten per centum per annum; and on their payment to the purchaser of the land aforesaid, a compensation for all improvements he may have made on the premises, subsequent to his purchase, the value of which improvements to be ascertained by three or more neighboring freeholders, to be appointed by the clerk aforesaid, who, on actual view of the premises, shall assess the value of such improvements, on their oaths, and make a return of such valuation to the clerk immediately. And the clerk of the court shall receive such compensation for his services herein, to be paid by, and received from, the parties, like costs of suit, as the judge of the district court shall, in that respect, tax and allow.

Sec. 31. *And be it further enacted,* That the several collectors shall, at the expiration of every month after they shall, respectively, commence their collections, in the next and every ensuing year, transmit to the Secretary of the Treasury a statement of the collections made by them, respectively, within the month, and pay over, quarterly, or sooner, if required by the Secretary of the Treasury, the moneys by them respectively collected within the said term ; and each of the said collectors shall complete the collection of all sums annually assigned to him for collection as aforesaid, shall pay over the same into the Treasury, and shall render his final account to the Treasury Department, within six months from and after the day when he shall have received the collection lists from the said board of principal assessors, or the said requisition of the Secretary of the Treasury as aforesaid: *Provided, however,* That the period of one year and three months, from the said annual day, shall be annually allowed to the collector designated in each State as aforesaid by the Secretary of the Treasury, with respect to the taxes contained in the list transmitted to him by the other collectors as aforesaid.

Sec. 32. *And be it further enacted,* That each collector shall be charged with the whole amount of taxes by him receipted, whether contained in the lists delivered to him by the principal assessors, respectively, or transmitted to him by other collectors; and shall be allowed credit for the amount of taxes contained in the lists transmitted in the manner above provided to other collectors, and by them receipted as aforesaid, and also for the taxes of such persons as may have absconded, or become insolvent, subsequent to the date of the assessment, and prior to the day when the tax ought, according to the provisions of this act, to have been collected: *Provided,* That it shall be proven, to the satisfaction of the Comptroller of the Treasury, that due diligence was used by the collector from, that no property was left from which the tax could have been recovered. And each collector, designated in each State as aforesaid by the Secretary of the Treasury, shall receive credit for the taxes due for all tracts of land which, after being offered by him for sale in manner aforesaid, shall or may have been purchased by him in behalf of the United States.

Sec. 33. *And be it further enacted,* That if any collector shall fail, either to collect or to render his account, or to pay over in the manner, or within the times, hereinbefore provided, it shall be the duty of the Comptroller of the Treasury, and he is hereby authorized and required, immediately after such delinquency, to issue a warrant of distress against such delinquent collector and his sureties, directed to the marshal of the district, therein expressing the amount of the taxes with which the said collector is chargeable, and the sums, if any, which have been paid. And the said marshal, himself, or by his deputy, immediately proceed to levy and collect the sum which may remain due, by distress and sale of the goods and chattels, or any personal effects, of the delinquent collector; and for want of goods, chattels, or effects, aforesaid, sufficient to satisfy the said warrant, the same may be levied on the person of the collector, who may be committed to prison, there to remain until discharged in due course of law: And furthermore, notwithstanding the commitment of the collector to prison as aforesaid, or if he abscond, and goods, chattels, and effects, cannot be found sufficient to satisfy the

said warrant, the said marshal, or his deputy, shall and may proceed to levy and collect the sum which remains due, by distress and sale of the goods and chattels, or any personal effects, of the surety or sureties of the delinquent collector. And the amount of the sums due from any collector, as aforesaid, shall, and the same are hereby declared to be, a lien upon the lands and real estate of such collector and his sureties, until the same shall be discharged according to law. And for want of goods and chattels, or other personal effects of such collector, or his sureties, sufficient to satisfy any warrant of distress, issued pursuant to the preceding section of this act, the lands and real estate of such collector and his sureties, or so much thereof as may be necessary for satisfying the said warrant, after being advertised for at least three weeks, in not less than three public places in the collection district, and in one newspaper printed in the county or district, if any there be, prior to the proposed time of sale, may and shall be sold by the marshal or his deputy; and for all lands and real estate, sold in pursuance of the authority aforesaid, the conveyances of the marshals, or their deputies, executed in due form of law, shall give a valid title against all persons claiming under delinquent collector, or their sureties, aforesaid. And all moneys that may remain of the proceeds of such sale, after satisfying the said warrant of distress, and paying the reasonable costs and charges of sale, shall be returned to the proprietor of the lands or real estate sold as aforesaid.

Sec. 34. *And be it further enacted,* That each and every collector, or his deputy, who shall exercise or be guilty of any extortion or oppression, under color of this act, or shall demand other or greater sums than shall be authorized by this act, shall be liable to pay a sum not exceeding two thousand dollars, to be recovered, by and for the use of the party injured with costs of suit, in any court having competent jurisdiction; and each and every collector or his deputies shall give receipts for all sums by them collected and retained in pursuance of this act.

Sec. 35. *And be it further enacted,* That there shall be allowed and paid, for the services performed under this act, to each principal assessor, two dollars for every day employed in making the necessary arrangements and giving the necessary instructions to the assistant assessors for the valuations; three dollars for every day employed in making revised valuations and tax lists, where an assessment and valuation have heretofore been made, and in hearing appeals and making out lists, agreeably to the provisions of this act, upon original assessments and valuations; and five dollars for every hundred taxable persons contained in the tax list, as delivered by him to the said board of principal assessors; to each assistant assessor, two dollars for every day actually employed in collecting lists and making valuations, the number of days necessary for that purpose being certified by the principal assessor, and approved by the Comptroller of the Treasury; and three dollars for every hundred taxable persons contained in the tax list, as completed and delivered by him to the principal assessor; to each of the principal assessors constituting the board of principal assessors as aforesaid, for every day's actual attendance at the said board, the sum of three dollars, and for travelling to and from the place designated by the Secretary of the Treasury, three dollars for each thirty miles. And to each of the clerks of the said board, three dollars for every day's actual attendance thereon. And the said board of principal assessors, and the said assessors, severally and respectively, shall be allowed their necessary and reasonable charges for books and stationery used in the execution of their duties; and the compensation herein allowed shall be in full for all other expenses not particularly specified.

Sec. 36. *And be it further enacted,* That the compensation hereinbefore provided for the services of the principal assessors and their assistants, and for the board of principal assessors and their clerks, shall be paid at the Treasury; and there is hereby appropriated, for that purpose the sum of two hundred thousand dollars, to be paid out of any money not otherwise appropriated. And the President of the United States shall be, and he is hereby, authorized to augment, in cases where he shall deem it necessary, the compensation authorized by this act for the principal assessors and their assistants: *Provided,* That no principal assessor shall, in any case, receive more than three hundred dollars, and no assistant assessor shall receive more than one hundred and fifty dollars; and for such augmented compensation, and the expense of carrying this act annually into effect, there is further hereby appropriated an annual sum of one hundred and fifty thousand dollars, to be paid out of any money in the Treasury, not otherwise appropriated.

Sec. 37. *And be it further enacted,* That in cases where principal assessors have not been, or shall not, during the present session of Congress, be appointed, and in cases where vacancies shall occur in the office of principal assessor, the President of the United States is hereby authorized to make appointments during the recess of the Senate by granting commissions, which shall expire at the end of the next session. And where no person can be found in any collection district, or assessment district, to serve either as collector, principal assessor, or assistant assessor, respectively, the President of the United States is hereby authorized to appoint one of the deputy postmasters in such district, to serve as collector, or assessor, as the case may be. And it shall be the duty of such deputy postmaster to perform, accordingly, the duties of such officer.

Sec. 38. *And be it further enacted,* That separate accounts shall be kept at the Treasury, of all moneys received from the direct tax and from the internal duties, in each of the respective States, Territories, and collection districts; and that separate accounts shall be kept of the amount of each species of duty that shall accrue, with the moneys paid to the collectors, assessors, and assistant assessors, and to the other officers employed, in each of the respective States, Territories, and collection districts, which accounts it shall be the duty of the Secretary of the Treasury, annually, in the month of December, to lay before Congress.

Sec. 39. *And be it further enacted,* That the principal assessors, respectively, shall, yearly, and every year, after the year one thousand eight hundred and fifteen, in the month of January, inquire and ascertain, in the manner by the sixth section of this act provided, what transfers and changes of property in lands, lots of ground, dwelling-houses, and slaves, have been made and effected in their respective districts, subsequent to the next preceding valuation, assessment, and apportionment of the direct tax, by this act laid; and, within twenty days thereafter, they shall make out three lists of such transfers and changes, and transmit one list to the Secretary of the Treasury another list to the commissioner of the revenue, and the third shall be delivered to the collector of the collection district. And it shall, yearly, and every year, after the said year one thousand eight hundred and fifteen, be the duty of the Secretary of the Treasury to notify the collectors of the several collection districts, a day in the month of February, on which it shall be the duty of the said collectors to commence laying and collecting the annual direct tax by this act laid and imposed, according to the assessment of the tax lists to them delivered by the said principal assessors, as aforesaid, subject only to such alterations therein as shall be just and proper, in the opinion of the Secretary of the Treasury, to conform to the transfers and changes aforesaid, ascertained by the principal assessors as aforesaid; and the said collectors shall, annually, in all respects, proceed in, and conclude, the collection of the said direct tax, in the same manner, and within the time, hereinbefore provided and prescribed.

Sec. 40. *And be it further enacted,* That each State may pay its quota of the direct tax by this act laid, into the Treasury of the United States, for the first, and for any and every succeeding year; and, in consideration of such payment, the State shall be entitled to a deduction of fifteen per centum, if paid before the first day of May, and ten per centum, if paid before the first day of October, in the year to which the payment relates: *Provided,* That notice of the intention to make such payment be given to the Secretary of the Treasury, on or before the first day of April in each year: *And provided,* That such notice and payment shall not in any wise prevent or discontinue the proceedings under this act, to make the valuations, assessments, and apportionments, herein authorized and directed, but shall only prevent or discontinue the collection of the quota of the State giving such notice and making such payment.

Sec. 41. *And be it further enacted,* That, towards establishing an adequate revenue to provide for the payment of the expenses of Government; for the punctual payment of the public debt, principal and interest, contracted and to be contracted, according to the terms of the contracts, respectively; and for creating an adequate sinking fund, gradually to redoce, and eventually to extingush, the public debt, contracted, and to be contracted, the direct tax by this act laid shall continue to be laid, levied, and collected, during the present war between the United States and Great Britain, and until the purposes aforesaid shall be completely accomplished, anything in the said act of Congress to the contrary thereof, in anywise notwithstanding. And, for the effectual application of the revenue to be raised by and from the said direct tax laid by this act, and also by and from the direct tax laid by the said act of Congress, entitled "An act to lay and collect a direct tax within the United States," to the purposes aforesaid, in due form of law, the faith of tne United States is hereby pledged: *Provided always,* That whenever Congress shall deem it expedient to alter, reduce, or change, the said direct tax, by this act laid, it shall be lawful so to do, upon providing and substituting by law, at the said time, and for the same purposes, other taxes or duties, which shall be equally productive with the direct tax so altered, reduced, or changed: *And provided further,* That nothing in this act contained shall be deemed or construed, in anywise, to rescind or impair any specific appropriation of the said direct taxes, or either of them; but such appropriation shall remain and be carried into effect, according to the true intent and meaning of the law and laws making the same, anything in this act to the contrary thereof, in anywise, notwithstanding.

SEC. 42. *And be it further enacted,* That it shall be lawful for the President of the United States to authorize the Secretary of the Treasury to anticipate the collection and receipt of the direct tax, laid and imposed by this act, and by the said act of Congress, entitled "An act to lay and collect a direct tax within the United States," by obtaining a loan upon the pledge of the said direct taxes, or either of them for the reimbursement thereof, to an amount not exceeding six millions of dollars, and at a rate of interest not exceeding six per centum per annum. And any bank or banks now incorporated, or which may hereafter be incorporated, under the authority of the United States, is, and are hereby, authorized to make such loan: *Provided always, and it is expressly declared,* That the money so obtained upon loan shall be applied to the purposes aforesaid, to which the said direct taxes, so to be pledged, are by this act applied and appropriated, and to no other purposes whatsoever.

Approved, January 9, 1815.

An Act to provide additional revenues for defraying the expenses of Government, and maintaining the public credit, by laying duties on various goods, wares, and merchandise, manufactured within the United States.

Be it enacted, &c., That, from and after the expiration of ninety days subsequent to the passing of this act, there shall be paid upon all goods, wares, and merchandise, of the following descriptions, which shall thereafter be manufactured or made for sale within the United States,

or the Territories thereof, the respective duties following, that is to say:

Pig iron, per ton, one dollar.

Castings of iron, per ton, one dollar and fifty cents.

Bar iron, per ton, one dollar.

Rolled or slit iron, per ton, one dollar.

Nails, brads, and sprigs, other than those usually denominated wrought, per pound, one cent.

Candles of white wax, or in part of white and other wax, per pound five cents.

Mould candles of tallow, or of wax, other than white, or in part of each, per pound three cents.

Hats and caps, in whole or in part of leather, wool, or furs; bonnets in whole or in part of wool or fur, if above two dollars in value, eight per centum ad valorem.

Hats of chip or wood, covered with silk or other materials, or not covered, if above two dollars in value, eight per centum ad valorem.

Umbrellas and parasols, if above the value of two dollars, eight per centum ad valorem.

Paper, three per centum ad valorem.

Playing and visiting cards, fifty per centum ad valorem.

Saddles and bridles, six per centum ad valorem.

Boots and bootees, exceeding five dollars per pair in value, five per centum ad valorem.

Beer, ale, and porter, six per centum ad valorem.

Tobacco, manufactured cigars, and snuff, twenty per centum ad valorem.

Leather, including therein all hides and skins, whether tanned, tawed, dressed, or otherwise made, on the original manufacture thereof, five per centum ad valorem; which said duties shall be paid by the owner or occupier of the buildings or vessels in which, or of the machines, implements, or utensils, wherewith the said goods, wares, and merchandise, shall have been manufactured or made, or by the agent or superintendent thereof; the amount thereof payable by any one person, at any one time, if not exceeding twenty dollars shall, and if exceeding twenty dollars may, be paid in money, with a deduction of two per centum, at the time of rendering the accounts of the articles so chargeable with duty, required to be rendered by the second section of this act, or without deduction at the next subsequent time prescribed for rendering such account.

SEC. 2. *And be it further enacted,* That every person who, from and after the expiration of ninety days subsequent to the passing of this act, shall be the owner or occupier of any building or vessel, or machine, implement, or utensil, and or intended to be used for the manufacturing or making of such goods, wares, and merchandise, or either of them, or who shall have such building, or vessel, or machine, implement, or utensil, under his superintendence, either as agent for the owner, or on his own account, shall, before the expiration of the said ninety days, and every person who, after the expiration of the said ninety days, shall use, or intend to use, any building, vessel, or machine, implement, or utensil, as aforesaid, either as owner, occupier, agent, or otherwise, shall, before he shall begin so to use, or cause the same so to be used, give bond, with at least two sureties, to the satisfaction of the collector of internal duties for the district in which the same shall be situate, in a sum not less than the computed duties for one year, nor less than one hundred dollars, that he will before using, or causing the same to be used, make true and exact entry and report, in writing. to the said collector, of every such building, or vessel, machine, implement, or utensil, owned, occupied, or superintended by him, with the size thereof, the names of the owner, occupier, agent, and superintendent, the place where situate, and the manner in which, and the time for which, not exceeding one year, it is intended to employ the same, with the denominations and quantities of the articles manufactured or made as aforesaid, which he may have on hand, with the value thereof; that he will, thereafter, before using, or causing the same to be used, make like entry and report of any other building, or vessel, machine, implement, or utensil. used, or intended to be used, as aforesaid, that he may own, occupy, or have the agency or superintendence of, with the size thereof, the names of the owner, occupier, agent, and superintendent, the place where situate, and the manner in which, and the time for which, not exceeding one year, it is intended to employ the same, with information, from time to time, of any change in the form size, agency, ownership, occupancy, or superintendence, which all or either of the said buildings, or vessels, machines, implements, or utensils, may undergo; that he will, from day to day, so long as he may use the same, enter, or cause to be entered, in a book or books to be kept by him for that purpose, and which shall be open at all times, between the rising and setting of the sun, for the inspection of the said collector, who may take any minutes, memorandums, or transcripts thereof, the denominations and quantities of the articles manufactured or made, and will render to the said collector, on the first day of January, April, July, and October in each year, or within ten days thereafter, a general account in writing, taken from his books, of the denominations and quantities of the said articles, with the aggregate value thereof, for three months preceding said days, or for such portion thereof as may have elapsed from the date of said entry and report to the said day which shall next ensue; that he will, at the said times, deliver to the said collector the original book of entries, which book shall be retained by said officer; that he will likewise, from day to day, enter or cause to be entered, in a book or books to be kept by him for that purpose, and which shall be open at all times, between the rising and setting of the sun, for the inspection of the said collector, who may take any minutes, memorandums, or transcripts, thereof, the denominations and quantities of all the hereinbefore enumerated manufactured articles sold, with the price for which the same were sold, specifying in each sale, the name of the person to whom sold, where the amount sold shall exceed ten dollars in value; and 'that he will render to the said collector, at the time of rendering the said general accounts, a statement in writing, taken from said book or books, in which there shall be specified the denominations and quantities of all such manufactured articles sold on each day, stating distinctly each sale, with the name of the purchaser, and the denominations and quantities sold, and price, where the same shall exceed ten dollars, and the aggregate denominations and quantities, with the aggregate value of all other sales; that he will verify, or cause to be verified, the said entries, reports, books, general accounts, and statements. on oath or affirmation, to be taken before the collector, or some officer authorized by law to administer the same, according to the form required by this act, where the same is prescribed; and that he will pay to the said collector the duties which by this act ought to be paid on the articles so manufactured, and in the said account mentioned, if not exceeding twenty dollars, at the time of rendering an account thereof, with a deduction of two per centum, and if exceeding twenty dollars, either at said time, with a like deduction, or at the next subsequent time prescribed for rendering such accounts, without deduction; and the said bond may, from time to time, at the discretion of the collector, be renewed or changed, in regard to the sureties and penalties thereof. And every such person, whether owner, occupier, agent, or superintendent, as aforesaid, shall, at the time of making the entry and report, first before stated, obtain, agreeably thereto, a license for employing, for a term not exceeding one year, such buildings, or vessels, or machines, implements, or utensils, describing the same, with the use to which they are to be applied, the place where situate, the name of the owner, occupier, agent, or superintendent, and the term for which it is intended to use the same; which license the said collector is hereby empowered and directed to grant. And a like license, for any term not exceeding a year, shall be obtained and granted on a like report and entry made at any time thereafter, without requiring a new bond, so long as the bond aforesaid shall remain in force. · Which licenses shall be signed by the commissioner of the revenue, and countersigned by the collector who shall issue the same.

SEC. 3. *And be it further enacted,* That the entries made in the books required to be kept by the second section of this act, shall, on the said first days of January, April, July, and October. or within ten days after each of the said days, be verified by the oath or affirmation, to be taken as aforesaid, of the person or persons by whom such entries shall have been made; which qualification shall be certified at the end of such entries by the collector, or other officer administering the same, and shall be, in substance, as follows: "I (or we) do swear (or affirm) that the foregoing entries were made by me (or us) on the respective days specified, and that they state, according to the best of —— knowledge and belief, the whole quantities and denominations, with the value thereof, of the —— manufactured (or sold, as the case may be) by ——, in the —— of ——."

Public Acts of Congress.

Sec. 4. *And be it further enacted,* That the owner, occupier, agent, or superintendent, aforesaid, shall, in case the original entries required to be made in his books by the second section of this act, shall not be made by himself, subjoin to the oath or affirmation of the person by whom they were made, the following oath or affirmation to be taken as aforesaid: "—— do solemnly swear (or affirm) that, to the best of —— knowledge and belief, the foregoing entries are just and true, and that —— have taken all the means in —— power to make them so."

Sec. 5. *And be it further enacted,* That in all cases in which the duties aforesaid shall not be duly paid, the person chargeable therewith shall pay, in addition, ten per centum on the amount thereof; and in case such duties, with said addition, shall not be paid within three months from the time the said duties ought to be paid, the collector for the district shall make a personal demand of the same from such person, or by notice in writing left at his dwelling, if within the collection district, and, if not, at the manufactory owned or superintended by such person; and in case of refusal or neglect to pay the said duties, with the addition, within ten days after such demand or notice, the amount thereof shall be recovered by distress and sale of the goods, chattels, and effects of the delinquent; and, in case of such distress, it shall be the duty of the officer charged with the collection to make, or cause to be made, an account of the goods or chattels which may be distrained, a copy of which, signed by the officer making such distress, shall be left with the owner or possessor of such goods, chattels, or effects, at his or her dwelling, with a note of the sum demanded, and the time and place of sale; and the said officer shall forthwith cause a notification to be publicly posted up, at two of the taverns nearest to the residence of the person whose property shall be distrained, or at the courthouse of the same county, if not more than ten miles distant; which notice shall specify the articles distrained, and the time and place proposed for the sale thereof; which time shall not be less than ten days from the date of such notification, and the place proposed for sale not more than five miles distant from the place of making such distress: *Provided,* That in any case of distress for the payment of the duties aforesaid, the goods, chattels, or effects, so distrained, shall and may be restored to the owner or possessor, if, prior to the day assigned for the sale thereof, payment, or tender thereof, shall be made to the proper officer charged with the collection, of the full amount demanded, together with such fee for levying, and such sum for the necessary and reasonable expenses of removing and keeping the goods, chattels, or effects, so distrained, as may be allowed, in like cases, by the laws or practice of the State or Territory wherein the distress shall have been made; but in case of non-payment or tender, as aforesaid, the said officer shall proceed to sell the said goods, chattels, or effects, at public auction, and shall and may retain, from the proceeds of such sales, the amount demandable for the use of the United States, with the necessary and reasonable expenses of distress and sale, and a commission of eight per centum thereon for his own use, rendering the overplus, if any there be to the person whose goods, chattels, or effects, shall have been distrained: *Provided,* That it shall not be lawful to make distress of beasts of the plough necessary for the cultivation of improved lands, arms, or household furniture, or apparel necessary for a family.

Sec. 6. *And be it further enacted,* That all goods, wares, and merchandise, which shall be manufactured or made within the United States, or the Territories thereof, the duties on which shall not have been duly paid, or secured, according to the true intent and meaning of this act, shall, together with the vessels containing the same, be forfeited, and may be seized and secured by any collector of the internal duties, and held by him until a decision shall be had thereon according to law: *Provided,* That said goods, wares, and merchandise, shall not be liable to be forfeited in the hands of a bona fide purchaser, who shall have purchased the same without knowledge of the duties not being paid, or secured to be paid. And if any person shall conceal or buy any goods, wares, and merchandise, as aforesaid, knowing them to be liable to seizure and forfeiture under this act, such person shall, on conviction thereof, forfeit and pay a sum double the value of the goods so concealed or purchased.

Sec. 7. *And be it further enacted,* That the owner, occupier, agent, or superintendent, aforesaid, of or for any such building, or vessel, machine, implement, or utensil, used in the manufacture or making of any of the said goods, wares, and merchandise, who shall wilfully neglect or refuse to make true and exact entry and report of the same, or to do, or cause to be done, any of the things by this act required to be done as aforesaid, excepting to pay the duties hereby laid in cases where the bond required by the second section of this act has been given, shall forfeit, for every such neglect or refusal, all the goods, wares, and merchandise, manufactured or made by or for him, with the vessels containing the same, and the vessels, machines, implements, or utensils, used in said manufacture or making, together with the sum of five hundred dollars, to be recovered with costs of suit; which said goods, wares, and merchandise, with the vessels, or such implements, or utensils, so used, may be seized by any collector of the internal duties, and may be held by him until a decision shall be had thereon according to law: *Provided,* Such seizure be made within three months after the cause for the same shall have occurred, and that a prosecution or suit thereupon shall have commenced by such collector within sixty days after such seizure.

Sec. 8. *And be it further enacted,* That if the duties aforesaid shall not be paid or secured, agreeably to the provisions of this act, or if any acts shall be done contrary to, or if omitted that are required to be done by said act, to be given as aforesaid, or the penalties thereby shall not be recovered, the said act,

be deemed forfeited, and shall be put in suit by the collector, for the recovery of the amount of the said duties, with the addition thereon, penalties, and costs, or either, as the case may be; and judgment thereon shall and may be taken at the return term, on motion to be made in open court, unless sufficient cause to the contrary be shown to, and allowed by, the court: *Provided,* That the writ or process in such case shall have been executed at least fourteen days before the return day thereof.

Sec. 9. *And be it further enacted,* That the duties imposed by this act shall be considered as applying solely to articles manufactured for sale, and shall not be considered as including any articles manufactured exclusively for the use of the person manufacturing the same.

Sec. 10. *And be it further enacted,* That the duties laid by this act shall be payable on all the goods, wares, and merchandise, aforesaid, the manufacture or making of which shall not, within ninety days from the passing thereof, be fully completed, or which shall not be then in the condition in which they usually are when offered for sale.

Sec. 11. *And be it further enacted,* That any owner, occupier, agent, or superintendent, as aforesaid, who may have given bond as required in the second section of this act, who shall, after thirty days' notice given him in writing by the collector, fail to renew or change the same, in regard to the sureties and penalties thereof, as is in the same section provided, shall thereafter incur the penalties attached to employing the said buildings, or vessels, or machines, implements, or utensils, without having a license therefor.

Sec. 12. *And be it further enacted,* That the forms of the bond required to be given by the second section of this act, as well as the forms of the several oaths, reports, entries, statements, and accounts, by this act required to be taken, kept, and rendered, shall be prescribed by the Treasury Department, agreeably to which the aforesaid specification of the buildings or vessels in which, or of the machines, implements, or utensils, wherewith the aforesaid goods, wares, and merchandise, shall be manufactured or made, shall be rendered by the owner, occupier, agent, or superintendent thereof.

Sec. 13. *And be it further enacted,* That the value of the manufactured or made goods, wares, and merchandise, required to be stated as aforesaid, shall be regulated by the average of the actual sales by the manufacturer of the like goods, wares, and merchandise, during the quarter, where such actual sales may have been made; and where no such actual sales have been made, such value, as far as respects a manufacturer selling exclusively by wholesale, shall be regulated by the average of the market wholesale sales of the like goods, wares, and merchandise, and so far as respects a manufacturer selling by retail, by the market sales by retail in like manner.

Sec. 14. *And be it further enacted,* That if any person shall forcibly obstruct or hinder a collector in the execution of this act, or of any of the powers or authorities hereby vested in him, or shall forcibly rescue, or cause to be rescued, any goods, wares, or merchandise, or vessels, machines, implements, or utensils, aforesaid, after the same shall have been seized by him, or shall attempt or endeavor so to do, the person so offending shall, for every such offence, forfeit and pay the sum of five hundred dollars.

Sec. 15. *And be it further enacted,* That a collector shall be authorized to enter, at any time between the rising and setting of the sun, any building or place where any vessel, machine, implement, or utensil, as aforesaid, is kept within his collection district, for the purpose of examining, measuring, or describing the same, or of inspecting the accounts of the goods, wares, and merchandise, from time to time manufactured or made. And every owner or occupier of such building, machine, implement, or utensil, or person having the agency or superintendence of the same, who shall refuse to admit such officer, or to suffer him to examine, measure, or describe the same, or to inspect said accounts, shall, for every such refusal, forfeit and pay the sum of five hundred dollars.

Sec. 16. *And be it further enacted,* That any person who shall be convicted of wilfully taking a false oath or affirmation, in any of the cases in which an oath or affirmation is required to be taken in virtue of this act, shall be liable to the pains and penalties to which persons are liable for wilful and corrupt perjury, and shall, moreover, forfeit the sum of five hundred dollars.

Sec. 17. *And be it further enacted,* That no person who shall have refused or neglected to comply with the provisions of this act, shall be entitled, while such refusal or neglect continues, to receive a license as aforesaid, or shall be entitled to credit for any internal duties whatever that may have accrued.

Sec. 18. *And be it further enacted,* That every collector shall give receipts for all sums by him collected under this act.

Sec. 19. *And be it further enacted,* That if it shall appear, to the satisfaction of the collector for the district, that any owner, occupier, agent, or superintendent, as aforesaid, of any buildings, vessels, or machines, implements, or utensils, as aforesaid, who shall have given bond agreeably to the second section of this act, and shall have ceased to use the same for one year, and made oath or affirmation thereof, to be lodged with said collector, hath acted agreeably to the condition of such bond, the collector shall cause such bond to be delivered to said owner, occupier, agent, or superintendent.

Sec. 20. *And be it further enacted,* That the several provisions of "An act making further provision for the collection of internal duties, and for the appointment and compensation of assessors," passed the second of August, one thousand eight hundred and thirteen, shall, and are hereby declared to apply in full force to the duties laid by, and to be collected under, this act, the same as if such duties and this act were recognised therein; which said duties shall be collected by the same collectors, in the same manner, for the same commissions, and under the same directions, as are thereby established in relation to the other internal duties; and all the obligations, duties, and penalties thereby imposed upon collectors, are hereby imposed upon the collectors of the duties laid by this act.

SEC. 21. *And be it further enacted,* That it shall be the duty of the collectors aforesaid, in their respective districts, and they are hereby authorized, to collect the duties imposed by this act, and to prosecute for the recovery of the same, and for the recovery of any sum or sums which may be forfeited by virtue of this act; and all fines, penalties, and forfeitures, which shall be incurred by force of this act, shall and may be sued for and recovered in the name of the United States, or of the collector within whose district any such fine, penalty, or forfeiture shall have been incurred, by bill, plaint, or information, one moiety thereof to the use of the United States, and the other moiety thereof to the use of the person, who, if a collector, shall first discover, if other than a collector shall first inform of the cause, matter, or thing, whereby any such fine, penalty, or forfeiture shall have been incurred; and where the cause of action or complaint shall arise or accrue more than fifty miles distant from the nearest place by law established for the holding of a district court, within the district in which the same shall arise or accrue, such suit and recovery may be had before any court of the State bolden within the said district, having jurisdiction in like cases.

SEC. 22. *And be it further enacted,* That the collector shall furnish one copy of this act to each person liable to pay a duty under the same, within the collection district, that may apply therefor, and shall advertise in a newspaper, or post up notices at the court-houses therein, of his instructions to furnish the same.

SEC. 23. *And be it further enacted,* That, towards establishing an adequate revenue to provide for the payment of the expenses of Government; for the punctual payment of the public debt, principal and interest, contracted, and to be contracted, according to the terms of the contracts, respectively; and for creating an adequate sinking fund, gradually to reduce, and eventually to extinguish, the public debt, contracted and to be contracted; the rates and duties laid and imposed by this act shall continue to be laid, levied, and collected, during the present war between the United States and Great Britain, and until the purposes aforesaid shall be completely accomplished. And for the effectual application of the revenue, to be raised by and from the said duties to the purposes aforesaid, in due form of law, the faith of the United States is hereby pledged: *Provided always,* That whenever Congress shall deem it expedient to alter, reduce, or change, the said duties, or either of them, it shall be lawful so to do, upon providing and substituting by law at the same time, and for the same purposes, other duties, which shall be equally productive with the duties so altered, reduced, or changed.

SEC. 24. *And be it further enacted,* That so

long as the duties herein imposed on each of the foregoing descriptions of goods, wares, and merchandise, shall continue to be laid the duties at present payable on the like descriptions of goods, wares, and merchandise, imported into the United States, shall not be discontinued or diminished and the faith of the United States is hereby pledged for the continuance of the same until this act shall be repealed.

Approved, January 18, 1815.

An Act to provide additional revenue for defraying the expenses of Government, and maintaining the public credit, by laying duties on household furniture, and on gold and silver watches.

Be it enacted, &c., That there shall be, and hereby is, imposed an annual duty on all household furniture kept for use, the value of which, in any one family, with the exception of beds, bedding, kitchen furniture, family pictures, and articles made in the family from domestic materials, shall exceed two hundred dollars in money, according to the following scale:

If not exceeding four hundred dollars, one dollar.

If above four hundred, and not exceeding six hundred dollars, one dollar and fifty cents.

If above six hundred, and not exceeding one thousand dollars, three dollars.

If above one thousand, and not exceeding fifteen hundred dollars, six dollars.

If above fifteen hundred, and not exceeding two thousand dollars, ten dollars.

If above two thousand, and not exceeding three thousand dollars, seventeen dollars.

If above three thousand, and not exceeding four thousand dollars, twenty-eight dollars.

If above four thousand, and not exceeding six thousand dollars, forty-five dollars.

If above six thousand, and not exceeding nine thousand dollars, seventy-five dollars.

If above nine thousand dollars, one hundred dollars; which duty shall be paid by the owner of the said household furniture.

That there shall be, and hereby is, likewise imposed, an annual duty of two dollars on every gold watch kept for use, and of one dollar on every silver watch kept for use, which duty shall be paid by the owner thereof.

SEC. 2. *And be it further enacted,* That whenever lists of property shall hereafter be taken in any collection district, under a general assessment therein by the assistant assessors as required by the "Act for the assessment and collection of direct taxes and internal duties," passed July the twenty-second, one thousand eight hundred and thirteen, or by any other act, passed or to be passed, lists of the value of the household furniture, as classed by the first section of this act, with the number and description of watches within such collection district, belonging to each person therein taxable as aforesaid, verified by name of the owner or agent, shall be given in writing by such person or his agent, as delivered to the assistant assessor, at the time of the application therefor, which shall be the same time as that prescribed in the act then in force for the delivery of the lists therein required to be delivered; and the said assistant assessor is hereby empowered and directed to apply therefor at the dwelling of said person, or his agent, at the said time.

SEC. 3. *And be it further enacted,* That if any person or agent, as aforesaid, shall not be prepared to exhibit a written list when required, and shall consent to disclose the value of any and all the said household furniture, and the number of watches, as aforesaid, in such case it shall be the duty of the assistant assessor to make such list, which, being distinctly read and assented to, shall be received as the list aforesaid of such person, and be certified as such by the said assistant assessor.

SEC. 4. *And be it further enacted,* That if any such person or agent shall deliver or disclose to any assessor any false or fraudulent list, with intent to defeat or evade the purposes of this act, such person or agent shall forfeit and pay the sum of one hundred dollars, to be recovered in any court having competent jurisdiction.

SEC. 5. *And be it further enacted,* That in case any person, whether owner or agent as aforesaid, shall be absent from his place of residence at the time an assistant assessor shall apply to receive the list of such person, it shall be the duty of such assessor to leave, at the house or place of residence of such person, a written note or memorandum, requiring him to present to such assessor the list aforesaid, within ten days from the date of such note or memorandum; and if any person, on being notified or required as aforesaid, shall refuse or neglect to give such list as aforesaid, within such time, it shall be the duty of the said assessor to make, according to the best information which he can obtain, such lists, which lists, so made and subscribed by such assessor, shall be received as the lists aforesaid of such person; and the person so failing or neglecting, unless in case of sickness or absence from home, shall, moreover, forfeit and pay the sum of fifty dollars.

SEC. 6. *And be it further enacted,* That the several assistant assessors in each of the said collection districts shall deliver the lists aforesaid to the principal assessor, within the time prescribed by the thirteenth section of the "Act for the assessment and collection of direct taxes and internal duties," passed twenty-second of July, eighteen hundred and thirteen, for the delivery of the lists therein designated: *Provided,* That if the said time be altered by any act subsequently passed, such delivery shall be within the time at prescribed therefor.

SEC. 7. *And be it further enacted,* That the respective principal assessors shall make out, according to the lists received from the assistant assessors, a general list or lists of all persons taxable as aforesaid, specifying the name of the owner or agent, the valuation of the household furniture, with the number and description of the watches as aforesaid, and the duty payable on each; which list or lists shall be made out in alphabetical order, for each county or smaller division of a collection district, as may be directed by the Secretary of the Treasury.

SEC. 8. *And be it further enacted,* That each of the collectors of the direct taxes and internal duties, for the collection districts aforesaid, shall, within sixty days from the day on which the principal assessor shall have received the said lists from the assistant assessors, be furnished by the principal assessor with one or more of the lists, prepared in conformity with the preceding section by the principal assessor, signed and certified by him. And each collector, on receiving a list as aforesaid, shall subscribe three receipts; one of which shall be given on a full and correct copy of such list, which list and receipt shall remain with the principal assessor, and be open to the inspection of any person who may apply to inspect the same: and the other two receipts shall be given on aggregate statements of the lists aforesaid, exhibiting the gross amount of each of the aforesaid duties, to be collected in each county or State district contained in the collection district, one of which aggregate statements and receipts shall be transmitted to the Commissioner of the Revenue, and the other to the Comptroller of the Treasury.

SEC. 9. *And be it further enacted,* That each of the said collectors, or his deputies, shall, within ten days after receiving his list, agreeably to the "Act for the assessment and collection of direct taxes and internal duties," passed twenty-second July, eighteen hundred and thirteen, or agreeably to any act subsequently passed, or to be passed, advertise, in one newspaper printed in his collection district, if any there be, and by notifications to be posted up in at least four public places in his collection district, that the said duties have become due and payable, and state the times and places at which he or they will attend to receive the same, which shall be within twenty days after such notification: and with respect to persons who shall not attend, according to such notification, it shall be the duty of each collector, in person or by deputy, to apply once at their respective dwellings within such district, and there demand the duties payable by such persons, which application shall be made within sixty days after the receipt of the said lists by the collector; and if the said duties shall not be then paid, or within twenty days thereafter, it shall be the duty of such collector and his deputies to proceed to collect the said duties by distress and sale of the goods, chattels, or effects, of the persons delinquent; and in case of such distress, it shall be the duty of the officer charged with the collection to make, or cause to be made, an account of the goods or chattels which may be distrained, a copy of which, signed by the officer making such distress, shall be left with the owner or possessor of such goods, chattels, or effects, or at his dwelling, with a note of the sum demanded, and the time and place of sale; and the said officer shall forthwith cause a notification to be publicly posted up at two of the taverns nearest to the residence

Public Acts of Congress.

of the person whose property shall be distrained, or of his agent, or at the court-house of the same county, if not more than ten miles distant, which notice shall specify the articles distrained, and the time or place proposed for the sale thereof; which time shall be less than ten days from the date of such notification, and the place proposed for sale not more than five miles distant from the place of making such distress: *Provided,* That in any case of distress for the payment of the duties aforesaid, the goods, chattels, or effects, so distrained, shall and may be restored to the owner or possessor, if, prior to the sale thereof, payment, or tender thereof, shall be made to the proper officer charged with the collection, of the full amount demanded, together with such fee for levying, and such sum for the necessary and reasonable expenses of removing and keeping the goods, chattels, or effects, so distrained, as may be allowed in like cases by the laws or practice of the State or Territory wherein the distress shall have been made; but in case of nonpayment, or tender, as aforesaid, the said officer shall proceed to sell the said goods, chattels, or effects, at public auction, and shall and may retain, from the proceeds of such sales, the amount demandable for the use of the United States, with the necessary and reasonable expenses of distress and sale, and a commission of five per centum thereon for his own use, rendering the overplus, if any there be, to the person whose goods, chattels, or effects, shall have been distrained, or to his agent: *Provided,* That it shall not be lawful to make distress of the tools or implements of a trade or profession, beasts of the plough necessary for the cultivation of improved lands, arms, or apparel necessary for a family.

Sec. 10. *And be it further enacted,* That it shall be the duty of every owner, or his agent, of household furniture, or watches as aforesaid, within a collection district of any State in which said collection district lists of property shall not, under a general assessment therein, have been directed by law to be taken previously to the month of February in any year, by the assistant assessors, conformably to the act, entitled "An act for the assessment and collection of direct taxes and internal duties," passed the twenty-second of July, one thousand eight hundred and thirteen, or to any act subsequently passed, to transmit, during the said month of February, in said year, to the principal assessor for the said collection district, a list in writing, stating the value of the household furniture, with the number and description of watches, owned or possessed by such person; on failure to do which, every such person, whether owner or agent, shall forfeit and pay the sum of one hundred dollars. And it shall be the duty of the principal assessor to cause a written or printed notice to be left, previous to the said month, in the year one thousand eight hundred and fifteen, at every inhabited house within the collection district, requiring every person to make out and render the lists annually as aforesaid. And it shall be the duty of the principal assessor, every year, within sixty days after the expiration

of the said month, to make out, and deliver to the collector, lists in the manner prescribed by the seventh and eighth sections of this act, and of the collector, thereupon, to proceed in all respects, as is required by the eighth and ninth sections of this act, in cases where lists as aforesaid shall have been taken by the assistant assessors, excepting so far as regards the times of paying the said duties, and of notifying and applying for the same, all of which shall be the same as those fixed in relation to the then existing direct tax becoming due.

Sec. 11. *And be it further enacted,* That the provisions of the preceding section of this act shall, under the penalty thereby provided, be observed in, and shall apply to, the several collection districts within the Territories, or districts, wherein no direct tax is laid, excepting that the collectors therein shall perform all the duties required thereby to be performed by the principal assessors: *Provided,* That, instead of the receipt of the collector, to the lists received from the principal assessor, the collector shall affix thereto a certificate, that the same is correct, and shall lodge, with the marshal for the district, the copy of the general list, which would otherwise have remained with the principal assessor, which list shall remain with the marshal, and be open to the inspection of any person who may apply to inspect the same: *And provided,* That the times for paying the said duties in such collection district, and of notifying and applying for the same, shall be the same, relatively to the date of such certificate, as in the other collection districts they are required to be relatively to the date of the collector's receipt.

Sec. 12. *And be it further enacted,* That in case any person shall be the owner of household furniture, a part of which shall be in one house and a part in another, the valuation of each part thereof shall be distinctly made.

Sec. 13. *And be it further enacted,* That, within the meaning of this act, household furniture shall be considered as including pictures, plate, clocks, and time pieces, (except watches) and as excluding books, maps, and philosophical apparatus.

Sec. 14. *And be it further enacted,* That the objects taxed as aforesaid, which shall belong to any charitable, religious, or literary institution, or which shall belong to the United States, or any State or Territory, or shall be permanently or specially exempted from taxation, at the time of passing this act, by the laws of the State or Territory wherein the same may be situate, shall be exempted from the aforesaid valuation and specification, and from the duties aforesaid.

Sec. 15. *And be it further enacted,* That, in cases in which it may be doubtful who is chargeable with the duties aforesaid, they shall be paid by the person in whose possession the articles taxed shall have been at the time of ascertaining the said duties, except where such person, his agent cannot, at the time of collecting the same, be found within the collection district in which they were ascertained, in which case any shall be paid by the person then in possession of such articles.

Sec. 16. *And be it further enacted,* That, in case any errors shall be committed in collecting, making out, or rendering, the lists aforesaid, by the assistant or principal assessors, or the collectors, the same may and shall be corrected in such way, and within such time, as shall be prescribed by the Secretary of the Treasury.

Sec. 17. *And be it further enacted,* That every collector shall give receipts for all sums by him collected under this act, which shall specify the value of the household furniture, with the number and description of watches, for which a duty shall have been paid,

Sec. 18. *And be it further enacted,* That the forms of lists and notifications required by this act, shall be prescribed by the Treasury Department.

Sec. 19. *And be it further enacted,* That if any person shall forcibly obstruct or hinder any officer in the execution of this act, or of any of the powers or authorities hereby vested in him, the person so offending shall forfeit and pay the sum of two hundred dollars.

Sec. 20. *And be it further enacted,* That any assistant assessor who shall wilfully neglect or fail to perform any of the duties herein required to be performed, shall, for every such neglect or failure, forfeit and pay a sum not exceeding one hundred dollars; and any principal assessor or collector who shall wilfully fail or neglect to perform any of the duties herein required to be performed by him, shall, for every such neglect or failure, forfeit and pay a sum not exceeding five hundred dollars.

Sec. 21. *And be it further enacted,* That, for performing the duties herein required, there shall be annually allowed and paid, to each principal assessor, at the rate of two dollars and fifty cents for every thousand persons in his collection district, according to the previous census; to each collector, in districts in which the direct tax is not laid, there shall be annually allowed and paid, at the same rate; and to each assistant assessor, where the lists aforesaid shall be taken, there shall be allowed and paid, for taking the same, at the rate of five dollars for every hundred lists delivered to the principal assessor, each of which lists shall contain the several objects herein taxed; besides which there shall be allowed and paid to each principal assessor or collector, for collection districts in which lists as aforesaid, under a general assessment therein, shall not be made by the assistant assessors, five dollars for every thousand persons in his collection district, according to the previous census, for delivering the notices required to be left in the year one thousand eight eight hundred and fifteen, at each 'inhabited house: *Provided,* That no additional allowance shall be made to the said officers for any contingent expenses, other than for advertising, printing, and paper, that may be incurred by them in the discharge of the duties hereby required to be performed; for the payment of which allowances, as well as those hereinafter authorized, seventy

thousand dollars, to be paid out of any money in the Treasury, not otherwise appropriated, are hereby annually appropriated.

Sec. 22. *And be it further enacted,* That, in cases where persons cannot be found to serve as principal or assistant assessors for the foregoing compensation, the President of the United States is hereby empowered to make an additional allowance: *Provided,* That the whole sum so allowed shall not, in any one year, exceed ten thousand dollars.

Sec. 23. *And be it further enacted,* That the several provisions of "An act making further provision for the collection of internal duties, and for the appointment and compensation of assessors," passed the second of August, one thousand eight hundred and thirteen, shall and are hereby declared to apply in full force to the duties laid by, and to be collected under, 'this act, the same as if such duties and this act were recognised therein; which said duties shall be collected by the same collectors, in the same manner, for the same commissions, and under the same directions, as are thereby established in relation to the other internal duties; and all the obligations, duties, and penalties, thereby imposed upon collectors, are hereby imposed upon the collectors of the duties laid by this act.

Sec. 24. *And be it further enacted,* That it shall be the duty of the collectors aforesaid, in their respective districts, and they are hereby authorized, to collect the duties imposed by this act, and to prosecute for the recovery of the same, and for the recovery of any sum or sums which may be forfeited by virtue of this act. And all fines, penalties, and forfeitures, which shall be incurred by force of this act, shall and may be sued for and recovered in the name of the United States, or of the collector within whose district any such fine, penalty, or forfeiture, shall have been incurred, by bill, plaint, or information, one moiety thereof to the use of the United States, and the other moiety thereof to the use of the person who, if a collector, shall first discover, if other than a collector, shall first inform, of the cause, matter, or thing, whereby any such fine, penalty, or forfeiture, shall have been incurred; and where the cause of action or complaint shall arise or accrue more than fifty miles distant from the nearest place by law established for the holding of a district court, within the district in which the same shall arise or accrue, such suit and recovery may be had before any court of the State, holden within the said district, having jurisdiction in like cases.

Sec. 25. *And be it further enacted,* That, towards establishing an adequate revenue to provide for the payment of the expenses of Government; for the punctual payment of the public debt, principal and interest, contracted, and to be contracted, according to the terms of the contracts, respectively; and for creating an adequate sinking fund, gradually to reduce, and eventually to extinguish, the public debt, contracted and to be contracted; the duties laid and imposed by this act shall continue to be laid, levied, and collected, during the present war between the United States and Great Britain, and until the purposes aforesaid shall be completely accomplished. And, for the effectual application of the revenue to be raised by and from the said duties to the purposes aforesaid, in due form of law, the faith of the United States is hereby pledged: *Provided always,* That whenever Congress shall deem it expedient to alter, reduce, or change, the said duties, or either of them, it shall be lawful so to do, upon providing and substituting. by law, at the same time, and for the same purposes, other duties, which shall be equally productive with the duties so altered, reduced. or changed.

Approved, January 18, 1815.

An Act supplementary to the act, entitled " An act providing for the indemnification of certain claimants of public lands in the Mississippi Territory."

Be it enacted, &c., That the President of the United States be, and he is hereby, authorized, by and with the advice and consent of the Senate, to appoint three fit and disinterested persons, to be and act as commissioners, by virtue of an act, entitled "An act providing for the indemnification of certain claimants of public lands in the Mississippi Territory," in the place of the Secretary of State, the Secretary of the Treasury, and the Attorney General of the United States, for the time being; and the said persons are hereby constituted and appointed a board of commissioners, any two of whom may act as a quorum, as in and by the act aforesaid is provided. Which board is hereby declared to be intended to effect the same purposes and services as the said original board; and is, in every respect, substituted for the same; and is hereby authorized to execute all the powers granted to, and directed to perform all the duties enjoined upon, the said original board of commissioners, according to the intent and provisions of the act aforesaid.

Sec. 2. *And be it further enacted,* That the commissioners to be appointed in pursuance of this act, shall meet at some suitable place within the District of Columbia, on the fourth Monday of January current, or as soon thereafter as may be, to enter on the duties assigned them. And that they shall proceed therein, as expeditiously as may be, and from time to time shall certify and report to the President of the United States, as to the sufficiency of the releases that shall have been made, and the claims they shall have finally adjudged and allowed, agreeably to the third section of the act to which this act is supplementary.

Sec. 3. *And be it further enacted,* That each of the said commissioners, before they proceed to execute their duties as such, shall take the following oath, or affirmation, to wit: "I, A B, do solemnly swear (or affirm) that I am not interested in the event of any decision that may be made by this board of commissioners, and that I will faithfully and impartially discharge and perform all the duties incumbent on me as a member thereof: and will adjudge and determine all the matters, claims, and controversies, subject to the adjudication and determination of this board, according to the best of my abilities, agreeably to the laws of the United States, and the principles of justice and equity."

Sec. 4. *And be it further enacted,* That the said board of commissioners shall have power and authority to appoint a secretary, whose duty it shall be to receive, file, and preserve, the papers, documents, and claims, that may be presented to, and received by, said board of commissioners, and to enter and record all the orders, proceedings, judgments, and determinations, of said board of commissioners. And one of said commissioners shall administer an oath to such secretary, for the faithful discharge of his duty. And there shall be allowed and paid, out of the Treasury of the United States, to each of the said commissioners, as well as to the secretary by them to be appointed, as a compensation for their respective services under this act, and in full for the same, the sum of fifteen hundred dollars.

Sec. 5. *And be it further enacted,* That further time be, and hereby is, allowed to deposite in the office of the Secretary of State, releases to the United States, of claims under the act, or pretended act, of the State of Georgia, passed on the seventh day of January, seventeen hundred and ninety-five, and assignments of rights or claims to moneys paid into the treasury of the State of Georgia, and power to sue therefor; and also for recording, in the office of the Secretary of State, any deed or evidence of any title or claim that hath been released to the United States, or that shall be released on or before the day hereby appointed, to wit: the third Monday in March next. And so much of the act of Congress, passed the third day of March, one thousand eight hundred and three, entitled "An act regulating the grants of lands of the United States south of the State of Tennessee," and so much of the act to which this is supplementary, as exclude claimants from recording their claims after the first day of January, one thousand eight hundred and four, be, and the same are hereby, repealed.

Sec. 6. *And be it further enacted,* That the said commissioners be, and hereby are, authorized and empowered to consider and determine all claims, that shall have been duly released to the United States, on or before the said third Monday of March, which may be made and preferred by assignees of bankrupts, or executors, or administrators on estates of deceased persons, which may be insolvent, and subject to distribution among the creditors of the persons so deceased.

Approved, January 23, 1815.

An Act to authorize the President of the United States to accept the services of State troops and of volunteers.

Be it enacted, &c., That the President of the United States be, and he is hereby, authorized and required to receive into the service of the United States any corps of troops which may have been, or may be, raised, organized, and of-ferred, under the authority of any of the States, whose term of service shall not be less than twelve months; which corps, when received into the service of the United States, shall be subject to the rules and articles of war, and employed in the State raising the same, or in the adjoining State, and not elsewhere, except with the assent of the Executive of the State so raising the same: *Provided*, That said corps shall not contain in the whole, exclusive of officers, more than forty thousand men; and that the number to be received in any State shall not exceed the number hereby apportioned to such State: that is to say, in New Hampshire, one thousand three hundred and eighteen. In Massachusetts, four thousand three hundred and ninety-five. In Vermont, one thousand three hundred and eighteen. In Rhode Island, four hundred and forty. In Connecticut, one thousand five hundred and forty. In New York, five thousand nine hundred and thirty-three. In New Jersey, one thousand three hundred and eighteen. In Pennsylvania, five thousand and fifty-five. In Delaware, four hundred and forty. In Maryland, one thousand nine hundred and eighty. In Virginia, five thousand and fifty-five. In North Carolina, two thousand eight hundred and fifty-eight. In South Carolina, one thousand nine hundred and eighty. In Georgia, one thousand three hundred and eighteen. In Kentucky, two thousand one hundred and ninety-six. In Ohio, one thousand three hundred and eighteen. In Tennessee, one thousand three hundred and eighteen. In Louisiana, two hundred and twenty. *And be it further provided*, That in case the President of the United States shall hereafter call on the Executives of the several States, to hold in readiness their respective quotas of militia for service, he shall consider the corps of State troops, raised in any State, as part of the quota of such State.

Sec. 2. *And be it further enacted*, That the corps as aforesaid, accepted under this act, shall be armed and equipped at the expense of the United States, and shall be entitled to the same pay, clothing, rations, forage, and emoluments of every kind, and (bounty excepted) to the same benefits and allowances as the regular troops of the United States.

Sec. 3. *And be it further enacted*, That the President of the United States be, and he is hereby, authorized to receive into the service of the United States, any volunteers who may offer their services, to be organized in conformity to the laws respecting the organization of the Military Establishment of the United States: *Provided*, That the whole number of such volunteers, who may be in service at any one time, exclusive of officers, shall not exceed forty thousand men.

Sec. 4. *And be it further enacted*, That the officers of the said volunteers shall be commissioned by the President of the United States; and, while in actual service, the said volunteers shall be entitled to the same pay, rations, forage, and emoluments of every kind, and (bounty excepted) to the same benefits and allowances as

the regular troops of the United States, and shall be subject to the rules and articles of war.

Sec. 5. *And be it further enacted*, That the said volunteers may, at their option, be armed and equipped by the United States, or at their own expense; and in case they arm and equip themselves, to the satisfaction of the President of the United States, they shall each be entitled to receive six and one-quarter cents per day, while in actual service, for the use and risk of such arms and equipments: *Provided*, That the compensation thus allowed shall not in any case exceed twenty-four dollars: *And provided also*, That no rifle shall be received into the service of the United States, whose calibre shall be formed to carry a ball of a smaller size than at the rate of seventy balls to a pound weight.

Sec. 6. *And be it further enacted*, That the said volunteers, if employed in service for a term not less than twelve months, may, at their option, be clothed at their own expense or by the United States; and in case they furnish their own clothing, they shall be entitled to receive in money a sum equal to the cost of the clothing allowed to the regular troops of the United States.

Sec. 7. *And be it further enacted*, That whenever any noncommissioned officer, musician, or private, having served in any of the corps of State troops or volunteers, raised by virtue of this act, during two years, or who, having engaged to serve two years, shall have been discharged in consequence of the termination of the present war, shall have obtained from the commanding officer of his company, battalion, or regiment, a certificate that he had faithfully performed his duty whilst in service, he shall be allowed, in addition to the emoluments allowed in this act, one hundred and sixty acres of land: and the widow and children, and if there be no widow or child, then the parents of such noncommissioned officers, musicians, and privates, as may have engaged for a term of service not less than two years, and who may be killed in action or die in the service, shall likewise be allowed the said quantity of one hundred and sixty acres of land, which shall be surveyed and granted in the manner provided by the act, entitled "An act to provide for the designating, surveying, and granting, the military bounty lands."

Sec. 8. *And be it further enacted*, That the appointment of the officers of the said volunteers, if received into the service of the United States for the term of twelve months, or for a longer term, shall be submitted to the Senate for their advice and consent, at their next session, after commissions for the same shall have been issued.

Sec. 9. *And be it further enacted*, That, if the whole number of forty thousand men, authorized by the first section of this act, shall not be furnished by the States, it shall be lawful for the President of the United States to supply the deficiency, by accepting the services of volunteers to the number of such deficiency: *Provided*, That the whole number of State troops and volunteers together, accepted under the provisions of this act, shall not exceed eighty thousand men.

Sec. 10. *And be it further enacted,* That the expenses incurred under this act, shall be defrayed out of the appropriations which are, or which may be, authorized, for defraying the expenses of calling out the militia for the defence of the United States.

Approved, January 27, 1815.

An Act to prohibit Intercourse with the Enemy, and for other purposes.

Be it enacted, &c., That it shall be lawful for any collector, naval officer, surveyor, or inspector of the customs, as well in an adjoining district as that to which he belongs, to enter on board, search, and examine, any ship, vessel, boat, or raft, and if he shall find on board the same any goods, wares, or merchandise, which he shall have probable cause to believe are subject to duty, the payment of which is intended to be evaded, or have been imported into the United States in any manner contrary to law, it shall be his duty to seize and secure the same for trial.

Sec. 2. *And be it further enacted,* That it shall be lawful for any collector, naval officer, surveyor, or inspector of the customs, as well in any adjoining district, as that to which he belongs, to stop, search, and examine, any carriage or vehicle of any kind whatsoever, and to stop any person travelling on foot, or beast of burden, on which he shall suspect there are any goods, wares, or merchandise, which are subject to duty, or which shall have been introduced into the United States in any manner contrary to law; and if such officer shall find any goods, wares, or merchandise, on any such carriage, vehicle, person travelling on foot, or beast of burden, which he shall have probable cause to believe are subject to duty, or have been unlawfully introduced into the United States, he shall seize and secure the same for trial. And if any of the said officers of the customs shall suspect that any goods, wares, or merchandise, which are subject to duty, or which shall have been introduced into the United States contrary to law, are concealed in any particular dwelling-house, store, or other building, he shall, upon proper application, on oath, to any judge or justice of the peace, be entitled to a warrant, directed to such officer, who is hereby authorized to serve the same, to enter such house, store, or other building, in the day time only, and there to search and examine whether there are any such goods, wares, or merchandise, which are subject to duty, or have been unlawfully imported; and if, on such search or examination, any such goods, wares, or merchandise, shall be found, which there shall be probable cause, for the officer making such search or examination, to believe are subject to duty, or have been unlawfully introduced into the United States, he shall seize and secure the same for trial.

Sec. 3. *And be it further enacted,* That if any citizen or citizens of the United States, or any person or persons inhabiting the same, shall transport, or attempt to transport, over land, or by water, in whatsoever way, or by whatso-ever means, naval or military stores, arms, or munitions of war, cattle, live stock, any articles of provisions, cotton, tobacco, goods, money, or supplies of any kind, from any place in the United States, to any of the provinces or territory belonging to the enemy, or of which they may be in possession, such naval or military stores, arms, or the munitions of war, cattle, live stock, articles of provisions, cotton, tobacco, goods, money, or other supplies, together with the carriage or wagon, cart, sleigh, vessel, boat, raft, or vehicle, of whatsoever kind, or horse, or other beast, by which they, or any of them, are transported, or attempted to be transported, shall be forfeited to the use of the United States, and the person or persons so offending, or aiding or privy to the same, shall forfeit and pay, to the use of the United States, a sum equal in value to the said enumerated articles, or other supplies, forfeited as aforesaid, as well as of the carriage, wagon, cart, sleigh, vessel, boat, raft, or other vehicle, or beast used to transport the same; and the said citizens and persons so offending, their aiders and abettors, and also the owner or owners of any of the said enumerated articles, or other supplies, knowing of such illegal act, and the owner or owners of the carriage, wagon, cart, sleigh, vessel, boat, raft, or other vehicle, or beast, used with his, or her, or their, knowledge and consent, to transport the same, shall, moreover, be considered as guilty of a misdemeanor, and be liable to be fined, in any sum not exceeding one thousand dollars, and imprisoned for a term not exceeding three years: *Provided,* That nothing herein shall be construed to prohibit any transportation, for the use or account of the United States, or any of them, or the supply of their troops or armies, whatsoever they may be.

Sec. 4. *And be it further enacted,* That every collector, naval officer, surveyor, and inspector of the customs, shall, on probable cause, have full power and authority to seize, stop, search for, detain, and keep in custody, until it shall have been ascertained whether the same shall have been forfeited or not, all naval or military stores, arms, or the munitions of war, cattle, live stock, articles of provisions, cotton, tobacco, goods, money, or other supplies, transported, or attempted to be transported, contrary to the provisions of the next preceding section of this act, as well as the carriage, wagon, cart, sleigh, vessel, boat, raft, or other vehicles, beast or beasts, used to transport the same. And if the officers authorized as aforesaid, or any of them, shall have probable cause to suspect a concealment in any particular dwelling-house, store, or building, of any naval or military stores, arms, or munitions of war, cattle, live stock, articles of provisions, cotton, tobacco, goods, money, or other supplies, with intent to be conveyed or transported, contrary to the provisions of the next preceding section of this act, they, or either of them, shall, upon proper application, supported by oath or affirmation, to any judge or justice of the peace, be entitled to a warrant, directed to such officer, who is hereby authorized to serve the same, to

Public Acts of Congress.

enter such dwelling-house, store or other building, in day time only, and there to search for such said enumerated articles or other supplies, as aforesaid; and in case any be found, to seize, detain, and keep in custody, until it shall have been forfeited or not; and if such unlawful intent exist, as aforesaid, any judge or justice, acting upon probable cause, aforesaid, is hereby authorized and required, on the owner or owners of such enumerated articles, or other supplies, being brought, on due process, before him, to hold him or them to security in a sufficient sum, with sufficient bail for his or their good behaviour, as a person or persons suspected, upon probable cause, as aforesaid, of carrying on trade or intercourse with the enemy; the said authority to bind to good behaviour, to extend also to the persons having the custody or charge of such prohibited articles or other supplies, with knowledge of the criminal intention to transport them as aforesaid; *Provided always,* That the necessity of a search warrant, arising under this act, shall in no case be considered as applicable to any carriage, wagon, cart, sleigh, vessel, boat, or other vehicle, of whatever form or construction, employed as a medium of transportation, or to packages, on any animal or animals, or carried by man on foot. *And provided also,* That all the said enumerated articles or other supplies, which shall be seized by virtue of this act, shall be put into, and remain in the custody of the collector, or such other person as he shall appoint for that purpose, until it shall have been ascertained whether the same have been forfeited or not.

Sec. 5. *And be it further enacted,* That every collector of the customs shall have authority, with the approbation of the principal officer of the Treasury Department, to employ, within his district, such number of proper persons, as inspectors of the customs, as he shall judge necessary, who are hereby declared to be officers of the customs; and the said inspectors, before they enter on the duties of their offices, shall take and subscribe, before the collectors appointing them, or before some magistrate, within their respective districts, authorized by law to administer oaths, the following oath or affirmation, to wit: "I———, having been appointed an inspector of the customs, within and for the district, of ——, do solemnly, sincerely, and truly, swear or affirm (as the case may be,) that I will diligently and faithfully execute the duties of the said office of inspector, and will use my best endeavors to prevent and detect frauds and violations against the laws of the United States; I further swear, or affirm, that I will support the Constitution of the United States."

Sec. 6. *And be it further enacted,* That any collector, naval officer, surveyor, or inspector, when proceeding to make any search or seizure authorized by this act, shall be, and is hereby, empowered to command any person who shall be within ten miles of the place where such search or seizure shall be made, to aid and assist such officer in the discharge and performance of his duty therein; and if any person, being so commanded, shall neglect or refuse to aid and assist such officer in making such search or seizure, the person so neglecting or refusing shall forfeit and pay a sum not exceeding two hundred dollars, and not less than fifty dollars. And such officer may also demand, in cases of resistance, the assistance of the marshal of the district, or any of his deputies, who shall call upon the posse of the district, if necessary, in his or their judgment, to render effectual the execution of this act; and all citizens or inhabitants of the district above the age of eighteen years, and able to travel, who refuse or neglect, on proper notice from the marshal, or any of his deputies, to join such posse, shall be considered guilty of a misdemeanor, and be liable to be fined, in any sum not exceeding three hundred dollars, and be imprisoned, for any term not exceeding three months.

Sec. 7. *And be it further enacted,* That the forfeitures and penalties mentioned in this act shall be sued for, prosecuted, and recovered, or inflicted, by action of debt, or by information or indictment, in any court competent to take cognizance thereof and try the same; and that all forfeitures and penalties, so recovered, by virtue of this act, shall, after deducting all proper costs and charges, be disposed of as follows: one moiety shall be for the use of the United States, and be paid into the Treasury thereof, by the collector recovering the same; the other moiety shall be divided between, and paid in equal proportions to, the collector and naval officer of the district, and surveyor of the port, wherein the same shall have been incurred, or to such of the said officers as there may be in the said district; and in districts where only one of the aforesaid offices shall have been established, the said moiety shall be given to such officer: *Provided,* That where the seizure shall have been made by any inspector or inspectors, out of the presence of the collector, naval officer, or surveyor, such inspector or inspectors shall be entitled, in addition to such other compensation as may be allowed them, to twenty-five per cent. on the moiety herein given to the collector, naval officer, and surveyor, as aforesaid, or to either of them: *And provided also,* That in all cases where such penalties and forfeitures shall be recovered, in pursuance of information given to such collector, naval officer, or surveyor, by any private informer, the one-half of such moiety shall be given to such informer, and the remainder thereof shall be disposed of between the collector, naval officer, and surveyor, in manner aforesaid, and the same allowance of twenty-five per cent. to inspectors, when the seizure is made by them as aforesaid: *And provided likewise,* That whenever the value of the property seized, condemned, and sold, under this act, shall be less than two hundred and fifty dollars, that part of the forfeiture which accrues to the United States, or so much thereof as may be necessary, shall be applied to the payment of the costs of prosecution: *And it is further provided,* That if any officer, or other person, entitled to a part or share of any of the penalties or forfeitures incurred in virtue of this act, shall be necessary as a witness, on the trial for such penalty or forfeiture, such officer or other person may be a witness upon the said trial, but in such case he shall not receive, or be entitled to, any part or share of the said penalty or forfeiture, and the part or share to which he otherwise would have been entitled shall revert to the United States.

SEC. 8. *And be it further enacted,* That if any suit or prosecution be commenced in any State court, against any collector, naval officer, surveyor, inspector, or any other officer, civil or military, or any other person aiding or assisting, agreeable to the provisions of this act, or under color thereof, for anything done, or omitted to be done, as an officer of the customs, or for anything done by virtue of this act, or under color thereof, and the defendant shall, at the time of entering his appearance in such court, file a petition for the removal of the cause for trial at the next circuit court of the United States to be holden in the district where the suit is pending, and offer good and sufficient surety for his entering bail in such court, on the first day of its session, copies of said process against him, and also for his there appearing at the court and entering special bail in the cause, if special bail was originally required therein, it shall then be the duty of the State court to accept the surety, and proceed no further in the cause, and the bail that shall have been originally taken shall be discharged; and such copies being entered as aforesaid in such court of the United States, the cause shall there proceed in the same manner as if it had been brought there by original process, whatever may be the amount of the sum in dispute, or damages claimed, or whatever the citizenship of the parties, any former law to the contrary notwithstanding: and any attachment of the goods or estate of the defendant, by the original process, shall hold the goods or estate so attached to answer the final judgment, in the same manner as by the laws of such State they would have been holden to answer final judgment, had it been rendered by the court in which the suit was commenced. And it shall be lawful, in any action or prosecution which may be now pending, or hereafter commenced, before any State court whatever, for anything done, or omitted to be done, by the defendant, as an inspector or other officer of the customs, after final judgment, for either party to remove and transfer, by appeal, such decision, during the session or term of said court, at which the same shall have taken place, from such court to the next circuit court of the United States, to be held in the district in which such appeal shall be taken in manner aforesaid; and it shall be the duty of the person taking such appeal, to produce and enter in the said circuit court attested copies of the process, proceedings, and judgment, in such cause; and it shall also be competent for either party, within six months of the rendition of a judgment in any such cause, by writ of error, or other process, to remove the same to the circuit court of the United States of that district in which such judgment shall have been rendered, and the said circuit court shall thereupon proceed to try and determine the facts and the law in such

action, in the same manner as if the same had been there originally commenced; the judgment in such case notwithstanding. And any bail which may have been taken, or property attached, shall be holden on the final judgment of the said circuit court in such action, in the same manner as if no such removal and transfer had been made as aforesaid; and the State court from which any such action may be removed and transferred as aforesaid, upon the party's giving good and sufficient security for the prosecution thereof, shall allow the same to be removed and transferred, and proceed no further in the case: *Provided, however,* That if the party aforesaid shall fail duly to enter the removal and transfer as aforesaid in the circuit court, agreeable to this act, the State court, by which judgment shall have been rendered, and from which the transfer and removal shall have been made as aforesaid, shall be authorized, on motion for that purpose, to issue execution, and to carry into effect any such judgment, the same as if no such removal and transfer had been made: *Provided nevertheless,* That this act shall not be construed to apply to any prosecution for an offence involving corporal punishment. *And provided also,* That no such appeal shall be allowed in any criminal action or prosecution, where final judgment shall have been rendered in favor of the defendant, or respondent, by the State court; and in any action or prosecution against any person as aforesaid, it shall be lawul for such person to plead the general issue, and give this act and any special matter in evidence. And if, in any such suit, the plaintiff is nonsuit, or judgment pass against him, the defendant shall recover double costs.

SEC. 9. *And be it further enacted,* That in any suit or prosecution against any person, for any act or thing done as an officer of the customs, or any person aiding or assisting such officer therein, and judgment shall be given against the defendant or respondent, if it shall appear to the court, before which such suit or prosecution shall be tried, that there was probable cause for doing such act or thing, such court shall order a proper certificate or entry to be made thereof, and in such case the defendant or respondent shall not be liable for costs, nor shall he be liable to execution, or to any action of damages, or to any other mode of prosecution for the act done by him as aforesaid: *Provided,* That such property or articles may be held in custody by the defendant, if any be, after judgment, forthwith returned to the claimant or claimants, his, her, or their, agent or agents.

SEC. 10. *And be it further enacted,* That no citizen, or person usually residing within the United States, shall be permitted to cross the frontier into any of the provinces or territory belonging to the enemy, or of which he may be possessed, without a passport first obtained from the Secretary of State, the Secretary of War, or other officer, civil or military, authorized by the President of the United States to grant the same, or from the Governor of a State or Territory; nor shall any citizen, or person residing as aforesaid, of his own accord, upon any pretence whatsoever, be permitted, without such passport, to go on board of any of the ships, or vessels, or boats, of the enemy, on the Lakes, along the seaboard, or elsewhere within the bays, sounds, rivers, or waters, of the United States, or to hold any intercourse with such enemy, or with any officer thereof; nor shall any citizen, or person residing as aforesaid, be permitted, without such passport, to visit or go to any camp of the enemy established within the limits of the United States, or elsewhere, or to hold any intercourse with the same, or with any officer belonging thereto; and whosoever shall voluntarily offend against any of the prohibitions aforesaid, mentioned in this section, shall be considered guilty of a misdemeanor, and liable to be fined in any sum not exceeding one thousand dollars, and to imprisonment for any term not exceeding three years. And every person coming from any of the enemy's provinces or territory, into the United States, shall report himself forthwith, or as soon as practicable thereafter, to the military commander, or to the collector, or other chief officer of the customs, of the district within which he may first arrive, upon pain, wherever the same is omitted, of being liable to the same prosecution and punishment, as is above provided in cases of unlawful intercourse with the enemy, without the authority of a passport.

SEC. 11. *And be it further enacted,* That any person or persons found hovering upon the frontier, near any of the provinces or territory belonging to the enemy, or of which he may be possessed, or travelling towards and near the same, at a distance from his or their usual place of abode or residence, and without any lawful business requiring his or their attendance there, and without a passport, shall be liable to be held to security for his or their good behaviour, in the manner pointed out in the fourth section of this act, as a person or persons suspected, upon probable cause, of being engaged in unlawful trade or intercourse with the enemy: *Provided always,* That nothing contained in any part of this act shall be construed to alter, in any respect, the law of treason.

SEC. 12. *And be it further enacted,* That it shall be lawful for the President of the United States, or such other person as he shall have empowered for that purpose, to employ, under proper instructions, to be by him given, in cases of resistance, such part of the land and naval forces of the United States, or the militia thereof, as shall be judged necessary, for the purpose of aiding and co-operating with the officers of the customs, and all other civil magistrates, in seizing and securing persons engaged, or suspected, upon probable cause as aforesaid, to be engaged, in unlawful trade or intercourse with the enemy as aforesaid, together with the articles or supplies, or vessels, boats, vehicles, or animals, employed as aforesaid, in such trade or intercourse, and searching for and seizing any property subject to duty, or which has been unlawfully imported.

SEC. 13. *And be it further enacted,* That this act shall continue in force during the continuance of the present war between the United States and Great Britain, and no longer: *Provided,* That the termination of the said war shall not be construed to stop or annul any proceedings that may theretofore have been commenced, or concluded, or in any way destroy or impair any rights or privileges accruing under, secured, or given, by virtue of this act, but applicable to any transaction prior thereto, the same proceedings shall and may be had as though this act were in full force.

Approved, February 4, 1815.

An Act supplementary to the act, entitled "An act to amend the act laying duties on licenses to retailers of wines, spirituous liquors, and foreign merchandise, and for other purposes."

Be it enacted, &c., That the fourth section of the act, entitled "An act to amend the act laying duties on licenses to retailers of wines, spirituous liquors, and foreign merchandise, and for other purposes," shall be construed to extend to and include any still, boiler, or other vessel, used in distillation, burnt or otherwise destroyed, whether the burning or destruction have taken place before or since the passage of the above recited act.

Approved, February 4, 1815.

An Act attaching to the Canton District, in the State of Ohio, the tract of land lying between the foot of the rapids of the Miama of Lake Erie and the Connecticut western reserve.

Be it enacted, &c., That all that tract of land lying between the foot of the rapids of the river Miami of Lake Erie and the Western line of the Connecticut reserve, in the State of Ohio, which was ceded to the United States, by certain tribes of Indians, at a treaty concluded at Brownstown, in the Michigan Territory, on the twenty-fifth day of November, one thousand eight hundred and eight, shall be attached to, and made a part of, the district of Canton.

SEC. 2. *And be it further enacted,* That in surveying and dividing the lands by this act attached to the district of Canton, the ordinary mode of surveying the public lands shall be so far deviated from, that the boundary lines of the tracts to be laid off therein shall be run parallel to, and at right angles with, the road laid out in conformity with the said treaty, and in every other respect the surveys shall be made in the same manner, and for the same compensation allowed for the surveying, the other public lands northwest of the river Ohio.

SEC. 3. *And be it further enacted,* That all the lands by this act attached to the district of Canton, shall be offered for sale to the highest bidder, under the direction of the register of the land office and the receiver of public moneys of the said district, at such time and place as the President of the United States shall designate by proclamation for that purpose; and the sales shall remain open one week, and no longer; and the said lands shall, in every respect, be sold on the same terms and conditions as have been provided for the sale of other lands of the United States. All the lands in the said tract, remaining unsold at the close of the said sales, may be disposed of at private sale by the register of the land office of the said district, on the same terms and conditions as are provided for the sale of other public lands in the same district; and patents shall be obtained in the same manner as in case of other lands of the United States.

Sec. 4. *And be it further enacted,* That the aforesaid register and receiver of public moneys shall, each, receive four dollars per day for each day's attendance on the public sales directed by this act.

Approved, February 4, 1815.

An Act for giving further time to the purchasers of public lands to complete their payments.

Be it enacted, &c., That every person who, after the first day of April, one thousand eight hundred and ten, and prior to the first day of April, one thousand eight hundred and eleven, had purchased any tract or tracts of land of the United States, not exceeding in the whole six hundred and forty acres, at any of the land offices of the United States, and whose lands have not already been actually sold or reverted to the United States, for non-payment of part of the purchase money, shall be, and they hereby are, allowed the further time of three years, from and after the expiration of the period already given by law, for completing the payment of the purchase money aforesaid; which further time of three years shall be allowed only on the following conditions: first, all arrears of interest on the purchase money shall be paid on or before the expiration of the time for completing the payment of the purchase money according to former laws: *Provided,* That in all cases in which the time for completing the payment of the purchase money may have expired, or shall expire, before the first day of June next, the interest may be paid on or before that day: second, the residue of the sum due on account of the principal of such purchase shall be paid, with interest thereon, in three equal annual payments, as follows, viz: one-third of the said sum, with the interest due thereon, within one year; one-third of the said sum, with the interest due thereon, within two years; and the residue, with the interest due thereon, within three years, after the expiration of the time for completing the payments on such purchases according to law. And in case of failure to pay the arrears of interest, or any of the three instalments of principal, with the accruing interest, at the time above-mentioned, the tract of land shall be forthwith advertised and offered for sale, in the manner and on the terms directed by law in case of lands not paid within the time limited by law, and shall revert to the United States in like manner, if the same is not sold at such sale.

Approved, February 4, 1815.

An Act to alter and amend the several acts for establishing a Navy Department, by adding thereto a Board of Commissioners.

Be it enacted, &c., That the President of the United States be, and he is hereby, authorized, by and with the advice and consent of the Senate, to appoint three officers of the Navy, whose rank shall not be below a post captain, who shall constitute a Board of Commissioners for the Navy of the United States; and shall have power to adopt such rules and regulations for the government of their meetings as they may judge expedient; and the board so constituted shall be attached to the office of the Secretary of the Navy, and, under his superintendence, shall discharge all the ministerial duties of said office, relative to the procurement of naval stores and materials, and the construction, armament, equipment, and employment of vessels of war, as well as all other matters connected with the Naval Establishment of the United States. And the said board shall appoint their own secretary, who shall receive, in compensation for his services, a sum not exceeding two thousand dollars per annum, who shall keep a fair record of their proceedings, subject at all times to the inspection of the President of the United States and the Secretary of the Navy.

Sec. 2. *And be it further enacted,* That the said Board of Commissioners, by and with the consent of the Secretary of the Navy, be, and are hereby, authorized to prepare such rules and regulations as shall be necessary for securing an uniformity in the several classes of vessels and their equipments, and for repairing and refitting them, and for securing responsibility in the subordinate officers and agents; which regulations, when approved by the President of the United States, shall be respected and obeyed until altered and revoked by the same authority, and the said rules and regulations, thus prepared and approved, shall be laid before Congress at their next session. It shall also be the duty of said board, upon the requisition of the Secretary of the Navy, to furnish all the estimates of expenditure which the several branches of the service may require, and such other information and statements as he may deem necessary.

Sec. 3. *And be it further enacted,* That the officer of the said board holding the oldest commission shall preside; and each Commissioner shall be entitled to receive, in compensation for his services, three thousand five hundred dollars per annum, in lieu of wages, rations, and other emoluments, as naval officers; and all letters and packets to and from the said Commissioners, which relate to their official duties, shall be free from postage.

Sec. 4. *And be it further enacted,* That nothing in this act shall be construed to take from the Secretary of the Navy his control and direction of the naval forces of the United States, as now by law possessed.

Approved, February 7, 1815.

An Act to authorise the purchase of a tract of land for the use of the United States.

Be it enacted, &c., That it shall be lawful for the President of the United States, and he is hereby authorized, to cause to be purchased, for the use of the United States, the whole, or such part, of that tract of land situate adjoining the village of Plattsburg, in the State of New York, on which Forts Moreau and Brown, and other works, barracks, arsenals, hospitals, and other public buildings now stand, as shall be by him judged requisite for the military purposes of the United States.

Approved, February 8, 1815.

An Act for the better regulation of the Ordnance Department.

Be it enacted, &c., That, from and after the passage of this act, the Ordnance department shall consist of one colonel, one lieutenant colonel, two majors, ten captains, ten first lieutenants, ten second lieutenants, and ten third lieutenants.

SEC. 2. *And be it further enacted,* That the Colonel, or senior officer of the Ordnance department, is authorized to enlist, for the service of that department, for five years, as many master armorers, master carriage makers, master black-smiths, artificers, armorers, carriage makers, black-smiths, and laborers, as the public service, in his judgment, under the directions of the Secretary for the Department of War, may require.

SEC. 3. *And be it further enacted,* That it shall be the duty of the Colonel of the Ordnance department to direct the inspection and proving of all pieces of ordnance, cannon balls, shot, shells, small arms, and side arms, and equipments, procured for the use of the armies of the United States; and to direct the construction of all cannon and carriages, and every implement and apparatus for ordnance, and all ammunition wagons, travelling forges, and artificer's wagons, the inspection and proving of powder, and the preparation of all kinds of ammunition and ordnance stores. And it shall also be the duty of the Colonel, or senior officer of the Ordnance department, to furnish estimates, and, under the direction of the Secretary for the Department of War, to make contracts and purchases for procuring the necessary supplies of arms, equipments, ordnance, and ordnance stores.

SEC. 4. *And be it further enacted,* That the Colonel of the Ordnance department shall organize and attach to regiments, corps, or garrisons, such number of artificers, with proper tools, carriages, and apparatus, under such regulations and restrictions relative to their government and number, as, in his judgment, with the approbation of the Secretary for the Department of War, may be considered necessary.

SEC. 5. *And be it further enacted,* That the Colonel of the Ordnance department, or senior officer of that department of any district, shall execute all orders of the Secretary for the Department of War, and, in time of war, the orders of any General, or field officer, commanding any army, garrison, or detachment, for the supply of all arms, ordnance, ammunition, carriages, forges, and apparatus, for garrison, field, or siege service.

SEC. 6. *And be it further enacted,* That the keepers of all magazines and arsenals shall, quarterly, or oftener, if so directed, and in such manner as directed by the Colonel of the Ordnance department, make correct returns to the Colonel, or senior officer, of the Ordnance department, of all ordnance, arms, and ordnance stores, they may have in charge.

SEC. 7. *And be it further enacted,* That the costs of repairs of damages done to arms, equipments, or implements, in the use of the armies of the United States, shall be deducted from the pay of any officer or soldier in whose care or use the said arms, equipments, or implements were when the said damages occurred: *Provided,* The said damages were occasioned by the abuse or negligence of the said officer or soldier. And it is hereby made the duty of every officer commanding regiments, corps, garrisons, or detachments, to make, once every two months, or oftener if so directed, a written report to the Colonel of the Ordnance department, stating all damages to arms, equipments, and implements, belonging to his command, noting those occasioned by negligence or abuse, and naming the officer or soldier by whose negligence or abuse the said damages were occasioned.

SEC. 8. *And be it further enacted,* That the Colonel of the Ordnance department shall make, half yearly, to the War Department, or oftener, if the Secretary for that Department shall so direct, a correct report of the officers, and all artificers, and laborers in his Department; also, of all ordnance, arms, military stores, implements, and apparatus, of every description, and in such form as the Secretary for the Department of War shall direct.

SEC. 9. *And be it further enacted,* That to insure system and uniformity in the different public armories, they are hereby placed under the direction of the Ordnance department. And the Colonel of the Ordnance department, under the direction of the Secretary for the Department of War, is hereby authorized to establish depots of arms, ammunition, and ordnance stores, in such parts of the United States, and in such numbers, as may be deemed necessary.

SEC. 10. *And be it further enacted,* That the Colonel of the Ordnance department, under the direction of the Secretary for the Department of War, is hereby authorized to draw up a system of regulations for the government of the Ordnance department, forms of returns and reports, and for the uniformity of manufactures of all arms, ordnance, ordnance stores, implements, and apparatus, and for the repairing and better preservation of the same.

SEC. 11. *And be it further enacted,* That the pay, emoluments, and allowances, for the officers of the Ordnance department, shall be the same as the pay, emoluments, and allowances, now allowed to officers of similar grades, respectively, in the artillery of the United States. And that the pay of a master armorer shall be thirty dollars per month, and one and a half rations per day; of a master carriage maker, thirty dollars per month, and one and a half rations per day; of a master blacksmith, thirty dollars per month, and one and a half rations per day. The pay of armorers, carriage makers, or blacksmiths, each, sixteen dollars per month, and one and a half rations per day; the pay of artificers, thirteen dollars per month, and one ration per day; and the pay of laborers, nine dollars per month, and one ration per day; and to all of the said workmen, artificers, and laborers, the same clothing, and other allowances, as are allowed to privates of infantry in the Army of the United States, except clothing to the master workmen.

Sec. 12. *And be it further enacted,* That the President of the United States is hereby authorized to continue in the service, under this act, all the officers of the Ordnance department in service on the passage of the same, or to transfer them to other corps of the Army of the United States.

Sec. 13. *And be it further enacted,* That the Colonel of the Ordnance department is hereby allowed, at the rate of one thousand dollars per year, for clerks, and such books and stationery as may be necessary to his department.

Sec. 14. *And be it further enacted,* That the act passed May the fourteenth, one thousand eight hundred and twelve, entitled "An act for the better regulation of the Ordnance department," and the sections of any other acts, coming within the purview of any of the sections of this act, be, and the same are hereby, repealed.

Approved, February 8, 1815.

An Act to amend the act laying duties on licenses to retailers of wines, spirituous liquors, and foreign merchandise.

Be it enacted, &c., That nothing contained in the first section of the act laying duties on licenses to retailers of wines, spirituous liquors, and foreign merchandise, shall be construed to extend to vine dressers who sell, at the place where the same is made, wine of their own growth, nor shall any vine dresser, for vending solely at the place where the same is made, wine of his own growth, be compelled to take out license as a retailer of wine.

Approved, February 8, 1815.

An Act making appropriations for repairing or rebuilding the public buildings within the City of Washington.

Be it enacted, &c., That the President of the United States cause to be repaired, or rebuilt, forthwith, the President's house, Capitol, and public offices, on their present sites, in the City of Washington, and that he be authorized to borrow, at an interest not exceeding six per centum per annum, from any bank or banks within the District of Columbia, or from any individual or individuals, a sum not exceeding five hundred thousand dollars, to be applied exclusively to that object.

Approved, February 13, 1815.

An Act in addition to the act to regulate the laying out and making a road from Cumberland, in the State of Maryland, to the State of Ohio.

Be it enacted, &c., That, in addition to the unexpended balance of the sum heretofore appropriated for laying out and making a road from Cumberland, in the State of Maryland, to the State of Ohio, the sum of one hundred thousand dollars be, and the same is hereby, appropriated, to be paid out of any money in the Treasury not otherwise appropriated, and to be expended, under the direction of the President of the United States, in making said road between Cumberland, in the State of Maryland, and Brownsville, in the State of Pennsylvania, commencing at Cumberland; which sum of one hundred thousand dollars shall be repaid out of the fund reserved for laying out and making roads to the State of Ohio, by virtue of the seventh section of an act, passed on the thirtieth day of April, one thousand eight hundred and two, entitled "An act to enable the people of the eastern division of the Territory Northwest of the river Ohio to form a constitution and State government, and for the admission of such State into the Union on an equal footing with the original States, and for other purposes."

Approved, February 14, 1815.

An Act making appropriations for the support of Government, for the year one thousand eight hundred and fifteen.

Be it enacted, &c., That, for the expenditure of the civil list in the present year, including the contingent expenses of the several departments and offices; for the compensation of the several loan officers and their clerks, and for books and stationery for the same; for the payment of annuities and grants, for the support of the Mint establishment; for the expense of intercourse with foreign nations; for the support of light-houses, beacons, buoys, and public piers; and for satisfying certain miscellaneous claims, the following sums be, and the same are hereby, respectively appropriated; that is to say:

For compensation granted by law to the members of the Senate and House of Representatives, their officers, and attendants, three hundred and eighteen thousand and four dollars.

For the expense of firewood, stationery, printing, and all other contingent expenses of the two Houses of Congress, fifty-two thousand eight hundred dollars.

For the expenses of the Library of Congress, including the Librarian's allowance, for the year one thousand eight hundred and fifteen, eight hundred dollars.

For compensation to the President of the United States, twenty-five thousand dollars.

For compensation to the Secretary of State, clerks, and persons employed in that department including a clerk on old records, and a clerk and messenger in the Patent Office, fifteen thousand nine hundred and thirty-eight dollars.

For additional compensation to the clerks in said department, not exceeding fifteen per centum on the sum allowed by the act, entitled "An act to regulate and fix the compensation of clerks, and to authorize the laying out certain public roads, and for other purposes," one thousand seventy-two dollars and fifty cents.

For the incidental and contingent expenses of the said department, including the expense of printing and distributing ten thousand four hundred copies of the laws of the third session of the thirteenth Congress, and printing the laws in newspapers, twelve thousand eight hundred and seventy dollars.

For the cost of one thousand copies of a new edition of the laws of the United States, as authorized by the act of the eighteenth of April, one thousand eight hundred and fourteen, including an additional volume, to be comprised in the said edition, eighteen thousand seven hundred and fifty dollars.

For the expense of reprinting five hundred and sixteen copies of the laws of the first and second sessions of the thirteenth Congress, captured by the enemy, seven hundred and seventy-four dollars.

For compensation to the Secretary of the Treasury, clerks, and persons employed in his office, including one thousand dollars for an additional clerk, authorized by the act of the eighteenth of April, one thousand eight hundred and fourteen, fourteen thousand two hundred ninety-nine dollars and eighty-one cents.

For expense of translating foreign languages, allowance to the person employed in transmitting passports and sea letters, and for stationery and printing in the office of the Secretary of the Treasury, one thousand five hundred dollars.

For compensation to the Comptroller of the Treasury, clerks, and persons employed in his office, including the sum of two thousand eight hundred and eighty-nine dollars for compensation to his clerks, in addition to the sum allowed by the act of the twenty-first of April, one thousand eight hundred and six, fifteen thousand eight hundred and sixty-six dollars.

For expense of stationery and printing, and contingent expenses, in the Comptroller's office, eight hundred dollars.

For compensation to the Auditor of the Treasury, clerks, and persons employed in his office, including the sum of one thousand dollars, for compensation to his clerks, in addition to the sum allowed by the act of the twenty-first of April, one thousand eight hundred and six, thirteen thousand two hundred and twenty-one dollars.

For expense of stationery and printing, and contingent expenses, in the Auditor's office, five hundred dollars.

For compensation to the Treasurer, clerks, and persons employed in his office, including the sum of one thousand dollars, for compensation to his clerks, in addition to the sum allowed by the act

of the twenty first of April, one thousand eight hundred and six, seven thousand two hundred twenty-seven dollars and forty-five cents.

For expense of stationery and printing, and contingent expenses, in the Treasurer's office, six hundred dollars.

For compensation to the Commissioner of the General Land Office, clerks, and persons employed in his office, including the sum of three thousand dollars, for compensation to his clerks, in addition to the sum allowed by the act of the twenty-fifth of April, one thousand eight hundred and twelve, thirteen thousand four hundred and ten dollars.

For expense of stationery and printing, and contingent expenses of the General Land Office, three thousand seven hundred dollars.

For compensation to the Commissioner of the Revenue, clerks, and persons employed in his office, twelve thousand four hundred and ten dollars.

For expense of stationery and printing, and contingent expenses of the Revenue Office, six thousand six hundred and fifty dollars.

For compensation to the Register of the Treasury clerks, and persons employed in his office, including the sum of one thousand dollars, for compensation to his clerks, in addition to the sum allowed by the act of the twenty-first of April, one thousand eight hundred and six, seventeen thousand and fifty-two dollars and two cents.

For additional compensation to the clerks in the Treasury Department, not exceeding fifteen per centum on the sum allowed by the act, entitled "An act to regulate and fix the compensation of clerks, and to authorize the laying out certain public roads, and for other purposes," six thousand six hundred and thirty-four dollars and nine cents.

For compensation to the messenger of the Register's office, for stamping and arranging ship's registers, ninety dollars.

For expense of stationery and printing, and contingent expenses of the Register's office, three thousand eight hundred dollars.

For fuel, and other contingent expenses of the Treasury Department, including rent of the houses occupied by the said department during a part of the year one thousand eight hundred and fourteen, and the whole of the year one thousand eight hundred and fifteen, and compensation of a superintendent and two watchmen, employed for the security of the Treasury buildings, six thousand nine hundred and twenty dollars.

For the purchase of fire engine and fire buckets for the Treasury Department, one thousand dollars.

For the purchase of books, maps, and charts, for the Treasury Department, four hundred dollars.

For compensation to the Secretary of the Commissioners of the Sinking Fund, two hundred and fifty dollars.

For compensation to the Secretary of War, clerks, and persons employed in his office, including the sum of three thousand nine hundred and sixty dollars, for compensation to his clerks, in addition to the sum allowed by the act of the twenty-first of April, one thousand eight hundred and six, and the sum of three hundred dollars for assistant messengers, twenty thousand five hundred and ten dollars.

For expense of stationery, printing, fuel, and other contingencies, in the office of the Secretary of War, including office rent, three thousand dollars.

For compensation to the Accountant of the War Department, clerks, and persons employed in his office, including the sum of fourteen thousand two hundred and seventy-five dollars, for compensation of his clerks, in addition to the sum allowed by the act of the twenty-first of April, one thousand eight hundred and six, twenty-five thousand eight hundred and twenty-five dollars.

For contingent expenses in the office of the Accountant of the War Department, one thousand dollars.

For additional compensation to the clerks in the War Department, not exceeding fifteen per centum on the sum allowed by the act, entitled "An act to regulate and fix the compensation of clerks, and to authorize the laying out certain public roads, and for other purposes," two thousand two hundred and twenty-six dollars.

For compensation to the Paymaster of the Army, clerks, and persons employed in his office, fifteen thousand seven hundred and ten dollars.

For contingent expenses in the office of the Paymaster of the Army, two thousand two hundred and fifty dollars.

For compensation to the Superintendent General of Military Supplies, clerks, and persons employed in his office, ten thousand four hundred and ten dollars.

For contingent expenses in the office of the Superintendent General of Military Supplies, one thousand dollars.

For compensation to the clerks in the Adjutant and Inspector General's office, one thousand eight hundred dollars.

For compensation to the Commissary General of Purchases, and the clerks in his office, ten thousand dollars.

For contingent expenses in the office of the Commissary General of Purchases, one thousand dollars.

For compensation to the Secretary of the Navy, clerks, and persons employed in his office, including the sum of one thousand six hundred dollars, for compensation of his clerks, in addition to the sum allowed by the act of the twenty-first of April, one thousand eight hundred and six, eleven thousand four hundred and ten dollars.

For contingent expenses in the office of the Secretary of the Navy, including office rent, three thousand three hundred dollars.

For compensation to the Accountant of the Navy, clerks, and persons employed in his office, including the sum of three thousand dollars for compensation of his clerks, in addition to the sum allowed by the act of the twenty-first of April, one thousand eight hundred and six, thirteen thousand four hundred and ten dollars.

For contingent expenses in the office of the Accountant of the Navy, including house rent, one thousand two hundred and fifty dollars.

For additional compensation to the clerks in the Navy Department, not exceeding fifteen per centum on the sum allowed by the act, entitled "An act to regulate and fix the compensation of clerks, and to authorize the laying out certain public roads, and for other purposes," one thousand nine hundred and thirty-five dollars.

For compensation to the Postmaster General, Assistant Postmasters General, clerks, and persons employed in the General Post Office, including the sum of five thousand seven hundred and fifty-five dollars, for compensation of the clerks in the General Post Office, in addition to the sum allowed by the act of the twenty-first of April, one thousand eight hundred and six, twenty-two thousand and ten dollars.

For contingent expenses of the General Post Office, two thousand eight hundred dollars.

For additional compensation to the clerks in the General Post Office, not exceeding fifteen per centum on the sum allowed by the act, entitled "An act to regulate and fix the compensation of clerks, and to authorize the laying out certain public roads, and for other purposes," one thousand four hundred and one dollars and seventy-five cents.

For compensation to the several Commissioners of Loans, and for allowance to certain Commissioners of Loans in lieu of clerk hire, fourteen thousand five hundred and fifty dollars.

For compensation to the clerks of sundry Commissioners of Loans, including a sum of three thousand dollars, in addition to the amount heretofore allowed by law, and to defray the authorized expenses of the several Loan Offices, thirteen thousand seven hundred dollars.

For compensation to the Surveyor General and his clerks, three thousand five hundred dollars.

For compensation to the Surveyor of Lands South of Tennessee, and his clerks, and for the contingent expenses of his office, three thousand two hundred dollars.

For compensation to the officers and clerks of the Mint, ten thousand one hundred dollars.

For wages to the persons employed in the different operations of the Mint, including the sum of six hundred dollars allowed to an assistant engraver, seven thousand five hundred dollars.

For repairs of furnaces, cost of iron and machinery, rents, and other contingent expenses of the Mint, three thousand eight hundred dollars.

For allowance of wastage in the gold and silver coinage, three thousand dollars.

For compensation to the Governor, Judges, and Secretary of the Mississippi Territory, nine thousand dollars.

For stationery, office-rent, and other contingent expenses of said Territory, three hundred and fifty dollars.

For compensation to the Governor, Judges and Secretary of the Indiana Territory, six thousand six hundred dollars.

For stationery, office-rent, and other contingent

expenses of said Territory, three hundred and fifty dollars.

For compensation to the Governor, Judges, and Secretary of the Missouri Territory, seven thousand eight hundred dollars.

For stationery, office-rent, and other contingent expenses of said Territory, three hundred and fifty dollars.

For compensation to the Governor. Judges, and Secretary of the Michigan Territory, six thousand six hundred dollars.

For stationery, office-rent, and other contingent expenses of said Territory, three hundred and fifty dollars.

For compensation to the Governor, Judges, and Secretary of the Illinois Territory, six thousand six hundred dollars.

For stationery, office-rent, and other contingent expenses of said Territory, three hundred and fifty dollars.

For the discharge of such demands against the United States, on account of the civil department, not otherwise provided for, as shall have been admitted in due course of settlement at the Treasury, two thousand dollars.

For compensation granted by law to the Chief Justice, the Associate Judges, and District Judges, of the United States, including the Chief Justice and Associate Judges of the District of Columbia, and the Attorney General; and also including the sum of one thousand dollars, short appropriated in the year one thousand eight hundred and fourteen, for the salary of the District Judge of Louisiana, sixty-four thousand dollars.

For the compensations of sundry District Attorneys and Marshals, as granted by law, including those in the several Territories, seven thousand eight hundred and fifty dollars.

For defraying the expenses of the Supreme, Circuit, and District Courts of the United States, including the District of Columbia, and of jurors, and witnesses, in aid of the funds arising from fines, penalties, and forfeitures, and for defraying the expenses of prosecutions for offences against the United States, and for the safekeeping of prisoners, forty thousand dollars.

For the payment of sundry pensions, granted by the late Government, eight hundred and sixty dollars.

For the payment of the annual allowance to the invalid pensioners of the United States, ninety-eight thousand dollars.

For the relief and support of sick and disabled seamen, in addition to the funds already appropriated by law, twenty thousand dollars.

For the maintenance and support of lighthouses, beacons, buoys, and public piers, stakeages of channels, bars, and shoals, including repairs and improvements, and contingent expenses, twenty-four thousand two hundred and ninety-nine dollars and eleven cents.

For the support and safekeeping of prisoners of war, five hundred thousand dollars.

For defraying the expenses of ascertaining land titles in Louisiana, eight thousand dollars.

For the salaries, allowances, and contingent expenses of Ministers to foreign nations, and of Secretaries of Legation, one hundred and nine thousand two hundred and fifty dollars.

For the contingent expenses of intercourse between the United States and foreign nations, fifty thousand dollars.

For the expenses of intercourse with the Barbary Powers, ten thousand dollars.

For the relief and protection of distressed American seamen in foreign countries, fifty thousand dollars.

For expenses of agents at Paris and Copenhagen, in relation to prize causes and captures of American vessels, four thousand dollars.

For the discharge of such miscellaneous claims against the United States, not otherwise provided for, as shall have been admitted in due course of settlement at the Treasury, four thousand dollars.

For paying to Augustus McKinney and Lazel Bancroft the amount of a judgment remitted by act of Congress, one thousand dollars.

For compensation to the board of commissioners appointed to carry into effect the act of the thirty-first of March, one thousand eight hundred and fourteen, for indemnifying certain claimants of public land in the Mississippi Territory, six thousand dollars.

For stationery, office rent, and other contingent expenses, of the last mentioned board of commissioners, a sum not exceeding twelve hundred dollars.

For the discharge of the claim of Farrington Barkelow, granted him by act of Congress for his relief, one thousand one hundred and sixty-eight dollars and twenty-five cents.

For the compensation of the Commissioners of the Navy Board, ten thousand five hundred dollars.

For compensation to the secretary of the Navy Board, two thousand dollars.

Sec. 2. *And be it further enacted,* That the several appropriations hereinbefore made shall be paid and discharged out of the fund of six-hundred thousand dollars, reserved by the act making provision for the debt of the United States, and out of any moneys in the Treasury not otherwise appropriated.

Approved, February 16, 1815.

An Act for the relief of the inhabitants of the late county of New Madrid, in the Missouri Territory, who suffered by earthquakes.

Be it enacted, &c., That any person or persons owning lands in the county of New Madrid, in the Missouri Territory, with the extent the said county had on the tenth day of November, one thousand eight hundred and twelve, and whose lands have been materially injured by earthquakes, shall be, and they are hereby, authorized to locate the like quantity of land on any of the public lands of the said Territory, the sale of which is authorized by law: *Provided,* That no person shall be permitted to locate a greater quantity of land under this act, than the quantity confirmed to him, except the owners of lots of ground or tracts of land of less quantity than one hundred and sixty acres, who are hereby authorized to locate and obtain any quantity of land, not exceeding one hundred and sixty acres, nor shall any person be entitled to locate more than six hundred and forty acres, nor shall any such location include any lead mine or salt spring: *And provided, also,* That in every case where such location shall be made according to the provisions of this act, the title of the person or persons to the land injured as aforesaid, shall revert to, and become absolutely vested in, the United States.

SEC. 2. *And be it further enacted,* That whenever it shall appear to the recorder of land titles for the Territory of Missouri, by the oath or affirmation of a competent witness, or witnesses, that any person or persons are entitled to a tract or tracts of land under the provisions of this act, it shall be the duty of the said recorder to issue a certificate thereof to the claimant or claimants; and upon such certificate being issued, and the location made, on the application of the claimants, by the principal deputy surveyor for said Territory, or under his direction, whose duty it shall be to cause a survey thereof to be made, and to return a plat of each location made to the said recorder, together with a notice in writing, designating the tract or tracts thus located, and the name of the claimant on whose behalf the same shall be made; which notice and plat the said recorder shall cause to be recorded in his office, and shall receive from the claimant, for his services on each claim, the sum of two dollars, for receiving the proof, issuing the certificate, and recording the notice and plat, as aforesaid; and the surveyor shall be entitled to the same compensation for his services from the party applying, as is allowed for surveying the public lands of the United States.

SEC. 3. *And be it further enacted,* That it shall be the duty of the recorder of land titles to transmit a report of the claims allowed, and locations made, under this act, to the Commissioner of the General Land Office, and shall deliver to the party a certificate, stating the circumstances of the case, and that he is entitled to a patent for the tract therein designated; which certificate shall be filed with the said recorder within twelve months after date, and the recorder shall thereupon issue a certificate in favor of the party, which certificate, being transmitted to the Commissioner of the General Land Office, shall entitle the party to a patent, to be issued in like manner as is provided by law for other public lands of the United States.

Approved, February 17, 1815.

An Act giving further time to complete the surveys, and obtain the patents, for lands located under Virginia resolution warrants.

Be it enacted, &c., That the officers and soldiers of the Virginia line on Continental establishment, or their legal representatives, to whom land warrants have issued by virtue of any resolution of the Legislature of Virginia, as a bounty for services which, by the laws of Virginia, passed prior

to the cession of the Northwestern Territory to the United States, entitled such officers and soldiers to bounty lands, and whose location of such warrants shall have been made prior to the twenty-third day of March, one thousand eight hundred and eleven, shall be allowed the further time of two years from the passing of this act to complete their surveys and obtain their patents for the land located as aforesaid: *Provided,* That surveys shall be made, and patents granted on the aforesaid locations, under the same regulations, restrictions, and provisions, in every respect, as were prescribed for the making of surveys and granting of patents by the act, entitled "An act authorizing patents to issue for lands located and surveyed by virtue of certain Virginia resolution warrants," passed on the third day of March, one thousand eight hundred and seven.

Approved, February 22, 1815.

An Act requiring the Secretary of the Senate and Clerk of the House of Representatives, in the Congress of the United States, to give security for the faithful application and disbursement of the contingent funds of the Senate and House of Representatives.

Be it enacted, &c., That it shall be the duty of the Secretary of the Senate, and Clerk of the House of Representatives, respectively, within ten days after the passage of this act, to give bond to the United States, with one or more sureties, to be approved by the Comptroller of the Treasury; each bond in the penal sum of twenty thousand dollars, with condition for the faithful application and disbursement of such contingent funds of the respective Houses as shall come into their hands, which bonds shall be deposited in the Comptroller's office. And it shall be the duty of each and every Secretary of the Senate, and Clerk of the House of Representatives, who may hereafter be chosen, to give bond as aforesaid, within thirty days after he enters upon the discharge of the duties of his said office.

SEC. 2. *And be it further enacted,* That, from and after the passage of this act, it shall be the duty of the Secretary of the Senate, and the Clerk of the House of Representatives, to deposite all money belonging to the United States, which may come into their hands, in one of the banks in the District of Columbia; and all debts payable by said Secretary or Clerk, on account of the Senate or House of Representatives, shall be paid by a draft, in favor of each creditor, on the bank where the money of Government may be deposited.

Approved, February 23, 1815.

An Act for the regulation of the Courts of Justice of Indiana.

Be it enacted, &c., That the Judges of the General Court of the Indiana Territory shall, in one and every year, hold two sessions of the said court, at Vincennes, in the county of Knox, on the first Mondays in February and September; of do, in the county of Harrison, on the third Mondays in February and September; and at Brookville, in the county of Franklin, on the first Mondays next succeeding the fourth Mondays of February and September; which courts, respectively, shall be composed of at least two of the judges appointed by the Government of the United States; and no person or persons, acting under the authority and appointment of the said Territory, shall be associated with the said judges.

Approved, February 24, 1815.

An Act to authorize the issuing of Treasury Notes, for the service of the year one thousand eight hundred and fifteen.

Be it enacted, &c., That the Secretary of the Treasury, with the approbation of the President of the United States, be, and he is hereby authorized to cause Treasury notes, for a sum not exceeding twenty-five millions of dollars, to be prepared, signed, and issued, at the Treasury of the United States, in the manner hereafter provided.

SEC. 2. *And be it further enacted,* That the said Treasury notes shall be, respectively, signed in behalf of the United States by persons to be appointed for that purpose by the President of the United States, two of whom shall sign each note; and they shall receive, as a compensation for that service, at the rate of seventy-five cents for every hundred notes thus signed by them, respectively; and the said notes shall likewise be countersigned by the Register of the Treasury, or, in case of his sickness or absence, by the Treasurer of the United States.

SEC. 3. *And be it further enacted,* That the said Treasury notes shall be prepared of such denominations as the Secretary of the Treasury, with the approbation of the President of the United States shall, from time to time, direct; and such of said notes as shall be of a denomination less than one hundred dollars shall be payable to bearer, and be transferable by delivery alone, and shall bear no interest; and such of the said notes as shall be of the denomination of one hundred dollars, or upwards, may be made payable to order, and transferable by delivery and assignment, endorsed on the same, and bearing an interest from the day on which they shall be issued, at the rate of five and two-fifths per centum per annum; or they may be made payable to bearer, and transferable by delivery alone, and bearing no interest, as the Secretary of the Treasury, with the approbation of the President of the United States, shall direct.

SEC. 4. *And be it further enacted,* That it shall be lawful for the holders of the aforesaid Treasury notes not bearing an interest, and of the Treasury notes bearing an interest at the rate of five and two-fifths per centum per annum, to present them at any time, in sums not less than one hundred dollars, to the Treasury of the United States, or to any commissioner of loans; and the holders of said Treasury notes not bearing an interest, shall be entitled to receive therefor the amount of the said notes in a certificate or certificates of funded stock, bearing interest at seven per

13th CON. 3d SESS.—61

centum per annum, and the holders of the aforesaid Treasury notes bearing an interest at the rate of five and two-fifths per centum, shall be entitled to receive therefor the amount of the said notes, including the interest due on the same, in a like certificate or certificates of funded stock, bearing an interest of six per centum per annum, from the first day of the calendar month next ensuing that in which the said notes shall thus be, respectively, presented, and payable quarter yearly, on the same days whereon the interest of the funded debt is now payable. And the stock thus to be issued shall be transferable in the same manner as the funded stock of the United States; the interest on the same, and its eventual reimbursement, shall be effected out of such fund as has been, or shall be, established by law for the payment and reimbursement of the funded public debt contracted since the declaration of war with Great Britain. And the faith of the United States is hereby pledged to establish sufficient revenues, and to appropriate them, as an addition to the said fund, if the same shall, at any time hereafter, become inadequate for effecting the purpose aforesaid: *Provided, however, and be it further enacted,* That it shall be lawful for the United States to reimburse the stock thus created, at any time after the last day of December, one thousand eight hundred and twenty-four.

SEC. 5. *And be it further enacted,* That it shall be lawful for the Secretary of the Treasury to cause the Treasury notes which, in pursuance of the preceding section, shall be delivered up and exchanged for funded stock, and also the Treasury notes which shall have been paid to the United States for taxes, duties, or demands, in the manner hereinafter provided, to be reissued, and applied anew, to the same purposes, and in the same manner, as when originally issued.

SEC. 6. *And be it further enacted,* That the Treasury notes authorized to be issued by this act, shall be everywhere received in all payments to the United States. On every such payment the note or notes shall be received for the amount of both the principal and the interest, which, on the day of such payment, may appear due on such of the notes as shall bear interest, thus given in payment; and the interest on the said notes bearing an interest shall, on such payments, be computed at the rate of one cent and one-half of a cent per day, on every hundred dollars of principal; and each month shall be computed as containing thirty days.

SEC. 7. *And be it further enacted,* That any person making payment to the United States in the said Treasury notes, into the hands of any collector, receiver of public moneys, or other public officer or agent, shall, on books kept according to such forms as shall be prescribed by the Secretary of the Treasury, give duplicate certificates of the number and respective amount of each and every Treasury note, and of the interest thereon, in case the same shall bear interest, thus paid by such person: and every collector, receiver of public moneys, or other public officer or agent, who shall thus receive in payment any of the said

Treasury notes bearing interest, shall, on payment of the same into the Treasury, or into one of the banks where the public moneys are or may be deposited, receive credit, both for the principal and for the interest, computed as aforesaid, which, on the day of such last mentioned payment, shall appear due on the note or notes thus paid in: *Provided always*, That in the settlement of his accounts he shall be charged for the interest accrued on such note or notes, from the day on which the same shall have been received by him in payment as aforesaid to the day on which the same shall be paid by him as aforesaid: *And provided, also*, That no charge or deduction, on account of interest, shall be made in respect to any bank into which payments as aforesaid may be made to the United States, either by individuals, or by collectors, receivers, or other public officers or agents, and which payments shall be received by such bank as specie, and credit given to the Treasurer of the United States for the amount thereof, including the interest accrued and due on such notes, from the day on which the same shall have been received by such bank, on account of the United States.

Sec. 8. *And be it further enacted*, That the Secretary of the Treasury be, and he is hereby, authorized, with the approbation of the President of the United States, to cause the said Treasury notes to be issued at the par value thereof, in payment of services, of supplies, or of debts, for which the United States are or may be answerable by law, to such person and persons as shall be willing to accept the same in payment; and to deposite portions of the said notes in the loan offices, or in State banks, for the purpose of paying the same to the public creditors as aforesaid; and to borrow money on the credit of the said notes; or to sell the same, at a rate not under par; and it shall be a good execution of this provision, to pay such notes to such bank or banks as will receive the same at par, and give credit to the Treasurer of the United States for the amount thereof, on the day on which the said notes shall thus be issued and paid to such bank or banks, respectively.

Sec. 9. *And be it further enacted*, That it shall and may be lawful for the holder of any Treasury notes issued, or authorized to be issued, under any laws heretofore passed, to convert the same into certificates of funded debt, upon the same terms, and in the same manner, hereinbefore provided, in relation to the Treasury notes authorized by this act, bearing an interest of five and two-fifths per centum.

Sec. 10. *And be it further enacted*, That a sum of forty thousand dollars, to be paid out of any money in the Treasury, not otherwise appropriated, be, and the same is hereby, appropriated, for defraying the expense of preparing, printing, engraving, signing, and otherwise incident to the issuing, of the Treasury notes authorized by this act.

Sec. 11. *And be it further enacted*, That if any person shall falsely make, forge, or counterfeit, or cause or procure to be falsely made, forged, or counterfeited, or willingly aid or assist in falsely making, forging, or counterfeiting, any note, in imitation of, or purporting to be, a Treasury note as aforesaid; or shall falsely alter, or cause or procure to be falsely altered, or willingly aid or assist in falsely altering, any Treasury note, issued as aforesaid; or shall pass, utter, or publish, or attempt to pass, utter, or publish, as true, any false, forged, or counterfeited, note, purporting to be a Treasury note as aforesaid, knowing the same to be falsely made, forged, or counterfeited; or shall pass, utter, or publish, or attempt to pass, utter, or publish, as true, any falsely altered Treasury note, issued as aforesaid, knowing the same to be falsely altered; or shall be, directly or indirectly, knowingly concerned in any of the offences aforesaid, every such person shall be deemed and adjudged guilty of felony; and, being thereof convicted by due course of law, shall be sentenced to be imprisoned and kept to hard labor, for a period not less than three years, nor more than ten years, and be fined in a sum not exceeding five thousand dollars.

Approved, February 24, 1815.

An Act to provide additional revenue for defraying the expenses of Government, and maintaining the public credit, by laying a direct tax upon the District of Columbia.

Be it enacted, &c., That a direct tax of nineteen thousand nine hundred and ninety-eight dollars and forty cents be, and is hereby, annually laid upon the District of Columbia, which shall be assessed and laid upon the same descriptions of property in the same manner, and be collected and accounted for likewise in the same manner, as is provided by the "Act to provide additional revenues for defraying the expenses of Government, and maintaining the public credit, by laying a direct tax upon the United States, and to provide for assessing and collecting the same," and the several acts referred to therein, or which may be passed amendatory thereof; for which purpose there shall be appointed a principal assessor for the District of Columbia, who, with such deputies as he may appoint, shall have the like qualifications and powers, receive the like compensations, discharge the like duties, and be subject to the like penalties, with the other principal or assistant assessors: *Provided*, That the said principal assessor shall, in addition to the powers of the other principal assessors, exercise the same powers and discharge the same duties devolved on the board of principal assessors, established by the said act; and the tax lists, made out by him conformably thereto, shall be delivered to the collector within one hundred and twenty days from the first day of April, in the year one thousand eight hundred and fifteen, on which day the said principal assessor shall direct and cause the several assistant assessors in his district, to inquire after and concerning all lands, lots of ground, with their improvements, dwelling-houses, and slaves, liable to taxation: *And provided*, That the collector of the said district shall, himself, retain the list of property lying within the said district, not owned occupied, or superintended, by some person residing therein ; and shall proceed to discharge the like duties that are performed in the respective States, by the collectors designated by the Secretary of the Treasury for receiving said list.

Sec. 2. *And be it further enacted,* That the principal assessor and assistant assessors for the District of Columbia, shall discharge the like duties required by the "Act to provide additional revenues for defraying the expenses of Government, and maintaining the public credit, by laying duties on household furniture, and on gold and silver watches," to be performed in the respective States by the assessors, anything in the tenth section of the said act to the contrary notwithstanding ; which said duties, and all other acts therein required to be done, as well by the said officers as by individuals, subject to the said act, shall be performed within the District of Columbia, under the penalties, for neglect or omission, thereby prescribed, and in point of time, relatively to the said first day of April, in the year one thousand eight hundred and fifteen, and in every year thereafter, relatively to such day as may be fixed by law for the performance of the like duties and acts in the several States.

Approved, February 27, 1815.

An Act to provide additional revenues for defraying the expenses of Government, and maintaining the public credit, by laying a duty on gold, silver, and plated ware, and jewelry and paste work, manufactured within the United States.

Be it enacted, &c., That, from and after the eighteenth day of April next, there shall be paid upon all gold, silver, and plated ware, and jewelry and paste work, except time pieces, which shall thereafter be manufactured or made for sale within the United States, or the Territories thereof, a duty of six per centum ad valorem, by the manufacturer thereof.

Sec. 2. *And be it further enacted,* That the duty aforesaid shall be imposed, paid, collected, and accounted for, in like manner, and subject to the like provisions and penalties, as the duties imposed by the "Act to provide additional revenues for defraying the expenses of Government, and maintaining the public credit, by laying duties on various goods, wares, and merchandise, manufactured within the United States," passed the eighteenth day of January, one thousand eight hundred and fifteen, all the provisions of which act shall apply to the duty hereby imposed, and to those by whom it shall be payable, the same as if it were specifically inserted among the dutiable objects enumerated in the first section thereof.

Approved, February 27, 1815.

An Act to repeal certain acts concerning the flotilla service, and for other purposes.

Be it enacted, &c., That, from and after the first day of April next, the act, entitled "An act authorizing the President of the United States to cause to be built barges, for the defence of the ports and harbors of the United States," passed the fifth day of July, in the year one thousand eight hundred and thirteen ; and also an act, entitled "An act authorizing the appointment of certain officers for the flotilla service," passed the sixteenth day of April, in the year one thousand eight hundred and fourteen, shall be repealed and cease to be in force.

Sec. 2. *And be it further enacted,* That the barges and other vessels composing the flotilla establishment, (they being first divested of their guns and military stores, which are to be carefully preserved,) shall be sold or laid up under the direction of the President of the United States, and the moneys arising therefrom paid into the Treasury thereof.

Sec. 3. *And be it further enacted,* That all the commissioned and warrant officers, and all the privates, who shall be discharged in consequence of the repeal of the acts aforesaid, shall be entitled to receive four months' pay, over and above what may be due to them, respectively, at the time of their discharge.

Sec. 4. *And be it further enacted,* That the President of the United States be, and he hereby is, authorized to cause all the armed vessels thereof on the Lakes, except such as he may deem necessary to enforce the proper execution of the revenue laws, to be sold or laid up, as he may judge most conducive to the public interest ; such vessels being first divested of their armament, tackle, and furniture, which are to be carefully preserved.

Sec. 5. *And be it further enacted,* That the act entitled "An act authorizing the President of the United States to cause to be built, or purchased, the vessels therein mentioned," passed the fifteenth day of November, in the year one thousand eight hundred and fourteen, be, and the same is hereby, repealed ; and the President of the United States is hereby, authorized to cause to be sold such of the vessels acquired under the said act as he may deem inexpedient to be retained in the public service ; and to cause the moneys arising therefrom to be paid into the public Treasury.

Sec. 6. *And be it further enacted,* That the President of the United States be, and he is hereby, authorized to cause to be sold, they being first divested of their guns and military stores, which are to be carefully preserved, such and so many of the gunboats belonging to the United States, as in his judgment may no longer be necessary to be retained for the public service ; and such of the warrant officers and privates as may be discharged in consequence of such sale, shall be entitled to receive four months' pay, over and above what may be due to them at the time of their discharge.

Approved, February 27, 1815.

An Act to amend and extend the provisions of the act of the sixteenth of April, one thousand eight hundred and fourteen, entitled "An act confirming certain claims to land in the Illinois Territory, and providing for their location."

Be it enacted, &c., That the western boundary

Public Acts of Congress.

of the tract of country set apart by the act of the sixteenth of April, one thousand eight hundred and fourteen, entitled "An act confirming certain claims to land in the Illinois Territory, and providing for their location," be extended upon the river Mississippi, to the middle thereof, so as to include all islands in said river, between the middle and eastern margin, throughout the length of said line; and that all or any of the said islands shall be subject to be appropriated under the said recited act.

Sec. 2. *And be it further enacted,* That the proviso contained in the fourth section of the before recited act be repealed, so far as it regards persons settled on fractions of sections or quarter sections containing less than one hundred and sixty acres; and that such persons, under the like circumstances, shall be considered as entitled to all the rights, benefits, and advantages, specified in the said fourth section, as those settled on sections or quarter sections, and also to any right, privilege, or advantage, secured by this act: *Provided, however,* That such persons shall not be permitted, in such cases, to take less than the whole quantity of such fractional quarter section on which they are respectively settled.

Sec. 3. *And be it further enacted,* That every person or persons, who settled on and improved any of the lands in the said Territory, reserved for the use of schools or seminaries of learning, before the fifth day of February, one thousand eight hundred and thirteen, and who would have had the right of pre-emption thereto had not the same been reserved as aforesaid, shall be entitled to the pre-emption of the like quantity of other land, upon the same terms, and under the same restrictions, provided by the fourth section of the said recited act, to be located on any lands within the boundary specified in this and the said recited act, not otherwise appropriated; and such persons shall also be entitled to the benefit of, and subject to, the restrictions contained in this act.

Sec. 4. *And be it further enacted,* That all and every person or persons entitled to the pre-emption of lands, under the fourth section of the before recited act, who failed to locate their claims within the time limited in said act, and which lands have been appropriated by others, shall be entitled to the pre-emption of the like quantity as they could have appropriated under the said act, or under the provisions of this act, to be located on any land within the boundary specified in this and the said recited act, not previously appropriated.

Sec. 5. *And be it further enacted,* That all and every person or persons, entitled to the pre-emption of lands under the provisions of this act, shall conform to, and be governed by, the rules prescribed in the said recited act, in locating, proving, and completing, their titles respectly, except in cases where the same is changed by this act.

Sec. 6. *And be it further enacted,* That it shall be the duty of the register of the land office for the district of Kaskaskia to give notice, by an advertisement inserted, for one month, in at least one newspaper published in the said Territory, to all persons entitled to pre-emption in the purchase of any tract of land, by virtue of this or the before recited act, that they may make such purchase, on application to him at his office, on or before the first day of May, in the year one thousand eight hundred and sixteen; and every person failing or refusing to enter, with the said register, the land to which the right of pre-emption is so secured, notice being given as before mentioned, within the time aforesaid, shall lose his, her, or their, right of pre-emption.

Sec. 7. *And be it further enacted,* That the locations of any confirmed claim, made by virtue of any authority given by the commissioners appointed to examine the claims of persons to land in the Illinois Territory, shall be, and the same are hereby, confirmed: *Provided,* That the provisions of this section shall not be so construed as to extend to any locations made by any person or persons without any authority from the commissioners aforesaid; nor shall it affect the claims of any other person or persons.

Sec. 8. *And be it further enacted,* That the register and receiver of public moneys of the land office at Kaskaskia shall be allowed the same commission, respectively, on the confirmed claims, which have been or shall be received in payment for land entered at the said office, as they are now entitled to on moneys received in payment for lands sold, calculating the *value of the* confirmed claims at the rate of two dollars per acre.

Sec. 9. *And be it further enacted,* That it shall be lawful for Ann Gilham to locate any unappropriated quarter section within the Illinois Territory; and whenever the said Ann Gilham shall enter, with the register of the land office at Kaskaskia, any unappropriated quarter section, it *shall* be the duty of the register to issue, to the said Ann Gilham, a certificate specifying therein the quarter section so located; and it *shall be the* duty of the Commissioner of the General Land Office to issue a patent for the land so located, whenever the certificate aforesaid shall be presented to him for that purpose.

Approved, February 27, 1815.

An Act to repeal certain acts therein mentioned.

Be it enacted, &c., That the act, entitled "An act to authorize the President of the United States to accept the services of State troops, and of volunteers," and the act, entitled "An act to authorize the raising a corps of sea fencibles," &c. and the same are hereby, repealed.

Approved, February 27, 1815.

An Act in addition to the act regulating the Post Office Establishment.

Be it enacted, &c., That the Postmaster General be, and is hereby, authorized to allow to the postmasters, respectively, such commission on the moneys arising from the postage of letters, newspapers, and packets, as shall be adequate to their respective services and expenses: *Provided* that the said commission shall not exceed the following several rates on the amount collected in one quarter; that is to say:

On a sum not exceeding one hundred and fifty dollars, twenty per cent.

On a sum not exceeding four hundred and fifty dollars, seventeen per cent.

On a sum not exceeding three thousand dollars, thirteen per cent.

On any sum over three thousand six hundred dollars, five per cent.

He may also allow the postmasters at distributing post offices, a commission of four per cent. on any sum of postages distributed, not exceeding four thousand dollars, and a commission of three per cent. on any sum of postages distributed over four thousand dollars.

He may also allow to such postmasters as receive and despatch foreign mails, a sum not exceeding twenty-five dollars per quarter year, for that service; and he may augment the commission of those postmasters who receive the mail regularly between the hours of nine o'clock in the evening and five o'clock in the morning, from twenty to thirty-three and one-third per cent. on one hundred and fifty dollars received in each quarter.

He may also allow to each postmaster one cent for each free letter delivered out of his office, and one cent for each free letter originally received by him and forwarded by mail.

He may also allow to each postmaster ten cents for every monthly register of the arrival and departure of the mail, returned to the General Post Office. The Postmaster General may also allow to the postmasters, respectively, a commission of thirty-three and one-third per cent. on the amount of postages which they shall collect on newspapers, magazines, and pamphlets; but no allowance for distribution, or for free letters, shall be made to any postmaster who shall collect postages to the amount of five thousand dollars in one quarter.

Sec. 2. *And be it further enacted,* That this act shall be in force on and after the first day of April next, and thereupon all other acts and clauses thereof, providing compensation or allowance to any postmaster or postmasters, shall cease to have effect, and are hereby repealed: *Provided,* That nothing herein contained shall be construed to affect, alter, or repeal, the provisions of the fortieth section of the act regulating the Post Office Establishment.

Sec. 3. *And be it further enacted,* That the Postmaster General be authorized to have the mail carried in any steamboat, or other vessel, which shall be used as a packet, in any of the waters of the United States, on such terms and conditions as shall be considered expedient: *Provided,* That he do not pay more than three cents for each letter, and each packet, and more than one half cent for each newspaper, conveyed in such mail.

Sec. 4. *And be it further enacted,* That it shall be the duty of every master or manager of any steamboat, packet, or other vessel, which shall pass from one part or place to another part or place, in the United States, where a post office is established, to deliver, within three hours after his arrival, if in the day time, and within two hours after the next sunrise, if the arrival be in the night, all letters and packets addressed to, or destined for, such port or place, to the postmaster there, for which he shall be entitled to receive of such postmaster two cents for every letter or packet so delivered, unless the same shall be carried or conveyed under a contract with the Postmaster General; and if any master or manager of a steamboat, or other vessel, shall fail so to deliver any letter, or packet, which shall have been brought by him, or shall have been in his care, or within his power, he shall incur a penalty of thirty dollars for every such failure.

Sec. 5. *And be it further enacted,* That every person employed on board any steamboat, or other vessel employed as a packet, shall deliver every letter, and packet of letters, intrusted to such person, to the master or manager of such steamboat, or other vessel, and before the said vessel shall touch at any other port or place; and for every failure, or neglect so to deliver, a penalty of ten dollars shall be incurred for each letter and packet.

Approved, February 27, 1815.

An Act to alter and establish certain Post Roads.

Be it enacted, &c., That the following post roads be, and the same are hereby, discontinued; that is to say: From Columbia, by Shelbyville, and Winchester, to Fayetteville, in Tennessee. From Tellico, in Tennessee, by Amoy river, Vanstown, and Tuckeytown, to Fort Stoddard, in Mississippi Territory; and from Tuckabatchy, by Tensaw, and Fort Stoddard, to Pascagoola river, in Mississippi Territory; from Cynthiana to Georgetown, in Kentucky. In North Carolina, from Washington to Lake Landing, on Motamuskeet. From Concord, by Loudon, Gilmanton, Meredith, New Holderness, to Plymouth; thence, by New Hampton, Sanbornton, Northfield, and Canterbury, to Concord.

Sec. 2. *And be it further enacted,* That the following be established post roads; that is to say:

In New Hampshire.—From Concord to Fryeburgh, in Maine. From Concord, by Salisbury, Andover, New Chester, Bridgewater, Plymouth, thence by New Holderness, New Hampton, Sanbornton, Salisbury, to Concord. From Exeter, by Brentwood, Poplin, Raymond, Candia, and Pembroke, to Concord.

In Vermont.—From Chester South village, by Andover, Weston, Land Grove, and Peru, to Manchester. From Salem, New York, by Rupert, Paulet, Middleton, and Ira, to Rutland.

In Maine.—From Kennebunk to Alfred; from Prospect, by Mount Ephraim, to Frankfort.

In Massachusetts.—From Hosack, New York, by Pawnal, Vermont, to Williamstown. From Northampton, by Hadley, Sunderland, and Montague, to Northfield. From Foxborough, by Mansfield, and Norton, to Taunton.

In Connecticut.—That the post road from Norwalk, by Reading, to Danbury, pass through Saugatock, and by the town-house in Reading.

In New York.—From Hadley Landing, in Sar-

Public Acts of Congress.

atoga, to Luzern, in Warren county. From Hamilton village, by Guilderland, Berne, Schoharie Courthouse, the Brick Church in Cobleskill, Colonel I. Steward's, and Maryland, to Milford. From West Point to Haverstraw. From Burrage Mills, in Coventry, to Oxford. That the mail from Huntington be carried by the north road to Smithtown, instead of the south road. From Stillwater, by Dunning street, in Malta, and the south end of Saratoga Lake, to Ballston Springs, thence, by the north end of Saratoga Lake, and by Rogers' Mills, to Stillwater. From Manlius, in Onondaga county, to Elbridge, in Camillus, thence to Auburn, in Cayuga county. From Bainbridge, through Coventry, to Green.

In New Jersey.—From Newark, by Orange Dale, and Hanover, to Morristown. From Asbury, in Mansfield township, by Hacketstown, Greenville, Newtown, and Frankfort, to Deekerstown.

In Pennsylvania.—From Huntington, by Woodcock Valley, Bedford, and Cumberland Valley, to Cumberland, in Maryland. From Mercer to New Castle. From Lancaster to Lebanon. From York, by Dover, Rosstown, Lewisburg, and Lisburn, to Carlisle.

In Ohio.—From Zanesville to Coshocton.—From Wheeling, in Virginia, by Stephen Scott's, at the mouth of Fishing Creek, to Marietta. From Delaware, in Ohio, by Norton, Upper Sandusky, and Lower Sandusky, to Fort Meigs. From Lebanon to Hamilton.

In Maryland.—From Baltimore, by Queenstown, Hillsborough, and Denton, to Milford. From Westminster, in Frederick county, through Uniontown, Middleburgh, Greenham, Mechanickstown, and Cavetown, to Hagerstown. From Elkton, by Sabinton, to Georgetown Cross Roads.

In Virginia.—From Lindsay's store, by Barboursville and Stannardsville, to Harrisonburg. From Richmond to Lindsay's store, in Albemarle county. From Colesville, in Chesterfield county, by Halcomb's and Dennis's, to Amelia Courthouse, in lieu of the present route from Colesville to Amelia Courthouse. From Parkersburg, in Wood county, to Point Pleasant; that the route from Hopkins' tavern to Powhatan Courthouse, pass by way of Genito Bridge. That the Postmaster General be authorized to send a mail from Port Tobacco, in Maryland, to Hanover town, so long as a stage shall run on that route. From the town of Petersburg, Virginia, by the Double Bridges, and John Key's tavern, in the county of Lunenburg, to Charlotte Courthouse. From Williesburg, in Charlotte county, by Doctor Snead's; in Halifax county, to Cunningham's store, in Person county, North Carolina.

In Kentucky.—From Cynthiana, by Paris, and Winchester, to Richmond. From Isbelville to Clarksville, Tennessee. From Lexington to Georgetown. From Cincinnati, by Kennedy's, Gaines', and Arnold's, on the Ridge road, to Georgetown. From Glasgow to Allen Courthouse, and from Allen Courthouse to Bowling Green. From Middletown to Westport.

In North Carolina.—From Washington, by Bath, John Adams's, the Log House Landing, on Pungo river, and Germantown, to the Lake Landing, in Matamuskeet. From Tarborough to Cobb's Bridge, in Edgecomb county. From Bryant's Cross Roads to Windsor. From Tarborough to Scotland Neck. From Pittsborough, by Liberty, and Gardner's store, to Lexington.

In Tennessee.—From Nashville, by Harpeth Settlement, and Shelbyville, to Fayetteville. From Rhea Courthouse, by Highways Garrison, Ross Fort, and Fort Jackson, to Fort St. Stephens.

In South Carolina.—From Marion Courthouse, by Harleysville, to Marlborough, to return by Brownsville, to Marion Courthouse. From Cheraw Courthouse, by the Burnt Saw Mills, on Lynch's creek, Williamsburg Courthouse, and Murray's Ferry, on Santee, to Monk's Corner.

In the Mississippi Territory.—From the Choctaw agency, by John Ford's, on Pearl river, to New Orleans, in the State of Louisiana.

In the Illinois Territory.—From Johnson Courthouse to Salem, in Kentucky.

Approved, March 1, 1815.

An Act making appropriations for the support of the Military Establishment for the year one thousand eight hundred and fifteen.

Be it enacted, &c., That, for defraying the expenses of the Military Establishment of the United States, for the year one thousand eight hundred and fifteen, for ordnance, fortifications, and the Indian department, the following sums be, and the same are hereby, respectively, appropriated; that is to say:

For the pay of the Army of the United States, including the private servants kept by officers, nine hundred thousand dollars.

For forage to officers, one hundred and twenty-five thousand dollars.

For subsistence of the Army, seven hundred thousand dollars.

For the medical and hospital department, fifty thousand dollars.

For clothing, three hundred and twenty-five thousand dollars.

For the Quartermaster's department, two hundred thousand dollars.

For purchasing horses for artillery, one hundred thousand dollars.

For ordnance and ordnance stores, including arsenals, magazines, and armories, nine hundred and thirty-eight thousand three hundred and thirty-eight dollars.

For fortifications, four hundred thousand dollars.

For contingencies, two hundred thousand dollars.

For the Indian department, two hundred thousand dollars.

For advancing three months' pay to the officers deranged, and noncommissioned officers and privates discharged, one million two hundred thousand dollars.

SEC. 2. *And be it further enacted,* That the several appropriations hereinbefore made, shall

Public Acts of Congress.

be paid out of any moneys in the Treasury, not otherwise appropriated.

Approved, March 3, 1815.

An Act making further provision for completing the public buildings at West Point for the accommodation of the Military Academy.

Be it enacted, &c., That the sum of twenty thousand dollars be and the same is hereby appropriated, to be paid out of any money in the Treasury, not otherwise appropriated, for completing buildings, and for providing an apparatus, a library, and all necessary implements, and for such contingent expenses as may be necessary and proper, in the judgment of the President of the United States, for the better support and accommodation of the Military Academy at West Point.

Approved, March 3, 1815.

An Act making appropriations for the support of the Navy of the United States for the year one thousand eight hundred and fifteen.

Be it enacted, &c., That, for defraying the expenses of the Navy, for the year one thousand eight hundred and fifteen, the following sums be and are hereby, respectively, appropriated; that is to say:

For pay and subsistence of the officers, and pay of the seamen, one million five hundred thirty-eight thousand three hundred sixty-four dollars and fifty cents.

For provisions, six hundred and seventy-three thousand nine hundred and seventy-two dollars and fifty cents.

For medicine, hospital stores, and all expenses on account of the sick, forty thousand dollars.

For repairs of vessels, five hundred thousand dollars.

For contingent expenses, including freight, transportation, and recruiting expenses, five hundred and fifty thousand dollars.

For ordnance, ammunition, and military stores, three hundred thousand dollars.

For navy yards, docks, and wharves, one hundred and sixty thousand dollars.

For pay and subsistence of the Marine Corps, one hundred and ninety thousand and twenty dollars.

For clothing for the same, sixty thousand three hundred and fifty-seven dollars.

For military stores for the same, one thousand six hundred dollars.

For contingent expenses for the same, eighteen thousand seven hundred and eight dollars.

For the purchase of the vessels captured by Commodore Macdonough, on Lake Champlain, such sum as shall be agreed upon, with the approbation of the President, not exceeding four hundred thousand dollars.

SEC. 2. *And be it further enacted,* That the several appropriations hereinbefore made, shall be paid out of any moneys in the Treasury, not otherwise appropriated.

Approved, March 3, 1815.

An Act to repeal so much of the several acts imposing duties on the tonnage of ships and vessels, and on goods, wares, and merchandise, imported into the United States, as imposes a discriminating duty on tonnage, between foreign vessels and vessels of the United States, and between goods imported into the United States in foreign vessels and vessels of the United States.

Be it enacted, &c., That so much of the several acts imposing duties on the tonnage of ships and vessels, and on goods, wares, and merchandise, imported into the United States, as imposes a discriminating duty of tonnage, between foreign vessels and vessels of the United States, and between goods imported into the United States in foreign vessels and vessels of the United States, be, and the same are hereby, repealed, so far as the same respects the produce or manufacture of the nation to which such foreign ships or vessels may belong. Such repeal to take effect in favor of any foreign nation, whenever the President of the United States shall be satisfied that the discriminating or countervailing duties of such foreign nation, so far as they operate to the disadvantage of the United States, have been abolished.

Approved, March 3, 1815.

An Act for fixing the Military Peace Establishment of the United States.

Be it enacted, &c., That the Military Peace Establishment of the United States shall consist of such proportions of artillery, infantry, and riflemen, not exceeding, in the whole, ten thousand men, as the President of the United States shall judge proper, and that the corps of engineers, as at present established, be retained.

SEC. 2. *And be it further enacted,* That the corps of artillery shall have the same organization as is prescribed by the act passed the thirtieth of March, one thousand eight hundred and fourteen; and the regiment of light artillery the same organization as is prescribed by the act passed the twelfth day of April, one thousand eight hundred and eight; and that each regiment of infantry and riflemen shall consist of one colonel, one lieutenant colonel, one major, one adjutant, one quartermaster, one paymaster, one surgeon, and two surgeons' mates, one sergeant major, one quartermaster sergeant, two principal musicians, and ten companies; each company to consist of one captain, one first lieutenant, and one second lieutenant, four sergeants, four corporals, two musicians, and sixty-eight privates.

SEC. 3. *And be it further enacted,* That there shall be two major generals, and four brigadier generals: the major generals to be entitled to two aids-de-camp, and the brigadier generals to one aid-de-camp, each, to be taken from the subalterns of the line; four brigade inspectors, and four brigade quartermasters, and such number of hospital surgeons and surgeon's mates, as the service may require, not exceeding five surgeons and fifteen mates, with one steward and one wardmaster to each hospital. The brigade inspectors, appointed under this act, shall be taken from the line, and the brigade quartermasters, the adjutants, regimental quartermasters, and paymasters, from the subalterns of the line.

Sec. 4. *And be it further enacted,* That the compensation, subsistence, and clothing, of the officers, cadets, non-commissioned officers, musicians, artificers, and privates, composing the Military Peace Establishment, shall be the same as are prescribed by the act, entitled "An act fixing the Military Peace Establishment of the United States," passed sixteenth March, one thousand eight hundred and two, and the act, entitled "An act to raise, for a limited time, an additional military force," passed twelfth April, one thousand eight hundred and eight; and that the major generals shall be entitled to the same compensation as is provided by an act, entitled "An act to raise an additional military force," passed eleventh January, one thousand eight hundred and twelve.

Sec. 5. *And be it further enacted,* That the President of the United States cause to be arranged, the officers, non-commissioned officers, musicians, and privates, of the several corps of troops now in the service of the United States, in such a manner as to form and complete out of the same the corps authorized by this act, and cause the supernumerary officers, non-commissioned officers, musicians, and privates, to be discharged from the service of the United States, from and after the first day of May next, or as soon as circumstances may permit.

Sec. 6. *And be it further enacted,* That to each commissioned officer, who shall be deranged by virtue of this act, there shall be allowed and paid, in addition to the pay and emoluments to which they will be entitled by law at the time of his discharge, three months' pay.

Sec. 7. *And be it further enacted,* That the several corps authorized by this act, shall be subject to the rules and articles of war, be recruited in the same manner, and with the same limitations; and that officers, non-commissioned officers, musicians, and privates, shall be entitled to the same provision for wounds and disabilities, the same provision for widows and children, and the same benefits and allowances in every respect, not inconsistent with the provisions of this act, as are authorized by the act of sixteenth March, one thousand eight hundred and two, entitled "An act fixing the Military Peace Establishment of the United States," and the act of the 12th April, one thousand eight hundred and eight, entitled "An act to raise, for a limited time, an additional military force;" and that the bounty to the recruit, and compensation to the recruiting officer, shall be the same as are allowed by the aforesaid act of the the 12th of April, one thousand eight hundred and eight.

Approved, March 3, 1815.

An Act concerning Invalid Pensioners.

Be it enacted, &c., That the Secretary of War be, and he is hereby, directed to place the following named persons, whose claims have been trans-

mitted to Congress, pursuant to a law passed the tenth day of April, eighteen hundred and six, on the pension list of invalid pensioners of the United States, according to the rates, and to commence at the times, herein mentioned; that is to say:

Robert Holberd, at the rate of five dollars per month, to commence on the thirtieth day of March, one thousand eight hundred and fourteen.

Eli Short, at the rate of three dollars and seventy-five cents per month, to commence the thirtieth day of March, one thousand eight hundred and fourteen.

Spencer Darnell, at the rate of five dollars per month, to commence on the fourteenth day of February, eighteen hundred and fourteen.

Abraham Estes, at the rate of three dollars and seventy-five cents per month, to commence the seventeenth day of April, eighteen hundred and fourteen.

Willis Tandy, at the rate of one dollar and twenty-five cents per month, to commence the seventeenth day of April, eighteen hundred and fourteen.

Samuel Sharon, at the rate of two dollars and fifty cents per month, to commence the seventeenth day of August, eighteen hundred and fourteen.

Alexander Naismith, at the rate of two dollars and fifty cents per month, to commence the twentieth day of August, eighteen hundred and fourteen.

Isaac Gray, at the rate of six dollars and sixty-six cents per month, to commence the twenty-second day of September, eighteen hundred and fourteen.

Thomas Williams, at the rate of two dollars and fifty cents per month, to commence the twenty-seventh day of July, eighteen hundred and fourteen.

John R. Rappleye, at the rate of five dollars per month, to commence the second day of September, eighteen hundred and fourteen.

John Sweeny, at the rate of seven dollars and fifty cents per month, to commence the seventeenth of March, eighteen hundred and fourteen.

Joshua Merrill, at the rate of two dollars and fifty cents per month, to commence the fourth of August, eighteen hundred and fourteen.

Grieve Drummond, at the rate of five dollars per month, to commence the twenty-eighth day of January, eighteen hundred and fifteen.

John Ward, at the rate of two dollars and fifty cents per month, to commence the thirtieth of November, eighteen hundred and fourteen.

Charles Rumsey, at the rate of five dollars per month, to commence the twelfth day of July, eighteen hundred and fourteen.

Grant Taylor, at the rate of five dollars per month, to commence the twenty-fourth day of November, eighteen hundred and fourteen.

Henry Bateman, at the rate of five dollars per month, to commence the seventeenth day of March, eighteen hundred and fourteen.

John Norton, at the rate of two dollars and fifty cents per month, to commence the second day of May, eighteen hundred and fourteen.

Jesse Young, at the rate of five dollars per month, to commence the sixth day of August, one thousand eight hundred and fourteen.

Daniel Averill, at the rate of two dollars and fifty cents per month, to commence the third day of January, eighteen hundred and fourteen.

John Bell, at the rate of ten dollars per month, to commence the ninth day of September, eighteen hundred and fourteen.

Minny Ryneason, at the rate of two dollars and fifty cents per month, to commence the sixth day of January, eighteen hundred and fifteen.

William Bond, at the rate of five dollars per month, to commence the eighth day of December, eighteen hundred and fourteen.

Richard Osburn, at the rate of two dollars and fifty cents per month, to commence the fifth day of September, eighteen hundred and fourteen.

Julius Turner, at the rate of three dollars and seventy-five cents per month, to commence the eighteenth day of August, eighteen hundred and fourteen.

William Cook, at the rate of two dollars and fifty cents per month, to commence the eighteenth day of August, eighteen hundred and fourteen.

John Frazer, at the rate of three dollars and seventy-five cents per month, to commence the sixteenth day of November, eighteen hundred and fourteen.

Christopher Sites, at the rate of two dollars and fifty cents per month, to commence the seventeenth day of February, eighteen hundred and fifteen.

William Barton, at the rate of thirty dollars per month, to commence the first day of January, eighteen hundred and fifteen.

William Berry, at the rate of five dollars per month, to commence the thirty-first day of March, eighteen hundred and fourteen.

James McNeal, at the rate of five dollars per month, to commence on the thirteenth day of September, eighteen hundred and fourteen.

Emanuel Kent, junior, at the rate of five dollars per month, to commence the thirteenth day of September, eighteen hundred and fourteen.

Jeremiah Searcy, of South Carolina, at the rate of five dollars per month, to commence from the third of March, eighteen hundred and fifteen.

Sec. 2. *And be it further enacted,* That the pensions of the following persons, already placed on the pension list of the United States, whose claims for an increase of pension have been transmitted to Congress pursuant to the act aforesaid, be increased to the sums herein respectively annexed to their names. The said increase to commence at the times herein mentioned; that is to say:

Charles Hunton, at the rate of two dollars and fifty cents per month, to commence the fourteenth day of November, eighteen hundred and fourteen.

Thomas Williams, at the rate of five dollars per month, to commence the twenty-ninth of October, eighteen hundred and fourteen.

Samuel White, at the rate of three dollars and seventy-five cents per month, to commence the twenty-eighth day of December, eighteen hundred and fourteen.

Thomas Machin, at the rate of twenty dollars per month, to commence the twenty-ninth day of October, eighteen hundred and fourteen.

John McClennon, at the rate of five dollars per month, to commence the third day of November, eighteen hundred and fourteen.

Richard Gressum, at the rate of five dollars per month, to commence the eighth day of November, eighteen hundred and fourteen.

Approved, March 3, 1815.

An Act to provide a library room, and for transporting the library lately purchased.

Be it enacted, &c., That the President of the United States be, and he is hereby, authorized to cause a proper apartment to be immediately selected and prepared for a library room, and to cause the library, lately purchased from Thomas Jefferson, to be placed therein during the ensuing recess of Congress.

Sec. 2. *And be it further enacted,* That the accounting officers of the Treasury be, and they are hereby, authorized and directed to settle the account of the expenditures incurred under this act; and that the amount so settled shall be paid out of any moneys in the Treasury, not otherwise appropriated.

Approved, March 3, 1815.

An Act concerning the Naval Establishment.

Be it enacted, &c., That in addition to the sums heretofore appropriated for that purpose, the sum of two hundred thousand dollars be, and the same is hereby, appropriated, annually, for three years, towards the purchase and supply of a stock of every description of timber required for ship building, and other naval purposes, to be paid out of any moneys in the Treasury, not otherwise appropriated.

Approved. March 3, 1815.

An Act to repeal certain acts therein mentioned.

Be it enacted, &c., That all acts, or parts of acts, which prohibit the entrance of the vessels of any foreign nation into the harbors or waters under the jurisdiction of the United States, be, and the same are hereby, repealed.

Sec. 2. *And be it further enacted,* That the "Act to prohibit American vessels from proceeding to, or trading with, the enemies of the United States, and for other purposes," passed the sixth day of July, eighteen hundred and twelve, be, and the same is hereby, repealed.

Sec. 3. *And be it further enacted,* That the "Act to prohibit the use of licenses or passes, granted by the authority of the Government of the United Kingdom of Great Britain and Ireland," passed the second day of August, eighteen hundred and thirteen, be, and the same is hereby, repealed.

Public Acts of Congress.

Sec. 4. *And be it further enacted,* That all penalties and forfeitures which have been incurred by virtue of the acts, or parts of acts, repealed, shall be hereby recovered and distributed in like manner as if the same had continued in full force.

Approved, March 3, 1815.

An Act increasing the compensation allowed the Sergeants-at-Arms of the Senate and House of Representatives, and of the Doorkeeper and Assistant Doorkeeper of the Senate and House of Representatives.

Be it enacted, &c., That, in addition to the sum already allowed by law to the Sergeants-at-Arms of the Senate and House of Representatives, and the Doorkeeper and Assistant Doorkeeper of the Senate and House of Representatives, be entitled to receive, annually, the sum of five hundred and fifty dollars, respectively, and that the additional compensation here allowed be considered to take effect from the first day of January, one thousand eight hundred and fourteen.

Approved, March 3, 1815.

An Act to authorize a loan for a sum not exceeding eighteen millions four hundred and fifty-two thousand eight hundred dollars.

Be it enacted, &c., That the President of the United States be, and he is hereby, authorized to borrow, on the credit of the United States, a sum not exceeding eighteen millions four hundred fifty-two thousand eight hundred dollars, to be applied, in addition to the moneys now in the Treasury, or which may be received from other sources, to defray any expenses which have been, or, during the present year, may be, authorized by law, and for which appropriations have been, or, during the present year, may be, made by law: *Provided,* That no engagement or contract shall be entered into, which shall preclude the United States from reimbursing any sum or sums thus borrowed, at any time after the expiration of twelve years from the last day of December next.

Sec. 2. *And be it further enacted,* That the Secretary of the Treasury, with the approbation of the President of he United States, be, and he is hereby, authorized to cause to be constituted certificates of stock, signed by the Register of the Treasury, or by a commissioner of loans, for the sum to be borrowed by this act, or for any part thereof, and the same to be sold. And the Secretary of the Treasury shall lay before Congress, during the first week in the month of February, one thousand eight hundred and sixteen, an account of all the moneys obtained by the sale of the certificates of stock, in manner aforesaid, together with a statement of the rate at which the same may have been sold.

Sec. 3. *And be it further enacted,* That the Secretary of the Treasury be, and he is hereby, authorized, with the approbation of the President of the United States, to employ an agent or agents, for the purpose of obtaining subscriptions to the loan authorized by this act, or of selling any part of the stock to be created by virtue thereof. A commission, not exceeding one-quarter of one per centum, on the amount thus sold, or for which subscriptions shall have been thus obtained, may, by the Secretary of the Treasury, be allowed to such agent or agents; and a sum not exceeding thirty thousand dollars, to be paid out of any moneys in the Treasury, not otherwise appropriated, is hereby appropriated, for paying the amount of such commission or commissions as may be thus allowed, and also for defraying the expenses of printing and issuing the subscription certificates, and certificates of stock, and other expenses incident to the completing of the loan authorized by this act.

Sec. 4. *And be it further enacted,* That so much of the funds constituting the annual appropriation of eight millions of dollars, for the payment of the principal and interest of the public debt of the United States, as may be wanted for that purpose, after satisfying the necessary sums for the payment of the interest, and such part of the principal, of the said debt, as the United States are now pledged annually to pay or reimburse, is hereby pledged and appropriated for the payment of the interest, and for the reimbursement of the principal, of the stock which may be created by virtue of this act. It shall, accordingly, be the duty of the Commissioners of the Sinking Fund, to cause to be applied and paid, out of the said fund, yearly, such sum and sums as may be annually wanted to discharge the interest accruing on the said stock, and to reimburse the principal, as the same may become due and may be discharged in conformity with the terms of the loan. And they are further authorized to apply, from time to time, such sum or sums, out of the said fund, as they may think proper, towards redeeming, by purchase, and at a price not above par, the principal of the said stock, or any part thereof. And the faith of the United States is hereby pledged to establish sufficient revenues for making good any deficiency that may hereafter take place in the funds hereby appropriated for paying the said interest and principal sums, or any of them, in manner aforesaid.

Sec. 5. *And be it further enacted,* That it shall be lawful for any of the banks in the District of Columbia, to lend any part of the sum authorized to be borrowed by virtue of this act, anything in any of their charters to the contrary notwithstanding.

Sec. 6. *And be it further enacted,* That it shall be lawful for the Secretary of the Treasury to accept, in payment of any loan obtained in virtue of this act, such Treasury notes as have been actually issued before the passing of this act, and which were made by law a charge upon the sinking fund, such Treasury notes to be credited for the principal thereof and the amount of interest actually accrued at the time of the payment.

Sec. 7. *And be it further enacted,* That it shall be lawful for the Secretary of the Treasury to cause to be paid the interest upon the Treasury notes which have become due, and remain unpaid, as well with respect to the time elapsed before they became due, as with respect to the time that shall elapse after they become due, and until funds shall be assigned for the payment of the said Treasury notes, and notice thereof shall be given by the Secretary of the Treasury.

Approved, March 3, 1815.

An Act to provide for the ascertaining and surveying of the boundary lines fixed by the Treaty with the Creek Indians, and for other purposes.

Be it enacted, &c., That the President of the United States be, and he is hereby, authorized to cause to be ascertained and surveyed the boundary line designated by the Treaty with the Creek nation of Indians, concluded on the ninth day of August, one thousand eight hundred and fourteen; and that the same be distinctly marked, in all such places, except where water-courses are described, as the boundary by the said treaty; and for this purpose the President of the United States shall have power to appoint, by and with the advice and consent of the Senate, three commissioners, whose compensation shall not exceed, exclusive of travelling expenses, the rate of eight dollars per day, during the time of actual service of such commissioners, in ascertaining and surveying the said boundary line; they shall have power to employ a skilful surveyor, who shall be allowed five dollars per day, and two chainmen and a marker, who shall each be allowed two dollars per day, in full for their services.

Sec. 2. *And be it further enacted,* That the said commissioners, on completing the ascertainment and survey aforesaid, shall make out three accurate plats of the survey of the said boundary line, one of which they shall transmit to the Secretary of State, one to the Surveyor of the lands south of the State of Tennessee, and the other to the Chiefs of the Creek nation of Indians.

Sec. 3. *And be it further enacted,* That all the public lands of the United States to which the Indian title was extinguished by the aforesaid treaty, shall be, and are hereby, formed into a land district; and for the disposal thereof a land office shall be established, which shall be kept at such convenient place as the President of the United States may direct; and, for the said land office, a register, and receiver of public moneys, shall be appointed, who shall give security in the same manner, in the same sums, and whose compensation, emoluments, duties, and authority, shall, in every respect, be the same, in relation to the lands which shall be disposed of at their office, as are or may be provided by law in relation to the registers and receivers of public moneys, in the several land offices established for the disposal of the other public lands of the United States.

Sec. 4. *And be it further enacted,* That the powers vested by law in the Surveyor of the lands of the United States south of the State of Tennessee, shall extend over all the public lands of the United States to which the Indian title was extinguished by the aforesaid treaty, and the same shall be surveyed in the manner, and for the same compensation, as other public lands in the Mississippi Territory.

Sec. 5. *And be it further enacted,* That the President of the United States is hereby authorized, whenever he shall think it proper, to direct so much of the public lands, lying in the said district, as shall have been surveyed in conformity to this act, to be offered for sale. All such lands shall, with the exception of the section numbered sixteen, which shall be reserved in each township for the support of schools within the same, with exception also of one entire township, to be located by the Secretary of the Treasury, for the use of a seminary of learning, and with the exception of any tracts of land reserved to the Indians by the said treaty, shall be offered to the highest bidder, under the direction of the register and receiver of public moneys of the said land office, on such day or days as shall, by a public proclamation of the President of the United States, be designated for that purpose. The public sales shall remain open for three weeks, and no longer; and the lands shall be sold for a price not less than that which has been, or may be, fixed by law, for the public lands in the Mississippi Territory; and shall, in every other respect, be sold in tracts of the same size, on the same terms and conditions, as have been, or may be, by law provided for the other public lands in the Mississippi Territory. The superintendents of the said public sales shall receive six dollars, each, for each day's attendance on the said sales. All lands, other than those reserved as aforesaid, and excepted as abovementioned, remaining unsold at the closing of the public sales, and which had been offered at the said sales, may be disposed of at private sale, by the register of the land office, in the same manner, under the same regulations, for the same price, and on the same terms and conditions, as are or may be provided by law for the sale of the other public lands of the United States in the Mississippi Territory. And patents shall be obtained for the lands sold in the said district in the same manner, and on the same terms, as for other public lands sold in the Mississippi Territory.

Sec. 6. *And be it further enacted,* That the President of the United States shall have power to appoint any or all of the aforesaid commissioners during the recess of the Senate.

Sec. 7. *And be it further enacted,* That a sum, not exceeding twenty-five thousand dollars, be, and the same is hereby, appropriated, to be paid out of any moneys in the Treasury, not otherwise appropriated, for the purpose of carrying this act into effect.

Approved, March 3, 1815.

An Act authorizing the purchase of the Vessels captured on Lake Champlain.

Be it enacted, &c., That the President of the United States be and he is hereby authorized to cause to be purchased the British vessels which were captured on Lake Champlain by the American squadron, on the eleventh day of September, in the year eighteen hundred and fourteen; and the amount of the valuation of such captured vessels, when duly made and returned to the

Navy Department, shall be distributed as prize money among the captors or their heirs.

Approved, March 3, 1815.

An Act for the protection of the Commerce of the United States against the Algerine Cruisers.

Whereas the Dey of Algiers, on the coast of Barbary, has commenced a predatory warfare against the United States—

Be it enacted, &c., That it shall be lawful fully to equip, officer, man, and employ, such of the armed vessels of the United States as may be judged requisite by the President of the United States for protecting effectually the commerce and seamen thereof on the Atlantic ocean, the Mediterranean, and adjoining seas.

Sec. 2. *And be it further enacted,* That it shall be lawful for the President of the United States to instruct the commanders of the respective public vessels aforesaid, to subdue, seize, and make prize of, all vessels, goods, and effects, of or belonging to the Dey of Algiers, or to his subjects, and to bring or send the same into port, to be proceeded against and distributed according to law; and, also, to cause to be done all such other acts of precaution or hostility, as the state of war will justify, and may, in his opinion, require.

Sec. 3. *And be it further enacted,* That, on the application of the owners of private armed vessels of the United States, the President of the United States may grant them special commissions, in the form which he shall direct, under the seal of the United States; and such private armed vessels, when so commissioned, shall have the like authority for subduing, seizing, taking, and bringing into port, any Algerine vessel, goods, or effects, as the beforementioned public armed vessels may by law have; and shall therein be subject to the instructions which may be given by the President of the United States for the regulation of their conduct; and their commissions shall be revocable at his pleasure: *Provided,* That before any commission shall be granted as aforesaid, the owner or owners of the vessels for which the same may be requested, and the commander thereof for the time being, shall give bond to the United States, with at least two responsible sureties, not interested in such vessel, in the penal sum of seven thousand dollars, or, if such vessel be provided with more than one hundred and fifty men, in the penal sum of fourteen thousand dollars, with condition for observing the treaties and laws of the United States, and the instructions which may be given as aforesaid, and also for satisfying all damages and injuries which shall be done contrary to the tenor thereof, by such commissioned vessel, and for delivering up the commission when revoked by the President of the United States.

Sec. 4. *And be it further enacted,* That any Algerine vessel, goods, or effects, which may be so captured and brought into port, by any private armed vessel of the United States, duly commissioned as aforesaid, may be adjudged good prize, and thereupon shall accrue to the owners, and officers, and men, of the capturing vessel, and shall be distributed according to the agreement which shall have been made between them, or, in failure of such agreement, according to the discretion of the court having cognizance of the capture.

Approved, March 3, 1815.

An Act to amend the act, entitled "An act to provide additional revenues for defraying the expenses of Government, and maintaining the public credit, by laying a direct tax upon the United States, and to provide for assessing and collecting the same," and the act, entitled "An act to provide additional revenues for defraying the expenses of Government, and maintaining the public credit, by laying duties on household furniture, and on gold and silver watches."

Be it enacted, &c., That, instead of the first day of February next, prescribed, by the "act to provide additional revenues for defraying the expenses of Government, and maintaining the public credit, by laying a direct tax upon the United States, and to provide for assessing and collecting the same," to the principal assessors to direct and cause the several assistant assessors to inquire after and concerning all lands and other objects taxed, the first day of April next be and the same is hereby prescribed for that purpose. And that the time prescribed, in the thirty-sixth section of the said act, to the Secretary of the Treasury, to notify the collectors of the several collection districts to proceed to the collection of the direct tax, after the current year, shall be some day in the month of May, instead of the month of February.

Sec. 2. *And be it further enacted,* That the thirteenth section of the "act to provide additional revenues for defraying the expenses of Government, and maintaining the public credit, by laying duties on household furniture, and on gold and silver watches," be, and the same is hereby, so amended, as that the several acts required to be performed previously to or during the month of February, in any year, may and shall be performed previously to or during the month of May, in any year, as the case may be, which last month, instead of February, shall be taken as the time referred to therein for taking the lists of property under a general assessment; and it shall be the duty of the principal assessor, in every year, within thirty days after the expiration of the said month of May, to make out and deliver to the collector, the lists as is required to be rendered by the said last mentioned act, to which this act is a supplement, and the like alteration hereby made in the tenth section of the said act shall and hereby is made in the other sections thereof, so far as any acts depending thereon are thereby required to be done.

Sec. 3. *And be it further enacted,* That a publication to be made by the collectors, to be designated by the Secretary of the Treasury for that purpose, as prescribed and required in the twenty-eighth and twenty-ninth sections of the act to which this act is a supplement, shall, in stead of being printed for sixty days, in at least one newspaper published in the State, as therein provided, be printed, at least once a week, for eight weeks in succession, in every newspaper within the State in which the laws of the United States are by public authority published; and for which printing the Secretary of the Treasury shall be and he is hereby authorized to pay and allow a price proportionate to the price of the other public printing done in said papers, and no more.

Approved, March 3, 1815.

An Act authorizing the Board of Navy Commissioners to appoint Clerks.

Be it enacted, &c., That the Board of Navy Commissioners be, and they are hereby, authorized to appoint two clerks, to be attached to their office, who shall receive for their services a sum not exceeding one thousand dollars each per annum.

SEC. 2. *And be it further enacted,* That for this purpose the sum of two thousand dollars is hereby appropriated, to be paid out of any moneys in the Treasury, not otherwise appropriated.

Approved, March 3, 1815.

An Act further to provide for the collection of duties on Imports and Tonnage.

Be it enacted, &c., That it shall be lawful for any collector, naval officer, surveyor, or inspector, of the customs, as well in an adjoining district as that to which he belongs, to enter on board, search, and examine, any ship, vessel, boat, or raft, and if he shall find on board the same any goods, wares, or merchandise, which he shall have probable cause to believe are subject to duty, the payment of which is intended to be evaded, or have been imported into the United States in any manner contrary to law, it shall be his duty to seize and secure the same for trial.

SEC. 2. *And be it further enacted,* That it shall be lawful for any collector, naval officer, surveyor, or inspector of the customs, as well in any adjoining district as that to which he belongs, to stop, search, and examine, any carriage or vehicle, of any kind whatsoever, and to stop any person travelling on foot, or beast of burden, on which he shall suspect there are goods, wares, or merchandise, which are subject to duty, or which shall have been introduced into the United States in any manner contrary to law; and if such officer shall find any goods, wares, or merchandise, on any such carriage, vehicle, person travelling on foot, or beast of burden, which he shall have probable cause to believe are subject to duty, or have been unlawfully introduced into the United States, he shall seize and secure the same for trial. And if any of the said officers of the customs shall suspect that any goods, wares, or merchandise, which are subject to duty, or shall have been introduced into the United States contrary to law, are concealed in any particular dwelling-house, store, or other building, he shall,

upon proper application, on oath, to any judge or justice of the peace, be entitled to a warrant, directed to such officer, who is hereby authorized to serve the same, to enter such house, store, or other building, in the day time only, and there to search and examine whether there are any goods, wares, or merchandise, which are subject to duty, or have been unlawfully imported; and if, on such search or examination, any such goods, wares, or merchandise, shall be found, which there shall be probable cause for the officer making such search or examination to believe are subject to duty, or have been unlawfully introduced into the United States, he shall seize and secure the same for trial: *Provided always,* That the necessity of a search warrant, arising under this act, shall, in no case, be considered as applicable to any carriage, wagon, cart, sleigh, vessel, boat, or other vehicle, of whatever form or construction, employed as a medium of transportation, or to packages on any animal or animals, or carried by man on foot.

SEC. 3. *And be it further enacted,* That every collector of the customs shall have authority, with the approbation of the principal officer of the Treasury Department, to employ, within his district, such number of proper persons, as inspectors of the customs, as he shall judge necessary, who are hereby declared to be officers of the customs; and the said inspectors, before they enter on the duties of their offices, shall take and subscribe, before the collectors appointing them, or before some magistrate within their respective districts, authorized by law to administer oaths, the following oath or affirmation, to wit: " I, ————, having been appointed an inspector of the customs, within and for the district of ——, do solemnly, sincerely, and truly, swear, (or affirm. as the case may be,) that I will diligently and faithfully execute the duties of the said office of inspector, and will use my best endeavors to prevent and detect frauds and violations against the laws of the United States. I further swear (or affirm) that I will support the Constitution of the United States."

SEC. 4. *And be it further enacted,* That any collector, naval officer, surveyor, or inspector, when proceeding to make any search or seizure, authorized by this act, shall be, and he is hereby, empowered to command any person who shall be within ten miles of the place where such search or seizure shall be made, to aid and assist such officer in the discharge of his duty therein; and if any person, being so commanded, shall neglect or refuse to aid and assist such officer in making such search or seizure, the person so neglecting or refusing shall forfeit and pay a sum not exceeding two hundred dollars, and not less than fifty dollars. And such officer may also demand, in cases of resistance, the assistance of the marshal of the district or any of his deputies, who shall call upon the posse of the district, if necessary, in his or their judgment, to render effectual the execution of this act; and all citizens or inhabitants of the district, above the age of eighteen years, and able to travel, who refuse or neglect, upon proper notice from the marshal, or any of his deputies, to join such posse, shall be considered guilty of a misdemeanor, and be liable to be fined in any sum not exceeding three hundred dollars, and be imprisoned for any term not exceeding three months.

Sec. 5. *And be it further enacted,* That the forfeitures and penalties mentioned in this act, shall be sued for, prosecuted, and recovered, or inflicted, by action of debt, or by information or indictment, in any court competent to take cognizance thereof and try the same; and that all forfeitures and penalties, so recovered by virtue of this act, shall, after deducting all proper costs and charges, be disposed of as follows: one moiety shall be for the use of the United States, and paid into the Treasury thereof by the collector recovering the same; the other moiety shall be divided between, and paid in equal proportions to, the collector and naval officer of the district and surveyor of the port, wherein the same shall have been incurred, to such of the said officers as there may be in the said district: and in districts where only one of the aforesaid offices shall have been established, the said moiety shall be given to such officer: *Provided,* That where the seizure shall have been made by any inspector or inspectors out of the presence of the collector, naval officer, or surveyor, such inspector or inspectors shall be entitled, in addition to such other compensation as may be allowed them, to twenty-five per cent. on the moiety herein given to the collector, naval officer, and surveyor, as aforesaid, or to either of them: *And provided also,* That in all cases where such forfeitures and penalties shall be recovered, in pursuance of information given to such collector, naval officer, or surveyor, by any private informer, the one-half of such moiety shall be given to such informer, and the remainder thereof shall be disposed of between the collector, naval officer, and surveyor, in manner aforesaid, and the same allowance of twenty-five per cent. to inspectors, when the seizure is made by them as aforesaid: *And provided likewise,* That whenever the value of the property seized, condemned, and sold, under this act, shall be less than two hundred and fifty dollars, that part of the forfeiture which accrues to the United States, or so much thereof as may be necessary, shall be applied to the payment of the costs of prosecution: *And it is further provided,* That if any officer or other person, entitled to a part or share of any of the penalties or forfeitures incurred in virtue of this act, shall be necessary as a witness on the trial for such penalty or forfeiture, such officer or other person may be a witness upon the said trial, but in such case he shall not receive or be entitled to any part or share of the said penalty or forfeiture; and the part or share, to which he otherwise would have been entitled, shall revert to the United States.

Sec. 6. *And be it further enacted,* That if any suit or prosecution be commenced in any State court against any collector, naval officer, surveyor, inspector, or any other officer civil or military, or any other person aiding or assisting agreeable to the provisions of this act, or under

color thereof, for anything done, or omitted to be done, as an officer of the customs, or for anything done by virtue of this act, or under color thereof and the defendant shall, at the time of entering his appearance in such court, file a petition for the removal of the cause for trial at the next circuit court of the United States, to be holden in the district where the suit is pending, and offer good and sufficient surety for his entering in such court, on the first day of its session, copies of said process against him, and also for his there appearing at the court and entering special bail in the cause, if special bail was originally required therein, it shall then be the duty of the State court to accept the surety, and proceed no farther in the cause, and the bail that shall have been originally taken shall be discharged: and such copies being entered as aforesaid in such court of the United States, the cause shall there proceed in the same manner as if it had been brought there by original process, whatever may be the amount of the sum in dispute or damages claimed, or whatever the citizenship of the parties, any former law to the contrary notwithstanding; and any attachment of the goods or estate of the defendant by the original process, shall hold the goods or estate so attached to answer the final judgment, in the same manner as *by the laws of such State* they would have been holden to answer the final judgment had it been rendered by the court in which the suit was commenced. And it shall be lawful, in any action or prosecution which may be now pending, or hereafter commenced, before any State court whatever, for anything done, or omitted to be done, by the defendant, as an inspector or other officer of the customs, after final judgment, for either party to remove and transfer by appeal, such decision, during the session or term of said court at which the same shall have taken place, from such court to the next circuit court of the United States, to be held in the district in which such appeal shall be taken in manner aforesaid; and it shall be the duty of the person taking such appeal, to produce and enter in the said circuit court attested copies of the process, proceedings, and judgment in such cause; and it shall also be competent for either party, within six months of the rendition of a judgment in any such cause, by writ of error, or other process, to the circuit court of the United States of that district in which such judgment shall have been rendered; and the said court shall thereupon proceed to try and determine the facts and the law in such action, in the same manner as if the same had been there originally commenced, the judgment in such case notwithstanding. And any bail which may have been taken, or property attached, shall be holden on the final judgment of the said circuit court in such action in the same manner as if no such removal or transfer had been made as aforesaid. And any State court from which any such action may be removed and transferred as aforesaid, upon the party's giving good and sufficient security for the prosecution thereof, shall allow the same to be removed and transferred, and proceed no farther

Public Acts of Congress.

in the case : *Provided, however,* That if the party aforesaid shall fail duly to enter the removal and transfer as aforesaid in the circuit court, agreeable to this act, the State court, by which judgment shall have been rendered, and from which the transfer and removal shall have been made as aforesaid, shall be authorized, on motion for that purpose, to issue execution, and to carry into effect any such judgment, the same as if no such removal and transfer had been made : *Provided, nevertheless,* That this act shall not be construed to apply to any prosecution for an offence involving corporal punishment. *And provided also,* That no such appeal shall be allowed in any criminal action or prosecution, where final judgment shall have been rendered in favor of the defendant or respondent, by the State court ; and in any action or prosecution against any person as aforesaid, it shall be lawful for such person to plead the general issue, and give this act, and any special matter in evidence. And if in any suit the plaintiff is nonsuit, or judgment pass against him, the defendant shall recover double costs.

Sec. 7. *And be it further enacted,* That in any suit or prosecution against any person, for any act or thing done as an officer of the customs, or any person aiding or assisting such officer therein, and judgment shall be given against the defendant, or respondent, if it shall appear to the court, before which such suit or prosecution shall be tried, that there was probable cause for doing such act or thing, such court shall order a proper certificate or entry to be made thereof, and in such case the defendant or respondent shall not be liable for costs, nor shall he be liable to execution, or to any action for damages, or to any other mode of prosecution, for the act done by him as aforesaid : *Provided,* That such property or articles as may be held in custody by the defendant, if any, be, after judgment, forthwith returned to the claimant or claimants, his, her, or their agent or agents.

Sec. 8. *And be it further enacted,* That this act shall continue in force for one year, and no longer ; *Provided,* That all fines, penalties, and forfeitures, which shall have been incurred before the expiration of the act, shall be recovered and distributed, and may be mitigated or remitted, in the same manner as if it had not expired.

Approved, March 3, 1815.

An Act supplementary to an act, entitled "An act for the better organization of the Courts of the United States, within the State of New York."

Be it enacted, &c., That the President of the United States, by and with the advice and consent of the Senate, be, and hereby is authorized to appoint one person as marshal, and one as district attorney, for the northern judicial district of the United States within the State of New York, created by the act to which this act is a supplement, bearing date the ninth day of April, in the year one thousand eight hundred and fourteen ; and that the terms of appointment and service, together with the duties, responsibilities, and emoluments of the said marshal and district at-

torney, respectively, for the district aforesaid, be, in all respects, the same, within their said district, as the terms of appointment and service, the duties, responsibilities, and emoluments of all other marshals and district attorneys, respectively, within their respective districts in the United States of America.

Approved, March 3, 1815.

An Act making additional appropriation for the service of the year one thousand eight hundred and fifteen.

Be it enacted, &c., That, for defraying the expense of preparing certificates of registry for ships and vessels, and for furnishing lists of crews, the sum of five thousand dollars be, and the same are hereby, appropriated, to be paid out of any money in the Treasury, not otherwise appropriated.

Approved, March 3, 1815.

An Act further supplementary to an act, entitled "An act providing for the indemnification of certain claimants of public lands in the Mississippi Territory."

Be it enacted, &c., That the commissioners appointed by virtue of the act, entitled "An act supplementary to an act, entitled 'An act providing for the indemnification of certain claimants of public lands in the Mississippi Territory,'" shall be, and they are hereby, authorized to decide, in a summary way, upon the quantity or boundary of land contained in any grant or deed exhibited before them, by any of the claimants of lands released to the United States, agreeably to the said act, according to such maps, surveys, or other evidence, as now exist, or which they may be now able to procure, without requiring or permitting any other survey to be made.

Sec. 2. *And be it further enacted,* That the said commissioners shall be, and they are hereby, authorized to allow and receive, in all cases, except those where femmes couvertes are parties, as sufficient legal releases, assignments, and powers, required by said act, and the supplement thereto, and as lawful conveyances, all such instruments as may be executed by the party, or his, her, or their attorney or attorneys, lawfully empowered, and either acknowledged by the party making the same, before some judge, or justice of the peace, notary public, mayor, recorder, or alderman, of a corporation, or master in chancery, or one of the said commissioners, or proved, by other evidence, to the satisfaction of the commissioners, to have been duly executed by the party.

Sec. 3. *And be it further enacted,* That the said commissioners shall be, and they are hereby, authorized, in all cases where the releases, assignments, and powers, required by the act aforesaid, already presented, or which may be presented on or before the third Monday in March instant, or powers of attorney by which said releases shall have been, or shall be, made, shall be, in the judgment of the commissioners aforesaid, defectively drawn or executed, to allow a further time, not exceeding two months, from and after the said third Monday in March instant, to perfect the same.

Public Acts of Congress.

Sec. 4. *And be it further enacted,* That the said commissioners shall be, and they are hereby, authorized to admit and finally settle all such claims as have been, or may be, within the time limited, duly released, assigned, and transferred, to the United States, anything in the said original act, or any supplement thereto, to the contrary notwithstanding ; and to administer oaths, or take affirmations, and to compel the attendance of witnesses, in all cases where necessary.

Sec. 5. *And be it further enacted,* That the President of the United States shall be, and he is hereby, authorized, from time to time, to cause to be issued such certificates of stock as are specified in the said original act, and supplement thereto, to such claimant or claimants, whose claim may be decided on and reported by the commissioners, on receiving such report, in relation to such claim, from the said commissioners.

Sec. 6. *And be it further enacted,* That the releases, assignments, and powers, required by the act aforesaid, and the supplement thereto, now received, and which may be hereafter received, shall be recorded by the secretary of the said commissioners, and the said records returned, with all other papers and documents in relation to said claims, when the business of the said commissioners shall be closed, to the office of the Secretary of State ; and that the said secretary shall be paid by the Secretary of the Treasury of the United States, out of any money not otherwise appropriated, at the rate of twelve and a half cents for each and every hundred words contained in each instrument so recorded.

Sec. 7. *And be it further enacted,* That on the dissolution of the said board of commissioners, and the performance of the duties assigned them, the President of the United States shall be, and he is hereby, authorized, if in his judgment he shall consider the said commissioners entitled to any further additional compensation for their services than is now provided for, to cause them to be paid such other and further sums, out of any money in the Treasury not otherwise appropriated, as he shall think just and reasonable : *Provided,* That such additional compensation shall not exceed fifty cents to each commissioner, for every deed or evidence of title which shall be submitted to their examination and decision, in pursuance of the provisions of the said original act, and the supplements thereto.

Approved, March 3, 1815.

An Act regulating and defining the duties of the United States' Judges for the Territory of Illinois.

Be it enacted, &c., That the Illinois Territory shall be divided into three circuits, in the manner, and for the purposes, hereinafter mentioned.

Sec. 2. *And be it further enacted,* That the counties of Madison and St. Clair shall compose the first circuit, the counties of Randolph and Johnson shall compose the second circuit, and the counties of Gallatin and Edwards shall compose the third circuit.

Sec. 3. *And be it further enacted,* That the judges heretofore appointed. or which may hereafter be appointed, for the Illinois Territory, under the authority of the Government of the United States, shall, previous to the time prescribed by this act for holding the first court in the said Territory, proceed to allot amongst themselves the circuit in which they shall respectively preside, which allotment shall continue in force for and during the term of one year thereafter; and such allotment shall be annually renewed ; and which allotment, in writing, signed by the said judges, or a majority of them, shall be entered of record in the said courts, respectively, by the clerks thereof, at the commencement of the term next after such allotment shall have been made.

Sec. 4. *And be it further enacted,* That it shall be the duty of the said judges, respectively, to hold two terms annually in each county in their respective circuits, in conformity with the preceding sections of this act, which shall commence at the times hereinafter mentioned, that is to say : in the county of Madison, on the last Mondays in May and September; in the county of St. Clair, on the second Mondays in June and October; in the county of Randolph, on the third Mondays in June and October; in the county of Johnson, on the fourth Mondays in June and October; *in the* county of Gallatin, on the first *Mondays in July* and November; and, in the *county of Edwards,* on the second Mondays in July and November, in each year ; and the said courts shall be styled Circuit Courts for the counties in which such courts shall be held, respectively.

Sec. 5. *And be it further enacted,* That the said courts shall be holden at the respective courthouses of said counties ; and the said judges, respectively, shall, in their respective circuits, have jurisdiction over all causes, matters, or things, at common law or in chancery, arising in each of said counties, except in cases where the debt or demand shall be under twenty dollars, in which cases they shall have no jurisdiction.

Sec. 6. *And be it further enacted,* That the said judges shall be conservators of the peace, and the said circuit courts, in term time, or the judges thereof in vacation, shall have power to award injunctions, writs of ne exeat, habeas corpus, and all other writs and process that may be necessary to the execution of the power with which they are or may be vested.

Sec. 7. *And be it further enacted,* That the said circuit courts, respectively, shall have power to hear and determine all treasons, felonies. and other crimes and misdemeanors, that may be committed within the respective counties aforesaid. and that may be brought before them, respectively, by any rules or regulations prescribed by law.

Sec. 8. *And be it further enacted,* That a suits shall be tried in the counties in which the originate, unless in cases that are or may be specially provided for by law.

Sec. 9. *And be it further enacted,* That if the circuit judge shall not attend on the first day of any court, or if a quorum of the court hereafter mentioned shall not attend in like manner, such court shall stand adjourned from day to day until a court shall be made, if that shall happen before four o'clock in the afternoon of the third day.

SEC. 10. *And be it further enacted,* That if either a circuit court, or the court hereinafter mentioned, shall not sit in any term, or shall not continue to sit the whole term, or before the end of the term shall not have heard and determined all matters ready for its decision, all such matters and things depending in court, and undetermined, shall stand continued until the next succeeding term.

SEC. 11. *And be it further enacted,* That if, from any cause, either of the said courts shall not sit on any day in a term after it shall have been opened, there shall be no discontinuance, but so soon as the cause is removed the court shall proceed to business until the end of the term, if the business depending before it be not sooner despatched.

SEC. 12. *And be it further enacted,* That the judicial term of the said circuit courts shall consist of six days in each county, during which time the court shall sit, unless the business before it shall be sooner determined.

SEC. 13. *And be it further enacted,* That a clerk shall be appointed by the said circuit courts, respectively, in each county, whose duty it shall be to issue process in all cases originating in his county, to keep and preserve the records of all the proceedings of the court therein, and to do and perform in the county all the duties which may be enjoined on him by law.

SEC. 14. *And be it further enacted,* That, in the cases that were, on the thirty-first day of December, in the year one thousand eight hundred and fourteen, depending in the courts of common pleas in the respective counties, the parties, or their attorneys, shall be permitted to take all such measures for bringing them to trial that might have been taken if no change had taken place; and the said circuit courts, respectively, shall, as far as possible, proceed to the trial thereof in the same manner that the said courts of common pleas might legally have done, had no other change than a mere alteration of the terms taken place.

SEC. 15. *And be it further enacted,* That the said judges, appointed as aforesaid, or a majority of them, shall constitute a court, to be styled the Court of Appeals for Illinois Territory, and shall hold two sessions annually at the town of Kaskaskia, which shall commence on the first Mondays in March and August, in every year, and continue in session until the business before them shall be completed; which court shall have appellate jurisdiction only, and to which appeals shall be allowed, and from which writs of error, according to the principles of the common law, and conformably to the laws and usages of the said Territory, may be prosecuted for the reversal of the judgments and decrees, as well of the said circuit courts, as of any inferior courts which now are, or hereafter may be, established by the laws of the said Territory.

SEC. 16. *And be it further enacted,* That a clerk

shall be appointed by the said court of appeals, whose duty it shall be to issue process in all cases brought before the said court where process ought to issue, and to keep and preserve the records of all the proceedings of the said court therein, and to do and perform all the duties as may be enjoined on him by law.

SEC. 17. *And be it further enacted,* That in all cases that were, on the said thirty-first day of December, eighteen hundred and fourteen, depending in the General Court of said Territory, the parties or their attorneys shall be permitted to take all such measures for bringing them to a final decision that might have been taken if no change had taken place, and the said court of appeals shall, as far as practicable, proceed to the final determination thereof, in the same manner that the said General Court might legally have done, had no other change than a mere alteration of the terms taken place.

SEC. 18. *And be it further enacted,* That appeals may be prayed, and writs of error taken out, upon matters of law only, in all cases wherein they are now allowed by law, to the said court of appeals, and all writs of error shall be issued by the clerk of the said court of appeals, and made returnable to the said court of Kaskaskia; but no question upon appeal or writ of error shall be decided without the concurrence of two judges at least.

SEC. 19. *And be it further enacted,* That the Legislature of the said Territory shall have power to change the times of holding any of the courts required to be holden by this act: *Provided, however,* That the said Legislature shall not have authority to increase the number of sessions to be held by the said courts respectively, in conformity with the provisions of the preceding sections of this act.

SEC. 20. *And be it further enacted,* That no judge or justice, appointed under the authority of the government of the said Territory, shall be associated with the aforesaid United States judges when sitting as circuit court judges as aforesaid. This act to commence and be in force from and after the first day of April next.

Approved, March 3, 1815.

An Act to continue in force, for a limited time, the act entitled "An act for establishing trading houses with the Indian tribes."

Be it enacted, &c., That the act, entitled "An act for establishing trading houses with the Indian tribes," approved on the second day of March, eighteen hundred and eleven, shall be, and the same is hereby, continued in force until the fourth day of March, eighteen hundred and seventeen, and no longer.

Approved, March 3, 1815.

An Act to fix the compensations, and increase the responsibility, of the collectors of the direct tax and internal duties; and for other purposes connected with the collection thereof.

Be it enacted, &c., That the collectors of the

Public Acts of Congress.

direct tax and internal duties shall be entitled to receive the same commissions which are now allowed by law, until the first day of July, one thousand eight hundred and fifteen : *Provided,* That the commissions accruing to any one collector, upon the moneys collected and paid into the Treasury, between the thirty-first of December, one thousand eight hundred and fourteen, and the first day of July, one thousand eight hundred and fifteen, shall not exceed the sum of three thousand dollars ; and the said collectors shall, from and after the said first day of July, be allowed, in lieu of the commission now allowed by law, four and one-half per centum upon all moneys accounted for and paid into the Treasury, from the first July, one thousand eight hundred and fifteen, until the first of January, one thousand eight hundred and sixteen, not exceeding fifty thousand dollars ; and one per centum upon all sums over and above that amount.

Sec. 2. *And be it further enacted,* That each collector, whose commission in any one calendar year shall not exceed one thousand dollars, shall be allowed, at the end of the year, in addition to such commission, the sum of two hundred dollars.

Sec. 3. *And be it further enacted,* That the collectors heretofore, or hereafter, designated by the Secretary of the Treasury, to receive the lists of property lying within collection districts not owned, occupied, or superintended, by some person residing therein, shall, respectively, in addition to their other commissions and compensations, be allowed a commission of five per centum on the moneys received for taxes thereon accounted for and paid by them into the Treasury.

Sec. 4. *And be it further enacted,* That it shall be lawful for the President of the United States to apportion and distribute, annually, a sum not exceeding, in the whole, twenty-five thousand dollars, or to any one collector five hundred dollars, among such collectors, as, for the execution of the public service, it shall appear to him necessary so to compensate, in addition to the other emoluments to which they are entitled.

Sec. 5. *And be it further enacted,* That in case a collector shall die, resign, or be removed from office, he shall be entitled to a commission equal to the average rate of that allowed to the collector of the same district the preceding calendar year, and no more ; and his successor shall, for the residue of the year, be allowed a commission equal to the sum that may remain, after deducting the sum allowed to his predecessor, from the whole amount of commission that would have been allowed had there been no such death, resignation, or removal, and no more : *Provided,* That either of the said collectors shall be entitled to the benefits of the provision contained in the fourth section of this act.

Sec. 6. *And be it further enacted* That it shall be the duty of each of the collectors, within ninety days from the end of every calendar year, to draw out a statement, exhibiting, in alphabetical order, the names of persons who may have paid, during the preceding calendar year, to him, or his deputies, any one or more of the internal duties, ex-

cept those on household furniture and on stamps, with the aggregate amount so paid, annexed to each name, and forthwith to cause one hundred copies of the same to be printed, to transmit one copy thereof to the commissioner of the revenue, to lodge one copy with the principal assessor, and one copy with the clerk of each town, county, and district, within his collection district, to post up one copy at each of the court-houses in his district, to post up the remaining copies at the other most public places in his district, the reasonable expenses incurred in the preparing, printing, and posting up, of which shall be allowed ; and any collector who shall purposely or negligently fail to discharge this duty, shall be deemed guilty of a misdemeanor in office, and, on conviction thereof, shall be fined a sum not less than five hundred dollars, nor more than ten thousand dollars.

Sec. 7. *And be it further enacted,* That all letters to and from the said collectors, relative to their official duties, shall be conveyed free of postage. And any collector who shall put his frank upon any other letter, shall, for every such act, forfeit and pay the sum of one hundred dollars, and the whole of which shall be for the use of the person who shall give information thereof.

Sec. 8. *And be it further enacted,* That it shall be the duty of the collectors to keep their offices open for the transaction of business every day, except on established holydays, between the hours of nine in the morning and three in the afternoon, and to attend therein themselves, or by deputy ; which said offices shall, after the present year, be kept at such places, in the respective districts, as may be designated by the commissioner of the revenue, in all cases in which such designation shall be thought expedient.

Sec. 9. *And be it further enacted,* That the amount of all taxes or duties collected by any deputy collector, until paid over to the collector, shall, and hereby is declared to, be a lien upon the lands and real estate of such deputy collector, and of his sureties, if he shall have given bond, from the time when a suit shall be instituted for recovering the same ; and for want of goods and chattels, or other personal effects of such deputy collector, or his sureties, to satisfy any judgment which shall or may be recovered against them, respectively, such lands and real estates may be sold at public auction, after being advertised for at least three weeks, in not less than three public places within the collection district, and in one newspaper printed in the county, if any there be, at least six weeks prior to the time of sale ; and for lands or real estate sold in pursuance of the authority aforesaid, the conveyances of the marshals, or their deputies, executed in due form of law, shall give a valid title against all persons claiming under such deputy collector, or his sureties, respectively. And in every case it shall and may be lawful for a principal collector to maintain and prosecute his action against a deputy collector and his sureties, or any of them, if a bond with sureties shall have been given, in the circuit court of the United States, for the recovery of all taxes collected by said deputy, and not paid over according to his engagement, or for the penalty of the bond which may have been given to secure the payment thereof: *Provided always,* That all moneys recovered in such suits shall be for the use of the United States, until the whole amount of the taxes collected and received by the deputy collector shall be otherwise paid to the United States by the deputy collector, or by the principal collector instituting such suits.

Sec. 10. *And be it further enacted,* That if any collector, or his deputy, shall have cause to suspect a concealment of any goods, wares, or merchandise, in respect to which the respective provisions of the acts imposing an internal duty thereon have not been complied with, in any particular dwelling-house, store, building, or place, (other than the manufactory in which the same were made,) they, or either of them, shall, upon proper application, on oath, to any justice of the peace, be entitled to a warrant to enter such house, store, or place, (in the day time only,) and there to search for such goods; and, if any shall be found, to seize and secure the same for trial.

Sec. 11. *And be it further enacted,* That all goods, wares, or merchandise, or other objects, which shall be seized by virtue of this act, or of any act relative to internal duties, shall be put into, and remain in, the custody of the collector, or such other person as he shall appoint for that purpose, until such proceedings shall be had as are legally required, to ascertain whether the same have been forfeited or not; and if it shall be adjudged that they are not forfeited, they shall be forthwith restored to the owner or claimant thereof; and if any person shall conceal or buy any such goods, wares, or merchandise, or other object, knowing them to be liable to seizure and forfeiture, such person shall, on conviction thereof, forfeit and pay a sum double the value of the goods, wares, or merchandise, or other objects so concealed and purchased, one moiety of which shall be for the use of the informer, and the other for the use of the United States.

Sec. 12. *And be it further enacted,* That it shall be the duty of the several collectors to make seizure of, and secure, any goods, wares, or merchandise, or other objects liable to seizure by virtue of this or any other act relating to the internal duties, as well without as within their respective districts.

Sec. 13 *And be it further enacted,* That if any officer or other person executing or aiding or assisting in the seizure of goods, wares, or merchandise, or other objects as aforesaid, shall be sued or molested for anything done in virtue of the powers given by this act, or of any other act, or by virtue of a warrant granted by any judge or justice, pursuant to law, such officer or other person may plead the general issue, and give this act and the special matter in evidence; and if in such suit the plaintiff is nonsuited, or judgment pass against him, the defendant shall recover double costs; and in actions, suits, or information, to be brought where any seizure shall be made pursuant to this act, or any other act relative to inter-

nal duties, if the property be claimed by any person, in every such case the onus probandi shall be upon such claimant: but the onus probandi shall lie on the claimant only when probable cause is shown for such prosecution, to be judged of by the court before whom the prosecution is had.

Sec. 14. *And be it further enacted,* That all penalties accruing by any breach of this act, or of any act relative to internal duties, shall be sued for and recovered, with costs of suit, in the name of the United States of America, or of the collector, in any court competent to try the same, and the trial of any fact which may be put in issue, shall be within the judicial district in which any such penalty shall have accrued, or seizure been made; and the collector within whose district the seizure shall be made, or forfeiture incurred, is hereby enjoined to cause suits for the same to be commenced without delay, and prosecuted to effect; and is, moreover, authorized to receive from the court before whom such trial is had, or from the proper officer thereof, the sum or sums so recovered, after deducting all proper charges, to be allowed by the said court, and on receipt thereof, the said collector shall pay and distribute the same, without delay, according to law, and transmit, quarter yearly, to the commissioner of the revenue, an account of all moneys by him received for fines, penalties, and forfeitures, during such quarter. And all goods, wares, and merchandise, or other objects, which shall become forfeited in virtue of this act, or of any act relative to internal duties, shall be seized and prosecuted for as aforesaid, before the proper court, which court shall cause fourteen days' notice to be given of such seizure, setting forth the articles seized, with the time and place appointed for trial, to be inserted in some newspaper published near the place of seizure, if any such there be, and also by posting up the same in the most public manner, for the space of fourteen days, at or near the place of trial, for which advertisement a sum not exceeding ten dollars shall be paid. And if no person shall appear and claim such articles, and give bond to defend the prosecution thereof, and to respond the costs, in case he shall not support his claim, the court shall proceed to hear and determine the cause according to law; and upon the prayer of any claimant, that any articles, so seized and prosecuted, or any part thereof, should be delivered to him, it shall be lawful for the court to appoint three proper persons to appraise such articles, who shall be sworn for the faithful discharge of their duty; and such appraisement shall be made at the expense of the party on whose prayer it is granted; and on the return of such appraisement, if the claimant shall, with one or more sureties, to be approved by the court, execute a bond in the usual form, to the United States, for the payment of a sum equal to the sum at which the articles, so prayed to be delivered, are appraised, which bond shall be lodged with the proper officer of the court, the said court shall order the said articles to be delivered to the said claimant; and if judgment shall pass in favor of the claimant, the said bond shall be cancelled; but if judgment shall pass against the claimant, as to the whole, or any part, of such articles, and the claimant shall not, within twenty days thereafter, pay into the court, or to the proper officer thereof, the amount of the appraised value of such articles so condemned, with the costs, judgment shall and may be granted upon the bond without further delay. And where any prosecution shall be commenced on account of the seizure of any such goods, wares, and merchandise, or other objects, and judgment shall be given for the claimant, if it shall appear to the court before whom such prosecution shall be tried, that there was reasonable cause of seizure, the said court shall cause a proper certificate or entry to be made thereof, and in such case the claimant shall not be entitled to costs, nor shall the person who made the seizure, or the prosecutor, be liable to action, suit, or judgment, on account of such seizure and prosecution: *Provided,* That the said goods, wares, and merchandise, or other objects, be, after judgment, forthwith returned to such claimant, or his agent: *And provided,* That no action or prosecution shall be maintained in any case under this act, or any act relative to internal duties, unless the same shall have been commenced within one year after the penalty or forfeiture was incurred, or within the time in such act prescribed, as the case may be.

Sec. 15. *And be it further enacted,* That all goods, wares, or merchandise, or other objects, which shall be condemned by virtue of this act, or of any other act relative to internal duties, and for which bond shall have been given by the claimant, agreeably to the provisions for that purpose in the foregoing section, shall be sold by the marshal, or other proper officer of the court before whom condemnation shall be had, to the highest bidder, at public auction, by order of such court, and at such place as the said court may appoint, giving at least fifteen days' notice, (except in case of perishable goods,) in one or more of the public newspapers of the place where such sale shall be; or, if no paper is published in such place, in one or more of the papers published in the nearest place thereto; for which advertising a sum not exceeding five dollars shall be paid. And the amount of such sales, deducting all proper charges, shall be paid within ten days after such sale, by the person selling the same, to the clerk, or other proper officer, of the court, directing such sale, to be by him, after deducting the charges allowed by the court, paid to the collector of the district in which such seizure or forfeiture has taken place, as hereinbefore directed.

Sec. 16. *And be it further enacted,* That the foregoing provisions of this act shall be applicable, in all respects, as well to all acts that may hereafter be passed, relative to internal duties, as to those heretofore passed and now in force.

Sec. 17. *And be it further enacted,* That any collector or his deputy, who shall directly or indirectly take or receive any bribe, reward, or recompense, or shall connive at any false entry, application, report, account, or statement, required to be made or rendered by any act relative to internal duties, and shall be convicted thereof, shall forfeit and pay a sum not less than two hundred, nor more than two thousand dollars for each offence; and any person giving or offering any bribe, reward, or recompense, for any such deception, collusion, or fraud, shall forfeit and pay a sum not less than two hundred, nor more than two thousand dollars, for each offence; one moiety whereof shall be to the use of the informer, and the other moiety for the use of the United States.

Sec. 18. *And be it further enacted,* That on all bonds given for internal duties an interest shall be paid, at the rate of six per centum per annum, from the time when the said bonds became due until the payment thereof.

Sec. 19. *And be it further enacted,* That any person, to whom a license for a still, or boiler, or other vessel used in the distillation of spirituous liquors, may have been, or may hereafter be, granted, who shall so alter the same as to increase its capacity, on application in writing to the collector who issued the said license, stating such increase of capacity, and on paying or securing, previous to using the same, the duty arising thereon for the unexpired period of the license, at the rate of duty prescribed for such term for which a license may be granted as is next below such period, shall be authorized to employ the still, boiler, or other vessel, so altered, on adducing the said license, and obtaining an endorsement thereon, under the hand of the said collector, which he is hereby required to make, specifying such increase of capacity, and that the duty thereon has been paid or secured.

Sec. 20. *And be it further enacted,* That any person who shall, after the thirtieth day of June next, erect, or cause to be erected, any still, or boiler, or other vessel, used or intended to be used in the distillation of spirituous liquors, or who shall so use any still, or boiler, or other vessel, in any part of the United States beyond the then existing boundary line established by law between the United States and the Indian tribes, or who shall be the owner, agent, or superintendent thereof, shall forfeit and pay the sum of five thousand dollars, together with the said still, boiler, or other vessel, and the spirits distilled therein: one moiety of which shall be for the use of the informer, and the other for the use of the United States. And for any violations hereof, the same course may and shall be pursued that is prescribed by the act passed the thirtieth of March, one thousand eight hundred and two, entitled "An act to regulate trade and intercourse with the Indian tribes, and to preserve peace on the frontiers," for violations thereof; and the courts specified therein shall have like jurisdiction. And the same authority that is given by the said act to apprehend and remove persons found in violation thereof, shall apply and extend to the said stills, boilers, or other vessels, and the spirits distilled therein, which may be seized and removed in like manner. And all spirits such shall have been, or which hereafter shall be so distilled, beyond the said boundary line, which shall be brought into the limits of a collection district, may and shall be seized and forfeited, and the person so introducing the same shall, moreover, forfeit and pay one thousand dollars; one moiety of which shall be to the use of the informer, and the other for the use of the United States: *Provided, nevertheless,* That no person who shall have removed his still out of one collection district into another, shall be liable to take out another license during the period of any existing license obtained for the same.

SEC. 21. *And be it further enacted,* That it shall be the duty of the collectors of the direct tax and internal duties, to prosecute for breaches of the provisions contained in the two preceding sections.

SEC. 22. *And be it further enacted,* That nothing contained in the act or acts imposing a duty on sales at auction of goods, wares, and merchandise, shall be construed to apply to the sale of any goods or chattels other than merchandise.

Approved, March 3, 1815.

An Act to vest more effectually in the State Courts' and in the District Courts of the United States' jurisdiction therein mentioned.

Be it enacted, &c., That the respective State or county courts, within or next adjoining a collection district, established by any act of Congress now in being, or hereafter to be passed, for the collection of any direct tax or internal duties of the United States, shall be, and are hereby, authorized to take cognizance of all complaints, suits, and prosecutions, for taxes, duties, fines, penalties, and forfeitures, arising and payable under any of the acts passed, or to be passed, as aforesaid, or where bonds are given under the said acts; and the district attorneys of the United States are hereby authorized and directed to appoint, by warrant, an attorney, as their substitute or deputy, in all cases where necessary to sue or prosecute for the United States, in any of the said State or county courts, within the sphere of whose jurisdiction the said district attorneys do not themselves reside or practice; and the said substitute or deputy shall be sworn or affirmed to the faithful execution of his duty.

SEC. 2. *And be it further enacted,* That the jurisdiction conferred by the foregoing section shall be considered as attaching, in the cases therein specified without regard to the amount or sum in controversy, and that it shall be concurrent with the jurisdiction of the district courts of the United States; but may, nevertheless, be exercised in cases where the fine, penalty, or forfeiture, may have been incurred, or the cause of action or complaint have arisen, at a less, as well as a greater distance than fifty miles from the nearest place by law established for the holding of a district court of the United States. But in all suits or prosecutions instituted by or on behalf of the United States in any State or county court, the process, proceedings, judgment, and execution therein shall not be delayed, suspended, or in any

way barred or defeated, by reason of any law of any State authorizing or directing a stay or suspension of process, proceedings, judgment, or execution : *Provided,* That final decrees and judgments in civil actions, passed or rendered in any State court by virtue hereof, may be re-examined in the circuit court of the United States, in the same manner, and under the same limitations, as are prescribed by the twenty-second section of the act to establish the judicial courts of the United States, passed the twenty-fourth of September, seventeen hundred and eighty-nine.

SEC. 3. *And be it further enacted,* That the state or county courts aforesaid, and the principal or presiding judge of any such court, shall be, and are hereby, authorized to exercise all and every power, in cases cognizable before them by virtue of this act, for the purpose of obtaining a mitigation or remission of any fine, penalty, or forfeiture, which may be exercised by the judges of the district courts of the United States, in cases brought before them by virtue of the law of the United States, passed on the third of March, one thousand seven hundred and ninety-seven, entitled "An act to provide for mitigating or remitting the forfeitures, penalties, and disabilities, accruing in certain cases therein mentioned ;" and in the exercise of the authority by this section given to the said State or county courts, or the principal or presiding judge as aforesaid, they shall be governed, in every respect, by the provisions of the law last mentioned, with this difference only, that instead of notifying the district attorneys of the United States, the said courts, or the presiding judge as aforesaid, shall, before exercising said authorities, cause reasonable notice to be given to the substitute or deputy, who may have been appointed to sue or prosecute for the United States, as aforesaid, that he may have an opportunity of showing cause against the mitigation or remission of such fine, penalty, or forfeiture.

SEC. 4. *And be it further enacted,* That the district court of the United States shall have cognizance, concurrent with the courts and magistrates of the several States, and the circuit courts of the United States, of all suits at common law, where the United States, or any officer thereof, under the authority of any act of Congress, shall sue, although the debt, claim, or other matter in dispute, shall not amount to one hundred dollars.

Approved, March 3, 1815.

RESOLUTIONS.

Resolutions, expressive of the sense of Congress of the gallant conduct of Captain Thomas Macdonough, the officers, seamen, marines, and infantry serving as marines, on board the United States' squadron on Lake Champlain.

Resolved, by the Senate and House of Representatives of the United States of America in Congress assembled, That the thanks of Congress be, and the same are hereby, presented to

Resolutions.

Captain Thomas Macdonough, and, through him, to the officers, petty officers, seamen, marines, and infantry serving as marines, attached to the squadron under his command, for the decisive and splendid victory gained on Lake Champlain, on the eleventh of September, in the year one thousand eight hundred and fourteen, over a British squadron of superior force.

Resolved, That the President of the United States be requested to cause gold medals to be struck, emblematical of the action between the two squadrons, and to present them to Captain Macdonough and Captain Robert Henly, and also to Lieutenant Stephen Cassin, in such manner as may be most honorable to them; and that the President be further requested to present a silver medal, with suitable emblems and devices, to each of the commissioned officers of the Navy and Army serving on board, and a sword to each of the midshipmen and sailingmasters, who so nobly distinguished themselves in that memorable conflict.

Resolved, That the President of the United States be requested to present a silver medal, with like emblems and devices, to the nearest male relative of Lieutenant Peter Gamble, and of Lieutenant John Stansbury, and to communicate to them the deep regret which Congress feel for the loss of those gallant men, whose names ought to live in the recollection and affection of a grateful country.

Resolved, That three months' pay be allowed, exclusively of the common allowance, to all the petty officers, seamen, marines, and infantry serving as marines, who so gloriously supported the honor of the American flag on that memorable day.

Approved, October 20, 1814.

Resolution, empowering the Joint Library Committee of Congress to contract for the purchase of Mr. Jefferson's library.

Resolved, &c., That the Joint Library Committee of the two Houses of Congress be, and they are hereby, authorized and empowered to contract. on their part, for the purchase of the library of Mr. Jefferson, late President of the United States, for the use of both Houses of Congress; and that the committee lay the terms of said contract before Congress, for their ratification.

Approved, October 21, 1814.

Resolution, expressive of the sense of Congress relative to the victory of the Peacock over the Epervier.

Resolved, &c., That the President of the United States be requested to present to Captain Lewis Warrington, of the sloop of war Peacock, a gold medal, with suitable emblems and devices, and a silver medal, with like emblems and devices, to each of the commissioned officers, and a sword to each of the midshipmen, and to the sailing master, of the said vessel, in testimony of the high sense entertained by Congress of the gallantry and good conduct of the officers and crew,

in the action with the British brig Epervier, on the twenty-ninth day of April, in the year one thousand eight hundred and fourteen, in which action the decisive effect and great superiority of the American gunnery were so signally displayed.

Approved, October 21, 1814.

Resolution, expressive of the sense of Congress relative to the capture of the British sloop Reindeer, by the American sloop Wasp.

Resolved, &c., That the President of the United States be requested to present to Captain Johnston Blakely, of the sloop Wasp, a gold medal, with suitable devices, and a silver medal, with like devices, to each of the commissioned officers, and also a sword to each of the midshipmen, and the sailingmaster, of the aforesaid vessel, in testimony of the high sense entertained by Congress of the gallantry and good conduct of the officers and crew, in the action with the British sloop of war Reindeer, on the twenty-eighth of June, in the year one thousand eight hundred and fourteen; in which action determined bravery and cool intrepidity, in nineteen minutes, obtained a decisive victory, by boarding.

Approved, November 3, 1814.

Resolutions, expressive of the sense of Congress of the gallantry and good conduct with which the reputation of the arms of the United States has been sustained by Major General Brown, Major General Scott, Major General Porter, Major General Gaines, Major General Macomb, and Brigadiers Ripley and Miller.

Resolved, &c., That the thanks of Congress be, and they are hereby, presented to Major General Brown, and, through him, to the officers and men, of the regular army, and of the militia, under his command, for their gallantry and good conduct in the successive battles of Chippewa, Niagara, and Erie, in Upper Canada, in which British veteran troops were beaten and repulsed by equal or inferior numbers; and that the President of the United States be requested to cause a gold medal to be struck, emblematical of these triumphs, and presented to Major General Brown.

Resolved, That the President of the United States be requested to cause a gold medal to be struck, with suitable emblems and devices, and presented to Major General Scott, in testimony of the high sense entertained by Congress of his distinguished services in the conflicts of Chippewa and Niagara, and of his uniform gallantry and good conduct in sustaining the reputation of the arms of the United States.

Resolved, That the President of the United States be requested to cause gold medals to be struck, with suitable emblems and devices, and presented to Brigadier General Ripley, Brigadier General Miller, and Major General Porter, in testimony of the high sense entertained by Congress of their gallantry and good conduct in the several conflicts of Chippewa, Niagara, and Erie.

Resolutions.

Resolved, That the thanks of Congress be, and they are hereby, presented to Major General Gaines, and, through him, to the officers and men under his command, for their gallantry and good conduct, in defeating the enemy at Erie on the fifteenth of August; repelling, with great slaughter, the attack of a British veteran army, superior in number; and that the President of the United States be requested to cause a gold medal to be struck, emblematical of this triumph, and presented to Major General Gaines.

Resolved, That the thanks of Congress be, and they are hereby, presented to Major General Macomb, and, through him, to the officers and men of the regular army under his command, and to the militia and volunteers of New York and Vermont, for their gallantry and good conduct in defeating the enemy at Plattsburg, on the eleventh of September; repelling, with one thousand five hundred men, aided by a body of militia and volunteers from New York and Vermont, a British veteran army, greatly superior in number; and that the President of the United States be requested to cause a gold medal to be struck, emblematical of this triumph, and presented to Major General Macomb.

Approved, November 3, 1814.

Resolution, requesting the President of the United States to recommend a day of public humiliation, fasting, and prayer.

It being a duty, peculiarly incumbent in a time of public calamity and war, humbly and devoutly to acknowledge our dependence on Almighty God, and to implore his aid and protection: Therefore,

Resolved, by the Senate and House of Representatives of the United States of America in Congress assembled, That a joint committee of both Houses wait on the President of the United States, and request that he recommend a day of public humiliation, prayer, and fasting, to be observed by the people of the United States with religious solemnity, and the offering of fervent supplications to Almighty God for the safety and welfare of these States, his blessing on their arms, and a speedy restoration of peace.

Resolution, for furnishing the American Antiquarian Society with a copy of the Journals of Congress, and of the documents published under their order.

Resolved, &c., That one copy of the public Journals of the Senate and House of Representatives, and of the documents published under the orders of the Senate and House of Representatives, respectively, which have been, or shall be, published by virtue of a resolution of the Senate and House of Representatives, passed at the last session of Congress, be transmitted to the Executive of the Commonwealth of Massachusetts, for the use and benefit of the American Antiquarian Society of the said Commonwealth.

Approved, December 1, 1814.

Resolutions, expressive of the high sense entertained by Congress of the patriotism and good conduct of the people of Louisiana and of New Orleans, during the late military operations before that city.

Resolved, &c., That Congress entertain a high sense of the patriotism, fidelity, zeal, and courage, with which the people of the State of Louisiana promptly and unanimously stepped forth, under circumstances of imminent danger from a powerful invading army, in the defence of all the individual, social, and political rights held dear by man. Congress declare and proclaim that the brave Louisianians deserve well of the whole people of the United States.

Resolved, That Congress entertain a high sense of the generosity, benevolence, and humanity, displayed by the people of New Orleans, in voluntarily affording the best accommodations in their power, and giving the kindest attentions, to the wounded, not only of our own army, but also to the wounded prisoners of a vanquished foe.

Resolved, That the President of the United States be requested to cause the foregoing resolutions to be communicated to his Excellency, the Governor of Louisiana, accompanied with a request that he cause the greatest possible publicity to be given to them, for the information of the whole people of Louisiana.

Approved, February 22, 1815.

Resolutions, expressive of the high sense entertained by Congress of the gallantry and good conduct of Commodore D. T. Patterson, and Major D. Carmick, and of the officers, seamen, and marines, under their command, in the defence of New Orleans.

Resolved, &c., That Congress entertain a high sense of the valor and good conduct of Commodore D. T. Patterson, of the officers, petty officers, and seamen, attached to his command, for their prompt and efficient co-operation with General Jackson, in the late gallant and successful defence of the city of New Orleans, when assailed by a powerful British force.

Resolved, That Congress entertain a high sense of the valor and good conduct of Major Daniel Carmick, of the officers, non-commissioned officers, and marines, under his command, in the defence of the said city, on the late memorable occasion.

Approved, February 22, 1815.

Resolutions, expressive of the thanks of Congress to Major General Jackson, and the troops under his command, for their gallantry and good conduct in the defence of New Orleans.

Resolved, &c., That the thanks of Congress be, and they are hereby, given to Major General Jackson, and, through him, to the officers and soldiers of the regular army, of the militia, and of the volunteers, under his command, the greater proportion of which troops consisted of militia and volunteers, suddenly collected together, for their uniform gallantry and good conduct, conspicuously displayed against the enemy, from the time of his landing before New Orleans until his

Resolutions.

final expulsion therefrom; and particularly for the valor, skill, and good conduct, on the eighth of January last, in repulsing, with great slaughter, a numerous British army, of chosen veteran troops, when attempting, by a bold and daring attack, to carry by storm the works hastily thrown up for the protection of New Orleans; and thereby obtaining a most signal victory over the enemy, with a disparity of loss, on his part, unexampled in military annals.

Resolved, That the President of the United States be requested to cause to be struck, a gold medal, with devices emblematical of this splendid achievement, and presented to Major General Jackson, as a testimony of the high sense entertained by Congress of his judicious and distinguished conduct on that memorable occasion.

Resolved, That the President of the United States be requested to cause the foregoing resolutions to be communicated to Major General Jackson, in such terms as they may deem best calculated to give effect to the objects thereof.

Approved, February 27, 1815.

A Resolution, directing the manner of providing stationery, and procuring the printing, for the Senate and House of Representatives.

Resolved, &c., That the Secretary of the Senate and the Clerk of the House of Representatives be directed, immediately after the adjournment of the present, and each succeeding, Congress, to advertise, three weeks successively, in two newspapers printed in the District of Columbia, for proposals for supplying the Senate and House of Representatives, during the succeeding Congress, with the necessary stationery and printing; which advertisement shall describe the kind of stationery and printing required; and that the proposals to be made be accompanied with sufficient security for their performance. And it shall be the duty of the Secretary and Clerk

aforesaid, in the month of April thereafter, to notify the lowest bidder or bidders (whose securities are deemed sufficient) of the acceptance of his or their proposals: *Provided,* That this resolution shall not be so construed, as to prevent the Secretary and Clerk aforesaid from contracting for separate parts of the supplies of stationery and printing required to be furnished.

Approved, March 3, 1815.

Resolutions, relative to the distribution of the *Laws of the United States.*

Resolved, &c., That the Secretary of State cause to be distributed, among the members of the present Congress, copies of the laws of the United States, ordered by law to be printed, as soon as the same shall be completed.

Resolved, That so many of the remaining copies of the laws as are not already directed to be distributed, be deposited in the Congressional Library.

Approved, March 3, 1815.

Resolution, for the appointment of a *joint committee* to wait upon the President, and request that he recommend a day of thanksgiving to *Almighty God,* for restoring to these United States the *blessings of* peace.

Resolved, &c., That a joint committee of both Houses wait upon the President of the United States, and request that he recommend a day of thanksgiving, to be observed by the people of the United States, with religious solemnity, and the offering of devout acknowledgments to Almighty God, for his great goodness, manifested in restoring to these United States the blessing of peace.

LANGDON CHEVES,
Speaker of the House.
JOHN GAILLARD,
President of the Senate.

INDEX

TO THE PROCEEDINGS AND DEBATES OF THE THIRD SESSION OF THE THIRTEENTH CONGRESS.

SENATE.—THIRD SESSION.

Senate Proceedings and Debates.

Senate Proceedings and Debates.

Senate Proceedings and Debates.

Senate Proceedings and Debates.

Senate Proceedings and Debates.

Senate Proceedings and Debates.

Senate Proceedings and Debates.

House Proceedings and Debates.

HOUSE OF REPRESENTATIVES AND APPENDIX.

House Proceedings and Debates.

House Proceedings and Debates.

House Proceedings and Debates.

House Proceedings and Debates.

House Proceedings and Debates.

House Proceedings and Debates.

House Proceedings and Debates.

House Proceedings and Debates.

House Proceedings and Debates.

House Proceedings and Debates.

Public Acts and Resolutions.

PUBLIC ACTS AND RESOLUTIONS.

Public Acts and Resolutions.

Public Acts and Resolutions.

Lightning Source UK Ltd.
Milton Keynes UK
UKHW010644100119
335176UK00006B/124/P